THE Java™ Class Libraries

Second Edition, Volume 1

The Java™ Series

Lisa Friendly, Series Editor
Tim Lindholm, Technical Editor
Please see our web site (http://www.awl.com /cseng/javaseries) for more information on these titles.

Ken Arnold and James Gosling, *The Java™ Programming Language, Second Edition*
ISBN 0-201-31006-6

Mary Campione and Kathy Walrath, *The Java™ Tutorial, Second Edition: Object-Oriented Programming for the Internet* (Book/CD)
ISBN 0-201-31007-4

Patrick Chan, *The Java™ Developers Almanac*
ISBN 0-201-37967-8

Patrick Chan and Rosanna Lee, *The Java™ Class Libraries, Second Edition, Volume 2: java.applet, java.awt, java.beans*
ISBN 0-201-31003-1

Patrick Chan, Rosanna Lee, and Doug Kramer, *The Java™ Class Libraries, Second Edition, Volume 1: java.io, java.lang, java.math, java.net, java.text, java.util*
ISBN 0-201-31002-3

James Gosling, Bill Joy, and Guy Steele, *The Java™ Language Specification*
ISBN 0-201-63451-1

James Gosling, Frank Yellin, and The Java Team, *The Java™ Application Programming Interface, Volume 1: Core Packages*
ISBN 0-201-63453-8

James Gosling, Frank Yellin, and The Java Team, *The Java™ Application Programming Interface, Volume 2: Window Toolkit and Applets*
ISBN 0-201-63459-7

Graham Hamilton, Rick Cattell, and Maydene Fisher, *JDBC™ Database Access with Java™: A Tutorial and Annotated Reference*
ISBN 0-201-30995-5

Jonni Kanerva, *The Java™ FAQ*
ISBN 0-201-63456-2

Doug Lea, *Concurrent Programming in Java™: Design Principles and Patterns*
ISBN 0-201-69581-2

Tim Lindholm and Frank Yellin, *The Java™ Virtual Machine Specification*
ISBN 0-201-63452-X

Henry Sowizral, Kevin Rushforth, and Michael Deering, *The Java™ 3D API Specification*
ISBN 0-201-32576-4

THE Java™ Class Libraries

Second Edition, Volume 1

java.io, java.lang, java.math java.net, java.text, java.util

Patrick Chan
Rosanna Lee
and
Douglas Kramer

ADDISON-WESLEY

An imprint of Addison Wesley Longman, Inc.

Reading, Massachusetts • Harlow, England • Menlo Park, California
Berkeley, California • Don Mills, Ontario • Sydney
Bonn • Amsterdam • Tokyo • Mexico City

The publisher offers discounts on this book when ordered in quantity for special sales. For more information, please contact:

Corporate, Government, and Special Sales Group
Addison Wesley Longman
One Jacob Way
Reading, Massachusetts 01867

Library of Congress Cataloging-in-Publication Data

Chan, Patrick, 1961-
The Java class libraries / Patrick Chan,
Rosanna Lee, and Douglas Kramer -- 2nd ed.
p. cm. -- (The Java series)
Includes index.
ISBN 0-201-31002-3
1. Java (Computer program language) I. Lee, Rosanna, 1960-, Kramer, Douglas, 1950-
II. Title. III. Series.
QA76.73.J38C47 1998
005.13'3--dc21 97-33423
CIP

ISBN 0-201-31002-3

3 4 5 6 7 8 CRW 01 00 99 98

3rd Printing July, 1998

To our parents

Agatha and Fai Chan
Patricia and Warren Lee
—P.C. & R.L.

To my new friends

Georgeanna
'Min
—D.K.

Contents

List of Figures xv
List of Tables xix
Preface xxi

Package Overviews

java.io 1
java.lang 10
java.lang.reflect 19
java.math 21
java.net 22
java.text 26
java.util 32
java.util.zip 36

Alphabetical Reference of Classes

AbstractMethodError 39
Adler32 41
ArithmeticException 45
Array 47
ArrayIndexOutOfBoundsException 70
ArrayStoreException 72

BigDecimal 74
BigInteger 99
BindException 134
BitSet 136
Boolean 144
BreakIterator 150
BufferedInputStream 176
BufferedOutputStream 185
BufferedReader 190
BufferedWriter 199

Byte 205
ByteArrayInputStream 216
ByteArrayOutputStream 224

Calendar 232
Character 282
CharacterIterator 305
CharArrayReader 315
CharArrayWriter 323
CharConversionException 331
CheckedInputStream 333
CheckedOutputStream 339
Checksum 343
ChoiceFormat 346
Class 365
ClassCastException 407
ClassCircularityError 409
ClassFormatError 411
ClassLoader 413
ClassNotFoundException 426
Cloneable 428
CloneNotSupportedException 431
CollationElementIterator 434
CollationKey 441
Collator 447
Compiler 470
ConnectException 473
Constructor 475
ContentHandler 487
ContentHandlerFactory 490
CRC32 493

DataFormatException 497
DatagramPacket 499
DatagramSocket 506
DatagramSocketImpl 516
DataInput 526
DataInputStream 534
DataOutput 546
DataOutputStream 552
Date 562
DateFormat 580
DateFormatSymbols 610

DecimalFormat 626
DecimalFormatSymbols 665
Deflater 679
DeflaterOutputStream 695
Dictionary 702
Double 709

EmptyStackException 721
Enumeration 723
EOFException 725
Error 727
EventListener 729
EventObject 731
Exception 737
ExceptionInInitializerError 741
Externalizable 743

Field 749
FieldPosition 774
File 782
FileDescriptor 802
FileInputStream 807
FilenameFilter 814
FileNameMap 816
FileNotFoundException 819
FileOutputStream 821
FileReader 827
FileWriter 830
FilterInputStream 834
FilterOutputStream 842
FilterReader 847
FilterWriter 855
Float 860
Format 872

GregorianCalendar 882
GZIPInputStream 896
GZIPOutputStream 902

Hashtable 913
HttpURLConnection 923

IllegalAccessError 939
IllegalAccessException 942
IllegalArgumentException 945
IllegalMonitorStateException 947
IllegalStateException 949
IllegalThreadStateException 951
IncompatibleClassChangeError 953
IndexOutOfBoundsException 955
InetAddress 957
Inflater 965
InflaterInputStream 976
InputStream 983
InputStreamReader 990
InstantiationError 997
InstantiationException 999
Integer 1001
InternalError 1015
InterruptedException 1017
InterruptedIOException 1019
InvalidClassException 1022
InvalidObjectException 1026
InvocationTargetException 1028
IOException 1031

LineNumberInputStream 1033
LineNumberReader 1040
LinkageError 1049
ListResourceBundle 1051
Locale 1054
Long 1069

MalformedURLException 1082
Math 1084
Member 1095
MessageFormat 1102
Method 1123
MissingResourceException 1140
Modifier 1143
MulticastSocket 1153

NegativeArraySizeException 1164
NoClassDefFoundError 1166
NoRouteToHostException 1168

NoSuchElementException 1170
NoSuchFieldError 1172
NoSuchFieldException 1174
NoSuchMethodError 1176
NoSuchMethodException 1178
NotActiveException 1181
NotSerializableException 1183
NullPointerException 1185
Number 1187
NumberFormat 1192
NumberFormatException 1213

Object 1215
ObjectInput 1226
ObjectInputStream 1230
ObjectInputValidation 1256
ObjectOutput 1259
ObjectOutputStream 1262
ObjectStreamClass 1283
ObjectStreamException 1288
Observable 1290
Observer 1296
OptionalDataException 1299
OutOfMemoryError 1302
OutputStream 1304
OutputStreamWriter 1308

ParseException 1314
ParsePosition 1317
PipedInputStream 1323
PipedOutputStream 1332
PipedReader 1337
PipedWriter 1342
PrintStream 1346
PrintWriter 1354
Process 1363
Properties 1370
PropertyResourceBundle 1378
ProtocolException 1381
PushbackInputStream 1383
PushbackReader 1392

Random 1399
RandomAccessFile 1406
Reader 1426
ResourceBundle 1435
RuleBasedCollator 1447
Runnable 1464
Runtime 1466
RuntimeException 1477

SecurityException 1479
SecurityManager 1481
SequenceInputStream 1503
Serializable 1508
ServerSocket 1515
Short 1530
SimpleDateFormat 1541
SimpleTimeZone 1559
Socket 1571
SocketException 1590
SocketImpl 1592
SocketImplFactory 1604
Stack 1606
StackOverflowError 1610
StreamCorruptedException 1612
StreamTokenizer 1614
String 1632
StringBuffer 1655
StringBufferInputStream 1665
StringCharacterIterator 1671
StringIndexOutOfBoundsException 1688
StringReader 1690
StringTokenizer 1697
StringWriter 1703
SyncFailedException 1708
System 1710

Thread 1723
ThreadDeath 1750
ThreadGroup 1751
Throwable 1769
TimeZone 1774
TooManyListenersException 1787

UnknownError 1790
UnknownHostException 1792
UnknownServiceException 1794
UnsatisfiedLinkError 1796
UnsupportedEncodingException 1798
URL 1800
URLConnection 1819
URLEncoder 1849
URLStreamHandler 1852
URLStreamHandlerFactory 1857
UTFDataFormatException 1860

Vector 1862
VerifyError 1878
VirtualMachineError 1880
Void 1882

WriteAbortedException 1883
Writer 1887

ZipEntry 1892
ZipException 1904
ZipFile 1906
ZipInputStream 1914
ZipOutputStream 1920

List of Figures

Package Overviews

Figure 1: Composing IO Streams. 4
Figure 2: Object Serialization and Deserialization. 4
Figure 3: `Socket` and `ServerSocket`. 23
Figure 4: Use of `URL` and `URLConnection` to Access Web Services. 24
Figure 5: Object Formatting and String Parsing. 27
Figure 6: User Characters. 28

Alphabetical Reference of Classes

Figure 7: A Rounded Big Decimal Value. 75
Figure 8: Simple Stack-Based Calculator. 77
Figure 9: `BitSet.set()`. 142
Figure 10: `Character` boundary. 150
Figure 11: User characters. 152
Figure 12: The Four Break Iterators. 157
Figure 13: Japanese Break Iterators. 160
Figure 14: Line Break Iterator. 166
Figure 15: `BufferedReader`. 191
Figure 16: `ByteArrayInputStream`. 216
Figure 17: `ByteArrayOutputStream`. 224
Figure 18: `Calendar`. 238
Figure 19: `UnicodeViewer`.. 256
Figure 20: Infinitely Long Contiguous Calendar. 277
Figure 21: `CharacterIterator`. 305
Figure 22: `CharArrayReader`. 315
Figure 23: `CharArrayWriter`. 323
Figure 24: `ChoiceFormat` pattern. 347
Figure 25: Breaking up a Number Line into Ranges. 348
Figure 26: Number Line for `ChoiceFormat` Pattern with Six Limits. 351

Figure 27: Number Line for ChoiceFormat with Seven Limits. 352
Figure 28: Number Line of ChoiceFormat For Singular and Plural Choices. 354
Figure 29: Examples of Classes. 365
Figure 30: A File System-Based ClassLoader and a Network-Based ClassLoader. 413
Figure 31: Unicast DatagramSocket. 506
Figure 32: DataOutputStream and DataInputStream. 534
Figure 33: DataOutputStream and DataInputStream. 552
Figure 34: DateFormatSymbols. 614
Figure 35: DecimalFormat format() and parse() Methods. 626
Figure 36: DecimalFormat. 627
Figure 37: Localized and Nonlocalized Patterns. 631
Figure 38: DecimalFormatSymbols. 667
Figure 39: setDigit(). 674
Figure 40: DeflaterOutputStream. 695
Figure 41: Dictionary. 703
Figure 42: Event Source, Event Object, and Event Listeners. 729
Figure 43: Event Source, Event Object, and Event Listeners. 731
Figure 44: Externalization and Restoration of an Object. 743
Figure 45: FieldPosition. 774
Figure 46: Directory Browser. 784
Figure 47: FileInputStream. 807
Figure 48: FileOutputStream. 821
Figure 49: FileReader. 827
Figure 50: FileWriter. 830
Figure 51: FilterInputStream. 834
Figure 52: FilterOutputStream. 842
Figure 53: FilterReader. 847
Figure 54: FilterWriter. 855
Figure 55: Formatting and parsing. 872
Figure 56: GZIPInputStream. 896
Figure 57: GZIPOutputStream. 902
Figure 58: Thumbnail Image Viewer Using GZIPOutputStream. 903
Figure 59: Hashtable. 913
Figure 60: InflaterInputStream. 976
Figure 61: InputStream. 983
Figure 62: InputStreamReader. 990
Figure 63: Reading UTF-8 from a File. 992
Figure 64: LineNumberReader. 1040
Figure 65: The Components of a Locale. 1054

Figure 66: MessageFormat. 1102
Figure 67: ObjectInputStream and ObjectOutputStream. 1230
Figure 68: ObjectInputStream and ObjectOutputStream. 1262
Figure 69: Observable and Observer Objects. 1290
Figure 70: Observable and Observer Objects. 1296
Figure 71: OutputStream and FilterOutputStream. 1304
Figure 72: OutputStreamWriter. 1308
Figure 73: ParsePosition. 1317
Figure 74: PipedInputStream and PipedOutputStream. 1323
Figure 75: PipedInputStream and PipedOutputStream. 1332
Figure 76: PipedReader and PipedWriter. 1337
Figure 77: PipedReader and PipedWriter. 1342
Figure 78: PrintStream. 1346
Figure 79: PrintWriter. 1354
Figure 80: Communicating with a Process through Standard IO. 1363
Figure 81: PushbackInputStream. 1383
Figure 82: How Bytes Are Pushed Back. 1384
Figure 83: How Characters Are Pushed Back. 1392
Figure 84: Reader. 1426
Figure 85: Rules Containing a Reset Character. 1449
Figure 86: SequenceInputStream. 1503
Figure 87: Object Serialization and Deserialization. 1508
Figure 88: Required Data and Optional Data. 1509
Figure 89: Socket (a) and ServerSocket (b). 1515
Figure 90: “Talk” Program. 1517
Figure 91: Socket and ServerSocket. 1572
Figure 92: Mail Notifier. 1575
Figure 93: Stack. 1606
Figure 94: StreamTokenizer. 1614
Figure 95: StringBuffer. 1655
Figure 96: StringCharacterIterator. 1671
Figure 97: Using StringCharacterIterator. 1674
Figure 98: StringReader. 1690
Figure 99: StringTokenizer. 1697
Figure 100: StringWriter. 1703
Figure 101: Thread Viewer. 1726
Figure 102: ThreadGroup. 1751
Figure 103: Thread Group Viewer. 1753
Figure 104: Threadgroup.suspend(). 1765

Figure 105: Travel Clock. 1777
Figure 106: Use of URL and URLConnection to Access Web Services. 1801
Figure 107: URL.getContent(). 1808
Figure 108: URLConnection. 1819
Figure 109: URLEncoder. 1850
Figure 110: Writer and FilterWriter. 1887
Figure 111: ZipFile and ZipEntry. 1906
Figure 112: ZIP File Viewer. 1907
Figure 113: ZipInputStream. 1914
Figure 114: ZipOutputStream. 1920

List of Tables

Package Overviews

Table 1: Locale-Sensitive Classes. 28

Alphabetical Reference of Classes

Table 2: Valid Array Types for the Get Methods. 48
Table 3: Valid Array Types for the Set Methods. 48
Table 4: Sign Bits in the Two's Complement and Their Minimal Representations. 100
Table 5: Values of Month and Day-of-Week Constants. 234
Table 6: Steps to Follow when Updating Calendar Fields. 270
Table 7: Unicode Category Types. 289
Table 8: Unicode Digit Characters. 291
Table 9: Ignorable Characters for Java and Unicode Identifiers. 292
Table 10: Ranges in a `ChoiceFormat` Pattern. 349
Table 11: Converting Symbols to `ChoiceFormat` Symbols. 349
Table 12: Format Variable Assignments. 354
Table 13: Type Descriptors of Primitive Types. 366
Table 14: Examples of Type Descriptors of Primitive Type Arrays. 367
Table 15: Examples of Type Descriptors of Class and Interface Arrays. 367
Table 16: Primitive Types and Their Wrapper Classes and Class Objects. 368
Table 17: Class Objects for Java Primitive Types. 403
Table 18: Ordering Strength for Latin-Based Languages. 448
Table 19: Getting a `Constructor` from a `Class` Object. 475
Table 20: Styles for Date and Time Formats. 582
Table 21: The Local Pattern Characters. 611
Table 22: Elements of the zoneStrings Array. 613
Table 23: Symbols Used with `DecimalFormat` Objects. 630
Table 24: Symbols in the U.S. English `DecimalFormatSymbols` Object. 665
Table 25: Getting a `Field` from a `Class` Object. 749
Table 26: Valid Field Types for the Get Methods. 751
Table 27: Valid Field Types for the Set Methods. 751
Table 28: HTTP Request Method Tokens. 924
Table 29: HTTP Response Codes. 925

Table 30: Methods That Throw an `IllegalThreadStateException`. 951
Table 31: Predefined Locales and Their Codes. 1056
Table 32: Valid Modifiers for Member Object Types. 1095
Table 33: Methods for Creating `Method` Objects. 1123
Table 34: Valid Modifiers for Java Entities. 1143
Table 35: Java System Properties. 1371
Table 36: Pattern Letters for the `SimpleDateFormat` Class. 1542
Table 37: Pattern Examples Using the U.S. Locale. 1543
Table 38: Syntactic Elements of a Stream Tokenizer. 1614
Table 39: Mapping of Escaped Character Sequences to a `char` Value. 1625
Table 40: Character to Byte Encoding Identifiers. 1639
Table 41: Byte to Character Encoding Identifiers. 1648
Table 42: Java System Properties. 1711
Table 43: Time Zone IDs and their Raw Offsets from GMT. 1775
Table 44: HTTP Request Header Fields. 1821
Table 45: HTTP Response Header Fields. 1822
Table 46: `ZipEntry` Properties. 1892

Preface

How to Use This Book

This book is intended as a reference rather than a tutorial. Its format is similar to a dictionary's in that it is designed to optimize the time it takes for you to look up information on a class or class member. For a tutorial-style presentation of the class libraries, see *The Java™ Tutorial*, by Mary Campione and Kathy Walrath. *The Java™ Class Libraries* does not explain any part of the Java language. There are several books you can use to learn the language. These include *The Java™ Programming Language*, by Ken Arnold and James Gosling, and *The Java™ Language Specification*, by James Gosling, Bill Joy, and Guy Steele.

Following is an overview of this book.

Package Overviews

This part briefly describes each package and all of the classes in it. Also included are diagrams that show the inheritance hierarchy of the classes that appear in a package.

Alphabetical Reference of Classes

This part covers the alphabetical listing of the classes from the following packages:

```
java.io
java.lang
java.lang.reflect
java.math
java.net
java.text
java.util
java.util.zip
```

Probably the most notable aspect about the structure of this book is the order in which the classes appear. Most Java books that contain an API alphabetically order the classes within a package and then alphabetically order the packages. The problem with this format is that it always takes two or more steps to locate a class. If you do not know which package contains the class you're looking for, you basically need to review each package looking for the class. If you do know which package, you first need to find the package and then find the class.

The classes in this book are ordered alphabetically without regard to package name. This makes looking up a class as straightforward as looking up a word in a dictionary.

Each class is described in its own chapter. Each chapter contains a picture of the class hierarchy, a class description, a class example, a member summary, and descriptions for every member in the class.

Class Hierarchy Diagrams

We include a class diagram for each class in the Java API. The class diagram shows all of the ancestors of the class, its siblings, its immediate descendents, and any interfaces that the class implements. In these diagrams, if a package name precedes a class or interface name, the class or interface is not in the same package as the current class.

In the diagrams, we visually distinguish the different kinds of Java entities, as follows:

1. The interface: A rounded rectangle
2. The class: A rectangle
3. The abstract class: A rectangle with an empty dot
4. The final class: A rectangle with a black dot
5. Classes with subclasses: A rectangle with a small black triangle on the lower right corner

Most of these elements are shown in Figure i. The class or interface being described in the current chapter is shaded grey. A solid line represents `extends`, while a dotted line represents `implements`.

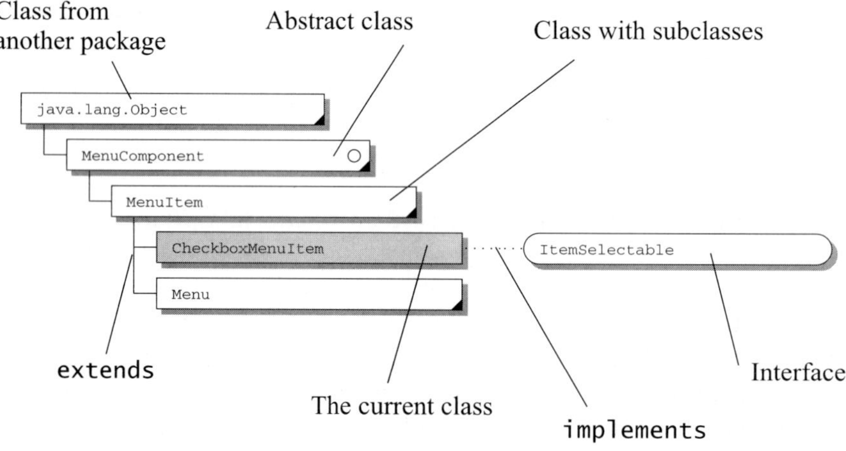

FIGURE i: Class Hierarchy Diagram.

Class Descriptions

In the class descriptions, we describe all of the properties of the class. For example, the properties of the `Graphics` class include the current color, font, paint mode, origin, and clipping area. Describing in one place all of a class's available properties and how the properties behave makes learning all of the capabilities of a class much easier than if the property descriptions were scattered throughout the member descriptions.

Any terminology used in the member descriptions is introduced and described in the class descriptions. If you find that the member description lacks detail, go to the class description for more information.

Class Examples

Ideally, we would have included a unique example for every single member in the Java API. We simply did not have enough time. So we tried to make sure that every member appeared in at least one example.

We worked to make the examples as useful as possible so that they demonstrate the member as it would typically be used. For example, in the example for a button we not only show how a button is created; we also show how button events are handled. In some cases, we also try to demonstrate some other class in the Java API. For example, in the `Graphics.drawOval()` example, we demonstrate not only how to draw an oval; we also show how to use the `BufferedReader` class to read integers from standard input that are used to locate the oval. We feel that gently introducing other classes in the Java API is a good way to help you become aware of all available classes in the Java API, as long as the introduction does not confuse the example.

Member Summaries

The Member Summary section for each class is intended to help the reader quickly grasp the key points of the class. It groups the members of the class into categories that are specific to that class. For example, in the `List` class the Selection Methods category lists all methods having to do with selections. It is meant to be a quick summary of the class's members, so it does not contain any syntax information other than the name of the member.

Member Descriptions

The member descriptions appear in alphabetical order within a class chapter regardless of what kind of method or field they are. This was done to make locating a member proceed as fast as possible.

Overloaded methods are placed together in one member description because they share very similar functionality. The different overloaded forms are typically provided as a convenience for the programmer when specifying parameters. For instance, some overloads eliminate parameters by providing common defaults. To describe overloads with missing parameters, we use a phrase of the form "if the parameter `p` is not specified, it defaults to the value `3.14`." Other overloads take different representations of a value. For example, one overload could take a particular parameter as an integer, while another could take the same parameter as a string containing an integer.

Each member description contains some or all of the following fields:

PURPOSE	A brief description of the purpose of this member
SYNTAX	The syntactic declaration of this member

DESCRIPTION	A full description of this member
PARAMETERS	The parameters accepted by this member, if any, listed in alphabetical order
RETURNS	The value and its range returned by this member, if any
EXCEPTIONS	The exceptions and errors thrown by this member, if any, listed in alphabetical order
SEE ALSO	Other related classes or members, if any, listed in alphabetical order
OVERRIDES	The method that this member overrides, if any
EXAMPLE	A code example that illustrates how this member is used. This is sometimes a reference to an example that illustrates the use of this method in another member example or class example.

Deprecation

A method or class is *deprecated* if its use is no longer recommended. A deprecated method appears in the Member Summary under the Deprecated Methods section. In the chapter body, the deprecated method is annotated by a "deprecated" tag in its method heading. For example, `Component.size()` is a deprecated method. It has the following method heading:

size() *DEPRECATED*

If not all of the overloaded forms of the method are deprecated, a "deprecated" tag appears beside the syntax of the deprecated forms. For example, one of the two forms of `BorderLayout.addLayoutComponent()` is deprecated. The second form shown below—the one with the "deprecated" tag—is deprecated.

SYNTAX
```
            public void addLayoutComponent(Component comp, Object location)
DEPRECATED  public void addLayoutComponent(String location, Component comp)
```

The method description contains a deprecation section with instructions on how to replace the usage of the deprecated method, like this:

DEPRECATION	A description of how to replace the usage of this deprecated method

How to Access the Examples

All of the code examples in this book have been compiled and run on the FCS version of Java 1.1.4, either on Solaris or Windows NT or both. Most of the complete examples are available on-line. You can access them and other information about this book by using the URL

```
http://java.sun.com/books/Series
```

Conventions Used in This Book

`Lucida Sans Typewriter` is used for examples, syntax declarations, class names, method names, values, and field names. *Italic* is used when defining a new term and for emphasis.

Acknowledgments

We want to thank the many people who made this book possible.

Mike Hendrickson, the Executive Editor for this book, helped coordinate the many tasks and people needed to complete this book.

Lisa Friendly, the series editor, was relentless in garnering reviewers for this book and providing all kinds of cheerful assistance.

The accuracy and quality of this book were improved immensely as the result of the astonishingly thorough reviews by the following individuals: Steve Byrne, John Rose, Joshua Bloch, Joseph Fialli, and Roger Riggs. Other reviewers who gave us helpful feedback include Calvin Austin, David Connelly, Li Gong, Brian Preston, Mark Reinhold, Nakul Saraiya, Roland Schemers, and Kathy Walrath.

Laura Michaels persevered through over 1,900 pages of manuscript under tremendous time pressure to improve the readability of this book. Sarah Weaver, Rosemary Simpson, Tracy Russ, Marina Lang, and Jason Jones all played a part in the production of this book and were wonderful to work with.

Patrick Chan
Rosanna Lee
Palo Alto, California
December, 1997

I have many people to thank for supporting me in contributing the `java.text` package to this book.

First, my co-authors, Patrick and Rosanna, flattered me by asking me to contribute to this book. I considered their previous edition to be the very best reference available on the Java API, bar none. So I feel very fortunate and honored to add to their accomplishments.

Lisa Friendly is my manager at JavaSoft and has fully supported not only my efforts at work, but also this extracurricular project to dig in and really learn Java. You couldn't ask for a more supportive and encouraging manager. Thank you, Lisa.

The Internationalization team helped improve the quality of this book immeasurably. Mark Davis of the Unicode Consortium personally contributed time, words, and instruction. The Taligent team, headed up by Mark, provided very detailed and constructive feedback. This includes Alan Liu, Helena Shih, Rich Gillam, and Laura Werner. The JavaSoft engineers also helped at key times, giving direction and answering questions: Brian Beck, Norbert Lindenberg, John O'Conner, and our tester, Cindy Cjao.

Some Japanese text was contributed by Etsuko Ishida. French translations were provided by Isabelle and Lionel Gilet. Writing is a very detailed, exacting, and laborious task. Lady, my precious dog, and those to whom I have dedicated the book have been my joy throughout these exhausting times.

I also thank Mike Hendrickson and the same production team that Patrick and Rosanna have mentioned previously.

Lastly, the other book authors in my family: my father and mother, Chuck and Jan. They have inspired me to be the best I can be, both in love and at work.

Douglas Kramer
Palo Alto, California
December, 1997

java.io

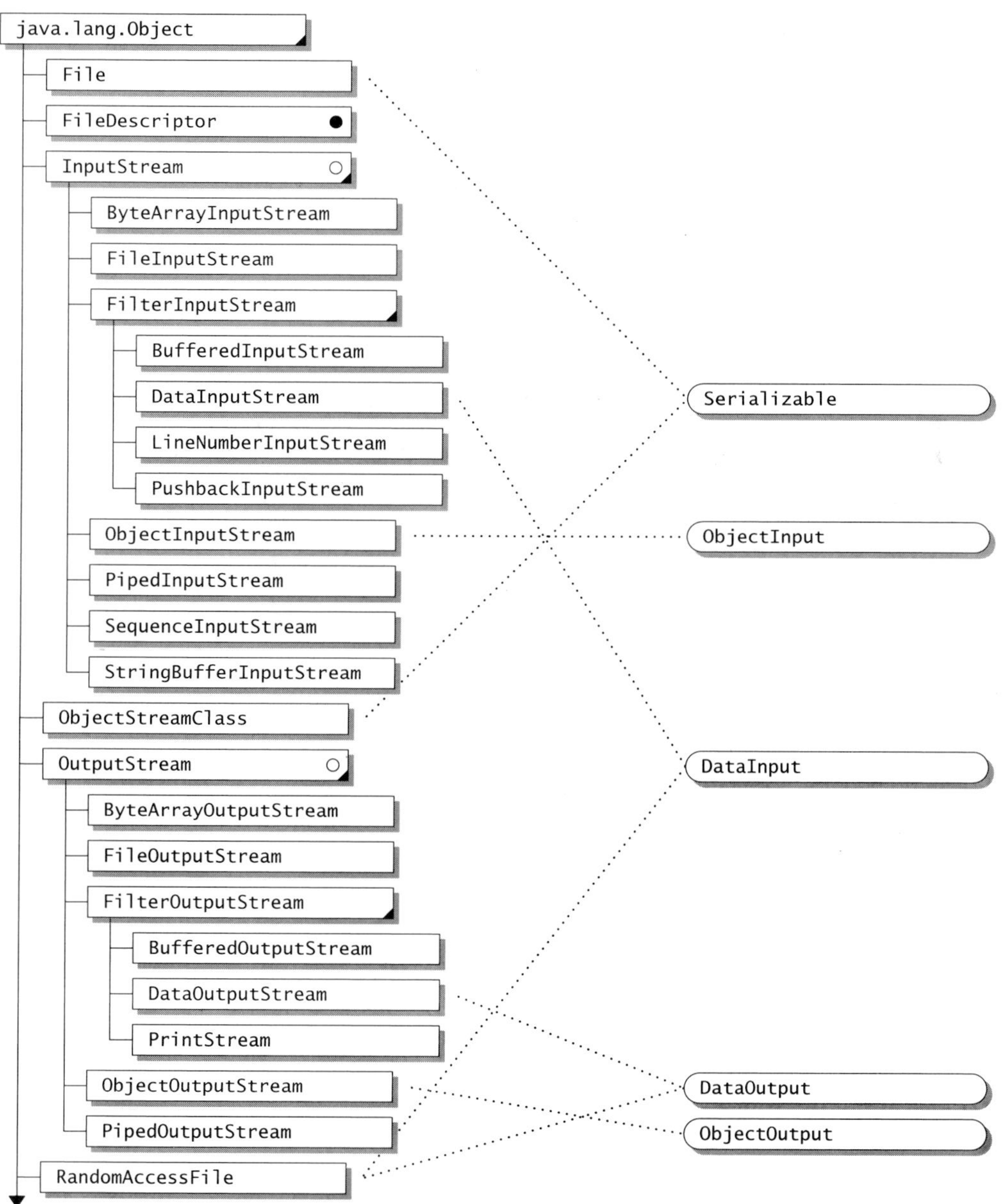
java.lang.Object
File
FileDescriptor
InputStream
ByteArrayInputStream
FileInputStream
FilterInputStream
BufferedInputStream
DataInputStream
LineNumberInputStream
PushbackInputStream
ObjectInputStream
PipedInputStream
SequenceInputStream
StringBufferInputStream
ObjectStreamClass
OutputStream
ByteArrayOutputStream
FileOutputStream
FilterOutputStream
BufferedOutputStream
DataOutputStream
PrintStream
ObjectOutputStream
PipedOutputStream
RandomAccessFile
Serializable
ObjectInput
DataInput
DataOutput
ObjectOutput

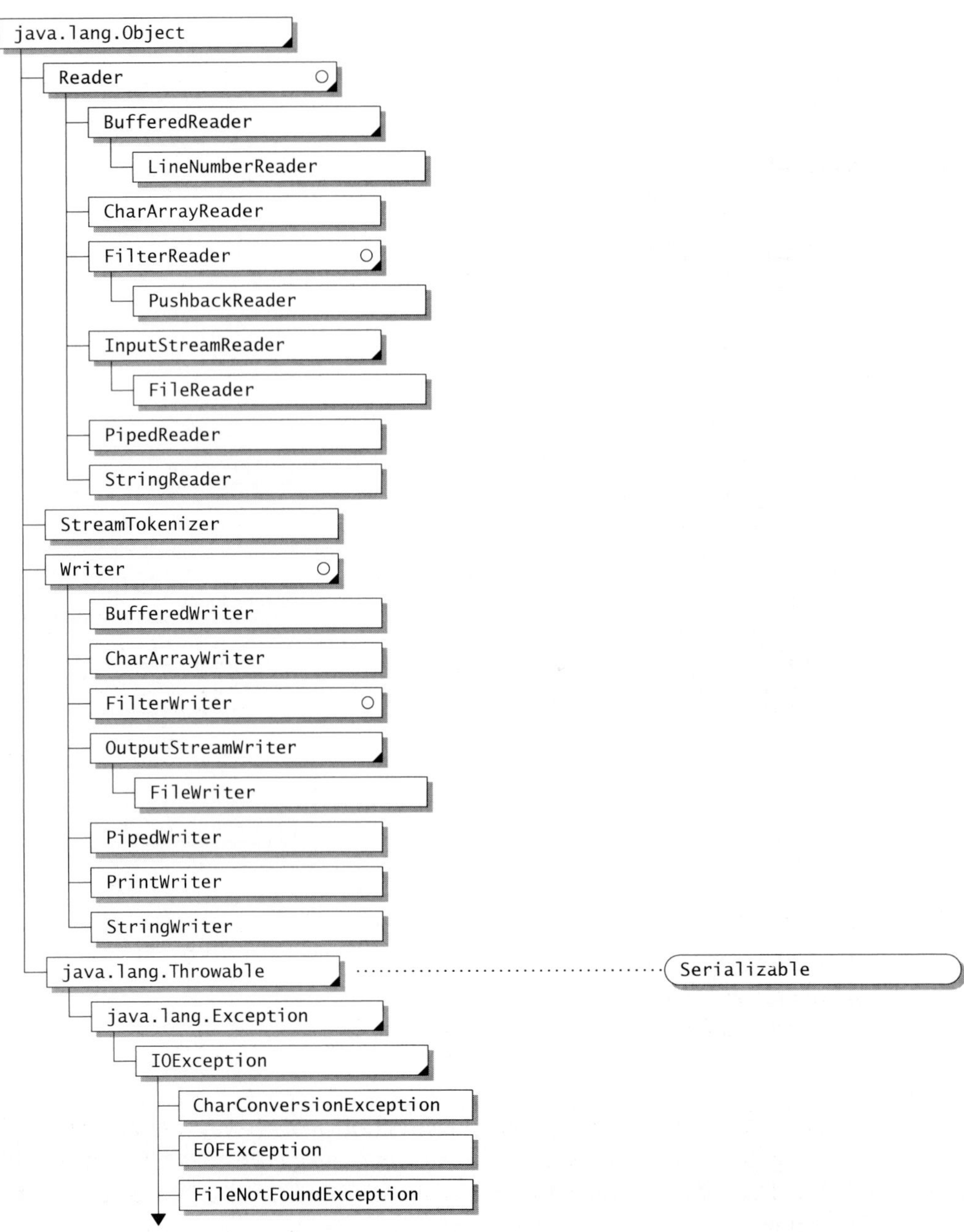
java.lang.Object
Reader
BufferedReader
LineNumberReader
CharArrayReader
FilterReader
PushbackReader
InputStreamReader
FileReader
PipedReader
StringReader
StreamTokenizer
Writer
BufferedWriter
CharArrayWriter
FilterWriter
OutputStreamWriter
FileWriter
PipedWriter
PrintWriter
StringWriter
java.lang.Throwable
Serializable
java.lang.Exception
IOException
CharConversionException
EOFException
FileNotFoundException

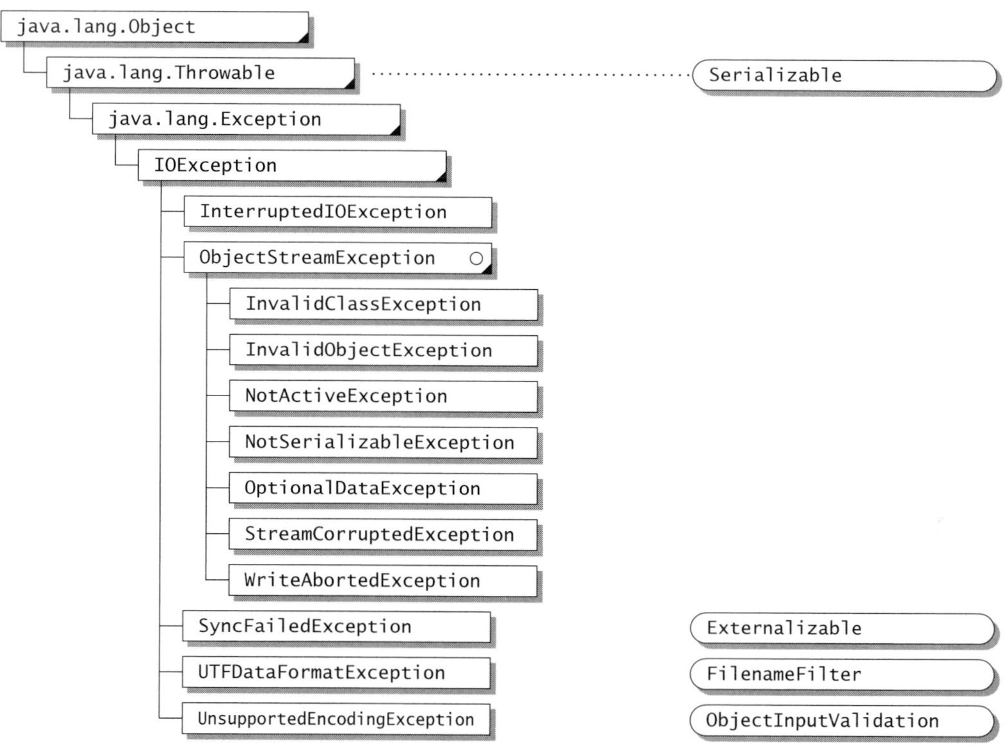

Description

This package contains three main groups of classes and interfaces:

- Classes for building data streams
- Classes and interfaces for serialization
- Classes and interfaces for dealing with the file system

Data Streams

A data stream is either an *input* stream for reading values from a data source, such as an HTTP server or a Java string, or an *output* stream for writing values to a data repository such as a file or an array of bytes. The data can be bytes or characters. The `java.io` package contains separate classes for dealing with byte streams and character streams. It also has classes for converting between byte streams and character streams.

A data container such as a file typically provides a method that returns an input stream for reading its contents or an output stream for storing values to it. These streams can be composed to form a chain of streams through which data flows and can be transformed by each stream. For example, after an input stream is obtained for a file, a data input stream could be added that transforms a stream of bytes into higher-level Java types, such as strings and integers, as shown in Figure 1.

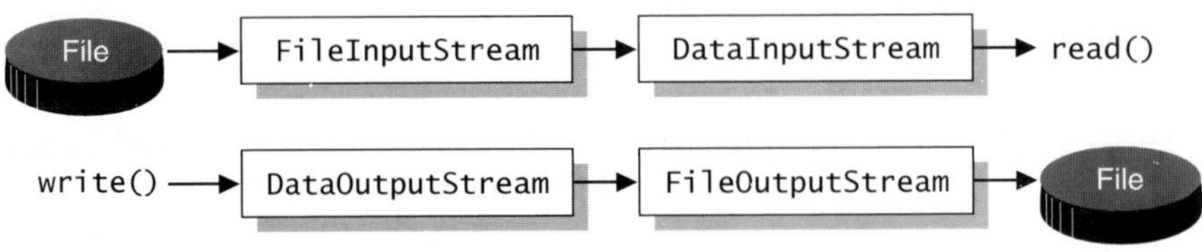

FIGURE 1: Composing IO Streams.

Serialization

To serialize an object means to convert its state into a byte stream in such a way that the byte stream can be restored into a copy of the object. Not all objects can be serialized. An object that can be serialized is *serializable*. A Java object is serializable if its class or any of its superclasses implement the `Serializable` interface or its subinterface `Externalizable`.

Deserialization is the process of converting the serialized form of an object into a copy of the object.

Data values that are of Java primitive types, arrays, strings, and objects can all be serialized. Figure 2 shows how object serialization and deserialization works. Primitive types can be serialized/deserialized by using methods in the `DataInputStream`/`DataOutputStream` classes.

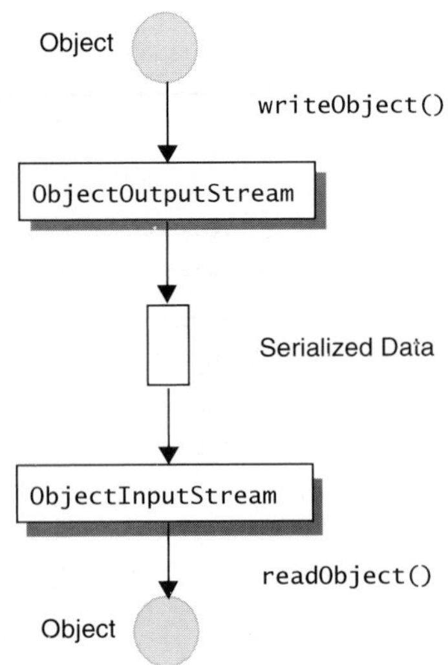

FIGURE 2: Object Serialization and Deserialization.

Files

The `java.io` package also contains classes for operating on files, such as creating and removing files, in a platform-independent way. Data in files can be treated as bytes or characters.

Class and Interface Summary

Superclasses

The following abstract classes define a minimum set of operations that a stream must implement. `InputStream` and `OutputStream` are for byte streams, while `Reader` and `Writer` are for character streams.

`InputStream`	The superclass of all byte input streams. Provides basic input methods for reading data from a byte stream.
`OutputStream`	The superclass of all byte output streams. Provides basic output methods for writing data to a byte stream.
`Reader`	The superclass of all character input streams. Provides basic input methods for reading characters from a character stream.
`Writer`	The superclass of all character output streams. Provides basic output methods for writing characters to a character stream.

Byte Stream-to-Character Stream Converters

The following classes allow a program to convert a byte stream into a character stream.

`InputStreamReader`	Reads bytes from a byte stream and converts them into characters.
`OutputStreamWriter`	Converts characters to a byte encoding and writes them to a byte stream.

Filter Streams

Filter streams perform some "processing," or "filtering," as data is passed through them. A filter output stream performs processing on the data *before* it is written to its eventual destination, while a filter input stream performs processing on the data *after* reading it from its original source. `FilterInputStream` and `FilterOutputStream` are for byte streams, while `FilterReader` and `FilterWriter` are for character streams.

`FilterInputStream`	The superclass of all byte input filter streams.
`FilterOutputStream`	The superclass of all byte output filter streams.
`FilterReader`	The superclass of all character input filter streams.
`FilterWriter`	The superclass of all character output filter streams.

Buffered Streams

Buffered streams are filter streams that *buffer* the data that flows through them in order to improve the performance of small read and write operations. `BufferedInputStream` and `BufferedOutputStream` are for byte streams, while `BufferedReader` and `BufferedWriter` are for character streams.

`BufferedInputStream`	A filter input stream that maintains a buffer of bytes read from the original input stream.
`BufferedOutputStream`	A filter output stream that maintains a buffer of bytes to be written to its destination output stream.
`BufferedReader`	A filter input stream that maintains a buffer of characters read from the original character input stream.
`BufferedWriter`	A filter output stream that maintains a buffer of characters to be written to its destination character output stream.

Files

The following classes provide file-related operations available in Java. `FileInputStream` and `FileOutputStream` are for reading/writing bytes to files, while `FileReader` and `FileWriter` are for reading/writing characters to files. The `RandomAccessFile` class allows random access to the contents of a file.

`File`	Represents a file that has methods for operating on a file.
`FileDescriptor`	Represents a handle to an open file.
`FileInputStream`	A filter input stream for reading bytes from a file.
`FileOutputStream`	A filter output stream for writing bytes to a file.
`FilenameFilter`	An interface for defining selection criteria for a list of filenames.
`FileReader`	A filter input stream for reading characters from a file.
`FileWriter`	A filter output stream for writing characters to a file.
`RandomAccessFile`	Used for accessing the contents of a file nonsequentially.

Serialization

The following classes are used to serialize (and deserialize) Java primitive data, arrays, strings, and objects in a compact binary form. They are typically used to save and retrieve values and objects in a file or exchange them via a network connection. The `DataInput`/`DataOutput`-related methods are for serializing/deserializing Java primitive types. The `ObjectInput`/`ObjectOutput`-related methods are for serializing/deserializing Java objects.

`DataInput`	An interface for deserializing Java primitive data.
`DataInputStream`	A filter input stream for deserializing Java primitive data.
`DataOutput`	An interface for serializing Java primitive data.
`DataOutputStream`	A filter output stream for serializing Java primitive data.
`Externalizable`	An interface to indicate that instances of a class can be serialized into a class-specific "external" format.
`ObjectInput`	An interface for deserializing Java primitive data and objects.
`ObjectInputStream`	An input stream for deserializing Java primitive data and objects.
`ObjectInputValidation`	An interface for validating a deserialized object.
`ObjectStreamClass`	Represents a class descriptor.
`ObjectOutput`	An interface for serializing Java primitive data and objects.
`ObjectOutputStream`	An output stream for serializing Java primitive data and objects.
`Serializable`	An interface to indicate that instances of a class can be serialized.

In-Memory Streams

The following classes use in-memory data structures as IO streams.

`ByteArrayInputStream`	An input stream that reads data from a `byte` array.
`ByteArrayOutputStream`	An output stream that writes its data to a `byte` array.
`CharArrayReader`	An input stream that reads data from a `char` array.
`CharArrayWriter`	An output stream that writes its data to a `char` array.
`StringReader`	An input stream that reads data from a `StringBuffer`.
`StringWriter`	An output stream that writes its data to a `StringBuffer`.

Pipes

The following two pairs of classes can be used to create a stream of data between two threads. Such a stream of data is called a *pipe*. One thread can write into one end of the pipe, while the other thread can read from the other end of the pipe. `PipedInputStream` and `PipedOutputStream` are for byte streams, while `PipedReader` and `PipedWriter` are for character streams.

`PipedInputStream`	An input stream for reading bytes from a pipe.
`PipedOutputStream`	An output stream for writing bytes to a pipe.
`PipedReader`	An input stream for reading input from a pipe.
`PipedWriter`	An output stream for writing output to a pipe.

Streams for Parsing

The following classes are useful when building parsers.

`PushbackInputStream`	A filter input stream that allows bytes to be unread from the stream.
`PushbackReader`	A filter input stream that allows characters to be unread from the stream.
`StreamTokenizer`	A filter input stream for parsing the stream into a sequence of tokens.

Input Stream Sequence

The following class is used to combine a sequence of input streams into a single input stream. When one input stream is exhausted, the class seamlessly starts reading from the next input stream.

`SequenceInputStream`	Creates a single input stream from two or more input streams.

Miscellaneous Filter Streams

The following classes implement various useful streams.

`LineNumberReader`	A buffered character input stream for counting the number of lines.
`PrintStream`	A filter output stream for converting Java primitive types and objects to a printable form.
`PrintWriter`	A character output stream for converting Java primitive types and objects to a printable form.

Serialization-Related Exceptions

The following are the serialization-related exceptions declared in this package. They are not subclasses of `RuntimeException`, so they must be either caught or declared in the `throws` clause.

`InvalidClassException`	Thrown if a problem related to the class of object being serialized/deserialized occurs.
`InvalidObjectException`	Thrown if validation of the deserialized object fails.

`NotActiveException`	Thrown if certain methods in `ObjectInputStream`/`ObjectOutputStream` are invoked when an object is not being serialized/deserialized.
`NotSerializableException`	Thrown if trying to serialize an object that does not implement the `Serializable` or `Externalizable` interface.
`ObjectStreamException`	The superclass of serialization-related exceptions.
`OptionalDataException`	Thrown if unexpected data is encountered in the serialization stream.
`StreamCorruptedException`	Thrown if data in the serialization stream does not match its associated control data.
`WriteAbortedException`	Thrown when the stream indicates that it contains incomplete serialization data because the writer aborted the serialization process.

All Other IO Exceptions

The following are the nonserialization-related exceptions declared in this package. They are not subclasses of `RuntimeException`, so they must be either caught or declared in the `throws` clause.

`CharConversionException`	Thrown if the byte-to-character or character-to-byte conversion fails.
`EOFException`	Thrown if end-of-file has been reached when reading from a data input stream.
`FileNotFoundException`	Thrown if attempting to access a nonexistent file.
`IOException`	The superclass of the other IO exceptions in this package.
`InterruptedIOException`	Thrown if a stream operation has been interrupted.
`SyncFailedException`	Thrown if the attempt to flush internal system buffers to the corresponding physical device has failed.
`UnsupportedEncodingException`	Thrown if the specified character-to-byte or byte-to-character encoding is not supported.
`UTFDataFormatException`	Thrown if a Unicode string in a malformed Unicode Transfer Format has been encountered.

Deprecated Classes

The following classes have been deprecated.

`LineNumberInputStream`	Replaced by `LineNumberReader`.
`StringBufferInputStream`	Replaced by `StringReader`.

java.lang

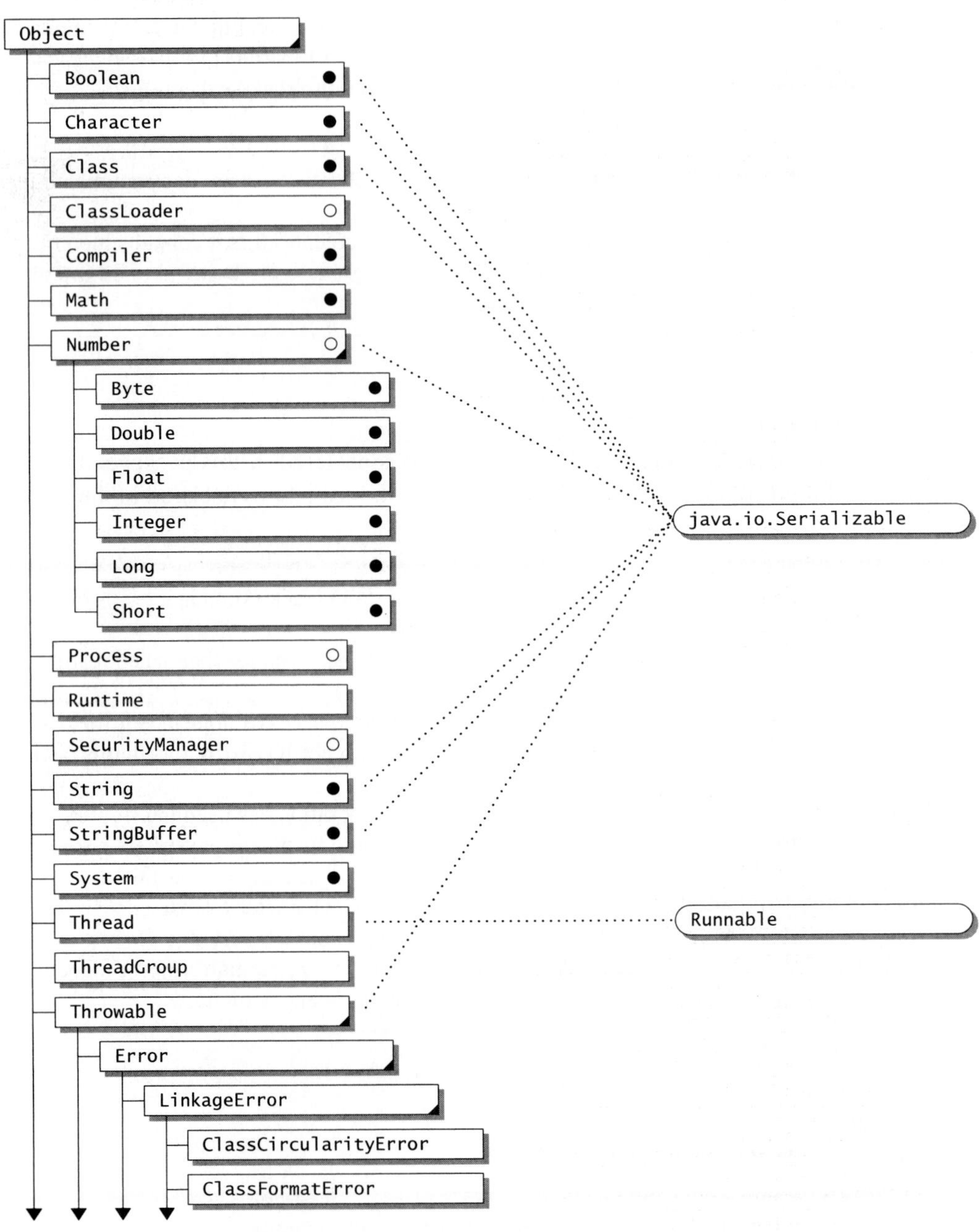
Object
Boolean
Character
Class
ClassLoader
Compiler
Math
Number
Byte
Double
Float
Integer
Long
Short
Process
Runtime
SecurityManager
String
StringBuffer
System
Thread
ThreadGroup
Throwable
Error
LinkageError
ClassCircularityError
ClassFormatError
java.io.Serializable
Runnable

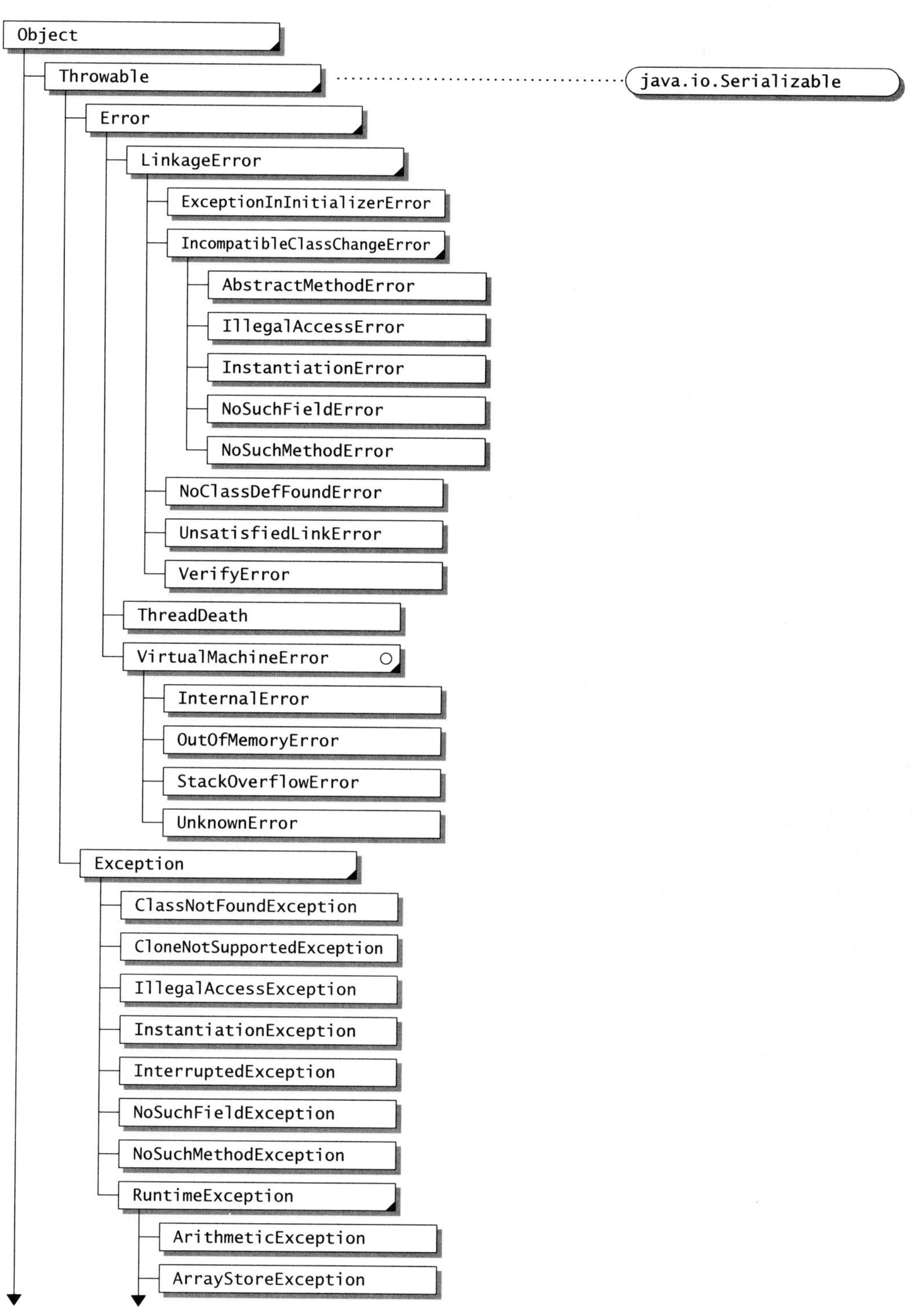
Object
Throwable
java.io.Serializable
Error
LinkageError
ExceptionInInitializerError
IncompatibleClassChangeError
AbstractMethodError
IllegalAccessError
InstantiationError
NoSuchFieldError
NoSuchMethodError
NoClassDefFoundError
UnsatisfiedLinkError
VerifyError
ThreadDeath
VirtualMachineError
InternalError
OutOfMemoryError
StackOverflowError
UnknownError
Exception
ClassNotFoundException
CloneNotSupportedException
IllegalAccessException
InstantiationException
InterruptedException
NoSuchFieldException
NoSuchMethodException
RuntimeException
ArithmeticException
ArrayStoreException

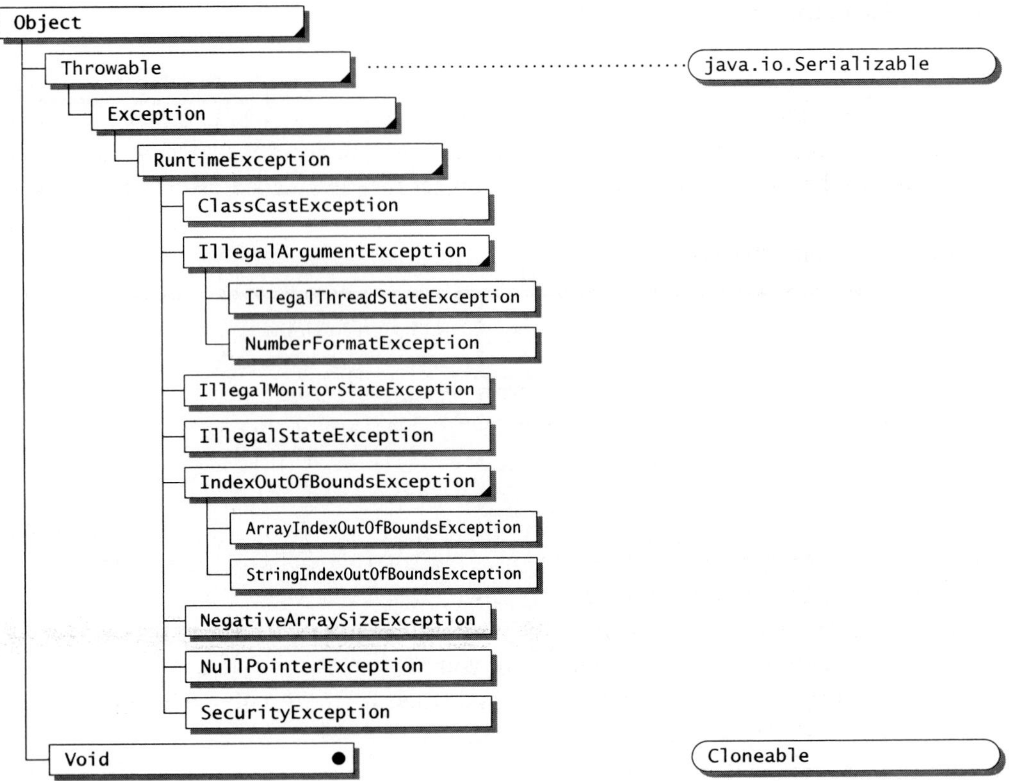

Description

This package contains classes that are integral to the Java language. These include `Object`, `Throwable`, `String`, and `Thread`. If any class in this package is missing, the runtime will not start. The classes in this package are automatically imported into every Java program, so there is no need to explicitly import them.

All errors and exceptions that can be thrown by the Java virtual machine appear in this package. Also included are classes for accessing system resources, primitive type object wrappers, a math class, and a security class.

Class and Interface Summary

Root Classes

The `Object` class is the superclass of all classes, so the methods defined in this class are inherited by all other classes. A `Class` object encapsulates information about a Java class that has been loaded into the system; there is one `Class` object for each loaded class. The `Throwable` class is the root of all Java errors and exceptions. A class that represents an error or an exception must inherit from `Throwable`.

`Class`	Used to obtain information about a Java class.
`Object`	The superclass of all Java objects.
`Throwable`	The superclass of all Java errors and exceptions.

Strings

The following classes provide Java's string manipulation capabilities. A `String` object is immutable. This means that any operation on it always results in a new `String` object, with the original object left intact. A `StringBuffer` object maintains an expandable sequence of characters and should be used in applications where you expect to modify a string a lot. In most applications, `String` objects are typically used and result in fewer programming errors. Consider using a `StringBuffer` object only if efficiency becomes an issue.

`String`	An immutable sequence of characters with lots of string-related operations.
`StringBuffer`	A mutable, expandable sequence of characters with lots of string-related operations.

Math

`Math`	A collection of mathematical operations for doing trigonometry, for rounding, and for finding logs and square roots.

System

The following classes are used to access system-related services such as the current time, processes, garbage collector, and memory management.

`ClassLoader`	Used to load Java classes and define loading policies.
`Process`	Used to obtain information about and communicate with processes spawned to execute system programs.
`Runtime`	Used to perform environment-related and system-related operations, such as loading libraries, executing system programs, and performing garbage collection.
`System`	Used to examine and manipulate system-related information such as the current time and system properties in a platform-independent manner. Contains fields for standard input, output, and error.

Threads

Threads allow a program to have multiple threads of execution occurring concurrently. The following classes provide the support for defining, creating, and manipulating Java threads.

`Runnable`	An interface that a class can implement to be runnable by a thread.
`Thread`	Used to define, create, and manipulate a thread.
`ThreadGroup`	Used to create and manipulate a set of threads.

Cloneable

The `Cloneable` interface is used by classes that want to support the `clone()` method. Unless a class implements this interface, an attempt to clone an object will result in a `CloneNotSupportedException` being thrown.

`Cloneable`	An interface that a class must implement in order to support the `clone()` method.

Primitive Type Wrappers

The following classes are used to work around the fact that primitive types such as `int` and `float` are not Java objects and that Java does not support templates. For example, classes that implement a data structure such as a tree or a hash table are typically implemented to handle objects so as to achieve maximal reusability. This means that a primitive type like `int` cannot be used with the class. When an `Integer` object is wrapped around an `int` value, the `int` value can then be used by the class. Of course, this introduces some overhead, so if efficiency is absolutely critical, you'll need to implement a version of the data structure specifically for the desired primitive type.

`Boolean`	An object wrapper for a `boolean` value.
`Byte`	An object wrapper for a `byte` value.
`Character`	An object wrapper for a `char` value.
`Double`	An object wrapper for a `double` value.
`Float`	An object wrapper for a `float` value.
`Integer`	An object wrapper for an `int` value.
`Long`	An object wrapper for a `long` value.
`Number`	The abstract superclass for the number objects (`Byte`, `Double`, `Float`, `Integer`, `Long`, `Short`, `BigDecimal`, and `BigInteger`).
`Short`	An object wrapper for a `short` value.
`Void`	Holds a reference to a `Class` object for `void`. Cannot be instantiated.

Security

The `SecurityManager` class is used to define the security policies of a Java application. It controls what a Java application or applet can and cannot do. It is typically used by an application that executes Java applets, such as a Web browser. It can be set once and cannot be removed. If an applet or application fails a security check, a `SecurityException` is thrown.

`SecurityException`	A runtime exception that is thrown when the program is denied access to perform an operation due to security reasons.
`SecurityManager`	Used to define the security policy for a Java program.

Compiler

The `Compiler` class is used to control a compiler that compiles Java byte codes directly into machine code for a particular platform. Such a compiler is not included in the Java development kit from Sun Microsystems and must be obtained from a third-party source.

`Compiler`	Used to compile Java byte codes into machine code.

Errors

A Java *error* is a type of exception thrown by the Java virtual machine to indicate that an unrecoverable erroneous condition has occurred. For example, an error would be thrown if there was an attempt to load a corrupted class.

`AbstractMethodError`	Thrown if attempting to invoke an abstract method.
`ClassCircularityError`	Thrown if attempting to load classes that have cyclic class inheritance.
`ClassFormatError`	Thrown if attempting to load a class that is not in an acceptable format.
`Error`	The superclass of all error classes.
`ExceptionInInitializerError`	Thrown if an exception is encountered in a static initializer.
`IllegalAccessError`	Thrown if attempting to access a member of a class to which it does not have access (such as a `protected` method).
`IncompatibleClassChangeError`	The superclass of errors that are thrown if attempting to access a member of a class in a way that violates Java language semantics.
`InstantiationError`	Thrown if attempting to instantiate an abstract class or an interface.
`InternalError`	Thrown if the Java virtual machine encounters an unrecoverable error that involves the virtual machine's internal logic.
`LinkageError`	The superclass of errors that result when attempting to load a class that has changed in an incompatible manner and consequently cannot be loaded.
`NoClassDefFoundError`	Thrown if the system's default class loader cannot find the class to load.
`NoSuchFieldError`	Thrown if attempting to access a nonexistent field of a class.
`NoSuchMethodError`	Thrown if attempting to access a nonexistent method of a class.

`OutOfMemoryError`	Thrown if the Java runtime runs out of memory and consequently cannot continue execution.
`StackOverflowError`	Thrown if the Java execution stack limit has been exceeded during the execution of a thread.
`ThreadDeath`	Thrown by the runtime to indicate that the current thread is about to be terminated.
`UnknownError`	Thrown if a condition that cannot be described by any other error has occurred.
`UnsatisfiedLinkError`	Thrown if a library cannot be loaded and linked successfully.
`VerifyError`	Thrown if a class cannot be loaded because it violates the Java byte code specification.
`VirtualMachineError`	The superclass of errors that are thrown if the Java virtual machine encounters an unrecoverable error, such as lack of memory or lack of stack size.

Runtime Exceptions

The following exceptions inherit from `RuntimeException`, so it is not necessary to catch them or declare them in a `throws` clause. However, exceptions of this type are considered programming bugs and should be corrected.

`ArithmeticException`	Thrown if attempting to perform an illegal arithmetic operation (such as division by zero).
`ArrayIndexOutOfBoundsException`	Thrown if attempting to access an array element with an index that is outside of the array bounds.
`ArrayStoreException`	Thrown if attempting to store an object of the wrong type in an array.
`ClassCastException`	Thrown if attempting to cast an object to an incompatible class.
`IllegalArgumentException`	Thrown if an illegal argument has been passed to a method.
`IllegalMonitorStateException`	Thrown if a thread calls an object's synchronized method but does not own the object's lock.
`IllegalStateException`	Thrown if invoking a method on an object while it is in an unsuitable state.
`IllegalThreadStateException`	Thrown if attempting to perform an operation on a thread while the thread is in a state unsuitable for that operation.

Continued

`IndexOutOfBoundsException`	The superclass of exceptions that are thrown when accessing an element with an index that is out of bounds.
`NegativeArraySizeException`	Thrown if attempting to create an array that has a negative size.
`NullPointerException`	Thrown if attempting to dereference a `null` reference.
`NumberFormatException`	Thrown if a string is not in a format that can be parsed into a number of the desired type.
`RuntimeException`	The superclass of all runtime exceptions that indicate a programming error.
`StringIndexOutOfBoundsException`	Thrown if attempting to access an element of a string using an index that is outside of the bounds of the string.

Exceptions

Thee following exceptions directly inherit from `Exception`, so they must be either caught or declared in the `throws` clause. Exceptions of this type typically indicate some error condition that can sometimes arise in an operation. For example, when loading a class the operation normally returns a reference to the class. However, if the class cannot be found, the `ClassNotFoundException` is raised. A program should catch this error, notify the user of the error, and then continue running.

`ClassNotFoundException`	Thrown if a class loader cannot find the class to load on explicit instructions from the program (rather than implicitly by the runtime, which loads classes as they are referenced).
`CloneNotSupportedException`	Thrown if attempting to clone an object that belongs to a class that does not implement the `Cloneable` interface.
`Exception`	The superclass used for representing exceptional conditions that must be caught.
`IllegalAccessException`	Thrown if not permitted to access a member of a class.
`InstantiationException`	Thrown if attempting to instantiate an abstract class or an interface.
`InterruptedException`	Thrown when a thread receives an interrupt invoked by another thread.
`NoSuchMethodException`	Thrown if attempting to access a nonexistent method of an object.
`NoSuchFieldException`	Thrown if attempting to access a nonexistent field of an object.

java.lang.reflect

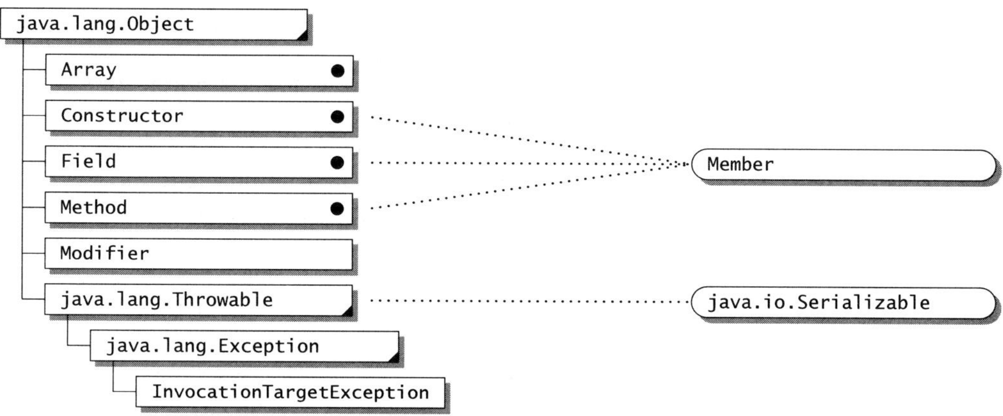

Description

This package provides classes and interfaces for obtaining *reflective* information about Java classes and objects. Reflective information includes information about the members that a class has, the signatures of a class's constructors and methods, and the types of its fields. With it, you also can create new objects, access and change an object's fields, and invoke an object's methods.

This package is typically used by programs such as debuggers, interpreters, object inspectors, and class browsers and by Java runtime services such as Object Serialization and JavaBeans.

Security

An application can get reflective information about a class or object only if it has been granted permission to do so by the security manager. If it does not have permission, a `SecurityException` is thrown. See `java.lang.SecurityManager.checkMemberAccess()`.

In addition, gaining access to reflective information does not automatically grant the holder of that information special privileges as far as the Java language is concerned. Specifically, the holder can access nonpublic members if, and only if, it was able to do so without using reflection.

Class and Interface Summary

Members

Instances of `Constructor`, `Field`, and `Method` are created only by the Java virtual machine. They are returned by methods in the `java.lang.Class`.

`Constructor`	Represents a constructor in a class.
`Field`	Represents a field in a class.
`Member`	The interface containing methods common to `Constructor`, `Field`, and `Method`.
`Method`	Represents a method in a class.

Utility Classes

The following classes are useful for dealing with Java arrays and modifiers.

`Array`	Used to create, access, and modify arrays. Cannot be instantiated.
`Modifier`	Used to decode the modifiers associated with a class and members of a class. Cannot be instantiated.

Exception

There is one exception declared in this package. It extends directly from `Exception`, so it must be either caught or declared in the `throws` clause.

`InvocationTargetException`	Thrown if the invoked method or constructor throws an exception.

java.math

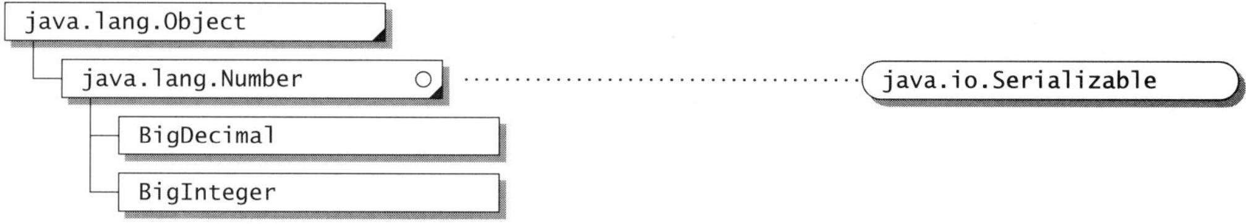

Description

This package contains classes for performing arithmetic and bit manipulation on arbitrary-precision decimal and integer numbers. `BigInteger` and `BigDecimal` are analogous to Java's primitive types—`double` and `long`, respectively—except `BigInteger` and `BigDecimal` have arbitrary precision. Hence, operations on them do not overflow or lose precision.

Class Summary

BigInteger

A `BigInteger` is represented in two's-complement notation. The class provides corresponding methods for all Java operations on `int` and `long`. The semantics of these operations are analogous to those of corresponding Java operations on `int` and `long`, except that operations on `BigInteger` do not overflow.

`BigInteger` also provides methods for modular arithmetic, GCD calculation, primality testing, prime generation, single-bit manipulation, and many methods corresponding to those in `java.lang.Math`.

`BigInteger`	Represents an arbitrary-precision integer.

BigDecimal

A `BigDecimal` represents an arbitrary-precision decimal number consisting of an arbitrary-precision integer value and a nonnegative integer *scale*. The scale represents the number of decimal digits to the right of the decimal point. This class provides operations for basic arithmetic, scale manipulation, comparison, format conversion, and hashing.

`BigDecimal`	Represents an arbitrary-precision decimal number.

java.net

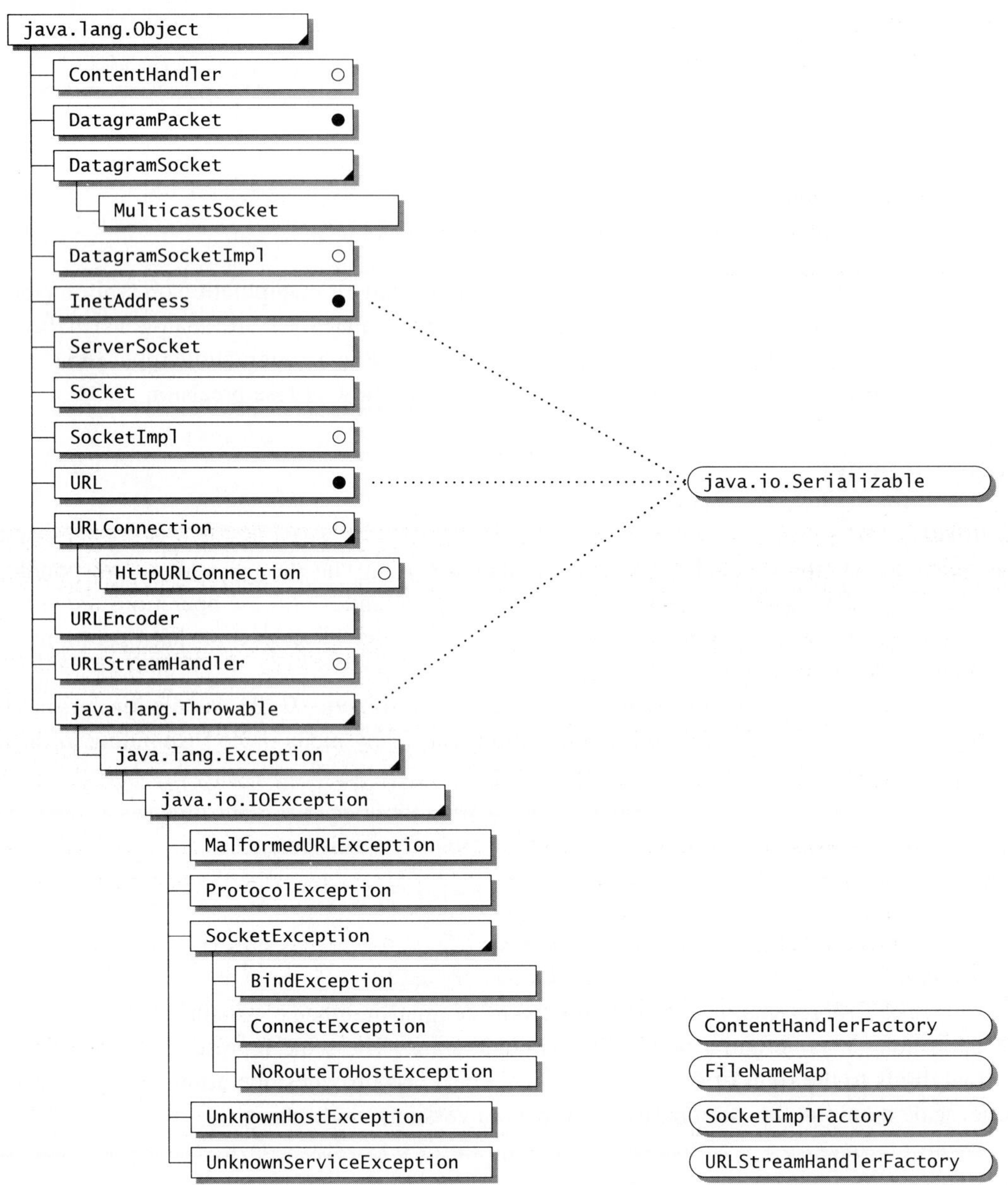

java.lang.Object
ContentHandler
DatagramPacket
DatagramSocket
MulticastSocket
DatagramSocketImpl
InetAddress
ServerSocket
Socket
SocketImpl
URL
URLConnection
HttpURLConnection
URLEncoder
URLStreamHandler
java.lang.Throwable
java.lang.Exception
java.io.IOException
MalformedURLException
ProtocolException
SocketException
BindException
ConnectException
NoRouteToHostException
UnknownHostException
UnknownServiceException
java.io.Serializable
ContentHandlerFactory
FileNameMap
SocketImplFactory
URLStreamHandlerFactory

Description

This package contains classes for implementing networking applications. Using the socket classes, you can communicate with any server on the Internet or implement your own Internet server.[1] A number of classes are provided to make it convenient to use *Universal Resource Locators* (URLs) to retrieve data on the Internet.

Class and Interface Summary

Host Name Resolution

The `InetAddress` class is used to resolve a host name to an Internet address.

`InetAddress`	Represents an Internet address with methods for resolving a host name to an Internet address.

Sockets

The following classes provide the necessary functionality for communicating with servers on the Internet. These classes can also be used to implement an Internet server. See Figure 3.

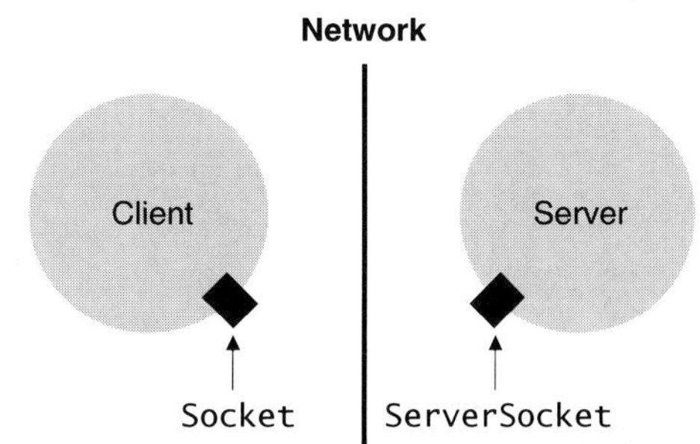

FIGURE 3: Socket and ServerSocket.

`DatagramPacket`	A datagram used in a connectionless protocol such as UDP.
`DatagramSocket`	Used for sending and receiving datagrams.
`DatagramSocketImpl`	The abstract superclass for a datagram socket implementation. Not directly used.
`MulticastSocket`	Used for sending and receiving multicast datagrams.
`ServerSocket`	Used by a server in a connection-oriented protocol such as TCP.

Continued

1. Restrictions may be placed by the security manager as to which servers you can communicate with. For example, some Web browsers allow applets to communicate only with the server from which the applet was loaded.

`Socket`	Used by a client or server in connectionless or connection-oriented protocols.
`SocketImpl`	The abstract superclass for a stream socket implementation. Not directly used.
`SocketImplFactory`	A factory that creates `SocketImpl` objects. Not directly used.

URL

The following classes make it convenient to use URLs to retrieve data on the Internet. The data can be retrieved as a complete object or as a stream. Figure 4 shows the use of the `URL` and `URLConnection` classes in accessing Web services.

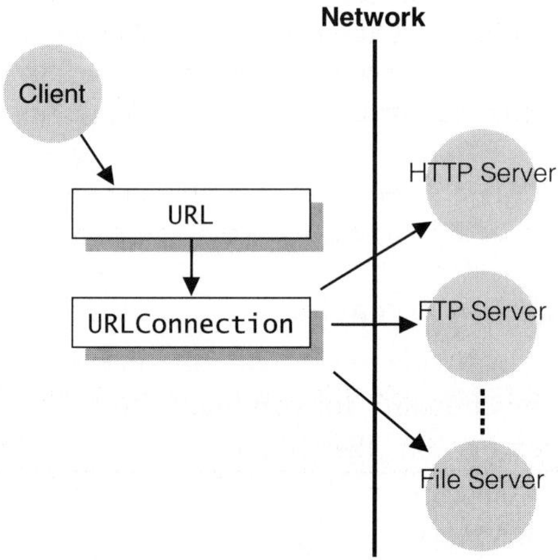

FIGURE 4: Use of `URL` and `URLConnection` to Access Web Services.

`ContentHandler`	The abstract superclass of content handlers for producing an object based on a MIME type. Not directly used.
`ContentHandlerFactory`	A factory that returns a new `ContentHandler` object based on a MIME type. Not directly used.
`FileNameMap`	An interface for mapping a filename to a MIME type.
`HttpURLConnection`	Used for creating an HTTP connection.
`URL`	Represents a URL with methods for parsing the URL and creating a connection to the URL's host.
`URLConnection`	Used for creating a connection to a URL's host and retrieving the data.
`URLEncoder`	Used for encoding a string in `x-www-form-urlencoded` format.
`URLStreamHandler`	The abstract superclass for URL protocol handlers (e.g., "http," "ftp," and "telnet"). Not directly used.
`URLStreamHandlerFactory`	A factory that creates instances of `URLStreamHandler` for different URL protocols. Not directly used.

Exceptions

The following are the exceptions declared in this package. They are not subclasses of `RuntimeException`, so they must be either caught or declared in the `throws` clause.

`BindException`	Thrown when attempting to bind a socket to a local address and port, but they cannot be assigned to the requesting program.
`ConnectException`	Thrown when attempting to connect a socket to a remote address and port.
`MalformedURLException`	Thrown if arguments to the `URL` constructor are invalid.
`NoRouteToHostException`	Thrown if the machine cannot be reached because there is no route to it.
`ProtocolException`	Thrown if attempting to connect to a socket of the wrong type.
`SocketException`	Thrown if attempting to create a socket to an unsupported service or if attempting to install a socket implementation factory when one has already been installed.
`UnknownHostException`	Thrown if a host name to an Internet address cannot be resolved.
`UnknownServiceException`	Thrown if attempting to use a service that is not supported by a URL connection.

java.text

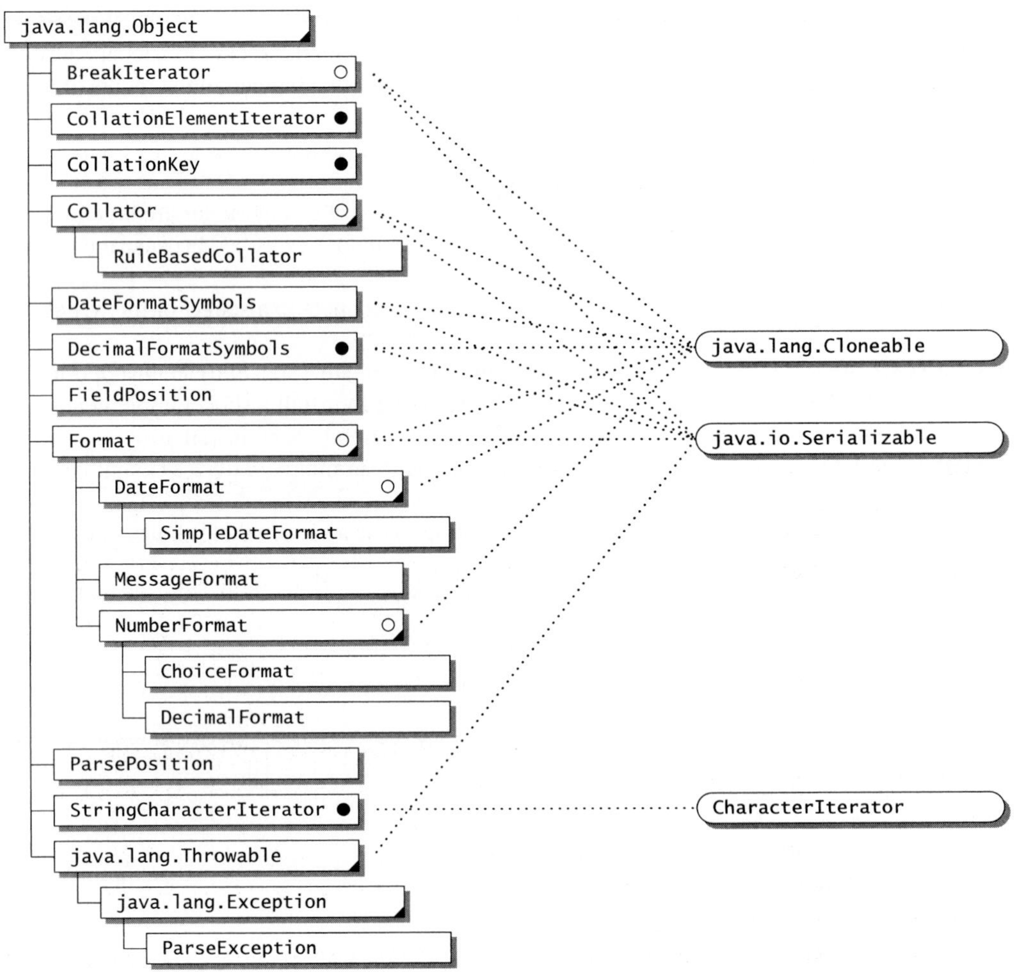

java.text

Description

This package contains classes and interfaces for handling text, dates, numbers, and messages in a manner independent of natural languages. This means your main application or applet can be written either to be language-independent and to call upon separate, dynamically linked localized resources. This allows the flexibility of adding localizations for new languages at any time.

These classes are capable of formatting dates, numbers, and messages, parsing; searching and sorting strings; and iterating over characters, words, sentences, and line breaks. This package contains three main groups of classes and interfaces:

- Classes for formatting and parsing
- Classes for string collation
- Classes for string iteration

Formatting and Parsing

As shown in Figure 5, *formatting* is basically the conversion of number and date objects to strings, while *parsing* is the reverse operation of converting strings to number and date objects.

Dates and numbers are represented internally in a locale-independent way. For example, dates are kept as milliseconds since epoch (January 1, 1970, 00:00:00 GMT). When these objects are printed or displayed, they must be converted to localized strings. The locale-specific parts of a date string, such as the time zone string, are separately imported from a locale-specific resource bundle.

The `format()` method converts the `Date` object from –604656780000 milliseconds to the form "Tuesday, November 3, 1997 9:47am CST" for the U. S. English locale. Figure 5 shows how the `format()` method of subclasses of `Format` enable instances of `Number`, `Date`, `String`, and other objects to be formatted to locale-specific strings.

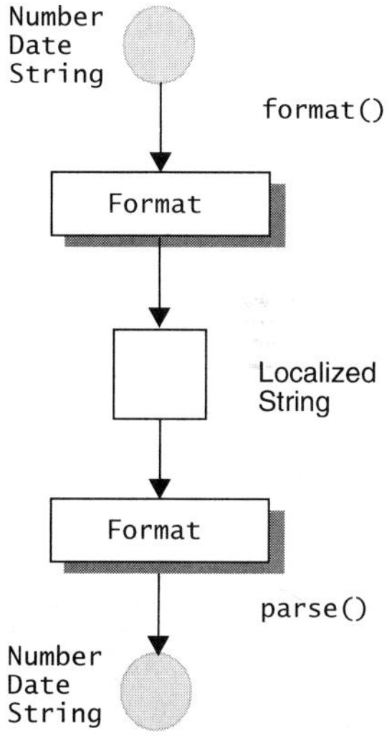

FIGURE 5: Object Formatting and String Parsing.

Conversely, the `parseObject()` method (and `parse()` method in subclasses) perform the reverse operation of parsing localized strings and converting them to `Number`, `Date`, and `String` objects. Figure 5 shows how the `parse()` method is complementary to `format()`. Any `String` formatted by `format()` is guaranteed to be parseable by `parseObject()`.

Java provides six subclasses of `Format` for formatting dates, numbers, and messages: `DateFormat`, `SimpleDateFormat`, `NumberFormat`, `DecimalFormat`, `ChoiceFormat`, and `MessageFormat`.

String Collation

The term *collate* means to determine the proper sort sequence for two or more strings. It can also tell if two strings are equal, for searching. The `Collator` class and its subclass `RuleBasedCollator` perform locale-sensitive string comparison. You use these classes to build searching and alphabetical sorting routines for natural language text. They can distinguish characters based on base character, accent marks, and uppercase/lowercase properties.

Collator is an abstract base class. Subclasses implement specific collation strategies. One subclass, RuleBasedCollator, is currently provided and is applicable to a wide set of languages. Other subclasses may be created to handle more specialized needs. CollationElementIterator provides an iterator for stepping through each character of a locale-specific string according to the rules of a specific Collator object. CollationKey enables fast sorting of strings by representing a string as a sort key under the rules of a specific Collator object.

String Iteration

While the Java types char and Character represent Unicode characters, sometimes Unicode characters combine to form a more complex character, called a *user character*, which has its own semantic value. The BreakIterator class makes it possible to iterate over these user characters. A break iterator can find the location of a character, word, or sentence boundary or potential line-break boundary. This makes it possible for a program to properly select characters for text operations such as highlighting a character, cutting a word, moving to the next sentence, or word-wrapping at a line ending. These operations are performed in a locale-sensitive manner, meaning that they honor the boundaries of text for a particular locale.

Figure 6 shows how the French word "théâtre" with seven user characters could be constructed of nine Unicode characters. A user character can be made of one stroke or multiple, disconnected strokes. In Latin languages (with the alphabet A–Z), a character is part of a larger word, but in ideographic languages (e.g., Chinese, Japanese, and Korean), a character can carry a complete idea or may be part of a larger word. Examples of user characters include "ä" (accent mark) and characters in some Middle East and Asian languages.

User Characters	|t|h|é|â|t|r|e|
Unicode Characters	|t|h|e|'|a|^|t|r|e|

FIGURE 6: User Characters.

Locale-Sensitive Classes

Most, but not all, of the classes in java.text are locale-sensitive, meaning you have to create a different one for each locale. Table 1 lists those classes.

Locale-Sensitive Classes		**Locale-Independent Classes**
NumberFormat	Collator	Format
DecimalFormat	RuleBasedCollator	ChoiceFormat
DecimalFormatSymbols	CollationElementIterator	FieldPosition
MessageFormat	CollationKey	ParsePosition
DateFormat	BreakIterator	ParseException
SimpleDateFormat	Collator	StringCharacterIterator
DateFormatSymbols		CharacterIterator

TABLE 1: Locale-Sensitive Classes.

Class and Interface Summary

General Format

The `Format` class defines the operations for formatting a `Date` or `Number` object (or number primitive) to a localized string and parsing a localized string to a `Number`, `Date`, `String`, or other object. The `format()` methods accept a `FieldPosition` object as a parameter. Some syntax forms of the `parse()` methods accept a `ParsePosition` object.

`Format`	The abstract superclass of all format classes. Provides the basic methods for formatting and parsing numbers, dates, strings, and other objects.
`FieldPosition`	A concrete class for holding the field constant and the begin and end indices for number and date fields.
`ParsePosition`	A concrete class for holding the current position in a string during parsing.

Number Format

The following classes define the operations for formatting a `Number` object or number primitive to a localized string and parsing a localized string to a `Number` object. `NumberFormat` is the abstract superclass; `DecimalFormat` and `ChoiceFormat` are its subclasses. `DecimalFormat` uses `DecimalFormatSymbols`.

`NumberFormat`	The abstract superclass that provides the basic fields and methods for formatting `Number` objects and number primitives to localized strings and parsing localized strings to `Number` objects.
`DecimalFormat`	A concrete class for formatting `Number` objects and number primitives to localized strings and parsing localized strings to `Number` objects.
`DecimalFormatSymbols`	A concrete class for accessing localized number strings, such as the grouping separators, decimal separator, and percent sign. Used by `DecimalFormat`.
`ChoiceFormat`	A concrete class for mapping strings to ranges of numbers and for handling plurals and names series in user messages.

Date and Time Formats

These classes define the operations for formatting a `Date` object to a localized string and parsing a localized string to a `Date` object. `DateFormat` is the abstract superclass, and `SimpleDateFormat` is its subclass.

`DateFormat`	The abstract superclass that provides the basic fields and methods for formatting `Date` objects to localized strings and parsing date and time strings to `Date` objects.
`SimpleDateFormat`	A concrete class for formatting `Date` objects to localized strings and parsing date and time strings to `Date` objects.
`DateFormatSymbols`	A concrete class for accessing localized date-time formatting strings, such as names of the months, days of the week, and the time zone. Used by `DateFormat`.

Message Format

The `Message` class is for producing language-specific user messages. It is a subclass of `Format`.

`MessageFormat`	A concrete class for producing a language-specific user message that contain numbers, currency, percentages, date, time, and string variables.

Exception

The `ParseException` exception is the only exception declared in this package. It is not a subclass of `RuntimeException`, so it must be either caught or declared in the `throws` clause.

`ParseException`	Thrown when an unexpected error has been encountered while parsing a string.

String Collation

These classes define the operations for performing locale-sensitive string comparisons for searching and alphabetical sorting for natural language text. `Collator` is the abstract superclass, and `RuleBasedCollator` is its subclass. `RuleBasedCollator` uses both `CollationElementIterator` and `CollationKey`.

`Collator`	The abstract superclass for performing locale-sensitive string comparisons for searching and alphabetical sorting for natural language text.
`RuleBasedCollator`	A concrete class for performing locale-sensitive string comparisons for searching and alphabetical sorting for natural language text.
`CollationElementIterator`	A concrete iterator class used to step through each character of a locale-specific string according to the rules of a specific `Collator` object.
`CollationKey`	A concrete class that represents a sort key for a string under the rules of a specific `Collator` object. Used for fast sorting of strings.

String Iteration

The following classes define the operations for finding and getting the position of logical breaks in a string of text based on user characters.

`BreakIterator`	An abstract class that defines the operations for finding and getting the position of logical breaks in a string of text: characters, words, sentences, and potential line breaks.
`StringCharacterIterator`	A concrete class for forward and backward iteration over a string of Unicode characters. Implements `CharacterIterator`.
`CharacterIterator`	An interface for forward and backward iteration over a string of Unicode characters.

java.util

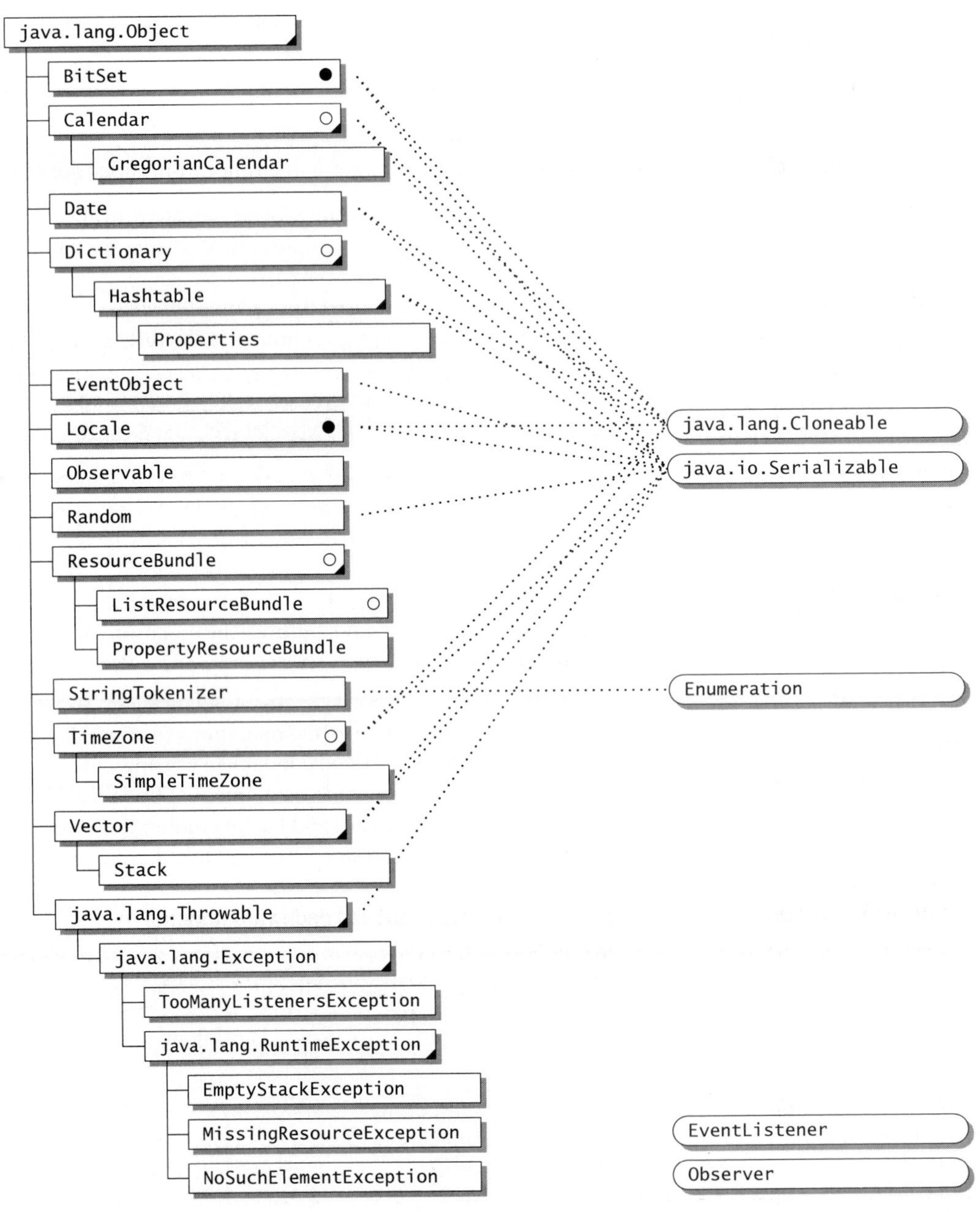
java.lang.Object
BitSet
Calendar
GregorianCalendar
Date
Dictionary
Hashtable
Properties
EventObject
Locale
Observable
Random
ResourceBundle
ListResourceBundle
PropertyResourceBundle
StringTokenizer
TimeZone
SimpleTimeZone
Vector
Stack
java.lang.Throwable
java.lang.Exception
TooManyListenersException
java.lang.RuntimeException
EmptyStackException
MissingResourceException
NoSuchElementException
java.lang.Cloneable
java.io.Serializable
Enumeration
EventListener
Observer

java.util

Description

This package contains several utility classes that are useful in typical Java programs, as follows:

- Classes that implement useful data structures
- Date- and time-related classes
- Internationalization and localization classes
- Root interfaces for events
- Miscellaneous classes including a simple string tokenizer and a random-number generator

Class and Interface Summary

Data Structures

The following classes implement a few data structures that are often used by a typical Java application. The `Enumeration` class provides a convenient way to visit all of the elements in a data structure. This is particularly useful for data structures whose elements cannot be retrieved with an index, such as a hash table.

`BitSet`	A space-efficient bit vector that automatically expands.
`Dictionary`	The abstract superclass for data structures that maintain a set of key/value pairs.
`Enumeration`	An interface consisting of methods for enumerating a list of objects.
`Hashtable`	A hash table for efficiently associating an object with another object.
`Stack`	A last-in/first-out stack of objects.
`Vector`	An array of objects that automatically expands.

Date and Time

The following classes are used to represent date- and time-related information.

`Calendar`	The abstract superclass for extracting calendar-related attributes from a `Date` value.
`Date`	Represents a date and time with the resolution of milliseconds.
`GregorianCalendar`	Represents a Gregorian calendar.
`SimpleTimeZone`	Represents a time zone for use with a Gregorian calendar.
`TimeZone`	The abstract superclass for representing a time zone.

Root Event Interfaces

The `EventObject` class is the superclass of all events (such as `AWTEvent`). `EventListener` is the interface from which all event listener interfaces extend.

`EventListener`	An interface to indicate that a class is an event listener.
`EventObject`	Represents an event fired by objects.

Internalization and Localization

A *resource bundle* is a set of resources such as strings and images. It is the primary means for localizing Java applications. A *locale* is Java's standard means of identifying a language for the purposes of internationalization.

`ListResourceBundle`	An abstract class representing a resource bundle whose values are known at the time the bundle is instantiated. Not used directly.
`Locale`	Used to identify a language and dialect for the purposes of internalization and localization.
`PropertyResourceBundle`	Represents a resource bundle whose values are stored in a properties file.
`ResourceBundle`	An abstract class representing a set of resources used for localizing an application.

Observer

An *observable object* is an object that holds some data that is constantly modified. An observer is an object that when registered with an observable object, gets notifications whenever the data held by the observable object changes.

`Observable`	The superclass of observable objects.
`Observer`	The interface that an observer must implement.

Properties

A *property* is a key/value pair; both the key and value are strings. This class is used to implement system properties (`java.lang.System.getProperties()`), as well as `PropertyResourceBundle`. The `Properties` class contains methods for saving and retrieving all of the data to/from a properties file.

`Properties`	A set of properties that has methods for saving and retrieving those properties.

Random Numbers

The `Random` class is used to generate pseudorandom numbers of the Java primitive number types.

`Random`	Used to generate pseudorandom numbers.

Parser

The `Parser` class is used to separate a string into smaller strings based on a set of characters that define the separators. The separators are typically whitespace characters, such as the space and the tab.

`StringTokenizer`	Used to parse a string to a sequence of tokens.

Exceptions

The following are the exceptions declared in this package. They are subclasses of `RuntimeException` and so should not be caught.

`EmptyStackException`	Thrown if attempting to access an element on an empty stack.
`MissingResourceException`	Thrown if a resource bundle or a resource could not be found.
`NoSuchElementException`	Thrown if attempting to access an element in an enumeration after the enumeration is exhausted.
`TooManyListenersException`	Thrown if attempting to add a listener to an object that does not support multiple listeners.

java.util.zip

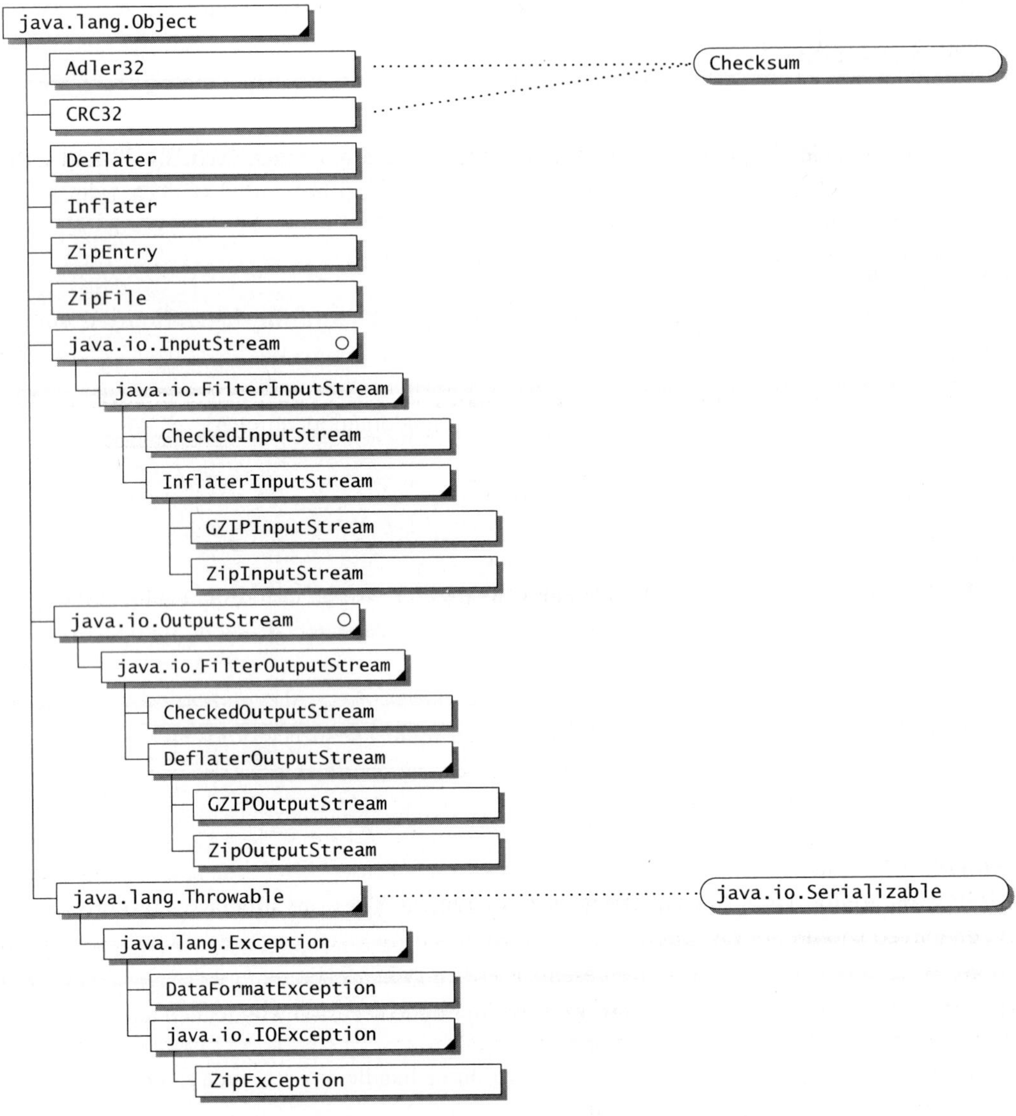

Description

This package contains classes for computing checksums of data and for compressing and decompressing data.

Class and Interface Summary

Checksum

This package provides implementations for two checksum algorithms: ADLER-32 and CRC-32. The ADLER-32 algorithm is faster than the CRC-32 algorithm, but CRC-32 produces better-quality checksums. `CheckedInputStream` and `CheckedOutputStream` use one of these algorithms in order to compute a checksum for data read from or written to a stream.

If you want to implement your own checksum algorithm, declare a class that implements `Checksum`. This allows your checksum algorithm to be used with `CheckedInputStream` and `CheckedOutputStream`.

`Adler32`	Implements the ADLER-32 algorithm for computing checksums.
`CheckedInputStream`	Computes the checksum of bytes read from a stream.
`CheckedOutputStream`	Computes the checksum of bytes written to a stream.
`Checksum`	The interface for checksums.
`CRC32`	Implements the CRC-32 algorithm for computing checksums.

ZIP File

A ZIP file consists of one or more compressed (or uncompressed) pieces of data. Each piece of data is represented by a *ZIP entry*. The ZIP entry contains information about the data, such as its uncompressed size, its checksum value, and its location in the ZIP file. `ZipFile` is used to read ZIP files, while `ZipOutputStream` is used to create ZIP files.

`ZipEntry`	Represents a ZIP entry in a ZIP file.
`ZipFile`	Used to read the contents of a ZIP file.

Compression

This package contains the following classes for *deflating* (compressing) data. A *deflater* is used to compress data. It is typically used with the `DeflaterOutputStream` class to compress a stream of data.

`GZIPOutputStream` and `ZipOutputStream` are subclasses of `DeflaterOutputStream` that produce compressed output in a specific format. A GZIP file differs from a ZIP file in that it contains only one piece of data, while a ZIP file can contain multiple pieces of data. Each piece of data in a ZIP file can be either compressed or uncompressed. See the `GZIPOutputStream` and `ZipEntry` for more information about these formats.

`Deflater`	Compresses a data stream of arbitrary length using the DEFLATE compression algorithm and data format.
`DeflaterOutputStream`	An output stream for compressing data using `Deflater`.
`GZIPOutputStream`	An output stream for creating a compressed file in GZIP format.
`ZipOutputStream`	An output stream for creating a ZIP file.

Decompression

This package contains the following classes for *inflating* (decompressing) data. An *inflater* is used to decompress data. It is typically used with the `InflaterOutputStream` class to decompress a stream of compressed data.

`GZIPInputStream` and `ZipInputStream` are subclasses of `InflaterOutputStream` that read and decompress compressed data in a specific format. A GZIP file differs from a ZIP file in that it contains only one piece of data, while a ZIP file can contain multiple pieces of data. Each piece of data in a ZIP file can be either compressed or uncompressed. See the `GZIPOutputStream` and `ZipEntry` for more information about these formats.

`Inflater`	Decompresses a data stream that was compressed using the DEFLATE compression algorithm and data format.
`InflaterInputStream`	An input stream for decompressing data using the `Inflater` class.
`GZIPInputStream`	An input stream for reading and decompressing a compressed file in GZIP format.
`ZipInputStream`	An input stream for reading a ZIP file.

Exceptions

There are two exception declared in this package. They extend directly from `Exception`, so they must be either caught or declared in the `throws` clause.

`DataFormatException`	Thrown if the compressed data is invalid or corrupted.
`ZipException`	Thrown if the data is not in ZIP format or if an error occurs while creating a new ZIP file.

AbstractMethodError

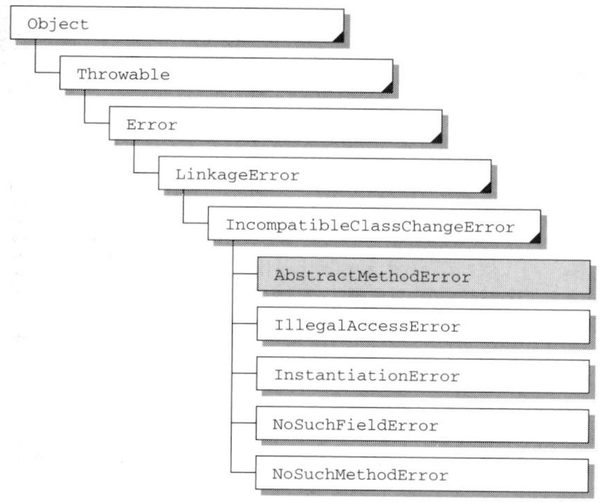

Syntax

```
public class AbstractMethodError extends IncompatibleClassChangeError
```

Description

`AbstractMethodError` is a runtime linkage error that is thrown when the Java virtual machine detects that the program is trying to invoke an abstract method. Normally, when you compile a program that attempts to invoke an abstract method, you get a compilation error pinpointing the problem so that a linkage error at runtime will not occur. However, the problem could be introduced when classes used by the program become inconsistent, for example by making an incompatible change and then recompiling only some of its classes.

`AbstractMethodError` should not be caught or declared in the `throws` clause of a method.

MEMBER SUMMARY	
Constructor	
`AbstractMethodError()`	Constructs an `AbstractMethodError` instance.

See Also

`Error`, `IncompatibleClassChangeError`.

Example

In this example, method1() in class B used to be nonabstract. The following main program compiled fine with it.

Main.java

```
class A extends B {
    public void method2(int i) {
        System.out.println(i);
    }
}
class Main {
    public static void main(String[] args) {
        System.out.println("AbstractMethodError example");
        A a = new A();
        a.method1(0);
    }
}
```

B.java

```
abstract class B {
    public void method1(int i) {
        System.out.println("method1:" + i);
    }
    abstract public void method2(int i);
}
```

However, if method1() is subsequently made abstract (by adding the abstract keyword and removing its body), running main() would throw AbstractMethodError.

Modified B.java

```
abstract class B {
    abstract public void method1(int i);
    abstract public void method2(int i);
}
```

AbstractMethodError()

PURPOSE Constructs an AbstractMethodError instance.

SYNTAX
```
public AbstractMethodError()
public AbstractMethodError(String msg)
```

DESCRIPTION These constructors construct an instance of AbstractMethodError. An optional string msg can be supplied that describes this particular instance of the error. If msg is not specified, it defaults to null.

PARAMETERS

msg A possibly null string that gives details about this error.

SEE ALSO Throwable.getMessage().

A B C D E F G H I J K L M N O P Q R S T U V W X Y Z

Adler32

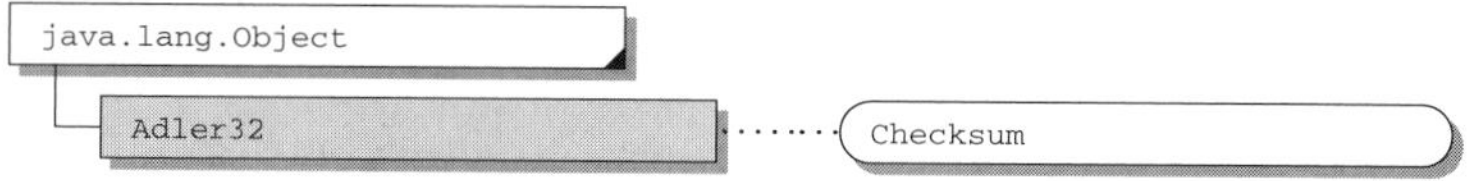

Syntax

```
public class Adler32 implements Checksum
```

Description

The `Adler32` class implements the ADLER-32 algorithm that is used to produce a checksum value on a stream of data. See `Checksum` for more information. The ADLER-32 algorithm is described in *RFC 1950*, which can be found at `http://ds.internic.net/rfc/rfc1950.txt`.

The `java.util.zip` package provides implementations of two different checksum algorithms: ADLER-32 and CRC-32 (see `CRC32`). The CRC-32 algorithm produces better-quality checksum values, but the ADLER-32 algorithm is faster.

Usage

To use this class to compute the checksum of a data set, you first must create an instance of this class. You then must call the new object's `update()` with the bytes of the data set. It is important to be consistent with the order of the bytes supplied to `update()`. Supplying the bytes in a different order will produce a different checksum. After all of the bytes have been given to `update()`, you call `getValue()` to retrieve the checksum value. To compute the checksum of another set of data, you can either create a new `ADLER32` object or simply call the current object's `reset()` method.

This class is typically used in conjunction with the `CheckedInputStream` and `CheckedOutputStream` classes, which make it convenient to compute the checksum on streaming data. See these classes for examples.

MEMBER SUMMARY	
Constructor	
`Adler32()`	Constructs an instance of `Adler32`.
Checksum Methods	
`getValue()`	Retrieves the current checksum value.
`reset()`	Resets this object to its initial state.
`update()`	Updates checksum with one or more bytes.

See Also

`CheckedInputStream`, `CheckedOutputStream`, `Checksum`, `CRC32`.

Example

This example implements a program that walks a tree of files and computes and prints the ADLER-32 checksum for each file.

```
import java.io.*;
import java.util.*;
import java.util.zip.*;

class Main implements Observer {
    // Use instance variable so that we can reuse it by calling reset().
    Adler32 checksum = new Adler32();

    Main(File dir) {
        FileWalker fw = new FileWalker();

        fw.addObserver(this);
        fw.walk(dir, false);
    }

    // This method is called for each file that the file walker discovers.
    public void update(Observable o, Object arg) {
        File f = (File)arg;
        checksum.reset();
        try {
            BufferedInputStream is = new BufferedInputStream(
                new FileInputStream(f));
            byte[] bytes = new byte[1024];
            int len = 0;

            // Read the file and compute the checksum.
            while ((len = is.read(bytes)) >= 0) {
                checksum.update(bytes, 0, len);
            }

            // Print the filename and checksum.
            System.out.println(f.getCanonicalPath()
                + " (" + checksum.getValue() + ")");
            is.close();
        } catch (IOException e) {
            e.printStackTrace();
        }
    }

    public static void main(String[] args) {
        if (args.length != 1) {
            System.err.println("Usage: java Main <directory>");
        } else {
            new Main(new File(args[0]));
        }
    }
}

class FileWalker extends Observable {
    void walk(File dir, boolean includeDirectories) {
```

```
            if (dir.isDirectory()) {
                if (includeDirectories) {
                    // Notify the observers.
                    setChanged();
                    notifyObservers(dir);
                }
                String[] filenames = dir.list();

                // Visit each file in this directory.
                for (int i=0; i < filenames.length; i++) {
                    walk(new File(dir, filenames[i]), includeDirectories);
                }
            } else {
                setChanged();
                notifyObservers(dir);
            }
        }
    }
```


Adler32()

PURPOSE Constructs an instance of `Adler32`.

SYNTAX `public Adler32()`

DESCRIPTION The checksum value of a new `Adler32` instance is `1`.

EXAMPLE See the class example.

getValue()

PURPOSE Retrieves the current checksum value.

SYNTAX `public long getValue()`

DESCRIPTION Each time `update()` is called, the checksum value maintained by this object is updated. This method returns the current value of the checksum.

RETURNS The current checksum value.

EXAMPLE See the class example.

reset()

PURPOSE Resets this object to its initial state.

SYNTAX `public void reset()`

DESCRIPTION After this object is used to compute a checksum value for a data set, it can be reused to compute the checksum of a new data set. The program first calls `reset()` to reset the checksum's value (to `1`) and then calls `update()` on the bytes of the new data set.

EXAMPLE See the class example.

update()

PURPOSE Updates checksum with one or more bytes.

SYNTAX

```
public void update(int bval)
public void update(byte[] buf)
public native void update(byte[] buf, int off, int len)
```

DESCRIPTION Calling this method updates the current checksum value using the byte value `bval` or the bytes in `buf`. If `buf` is specified, only `len` bytes starting from `buf[off]` are to be used to update the checksum value. If `off` is not specified, it defaults to `0`. If `len` is not specified, it defaults to `buf.length`.

PARAMETERS

`buf` A non-`null` array of `byte` values.
`bval` A `byte` value. Only the low-order byte of `bval` is used.
`len` The number of bytes to use starting from `buf[off]`. `0` ≤ `len` ≤ `buf.length-off`.
`off` The `0`-based index of the first byte in `buf` to use. `0` ≤ `off` < `buf.length`.

EXAMPLE See the class example.

java.lang
ArithmeticException

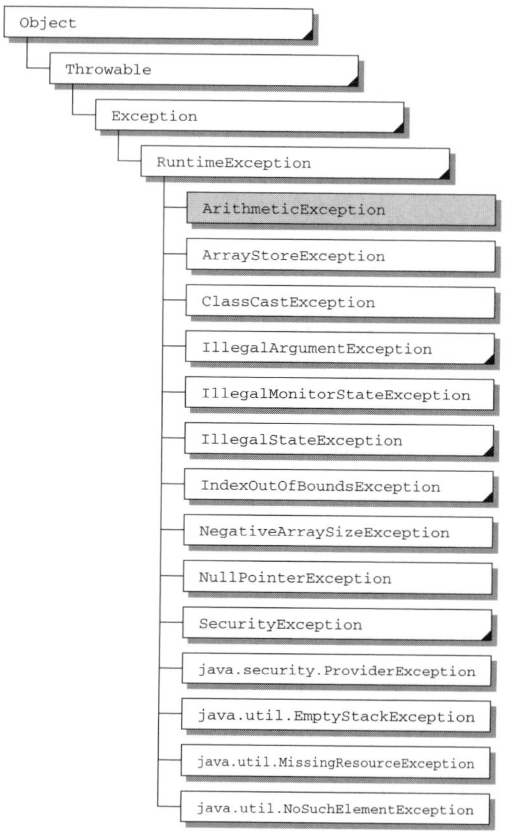

Syntax

`public class ArithmeticException extends RuntimeException`

Description

`ArithmeticException` is a runtime exception that is thrown when the program attempts to perform an illegal arithmetic operation. It should not be caught or declared in the `throws` clause of a method.

MEMBER SUMMARY	
Constructor	
`ArithmeticException()`	Constructs an `ArithmeticException` instance.

Example

The following code is attempting to divide by `0`. It throws an `ArithmeticException`.

```
class Main {
    public static void main(String[] args) {
        System.out.println("ArithmeticException Example");

        int a = 100;
        a /= 0;
    }
}
```

ArithmeticException()

PURPOSE Constructs an `ArithmeticException` instance.

SYNTAX
```
public ArithmeticException()
public ArithmeticException(String msg)
```

DESCRIPTION This constructor constructs an instance of `ArithmeticException`. An optional string `msg` can be supplied that describes this particular instance of the exception. If `msg` is not specified, it defaults to `null`.

PARAMETERS

`msg` A possibly `null` string that gives details about this exception.

SEE ALSO `Throwable.getMessage()`.

A B C D E F G H I J K L M N O P Q R S T U V W X Y Z

Syntax

```
public final class Array
```

Description

This class is used to dynamically create, access, and modify Java arrays. It is most often used when dealing with arrays whose component type is unknown. For example, with this class you could implement a method that takes any arbitrary array and return a copy of the array that is twice the original's size.

Usage

The `Array` class is a collection of static methods. It cannot be instantiated. To use a method, you need to supply a reference to an array object. For example, to get the length of an unknown array object `ar`, you would write

```
Array.getLength(ar);
```

Arrays as Objects

All arrays are objects, so they can be cast into the type `Object` at any time. For example:

```
int[] ints = new int[10];
Object a = ints;
```

To determine if an object is an array, use `Class.isArray()` on its class.

The Component Type

The type of an array's elements is called the *component type*. For example, the component type of `colors` in the following line is `Color`:

```
Color[] colors = new Color[8];
```

Component types can also be arrays. For example, in the following line the component type of `map` is `int[]`:

```
int[][] map = new int[100][100];
```

The component type of array `int[]` is `int`. The component type of an array can be retrieved by calling `Class.getComponentType()` on its class.

Widening Primitive Conversions

The various array element get and set methods will automatically perform widening conversions on primitive types if necessary. For example, if `getLong()` is invoked on a `byte` array, the method will automatically widen the `byte` value to a `long` value. If `setByte()` is invoked on a `long` array, the same widening conversion will take place.

Narrowing conversions are not permitted. Also, even if two primitive types are the same size, a conversion may not be permitted. For example, you cannot call `getChar()` on a `short` array. To achieve this conversion, you need to use the Java language's casting operators before calling the methods in this class.

The automatic conversions that are allowed exactly match the automatic widening conversions as defined in *The Java Language Specification*. Tables 2 and 3 show a complete listing of all valid array types for all of the get and set methods, respectively.

Get Method	Input Array Type
`getBoolean()`	`boolean[]`
`getChar()`	`char[]`
`getByte()`	`byte[]`
`getShort()`	`byte[], short[]`
`getInt()`	`byte[], short[], char[], int[]`
`getLong()`	`byte[], short[], char[], int[], long[]`
`getFloat()`	`byte[], short[], char[], int[], long[], float[]`
`getDouble()`	`byte[], short[], char[], int[], long[], float[], double[]`

TABLE 2: Valid Array Types for the Get Methods.

Set Method	Input Array Type
`setBoolean()`	`boolean[]`
`setChar()`	`double[], float[], long[], int[], char[]`
`setByte()`	`double[], float[], long[], int[], short[], byte[]`
`setShort()`	`double[], float[], long[], int[], short[]`
`setInt()`	`double[], float[], long[], int[]`
`setLong()`	`double[], float[], long[]`
`setFloat()`	`double[], float[].`
`setDouble()`	`double[]`

TABLE 3: Valid Array Types for the Set Methods.

See Also

`java.lang.Class.getComponentType(), java.lang.Class.isArray().`

MEMBER SUMMARY

Creation Method	
`newInstance()`	Creates an array that has the specified component type and length.
Length Method	
`getLength()`	Retrieves the length of an array.
Get Methods	
`get()`	Retrieves the value of an element in an array.
`getBoolean()`	Retrieves the value of an element in a `boolean` array.
`getByte()`	Retrieves a `byte` value from a `byte` array.
`getChar()`	Retrieves a `char` value from a `char` array.
`getDouble()`	Retrieves a `double` value from a numerical array.
`getFloat()`	Retrieves a `float` value from a numerical array.
`getInt()`	Retrieves an `int` value from a numerical array.
`getLong()`	Retrieves a `long` value from a numerical array.
`getShort()`	Retrieves a `short` value from a numerical array.
Set Methods	
`set()`	Sets an element of an array to a value.
`setBoolean()`	Sets an element of a `boolean` array to a `boolean` value.
`setByte()`	Sets an element of a numerical array to a `byte` value.
`setChar()`	Sets an element of a numerical array to a `char` value.
`setDouble()`	Sets an element of a numerical array to a `double` value.
`setFloat()`	Sets an element of a numerical array to a `float` value.
`setInt()`	Sets an element of a numerical array to an `int` value.
`setLong()`	Sets an element of a numerical array to a `long` value.
`setShort()`	Sets an element of a numerical array to a `short` value.

Example

This example implements the quick-sort algorithm. It is designed to operate on any arbitrary array type. All that's necessary to sort the array is to provide quick-sort with a means to compare the elements of the array. In particular, you need to supply quick-sort with a class that implement the `Comparable` interface.

The program generates a set of random `double` values, sorts the set, and then prints out the values.

Main.java

```
import java.lang.reflect.*;

class Main {
    Main() {
```

```
            double[] ds = new double[12];

            // Fill with random numbers.
            for (int i=0; i<ds.length; i++) {
                ds[i] = Math.random();
            }

            // Sort it.
            QuickSort.sort(ds, new Compare());

            // Print sorted list.
            for (int i=0; i<ds.length; i++) {
                System.out.println(ds[i]);
            }
        }

        class Compare implements Comparator {
            public int compare(Object a, Object b) {
                double i = ((Double)a).doubleValue();
                double j = ((Double)b).doubleValue();
                if (i < j) {
                    return -1;
                } else if (i > j) {
                    return 1;
                } else {
                    return 0;
                }
            }
        }

        public static void main(String[] args) {
            new Main();
        }
    }
```

Comparator.java

```
public interface Comparator {
    // Returns -1 if o1 < o2, 0 if o1 == o2, 1 if o1 > o2.
    int compare(Object o1, Object o2);
}
```

QuickSort.java

```
import java.lang.reflect.*;

class QuickSort {
    // Main sort routine.
    // If a is an array of primitive types, cmp.compare will be called
    // with the appropriate wrapper.
    public static void sort(Object a, Comparator cmp) {
        sort(a, 0, Array.getLength(a) - 1, cmp);
    }

    // Private recursive routine.
    private static void sort(Object a, int lo0, int hi0, Comparator cmp) {
        int lo = lo0;
        int hi = hi0;
        Object mid;
```

```
        if (hi0 > lo0) {
            mid = Array.get(a, (lo0 + hi0) / 2);

            // Loop through the array until indices cross.
            while(lo <= hi) {
                while(lo < hi0 && cmp.compare(Array.get(a, lo), mid) < 0) {
                    ++lo;
                }

                while(hi > lo0 && cmp.compare(Array.get(a, hi), mid) > 0) {
                    --hi;
                }

                // if the indexes have not crossed, swap
                if(lo <= hi) {
                    swap(a, lo, hi);
                    ++lo;
                    --hi;
                }
            }

            if(lo0 < hi) {
                sort(a, lo0, hi, cmp);
            }

            if(lo < hi0) {
                sort(a, lo, hi0, cmp);
            }
        }
    }

    // Swap a[i] and a[j].
    private static void swap(Object a, int i, int j) {
        Object t = Array.get(a, i);
        Array.set(a, i, Array.get(a, j));
        Array.set(a, j, t);
    }
}
```


get()

PURPOSE
Retrieves the value of an element in an array.

SYNTAX
```
public static native Object get(Object ar, int ix) throws
    IllegalArgumentException, ArrayIndexOutOfBoundsException
```

DESCRIPTION
This method retrieves the value of an element stored in `ar` at index `ix` as an object. If the component type of `ar` is primitive, the returned object is a wrapper around the value. For example, if `ar` is a `byte` array, the returned object is a `Byte` object.

PARAMETERS

`ar`	The non-`null` array.
`ix`	The `0`-based index of the desired element in `ar`.

RETURNS The possibly `null` object of the `ix`'th element of `ar`.

EXCEPTIONS

`ArrayIndexOutOfBoundsException`
: If `ix` is negative or greater than `Array.getLength(ar)-1`.

`IllegalArgumentException`
: If `ar` is not an array.

SEE ALSO `set()`.

EXAMPLE This example defines a method for randomizing the elements of an array. The randomizing method works with arrays of any component type.

```
import java.lang.reflect.*;

class Main {
    public static void main(String[] args) {
        char[] charArray = {'a', 'b', 'c', 'd'};
        randomizeArray(charArray);
        printArray(charArray);

        int[] intArray = {0, 1, 2, 3, 4};
        randomizeArray(intArray);
        printArray(intArray);

        String[] stringArray = {"A", "B", "C", "D", "E"};
        randomizeArray(stringArray);
        printArray(stringArray);
    }

    static void randomizeArray(Object a) {
        int len = Array.getLength(a);

        for (int i=0; i<len/2; i++) {
            int ix1 = (int)Math.floor(Math.random()*len);
            int ix2 = (int)Math.floor(Math.random()*len);
            Object o = Array.get(a, ix1);

            // Swap elements.
            Array.set(a, ix1, Array.get(a, ix2));
            Array.set(a, ix2, o);
        }
    }

    static void printArray(Object a) {
        for (int i=0; i<Array.getLength(a); i++) {
            System.out.print(Array.get(a, i) + " ");
        }
        System.out.println();
    }
}
```

getBoolean()

PURPOSE Retrieves the value of an element in a `boolean` array.

SYNTAX `public static native boolean getBoolean(Object ar, int ix) throws IllegalArgumentException, ArrayIndexOutOfBoundsException`

DESCRIPTION This method retrieves the value of the `ix`'th element in the `boolean` array `ar`.

PARAMETERS

`ar` The non-`null` `boolean` array.

`ix` The `0`-based index of the desired element in `ar`.

RETURNS The `boolean` value at index `ix` in `ar`.

EXCEPTIONS

`ArrayIndexOutOfBoundsException`

If `ix` is negative or greater than `Array.getLength(ar)-1`.

`IllegalArgumentException`

If `ar` is not a `boolean` array.

SEE ALSO `setBoolean()`.

EXAMPLE This example demonstrates how to use the `Array` methods to create and modify a `boolean` array. It also demonstrates that the object created by `newInstance()` is really an object of type `boolean[]`. Notice also that the `Array` methods can work on the array either as type `Object` or as type `boolean[]`.

```
import java.lang.reflect.*;

class Main {
    public static void main(String[] args) {
        // Create a new boolean array.
        Object a = Array.newInstance(boolean.class, 7);

        // Set an element.
        Array.setBoolean(a, 2, Math.random() > .5);

        // Print the element.
        System.out.println(Array.getBoolean(a, 2));

        // Show that a is really an object of type boolean[]
        boolean[] b = (boolean[])a;
        Array.setBoolean(b, 3, Math.random() > .5);
        System.out.println(Array.getBoolean(b, 3));
    }
}
```

getByte()

PURPOSE Retrieves a byte value from a byte array.

SYNTAX `public static native byte getByte(Object ar, int ix) throws IllegalArgumentException, ArrayIndexOutOfBoundsException`

DESCRIPTION This method retrieves the ix'th element in the array ar as a byte value. The component type of ar must be byte.

PARAMETERS

ar The non-null byte array.

ix The 0-based index of the desired element in ar.

RETURNS The byte value at index ix in ar.

EXCEPTIONS

ArrayIndexOutOfBoundsException
If ix is negative or greater than Array.getLength(ar)-1.

IllegalArgumentException
If ar is not a byte array.

SEE ALSO setByte().

EXAMPLE This example demonstrates the set of array types on which getByte() and setByte() can operate.

```
import java.lang.reflect.*;

class Main {
    public static void main(String[] args) {
        byte[] bytes = new byte[1];
        char[] chars = new char[1];
        short[] shorts = new short[1];
        int[] ints = new int[1];
        long[] longs = new long[1];
        float[] floats = new float[1];
        double[] doubles = new double[1];

        // The set of array types on which getByte() can operate.
        Array.getByte(bytes, 0);

        // The set of array types on which setByte() can operate.
        Array.setByte(bytes, 0, (byte)1);
        Array.setByte(shorts, 0, (byte)1);
        Array.setByte(ints, 0, (byte)1);
        Array.setByte(longs, 0, (byte)1);
        Array.setByte(floats, 0, (byte)1);
        Array.setByte(doubles, 0, (byte)1);
    }
}
```

getChar()

PURPOSE Retrieves a char value from an array.

SYNTAX `public static native char getChar(Object ar, int ix) throws IllegalArgumentException, ArrayIndexOutOfBoundsException`

DESCRIPTION This method retrieves the ix'th element in the array ar as a char value. The component type of ar must be char.

PARAMETERS

ar The non-null char array.

ix The 0-based index of the desired element in ar.

RETURNS The char value at index ix in ar.

EXCEPTIONS

ArrayIndexOutOfBoundsException

If ix is negative or greater than Array.getLength(ar)-1.

IllegalArgumentException

If ar is not a char array.

SEE ALSO setChar().

EXAMPLE This example demonstrates the set of array types on which getChar() and setChar() can operate.

```
import java.lang.reflect.*;

class Main {
    public static void main(String[] args) {
        byte[] bytes = new byte[1];
        char[] chars = new char[1];
        short[] shorts = new short[1];
        int[] ints = new int[1];
        long[] longs = new long[1];
        float[] floats = new float[1];
        double[] doubles = new double[1];

        // The set of array types on which getChar() can operate.
        Array.getChar(chars, 0);

        // The set of array types on which setChar() can operate.
        Array.setChar(chars, 0, 'a');
        Array.setChar(ints, 0, 'a');
        Array.setChar(longs, 0, 'a');
        Array.setChar(floats, 0, 'a');
        Array.setChar(doubles, 0, 'a');
    }
}
```

getDouble()

PURPOSE Retrieves a `double` value from a numerical array.

SYNTAX `public static native double getDouble(Object ar, int ix) throws IllegalArgumentException, ArrayIndexOutOfBoundsException`

DESCRIPTION This method retrieves the `ix`'th element in the array `ar` as a `double` value. The component type of `ar` must be one of `byte`, `short`, `char`, `int`, `long`, `float`, or `double`.

PARAMETERS

`ar` The non-`null` numerical array.

`ix` The `0`-based index of the desired element in `ar`.

RETURNS The `double` value at index `ix` in `ar`.

EXCEPTIONS

`ArrayIndexOutOfBoundsException`

If `ix` is negative or greater than `Array.getLength(ar)-1`.

`IllegalArgumentException`

If `ar` is not an array or if the component type of `ar` is not one of `byte`, `short`, `char`, `int`, `long`, `float`, or `double`.

SEE ALSO `setDouble()`.

EXAMPLE This example demonstrates the set of array types on which `getDouble()` and `setDouble()` can operate.

```
import java.lang.reflect.*;

class Main {
    public static void main(String[] args) {
        byte[] bytes = new byte[1];
        char[] chars = new char[1];
        short[] shorts = new short[1];
        int[] ints = new int[1];
        long[] longs = new long[1];
        float[] floats = new float[1];
        double[] doubles = new double[1];

        // The set of array types on which getDouble() can operate.
        Array.getDouble(bytes, 0);
        Array.getDouble(shorts, 0);
        Array.getDouble(chars, 0);
        Array.getDouble(ints, 0);
        Array.getDouble(longs, 0);
        Array.getDouble(floats, 0);
        Array.getDouble(doubles, 0);

        // The set of array types on which setDouble() can operate.
        Array.setDouble(doubles, 0, 1L);
    }
}
```

getFloat()

PURPOSE
Retrieves a `float` value from a numerical array.

SYNTAX

```
public static native float getFloat(Object ar, int ix) throws
    IllegalArgumentException, ArrayIndexOutOfBoundsException
```

DESCRIPTION
This method retrieves the `ix`'th element in the array `ar` as a `float` value. The component type of `ar` must be one of `byte`, `short`, `char`, `int`, `long`, or `float`.

PARAMETERS

`ar` The non-`null` numerical array.

`ix` The `0`-based index of the desired element in `ar`.

RETURNS
The `float` value at index `ix` in `ar`.

EXCEPTIONS

`ArrayIndexOutOfBoundsException`
If `ix` is negative or greater than `Array.getLength(ar)-1`.

`IllegalArgumentException`
If `ar` is not an array or if the component type of `ar` is not one of `byte`, `short`, `char`, `int`, `long`, or `float`.

SEE ALSO
`setFloat()`.

EXAMPLE
This example demonstrates the set of array types on which `getFloat()` and `setFloat()` can operate.

```
import java.lang.reflect.*;

class Main {
    public static void main(String[] args) {
        byte[] bytes = new byte[1];
        char[] chars = new char[1];
        short[] shorts = new short[1];
        int[] ints = new int[1];
        long[] longs = new long[1];
        float[] floats = new float[1];
        double[] doubles = new double[1];

        // The set of array types on which getFloat() can operate.
        Array.getFloat(bytes, 0);
        Array.getFloat(shorts, 0);
        Array.getFloat(chars, 0);
        Array.getFloat(ints, 0);
        Array.getFloat(longs, 0);
        Array.getFloat(floats, 0);

        // The set of array types on which setFloat() can operate.
        Array.setFloat(floats, 0, 1L);
        Array.setFloat(doubles, 0, 1L);
    }
}
```

getInt()

PURPOSE Retrieves an `int` value from a numerical array.

SYNTAX `public static native int getInt(Object ar, int ix) throws IllegalArgumentException, ArrayIndexOutOfBoundsException`

DESCRIPTION This method retrieves the `ix`'th element in the array `ar` as an `int` value. The component type of `ar` must be one of `byte`, `short`, `char`, or `int`.

PARAMETERS

`ar` The non-`null` numerical array.

`ix` The `0`-based index of the desired element in `ar`.

RETURNS The `int` value at index `ix` in `ar`.

EXCEPTIONS

`ArrayIndexOutOfBoundsException`
If `ix` is negative or greater than `Array.getLength(ar)-1`.

`IllegalArgumentException`
If `ar` is not an array or if the component type of `ar` is not one of `byte`, `short`, `char`, or `int`.

SEE ALSO `setInt()`.

EXAMPLE This example demonstrates the set of array types on which `getInt()` and `setInt()` can operate.

```
import java.lang.reflect.*;

class Main {
    public static void main(String[] args) {
        byte[] bytes = new byte[1];
        char[] chars = new char[1];
        short[] shorts = new short[1];
        int[] ints = new int[1];
        long[] longs = new long[1];
        float[] floats = new float[1];
        double[] doubles = new double[1];

        // The set of array types on which getInt() can operate.
        Array.getInt(bytes, 0);
        Array.getInt(shorts, 0);
        Array.getInt(chars, 0);
        Array.getInt(ints, 0);

        // The set of array types on which setInt() can operate.
        Array.setInt(ints, 0, 1);
        Array.setInt(longs, 0, 1);
        Array.setInt(floats, 0, 1);
        Array.setInt(doubles, 0, 1);
    }
}
```

getLength()

PURPOSE Retrieves the length of an array.

SYNTAX `public static native int getLength(Object ar) throws IllegalArgumentException`

PARAMETERS

`ar` The non-`null` array.

RETURNS The non-negative length of `ar`.

EXCEPTIONS

`IllegalArgumentException`

If `ar` is not an array.

SEE ALSO `Class.isArray()`.

EXAMPLE This example implements a method for doubling the size of any arbitrary array. It fetches the component type of the array and then creates an instance of the array that is twice as big as the original. The method then copies the original values to the array.

```
import java.lang.reflect.*;

class Main {
    // Returns an array with the same contents but double in size.
    public static Object expand(Object array) {
        Object result = Array.newInstance(array.getClass().getComponentType(),
            Array.getLength(array)*2);

        // Copy the old contents to the new array.
        for (int i=0; i<Array.getLength(array); i++) {
            Array.set(result, i, Array.get(array, i));
        }

        // A faster alternative would be
        //System.arraycopy(array, 0, result, 0, Array.getLength(array));

        return result;
    }

    public static void main(String[] args) {
        int[] ints = {5, 4, 6, 9, 1};
        char[] chars = {'j', 'a', 'v', 'a'};

        ints = (int[])expand(ints);
        chars = (char[])expand(chars);
    }
}
```

A B C D E F G H I J K L M N O P Q R S T U V W X Y Z

getLong()

PURPOSE Retrieves a `long` value from a numerical array.

SYNTAX
```
public static native long getLong(Object ar, int ix) throws
    IllegalArgumentException, ArrayIndexOutOfBoundsException
```

DESCRIPTION This method retrieves the `ix`'th element in the array `ar` as a `long` value. The component type of `ar` must be one of `byte`, `short`, `char`, `int`, or `long`.

PARAMETERS

`ar` The non-`null` numerical array.

`ix` The `0`-based index of the desired element in `ar`.

RETURNS The `long` value at index `ix` in `ar`.

EXCEPTIONS

`ArrayIndexOutOfBoundsException`
If `ix` is negative or greater than `Array.getLength(ar)-1`.

`IllegalArgumentException`
If `ar` is not an array or if the component type of `ar` is not one of `byte`, `short`, `char`, `int`, or `long`.

SEE ALSO `setLong()`.

EXAMPLE This example demonstrates the set of array types on which `getLong()` and `setLong()` can operate.

```
import java.lang.reflect.*;

class Main {
    public static void main(String[] args) {
        byte[] bytes = new byte[1];
        char[] chars = new char[1];
        short[] shorts = new short[1];
        int[] ints = new int[1];
        long[] longs = new long[1];
        float[] floats = new float[1];
        double[] doubles = new double[1];

        // The set of array types on which getLong() can operate.
        Array.getLong(bytes, 0);
        Array.getLong(shorts, 0);
        Array.getLong(chars, 0);
        Array.getLong(ints, 0);
        Array.getLong(longs, 0);

        // The set of array types on which setLong() can operate.
        Array.setLong(longs, 0, 1L);
        Array.setLong(floats, 0, 1L);
        Array.setLong(doubles, 0, 1L);
    }
}
```

getShort()

PURPOSE
Retrieves a `short` value from a numerical array.

SYNTAX

```
public static native short getShort(Object ar, int ix) throws
    IllegalArgumentException, ArrayIndexOutOfBoundsException
```

DESCRIPTION
This method retrieves the `ix`'th element in the array `ar` as a `short` value. The component type of `ar` must be either `short` or `byte`.

PARAMETERS

`ar` The non-`null` numerical array.

`ix` The `0`-based index of the desired element in `ar`.

RETURNS
The `short` value at index `ix` in `ar`.

EXCEPTIONS

`ArrayIndexOutOfBoundsException`
If `ix` is negative or greater than `Array.getLength(ar)-1`.

`IllegalArgumentException`
If `ar` is not an array or if the component type of `ar` is not one of `byte` or `short`.

SEE ALSO
`setShort()`.

EXAMPLE
This example demonstrates the set of array types on which `getShort()` and `setShort()` can operate.

```
import java.lang.reflect.*;

class Main {
    public static void main(String[] args) {
        byte[] bytes = new byte[1];
        char[] chars = new char[1];
        short[] shorts = new short[1];
        int[] ints = new int[1];
        long[] longs = new long[1];
        float[] floats = new float[1];
        double[] doubles = new double[1];

        // The set of array types on which getShort() can operate.
        Array.getShort(bytes, 0);
        Array.getShort(shorts, 0);

        // The set of array types on which setShort() can operate.
        Array.setShort(shorts, 0, (short)1);
        Array.setShort(ints, 0, (short)1);
        Array.setShort(longs, 0, (short)1);
        Array.setShort(floats, 0, (short)1);
        Array.setShort(doubles, 0, (short)1);
    }
}
```

A B C D E F G H I J K L M N O P Q R S T U V W X Y Z

newInstance()

PURPOSE Creates an array that has the specified component type and length.

SYNTAX
```
public static Object newInstance(Class componentType, int len)
   throws NegativeArraySizeException
public static Object newInstance(Class componentType, int[] dims)
   throws IllegalArgumentException, NegativeArraySizeException
```

DESCRIPTION This method creates an array. If `len` is specified, this method creates a one-dimensional array of length `len` whose component type is `componentType`. In this case, the returned array is indistinguishable from one created using the `new` operator:

```
new componentType[len]
```

If `dims` is specified, the returned array has dimensions equals to `dims.length`. For example, if `dims.length` is `2`, the array is two-dimensional. The effect is equivalent to this array creation expression:

```
new componentType[dims[0]]...[dims[dims.length-1]]
```

To create an array when the tail dimensions are not defined, you need to supply an array as the component type. For example, to use `newInstance()` to duplicate the expression

```
int[][] ints = new int[10][];
```

you would say

```
int[] dims = {10};
int[][] ints =
    (int[][])Array.newInstance(int[].class, dims);
```

PARAMETERS

`componentType`
The non-`null` `Class` object representing the new array's component type.

`dims` A non-`null` array of `int`s representing the dimensions of the new array.

`len` The non-negative length of the new array.

RETURNS The non-`null` new array.

EXCEPTIONS

`IllegalArgumentException`
If `dims.length` is `0` or if `dims.length` exceeds the maximum array dimension limit (typically `255`).

`NegativeArraySizeException`
If `len` is negative.

EXAMPLE This is a simple example of using `newInstance()` to create multidimensional arrays.

```
import java.lang.reflect.*;

class Main {
    public static void main(String[] args) {
        // Creates an int array with 0 elements.
        int[] d0 = {0};
        int[] a0 = (int[])Array.newInstance(int.class, d0);

        // Do the same, this time using just an integer.
        int[] b0 = (int[])Array.newInstance(int.class, 0);

        // Create a 10x10 array of strings.
        int[] d1 = {10, 10};
        String[][] a1 = (String[][])Array.newInstance(String.class, d1);

        // Create an array of 10 int arrays.
        int[] d2 = {10};
        int[][] a2 = (int[][])Array.newInstance(int[].class, d2);

        // Do the same, this time using just an integer.
        int[][] b2 = (int[][])Array.newInstance(int[].class, 10);

        // Create a 10x10 array of 10 int arrays.
        int[] d3 = {10, 10};
        int[][][] a3 = (int[][][])Array.newInstance(int[].class, d3);
    }
}
```

set()

PURPOSE Sets an element of an array to a value.

SYNTAX

```
public static native void set(Object ar, int ix, Object val)
    throws IllegalArgumentException,
    ArrayIndexOutOfBoundsException
```

DESCRIPTION This method sets the `ix`'th element in the array `ar` to `val`. If `ar` is an array of object references, `val` must be assignable to the array component type. If the component type of `ar` is primitive, `val` must be a wrapper object of the appropriate type. When `val` is unwrapped, its value may be automatically widened. For example, if `ar` is an `int` array, `val` may be an `Integer`, a `Short`, a `Character`, or a `Byte`. See Table 3 in the class description for the list of allowed primitive conversions.

PARAMETERS

`ar`	The non-`null` `boolean` array.
`ix`	The `0`-based index of the desired element in `ar`.
`val`	The new value.

A B C D E F G H I J K L M N O P Q R S T U V W X Y Z

EXCEPTIONS

`ArrayIndexOutOfBoundsException`
: If `ix` is negative or greater than `Array.getLength(ar)-1`.

`IllegalArgumentException`
: If `ar` is not an array or if the value cannot be converted to `ar`'s component type.

EXAMPLE This example shows how to access and modify arrays that have object references and primitive component types.

```
import java.lang.reflect.*;

class Main {
    public static void main(String[] args) {
        boolean[] booleans = new boolean[1];
        byte[] bytes = new byte[1];
        char[] chars = new char[1];
        short[] shorts = new short[1];
        int[] ints = new int[1];
        long[] longs = new long[1];
        float[] floats = new float[1];
        double[] doubles = new double[1];
        Object[] objects = new Object[1];
        String[] strings = new String[1];

        // Different ways that set() can be used.
        Array.set(booleans, 0, Boolean.TRUE);
        Array.set(bytes, 0, new Byte((byte)1));
        Array.set(chars, 0, new Character('a'));
        Array.set(shorts, 0, new Short((short)1));
        Array.set(ints, 0, new Integer(1));
        Array.set(longs, 0, new Long(1L));
        Array.set(floats, 0, new Float(1.0f));
        Array.set(doubles, 0, new Double(1));
        Array.set(objects, 0, System.out);
        Array.set(strings, 0, "abc");

        // Different ways that get() can be used.
        Boolean bool = (Boolean)Array.get(booleans, 0);
        Byte b = (Byte)Array.get(bytes, 0);
        Character c = (Character)Array.get(chars, 0);
        Short s = (Short)Array.get(shorts, 0);
        Integer i = (Integer)Array.get(ints, 0);
        Long l = (Long)Array.get(longs, 0);
        Float f = (Float)Array.get(floats, 0);
        Double d = (Double)Array.get(doubles, 0);
        Object obj = (Object)Array.get(objects, 0);
        String str = (String)Array.get(strings, 0);

        // Demonstration of widening conversions.
        Array.set(ints, 0, new Byte((byte)1));
        Array.set(doubles, 0, new Integer(1));
    }
}
```

setBoolean()

PURPOSE Sets an element of a `boolean` array to a `boolean` value.

SYNTAX
```
public static native void setBoolean(Object ar, int ix, boolean
   bval) throws IllegalArgumentException,
   ArrayIndexOutOfBoundsException
```

DESCRIPTION This method sets the `ix`'th element in the `boolean` array `ar` to `bval`.

PARAMETERS

`ar`	The non-`null` `boolean` array.
`bval`	The new `boolean` value.
`ix`	The `0`-based index of the desired element in `ar`.

EXCEPTIONS

`ArrayIndexOutOfBoundsException`
If `ix` is negative or greater than `Array.getLength(ar)-1`.

`IllegalArgumentException`
If `ar` is not a `boolean` array.

SEE ALSO `getBoolean()`.

EXAMPLE See `getBoolean()`.

setByte()

PURPOSE Sets an element of a numerical array to a `byte` value.

SYNTAX
```
public static native void setByte(Object ar, int ix,
   byte bval) throws IllegalArgumentException,
   ArrayIndexOutOfBoundsException
```

DESCRIPTION This method can be used to update arrays of the following component types: `byte`, `short`, `int`, `long`, `float`, and `double`.

PARAMETERS

`ar`	The non-`null` numerical array.
`bval`	The new `byte` value.
`ix`	The `0`-based index of the desired element in `ar`.

EXCEPTIONS

`ArrayIndexOutOfBoundsException`
If `ix` is negative or greater than `Array.getLength(ar)-1`.

`IllegalArgumentException`
If `ar` is not an array or if the component type of `ar` is not one of `byte`, `short`, `int`, `long`, `float`, or `double`.

SEE ALSO getByte().

EXAMPLE See getByte().

A B C D E F G H I J K L M N O P Q R S T U V W X Y Z

setChar()

PURPOSE Sets an element of a numerical array to a char value.

SYNTAX
```
public static native void setChar(Object ar, int ix, char ch)
   throws IllegalArgumentException,
   ArrayIndexOutOfBoundsException
```

DESCRIPTION This method can be used to update arrays of the following component types: char, int, long, float, and double.

PARAMETERS

ar The non-null numerical array.
ch The new char value.
ix The 0-based index of the desired element in ar.

EXCEPTIONS

ArrayIndexOutOfBoundsException
If ix is negative or greater than Array.getLength(ar)-1.

IllegalArgumentException
If ar is not an array or if the component type of ar is not one of char, int, long, float, or double.

SEE ALSO getChar().

EXAMPLE See getChar().

setDouble()

PURPOSE Sets an element of a numerical array to a double value.

SYNTAX
```
ublic static native void setDouble(Object ar, int ix,
   double dval) throws IllegalArgumentException,
   ArrayIndexOutOfBoundsException
```

DESCRIPTION This method can be used to update double arrays.

PARAMETERS

ar The non-null numerical array.
dval The new double value.
ix The 0-based index of the desired element in ar.

EXCEPTIONS

`ArrayIndexOutOfBoundsException`
If `ix` is negative or greater than `Array.getLength(ar)-1`.

`IllegalArgumentException`
If `ar` is not a `double` array.

SEE ALSO `getDouble()`.

EXAMPLE See `getDouble()`.

setFloat()

PURPOSE Sets an element of a numerical array to a `float` value.

SYNTAX

```
public static native void setFloat(Object ar, int ix,
   float fval) throws IllegalArgumentException,
   ArrayIndexOutOfBoundsException
```

DESCRIPTION This method can be used to update `float` and `double` arrays.

PARAMETERS

`ar` The non-`null` numerical array.
`fval` The new `float` value.
`ix` The `0`-based index of the desired element in `ar`.

EXCEPTIONS

`ArrayIndexOutOfBoundsException`
If `ix` is negative or greater than `Array.getLength(ar)-1`.

`IllegalArgumentException`
If `ar` is not a `double` or `float` array.

SEE ALSO `getFloat()`.

EXAMPLE See `getFloat()`.

setInt()

PURPOSE Sets an element of a numerical array to an `int` value.

SYNTAX

```
public static native void setInt(Object ar, int ix, int ival)
   throws IllegalArgumentException,
   ArrayIndexOutOfBoundsException
```

DESCRIPTION This method can be used to update arrays of the following component types: `int`, `long`, `float`, and `double`.

PARAMETERS

`ar`	The non-`null` numerical array.
`ival`	The new `long` value.
`ix`	The `0`-based index of the desired element in `ar`.

EXCEPTIONS

`ArrayIndexOutOfBoundsException`
If `ix` is negative or greater than `Array.getLength(ar)-1`.

`IllegalArgumentException`
If `ar` is not an array of one of the following component types: `int`, `long`, `float`, or `double`.

SEE ALSO `getLong()`.

EXAMPLE See `getLong()`.

setLong()

PURPOSE Sets an element of a numerical array to a `long` value.

SYNTAX

```
public static native void setLong(Object ar, int ix,
   long lval) throws IllegalArgumentException,
   ArrayIndexOutOfBoundsException
```

This method can be used to update arrays of the following component types: `long`, `float`, and `double`.

PARAMETERS

`ar`	The non-`null` numerical array.
`ix`	The `0`-based index of the desired element in `ar`.
`lval`	The new `long` value.

EXCEPTIONS

`ArrayIndexOutOfBoundsException`
If `ix` is negative or greater than `Array.getLength(ar)-1`.

`IllegalArgumentException`
If `ar` is not an array of one of the following component types: `long`, `float`, or `double`.

SEE ALSO `getLong()`.

EXAMPLE See `getLong()`.

setShort()

PURPOSE Sets an element of a numerical array to a `short` value.

SYNTAX
```
public static native void setShort(Object ar, int ix,
   short sval) throws IllegalArgumentException,
   ArrayIndexOutOfBoundsException
```

DESCRIPTION This method can be used to update arrays of the following component types: `short`, `int`, `long`, `float`, and `double`.

PARAMETERS

`ar`	The non-`null` numerical array.
`ix`	The `0`-based index of the desired element in `ar`.
`sval`	The new `short` value.

EXCEPTIONS

`ArrayIndexOutOfBoundsException`
If `ix` is negative or greater than `Array.getLength(ar)-1`.

`IllegalArgumentException`
If `ar` is not an array of one of the following component types: `short`, `int`, `long`, `float`, or `double`.

SEE ALSO `getShort()`.

EXAMPLE See `getShort()`.

java.lang
ArrayIndexOutOfBoundsException

A
B
C
D
E
F
G
H
I
J
K
L
M
N
O
P
Q
R
S
T
U
V
W
X
Y
Z

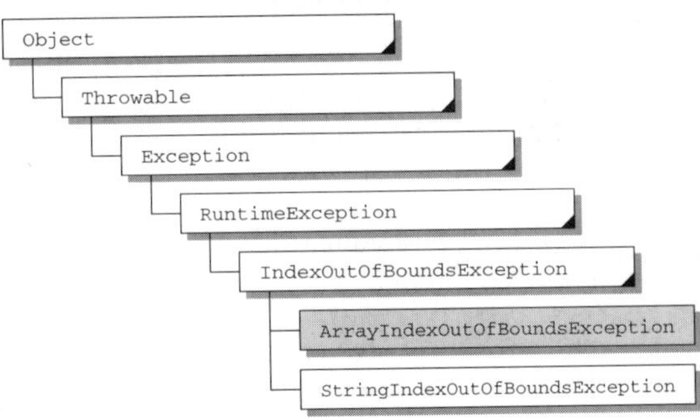

Syntax

```
public class ArrayIndexOutOfBoundsException extends IndexOutOfBoundsException
```

Description

`ArrayIndexOutOfBoundsException` is a runtime exception that is thrown when the program attempts to access an element within an array by using an index that is not within the bounds of the array. Because array indices use a zero-based numbering scheme, the index is usually either negative or a number greater than or equal to the array's length.

`ArrayIndexOutOfBoundsException` is a runtime exception that should not be caught or declared in the `throws` clause of a method.

MEMBER SUMMARY	
Constructor	
`ArrayIndexOutOfBoundsException()`	Constructs an instance of `ArrayIndexOutOfBoundsException`.

See Also

`IndexOutOfBoundsException`, `RuntimeException`.

Example

This example throws an ArrayIndexOutOfBoundsException.

```
class Main {
    public static void main(String[] args) {
        System.out.println("ArrayIndexOutOfBoundsException example");

        char[] buf = {'a', 'b', 'c'};
        int i;

        for (i = 0; i < buf.length; i++)
            System.out.println(buf[i]);

        System.out.println(buf[i]); // index out of bounds
    }
}
```

ArrayIndexOutOfBoundsException()

PURPOSE Constructs an ArrayIndexOutOfBoundsException instance.

SYNTAX

```
public ArrayIndexOutOfBoundsException()
public ArrayIndexOutOfBoundsException(int idx)
public ArrayIndexOutOfBoundsException(String msg)
```

DESCRIPTION These constructors construct an instance of ArrayIndexOutOfBoundsException. An optional string msg can be supplied that describes this particular instance of the exception. Alternatively, the index idx that caused the exception can be supplied to the constructor, which will use idx to construct a message for describing this exception. If neither msg nor idx is supplied, the message defaults to null.

PARAMETERS

idx The index that caused the exception.

msg A possibly null string that gives details about this exception.

SEE ALSO Throwable.getMessage().

java.lang
ArrayStoreException

A B C D E F G H I J K L M N O P Q R S T U V W X Y Z

- Object
  - Throwable
    - Exception
      - RuntimeException
        - ArrayStoreException
        - ArithmeticException
        - ClassCastException
        - IllegalArgumentException
        - IllegalMonitorStateException
        - IllegalStateException
        - IndexOutOfBoundsException
        - NegativeArraySizeException
        - NullPointerException
        - SecurityException
        - java.security.ProviderException
        - java.util.EmptyStackException
        - java.util.MissingResourceException
        - java.util.NoSuchElementException

Syntax

```
public class ArrayStoreException extends RuntimeException
```

Description

`ArrayStoreException` is a runtime exception that is thrown when the program attempts to store an object of the wrong type into an array. It should not be caught or declared in the `throws` clause of a method.

MEMBER SUMMARY	
Constructor	
`ArrayStoreException()`	Constructs an `ArrayStoreException` instance.

See Also

`RuntimeException`.

Example

This example throws an `ArrayStoreException` when it tries to store a `String` instance in an `Integer` array.

```
class Main {
    private static void storeItem(Object[]a, int i, Object item) {
        a[i] = item;
    }
    public static void main(String[] args) {
        System.out.println("ArrayStoreException Example");

        Integer[] a = new Integer[3];
        storeItem(a, 2, new String("abc"));
    }
}
```

ArrayStoreException()

PURPOSE
Constructs an `ArrayStoreException` instance.

SYNTAX
```
public ArrayStoreException()
public ArrayStoreException(String msg)
```

DESCRIPTION
These constructors construct an instance of `ArrayStoreException`. An optional string `msg` can be supplied that describes this particular instance of the exception. If `msg` is not supplied, it defaults to `null`.

PARAMETERS

`msg` A possibly `null` string that gives details about this exception.

SEE ALSO
`Throwable.getMessage()`.

java.math
BigDecimal

java.lang.Object
- java.lang.Number
  - BigDecimal
  - BigInteger
  - java.lang.Byte
  - java.lang.Double
  - java.lang.Float
  - java.lang.Integer
  - java.lang.Long
  - java.lang.Short

A B C D E F G H I J K L M N O P Q R S T U V W X Y Z

Syntax

```
public class BigDecimal extends Number
```

Description

A `BigDecimal` object represents an arbitrary-precision decimal number. The *scale* of a big decimal value is the number of digits to the right of the decimal point. For example, in the value `123.4560`, the scale is 4. Zeros at the end of the fractional part of a big decimal value are significant and are never automatically truncated to reduce the scale. For example, some operators do not consider `1.0` to be equal to `1.00`.

A `BigDecimal` object is immutable. That is, it contains a value that cannot be changed. Most big decimal operations yield a new `BigDecimal` object that holds the result of the operation. Big decimal values never overflow.

Usage

To perform big decimal arithmetic, you first must create `BigDecimal` objects that contain the values of the operands and then use the methods in this class to operate on those objects. For example, to multiply the values `1.2` and `3.4`, you create two `BigDecimal` objects, one for `1.2` and one for `3.4`. Then, you call `multiply()` using one object while passing in the other object. The result of `multiply()` is a new `BigDecimal` object containing the value `4.08`.

Scale

The scale of a big decimal value is the location of the decimal point counting from the right. It cannot be negative. The scale of the resulting big decimal value of an operation depends on the operation and the scales of the operands. For example, when two big decimal values are added together, the scale of the sum is the maximum of the scale of the two operands so that the addition yields an exact answer.

The scale of a big decimal value can be increased at any time; doing so never reduces the precision of the value. The scale also can be decreased, but when precision is lost, a rounding mode must be specified. See later in this class for more details on rounding.

Rounding Modes

Whenever an operation causes the big decimal value to lose precision, a rounding mode must be supplied to specify how the lost digits are to affect the remaining significant digits. In Figure 7, the value `123.4567890` is truncated to `123.456`. Digit `6` is called the *new tail digit*. The lost digits are converted to a fraction by prefixing the lost digits with a decimal point. The resulting fraction is called the *lost fraction*. The lost fraction of this example is `.7890`.

The rounding modes may use the value of the lost fraction, the tail digit itself, and the sign to determine how to affect the new tail digit. For example, in the `ROUND_CEILING` rounding mode, if the lost fraction is greater than `0`, the tail digit is incremented by `1`.

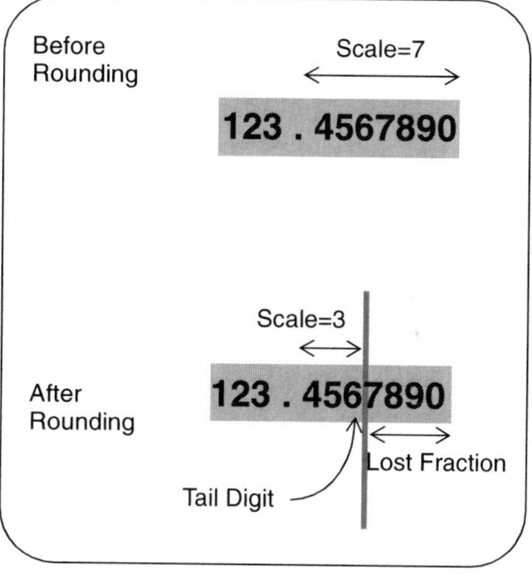

FIGURE 7: A Rounded Big Decimal Value.

Infinity and NaN

Big decimal values cannot be created from either the Infinity or `NaN` values. Moreover, none of the big decimal operations yield either the Infinity or `NaN` values.

MEMBER SUMMARY	
Constructor	
`BigDecimal()`	Constructs a `BigDecimal` instance.
Math Methods	
`abs()`	Calculates the absolute value of this big decimal value.
`add()`	Calculates the sum of this big decimal value and another.
`divide()`	Calculates the result of dividing this big decimal value by another.
`max()`	Compares this big decimal value with another and returns the greater of the two.
`min()`	Compares this big decimal value with another and returns the lesser of the two.

Continued

A B C D E F G H I J K L M N O P Q R S T U V W X Y Z

MEMBER SUMMARY	
Math Methods *(Continued)*	
`movePointLeft()`	Returns the result of moving the decimal point to the left.
`movePointRight()`	Returns the result of moving the decimal point to the right.
`multiply()`	Calculates the product of this big decimal value and another.
`negate()`	Calculates the product of this big decimal value and `-1`.
`signum()`	Determines the sign of this big decimal value.
`subtract()`	Calculates the difference of this big decimal value and another.
Comparison Methods	
`equals()`	Determines if this big decimal value is equal to another object.
`compareTo()`	Compares this big decimal value with another.
Conversion Methods	
`doubleValue()`	Converts this big decimal value to a `double` value.
`floatValue()`	Converts this big decimal value to a `float` value.
`intValue()`	Converts this big decimal value to an `int` value.
`longValue()`	Converts this big decimal value to a `long` value.
`toBigInteger()`	Converts this big decimal value to a big integer value.
`valueOf()`	Returns a `BigDecimal` instance for a primitive integer value.
Scaling Methods	
`scale()`	Retrieves the scale of this big decimal value.
`setScale()`	Returns the result of changing the scale of this big decimal value.
Rounding Mode Constants	
`ROUND_CEILING`	Rounding mode that specifies rounding toward positive Infinity.
`ROUND_DOWN`	Rounding mode that specifies rounding toward zero.
`ROUND_FLOOR`	Rounding mode that specifies rounding toward negative Infinity.
`ROUND_HALF_DOWN`	Rounding mode that specifies rounding toward the nearest neighbor; if equidistant, rounding is toward zero.
`ROUND_HALF_EVEN`	Rounding mode that specifies rounding toward the nearest neighbor; if equidistant, rounding is toward the even new tail digit.
`ROUND_HALF_UP`	Rounding mode that specifies rounding toward the nearest neighbor; if equidistant, rounding is away from zero.
`ROUND_UNNECESSARY`	Rounding mode that specifies that loss of precision must not occur.
`ROUND_UP`	Rounding mode that specifies rounding away from zero.
Object Methods	
`hashCode()`	Computes the hash code for this big decimal value.
`toString()`	Generates a string representing this big decimal value.

A B C D E F G H I J K L M N O P Q R S T U V W X Y Z

See Also

`BigInteger`.

Example

This example implements a simple stack-based calculator. To use it, you first enter a value and then press the ENT key to push the value onto the stack. You then enter another value and press the desired operation key. For example, to divide 1 by 3, you press 1, then ENT, then 3, and then `/`. See Figure 8.

The calculator maintains an internal scale of 50 digits used for all calculations done by the calculator. The calculator also maintains a scale for displaying values. This output scale can be increased or decreased by hitting the >P and <P keys, respectively.

FIGURE 8: Simple Stack-Based Calculator.

```
import java.awt.*;
import java.awt.event.*;
import java.math.*;
import java.util.*;

class Main extends Frame implements ActionListener {
    // Used to show the current values.
    TextField display = new TextField();

    // Scale used internally for calculations.
    int inScale = 50;

    // Scale used to display answers.
    int outScale = 3;

    Main() {
        super("BigDecimal Example");
        Panel p = new Panel(new GridLayout(0, 4));
        String[] keys = {"ABS", "NEG", ">P", "<P",
                         "7", "8", "9", "/",
                         "4", "5", "6", "*",
                         "1", "2", "3", "-",
                         "MIN", "0", ".", "+",
                         "MAX", "CE", "POP", "ENT" };

        // Create the panel.
        for (int i=0; i<keys.length; i++) {
            Button b = new Button(keys[i]);
            b.addActionListener(this);
            p.add(b);
        }
        add(p, BorderLayout.CENTER);

        // Add the display and show the frame.
        add(display, BorderLayout.NORTH);
        display.setEditable(false);
        pack();
```

```
        show();
    }

    // Stack of values.
    Stack stack = new Stack();

    // If the stack is empty return 0.
    BigDecimal pop() {
        if (stack.empty()) {
            return BigDecimal.valueOf(0, inScale);
        }
        return (BigDecimal)stack.pop();
    }

    BigDecimal getDisplayValue() {
        if (display.getText() == null
                || display.getText().length() == 0
                || display.getText().equals(".")) {
            return BigDecimal.valueOf(0, inScale);
        }
        BigDecimal n = new BigDecimal(display.getText());
        return n.setScale(Math.max(inScale, n.scale()));
    }

    // If true, all digits, periods will be appended to the value
    // on the display.
    boolean inputMode;

    public void actionPerformed(ActionEvent evt) {
        BigDecimal n = getDisplayValue();
        String key = ((Button)evt.getSource()).getLabel();
        char c = key.charAt(0);
        boolean newInputMode = false;

        if ((c >= '0' && c <= '9') || c == '.') {
            if (!inputMode) {
                stack.push(n);
                inputMode = true;
            } else {
                key = display.getText() + key;
            }
            display.setText(key);
            return;
        }

        if (key.equals("+")) {
            n = pop().add(n);
        } else if (key.equals("-")) {
            n = pop().subtract(n);
        } else if (key.equals("*")) {
            n = pop().multiply(n).setScale(inScale, BigDecimal.ROUND_HALF_UP);
        } else if (key.equals("/")) {
            n = pop().divide(n, BigDecimal.ROUND_HALF_UP);
        } else if (key.equals("ABS")) {
            n = n.abs();
            newInputMode = inputMode;
        } else if (key.equals("NEG")) {
            n = n.negate();
            newInputMode = inputMode;
        } else if (key.equals("<P")) {
```

```
                outScale = Math.max(0, outScale-1);
                newInputMode = inputMode;
            } else if (key.equals(">P")) {
                outScale++;
                newInputMode = inputMode;
            } else if (key.equals("MIN")) {
                n = pop().min(n);
            } else if (key.equals("MAX")) {
                n = pop().max(n);
            } else if (key.equals("CE")) {
                n = new BigDecimal(0).setScale(inScale);
            } else if (key.equals("POP")) {
                n = pop();
            } else if (key.equals("STO")) {
                stack.push(n);
            }

            inputMode = newInputMode;

            if (!inputMode) {
                // Display the number using the display scale.
                display.setText("" +
                    n.setScale(outScale, BigDecimal.ROUND_HALF_UP));
            }
        }

        public static void main(String[] args) {
            new Main();
        }
    }
```

abs()

PURPOSE Calculates the absolute value of this big decimal value.

SYNTAX `public BigDecimal abs()`

DESCRIPTION If N is $\geq$ `0`, the absolute value of N is N. If $N <$ `0`, the absolute value of N is $-N$. This method calculates and returns a `BigDecimal` object that contains the absolute value of this big decimal value.

The scale of the result is the same as for this big decimal value.

RETURNS A non-`null` `BigDecimal` object containing the absolute value of this big decimal value.

EXAMPLE

```
BigDecimal a = new BigDecimal("1.23");
System.out.println(a.abs());                    // 1.23

a = new BigDecimal(-6.25);
System.out.println(a);// -6.25

System.out.println(a.abs());                    // 6.25
```

add()

PURPOSE Calculates the sum of this big decimal value and another.

SYNTAX `public BigDecimal add(BigDecimal val)`

DESCRIPTION This method calculates the sum of adding `val` to this big decimal value and returns a `BigDecimal` that represents the sum. The return value is *exactly* equal to the sum with no loss of precision. The scale of the return value is

`Math.max(this.scale(), val.scale()).`

This is sufficient to represent the sum without loss of precision. Neither the value of `val` nor that of this big decimal is changed.

PARAMETERS

`val` A non-`null` `BigDecimal` object.

RETURNS A non-`null` `BigDecimal` object containing this big decimal value plus `val`.

EXAMPLE This example implements Newton's algorithm for approximating square roots.

```
import java.math.*;

class Main {
    public static void main(String[] args) {
        for (int i=0; i<args.length; i++) {
            System.out.println("sqrt("+args[i]+") = " +
                sqrt(BigDecimal.valueOf(Integer.parseInt(args[i]))));
        }
    }

    public static BigDecimal sqrt(BigDecimal n) {
        BigDecimal TWO = BigDecimal.valueOf(2);

        // First approximation.
        BigDecimal x = n.divide(BigDecimal.valueOf(3), 20,
            BigDecimal.ROUND_DOWN);
        BigDecimal lastX = BigDecimal.valueOf(0);

        for (int i=0; i<50; i++) {
            x = n.add(x.multiply(x)).divide(x.multiply(TWO), 20,
                BigDecimal.ROUND_DOWN);
            if (x.compareTo(lastX) == 0) {
                break;
            }
            lastX = x;
        }
        return x;
    }
}
```

Output

```
sqrt(2) = 1.41421356237309504880
sqrt(3) = 1.73205080756887729352
sqrt(4) = 2.00000000000000000000
```

A B C D E F G H I J K L M N O P Q R S T U V W X Y Z

```
sqrt(5) = 2.23606797749978969640
sqrt(6) = 2.44948974278317809819
```

BigDecimal()

PURPOSE Constructs a `BigDecimal` instance.

SYNTAX

```
public BigDecimal(BigInteger bval)
public BigDecimal(double dval) throws NumberFormatException
public BigDecimal(String sval) throws NumberFormatException
public BigDecimal(BigInteger bval, int scale) throws
   NumberFormatException
```

DESCRIPTION The first form of the constructor creates a new `BigDecimal` object initialized with the value in `bval`. The scale of the result is `0`.

The second form of the constructor creates a new `BigDecimal` object initialized with the value `dval`. `dval` cannot be Infinity, negative Infinity, or `NaN`. Note that the numerical value of a `double` is sometimes not exactly the value declared by the program. For example, with a declaration of

```
double d = 1.23;
```

the value of `d` might be `1.2299999....` (see the example). To avoid such unintended imprecision, use the third form of the constructor.

The third form of the constructor creates a new `BigDecimal` object initialized with the radix 10 value specified in the string. The string may contain only an optional leading negative sign, digits, and one decimal point (period); it may not contain any whitespaces.

The fourth form of the constructor creates a new `BigDecimal` object initialized with the value `bval/10^scale`. The scale of the new object is `scale`. See `valueOf()` for a convenient method for creating `BigDecimal` objects from primitive integer values (`long`, `int`, `short`, and `byte`).

PARAMETERS

`bval`	A non-`null` `BigDecimal` object.
`dval`	A `double` value whose value is not Infinity, negative Infinity, or `NaN`.
`scale`	The nonnegative scale of the new big decimal value.
`sval`	A non-`null` `String` containing a valid number in radix 10.

EXCEPTIONS

`NumberFormatException`
If `dval`, `sval`, or `scale` is not a valid number.

SEE ALSO `Double.isInfinite()`, `Double.isNaN()`, `valueOf()`.

A B C D E F G H I J K L M N O P Q R S T U V W X Y Z

EXAMPLE

Note that the `BigDecimal` created from the `double` `1.23` (`1.2299999...`) is the exact value of the closest `double` to `1.23`. To obtain a `BigDecimal` with an exact value of `1.23`, use the constructor with the string "1.23".

```
BigDecimal a = new BigDecimal(1.23);
System.out.println(a);
    // 1.229999999999999982236431605997495353221893310546875

double d = Double.MAX_VALUE * Double.MAX_VALUE;
// a = new BigDecimal(d);                          // NumberFormatException

a = new BigDecimal("-123.456");
System.out.println(new BigDecimal("123."));        // 123
System.out.println(new BigDecimal(".123"));        // 0.123
System.out.println(new BigDecimal(".0"));          // 0.0
System.out.println(new BigDecimal("0."));          // 0
// a = new BigDecimal(" 123.456");                 // NumberFormatException
// a = new BigDecimal("123.456 ");                 // NumberFormatException
// a = new BigDecimal("+123.456");                 // NumberFormatException
// a = new BigDecimal(".");                        // NumberFormatException

a = new BigDecimal(new BigInteger("123"), 2);
System.out.println(a);                             // 1.23
```

compareTo()

PURPOSE

Compares this big decimal value with another.

SYNTAX

`public int compareTo(BigDecimal val)`

DESCRIPTION

If this big decimal value is less than `val`, `-1` is returned. If this big decimal value is equal to `val`, `0` is returned. If this big decimal value is greater than `val`, `1` is returned.

The equals test used in this method differs from `equals()`. In particular, with `equals()`, not only must the values be numerically equal, but so must their scales. For example, `equals()` would not consider `1.0` and `1.00` equal. `compareTo()` compares only the numerical values and hence would consider `1.0` and `1.00` to be equal.

PARAMETERS

`val` A non-`null` `BigDecimal` object.

RETURNS

`-1`, `0`, or `1`, depending on how this big decimal value compares with `val`.

SEE ALSO

`equals()`.

EXAMPLE

```
BigDecimal a = new BigDecimal("1.23");
BigDecimal b = new BigDecimal("1.234");
System.out.println(a.compareTo(b));          // -1
System.out.println(b.compareTo(a));          // 1
```

A B C D E F G H I J K L M N O P Q R S T U V W X Y Z

```
a = new BigDecimal("1.23");
b = new BigDecimal("1.2300");
System.out.println(a.compareTo(b));          // 0
System.out.println(a.equals(b));             // false
```


divide()

PURPOSE Calculates the result of dividing this big decimal value by another.

SYNTAX

```
public BigDecimal divide(BigDecimal val, int roundingMode) throws
    ArithmeticException, IllegalArgumentException
public BigDecimal divide(BigDecimal val, int newScale, int
    roundingMode) throws ArithmeticException,
    IllegalArgumentException
```

DESCRIPTION This method divides this big decimal value by `val` and returns a `BigDecimal` that represents the result. The scale of the result is `newScale`. If `newScale` is not specified, it defaults to the scale of this object. If there is a loss of precision in the result, the specified rounding mode is used to determine how the lost fraction affects the remaining value. See the various rounding modes for more details.

Neither the value of `val` nor that of this big decimal is changed.

PARAMETERS

`newScale` A nonnegative integer that specifies the scale of the result.

`roundingMode`
One of the eight possible rounding modes.

`val` A non-`null` `BigDecimal` object.

RETURNS A non-`null` `BigDecimal` object containing this big decimal value divided by `val`.

EXCEPTIONS

`ArithmeticException`
If `val` is equal to `0` or if the rounding mode is `ROUND_UNNECESSARY` and rounding occurs.

`IllegalArgumentException`
If `roundingMode` is not a valid rounding mode.

SEE ALSO `java.lang.ArithmeticException`.

EXAMPLE

```
import java.math.*;
class Main {
    public static void main(String[] args) {
        BigDecimal a = new BigDecimal("10.00");
```

```
            print(a.divide(new BigDecimal("5"), BigDecimal.ROUND_UNNECESSARY));
                                                        // 2.00

            //print(a.divide(new BigDecimal("3"), BigDecimal.ROUND_UNNECESSARY));
                                                        // ArithmeticException

            print(a.divide(new BigDecimal("3"), BigDecimal.ROUND_DOWN));
                                                        // 3.33

            print(a.divide(new BigDecimal("3"), 10, BigDecimal.ROUND_DOWN));
                                                        // 3.3333333333

            print(a.divide(new BigDecimal("3"), 10, BigDecimal.ROUND_CEILING));
                                                        // 3.3333333334
        }

        static void print(BigDecimal a) {
            System.out.println(a);
        }
    }
```

doubleValue()

PURPOSE Converts this big decimal value to a `double` value.

SYNTAX `public double doubleValue()`

DESCRIPTION The returned `double` value is an approximation of this big decimal value. If the magnitude of this big decimal value is larger than what can be represented by a `double` value, a value of either Infinity or negative Infinity is returned.

RETURNS A `double` value approximating this big decimal value.

SEE ALSO `Number.doubleValue()`.

EXAMPLE

```
BigDecimal a = new BigDecimal(1.23);
System.out.println(a.doubleValue());        // 1.23

// Make a very large number.
a = new BigDecimal(Double.MAX_VALUE);
a = a.add(a);
System.out.println(a.doubleValue());        // Infinity
```

equals()

PURPOSE Determines if this big decimal value is equal to another object.

SYNTAX `public boolean equals(Object val)`

DESCRIPTION This method returns `true` only if `val` is an instance of `BigDecimal`, this big decimal value is numerically equal to `val`, and the scales of both big decimal values are equal. For example, `1.0` is equal to `1.0` but is not equal to `1.00`. This method differs from `compareTo()` in that `compareTo()` compares only the numerical values; the scales need not be the same.

PARAMETERS

`val` A possibly `null` object.

RETURNS `true` if `val` is a `BigDecimal` and both the value and scale of this big decimal value and `val` are the same.

OVERRIDES `java.lang.Object.equals()`.

SEE ALSO `compareTo()`, `hashCode()`.

EXAMPLE

```
BigDecimal a = new BigDecimal("-123.45");
BigDecimal b = new BigDecimal("123.45");
System.out.println(a.negate().equals(b));     // true

a = new BigDecimal("1.23");
b = new BigDecimal("1.230");
System.out.println(a.equals(b));              // false

System.out.println(a.compareTo(b));           // 0
```

floatValue()

PURPOSE Converts this big decimal value to a `float` value.

SYNTAX `public float floatValue()`

DESCRIPTION The returned `float` value is an approximation of this big decimal value. If the magnitude of this big decimal value is larger than what can be represented by a `float` value, a value of either Infinity or negative Infinity is returned.

RETURNS A `float` value approximating this big decimal value.

SEE ALSO `Number.floatValue()`.

EXAMPLE

```
BigDecimal a = new BigDecimal("1.99");
System.out.println(a.floatValue());  // 1.99

a = new BigDecimal(Double.MAX_VALUE);
System.out.println(a.floatValue());  // Infinity

a = new BigDecimal(-Double.MAX_VALUE);
System.out.println(a.floatValue());  // -Infinity
```

A
B
C
D
E
F
G
H
I
J
K
L
M
N
O
P
Q
R
S
T
U
V
W
X
Y
Z

hashCode()

PURPOSE Computes the hash code for this big decimal value.

SYNTAX `public int hashCode()`

DESCRIPTION The big decimal value's hash code is an integer that is calculated from the value and scale. Two big decimal values whose numerical values and scales are equal will have the same hash code. However, unequal big decimal values might also have the same hash code, although the hash code algorithm minimizes this possibility. The hash code is typically used as the key in a hash table.

Note that two numerically equal big decimal values that have different scales generally do not have the same hash code. For example, `1.0` and `1.00` have different hash codes.

RETURNS The big decimal value's hash code.

OVERRIDES `java.lang.Object.hashCode()`.

SEE ALSO `equals()`, `java.util.Hashtable`.

EXAMPLE See `java.lang.Object.hashCode()`.

intValue()

PURPOSE Converts this big decimal value to an `int` value.

SYNTAX `public int intValue()`

DESCRIPTION The fractional part of this big decimal value is truncated and the remaining integer part is converted to an `int`. Only the lower-order 32-bits of this big decimal value are used.

RETURNS An `int` representing this big decimal value.

SEE ALSO `Number.intValue()`.

EXAMPLE

```
BigDecimal a = new BigDecimal("1.99");

System.out.println(a.intValue());  // 1

a = new BigDecimal("2342341908309182309128393 3");
System.out.println(a.intValue());  // -249268259
```

longValue()

PURPOSE Converts this big decimal value to a `long` value.

SYNTAX `public long longValue()`

DESCRIPTION The fractional part of this big decimal value is truncated and the remaining integer part is converted to a `long`. Only the lower-order 64-bits of this big decimal value are used.

RETURNS A `long` representing this big decimal value.

SEE ALSO `Number.longValue()`.

EXAMPLE

```
BigDecimal a = new BigDecimal("1.99");
System.out.println(a.longValue());  // 1

a = new BigDecimal("313234234234190830918230912839933");
System.out.println(a.longValue());  // -5251313250005125155
```

max()

PURPOSE Compares this big decimal value with another and returns the greater of the two.

SYNTAX `public BigDecimal max(BigDecimal val)`

DESCRIPTION This method returns either this `BigDecimal` object or `val`, whichever is greater. If they are equal, `val` is returned. The scale of the returned object is not modified. The scales of the big decimal values are ignored for the purpose of the comparison.

PARAMETERS

`val` A non-`null` `BigDecimal` object.

RETURNS Either this object or `val`, whichever is greater.

EXAMPLE

```
out.println(new BigDecimal("1.23").max(new BigDecimal("1.234")));  // 1.234
out.println(new BigDecimal("1.23").max(new BigDecimal("1.230")));  // 1.230
out.println(new BigDecimal("1.2300").max(new BigDecimal("1.23"))); // 1.23
```

min()

PURPOSE Compares this big decimal value with another and returns the lesser of the two.

SYNTAX `public BigDecimal min(BigDecimal val)`

DESCRIPTION This method returns either this `BigDecimal` object or `val`, whichever is less. If they are equal, `val` is returned. The scale of the returned object is not modified. The scales of the big decimal values are ignored for the purpose of the comparison.

PARAMETERS

`val` A non-null `BigDecimal` object.

RETURNS Either this `object` or `val`, whichever is less.

EXAMPLE

```
out.println(new BigDecimal("1.23").min(new BigDecimal("1.234")));  // 1.23
out.println(new BigDecimal("1.23").min(new BigDecimal("1.230")));  // 1.230
out.println(new BigDecimal("1.2300").min(new BigDecimal("1.23"))); // 1.23
```

movePointLeft()

PURPOSE Returns the result of moving the decimal point to the left.

SYNTAX `public BigDecimal movePointLeft(int n)`

DESCRIPTION This method returns a `BigDecimal` that is the same as this big decimal value, except that the decimal point is moved to the left by `n` places. If `n` is negative, the decimal point is moved to the right by –`n` places. This method is equivalent to multiplying this big decimal value by `10^-n`.

The scale of the result is `Math.max(0, this.scale()+n)`. The value of this big decimal is not changed.

PARAMETERS

`n` The number of places to the left to move the decimal point. If negative, the number of places to move the decimal point to the right.

RETURNS A non-null `BigDecimal` object containing this big decimal value multiplied by `10^-n`.

EXAMPLE

```
BigDecimal a = new BigDecimal("1.00");

System.out.println(a.scale());      // 2

a = a.movePointLeft(1);
System.out.println(a);              // 0.100
System.out.println(a.scale());      // 3

a = a.movePointLeft(-2);
System.out.println(a);              // 10.0
System.out.println(a.scale());      // 1
```

movePointRight()

PURPOSE Returns the result of moving the decimal point to the right.

SYNTAX `public BigDecimal movePointRight(int n)`

DESCRIPTION This method returns a `BigDecimal` that is the same as this decimal, except that the decimal point is moved to the right by `n` places. If `n` is negative, the decimal point is moved to the left by –`n` places. This method is equivalent to multiplying this big decimal value by `10^n`.

The scale of the result is `Math.max(0, this.scale()-n)`. The value of this big decimal is not changed.

PARAMETERS

`n` The number of places to the right to move the decimal point. If negative, the number of places to the left to move the decimal point.

RETURNS A non-`null` `BigDecimal` object containing this big decimal value multiplied by `10^n`.

EXAMPLE

```
BigDecimal a = new BigDecimal("1.0");

System.out.println(a.scale());      // scale 1

a = a.movePointRight(2);
System.out.println(a);              // 100
System.out.println(a.scale());      // scale 0

a = a.movePointRight(-3);
System.out.println(a);              // .100
System.out.println(a.scale());      // scale 3
```

multiply()

PURPOSE Calculates the product of this big decimal value and another.

SYNTAX `public BigDecimal multiply(BigDecimal val)`

DESCRIPTION This method multiplies the value of `val` with this big decimal value and returns a `BigDecimal` that represents the product. The scale used in the calculation is `this.scale()+val.scale()`. This is also the scale of the returned big decimal value. Neither the value of `val` nor that of this big decimal value is changed.

PARAMETERS

`val` A non-`null` `BigDecimal` object.

RETURNS A non-`null` `BigDecimal` object containing this big decimal value times `val`.

EXAMPLE Ever wonder what the square of the largest `double` value is?

```
System.out.println(
    new BigDecimal(Double.MAX_VALUE).multiply(
        new BigDecimal(Double.MAX_VALUE)));
```

Output

```
323170060713110001248980312245795738430907116738220374205158864782928239949931
```

A
B
C
D
E
F
G
H
I
J
K
L
M
N
O
P
Q
R
S
T
U
V
W
X
Y
Z

negate()

PURPOSE Calculates the product of this big decimal value and `-1`.

SYNTAX `public BigDecimal negate()`

DESCRIPTION This method multiplies this big decimal value by `-1` and returns a `BigDecimal` that represents the product. The scale of the result is the same as that of this big decimal value. This big decimal value is not changed.

RETURNS A non-`null` `BigDecimal` object containing this big decimal value multiplied by `-1`.

EXAMPLE

```
System.out.println(new BigDecimal("-1.23").negate()); // 1.23
```

ROUND_CEILING

PURPOSE Rounding mode that specifies rounding toward positive Infinity.

SYNTAX `public final static int ROUND_CEILING`

DESCRIPTION If the value is positive and the lost fraction is > `0`, the new tail digit is incremented by 1. If the value is negative, the new tail digit is not affected.

With this rounding mode, the resulting value is never less than the current value. For example, `1.5` rounds to `2` and `-1.5` rounds to `-1`.

See the class description for more information about rounding modes.

SEE ALSO `setScale()`, `divide()`.

EXAMPLE See `setScale()`.

ROUND_DOWN

PURPOSE Rounding mode that specifies rounding toward zero.

SYNTAX `public final static int ROUND_DOWN`

DESCRIPTION With this rounding mode, the lost fraction is simply dropped and does not affect the new tail digit. For example, `1.5` rounds to `1` and `-1.5` rounds to `-1`.

See the class description for more information about rounding modes.

SEE ALSO `setScale(), divide().`

EXAMPLE See `setScale()`.

ROUND_FLOOR

PURPOSE Rounding mode that specifies rounding toward negative Infinity.

SYNTAX `public final static int ROUND_FLOOR`

DESCRIPTION If the value is positive, the lost fraction does not affect the tail digit. If the value is negative and the lost fraction is > 0, the new tail digit is incremented by 1.

With this rounding mode, the resulting value is never greater than the current value. For example, `1.5` rounds to `1` and `-1.5` rounds to `-2`.

See the class description for more information about rounding modes.

SEE ALSO `setScale(), divide().`

EXAMPLE See `setScale()`.

ROUND_HALF_DOWN

PURPOSE Rounding mode that specifies rounding toward the nearest neighbor; if equidistant, rounding is toward zero.

SYNTAX `public final static int ROUND_HALF_DOWN`

DESCRIPTION If the lost fraction is ≤ `.5`, the big decimal value is rounded toward zero. If the lost fraction is > `.5`, the big decimal value is rounded away from zero. For example,

`1.1` rounds to `1`
`1.5` rounds to `1`
`1.9` rounds to `2`
`-1.1` rounds to `-1`
`-1.5` rounds to `-1`
`-1.9` rounds to `-2`

See the class description for more information about rounding modes.

SEE ALSO `setScale(), divide().`

EXAMPLE See `setScale()`.

ROUND_HALF_EVEN

PURPOSE Rounding mode that specifies rounding toward the nearest neighbor; if equidistant, rounding is toward the even new tail digit.

SYNTAX `public final static int ROUND_HALF_EVEN`

DESCRIPTION Rounding behaves as for `ROUND_HALF_UP` if the digit to the left of the discarded fraction is odd; it behaves as for `ROUND_HALF_DOWN` if that digit is even. (That is, rounding is toward the "nearest neighbor" unless both neighbors are equidistant, in which case, rounding is toward the even neighbor.)

If the lost fraction is < `.5`, the value is rounded toward zero. If the lost fraction is > `.5`, the value is rounded away from zero. If the lost fraction is equal to `.5`, the new tail digit is made even if it is not already even. For example,

`1.1` rounds to `1`
`1.5` rounds to `2`
`1.9` rounds to `2`
`2.5` rounds to `2`
`-1.1` rounds to `-1`
`-1.5` rounds to `-2`
`-1.9` rounds to `-2`
`-2.5` rounds to `-2`

See the class description for more information about rounding modes.

SEE ALSO `setScale(), divide().`

EXAMPLE See `setScale()`.

ROUND_HALF_UP

PURPOSE Rounding mode that specifies rounding toward the nearest neighbor; if equidistant, rounding is away from zero.

SYNTAX `public final static int ROUND_HALF_UP`

DESCRIPTION If the lost fraction is < `.5`, the value is rounded toward zero. If the lost fraction is ≥ `.5`, the value is rounded away from zero. For example,

`1.1` rounds to `1`
`1.5` rounds to `2`
`1.9` rounds to `2`
`-1.1` rounds to `-1`
`-1.5` rounds to `-2`
`-1.9` rounds to `-2`

See the class description for more information about rounding modes.

SEE ALSO `setScale(), divide().`

EXAMPLE See `setScale()`.

ROUND_UNNECESSARY

PURPOSE Rounding mode that specifies that loss of precision must not occur.

SYNTAX
```
public final static int ROUND_UNNECESSARY
```

DESCRIPTION When the scale of an operation's result might be reduced from that of the operation's operands, a rounding mode must be supplied to specify how the lost digits are to affect the remaining significant digits. However, if no loss of precision is expected (that is, the lost fraction is equal to `0`), `ROUND_UNNECESSARY` can be used as the rounding mode. With this rounding mode, should a loss of precision occur, the operation will result in an `ArithmeticException`.

SEE ALSO `java.lang.ArithmeticException.`

EXAMPLE See `setScale()`.

ROUND_UP

PURPOSE Rounding mode that specifies rounding away from zero.

SYNTAX
```
public final static int ROUND_UP
```

DESCRIPTION If the lost fraction is greater than `0`, the tail digit is incremented by `1`. For example, `1.5` rounds to `2` and `-1.5` rounds to `-2`.

See the class description for more information about rounding modes.

SEE ALSO `setScale(), divide().`

EXAMPLE See `setScale()`.

scale()

PURPOSE Retrieves the scale of this big decimal value.

SYNTAX
```
public int scale()
```

DESCRIPTION The scale of a big decimal value is the number of digits to the right of the decimal point.

RETURNS A nonnegative integer indicating the scale of this value.

SEE ALSO `setScale()`.

EXAMPLE See `movePointLeft()`.

A B C D E F G H I J K L M N O P Q R S T U V W X Y Z

setScale()

PURPOSE Returns the result of changing the scale of this big decimal value.

SYNTAX
```
public BigDecimal setScale(int newScale) throws
   ArithmeticException, IllegalArgumentException
public BigDecimal setScale(int newScale, int roundingMode) throws
   ArithmeticException, IllegalArgumentException
```

DESCRIPTION This method is used to obtain a big decimal value that has the same numerical value as this big decimal value but a different scale. If `newScale` is greater than the current scale, zeroes are appended to the end of the fractional part of this big decimal value. For example, changing the scale of `1.23` to `3` produces a value of `1.230`. Increasing the scale never changes the big decimal's numerical value.

If `newScale` is less than the current scale, the resulting big decimal value may lose precision. This means that a rounding mode must be supplied to specify how the lost fraction is to affect the remaining value. For example, changing the scale of `1.23` to `1` may produce a value of either `1.2` or `1.3`, depending on the rounding mode used. See the class description for more information about rounding modes.

If `roundingMode` is not specified, it defaults to `ROUND_UNNECESSARY`.

This big decimal value is not changed by this method.

PARAMETERS

`newScale` The new nonnegative scale of the resulting big decimal value.

`roundingMode`
One of the eight possible rounding modes.

RETURNS A non-`null` big decimal value with the same numeric value as this big decimal value but a scale of `newScale`.

EXCEPTIONS

`ArithmeticException`
If `newScale <0` or if `roundingMode` is `ROUND_UNNECESSARY` and rounding occurs.

`IllegalArgumentException`
If `roundingMode` is not a valid rounding mode.

SEE ALSO `java.lang.ArithmeticException`.

EXAMPLE

```
import java.math.*;

class Main {
    static void round(String num, int scale, int roundingMode) {
        System.out.println(new BigDecimal(num).setScale(scale, roundingMode));
    }

    public static void main(String[] args) {
        // Increasing the scale.
        BigDecimal a = new BigDecimal("1.23");
        System.out.println(a.setScale(3));                    // 1.230

        // Decreasing the scale.
        round(".5", 0, BigDecimal.ROUND_CEILING);             // 1
        round(".5", 0, BigDecimal.ROUND_DOWN);                // 0
        round(".5", 0, BigDecimal.ROUND_FLOOR);               // 0
        round(".5", 0, BigDecimal.ROUND_HALF_DOWN);           // 0
        round(".5", 0, BigDecimal.ROUND_HALF_EVEN);           // 0
        round(".5", 0, BigDecimal.ROUND_HALF_UP);             // 1
        round(".4", 0, BigDecimal.ROUND_HALF_UP);             // 0
        round(".4", 0, BigDecimal.ROUND_UP);                  // 1
       //round(".5", 0, BigDecimal.ROUND_UNNECESSARY);       // ArithmeticException
        round("1.0", 0, BigDecimal.ROUND_UNNECESSARY);        // 1

        round("-.5", 0, BigDecimal.ROUND_CEILING);            // 0
        round("-.5", 0, BigDecimal.ROUND_DOWN);               // 0
        round("-.5", 0, BigDecimal.ROUND_FLOOR);              // -1
        round("-.5", 0, BigDecimal.ROUND_HALF_DOWN);          // 0
        round("-.5", 0, BigDecimal.ROUND_HALF_EVEN);          // 0
        round("-.5", 0, BigDecimal.ROUND_HALF_UP);            // -1
        round("-.4", 0, BigDecimal.ROUND_HALF_UP);            // 0
        round("-.4", 0, BigDecimal.ROUND_UP);                 // -1
       //round("-.5", 0, BigDecimal.ROUND_UNNECESSARY);      // ArithmeticException
        round("-1.0", 0, BigDecimal.ROUND_UNNECESSARY);       // -1
    }
}
```

signum()

PURPOSE Determines the sign of this big decimal value.

SYNTAX `public int signum()`

DESCRIPTION If the value of this big decimal is negative, this method returns `-1`. If the value is `0`, this method returns `0`. If the value is greater than `0`, this method returns `1`.

RETURNS `-1`, `0`, or `1`, depending on the sign of this big decimal value.

EXAMPLE

```
BigDecimal a = new BigDecimal(-1.23);
System.out.println(a.signum());      // -1

a = new BigDecimal(0);
System.out.println(a.signum());      // 0
```

```
a = new BigDecimal(1.23);
System.out.println(a.signum());     // 1
```


subtract()

PURPOSE Calculates the difference of this big decimal value and another.

SYNTAX `public BigDecimal subtract(BigDecimal val)`

DESCRIPTION This method subtracts `val` from this big decimal value and returns a `BigDecimal` that represents the difference. The return value is *exactly* equal to the difference, with no loss of precision. The scale of the return value is

`Math.max(this.scale(), val.scale()).`

This is sufficient to represent the difference without loss of precision. Neither the value of `val` nor that of this big decimal is changed.

PARAMETERS

`val` A non-`null` `BigDecimal` object.

RETURNS A non-`null` `BigDecimal` object containing this big decimal value minus `val`.

EXAMPLE

```
System.out.println(
    new BigDecimal("1.23").subtract(new BigDecimal("1.234"))); // -0.004
```

toBigInteger()

PURPOSE Converts this big decimal value to a big integer value.

SYNTAX `public BigInteger toBigInteger()`

DESCRIPTION This method converts this big decimal number into a big integer value by discarding the fractional part of this big decimal number.

RETURNS A non-`null` `BigInteger` object containing the nonfractional part of this big decimal value.

SEE ALSO `BigInteger`.

EXAMPLE

```
System.out.println(new BigDecimal("-123.45").toBigInteger()); // -123
System.out.println(new BigDecimal("123.45").toBigInteger());  // 123
```

toString()

PURPOSE

Generates a string representing this big decimal value.

SYNTAX

`public String toString()`

DESCRIPTION

This method returns a string representing this big decimal value in radix 10. The scale of the value is preserved. If the big decimal value is negative, a negative sign precedes the value. The resulting string can be used in the `BigDecimal()` constructor to create a new `BigDecimal` object that has the same value and scale as this object.

If the value is between `0` and `1`, the returned string includes a `0` that precedes the decimal point. For example, the value `.123` produces the string "0.123".

RETURNS

A non-`null` string containing this big decimal value in radix 10.

OVERRIDES

`java.lang.Object.toString()`.

EXAMPLE

```
// The scale is preserved.
BigDecimal a = new BigDecimal("-123.000");
System.out.println(a.toString());     // "-123.000"

a = new BigDecimal(new BigInteger("123", 10), 5);
String s = a.toString();
System.out.println(s);                // "0.00123"

// Use the string to create an identical big decimal value.
a = new BigDecimal(s);
System.out.println(a);                // "0.00123"
```

valueOf()

PURPOSE

Returns a `BigDecimal` instance for a primitive integer value.

SYNTAX

```
public static BigDecimal valueOf(long val)
public static BigDecimal valueOf(long val, int scale) throws
   NumberFormatException
```

DESCRIPTION

This method returns a `BigDecimal` instance containing the value `val/10^scale`. If `scale` is not specified, it defaults to `0`.

This method is very similar to the `BigDecimal` constructor for creating big decimal values. Unlike the `BigDecimal` constructor, this method maintains a list of precreated `BigDecimal` objects for common values such as `0` and `1` and returns these objects instead of creating new ones.

PARAMETERS

`scale` The scale of the resulting big decimal value.

`val` The resulting big decimal value is `val*10^scale`.

RETURNS A `BigDecimal` instance.

EXCEPTIONS

`NumberFormatException`
If `scale` < `0`.

SEE ALSO `BigDecimal()`.

EXAMPLE

```
BigDecimal a = BigDecimal.valueOf(0);
BigDecimal b = BigDecimal.valueOf(1);

System.out.println(a.subtract(b));             // -1

System.out.println(BigDecimal.valueOf(1, 3));  // 0.001
```

BigInteger

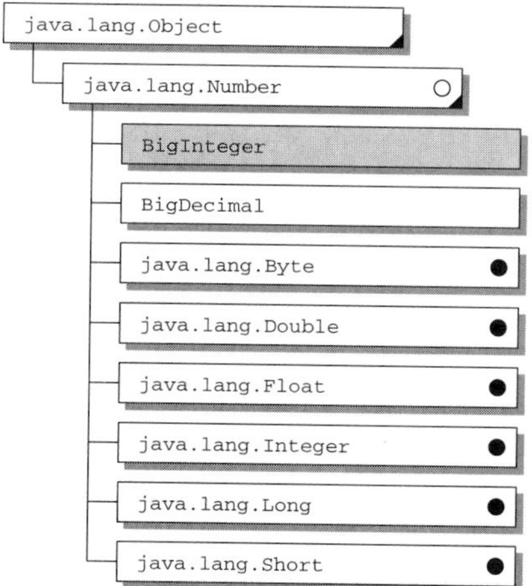

Syntax

`public class BigInteger extends Number`

Description

A `BigInteger` object represents an arbitrary-precision integer. A big integer value provides a means to do calculation on a value that is too big to be represented by a 64-bit `long` value. The operations in this class provide the same kind of operations (and more) that are available for `long` values. They are semantically identical to the Java integer operations, except that big integer values never overflow. See *The Java Language Specification, First Edition*, for details about Java integer operations.

A `BigInteger` object is immutable. That is, it contains a value that cannot be changed. Most big integer operations yield a new `BigInteger` object that holds the result of the operation.

Usage

To do big integer arithmetic, you first must create `BigInteger` objects containing the values of the operands and then use the methods in this class to operate on those objects. For example, to multiply the values `12` and `34`, you create two `BigInteger` objects, one for `12` and one for `34`. You then call `multiply()` using one object while passing in the other object. The result of `multiply()` is a new `BigInteger` object containing the value of `408`.

Bit Representation and Sign Bits

This class provides bit manipulation operations for big integer values. These bit manipulation operations use the two's complement form of this value when manipulating the bits. For example, the value 3 has the bit pattern 11.

In the case of negative numbers, the bit manipulation operations operate as if there are an infinite number of 1 bits preceding the value. For example, the value -3 has the bit pattern ...111101, where the ... indicates an infinite number of ones. This infinite number of ones is called the *sign bits* for the number –3. In the case of positive numbers, the bit manipulation operations operate as if there are an infinite number of 0 bits preceding the value. For example, the value 5 has the bit pattern ...000101. The infinite number of zero bits is called the sign bits for the number 5. Table 4 contains examples of the two's complement representation of some numbers. The italicized digits are the sign bits.

Note that manipulating a single bit can never change the sign of a big integer value.

Number	Two's Complement Representation	Minimal Representation
5	`...`*`000`*`101`	*`0`*`101`
-3	`...`*`111`*`101`	*`1`*`01`
0	`...`*`000000`*	*`0`*
-1	`...`*`111111`*	*`1`*

TABLE 4: Sign Bits in the Two's Complement and Their Minimal Representations.

Minimal Representation

The minimal representation of a big integer value is its two's complement representation with all but one sign bit removed. The minimal representation always has at least one digit. Table 4 contains examples of the minimal representation of some big integer values. The italicized digits are the sign bits.

Use of BigInteger as a Bit Vector

`BigInteger` can be used as a bit vector. It has methods for setting and clearing bits in its two's complement representation, as well as logical bit manipulation methods such as AND, OR, and XOR. A `BigInteger` is immutable, so invoking these methods on `BigInteger` may result in the generation of a new instance of the object. You should consider the performance consequences when using `BigInteger` in this way.

MEMBER SUMMARY	
Constructor	
`BigInteger()`	Constructs a `BigInteger` instance.
Math Methods	
`abs()`	Calculates the absolute value of this big integer value.
`add()`	Calculates the sum of this big integer value and another.
`divide()`	Calculates the result of this big integer value divided by another.
`divideAndRemainder()`	Calculates the quotient and remainder of two big integers.
`gcd()`	Calculates the greatest common denominator of this big integer value and another.
`isProbablePrime()`	Guesses whether this big integer value is prime.
`max()`	Compares this big integer value with another and return the greater of the two.
`min()`	Compares this big integer value with another and return the lesser of the two.
`mod()`	Calculates the residue of this big integer modulo another.
`modInverse()`	Calculates the modular multiplicative inverse of this big integer value.
`modPow()`	Calculates the residue of this big integer value raised to a power and modulo another big integer.
`multiply()`	Calculates the product of this big integer value and another.
`negate()`	Calculates the product of `-1` and this big integer value.
`pow()`	Calculates the result of raising this big integer value to a power.
`remainder()`	Calculates the remainder of dividing this big integer value by another.
`signum()`	Determines the sign of this big integer value.
`subtract()`	Calculates the difference between this big integer value and another.
Bit Methods	
`and()`	AND's this big integer value with another bit integer value.
`andNot()`	AND's this big integer value with the inverse of another big integer value.
`bitCount()`	Counts the number of zeroes or ones in the two's complement representation of this big integer value.
`bitLength()`	Determines the number of bits in the minimal representation of this big integer value exclusive of sign bits.
`clearBit()`	Returns the result of clearing a bit in the two's complement representation of this big integer value.
`flipBit()`	Returns the result of reversing a bit in this big integer value.
`getLowestSetBit()`	Finds the rightmost 1 bit in the two's complement representation of this big integer value.

Continued

MEMBER SUMMARY	
Bit Methods *(Continued)*	
`not()`	Complements all of the bits in this big integer value.
`or()`	OR's the bits in this big integer value with another.
`setBit()`	Returns the result of setting a bit in the two's complement representation of this big integer value.
`shiftLeft()`	Shifts to the left the bits in the two's complement representation of this big integer value.
`shiftRight()`	Shifts to the right the bits in the two's complement representation of this big integer value.
`testBit()`	Determines if some bit is set in the two's complement representation of this big integer value.
`xor()`	XOR's this big integer value with another big integer value.
Conversion Methods	
`doubleValue()`	Converts this big integer value to a `double` value.
`floatValue()`	Converts this big integer value to a `float` value.
`intValue()`	Converts this big integer value to an `int` value.
`longValue()`	Converts this big integer value to a `long` value.
`toByteArray()`	Creates an array containing the bits of this big integer value.
`valueOf()`	Returns a `BigInteger` instance for a primitive integer value.
Comparison Methods	
`compareTo()`	Compares this big integer value with another.
`equals()`	Determines if this big integer value is equal to an object.
Object Methods	
`hashCode()`	Computes the hash code for this big integer value.
`toString()`	Generates a string representing this big integer value.

See Also

`BigDecimal.`

Example

This example demonstrates a simple use of big integers. This program runs in an infinite loop, printing out Fibonacci numbers.

```
import java.math.*;

class Main {
    public static void main(String[] args) {
        BigInteger f1 = BigInteger.valueOf(1);
        BigInteger f2 = f1;
```

```
            // Print first two Fibonacci nubmers.
            System.out.println(1);
            System.out.println(1);

            // Print the remaining Fibonacii numbers.
            while (true) {
                BigInteger sum = f1.add(f2);
                f1 = f2;
                f2 = sum;
                System.out.println(sum);
            }
        }
    }
```

Output

```
1
1
2
3
5
8
13
21
34
55
89
144
233
```

abs()

PURPOSE Calculates the absolute value of this big integer value.

SYNTAX `public BigInteger abs()`

DESCRIPTION If N is $\geq$ `0`, the absolute value of N is N. If $N <$ `0`, the absolute value of N is $-N$. This method calculates and returns a `BigInteger` object containing the absolute value of this big integer value. The value of this big integer is not changed.

RETURNS A non-`null` `BigInteger` object containing the absolute value of this big integer value.

EXAMPLE

```
BigInteger a = new BigInteger("123");
System.out.println(a.abs());            // 123

a = new BigInteger("-123");
System.out.println(a.abs());            // 123
```

A B C D E F G H I J K L M N O P Q R S T U V W X Y Z

add()

PURPOSE Calculates the sum of this big integer value and another.

SYNTAX `public BigInteger add(BigInteger val) throws ArithmeticException`

DESCRIPTION This method calculates the sum of adding `val` to this big integer value and returns a `BigInteger` that represents the sum. Neither the value of `val` nor that of this big integer is changed.

PARAMETERS

`val` A non-`null` `BigInteger` object.

RETURNS A non-`null` `BigInteger` object that is the sum of this big integer value and `val`.

EXAMPLE This example prints the sum of all integers supplied on the command line.

```
import java.math.*;

class Main {
    public static void main(String[] args) {
        BigInteger sum = BigInteger.valueOf(0);

        for (int i=0; i<args.length; i++) {
            sum = sum.add(new BigInteger(args[i]));
        }
        System.out.println(sum);
    }
}
```

Output

```
>java Main 89985897459834234234 90384293847293487839
180370191307127722073
```

and()

PURPOSE AND's this big integer value with another big integer value.

SYNTAX `public BigInteger and(BigInteger val)`

DESCRIPTION This method AND's `val` to this big integer value and returns a `BigInteger` that represents the result. This method is equivalent to taking the bit vector intersection of `val` and this big integer value. This operation is similar to the Java & operator for primitive number types. Note that the return value is negative only if both `val` and this big integer value are negative. Neither the value of `val` nor that of this big integer is changed.

PARAMETERS

`val` A non-`null` `BigInteger` object.

RETURNS A non-null `BigInteger` object containing this big integer value AND'ed with `val`.

SEE ALSO `andNot, not(), or(), xor().`

EXAMPLE

```
BigInteger a = new BigInteger("110111", 2);    //      110111
BigInteger b = new BigInteger("101010", 2);    //      101010
System.out.println(a.and(b).toString(2));      //      100010

a = new BigInteger( "-0111", 2);               // ...11111001
b = new BigInteger("101010", 2);               // ...00101010
System.out.println(a.and(b).toString(2));      //      101000
```

andNot()

PURPOSE AND's this big integer value with the inverse of another big integer value.

SYNTAX `public BigInteger andNot(BigInteger val)`

DESCRIPTION This method first inverts all of the bits in `val` and then AND's the result of doing that to this big integer value. This method is equivalent to taking the bit vector set difference of this big integer value and `val`. The result is negative only if this big integer value is negative and `val` is nonnegative. Neither the value of `val` nor that of this big integer is changed.

PARAMETERS

`val` A non-null `BigInteger` object.

RETURNS A non-null `BigInteger` object containing this big integer value AND'ed with `not(val)`.

SEE ALSO `and(), not(), or(), xor().`

EXAMPLE

```
BigInteger a = new BigInteger("110111", 2);    //                110111
BigInteger b = new BigInteger(  "1010", 2);    //    (~b)   ...11110101
System.out.println(a.andNot(b).toString(2));   //  110101        110101

a = new BigInteger("-0111", 2);                //           ...11111001
b = new BigInteger( "1010", 2);                //    (~b)   ...11110101
System.out.println(a.andNot(b).toString(2));   //   -1111   ...11110001
```

BigInteger()

PURPOSE Constructs a `BigInteger` instance.

SYNTAX `public BigInteger(String sval) throws NumberFormatException`

```
public BigInteger(String sval, int rdx) throws
    NumberFormatException
public BigInteger(byte[] bval) throws NumberFormatException
public BigInteger(int sign, byte[] magnitude) throws
    NumberFormatException
public BigInteger(int numBits, Random rnd) throws
    IllegalArgumentException
public BigInteger(int bitLength, int certainty, Random rnd)
```

DESCRIPTION

In the first form of the constructor, the value in `sval` is parsed as a radix 10 number to obtain the big integer value. The first character optionally can be a negative sign, thereby indicating that the value is negative. `sval` must not contain any spaces and must contain at least one digit. The `sval` format is compatible with the strings generated by `toString()`.

In the second form of the constructor, the value in `sval` is parsed as a radix `rdx` number to obtain the big integer value. The first character optionally can be a negative sign, thereby indicating that the value is negative. `sval` must not contain any spaces and must contain at least one digit. The method `Character.digit()` is used to convert the digits in `sval`. The `sval` format is compatible with the strings generated by `toString(rdx)`.

In the third form of the constructor, the big integer value is taken from the `byte` array `bval`, which contains an integer in two's complement form. The bits are assumed to be in big-endian order. That is, `bval[0]` contains the most-significant byte and `bval[bval.length-1]` contains the least-significant byte. If the most-significant bit of `bval[0]` is a 1, the result is negative. If `bval.length` is `0`, `NumberFormatException` is thrown. The `bval` format is compatible with the `byte` arrays generated by `toByteArray()`.

In the fourth form of the constructor, the big integer value is taken from the `byte` array `magnitude`, which contains a nonnegative binary number. The bits are assumed to be in big-endian order. That is, `magnitude[0]` contains the most-significant byte and `magnitude[bval.length-1]` contains the least-significant byte. If `sign` is `-1`, the result is negative. If `sign` is `0`, `magnitude` must contain only zeros. If `sign` is `1`, the result is positive.

In the fifth form of the constructor, the big integer value is initialized with `numBits` number of random bits. `rnd` is used to generate the random bits. The value is never negative and is in the range `[0 .. 2^numBits - 1]`.

In the sixth form of the constructor, the big integer value is initialized with `numBits` number of random bits. `rnd` is used to generate the random bits. The probability that the result is prime is controlled by `certainty`; larger values increase the probability of a prime number's being obtained. More precisely, the probability that the result is prime is ≥ `1-.5^certainty`. The larger the size of `certainty`, the longer this constructor takes to complete.

PARAMETERS

`bitLength`	Specifies the number of random bits. `bitLength` ≥ `2`.
`bval`	A non-`null` array containing the "signed" bytes of the value in big-endian order. `bval.length` > `0`.
`certainty`	A nonnegative integer specifying that the probability of the result's being prime should be greater than `1-.5^certainty`.
`magnitude`	A non-`null` array containing the bytes of the magnitude in big-endian order.
`numBits`	Specifies the number of random bits. `numBits` ≥ `0`.
`rdx`	The radix of `sval`. `Character.MIN_RADIX` ≤ `rdx` ≤ `Character.MAX_RADIX`.
`rnd`	A non-`null` `Random` object.
`sign`	`-1` if the result is negative, `0` if the result is `0`, or `1` if the result is positive.
`sval`	A non-`null` string containing an optional leading negative sign and at least one digit. The digits must not be larger than the ones allowed by `rdx`. No space characters (leading, trailing, or embedded) are allowed.

EXCEPTIONS

`ArithmeticException`
If `bitLength` < `2`.

`IllegalArgumentException`
If `numBits` < `0`.

`NumberFormatException`
If `bval.length` is `0`; or if `sign` is not `-1`, `0`, or `1`; or if `rdx` is invalid; or if `sval` is empty or invalid.

SEE ALSO `toByteArray()`, `toString()`.

EXAMPLE This example demonstrates all of the forms of the constructor.

```
// BigInteger(byte[] bval)
    BigInteger a = new BigInteger(new byte[]{0x1, 0});
    System.out.println(a);                                  // 256

    a = new BigInteger(new byte[]{(byte)128});
    System.out.println(a);                                  // -128

// BigInteger(int signum, byte[] magnitude)
    a = new BigInteger(1, new byte[]{(byte)128});
    System.out.println(a);                                  // 128

    a = new BigInteger(0, new byte[]{(byte)0});
    System.out.println(a);                                  // 0
    a = new BigInteger(0, new byte[]{});
    System.out.println(a);                                  // 0
    //a = new BigInteger(0, new byte[]{(byte)128});         // NumberFormatEx

    a = new BigInteger(-1, new byte[]{(byte)128});
    System.out.println(a);                                  // -128

// BigInteger(int numBits, Random rnd)
    a = new BigInteger(0, new Random());
    System.out.println(a);                                  // 0
```

```
        a = new BigInteger(1, new Random());
        System.out.println(a);                          // 1

        // a = new BigInteger(-1, new Random());        // IllegalArgumentEx

        a = new BigInteger(32, new Random());
        System.out.println(a);                          // 17950393

    // BigInteger(int numBits, int certainty, Random rnd)
        a = new BigInteger(32, 0, new Random());
        System.out.println(a);                          // 3681762179

        a = new BigInteger(32, 1000, new Random());
        System.out.println(a);                          // 2473873543

        a = new BigInteger(32, -10, new Random());
        System.out.println(a);                          // 3821485007
```


bitCount()

PURPOSE Counts the number of zeroes or ones in the two's complement representation of this big integer value.

SYNTAX `public int bitCount()`

DESCRIPTION If this big integer value is nonnegative, this method returns the number of bits that have the value `1`. If this big integer value is negative, this method returns the number of bits that have the value `0`.

RETURNS The number of `0` bits if this value is nonnegative; the number of `1` bits if this value is negative.

EXAMPLE

```
System.out.println(new BigInteger("0", 2).bitCount());      // 0
System.out.println(new BigInteger("1", 2).bitCount());      // 1
System.out.println(new BigInteger("10", 2).bitCount());     // 1
System.out.println(new BigInteger("1010", 2).bitCount());   // 2
System.out.println(new BigInteger("-1", 2).bitCount());     // 0
System.out.println(new BigInteger("-10", 2).bitCount());    // 1
System.out.println(new BigInteger("-1010", 2).bitCount()); // 2
```

bitLength()

PURPOSE Determines the number of bits in the minimal representation of this big integer value, exclusive of sign bits.

SYNTAX `public int bitLength()`

DESCRIPTION The minimal representation of a big integer value is its two's complement representation with all but one sign bit removed. See the class description for more details. This method returns the number of bits in the minimal representation with all sign bits removed.

RETURNS The number of bits in the minimal representation of this big integer value, exclusive of sign bits. This number is nonnegative.

EXAMPLE This example prints out the minimal representation of some big integers. The size of the minimal representation is `bitLength()+1` (plus 1 for the sign bit).

```
import java.math.*;

class Main {
    // Print the minimal representation of val
    static void printMinRep(long val) {
        BigInteger n   = BigInteger.valueOf(val);
        int blen = n.bitLength();
        System.out.print(n.signum() < 0 ? "1" : "0");
        for(int i=blen-1; i>=0; i--) {
            System.out.print(n.testBit(i) ? "1" : "0");
        }
        System.out.println();
    }

    public static void main(String[] args) {
        printMinRep(0);      // 0
        printMinRep(1);      // 01
        printMinRep(0xff);   // 011111111
        printMinRep(-1);     // 1
        printMinRep(-0xff);  // 100000001
        printMinRep(-3);     // 101
        printMinRep(5);      // 0101
    }
}
```

clearBit()

PURPOSE Returns the result of clearing a bit in the two's complement representation of this big integer value.

SYNTAX `public BigInteger clearBit(int n) throws ArithmeticException`

DESCRIPTION This method returns a copy of this `BigInteger` with the bit at position `n` set to `0`. This method is equivalent to

`and(BigInteger.valueOf(1).shiftLeft(n).not())`.

The value of this big integer is not changed.

PARAMETERS

`n` The `0`-based position of the bit in this big integer value to set to `0`.

RETURNS A non-null BigInteger with the same value as this big integer, except that the nth bit has been set to 0.

EXCEPTIONS

ArithmeticException
If n < 0.

SEE ALSO setBit(), testBit().

EXAMPLE

```
import java.math.*;

class Main {
    public static void main(String[] args) {
        BigInteger a = new BigInteger("101010", 2);     // 101010
        System.out.println(a.clearBit(1).toString(2)); // 101000

        a = new BigInteger("-0111", 2);                 //            ...11111001
        System.out.println(a.clearBit(5).toString(2)); // -100111   ...11011001
    }
}
```

compareTo()

PURPOSE Compares this big integer value with another.

SYNTAX `public int compareTo(BigInteger val)`

DESCRIPTION If this big integer value is less than val, -1 is returned. If this big integer value is equal to val, 0 is returned. If this big integer value is greater than val, 1 is returned.

PARAMETERS

val A non-null BigInteger object.

RETURNS -1, 0, or 1, depending on how this big integer value compares with val.

SEE ALSO equals().

EXAMPLE This example reads a list of big integers from standard input, sorts the big integers, and then prints them to standard output. This example uses the QuickSort and Comparable classes from the java.lang.reflect.Array class example.

```
import java.math.*;
import java.io.*;
import java.lang.reflect.*;
import java.util.*;

class Main {
    static class Compare implements Comparable {
        public int compare(Object a, Object b) {
            return ((BigInteger)a).compareTo((BigInteger)b);
```

```
            }
        }

        public static void main(String[] args) {
            BufferedReader is =
                new BufferedReader(new InputStreamReader(System.in));
            String line;
            Vector v = new Vector();

            // Save the string numbers in v.
            try {
                while ((line = is.readLine()) != null) {
                    v.addElement(line);
                }
            } catch (Exception e) {
                e.printStackTrace();
            }

            // Copy v into an array of big nums.
            BigInteger[] nums = new BigInteger[v.size()];
            for (int i=0; i<nums.length; i++) {
                nums[i] = new BigInteger((String)v.elementAt(i));
            }

            // Sort the list.
            QuickSort.sort(nums, new Compare());

            // Print sorted list.
            for (int i=0; i<nums.length; i++) {
                System.out.println(nums[i]);
            }
        }
    }
```


divide()

PURPOSE

Calculates the result of dividing this big integer value by another.

SYNTAX

```
public BigInteger divide(BigInteger val) throws
    ArithmeticException
```

DESCRIPTION

This method divides this big integer value by `val` and returns a `BigInteger` representing the result. The fractional part of the result is discarded. That is, the result is rounded toward `0`. The sign of the quotient is positive if both `val` and this big integer have the same sign; it is negative otherwise. Neither the value of `val` nor that of this big integer is changed.

PARAMETERS

`val` A non-`null` `BigInteger` object.

RETURNS

A non-`null` `BigInteger` object containing the integral part of this big integer value divided by `val`.

EXCEPTIONS

`ArithmeticException`
If `val` equals `0`.

SEE ALSO `divideAndRemainder()`, `remainder()`.

EXAMPLE

```
BigInteger a = BigInteger.valueOf(10);
BigInteger b = BigInteger.valueOf(3);

System.out.println(a.divide(b));                // 3
System.out.println(a.divide(b.negate()));       // -3
```

divideAndRemainder()

PURPOSE Calculates the quotient and remainder of two big integers.

SYNTAX

```
public BigInteger[] divideAndRemainder(BigInteger divisor)
    throws ArithmeticException
```

DESCRIPTION This method divides this big integer value by `divisor` and returns both the quotient and remainder. The quotient is the integral part of this big integer value divided by `divisor`. The remainder is this big integer value modulo `divisor`. The sign of the quotient is positive if both `divisor` and this big integer have the same sign; it is negative otherwise. The sign of the remainder is the same as the sign of this big integer, except that if the remainder is 0, in which case the sign is positive.

In summary, this big integer value equals the quotient * `divisor` + remainder. Neither the value of `divisor` nor that of this big integer is changed.

PARAMETERS

`divisor` A non-`null` `BigInteger` object.

RETURNS A non-`null` two-element `BigInteger` array in which the first element contains the quotient and the second element contains the remainder.

EXCEPTIONS

`ArithmeticException`
If `val` equals `0`.

SEE ALSO `divide()`, `remainder()`.

EXAMPLE

```
BigInteger[] ans;
BigInteger a = BigInteger.valueOf(5);
BigInteger b = BigInteger.valueOf(3);

ans = a.divideAndRemainder(b);                  // 5/3
System.out.println(ans[0]+" "+ans[1]);          // 1 2
```

```
ans = a.divideAndRemainder(b.negate());          // 5/-3
System.out.println(ans[0]+" "+ans[1]);           // -1 2

ans = a.negate().divideAndRemainder(b);          // -5/3
System.out.println(ans[0]+" "+ans[1]);           // -1 -2

ans = a.negate().divideAndRemainder(b.negate()); // -5/-3
System.out.println(ans[0]+" "+ans[1]);           // 1 -2

//ans = a.divideAndRemainder(BigInteger.valueOf(0)); // ArithmeticException
```

A B C D E F G H I J K L M N O P Q R S T U V W X Y Z

doubleValue()

PURPOSE Converts this big integer value to a `double` value.

SYNTAX `public double doubleValue()`

DESCRIPTION The returned `double` value is an approximation of this big integer value. If the magnitude of this big integer value is larger than what can be represented by a `double` value, then a value of either Infinity or negative Infinity is returned.

RETURNS A `double` value approximating this big integer value.

SEE ALSO `java.lang.Number.doubleValue()`.

EXAMPLE

```
BigInteger a = BigInteger.valueOf(-Long.MAX_VALUE);
System.out.println(a.doubleValue());          // -9.223372036854776E18

// Make a number with a very large magnitude.
a = a.pow(99);
System.out.println(a.doubleValue());          // -Infinity

// Make a number with a very large magnitude.
a = a.pow(2);
System.out.println(a.doubleValue());          // Infinity
```

equals()

PURPOSE Determines if this big integer value is equal to an object.

SYNTAX `public boolean equals(Object val)`

DESCRIPTION This method returns `true` only if `val` is an instance of `BigInteger` and this big integer value is numerically equal to the value of `val`.

PARAMETERS

`val` A possibly `null` object.

RETURNS `true` if `val` is not `null` and this big integer value is the same as `val`'s.

OVERRIDES java.lang.Object.equals().

SEE ALSO compareTo(), hashCode().

EXAMPLE

```
BigInteger a = BigInteger.valueOf(1);
BigInteger b = BigInteger.valueOf(2);

System.out.println(a.equals(b.add(b)));    // true
System.out.println(a.equals(null));        // false
```

A B C D E F G H I J K L M N O P Q R S T U V W X Y Z

flipBit()

PURPOSE Returns the result of reversing a bit in this big integer value.

SYNTAX `public BigInteger flipBit(int pos) throws ArithmeticException`

DESCRIPTION This method makes a copy of this `BigInteger` with the bit at position `pos` reversed. The value of this big integer is not changed.

PARAMETERS

`pos` `0`-based bit position of the big integer value to flip. The least-significant bit has bit position `0`.

RETURNS A non-`null` `BigInteger` object containing this big integer value with the `pos`th bit reversed.

EXCEPTIONS

`ArithmeticException`
If `n` < `0`.

SEE ALSO `java.lang.ArithmeticException`.

EXAMPLE

```
BigInteger a = BigInteger.valueOf(0);

a = a.flipBit(100);
System.out.println(a);       // 1267650600228229401496703205376

a = a.flipBit(100);
System.out.println(a);       // 0
```

floatValue()

PURPOSE Converts this big integer value to a `float` value.

SYNTAX `public float floatValue()`

DESCRIPTION The returned float value is an approximation of this big integer value. If the magnitude of this big integer value is larger than what can be represented by a float value, then a value of either Infinity or negative Infinity is returned.

RETURNS A float value approximating this big integer value.

SEE ALSO java.lang.Number.floatValue().

EXAMPLE

```
BigInteger a = BigInteger.valueOf(-Long.MAX_VALUE);
System.out.println(a.floatValue());          // -9.223372E18

// Make a number with a very large magnitude.
a = a.pow(99);
System.out.println(a.floatValue());          // -Infinity

// Make a number with a very large magnitude.
a = a.pow(2);
System.out.println(a.floatValue());          // Infinity
```

gcd()

PURPOSE Computes the greatest common denominator of this big integer value and another.

SYNTAX `public BigInteger gcd(BigInteger val)`

DESCRIPTION The greatest common denominator (gcd) is the largest value that evenly divides this big integer value and val (with remainders equal to 0). The calculation uses the absolute value of this big integer and of val.

The gcd is never negative. If this big integer value is 0 and val is 0, this method returns 0.

PARAMETERS

val A non-null BigInteger object.

RETURNS A non-null BigInteger object containing the gcd of this big integer value and val.

EXAMPLE

```
import java.math.*;
import java.util.Random;

class Main {
    // Returns gcd(x, y).
    static void printGCD(long x, long y) {
        System.out.println(BigInteger.valueOf(x).gcd(BigInteger.valueOf(y)));
    }

    public static void main(String[] args) {
        printGCD(0, 0);     // 0
        printGCD(1, 0);     // 1
```

```
            printGCD(0, 1);      // 1
            printGCD(1, 1);      // 1

            printGCD(5, 3);      // 1
            printGCD(25, 10);    // 5
            printGCD(-25, 10);   // 5

            Random rnd = new Random();
            while (true) {
                BigInteger a = new BigInteger(64, rnd);
                BigInteger b = new BigInteger(64, rnd);

                System.out.println("gcd("+a+","+b+")="+a.gcd(b));
            }
                    // ... <sample output>
                    // gcd(16952353143335189504,3481913592572825989)=1
                    // gcd(4617725947040842835,16363096468092271150)=5
                    // gcd(215684152070057280,10999101742231209159)=3
                    // gcd(16492901384184808671,13519219882357115807)=1
                    // gcd(18321175869446016956,16791079565960874729)=1
        }
    }
```

getLowestSetBit()

PURPOSE Finds the rightmost 1 bit in the two's complement representation of this big integer value.

SYNTAX `public int getLowestSetBit()`

DESCRIPTION This method finds the rightmost 1 bit in its two's complement representation and returns the bit's position.

RETURNS The `0`-based position of the rightmost `1` bit or `-1` if there is none.

EXAMPLE

```
System.out.println(new BigInteger("0", 2).getLowestSetBit());      // -1
System.out.println(new BigInteger("1", 2).getLowestSetBit());      // 0
System.out.println(new BigInteger("1000", 2).getLowestSetBit());   // 3
System.out.println(new BigInteger("-1", 2).getLowestSetBit());     // 0
System.out.println(new BigInteger("-1000", 2).getLowestSetBit()); // 3
```

hashCode()

PURPOSE Computes the hash code for this big integer value.

SYNTAX `public int hashCode()`

DESCRIPTION The big integer value's hash code is an integer that is calculated from the value. Two big integer values whose numerical values are equal will have the same hash code. However, unequal big integer values might also have the same hash code, although the hash code algorithm minimizes this possibility. The hash code is typically used as the key in a hash table.

RETURNS The big integer value's hash code.

OVERRIDES `java.lang.Object.hashCode()`.

SEE ALSO `equals()`, `java.util.Hashtable`.

EXAMPLE See `java.lang.Object.hashCode()`.

intValue()

PURPOSE Converts this big integer value to an `int` value.

SYNTAX `public int intValue()`

DESCRIPTION This method converts the low-order 32-bits of this big integer value into an `int` value.

RETURNS An `int` representing this big integer value.

SEE ALSO `java.lang.Number.intValue()`.

EXAMPLE

```
BigInteger a = new BigInteger("123");

System.out.println(a.intValue());  // 123

a = new BigInteger("23423419083091823091283933");
System.out.println(a.intValue());  // -249268259
```

isProbablePrime()

PURPOSE Guesses whether this big integer value is prime.

SYNTAX `public boolean isProbablePrime(int certainty)`

DESCRIPTION This method guesses whether this big integer value is prime. If this method returns `false`, this value is definitely composite. However, if this method returns `true`, there is a probability that this value is prime. This probability can be controlled by `certainty`. In particular, this method returns `true` if the probability that this number is prime ≥ `1-.5^certainty`. The larger the size of `certainty`, the longer this method takes to complete.

PARAMETERS

`certainty` A nonnegative integer controlling the accuracy of this method.

RETURNS `true` if this big integer value may be a prime; `false` if it is definitely a composite number.

EXAMPLE This example uses a certainty value of 20 to find the primes between a range of numbers. The output shows the primes found between 1,000,000 and 1,000,500.

```
import java.math.*;

class Main {
    public static void main(String[] args) {
        int start = Integer.parseInt(args[0]);
        int len = start + Integer.parseInt(args[1]);
        for (int i=start; i < len; i++) {
            // Do the check.
            if (BigInteger.valueOf(i).isProbablePrime(20)) {
                System.out.print(i + " ");
            }
        }
        System.out.println();
    }
}
```

Output

```
> java Main 1000000 500
1000003 1000033 1000037 1000039 1000081 1000099 1000117 1000121 1000133 1000151
1000159 1000171 1000183 1000187 1000193 1000199 1000211 1000213 1000231 1000249
1000253 1000273 1000289 1000291 1000303 1000313 1000333 1000357 1000367 1000381
1000393 1000397 1000403 1000409 1000423 1000427 1000429 1000453 1000457
```

longValue()

PURPOSE Converts this big integer value to a `long` value.

SYNTAX `public long longValue()`

DESCRIPTION This method converts the low-order 64-bits of this big integer into a `long` value.

RETURNS A `long` representing this big integer value.

SEE ALSO `java.lang.Number.longValue()`.

EXAMPLE

```
BigInteger a = new BigInteger("123");
System.out.println(a.longValue());  // 123

a = new BigInteger("3132342342341908309182309128393 3");
System.out.println(a.longValue());  // -5251313250005125155
```

max()

PURPOSE
Compares this big integer value with another and returns the greater of the two.

SYNTAX
`public BigInteger max(BigInteger val)`

DESCRIPTION
This method returns either this `BigInteger` object or `val`, whichever is greater. If they are equal, `val` is returned.

PARAMETERS

`val` A non-`null` `BigInteger` object.

RETURNS
Either this object or `val`, whichever is greater.

EXAMPLE

```
System.out.println(BigInteger.valueOf("123").max(BigInteger.valueOf("1234")));
                                                                    // 1234
```

min()

PURPOSE
Compares this big integer value with another and returns the lesser of the two.

SYNTAX
`public BigInteger min(BigInteger val)`

DESCRIPTION
This method returns either this `BigInteger` object or `val`, whichever is less. If they are equal, `val` is returned.

PARAMETERS

`val` A non-`null` `BigInteger` object.

RETURNS
Either this object or `val`, whichever is less.

EXAMPLE

```
System.out.println(BigInteger.valueOf("123").min(BigInteger.valueOf("1234")));
                                                                    // 123
```

mod()

PURPOSE
Calculates the residue of this big integer modulo another.

SYNTAX
`public BigInteger mod(BigInteger m)`

DESCRIPTION
This method calculates the residue of this big integer value modulo `m`. The result is never negative. Neither the value of `m` nor that of this big integer is changed.

PARAMETERS

`m` The nonnegative modulus.

RETURNS This big integer value modulo m.

EXCEPTIONS

ArithmeticException
If m ≤ 0.

SEE ALSO modInverse(), modPow().

EXAMPLE

```
BigInteger a = BigInteger.valueOf(5);
BigInteger b = BigInteger.valueOf(3);

System.out.println(a.mod(b));                       // 5%3 = 2
System.out.println(a.negate().mod(b));              // -5%3 = 1
//System.out.println(a.mod(b.negate()));            // ArithmeticException
//System.out.println(a.mod(BigInteger.valueOf(0))); // ArithmeticException
```

modInverse()

PURPOSE Calculates the modular multiplicative inverse of this big integer value.

SYNTAX

```
public BigInteger modInverse(BigInteger m) throws
    ArithmeticException
```

DESCRIPTION The modular multiplicative inverse *i* of a number *n* modulo m is a value such that (*i***n*)(mod m) = 1. The result is always < m. A modular multiplicative inverse exists if and only if gcd(m) equals 1. Neither the value of m nor that of this big integer is changed.

PARAMETERS

m The nonnegative modulus.

RETURNS The modular multiplicative inverse of this big integer value modulo m.

EXCEPTIONS

ArithmeticException
If m ≤ 0 or no modular multiplicative inverse exists.

SEE ALSO mod(), modPow().

EXAMPLE

```
import java.math.*;
import java.util.Random;

class Main {
    // Prints x.modInverse(m).
    static void printModInverse(int x, int m) {
        BigInteger a = BigInteger.valueOf(x);
        System.out.println(a.modInverse(BigInteger.valueOf(m)));
    }

    public static void main(String[] args) {
        printModInverse(0, 1);       // 0
```

```
        printModInverse(1, 1);        // 0
        printModInverse(5, 3);        // 2
        printModInverse(10, 3);       // 1
        printModInverse(9, 7);        // 4
        //printModInverse(10, 5);     // ArithmeticException
        //printModInverse(5, 0);      // ArithmeticException

        Random rnd = new Random();
        BigInteger ONE = BigInteger.valueOf(1);
        while (true) {
            BigInteger a = new BigInteger(32, rnd);
            BigInteger m = new BigInteger(32, rnd);

            if (a.gcd(m).intValue() == 1) {
                BigInteger inv = a.modInverse(m);
                System.out.println(
                    a + " * " + inv + " (mod " + m + ") = " +
                        a.multiply(inv).mod(m));
            }
        }
                // 1571004015 * 385084739 (mod 1370659187) = 1
                // 603331458 * 255317344 (mod 1317188219) = 1
                // 1424330431 * 72896381 (mod 206427394) = 1
                // 1160587373 * 532755746 (mod 1370179997) = 1
                // 488707349 * 2846222921 (mod 4190656154) = 1
                // 4290966619 * 1930549735 (mod 3246793271) = 1
                // 487989081 * 1489938937 (mod 3169209884) = 1
                // 3717708439 * 252962773 (mod 533163014) = 1
                // 3988371331 * 1266113047 (mod 1511544858) = 1
    }
}
```

modPow()

PURPOSE
: Calculates the result of this big integer value raised to a power and modulo another big integer.

SYNTAX
: `public BigInteger modPow(BigInteger exp, BigInteger m)`

DESCRIPTION
: This method raises this big integer value to the power `exp` and returns a `BigInteger` that represents the result modulo `m`. The result is always ≤ `m`. Neither the value of `exp` or `m` nor that of this big integer is changed.

If `exp = 1`, the result is equivalent to `mod(m)`. If `exp` < `0`, the result is the modular multiplicative inverse of this big integer value modulo `m` (see `modInverse()`).

PARAMETERS

`exp` The nonnegative exponent.

`m` The nonnegative modulus.

EXCEPTIONS

`ArithmeticException`

If `m` ≤ `0`.

RETURNS A non-null `BigInteger` object containing this big integer value raised to the power exp, modulo `m`.

SEE ALSO `mod()`, `modInverse()`.

EXAMPLE

```
import java.math.*;

class Main {
    // Prints x.modPow(y, m).
    static void printModPow(int x, int y, int m) {
        BigInteger a = BigInteger.valueOf(x);
        BigInteger b = BigInteger.valueOf(y);
        BigInteger mod = BigInteger.valueOf(m);

        System.out.println(a.modPow(b, mod));
    }
    public static void main(String[] args) {
        printModPow(0, 0, 7);     // 1        0^0 (mod 7) == 1
        printModPow(11, 1, 7);    // 4        11^1 (mod 7) == 4
        printModPow(11, 2, 7);    // 2        11^2 (mod 7) == 2
        printModPow(11, 3, 7);    // 1        11^3 (mod 7) == 1
        printModPow(11, 4, 7);    // 4        11^4 (mod 7) == 4
        printModPow(11, 5, 7);    // 2        11^5 (mod 7) == 2


    // mod() behavior
        printModPow(0, 1, 7);     // 0         0 (mod 3)
        printModPow(-1, 1, 7);    // 6        -1 (mod 7) == 6
        printModPow(10, 1, 7);    // 3        10 (mod 7) == 3

    // modInverse() behavior
        //printModPow(0, -1, 7); // ArithmeticException: not invertible.
        printModPow(11, -1, 7);  // 2        2*11 (mod 7) == 1
        printModPow(-1, -1, 7);  // 6        6*-1 (mod 7) == 1
    }
}
```

multiply()

PURPOSE Calculates the product of this big integer value and another.

SYNTAX `public BigInteger multiply(BigInteger val)`

DESCRIPTION This method multiplies `val` by this big integer value and returns a `BigInteger` that represents the product. Neither the value of `val` nor that of this big integer is changed.

PARAMETERS

`val` A non-null `BigInteger` object.

RETURNS A non-null `BigInteger` object containing this big integer value times `val`.

EXAMPLE This example implements the factorial function. It takes an integer supplied on the command line and prints the factorial of that integer.

```
import java.math.*;

class Main {
    public static void main(String[] args) {
        int n = Integer.parseInt(args[0]);
        BigInteger prod = BigInteger.valueOf(1);

        for (int i=1; i<=n; i++) {
            prod = prod.multiply(BigInteger.valueOf(i));
        }
        System.out.println(prod);
    }
}
```

Output

```
> java Main 194
1329178992900849493067173151582273301498507986642340916517522614087804962588
5933295500097441431699945742094900688204258245034244273441204766216569397389533
5571294880851102985058827022038890413030589601300725778799567469868524038465999
2088208002817053322111541235006824394497130022759529535022888837623252086897500
8352000000000000000000000000000000000000000000000
```

negate()

PURPOSE Calculates the product of -1 and this big integer value.

SYNTAX `public BigInteger negate()`

DESCRIPTION This method multiplies this big integer value by -1 and returns a `BigInteger` that represents the result. This method is equivalent to calling `not().add(BigInteger.valueOf(1))`. The value of this big integer is not changed.

RETURNS A non-`null` `BigInteger` object containing this big integer value multiplied by -1.

EXAMPLE

```
System.out.println(new BigInteger("-123").negate()); // 123
```

not()

PURPOSE Complements all of the bits in this big integer value.

SYNTAX `public BigInteger not()`

DESCRIPTION This method complements (inverts) all of the bits in this big integer value and returns a `BigInteger` that represents the result. This operation is similar to the

A B C D E F G H I J K L M N O P Q R S T U V W X Y Z

Java ~ operator for primitive number types. The result is negative only if this big integer value is nonnegative. The value of this big integer is not changed.

RETURNS A non-null `BigInteger` object containing this big integer value with all of the bits inverted.

SEE ALSO `and(), andNot, or(), xor().`

EXAMPLE

```
BigInteger a = BigInteger.valueOf(0);          //
System.out.println(a.not().toString(2));       //      -1    ...111111111

a = new BigInteger("101010", 2);               //                 101010
System.out.println(a.not().toString(2));       // -101011    ...111010101

a = new BigInteger("-101", 2);                 //            ...111111011
System.out.println(a.not().toString(2));       //     100             100
```

A B C D E F G H I J K L M N O P Q R S T U V W X Y Z

or()

PURPOSE OR's the bits in this big integer value with another.

SYNTAX `public BigInteger or(BigInteger val)`

DESCRIPTION This method OR's all of the bits in this big integer value with `val` and returns a `BigInteger` representing the result. This operation is similar to the Java | operator for primitive number types. The result is negative if either `val` or this big integer value is negative. Neither the value of `val` nor that of this big integer is changed.

PARAMETERS

`val` A non-null `BigInteger` object.

RETURNS A non-null `BigInteger` object containing this big integer value OR'ed with `val`.

SEE ALSO `and(), andNot, not(), xor().`

EXAMPLE

```
BigInteger a = new BigInteger("110111", 2);     // 110111
BigInteger b = new BigInteger("101010", 2);     // 101010
System.out.println(a.or(b).toString(2));        // 111111

a = new BigInteger("-0111", 2);                 // 111001
b = new BigInteger("101010", 2);                // 101010
System.out.println(a.or(b).toString(2));        // -101
```

pow()

PURPOSE Calculates the result of raising this big integer value to a power.

SYNTAX `public BigInteger pow(int exp) throws ArithmeticException`

DESCRIPTION This method raises this big integer value to the power `exp` and returns a `BigInteger` representing the result. `exp` must be ≥ `0`. The value of this big integer is not changed.

PARAMETERS

`exponent` The nonnegative exponent.

RETURNS A non-`null` `BigInteger` object containing this big integer value raised to the power `exp`.

EXCEPTIONS

`ArithmeticException`

If `exp` < `0`.

SEE ALSO `java.lang.ArithmeticException`.

EXAMPLE

```
import java.math.*;

class Main {
    // Returns x raised to the power of y.
    static void printPow(int x, int y) {
        System.out.println(BigInteger.valueOf(x).pow(y));
    }

    public static void main(String[] args) {
        printPow(0, 0);      // 1
        printPow(1, 0);      // 1
        printPow(-1, 0);     // 1
        printPow(1, 1);      // 1
        printPow(0, 1);      // 0
        //printPow(2, -1);   // ArithmeticException

        printPow(2, 3);      // 8
        printPow(-2, 3);     // -8

        printPow(12, 34);    // 4922235242952026704037113243122008064
    }
}
```

remainder()

PURPOSE Calculates the remainder by dividing this big integer value by another.

SYNTAX `public BigInteger remainder(BigInteger val) throws ArithmeticException`

A B C D E F G H I J K L M N O P Q R S T U V W X Y Z

DESCRIPTION
This method divides this big integer value by `val` and returns the remainder. This operation is identical to the Java % operator for primitive integer types. The sign of the remainder is the same as the sign of this big integer value, except if the remainder is 0, in which case the sign is positive. Neither the value of `val` nor that of this big integer is changed.

PARAMETERS

`val` A non-`null` `BigInteger` object.

EXCEPTIONS

`ArithmeticException`
If `val` is `0`.

SEE ALSO `divide()`, `divideAndRemainder()`.

EXAMPLE

```
BigInteger a = BigInteger.valueOf(5);
BigInteger b = BigInteger.valueOf(3);

BigInteger ans = a.remainder(b);             // 5%3
System.out.println(ans);                     // 2

ans = a.remainder(b.negate());               // 5%-3
System.out.println(ans);                     // 2

ans = a.negate().remainder(b);               // -5%3
System.out.println(ans);                     // -2

ans = a.negate().remainder(b.negate());      // -5%-3
System.out.println(ans);                     // -2

//ans = a.remainder(BigInteger.valueOf(0)); // ArithmeticException
```

setBit()

PURPOSE
Returns the result of setting a bit in the two's complement representation of this big integer value.

SYNTAX
`public BigInteger setBit(int n) throws ArithmeticException`

DESCRIPTION
This method sets to `1` the bit at bit position `n` in this big integer value. This method is equivalent to `or(BigInteger.valueOf(1).shiftLeft(n))`. The value of this big integer is not changed.

PARAMETERS

`n` The `0`-based position of the bit in this big integer value to set to `1`.

RETURNS
A non-`null` `BigInteger` with the same value as this big integer, except that the `n`th bit has been set to `1`.

EXCEPTIONS

`ArithmeticException`
If `n` < `0`.

SEE ALSO `clearBit()`, `testBit()`.

EXAMPLE

```
import java.math.*;

class Main {
    public static void main(String[] args) {
        BigInteger a = new BigInteger("101010", 2);    // 101010
        System.out.println(a.setBit(2).toString(2));  // 101110

        a = new BigInteger("-111", 2);                 //             ...11111001
        System.out.println(a.setBit(2).toString(2));  //    -11      ...11111101
    }
}
```


shiftLeft()

PURPOSE Shifts to the left the bits in the two's complement representation of this big integer value.

SYNTAX `public BigInteger shiftLeft(int n)`

DESCRIPTION This method shifts all of the bits in this big integer value left by `n` places. The values of the bits in positions `0` to `n-1` after the shift are `0`.

If `n` < `0`, the bits are shifted right. If this big integer value is negative, the logically infinite number of leading ones are shifted right as well.

The value of this big integer is not changed.

PARAMETERS

`n` The number of places to shift to the left (or right, if negative).

RETURNS A non-`null` `BigInteger` object containing this big integer value multiplied by `2^n`.

EXAMPLE See `shiftRight()`.

shiftRight()

PURPOSE Shifts to the right the bits in the two's complement representation of this big integer value.

SYNTAX `public BigInteger shiftRight(int n)`

DESCRIPTION If this big integer value is negative, the logically infinite number of leading ones are shifted right. Therefore the largest value that a negative number can be after an arbitrary number of shifts is -1.

If n < 0, the bits are shifted to the left. In this case, the values of the bits in positions 0 to n-1 after the shift are 0.

PARAMETERS

n The number of places to shift to the right (or left, if negative).

RETURNS A non-null BigInteger object containing this big integer value divided by 2^n.

EXAMPLE

```
BigInteger a = BigInteger.valueOf(123);
System.out.println(a.shiftRight(1));   // 61
System.out.println(a.shiftRight(100)); // 0

a = BigInteger.valueOf(-123);
System.out.println(a.shiftRight(1));   // -62
System.out.println(a.shiftRight(100)); // -1

a = BigInteger.valueOf(123);
System.out.println(a.shiftLeft(1));    // 246
System.out.println(a.shiftLeft(100));  // 155921023828072216384094494261248

a = BigInteger.valueOf(-123);
System.out.println(a.shiftLeft(1));    // -246
System.out.println(a.shiftLeft(100));  // -155921023828072216384094494261248

// Shift with negative values.
a = BigInteger.valueOf(123);
System.out.println(a.shiftRight(-1));  // 246
System.out.println(a.shiftLeft(-1));   // 61
```

signum()

PURPOSE Determines the sign of this big integer value.

SYNTAX `public int signum()`

DESCRIPTION If the value of this big integer is negative, this method returns -1. If the value is 0, this method returns 0. If the value is greater than zero, this method returns 1.

RETURNS -1, 0, or 1, depending on the sign of this big integer value.

EXAMPLE

```
BigInteger a = BigInteger.valueOf(-1);
System.out.println(a.signum());     // -1

a = BigInteger.valueOf(0);
System.out.println(a.signum());     // 0
```

```
a = BigInteger.valueOf(123);
System.out.println(a.signum());     // 1
```

subtract()

PURPOSE
Calculates the difference between this big integer value and another.

SYNTAX
`public BigInteger subtract(BigInteger val)`

DESCRIPTION
This method subtracts the value of `val` from this big integer value and returns a `BigInteger` that represents the difference. Neither the value of `val` nor that of this big integer is changed.

PARAMETERS

`val` A non-`null` `BigInteger` object.

RETURNS
A non-`null` `BigInteger` object containing this big integer value minus `val`.

EXAMPLE

```
System.out.println(new BigInteger("123").subtract(new BigInteger("1234")));
// -1111
```

testBit()

PURPOSE
Determines if some bit is set in the two's complement representation of this big integer value.

SYNTAX
`public boolean testBit(int n) throws ArithmeticException`

DESCRIPTION
This method returns `true` if the bit at bit position `n` in this big integer value has the value `1`.

PARAMETERS

`n` The `0`-based position of the bit to be tested.

RETURNS
`true` if the bit at `n` has the value `0`; `false` otherwise.

EXCEPTIONS

`ArithmeticException`
If `n` < `0`.

SEE ALSO
`clearBit()`, `setBit()`.

EXAMPLE
This example implements a routine that prints the two's complement representation of a big integer value.

```
import java.math.*;
import java.util.Random;
```

```
class Main {
    // Print the low-order 32-bits of n.
    static void print(BigInteger n) {
        for(int i=31; i>=0; i--) {
            System.out.print(n.testBit(i) ? "1" : "0");
        }
        System.out.println();
    }

    public static void main(String[] args) {
        print(BigInteger.valueOf(0));       // 00000000000000000000000000000000
        print(BigInteger.valueOf(1));       // 00000000000000000000000000000001
        print(BigInteger.valueOf(-1));      // 11111111111111111111111111111111
        print(BigInteger.valueOf(65536));   // 00000000000000010000000000000000
        print(BigInteger.valueOf(-65536));  // 11111111111111110000000000000000

        print(new BigInteger(32, new Random()));
                                            // 10111010100011101001001101110010
    }
}
```

toByteArray()

PURPOSE Creates an array containing the bits of this big integer value.

SYNTAX `public byte[] toByteArray()`

DESCRIPTION This method creates the smallest `byte` array large enough to contain the minimal bit representation of this big integer value (see the class description for details). The bits in the *result* byte area are stored in two's complement form. The bits are in big-endian order; that is, *result*`[0]` contains the most-significant byte and *result*`[bval.length-1]` contains the least-significant byte. The representation contains enough sign bits to fill *result*`[0]`.The resulting `byte` array can be used in the `BigInteger()` constructor to create a new `BigInteger` object with the identical value as this object.

The size of the array is exactly `ceil((bitLength()+1)/8)`.

RETURNS A non-`null` `byte` array containing the bits of this big integer value. The length of the array is ≥ 1.

SEE ALSO `BigInteger()`.

EXAMPLE

```
import java.math.*;

class Main {
    // Creates a BigInteger object, calls toByteArray() and prints the result.
    static void print(int n) {
        byte[] buf = BigInteger.valueOf(n).toByteArray();

        System.out.print("new byte[]{");
        for (int i=0; i<buf.length; i++) {
```

```
            if (i>0) {
                System.out.print(" ,");
            }
            System.out.print("0x"+Integer.toHexString(buf[i]&0xff));
        }
        System.out.println("}");
    }

    public static void main(String[] args) {
        print(0);       // new byte[]{0x0}
        print(1);       // new byte[]{0x1}
        print(-1);      // new byte[]{0xff}
        print(0x80);    // new byte[]{0x0 ,0x80}
        print(-0x80);   // new byte[]{0x80}
    }
}
```


toString()

PURPOSE Generates a string representing this big integer value.

SYNTAX

```
public String toString()
public String toString(int rdx)
```

DESCRIPTION This method returns a string representing this big integer value in radix `rdx`. If the big integer value is negative, a negative sign precedes the returned string. The resulting string can be used in the `BigInteger()` constructor to create a new `BigInteger` object that has the same value as this big integer object.

`rdx` should be in the range `Character.MIN_RADIX` to `Character.MAX_RADIX`. If `rdx` is outside that range, it is set to 10. The method `Character.forDigit()` is used to convert a base `rdx` digit to a printable character. If `rdx` is not specified, it defaults to 10.

Note that when the value is negative and `rdx` is 2, this method does not produce a value in two's complement form. For example, if the value is `-5`, the two's complement form is ...111011; this method instead produces -101.

PARAMETERS

`rdx` The radix of the generated string. `Character.MIN_RADIX` ≤ `rdx` ≤ `Character.MAX_RADIX`. If `rdx` is outside this range, radix 10 is used.

RETURNS A non-`null` string containing this big integer value in radix `rdx`.

SEE ALSO `Character.MAX_RADIX`, `Character.MIN_RADIX`.

EXAMPLE This example implements a radix converter. The in and out radixes are supplied on the command line. The program reads input value from standard input and writes the conversions on standard output.

```
import java.math.*;
import java.io.*;

class Main {
    public static void main(String[] args) {
        if (args.length < 2) {
            System.err.println("Usage: java Main <in-radix> <out-radix>");
            System.exit(1);
        }

        int inradix = Integer.parseInt(args[0]);
        int outradix = Integer.parseInt(args[1]);

        BufferedReader is =
            new BufferedReader(new InputStreamReader(System.in));
        String line;
        try {
            // Read numbers from standard input.
            while ((line = is.readLine()) != null) {
                BigInteger a = new BigInteger(line, inradix);
                System.out.println(a.toString(outradix));
            }
        } catch (Exception e) {
            e.printStackTrace();
        }
    }
}
```

Output

```
> java Main 10 26
12345678
110alk
> java Main 10 2
-2
-10
```

valueOf()

PURPOSE Returns a `BigInteger` instance for a primitive integer value.

SYNTAX `public static BigInteger valueOf(long val)`

DESCRIPTION This method returns a `BigInteger` instance containing the value `val`.

This method is very similar to the `BigInteger` constructor for creating big integer values. The difference is that this method maintains a list of precreated `BigInteger` objects for common values such as `0` and `1` and, where possible, returns these objects instead of creating new ones.

PARAMETERS

`val` The resulting big integer's value.

RETURNS A non-`null` `BigInteger` representing the value `val`.

SEE ALSO `BigInteger()`.

EXAMPLE See `remainder()`.

xor()

PURPOSE XOR's this big integer value with another big integer value.

SYNTAX `public BigInteger xor(BigInteger val)`

DESCRIPTION This method XOR's `val` with this big integer value and returns a `BigInteger` that represents the result. This operation is similar to the Java ^ operator for primitive number types. The result is negative if either this big integer value or `val` is negative (but not both). Neither the value of `val` nor that of this big integer is changed.

A property of the XOR operation is that `a.xor(b).xor(b).equals(a)` is `true`.

PARAMETERS

`val` A non-`null` `BigInteger` object.

RETURNS A non-`null` `BigInteger` object containing this big integer value XOR'ed with `val`.

SEE ALSO `and()`, `andNot()`, `not()`, `or()`.

EXAMPLE

```
BigInteger a = new BigInteger("110111", 2);  //              110111
BigInteger b = new BigInteger("101010", 2);  //              101010
System.out.println(a.xor(b).toString(2));    //   11101      011101

a = new BigInteger(  "-111", 2);             //          ...11111001
b = new BigInteger("101010", 2);             //             00101010
System.out.println(a.xor(b).toString(2));    // -101101  ...11010011

a = new BigInteger(   "-111", 2);            //          ...11111001
b = new BigInteger("-101010", 2);            //          ...11010110
System.out.println(a.xor(b).toString(2));    //  101111     00101111
```

java.net
BindException

```
java.lang.Object
  java.lang.Throwable
    java.lang.Exception
      java.io.IOException
        SocketException
          BindException
          ConnectException
          NoRouteToHostException
```

A B C D E F G H I J K L M N O P Q R S T U V W X Y Z

Syntax

```
public class BindException extends SocketException
```

Description

`BindException` is an exception that is thrown when the program attempts to bind a socket to a local address and port. It is thrown when the local address and port cannot be assigned to the requesting program. Two reasons the address and port cannot be assigned are that they are already in use or they are reserved for system-level (supervisor-level) programs.

MEMBER SUMMARY	
Constructor	
`BindException()`	Constructs a `BindException` instance.

See Also

`DatagramSocket.DatagramSocket()`, `DatagramSocketImpl.bind()`, `ServerSocket.ServerSocket()`, `SocketException`, `SocketImpl.bind()`, `Socket.Socket()`.

Example

This example raises `BindException` when the second server socket is created because both server sockets are attempting to bind to the same port.

```
import java.net.ServerSocket;
import java.io.IOException;

class Main {
  public static void main(String[] args) {
    System.out.println("BindException example");
    try {
      // create server socket for port 2040
      ServerSocket srv = new ServerSocket(2040, 50);
      System.out.println("server socket created" + srv.toString());

      // create another one for same port will throw BindException
      ServerSocket srv2 = new ServerSocket(2040, 50);
      System.out.println("server socket created" + srv2.toString());

    } catch (IOException e) {
      e.printStackTrace();
    }
  }
}
```

BindException()

PURPOSE Constructs a `BindException` instance.

SYNTAX

```
public BindException()
public BindException(String msg)
```

DESCRIPTION This constructor constructs an instance of `BindException`. An optional string `msg` can be supplied that describes this particular instance of the exception. If `msg` is not specified, it defaults to `null`.

PARAMETERS

`msg` A possibly `null` string that gives details about this exception.

SEE ALSO `java.lang.Throwable.getMessage()`.

java.util

BitSet

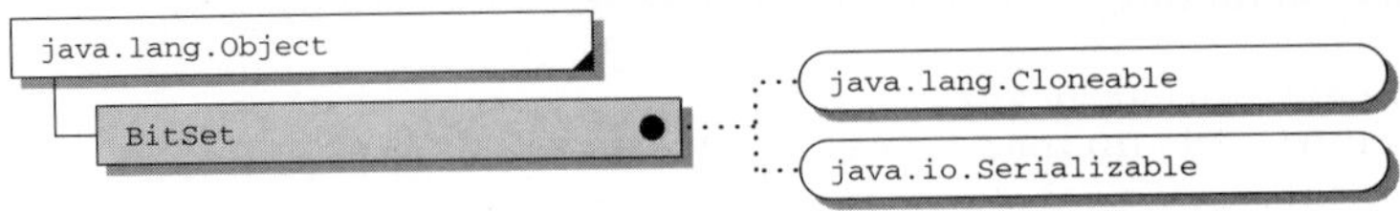

Syntax

```
public final class BitSet implements Cloneable, Serializable
```

Description

The `BitSet` class is used to represent a bit set.[1] Each element in the bit set is a bit that is either set (`1`) or cleared (`0`). You create a bit set with an initial size. The bit set will grow automatically as bits beyond its initial size are set/cleared. You can access and update the bits in the set individually by their indices, and you can perform bitwise logical operations on the entire set.

You can use a bit set as a compact way of representing a set of `boolean` flags. You can also use a bit set to record `boolean` information about an array of objects, for example, on/off switch settings on a bank of lights.

MEMBER SUMMARY	
Constructor	
`BitSet()`	Constructs a `BitSet` instance with all bits initialized to `0`.
Bit Manipulation Methods	
`and()`	Applies the logical AND of this bit set with another bit set.
`clear()`	Clears a bit in this bit set.
`get()`	Retrieves a bit from this bit set.
`or()`	Applies logical OR of this bit set with another bit set.
`set()`	Sets a bit in this bit set.
`size()`	Determines the number of bits in this bit set.
`xor()`	Applies logical XOR of this bit set with another bit set.
Object Override Methods	
`clone()`	Makes a copy of this bit set.
`equals()`	Compares this bit set with another object for equality.
`hashCode()`	Computes the hash code for this bit set.
`toString()`	Generates the string representation of this bit set.

1. `BitSet` is a misnomer because "sets" are unordered. `BitVector` would be a more correct class name.

See Also

`java.io.Serializable`, `Vector`.

Example

This example shows the use of two `BitSet` instances, `english` and `french`, to represent whether a person in a group speaks English and/or French, respectively. These two instances are then used to determine which persons are bilingual and which are unilingual. The example uses the bitwise logical methods as well as `set()/get()` methods on the bit sets.

```
import java.util.BitSet;

class Main {
    private static void initBitSets(BitSet e, BitSet f) {
        for(int i = 0; i < 10; i++)
            e.set(i);
        for (int i = 5; i <15; i++)
            f.set(i);
        System.out.println("english: " + e);
        System.out.println("french: " + f);
    }
    public static void main(String[] args) {
        BitSet english = new BitSet(100);  // tracks English speakers
        BitSet french = new BitSet(100);   // tracks French speakers

        // initialize bit arrays with data
        initBitSets(english, french);

        BitSet bilingual = (BitSet)english.clone();
        bilingual.and(french);

        if (bilingual.equals(english))
            // this means entire English class is bilingual
            System.out.println("Completely bilingual class");
        else
            System.out.println("Bilingual: " + bilingual.toString());

        BitSet either = (BitSet)english.clone();
        either.or(french);
        int eitherCount = 0;

        // count how many speak either English or French or both
        for (int i=0; i < either.size(); i++) {
            if (either.get(i))
                ++eitherCount;
        }
        System.out.println("Either(" + eitherCount + "):" + either);

        // find those who speak just either French or English but not both
        BitSet one = (BitSet)english.clone();
        one.xor(french);
        System.out.println("One: " + one);

        // Another ways to do this is to take 'either' and
        // eliminate those who are bilingual

        // fast way
```

```
            one = (BitSet)either.clone();
            one.xor(bilingual);
            System.out.println("One:" + one);

            // slow way
            one = (BitSet)either.clone();
            for (int i = 0; i < one.size(); i++)
                if (bilingual.get(i))
                    one.clear(i);
            System.out.println("One:" + one);
        }
    }
```


and()

PURPOSE Applies logical AND of this bit set with another bit set.

SYNTAX `public void and(BitSet bs)`

DESCRIPTION This method applies logical AND of this bit set with the bit set `bs`. For all indices of this bit set, if the *i*th bit in this bit set and the *i*th bit in `bs` are both set, the *i*th bit of this set will remain set. Otherwise the *i*th bit will be cleared. If `bs` has fewer bits than this bit set, the rest of the bits in this bit set that are not ANDed are set to `0`. If `bs` has more bits than this bit set does, the extra bits are not used.

PARAMETERS

`bs` The non-`null` bit set with which to logically AND.

SEE ALSO `or()`, `xor()`.

EXAMPLE See the class example.

BitSet()

PURPOSE Constructs a `BitSet` instance with bits initialized to `0`.

SYNTAX `public BitSet()`
`public BitSet(int nbits)`

DESCRIPTION There are two forms of the constructor for the `BitSet` class. The first form constructs a bit set with a default initial size of 64 bits. The second form constructs a bit set with the initial size of `nbits` bits, which is always rounded up to the next 64-bit increment. For example, if `nbits` is 8 the size of the bit set is 64. For both forms of the constructor, the bit set will automatically grow if bits in positions higher than this initial size are set (by `clear()` or `set()`).

Also for both forms of the constructor, all bits in the new bit set are initialized to `0`.

PARAMETERS

`nbits` The initial size of the bit set. `nbits` ≥ `0`.

EXCEPTIONS

`NegativeArraySizeException`
If `nbits` < `0`.

SEE ALSO `clear()`, `set()`.

EXAMPLE See the class example and `hashCode()`.

A B C D E F G H I J K L M N O P Q R S T U V W X Y Z

clear()

PURPOSE Clears a bit in this bit set.

SYNTAX `public void clear(int pos)`

DESCRIPTION This method sets the bit at index `pos` in this bit set to `0`. If `pos` is beyond the size of this bit set, the bit set is grown automatically so that `pos` identifies a bit in the new, larger bit set. Any new bits added are initialized to `0`.

PARAMETERS

`pos` The `0`-based index of the bit to clear. `pos` ≥ `0`.

EXCEPTIONS

`IndexOutOfBoundsException`
If `pos` < `0`.

SEE ALSO `set()`.

EXAMPLE See the class example.

clone()

PURPOSE Makes a copy of this bit set.

SYNTAX `public Object clone()`

DESCRIPTION This method makes a copy of all bits in this bit set.

RETURNS A new non-`null` bit set that has the same bits as this bit set.

OVERRIDES `java.lang.Object.clone()`.

EXAMPLE See the class example.

equals()

PURPOSE Compares this bit set with another object for equality.

SYNTAX `public boolean equals(Object obj)`

DESCRIPTION This method compares the bits in this bit set with the bits in `obj` for equality. If `obj` is `null` or if `obj` is not a `BitSet`, `equals()` returns `false`. If all of the bits in this bit set are identical to those in `obj`, this method returns `true`. If one bit set is longer than the other, the extra bits in the longer bit set are logically ANDed with zero bits. If not all of the bits are identical, `equals()` returns `false`.

PARAMETERS

`obj` The possibly `null` object with which to compare.

RETURNS `true` if `obj` is a bit set and has the same bits as this bit set; `false` otherwise.

OVERRIDES `java.lang.Object.equals()`.

SEE ALSO `hashCode()`.

EXAMPLE See the class example.

get()

PURPOSE Retrieves a bit from this bit set.

SYNTAX `public boolean get(int pos)`

DESCRIPTION This method retrieves the bit at index `pos` of this bit set. It returns `true` if the bit has been set (to `1`) and `false` if the bit has been cleared (set to `0`). If `pos` is beyond the size of this bit set, `false` is returned.

PARAMETERS

`pos` The `0`-based index of the bit to retrieve. `pos` ≥ `0`.

RETURNS The `boolean` value of the specified bit in this bit set.

EXCEPTIONS

`IndexOutOfBoundsException`
If `pos` < `0`.

SEE ALSO `clear()`, `set()`.

EXAMPLE See the class example.

hashCode()

PURPOSE Computes the hash code for this bit set.

SYNTAX `public int hashCode()`

DESCRIPTION This method computes and returns the hash code for this bit set. The hash code is calculated using an algorithm involving all of the bits in this bit set.

RETURNS The hash code of this bit set.

OVERRIDES `java.lang.Object.hashCode().`

SEE ALSO `equals(), java.util.Hashtable.`

EXAMPLE

```
BitSet bs = new BitSet(128);
...
int[] hits = new int[13];
int hashval = bs.hashCode();             // generate hash code
++hits[Math.abs(hashval%hits.length)];   // count hits
```

or()

PURPOSE Applies logical OR of this bit set with another bit set.

SYNTAX `public void or(BitSet bs)`

DESCRIPTION This method applies logical OR of this bit set with the bit set `bs`. For all indices of this bit set, if the *i*th bit in `bs` is set, the *i*th bit of this set will be set. Otherwise, the *i*th bit in this bit set remains unchanged (if it was `0` before, it will remain `0`; if it was set before, it will remain set). If `bs` has fewer bits than this bit set, the extra bits in this bit set are left unchanged. If `bs` has more bits than this bit set, the extra bits are not used.

PARAMETERS

`bs` The non-`null` bit set with which to logically OR.

SEE ALSO `and(), xor().`

EXAMPLE See the class example.

set()

PURPOSE Sets a bit in this bit set.

SYNTAX `public void set(int pos)`

DESCRIPTION This method sets the bit at index pos in this bit set to 1. If pos is beyond the size of this bit set, the bit set is grown automatically so that pos identifies a bit in the new, larger bit set. Except for the bit at pos, any new bits added are initialized to 0, as shown in Figure 9.

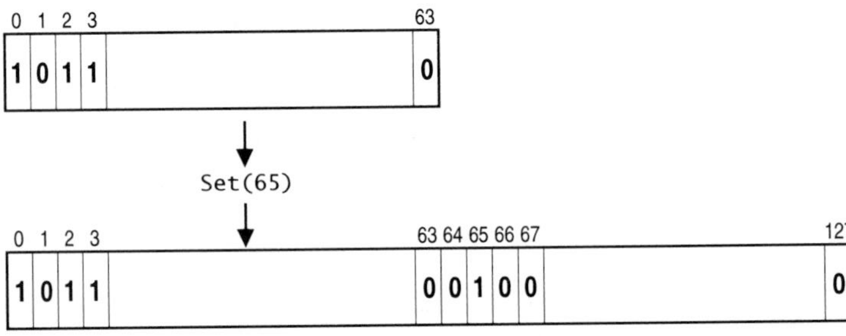

FIGURE 9: `BitSet.set()`.

PARAMETERS

pos The 0-based index of the bit to set pos ≥ 0.

EXCEPTIONS

IndexOutOfBoundsException
If pos < 0.

SEE ALSO clear().

EXAMPLE

```
import java.util.BitSet;

class Main {
    public static void main(String[] args) {
        BitSet bs = new BitSet();
        System.out.println("Original size: " + bs.size());    // 64
        // Set bit at 65
        bs.set(65);
        System.out.println("New size: " + bs.size());         // 128
    }
}
```

size()

PURPOSE Determines the number of bits in this bit set.

SYNTAX `public int size()`

DESCRIPTION The number of bits in a bit set is always rounded up to its closest 64-bit increment. For example, creating a bit set with an initial size of 8 bits actually creates one that is 64 bits. Creating a bit set with an initial size of 65 bits actually creates one that is 128 bits. This method returns the number of bits in this bit set.

RETURNS The number of bits in this bit set.

SEE ALSO `BitSet()`, `clear()`, `set()`.

EXAMPLE See class example.

toString()

PURPOSE Generates the string representation for this bit set.

SYNTAX `public String toString()`

DESCRIPTION The string representation of a bit set consists of a comma-separated list of the indices of the bits in the bit set that have been set (to `1`). The indices of the bits that are clear are not included in the string. This method returns this string representation.

RETURNS The non-`null` string representation of this bit set.

OVERRIDES `java.lang.Object.toString()`.

EXAMPLE See class example.

xor()

PURPOSE Applies logical XOR of this bit set with another bit set.

SYNTAX `public void xor(BitSet bs)`

DESCRIPTION This method applies logical XOR of this bit set with the bit set `bs`. For all indices in this set, if the *i*th bit in this bit set and the *i*th bit in `bs` are the same, the *i*th bit in this bit set is cleared. If the two *i*th bits are different (one is set and the other is not), the *i*th bit is set. If `bs` has fewer bits than this bit set, the extra bits in this bit set are left unchanged. If `bs` has more bits than this bit set, the extra bits are not used.

PARAMETERS

`bs` The non-`null` bit set with which to logically XOR.

SEE ALSO `and()`, `or()`.

EXAMPLE See the class example.

Boolean

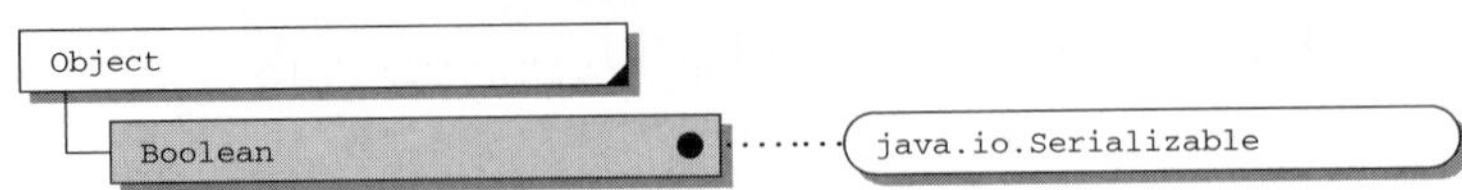

A
B
C
D
E
F
G
H
I
J
K
L
M
N
O
P
Q
R
S
T
U
V
W
X
Y
Z

Syntax

```
public final class Boolean extends Object implements Serializable
```

Description

The `Boolean` class provides an object wrapper for `boolean` data values. This wrapper allows `boolean`s to be passed to methods in Java class libraries that accept Java objects as parameters.

Usage

`Boolean` instances are used to pass `boolean` values to methods that accept Java objects as parameters. They cannot be used in boolean expressions in place of `boolean`. For example, the following is not allowed:

```
Boolean b1 = new Boolean(true);
if (b1) ...
```

To perform logical tests using a `Boolean` instance, you must first obtain its `boolean` value, as follows:

```
if (b1.booleanValue()) ...
```

MEMBER SUMMARY	
Constructor	
`Boolean`	Constructs a `Boolean` object using its string representation or `boolean` value.
Constant Fields	
`FALSE`	A `Boolean` object that has the `boolean` value `false`.
`TRUE`	A `Boolean` object that has the `boolean` value `true`.
`TYPE`	The `Class` object representing the primitive type `boolean`.
Conversion Methods	
`booleanValue()`	Retrieves the `boolean` value of this `Boolean` object.
`getBoolean()`	Retrieves the `boolean` value of a system property.
`valueOf()`	Creates a `Boolean` object using its string representation.

MEMBER SUMMARY

Object Methods	
`equals()`	Compares this object with another object for equality.
`hashCode()`	Computes the hash code for this object.
`toString()`	Generates the string representation of this object.

See Also

`java.io.Serializable`.

Example

```
class Main {
    public static void main(String args[]) {
        Boolean tb = new Boolean(true);
        Boolean fb = new Boolean(false);

        if (tb.booleanValue() && fb.booleanValue())
            System.err.println("logic error");

        if (tb.equals(Boolean.TRUE) && fb.equals(Boolean.FALSE))
            System.err.println("expected behavior");

        System.out.println("tb :" + tb.toString());
        System.out.println("fb :" + fb.toString());
    }
}
```

Boolean()

PURPOSE Constructs a `Boolean` object using its string representation or `boolean` value.

SYNTAX
```
public Boolean(boolean boolVal)
public Boolean(String strVal)
```

DESCRIPTION These constructors construct a `Boolean` object using a `boolean` value `boolVal` or a string representation of the `boolean` value `strVal`.

PARAMETERS

`boolVal` The `boolean` value that the new object will have.

`strVal` The non-`null` string representation of the `boolean` value that the new object will have. If `strVal` is the case-insensitive equivalent of the string "true", the `boolean` value of the new object will be `true`; otherwise, the `boolean` value will be `false`.

SEE ALSO `valueOf()`.

EXAMPLE

```
Boolean status = new Boolean(true);         // true
Boolean b1 = new Boolean("True");           // true
Boolean b2 = new Boolean("false");          // false
Boolean b3 = new Boolean("neither");        // false
```


booleanValue()

PURPOSE Retrieves the `boolean` value of this `Boolean` object.

SYNTAX `public boolean booleanValue()`

RETURNS The `boolean` value of this object.

EXAMPLE

```
Boolean status = new Boolean(false);
boolean bval = status.booleanValue();
if (bval)
    return (-1);
```

equals()

PURPOSE Compares this object with another object for equality.

SYNTAX `public boolean equals(Object obj)`

DESCRIPTION This method compares the `boolean` value of this object with the `boolean` value of `obj`. It returns `true` if the two values are equal. It returns `false` if the two values are not equal or if `obj` is `null` or not a `Boolean` object.

PARAMETERS

`obj` The possibly `null` object against which this object will be compared.

RETURNS `true` if `obj` has the same `boolean` value as this object; `false` otherwise.

OVERRIDES `Object.equals()`.

SEE ALSO `hashCode()`.

EXAMPLE

```
Object obj1 = new Boolean(true);
Object obj2 = new Boolean(false);
if (obj1.equals(obj2))
    return (-1);
```

FALSE

PURPOSE A `Boolean` object that has the `boolean` value `false`.

SYNTAX `public static final Boolean FALSE`

SEE ALSO `TRUE`.

EXAMPLE

```
Boolean status = new Boolean(true);
...
// Returns -1 if status is false
if(status.equals(Boolean.FALSE))
    return (-1);
```

getBoolean

PURPOSE Retrieves the `boolean` value of a system property.

SYNTAX `public static boolean getBoolean(String property)`

DESCRIPTION This method retrieves the system property identified by `property` and parses its value to determine whether it has the case-insensitive string value "true". It returns `true` if the string value is "true". If the string value is not "true" or if the property is not found, this method returns `false`.

PARAMETERS

`property` The non-`null` string name of the property of interest.

RETURNS A `boolean` value indicating whether the specified property has the string value "true".

SEE ALSO `java.util.Properties`, `System.getProperty()`.

EXAMPLE

```
if (Boolean.getBoolean("os.password.required")) {
    password = Login.getPassword("Password:");
}
```

hashCode()

PURPOSE Computes the hash code for this object.

SYNTAX `public int hashCode()`

DESCRIPTION This method returns the hash code for this object. The hash code of a `Boolean` object is calculated using its `boolean` value. `Boolean` objects with the same `boolean` value have the same hash value.

RETURNS An `int` representing the hash code of this object.

OVERRIDES `Object.hashCode()`.

SEE ALSO `equals()`, `java.util.Hashtable`.

EXAMPLE

```
Boolean b1 = new Boolean("true");        // true
Boolean b2 = new Boolean(false);
Boolean b3 = new Boolean(true);

if (b1.hashCode() == b3.hashCode())      // equal
    System.out.println("hash equal");
else
    System.out.println("hash different");

if (b1.hashCode() == b2.hashCode())      // different
    System.out.println("hash equal");
else
    System.out.println("hash different");
```


toString()

PURPOSE Generates the string representation of this object.

SYNTAX `public String toString()`

DESCRIPTION This method generates and returns the string representation of this `Boolean` object. The string representation of a `Boolean` object is either "true" or "false", depending on the object's `boolean` value.

RETURNS The non-`null` string representation of this `Boolean` object's `boolean` value.

OVERRIDES `Object.toString()`.

SEE ALSO `valueOf()`.

EXAMPLE

```
Boolean status = new Boolean(true);
String strval = status.toString();
System.out.println("Value of status is: " + strval); // "true"
```

TRUE

PURPOSE A `Boolean` object that has the `boolean` value `true`.

SYNTAX `public static final Boolean TRUE`

SEE ALSO `FALSE`.

EXAMPLE

```
Boolean status = new Boolean(true);
...
if(status.equals(Boolean.TRUE))
    return (-1);
```

TYPE

PURPOSE The Class object representing the primitive type boolean.

SYNTAX `public static final Class TYPE`

DESCRIPTION This constant can be used where the Class object— boolean.class—of the primitive type boolean is required, such as for reflection. Although there are no restrictions on the use of Boolean.TYPE, the preferred syntax for naming the class is boolean.class.

SEE ALSO Class.

EXAMPLE

```
public static void main(String[] args) {
    Class c = Boolean.TYPE;
    System.out.println("TYPE: " + c);
    System.out.println("isPrimitive: " + c.isPrimitive());
    System.out.println("superclass: " + c.getSuperclass());
    try {
        Object obj = c.newInstance();  // ERROR
        System.out.println("boolean: " + obj);
    } catch (InstantiationException e) {
        e.printStackTrace();
    } catch (IllegalAccessException e) {
        e.printStackTrace();
    }
}
```

valueOf()

PURPOSE Creates a Boolean object using its string representation.

SYNTAX `public static Boolean valueOf(String str)`

DESCRIPTION This method creates a Boolean object by parsing the string str. If str contains the string "true" (case is not significant), the resulting object has the boolean value true; otherwise, its value is false.

PARAMETERS

str The non-null string representation of a boolean value (i.e., "true" or "false").

RETURNS A new Boolean object that has the boolean value represented by str.

SEE ALSO toString().

EXAMPLE

```
Boolean b1 = Boolean.valueOf("TrUE");
if (b1.booleanValue())
    System.out.println("correct");
```

BreakIterator

java.lang.Object
BreakIterator
SimpleTextBoundary
java.lang.Cloneable
java.io.Serializable

Syntax

```
public abstract class BreakIterator extends Object implements Cloneable,
    Serializable
```

Description

`BreakIterator` is an abstract class that indirectly implements methods for finding and getting the position of four different kinds of logical breaks, or boundaries, in a string of text, based on user characters (rather than Unicode characters).

As shown in Figure 10, a *character boundary* is a location between characters. A break iterator has an imaginary cursor that tracks the current boundary. A break iterator can find the location of a character, word, or sentence boundary, as well as potential line-break boundaries. Hence, a program is able to properly select characters for text operations, such as highlighting a character, cutting a word, moving to the next sentence, or word-wrapping at a line ending. These operations are performed in a locale-sensitive manner, meaning that they honor the text boundary semantics for a particular locale.

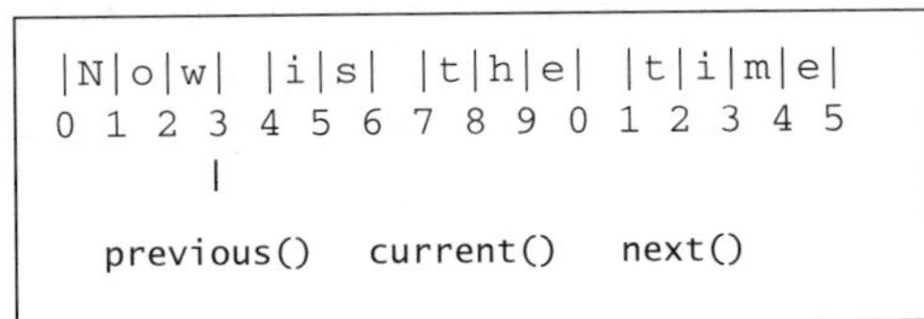

FIGURE 10: Character boundary.

Another typical use of a break iterator is when searching for a *whole* word, checking whether the start and end are at word boundaries. For example, a search for "depend" would initially stop on "independent," but a test for word boundaries at either end of the match "in|depend|ent" would indicate this is not a whole word match.

It's important to note that all built-in `BreakIterator` objects stop only between user characters, not between just any Unicode characters. A user character can be composed of more than one Unicode characters. For example, the user character "é" can be composed of the two Unicode characters, |e|´|. Thus the word "frappé" when decomposed to the Unicode characters |f|r|a|p|p|e|´|, has word breaks at |frappe´| and not |frappe|´.

`BreakIterator` is intended for use with natural languages only. Do not use this class to tokenize a programming language.

Usage

When writing a program to use `BreakIterator`, you first determine which kinds of break iterators you need to create. When creating a break iterator, you specify which of the four kinds you want, either character, word, or sentence boundary or potential line-break boundaries. You do this by using the appropriate creation method—`getCharacterInstance()`, `getWordInstance()`, `getSentenceInstance()`, or `getLineInstance()`—to create a break iterator that performs the desired boundary analysis. Do not try calling the constructor (it is protected and automatically called as needed). A single instance of `BreakIterator` can work on only one kind of boundary, so if you want to iterate over different kinds of boundaries, you must create a different break iterator for each one.

The break iterator creation methods can take a specific locale or will use the default locale. Choosing `getAvailableLocales()` allows you to determine if the locale you want is installed. Once the break iterator is created, use `setText()` to assign either a string or a `CharacterIterator` object to that break iterator.

Calling a movement method causes the break iterator to scan through the text, analyzing the sequence of characters and looking for the kind of boundary in which it specializes. For example, calling `next()` on a word-break iterator causes the iterator to start scanning forward from the current position and analyze characters using the word boundary rules (mentioned later in this discussion) until either it finds a position that satisfies the definition of a word boundary or it can move no further. It then returns an integer indicating the position of the boundary. This integer is the index of the character that would follow it. In contrast, calling the same method `next()` on a sentence-break iterator finds the next sentence boundary.

In general, a movement method returns the position of the boundary found. If the iterator is at either end of its range and `next()`, `previous()`, or `following()` attempts to move the cursor beyond the end of the text, then the method instead returns `BreakIterator.DONE` and does not move the cursor.

Unicode Characters

A *Unicode character* is a 16-bit encoding for written characters. The Unicode set of over 38,000 characters enables the writing of multilingual text. A Unicode character can be either a base character or combining character. A *base character* is one that does not graphically combine with any preceding character, which is characteristic of most Unicode characters. A *combining character* is one that graphically combines with a preceding base character. A combining character does not stand alone unless it is being described. Accents are examples of combining characters. A *combining character sequence* consists of a base character and zero or more combining characters. The base and combining characters are dynamically composed at printout time to a user character. Unicode characters are devoid of any style richness, such as font, weight, or point size. A pure Unicode sequence of characters corresponds to plain text.

User Characters

So what are user characters and how do they differ from Unicode characters? All built-in `BreakIterator` objects created with `getXXXInstance()` methods stop only *between* user characters for all locales, not between just any Unicode characters. Such iterators will never stop in the middle of a user character. This is the proper iterator behavior that users expect.

While the Java types `char` and `Character` represent Unicode characters, some Unicode characters combine to form a more complex character, called a *user character*, as shown in Figure 11. A user character has its own semantic value for such things as accented characters, ligatures, and combining characters required for languages of the Middle East and South Asia. Theoretically, developers can subclass `BreakIterator` with their own iterators that do stop in the middle of user characters.

```
User characters       |t|h|é|â|t|r|e|
Unicode characters    |t|h|e|’|a|^|t|r|e|
```

FIGURE 11: User characters.

A user character is the smallest component of written language that has semantic value to a native-language user. It can be made of one stroke or multiple, disconnected strokes. For example, in Latin languages (with the alphabet A–Z), a character is part of a larger word, but in ideographic languages (e.g., Chinese, Japanese, and Korean), a character can carry a complete idea or may be part of a larger word. Examples of user characters include “ä” (accent mark) and characters in some Middle East and Asian languages. It does not include ligatures (such as “fi”) because users think of these as two characters represented by a single glyph. A user character carries no font information; a font is necessary to render it.

Break iterators treat combining character sequences as a single user character. In other words, a break will never occur between the characters in a combining character sequence. A character break iterator would step through these as a single character. This feature is necessary for meeting user expectations about characters. For example, when stepping through characters in the French word “théâtre,” it would treat each accented character as a single character. Figure 11 shows how the French word “théâtre”, with seven user characters, could be constructed of nine Unicode characters. The letter “â” can be produced from a base letter (a) plus a diacritical mark (^), as two separate Unicode characters.

The previous example is contrived because the letter “â” is actually precomposed as the single Unicode character `\u00E2`. This is true for the most common user characters for the Latin-based languages. Combining character sequences are required for languages in the Middle East and for South Asia. Real-life examples are from Arabic, such as these:

```
\u0628\u064B (ARABIC BEH + ARABIC FATHATAN)
```

and from Devangari, such as these:

```
\u0915\u0941 (DEVANAGARI KA + DEVANAGARI VOWEL SIGN U)
```

In addition, special combining marks are used to aid with stress and pronunciation in dictionaries and language books. For example, in books teaching Italian, it is common to mark unusual stress with a dot under the vowel; for example:

```
a\u0307 (A + COMBINING DOT BELOW)
```


Locale

Break iterators are locale-sensitive because the conventions on where to break characters, words, lines, and sentences vary by language. You specify a locale (or use the default locale) when you create an instance of a break iterator.

Boundary

A break iterator has a single string of text that it can iterate over. A *boundary* is a location between characters or at the start or end of the string, as shown in Figure 10. Boundaries break the string into logical groups of characters. Four different kinds of boundaries exist, corresponding to the four kinds of break iterators: character boundaries, word boundaries, sentence boundaries, and line-break boundaries. A character has a character boundary on each side, a word has a word boundary on each side, and so on. A boundary is also called a *text break*. By definition, all four kinds of boundaries exist at the start and end of a string. Therefore the end of a string is considered the end of a sentence even if the string does not end with a period.

Boundary Position

Each boundary has a *boundary position* in the string—an integer given by the index of the character that would follow it. Thus the boundary between characters 3 and 4 has a position of 4. Since character indexes are zero-based, boundary positions are also zero-based. The first boundary in text is typically at position 0, and the last one is at the string's length, `str.length()`. The trivial case of text composed of an empty string has a single boundary at boundary position 0. See `first()` for a description of text subranges.

Notice that these offsets are the same used by `String.substring(int, int)`.

Boundary Rules

Developers have no direct control over the rules the break iterators use when analyzing text to determine breaks, although they could subclass `BreakIterator` and define their own rules for `next()`, `previous()`, and `following()`. The rules are rather complex, so this section states only the general rules. Boundary rules are likely to change in future releases of `BreakIterator`, so the details are not to be considered a spec.

As a break iterator is determining where a boundary is located, it takes into account the order of characters, their case (uppercase / lowercase / no case), and whether they are punctuation, symbols, or whitespace. It recognizes a break by the combination of these factors, including look-ahead, when determining whether it has reached a boundary. Here are the general rules for all boundaries:

- All four kinds of boundaries exist at the start and end of a string. For example, in English, the end of a string is considered the end of a sentence even if the string does not end with a period.
- Newlines (`\n`, `\r`, and `\r\n`) and many control characters (such as `\t`) are boundaries for all break iterators.

Descriptions of the four kinds of boundaries follow and are illustrated using this sentence:

```
He's from Africa. "Mr. Livingston, I presume?" Yes.
```

Character Boundary Analysis

Character boundary analysis locates the boundaries between user characters in a string. When it encounters a combining character sequence, it treats that sequence as a single character. Thus character boundary analysis provides the expected navigation through character strings, regardless of whether the character is encoded as one or more Unicode characters. In the following, the vertical bars indicate character boundaries:

```
|H|e|'|s| |f|r|o|m| |A|f|r|i|c|a|.| |"|M|r|.| |L|i|v|i|n|g|s|t|o|n|,| |I|
|p|r|e|s|u|m|e|?|"| |Y|e|s|.|
```

Word Boundary Analysis

Word boundary analysis provides expected interpretation of whitespace and punctuation marks within and following words. In general, here are the rules:

- Characters that are not part of a word, such as spaces, tabs, some symbols, and some punctuation marks, have word breaks on both sides.
- A sequence of spaces is considered a single word, for example:

```
|He's| |from| |Africa|.| |"|Mr|.| |Livingston|,| |I| |presume|?|"| |Yes.|
```

Note: There is no word boundary before the last period, but there should be. This is a known bug in Java 1.1.5 and earlier versions.

Sentence Boundary Analysis

In many written languages, the sentence terminator is a period. However, that same character is also used to terminate abbreviations and as a decimal separator. The result can be unresolvable ambiguities. Thus boundary analysis for sentences cannot be perfect. Here are the general rules for determining sentence boundaries:

- When a period is followed by whitespace and an uppercase letter, a sentence boundary is defined to be the end of the whitespace.
- Any parentheses and quotations between the period and uppercase letter are properly handled; for example: `|He said, "Hello." |(Yes, he did.)|.`

In the following, the vertical bars indicate sentence boundaries:

```
|He's from Africa. |"Mr. |Livingston, I presume?" |Yes.|
```

Notice that the sentence-break iterator mistakenly interprets "Mr." as being at the end of a sentence because the next word ("Livingston") begins with a capital letter.

Line-Break Boundary Analysis

Line-break boundary analysis determines possible locations where text could break to continue on the next line. That is, this analysis finds the boundaries of nonbreakable substrings. Here are the general rules for determining potential line-break boundaries:

- A line-break boundary falls after the end of a sequence of whitespace (e.g., space, tab, newline).
- A line-break boundary falls after both soft and hard hyphens in hyphenated words.

A hard hyphen is a hyphen that always appears regardless of where the word falls on the line, as in the expression "short-lived." A soft hyphen appears at the end of a line only when a word splits and continues on the next line.

Note that the movement methods move the cursor to the *potential* line-breaks, not the actual line breaks that might be visibly displayed on-screen. In the following, the vertical bars indicate line breaks:

```
|He's |from |Africa. |"Mr. |Livingston, |I |presume?" |Yes.|
```

Cursor and Current Position

Each iterator has a *cursor*. This cursor is conceptually the same as the caret described in `TextComponent`, except that it is not visible. The cursor can be positioned at any of the boundary positions in the text and has a *current position*. The movement methods can move the cursor in the text, in either direction, ranging from boundary position 0 to the length of the string `str.length()`, each time returning the new current position. Each iterator has its own separate cursor, even if the iterators point to the same text. Thus a word-break iterator and a line-break iterator operating on the same text will have different cursors. For a given iterator, the cursor must be at one of that iterator's boundaries.

Convenience Methods: isBoundary() and preceding()

The following two convenience methods are not part of the current API but are commonly used and may be added to `BreakIterator` in a later release. Feel free to use them.

- **`isBoundary()`**. Checks whether the current position is at a boundary. If so, returns `true`; otherwise, returns `false` .

```
public boolean isBoundary(int pos) {
    if (pos == 0) return true;
        return following(pos-1) == pos;
}
```

- **`preceding()`**. Returns the index of the closest boundary before the specified position.

```
public int preceding(int pos) {
    if (following(pos) != BreakIterator.DONE) {
```

```
            while (previous() >= pos)
                ;
            return current();
        } else {
            last();
            while (previous() >= pos)
                ;
            return current();
        }
    }
```


MEMBER SUMMARY

Constructor	
`BreakIterator()`	Constructor used by subclasses.
Break Iterator Creation Methods	
`getCharacterInstance()`	Creates a new break iterator for character boundaries.
`getLineInstance()`	Creates a new break iterator for line-break boundaries.
`getSentenceInstance()`	Creates a new break iterator for sentence boundaries.
`getWordInstance()`	Creates a new break iterator for word-break boundaries.
Locale Method	
`getAvailableLocales()`	Gets the locales for which break iterators are installed.
Movement Methods	
`current()`	Retrieves the current position of the cursor.
`first()`	Moves the cursor to the first boundary in the text and retrieves the position.
`following()`	Moves the cursor to the first boundary following a boundary position and retrieves the position.
`last()`	Moves the cursor to the last boundary in the text and retrieves the position.
`next()`	Moves the cursor forward a fixed number of boundaries in the text and retrieves the position.
`previous()`	Moves the cursor backward one boundary in the text and retrieves that position.
Text Methods	
`getText()`	Gets the character iterator for the text being scanned.
`setText()`	Sets a new string to be scanned for text boundaries.
Termination Constant	
`DONE`	Returned when this iterator tries to go beyond the end of text.
Object Methods	
`clone()`	Creates a copy of this `BreakIterator` object.

See Also

`CharacterIterator`, `StringCharacterIterator`, `CollationElementIterator`.

Example 1

This example demonstrates all four types of break iterators. To run this program, supply the filename of a text file you want to test. This brings up the text area shown in Figure 12. The cursor is initially at position 0. Press the letters indicated at the bottom of the text area to move the cursor, using the Shift key to move backward. You also can click with the mouse to move to a new position.

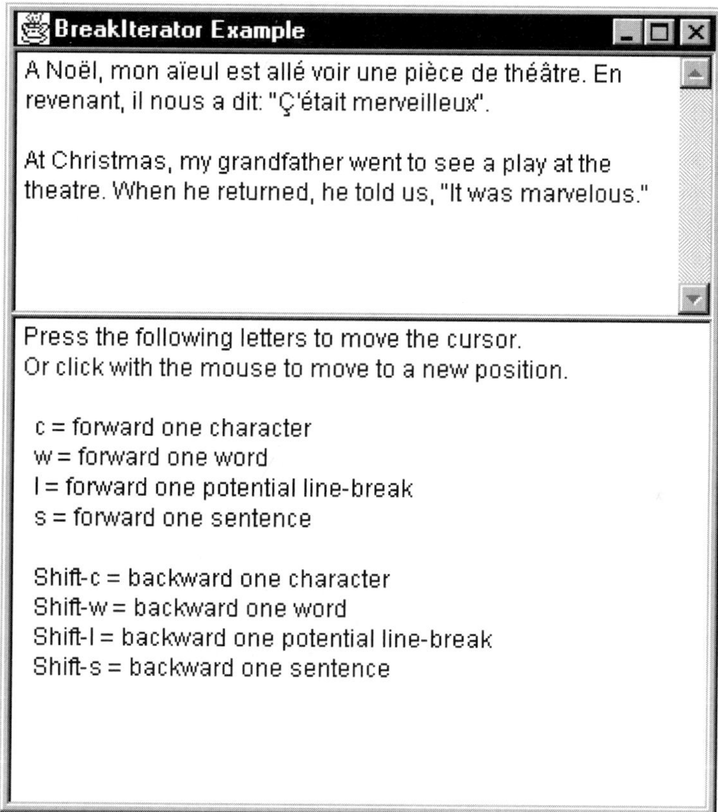

FIGURE 12: The Four Break Iterators.

Main.java

```
import java.awt.*;
import java.awt.event.*;
import java.io.*;
import java.util.*;
import java.text.*;

class Main extends Frame {
```

```
// Create text area and four break iterators
TextArea tArea =
    new TextArea("", 15, 50, TextArea.SCROLLBARS_VERTICAL_ONLY);
TextArea message =
    new TextArea("", 15, 50, TextArea.SCROLLBARS_NONE);

BreakIterator charBI = BreakIterator.getCharacterInstance();
BreakIterator wordBI = BreakIterator.getWordInstance();
BreakIterator sentBI = BreakIterator.getSentenceInstance();
BreakIterator lineBI = BreakIterator.getLineInstance();

Main(String s, String sNative) {
    super("BreakIterator Example");

    // Initialize various objects with the text.
    tArea.setText(s);
    charBI.setText(sNative);
    wordBI.setText(sNative);
    sentBI.setText(sNative);
    lineBI.setText(sNative);

    message.setText(
      "Press the following letters to move the cursor.\n" +
      "Or click with the mouse to move to a new position.\n" +
      "\n" +
      "   c = forward one character\n" +
      "   w = forward one word\n" +
      "   l = forward one potential line-break\n" +
      "   s = forward one sentence\n" +
      "\n" +
      "   Shift-c = backward one character\n" +
      "   Shift-w = backward one word\n" +
      "   Shift-l = backward one potential line-break\n" +
      "   Shift-s = backward one sentence\n"
    );

    message.setEditable(false);

    // Add layout to text area and listen for key events.
    add(tArea, BorderLayout.CENTER);
    add(message, BorderLayout.SOUTH);
    tArea.addKeyListener(new KeyEventHandler());

    setSize(400, 400);
    pack();
    show();
}

class KeyEventHandler extends KeyAdapter {
    public void keyPressed(KeyEvent evt) {
        BreakIterator bi = null;
        int sel = tArea.getSelectionStart();

        switch (Character.toLowerCase(evt.getKeyChar())) {
          case 'c':
            bi = charBI;
            break;
          case 'w':
            bi = wordBI;
            break;
```

```
                case 'l':
                  bi = lineBI;
                  break;
                case 's':
                  bi = sentBI;
                  break;
              }

              if (bi != null) {
                  // Get the length of text
                  int end = bi.getText().getEndIndex();
                  System.out.println(sel);
                  if (sel < end) {
                     // Move using absolute position
                     bi.following(sel);
                  }
                  if (sel <= end) {
                      // Are we moving to a previous boundary?
                      if (Character.isUpperCase(evt.getKeyChar())) {
                          bi.previous();
                          if (bi.current() >= sel) {
                              bi.previous();
                          }
                      }
                  }
                  tArea.select(bi.current(), bi.current());
              }
              evt.consume();
          }
      }

      public static void main(String[] args) {
          if (args.length != 1) {
              System.err.println("Usage: java Main <filename>");
              System.exit(1);
          }
          try {
              // To workaround a TextArea bug, create two versions
              // of the text:
              // - one with '\n' for newlines (to display in text area)
              // - the other with native newlines (to iterate over)
              // Read in the entire contents of the file.
              BufferedReader rd = new BufferedReader(new FileReader(args[0]));
              String sep = System.getProperty("line.separator");
              String line;
              StringBuffer sbuf = new StringBuffer();
              StringBuffer sbufNative = new StringBuffer();

              while ((line = rd.readLine()) != null) {
                  sbuf.append(line);
                  sbuf.append('\n');
                  sbufNative.append(line);
                  sbufNative.append(sep);
              }
              rd.close();
              new Main(new String(sbuf), new String(sbufNative));
          } catch (Exception e) {
              e.printStackTrace();
          }
      }
}
```

Example 2

This example uses the text area from the previous example but uses Japanese characters instead. See Figure 13. The text is contained inside the source file rather than imported from a file. This example displays output properly only if you have Japanese fonts installed on your system.

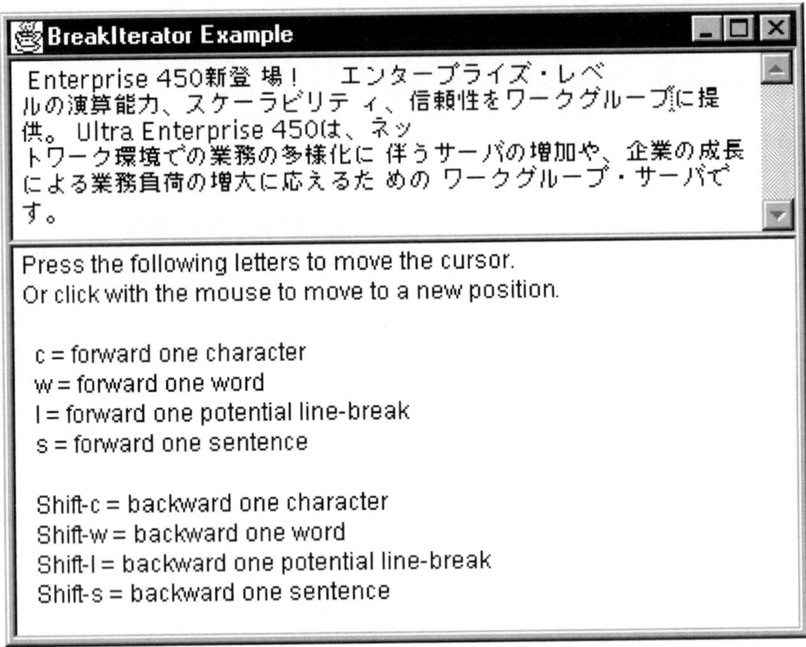

FIGURE 13: Japanese Break Iterators.

MainJapan.java

```
import java.awt.*;

class MainJapan extends Frame {

    public static void main(String[] args) {

        StringBuffer sbuf = new StringBuffer();

        sbuf = new
StringBuffer("\u7956\u7236\u304c\u30af\u30ea\u30b9\u30de\u30b9\u306b\u829d\u5c
45\u3092\u898b\u306b\u884c\u304d\u3001\u3068\u3066\u3082\u611f\u6fc0\u3057\u30
5f\u3068\u3044\u3063\u3066\u307e\u3057\u305f\u3002");

        new Main(new String(sbuf), new String(sbuf));
    }
}
```

BreakIterator()

PURPOSE Constructor used by subclasses.

SYNTAX `protected BreakIterator()`

DESCRIPTION The `BreakIterator` class is stateless and has no default behavior. This constructor is protected; do not call it directly. Instead, use the break iterator creation methods, listed below.

SEE ALSO `getCharacterInstance()`, `getLineInstance()`, `getSentenceInstance()`, `getWordInstance()`.

EXAMPLE See the class example.

clone()

PURPOSE Creates a copy of this `BreakIterator` object.

SYNTAX `public Object clone()`

DESCRIPTION This method makes a copy of this break iterator. The copy points to the same text and has the same current cursor position.

OVERRIDES `java.lang.Object.clone()`.

RETURNS A copy of this break iterator.

EXAMPLE This example demonstrates the use of `clone()` to copy a word-break iterator. Note that the copy has the same `current()` cursor position (5) and current character ("w") as the original.

```
import java.text.BreakIterator;

class Main {

    public static void main(String args[]) {

        String str = "Hello world";

        // create word break iterator
        BreakIterator wb = BreakIterator.getWordInstance();
        wb.setText(str);
        wb.next();
        printValues(wb);        // prints '5' and 'w'

        // create a clone
        BreakIterator wbCopy = (BreakIterator)wb.clone();
        printValues(wbCopy);    // prints '5' and 'w'
    }

    public static void printValues(BreakIterator b) {
        System.out.println(b.current());
        System.out.println(b.getText().current());
    }
}
```

current()

PURPOSE Retrieves the current position of the cursor.

SYNTAX `public abstract int current()`

DESCRIPTION This method retrieves the current position of this break iterator's cursor in its string of text. This position can be moved with the movement methods. When a break iterator is first created, this value is initially equal to `first()`.

RETURNS The current cursor position of this break iterator.

EXAMPLE This example prints the boundary position that is after the first word in a string.

```
import java.text.BreakIterator;

class Main {
    public static void main(String args[]) {

        String str = "Thank you very much.";

        // create word break iterator
        BreakIterator wb = BreakIterator.getWordInstance();
        wb.setText(str);

        // next boundary after current position
        int pos = wb.next();
        System.out.println(wb.current());  // prints 5
    }
}
```

DONE

PURPOSE Returned when this iterator tries to go beyond the end of text.

SYNTAX `public final static int DONE`

DESCRIPTION This class constant is returned by `previous()`, `next()`, or `following()` when this iterator attempts to step past the first or last boundary. This is useful for testing when to stop while iterating to the end of the text.

SEE ALSO `previous()`, `next()`, `following()`.

EXAMPLE See the class example.

first()

PURPOSE
Moves the cursor to the first boundary in the text and retrieves the position.

SYNTAX
`public abstract int first()`

DESCRIPTION
This method moves this break iterator's cursor to the first boundary in the text and returns the value of that text boundary. The first position can be either 0, if the break iterator was created from a string, or greater than 0, if the break iterator was created from a substring using `setText()` from `BreakIterator`: `setText(new StringCharacterIterator(text, begin, end, pos))`.

RETURNS
The position of the first text boundary, which is greater than or equal to 0.

SEE ALSO
`last()`.

EXAMPLE
See `next()`.

following()

PURPOSE
Moves the cursor to the first boundary following a character position and retrieves the position.

SYNTAX
`public abstract int following(int pos)`

DESCRIPTION
This method moves this break iterator's cursor to the position of the first boundary following the character position `pos` and returns that new position. For example, if the character position `pos` is in the middle of a sentence, this method, when called on a sentence-break iterator, will move the cursor to the end of that sentence. The return value is either greater than the specified position or the value `BreakIterator.DONE`.

Compare to `next()`, which also moves the position ahead, but the argument `n` is relative to the current position, rather than absolute.

PARAMETERS

`pos`
The character position from which to begin scanning forward. The value `pos` must be within the iterator range within the text, excluding the last boundary. That is, `first()` ≤ `pos` ≤ `last()-1` or an `IllegalArgumentException` is thrown.

RETURNS
The position of the first boundary following `pos`.

EXAMPLE
See `next()`.

A B C D E F G H I J K L M N O P Q R S T U V W X Y Z

getAvailableLocales()

PURPOSE Gets the set of locales for which break iterators are installed.

SYNTAX `public static synchronized Locale[] getAvailableLocales()`

DESCRIPTION This method queries the system and returns the set of locales for which break iterators are installed.

RETURNS Array of available locales.

EXAMPLE This example displays the list of available locales. The output list has been abbreviated from the 50 locales actually printed out.

```
import java.text.BreakIterator;
import java.util.Locale;

class Main {
    public static void main(String args[]) {

        // get list of installed locales with break iterators
        Locale locales[] = BreakIterator.getAvailableLocales();

        // print all locales
        for (int i = 0; i < locales.length; i++) {
            System.out.println(locales[i].getDisplayName());
        }
    }
}
```

Output

```
> java Main
Arabic (Egypt)
Belorussian (Belarus)
Bulgarian (Bulgaria)
Catalan (Spain)
Czech (Czech Republic)
Danish (Denmark)
German (Germany)
German (Austria)
German (Switzerland)
Greek (Greece)
English (Canada)
English (United Kingdom)
English (Ireland)
English (United States)
...
```

getCharacterInstance()

PURPOSE
Creates a new break iterator for character boundaries.

SYNTAX
```
public static BreakIterator getCharacterInstance()
public static BreakIterator getCharacterInstance(Locale loc)
```

DESCRIPTION
This method creates a new character-break iterator with the locale `loc`. The locale determines precisely how character boundary analysis is done, which can differ for different languages. If `loc` is not specified, the default locale is used. Breaks are between user characters, not Unicode characters.

Note: This method would be better named `getUserCharacterInstance()` to indicate that it iterates over *user* characters.

PARAMETERS

`loc` The locale for the character-break iterator. If a character-break iterator is not available for the specified locale, a default character-break iterator is used.

RETURNS
An instance of `BreakIterator` that finds character boundaries.

SEE ALSO
`java.util.Locale.getDefault()`.

EXAMPLE
See the class example.

getLineInstance()

PURPOSE
Creates a new break iterator for line-break boundaries.

SYNTAX
```
public static BreakIterator getLineInstance()
public static BreakIterator getLineInstance(Locale loc)
```

DESCRIPTION
This method creates a new line-break iterator with the locale `loc`. The locale determines precisely how line-break boundary analysis is done, which can differ for different languages. If `loc` is not specified, the default locale is used.

Note that if the text is displayed, such as in a text area, the movement methods move the cursor to any of the *potential* line-breaks. The break iterator does not know where the lines are visibly broken.

A line-break iterator is useful for determining the possible places where a text string can be broken at the end of a line (word-wrapping).

PARAMETERS

`loc` The locale for the line-break iterator. If a line-break iterator is not available for the specified locale, a default line-break iterator is used.

RETURNS
An instance of `BreakIterator` that finds potential line-break boundaries.

SEE ALSO
`java.util.Locale.getDefault()`.

EXAMPLE

This example implements a program that displays the contents of a text file. The program uses a line-break iterator to break long lines. Try changing the width of the window and watch it break at different places. See Figure 14.

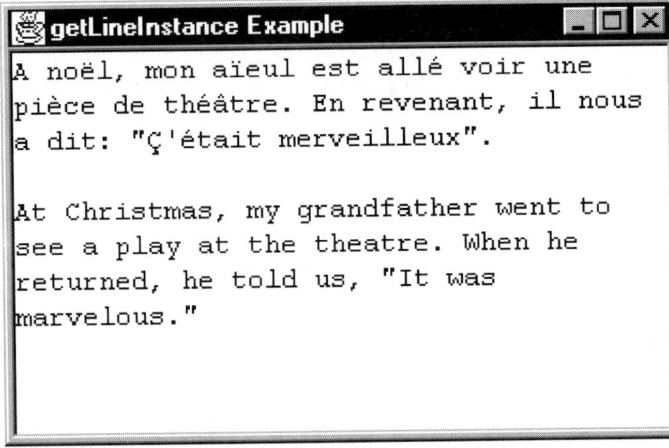

FIGURE 14: Line Break Iterator.

The program first reads in the contents of a file and breaks it up into lines. Then it takes each line and breaks it up into substrings (we'll call them *segments*) that are determined by the line-break boundaries of a line-break iterator. These nonbreakable segments are all stored in a vector called segments. To record the end of each line in segments, a string containing a newline is added after the last segment of every line. This enables the painting routine to detect the occurrence of a newline and then start painting a new line.

A scrollpane is used to allow the text display to be scrolled vertically. However, for the scrollpane to work, the text canvas must report the full dimensions of text display in `getPreferredSize()`. This means that `getPreferredSize()` must determine the height of the text display based on the current width of the scrollpane's viewport. This algorithm to calculate the height is similar to the algorithm to actually paint the text.

Note: This program builds a vector of all possible line-break positions in the document—not an efficient way to go, as it wastes both memory and time. A more efficient technique is to keep a vector of actual line start positions and rebuild it every time you detect a width change.

```
import java.awt.*;
import java.io.*;
import java.util.*;
import java.text.*;

class Main extends Frame {
    Main(Vector lines) {
        super("getLineInstance Example");
        ScrollPane sp = new ScrollPane();
        TextCanvas cv = new TextCanvas(lines, sp);

        // Setup the components and show the frame.
```

```
        sp.add(cv);
        add(sp, BorderLayout.CENTER);
        setSize(400, 400);
        show();
    }

    public static void main(String[] args) {
        if (args.length != 1) {
            System.err.println("Usage: java Main <filename>");
            System.exit(1);
        }
        try {
            // Read in the entire contents of the file.
            // Each line is placed into 'v'.
            BufferedReader rd = new BufferedReader(new FileReader(args[0]));
            Vector v = new Vector();
            String line;

            while ((line = rd.readLine()) != null) {
                v.addElement(line);
            }
            rd.close();
            new Main(v);
        } catch (Exception e) {
            e.printStackTrace();
        }
    }
}

class TextCanvas extends Component {
    BreakIterator bi = BreakIterator.getLineInstance();
    Vector segments = new Vector();
    Font f = new Font("Monospaced", Font.PLAIN, 14);
    FontMetrics fm;
    ScrollPane scrollpane;

    TextCanvas(Vector lines, ScrollPane sp) {
        scrollpane = sp;
        fm = getFontMetrics(f);

        for (int i=0; i<lines.size(); i++) {
            int start = 0;
            String line = (String)lines.elementAt(i);
            bi.setText(line);

            while (bi.next() != bi.DONE) {
                segments.addElement(line.substring(start, bi.current()));
                start = bi.current();
            }
            segments.addElement("\n");
        }
    }

    // Determines the dimensions of the component given
    // the width of the scrollpane viewport.
    public Dimension getPreferredSize() {
        int x = 0;
        int y = 0;
        int w = scrollpane.getViewportSize().width;
```

```
            for (int i=0; i<segments.size(); i++) {
                String word = (String)segments.elementAt(i);

                if (word.equals("\n")) {
                    // Start a new line.
                    x = 0;
                    y++;
                } else {
                    int sw = fm.stringWidth(word);

                    // Need to break?
                    if (x + sw > w) {
                        x = 0;
                        y++;
                    }
                    x += sw;
                }
            }
            return new Dimension(w, y * fm.getHeight());
        }

        public void paint(Graphics g) {
            int x = 0;
            int y = fm.getAscent();
            int w = getSize().width;

            g.setFont(f);
            for (int i=0; i<segments.size(); i++) {
                int start = 0;
                String word = (String)segments.elementAt(i);

                if (word.equals("\n")) {
                    // Start a new line.
                    x = 0;
                    y += fm.getHeight();
                } else {
                    int sw = fm.stringWidth(word);

                    // Need to break?
                    if (x + sw > w) {
                        x = 0;
                        y += fm.getHeight();
                    }
                    g.drawString(word, x, y);

                    x += sw;
                }
            }
        }
    }
```

getSentenceInstance()

PURPOSE
Creates a new break iterator for sentence boundaries.

SYNTAX
```
public static BreakIterator getSentenceInstance()
public static BreakIterator getSentenceInstance(Locale loc)
```

DESCRIPTION
This method creates a new sentence-break iterator with the locale `loc`. The locale determines precisely how sentence boundary analysis is done, which can differ for different languages. If `loc` is not specified, the default locale is used.

PARAMETERS

`loc` The locale for the sentence-break iterator. If a sentence-break iterator is not available for the specified locale, a default sentence-break iterator is used.

RETURNS
An instance of `BreakIterator` that finds sentence boundaries.

SEE ALSO
`java.util.Locale.getDefault()`.

EXAMPLE
See the class example.

getText()

PURPOSE
Gets the character iterator for the text being scanned.

SYNTAX
```
public abstract CharacterIterator getText()
```

DESCRIPTION
This method gets the character iterator for the text being scanned by this break iterator.

To get the actual character at this position, you cannot reliably call `current()` on that character iterator. A `BreakIterator` object doesn't keep its character iterator up-to-date. Hence, its character iterator does not always points to the same character that the `BreakIterator` object's method `current()` points to. So calling `getText().current()` is not guaranteed to give you the character you expect. If you have a separate reference to the string you're iterating over (you usually do), then you can get the character using

```
string.charAt(bi.current())
```

where `bi` is the `BreakIterator` object. If you don't have a separate reference to the string or the string isn't a `String` object, you have to manually set the iterator you get back from `getText()` to point to the right character:

```
bi.getText().setIndex(bi.current())
```

RETURNS
The character iterator for the text being iterated over.

SEE ALSO
`CharacterIterator`.

EXAMPLE This example demonstrates how to get to the text through its character iterator. It prints the text by iterating with the character iterator rather than using the original word-break iterator.

```
import java.text.StringCharacterIterator;
import java.text.CharacterIterator;
import java.text.BreakIterator;

class Main {
    public static void main(String args[]) {

        String str = "Hello world.";

        // Create the word break iterator.
        BreakIterator wb = BreakIterator.getWordInstance();
        wb.setText(str);

        // Get the text from the boundary.
        CharacterIterator ci = wb.getText();

        // Print the text.
        printText(ci);

        // Now set the text using a string character iterator.
        // Notice the start and begin are set to pick up "bye"
        wb.setText(new StringCharacterIterator("Goodbye world.", 4, 7, 4));

        // Get the text from the boundary.
        ci = wb.getText();

        // Print the text again.
        printText(ci);
    }

    public static void printText(CharacterIterator ci){
        // print the entire text using the character iterator
        do {
            System.out.print(ci.current());
            ci.next();
        } while (ci.current() != CharacterIterator.DONE) ;
        System.out.println("");
    }
}
```

Output

```
>java Main
Hello world.
bye
```

getWordInstance()

PURPOSE
Creates a new break iterator for word-break boundaries.

SYNTAX
```
public static BreakIterator getWordInstance()
public static BreakIterator getWordInstance(Locale loc)
```

DESCRIPTION
This method creates a new word-break iterator with the locale `loc`. The locale determines precisely how word boundary analysis is done, which can differ for different languages. If `loc` is not specified, the default locale is used. One use for a word-break iterator is to find the boundaries on either side of a word so that it can be highlighted when double-clicked by a mouse.

PARAMETERS

`loc`
The locale for the word-break iterator. If a word-break iterator is not available for the specified locale, a default word-break iterator is used.

RETURNS
An instance of `BreakIterator` that finds word boundaries.

SEE ALSO
`java.util.Locale.getDefault()`.

EXAMPLE
See the class example.

last()

PURPOSE
Moves the cursor to the last boundary in the text and retrieves the position.

SYNTAX
```
public abstract int last()
```

DESCRIPTION
This method moves this break iterator's cursor to the last boundary in the text and returns that boundary position. The last position can be either `text.length()`, if the break iterator was created from a string, or a smaller value, if the break iterator was created from a substring using `setText()` from this class:

```
setText(new StringCharacterIterator(text, begin, end, pos))
```

RETURNS
The position of the last text boundary, which is less than or equal to `text.length()`, the length of the string.

EXAMPLE
See `next()`.

next()

PURPOSE Moves the cursor forward a fixed number of boundaries in the text and retrieves the position.

SYNTAX
```
public abstract int next()
public abstract int next(int n)
```

DESCRIPTION This method moves the cursor `n` boundaries forward (n>0) or backward (n<0) relative to its current position and returns the new boundary position. If calling this method would move the cursor *past* either end, the method positions the cursor at that end and returns `BreakIterator.DONE`. If `n` is not specified, it defaults to `1`.

As with other movement methods, what `next()` considers a boundary depends on the kind of iterator this is. The `next()` method can move by characters, words, sentences, or potential line breaks.

PARAMETERS

`n` The number of boundaries to move forward, relative to the current position of the cursor. A value of `0` does nothing. Negative values move backward through the text, and positive values move forward.

RETURNS The position of the `n`th boundary moving forward, or `BreakIterator.DONE`.

EXAMPLE This example demonstrates different movement operations on a word-break iterator. Notice that `wb.next()` counts "We" as the first word and whitespace as the second word. On the other hand, `lb.next()` counts "We" (including the trailing whitespace) as the first word.

```
import java.text.BreakIterator;

class Main {
    public static void main(String args[]) {

        String str = "We want to thank you.";

        // create word-break iterator
        BreakIterator wb = BreakIterator.getWordInstance();
        wb.setText(str);

        // create line-break iterator
        BreakIterator lb = BreakIterator.getLineInstance();
        lb.setText(str);

        System.out.println("'wb' is word-break iterator");
        System.out.println("'lb' is line-break iterator");

        // initial current position
        int rtn = wb.current();
        System.out.print("wb.current():      ");
        printCurrentBoundary(wb, str, rtn);
```

```
// next boundary after current position
rtn = wb.next();
        System.out.print("wb.next():          ");
printCurrentBoundary(wb, str, rtn);

// move 2 word boundaries ahead
rtn = wb.next(2);
System.out.print("wb.next(2):         ");
printCurrentBoundary(wb, str, rtn);

// initial current position
rtn = lb.current();
System.out.print("lb.current():       ");
printCurrentBoundary(lb, str, rtn);

// move 4 line boundaries ahead
rtn = lb.next(4);
System.out.print("lb.next(4):         ");
printCurrentBoundary(lb, str, rtn);

// move one boundary ahead
rtn = lb.next();
System.out.print("lb.next():          ");
printCurrentBoundary(lb, str, rtn);

// move one boundary ahead
rtn = lb.next();
System.out.print("lb.next():          ");
printCurrentBoundary(lb, str, rtn);

// move to previous boundary
rtn = lb.previous();
System.out.print("lb.previous():      ");
printCurrentBoundary(lb, str, rtn);

// move 100 boundaries ahead
rtn = lb.next(100);
System.out.print("lb.next(100):       ");
printCurrentBoundary(lb, str, rtn);

// move to boundary following character position 8
rtn = lb.following(8);
System.out.print("lb.following(8):    ");
printCurrentBoundary(lb, str, rtn);

// move to the boundary following the next-to-last boundary
int nextToLast = lb.last() - 1;
rtn = lb.following(nextToLast);
System.out.print("lb.following(" + nextToLast + "):  ");
printCurrentBoundary(lb, str, rtn);

// move to first boundary
rtn = lb.first();
System.out.print("lb.first():         ");
printCurrentBoundary(lb, str, rtn);

// move to last boundary
rtn = lb.last();
System.out.print("lb.last():          ");
printCurrentBoundary(lb, str, rtn);
```

```
        }

        // Print the text with a separator '|' at the current position
        public static void printCurrentBoundary(BreakIterator b,
                                                String src,
                                                int rtn) {
            int pos = b.current();
            System.out.print("\"" + src.substring(0,pos));
            System.out.print("|");
            System.out.print(src.substring(pos,src.length()) + "\"");
            if (rtn == BreakIterator.DONE)
                System.out.println("   returns " + "DONE");
            else
                System.out.println("   returns \"" + rtn + "\"");
        }
    }
```

Output

```
> java Main
'wb' is word-break iterator
'lb' is line-break iterator
wb.current():       "|We want to thank you."   returns "0"
wb.next():          "We| want to thank you."   returns "2"
wb.next(2):         "We want| to thank you."   returns "7"
lb.current():       "|We want to thank you."   returns "0"
lb.next(4):         "We want to thank |you."   returns "17"
lb.next():          "We want to thank you.|"   returns "21"
lb.next():          "We want to thank you.|"   returns DONE
lb.previous():      "We want to thank |you."   returns "17"
lb.next(100):       "We want to thank you.|"   returns DONE
lb.following(8):    "We want to |thank you."   returns "11"
lb.following(20):   "We want to thank you.|"   returns "21"
lb.first():         "|We want to thank you."   returns "0"
lb.last():          "We want to thank you.|"   returns "21"
```

previous()

PURPOSE Moves the cursor backward one boundary in the text and retrieves that position.

SYNTAX `public abstract int previous()`

DESCRIPTION This method moves the cursor backward one boundary in the text relative to its current position and returns the new boundary position. If the cursor is at the start of the iteration range, then calling this method returns `BreakIterator.DONE` and does not move the cursor.

As with other movement methods, what `previous()` considers a boundary depends on what kind of iterator this is. The `previous()` method can move by characters, words, sentences, or potential line breaks.

RETURNS The position of the closest boundary moving backward, or `BreakIterator.DONE`.

EXAMPLE See `next()`.

setText()

PURPOSE Sets a new string to be scanned for text boundaries.

SYNTAX
```
public void setText(String newText)
public abstract void setText(CharacterIterator newText)
```

DESCRIPTION This method assigns a new text string to this break iterator and sets the current position to `first()`. It accepts either a string or a character iterator for `newText`. Note that an instance of `StringCharacterIterator` is an implementation of `CharacterIterator` and has a string associated with it. If a string is passed in, this method internally creates an instance of `StringCharacterIterator` from it.

PARAMETERS

`newText` The new string to iterate over.

EXAMPLE See `getText()`. `CharacterIterator`, `StringCharacterIterator`.

A
B
C
D
E
F
G
H
I
J
K
L
M
N
O
P
Q
R
S
T
U
V
W
X
Y
Z

BufferedInputStream

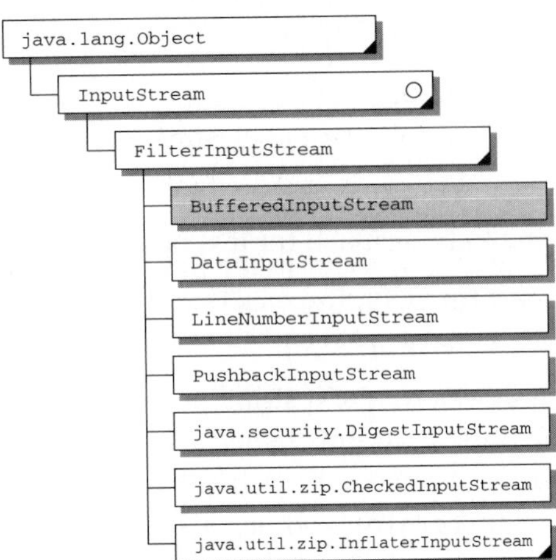

Syntax

```
public class BufferedInputStream extends FilterInputStream
```

Description

`BufferedInputStream` implements a *buffered input stream.* A buffered input stream is a filter input stream. You can compose it with an existing input stream to allow buffering of input when reading from that stream. The buffered input stream maintains a buffer of bytes read from the original input stream. Requests to read from the buffered input stream retrieve bytes from this buffer, rather than performing read operations on the original input stream. When all bytes from the buffer have been read, the buffer is refilled with input from the original input stream.

If read operations on the original input stream have a high per-read overhead, buffering the stream can improve the performance significantly because it can reduce the number of read operations on the original input stream. The buffered input stream incurs extra memory overhead because it must maintain the buffer. It also incurs an extra level of copying because bytes must first be copied into the buffer.

Usage

You create a `BufferedInputStream` by supplying its constructor with the stream for which it is providing buffering. You then can read and otherwise use the `BufferedInputStream` just like any other input stream. The following code creates a `BufferedInputStream` for reading from a socket:

```
Socket sock = new Socket("somehost", port);
BufferedInputStream in = new BufferedInputStream(sock.getInputStream());
```

```
for (int ch=in.read(); ch >= 0; ch = in.read()) {
    ...
}
```

Current Read Position and Mark/Reset

You can mark a buffered input stream using a stream *mark*. A mark marks a position in the input stream so that you can subsequently return to it. Stream marks are intended for situations in which you need to read ahead a little to see what is in the stream. Parsers often make use of this feature instead of remembering the read data itself. When you set the mark, you supply a *read limit,* which indicates the number of bytes in the input stream from the marked position that are to be saved. If you subsequently read beyond this read limit, the mark becomes *invalidated* and you cannot return the stream to its mark.

The `BufferedInputStream` provides implementations for the `mark()` and `reset()` methods (declared in the `InputStream` class).

BufferedInputStream versus BufferedReader

`BufferedInputStream` is meant for byte streams. Its methods read bytes (0–255). `BufferedReader` is for character input streams.

A B C D E F G H I J K L M N O P Q R S T U V W X Y Z

MEMBER SUMMARY	
Constructor	
`BufferedInputStream()`	Constructs a `BufferedInputStream` instance for an input stream.
Input Methods	
`read()`	Reads bytes from this buffered input stream.
`skip()`	Skips the specified number of bytes in this buffered input stream.
Mark/Reset Methods	
`mark()`	Marks the current position in the buffered input stream.
`markSupported()`	Determines whether this stream supports rereading of its data.
`reset()`	Repositions the buffered input stream to the last marked position.
Stream Method	
`available()`	Determines the number of bytes that can be read without being blocked.
Protected Fields	
`buf`	The buffer that stores the input stream data.
`count`	The number of bytes in the buffer.
`marklimit`	The maximum read-ahead allowed before the mark is invalidated.
`markpos`	The position in the buffer of the current mark.
`pos`	The current read position in the buffer.

See Also

`BufferedOutputStream`, `BufferedReader`, `FilterInputStream`, `InputStream`.

Example

This example shows the use of a buffered input stream to read in a file and print it out twice to standard output. It uses the mark/reset of the buffered input stream to avoid reading the file twice.

```
import java.io.*;

// reads in a file and sends it to standard output 2 times
class Main {
    public static void main(String[] args) {
        if (args.length != 1) {
            System.err.println("Usage: java Main <file>");
            System.exit(-1);
        }
        try {
            File f = new File(args[0]);
            FileInputStream in = new FileInputStream(f);
            // create buffered input stream for 'in'
            BufferedInputStream bufin = new BufferedInputStream(in);
            if (bufin.markSupported()) {
                int limit;
                // create mark for size of file
                bufin.mark(limit=(int)f.length());

                // first copy; read just before EOF
                for (int i = 0; i < limit; i++)
                    System.out.print((char)(bufin.read()));
                // reset to beginning of file
                bufin.reset();
            }
            int c;
            while ((c=bufin.read()) >= 0)    // second copy
                System.out.print((char)c);
            bufin.close();
        } catch (IOException e) {
            e.printStackTrace();
        }
    }
}
```

available()

PURPOSE Determines the number of bytes that can be read without being blocked.

SYNTAX `public synchronized int available() throws IOException`

DESCRIPTION This method returns the number of bytes that can be read without being blocked. This number is the sum of the number of unread bytes in the buffer and the number of bytes available from the input stream.

RETURNS The number of bytes that can be read without being blocked.

EXCEPTIONS

`IOException`

If an IO error occurred while attempting to determine the number of bytes available.

OVERRIDES `FilterInputStream.available()`.

SEE ALSO `InputStream.available()`.

EXAMPLE See `InputStream.available()`.

buf

PURPOSE The buffer that stores the input stream data.

SYNTAX `protected byte[] buf`

DESCRIPTION This field stores the input stream data. It is allocated when the buffer input stream is first created. It may expand as required to support marking with a read limit larger than its current buffer size.

`buf` is filled from bytes read from the underlying input stream. Bytes that are read from this buffer input stream are retrieved from `buf`.

SEE ALSO `count`, `pos`.

BufferedInputStream()

PURPOSE Constructs a `BufferedInputStream` instance for an input stream.

SYNTAX

```
public BufferedInputStream(InputStream in)
public BufferedInputStream(InputStream in, int size)
```

DESCRIPTION There are two forms of the constructor for `BufferedInputStream`. The first form constructs for the input stream `in` a buffered input stream that has the default buffer size of 2K. The second form constructs a buffered input stream for `in` that has the buffer size `size`. The buffer size may increase after the stream has been constructed if the stream is asked to support a read limit that exceeds its current buffer size.

A buffer of the specified size is created to cache the bytes read. The larger the buffer, the more bytes that can be retrieved from each read operation from the actual input stream in; thus fewer reads are required from in. If read operations on in are slow, a bigger buffer might result in significant performance improvements. However, a bigger buffer also means more memory is required to store the bytes. Thus you should select a buffer size that balances performance requirements and memory demands.

PARAMETERS
- `in` The non-null input stream.
- `size` The buffer size.

SEE ALSO `BufferedOutputStream`.

EXAMPLE See the class example and `skip()`.

count

PURPOSE The number of bytes in the buffer.

SYNTAX `protected int count`

DESCRIPTION This field records the total number of bytes, read and unread, in the buffer `buf`.

SEE ALSO `pos`, `markpos`.

mark()

PURPOSE Marks the current position in the buffered input stream.

SYNTAX `public synchronized void mark(int readlimit)`

DESCRIPTION Buffered input streams support marks and resets. This method marks the current position in the input stream and records that `readlimit` of bytes can be read or skipped from this position before this marked position becomes invalidated (i.e., the stream can no longer reset to this mark). A subsequent call to `reset()` will reposition the stream at the last marked position so that later reads will reread the same bytes.

PARAMETERS
- `readlimit` The number of bytes that can be read or skipped from this marked position before the mark becomes invalidated.

OVERRIDES `FilterInputStream.mark()`.

SEE ALSO `marklimit`, `markpos`, `reset()`.

EXAMPLE See the class example.

marklimit

PURPOSE The maximum read-ahead allowed before the mark is invalidated.

SYNTAX `protected int marklimit`

DESCRIPTION When you set a mark on the input stream by calling `mark()`, you specify the number of bytes that can be read or skipped before the mark is invalidated. This number is recorded in the field `marklimit`. If you subsequently read or skip beyond `marklimit` number bytes, a later call to `reset()` will not reset the read position to that previously marked.

SEE ALSO `mark()`, `markpos`, `read()`, `skip()`, `reset()`.

EXAMPLE This example is taken from the source of `BufferedInputStream`. It shows how `mark()` sets the fields `marklimit` and `markpos`.

```
public synchronized void mark(int readlimit) {
    marklimit = readlimit;
    markpos = pos;
}
```

markpos

PURPOSE The position in the buffer of the current mark.

SYNTAX `protected int markpos`

DESCRIPTION When you set a mark on the input stream by calling `mark()`, the current read position is recorded in the field `markpos`. When `reset()` is invoked, the current read position is reset to `markpos`. If no mark has been set, the value of `markpos` is `-1`.

SEE ALSO `mark()`, `pos`, `reset()`.

EXAMPLE See `marklimit`.

markSupported()

PURPOSE Determines whether this stream supports rereading of its data.

SYNTAX `public boolean markSupported()`

DESCRIPTION This method returns whether this stream supports rereading of its data (i.e., mark/reset). Buffered input streams support this feature. Hence, this method always returns `true`.

RETURNS `true`.

OVERRIDES `FilterInputStream.markSupported()`.

SEE ALSO `mark()`, `reset()`.

EXAMPLE See the class example.

A B C D E F G H I J K L M N O P Q R S T U V W X Y Z

pos

PURPOSE The current read position in the buffer.

SYNTAX `protected int pos`

DESCRIPTION This field records the current read position in the buffer. `read()` and `skip()` methods start from this position when reading or skipping bytes from this stream.

SEE ALSO `read()`, `skip()`.

read()

PURPOSE Reads bytes from this buffered input stream.

SYNTAX
```
public synchronized int read() throws IOException
public synchronized int read(byte[] buffer, int offset, int count)
    throws IOException
```

DESCRIPTION The `read()` method has two forms. It reads bytes from this buffered input stream, starting at the current read position. If all of the bytes buffered earlier have been read, the buffer is refilled with data from this buffered input stream's original input stream. The current read position is usually that of the next byte after the last byte read during the previous `read()` or `skip()` invocation. However, the current read position can be changed using `reset()`.

The first form of `read()` returns the byte in the current read position in this buffered input stream. If the end of the stream has been reached, this method returns `-1`.

The second form of `read()` reads `count` bytes from this buffered input stream starting at the current read position and stores the bytes read into the `byte` array `buffer` starting at index `offset`. The actual number of bytes read is returned. This number could differ from `count` (when the number of bytes available is less than that requested). If no bytes can be read because the end of the stream has been reached, this method returns `-1`.

PARAMETERS

`buffer` The non-`null` buffer into which the bytes are stored.

`count` The number of bytes to read. `0` ≤ `count` ≤ `buffer.length-offset`.

`offset` The index in `buffer` at which to start storing the bytes read. `0` ≤ `offset` < `buffer.length`.

RETURNS The first form returns the byte read; the second returns the actual number of bytes read. Both forms return `-1` when end-of-stream is reached.

EXCEPTIONS

`ArrayIndexOutOfBoundsException`
If `count` or `offset` is outside of the specified bounds.

`IOException`
If an IO error occurred while attempting to read the requested bytes.

OVERRIDES `FilterInputStream.read()`.

SEE ALSO `mark()`, `reset()`, `skip()`.

EXAMPLE See the class example and `skip()`.

reset()

PURPOSE Repositions the buffered input stream to the last marked position.

SYNTAX `public synchronized void reset() throws IOException`

DESCRIPTION This method repositions the stream to the last marked position. If the stream has not been marked or if the mark has been invalidated by reading or skipping beyond the mark, an `IOException` is thrown.

EXCEPTIONS

`IOException`
If the stream has not been marked or if the mark has been invalidated.

OVERRIDES `FilterInputStream.reset()`.

SEE ALSO `mark()`.

EXAMPLE See the class example.

skip()

PURPOSE Skips the specified number of bytes in this buffered input stream.

SYNTAX `public synchronized long skip(long count) throws IOException`

DESCRIPTION This method skips `count` number of bytes of this buffered input stream, starting at the current read position. It returns the actual number of bytes skipped, which differs from `count` if there are fewer bytes available in the stream. The current read position is updated to reflect the number of bytes skipped. The next `read()` will not return those skipped bytes.

It returns `0` if it cannot skip any bytes.

PARAMETERS

`count` The number of bytes to be skipped. If `count` < `0`, this method just returns `0` without doing anything.

RETURNS The actual number of bytes skipped.

EXCEPTIONS

`IOException`
If an IO error occurred while attempting to skip.

OVERRIDES `FilterInputStream.skip()`.

EXAMPLE This example reads in a file and skips the first half before echoing the second half to standard output.

```
import java.io.*;

//  read a file and skips first half, and echos rest
class Main {
    public static void main(String[] args) {
        if (args.length != 1) {
            System.err.println("Usage: java Main <file>");
            System.exit(-1);
        }
        try {
            File f = new File(args[0]);
            FileInputStream in = new FileInputStream(f);
            // create buffered input stream with initial buffer
            BufferedInputStream bufin = new BufferedInputStream(in, 1024);
            int count;
            long half = f.length()/2;

            bufin.skip(half);        // skip first half of file

            // echo the rest
            byte[] buf = new byte[1024];
            while ((count=bufin.read(buf, 0, buf.length)) > 0)
                for (int i = 0; i<count; i++)
                    System.out.print((char)buf[i]);

            System.out.flush();
            bufin.close();
        } catch (IOException e) {
            e.printStackTrace();
        }
    }
}
```

BufferedOutputStream

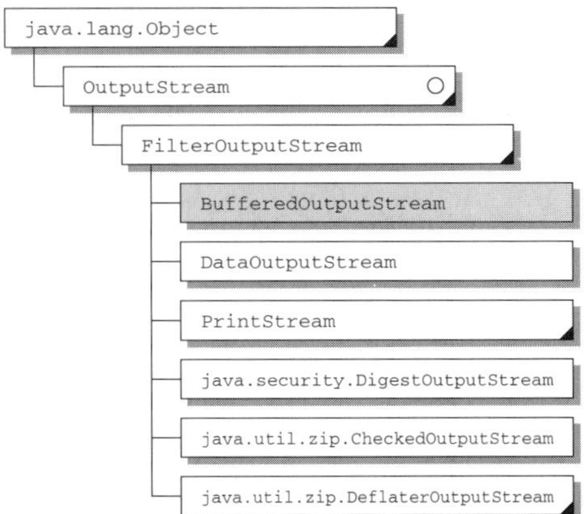

Syntax

```
public class BufferedOutputStream extends FilterOutputStream
```

Description

`BufferedOutputStream` implements a *buffered output stream.* A buffered output stream is a filter output stream. You can compose it with an existing output stream to allow buffering of output when writing to that stream. The buffered output stream maintains a buffer of bytes to be written to the original output stream. Requests to write to the buffered output stream result in the bytes being stored in a buffer, rather than write operations being performed on the original output stream. When the buffer becomes full or when the stream is flushed, the bytes in it are written out to the original output stream.

If write operations to the original output stream have a high per-operation overhead, buffering the stream can improve the performance significantly because it can reduce the number of write operations on the original output stream. However, the buffered output stream incurs extra memory overhead because it must maintain the buffer. It also incurs an extra level of copying because the bytes must first be copied to the buffer.

Usage

`BufferedOutputStream` provides buffering for the stream that it is filtering. The following code creates a `BufferedOutputStream` for writing to a socket:

```
Socket sock = new Socket("somehost", port);
BufferedOutputStream out =
    new BufferedOutputStream(sock.getOutputStream());
out.write(bytes);
...
out.flush(); // flush data written so far
```

BufferedOutputStream versus BufferedWriter

`BufferedOutputStream` is meant for byte streams. Its methods write bytes (0–255). `BufferedWriter` is for character output streams.

MEMBER SUMMARY	
Constructor	
`BufferedOutputStream()`	Constructs a `BufferedOutputStream` instance for an output stream.
Output Method	
`write()`	Writes bytes to the buffered output stream.
Stream Method	
`flush()`	Flushes the buffered bytes into the output stream.
Protected Fields	
`buf`	The buffer in which data is stored.
`count`	The number of bytes stored in the buffer.

See Also

`BufferedInputStream`, `BufferedWriter`, `FilterOutputStream`, `OutputStream`.

Example

This example shows how a buffered output stream can be used with a socket. Operations on sockets are relatively expensive, so putting a buffer in front of the socket helps cut down the cost of using the socket.

```
import java.io.OutputStream;
import java.io.BufferedOutputStream;
import java.io.IOException;
import java.net.Socket;

class Main {
    public static void main(String[] args) {
        try {
            //  9 == 'discard' port
            Socket sock = new Socket("localhost", 9);

            OutputStream so = sock.getOutputStream();
            BufferedOutputStream out = new BufferedOutputStream(so, 8192);

            String msg = "this is a test";
            byte[] ob = msg.getBytes();

            for (int i = 0; i < 5000; i++)
```

```
                out.write(ob, 0, ob.length);

            out.flush();
            out.close();
            sock.close();
        } catch (IOException e) {
            e.printStackTrace();
        }
    }
}
```


buf

PURPOSE The buffer in which data is stored.

SYNTAX `protected byte[] buf`

DESCRIPTION This field is used to store the bytes written to the buffered output stream before they get written to the output stream of this buffered output stream.

SEE ALSO `count`.

EXAMPLE This example is taken from the source of `BufferedOutputStream`. It shows how the `write()` method uses the fields `buf` and `count`.

```
public synchronized void write(int b) throws IOException {
    if (count >= buf.length) {
        flushBuffer();
    }
    buf[count++] = (byte)b;
}
```

BufferedOutputStream()

PURPOSE Constructs a `BufferedOutputStream` instance for an output stream.

SYNTAX
```
public BufferedOutputStream(OutputStream out)
public BufferedOutputStream(OutputStream out, int size)
```

DESCRIPTION There are two forms of the constructor for `BufferedOutputStream`. The first form constructs for the output stream `out` a buffered output stream that has the default buffer size of 512 bytes. The second form constructs a buffered output stream for `out` that has the buffer size `size`.

A buffer of the specified size is created to cache the bytes to be written. The larger the buffer, the more bytes that can be cached before being written to `out`. If write operations on `out` are slow, a bigger buffer might result in significant performance improvements. However, a bigger buffer also means more memory is required to store the bytes. Thus you should select a buffer size that is balanced between performance requirements and memory demands.

The buffered output is written to `out` either when the buffer becomes full or when `flush()` is invoked.

PARAMETERS

`out`	The non-`null` output stream.
`size`	The buffer size. `size` ≥ `0`.

SEE ALSO `FilterOutputStream`.

EXAMPLE See the class example.

A B C D E F G H I J K L M N O P Q R S T U V W X Y Z

count

PURPOSE The number of bytes stored in the buffer.

SYNTAX `protected int count`

DESCRIPTION This field records the number of bytes that are stored in this buffer and that have yet to be written to the output stream of this buffered output stream.

SEE ALSO `buf`, `flush()`.

EXAMPLE See `buf`.

flush()

PURPOSE Flushes the buffered bytes into the output stream.

SYNTAX `public synchronized void flush() throws IOException`

DESCRIPTION This method writes any buffered bytes to the output stream (`out`) of this buffered output stream and clears the buffer. `out` is then flushed. This, in turn, flushes the next stream downstream, and so on. Hence, this method effectively flushes this stream and all of the streams "downstream."

EXCEPTIONS

`IOException`
If an IO error occurred while attempting to flush the stream.

OVERRIDES `FilterOutputStream.flush()`.

SEE ALSO `buf`, `count`, `write()`.

EXAMPLE See the class example.

write()

PURPOSE Writes bytes to the buffered output stream.

SYNTAX
```
public synchronized void write(int oneByte)
public synchronized void write(byte[] buffer, int offset, int
   count) throws IOException
```

DESCRIPTION The `write()` method writes the specified byte or bytes to this buffered output stream. The first form writes a single byte `oneByte` to the buffered output stream. The second form writes `count` bytes from the buffer `buffer` starting at index `offset` to the buffered output stream.

If there is room in the buffer of this stream to hold the bytes, they are buffered. Otherwise, any buffered bytes and these new bytes are written to the output stream of this buffered output stream. This clears the buffer and allows bytes in subsequent `write()` calls to be buffered.

PARAMETERS

`buffer` The non-`null` buffer containing data to be written.

`count` The number of bytes from `buffer` to be written. `0` ≤ `count` ≤ `buffer.length-offset`.

`offset` The index in `buffer` of the bytes to be written. `0` ≤ `offset` < `buffer.length`.

`oneByte` The byte to be written. The low-order byte of `oneByte` is written.

EXCEPTIONS

`ArrayIndexOutOfBoundsException`

If `count` or `offset` is outside of the specified bounds.

`IOException`

If an IO error occurred while attempting to write the bytes.

OVERRIDES `FilterOutputStream.write()`.

SEE ALSO `flush()`.

EXAMPLE See the class example.

java.io

BufferedReader

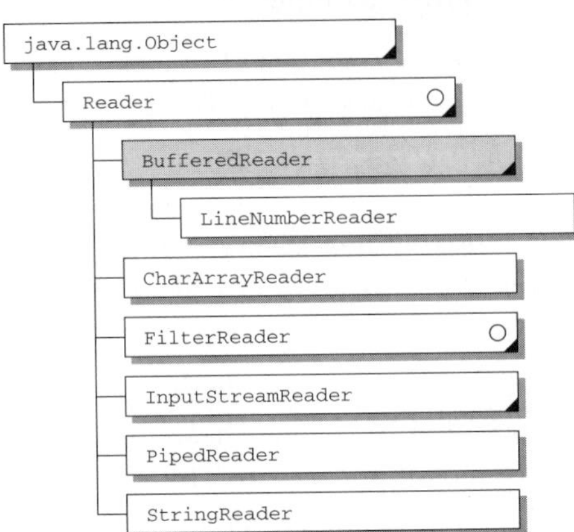

Syntax

```
public class BufferedReader extends Reader
```

Description

`BufferedReader` implements a buffered character input stream, or *buffered reader.* A buffered reader is a filter reader. You can compose it with an existing reader to allow buffering of characters read from that original reader. The buffered reader maintains a `char` buffer for storing characters read from the original reader. Requests to read from the buffered reader retrieve characters from this buffer rather than perform read operations directly on the original reader (except under special conditions; see *Bypassing Copying* later in this section for details). When all of the characters from the buffer have been read, the buffer is refilled with input from the original reader.

A `BufferedReader` is useful for enhancing performance when read operations on a reader have a high per-read overhead. When a `BufferedReader` is used, the application need not worry about minimizing the number of read operations. The application should, however, be aware that the `BufferedReader` imposes an extra level of copying and incurs extra memory overhead due to allocation of the buffer,

Usage

You create a `BufferedReader` by supplying its constructor with the reader for which it is providing buffering. You then can read from and otherwise use the `BufferedReader` just like any other reader. The following code creates a `BufferedReader` for reading from a file:

```
BufferedReader in = new BufferedReader(new FileReader("inputfile"));
String str = in.readLine();
```

Current Read Position and Mark/Reset

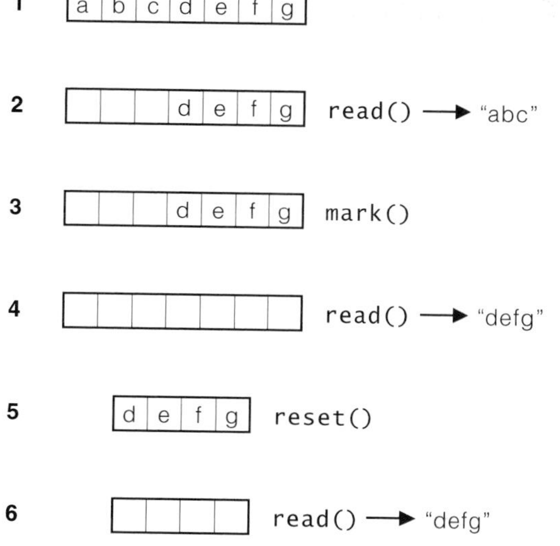

FIGURE 15: **`BufferedReader`.**

You can mark a buffered reader using a stream *mark*. A mark marks a position in the reader so that you can subsequently return to it. Stream marks are intended for situations in which you need to read ahead a little for a preview of what will be read by the reader. Parsers often make use of this feature instead of remembering the read data itself. When you set the mark, you supply a *read limit* to indicate the number of characters that the reader should save starting from the marked position. If you subsequently read beyond this read limit, the mark becomes invalidated and you cannot return the stream to its mark.

The `BufferedReader` provides implementations for the `mark()` and `reset()` methods. In Figure 15, the buffered reader initially contains the characters "`abcdefg`". `mark()` is called after the first three characters are read. After four more characters ("`defg`") are read, `reset()` is called. This method resets the read pointer back four positions, after which "`defg`" can then be reread.

Bypassing Copying

Typically, when you perform a read operation, the buffered reader retrieves the characters from its internal buffer. If the internal buffer is empty, the buffered reader will read characters from the reader being filtered, copy them to the buffer, and return the characters requested.

However, if the requested number of characters is larger than the size of the internal buffer and the buffer is empty, the internal buffer will be bypassed so that characters are read directly from the reader being filtered. If the reader has been marked, this bypass is not done because doing so would disable the support for mark/reset.

BufferedInputStream versus BufferedReader

`BufferedInputStream` is meant for byte streams. Its methods read bytes (0–255). `BufferedReader` is for character input streams.

A B C D E F G H I J K L M N O P Q R S T U V W X Y Z

MEMBER SUMMARY	
Constructor	
`BufferedReader()`	Constructs a `BufferedReader` instance.
Input Methods	
`read()`	Reads one or more characters from this buffered reader.
`readLine()`	Reads a sequence of characters terminated by a line terminator.
`skip()`	Skips characters from this buffered reader.
Mark/Reset Methods	
`mark()`	Marks the current read position in this buffered reader.
`markSupported()`	Determines whether this buffered reader supports mark/reset.
`reset()`	Repositions this buffered reader to the last marked position.
Stream Methods	
`close()`	Closes this buffered reader.
`ready()`	Determines whether this buffered reader is ready to be read without being blocked.

See Also

`BufferedInputStream`, `BufferedOutputStream`, `BufferedWriter`.

Example

This example uses a `BufferedReader` to read and echo the contents of a text file to standard output.

```
import java.io.*;

class Main {
    public static void main(String[] args) {
        if (args.length != 1) {
            System.err.println("Usage: java Main <file>");
            System.exit(-1);
        }
        try {
            // Create buffered reader
            BufferedReader in = new BufferedReader(new FileReader(args[0]));
            String str;
            while ((str = in.readLine()) != null) {
                System.out.println(str);
            }
            in.close();
        } catch (IOException e) {
            e.printStackTrace();
        }
    }
}
```

BufferedReader()

PURPOSE
Constructs a `BufferedReader` instance.

SYNTAX
```
public BufferedReader(Reader in)
public BufferedReader(Reader in, int size)
```

DESCRIPTION
There are two forms of the constructor for `BufferedReader`. The first form constructs for the reader `in` a buffered reader that has the default buffer size of 8K characters. The second form constructs a buffered reader for `in` that has the buffer size `size`. The buffer size may increase after the reader has been constructed if the reader is asked to support a mark read limit larger than its current buffer size.

A buffer of the specified size is created to cache the characters read. The larger the buffer, the more characters that can be retrieved from each read operation from the actual reader `in`; thus fewer reads are required from `in`. If read operations on `in` are slow, a bigger buffer might result in significant performance improvements. However, a bigger buffer also means more memory is required to store the characters. Thus you should select a buffer size that balances performance requirements and memory demands.

PARAMETERS

`in` A non-`null` reader from which to read data.

`size` The nonnegative size of the buffer to use.

EXCEPTIONS

`IllegalArgumentException`

If `size` ≤ `0`.

SEE ALSO
`BufferedWriter`.

EXAMPLE
See the class example.

close()

PURPOSE
Closes this buffered reader.

SYNTAX
```
public void close() throws IOException
```

DESCRIPTION
This method closes this buffered reader by closing the reader that it is filtering (`in`) and releasing the buffer used by this buffered reader. All readers "downstream" from this reader are consequently closed as well. If this buffered reader has already been closed, this method does nothing.

EXCEPTIONS

`IOException`

If an IO error occurs while attempting to close `in`.

OVERRIDES `FilterReader.close()`.

SEE ALSO `flush()`.

EXAMPLE See the class example.

mark()

PURPOSE Marks the current read position in this buffered reader.

SYNTAX `public void mark(int readLimit) throws IOException`

DESCRIPTION This method marks the current position in this reader so that a subsequent call to `reset()` will reposition the read position of the stream to this marked position. This marked position becomes invalid if you read more than `readLimit` number of characters beyond this marked position.

PARAMETERS

`readLimit` The nonnegative number of characters that can be read before this mark is invalidated.

EXCEPTIONS

`IllegalArgumentException`
If `readLimit` is < `0`.

`IOException`
If an IO error occurs.

OVERRIDES `FilterReader.mark()`.

SEE ALSO `markSupported()`, `reset()`.

EXAMPLE See `skip()`.

markSupported()

PURPOSE Determines whether this buffered reader supports mark/reset.

SYNTAX `public boolean markSupported()`

DESCRIPTION This method returns whether this reader supports rereading of its data (i.e., mark/reset). Buffered readers support this feature. Hence, this method always returns `true`.

RETURNS `true`.

OVERRIDES `FilterReader.markSupported()`.

SEE ALSO `mark()`, `reset()`.

EXAMPLE See `skip()`.

read()

PURPOSE
Reads one or more characters from this buffered reader.

SYNTAX
```
public int read() throws IOException
public int read(char buf[], int offset, int count) throws
    IOException
```

DESCRIPTION
The first form of this method reads a single character from this buffered reader. If all of the characters buffered earlier have been read, the buffer is refilled with more characters from the reader being filtered (`in`) and the first unread character returned. If no character can be read before end-of-stream is reached, `-1` is returned.

The second form of this method reads characters from this buffered reader, starting at the current read position. If all of the characters buffered earlier have been read, no mark has been set (or the mark has been invalidated), and the requested number of characters (`count`) is larger than the reader's internal buffer size, the characters are read directly from the reader being filtered (`in`) and copied into `buf`, bypassing the buffer maintained by this reader. Otherwise, characters are copied from the buffer maintained by this reader into `buf`. The number of characters actually read is returned. If no character can be read because end-of-stream is reached, `-1` is returned.

PARAMETERS

`buf` The buffer into which the characters read are stored.

`count` The number of characters to read. `0` ≤ `count` ≤ `buf.length-offset`.

`offset` The index in `buf` at which to start storing the characters read. `0` ≤ `offset` < `buf.length`.

RETURNS
The first form returns the character read; the second returns the actual number of characters read. Both forms return `-1` when end-of-stream is reached before any character is read.

OVERRIDES
`FilterReader.read()`.

EXCEPTIONS

`ArrayIndexOutOfBoundsException`
If `count` or `offset` is outside of the specified bounds.

`IOException`
If an IO error occurs.

EXAMPLE
See `skip()`.

A
B
C
D
E
F
G
H
I
J
K
L
M
N
O
P
Q
R
S
T
U
V
W
X
Y
Z

readLine()

PURPOSE
Reads a sequence of characters terminated by a line terminator.

SYNTAX
`public String readLine() throws IOException`

DESCRIPTION
This method reads a line of characters and returns it as a string. A line is defined as a sequence of characters terminated by a newline (`\n`), return (`\r`), newline-return (`\r\n`), or end-of-stream. The string does not include the line terminator character. This method blocks until a complete line has been read.

The read position is updated accordingly.

RETURNS
A `String` containing the contents of the line. `null` if no character is read before end-of-stream is reached.

EXCEPTIONS
`IOException`
If an IO error occurs while attempting to read.

SEE ALSO
`DataInputStream.readLine()`.

EXAMPLE
See the class example.

ready()

PURPOSE
Determines whether this buffered reader is ready to be read without being blocked.

SYNTAX
`public boolean ready() throws IOException`

DESCRIPTION
This method determines if the buffered reader can be read without being blocked. The buffered reader is ready to be read without being blocked if there are unread characters in its buffer or if the reader being filtered (`in`) is ready to be read.

RETURNS
`true` if this reader is ready to be read without being blocked.

OVERRIDES
`FilterReader.ready()`.

EXCEPTIONS
`IOException`
If this reader has already been closed or if an IO error was encountered while determining whether the underlying reader being filtered is ready.

EXAMPLE
See `Reader.ready()`.

reset()

PURPOSE
Repositions this buffered reader to the last marked position.

SYNTAX
`public void reset() throws IOException`

DESCRIPTION
This method repositions the reader to the last marked position. If the reader has not been marked or if the mark has been invalidated by reading or skipping beyond the mark, an `IOException` is thrown.

OVERRIDES
`FilterReader.reset()`.

EXCEPTIONS

`IOException`

If this reader has never been marked or if the mark has been invalidated.

EXAMPLE
See `skip()`.

skip()

PURPOSE
Skips characters from this buffered reader.

SYNTAX
`public long skip(long count) throws IOException`

DESCRIPTION
This method skips `count` number of characters of this reader, starting at the current read position. It returns the actual number of characters skipped, which differs from `count` if there are fewer characters available in the reader. The current read position is updated to reflect the number of characters skipped. The next `read()` or `readLine()` will not return those skipped characters.

PARAMETERS

`count` The number of characters to skip.

RETURNS
The nonnegative number of characters actually skipped.

OVERRIDES
`FilterReader.skip()`.

EXCEPTIONS

`IOException`

If this reader has already been closed or some other IO error has occurred.

EXAMPLE
This example reads in a file by using a buffered reader. It prints the second half of the file before printing the first half.

```
import java.io.*;

// Second half first
class Main {
    public static void main(String[] args) {
        if (args.length != 1) {
            System.err.println("Usage: java Main <inputfile>");
```

A B C D E F G H I J K L M N O P Q R S T U V W X Y Z

```
            System.exit(-1);
        }
        try {
            File f = new File(args[0]);
            BufferedReader in = new BufferedReader(new FileReader(f));
            if (!in.markSupported()) {
                System.err.println("Mark not supported");
                System.exit(-1);
            }
            long limit  = f.length();        // get file size
            // create mark for size of file
            in.mark((int)limit);

            // first copy; read just before EOF
            in.skip(limit/2);
            char[] buf = new char[(int)(limit/2)+1];
            int howmany = in.read(buf);
            PrintWriter out = new PrintWriter(System.out, true);
            out.write(buf, 0, howmany);

            // reset to beginning of file
            in.reset();
            howmany = in.read(buf, 0, (int)limit/2);
            out.write(buf, 0, howmany);
            out.flush();
            in.close();
        } catch (IOException e) {
            e.printStackTrace();
        }
    }
}
```

BufferedWriter

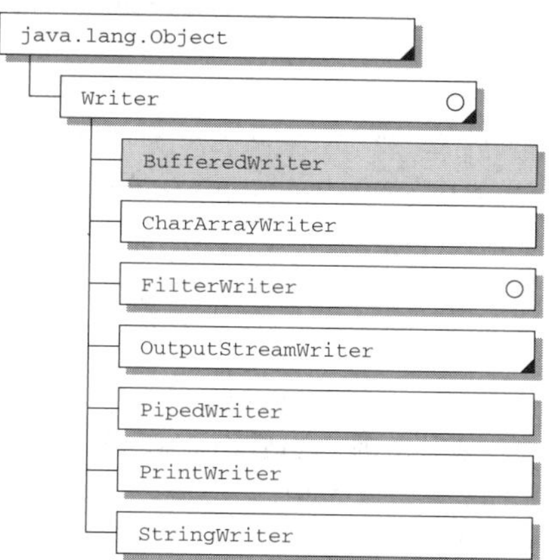

Syntax

`public class BufferedWriter extends Writer`

Description

`BufferedWriter` implements a buffered character output stream, or *buffered writer.* A buffered writer is a filter writer. You can compose it with an existing writer to allow buffering of characters before they are written to the target writer. The buffered writer maintains a `char` buffer for storing characters to be written to the target writer. Requests to write to the buffered writer results in the characters' being stored in the buffered writer's internal buffer rather than being written directly to the target writer (except under special conditions; see *Bypassing Copying* later in this section for details). When the internal buffer becomes full, its contents are flushed in the order in which they were written to the target writer.

`BufferedWriters` are useful for enhancing performance when write operations on a writer has a high per-write overhead. When a `BufferedWriter` is used, the application need not worry about minimizing the number of write operations. The application should, however, be aware that in most cases the `BufferedWriter` imposes an extra level of copying and incurs extra memory overhead due to the allocation of the buffer,

Usage

You create a `BufferedWriter` by supplying its constructor with the writer for which the output is destined. You then can write and otherwise use the `BufferedWriter` just like any other writer. The following code creates a `BufferedWriter` for writing characters to a file:

```
BufferedWriter out = new BufferedWriter(new FileWriter("outputfile"));
out.write("this is an example");
out.write("more characters");
...
out.flush();  // flushes the buffered characters to file
```

A B C D E F G H I J K L M N O P Q R S T U V W X Y Z

Bypassing Copying

Typically, when you perform a write operation, the buffered writer copies to its internal buffer the characters to be written. When the internal buffer becomes full, the characters are written to the target writer.

However, if the number of characters from a `char` array to be written is larger than the size of the internal buffer, the internal buffer is flushed and the `char` array is used directly to write characters to the target writer, thus bypassing the copying to the writer's internal buffer.

Writing Line Separators

`BufferedWriter` contains a `newLine()` method for writing a line separator as defined by the system property line.separator. This is the recommended way of writing a line separator, instead of embedding platform-dependent newline characters into the character stream or strings to be written.

BufferedOutputStream versus BufferedWriter

`BufferedOutputStream` is meant for byte streams. Its methods write bytes (0–255). `BufferedWriter` is for character output streams.

MEMBER SUMMARY	
Constructor	
`BufferedWriter()`	Constructs a `BufferedWriter` instance.
Output Methods	
`newLine()`	Writes a line separator to this buffered writer.
`write()`	Writes one or more characters to this buffered writer.
Stream Methods	
`close()`	Closes this buffered writer.
`flush()`	Flushes this buffered writer.

See Also

`BufferedOutputStream`, `BufferedReader`, `FilterWriter`.

Example

This example creates a `BufferedWriter` using the standard output stream `System.out` and writes to it a string followed by a line terminator.

```
import java.io.*;

class Main {
    public static void main(String[] args) {
```

```
            try {
                BufferedWriter out =
                    new BufferedWriter(new OutputStreamWriter(System.out));

                out.write("This is a test.");
                out.newLine();
                out.flush();   // not needed; for example only; close will flush
                out.close();
            } catch (IOException e) {
                e.printStackTrace();
            }
        }
    }
```


BufferedWriter()

PURPOSE Constructs a `BufferedWriter` instance.

SYNTAX
```
public BufferedWriter(Writer out)
public BufferedWriter(Writer out, int size)
```

DESCRIPTION There are two forms of the constructor for `BufferedWriter`. The first form constructs for the writer `out` a new buffered writer that has the default buffer size of 8K characters. The second form constructs a buffered writer for `out` that has the buffer size `size`.

A buffer of the specified size is created to cache the characters before they are written to `out`. When the buffer becomes full, or if the writer is flushed, the contents of the buffer are written to `out`. The larger the buffer, the more characters that can be cached before an actual write operation is performed. If write operations on `out` are slow, this results in significant performance improvements. However, it also means more memory is required to store the characters. Thus you should select a buffer size that balances performance requirements and memory demands.

PARAMETERS

`out` A non-`null` writer to which buffered characters are eventually written.

`size` The nonnegative size of the buffer to use.

EXCEPTIONS

`IllegalArgumentException`

If `size` ≤ `0`.

SEE ALSO `BufferedReader`.

EXAMPLE See the class example.

A
B
C
D
E
F
G
H
I
J
K
L
M
N
O
P
Q
R
S
T
U
V
W
X
Y
Z

close()

PURPOSE Closes this buffered writer.

SYNTAX `public void close() throws IOException`

DESCRIPTION This method closes this buffered writer by closing the writer that it is filtering (`out`) and releasing the buffer used by this buffered writer. All writers "downstream" from this writer are consequently closed as well. If this buffered writer has already been closed, this method does nothing.

EXCEPTIONS

`IOException`

If an IO error occurs while attempting to close `out`.

OVERRIDES `FilterWriter.close()`.

SEE ALSO `flush()`.

EXAMPLE See the class example.

flush()

PURPOSE Flushes this buffered writer.

SYNTAX `public void flush() throws IOException`

DESCRIPTION This method writes any buffered characters to the writer (`out`) being filtered and clears the buffer. It then flushes `out`. This, in turn, will flush all of the writers "downstream."

EXCEPTIONS

`IOException`

If an IO error occurs while attempting to flush `out`.

OVERRIDES `FilterWriter.flush()`.

SEE ALSO `close()`.

EXAMPLE See the class example.

newLine()

PURPOSE Writes a line separator to this buffered writer.

SYNTAX `public void newLine() throws IOException`

DESCRIPTION The line separator printed is defined by the system property line.separator. On Solaris, it is `\n`; on Windows NT, it is `\r\n`. Writing a line separator has no implication regarding when the buffer will be flushed.

EXCEPTIONS

`IOException`

If an IO error occurs while attempting to write the line separator.

SEE ALSO `BufferedReader.readLine()`.

EXAMPLE See the class example.

write()

PURPOSE Writes one or more characters to this buffered writer.

SYNTAX

```
public void write(int oneChar) throws IOException
public void write(char buf[], int offset, int count) throws
    IOException
public void write(String str, int offset, int count) throws
    IOException
```

DESCRIPTION The first form of this method writes a single character to this buffered writer. The low order 2 bytes of `oneChar` are used. If this writer's internal buffer becomes full as a result of this write, the contents of the internal buffer are flushed to the writer being filtered (`out`).

The second form of this method writes `count` number of characters starting at index `offset` from the `char` array `buf` to this buffered writer. If `count` is greater than the size of this writer's internal buffer, the contents of the internal buffer are flushed to `out` and the characters from `buf` are written directly to `out`. If `count` is less than the size of this writer's internal buffer, the characters from `buf` are first copied to this writer's internal buffer. If this causes the internal buffer to become full, the contents of the internal buffer are flushed to `out`.

The third form of this method writes `count` number of characters starting at index `offset` from the string `str` to this buffered writer. The characters are first copied to this writer's internal buffer. If this causes the internal buffer to become full, the contents of the internal buffer are flushed to `out`.

PARAMETERS

`buf`	The non-`null` `char` array containing the characters to be written.
`count`	The number of characters from `buf` or `str` to write. `0` ≤ `count` ≤ `buf.length` or `0` ≤ `count` ≤ `str.length()`.
`offset`	The index in `buf` or `str` at which to start fetching the characters to be written. `0` ≤ `offset` < `buf.length` or `0` ≤ `offset` < `str.length()`.
`str`	The non-`null` string containing the characters to be written.
`oneChar`	The low-order 2 bytes of `oneChar` is written.

OVERRIDES `FilterWriter.write()`.

EXCEPTIONS

`ArrayIndexOutOfBoundsException`
If `count` or `offset` is outside of the specified bounds.

`IOException`
If an IO error occurs while attempting to write the characters.

EXAMPLE See the class example.

Byte

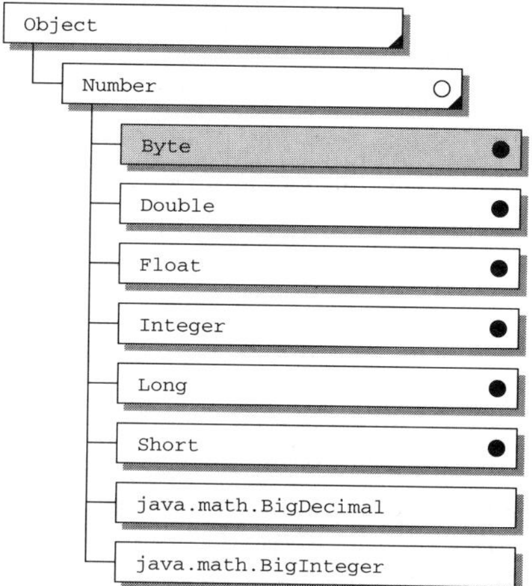

Syntax

```
public final class Byte extends Number
```

Description

A *byte* in Java is a 8-bit signed integer. The `Byte` class provides an object wrapper for `byte` data values. This allows bytes to be passed to methods in Java class libraries that accept Java objects as parameters. In addition, the `Byte` class provides methods that convert values to and from `byte` values.

Usage

A `Byte` instance is used to pass a `byte` value to a method that accepts Java objects as parameters. It cannot be used in arithmetic expressions in place of `byte`. For example, the following is not allowed:

```
Byte b1 = new Byte((byte)10);
Byte b2 = new Byte((byte)-2);
Byte b3 = b1 + b2; // Illegal
```

To perform arithmetic operations using a `Byte` instance, you first must use access methods defined in the `Byte` class to obtain the instance's numeric value, as follows:

```
byte b3 = b1.byteValue() * b2.byteValue();
double d1 = b1.doubleValue() + b2.shortValue();
```

A B C D E F G H I J K L M N O P Q R S T U V W X Y Z

MEMBER SUMMARY	
Constructor	
`Byte()`	Constructs a `Byte` object using a `byte` value or a string.
Number Methods	
`byteValue()`	Retrieves the value of this object as a `byte`.
`doubleValue()`	Retrieves the value of this object as a `double`.
`floatValue()`	Retrieves the value of this object as a `float`.
`intValue()`	Retrieves the value of this object as an `int`.
`longValue()`	Retrieves the value of this object as a `long`.
`shortValue()`	Retrieves the value of this object as a `short`.
`byte`-Related Constants	
`MAX_VALUE`	The minimum value a `byte` can have.
`MIN_VALUE`	The maximum value a `byte` can have.
`TYPE`	The `Class` object representing the primitive type `byte`.
String Conversion Methods	
`decode()`	Parses the string representation of an 8-bit signed integer into a `Byte`.
`parseByte()`	Parses the string representation of an integer into a `byte`.
`valueOf()`	Creates a `Byte` object using its string representation.
`toString()`	Generates the string representation of a `byte` or a `Byte` object.
Object Methods	
`equals()`	Compares this object with another object for equality.
`hashCode()`	Computes the hash code for this object.

See Also

`Double`, `Float`, `Long`, `Integer`, `Number`, `Short`.

Byte()

PURPOSE Constructs a `Byte` object using a `byte` value or a string.

SYNTAX
```
public Byte(byte value)
public Byte(String str) throws NumberFormatException
```

DESCRIPTION This first form of this constructor constructs a `Byte` object using `value`. The second form parses `str`, the string representation of an integer, and uses its numeric value to create the `Byte` object. The string consists of a sequence of digits in radix 10 and an optional minus character (–) as a prefix to indicate a negative number.

PARAMETERS

`str` The non-`null` string representation of an integer in radix 10.

`value` The numeric value to use as the object's value.

EXCEPTIONS

`NumberFormatException`

If `str` cannot be parsed into an 8-bit signed integer.

SEE ALSO `decode()`, `parseByte()`, `valueOf()`.

EXAMPLE

```
Byte width = new Byte((byte)12);         // using integer
try {
    Byte height = new Byte("22");        // using string
    int area = width.intValue() * height.shortValue();
} catch (NumberFormatException e) {
  ...
}
```

byteValue()

PURPOSE Retrieves the value of this object as a `byte`.

SYNTAX `public byte byteValue()`

RETURNS The value of this object as a `byte`.

SEE ALSO `doubleValue()`, `floatValue()`, `intValue()`, `longValue()`, `Number`, `shortValue()`.

EXAMPLE See `doubleValue()`.

decode()

PURPOSE Parses the string representation of an 8-bit signed integer into a `Byte`.

SYNTAX `public static Byte decode(String str) throws NumberFormatException`

DESCRIPTION The string may be in hexadecimal format (with a `0x` or `#` prefix), in octal format (with a zero character (`0`) prefix), or in decimal format (radix 10 digits preceded by an optional minus character (–)).

`decode()` is similar to `valueOf()`, except that `valueOf()` accepts a radix argument so as to determine the radix, while `decode()` examines the string's format so as to determine the radix. `decode()` also is similar to `parseByte()`, except that parseByte() returns a byte, while decode() returns a Byte object. parseByte(), like valueOf(), accepts a radix argument.

PARAMETERS

str — The non-null string to parse.

EXCEPTIONS

NumberFormatException
If str cannot be parsed into an 8-bit signed integer.

SEE ALSO Byte(), parseByte(), valueOf().

EXAMPLE This example uses decode() to convert some strings into Byte objects.

```
class Main {
    public static void main(String[] args) {
        try {
            Byte b_dec = Byte.decode("25");
            Byte b_oct = Byte.decode("065");        // octal
            Byte b_hex1 = Byte.decode("0x1f");      // hex
            Byte b_hex2 = Byte.decode("#1e");       // hex
            // Byte b_big = Byte.decode("255");     // ERROR: too big

            System.out.println("parsed: " +
                b_dec + "," + b_oct + "," + b_hex1 + ","  + b_hex2);
        } catch (NumberFormatException e) {
            e.printStackTrace();
        }
    }
}
```

doubleValue()

PURPOSE Retrieves the value of this object as a double.

SYNTAX `public double doubleValue()`

DESCRIPTION This method returns the value of this object as a double by casting its value to a double.

RETURNS The value of this object as a double.

SEE ALSO byteValue(), floatValue(), intValue(), longValue(), Number, shortValue().

EXAMPLE

```
Byte iobj = new Byte((byte)118);

byte bval = iobj.byteValue();     // 118.0
double dval = iobj.doubleValue(); // 118.0
float fval = iobj.floatValue();   // 118
int ival = iobj.intValue();       // 118
long lval = iobj.longValue();     // 118
short sval = iobj.shortValue();   // 118
```

equals()

PURPOSE Compares this object with another object for equality.

SYNTAX `public boolean equals(Object obj)`

DESCRIPTION This method compares the `byte` value of this object with that of `obj`. It returns `true` if the two values are equal; it returns `false` otherwise. It also returns `false` if `obj` is `null` or is not a `Byte` object.

PARAMETERS

`obj` The possibly `null` object against which this object will be compared.

RETURNS `true` if `obj` has the same `byte` value as this object; `false` otherwise.

OVERRIDES `Object.equals()`.

SEE ALSO `hashCode()`.

EXAMPLE

```
Byte b1 = new Byte((byte)92);
Byte b2 = new Byte((byte)92);

// Check whether the value of two Integers are equal
if (b1.equals(b2))
    System.out.println("equal");
```

floatValue()

PURPOSE Retrieves the value of this object as a `float`.

SYNTAX `public float floatValue()`

DESCRIPTION This method returns the value of this object as a `float` by casting its value to a `float`.

RETURNS The value of this object as a `float`.

SEE ALSO `byteValue()`, `doubleValue()`, `intValue()`, `longValue()`, `Number`, `shortValue()`.

EXAMPLE See `doubleValue()`.

hashCode()

PURPOSE Computes the hash code for this object.

SYNTAX `public int hashCode()`

DESCRIPTION The hash code for this object is calculated using its `byte` value. Two `Byte` objects with the same `byte` value will have the same hash code.

RETURNS An int representing the hash code.

OVERRIDES Object.hashCode().

SEE ALSO equals(), java.util.Hashtable.

EXAMPLE

```
Byte b0 = new Byte((byte)39);
int hashval = b0.hashCode();          // generate hash code
++hits[Math.abs(hashval%tabsize)];    // count hits
```


intValue()

PURPOSE Retrieves the value of this object as an int.

SYNTAX `public int intValue()`

DESCRIPTION This method retrieves the value of this object as an int by casting its value to an int.

RETURNS The value of this object as an int.

SEE ALSO byteValue(), doubleValue(), floatValue(), longValue(), Number, shortValue().

EXAMPLE See doubleValue().

longValue()

PURPOSE Retrieves the value of this object as a long.

SYNTAX `public long longValue()`

DESCRIPTION This method retrieves the value of this object as a long by casting its value to a long.

RETURNS The value of this object as a long.

SEE ALSO byteValue(), doubleValue(), floatValue(), intValue(), Number, shortValue().

EXAMPLE See doubleValue().

MAX_VALUE

PURPOSE The maximum value a byte can have.

SYNTAX `public static final byte MAX_VALUE`

DESCRIPTION This constant represents the maximum value a byte can have, which is 127.

SEE ALSO MIN_VALUE.

EXAMPLE

```
// test if number is less than MAX_VALUE
byte b0 = 32;
if (b0 < Byte.MAX_VALUE)
    b0 += 5;
```

MIN_VALUE

PURPOSE The minimum value a byte can have.

SYNTAX `public static final byte MIN_VALUE`

DESCRIPTION This constant represents the minimum value a byte can have, which is -128.

SEE ALSO MAX_VALUE.

EXAMPLE

```
// test if number is greater than MIN_VALUE
byte b0 = -12;
if (b0 > Byte.MIN_VALUE)
    b0 -= 5;
```

parseByte()

PURPOSE Parses the string representation of an integer into a byte.

SYNTAX

```
public static byte parseByte(String str) throws
   NumberFormatException
public static byte parseByte(String str, int radix) throws
   NumberFormatException
```

DESCRIPTION This method parses the string str into an integer and returns it as a byte. If no radix is given, the radix used to parse str is 10. A positive integer consists of digits in the specified radix; a negative integer has a leading minus (–) character in addition to digits in the specified radix.

parseByte() is similar to valueOf(), except that parseByte() returns a byte, while valueOf() returns a Byte object. parseByte() also is similar to decode(), except that decode() returns a Byte object and examines the string's format so as to determine its radix. Note that strings with 0x and # prefixes accepted by decode() are illegal in parseByte() and the 0 prefix for denoting octal numbers is ignored by parseByte(). See the example.

PARAMETERS

radix The radix to use when parsing str. Character.MIN_RADIX ≤ radix ≤ Character.MAX_RADIX.

str — The non-null string containing the integer.

RETURNS — A byte containing the numeric value of the integer represented by str.

EXCEPTIONS

NumberFormatException
If str cannot be parsed into an 8-bit signed integer of the specified radix.

SEE ALSO — Character.MAX_RADIX, Character.MIN_RADIX, decode(), toString(), valueOf().

EXAMPLE — This example uses parseByte() to convert strings into byte values. Note that octal strings acceptable to decode() are treated as decimal strings here and that hexadecimal strings acceptable to decode() throw NumberFormatException.

```
class Main {
    public static void main(String[] args) {
        try {
            byte b_dec = Byte.parseByte("25");          // decimal
            byte b_oct = Byte.parseByte("65", 8);       // octal
            byte b_hex1 = Byte.parseByte("1f", 16);     // hex
            byte b_hex2 = Byte.parseByte("1e", 16);     // hex
            byte b_oct2 = Byte.parseByte("033");        // leading 0 ignored
            // byte b_hex3 = Byte.parseByte("0x1e");    // ERROR: format
            // byte b_hex4 = Byte.parseByte("0x1e", 16);// ERROR: format

            System.out.println("parsed: " + b_dec + "," + b_oct + "," + b_hex1
                         + ","  + b_hex2 + "," + b_oct2);
        } catch (NumberFormatException e) {
            e.printStackTrace();
        }
    }
}
```

shortValue()

PURPOSE — Retrieves the value of this object as a short.

SYNTAX — public short shortValue()

DESCRIPTION — This method retrieves the value of this object as a short by casting its value to a short.

RETURNS — The value of this object as a short.

SEE ALSO — byteValue(), doubleValue(), floatValue(), intValue(), Number, longValue().

EXAMPLE — See doubleValue().

toString()

PURPOSE
Generates the string representation of a `byte` or a `Byte` object.

SYNTAX
```
public String toString()
public static String toString(byte bval)
```

DESCRIPTION
The first form of this method returns the string representation of the `byte` value of this `Byte` object. The second form of this method returns the string representation of the `byte` value `bval`. For both forms, the radix 10 is used.

The string consists of digits from radix 10 ("0123456789") that represents the numeric value of the number. If the number is negative, a leading negative sign precedes the digits.

PARAMETERS

`bval` The `byte` value for which to generate the string representation.

RETURNS
The non-`null` string representation of this `Byte` object, or `bval`.

OVERRIDES
`Object.toString()`.

SEE ALSO
`decode()`, `parseByte()`, `String.valueOf()`, `valueOf()`.

EXAMPLE
```
class Main {
    public static void main(String[] args) {
        byte bval = 12;
        Byte bobj = new Byte((byte)34); // cast to byte needed

        System.out.println(Byte.toString(bval));
        System.out.println(bobj.toString());
    }
}
```

TYPE

PURPOSE
The `Class` object representing the primitive type `byte`.

SYNTAX
```
public static final Class TYPE
```

DESCRIPTION
This constant can be used where the `Class` object—`byte.class`—of the primitive type `byte` is required, such as for reflection. Although there are no restrictions on the use of `Byte.TYPE`, the preferred syntax for naming the class is `byte.class`.

SEE ALSO
`Class`.

EXAMPLE
```
public static void main(String[] args) {
    Class c = Byte.TYPE;
    System.out.println("TYPE: " + c);
    System.out.println("isPrimitive: " + c.isPrimitive());
```

```
        System.out.println("superclass: " + c.getSuperclass());
        try {
            Object obj = c.newInstance();  // ERROR
            System.out.println("byte: " + obj);
        } catch (InstantiationException e) {
            e.printStackTrace();
        } catch (IllegalAccessException e) {
            e.printStackTrace();
        }
    }
```


valueOf()

PURPOSE Creates a `Byte` object using its string representation.

SYNTAX
```
public static Byte valueOf(String str) throws
   NumberFormatException
public static Byte valueOf(String str, int radix) throws
   NumberFormatException
```

DESCRIPTION This method parses the string `str` into an integer and returns a `Byte` object constructed using the integer. If no radix is given, the radix used to parse `str` is 10. A positive integer consists of digits in the specified radix. A negative integer has a leading negative (–) character followed by digits in the specified radix.

This method is similar to `parseByte()`, except `parseByte()` returns a `byte`, while `valueOf()` returns a `Byte` object. This method is similar to `decode()`, except that `valueOf()` accepts a radix argument to determine the radix, while `decode()` examines the string's format so as to determine the radix. Note that strings with a `0x` or `#` prefix accepted by `decode()` are illegal in `valueOf()`, and the `0` prefix for denoting octal numbers is ignored by `valueOf()`. See the example.

PARAMETERS

`radix` The radix to use when parsing `str`. `Character.MIN_RADIX` ≤ `radix` ≤ `Character.MAX_RADIX`.

`str` The non-`null` string containing the integer.

EXCEPTIONS

`NumberFormatException`
If `str` cannot be parsed into an 8-bit signed integer of the specified radix.

SEE ALSO `Character.MAX_RADIX`, `Character.MIN_RADIX`, `decode()`, `parseByte()`, `String.valueOf()`, `toString()`.

EXAMPLE This example uses `valueOf()` to convert strings into `Byte` objects. Note that octal strings acceptable to `decode()` are treated as decimal strings here and that hexadecimal strings acceptable to decode() throw NumberFormat-Exception.

```
class Main {
    public static void main(String[] args) {
        try {
            Byte b_dec = Byte.valueOf("25");          // decimal
            Byte b_oct = Byte.valueOf("65", 8);       // octal
            Byte b_hex1 = Byte.valueOf("1f", 16);     // hex
            Byte b_hex2 = Byte.valueOf("1e", 16);     // hex
            Byte b_oct2 = Byte.valueOf("033");        // leading 0 ignored
            // Byte b_hex3 = Byte.valueOf("0x1e");    // ERROR: format
            // Byte b_hex4 = Byte.valueOf("0x1e", 16);// ERROR: format

            System.out.println("parsed: " + b_dec + "," + b_oct + "," + b_hex1
                                  + ","  + b_hex2 + "," + b_oct2);
        } catch (NumberFormatException e) {
            e.printStackTrace();
        }
    }
}
```

ByteArrayInputStream

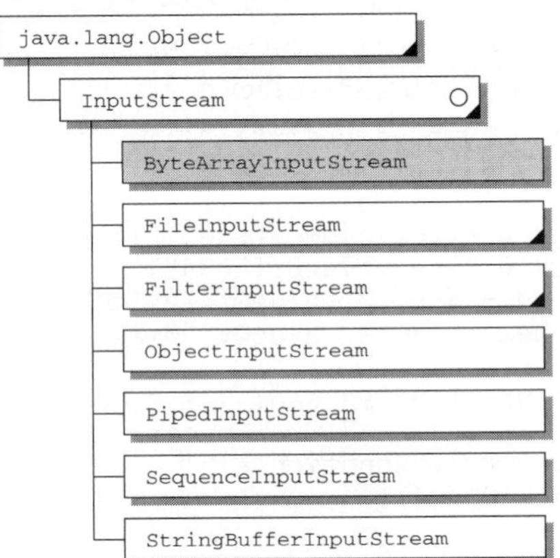

A B C D E F G H I J K L M N O P Q R S T U V W X Y Z

Syntax

```
public class ByteArrayInputStream extends InputStream
```

Description

`ByteArrayInputStream` implements a byte array input stream. You can use this stream to turn a `byte` array into an input stream on which you can perform read operations. Requests to read from the stream retrieve bytes from the original `byte` array (see Figure 16).

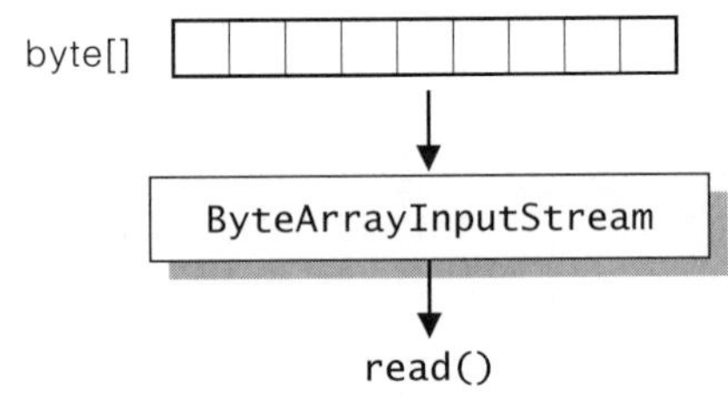

FIGURE 16: **`ByteArrayInputStream.`**

CharArrayReader and StringReader

`CharArrayReader` provides similar functionality for `char` arrays. See `CharArrayReader` for details. `StringReader` provides similar functionality as `CharArrayReader`, except instead of reading from a `char` array, you read characters from a `StringBuffer` that behaves like a reader.

MEMBER SUMMARY	
Constructor	
`ByteArrayInputStream()`	Constructs a `ByteArrayInputStream` using a `byte` array.
Input Methods	
`read()`	Reads bytes from this byte array input stream.
`skip()`	Skips the specified number of bytes in this byte input stream.

MEMBER SUMMARY	
Mark/Reset Methods	
`mark()`	Marks the current position in the byte array input stream.
`markSupported()`	Determines whether this stream supports rereading of its data.
`reset()`	Resets the buffer to the previously marked position of the `byte` array.
Stream Method	
`available()`	Determines the number of unread bytes in this byte array input stream.
Protected Fields	
`buf`	The `byte` array containing the bytes to be read.
`count`	The ending index of the `byte` array to be read.
`mark`	The position of the mark.
`pos`	The current read position in the `byte` array.

See Also

`ByteArrayOutputStream`, `CharArrayReader`, `FilterOutputStream`, `OutputStream`.

Example

This example exercises all of the methods in the `ByteArrayInputStream` class. It reads all of the bytes from the stream, resets the stream, skips 3 bytes, and then reads the rest of the bytes from the stream.

```
import java.io.ByteArrayInputStream;

class Main {
    public static void main(String[] args) {
        byte[] inputbytes = { 'a', 'b', 'c', 'd', 'e'};
        ByteArrayInputStream in = new ByteArrayInputStream(inputbytes);

        System.out.println("Available: " + in.available());
        int b;

        while ((b=in.read()) >= 0)          // reads "abcde"
            System.out.print((char)b);
        in.reset();
        System.out.println();

        in.skip(3);                         // skip "abc"

        while ((b=in.read()) >= 0)          // reads "de"
            System.out.print((char)b);
        System.out.println();
    }
}
```

available()

PURPOSE Determines the number of unread bytes in this byte array input stream.

SYNTAX `public synchronized int available()`

DESCRIPTION This method returns the number of bytes that have yet to be read from this byte array input stream.

RETURNS The number of bytes yet to be read from this stream.

OVERRIDES `InputStream.available()`.

EXAMPLE See the class example.

buf

PURPOSE The `byte` array containing the bytes to be read.

SYNTAX `protected byte[] buf`

DESCRIPTION `buf` is a reference to the `byte` array used to create this byte array input stream. Because this is a reference, any changes to the original `byte` array are reflected in this byte array input stream.

SEE ALSO `count`, `pos`.

EXAMPLE This example is taken from the source of `ByteArrayInputStream`. It shows the usage of all of the three protected fields of `ByteArrayInputStream`.

```
public synchronized int read() {
    return (pos < count) ? (buf[pos++] & 0xff) : -1;
}
```

ByteArrayInputStream()

PURPOSE Constructs a `ByteArrayInputStream` using a `byte` array.

SYNTAX `public ByteArrayInputStream(byte[] buffer)`
`public ByteArrayInputStream(byte[] buffer, int offset, int count)`

DESCRIPTION The two forms of this constructor construct a byte array input stream using an existing `byte` array `buffer`. `buffer` is used directly and not copied, so any changes to `buffer` after the creation of this stream also affect this input stream. The bytes to be read from `buffer` are the `count` number of bytes starting at index `offset`. If `offset` and `count` are not specified, all of the bytes in the entire buffer will be read.

PARAMETERS

`buffer` The non-`null` buffer containing the bytes to be read (not copied).

`count` The number of bytes that can be read from `buffer`. If `count` + `offset` exceeds `buffer.length`, `count` is automatically lowered to the limit imposed by `buffer`.

`offset` The index in `buffer` from which to start reading.

EXAMPLE See the class example.

count

PURPOSE The ending index of the `byte` array to be read.

SYNTAX `protected int count`

DESCRIPTION This field records the exclusive ending index of the `byte` array to be read. It is calculated initially when the byte array input stream is first created, and it remains unchanged. See the constructor for how it is initialized.

SEE ALSO `pos`, `ByteArrayInputStream()`.

EXAMPLE See `buf`.

mark

PURPOSE The position of the mark.

SYNTAX `protected int mark`

DESCRIPTION When you set a mark on this byte array input stream by calling `mark()`, the current read position is recorded in the field `mark`. When `reset()` is invoked, the current read position is reset to `mark`. If no mark has been set, the value of `mark` is the value of `offset` passed to the constructor (or `0` if the offset was not supplied). This field should not be used directly. `mark()` should be used to change its value.

Note: In Java 1.1.4, the constructor does not use the offset supplied to set `mark`. `mark` is always initialized to `0`.

SEE ALSO `mark()`, `pos`, `reset()`.

A B C D E F G H I J K L M N O P Q R S T U V W X Y Z

mark()

PURPOSE Marks the current position in the `byte` array input stream.

SYNTAX `public synchronized void mark(int readlimit)`

DESCRIPTION Byte array input streams support marks and resets. This method marks the current position in the input stream. A subsequent call to `reset()` will reposition the stream at this marked position so that later reads will reread the same bytes.

PARAMETERS

`readlimit` This parameter is ignored.

OVERRIDES `InputStream.mark()`.

SEE ALSO `mark`, `markSupported()`, `reset()`.

EXAMPLE This example creates a byte array input stream that has five characters. It reads the first three characters, sets a mark, completes reading the stream, and then returns to the mark and rereads the rest of the stream. Note that the argument (`0`) to `mark()` is ignored.

```
import java.io.ByteArrayInputStream;

class Main {
    public static void main(String[] args) {
        byte[] inputbytes = { 'a', 'b', 'c', 'd', 'e'};
        ByteArrayInputStream in = new ByteArrayInputStream(inputbytes);

        System.out.println("Available: " + in.available());
        int b;

        for (int i = 0; i < 3; i++) {
            b=in.read();                    // reads "abc"
            System.out.print((char)b);
        }
        System.out.println();
        in.mark(0);                         // mark position
        while ((b=in.read()) >= 0)          // reads "de"
            System.out.print((char)b);
        System.out.println();

        in.reset();                         // go back to mark
        while ((b=in.read()) >= 0)          // reads "de"
            System.out.print((char)b);
        System.out.println();
    }
}
```

markSupported()

PURPOSE Determines whether this stream supports rereading of its data.

SYNTAX `public boolean markSupported()`

DESCRIPTION This method returns whether this stream supports rereading of its data (i.e., mark/reset). Byte array input streams support this feature. Hence, this method always returns `true`.

RETURNS `true`.

OVERRIDES `InputStream.markSupported()`.

SEE ALSO `mark()`, `reset()`.

pos

PURPOSE The current read position in the `byte` array.

SYNTAX `protected int pos`

DESCRIPTION This field records the current read position in the `byte` array of this byte array input stream. The next `read()` or `skip()` operation will start reading from this position. This field is set initially when the byte array input stream is first created and is updated during `read()` and `skip()` operations to record which byte to read next. `reset()` sets `pos` to the previous marked position (see `mark()`) so that subsequent reading and skipping will start at the marked position.

`pos` is a `0`-based index of `buf`. It is initialized to the value of `offset` supplied in the `ByteArrayInputStream()` constructor (or to `0` if not supplied).

SEE ALSO `count`.

EXAMPLE See `buf`.

read()

PURPOSE Reads bytes from this byte array input stream.

SYNTAX
```
public synchronized int read()
public synchronized int read(byte[] buffer, int offset, int count)
```

DESCRIPTION The `read()` method reads bytes from this byte array input stream, starting at the current read position. The current read position is usually that of the next byte after the last byte read during the previous `read()` or `skip()` invocation. However, the current read position can be changed using `reset()`.

The first form of `read()` returns the byte at the current read position in this byte array input stream. If end-of-stream has been reached, this method returns `-1`.

The second form of `read()` reads `count` bytes from this byte array input stream starting at the current read position and stores the bytes read into the byte array buffer starting at index offset. The actual number of bytes read is returned. This number could differ from count when the number of bytes available is less than that requested. If no bytes can be read because end-of-stream has been reached, this method returns -1.

A B C D E F G H I J K L M N O P Q R S T U V W X Y Z

PARAMETERS

buffer	The non-null buffer into which the data is read.
count	The number of bytes to read. 0 ≤ count ≤ buffer.length-offset.
offset	The index in buffer at which to start storing the bytes read. 0 ≤ offset < buffer.length.

RETURNS The first form returns the byte read. The second returns the actual number of bytes read. Both forms return -1 when end-of-stream is reached.

EXCEPTIONS

ArrayIndexOutOfBoundsException
If count or offset is outside of the specified bounds.

IOException
If an IO error occurred while attempting to read the requested bytes.

OVERRIDES InputStream.read().

SEE ALSO reset(), skip().

EXAMPLE See the class example.

reset()

PURPOSE Resets the buffer to the previously marked position of the byte array.

SYNTAX `public synchronized void reset()`

DESCRIPTION This method resets the current read position of this stream to the previously marked position. If no mark has been set, it is set to the offset specified in the constructor (or to 0 if no offset was specified). The ending index of the byte array to read (that calculated originally using offset and count arguments to the constructor) remains unchanged.

Note: In Java 1.1.4, the offset specified in the constructor is not used by reset(). If no mark has been set, reset() always resets to the beginning of the byte array (0). For example, regardless of whether offset was 10 or 0, reset() always sets the current read position to 0.

OVERRIDES InputStream.reset().

SEE ALSO count, pos, mark, mark(), read(), skip().

EXAMPLE See the class example.

skip()

PURPOSE Skips the specified number of bytes in this byte array input stream.

SYNTAX `public synchronized long skip(long count)`

DESCRIPTION This method skips `count` number of bytes of this byte array input stream starting at the current read position. It returns the actual number of bytes skipped, which may differ from `count` if there are fewer bytes available in the stream. The current read position is updated to reflect the number of bytes skipped. The next `read()` will not return those bytes skipped.

It returns `0` if it cannot skip any bytes.

PARAMETERS

`count` The number of bytes to be skipped.

RETURNS The actual number of bytes skipped.

OVERRIDES `InputStream.skip()`.

SEE ALSO `read()`.

EXAMPLE See the class example.

ByteArrayOutputStream

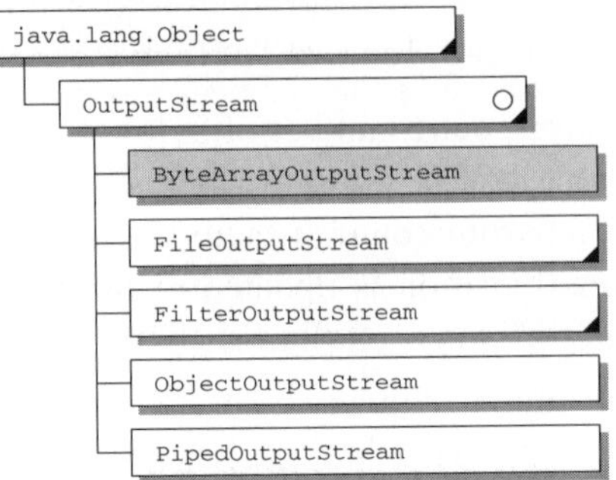

A B C D E F G H I J K L M N O P Q R S T U V W X Y Z

Syntax

```
public class ByteArrayOutputStream extends OutputStream
```

Description

`ByteArrayOutputStream` implements a byte array output stream. You can use a byte array output stream to treat a `byte` array as an output stream on which you can perform write operations. Requests to write bytes to the stream store the bytes into an automatically expandable `byte` array whose contents can later be retrieved as a `byte` array or as a string. This is helpful when you want to capture output from methods that operate on output streams in the form of a `byte` array. See Figure 17.

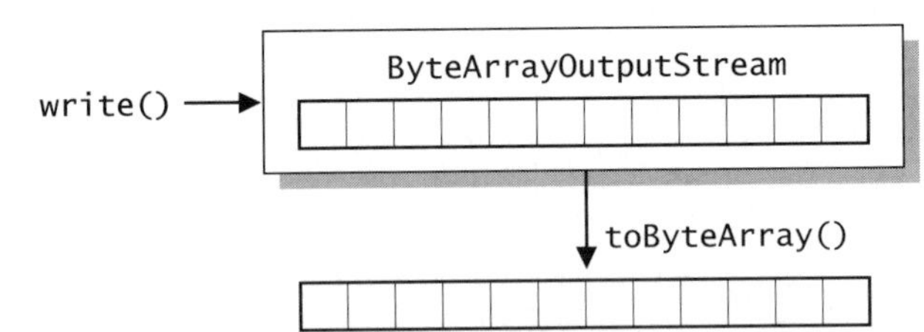

FIGURE 17: **`ByteArrayOutputStream`.**

CharArrayWriter

`CharArrayWriter` provides similar functionality for `char` arrays. `StringWriter` provides similar functionality for `StringBuffer`.

MEMBER SUMMARY	
Constructor	
`ByteArrayOutputStream()`	Constructs a `ByteArrayOutputStream` instance.
Output Method	
`write()`	Writes bytes to this byte array output stream.

MEMBER SUMMARY

Stream Methods	
`reset()`	Resets this stream so that it can be reused.
`size()`	Retrieves the number of bytes in this stream.
Externalizing Methods	
`toByteArray()`	Retrieves the contents of this stream as a `byte` array.
`toString()`	Retrieves the contents of this stream as a string.
`writeTo()`	Writes the contents of this stream to another stream.
Protected Fields	
`buf`	The buffer in which data of this stream is stored.
`count`	The number of bytes in this stream.

A B C D E F G H I J K L M N O P Q R S T U V W X Y Z

See Also

`ByteArrayInputStream`, `CharArrayWriter`, `StringWriter`, `OutputStream`.

Example

This example shows the use of a byte array output stream to collect the compressed bytes of a file and write the compressed bytes to another file.

```
import java.io.*;
import java.util.zip.*;

class Main {
    public static void main(String[] args) {
        if (args.length != 2) {
            System.err.println("Usage: java Main <input> <output>");
            System.exit(-1);
        }
        try {
            FileInputStream in = new FileInputStream(args[0]);

            // Create compressed stream that writes to byte array output stream
            ByteArrayOutputStream b = new ByteArrayOutputStream();
            GZIPOutputStream out = new GZIPOutputStream(b);

            byte[] buf = new byte[512];
            int howmany;
            while ((howmany = in.read(buf)) > 0) {
                out.write(buf, 0, howmany);
            }
            in.close();
            out.flush();
            byte[] compressedBytes = b.toByteArray(); // get byte array
            b.writeTo(new FileOutputStream(args[1])); // write to file
            out.close();                              // closes both out and b
            System.out.println("compressed size: " + compressedBytes.length);
```

```
                // ... do something with byte array

            } catch (IOException e) {
                System.out.println(e);
            }
        }
    }
```

A B C D E F G H I J K L M N O P Q R S T U V W X Y Z

buf

PURPOSE The buffer in which data of this stream is stored.

SYNTAX `protected byte[] buf`

DESCRIPTION This field is used to store the bytes written to the byte array output stream. `buf`'s initial size is determined by the arguments to the `ByteArrayOutputStream()` constructor, but it is expanded as needed as more bytes are written to the stream.

SEE ALSO `count`, `size()`.

EXAMPLE This example is taken from the source of `ByteArrayOutputStream`. It shows the use of the protected fields `buf` and `count` in the `write()` method.

```
public synchronized void write(int b) {
    int newcount = count + 1;
    if (newcount > buf.length) {
        byte newbuf[] = new byte[Math.max(buf.length << 1, newcount)];
        System.arraycopy(buf, 0, newbuf, 0, count);
        buf = newbuf;
    }
    buf[count] = (byte)b;
    count = newcount;
}
```

ByteArrayOutputStream()

PURPOSE Constructs a `ByteArrayOutputStream` instance.

SYNTAX
```
public ByteArrayOutputStream()
public ByteArrayOutputStream(int size)
```

DESCRIPTION There are two forms of the constructor for `ByteArrayOutputStream`. The first form constructs a byte array output stream that has the default buffer size of 32 bytes. The second form constructs a byte array output stream buffer of size `size`.

A buffer of the specified size is created to store the bytes written to this stream. As the number of bytes written to this stream exceeds the buffer size, the buffer will be grown automatically to accommodate the additional bytes.

PARAMETERS

size — The initial buffer size. `size` > `0`.

SEE ALSO — `size()`.

EXAMPLE — See the class example.

count

PURPOSE — The number of bytes in this stream.

SYNTAX — `protected int count`

DESCRIPTION — This field records the number of bytes that have been written to this stream since its most recent reset or since it was created if it has never reset. This number is incremented as more bytes are written to this stream and is set to `0` when `reset()` is invoked.

RETURNS — The number of bytes in this stream.

SEE ALSO — `reset()`, `size()`.

EXAMPLE — See `buf`.

reset()

PURPOSE — Resets this stream so that it can be reused.

SYNTAX — `public synchronized void reset()`

DESCRIPTION — This method resets the current write position of this stream to be the beginning of the `byte` array. The size of this stream becomes `0`, and all bytes written earlier to the current stream are lost. Subsequent write operations to this stream start at the beginning of the `byte` array.

OVERRIDES — `OutputStream.reset()`.

SEE ALSO — `write()`, `writeTo()`.

EXAMPLE — This example writes data to a byte array output stream and computes its checksum. It then resets the checksum and the byte array output stream and computes the checksum for another set of data values.

```
import java.io.*;
import java.util.zip.Adler32;

class Main {
    public static void main(String[] args) {
        ByteArrayOutputStream buf = new ByteArrayOutputStream();
        Adler32 checksum = new Adler32();
```

```
            for (int i = 0; i < 26; i++) {
                buf.write('a'+i);
            }

            // Compute checksum of 'a' - 'z'
            checksum.update(buf.toByteArray(), 0, buf.size());
            System.out.println("first checksum: " + checksum.getValue());

            // Reset buffer and checksum
            checksum.reset();
            buf.reset();

            for (int i = 0; i < 10; i++) {
                buf.write('0'+i);
            }

            checksum.update(buf.toByteArray(), 0, buf.size());
            System.out.println("second checksum: " + checksum.getValue());
        }
    }
```


size()

PURPOSE Retrieves the number of bytes in this stream.

SYNTAX `public int size()`

DESCRIPTION This method returns the number of bytes that have been written to this stream since its most recent reset or since it was created if it has never been reset. This number is incremented as more bytes are written to this stream and is set to `0` when `reset()` is invoked.

RETURNS The number of bytes in this stream.

SEE ALSO `count`, `reset()`.

EXAMPLE See `reset()`.

toByteArray()

PURPOSE Retrieves the contents of this stream as a `byte` array.

SYNTAX `public synchronized byte[] toByteArray()`

DESCRIPTION This method is used to retrieve the contents of this stream as a `byte` array. The contents of this stream are copied to a newly created `byte` array, and this new `byte` array is returned. Subsequent changes to this stream do not affect the `byte` array that is returned.

RETURNS A new non-`null` `byte` array containing the contents of this stream.

EXAMPLE See the class example.

toString()

PURPOSE Retrieves the contents of this stream as a string.

SYNTAX

```
public String toString()
public String toString(String enc) throws
   UnsupportedEncodingException
```

DEPRECATED `public String toString(int hibyte)`

DESCRIPTION This method creates a string using the contents of this byte array output stream. The string that is returned is a snapshot of the current contents of this stream. It is not affected by any subsequent changes to this stream.

If `enc` is not supplied, the high-order byte of each character is `0`. If `enc` is supplied, it is an identifier specifying the encoding scheme to use when translating the bytes in this `byte` array into characters. See `String.String()` for details about encoding identifiers.

PARAMETERS

`enc` The non-`null` string identifying the encoding to use when converting the bytes to Unicode.

`hibyte` The byte used as the high-order byte of each character in the resulting string.

RETURNS The non-`null` string representation of this stream.

EXCEPTIONS

`UnsupportedEncodingException`
If no byte-to-character converter is found for the encoding identified by `enc`.

DEPRECATION If `hibyte` is supplied, the high-order byte of each 16-bit Unicode character of the string is set to `hibyte`. Use of this form of `toString()` is deprecated because it does not properly convert bytes into characters in general. Replace the usage of this form of the method, as in

```
ByteArrayOutputStream out = ...;
String s1 = out.toString(hibyte);
```

with

```
String s1 = out.toString("ISO-Latin-1"); // or appropriate encoder
```

OVERRIDES `java.lang.Object.toString()`.

SEE ALSO `java.lang.String.String()`, `toByteArray()`.

EXAMPLE

```
import java.io.*;

class Main {
    public static void main(String[] args) {
        ByteArrayOutputStream out = new ByteArrayOutputStream();
        out.write('a');
        out.write('b');
        out.write('c');
```

A B C D E F G H I J K L M N O P Q R S T U V W X Y Z

```
            System.out.println(out.toString());   // abc
        }
    }
```

A B C D E F G H I J K L M N O P Q R S T U V W X Y Z

write()

PURPOSE Writes bytes to this byte array output stream.

SYNTAX

```
public synchronized void write(int oneByte)
public synchronized void write(byte[] buffer, int offset, int
   count)
```

DESCRIPTION The `write()` method writes the specified byte or bytes to this byte array output stream. The first form writes a single byte `oneByte` to this stream. The second form writes to this stream `count` bytes from the `byte` array `buffer` starting at index `offset`.

The bytes written are copied to the stream starting at the current write position. The current write position is usually the next index after the point at which the last byte from the previous `write()` occurred, unless set to `0` via `reset()`. The current write position is incremented to reflect the new bytes written. The internal `byte` array used to hold the contents of the stream expands dynamically as required to hold all of the new data.

PARAMETERS

`buffer` The non-`null` `byte` array containing data to be written.

`count` The number of bytes from `buffer` to be written. `0` ≤ `count` ≤ `buffer.length-offset`.

`offset` The index in `buffer` of the bytes to be written. `0` ≤ `offset` < `buffer.length`.

`oneByte` The byte to be written. The low-order byte of `oneByte` is written.

EXCEPTIONS

`ArrayIndexOutOfBoundsException`
If `count` or `offset` is outside of the specified bounds.

OVERRIDES `OutputStream.write()`.

SEE ALSO `reset()`.

EXAMPLE See the class example and `toString()`.

writeTo()

PURPOSE Writes the contents of this stream to another stream.

SYNTAX

```
public synchronized void writeTo(OutputStream out) throws
    IOException
```

DESCRIPTION This method writes the entire contents of this stream to the output stream `out`. The output consists of all of the bytes from the beginning of this stream to the current write position of this stream. This method does not change the current write position.

PARAMETERS

`out` The non-`null` stream to which to write.

EXCEPTIONS

`IOException`

If an IO error occurred while attempting to write to `out`.

SEE ALSO `OutputStream`.

EXAMPLE See the class example.

Calendar

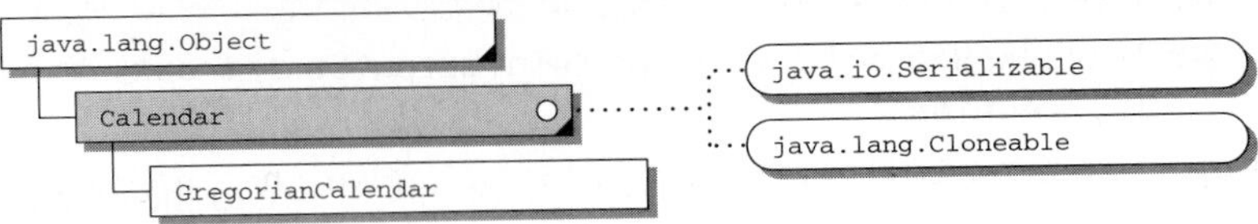

Syntax

```
public abstract class Calendar implements Serializable, Cloneable
```

Description

Java represents a date and time using a single `long` value called a *Date value*. The `Date` class is used to represent a `Date` value. There is no practical limit to the dates represented by a `Date` value because it can represent dates hundreds of millions of years in the past and in the future. A `Date` value contains information about the time of day down to the millisecond. A `Date` value is always relative to GMT and so is independent of time zones. See the `Date` class for more information.

The `Calendar` class is used to extract calendar-related attributes from a `Date` value. For example, if you obtained a `Date` value and wanted to know what year it represented, you would create a `Calendar` object initialized with the `Date` value and then call a method to determine the `Date` value's year.

You can also initialize a `Calendar` object using a valid combination of calendar-related attributes rather than a `Date` value. For example, you could initialize a `Calendar` object with a year and one of the 365 days in the year. The combination must be sufficient to represent a particular day on a calendar. For example, a year and a day-of-week is not sufficient to represent a day.

Once a `Calendar` object has properly been initialized with a date, you can either convert it to a `Date` value (see `getTime()`) or use it to determine any other calendar-related attributes of the date. For example, if you initialized a `Calendar` object with the year, month, and day, you could determine its day-of-week or week-in-year.

At the moment, the descriptions in this class frequently refer to the `GregorianCalendar` class. As more calendar classes are added in the future, the descriptions in this class will become more generic.

The Superclass of Calendars

The `Calendar` class is designed to support different kinds of current calendar systems. The idea is for this class to provide functionality that is common to most calendar systems and to make that functionality available to subclasses. The subclasses then can override and add details that are specific to a calendar system. Java 1.1.4 provides only one subclass of this class—`GregorianCalendar`.

Usage

To create a Calendar object, you determine which calendar system you want to use and then construct an instance of the class that represents that system. In Java 1.1.4, only one calendar system is supported—the Gregorian system, which is represented by the GregorianCalendar class.

Another way to create a Calendar object is to use the getInstance() method in this class. This method returns a Calendar object based on the current locale and time zone. In Java 1.1.4, it returns only GregorianCalendar objects.

By default, the Calendar object is initialized with the current date and time. You can then call the get() method to determine any of the calendar-related attributes of the current date and time.

If the current date is not the desired date, you can change the Calendar object's date by setting a new Date value (see setTime()) or by changing any of the calendar's attributes (see set()).

Calendar Fields and the Date Value

A Calendar object contains 17 *calendar fields*. These calendar fields represent the calendar-related attributes of a date. Examples of calendar fields are the year, month, and hour.

A calendar field can be set or cleared. When a calendar field is cleared, it is not used when the fields are converted into a Date value. When get() is invoked, all cleared calendar fields are recomputed before the result is returned. Therefore all cleared fields become set whenever a call to get() is made.

As mentioned, the Calendar class can be used to convert a set of calendar fields into a Date value. One reason why you might want to do this is that the Date value is a compact and typical way of saving or exchanging dates between programs.

When converting a set of calendar fields to a Date value, note that not all calendar fields are necessary to do the conversion. For example, if the year, month, and day are available, none of the other date-related calendar fields are used. However, if the month value is cleared (not set), the day-of-year calendar field is used in the conversion. If the day-of-year field is cleared, other possible calendar fields are examined. In short, the algorithm that converts calendar field values to a Date value looks for a set of calendar fields in a particular order until they resolve to a particular day.

The order in which calendar fields are examined is very important. In particular, if you were to set the day-of-year field hoping to change the current date of a Calendar object, it would be ignored if the year, month, and date fields were set. To force the Calendar object to notice the new day-of-year value, you need to clear the month field. The set() method describes this information in detail.

Leniency

A calendar that is not *lenient* does not allow you to set a calendar field that is outside of that field's normal range. For example, the month of the Gregorian calendar has a range of 1 to 12. Therefore you cannot set the month calendar field to a value less than 1 or greater than 12.

A lenient calendar allows you to set a calendar field to a value outside of the field's normal range. For example, in a lenient Gregorian calendar, if you set a month of `13`, the calendar's year field would advance by one year and the month field will have the value `1` (January). For information on how values outside a calendar field's normal range affect the calendar's other fields, see the description of the calendar field's constant (`MONTH`, `YEAR`, and so on).

A calendar can be set at any time to be lenient or nonlenient.

Time Zone and Locale

`Date` values are independent of time zones but a `Calendar` object is not. When a `Calendar` object is initialized with a `Date` value, the time fields are computed based on a time zone. By default, `Calendar` objects use the default time zone (see `TimeZone.getDefault()`), but it can be changed to any time zone.

Two of the calendar properties are locale-dependent: the first day-of-week (see `getFirstDayOfWeek()`) and the minimal number of days in the first week (see `getMinimalDaysInFirstWeek()`). For example, the first day-of-week in the United States is Sunday while in France, it is Monday.

Formatting Dates

This class is not used to create formatted date and time strings. See `DateFormat` and `SimpleDateFormat` for complete information about formatting date and time strings.

Calendar Constants

To reduce space, there are no descriptions for the month and day-of-week calendar constants. The month constants are used by the `MONTH` field; see the `MONTH` member for an example that uses these constants. The day-of-week constants are used by the `DAY_OF_WEEK` field; see the class example for an example of their usage. Table 5 summarizes their values. For an example that demonstrates these constants, see the class example.

Month Constants				Day-of-Week Constants	
JANUARY	0	AUGUST	7	SUNDAY	1
FEBRUARY	1	SEPTEMBER	8	MONDAY	2
MARCH	2	OCTOBER	9	TUESDAY	3
APRIL	3	NOVEMBER	10	WEDNESDAY	4
MAY	4	DECEMBER	11	THURSDAY	5
JUNE	5	UNDECIMBER	12	FRIDAY	6
JULY	6			SATURDAY	7

TABLE 5: Values of Month and Day-of-Week Constants.

MEMBER SUMMARY

Constructor	
`Calendar()`	Used by a subclass to construct a `Calendar` instance.
Creation Method	
`getInstance()`	Creates a `Calendar` object.
Month Constants	
`APRIL`	Specifies April.
`AUGUST`	Specifies August.
`DECEMBER`	Specifies December.
`FEBRUARY`	Specifies February.
`JANUARY`	Specifies January.
`JULY`	Specifies July.
`JUNE`	Specifies June.
`MARCH`	Specifies March.
`MAY`	Specifies May.
`NOVEMBER`	Specifies November.
`OCTOBER`	Specifies October.
`SEPTEMBER`	Specifies September.
`UNDECIMBER`	Artificial name specifying the thirteenth month for lunar calendars.
Day-of-Week Constants	
`FRIDAY`	Specifies Friday.
`MONDAY`	Specifies Monday.
`SATURDAY`	Specifies Saturday.
`SUNDAY`	Specifies Sunday.
`THURSDAY`	Specifies Thursday.
`TUESDAY`	Specifies Tuesday.
`WEDNESDAY`	Specifies Wednesday.
Calendar Field Constants	
`AM_PM`	Specifies the AM/PM field.
`DATE`	Specifies the date calendar field.
`DAY_OF_MONTH`	Specifies the day-of-month calendar field.
`DAY_OF_WEEK`	Specifies the day-of-week calendar field.
`DAY_OF_WEEK_IN_MONTH`	Specifies the day-of-week-in-month calendar field.
`DAY_OF_YEAR`	Specifies the day-of-year calendar field.
`DST_OFFSET`	Specifies the daylight-savings-time calendar field.
`ERA`	Specifies the era calendar field.
`FIELD_COUNT`	Specifies the number of calendar fields.
`HOUR`	Specifies the hour (12-hour clock) calendar field.

Continued

A B C D E F G H I J K L M N O P Q R S T U V W X Y Z

MEMBER SUMMARY

Calendar Field Constants *(Continued)*

`HOUR_OF_DAY`	Specifies the hour-of-day (24-hour clock) calendar field.
`MILLISECOND`	Specifies the millisecond calendar field.
`MINUTE`	Specifies the minute calendar field.
`MONTH`	Specifies the month calendar field.
`SECOND`	Specifies the second calendar field.
`WEEK_OF_MONTH`	Specifies the week-of-month calendar field.
`WEEK_OF_YEAR`	Specifies the week-of-year calendar field.
`YEAR`	Specifies the year calendar field.
`ZONE_OFFSET`	Specifies the zone-offset calendar field.

Time Constants

`AM`	Represents A.M. in a 12-hour clock.
`PM`	Represents P.M. in a 12-hour clock.

Calendar Property Methods

`getFirstDayOfWeek()`	Retrieves this `Calendar` object's first day-of-week.
`getMinimalDaysInFirstWeek()`	Retrieves the minimal number of days required in the first week of the year.
`isLenient()`	Determines if this `Calendar` object is lenient.
`setFirstDayOfWeek()`	Sets this `Calendar` object's first day-of-week.
`setLenient()`	Sets the leniency property of this `Calendar` object.
`setMinimalDaysInFirstWeek()`	Sets the minimal number of days required in the first week of the year.

Calendar Field Methods

`add()`	Increments/decrements a calendar field.
`clear()`	Clears the values of time fields.
`get()`	Retrieves the value of a calendar field.
`getTime()`	Computes this `Calendar` object's `Date` value.
`isSet()`	Determines if a calendar field has been set.
`roll()`	Rolls a calendar field.
`set()`	Sets the values for the year, month, date, hour, minute, and second fields.
`setTime()`	Sets this `Calendar` object's current date and time.

Comparison Methods

`after()`	Determines if the time of this `Calendar` object is later than another time.
`before()`	Determines if the time of this `Calendar` object is before another time.

MEMBER SUMMARY	
Range Methods	
`getGreatestMinimum()`	Retrieves the greatest minimum value for a calendar field.
`getLeastMaximum()`	Retrieves the least maximum value for a calendar field.
`getMaximum()`	Retrieves the maximum value for a calendar field.
`getMinimum()`	Retrieves the minimum value for a calendar field.
Locale Method	
`getAvailableLocales()`	Retrieves the set of locales in which the current date can be printed.
Time Zone Methods	
`getTimeZone()`	Retrieves this `Calendar` object's time zone.
`setTimeZone()`	Sets the time zone.
Protected Methods	
`complete()`	Computes either the `Date` value or the calendar fields.
`computeFields()`	Computes the values for the calendar fields from this `Calendar` object's `Date` value.
`computeTime()`	Converts the calendar fields into a `Date` value.
`getTimeInMillis()`	Computes this `Calendar` object's `Date` value and returns it as a long.
`internalGet()`	Retrieves the current value of a calendar field.
`setTimeInMillis()`	Sets this `Calendar` object's current date time.
Protected Fields	
`areFieldsSet`	Indicates whether any fields have been cleared.
`fields`	Holds the calendar field values.
`isSet`	Holds the set state of each calendar field.
`isTimeSet`	Indicates if the time field is valid.
`time`	Holds this `Calendar` object's current date and time.
Object Methods	
`clone()`	Creates a clone of this `Calendar` object.
`equals()`	Determines if this `Calendar` object is equal to another object.

See Also

`Date`, `GregorianCalendar`, `java.text.DateFormat`, `java.text.SimpleDateFormat`, `Locale`, `TimeZone`.

Example

This example displays the calendar for a particular year. The year is supplied on the command line. If no year is supplied, a calendar for the current year is displayed. See Figure 18. The calendar displays locale-dependent names and is sensitive to the first day-of-week.

If you click any date, the specifics of that date are printed to standard output.

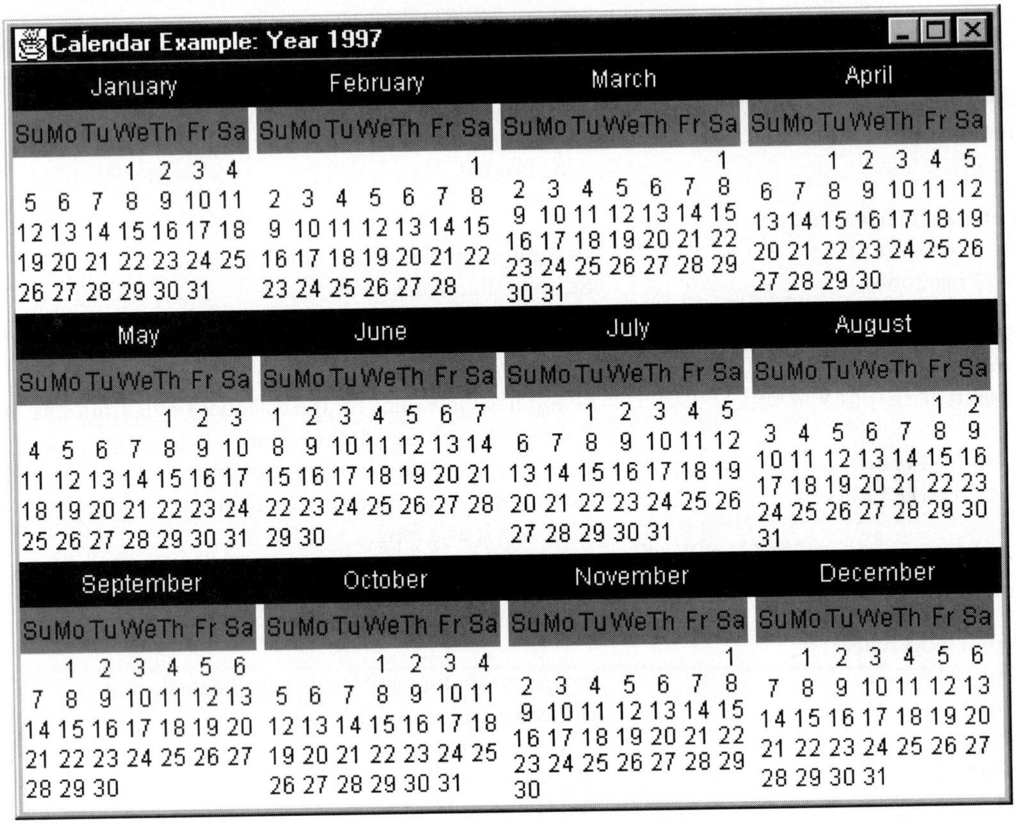

FIGURE 18: `Calendar.`

```
import java.awt.*;
import java.awt.event.*;
import java.text.*;
import java.util.*;

class Main extends Frame {
    Main(int year) {
        super("Calendar Example: Year " + year);
        setLayout(new GridLayout(3, 4));

        Calendar cal = Calendar.getInstance();
        for (int i=cal.getMinimum(Calendar.MONTH);
             i<=cal.getMaximum(Calendar.MONTH); i++) {
            cal.set(year, i, 1);
            add(new MonthCanvas(cal));
```

```
        }
        setSize(500, 400);
        show();
    }
    public static void main(String[] args) {
        if (args.length < 1) {
            new Main(Calendar.getInstance().get(Calendar.YEAR));
        } else {
            new Main(Integer.parseInt(args[0]));
        }
    }
}

class MonthCanvas extends Container {
    static String[] monthNames;
    static String[] weekNames;

    MonthCanvas(Calendar cal) {
        setLayout(new BorderLayout());

        // Add the month label.
        Panel p = new Panel(new GridLayout(2, 1));
        Label l = new Label(monthNames[cal.get(Calendar.MONTH)], Label.CENTER);
        l.setBackground(Color.black);
        l.setForeground(Color.white);
        p.add(l);

        // Add the day of the week labels.
        Panel q = new Panel(new GridLayout(1, weekNames.length));
        for (int i=0; i<weekNames.length; i++) {
            l = new Label(weekNames[i], Label.CENTER);
            l.setBackground(Color.gray);
            q.add(l);
        }
        p.add(q);
        add(p, BorderLayout.NORTH);

        // Create a grid for the days.
        p = new Panel(new GridLayout(0, weekNames.length));

        // Get the day of the week of the first day.
        cal.set(Calendar.DAY_OF_MONTH, 1);
        int dayOfWeek = cal.get(Calendar.DAY_OF_WEEK);

        // Fill the first few cells with blanks.
        for (int i=cal.getFirstDayOfWeek(); i<dayOfWeek; i++) {
            p.add(new Label());
        }

        // Add the days.
        for (int i=cal.getMinimum(Calendar.DAY_OF_MONTH);
                i<=cal.getMaximum(Calendar.DAY_OF_MONTH); i++) {
            Calendar c = Calendar.getInstance();
            c.set(cal.get(Calendar.YEAR), cal.get(Calendar.MONTH), i);

            // Make sure we haven't skipped to the next month.
            if (c.get(Calendar.MONTH) != cal.get(Calendar.MONTH)) {
                break;
            }
            p.add(new DayCanvas(c));
```

```
        }
        add(p, BorderLayout.CENTER);
    }

    static {
        // Initialize month names.
        Calendar cal = Calendar.getInstance();
        monthNames = new String[cal.getMaximum(Calendar.MONTH) -
                                cal.getMinimum(Calendar.MONTH) + 1];

        // Roll the calendar until it uses the first month.
        while (cal.get(Calendar.MONTH) != cal.getMinimum(Calendar.MONTH)) {
            cal.roll(Calendar.MONTH, false);
        }

        // Use SimpleDateFormat to fill monthNames.
        for (int i=0; i<monthNames.length; i++) {
            SimpleDateFormat sdf = new SimpleDateFormat("MMMM");
            monthNames[i] = sdf.format(cal.getTime());
            cal.roll(Calendar.MONTH, true);
        }

        // Initialize day of week names.  The first element contains the name
        // of getFirstDayOfWeek().
        weekNames = new String[cal.getMaximum(Calendar.DAY_OF_WEEK) -
                               cal.getMinimum(Calendar.DAY_OF_WEEK) + 1];

        // Roll the calendar until it uses the first day of week.
        while (cal.get(Calendar.DAY_OF_WEEK) != cal.getFirstDayOfWeek()) {
            cal.roll(Calendar.DAY_OF_WEEK, false);
        }

        // Use SimpleDateFormat to fill weekNames.
        for (int i=0; i<weekNames.length; i++) {
            SimpleDateFormat sdf = new SimpleDateFormat("E");
            weekNames[i] = sdf.format(cal.getTime());

            // Only take the first two characters.
            if (weekNames[i].length() > 2) {
                weekNames[i] = weekNames[i].substring(0, 2);
            }
            cal.roll(Calendar.DAY_OF_WEEK, true);
        }
    }
}

class DayCanvas extends Component implements MouseListener {
    int day;
    Calendar cal;

    DayCanvas(Calendar cal) {
        this.cal = cal;
        addMouseListener(this);
    }

    public void paint(Graphics g) {
        int day = cal.get(Calendar.DAY_OF_MONTH);
        FontMetrics fm = g.getFontMetrics();

        g.setColor(Color.black);
```

```
            g.drawString("" + day,
                (getSize().width-fm.stringWidth(""+day))/2,
                (getSize().height-fm.getHeight())/2+fm.getAscent());
        }

        // Event handling methods.
        int[] fieldValues = {
            Calendar.ERA, Calendar.YEAR, Calendar.MONTH,
            Calendar.DAY_OF_MONTH, Calendar.DAY_OF_WEEK,
            Calendar.DAY_OF_WEEK_IN_MONTH, Calendar.DAY_OF_YEAR,
            Calendar.WEEK_OF_MONTH, Calendar.WEEK_OF_YEAR,
            Calendar.HOUR, Calendar.HOUR_OF_DAY, Calendar.AM_PM,
            Calendar.MILLISECOND, Calendar.MINUTE, Calendar.SECOND,
            Calendar.ZONE_OFFSET, Calendar.DST_OFFSET,};
        String[] fieldNames = {
            "ERA", "YEAR", "MONTH",
            "DAY_OF_MONTH", "DAY_OF_WEEK",
            "DAY_OF_WEEK_IN_MONTH", "DAY_OF_YEAR",
            "WEEK_OF_MONTH", "WEEK_OF_YEAR",
            "HOUR", "HOUR_OF_DAY", "AM_PM",
            "MILLISECOND", "MINUTE", "SECOND",
            "ZONE_OFFSET", "DST_OFFSET", };

        public void mousePressed(MouseEvent e) {
            System.out.println("--------------------------------");
            for (int i=0; i<Calendar.FIELD_COUNT; i++) {
                System.out.print(fieldNames[i] + "=" + cal.get(fieldValues[i]));
                System.out.println("        ("+cal.getMaximum(fieldValues[i])+")");
            }
        }
        public void mouseClicked(MouseEvent e) {}
        public void mouseReleased(MouseEvent e) {}
        public void mouseEntered(MouseEvent e) {}
        public void mouseExited(MouseEvent e) {}
    }
```

Output The following output is generated by clicking January 1 1997:

```
--------------------------------
ERA=1        (1)
YEAR=1997        (5000000)
MONTH=0        (11)
DAY_OF_MONTH=1        (31)
DAY_OF_WEEK=4        (7)
DAY_OF_WEEK_IN_MONTH=1        (6)
DAY_OF_YEAR=1        (366)
WEEK_OF_MONTH=1        (6)
WEEK_OF_YEAR=1        (54)
HOUR=3        (12)
HOUR_OF_DAY=3        (23)
AM_PM=0        (1)
MILLISECOND=550        (999)
MINUTE=33        (59)
SECOND=44        (59)
ZONE_OFFSET=-28800000        (43200000)
DST_OFFSET=0        (3600000)
```

add()

PURPOSE Increments/decrements a calendar field.

SYNTAX `abstract public void add(int fld, int amount)`

DESCRIPTION This method increments the calendar field `fld` by `amount`. Modifying the calendar field can also affect other calendar fields. For example, if the current date is January 31 and the `DATE` field is incremented by `1`, the month is changed to February.

The leniency of this `Calendar` object has no effect on this method. `fld` cannot be either `DST_OFFSET` or `ZONE_OFFSET`.

PARAMETERS

`amount` The amount of date or time to be added to the field.

`fld` One of the valid calendar field constants.

EXCEPTIONS

`IllegalArgumentException`

If `fld` is either `DST_OFFSET` or `ZONE_OFFSET`.

SEE ALSO `roll()`.

EXAMPLE

```
import java.text.*;
import java.util.*;

class Main {
    public static void main(String[] args) {
        Calendar cal = Calendar.getInstance();
        DateFormat df = DateFormat.getInstance();

        System.out.println(df.format(cal.getTime()));       // 6/2/97 9:35 AM
        cal.add(Calendar.MONTH, 12);
        System.out.println(df.format(cal.getTime()));       // 6/2/98 9:35 AM
        cal.add(Calendar.DATE, 40);
        System.out.println(df.format(cal.getTime()));       // 7/12/98 9:35 AM
        cal.add(Calendar.HOUR, -12);
        System.out.println(df.format(cal.getTime()));       // 7/11/98 9:35 PM

        //cal.add(Calendar.DST_OFFSET, 1);                  // IllegalArgumentEx
        //cal.add(Calendar.ZONE_OFFSET, 1);                 // IllegalArgumentEx
    }
}
```

after()

PURPOSE Determines if the time of this `Calendar` object is later than another time.

SYNTAX `abstract public boolean after(Object cal)`

DESCRIPTION This method returns `true` if `cal` is an instance of this `Calendar` object and `getTimeInMillis() > cal.getTimeInMillis()`. Note that the comparison is independent of the time zone.

As needed, this method recomputes the time fields of this `Calendar` object and `cal` using their calendar fields before doing the comparison.

PARAMETERS

`cal` A possibly `null` object.

RETURNS `true` if this `Calendar` object's time is later than `cal`'s time.

EXCEPTIONS

`IllegalArgumentException`

If there is insufficient information to recompute the calendar fields of this `Calendar` object and `cal`.

SEE ALSO `before()`.

EXAMPLE

```
Calendar cal1 = Calendar.getInstance();
Calendar cal2 = Calendar.getInstance(TimeZone.getTimeZone("GMT"));

// Make sure both calendars have identical times.
Date date = new Date();
cal1.setTime(date);
cal2.setTime(date);

// Demonstrates that calendar times are independent to the time zone.
System.out.println(cal1.after(cal2));        // false
System.out.println(cal2.after(cal1));        // false

cal2.set(1000, Calendar.JANUARY, 1);
System.out.println(cal1.after(cal2));        // true

cal2.set(3000, Calendar.JANUARY, 1);
System.out.println(cal1.after(cal2));        // false
```

AM

PURPOSE Calendar field value representing A.M. in a 12-hour clock.

SYNTAX `public final static int AM`

DESCRIPTION This constant (value `0`) represents A.M. in a 12-hour clock. Midnight is A.M., and noon is P.M.

EXAMPLE See `AM_PM`.

AM_PM

PURPOSE Calendar constant specifying the A.M./P.M. field.

SYNTAX `public final static int AM_PM`

DESCRIPTION This constant is used in a call to `get()` or `set()` to retrieve or set the A.M./P.M. of a `Calendar` object. There are only two possible values for this field: `AM` (`0`) and `PM` (1).

Midnight is A.M., and noon is P.M.

SEE ALSO `AM, get(), PM, set().`

EXAMPLE

```
import java.util.*;

class Main {
    public static void main(String[] args) {
        Calendar cal = Calendar.getInstance();
        cal.setTimeZone(TimeZone.getTimeZone("GMT"));

        // Is midnight am or pm?
        cal.setTime(new Date(0));
        System.out.println(cal.get(Calendar.AM_PM));     // 0          <AM>

        // A millisecond before midnight?
        cal.setTime(new Date(-1));
        System.out.println(cal.get(Calendar.AM_PM));     // 1          <PM>

        // How about noon?
        cal.setTime(new Date(12*60*60*1000));
        System.out.println(cal.get(Calendar.AM_PM));     // 1          <PM>

        // Add 12 hours to the current time.
        cal = Calendar.getInstance();
        System.out.println(cal.get(Calendar.AM_PM));     // 0          <AM>
        cal.add(Calendar.HOUR, 12);
        System.out.println(cal.get(Calendar.AM_PM));     // 1          <PM>
    }
}
```

areFieldsSet

PURPOSE Indicates whether any fields have been cleared.

SYNTAX `protected boolean areFieldsSet`

DESCRIPTION If all calendar fields are set, this flag is `true`. If some calendar field is cleared (see `clear()`), it is `false`.

before()

PURPOSE Determines if the time of this `Calendar` object is before another time.

SYNTAX `abstract public boolean before(Object cal)`

DESCRIPTION This method returns `true` if `cal` is an instance of this `Calendar` object and `getTimeInMillis()` < `cal.getTimeInMillis()`. Note that the comparison is independent of the time zone.

As needed, this method recomputes the time fields of this `Calendar` object and `cal` using their calendar fields before doing the comparison.

PARAMETERS

`cal` A possibly `null` object.

RETURNS `true` if this `Calendar` object's time is earlier than `cal`'s time.

EXCEPTIONS

`IllegalArgumentException`

If there is insufficient information to recompute the calendar fields of this `Calendar` object and `cal`.

SEE ALSO `after()`.

EXAMPLE

```
Calendar cal1 = Calendar.getInstance();
Calendar cal2 = Calendar.getInstance(TimeZone.getTimeZone("GMT"));

// Make sure both calendars have identical times.
Date date = new Date();
cal1.setTime(date);
cal2.setTime(date);

// Demonstrates that calendar times are independent to the time zone.
System.out.println(cal1.before(cal2));          // false
System.out.println(cal2.before(cal1));          // false

cal2.set(1000, Calendar.JANUARY, 1);
System.out.println(cal1.before(cal2));          // false

cal2.set(3000, Calendar.JANUARY, 1);
System.out.println(cal1.before(cal2));          // true
```

Calendar()

PURPOSE Used by a subclass to construct a `Calendar` instance.

SYNTAX
```
protected Calendar()
protected Calendar(TimeZone tz, Locale loc)
```

DESCRIPTION This constructor is used by the constructors in Calendar subclasses to initialize the calendar's time zone to tz and locale to loc. If tz and loc are not specified, it defaults to TimeZone.getDefault() and Locale.getDefault(), respectively. The time zone affects the values of the calendar fields. For example, if one Calendar object was created with GMT and another with ECT, the calendar fields of the ECT Calendar object would all be 1 hour later.

The locale affects various calendar properties such as the first day-of-week (see getFirstDayOfWeek()) and the minimal days in the first week-of-the-year (see getMinimalDaysInFirstWeek()).

To create a Calendar instance, use getInstance().

PARAMETERS

tz A non-null TimeZone object.

loc A non-null Locale object.

SEE ALSO getInstance(), Locale.getDefault(), TimeZone.getDefault().

clear()

PURPOSE Clears the values of time fields.

SYNTAX

```
public final void clear()
public final void clear(int fld)
```

DESCRIPTION This method clears the calendar field fld. Hence, isSet[fld] will be false. The new value of the calendar field fld is 0 (that is, fields[fld] = 0).

This method is normally used to force the Calendar object to recompute its Date value when a calendar field has been modified. When certain calendar fields are modified, the Calendar object does not recompute the Date value; this is done for efficiency reasons. By clearing particular fields, you can cause the Calendar object to recompute the Date value. See set() for details.

If fld is not specified, this method clears all of the calendar fields.

This method also sets areFieldsSet to false.

PARAMETERS

fld One of the valid calendar field constants.

SEE ALSO areFieldsSet, fields, set().

EXAMPLE This example demonstrates that setting certain calendar fields in a Calendar object does not trigger a recomputation of the date. In the example, modifying DAY_OF_YEAR has no effect. To force the Calendar object to recompute the date, you would have to clear the month field.

```
import java.text.*;
import java.util.*;

class Main {
    static void printDate(Calendar cal) {
        System.out.println(new SimpleDateFormat("yyyy/M/dd").format(
            cal.getTime()));
    }

    public static void main(String[] args) {
        Calendar cal = Calendar.getInstance();

        cal.clear();
        cal.set(Calendar.YEAR, 1997);
        // printDate(cal);                              // IllegalArgumentEx
        cal.set(Calendar.MONTH, Calendar.DECEMBER);
        // printDate(cal);                              // IllegalArgumentEx
        cal.set(Calendar.DATE, 25);
        printDate(cal);                                 // 1997/12/25

        // This sequence does not produce the correct date.
        cal = Calendar.getInstance();
        cal.set(Calendar.DAY_OF_YEAR, 100);
        printDate(cal);                                 // 1997/10/29

        // This prints the correct date.
        cal.clear(Calendar.MONTH);
        cal.set(Calendar.DAY_OF_YEAR, 100);
        printDate(cal);                                 // 1997/4/09
    }
}
```

clone()

PURPOSE Creates a clone of this `Calendar` object.

SYNTAX `public Object clone()`

DESCRIPTION This method creates a clone of this `Calendar` object. The property values of the returned clone are identical to this object. The values of the calendar fields and `isSet` fields are also copied to the clone.

RETURNS A non-`null` `GregorianCalendar` object.

SEE ALSO `fields`, `isSet`.

EXAMPLE See `GregorianCalendar.equals()`.

complete()

PURPOSE Computes either the `Date` value or the calendar fields.

SYNTAX `protected void complete()`

DESCRIPTION This method is called by `get()` in case the `Date` value or calendar fields need to be recomputed. The default implementation does the following:

```
if (!isTimeSet)
    computeTime();
if (!areFieldsSet)
    computeFields();
```

SEE ALSO `areFieldsSet, get(), isTimeSet.`

A B C D E F G H I J K L M N O P Q R S T U V W X Y Z

computeFields()

PURPOSE Computes the values for the calendar fields from this `Calendar` object's `Date` value.

SYNTAX `protected abstract void computeFields()`

DESCRIPTION If `areFieldsSet` is `false`, an override of this method should use the `Date` value in the time field to initialize the array `fields`. If successful, this method must set `areFieldsSet` and all elements of the array `isSet` to `true`.

If `areFieldsSet` and `isTimeSet` are both `false`, the override should throw an `IllegalArgumentException`.

SEE ALSO `areFieldsSet, fields, isSet, isTimeSet.`

computeTime()

PURPOSE Converts the calendar fields into a `Date` value.

SYNTAX `protected abstract void computeTime()`

DESCRIPTION If `isTimeSet` is `false`, an override of this method should convert the values in `fields` into a `Date` value and set the field `time` with this value. The `Date` value is the number of milliseconds from epoch (January 1, 1970 00:00:00 UTC). See the `Date` class for details on this value.

Not all of the values in `fields` need to be set. Which fields are used in the computation is calendar-specific.

If the calendar is not lenient, this method should also ensure that the calendar fields are consistent. In particular, if the value of a calendar field set by calling `set()` is not within the bounds of the calendar field, an `IllegalArgument-Exception` should be thrown. For example, if the override discovered that the `MONTH` field was set to `100`, it should throw the exception.

If successful, this method must set `isTimeSet` to `true`.

EXCEPTIONS
`IllegalArgumentException`
If insufficient calendar fields were set to determine a `Date` value.

SEE ALSO `fields`, `isLenient()`, `isTimeSet`, `time`.

DATE

PURPOSE Specifies the date calendar field.

SYNTAX `public final static int DATE`

DESCRIPTION This constant is used in a call to `get()` or `set()` to retrieve or set the day-of-month of a `Calendar` object. There are at most 31 days in a month. The values returned by `get()` or set using `set()` must be in the (inclusive) range `1` to `31`.

This constant is identical to `DAY_OF_MONTH`.

SEE ALSO `DAY_OF_MONTH`, `get()`, `set()`.

EXAMPLE See the class example.

DAY_OF_MONTH

PURPOSE Specifies the day-of-month calendar field.

SYNTAX `public final static int DAY_OF_MONTH`

DESCRIPTION This constant is used in a call to `get()` or `set()` to retrieve or set the day-of-month of a `Calendar` object. In the Gregorian calendar, there are at most 31 days in a month.

If this `Calendar` object is not lenient (see `isLenient()`), the day-of-month field can be set only with values between `1` and the last day of the current month. For example, setting a day-of-month value of `30` for the month of February results in an `IllegalArgumentException`.

If this `Calendar` object is lenient, the day-of-month field can be set to any integer value. However, setting values to less than `1` or greater than the number of days in the current month will affect the month field. For example, suppose the day-of-month is set to *D*. The simplest way to understand the effect is to assume that the current day-of-month is `1` and that *D — 1* days are added to `1`. Therefore, if the current month is January then setting day-of-month to `32` causes the month to become February and the day-of-month to be `1`. On the other hand, if day-of-month was set to `0`, the month changes to December and the day-of-month becomes `31`.

SEE ALSO `get()`, `isLenient()`, `set()`.

EXAMPLE See the class example.

DAY_OF_WEEK

PURPOSE Specifies the day-of-week calendar field.

SYNTAX `public final static int DAY_OF_WEEK`

DESCRIPTION This constant is used in a call to `get()` or `set()` to retrieve or set the day-of-week for a `Calendar` object. The possible values returned by `get()` and set using `set()` are `SUNDAY` (1), `MONDAY` (2), `TUESDAY` (3), `WEDNESDAY` (4), `THURSDAY` (5), `FRIDAY` (6), or `SATURDAY` (7).

SEE ALSO `get()`, `set()`.

EXAMPLE See the class example.

DAY_OF_WEEK_IN_MONTH

PURPOSE Specifies the day-of-week-in-month calendar field.

SYNTAX `public final static int DAY_OF_WEEK_IN_MONTH`

DESCRIPTION The day-of-week-in-month is the *n*th time the current day-of-week has occurred in the current month. For example, if the day-of-week is `MONDAY` and is the second Monday of the month, the day-of-week-in-month is `2`. This constant is used in a call to `get()` or `set()` to retrieve or set the day-of-week-in-month field for a `Calendar` object.

If the day-of-week-in-month calendar field is set to a negative value, it means "the last *n*th week of the day-of-week." For example, if the day-of-week is Sunday and the month is January, then the setting of day-of-week-in-month to `-2` means the second to last Sunday in January.

SEE ALSO `get()`, `set()`.

EXAMPLE

```
import java.util.*;
import java.text.*;

class Main {
    // Prints the date of the n'th dayOfWeek in month, year.
    static void printDate(int n, int dayOfWeek, int month, int year) {
        DateFormat formatter = new SimpleDateFormat("MMM dd yyyy");
        Calendar cal = Calendar.getInstance();

        cal.clear();
```

```
            cal.set(Calendar.DAY_OF_WEEK_IN_MONTH, n);
            cal.set(Calendar.DAY_OF_WEEK, dayOfWeek);
            cal.set(Calendar.MONTH, month);
            cal.set(Calendar.YEAR, year);
            System.out.println(formatter.format(cal.getTime()));
        }

        public static void main(String[] args) {
            // 1st Sunday of Jan 1997
            printDate(1, Calendar.SUNDAY, Calendar.JANUARY, 1997);    // Jan 05 1997
            // 4th Sunday of Jan 1997
            printDate(4, Calendar.SUNDAY, Calendar.JANUARY, 1997);    // Jan 26 1997
            // 9th Sunday of Jan 1997
            printDate(8, Calendar.SUNDAY, Calendar.JANUARY, 1997);    // Feb 23 1997

            // last Sunday of Jan 1997
            printDate(-1, Calendar.SUNDAY, Calendar.JANUARY, 1997);   // Jan 26 1997
            // 4th to last Sunday of Jan 1997
            printDate(-4, Calendar.SUNDAY, Calendar.JANUARY, 1997);   // Jan 05 1997
            // 8th to last Sunday of Jan 1997
            printDate(-8, Calendar.SUNDAY, Calendar.JANUARY, 1997);   // Dec 08 1996
        }
    }
```

DAY_OF_YEAR

PURPOSE Specifies the day-of-year calendar field.

SYNTAX `public final static int DAY_OF_YEAR`

DESCRIPTION This constant is used in a call to `get()` or `set()` to retrieve or set the day-of-year of a `Calendar` object. In the Gregorian calendar, there are at most `366` days in a year.

SEE ALSO `DATE`, `get()`, `set()`.

EXAMPLE See the class example.

DST_OFFSET

PURPOSE Specifies the daylight-savings-time calendar field.

SYNTAX `public final static int DST_OFFSET`

DESCRIPTION If the current date is not daylight savings time, the `DST_OFFSET` calendar field is `0`. Otherwise, the calendar field contains the number of milliseconds of the daylight savings time shift. For example, if the current date is in daylight savings time and the time shift is 1 day, then the `DST_OFFSET` is `24*60*60*1000` milliseconds.

Note: In Java 1.1.4 version of the `GregorianCalendar`, there are many bugs involving the use of this field. In particular, the computations used in determining the calendar fields from the internal `Date` value ignore this calendar field and instead determine the `DST_OFFSET` from the `TimeZone` object returned by `getTimeZone()`. To work around these bugs, instead of setting this calendar field, create a `TimeZone` object that has the desired values and then call `setTimeZone()` with it.

SEE ALSO `DST_OFFSET`, `get()`, `getTimeZone()`, `set()`, `setTimeZone()`.

A B C D E F G H I J K L M N O P Q R S T U V W X Y Z

equals()

PURPOSE Determines if this `Calendar` object is equal to another object.

SYNTAX `abstract public boolean equals(Object obj)`

DESCRIPTION This method should return `true` if `obj` is a `Calendar` object whose class is an instance of this class and its properties are identical.

PARAMETERS
`obj` A possibly `null` object.

RETURNS `true` if `obj` is a `Calendar` object and has properties that are identical to this; `false` otherwise.

EXAMPLE See `GregorianCalendar.equals()`.

ERA

PURPOSE Specifies the era calendar field.

SYNTAX `public final static int ERA`

DESCRIPTION This constant is used in a call to `get()` or `set()` to retrieve or set the era of a `Calendar` object. In the Gregorian calendar, only two values are possible: `GregorianCalendar.BC` (`0`) and `GregorianCalendar.AD` (`1`).

The effect of setting a negative year depends on the value of the era calendar field. See `YEAR` for details.

SEE ALSO `get()`, `set()`, `YEAR`.

EXAMPLE

```
import java.text.*;
import java.util.*;

class Main {
    static void printDate(Calendar cal) {
```

```
        System.out.println(new SimpleDateFormat("yyyy/M/dd EE G").format(
            cal.getTime()));
    }

    public static void main(String[] args) {
        Calendar cal = Calendar.getInstance();
        printDate(cal);                              // 1997/6/03 Tue AD

        // Change the era.
        cal.set(Calendar.ERA, GregorianCalendar.BC);
        printDate(cal);                              // 1997/6/03 Mon BC

        cal.set(Calendar.YEAR, 0);
        printDate(cal);                              // 0001/6/03 Fri AD

        cal.set(Calendar.YEAR, -1000);
        printDate(cal);                              // 1001/6/03 Tue AD

        cal.set(Calendar.YEAR, 1000);
        printDate(cal);                              // 1000/6/03 Mon BC
    }
}
```

FIELD_COUNT

PURPOSE Specifies the number of calendar fields.

SYNTAX `public final static int FIELD_COUNT`

DESCRIPTION This constant (value 17) specifies the number of calendar fields. It is typically useful only to the subclasses of this class.

EXAMPLE See the class example.

fields

PURPOSE Holds the calendar field values.

SYNTAX `protected int[] fields`

DESCRIPTION This array is used to hold each of the calendar field values. If `isSet[fld]` is `false`, `fields[fld]` does not contain a valid value and should be recomputed using `computeFields()`. The size of this array is exactly `FIELD_COUNT`.

SEE ALSO `computeFields()`.

get()

PURPOSE Retrieves the value of a calendar field.

SYNTAX `public final int get(int fld)`

DESCRIPTION This method retrieves the value of the calendar field `fld`. The field is recomputed if necessary. See `set()` for details on how calendar fields are recomputed.

The default implementation of this method is

```
complete();
return fields[field];
```

PARAMETERS

`fld` One of the valid calendar field constants.

RETURNS The value for the calendar field `fld`.

EXCEPTIONS

`IllegalArgumentException`
If there is insufficient information to recompute the calendar field.

SEE ALSO `complete()`, `fields`, `set()`.

EXAMPLE This example is a simple demonstration of retrieving a calendar field. It demonstrates that if there is an insufficient date to recompute the field, `IllegalArgumentException` is thrown. See the class example for a more elaborate example.

```
import java.util.*;

class Main {
    public static void main(String[] args) {
        Calendar cal = Calendar.getInstance();

        System.out.println(cal.get(Calendar.YEAR));     // 1997

        cal.clear();
        cal.set(Calendar.YEAR, 2000);
        // Not enough information in cal to resolve to a date.
        // System.out.println(cal.get(Calendar.DATE));  // IllegalArgumentEx
    }
}
```

getAvailableLocales()

PURPOSE Retrieves the set of locales in which the current date can be printed.

SYNTAX `public static synchronized Locale[] getAvailableLocales()`

DESCRIPTION

This method returns the available locales in which the current date can be printed. The default implementation of this method returns `DateFormat.getAvailableLocales()`.

Use the `DateFormat` class to print the dates in the available locales.

RETURNS

The non-`null` set of locales in which the current date can be printed.

SEE ALSO

`java.text.DateFormat`.

EXAMPLE

This example retrieves the available locales and displays the current date in each of the locales. `Main.java` contains writes the dates into a file, while `UnicodeViewer.java` reads the dates from a file and displays them. See Figure 19.

Main.java

```
import java.io.*;
import java.text.*;
import java.util.*;

class Main {
    public static void main(String[] args) {
        if (args.length != 1) {
            System.err.println("Usage: java Main <outputfile>");
            System.exit(1);
        }

        Locale[] locs = Calendar.getAvailableLocales();
        Date date = new Date();
        try {
            BufferedWriter wr = new BufferedWriter(new OutputStreamWriter(
                new FileOutputStream(args[0]), "UTF8"));

            for (int i=0; i<locs.length; i++) {
                DateFormat df = DateFormat.getDateTimeInstance(
                        DateFormat.FULL, DateFormat.FULL, locs[i]);
                wr.write(locs[i] + ": " + df.format(date));
                wr.newLine();
            }
            wr.close();
        } catch (IOException e) {
            e.printStackTrace();
            System.exit(1);
        }
    }
}
```

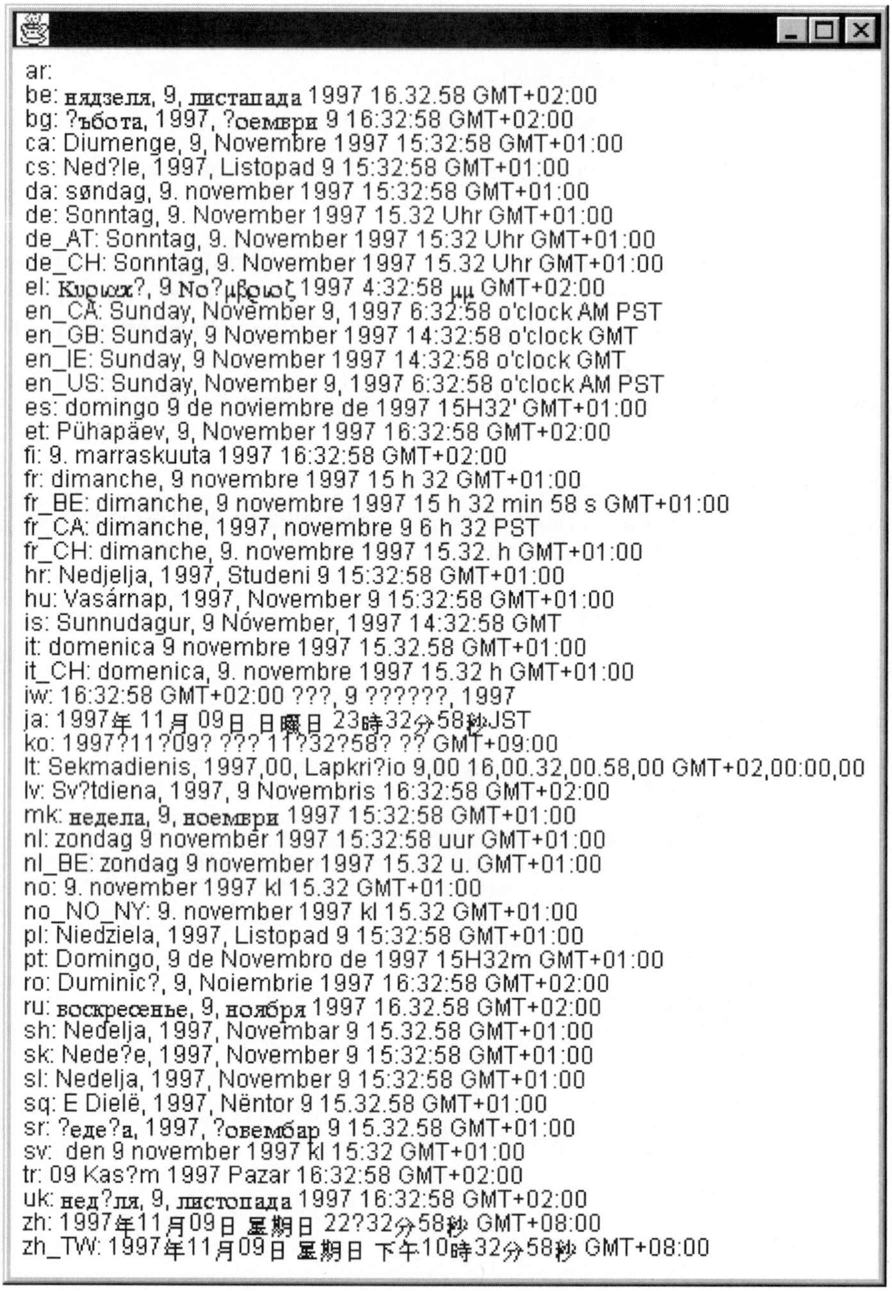

```
ar:
be: нядзеля, 9, лістапада 1997 16.32.58 GMT+02:00
bg: ?ъбота, 1997, ?оември 9 16:32:58 GMT+02:00
ca: Diumenge, 9, Novembre 1997 15:32:58 GMT+01:00
cs: Ned?le, 1997, Listopad 9 15:32:58 GMT+01:00
da: søndag, 9. november 1997 15:32:58 GMT+01:00
de: Sonntag, 9. November 1997 15.32 Uhr GMT+01:00
de_AT: Sonntag, 9. November 1997 15:32 Uhr GMT+01:00
de_CH: Sonntag, 9. November 1997 15.32 Uhr GMT+01:00
el: Κυριακ?, 9 Νο?μβριος 1997 4:32:58 μμ GMT+02:00
en_CA: Sunday, November 9, 1997 6:32:58 o'clock AM PST
en_GB: Sunday, 9 November 1997 14:32:58 o'clock GMT
en_IE: Sunday, 9 November 1997 14:32:58 o'clock GMT
en_US: Sunday, November 9, 1997 6:32:58 o'clock AM PST
es: domingo 9 de noviembre de 1997 15H32' GMT+01:00
et: Pühapäev, 9, November 1997 16:32:58 GMT+02:00
fi: 9. marraskuuta 1997 16:32:58 GMT+02:00
fr: dimanche, 9 novembre 1997 15 h 32 GMT+01:00
fr_BE: dimanche, 9 novembre 1997 15 h 32 min 58 s GMT+01:00
fr_CA: dimanche, 1997, novembre 9 6 h 32 PST
fr_CH: dimanche, 9. novembre 1997 15.32. h GMT+01:00
hr: Nedjelja, 1997, Studeni 9 15:32:58 GMT+01:00
hu: Vasárnap, 1997, November 9 15:32:58 GMT+01:00
is: Sunnudagur, 9 Nóvember, 1997 14:32:58 GMT
it: domenica 9 novembre 1997 15.32.58 GMT+01:00
it_CH: domenica, 9. novembre 1997 15.32 h GMT+01:00
iw: 16:32:58 GMT+02:00 ???, 9 ??????, 1997
ja: 1997年 11月 09日 日曜日 23時32分58秒JST
ko: 1997?11?09? ??? 11?32?58? ?? GMT+09:00
lt: Sekmadienis, 1997,00, Lapkri?io 9,00 16,00.32,00.58,00 GMT+02,00:00,00
lv: Sv?tdiena, 1997, 9 Novembris 16:32:58 GMT+02:00
mk: недела, 9, ноември 1997 15:32:58 GMT+01:00
nl: zondag 9 november 1997 15:32:58 uur GMT+01:00
nl_BE: zondag 9 november 1997 15.32 u. GMT+01:00
no: 9. november 1997 kl 15.32 GMT+01:00
no_NO_NY: 9. november 1997 kl 15.32 GMT+01:00
pl: Niedziela, 1997, Listopad 9 15:32:58 GMT+01:00
pt: Domingo, 9 de Novembro de 1997 15H32m GMT+01:00
ro: Duminic?, 9, Noiembrie 1997 16:32:58 GMT+02:00
ru: воскресенье, 9, ноября 1997 16.32.58 GMT+02:00
sh: Nedelja, 1997, Novembar 9 15.32.58 GMT+01:00
sk: Nede?e, 1997, November 9 15:32:58 GMT+01:00
sl: Nedelja, 1997, November 9 15:32:58 GMT+01:00
sq: E Dielë, 1997, Nëntor 9 15.32.58 GMT+01:00
sr: ?еде?а, 1997, ?овембар 9 15.32.58 GMT+01:00
sv:  den 9 november 1997 kl 15:32 GMT+01:00
tr: 09 Kas?m 1997 Pazar 16:32:58 GMT+02:00
uk: нед?ля, 9, листопада 1997 16:32:58 GMT+02:00
zh: 1997年11月09日 星期日 22?32分58秒 GMT+08:00
zh_TW: 1997年11月09日 星期日 下午10時32分58秒 GMT+08:00
```

FIGURE 19: `UnicodeViewer.`

A B C D E F G H I J K L M N O P Q R S T U V W X Y Z

UnicodeViewer.java

```
import java.awt.*;
import java.io.*;
import java.util.*;

class UnicodeViewer extends Frame {
    UnicodeViewer(Vector lines) {
        add(BorderLayout.CENTER, new TextCanvas(lines));

        setSize(400, 400);
        show();
    }

    public static void main(String[] args) {
        if (args.length != 1) {
            System.err.println("Usage: java Main <inputfile>");
            System.exit(1);
        }
        try {
            // Read in the entire contents of the file.
            BufferedReader rd = new BufferedReader(
                new InputStreamReader(new FileInputStream(args[0]), "UTF8"));
            String line;
            Vector lines = new Vector();

            while ((line = rd.readLine()) != null) {
                    lines.addElement(line);
            }

            rd.close();
            new UnicodeViewer(lines);
        } catch (Exception e) {
            e.printStackTrace();
        }
    }
}

class TextCanvas extends Component {
    FontMetrics fontM;
    Font font = new Font("Monospaced", Font.PLAIN, 10);
    Vector lines;
    TextCanvas(Vector lines) {
        this.lines = lines;
    }

    public void paint(Graphics g) {
        if (fontM == null) {
            fontM = g.getFontMetrics(font);
        }
        setFont(font);

        int x = fontM.getHeight()/2;
        int y = fontM.getHeight()/2 + fontM.getAscent();

        for (int i=0; i<lines.size(); i++) {
            g.drawString((String)lines.elementAt(i), x, y);
            y += fontM.getHeight();
        }
    }
}
```

getFirstDayOfWeek()

PURPOSE Retrieves this Calendar object's first day-of-week.

SYNTAX `public int getFirstDayOfWeek()`

DESCRIPTION The first-day-of-week determines which weekday to display in the leftmost column of a calendar. This value is locale-dependent. For example, the first day-of-week in the United States is Sunday, while in France, it is Monday.

RETURNS One of the seven days of the week constants. It must be ≥ `Calendar.SUNDAY` and ≤ `Calendar.SATURDAY`.

SEE ALSO `setFirstDayOfWeek()`.

EXAMPLE See the class example.

getGreatestMinimum()

PURPOSE Retrieves the greatest minimum value for a calendar field.

SYNTAX `abstract public int getGreatestMinimum(int fld)`

DESCRIPTION This method returns the greatest minimum value for the calendar field `fld`.

PARAMETERS

`fld` One of the valid calendar field constants.

RETURNS The greatest minimum value for the calendar field `fld`.

SEE ALSO `getLeastMaximum()`, `getMaximum()`, `getMinimum()`.

EXAMPLE See `GregorianCalendar.getMinimum()`.

getInstance()

PURPOSE Creates a `Calendar` object.

SYNTAX

```
public static synchronized Calendar getInstance()
public static synchronized Calendar getInstance(TimeZone zone)
public static synchronized Calendar getInstance(Locale aLocale)
public static synchronized Calendar getInstance(TimeZone zone,
   Locale aLocale)
```

DESCRIPTION This class contains a `getInstance()` method that returns a `Calendar` object that best represents the current locale. In Java 1.1.4, this method returns only `GregorianCalendar` objects.

The new `Calendar` object is initialized with the current date and time.

If zone is not specified, it defaults to TimeZone.getDefault(). If aLocale is not specified, it defaults to Locale.getDefault().

PARAMETERS

aLocale — A non-null Locale object.

zone — A non-null TimeZone object.

RETURNS — A new non-null Calendar object initialized to the current date and time.

EXAMPLE — See the class example.

getLeastMaximum()

PURPOSE — Retrieves the least maximum value for a calendar field.

SYNTAX

```
abstract public int getLeastMaximum(int fld)
```

DESCRIPTION — This method returns the lowest maximum value for the calendar field fld. For example, the lowest maximum value for the DAY_OF_MONTH field in a Gregorian calendar is 28.

PARAMETERS

fld — One of the valid calendar field constants.

RETURNS — The lowest maximum value for the calendar field fld.

SEE ALSO — getGreatestMinimum(), getMaximum(), getMinimum().

EXAMPLE — See the class example.

getMaximum()

PURPOSE — Retrieves the maximum value for a calendar field.

SYNTAX

```
abstract public int getMaximum(int fld)
```

DESCRIPTION — This method returns the maximum value for the calendar field fld. For example, the maximum value for the DAY_OF_MONTH field in a Gregorian calendar is 31.

PARAMETERS

fld — One of the valid calendar field constants.

RETURNS — The maximum value for the calendar field fld.

SEE ALSO — getGreatestMinimum(), getLeastMaximum(), getMinimum().

EXAMPLE — See the class example.

getMinimalDaysInFirstWeek()

PURPOSE Retrieves the minimal number of days required in the first week of the year.

SYNTAX `public int getMinimalDaysInFirstWeek()`

DESCRIPTION This method returns the minimal number of days required in the first week of the year. For example, if the first week is defined as containing the first day of the first month of a year, this method returns `1`. If the minimal days required must be a full week, this method returns `7`.

RETURNS The minimal days required in the first week of the year.

SEE ALSO `setMinimalDaysInFirstWeek()`.

getMinimum()

PURPOSE Retrieves the minimum value for a calendar field.

SYNTAX `abstract public int getMinimum(int fld)`

DESCRIPTION This method returns the minimum value for the calendar field `fld`. For example, the minimum value for the `DAY_OF_MONTH` field in a Gregorian calendar is `1`.

PARAMETERS

`fld` One of the valid calendar field constants.

RETURNS The minimum value for the calendar field `fld`.

SEE ALSO `getGreatestMinimum()`, `getLeastMaximum()`, `getMaximum()`.

EXAMPLE See the class example.

getTime()

PURPOSE Computes this `Calendar` object's `Date` value.

SYNTAX `public final Date getTime()`

DESCRIPTION If this `Calendar`'s `Date` value is not valid (for example, a calendar field was modified), then the `Calendar` object computes a new `Date` value based on the values of the calendar fields. See `set()` for details on the computation process.

By default, this method calls `getTimeInMillis()` and returns the result in a new `Date` object.

RETURNS The non-`null` `Date` value of this `Calendar` object.

SEE ALSO `Date`, `getTimeInMillis()`, `setTime()`.

EXCEPTIONS

`IllegalArgumentException`

If insufficient calendar fields were set to determine a `Date` value.

EXAMPLE

```
Date xmas = (new GregorianCalendar(1997, Calendar.DECEMBER, 25)).getTime();
```


getTimeInMillis()

PURPOSE Computes this `Calendar` object's `Date` value and returns it as a `long`.

SYNTAX `protected long getTimeInMillis()`

DESCRIPTION If this `Calendar`'s `Date` value is not valid (for example, a calendar field was modified), then the `Calendar` object computes a new `Date` value based on the values of the calendar fields. See `set()` for details on the computation process. The new `Date` value is returned as a `long`. It is the number of milliseconds from epoch (January 1, 1970 00:00:00 UTC). See `Date` for details on this `long` value.

By default, this method is called by `getTime()` and calls `computeTime()` if `isTimeSet` is `false`.

Note: The `GregorianCalendar` class does not take into account leap seconds, so the result is not exactly UTC. See the `Date` class description for more details.

RETURNS A `long` value representing the `Date` value of this `Calendar` object.

SEE ALSO `computeTime()`, `getTime()`, `isTimeSet`, `setTimeInMillis()`.

EXCEPTIONS

`IllegalArgumentException`

If insufficient calendar fields were set to determine a `Date` value.

getTimeZone()

PURPOSE Retrieves this `Calendar` object's time zone.

SYNTAX `public TimeZone getTimeZone()`

RETURNS A non-`null` `TimeZone` object.

SEE ALSO `setTimeZone()`, `TimeZone`.

EXAMPLE

```
import java.util.*;

class Main {
    public static void main(String[] args) {
        Calendar cal = Calendar.getInstance();

        TimeZone tz = cal.getTimeZone();
        System.out.println(tz.getID());              // PST
    }
}
```

A B C D E F G H I J K L M N O P Q R S T U V W X Y Z

HOUR

PURPOSE Specifies the hour (12-hour clock) calendar field.

SYNTAX `public final static int HOUR`

DESCRIPTION This constant is used in a call to `get()` or `set()` to retrieve or set the hour of a `Calendar` object. This calendar field represents the hour of a 12-hour clock and, when used in conjunction with the `AM_PM` calendar field, indicates an hour in the day. `0` A.M. is midnight, and `0` P.M. is noon. The value returned from a call to `get()` is always in the range `0` to `11`.

If this `Calendar` object is not lenient (see `isLenient()`), the hour field can be set only with values in the range `0` to `11`. Otherwise, the hour field can be set to any integer value. However, setting values to less than `0` or greater than `23` changes the day. In particular, if the hour field is set to *H*, this `Calendar` object is increased by `Math.floor(H/24)` days. Also, the hour field is set to *H* `mod` `12`. Finally, the `AM_PM` field is set to `AM` if *H* `mod 24` < `12` and to `PM` if *H* `mod 24` ≥ `12`.

SEE ALSO `AM_PM`, `clear()`, `get()`, `HOUR_OF_DAY`, `isLenient()`, `set()`.

EXAMPLE This example shows how to set and get the hour field of a `Calendar` object. The simplest method is to use the `HOUR_OF_DAY` field. However, if it is necessary to modify the `HOUR` field, you need to clear the `HOUR_OF_DAY` field (see `clear()`).

Notice that when the hour field is set to `24`, the day of the `Calendar` object is advanced by 1 day.

```
Calendar cal = Calendar.getInstance();
SimpleDateFormat df = new SimpleDateFormat("MMM d  K a / H");

cal.set(Calendar.HOUR_OF_DAY, 0);
System.out.println(df.format(cal.getTime()));     // Nov 1  0 AM / 0
cal.set(Calendar.HOUR_OF_DAY, 13);
System.out.println(df.format(cal.getTime()));     // Nov 1  1 PM / 13
cal.set(Calendar.HOUR_OF_DAY, 24);
System.out.println(df.format(cal.getTime()));     // Nov 2  0 AM / 0
```

```
cal.set(Calendar.HOUR_OF_DAY, -1);
System.out.println(df.format(cal.getTime()));     // Oct 31  11 PM / 23

// The hour can be set using the HOUR calendar field.
cal.set(Calendar.HOUR, 13);
cal.clear(Calendar.HOUR_OF_DAY);
System.out.println(df.format(cal.getTime()));     // Nov 2  1 AM / 13
```


HOUR_OF_DAY

PURPOSE Specifies the hour-of-day (24-hour clock) calendar field.

SYNTAX `public final static int HOUR_OF_DAY`

DESCRIPTION This constant is used in a call to `get()` or `set()` to retrieve or set the hour-of-day of a `Calendar` object. This calendar field represents an hour of a 24-hour clock. The value returned from a call to `get()` is always in the range `0` to `23`.

If this `Calendar` object is not lenient (see `isLenient()`), the hour-of-day field can be set only with values in the range `0` to `23`. Otherwise, the hour-of-day field can be set to any integer value. However, setting values to less than `0` or greater than `23` changes the day. In particular, if the hour field is set to *H*, this `Calendar` object is increased by `Math.floor(H/24)` days. Also, the hour field is set to *H* `mod 24`.

SEE ALSO `AM_PM`, `clear()`, `get()`, `HOUR`, `isLenient()`, `set()`.

EXAMPLE See `HOUR`.

internalGet()

PURPOSE Retrieves the current value of a calendar field.

SYNTAX `protected final int internalGet(int fld)`

DESCRIPTION This method simply returns `fields[fld]`. It does not care if the calendar field is clear (see `clear()`) or if the calendar field needs to be recomputed.

PARAMETERS

`fld` One of the valid calendar field constants.

RETURNS The value for the calendar field `fld`.

SEE ALSO `clear()`, `fields`, `get()`.

A B C D E F G H I J K L M N O P Q R S T U V W X Y Z

isLenient()

PURPOSE Determines if this `Calendar` object is lenient.

SYNTAX `public boolean isLenient()`

DESCRIPTION A calendar that is not lenient does not allow you to set a calendar field that is outside of that field's normal range. See the class description for more information.

RETURNS `true` if this `Calendar` object is lenient; `false` otherwise.

SEE ALSO `setLenient()`.

EXAMPLE See `setLenient()`.

isSet()

PURPOSE Determines if a calendar field has been set.

SYNTAX `public final boolean isSet(int fld)`

DESCRIPTION This method simply returns `isSet[fld]`.

PARAMETERS
`fld` One of the valid calendar field constants.

RETURNS `isSet[fld]`.

SEE ALSO `isSet, set()`.

isSet

PURPOSE Holds the set state of each calendar field.

SYNTAX `protected boolean[] isSet`

DESCRIPTION This array is used to record the set state (see `clear()`) of a field. If `isSet[fld]` is `false`, the calendar field `fld` is cleared. The size of this array is exactly `FIELD_COUNT`.

SEE ALSO `isSet()`.

isTimeSet

PURPOSE Indicates if the time field is valid.

SYNTAX `protected boolean isTimeSet`

DESCRIPTION If `true`, the time field is valid. Otherwise, the time field can be made `true` by calling `computeTime()`.

SEE ALSO `computeTime()`, `time`.

MILLISECOND

PURPOSE Specifies the millisecond calendar field.

SYNTAX `public final static int MILLISECOND`

DESCRIPTION This constant is used in a call to `get()` or `set()` to retrieve or set the millisecond of a `Calendar` object. The value returned from a call to `get()` is always in the range `0` to `999`.

If this `Calendar` object is not lenient (see `isLenient()`), the millisecond field can be set only with values in the range `0` to `999`. Otherwise, the millisecond field can be set to any integer value. However, setting values to less than `0` or greater than `999` changes the second calendar field. In particular, if the millisecond field is set to *S*, this `Calendar` object is increased by `Math.floor(S/1000)` seconds. Also, the millisecond field is set to *S* `mod 1000`.

SEE ALSO `AM_PM`, `clear()`, `get()`, `SECOND`, `isLenient()`, `set()`.

EXAMPLE This example shows how to set and get the millisecond field of a `Calendar` object. Notice that when the millisecond field is set to `1000`, the second field of the `Calendar` object is advanced by 1 second. Also, when the millisecond field is set to `-1`, the second field is decreased by 1 second.

```
Calendar cal = Calendar.getInstance();
SimpleDateFormat df = new SimpleDateFormat("mm:ss:SSS");

cal.set(Calendar.MILLISECOND, 12);
System.out.println(df.format(cal.getTime()));      // 25:54:012
cal.set(Calendar.MILLISECOND, 1000);
System.out.println(df.format(cal.getTime()));      // 25:55:000
cal.set(Calendar.MILLISECOND, -1);
System.out.println(df.format(cal.getTime()));      // 25:53:999
```

MINUTE

PURPOSE Specifies the minute calendar field.

SYNTAX `public final static int MINUTE`

DESCRIPTION This constant is used in a call to get() or set() to retrieve or set the minute of a Calendar object. The value returned from a call to get() is always in the range 0 to 59.

If this Calendar object is not lenient (see isLenient()), the minute field can be set only with values in the range 0 to 59. Otherwise, the minute field can be set to any integer value. However, setting values to less than 0 or greater than 59 changes the hour field. In particular, if the minute field is set to *M*, this Calendar object is increased by Math.floor(M/60) hours. Also, the minute field is set to *S* mod 60.

SEE ALSO AM_PM, clear(), get(), HOUR, isLenient(), set().

EXAMPLE This example shows how to set and get the minute field of a Calendar object. Notice that when the minute field is set to 1000, the hour field of the Calendar object is advanced by 1 hour. Also, when the minute field is set to -1, the hour field is decreased by 1 hour.

```
Calendar cal = Calendar.getInstance();
DateFormat df = DateFormat.getInstance();

cal.set(Calendar.MINUTE, 12);
System.out.println(df.format(cal.getTime()));     // 11/1/97 7:12 PM
cal.set(Calendar.MINUTE, 60);
System.out.println(df.format(cal.getTime()));     // 11/1/97 8:00 PM
cal.set(Calendar.MINUTE, -1);
System.out.println(df.format(cal.getTime()));     // 11/1/97 6:59 PM
```

MONTH

PURPOSE Specifies the month calendar field.

SYNTAX `public final static int MONTH`

DESCRIPTION This constant is used in a call to get() or set() to retrieve or set the month of a Calendar object. In the Gregorian calendar, there are exactly 12 months in a year.

If this Calendar object is not lenient (see isLenient()), the month field can be set only with values in the range 0 and 11. Otherwise, the month field can be set to any integer value. However, setting values to less than 0 or greater than 11 changes the year. In particular, if the month is set to *M*, this Calendar object is increased by Math.floor(M/12) years. Also, the month field is set to *M* mod 12.

SEE ALSO isLenient(), get(), set().

EXAMPLE This example implements a utility for determining the number of days in a particular month in a particular year.

```
import java.util.*;

class Main {
    static int daysIn(int year, int month) {
        Calendar cal = Calendar.getInstance();
        cal.set(year, month, cal.getMaximum(Calendar.DAY_OF_MONTH));

        while (cal.get(Calendar.MONTH) != month) {
            cal.add(Calendar.DAY_OF_MONTH, -1);
        }
        return cal.get(Calendar.DAY_OF_MONTH);
    }

    public static void main(String[] args) {
        System.out.println(daysIn(2000, Calendar.FEBRUARY));
        System.out.println(daysIn(2001, Calendar.FEBRUARY));

        for (int i=Calendar.JANUARY; i<=Calendar.DECEMBER; i++) {
            System.out.print(daysIn(1997, i) + " ");
        }
        System.out.println();             // 31 28 31 30 31 30 31 31 30 31 30 31
    }
}
```

PM

PURPOSE Represents P.M. in a 12-hour clock.

SYNTAX `public final static int PM`

DESCRIPTION This constant (value `0`) represents P.M. in a 12-hour clock. Midnight is A.M., and noon is P.M.

EXAMPLE See `AM_PM`.

roll()

PURPOSE Rolls a calendar field.

SYNTAX `abstract public void roll(int fld, boolean up)`

DESCRIPTION This method increments or decrements the calendar field `fld` by `1`.

If `up` is `true` and `get(fld) == getMaximum(fld)`, the calendar field is set to `getMinimum(fld)`. If `up` is `false` and `get(fld) == getMinimum(fld)`, the calendar field is set to `getMaximum(fld)`. This process is called *rolling*.

Rolling the calendar field can also affect other calendar fields. For example, if the current date is January 31 and the WEEK_OF_MONTH field is 5, rolling up the DATE field causes the WEEK_OF_MONTH field to be 1.

The leniency of this Calendar object has no effect on this method. fld cannot be either DST_OFFSET or ZONE_OFFSET.

PARAMETERS

fld One of the valid calendar field constants.

up If true, rolls the calendar field up; if false, rolls the calendar field down.

EXCEPTIONS

IllegalArgumentException
If fld is either DST_OFFSET or ZONE_OFFSET.

SEE ALSO add().

EXAMPLE

```
import java.util.*;
import java.text.*;

class Main {
    public static void main(String[] args) {
        Calendar cal = Calendar.getInstance();
        DateFormat df = DateFormat.getInstance();

        cal.set(1997, Calendar.JANUARY, 31);

        System.out.println(df.format(cal.getTime()));     // 1/31/97 9:54 AM
        cal.roll(Calendar.MONTH, false);
        System.out.println(df.format(cal.getTime()));     // 12/31/97 9:54 AM
        cal.roll(Calendar.DATE, true);
        System.out.println(df.format(cal.getTime()));     // 12/1/97 9:54 AM

        //cal.roll(Calendar.DST_OFFSET, true);            // IllegalArgumentEx
        //cal.roll(Calendar.ZONE_OFFSET, true);           // IllegalArgumentEx
    }
}
```

SECOND

PURPOSE Specifies the second calendar field.

SYNTAX `public final static int SECOND`

DESCRIPTION This constant is used in a call to get() or set() to retrieve or set the second of a Calendar object. The value returned from a call to get() is always in the range 0 to 59.

If this Calendar object is not lenient (see isLenient()), the second field can be set only with values in the range 0 to 59. Otherwise, the second field can be set to any integer value. However, setting values to less than `0` or greater than `59` changes the minute field. In particular, if the second field is set to *S*, this `Calendar` object is increased by `Math.floor(S/60)` minutes. Also, the second field is set to *S* `mod 60`.

SEE ALSO `AM_PM, clear(), get(), MINUTE, isLenient(), set().`

EXAMPLE This example shows how to set and get the second field of a `Calendar` object. Notice that when the second field is set to `60`, the minute field of the `Calendar` object is advanced by 1 minute. Also, when the second field is set to `-1`, the minute field is decreased by 1 minute.

```
Calendar cal = Calendar.getInstance();
SimpleDateFormat df = new SimpleDateFormat("HH:mm:ss");

cal.set(Calendar.SECOND, 12);
System.out.println(df.format(cal.getTime()));      // 19:39:12
cal.set(Calendar.SECOND, 60);
System.out.println(df.format(cal.getTime()));      // 19:40:00
cal.set(Calendar.SECOND, -1);
System.out.println(df.format(cal.getTime()));      // 19:38:59
```

set()

PURPOSE Sets the values for the year, month, date, hour, minute, and second fields.

SYNTAX

```
public final void set(int fld, int newValue)
public final void set(int year, int month, int date)
public final void set(int year, int month, int date, int
   hourOfDay, int minute)
public final void set(int year, int month, int date, int
   hourOfDay, int minute, int second)
```

DESCRIPTION The first form of this method sets the calendar `fld` to `newValue`. The range of `newValue` depends on whether the calendar is lenient (see the class description for details on leniency). If the calendar is not lenient, the range of `newValue` is restricted; otherwise, `newValue` can usually be any integer value. See the description for the `fld` constant for details.

The other forms of this method are convenience methods for setting a set of calendar fields. In particular, the `YEAR` field is set to the year; the `MONTH` field is set to the month; the `DATE` field is set to the date; `HOUR_OF_DAY` field is set to the `hourOfDay`; the `MINUTE` field is set to the minute; the `SECOND` field is set to the second.

It is important to note that when a calendar field is set, this may not cause the other calendar fields to be updated. For example, setting the `DAY_OF_YEAR` calendar field has no effect on the other calendar fields. This is because when a

Calendar object recomputes the date, it does so by examining the calendar fields in a particular order. If it discovers a set that is sufficient to produce a date, it stops looking at the other calendar fields. In the case of the DAY_OF_YEAR calendar field, the Calendar object first examines the YEAR, MONTH, and DATE fields. When it discovers that they are all set, it simply uses their values; it does not even examine the DAY_OF_YEAR calendar field. To force the modified DAY_OF_YEAR calendar field to take effect, you must clear the MONTH calendar field.

The following list shows the order in which the calendar fields are examined to determine the date. In any step, if one of the calendar fields is cleared (see clear()), the next set of calendar fields is examined. For example, in step one, if DAY_OF_MONTH is cleared, the conversion algorithm then goes to step two and examines the WEEK_OF_MONTH and DAY_OF_WEEK fields.

- YEAR, MONTH, DAY_OF_MONTH
- YEAR, MONTH, WEEK_OF_MONTH, DAY_OF_WEEK
- YEAR, MONTH, DAY_OF_WEEK_IN_MONTH, DAY_OF_WEEK
- YEAR, DAY_OF_YEAR
- YEAR, DAY_OF_WEEK, WEEK_OF_YEAR

The following list shows the order in which the calendar fields are examined to determine the time.

- HOUR_OF_DAY
- AM_PM, HOUR

Table 6 shows each calendar field and the steps that are needed if a calendar field is modified. The steps force the Calendar object to use the new value of the modified calendar field. Note that when a step says to set a calendar field, it is fine to leave it as the current value; it is only necessary that the mentioned field be not cleared.

Modified Calendar Field	Steps
AM_PM	Clear HOUR_OF_DAY and set HOUR.
DATE	None.
DAY_OF_MONTH	None.
DAY_OF_WEEK	Clear DAY_OF_MONTH and set WEEK_OF_MONTH (or clear MONTH and DAY_OF_YEAR and set WEEK_OF_YEAR).
DAY_OF_WEEK_IN_MONTH	Clear DAY_OF_MONTH and WEEK_OF_MONTH and set DAY_OF_WEEK.
DAY_OF_YEAR	Clear MONTH.
DST_OFFSET	None.

TABLE 6: Steps to Follow when Updating Calendar Fields.

Modified Calendar Field	Steps
ERA	None.
HOUR	Clear HOUR_OF_DAY and set AM_PM.
HOUR_OF_DAY	None.
MILLISECOND	None.
MINUTE	None.
MONTH	None.
SECOND	None.
WEEK_OF_MONTH	Clear DAY_OF_MONTH and set DAY_OF_WEEK.
WEEK_OF_YEAR	Clear MONTH and DAY_OF_YEAR and set DAY_OF_WEEK.
YEAR	None.
ZONE_OFFSET	None.

TABLE 6: Steps to Follow when Updating Calendar Fields.

PARAMETERS

`date`	The new value of the DATE field.
`fld`	The field to modify. Must be one of the valid calendar field constants.
`hourOfDay`	The new value of the HOUR_OF_DAY field.
`minute`	The new value of the MINUTE field.
`month`	The new value of the MONTH field.
`newValue`	The new value of the field `fld`.
`second`	The new value of the SECOND field.
`year`	The new value of the YEAR field.

SEE ALSO `clear()`, `get()`, `isLenient()`, `setLenient()`.

EXAMPLE This example modifies those calendar fields that require the clearing of other calendar fields in order to take effect.

```
import java.util.*;
import java.text.*;

class Main {
    public static void main(String[] args) {
        Calendar oldCal = Calendar.getInstance();
        DateFormat df = DateFormat.getInstance();

        System.out.println(df.format(oldCal.getTime()));    // 11/8/97 7:45 PM

    // Modify AM_PM
        Calendar cal = (Calendar)oldCal.clone();
        cal.set(Calendar.AM_PM, Calendar.AM);
        cal.clear(Calendar.HOUR_OF_DAY);
        System.out.println(df.format(cal.getTime()));       // 11/8/97 7:45 AM
    // Modify DAY_OF_WEEK and use WEEK_OF_MONTH
        cal = (Calendar)oldCal.clone();
```

```
            cal.set(Calendar.DAY_OF_WEEK, Calendar.SUNDAY);
            cal.clear(Calendar.DAY_OF_MONTH);
            System.out.println(df.format(cal.getTime()));         // 11/2/97 7:45 PM

        // Modify DAY_OF_WEEK and use WEEK_OF_YEAR
            cal = (Calendar)oldCal.clone();
            cal.set(Calendar.DAY_OF_WEEK, Calendar.SUNDAY);
            cal.clear(Calendar.MONTH);
            cal.clear(Calendar.DAY_OF_YEAR);
            System.out.println(df.format(cal.getTime()));         // 11/2/97 7:45 PM

        // Modify DAY_OF_WEEK_IN_MONTH
            cal = (Calendar)oldCal.clone();
            cal.set(Calendar.DAY_OF_WEEK_IN_MONTH, -1);
            cal.clear(Calendar.DAY_OF_MONTH);
            cal.clear(Calendar.WEEK_OF_MONTH);
            System.out.println(df.format(cal.getTime()));         // 11/29/97 7:45 PM

        // Modify DAY_OF_YEAR
            cal = (Calendar)oldCal.clone();
            cal.set(Calendar.DAY_OF_YEAR, 32);
            cal.clear(Calendar.MONTH);
            System.out.println(df.format(cal.getTime()));         // 2/1/97 7:45 PM

        // Modify HOUR
            cal = (Calendar)oldCal.clone();
            cal.set(Calendar.HOUR, 13);
            cal.clear(Calendar.HOUR_OF_DAY);
            System.out.println(df.format(cal.getTime()));         // 11/9/97 1:45 AM
              // Since AM_PM field is PM, the time is 1:34 am the next day.
              // If the AM_PM field were AM, the time would be 1:34 pm the same day.

        // Modify WEEK_OF_MONTH
            cal = (Calendar)oldCal.clone();
            cal.set(Calendar.WEEK_OF_MONTH, 4);
            cal.clear(Calendar.DAY_OF_MONTH);
            System.out.println(df.format(cal.getTime()));         // 11/22/97 7:45 PM

        // Modify WEEK_OF_YEAR
            cal = (Calendar)oldCal.clone();
            cal.set(Calendar.WEEK_OF_YEAR, 5);
            cal.clear(Calendar.MONTH);
            cal.clear(Calendar.DAY_OF_YEAR);
            System.out.println(df.format(cal.getTime()));         // 2/1/97 7:45 PM
        }
    }
```

setFirstDayOfWeek()

PURPOSE Sets this Calendar object's first day-of-week.

SYNTAX `public void setFirstDayOfWeek(int value)`

DESCRIPTION The first-day-of-week determines which weekday to display in the leftmost column of a calendar. This value is locale-dependent. For example, the first day of week in the United States is Sunday, while in France, it is Monday.

PARAMETERS

`value` One of the seven days of the week constants. It must be ≥ `Calendar.SUNDAY` and ≤ `Calendar.SATURDAY`.

SEE ALSO `getFirstDayOfWeek()`.

EXAMPLE See `WEEK_OF_MONTH`.

A B C D E F G H I J K L M N O P Q R S T U V W X Y Z

setLenient()

PURPOSE Sets the leniency property of this `Calendar` object.

SYNTAX `public void setLenient(boolean lenient)`

DESCRIPTION This method sets the leniency of this `Calendar` object to `lenient`. A calendar that is not lenient does not allow you to set a calendar field that is outside of that field's normal range. See the class description for more information.

PARAMETERS

`lenient` The new leniency of this `Calendar` object.

SEE ALSO `isLenient()`.

EXAMPLE

```
import java.util.*;

class Main {
    public static void main(String[] args) {
        Calendar cal = Calendar.getInstance();

        System.out.println(cal.isLenient());                // true
        cal.set(Calendar.MONTH, 100);
        System.out.println(cal.get(Calendar.MONTH));        // 4
        cal.set(Calendar.DATE, -100);
        System.out.println(cal.get(Calendar.DATE));         // 20

        cal.setLenient(false);
        cal.set(Calendar.MONTH, 100);
        //System.out.println(cal.get(Calendar.MONTH));      // IllegalArgumentEx
        cal.set(Calendar.DATE, -100);
        //System.out.println(cal.get(Calendar.DATE));       // IllegalArgumentEx
    }
}
```

setMinimalDaysInFirstWeek()

PURPOSE Sets the minimal number of days required in the first week of the year.

SYNTAX `public void setMinimalDaysInFirstWeek(int value)`

DESCRIPTION This method sets the minimal number of days required in the first week of the year. For example, if the first week is defined as containing the first day of the first month of a year, `value` should be `1`. If the minimal days required must be a full week, `value` should be `7`.

PARAMETERS

`value` The new minimal days required in the first week of the year.

SEE ALSO `getMinimalDaysInFirstWeek()`.

setTime()

PURPOSE Sets this `Calendar` object's current date and time.

SYNTAX `public final void setTime(Date date)`

DESCRIPTION This method sets this `Calendar` object's current date to `date`. This method also recomputes the time fields.

By default, this method calls `setTimeInMillis(date.getTime())`.

PARAMETERS

`date` A non-`null` `Date`.

SEE ALSO `getTime()`, `setTimeInMillis()`.

EXAMPLE This example prints the day-of-week at epoch (time `0`, which is January 1, 1970 00:00:00 UTC). It also demonstrates that time can be negative and prints the day-of-week 1 day earlier.

```
import java.util.*;
import java.text.*;

class Main {
    public static void main(String[] args) {
        Calendar cal = Calendar.getInstance();

        // We are interested in the time at GMT.
        cal.setTimeZone(TimeZone.getTimeZone("GMT"));

        // Print the date at GMT at time 0.
        cal.setTime(new Date(0));
        System.out.println(cal.get(Calendar.DAY_OF_WEEK));   // 5    <THURSDAY>

        // Print the date at GMT at time -1 day.
        cal.setTime(new Date(-24*60*60*1000));
        System.out.println(cal.get(Calendar.DAY_OF_WEEK));   // 4    <WEDNESDAY>
    }
}
```

setTimeInMillis()

PURPOSE Sets this `Calendar` object's current date time.

SYNTAX `protected void setTimeInMillis(long millis)`

DESCRIPTION This method sets this `Calendar` object's current date to `millis` which is the number of milliseconds from epoch (January 1, 1970 00:00:00 UTC). See `Date` for details on this `long` value.

If `millis` is positive, it means the number of milliseconds *since* epoch. If it is negative, it means the number of milliseconds *before* epoch. This method also recomputes the time fields.

Note: The `GregorianCalendar` class does not take into account leap seconds, so `millis` is not interpreted exactly as UTC. See the `Date` class description for more details.

PARAMETERS

`millis` The number of milliseconds from epoch.

SEE ALSO `Date.getTime()`, `getTimeInMillis()`, `setTime()`.

setTimeZone()

PURPOSE Sets the time zone.

SYNTAX `public void setTimeZone(TimeZone tz)`

DESCRIPTION This method sets the time zone for this `Calendar` object to `tz`. The new time zone does not affect the fields until the fields are recomputed. See the class description for information about how to cause the fields to be recomputed.

PARAMETERS

`tz` A non-`null` `TimeZone` object.

SEE ALSO `getTimeZone()`.

EXAMPLE This example prints the time in the local time zone. The program then sets the time zone to `GMT` and prints the same time in `GMT`.

```
import java.util.*;

class Main {
    // Pads the value with a zero on the left if val is a single digit.
    static void printTwoDigits(int val) {
        if (val < 10) {
            System.out.print("0");
        }
        System.out.print(val);
    }
```

```
        // Prints the time.
        static void printTime(Calendar cal) {
            printTwoDigits(cal.get(Calendar.HOUR));
            System.out.print(":");
            printTwoDigits(cal.get(Calendar.MINUTE));
            System.out.print(":");
            printTwoDigits(cal.get(Calendar.SECOND));

            System.out.println(
                (cal.get(Calendar.AM_PM) == Calendar.AM) ? " am" : " pm");
        }

        public static void main(String[] args) {
            Calendar cal = Calendar.getInstance();
            printTime(cal);                                    // 07:08:40 pm

            // Set the new time zone.
            cal.setTimeZone(TimeZone.getTimeZone("GMT"));

            // This step causes the calendar object to recompute all the fields.
            cal.setTime(cal.getTime());
            printTime(cal);                                    // 02:08:40 am
        }
    }
```

time

PURPOSE Holds this `Calendar` object's current date and time.

SYNTAX `protected long time`

DESCRIPTION This field holds this `Calendar` object's current date and time as a single `long` value. This `long` value is the number of milliseconds since epoch (January 1, 1970 00:00:00 UTC). See the `Date` class for details on this `long` value.

This field is valid only if `isTimeSet` is `true`. If `isTimeSet` is `false`, `computeTime()` must be called before the value in this field is valid.

SEE ALSO `computeTime()`, `Date.getTime()`, `isTimeSet`.

WEEK_OF_MONTH

PURPOSE Specifies the week-of-month calendar field.

SYNTAX `public final static int WEEK_OF_MONTH`

DESCRIPTION The week-of-month refers to the *n*th week of the current month. This constant is used in a call to `get()` or `set()` to retrieve or set the week-of-month of a `Calendar` object. When setting this field, you must also set the `DAY_OF_WEEK` field (or keep the current one). In addition, you must clear the `DAY_OF_MONTH` field; otherwise, the new `WEEK_OF_MONTH` value will not take effect. See `set()` for more information.

If this `Calendar` object is not lenient (see `isLenient()`), the week-of-month field can be set only with values in the range `1` to the maximum number of weeks for all months. In the Gregorian calendar, the minimum value is `1` and the maximum value is `6`. Note that this is different from calendar fields such as `DAY_OF_MONTH` whose maximum value cannot exceed the last day of the current month.

The week-of-month is affected by the value of `getFirstDayOfWeek()`. For example, suppose the first of January falls on a Monday. If `getFirstDayOfWeek()` returns `SUNDAY`, then the week-of-month for the seventh will be `2`. However, if the `getFirstDayOfWeek()` returns `MONDAY`, then the week-of-month for the seventh will be `1`.

Note that setting this field can change the month calendar field. For example, if the `getFirstDayOfWeek()` is `SUNDAY` and the first day-of-month falls on a Monday, then setting the week-of-month to `1` and the day-of-week to `SUNDAY` causes the month to be the previous month and the week-of-month to be the last week of that month.

If this `Calendar` object is lenient, the week-of-month field can be set to any integer value. The simplest way to understand the effects of setting this calendar field is to imagine an infinite calendar arranged contiguously, as in Figure 20. The first column of this calendar must be `getFirstDayOfWeek()`.

```
Su Mo Tu We Th Fr Sa
...
23 24 25 26 27 28 29
30 31  1  2  3  4  5  April
 6  7  8  9 10 11 12
13 14 15 16 17 18 19
20 21 22 23 24 25 26
27 28 29 30  1  2  3  May
 4  5  6  7  8  9 10
...
```

FIGURE 20: Infinitely Long Contiguous Calendar.

Now imagine the current week pointer pointing at the week containing the first of the current month. If the first day of that week does not fall in the first column, the current week will contain the final days of the previous month. If the week-of-month is set to *W*, move the current week pointer down/up *W* – `1` lines. Next, choose a day in the current week based on the day-of-week field. The month field will be set to the month that contains that day. Also, the week-of-month field will be modified if necessary to be `1`-based *n*th week of that month.

For example, in Figure 20, if the month is May, then the current week pointer is at the week containing the first of May. If the week-of-month is set to `-1`, then move the pointer up 2 places (`-1-1` = –2). If the day-of-week is Sunday,

A B C D E F G H I J K L M N O P Q R S T U V W X Y Z

then the week-of-month field will be set to 3 (and the calendar field will be set to 13).

SEE ALSO DAY_OF_WEEK_IN_MONTH, isLenient(), get(), set().

EXAMPLE This example implements a utility for determining the number of weeks in a particular month in a particular year. It also implements a utility to determine the date based on a particular year, month, week-of-month, and day-of-week.

Notice that the first week in February does not contain a Sunday, so the resulting date is the last Sunday in January.

```
import java.text.*;
import java.util.*;

class Main {
    // Returns the number of week in the given month.
    static int weeksIn(Calendar cal, int month) {
        cal.set(Calendar.MONTH, month);
        cal.set(Calendar.DAY_OF_MONTH, cal.getMaximum(Calendar.DAY_OF_MONTH));

        while (cal.get(Calendar.MONTH) != month) {
            cal.add(Calendar.DAY_OF_MONTH, -1);
        }
        return cal.get(Calendar.WEEK_OF_MONTH);
    }

    // Print the date of the given month, week-of-month, and day-of-week.
    static void dayInWeek(Calendar cal, int month, int week_of_month,
                int day_of_week) {
        cal.clear(Calendar.DAY_OF_MONTH);
        cal.set(Calendar.MONTH, month);
        cal.set(Calendar.DAY_OF_WEEK, day_of_week);
        cal.set(Calendar.WEEK_OF_MONTH, week_of_month);
        System.out.println(DateFormat.getInstance().format(cal.getTime()));
    }

    public static void main(String[] args) {
        Calendar cal = Calendar.getInstance();

        cal.setFirstDayOfWeek(Calendar.SUNDAY);
        for (int i=Calendar.JANUARY; i<=Calendar.DECEMBER; i++) {
            System.out.print(weeksIn(cal, i) + " ");
        }
        System.out.println();                    // 5 5 6 5 5 5 5 6 5 5 6 5

        cal.setFirstDayOfWeek(Calendar.MONDAY);
        for (int i=Calendar.JANUARY; i<=Calendar.DECEMBER; i++) {
            System.out.print(weeksIn(cal, i) + " ");
        }
        System.out.println();                    // 5 5 6 5 5 6 5 5 5 5 5 5

        // What day is Sunday in the 1st week in February?
        dayInWeek(cal, Calendar.FEBRUARY, 1, Calendar.SUNDAY);//1/26/97 1:08 AM

        // What day is Sunday in the 6th week in February?
        dayInWeek(cal, Calendar.FEBRUARY, 6, Calendar.SUNDAY);//3/2/97 1:08 AM
```

```
        // What day is Sunday in the 0th week in February?
        dayInWeek(cal, Calendar.FEBRUARY, 0, Calendar.SUNDAY);//1/19/97 1:08 AM
    }
}
```


WEEK_OF_YEAR

PURPOSE Specifies the week-of-year calendar field.

SYNTAX `public final static int WEEK_OF_YEAR`

DESCRIPTION The week-of-year refers to the *n*th week of the year. This constant is used in a call to `get()` or `set()` to retrieve or set the week-of-year of a `Calendar` object. When you set this calendar field, you also must set the `DAY_OF_WEEK` field (or keep the current one). In addition, you must clear both the `MONTH` and `DAY_OF_YEAR` fields; otherwise, the new `WEEK_OF_YEAR` value will not take effect. See `set()` for more information.

In the Gregorian calendar, the maximum number of weeks in a year is `54`.

SEE ALSO `get()`, `set()`.

EXAMPLE This example prints all of the years between `1000` and `2000` that have `54` weeks.

```
import java.text.*;
import java.util.*;

class Main {
    // Returns number of weeks in a year.
    static int numWeeksInYear(int year) {
        Calendar cal = Calendar.getInstance();

        cal.clear(Calendar.MONTH);
        cal.clear(Calendar.DAY_OF_YEAR);
        cal.set(Calendar.YEAR, year);
        cal.set(Calendar.DAY_OF_WEEK, Calendar.SUNDAY);
        cal.set(Calendar.WEEK_OF_YEAR, cal.getMaximum(Calendar.WEEK_OF_YEAR));

        while (cal.get(Calendar.YEAR) != year) {
            cal.add(Calendar.WEEK_OF_YEAR, -1);
        }
        return cal.get(Calendar.WEEK_OF_YEAR);
    }

    public static void main(String[] args) {
        for (int i=1000; i<2000; i++) {
            int n = numWeeksInYear(i);
            if (n == 54) {
                System.out.print(i + " ");
            }
        }
// 1004 1032 1060 1088 1116 1144 1172 1200 1228 1256 1284 1312 1340 1368 1396
```

```
// 1424 1452 1480 1508 1536 1564 1600 1628 1656 1684 1724 1752 1780 1820 1848
// 1876 1916 1944 1972
    }
}
```

A B C D E F G H I J K L M N O P Q R S T U V W X Y Z

YEAR

PURPOSE Specifies the year calendar field.

SYNTAX `public final static int YEAR`

DESCRIPTION This constant is used in a call to `get()` or `set()` to retrieve or set the year of a `Calendar` object.

In the Gregorian calendar, there is no year `0`. Retrieving the year from a `GregorianCalendar` object always yields a value greater than `0`. If you set a year *Y* of `0` or less, the era will be "flipped" and the year set to $-Y + 1$. For example, if the current era is `BC` and the year is `-1`, the new era will be `AD` and the new year will be `2`.

Note: Setting a negative year does not affect the internal era value. That is, if you set the era to `BC` and set a negative year, the internal era value is still `BC`, but retrieving the era value yields `AD`. This is important because the effect of negative years on the era depends on the internal era value. This means that the era does not keep flipping every time you set a negative year.

SEE ALSO `get()`, `set()`.

EXAMPLE

```
import java.text.*;
import java.util.*;

class Main {
    static void printDate(Calendar cal) {
        System.out.println(new SimpleDateFormat("yyyy/M/dd G").format(
            cal.getTime()));
    }

    public static void main(String[] args) {
        Calendar cal = Calendar.getInstance();

        cal.set(Calendar.YEAR, -1000);
        printDate(cal);                                   // 1001/10/29 BC
        cal.set(Calendar.YEAR, -1);
        printDate(cal);                                   // 0002/10/29 BC
        cal.set(Calendar.YEAR, 0);
        printDate(cal);                                   // 0001/10/29 BC
        cal.set(Calendar.YEAR, 1);
        printDate(cal);                                   // 0001/10/29 AD
        cal.set(Calendar.YEAR, 2000);
        printDate(cal);                                   // 2000/10/29 AD
```

```
        cal = Calendar.getInstance();
        cal.set(Calendar.ERA, GregorianCalendar.BC);
        cal.set(Calendar.YEAR, 0);
        printDate(cal);                                  // 0001/10/29 AD

        // Print out some years in which March 15th falls on a Sunday.
        cal.set(0, Calendar.MARCH, 15);
        for (int i=2000; i<=2050; i++) {
            cal.set(Calendar.YEAR, i);
            if (cal.get(Calendar.DAY_OF_WEEK) == Calendar.SUNDAY) {
                System.out.print(i + " ");
            }
        }
        System.out.println();          // 2001 2006 2012 2023 2029 2034 2040
    }
}
```

ZONE_OFFSET

PURPOSE Specifies the zone-offset calendar field.

SYNTAX `public final static int ZONE_OFFSET`

DESCRIPTION This constant is used in a call to `get()` or `set()` to retrieve or set the zone-offset of a `Calendar` object. The `ZONE_OFFSET` calendar field contains the difference in time of a time zone compared with `GMT`. In particular, it contains the number of milliseconds the time zone differs from `GMT`. For example, `PST` differs by `-8*1000*60*60` milliseconds from `GMT`. The `ZONE_OFFSET` calendar field is based on standard time (that is, the effects of daylight savings time are ignored.) Daylight savings time effects are handled by the `DST_OFFSET` field.

Note: In the Java 1.1.4 version of the `GregorianCalendar`, there are many bugs involving the use of this field. In particular, the computations used in determining the calendar fields from the internal `Date` value ignore this field and instead determine the `ZONE_OFFSET` from the `TimeZone` object returned by `getTimeZone()`. To work around these bugs, instead of setting this calendar field, create a new `TimeZone` object that has the desired values and then call `setTimeZone()` with it.

SEE ALSO `DST_OFFSET`, `get()`, `getTimeZone()`, `set()`, `setTimeZone()`.

java.lang

Character

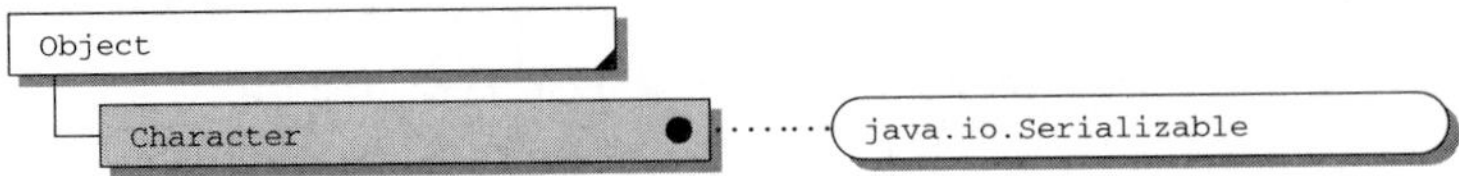

Syntax

```
public final class Character extends Object implements Serializable
```

Description

A `char` value in Java represents a Unicode character. Information about the Unicode 2.0 Standard is available at `http://www.unicode.org`. Detailed descriptions about characters are available from *The Java Language Specification, First Edition*, Section 20.5.

The `Character` class provides an object wrapper for `char` data values. This wrapper allows characters to be passed to methods in Java class libraries that accept Java objects as parameters. In addition, the `Character` class provides methods that operate on characters, such as determining whether a character is uppercase or lowercase and converting a character to its numeric value.

Usage

A `Character` instance is used to pass `char` values to methods that accept Java objects as parameters. To use one in character manipulation operations, you first must obtain the `Character` instance's `char` value from the `Character` instance:

```
Character charobj = new Character('A');
char[] str = new char[3];
 ...
str[2] = charobj.charValue();
 ...
if (charobj.equals(anotherObject))
    return 0;
```

Unicode Categories

The `Character` class uses the Unicode Standard extensively for determining the attributes of a character. For example, the definitions of letter cases, spaces, and identifiers used are those defined by the Standard. We briefly summarize the definitions here. The full definitions are available from the Standard. Refer to the Unicode attribute table for the specifications of the attributes, in `ftp://unicode.org/pub/MappingTables/UnicodeData1.1.5.txt`.

Digit Characters

A *digit character* is a character that represents a digit in a number system. The *base*, or *radix*, of the number system determines the numeric value of a digit. For example, in radix 16, the numeric value of the digit character "A" (or "a") is 10.

The `Character` class provides methods that convert a digit character to and from its numeric value, as well as a method to determine whether a character is a digit character.

Character Case

Many Roman character sets support the notion of *uppercase* and *lowercase* characters. For example, "A" and "a" are uppercase and lowercase characters, respectively, in the ISO-LATIN-1 character set. In addition, Java supports the notion of *titlecase*, which some characters have for displaying the character as the first character in a title. There are only four characters in the Unicode character set with a true titlecase form. For characters that have only uppercase and no titlecase forms, the uppercase forms are used as the titlecase.

The `Character` class provides methods for converting a character to and from the cases and for determining the case of a character.

Space Characters

There are three types of space characters: Unicode space characters, ISO-LATIN-1 space characters, and characters that Java considers space. Unicode space characters are the line separators, paragraph separators, and space separators. ISO-LATIN-1 space characters, sometimes referred to as *whitespace* characters, include blanks, tabs, line feed characters, form feed characters, and newline characters.

The `Character` class contains methods to determine whether a character is a space character as defined by these definitions of "space."

Unicode Identifiers

The Unicode 2.0 Standard defines a syntax for *identifiers* so that parsers written for Unicode-based parsers can share the same rules. A Unicode identifier must lead with a letter and be followed by any number of letters, digits, connecting punctuation characters (e.g., _), combining marks, nonspacing marks, and/or ignorable control characters. See `isUnicodeIdentifierStart()` and `isUnicodeIdentifierPart()` for details.

Java Identifiers

Java defines a syntax for Java identifiers. A Java identifier must lead with a letter, a currency symbol (e.g., $), or a connecting punctuation character (e.g., _). It must then be followed by zero or more letters, currency symbols, connecting punctuation characters, digits, numeric letters, combining marks, nonspacing marks, or ignorable control characters. See `isJavaIdentifierStart()` and `isJavaIdentifierPart()` for details.

MEMBER SUMMARY

Constructor	
`Character()`	Constructs a `Character` object using a `char` value.
Digit Character Fields and Methods	
`digit()`	Retrieves the numeric value of a digit character in the specified radix.
`forDigit()`	Retrieves the `char` value (digit character) of a number in the specified radix.
`getNumericValue()`	Retrieves the Unicode numeric value of a character.
`isDigit()`	Determines whether a character is a digit character.
`MAX_RADIX`	The maximum radix available for converting a digit character to or from a number.
`MIN_RADIX`	The minimum radix available for converting a digit character to or from a number.
Case Methods	
`isLowerCase()`	Determines whether a character is lowercase.
`isTitleCase()`	Determines whether a character is a titlecase character.
`isUpperCase()`	Determines whether a character is uppercase.
`toLowerCase()`	Retrieves the lowercase form of a character.
`toTitleCase()`	Retrieves the titlecase form of a character.
`toUpperCase()`	Retrieves the uppercase form of a character.
Space Methods	
`isSpaceChar()`	Determines whether a character is a Unicode space character.
`isWhitespace`	Determines whether a character is an ISO-LATIN-1 space character.
Character Value Fields and Method	
`charValue()`	Retrieves the value of this object as a `char`.
`MAX_VALUE`	The maximum value that a `char` can have.
`MIN_VALUE`	The minimum value that a `char` can have.
Comparison Methods	
`equals()`	Compares this object with another object for equality.
`isDefined()`	Determines whether a character is defined in Unicode.
`isJavaIdentifierStart()`	Determines whether a character is a valid first character in a Java identifier.
`isJavaIdentifierPart()`	Determines whether a character is a valid nonfirst character in a Java identifier.
`isIdentifierIgnorable()`	Determines whether a character is ignorable in a Java or Unicode identifier.

MEMBER SUMMARY	
`isISOControl()`	Determines whether a character is an ISO control character.
`isLetter()`	Determines whether a character is a letter.
`isLetterOrDigit()`	Determines whether a character is a letter or a digit.
`isUnicodeIdentifierStart()`	Determines whether a character is a valid first character in a Unicode identifier.
`isUnicodeIdentifierPart()`	Determines whether a character is a valid nonfirst character in a Unicode identifier.
Unicode Category Method	
`getType()`[a]	Retrieves the Unicode category of a character.
Object Methods	
`hashCode()`	Computes the hash code for this object.
`toString()`	Generates the string representation of this object.
`TYPE`	The `Class` object for the primitive type `char`.
Deprecated Methods	
`isJavaLetter()`	Replaced by `isJavaIdentifierStart()`.
`isJavaLetterOrDigit()`	Replaced by `isJavaIdentifierPart()`.
`isSpace()`	Replaced by `isWhitespace()`.

a. The constants defined in the `Character` class returned by `getType()` are not listed in this Member Summary. They can be found in Table 7.

Character()

PURPOSE Constructs a `Character` object using a `char` value.

SYNTAX `public Character(char ch)`

DESCRIPTION This constructor creates a `Character` object using the `char` value `ch`.

PARAMETERS

`ch` The value that the `Character` object will have.

EXAMPLE

```
Character newch = new Character('A');
```

charValue()

PURPOSE Retrieves the value of this object as a `char`.

SYNTAX `public char charValue()`

RETURNS The `char` value of this object.

SEE ALSO `MAX_VALUE`, `MIN_VALUE`.

EXAMPLE

```
Character charobj = new Character('A');
char ch = charobj.charValue(); // returns ('A');
```

digit()

PURPOSE Retrieves the numeric value of a digit character in the specified radix.

SYNTAX `public static int digit(char ch, int radix)`

DESCRIPTION This method returns the numeric value of the given digit character `ch` using the specified radix `radix`. If `radix` is not a valid radix or if `ch` is not a valid digit character in radix `radix`, this method returns `-1`. This method is the inverse of `forDigit()`.

PARAMETERS

`ch` The digit character for which to get the numeric value.

`radix` The radix of the number system to use.

RETURNS The numeric value of `ch` in radix `radix`. This method returns `-1` if `ch` is not a valid digit character in radix `radix`.

SEE ALSO `forDigit()`, `isDigit()`, `getNumericValue()`, `MAX_RADIX`, `MIN_RADIX`.

EXAMPLE

```
// Given a char array and radix, return its numeric value
// Assume array contains only valid digits
static int charsToNumber(char[] str, int radix) {
    int number = 0;
    for (int magnitude = 1, i = str.length - 1;
         i >= 0;
         magnitude *= radix, i--)
        number += (Character.digit(str[i], radix)) * magnitude;
    return number;
}
```

equals()

PURPOSE Compares this object with another object for equality.

SYNTAX `public boolean equals(Object obj)`

DESCRIPTION This method compares the `char` value of this object against that of the object `obj`. It returns `true` if the two values are equal. It returns `false` if the two values are not equal or if `obj` either is `null` or is not a `Character` object.

PARAMETERS

`object` The possibly `null` object against which this object will be compared.

RETURNS `true` if `obj` has the same `char` value as this object; `false` otherwise.

OVERRIDES `Object.equals()`.

SEE ALSO `hashCode()`.

EXAMPLE

```
Character c1 = new Character('\u23f3');
Character c2 = new Character('A');
if (c1.equals(c2))
          ...
```

forDigit()

PURPOSE Retrieves the `char` value (digit character) of a number in the specified radix.

SYNTAX `public static char forDigit(int d, int rdx)`

DESCRIPTION This method returns the character representation of the digit `d` in the radix `rdx`. For example, the character representation of the digit `10` in radix 16 is "A".

This method is the inverse of `digit()`.

PARAMETERS

`d` The digit for which to generate the digit character. `0` ≤ `d` < `rdx`.

`rdx` The radix of the number system to use. `MIN_RADIX` ≤ `rdx` ≤ `MAX_RADIX`.

RETURNS The character representation of `d` in radix `rdx`. If either `d` or `rdx` is outside of the ranges specified here, the null character (\0) is returned.

SEE ALSO `digit()`, `isDigit()`, `MAX_RADIX`, `MIN_RADIX`.

EXAMPLE

```
char ch = Character.forDigit(10, 16); // returns 'A'
```

getNumericValue()

PURPOSE Retrieves the Unicode numeric value of a character.

SYNTAX `public static int getNumericValue(ch)`

DESCRIPTION This method is a more generalized version of `digit()`. It returns the numeric value of a character that can be used to represent a digit, regardless of the radix. It is possible for different values of `ch` to return the same result. For example, different representations of 1 all return `1`.

If a character does not have a numeric value, `-1` is returned. If a character has a numeric value but not one that can be represented as a positive integer, `-2` is returned. Examples of these are the fractional characters (`\u2153-\u215e` and `\u00bd-\u00be`).

PARAMETERS

`ch` The character for which to get the numeric value.

RETURNS The numeric value of ch.

SEE ALSO `digit()`.

EXAMPLE

```
System.out.println(Character.getNumericValue('1'));      // 1
System.out.println(Character.getNumericValue('2'));      // 2
System.out.println(Character.getNumericValue('3'));      // 3
System.out.println(Character.getNumericValue('4'));      // 4
System.out.println(Character.getNumericValue('5'));      // 5
System.out.println(Character.getNumericValue('a'));      // 10
System.out.println(Character.getNumericValue('i'));      // 18
System.out.println(Character.getNumericValue('\u216c')); // 50
System.out.println(Character.getNumericValue('\u221e')); // -1 (infinity)
System.out.println(Character.getNumericValue(' '));      // -1
System.out.println(Character.getNumericValue(','));      // -1
System.out.println(Character.getNumericValue('\u2155')); // -2 (1/5)
System.out.println(Character.getNumericValue('\u215f')); // 1
System.out.println(Character.getNumericValue('\u00be')); // -2 (3/4)
```

getType()

PURPOSE Determines the Unicode category of a character.

SYNTAX `public static int getType(char ch)`

DESCRIPTION This method returns the Unicode category to which `ch` belongs. These categories are described in detail in the Unicode 2.0 Standard.

PARAMETERS

`ch` The character to check.

RETURNS One of the categories in Table 7 to which `ch` corresponds.

Constant Name	Value	Constant Name	Value
Space		**Punctuations**	
SPACE_SEPARATOR	12	DASH_PUNCTUATION	20
LINE_SEPARATOR	13	START_PUNCTUATION	21
PARAGRAPH_SEPARATOR	14	END_PUNCTUATION	22
Letters		CONNECTOR_PUNCTUATION	23
UPPERCASE_LETTER	1	OTHER_PUNCTUATION	24
LOWERCASE_LETTER	2	**Symbols**	
TITLECASE_LETTER	3	MATH_SYMBOL	25
MODIFIER_LETTER	4	CURRENCY_SYMBOL	26
OTHER_LETTER	5	MODIFIER_SYMBOL	27
Numbers		OTHER_SYMBOL	28
DECIMAL_DIGIT_NUMBER	9	**Format Controls**	
LETTER_NUMBER	10	CONTROL	15
OTHER_NUMBER	11	FORMAT	18
Marks		**Others**	
NON_SPACING_MARK	6	UNASSIGNED	0
ENCLOSING_MARK	7	PRIVATE_USE	18
COMBINING_SPACING_MARK	8	SURROGATE	19

TABLE 7: Unicode Category Types.

SEE ALSO `isDigit()`, `isISOControl()`, `isSpaceChar()`.

EXAMPLE

```
System.out.println(Character.getType('a'));       // LOWERCASE_LETTER
System.out.println(Character.getType('5'));       // DECIMAL_DIGIT_NUMBER
System.out.println(Character.getType('A'));       // UPPERCASE_LETTER
System.out.println(Character.getType('\n'));      // CONTROL
System.out.println(Character.getType(' '));       // SPACE_SEPARATOR
System.out.println(Character.getType('\u2029'));  // PARAGRAPH_SEPARATOR
System.out.println(Character.getType(';'));       // OTHER_PUNCTUATION
System.out.println(Character.getType('_'));       // CONNECTOR_PUNCTUATION
System.out.println(Character.getType('i'));       // LOWERCASE_LETTER
System.out.println(Character.getType('$'));       // CURRENCY_SYMBOL
System.out.println(Character.getType('<'));       // MATH_SYMBOL
```

hashCode()

PURPOSE Computes the hash code for this object.

SYNTAX `public int hashCode()`

DESCRIPTION This method returns the hash code for this `Character` object. The hash code is calculated using this object's `char` value. Two `Character` objects with the same `char` values have the same hash code.

RETURNS An `int` representing this object's hash code.

OVERRIDES `Object.hashCode()`.

SEE ALSO `equals()`, `java.util.Hashtable`.

EXAMPLE

```
int[] hits = new int[1023];
Character cobj = new Character('A');
int hashval = cobj.hashCode();          // generate hash code
++hits[Math.abs(hashval%hits.length)]; // count hits
```

isDefined()

PURPOSE Determines whether a character is defined in Unicode.

SYNTAX `public static boolean isDefined(char ch)`

DESCRIPTION This method returns `true` if `ch` is defined in Unicode. Some characters in the range `MIN_VALUE` and `MAX_VALUE` do not have a meaning in Unicode.

`ch` is defined if it has an entry in the Unicode attribute table (see the class description) or if `\u3040` ≤ `ch` ≤ `\u9fa5` or if `\uf900` ≤ `ch` ≤ `\ufa2d`.

PARAMETERS

`ch` The character to check.

RETURNS `true` if `ch` is defined in Unicode; `false` otherwise.

SEE ALSO `isDigit()`, `isLetter()`, `isLetterOrDigit()`, `isUpperCase()`, `isLowerCase()`, `isTitleCase()`, `MAX_VALUE`, `MIN_VALUE`.

EXAMPLE See `isLetter()`.

isDigit()

PURPOSE Determines whether a character is a digit character.

SYNTAX `public static boolean isDigit(char ch)`

DESCRIPTION This method determines whether the character `ch` is a digit character. A digit character is one of the ISO-LATIN-1 characters 0–9 or one of the Unicode characters representing digits in other languages (such as Arabic-Indic digits).

Unicode Range	Description
\u0030 - \u0039	ISO-Latin-1 digits (0–9).
\u0660 - \u0669	Arabic-Indic digits.
\u06f0 - \u06f9	Extended Arabic-Indic digits.
\u0966 - \u096f	Devanagari digits.
\u09e6 - \u09ef	Bangali digits.
\u0a66 - \u0a6f	Gurmukhi digits.
\u0ae6 - \u0aef	Gujarati digits.
\u0b66 - \u0b6f	Oriya digits.
\u0be7 - \u0bef	Tamil digits.
\u0c66 - \u0c6f	Telugu digits.
\u0ce6 - \u0cef	Kannada digits.
\u0d66 - \u0d6f	Malayalam digits.
\u0e50 - \u0e59	Thai digits.
\u0ed0 - \u0ed9	Lao digits.
\u0f20 - \u0f29	Tibetan digits.
\uff10 - \uff19	Fullwidth digits.

TABLE 8: Unicode Digit Characters.

PARAMETERS

`ch` The character being checked.

RETURNS `true` if `ch` is a digit character; `false` otherwise.

SEE ALSO `digit()`, `forDigit()`, `getNumericValue()`.

EXAMPLE

```
if (Character.isDigit(ch))
    number += Character.digit(ch, 10);
```

isIdentifierIgnorable()

PURPOSE Determines whether a character is ignorable in a Java or Unicode identifier.

SYNTAX `public static boolean isIdentifierIgnorable(Character ch)`

DESCRIPTION A character is ignorable in a Java or Unicode identifier if `ch` is one of the characters in Table 9.

Unicode Range	Description
`\u0000 - \u0008`	ISO control characters that are not whitespace.
`\u000e - \u001b`	ISO control characters that are not whitespace.
`\u200c - \u200f`	Join controls.
`\u200a - \u200e`	Bidirectional controls.
`\u206a - 0x206f`	Format controls.
`\ufeff`	Zero-width no-break space.

TABLE 9: Ignorable Characters for Java and Unicode Identifiers.

PARAMETERS
`ch` The character to check.

RETURNS `true` if `ch` is ignorable; `false` otherwise.

SEE ALSO `isJavaIdentifierPart()`, `isJavaIdentifierStart()`, `isUnicodeIdentifierPart()`, `isUnicodeIdentifierStart()`.

isISOControl()

PURPOSE Determines whether a character is an ISO control character.

SYNTAX `public static boolean isDigit(char ch)`

DESCRIPTION A character `ch` is an ISO control character if `\u0000` ≤ `ch` ≤ `\u001f` or if `\u007f` ≤ `ch` ≤ `\u009f`.

PARAMETERS
`ch` The character being checked.

RETURNS `true` if `ch` is an ISO control character; `false` otherwise.

isJavaIdentifierPart()

PURPOSE Determines whether a character is a valid nonfirst character in a Java identifier.

SYNTAX `public static boolean isJavaIdentifierPart(char ch)`

DESCRIPTION — This method determines whether the character `ch` is valid as a character in a Java identifier when the character does not occur at the start of the identifier. It is a valid Java identifier character if it is one of the following:

- A letter
- A currency symbol (e.g., $)
- A connecting punctuation character (e.g., _)
- A digit or a numeric letter
- A combining mark
- A nonspacing mark
- An ignorable control character

PARAMETERS

`ch` — The character being checked.

RETURNS — `true` if `ch` is valid as the nonfirst character in a Java identifier; `false` otherwise.

SEE ALSO — `isDigit()`, `isJavaIdentifierStart()`, `isLetter()`, `isLetterOrDigit()`, `isUnicodeIdentifierPart()`.

EXAMPLE — See `isJavaIdentifierStart()`.

isJavaIdentifierStart()

PURPOSE — Determines whether a character is a valid first character in a Java identifier.

SYNTAX — `public static boolean isJavaIdentifierStart(char ch)`

DESCRIPTION — This method determines whether the character `ch` is valid as the first character in a Java identifier. It is valid if it is one of the following:

- A letter
- A currency symbol (e.g., $)
- A connecting punctuation character (e.g., _)

DESCRIPTION

`ch` — The character being checked.

RETURNS — `true` if `ch` is valid as the first character in a Java identifier; `false` otherwise.

SEE ALSO — `isJavaIdentifierPart()`, `isLetter()`, `isUnicodeIdentifierStart()`.

EXAMPLE — This example defines a function that checks whether a string is a valid Java identifier.

```
class Main {
    public static boolean validJavaIdentifier(String str) {
        char[] buf = new char[str.length()];
        str.getChars(0, buf.length, buf, 0);
```

```
            if (!Character.isJavaIdentifierStart(buf[0]))
                return false;

            for (int i = 1; i < buf.length; i++) {
                if (!Character.isJavaIdentifierPart(buf[i]))
                    return false;
            }
            return true;
        }

        public static void main(String[] args) {
            for (int i = 0; i < args.length; i++)
                System.out.println(args[i] + ":" +
                    (validJavaIdentifier(args[i]) ? "OK" : "Invalid"));
        }
    }
```


isJavaLetter()

PURPOSE: Replaced by `isJavaIdentifierStart()`.

SYNTAX: `public static boolean isJavaLetter(char ch)`

PARAMETERS
`ch` The character being checked.

RETURNS: `true` if `ch` is valid as the first character in a Java identifier; `false` otherwise.

DEPRECATION: Replace the usage of this deprecated method, as in

```
if (Character.isJavaLetter('A')) ...
```

with

```
if (Character.isJavaIdentifierStart('A')) ...
```

isJavaLetterOrDigit() *DEPRECATED*

PURPOSE: Replaced by `isJavaIdentifierPart()`.

SYNTAX: `public static boolean isJavaLetter(char ch)`

PARAMETERS
`ch` The character being checked.

RETURNS: `true` if `ch` is valid as the nonfirst character in a Java identifier; `false` otherwise.

DEPRECATION: Replace the usage of this deprecated method, as in

```
if (Character.isJavaLetterOrDigit('A')) ...
```

with

```
if (Character.isJavaIdentifierPart('A')) ...
```

isLetter()

PURPOSE Determines whether a character is a letter.

SYNTAX `public static boolean isLetter(char ch)`

DESCRIPTION This method determines whether the character `ch` is a letter. A letter is defined as one of the ISO-LATIN-1 characters "a" to "z" or "A" to "Z" or one of the Unicode characters representing letters in other languages (such as extended Latin sets and Basic Arabic). A character is defined in Unicode as being a letter if it is in one of the categories "Lu," "Ll," "Lt," "Lm," or "Lo."

Although Roman character sets have the notion of uppercase and lowercase, some character sets, such as Asian or Arabic character sets, do not.

PARAMETERS

`ch` The character being checked.

RETURNS `true` if `ch` is a letter; false otherwise.

SEE ALSO `isDigit()`, `isJavaLetter()`, `isJavaLetterOrDigit()`, `isLetterOrDigit()`, `isLowerCase()`, `isTitleCase()`, `isUpperCase()`.

EXAMPLE This example defines a function that prints out information about a particular character. It demonstrates the use of `isDefined()`, `isLowerCase()`, `isUpperCase()`, `isTitleCase()`, `isLetter()`, `isDigit()`, and `isWhitespace()`.

```
class WhatCase {
    public static void charInfo(char ch) {
        System.out.print("'" + ch + "': ");
        if (!Character.isDefined(ch)) {
            System.out.println("**");
            return;
        }
        // case
        if (Character.isLowerCase(ch))
            System.out.print('l');
        else if (Character.isUpperCase(ch))
            System.out.print('u');
        else if (Character.isTitleCase(ch))
            System.out.print('t');
        else
            System.out.print('-');

        // letter or digit or space
        if (Character.isLetter(ch))
            System.out.println('l');
        else if (Character.isDigit(ch))
            System.out.println('d');
        else if (Character.isWhitespace(ch))
            System.out.println('s');
        else System.out.print('-');
        System.out.println();
    }
```

```
        public static void main(String[] args) {
            char[] buf = {'a', 'b', 'T', '5', '\t'};
            for (int i = 0; i < buf.length; i++)
                charInfo(buf[i]);
        }
    }
```


isLetterOrDigit()

PURPOSE Determines whether a character is a letter or a digit.

SYNTAX `public static boolean isLetterOrDigit(char ch)`

DESCRIPTION This method determines whether the character `ch` is a letter character (`isLetter()`) or a digit character (`isDigit()`). It returns `true` if `ch` is a letter character or a digit character; `false` otherwise.

PARAMETERS

`ch` The character being checked.

RETURNS `true` if `ch` is a letter character or a digit character; `false` otherwise.

SEE ALSO `isDigit()`, `isJavaLetter()`, `isJavaLetterOrDigit()`, `isLetter()`.

EXAMPLE Usage of `isLetterOrDigit()` is similar to that of `isLetter()`. See `isLetter()` for a similar usage of `isLetter()`.

isLowerCase()

PURPOSE Determines whether a character is lowercase.

SYNTAX `public static boolean isLowerCase(char ch)`

DESCRIPTION This method determines whether the character `ch` is lowercase. `ch` is a lowercase character if, and only if, all of the following are true:

- `ch` < `\u2000` or `ch` > `\u2fff`.
- The Unicode attribute table does not specify a lowercase mapping for `ch`.
- The Unicode attribute table specifies an uppercase mapping for `ch`, or the name of `ch` in the Unicode attribute table contains the words `SMALL LETTER` or `SMALL LIGATURE`.

PARAMETERS

`ch` The character being tested.

RETURNS `true` if `ch` is a lowercase character; `false` otherwise.

SEE ALSO `isTitleCase()`, `isUpperCase()`, `toLowerCase()`.

EXAMPLE See also the `isLetter()` example.

```
if (Character.isLowerCase(ch))
    return (Character.toUpperCase(ch));
```

isSpace()

DEPRECATED

PURPOSE Replaced by `isWhitespace()`.

SYNTAX `public static boolean isSpace(char ch)`

PARAMETERS

`ch` The character being tested.

RETURNS `true` if `ch` is \n, \t, \f, \r, or ' ' (space); `false` otherwise.

DEPRECATION Replace the usage of this deprecated method, as in

```
if (Character.isSpace('A')) ...
```

with

```
if (Character.isWhitespace('A')) ...
```

isSpaceChar()

PURPOSE Determines whether a character is a Unicode space character.

SYNTAX `public static boolean isWhitespace(char ch)`

DESCRIPTION The Unicode 2.0 Standard specifies that the characters in the following categories are space characters: space separators, line separators, and paragraph separators. These are the Unicode categories "Zs," "Zl," and "Zp," respectively. See the Standard for a complete list of space characters.

PARAMETERS

`ch` The character being tested.

RETURNS `true` if `ch` is a Unicode space character; `false` otherwise.

SEE ALSO `isWhitespace()`.

EXAMPLE

```
System.out.println("Uspace: " + Character.isSpaceChar('\u0020')); // True
System.out.println("Uline: " + Character.isSpaceChar('\u2028'));  // True
System.out.println("Upara: " + Character.isSpaceChar('\u2029'));  // True

System.out.println("space: " + Character.isSpaceChar(' '));        // True
System.out.println("newline: " + Character.isSpaceChar('\n'));     // False
System.out.println("tab: " + Character.isSpaceChar('\t'));         // False
System.out.println("return: " + Character.isSpaceChar('\r'));      // False
System.out.println("form feed: " + Character.isSpaceChar('\f'));   // False
```

isTitleCase()

PURPOSE Determines whether a character is a titlecase character.

SYNTAX `public static boolean isTitleCase(char ch)`

DESCRIPTION This method determines whether the character `ch` is a titlecase character. In Unicode, there are only four characters that are titlecase characters: `\u01c5`, `\u01c8`, `\u01cb`, and `\u01f2`.

This method returns `true` if `ch` is one of these; `false` otherwise.

PARAMETERS

`ch` The character being checked.

RETURNS `true` if `ch` is a titlecase character; `false` otherwise.

SEE ALSO `isLowerCase()`, `isUpperCase()`, `toTitleCase()`, `toUpperCase()`.

EXAMPLE See `isLetter()`.

isUnicodeIdentifierPart()

PURPOSE Determines whether a character is a valid nonfirst character in a Unicode identifier.

SYNTAX `public static boolean isUnicodeIdentifierPart(char ch)`

DESCRIPTION This method determines whether the character `ch` is valid as a character in a Unicode identifier when the character does not occur at the start of the identifier. It is valid if it is one of the following:

- A letter
- A connecting punctuation character (e.g., _)
- A digit or a numeric letter
- A combining mark
- A nonspacing mark
- An ignorable control character

PARAMETERS

`ch` The character being checked.

RETURNS `true` if `ch` is valid as the nonfirst character in a Unicode identifier; `false` otherwise.

SEE ALSO `isDigit()`, `isJavaIdentifierPart()`, `isLetter()`, `isLetterOrDigit()`, `isUnicodeIdentifierStart()`.

EXAMPLE Usage of `isUnicodeIdentifierPart()` is similar to that of `isJavaIdentifierPart()`. See `isJavaIdentifierStart()` for a similar usage of `isJavaIdentifierPart()`.

isUnicodeIdentifierStart()

PURPOSE
Determines whether a character is a valid first character in a Unicode identifier.

SYNTAX
`public static boolean isUnicodeIdentifierStart(char ch)`

DESCRIPTION
This method determines whether the character `ch` is valid as the first character in a Unicode identifier. It is valid if it is a letter (`isLetter()`).

PARAMETERS

`ch` The character being checked.

RETURNS
`true` if `ch` is valid as the first character in a Unicode identifier; `false` otherwise.

SEE ALSO
`isJavaIdentifierStart()`, `isLetter()`, `isUnicodeIdentifierPart()`.

EXAMPLE
Usage of `isUnicodeIdentifierStart()` is similar to that of `isJavaIdentifierStart()`. See `isJavaIdentifierStart()` for a similar usage of `isJavaIdentifierStart()`.

isUpperCase()

PURPOSE
Determines whether a character is uppercase.

SYNTAX
`public static boolean isUpperCase(char ch)`

DESCRIPTION
This method determines whether the character `ch` is an uppercase character. `ch` is an uppercase character if, and only if, all of the following are true:

- `ch < \u2000` or `ch > \u2fff`.
- The Unicode attribute table does not specify an uppercase mapping for `ch`.
- The Unicode attribute table specifies a lowercase mapping for `ch`, or the name of `ch` in the Unicode attribute table contains the words `CAPITAL LETTER` or `CAPITAL LIGATURE`.

PARAMETERS

`ch` The character being checked.

RETURNS
`true` if `ch` is an uppercase character; `false` otherwise.

SEE ALSO
`isLowerCase()`, `isTitleCase()`, `toUpperCase()`.

EXAMPLE

```
if (Character.isUpperCase(ch))
    return (Character.toLowerCase(ch));
```

A B C D E F G H I J K L M N O P Q R S T U V W X Y Z

isWhitespace()

PURPOSE Determines whether a character is a Java whitespace character.

SYNTAX `public static boolean isWhitespace(char ch)`

DESCRIPTION A whitespace character is one of the following:

- A Unicode space separator (category "Zs"), except `\u00a0` and `\ufeff`
- A Unicode line separator (category "Zl")
- A Unicode paragraph separator (category "Zp")
- `\u0009` (horizontal tab)
- `\u000a` (line feed)
- `\u000b` (vertical tab)
- `\u000c` (form feed)
- `\u000d` (carriage return)
- `\u001c` (file separator)
- `\u001d` (group separator)
- `\u001e` (record separator)
- `\u001f` (unit separator)

PARAMETERS

`ch` The character being tested.

RETURNS `true` if `ch` is a Java whitespace character; `false` otherwise.

SEE ALSO `isSpaceChar()`.

EXAMPLE

```
// Returns the number of white space characters in char array
static int countWhitespaces(char[] str) {
    int count = 0;
    for (int i = 0; i < str.length; i++)
        if (Character.isWhitespace(str[i]))
                ++count;
    return (count);
}
```

MAX_RADIX

PURPOSE The maximum radix available for converting a digit character to or from a number.

SYNTAX `public static final int MAX_RADIX`

DESCRIPTION This constant is the maximum radix available for converting a digit character or a string consisting of digit characters to or from its numeric value. The value of this field is `36`.

SEE ALSO `digit()`, `forDigit()`, `Integer.toString()`, `MIN_RADIX`, `valueOf()`.

EXAMPLE

```
if (radix >= Character.MIN_RADIX &&
    radix <= Character.MAX_RADIX)
    number = Character.digit(ch, radix);
```

MAX_VALUE

PURPOSE The maximum value that a char can have.

SYNTAX `public static final char MAX_VALUE`

DESCRIPTION A char value in Java represents a Unicode character. MAX_VALUE represents the maximum value that a char can have, which is \uffff.

SEE ALSO MIN_VALUE.

EXAMPLE

```
char ch = 'a';
          ...
if (ch <= Character.MAX_VALUE && ch >= Character.MIN_VALUE)
          ...
```

MIN_RADIX

PURPOSE The minimum radix available for converting a digit character to or from a number.

SYNTAX `public static final int MIN_RADIX`

DESCRIPTION This constant is the minimum radix available for converting a digit character or a string consisting of digit characters to or from its numeric value. The value of this field is 2.

SEE ALSO digit(), forDigit(), Integer.toString(), MAX_RADIX, valueOf().

EXAMPLE See MAX_RADIX.

MIN_VALUE

PURPOSE The minimum value that a char can have.

SYNTAX `public static final char MIN_VALUE`

DESCRIPTION A char value in Java represents a Unicode character. MIN_VALUE represents the minimum value that a char can have, which is \u0000.

SEE ALSO MAX_VALUE.

EXAMPLE See MAX_VALUE.

toLowerCase()

PURPOSE Retrieves the lowercase form of a character.

SYNTAX `public static char toLowerCase(char ch)`

DESCRIPTION This method returns the lowercase form of ch. If ch does not have a lowercase form, ch is returned unmodified.

PARAMETERS

ch The character for which to get the lowercase form.

RETURNS The lowercase form of ch if it has one; ch otherwise.

SEE ALSO isLowerCase(), toTitleCase(), toUpperCase().

EXAMPLE See also the toTitleCase() example.

```
// Make all characters in the char array 'name' lowercase
for (int i = 0; i < name.length; i++)
    name[i] = Character.toLowerCase(name[i]);
```

toString()

PURPOSE Generates the string representation of this object.

SYNTAX `public String toString()`

DESCRIPTION This method returns the string representation of a Character object. The string representation of a Character object is its char value.

RETURNS The non-null string containing this Character object's char value.

OVERRIDES Object.toString().

EXAMPLE

```
Character ch = new Character('A');
String chstr = ch.toString();
System.out.println("Value of ch is " + chstr);
```

toTitleCase()

PURPOSE Retrieves the titlecase form of a character.

SYNTAX `public static char toTitleCase(char ch)`

DESCRIPTION This method returns the titlecase form of ch. If ch does not have a true titlecase form, its uppercase form is returned. If ch has no uppercase form, ch is returned unmodified.

PARAMETERS

ch The character for which to get the titlecase form.

RETURNS The titlecase form of ch if it has one; ch otherwise.

SEE ALSO isTitleCase(), toLowerCase(), toUpperCase().

EXAMPLE This example shows the use of toTitleCase() in returning the titlecase form of a string. It capitalizes the first character of each word.

```
class CMain {
    public static String makeTitle(String name) {
        char[] buf = new char[name.length()];
        boolean title = true;
        name.getChars(0, name.length(), buf, 0);

        // Capitalize first letter of each word

        for (int i = 0; i < buf.length; i++) {
            if (title)
                buf[i] = Character.toTitleCase(buf[i]);
            else
                buf[i] = Character.toLowerCase(buf[i]);
            title = Character.isWhiteSpace(buf[i]);
        }
        return (new String(buf));
    }

    public static void main(String[] args) {
        if (args.length == 1)
            System.out.println(makeTitle(args[0]));
        else
            System.out.println(makeTitle("this is a tEst"));
    }
}
```

toUpperCase()

PURPOSE Retrieves the uppercase form of a character.

SYNTAX `public static char toUpperCase(char ch)`

DESCRIPTION This method returns the uppercase form of ch. If ch does not have an uppercase form, ch is returned unmodified.

PARAMETERS

ch The character for which to get the uppercase form.

RETURNS The uppercase form of ch if it has one; ch otherwise.

SEE ALSO `isUpperCase(), toLowerCase(), toTitleCase().`

EXAMPLE

```
// Make all characters in the char array 'name' uppercase
for (int i = 0; i < name.length; i++)
    name[i] = Character.toUpperCase(name[i]);
```


TYPE

PURPOSE The `Class` object for the primitive type `char`.

SYNTAX `public static final Class TYPE`

DESCRIPTION This constant can be used where the `Class` object—`char.class`—of the primitive type `char` is required, such as for reflection. Although there are no restrictions on the use of `Character.TYPE`, the preferred syntax for naming the class is `char.class`.

SEE ALSO `Class.`

EXAMPLE

```
public static void main(String[] args) {
    Class c = Character.TYPE;
    System.out.println("TYPE: " + c);
    System.out.println("isPrimitive: " + c.isPrimitive());
    System.out.println("superclass: " + c.getSuperclass());
    try {
        Object obj = c.newInstance();  // ERROR
        System.out.println("char: " + obj);
    } catch (InstantiationException e) {
        e.printStackTrace();
    } catch (IllegalAccessException e) {
        e.printStackTrace();
    }
}
```

CharacterIterator

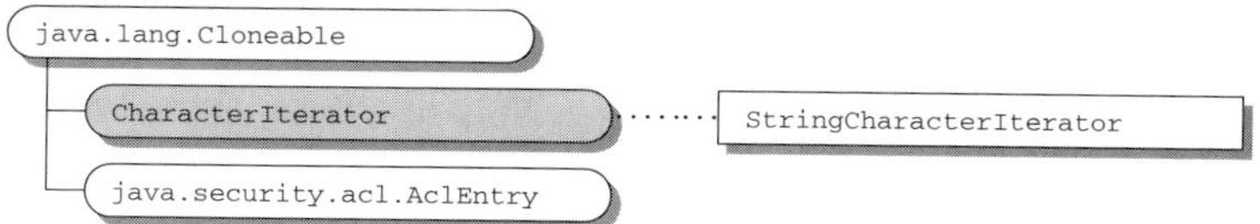

Syntax

```
public interface CharacterIterator extends Cloneable
```

Description

`CharacterIterator` is an interface that defines a protocol for iterating forward and backward over Unicode characters. A class should implement this interface if it wants to move about within a range of text and return individual Unicode characters or their index values.

This interface enables text iterator operations to work indirectly not only on `String` but also on classes other than `String`. When you want to pass text into a method, you should make the parameter type `CharacterIterator` so that the operation can be independent of text storage. For example, if text is stored in a remote database, a character iterator can make it appear local. Another example is the `setText()` method of `BreakIterator`.

As shown in Figure 21, a character iterator has a cursor that keeps track of the current index, or position, in the text. The iterator's movement methods can control the position of the cursor; they either jump to an absolute position or jump relative to the current position. These methods can return the character or its index at the new position. A `CharacterIterator` object has its own range of characters that it is restricted to that may be either the entire range or a subrange of the larger text. In other words, it can iterate over a nonzero-based range of characters; `getBeginIndex()` need not return `0`.

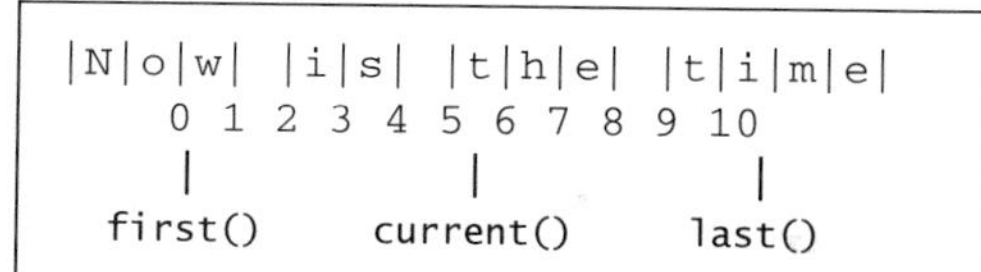

FIGURE 21: **`CharacterIterator`.**

For an implementation of `CharacterIterator`, see the class `StringCharacterIterator`. This class implements the `CharacterIterator` interface for iterating over characters in a string. You might create another implementation of `CharacterIterator` if you were to store characters in an object other than `String`. For example, for large amounts of text you might create a new class `LargeString` that stores characters in a file and has a buffer to hold a reasonable set of characters. Conforming to the `CharacterIterator` interface would ensure that `BreakIterator`, a class that uses `CharacterIterator`, would work the same when iterating through words and sentences, regardless of whether they were stored in `String` or `LargeString` objects.

A B C D E F G H I J K L M N O P Q R S T U V W X Y Z

Usage

To create an object that can do character iteration, create a class that implements the `CharacterIterator` interface, such as `StringCharacterIterator`. Then create an instance of that class. You can implement the subclass to allow iteration over a restricted subrange of text. The iterator is unaware of any text outside this subrange. This subrange includes characters having index values from `getBeginIndex()` through `getEndIndex() - 1`. The index of the current character can be retrieved by calling `getIndex()`.

Calling a movement method on this character iterator causes its cursor to move to the specified position in that subrange. The methods `next()` and `previous()` move relative to the current position. If either method would move the cursor beyond either end of the subrange, the method instead returns `CharacterIterator.DONE`, thereby signaling that the iterator cannot go any further. The methods `first()`, `last()`, and `setIndex(int)` move to absolute positions, independent of the current position. All five movement methods return the character at the new position. The getter methods with names containing "index" return index values: `getBeginIndex()`, `getEndIndex()`, and `getIndex()`.

Index

The position of each character is identified by its *index*, which is 0-based, starting with the first character, independent of any subrange. Thus a given character has a fixed index regardless of the begin and end indexes of the subrange.

Subrange

An iterator has its own range of characters that it can iterate over. This range can be a *subrange* of the full text. To be precise, the iterator allows the current index to travel over the range from `getBeginIndex()` to `getEndIndex() - 1`.

The integer returned by `getEndIndex()` is the index of the first character *following* the end of the iterable range. Another way to look at this is that the iterator's range includes the first character `getBeginIndex()` and excludes the last character `getEndIndex()`. Thus, if the text subrange can iterate over character index 5 to 10 inclusive, `getEndIndex()` returns `11`.

`CharacterIterator` has no methods for setting a subrange. Implementors of this interface can set subranges by creating a constructor that accepts the begin and end positions of a subrange. Then the start and end index values of this subrange can be returned by `getBeginIndex()` and `getEndIndex()`.

Cursor and Current Index

The *current index* is that index where the iterator is currently positioned in the characters. This position is marked by an imaginary *cursor* just ahead of the character at the current index and positioned between characters. Calling the movement methods moves the cursor and current index from one position to another, in either direction. This cursor is conceptually the same as the caret described in `TextComponent`, except that it is not visible.

MEMBER SUMMARY	
Movement Methods	
`first()`	Moves the index to the beginning of the text subrange and retrieves that character.
`last()`	Moves the index to the end of the text subrange and retrieves that character.
`next()`	Increments the index by 1 and retrieves that character.
`previous()`	Decrements the index by 1 and retrieves that character.
`setIndex()`	Moves the index to a position and retrieves that character.
Character and Index Getter Methods	
`current()`	Retrieves the character at the current index.
`getIndex()`	Retrieves the current index.
`getBeginIndex()`	Retrieves the index at the beginning of the text subrange.
`getEndIndex()`	Retrieves the index at the end of the text subrange.
Constant	
`DONE`	Returned when this iterator tries to go beyond either end of text.
Object Method	
`clone()`	Creates a copy of this `CharacterIterator`.

See Also

`StringCharacterIterator`.

Example

This example creates a class `StrCharacterIterator` that implements all methods in the interface `CharacterIterator`. This example is taken from the Java class `StringCharacterIterator`. The `main` method creates an instance of `StrCharacterIterator` and prints out a string of text in three ways: forward, backward, and from the center of the string.

```
import java.text.CharacterIterator;

class StrCharacterIterator implements CharacterIterator {
    private String text;
    private int begin;
    private int end;
    private int pos;

    public StrCharacterIterator(String text) {
      // this(text, 0);

        if (text == null)
            throw new NullPointerException();
        this.text = text;
```

```
        this.begin = 0;
        this.end = text.length();
        this.pos = 0;
    }

    public char first() {
        pos = begin;
        return text.charAt(pos);
    }

    public char last() {
        pos = end - 1;
        return text.charAt(pos);
    }

    public char setIndex(int p) {
        if (p < begin || p >= end)
            throw new IllegalArgumentException("Invalid index");
        pos = p;
        return text.charAt(p);
    }

    public char current() {
        if (pos >= begin && pos < end) {
            return text.charAt(pos);
        }
        else {
            return DONE;
        }
    }

    public char next() {
        if (++pos < end) {
            return text.charAt(pos);
        }
        else {
            return DONE;
        }
    }

    public char previous() {
        if (pos > begin) {
            return text.charAt(--pos);
        }
        else {
            return DONE;
        }
    }

    public int getBeginIndex() {
        return begin;
    }

    // the index returned is the index of the
    // first character following the end of the text.
    public int getEndIndex() {
        return end;
    }
```

```
    public int getIndex() {
        return pos;
    }


    public Object clone() {
        try {
            StrCharacterIterator other
            = (StrCharacterIterator) super.clone();
                return other;
        }
        catch (CloneNotSupportedException e) {
                throw new InternalError();
        }
    }
}

class Main {
    public static void main(String args[]) {

        String str = "Hello world";

        StrCharacterIterator iter = new StrCharacterIterator(str);

        traverseForward(iter);              // Hello world
        traverseBackward(iter);             // dlrow olleH
        traverseOut(iter, 5);               //  world olleH
    }


    // Traverse the text forward, from start to end.
    public static void traverseForward(StrCharacterIterator iter) {
        for(char c = iter.first();
            c != StrCharacterIterator.DONE;
            c = iter.next()) {
            System.out.print(c);
        }
        System.out.println();
    }

    // Traverse the text backwards, from end to start.
    public static void traverseBackward(StrCharacterIterator iter) {
        for(char c = iter.last();
            c != CharacterIterator.DONE;
            c = iter.previous()) {
            System.out.print(c);
        }
        System.out.println();
    }

    // Traverse from a given position forward to end and then
    // from that same given position backward to start.
    public static void traverseOut(StrCharacterIterator iter, int pos) {
        for (char c = iter.setIndex(pos);
             c != CharacterIterator.DONE;
             c = iter.next()) {
             System.out.print(c);
        }
        int end = iter.getIndex();
```

```
            for (char c = iter.setIndex(pos);
                 c != CharacterIterator.DONE;
                 c = iter.previous()) {
                 System.out.print(c);
            }
        }
    }
```

Output

```
> java Main
Hello world
dlrow olleH
 world olleH
```


clone()

PURPOSE Creates a copy of this character iterator.

SYNTAX `public abstract Object clone()`

DESCRIPTION This method makes a copy of this character iterator. The copy points to the same text and has the same current index as the original.

RETURNS A copy of this character iterator.

OVERRIDES `java.lang.Object.clone()`.

EXAMPLE See `StringCharacterIterator.clone`.

current()

PURPOSE Retrieves the character at the current index.

SYNTAX `public abstract char current()`

DESCRIPTION This method gets the character at the current index. This is the same index as returned by `getIndex()`. This method does not move the current index.

RETURNS The character at the current index.

SEE ALSO `getIndex()`.

EXAMPLE See `StringCharacterIterator.next()`.

DONE

PURPOSE Returned when this iterator tries to go beyond either end of text.

SYNTAX `public final static char DONE`

DESCRIPTION This constant is returned by `previous()` or `next()` when this iterator attempts to step past the first or last character. It is useful for testing that these methods return `DONE` to determine when to stop, while iterating to the end of the text.

`DONE` has the Unicode value of `\uFFFF`. The Unicode 2.0 standard states that `\uFFFF` is an invalid Unicode value and should not occur in any valid Unicode string.

SEE ALSO `previous()`, `next()`.

EXAMPLE See `StringCharacterIterator.next()`.

first()

PURPOSE Moves the index to the beginning of the text subrange and retrieves that character.

SYNTAX `public abstract char first()`

DESCRIPTION This method moves the current index to the beginning of the text subrange and returns the character at that position. This new index is the same as returned by `getBeginIndex()`.

RETURNS The first character in the text subrange.

SEE ALSO `getBeginIndex()`.

EXAMPLE See `StringCharacterIterator.next()`.

getBeginIndex()

PURPOSE Retrieves the index at the beginning of the text subrange.

SYNTAX `public abstract int getBeginIndex()`

DESCRIPTION This method returns the index at the beginning of the iterable text subrange. It does not move the current index.

RETURNS The index at which the text subrange begins.

SEE ALSO `first()`.

EXAMPLE See `StringCharacterIterator.next()`.

getEndIndex()

PURPOSE Retrieves the index at the end of the text subrange.

SYNTAX `public abstract int getEndIndex()`

DESCRIPTION This method retrieves the index of the first character that follows the end of the text subrange. Thus, if the text subrange includes characters with index `5` to `10`, this method returns `11`. This method does not move the current index.

RETURNS The index at which the text subrange ends.

EXAMPLE See `StringCharacterIterator.next()`.

getIndex()

PURPOSE Retrieves the current index.

SYNTAX `public abstract int getIndex()`

DESCRIPTION This method gets the current index without moving it.

RETURNS The current index.

EXAMPLE See `StringCharacterIterator.next()`.

last()

PURPOSE Moves the index to the end of the text subrange and retrieves that character.

SYNTAX `public abstract char last()`

DESCRIPTION This method moves the current index to the end of the text subrange and returns the character at that position. This new index is the same as returned by `getEndIndex() - 1`.

RETURNS The last character in the text subrange.

SEE ALSO `getEndIndex()`.

EXAMPLE See `StringCharacterIterator.next()`.

next()

PURPOSE Increments the index by 1 and retrieves that character.

SYNTAX `public abstract char next()`

DESCRIPTION This method increments the current index by 1 and returns the character at the new index. If the iterator attempts to increment past the end of the text subrange, the current index remains at that position and a value of `CharacterIterator.DONE` is returned.

RETURNS The character at the new index or `CharacterIterator.DONE`.

SEE ALSO `CharacterIterator.DONE`.

EXAMPLE See `StringCharacterIterator.next()`.

A B C D E F G H I J K L M N O P Q R S T U V W X Y Z

previous()

PURPOSE Decrements the index by 1 and retrieves that character.

SYNTAX `public abstract char previous()`

DESCRIPTION This method decrements the current index by 1 and returns the character at the new index. If the iterator attempts to decrement past the beginning of its range, `getBeginIndex()`, the current index remains at that position and `CharacterIterator.DONE` is returned.

RETURNS The character at the new index, or `CharacterIterator.DONE`.

SEE ALSO `CharacterIterator.DONE`.

EXAMPLE See `StringCharacterIterator.next()`.

setIndex()

PURPOSE Moves the index to a position and retrieves that character.

SYNTAX `public abstract char setIndex(int idx)`

DESCRIPTION This method sets the current index to `idx` and returns the character at that new index. Currently, if a value outside of the subrange is passed in, it throws an error; this behavior may change in future versions.

Note: In JDK 1.1.x, the call `iterator.setIndex(iterator.getEndIndex())` throws an exception. This is considered a bug. Starting with JDK 1.2, this will be a valid call. Because it is a change in semantics, it will not be fixed in the JDK 1.1.x series.

PARAMETERS

`idx` The position within the text. Valid values are in the range `getBeginIndex()` ≤ `idx` < `getEndIndex()`. An `IllegalArgumentException` is thrown if an invalid value is supplied.

Note: In JDK 1.1.x, a value of `idx` equal to `end` is invalid. This is considered a bug. Starting in JDK 1.2 it will be valid.

RETURNS The character at the specified position.

EXCEPTIONS

`IllegalArgumentException`

If `idx` is outside of its valid range. This behavior of throwing an error for values outside of the subrange may change in future versions.

EXAMPLE See `StringCharacterIterator.next()`.

CharArrayReader

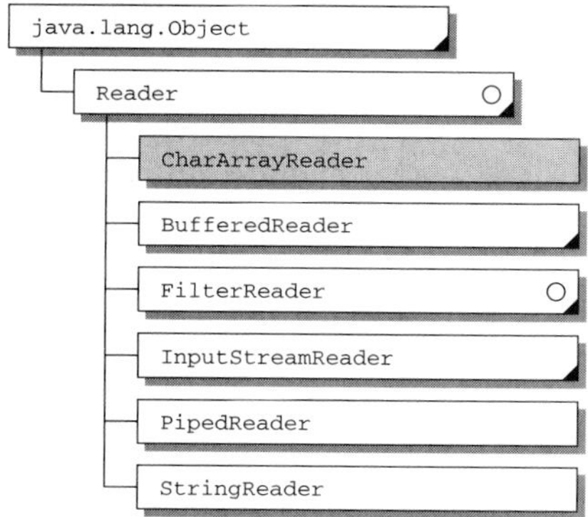

Syntax

```
public class CharArrayReader extends Reader
```

Description

`CharArrayReader` implements a char array input stream, or *char array reader*. You can use a char array reader to turn a `char` array into an input stream on which you can perform character-read operations. Requests to read from the char array reader retrieve characters from the original `char` array (see Figure 22).

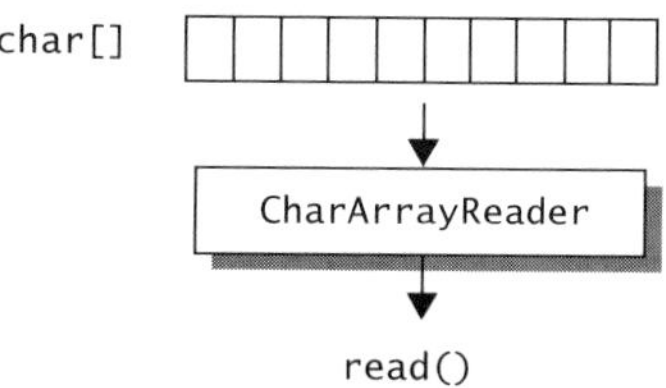

FIGURE 22: `CharArrayReader`.

ByteArrayInputStream and StringReader

`ByteArrayInputStream` provides similar functionality for `byte` arrays. See `ByteArrayInputStream` for details. `StringReader` provides similar functionality, except that instead of reading from a `char` array, you read characters from a `StringBuffer` that behaves like a reader.

MEMBER SUMMARY	
Constructor	
`CharArrayReader()`	Constructs a `CharArrayReader` instance using a `char` array.
Input Methods	
`read()`	Reads one or more characters from this char array reader.
`skip()`	Skips a specified number of characters in this char array reader.

Continued

MEMBER SUMMARY	
Mark/Reset Methods	
`mark()`	Marks the current position in this char array reader.
`markSupported()`	Determines whether this char array reader supports rereading of its data.
`reset()`	Resets to the previously marked position of the char array reader.
Stream Methods	
`close()`	Closes this char array reader.
`ready()`	Determines whether this reader is ready to be read without being blocked.
Protected Fields	
`buf`	The `char` array containing the characters to be read.
`count`	The ending index of the `char` array to be read.
`markedPos`	The position of the mark.
`pos`	The current read position in the `char` array.

See Also

`ByteArrayInputStream`, `CharArrayWriter`, `FilterWriter`, `StringWriter`, `Writer`.

Example

This example exercises all of the methods in the `CharArrayReader` class. It reads all of the characters from the reader, resets the reader, skips three characters, and then reads the rest of the characters from the reader.

```
import java.io.*;

class Main {
    public static void main(String[] args) {
        char[] input = { 'a', 'b', 'c', 'd', 'e'};
        CharArrayReader in = new CharArrayReader(input);

        int ch;

        try {
            while ((ch=in.read()) >= 0)        // reads "abcde"
                System.out.print((char)ch);
            in.reset();
            System.out.println();

            in.skip(3);                        // skip "abc"

            while ((ch=in.read()) >= 0)        // reads "de"
                System.out.print((char)ch);
            System.out.println();
```

```
            in.close();
        } catch (IOException e) {
            e.printStackTrace();
        }
    }
}
```


buf

PURPOSE The char array containing the characters to be read.

SYNTAX `protected char[] buf`

DESCRIPTION `buf` is a reference to the `char` array used to create this char array reader. Because this is a reference, any changes to the original `char` array are reflected in this char array reader.

SEE ALSO `count`, `pos`.

CharArrayReader()

PURPOSE Constructs a `CharArrayReader` instance using a `char` array.

SYNTAX

```
public CharArrayReader(char[] buffer)
public CharArrayReader(char[] buffer, int offset, int count)
```

DESCRIPTION These constructors are used to create a char array reader using an existing `char` array `buffer`. `buffer` is used directly and not copied, so any changes to `buffer` after the creation of this reader also affect this reader. The characters to be read from `buffer` are the `count` number of characters starting at index `offset`. If `offset` and `count` are not specified, all of the characters in the entire buffer will be read.

PARAMETERS

`buffer` The non-`null` buffer containing the characters to be read (not copied).

`count` The number of characters that can be read from `buffer`. If `count + offset` exceeds `buffer.length`, `count` is automatically lowered to the limit imposed by `buffer`.

`offset` The index in `buffer` from which to start reading.

EXAMPLE See the class example.

close()

PURPOSE Closes this char array reader.

SYNTAX `public void close()`

DESCRIPTION This method closes this reader by releasing its buffer (setting `buf` to `null`). `close()` is idempotent; that is, only the first `close()` has any effect and subsequent invocations of it do nothing. Once a reader has been closed, attempts to invoke other methods on the reader, other than the `close()` method, will throw an `IOException`.

EXAMPLE See the class example.

count

PURPOSE The ending index of the `char` array to be read.

SYNTAX `protected int count`

DESCRIPTION This field records the exclusive ending index of the `char` array to be read. It is calculated initially when the char array reader is first created, and it remains unchanged. See the constructor for how `count` is initialized.

SEE ALSO `pos`, `CharArrayReader()`.

mark()

PURPOSE Marks the current position in this char array reader.

SYNTAX `public void mark(int readlimit) throws IOException`

DESCRIPTION Char array readers support marks and resets. This method marks the current position in this char array reader. A subsequent call to `reset()` will reposition this reader at this marked position so that subsequent reads will reread the same characters.

PARAMETERS

`readlimit` This parameter is ignored.

OVERRIDES `Reader.mark()`.

SEE ALSO `markedPos`, `markSupported()`, `reset()`.

EXAMPLE This example creates a char array reader that has five characters. It skips the first three characters, sets a mark, completes reading, and then returns to the mark and rereads the rest of the reader. Note that the argument (`0`) to `mark()` is ignored.

```
import java.io.*;

class Main {
    public static void main(String[] args) {
        char[] input = { 'a', 'b', 'c', 'd', 'e'};
        CharArrayReader in = new CharArrayReader(input);

        int ch;

        try {
            in.skip(3);                        // skip "abc"
            in.mark(0);
            while ((ch=in.read()) >= 0)        // reads "de"
                System.out.print((char)ch);
            in.reset();
            System.out.println();

            while ((ch=in.read()) >= 0)        // reads "de"
                System.out.print((char)ch);
            System.out.println();
            in.close();
        } catch (IOException e) {
            e.printStackTrace();
        }
    }
}
```

markedPos

PURPOSE The position of the mark.

SYNTAX `protected int mark`

DESCRIPTION When you set a mark on this char array input stream by calling `mark()`, the current read position is recorded in the field `markedPos`. When `reset()` is invoked, the current read position is reset to `mark`. If no mark has been set, the value of `markedPos` is the offset supplied to the constructor (or `0` if the offset was not supplied). This field should not be used directly. `mark()` should be used to change its value.

Note: In Java 1.1.4, the constructor does not use the offset supplied to set `markedPos`. `markedPos` is always initialized to `0`.

SEE ALSO `mark()`, `pos`, `reset()`.

A B C D E F G H I J K L M N O P Q R S T U V W X Y Z

markSupported()

PURPOSE Determines whether this char array reader supports rereading of its data.

SYNTAX

```
public boolean markSupported()
```

DESCRIPTION This method returns whether this char array input stream supports rereading of its data (i.e., mark/reset). Char array readers support this feature. Hence, this method always returns `true`.

RETURNS `true`.

OVERRIDES `Reader.markSupported()`.

SEE ALSO `mark()`, `reset()`.

pos

PURPOSE The current read position in the `char` array.

SYNTAX

```
protected int pos
```

DESCRIPTION This field records the current read position in the `char` array of this reader. The next `read()` or `skip()` operation will start reading from this position. This field is set initially when this reader is first created and is updated during `read()` and `skip()` operations to record which character to read next. `reset()` sets `pos` to the previously marked position (see `mark()`) so that subsequent reading and skipping will start at the marked position.

`pos` is a `0`-based index of `buf`. It is initialized to the value of `offset` supplied in the `CharArrayReader()` constructor (or to `0` if the value is not supplied).

SEE ALSO `count`.

read()

PURPOSE Reads one or more characters from this char array reader.

SYNTAX

```
public int read()
public int read(char[] buffer, int offset, int count)
```

DESCRIPTION The `read()` method reads characters from this char array reader, starting at the current read position. The current read position is usually that of the next character after the last character read during the previous `read()` or `skip()` invocation. However, the current read position can be changed using `reset()`.

The first form of `read()` returns the character at the current read position in this char array reader. The high-order 2 bytes of the `int` returned are set to `0`. If end-of- stream has been reached, this method returns `-1`.

The second form of `read()` reads `count` characters from this reader starting at the current read position and stores the characters read into the `char` array `buffer` starting at index `offset`. The actual number of characters read is returned. This number could differ from `count` when the number of characters available is less than that requested. If no characters can be read because end-of-stream has been reached, this method returns `-1`.

PARAMETERS

`buffer`	The non-`null` buffer into which the data is read.
`count`	The number of characters to read. `0` ≤ `count` ≤ `buffer.length`.
`offset`	The index in `buffer` at which to start storing the characters read. `0` ≤ `offset` < `buffer.length`.

RETURNS The first form returns the characters read. The second returns the actual number of characters read. Both forms return `-1` if end-of-stream has been reached.

EXCEPTIONS

`ArrayIndexOutOfBoundsException`

If `count` or `offset` is outside of the specified bounds.

`IOException`

If an IO error occurred while attempting to read the requested characters.

OVERRIDES `Reader.read()`.

SEE ALSO `reset()`, `skip()`.

EXAMPLE See the class example.

ready()

PURPOSE Determines whether this reader is ready to be read without being blocked.

SYNTAX `public boolean ready() throws IOException`

DESCRIPTION This method determines whether this reader is ready to be read without being blocked. Char array readers can always be read without being blocked. Hence, this method always returns `true`.

RETURNS `true`.

EXCEPTIONS

`IOException`

If this reader has already been closed.

EXAMPLE See `Reader.ready()`.

reset()

PURPOSE Resets the buffer to the previously marked position of the char array reader.

SYNTAX `public void reset() throws IOException`

DESCRIPTION This method resets the current read position of this char array reader to the previously marked position. If no mark has been set, it is set to the offset specified in the constructor (or to `0` if no offset was specified). The ending index of this reader (the index calculated originally using the `offset` and `count` arguments to the constructor) remains unchanged.

Note: In Java 1.1.4, the offset specified in the constructor is not used by `reset()`. If no mark has been set, `reset()` always resets to the beginning of the `char` array (`0`). For example, regardless of whether `offset` was `10` or `0`, `reset()` always sets the current read position to `0`.

OVERRIDES `Reader.reset()`.

SEE ALSO `count, pos, markedPos, mark(), read(), skip()`.

EXAMPLE See the class example.

skip()

PURPOSE Skips a specified number of characters in this char array reader.

SYNTAX `public long skip(long count) throws IOException`

DESCRIPTION This method skips `count` number of characters of this char array reader starting at the current read position. It returns the actual number of characters skipped, which may differ from `count` if there are fewer characters available in the stream. The current read position is updated to reflect the number of characters skipped. The next `read()` will not return those characters skipped.

It returns `0` if it cannot skip any characters.

PARAMETERS
`count` The number of characters to be skipped.

RETURNS The actual number of characters skipped.

OVERRIDES `Reader.skip()`.

SEE ALSO `read()`.

EXAMPLE See the class example.

CharArrayWriter

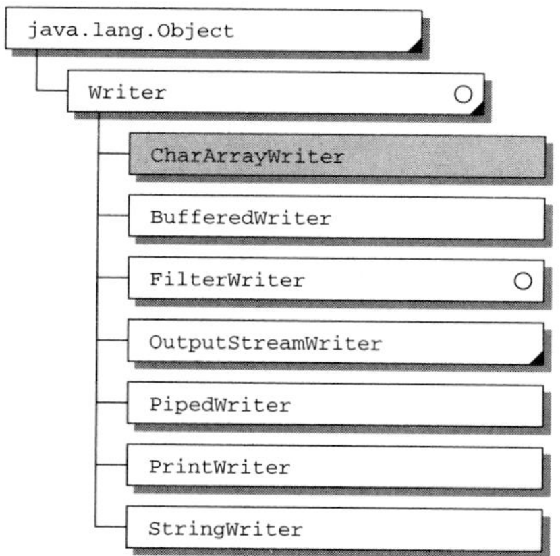

Syntax

```
public class CharArrayWriter extends Writer
```

Description

`CharArrayWriter` implements a character array output stream, or *char array writer.* You can use a char array writer to treat a `char` array as a writer on which you can perform write operations. Requests to write characters to the writer store the characters in an automatically expandable `char` array whose contents can later be retrieved as a `char` array or as a string. This is helpful when you want to capture output from methods that operate on writers in the form of a `char` array. See Figure 23.

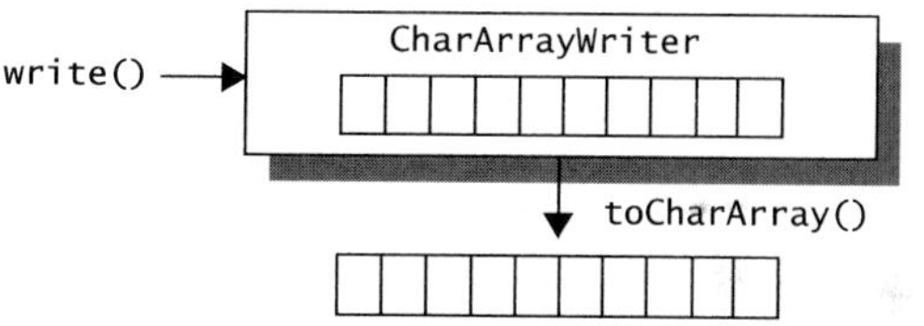

FIGURE 23: **`CharArrayWriter.`**

StringWriter and ByteArrayOutputStream

Classes that perform similar functions are `StringWriter` and `ByteArrayOutputStream`. `StringWriter` provides similar functionality, except that instead of writing to a `char` array, you write to a `StringBuffer`. `ByteArrayOutputStream` provide similar functionality for `byte` arrays.

MEMBER SUMMARY	
Constructor	
`CharArrayWriter()`	Constructs a `CharArrayWriter` instance.
Output Method	
`write()`	Writes characters to this char array writer.
Stream Methods	
`close()`	This method does nothing.
`flush()`	This method does nothing.
`reset()`	Resets this char array writer so that it can be reused.
`size()`	Retrieves the number of characters in this char array writer.
Externalizing Methods	
`toCharArray()`	Retrieves the contents of this char array writer as a `char` array.
`toString()`	Retrieves the contents of this char array writer as a string.
`writeTo()`	Writes the contents of this writer to another writer.
Protected Fields	
`buf`	The buffer in which data of this char array writer is stored.
`count`	The number of characters in this char array writer.

See Also

`ByteArrayOutputStream`, `CharArrayReader`, `StringWriter`, `OutputStream`.

Example

This example shows the use of a char array writer to add a backslash character to escape meta characters that appear in a string.

```
import java.io.CharArrayWriter;

class Main {
    // for any meta character that appear in the string 's',
    // escape it with the backslash.
    public static String encode(String s, char[] metachars) {
        // start off with length of string; stream will grow automatically
        CharArrayWriter out = new CharArrayWriter(s.length());

        for (int i = 0; i < s.length(); i++) {
            int c = (int)s.charAt(i);
            for (int j = 0; j < metachars.length; j++) {
                if (c == metachars[j]) {
                    out.write('\\');
                    break;
                }
            }
```

```
            out.write(c);
        }
        return out.toString();
    }
    public static void main(String[] args) {
        char[] meta = {'\\', '\''};
        String raw = "'abc'\\b2+3";
        String answer = encode(raw, meta);

        System.out.println("Raw: " + raw);
        System.out.println("Encoded: " + answer);
    }
}
```


buf

PURPOSE The buffer in which data of this char array writer is stored.

SYNTAX `protected char[] buf`

DESCRIPTION This field is used to store the characters written to the char array writer. `buf`'s initial size is determined by the arguments to the `CharArrayWriter()` constructor, but it is expanded as needed as more characters are written to the writer.

SEE ALSO `count`, `size()`.

CharArrayWriter()

PURPOSE Constructs a `CharArrayWriter` instance.

SYNTAX
```
public CharArrayWriter()
public CharArrayWriter(int size)
```

DESCRIPTION There are two forms of the constructor for `CharArrayWriter`. The first form constructs a char array writer that has the default buffer size of 32 characters. The second form constructs a char array writer buffer of size `size`.

A buffer of the specified size is created to store the characters written to this writer. As the number of characters written to this writer exceeds the buffer size, the buffer will be grown automatically to accommodate the additional characters.

PARAMETERS

`size` The initial buffer size. `size` > `0`.

SEE ALSO `size()`.

EXAMPLE See the class example and `reset()`.

A B C D E F G H I J K L M N O P Q R S T U V W X Y Z

close()

PURPOSE This method does nothing.

SYNTAX `public void close()`

DESCRIPTION This method implements the abstract method declared in `Writer`.

SEE ALSO `Writer.close()`.

count

PURPOSE The number of characters in this char array writer.

SYNTAX `protected int count`

DESCRIPTION This field records the number of characters that have been written to this writer since its most recent reset or since it was created if it has never reset. This number is incremented as more characters are written to this writer and is set to `0` when `reset()` is invoked.

RETURNS The number of characters in this writer.

SEE ALSO `reset()`, `size()`.

EXAMPLE See `buf`.

flush()

PURPOSE This method does nothing.

SYNTAX `public void flush()`

DESCRIPTION This method implements the abstract method declared in `Writer`.

SEE ALSO `Writer.flush()`.

reset()

PURPOSE Resets this char array writer so that it can be reused.

SYNTAX `public synchronized void reset()`

DESCRIPTION This method resets the current write position of this writer to be the beginning of the `char` array. The size of this writer becomes `0`, and all characters written earlier to the current writer are lost. Subsequent write operations to this writer start at the beginning of the `char` array.

OVERRIDES `Writer.reset()`.

SEE ALSO `write()`, `writeTo()`.

EXAMPLE This example shows the use of `reset()` and `writeTo()` to write a list of HTML anchors when their descriptions and references are provided. It uses the char array writer to construct each anchor and then writes the result to the output writer. Before processing the next anchor, it resets the char array writer.

```
import java.io.*;

class Main {
    // writes out an HTML anchor:    <A HREF="ref"> desc </A>
    static CharArrayWriter buf = new CharArrayWriter();
    static String prefix = "<A HREF=\"";
    static String suffix = " </A>\n";

    public static void anchor(String[] desc, String[] ref, Writer out)
    throws IOException{

        for (int a = 0; a < desc.length; a++) {
                buf.write(prefix, 0, prefix.length());
                buf.write(ref[a], 0, ref[1].length());

                buf.write("\"> ", 0, 3);
                buf.write(desc[a], 0, desc[a].length());

                buf.write(suffix, 0, suffix.length());
                buf.writeTo(out);
                buf.reset();        // reset stream to start of buffer
        }
    }
    public static void main(String[] args) {
        String[] desc = {"Preface", "Table of Contents",
                         "Index", "Glossary"};
        String[] ref = {"preface.htm", "toc.htm",
                        "index.htm", "glossary.htm"};
        Writer out = new OutputStreamWriter(System.out);
        try {
            anchor(desc, ref, out);
            out.flush();
        } catch (IOException e) {
            e.printStackTrace();
        }
    }
}
```

size()

PURPOSE Retrieves the number of characters in this char array writer.

SYNTAX `public int size()`

A B C D E F G H I J K L M N O P Q R S T U V W X Y Z

DESCRIPTION This method returns the number of character that have been written to this char array writer since its most recent reset or since it was created if it has never reset. This number is incremented as more characters are written to this writer and is set to `0` when `reset()` is invoked.

RETURNS The number of characters in this char array writer.

SEE ALSO `count`, `reset()`.

EXAMPLE This example shows the use of a char array writer to concatenate the string representations of a vector of objects. It returns the result as a `char` array.

```
import java.util.Vector;
import java.io.*;

class Main {
    public static char[] concat(Vector objs, boolean printSize) {
        CharArrayWriter out = new CharArrayWriter();

        for (int i = 0; i < objs.size(); i++) {
            String str = objs.elementAt(i).toString();
            out.write(str, 0, str.length());
        }
        if (printSize)
            System.out.println("Size: " + out.size());
        return (out.toCharArray());
    }
    public static void main(String[] args) {
        Vector objs = new Vector(args.length);

        for (int i = 0; i < args.length; i++)
            objs.addElement(args[i]);

        char[] all = concat(objs, true); // print size of total string

        for (int i = 0; i < all.length; i++)
            System.out.print(all[i]);
        System.out.println();
    }
}
```

toCharArray()

PURPOSE Retrieves the contents of this char array writer as a char array.

SYNTAX `public char[] toCharArray()`

DESCRIPTION This method is used to retrieve the contents of this char array writer as a `char` array. The contents of this writer are copied to a newly created `char` array, and this new `char` array is returned. Subsequent changes to this writer do not affect the `char` array that is returned.

RETURNS A new non-`null` `char` array containing the contents of this writer.

EXAMPLE See `size()`.

toString()

PURPOSE Retrieves the contents of this char array writer as a string.

SYNTAX

```
public String toString()
```

DESCRIPTION This method creates a string using the contents of this char array writer. The string that is returned is a snapshot of the current contents of this writer. It is not affected by any subsequent changes to this writer.

RETURNS The non-`null` string representing the contents of this char array writer.

OVERRIDES `java.lang.Object.toString()`.

SEE ALSO `java.lang.String.String()`, `toCharArray()`.

EXAMPLE See the class example.

write()

PURPOSE Writes one or more characters to this char array writer.

SYNTAX

```
public void write(int oneChar)
public void write(char[] buffer, int offset, int count)
public void write(String str, int offset, int count)
```

DESCRIPTION The `write()` method writes one or more characters to this char array writer. The first form writes a single character `oneChar` to this writer. The second and third forms write to this writer either `count` characters from the `char` array `buffer` or the string `str` starting at index `offset`.

The characters written are copied to the writer starting at the current write position. The current write position is usually the next index after the point at which the last character from the previous `write()` occurred, unless set to `0` via `reset()`. The current write position is incremented to reflect the new characters written. The internal `char` array used to hold the contents of the writer expands dynamically as required to hold all of the new data.

PARAMETERS

`buffer` The non-`null` `char` array containing the characters to be written.

`count` The number of characters from `buffer` or `str` to be written.
`0` ≤ `count` ≤ `buffer.length-offset` or `0` ≤ `count` ≤ `str.length()-offset`.

offset — The index in `buffer` or `str` of the first character to be written. $0 \le$ `offset` $<$ `buffer.length` or $0 \le$ `offset` $<$ `str.length()`.

oneChar — The character to be written. The low-order 2 bytes of `oneChar` are used.

str — The non-`null` string containing the characters to be written.

A B C D E F G H I J K L M N O P Q R S T U V W X Y Z

EXCEPTIONS

`ArrayIndexOutOfBoundsException`
If `count` or `offset` is outside of the specified bounds.

OVERRIDES `Writer.write()`.

SEE ALSO `reset()`, `writeTo()`.

EXAMPLE See the class example and `size()`.

writeTo()

PURPOSE Writes the contents of this writer to another writer.

SYNTAX `public void writeTo(Writer out) throws IOException`

DESCRIPTION This method writes the entire contents of this writer to the writer `out`. The output consists of all of the characters that have been written to this writer since its most recent reset or since it was created if it has never reset.

This method does not change the current write position.

PARAMETERS

out — The non-`null` writer to which to write.

EXCEPTIONS

`IOException`
If an IO error occurred while attempting to write to `out`.

SEE ALSO `write()`, `Writer`.

EXAMPLE See `size()`.

CharConversionException

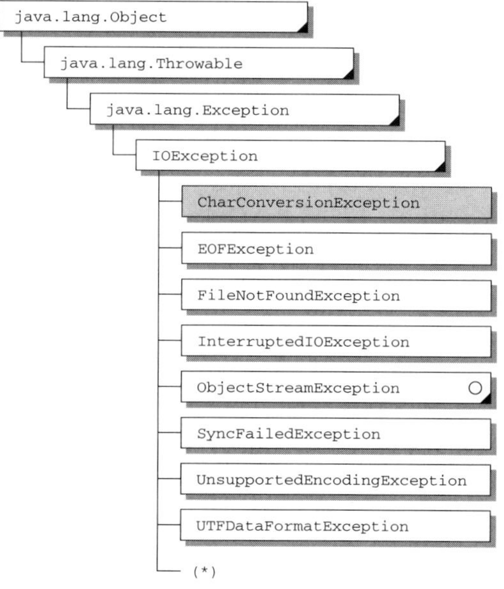

(*) 7 classes from other packages not shown.

Syntax

```
public class CharConversionException extends IOException
```

Description

The `CharConversionException` exception is thrown when there is a problem converting a character to its byte encoding. This can happen if the character cannot be converted because the buffer being used for the conversion becomes full before all of the characters have been converted. Also, it can happen if the sequence of characters being converted is malformed. It can also happen if a character cannot be converted because no mapping for it can be found.

A method that throws `CharConversionException` must declare it or any of its superclasses in the method's `throws` clause.

MEMBER SUMMARY	
Constructor	
`CharConversionException()`	Constructs an instance of `CharConversionException`.

See Also

`OutputStreamWriter.write()`.

Example

In Java 1.1.4, the only place where `CharConversionException` is thrown directly is `OutputStreamWriter.write()`, when it runs of buffer space to do the conversion.

A B C D E F G H I J K L M N O P Q R S T U V W X Y Z

CharConversionException()

PURPOSE	Constructs an instance of `CharConversionException`
SYNTAX	`public CharConversionException()` `public CharConversionException(String s)`
DESCRIPTION	The two forms of this constructor construct an instance of `CharConversionException`. An optional string `msg` can be supplied that describes this particular instance of the exception. If `msg` is not supplied, it defaults to `null`.
PARAMETERS	
`msg`	A possibly `null` string that gives details about this exception.
SEE ALSO	`java.lang.Throwable.getMessage()`.

CheckedInputStream

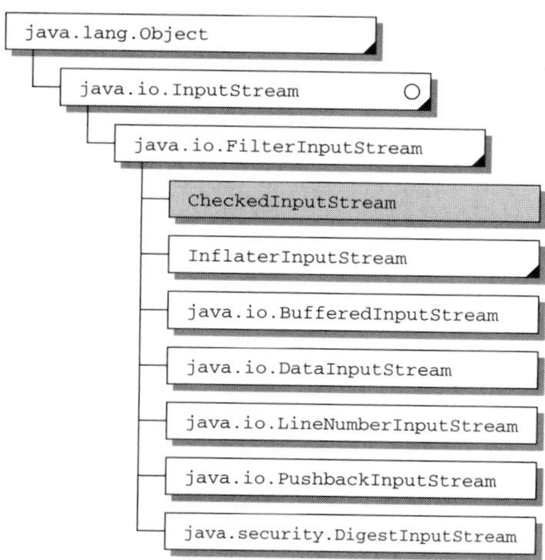

A B C D E F G H I J K L M N O P Q R S T U V W X Y Z

Syntax

```
public class CheckedInputStream extends FilterInputStream
```

Description

A checked input stream computes a checksum value based on the data that flows through it. See `Checksum` for more information about checksum values and `InputStream` for more information about input streams.

Usage

A checked input stream is a filter input stream, so it can be included in any part of the input stream pipeline (see `FilterInputStream` for more details). After all of the data has flowed through the checked input stream, use `getChecksum()` to retrieve the checksum value.

MEMBER SUMMARY	
Constructor	
`CheckedInputStream()`	Constructs a `CheckedInputStream` instance.
Checksum Value Method	
`getChecksum()`	Retrieves this checked input stream's checksum object.
Stream Methods	
`read()`	Reads bytes from this checked input stream.
`skip()`	Skips bytes from this checked input stream.

See Also

Adler32, CheckedOutputStream, CRC32, java.io.FilterInputStream, java.io.InputStream.

Example

This example implements a program that periodically checks a set of URLs for any changes. For each URL, the program reads in the URL contents through a checked input stream and then retrieves its checksum value. A checksum value that differs from the value retrieved the previous time means the URL contents have changed; the user is notified. Note that this is not the most efficient means of detecting change, but it works for all protocols.

The checksum value for each URL is stored in a properties file.

One useful enhancement to this program is to send mail whenever a change to a URL is detected. The mail message could include URLs that changed.

```
import java.net.*;
import java.io.*;
import java.util.*;
import java.util.zip.*;

class Main implements Runnable {
    Vector urls;
    int period = 60 * 60 * 1000;     // One hour.

    Main(Vector urls, String periodStr) {
        this.urls = urls;

        // Get time units.
        char c = periodStr.charAt(periodStr.length()-1);
        double p = Double.valueOf(
            periodStr.substring(0, periodStr.length()-1)).doubleValue();

        if (c == 's') {                                      // seconds
            period = (int)(p * 1000);
        } else if (c == 'd') {                               // days
            period = (int)(p * 24 * 60 * 60 * 1000);
        } else if (c == 'h') {                               // hours
            period = (int)(p * 60 * 60 * 1000);
        } else if (c == 'm') {                               // minutes
            period = (int)(p * 60 * 1000);
        }

        (new Thread(this)).start();
    }

    public void run() {
        Adler32 adler = new Adler32();
        Properties prop = getChecksums();

        while (true) {
            try {
                for (int i=0; i<urls.size(); i++) {
                    URL url = new URL((String)urls.elementAt(i));
                    CheckedInputStream is =
                        new CheckedInputStream(
```

```
                    new BufferedInputStream(url.openStream()), adler);

                // Use skip().
                while (is.skip(100000) > 0) {
                }

                // Or use read().
                //byte[] buf = new byte[1024];
                //while (is.read(buf, 0, buf.length) >= 0) {
                //}
                is.close();

                // Compare the current checksum with the previous checksum.
                String s = (String)prop.get(
                    URLEncoder.encode(url.toString()));
                if (s == null
                    || !s.equals(""+is.getChecksum().getValue())) {
                    System.out.println(
                        url.toString() + " has been updated.");
                }
                prop.put(URLEncoder.encode(url.toString()),
                    ""+is.getChecksum().getValue());

                // Reset since it will be used again.
                adler.reset();
            }
            // Save the latest set of checksums.
            saveChecksums(prop);

            // Sleep for the specified period.
            Thread.sleep(period);
        } catch (Exception e) {
            e.printStackTrace();
        }
    }
}

// Read and return the checksum values.
Properties getChecksums() {
    Properties prop = new Properties();
    try {
        FileInputStream fis = new FileInputStream("urls.properties");
        prop.load(fis);
        fis.close();
    } catch (IOException e) {
    }
    return prop;
}

// Save and return the checksum values.
void saveChecksums(Properties prop) {
    FileInputStream fis;
    Properties properties = new Properties();
    try {
        FileOutputStream fos = new FileOutputStream("urls.properties");
        prop.save(fos, "Checksum of URLs");
        fos.close();
    } catch (IOException e) {
        e.printStackTrace();
    }
```

```
    }

    public static void main(String[] args) {
        if (args.length < 2) {
            System.err.println("Usage: java Main <file of URLs> <Ns|Nm|Nh|Nd>");
            System.exit(1);
        }

        // Read file of URLs
        Vector urls = new Vector();
        try {
            // Create the input stream.
            BufferedReader is = new BufferedReader(new FileReader(args[0]));

            // Read the input stream.
            String line = null;
            while ((line = is.readLine()) != null) {
                urls.addElement(line);
            }
            is.close();
        } catch (IOException e) {
            e.printStackTrace();
        }
        new Main(urls, args[1]);
    }
}
```

urls.properties

```
#Checksum of URLs
#Wed Nov 05 10:20:18 CST 1997
http%3A%2F%2Fwww.xeo.com%2F=3972502904
http%3A%2F%2Fwww.sun.com%2F=1029482416
http%3A%2F%2Fwww.cnet.com%2F=290411809
http%3A%2F%2Fwww.amazon.com%2Fexec%2Fobidos%2FISBN%3D0201310031%2F5524-
8081340-507344=398532795
http=//www.sun.com/=1029482416
http%3A%2F%2Fwww.webweek.com%2F=3295535806
http%3A%2F%2Fwww.yahoo.com%2F=175549173
http%3A%2F%2Fjava.sun.com%2F=224182184
```

CheckedInputStream()

PURPOSE Constructs a `CheckedinputStream` instance.

SYNTAX `public CheckedInputStream(InputStream in, Checksum cksum)`

DESCRIPTION This constructor constructs a filter input stream for `in` using the checksum algorithm encapsulated by `cksum`.

PARAMETERS

`cksum` A non-`null` checksum object.

`in` A non-`null` input stream.

SEE ALSO `Adler32`, `CRC32`.

EXAMPLE See the class example.

getChecksum()

PURPOSE Retrieves this checked input stream's checksum object.

SYNTAX
```
public Checksum getChecksum()
```

DESCRIPTION Each value that passes through this checked input stream is also given to the checksum object. The checksum object uses the value to update its checksum value. Use this method to retrieve the input stream's checksum object, which can then be used to retrieve the checksum value. The returned checksum object is the same one specified in the constructor.

RETURNS The non-`null` checksum object.

SEE ALSO `CheckedInputStream`, `Checksum.getValue()`.

EXAMPLE See the class example.

read()

PURPOSE Reads bytes from this checked input stream.

SYNTAX
```
public int read() throws IOException
public int read(byte[] buf, int off, int len) throws IOException
```

DESCRIPTION This method reads at most `len` bytes from this input stream and places them in `buf` starting at `buf[off]`. The blocking behavior of this method depends on the input streams from which it reads. In general, this method blocks until some bytes (possibly less than `len`) are read.

If no parameters are specified, this method returns a single byte from this input stream.

Note that `mark()` should not be used with this input stream; the repeated reads will affect the checksum value.

PARAMETERS

`buf` The non-`null` buffer in which to read the data.

`len` The maximum number of bytes to read into `buf` starting at `buf[off]`. `0` ≤ `len` ≤ `buf.length-off`.

`off` The `0`-based starting offset of the data in `buf`. `0` ≤ `off` < `buf.length`.

RETURNS If `-1` is returned, the end of the stream is reached. If no parameters are specified, the read byte is returned in the low-order byte of an `int` (the high-order 3 bytes are set to 0); otherwise, the number of read bytes is returned.

EXCEPTIONS
`IOException`
If an IO error occurs while reading bytes.

OVERRIDES `java.io.FilterInputStream.read()`.

SEE ALSO `java.io.IOException`, `java.io.InputStream.mark()`.

EXAMPLE See the class example.

A B C D E F G H I J K L M N O P Q R S T U V W X Y Z

skip()

PURPOSE Skips bytes from this checked input stream.

SYNTAX `public long skip(long n) throws IOException`

DESCRIPTION This method skips `n` bytes from the input stream. This method will block until at least `n` bytes have been skipped or the end of stream has been reached. The skipped bytes are still used in computation of the checksum value. If `n > 0` and the return value is `0`, the end of the stream has been reached.

PARAMETERS
`n` The nonnegative number of bytes to skip.

RETURNS The possibly zero number of bytes skipped.

EXCEPTIONS
`IOException`
If an IO error occurs while skipping bytes.

OVERRIDES `java.io.FilterInputStream.read()`.

SEE ALSO `java.io.IOException`.

EXAMPLE See the class example.

CheckedOutputStream

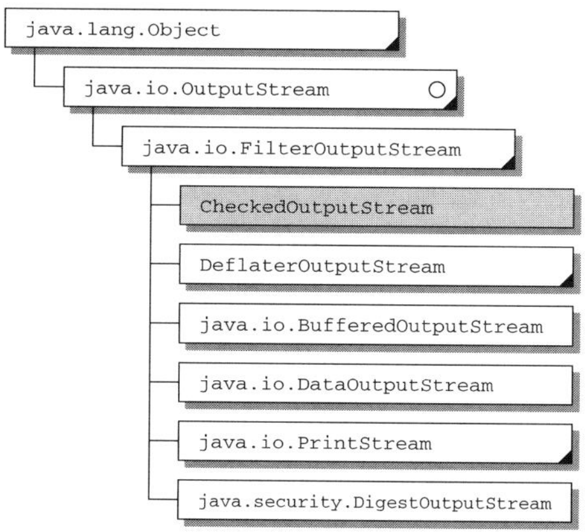

Syntax

```
public class CheckedOutputStream extends FilterOutputStream
```

Description

A checked output stream computes a checksum value based on the data that flows through it. See `Checksum` for more information about checksum values and `OutputStream` for more information about output streams.

Usage

A checked output stream is a filter output stream can be included in any part of the output stream pipeline (see `FilterOutputStream` for more details). After all of the data has flowed through the checked output stream, use `getChecksum()` to retrieve the checksum value.

MEMBER SUMMARY	
Constructor	
`CheckedOutputStream()`	Constructs a `CheckedOutputStream` instance.
Checksum Value Method	
`getChecksum()`	Retrieves this checked output stream's checksum object.
Stream Method	
`write()`	Writes bytes to this checked output stream.

See Also

Adler32, CRC32, java.io.OutputStream.

Example

A B C D E F G H I J K L M N O P Q R S T U V W X Y Z

This example is a simple demonstration of how to use a checked output stream. This example reads a file and writes a compressed version of it. A checked input stream is used to compute a checksum of the uncompressed file. A checked output stream is used to compute the checksum value of the compressed file. Both checksums are printed.

```
import java.io.*;
import java.util.zip.*;

class Main {

    public static void main(String[] args) {
        if (args.length != 1) {
            System.err.println("Usage: java Main <file>");
            System.exit(1);
        }

        try {
            // Create the input streams.
            CheckedInputStream cis = new CheckedInputStream(
                new BufferedInputStream(
                new FileInputStream(args[0])), new Adler32());

            // Create the output streams.
            CheckedOutputStream cos = new CheckedOutputStream(
                new FileOutputStream(args[0]+".zip"), new Adler32());
            OutputStream os = new BufferedOutputStream(
                new GZIPOutputStream(cos));

            byte[] buf = new byte[1024];
            int len;

            // Transfer from the input stream to the output stream.
            while ((len = cis.read(buf)) >= 0) {
                os.write(buf, 0, len);
            }

            // Print the checksum value of the compressed output stream.
            System.out.println("input:  "+cis.getChecksum().getValue());
            System.out.println("output: "+cos.getChecksum().getValue());

            // Clean up.
            cis.close();
            os.close();
        } catch (IOException e) {
            e.printStackTrace();
        }
    }
}
```

CheckedOutputStream()

PURPOSE Constructs a `CheckedOutputStream` instance.

SYNTAX
```
public CheckedOutputStream(OutputStream out, Checksum cksum)
```

DESCRIPTION This constructor constructs a filter output stream for `out` using the checksum algorithm encapsulated by `cksum`.

PARAMETERS

`cksum` A non-`null` checksum object.

`out` A non-`null` output stream.

SEE ALSO `Adler32`, `CRC32`.

EXAMPLE See the class example.

getChecksum()

PURPOSE Retrieves this checked output stream's checksum object.

SYNTAX
```
public Checksum getChecksum()
```

DESCRIPTION Each value that passes through this checked output stream is also given to the checksum object. The checksum object uses the value to update its checksum value. Use this method to retrieve the output stream's checksum object, which can then be used to retrieve the checksum value. The returned checksum object is the same one specified in the constructor.

RETURNS The non-`null` checksum object.

SEE ALSO `CheckedOutputStream`, `Checksum.getValue()`.

EXAMPLE See the class example.

write()

PURPOSE Writes bytes to this checked output stream.

SYNTAX
```
public void write(int bval) throws IOException
public void write(byte[] buf, int off, int len) throws
    IOException
```

DESCRIPTION In the first form of this method, the `byte` value `(byte)bval` (that is, the least-significant 8 bits) is written to this checked output stream. In the second form, `len` bytes starting from `buf[off]` are written to this checked output stream. In both cases, this method blocks until all of the specified bytes have been written to the output stream.

PARAMETERS

`buf`	The non-`null` buffer containing the data to write.
`bval`	The `byte` to be written. The low-order byte of `bval` is written.
`len`	The number of bytes to write starting from `buf[off]`. `0` ≤ `len` ≤ `buf.length-off`.
`off`	The starting offset of the data in `buf`. `0` ≤ `off` < `buf.length`.

EXCEPTIONS

`IOException`
If an IO error occurs while writing.

OVERRIDES `java.io.FilterOutputStream.write()`.

SEE ALSO `java.io.IOException`.

EXAMPLE See the class example.

Checksum

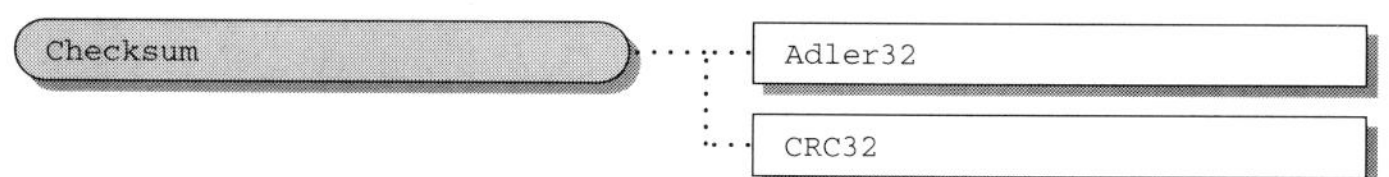

Syntax

```
public interface Checksum
```

Description

A checksum is an algorithm that takes a data set (an arbitrary sequence of bytes) and computes a single value (checksum value) to represent the data set. The goal of the checksum algorithm is to compute a different value if there are any changes to the data set. That is, with a better checksum algorithm, there is a higher probability of different checksum values for different data sets.

Checksums are most often used to verify the integrity of data. For example, in some communications protocols, a checksum value is computed and added to each packet delivered to the receiver. The receiver can recompute the checksum value of the packet data and compare it with the checksum value computed by the sender. If the checksum values are not equal, the packet data is definitely corrupted. If the checksum values are equal, there is a very high probability that the data is correct.

Usage

The `java.util.zip` package provides implementations for two different checksum algorithms: ADLER-32 (see `Adler32`) and CRC-32 (see `CRC32`). The CRC-32 algorithm produces better-quality checksum values, but the ADLER-32 algorithm is faster. Both classes implement this interface.

The `CheckedInputStream` and `CheckedOutputStream` classes use `Checksum` objects and make it easy to compute a checksum on a stream of data. If you need to implement your own checksum algorithm, you can take advantage of these classes by implementing this interface.

MEMBER SUMMARY	
Checksum Value Get Method	
`getValue()`	Retrieves the current checksum value.
Checksum Value Update Methods	
`reset()`	Resets this object to its initial state.
`update()`	Updates the checksum with one or more bytes.

See Also

`Adler32`, `CheckedInputStream`, `CheckedOutputStream`, `CRC32`.

Example

This example demonstrates how to build your own checksum class. The example declares the `XorChecksum` class, which implements a very simple algorithm that XOR's together every byte (this is not a particularly good algorithm). The program then uses the `XorChecksum` class in a checked input stream to compute the checksum of the data read from standard input.

```
import java.io.*;
import java.util.zip.*;

class Main {
    public static void main(String[] args) {
        if (args.length != 1) {
            System.err.println("Usage: java Main <file>");
            System.exit(1);
        }

        try {
            CheckedInputStream is = new CheckedInputStream(
                new BufferedInputStream(
                new FileInputStream(args[0])), new XorChecksum());
            byte[] bytes = new byte[1024];
            int len = 0;

            // Read the file and compute the checksum.
            while ((len = is.read(bytes)) >= 0) {
            }
            is.close();
            System.out.println(is.getChecksum().getValue());
        } catch (IOException e) {
            e.printStackTrace();
        }
    }
}

class XorChecksum implements Checksum {
    long chksum = 0;

    public long getValue() {
        return chksum;
    }
    public void update(int b) {
        chksum ^= (b & 0xFF);
    }
    public void update(byte[] b, int off, int len) {
        for (int i=0; i<len; i++) {
            chksum ^= (b[off+i] & 0xFF);
        }
    }
    public void reset() {
        chksum = 0;
    }
}
```

getValue()

PURPOSE Retrieves the current checksum value.

SYNTAX
```
public long getValue()
```

DESCRIPTION Each time `update()` is called, the checksum value maintained by this object is updated. This method returns the current value of the checksum.

RETURNS The current checksum value.

EXAMPLE See the class example.

reset()

PURPOSE Resets this object to its initial state.

SYNTAX
```
public void reset()
```

DESCRIPTION After this object is used to compute a checksum value for a data set, it can be reused to compute the checksum of a new data set. The program first calls `reset()` to reset the checksum's value and then calls `update()` on the bytes of the new data set.

EXAMPLE See the class example.

update()

PURPOSE Updates the checksum with one or more bytes.

SYNTAX
```
public void update(int bval)
public void update(byte[] buf, int off, int len)
```

DESCRIPTION Calling this method updates the current checksum value with the `byte` value `bval` or the bytes in `buf`. If `buf` is specified, only `len` bytes starting from `buf[off]` are used to update the checksum value. If `off` is not specified, it defaults to `0`. If `len` is not specified, it defaults to `buf.length`.

PARAMETERS

`buf`	A non-`null` array of `byte` values.
`bval`	A `byte` value. Only the low-order byte of `bval` is used.
`len`	The number of bytes to use starting from `buf[off]`. `0` ≤ `len` ≤ `buf.length-off`.
`off`	The `0`-based index of the first byte in `buf` to use. `0` ≤ `off` < `buf.length`.

EXAMPLE See the class example.

ChoiceFormat

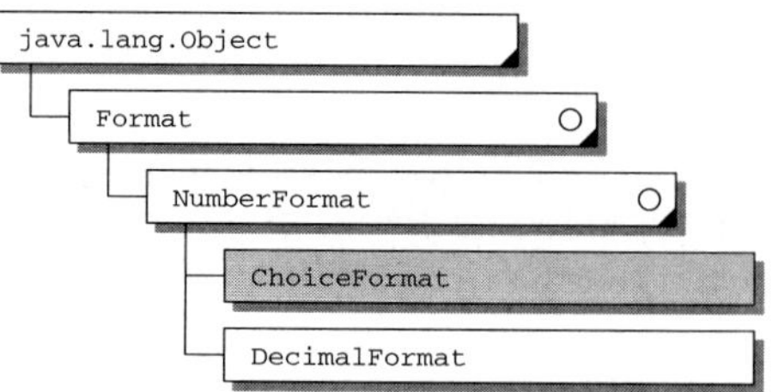

Syntax

```
public class ChoiceFormat extends NumberFormat
```

Description

A `ChoiceFormat` is like a switch statement for choosing strings, whereby a numeric value determines which string is chosen. First, you define ranges along the number line and assign strings to those ranges. Then, the `format()` method generates an output string from a number based on which range that number falls in.

`ChoiceFormat` is generally used in a `MessageFormat` for handling plurals ("1 file", "2 files") or a named series ("Sun", "Mon", "Tue", and so on) in user messages. With plurals, variations of a word that is displayed ("file") are chosen to correspond to the number that modifies it (1 or 2). Likewise, a named series allows the mapping of any number, such as a `double`, to days of the week. This is useful when you compute a number and map that number into a day of the week. For example, if you calculate that you are 37% the way through the week, which day would that correspond to? The term "choice" refers to the fact that a different string is chosen for each range.

The internal model of a `ChoiceFormat` is to break all numbers down into ranges by way of an array of limits and a corresponding array of strings.

The limits and strings Arrays

When creating a `ChoiceFormat`, you can specify either (1) a pattern or (2) two arrays, `strings` and `limits`. The lengths of these two arrays must be the same. `limits` is an array of `doubles` that represents ranges, while `strings` is an array that represents the string objects corresponding to those ranges. The limits must be in ascending order. For example:

```
double[] limits = {1,2,3,4,5,6,7};
String[] strings = {"Sun","Mon","Tue","Wed","Thu","Fri","Sat"};
```

These two arrays are equivalent to the following pattern:

```
1.0#Sun|2.0#Mon|3.0#Tue|4.0#Wed|5.0#Thu|6.0#Fri|7.0#Sat
```

The `ChoiceFormat` instance maps the member of the limits and strings arrays directly to each other. You can then convert in either direction—format a number to a string, or parse a string to a number.

Pattern

The choice *pattern* determines the ranges and string choices for the message. The pattern can be passed in with the constructor or set with `applyPattern()`. The pattern is of this form:

```
double "#" string ("|" double ("#" | "<") string)*
```

You can use the character ≤ (`\u2264`, less-than-or-equal-to) instead of # if you are editing Unicode text. (Note that in the previous expression, the vertical bar (|) inside the double quotation marks means the literal character, while the same character without quotation marks means "or.")

The `strings` and `doubles` in the pattern map to the `strings` and `limits` arrays as following. (The # sign is shown for convenience; it could be replaced by <.)

```
limits[0]#string[0]|limits[1]#string[1]|limits[2]#string[2]|...
```

For example, from the previous example:

```
1.0#Sun|2.0#Mon|3.0#Tue|4.0#Wed|5.0#Thu|6.0#Fri|7.0#Sat
```

To help remember how this works, you can think of the hash sign (#) as meaning "less than or equal" symbol (≤), as here:

```
1.0≤Sun|2.0≤Mon|3.0≤Tue|4.0≤Wed|5.0≤Thu|6.0≤Fri|7.0≤Sat
```

This corresponds to Figure 24. Notice that the region below 1.0 is also mapped to the value `Sun` at 1.0.

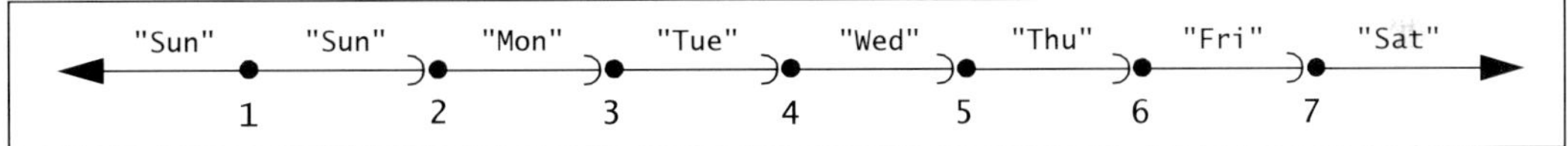

FIGURE 24: `ChoiceFormat` pattern.

Usage: Formatting

When formatting, you are given a number `num` to map to a string. Call `format(num)` to do the conversion, where `num` is promoted internally to a `double`. The `format()` method returns the string corresponding to that number. The `format()` method maps the number to the string by first determining in which range the number is. It does this by determining for which index `j` the following is true:

```
limit[j] ≤ num < limit[j+1]
```

In words, the `double num` corresponds to index `j` if and only if `num` is equal to or greater than `limit[j]` and less than `limit[j+1]`. If `num` is less than `limit[0]`, then index `0` is used. If `num` is greater than `limit[limit.length - 1]`, then index `limit.length - 1` is used.

The `format()` method then uses the string from the string array `strings[j]` to produce the final string, which is then returned.

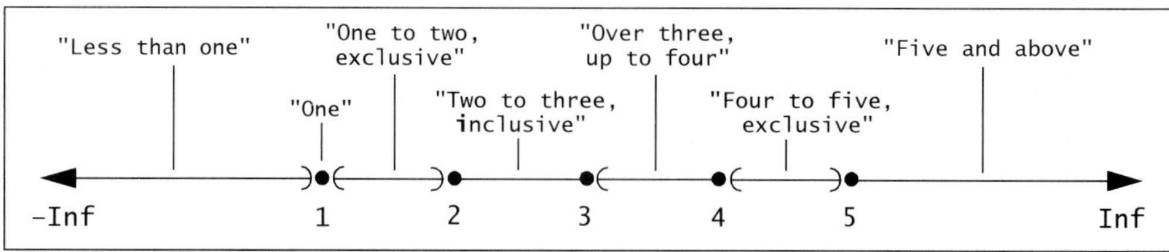

FIGURE 25: Breaking up a Number Line into Ranges.

Usage: Parsing

When parsing, you are given a string to map to a number. You call `parse(string, pos)` to do the conversion, where `pos` is an instance of `ParsePosition`, which tracks the string index during parsing. If there is no match, `Double.NaN` is returned.

Note: `ChoiceFormat` differs from `NumberFormat` classes in that you create a `ChoiceFormat` object with its constructor (not with a `getInstance()` style creation method). The creation methods aren't necessary because `ChoiceFormat` doesn't require any complex setup for a given locale. In fact, `ChoiceFormat` doesn't implement any locale-specific behavior.

Usage: Constructing a Pattern

Constructing a pattern requires three steps. Starting with the number line, you first break it up into ranges and define the strings you want for each range. Next, you convert the symbols to those allowed in patterns. Finally, you produce the pattern string.

1. **Figure out the ranges.**

   Write down the ranges you want using <= (less than or equal) and < (less than), with the string results for each range. Make sure that the following holds:

   - There are *no* gaps or overlaps. That is, every number from –infinity to +infinity belongs to *exactly* one range.
   - The ranges are in ascending order.

   Example: This example shows every combination of ranges using ≤ and <. See Figure 25 and Table 10. Note that if you want exactly one number, you use two ≤ signs, as shown in the second and last rows in Table 10.

Lower Limit	Lower Relation	String Result	Upper Relation	Upper Limit
`-Infinity`	≤	`"Less than one"`	<	`1.0`
`1.0`	≤	`"One"`	≤	`1.0`
`1.0`	<	`"One to two, exclusive"`	<	`2.0`
`2.0`	≤	`"Two to three, inclusive"`	≤	`3.0`
`3.0`	<	`"Over three, up to four"`	≤	`4.0`
`4.0`	<	`"Four to five, exclusive"`	<	`5.0`
`5.0`	≤	`"Five and above"`	≤	`Infin-ity`

TABLE 10: Ranges in a `ChoiceFormat` Pattern.

2. Convert the symbols to those allowed in patterns.

a. Drop the uppermost relation and upper bound.

b. For ≤, substitute either # or `\u2064` (the Unicode symbol for ≤).

c. (Optional) In place of –Infinity, you can choose any valid number in the first range. This will be the number returned by the `parse()` method.

Table 11 continues with the same example.

Lower Limit	Lower Relation	String Result
`-1.0`	#	`"Less than one"`
`1.0`	#	`"One"`
`1.0`	<	`"One to two, exclusive"`
`2.0`	#	`"Two to three, inclusive"`
`3.0`	<	`"Over three, up to four"`
`4.0`	<	`"Four to five, exclusive"`
`5.0`	#	`"Five and above"`

TABLE 11: Converting Symbols to `ChoiceFormat` Symbols.

3. Compose the pattern string by appending each range, with strings separated from each other by a |.

Example:

```
pattern = "-1.0#Less than one"
        + "|1.0#One"
        + "|1.0<One to two, exclusive"
        + "|2.0#Two to three, inclusive"
        + "|3.0<Over three, up to four"
        + "|4.0<Four to five, exclusive"
        + "|5.0#Five and above";
```

For clarity, this example is shown broken up on separate lines.

If you want to do the reverse and figure out *exactly* what a complicated pattern means, just reverse this process to find the original ranges.

Note: You can always figure out what the missing upper elements in the range are like this:

- The upper bound is always the same as the next lower bound.
- The upper relation is always the opposite of the next lower relation (for example, < and # or # and <).

Other examples of patterns follow. In each case, the text in the string indicates the range it covers.

```
"-INF#Negative|0.0#Zero|0.0<Positive"
"-INF#Non-Positive|0.0<Positive"
"-INF#Negative|0.0#Non-Negative"
```

MEMBER SUMMARY

Constructor	
`ChoiceFormat()`	Constructs a `ChoiceFormat` instance with limits and strings.
Parse and Format Methods	
`format()`	Formats this `ChoiceFormat` object to produce a string.
`parse()`	Parses a string to a number.
Pattern, Format, and Limit Methods	
`applyPattern()`	Applies a pattern to this `ChoiceFormat` object.
`getFormats()`	Gets the array of strings for this `ChoiceFormat` object.
`getLimits()`	Gets the array of limits for this `ChoiceFormat` object.
`setChoices()`	Sets the choices to be used in formatting.
`toPattern()`	Produces a string of the current pattern.
Double Methods	
`nextDouble()`	Finds the closest `double` greater than a `double`.
`previousDouble()`	Finds the closest `double` less than a `double`.

MEMBER SUMMARY	
Object Methods	
`clone()`	Creates a copy of this `ChoiceFormat` object.
`equals()`	Compares two `ChoiceFormat` objects for equality.
`hashCode()`	Computes the hash code for this `ChoiceFormat` object.

See Also

`DecimalFormat`, `MessageFormat`.

Example 1

In this example, a pattern is defined with six limits: –1, 0, 1, 1.0, 2, and 2 (see Figure 26). Notice that the hash mark (#) means "is exactly" only if the next term is a less-than symbol (<), as is the case for 1 and 2. Otherwise, it means that the value is greater than or equal to the limit.

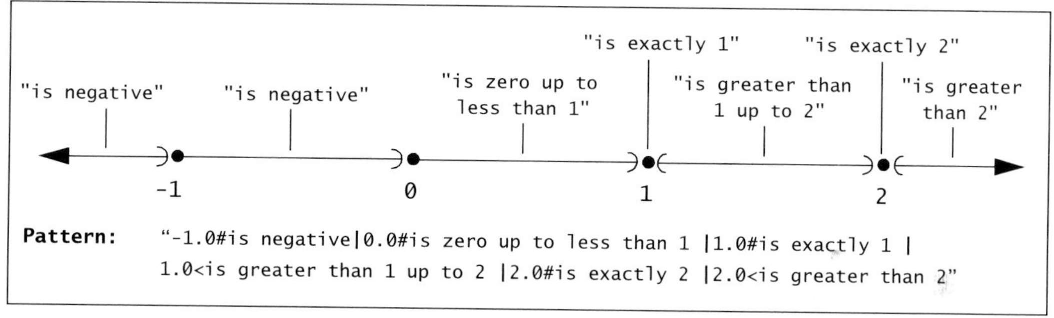

FIGURE 26: Number Line for `ChoiceFormat` Pattern with Six Limits.

Main1.java

```
import java.text.*;
import java.util.*;

public class Main1 {
    public static void main (String args[])
    {
        ChoiceFormat fmt = new ChoiceFormat(
            "-1#is negative|" +
            "0#is zero up to less than 1 |" +
            "1#is exactly 1 |" +
            "1.0<is greater than 1 up to 2 |" +
            "2#is exactly 2 |" +
            "2<is greater than 2");

        System.out.println("Pattern : " + fmt.toPattern() + "\n");

        print(Double.NaN, fmt);               // "is negative"
        print(Double.NEGATIVE_INFINITY, fmt); // "is negative"
```

```
            print(-1.0, fmt);                        // "is negative"
            print(-0.5, fmt);                        // "is negative"
            print(0, fmt);                           // "is zero up to less than 1"
            print(0.9, fmt);                         // "is zero up to less than 1"
            print(1.0, fmt);                         // "is exactly 1"
            print(1.5, fmt);                         // "is greater than 1 up to 2"
            print(2, fmt);                           // "is exactly 2"
            print(2.1, fmt);                         // "is greater than 2"
            print(Double.POSITIVE_INFINITY, fmt);    // "is greater than 2"
        }

        static void print(double value, ChoiceFormat cf) {
            String str = "format(" + value + "):";
            System.out.print(str);
            for (int i = 0; i < 22 - str.length(); i++) {
                System.out.print(" ");
            }
            System.out.println(cf.format(value));
        }
    }
```

Example 2

In this example (see Figure 27), seven limits are defined to map to the 7 days of the week. For simplicity, this example is not globalized (the user messages are not in resource bundles). the example is globalized. Notice that the `limits` array defines eight ranges: one range for each member, plus another range for numbers below 1.

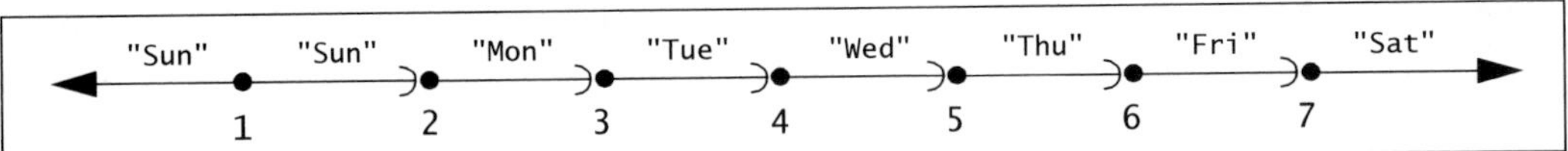

FIGURE 27: Number Line for `ChoiceFormat` with Seven Limits.

This example loops through numbers along the range, printing each number, its formatted string, and then the parsed version of the string.

Main2.java

```
import java.text.ChoiceFormat;
import java.text.ParsePosition;

class Main2 {
    static public void main(String[] args) {

        // Define the integer ranges.
        double[] limits = {1,2,3,4,5,6,7};

        // Define the strings that map to the ranges.
        String[] dayNames = {"Sun","Mon","Tue","Wed","Thu","Fri","Sat"};

        // Create a choice format based on the limits and dayName arrays.
        ChoiceFormat form = new ChoiceFormat(limits, dayNames);

        // Diagnostics - print the pattern.
        System.out.println("Pattern: " + form.toPattern());
```

```
            // Create a parse position for parsing.
            ParsePosition pos = new ParsePosition(0);

            // Print a heading.
            System.out.println("\n" + "Formatting | Parsing");

            // Loop over the range, formatting and parsing.
            for (double num = 0.0; num <= 8.0; num = num + .5) {
                pos.setIndex(0);

                System.out.print(num);

                System.out.print("  ->   ");

                // Format the number and print the resulting string.
                System.out.print(form.format(num));

                // Print an arrow.
                System.out.print("  ->   ");

                // Parse the formatted output back to a number.
                System.out.println(form.parse(form.format(num), pos));
            }
        }
}
```

Output

```
> java Main2
Pattern: 1.0#Sun|2.0#Mon|3.0#Tue|4.0#Wed|5.0#Thu|6.0#Fri|7.0#Sat

Formatting | Parsing
0.0  ->   Sun  ->   1.0
0.5  ->   Sun  ->   1.0
1.0  ->   Sun  ->   1.0
1.5  ->   Sun  ->   1.0
2.0  ->   Mon  ->   2.0
2.5  ->   Mon  ->   2.0
3.0  ->   Tue  ->   3.0
3.5  ->   Tue  ->   3.0
4.0  ->   Wed  ->   4.0
4.5  ->   Wed  ->   4.0
5.0  ->   Thu  ->   5.0
5.5  ->   Thu  ->   5.0
6.0  ->   Fri  ->   6.0
6.5  ->   Fri  ->   6.0
7.0  ->   Sat  ->   7.0
7.5  ->   Sat  ->   7.0
8.0  ->   Sat  ->   7.0
```

Example 3

This example provides variations on the text "There is 1 file" for singular and plural. It is properly set up with the text in resources files, one for `US` English and another for `FR` French. It creates a message format and then gets the resource bundle. Then it creates, from the resource bundle, an array of limits and an array of strings, passing both into the `ChoiceFormat()` constructor. Next, it creates an array of formats `formats` to hold `fileformat` (the instance of `ChoiceFormat`) and the number format. These are members `formats[0]` and `formats[2]`, which correspond to the argument numbers in the fully expanded pattern. The pattern (in US English) is

```
"There {0} on {1}"
```

In the plural case in `MyResources.java`, where `{0}` expands to "`are {2} files`", the pattern expands to

```
"There are {2} files on {1}"
```

Therefore, the formats maps to the variables as shown in Table 12 and Figure 28.

Array Element	Content	Applies to
`formats[0]`	`fileformat`	variable `{0}`
`formats[1]`	`null`	variable `{1}`
`formats[2]`	`NumberFormat`	variable `{2}`

TABLE 12: Format Variable Assignments.

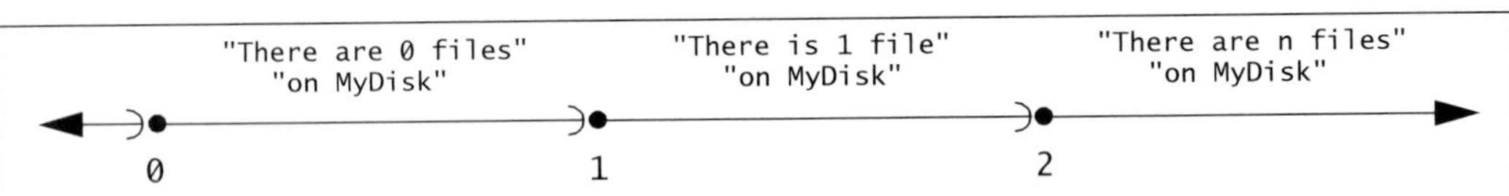

FIGURE 28: Number Line of `ChoiceFormat` For Singular and Plural Choices.

Main3.java

```
import java.text.*;
import java.util.*;

class Main3 {
    static public void main(String[] args) {

        Locale[] locArray = {Locale.ENGLISH, Locale.FRENCH};

        MessageFormat mf;

        for (int i = 0; i < locArray.length; ++i) {

            Locale loc = locArray[i];

            // Create a message format and set its locale.
            mf = new MessageFormat("");
            mf.setLocale(loc);

            // Create a resource bundle object and load the bundle.
```

```
            ResourceBundle myResources = null;
            myResources = ResourceBundle.getBundle("MyResources", loc);

            // Define the integer ranges
            double[] filelimits = {0,1,2};

            // Get locale-specific strings
            String[] fileparts = { myResources.getString("are no files"),
                                   myResources.getString("is one file"),
                                   myResources.getString("are X files") };

            // Create a choice format based on the filelimits and fileparts
            ChoiceFormat fileformat = new ChoiceFormat(filelimits, fileparts);

            // Create an array of formats
            Format[] formats = {fileformat, null, NumberFormat.getInstance()};

            // Get the pattern from resource bundle:  "There {0} on {1}"
            String pattern = myResources.getString("pattern");

            // Apply the pattern and set the formats to mf.
            mf.applyPattern(pattern);
            mf.setFormats(formats);

            // Create an array of objects to be formatted
            Object[] arguments = {null, "MyDisk", null};

            // Loop over the range. formatting and printing
            for (int num = 0; num < 4; num++) {
                arguments[0] = new Integer(num);
                arguments[2] = arguments[0];
                System.out.println(mf.format(arguments));
            }
            System.out.println();
        }
    }
}
```

MyResources.java

```
import java.util.ListResourceBundle;

public class MyResources extends ListResourceBundle {
    public Object[][] getContents() {
        return contents;
    }

    static final Object[][] contents = {
        // LOCALIZE THE FOLLOWING
        {"are no files", "are no files"},
        {"is one file", "is one file"},
        {"are X files", "are {2} files"},
        {"pattern", "There {0} on {1}."}
        // END OF MATERIAL TO LOCALIZE
    };
}
```

MyResources_fr.java

```
import java.util.ListResourceBundle;

public class MyResources_fr extends ListResourceBundle {
    public Object[][] getContents() {
        return contents;
    }

    static final Object[][] contents = {
        // LOCALIZE THE FOLLOWING
        {"are no files", "n' y a pas des fichiers",},
        {"is one file", "y a un fichier"},
        {"are X files", "y a {2} fichiers"},
        {"pattern", "Il {0} sur {1}."}
        // END OF MATERIAL TO LOCALIZE
    };
}
```

Output

```
> java Main3
There are no files on MyDisk.
There is one file on MyDisk.
There are 2 files on MyDisk.
There are 3 files on MyDisk.

Il n' y a pas des fichiers sur MyDisk.
Il y a un fichier sur MyDisk.
Il y a 2 fichiers sur MyDisk.
Il y a 3 fichiers sur MyDisk.
```

applyPattern()

PURPOSE Applies a pattern to this `ChoiceFormat` object.

SYNTAX `public void applyPattern(String newPattern)`

DESCRIPTION This method sets the pattern of this `ChoiceFormat` object to `newPattern`.

PARAMETERS

`newPattern` A non-`null` pattern string.

EXAMPLE This example is similar to Example 2, except that it uses the first form of the constructor that takes a pattern. Also, it then uses `applyPattern()`, rather than specifying `limits` and `dayNames` arrays. It formats only one number rather than looping over a range.

```
import java.text.ChoiceFormat;

class Main {
    static public void main(String[] args) {

        // Create a choice format using that pattern.
        ChoiceFormat form = new ChoiceFormat("");
```

```
            // Create the pattern string.
            String pattern =
                "1.0#Sun|2.0#Mon|3.0#Tue|4.0#Wed|5.0#Thu|6.0#Fri|7.0#Sat";

            // Apply the pattern.
            form.applyPattern(pattern);

            // Diagnostics - iterate over the arrays.
            for (int i = 0; i < form.getFormats().length; i++) {

                // Get the formats.
                System.out.print((form.getFormats())[i] + "  ");

                // Get the limits.
                System.out.println((form.getLimits())[i]);
            }

            // Format the number 2.5
            double num = 2.5;

            // Format the number and print the result.
            System.out.println("\n" + form.format(num));        // "Mon"
        }
    }
```

Output

```
Sun  1.0
Mon  2.0
Tue  3.0
Wed  4.0
Thu  5.0
Fri  6.0
Sat  7.0

Mon
```

ChoiceFormat()

PURPOSE Constructs a `ChoiceFormat` instance with limits and strings.

SYNTAX

```
public ChoiceFormat(String newPattern)
public ChoiceFormat(double[] limits, String[] strings)
```

DESCRIPTION There are two forms of the constructor for `ChoiceFormat`. The first form constructs an instance of `ChoiceFormat` based on a pattern. The second form constructs an instance of `ChoiceFormat` with limits and corresponding strings.

PARAMETERS

- `limits` A non-`null` array of `double`s.
- `newPattern` A non-`null` pattern string to be applied to the new `ChoiceFormat` object.
- `strings` A non-`null` array of strings.

SEE ALSO `setChoices()`

EXAMPLE This example is similar to Example 2, except that it uses the first form of the constructor that takes a pattern, rather than specifying `limits` and `dayNames` arrays. It formats only one number (2.5) rather than looping over a range.

```
import java.text.ChoiceFormat;

class Main {
    static public void main(String[] args) {

        // Create the pattern string.
        String pattern =
            "1.0#Sun|2.0#Mon|3.0#Tue|4.0#Wed|5.0#Thu|6.0#Fri|7.0#Sat";

        // Create a choice format using that pattern.
        ChoiceFormat form = new ChoiceFormat(pattern);

        // Format the number 2.5
        double num = 2.5;

        // Format the number and print the result.
        System.out.print(form.format(num));          // "Mon"
    }
}
```

clone()

PURPOSE Creates a copy of this `ChoiceFormat` object.

SYNTAX `public Object clone()`

DESCRIPTION This method makes a copy of this `ChoiceFormat` object. The new `ChoiceFormat` object has a complete copy of the limits and strings arrays (that is, the pattern). Changing any value in the new `ChoiceFormat` object will not affect the original instance.

RETURNS A non-`null` copy of this object.

OVERRIDES `NumberFormat.clone()`

EXAMPLE This example illustrates the use of `clone()` to copy a `ChoiceFormat` object. Note that the copy has the same pattern as the original.

```
import java.text.ChoiceFormat;

class Main {
    public static void main(String args[]) {

        // Create choice format.
        ChoiceFormat cf = new ChoiceFormat("1.0#Yes|2.0#No");

        // Print pattern.
        System.out.println("Original pattern: " + cf.toPattern());

        // Create a clone.
```

```
            ChoiceFormat cfCopy = (ChoiceFormat)cf.clone();

            // Print pattern.
            System.out.println("Copy's pattern:    " + cf.toPattern());

            // Test for equality.
            if (cf.equals(cfCopy)) {
                System.out.println("Clone is equal to original");
            }

            // Compute hashcode.
            int hc = cf.hashCode();
            System.out.println("Hash code:         " + hc);
        }
    }
```

Output

```
> java Main
Original pattern: 1.0#Yes|2.0#No
Copy's pattern:   1.0#Yes|2.0#No
Clone is equal to original
Hash code:        2999
```

equals()

PURPOSE Compares two `ChoiceFormat` objects for equality.

SYNTAX `public boolean equals(Object obj)`

DESCRIPTION This method compares this `ChoiceFormat` object with `obj` for equality. If `obj` is a `ChoiceFormat` object and if its `limits` and `strings` arrays are equal (that is, if its pattern is equal) to those of this `ChoiceFormat` object, then the objects are equal and this method returns `true`.

PARAMETERS

`obj` The possibly `null` object with which to compare.

RETURNS `true` if `obj` is equal to this object; `false` otherwise.

OVERRIDES `NumberFormat.equals()`.

SEE ALSO `hashCode()`.

EXAMPLE See `clone()`.

format()

PURPOSE Formats this `ChoiceFormat` object to produce a string.

SYNTAX

```
public StringBuffer format(long num, StringBuffer appendBuf,
    FieldPosition pos)
public StringBuffer format(double num, StringBuffer appendBuf,
    FieldPosition pos)
```

DESCRIPTION This method formats the `long` or `double num` to produce a string, which is appended to the buffer `appendBuf`. The `appendbuf` value is returned. Returning the full result allows chaining, as with `StringBuffer.append()`.

Internally, this method calls `format(double, StringBuffer, FieldPosition)`. Thus the range of `long`s that are supported is equal only to the range that can be stored by `double`.

The field position `pos` is ignored and has absolutely no effect. You can pass in the value of `null`.

PARAMETERS

`appendBuf`	The non-`null` string buffer in which the resulting string is to be appended.
`num`	The number to format.
`pos`	This parameter is ignored. You can pass in `null`.

RETURNS The non-`null` string passed in as `appendBuf` with the newly formatted string appended to it.

OVERRIDES `format() in class NumberFormat.`

EXAMPLE See Example 2 and Example 3 in the class examples.

getFormats()

PURPOSE Gets the array of strings for this `ChoiceFormat` object.

SYNTAX `public Object[] getFormats()`

RETURNS The non-`null` strings array belonging to this `ChoiceFormat` object.

EXAMPLE See `applyPattern()`.

getLimits()

PURPOSE Gets the array of limits for this `ChoiceFormat` object.

SYNTAX `public double[] getLimits()`

RETURNS The non-`null` array of `double`s belonging to this `ChoiceFormat` object.

EXAMPLE See `applyPattern()`.

hashCode()

PURPOSE Computes the hash code for this `ChoiceFormat` object.

SYNTAX `public int hashCode()`

DESCRIPTION This method computes the hash code for this `ChoiceFormat` object based on the limits and strings arrays of this `ChoiceFormat` object. Two `ChoiceFormat` objects with the same properties will have the same hash code. However, two `ChoiceFormat` objects that do not have the same properties might also have the same hash code, although the hash code algorithm minimizes this possibility. The hash code is typically used as the key in a hash table.

RETURNS An `int` representing the hash code of this `ChoiceFormat` object.

OVERRIDES `NumberFormat.hashCode()`.

SEE ALSO `equals()`, `java.util.Hashtable`.

EXAMPLE See `clone()`.

A B C D E F G H I J K L M N O P Q R S T U V W X Y Z

nextDouble()

PURPOSE Finds the closest `double` greater than a `double`.

SYNTAX
```
public final static double nextDouble(double d)
public static double nextDouble(double d, boolean next)
```

DESCRIPTION This method finds the next `double` greater than `d`. If `d` is `NaN`, it returns the same value. This method is used to make half-open intervals.

If the `boolean next` is `true`, then it performs the operation just described. If `next` is `false`, it performs `previousDouble()`.

PARAMETERS

`d` The `double` at which to start to find the next `double`.

`next` If `true`, performs the `nextDouble(double)` operation; if `false`, performs the `previousDouble(double)` operation.

RETURNS The closest `double` greater than `d`.

SEE ALSO `previousDouble()`.

EXAMPLE This example demonstrates both `nextDouble()` and `previousDouble()`.

```
import java.text.ChoiceFormat;

class Main {
    static public void main(String[] args) {

        // Define the integer ranges.
        double[] limits = {Double.NEGATIVE_INFINITY,
```

```
                                        1.0,
                                        ChoiceFormat.nextDouble(1.0)};

            // Define the strings that map to the ranges.
            String[] strings = {"Less than one","One","Greater than one"};

            // Create a choice format based on the limits and dayName arrays.
            ChoiceFormat form = new ChoiceFormat(limits, strings);

            // Diagnostics - print the pattern and nextDouble
            System.out.println("pattern: " + form.toPattern());
            System.out.println("nextDouble(1.0): " + ChoiceFormat.nextDouble(1.0));

            // Print a heading.
            System.out.println("\n" + "num   format(num)");
            System.out.println("---   -------------");

            // Loop over the range, formatting and parsing.
            for (double num = 0.5; num <= 1.5; num = num + .5) {

                System.out.print(num + "   ");

                // Format the number and print the resulting string.
                System.out.println(form.format(num));
            }
        }
    }
```

Output

```
pattern: -Infinity<Less than one|1.0#One|1.0<Greater than one
nextDouble(1.0): 1.0000000000000002

num   format(num)
---   -------------
0.5   Less than one
1.0   One
1.5   Greater than one
```

parse()

PURPOSE Parses a string to a number.

SYNTAX `public Number parse(String sourceStr, ParsePosition pos)`

DESCRIPTION Always returns a `Double` object.

PARAMETERS

`pos` The non-`null` parse position that determines where the parse begins.

`sourceStr` The non-`null` string to be parsed.

RETURNS A non-`null` instance of `Double` with the parsed value, or `Double.NaN` if no choice is matched.

OVERRIDES `NumberFormat.parse()`.

EXAMPLE See Example 2 and Example 3 in the class examples.

previousDouble()

PURPOSE Finds the closest `double` less than a `double`.

SYNTAX `public final static double previousDouble(double d)`

DESCRIPTION This method finds the previous `double` less than `d`. If `d` is `NaN`, returns the same value.

PARAMETERS

`d` The `double` at which to start to find the previous `double`.

RETURNS The closest `double` less than `d`.

SEE ALSO `nextDouble()`

EXAMPLE See `nextDouble()`.

setChoices()

PURPOSE Sets the choices to be used in formatting.

SYNTAX `public void setChoices(double[] limits, String[] strings)`

DESCRIPTION This method applies the `limits` and `strings` arrays to this `ChoiceFormat` object. You would use this method if the `ChoiceFormat` object were already created and you wanted to change its `limits` and `strings` values.

PARAMETERS

`limits` A non-`null` array of `doubles` that define the choice ranges. The `doubles` should be in ascending order.

`strings` A non-`null` array of `String` objects that correspond to the `limits`.

EXAMPLE This example uses `setChoices()` to set the `limits` and `strings` arrays.

```
import java.text.ChoiceFormat;

class Main {
    static public void main(String[] args) {

        // Create an empty choice format.
        ChoiceFormat form = new ChoiceFormat("");

        // Define the integer ranges.
        double[] limits = {1,2,3,4,5,6,7};

        // Define the strings that map to the ranges.
        String[] dayNames = {"Sun","Mon","Tue","Wed","Thu","Fri","Sat"};

        // Apply the limits and dayNames.
        form.setChoices(limits, dayNames);

        // Format the number 2.5
```

```
            double num = 2.5;

            // Format the number and print the result.
            System.out.print(form.format(num));          // "Mon"
        }
    }
```


toPattern()

PURPOSE Produces a string of the current pattern.

SYNTAX `public String toPattern()`

RETURNS The non-`null` pattern from this `ChoiceFormat` object.

EXAMPLE See Example 2 in the class examples.

Class

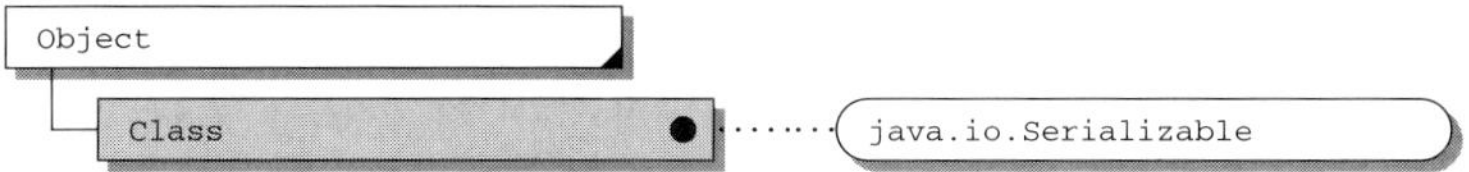

A B C D E F G H I J K L M N O P Q R S T U V W X Y Z

Syntax

```
public final class Class implements Serializable
```

Description

Every object in Java is an instance of a class. For each class, Java maintains an immutable `Class` object that contains information about the class. We say that the `Class` object *represents* or *reflects* the class.

The `Class` object contains information that includes the class's string name, the superclass that it extends, the interfaces that it implements, and the class loader used to load this class. The `Class` class provides methods that return this information about a class, as well as a method to generate new instances of the class.

The `Class` object is also used to give information about interfaces, although an interface does differ from a class. When talking about a `Class` object, we will often loosely speak of the "class" it reflects, with the understanding that the `Class` object may in fact reflect an interface, not a class.

Figure 29 shows that each class file (`Component.class`, `Button.class`, and so on) that has been loaded has a corresponding `Class` object. When you invoke `getSuperclass()` on the `Button` class's `Class` object, you get back the `Class` object for `Component`. When you invoke `getClass()` on an instance of a `Button` object, you get back the `Class` object for `Button`.

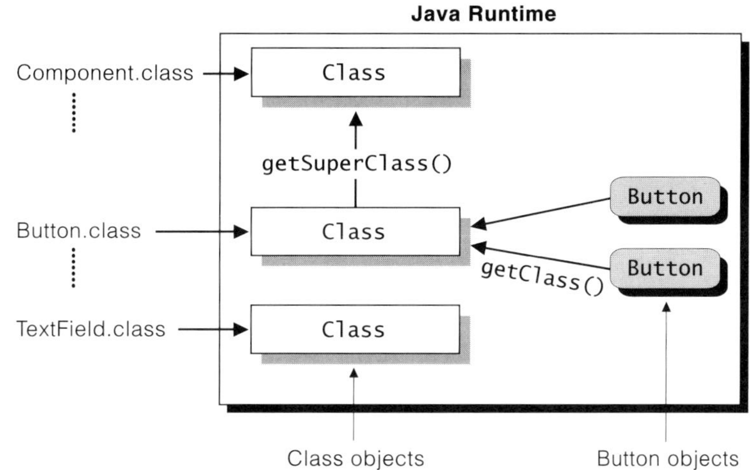

FIGURE 29: Examples of Classes.

Type Descriptors

Every `Class` object has a unique string representation called the *type descriptor*. The type descriptor of a `Class` object is obtained by calling its `getName()` method. Except for primitive types, a type descriptor can be used to retrieve its corresponding `Class` object by using the `forName()` method. Following are descriptions of the type descriptors for each Java entity.

Classes and Interfaces

The type descriptor of a class or interface is the fully qualified name of the class or interface. For example,

```
java.lang.String
java.lang.Cloneable
```

The type descriptor of an *inner* class or interface is the fully qualified name of the inner class or interface. The name of the inner class is separated from the name of its parent class by a dollar sign ($) rather than a dot (.). For example,

```
pkg1.pkg2.Main$InnerClass
pkg1.pkg2.Main$InnerInterface
pkg1.pkg2.Main$InnerClass$DeeperInnerClass
```

Primitive Types

The type descriptor of primitive types are shown in Table 13. The `Class` object for a primitive type is not obtained using `forName()`. Instead, Java provides a "wrapper class" for each primitive type. See Table 16 for details.

Primitive Type	Type Descriptor
`boolean`	`Z`
`byte`	`B`
`char`	`C`
`short`	`S`
`int`	`I`
`long`	`J`
`float`	`F`
`double`	`D`

TABLE 13: Type Descriptors of Primitive Types.

Arrays

The type descriptor of a primitive type array contains a left brace ([) for each dimension of the array. Table 14 contains some examples of primitive type arrays.

The type descriptor of a class or interface array also contains a left brace ([) for each dimension of the array. However, the type descriptor of the class or interface is prefixed with an "L" and appended with a semicolon (;). Table 15 shows some examples of class and interface arrays.

Primitive Type Array	Type Descriptor
`boolean[]`	`[B`
`boolean[][]`	`[[B`
`double[][]`	`[[D`

TABLE 14: Examples of Type Descriptors of Primitive Type Arrays.

Class or Interface Array	Type Descriptor
`java.lang.String[]`	`[Ljava.lang.String;`
`java.lang.String[][]`	`[[Ljava.lang.String;`
`java.lang.Cloneable[]`	`[Ljava.lang.Cloneable;`
`pkg1.pkg2.Main.InnerClass[]`	`[Lpkg1.pkg2.Main$InnerClass;`

TABLE 15: Examples of Type Descriptors of Class and Interface Arrays.

Retrieving Class Objects

You can use any of five ways to retrieve the `Class` objects for a class, as follows:

1. **Use `Object.getClass()`**

   If you already have an object of the class, you can retrieve its `Class` object by invoking `getClass()` on it. Here is an example of getting the `Class` object for a `String` object:

   ```
   String str = "abc";
   Class c1 = str.getClass();
   ```

2. **Use `Class.getSuperclass()`**

   If you already have a `Class` object, you can retrieve the `Class` object of its superclass by using `getSuperclass()`. Here is an example of getting the `Class` object for `Component` by using one of its subclasses, `Button`:

   ```
   Button b = new Button();
   Class c1 = b.getClass();
   Class c2 = c1.getSuperclass(); // Class object for Component
   ```

3. **Use the `.class` Syntax**

   If you know the name of the class, interface, or primitive type at the time the program is written, you can retrieve its `Class` object by appending `.class` to the name. Here are some examples that use this syntax:

   ```
   Class c1 = String.class;
   Class c2 = java.awt.Button.class;
   Class c3 = Main.InnerClass.class;
   Class c4 = int.class;
   Class c5 = int[].class;
   Class c6 = int[][].class;
   Class c7 = String[].class;
   ```

4. **Use `Class.forName()`**
If you don't know the name of the class at the time the program is written, you need to use `forName()`. Here are some examples of this method. See `forName()` for more details.

```
Class c1 = Class.forName("java.lang.String");
Class c2 = Class.forName("[Ljava.awt.String;");
Class c3 = Class.forName("[I");
Class c4 = Class.forName("Main$InnerClass");
```

5. **Use Primitive Type Wrappers**
Primitive types are not objects (that is, they are not subclasses of `Object`), so Java provides a "wrapper class" for each primitive type. Each wrapper class contains a constant field that refers to the `Class` object of its associated primitive type. Table 16 shows each primitive type and `void` (which is not a type) along with its wrapper class and the name field containing the type's `Class` object. Although there are no restrictions on the use of a wrapper's `TYPE` constant, the preferred syntax for naming the class associated with a primitive type is the `.class` syntax.

Primitive Type	Wrapper Class	Class Object
`boolean`	`Boolean`	`Boolean.TYPE`
`byte`	`Byte`	`Byte.TYPE`
`char`	`Character`	`Character.TYPE`
`short`	`Short`	`Short.TYPE`
`int`	`Integer`	`Integer.TYPE`
`long`	`Long`	`Long.TYPE`
`float`	`Float`	`Float.TYPE`
`double`	`Double`	`Double.TYPE`
`void`	`Void`	`Void.TYPE`

TABLE 16: Primitive Types and Their Wrapper Classes and Class Objects.

MEMBER SUMMARY

Class Retrieval Methods

`forName()`	Retrieves the `Class` object specified by the class's type descriptor.
`getClasses()`	Retrieves an array of `Class` objects for all public class and interface members. Not implemented.
`getDeclaredClasses()`	Retrieves an array of `Class` objects for all class and interface members. Not implemented.
`getSuperclass()`	Retrieves the superclass that this class extends.

MEMBER SUMMARY

Reflection Methods	
`getComponentType()`	Retrieves the component type of an array.
`getConstructor()`	Retrieves a `Constructor` object for a public constructor.
`getConstructors()`	Retrieves `Constructor` objects for all public constructors.
`getDeclaredConstructor()`	Retrieves a `Constructor` object for a constructor.
`getDeclaredConstructors()`	Retrieves `Constructor` objects for all constructors.
`getDeclaredField()`	Retrieves a `Field` object for a declared field.
`getDeclaredFields()`	Retrieves `Field` objects for all declared fields.
`getDeclaredMethod()`	Retrieves a `Method` object for a declared method.
`getDeclaredMethods()`	Retrieves `Method` objects for all declared methods.
`getDeclaringClass()`	Retrieves the declaring class of this `Class` object. Not implemented.
`getField()`	Retrieves a `Field` object for an accessible public field.
`getFields()`	Retrieves `Field` objects for all accessible public fields.
`getInterfaces()`	Retrieves the interfaces being implemented by this class.
`getMethod()`	Retrieves a `Method` object for an accessible public method.
`getMethods()`	Retrieves `Method` objects for all accessible public methods.
`getModifiers()`	Retrieves the Java language modifiers for the class represented by this `Class` object.
`getName()`	Retrieves the type descriptor for this `Class` object.
Resource Methods	
`getResource()`	Finds a resource associated with the class represented by this `Class` object.
`getResourceAsStream()`	Finds and creates an input stream on a resource associated with the class represented by this `Class` object.
Security Method	
`getSigners()`	Retrieves the signers of this class.
Object Type Query Methods	
`isArray()`	Determines if this `Class` object represents an array type.
`isAssignableFrom()`	Determines if the class represented by this `Class` object is a superclass of a class.
`isInstance()`	Determines if an object is an instance of the class represented by this `Class` object.
`isInterface()`	Determines if this `Class` object represents an interface.
`isPrimitive()`	Determines if this `Class` object represents a primitive Java type.
Instance Creation Method	
`newInstance()`	Constructs an instance of the class represented by this `Class` object.

Continued

MEMBER SUMMARY	
Class Loader Method	
`getClassLoader()`	Retrieves the class loader for this class.
Object Method	
`toString()`	Generates the string representation of this class.

See Also

`ClassLoader`, `java.lang.reflect.Array`, `java.lang.reflect.Constructor`, `java.lang.reflect.Field`, `java.lang.reflect.Method`, `java.lang.reflect.Modifier`, `java.net.URL`, `Object.getClass()`.

Example

See the method examples for various uses of `Class`.

forName()

PURPOSE
Retrieves the `Class` object specified by the class's type descriptor.

SYNTAX
```
public static native Class forName(String className) throws
    ClassNotFoundException
```

DESCRIPTION
This method retrieves the `Class` object specified by the type descriptor in `className`. The syntax of `className` is that of the string returned by `getName()`. See the class description for details on the type descriptors of `Class` objects.

This method cannot be used to retrieve the `Class` objects for primitive types. See the class description for ways to do this.

This method causes the class to be loaded using the class loader of the calling method. For example, if the calling method's class was loaded using the default system class loader, `className` will also be loaded using the default system class loader. The static initializer of the class may or may not be run as part of `forName()`. Any failure during this process causes a `ClassNotFoundException` to be thrown.

PARAMETERS
`className` The non-`null` type descriptor of a `Class` object (e.g., "java.lang.String"). See the class description for details.

RETURNS
The non-`null` `Class` object represented by `className`.

EXCEPTIONS

`ClassNotFoundException`
If the class for `className` could not be found.

`IllegalArgumentException`
If `className`'s syntax is incorrect.

SEE ALSO `ClassLoader`, `getName()`.

EXAMPLE

```
System.out.println(Class.forName("java.lang.String"));
                                       // class java.lang.String
System.out.println(Class.forName("java.lang.Cloneable"));
                                       // interface java.lang.Cloneable
//System.out.println(Class.forName("String"));    // ClassNotFoundException

// Inner classes and interfaces.
System.out.println(Class.forName("Main$InnerC")); // class Main$InnerC
System.out.println(Class.forName("Main$InnerI")); // interface Main$InnerI

// Primitive types.
//System.out.println(Class.forName("int"));       // ClassNotFoundException
//System.out.println(Class.forName("I"));         // ClassNotFoundException

// Arrays
System.out.println(Class.forName("[I"));          // class [I
System.out.println(Class.forName("[[I"));         // class [[I
System.out.println(Class.forName("[Ljava.lang.String;"));
                                       // class [Ljava.lang.String;
System.out.println(Class.forName("[LMain$InnerC;")); // class [LMain$InnerC;
System.out.println(Class.forName("[LMain$InnerI;")); // class [LMain$InnerI;

// A roundabout way of getting the Class object for a primitive type.
System.out.println(Class.forName("[I").getComponentType());  // int
```

getClasses()

PURPOSE Retrieves an array of `Class` objects for all public class and interface members. Not implemented.

SYNTAX `public Class[] getClasses()`

DESCRIPTION This method retrieves an array containing `Class` objects for all of the public classes and interfaces that are members of the class represented by this `Class` object. This includes public class and interface members inherited from superclasses and public class and interface members declared by the class.

RETURNS A non-`null` array of `Class` objects.

SEE ALSO `getDeclaredClasses()`.

getClassLoader()

PURPOSE Retrieves the class loader for this class.

SYNTAX `public native ClassLoader getClassLoader()`

DESCRIPTION Each class is loaded into the runtime system using a *class loader.* A class loader can be used to enforce policies related to loading classes (e.g., determining where to find class files if the classes are contained in files, getting classes from network sockets, and getting classes from secure network sockets). A class loader is represented in the system by using a `ClassLoader` object. This method retrieves the `ClassLoader` object used to load this `Class` object. A value of `null` indicates that the default system class loader was used to load this class.

RETURNS A `ClassLoader` object for this `Class` object; `null` if the default system class loader was used.

SEE ALSO `ClassLoader`.

EXAMPLE

```
Class c = obj.getClass();
ClassLoader loader = c.getClassLoader();
if (loader == null)
    System.out.println("Default system class loader");
else
    System.out.println(loader);
```

getComponentType()

PURPOSE Retrieves the component type of an array.

SYNTAX `public native Class getComponentType()`

DESCRIPTION The type of an array's elements is called the *component type*. For example, the component type of `colors` in this line is `Color`:

```
Color[] colors = new Color[8];
```

Component types can also be arrays. For example, in the following line the component type of `map` is `int[]`:

```
int[][] map = new int[100][100];
```

The component type of array `int[]` is `int`.

If this object represents an array, this method returns the array's component type. Otherwise, it returns `null`.

RETURNS A possibly `null` `Class` object.

SEE ALSO `java.lang.reflect.Array`.

EXAMPLE

```
class Main {
    static void printComponentType(Class c) {
        System.out.println(c.getComponentType());
    }

    public static void main(String[] args) {
        // printComponentType(null);              // NullPointerException
        printComponentType(int.class);           // null
        printComponentType(int[].class);         // int
        printComponentType(int[][].class);       // class [I
        printComponentType(String[].class);      // class java.lang.String
    }
}
```

getConstructor()

PURPOSE Retrieves a `Constructor` object for a public constructor.

SYNTAX

```
public Constructor getConstructor(Class[] parameterTypes) throws
    NoSuchMethodException, SecurityException
```

DESCRIPTION This method retrieves a `Constructor` instance reflecting the constructor of this `Class` object with the parameter list specified by `parameterTypes`. The constructor must be public; otherwise, a `NoSuchMethodException` is thrown.

`parameterTypes` represents the parameter types of the constructor. It is an array of `Class` objects, one for each parameter. The first element of the array refers to the type of the first parameter, the second element refers to the type of the second parameter, and so on. For example, in the following constructor signature:

```
public Label(String text, int alignment)
```

an array with the following `Class` objects is produced:

```
java.lang.String.class, int.class
```

Note: The specified parameter types must match exactly those of the constructor. This method does not emulate the compiler in choosing the best match among overloadings.

PARAMETERS

`parameterTypes`

A non-`null` array of `Class` objects, one for each parameter.

RETURNS A non-`null` `Constructor` object reflecting the constructor whose parameter list matches `parameterTypes`.

EXCEPTIONS

`NoSuchMethodException`
If a constructor with the parameters specified by `parameterTypes` does not exist or is not public.

`SecurityException`
If access to the information is denied.

SEE ALSO `getConstructors()`, `getDeclaredConstructor()`, `getDeclaredConstructors()`, `java.lang.reflect.Constructor`.

EXAMPLE

```
import java.lang.reflect.*;

class Main {
    static void printConstructor(Class c, Class[] paramTypes) {
        try {
            System.out.println(c.getConstructor(paramTypes));
        } catch (NoSuchMethodException e) {
            System.out.println(e);
        }
    }
    public static void main(String[] args) {
        printConstructor(String.class, new Class[]{});
                                  // public java.lang.String()

        printConstructor(String.class, new Class[]{String.class});
                                  // public java.lang.String(java.lang.String)

        printConstructor(String.class, new Class[]{char[].class});
                                  // public java.lang.String(char[])

        printConstructor(String.class, new Class[]{char[].class, int.class,
            int.class});
                                  // public java.lang.String(char[],int,int)

        printConstructor(String.class, new Class[]{char[].class, int.class,
            int.class});
                                  // public java.lang.String(char[],int,int)

        printConstructor(Main.InnerC.class, new Class[]{});
                                  // public Main$InnerC()

        printConstructor(Main.InnerC.class, new Class[]{int.class});
                                  // NoSuchMethodException
    }

    static class InnerC {
        public InnerC() {}
        InnerC(int i) {}
    }
}
```

getConstructors()

PURPOSE Retrieves `Constructor` objects for all public constructors.

SYNTAX `public Constructor[] getConstructors() throws SecurityException`

DESCRIPTION This method retrieves an array containing a `Constructor` object for each public constructor in the class represented by this `Class` object.

RETURNS A non-`null` array containing `Constructor` objects.

EXCEPTIONS

`SecurityException`

If access to the information is denied.

SEE ALSO `getConstructor()`, `getDeclaredConstructor()`, `getDeclaredConstructors()`, `java.lang.reflect.Constructor`.

EXAMPLE

```
import java.lang.reflect.*;

class Main {
    static void printConstructors(Constructor[] cons) {
        for (int i=0; i<cons.length; i++) {
            System.out.println(cons[i]);
        }
    }
    public static void main(String[] args) {
        printConstructors(StringBuffer.class.getConstructors());
            // public java.lang.StringBuffer()
            // public java.lang.StringBuffer(int)
            // public java.lang.StringBuffer(java.lang.String)

        printConstructors(InnerC.class.getConstructors());
            // public Main$InnerC()

        printConstructors(java.lang.Cloneable.class.getConstructors());

        printConstructors(int.class.getConstructors());
    }

    static class InnerC {
        public InnerC() {}
        InnerC(int i) {}
    }
}
```

getDeclaredClasses()

PURPOSE Retrieves an array of `Class` objects for all class and interface members. Not implemented.

SYNTAX `public Class[] getDeclaredClasses() throws SecurityException`

DESCRIPTION This method retrieves an array containing `Class` objects for all of the classes and interfaces that are declared as members of the class represented by this `Class` object.

RETURNS A non-`null` array of `Class` objects.

SEE ALSO `getClasses()`.

EXCEPTIONS

`SecurityException`
If access to the information is denied.

A B C D E F G H I J K L M N O P Q R S T U V W X Y Z

getDeclaredConstructor()

PURPOSE Retrieves a `Constructor` object for a constructor.

SYNTAX

```
public Constructor getDeclaredConstructor(Class[]
   parameterTypes) throws NoSuchMethodException,
   SecurityException
```

DESCRIPTION This method retrieves a constructor of this `Class` object with the parameter list as specified by `parameterTypes`. Unlike `getConstructor()`, the constructor need not be public. Moreover, `getDeclaredConstructor()` is subjected to more stringent security access checks than `getConstructor()` and consequently does not work in applets. See `SecurityManager.checkMemberAccess()` for details.

See `getConstructor()` for details about `parameterTypes`.

PARAMETERS

`parameterTypes`
A non-`null` array of `Class` objects, one for each parameter.

RETURNS A non-`null` `Constructor` object representing a constructor whose parameter list matches `parameterTypes`.

EXCEPTIONS

`NoSuchMethodException`
If a constructor with the parameters specified by `parameterTypes` does not exist or is not public.

`SecurityException`
If access to the information is denied.

SEE ALSO `getConstructor()`, `getConstructors()`, `getDeclaredConstructors()`, `java.lang.reflect.Constructor`, `SecurityManager.checkMemberAccess()`.

EXAMPLE

```
import java.lang.reflect.*;

class Main {
    static void printConstructor(Class c, Class[] paramTypes) {
        try {
            System.out.println(c.getDeclaredConstructor(paramTypes));
        } catch (NoSuchMethodException e) {
            System.out.println(e);
        }
    }
    public static void main(String[] args) {
        printConstructor(String.class, new Class[]{});
                                        // public java.lang.String()

        printConstructor(String.class,
            new Class[]{int.class, int.class, char[].class});
                                       // private java.lang.String(int,int,char[])

        printConstructor(Main.InnerC.class, new Class[]{});
                                        // public Main$InnerC()

        printConstructor(Main.InnerC.class, new Class[]{int.class});
                                        // Main$InnerC(int)

        printConstructor(Main.InnerC.class, new Class[]{float.class});
                                        // Main$InnerC(float)
    }

    static class InnerC {
        public InnerC() {}
        InnerC(int i) {}
        private InnerC(float i) {}
    }
}
```

getDeclaredConstructors()

PURPOSE Retrieves `Constructor` objects for all constructors.

SYNTAX `public Constructor[] getDeclaredConstructors() throws SecurityException`

DESCRIPTION This method retrieves an array containing a `Constructor` object for every constructor in the class represented by this `Class` object. Unlike `getConstructors()`, this method retrieves all constructors, including private and package-protected ones. Moreover, `getDeclaredConstructors()` is subjected to more stringent security access checks than `getConstructors()` and consequently does not work in applets. See `SecurityManager.checkMemberAccess()` for details.

RETURNS A non-`null` array containing `Constructor` objects.

EXCEPTIONS

`SecurityException`
If access to the information is denied.

SEE ALSO `getConstructor()`, `getConstructors()`, `getDeclaredConstructor()`, `java.lang.reflect.Constructor`, `SecurityManager.checkMemberAccess()`.

EXAMPLE

```
import java.lang.reflect.*;

class Main {
    static void printConstructors(Constructor[] cons) {
        for (int i=0; i<cons.length; i++) {
            System.out.println(cons[i]);
        }
    }

    public static void main(String[] args) {
        printConstructors(java.lang.String.class.getDeclaredConstructors());
            // public java.lang.String()
            // public java.lang.String(java.lang.String)
            // public java.lang.String(char[])
            // public java.lang.String(char[],int,int)
            // public java.lang.String(byte[],int,int,int)
            // public java.lang.String(byte[],int)
            // private java.lang.String(byte[],int,int,
            //     sun.io.ByteToCharConverter)
            // public java.lang.String(byte[],int,int,java.lang.String)
            //     throws java.io.UnsupportedEncodingException
            // public java.lang.String(byte[],java.lang.String)
            //     throws java.io.UnsupportedEncodingException
            // public java.lang.String(byte[],int,int)
            // public java.lang.String(byte[])
            // public java.lang.String(java.lang.StringBuffer)
            // private java.lang.String(int,int,char[])

        printConstructors(InnerC.class.getDeclaredConstructors());
            // public Main$InnerC()
            // Main$InnerC(int)
            // private Main$InnerC(double)
    }

    static class InnerC {
        public InnerC() {}
        InnerC(int i) {}
        private InnerC(double i) {}
    }
}
```

getDeclaredField()

PURPOSE Retrieves a `Field` object for a declared field.

SYNTAX

```
public Field getDeclaredField(String fieldName) throws
    NoSuchFieldException, SecurityException
```

DESCRIPTION This method retrieves a `Field` object for a field in the class represented by this `Class` object. The field must be declared by this class, not one declared by any of the class's superclasses or implemented interfaces.

Unlike `getField()`, the field need not be public; it can be a public, private, protected, or package-protected field. Moreover, `getDeclaredField()` is subjected to more stringent security access checks than `getField()` and consequently does not work in applets. See `SecurityManager.checkMemberAccess()` for details.

PARAMETERS

`fieldName` A non-`null` string containing the unqualified name of a field.

RETURNS A non-`null` `Field` object.

EXCEPTIONS

`NoSuchFieldException`

If `fieldName` is not found or is not accessible.

`SecurityException`

If access to the information is denied.

SEE ALSO `getDeclaredFields()`, `getField()`, `getFields()`, `java.lang.reflect.Field`, `SecurityManager.checkMemberAccess()`.

EXAMPLE

```
import java.lang.reflect.Field;

class Main {
    static void print(Field f) {
        System.out.println(f);
    }

    public static void main(String[] args) {
        try {
            print(D.class.getDeclaredField("g"));        // public int D.ci
            print(D.class.getDeclaredField("ci"));       // public int D.ci

        // print(D.class.getDeclaredField("D.g"));    // NoSuchFieldException
        // print(D.class.getDeclaredField("C.ci"));   // NoSuchFieldException
        // print(D.class.getDeclaredField("X"));      // NoSuchFieldException
        // print(D.class.getDeclaredField("Q"));      // NoSuchFieldException
        } catch (NoSuchFieldException e) {
            e.printStackTrace();
        }
    }
}
```

```
class C {
    public int ci;
    public int cj;
}

class D extends C implements I {
    float g;
    public int ci;
}

interface I {
    int X = 99;
}
```

A B C D E F G H I J K L M N O P Q R S T U V W X Y Z

getDeclaredFields()

PURPOSE Retrieves `Field` objects for all declared fields.

SYNTAX `public Field[] getDeclaredFields() throws SecurityException`

DESCRIPTION This method retrieves an array containing a `Field` object for every field in the class represented by this `Class` object. It retrieves only fields declared by the class, not those declared by any of the class's superclasses or implemented interfaces.

Unlike `getFields()`, the return value includes all fields, including public, private, protected, and package-protected fields. Moreover, `getDeclaredFields()` is subjected to more stringent security access checks than `getFields()` and consequently does not work in applets. See `SecurityManager.checkMemberAccess()` for details.

A non-`null` array containing `Field` objects.

EXCEPTIONS

`SecurityException`
If access to the information is denied.

SEE ALSO `getDeclaredField()`, `getField()`, `getFields()`, `java.lang.reflect.Field`.

EXAMPLE

```
import java.lang.reflect.*;

class Main {
    static void printFields(Field[] fields) {
        for (int i=0; i<fields.length; i++) {
            System.out.println(fields[i]);
        }
    }

    public static void main(String[] args) {
        printFields(java.awt.Point.class.getDeclaredFields());
                                // public int java.awt.Point.x
```

```
                        // public int java.awt.Point.y
                // private static final long java.awt.Point.serialVersionUID

        printFields(C.class.getDeclaredFields());
                        // float C.f
                        // public int C.ci
                        // public int C.cj

        printFields(D.class.getDeclaredFields());
                        // float D.g
                        // public int D.ci
                        // public int D.x

        printFields(I.class.getDeclaredFields());
                        // public static final int I.X
    }
}

class C implements I {
    float f;
    public int ci;
    public int cj;
}

class D extends C {
    float g;
    public int ci;
    public int x;
}

interface I {
    int X = 99;
}
```

getDeclaredMethod()

PURPOSE Retrieves a `Method` object for a declared method.

SYNTAX

```
public Method getDeclaredMethod(String methodName, Class[]
   parameterTypes) throws NoSuchMethodException,
   SecurityException
```

DESCRIPTION This method retrieves a `Method` object for a method in the class represented by this `Class` object. The method must be declared by this class, not one declared by any of the class's superclasses or implemented interfaces. The returned method has the name `methodName` and a parameter list that matches `parameterTypes`. See `getConstructor()` for details about `parameterTypes`.

Unlike `getMethod()`, the method need not be public; it can be a public, private, protected, or package-protected method. Moreover, `getDeclaredMethod()` is subjected to more stringent security access checks than `getMethod()` and consequently does not work in applets. See `SecurityManager.checkMemberAccess()` for details.

PARAMETERS

`methodName` A non-`null` string containing the unqualified name of a method.

RETURNS A non-`null` `Method` object.

EXCEPTIONS

`NoSuchFieldException`
If `methodName` is not found or is not accessible.

`SecurityException`
If access to the information is denied.

SEE ALSO `getDeclaredMethods()`, `getMethod()`, `getMethods()`, `java.lang.reflect.Method`, `SecurityManager.checkMemeberAccess()`.

EXAMPLE

```
import java.lang.reflect.*;

class Main {
    // Prints all the methods except for ones from Object.
    static void print(Method m) {
        System.out.println(m);
    }

    public static void main(String[] args) {
        Class[] pt = new Class[]{};
        try {
            print(C.class.getDeclaredMethod("c_prv", pt));
                                        // private void c_prv()
            print(C.class.getDeclaredMethod("c_pub1", pt));
                                        // public void C.c_pub1()
            print(C.class.getDeclaredMethod("c_pub1", pt));
                                        // public void C.c_pub1()

            print(D.class.getDeclaredMethod("c_pub1", pt));
                                        // public void D.c_pub1()
            //print(D.class.getDeclaredMethod("c_pub2", pt));
                                        // NoSuchMethodException
            print(D.class.getDeclaredMethod("d_pub", pt));
                                        // public void D.d_pub()

            print(I.class.getDeclaredMethod("i_m", pt));
                                        // public abstract void I.i_m()
            //print(J.class.getDeclaredMethod("i_m", pt));
                                        // NoSuchMethodException
            print(J.class.getDeclaredMethod("j_m", pt));
                                        // public abstract void J.j_m()
        } catch (NoSuchMethodException e) {
            e.printStackTrace();
        }
    }
}

class C {
    private void c_prv() {}
    public void c_pub1() {}
    public void c_pub2() {}
}
```

```
class D extends C {
    private void d_prv() {}
    public void c_pub1() {}    // override
    public void d_pub() {}
}

interface I {
    void i_m();
}

interface J extends I {
    void j_m();
}
```

getDeclaredMethods()

PURPOSE Retrieves `Method` objects for all declared methods.

SYNTAX `public Method[] getDeclaredMethods() throws SecurityException`

DESCRIPTION This method retrieves an array containing a `Method` object for every method in the class represented by this `Class` object. It retrieves only methods declared by the class, not those declared by any of the class's superclasses or implemented interfaces.

Unlike `getMethods()`, the return value includes all methods, including private, protected, and package-protected methods. Moreover, `getDeclaredMethods()` is subjected to more stringent security access checks than `getMethods()` and consequently does not work in applets. See `SecurityManager.checkMemberAccess()` for details.

RETURNS A non-`null` array containing `Method` objects.

EXCEPTIONS

`SecurityException`

If access to the information is denied.

SEE ALSO `getDeclaredMethod()`, `getMethod()`, `getMethods()`, `java.lang.reflect.Method`, `SecurityManager.checkMemberAccess()`.

EXAMPLE

```
import java.lang.reflect.*;

class Main {
    // Prints all the methods except for ones from Object.
    static void printMethods(Method[] methods) {
        for (int i=0; i<methods.length; i++) {
            if (methods[i].getDeclaringClass() != Object.class) {
                System.out.println(methods[i]);
            }
        }
    }
```

```
    public static void main(String[] args) {
        printMethods(C.class.getDeclaredMethods());
                                            // private void C.c_prv()
                                            // public void C.c_pub1()
                                            // public void C.c_pub2()
        printMethods(D.class.getDeclaredMethods());
                                            // private void D.d_prv()
                                            // public void D.c_pub1()
                                            // public void D.d_pub()
        printMethods(I.class.getDeclaredMethods());
                                            // public abstract void I.i_m()
        printMethods(J.class.getDeclaredMethods());
                                            // public abstract void J.j_m()
    }
}

class C {
    private void c_prv() {}
    public void c_pub1() {}
    public void c_pub2() {}
}

class D extends C {
    private void d_prv() {}
    public void c_pub1() {}     // override
    public void d_pub() {}
}

interface I {
    void i_m();
}

interface J extends I {
    void j_m();
}
```

getDeclaringClass()

PURPOSE Retrieves the declaring class of this `Class` object. Not implemented.

SYNTAX `public Class getDeclaringClass()`

DESCRIPTION If the class or interface represented by this `Class` object is a member of another class, this method retrieves the `Class` object representing the class of which it is a member (its declaring class). This method returns `null` if this class or interface is not a member of any other class.

RETURNS A possibly `null` `Class` object.

SEE ALSO `getClass()`.

getField()

PURPOSE Retrieves a `Field` object for an accessible public field.

SYNTAX
```
public Field getField(String fieldName) throws
   NoSuchFieldException, SecurityException
```

DESCRIPTION This method retrieves a `Field` object that has the name `fieldName`. The object comes from the set of public fields accessible from the class represented by this `Class` object. More specifically, the accessible set of public fields includes all public fields of the following:

- This class or interface
- All superclasses of this class or interface
- Interfaces implemented by this class
- Interfaces extended from interfaces implemented by this class

An attempt to retrieve a `Field` object for a field not in this set results in a `NoSuchFieldException`.

PARAMETERS

`fieldName` A non-`null` string containing the unqualified name of a field.

RETURNS A non-`null` `Field` object.

EXCEPTIONS

`NoSuchFieldException`
If `fieldName` is not found or is not accessible.

`SecurityException`
If access to the information is denied.

SEE ALSO `getDeclaredField()`, `getDeclaredFields()`, `getFields()`, `java.lang.reflect.Field`, `SecurityManager.checkMemberAccess()`.

EXAMPLE
```
import java.lang.reflect.Field;

class Main {
    static void print(Field f) {
        System.out.println(f);
    }

    public static void main(String[] args) {
        try {
            // print(D.class.getField("f"));     // NoSuchFieldException
            print(D.class.getField("ci"));       // public int D.ci
            // print(D.class.getField("C.ci")); // NoSuchFieldException
            print(D.class.getField("cj"));       // public int C.cj
            print(D.class.getField("X"));        // public static final int I.X
            print(D.class.getField("Y"));        // public static final int J.Y

            print(C.class.getField("ci"));       // public int C.ci
            // print(C.class.getField("Q"));     // NoSuchFieldException
        } catch (NoSuchFieldException e) {
```

A B C D E F G H I J K L M N O P Q R S T U V W X Y Z

```
                e.printStackTrace();
            }
        }
    }

    class C implements J {
        float f;
        public int ci;
        public int cj;
    }

    class D extends C {
        float g;
        public int ci;
    }

    interface I {
        int X = 99;
    }

    interface J extends I {
        int Y = 99;
    }
```

getFields()

PURPOSE Retrieves `Field` objects for all accessible public fields.

SYNTAX `public Field[] getFields() throws SecurityException`

DESCRIPTION This method retrieves an array containing `Field` objects for every field in the set of public fields accessible from the class represented by this `Class` object. More specifically, the accessible set of public fields includes all public fields of the following:

- This class or interface
- All superclasses of this class or interface
- Interfaces implemented by this class
- Interfaces extended from interfaces implemented by this class

If the class represented by this `Class` object is an array or primitive type, this method retrieves an array of length zero. In particular, the implicit length field of arrays are not returned.

RETURNS A non-`null` array containing `Field` objects.

EXCEPTIONS

`SecurityException`
If access to the information is denied.

SEE ALSO `getDeclaredField()`, `getDeclaredFields()`, `getField()`, `java.lang.reflect.Field`, `Security.checkMemberAccess()`.

EXAMPLE

```
import java.lang.reflect.*;

class Main {
    static void printFields(Field[] fields) {
        for (int i=0; i<fields.length; i++) {
            System.out.println(fields[i]);
        }
    }

    public static void main(String[] args) {
        printFields(java.awt.Point.class.getFields());
                              // public int java.awt.Point.x
                              // public int java.awt.Point.y

        printFields(C.class.getFields());
                              // public static final int I.X
                              // public static final int J.Y
                              // public int C.ci
                              // public int C.cj

        printFields(D.class.getFields());
                              // public static final int I.X
                              // public static final int J.Y
                              // public int C.ci
                              // public int C.cj
                              // public int D.ci
                              // public int D.x

        printFields(I.class.getFields());
                              // public static final int I.X

        printFields(J.class.getFields());
                              // public static final int I.X
                              // public static final int J.Y
    }
}

class C implements J {
    float f;
    public int ci;
    public int cj;
}

class D extends C {
    float g;
    public int ci;
    public int x;
}

interface I {
    int X = 99;
}

interface J extends I {
    int Y = 99;
}
```

getInterfaces()

PURPOSE Retrieves the interfaces being implemented by this class.

SYNTAX `public native Class[] getInterfaces()`

DESCRIPTION If this `Class` object represents a class, this method retrieves exactly those interfaces that appear on the class's `implements` clause. This list does not include any interfaces that a superclass may implement. Moreover, there is no attempt to minimize the entries in the list. For example, an interface in the list may already be extended by another in the list.

The order of the interfaces in the returned list is exactly the order in which they appear on the `implements` clause.

If this `Class` object represents an interface, this method retrieves exactly those interfaces that appear on its `extends` clause. The contents and order of the entries in the list are identical to the interface list of a class.

RETURNS A non-`null` array of `Class` objects of interfaces implemented by this class. An array of length `0` is returned if this class does not implement any interfaces.

EXAMPLE

```
class Main {
    static void printInterfaces(Class c) {
        for (int i=0; i<c.getInterfaces().length; i++) {
            System.out.print(c.getInterfaces()[i].getName()+" ");
        }
    System.out.println();
    }
    public static void main(String[] args) {
        printInterfaces(C.class);     // I
        printInterfaces(D.class);     //
        printInterfaces(E.class);     // I J
        printInterfaces(I.class);     // J
        printInterfaces(J.class);     //
    }
}

class C implements I {}

class D extends C {}

class E implements I, J {}

interface I extends J {}

interface J {}
```

getMethod()

PURPOSE Retrieves a `Method` object for an accessible public method.

SYNTAX
```
public Method getMethod(String methodName, Class[]
   parameterTypes) throws NoSuchMethodException,
   SecurityException
```

DESCRIPTION This method retrieves a `Method` object for an accessible public method. The method can be declared or inherited in the class or interface represented by this `Class` object. The returned method has the name `methodName` and a parameter list that matches `parameterTypes`. See `getConstructor()` for details about `parameterTypes`.

PARAMETERS

`methodName` A non-`null` string containing an unqualified method name.

`parameterTypes`
A non-`null` array of `Class` objects, one for each parameter.

RETURNS A non-`null` `Method` object representing a method whose parameter list matches `parameterTypes`.

EXCEPTIONS

`NoSuchMethodException`
If `methodName` with the parameters specified by `parameterTypes` does not exist or is not public.

`SecurityException`
If access to the information is denied.

SEE ALSO `getDeclaredMethod()`, `getDeclaredMethods()`, `getMethods()`, `java.lang.reflect.Method`, `SecurityManager.checkMemberAccess()`.

EXAMPLE
```
import java.lang.reflect.*;

class Main {
    static void print(Method m) {
    System.out.println(m);
    }

    public static void main(String[] args) {
        try {
            // print(C.class.getMethod("c_prv", new Class[]{}));
                                            // NoSuchMethodException
            print(C.class.getMethod("c_pub1", new Class[]{}));
                                            // public void C.c_pub1()
            print(C.class.getMethod("c_pub1", new Class[]{}));
                                            // public void C.c_pub1()

            print(D.class.getMethod("c_pub1", new Class[]{}));
                                            // public void D.c_pub1()
            print(D.class.getMethod("c_pub2", new Class[]{}));
                                            // public void C.c_pub2()
```

```
                print(D.class.getMethod("d_pub", new Class[]{}));
                                                // public void D.d_pub()

                print(I.class.getMethod("i_m", new Class[]{}));
                                                // public abstract void I.i_m()
                print(J.class.getMethod("i_m", new Class[]{}));
                                                // public abstract void I.i_m()
                print(J.class.getMethod("j_m", new Class[]{}));
                                                // public abstract void J.j_m()
            } catch (NoSuchMethodException e) {
                e.printStackTrace();
        }
        }
    }

    class C {
        private void c_prv() {}
        public void c_pub1() {}
        public void c_pub2() {}
    }

    class D extends C {
        private void d_prv() {}
        public void c_pub1() {}     // override
        public void d_pub() {}
    }

    interface I {
        void i_m();
    }

    interface J extends I {
        void j_m();
    }
```

getMethods()

PURPOSE Retrieves `Method` objects for all accessible public methods.

SYNTAX `public Method[] getMethods() throws SecurityException`

DESCRIPTION This method retrieves an array containing `Method` objects for every accessible public method. The methods are declared or inherited in the class or interface represented by this `Class` object.

RETURNS A non-`null` array containing `Method` objects.

EXCEPTIONS

`SecurityException`
If access to the information is denied.

SEE ALSO `getDeclaredMethod()`, `getDeclaredMethods()`, `getMethod()`, `java.lang.reflect.Method`, `SecurityManager.checkMemberAccess()`.

EXAMPLE

```
import java.lang.reflect.*;

class Main {
    // Prints all the public methods except for ones from Object.
    static void printMethods(Method[] methods) {
        for (int i=0; i<methods.length; i++) {
            if (methods[i].getDeclaringClass() != Object.class) {
                System.out.println(methods[i]);
            }
        }
    }

    public static void main(String[] args) {
        printMethods(C.class.getMethods());
                                        // public void C.c_pub1()
                                        // public void C.c_pub2()
        printMethods(D.class.getMethods());
                                        // public void D.c_pub1()
                                        // public void C.c_pub2()
                                        // public void D.d_pub()
        printMethods(I.class.getMethods());
                                        // public abstract void I.i_m()
        printMethods(J.class.getMethods());
                                        // public abstract void I.i_m()
                                        // public abstract void J.j_m()
    }
}

class C {
    private void c_prv() {}
    public void c_pub1() {}
    public void c_pub2() {}
    protected void c_prot() {}
}

class D extends C {
    private void d_prv() {}
    public void c_pub1() {}
    public void d_pub() {}
}

interface I {
    void i_m();
}

interface J extends I {
    void j_m();
}
```

getModifiers()

PURPOSE Retrieves the Java language modifiers for the class represented by this `Class` object.

SYNTAX `public native int getModifiers()`

DESCRIPTION This method retrieves an `int` encoding the modifiers of the class or interface represented by this `Class` object. The possible list of class modifiers are `public`, `abstract`, and `final`. The only possible interface modifier is `public`. If this `Class` object is an interface, the `Modifier.INTERFACE` also appears in the modifier set.

To process the encoding, use the methods and constants in `Modifier`.

RETURNS An `int` representing the modifiers specified for this class.

SEE ALSO `java.lang.reflect.Modifier`.

EXAMPLE Note that the `synchronized` modifier appears in the modifier set for some classes. This is because the Java virtual machine uses the bit position for its own purposes. This modifier should be ignored.

Also note that for an interface, the `interface` modifier appears in the modifier set. This modifier also should be ignored.

```
import java.lang.reflect.*;

class Main {
    static void printModifiers(int mods) {
        System.out.println(Modifier.toString(mods));
    }

    public static void main(String[] args) {
        printModifiers(String.class.getModifiers());
                                            // public final synchronized
        printModifiers(Cloneable.class.getModifiers());
                                            // public interface
        printModifiers(java.awt.Component.class.getModifiers());
                                            // public abstract synchronized

        // Inner classes
        printModifiers(Main.InnerA.class.getModifiers());
                                            // abstract
        printModifiers(Main.InnerB.class.getModifiers());
                                            // final
        printModifiers(Main.InnerC.class.getModifiers());
                                            // public
    }

    static abstract class InnerA {}
    static final private class InnerB {}
    static public class InnerC {}
}
```

getName()

PURPOSE Retrieves the type descriptor for this `Class` object.

SYNTAX `public native String getName()`

DESCRIPTION Every `Class` object has a unique type descriptor. See the class descriptions for details on type descriptors.

RETURNS The non-`null` type descriptor for this `Class` object.

SEE ALSO `forName()`, `toString()`.

EXAMPLE

```
import java.lang.reflect.Array;

class Main {
    public static void main(String[] args) {
        System.out.println(String.class.getName());      // java.lang.String
        System.out.println(Cloneable.class.getName());
                                            // java.lang.Cloneable
        // Inner classes and interfaces.
        System.out.println(Main.InnerC.class.getName());  // Main$InnerC
        System.out.println(Main.InnerI.class.getName());  // Main$InnerC

        // Primitive types.
        System.out.println(int.class.getName());          // int
        System.out.println(Void.TYPE.getName());          // void

        // Arrays
        System.out.println(String[].class.getName());
                                            // [Ljava.lang.String;
        System.out.println(Main.InnerC[].class.getName());// [LMain$InnerC;
        System.out.println(Main.InnerI[].class.getName());// [LMain$InnerI;
        System.out.println(int[].class.getName());        // [I
    }

    static class InnerC {}
    interface InnerI {}
}
```

getResource()

PURPOSE Finds a resource associated with the class represented by this `Class` object.

SYNTAX `public URL getResource(String resourceName)`

DESCRIPTION This method finds the resource with the name `resourceName` and returns its URL. The URL can then be used in a class to `URL.getContent()` to retrieve the resource. `null` is returned if the resource cannot be found.

To find the resource, this method uses the class loader of the class represented by this `Class` object. In particular, it calls `ClassLoader.getResource()`. If this Class object refers to an array, the class loader of the array's component type is used to find the resource.

How a class loader uses resourceName to locate the resource depends on the class loader. However, most class loaders will try to behave like the system class loader whenever possible. Following is a description of the behavior of the default system class loader.

Suppose that a class C is in a package P.Q, where Q is a subpackage of package P. This method maps this package/class structure (P.Q.C) into a directory/file structure of the form "DIR/P/Q/C," where "DIR," "P," and "Q" are all directories and "C" is a class file.

If resourceName does not start with a forward slash (/), it is interpreted relative to the directory "DIR/P/Q." For example, if resourceName is "data.txt" it refers to a file at "DIR/P/Q/data.txt." If resourceName is "R/data.txt," it refers to a file at "DIR/P/Q/R/data.txt."

If resourceName does start with a forward slash, it is interpreted relative to "DIR." For example, if resourceName is "/data.txt" it refers to a file at "DIR/data.txt." If resourceName is "/P/data.txt," it refers to a file at "DIR/P/data.txt." If resourceName is "/P/Q/R/data.txt," it refers to a file at "DIR/P/Q/R/data.txt."

In this example, the name "data.txt" is equivalent to "/P/Q/data.txt."

PARAMETERS

resourceName
: A non-null string containing the name and location of the resource.

RETURNS
: A possibly null URL object with the name resourceName.

SEE ALSO
: ClassLoader, getResourceAsStream(), java.net.URL, java.net.URL.getContent().

EXAMPLE
: This example demonstrates how to read a text file using getResourceAsStream(). As a demonstration of the effect that packages have on this method, the Main class is declared in a package called pkg. Moreover, three resource files are placed in three different packages: one in the top-level (unnamed) package, one in the package pkg, and one in the subpackage subpkg.

Also included is some example code for reading an image resource. The object type that is returned by URL.getContent() is platform-dependent. In the program, we test for two possibilities: one as an Image object and the other as a FileImageSource. Unfortunately, in the latter case undocumented classes from the sun.* packages are necessary to create the image. These undocumented classes may be changed in a future release; nevertheless, we hope you find the code useful for the present version.

pkg/Main.java

```
package pkg;

import java.awt.*;
import java.io.*;
import java.net.*;

class Main {
    static String getResource(String rsrcName) {
        String result = "";

        try {
            // Find the text file.
            URL url =
                Main.class.getResource(rsrcName); // Main[].class also works.
            if (url == null) {
                return null;
            }

            // Read the text file.
            BufferedReader rd = new BufferedReader(
                new InputStreamReader(url.openStream()));

            // Read each line and print it.
            String line;
            while ((line = rd.readLine()) != null) {
                result += line;
            }
            rd.close();
        } catch (IOException e) {
            System.out.println(e);
        } catch (Exception e) {
            System.out.println(e);
        }
        return result;
    }

    public static void main(String[] args) {
        System.out.println(getResource("/input.txt"));
                                        // The Java Class Libraries.
        System.out.println(getResource("input.txt"));
                                        // null

        System.out.println(getResource("resource.txt"));
                                        // Have a nice day.
        System.out.println(getResource("/pkg/resource.txt"));
                                        // Have a nice day.
        System.out.println(getResource("/pkg.resource.txt"));
                                        // null
        System.out.println(getResource("/resource.txt"));
                                        // null

        System.out.println(getResource("subpkg/data.txt"));
                                        // Humpty Dumpty.
        System.out.println(getResource("/pkg/subpkg/data.txt"));
                                        // Humpty Dumpty.
        System.out.println(getResource("data.txt"));
                                        // null

        // Read an image
```

```
            try {
                URL url = Main.class.getResource("duke.gif");
                Object o = url.getContent();

                // Determine what type of object is returned.
                Image image = null;
                if (o instanceof Image) {
                    image = (Image)o;
                } else if (o instanceof sun.awt.image.FileImageSource) {
                    image = Toolkit.getDefaultToolkit().createImage(
                        new sun.awt.image.URLImageSource(url));
                }
                System.out.println(image);
            } catch (IOException e) {
                System.out.println(e);
            }
        }
    }
```

input.txt

```
The Java Class Libraries.
```

pkg/resource.txt

```
Have a nice day.
```

pkg/subpkg/data.txt

```
Humpty Dumpty.
```

getResourceAsStream()

PURPOSE
Finds and creates an input stream on a resource associated with the class represented by this `Class` object.

SYNTAX
`public InputStream getResourceAsStream(String resourceName)`

DESCRIPTION
This method finds the resource with the name `resourceName` and returns an input stream that can be used to retrieve the contents of the resource. `null` is returned if the resource cannot be found.

This method behaves similarly to `getResource()`. It is essentially equivalent to

```
getResource(resourceName).openStream();
```

See `getResource()` for details on how `resourceName` is used.

PARAMETERS

`resourceName`
A non-`null` string containing the name and location of the resource.

RETURNS
A possibly `null` `InputStream` object that can be used to read the resource with the name `resourceName`.

SEE ALSO `ClassLoader`, `getResource()`, `java.net.URL`, `java.net.URL.getContent()`.

EXAMPLE This example demonstrates how to read a text file using `getResourceAsStream()`. As a demonstration of the effect that packages have on this method, the `Main` class is declared in a package called `pkg`. Moreover, three resource files are placed in three different packages—one in the top-level (unnamed) package, one in the package `pkg`, and one in the subpackage `subpkg`.

pkg/Main.java

```
package pkg;

import java.awt.*;
import java.io.*;
import java.net.*;

class Main {
    static String getResource(String rsrcName) {
        String result = "";

        try {
            // Get an input stream on the resource.
            InputStream is = Main.class.getResourceAsStream(rsrcName);
                        // Main[].class also works.
            if (is == null) {
                return null;
            }

            // Convert the input stream into a reader.
            BufferedReader rd = new BufferedReader(new InputStreamReader(is));

            // Read each line and print it.
            String line;
            while ((line = rd.readLine()) != null) {
                result += line;
            }
            is.close();
        } catch (IOException e) {
            System.out.println(e);
        } catch (Exception e) {
            System.out.println(e);
        }
        return result;
    }

    public static void main(String[] args) {
        System.out.println(getResource("/input.txt"));
                                                // The Java Class Libraries.
        System.out.println(getResource("input.txt"));
                                                // null

        System.out.println(getResource("resource.txt"));
                                                // Have a nice day.
        System.out.println(getResource("/pkg/resource.txt"));
                                                // Have a nice day.
        System.out.println(getResource("/pkg.resource.txt"));
                                                // null
        System.out.println(getResource("/resource.txt"));
                                                // null
```

```
            System.out.println(getResource("subpkg/data.txt"));
                                                // Humpty Dumpty.
            System.out.println(getResource("/pkg/subpkg/data.txt"));
                                                // Humpty Dumpty.
            System.out.println(getResource("data.txt"));
                                                // null
        }
    }
```

input.txt

```
The Java Class Libraries.
```

pkg/resource.txt

```
Have a nice day.
```

pkg/subpkg/data.txt

```
Humpty Dumpty.
```

getSigners()

PURPOSE Retrieves the signers of this class.

SYNTAX `public native Object[] getSigners()`

DESCRIPTION If a class loader supports signing of classes, it records the signature[1] information of a class that it has loaded by invoking `ClassLoader.setSigners()`. The program subsequently retrieves this information using `getSigners()`. For example, a Web browser might use the signature information to determine whether an applet thus signed is allowed to execute.

If this class has not been signed, `null` is returned.

RETURNS A possibly `null` array of signers. The component type of the resulting array is of class `Identity`.

SEE ALSO `ClassLoader.setSigners()`, `java.security.Identity`, `java.security.Signer`.

EXAMPLE This example uses the signed applet example at

`http://java.sun.com/security/signExample/index.html`.

It calls `getSigners()` on the `writeFile` class. The output of this method is shown after the code.

```
public void showSigners() {
    try {
        Class c = Class.forName("writeFile");
        Object[] signers = c.getSigners();
```

1. "Signature" here refers to security-related information rather than the signature of methods or classes. See the class description of `Class` for details.

```
            if (signers == null) {
                System.out.println("null signers");
            } else {
                for (int i = 0; i < signers.length; i++) {
                    System.out.println("signer[" + i + "]:" + signers[i]);
                    System.out.println(signers[i].getClass());
            }
            }
        } catch (Exception e) {
            e.printStackTrace();
        }
    }
```

Output

```
> appletviewer signedWriteFile.html
signer[0]:Duke[identitydb.obj][trusted]
class sun.security.provider.SystemIdentity
```

getSuperclass()

PURPOSE Retrieves the superclass that this class extends.

SYNTAX `public native Class getSuperclass()`

DESCRIPTION This method retrieves the superclass that this class extends. If this `Class` object is that of `Object`, a primitive type, or an interface, `null` is returned.

RETURNS The `Class` object for the superclass of this `Class` object; `null` if this `Class` is that of `Object`, an interface or a primitive type.

SEE ALSO `Object.getClass()`.

EXAMPLE

```
class Main {
    public static void main(String[] args) {
        System.out.println(java.lang.String.class.getSuperclass());
            // class java.lang.String
        System.out.println(java.awt.Button.class.getSuperclass());
            // class java.awt.Component

        System.out.println(java.awt.LayoutManager.class.getSuperclass());
            // null
        System.out.println(java.awt.LayoutManager2.class.getSuperclass());
            // null
    }
}
```

isArray()

PURPOSE Determines if this `Class` object represents an array type.

SYNTAX `public native boolean isArray()`

RETURNS true if this Class object represents an array type; false otherwise.

EXAMPLE

```
class Main {
    static void printIsArray(Object o) {
        System.out.println(o.getClass().isArray());
    }

    public static void main(String[] args) {
        printIsArray(new String());              // false
        printIsArray(new String[0]);             // true
        printIsArray(new String[0][0]);          // true
        printIsArray(new int[0]);                // true
    }
}
```

isAssignableFrom()

PURPOSE Determines if the class represented by this Class object is a superclass of a class.

SYNTAX `public native boolean isAssignableFrom(Class cls)`

DESCRIPTION If one of the following is true, this method returns true:

- This Class object represents a class and is equal to cls.
- This Class object represents a class and is a superclass of cls.
- This Class object represents an interface and is implemented by cls.
- This Class object represents an interface and is extended by cls.

If this Class object or cls represents a primitive type, this method returns true only if cls is equal to this object.

PARAMETERS

cls A non-null Class object.

RETURNS true if an object of type cls can be assigned to objects of this class; false otherwise.

SEE ALSO isInstance().

EXAMPLE

```
class Main {
    static void printIsAssignableFrom(Class a, Class b) {
        System.out.println(a.isAssignableFrom(b));
    }

    public static void main(String[] args) {
        printIsAssignableFrom(C.class, Object.class);          // false
        printIsAssignableFrom(C.class, C.class);               // true
        printIsAssignableFrom(C.class, D.class);               // true
        printIsAssignableFrom(D.class, C.class);               // false

        printIsAssignableFrom(Object.class, int[].class);      // true
```

```
        printIsAssignableFrom(int[].class, int[].class);       // true
        printIsAssignableFrom(C[].class, D.class);             // false
        printIsAssignableFrom(C[].class, D[].class);           // true
        printIsAssignableFrom(C[].class, C[][].class);         // false

        printIsAssignableFrom(Object.class, I.class);          // true
        printIsAssignableFrom(I.class, I.class);               // true
        printIsAssignableFrom(D.class, I.class);               // false
        printIsAssignableFrom(I.class, D.class);               // true

        printIsAssignableFrom(D.class, J.class);               // false
        printIsAssignableFrom(J.class, D.class);               // false

        printIsAssignableFrom(I.class, J.class);               // true
        printIsAssignableFrom(J.class, J.class);               // true
        printIsAssignableFrom(J.class, I.class);               // false

        // Returns true iff both Class objects are equal.
        printIsAssignableFrom(long.class, long.class);         // true

        // Does not work for primitive types in general.
        printIsAssignableFrom(long.class, int.class);          // false
    }
}

class C {}
class D extends C implements I {}
interface I {}
interface J extends I {}
```

isInstance()

PURPOSE

Determines if an object is an instance of the class represented by this `Class` object.

SYNTAX

`public native boolean isInstance(Object obj)`

DESCRIPTION

This method is equivalent to

```
obj instanceof this
```

This method returns `true` if `obj` is non-`null` and can be cast to the type represented by this `Class` object. If this `Class` object is an interface, this method returns `true` if `obj`'s class or one of its superclasses implements the interface. If this `Class` object represents a primitive type, this method returns `false`. If `obj` is `null`, this method returns `false`.

PARAMETERS

`obj` A possibly `null` object.

RETURNS

`true` if the expression (`obj instanceof this`) evaluates to `true`; `false` otherwise.

SEE ALSO

`isAssignableFrom()`.

EXAMPLE

```
class Main {
    static void printIsInstance(Object a, Object b) {
        // Prints b instanceof a.getClass().
        System.out.println(a.getClass().isInstance(b));
    }

    public static void main(String[] args) {
        C c = new C();
        D d = new D();

        printIsInstance(c, null);                 // false
        printIsInstance(c, c);                    // true
        printIsInstance(c, d);                    // true
        printIsInstance(d, c);                    // false

        printIsInstance(new Object(), new int[1]);        // true
        printIsInstance(new int[1], new int[1]);          // true
        printIsInstance(new C[1], d);                     // false
        printIsInstance(new C[1], new D[1]);              // true
        printIsInstance(new C[1], new C[1][1]);           // false

        System.out.println(I.class.isInstance(c));        // false
        System.out.println(I.class.isInstance(d));        // true
        System.out.println(I.class.isInstance(new D[1])); // false
    }
}

class C {}
class D extends C {}
interface I {}
```

isInterface()

PURPOSE Determines if this `Class` object represents an interface.

SYNTAX `public native boolean isInterface()`

DESCRIPTION A `Class` object is used to represent either a Java class or a Java interface. This method returns whether this `Class` object is for an interface or for a class.

RETURNS `true` if this `Class` object represents an interface; `false` otherwise.

SEE ALSO `isPrimitive()`, `toString()`.

EXAMPLE

```
class Main {
    public static void main(String[] args) {
        System.out.println(Main.class.isInterface());                 // false
        System.out.println(java.lang.Cloneable.class.isInterface()); // true
        System.out.println(Main.InnerI.class.isInterface());         // true
        System.out.println(int.class.isInterface());                 // false
    }

    interface InnerI {}
}
```

isPrimitive()

PURPOSE Determines if this `Class` object represents a primitive Java type.

SYNTAX `public native boolean isPrimitive()`

DESCRIPTION There are eight primitive Java types: `boolean`, `char`, `byte`, `short`, `int`, `long`, `float`, and `double`. Calling this method on `Class` objects representing these types yields `true`. There is actually a ninth kind of `Class` object whose `isPrimitive()` method returns `true`. It is `void.class`, which represents the return type for methods that do not return anything.

The primitive type `Class` objects can be retrieved using the `.class` syntax or through the equivalent wrapper classes. Table 17 shows both means of retrieving primitive Java type `Class` objects. The preferred syntax for naming the class is the `.class` syntax.

Using *primitiveType*.class	Using *Wrapper*.TYPE
`boolean.class`	`Boolean.TYPE`
`char.class`	`Character.TYPE`
`byte.class`	`Byte.TYPE`
`short.class`	`Short.TYPE`
`int.class`	`Integer.TYPE`
`long.class`	`Long.TYPE`
`float.class`	`Float.TYPE`
`double.class`	`Double.TYPE`
`void.class`	`Void.TYPE`

TABLE 17: Class Objects for Java Primitive Types.

RETURNS `true` if this `Class` represents a primitive Java type; `false` otherwise.

EXAMPLE

```
class Main {
    public static void main(String[] args) {
        System.out.println(String.class.isPrimitive());     // false
        System.out.println(int.class.isPrimitive());        // true
        System.out.println(int[].class.isPrimitive());      // false
        System.out.println(Integer.TYPE.isPrimitive());     // true
        System.out.println(Void.TYPE.isPrimitive());        // true

        System.out.println(int.class == Integer.TYPE);      // true
    }
}
```

newInstance()

PURPOSE Constructs an instance of the class represented by this `Class` object.

SYNTAX
```
public native Object newInstance() throws
    InstantiationException, IllegalAccessException
```

A B C D E F G H I J K L M N O P Q R S T U V W X Y Z

DESCRIPTION This method constructs an instance of the class represented by this `Class` object. It uses the constructor that takes no parameters to construct the new object.

To create objects using constructors other than the constructor that takes no parameters, see `Constructor.newInstance()`.

Instances of abstract classes, interfaces, and primitive types cannot be created using `newInstance()`.

RETURNS A new non-`null` instance of the class represented by this `Class` object.

EXCEPTIONS

`IllegalAccessException`
If the class or initializer for the instance is not accessible. For example, when a new instance of a class is being created in another package, this exception will occur if either the class or the constructor that takes no parameters is not declared `public`.

`InstantiationException`
If the object could not be instantiated because the class is an abstract class, if the class is an interface or a primitive type, or because of some other reason.

`NoSuchMethodException`
If the class does not have a constructor that takes no parameters.

SEE ALSO `java.lang.reflect.Constructor`.

EXAMPLE This example uses `newInstance()` to create a new `StringBuffer` object. The example also demonstrates three different situations in which this method will throw an exception.

```
class Main {
    public static void main(String[] args) {
        try {
            StringBuffer buf = (StringBuffer)StringBuffer.class.newInstance();
            buf.append("Java");
            System.out.println(buf);            // Java

            // No null constructor.
            //Boolean.class.newInstance();      // NoSuchMethodException

            // Constructor is private
            //Class.class.newInstance();        // IllegalAccessException

            // Abstract class
            //Number.class.newInstance();       // InstantiationException
```

```
        } catch (InstantiationException e) {
            System.out.println(e);
        } catch (IllegalAccessException e) {
            System.out.println(e);
        }
    }
}
```

A B C D E F G H I J K L M N O P Q R S T U V W X Y Z

toString()

PURPOSE Generates the string representation of this class.

SYNTAX `public String toString()`

DESCRIPTION If this `Class` object represents a class or an array type, the string "class *type-descriptor*" is generated. If this `Class` object represents an interface, the string "interface *type-descriptor*" is generated. See the class description for details on type descriptors.

If this `Class` object represents a primitive Java type, this method returns the name of the primitive type (e.g., "int" or "byte").

Note that the result of `toString()` cannot be passed to `forName()`; use the result of `getName()` instead. See `forName()` for details.

RETURNS A non-`null` string containing the string representation of this class.

OVERRIDES `Object.toString()`.

SEE ALSO `getName()`, `isInterface()`.

EXAMPLE

```
import java.lang.reflect.Array;

class Main {
    public static void main(String[] args) {
        System.out.println(String.class.toString());
                                        // class java.lang.String
        System.out.println(Cloneable.class.toString());
                                        // interface java.lang.Cloneable

        // Inner classes and interfaces.
        System.out.println(Main.InnerC.class.toString());
                                        // class Main$InnerC
        System.out.println(Main.InnerI.class.toString());
                                        // interface Main$InnerC

        // Primitive types.
        System.out.println(int.class.toString());           // int
        System.out.println(Void.TYPE.toString());           // void

        // Arrays
        System.out.println(String[].class.toString());
                                        // class [Ljava.lang.String;
```

```
            System.out.println(Main.InnerC[].class.toString());
                                                // class [LMain$InnerC;
            System.out.println(Main.InnerI[].class.toString());
                                                // class [LMain$InnerI;
            System.out.println(int[].class.toString());
                                                // class [I
        }

        static class InnerC {}
        interface InnerI {}
    }
```

java.lang

ClassCastException

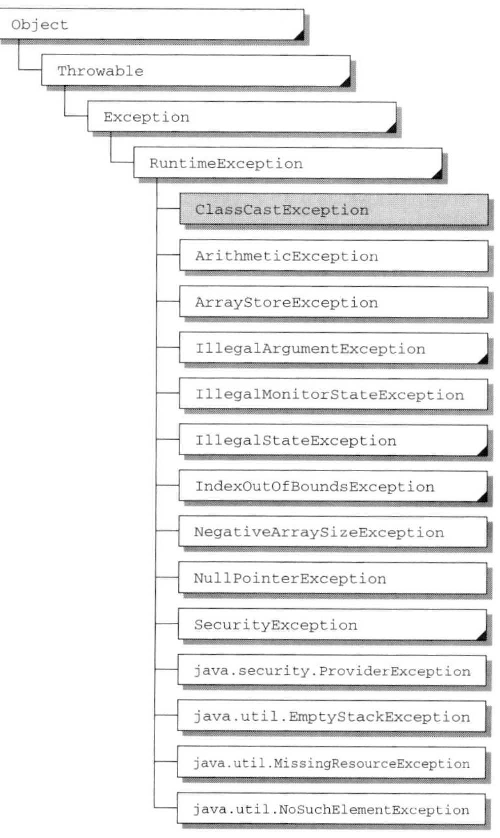

Syntax

```
public class ClassCastException extends RuntimeException
```

Description

`ClassCastException` is a runtime exception that is thrown when the program attempts to cast an instance of a class to another class and that cast is not allowed.

`ClassCastException` should not be caught or declared in the `throws` clause of a method.

MEMBER SUMMARY	
Constructor	
`ClassCastException()`	Constructs a `ClassCastException` instance.

See Also

`RuntimeException.`

Example

This example throws a `ClassCastException` when it attempts to cast a `String` instance to an `Integer` instance:

```
class Main {
    private static void storeItem(Integer[]a, int i, Object item) {
        a[i] = (Integer) item;
    }
    public static void main(String[] args) {
        System.out.println("ClassCastException Example");

        Integer[] a = new Integer[3];
        storeItem(a, 2, new String("abc"));
    }
}
```

A B C D E F G H I J K L M N O P Q R S T U V W X Y Z

ClassCastException()

PURPOSE Constructs a `ClassCastException` instance.

SYNTAX
```
public ClassCastException()
public ClassCastException(String msg)
```

DESCRIPTION These two forms of the constructor construct an instance of `ClassCastException`. An optional string `msg` can be supplied that describes this particular instance of the exception. If `msg` is not specified, it defaults to `null`.

PARAMETERS

`msg` A possibly `null` string that gives details about this exception.

SEE ALSO `Throwable.getMessage().`

ClassCircularityError

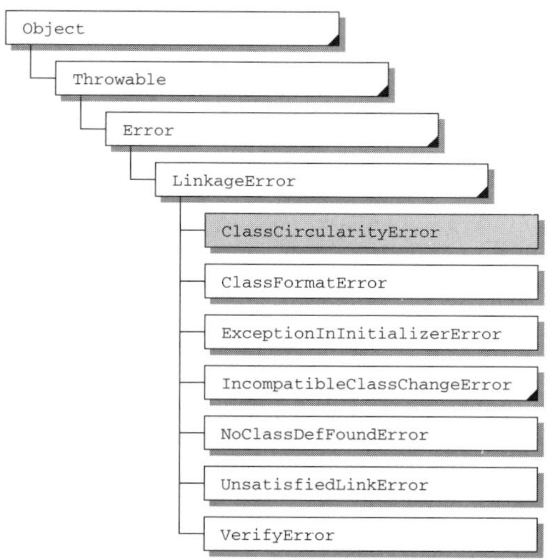

Syntax

```
public class ClassCircularityError extends LinkageError
```

Description

`ClassCircularityError` is a runtime linkage error that is thrown when the class loader attempts to load in classes that have cyclic class inheritance. Normally, when you compile classes that have cyclic class inheritance, you get a compilation error pinpointing the problem so that a linkage error at runtime does not occur. However, the circularity could be introduced when classes of a program become inconsistent, for example by making an incompatible change and then recompiling only some of the classes.

`ClassCircularityError` should not be caught or declared in the `throws` clause of a method.

MEMBER SUMMARY	
Constructor	
`ClassCircularityError()`	Constructs a `ClassCircularityError` instance.

See Also

`Error`, `LinkageError`.

Example

The following code is an example of two classes that would throw a `ClassCircularityError`:

```
class A extends B {
}

class B extends A {
}
```


ClassCircularityError()

PURPOSE Constructs a `ClassCircularityError` instance.

SYNTAX
```
public ClassCircularityError()
public ClassCircularityError(String msg)
```

DESCRIPTION These two forms of the constructor construct an instance of `ClassCircularityError`. An optional string `msg` can be supplied that describes this particular instance of the error. If `msg` is not specified, it defaults to `null`.

PARAMETERS

`msg` A possibly `null` string that gives details about this error.

SEE ALSO `Throwable.getMessage()`.

ClassFormatError

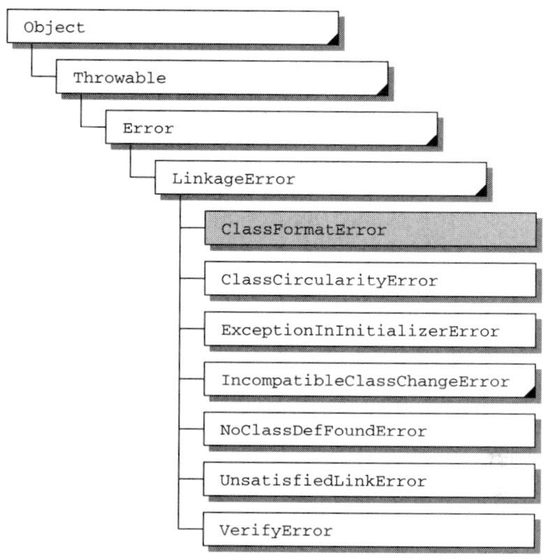

Syntax

```
public class ClassFormatError extends LinkageError
```

Description

`ClassFormatError` is a runtime linkage error that is thrown when the class loader attempts to load in a class that is not in a format that it accepts. This can happen, for example, if the class file in which the class is stored becomes corrupted or if the class is being loaded across a network and the server sending the class is not sending it in an acceptable format.

`ClassFormatError` should not be caught or declared in the `throws` clause of a method.

MEMBER SUMMARY	
Constructor	
`ClassFormatError()`	Constructs a `ClassFormatError` instance.

See Also

`Error`, `LinkageError`.

ClassFormatError()

PURPOSE Constructs a `ClassFormatError` instance.

SYNTAX
```
public ClassFormatError()
public ClassFormatError(String msg)
```

PURPOSE These two forms of the constructor construct an instance of `ClassFormatError`. An optional string `msg` can be supplied that describes this particular instance of the error. If `msg` is not supplied, it defaults to `null`.

PARAMETERS

`msg` A possibly `null` string that gives details about this error.

SEE ALSO `Throwable.getMessage()`.

ClassLoader

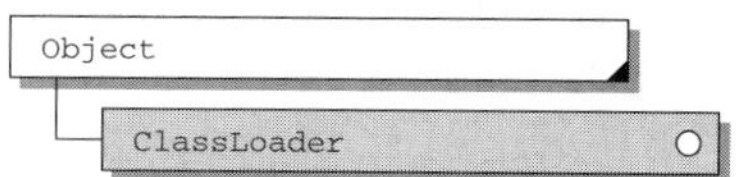

Syntax

```
public abstract class ClassLoader
```

Description

`ClassLoader` is an abstract class that can be used to define policies for loading Java classes into the runtime environment. Such policies include the format that the classes are stored in (e.g., bytecode, ZIP, compressed), the source for the classes (e.g., file system, network), how to locate the classes within the source (e.g., the directories to search, the JAR files to use, the machines to contact), and security conditions to apply when loading the classes. Figure 30 shows examples of two different implementations of `ClassLoader`. One loads classes from the network, while the other loads classes from the file system.

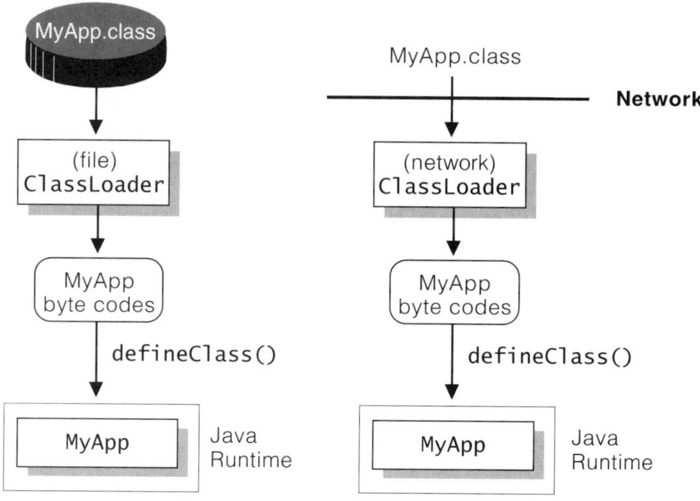

FIGURE 30: A File System-Based `ClassLoader` and a Network-Based `ClassLoader`.

Class Files

The definition of a Java class or interface is represented by a *class file*. Each class file contains the byte codes of the class or interface. See *The Java Virtual Machine Specification*, Chapter 4, for a description of the class file format.

ZIP Files

You can package class files into a *ZIP file*. A ZIP file is made up of one or more compressed (or uncompressed) pieces of data. Each piece of data is represented by a *ZIP entry*. The ZIP entry contains information about the data, such as its uncompressed size, its checksum value, and its location in the ZIP file. The format of a ZIP file is described in detail in the documents at `ftp://ftp.uu.net/pub/archiving/zip/doc/`.

A ZIP file's name has a `.zip` file extension. The ZIP file can be created by using any ZIP tool that supports long filenames.

Older versions of the JDK do not support compressed ZIP files. Therefore, you should turn compression off when producing a ZIP file for class files to be used by the JDK.

Archives

An applet, application, or class library may consist of multiple class files and may make use of resources such as images and audio clips. You can package related class files and resources into an *archive*. Java Archive (JAR) specifies a platform-independent file format for archives. The Java archive tool, `jar`, available on Solaris and Windows platforms, allows you to create a JAR archive using multiple class and resource (such as image and sound) files.

A JAR file's name has a `.jar` file extension.

See `http://java.sun.com/products/jdk/1.1/docs/guide/jar/` for details on JAR and the `jar` command.

Digests and Signed Archives

JAR allows you not only to package multiple files into a single archive for quicker downloads, but also to sign or provide a digest of individual files within the archive. This allows a class loader to verify the integrity of individual files and/or determine the identity of the supplier of the file.

A message digest algorithm accepts a sequence of bytes and produces a compact representation of it, called a *digest*. You cannot reproduce the original stream of bytes from the digest, but you can use the digest to verify whether a sequence of bytes has been modified (by recalculating the sequence's digest and comparing it with the original digest). Popular message digest algorithms supported by JAR include MD5 and SHA. A single file can have both MD5 and SHA digests.

Supplying a digest with a file allows the receiver of the file to verify its integrity. However, someone could have substituted both the file and its digest, thereby providing to the receiver information different from what was intended by its supplier. JAR also provides support for signing individual files within an archive. Signature specifications supported by JAR include RSA, DSA, and PGP. Using one of these algorithms, the sender can "sign" the file with a digital signature. The signed file contains information that can subsequently be used to verify the identity of the signer.

Default System Class Loader

The default system class loader loads classes from files in directories, JAR files, or ZIP files specified by the `java.class.path` system property, which in turn is initialized by the *Java Runtime Environment* (JRE). `java.class.path` contains an ordered list of directory names, JAR files, or ZIP files in which to search for a given class. It is a read-only property that cannot be changed once it has been initialized by the JRE.

The JRE initializes `java.class.path` by appending the following list to the ordered list specified by the `CLASSPATH` environment variable.

```
$JAVA_HOME/classes
$JAVA_HOME/lib/classes.zip
$JAVA_HOME/lib/classes.jar
$JAVA_HOME/lib/rt.jar
$JAVA_HOME/lib/i18n.jar
```

`$JAVA_HOME` is the directory in which the JDK has been installed (for example `$JAVA_HOME/bin/java` is the location of the Java interpreter).

For example, if you set `CLASSPATH` to ".", which means to look for class files in directory in which the Java application is run, "." will be inserted at the front of the list, followed by the rest of the items in the default list.

Commands such as the Java interpreter and compiler have a `-classpath` option that allows you to override how the JRE initializes the `java.class.path` environment variable. See the documentation for these commands to see how to set the `-classpath` option.

Creating New Class Loaders

A new class loader can be created by defining a subclass of `ClassLoader` and providing an implementation for the abstract method `loadClass()`. Some examples of class loading policies are loading classes from a network socket, from a secure network socket, from files in a particular directory, or from a stream generated by a program.

Any subclass of `ClassLoader` must provide an implementation of the `loadClass()` method. `loadClass()` defines the policy regarding where the definition of classes are found and how to load them.

The `ClassLoader` class defines methods that can be used by subclasses of `ClassLoader` in the implementations of their own `loadClass()` methods. These include methods to obtain a `Class` object given the definition of the class in byte code form, to resolve classes referenced by a given class, and to load a class using the default system class loader.

Resources and System Resources

Applications and applets often use resources such as images and audio files in addition to byte codes. `ClassLoader` contains static methods for obtaining *system resources*. System resources are retrieved using the same policy used by the default system class loader to load classes. Subclasses of `ClassLoader` provide methods for retrieving resources for classes loaded by that class loader.

MEMBER SUMMARY	
Constructor	
`ClassLoader()`	Constructs a `ClassLoader` instance.
Method Provided by Subclass	
`loadClass()`	Loads a class using the policy defined by this class loader.
Helper Methods	
`defineClass()`	Generates a `Class` object using an array of byte codes.
`findLoadedClass()`	Finds a class previously loaded by this class loader.
`findSystemClass()`	Loads and links a class using the default system class loader.
`resolveClass()`	Links a class so that it can be executed.
Security Method	
`setSigners()`	Records the signers for a class.
Resource Methods	
`getResource()`	Retrieves a resource using this class loader.
`getResourceAsStream()`	Retrieves a resource as a stream using this class loader.
`getSystemResource()`	Retrieves a system resource using the policy of the default system class loader.
`getSystemResourceAsStream()`	Retrieves a system resource as a stream, using the policy of the default system class loader.

See Also

`Class`, `Object`, `System.getProperties()`.

Example

This example implements a class loader that loads byte codes from files in a directory. Note that no subdirectories are allowed within the directory. If a class is from a package, the package name is stripped from the class's name before the class's name is used to construct the name of the class file from which the byte codes will be read.

```
import java.io.*;
import java.net.*;

// Class loader for loading bytes codes from a file.
public class FileClassLoader extends ClassLoader {
    String path;

    public FileClassLoader(String path) {
        this.path = path;
    }

    // Loads the bytes from file
    Class loadIt(String classname) throws ClassNotFoundException {
```

```
        // To get file name, remove the package name, if any.
        String filename;
        if (classname.indexOf(".") >= 0) {
            filename = classname.substring(classname.lastIndexOf(".")+1);
        } else {
            filename = classname;
        }
        // Make sure the filename ends with .class
        filename += ".class";

        File fullname = new File(path, filename);
        System.out.println("class file name: " + fullname);
        try {
            // Read in the byte codes.
            InputStream is = new FileInputStream(fullname);
            int bufsize = (int)fullname.length();
            byte buf[] = new byte[bufsize];
            is.read(buf, 0, bufsize);
            is.close();

            // Define the class
            return defineClass(classname, buf, 0, buf.length);
        } catch (Exception e) {
            throw new ClassNotFoundException(classname);
        }
    }

    protected synchronized Class loadClass(String name, boolean resolve)
            throws ClassNotFoundException {
        // Try to find it from the cache
        Class c = findLoadedClass(name);
        System.out.println(name + ((c == null) ? " not " : " ") + "in cache");

        // Not in cache
        if (c == null) {
            // See if it can be loaded by system class loader
            try {
                // No need to call resolveClass() on the result
                // because findSystemClass() loads and links the class.
                return findSystemClass(name);
            } catch (ClassNotFoundException e) {
            }

            // Try to get it from file
            c = loadIt(name);
        }

        // Link class if asked to do so
        if (c != null && resolve) {
        System.out.println("Resolving class: " + name);
            resolveClass(c);
        }
        return c;
    }

    // Returns a URL containing the location of the named resource.
    public URL getResource(String name) {
        try {
            File file = new File(path, name);
            String absPath =
```

A B C D E F G H I J K L M N O P Q R S T U V W X Y Z

```
                    file.getAbsolutePath().replace(file.separatorChar, '/');

                // If leading character is not '/', add for URL.
                if (absPath.charAt(0) != '/') {
                    absPath = '/' + absPath;
                }

                System.out.println("resource name: " + absPath);
                return new URL("file:" + absPath);
            } catch (MalformedURLException e) {
                e.printStackTrace();
            }
            return null;
        }

        // Returns an input stream to the named resource.
        public InputStream getResourceAsStream(String name) {
            try {
                return new FileInputStream(new File(path, name));
            } catch (FileNotFoundException e) {
                e.printStackTrace();
            }
            return null;
        }
    }
```

ClassLoader()

PURPOSE Constructs a `ClassLoader` instance.

SYNTAX `protected ClassLoader()`

EXAMPLE See the class example. `FileClassLoader`'s constructor automatically calls this protected `ClassLoader` constructor.

defineClass()

PURPOSE Generates a `Class` object using an array of byte codes.

SYNTAX
```
protected final Class defineClass(String className, byte[]
    bytecode, int offset, int length)
```
DEPRECATED
```
protected final Class defineClass(byte[] bytecodes, int offset,
    int length)
```

DESCRIPTION The Java compiler compiles Java programs into a machine-independent representation called *byte codes* to be used by the Java interpreter and runtime system. `defineClass()` converts byte codes into a `Class` object. In addition, `defineClass()` places the resulting `Class` object into a cache so that the class can be retrieved later by using `findLoadedClass()`.

When a new `ClassLoader` is defined, the implementation of `loadClass()` should use `defineClass()` to turn the byte codes that it loads into `Class` objects.

The format of the byte codes is defined in *The Java Virtual Machine Specification*.

PARAMETERS

`bytecodes` A non-`null` array of bytes containing the byte codes for the class.

`className` The possibly `null` name of the class being defined. This is the fully qualified class name (e.g., "java.lang.String").

`offset` The start position in `bytecodes` of the class's byte codes. `0` ≤ `offset` < `bytecodes.length`.

`length` The number of bytes occupied by the class's byte codes. `0` ≤ `length` ≤ `bytecodes.length-offset`.

RETURNS A non-`null` `Class` object generated by using given byte codes.

EXCEPTIONS

`ClassFormatError`
If the bytes in `bytecodes` are not in the correct format.

DEPRECATION The form of this method that does not accept a class name has been deprecated. Use the first form instead. If the class name is not known, supply `null` as the name. For example, instead of using

```
Class c = defineClass(buf, 0, buf.length);
```

use

```
Class c = defineClass(className, buf, 0, buf.length);
```

or

```
Class c = defineClass(null, buf, 0, buf.length);
```

SEE ALSO `findLoadedClass()`, `loadClass()`, `Class`.

EXAMPLE See the class example.

findLoadedClass()

PURPOSE Finds a class previously loaded by this class loader.

SYNTAX `protected final Class findLoadedClass(String className)`

DESCRIPTION When a class is loaded using this class loader, the resulting `Class` object is put into a cache. The class may have been loaded when the program explicitly invoked `loadClass()`, or loaded by the Java virtual machine while loading another class in order to complete its loading.

A class loader implementing `loadClass()` should use `findLoadedClass()` first before attempting to load a class.

Note that the class may or may not have been linked (depending on whether the previous call to load it requested that it be linked). The caller of `findLoadedClass()` should call `resolveClass()` on the resulting class if the class needs to be linked before being returned.

PARAMETERS

`className` A non-`null` string containing the fully qualified name of the class to load (e.g., "java.lang.String").

RETURNS The `Class` object for `className`; `null` if not found in the cache.

SEE ALSO `defineClass()`, `resolveClass()`.

EXAMPLE See the class example.

A B C D E F G H I J K L M N O P Q R S T U V W X Y Z

findSystemClass()

PURPOSE Loads and links a class by using the default system class loader.

SYNTAX

```
protected final Class findSystemClass(String className) throws
    ClassNotFoundException
```

DESCRIPTION The default system class loader loads classes from files in directories, JAR files, and ZIP files specified by the `java.class.path` system property.

`findSystemClass()` uses this default system class loader to load the class named by `className` and then links the resulting class (see `resolveClass()`).

PARAMETERS

`className` A non-`null` string containing the fully qualified name of the class to load (e.g., "java.lang.String").

RETURNS A new `Class` object with the name `className`.

EXCEPTIONS

`ClassNotFoundException`
If a class with the name `className` was not found in the directories, JAR files, and ZIP files specified by the `java.class.path` system property.

SEE ALSO `Class`, `loadClass()`, `resolveClass()`.

EXAMPLE See the class example.

getResource()

PURPOSE
Retrieves a resource using this class loader.

SYNTAX
`public URL getResource(String resName)`

DESCRIPTION
The default implementation of this method does nothing; it simply returns `null`. Subclasses of `ClassLoader` should override this method to retrieve the resource as specified by `resName`. The caller of `getResource()` should invoke `getContent()` on the result in order to get the resource.

PARAMETERS

`resName` The non-`null` name of the resource to retrieve.

RETURNS
A possibly `null` `URL` instance from which the resource could be gotten.

SEE ALSO
`java.net.URL`, `java.net.URL.getContents()`, `getResourceAsStream()`, `getSystemResource()`.

EXAMPLE
See the class example, `loadClass()`.

getResourceAsStream()

PURPOSE
Retrieves a resource as a stream using this class loader.

SYNTAX
`public InputStream getResourceAsStream(String resName)`

DESCRIPTION
The default implementation of this method does nothing; it simply returns `null`. Subclasses of `ClassLoader` should override this method to retrieve the input stream of the resource as specified by `resName`. This method is equivalent to invoking `openStream()` on the result of `getResource()`.

```
try {
    URL url = classloader.getResource("someImage");
    return url.openStream();
} catch (IOException) {
    return null;
}
```

PARAMETERS

`resName` The non-`null` name of the resource for which to get the input stream.

RETURNS
A possibly `null` input stream from which the resource could be obtained.

SEE ALSO
`java.net.URL`, `java.net.URL.getContents()`, `java.net.URL.openStream()`, `getResource()`, `getSystemResourceAsStream()`.

EXAMPLE
See the class example and `loadClass()`.

getSystemResource()

PURPOSE
Retrieves a system resource using the policy of the default system class loader.

SYNTAX
```
public static final URL getSystemResource(String resName)
```

DESCRIPTION
System resources are retrieved using the same policy used by the default system class loader to load classes. Specifically, the default system class loader retrieves resources from files in directories, ZIP files, and JAR files specified by the `java.class.path` system property. For example, if `java.class.path` includes the directory `/a/b/c`, the default system class loader would attempt to retrieve the resource `resName` from the `/a/b/c`.

The caller of `getSystemResource()` should invoke `getContent()` on the result in order to get the resource.

PARAMETERS

`resName` The non-`null` name of the resource to retrieve.

RETURNS
A possibly `null` `URL` instance from which the resource could be obtained.

SEE ALSO
`java.net.URL`, `java.net.URL.getContents()`, `getResource()`, `getSystemResourceAsStream()`.

EXAMPLE
See `loadClass()` for a similar usage of `getResource()`.

getSystemResourceAsStream()

PURPOSE
Retrieves a system resource as a stream, using the policy of the default system class loader.

SYNTAX
```
public static final InputStream getResourceAsStream(String
    resName)
```

DESCRIPTION
System resources are retrieved using the same policy used by the default system class loader to load classes. Specifically, the default system class loader retrieves resources from files in directories, ZIP files, and JAR files specified by the `java.class.path` system property. For example, if `java.class.path` includes the directory `/a/b/c`, the default system class loader would attempt to retrieve the resource `resName` from the `/a/b/c`.

This method is equivalent to invoking `openStream()` on the result of `getSystemResource()`.

```
try {
    URL url = classloader.getSystemResource("someImage");
    return url.openStream();
} catch (IOException) {
    return null;
}
```

PARAMETERS

resName — The non-null name of the resource for which to get the input stream.

RETURNS — A possibly null input stream from which the resource could be obtained.

SEE ALSO — java.net.URL, java.net.URL.getContents(), java.net.URL.openStream(), getResourceAsStream(), getSystemResource().

EXAMPLE — See loadClass() for a similar usage of getResourceAsStream().

A B C D E F G H I J K L M N O P Q R S T U V W X Y Z

loadClass()

PURPOSE — Loads a class using the policy defined by this ClassLoader.

SYNTAX

```
protected abstract Class loadClass(String className, boolean
   resolve) throws ClassNotFoundException
public Class loadClass(String name) throws ClassNotFoundException
```

DESCRIPTION — The first form of this method loads the specified class className by using the policy defined by this class loader. This is an abstract method that must be defined by the subclass of ClassLoader. When defined by a subclass, this method should be declared synchronized because it may be invoked recursively as explained later.

The general flow of loadClass() is first to obtain the byte codes for the specified class and then to call defineClass() to turn the byte codes into a Class object. Then, if resolve is true, loadClass() should call resolveClass() to "link" the class being loaded. The caller of loadClass() sets resolve depending on how the resulting class is intended to be used. resolve should be set to true when an instance of the class being requested is being created or if the class's methods are to be invoked. resolve can be set to false if the class is being loaded simply to check its existence or to get its superclasses.

In the process of loading the class specified by className, the Java virtual machine may require additional classes to be loaded. Such classes are loaded using the loadClass() method of this class loader. Therefore, loadClass() must ensure that it is able to load all the classes referenced directly or indirectly by classes that it loads. For example if a class references system classes (such as java.lang.Object), loadClass() might use findSystemClass() to load them.

The second form of this method calls the first form with resolve set to true.

PARAMETERS

className — A non-null string containing the fully qualified name of the class to load (e.g., "java.lang.String").

resolve — true if the classes referenced by this class need to be loaded; false otherwise.

RETURNS A non-null new Class object with the name className.

EXCEPTIONS

ClassNotFoundException
If a class with the name className could not be found according to the policy of this class loader.

SEE ALSO findSystemClass(), defineClass(), Hashtable, resolveClass().

EXAMPLE The following code shows how to load a class and retrieve resources using the FileClassLoader from the class example. Notice that the Java virtual machine uses the same class loader to load classes referred to by the initial class (Class1).

```
import java.net.*;
import java.io.*;

class Main {
    public static void main(String[] args) {
        if (args.length != 3) {
            System.err.println(
                "usage: java Main <dir> <classname> <resource>");
            System.exit(-1);
        }

        try {
            ClassLoader cl = new FileClassLoader(args[0]);
            Class c = cl.loadClass(args[1]);

            System.out.println("Class: " + c);
            System.out.println("Resource: " + cl.getResource(args[2]));
            System.out.println("Resource Stream: " +
                cl.getResourceAsStream(args[2]));
        } catch (ClassNotFoundException e) {
            e.printStackTrace();
        }
    }
}
```

Output

```
> java Main /book/vol1/ioser/Serializable Class1 frame.txt
Class1 not in cache
class file name: /book/vol1/ioser/Serializable\Class1.class
java.lang.Object not in cache
java.io.Serializable not in cache
resource name: /book/vol1/ioser/Serializable/frame.txt
Class: class Class1
Resource: file:/book/vol1/ioser/Serializable/frame.txt
Resource Stream: java.io.FileInputStream@1ee7f3
```

resolveClass()

PURPOSE
Links a class so that it can be executed.

SYNTAX

```
protected final void resolveClass(Class c)
```

DESCRIPTION
This method links the class `c`. Linking a class effectively introduces it into the Java runtime so that it can be executed. A class must be linked before an instance of it can be created or methods can be invoked on it. Linking involves verification of the class, creating the static fields of the class, and resolution of symbolic references of members from other classes and interfaces. Details of linking can be found in *The Java Language Specification, First Edition*, Section 12.3.

In the process of linking the class `c`, the Java virtual machine may require additional classes to be loaded. Such classes are loaded using the `loadClass()` method of this class loader.

If `c` has previously been linked, calling `resolveClass()` on it does nothing.

PARAMETERS

`c` The non-`null` class being linked.

SEE ALSO
`defineClass()`, `loadClass()`.

EXAMPLE
See the class example.

setSigners()

PURPOSE
Records the signers for a class.

SYNTAX

```
protected final void setSigners(Class cl, Object[] signers)
```

DESCRIPTION
If a class loader supports signing of classes, then after `defineClass()` has been called on the object, the class loader should call `setSigners()` on the resulting class. Setting the signers of a class allows the program to subsequently retrieve the class's signers using `Class.getSigners()`. For example, a Web browser might use the signer information to determine whether an applet thus signed is allowed to execute.

PARAMETERS

`cl` The non-`null` class object for which to record signers.

`signers` A non-`null` array of signers. The elements of `signers` are of class `Identity`.

SEE ALSO
`Class.getSigners()`, `java.security.Identity`, `java.security.Signer`.

ClassNotFoundException

A
B
C
D
E
F
G
H
I
J
K
L
M
N
O
P
Q
R
S
T
U
V
W
X
Y
Z

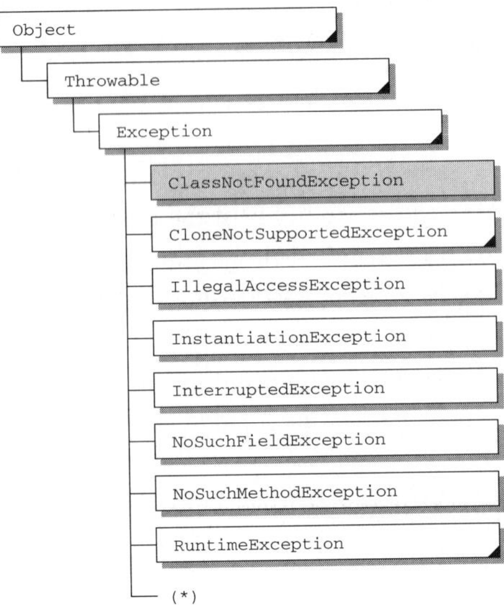

Syntax

```
public class ClassNotFoundException extends Exception
```

Description

`ClassNotFoundException` is an exception that is thrown when a class loader cannot find the class to load. This can happen if you define a class loader and it fails to find the class defined.

`ClassNotFoundException` and `NoClassDefFoundError` both report the same error; that is, the requested class cannot be found. They differ in that `ClassNotFoundException` is an exception thrown by a program-defined class loader or the user's invocation of a method to find a class (such as the use of `Class.forName()` and `ClassLoader.findSystemClass()`). On the other hand, `NoClassDefFoundError` is a runtime linkage error thrown by the Java virtual machine when it is attempting to load and resolve class references.

A method that throws `ClassNotFoundException` must declare it or any of its superclasses in the method's `throws` clause.

MEMBER SUMMARY	
Constructor	
`ClassNotFoundException()`	Constructs a `ClassNotFoundException` instance.

See Also

`Class`, `Class.forName()`, `ClassLoader.loadClass()`, `ClassLoader.findSystemClass()`, `NoClassDefFoundError`.

Example

This program defines a class `DebugClassLoader` that just echoes the class being loaded. You can make this program throw `ClassNotFoundException` by giving it a bogus class name. A valid class name is qualified by its package name (e.g., `java.lang.String`).

```
class DebugClassLoader extends ClassLoader {
    public synchronized Class loadClass(String name, boolean resolve)
        throws ClassNotFoundException {
            System.out.println("Loading " + name);
            return (findSystemClass(name));
        }
}
class Main {
    public static void main(String[] args) {
        System.out.println("ClassNotFound Example");
        if (args.length != 1) {
            System.err.println("usage: java Main <classname>");
            System.exit(1);
        }
        DebugClassLoader loader = new DebugClassLoader();
        try {
            loader.loadClass(args[0], true);
        } catch (ClassNotFoundException e) {
            e.printStackTrace();
        }
    }
}
```

ClassNotFoundException()

PURPOSE Constructs a `ClassNotFoundException` instance.

SYNTAX
```
public ClassNotFoundException()
public ClassNotFoundException(String msg)
```

DESCRIPTION These constructors construct an instance of `ClassNotFoundException`. An optional string `msg` can be supplied that describes this particular instance of the exception. If `msg` is not supplied, it defaults to `null`.

PARAMETERS

`msg` A possibly `null` string that gives details about this exception.

SEE ALSO `Throwable.getMessage()`.

Cloneable

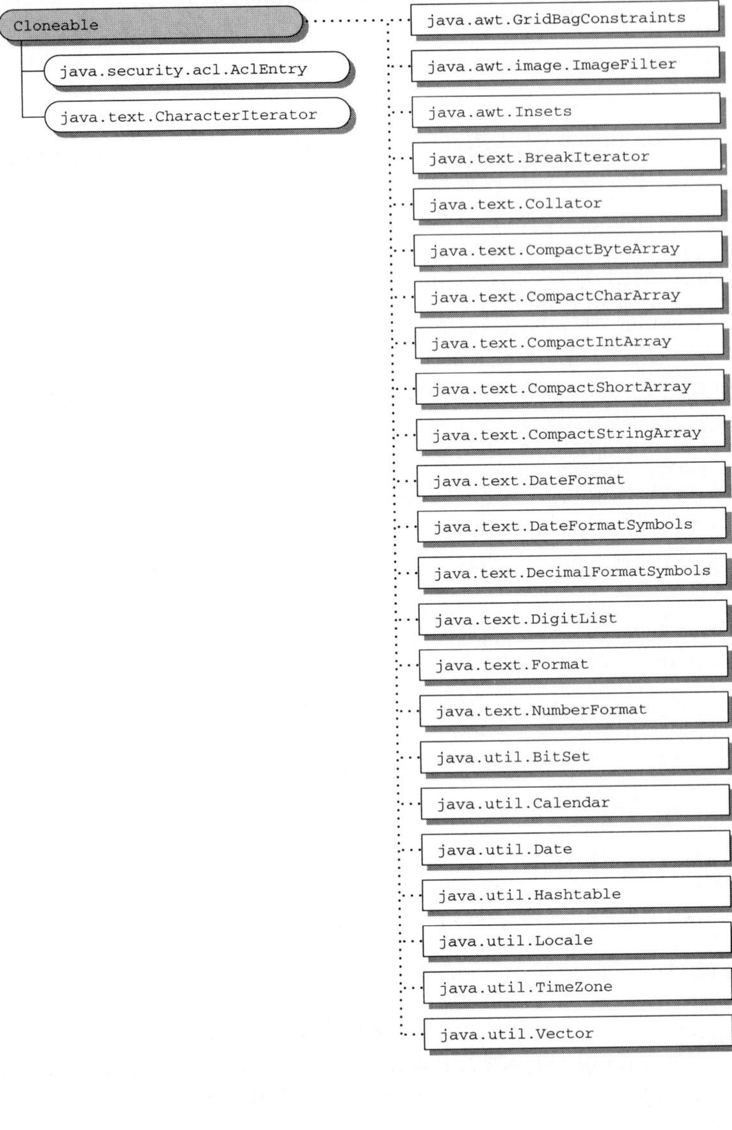
Cloneable
java.security.acl.AclEntry
java.text.CharacterIterator
java.awt.GridBagConstraints
java.awt.image.ImageFilter
java.awt.Insets
java.text.BreakIterator
java.text.Collator
java.text.CompactByteArray
java.text.CompactCharArray
java.text.CompactIntArray
java.text.CompactShortArray
java.text.CompactStringArray
java.text.DateFormat
java.text.DateFormatSymbols
java.text.DecimalFormatSymbols
java.text.DigitList
java.text.Format
java.text.NumberFormat
java.util.BitSet
java.util.Calendar
java.util.Date
java.util.Hashtable
java.util.Locale
java.util.TimeZone
java.util.Vector

Syntax

`public interface Cloneable`

Description

A class implements the `Cloneable` interface to indicate that instances of that class can be cloned. The definition of "clone" may differ for different classes. In general, it means that a copy of the object is created and returned. The degree to which the internal data structure associated with the object is copied depends on the class definition of the object.

Object.clone()

The default implementation of `Object.clone()` implements cloning of an object by performing a field-by-field copy of the object being cloned. The objects contained in the fields themselves are not cloned. For a class to use the default implementation of `Object.clone()`, it must implement the `Cloneable` interface. If the class does not implement `Cloneable`, a `CloneNotSupportedException` is thrown.

A class whose `clone()` method does not use the default implementation of `Object.clone()` need not implement `Cloneable`. However, it is good programming practice for any class that provides an implementation for `clone()` to implement `Cloneable`.

Making an Object Cloneable

A class that is cloneable should declare that it implements the `Cloneable` interface. If `clone()` is not overridden, then `super.clone()` is used for that class.

You can override `clone()` to perform tasks specific to the cloning of that class. There is no requirement that the method make use of `super.clone()` or `Object.clone()`.

It is common also for cloneable classes to override `clone()` so as to make it `public` rather than `protected`. This is done so that the `clone()` method can be accessed by other classes.

See Also

`CloneNotSupportedException`, `Object.clone()`.

Example

This example shows a class `A` that implements the `Cloneable` interface. It overrides the `clone()` method by calling `Object.clone()`. `Object.clone()` creates an instance of the object and performs a field-to-field copy of the original object.

```
class A implements Cloneable {
    int a;
    public A(int i) {
        a = i;
    }
    public Object clone() throws CloneNotSupportedException {
        // Use default cloning of field-to-field copy
        return super.clone();
    }
}
```

```
public class Main {
    public static void main(String[] args) {
        System.out.println("Cloneable example");
        A i = new A(10);

        try {
            A j = (A)(i.clone());
            System.out.println(j.a);
        } catch (CloneNotSupportedException e) {
            e.printStackTrace();
        }
    }
}
```

CloneNotSupportedException

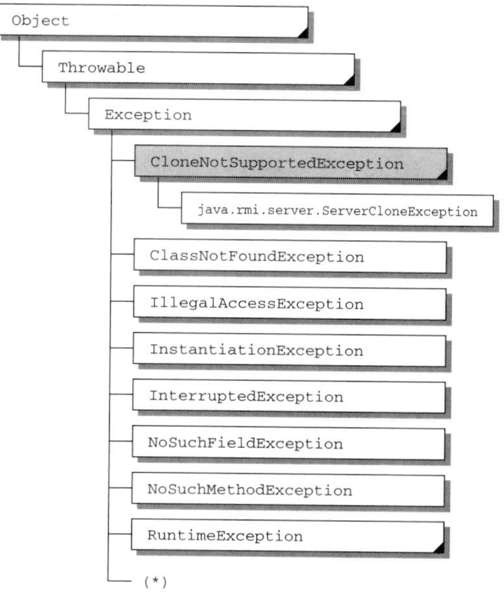

(*) 21 classes from other packages not shown.

Syntax

```
public class CloneNotSupportedException extends Exception
```

Description

`CloneNotSupportedException` is an exception that is thrown to indicate that an instance of a class cannot be cloned.

The default implementation of `Object.clone()` implements the cloning of an object by performing a field-by-field copy of the object being cloned. The objects contained in the fields themselves are not cloned. A class whose `clone()` method uses this default implementation of `Object.clone()` to clone itself must implement the `Cloneable` interface.[1] If the class does not implement `Cloneable`, a `CloneNotSupportedException` is thrown.

A class can override `clone()` to throw a `CloneNotSupportedException` to indicate that instances of that class cannot be cloned.

A method that throws a `CloneNotSupportedException` must declare it or any of its superclasses in the method's `throws` clause.

---

1. A class whose `clone()` method does not use the default implementation of `Object.clone()` need not implement `Cloneable`. However, it is good programming practice for any class that provides an implementation for `clone()` to implement `Cloneable`.

MEMBER SUMMARY	
Constructor	
`CloneNotSupportedException()`	Constructs a `CloneNotSupportedException` instance.

A B C D E F G H I J K L M N O P Q R S T U V W X Y Z

See Also

`Cloneable`, `Object.clone()`.

Example

This example throws a `CloneNotSupportedException` because `A.clone()` uses `Object.clone()` but the class `A` does not implement the `Cloneable` interface. See `Cloneable` for an example in which `A` is cloneable.

```
class A {
    int a;
    public A(int i) {
        a = i;
    }
    public Object clone() throws CloneNotSupportedException {
        // Use default Object.clone() (field-to-field copy)
        return super.clone();
    }
}

public class Main {
    public static void main(String[] args) {
        System.out.println("CloneNotSupportedException example");
        A i = new A(10);

        try {
            A j = (A)(i.clone());
            System.out.println(j.a);
        } catch (CloneNotSupportedException e) {
            e.printStackTrace();
        }
    }
}
```

CloneNotSupportedException()

PURPOSE Constructs a `CloneNotSupportedException` instance.

SYNTAX
```
public CloneNotSupportedException()
public CloneNotSupportedException(String msg)
```

DESCRIPTION These constructors construct an instance of `CloneNotSupportedException`. An optional string `msg` can be supplied that describes this particular instance of the exception. If `msg` is not supplied, it defaults to `null`.

PARAMETERS

`msg` A string that gives details about this exception.

SEE ALSO `Throwable.getMessage()`.

java.text
CollationElementIterator

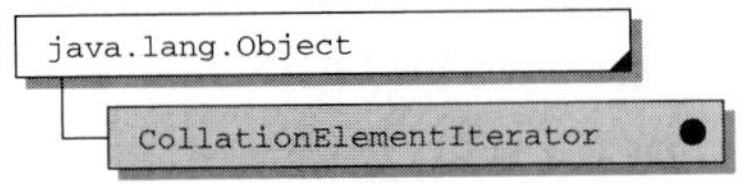

Syntax

```
public final class CollationElementIterator extends Object
```

Description

The `CollationElementIterator` class is an iterator used to walk through the decomposed characters of a locale-specific string according to the rules of a specific `Collator` object. This class is used primarily to search through strings. The iterator returns the collation element of the positioned character. This collation element contains properties that define how a character is collated by the given `Collator` object. These properties include sorting order based on accents and uppercase/lowercase characters.

This class is used by the `compare()` method of `RuleBasedCollator`. A separate iterator is created for the source and target strings. The `compare()` method iterates through each character, comparing order properties and determining which string should sort first, based on the primary, secondary, and tertiary orders.

Usage

When you call `compare(String, String)` on a built-in `Collator` object, such as `RuleBased-Collator`, each string is decomposed and a `CollationElementIterator` object is created automatically for each string. You would explicitly create a `CollationElementIterator` object only if you want to create your own collation rules that need access to the particular values of the primary, secondary, and tertiary orders.

A `CollationElementIterator` object relies on a particular `Collator` object for its collation order. `CollationElementIterator` has no public constructor or creation methods. The method to create one is `getCollationElementIterator()`, which is a member of `RuleBased-Collator`.

To create an instance of a `CollationElementIterator`, you create an instance of `Rule-BasedCollator` and then call `getCollationElementIterator()` on the string over which you want to iterate. Calling `next()` the first time goes to the first character and returns the *collation element* (also called *collation order*) of that character, an integer. A collation element consists of the primary, secondary, and tertiary orders. Calling one of the order methods, such as `pri-maryOrder()`, returns that value.

```
Collator collator = Collator.getInstance(Locale.FRENCH);
if (collator instanceof RuleBasedCollator) {
    // Cast to the subclass.
    RuleBasedCollator rbc = (RuleBasedCollator)collator;
```

```
        // Get the iterator for the string.
        CollationElementIterator cei =
            rbc.getCollationElementIterator("Test string");

        // Iterate to first character and get its collation element.
        int collationOrder = cei.next();

        // Get the primary order from the collation element.
        int primaryOrder =
            CollationElementIterator.primaryOrder(collationOrder);
}
```


Iteration Over Characters

Collation rules vary by language. `CollationElementIterator` takes into account the language-specific traits of characters. Calling `next()` can result in iterating over one or more characters, depending on these traits. Some languages condense several characters into a single one for sorting. For example, consider the following in traditional Spanish collation, where "ch" is condensed to a single character for sorting so that the following holds:

"ca" sorts first on "c" and second on "a"
"cha" sorts first on "ch" and second on "a"

Some languages expand a single character (with an accent) into multiple characters for sorting. For example, in traditional German collation, the "ä" is expanded to "ae" for sorting, so that

"äb" sorts first on "a", second on "e", and third on "b"

Note: Starting with JDK 1.1.6, the default behavior in Spanish is to treat "ch" as two letters, and the default behavior in German is for "ä" not to expand to "ae".

Primary, Secondary, and Tertiary Order Properties

The *primary order*, *secondary order*, and *tertiary order* properties are related to the ordering strengths `PRIMARY`, `SECONDARY`, and `TERTIARY` in `Collator`. Primary order has a higher sort priority than secondary order, which has a higher priority than tertiary order. The collator comparison methods sort strings first using the primary order. If the entire string has identical primary orders, it sorts on secondary orders. And for strings that have identical secondary order, it sorts on the tertiary order. Primary order is determined only by the base character; it ignores accents and uppercase/lowercase differences between characters. For Western languages, the secondary order is determined by accents and the tertiary order is determined by uppercase/lowercase characters, such as "a" versus "A".

Internally, you can think of a `CollationElementIterator` object as having a *collation element*, which defines the ordering strength. This collation element consists of three fields packed into an integer. To extract the fields, you can use one of these methods:

```
primaryOrder(int)
secondaryOrder(int)
tertiaryOrder(int)
```

When doing language-sensitive searching, you generally allow the user to specify "weak" matches. The weakest match is one that results, for example, from searching for the letter "a" and it matches "a", "A", "à", "â", or "ä"—that is, it ignores uppercase/lowercase and accents. This search considers only the primary order. A stronger match is one whereby uppercase/lowercase is ignored but accents are not. This search considers the primary and secondary orders. If all of the fields of a collation element that you are considering are zero, then you should ignore that collation element completely when searching.

Whenever you find a match, you should double-check that the string you found is on user character boundaries. You do this by using a break iterator from `BreakIterator.getCharacterInstance()`. If you don't do this, then you may be including only half a user character! You can also give the user the choice of "whole words only" by instead using the break iterator from `BreakIterator.getWordInstance()`.

MEMBER SUMMARY	
End-of-String Constant	
`NULLORDER`	Returned by `next()` when end-of-string is reached.
Iterator Methods	
`next()`	Moves the iterator to the next decomposed character in the string and retrieves its collation element.
`reset()`	Resets the iterator to the beginning of the string.
Order Methods	
`primaryOrder()`	Retrieves the primary order value from a collation element.
`secondaryOrder()`	Retrieves the secondary order value from a collation element.
`tertiaryOrder()`	Retrieves the tertiary order value from a collation element.

See Also

`Collator`, `RuleBasedCollator`.

Example

This example creates a `RuleBasedCollator` object for the French locale and then calls `getCollationElementIterator()` on a string to produce a `CollationElementIterator` object for that string. It iterates over the string by calling `next()`, which returns the collation element, an integer. It then calls the three order methods (`primaryOrder()`, `secondaryOrder()`, and `tertiaryOrder()`) and prints out their values.

The eight-character string "abcABCàÀ" is decomposed into ten characters because two of the characters have accents. You can uncomment the line that sets the collator to

NO_DECOMPOSITION to see that changing the decomposition mode changes the values of the primary and secondary orders for accented characters.

```
import java.text.CollationElementIterator;
import java.text.Collator;
import java.text.RuleBasedCollator;
import java.util.Locale;

public class Main {

    public static void main(String[] args) {
        Locale loc = Locale.FRENCH;
        int element;

        // Set up string to iterate over.
        // String str = "abcàâäéèêëîïôöùûüçÁÀÄÉÈÊËÎÏÔÖÙÚÜÇ";
        String str = "abcABCàÀ";
        System.out.println("String: " + str + "\n");

        // Create an instance of a subclass of collator.
        Collator collator = Collator.getInstance(loc);

        if (collator instanceof RuleBasedCollator) {

            // Cast to the subclass.
            RuleBasedCollator rbc = (RuleBasedCollator)collator;

            // Try changing the decomposition mode.
            // rbc.setDecomposition(Collator.NO_DECOMPOSITION);

            // Get the first key of the string.
            CollationElementIterator cei =
                rbc.getCollationElementIterator(str);

            System.out.println("collation  primary  secondary  tertiary");
            System.out.println(" element    order     order      order");
            System.out.println("  (hex)");

            // Iterate to next character and get collation element.
            while ((element = cei.next()) !=
                    CollationElementIterator.NULLORDER) {

                System.out.print(" ");
                printInColumn(Integer.toHexString(element), 12);

                // Print the primary, secondary and tertiary orders.
                printInColumn(
                    CollationElementIterator.primaryOrder(element), 11
                );

                printInColumn(
                    CollationElementIterator.secondaryOrder(element), 11
                );

                printInColumn(
                    CollationElementIterator.tertiaryOrder(element), 0
                );
                System.out.println();
            }
```

```
            }
        }

        // Print string in a particular vertical column
        static void printInColumn(String str, int col) {
            System.out.print(str);
            for (int p = str.length(); p < col; ++p) {
                System.out.print(" ");
            }
        }

        // Print integer in a particular vertical column
        static void printInColumn(int integer, int col) {
            System.out.print(integer);
            for (int p = Integer.toString(integer).length(); p < col; ++p) {
                System.out.print(" ");
            }
        }
    }
```

Output

```
> java Main
String: abcABCàÀ

collation  primary  secondary  tertiary
 element    order     order      order
  (hex)
 450000       69      0           0
 460000       70      0           0
 470000       71      0           0
 450001       69      0           1
 460001       70      0           1
 470001       71      0           1
 450000       69      0           0
 1600         0       22          0
 450001       69      0           1
 1600         0       22          0
```

Note: This is the output as generated by JDK 1.1.6. A known bug in earlier versions produces different output for accented characters.

next()

PURPOSE Moves the iterator to the next decomposed character in the string and retrieves its collation element.

SYNTAX `public int next()`

DESCRIPTION This method operates over the decomposed character and returns its collation element. The first time you call `next()`, it moves to the first character. Subsequent calls move it to subsequent characters.

RETURNS The next character's collation element. Returns `NULLORDER` if end-of-string is reached.

EXAMPLE See the class example.

NULLORDER

PURPOSE A constant returned by `next()` when end-of-string is reached.

SYNTAX `public final static int NULLORDER`

DESCRIPTION `NULLORDER` is returned by `next()` to indicate the end of string has been reached by the iterator. The value of `NULLORDER` is `0xffffffff`.

EXAMPLE See the class example.

primaryOrder()

PURPOSE Retrieves the primary order value from a collation element.

SYNTAX `public final static int primaryOrder(int order)`

DESCRIPTION Gets the primary order of a collation element.

PARAMETERS
`order` A collation element returned from `next()`.

RETURNS The primary order of a collation element.

EXAMPLE See the class example.

reset()

PURPOSE Resets the iterator to the beginning of the string.

SYNTAX `public void reset()`

DESCRIPTION This method resets this `CollationElementIterator` to the beginning of the string.

Note: JDK 1.1.6 fixes a known bug whereby calling `reset()` and iterating over the same string again does not give the same results. The workaround is to create a new instance of `CollationElementIterator` for each pass.

secondaryOrder()

PURPOSE Retrieves the secondary order value from a collation element.

SYNTAX `public final static short secondaryOrder(int order)`

DESCRIPTION Gets the secondary order of a collation element.

PARAMETERS

`order` A collation element returned from `next()`.

RETURNS The secondary order of a collation element.

EXAMPLE See the class example.

tertiaryOrder()

PURPOSE Retrieves the tertiary order value from a collation element.

SYNTAX `public final static short tertiaryOrder(int order)`

PARAMETERS

`order` A collation element returned from `next()`.

RETURNS The tertiary order of a collation element.

EXAMPLE See the class example.

CollationKey

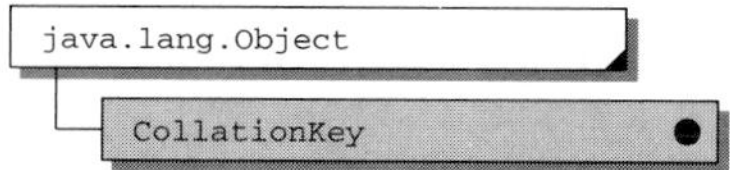

Syntax

```
public final class CollationKey extends Object
```

Description

The `CollationKey` class represents a sort key for a `String` object under the rules of a specific `Collator` object. Thus creating a `CollationKey` object produces a key from a string. These keys can then be compared; comparing two keys returns the relative order of the strings they represent. Once keys have been created, using `compareTo()` with `CollationKey` objects is generally a faster way of comparing than using the `compare()` method of `Collator`. Thus, when the strings must be compared multiple times, for example when sorting a list of strings, it's more efficient to use `CollationKey` objects.

Usage

A particular collator produce a `CollationKey` object. `CollationKey` has no public constructor or creation methods. The method to create a `CollationKey` object is `getCollationKey()`, a member of the `Collator` class.

To create an instance of `CollationKey` for a given string you want to compare (call it `string`) and `Collator` object (call it `collator`), call:

```
collator.getCollationKey(string)
```

When comparing multiple strings, all of their `CollationKey` objects must be generated from the same collator object. You then use `compareTo()` to compare `CollationKey` objects from two strings. Alternatively, you can use `toByteArray()` and then call a bitwise comparison operation.

A collator has a strength and a decomposition mode, as described in the `Collator` class. The strength of a `CollationKey` object is derived from the strength of its associated `Collator` object. Never compare `CollationKey` objects that come either from different collators or from the same collator but with different strength or decomposition settings.

If the strength of the `Collator` object associated with a `CollationKey` object is set to `Collator.IDENTICAL`, then `compare()` and `compareTo()` will return `0` if, and only if, the compared strings are canonically equivalent (see *The Unicode Standard*, version 2.0).

Generating a `CollationKey` object for a string involves examining the entire string and converting the string to a series of bits that can be compared bitwise. This allows for fast comparisons once the keys are generated. The cost of generating keys is recouped in faster comparisons when strings need to be compared many times. On the other hand, the result of a comparison is often determined by the first couple of characters of each string. The `compare()` method in `Collator` examines only as many characters as it needs. This allows it to do single comparisons faster.

The following example shows how `CollationKey` objects might be used to sort a list of strings:

```
// Create an array of CollationKey objects for the strings to be sorted.
Collator myCollator = Collator.getInstance();
CollationKey[] keys = myCollator.getCollationKey[3];
keys[0] = myCollator.getCollationKey("Tom");
keys[1] = myCollator.getCollationKey("Dick");
keys[2] = myCollator.getCollationKey("Harry");
sort( keys );
//...
// Inside body of sort routine, compare keys this way
if( keys[i].compareTo( keys[j] ) > 0 ) {
    // swap keys[i] and keys[j]
}
//...
// Finally, when we've returned from sort.
System.out.println( keys[0].getSourceString() );
System.out.println( keys[1].getSourceString() );
System.out.println( keys[2].getSourceString() );
```

MEMBER SUMMARY

Comparison Method	
`compareTo()`	Compares this `CollationKey` object to the target `CollationKey` object.
String Getter Method	
`getSourceString()`	Retrieves the original string used to create this `CollationKey` object.
Byte Method	
`toByteArray()`	Converts this `CollationKey` object to an array of bytes.
Object Methods	
`equals()`	Compares this `CollationKey` object with another object for equality.
`hashCode()`	Creates the hash code for this `CollationKey` object.

See Also

`Collator`, `RuleBasedCollator`.

Example

This example creates keys for three strings and then calls `compareTo()` in a sort routine.

```
import java.text.CollationKey;
import java.text.Collator;
import java.util.Locale;

public class Main {

    public static void main(String[] args) {
        Locale loc = Locale.FRENCH;

        // Create an instance of a subclass of collator.
        Collator myCollator = Collator.getInstance(loc);

        // Create array of collation keys for strings to be sorted.
        CollationKey[] keys = new CollationKey[3];
        keys[0] = myCollator.getCollationKey("Tom");
        keys[1] = myCollator.getCollationKey("Dick");
        keys[2] = myCollator.getCollationKey("Harry");

        // Sort keys and print strings.
        sortArray(keys);
        printArray(keys);              // "Dick" "Harry" "Tom"
    }

    // Sort collation keys.
    public static void sortArray(CollationKey[] keys) {
        CollationKey tmp;

        // Sort the keys by comparing two at a time.
        for (int i = 0; i < keys.length; i++) {
            for (int j = i + 1; j < keys.length; j++) {

                // Compare keys .
                if( keys[i].compareTo( keys[j] ) > 0 ) {
                    //swap keys[i] and keys[j]
                    tmp = keys[i];
                    keys[i] = keys[j];
                    keys[j] = tmp;
                }
            }
        }
    }

    // Print contents of an array
    static void printArray(CollationKey[] a) {
        for (int i = 0; i < a.length; i++) {
            if (a[i].getSourceString().length() == 0) {
                System.out.println("(empty)" + "  ");
            } else {
                System.out.println(a[i].getSourceString() + "  ");
            }
        }
    }
}
```

compareTo()

PURPOSE Compares this `CollationKey` object to the target `CollationKey` object.

SYNTAX `public int compareTo(CollationKey target)`

DESCRIPTION This method compares this `CollationKey` object to the `target` `CollationKey` object and returns an integer indicating which should be sorted first. The collation rules of the `Collator` object that created these keys apply.

If the strength of two `CollationKey` objects is identical, then `compareTo()` returns `0` if, and only if, the strings are canonically equivalent (see *The Unicode Standard*, version 2.0).

Note: `CollationKey` objects created by different collators cannot be compared. Nor can `CollationKey` objects be compared if they are from the same collator but have different strengths or decomposition settings.

PARAMETERS

`target` A `CollationKey` object to compare.

RETURNS An `int` that is less than `0` if this `CollationKey` object is less than `target`, `0` if they are equal, and greater than `0` if this `CollationKey` object is greater than `target`.

SEE ALSO `Collator.compare()`.

EXAMPLE See the class example.

equals()

PURPOSE Compares this `CollationKey` object with another object for equality.

SYNTAX `public boolean equals(Object obj)`

DESCRIPTION This method compares this `CollationKey` object with `obj` for equality. If `obj` is a `CollationKey` object and if its key is equal to that of this `CollationKey` object, then the objects are equal and this method returns `true`. It is not necessary for the strings from which the keys were created to be equal.

The collation rules of the collator object that created these keys are applied. *Note:* `CollationKey` objects created by different collators cannot be compared.

PARAMETERS

`obj` A possibly `null` object.

RETURNS `true` if this collator is equal to `obj`; `false` otherwise.

OVERRIDES `java.lang.Object.equals()`.

SEE ALSO `hashCode()`.

EXAMPLE See `clone()`.

getSourceString()

PURPOSE Retrieves the original string used to create this `CollationKey` object.

SYNTAX `public String getSourceString()`

RETURNS The original string from which this `CollationKey` object was created.

EXAMPLE See the class example.

hashCode()

PURPOSE Computes the hash code of this `CollationKey` object.

SYNTAX `public int hashCode()`

DESCRIPTION This method computes the hash code based on the key of this `CollationKey` object, not the string from which the key was created. Two `CollationKey` objects with the same keys will have the same hash code. However, two `CollationKey` objects that do not have the same keys might also have the same hash code, although the hash code algorithm minimizes this possibility. The hash code is typically used as the key in a hash table.

If `ck1` and `ck2` are instances of `CollationKey` and if `ck1.equals(ck2)` is true, then `ck1.hashCode() == ck2.hashCode()`. This allows language-sensitive comparison in a hash table.

RETURNS The `CollationKey` object's hash code, an integer.

OVERRIDES `java.lang.Object.hashCode()`.

SEE ALSO `equals()`.

EXAMPLE See `clone()`.

toByteArray()

PURPOSE Converts this `CollationKey` object to an array of bytes.

SYNTAX `public byte[] toByteArray()`

DESCRIPTION This method converts this `CollationKey` object to a `byte` array. If two `CollationKey` objects could be legitimately compared, then one could compare the byte arrays of each of those keys to obtain the same result. Each byte array is organized by most-significant byte first.

Therefore, as an alternative to compareTo(), you can use toByteArray() and then call a bitwise comparison operation. Java doesn't have a built-in bitwise comparison operation. This method is useful when storing a CollationKey object in some sort of external form: a flat file, a database, or whatever. If a database application can cache the generated keys and reuse them in a table of contents, then using the byte array and doing bitwise comparison speeds up the comparing time. If you're writing a pure Java application that doesn't have to share CollationKey objects with the outside world, compareTo() is faster and easier.

RETURNS An array of bytes.

Collator

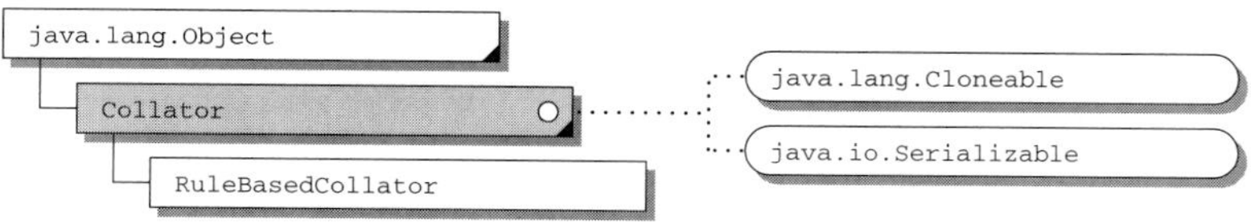

Syntax

```
public abstract class Collator extends Object implements Cloneable, Serializable
```

Description

The `Collator` class performs locale-sensitive string comparison. You use this class to build searching and alphabetical sorting routines for natural language text. The term *collate* means to determine the proper sort sequence for two or more strings.

`Collator` is an abstract base class. Subclasses implement specific collation strategies. One subclass, `RuleBasedCollator`, is currently provided and is applicable to a wide set of languages. Other subclasses may be created to handle more specialized needs.

Usage

As with other locale-sensitive classes, you use the static creation method `getInstance(Locale)` to obtain the appropriate instance of a `Collator` subclass for a given locale. This method is demonstrated below under sorting. You do not need to understand the particular sorting rules for the locales that Java supports. You simply create a `Collator` instance for either the default locale or a particular locale. If you need to understand the details of a particular collation strategy or if you need to modify that strategy, you need to look at the subclasses of `Collator`.

At the heart of the collator is the `compare()` method, which compares two strings. You can make the comparison more or less strict by setting the strength and the decomposition mode of the collator. The decomposition mode determines whether (and how much) the strings are decomposed before doing the comparison. These are both discussed further in a later subsection. Strength is discussed in the next subsection.

The two natural uses for `Collator` are for sorting and searching.

- **Sorting.** An important operation of collation is comparing two strings to see in what order they would sort. The following example shows how to use the `compare()` method on two strings for the default locale:

```
Collator myCollator = Collator.getInstance();
if ( myCollator.compare("abc", "ABC") < 0 ) {
    System.out.println("abc is less than ABC");
} else {
    System.out.println("abc is greater than ABC");
}
```

- **Searching.** In a search routine you compare two strings for equality to see if they are equal. Use `CollationElementIterator` for searching.

For comparing strings exactly once, the `compare()` method provides the best performance. For sorting a list of `Strings` however, it is generally necessary to compare each string multiple times. In this case, `CollationKey` provides the better performance.

The `CollationKey` class converts a `String` object to a series of bits that can be compared bitwise against other `CollationKey` objects. A `CollationKey` object is created by a `Collator` object for a given `String` object. *Note*: `CollationKey` objects from different `Collator` objects cannot be compared. See the class description for `CollationKey` for an example using `CollationKey`.

Strength Property

The *strength* property determines the minimum level of difference between two strings considered significant during comparison. This is also called the *ordering strength*. Some languages do not have characters with accents or with uppercase and lowercase differences. However, for those that do, following are the typical definitions of strengths. See also Table 18.

When doing language-sensitive searching, you generally allow the user to specify "weak" matches. The weakest match is one where searching for the letter "a" matches "a", "A", "à", "â", or "ä". That is, uppercase/lowercase and accents are ignored; only base letters are compared. This search employs the `PRIMARY` strength. A stronger match is one in which uppercase/lowercase is ignored, but accents are not. This search employs a `SECONDARY` strength. `TERTIARY` strength applies when all properties match except the "bits" are different. `IDENTICAL` strength means all differences are significant; the only way for a comparison to return `0` is if the strings are either bit-for-bit identical or canonically equivalent (see *The Unicode Standard, Vol. 2*). For the vast majority of strings, the difference will be either primary, secondary, or tertiary, with `IDENTICAL` not coming into play.

<table>
<tr><th>Strength</th><th>Primary</th><th>Secondary</th><th>Tertiary</th><th>Identical</th></tr>
<tr><td>Base Character
"a" versus "b"</td><td>Equal if same base character.</td><td rowspan="2">Equal if same base char and accent.</td><td rowspan="3">Equal if same base char, accent, and case.</td><td rowspan="4">Equal if same bits.</td></tr>
<tr><td>Accent
"a" versus "á"</td><td rowspan="3">Accent, case and bits can differ.</td></tr>
<tr><td>Upper/ lowercase
"a" versus "A"</td><td rowspan="2">Case and bits can differ.</td></tr>
<tr><td>Bits Identical</td><td>Bits can differ.</td></tr>
</table>

TABLE 18: Ordering Strength for Latin-Based Languages.

Note: The `IDENTICAL` constant cannot be used in JDK 1.1.5 or earlier because it was not yet fully implemented. In those versions, calling `setStrength(Collator.IDENTICAL)` throws an illegal argument exception. This is fixed in JDK 1.1.6.

With `PRIMARY` and `SECONDARY` strengths, words that differ only in case and accents will compare as exactly the same string. Therefore, in sorting, the order of the words is determined basically by their original order and how the sorting algorithm treats equivalent words, not by any intrinsic differences in the words themselves.

With `SECONDARY` or `TERTIARY` strength, an unaccented base character sorts before an accented version of the same base character. However, some languages with accents, such as French, sort from left to right on the base characters and then sort from right to left on the accents, for example:

French sort order:

```
pêche
péché
```

The rules in some languages are not always clear-cut. Sometimes accent marks have primary strength because the accent represents a new character. For example, traditional German sorts the letter "ö" (o-umlaut) as if it were two characters, "oe". The extra character raises this difference to primary strength. *Note:* Starting with JDK 1.1.6, the default behavior in German is for "ö" not to expand to "oe."

The following examples illustrate `IDENTICAL` strength:

- **Example 1**
  Control characters `\u0001` and `\u0002` are ignored at a primary, secondary, and tertiary level. At these levels, the following returns `0`:

  ```
  myCollator.compare("ab\u0001c", "ab\u0002c")
  ```

  However, when the strength is set to `IDENTICAL`, the comparison includes the character codes, thus returning `-1`, since `0x0001` < `0x0002`.

- **Example 2**
  "à" (`\u00E0`) and the combination "a" + " ‘ " (`\u0061` + `\u0300`) are canonical equivalents in Unicode, and, on the primary, secondary, and tertiary levels, compare as equal. That is, with decomposition left at the default of `CANONICAL_DECOMPOSITION`, the following returns `0`:

  ```
  myCollator.compare("\u00E0", "\u0061\u0300")
  ```

  However, when the strength is set to `IDENTICAL` and decomposition is set to `NO_DECOMPOSITION`, these strings compare as not equal, since the character codes are not the same. This method returns `1`, since `0x00E0` > `0x0061`.

  This is the behavior for the current implementation, `RuleBasedCollator`. You can build your own collator that has different strength criteria.

Decomposition

The *decomposition mode* determines how Unicode composed characters are decomposed prior to comparison. Basically, decomposition converts precomposed characters like a-grave (`\u00E0`) into a sequence of combining characters, in this case "`a\u0300`". This is done because these two strings are really the same as far as Unicode is concerned; `\u00e0` is defined to be exactly equivalent to "`a\u0300`". So if both strings are decomposed before being compared, the strings will compare as equal, which is what is desired. However, decomposing takes time. If you know that both of your strings contain only precomposed characters or that they both contain no precomposed characters, then you can turn off decomposition and thereby make the comparison go faster.

Alternatively, you can adjust the decomposition mode to allow the user to select between faster and more complete collation behavior. For Latin languages, "No decomposition" is not a useful mode unless you know that the text contains no accents. "Canonical decomposition" is somewhat slower than no decomposition, but it handles accents correctly. "Full decomposition" handles compatibility characters, such as half-width Katakana. For more details on decomposition, see *The Unicode Standard, Vol. 2.*

MEMBER SUMMARY	
Constructor	
`Collator()`	Constructor called by subclasses.
Creation Method	
`getInstance()`	Creates and returns a `Collator` object for a locale.
Decomposition Constants	
`CANONICAL_DECOMPOSITION`	Indicates characters that are Unicode canonical variants will be decomposed for collation.
`FULL_DECOMPOSITION`	Indicates all characters that are Unicode variants will be decomposed for collation.
`NO_DECOMPOSITION`	Indicates accented characters will not be decomposed for collation.
Comparison Constants	
`PRIMARY`	Indicates comparisons should consider only primary differences.
`SECONDARY`	Indicates comparisons should consider only secondary and greater differences.
`TERTIARY`	Indicates comparisons should consider only tertiary and greater differences.
`IDENTICAL`	Indicates comparisons should consider all differences.

MEMBER SUMMARY	
Comparison Method	
`compare()`	Compares two strings according to this `Collator` object's rules and returns an integer indicating which should be sorted first.
Collation Method	
`getCollationKey()`	Transforms a string into a collation key for bitwise comparison with other collation keys.
Decomposition Methods	
`getDecomposition()`	Retrieves the mode that determines how Unicode composed characters are separated prior to comparison.
`setDecomposition()`	Sets the mode that determines how Unicode composed characters are separated prior to comparison.
Strength Methods	
`getStrength()`	Sets the minimum level of difference considered significant during comparison.
`setStrength()`	Retrieves the minimum level of difference considered significant during comparison.
Locale Method	
`getAvailableLocales()`	Gets the set of locales for which `Collator` objects are installed.
Object Methods	
`clone()`	Creates a copy of this `Collator` object.
`equals()`	Compares this `Collator` object with another object for equality.
`hashCode()`	Computes the hash code for this `Collator` object.

See Also

`RuleBasedCollator`, `CollationKey`, `CollationElementIterator`, `Locale`.

Example

This example compares and sorts the lines read in from a file.

```
import java.text.Collator;
import java.util.Locale;
import java.util.Vector;
import java.io.*;

class Main {
```

```
Main (String[] array) {
    Locale loc = Locale.FRENCH;

    // Create an instance of a subclass of collator.
    Collator collator = Collator.getInstance(loc);

    // Find out what kind of subclass it is.
    System.out.println(collator.getClass() + "\n");
                                    // java.text.RuleBasedcollator
    // Sort and print the array.
    sortArray(collator, array);
    printArray(array);
}

// Sort strings.
public static void sortArray(Collator collator, String[] strArray) {
    String tmp;
    // Sort the string array.
    for (int i = 0; i < strArray.length; i++) {
        for (int j = i + 1; j < strArray.length; j++) {
            // Compare members of the array two at a time.
            if( collator.compare(strArray[i], strArray[j] ) > 0 ) {
                //swap strArray[i] and strArray[j]
                tmp = strArray[i];
                strArray[i] = strArray[j];
                strArray[j] = tmp;
            }
        }
    }
}

// Print the contents of an array
static void printArray(String[] a) {
    for (int i = 0; i < a.length; i++) {
        if (a[i].length() == 0) {
            System.out.println("(empty)" + "  ");
        } else {
            if (a[i] == null) {
                System.out.println("(null)" + "  ");
            } else {
                System.out.println(a[i] + "  ");
            }
        }
    }
}

public static void main(String[] args) {
    // Accept a string as an argument
    if (args.length != 1) {
        System.err.println("This program sorts lines in a file");
        System.err.println("Usage: java Main input.txt");
        System.exit(1);
    }

    try {
        // Read in the entire contents of the file.
        BufferedReader rd = new BufferedReader(new FileReader(args[0]));
        String line;

        // Create a vector to hold the strings read in.
```

```
            Vector tmpVector = new Vector();

            int i = 0;
            try {
                while ((line = rd.readLine()) != null) {
                    tmpVector.insertElementAt(line, i);
                    ++i;
                }
            } catch (ArrayIndexOutOfBoundsException e) {
                System.out.println(e);
            }

            rd.close();

            // Copy the vector to an array of strings.
            String[] newArray = new String[i];
            tmpVector.copyInto((Object[])newArray);

            // Call the constructor passing in the array.
            new Main(newArray);

        } catch (Exception e) {
            e.printStackTrace();
        }
    }
}
```

Output

```
> java Main input.txt
class java.text.RuleBasedCollator

Cinnamon
dogs
Doug
friends
Lady
Linda
pêche
péché
pécher
pêcher
toad
toed
tofu
töne
tots
```


CANONICAL_DECOMPOSITION

PURPOSE Indicates characters that are Unicode canonical variants will be decomposed for collation.

SYNTAX `public final static int CANONICAL_DECOMPOSITION`

DESCRIPTION This constant is a decomposition value that indicates that characters that are Unicode canonical variants will be decomposed for collation. With decomposition set to CANONICAL_DECOMPOSITION, characters that are canonical variants according to Unicode 2.0 will be decomposed for collation. This is the default setting and should be used to get correct collation of accented characters. The integer value of CANONICAL_DECOMPOSITION is 1.

SEE ALSO getDecomposition(), setDecomposition().

EXAMPLE See setDecomposition().

clone()

PURPOSE Creates a copy of this Collator object.

SYNTAX `public Object clone()`

DESCRIPTION This method makes a copy of this Collator object. The new Collator object is a complete copy of the original, including its properties. Changing any value in the new Collator object will not affect the original instance.

RETURNS A copy of this Collator object.

OVERRIDES java.lang.Object.clone().

EXAMPLE This example illustrates the use of clone() to copy a RuleBasedCollator object. Note that the copy has the same rules as the original.

```
import java.text.RuleBasedCollator;
import java.text.ParseException;

class Main {
    public static void main(String args[]) {

        // Create a simple collator rule.
        String rules = "< a < b < c < d";

        // Create a rule-based collator.
        try {
            RuleBasedCollator rbc = new RuleBasedCollator(rules);

            // Create a clone.
            RuleBasedCollator rbcCopy = (RuleBasedCollator)rbc.clone();
            System.out.println("Copy's rules:" + "\n" + rbc.getRules());

            // Tests for equality.
            if (rbc.equals(rbcCopy)) {
                System.out.println("Clone is equal to original");
            }

            // Compute hashcode.
            int hc = rbc.hashCode();
            System.out.println("Hash code:        " + hc);
```

```
                } catch (ParseException pe) {
                System.out.println("Parse exception for rules");
            }
        }
    }
```


Collator()

PURPOSE
Constructor called by subclasses.

SYNTAX
`protected Collator()`

DESCRIPTION
Do not call this constructor directly. You typically create an instance of a `Collator` subclass by calling the creation method `getInstance()`. This constructor is protected so that only subclasses can access it.

The default strength is `TERTIARY`. The default decomposition mode is `CANONICAL_DECOMPOSITION`.

SEE ALSO
`getInstance()`.

compare()

PURPOSE
Compares two strings according to this `Collator` object's rules and returns an integer indicating which should be sorted first.

SYNTAX
`public abstract int compare(String source, String target)`

DESCRIPTION
This method compares the `source` string to the `target` string character-by-character according to the collation rules for this `Collator` object. It returns an integer less than, equal to, or greater than zero, depending on whether `source` is less than, equal to, or greater than `target`.

For a one-time comparison, this method has the best performance. However, if a given string will be involved in multiple comparisons, `compareTo()` in `CollationKey` has the best performance. See the `CollationKey` class description for an example.

PARAMETERS
`source` A string to compare.
`target` A string to compare.

RETURNS
An `int` that is less than `0` if `source` is less than `target`, `0` if `source` and `target` are equal, and greater than `0` if `source` is greater than `target`.

SEE ALSO
`CollationKey`, `getCollationKey()`.

EXAMPLE
See the class example.

A B C D E F G H I J K L M N O P Q R S T U V W X Y Z

equals()

PURPOSE Compares this `Collator` object with another object for equality.

SYNTAX
```
public boolean equals(Object obj)
public boolean equals(String source, String target)
```

DESCRIPTION The first form of this method compares the equality of this `Collator` object with another object `obj`. Two `Collator` objects are equal only if their decomposition mode and strength are equal.

The second form is a convenience method for comparing the equality of two strings, `source` and `target`, based on this `Collator` object's collation rules.

Subclasses override this method to compare their own data as well. So if you compare two `RuleBasedCollator` objects, this method will compare the strength, the decomposition mode, and the collation rules.

PARAMETERS

`obj` A possibly `null` object.
`source` A source string with which to be compared.
`target` A target string with which to be compared.

RETURNS The first form returns `true` if this collator is the same as the `obj` collator; `false` otherwise.

The second form returns `true` if the strings are equal according to the collation rules; `false` otherwise.

OVERRIDES `java.lang.Object.equals()`.

SEE ALSO `hashCode()`.

EXAMPLE See `clone()`.

FULL_DECOMPOSITION

PURPOSE Indicates all characters that are Unicode variants will be decomposed for collation.

SYNTAX
```
public final static int FULL_DECOMPOSITION
```

DESCRIPTION This constant is a decomposition value that indicates that all characters that are Unicode variants will be decomposed for collation. With decomposition set to `FULL_DECOMPOSITION`, both Unicode canonical variants and Unicode compatibility variants will be decomposed for collation. This not only causes accented characters to be collated, but also causes characters that have special formats to be collated with their norminal form. For example, the half-width and full-width ASCII and Katakana characters are collated together.

FULL_DECOMPOSITION is the most complete and therefore the slowest decomposition mode. The integer value of FULL_DECOMPOSITION is 2.

SEE ALSO getDecomposition(), setDecomposition().

EXAMPLE See setDecomposition().

getAvailableLocales()

PURPOSE Gets the set of locales for which collators are installed.

SYNTAX `public static synchronized Locale[] getAvailableLocales()`

DESCRIPTION This method queries the system and returns the set of locales for which collators are installed.

RETURNS An array of the available locales.

EXAMPLE This example displays the list of available locales. The output list has been abbreviated from the 50 locales actually printed out.

```
import java.text.Collator;
import java.util.Locale;

class Main {
    public static void main(String args[]) {

        // Get list of installed locales with collators.
        Locale locales[] = Collator.getAvailableLocales();

        // Print all locales.
        for (int i = 0; i < locales.length; i++) {
            System.out.println(locales[i].getDisplayName());
        }
    }
}
```

Output

```
> java Main
Arabic (Egypt)
Belorussian (Belarus)
Bulgarian (Bulgaria)
Catalan (Spain)
Czech (Czech Republic)
Danish (Denmark)
German (Germany)
German (Austria)
German (Switzerland)
Greek (Greece)
English (Canada)
English (United Kingdom)
English (Ireland)
English (United States)
...
```

getCollationKey()

PURPOSE Transforms a string into a collation key for bitwise comparison with other collation keys.

SYNTAX `public abstract CollationKey getCollationKey(String source)`

DESCRIPTION This method transforms the `source` string into a series of bits (in an instance of `CollationKey`) that can be compared bitwise using `compareTo()` in `CollationKey` to other `CollationKey` instances. The rules for this conversion are based on this collator's collation rules. A `CollationKey` object provides better performance than `compare()` when strings are involved in multiple comparisons.

PARAMETERS

`source` The string to be transformed into a collation key.

RETURNS The instance of `CollationKey` for the `source` string. If `source` is `null`, a `null` `CollationKey` object is returned.

SEE ALSO `CollationKey`, `compare()`.

EXAMPLE This example uses `getCollationKey()` to convert strings into collation keys and then calls `compareTo()` from `CollationKey` to compare them.

```
import java.text.Collator;
import java.text.CollationKey;
import java.util.Locale;

class Main {
    public static void main(String args[]) {
        Locale loc = Locale.FRENCH;

        // Create an instance of a subclass of collator.
        Collator collator = Collator.getInstance(loc);

        // Find out what kind of subclass it is.
        System.out.println(collator.getClass() + "\n");
                                    // java.text.RuleBasedcollator

        // Create array of collation keys for the strings to be sorted.
        CollationKey[] keys = new CollationKey[3];

        // Create collation keys from the two strings.
        keys[0] = collator.getCollationKey("Tom");
        keys[1] = collator.getCollationKey("Dick");
        keys[2] = collator.getCollationKey("Harry");

        // Sort and print the array of keys.
        sortArray(keys);
        printArray(keys);
    }

    // Sort collation keys.
    public static void sortArray(CollationKey[] keys) {
```

```
            CollationKey tmp;

            // Sort the keys by comparing two at a time.
            for (int i = 0; i < keys.length; i++) {
                for (int j = i + 1; j < keys.length; j++) {

                    // Compare keys .
                    if( keys[i].compareTo( keys[j] ) > 0 ) {
                        //swap keys[i] and keys[j]
                        tmp = keys[i];
                        keys[i] = keys[j];
                        keys[j] = tmp;
                    }
                }
            }
        }

        // Print contents of an array
        static void printArray(CollationKey[] a) {
            for (int i = 0; i < a.length; i++) {
                if (a[i].getSourceString().length() == 0) {
                    System.out.println("(empty)" + "  ");
                } else {
                    System.out.println(a[i].getSourceString() + "  ");
                }
            }
        }
    }
```

Output

```
> java Main
class java.text.RuleBasedCollator

Dick
Harry
Tom
```

getDecomposition()

PURPOSE Retrieves the mode that determines how Unicode composed characters are separated prior to comparison.

SYNTAX `public synchronized int getDecomposition()`

DESCRIPTION This method gets the decomposition mode of this collator. See `setDecomposition()` for a description of decomposition mode.

RETURNS The decomposition mode of this collator.

SEE ALSO `setDecomposition`, `NO_DECOMPOSITION`, `CANONICAL_DECOMPOSITION`, `FULL_DECOMPOSITION`.

EXAMPLE See `setDecomposition()`.

A B C D E F G H I J K L M N O P Q R S T U V W X Y Z

getInstance()

PURPOSE Creates and returns a `Collator` for a locale.

SYNTAX
```
public static synchronized Collator getInstance()
public static synchronized Collator getInstance(Locale loc)
```

DESCRIPTION This method creates and returns a `Collator` for the locale `loc`. Currently, this creates an instance of `RuleBasedCollator`, the only current subclass of `Collator`. It also loads the associated resource bundle. Omitting the locale uses the default locale, which is determined by `java.util.Locale.getDefault()`.

PARAMETERS
`loc` The locale for the new collator.

RETURNS The collator for the locale.

SEE ALSO `java.util.Locale`, `ResourceBundle`, `java.util.Locale.getDefault()`.

EXAMPLE See the class example.

getStrength()

PURPOSE Retrieves the minimum level of difference considered significant during comparison.

SYNTAX
```
public synchronized int getStrength()
```

DESCRIPTION This method returns this collator's strength property. The strength property determines the minimum level of difference considered significant during comparison.

RETURNS This collator's current strength property.

SEE ALSO `setStrength()`, `PRIMARY`, `SECONDARY`, `TERTIARY`, `IDENTICAL`.

EXAMPLE See `setStrength()`.

hashCode()

PURPOSE Computes a hash code of this `Collator`.

SYNTAX
```
public synchronized abstract int hashCode()
```

DESCRIPTION This method computes that hash code of `Collator` based on the pattern of this `Collator`. Two `Collator` objects with the same properties will have the same hash code. However, two `Collator` objects that do not have the same properties might also have the same hash code, although the hash code algorithm minimizes this possibility. The hash code is typically used as the key in a hash table.

RETURNS The `Collator`'s hash code, an integer.

OVERRIDES `java.lang.Object.hashCode()`.

SEE ALSO `equals()`.

EXAMPLE See `clone()`.

A B C D E F G H I J K L M N O P Q R S T U V W X Y Z

IDENTICAL

PURPOSE Indicates comparisons should consider all differences.

SYNTAX `public final static int IDENTICAL`

DESCRIPTION This constant is a strength value for collators that indicates that comparisons should consider all differences. If the strength is set to `IDENTICAL`, then the only way for a comparison to return `0` is if the strings are either bit-for-bit identical or canonically equivalent. This is the behavior for the current implementation in `RuleBasedCollator`; you can build your own collator that has different rules.

A common example is for control characters (`\u0001 versus \u0002`) to be considered equal at the `PRIMARY`, `SECONDARY`, and `TERTIARY` levels but different at the `IDENTICAL` level. Also, if decomposition is set to `NO_DECOMPOSITION`, differences between precomposed accents such as `\u00C0` (A-grave) and combining accents such as "`A\u0300`" (A, combining-grave) will be considered significant at the `TERTIARY` level. The integer value of `IDENTICAL` is `3`.

Note: The `IDENTICAL` constant cannot be used in JDK 1.1.5 or earlier because it was not yet fully implemented. Calling `setStrength(Collator.IDENTICAL)` throws an illegal argument exception in those versions. This is fixed in JDK 1.1.6.

SEE ALSO `setStrength()`, `getStrength()`.

EXAMPLE See `setStrength()`.

NO_DECOMPOSITION

PURPOSE Indicates accented characters will not be decomposed for collation.

SYNTAX `public final static int NO_DECOMPOSITION`

DESCRIPTION This constant is a decomposition value that indicates that accented characters will not be decomposed for collation. With decomposition set to

NO_DECOMPOSITION, a base character and its accent will remain as a single character. This provides the fastest collation but will produce correct results only for languages that do not use accents. The integer value of NO_DECOMPOSITION is 0. Do not use this mode unless you know what you are doing!

SEE ALSO getDecomposition(), setDecomposition().

EXAMPLE See setDecomposition().

PRIMARY

PURPOSE Indicates comparisons should consider only primary differences.

SYNTAX `public final static int PRIMARY`

DESCRIPTION This constant is a strength value for collators that indicates that only primary differences are to be considered significant during comparison. The assignment of strengths to language features is locale-dependent. A common example is for different base letters ("a" versus "b") to be considered a PRIMARY difference. The integer value of PRIMARY is 0.

SEE ALSO setStrength(), getStrength().

EXAMPLE See setStrength().

SECONDARY

PURPOSE Indicates comparisons should consider only secondary and greater differences.

SYNTAX `public final static int SECONDARY`

DESCRIPTION This constant is a strength value for collators that indicates that only SECONDARY and greater differences are considered significant during comparison. The assignment of strengths to language features is locale-dependent. A common example is for different accented forms of the same base letter ("a" versus "á") to be considered a having a SECONDARY difference. The integer value of SECONDARY is 1.

SEE ALSO setStrength(), getStrength().

EXAMPLE See setStrength().

setDecomposition()

PURPOSE Sets the mode that determines how Unicode composed characters are separated prior to comparison.

SYNTAX `public synchronized void setDecomposition(int mode)`

DESCRIPTION This method set the decomposition mode of this `Collator`. The decomposition mode determines how Unicode composed characters are decomposed prior to comparison. Adjusting the decomposition mode allows you to select between faster and more complete collation behavior.

The three values for decomposition mode are `NO_DECOMPOSITION`, `CANONICAL_DECOMPOSITION`, and `FULL_DECOMPOSITION`. See the documentation for these three constants for a description of their meanings.

PARAMETERS

`mode` The new decomposition mode. Valid values are the static constants `NO_DECOMPOSITION`, `CANONICAL_DECOMPOSITION`, `FULL_DECOMPOSITION`.

EXCEPTIONS

`IllegalArgumentException`
If the given value is not a valid decomposition mode.

SEE ALSO `getDecomposition()`, `NO_DECOMPOSITION`, `CANONICAL_DECOMPOSITION`, `FULL_DECOMPOSITION`.

EXAMPLE This example performs sorting with the three different modes of decomposition to demonstrate how the sort can differ. It prints out the result to standard output, and also displays the results in a text area. It includes some Unicode characters that your system font may not be able to display, including accents and Katakana.

```
import java.awt.*;
import java.util.*;
import java.text.*;

class Main extends Frame {
    static int COLWIDTH = 10;

    // Create text area
    TextArea tArea =
        new TextArea("", 49, 50, TextArea.SCROLLBARS_VERTICAL_ONLY);

    Main(String s) {
        super("Collator Example");

        // Initialize various objects with the text.
        tArea.setText(s);
        tArea.setEditable(false);
        tArea.setFont(new Font("Courier", Font.PLAIN, 12));

        // Add layout to text area and listen for key events.
```

```
        add(tArea, BorderLayout.CENTER);

        setSize(400, 400);
        pack();
        show();
    }

    public static void main(String[] args) {
        Locale loc = Locale.FRENCH;

        // Create an instance of a subclass of collator.
        Collator collator = Collator.getInstance(loc);

        int[] decompositions = {
                                Collator.NO_DECOMPOSITION,
                                Collator.CANONICAL_DECOMPOSITION,
                                Collator.FULL_DECOMPOSITION
                            };

        // Set up strings to sort.
        String[] array = new String[] {
                    "ábc",
                    "Ábc",
                    "àbc",
                    "Abc",
                    "äbc",
                    "Àbc",
                    "abc",
                    "Äbc",
            //      "A\u0300bc",     // A grave b c
                    "\u00b5",        // u - MICRON SIGN
                    "\u0041",        // A - LATIN CAPITAL LETTER A
                    "\u30ab",        // ? - KATAKANA LETTER KA
                    "\u03bc",        // u - GREEK SMALL LETTER MU
                    "\uff21",        // A - FULLWIDTH CAPITAL LETTER A
                    "\uff76"         // ? - HALFWIDTH KATAKANA LETTER KA
        };

        // Set up strings to sort.
        String[] arrayLabel = new String[] {
                    "a-acute b c",
                    "A-acute b c",
                    "a-grave b c",
                    "A b c",
                    "a-umlaut b c",
                    "A-grave b c",
                    "a b c",
                    "A-umlaut b c",
            //      "A\\u0300bc -  A grave b c",
                    "\\u00b5 - MICRON SIGN",
                    "\\u0041 - LATIN CAPITAL LETTER A",
                    "\\u30ab - KATAKANA LETTER KA",
                    "\\u03bc - GREEK SMALL LETTER MU",
                    "\\uff21 - FULLWIDTH CAPITAL LETTER A",
                    "\\uff76 - HALFWIDTH KATAKANA LETTER KA"
        };

        StringBuffer strbuf = new StringBuffer("");

        for (int i=0; i < decompositions.length; i++) {
```

```
            collator.setDecomposition(decompositions[i]);
            int decomp = collator.getDecomposition();

            switch (decomp) {
                case(0):
                    System.out.print("No Decomposition: ");
                    strbuf.append("No Decomposition: ");
                    System.out.println(" (Do not use this mode)");
                    strbuf.append(" (Do not use this mode)");
                    break;
                case(1):
                    System.out.print("Canonical Decomposition: ");
                    strbuf.append("Canonical Decomposition: ");
                    System.out.println(" ---------------------");
                    strbuf.append(" ---------------------");
                    break;
                case(2):
                    System.out.print("Full Decomposition: ");
                    strbuf.append("Full Decomposition: ");
                    System.out.println(" --------------------------");
                    strbuf.append(" --------------------------");
                    break;
            }
            strbuf.append("\n");

            // Sort and append the strings to the string buffer.
            sortArray(collator, array, arrayLabel);
            appendArrayToStrBuf(array, arrayLabel, strbuf);
        }
        new Main(new String(strbuf));
    }

    // Sort strings.
    public static void sortArray(Collator collator,
                                 String[] strArray,
                                 String[] strArrayLabel) {
        String tmp;
        // Sort the string array.
        for (int i = 0; i < strArray.length; i++) {
            for (int j = i + 1; j < strArray.length; j++) {
                // Compare members of the array two at a time.
                if( collator.compare(strArray[i], strArray[j] ) > 0 ) {
                    // Swap strArray[i] and strArray[j].
                    tmp = strArray[i];
                    strArray[i] = strArray[j];
                    strArray[j] = tmp;

                    // Swap the same items in the label array
                    tmp = strArrayLabel[i];
                    strArrayLabel[i] = strArrayLabel[j];
                    strArrayLabel[j] = tmp;
                }
            }
        }
    }

    // Print the contents of a 1-dimensional array of strings
    // plus its label array.
    static void appendArrayToStrBuf(String[] a,
                                    String[] aLabel,
```

```
                                            StringBuffer strbuf) {
            for (int i = 0; i < a.length; i++) {
                if (a[i].length() == 0) {
                    strbuf.append("(empty)" + "\n");
                    System.out.println("(empty)");
                } else {
                    if (a[i] == null) {
                        strbuf.append("(null)" + "\n");
                        System.out.println("(null)");
                    } else {
                        strbuf.append(a[i]
                                  + appendSpaces(COLWIDTH - a[i].length())
                                  + aLabel[i] + "\n");
                        System.out.println(a[i]
                                  + appendSpaces(COLWIDTH - a[i].length())
                                  + aLabel[i]);
                    }
                }
            }
            strbuf.append("\n");
            System.out.println();
        }

        // Print spaces.
        static String appendSpaces(int count) {
            String strTmp = "";
            for (int i = 0; i < count; i++) {
                strTmp = strTmp + " ";
            }
            return strTmp;
        }
    }
```

Output

```
> java Main
No Decomposition:  (Do not use this mode)
u          \u00b5 - MICRON SIGN
A          \u0041 - LATIN CAPITAL LETTER A
abc        a b c
Abc        A b c
Àbc        A-grave b c
Ábc        A-acute b c
Äbc        A-umlaut b c
àbc        a-grave b c
ábc        a-acute b c
äbc        a-umlaut b c
?          \u03bc - GREEK SMALL LETTER MU
?          \u30ab - KATAKANA LETTER KA
?          \uff21 - FULLWIDTH CAPITAL LETTER A
?          \uff76 - HALFWIDTH KATAKANA LETTER KA

Canonical Decomposition:  ----------------
u          \u00b5 - MICRON SIGN
A          \u0041 - LATIN CAPITAL LETTER A
abc        a b c
Abc        A b c
ábc        a-acute b c
Ábc        A-acute b c
àbc        a-grave b c
```

```
Àbc       A-grave b c
äbc       a-umlaut b c
Äbc       A-umlaut b c
?         \u03bc - GREEK SMALL LETTER MU
?         \u30ab - KATAKANA LETTER KA
?         \uff21 - FULLWIDTH CAPITAL LETTER A
?         \uff76 - HALFWIDTH KATAKANA LETTER KA

Full Decomposition:  --------------------
A         \u0041 - LATIN CAPITAL LETTER A
?         \uff21 - FULLWIDTH CAPITAL LETTER A
abc       a b c
Abc       A b c
ábc       a-acute b c
Ábc       A-acute b c
àbc       a-grave b c
Àbc       A-grave b c
äbc       a-umlaut b c
Äbc       A-umlaut b c
?         \u03bc - GREEK SMALL LETTER MU
u         \u00b5 - MICRON SIGN
?         \u30ab - KATAKANA LETTER KA
?         \uff76 - HALFWIDTH KATAKANA LETTER KA
```

A B C D E F G H I J K L M N O P Q R S T U V W X Y Z

setStrength()

PURPOSE Sets the minimum level of difference considered significant during comparison.

SYNTAX `public synchronized void setStrength(int strength)`

DESCRIPTION This method sets this collator's strength property. The strength property determines the minimum level of difference between two strings considered significant during comparison.

PARAMETERS

`strength` A new strength value. Valid values are the static constants `PRIMARY`, `SECONDARY`, `TERTIARY`, and `IDENTICAL`.

EXCEPTIONS

`IllegalArgumentException`

If the new strength value is not valid.

SEE ALSO `getStrength()`, `PRIMARY`, `SECONDARY`, `TERTIARY`, `IDENTICAL`.

EXAMPLE This example performs sorting with different values of strength to demonstrate how the sort can differ.

```
import java.text.Collator;
import java.util.Locale;

class Main {
```

```
    public static void main(String args[]) {
        Locale loc = Locale.FRENCH;

        // Create an instance of a subclass of collator.
        Collator collator = Collator.getInstance(loc);

        int[] strengths = {  Collator.PRIMARY,
                             Collator.SECONDARY,
                             Collator.TERTIARY
                          // Collator.IDENTICAL  // BUG: Throws exception
                          };

        // Set up strings to sort.
        String[] array = new String[] {
            "Äbc",
            "äbc",
            "Àbc",
            "àbc",
            "Ábc",
            "ábc ",
            "Abc",
            "abc"
        };

        for (int i=0; i < strengths.length; i++) {
            collator.setStrength(strengths[i]);
            System.out.print("Strength: ");
            System.out.println(collator.getStrength());

            // Sort and print the string array.
            sortArray(collator, array);
            printArray(array);
        }
    }

    // Sort strings.
    public static void sortArray(Collator collator, String[] strArray) {
        String tmp;
        // Sort the string array.
        for (int i = 0; i < strArray.length; i++) {
            for (int j = i + 1; j < strArray.length; j++) {
                // Compare members of the array two at a time.
                if( collator.compare(strArray[i], strArray[j] ) > 0 ) {
                    //swap strArray[i] and strArray[j]
                    tmp = strArray[i];
                    strArray[i] = strArray[j];
                    strArray[j] = tmp;
                }
            }
        }
    }

    // Print the contents of a 1-dimensional array
    static void printArray(String[] a) {
        for (int i = 0; i < a.length; i++) {
            if (a[i].length() == 0) {
                System.out.println("(empty)" + "  ");
            } else {
                if (a[i] == null) {
                    System.out.println("(null)" + "  ");
```

```
                } else {
                    System.out.println(a[i] + "  ");
                }
            }
        }
        System.out.println();
    }
}
```

Output

```
>java Main
Strength: 0
Äbc
äbc
Àbc
àbc
Ábc
ábc
Abc
abc

Strength: 1
Abc
abc
Ábc
àbc
Àbc
äbc
Äbc
ábc

Strength: 2
abc
Abc
Ábc
àbc
Àbc
äbc
Äbc
ábc
```

TERTIARY

PURPOSE Indicates comparisons should consider only tertiary and greater differences.

SYNTAX `public final static int TERTIARY`

DESCRIPTION This constant is a strength value for collators that indicates that only tertiary and greater differences are considered significant during comparison. The assignment of strengths to language features is locale-dependent. A common example is for case differences (“a” versus “A”) to be considered a TERTIARY difference. The integer value of TERTIARY is 2.

SEE ALSO `setStrength()`, `getStrength()`.

EXAMPLE See `setStrength()`.

java.lang
Compiler

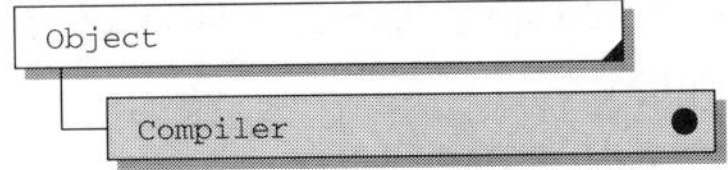

Syntax

```
public final class Compiler
```

Description

The `Compiler` class is used to control a compiler that compiles Java byte codes directly into machine code for a particular platform. Such a compiler is not included in the Java Development Kit (JDK) from Sun Microsystems, Inc.; it must be obtained from a third-party source.

If the system property `java.compiler` exists, it defines the name of the library that contains the compiler. The value of the `java.compiler` property is passed into `System.loadLibary()` to load the library. When a class is compiled into machine code, the machine code is not returned. Rather, the Java runtime maintains the compiled machine code and runs it automatically whenever a method in the class is called.

MEMBER SUMMARY	
Compiler Methods	
`command()`	Sends a command to the compiler.
`compileClass()`	Compiles a class into machine code.
`compileClasses()`	Compiles classes by name into machine code.
`disable()`	Disables the compiler.
`enable()`	Enables the compiler.

command()

PURPOSE Sends a command to the compiler.

SYNTAX `public static native Object command(Object arg)`

DESCRIPTION This method allows an application to communicate with the compiler. Since different compilers will have different commands to which they respond, you need to read the documentation supplied by the compiler vendor to determine the commands that are available.

PARAMETERS

`arg` A compiler-specific argument.

RETURNS A compiler-specific return value. `null` is returned if the compiler is not loaded or is disabled.

SEE ALSO `disable()`, `enable()`.

A B C D E F G H I J K L M N O P Q R S T U V W X Y Z

compileClass()

PURPOSE Compiles a class into machine code.

SYNTAX `public static native boolean compileClass(Class oneClass)`

DESCRIPTION This method compiles the class `oneClass` into machine code.

PARAMETERS

`oneClass` The non-`null` class to compile.

RETURNS `true` if the compilation succeeds; `false` otherwise. `false` is also returned if the compiler is not loaded or is disabled.

SEE ALSO `disable()`, `enable()`.

compileClasses()

PURPOSE Compiles classes by name into machine code.

SYNTAX `public static native boolean compileClasses(String classNames)`

DESCRIPTION The string `classNames` specifies the names of the classes to compile. In the simple case, `classNames` names a single class. To name more than one class, check with the compiler documentation to determine how multiple class names are specified.

PARAMETERS

`classNames` The non-`null` string containing the name of the classes to compile.

RETURNS `true` if the compilation of all of the classes succeed; `false` otherwise. `false` is also returned if the compiler is not loaded or is disabled.

SEE ALSO `disable()`, `enable()`.

disable()

PURPOSE Disables the compiler.

SYNTAX `public static native void disable()`

DESCRIPTION This method disables the compiler. Once the compiler has been disabled, `command()` returns `null`, while `compileClass()` and `compileClasses()` return `false`.

SEE ALSO `command()`, `compileClass()`, `compileClasses()`.

enable()

PURPOSE Enables the compiler.

SYNTAX `public static native void enable()`

DESCRIPTION This method enables the compiler so that classes can be compiled.

SEE ALSO `command()`, `compileClass()`, `compileClasses()`.

ConnectException

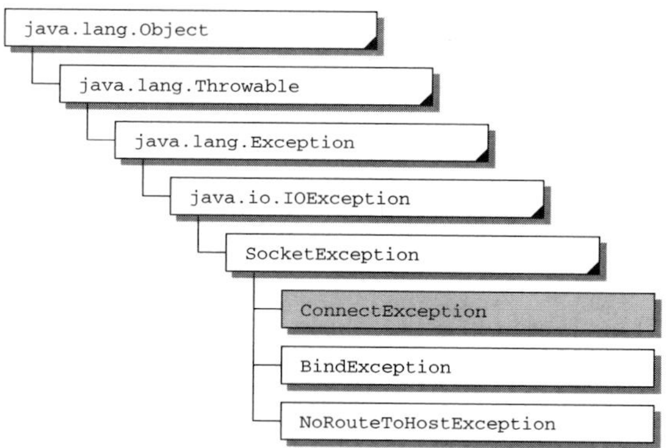

Syntax

`public class ConnectException extends SocketException`

Description

`ConnectException` is an exception that is thrown when the program attempts to connect a socket to a remote address and port. It indicates that the connection could not be established at the specified remote address and port, for example because no process was listening on the remote address/port.

MEMBER SUMMARY	
Constructor	
`ConnectException()`	Constructs a `ConnectException` instance.

See Also

`Socket.Socket()`, `SocketImpl.connect()`.

Example

This example connects to a unbound port on the local machine and gets a `ConnectException`.

```
import java.net.Socket;
import java.net.InetAddress;
import java.io.IOException;
import java.io.InputStream;
```

```
class Main {
  public static void main(String[] args) {
    System.out.println("ConnectionException example");
    try {
      // pick some random port number on local machine
      Socket sock = new Socket(InetAddress.getLocalHost(), 1997);

      InputStream in = sock.getInputStream();

      for (int ch = in.read(); ch >= 0; ch = in.read()) {
        System.out.print((char)(ch));
      }
    } catch (IOException e) {
      e.printStackTrace();
    }
  }
}
```


ConnectException()

PURPOSE Constructs a `ConnectException` instance.

SYNTAX `public ConnectException(String msg)`

DESCRIPTION The two forms of this constructor construct an instance of `ConnectException`. An optional string `msg` can be supplied that describes this particular instance of the exception. If `msg` is not supplied, it defaults to `null`.

PARAMETERS

`msg` A possibly `null` string that gives details about this exception.

SEE ALSO `java.lang.Throwable.getMessage()`.

Constructor

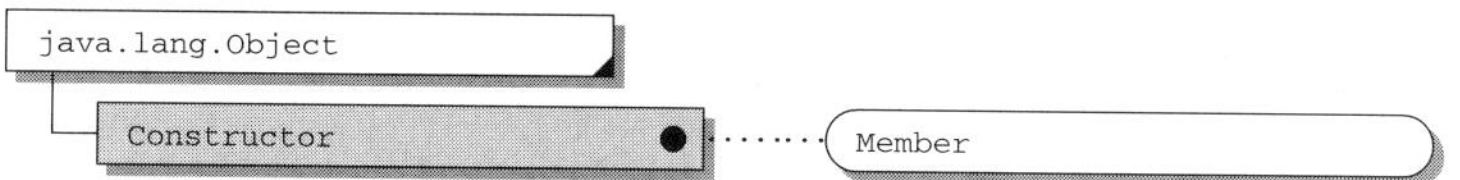

Syntax

```
public final class Constructor implements Member
```

Description

A `Constructor` object represents a constructor in a class. It can be used to discover the constructor's list of attributes—its name, set of modifiers, parameter types, and set of throwable exceptions. The `Constructor` object can also be used to create a new instance of the `Constructor` object's class that is exactly like the `new` operator.

Usage

This class cannot be instantiated (since you can't create a constructor). Instead, you need first to obtain a `Class` object for the class that has the desired constructor. For example,

```
Class.forName("java.awt.Point")
```

or

```
java.awt.Point.class
```

With this `Class` object, you then call one of the methods in Table 19 to obtain a `Constructor` object for the desired constructor.

Method	Description
`Class.getConstructor()`	Retrieves a `Constructor` object for a public constructor in a class.
`Class.getConstructors()`	Retrieves `Constructor` objects for all public constructors in a class.
`Class.getDeclaredConstructor()`	Retrieves a `Constructor` object for a constructor in a class.
`Class.getDeclaredConstructors()`	Retrieves a `Constructor` object for all constructors in a class.

TABLE 19: Getting a `Constructor` from a `Class` Object.

The Name

The name of a `Constructor` object is the string used to name the constructor in the source code. Unlike `Field` and `Method` objects, this method returns a fully qualified name. For example, the constructor signature of the `Point` class is

```
public Point()
```

and its name is `java.awt.Point`. All `Constructor` objects have a name.

The Modifiers

The modifiers of a constructor can be retrieved from a `Constructor` object by using `getModifiers()` and methods in the `Modifier` class. A constructor can have at most one access modifier—`public`, `protected`, or `private`. For example, in the following constructor signature, the modifier is `private`:

```
private Point()
```

The Parameter Types

The parameter types of a `Constructor` object are represented by an array of `Class` objects, one for each parameter. The first element of the array refers to the type of the first parameter, the second element refers to the type of the second parameter, and so on. For example, in the following constructor signature:

```
public Label(String text, int alignment)
```

an array with the following `Class` objects is produced:

```
java.lang.String.class, int.class
```

The Exception Types

The exception types of a `Constructor` object are represented by an array of `Class` objects, one for each declared exception. For example, in the following constructor signature:

```
public C() throws IllegalAccessException,
                  IllegalArgumentException, InvocationTargetException
```

an array with the following `Class` objects is produced:

```
java.lang.IllegalAccessException.class,
java.lang.IllegalArgumentException.class,
java.lang.reflect.InvocationTargetException.class
```

The order of the elements in the array does not necessarily match the order in which the exceptions are declared.

The Declaring Class

Unlike fields and methods, a constructor cannot be inherited. Hence, the declaring class of a `Constructor` object is always the `Class` object used to create the `Constructor` object. For example, in the following example the declaring class for the `C()` constructor is `C.class`:

```
class C {
    public C(int i) {
    }
}
```


MEMBER SUMMARY

Creation Method	
`newInstance()`	Creates an instance of this `Constructor` object's class.
Get Attribute Methods	
`getDeclaringClass()`	Retrieves this `Constructor` object's declaring `Class` object.
`getExceptionTypes()`	Retrieves this `Constructor` object's list of declared exceptions.
`getModifiers()`	Retrieves the `Constructor` modifiers for this `Constructor` object.
`getName()`	Retrieves this `Constructor` object's fully qualified name.
`getParameterTypes()`	Retrieves the type of each parameter in this `Constructor` object's parameter list.
Object Methods	
`equals()`	Compares this `Constructor` object with another `Constructor` object.
`hashCode()`	Computes the hash code for this `Constructor` object.
Debugging Method	
`toString()`	Generates a string representing this `Constructor` object.

See Also

`java.lang.Class`, `Modifier`.

Example

This example demonstrates how to retrieve a `Constructor` object which reflects a constructor with no arguments, use it to instantiate that constructor's class, and then serialize the object.

```
import java.lang.reflect.*;
import java.io.*;
```

```
class Main {
    Main(Class c) {
        Constructor con = null;
        Object obj = null;

        // Get the constructor that takes no arguments
        try {
            con = c.getConstructor(new Class[] {});
        } catch (NoSuchMethodException e) {
            System.out.println(
                "\nThere is no constructor that takes no arguments.");
            return;
        }

        // Another way of getting the constructor with no arguments
        boolean found = false;
        Constructor[] cons = c.getConstructors();
        for (int i=0; i<cons.length && !found; i++) {
            if (cons[i].getParameterTypes().length == 0) {
                con = cons[i];
                found = true;
            }
        }
        if (!found) {
            System.out.println(
                "\nThere is no constructor that takes no arguments.");
            return;
        }

        try {
            // Now create object.
            obj = con.newInstance(new Object[] {});
        } catch (InstantiationException e) {
            e.printStackTrace();
            return;
        } catch (InvocationTargetException e) {
            e.getTargetException().printStackTrace();
            return;
        } catch (IllegalAccessException e) {
            e.printStackTrace();
            return;
        }

        try {
            // Print message
            System.out.print(
                "Serializing " + con.getDeclaringClass().getName()
                + " to " + con.getName() + ".ser ... ");

            ObjectOutputStream os = new ObjectOutputStream(
                new FileOutputStream(con.getName() + ".ser"));
            os.writeObject(obj);
            os.close();

            System.out.println("done");
        } catch (IOException e) {
            e.printStackTrace();
        }
    }
```

```
    public static void main(String[] args) {
        if (args.length != 1) {
            System.err.println("Usage: java Main <classname>");
        } else {
            try {
                new Main(Class.forName(args[0]));
            } catch (ClassNotFoundException e) {
                e.printStackTrace();
            }
        }
    }
}
```

Output

```
> java Main java.lang.reflect.Constructor
The is no constructor that takes no arguments.
> java Main java.awt.Point
Serializing java.awt.Point to java.awt.Point.ser ... done
```

equals()

PURPOSE Compares this `Constructor` object with another `Constructor` object.

SYNTAX `public boolean equals(Object obj)`

DESCRIPTION Two `Constructor` objects are equal only if they both refer to exactly the same constructor in the same class.

PARAMETERS

`obj` A possibly `null` `Constructor` object.

OVERRIDES `java.lang.Object.equals()`.

SEE ALSO `hashCode()`.

EXAMPLE This example demonstrates that two `Constructor` objects created on the same constructor cannot be compared for equality by comparing their references.

```
import java.lang.reflect.*;

class Main {
    public static void main(String[] args) {
        try {
            Constructor c0 = C.class.getConstructor(new Class[] {});
            Constructor c1 = C.class.getConstructor(new Class[] {});

            System.out.println("c0 == c1:       " + (c0==c1));         // false
            System.out.println("c0.equals(c1): " + (c0.equals(c1))); // true
        } catch (NoSuchMethodException ext) {
            ext.printStackTrace();
        }
    }
}

class C {
    public C() {}
}
```

getDeclaringClass()

PURPOSE Retrieves this `Constructor` object's declaring class object.

SYNTAX `public Class getDeclaringClass()`

DESCRIPTION Unlike fields and methods, a constructor cannot be inherited. Hence, the declaring class of a `Constructor` object is always the `Class` object used to create the `Constructor` object.

The name of the `Constructor` object's declaring class is always identical to the `Constructor` object's name.

RETURNS The non-`null` declaring class object of this `Constructor` object.

EXAMPLE See the class example.

getExceptionTypes()

PURPOSE Retrieves this `Constructor` object's list of declared exceptions.

SYNTAX `public Class[] getExceptionTypes()`

RETURNS A non-`null` array with a length equal to the number of declared exceptions in this constructor.

EXAMPLE

```
import java.lang.reflect.*;
import java.util.NoSuchElementException;

class Main {
    public static void main(String[] args) {
        Constructor[] cons = ClassX.class.getConstructors();

        // Scan each method.
        for (int i=0; i<cons.length; i++) {
            Class[] es = cons[i].getExceptionTypes();

            // Print out each exception
            for (int j=0; j<es.length; j++) {
                System.out.println(es[j]);
            }
        }
    }
}

class ClassX {
    public ClassX() throws NoSuchElementException, IllegalArgumentException {
    }
}
```

Output

```
> java Main
class java.util.NoSuchElementException
class java.lang.IllegalArgumentException
```


getModifiers()

PURPOSE Retrieves the `Constructor` modifiers for this `Constructor` object.

SYNTAX `public native int getModifiers()`

DESCRIPTION This method retrieves this `Constructor` object's set of constructor modifiers, bit-encoded in an `int`. The possible constructor modifiers are `public`, `protected`, and `private`. To process the encoding, use the methods and constants in `Modifier`.

RETURNS An `int` representing the `Constructor` object's set of modifiers.

SEE ALSO `Modifier`.

EXAMPLE See the class example.

getName()

PURPOSE Retrieves this `Constructor` object's fully qualified name.

SYNTAX `public String getName()`

DESCRIPTION The name of a `Constructor` object is the string used to name the constructor in the source code. This name is the same as the name of the `Constructor` object's declaring class. Unlike with `Field` and `Method` objects, this method retrieves a fully qualified name.

RETURNS A non-`null` string containing this `Constructor` object's name.

EXAMPLE See the class example.

getParameterTypes()

PURPOSE Retrieves the type of each parameter in this `Constructor` object's parameter list.

SYNTAX `public Class[] getParameterTypes()`

DESCRIPTION This method retrieves an array containing one `Class` object for each of this constructor's parameters. The first element of the resulting array refers to the type of the first parameter, the second element refers to the type of the second parameter, and so on.

RETURNS A non-`null` array with a length equal to the number of parameters in this constructor.

EXAMPLE See the class example.

hashCode()

PURPOSE Computes the hash code for this `Constructor` object.

SYNTAX `public int hashCode()`

DESCRIPTION The `Constructor` object's hash code is an integer calculated from the `Constructor` object's declaring class name. Two equal `Constructor` objects will have the same hash code. However, unequal `Constructor` objects might also have the same hash code, although the hash code algorithm minimizes this possibility. The hash code is typically used as the key in a hash table.

RETURNS The `Constructor` object's hash code.

OVERRIDES `java.lang.Object.hashCode()`.

SEE ALSO `equals(), java.util.Hashtable`.

EXAMPLE This example creates a `Constructor` object and inserts it into a hash table.

```
import java.awt.*;
import java.util.*;
import java.lang.reflect.*;

class Main {
    public static void main(String[] args) {
        Hashtable ht = new Hashtable();
        try {
            Constructor f = Point.class.getConstructor(new Class[] {});
            ht.put(f, f);
        } catch (NoSuchMethodException e) {
            e.printStackTrace();
        }
    }
}
```

newInstance()

PURPOSE
Creates an instance of this `Constructor` object's class.

SYNTAX
```
public native Object newInstance(Object[] args) throws
   InstantiationException, IllegalAccessException,
   IllegalArgumentException, InvocationTargetException
```

DESCRIPTION
This method is used to create an instance of this `Constructor` object's declaring class.

`args` contains the values to be passed as arguments to the constructor. The length must be equal to the number of parameters accepted by the constructor. If a parameter type is an object reference, the type of the corresponding value in `args` must be assignable to the parameter type. If a parameter type is primitive, the corresponding value in `args` must be an object wrapper of the appropriate type. When the value is unwrapped, it may be automatically widened. For example, if the type of the second parameter is `int`, `args[1]` must be an `Integer`, a `Short`, a `Character`, or a `Byte`. If `args[1]` is a `Short`, a `Character`, or a `Byte`, its unwrapped value is automatically widened to an `int`. More information about valid widening conversions are described in Table 27 in the `Field` class and *The Java Language Specification, First Edition*, Section 5.1.4. Automatic narrowing conversions are never done. If an attempt to widen a value to a parameter type fails, an `IllegalArgumentException` is thrown.

If the constructor throws an exception, this method wraps the exception with `InvocationTargetException` and throws it. You can retrieve the exception that was thrown by the constructor by calling `InvocationTargetException.getTargetException()`.

`newInstance()` does not use the types of the arguments to select an overloading. It is always invoked on a specific overloading of the constructor, previously selected by a call to `getConstructor()` or other means. The reflection package does not automatically choose between overloadings.

When `newInstance()` is called, the Java virtual machine performs the access checks described in *The Java Language Specification, First Edition*, Section 6.6.1. These checks compare the identity of the caller of `newInstance()` with the access permission and identity of the constructor being called. It is as if the caller of `newInstance()` had a statically-compiled call to the selected constructor. The access check takes into account both the accessibility of the constructor itself and the accessibility of its class.

PARAMETERS

`args`
The non-`null` array containing the argument values to be passed to the constructor.

RETURNS A new non-null instance of this Constructor object's declaring class.

EXCEPTIONS

IllegalAccessException
If the calling class does not have permission to call this constructor.

IllegalArgumentException
If this Constructor object's class does not inherit or declare this constructor, or if args is not compatible with the constructor's parameter type list.

InstantiationException
If the constructor's class is abstract.

InvocationTargetException
If the constructor throws an exception.

SEE ALSO InvocationTargetException.getTargetException().

EXAMPLE This example demonstrates how to create a Constructor object and how to create an object using the Constructor object.

```
import java.lang.reflect.*;

class Main {
    public static void main(String[] args) {
        try {
            // Demonstrate that if a class does not define any constructors,
            // a constructor without any parameters is automatically defined.
            Constructor cons = C.class.getDeclaredConstructor(new Class[] {});
            C c = (C)cons.newInstance(new Object[] {});

            // Demonstrate that a value must be wrapped in an object wrapper
            // if the parameter type is primitive.
            cons = D.class.getDeclaredConstructor(new Class[] {int.class});
            D d = (D)cons.newInstance(new Object[] {new Integer(0)});

            // Demonstrate that a byte parameter is automatically
            // widened to an int.
            d = (D)cons.newInstance(new Object[] {new Byte((byte)0)});

            // Demonstrate how to handle an exception thrown by the constructor.
            d = (D)cons.newInstance(new Object[] {new Integer(-1)});
        } catch (InstantiationException e) {
            e.printStackTrace();
        } catch (InvocationTargetException e) {
            e.getTargetException().printStackTrace();
        } catch (IllegalAccessException e) {
            e.printStackTrace();
        } catch (NoSuchMethodException e) {
            e.printStackTrace();
        }
    }
}

class C {
}
class D {
    D(int i) throws IllegalArgumentException {
```

```
            if (i < 0) {
                throw new IllegalArgumentException();
            }
        }
    }
```


toString()

PURPOSE — Generates a string representing this `Constructor` object.

SYNTAX — `public String toString()`

DESCRIPTION — This method generates a string containing this `Constructor` object's set of modifiers, fully qualified name, parameter types, and declared exceptions. The order of the modifiers matches the canonical order as defined in *The Java Language Specification*. The canonical ordering is `public`, `protected`, and `private`.

OVERRIDES — `java.lang.Object.toString()`.

EXAMPLE — This example implements a program that takes a fully qualified class name, instantiates it, and prints out all of its constructors. Note that `getDeclaredConstructors()` retrieves all public, protected, private and default (package) access constructors and hence is subject to access checks by the security manager. Therefore an example such as this may not work in applets.

```
import java.lang.reflect.*;
import java.io.*;
import java.util.*;

class Main {
    Main(Class c) {
        Constructor cons[] = c.getDeclaredConstructors();

        for (int i=0; i<cons.length; i++) {
            System.out.println(cons[i].toString());
        }
    }

    public static void main(String[] args) {
        if (args.length != 1) {
            System.err.println("Usage: java Main <classname>");
        } else {
            try {
                new Main(Class.forName(args[0]));
            } catch (ClassNotFoundException e) {
                e.printStackTrace();
            }
        }
    }
}
```

Output

```
> java Main java.lang.String
public java.lang.String()
public java.lang.String(java.lang.String)
public java.lang.String(char[])
public java.lang.String(char[],int,int)
public java.lang.String(byte[],int,int,int)
public java.lang.String(byte[],int)
private java.lang.String(byte[],int,int,sun.io.ByteToCharConverter)
public java.lang.String(byte[],int,int,java.lang.String)
    throws java.io.UnsupportedEncodingException
public java.lang.String(byte[],java.lang.String)
    throws java.io.UnsupportedEncodingException
public java.lang.String(byte[],int,int)
public java.lang.String(byte[])
public java.lang.String(java.lang.StringBuffer)
private java.lang.String(int,int,char[])
```

ContentHandler

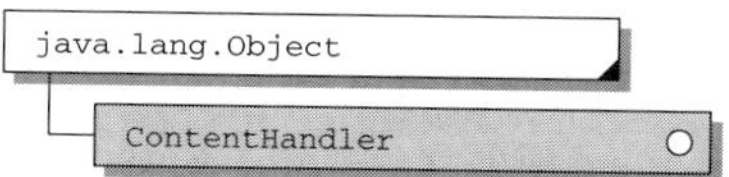

Syntax

```
abstract public class ContentHandler
```

Description

A *content handler* is responsible for converting a document of a certain format into a Java object. For example, there is a content handler responsible for converting a GIF file into an `Image` object. The different content handlers available are platform-dependent. Content handlers are created by a *content handler factory* (see `ContentHandlerFactory`).

Usage

Content handlers are typically not used directly by programs. If you use `URL.getContent()` or `URLConnection.getContent()`, these methods will automatically create the content handler corresponding to the document named by the URL and return to you an object that represents the contents of the document.

Document Header and Content Type

Each document returned by an HTTP server has a document header. This header describes various properties about the document's contents (see *RFC 2045*). One such property is the document's *content type*, which describes the format of the document. The content type—also referred to as the *MIME type*—is specified using MIME (*RFC 2046*) and consists of a media type and a subtype. For example, an HTML document has a content type "text/html" consisting of the media type "text" and subtype "html", while a movie might have a content type of "video/mpeg" consisting of the media type "video" and subtype "mpeg".

Content Handler Factory

A content handler factory is responsible for creating a content handler for a document by using the document's content type. The factory decides which subclass of `ContentHandler` to create by examining the content type of the document read from the HTTP server. For example, if the content type is "text/html", the factory will create a content handler that reads an HTML document and returns a `String` object. If the content type is "video/mpeg", the factory will create a content handler that reads the image and returns an `Image` object. The policy for determining which content handler to create is determined by the factory.

The application can set the content handler factory that is to be to used (if permitted by the security manager) by using `URLConnection.setContentHandlerFactory()`. If no factory has been set, the system uses the default policy for creating content handlers described in the next section. There is no "default" content handler factory object that you can access; `URLConnection.getContent()` basically implements the default policy described here.

There can be only one content handler factory installed in an application at any one time. Once installed, the content handler factory cannot be replaced.

Default Policy for Creating Content Handlers

If no content handler factory has been installed, the system searches for a class with the class name

packagePrefix "." *mediaType* "." *subType*

packagePrefix is obtained from the system property `java.content.handler.pkgs`, which is a |-separated list of package prefixes. If the class is not found using these prefixes, the package prefix `sun.net.www.content` is tried. For example, if the `java.content.handler.pkgs` system property contains "com.widget.content|com.wiz" and the content type is "image/gif", the system would attempt to load each of the following classes in turn until one is successfully instantiated:

```
com.widget.content.image.gif
com.wiz.image.gif
sun.net.www.content.image.gif
```

If no class can be instantiated this way, the system returns a content handler for dealing with unknown content types. The content handler returns as the object the input stream for reading the document.

This default policy allows an application to create its own content handlers, add them to the application's class path, and have them be used when `URL.getContent()` or `URLConnection.getContent()` is invoked.

Turning Document Data into a Java Object

Once a content handler has been created, either by using a content handler factory or by using the system's default policy, the `getContent()` method is invoked on it with the URL connection from which to get the document as the argument. How the content handler uses the URL connection is implementation-specific to the content handler. Typically, the process involves reading from the input stream associated with the connection.

MEMBER SUMMARY	
Communication Method	
`getContent()`	Generates an object by reading its representation from a URL connection.

See Also

`ContentHandlerFactory`, `URL`, `URLConnection.getContent()`.

Example

This example shows an implementation of a content handler that reads the contents from the connection and returns the contents read in the form of a string. See related examples in `ContentHandlerFactory` and `URLConnection.setContentHandlerFactory()`.

```
import java.net.*;
import java.io.*;

// Content handler that reads input stream and returns a String
class SimpleStringHandler extends ContentHandler {
    public Object getContent(URLConnection conn) throws IOException {
        InputStream input = conn.getInputStream();
        StringBuffer buf = new StringBuffer();
        int c;
        while ((c = input.read()) >= 0) {
            buf.append((char) c);
        }
        input.close();
        return (buf.toString());
    }
}
```

getContent()

PURPOSE Generates an object by reading its representation from a URL connection.

SYNTAX

```
abstract public Object getContent(URLConnection urlconn) throws
   IOException
```

DESCRIPTION This method reads, from the URL connection `urlconn`, the representation of an object whose type is expected by this particular `ContentHandler` class. If the representation is not in the correct format expected for this particular `ContentHandler` class, an `IOException` is thrown.

This method is invoked by `URLConnection.getContent()` on the content handler. It is not invoked directly by the application.

PARAMETERS

`urlconn` The URL connection from which to read the object.

EXCEPTIONS

`IOException`

If the object is not in the format expected by this content handler or if an IO error occurred while the object was being read.

SEE ALSO `ContentHandlerFactory`, `URL`, `URL.getContent()`, `URLConnection.getContent()`.

EXAMPLE See the class example.

ContentHandlerFactory

ContentHandlerFactory

Syntax

```
public interface ContentHandlerFactory
```

Description

A *content handler factory* is responsible for creating *content handlers*, which are objects that convert documents into Java objects. For example, there is a content handler responsible for converting a GIF file into an `Image` object. The different content handlers available are platform-dependent.

Usage

An application such as a Web browser installs a content handler factory in order to control the type of content handler created for different types of documents. It does this by creating an object that implements the `ContentHandlerFactory` interface and installing the interface, as follows:

```
ContentHandlerFactory factory = new SampleFactory();
URLConnection.setContentHandlerFactory(factory);
```

Subsequent invocations of `URL.getContent()` or `URLConnection.getContent()` will automatically create content handlers using this factory.

Document Header and Content Type

Each document returned by an HTTP server has a document header. This header describes various properties about the document's contents (see *RFC 2045*). One such property is the document's *content type*, which describes the format of the document. The content type—also referred to as the *MIME type*—is specified using MIME (*RFC 2046*) and consists of a media type and a subtype. For example, an HTML document has a content type "text/html" consisting of the media type "text" and subtype "html", while a movie might have a content type of "video/mpeg" consisting of the media type "video" and subtype "mpeg".

Content Handler Factory

A content handler factory creates a content handler for a document by using its content type. The factory decides which subclass of `ContentHandler` to create by examining the content type of the document read from the HTTP server. For example, if the content type is "text/html", the factory will create a content handler that reads an HTML document and returns a `String` object. If the content type is "video/mpeg", the factory will create a content handler that reads the image and returns an `Image` object. The policy of which content handler to create is determined by the factory.

The application can set the content handler factory that is to be used (if permitted by the security manager) by using `URLConnection.setContentHandlerFactory()`. If no factory has been set, the system uses the default policy for creating content handlers described in the class description of `ContentHandler`. There is no "default" content handler factory object that you can access; `URLConnection.getContent()` basically implements the default policy described here.

There can be only one content handler factory installed in a program at any one time. Once installed, the content handler factory cannot be replaced.

MEMBER SUMMARY	
Handler Creation Method	
`createContentHandler()`	Creates a content handler for documents of a content type.

See Also

`ContentHandler`, `URL`, `URLConnection.setContentHandlerFactory()`, `URLStreamHandler`.

Example

The following is an example of a `ContentHandlerFactory` implementation. See related examples in `ContentHandler` and `URLConnection.setContentHandlerFactory()`.

```
class SampleFactory implements ContentHandlerFactory {
    Hashtable handlers = new Hashtable();
    static private ContentHandler defaultHandler = new SimpleStringHandler();

    // Construct class name for content handler for contentType
    // "majorType/minorTYpe" -> majorType.minorType
    private String mapContentTypeToClassName(String contentType) {
        int len = contentType.length();
        char className[] = new char[len];
        contentType.getChars(0, len, className, 0);
        for (int j = 0; j < len; j++) {
            char c = className[j];
            // turn '/' to '.'; nonletter and nondigits to '_'
            if (c == '/') {
                className[j] = '.';
            } else if (!Character.isLetterOrDigit(c)) {
                className[j] = '_';
            }
        }
        return (new String(className));
    }

    public ContentHandler createContentHandler(String contentType) {
        ContentHandler handler = null;
        if (contentType == null)
```

A B C D E F G H I J K L M N O P Q R S T U V W X Y Z

```
                return defaultHandler;        // no type specified

            // Check cache first
            handler = (ContentHandler)handlers.get(contentType);
            if (handler != null)
                return handler;

            // Get class name from content
            String className = mapContentTypeToClassName(contentType);
            try {
                handler = (ContentHandler)Class.forName(className).newInstance();
            } catch(Exception e) {
                // cannot get handler, just use default
                handler = defaultHandler;
            }

            // Add newly found handler to cache
            handlers.put(contentType, handler);
            return handler;
        }
    }
```


createContentHandler()

PURPOSE Creates a content handler for documents of a content type.

SYNTAX `ContentHandler createContentHandler(String contentType)`

DESCRIPTION This method creates a new content handler for processing documents with the content type `contentType`. Content type is described in the class description. If no content handler can be created for `contentType`, this method returns `null`.

This method is invoked by `URLConnection.getContent()` on the installed content handler factory. It is not invoked directly by the application.

PARAMETERS

`contentType` A non-`null` string containing the content type for which to create the content handler.

RETURNS A new content handler for `contentType`; `null` if cannot create content handler for `contentType`.

SEE ALSO `ContentHandler`, `URL`, `URL.getContent()`, `URLConnection.getContent()`.

EXAMPLE See the class example.

CRC32

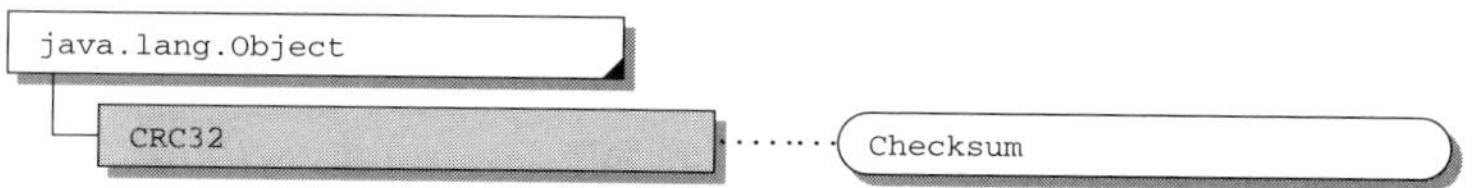

A B C D E F G H I J K L M N O P Q R S T U V W X Y Z

Syntax

```
public class CRC32 implements Checksum
```

Description

The CRC-32 class implements the CRC-32 algorithm, which is used to produce a checksum value on a stream of data. See Checksum for more information on checksums. The CRC-32 algorithm is specified in the documents *ISO 3309* (Section 8.1.1.6.2) and *ITU-T V.42*. http://www.iso.ch contains information for ordering ISO documents.

The java.util.zip package provides implementations for two different checksum algorithms: ADLER-32 (see Adler32) and CRC-32. The CRC-32 algorithm produces better-quality checksum values, but the ADLER-32 algorithm is faster.

Usage

To use this class to compute the checksum of a data set, you first must create an instance of this class. You then must call the new object's update() method with every byte of the data set. It is important to be consistent with the order of the bytes supplied to update(). Supplying the bytes in a different order will produce a different checksum. After all of the bytes have been given to update(), you call getValue() to retrieve the checking value. To compute the checksum of another set of data, you can either create a new CRC32 object or simply call the object's reset() method.

This class is typically used in conjunction with the CheckedInputStream and CheckedOutputStream classes, which make it convenient to compute the checksum on streaming data. See these classes for examples.

MEMBER SUMMARY	
Constructor	
CRC32()	Constructs a CRC32 instance.
Checksum Methods	
getValue()	Retrieves the current checksum value.
reset()	Resets this object to its initial state.
update()	Updates the checksum with one or more bytes.

See Also

Adler32, CheckedInputStream, CheckedOutputStream, Checksum.

Example

This example runs both the ADLER-32 and CRC-32 checksum algorithms on a file. Both the checksum result and the time it took to run the checksum algorithm is returned.

```
import java.io.*;
import java.util.zip.*;

class Main {
    static long getChecksumValue(Checksum checksum, String fname) {
        try {
            BufferedInputStream is = new BufferedInputStream(
                new FileInputStream(fname));
            byte[] bytes = new byte[1024];
            int len = 0;

            // Read the file and compute the checksum.
            while ((len = is.read(bytes)) >= 0) {
                checksum.update(bytes, 0, len);
            }
            is.close();
        } catch (IOException e) {
            e.printStackTrace();
        }
        return checksum.getValue();
    }
    public static void main(String[] args) {
        if (args.length != 1) {
            System.err.println("Usage: java Main <file>");
            System.exit(1);
        }

        // Measure the performance of CRC32.
        long time = System.currentTimeMillis();
        long cv = getChecksumValue(new CRC32(), args[0]);
        time = System.currentTimeMillis() - time;
        System.out.println("crc32");
        System.out.println("    checksum: " + cv);
        System.out.println("    time    : " + time + "ms");

        // Measure the performance of Adler32.
        time = System.currentTimeMillis();
        cv = getChecksumValue(new Adler32(), args[0]);
        time = System.currentTimeMillis() - time;
        System.out.println("adler32");
        System.out.println("    checksum: " + cv);
        System.out.println("    time    : " + time + "ms");
    }
}
```

Output

```
crc32
    checksum: 2964640970
    time    : 5270ms
```

```
adler32
    checksum: 2851388021
    time    : 3240ms
```

CRC32()

PURPOSE Constructs a CRC32 instance.

SYNTAX `public CRC32()`

DESCRIPTION The checksum value of a new CRC32 instance is 0.

EXAMPLE See the class example.

getValue()

PURPOSE Retrieves the current checksum value.

SYNTAX `public long getValue()`

DESCRIPTION Each time update() is called, the checksum value maintained by this object is updated. This method returns the current value of the checksum.

RETURNS The current checksum value.

EXAMPLE See the class example.

reset()

PURPOSE Resets this object to its initial state.

SYNTAX `public void reset()`

DESCRIPTION After this object is used to compute a checksum value for a data set, it can be reused by calling this method. The program first calls reset() to reset the checksum's value (to 0) and then calls update() on the bytes of the new data set.

EXAMPLE See the class example.

update()

PURPOSE Updates the checksum with one or more bytes.

SYNTAX `public void update(int bval)`

```
public void update(byte[] buf)
public native void update(byte[] buf, int off, int len)
```

DESCRIPTION Calling this method updates the current checksum value with the byte value bval or the bytes in buf. If buf is specified, only len bytes starting from buf[off] are used to update the checksum value. If off is not specified, it defaults to 0. If len is not specified, it defaults to buf.length.

PARAMETERS

buf A non-null array of byte values.

bval A byte value. Only the low-order byte of bval is used.

len The number of bytes to use starting from buf[off]. 0 ≤ len ≤ buf.length-off.

off The 0-based index of the first byte in buf to use. 0 ≤ off < buf.length.

EXAMPLE See the class example.

DataFormatException

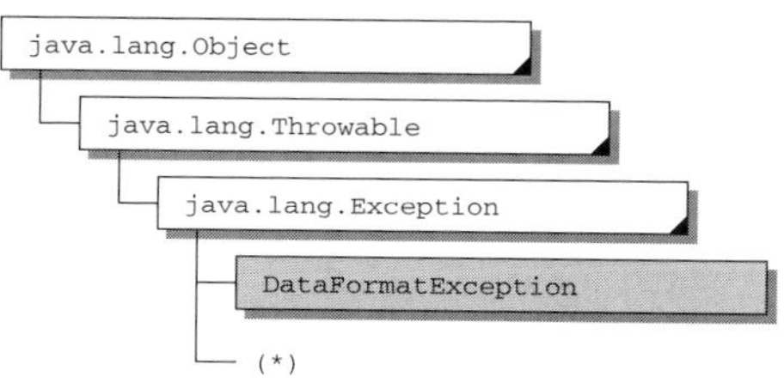

(*) 28 classes from other packages not shown.

Syntax

```
public class DataFormatException extends Exception
```

Description

The `DataFormatException` exception is thrown by the `Inflater` class if the compressed data is invalid or has been corrupted.

MEMBER SUMMARY	
Constructor	
`DataFormatException()`	Constructs a `DataFormatException` instance.

See Also

`Inflater`.

Example

This example is a simple demonstration of how a `DataFormatException` can be thrown by the `Inflater` class. An invalid buffer of data is given to the inflater. When an attempt is made to read the decompressed data, the inflater discovers that the input is invalid and throws the exception.

```
import java.util.zip.*;

class Main {
    public static void main(String[] args) {
        Inflater inf = new Inflater();
        byte[] buf = new byte[]{'0', '1', '2'};

        inf.setInput(buf);
```

```
            try {
                inf.inflate(buf);
            } catch (DataFormatException e) {
                System.err.println("The compressed data is invalid");
            }
        }
    }
```


DataFormatException()

PURPOSE Constructs a `DataFormatException` instance.

SYNTAX
```
public DataFormatException()
public DataFormatException(String msg)
```

DESCRIPTION This constructor constructs an instance of `DataFormatException`. An optional string `msg` can be supplied that describes this particular instance of the exception. If `msg` is not supplied, it defaults to `null`.

PARAMETERS

`msg` A possibly `null` message containing details that caused the exception.

SEE ALSO `java.lang.Throwable.getMessage()`.

DatagramPacket

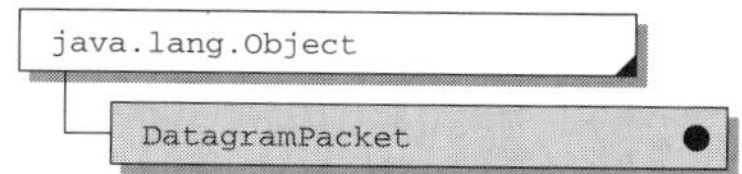

Syntax

```
public final class DatagramPacket
```

Description

All protocols can be classified as either *connection-oriented* or *connectionless*. In a connection-oriented protocol, a *connection* is established between the communicating parties such that data sent from one party to the other party is received in the same order in which it was sent. Furthermore, that data behaves like a *stream*. That is, if any piece of data—called a *packet*—is lost in transmission, the sending party will retransmit that packet to ensure that the receiver gets it. The sending and receiving parties keep track of what packets have been sent and received, thus maintaining a logical stream of the data.

In a connectionless protocol, no state is kept about each packet that is sent. The receiver cannot tell whether a packet is missing or whether a packet has been received twice. Each packet—called a *datagram packet*—is a separate, self-contained unit that has no relationship to other packets being sent and received. Data sent between the communicating parties is limited to the size of the datagram packet.

The `DatagramPacket` class represents datagram packets in a connectionless protocol. A datagram packet that is sent contains the address of its destination and its contents. A datagram packet that is received contains the address of its source and its contents. Datagram packets can be used for both single-client to single-server communication (*unicast*) and single-client to multiple-server communication (*multicast*). The only difference between the two modes of communication is that with unicast, the destination in the datagram packet is the address of a single machine, while with multicast, the destination in the datagram packet is a multicast group address.

MEMBER SUMMARY	
Constructor	
`DatagramPacket()`	Constructs a `DatagramPacket` instance for sending/receiving datagram packets.
Field Access Methods	
`getAddress()`	Retrieves the destination address or source address of this datagram packet.

Continued

MEMBER SUMMARY	
Field Access Methods (Continued)	
`getData()`	Retrieves the contents of this datagram packet.
`getLength()`	Retrieves the length of this datagram packet.
`getPort()`	Retrieves the destination port or source port of this datagram packet.
Field Update Methods	
`setAddress()`	Sets the destination address or source address of this datagram packet.
`setData()`	Sets the contents of this datagram packet.
`setLength()`	Sets the length of this datagram packet.
`setPort()`	Sets the destination port or source port of this datagram packet.

See Also

`DatagramSocket`, `MulticastSocket`.

Example

The following example is a standalone program that makes a datagram packet exchange using `DatagramPacket`. By default, it uses port 13 (the `daytime` port) on the local machine. You can supply a port number of any datagram service (either your own or standard ones like `echo` (port 7)) that sends a request and then expects a reply (in string format).

```
import java.net.*;
import java.io.*;

class Main {
    public static String dgExchange(String msg, InetAddress dst, int port) {
        byte[] outbuf = msg.getBytes();
        byte[] inbuf = new byte[256];  // default size

        try {
            // Send datagram
            DatagramPacket request =
                new DatagramPacket(outbuf, outbuf.length, dst, port);
            DatagramSocket sock = new DatagramSocket();
            sock.send(request);

            // Wait for reply
            DatagramPacket reply = new DatagramPacket(inbuf, inbuf.length);
            sock.receive(reply);

            System.out.println(
                "Received packet from:" + reply.getAddress() +
                " port: " + reply.getPort() +
                " length: " + reply.getLength());
```

```
            sock.close();
            return (new String(reply.getData()));
        } catch (SocketException e) {
            e.printStackTrace();
        } catch (IOException e) {
            e.printStackTrace();
        }
        return (null);
    }

    public static void main(String[] args) {
        try {
            String msg = "\n";
            int port = 13;
            InetAddress dst = InetAddress.getLocalHost();

            if (args.length > 0) {
                port = Integer.parseInt(args[0]);
                if (args.length >= 2)
                    msg = args[1];
                if (args.length == 3)
                    dst = InetAddress.getByName(args[2]);
            }

            System.out.println(dgExchange(msg, dst, port));
        } catch (UnknownHostException e) {
            e.printStackTrace();
        }
    }
}
```

DatagramPacket()

PURPOSE

Constructs a `DatagramPacket` instance for sending/receiving datagram packets.

SYNTAX

```
public DatagramPacket(byte[] inBuffer, int max)
public DatagramPacket(byte[] outBuffer, int count, InetAddress
    dst, int port)
```

DESCRIPTION

This class has two constructor forms. The first form constructs a `DatagramPacket` instance for receiving a datagram packet. You specify an existing buffer `inBuffer` in which to put the incoming datagram packet, and you specify the maximum number of bytes, `max`, you expect to receive into `inBuffer`.

The second form constructs a `DatagramPacket` instance for sending a datagram packet. You specify the buffer `outBuffer` that contains the bytes to be sent, the number of bytes to send (`count`), and the destination of the datagram packet (`dst` and `port`). Any direct updates to `outBuffer` after this `DatagramPacket` has been created affects the contents of this datagram packet as well.

The fields of a datagram packet can be changed after the datagram packet has been created using the appropriate `set` methods.

PARAMETERS

`count`	The number of bytes in `outBuffer` to send. `count` ≤ `outBuffer.length`.
`dst`	The non-`null` destination address to which to send the datagram packet.
`inBuffer`	The non-`null` buffer in which to receive the data.
`max`	The maximum number of bytes to receive into `inBuffer`. `max` ≤ `inBuffer.length`.
`outBuffer`	The non-`null` buffer containing the data to send.
`port`	The port to which to send the datagram packet. `0` ≤ `port` ≤ `65535`.

EXCEPTIONS

`IllegalArgumentException`
If `count`, `max`, or `port` are not within the specified bounds.

SEE ALSO `DatagramSocket.receive()`, `DatagramSocket.send()`, `InetAddress`, `MulticastSocket.send()`, `setAddress()`, `setData()`, `setLength()`, `setPort()`.

EXAMPLE See the class example.

getAddress()

PURPOSE Retrieves the destination address or source address of this datagram packet.

SYNTAX `public synchronized InetAddress getAddress()`

DESCRIPTION If this is an outgoing datagram packet, `getAddress()` returns the destination address of the datagram packet. If this is an incoming datagram packet, `getAddress()` returns the source address of the datagram packet (i.e., who sent the datagram packet). The address of a datagram packet is its IP address.

RETURNS The destination address or source address of this datagram packet; `null` if this datagram packet is for receiving data and no data has been received yet.

SEE ALSO `getPort()`, `InetAddress`, `setAddress()`.

EXAMPLE See the class example.

getData()

PURPOSE Retrieves the contents of this datagram packet.

SYNTAX `public synchronized byte[] getData()`

RETURNS The non-`null` `byte` array containing the data to be sent or the data received.

Any changes to this byte array also affect the DatagramPacket from which it came.

SEE ALSO `getLength(), setData().`

EXAMPLE See the class example.

getLength()

PURPOSE Retrieves the length of this datagram packet.

SYNTAX `public synchronized int getLength()`

DESCRIPTION If this is an outgoing datagram packet, `getLength()` returns the number of bytes in this datagram packet. If this is an incoming datagram packet, `getLength()` returns the number of bytes received into this datagram packet.

RETURNS The number of bytes in this datagram packet.

SEE ALSO `getData(), setLength().`

EXAMPLE See the class example.

getPort()

PURPOSE Retrieves the destination port or source port of this datagram packet.

SYNTAX `public synchronized int getPort()`

DESCRIPTION Each machine has an IP address that contains network addressing information that allows datagram packets to be routed to the machine. On a single machine, there can be many logical entities (called *servers*) that perform different functions. For example, there can be a time server, a file server, and a calendar server, all on the same machine. A client application is typically interested in communicating with a particular server on a machine. Hence, it must identify the server within the machine. A *port number* is a logical address within a machine. Each server uses a port number so that it can be further identified within the machine. Once a datagram packet reaches a machine, the port number is used to route the datagram packet to the appropriate server.

For an outgoing datagram packet, `getPort()` returns the port number on the destination machine to which to send this datagram packet. For an incoming datagram packet, `getPort()` returns the port number in the sending machine from which this datagram packet was sent.

RETURNS The destination or source port of this datagram packet. $0 \leq$ port ≤ 65535, unless this is a datagram packet for receiving data and no data has been received yet, in which case `-1` is returned.

SEE ALSO getAddress(), DatagramSocket.getLocalPort(), setPort().

EXAMPLE See the class example.

A B C D E F G H I J K L M N O P Q R S T U V W X Y Z

setAddress()

PURPOSE Sets the destination address or source address of this datagram packet.

SYNTAX `public synchronized void setAddress(InetAddress newaddr)`

DESCRIPTION This method sets the address field of this datagram packet to be the IP address `newaddr`.

PARAMETERS

`newaddr` The non-`null` destination address or source address of this datagram packet.

SEE ALSO `getAddress()`, `getPort()`, `InetAddress`.

EXAMPLE See `setPort()`.

setData()

PURPOSE Sets the contents of this datagram packet.

SYNTAX `public synchronized void setData(byte[] newbuf)`

DESCRIPTION This method replaces the buffer being used by this datagram packet with the new buffer `newbuf`. The datagram packet length remains unchanged until `setLength()` is called.

PARAMETERS

`newbuf` A non-`null` `byte` array containing the data to be sent or the data received.

SEE ALSO `getData()`, `getLength()`, `setLength()`.

EXAMPLE See `setPort()`.

setLength()

PURPOSE Sets the length of this datagram packet.

SYNTAX `public synchronized void setLength(int newlen)`

DESCRIPTION This method sets the number of bytes in this datagram packet to be `newlen`.

PARAMETERS

`newlen` The number of bytes in this datagram packet. `newlen` ≤ `getData().length`.

EXCEPTIONS

`IllegalArgumentException`

If `newlen` > `getData().length`.

SEE ALSO getData(), getLength(), setData().

EXAMPLE See setPort().

setPort()

PURPOSE Sets the destination port or source port of this datagram packet.

SYNTAX `public synchronized void setPort(int newport)`

DESCRIPTION This method sets the port number of this datagram packet to be `newport`.

PARAMETERS

`newport` The new port number of this datagram packet. `0` ≤ `newport` ≤ `65535`.

EXCEPTIONS

`IllegalArgumentException`

If `newport` > `65535` or `newport` < `0`.

SEE ALSO getPort().

EXAMPLE This example illustrates how the set methods are used by a socket implementation to update the contents of a datagram packet.

```
import java.net.DatagramSocketImpl;
import java.net.InetAddress;
import java.net.DatagramPacket;
import java.io.IOException;

class SomeDatagramSocketImpl extends DatagramSocketImpl {
  int fd;
  int senderPort;
  InetAddress senderAddr;
  byte[] incoming;
        ...

  private native void receiveImpl() throws IOException;

  public synchronized void receive(DatagramPacket dg) throws IOException {
    receiveImpl();      // sets sender information and incoming buffer

    dg.setPort(senderPort);
    dg.setAddress(senderAddr);
    dg.setData(incoming);        // do this before setLength()
    dg.setLength(incoming.length);
  }
}
```

java.net
DatagramSocket

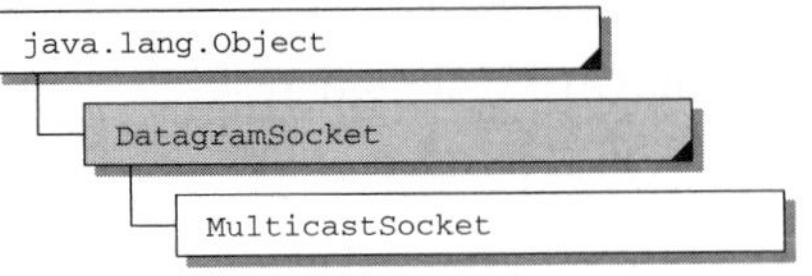

A B C D E F G H I J K L M N O P Q R S T U V W X Y Z

Syntax

```
public class DatagramSocket
```

Description

A *socket* is a communications endpoint. A *datagram socket* is an endpoint for sending and receiving *datagram packets* between applications. The `DatagramSocket` class is used to represent a datagram socket.

Unicast

In a client/server application that uses datagram sockets to communicate, the server creates a datagram socket for a "well-known" port. Clients learn about these ports either by convention or through a naming service that maps service names to port numbers. The server then waits for clients to send datagram packets to this port (on its machine). When the server receives a datagram packet, it processes the datagram packet and, if appropriate, sends a reply to the client.

The client interacts with the server by creating a datagram packet with the server's address (machine address plus port number) in it and then filling it with the contents of the request to be sent to the server. The client then creates a datagram socket and sends this packet through the socket to the server (see Figure 31). The server can receive the packet using either a `Socket` or a `DatagramSocket`. If the client is expecting a reply, it waits until the server sends a reply.

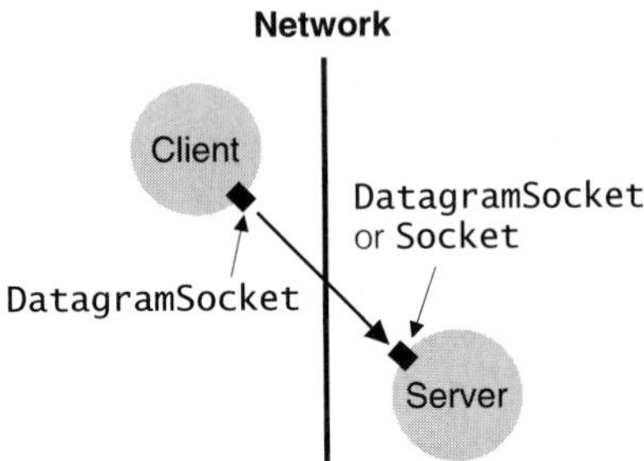

FIGURE 31: Unicast `DatagramSocket`.

In this mode of communication, the client sends a single datagram packet to a single designated server. This is called *unicast* communication.

Multicast

A client can also communicate by sending a *single* datagram packet to a *multicast group* comprising zero or more members. The group is identified by a *multicast address*—an IP address to which group members subscribe. The client program can use either `DatagramSocket` or

MulticastSocket to send the datagram packet. See send() and the MulticastSocket class for details.

Datagram Socket Implementation

The actual implementation of a datagram socket is supplied by a subclass of DatagramSocket-Impl. When the application creates an instance of DatagramSocket, a corresponding instance of DatagramSocketImpl is created. The particular subclass of DatagramSocketImpl to use is configurable by the application or the user of the application by setting the impl.prefix system property. The subclass's class name is java.net.*prefix*DatagramSocketImpl, where *prefix* is the setting of the impl.prefix system property. If impl.prefix has not been set, the default prefix is Plain.[1]

This indirection allows a datagram socket implementation to be chosen at runtime depending on the properties of the network.

Socket Time-Out Period

By default, when the application requests to receive data from a datagram socket, it blocks indefinitely until a datagram packet arrives. The application can specify a time-out period for the datagram socket such that the receive request will block only until either a datagram packet arrives or the time-out period expires.

MEMBER SUMMARY	
Constructor	
DatagramSocket()	Constructs a DatagramSocket instance.
Communication Methods	
close()	Closes this datagram socket.
receive()	Receives a datagram packet from this datagram socket.
send()	Sends a datagram packet to its destination using this datagram socket.
Socket Time-Out Methods	
getSoTimeout()	Retrieves the time-out period of this datagram socket.
setSoTimeout()	Sets the time-out period of this datagram socket.
Field Access Methods	
getLocalPort()	Retrieves the local port to which this datagram socket is bound.
getLocalAddress()	Retrieves the local address to which this datagram socket is bound.

1. PlainDatagramSocketImpl is a java.net package-private implementation of datagram sockets with no security checks.

See Also

DatagramPacket, DatagramSocketImpl, InetAddress, MulticastSocket, ServerSocket, Socket.

Example

This example shows the use of DatagramSocket by both the server and the client. The server implements EchoServer, which creates a DatagramSocket and waits for requests. When it receives a request, it sends back to the client a copy of the datagram packet that it received. The client implements the echo() method, which creates a DatagramSocket to communicate with the server.

```
class EchoServer extends Thread {
    private DatagramSocket sock = null;
    EchoServer(int port) {
        try {
            sock = new DatagramSocket(port);
        } catch (SocketException e) {
            e.printStackTrace();
        }
    }
    public void run() {
        if (sock == null)
            return;

        byte[] inbuf = new byte[1024];
        DatagramPacket request = new DatagramPacket(inbuf, inbuf.length);
        try {
            while (true) {
                sock.receive(request);
                sock.send(request); // just return what was sent
            }
        } catch (IOException e) {
            e.printStackTrace();
        }
    }
}

public static void echo(String msg, InetAddress dst, int port) {
    byte[] inbuf = new byte[1024];  // default size
    byte[] outbuf = msg.getBytes();

    try {
        DatagramSocket client = new DatagramSocket(); // any port
        DatagramPacket request = new DatagramPacket(outbuf, outbuf.length,
            dst, port);
        DatagramPacket reply = new DatagramPacket(inbuf, inbuf.length);
        client.send(request);
        client.receive(reply);
        client.close();
        System.out.println(new String(reply.getData()));
    } catch (SocketException e) {
        e.printStackTrace();
    } catch (IOException e) {
        e.printStackTrace();
    }
}
```

close()

PURPOSE Closes this datagram socket.

SYNTAX

```
public void close()
```

DESCRIPTION This method closes this datagram socket. It should be used when the datagram socket is no longer needed. Closing a datagram socket frees the port that it was bound to and frees any resources (like file descriptors) associated with the datagram socket. After the datagram socket has been closed, it can no longer be used.

SEE ALSO `DatagramSocket()`, `DatagramSocketImpl.close()`.

EXAMPLE See the class example.

A B C D E F G H I J K L M N O P Q R S T U V W X Y Z

DatagramSocket()

PURPOSE Constructs a `DatagramSocket` instance.

SYNTAX

```
public DatagramSocket() throws SocketException
public DatagramSocket(int port) throws SocketException
public DatagramSocket(int port, InetAddress localAddr) throws
   SocketException
```

DESCRIPTION This constructor creates a datagram socket and binds it to the specified local port `port` and local address `localAddr`. If `port` is not supplied or if `port` is `0`, the new datagram socket is bound to any locally available port. Use of certain ports is restricted (for example, those well-known ports for Internet protocols like FTP, Telnet, SMTP, and so on), and use of *any* port is permitted only if allowed by the security manager.

`localAddr` is useful when creating datagram socket on a multihomed host for specifying which one of the multiple addresses of the local machine to use. If `localAddr` is not specified, any address associated with the local machine is used. The address chosen is implementation-dependent.

The actual implementation of the `DatagramSocket` class is supplied by a subclass of `DatagramSocketImpl`. See the class description for details.

PARAMETERS

`localAddr` The local address to which to bind this datagram socket.

`port` The local port to which to bind this datagram socket. `0` ≤ `port` ≤ `65535`. If `port` is `0` or unspecified, use any available port.

EXCEPTIONS

`IllegalArgumentException`

If `port` < `0` or `port` > `65535`.

`SecurityException`
If cannot use `port` due to security reasons.

`SocketException`
If cannot create a datagram socket using `port` and/or `localAddr`.

SEE ALSO `BindException`, `DatagramSocketImpl.create()`, `DatagramSocketImpl.bind()`, `java.lang.IllegalArgumentException`, `java.lang.SecurityException`, `java.lang.SecurityManager.checkListen()`.

EXAMPLE See the class example.

getLocalAddress()

PURPOSE Retrieves the local address to which this datagram socket is bound.

SYNTAX `public InetAddress getLocalAddress()`

DESCRIPTION A datagram socket has two endpoints: the sending end and the receiving end. Each end is identified by the IP address of the machine to which it is connected and the port on the machine being used. `getLocalAddress()` returns the address (containing both the IP address and machine name) that is being used by this datagram socket on the local machine to send and receive data.

If the current execution context is not allowed to connect to the local machine via the network interface that is bound to the datagram socket, the address of any one of the local machine's network interfaces is returned.

RETURNS The address of the interface being used for the datagram socket on the local machine, or any local address if the current execution context is not allowed to connect to the network interface that is actually bound to the datagram socket.

SEE ALSO `DatagramPacket.getAddress()`, `getLocalPort()`, `InetAddress`, `java.lang.SecurityManager.checkConnect()`.

EXAMPLE See `getLocalPort()`.

getLocalPort()

PURPOSE Retrieves the local port to which this datagram socket is bound.

SYNTAX `public int getLocalPort()`

DESCRIPTION A datagram socket has two endpoints: the sending end and the receiving end. Each endpoint is identified by the IP address of the machine to which it is connected and the port on the machine being used. `getLocalPort()` returns the port number that is being used by this datagram socket on the local machine to send and receive data.

RETURNS The port number being used for the datagram socket on the local machine.

SEE ALSO `DatagramPacket.getPort()`, `getLocalAddress()`.

EXAMPLE

```
try {
    DatagramSocket client = new DatagramSocket();
    System.out.println("Using port number " + client.getLocalPort());
    System.out.println("Using address " + client.getLocalAddress());
        ...
    client.close();
} catch (SocketException e) {
    e.printStackTrace();
}
```


getSoTimeout()

PURPOSE Retrieves the time-out period of this datagram socket.

SYNTAX `public synchronized int getSoTimeout() throws SocketException`

DESCRIPTION A datagram socket's time-out period specifies the maximum number of milliseconds that `receive()` will block when waiting to receive a datagram packet. If the time-out period is `0`, `receive()` will block indefinitely until a datagram packet is received. If the time-out period is greater than `0`, subsequent invocations of `receive()` will unblock either when the caller of `receive()` receives a datagram packet within the time-out period or when the time-out period expires, at which time `InterruptedIOException` will be thrown.

`getSoTimeout()` retrieves the time-out period of this datagram socket.

RETURNS A positive number specifying the maximum number of milliseconds that `receive()` will block. If `0`, `receive()` will block indefinitely when waiting for datagram packets.

EXCEPTIONS

`SocketException`

If an error occurred while attempting to get the datagram socket's time-out period.

SEE ALSO `DatagramSocketImpl.getOption()`, `setSoTimeout()`, `SocketException`.

EXAMPLE See `setSoTimeout()`.

A B C D E F G H I J K L M N O P Q R S T U V W X Y Z

receive()

PURPOSE Receives a datagram packet from this datagram socket.

SYNTAX

```
public synchronized void receive(DatagramPacket dgram) throws
    IOException
```

DESCRIPTION This method reads a datagram packet `dgram` from this datagram socket. It blocks until `dgram` is read. `dgram` must contain a preallocated buffer in which to receive the incoming data. Upon return, `dgram` will contain the incoming data, as well as the address of the sender of the datagram packet.

Because the socket is a datagram socket, there is no guarantee that the same packet `dgram` will arrive just once. There also is no guarantee that successive calls to `receive()` will retrieve the datagram packets in the same order in which they were sent or even that a datagram packet will arrive at all.

Datagram packets sent to this datagram socket from senders disallowed by the receiving program's security manager are silently ignored.

PARAMETERS

`dgram` The non-`null` datagram packet into which to receive the data. Upon return, `dgram` will contain the data of the packet and the address of the sender. The buffer in `dgram` for holding the data must have been preallocated. If the amount of data exceeds the buffer's size, the excess is ignored.

EXCEPTIONS

`InterruptedIOException`
If the time-out period for this datagram socket has expired before a datagram packet was received. This datagram socket may still receive future datagram packets.

`IOException`
If an I/O error occurred while receiving the datagram packet.

SEE ALSO `DatagramPacket`, `DatagramSocketImpl.receive()`, `getSoTimeout()`, `java.io.InterruptedIOException`, `java.io.IOException`, `java.lang.SecurityManager.checkConnect()`, `java.lang.SecurityManager.checkMulticast()`, `MulticastSocket.send()`, `send()`, `setSoTimeout()`.

EXAMPLE See the class example.

send()

PURPOSE Sends a datagram packet to its destination using this datagram socket.

SYNTAX

```
public void send(DatagramPacket dgram) throws IOException
```

DESCRIPTION

This method uses this datagram socket to send the datagram packet `dgram` to the destination address found inside `dgram`. Delivery of `dgram` to its destination is not guaranteed because datagram protocols have unreliable delivery.

If the destination address is a multicast address, `dgram` is sent to the multicast address and may be received by multiple receivers. This datagram socket sends `dgram` using the default time-to-live value,[1] which is determined by this datagram socket's `DatagramSocketImpl`. Most implementations use a default of one, which means to multicast on the local network. If this datagram socket is a subclass of `MulticastSocket`, `MulticastSocket.getTTL()` is used as the time-to-live value. Use `MulticastSocket.send()` for specifying the time-to-live value on a per packet basis.

This method can be executed only if the security manager permits communication with the destination specified in `dgram`.

PARAMETERS

`dgram` The non-`null` datagram packet being sent through this datagram socket. `dgram` contains the address of the destination as well as the packet contents to send.

EXCEPTIONS

`IOException`

If an I/O error occurred during the transmission of the datagram packet.

`SecurityException`

If not allowed to communicate with the destination specified in `dgram` due to security reasons.

SEE ALSO

`ConnectException`, `DatagramPacket`, `DatagramSocketImpl.getTTL()`, `DatagramSocketImpl.send()`, `DatagramSocketImpl.setTTL()`, `receive()`, `NoRouteToHostException`, `java.io.IOException`, `java.lang.SecurityException`, `java.lang.SecurityManager.checkConnect()`, `java.lang.SecurityManager.checkMulticast()`, `MulticastSocket.send()`.

EXAMPLE

See the class example.

1. If the time-to-live value of a datagram packet is one, the datagram packet is transmitted using the local network multicast which reaches all immediately-neighboring members of the sender. If the datagram packet's time-to-live value is greater than one, the datagram packet is also forwarded by *multicast routers* to all other networks that have members of the multicast group. If the datagram packet's time-to-live value is greater than two, the datagram packet is again forwarded from those networks, and so on.

setSoTimeout()

PURPOSE Sets the time-out period of this datagram socket.

SYNTAX

```
public synchronized void setSoTimeout(int timeout) throws
    SocketException
```

DESCRIPTION A datagram socket's time-out period specifies the maximum number of milliseconds that `receive()` will block when waiting to receive a datagram packet. If the time-out period is `0`, `receive()` will block indefinitely until a datagram packet is received. If the time-out period is greater than `0`, subsequent invocations of `receive()` will unblock either when the caller of `receive()` receives a datagram packet within the time-out period or when the time-out period expires, at which time `InterruptedIOException` will be thrown.

`setSoTimeout()` sets the time-out period of this datagram socket and affects only subsequent `receive()` calls.

PARAMETERS

`timeout` A positive number specifying the maximum number of milliseconds that `receive()` will block. If `0`, `receive()` will block indefinitely when waiting for datagram packets.

EXCEPTIONS

`SocketException`
If an error occurred while attempting to set the datagram socket's time-out period.

SEE ALSO `DatagramSocketImpl.setOption()`, `getSoTimeout()`, `SocketException`.

EXAMPLE This example is a variation of the `EchoServer` class in the class example. It sets the datagram socket's time-out to be 1 second and displays a message each time the time-out expires without receiving a datagram packet.

```
class TimedEchoServer extends Thread {
    private DatagramSocket sock = null;
    TimedEchoServer(int port) {
        try {
            sock = new DatagramSocket(port);
        } catch (SocketException e) {
            e.printStackTrace();
        }
    }
    public void run() {
        if (sock == null)
            return;

        byte[] inbuf = new byte[1024];
        DatagramPacket request = new DatagramPacket(inbuf, inbuf.length);

        try {
            sock.setSoTimeout(1000);            // set timeout to be 1 sec
```

```
            while (true) {
                try {
                    sock.receive(request);
                    sock.send(request);         // just return what was sent
                } catch (InterruptedIOException e) {
                    System.err.println("No message for " +
                        sock.getSoTimeout() + "ms");
                }
            }
        } catch (IOException e) {
            e.printStackTrace();
        }
    }
}
```

java.net

DatagramSocketImpl

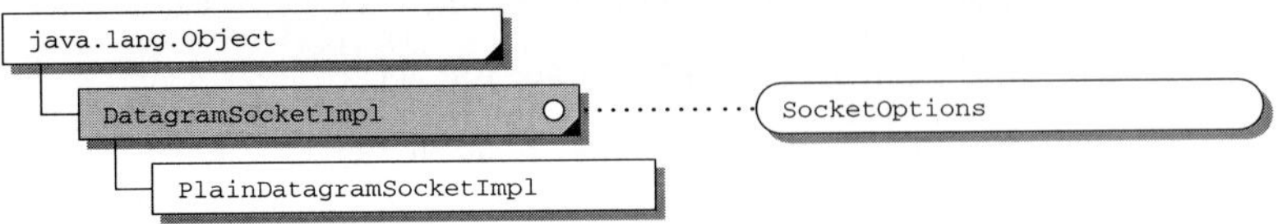

A
B
C
D
E
F
G
H
I
J
K
L
M
N
O
P
Q
R
S
T
U
V
W
X
Y
Z

Syntax

```
public abstract class DatagramSocketImpl implements SocketOptions
```

Description

The Java programmer uses the methods in the `DatagramSocket` and `MulticastSocket` classes for writing applications that communicate with each other using datagram packets. The actual implementations of the `DatagramSocket` and `MulticastSocket` classes are configurable at runtime and are supplied by a subclass of `DatagramSocketImpl`. `DatagramSocketImpl` contains the methods necessary for implementing both unicast and multicast datagram sockets.

Usage

The methods in `DatagramSocketImpl` are invoked from `DatagramSocket` and `MulticastSocket` and are not invoked directly by the program. To define a datagram socket implementation, you define a subclass of `DatagramSocketImpl` that provides implementations for its abstract methods.

Selecting the Implementation

A program selects the datagram socket implementation to use by setting the system property `impl.prefix`. The value of this property is used in determining the class name of the implementation:

`java.net.`*`prefix`*`DatagramSocketImpl`

This implementation class is used for both `DatagramSocket` and `MulticastSocket`.

MEMBER SUMMARY	
Methods for Changing Datagram Socket State	
`bind()`	Binds this datagram socket to the local port and address.
`close()`	Closes this datagram socket.
`create()`	Creates an unconnected datagram socket.
Methods for Communicating	
`peek()`	Looks in a datagram packet sent to this datagram socket for the sender's address.

MEMBER SUMMARY	
`receive()`	Receives a datagram packet from this datagram socket.
`send()`	Sends a datagram packet using this datagram socket.
Multicast Methods	
`getTTL()`	Retrieves the time-to-live for multicast packets sent from this datagram socket.
`join()`	Makes this datagram socket join a multicast group.
`leave()`	Makes this datagram socket leave a multicast group.
`setTTL()`	Sets the time-to-live for multicast packets sent from this datagram socket.
Datagram Socket Information Fields	
`fd`	This datagram socket's file descriptor.
`localPort`	This datagram socket's local port number.
Datagram Socket Information Methods	
`getFileDescriptor()`	Retrieves this datagram socket's file descriptor.
`getLocalPort()`	Retrieves this datagram socket's local port number.

See Also

`DatagramSocket`, `InetAddress`, `MulticastSocket`, `SocketImpl`.

Example

The JDK contains a package-private class `PlainDatagramSocketImpl` that implements datagram sockets using native methods that have no security checks. This is the implementation that is used when no datagram socket implementation has been selected (via the `impl.prefix` system property). Typically, the application (e.g., a Web browser) installs its own datagram socket implementation and this plain implementation is not used. `PlainDatagramSocketImpl` gives you a good idea of how to build datagram socket implementations. The following example extends `PlainDatagramSocketImpl` to give some debugging output. Because this new class is being added to the `java.net` package, the class file for the following must be installed in `$JAVA_HOME/classes/java/net`:

```
package java.net;

import java.net.*;
import java.io.IOException;
import java.net.PlainDatagramSocketImpl;

/**
 * Wrapper around default datagram socket implementation that
 * provides debugging information.
```

```
 */

public class DebugDatagramSocketImpl extends PlainDatagramSocketImpl {
  protected synchronized void create() throws SocketException {
    super.create();
    System.err.println("Created socket using file descriptor " + fd);
  }
  protected synchronized void bind(int lport, InetAddress laddr)
    throws SocketException {
    System.err.println("Binding to local address: " + laddr + "/" + lport);
    super.bind(lport, laddr);
  }
  protected synchronized void send(DatagramPacket p) throws IOException {
    System.err.println("Sending packet to: " + p.getAddress() + "/" + p.get-
Port());
    super.send(p);
  }
  protected int peek(InetAddress i) throws IOException {
    int port = super.peek(i);
    System.err.println("Peeking " + i + "/" + port);
    return port;
  }
  protected synchronized void receive(DatagramPacket p) throws IOException {
    super.receive(p);
    System.err.println("Received packet from " + p.getAddress() + "/" + p.get-
Port());
  }
  protected void setTTL(byte ttl) throws IOException {
    System.err.println("Setting TTL to " + ttl);
    super.setTTL(ttl);
  }
  protected byte getTTL() throws IOException {
    byte ttl = super.getTTL();
    System.err.println("TTL is " + ttl);
    return ttl;
  }
  protected void join(InetAddress inetaddr) throws IOException {
    System.err.println("Joining " + inetaddr);
    super.join(inetaddr);
  }
  protected void leave(InetAddress inetaddr) throws IOException {
    System.err.println("Leaving " + inetaddr);
    super.leave(inetaddr);
  }
  protected void close() {
    System.err.println("Closing socket");
    super.close();
  }

  /* methods from SocketOptions */
  public void setOption(int optID, Object o) throws SocketException {
    super.setOption(optID, o);
    System.err.println("Set option " + optID + " to " + o);
  }
  public Object getOption(int optID) throws SocketException {
    Object optRes = super.getOption(optID);
    System.err.println("Option " + optID + " is " + optRes);
    return optRes;
  }
}
```

bind()

PURPOSE Binds a datagram socket to a local port and address.

SYNTAX
```
protected abstract void bind(int localPort, InetAddress
    localAddr) throws SocketException
```

DESCRIPTION This method binds this datagram socket to the specified local port `localPort` and local address `localAddr`.

PARAMETERS

`localAddr` The non-`null` local address to which to bind this datagram socket.

`localPort` The local port to which to bind this datagram socket. `0` ≤ `localPort` ≤ `65535`.

EXCEPTIONS

`SocketException`

If a problem occurred while attempting to bind to `localAddr` and `localPort`. This can occur, for example, if `localPort` is already in use.

SEE ALSO `BindException`, `DatagramSocket.DatagramSocket()`.

EXAMPLE See `create()`.

close()

PURPOSE Closes this datagram socket.

SYNTAX
```
protected abstract void close()
```

DESCRIPTION This method closes this datagram socket. It typically frees up the resources used for this datagram socket, such as its file descriptor and local port number.

SEE ALSO `DatagramSocket.close()`.

EXAMPLE See the class example.

create()

PURPOSE Creates a new unconnected datagram socket.

SYNTAX
```
protected abstract void create() throws SocketException
```

DESCRIPTION This method creates a new unconnected datagram socket. Creating a datagram socket typically involves allocation of some local resources, such as a file descriptor to be used for the datagram socket. This unconnected datagram socket needs to be bound locally before being used for sending or receiving datagram packets.

EXCEPTIONS

SocketException
If a problem was encountered while attempting to create a new unconnected datagram socket. This can occur, for example, if no more file descriptors are available.

SEE ALSO `bind()`, `DatagramSocket.DatagramSocket()`.

EXAMPLE This code fragment shows the typical steps involved in setting up a datagram socket.

```
DatagramSocketImpl impl = (DatagramSocketImpl) implClass.newInstance();
impl.create();
impl.bind(localPort, localAaddr);
```

fd

PURPOSE This datagram socket's file descriptor.

SYNTAX `protected FileDescriptor fd`

SEE ALSO `getFileDescriptor()`, `java.io.FileDescriptor`.

getFileDescriptor()

PURPOSE Retrieves this datagram socket's file descriptor.

SYNTAX `protected FileDescriptor getFileDescriptor()`

DESCRIPTION A datagram socket has a file descriptor associated with it for doing IO. It is allocated at the time the datagram socket is created and freed when the datagram socket is closed. This method returns this datagram socket's file descriptor.

RETURNS This datagram socket's file descriptor; `null` if this datagram socket is closed or unbound.

SEE ALSO `close()`, `create()`, `fd`, `java.io.FileDescriptor`.

getLocalPort()

PURPOSE Retrieves this datagram socket's local port number.

SYNTAX `protected int getLocalPort()`

DESCRIPTION A datagram socket must be bound locally before it is used. This method returns the local port number being used by this datagram socket.

RETURNS This datagram socket's local port number.

SEE ALSO `localPort`, `bind()`.

getTTL()

PURPOSE Retrieves the time-to-live for multicast packets sent from this datagram socket.

SYNTAX `protected abstract byte getTTL() throws IOException`

DESCRIPTION A multicast packet sent from this datagram socket has a time-to-live value that specifies the transmission range of the packet.[1] The higher the time-to-live value, the higher the potential coverage of the multicast packet. The default time-to-live value is determined by `setTTL()`. If `setTTL()` has never been invoked on this socket, `getTTL()` returns an implementation-dependent default. Most implementations use a default of one, which means to multicast on the local network.

`getTTL()` returns the default time-to-live value used for packets sent from this datagram socket.

RETURNS An unsigned 8-bit number specifying the time-to-live value for multicast packets sent from this datagram socket. `0` < time-to-live ≤ `0xFF`.

EXCEPTIONS

`IOException`

If an error occurred while attempting to retrieve this datagram socket's time-to-live value.

SEE ALSO `DatagramSocket.send()`, `java.io.IOException`, `MulticastSocket.getTTL()`, `MulticastSocket.send()`, `setTTL()`.

1. If the time-to-live value of a datagram packet is one, the datagram packet is transmitted using the local network multicast which reaches all immediately-neighboring members of the sender. If the datagram packet's time-to-live value is greater than one, the datagram packet is also forwarded by *multicast routers* to all other networks that have members of the multicast group. If the datagram packet's time-to-live value is greater than two, the datagram packet is again forwarded from those networks, and so on.

join()

PURPOSE Makes this datagram socket join a multicast group.

SYNTAX
```
protected abstract void join(InetAddress groupAddr) throws
   IOException
```

DESCRIPTION When a datagram socket is a member of a multicast group, it receives any datagram packet sent to the multicast group (within the datagram packet's time-to-live setting). Members of a multicast group can span different networks. This method makes this datagram socket a member of the multicast group that has the multicast address `groupAddr`. After this method is called, this datagram socket will receive datagram packets sent to `groupAddr`.

A datagram socket can join more than one group, but cannot join a group in which it is already a member.

PARAMETERS

`groupAddr` The non-`null` address of the multicast group.

EXCEPTIONS

`IOException`
If an IO error occurred while a datagram socket is attempting to join the multicast group.

SEE ALSO `leave()`, `MulticastSocket`.

leave()

PURPOSE Makes this datagram socket leave a multicast group.

SYNTAX
```
protected abstract void leave(InetAddress groupAddr) throws
   IOException
```

DESCRIPTION When a datagram socket is a member of a multicast group, it receives any datagram packet sent to the multicast group (within the datagram packet's time-to-live setting). Members of a multicast group can span different networks. This method removes this datagram socket from the group that has the multicast address `groupAddr`. After this method is called, this datagram socket will no longer receive datagram packets sent to `groupAddr`.

If this datagram socket is not a member of `groupAddr`, an exception is thrown.

PARAMETERS

`groupAddr` The non-`null` address of the multicast group.

EXCEPTIONS

`IOException`

If an IO error occurred while attempting to leave the multicast group.

SEE ALSO `join()`, `MulticastSocket`.

localPort

PURPOSE This datagram socket's local port number.

SYNTAX `protected int localPort`

SEE ALSO `getLocalPort()`.

peek()

PURPOSE Looks in a datagram packet sent to this datagram socket for the sender's address.

SYNTAX

```
protected abstract int peek(InetAddress sender) throws
   IOException
```

DESCRIPTION This method examines the next datagram packet arriving in this datagram socket and sets `sender` to be the datagram packet's sender address. It blocks until a datagram packet arrives, or, if the datagram socket has a nonzero socket time-out set, until the socket time-out expires. If the socket time-out expires, `InterruptedIOException` is thrown.

`peek()` is typically used by the datagram socket implementation to check whether the caller is allowed to receive a datagram packet from the sender prior to retrieving the contents of the datagram packet.

PARAMETERS

`sender` A new non-`null` IP address whose contents will be updated upon return from `peek()`.

RETURNS The port number of the sender's address.

EXCEPTIONS

`InterruptedIOException`

If the datagram socket times out before a datagram packet has been received.

`IOException`

If an IO error occurred while attempting to retrieve the datagram packet's address.

SEE ALSO `DatagramSocket.getSoTimeout()`, `DatagramSocket.receive()`, `DatagramSocket.setSoTimeout()`.

A B C D E F G H I J K L M N O P Q R S T U V W X Y Z

receive()

PURPOSE Receives a datagram packet from this datagram socket.

SYNTAX
```
protected abstract void receive(DatagramPacket dgram) throws
    IOException
```

DESCRIPTION This method reads a datagram packet `dgram` from this datagram socket. It blocks until a datagram packet arrives, or, if the datagram socket has a nonzero socket time-out set, until the socket time-out expires. If the socket time-out expires, `InterruptedIOException` is thrown.

PARAMETERS

`dgram` The non-`null` datagram packet into which to receive data. `dgram` must contain a preallocated buffer in which to store the contents of incoming data. If the size of the incoming data exceeds the buffer's size, the excess bytes are ignored.

EXCEPTIONS

`InterruptedIOException`
If the socket time-out expires prior to a datagram packet's arriving.

`IOException`
If an IO error was encountered while attempting to receive a datagram packet.

SEE ALSO `DatagramSocket.getSoTimeout()`, `DatagramSocket.receive()`, `DatagramSocket.setSoTimeout()`.

send()

PURPOSE Sends a datagram packet using this datagram socket.

SYNTAX
```
protected abstract void send(DatagramPacket dgram) throws
    IOException
```

DESCRIPTION This method sends the datagram packet `dgram` to the destination specified in `dgram`. The destination may be a single host address or a multicast group address. If the address is a multicast group address, the time-to-live value (retrieved using `getTTL()`) is used to control coverage of the multicast packet.

PARAMETERS

`dgram` The non-`null` datagram packet to send. It contains the address of the destination as well as the packet contents to send.

EXCEPTIONS

`IOException`
If an IO error occurred while attempting to send the packet.

SEE ALSO `DatagramSocket.send()`, `getTTL()`, `MulticastSocket.send()`, `setTTL()`.

setTTL()

PURPOSE Sets the time-to-live for multicast packets sent from this datagram socket.

SYNTAX `protected abstract void setTTL(byte ttl) throws IOException`

DESCRIPTION A multicast packet sent from this datagram socket has a time-to-live value that specifies the transmission range of the packet.[1] The higher the time-to-live value, the higher the potential coverage of the multicast packet.

This method sets the time-to-live value used for packets sent from this datagram socket to be `ttl`. Subsequent calls to `send()` will use this time-to-live value. Subsequent calls to `getTTL()` will return this time-to-live value.

PARAMETERS

`ttl` An unsigned 8-bit number specifying the time-to-live for packets sent from this datagram socket. `0` < `ttl` ≤ `0xFF`.

EXCEPTIONS

`IOException`

If an IO error occurred while attempting to set the time-to-live of this datagram socket.

SEE ALSO `getTTL()`, `java.io.IOException`, `MulticastSocket.setTTL()`, `send()`.

A B C D E F G H I J K L M N O P Q R S T U V W X Y Z

1. If the time-to-live value of a datagram packet is one, the datagram packet is transmitted using the local network multicast which reaches all immediately-neighboring members of the sender. If the datagram packet's time-to-live value is greater than one, the datagram packet is also forwarded by *multicast routers* to all other networks that have members of the multicast group. If the datagram packet's time-to-live value is greater than two, the datagram packet is again forwarded from those networks, and so on.

java.io
DataInput

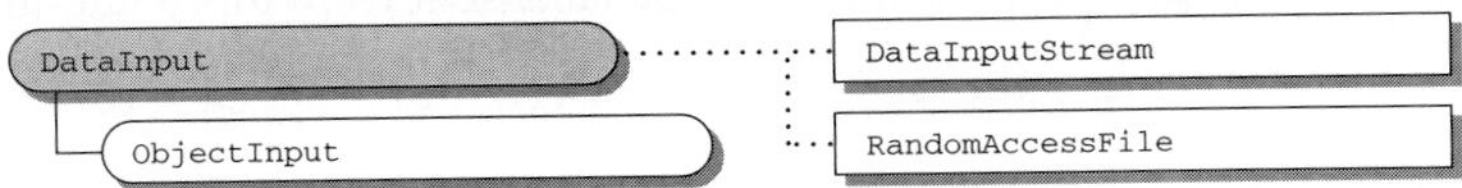

A B C D E F G H I J K L M N O P Q R S T U V W X Y Z

Syntax

```
public interface DataInput
```

Description

`DataInput` is an interface that declares methods for reading in data values and returning them as Java primitive data types. The format of the data values read is determined by the class that implements the `DataInput` interface. The types supported include `byte`, 16-bit Unicode `char`, 16-bit `short`, 32-bit `int`, 32-bit `float`, 64-bit `long`, 64-bit `double`, byte strings, and Unicode strings.

See `ObjectInput` for methods that read in Java objects.

MEMBER SUMMARY

Methods for Reading a Boolean, a Byte, a Character, or a Number

`readBoolean()`	Reads a `boolean`.
`readByte()`	Reads an 8-bit `byte`.
`readChar()`	Reads a 16-bit `char`.
`readDouble()`	Reads a 64-bit `double`.
`readFloat()`	Reads a 32-bit `float`.
`readInt()`	Reads a 32-bit `int`.
`readLong()`	Reads a 64-bit `long`.
`readShort()`	Reads a 16-bit `short`.
`readUnsignedByte()`	Reads an unsigned 8-bit `byte`.
`readUnsignedShort()`	Reads an unsigned 16-bit `short`.

Methods for Reading or Skipping Bytes

`readFully()`	Reads the requested number of bytes.
`skipBytes()`	Skips the requested number of bytes.

Methods for Reading a String

`readLine()`	Reads in a sequence of bytes terminated by a line terminator.
`readUTF()`	Reads in a Unicode string.

See Also

`DataInputStream`, `DataOutput`, `EOFException`, `ObjectInput`, `RandomAccessFile`.

Example

See the class examples of `DataInputStream` and `RandomAccessFile`.

A B C D E F G H I J K L M N O P Q R S T U V W X Y Z

readBoolean()

PURPOSE Reads a `boolean`.

SYNTAX `boolean readBoolean() throws IOException`

DESCRIPTION This method reads a `boolean` value. A `boolean` is represented as a single byte. If the byte is nonzero, the `boolean` value is `true`. If the byte is 0, the `boolean` value is `false`.

RETURNS The `boolean` read.

EXCEPTIONS

`EOFException`
If end-of-file was reached.

`IOException`
If an IO error occurred.

SEE ALSO `Dataoutput.writeBoolean()`.

readByte()

PURPOSE Reads an 8-bit `byte`.

SYNTAX `byte readByte() throws IOException`

RETURNS The 8-bite signed `byte` read.

EXCEPTIONS

`EOFException`
If end-of-file was reached.

`IOException`
If an IO error occurred.

SEE ALSO `DataOutput.writeByte()`, `DataOutput.writeBytes()`, `readUnsignedByte()`.

readChar()

PURPOSE Reads a 16-bit char.

SYNTAX `char readChar() throws IOException`

DESCRIPTION A Unicode `char` is represented by a 16-bit unsigned integer. This method reads a `char` by reading two consecutive bytes and then interpreting those as a 16-bit unsigned integer (the first byte read is the high-order byte) to be used as the value of the `char`.

RETURNS The `char` read.

EXCEPTIONS

`EOFException`
If end-of-file was reached.

`IOException`
If an IO error occurred.

SEE ALSO `DataOutput.writeChar()`, `DataOutput.writeChars()`.

readDouble()

PURPOSE Reads a 64-bit `double`.

SYNTAX `double readDouble() throws IOException`

DESCRIPTION This method reads 8 bytes and returns the `double` value represented by the bits of those 8 bytes. The 8 bytes are in the format expected by `Double.longBits-ToDouble()`.

RETURNS The 64-bit `double` read.

EXCEPTIONS

`EOFException`
If end-of-file was reached.

`IOException`
If an IO error occurred.

SEE ALSO `DataOutput.writeDouble()`, `readFloat()`.

readFloat()

PURPOSE Reads a 32-bit `float`.

SYNTAX `float readFloat() throws IOException`

DESCRIPTION

This method reads 4 bytes and returns the `float` value represented by the bits of those 4 bytes. The 4 bytes are in the format expected by `Float.intBitsToFloat()`

RETURNS

The 32-bit `float` read.

EXCEPTIONS

`EOFException`

If end-of-file was reached.

`IOException`

If an IO error occurred.

SEE ALSO

`DataOutput.writeFloat()`, `readDouble()`.

readFully()

PURPOSE

Reads the requested number of bytes.

SYNTAX

```
void readFully(byte[] buffer) throws IOException
void readFully(byte[] buffer, int offset, int count) throws
   IOException
```

DESCRIPTION

This method reads bytes to store into the `byte` array `buffer`, blocking until the requested number of bytes have been read. The first form of the method reads `buffer.length` number of bytes and stores them starting at index `0`. The second form reads `count` number of bytes and stores them starting at index `offset`.

PARAMETERS

`buffer` The buffer into which the data is read.

`count` The number of bytes to read.

`offset` The index in `buffer` at which to start storing the data read.

EXCEPTIONS

`EOFException`

If end-of-file was reached.

`IOException`

If an IO error occurred.

SEE ALSO

`DataOutput.writeByte()`, `DataOutput.writeBytes()`, `skipBytes()`.

readInt()

PURPOSE

Reads a 32-bit `int`.

SYNTAX

```
int readInt() throws IOException
```

A B C D E F G H I J K L M N O P Q R S T U V W X Y Z

DESCRIPTION This method reads 4 bytes and returns the `int` value represented by the bits of those 4 bytes. The higher-order bytes are read in order from the input source.

RETURNS The `int` read.

EXCEPTIONS

`EOFException`
If end-of-file was reached.

`IOException`
If an IO error occurred.

SEE ALSO `DataOutput.writeInt()`, `readLong()`, `readShort()`, `readUnsignedShort()`.

readLine()

PURPOSE Reads in a sequence of bytes terminated by a line terminator.

SYNTAX `String readLine() throws IOException`

DESCRIPTION A line is a sequence of bytes terminated by `\n`, `\r`, `\r\n`, or end-of-stream. Each byte read is converted to a character by setting the high-order byte of each character to `0`. This method blocks until a complete line has been read.

RETURNS A string containing the bytes of the line read (not including the line terminating character). `null` if no bytes are read before end-of-stream is reached.

EXCEPTIONS

`EOFException`
If end-of-file was reached.

`IOException`
If an IO error occurred.

SEE ALSO `DataInputStream.readLine()`, `DataOutput.writeLine()`, `ObjectInputStream.readLine()`, `readUTF()`.

readLong()

PURPOSE Reads a 64-bit `long`.

SYNTAX `long readLong() throws IOException`

DESCRIPTION This method reads 8 bytes and returns the `long` value represented by the bits of those 8 bytes. The higher-order bytes are read in order from the input source.

RETURNS The 64-bit `long` read.

EXCEPTIONS

`EOFException`

If end-of-file was reached.

`IOException`

If an IO error occurred.

SEE ALSO `DataOutput.writeLong()`, `readInt()`.

readShort()

PURPOSE Reads a 16-bit `short`.

SYNTAX `short readShort() throws IOException`

DESCRIPTION This method reads 2 bytes and returns the `short` value represented by the bits of those 2 bytes. The higher-order byte is read first from the input source.

RETURNS The `short` value read.

EXCEPTIONS

`EOFException`

If end-of-file was reached.

`IOException`

If an IO error occurred.

SEE ALSO `DataOutput.writeShort()`, `readUnsignedShort()`.

readUnsignedByte()

PURPOSE Reads an unsigned 8-bit `byte`.

SYNTAX `int readUnsignedByte() throws IOException`

DESCRIPTION This method reads an 8-bit byte and returns it as an unsigned number. The only difference between this method and `readByte()` is that `readByte()` returns the value read as a `byte`, while this method returns the value as an `int`. The higher-order 3 bytes of an `int` are unused and zeroed when an `int` is used to store an 8-bit byte; hence, the `int` is always unsigned.

RETURNS An `int` containing the 8 bits read.

EXCEPTIONS

`EOFException`

If end-of-file was reached.

`IOException`

If an IO error occurred.

SEE ALSO `DataOutput.writeByte()`, `DataOutput.writeBytes()`, `readByte()`, `readInt()`, `readUnsignedShort()`.

readUnsignedShort()

PURPOSE Reads an unsigned 16-bit `short`.

SYNTAX `int readUnsignedShort() throws IOException`

DESCRIPTION This method reads 16 bits and returns them as an unsigned number. The only difference between this method and `readShort()` is that `readShort()` returns the value read as a `short`, while this method returns the value as an `int`. The higher-order 2 bytes of an `int` are unused and zeroed when an `int` is used to store a 16-bit `short`; hence, the `int` is always unsigned.

RETURNS An `int` containing the 16 bits read.

EXCEPTIONS

`EOFException`
If end-of-file was reached.

`IOException`
If an IO error occurred.

SEE ALSO `DataOutput.writeShort()`, `readInt()`, `readShort()`.

readUTF()

PURPOSE Reads in a Unicode string.

SYNTAX `String readUTF() throws IOException`

DESCRIPTION This method reads a UTF-encoded sequence of characters and returns it as a string. UTF stands for Unicode Transfer Format, a character encoding scheme for Unicode characters. UTF strings are restricted to have an encoded length less than or equal to 65535. See *The Java Language Specification, First Edition*, Section 22.1.15, for details of UTF.

RETURNS A string containing the characters read.

EXCEPTIONS

`EOFException`
If end-of-file was reached.

`IOException`
If an IO error occurred.

SEE ALSO `DataOutput.writeUTF()`, `readLine()`.

skipBytes()

PURPOSE Skips the requested number of bytes.

SYNTAX `int skipBytes(int count) throws IOException`

DESCRIPTION This method skips `count` number of bytes. It blocks until `count` number of bytes have been skipped.

PARAMETERS

`count` The number of bytes to skip.

RETURNS The actual number of bytes skipped.

EXCEPTIONS

`EOFException`

If end-of-file was reached.

`IOException`

If an IO error occurred.

SEE ALSO `DataOutput.writeByte()`, `DataOutput.writeBytes()`, `readByte()`, `readFully()`, `readUnsignedByte()`.

java.io
DataInputStream

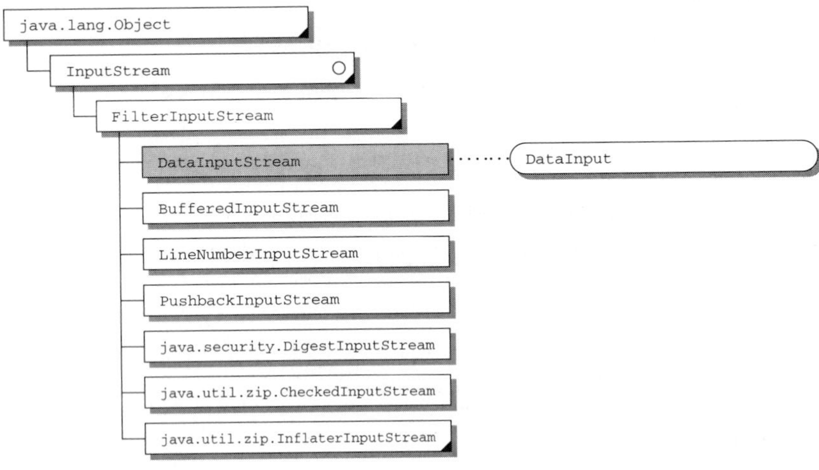

Syntax

```
public class DataInputStream extends FilterInputStream implements DataInput
```

Description

The `DataInputStream` class is a filter input stream that implements the `DataInput` interface. It can be composed with another input stream to allow data from that other stream to be read and interpreted (through this filter input stream) as representations of Java primitive data types. The types supported include `byte`, 16-bit Unicode `char`, 16-bit `short`, 32-bit `int`, 32-bit `float`, 64-bit `long`, 64-bit `double`, byte strings, and Unicode strings.

Typically, you use a `DataInputStream` to read data created by using a `DataOutputStream` (see Figure 32).

See `ObjectInput` and `ObjectInputStream` for details on reading in Java objects.

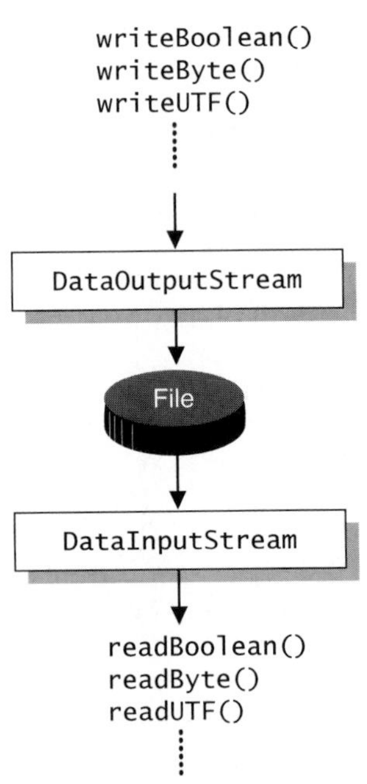

FIGURE 32: `DataOutputStream` and `DataInputStream`.

MEMBER SUMMARY	
Constructor	
`DataInputStream()`	Constructs a `DataInputStream` instance from an existing input stream.
Methods for Reading a Boolean, a Byte, a Character, or a Number	
`readBoolean()`	Reads a `boolean` from this input stream.
`readByte()`	Reads a `byte` from this input stream.
`readChar()`	Reads a 16-bit Unicode `char` from this input stream.
`readDouble()`	Reads a 64-bit `double` from this input stream.
`readFloat()`	Reads a 32-bit `float` from this input stream.
`readInt()`	Reads a 32-bit `int` from this input stream.
`readLong()`	Reads a 64-bit `long` from this input stream.
`readShort()`	Reads a 16-bit `short` from this input stream.
`readUnsignedByte()`	Reads an unsigned 8-bit `byte` from this input stream.
`readUnsignedShort()`	Reads an unsigned 16-bit `short` from this input stream.
Methods for Reading or Skipping Bytes	
`read()`	Reads bytes from this input stream into an array of bytes.
`readFully()`	Reads the requested number of bytes from this input stream.
`skipBytes()`	Skips the requested number of bytes from this input stream.
Method for Reading a String	
`readUTF()`	Reads a Unicode string from this input stream.
Deprecated Method	
`readLine()`	Replaced by `BufferedReader.readLine()`.

See Also

`BufferedReader.readLine()`, `DataInput`, `DataOutputStream`, `InputStream`, `InputStreamReader`, `ObjectInput`, `ObjectInputStream`, `RandomAccessFile`.

Example

This example shows the use of the methods in `DataInputStream`. It reads in a file generated by the class example of `DataOutputStream` and prints out what was read.

```
import java.io.*;

class Main {
    public static void main(String[] args) {
        if (args.length != 1) {
            System.err.println(
                "Usage: java Main <output from DataOutput example>");
            System.exit(-1);
```

```
            }
            FileInputStream file_in;
            DataInputStream data_in;

            try {
                file_in = new FileInputStream(args[0]);
                data_in = new DataInputStream(file_in);

                System.out.println("Available: " + data_in.available());

                byte b;
                byte[] b2 = new byte[1];
                b = data_in.readByte();
                System.out.println("Byte: " + b);
                data_in.read(b2);
                System.out.println("Byte[0]: " + (char)b2[0]);
                data_in.read(b2, 0, b2.length);
                System.out.println("Byte[0]: " + (char)b2[0]);
                int ub = data_in.readUnsignedByte();
                System.out.println("Unsigned Byte: " + b);
                System.out.println("Boolean: " + data_in.readBoolean());
                char a = data_in.readChar();
                System.out.println("Char: " + a);

                byte[] b3 = new byte[3];
                data_in.readFully(b3);
                System.out.println("readFully: " + (char)b3[0] + (char)b3[1] +
                                   (char)b3[2]);
                data_in.skipBytes(6); // skip string 'abc'
                double d1 = data_in.readDouble();
                float f1 = data_in.readFloat();
                int i = data_in.readInt();
                long l = data_in.readLong();
                short s = data_in.readShort();
                String str = data_in.readUTF();
                ub = data_in.readUnsignedByte();
                int us = data_in.readUnsignedShort();
                System.out.println("UTF String" + str);
            } catch (IOException e) {
                System.out.println(e);
            }
        }
    }
```

DataInputStream()

PURPOSE Constructs a `DataInputStream` instance from an existing stream.

SYNTAX `public DataInputStream(InputStream in)`

DESCRIPTION This constructor constructs a data input stream for an existing input stream `in`. The input for this new data input stream comes from the input stream `in`. When a read operation is performed on this data input stream, the stream reads bytes from `in` and returns the answer in the data type requested.

PARAMETERS

`in` The non-`null` input stream from which the data values will be read.

SEE ALSO `FilterInputStream`.

EXAMPLE See the class example.

read()

PURPOSE Reads bytes from this input stream into an array of bytes.

SYNTAX

```
public final int read(byte[] buffer) throws IOException
public final int read(byte[] buffer, int offset, int count) throws
   IOException
```

DESCRIPTION This method reads bytes from the data input stream and copies them into the byte array `buffer`. If `offset` and `count` are specified, `count` bytes are read and placed into `buffer` starting at index `offset`. Otherwise, `buffer.length` bytes are read and placed into `buffer` starting at index `0`. This method might block if no bytes are available to be read. Also, the requested number of bytes to be read (either `count` or `buffer.length`) might not all be read if that number is not available. If you want to block waiting for all of the number of bytes requested, use `readFully()`.

PARAMETERS

`buffer` The non-`null` `byte` array into which the data is read.

`count` The maximum number of bytes to read. `0` ≤ `count` ≤ `buffer.length-offset`.

`offset` The index in `buffer` to start storing the bytes read. `0` ≤ `offset` < `buffer.length`.

RETURNS The actual number of bytes read. `-1` is returned when no bytes are read because end-of-stream has been reached.

EXCEPTIONS

`ArrayIndexOutOfBoundsException`

If `count` or `offset` is outside of the specified bounds.

`IOException`

If an IO error occurred while attempting to read from this stream.

OVERRIDES `FilterInputStream.read()`.

SEE ALSO `DataOutputStream.write()`, `DataOutputStream.writeByte()`, `readByte()`, `readLine()`, `readFully()`, `readUnsignedByte()`.

EXAMPLE See the class example.

A B C D E F G H I J K L M N O P Q R S T U V W X Y Z

readBoolean()

PURPOSE Reads a `boolean` from this input stream.

SYNTAX `public final boolean readBoolean() throws IOException`

DESCRIPTION This method reads a `boolean` value from the input stream. A `boolean` is represented as a single byte. If the byte is nonzero, the `boolean` value is `true`. If the byte is 0, the `boolean` value is `false`.

RETURNS The `boolean` value read (`true` or `false`).

EXCEPTIONS

`EOFException`
If end-of-file was reached while attempting to read from this stream.

`IOException`
If an IO error occurred while attempting to read from this stream.

SEE ALSO `DataOutputStream.writeBoolean()`.

EXAMPLE See the class example.

readByte()

PURPOSE Reads a `byte` from this input stream.

SYNTAX `public final byte readByte() throws IOException`

RETURNS The 8-bit `byte` read.

EXCEPTIONS

`EOFException`
If end-of-file was reached while attempting to read from this stream.

`IOException`
If an IO error occurred while attempting to read from this stream.

SEE ALSO `DataOutputStream.writeByte()`, `DataOutputStream.writeBytes()`, `readUnsignedByte()`.

EXAMPLE See the class example.

readChar()

PURPOSE Reads a 16-bit Unicode `char` from this input stream.

SYNTAX `public final char readChar() throws IOException`

DESCRIPTION A Unicode `char` is represented by a 16-bit unsigned integer. This method reads a `char` by reading two consecutive bytes from the input stream and then interpreting them as a 16-bit unsigned integer (the first byte read is the high-order byte) to be used as the value of the `char`.

RETURNS The `char` read.

EXCEPTIONS

`EOFException`

If end-of-file was reached while attempting to read from this stream.

`IOException`

If an IO error occurred while attempting to read from this stream.

SEE ALSO `DataOutputStream.writeChar()`, `DataOutputStream.writeChars()`.

EXAMPLE See the class example.

readDouble()

PURPOSE Reads a 64-bit `double` from this input stream.

SYNTAX `public final double readDouble() throws IOException`

DESCRIPTION This method reads 8 bytes from the input stream and returns the `double` value represented by the bits of those 8 bytes. The 8 bytes are in the format expected by `Double.longBitsToDouble()`.

RETURNS The `double` value read.

EXCEPTIONS

`EOFException`

If end-of-file was reached while attempting to read from this stream.

`IOException`

If an IO error occurred while attempting to read from this stream.

SEE ALSO `DataOutputStream.writeDouble()`,`java.lang.Double.longBitsToDouble()`.

EXAMPLE See the class example.

readFloat()

PURPOSE Reads a 32-bit `float` from this input stream.

SYNTAX `public final float readFloat() throws IOException`

DESCRIPTION This method reads 4 bytes from the input stream and returns the `float` value represented by the bits of those 4 bytes. The 4 bytes are in the format expected by `Float.intBitsToFloat()`.

RETURNS The `float` value read.

EXCEPTIONS

`EOFException`
If end-of-file was reached while attempting to read from this stream.

`IOException`
If an IO error occurred while attempting to read from this stream.

SEE ALSO `DataOutputStream.writeFloat()`, `Float.intBitsToFloat()`.

EXAMPLE See the class example.

readFully()

PURPOSE Reads the requested number of bytes from this input stream.

SYNTAX

```
public final void readFully(byte[] buffer) throws IOException
public final void readFully(byte[] buffer, int offset, int count)
   throws IOException
```

DESCRIPTION This method reads bytes from the data input stream and copies them into the `byte` array `buffer`. If `offset` and `count` are specified, `count` bytes are read and placed into `buffer` starting at index `offset`. If they are not specified, `buffer.length` bytes are read and placed into `buffer` starting at index `0`. These methods will block waiting for all of the requested number of bytes to be read (either `count` or `buffer.length`).

PARAMETERS

`buffer` The `byte` array into which the data is read.
`count` The maximum number of bytes to read. `0` ≤ `count` ≤ `buffer.length-offset`.
`offset` The index in `buffer` at which to start storing the bytes read. `0` ≤ `offset` < `buffer.length`.

EXCEPTIONS

`ArrayIndexOutOfBoundsException`
If `count` or `offset` is outside of the specified bounds.

`EOFException`
If end-of-file was reached while attempting to read from this stream.

`IOException`
If an IO error occurred while attempting to read from this stream.

EXAMPLE See the class example.

readInt()

PURPOSE Reads a 32-bit `int` from this input stream.

SYNTAX `public final int readInt() throws IOException`

DESCRIPTION This method reads 4 bytes from the input stream and returns the `int` value represented by the bits of those 4 bytes. The higher-order bytes are read in order from the input stream.

RETURNS The `int` value read.

EXCEPTIONS

`EOFException`

If end-of-file was reached while attempting to read from this stream.

`IOException`

If an IO error occurred while attempting to read from this stream.

SEE ALSO `DataOutputStream.writeInt()`.

EXAMPLE See the class example.

readLine() *DEPRECATED*

PURPOSE Replaced by `BufferedReader.readLine()`.

SYNTAX `public final String readLine() throws IOException`

RETURNS A string copy of a line from the input stream; `null` if no byte is read before end-of-file is reached.

EXCEPTIONS

`IOException`

If an IO error occurred while attempting to read from this stream.

DEPRECATION This method reads in from the input stream a sequence of bytes terminated by a line terminator. A line is defined as a sequence of bytes terminated by a newline (`\n`), return (`\r`), newline-return (`\r\n`), or end-of-file. The high-order byte of each character in the string is set to 0. The string does not include the line terminator character. The usage of this method is deprecated because, in general, it does not convert the bytes read into strings properly. The following example uses `readLine()` to read strings from a file.

```
import java.io.*;

class Old {
    public static void main(String[] args) {
        if (args.length == 0) {
            System.err.println("java Old <inputfile>");
            System.exit(-1);
        }
```

A B C D E F G H I J K L M N O P Q R S T U V W X Y Z

```
        try {
            DataInputStream in =
                new DataInputStream(new FileInputStream(args[0]));

            String line;
            while ((line=in.readLine()) != null) {
                System.out.println(line);
            }
            in.close();
        } catch (IOException e) {
            e.printStackTrace();
        }
    }
}
```

Replace its usage with `BufferedReader.readLine()` as follows:

```
import java.io.*;

class New {
    public static void main(String[] args) {
        if (args.length == 0) {
            System.err.println("java New <inputfile>");
            System.exit(-1);
        }
        try {
            BufferedReader in = new BufferedReader(new
FileReader(args[0]));

            String line;
            while ((line=in.readLine()) != null) {
                System.out.println(line);
            }
            in.close();
        } catch (IOException e) {
            e.printStackTrace();
        }
    }
}
```

readLong()

PURPOSE Reads a 64-bit `long` from this input stream.

SYNTAX `public final long readLong() throws IOException`

DESCRIPTION This method reads 8 bytes from the input stream and returns the `long` value represented by the bits of those 8 bytes. The higher-order bytes are read in order from the input stream.

RETURNS The `long` value read.

EXCEPTIONS

`EOFException`

If end-of-file was reached while attempting to read from this stream.

`IOException`

If an IO error occurred while attempting to read from this stream.

SEE ALSO `DataOutputStream.writeLong()`.

EXAMPLE See the class example.

readShort()

PURPOSE Reads a 16-bit `short` from this input stream.

SYNTAX `public final short readShort() throws IOException`

DESCRIPTION This method reads 2 bytes from the input stream and returns the `short` value represented by the bits of those 2 bytes. The higher-order byte is read first from the input stream.

RETURNS The `short` value read.

EXCEPTIONS

`EOFException`

If end-of-file was reached while attempting to read from this stream.

`IOException`

If an IO error occurred while attempting to read from this stream.

SEE ALSO `DataOutputStream.writeShort()`, `readUnsignedShort()`.

EXAMPLE See the class example.

readUnsignedByte()

PURPOSE Reads an unsigned 8-bit byte from this input stream.

SYNTAX `public final int readUnsignedByte() throws IOException`

DESCRIPTION This method reads a byte from this input stream and returns it as the lowest byte in an `int`. The only difference between this method and `readByte()` is that this method returns the byte in an `int`, while `readByte()` returns the byte in a `byte`. Because `byte` is a signed type, the highest-order bit will determine the sign of the value. When a byte is returned in an `int`, the higher-order 3 bytes are unused (0). Hence, the `int` value returned is always unsigned.

RETURNS An `int` containing the byte read.

EXCEPTIONS

`EOFException`

If end-of-file was reached while attempting to read from this stream.

`IOException`

If an IO error occurred while attempting to read from this stream.

SEE ALSO `DataOutputStream.writeByte(), readByte().`

EXAMPLE See the class example.

readUnsignedShort()

PURPOSE Reads an unsigned 16-bit `short` from this input stream.

SYNTAX

```
public final int readUnsignedShort() throws IOException
```

DESCRIPTION This method reads 2 bytes from this input stream and returns the unsigned integer value represented by the bits of those 2 bytes. The higher-order byte is read first from the input stream. The only difference between this method and `readShort()` is that this method returns the result as an `int`, while `readShort()` returns the result as a `short`.

DESCRIPTION Because `short` is a signed type, the highest-order bit will determine the sign of the value. When a `short` is returned in an `int`, it occupies the lower-order 2 bytes of the `int`; the higher-order 2 bytes are unused (0). Hence, the `int` value returned is always unsigned.

RETURNS An `int` containing the 16-bit `short` value read.

EXCEPTIONS

`EOFException`
If end-of-file was reached while attempting to read from this stream.

`IOException`
If an IO error occurred while attempting to read from this stream.

SEE ALSO `DataOutputStream.writeShort(), readShort().`

EXAMPLE See the class example.

readUTF()

PURPOSE Reads a Unicode string from this data input stream.

SYNTAX

```
public final String readUTF() throws IOException
public final static String readUTF(DataInput in) throws
    IOException
```

DESCRIPTION This method reads a Unicode string and returns it as a `String`. The first form of this method reads the string from this data input stream. The second form reads the string from the data input stream `in`.

UTF stands for Unicode Transfer Format. It is an encoding scheme for Unicode characters. The size of the string is specified in the encoded form. UTF strings are restricted to have an encoded length ≤ 65535. When writing a string to a data stream, use `DataOutputStream.writeUTF()` and read it back using `readUTF()`.

See *The Java Language Specification, First Edition*, Section 22.1.15, for details of UTF.

PARAMETERS

`in` The non-`null` stream from which to read the string.

RETURNS The Unicode string read as a `String`.

EXCEPTIONS

`EOFException`
If end-of-file was reached while attempting to read the string.

`IOException`
If an IO error occurred while attempting to read the string.

`UTFDataFormatException`
If the string being read is a malformed UTF string.

SEE ALSO `DataOutputStream.writeUTF()`.

EXAMPLE See the class example.

skipBytes()

PURPOSE Skips the requested number of bytes from this input stream.

SYNTAX `public final int skipBytes(int count) throws IOException`

DESCRIPTION This method skips `count` number of bytes from the input stream. It blocks until all `count` number of bytes are skipped.

PARAMETERS

`count` The number of bytes to be skipped.

RETURNS The actual number of bytes skipped.

EXCEPTIONS

`EOFException`
If end-of-file was reached while attempting to skip the requested number of bytes.

`IOException`
If an IO error occurred while attempting to skip the requested number of bytes.

EXAMPLE See the class example.

java.io

DataOutput

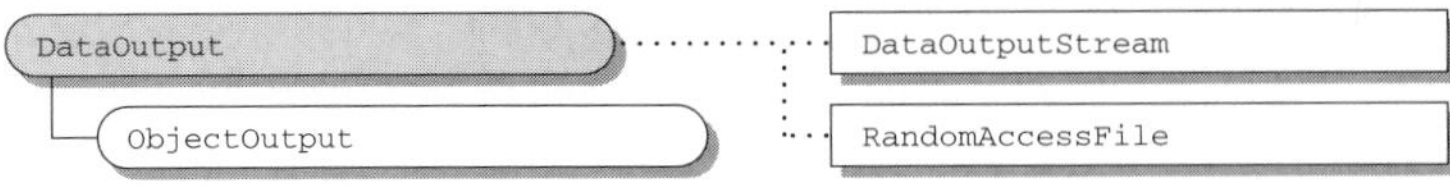

Syntax

```
public interface DataOutput
```

Description

`DataOutput` is an interface that declares methods for writing Java primitive data values. The format of the data values written is determined by the class that implements the `DataOutput` interface. The types supported include `byte`, 16-bit Unicode `char`, 16-bit `short`, 32-bit `int`, 32-bit `float`, 64-bit `long`, 64-bit `double`, byte strings, and Unicode strings.

See `ObjectOutput` for details on writing out Java objects.

MEMBER SUMMARY

Methods for Writing a Byte, a Boolean, a Character, or a Number

`writeBoolean()`	Writes a `boolean`.
`writeByte()`	Writes an 8-bit `byte`.
`writeChar()`	Writes a 16-bit `char`.
`writeDouble()`	Writes a 64-bit `double`.
`writeFloat()`	Writes a 32-bit `float`.
`writeInt()`	Writes a 32-bit `int`.
`writeLong()`	Writes a 64-bit `long`.
`writeShort()`	Writes a 16-bit `short`.

Method for Writing Bytes

`write()`	Writes a single byte or an array of bytes.

Methods for Writing a String

`writeBytes()`	Writes a string as a sequence of bytes.
`writeChars()`	Writes a string as a sequence of `char`s.
`writeUTF()`	Writes a string in UTF.

See Also

`DataInput`, `DataOutputStream`, `ObjectOutput`, `RandomAccessFile`.

Example

See the class examples of `DataOutputStream` and `RandomAccessFile`.

write()

PURPOSE Writes a single byte or an array of bytes.

SYNTAX
```
void write(int oneByte) throws IOException
void write(byte[] buffer) throws IOException
void write(byte[] buffer, int offset, int count) throws
   IOException
```

DESCRIPTION This method writes bytes. The first form writes the low-order byte of `oneByte`. The second form writes all of the bytes from the `byte` array `buffer`. The third form writes `count` number of bytes starting at the index `offset` from the `byte` array `buffer`.

PARAMETERS

- `buffer` The non-`null` `byte` array containing the bytes to be written.
- `count` The number of bytes to be written. `0` ≤ `count` ≤ `buffer.length-offset`.
- `offset` The index in `buffer` from which to get the bytes to be written. `0` ≤ `offset` < `buffer.length`.
- `oneByte` The byte to be written.

EXCEPTIONS

`IOException`
If an IO error occurred.

SEE ALSO `DataInput.readByte()`, `writeByte()`, `writeBytes()`.

writeBoolean()

PURPOSE Writes a `boolean`.

SYNTAX
```
void writeBoolean(boolean val) throws IOException
```

DESCRIPTION This method writes the `boolean` value `val`. The output consists of a single byte whose value is `1` if `val` is `true` and `0` if `val` is `false`.

PARAMETERS

- `val` The `boolean` value to be written.

EXCEPTIONS

`IOException`
If an IO error occurred while attempting to write.

SEE ALSO `DataInput.readBoolean()`.

writeByte()

PURPOSE Writes an 8-bit byte.

SYNTAX `void writeByte(int val) throws IOException`

DESCRIPTION This method writes an 8-bit byte. The output consists of a single byte whose value is the lowest-order byte of `val`.

PARAMETERS

`val` The `byte` value to be written.

EXCEPTIONS

`IOException`

If an IO error occurred while attempting to write.

SEE ALSO `DataInput.readByte(), DataInput.readUnsignedByte(), write(), writeBytes().`

writeBytes()

PURPOSE Writes a string as a sequence of bytes.

SYNTAX `void writeBytes(String str) throws IOException`

DESCRIPTION This method writes the string `str` as a sequence of 8-bit bytes. Because a string consists of 16-bit Unicode `char`s, only the lower-order 8 bits of each `char` are written; the higher-order 8 bits are lost (and not written). Use `writeChar()` and `writeChars()` to write all 16 bits of a Unicode `char` or `char` string.

PARAMETERS

`str` The non-`null` string of bytes to be written.

EXCEPTIONS

`IOException`

If an IO error occurred.

SEE ALSO `DataInput.readByte(), DataInput.readFully(), writeChars(), writeUTF().`

writeChar()

PURPOSE Writes a 16-bit `char`.

SYNTAX `void writeChar(int val) throws IOException`

DESCRIPTION This method writes `val` as a 16-bit `char`. Because an `int` is a 32-bit entity, only the lower-order 16 bits of `val` are written.

PARAMETERS

`val` The `char` value to be written.

EXCEPTIONS

`IOException`

If an IO error occurred.

SEE ALSO `DataInput.readChar()`, `writeByte()`, `writeChars()`.

writeChars()

PURPOSE Writes a string as a sequence of `char`s.

SYNTAX `void writeChars(String str) throws IOException`

DESCRIPTION This method writes the string `str` as a sequence of 16-bit `char` values. Each `char` written consists of 2 bytes (higher-order written first), which represent its Unicode value.

PARAMETERS

`str` The non-`null` string to be written.

EXCEPTIONS

`IOException`

If an IO error occurred.

SEE ALSO `DataInput.readChar()`, `writeBytes()`, `writeChar()`, `writeUTF()`.

writeDouble()

PURPOSE Writes a 64-bit `double`.

SYNTAX `void writeDouble(double val) throws IOException`

DESCRIPTION This method writes the `double` value `val`. The output generated consists of 8 bytes in the format produced by `Double.doubleToLongBits()`.

PARAMETERS

`val` The `double` value to be written.

EXCEPTIONS

`IOException`

If an IO error occurred.

SEE ALSO `DataInput.readDouble()`, `java.lang.Double.doubleToLongBits()`, `writeFloat()`.

writeFloat()

PURPOSE Writes a 32-bit `float`.

SYNTAX `void writeFloat(float val) throws IOException`

DESCRIPTION This method writes the `float` value `val`. The output generated consists of 4 bytes in the format produced by `Float.floatToIntBits()`.

PARAMETERS

`val` The `float` value to be written.

EXCEPTIONS

`IOException`

If an IO error occurred.

SEE ALSO `DataInput.readFloat()`, `java.lang.Float.floatToIntBits()`, `writeDouble()`.

writeInt()

PURPOSE Writes a 32-bit `int`.

SYNTAX `void writeInt(int val) throws IOException`

DESCRIPTION This method writes the `int` value `val`. The output generated consists of 4 bytes, highest-to-lowest byte order, that represent the value of `val`.

PARAMETERS

`val` The `int` value to be written.

EXCEPTIONS

`IOException`

If an IO error occurred.

SEE ALSO `DataInput.readInt()`, `writeLong()`, `writeShort()`.

writeLong()

PURPOSE Writes a 64-bit `long`.

SYNTAX `void writeLong(long val) throws IOException`

DESCRIPTION This method writes the `long` value `val`. The output generated consists of 8 bytes, highest-to-lowest byte order, that represent the value of `val`.

PARAMETERS

`val` The `long` value to be written.

EXCEPTIONS

`IOException`

If an IO error occurred.

SEE ALSO `DataInput.readLong()`, `writeInt()`, `writeShort()`.

A B C D E F G H I J K L M N O P Q R S T U V W X Y Z

writeShort()

PURPOSE Writes a 16-bit `short`.

SYNTAX `void writeShort(int val) throws IOException`

DESCRIPTION This method writes the `short` value `val`. Because a `short` is only 16 bits, only the lower-order 2 bytes of `val` are written. The output generated consists of 2 bytes, with the higher-order byte written first.

PARAMETERS

`val` The `short` value to be written.

EXCEPTIONS

`IOException`

If an IO error occurred.

SEE ALSO `DataInput.readShort()`, `DataInput.readUnsignedShort()`, `writeInt()`, `writeLong()`.

writeUTF()

PURPOSE Writes a string in UTF.

SYNTAX `void writeUTF(String str) throws IOException`

DESCRIPTION This method writes out the string `str` in UTF. UTF stands for Unicode Transfer Format, an encoding scheme for Unicode characters. UTF strings are restricted to have an encoded length ≤ 65535. See *The Java Language Specification, First Edition*, Section 22.2.14, for details on UTF.

PARAMETERS

`str` The non-`null` string to be written.

EXCEPTIONS

`IOException`

If an IO error occurred.

`UTFDataFormatException`

If the resulting UTF data size would exceed `65535` bytes.

SEE ALSO `DataInput.readUTF()`, `writeChars()`.

java.io
DataOutputStream

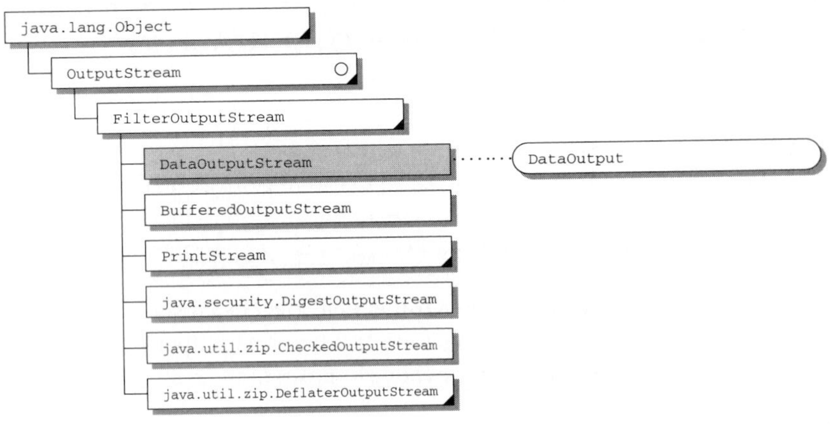

A B C D E F G H I J K L M N O P Q R S T U V W X Y Z

Syntax

```
public class DataOutputStream extends FilterOutputStream implements DataOutput
```

Description

The `DataOutputStream` class is a filter that implements the `DataOutput` interface. It can be composed with another stream so that you can use this data output stream to write typed data to that stream. The types supported include `byte`, 16-bit Unicode `char`, 16-bit `short`, 32-bit `int`, 32-bit `float`, 64-bit `long`, 64-bit `double`, byte strings, and Unicode strings.

Typically, you use `DataOutputStream` to generate the output that will be read subsequently using a `DataInputStream` (see Figure 33).

See `ObjectOutput` and `ObjectOutputStream` for details on writing out Java objects.

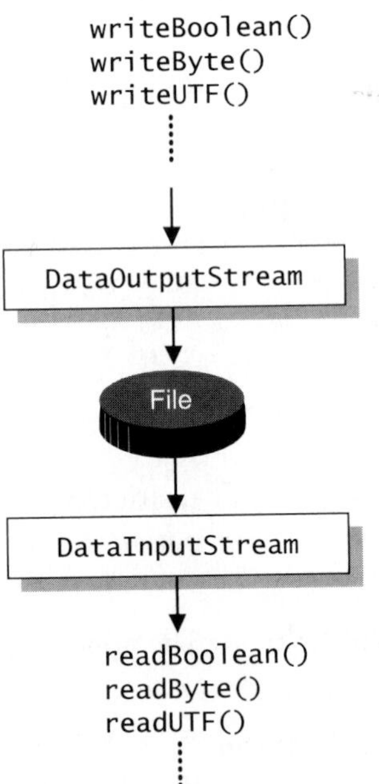

FIGURE 33: `DataOutputStream` and `DataInputStream`.

MEMBER SUMMARY

Constructor

`DataOutputStream()`	Constructs a `DataOutputStream` instance for an existing output stream.

Methods for Writing a Byte, a Boolean, a Character, or a Number

`writeBoolean()`	Writes a `boolean` to this output stream.
`writeByte()`	Writes an 8-bit `byte` to this output stream.
`writeChar()`	Writes a 16-bit `char` to this output stream.
`writeDouble()`	Writes a 64-bit `double` to this output stream.
`writeFloat()`	Writes a 32-bit `float` to this output stream.
`writeInt()`	Writes a 32-bit `int` to this output stream.
`writeLong()`	Writes a 64-bit `long` to this output stream.
`writeShort()`	Writes a 16-bit `short` to this output stream.

Method for Writing Bytes

`write()`	Writes bytes to this output stream.

Methods for Writing a String

`writeBytes()`	Writes a string as a sequence of bytes to this output stream.
`writeChars()`	Writes a string as a sequence of `char`s to this output stream.
`writeUTF()`	Writes a string in UTF to this output stream.

Size and Flush Methods

`flush()`	Writes any buffered output to this output stream.
`size()`	Determines the number of bytes written to this stream so far.

Protected Field

`written`	The number of bytes written to this stream so far.

See Also

`BufferedWriter`, `DataInputStream`, `DataOutput`, `ObjectOutput`, `ObjectOutputStream`, `OutputStream`, `OutputStreamWriter`.

Example

This example shows the use of the methods in `DataOutputStream`. It generates a file that can be read back in using the class example of `DataInputStream`.

```
import java.io.*;

class Main {
    public static void main(String[] args) {
        if (args.length != 1) {
            System.err.println("Usage: java Main <output file>");
```

```
            System.exit(-1);
        }
        FileOutputStream file_out;
        DataOutputStream data_out;

        try {
            file_out = new FileOutputStream(args[0]);
            data_out = new DataOutputStream(file_out);

            char a = 'a';
            byte b = 2;
            String c = "abc";
            short d = 4;
            byte[] b2 = {'a', 'b', 'c'};

            data_out.write(b);
            data_out.write(b2, 0, b2.length);
            data_out.writeBoolean(true);
            data_out.writeChar(a);
            data_out.writeBytes(c);
            data_out.writeChars(c);
            data_out.writeDouble(123.456);
            data_out.writeFloat(123.456f);
            data_out.writeInt(678);
            data_out.writeLong(678l);
            data_out.writeShort(d);
            data_out.writeUTF(c);
            data_out.writeUTF("abc\n");
            data_out.write(b);
            data_out.writeShort(d);
            data_out.flush();
            System.out.println("Size of file written: " + data_out.size());
            data_out.close();
        } catch (IOException e) {
            System.out.println(e);
        }
    }
}
```

A B C D E F G H I J K L M N O P Q R S T U V W X Y Z

DataOutputStream()

PURPOSE Constructs a `DataOutputStream` instance for an existing output stream.

SYNTAX `public DataOutputStream(OutputStream out)`

DESCRIPTION This constructor constructs a data output stream (filter) for the existing output stream `out`. You can use the methods of this newly created data output stream to write typed output to `out`.

PARAMETERS

`out` this output stream to which data will be written.

SEE ALSO `FilterOutputStream`.

EXAMPLE See the class example.

flush()

PURPOSE Writes any buffered output to this output stream.

SYNTAX `public void flush() throws IOException`

DESCRIPTION `DataOutputStream` is simply a filter stream that passes data written onto its output stream. It does no buffering. Calling `flush()` on this data output stream invokes `flush()` on this output stream associated with this data output stream. If this output stream (or any of its filters) does any buffering, any unwritten output will be written out. This method effectively flushes this stream and all of the streams "downstream."

EXCEPTIONS

`IOException`

If an IO error occurred while attempting to flush this output stream.

OVERRIDES `FilterOutputStream.flush()`.

EXAMPLE See the class example.

size()

PURPOSE Determines the number of bytes written to this stream so far.

SYNTAX `public final int size()`

DESCRIPTION The data output stream keeps track of how many bytes have been written to this output stream so far. This number is updated after each write operation. `size()` returns this number.

RETURNS The number of bytes written to this stream so far.

SEE ALSO `written`.

EXAMPLE See the class example.

write()

PURPOSE Writes bytes to this output stream.

SYNTAX

```
public synchronized void write(int oneByte) throws IOException
public synchronized void write(byte[] buffer, int offset, int
   count) throws IOException
```

DESCRIPTION The `write()` method writes the specified byte or bytes to this data output stream. The first form of `write()` writes a single byte `oneByte` to this stream.

The second form writes count bytes from the byte array buffer starting at index offset to this stream.

PARAMETERS

buffer — The non-null byte array containing data to be written.

count — The number of bytes from buffer to be written. 0 ≤ count ≤ buffer.length-offset.

offset — The index in buffer of the bytes to be written. 0 ≤ offset < buffer.length.

oneByte — The byte to be written. The low-order byte from oneByte is written.

EXCEPTIONS

ArrayIndexOutOfBoundsException
If count or offset is outside of the specified bounds.

IOException
If an IO error occurred while attempting to write.

OVERRIDES — FilterOutputStream.write().

SEE ALSO — DataInputStream.readByte(), DataInputStream.readLine(), DataInputStream.readFully(), DataInputStream.readUnsignedByte(), writeByte(), writeBytes().

EXAMPLE — See the class example.

writeBoolean()

PURPOSE — Writes a boolean to this output stream.

SYNTAX

```
public final void writeBoolean(boolean val) throws IOException
```

DESCRIPTION — This method writes the boolean value val to this output stream. The output consists of a single byte whose value is 1 if val is true and 0 if val is false.

PARAMETERS

val — The boolean value to be written.

EXCEPTIONS

IOException
If an IO error occurred while attempting to write.

SEE ALSO — DataInputStream.readBoolean().

EXAMPLE — See the class example.

writeByte()

PURPOSE
Writes an 8-bit byte to this output stream.

SYNTAX
```
public final void writeByte(int val) throws IOException
```

DESCRIPTION
This method writes the 8-bit byte (in the lowest-order byte of `val`) to this output stream. The output consists of a single byte whose value is the lowest-order byte of `val`.

PARAMETERS

`val` The `byte` value to be written.

EXCEPTIONS

`IOException`

If an IO error occurred while attempting to write.

SEE ALSO
`DataInputStream.read()`, `DataInputStream.readByte()`, `DataInputStream.readFully()`, `DataInputStream.readLine()`, `DataInputStream.readUnsignedByte()`, `write()`.

EXAMPLE
See the class example.

writeBytes()

PURPOSE
Writes a string as a sequence of bytes to this output stream.

SYNTAX
```
public final void writeBytes(String str) throws IOException
```

DESCRIPTION
This method writes the string `str` to this output stream as a sequence of bytes (8 bits). Because a string consists of 16-bit Unicode `char` values, only the lower-order 8 bits of each `char` is written; the higher-order 8 bits are lost (and not written). Use `writeChar()` and `writeChars()` to write all 16 bits of a Unicode `char` or `char` string.

PARAMETERS

`str` The non-`null` string to be written.

EXCEPTIONS

`IOException`

If an IO error occurred while attempting to write.

SEE ALSO
`DataInputStream.read()`, `DataInputStream.readByte()`, `DataInputStream.readFully()`, `DataInputStream.readLine()`, `DataInputStream.readUnsignedByte()`, `write()`, `writeChar()`, `writeChars()`.

EXAMPLE
See the class example.

writeChar()

PURPOSE Writes a 16-bit `char` to this output stream.

SYNTAX `public final void writeChar(int val) throws IOException`

DESCRIPTION This method writes a 16-bit Unicode `char val` to this output stream. Only the lower-order 2 bytes of `val` are written; the higher-order 2 bytes are ignored. The output consists of 2 bytes (higher-order written first), which represent the Unicode value of `val`.

PARAMETERS

`val` The `char` value to be written.

EXCEPTIONS

`IOException`

If an IO error occurred while attempting to write.

SEE ALSO `BufferedWriter.write()`, `DataInputStream.readChar()`, `writeByte()`, `writeChars()`.

EXAMPLE See the class example.

writeChars()

PURPOSE Writes a string as a sequence of `chars` to this output stream.

SYNTAX `public final void writeChars(String str) throws IOException`

DESCRIPTION This method writes the string `str` to this output stream as a sequence of `chars` (16 bits). Each `char` written consists of 2 bytes (higher-order written first), which represent its Unicode value.

PARAMETERS

`str` The non-`null` string to be written.

EXCEPTIONS

`IOException`

If an IO error occurred while attempting to write.

SEE ALSO `BufferedWriter.write()`, `DataInputStream.readChar()`, `writeChar()`, `writeBytes()`.

EXAMPLE See the class example.

writeDouble()

PURPOSE Writes a 64-bit `double` to this output stream.

SYNTAX `public final void writeDouble(double val) throws IOException`

DESCRIPTION This method writes the `double` value `val` to this output stream. The output generated consists of 8 bytes in the format produced by `Double.doubleToLongBits()`.

PARAMETERS

`val` The `double` value to be written.

EXCEPTIONS

`IOException`

If an IO error occurred while attempting to write.

SEE ALSO `DataInputStream.readDouble()`, `java.lang.Double.doubleToLongBits()`.

EXAMPLE See the class example.

writeFloat()

PURPOSE Writes a 32-bit `float` to this output stream.

SYNTAX `public final void writeFloat(float val) throws IOException`

DESCRIPTION This method writes the `float` value `val` to this output stream. The output generated consists of 4 bytes in the format produced by `Float.floatToIntBits()`.

PARAMETERS

`val` The `float` value to be written.

EXCEPTIONS

`IOException`

If an IO error occurred while attempting to write.

SEE ALSO `DataInputStream.readFloat()`, `java.lang.Float.floatToIntBits()`.

EXAMPLE See the class example.

writeInt()

PURPOSE Writes a 32-bit `int` to this output stream.

SYNTAX `public final void writeInt(int val) throws IOException`

DESCRIPTION This method writes the `int` value `val` to this output stream. The output generated consists of 4 bytes, highest-to-lowest byte order, that represent the value of `val`.

PARAMETERS

val — The `int` value to be written.

EXCEPTIONS

IOException — If an IO error occurred while attempting to write.

SEE ALSO — `DataInputStream.readInt()`.

EXAMPLE — See the class example.

writeLong()

PURPOSE — Writes a 64-bit `long` to this output stream.

SYNTAX — `public final void writeLong(long val) throws IOException`

DESCRIPTION — This method writes the `int` value `val` to this output stream. The output generated consists of 8 bytes, highest-to-lowest byte order, that represent the value of `val`.

PARAMETERS

val — The `long` value to be written.

EXCEPTIONS

IOException — If an IO error occurred while attempting to write.

SEE ALSO — `DataInputStream.readLong()`.

EXAMPLE — See the class example.

writeShort()

PURPOSE — Writes a 16-bit `short` to this output stream.

SYNTAX — `public final void writeShort(int val) throws IOException`

DESCRIPTION — This method writes the `short` value `val` to this output stream (the lower-order 2 bytes of `val` are used). The output generated consists of 2 bytes, with the higher-order byte written first.

PARAMETERS

val — The value to be written. The 2 lower-order bytes of `val` are used as the value of the `short` to be written.

EXCEPTIONS

`IOException`

If an IO error occurred while attempting to write.

SEE ALSO `DataInputStream.readShort()`, `DataInputStream.readUnsignedShort()`.

EXAMPLE See the class example.

A B C D E F G H I J K L M N O P Q R S T U V W X Y Z

writeUTF()

PURPOSE Writes a string in UTF to this output stream.

SYNTAX `public final void writeUTF(String str) throws IOException`

DESCRIPTION This method writes a string `str` to this output stream in UTF. UTF stands for Unicode Transfer Format, an encoding scheme for Unicode characters. UTF strings are restricted to have an encoded length ≤ 65535. When writing a string to a data stream, use the `writeUTF()` method and read it back using `DataInputStream.readUTF()`. See *The Java Language Specification, First Edition*, Section 22.2.14, for details on UTF.

PARAMETERS

`str` The non-`null` string to be written.

EXCEPTIONS

`IOException`

If an IO error occurred while attempting to write.

`UTFDataFormatException`

If the resulting UTF data size would exceed 65535 bytes.

SEE ALSO `DataInputStream.readUTF()`, `writeBytes()`, `writeChars()`.

EXAMPLE See the class example.

written

PURPOSE The number of bytes written to this stream so far.

SYNTAX `protected int written`

DESCRIPTION This field records the number of bytes written to this stream so far. It is updated after each write operation.

SEE ALSO `size()`.

EXAMPLE See the class example.

Date

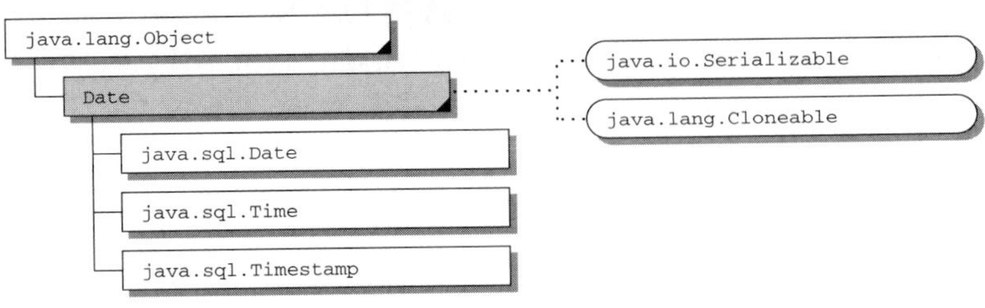

A
B
C
D
E
F
G
H
I
J
K
L
M
N
O
P
Q
R
S
T
U
V
W
X
Y
Z

Syntax

```
public class Date
```

Description

The `Date` class is used to represent a particular date and time with the resolution of milliseconds.

Usage

To create a `Date` instance for the current date and time, you use the constructor that takes no parameters. The following code creates and displays the current date and time:

```
System.out.println(new Date());  // Sun Nov 09 15:19:09 CST 1997
```

You can also use the `getTime()` method from `Calendar` to get a `Date` instance. The following code creates a `GregorianCalendar` instance and gets a `Date` instance from it.

```
Calendar xmas = new GregorianCalendar(1997, Calendar.DECEMBER, 25);
Date d = xmas.getTime();
```

`Date` provides methods to update the date and time in a `Date` instance, compare two `Date` instances, and obtain the canonical string representation.

Use the `Calendar` class to convert a date to a `Date` object and to extract calendar-related values (e.g., month and year) from a `Date` object.

Coordinated Universal Time—UTC

The `Date` class is intended to represent *Coordinated Universal Time* (UTC), a standard for keeping time using atomic clocks. UTC is very close to the conventional system people use for keeping time: 60 seconds per minute, 60 minutes per hour, and 24 hours per day. However, in UTC, every one or two years, there is an extra second—called a *leap second*—added after the last second of the day on either December 31 or June 30. Most computers do not keep track of these leap second updates. Therefore `Date` on most systems is just a very close approximation of UTC.

Number of Milliseconds Since Epoch

A `Date` instance can be compactly represented in a single `long` value. The value counts the number of elapsed milliseconds from *epoch* (January 1, 1970 00:00:00 UTC). If the value is positive, it means the number of milliseconds *since* epoch. If it is negative, it means the number of milliseconds *before* epoch.

The methods `Date()`, `getTime()`, and `setTime()` use this representation.

Specifying the Date and Time

You can create a `Date` instance that contains the current date and time using the constructor that takes no parameters. You can also create a `Date` instance for a specific date and time by specifying the number of milliseconds from epoch.

By using the `Calendar` class, you can specify a date and time using calendar-related values such as the month, year, and day. See `Calendar` for more details.

The `Date` class has other constructors for specifying the date and time. However, they have been deprecated because they are not always correct in international environments. See the individual methods for how to replace their usages.

Displaying the Date and Time

The `Date` class provides a `toString()` method for displaying the date's value in canonical form, such as:

```
Sat Apr 20 09:32:58 EST 1996
```

There are different formats for displaying the date value in a string form. Also, different locales may have different ways of displaying the date and time. Here are two examples of different string representations of dates:

```
August 1, 1981 15:32:44 PST
18 Feb 1978 00:06:23 GMT 0430
```

Except for `toString()`, the usage of the other string conversion methods in the `Date` class have been deprecated. See the `DateFormat` class for details on how to display `Date` values in different formats and locales.

Modifying the Date and Time

After creating a `Date` object, you can modify the date and time it represents by setting its date value (its number of milliseconds since epoch). Modifying a `Date` object updates only the `Date` object itself and does not affect the system's clock (date).

The `Date` class contains methods for setting any or all of a date's component (year, month, day, hour, minutes, and seconds). However, these methods have been deprecated because they do not, in general, function correctly in international environments. See the individual methods for how to replace their usages.

A B C D E F G H I J K L M N O P Q R S T U V W X Y Z

MEMBER SUMMARY

Constructor

`Date()`	Constructs a `Date` instance.

Getting and Setting Date and Time Value

`getTime()`	Retrieves the value of this `Date` in milliseconds since epoch.
`setTime()`	Sets the value of this `Date` in milliseconds since epoch.

Comparison Methods

`after()`	Determines whether this `Date` comes after another `Date`.
`before()`	Determines whether this `Date` comes before another `Date`.
`equals()`	Compares this `Date` object with another object for equality.

Object Methods

`hashCode()`	Computes the hash code for this `Date`.
`toString()`	Generates the string representation of this `Date` using UNIX `ctime` convention.

Deprecated Date Field Access Methods

`getDate()`	Replaced by `Calendar.get(Calendar.DAY_OF_MONTH)`.
`getDay()`	Replaced by `Calendar.get(Calendar.DAY_OF_WEEK)-1`.
`getHours()`	Replaced by `Calendar.get(Calendar.HOUR_OF_DAY)`.
`getMinutes()`	Replaced by `Calendar.get(Calendar.MINUTE)`.
`getMonth()`	Replaced by `Calendar.get(Calendar.MONTH)`.
`getSeconds()`	Replaced by `Calendar.get(Calendar.SECOND)`.
`getTimezoneOffset()`	Replaced by `Calendar.get(Calendar.ZONE_OFFSET)` and `Calendar.get(Calendar.DST_OFFSET)`.
`getYear()`	Replaced by `Calendar.get(Calendar.YEAR)-1900`.

Deprecated Update Methods

`setDate()`	Replaced by `Calendar.set(Calendar.DAY_OF_MONTH, int)`.
`setHours()`	Replaced by `Calendar.set(Calendar.HOUR_OF_DAY, int)`.
`setMinutes()`	Replaced by `Calendar.set(Calendar.MINUTE, int)`.
`setMonth()`	Replaced by `Calendar.set(Calendar.MONTH, int)`.
`setSeconds()`	Replaced by `Calendar.set(Calendar.SECOND, int)`.
`setYear()`	Replaced by `Calendar.set(Calendar.YEAR, int)`.

Deprecated Date Format Methods

`parse()`	Replaced by `SimpleDateFormat.parse()`.
`toGMTString()`	Replaced by `SimpleDateFormat.format(this)`.
`toLocaleString()`	Replaced by `DateFormat.getDateTimeInstance().format(this)`.
`UTC()`	Replaced by `GregorianCalendar().getTime().getTime()`.

See Also

`Calendar`, `GregorianCalendar`, `java.text.DateFormat`, `java.text.SimpleDateFormat`, `System.currentTimeMillis()`, `SimpleTimeZone`, `TimeZone`.

Example

See the *Usage* section.

A B C D E F G H I J K L M N O P Q R S T U V W X Y Z

after()

PURPOSE Determines whether this `Date` comes after another `Date`.

SYNTAX `public boolean after(Date when)`

DESCRIPTION This method determines whether this `Date` comes after `when`. If this `Date` comes after `when`, this method returns `true`; otherwise, it returns `false`.

PARAMETERS

`when` The non-`null` `Date` against which to compare.

RETURNS `true` if this `Date` comes after `when`; `false` otherwise.

SEE ALSO `before()`.

EXAMPLE

```
import java.util.Date;

class Main {
    public static void main(String[] args) {
        Date d1 = new Date();                      // now
        Date d2 = new Date(d1.getTime()+1000);     // add one second

        System.out.println(d1.equals(d2));         // false
        System.out.println(d1.after(d2));          // false
        System.out.println(d1.before(d2));         // true
    }
}
```

before()

PURPOSE Determines whether this `Date` comes before another `Date`.

SYNTAX `public boolean before(Date when)`

DESCRIPTION This method determines whether this `Date` comes before `when`. If this `Date` comes before `when`, this method returns `true`; otherwise, it returns `false`.

PARAMETERS

when — The non-null Date against which to compare.

RETURNS — true if this Date comes before when; false otherwise.

SEE ALSO — after().

EXAMPLE — See after().

Date()

PURPOSE — Constructs a Date instance.

SYNTAX

```
public Date()
public Date(long msSinceEpoch)
DEPRECATED public Date(int year, int month, int day)
DEPRECATED public Date(int year, int month, int day, int hours, int minutes)
DEPRECATED public Date(int year, int month, int day, int hours, int minutes,
    int seconds)
DEPRECATED public Date (String dateStr)
```

DESCRIPTION — This constructor constructs a Date object. The first form constructs a Date object for the current date and time.

The second form constructs a Date object for the date and time represented by the number of milliseconds from epoch, msSinceEpoch. If it is positive, it means the number of milliseconds *since* epoch. If it is negative, it means the number of milliseconds *before* epoch.

The usage of all other forms of the constructor is deprecated.

PARAMETERS

day	The day of the month. 1 ≤ day ≤ 31.
dateStr	The non-null string representation of the date and time.
hours	The hour of the day. 0 ≤ hours ≤ 23.
minutes	The minute of the hour. 0 ≤ minutes ≤ 59.
month	The month of the year. 0 ≤ month ≤ 11; January=0.
msSinceEpoch	The date and time as specified by the number of milliseconds from epoch.
seconds	The second within the minute. 0 ≤ seconds ≤ 59.
dateStr	A string representing the date and time in a syntax accepted by parse().
year	The year. year must be a positive number. It is added to 1900 to get the complete year number (e.g., 97 means 1997).

SEE ALSO — java.lang.System.currentTimeMillis().

EXAMPLE — See after().

DEPRECATION — The third, fourth, and fifth forms of this constructor create a Date object for the date and time specified using year/month/day and, optionally, hours/minutes/

seconds. The usage of these forms should be replaced using the `Gregorian-Calendar` class. The last form constructs a `Date` object for the date and time as specified using a string `dateStr`. You should replace the usage of this form with `SimpleDateFormat` or `DateFormat`.

The following usages are deprecated:

```
Date ymd = new Date(89, 9, 17);                 // Oct 17, 1989
Date ymdhm = new Date(89, 9, 17, 17, 4);        // Oct 17, 1989,
5:04pm
Date ymdhms = new Date(89, 9, 17, 17, 4, 15);
                                    // Oct 17, 1989, 5:04:15pm

Date s1 = new Date("17 Oct 1989 17:04:15");
Date s2 = new Date("17 Oct 1989");
Date s3 = new Date("Thu, 2 Nov 1995");
Date s4 = new Date("Sat, 12 Aug 1995 13:30:00 GMT");
```

You can replace them with the following:

```
Date ymd =                        // Oct 17, 1989
    (new GregorianCalendar(1989, Calendar.OCTOBER, 17)).getTime();
Date ymdhm =                      // Oct 17, 1989, 5:04pm
    (new GregorianCalendar(1989, Calendar.OCTOBER, 17, 17, 4)).
        getTime();
Date ymdhms =                     // Oct 17, 1989, 5:04:15pm
    (new GregorianCalendar(1989, Calendar.OCTOBER, 17, 17, 4, 15)).
        getTime();
try {
    DateFormat f1 = new SimpleDateFormat("dd MMM yyyy HH:mm:ss");
    DateFormat f2 = new SimpleDateFormat("dd MMM yyyy");
    DateFormat f3 = new SimpleDateFormat("EEE, dd MMM yyyy");
    DateFormat f4 = new SimpleDateFormat(
        "EEE, dd MMM yyyy HH:mm:ss 'GMT'");

    Date s1 = f1.parse("17 Oct 1989 17:04:15");
    Date s2 = f2.parse("17 Oct 1989");
    Date s3 = f3.parse("Thu, 2 Nov 1995");
    Date s4 = f4.parse("Sat, 12 Aug 1995 13:30:00 GMT");
} catch (ParseException e) {
    e.printStackTrace();
}
```

equals()

PURPOSE Compares this `Date` object with another object for equality.

SYNTAX `public boolean equals(Object obj)`

DESCRIPTION This method compares this `Date` with `obj` for equality. If `obj` is a `Date` object and if it has the same `Date` value as this `Date`, the objects are equal and this method returns `true`. If the `Date` values are not equal or if `obj` is `null` or not a `Date` object, this method returns `false`.

PARAMETERS

obj — The object with which to compare. `obj` can be `null`.

RETURNS — `true` if the objects are the same; `false` otherwise.

OVERRIDES — `java.lang.Object.equals()`.

SEE ALSO — `hashCode()`.

EXAMPLE — See `after()`.

getDate() *DEPRECATED*

PURPOSE — Replaced by `Calendar.get(Calendar.DAY_OF_MONTH)`.

SYNTAX — `public int getDate()`

RETURNS — The day of the month of this `Date`. It is a number in the range `1` to `31`, inclusive.

DEPRECATION — This example shows how to write a date and time printing routine that makes use of the various access methods to display the date and time in a user-friendly format. The use of the access methods in the `Date` class is deprecated. Note also that the time zone offset returned by `Date.getTimezoneOffset()` is that *west* of the Greenwich meridian (GMT) (normally, the time zone offset is *east* of GMT).

```
import java.util.Date;

class Old {
    private final static String[] WeekDays =
        {"Sun", "Mon", "Tue", "Wed", "Thu", "Fri", "Sat"};
    private final static String[] Months =
        {"Jan", "Feb", "Mar", "Apr", "May", "Jun",
         "Jul", "Aug", "Sep", "Oct", "Nov", "Dec"};
    private static String fixWidth(int num) {
        if (num == 0)
            return "00";
        if (num < 10)
            return ("0" + num);
        return (Integer.toString(num, 10));
    }
    // prints out date in the form
    // Tue Oct 17 1995 hh:mm:ss GMT+HHMM
    private static String dateToString(Date d) {
        String buf = WeekDays[d.getDay()] + " " +
            Months[d.getMonth()] + " " +
            d.getDate() + " " +
            (d.getYear() + 1900) + " " +
            d.getHours() + ":" +
            d.getMinutes() + ":" +
            d.getSeconds() + " GMT" +
            ((d.getTimezoneOffset() >= 0) ? "+" : "-") +
            fixWidth((d.getTimezoneOffset()/60)) +
```

```
            fixWidth((d.getTimezoneOffset()%60));
        return (buf);
    }
    public static void main(String[] args) {
        Date d = new Date();
        System.out.println("today: " + dateToString(d));
    }
}
```


This program can be rewritten using methods from the `Calendar` class as follows. It can also be reduced to just a few lines using `SimpleDateFormat`, as shown below also. The time zone offset displayed is the offset from GMT (which has the opposite sign as that of "west of the Greenwich meridian," as returned by `Date.getTimezoneOffset()`).

```
import java.util.*;
import java.text.SimpleDateFormat;

class New {
    private final static String[] WeekDays =
        {"Sun", "Mon", "Tue", "Wed", "Thu", "Fri", "Sat"};
    private final static String[] Months =
        {"Jan", "Feb", "Mar", "Apr", "May", "Jun",
         "Jul", "Aug", "Sep", "Oct", "Nov", "Dec"};
    private static String fixWidth(int num) {
        if (num == 0)
            return "00";
        if (num < 10)
            return ("0" + num);
        return (Integer.toString(num, 10));
    }
    // prints out date in the form
    // Tue Oct 17 1995 hh:mm:ss GMT+HHMM
    private static String dateToString(Date d) {
        GregorianCalendar cal = new GregorianCalendar();
        int offset = (cal.get(Calendar.ZONE_OFFSET)+
            cal.get(Calendar.DST_OFFSET))/60000;
        cal.setTime(d);
        String buf = WeekDays[cal.get(Calendar.DAY_OF_WEEK)-1] +
            " " + Months[cal.get(Calendar.MONTH)] + " " +
            cal.get(Calendar.DAY_OF_MONTH) + " " +
            cal.get(Calendar.YEAR) + " " +
            cal.get(Calendar.HOUR_OF_DAY) + ":" +
            cal.get(Calendar.MINUTE) + ":" +
            cal.get(Calendar.SECOND) + " GMT" +
            ((offset >= 0) ? "+" : "-") +
                fixWidth(Math.abs(offset/60)) +
                fixWidth(Math.abs(offset%60));
        return (buf);
    }
    public static void main(String[] args) {
        Date d = new Date();
        System.out.println("today: " + dateToString(d));
        SimpleDateFormat df =
            new SimpleDateFormat("EEE MMM d yyyy HH:mm:ss zzz");
        System.out.println(df.format(d));
    }
}
```

A B C D E F G H I J K L M N O P Q R S T U V W X Y Z

getDay() *DEPRECATED*

PURPOSE Replaced by `Calendar.get(Calendar.DAY_OF_WEEK)-1`.

SYNTAX `public int getDay()`

RETURNS The day of the week of this `Date`. It is a number in the range `0`–`6`, inclusive, with Sunday = `0`.

DEPRECATION See `getDate()`.

getHours() *DEPRECATED*

PURPOSE Replaced by `Calendar.get(Calendar.HOUR_OF_DAY)`.

SYNTAX `public int getHours()`

RETURNS The hour of the day of this `Date`. It is a number in the range `0`–`23`, inclusive, with midnight = `0`.

DEPRECATION See `getDate()`.

getMinutes() *DEPRECATED*

PURPOSE Replaced by `Calendar.get(Calendar.MINUTE)`.

SYNTAX `public int getMinutes()`

RETURNS The minute of the hour of this `Date`. It is a number in the range `0`–`59`, inclusive.

DEPRECATION See `getDate()`.

getMonth() *DEPRECATED*

PURPOSE Replaced by `Calendar.get(Calendar.MONTH)`.

SYNTAX `public int getMonth()`

RETURNS The month of the year of this `Date`. It is a number in the range `0`–`11`, inclusive, with January = `0`.

DEPRECATION See `getDate()`.

getSeconds() *DEPRECATED*

PURPOSE Replaced by `Calendar.get(Calendar.SECOND)`.

SYNTAX `public int getSeconds()`

RETURNS The second within the minute of this `Date`. It is a number in the range `0–59`, inclusive.

DEPRECATION See `getDate()`.

getTime()

PURPOSE Retrieves the value of this `Date` in milliseconds since epoch.

SYNTAX `public long getTime()`

RETURNS The number of milliseconds from epoch of this `Date`. If it is positive, it means the number of milliseconds *since* epoch. If it is negative, it means the number of milliseconds *before* epoch.

SEE ALSO `setTime()`.

EXAMPLE

```
import java.util.Date;
import java.io.DataInputStream;
import java.io.IOException;

class Test {
    public static void tests() {
        try {
            Thread.sleep(5);
        } catch (InterruptedException e) {
        }
    }
}
class Main {
    public static void main(String[] args) {
        Date startTime = new Date();
        Test.tests();
        Date endTime = new Date();
        System.out.println("Tests took: " +
                           (endTime.getTime() - startTime.getTime()) +
                           " ms");
    }
}
```

getTimezoneOffset() *DEPRECATED*

PURPOSE Replaced by `Calendar.get(Calendar.ZONE_OFFSET)` and `Calendar.get(Calendar.DST_OFFSET)`.

SYNTAX `public int getTimezoneOffset()`

RETURNS The time zone offset west of GMT in number of minutes.

DEPRECATION — This method is equivalent to

```
-(Calendar.get(Calendar.ZONE_OFFSET)+
    Calendar.get(Calendar.DST_OFFSET))/(60*1000))
```

See getDate(). Note that the value returned by getTimezoneOffset() is opposite that of the offset from GMT.

getYear() *DEPRECATED*

PURPOSE — Replaced by `Calendar.get(YEAR)-1900`.

SYNTAX — `public int getYear()`

RETURNS — The year of this `Date`. It is added to 1900 to get the complete year number (e.g., 97 means 1997).

DEPRECATION — See `getDate()`.

hashCode()

PURPOSE — Computes the hash code for this `Date`.

SYNTAX — `public int hashCode()`

DESCRIPTION — The hash code of a `Date` object is computed using its time value (`getTime()`). Two `Date` objects with the same time value have the same hash code. However, two `Date` objects with the same hash code may not necessarily have the same time value.

RETURNS — The hash code of this `Date`.

OVERRIDES — `java.lang.Object.hashCode()`.

SEE ALSO — `equals()`, `getTime()`.

EXAMPLE — See `java.lang.Object.hashCode()`.

parse() *DEPRECATED*

PURPOSE — Replaced by `SimpleDateFormat.parse()`.

SYNTAX — `public static long parse(String str)`

PARAMETERS

`str` — The string to be parsed in some common date and time formats.

RETURNS — The `Date` value of `str` in number of seconds since epoch.

EXCEPTIONS

`IllegalArgumentException`

If `str` does not contain a date and time representation that can be parsed.

DEPRECATION This method parses the string `str` and computes its corresponding date and time value in the number of milliseconds since epoch. Replace the usage of this method with `SimpleDateFormat` and `DateFormat`.

This example contains the usage of the deprecated methods `UTC()`, `parse()`, `toGMTString()`, and `toLocaleString()` (as well as some deprecated constructors).

```
import java.util.Date;

class Old {
    public static void main(String[] args) {
        long utcTime = Date.UTC(95,10,2,10,30,4);
        long parsedTime = Date.parse("11 November 1996");

        Date utcDate = new Date(utcTime);
        Date parsedDate = new Date("11 Nov 1996");
        int tracker;

        if (utcDate.before(parsedDate)) {
            tracker = -1;
            utcDate.setTime(parsedTime); // reset
        } else if (utcDate.after(parsedDate)) {
            tracker = 1;
            utcDate.setTime(parsedTime); // reset
        } else if (utcDate.equals(parsedDate))
            tracker = 0;
        // Print the date in the three formats
        System.out.println("GMT: " + utcDate.toGMTString());
        System.out.println("Locale: " + utcDate.toLocaleString());
        System.out.println("ctime: " + utcDate.toString());
    }
}
```

Replace the usage of these deprecated methods with corresponding methods from `Calendar` (`GregorianCalendar`), `SimpleDateFormat`, and `DateFormat`:

```
import java.util.*;
import java.text.*;

class New {
    public static void main(String[] args) {
        try {
        long utcTime = (new GregorianCalendar(1995,10,2,10,30,4)).
                getTime().getTime();
        SimpleDateFormat df = new SimpleDateFormat("d MMMM yyyy");
        long parsedTime = (df.parse("11 November 1996")).getTime();

        Date utcDate = new Date(utcTime);
        SimpleDateFormat df2 = new SimpleDateFormat("d MMM yyyy");
        Date parsedDate = df2.parse("11 Nov 1996");
        int tracker;
```

```
                if (utcDate.before(parsedDate)) {
                    tracker = -1;
                    utcDate.setTime(parsedTime); // reset
                } else if (utcDate.after(parsedDate)) {
                    tracker = 1;
                    utcDate.setTime(parsedTime); // reset
                } else if (utcDate.equals(parsedDate))
                    tracker = 0;

                // Print the date in the three formats
                SimpleDateFormat df3 =
                    new SimpleDateFormat("d MMM yyyy HH:mm:ss 'GMT'",
                        Locale.US);
                df3.setTimeZone(TimeZone.getTimeZone("GMT"));
                System.out.println("GMT: " + df3.format(utcDate));

                DateFormat df4 = DateFormat.getDateTimeInstance();
                df4.setTimeZone(TimeZone.getDefault());
                System.out.println("Locale: " + df4.format(utcDate));

                System.out.println("ctime: " + utcDate.toString());
            } catch (ParseException e) {
                e.printStackTrace();
            }
            }
        }
```

setDate() *DEPRECATED*

PURPOSE Replaced by `Calendar.set(Calendar.DAY_OF_MONTH, int)`.

SYNTAX `public void setDate(int day)`

PARAMETERS

`day` The day of the month to which to set this `Date`. `day` must be a number in the range 1–31, inclusive.

DEPRECATION Replace the usage of this deprecated method, as in

```
Date date = new Date();
d.setDate(day);
```

with the following:

```
Calendar cal = new GregorianCalendar();
cal.set(Calendar.DAY_OF_MONTH, day);
Date d = cal.getTime();
```

Note that these are not identical because using `Date.setDate()` updates the `Date` instance, while the second code snippet updates the `Calendar` instance and gets a new `Date` from it. Typically, if you are dealing with `Calendar`, you will continue to use the `Calendar` instance until you need to get a `Date` instance from it.

setHours()

DEPRECATED

PURPOSE Replaced by `Calendar.set(Calendar.HOUR_OF_DAY, int)`.

SYNTAX `public void setHours(int hour)`

PARAMETERS

`hour` The hour to which to set this `Date`. `hour` must be in the range `0`–`23`, inclusive, with midnight = `0`.

DEPRECATION Replace the usage of this deprecated method, as in

```
Date date = new Date();
d.setHours(hour);
```

with the following:

```
Calendar cal = new GregorianCalendar();
cal.set(Calendar.HOUR_OF_DAY, hour);
Date d = cal.getTime();
```

Note that these are not identical because using `Date.setHours()` updates the `Date` instance, while the second code snippet updates the `Calendar` instance and gets a new `Date` from it. Typically, if you are dealing with `Calendar`, you will continue to use the `Calendar` instance until you need to get a `Date` instance from it.

setMinutes()

DEPRECATED

PURPOSE Replaced by `Calendar.set(Calendar.MINUTE, int)`.

SYNTAX `public void setMinutes(int minute)`

PARAMETERS

`minute` The minute of the hour to which to set this `Date`. `minute` must be in the range `0`–`59`, inclusive.

DEPRECATION Replace the usage of this deprecated method, as in

```
Date date = new Date();
d.setMinutes(minute);
```

with the following:

```
Calendar cal = new GregorianCalendar();
cal.set(Calendar.MINUTE, minute);
Date d = cal.getTime();
```

Note that these are not identical because using `Date.setMinutes()` updates the `Date` instance, while the second code snippet updates the `Calendar` instance and gets a new `Date` from it. Typically, if you are dealing with `Calendar`, you will continue to use the `Calendar` instance until you need to get a `Date` instance from it.

setMonth() *DEPRECATED*

PURPOSE Replaced by `Calendar.set(Calendar.MONTH, int)`.

SYNTAX `public void setMonth(int month)`

PARAMETERS

`month` The month of the year to which to set this `Date`. `month` must be in the range `0`–`11`, inclusive, with January = `0`.

DEPRECATION Replace the usage of this deprecated method, as in

```
Date date = new Date();
d.setMonth(month);
```

with the following:

```
Calendar cal = new GregorianCalendar();
cal.set(Calendar.MONTH, month);
Date d = cal.getTime();
```

Note that these are not identical because using `Date.setMonth()` updates the `Date` instance, while the second code snippet updates the `Calendar` instance and gets a new `Date` from it. Typically, if you are dealing with `Calendar`, you will continue to use the `Calendar` instance until you need to get a `Date` instance from it.

setSeconds() *DEPRECATED*

PURPOSE Replaced by `Calendar.set(Calendar.SECOND, int)`.

SYNTAX `public void setSeconds(int second)`

PARAMETERS

`second` The second of the minute to which to set this `Date`. `second` must be in the range `0`–`59`, inclusive.

DEPRECATION Replace the usage of this deprecated method, as in

```
Date date = new Date();
d.setSeconds(second);
```

with the following:

```
Calendar cal = new GregorianCalendar();
cal.set(Calendar.SECOND, second);
Date d = cal.getTime();
```

Note that these are not identical because using `Date.setSeconds()` updates the `Date` instance, while the second code snippet updates the `Calendar` instance and gets a new `Date` from it. Typically, if you are dealing with `Calendar`, you will continue to use the `Calendar` instance until you need to get a `Date` instance from it.

setTime()

PURPOSE Sets the value of this `Date` in milliseconds since epoch.

SYNTAX `public void setTime(long msSinceEpoch)`

DESCRIPTION This method sets the date and time values of this `Date` to be `msSinceEpoch` in milliseconds since epoch. If `msSinceEpoch` is `0`, this corresponds to epoch (January 1, 1970 00:00:00 UTC). If it is positive, it means the number of milliseconds *since* epoch. If it is negative, it means the number of milliseconds *before* epoch.

This method causes the value of this `Date` to be recalculated. This does not affect the system's clock.

PARAMETERS

`msSinceEpoch` The new date and time values in milliseconds from epoch.

SEE ALSO `getTime()`.

EXAMPLE

```
Date d = new Date();
Date d2 = new Date();
d2.setTime(d.getTime()-5000); // set d2 to be 5 seconds behind d1
```

setYear() *DEPRECATED*

PURPOSE Replaced by `Calendar.set(Calendar.YEAR, int)`.

SYNTAX `public void setYear(int year)`

PARAMETERS

`year` The year to which to set this `Date`. `year` must be a positive number. It is added to 1900 to get the complete year number (e.g., 95 means 1995).

DEPRECATION Replace the usage of this deprecated method, as in

```
Date date = new Date();
d.setYear(year);
```

with the following:

```
Calendar cal = new GregorianCalendar();
cal.set(Calendar.YEAR, year+1900);
Date d = cal.getTime();
```

Note that `Date.setYear()` will automatically add 1900 to `year`, but `Calendar`'s `set()` method will not.

Note also that these are not identical because using `Date.setYear()` updates the `Date` instance, while the second code snippet updates the `Calendar` instance and gets a new `Date` from it. Typically, if you are dealing with `Calendar`, you will continue to use the `Calendar` instance until you need to get a `Date` instance from it.

A B C D E F G H I J K L M N O P Q R S T U V W X Y Z

toGMTString() *DEPRECATED*

PURPOSE Replaced by `SimpleDateFormat.format()`.

SYNTAX `public String toGMTString()`

RETURNS The non-`null` string representation of this `Date` using GMT convention.

DEPRECATION The Internet GMT string representation of a date and time has the following format:

Day Month Year HH:*MM*:*SS GMT*

where the following holds:

- *Day* is the day of the month (01–31).
- *Month* is the abbreviated string name of the month (e.g., “Jan”).
- *Year* is the year (e.g., 1995).
- *HH* is the hour (00–23).
- *MM* is the minutes (00–59).
- *SS* is the seconds (00–59).

See `parse()` to see how to replace the usage of this deprecated method.

toLocaleString() *DEPRECATED*

PURPOSE Replaced by `DateFormat.getDateTimeInstance().format()`.

SYNTAX `public String toLocaleString()`

RETURNS The non-`null` string representation of this `Date` using local conventions.

DEPRECATION See `parse()` to see how to replace the usage of this deprecated method.

toString()

PURPOSE Generates the string representation of this `Date` using UNIX `ctime` convention.

SYNTAX `public String toString()`

DESCRIPTION This method returns the string representation of this `Date` using the UNIX `ctime` convention. This format is

Wday Month Mday HH:*MM*:*SS TZone Year*

where the following holds:

- *Wday* is the weekday abbreviated string (e.g., “Wed”).
- *Month* is the abbreviated string of the month (e.g., “Jan”).
- *Mday* is the day of the month (01–31).
- *HH* is the hour (00–23).

- *MM* is the minutes (`00–59`).
- *SS* is the seconds (`00–59`).
- *TZone* is the time zone (e.g., "PDT").
- *Year* is the year (e.g., `1995`).

All fields have constant width.

The following is an example of a `ctime` string:

```
Sat Aug 12 02:00:00 PDT 1995
```

RETURNS The non-`null` string representation of this `Date` using UNIX `ctime` convention.

OVERRIDES `java.lang.Object.toString()`.

EXAMPLE See `getTime()`.

UTC()

DEPRECATED

PURPOSE Replaced by `GregorianCalendar().getTime().getTime()`.

SYNTAX

```
public static long UTC(int year, int month, int day, int hours,
   int minutes, int seconds)
```

PARAMETERS

`day` The day of the month. `day` must be in the range `1–31`, inclusive.

`hours` The hour of the day. `hours` must be in the range `0–23`, inclusive.

`minutes` The minute of the hour. `minutes` must be in the range `0–59`, inclusive.

`month` The month of the year. `month` must be in the range `0–11`, inclusive; January = `0`.

`seconds` The second within the minute. `seconds` must be in the range `0–59`, inclusive.

`year` The year. `year` must be a positive number. It is added to 1900 to get the complete year number (e.g., 95 means 1995).

RETURNS The date and time in milliseconds since epoch.

DEPRECATION See `parse()` to see how to replace the usage of this deprecated method.

java.text

DateFormat

Syntax

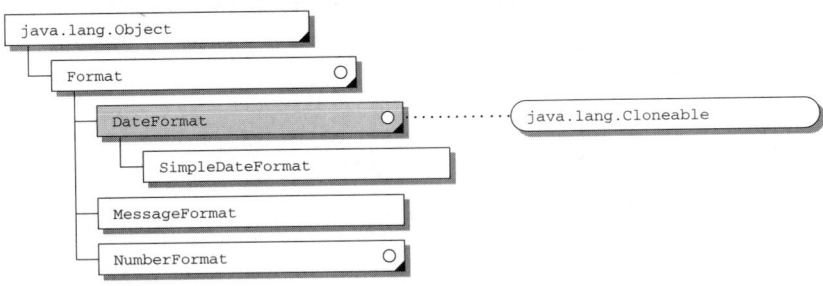

```
public class DateFormat extends Format implements Cloneable
```

Description

`DateFormat` is an abstract base class that defines the programming interface for formatting and parsing a date and time in a locale-sensitive manner. A `DateFormat` object ultimately operates on a `Date` object, which holds information about both date and time. Dates and times can be formatted or parsed either together or separately.

Subclasses of `DateFormat`, such as `SimpleDateFormat`, allow for formatting (milliseconds to text), parsing (text to milliseconds), and normalization.

`DateFormat` enables you to format and parse dates for any locale. Your code can be completely independent of the local conventions for months, days of the week, or even the calendar format (lunar versus solar).

`DateFormat` provides many class methods for obtaining default date and time formatters based on the default locale or a specified locale and a number of formatting styles. The formatting styles include `FULL`, `LONG`, `MEDIUM`, `SHORT`, and `DEFAULT`. More details about and examples of using these styles are provided in the method descriptions.

Usage: Subclassing

Concrete subclasses of `DateFormat` *must* implement (or inherit implementations of) the two methods `format()` and `parseObject()` that `Format` requires, plus this method:

```
public StringBuffer format(Date date, StringBuffer appendBuf,
    FieldPosition pos)
```

Usage: Creating a DateFormat Object

To create a `DateFormat` object, you use one of the following format creation static methods. Determine whether you want to format a date, a time, or both, then decide on the style and the locale, and finally call the appropriate method:

- Use `getDateInstance()` to get the date format.
- Use `getTimeInstance()` to get the time format.
- Use `getDateTimeInstance()` or `getInstance()` to get a date and time format.

These all return an instance of `DateFormat`. For the majority of locales (actually, all locales in JDK 1.1.6), the return object is also an instance of `SimpleDateFormat`. Once created, you cannot change the style or locale of a `DateFormat` object. Calling these methods with no parameters returns a format using the default style (`MEDIUM`) and current locale. To specify a style, pass it in, as follows:

```
DateFormat df = DateFormat.getDateInstance(DateFormat.LONG);
```

To specify a style and locale, pass them both in, as follows:

```
DateFormat df =
    DateFormat.getDateInstance(DateFormat.LONG, Locale.FRANCE);
```

You can also set the time zone on the format if you wish by using `setTimeZone()`.

Usage: Formatting

To convert a date to a string, call `format()` on an instance of `Date`. For example, to format the current date, do this:

```
String myStr =
    DateFormat.getDateInstance(DateFormat.LONG).format(new Date());
// November 21, 1997
```

The following example calls `format()` on an instance of `Date` to format the current date using the `LONG` style for France:

```
String myStr = DateFormat.getDateInstance(
    DateFormat.LONG, Locale.FRANCE).format(new Date());
// 21 novembre 1997
```

Usage: Parsing

You can use a `DateInstance` object to do the reverse operation of formatting. That is, for a string in the form of a date, to parse the string to a date object:

```
myDate = df.parse(myString);
```

Forms of the `parse` methods allow passing in a `ParsePosition`, thereby enabling you to progressively parse through pieces of a string.

Casting to SimpleDateFormat

If you want even more control over the format or parsing (or you want to give your users more control), try casting the `DateFormat` object you get from the creation methods to a `SimpleDateFormat`, as shown in the following code. This will work for most countries. Just remember first to test that it is an instance of `SimpleDateFormat`, in case you encounter an unusual subclass of `DateFormat`.

```
DateFormat df = DateFormat.getInstance();
if (df instanceof SimpleDateFormat) {
    SimpleDateFormat sdf = (SimpleDateFormat)df;
    // Call format() or parse() here.
}
```

Alternatively, the cast could be executed inside a `try` block, catching a `ClassCastException`.

Formatting Styles

The formatting styles control how abbreviated the dates and times are. Table 20 gives the general format produced by the different styles—different locales give different results.

Note: The `FULL` date should contain milliseconds. It is a known bug in Java 1.1.5 and earlier that the `FULL` date does not contain milliseconds. `FULL` formats should contain enough information to allow a round trip from `Date` object to a string and back.

Style	General Date	Date (U.S. English)	General Time	Time (U.S. English)
`SHORT`	Purely numeric.	2/10/62	hour, mins	1:30 PM
`MEDIUM`	Abbreviated month.	10-Feb-62	hour, mins, secs	1:30:15 PM
`LONG`	Full month.	February 10, 1962	hour, min, sec, time zone	1:30:15 PM PST
`FULL`	Adds day of week and era.	Tuesday, February 10, 1962	hour, min, sec, text, time zone	1:30:15;45 o'clock PM PST

TABLE 20: Styles for Date and Time Formats.

FieldPosition and Alignment

The constants that end in `FIELD` are useful for aligning a column of formatted dates on that field and for finding out where the field is for selection on the screen. For example, you can align a column of dates on the month or on the year. To do this, use the `FieldPosition` class; refer to that class for more information.

When `format(Date date, StringBuffer appendBuf, FieldPosition pos)` is called, the begin and end index values of `pos` are updated with the position of the `pos` field. For example, if that method produced the time string "1996.07.10 AD at 15:08:56 PDT", and if the given `pos` is `DateFormat.YEAR_FIELD`, the offsets `pos.beginIndex()` and `pos.getEndIndex()` return `0` and `4`, respectively (corresponding to "1996").

Notice that if the same time field appears more than once in a pattern, the `FieldPosition` object will be set for the first occurrence of that time field. For instance, suppose you format a `Date` to the time string "1 PM PDT (Pacific Daylight Time)" using the pattern "`h a z (zzzz)`" and the alignment field `DateFormat.TIMEZONE_FIELD`. In this case, the offsets pos.getBeginIndex() and pos.getEndIndex() will return to 5 and 8, respectively, for the first occurrence of the time-zone pattern character "z" (corresponding to "PDT").

Normalization

You can *normalize* Date objects to a particular style or to normal values. This usually involves the round trip of parsing a non-normalized string to a Date object and then formatting it back to a normalized string.

A typical way to normalize a style is to parse dates of any style (SHORT, MEDIUM, LONG, or FULL) and format to one style. For example, "March 8, 1997", "3/8/1997", and "1997-8-3" could normalize to "03/08/97".

The other way to normalize is on value. A normalized value is a value in the normal, expected range. The string "April 37" is not a normalized date, since April has only 30 days. You have the choice of interpreting this date either as an error or as 7 days after April 30. In the latter case, you can parse and then format it, yielding "May 7". Normalization on value is controlled by the *lenient* property of the Calendar object that is used by the DateFormat object. The default state of a Calendar object is for the lenient property to be set to true, which allows for normalization. If lenient is set to false, a ParseException would be thrown. See the setLenient(true) method in the Calendar object for more information.

MEMBER SUMMARY	
Constructor	
DateFormat()	Constructor called by subclasses.
Format Creation Methods	
getDateInstance()	Creates a date (not time) format with a style, for a locale.
getDateTimeInstance()	Creates a date and time format with a style, for a locale.
getInstance()	Creates a date and time format for the default locale.
getTimeInstance()	Creates a time format with a style, for a locale.
Format and Parse Methods	
format()	Formats an Number or Date object to produce a string.
parse()	Parses a date-time string to produce a Date object.
parseObject()	Parses a date-time string to produce an object.
Parsing Leniency Methods	
isLenient()	Determines if parsing is set to lenient for this DateFormat object.
setLenient()	Sets parsing to be lenient for this DateFormat object.
Number Format Methods	
getNumberFormat()	Retrieves the NumberFormat object used to format and parse a date-time.
setNumberFormat()	Sets the NumberFormat object used to format and parse a date-time.

Continued

MEMBER SUMMARY	
Format Constant	
`numberFormat`	The `NumberFormat` object this `DateFormat` object uses.
Calendar Methods	
`getCalendar()`	Retrieves the `Calendar` object used with this `DateFormat` object.
`setCalendar()`	Sets the `Calendar` object used with this `DateFormat` object.
Calendar Constant	
`calendar`	The `Calendar` object this `DateFormat` object uses.
Date-Time Style Constants	
`DEFAULT`	The default style of the date or time.
`FULL`	The full, unabbreviated style of the date or time.
`LONG`	The long style of the date or time.
`MEDIUM`	The medium-length style of the date or time.
`SHORT`	The short style of the date or time.
FieldPosition Field Constants	
`AM_PM_FIELD`	Specifies the `AM_PM` field.
`DATE_FIELD`	Specifies the `DATE` field.
`DAY_OF_WEEK_FIELD`	Specifies the `DAY_OF_WEEK` field.
`DAY_OF_WEEK_IN_MONTH_FIELD`	Specifies the `DAY_OF_WEEK_IN_MONTH` field.
`DAY_OF_YEAR_FIELD`	Specifies the `DAY_OF_YEAR` field.
`ERA_FIELD`	Specifies the `ERA` field.
`HOUR0_FIELD`	Specifies the zero-based `HOUR` field.
`HOUR1_FIELD`	Specifies the one-based `HOUR` field.
`HOUR_OF_DAY0_FIELD`	Specifies the zero-based `HOUR_OF_DAY` field.
`HOUR_OF_DAY1_FIELD`	Specifies the one-based `HOUR_OF_DAY` field.
`MILLISECOND_FIELD`	Specifies the `MILLISECOND` field.
`MINUTE_FIELD`	Specifies the `MINUTE` field.
`MONTH_FIELD`	Specifies the `MONTH` field.
`SECOND_FIELD`	Specifies the `SECOND` field.
`TIMEZONE_FIELD`	Specifies the `TIMEZONE` field.
`WEEK_OF_MONTH_FIELD`	Specifies the `WEEK_OF_MONTH` field.
`WEEK_OF_YEAR_FIELD`	Specifies the `WEEK_OF_YEAR` field.
`YEAR_FIELD`	Specifies the `YEAR` field.
Time Zone Methods	
`getTimeZone()`	Retrieves the time zone from the `Calendar` object of this `DateFormat` object.
`setTimeZone()`	Sets the time zone for the `Calendar` object of this `DateFormat` object.

MEMBER SUMMARY	
Locale Methods	
`getAvailableLocales()`	Retrieves the list of currently installed locales for `DateFormat`.
Object Methods	
`clone()`	Creates a copy of this `DateFormat` object.
`equals()`	Compares this `DateFormat` with another object for equality.
`hashCode()`	Computes the hash code for this `DateFormat` object.

See Also

`Format`, `NumberFormat`, `SimpleDateFormat`, `Calendar`, `GregorianCalendar`, `TimeZone`.

Example

This example calls all of the creation methods for each style for all available locales and then prints them all.

```
import java.text.DateFormat;
import java.util.Date;
import java.util.Locale;

class Main {

    public static void main(String args[]) {
        int COL1WIDTH = 19;
        int COL2WIDTH = 10;
        String myString;
        Date date = new Date();
        Locale[] locArray = DateFormat.getAvailableLocales();
        int[] styles = { DateFormat.SHORT,
                         DateFormat.MEDIUM,
                         DateFormat.LONG,
                         DateFormat.FULL,
                         DateFormat.DEFAULT };

        String[] styleNames = { "SHORT", "MEDIUM", "LONG", "FULL", "DEFAULT" };

        // Loop over the locales.
        for (int i = 0; i < locArray.length; ++i) {
            Locale loc = locArray[i];

            System.out.println("\n" + "---------------------------------");
            System.out.println(loc.getDisplayName() + "\n");

            System.out.println("getDateInstance()");

          // Create a instance of the current date in each style and print it.
            for (int s = 0; s < styles.length; s++) {
                myString =
```

```
                DateFormat.getDateInstance(styles[s], loc).format(date);

                printInColumn("  Date", COL1WIDTH);
                printInColumn(styleNames[s], COL2WIDTH);
                System.out.println(myString);
            }

            System.out.println();
            System.out.println("getTimeInstance()");

            for (int s = 0; s < styles.length; s++) {
                myString =
                DateFormat.getTimeInstance(styles[s], loc).format(date);

                printInColumn("  Time", COL1WIDTH);
                printInColumn(styleNames[s], COL2WIDTH);
                System.out.println(myString);
            }

            System.out.println();
            System.out.println("getDateTimeInstance()");

            for (int s = 0; s < styles.length; s++) {

                myString =
                DateFormat.getDateTimeInstance(styles[s],
                                               styles[s], loc).format(date);

                printInColumn("  Date and Time", COL1WIDTH);
                printInColumn((styleNames[s]), COL2WIDTH);
                System.out.println(myString);
            }

            System.out.println();
            System.out.println("getInstance()");

            myString =
            DateFormat.getInstance().format(date);

            printInColumn("  Default", COL1WIDTH);
            printInColumn("SHORT", COL2WIDTH);
            System.out.println(myString);
        }
    }

    static void printInColumn(String str, int col) {
        System.out.print(str);
        for (int p = str.length(); p < col; ++p) {
            System.out.print(" ");
        }
    }
}
```

Output

```
> java Main

--------------------------------------
English (United States)
```

```
getDateInstance()
  Date              SHORT          11/23/97
  Date              MEDIUM         23-Nov-97
  Date              LONG           November 23, 1997
  Date              FULL           Sunday, November 23, 1997
  Date              DEFAULT        23-Nov-97

getTimeInstance()
  Time              SHORT          1:27 AM
  Time              MEDIUM         1:27:06 AM
  Time              LONG           1:27:06 AM PST
  Time              FULL           1:27:06 o'clock AM PST
  Time              DEFAULT        1:27:06 AM

getDateTimeInstance()
  Date and Time     SHORT          11/23/97 1:27 AM
  Date and Time     MEDIUM         23-Nov-97 1:27:06 AM
  Date and Time     LONG           November 23, 1997 1:27:06 AM PST
  Date and Time     FULL           Sunday, November 23, 1997 1:27:06 o'clock AM PST
  Date and Time     DEFAULT        23-Nov-97 1:27:06 AM

getInstance()
  Default           SHORT          11/23/97 1:27 AM

-------------------------------------
French (France)

getDateInstance()
  Date              SHORT          23/11/97
  Date              MEDIUM         23 nov 97
  Date              LONG           23 novembre 1997
  Date              FULL           dimanche, 23 novembre 1997
  Date              DEFAULT        23 nov 97

getTimeInstance()
  Time              SHORT          10:27
  Time              MEDIUM         10:27:06
  Time              LONG           10:27:06 GMT+01:00
  Time              FULL           10 h 27 GMT+01:00
  Time              DEFAULT        10:27:06

getDateTimeInstance()
  Date and Time     SHORT          23/11/97 10:27
  Date and Time     MEDIUM         23 nov 97 10:27:06
  Date and Time     LONG           23 novembre 1997 10:27:06 GMT+01:00
  Date and Time     FULL           dimanche, 23 novembre 1997 10 h 27 GMT+01:00
  Date and Time     DEFAULT        23 nov 97 10:27:06

getInstance()
  Default           SHORT          11/23/97 1:27 AM
```

[The other locales are not shown here.]

AM_PM_FIELD

PURPOSE Specifies the AM_PM field.

SYNTAX `public final static int AM_PM_FIELD`

DESCRIPTION This constant is passed into the FieldPosition constructor to signify that the AM_PM part of this date should be located. The FieldPosition object can then be passed into format(). Its value is 14.

SEE ALSO FieldPosition.

EXAMPLE Similar to INTEGER_FIELD in the class example in FieldPosition.

calendar

PURPOSE The Calendar object this DateFormat object uses.

SYNTAX `protected Calendar calendar`

DESCRIPTION This field holds the Calendar object that this DateFormat object uses to produce the date and time values. Subclasses should initialize this to the default Calendar object to be used with this DateFormat object.

EXAMPLE This example creates a subclass of DateFormat and sets the calendar and numberFormat fields.

```
import java.text.*;
import java.util.*;

public class Main extends DateFormat {

    public Main(Locale loc) {
        initialize(loc);
    }

    // Required when subclassing DateFormat.
    public StringBuffer format(Date d, StringBuffer buf, FieldPosition pos) {
        // Some implementation goes here.
        return buf;
    }

    // Required when subclassing DateFormat.
    public Date parse(String sourceStr, ParsePosition pos) {
        // Some implementation goes here.
        return (new Date());
    }

    // Required when subclassing Format.
    public Object parseObject(String sourceStr, ParsePosition pos) {
        // Some implementation goes here.
        return (new Date());
    }
```

```
    private void initialize(Locale loc) {
        calendar = Calendar.getInstance(TimeZone.getTimeZone("PST"));
        numberFormat = NumberFormat.getInstance(loc);

        System.out.println(calendar);          // java.util.GregorianCalendar@0
        System.out.println(numberFormat);      // java.text.DecimalFormat@2a796
    }

    public static void main(String args[]) {

        // Create a date format.
        DateFormat df = DateFormat.getInstance();

        new Main(Locale.FRANCE);
    }
}
```

clone()

PURPOSE Creates a copy of this `DateFormat` object.

SYNTAX `public Object clone()`

DESCRIPTION This method creates a clone of this `DateFormat` object by making a copy of the entire object. If you make changes to the new copy, they will not affect this original `DateFormat` object.

RETURNS A copy of this `DateFormat` object.

OVERRIDES `Format.clone()`.

EXAMPLE This example illustrates the use of `clone()` to copy a `DateFormat` object. It then uses `equals()` to compare them and prints out `hashcode()`. Note that the copy is equal to the original.

```
import java.text.DateFormat;
import java.util.Calendar;

class Main {

    public static void main(String args[]) {

        // Create a date format.
        DateFormat df = DateFormat.getInstance();

        // Get the day of week from calendar.
        System.out.println(df.getCalendar().get(Calendar.DAY_OF_WEEK));

        // Create a clone.
        DateFormat dfCopy = (DateFormat)df.clone();

        // Get the day of week from clone's calendar.
        System.out.println(dfCopy.getCalendar().get(Calendar.DAY_OF_WEEK));
```

```
            if(df.equals(dfCopy)) {
                System.out.println("Copy is equal to original");
            } else {
                System.out.println("Copy is not equal to original");
            }

            // Compute hashcode.
            int hc = df.hashCode();
            System.out.println("Hash code is: " + hc);
        }
    }
```

Output

```
> java Main
3
3
Copy is equal to original
Hash code is: 1137591166
```

A B C D E F G H I J K L M N O P Q R S T U V W X Y Z

DATE_FIELD

PURPOSE Specifies the DATE field.

SYNTAX `public final static int DATE_FIELD`

DESCRIPTION This constant is passed in to the `FieldPosition` constructor to signify that the `DATE` part of this date should be located. The `FieldPosition` object can then be passed into `format()`. Its value is 3.

SEE ALSO `FieldPosition`.

EXAMPLE Similar to `INTEGER_FIELD` in the class example in `FieldPosition`.

DateFormat()

PURPOSE Constructor called by subclasses.

SYNTAX `protected DateFormat()`

DESCRIPTION Do not call this constructor directly. You typically create an instance of a `DateFormat` subclass by calling one of the format creation methods listed below, such as `getInstance()`. This constructor is protected so that only subclasses can access it.

SEE ALSO `getInstance()`, `getDateInstance()`, `getTimeInstance()`, `getDateTimeInstance()`.

DAY_OF_WEEK_FIELD

PURPOSE Specifies the DAY_OF_WEEK field.

SYNTAX `public final static int DAY_OF_WEEK_FIELD`

DESCRIPTION This constant is passed in to the FieldPosition constructor to signify that the DAY_OF_WEEK part of this date should be located. The FieldPosition object can then be passed into format(). Its value is 9.

SEE ALSO FieldPosition.

EXAMPLE Similar to INTEGER_FIELD in the class example in FieldPosition.

DAY_OF_WEEK_IN_MONTH_FIELD

PURPOSE Specifies the DAY_OF_WEEK_IN_MONTH field.

SYNTAX `public final static int DAY_OF_WEEK_IN_MONTH_FIELD`

DESCRIPTION This constant is passed in to the FieldPosition constructor to signify that the DAY_OF_WEEK_IN_MONTH part of this date should be located. The FieldPosition object can then be passed into format(). Its value is 11.

SEE ALSO FieldPosition.

EXAMPLE Similar to INTEGER_FIELD in the class example in FieldPosition.

DAY_OF_YEAR_FIELD

PURPOSE Specifies the DAY_OF_YEAR field.

SYNTAX `public final static int DAY_OF_YEAR_FIELD`

DESCRIPTION This constant is passed into the FieldPosition constructor to signify that the DAY_OF_YEAR part of this date should be located. The FieldPosition object can then be passed into format(). Its value is 10.

SEE ALSO FieldPosition.

EXAMPLE Similar to INTEGER_FIELD in the class example in FieldPosition.

DEFAULT

PURPOSE Specifies the default style of the date or time.

SYNTAX `public final static int DEFAULT`

DESCRIPTION This constant is the default style pattern. Its value is `MEDIUM`.

SEE ALSO `SHORT, MEDIUM, LONG, FULL.`

EXAMPLE See `FULL`.

A B C D E F G H I J K L M N O P Q R S T U V W X Y Z

ERA_FIELD

PURPOSE Specifies the `ERA` field.

SYNTAX `public final static int ERA_FIELD`

DESCRIPTION This constant is passed in to the `FieldPosition` constructor to signify that the `ERA` part of this date should be located. The `FieldPosition` object can then be passed into `format()`. Its value is `0`.

SEE ALSO `FieldPosition.`

EXAMPLE Similar to `INTEGER_FIELD` in the class example in `FieldPosition`.

equals()

PURPOSE Compares this `DateFormat` with another object for equality.

SYNTAX `public boolean equals(Object obj)`

DESCRIPTION This method compares this `DateFormat` with another object for equality. If `obj` is a `DateFormat` object and if it has the same `Calendar` object and `NumberFormat` object as this `DateFormat` object, the objects are equal and this method returns `true`. If the `Calendar` object and `NumberFormat` object are not equal or if `obj` is `null` or is not a `DateFormat` object, the method returns `false`.

PARAMETERS

`obj` A possibly `null` object with which to compare.

RETURNS `true` if the objects are equal; `false otherwise`.

OVERRIDES `java.lang.Object.equals().`

SEE ALSO `hashCode().`

EXAMPLE See `clone()`.

format()

PURPOSE Formats a `Number` or `Date` object to produce a string.

SYNTAX

```
public final StringBuffer format(Object obj,
   StringBuffer appendBuf, FieldPosition pos)
public abstract StringBuffer format(Date date,
   StringBuffer appendBuf, FieldPosition pos)
public final String format(Date date)
```

DESCRIPTION

This method formats a Number or Date object to produce a string, which is appended to the buffer appendbuf. The appendBuf value is returned. Returning the full result allows chaining. If appendBuf is not specified, the produced string is simply returned.

When formatting a Number object, that number represents the number of milliseconds from the start of the epoch. See Date for a description of epoch.

The FieldPosition object pos has absolutely no effect on the formatted result. Its purpose is to determine where in the string the range of characters are for a given field so that the strings can be aligned in a column on that particular field. If you don't care about column alignment, set pos to any valid FieldPosition object.

The FieldPosition object works as follows. Create an instance of FieldPosition using the field constant for the field you want to align. For example, if you are formatting dates and want to output them in a column and align the months, create the FieldPosition object with the field constant DateFormat.MONTH_FIELD. When you call format(), the begin and end index values of the FieldPosition object pos are updated to the month range in the resulting string. You can then use these values to get the length of the month portion and then use that to position the string horizontally. For an example of this, see the class example in the FieldPosition class.

PARAMETERS

appendBuf
The string buffer in which to append the resulting string.

date
A Date to be formatted into a date-time string.

obj
A Number or a Date object to be converted to a string. A Number object represents the number of milliseconds from the start of epoch (January 1, 1970 00:00:00 UTC).

pos
A FieldPosition object whose field you want to eventually align in a column.

RETURNS

The formatted date-time string, either a String object or a StringBuffer object.

OVERRIDES

Format.format().

SEE ALSO

Format.

EXAMPLE

See the class example.

FULL

PURPOSE Specifies the full, unabbreviated style of the date or time.

SYNTAX `public final static int FULL`

DESCRIPTION This is the constant for the full, unabbreviated style pattern. Its value is `0`.

Note: The `FULL` date should contain milliseconds. It is a known bug in Java 1.1.5 and earlier that the `FULL` date does not contain milliseconds. `FULL` formats should contain enough information to allow a round trip from the `Date` object to the string and back.

SEE ALSO `SHORT`, `MEDIUM`, `LONG`, `DEFAULT`.

EXAMPLE This example prints out the current date using each different style.

```
import java.text.DateFormat;
import java.util.Date;

class Main {

    public static void main(String args[]) {

        String myString;

        int[] styles = { DateFormat.SHORT,
                         DateFormat.MEDIUM,
                         DateFormat.LONG,
                         DateFormat.FULL,
                         DateFormat.DEFAULT };

        // Create a instance of the current date in each style and print it.
        for (int i = 0; i < styles.length; i++) {
            myString =
                DateFormat.getDateInstance(styles[i]).format(new Date());

            System.out.println(myString);

        }
    }
}
```

Output

```
> java Main
11/21/97
21-Nov-97
November 21, 1997
Friday, November 21, 1997
21-Nov-97
```

getAvailableLocales()

PURPOSE Retrieves the list of currently installed locales for `DateFormat`.

SYNTAX
```
public static Locale[] getAvailableLocales()
```

DESCRIPTION This method queries the system and gets the set of `Locale` instances for which `DateFormat` instances are installed for this virtual machine.

RETURNS An array of locales for which `DateFormat` resources are installed.

EXAMPLE See the class example.

getCalendar()

PURPOSE Retrieves the `Calendar` object used with this `DateFormat` object.

SYNTAX
```
public Calendar getCalendar()
```

RETURNS The `Calendar` object associated with this `DateFormat` object.

EXAMPLE See `setCalendar()`.

getDateInstance()

PURPOSE Creates a date (not time) format with a style, for a locale.

SYNTAX
```
public final static DateFormat getDateInstance()
public final static DateFormat getDateInstance(int style)
public final static DateFormat getDateInstance(int style,
   Locale loc)
```

DESCRIPTION This method creates and returns an instance of `DateFormat` that formats and parses dates, not times, using the formatting style `style` for the locale `loc`. For example, `SHORT` means "M/d/yy" in the U.S. locale. If the style or locale is not specified, the `DEFAULT` style is used.

PARAMETERS

`loc` A locale for this `DateFormat` object.

`style` A formatting style.

RETURNS A `DateFormat` object that formats and parses dates.

EXAMPLE See the class example.

getDateTimeInstance()

PURPOSE Creates a date and time format with a style, for a locale.

SYNTAX
```
public final static DateFormat getDateTimeInstance()
public final static DateFormat getDateTimeInstance(int dateStyle,
   int timeStyle)
public final static DateFormat getDateTimeInstance(int dateStyle,
   int timeStyle, Locale loc)
```

DESCRIPTION This method creates and returns an instance of `DateFormat` that formats and parses dates and times using the formatting style `style` for the locale `loc`. For example, `SHORT` for both `dateStyle` and `timeStyle` means "M/d/yy h:mm a" in the U.S. locale. If the style or locale is omitted, the `DEFAULT` style is used.

PARAMETERS

`dateStyle` A `DateFormat` formatting style.

`loc` A locale for this format.

`timeStyle` A time formatting style.

RETURNS The `DateFormat` object that formats and parses dates and times.

EXAMPLE See the class example.

getInstance()

PURPOSE Creates a date and time format for the default locale.

SYNTAX
```
public final static DateFormat getInstance()
```

DESCRIPTION This method creates and returns an instance of `DateFormat` that formats and parses dates and times using a particular formatting style for the default locale. For Java 1.1.5 and earlier, the `SHORT` style is used.

Note: This style may change in future versions of Java.

RETURNS The default `DateFormat` object that uses the `SHORT` style for both the date and the time.

EXAMPLE See the class example.

getNumberFormat()

PURPOSE Retrieves the `NumberFormat` object used to format and parse a date-time.

SYNTAX
```
public NumberFormat getNumberInstance()
```

RETURNS The `NumberFormat` object this `DateFormat` object uses when formatting and parsing.

EXAMPLE See `setNumberFormat()`.

getTimeInstance()

PURPOSE Creates a time format with a style, for a locale.

SYNTAX
```
public final static DateFormat getTimeInstance()
public final static DateFormat getTimeInstance(int style)
public final static DateFormat getTimeInstance(int style,
   Locale loc)
```

DESCRIPTION This method creates and returns an instance of `DateFormat` that formats and parses times (not dates) using the formatting style `style` for the locale `loc`. For example, `SHORT` means "h:mm a" in the U.S. locale. If the style or locale is omitted, the `DEFAULT` style is used.

PARAMETERS
`loc` A locale for this `DateFormat` object.
`style` A formatting style.

RETURNS A `DateFormat` object that formats and parses times.

EXAMPLE See the class example.

getTimeZone()

PURPOSE Retrieves the time zone from the `Calendar` object of this `DateFormat` object.

SYNTAX
```
public TimeZone getTimeZone()
```

RETURNS The time zone associated with the `Calendar` object of `DateFormat`.

EXAMPLE See `setTimeZone()`.

hashCode()

PURPOSE Computes the hash code for this `DateFormat` object.

SYNTAX
```
public int hashCode()
```

DESCRIPTION This method computes the hash code for the `DateFormat` object. Two `DateFormat` objects with the same properties will have the same hash code. However, two `DateFormat` objects that do not have the same properties might also have the same hash code, although the hash code algorithm minimizes this possibility. The hash code is typically used as the key in a hash table.

RETURNS The `DateFormat` object's hash code, an integer.

OVERRIDES `java.lang.Object.hashCode()`.

SEE ALSO `equals()`.

EXAMPLE See `clone()`.

HOUR_OF_DAY0_FIELD

PURPOSE Specifies the zero-based `HOUR_OF_DAY` field.

SYNTAX `public final static int HOUR_OF_DAY0_FIELD`

DESCRIPTION This constant is passed in to the `FieldPosition` constructor to signify that the `HOUR_OF_DAY0` part of this date should be located. The `FieldPosition` object can then be passed into `format()`. Its value is `5`. A zero-based 24-hour clock has 0:00 as its first hour. For example, 23:59 + 1 hour results in 0:59.

SEE ALSO `FieldPosition`.

EXAMPLE Similar to `INTEGER_FIELD` in the class example in `FieldPosition`.

HOUR_OF_DAY1_FIELD

PURPOSE Specifies the one-based `HOUR_OF_DAY` field.

SYNTAX `public final static int HOUR_OF_DAY1_FIELD`

DESCRIPTION This constant is passed into the `FieldPosition` constructor to signify that the `HOUR_OF_DAY1` part of this date should be located. The `FieldPosition` object can then be passed in to `format()`. Its value is `4`. A one-based 24-hour clock has 1:00 as its first hour. For example, 23:59 + 1 hour results in 24:59.

SEE ALSO `FieldPosition`.

EXAMPLE Similar to `INTEGER_FIELD` in the class example in `FieldPosition`.

HOUR0_FIELD

PURPOSE Specifies the zero-based `HOUR` field.

SYNTAX `public final static int HOUR0_FIELD`

DESCRIPTION This constant is passed into the `FieldPosition` constructor to signify that the `HOUR0` part of this date should be located. The `FieldPosition` object can then be passed in to `format()`. Its value is `16`. A zero-based 12-hour clock has 0:00 as its first hour. For example, 11:30 P.M. + 1 hour results in 0:30 A.M.

SEE ALSO `FieldPosition`.

EXAMPLE Similar to `INTEGER_FIELD` in the class example in `FieldPosition`.

HOUR1_FIELD

PURPOSE Specifies the one-based `HOUR` field.

SYNTAX `public final static int HOUR1_FIELD`

DESCRIPTION This constant is passed into the `FieldPosition` constructor to signify that the `HOUR1` part of this date should be located. The `FieldPosition` object can then be passed into `format()`. Its value is 15. A one-based 12-hour clock has 12:00 as its first hour. For example, 11:30 P.M. + 1 hour results in 12:30 A.M.

SEE ALSO `FieldPosition`.

EXAMPLE Similar to `INTEGER_FIELD` in the class example in `FieldPosition`.

isLenient()

PURPOSE Determines if parsing is set to lenient for this `DateFormat` object.

SYNTAX `public boolean isLenient()`

RETURNS `true` if the date and time parsing is set to lenient; `false` otherwise.

EXAMPLE See `setLenient()`.

LONG

PURPOSE Used for a long style of the date or time.

SYNTAX `public final static int LONG`

DESCRIPTION This is the constant for the long style pattern. Its value is `1`.

SEE ALSO `SHORT`, `MEDIUM`, `FULL`, `DEFAULT`.

EXAMPLE See `FULL`.

MEDIUM

PURPOSE Specifies the medium-length style of the date or time.

SYNTAX `public final static int MEDIUM`

DESCRIPTION This is the constant for the medium style pattern. Its value is 2.

SEE ALSO SHORT, LONG, FULL, DEFAULT.

EXAMPLE See FULL.

A B C D E F G H I J K L M N O P Q R S T U V W X Y Z

MILLISECOND_FIELD

PURPOSE Specifies the MILLISECOND field.

SYNTAX `public final static int MILLISECOND_FIELD`

DESCRIPTION This constant is passed into the FieldPosition constructor to signify that the MILLISECOND part of this date should be located. The FieldPosition object can then be passed in to format(). Its value is 8.

SEE ALSO FieldPosition.

EXAMPLE Similar to INTEGER_FIELD in the class example in FieldPosition.

MINUTE_FIELD

PURPOSE Specifies the MINUTE field.

SYNTAX `public final static int MINUTE_FIELD`

DESCRIPTION This constant is passed in to the FieldPosition constructor to signify that the MINUTE part of this date should be located. The FieldPosition object can then be passed into format(). Its value is 6.

SEE ALSO FieldPosition.

EXAMPLE Similar to INTEGER_FIELD in the class example in FieldPosition.

MONTH_FIELD

PURPOSE Specifies the MONTH field.

SYNTAX `public final static int MONTH_FIELD`

DESCRIPTION This constant is passed into the `FieldPosition` constructor to signify that the `MONTH` part of this date should be located. The `FieldPosition` object can then be passed in to `format()`. Its value is 2.

SEE ALSO `FieldPosition`.

EXAMPLE Similar to `INTEGER_FIELD` in the class example in `FieldPosition`.

numberFormat

PURPOSE The `NumberFormat` object this `DateFormat` object uses.

SYNTAX

```
protected NumberFormat numberFormat
```

DESCRIPTION This field is the `NumberFormat` object that this `DateFormat` object uses to format numbers in dates and times. Subclasses should initialize this to the default `NumberFormat` object for the locale associated with this `DateFormat` object.

EXAMPLE See `calendar` field.

parse()

PURPOSE Parses a date-time string to produce a `Date` object.

SYNTAX

```
public Date parse(String sourceStr) throws ParseException
public abstract Date parse(String sourceStr, ParsePosition pos)
```

DESCRIPTION This method parses a string starting at the parse position `pos` looking for the pattern of this `DateFormat` object. If this pattern is found at that position, an instance of `Date` is produced and the begin index of the parse position is updated to this position. If this pattern is not found, the syntax form that takes a parse position returns `null` and the parse position does not advance; the form that takes only a string throws a `ParseException`.

For example, the string "07/10/96 4:50 PM, PDT" will be parsed into an instance of `Date` that is equivalent to `new Date(837039928046)`.

By default, parsing is lenient. That is, if, for example, the input is January 32, the parse will still succeed, treating it as February 1. Clients may insist on strict adherence to the format by calling `setLenient(false)`.

Omitting the parse position `pos` causes the parse to begin at the start of `sourceStr`.

PARAMETERS

`pos` The parse position that determines where the parse begins. If `parse()` succeeds, the begin index is updated to the position at which parsing terminated.

`sourceStr`	The string to be parsed.
RETURNS	An instance of `Date`, or `null` if the input could not be parsed.

EXCEPTIONS

`ParseException`
For `parse(String)`, if the given string cannot be parsed as a date.

SEE ALSO `setLenient()`, `parseObject()`.

EXAMPLE This example parses a paragraph for all of the short dates it can find. You could find all of the other dates as well (medium, long, full) by creating an array of `DateFormat` objects and iterating through them.

```
import java.text.*;
import java.io.*;
import java.util.*;

class Main {
    // Create a date format.
    static DateFormat dateForm = DateFormat.getDateInstance(DateFormat.SHORT);

    // Create a parse position object for tracking the parse.
    static ParsePosition parsePos = new ParsePosition(0);

    Main (String str) {
        // Print out original text.
        System.out.println(str);

        // Parse through text for short dates.
        System.out.println("Finding all short dates in the above text:");
        parseDate(str);
    }

    static void parseDate(String str) {
        int beginParseIndex;
        int endParseIndex;
        int intLength;
        Date d = null;
        dateForm.setLenient(false);

        while (parsePos.getIndex() < str.length()) {
            beginParseIndex = parsePos.getIndex();

            // Parse the string for a date starting at parsePos.
            d = dateForm.parse(str, parsePos);

            endParseIndex = parsePos.getIndex();

            if (d != null) {
                // Count length of index for printing spaces.
                intLength =
                    ((new Integer(beginParseIndex)).toString()).length();
                System.out.print("Index: ");
                printSpaces(4 - intLength);
                System.out.print(beginParseIndex);
                printSpaces(4);
```

```
                // Count length of date for printing spaces.
                System.out.print("Number: ");
                printSpaces(10 - dateForm.format(d).length());
                System.out.println(dateForm.format(d));
            }
            parsePos.setIndex(endParseIndex + 1);
        }
        // Reset parse position to 0 for next loop.
        parsePos.setIndex(0);
    }

    // Print spaces.
    static void printSpaces(int count) {
        for (int p = 0; p < count; ++p) {
            System.out.print(" ");
        }
    }

    public static void main(String[] args) {
        // Accept an input text file
        if (args.length != 1) {
            System.err.println("This program parses text for dates");
            System.err.println("Usage: java Main input.txt");
            System.exit(1);
        }

        try {
            // Read the text into a buffered reader
            // with '\n' for newlines
            BufferedReader rd = new BufferedReader(new FileReader(args[0]));
            String line;
            StringBuffer sbuf = new StringBuffer();

            while ((line = rd.readLine()) != null) {
                sbuf.append(line);
                sbuf.append('\n');
            }
            rd.close();

            // Call the constructor Main with the input string
            new Main(new String(sbuf));

        } catch (Exception e) {
            e.printStackTrace();
        }
    }
}
```

Output

```
> java Main input.txt
Jan 1, 1998.  It's hard to find a system on 2/10/98 under $1200 that is
100%-reliable.  Starting March 1, 1998, the price of $1,100.00 will
include 3 required $50 add-ons.  The price is going up 10 - 15% on
November 3, 1998 at 5:25pm.  Wait for 12/31/98.

Finding all short dates in the above text:
Index:   44    Number:    2/10/98
Index:  248    Number:   12/31/98
```

parseObject()

PURPOSE Parses a date-time string to produce an object.

SYNTAX `public Object parseObject(String sourceStr, ParsePosition pos)`

DESCRIPTION This method parses a string starting at the parse position `pos` looking for the pattern of this `DateFormat` object. If this pattern is found at that position, an object is produced and the begin index of the parse position is updated to this position. If this pattern is not found, it returns `null` and the parse position does not advance.

This convenience method simply calls `parse(String, ParsePosition)`.

PARAMETERS

`pos` The parse position that determines where the parse begins. If `parse()` succeeds, the begin index is updated to the position at which parsing terminated.

`sourceStr` The string to be parsed.

RETURNS An object if the parse succeeds, or `null` if the input could not be parsed.

OVERRIDES `Format.parseObject()`.

SEE ALSO `parse()`.

EXAMPLE See the class example in `Format` for an example of `parseObject()`.

SECOND_FIELD

PURPOSE Specifies the `SECOND` field.

SYNTAX `public final static int SECOND_FIELD`

DESCRIPTION This constant is passed into the `FieldPosition` constructor to signify that the `SECOND` part of this date should be located. The `FieldPosition` object can then be passed into `format()`. Its value is 7.

SEE ALSO `FieldPosition`.

EXAMPLE Similar to `INTEGER_FIELD` in the class example in `FieldPosition`.

setCalendar()

PURPOSE Sets the `Calendar` object used with this `DateFormat` object.

SYNTAX `public void setCalendar(Calendar newCalendar)`

DESCRIPTION This method sets the `Calendar` object to be used by this `DateFormat` object.

Initially, when an instance of DateFormat is created, the default Calendar object for the specified or default locale is used. This method enables you to change the Calendar object.

PARAMETERS

newCalendar A new Calendar object.

EXAMPLE This example creates a DateFormat object, then creates a new Calendar object, and then sets the new Calendar object to the DateFormat object.

```
import java.text.DateFormat;
import java.util.Calendar;
import java.util.TimeZone;

class Main {

    public static void main(String args[]) {

        // Create a date format.
        DateFormat df = DateFormat.getInstance();

        // Create a new calendar.
        Calendar newCalendar =
            Calendar.getInstance(TimeZone.getTimeZone("PST"));

        // Set the new calendar to this date format.
        df.setCalendar(newCalendar);

        // Print the new calendar.
        System.out.print(df.getCalendar());    // "java.util.GregorianCalendar"
    }
}
```

setLenient()

PURPOSE Sets parsing to be lenient for this DateFormat object.

SYNTAX `public void setLenient(boolean lenient)`

DESCRIPTION This method sets whether date-time parsing is lenient. When lenient is set to true, the parser allows out-of-range values such as Jan 32 (which is interpreted as Feb 1). If lenient is set to false, for strict parsing, then out-of-range values trigger a ParseException. (IllegalArgumentException prior to JDK 1.1.6).

PARAMETERS

lenient If true, the parsing is lenient; otherwise, it is strict.

SEE ALSO java.util.Calendar.setLenient().

EXAMPLE This method prints out a date in the normal range (February 10) and one outside of the normal range (February 38), first with lenient as `true` and then with lenient as `false`.

```
import java.text.DateFormat;
import java.text.ParsePosition;

class Main {

    // Create a parse position object to track parsing.
    static ParsePosition pos = new ParsePosition(0);

    public static void main(String args[]) {

        // Create a date format.
        DateFormat df = DateFormat.getDateInstance(DateFormat.MEDIUM);

        System.out.println(df.isLenient());    // true

        // Print normal date.
        print(df.parse("10-Feb-98", pos));     // Tue Feb 10 00:00:00 PST 1998

        // Reset parse position to start.
        pos.setIndex(0);

        // Print date outside of normal range.
        print(df.parse("38-Feb-98", pos));     // Tue Mar 10 00:00:00 PST 1998

        // Turn off lenient.
        df.setLenient(false);

        // Reset parse position to start.
        pos.setIndex(0);

        // Print dates with lenient false.
        print(df.parse("10-Feb-98", pos));     // Tue Feb 10 00:00:00 PST 1998

        // Reset parse position to start.
        pos.setIndex(0);

        print(df.parse("31-Feb-98", pos));
                                   // IllegalArgumentException (JDK 1.1.5)
                                   // ParseException           (JDK 1.1.6)
    }

    static void print(Object s) {
        System.out.println(s);
    }
}
```

setNumberFormat()

PURPOSE Sets the `NumberFormat` object used to format and parse a date-time.

SYNTAX `public void setNumberFormat(NumberFormat numFormat)`

DESCRIPTION

This method sets the instance of `NumberFormat` used with this `DateFormat` object for formatting and parsing dates. It is set up to not use grouping separators, since dates do not use them. It is also set to parse only integers so that it can handle decimal separators inside of dates, such as "dd.mm.yy".

PARAMETERS

`numFormat` The new `NumberFormat` to be set.

EXAMPLE

This example creates a `DateFormat` object, then creates a new `NumberFormat` object, and then applies the new `NumberFormat` object to the `DateFormat` object using `setNumberFormat()`.

```
import java.text.DateFormat;
import java.text.NumberFormat;
import java.util.Locale;

class Main {

    public static void main(String args[]) {

        // Create a date format.
        DateFormat df = DateFormat.getInstance();

        // Create a new number format.
        NumberFormat numFormat = NumberFormat.getNumberInstance(Locale.FRANCE);

        // Set the new calendar to this date format.
        df.setNumberFormat(numFormat);

        // Print the new number instance.
        System.out.print(df.getNumberFormat());   // "java.text.DecimalFormat"
    }
}
```

setTimeZone()

PURPOSE

Sets the time zone for the `Calendar` object of this `DateFormat` object.

SYNTAX

`public void setTimeZone(TimeZone zone)`

PARAMETERS

`zone` The new time zone to be set.

EXAMPLE

This example sets the time zone and then gets it.

```
import java.text.DateFormat;
import java.util.TimeZone;

class Main {

    public static void main(String args[]) {
```

```
            // Create a date format.
            DateFormat df = DateFormat.getInstance();

            // Set the time zone of the calendar.
            df.setTimeZone(TimeZone.getTimeZone("PST"));

            // Get the time zone from the calendar.
            TimeZone tz = df.getTimeZone();

            // Print the time zone string.
            System.out.println(tz.getID());     // "PDT"
        }
    }
```

A B C D E F G H I J K L M N O P Q R S T U V W X Y Z

SHORT

PURPOSE Specifies the short style of the date or time.

SYNTAX `public final static int SHORT`

DESCRIPTION This is the constant for the short style pattern. Its value is 3.

SEE ALSO `MEDIUM`, `LONG`, `FULL`, `DEFAULT`.

EXAMPLE See `FULL`.

TIMEZONE_FIELD

PURPOSE Specifies the `TIMEZONE` field.

SYNTAX `public final static int TIMEZONE_FIELD`

DESCRIPTION This constant is passed in to the `FieldPosition` constructor to signify that the `TIMEZONE` part of this date should be located. The `FieldPosition` object can then be passed into `format()`. Its value is 17.

SEE ALSO `FieldPosition`.

EXAMPLE Similar to `INTEGER_FIELD` in the class example in `FieldPosition`.

WEEK_OF_YEAR_FIELD

PURPOSE Specifies the `WEEK_OF_YEAR` field.

SYNTAX `public final static int WEEK_OF_YEAR_FIELD`

DESCRIPTION This constant is passed in to the `FieldPosition` constructor to signify that the `WEEK_OF_YEAR` part of this date should be located. The `FieldPosition` object can then be passed in to `format()`. Its value is `12`.

SEE ALSO `FieldPosition`.

EXAMPLE Similar to `INTEGER_FIELD` in the class example in `FieldPosition`.

WEEK_OF_MONTH_FIELD

PURPOSE Specifies the `WEEK_OF_MONTH` field.

SYNTAX `public final static int WEEK_OF_MONTH_FIELD`

DESCRIPTION This constant is passed in to the `FieldPosition` constructor to signify that the `WEEK_OF_MONTH` part of this date should be located. The `FieldPosition` object can then be passed in to `format()`. Its value is `13`.

SEE ALSO `FieldPosition`.

EXAMPLE Similar to `INTEGER_FIELD` in the class example in `FieldPosition`.

YEAR_FIELD

PURPOSE Specifies the `YEAR` field.

SYNTAX `public final static int YEAR_FIELD`

DESCRIPTION This constant is passed into the `FieldPosition` constructor to signify that the `YEAR` part of this date should be located. The `FieldPosition` object can then be passed into `format()`. Its value is `1`.

SEE ALSO `FieldPosition`.

EXAMPLE Similar to `INTEGER_FIELD` in the class example in `FieldPosition`.

java.text
DateFormatSymbols

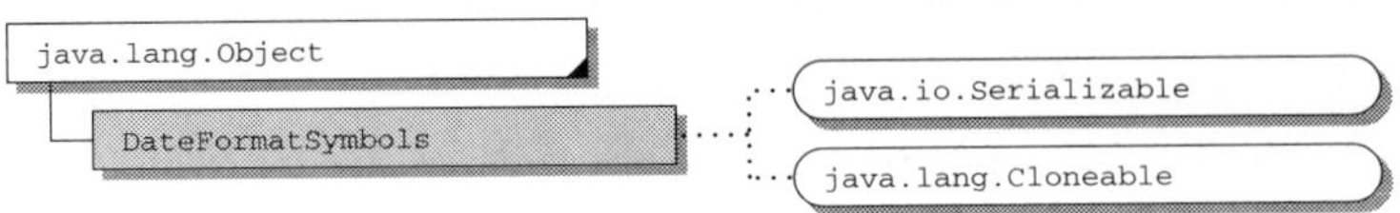

A B C D E F G H I J K L M N O P Q R S T U V W X Y Z

Syntax

```
public class DateFormatSymbols extends Object implements Serializable, Cloneable
```

Description

`DateFormatSymbols` is a class for accessing localizable date-time formatting strings, such as the names of the months, the names of the days of the week, and the time-zone strings. `DateFormat` and `SimpleDateFormat` both use `DateFormatSymbols` to access this information.

Usage

Typically you shouldn't use `DateFormatSymbols` directly. Rather, you are encouraged to create a date-time formatter with the `DateFormat` class's creation methods: `getInstance()`, `getTimeInstance()`, `getDateInstance()`, or `getDateTimeInstance()`. These methods automatically create an instance of `DateFormatSymbols` for the formatter so that you don't have to. After the formatter is created, you may modify its format pattern using the `setPattern()` method. For more information about creating formatters using `DateFormat`'s creation methods, see `DateFormat`.

If you want to create a date-time formatter with a specific format pattern for a specific locale, you can do so with the following:

```
new SimpleDateFormat(aPattern, new DateFormatSymbols(aLocale)).
```

`DateFormatSymbols` objects are cloneable. You can modify the date-time formatting data of such an object. For instance, you can replace the localized date-time format pattern characters with ones that are easy for you to remember.

Localization and Subclassing

To add date format symbols for locales that use the Gregorian calendar, you create resource bundles like those already set up in Java. To create symbols for a different kind of calendar, such as the Hindi calendar, you could subclass `DateFormatSymbols` with `HindiDateFormatSymbols`. In this case, `DateFormatSymbols` is just a wrapper class to get access to the resource bundle. Likewise, you would subclass `DateFormat` with `HindiDateFormat`.

Local Pattern Characters Property

The characters used in `SimpleDateFormat` are held in a string that is referred to as *LocalPatternChars*. Unlike the other properties, these characters are not normally part of a message displayed to a user. Rather, they are part of a pattern that is interpreted by date format classes to produce a date string. In U.S. English, it holds the following:

```
GyMdkHmsSEDFwWahKz
```

For example, the "h," "m," "s," and "a" characters mean hours, minutes, seconds, and A.M./P.M. These are used to specify the pattern "hh:mm:ss a", which could produce the string "10:15:00 AM". See the `SimpleDateFormat` class for a definition of each character.

Table 21 shows the meaning of the characters. For a fuller description, see the corresponding table in `SimpleDateFormat`.

Pattern Letter	Meaning	Date/Time	Example	
`G`	Era designator	Date	`AD`	
`y`	Year	Date	`97`	(last 2 digits of year)
`M`	Month in year	Date	`7`	(7th month)
`d`	Day in month	Date	`5`	(5th day in month)
`k`	Hour in day (1–24)	Time	`24`	
`H`	Hour in day (0–23)	Time	`0`	
`m`	Minute in hour	Time	`30`	
`s`	Second in minute	Time	`55`	
`S`	Millisecond	Time	`978`	
`E`	Day in week	Date	`Tues`	
`D`	Day in year	Date	`89`	(89th day)
`F`	Day of week in month	Date	`2`	(2nd Wed in July)
`w`	Week in year	Date	`27`	
`W`	Week in month	Date	`2`	
`a`	A.M./P.M. marker	Time	`PM`	
`h`	Hour in A.M./P.M. (1–12)	Time	`12`	
`K`	Hour in A.M./P.M. (0–11)	Time	`0`	
`z`	Time zone	Time	`PST`	

TABLE 21: The Local Pattern Characters.

AM/PM Strings Property

The two strings representing the two 12-hour time periods measured by a 12-hour clock. In U.S. English, it holds the strings "AM" (ante meridiem), meaning before noon, and "PM" (post meridiem), meaning at or after noon. For example, 10:00 A.M. is in the morning and 10:00 P.M. is in the evening. Midnight is A.M., and noon is P.M.

Eras Property

The *eras* property is an array that holds the strings representing the eras before and after Christ in the Gregorian calendar. In U.S. English, it holds "AD" (Anno Domini) for the era after Christ and "BC" (Before Christ).

Months and Short Months Properties

The *months* and *shortMonths* properties are arrays that hold the string names for the 12 months of the year, plus one for a possible thirteenth month for the lunar year. In U.S. English, they hold the following, where `(empty)` represents the empty string:

months:

```
January, February, March, April, May, June, July, August, September,
October, November, December, (empty)
```

shortMonths:

```
Jan, Feb, Mar, Apr, May, Jun, Jul, Aug, Sep, Oct, Nov, Dec, (empty)
```

Weekdays and Short Weekdays Properties

The *weekdays* and *shortWeekdays* properties are arrays that hold the string names for the 7 days of the week. They are held in an 8-member array so that they can be one-based. In U.S. English, they hold the following, where `(empty)` means the string is empty:

weekdays:

```
(empty), Sunday, Monday, Tuesday, Wednesday, Thursday, Friday, Saturday
```

shortWeekdays:

```
(empty), Sun, Mon, Tue, Wed, Thu, Fri, Sat
```

Time Zone Strings Property

The *zoneStrings* property is a two-dimensional array of strings used when displaying time-zone data. It is an n x 6 array, shown in Table 22. `ID` is not localized but is used to look up the localized time-zone data internally. The 6th dimension is one string for each city per time zone. The purposes of these cities was to help identify the time zones. An example would be "San Francisco" for the Pacific Standard Time zone. Localizers can localize any time-zone strings of the time zone except the `ID`. The `setZoneStrings()` method sets the time-zone strings, and the `getZoneStrings()` method gets the strings.

Note: In JDK 1.2 the zoneStrings property might change to an n x 5 array, where the representative city is removed.

ID	Standard Time-Zone Name		Daylight Time-Zone Name		Representative City
	Long	Short	Long	Short	
PST	Pacific Standard Time	PST	Pacific Daylight Time	PDT	San Francisco
MST	Mountain Standard Time	MST	Mountain Daylight Time	MDT	Denver
PNT	Mountain Standard Time	MST	Mountain Standard Time	MST	Phoenix
CST	Central Standard Time	CST	Central Daylight Time	CDT	Chicago
EST	Eastern Standard Time	EST	Eastern Daylight Time	EDT	New York
IET	Eastern Standard Time	EST	Eastern Standard Time	EST	Indianapolis
PRT	Atlantic Standard Time	AST	Atlantic Daylight Time	ADT	Halifax
HST	Hawaii Standard Time	HST	Hawaii Daylight Time	HDT	Honolulu
AST	Alaska Standard Time	AST	Alaska Daylight Time	ADT	Anchorage

TABLE 22: Elements of the zoneStrings Array.

MEMBER SUMMARY

Constructors

`DateFormatSymbols()`	Constructs a `DateFormatSymbols` instance by loading format data from resources for a locale.

Pattern Methods

`getLocalPatternChars()`	Retrieves the localized date-time pattern characters.
`setLocalPatternChars()`	Sets the localized date-time pattern characters.

Date-Time String Getter Methods

`getAmPmStrings()`	Retrieves the array of A.M.-P.M. strings.
`getEras()`	Retrieves the array of era strings.
`getMonths()`	Retrieves the array of month strings.
`getShortMonths()`	Retrieves the array of short month strings.
`getShortWeekdays()`	Retrieves the array of short weekday strings.
`getWeekdays()`	Retrieves the array of weekday strings.
`getZoneStrings()`	Retrieves the array of time-zone strings.

Date-Time String Setter Methods

`setAmPmStrings()`	Sets the array of A.M.-P.M. strings.
`setEras()`	Sets the array of era strings.
`setMonths()`	Sets the array of month strings.
`setShortMonths()`	Sets the array of short month strings.
`setShortWeekdays()`	Sets the array of short weekday strings.
`setWeekdays()`	Sets the array of weekday strings.
`setZoneStrings()`	Sets the array of time-zone strings.

Continued

MEMBER SUMMARY

Object Methods	
`clone()`	Creates a copy of this `DateFormatSymbols` object.
`equals()`	Compares this `DateFormatSymbols` object with another object for equality.
`hashCode()`	Computes the hash code for this `DateFormatSymbols` object.

See Also

`DateFormat`, `SimpleDateFormat`, `SimpleTimeZone`.

Example

This example displays in a scrolling text area all of the date format symbols for all available locales. It adds the default locale to the start of the locales array so that it is the first one to appear at the top of the scrolling text area. See Figure 34.

Note that all properties are one-dimensional arrays except zone strings, which are in a two-dimensional array, and local pattern characters, which are in a string.

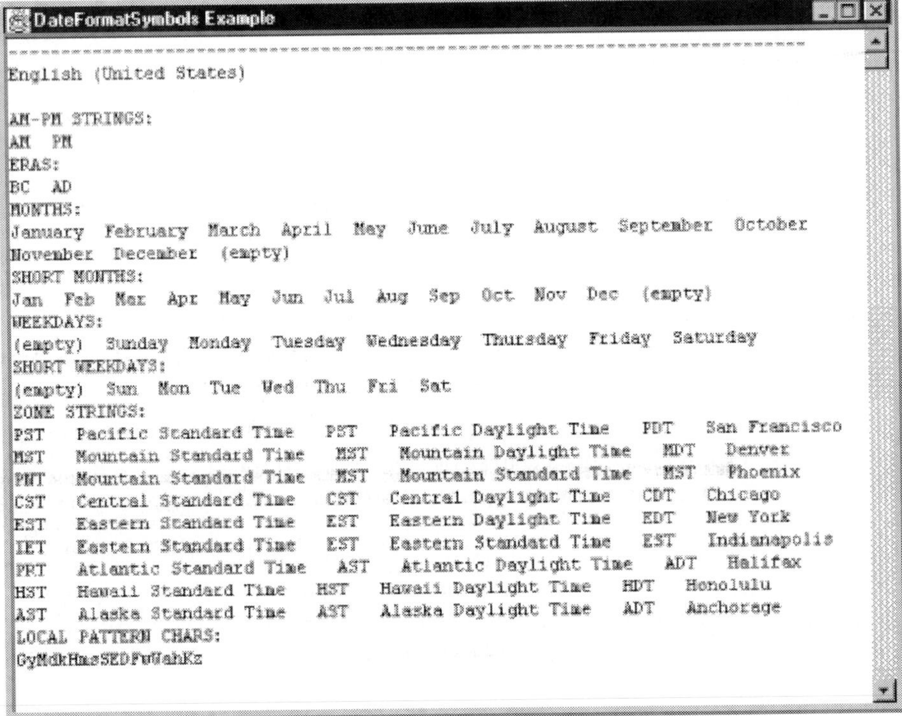

FIGURE 34: `DateFormatSymbols.`

```
import java.text.DateFormat;
import java.text.DateFormatSymbols;
import java.util.*;
import java.awt.*;

class Main extends Frame {
    TextArea textArea =
        new TextArea("", 30, 100, TextArea.SCROLLBARS_VERTICAL_ONLY);

    Main(StringBuffer strbuf) {
        super("DateFormatSymbols Example");

        // Set the text and add the layout to text area.
        textArea.setText(strbuf.toString());
        add(textArea, BorderLayout.CENTER);

        // Set size and show window.
        Font f = new Font("Courier", Font.PLAIN, 12);
        textArea.setFont(f);
        textArea.setEditable(false);
        setSize(600, 480);
        show();
    }

    public static void main(String[] args) {
        StringBuffer strbuf = new StringBuffer(1500);

        // Create an array of all available locales.
        Locale[] locales = DateFormat.getAvailableLocales();

        // Add the default locale to the beginning so it's displayed first.
        Locale[] localesPlusDefault = new Locale[locales.length + 1];
        System.arraycopy(locales, 0, localesPlusDefault, 1, locales.length);
        localesPlusDefault[0] = Locale.getDefault();

        // Loop through all locales.
        for (int i = 0; i < localesPlusDefault.length; ++i) {

            // Build up string to display in a string buffer
            strbuf.append("------------------------------------");
            strbuf.append("------------------------------------\n");
            strbuf.append(localesPlusDefault[i].getDisplayName());
            strbuf.append("\n\n");

            // Create a new date format symbols for US
            DateFormatSymbols dfs =
                               new DateFormatSymbols(localesPlusDefault[i]);

            strbuf.append("AM-PM STRINGS:" + "\n");
            appendArray(dfs.getAmPmStrings(), strbuf);
            strbuf.append("ERAS:" + "\n");
            appendArray(dfs.getEras(), strbuf);
            strbuf.append("MONTHS:" + "\n");
            appendArray(dfs.getMonths(), strbuf);
            strbuf.append("SHORT MONTHS: " + "\n");
            appendArray(dfs.getShortMonths(), strbuf);
            strbuf.append("WEEKDAYS:" + "\n");
            appendArray(dfs.getWeekdays(), strbuf);
            strbuf.append("SHORT WEEKDAYS: " + "\n");
```

```
                appendArray(dfs.getShortWeekdays(), strbuf);
                strbuf.append("ZONE STRINGS:" + "\n");
                appendDeepArray(dfs.getZoneStrings(), strbuf);
                strbuf.append("LOCAL PATTERN CHARS: " + "\n");
                strbuf.append(dfs.getLocalPatternChars() + "\n\n");
            }
            new Main(strbuf);
        }

        // Append the contents of a 1-dimensional array to a string
        static void appendArray(Object[] a, StringBuffer strbuf) {
            for (int i=0; i<a.length; i++) {
                if (a[i].toString().length() == 0) {
                    strbuf.append("(empty)" + "  ");
                } else {
                    strbuf.append(a[i] + "  ");
                }
            }
            strbuf.append("\n");
        }

        // Print out the contents of a 2-dimensional array.
        static void appendDeepArray(Object[][] a, StringBuffer strbuf) {
            for (int i=0; i<a.length; i++) {
                for (int j=0; j<a[i].length; j++) {
                    strbuf.append(a[i][j] + "   ");
                }
                strbuf.append("\n");
            }
        }
    }
```

clone()

PURPOSE Creates a copy of this `DateFormatSymbols` object.

SYNTAX `public Object clone()`

DESCRIPTION This method makes a copy of this date format symbols object.

OVERRIDES `java.lang.Object.clone()`.

EXAMPLE This example illustrates the use of `clone()` to copy a `DateFormatSymbols` object. It then uses `equals()` to compare the two objects and then prints out `hashcode()`. Note that the copy is equal to the original.

```
    import java.text.DateFormatSymbols;

    class Main {

        public static void main(String args[]) {

            // Create a date format symbols.
            DateFormatSymbols dfs = new DateFormatSymbols();
```

```
        // Get the localized pattern.
        System.out.println(dfs.getLocalPatternChars());

        // Create a clone.
        DateFormatSymbols dfsCopy = (DateFormatSymbols)dfs.clone();

        // Get the the localized pattern from the clone.
        System.out.println(dfsCopy.getLocalPatternChars());

        if(dfs.equals(dfsCopy)) {
            System.out.println("Copy is equal to original");
        } else {
            System.out.println("Copy is not equal to original");
        }

        // Compute hashcode.
        int hc = dfs.hashCode();
        System.out.println("Hash code is: " + hc);
    }
}
```

Output

```
> java Main
GyMdkHmsSEDFwWahKz
GyMdkHmsSEDFwWahKz
Copy is equal to original
Hash code is: -1778325794
```

DateFormatSymbols()

PURPOSE Creates a `DateFormatSymbols` object for a locale.

SYNTAX

```
public DateFormatSymbols()
public DateFormatSymbols(Locale loc)
```

DESCRIPTION This constructor creates a `DateFormatSymbols` object by loading format strings from resource files for the locale `loc`. Omitting `loc` uses the default locale.

PARAMETERS

`loc` The locale for the date format symbols.

EXCEPTIONS

`MissingResourceException`

If the resources for the default locale cannot be found or cannot be loaded.

EXAMPLE See the class example.

A B C D E F G H I J K L M N O P Q R S T U V W X Y Z

equals()

PURPOSE Compares this `DateFormatSymbols` object with another object for equality.

SYNTAX `public boolean equals(Object obj)`

DESCRIPTION This method compares this `DateFormatSymbols` object with another object for equality. If `obj` is a `DateFormatSymbols` object and if all of its properties are equal to those in this `DateFormatSymbols` object, the objects are equal and this method returns `true`. If the properties are not equal or if `obj` is `null` or is not a `DateFormatSymbols` object, the method returns `false`.

PARAMETERS

`obj` A possibly `null` object.

RETURNS `true` if obj is equal to this object; `false` otherwise.

OVERRIDES `java.lang.Object.equals()`.

SEE ALSO `hashCode()`.

EXAMPLE See `clone()`.

getAmPmStrings()

PURPOSE Retrieves the array of A.M.-P.M. strings.

SYNTAX `public String[] getAmPmStrings()`

RETURNS An array of A.M.-P.M. strings. For example, "`AM`" and "`PM`".

EXAMPLE See the class example or `setAmPmStrings()`.

getEras()

PURPOSE Retrieves the array of era strings.

SYNTAX `public String[] getEras()`

RETURNS An array of era strings. For example, "`AD`" and "`BC`" for U.S. English.

EXAMPLE See the class example or `setAmPmStrings()`.

getLocalPatternChars()

PURPOSE Retrieves the localized date-time pattern characters.

SYNTAX `public String getLocalPatternChars()`

DESCRIPTION Gets localized date-time pattern characters. These characters are used individually in the pattern of a `SimpleDateFormat` instance. See `SimpleDateFormat` for their

RETURNS Localized date-time pattern characters. For U.S. English, they are: "`GyMdkHmsSEDFwWahKz`"

EXAMPLE See the class example or `setAmPmStrings()`.

getMonths()

PURPOSE Retrieves the array of month strings.

SYNTAX `public String[] getMonths()`

RETURNS An array with 13 month strings, where the thirteenth one is for a lunar year. For U.S. English they are:

"January", "February", "March", "April", "May", "June", "July", "August", "September", "October", "November", "December", ""

EXCEPTIONS See the class example or `setAmPmStrings()`.

getShortMonths()

PURPOSE Retrieves the array of short month strings.

SYNTAX `public String[] getShortMonths()`

RETURNS Abbreviated month strings. For U.S. English, they are:

"Jan", "Feb", "Mar", "Apr", "May", "Jun", "Jul", "Aug", "Sep", "Oct", "Nov", "Dec", ""

EXAMPLE See the class example or `setAmPmStrings()`.

getShortWeekdays()

PURPOSE Retrieves the array of short weekday strings.

SYNTAX `public String[] getShortWeekdays()`

RETURNS An array with 8 abbreviated weekday strings. The first element is empty so the days can be 1-based. For U.S. English, they are:

"", "Sun", "Mon", "Tue", "Wed", "Thu", "Fri", "Sat"

EXAMPLE See the class example or `setAmPmStrings()`.

getWeekdays()

PURPOSE Retrieves the array of weekday strings.

SYNTAX `public String[] getWeekdays()`

RETURNS An array with 8 weekday strings. The first element is empty so the days can be 1-based. For U.S. English, they are:

"", "Sunday", "Monday", "Tuesday", "Wednesday", "Thursday", "Friday", "Saturday"

EXAMPLE See the class example or `setAmPmStrings()`.

getZoneStrings()

PURPOSE Retrieves the array of time-zone strings.

SYNTAX `public String[][] getZoneStrings()`

RETURNS Time-zone strings.

EXAMPLE See the class example or `setAmPmStrings()`.

hashCode()

PURPOSE Computes the hashcode for this `DateFormatSymbols` object.

SYNTAX `public int hashCode()`

DESCRIPTION This method computes the hash code for the `DateFormatSymbols` object. Two `DateFormatSymbols` objects with the same properties will have the same hash code. However, two `DateFormatSymbols` objects that do not have the same properties might also have the same hash code, although the hash code algorithm minimizes this possibility. The hash code is typically used as the key in a hash table.

RETURNS The hash code of this `DateFormatSymbols` object, an integer.

OVERRIDES `java.lang.Object.hashCode()`.

SEE ALSO `equals()`.

EXAMPLE See `clone()`.

setAmPmStrings()

PURPOSE This method sets the array of A.M.-P.M. strings.

SYNTAX `public void setAmPmStrings(String[] newAmPms)`

DESCRIPTION This method sets A.M.-P.M. strings. For example: "A.M." and "P.M".

PARAMETERS

`newAmPms` An array of the new A.M.-P.M. strings.

EXAMPLE This example sets strings for all of the `DateFormatSymbols` and then prints them out. While this sets the symbols to those used in FR French, this is not how you typically would create date format symbols for a new locale. You would do that using resource bundles.

```
import java.text.DateFormatSymbols;
import java.util.*;

class Main {
    public static void main(String[] args) {
        Locale locale = Locale.US;

        // Create a new date format symbols for default locale.
        DateFormatSymbols dfs = new DateFormatSymbols();

        // Assign new arbitrary characters for symbols.

        System.out.println("AM-PM STRINGS:");
        dfs.setAmPmStrings(new String[] {"AM", "PM"});
        printArray(dfs.getAmPmStrings());

        System.out.println("ERAS:");
        dfs.setEras(new String[] {"BC", "ap. J.-C."});
        printArray(dfs.getEras());

        System.out.println("MONTHS:");
        dfs.setMonths(new String[]
                  {"janvier", "février", "mars", "avril", "mai", "juin",
                   "juillet", "août", "septembre", "octobre", "novembre",
                   "décembre"});
        printArray(dfs.getMonths());

        System.out.println("SHORT MONTHS:");
        dfs.setShortMonths(new String[]
                      {"jan", "fév", "mar", "avr", "mai", "jun",
                       "jul", "aoû", "sep", "oct", "nov", "déc"});
        printArray(dfs.getShortMonths());

        System.out.println("WEEKDAYS:");
        dfs.setWeekdays(new String[]
                  {"dimanche", "lundi", "mardi", "mercredi",
                   "jeudi", "vendredi", "samedi"});
        printArray(dfs.getWeekdays());

        System.out.println("SHORT WEEKDAYS:");
        dfs.setShortWeekdays(new String[]
```

```
                {"dim", "lun", "mar", "mer", "jeu", "ven", "sam"});
        printArray(dfs.getShortWeekdays());

        System.out.println("ZONE STRINGS:");
        dfs.setZoneStrings(new String[][]
        {
            {"ECT", "Central European Standard Time", "CEST",
             "Central European Daylight Time", "CEDT", "Paris"}
        });
        printDeepArray(dfs.getZoneStrings());

        System.out.println("LOCAL PATTERN CHARS:");
        dfs.setLocalPatternChars("GanjkHmsSEDFwWxhKz");
        System.out.println(dfs.getLocalPatternChars() + "\n");
    }

    // Print the contents of a 1-dimensional array
    static void printArray(Object[] a) {
        for (int i=0; i<a.length; i++) {
            if (a[i].toString().length() == 0) {
                System.out.print("(empty)" + "  ");
            } else {
                System.out.print(a[i] + "  ");
            }
        }
        System.out.print("\n\n");
    }

    // Print the contents of a 2-dimensional array.
    static void printDeepArray(Object[][] a) {
        for (int i=0; i<a.length; i++) {
            for (int j=0; j<a[i].length; j++) {
                System.out.print(a[i][j] + "   ");
            }
            System.out.print("\n");
        }
        System.out.print("\n");
    }
}
```

Output

```
> java Main

AM-PM STRINGS:
AM  PM

ERAS:
BC  ap. J.-C.

MONTHS:
janvier  février  mars  avril  mai  juin  juillet  août  septembre  octobre
novembre  décembre

SHORT MONTHS:
jan  fév  mar  avr  mai  jun  jul  aoû  sep  oct  nov  déc

WEEKDAYS:
dimanche  lundi  mardi  mercredi  jeudi  vendredi  samedi
```

```
SHORT WEEKDAYS:
dim  lun  mar  mer  jeu  ven  sam

ZONE STRINGS:
ECT   Central European Standard Time   CEST   Central European Daylight Time
CEDT   Paris

LOCAL PATTERN CHARS:
GanjkHmsSEDFwWxhKz
```

A B C D E F G H I J K L M N O P Q R S T U V W X Y Z

setEras()

PURPOSE Sets the array of era strings.

SYNTAX `public void setEras(String[] newEras)`

DESCRIPTION This method sets era strings. For example, "AD" and "BC".

PARAMETERS

`newEras` An array of the new era strings.

EXAMPLE See `setAmPmStrings()`.

setLocalPatternChars()

PURPOSE Sets the localized date-time pattern characters.

SYNTAX `public void setLocalPatternChars(String newLocalPatternChars)`

DESCRIPTION This method sets localized date-time pattern characters. These characters are used individually in the pattern of a `SimpleDateFormat` instance.

PARAMETERS

`newLocalPatternChars`
A string of the new localized date-time pattern characters.

EXAMPLE See `setAmPmStrings()`.

setMonths()

PURPOSE Sets the array of month strings.

SYNTAX `public void setMonths(String[] newMonths)`

DESCRIPTION This method sets month strings. For example, "January" and "February".

PARAMETERS

`newMonths` An array of the new month strings.

EXAMPLE See `setAmPmStrings()`.

setShortMonths()

PURPOSE Sets the array of short month strings.

SYNTAX `public void setShortMonths(String[] newShortMonths)`

DESCRIPTION This method sets short month strings. For example, "Jan" and "Feb".

PARAMETERS

`newShortMonths`
An array of the new short month strings.

EXAMPLE See `setAmPmStrings()`.

setShortWeekdays()

PURPOSE Sets the array of short weekday strings.

SYNTAX `public void setShortWeekdays(String[] newShortWeekdays)`

DESCRIPTION This method sets short weekday strings. For example, "Sun" and "Mon".

PARAMETERS

`newShortWeekdays`
An array of the new short weekday strings.

EXAMPLE See `setAmPmStrings()`.

setWeekdays()

PURPOSE Sets the array of weekday strings.

SYNTAX `public void setWeekdays(String[] newWeekdays)`

DESCRIPTION This method sets weekday strings. For example, "Sunday" and "Monday".

PARAMETERS

`newWeekdays` An array of the new weekday strings.

EXAMPLE See `setAmPmStrings()`.

setZoneStrings()

PURPOSE Sets the array of time-zone strings.

SYNTAX `public void setZoneStrings(String[][] newZoneStrings)`

DESCRIPTION This method sets time-zone strings in an n x 6 array as shown in the class description. `ID` is not localized but is used to look up the localized time-zone data internally. Localizers can localize any zone strings except for the ID of the time zone.

PARAMETERS

`newZoneStrings`
A two-dimensional array of the new time-zone strings.

EXAMPLE See `setAmPmStrings()`.

DecimalFormat

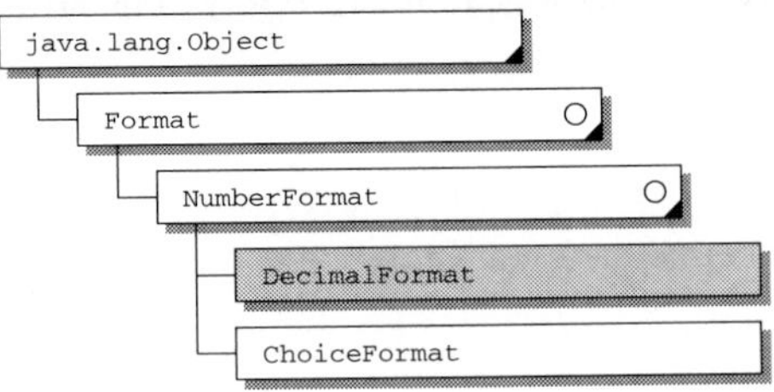

Syntax

```
public class DecimalFormat extends NumberFormat
```

Description

Numbers are represented internally in a locale-independent way without inherent formatting. When a number is printed or displayed, it must be converted to a string, which can be localized and formatted.

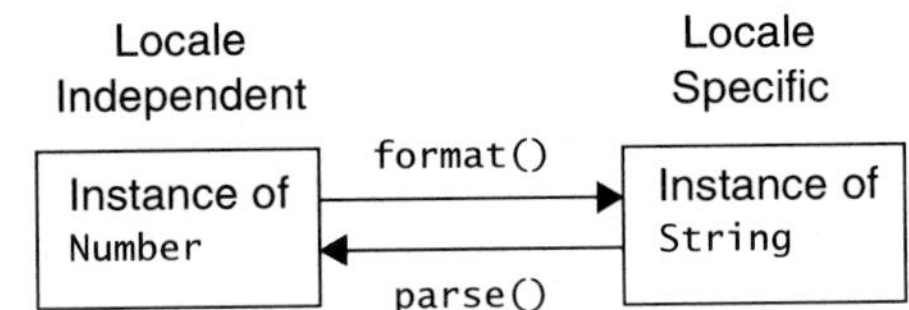

FIGURE 35: `DecimalFormat` `format()` and `parse()` Methods.

As shown in Figure 35, the `DecimalFormat` class enables decimal numbers to be formatted to locale-specific strings. It also enables locale-specific strings to be parsed into number objects.

A decimal number can be formatted in many different ways. For example, the following are different ways of formatting the number –1234.56 in the `US` locale:

```
-1234.56   // Prefix minus sign for negative value
-1234.6    // 1 decimal place. Notice rounding up.
-1,234.56  // Grouping separator for thousands
-01,234.560// Leading and trailing zero
-1234      // No decimal places or decimal separator
(1234.5)   // Parentheses to show negative value
1234.5-    // Suffix minus sign
-123,456%  // Percentage
```

`DecimalFormat` is a concrete subclass of `NumberFormat` for formatting and parsing decimal numbers. The methods `format()` and `parse()` are complements: The first converts a number to a string, while the second does the reverse, converting a string to a number. When formatting, this class can set the display precision (rounding of least-significant digits) and can display leading/trailing zeros, grouping separators, the decimal separator, and prefixes/suffixes for positive/negative values. It also can set the multiplier for percent and permill. This class allows for localization to Western, Arabic, and Indic numbers. For example, the symbol for zero in Arabic is a dot raised above the baseline.

See NumberFormat to format for currency and percent.

Figure 36 shows the relationship among the various methods in DecimalFormat. It shows how the DecimalFormat object contains only a single pattern. This pattern can be set or retrieved either as localized or nonlocalized.

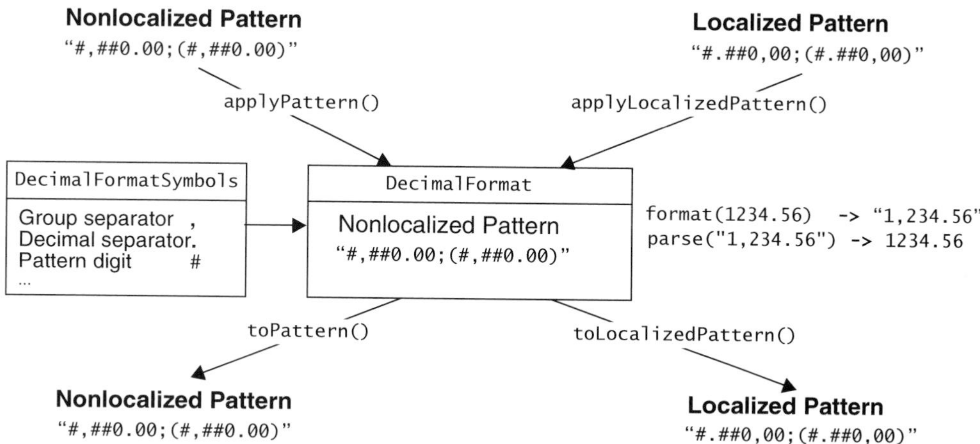

FIGURE 36: **DecimalFormat.**

Usage

In general, do not use the constructor DecimalFormat() because it creates a DecimalFormat object only for the default locale and is not localized. Instead, use one of the NumberFormat creation methods such as getInstance(), which takes a locale as an argument. You need a localized DecimalFormat object to format and parse native strings and numbers. You would create a different DecimalFormat object for each locale. You must test whether the object returned from getInstance() is an instance of DecimalFormat before casting it to one.

The DecimalFormat object has a pattern that is used both when formatting and parsing. You can use the default value or set your own. You can set the full pattern using one of the two "apply" methods or set individual properties using the setter methods. When applying a full pattern, use either applyLocalizedPattern(), if your pattern is localized, or applyPattern(), if it is not localized. (This is described later in this description under *Localized versus Nonlocalized Pattern*.) You can set separate patterns for positive and negative numbers; separate the patterns by a semicolon.

At this point, you can call format() and pass in a local number to produce a string. Or you can call parse() and pass in a native string to produce a number. The format() method uses the pattern to determine the appearance of the string, while parse() recognizes the pattern in a string and creates a number. Notice that format() always *produces* a native string, while parse() *operates* on a native string, regardless of whether the pattern was applied using applyLocalizedPattern() or applyPattern().

Here is the code to format a number with a localized pattern in the German locale. The method `getInstance()` is declared to return a `NumberFormat` object.

```
NumberFormat nf = NumberFormat.getInstance(Locale.GERMAN);
if (nf instanceof DecimalFormat) {
    DecimalFormat df = (DecimalFormat)nf;
}
```

This code first tests that the object returned from `getInstance()` is an instance of `DecimalFormat`. If it can, then it can be cast and assigned to an instance of `DecimalFormat`. In the most general case, the cast might fail if `getInstance()` returned in a format that is not an instance of `DecimalFormat`, such as a Roman numeral or a Chinese, Japanese, or Korean nondecimal number format.

Alternatively, the cast could be executed inside a `try` block, catching a `ClassCastException`.

When the grouping separator is a space, as in France, it is actually a hard (nonbreaking) space character, rather than a normal space. The meaning of # and 0 are described in the section *Decimal Format Symbols*. To include a pattern symbol in a prefix or suffix, put a single quotation mark on either side of the symbol. Parsing will be unreliable if any of the digit symbols or the grouping separator or decimal separator are the same or if any of them occur unquoted in the prefixes or suffixes.

The setter methods can change a single property. For example, in the previous code fragment, `setGroupingSize(3)` is equivalent to placing the group separator (the comma) three places from the decimal separator (the period).

You also can set a nonlocalized pattern using `applyPattern()`:

```
df.applyPattern("#,##0.00;(#,##0.00)");
```

You might do this if you wanted to apply the same pattern to several different locales and if the pattern itself was not visible to a user. It would likely confuse users to see a nonlocalized pattern, since the separator characters would not be what they expected. The nonlocalized pattern coincides with the U. S. locale.

The `DecimalFormat` class is designed for normal decimal values. (For very large or small numbers, in JDK 1.2 you will be able to use a format that can express exponential values.) This class handles only localized digits, where the ten digits are contiguous in Unicode, from 0 to 9. Other digits sets (such as superscripts) would need a different subclass.

To align columns of numbers on the decimal point, refer to the description in the `NumberFormat` class.

Pattern

A *pattern* is a shorthand specification for formatting properties of a decimal number and is represented as a string. The pattern is similar to that used in spreadsheet applications for formatting numbers in cells. A pattern can be localized or not. The pattern is used both for formatting and parsing. During formatting, it determines what the string will look like. During parsing, it determines what pattern of digits and other characters will be recognized as numbers.

The pattern determines the presence of leading/trailing zeroes, the symbols for the decimal separator and the grouping separator, the grouping size, and any prefix and suffix. The prefix and suffix can differ for positive and negative numbers and can include the single characters +, -, and % or the enclosing pairs [ ] and ( ). For example, here is a variety of patterns, along with their effects when formatting the negative number –1234.56:

```
Pattern         Formatted Number

-#0.##          -1234.56          // Prefix minus sign for negative value
-#0.#           -1234.6           // 1 decimal place. Notice rounding up
-#,##0.##       -1,234.56         // Grouping separator for thousands
-00,000.000     -01,234.560       // Leading and trailing zero
-####           -1234             // No decimal places or decimal separator
(###0.#)        (1234.5)          // Parentheses to show negative value
###0.#-         1234.5-           // Suffix minus sign
#,###%          -123,456%         // Percentage
```

As shown, a zero is typically included as the least-significant integer digit when the pattern contains a fraction. This causes a zero to appear in the integer part for fractions that have no integer part. For example, pattern "#.#" will format the number 0.1 as ".1", whereas "0.#" will format 0.1 as "0.1". The number 0 formats as "0" even if the pattern has no digits: ".".

The integer portion of the pattern does not limit the number of significant integer digits, since truncating significant digits is not typically the end-user desire. Use `setMaximumInteger()` in `NumberFormat` if you want to limit integer digits.

A pattern can have two parts, for positive and negative numbers, separated by a semicolon:

```
positivepattern;negativepattern

#,###.##;(#,###.##)                  // 1,234.56 (1,234.56)
```

In this example, negative numbers are shown in parentheses. The *negativepattern* uses the pattern specified by the *positivepattern*, but it can have a different prefix and suffix. Therefore the negative grouping, minimum count, and maximum count are ignored.

The following shows the BNF notation for the pattern:

```
pattern := pospattern{;negpattern;}
pospattern := subpattern;
negpattern := subpattern;
subpattern := {prefix}integer{.fraction}{suffix}
prefix := '\\u0000'..'\\uFFFD' - specialCharacters
suffix := '\\u0000'..'\\uFFFD' - specialCharacters
integer := '#'* '0' *
fraction := '0'* '#'*
```

If the # and 0 symbols are not in the order shown, an `IllegalArgumentException` is thrown. For example, "0,###.0" is invalid.

A grouping separator can occur inside the integer portion. The notation for the previous structure is

```
{X}        X is optional
X*         0 or more instances of X
X..Y       any character from X up to Y, inclusive.
S - T      characters in S, except those in T
```

Table 23 shows the special characters used in the parts of the subpattern, with notes on their meanings. Many of these are defined by the `DecimalFormatSymbols` class.

Symbol	Meaning
`0`	A digit; zero shows as 0 (default).
`#`	A digit; zero shows as absent.
`.`	Placeholder for the decimal separator.
`,`	Placeholder for the grouping separator.
`E`	Used to separate the mantissa and the exponent for exponential formats.[a]
`;`	Used to separate formats.
`-`	Signifies use the default negative prefix.
`%`	Signifies multiply by 100 and show as percentage.
`\u2030`	Signifies multiply by 1,000 and show as permill.
`\u00a4`	Represents the currency sign; replaced by currency symbol. If repeated twice, replaced by international currency symbol. If present in a pattern, the monetary decimal separator is used instead of the decimal separator.
`'X'`	Single quote is used to quote special characters in a prefix or suffix, such as `'#'`.
`X`	Signifies that any other characters can be used in the prefix or suffix.

TABLE 23: Symbols Used with `DecimalFormat` Objects.

a. In JDK 1.1.6, the symbol 'E' has been removed from the set of special characters that can be used in a subpattern. Therefore, avoid using it. It has been included in JDK 1.2.

Any characters besides those present in the integer, decimal separator, or fraction part can be used in the prefix or suffix.

Some of these symbols appear only in patterns (e.g., the digit, #; the pattern separator, ;). Some appear only in numbers (e.g., infinity, `NaN`). Others can appear in both (e.g., decimal separator, grouping separator, zero digit, minus sign, percent, permill).

If these symbols are visible to a user, you might want to change some or all to locale-specific values. The decimal and grouping separators vary from locale to locale; for example, the 0 digit is a centered dot in Arabic. The digit # and pattern separator ; symbols normally appear only in patterns and not in numbers or formatted strings, so they need not change from locale to locale. However, if you want to include either as a literal, quote it. For example, "`'#'#`" produces numbers like "`#1`", "`#2`", and so on.

Illegal patterns, such as "#.#.#" will cause a `ParseException` to be thrown.

Localized versus Nonlocalized Patterns

As shown in Figure 36, `DecimalFormat` has a single internal representation of its pattern. This pattern can be set either by using `applyPattern()` (for the nonlocalized pattern) or `applyLocalizedPattern()`. To get a pattern from a `DecimalFormat` object, use `toPattern()` or `toLocalizedPattern()`, as appropriate.

Note that while you can apply either a localized or nonlocalized pattern to the `DecimalFormat` object, `format()` always operates on numbers to produce localized strings, while `parse()` operates only on localized strings.

So which pattern should you use—localized or nonlocalized? Always use the nonlocalized pattern unless the pattern is shown to the user.

The localized pattern is available for the convenience of displaying the pattern to a user in a form the user will recognize. For example, it would confuse a German reader to see the nonlocalized pattern, since the decimal point and grouping separator differ from what's expected.

The nonlocalized pattern is locale-independent. This pattern can be relied on to have a fixed set of symbols regardless of locale settings. The nonlocalized pattern happens to also correspond to the pattern for the U. S. English locale.

A nonlocalized pattern is also useful for applying the same pattern to `DecimalFormat` objects of different locales. For example, use the nonlocalized pattern when holding the pattern in a variable that you may want to apply to more than one locale. In this way, the nonlocalized pattern is an "interchange format," where a `DecimalFormat` object is capable of converting one localized pattern to another, as shown in Figure 37. See the example in `toPattern()` for more details.

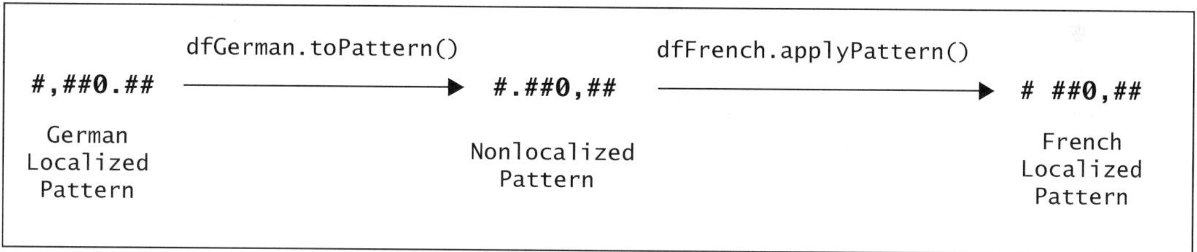

FIGURE 37: Localized and Nonlocalized Patterns.

Decimal Format Symbols

A *decimal format symbol* is a symbol that can appear in a pattern or in a formatted version of a decimal number. These symbols are represented in an instance of the `DecimalFormatSymbols` class; see that class for more details. Setting the pattern for a `DecimalFormat` object, using its setter methods, changes only the `DecimalFormat` object. It does not change the values in the `DecimalFormatSymbols` object; you would use setter methods in `DecimalFormatSymbols` to do that.

Grouping Size

For ease of reading, numbers of large magnitude can have their integer digits grouped and separated by group separators. For example, in the French locale, the integer portion of positive and negative numbers have groupings of three digits separated by hard spaces:

```
12 345,678
```

Here, the grouping separator is a hard space, the decimal separator is a comma (,) and the grouping size is 3. The group size can be set either with a pattern or with `setGroupingSize()`. The grouping separator character is defined in the `DecimalFormatSymbols` class. Whether the grouping separator is shown is controlled in the `NumberFormat` class.

The grouping separator is commonly used for thousands, but in some countries, it is used for ten-thousands. A pattern has one grouping size, such as 3 (for 100,000,000) or 4 (1,0000,0000). If you supply a pattern with multiple grouping sizes, the interval between the last one and the decimal separator is the one that is used. So "#,##,###,####" == "######,####" == "##,####,####".

Decimal Separator Always Shown

A decimal separator is always displayed in a number that has a fractional part. However, when the fractional part is not displayed, the decimal separator can be shown or hidden. This property is set with `setDecimalSeparatorAlwaysShown()`. The first example that follows has the decimal separator showing and the second has it hidden:

```
123.
123
```

Multiplier

A `DecimalFormat` object has two multipliers: the values used with percent (per 100) and the values used with permill (per 1000). The choice of multipliers is determined by the suffix character (% or ‰). See `setMultiplier()` for more details.

Prefix and Suffix

Positive and negative values can have prefixes and suffixes to distinguish them visually. For the parse to work, the prefix must be different from the suffix. For example, a positive number in the U. S. English locale can have a plus sign (+) prefix and no suffix:

```
+123
```

A negative number can be defined to be displayed within parentheses. Here, the opening parenthesis "(" is the prefix and the closing parenthesis ")" is the suffix:

```
(123)
```

If there is no explicit negative subpattern, a minus sign, –, is prefixed to the positive form. That is, the pattern "0.00" alone is equivalent to "0.00;–0.00".

NaN and Infinity

The values `NaN` and Infinity have their own ways of being formatted. `NaN` is formatted as a single character, typically `\uFFFD`. The value +infinity is formatted as a single character, typically `\u221E`, with the positive prefixes and suffixes. The value –infinity is formatted as the same character with the negative prefixes and suffixes. See the *Java Language Specification* for more details.

See Also

`Format`, `NumberFormat`, `ChoiceFormat`, `DecimalFormatSymbols`.

MEMBER SUMMARY	
Constructor	
`DecimalFormat()`	Constructs a `DecimalFormat` object with a pattern and symbols.
Format and Parse Methods	
`format()`	Formats this decimal number to produce a string.
`parse()`	Converts a string to `Number` object.
Full Pattern Methods	
`applyLocalizedPattern()`	Assigns a localized pattern to this `DecimalFormat` object.
`applyPattern()`	Assigns a nonlocalized pattern to this `DecimalFormat` object.
`toLocalizedPattern()`	Produces a string of the current localized pattern.
`toPattern()`	Produces a string of the current nonlocalized pattern.
Getter Methods	
`getDecimalFormatSymbols()`	Retrieves the decimal format symbols for this `DecimalFormat` object.
`getGroupingSize()`	Retrieves the number of digits between grouping separators.
`getMultiplier()`	Retrieves the multiplier used for percent or permill.
`getNegativePrefix()`	Retrieves the prefix for negative numbers.
`getNegativeSuffix()`	Retrieves the suffix for negative numbers.
`getPositivePrefix()`	Retrieves the prefix for positive numbers.
`getPositiveSuffix()`	Retrieves the suffix for positive numbers.
`isDecimalSeparatorAlwaysShown()`	Determines if the decimal separator is displayed with integers.

Continued

MEMBER SUMMARY

Setter Methods	
`setDecimalFormatSymbols()`	Sets the decimal format symbols for this `DecimalFormat` object.
`setDecimalSeparatorAlwaysShown()`	Sets the decimal separator display property for integers.
`setGroupingSize()`	Sets the number of digits between grouping separators.
`setMultiplier()`	Sets the multiplier for use in percent and permill.
`setNegativePrefix()`	Sets the prefix for negative numbers.
`setNegativeSuffix()`	Sets the suffix for negative numbers.
`setPositivePrefix()`	Sets the prefix for positive numbers.
`setPositiveSuffix()`	Sets the suffix for positive numbers.
Object Methods	
`clone()`	Creates a copy of this `DecimalFormat` object.
`equals()`	Compares two `DecimalFormat` objects for equality.
`hashCode()`	Computes the hash code for this `DecimalFormat` object.

Example

For each of the available locales, this example prints out the localized pattern and then formats the number 1234.56 to a string and parses the string back to a number. If a number appears as a question mark (?), your system may not have the font to be able to print it.

```
import java.text.NumberFormat;
import java.text.DecimalFormat;
import java.util.Locale;
import java.text.ParseException;

class Main {

    public static void main(String[] args) {
        Locale[] locales = NumberFormat.getAvailableLocales();
        double myNumber = 1234.56;
        NumberFormat numform;
        DecimalFormat decform = null;
        int WIDTHCOL1 = 33;
        int WIDTHCOL2 = 29;
        int WIDTHCOL3 = 14;
        int WIDTHCOL0 = 10;

        for (int j = 0; j < 3; ++j) {
            switch (j) {
            case 0:
```

```
        printInColumn("\n", 0);
        printInColumn("COUNTRY", WIDTHCOL1 - WIDTHCOL0);
        printInColumn("DECIMAL:", WIDTHCOL0);
        printInColumn("PATTERN", WIDTHCOL2);
        printInColumn("FORMATTED", WIDTHCOL3);
        printInColumn("PARSED\n", 0);
        break;
    case 1:
        printInColumn("\n", 0);
        printInColumn("COUNTRY", WIDTHCOL1 - WIDTHCOL0);
        printInColumn("PERCENT:", WIDTHCOL0);
        printInColumn("PATTERN", WIDTHCOL2);
        printInColumn("FORMATTED", WIDTHCOL3);
        printInColumn("PARSED\n", 0);
        break;
    default:
        printInColumn("\n", 0);
        printInColumn("COUNTRY", WIDTHCOL1 - WIDTHCOL0);
        printInColumn("CURRENCY:", WIDTHCOL0);
        printInColumn("PATTERN", WIDTHCOL2);
        printInColumn("FORMATTED", WIDTHCOL3);
        printInColumn("PARSED\n", 0);
        break;
    }
    for (int i = 0; i < locales.length; ++i) {

        printInColumn(locales[i].getDisplayName(), WIDTHCOL1);

        switch (j) {
        case 0:
            numform = NumberFormat.getInstance(locales[i]);
            break;
        case 1:
            numform = NumberFormat.getPercentInstance(locales[i]);
            break;
        default:
            numform = NumberFormat.getCurrencyInstance(locales[i]);
            break;
        }

        // Test numform is instance of DecimalFormat before casting.
        if (numform instanceof DecimalFormat) {

            // Cast numform to a decimal format.
            decform = (DecimalFormat)numform;

            try {
                // Print pattern.
                printInColumn((decform).toLocalizedPattern(),
                                                    WIDTHCOL2);

                // Print formatted number (a string).
                printInColumn(decform.format(myNumber), WIDTHCOL3);
            } catch (IllegalArgumentException iae) { }

            try {
                // Print the parsed string (a number).
                print(decform.parse(decform.format(myNumber)));
            } catch (ParseException pe) {
                print("Parse exception");
```

```
                }
            }
        }
    }
}

static void printInColumn(String str, int col) {
    System.out.print(str);
    for (int p = str.length(); p < col; ++p) {
        System.out.print(" ");
    }
}

static void print(Object obj) {
    System.out.println(obj);
}
}
```

Output

```
> java Main
COUNTRY                        DECIMAL:  PATTERN                         FORMATTED     PARSED
Arabic (Egypt)                           #,##0.###;#,##0.###-            ????????      1234.56
Belorussian (Belarus)                    #,##0.###                       1 234,56      1234.56
Bulgarian (Bulgaria)                     #,##0.###                       1.234,56      1234.56
Catalan (Spain)                          #,##0.###                       1.234,56      1234.56
Czech (Czech Republic)                   #,##0.###                       1.234,56      1234.56
Danish (Denmark)                         #,##0.###                       1.234,56      1234.56
German (Germany)                         #,##0.###                       1.234,56      1234.56
German (Austria)                         #,##0.###                       1.234,56      1234.56
German (Switzerland)                     #,##0.###                       1'234,56      1234.56
Greek (Greece)                           #,##0.###                       1.234,56      1234.56
English (Canada)                         #,##0.###                       1;234.56      1234.56
English (United Kingdom)                 #,##0.###                       1,234.56      1234.56
English (Ireland)                        #,##0.###                       1,234.56      1234.56
English (United States)                  #,##0.###                       1,234.56      1234.56
Spanish - Modern Sort (Spain)            #,##0.###                       1.234,56      1234.56
Estonian (Estonia)                       #,##0.###                       1 234,56      1234.56
Finnish (Finland)                        #,##0.###                       1 234,56      1234.56
French (France)                          #,##0.###                       1 234,56      1234.56
French (Belgium)                         #,##0.###                       1.234,56      1234.56
French (Canada)                          #,##0.###                       1 234,56      1234.56
French (Switzerland)                     #,##0.###                       1'234.56      1234.56
Croatian (Croatia)                       #,##0.###                       1.234,56      1234.56
Hungarian (Hungary)                      #,##0.###                       1 234,56      1234.56
Icelandic (Iceland)                      #,##0.###                       1.234,56      1234.56
Italian (Italy)                          #,##0.###                       1.234,56      1234.56
Italian (Switzerland)                    #,##0.###                       1'234.56      1234.56
Hebrew (Israel)                          #,##0.###                       1,234.56      1234.56
Japanese (Japan)                         #,##0.###                       1,234.56      1234.56
Korean (Korea)                           #,##0.###                       1,234.56      1234.56
Lithuanian (Lituania)                    #,##0.00                        1.234,56      1234.56
Latvian (Latvia)                         #,##0.###                       1 234,56      1234.56
Macedonian (Macedonia)                   #,##0.###;(#,##0.###)           1.234,56      1234.56
Dutch (Netherlands)                      #,##0.###                       1.234,56      1234.56
Dutch (Belgium)                          #,##0.###                       1.234,56      1234.56
Norwegian (Bokmål) (Norway)              #,##0.###                       1 234,56      1234.56
Norwegian (Nynorsk) (Norway,NY)          #,##0.###                       1 234,56      1234.56
Polish (Poland)                          #,##0.###                       1.234,56      1234.56
Portuguese (Portugal)                    #,##0.###                       1.234,56      1234.56
Romanian (Romania)                       #,##0.###                       1.234,56      1234.56
Russian (Russia)                         #,##0.###                       1.234,56      1234.56
Serbian (Latin) (Serbia)                 #,##0.###                       1.234,56      1234.56
Slovak (Slovakia)                        #,##0.###                       1 234,56      1234.56
Slovene (Slovenia)                       #,##0.###                       1.234,56      1234.56
Albanian (Albania)                       #,##0.###                       1.234,56      1234.56
Serbian (Cyrillic) (Serbia)              #,##0.###                       1 234,56      1234.56
Swedish (Sweden)                         #,##0.###                       1 234,56      1234.56
Turkish (Turkey)                         #,##0.###                       1.234,56      1234.56
Ukrainian (Ukraine)                      #,##0.###                       1.234,56      1234.56
Chinese (China)                          #,##0.###                       1,234.56      1234.56
Chinese (ROC)                            #,##0.###                       1,234.56      1234.56
```

COUNTRY	PERCENT: PATTERN	FORMATTED	PARSED
Arabic (Egypt)	#,##0%	???????%	1234.56
Belorussian (Belarus)	#,##0%	123 456%	1234.56
Bulgarian (Bulgaria)	#,##0%	123.456%	1234.56
Catalan (Spain)	#,##0%	123.456%	1234.56
Czech (Czech Republic)	#,##0%	123.456%	1234.56
Danish (Denmark)	#,##0%	123.456%	1234.56
German (Germany)	#,##0%	123.456%	1234.56
German (Austria)	#,##0%	123.456%	1234.56
German (Switzerland)	#,##0%	123'456%	1234.56
Greek (Greece)	#,##0%	123.456%	1234.56
English (Canada)	#,##0%	123;456%	1234.56
English (United Kingdom)	#,##0%	123,456%	1234.56
English (Ireland)	#,##0%	123,456%	1234.56
English (United States)	#,##0%	123,456%	1234.56
Spanish - Modern Sort (Spain)	#,##0%	123.456%	1234.56
Estonian (Estonia)	#,##0%	123 456%	1234.56
Finnish (Finland)	#,##0%	123 456%	1234.56
French (France)	#,##0%	123 456%	1234.56
French (Belgium)	#,##0%	123.456%	1234.56
French (Canada)	#,##0%	123 456%	1234.56
French (Switzerland)	#,##0%	123'456%	1234.56
Croatian (Croatia)	#,##0%	123.456%	1234.56
Hungarian (Hungary)	#,##0%	123 456%	1234.56
Icelandic (Iceland)	#,##0%	123.456%	1234.56
Italian (Italy)	#,##0%	123.456%	1234.56
Italian (Switzerland)	#,##0%	123'456%	1234.56
Hebrew (Israel)	#,##0%	123,456%	1234.56
Japanese (Japan)	#,##0%	123,456%	1234.56
Korean (Korea)	#,##0%	123,456%	1234.56
Lithuanian (Lituania)	#,##%	12.34.56%	1234.56
Latvian (Latvia)	#,##0%	123 456%	1234.56
Macedonian (Macedonia)	#,##0%	123.456%	1234.56
Dutch (Netherlands)	#,##0%	123.456%	1234.56
Dutch (Belgium)	#,##0%	123.456%	1234.56
Norwegian (Bokmål) (Norway)	#,##0%	123 456%	1234.56
Norwegian (Nynorsk) (Norway,NY)	#,##0%	123 456%	1234.56
Polish (Poland)	#,##0%	123.456%	1234.56
Portuguese (Portugal)	#,##0%	123.456%	1234.56
Romanian (Romania)	#,##0%	123.456%	1234.56
Russian (Russia)	#,##0%	123.456%	1234.56
Serbian (Latin) (Serbia)	#,##0%	123.456%	1234.56
Slovak (Slovakia)	#,##0%	123 456%	1234.56
Slovene (Slovenia)	#,##0%	123.456%	1234.56
Albanian (Albania)	#,##0%	123.456%	1234.56
Serbian (Cyrillic) (Serbia)	#,##0%	123 456%	1234.56
Swedish (Sweden)	#,##0%	123 456%	1234.56
Turkish (Turkey)	#,##0%	123.456%	1234.56
Ukrainian (Ukraine)	#,##0%	123.456%	1234.56
Chinese (China)	#,##0%	123,456%	1234.56
Chinese (ROC)	#,##0%	123,456%	1234.56

COUNTRY	CURRENCY: PATTERN	FORMATTED	PARSED
Arabic (Egypt)	? #,##0.###;?#,##0.###-	? ????????	1234.56
Belorussian (Belarus)	???#,##0.##	???1 234,56	1234.56
Bulgarian (Bulgaria)	Lv#,##0.##	Lv1.234,56	1234.56
Catalan (Spain)	Pts #,##0	Pts 1.235	1235
Czech (Czech Republic)	K? #,##0.##;-#,##0.## K?	K? 1.234,56	1234.56
Danish (Denmark)	kr #,##0.00;kr -#,##0.00	kr 1.234,56	1234.56
German (Germany)	#,##0.00 DM	1.234,56 DM	1234.56
German (Austria)	öS #,##0.00	öS 1.234,56	1234.56
German (Switzerland)	Fr. #,##0.00;Fr.-#,##0.00	Fr. 1'234,56	1234.56
Greek (Greece)	#,##0.00 ???	1.234,56 ???	1234.56
English (Canada)	$#,##0.00	$1;234.56	1234.56
English (United Kingdom)	£#,##0.00	£1,234.56	1234.56
English (Ireland)	IR£#,##0.00	IR£1,234.56	1234.56
English (United States)	$#,##0.00;($#,##0.00)	$1,234.56	1234.56
Spanish - Modern Sort (Spain)	#,##0.00 Pts	1.234,56 Pts	1234.56
Estonian (Estonia)	#,##0.### kr	1 234,56 kr	1234.56
Finnish (Finland)	#,##0.00 mk	1 234,56 mk	1234.56
French (France)	#,##0.00 F	1 234,56 F	1234.56
French (Belgium)	#,##0.00 FB	1.234,56 FB	1234.56
French (Canada)	#,##0.00 $;(#,##0.00$)	1 234,56 $	1234.56
French (Switzerland)	Fr. #,##0.00;Fr.-#,##0.00	Fr. 1'234.56	1234.56
Croatian (Croatia)	Din #,##0.##	Din 1.234,56	1234.56
Hungarian (Hungary)	FT#,##0.##	FT1 234,56	1234.56

```
Icelandic (Iceland)                 #,##0.## kr                     1.234,56 kr    1234.56
Italian (Italy)                     L. #,##0.00                     L. 1.234,56    1234.56
Italian (Switzerland)               Fr. #,##0.00;Fr.-#,##0.00       Fr. 1'234.56   1234.56
Hebrew (Israel)                     ??#,##0.##;??-#,##0.##          ??1,234.56     1234.56
Japanese (Japan)                    ¥#,##0                          ¥1,235         1235
Korean (Korea)                      ?#,##0.00                       ?1,234.56      1234.56
Lithuanian (Lituania)               #,##0.## Lt                     1.234,56 Lt    1234.56
Latvian (Latvia)                    #,##0.## Ls                     1 234,56 Ls    1234.56
Macedonian (Macedonia)              Den #,##0.##                    Den 1.234,56   1234.56
Dutch (Netherlands)                 F #,##0.00;F #,##0.00-          F 1.234,56     1234.56
Dutch (Belgium)                     #,##0.00 BF                     1.234,56 BF    1234.56
Norwegian (Bokmål) (Norway)         kr #,##0.00;kr #,##0.00-        kr 1 234,56    1234.56
Norwegian (Nynorsk) (Norway,NY)     kr #,##0.00;kr#,##0.00-         kr 1 234,56    1234.56
Polish (Poland)                     Z?#,##0.##                      Z?1.234,56     1234.56
Portuguese (Portugal)               #,##0.00 Esc.                   1.234,56 Esc.  1234.56
Romanian (Romania)                  #,##0.00 lei                    1.234,56 lei   1234.56
Russian (Russia)                    rub#.0##### ,.                  rub1234,56 ,.  1234.56
Serbian (Latin) (Serbia)            Din #,##0.00                    Din 1.234,56   1234.56
Slovak (Slovakia)                   K? #,##0.00 ;-#,##0.00 K?       K? 1 234,56    1234.56
Slovene (Slovenia)                  tol #,##0.##                    tol 1.234,56   1234.56
Albanian (Albania)                  Lek#,##0.###                    Lek1.234,56    1234.56
Serbian (Cyrillic) (Serbia)         Din #,##0.00                    Din 1 234,56   1234.56
Swedish (Sweden)                    #,##0.00 kr                     1 234,56 kr    1234.56
Turkish (Turkey)                    #,##0.00 TL                     1.234,56 TL    1234.56
Ukrainian (Ukraine)                 #,##0.## ???;-#,##0.##???       1.234,56 ???   1234.56
Chinese (China)                     ?#,##0.00                       ?1,234.56      1234.56
Chinese (ROC)                       NT$#,##0.00                     NT$1,234.56    1234.56
```

applyLocalizedPattern()

PURPOSE Assigns a localized pattern to this `DecimalFormat` object.

SYNTAX `public void applyLocalizedPattern(String pattern)`

DESCRIPTION This method applies the `pattern` string to this `DecimalFormat` object; the pattern is assumed to be in a localized notation. The properties of this pattern can also be changed individually through the various setter methods in this class.

If you set the positive and negative suffixes to % or ‰ and call `applyPattern()`, the multiplier will automatically be set to the appropriate value.

PARAMETERS

`pattern` A non-`null` localized pattern string.

EXCEPTIONS

`ParseException`
If the pattern is incorrect.

SEE ALSO `toLocalizedPattern()`.

EXAMPLE This example requires passing in a number as a parameter on the command line. It then applies both the nonlocalized and localized patterns to show that their effects are identical for the same `DecimalFormat` object. It displays the German formatting of the value passed in and of the negative of the value passed in.

```
import java.text.NumberFormat;
import java.text.DecimalFormat;
import java.text.ParseException;
```

```
import java.util.Locale;

class Main {

    public static void main(String[] args) {
        if (args.length != 1) {
            System.err.println("Usage: java Main <German number>");
            System.err.println("where <German number> is of form: 1234567,89");
            System.exit(1);
        }

        Locale loc = Locale.GERMAN;
        NumberFormat numform = NumberFormat.getInstance(loc);
        Number num = null;

        try {
            num = numform.parse(args[0]);
        } catch (ParseException pe) {
            System.out.println("Parse exception");
        }

        System.out.println("Locale:                 " + loc.getDisplayName());

        // Check that numform is a DecimalFormat.
        if (numform instanceof DecimalFormat) {

            DecimalFormat decform = (DecimalFormat)numform;

            System.out.println("\napplyPattern ---------------------------");

            decform.applyPattern("#,##0.00;(#,##0.00)");

            System.out.println("toLocalizedPattern:  "
                + decform.toLocalizedPattern());

            System.out.println("toPattern:           "
                + decform.toPattern());

            System.out.println("format:              "
                + decform.format(num));

            System.out.println("format (negative):   "
                + decform.format((-1) * num.doubleValue()));

            System.out.println("\napplyLocalizedPattern ------------------");

            decform.applyLocalizedPattern("#.##0,00;(#.##0,00)");

            System.out.println("toLocalizedPattern:  "
                + decform.toLocalizedPattern());

            System.out.println("toPattern:           "
                + decform.toPattern());

            System.out.println("format:              "
                + decform.format(num));

            System.out.println("format: (negative)   "
                + decform.format((-1) * num.doubleValue()));
```

```
            }
        }
    }
```

Output

```
> java Main 1234567,89
Locale:                German (Germany)

applyPattern --------------------------
toLocalizedPattern:  #.##0,00;(#.##0,00)
toPattern:           #,##0.00;(#,##0.00)
format:              1.234.567,89
format (negative):   (1.234.567,89)

applyLocalizedPattern -----------------
toLocalizedPattern:  #.##0,00;(#.##0,00)
toPattern:           #,##0.00;(#,##0.00)
format:              1.234.567,89
format: (negative)   (1.234.567,89)
```

applyPattern()

PURPOSE Assigns a nonlocalized pattern to this `DecimalFormat` object.

SYNTAX `public void applyPattern(String pattern)`

DESCRIPTION This method applies the string `pattern` to this `DecimalFormat` object; the pattern is assumed to be in a nonlocalized notation. The properties of this pattern can also be changed individually via the various setter methods.

If you set the positive and negative suffixes to % or ‰ and call `applyPattern()`, the multiplier will automatically be set to the appropriate value.

PARAMETERS

`pattern` The non-`null` nonlocalized string pattern to be applied.

EXCEPTIONS

`ParseException`

If the pattern is incorrect.

SEE ALSO `toPattern()`.

EXAMPLE This example prints out the same number –1234.56 starting with the default format and then applying many different formats.

```
import java.text.*;
import java.util.Locale;

class Main {
    // Create number format.
    static NumberFormat numform = NumberFormat.getInstance(Locale.US);
```

```
    static DecimalFormat decform;

    public static void main(String[] args) {

        // Test that numform is a decimal format before casting.
        if (numform instanceof DecimalFormat) {

            decform = (DecimalFormat)numform;

            // Default pattern
            print(decform.format(-1234.56));                      // -1,234.56

            // Apply patterns and format each one
            decform.applyPattern("0.##;-0.##");                   // 2 decimal places
            print(decform.format(-1234.56));                      // -1234.56

            decform.applyPattern("0.#;-0.#");                     // 1 decimal place
            print(decform.format(-1234.56));                      // -1234.6

            decform.applyPattern("#,##0.##;-#,##0.##");           // Group separator
            print(decform.format(-1234.56));                      // -1,234.56

            decform.applyPattern("00,000.000;-00,000.000");       // Lead/trail zeros
            print(decform.format(-1234.56));                      // -01,234.560

            decform.applyPattern("0;-0");                         // No decimal sep
            print(decform.format(-1234.56));                      // -1235

            decform.applyPattern("###0.#;(###0.#)");              // Paren for neg val
            print(decform.format(-1234.56));                      // (1234.6)

            decform.applyPattern("###0.#;###0.#-");               // Suffix minus sign
            print(decform.format(-1234.56));                      // 1234.6-

            decform.applyPattern("#,##0%;#,##0%");                // Percentage
            print(decform.format(-1234.56));                      // -123,456%
        }

    }

    // To help with readability.
    static void print(String s) {
        System.out.println(s);
    }
}
```

clone()

PURPOSE Creates a copy of this `DecimalFormat` object.

SYNTAX `public Object clone()`

DESCRIPTION This method makes a copy of this `DecimalFormat` object. The new `DecimalFormat` object has a complete copy of the entire pattern. Changing any value in the new `DecimalFormat` object will not affect the original instance.

RETURNS A non-`null` copy of this `DecimalFormat` object.

OVERRIDES `NumberFormat.clone()`.

EXAMPLE This example illustrates the use of `clone()` to copy a `DecimalFormat` object. Note that the copy has the same pattern as the original.

```
import java.text.DecimalFormat;

class Main {
    public static void main(String args[]) {

        // Create decimal format.
        DecimalFormat df = new DecimalFormat("#,###0.00");
        System.out.println("Original pattern: " + df.toPattern());

        // Create a clone.
        DecimalFormat dfCopy = (DecimalFormat)df.clone();
        System.out.println("Copy's pattern:   " + df.toPattern());

        // Tests for equality.
        if (df.equals(dfCopy)) {
            System.out.println("Clone is equal to original");
        }

        // Compute hashcode.
        int hc = df.hashCode();
        System.out.println("Hash code:        " + hc);
    }
}
```

DecimalFormat()

PURPOSE Constructs a `DecimalFormat` object with a pattern and symbols.

SYNTAX
```
public DecimalFormat()
public DecimalFormat(String pattern)
public DecimalFormat(String pattern, DecimalFormatSymbols
    symbols)
```

DESCRIPTION This constructor creates a `DecimalFormat` object with the string `pattern` and `symbols` for the default locale. This is a convenient way to obtain a `Decimal-`

Format object when it is sufficient to display the number in only the default locale. If pattern or symbols is omitted, the default value is used.

To obtain standard formats for a particular locale, use the creation methods on NumberFormat, such as getInstance(), getCurrencyInstance(), getNumberInstance(), and getPercentInstance(). These creation methods return the most appropriate subclass of NumberFormat for a given locale. If you need minor adjustments to a standard format, you can modify the format returned by a NumberFormat creation method.

PARAMETERS

pattern The default pattern string to be applied.

symbols The set of decimal format symbols to be used.

EXCEPTIONS

IllegalArgumentException

If the given pattern is invalid.

SEE ALSO NumberFormat.getInstance(), NumberFormat.getNumberInstance(), NumberFormat.getCurrencyInstance(), NumberFormat.getPercentInstance(), DecimalFormatSymbols

EXAMPLE This program takes a file as input, where the file starts with a pattern followed by a list of numbers. An instance of DecimalFormat is created from the pattern. Then the program formats each number with this DecimalFormat object and prints it. You can try supplying your own numbers in the input file.

```
import java.text.NumberFormat;
import java.text.DecimalFormat;
import java.text.ParseException;
import java.io.*;

class Main {

    Main(String myPattern, String[] myStrings) {
        NumberFormat form;

        DecimalFormat df = new DecimalFormat(myPattern);
        String pattern = df.toPattern();

        // Print the pattern.
        System.out.println("PATTERN");
        System.out.println(pattern);
        System.out.println("");

        // Print the numbers.
        System.out.print("ORIGINAL STRING");
        printSpaces("ORIGINAL STRING", 20);
        System.out.println("FORMATTED STRING");

        for (int i=0; ((myStrings[i] != null) & (i < myStrings.length)); i++) {
            System.out.print(myStrings[i]);
            printSpaces(myStrings[i], 20);
```

```
                System.out.println(df.format(new Double(myStrings[i])));
            }
        }

        public static void main(String[] args) {
            if (args.length != 1) {
                System.err.println("Usage: java Main <filename>");
                System.exit(1);
            }

            try {
                // Read in the entire contents of the file.
                // Convert the contents so that the new line is '\n'.
                BufferedReader rd = new BufferedReader(new FileReader(args[0]));
                String sep = System.getProperty("line.separator");
                String line;
                String[] myStrings = new String[100];
                String myPattern = null;

                // Read in the pattern.
                if ((line = rd.readLine()) != null) {
                    myPattern = line;
                }

                int i = 0;

                // Read in the numbers.
                while ((line = rd.readLine()) != null) {
                    myStrings[i] = new String(line);
                    i++;
                }
                rd.close();

                new Main(myPattern, myStrings);
            } catch (Exception e) {
                e.printStackTrace();
            }
        }

        static void printSpaces(String s, int column) {
            for (int i = s.length(); i < column; i++) {
                System.out.print(" ");
            }
        }
    }
```

Output

```
> java Main input.txt
PATTERN
#,#00.0#;(#,#00.0#)

ORIGINAL STRING      FORMATTED STRING
1234.5678            1,234.57
1234.567             1,234.57
1234.56              1,234.56
1234.5               1,234.5
1234.                1,234.0
123.                 123.0
12.                  12.0
```

```
1.                  01.0
1                   01.0
-1234.5678          (1,234.57)
-1234.567           (1,234.57)
-1234.56            (1,234.56)
-1234.5             (1,234.5)
-1234.              (1,234.0)
-123.               (123.0)
-12.                (12.0)
-1.                 (01.0)
-1                  (01.0)
0000.0000           00.0
0                   00.0
```

A B C D E F G H I J K L M N O P Q R S T U V W X Y Z

equals()

PURPOSE Compares two `DecimalFormat` objects for equality.

SYNTAX `public boolean equals(Object obj)`

DESCRIPTION This method compares this `DecimalFormat` object with `obj` for equality. If `obj` is a `DecimalFormat` object and if it has the same values of prefix, suffix, multiplier, grouping size, symbols, and decimal separator display state, then the objects are equal and this method returns `true`. If the `DecimalFormat` values are not equal or if `obj` is `null` or not a `DecimalFormat` object, this method returns `false`.

PARAMETERS

`obj` A possibly `null` object to which to compare.

RETURNS `true` if object `obj` is not `null` and is of type `DecimalFormat` and is equal to this `DecimalFormat` object; `false` otherwise.

OVERRIDES `NumberFormat.equals()`.

SEE ALSO `hashCode()`.

EXAMPLE See `clone()`.

format()

PURPOSE Formats this decimal number to produce a string.

SYNTAX

```
public StringBuffer format(double number, StringBuffer dest,
    FieldPosition fieldPos)
public StringBuffer format(long number, StringBuffer dest,
    FieldPosition fieldPos)
```

DESCRIPTION This method converts the `fieldPos` part of the decimal number to a string and appends it to the string buffer `dest`. This method performs the reverse operation of `parse()`, which converts a string to a number.

PARAMETERS

`dest`	The non-`null` string buffer to which the formatted string is appended.
`fieldPos`	The field position that identifies what part of the number to convert.
`number`	The `double` or `long` to convert to a string.

RETURNS A non-`null` string buffer representing the decimal number.

OVERRIDES `NumberFormat.format()`.

EXAMPLE This class formats the integer and fraction portions of a decimal number to two separate strings.

```
import java.text.*;
import java.io.*;
import java.util.*;

class Main {
    // Create field position objects for dates.
    static FieldPosition intPos =
        new FieldPosition(DecimalFormat.INTEGER_FIELD);
    static FieldPosition fractPos =
        new FieldPosition(DecimalFormat.FRACTION_FIELD);

    // Create number format.
    static NumberFormat numform = NumberFormat.getInstance(Locale.US);

    // Declare the decimal format.
    static DecimalFormat decform;
    public static void main(String[] args) {
        if (args.length != 1) {
            System.err.println("Usage: java Main <number>");
            System.err.println("where <number> is of form: 12345.678");
            System.exit(1);
        }

        if (numform instanceof DecimalFormat) {
            decform = (DecimalFormat)NumberFormat.getInstance(Locale.US);

            // Declare number.
            Number num = null;

            // Convert the string passed in to a number.
            try {
                num = decform.parse(args[0]);
            } catch (ParseException pe) {
                System.out.println("Parse exception");
            }

            // Create string buffer to hold decimal.
            StringBuffer sb = new StringBuffer("");

            // Format the integer portion of the number.
            decform.format(num, sb, intPos);
```

```
            System.out.println("\nDecimal:    " + sb);

            printIntegerValue(sb);
            sb.setLength(0);

            decform.format(num, sb, fractPos);
            printFractionValue(sb);
            sb.setLength(0);

            System.out.println("\nInteger field:  " + intPos.getField());
            System.out.println("Fraction field: " + fractPos.getField());
        }
    }
    static void printIntegerValue(StringBuffer sb) {
        System.out.print("Integer:    ");
        System.out.println(sb.toString().substring(intPos.getBeginIndex(),
                                                   intPos.getEndIndex()));
    }
    static void printFractionValue(StringBuffer sb) {
        System.out.print("Fraction:   ");
        System.out.println(sb.toString().substring(fractPos.getBeginIndex(),
                                                   fractPos.getEndIndex()));
    }
}
```

Output

```
> java Main 12345.678
Decimal:    12,345.678
Integer:    12,345
Fraction:   678

Integer field:  0
Fraction field: 1
```

getDecimalFormatSymbols()

PURPOSE Retrieves the decimal format symbols for this `DecimalFormat` object.

SYNTAX `public DecimalFormatSymbols getDecimalFormatSymbols()`

DESCRIPTION This method returns the decimal format symbols for this `DecimalFormat` object. These are symbols that can appear in a pattern and in the resulting formatted strings.

If the `DecimalFormat` object was created using the creation method `NumberFormat.getInstance(Locale loc)`, the `DecimalFormatSymbols` object will have the same locale `loc`.

To see the string representation of the symbols, call the getter methods in `DecimalFormatSymbols` on the returned object. Because each locale can have its own decimal format symbols, it is generally not necessary to change these symbols; however, you can change them with methods in the `DecimalFormatSymbols` class.

RETURNS The decimal format symbols for this `DecimalFormat` object.

SEE ALSO `setDecimalFormatSymbols()`, `DecimalFormatSymbols`.

EXAMPLE This example gets the decimal format symbols for each locale and prints them out.


```
import java.text.*;
import java.util.Locale;

class Main {

    public static void main(String[] args) {

        Locale[] locales = NumberFormat.getAvailableLocales();
        NumberFormat numform = null;
        DecimalFormat decform = null;
        DecimalFormatSymbols sym = null;
        int WIDTHCOL = 33;
        int WIDTHCOL1 = 29;

        for (int i = 0; i < locales.length; ++i) {

            // Print out language and country names.
            printAlignColumn(locales[i].getDisplayName(), WIDTHCOL);

            // Get the number format for the locale.
            numform = NumberFormat.getInstance(locales[i]);

            // Cast the number format to a decimal format.
            if (numform instanceof DecimalFormat) {

                decform = (DecimalFormat)numform;
                sym = decform.getDecimalFormatSymbols();

                                                     //-- US Values --
                print(sym.getZeroDigit());             //  0
                print(sym.getGroupingSeparator());     //  ,
                print(sym.getDecimalSeparator());      //  .
                print(sym.getPerMill());               //  \u2030
                print(sym.getPercent());               //  %
                print(sym.getDigit());                 //  #
                print(sym.getPatternSeparator());      //  ;
                print(sym.getInfinity());              //  \u221E
                print(sym.getNaN());                   //  \uFFFD
                print(sym.getMinusSign());             //  -
                print("\n");
            }
        }
    }

    static void printAlignColumn(String str, int col) {
        System.out.print(str);
        for (int p = str.length(); p < col; ++p) {
            System.out.print(" ");
        }
    }

    static void print(char ch) {
```

```
        System.out.print(ch);
    }

    static void print(String str) {
        System.out.print(str);
    }
}
```

Output

```
Arabic (Egypt)                      ?????#;??-
Belorussian (Belarus)               0 ,?%#;??-
Bulgarian (Bulgaria)                0.,?%#;??-
Catalan (Spain)                     0.,?%#;??-
Czech (Czech Republic)              0.,?%#;??-
Danish (Denmark)                    0.,?%#;??-
German (Germany)                    0.,?%#;??-
German (Austria)                    0.,?%#;??-
German (Switzerland)                0',?%#;??-
Greek (Greece)                      0.,?%#;??-
English (Canada)                    0;.?%#;??-
English (United Kingdom)            0,.?%#;??-
English (Ireland)                   0,.?%#;??-
English (United States)             0,.?%#;??-
Spanish - Modern Sort (Spain)       0.,?%#;??-
Estonian (Estonia)                  0 ,?%#;??-
Finnish (Finland)                   0 ,?%#;??-
French (France)                     0 ,?%#;??-
French (Belgium)                    0.,?%#;??-
French (Canada)                     0 ,?%#;??-
French (Switzerland)                0'.?%#;??-
Croatian (Croatia)                  0.,?%#;??-
Hungarian (Hungary)                 0 ,?%#;??-
Icelandic (Iceland)                 0.,?%#;??-
Italian (Italy)                     0.,?%#;??-
Italian (Switzerland)               0'.?%#;??-
Hebrew (Israel)                     0,.?%#;??-
Japanese (Japan)                    0,.?%#;??-
Korean (Korea)                      0,.?%#;??-
Lithuanian (Lituania)               0.,?%#;??-
Latvian (Latvia)                    0 ,?%#;??-
Macedonian (Macedonia)              0.,?%#;??-
Dutch (Netherlands)                 0.,?%#;??-
Dutch (Belgium)                     0.,?%#;??-
Norwegian (Bokmål) (Norway)         0 ,?%#;??-
Norwegian (Nynorsk) (Norway,NY)     0 ,?%#;??-
Polish (Poland)                     0.,?%#;??-
Portuguese (Portugal)               0.,?%#;??-
Romanian (Romania)                  0.,?%#;??-
Russian (Russia)                    0.,?%#;??-
Serbian (Latin) (Serbia)            0.,?%#;??-
Slovak (Slovakia)                   0 ,?%#;??-
Slovene (Slovenia)                  0.,?%#;??-
Albanian (Albania)                  0.,?%#;??-
Serbian (Cyrillic) (Serbia)         0 ,?%#;??-
Swedish (Sweden)                    0 ,?%#;??-
Turkish (Turkey)                    0.,?%#;??-
Ukrainian (Ukraine)                 0.,?%#;??-
Chinese (China)                     0,.?%#;??-
Chinese (ROC)                       0,.?%#;??-
```

getGroupingSize()

PURPOSE Retrieves the number of digits between grouping separators.

SYNTAX `public int getGroupingSize()`

DESCRIPTION This method returns the grouping size. Grouping size is the number of digits between grouping separators in the integer portion of a number. For example, in the number "123,456.78" the grouping size is 3.

RETURNS The number of digits in a group.

SEE ALSO `setGroupingSize()`.

EXAMPLE This example calls all of the grouping, prefix, and suffix getter methods and prints out the returned characters.

```
import java.text.*;
import java.util.Locale;

class Main {

    // Create number format.
    static NumberFormat numform  =
            (DecimalFormat)NumberFormat.getInstance(Locale.JAPANESE);

    // Declare decimal format.
    static DecimalFormat decform;

    public static void main(String[] args) {

        if (numform instanceof DecimalFormat) {
            decform = (DecimalFormat)numform;

            decform.applyPattern("#,##0.#;(#,##0.#)");      // Paren for neg val
            System.out.println(decform.format(-1234.56));  // (1,234.6)

            print(decform.getGroupingSize());              //  "3"
            print(decform.getNegativePrefix());            //  "("
            print(decform.getNegativeSuffix());            //  ")"
            print(decform.getPositivePrefix());            //  ""
            print(decform.getPositiveSuffix());            //  ""
        }
    }

    static String QUOTE = "\"";

    // To help with readability.
    static void print(Object s) {
        System.out.println(QUOTE + s + QUOTE);
    }

    static void print(int i) {
        System.out.println(QUOTE + i + QUOTE);
    }
}
```

getMultiplier()

PURPOSE Retrieves the multiplier used for percent or permill.

SYNTAX `public int getMultiplier()`

DESCRIPTION This method gets the multiplier for use in percent (per 100) and permill (per 1000). To get the percentage multiplier, set the positive and negative suffixes to % before calling `getMultiplier()`. (For Arabic, use the Arabic percent symbol.) To get the permill multiplier, set the suffixes to ‰ (`\u2030`) before calling `getMultiplier()`.

RETURNS The multiplier for percent or permill.

SEE ALSO `setMultiplier()`. `getPositiveSuffix()`, `getNegativeSuffix()`.

EXAMPLE See `setMultiplier()`.

getNegativePrefix()

PURPOSE Retrieves the prefix for negative numbers.

SYNTAX `public String getNegativePrefix()`

RETURNS The string prefix for negative numbers.

SEE ALSO `setNegativePrefix()`, `getNegativeSuffix()`.

EXAMPLE See `getGroupingSize()`.

getNegativeSuffix()

PURPOSE Retrieves the suffix for negative numbers.

SYNTAX `public String getNegativeSuffix()`

RETURNS The string suffix for negative numbers.

SEE ALSO `setNegativeSuffix()`, `getNegativePrefix()`.

EXAMPLE See `getGroupingSize()`.

getPositivePrefix()

PURPOSE Retrieves the prefix for positive numbers.

SYNTAX `public String getPositivePrefix()`

RETURNS The string prefix for positive numbers.

SEE ALSO `setPositivePrefix(), getPositiveSuffix().`

EXAMPLE See `getGroupingSize()`.

getPositiveSuffix()

PURPOSE Retrieves the suffix for positive numbers.

SYNTAX `public String getPositiveSuffix()`

RETURNS The string suffix for positive numbers.

SEE ALSO `setPositiveSuffix(), getPositivePrefix().`

EXAMPLE See `getGroupingSize()`.

hashCode()

PURPOSE Computes the hashcode for this `DecimalFormat` object.

SYNTAX `public int hashCode()`

DESCRIPTION This method computes the hash code for this `DecimalFormat` object based on the pattern of this object. Two `DecimalFormat` objects with the same properties will have the same hash code. However, two `DecimalFormat` objects that do not have the same properties might also have the same hash code, although the hash code algorithm minimizes this possibility. The hash code is typically used as the key in a hash table.

RETURNS The hash code of this `DecimalFormat` object (an integer).

OVERRIDES `NumberFormat.hashCode()`.

SEE ALSO `equals()`.

EXAMPLE See `clone()`.

isDecimalSeparatorAlwaysShown()

PURPOSE Determines if the decimal separator is displayed with integers.

SYNTAX `public boolean isDecimalSeparatorAlwaysShown()`

RETURNS `true` if the decimal separator is displayed with integers; `false` otherwise. (The decimal separator will always appear with decimal numbers.)

SEE ALSO `setDecimalSeparatorAlwaysShown()`.

EXAMPLE See `setDecimalSeparatorShown()`.

parse()

PURPOSE
Converts a string to `Number` object.

SYNTAX
`public Number parse(String str, ParsePosition pos)`

DESCRIPTION
This method begins parsing the string `str` starting at position `pos` and, if the string matches this `DecimalFormat` object's pattern, converts the matching string to a `Number` object. It parses locale-specific text using the locale of its associated `DecimalFormatSymbols` object. It returns a `Long` if it has no fractional part and is within the range of a `Long` (`Long.MIN_VALUE`, `Long.MAX_VALUE`). Otherwise, it returns a `Double`. This method performs the reverse operation of `format()`.

PARAMETERS
`pos` Position at which to begin parsing the string.
`str` String to be converted to a number.

RETURNS
A `Long` if within its range; otherwise, a `Double`, or `null` if the parse failed.

OVERRIDES
`NumberFormat.parse()`.

EXAMPLE
This example parses a paragraph for all of the numbers it contains. It parses only for decimal numbers. You could refine this program to further recognize decimal numbers as currency ($1,100.00) and percentages (15%) by including formats using `getCurrencyInstance()` and `getPercentInstance()`.

```
import java.text.*;
import java.io.*;
import java.util.*;

class Main {

    // Create a parse position object for tracking the parse.
    static ParsePosition parsePos = new ParsePosition(0);

    // Create a number format.
    static NumberFormat numForm = NumberFormat.getInstance();

    Main (String str) {
        // Print out original text.
        System.out.println(str);

        // Parse through text for numbers.
        System.out.println("Found all decimals numbers in the above text:");
        parseNum(str);
    }

    static void parseNum(String str) {
        int beginParseIndex;
        int endParseIndex;
        int intLength;
        Number num = null;
```

```
            while (parsePos.getIndex() < str.length()) {

                beginParseIndex = parsePos.getIndex();

                // Parse the string starting at parsePos for a number.
                num = numForm.parse(str, parsePos);

                endParseIndex = parsePos.getIndex();

                if (num != null) {

                    // Count length of integer portion for printing spaces.
                    intLength =
                        ((new Integer(beginParseIndex)).toString()).length();

                    System.out.print("Index: ");
                    printSpaces(4 - intLength);
                    System.out.print(beginParseIndex + "  ");

                    // Count length of integer portion for printing spaces.
                    intLength = countIntLength(numForm, num);

                    System.out.print("  Number: ");
                    printSpaces(7 - intLength);

                    // Format the output so the column aligns.
                    System.out.println(numForm.format(num));
                }
                parsePos.setIndex(endParseIndex + 1);
            }
            // Reset parse position to 0 for next loop.
            parsePos.setIndex(0);
        }

        // Count length of integer portion of number.
        static int countIntLength (NumberFormat numForm, Number num) {
            FieldPosition fp = new FieldPosition(NumberFormat.INTEGER_FIELD);
            StringBuffer strBuf = new StringBuffer("");
            long lg = num.longValue();
            numForm.format(lg, strBuf, fp);
            return (fp.getEndIndex() - fp.getBeginIndex());
        }

        // Print spaces.
        static void printSpaces(int count) {
            for (int p = 0; p < count; ++p) {
                System.out.print(" ");
            }
        }

        public static void main(String[] args) {

            // Accept an input text file
            if (args.length != 1) {
                System.err.println("This program parses text for numbers");
                System.err.println("Usage: java Main <filename>");
                System.exit(1);
            }
            try {
                // Read the text into a buffered reader
```

```
            // with '\n' for newlines
            BufferedReader rd = new BufferedReader(new FileReader(args[0]));
            String line;
            StringBuffer sbuf = new StringBuffer();

            while ((line = rd.readLine()) != null) {
                sbuf.append(line);
                sbuf.append('\n');
            }
            rd.close();

            // Call the constructor Main with the input string
            new Main(new String(sbuf));

        } catch (Exception e) {
            e.printStackTrace();
        }
    }
}
```

Output

```
> java Main input.txt
Jan 1, 1998.  It's hard to find a system under $1200 that is 100%-reliable.
The current price of $1,100.00 does not include 3 required $50 add-ons.
The price is going up 10 - 15% on November 3, 1998 at 5:25pm.  Wait for 12/31/
98.

Found all decimals numbers in the above text:
Index:    4     Number:      1
Index:    7     Number:  1,998
Index:   48     Number:  1,200
Index:   61     Number:    100
Index:   98     Number:  1,100
Index:  124     Number:      3
Index:  136     Number:     50
Index:  170     Number:     10
Index:  175     Number:     15
Index:  191     Number:      3
Index:  194     Number:  1,998
Index:  202     Number:      5
Index:  204     Number:     25
Index:  220     Number:     12
Index:  223     Number:     31
Index:  226     Number:     98
```

setDecimalFormatSymbols()

PURPOSE Sets the decimal format symbols for this `DecimalFormat` object.

SYNTAX `public void setDecimalFormatSymbols(DecimalFormatSymbols newSymbols)`

DESCRIPTION This method sets the decimal format symbols for this `DecimalFormat` object. These are the symbols that can appear in a pattern and in the resulting formatted strings.

When you call `applyLocalizedPattern()`, it uses the following symbols from the decimal format symbols: zero digit, grouping separator, decimal separator, percent sign, permill sign, pattern digit (#), and pattern separator.

To see the string representation of the symbols, call the getter methods in `DecimalFormatSymbols` on the decimal format symbols object. Because each locale can have its own decimal format symbols, it is generally not necessary to change these symbols. However, you can change them with methods in the `DecimalFormatSymbols` class.

PARAMETERS

`newSymbols` The decimal format symbols to be applied.

SEE ALSO `getDecimalFormatSymbols()`, `DecimalFormatSymbols`.

EXAMPLE This example creates a French `DecimalFormatSymbols` object and a `DecimalFormat` object and sets the former to the latter. Then it displays each of the values of the French symbols using the getter methods.

```
import java.text.*;
import java.util.Locale;

class Main {

    public static void main(String[] args) {

        Locale loc = Locale.FRENCH;
        NumberFormat numform = null;
        DecimalFormat decform = null;
        DecimalFormatSymbols sym = new DecimalFormatSymbols(loc);

        // Print out language and country names.
        System.out.println(loc.getDisplayName());

        // Get the number format for the locale.
        numform = NumberFormat.getInstance(loc);

        // Test before casting.
        if (numform instanceof DecimalFormat) {

            // Cast the number format to a decimal format.
            decform = (DecimalFormat)numform;

            // Set the symbols for the given locale.
            decform.setDecimalFormatSymbols(sym);
                                                  //--French Values--
            print(sym.getZeroDigit());             //  "0"
            print(sym.getGroupingSeparator());     //  " "
            print(sym.getDecimalSeparator());      //  ","
            print(sym.getPerMill());               //  \u2030
            print(sym.getPercent());               //  "%"
            print(sym.getDigit());                 //  "#"
            print(sym.getPatternSeparator());      //  ";"
            print(sym.getInfinity());              //  \u221E
            print(sym.getNaN());                   //  \uFFFD
            print(sym.getMinusSign());             //  "-"
```

```
            print("\n");
        }
    }

    static void print(char ch) {
        System.out.print(ch);
    }

    static void print(String str) {
        System.out.print(str);
    }
}
```

A B C D E F G H I J K L M N O P Q R S T U V W X Y Z

setDecimalSeparatorAlwaysShown()

PURPOSE Sets the decimal separator display property for integers.

SYNTAX `public void setDecimalSeparatorAlwaysShown(boolean newValue)`

DESCRIPTION This method determines whether the decimal separator is displayed with integers. If `newValue` is `true`, the decimal separator is displayed with integers; if `false`, the decimal separator is not shown with integers. The decimal separator will always appear if a fractional part exists.

PARAMETERS

`newValue` If `true`, the decimal separator is displayed with integers; if `false`, the decimal separator is not shown with integers.

SEE ALSO `isDecimalSeparatorAlwaysShown()`.

EXAMPLE This class formats and displays integers with the decimal separator both showing and hidden.

```
import java.text.*;
import java.util.Locale;

class Main {

    public static void main(String[] args) {

        NumberFormat nf = NumberFormat.getInstance(Locale.ITALIAN);
        DecimalFormat df = null;

        // Test before casting.
        if (nf instanceof DecimalFormat) {

            // Cast number format.
            df = (DecimalFormat)nf;

            long lg = 1234;

            df.setDecimalSeparatorAlwaysShown(true);
            System.out.println(df.format(lg));                   // 1.234,
```

```
                df.setDecimalSeparatorAlwaysShown(false);
                System.out.println(df.format(lg));                   // 1.234

                System.out.println(df.isDecimalSeparatorAlwaysShown());  // false
            }
        }
    }
```

A B C D E F G H I J K L M N O P Q R S T U V W X Y Z

setGroupingSize()

PURPOSE Sets the number of digits between grouping separators.

SYNTAX `public void setGroupingSize(int groupSize)`

DESCRIPTION This method sets the grouping size. Grouping size is the number of digits between grouping separators in the integer portion of a number. For example, in the number "123,456.78" the grouping size is 3.

PARAMETERS

`groupSize` The number of digits to be grouped together.

SEE ALSO `getGroupingSize()`, `NumberFormat.setGroupingUsed()`, `DecimalFormatSymbols.setGroupingSeparator()`.

EXAMPLE This example sets the grouping size, negative prefix/suffix, and the positive prefix/suffix.

```
import java.text.*;
import java.util.Locale;

class Main {

    static NumberFormat numform = NumberFormat.getInstance(Locale.FRANCE);
    static DecimalFormat decform;

    public static void main(String[] args) {

        // Test before casting.
        if (numform instanceof DecimalFormat) {

            decform = (DecimalFormat)numform;

            decform.applyPattern("#,##0.#;(#,##0.#)");      // Paren for neg val
            System.out.println(decform.format(12345.67));    // 12 345.7
            System.out.println(decform.format(-12345.67));   // (12 345.7)

            decform.setGroupingSize(4);
            decform.setNegativePrefix("[");
            decform.setNegativeSuffix("]");
            decform.setPositivePrefix("+");
            decform.setPositiveSuffix("+");
```

```
            print(decform.getGroupingSize());               //  "4"
            print(decform.getNegativePrefix());             //  "["
            print(decform.getNegativeSuffix());             //  "]"
            print(decform.getPositivePrefix());             //  "+"
            print(decform.getPositiveSuffix());             //  "+"

            System.out.println(decform.format(12345.67));   // +1 2345,7+
            System.out.println(decform.format(-12345.67));  // [1 2345,7]
        }
    }

    static String QUOTE = "\"";

    // To help with readability.
    static void print(Object s) {
        System.out.println(QUOTE + s + QUOTE);
    }

    static void print(int i) {
        System.out.println(QUOTE + i + QUOTE);
    }
}
```


setMultiplier()

PURPOSE Sets the multiplier for use in percent and permill.

SYNTAX `public void setMultiplier(int newValue)`

DESCRIPTION This method sets the multiplier for use in percent and permill. To set the percent multiplier, set the positive and negative suffixes to % and then call `setMultiplier()` on 100. (For Arabic, use the Arabic percent symbol.) To set the permill multiplier, set the suffixes to ‰ (`\u2030`) and then call `setMultiplier()` on the value you want, normally 1000. For all other suffixes, the multiplier is 1.

There should be no need to change the multipliers; they should be identical for all locales. However, the symbols might change.

For example, calling `format()` with a suffix of % and a multiplier of 100 causes the number 1.23 to be displayed as the string "123%".

PARAMETERS

`newValue` The integer to be used as a multiplier.

SEE ALSO `getMultiplier(). setPositiveSuffix(), setNegativeSuffix().`

EXAMPLE This example sets the suffixes and multipliers to the appropriate values for the `US` locale, doing it first with `setMultiplier()` and then with `applyPattern()`.

```
import java.text.*;
import java.util.Locale;

class Main {

    // Create number format.
    static NumberFormat numform = NumberFormat.getInstance(Locale.US);
    static DecimalFormat decform;

    public static void main(String[] args) {

        // Test before casting.
        if (numform instanceof DecimalFormat) {

            decform = (DecimalFormat)numform;

            printValue();                                   //  -1.23

            // Percent
            decform.setPositiveSuffix("%");
            decform.setNegativeSuffix("%");
            decform.setMultiplier(100);
            printValue();                                   //  -123%

            // Permill
            decform.setPositiveSuffix("\u2030");
            decform.setNegativeSuffix("\u2030");
            decform.setMultiplier(1000);
            printValue();                                   //  -1,230\u2030

            // Apply percent with a pattern
            decform.applyPattern("#,##0.#%;(#,##0.#%)");
            System.out.println(decform.getMultiplier());   //  100
            printValue();                                   //  (123%)
        }
    }

    static void printValue() {
        System.out.println(decform.format(-1.23));
    }
}
```

setNegativePrefix()

PURPOSE Sets the prefix for negative numbers.

SYNTAX `public void setNegativePrefix(String newValue)`

DESCRIPTION This method sets the prefix for negative numbers.

Examples include –123 and Fr–123. When used with the negative suffix, a negative number can be formatted with a set of parentheses, as in ($123).

PARAMETERS

`newValue` The string to appear ahead of a negative number.

SEE ALSO `getNegativePrefix()`.

EXAMPLE See `setGroupingSize()`.

setNegativeSuffix()

PURPOSE Sets the suffix for negative numbers.

SYNTAX `public void setNegativeSuffix(String newValue)`

DESCRIPTION This method sets the suffix for negative numbers; for example, the percent sign used with negative numbers: –123%. When used with the negative prefix, a negative number can be formatted with a set of parentheses, as in ($123).

PARAMETERS

`newValue` The string to appear after a negative number.

SEE ALSO `getNegativeSuffix()`.

EXAMPLE See `setGroupingSize()`.

setPositivePrefix()

PURPOSE Sets the prefix for positive numbers.

SYNTAX `public void setPositivePrefix(String newValue)`

DESCRIPTION This method sets the prefix for positive numbers; for example, +123, $123, and Fr123.

PARAMETERS

`newValue` The string to appear ahead of a positive number.

SEE ALSO `getPositivePrefix()`.

EXAMPLE See `setGroupingSize()`.

setPositiveSuffix()

PURPOSE Sets the suffix for positive numbers.

SYNTAX `public void setPositiveSuffix(String newValue)`

DESCRIPTION This method sets the suffix for positive numbers; for example, 123%.

PARAMETERS

`newValue` The string to appear after a positive number.

SEE ALSO `getPositiveSuffix()`.

EXAMPLE See `setGroupingSize()`.

toLocalizedPattern()

PURPOSE Produces a string of the current localized pattern.

SYNTAX `public String toLocalizedPattern()`

DESCRIPTION This method synthesizes a localized pattern string that represents the current pattern of this `DecimalFormat` object. It uses the locale of the number format (which you specify when creating the number format). This string should be used when displaying the pattern to a native user, so the familiar, native separators will be displayed.

RETURNS The localized string pattern for this `DecimalFormat` object.

SEE ALSO `applyLocalizedPattern()`.

EXAMPLE See `applyLocalizedPattern()`.

toPattern()

PURPOSE Produces a string of the current nonlocalized pattern.

SYNTAX `public String toPattern()`

DESCRIPTION This method synthesizes a nonlocalized pattern string that represents the current state of this `DecimalFormat` object. This pattern is independent of locales, so it can be applied to a `DecimalFormat` object in any locale by using `applyPattern()`.

This pattern happens to coincide with the pattern of the U.S. locale.

RETURNS The nonlocalized string pattern for this `DecimalFormat` object.

SEE ALSO `applyPattern()`.

EXAMPLE

This example first creates French and German `NumberFormat` objects. It then applies a nonlocalized pattern to the German format. Then it prints out the German pattern, the nonlocalized pattern, and the French pattern. See `applyLocalizedPattern()` for another example of the `toPattern()` method.

```
import java.text.NumberFormat;
import java.text.DecimalFormat;
import java.text.ParseException;
import java.util.Locale;

class Main {

    public static void main(String[] args) {

        NumberFormat numform_GERMAN = NumberFormat.getInstance(Locale.GERMAN);
        NumberFormat numform_FRENCH = NumberFormat.getInstance(Locale.FRENCH);
        Number num = null;

        DecimalFormat decform_GERMAN = null;
        DecimalFormat decform_FRENCH = null;

        // Temporary string for the pattern.
        String pattern = null;

        if (numform_GERMAN instanceof DecimalFormat) {

            decform_GERMAN = (DecimalFormat)numform_GERMAN;

            decform_GERMAN.applyPattern("#,##0.00;(#,##0.00)");

            // Print out the German pattern.
            print("toLocalizedPattern: (German) "
              + (decform_GERMAN.toLocalizedPattern()));  // #.##0,00;(#.##0,00)

            // Print out the non-localized pattern.
            pattern =  (decform_GERMAN).toPattern();
            print("toPattern:    (Non-localized) "
               + pattern);                              // #,##0.00;(#,##0.00)

        }

        if (numform_FRENCH instanceof DecimalFormat) {

            decform_FRENCH = (DecimalFormat)numform_FRENCH;

            decform_FRENCH.applyPattern(pattern);

            // Print out the French pattern.
            print("toLocalizedPattern: (French) "
              + (decform_FRENCH).toLocalizedPattern());  // # ##0,00;(# ##0,00)
        }
    }

    static void print(String s) {
        System.out.println(s);
    }
}
```

Output

```
> java Main
toLocalizedPattern: (German) #.##0,00;(#.##0,00)
toPattern:   (Non-localized) #,##0.00;(#,##0.00)
toLocalizedPattern: (French) # ##0,00;(# ##0,00)
```

DecimalFormatSymbols

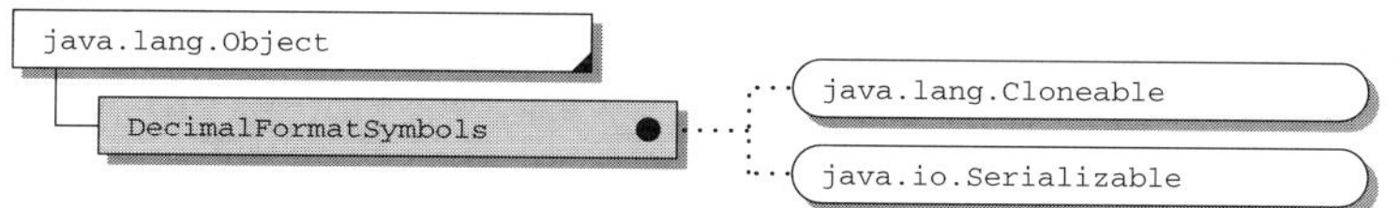

A B C D E F G H I J K L M N O P Q R S T U V W X Y Z

Syntax

```
public final class DecimalFormatSymbols extends Object implements Cloneable,
    Serializable
```

Description

The `DecimalFormatSymbols` class represents the set of symbols needed by `DecimalFormat` to format numbers. Each `DecimalFormatSymbols` object corresponds to a particular locale. The symbols are shown in Table 24 with their U. S English values.

U.S. English	Unicode	Symbol Name	Where Used
`0`	`\u0030`	Zero digit	In localized patterns and formatted strings.
`,`	`\u002C`	Grouping separator	In localized patterns and formatted strings.
`.`	`\u002E`	Decimal separator	In localized patterns and formatted strings.
`%`	`\u0025`	Percent sign	In localized patterns and formatted strings.
‰	`\u2030`	Per mill sign	In localized patterns and formatted strings.
–	`\u002D`	Minus sign	In localized patterns and formatted strings.
`#`	`\u0023`	Pattern digit	Only in localized patterns.
`;`	`\u003B`	Pattern separator	Only in localized patterns.
∞	`\u221E`	Infinity	Only in localized formatted strings.
�	`\uFFFD`	`NaN`	Only in localized formatted strings.

TABLE 24: Symbols in the U.S. English `DecimalFormatSymbols` Object.

These symbols appear in patterns generated using `applyLocalizedPattern()` in the `DecimalFormat` class. They also appear in formatted numbers produced from the `format()` method. This class contains setters for setting these symbols. The purpose of changing these symbols is to satisfy the requirements of a particular locale.

Usage

When you create an instance of `DecimalFormat`, it creates for itself an instance of `DecimalFormatSymbols` from its locale data. If you need to change any of these symbols, you can call getDecimalFormatSymbols() to get the DecimalFormatSymbols object from your decimal format and modify it.

Alternatively, you can call a constructor DecimalFormatSymbols() to create an instance directly. Use the constructor with no argument to create an instance of DecimalFormatSymbols based on the default locale.

If certain characters (e.g., NaN, Infinity, per mill) do not display properly, it may be because your system does not have the proper font. Java relies on system fonts and does not provide its own with Java 1.1.

A B C D E F G H I J K L M N O P Q R S T U V W X Y Z

MEMBER SUMMARY

Constructor	
DecimalFormatSymbols()	Constructs a DecimalFormatSymbols instance.
Symbol Getter Methods	
getDecimalSeparator()	Retrieves the character used for the decimal separator.
getDigit()	Retrieves the character used for a digit in a pattern.
getGroupingSeparator()	Retrieves the character used for the grouping separator.
getInfinity()	Retrieves the string used to represent infinity.
getMinusSign()	Retrieves the character used for the default minus sign.
getNaN()	Retrieves the string used to represent NaN.
getPatternSeparator()	Retrieves the character that separates positive and negative subpatterns.
getPercent()	Retrieves the character used for the percent sign.
getPerMill()	Retrieves the character used for the per mill sign.
getZeroDigit()	Retrieves the character used for the zero digit.
Symbol Setter Methods	
setDecimalSeparator(char)	Sets the character used for the decimal separator.
setDigit()	Sets the character used for a digit in a pattern.
setGroupingSeparator()	Sets the character used for the grouping separator.
setInfinity()	Sets the string that represents infinity.
setMinusSign()	Sets the character used for the minus sign.
setNaN()	Sets the string that represents NaN.
setPatternSeparator()	Sets the character that separates positive and negative subpatterns.
setPercent()	Sets the character used for the percent sign.
setPerMill()	Sets the character used for the per mill sign.
setZeroDigit()	Sets the character used for the zero digit.
Object Methods	
clone()	Creates a copy of this DecimalFormatSymbols object.
equals()	Compares two DecimalFormatSymbols objects for equality.
hashCode()	Computes the hashcode for this DecimalFormatSymbols object.

See Also

`DecimalFormat`, `java.util.Locale()`.

Example

This example creates a text area and displays in it all of the decimal format symbols for each available locale. See Figure 38.

Note: A character may not display properly if you do not have a font that supports it. In particular, on some systems the fonts don't display Infinity and `NaN` properly.

DecimalFormatSymbols Example

	zero digit	group sep	decimal sep	permill	percent	digit	pattern sep	nan	minus sign	infinity
Arabic (Egypt)	?	?	?	‰	%	#	;	?	-	8
Belorussian (Belarus)	0		,	‰	%	#	;	?	-	8
Bulgarian (Bulgaria)	0	.	,	‰	%	#	;	?	-	8
Catalan (Spain)	0	.	,	‰	%	#	;	?	-	8
Czech (Czech Republic)	0	.	,	‰	%	#	;	?	-	8
Danish (Denmark)	0	.	,	‰	%	#	;	?	-	8
German (Germany)	0	.	,	‰	%	#	;	?	-	8
German (Austria)	0	.	,	‰	%	#	;	?	-	8
German (Switzerland)	0	'	,	‰	%	#	;	?	-	8
Greek (Greece)	0	.	,	‰	%	#	;	?	-	8
English (Canada)	0	;	.	‰	%	#	;	?	-	8
English (United Kingdom)	0	,	.	‰	%	#	;	?	-	8
English (Ireland)	0	,	.	‰	%	#	;	?	-	8
English (United States)	0	,	.	‰	%	#	;	?	-	8

FIGURE 38: `DecimalFormatSymbols.`

```
import java.text.NumberFormat;
import java.text.DecimalFormatSymbols;
import java.util.Locale;
import java.awt.*;

class Main extends Frame {
    TextArea textArea = new TextArea("", 30, 100,
                                TextArea.SCROLLBARS_VERTICAL_ONLY);

    Main(StringBuffer strbuf) {
        super("DecimalFormatSymbols Example");
```

```
            // Set the text and add the layout to text area.
            textArea.setText(strbuf.toString());
            add(textArea, BorderLayout.CENTER);

            // Set size and show window.
            Font f = new Font("Courier", Font.PLAIN, 12);
            textArea.setFont(f);
            textArea.setEditable(false);
            setSize(700, 500);
            show();
        }

        public static void main(String[] args) {
            StringBuffer strbuf = new StringBuffer(1500);
            Locale[] locales = NumberFormat.getAvailableLocales();

            strbuf.append("                    ");
            strbuf.append("zero  group decimal permill percent digit " +
                                         "pattern  nan  minus infinity \n");
            strbuf.append("                    ");
            strbuf.append("digit  sep   sep                          " +
                                                 "sep        sign \n");
            for (int i = 0; i < locales.length; ++i) {
                strbuf.append(locales[i].getDisplayName()).append("\n");

                // Print decimal format symbols
                DecimalFormatSymbols dfs = new DecimalFormatSymbols(locales[i]);
                String spacer = "      ";
                strbuf.append("                    "
                              + dfs.getZeroDigit() + spacer
                              + dfs.getGroupingSeparator() + spacer
                              + dfs.getDecimalSeparator() + spacer
                              + dfs.getPerMill() + spacer
                              + dfs.getPercent() + spacer
                              + dfs.getDigit() + spacer
                              + dfs.getPatternSeparator() + spacer
                              + dfs.getNaN() + spacer
                              + dfs.getMinusSign() + spacer
                              + dfs.getInfinity() + "\n"
                );
            }
            new Main(strbuf);
        }
    }
```

clone()

PURPOSE Creates a copy of this `DecimalFormatSymbols` object.

SYNTAX `public Object clone()`

DESCRIPTION This method makes a copy of this `DecimalFormatSymbols` object. The new decimal format has a complete copy of all symbols. Changing any value in the new instance will not affect the original instance.

RETURNS A non-null copy of this DecimalFormatSymbols object.

OVERRIDES java.lang.Object.clone().

EXAMPLE This example illustrates the use of clone() to copy a DecimalFormatSymbols object. Note that the copy has the same symbols as the original.

```
import java.text.DecimalFormatSymbols;
import java.util.Locale;

class Main {

    public static void main(String args[]) {

        // Create decimal format symbols.
        DecimalFormatSymbols dfs = new DecimalFormatSymbols(Locale.ITALIAN);
        System.out.println("Original decimal sep: " +
                                          dfs.getDecimalSeparator());

        // Create a clone.
        DecimalFormatSymbols dfsCopy = (DecimalFormatSymbols)dfs.clone();
        System.out.println("Copy's decimal sep:   " +
                                          dfs.getDecimalSeparator());

        // Test for equality.
        if (dfs.equals(dfsCopy)) {
            System.out.println("Clone is equal to original");
        }

        // Compute hashcode
        int hc = dfs.hashCode();
        System.out.println("Hash code:            " + hc);
    }
}
```

DecimalFormatSymbols()

PURPOSE Constructs a DecimalFormatSymbols instance.

SYNTAX
```
public DecimalFormatSymbols()
public DecimalFormatSymbols(Locale loc)
```

DESCRIPTION This method used constructs a DecimalFormatSymbols object either for the default locale if loc is not passed in, or for a specific locale if loc is passed in.

PARAMETERS

loc The locale for the decimal format symbols.

EXAMPLE See the class example.

A B C D E F G H I J K L M N O P Q R S T U V W X Y Z

equals()

PURPOSE Compares two `DecimalFormatSymbols` objects for equality.

SYNTAX `public boolean equals(Object obj)`

DESCRIPTION This method compares this `DecimalFormatSymbols` object with `obj` for equality. If `obj` is a `DecimalFormatSymbols` object and if it has the same individual symbol values as this `DecimalFormatSymbols` object, the objects are equal and this method returns `true`. If the individual symbols are not equal or if `obj` is `null` or not a `DecimalFormatSymbols` object, this method returns `false`.

PARAMETERS

`obj` A possibly `null` object with which to compare.

RETURNS `true` if the objects are equal; `false` otherwise.

OVERRIDES `java.lang.Object.equals()`.

SEE ALSO `hashCode()`.

EXAMPLE See `clone()`.

getDecimalSeparator()

PURPOSE Retrieves the character used for the decimal separator.

SYNTAX `public char getDecimalSeparator()`

RETURNS The character used for the decimal sign in localized patterns and localized formatted numbers. Different for French, German, and other locales.

SEE ALSO `setDecimalSeparator()`.

EXAMPLE See `setDigit()`.

getDigit()

PURPOSE Retrieves the character used for a digit in a pattern.

SYNTAX `public char getDigit()`

RETURNS The character used as a placeholder for a digit in a localized pattern.

SEE ALSO `setDigit()`.

EXAMPLE See `setDigit()`.

getGroupingSeparator()

PURPOSE Retrieves the character used for the grouping separator.

SYNTAX `public char getGroupingSeparator()`

RETURNS The character used for thousands separator in localized patterns and localized formatted numbers. Different for French, German, and other locales.

SEE ALSO `setGroupingSeparator()`.

EXAMPLE See `setDigit()`.

getInfinity()

PURPOSE Retrieves the string used to represent infinity.

SYNTAX `public String getInfinity()`

RETURNS The character used to represent infinity in localized formatted numbers. This string is seldom changed.

SEE ALSO `setInfinity()`.

EXAMPLE See `setDigit()`.

getMinusSign()

PURPOSE Retrieves the character used for the default minus sign.

SYNTAX `public char getMinusSign()`

RETURNS The character used to represent the default minus sign in localized patterns and localized formatted numbers. If no explicit negative format is specified, one is formed by prefixing this minus sign to the positive format.

SEE ALSO `setMinusSign()`.

EXAMPLE See `setDigit()`.

getNaN()

PURPOSE Retrieves the string used to represent `NaN`.

SYNTAX `public String getNaN()`

RETURNS The character used to represent `NaN` (not-a-number) in localized formatted numbers.

SEE ALSO `setNaN()`.

EXAMPLE See `setDigit()`.

getPatternSeparator()

PURPOSE Retrieves the character that separates positive and negative subpatterns.

SYNTAX `public char getPatternSeparator()`

RETURNS The character used to separate positive and negative subpatterns in a localized pattern.

SEE ALSO `setPatternSeparator()`.

EXAMPLE See `setDigit()`.

getPercent()

PURPOSE Retrieves the character used for the percent sign.

SYNTAX `public char getPercent()`

RETURNS The character used for the percent sign in localized patterns and localized formatted numbers. Different for Arabic and other locales.

SEE ALSO `setPercent()`.

EXAMPLE See `setDigit()`.

getPerMill()

PURPOSE Retrieves the character used for the per mill sign.

SYNTAX `public char getPerMill()`

RETURNS The character used for the per mill sign in localized patterns and localized formatted numbers. Different for Arabic and other locales.

SEE ALSO `setPerMill()`.

EXAMPLE See `setDigit()`.

getZeroDigit()

PURPOSE Retrieves the character used for the zero digit.

SYNTAX `public char getZeroDigit()`

RETURNS The character used for the zero digit in localized patterns and localized formatted numbers. The zero for most western languages is 0. The Arabic zero is a dot above the baseline.

SEE ALSO `setZeroDigit()`.

EXAMPLE See `setDigit()`.

hashCode()

PURPOSE Computes the hashcode for this `DecimalFormatSymbols` object.

SYNTAX `public int hashCode()`

DESCRIPTION This method computes the hash code for this `DecimalFormatSymbols` object based on the zero digit, grouping separator, and decimal separator of this decimal format symbols object. Two `DecimalFormatSymbols` objects with the same properties will have the same hash code. However, two `DecimalFormatSymbols` objects that do not have the same properties might also have the same hash code, although the hash code algorithm minimizes this possibility. The hash code is typically used as the key in a hash table.

RETURNS The hash code of this `DecimalFormatSymbols` object (an integer).

OVERRIDES `java.lang.Object.hashCode()`.

SEE ALSO `equals()`.

EXAMPLE See `clone()`.

setDecimalSeparator()

PURPOSE Sets the character used for the decimal separator.

SYNTAX `public void setDecimalSeparator(char decimalSep)`

DESCRIPTION This method sets the character used for the decimal separator in localized patterns and localized formatted numbers. Different for Arabic and other locales.

PARAMETERS

`decimalSep` The character specifying the new decimal separator symbol.

EXAMPLE See `setDigit()`.

setDigit()

PURPOSE Sets the character used for a digit in a pattern.

SYNTAX `public void setDigit(char digit)`

DESCRIPTION This method sets the character used as a placeholder for a digit in a localized pattern.

PARAMETERS

`digit` The character specifying the new digit pattern symbol.

EXAMPLE This example sets arbitrary characters for each of the decimal format symbols. See Figure 39.

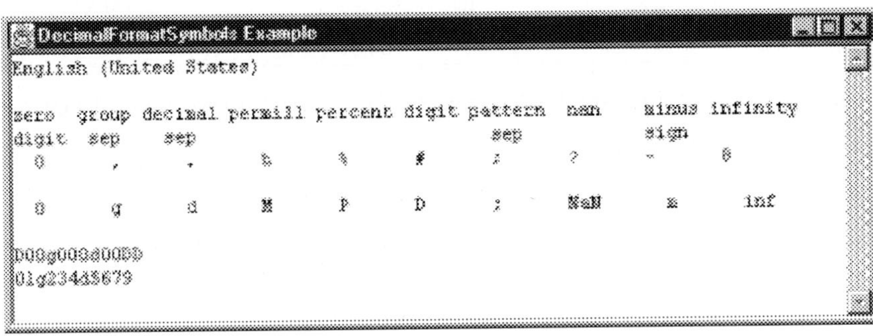

FIGURE 39: `setDigit()`.

```
import java.text.NumberFormat;
import java.text.DecimalFormat;
import java.text.DecimalFormatSymbols;
import java.util.Locale;
import java.awt.*;

class Main extends Frame {
    TextArea textArea =
        new TextArea("", 30, 100, TextArea.SCROLLBARS_VERTICAL_ONLY);

    Main(StringBuffer strbuf) {
        super("DecimalFormatSymbols Example");

        // Set the text and add the layout to text area.
        textArea.setText(strbuf.toString());
        add(textArea, BorderLayout.CENTER);

        // Set size and show window.
        Font f = new Font("Courier", Font.PLAIN, 12);
        textArea.setFont(f);
        setSize(600, 200);
        show();
    }

    public static void main(String[] args) {
        StringBuffer strbuf = new StringBuffer(1500);
```

```
Locale[] locales = NumberFormat.getAvailableLocales();

// Loop through all locales looking for US
for (int i = 0; i < locales.length; ++i) {

    // Skip if country is not US.
    if (!(locales[i].getCountry().equals("US"))) {
        continue;
    }

    // Build up string to display in a string buffer
    strbuf.append(locales[i].getDisplayName()).append("\n\n");
    strbuf.append("zero  group decimal permill percent digit " +
        "pattern  nan    minus infinity \n");
    strbuf.append("digit  sep    sep                         " +
        "  sep            sign \n");

    // Create a new decimal format symbols for US
    DecimalFormatSymbols dfs = new DecimalFormatSymbols(locales[i]);

    // Append characters to string buffer
    String spacer = "      ";
    strbuf.append("  "
                    + dfs.getZeroDigit() + spacer
                    + dfs.getGroupingSeparator() + spacer
                    + dfs.getDecimalSeparator() + spacer
                    + dfs.getPerMill() + spacer
                    + dfs.getPercent() + spacer
                    + dfs.getDigit() + spacer
                    + dfs.getPatternSeparator() + spacer
                    + dfs.getNaN() + spacer
                    + dfs.getMinusSign() + spacer
                    + dfs.getInfinity() + "\n\n"
    );

    // Assign new arbitrary characters for symbols.
    dfs.setZeroDigit('0');
    dfs.setGroupingSeparator('g');
    dfs.setDecimalSeparator('d');
    dfs.setPerMill('M');
    dfs.setPercent('P');
    dfs.setDigit('D');
    dfs.setPatternSeparator(';');
    dfs.setNaN("NaN");
    dfs.setMinusSign('m');
    dfs.setInfinity("inf");

    // Append characters to string buffer
    strbuf.append("  "
                    + dfs.getZeroDigit() + spacer
                    + dfs.getGroupingSeparator() + spacer
                    + dfs.getDecimalSeparator() + spacer
                    + dfs.getPerMill() + spacer
                    + dfs.getPercent() + spacer
                    + dfs.getDigit() + spacer
                    + dfs.getPatternSeparator() + spacer
                    + dfs.getNaN() + spacer
                    + dfs.getMinusSign() + spacer
                    + dfs.getInfinity() + "\n\n"
    );
```

```
                // Append formatted number (a string) to string buffer.
                NumberFormat form = NumberFormat.getInstance(locales[i]);

                try {
                    // Chinese, Japanese, Korean numbers cannot cast to decimals
                    DecimalFormat decform = (DecimalFormat)form;
                    decform.setDecimalFormatSymbols(dfs);
                    decform.applyLocalizedPattern("D00g000d00DD;mD00g000d00DD");

                    // Append pattern to string buffer.
                    strbuf.append(decform.toLocalizedPattern() + "\n");
                                                            // D00g000d00DD
                    strbuf.append(decform.format(1234.56789) + "\n");
                                                            //  01g234d5679
                } catch (ClassCastException e ) {
                    System.err.println("Exception casting a class");
                }
            }
            new Main(strbuf);
        }
    }
```

setGroupingSeparator()

PURPOSE Sets the character used for the grouping separator.

SYNTAX `public void setGroupingSeparator(char groupSep)`

DESCRIPTION This method sets `groupSep` to be the character used for the thousands separator in localized patterns and localized formatted numbers. Different for French, German, and other locales.

PARAMETERS

`groupSep` The character specifying the new grouping separator symbol.

EXAMPLE See `setDigit()`.

setInfinity()

PURPOSE Sets the string that represents infinity.

SYNTAX `public void setInfinity(String infinity)`

DESCRIPTION This method sets the string, normally a single character, used to represent infinity in localized formatted numbers. This string is seldom changed.

PARAMETERS

`infinity` The possibly `null` string containing the new infinity symbol.

EXAMPLE See `setDigit()`.

setMinusSign()

PURPOSE Sets the character used for the minus sign.

SYNTAX `public void setMinusSign(char minusSign)`

DESCRIPTION This method sets the character used to represent the default minus sign in localized patterns and localized formatted numbers. If no explicit negative format is specified, one is formed by prefixing this minus sign to the positive format.

PARAMETERS

`minusSign` The character specifying the new default minus sign.

EXAMPLE See `setDigit()`.

setNaN()

PURPOSE Sets the string that represents `NaN`.

SYNTAX `public void setNaN(String nan)`

DESCRIPTION This method gets the character used to represent `NaN` (not-a-number) in localized formatted numbers. `NaN` is part of the IEEE 754 standard that defines `NaN` to represent the result of certain operations like dividing zero by zero (0/0). This string is seldom changed.

PARAMETERS

`nan` The possibly `null` string containing the new `NaN` symbol.

EXAMPLE See `setDigit()`.

setPatternSeparator()

PURPOSE Sets the character that separates positive and negative subpatterns.

SYNTAX `public void setPatternSeparator(char patternSep)`

DESCRIPTION This method sets the character used to separate positive and negative subpatterns in a localized pattern.

PARAMETERS

`patternSep` The character specifying the new pattern separator symbol.

EXAMPLE See `setDigit()`.

setPercent()

PURPOSE Sets the character used for the percent sign.

SYNTAX `public void setPercent(char percent)`

DESCRIPTION This method sets the character used for the percent sign in localized patterns and localized formatted numbers. Different for Arabic and other locales.

PARAMETERS

`percent` The character specifying the new percent symbol.

EXAMPLE See `setDigit()`.

setPerMill()

PURPOSE Sets the character used for the per mill sign.

SYNTAX `public void setPerMill(char perMill)`

DESCRIPTION This method sets the character used for the per mill sign in localized patterns and localized formatted numbers. For the U.S. English locale, the symbol is ‰. Different for Arabic and other locales.

PARAMETERS

`perMill` The character specifying the new per mill symbol.

EXAMPLE See `setDigit()`.

setZeroDigit()

PURPOSE Sets the character used for the zero digit.

SYNTAX `public void setZeroDigit(char zeroDigit)`

DESCRIPTION This method sets the character used for the zero digit in localized patterns and localized formatted numbers. The zero for most Western languages is 0. The Arabic zero is a dot above the baseline.

PARAMETERS

`zeroDigit` The character specifying the new zero digit symbol.

EXAMPLE See `setDigit()`.

A B C D E F G H I J K L M N O P Q R S T U V W X Y Z

Deflater

A B C D E F G H I J K L M N O P Q R S T U V W X Y Z

Syntax

```
public class Deflater
```

Description

The `Deflater` class is used to compress a data stream of arbitrary length. The compressed data can be decompressed using the `Inflate` class. The DEFLATE compression algorithm and data format is described in *RFC 1951*, which can be found at `http://ds.internic.net/rfc/rfc1951.txt`.

This class uses the ZLIB compression library to perform the compression. Complete information about this library can be found at `ftp://ftp.uu.net/pub/archiving/zip/doc/`.

Usage

A deflater is typically used with the `DeflaterOutputStream` class, which makes it convenient to compress a stream of data.

To use a deflater to compress some data, you first must create a `Deflater` instance. Then you supply uncompressed data to the deflater by calling `setInput()`. After each call to `setInput()`, you must call `deflate()` to retrieve the compressed data. You must continually call `deflate()` until `needsInput()` returns `true`, at which point you can call `setInput()` again to supply more uncompressed data.

When all of the uncompressed data has been delivered to the deflater, call `finish()` to end the data stream. Finally, call `deflate()` to retrieve the remaining compressed data.

Prebuilt Dictionaries

As the deflater compresses data, it dynamically builds an internal dictionary that contains patterns that it encounters. Whenever the deflater encounters a pattern that is in the dictionary, it can represent the pattern with a smaller number of bits, thus resulting in a good compression ratio.

However, if the data is short or does not contain many repeats of the same pattern, the deflater cannot build a useful dictionary. In this case, the compression ratio may not be very good. To help with this situation, you can supply the deflater with a prebuilt dictionary. See `setDictionary()` for more on how to create a prebuilt dictionary.

Compression Level

The deflater can compress data at ten different levels. Generally, compression runs the fastest at the lowest level (level `0`), but this yields the worst compression ratio. On the other hand, compression runs the slowest at the highest level (level 9), thereby yielding the best compression ratio.

Compression Strategy

The compression strategy affects the compression algorithm used to compress the input data. Different compression strategies work better for different types of input. There are three available compression strategies: `DEFAULT_STRATEGY`, `FILTERED`, and `HUFFMAN_ONLY`. Here is an excerpt about these strategies in the ZLIB documentation (`ftp://ftp.uu.net/pub/archiving/zip/doc/`) by Jean-loup Gailly and Mark Adler:

> Use the value `DEFAULT_STRATEGY` for normal data, `FILTERED` for data produced by a filter (or predictor), and `HUFFMAN_ONLY` to force Huffman encoding only (no string match). Filtered data consists mostly of small values with a somewhat random distribution. In this case, the compression algorithm is tuned to compress them better. The effect of `FILTERED` is to force more Huffman coding and less string matching; it is somewhat intermediate between `DEFAULT_STRATEGY` and `HUFFMAN_ONLY`. The strategy parameter only affects the compression ratio but not the correctness of the compressed output even if it is not set appropriately.

ZLIB Header

The ZLIB header is described in *RFC 1950*. This specification is described in `http://ds.internic.net/rfc/rfc1950.txt`. The header is optional; neither the GZIP or ZIP formats use them. However, without the ZLIB header a prebuilt dictionary cannot be used.

MEMBER SUMMARY	
Constructor	
`Deflater()`	Constructs a `Deflater` instance.
Compression Method	
`deflate()`	Retrieves compressed data from this deflater.
Stream Methods	
`end()`	Frees all internal resources used by this deflater.
`finalize()`	Called by Java virtual machine to clean up this deflater's state when it is ready to be discarded.
`finish()`	Indicates the end of the uncompressed data.
`finished()`	Determines if any more compressed data is available.
`needsInput()`	Determines if the input buffer is empty.
`reset()`	Resets this deflater so that it can be reused.
Property Methods	
`getAdler()`	Retrieves the current checksum value of the uncompressed data written so far.
`getTotalIn()`	Retrieves the number of uncompressed bytes delivered to this deflater.

MEMBER SUMMARY	
getTotalOut()	Retrieves the number of compressed bytes read from this deflater.
setInput()	Delivers uncompressed data to this deflater to compress.
setLevel()	Sets the compression level of this deflater.
setStrategy()	Sets the compression strategy for this deflater.
Dictionary Method	
setDictionary()	Sets a prebuilt dictionary for compression.
Compression-Level Constants	
BEST_COMPRESSION	Specifies the smallest compressed size.
BEST_SPEED	Specifies the fastest compression speed.
DEFAULT_COMPRESSION	Specifies a default compression level.
NO_COMPRESSION	Specifies no compression.
Compression-Strategy Constants	
DEFAULT_STRATEGY	Specifies a default compression strategy.
FILTERED	Specifies less string matching and more Huffman encoding.
HUFFMAN_ONLY	Specifies only Huffman encoding.
Compression Method Constant	
DEFLATED	Specifies that zip entries should be compressed.

See Also

DeflaterOutputStream, Inflater.

Example

This example demonstrates how to use a deflater with and without a prebuilt dictionary. The JavaDeflater class extends the Deflater class. The JavaDeflater uses a prebuilt dictionary.

The program uses the JavaDeflater and Deflater classes to compress each file specified on the command line. The results of the compression are printed out.

Main.java

```
import java.io.*;
import java.util.zip.*;

class Main {
    static void deflate(Deflater def, InputStream in) throws IOException {
            byte[] inbuf = new byte[1024];
            byte[] outbuf = new byte[1024];
            int inlen;

            // Read and uncompressed data and give it to the deflater.
            while ((inlen = in.read(inbuf)) >= 0) {
```

```
                def.setInput(inbuf, 0, inlen);
                while (!def.needsInput()) {
                    // Read the deflated data and discard it.
                    def.deflate(outbuf);
                }
            }

            // There is no more uncompressed data.
            def.finish();

            // Read the rest of the compressed data.
            while (!def.finished()) {
                def.deflate(outbuf);
            }

            // Print statistics.
            System.out.println("   " + def.getTotalIn() + " -> " +
                                   def.getTotalOut());
            System.out.println("   adler: 0x" +
                                   Integer.toHexString(def.getAdler()));
        }

        public static void main(String[] args) {
            if (args.length == 0) {
                System.err.println("Usage: java Main <filename1>...");
                System.exit(1);
            }

            JavaDeflater javadef = new JavaDeflater();
            Deflater def = new Deflater();

            for (int i=0; i<args.length; i++) {
                try {
                    // Without dictionary.
                    System.out.println(args[i] + " (no dictionary)");
                    deflate(def, new FileInputStream(args[i]));

                    // With dictionary.
                    System.out.println(args[i] + " (with dictionary)");
                    deflate(javadef, new FileInputStream(args[i]));
                } catch (Exception e) {
                    e.printStackTrace();
                }

                // Reset the deflaters for another file.
                javadef.reset();
                def.reset();
            }
        }
    }
```

JavaDeflater.java

```
    import java.io.*;
    import java.util.zip.*;

    class JavaDeflater extends Deflater {
        public JavaDeflater() {
            super();
            init();
```

A B C D E F G H I J K L M N O P Q R S T U V W X Y Z

```
    }
    public JavaDeflater(int level) {
        super(level);
        init();
    }
    public JavaDeflater(int level, boolean noHeader) {
        super(level, noHeader);
        init();
    }

    void init() {
        byte[] buf = dictionary.getBytes();
        setDictionary(buf, 0, buf.length);
    }

    protected void finalize() {
        System.out.println("This deflater instance is no longer being used.");
        end();
    }

    // A dictionary of all Java keywords.
    String dictionary =
"newbooleanbytecharshortintlongfloatdoublestringvoidsuperprotected"
+"nulltruefalsethisifelseforwhiledoswitchcasedefaultbreakcontinuereturntry"
+"catchfinallythrowimportclassextendsimplementsinterfacepackageprivatepublic"
+"statictransientconstsynchronizednativefinalvolatileabstractthrowslength";
}
```

Output

```
> java Main Main.java Main.class
Main.java (no dictionary)
  2042 -> 684
  adler: 0xc51d14a3
Main.java (with dictionary)
  2042 -> 663
  adler: 0xc51d14a3
Main.class (no dictionary)
  1925 -> 1111
  adler: 0x86ecc941
Main.class (with dictionary)
  1925 -> 1111
  adler: 0x86ecc941
```

BEST_COMPRESSION

PURPOSE
Compression-level constant that specifies the smallest compressed size.

SYNTAX
`public static final int BEST_COMPRESSION`

DESCRIPTION
This constant (value 9) is used in `setLevel()` to specify compression to the smallest size. This default compression level in the current implementation is 6.

SEE ALSO
`BEST_SPEED`, `NO_COMPRESSION`, `setLevel()`.

EXAMPLE
See `ZipOutputStream.setLevel()`.

A B C D E F G H I J K L M N O P Q R S T U V W X Y Z

BEST_SPEED

PURPOSE Compression-level constant that specifies the fastest compression speed.

SYNTAX `public static final int BEST_SPEED`

DESCRIPTION This constant (value `1`) is used in `setLevel()` to specify compression at the fastest speed, thereby likely resulting in a sacrifice of compression size.

SEE ALSO `BEST_COMPRESSION`, `NO_COMPRESSION`, `setLevel()`.

EXAMPLE See `ZipOutputStream.setLevel()`.

DEFAULT_COMPRESSION

PURPOSE Compression-level constant that specifies a default compression level.

SYNTAX `public static final int DEFAULT_COMPRESSION`

DESCRIPTION This constant (value `-11`) is used in `setLevel()` to specify compression at a default level determined by the implementation. The default compression level in the current implementation is `6`. See the class description for more information about compression levels.

The default compression level in the current implementation is `6`.

EXAMPLE See `ZipOutputStream.setLevel()`.

DEFAULT_STRATEGY

PURPOSE Compression-strategy constant that specifies a default compression strategy.

SYNTAX `public static final int DEFAULT_STRATEGY`

DESCRIPTION This compression strategy constant (value `0`) specifies a default compression that works well for most types of data. See the class description for more details.

SEE ALSO `FILTERED`, `HUFFMAN_ONLY`, `setStrategy()`.

EXAMPLE See `setStrategy()`.

deflate()

PURPOSE Retrieves compressed data from this deflater.

SYNTAX
```
public int deflate(byte[] buf)
public synchronized native int deflate(byte[] buf, int off, int
   len)
```

DESCRIPTION After this deflater is given uncompressed data via `setInput()`, this method should be called to retrieve the compressed data. This method should be called continually until `needsInput()` returns `true`. See the class description for more information on how to use this method.

If `off` is not specified, it defaults to `0`. If `len` is not specified, it defaults to `buf.length`.

PARAMETERS

`buf` The non-`null` buffer into which the compressed data is stored.

`len` The maximum number of bytes to store into `buf` starting at `buf[off]`. `0` ≤ `len` ≤ `buf.length-off`.

`off` The `0`-based index in `buf` to start storing compressed bytes. `0` ≤ `off` < `buf.length`.

RETURNS The number of compressed bytes actually retrieved.

SEE ALSO `finished()`, `needsInput()`, `setInput()`.

EXAMPLE See the class example.

DEFLATED

PURPOSE Compression-method constant that specifies that zip entries should be compressed.

SYNTAX
```
public static final int DEFLATED
```

DESCRIPTION This constant (value `8`) is used in conjunction with `ZipOutputStream.setMethod()` to set the default compression method. `DEFLATED` specifies that subsequent zip entries should be compressed.

See `ZipOutputStream.setMethod()` for more details.

SEE ALSO `ZipOutputStream.setMethod()`, `ZipOutputStream.STORED`.

EXAMPLE `ZipOutputStream.finish()`.

A
B
C
D
E
F
G
H
I
J
K
L
M
N
O
P
Q
R
S
T
U
V
W
X
Y
Z

Deflater()

PURPOSE Constructs a `Deflater` instance.

SYNTAX
```
public Deflater()
public Deflater(int lvl)
public Deflater(int lvl, boolean noHeader)
```

DESCRIPTION The deflater's compression level is initialized to `lvl`. See `setLevel()` for more details about the compression level. If `lvl` is not specified, it defaults to `DEFAULT_COMPRESSION`.

`noHeader` controls whether the compressed data should be preceded by a ZLIB header (see the class description for more information about this header). If `noHeader` is `true`, the header is not included with the compressed data.

The `Inflater` class can be used to read data compressed by the `Deflater`. However, the values of the `noHeader` parameters in both the deflater and inflater must match. That is, if the compressed data is written without a ZLIB header, the inflater must be created with `noHeader` being `true`.

If `noHeader` is `true`, a dictionary cannot be used with this deflater. If `noHeader` is not specified, it defaults to `false`.

PARAMETERS
- `lvl` A compression level in the range `0` to `9`.
- `noHeader` If `true`, the ZLIB header is not written out.

SEE ALSO `Inflater.Inflater()`.

EXAMPLE See the class example.

end()

PURPOSE Frees all internal resources used by this deflater.

SYNTAX
```
public synchronized native void end()
```

DESCRIPTION This method discards any unprocessed input left in the deflater and frees all resources used by this deflater. After this method call, this deflater can no longer be used.

This method is automatically called by `finalize()` when the Java virtual machine reclaims this `Deflater` instance.

SEE ALSO `finalize()`.

EXAMPLE See the class example.

FILTERED

PURPOSE Compression-strategy constant that specifies less string matching and more Huffman encoding.

SYNTAX `public static final int FILTERED`

DESCRIPTION This compression-strategy constant (value `1`) specifies that the decompressor should use less string matching and more Huffman encoding. See the class description for more details.

SEE ALSO `DEFAULT_COMPRESSION`, `HUFFMAN_ONLY`, `setStrategy()`.

EXAMPLE See `setStrategy()`.

finalize()

PURPOSE Called by Java virtual machine to clean up this deflater's state when it is ready to be discarded..

SYNTAX `protected void finalize()`

DESCRIPTION This method should not be called directly. It is automatically called by the Java virtual machine when this `Deflater` instance is ready to be discarded.

This method calls `end()` by default. If you override this method, you should call `end()` to ensure the internal resources are freed.

SEE ALSO `end()`.

OVERRIDES `java.lang.Object.finalize()`.

EXAMPLE See the class example.

finish()

PURPOSE Indicates the end of the uncompressed data.

SYNTAX `public synchronized void finish()`

DESCRIPTION This method should be called when all of the uncompressed data has been given to this deflater via the `setInput()` method call. No more data can be given to this deflater after this call. To reuse this deflater, call `reset()`.

SEE ALSO `finished()`, `setInput()`.

EXAMPLE See the class example.

finished()

PURPOSE Determines if any more compressed data is available.

SYNTAX `public synchronized boolean finished()`

DESCRIPTION This method returns `true` when no more compressed data is available from this deflater. In particular, `setInput()` and `deflate()` should no longer be called. To reuse this method, call `reset()`.

RETURNS `true` if no more compressed data is available; `false` otherwise.

SEE ALSO `deflate(), reset(), setInput().`

EXAMPLE See the class example.

getAdler()

PURPOSE Retrieves the current checksum value of the uncompressed data written so far.

SYNTAX `public synchronized native int getAdler()`

DESCRIPTION The algorithm used to compute the checksum value is ADLER-32. See `Adler32` for more details.

After `setDictionary()` is called, this method may be called to determine the checksum value of the dictionary. If the deflater and the inflater use different dictionaries at different times, the inflater can retrieve this checksum value and use it to determine which dictionary the deflater used.

The return value is undefined if this deflater was created with the `noHeader` option. See `Deflater()` for more details.

RETURNS The checksum value of the uncompressed data.

SEE ALSO `Adler32, setDictionary().`

EXAMPLE See the class example.

getTotalIn()

PURPOSE Retrieves the number of uncompressed bytes delivered to this deflater.

SYNTAX `public synchronized native int getTotalIn()`

DESCRIPTION This method returns the number of uncompressed bytes delivered to this deflater via the `setInput()` method call.

RETURNS The number of bytes delivered to this deflater.

SEE ALSO `setInput()`.

EXAMPLE See the class example.

getTotalOut()

PURPOSE Retrieves the number of compressed bytes read from this deflater.

SYNTAX `public synchronized native int getTotalOut()`

DESCRIPTION This method returns the number of compressed bytes read from this deflater via the `deflate()` method call.

RETURNS The number of bytes read from this deflater.

SEE ALSO `deflate()`.

EXAMPLE See the class example.

HUFFMAN_ONLY

PURPOSE Compression-strategy constant that specifies only Huffman encoding.

SYNTAX `public static final int HUFFMAN_ONLY`

DESCRIPTION This compression-strategy constant (value `2`) specifies that the compressor should compress the data using only Huffman encoding. See the class description for more details.

SEE ALSO `DEFAULT_COMPRESSION`, `FILTERED`, `setStrategy()`.

EXAMPLE See `setStrategy()`.

needsInput()

PURPOSE Determines if the input buffer is empty.

SYNTAX `public boolean needsInput()`

DESCRIPTION The input buffer is the `byte` array of uncompressed data supplied to `setInput()`. This method returns `true` as long as there are unread bytes in the input buffer.

Note that this method will return `true` if `finished()` returns `true`.

RETURNS `true` if the input buffer is empty; `false` otherwise.

SEE ALSO `setInput()`.

EXAMPLE See the class example.

NO_COMPRESSION

PURPOSE Compression-level constant that specifies no compression.

SYNTAX `public static final int NO_COMPRESSION`

DESCRIPTION This constant (value `0`) is used in `setLevel()` to specify that the input data should not be compressed.

SEE ALSO `BEST_COMPRESSION`, `BEST_SPEED`, `setLevel()`.

EXAMPLE See `ZipOutputStream.setLevel()`.

reset()

PURPOSE Resets this deflater so that it can be reused.

SYNTAX `public synchronized native void reset()`

DESCRIPTION This method discards any data on which this deflater may be working. After this method is called, this deflater can be reused to deflate a new stream of data.

This method does not modify the current values of the compression level or of the compression strategy.

SEE ALSO `setLevel()`, `setStrategy()`.

EXAMPLE See the class example.

setDictionary()

PURPOSE Sets a prebuilt dictionary for compression.

SYNTAX
```
public void setDictionary(byte[] buf)
public synchronized native void setDictionary(byte[] buf, int
    off, int len)
```

DESCRIPTION This method sets a prebuilt dictionary to be used to compress the input data. See the class description for more information on when the use of a prebuilt dictionary is appropriate. The dictionary is a `byte` array that contain patterns of bytes that are likely to occur in the input stream. For example, if the 4-byte ASCII string “Java” is likely to appear in the input stream, the dictionary should contain the 4 bytes that make up the word “Java.” There is no need to separate the byte sequences that make up the patterns in the `buf`; they can all be concatenated together in the dictionary. For optimal performance, the more commonly used patterns should appear near the end of the dictionary.

This deflater copies `len` bytes in `buf`, starting from `buf[off]`, into its internal dictionary. Only the last 32K are used. If `off` is not specified, it defaults to `0`. If `len` is not specified, it defaults to `buf.length`.

The dictionary is not included in the compressed output stream. However, after this method is called, `getAdler()` can be called to retrieve a checksum value on the dictionary. This checksum value will be included in the compressed output stream and so will be available to the decompressor (see `Inflater`). In cases in which the decompressor can choose from more than one dictionary, the decompressor can use the checksum value to determine which dictionary to use.

The checksum value of the dictionary can also be computed by using the `Adler32` class:

```
Adler32 crc = new Adler32();
crc.update(buf, off, len);
crc.getValue();
```

PARAMETERS

`buf` A non-`null` `byte` array containing the prebuilt dictionary.

`len` The number of bytes to use starting from `buf[off]`. Only the last `0xFFFF` bytes will be used. `0` ≤ `len` ≤ `buf.length-off`.

`off` A nonnegative 0-based index specifying the first byte in `buf` to use. `0` ≤ `off` < `buf.length`.

SEE ALSO `Adler32`, `deflate()`, `getAdler()`.

EXAMPLE See the class example.

setInput()

PURPOSE Delivers uncompressed data to this deflater to compress.

SYNTAX

```
public void setInput(byte[] buf)
public synchronized void setInput(byte[] buf, int off, int len)
```

DESCRIPTION This method delivers `len` bytes starting from `buf[off]` to this deflater to compress. If `off` is not specified, it defaults to `0`. If `len` is not specified, it defaults to `buf.length`.

All of the uncompressed data must be delivered to this deflater using this method call. After each call to this method, `deflate()` must be called to retrieve the compressed data. See `deflate()` for more details. When all of the uncompressed data has been delivered to this deflater, `finish()` must be called.

If `needsInput()` returns `false`, then there are more uncompressed data in the input buffer and `setInput()` should not be called yet. If `needsInput()` returns `true`, the uncompressed data previously set have been used up and `setInput()` should be called to refill the input buffer.

PARAMETERS

`buf`	The non-`null` buffer containing the uncompressed data.
`off`	The starting offset of the data in `buf`. `0` ≤ `off` < `buf.length`.
`len`	The number of bytes in `buf` starting at `buf[off]`. `0` ≤ `len` ≤ `buf.length-off`.

SEE ALSO `deflate()`, `finish()`, `finished()`, `needsInput()`.

EXAMPLE See the class example.

setLevel()

PURPOSE Sets the compression level of this deflater.

SYNTAX `public synchronized void setLevel(int lvl)`

DESCRIPTION The deflater can compress data at ten different levels. Generally, compression runs the fastest at the lowest level (level `0`), but this yields the worst compression ratio. On the other hand, compression runs the slowest at the highest level (level `9`), thereby yielding the best compression ratio.

This method must be called before a new piece of data is compressed using `setInput()`. It can be called again after `reset()`.

Note: This method does not work in Java 1.1.4. In particular, this method does not change the compression level from `DEFAULT_COMPRESSION`.

PARAMETERS

`lvl`	A compression level in the range `0` to `9`.

EXCEPTIONS

`IllegalArgumentException`
If the compression level is invalid.

SEE ALSO `BEST_COMPRESSION`, `BEST_SPEED`, `DEFAULT_COMPRESSION`.

EXAMPLE See `ZipOutputStream.setLevel()`.

setStrategy()

PURPOSE Sets the compression strategy for this deflater.

SYNTAX `public synchronized void setStrategy(int stgy)`

DESCRIPTION The compression strategy affects the compression algorithm used to compress the input data. Different compression strategies work better for different types of input. There are three available compression strategies: `DEFAULT_STRATEGY`, `FILTERED`, and `HUFFMAN_ONLY`. See the class description for more details.

This method must be called before a new piece of data is compressed using `setInput()`. It can be called again after `reset()`.

PARAMETERS

`stgy` The new compression strategy that must be one of `DEFAULT_STRATEGY`, `FILTERED`, or `HUFFMAN_ONLY`.

EXCEPTIONS

`IllegalArgumentException`

If `stgy` is not one of the compression-strategy constants.

SEE ALSO `DEFAULT_STRATEGY`, `FILTERED`, `HUFFMAN_ONLY`.

EXAMPLE This example opens a file and compresses it using each of the three different compression strategies. The results are printed to standard output.

```
import java.io.*;
import java.util.zip.*;

class Main {

    static void zipit(InputStream is, int strategy)
        throws ZipException, IOException {
        // Create the entry and output streams.
        Deflater def = new Deflater();
        DeflaterOutputStream os = new DeflaterOutputStream(
            new NullOutputStream(), def);

        def.setStrategy(strategy);

        int len = 0;
        byte[] buf = new byte[1024];
        long time = System.currentTimeMillis();

        // Set compression level and write entry.

        // Write data.
        while ((len = is.read(buf)) >= 0) {
            os.write(buf, 0, len);
        }
        os.close();

        System.out.println("strategy: " + strategy);
        System.out.println("    " + def.getTotalIn() + " -> " +
```

```
                                 def.getTotalOut());
            System.out.println("    time: " +
                                 (System.currentTimeMillis()-time) + "ms");
        }

        public static void main(String[] args) {
            if (args.length != 1) {
                System.err.println("Usage: java Main <filename>");
            } else {
                try {
                    zipit(new FileInputStream(args[0]), Deflater.DEFAULT_STRATEGY);
                    zipit(new FileInputStream(args[0]), Deflater.FILTERED);
                    zipit(new FileInputStream(args[0]), Deflater.HUFFMAN_ONLY);
                } catch (Exception e) {
                    e.printStackTrace();
                }
            }
        }
    }

    class NullOutputStream extends OutputStream {
        public void write(int b) {}
        public void write(byte[] buf, int off, int len) {}
    }
```

Output

```
> java Main Main.java
strategy: 0
    1408 -> 645
    time: 220ms
strategy: 1
    1408 -> 684
    time: 0ms
strategy: 2
    1408 -> 955
    time: 60ms

> java Main Main.class
strategy: 0
    1745 -> 1014
    time: 110ms
strategy: 1
    1745 -> 1039
    time: 0ms
strategy: 2
    1745 -> 1317
    time: 0ms
```

DeflaterOutputStream

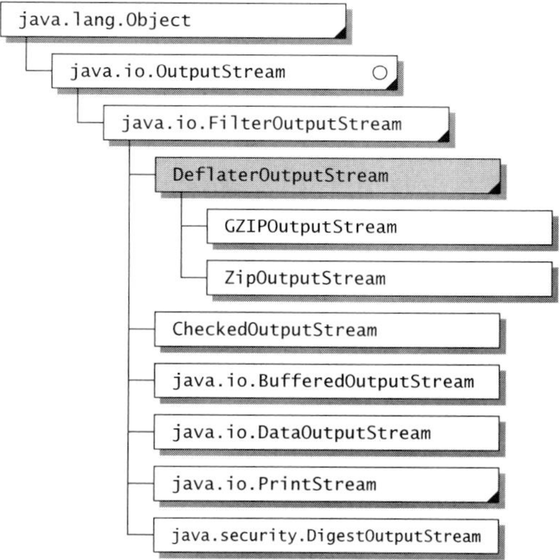

Syntax

```
public class DeflaterOutputStream extends FilterOutputStream
```

Description

The `DeflaterOutputStream` class implements an output stream filter for compressing data using the `Deflater` class. It makes it convenient to use a `Deflater` instance in a data streaming fashion. See the `Deflater` class for more information.

Usage

To use a deflater output stream, you create a `DeflaterOutputStream` instance on an existing output stream that will receive the compressed data. Then you write the uncompressed data to the deflater output stream using `write()`. See Figure 40.

When all of the uncompressed data has been written into the deflater output stream, it is necessary to call `close()` to force the deflater trailing information to be written out. When another data stream is to be written to the same deflater output stream, call `finish()` instead (see `finish()` for details).

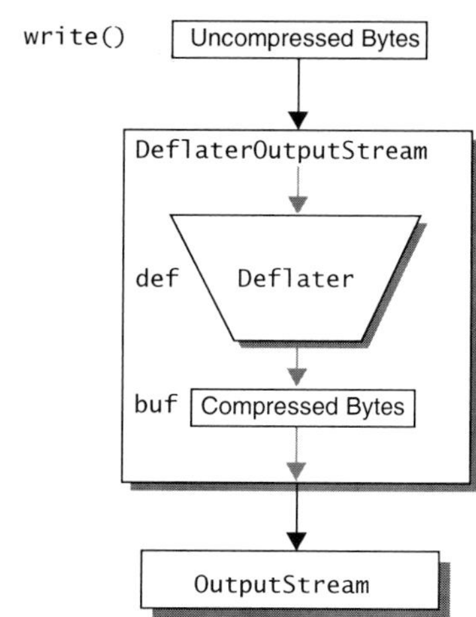

FIGURE 40: `DeflaterOutputStream`.

MEMBER SUMMARY	
Constructor	
`DeflaterOutputStream()`	Creates a `DeflaterOutputStream` instance.
Stream Methods	
`close()`	Writes the closing information of the compressed data and closes this stream.
`finish()`	Writes the closing information of the compressed data without closing this stream.
`write()`	Writes data to this deflater output stream to be compressed.
Protected Fields and Method	
`buf`	The buffer for retrieving compressed data from the deflater.
`def`	The deflater used to compress data.
`deflate()`	Compresses data and writes it to the underlying output stream.

See Also

`Deflater`, `java.io.FilterOutputStream`

Example

This example uses the deflater output stream to compress the pixels of an image as it is being serialized. See `InflaterInputStream` for an example that reads the serialized images created by this example.

Main.java

```
import java.awt.*;
import java.io.*;

class Main {
    public static void main(String[] args) {
        if (args.length < 1) {
            System.err.println("Usage: java Main <imagefile>...");
            System.exit(1);
        }

        for (int i=0; i<args.length; i++) {
            try {
                ObjectOutputStream os = new ObjectOutputStream(
                    new FileOutputStream(args[i]+".imgz"));

                System.out.println("Writing " + args[i] + ".imgz");
                os.writeObject(new SerImage(args[i]));
                os.close();
            } catch (IOException e) {
                e.printStackTrace();
            }
        }
```

```
        System.exit(0);
    }
}
```

SerImage.java

```
import java.awt.*;
import java.awt.image.*;
import java.io.*;
import java.util.zip.*;

public class SerImage implements Serializable {
    transient Image image;

    public SerImage(String filename) {
        image = Toolkit.getDefaultToolkit().getImage(filename);

        MediaTracker tracker = new MediaTracker(new Button());
        try {
            tracker.addImage(image, 0);
            tracker.waitForAll(0);
        } catch (Exception e) {
            throw new IllegalArgumentException("Could not create image.");
        }
    }

    private void writeObject(ObjectOutputStream out) throws IOException {
        Dimension d = new Dimension(image.getWidth(null),
                                    image.getHeight(null));
        DeflaterOutputStream dos = new DeflaterOutputStream(out);
        ObjectOutputStream os = new ObjectOutputStream(dos);

        // Write the dimensions of the image.
        os.writeObject(d);

        // Grab the image pixels.
        int[] pixels = new int[d.width * d.height];
        PixelGrabber pg = new PixelGrabber(
            image, 0, 0, d.width, d.height, pixels, 0, d.width);
        try {
            pg.grabPixels();
        } catch (Exception e) {
            throw new IOException("Could not grab pixels.");
        }

        // Write the pixel data to be compressed.
        os.writeObject(pixels);

        // Write closing information of compressed data.
        dos.finish();
    }

    private void readObject(ObjectInputStream in)
            throws IOException, ClassNotFoundException {
        ObjectInputStream is = new ObjectInputStream(
            new InflaterInputStream(in));

        // Read the Dimensions.
        Dimension d = (Dimension)is.readObject();
```

A B C D E F G H I J K L M N O P Q R S T U V W X Y Z

```
                // Read the pixels into a pixel array.
                int[] pixels = (int[])is.readObject();

                // Convert the pixels into an image.
                image = Toolkit.getDefaultToolkit().createImage(
                    new MemoryImageSource(d.width, d.height, pixels, 0, d.width));
            }
        }
```

A B C D E F G H I J K L M N O P Q R S T U V W X Y Z

buf

PURPOSE The buffer for retrieving compressed data from the deflater.

SYNTAX `protected byte[] buf`

DESCRIPTION This buffer is used by this stream to retrieve compressed data from its internal `Deflater` instance (see `def`). The compressed data is then written out to the underlying output stream.

The size of this buffer is determined by a parameter to the constructor.

SEE ALSO `DeflaterOutputStream()`.

close()

PURPOSE Writes the closing information of the compressed data and closes this stream.

SYNTAX `public void close() throws IOException`

DESCRIPTION This method calls `finish()` on this deflater output stream and closes it. All output streams downstream are also closed. This deflater output stream can no longer be used after this call.

EXCEPTIONS

`IOException`

If an IO error occurs while closing.

OVERRIDES `java.io.FilterOutputStream.close()`.

SEE ALSO `java.io.IOException`, `java.io.OutputStream.close()`, `finish()`.

EXAMPLE See the class example.

def

PURPOSE The deflater used to compress data.

SYNTAX `protected Deflater def`

DESCRIPTION This field holds a reference to the `Deflater` instance that this deflater output stream uses to compress the data written to this stream. This is the same `Deflater` instance that is supplied to the constructor.

SEE ALSO `Deflater.`

A B C D E F G H I J K L M N O P Q R S T U V W X Y Z

deflate()

PURPOSE Compresses data and writes it to the underlying output stream.

SYNTAX
```
protected void deflate() throws IOException
```

DESCRIPTION This method retrieves compressed data from the `Deflater` instance (see `def`) into `buf` (see `buf`) and writes it to the underlying output stream. This method is called every time `write()` is called.

EXCEPTIONS

`IOException`

If an IO error occurs while writing to the underlying output stream.

SEE ALSO `buf, def, java.io.IOException.`

DeflaterOutputStream()

PURPOSE Creates a `DeflaterOutputStream` instance.

SYNTAX
```
public DeflaterOutputStream(OutputStream out)
public DeflaterOutputStream(OutputStream out, Deflater defl)
public DeflaterOutputStream(OutputStream out, Deflater defl, int
    bufsize)
```

DESCRIPTION This constructor creates a deflater output stream around `out`. Data written to this new deflater output stream will be compressed by `defl` and then written to `out`. `defl` is assigned to the protected field `def` (see `def`). If `defl` is not specified, it defaults to a new instance of `Deflater`.

`bufsize` determines the size of the protected field `buf` (see `buf` for details). If `bufsize` is not specified, it defaults to `512`.

PARAMETERS

`bufsize` A nonnegative buffer size.
`defl` A non-`null` `Deflater` instance.
`out` A non-`null` output stream.

SEE ALSO `buf, def, Deflater.`

EXAMPLE See the class example.

finish()

PURPOSE Writes the closing information of the compressed data without closing this stream.

SYNTAX `public void finish() throws IOException`

DESCRIPTION This method must be called after all of the data has been written to this deflater output stream. It writes out necessary information that appears at the end of the compressed data. This deflater output stream can no longer be used after this call.

If it is necessary to write another compressed stream to the same underlying output stream, this method should be used instead of `close()`. In this case, a new deflater output stream must be created on the underlying stream. An example of where this feature might be used is in a client/server application that delivers many compressed pieces of data on the same connection.

EXCEPTIONS

`IOException`
If an IO error occurs while writing the closing information for the compressed data.

SEE ALSO `close()`, `java.io.IOException`.

EXAMPLE See the class example.

write()

PURPOSE Writes data to this deflater output stream to be compressed.

SYNTAX
```
public void write(int bval) throws IOException
public void write(byte[] buf, int off, int len) throws
   IOException
```

DESCRIPTION This method writes the byte `bval` or `len` bytes starting from `buf[off]` to this deflater output stream. This method blocks until all of the bytes have been written to this output stream.

PARAMETERS

`bval` A `byte` value to be written to this output stream. The low-order byte in `bval` is used.

`buf` A non-`null` `byte` array containing the data to be written.

`len` The number of bytes to write starting from `buf[off]`. `0` ≤ `len` ≤ `buf.length-off`.

`off` The `0`-based index of the first byte in `buf` to write. `0` ≤ `off` < `buf.length`.

EXCEPTIONS

`IOException`

If an IO error occurs while writing.

OVERRIDES `java.io.FilterOutputStream.write()`.

SEE ALSO `java.io.IOException`, `java.io.OutputStream.write()`.

EXAMPLE See the class example.

java.util
Dictionary

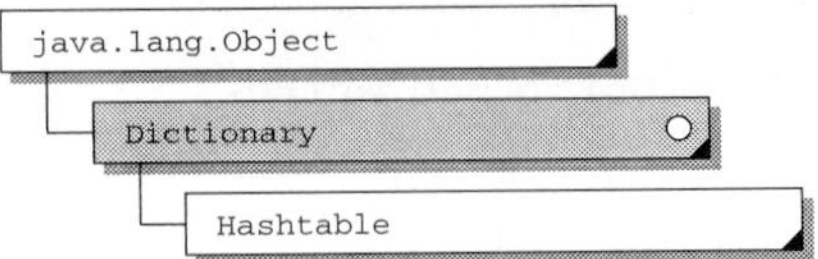

Syntax

```
public abstract class Dictionary
```

Description

`Dictionary` is an abstract class that provides methods for maintaining a set of *key/element* pairs. *key* is the non-`null` object used to find the pair in the dictionary. *element* is the non-`null` object associated with *key*. The `Dictionary` class provides methods for finding the element in a dictionary, enumerating the keys and elements in the dictionary, and adding, updating, and removing elements in the dictionary.

For example, a key/element pair could be an employee's name and his/her employee record. The dictionary would represent an employee database keyed on the employee's name. You can add an employee name/record to the dictionary, replace an existing record with a new one, or remove a record. In addition, you can enumerate all of the employees (names) in the dictionary and all of the employee records in the dictionary.

MEMBER SUMMARY	
Dictionary Methods	
`elements()`	Retrieves a list of all elements in this dictionary.
`get()`	Retrieves the element associated with a key in this dictionary.
`isEmpty()`	Determines whether this dictionary has any elements.
`keys()`	Retrieves a list of all keys in this dictionary.
`put()`	Adds a key/element pair to this dictionary.
`remove()`	Removes a key/element pair from this dictionary.
`size()`	Retrieves the number of elements in this dictionary.

See Also

`Hashtable`.

Example

This example implements a binary tree using the `Dictionary` class. There are three classes in this example, as shown in Figure 41. `Tree` is a binary tree implemented using the `Dictionary` class. Each node in the tree is represented by `TreeNode`, and the key in each node must be a string. The class `TreeEnumerator` is used when enumerating the nodes in a tree.

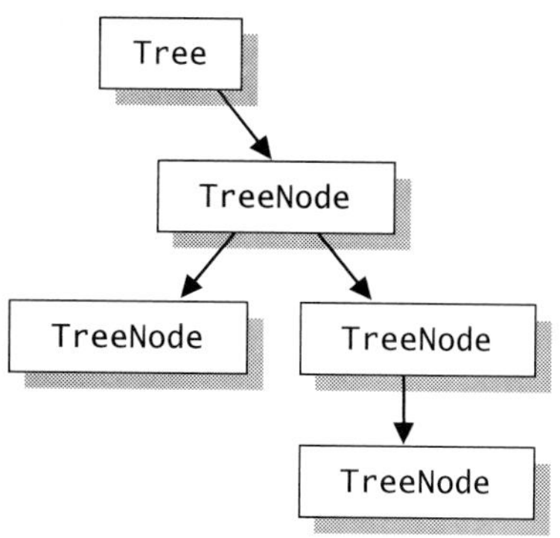

FIGURE 41: `Dictionary`.

```
import java.util.*;

class Main {
    static public void main(String[] args) {
        Tree t = new Tree();

        // Add 20 random numbers.
        for (int i=0; i<20; i++) {
            double r = Math.random();
            t.put(""+Math.floor(r * 10), new Double(r));
        }
        // Display the elements in the tree.
        String key;
        for (Enumeration e = t.keys(); e.hasMoreElements(); ) {
            key = (String)e.nextElement();
            System.out.print(key + ": ");
            System.out.println(t.get(key));
        }
    }
}

// This class implements a node in the binary tree.
// The node contains a reference to the key and element.
// The node also contains a reference to left and right branch
// of the tree.
class TreeNode {
    // 0 -> left, 1 -> right
    TreeNode[] branch = new TreeNode[2];
    String key;
    Object value;
    TreeNode(String k, Object v) {
        key = k;
        value = v;
    }
}

class Tree extends Dictionary {
    TreeNode root;
    int count;

    public int size() {
        return count;
    }

    public boolean isEmpty() {
        return root == null;
    }
```

```
    public Enumeration keys() {
        return new TreeEnumerator(this, true);
    }

    public Enumeration elements() {
        return new TreeEnumerator(this, false);
    }


    // Recurse the tree, looking for 'key'.
    public Object get2(TreeNode n, String key) {
        if (n == null) return null;
        int cmp = key.compareTo(n.key);

        if (cmp == 0) return n.value;
        return get2(n.branch[cmp = Math.min(1, Math.max(0, cmp))], key);
    }
    public Object get(Object key) {
        return get2(root, (String)key);
    }

    // n is never null.  Smaller elements are added to the left branch.
    public Object put2(TreeNode n, String key, Object value) {
        int cmp = key.compareTo(n.key);
        if (cmp == 0) {
            Object old = n.value;
            n.value = value;
            return old;
        }
        cmp = Math.min(1, Math.max(0, cmp));
        if (n.branch[cmp] != null) {
            return put2(n.branch[cmp], key, value);
        } else {
            n.branch[cmp] = new TreeNode(key, value);
            count++;
            return null;
        }
    }
    public Object put(Object key, Object value) {
        if (root == null) {
            root = new TreeNode((String)key, value);
            count++;
            return null;
        } else {
            return put2(root, (String)key, value);
        }
    }

    public Object remove(Object key) {
        // not implemented
        return null;
    }
}

// The enumerator create a list of tree nodes, large enough
// to hold all the tree nodes in the tree.  The enumerator
// then recurses the tree and places all tree nodes in the list.
class TreeEnumerator implements Enumeration {
    boolean keys;
```

A B C D E F G H I J K L M N O P Q R S T U V W X Y Z

```
        int index;
        TreeNode[] list;

        void traverse(TreeNode n) {
            if (n == null) return;
            traverse(n.branch[0]);
            list[index++] = n;
            traverse(n.branch[1]);
        }
        TreeEnumerator(Tree tree, boolean keys) {
            this.keys = keys;
            list = new TreeNode[tree.count];
            traverse(tree.root);
            index = 0;
        }
        public boolean hasMoreElements() {
            return index < list.length;
        }
        public Object nextElement() {
            if (keys) {
                return list[index++].key;
            } else {
                return list[index++].value;
            }
        }
    }
```

A B C D E F G H I J K L M N O P Q R S T U V W X Y Z

elements()

PURPOSE Retrieves a list of all elements in this dictionary.

SYNTAX `abstract public Enumeration elements()`

DESCRIPTION This method retrieves a list of all elements in this dictionary. This list can be enumerated using methods in the `Enumeration` class. There is no guaranteed relationship between the order in which elements are added to this dictionary and the order of elements in this list. Neither is there any guaranteed relationship between the order of this list and the order of the list generated using `keys()`. Any such relationships depend on the implementation of the subclass of `Dictionary`. The effects of modifying the dictionary while the dictionary is being enumerated also depends on the subclass.

RETURNS A non-`null` list of all the elements in this dictionary.

SEE ALSO `keys()`, `size()`, `Enumeration`.

EXAMPLE See the `Dictionary` and `Hashtable` class examples.

get()

PURPOSE Retrieves the element associated with a key in this dictionary.

SYNTAX `abstract public Object get(Object key)`

DESCRIPTION This method retrieves the element associated with the key `key` in this dictionary. It returns `null` if `key` is not in this dictionary.

PARAMETERS

`key` The non-`null` key for which to search.

RETURNS The element associated with `key` or `null` if `key` is not found in this dictionary.

SEE ALSO `put()`.

EXAMPLE See the class example and `Hashtable.get()`.

isEmpty()

PURPOSE Determines whether this dictionary has any elements.

SYNTAX `abstract public boolean isEmpty()`

RETURNS `true` if there are no elements in this dictionary; `false` if there are elements.

SEE ALSO `size()`.

EXAMPLE See the `Dictionary` and `Hashtable` class examples.

keys()

PURPOSE Retrieves a list of all keys in this dictionary.

SYNTAX `abstract public Enumeration keys()`

DESCRIPTION This method retrieves a list of all keys in this dictionary. This list can be enumerated using methods in the `Enumeration` class. There is no guaranteed relationship between the order in which keys are added to this dictionary and the order of keys in this list. Neither is there any guaranteed relationship between the order of this list and the order of the list generated using `elements()`. Any such relationships depend on the implementation of the subclass of `Dictionary`. The effects of modifying the dictionary while the dictionary is being enumerated also depends on the subclass.

RETURNS A non-`null` list of all keys in this dictionary.

SEE ALSO `elements()`, `size()`, `Enumeration`.

EXAMPLE See the `Dictionary` and `Hashtable` class examples.

put()

PURPOSE Adds a key/element pair to this dictionary.

SYNTAX `abstract public Object put(Object key, Object elem)`

DESCRIPTION This method adds the pair of key `key` and element `elem` to this dictionary. `put()` returns the element previously associated with `key`, if any; it returns `null` if `key` was not in the dictionary. Any existing entry with the key `key` is removed. After this call to `put()`, `elem` can be retrieved from this dictionary using the call

```
elem = dictionary.get(key);
```

or returned as part of the enumeration returned by `elements()`. `key` can be obtained as part of the enumeration returned by `keys()`.

PARAMETERS

`elem` The non-`null` element to add.

`key` The non-`null` key to add.

RETURNS The element previously associated with `key`; `null` if `key` was not in this dictionary.

SEE ALSO `elements()`, `get()`, `keys()`.

EXAMPLE See the `Dictionary` and `Hashtable` class examples.

remove()

PURPOSE Removes a key/element pair from this dictionary.

SYNTAX `abstract public Object remove(Object key)`

DESCRIPTION This method removes the element with the key `key` from this dictionary and returns the element. If `key` is not in this dictionary, this method returns `null`.

PARAMETERS

`key` The non-`null` key associated with the element to be removed.

RETURNS The element associated with `key`; `null` if key was not in the dictionary.

SEE ALSO `get()`, `put()`.

EXAMPLE See the class example and `Hashtable.get()`.

size()

PURPOSE Retrieves the number of elements in this dictionary.

SYNTAX `abstract public int size()`

RETURNS The number of elements in this dictionary.

SEE ALSO `elements()`, `keys()`.

EXAMPLE See the `Dictionary` and `Hashtable` class examples.

Double

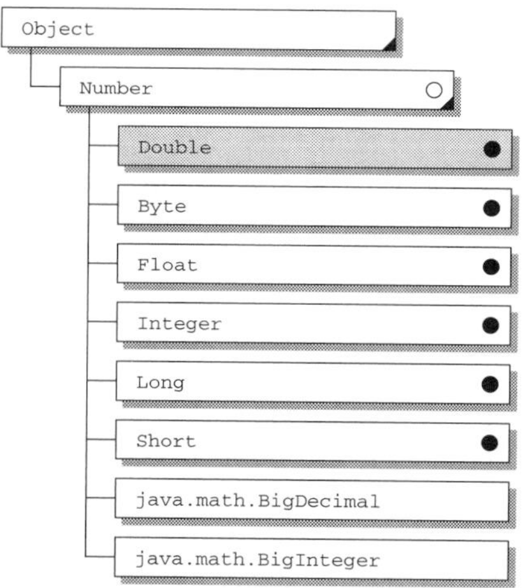

A B C D E F G H I J K L M N O P Q R S T U V W X Y Z

Syntax

```
public final class Double extends Number
```

Description

A `double` in Java is a 64-bit floating-point number. The `Double` class provides an object wrapper for `double` data values. This wrapper allows `double`s to be passed to methods in Java class libraries that accept Java objects as parameters. In addition, the `Double` class provides methods that convert values to and from `double`s and perform other operations on `double`s.

Usage

A `Double` instance cannot be used in an arithmetic expression in place of `double`. For example, the following is not allowed:

```
Double d1 = new Double(243.34);
Double d2 = new Double(5);
Double d3 = d1 * d2; // Illegal
```

To perform an arithmetic operation using a `Double` instance, you first must use access methods defined in the `Double` class to obtain its numeric value, as follows:

```
double d3 = d1.doubleValue() * d2.doubleValue();
long lnum = d1.longValue() + d2.intValue();
```

MEMBER SUMMARY	
Constructor	
`Double()`	Constructs a `Double` instance using a `double` or a string.
Constant Fields	
`MAX_VALUE`	The maximum value a `double` can have.
`MIN_VALUE`	The smallest positive value a `double` can have.
`NaN`	The special Not-a-Number (`NaN`) value.
`NEGATIVE_INFINITY`	Negative infinity for a `double`.
`POSITIVE_INFINITY`	Positive infinity for a `double`.
`TYPE`	The `Class` object representing the primitive type `double`.
Number Methods	
`byteValue()`	Retrieves the value of this object as a `byte`.
`doubleValue()`	Retrieves the value of this object as a `double`.
`floatValue()`	Retrieves the value of this object as a `float`.
`intValue()`	Retrieves the value of this object as an `int`.
`longValue()`	Retrieves the value of this object as a `long`.
`shortValue()`	Retrieves the value of this object as a `short`.
Conversion Methods	
`doubleToLongBits()`	Retrieves the bit representation of a `double`.
`longBitsToDouble()`	Retrieves the `double` corresponding to a given bit representation.
`toString()`	Generates the string representation of a `double` or a `Double` object.
`valueOf()`	Creates a `Double` object using its string representation.
Comparison Methods	
`equals()`	Compares this object with another object for equality.
`isInfinite()`	Determines whether a `double` is infinitely large in magnitude.
`isNaN()`	Determines whether a `double` is the special Not-a-Number (`NaN`) value.
Hash Code Method	
`hashCode()`	Computes the hash code for this object.

See Also

`Byte`, `Float`, `Integer`, `Number`, `Long`, `Short`.

byteValue()

PURPOSE Retrieves the value of this object as a `byte`.

SYNTAX `public byte byteValue()`

RETURNS This method retrieves the value of this object as a `byte` by casting its `double` to a `byte` value. If the `double` exceeds what a `byte` value can accommodate, the sign of the `byte` value might differ from that of the `double`. Their numeric values might be very different as a result of the cast.

SEE ALSO `doubleValue()`, `floatValue()`, `intValue()`, `longValue()`, `Number`, `shortValue()`.

EXAMPLE See `doubleValue()`.

Double()

PURPOSE Constructs a `Double` instance using a `double` or a string.

SYNTAX
```
public Double(double dVal)
public Double(String str) throws NumberFormatException
```

DESCRIPTION The first form of the constructor constructs an instance of `Double` using a `double dVal`. The second form constructs an instance of `Double` using its string representation `str`. The format of `str` is described in `valueOf()`.

PARAMETERS

`dVal` The `double` that the new object will have.

`str` The non-`null` string representation of the `double` that the new object will have.

EXCEPTIONS

`NumberFormatException`

If `str` contains an invalid string representation of a `double`.

SEE ALSO `valueOf()`.

EXAMPLE

```
// Create new Double object called 'pi'
Double pi = new Double(3.14159);
try {
    // Create new Double object using a string
    Double dobj = new Double("29.5");
    if (dobj.equals(pi))
        ...
} catch (NumberFormatException e) {
  ...
}
```

A B C D E F G H I J K L M N O P Q R S T U V W X Y Z

A
B
C
D
E
F
G
H
I
J
K
L
M
N
O
P
Q
R
S
T
U
V
W
X
Y
Z

doubleToLongBits()

PURPOSE Retrieves the bit representation of a `double`.

SYNTAX `public static native long doubleToLongBits(double value)`

DESCRIPTION A `double` is a 64-bit floating-point number. This method returns in a `long` (64-bit integer) the bit representation of the `double` value `value`. The bit representation is the IEEE standard format for 64-bit floating-point numbers. This method is the inverse of the method `longBitsToDouble()`.

PARAMETERS

`value` The `double` for which to get the bit representation.

RETURNS A `long` value containing the bit representation.

SEE ALSO `longBitsToDouble()`.

EXAMPLE

```
double dnum = 22.45915;
long bitrepr = Double.doubleToLongBits(dnum);       // get bit repr
double reconst = Double.longBitsToDouble(bitrepr); // reconstruct dnum

if (reconst == dnum) // should be true
    System.out.println("correct");
```

doubleValue()

PURPOSE Retrieves the value of this object as a `double`.

SYNTAX `public double doubleValue()`

RETURNS The value of this object as a `double`.

SEE ALSO `byteValue()`, `floatValue()`, `intValue()`, `longValue()`, `Number`, `shortValue()`.

EXAMPLE

```
Double dobj = new Double(1923311.47712);

double dval = dobj.doubleValue(); // 1923311.47712
float fval = dobj.floatValue();   // 1923311.5
int ival = dobj.intValue();       // 1923311
long lval = dobj.longValue();     // 1923311
byte bval = dobj.byteValue();     // -17
short sval = dobj.shortValue();   // 22767
```

equals()

PURPOSE Compares this object with another object for equality.

SYNTAX `public boolean equals(Object obj)`

DESCRIPTION This method compares the `double` of this `Double` object against that of the object `obj`. It returns `true` if the two values are equal. It returns `false` if the two values are not equal or if `obj` is `null` or is not a `Double` object. This method considers two `NaN` `doubles` to be equal so that a `Double` object containing `NaN` can be used in hash tables. This is contrary to the IEEE specification.

PARAMETERS

`obj` The possibly `null` object with which this object will be compared.

RETURNS `true` if `obj` has the same `double` as this object; `false` otherwise.

OVERRIDES `Object.equals()`.

SEE ALSO `hashCode()`.

EXAMPLE

```
Double d1 = new Double(4.8123);
Double d2 = new Double(4.8123);

// Check whether the value of two Doubles are equal
if (d1.equals(d2))
    System.out.println("equal");
```

floatValue()

PURPOSE Retrieves the value of this object as a `float`.

SYNTAX `public float floatValue()`

DESCRIPTION This method returns the value of this object as a `float` by casting its `double` to a `float` value. This might result in a loss of precision because `double` is a 64-bit floating-point value, while `float` is a 32-bit floating-point value.

RETURNS The value of this object as a `float`.

SEE ALSO `byteValue()`, `doubleValue()`, `intValue()`, `longValue()`, `Number`, `shortValue()`.

EXAMPLE See `doubleValue()`.

A B C D E F G H I J K L M N O P Q R S T U V W X Y Z

hashCode()

PURPOSE Computes the hash code for this object.

SYNTAX `public int hashCode()`

DESCRIPTION This method returns the hash code for this `Double` object. The hash code for a `Double` object is calculated using the object's `double`. Two `Doubles` with the same `double` have the same hash code. However, two `Doubles` with the same hash code may not necessarily have the same `double`.

RETURNS An `int` representing the hash code.

OVERRIDES `Object.hashCode()`.

SEE ALSO `equals()`, `java.util.Hashtable`.

EXAMPLE

```
// Keep track of hits on hash code
int[] hits = new int[1023];
Double dnum = new Double(1.61803);
int hashval = dnum.hashCode();
++hits[Math.abs(hashval%hits.length)];  // count hits
```

intValue()

PURPOSE Retrieves the value of this object as an `int`.

SYNTAX `public int intValue()`

DESCRIPTION This method returns the value of this object as an `int` by casting its `double` to an `int` value. If the `double` exceeds what an `int` value can accommodate, the sign of the `int` value might differ from that of the `double`. Their numeric values might be very different as a result of the cast.

RETURNS The value of this object as an `int`.

SEE ALSO `byteValue()`, `doubleValue()`, `floatValue()`, `longValue()`, `Number`, `shortValue()`.

EXAMPLE See `doubleValue()`.

isInfinite()

PURPOSE Determines whether a `double` is infinitely large in magnitude.

SYNTAX
```
public boolean isInfinite()
public static boolean isInfinite(double value)
```

DESCRIPTION

The first form of this method returns `true` if the `double` of this `Double` object is infinitely large in magnitude. It returns `false` otherwise. The second form returns `true` if the `double` value `value` is infinitely large in magnitude. It returns `false` otherwise.

PARAMETERS

`value` The `double` to check for infinity.

RETURNS

`true` if the `double` is infinitely large in magnitude; `false` otherwise.

SEE ALSO

`NEGATIVE_INFINITY`, `POSITIVE_INFINITY`.

EXAMPLE

```
Double dnum = new Double(1.6878);
 ...
if (dnum.isInfinite())        // method version
    throw new ArithmeticException();
if (Double.isInfinite(85.1))    // class version
    break;
```

isNaN()

PURPOSE

Determines whether a `double` is the special Not-a-Number (`NaN`) value.

SYNTAX

```
public boolean isNaN()
public static boolean isNaN(double value)
```

DESCRIPTION

The first form of this method returns `true` if the `double` of this `Double` object is the special `NaN` value. It returns `false` otherwise. The second form returns `true` if the `double` value `value` is the special `NaN` value. It returns `false` otherwise.

PARAMETERS

`value` The `double` to check whether it is `NaN`.

RETURNS

`true` if the `double` is `NaN`; `false` otherwise.

SEE ALSO

`NaN`.

EXAMPLE

```
Double dnum = new Double(1.523E24);
if (dnum.isNaN())                    // method version
    throw new ArithmeticException();
if (Double.isNaN(dnum.doubleValue())) // class version
 ...
```

longBitsToDouble()

PURPOSE Retrieves the `double` corresponding to a given bit representation.

SYNTAX `public static native double longBitsToDouble(long bits)`

DESCRIPTION This method returns the `double` corresponding to the bit representation `bits`. This method is the inverse of `doubleToLongBits()`.

PARAMETERS

`bits` The bits to use to generate the `double`.

RETURNS The `double` represented by `bits`.

SEE ALSO `doubleToLongBits()`.

EXAMPLE See `doubleToLongBits()`.

longValue()

PURPOSE Retrieves the value of this object as a `long`.

SYNTAX `public long longValue()`

DESCRIPTION This method returns the value of this object as a `long` by casting its `double` to a `long` value.

RETURNS The value of this object as a `long`.

SEE ALSO `byteValue()`, `doubleValue()`, `floatValue()`, `intValue()`, `Number`, `shortValue()`.

EXAMPLE See `doubleValue()`.

MAX_VALUE

PURPOSE The maximum value a `double` can have.

SYNTAX `public static final double MAX_VALUE`

DESCRIPTION This constant represents the maximum value a `double` can have, which is `1.79769313486231570e+308d`.

SEE ALSO `MIN_VALUE`.

EXAMPLE

```
// test if number is less than MAX_VALUE
double dnum = 3.1415927;
if (dnum < Double.MAX_VALUE)
    dnum *= 100;
```

MIN_VALUE

PURPOSE The smallest positive value a `double` can have.

SYNTAX `public static final double MIN_VALUE`

DESCRIPTION This constant represents the smallest positive value a `double` can have, which is `4.94065645841246544e-324`.

SEE ALSO `MAX_VALUE`.

EXAMPLE

```
// test if number is greater than MIN_VALUE
double dnum = 2.71828;
if (dnum > Double.MIN_VALUE)
    dnum = 1/dnum;
```

NaN

PURPOSE The special Not-a-Number value.

SYNTAX `public static final double NaN`

DESCRIPTION This constant represents the special Not-a-Number (`NaN`) value. The value of `NaN` is not equal to anything, including `NaN` itself. However, for `Double.equals()` to be useful in hash tables, `Double.equals()` considers two `NaN`s equal. This is contrary to the IEEE specification. The equals operator (==), however, is consistent with the IEEE; that is, two `NaN`s are not equal when the equals operator is used.

SEE ALSO `isNaN()`.

EXAMPLE

```
double dnum = Double.NaN;
// test if number is Not-A-Number
if (Double.isNaN(dnum))                 // succeeds
    System.out.println("correct");
if (Double.isNaN(Double.NaN))           // succeeds
    System.out.println("correct");

// A NaN is not equal to itself except when using equals()
if (dnum == Double.NaN)                 // fails
    System.out.println("incorrect");
Double d1 = new Double(Double.NaN);
Double d2 = new Double(Double.NaN);
if (d1.equals(d2))                      // succeeds
    System.out.println("correct");
```

NEGATIVE_INFINITY

PURPOSE Negative infinity for a `double`.

SYNTAX `public static final double NEGATIVE_INFINITY`

SYNTAX `isInfinite(), POSITIVE_INFINITY.`

EXAMPLE

```
double dnum;
 ...
// reset to 0 if number reached neg infinity
if (dnum == Double.NEGATIVE_INFINITY)
    dnum = 0;
```

POSITIVE_INFINITY

PURPOSE Positive infinity for a `double`.

SYNTAX `public static final double POSITIVE_INFINITY`

SEE ALSO `isInfinite(), NEGATIVE_INFINITY.`

EXAMPLE

```
double dnum;
 ...
// reset to 0 if number reached pos infinity
if (dnum == Double.POSITIVE_INFINITY)
    dnum = 0;
```

shortValue()

PURPOSE Retrieves the value of this object as a `short`.

SYNTAX `public short shortValue()`

RETURNS This method returns the value of this object as a `short` by casting its `double` to a `short`. If the `double` exceeds what a `short` can accommodate, the sign of the `short` might differ from that of the `double`. Their numeric values be very different as a result of the cast.

SEE ALSO `byteValue(), doubleValue(), floatValue(), intValue(), longValue(), Number.`

EXAMPLE See `doubleValue()`.

toString()

PURPOSE
Generates the string representation of a `double` or a `Double` object.

SYNTAX
```
public String toString()
public static native String toString(double dval)
```

DESCRIPTION
The two forms of this method return the string representation of a `double`. The first form returns the string representation of this `Double` object (basically, the string form of its `double`). The second form returns the string representation of `dval`.

The format of the string is a leading negative sign (if the number is negative) followed by a sequence of digits, a period character, more digits, and, optionally, an exponent. Special cases are made for `NaN`, `POSITIVE_INFINITY`, and `NEGATIVE_INFINITY`. See *The Java Language Specification, First Edition*, Section 20.10.15, for a full description of the string representation.

PARAMETERS

`dval` The `double` for which to return the string representation.

RETURNS
The non-`null` string representation of a `double`.

OVERRIDES
`Object.toString()`.

SEE ALSO
`valueOf()`.

EXAMPLE
```
Double dnum = new Double(0.843);
String str = dnum.toString();         // get string form of Double obj
String str2 = Double.toString(0.432); // string form of double
String pstr = "The values are " + str + ", " + str2;
```

TYPE

PURPOSE
The `Class` object representing the primitive type `double`.

SYNTAX
```
public static final Class TYPE
```

DESCRIPTION
This constant can be used where the `Class` object—`double.class`—of the primitive type `double` is required, such as for reflection. Although there are no restrictions on the use of `Double.TYPE`, the preferred syntax for naming the class is `double.class`.

SEE ALSO
`Class`.

EXAMPLE
```
public static void main(String[] args) {
    Class c = Double.TYPE;
    System.out.println("TYPE: " + c);
```

```
        System.out.println("isPrimitive: " + c.isPrimitive());
        System.out.println("superclass: " + c.getSuperclass());
        try {
            Object obj = c.newInstance();  // ERROR
            System.out.println("double: " + obj);
        } catch (InstantiationException e) {
            e.printStackTrace();
        } catch (IllegalAccessException e) {
            e.printStackTrace();
        }
    }
```

A B C D E F G H I J K L M N O P Q R S T U V W X Y Z

valueOf()

PURPOSE Creates a new `Double` object using its string representation.

SYNTAX `public static native Double valueOf(String str) throws NumberFormatException`

DESCRIPTION This method creates a new `Double` object by parsing `str` into a `double`. The format of the string is

[*Sign*] *Digits* **.** [*Digits*] [*ExponentPart*]

[*Sign*] **.** *Digits* [*ExponentPart*]

where *Sign* is a negative sign, *Digits* is a sequence of digits from "0123456789," and *ExponentPart* is one of "e" or "E" followed by a signed integer. Details of this format are in *The Java Language Specification, First Edition*, Section 20.10.16. Leading and trailing whitespace characters in `str` are ignored.

PARAMETERS

`str` The non-`null` string to be parsed.

RETURNS A new `Double` object with the `double` of the number parsed from `str`.

SEE ALSO `toString()`.

EXCEPTIONS

`NumberFormatException`
If `str` cannot be parsed into a `double`.

EXAMPLE

```
String str = "1.0871E3";
try {
    Double r = Double.valueOf(str);
    ...
} catch (NumberFormatException e) {
    System.err.println("Could not convert string to number " + str);
}
```

EmptyStackException

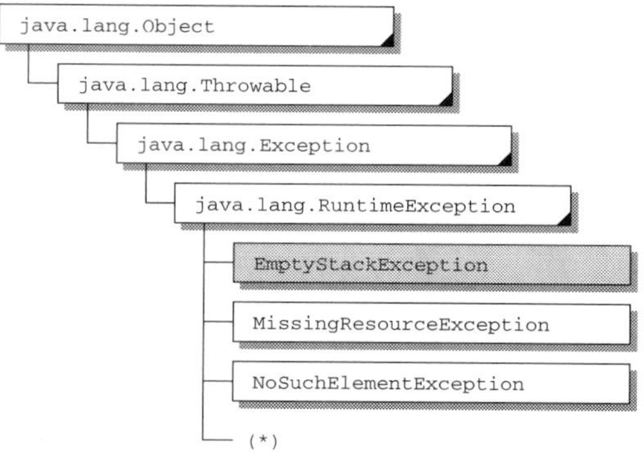

(*) 11 classes from other packages not shown.

A B C D E F G H I J K L M N O P Q R S T U V W X Y Z

Syntax

`public class EmptyStackException extends RuntimeException`

Description

`EmptyStackException` is a runtime exception that is thrown when the program attempts to access an item on a stack when the stack is empty (see the `Stack` class).

`EmptyStackException` should not be caught or declared in the `throws` clause of a method.

MEMBER SUMMARY	
Constructor	
`EmptyStackException()`	Constructs an `EmptyStackException` instance.

See Also

`java.lang.RuntimeException`, `Stack.pop()`, `Stack.peek()`.

Example

In this example, `main()` throws `EmptyStackException` when it attempts to pop an item off the stack the fourth time.

```
import java.util.Stack;

class Main {
    public static void main(String[] args) {
```

```
            System.out.println("EmptyStackException example");
            Stack s = new Stack();

            System.out.println("push: " + s.push(new Integer(1)));
            System.out.println("push: " + s.push(new Integer(2)));
            System.out.println("push: " + s.push(new Integer(3)));

            System.out.println("pop: " + s.pop());
            System.out.println("pop: " + s.pop());
            System.out.println("pop: " + s.pop());

            System.out.println("pop: " + s.pop()); // empty stack
        }
    }
```

A B C D E F G H I J K L M N O P Q R S T U V W X Y Z

EmptyStackException()

PURPOSE Constructs an `EmptyStackException` instance.

SYNTAX `public EmptyStackException()`

DESCRIPTION This constructor constructs an `EmptyStackException` instance with no detail message.

Enumeration

Enumeration ······ StringTokenizer

Syntax

`public interface Enumeration`

Description

The `Enumeration` interface provides methods for enumerating a list of objects. An individual object on this list to be enumerated is called an *element*. The order in which elements are enumerated depends on the subclass that implements `Enumeration`.

Usage

You typically use this interface in a `for` loop. Each step retrieves a single element from the enumeration via `nextElement()`. `hasMoreElements()` serves as the terminating condition for the loop. For example, the following code to print all elements of a vector `vec` typifies how the methods in the `Enumeration` interface are used:

```
for (Enumeration e = vec.elements(); e.hasMoreElements();) {
    System.out.println(e.nextElement());
}
```

Typically, `hasMoreElements()` should be invoked once each time before `nextElement()` is invoked. Some implementations (such as the `Enumeration` implemented by `Hashtable`) have side effects and depend on this behavior. For example, if you call `hasMoreElements()` twice in a row before calling `nextElement()`, you might miss one of the elements. Also, it is up to the class implementing `Enumeration` whether modifications to the object being enumerated (such as a dictionary) invalidates or has any effect on the enumeration in progress.

MEMBER SUMMARY	
Enumeration Methods	
`hasMoreElements()`	Determines whether there are more elements in the enumeration.
`nextElement()`	Retrieves the next element in the enumeration.

See Also

`Hashtable`, `Properties`, `SequenceInputStream`, `StringTokenizer`, `Vector`.

Example

In addition to the previous sample usage, see `TreeEnumerator` in the class example of `Dictionary` and see the class example of `Hashtable` for example implementations of `Enumeration`.

A B C D E F G H I J K L M N O P Q R S T U V W X Y Z

hasMoreElements()

PURPOSE Determines whether there are more elements in the enumeration.

SYNTAX `boolean hasMoreElements()`

RETURNS `true` if there are more elements in this enumeration; `false` otherwise.

SEE ALSO `nextElement()`.

EXAMPLE See the example in the class description.

nextElement()

PURPOSE Retrieves the next element in the enumeration.

SYNTAX `Object nextElement()`

DESCRIPTION This method returns the next element in this enumeration. You can retrieve all of the elements in this enumeration by successively calling `nextElement()` until `hasMoreElements()` returns `false`. If there are no more elements in the enumeration, a `NoSuchElementException` is thrown.

RETURNS The next element in this enumeration.

EXCEPTIONS

`NoSuchElementException`
If there are no more elements in this enumeration.

SEE ALSO `hasMoreElements()`.

EXAMPLE See the example in the class description.

java.io

EOFException

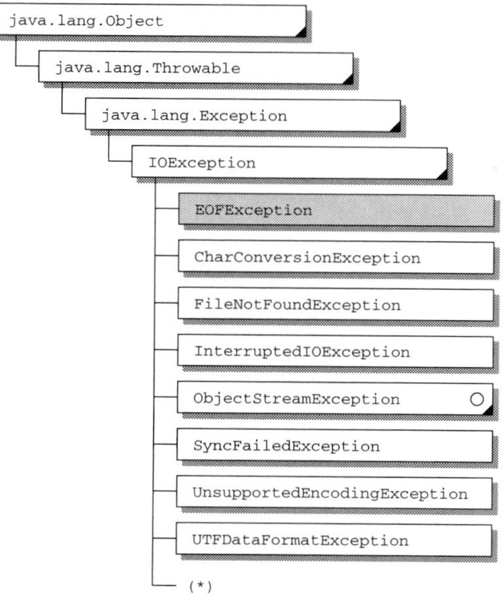

(*) 7 classes from other packages not shown.

Syntax

```
public class EOFException extends IOException
```

Description

`EOFException` is an IO exception that is thrown when a program reading from a `DataInput` stream reaches end-of-stream (through the use of either `DataInputStream`, `ObjectInputStream`, or `RandomAccessFile`). Other input streams in the Java IO library typically use a value of `-1` to indicate that end-of-stream has been reached. However, because read methods on streams that implement the `DataInput` interface can return negative values, including `-1`, these methods use the `EOFException` to denote that end-of-stream has been reached.

A method that throws `EOFException` must declare it or any of its superclasses in the method's `throws` clause.

MEMBER SUMMARY	
Constructor	
`EOFException()`	Constructs an `EOFException` instance.

See Also

DataInput, DataInputStream, IOException, ObjectInputStream, RandomAccessFile.

Example

This example writes out a string to a random access file and then reads it back and echoes its contents to standard output. When reading from the file, it catches the EOFException to terminate the reading.

```
import java.io.RandomAccessFile;
import java.io.EOFException;
import java.io.IOException;

class Main {
    public static void main(String[] args) {
        if (args.length != 1) {
            System.err.println("java Main <outputfile>");
            System.exit(-1);
        }
        try {
            RandomAccessFile raf = new RandomAccessFile(args[0], "rw");
            String str = "This is a test";
            raf.writeChars(str);
            raf.close();

            // read the stuff back
            raf = new RandomAccessFile(args[0], "r");
            try {
                while (true)
                    System.out.print(raf.readChar());
            } catch (EOFException e) {
                // end of file reached
                System.out.println();
            }
            raf.close();
        } catch (IOException e) {
            e.printStackTrace();
        }
    }
}
```

EOFException()

PURPOSE Constructs an EOFException instance.

SYNTAX
```
public EOFException()
public EOFException(String msg)
```

DESCRIPTION These constructors construct an instance of EOFException. An optional string msg can be supplied that describes this particular instance of the exception. If msg is not supplied, it defaults to null.

PARAMETERS

msg A possibly null string that gives details about this exception.

SEE ALSO java.lang.Throwable.getMessage().

Error

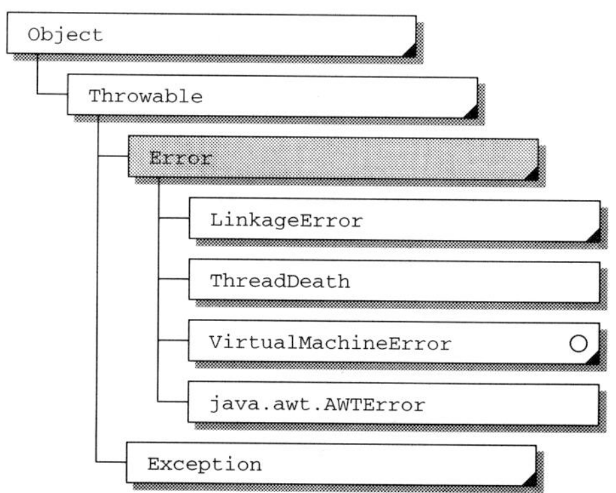

A B C D E F G H I J K L M N O P Q R S T U V W X Y Z

Syntax

```
public class Error extends Throwable
```

Description

The `Error` class is the superclass of classes used to represent erroneous or abnormal events. Errors are thrown only by the Java virtual machine. `Error` and its subclasses should not be thrown or subclassed by user programs. Nor should they be caught by user programs. Furthermore, `Error` and its subclasses need not be specified in the `throws` clause of a method, even if that method throws the `Error`.

MEMBER SUMMARY	
Constructor	
`Error()`	Constructs an `Error` object.

See Also

`Exception`, `RuntimeException`, `Throwable`.

Example

See examples for subclasses of `Error`.

Error()

PURPOSE Constructs an `Error` object.

SYNTAX
```
public Error()
public Error(String msg)
```

DESCRIPTION This class has two constructors. The first form constructs an `Error` object that has no additional description other than the class name of the `Error` object. The second form constructs an `Error` object using the string `msg`. `msg` provides information about the error in addition to the class name of the `Error` object. If `msg` is not specified, it defaults to `null`.

PARAMETERS

`msg` A possibly `null` string containing information about the error.

SEE ALSO `Throwable.getMessage()`.

EventListener

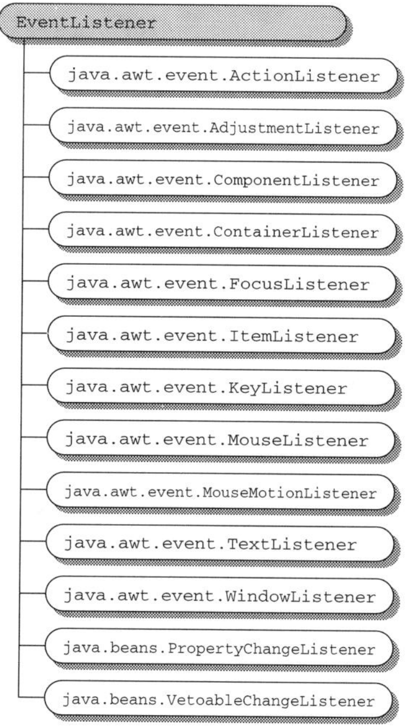

Syntax

```
public interface EventListener
```

Description

An *event listener* is an object that listens for events fired from an *event source*. Every type of event has a corresponding event listener interface used to listen for that particular event object type. For example, the listener interface for the `FocusEvent` is `FocusListener`. See `EventObject` for more information about event objects and event listeners. In Figure 42, an event source fires an event object, which is then dispatched to the event listeners.

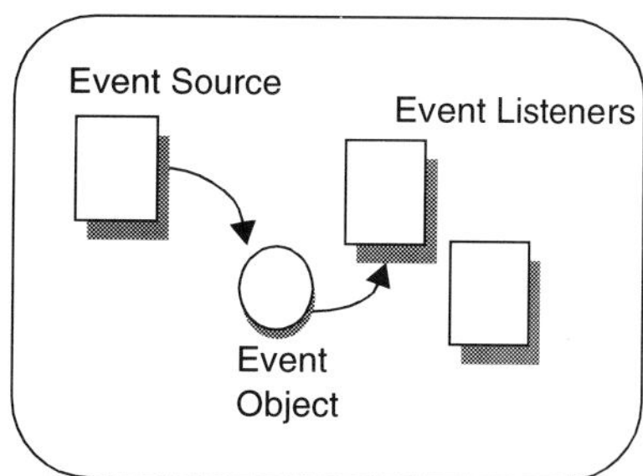

FIGURE 42: Event Source, Event Object, and Event Listeners.

Usage

This interface is typically used as the superclass of another interface. When a new event object type is created, a new corresponding event listener interface must be declared for the new event object type. The new event listener interface must extend this interface.

The new event listener interface declares one or more *listener methods*—callback methods called by the event source when it fires an event. For example, the FocusListener interface defines two listener methods, as follows:

```
public void focusGained(FocusEvent evt))
public void focusLost(FocusEvent evt)
```

focusGained() is called when the event source gains the focus. focusLost() is called when the event source loses the focus.

See EventObject for more information about event listeners.

See Also

EventObject, java.awt.event.*, TooManyListenersException.

Example

See the EventObject class example.

java.util
EventObject

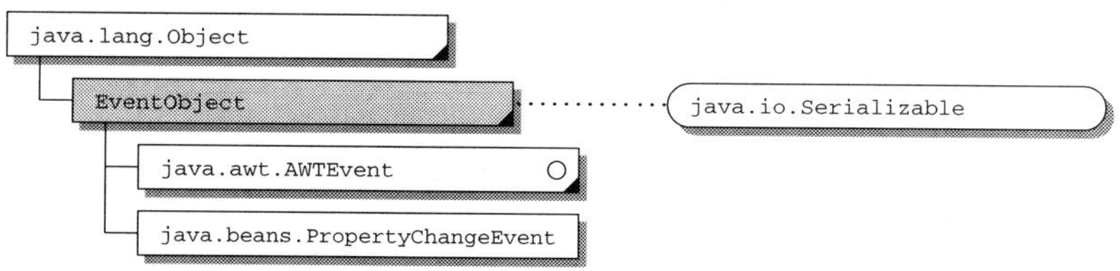

Syntax

```
public class EventObject implements java.io.Serializable
```

Description

An *event object* is used to represent events that are fired by objects. For example, a button fires an event object whenever the user presses the button.

Usage

This class is rarely used as is because most events have additional useful information about the event that cannot be carried along with this class. For example, when a `List` component fires an event because the user selected an item, the event should indicate which item was selected. Therefore an event source typically provides a subclass of `EventObject` with additional fields and field accessor methods to support the extra information. For example, the `List` component fires an `ItemEvent` event object that can hold the identity of the selected item. There are many examples of `EventObject` subclasses in the `java.awt.event` package.

There are many other details when declaring a new event object type and using event objects. These are described later in this class.

Event Source

The event source is the object that fires an event object. For example, when the user presses a button and causes an event object to be fired, the event source of the event button should be the button instance.

FIGURE 43: Event Source, Event Object, and Event Listeners.

Event Listeners

For every event object type, there must be a corresponding event listener interface used to listen for that event type. In Figure 43, an event source fires an event object, which is then dispatched to the event listeners.

For example, to listen to the `FocusEvent` event type that is fired whenever a component gains or loses a focus, a listener object must implement the `FocusListener` interface.

The `FocusListener` interface contains a group of callback methods (*listener methods*), one of which will be called when the event source fires an event. For example, the `FocusListener` interface defines two listener methods, as follows:

```
public void focusGained(FocusEvent e)
public void focusLost(FocusEvent e)
```

`focusGained()` is called when the event source gains the focus. `focusLost()` is called when the event source loses the focus.

Event Source Registration Methods

An event source should have a pair of methods for registering and removing listeners. For example, objects that fire focus events provide the following methods:

```
void addFocusListener(FocusListener listener)
void removeFocusListener(FocusListener listener)
```

`addFocusListener()` adds listener to its list of listeners. `removeFocusListener()` removes a listener from its list of listeners.

Too Many Listeners

Most event sources allow more than one listener to listen for events. In this case, when the event source fires an event, it creates and delivers a new event object for each listener. However, if an event source allows only a single listener, it's add listener method should declare the `TooManyListenersException` in its signature and throw that exception if an attempt is made to add more than one listener.

Signature Conventions

Following is a list of conventions that are recommended when you are designing event object and event listener pairs. All event objects and listeners in the Java class libraries follow these conventions. The conventions are used by the Beans introspector (see `java.beans.Introspector` in *Volume 2* for more information).

1. The name of the `EventObject` subclass should end with the string "Event". For example, the event object for focus events is called `FocusEvent`.
2. The name of the event listener for an event object type should be the name of the event object, except that the suffix "Event" is replaced with "Listener". For example, the event listener for focus events is called `FocusListener`.
3. The event listener interface must extend `EventListener`.
4. The listener methods in the event listener interface should not return a result and should take a single parameter—the event object to which it is associated. For example, `FocusListener` interface defines the following two listener methods, each taking a single parameter of the type `FocusEvent`:

```
public void focusGained(FocusEvent e)
public void focusLost(FocusEvent e)
```

5. An event source that can fire a particular event object type must supply two event listener registration methods. One method is used to add a listener and the other to remove a listener. The add listener method has the same name as the listener interface, with the prefix "add" included. It takes a single parameter—an object of the listener type—and does not return a value. The remove listener method has the same name as the listener interface, with the prefix "remove" included. It also takes a single parameter—an object of the listener type—and does not return a value. For example, the listener registration methods for the `FocusListener` are

```
void addFocusListener(FocusListener listener)
void removeFocusListener(FocusListener listener)
```

MEMBER SUMMARY	
Constructor	
`EventObject()`	Constructs an `EventObject` instance.
Event Source Methods	
`getSource()`	Retrieves the event source for this event object.
`source`	Holds the object firing this event.
Debugging Method	
`toString()`	Generates a string representation of this event object.

See Also

`EventListener`, `java.awt.event`, `TooManyListenersException`.

Example

This example demonstrates all of the steps taken when a new event object type is being declared—that is, declare the event listener registration methods and declare an event listener interface. The example declares a `Timer` object, which fires a `TickEvent` to all of its listeners. The tick event holds the time that the tick event was fired.

```
import java.util.*;

class Main implements TickListener {
    Main() {
        Timer timer = new Timer(3000);
        timer.addTickListener(this);
    }

    // Called whenever timer ticks.
    public void ticked(TickEvent evt) {
        System.out.println(evt.getTime());
    }
```

```
    public static void main(String[] args) {
        new Main();
    }
}

class Timer extends Thread {
    int period;
    Vector listeners = new Vector();

    Timer(int periodMillis) {
        period = periodMillis;
        start();
    }

    // Listener registration methods.
    void addTickListener(TickListener listener) {
        listeners.addElement(listener);
    }
    void removeTickListener(TickListener listener) {
        listeners.removeElement(listener);
    }

    public void run() {
        while (true) {
            try {
                // This avoids a race condition
                Vector v = (Vector)listeners.clone();

                // Deliver a TickEvent to all listeners.
                for (int i=0; i<v.size(); i++) {
                    ((TickListener)v.elementAt(i)).ticked(new TickEvent(this));
                }

                Thread.sleep(period);
            } catch (Exception e) {
                e.printStackTrace();
            }
        }
    }
}

class TickEvent extends EventObject {
    long time;

    TickEvent(Object source) {
        super(source);
        time = System.currentTimeMillis();
    }

    long getTime() {
        return time;
    }
}

interface TickListener {
    void ticked(TickEvent evt);
}
```

EventObject()

PURPOSE
Constructs an `EventObject` instance.

SYNTAX
```
public EventObject(Object source)
```

DESCRIPTION
This constructor creates an `EventObject` object with `source` as the event source.

PARAMETERS
`source` The non-`null` object firing this event.

EXAMPLE
See the class example.

getSource()

PURPOSE
Retrieves the event source for this event object.

SYNTAX
```
public Object getSource()
```

DESCRIPTION
The event source is the object that fired this event. This method returns the event source.

RETURNS
The non-`null` object firing this event.

EXAMPLE
See the class example.

source

PURPOSE
Holds the object firing this event.

SYNTAX
```
protected transient Object source
```

DESCRIPTION
The event source is the object that fired this event. This field is used to hold the non-`null` event source.

EXAMPLE
See the class example.

toString()

PURPOSE
Generates a string representation of this event object.

SYNTAX
```
public String toString()
```

DESCRIPTION
This method returns a string containing details of the event source. In particular, the string includes the result of `getSource().toString()`.

When this class is subclassed, this method should be overridden to include any extra state that the subclass adds.

RETURNS A non-`null` string containing details of the event source.

OVERRIDES `java.lang.Object.toString()`.

EXAMPLE See `java.lang.Object.toString()`.

Exception

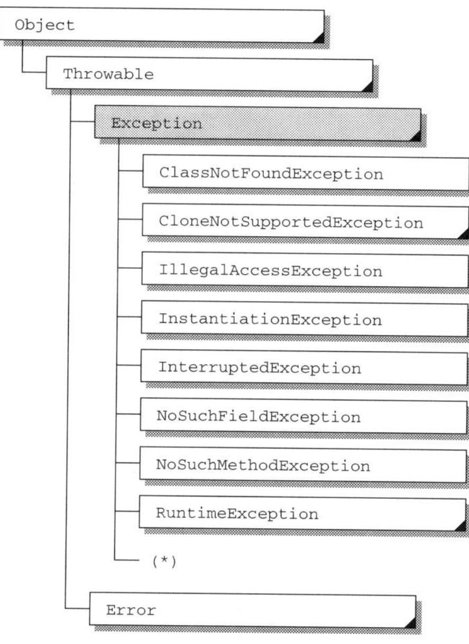

(*) 21 classes from other packages not shown.

Syntax

```
public class Exception extends Throwable
```

Description

The `Exception` class is the superclass of classes used to represent exceptional conditions. There are two types of exceptional conditions: (1) runtime exceptions thrown by the Java runtime system that are considered unrecoverable and should not be caught and (2) all others. The former is represented by `RuntimeException` and its subclasses and the latter by all other subclasses of `Exception`. This latter category includes exceptions thrown by the Java runtime system that are considered to be nonfatal. Even though they are thrown by the runtime system, these exceptions are not subclasses of `RuntimeException`. This is because they are recoverable by user programs and therefore must be declared in the `throws` clause of a method and caught by using `try/catch` statements.

Any method that throws any instance of `Exception` that is not a `RuntimeException` must declare the exception(s) in its `throws` clause as part of the method's declaration. This is a Java language requirement. Any method that calls this method must either catch the exception(s) by using `try/catch` statements or declare the exception(s) in its own `throws` clause. The Java compiler will generate a compilation error for any code that does not follow these rules.

RuntimeException and its subclasses should not be declared in a method's throws clause. Nor should they be caught by using try/catch statements. These exceptions should be allowed to percolate to the top level of the user's program, where they are dealt with by the Java runtime system. The system displays to the user executing the faulty program a stack trace of where the RuntimeException occurred. User programs should not subclass RuntimeException (or its subclasses); these are reserved for the Java runtime system.

MEMBER SUMMARY	
Constructor	
Exception()	Constructs an Exception instance.

See Also

Error, RuntimeException, Throwable.

Example

This example defines a stack and two exceptions: StackOverflow and StackUnderflow. StackOverflow is thrown when you attempt to push an item onto a full stack. StackUnderflow is thrown when you attempt to pop an item off of an empty stack.

```
// attempting to add to stack when it is full
class StackOverflow extends Exception {
};

// attempting to access stack when it is empty
class StackUnderflow extends Exception {
};

// A stack that has a 3 item limit
class threeDeep {
    static final int STACK_SIZE = 3;
    private int[] stack_store = new int[STACK_SIZE];
    private int stack_ptr = 0;

    // push item onto stack
    public void push(int item) throws StackOverflow {
        if (stack_ptr >= STACK_SIZE)
            throw new StackOverflow();
        else
            stack_store[stack_ptr++] = item;
    }

    // pop item off top of stack
    public int pop() throws StackUnderflow {
        if (stack_ptr == 0)
            throw new StackUnderflow();
        else
```

```
            return (stack_store[--stack_ptr]);
        }
    }

    threeDeep s = new threeDeep();
    try {
        s.push(i);
    } catch (StackOverflow e) {
        System.err.println("overflow " + i);
    }
     ...
    try {
        System.out.println("pop " + s.pop());
    } catch (StackUnderflow e) {
        System.err.println("underflow " + e);
    }
```


Exception()

PURPOSE Constructs an `Exception` instance.

SYNTAX
```
public Exception()
public Exception(String msg)
```

DESCRIPTION This class has two constructors. The first constructs an `Exception` instance with no detail message. The second constructs an `Exception` instance by using the string `msg`, which provides information about the exception. If `msg` is not supplied, it defaults to `null`.

Subclasses of `Exception` define their own constructors that use these constructors. In addition, subclasses can define new methods and instance variables that can be used to store state information about the exception, as appropriate.

PARAMETERS

`msg` A possibly `null` string containing information about the exception.

SEE ALSO `Throwable.getMessage()`.

EXAMPLE This example illustrates how an exception `PrinterOutOfPaperException` can be defined to include additional information about the exception. In this case, the exception records the time at which the exception occurred.

```
import java.util.Date;

class PrinterOutOfPaperException extends Exception {
    public Date when;
    public PrinterOutOfPaperException() {
        super();
        when = new Date();
    }
    public PrinterOutOfPaperException(String msg) {
        super(msg);
```

```
            when = new Date();
        }
    }

    try {
      ...
        throw new PrinterOutOfPaperException("ATTENTION");
    } catch (PrinterOutOfPaperException e) {
        System.err.println("Out of paper since " + e.when);
      ... <wait for paper and continue>
    }
```

ExceptionInInitializerError

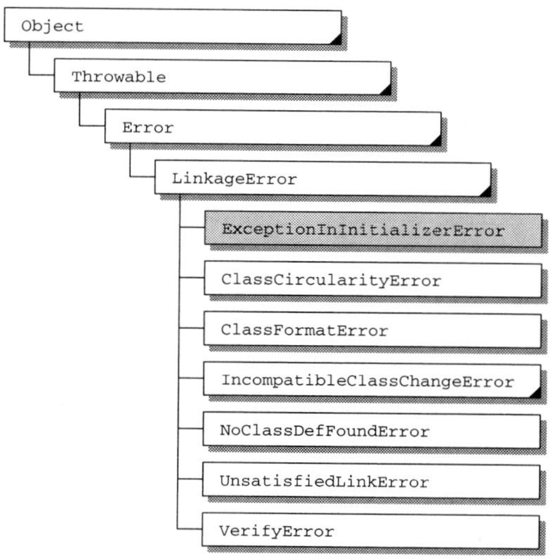

Syntax

`public class ExceptionInInitializerError extends LinkageError`

Description

`ExceptionInInitializerError` is a runtime linkage error that is thrown when an exception occurs while the Java runtime is initializing a static variable or a class's static initializer. If an `Error` or any of its subclasses is thrown during static initialization, the error itself is rethrown. If an exception (not a subclass of `Error`'s) is thrown, that exception is wrapped inside an `ExceptionInInitializerError` and then thrown by the initializer.

MEMBER SUMMARY	
Constructor	
`ExceptionInInitializerError()`	Constructs an `ExceptionInInitializerError` instance.
`getException()`	Retrieves the exception that caused the initializer to fail.

Example

Java 1.1.4 ignores exceptions and errors thrown during static initialization. Therefore it is not possible to produce an example that throws `ExceptionInInitializerError`.

ExceptionInInitializerError()

PURPOSE Constructs an `ExceptionInInitializerError` instance.

SYNTAX

```
public ExceptionInInitializerError()
public ExceptionInInitializerError(Throwable e)
public ExceptionInInitializerError(String msg)
```

DESCRIPTION This constructor constructs an instance of `ExceptionInInitializerError`. If no `Throwable` is supplied, it defaults to `null`. If no detailed message `msg` is supplied, it defaults to `null`.

PARAMETERS

`e` The possibly `null` exception thrown.

`msg` A possibly `null` string that gives details about this error.

SEE ALSO `getException()`, `Throwable.getMessage()`.

getException()

PURPOSE Retrieves the exception that caused the initializer to fail.

SYNTAX `public Throwable getException()`

RETURNS The possibly `null` exception that caused the initializer to fail.

Externalizable

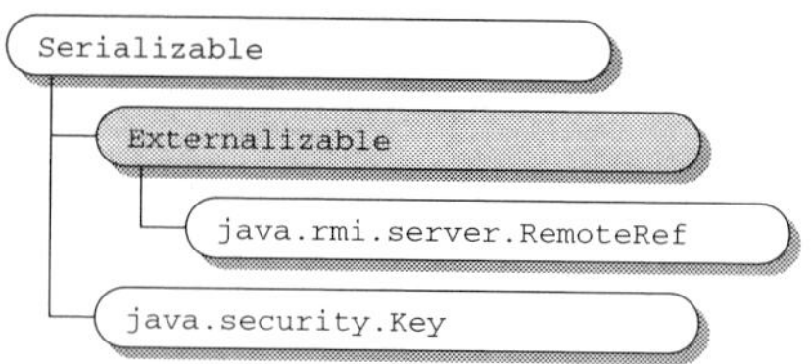

Syntax

```
public interface Externalizable extends java.io.Serializable
```

Description

Externalization is a way to gain more control over the data written into the stream when serializing an object's state.

When *default* serialization is used, the following is taken care of automatically.

- Restoration of the state of superclasses (some of which may be serializable)
- Support for compatible changes, such as the addition of fields and superclasses
- Formatting and versioning of all *serializable fields*. In Java 1.1, the *serializable* fields of a class are all of its nontransient and nonstatic fields.
- Skipping data written by an evolved version of `writeObject()` that an older version of `readObject()` does not know exists.

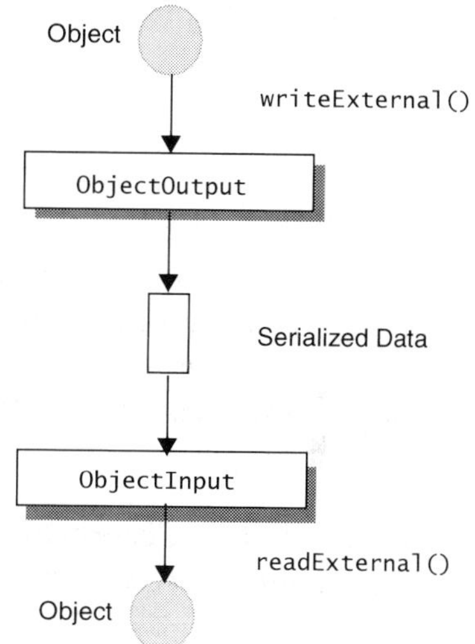

FIGURE 44: Externalization and Restoration of an Object.

When *customized* serialization is used, the class must take care of compatible changes and versioning. There is some support for versioning in terms of the Stream Unique Identifier (SUID), but the class's serialization methods must take care to maintain the format compatibility with the version identified by the SUID.

When externalization is used, the class must take care of all four tasks.

Usage

To make objects of a class externalizable, you declare the class to implement the `Externalizable` interface and implement the two methods in the `Externalizable` interface.

```
public class ClassE implements Externalizable {
    ...
    public ClassE() {
```

```
        ...
    }
    public void writeExternal(ObjectOutput out) throws IOException {
        ...
    }
    public void readExternal(ObjectInput in) throws IOException,
        ClassNotFoundException {
        ...
    }
}
```


This will make `ClassE` externalizable. You can serialize an instance of `ClassE` to any object that implements the `ObjectOutput` interface and then restore the object using an object that implements the `ObjectInput` interface. For the restoration to succeed, the class must have a public constructor that takes no parameters.

```
ObjectOutputStream out = ...;
out.writeObject(new ClassE());
ObjectInputStream in = ...
ClassE obj = (ClassE) in.readObject();
```

Externalization

The externalizable object is serialized using its `writeExternal()` method. `writeExternal()` must take care to record its complete state, including those of its superclass(es). It does not have special privileges as far as the Java language is concerned and therefore can serialize only accessible fields of its superclass(es).

When the serialized state of such an externalizable object is restored, first, its public constructor that takes no parameters is called. If the class does not have this constructor, a `NoSuchMethodError` is thrown. Next, the class's fields are restored via a call to its `readExternal()` method. Whether the superclass is serializable or nonserializable does not matter because the current class is completely responsible for restoring its state.

Effect of Subclassing

A class that subclasses an externalizable class is also externalizable. The subclass, by default, inherits its superclass's `writeExternal()` and `readExternal()` methods. If the subclass wants to serialize or restore state relevant for the subclass, it needs to override `writeExternal()` and `readExternal()`. If the superclass's state is relevant for the subclass, the subclass should first invoke methods to serialize and restore the superclass's state and then serialize and restore data relevant to the subclass. The recommended way of doing this is for the `writeExternal()` override to call `super.writeExternal()` first before writing the subclass's state and for the `readExternal()` override to call `super.readExternal()` before reading data for the subclass's state.

An Externalizable Object's Class

When a serializable object is serialized, its corresponding class descriptor (`ObjectStreamClass`) is also written out (see `Serializable`). Similarly, when an externalizable object is serialized, in addition to the data that is written using `writeExternal()`, its class descriptor is also written out. The only difference is that for an externalizable class, the names and type names of its serializable fields are *not* written.

Use of ObjectInputStream and ObjectOutputStream
Another difference between a class that implements `Serializable` and one that implements `Externalizable` is the type of objects that can be used to hold the state of the serialized data. `Serializable` objects are serialized to `ObjectOutputStreams` and deserialized from `ObjectInputStreams`. Externalizable objects are slightly more flexible. They are serialized to any object that implements the `ObjectOutput` interface and restored from any object that implements the `ObjectInput` interface.

Security Considerations
Declaring a class to be `Externalizable` is even more prone to abuse than declaring it `Serializable`. The `readExternal()` and `writeExternal()` methods are public, and hence, any code that holds a reference to an externalizable object can get its state by externalizing it. Such code can also easily reinitialize or corrupt an externalizable object by invoking `readExternal()` on it using data from any object that supports the `ObjectInput` interface.

Note that the field names and types are not written to the serialized stream for an externalizable class (unless the externalizable class has chosen to serialize the field names and types). This is a benefit, since it ensures that externalizable data is not as self-describing as serializable data is.

For more details on security-related issues relating to externalizable objects, see `http://java/sun.com/jdk/1.1/docs/guide/serialization`.

MEMBER SUMMARY	
Externalizable Methods	
`readExternal()`	Restores an object's state.
`writeExternal()`	Serializes this object's state.

See Also
`ObjectInput, ObjectOutput, Serializable.`

Example
This example declares a class `ClassE` that is externalizable. It writes it out to a file using `writeExternal()` and then reads it back using `readExternal()`.

```
import java.io.*;

class Main {
```

```
    public static void main(String[] args) {
        try {
            // Write it out
            FileOutputStream f = new FileOutputStream("ClassE.ser");
            ObjectOutput out = new ObjectOutputStream(f);

            out.writeObject(new ClassE(30, "Hello"));
            out.flush();
            out.close();

            // Read it back
            FileInputStream f2 = new FileInputStream("ClassE.ser");
            ObjectInputStream in = new ObjectInputStream(f2);
            ClassE eobj = (ClassE) in.readObject();
            in.close();
            System.out.println("eobj.field1 " + eobj.field1);
        } catch (IOException e) {
            e.printStackTrace();
        } catch (ClassNotFoundException e) {
            e.printStackTrace();
        }
    }
}

class ClassE  implements Externalizable {
    int field1;
    String field2;

    public ClassE(int i, String s) {
        field1 = i;
        field2 = s;
    }

    // Required for Externalizable
    public ClassE() {
    }

    public void writeExternal(ObjectOutput out) throws IOException {
        out.writeBytes(String.valueOf(field1));
        out.write('\n');
        out.writeBytes(field2);
        out.write('\n');
    }

    public void readExternal(ObjectInput in) throws IOException,
        ClassNotFoundException {
        field1 = Integer.parseInt(in.readLine());
        field2 = in.readLine();
    }
}
```

readExternal()

PURPOSE Restores this object's state.

SYNTAX

```
public void readExternal(ObjectInput in) throws IOException,
   ClassNotFoundException
```

DESCRIPTION This method restores an object's state by obtaining data from `in`. `in` need not be an instance of `ObjectInputStream`; it can be any object that implements the `ObjectInput` interface. The data read from `in` must match the data written by `writeExternal()`.

Note: This method must be able to read all future and previous compatible formats of this class.

PARAMETERS

`in` The `ObjectInput` object from which to obtain the data for restoring this object.

EXCEPTIONS

`ClassNotFoundException`
If an invocation of `readObject()` by `readExternal()` cannot deserialize an object because its corresponding class is not found. The class of the object being deserialized has already been found by the time `readExternal()` is called.

`IOException`
If an IO error was encountered while reading from `in`.

SEE ALSO `writeExternal()`.

EXAMPLE See the class example.

writeExternal()

PURPOSE Serializes this object's state.

SYNTAX

```
public void writeExternal(ObjectOutput out) throws IOException
```

DESCRIPTION This method writes the state of this object to `out`. `out` need not be an instance of `ObjectOutputStream`; it can be any object that implements the `ObjectOutput` interface. The data written by `writeExternal()` must match that expected by `readExternal()`.

Note: This method must produce a format that is readable by all existing and future `readExternal()` implementations for this class.

PARAMETERS

`out` The `ObjectOutput` object to which to write the state of this object.

EXCEPTIONS

`IOException`
If an IO error occurs while writing data to `out`.

SEE ALSO `readExternal()`.

EXAMPLE See the class example.

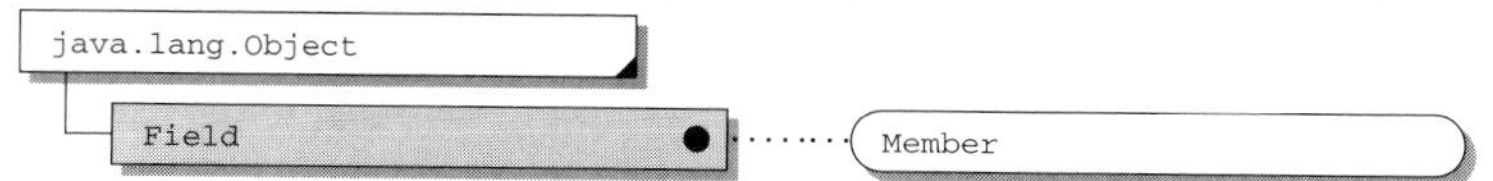

A B C D E F G H I J K L M N O P Q R S T U V W X Y Z

Syntax

```
public final class Field implements Member
```

Description

A `Field` object represents a field member in a class or an interface. It can represent a static (class) field or an instance field. Also, it can be used to discover the modifiers on a field (see `Modifier`) and to access and modify the contents of the field.

Usage

This class cannot be instantiated (since you can't create a field). Instead, you need first to obtain a `Class` object for the class that has the desired field. For example,

```
Class.forName("java.awt.Point")
```

or

```
java.awt.Point.class
```

With the `Class` object, you then call one of the methods in Table 25 to obtain a `Field` object for the desired field.

Method	Description
`Class.getField()`	Retrieves a `Field` object for a public inherited or declared field in a class.
`Class.getFields()`	Retrieves `Field` objects for all public inherited and declared fields in a class.
`Class.getDeclaredField()`	Retrieves a `Field` object for a declared field in a class.
`Class.getDeclaredFields()`	Retrieves `Field` objects for all declared fields in a class.

TABLE 25: Getting a `Field` from a `Class` Object.

See the method descriptions in `Class` for more details.

The Name

The name of a `Field` object is the string used to name the field in the source code. For example, in the following field declaration the name of the `Field` object is "allDone":

```
public boolean allDone
```

All `Field` objects have a name.

The Type

The type of a `Field` object is the field's type and is represented by a `Class` object. For example, in the following field declaration:

```
public boolean allDone
```

the type of the field is `boolean` and the type of the `Field` object is `boolean.class`. All `Field` objects have a type.

The Modifiers

The modifiers of a field can be retrieved from a `Field` object by using `getModifiers()` and methods in the `Modifier` class. A `Field` object can have any of these four modifiers—`static`, `final`, `volatile`, and `transient`—and at most one access modifier, either `public`, `protected`, or `private`. For example, in the following field declaration, the modifiers are `public`, `static`, and `final`:

```
public static final int ALL_DONE
```

The Value

The value of an instance or static field can be retrieved by using a `Field` object and the get methods in this class. For an instance field, you need to supply a reference to an object instance. There is no need for an object instance when retrieving the value of a static field.

The Declaring Class

The declaring class of a `Field` object is the class or interface that actually declares the field. For example, in the following code the declaring class of `D.x` is `C`:

```
class C {
    int x;
}
class D extends C {
}
```

Because fields are inherited, they can appear in classes that do not explicitly declare them. In the previous example, a `Field` object reflecting `C.x` is indistinguishable from one reflecting `D.x` because the two names refer to the same field. However, the two `Field` objects need not have identical references; you must use `equals()` to determine their equality.

When you create a `Field` object for an inherited field in a class, the identity of that class is lost (i.e., it cannot be retrieved from the `Field object`); only the `Field` object's declaring class is available.

To modify a field, say `C.x` as in the previous example, you can use a `Field` object reflecting either `C.x` or `D.x`, since they are equal. The same holds true if you want to modify `D.x`. See `setByte()` for an example.

Widening Primitive Conversions

The various `Field` object get and set methods will automatically perform widening conversions on primitive types if necessary. For example, if `getLong()` is invoked on a `byte` field, the method will automatically widen the `byte` value to a `long` value. Conversely, if `setByte()` is invoked on a `long` field, the same widening conversion will take place.

Narrowing conversions are not permitted. Also, even if two primitive types are the same size, a conversion may not be permitted. For example, you cannot call `getChar()` on a `short` field. To achieve this conversion, you need to use the Java language's casting operators before calling the methods in this class.

The automatic conversions that are allowed exactly match the automatic widening conversions defined in *The Java Language Specification*. Tables 26 and 27 show a complete listing of all valid field types for all of the get and set methods, respectively.

Get Method	Field Type
`getBoolean()`	`boolean`
`getChar()`	`char`
`getByte()`	`byte`
`getShort()`	`byte, short`
`getInt()`	`byte, short, char, int`
`getLong()`	`byte, short, char, int, long`
`getFloat()`	`byte, short, char, int, long, float`
`getDouble()`	`byte, short, char, int, long, float, double`

TABLE 26: Valid Field Types for the Get Methods.

Set Method	Field Type
`setBoolean()`	`boolean`
`setChar()`	`double, float, long, int, char`
`setByte()`	`double, float, long, int, short, byte`
`setShort()`	`double, float, long, int, short`
`setInt()`	`double, float, long, int`
`setLong()`	`double, float, long`
`setFloat()`	`double, float`
`setDouble()`	`double`

TABLE 27: Valid Field Types for the Set Methods.

Accessibility

When the get and set methods are invoked on a `Field` object, the Java virtual machine performs the access checks described in *The Java Language Specification, First Edition*, Section 6.6.1. For example, using a `Field` object, you cannot invoke `set()` on it if the field being reflected is final and you cannot invoke `get()` on it from another class if the field being reflected is private. These checks compare the identity of the caller with the access permission and identity of the field being accessed. It is as if the caller had statically-compiled code that accesses the field. The access check takes into account both the accessibility of the field itself and the accessibility of its class.

A B C D E F G H I J K L M N O P Q R S T U V W X Y Z

MEMBER SUMMARY	
Attribute Methods	
`getDeclaringClass()`	Retrieves this `Field` object's declaring class.
`getModifiers()`	Retrieves the field modifiers for this `Field` object.
`getName()`	Retrieves this `Field` object's name.
`getType()`	Retrieves this `Field` object's type.
Get Value Methods	
`get()`	Retrieves this `Field` object's value.
`getBoolean()`	Retrieves the value of this `boolean` field.
`getByte()`	Retrieves the value of this `byte` field.
`getChar()`	Retrieves the value of this `char` field.
`getDouble()`	Retrieves the contents of this numerical field as a `double` value.
`getFloat()`	Retrieves the contents of this numerical field as a `float` value.
`getInt()`	Retrieves the contents of this numerical field as an `int` value.
`getLong()`	Retrieves the contents of this numerical field as a `long` value.
`getShort()`	Retrieves the contents of this numerical field as a `short` value.
Set Value Methods	
`set()`	Sets the value of this `Field` object.
`setBoolean()`	Sets the value of this `boolean` field.
`setByte()`	Sets the value of this numerical field to a `byte` value.
`setChar()`	Sets the value of this field to a `char` value.
`setDouble()`	Sets the value of this `double` field.
`setFloat()`	Sets the value of this numerical field to a `float` value.
`setInt()`	Sets the value of this numerical field to an `int` value.
`setLong()`	Sets the value of this numerical field to a `long` value.
`setShort()`	Sets the value of this numerical field to a `short` value.
Object Methods	
`equals()`	Compares this `Field` object with another `Field` object.
`hashCode()`	Computes the hash code for this `Field` object.

MEMBER SUMMARY

Debug Method	
`toString()`	Generates a string representing this `Field` object.

A B C D E F G H I J K L M N O P Q R S T U V W X Y Z

See Also

`java.lang.Class`, `Modifiers`.

Example

This example is a simple demonstration of how to access and modify a field value. In particular, the program scans all of the `public` fields in class `C` and increments them by 1. It invokes the appropriate get and set method based on the field's type.

```
import java.lang.reflect.*;

class Main {
    // Print the names and values of all public fields in o.
    public static void printFields(Object o) {
        Field[] fields = o.getClass().getFields();

        try {
            for (int i=0; i<fields.length; i++) {
                System.out.println(fields[i].getName() + " = " +
                                   fields[i].get(o));
            }
        } catch (IllegalAccessException e) {
            e.printStackTrace();
        }
    }

    // Increment all public fields by 1.
    public static void incFields(Object o) {
        Field[] fields = o.getClass().getFields();

        try {
            for (int i=0; i<fields.length; i++) {
                if (fields[i].getType() == byte.class) {
                    fields[i].setByte(o, (byte)(fields[i].getByte(o) + 1));
                } else if (fields[i].getType() == short.class) {
                    fields[i].setShort(o, (short)(fields[i].getShort(o) + 1));
                } else if (fields[i].getType() == char.class) {
                    fields[i].setChar(o, (char)(fields[i].getChar(o) + 1));
                } else if (fields[i].getType() == int.class) {
                    fields[i].setInt(o, fields[i].getInt(o) + 1);
                } else if (fields[i].getType() == long.class) {
                    fields[i].setLong(o, (long)(fields[i].getLong(o) + 1));
                } else if (fields[i].getType() == float.class) {
                    fields[i].setFloat(o, (float)(fields[i].getFloat(o) + 1));
                } else if (fields[i].getType() == double.class) {
                    fields[i].setDouble(o,
                                        (double)(fields[i].getDouble(o) + 1));
```

```
                } else if (fields[i].getType() == String.class) {
                    fields[i].set(o, fields[i].get(o) + "1");
                }
            }
        } catch (IllegalAccessException e) {
            e.printStackTrace();
        }
    }

    public static void main(String[] args) {
        C c = new C();

        printFields(c);
        incFields(c);
        printFields(c);
    }
}

class C {
    public byte b = 1;
    public short s = 2;
    public char c = 'a';
    public int i = 3;
    public long j = 4;
    public float f = 5.0f;
    public double d = 6.0;

    // Field can be static.
    static public String str = "Java";
}
```

Output

```
> java Main
b = 1
s = 2
c = a
i = 3
j = 4
f = 5.0
d = 6.0
str = Java
b = 2
s = 3
c = b
i = 4
j = 5
f = 6.0
d = 7.0
str = Java1
```

equals()

PURPOSE Compares this `Field` object with another `Field` object.

SYNTAX `public boolean equals(Object fld)`

DESCRIPTION Two `Field` objects are equal only if both `Field` objects refer to exactly the same field in the same class. Note that a `Field` object reflecting an inherited field is equal to one reflecting a declared field.

PARAMETERS

`fld` A possibly `null` `Field` object.

OVERRIDES `java.lang.Object.equals()`.

SEE ALSO `hashCode()`.

EXAMPLE This example creates a number of `Field` objects and tests their equality. Notice that when a `Field` object is created for an inherited field, it is equal to the declared field (and in fact, the name of `dy` appears as `C.y`).

```
import java.lang.reflect.*;

class Main {
    public static void main(String[] args) {
        try {
            Field cx = C.class.getField("x");
            Field cy = C.class.getField("y");

            Field dx = D.class.getField("x");
            Field dy = D.class.getField("y");

            Field ex = E.class.getField("x");

            checkEquality(cx, dx);    // C.x != D.x
            checkEquality(cy, dy);    // C.y == C.y
            checkEquality(cx, ex);    // C.x != E.x
        } catch (NoSuchFieldException ext) {
            ext.printStackTrace();
        }
    }

    public static void checkEquality(Field f1, Field f2) {
    System.out.print(f1.getDeclaringClass().getName()+"."+f1.getName());
        if (f1.equals(f2)) {
            System.out.print(" == ");
        } else {
            System.out.print(" != ");
        }
    System.out.println(f2.getDeclaringClass().getName()+"."+f2.getName());
    }
}

class C {
    public int x;
    public int y;
}
class D extends C {
    public int x;
}
class E {
    public int x;
}
```

get()

PURPOSE

Retrieves this `Field` object's value.

SYNTAX

```
public native Object get(Object obj) throws
   IllegalArgumentException, IllegalAccessException
```

DESCRIPTION

This method retrieves the value in `obj` of the field reflected by this `Field` object. If the field is static, `obj` is ignored. If the field type is primitive, the returned object is a wrapper around the value. For example, if this `Field` object is a `byte` field, the returned object is a `Byte` object.

The caller must have permission to access the field reflected by this `Field` object. See the class description for details.

PARAMETERS

`obj` A non-`null` object whose class inherits or declares this field, or in the case of a static field, any possibly `null` value.

RETURNS

The value of this field. It is `null` if the field's value is `null`.

EXCEPTIONS

`IllegalAccessException`
If the caller does not have permission to access this field. See the class description for details.

`IllegalArgumentException`
If `obj`'s class does not inherit or declare this field.

`NullPointerException`
If this field is an instance field and `obj` is `null`.

EXAMPLE

This example creates `Field` objects on primitive types and uses them to retrieve the field values. It then prints out the `Class` object of the returned objects. The output indicates that the returned objects are wrapper objects.

```
import java.lang.reflect.*;

class Main {
    public static void main(String[] args) {
        try {
            C c = new C();
            Field fi = C.class.getField("i");
            Field ff = C.class.getField("f");
            Field fs = C.class.getField("s");

            System.out.println(fi.get(c).getClass());
            System.out.println(ff.get(c).getClass());
            System.out.println(fs.get(c).getClass());
        } catch (IllegalAccessException e) {
            e.printStackTrace();
        } catch (NoSuchFieldException e) {
            e.printStackTrace();
        }
```

```
        }
    }

    class C {
        public int i;
        public float f;
        public String s = "Java";
    }
```

Output

```
    class java.lang.Integer
    class java.lang.Float
    class java.lang.String
```

getBoolean()

PURPOSE Retrieves the value of this `boolean` field.

SYNTAX
```
public native boolean getBoolean(Object obj) throws
   IllegalArgumentException, IllegalAccessException
```

DESCRIPTION This method retrieves the value in `obj` of the `boolean` field reflected by this `Field` object. If the field is static, `obj` is ignored.

The caller must have permission to access the field reflected by this `Field` object. See the class description for details.

PARAMETERS

`obj` A non-`null` object whose class inherits or declares this field, or in the case of a static field, any possibly `null` value.

RETURNS `true` if the value of this field is `true`; `false` if the value of this field is `false`.

EXCEPTIONS

`IllegalAccessException`
If the caller does not have permission to access this field. See the class description for details.

`IllegalArgumentException`
If `obj`'s class does not inherit or declare this field or if this field type is not a `boolean`.

`NullPointerException`
If this field is an instance field and `obj` is `null`.

SEE ALSO `setBoolean()`.

EXAMPLE See the class example.

getByte()

PURPOSE Retrieves the value of this `byte` field.

SYNTAX
```
public native byte getByte(Object obj) throws
   IllegalArgumentException, IllegalAccessException
```

DESCRIPTION This method retrieves the value in `obj` of the `byte` field reflected by this `Field` object. If the field is static, `obj` is ignored.

The caller must have permission to access the field reflected by this `Field` object. See the class description for details.

PARAMETERS

`obj` A non-`null` object whose class inherits or declares this field, or in the case of a static field, any possibly `null` value.

RETURNS The value of this `byte` field.

EXCEPTIONS

`IllegalAccessException`
If the caller does not have permission to access this field. See the class description for details.

`IllegalArgumentException`
If `obj`'s class does not inherit or declare this field or if this field type is not `byte`.

`NullPointerException`
If this field is an instance field and `obj` is `null`.

SEE ALSO `setByte()`.

EXAMPLE See the class example.

getChar()

PURPOSE Retrieves the value of this `char` field.

SYNTAX
```
public native char getChar(Object obj) throws
   IllegalArgumentException, IllegalAccessException
```

DESCRIPTION This method retrieves the value in `obj` of the `char` field reflected by this `Field` object. If the field is static, `obj` is ignored.

The caller must have permission to access the field reflected by this `Field` object. See the class description for details.

PARAMETERS

`obj` A non-`null` object whose class inherits or declares this field, or in the case of a static field, any possibly `null` value.

RETURNS The value of this `char` field.

EXCEPTIONS

`IllegalAccessException`
: If the caller does not have permission to access this field. See the class description for details.

`IllegalArgumentException`
: If `obj`'s class does not inherit or declare this field or if this field type is not `char`.

`NullPointerException`
: If this field is an instance field and `obj` is `null`.

SEE ALSO `setChar()`.

EXAMPLE See the class example.

getDeclaringClass()

PURPOSE Retrieves this `Field` object's declaring class.

SYNTAX

```
public Class getDeclaringClass()
```

DESCRIPTION This method retrieves this `Field` object's declaring class. The declaring class of a `Field` object is the class or interface that actually declares the field. See the class description for more details.

RETURNS The non-`null` `Class` object of the declaring class of this `Field` object.

EXAMPLE See `equals()`.

getDouble()

PURPOSE Retrieves the contents of this numerical field as a `double` value.

SYNTAX

```
public native double getDouble(Object obj) throws
   IllegalArgumentException, IllegalAccessException
```

DESCRIPTION This method retrieves the value in `obj` of the numerical field reflected by this `Field` object. If the field is static, `obj` is ignored. The field type must be either `byte`, `short`, `char`, `int`, `long`, `float`, or `double`.

The caller must have permission to access the field reflected by this `Field` object. See the class description for details.

PARAMETERS

`obj`
: A non-`null` object whose class inherits or declares this field, or in the case of a static field, any possibly `null` value.

RETURNS A `double` representing the value of this field.

EXCEPTIONS

`IllegalAccessException`
: If the caller does not have permission to access this field. See the class description for details.

`IllegalArgumentException`
: If `obj`'s class does not inherit or declare this field or if this field type cannot be converted to `double`.

`NullPointerException`
: If this field is an instance field and `obj` is `null`.

SEE ALSO `setDouble()`.

EXAMPLE See the class example.

A B C D E F G H I J K L M N O P Q R S T U V W X Y Z

getFloat()

PURPOSE Retrieves the contents of this numerical field as a `float` value.

SYNTAX

```
public native float getFloat(Object obj) throws
    IllegalArgumentException, IllegalAccessException
```

DESCRIPTION This method retrieves the value in `obj` of the numerical field reflected by this `Field` object. If the field is static, `obj` is ignored. The field type must be either `byte`, `short`, `char`, `int`, `long`, or `float`.

The caller must have permission to access the field reflected by this `Field` object. See the class description for details.

PARAMETERS

`obj` A non-`null` object whose class inherits or declares this field, or in the case of a static field, any possibly `null` value.

RETURNS A `float` representing the value of this field.

EXCEPTIONS

`IllegalAccessException`
: If the caller does not have permission to access this field. See the class description for details.

`IllegalArgumentException`
: If `obj`'s class does not inherit or declare this field or if this field type cannot be converted to `float`.

`NullPointerException`
: If this field is an instance field and `obj` is `null`.

SEE ALSO `setFloat()`.

EXAMPLE See the class example.

getInt()

PURPOSE Retrieves the contents of this numerical field as an `int` value.

SYNTAX

```
public native int getInt(Object obj) throws
   IllegalArgumentException, IllegalAccessException
```

DESCRIPTION This method retrieves the value in `obj` of the numerical field reflected by this `Field` object. If the field is static, `obj` is ignored. The field type must be either `byte`, `short`, `char`, or `int`.

The caller must have permission to access the field reflected by this `Field` object. See the class description for details.

PARAMETERS

`obj` A non-`null` object whose class inherits or declares this field, or in the case of a static field, any possibly `null` value.

RETURNS An `int` representing the value of this field.

EXCEPTIONS

`IllegalAccessException`
If the caller does not have permission to access this field. See the class description for details.

`IllegalArgumentException`
If `obj`'s class does not inherit or declare this field or if this field type cannot be converted to `int`.

`NullPointerException`
If this field is an instance field and `obj` is `null`.

SEE ALSO `setInt()`.

EXAMPLE See the class example.

getLong()

PURPOSE Retrieves the contents of this numerical field as a `long` value.

SYNTAX

```
public native long getLong(Object obj) throws
   IllegalArgumentException, IllegalAccessException
```

DESCRIPTION This method retrieves the value in `obj` of a numerical field reflected by this `Field` object. If the field is static, `obj` is ignored. The field type must be either `byte`, `short`, `char`, `int`, or `long`.

The caller must have permission to access the field reflected by this `Field` object. See the class description for details.

PARAMETERS

`obj` A non-`null` object whose class inherits or declares this field, or in the case of a static field, any possibly `null` value.

RETURNS A `long` representing the value of this field.

EXCEPTIONS

`IllegalAccessException`
If the caller does not have permission to access this field. See the class description for details.

`IllegalArgumentException`
If `obj`'s class does not inherit or declare this field or if this field type cannot be converted to `long`.

`NullPointerException`
If this field is an instance field and `obj` is `null`.

SEE ALSO `setLong()`.

EXAMPLE See the class example.

A B C D E F G H I J K L M N O P Q R S T U V W X Y Z

getModifiers()

PURPOSE Retrieves the field modifiers for this `Field` object.

SYNTAX `public native int getModifiers()`

DESCRIPTION This method retrieves the field's set of modifiers bit-encoded as an `int`. The possible field modifiers are `public`, `protected`, `private`, `static`, `final`, `volatile`, and `transient`. To process the encoding, use the methods and constants in `Modifier`.

RETURNS An `int` representing the `Field` object's set of modifiers.

SEE ALSO `Modifier`.

EXAMPLE This example implements a program that prints all of the `public` fields (declared and inherited) of a class.

```
import java.lang.reflect.*;
import java.io.*;
import java.util.*;

class Main {
    Main(Class c) {
        Field fields[] = c.getFields();

        for (int i=0; i<fields.length; i++) {
            int mods = fields[i].getModifiers();
            System.out.print(Modifier.toString(mods & ~Modifier.PUBLIC));
            System.out.print(" ");
            System.out.print(fields[i].getType().getName());
```

```
                System.out.print(" ");
                System.out.println(fields[i].getName());
            }
        }

        public static void main(String[] args) {
            if (args.length != 1) {
                System.err.println("Usage: java Main <classname>");
            } else {
                try {
                    new Main(Class.forName(args[0]));
                } catch (ClassNotFoundException e) {
                    e.printStackTrace();
                }
            }
        }
    }
```

Output

```
> java Main java.awt.Point
int x
int y
> java Main java.lang.Thread
static final int MIN_PRIORITY
static final int NORM_PRIORITY
static final int MAX_PRIORITY
```

getName()

PURPOSE
Retrieves this `Field` object's name.

SYNTAX
`public String getName()`

DESCRIPTION
The name of a `Field` object is the string used to name the field in the source code. See the class description for more details.

RETURNS
A non-`null` string containing this `Field` object's name.

EXAMPLE
See `getModifiers()`.

getShort()

PURPOSE
Retrieves the contents of this numerical field as a `short` value.

SYNTAX
```
public native short getShort(Object obj) throws
   IllegalArgumentException, IllegalAccessException
```

DESCRIPTION
This method retrieves the value in `obj` of the numerical field reflected by this `Field` object. If the field is static, `obj` is ignored. The field type must be either `byte` or `short`.

The caller must have permission to access the field reflected by this `Field` object. See the class description for details.

PARAMETERS

`obj` A non-`null` object whose class inherits or declares this field, or in the case of a static field, any possibly `null` value.

RETURNS A `short` representing the value of this field.

EXCEPTIONS

`IllegalAccessException`
If the caller does not have permission to access this field. See the class description for details.

`IllegalArgumentException`
If `obj`'s class does not inherit or declare this field or if this field type cannot be converted to `short`.

`NullPointerException`
If this field is an instance field and `obj` is `null`.

SEE ALSO `setShort()`.

EXAMPLE See the class example.

getType()

PURPOSE Retrieves this `Field` object's type.

SYNTAX `public Class getType()`

DESCRIPTION This method retrieves this `Field` object's type. The type of a `Field` object is the field's type and is represented by a class object. See the class description for more details.

RETURNS A non-`null` `Class` object representing this `Field` object's type.

EXAMPLE See `getModifiers()`.

hashCode()

PURPOSE Computes the hash code for this `Field` object.

SYNTAX `public int hashCode()`

DESCRIPTION The `Field` object's hash code is an integer that is calculated from the `Field` object's name and declaring class name. Two equal `Field` objects will have the same hash code. Note that unequal `Field` objects might also have the same hash code, although the hash code algorithm minimizes this possibility. The hash code is typically used as the key in a hash table.

RETURNS The `Field` object's hash code.

OVERRIDES `java.lang.Object.hashCode()`.

SEE ALSO `equals()`, `java.util.Hashtable`.

EXAMPLE This example creates a `Field` object and inserts it into a hash table.

```
import java.awt.*;
import java.util.*;
import java.lang.reflect.*;

class Main {
    public static void main(String[] args) {
        Hashtable ht = new Hashtable();
        try {
            Field f = Point.class.getField("x");
            ht.put(f, f);
        } catch (NoSuchFieldException e) {
            e.printStackTrace();
        }
    }
}
```

set()

PURPOSE Sets the value of this `Field` object.

SYNTAX
```
public native void set(Object obj, Object val) throws
   IllegalArgumentException, IllegalAccessException
```

DESCRIPTION This method sets the value in `obj` of the field reflected by this `Field` object to the value of `val`. If the field is static, `obj` is ignored.

If the field holds a reference, `val` must be assignable to the field's type. If the field's type is primitive, `val` must be a wrapper object of the appropriate type. `val` is unwrapped and its value is automatically widened if necessary and assigned to the field. For example, if this is an `int` field, `val` must be an `Integer`, a `Short`, a `Character`, or a `Byte`. See Table 27 in the class description for the allowed primitive conversions.

The caller must have permission to update the field reflected by this `Field` object. See the class description for details.

PARAMETERS

`obj` A non-`null` object whose class inherits or declares this field, or in the case of a static field, any possibly `null` value.

`val` The possibly `null` new value.

EXCEPTIONS

`IllegalAccessException`
If this field is final or if the caller does not have permission to access this field. See the class description for details.

`IllegalArgumentException`
If `obj`'s class does not inherit or declare this field or if `val` cannot be converted to this field's type.

`NullPointerException`
If this field is an instance field and `obj` is `null` or if this field's type is primitive and `val` is `null`.

EXAMPLE This example demonstrates how to use an wrapper to set a field whose type is primitive.

```
import java.lang.reflect.*;

class Main {
    public static void main(String[] args) {
        try {
            C c = new C();
            Field fi = C.class.getField("i");
            Field ff = C.class.getField("f");
            Field fs = C.class.getField("s");

            fi.set(c, new Integer(10));
            ff.set(c, new Integer(10));
            fs.set(c, "Java");
            // fi.set(c, null); NullPointerException
        } catch (IllegalAccessException e) {
            e.printStackTrace();
        } catch (NoSuchFieldException e) {
            e.printStackTrace();
        }
    }
}

class C {
    public int i;
    public float f;
    public String s;
}
```

setBoolean()

PURPOSE Sets the value of this `boolean` field.

SYNTAX
```
public native void setBoolean(Object obj, boolean bval) throws
    IllegalArgumentException, IllegalAccessException
```

DESCRIPTION — This method sets the value in `obj` of the `boolean` field reflected by this `Field` object to `bval`. If the field is static, `obj` is ignored.

The caller must have permission to access the field reflected by this `Field` object. See the class description for details.

PARAMETERS

`bval` — The new `boolean` value.

`obj` — A non-`null` object whose class inherits or declares this field, or in the case of a static field, any possibly `null` value.

EXCEPTIONS

`IllegalAccessException`
If this field is final or if the caller does not have permission to access this field. See the class description for details.

`IllegalArgumentException`
If `obj`'s class does not inherit or declare this field or if this field's type is not `boolean`.

`NullPointerException`
If this field is an instance field and `obj` is `null`.

SEE ALSO — `getBoolean()`.

EXAMPLE — See `getByte()` and the class example.

setByte()

PURPOSE — Sets the value of this numerical field to a `byte` value.

SYNTAX

```
public native void setByte(Object obj, byte bval) throws
    IllegalArgumentException, IllegalAccessException
```

DESCRIPTION — This method sets the value in `obj` of the numerical field reflected by this `Field` object to `bval`. If the field is static, `obj` is ignored. This `Field` object's field type must be one of the following: `byte`, `short`, `int`, `long`, `float`, or `double`.

The caller must have permission to access the field reflected by this `Field` object. See the class description for details.

PARAMETERS

`bval` — The new `byte` value.

`obj` — A non-`null` object whose class inherits or declares this field, or in the case of a static field, any possibly `null` value.

EXCEPTIONS

`IllegalAccessException`
If this field is final or if the caller does not have permission to access this field. See the class description for details.

`IllegalArgumentException`
If `obj`'s class does not inherit or declare this field or if `bval` cannot be converted to this field's type.

`NullPointerException`
If this field is an instance field and `obj` is `null`.

SEE ALSO `getByte()`.

EXAMPLE This example demonstrates three things:

- `Field` objects on inherited fields are equal to `Field` objects on declared fields.
- The class from which you retrieve the Field is irrelevant.
- The `Field` object can be used to modify either a declared or an inherited field.
- The `byte` value is automatically widened to a `double` value.
- `set()` can be used with a wrapper in place of `setByte()`.

```
import java.lang.reflect.*;

class Main {
    public static void main(String[] args) {
        C c = new C();
        D d = new D();
        try {
            Field cf = C.class.getField("x");
            Field df = D.class.getField("x");

            System.out.println(cf.equals(df));          // true

            cf.setByte(d, (byte)8);
            cf.set(d, new Byte((byte)9));
            df.setByte(c, (byte)10);

            System.out.println(c.x);                    // 10.0
            System.out.println(d.x);                    // 9.0
        } catch (NoSuchFieldException e) {
            e.printStackTrace();
        } catch (IllegalAccessException e) {
            e.printStackTrace();
        }
    }
}

class C {
    public double x;
}
class D extends C {
}
```

setChar()

PURPOSE Sets the value of this field to a `char` value.

SYNTAX
```
public native void setChar(Object obj, char ch) throws
    IllegalArgumentException, IllegalAccessException
```

DESCRIPTION This method sets the value in `obj` of the field reflected by this `Field` object to `ch`. If the field is static, `obj` is ignored. This `Field` object's field type must be one of the following: `char`, `int`, `long`, `float`, or `double`.

The caller must have permission to access the field reflected by this `Field` object. See the class description for details.

PARAMETERS

`ch` The new `char` value.

`obj` A non-`null` object whose class inherits or declares this field, or in the case of a static field, any possibly `null` value.

EXCEPTIONS

`IllegalAccessException`

If this field is final or if the caller does not have permission to access this field. See the class description for details.

`IllegalArgumentException`

If `obj`'s class does not inherit or declare this field or if this field's type is not `char`.

`NullPointerException`

If this field is an instance field and `obj` is `null`.

SEE ALSO `getChar()`.

EXAMPLE See `getByte()` and the class example.

setDouble()

PURPOSE Sets the value of this `double` field.

SYNTAX
```
public native void setDouble(Object obj, double dval) throws
    IllegalArgumentException, IllegalAccessException
```

DESCRIPTION This method sets the value in `obj` of the `double` field reflected by this `Field` object to `dval`. If the field is static, `obj` is ignored.

The caller must have permission to access the field reflected by this `Field` object. See the class description for details.

PARAMETERS

`dval` The new `double` value.

obj — A non-null object whose class inherits or declares this field, or in the case of a static field, any possibly null value.

EXCEPTIONS

IllegalAccessException
: If this field is final or if the caller does not have permission to access this field. See the class description for details.

IllegalArgumentException
: If obj's class does not inherit or declare this field or if this field's type is not double.

NullPointerException
: If this field is an instance field and obj is null.

SEE ALSO getDouble().

EXAMPLE See getByte() and the class example.

setFloat()

PURPOSE Sets the value of this numerical field to a float value.

SYNTAX
```
public native void setFloat(Object obj, float fval) throws
   IllegalArgumentException, IllegalAccessException
```

DESCRIPTION This method sets the value in obj of the numerical field reflected by this Field object to fval. If the field is static, obj is ignored. This Field object's field type must be either float or double.

The caller must have permission to access the field reflected by this Field object. See the class description for details.

PARAMETERS

fval — The new float value.

obj — The possibly null object whose class inherits or declares this field. If null, field must be a static field.

EXCEPTIONS

IllegalAccessException
: If this field is final or if the caller does not have permission to access this field. See the class description for details.

IllegalArgumentException
: If obj's class does not inherit or declare this field or if fval cannot be converted to this field's type.

NullPointerException
: If this field is an instance field and obj is null.

SEE ALSO getFloat().

EXAMPLE See getByte() and the class example.

setInt()

PURPOSE
Sets the value of this numerical field to an `int` value.

SYNTAX
```
public native void setInt(Object obj, int ival) throws
   IllegalArgumentException, IllegalAccessException
```

DESCRIPTION
This method sets the value in `obj` of the numerical field reflected by this `Field` object to `ival`. If the field is static, `obj` is ignored. This `Field` object's field type must be one of the following: `int`, `long`, `float`, or `double`.

The caller must have permission to access the field reflected by this `Field` object. See the class description for details.

PARAMETERS

`ival` The new `int` value.

`obj` A non-`null` object whose class inherits or declares this field, or in the case of a static field, any possibly `null` value.

EXCEPTIONS

`IllegalAccessException`
If this field is final or if the caller does not have permission to access this field. See the class description for details.

`IllegalArgumentException`
If `obj`'s class does not inherit or declare this field or if `ival` cannot be converted to this field's type.

`NullPointerException`
If this field is an instance field and `obj` is `null`.

SEE ALSO
`getInt()`.

EXAMPLE
See `getByte()` and the class example.

setLong()

PURPOSE
Sets the value of this numerical field to a `long` value.

SYNTAX
```
public native void setLong(Object obj, long lval) throws
   IllegalArgumentException, IllegalAccessException
```

DESCRIPTION
This method sets the value in `obj` of the numerical field reflected by this `Field` object to `lval`. If the field is static, `obj` is ignored. This `Field` object's field type must be one of the following: `long`, `float`, or `double`.

The field being reflected must be accessible. See the class description for details.

PARAMETERS

`lval` The new `long` value.

`obj` A non-`null` object whose class inherits or declares this field, or in the case of a static field, any possibly `null` value.

EXCEPTIONS

`IllegalAccessException`
If this field is final or if the caller does not have permission to access this field. See the class description for details.

`IllegalArgumentException`
If `obj`'s class does not inherit or declare this field or if `lval` cannot be converted to this field's type.

`NullPointerException`
If this field is an instance field and `obj` is `null`.

SEE ALSO `getLong()`.

EXAMPLE See `getByte()` and the class example.

setShort()

PURPOSE Sets the value of this numerical field to a `short` value.

SYNTAX

```
public native void setShort(Object obj, short sval) throws
    IllegalArgumentException, IllegalAccessException
```

DESCRIPTION This method sets the value in `obj` of the numerical field reflected by this `Field` object to `sval`. If the field is static, `obj` is ignored. This `Field` object's field type must be one of the following: `short`, `int`, `long`, `float`, or `double`.

The caller must have permission to access the field reflected by this `Field` object. See the class description for details.

PARAMETERS

`obj` A non-`null` object whose class inherits or declares this field, or in the case of a static field, any possibly `null` value.

`sval` The new `short` value.

EXCEPTIONS

`IllegalAccessException`
If this field is final or if the caller does not have permission to access this field. See the class description for details.

`IllegalArgumentException`
If `obj`'s class does not inherit or declare this field or if `sval` cannot be converted to this field's type.

`NullPointerException`
If this field is an instance field and `obj` is `null`.

SEE ALSO `getShort()`.

EXAMPLE See `getByte()` and the class example.

toString()

PURPOSE Generates a string representing this `Field` object.

SYNTAX `public String toString()`

DESCRIPTION This method generates a string containing this `Field` object's name, type, and set of modifiers, as well as the fully qualified name of the declaring class. The order of the modifiers matches the canonical order as defined in *The Java Language Specification*. The canonical ordering is `public`, `protected`, `private`, `static`, `final`, `volatile`, and `transient`.

OVERRIDES `java.lang.Object.toString()`.

EXAMPLE This example creates two `Field` objects and uses `toString()` to print them out.

```
import java.lang.reflect.*;

class Main {
    public static void main(String[] args) {
        try {
            Field f1 = Thread.class.getField("MIN_PRIORITY");
            Field f2 = java.awt.Point.class.getField("x");

            System.out.println(f1.toString());
            System.out.println(f2.toString());

            // The following two lines are equivalent to the above two lines.
            // System.out.println(f1);
            // System.out.println(f2);
        } catch (NoSuchFieldException e) {
            e.printStackTrace();
        }
    }
}
```

Output

```
public static final int java.lang.Thread.MIN_PRIORITY
public int java.awt.Point.x
```

java.text
FieldPosition


```
java.lang.Object
  └─ FieldPosition
```

Syntax

```
public class FieldPosition extends Object
```

Description

Numbers and dates are made up of fields. A number can have an integer field and a fraction field. A date can have a year, month, week, day, hour, minute, and second field, among others.

The `FieldPosition` class holds the field constant that identifies a particular field and the begin index and end index of that field within a formatted number or date. This is useful for aligning a column of formatted numbers or dates on that field. For example, you can align numbers on a decimal point or dates on the year.

`FieldPosition` class identifies the position of a field in a formatted string by the characters from the begin index (inclusive) to the end index (exclusive).

If all you want is the contents of one or more date fields, use the `SimpleDateFormat` class instead. This gives you a simple way, using patterns, to get any combination of the day, month, year, hours, minutes, seconds, and so on.

Field position is not used when parsing a string to a number or date.

Usage

You call the constructor `FieldPosition()` to create a field position object, supplying the field constant for the field you want to format. For example, use `NumberFormat.INTEGER_FIELD` to identify the integer portion of a number. Then pass this field position as an input to the appropriate `format()` method for the number or date. The `format()` method formats the number or date and then locates the begin and end index values of the field in the resulting string. It then puts those values into the field position object.

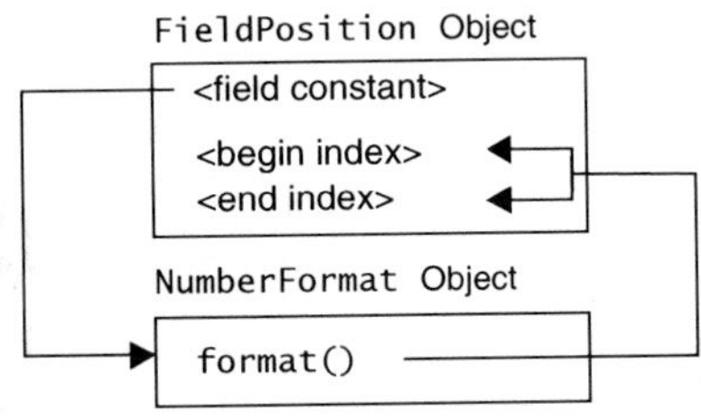

FIGURE 45: `FieldPosition`.

As shown in Figure 45, notice that the `FieldPosition` object holds the field constant that is used as input to the `format()` method. It also holds the resulting begin and end index values.

Field position objects are used by the `Format` family of classes. For example, a version of the `format()` method in the various `Format` classes requires a `FieldPosition` object as an argument. You use this `format` method to get the position of a field. For example, to update a field position object with the positions of the month field, do the following:

```
FieldPosition monthPos = new FieldPosition(DateFormat.MONTH_FIELD);
StringBuffer strbuf = new StringBuffer("");
Date date = new Date();
dateFormat.format(date, strbuf, monthPos);
```

The string buffer `strbuf` holds the entire formatted date string. The `monthPos` results in having its begin and end index values updated. See the class example for more detail.

Field Constants

Fields are identified by static constants, whose names typically end with `_FIELD`, defined in the various subclasses of `Format`. `NumberFormat` has only two fields: `INTEGER_FIELD` and `FRACTIONFIELD`. `DateFormat` has over a dozen fields, including `DATE_FIELD` and `YEAR_FIELD`. `MessageFormat` has no fields.

Index

An *index* is the zero-based position of a character in a string. The field ranges from `beginIndex()` (inclusive) to `endIndex()` (exclusive). Note that `endIndex()` has a value that is 1 greater than the last character in the field. These positions are updated after formatting to indicate where the field is located.

MEMBER SUMMARY	
Constructor	
`FieldPosition()`	Constructs a `FieldPosition` instance for a specific field.
Access Methods	
`getBeginIndex()`	Retrieves the index of the first character in this field.
`getEndIndex()`	Retrieves the index of the character following the last character in this field.
`getField()`	Retrieves the field identifier of this field.

See Also

`Format`, `DecimalFormat`, `NumberFormat`.

Example

This example prints a column of numbers aligned on the decimal point. It uses `FieldPosition` to get the begin and end index values of the integer portion of each number. It then subtracts that length from a constant, `COLUMNWIDTH`, and prints that many spaces ahead of the number.

```
import java.text.*;
import java.io.*;
import java.util.*;

class Main {
```

```
    // Width of column to the decimal separator
    static int COLUMNWIDTH = 7;

    // Create a parse position object for tracking the parse.
    static ParsePosition parsePos = new ParsePosition(0);

    // Create a number format.
    static NumberFormat numForm = NumberFormat.getInstance();


    Main (String str) {
        // Print out original text.
        System.out.println("Contents of input.txt:");
        System.out.println(str);

        // Parse through text for numbers.
        System.out.println("Aligned column of numbers:");
        parseNum(str);
    }

    static void parseNum(String str) {
        int beginParseIndex;
        int endParseIndex;
        int intLength;
        Number num = null;

        while (parsePos.getIndex() < str.length()) {

            beginParseIndex = parsePos.getIndex();


            // Parse the string starting at parsePos for a number.
            num = numForm.parse(str, parsePos);

            endParseIndex = parsePos.getIndex();

            if (num != null) {

                // Count length of integer portion for printing spaces.
                intLength =
                    ((new Integer(beginParseIndex)).toString()).length();

                // Count length of integer portion for printing spaces.
                intLength = countIntLength(numForm, num);

                printSpaces(COLUMNWIDTH - intLength);

                // Format the output so the column aligns.
                System.out.println(numForm.format(num));
            }
            parsePos.setIndex(endParseIndex + 1);
        }
        // Reset parse position to 0 for next loop.
        parsePos.setIndex(0);
    }

    // Count length of integer portion of number.
    static int countIntLength (NumberFormat numForm, Number num) {
        FieldPosition fp = new FieldPosition(NumberFormat.INTEGER_FIELD);
```

```
            StringBuffer strBuf = new StringBuffer("");
            long lg = num.longValue();
            numForm.format(lg, strBuf, fp);
            return (fp.getEndIndex() - fp.getBeginIndex());
        }

        // Print spaces.
        static void printSpaces(int count) {
            for (int p = 0; p < count; ++p) {
                System.out.print(" ");
            }
        }

        public static void main(String[] args) {

            // Accept an input text file
            if (args.length != 1) {
                System.err.println("This program aligns a column of numbers");
                System.err.println("Usage: java Main <filename>");
                System.exit(1);
            }
            try {
                // Read the text into a buffered reader
                // with '\n' for newlines
                BufferedReader rd = new BufferedReader(new FileReader(args[0]));
                String line;
                StringBuffer sbuf = new StringBuffer();

                while ((line = rd.readLine()) != null) {
                    sbuf.append(line);
                    sbuf.append('\n');
                }
                rd.close();

                // Call the constructor Main with the input string
                new Main(new String(sbuf));

            } catch (Exception e) {
                e.printStackTrace();
            }
        }
    }
```

Output

```
> java Main input.txt
Contents of input.txt:
1.000
19.48
1234.56
3847.2
294.93
2.483
0.2287
.8713
25

Aligned column of numbers:
      1
     19.48
```

A B C D E F G H I J K L M N O P Q R S T U V W X Y Z

```
1,234.56
3,847.2
  294.93
    2.483
    0.229
    0.871
   25
```

A B C D E F G H I J K L M N O P Q R S T U V W X Y Z

FieldPosition()

PURPOSE Constructs a `FieldPosition` instance for a specific field.

SYNTAX `public FieldPosition(int field)`

DESCRIPTION This method constructs an instance of `FieldPosition` for the field. Fields are identified by constants, whose names typically end with `_FIELD`, in the various subclasses of `Format`.

A field position object is passed in to some versions of the `format()` method in `NumberFormat` and `DateFormat`. A field position object holds the begin index and end indexes of the given field in the resulting format. Therefore, if a field position is created with an `HOUR_FIELD` and this field position object is passed into a `format()` method for a date, then `beginIndex()` and `endIndex()` will locate the hour substring in the date string.

Note: JDK 1.1.5 and earlier versions have a bug that does not allow these fields to be found in a date: `DATE_FIELD`, `DAY_OF_WEEK_IN_MONTH_FIELD`, and `DAY_OF_YEAR_FIELD`. This has been fixed in JDK 1.1.6.

PARAMETERS

`field` Any of the constants whose names typically end with `_FIELD` in subclasses of `Format`, namely in `DateFormat` and `NumberFormat`.

SEE ALSO `NumberFormat.INTEGER_FIELD`, `NumberFormat.FRACTION_FIELD`, `DateFormat.YEAR_FIELD`, `DateFormat.MONTH_FIELD`, and so on.

EXAMPLE See the class example.

getBeginIndex()

PURPOSE Retrieves the index of the first character in this field.

SYNTAX `public int getBeginIndex()`

RETURNS The index of the first character in this field.

EXAMPLE This example methodically prints out the begin and end index values for the day, month, and year fields for today's date. It first creates field position objects for the day, month, and year and the date format `fullDateForm`. It then uses the `format()` method to format the date and retrieve the begin and end index values for the individual day, month, and year fields of the date, as well as the content of those fields.

Note: This exhibits a bug in JDK 1.1.5, in which the `DATE_FIELD` is not properly found. This may be fixed in JDK 1.1.6.

See the class example for a more practical example of `getBeginIndex()`.

```
import java.text.*;
import java.io.*;
import java.util.*;

class Main {

    static String QUOTE = "\"";

    // Create field position objects for dates.
    static FieldPosition dayPos = new FieldPosition(DateFormat.DATE_FIELD);
    static FieldPosition monthPos = new FieldPosition(DateFormat.MONTH_FIELD);
    static FieldPosition yearPos = new FieldPosition(DateFormat.YEAR_FIELD);

    // Create date formats.
    static DateFormat fullDateForm =
           DateFormat.getDateInstance(DateFormat.FULL, Locale.US);

    public static void main(String[] args) {
        // Get the current date.
        Date date = new Date();

        // Create string buffer to hold date.
        StringBuffer strbuf = new StringBuffer("");

        // Format the date in full form
        fullDateForm.format(date, strbuf, dayPos);
        println("\nFull Date:     " + strbuf + "\n");

        System.out.print("Day:            ");
        printPositionValues(strbuf, dayPos);
        println("            (Bug)");
        strbuf.setLength(0);

        // Print the month
        System.out.print("Month:          ");
        fullDateForm.format(date, strbuf, monthPos);
        printPositionValues(strbuf, monthPos);
        println("");
        strbuf.setLength(0);

        // Print the year
        System.out.print("Year:           ");
        fullDateForm.format(date, strbuf, yearPos);
        printPositionValues(strbuf, yearPos);
        println("");
        strbuf.setLength(0);

        // Print the field constant values
```

```
        println("\nField contants");
        println("Day field:     " + dayPos.getField());         // 3
        println("Month field:   " + monthPos.getField());       // 2
        println("Year field:    " + yearPos.getField());        // 1

    }

    static String s;

    static void printPositionValues(StringBuffer strbuf, FieldPosition pos) {
        s = ("(" + pos.getBeginIndex() + ","
                            + pos.getEndIndex() + ")  ");
        print(s);
        printSpaces(10 - s.length());
        print(QUOTE + strbuf.toString().substring(pos.getBeginIndex(),
                            pos.getEndIndex()) + QUOTE);
    }


    static void print(String s) {
        System.out.print(s);
    }

    static void println(String s) {
        System.out.println(s);
    }

    // Print spaces.
    static void printSpaces(int count) {
        for (int p = 0; p < count; ++p) {
            System.out.print(" ");
        }
    }
}
```

Output

```
> java Main
Full Date:     Saturday, November 1, 1997

Day:           (0,0)     ""              (Bug)
Month:         (10,18)   "November"
Year:          (22,26)   "1997"

Field contants
Day field:     3
Month field:   2
Year field:    1
```

getEndIndex()

PURPOSE Retrieves the index of the character following the last character in this field.

SYNTAX `public int getEndIndex()`

RETURNS The index of the character following the last character in this field.

EXAMPLE See both the `getBeginIndex()` example and the class example.

getField()

PURPOSE Retrieves the field identifier of this field.

SYNTAX `public int getField()`

DESCRIPTION This method returns the field identifier of this field. This is an integer value of the field constant passed in to the `FieldPosition()` constructor. For example the following code fragment returns 2 (i.e. `DateFormat.MONTH_FIELD`).

```
(new FieldPosition(DateFormat.MONTH_FIELD)).getField()
```

RETURNS The field identifier.

EXAMPLE See the class example.

java.io
File

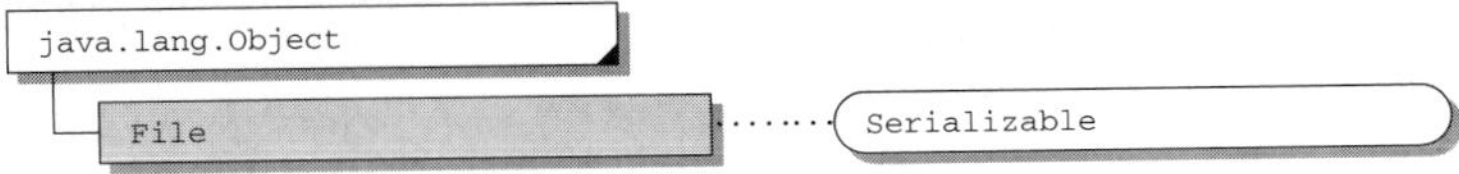

Syntax

```
public class File implements Serializable
```

Description

The `File` class represents a filename. The filename can be absolute, in which case it is resolved relative to the root directory of the file system. Or it can be relative, in which case it is resolved relative to the current directory in which the Java program is running. The filename is specified in the filename convention of the file system on which the Java program is running.

This class not only manipulates the filename itself. It also provides methods for performing file-related operations that actually interact with the underlying file system. Such operations include creating directories, obtaining the status of the file/directory, renaming the file, and checking permissions on the file.

Usage

The `File` class can be used to manipulate filenames; for example:

```
File f = new File("a:\\examples\\Main.java");
System.out.println(f.getParent());      // a:\examples
System.out.println(f.getName());        // Main.java
```

The `File` class can also be used to update the file system. The following code fragment renames a file in the file system.

```
File od = new File("a:\\examples");
File nd = new File("a:\\egs");
od.renameTo(nd);
```

MEMBER SUMMARY	
Constructor	
`File()`	Constructs an instance of `File`.
Filename Methods	
`getAbsolutePath()`	Generates the absolute (complete) pathname of this file.
`getCanonicalPath()`	Generates the absolute pathname of this file with all references resolved.
`getName()`	Retrieves the filename (no directory) of this file.

MEMBER SUMMARY	
`getParent()`	Retrieves the pathname of the parent directory of this file.
`getPath()`	Retrieves the pathname of this file.
`isAbsolute()`	Determines whether the pathname of this file is absolute.
`isDirectory()`	Determines whether this file names a directory.
`isFile()`	Determines whether this file names a regular file (nondirectory).
File Status Methods	
`canRead()`	Determines whether the current execution context is allowed to read this file.
`canWrite()`	Determines whether the current execution context is allowed to write to this file.
`exists()`	Determines whether this file exists.
`lastModified()`	Retrieves the last modification time of this file.
`length()`	Retrieves the size of this file in bytes.
File Namespace Methods	
`delete()`	Deletes this file or directory.
`list()`	Lists the files in the directory named by this file.
`mkdir()`	Creates a directory with the pathname of this file.
`mkdirs()`	Creates all directories in the pathname of this file.
`renameTo()`	Renames this file.
File System Property Fields (Static)	
`pathSeparator`	The path variable separator string of the operating system.
`pathSeparatorChar`	The path variable separator character of the operating system.
`separator`	The file directory separator string of the file system.
`separatorChar`	The file directory separator character of the file system.
Object Methods	
`equals()`	Compares this object with another object for equality.
`hashCode()`	Computes the hash code for the file.
`toString()`	Generates the string representation for this object.

See Also

`FileDescriptor`, `FileInputStream`, `FileOutputStream`, `FileReader`, `FileWriter`, `java.io.Serializable`.

Example

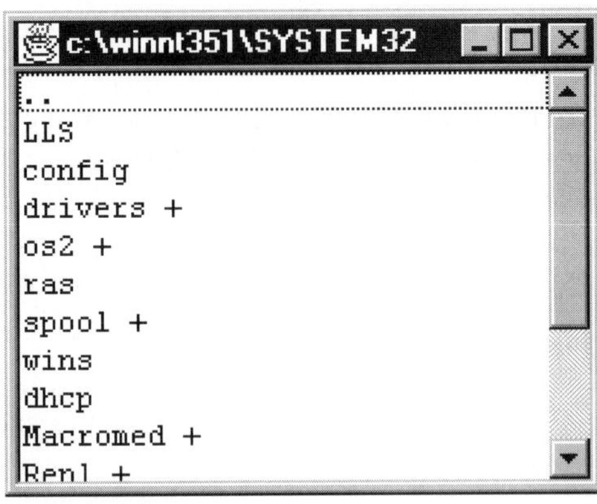

FIGURE 46: Directory Browser.

This example implements a simple directory browser. It shows only directories, not files. A directory with subdirectories has a + to the right of its name. Double-clicking a directory name moves the browser into that directory. If the directory name ".." is double-clicked, the browser moves up one directory.

```
import java.awt.*;
import java.awt.event.*;
import java.io.*;

class Main extends Frame implements
ActionListener {
    List list = new List();
    File curDir;

    Main(File dir) {
        curDir = dir;

        // Fill list with the directories in the current directory.
        display(null);

        // Listen for events.
        list.addActionListener(this);

        // Setup frame and display.
        setFont(new Font("Monospaced", Font.PLAIN, 12));
        add(list);
        setSize(300, 200);
        show();
    }

    // Fills list with the directories in the directory 'name'.
    void display(String name) {
        String[] filenames;
        if (name == null) {
            filenames = curDir.list();
        } else if (name.equals("..")) {
            curDir = new File(curDir.getParent());
        } else {
            curDir = new File(curDir, name);
        }

        // Get the filenames in curDir.
        filenames = curDir.list();

        if (filenames == null) {
            // This simplifies the subsequent code.
            filenames = new String[]{};
        }

        // Update the frame's title.
        setTitle(curDir.getAbsolutePath());
```

```
        for (int i=0; i<filenames.length; i++) {
            File f = new File(curDir, filenames[i]);

            // If f is a directory and has children, append a "+" to the name.
            if (f.isDirectory()) {
                String[] children = f.list();

                if (children != null) {
                    for (int j=0; j<children.length; j++) {
                        if ((new File(f, children[j])).isDirectory()) {
                            filenames[i] += " +";
                            break;
                        }
                    }
                }
            } else {
                filenames[i] = null;
            }
        }

        // Update the list component with the new filenames..
        list.removeAll();
        if (curDir.getParent() != null) {
            list.addItem("..");
        }
        for (int i=0; i<filenames.length; i++) {
            if (filenames[i] != null) {
                list.addItem(filenames[i]);
            }
        }
    }

    public void actionPerformed(ActionEvent evt) {
        String item = list.getSelectedItem();

        if (item != null && (item.equals("..") || item.endsWith(" +"))) {
            if (item.endsWith(" +")) {
                item = item.substring(0, item.length()-2);
            }
            // If item is a directory, update the list.
            display(item);
        }
    }

    public static void main(String[] args) {
        if (args.length == 1) {
            File dir = new File(args[0]);

            if (!dir.isDirectory()) {
                System.err.println(args[0] + " is not a directory.");
            } else if (!dir.exists()) {
                System.err.println(args[0] + " does not exist.");
            } else {
                new Main(new File(dir.getAbsolutePath()));
            }
        } else {
            System.err.println("Usage: java Main <directory>");
        }
    }
}
```

canRead()

PURPOSE Determines whether the current execution context is allowed to read this file.

SYNTAX `public boolean canRead()`

DESCRIPTION This method determines whether the current execution context is allowed, by the security manager and the underlying file system, to read this file. It returns `true` if allowed; `false` otherwise.

RETURNS `true` if allowed to read this file; `false` otherwise.

EXCEPTIONS

`SecurityException`
If this file cannot be read for security reasons.

SEE ALSO `java.lang.SecurityManager.checkRead()`.

EXAMPLE See `File()`.

canWrite()

PURPOSE Determines whether the current execution context is allowed to write to this file.

SYNTAX `public boolean canWrite()`

DESCRIPTION This method determines whether the current execution context is allowed, by the security manager and the underlying file system, to write to this file. It returns `true` if allowed; `false` otherwise.

RETURNS `true` if allowed to write to this file; `false` otherwise.

EXCEPTIONS

`SecurityException`
If this file cannot be written to for security reasons.

SEE ALSO `java.lang.SecurityManager.checkWrite()`.

EXAMPLE See `File()`.

delete()

PURPOSE Deletes this file or directory.

SYNTAX `public boolean delete()`

DESCRIPTION This method deletes this file or directory. If a directory, the directory must be empty before it can be removed. This method deletes only the file or directory if the current execution context is allowed by the security manager and the underlying file system to delete it.

RETURNS `true` if this file has been successfully deleted; `false` otherwise.

EXCEPTIONS

`SecurityException`

If this file cannot be deleted for security reasons.

SEE ALSO `java.lang.SecurityManager.checkDelete()`.

EXAMPLE This example shows the use of `delete()`, `mkdir()`, and `mkdirs()`. The program creates the specified directory (and any parent directories required) and a subdirectory beneath it.

```
import java.io.File;

class Main {
    public static void main(String[] args) {
        if (args.length != 1) {
            System.err.println("Usage: java Mods <newDirPath>");
            System.exit(-1);
        }

        File dir = new File(args[0]);
        if (dir.exists()) {
                System.out.println((dir.delete() ? "Deleted " :
                                    "Could not delete ") + dir.getPath());
        }
        if (dir.mkdirs()) {
            System.out.println("Created directory " + dir.getAbsolutePath());
            File subdir = new File(dir, "newSub");

            if (subdir.mkdir()) {
                System.out.println("Created subdirectory " +
                                   subdir.getAbsolutePath());
                System.out.println((subdir.delete() ? "Deleted " :
                                    "Could not delete ") + subdir.getPath());
            }
            else
                System.out.println("Could not create subdirectory " +
                                   subdir.getAbsolutePath());
            System.out.println((dir.delete() ? "Deleted " :
                                "Could not delete ") + dir.getPath());
        } else {
            System.out.println("Could not create directory " +
                               dir.getAbsolutePath());
        }
    }
}
```

equals()

PURPOSE Compares this object with another object for equality.

SYNTAX `public boolean equals(Object obj)`

DESCRIPTION This method determines whether this `File` object has the same path as that of `obj`. It returns `true` if the two paths are equal. It returns `false` if the two are not equal. It returns `false` if `obj` is `null` or is not a `File` object. The path comparison uses string comparison. Consequently, for file systems that support case-insensitive file pathnames, two paths that have characters that are the same but of different cases are not equal.

PARAMETERS

`obj` The possibly `null` object against which this object will be compared.

RETURNS `true` if `obj` has the same path as this object; `false` otherwise.

OVERRIDES `java.lang.Object.equals()`.

SEE ALSO `hashCode()`.

EXAMPLE See `renameTo()`.

exists()

PURPOSE Determines whether this file exists.

SYNTAX `public boolean exists()`

DESCRIPTION This method determines whether this file exists. The check can be made only if this current execution context is allowed, by the security manager and the underlying file system, to examine this file. It returns `true` if this file exists; `false` otherwise.

RETURNS `true` if this file exists; `false` otherwise.

EXCEPTIONS

`SecurityException`
If this file cannot be examined for security reasons.

SEE ALSO `java.lang.SecurityManager.checkRead()`.

EXAMPLE This example finds all of the drives that exists on a Windows NT machine (except for “a:” and “b:”).

```
import java.io.File;
class Main {
    public static void main(String[] args) {
        for (char ch='C'; ch<='Z'; ch++) {
            File f = new File(ch + ":");
```

```
            if (f.exists()) {
                System.out.println(f.toString());
            }
        }
    }
}
```


File()

PURPOSE Constructs an instance of File.

SYNTAX

```
public File(String path)
public File(String dirPath, String name)
public File(File dir, String name)
```

DESCRIPTION There are three forms of the constructor for the File class. The first form constructs an instance of File for the file pathname path. path can be absolute or relative (or even a single-component filename). If it is not an absolute pathname, it is taken to be relative to the current working directory of the program.

The second form constructs an instance of File using a file directory pathname dirPath and a pathname name to be taken relative to dirPath. dirPath and name are composed together (with the file directory separator in between) to obtain the path for the new File instance. dirPath can be an absolute pathname or a relative pathname. If dirPath is null, this form of the constructor is equivalent to new File(name).

The third form is similar to the second, except that it takes a File object as the directory to which name is relative.

PARAMETERS

dir The non-null File instance of the directory to which name is relative.

dirPath The possibly null pathname of the directory to which name is relative.

name The non-null file pathname relative to the directory specified (dirPath or dir).

path The non-null file pathname.

EXAMPLE This example shows the use of methods in the File class to print a detailed listing of files in a directory.

```
import java.io.File;
import java.util.Date;

class Main {
    public static void printOne(File f) {
        if (f.exists()) {
            System.out.print(f.canRead() ? "r" : "-");
            System.out.print(f.canWrite() ? "w" : "-");
            System.out.print(f.isDirectory() ? "x" : "-");
```

```
                System.out.print('\t');

                System.out.print(f.length());
                System.out.print('\t');

                System.out.print(new Date(f.lastModified()));
                System.out.print('\t');
            } else {
                System.out.print("\t\t\t\t\t");
            }
            System.out.println(f.getName());
        }
        public static void main(String[] args) {
            if (args.length != 1) {
                System.err.println("Usage: java Main <filepath>");
                System.exit(-1);
            }
            File f1 = new File(args[0]);
            String[] ls;
            int i;
            for (ls = f1.list(), i = 0;
                 ls != null && i < ls.length;
                 printOne(new File(f1, ls[i])), i++);
        }
    }
```

getAbsolutePath()

PURPOSE Generates the absolute (complete) pathname of this file.

SYNTAX `public String getAbsolutePath()`

DESCRIPTION An *absolute* pathname is a pathname that names a file starting at the root of the file system. Its precise definition is file system-dependent. This method generates the absolute pathname of this file. The actual file itself need not exist.

If this `File` instance was created with an absolute pathname, that pathname is returned. Otherwise, the current working directory of this program is composed with the pathname of this file (using the file directory separator) to generate the absolute pathname. The current working directory is determined using the system property `user.dir`.

RETURNS The non-`null` absolute file pathname of this file.

EXCEPTIONS

`SecurityException`

If not allowed to access the `user.dir` system property.

SEE ALSO `getPath()`, `isAbsolute()`, `java.lang.System.getProperty()`.

EXAMPLE This example shows the `getAbsolutePath()` method being used to obtain the absolute path for `File` instances that are created using absolute and relative pathnames on a Windows NT system.

```
System.out.println(new File("Main.java").getAbsolutePath());
                                        // e:\book\egs\io\File\Main.java
System.out.println(
    new File("c:\\frontpage_webs\\", "Content").getAbsolutePath());
                                        // c:\frontpage_webs\Content
System.out.println(
    new File("c:\\frontpage_webs", "Content").getAbsolutePath());
                                        // c:\frontpage_webs\Content
System.out.println(new File("\\tmp\\graphics").getAbsolutePath());
                                        // \tmp\graphics
```


getCanonicalPath()

PURPOSE Generates the absolute pathname of this file with all references resolved.

SYNTAX `public String getCanonicalPath() throws IOException`

DESCRIPTION An *absolute* pathname is a pathname that names a file starting at the root of the file system. Its precise definition is file system-dependent. A *canonical* pathname is an absolute pathname with all references resolved. Its precise definition is again file system-dependent. For example, some file systems support the notion of relative pathnames, where ".." is used to denote the parent directory. Calling `getCanonicalPath()` on such a file would resolve ".." to the name of its parent directory. If the actual file named by this `File` instance does not exist, the behavior of `getCanonicalPath()` is undefined. It might return the file's absolute pathname or throw an `IOException`.

RETURNS The non-`null` canonical file pathname of this file.

EXCEPTIONS

`IOException`

If an IO error occurred while attempting to determine the canonical pathname of the file.

`SecurityException`

If not allowed to access the `user.dir` system property.

SEE ALSO `getAbsolutePath()`, `getPath()`, `isAbsolute()`, `java.lang.System.getProperty()`.

EXAMPLE This example shows `getCanonicalPath()` being used to obtain the canonical path for `File` instances created using absolute and relative pathnames on a Unix system. In the third example, the names ".." and "." are resolved. In the last example, the `File` instance names a nonexistent file using the same ".."

and "." names; in this case, these names are not resolved and the absolute path is returned.

```
System.out.println(
    new File("Main.java").getCanonicalPath());
                                        // /home/rosanna/tmp/Main.java
System.out.println(
    new File("~rosanna").getCanonicalPath());
                                        // /home/rosanna/tmp/~rosanna
System.out.println(
    new File("/export/home/tmp/../java", ".").getCanonicalPath());
                                        // /export/home/java
System.out.println(
    new File("/notthere/home/tmp/../java", ".").getCanonicalPath());
                                        // /notthere/home/tmp/../java/.
```


getName()

PURPOSE Retrieves the filename (no directory) of this file.

SYNTAX `public String getName()`

DESCRIPTION This method returns the last (lowest-level) component of the pathname of this file. This is the name of the file (with no path/directory information).

RETURNS The non-`null` filename of this file.

SEE ALSO `getParent()`, `getPath()`.

EXAMPLE

```
System.out.println(new File("Main.java").getName());        // Main.java
System.out.println(
    new File("c:\\frontpage_webs\\", "Content").getName()); // Contents
System.out.println(new File("c:").getName());               // c:
System.out.println(new File("\\tmp\\graphics").getName());  // graphics
System.out.println(new File("\\tmp\\graphics\\").getName());// (empty string)
```

getParent()

PURPOSE Retrieves the pathname of the parent directory of this file.

SYNTAX `public String getParent()`

DESCRIPTION This method retrieves the pathname of the parent directory of this file. This is the pathname of the file, excluding the last (lowest-level) component. This method operates merely on the name of the file based on the arguments supplied to its original `File` constructor. For example, if no parent directory is supplied in the original pathname, `getParent()` returns `null`. This method does not use, for example, `getAbsolutePath()` to determine the parent directory. Neither does it check with the file system to see if the file has a parent by that name.

RETURNS The pathname of the parent directory; `null` if none is found.

SEE ALSO `getAbsolutePath()`, `getCanonicalPath()`, `getName()`, `getPath()`.

EXAMPLE

```
System.out.println(new File("Main.java").getParent());        // null
System.out.println(new File("c:").getParent());               // null
System.out.println(new File("c:\\").getParent());             // null
System.out.println(new File("c:\\tmp").getParent());          // c:\
System.out.println(new File("\\tmp").getParent());            // \
System.out.println(new File("\\tmp\\graphics").getParent());  // \tmp
System.out.println(new File("\\tmp\\graphics\\").getParent());// \tmp\graphics
```

A B C D E F G H I J K L M N O P Q R S T U V W X Y Z

getPath()

PURPOSE Retrieves the pathname of this file.

SYNTAX `public String getPath()`

DESCRIPTION The pathname of this file is the path with which this instance of `File` was created. Whereas `getAbsolutePath()` determines the complete path of the file, this method operates merely on the name of the file based on the arguments supplied to its original `File` constructor.

RETURNS The non-`null` pathname of this file.

SEE ALSO `File()`, `getAbsolutePath()`, `getCanonicalPath()`, `getName()`.

EXAMPLE

```
System.out.println(new File("Main.java").getPath());        // Main.java
System.out.println(new File("c:").getPath());               // c:
System.out.println(new File("c:\\tmp").getPath());          // c:\tmp
System.out.println(new File("\\tmp").getPath());            // \tmp
System.out.println(new File("\\tmp\\graphics").getPath());  // \tmp\graphics
System.out.println(new File("\\tmp\\graphics\\").getPath());// \tmp\graphics\
```

hashCode()

PURPOSE Computes the hash code for this file.

SYNTAX `public int hashCode()`

DESCRIPTION The hash code for a `File` object is calculated using the character values of its path. Two `Files` with the same path have the same hash code. However, two

Files with the same hash code may not necessarily have the same path. This method returns the hash code for this File object.

RETURNS The hash code of this file.

OVERRIDES java.lang.Object.hashCode().

SEE ALSO equals(), java.util.Hashtable.

EXAMPLE See renameTo().

A B C D E F G H I J K L M N O P Q R S T U V W X Y Z

isAbsolute()

PURPOSE Determines whether the pathname of this file is absolute.

SYNTAX `public native boolean isAbsolute()`

DESCRIPTION An *absolute* pathname is a pathname that names a file starting at the root of the file system. Its precise definition is file system-dependent. This method determines whether the pathname of this file is an absolute pathname.

On Unix, an absolute pathname has a leading separator. On Windows NT, an absolute pathname has either (a) a leading separator or a leading forward slash character (/) or (b) a drive specifier followed by a separator or forward slash. A driver specifier is a single letter followed by a colon (:). See the following examples.

RETURNS true if the pathname of this file is absolute; false otherwise.

SEE ALSO getAbsolutePath(), getPath(), separator.

EXAMPLE

```
System.out.println(new File("Main.java").isAbsolute());        // false
System.out.println(new File("c:").isAbsolute());               // false
System.out.println(new File("c:Main.java").isAbsolute());      // false
System.out.println(new File("c:/").isAbsolute());              // true
System.out.println(new File("c:\\").isAbsolute());             // true
System.out.println(new File("c:/tmp").isAbsolute());           // true
System.out.println(new File("c:\\tmp").isAbsolute());          // true
System.out.println(new File("/tmp").isAbsolute());             // true
System.out.println(new File("\\tmp").isAbsolute());            // true
System.out.println(new File("\\tmp\\graphics").isAbsolute());  // true
System.out.println(new File("\\tmp\\graphics\\").isAbsolute());// true
```

isDirectory()

PURPOSE Determines whether this file names a directory.

SYNTAX `public boolean isDirectory()`

DESCRIPTION This method determines from the file system whether this file names a directory. If the file does not exist, `false` is returned. This check can be made only if the current execution context is allowed, by the security manager and the underlying file system, to read this file.

RETURNS `true` if this file names a directory; `false` otherwise.

EXCEPTIONS

`SecurityException`

If this file cannot be examined due to security reasons.

SEE ALSO `isFile()`, `java.lang.SecurityManager.checkRead()`.

EXAMPLE

```
System.out.println(new File("Main.java").isDirectory());        // false
System.out.println(new File("c:").isDirectory());               // false
System.out.println(new File("e:Main.java").isDirectory());      // false
System.out.println(new File("c:\\").isDirectory());             // true
System.out.println(new File("c:\\notthere").isDirectory());     // false
System.out.println(new File("\\tmp").isDirectory());            // true
```

isFile()

PURPOSE Determines whether this file names a regular file (nondirectory).

SYNTAX `public boolean isFile()`

DESCRIPTION This method determines from the file system whether this file names a regular file (i.e., not a directory). If the file does not exist, `false` is returned. This check can be made only if the current execution context is allowed, by the security manager and the underlying file system, to read this file.

RETURNS `true` if this file names a regular file; `false` otherwise.

EXCEPTIONS

`SecurityException`

If this file cannot be examined due to security reasons.

SEE ALSO `isDirectory()`, `java.lang.SecurityManager.checkRead()`.

EXAMPLE

```
System.out.println(new File("Main.java").isFile());        // true
System.out.println(new File("c:").isFile());               // false
System.out.println(new File("e:Main.java").isFile());      // true
System.out.println(new File("c:\\").isFile());             // false
System.out.println(new File("c:\\notthere").isFile());     // false
System.out.println(new File("c:\\tmp").isFile());          // false
```

lastModified()

PURPOSE Retrieves the last modification time of this file.

SYNTAX `public long lastModified()`

DESCRIPTION This method retrieves the last modification time of this file. This method can be invoked only if the current execution context is allowed, by the security manager and the underlying file system, to read this file.

RETURNS The last modification time (in number of milliseconds since epoch).

EXCEPTIONS

`SecurityException`
If this file cannot be examined due to security reasons.

SEE ALSO `java.util.Date`, `java.lang.SecurityManager.checkRead()`.

EXAMPLE See `File()`.

length()

PURPOSE Retrieves the size of this file in bytes.

SYNTAX `public long length()`

DESCRIPTION This method retrieves the size of this file in bytes. It can be invoked only if the current execution context is allowed, by the security manager and the underlying file system, to read this file.

RETURNS The number of bytes in this file.

EXCEPTIONS

`SecurityException`
If this file cannot be examined due to security reasons.

SEE ALSO `java.lang.SecurityManager.checkRead()`.

EXAMPLE See `File()`.

list()

PURPOSE Lists the files in the directory named by this file.

SYNTAX

```
public String[] list()
public String[] list(FilenameFilter filter)
```

DESCRIPTION This method lists the files in the directory named by this file. If a filename filter `filter` is supplied, the names returned are the subset of files found in the directory that satisfy `filter`. If no filter is supplied, the names of all of the files found in this directory are returned.

If this file does not name a directory, `null` is returned. The names "." and ".." —which are used to indicate the current directory and parent directory, respectively—are not included in this list.

This method can be invoked only if the current execution context is allowed, by the security manager and the underlying file system, to read this file.

PARAMETERS

`filter` The filter used to select filenames.

RETURNS The possibly `null` filter-selected files in the directory named by this file.

EXCEPTIONS

`SecurityException`

If this file cannot be examined due to security reasons.

SEE ALSO `FilenameFilter`, `isDirectory()`, `java.lang.SecurityManager.checkRead()`.

EXAMPLE See the class examples of `File` and `FilenameFilter`.

mkdir()

PURPOSE Creates a directory with the pathname of this file.

SYNTAX `public boolean mkdir()`

DESCRIPTION This method creates a directory with the pathname of this file. All intermediate directories in the pathname of this file must already exist.

This method can be executed only if this current execution context is allowed, by the security manager and the underlying file system, to write to (create) this directory. This method returns `true` if the directory was created successfully. It returns `false` otherwise or if the directory already exists.

RETURNS `true` if the directory was created successfully; `false` otherwise.

EXCEPTIONS

`SecurityException`

If this directory could not be created due to security reasons.

SEE ALSO `mkdirs()`, `java.lang.SecurityManager.checkWrite()`.

EXAMPLE See `delete()`.

mkdirs()

PURPOSE Creates all directories in the pathname of this file.

SYNTAX `public boolean mkdirs()`

DESCRIPTION This method creates all directories in the pathname of this file, including this file itself. It returns `true` if all directories were successfully created. If any of the intermediate directories already exist, `mkdirs()` skips it and attempts the next directory below it. If the terminal directory itself exists, this method returns `false`.

This method can be executed only if this current execution context is allowed, by the security manager and the underlying file system, to write to (create) this directory.

RETURNS `true` if all directories in this path have been successfully created (or already exist); `false` otherwise.

SEE ALSO `mkdir()`, `java.lang.SecurityManager.checkWrite()`.

EXAMPLE See `delete()`.

A B C D E F G H I J K L M N O P Q R S T U V W X Y Z

pathSeparator

PURPOSE The path variable separator string of the operating system.

SYNTAX `public static final String pathSeparator`

DESCRIPTION *Path variables* are used by operating systems and programs to specify an ordered search path. For example, Java defines a CLASSPATH variable that specifies the search order for Java classes for the default Java class loader. Each item in the search path is separated by a *path variable separator* character. This character varies depending on the operating system. On UNIX, the separator is the colon (:). On Windows NT, it is the semicolon (;).

The `pathSeparator` field represents the path variable separator character of the operating system as a string. This field's value is determined by the `path.separator` system property.

SEE ALSO `pathSeparatorChar`, `java.lang.System.getProperty()`.

EXAMPLE This method parses a path variable string into its component.

```
import java.io.File;
import java.util.StringTokenizer;
import java.util.NoSuchElementException;

class Main {
    public static void main(String[] args) {
```

```
            if (args.length != 1) {
                System.err.println("Usage: java Main <path>");
                System.exit(-1);
            }
            StringTokenizer parser =
                new StringTokenizer(args[0], File.pathSeparator);
            System.out.println("\nInput: " + args[0]);
            System.out.println("There are " + parser.countTokens() +
                                   " entries in the path");
            try {
                while(parser.hasMoreTokens()) {
                    System.out.println(parser.nextToken());
                }
            } catch (NoSuchElementException e) {
                System.err.println(e);
            }
        }
    }
```

pathSeparatorChar

PURPOSE The path variable separator character of the operating system.

SYNTAX `public static final char pathSeparatorChar`

SEE ALSO `pathSeparator`, `java.lang.System.getProperty()`.

EXAMPLE The usage of this field is similar to that of `pathSeparator`.

renameTo()

PURPOSE Renames this file.

SYNTAX `public boolean renameTo(File dest)`

DESCRIPTION This method renames this file to the new filename `dest`. Successful renaming of this file does not affect the filename of this instance of `File`. For example, `getPath()` will still return the same string that it did before `renameTo()` was called.

This method can be executed only if this current execution context is allowed, by the security manager and the underlying file system, to rename this file to `dest`.

PARAMETERS

`dest` The new filename.

RETURNS `true` if this file has been successfully renamed to `dest`; `false` otherwise.

EXCEPTIONS

`SecurityException`
If this file cannot be renamed to `dest` for security reasons.

SEE ALSO `java.lang.SecurityManager.checkWrite()`.

EXAMPLE This example renames a file.

```
import java.io.File;

class Main {
    public static void main(String[] args) {
        if (args.length != 2) {
            System.err.println("Usage: java Main <file1> <file2>");
            System.exit(-1);
        }
        File f1 = new File(args[0]);
        File f2 = new File(args[1]);
        System.out.println("f1: " + f1.toString() + " " + f1.hashCode());
        System.out.println("f2: " + f2.toString() + " " + f2.hashCode());

        if (f1.equals(f2)) {
            System.err.println("Cannot rename a file to itself");
            System.exit(-1);
        }
        System.out.println(f1.getPath() +
           (f1.renameTo(f2) ? " renamed to " : " could not be renamed to ") +
                            f2.getPath());

        // check f1 and f2: their path and hash codes
        System.out.println("f1: " + f1.toString() + " " + f1.hashCode());
        System.out.println("f2: " + f2.toString() + " " + f2.hashCode());
    }
}
```

separator

PURPOSE The file directory separator string of the file system.

SYNTAX `public static final String separator`

DESCRIPTION Each directory name in a file pathname is separated by a *directory separator* character. This character is file system-dependent. On UNIX, the character is the forward slash (/). On Windows NT, it is the backward slash (\).

The `separator` field contains the directory separator character in a string. This field's value is determined by the `file.separator` system property.

SEE ALSO `separatorChar`, `java.lang.System.getProperty()`.

EXAMPLE

```
import java.io.File;
import java.util.*;
```

```
class Main {
    public static void main(String[] args) {
        if (args.length != 1) {
            System.err.println("Usage: java Main <filepath>");
            System.exit(-1);
        }
        String path = (new File(args[0])).getAbsolutePath();
        StringTokenizer parser = new StringTokenizer(path, File.separator);
        System.out.println("\nInput: " + path);
        System.out.println("There are " + parser.countTokens() +
                           " components in the file pathname");
        try {
            while(parser.hasMoreTokens()) {
                System.out.println(parser.nextToken());
            }
        } catch (NoSuchElementException e) {
            System.err.println(e);
        }
    }
}
```

separatorChar

PURPOSE The file directory separator character of the file system.

SYNTAX `public static final char separatorChar`

SEE ALSO `separator`, `java.lang.System.getProperty()`.

EXAMPLE This usage of this field is similar to that of `separator`.

toString()

PURPOSE Generates the string representation for this object.

SYNTAX `public String toString()`

DESCRIPTION The string representation of a `File` object is the file pathname with which it was created. This is the same as the result returned by `getPath()`. `toString()` returns this string representation.

RETURNS The non-`null` string representation of this file.

OVERRIDES `java.lang.Object.toString()`.

SEE ALSO `File()`, `getPath()`.

EXAMPLE See `renameTo()`.

java.io

FileDescriptor

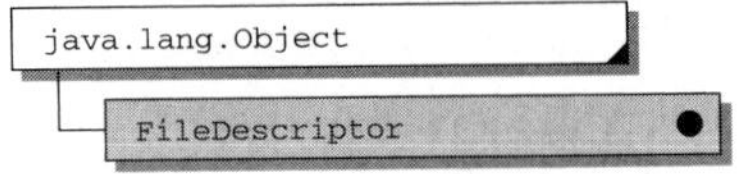

A
B
C
D
E
F
G
H
I
J
K
L
M
N
O
P
Q
R
S
T
U
V
W
X
Y
Z

Syntax

```
public final class FileDescriptor
```

Description

A *file descriptor* is a compact representation of information required to access and manipulate an open file or device (such as a socket). When you open a file, you get back a file descriptor for it. Thereafter, you use this file descriptor for reading from or writing to the file. The operations allowed on the file descriptor are determined by the mode in which you opened the file. For example, if you opened a file for reading, then the file descriptor you get back will allow read operations on the file.

The `FileDescriptor` class is used to represent a file descriptor.

Usage

In the Java class libraries, you typically need not manipulate file descriptors directly. Java defines IO stream classes for files and sockets that use file descriptors internally. Therefore, instead of using file descriptors directly, you typically use file/socket stream references to perform IO operations. However, for those special cases in which you want to use file descriptors directly, these IO classes provide constructors that accept a file descriptor as an argument.

Standard Input/Output

There are three open file descriptors associated with the three standard open files: input, output, and error output. Standard input is used by the program to read data input by the user who is running the program. Standard output is used by the program to print text output for display to the user. Standard error output is used by the program to print error messages to the user. The `FileDescriptor` class defines three fields that correspond to each of these standard descriptors: `in`, `out`, and `err`. You can use these fields directly when doing standard IO. However, you are advised to use the corresponding IO streams in `System` (`System.in`, `System.out`, and `System.err`); these provide a much easier-to-use abstraction for doing standard IO.

MEMBER SUMMARY	
Standard IO Fields	
err	File descriptor for standard error output.
in	File descriptor for standard input.
out	File descriptor for standard output.
File Descriptor Methods	
sync()	Flushes the changes to the corresponding physical device.
valid()	Determines whether this file descriptor is valid.

See Also

FileInputStream, FileOutputStream, RandomAccessFile, java.net.SocketImpl, SyncFailedException, java.lang.System.err, java.lang.System.in, java.lang.System.out.

Example

This example shows how standard in, out, and err can be accessed using file descriptors instead of using System.in, System.out, and System.err.

```
import java.io.*;

class Main {
    public static void main(String[] args) {
        FileOutputStream stderr =
            new FileOutputStream(FileDescriptor.err);
        FileOutputStream stdout =
            new FileOutputStream(FileDescriptor.out);
        FileInputStream stdin =
            new FileInputStream(FileDescriptor.in);
        try {
            StringBuffer sb = new StringBuffer();
            int c;
            while ((c=stdin.read()) > -1) {
                if (c == '\n' || c == '\r')
                    break;
                sb.append((char)c);
            }
            // print to standard out
            byte[] buf = sb.toString().getBytes();
            stdout.write(buf);
            stdout.write('\n');
            stdout.flush();
        } catch (IOException e) {
            e.printStackTrace();
        }
    }
}
```

A B C D E F G H I J K L M N O P Q R S T U V W X Y Z

in

PURPOSE File descriptor for standard input.

SYNTAX `public static final FileDescriptor in`

SEE ALSO `System.in`.

EXAMPLE See the class example.

out

PURPOSE File descriptor for standard output.

SYNTAX `public static final FileDescriptor out`

SEE ALSO `System.out`.

EXAMPLE See the class example.

err

PURPOSE File descriptor for standard error output.

SYNTAX `public static final FileDescriptor err`

SEE ALSO `System.err`.

EXAMPLE See the class example.

sync()

PURPOSE Flushes the changes to the corresponding physical device.

SYNTAX `public native void sync() throws SyncFailedException`

DESCRIPTION This method flushes to the corresponding physical device all of the updates made to the contents and attributes of the file associated with this file descriptor. This method blocks until all such changes have been flushed.

Calling `write()` and `flush()` on an output stream differs from calling `sync()` on a file descriptor. Calling `write()` and `flush()` typically writes any internal program data to system buffers, which hold the changes before they are written to the physical devices. Changes held in a system buffer may not always be written immediately to the buffer's corresponding physical device. If the system crashes before the physical device has been updated, the changes are lost. Calling `sync()` on the file descriptor pushes the changes from the system buffer to the physical device. When `sync()` returns, the program can be sure that its changes have been committed to the physical device.

EXCEPTIONS

`SyncFailedException`

If the updates cannot be flushed to the physical device or if the system cannot guarantee that the updates have been flushed.

EXAMPLE This example makes a copy of a file. Before closing the new file, the example gets the new file's file descriptor and calls `sync()` on it to make sure that the changes were written to the underlying file system.

```
import java.io.*;

class Main {
    public static void main(String[] args) {
        if (args.length == 0) {
            System.err.println("java Main <inputfile> <outputfile>");
            System.exit(-1);
        }
        try {
            FileInputStream in = new FileInputStream(args[0]);
            FileOutputStream out = new FileOutputStream(args[1]);

            byte[] buf = new byte[512];
            int count;
            while ((count = in.read(buf)) > 0) {
                out.write(buf, 0, count);
            }
            in.close();
            out.flush();               // Flush data
            out.getFD().sync();        // Commit changes to disk
            out.close();
        } catch (IOException e) {
            e.printStackTrace();
        }
    }
}
```

valid()

PURPOSE Determines whether this file descriptor is valid.

SYNTAX `public native boolean valid()`

DESCRIPTION A file descriptor is associated with an open file. A file descriptor is *valid* if it has not been closed. This method determines whether this file descriptor is valid.

RETURNS `true` if the file descriptor is valid; `false` otherwise.

EXAMPLE

```
import java.io.FileInputStream;
import java.io.IOException;
import java.io.FileDescriptor;

class Main {
    public static void main(String[] args) {
        if (args.length != 1) {
            System.err.println("Usage: java Main <input_file>");
            System.exit(-1);
        }
        try {
            FileInputStream in = new FileInputStream(args[0]);
            if (in.getFD().valid())
                System.out.println("got valid file descriptor");
            // ...

            in.close();
        } catch (IOException e) {
            e.printStackTrace();
        }
    }
}
```

FileInputStream

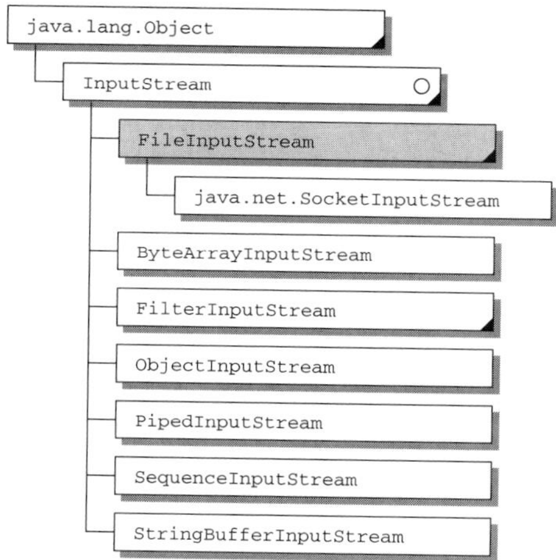

Syntax

```
public class FileInputStream extends InputStream
```

Description

The `FileInputStream` class provides methods for reading input from a file (Figure 47).

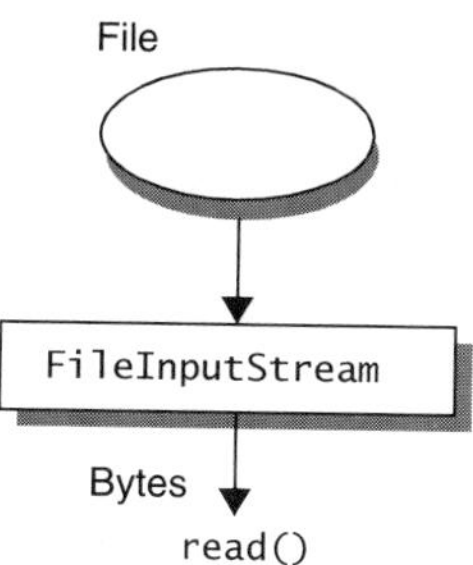

FIGURE 47: **`FileInputStream`.**

Usage

This class can be used directly to read data from a file, or it can be composed with other streams or readers to read data from a file. The following code uses `FileInputStream` directly:

```
FileInputStream in = newFileInputStream("inputfile");
byte[] buf = new byte[512];
while (in.read(buf) > 0) ...
```

The following code composes an `InputStreamReader` with a `FileInputStream` to read character files. `FileReader` can be used for the same purpose.

```
InputStreamReader in =
    new InputStreamReader(new FileInputStream("inputfile"));
char[] buf = new char[512];
while (in.read(buf) > 0) ...
```

FileInputStream versus FileReader

`FileInputStream` is meant for reading bytes (0–255) from a file. `FileReader` is a convenience class for reading characters from a file. If you are reading characters from a file that has a particular encoding, you can use `FileInputStream` with `InputStreamReader` as shown previously.

MEMBER SUMMARY

Constructor	
`FileInputStream()`	Constructs a `FileInputStream` instance.
Input Methods	
`read()`	Reads bytes from this file input stream.
`skip()`	Skips bytes from this file input stream.
Stream Methods	
`available()`	Determines the number of bytes that can be read without being blocked.
`close()`	Closes this file input stream.
`finalize()`	Called by the Java virtual machine to close this file input stream when it is ready to be discarded.
File Descriptor Method	
`getFD()`	Retrieves the file descriptor used by this file input stream.

See Also

`File`, `FileDescriptor`, `FileOutputStream`, `FileReader`, `FileWriter`, `InputStream`, `InputStreamReader`.

Example

This example shows the use of a file input stream to make a copy of a file.

```
import java.io.*;

class Main {
    public static void main(String[] args) {
        if (args.length != 2) {
            System.err.println("java Main <inputfile> <outputfile>");
            System.exit(-1);
        }
        try {
            FileInputStream in = new FileInputStream(args[0]);
            FileOutputStream out = new FileOutputStream(args[1]);

            byte[] buf = new byte[512];
```

```
                int count;
                while ((count = in.read(buf)) > 0) {
                    out.write(buf, 0, count);
                }
                in.close();
                out.close();
            } catch (IOException e) {
                e.printStackTrace();
            }
        }
    }
```

A B C D E F G H I J K L M N O P Q R S T U V W X Y Z

available()

PURPOSE — Determines the number of bytes that can be read without being blocked.

SYNTAX — `public native int available() throws IOException`

DESCRIPTION — This method returns the number of bytes that can be read from this file input stream without being blocked. This number is less than or equal to the number of bytes left to be read from the file.

RETURNS — The number of bytes that can be read without being blocked.

EXCEPTIONS

`IOException`

If an IO error occurred.

OVERRIDES — `InputStream.available()`.

EXAMPLE — See `InputStream.available()`.

close()

PURPOSE — Closes this file input stream.

SYNTAX — `public native void close() throws IOException`

DESCRIPTION — This method closes this file input stream. It releases any resources, such as file descriptors, used by this file input stream. If the file has already been closed, this method does nothing.

EXCEPTIONS

`IOException`

If an IO error occurred.

OVERRIDES — `InputStream.close()`.

EXAMPLE — See the class example.

FileInputStream()

PURPOSE Constructs a `FileInputStream` instance.

SYNTAX
```
public FileInputStream(String filename) throws
   FileNotFoundException
public FileInputStream(File file) throws FileNotFoundException
public FileInputStream(FileDescriptor fd)
```

DESCRIPTION There are three forms of this constructor for `FileInputStream`. The first form constructs a file input stream for the file that has the name `filename`. `filename` is a platform-dependent name of the file. It can be an absolute or a relative pathname of the file. If absolute, it is resolved relative to the root of the file system. If relative, it is resolved relative to the current directory in which the Java program was started. The second form constructs a file input stream for the file identified by the `File` object file. The third form constructs a file input stream using the open file descriptor `fd`.

The file input stream may be created only if the current execution context is allowed, by the security manager and the underlying file system, to read the specified file.

PARAMETERS
- `fd` The non-`null` open file descriptor of the file.
- `file` The non-`null` `File` object of the file.
- `filename` The non-`null` string name of the file.

EXCEPTIONS
- `FileNotFoundException`
  If the file is not found.
- `SecurityException`
  If the file cannot be read due to security reasons.

SEE ALSO `File, FileDescriptor, java.lang.SecurityManager.checkRead().`

EXAMPLE See the class example, `available()`.

finalize()

PURPOSE Called by the Java virtual machine to close this file input stream when it is ready to be discarded.

SYNTAX
```
protected void finalize() throws IOException
```

DESCRIPTION This method is called by the Java virtual machine when this object is ready to be discarded. See `Object.finalize()` for details.

OVERRIDES `java.lang.Object.finalize().`

SEE ALSO `close()`, `java.lang.System.gc()`, `java.lang.System.runFinalization()`, `java.lang.System.runFinalizersOnExit()`.

getFD()

PURPOSE Retrieves the file descriptor used by this file input stream.

SYNTAX `public final FileDescriptor getFD() throws IOException`

RETURNS The (non-`null`) file descriptor used by this file input stream.

EXCEPTIONS

`IOException`

If the file has already been closed and consequently no longer has a file descriptor.

SEE ALSO `FileDescriptor`.

EXAMPLE

```
FileInputStream in = new FileInputStream("somefilename");

// Creates stream using file descriptor of another stream
FileInputStream in2 = new FileInputStream(in.getFD());
```

read()

PURPOSE Reads bytes from this file input stream.

SYNTAX

```
public native int read() throws IOException
public int read(byte[] buffer) throws IOException
public int read(byte[] buffer, int offset, int count) throws
    IOException
```

DESCRIPTION This method reads bytes from this file input stream. The first form of this method reads a single byte (8 bits) from this file input stream and returns it as a 32-bit `int`. The first three bytes of the `int` are not used. `read()` blocks until a byte is available for reading from this input stream. If end-of-file is reached on this stream, `read()` returns `-1`.

The second and third forms read bytes from this file input stream and store the bytes read into the `byte` array `buffer`. If `count` is specified, it reads at most `count` number of bytes from this stream; otherwise, it reads at most `buffer.length` number of bytes. If `offset` is specified, `read()` stores the bytes read in `buffer` starting at `offset`; otherwise, the bytes are stored starting at index `0`. `read()` returns the number of bytes actually read from this stream.

If end-of-file is reached on this stream before any bytes are read, read() returns -1.

PARAMETERS

buffer The non-null byte array into which the data read is stored.

count The number of bytes to read. 0 ≤ count ≤ buffer.length-offset.

offset The index in buffer at which to start storing the bytes read. 0 ≤ offset < buffer.length.

RETURNS The first form returns the byte read. The second and third forms return the actual number of bytes read. All forms return -1 if end-of-file has been reached before any bytes have been read.

EXCEPTIONS

ArrayIndexOutOfBoundsException
If count or offset is outside of the specified bounds.

IOException
If an IO error occurred while attempting to read.

OVERRIDES InputStream.read().

SEE ALSO skip().

EXAMPLE See the class example and skip().

skip()

PURPOSE Skips bytes from this file input stream.

SYNTAX `public native long skip(long count) throws IOException`

DESCRIPTION This method skips count number of bytes from this file input stream. Bytes that are skipped will not be returned in subsequent read() calls. skip() returns the actual number of bytes skipped.

PARAMETERS

count The number of bytes to be skipped.

RETURNS The actual number of bytes skipped.

EXCEPTIONS

IOException
If an IO error occurred while attempting to read.

OVERRIDES InputStream.skip().

EXAMPLE This example demonstrates the use of available() and skip(). It opens a file and uses available() to determine the number of bytes in the file and then skips half of the file before echoing the rest to standard output.

```
import java.io.*;

class Main {
    public static void main(String[] args) {
        if (args.length != 1) {
            System.err.println("Usage: java Main <input_file>");
            System.exit(-1);
        }
        try {
            File f = new File(args[0]);
            FileInputStream in = new FileInputStream(f);
            long size = f.length();           // Get size of file.

            in.skip(size/2);                  // Skip half the file.

            int c;
            while ((c=in.read()) > -1)        // Echo the rest.
                System.out.print((char)c);

            in.close();                       // Close it.
            System.out.flush();
        } catch (FileNotFoundException e) {
            System.err.println(args[0] + " is not found");
        } catch (IOException e) {
            e.printStackTrace();
        }
    }
}
```

java.io
FilenameFilter

FilenameFilter

A B C D E F G H I J K L M N O P Q R S T U V W X Y Z

Syntax

`public interface FilenameFilter`

Description

Given a list of filenames, you can use a *filename filter* to obtain a subset of those filenames. The filename filter defines the properties that a filename must have in order to pass the filter. For example, a filename filter might only accept filenames that have a `.java` extension.

The `FilenameFilter` interface is used to create filename filters.

Usage

This interface is used to filter out filenames. For example, `File.list()` accepts a `FilenameFilter` to determine which filenames it should return.

MEMBER SUMMARY	
Filter Method	
`accept()`	Determines whether a filename passes this filename filter.

See Also

`File.list()`, `java.awt.FileDialog.getFilenameFilter()`, `java.awt.FileDialog.setFilenameFilter()`.

Example

This example defines a filename filter that accepts only files with the `.java` file extension.

```
import java.io.FilenameFilter;
import java.io.File;

class JavaSrcFilter implements FilenameFilter {
    public boolean accept(File dir, String name) {
        return (name.endsWith(".java"));
    }
}

class Main {
    public static void main (String[] args) {
        String dir = ".";
```

```
        if (args.length == 1)
            dir = args[0];

        File f1 = new File(dir);
        int i;
        String[] ls;
        FilenameFilter filter = new JavaSrcFilter();
        System.out.println("Java Source Files: " );
        for (ls = f1.list(filter), i = 0;
             ls != null && i < ls.length;
             System.out.println("\t" + ls[i++]));
    }
}
```

A B C D E F G H I J K L M N O P Q R S T U V W X Y Z

accept()

PURPOSE Determines whether a filename passes this filename filter.

SYNTAX `boolean accept(File dir, String name)`

DESCRIPTION This method determines whether a file from the directory `dir` with filename `name` has the properties required to pass this filename filter. It returns `true` if the filename passes the filter; `false` otherwise.

PARAMETERS

`dir` The possibly `null` directory in which the file is found. If `null`, `name` is relative to the current working directory in which the java program was invoked.

`name` The non-`null` name of the file.

RETURNS `true` if the specified file passes this filename filter; `false` otherwise.

SEE ALSO `File.list()`, `java.awt.FileDialog`.

EXAMPLE See the class example.

java.net
FileNameMap

FileNameMap

Syntax

```
public interface FileNameMap
```

Description

The `FileNameMap` interface is used to map a filename into its corresponding content type. The content type—also referred to as the *MIME type*—is specified using MIME (*RFC 2046*) and consists of a media type and a subtype. For example, an HTML document has a content type "text/html" consisting of the media type "text" and subtype "html", while a movie might have a content type of "video/mpeg" consisting of the media type "video" and subtype "mpeg".

Usage

`FileNameMap` is useful when implementing URL stream handlers—classes that load the contents of a URL using a particular protocol. The handler sends a request to the server identified by the URL and receives back data, or *content*. The handler must determine the type of the content in order to return an object of the appropriate class to the caller. The content's type is often explicitly specified in the response received by the handler. However, sometimes no content type is specified, in which case the handler must use heuristics to determine the content's type. One possible heuristic is to determine the content's type using the URL or the file's filename. The heuristics used are determined by the URL stream handler.

`FileNameMap` is an interface for determining the content type of a file by inspecting its name. The abstract class `URLConnection`, whose implementation is supplied by an individual URL stream handler, makes use of `FileNameMap` for determining content types.

MEMBER SUMMARY	
Determining Type Method	
`getContentTypeFor()`	Determines the MIME type of a filename.

See Also

`ContentHandler`, `URLConnection.FileNameMap`, `URLConnection.guessContentTypeFromName()`, `URLStreamHandler`.

getContentTypeFor()

PURPOSE Determines the MIME type of a filename.

SYNTAX `public String getContentTypeFor(String fileName)`

DESCRIPTION This method determines the MIME type of a filename or the filename component of a URL by examining the name itself. For example, an implementation could use a filename's extension to determine the content type, so that, for example, an extension of "html" or "htm" gets mapped to the MIME type "text/html".

PARAMETERS

`fileName` The non-`null` filename to check.

RETURNS The MIME type of the filename as a string. `null` if the type could not be determined.

SEE ALSO `URLConnection.guessContentTypeFromName()`.

EXAMPLE This example defines a table-driven implementation of `FileNameMap`.

```
import java.net.FileNameMap;
import java.util.Hashtable;
import java.io.File;

class TestMap implements FileNameMap {
    static Hashtable map = new Hashtable();
    static {
        // add a few entries for testing
        map.put("txt", "text/plain");
        map.put("text", "text/plain");
        map.put("htm", "text/html");
        map.put("html", "text/html");
        map.put("gif", "image/gif");
        map.put("mpg", "video/mpeg");
        map.put("mpeg", "video/mpeg");
    };

    public String getContentTypeFor(String filename) {
        // first get rid of fragment identifier of URL in case filename is URL
        int posn = filename.lastIndexOf('#');
        if (posn != -1)
            filename = filename.substring(0, posn - 1);

        File f = new File(filename);
        String atom = f.getName();          // get name without directory

        System.out.println("atom: " + atom);

        posn = atom.lastIndexOf('.');

        if (posn == -1)
            return null;        // don't know how to deal with no extension

        String typename = atom.substring(posn + 1);
```

```
            System.out.println("typename: " + typename);
            return (String) map.get(typename);
        }
    }

    class Main {
        public static void main(String args[]) {
            String target = "http://www.sun.com/homepage.gif";
            if (args.length > 0) {
                 target = args[0];
            }

            FileNameMap map = new TestMap();
            System.out.println("type is " + map.getContentTypeFor(target));
        }
    }
```

FileNotFoundException

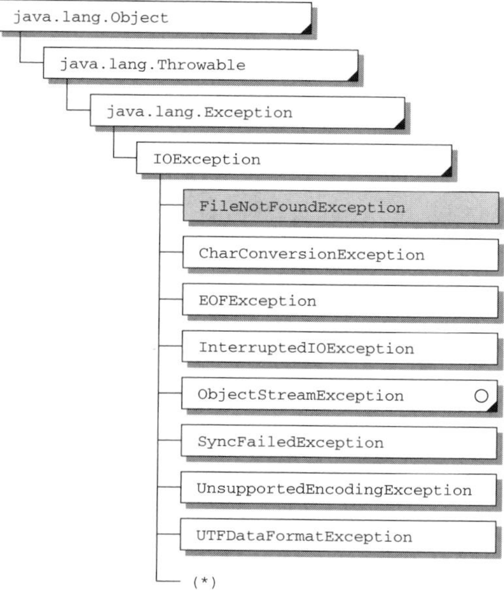

A B C D E F G H I J K L M N O P Q R S T U V W X Y Z

Syntax

`public class FileNotFoundException extends IOException`

Description

`FileNotFoundException` is an IO exception that is thrown when a program attempts to read from a nonexistent file or to write to a file in a nonexistent directory.

A method that throws `FileNotFoundException` must declare it or any of its superclasses in the method's `throws` clause.

MEMBER SUMMARY	
Constructor	
`FileNotFoundException()`	Constructs a `FileNotFoundException` instance.

See Also

`FileInputStream`, `FileOutputStream`, `FileReader`, `FileWriter`, `IOException`.

Example

This example echoes a file's contents, throwing `FileNotFoundException` if the file does not exist.

```
import java.io.FileInputStream;
import java.io.FileNotFoundException;
import java.io.IOException;

class Main {
    public static void main(String[] args) {
        if (args.length == 0) {
            System.err.println("java Main <inputfile>");
            System.exit(-1);
        }
        try {
            FileInputStream in = new FileInputStream(args[0]);
            // ...
        } catch (FileNotFoundException e) {
            System.err.println("File " + args[0] + " not found");
        } catch (IOException e) {
            e.printStackTrace();
        }
    }
}
```

FileNotFoundException()

PURPOSE Constructs a `FileNotFoundException` instance.

SYNTAX
```
public FileNotFoundException()
public FileNotFoundException(String msg)
```

DESCRIPTION There are two forms to the `FileNotFoundException` constructor. They construct an instance of `FileNotFoundException`. An optional string `msg` can be supplied that describes this particular instance of the exception. If `msg` is not supplied, it defaults to `null`.

PARAMETERS

`msg` A possibly `null` string that gives details about this exception.

SEE ALSO `java.lang.Throwable.getMessage()`.

A B C D E F G H I J K L M N O P Q R S T U V W X Y Z

FileOutputStream

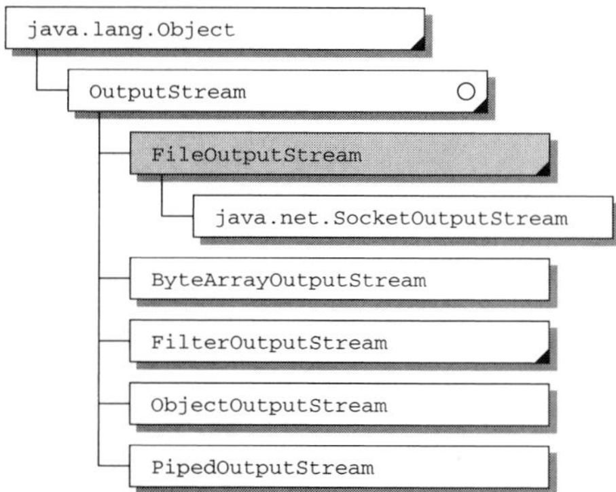

Syntax

```
public class FileOutputStream extends OutputStream
```

Description

The `FileOutputStream` class provides methods for writing data to a file (Figure 48).

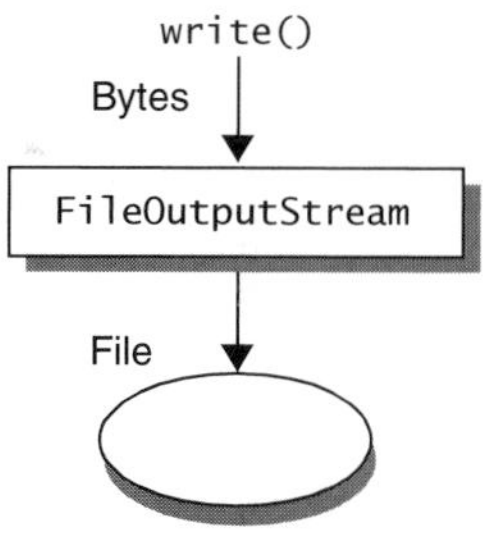

FIGURE 48: **`FileOutputStream`.**

Usage

This class can be used directly to write data to a file, or it can be composed with other streams or writers to write data to a file. The following code uses `FileOutputStream` directly:

```
FileOutputStream out = new FileOutputStream("temp");
byte[] buf = new byte[512];
    ...
out.write(buf);
```

The following code creates a `BufferedWriter` using an `OutputStreamWriter` and a `FileOutputStream` to write a string to a file. `FileWriter` can be used for the same purpose.

```
BufferedWriter out = new BufferedWriter(new OutputStreamWriter(
        new FileOutputStream("temp")));
String s = "hello";
out.write(s, 0, s.length);
```

FileOutputStream versus FileWriter

`FileOutputStream` is meant for writing bytes to a file. Its methods write bytes (0–255). `FileWriter` is a convenience class for writing characters to a file. If you are writing characters to a file using a particular encoding, you can use `FileOutputStream` with `OutputStreamWriter` as shown previously.

MEMBER SUMMARY	
Constructor	
`FileOutputStream()`	Constructs a `FileOutputStream` instance.
Output Method	
`write()`	Writes bytes to this file output stream.
Methods for Closing the Stream	
`close()`	Closes this file output stream.
`finalize()`	Called to close this file output stream when it is ready to be discarded.
File Descriptor Method	
`getFD()`	Retrieves the file descriptor used by this file output stream.

See Also

`File`, `FileDescriptor`, `FileInputStream`, `FileReader`, `FileWriter`, `OutputStream`, `OutputStreamWriter`.

Example

This example creates a `FileOutputStream` using the filename supplied in the command line. It then creates a second `FileOutputStream` using the file descriptor of the first `FileOutputStream`. Both of these point to the same file. A "hello" string is then written to each of these streams. The result is two lines of "`hello`" in the output file.

```
import java.io.FileOutputStream;
import java.io.IOException;

class Main {
    public static void main (String[] args) {
        if (args.length != 1) {
            System.err.println("Usage: java Main <output_file>");
            System.exit(-1);
        }
        try {
            FileOutputStream out = new FileOutputStream(args[0]);
            FileOutputStream out2 = new FileOutputStream(out.getFD());

            byte[] buf = {'h', 'e', 'l', 'l', 'o', '\n'};
            out.write(buf);
        out2.write(buf);
            out.close();    // closes out2 too
```

```
            } catch (IOException e) {
                e.printStackTrace();
            }
        }
    }
```

close()

PURPOSE Closes this file output stream.

SYNTAX `public native void close() throws IOException`

DESCRIPTION This method closes this file output stream. It releases any resources, such as file descriptors, used by this file output stream. If the file has already been closed, this method does nothing.

EXCEPTIONS

`IOException`

If an IO error occurred.

OVERRIDES `OutputStream.close()`.

EXAMPLE See the class example.

FileOutputStream()

PURPOSE Constructs a `FileOutputStream` instance.

SYNTAX

```
public FileOutputStream(String filename) throws IOException
public FileOutputStream(File file) throws IOException
public FileOutputStream(FileDescriptor fd)
public FileOutputStream(String filename, boolean append) throws
    IOException
```

DESCRIPTION There are four forms of this constructor for `FileOutputStream`. The first form constructs a file output stream for writing to the file that has the name `filename`. `filename` is a platform-dependent name of the file. It can be an absolute or a relative pathname of the file. If absolute, it is resolved relative to the root of the file system. If relative, it is resolved relative to the current directory in which the Java program was started.

The second form constructs a file output stream for the file identified by the `File` object `file`. The third form constructs a file output stream using the opened file descriptor `fd`.

For these first three forms, if the file specified already exists, any data contained therein is erased when the file output stream is created. If the file did not exist, it is created.

The `fourth` form of this method allows the write operations to the newly created stream to append data to the file rather than overwrite any existing data in the file. If `append` is `true`, data written to this stream is appended to any existing data in the file that has the name `filename`. If `append` is `false`, existing data in the file is cleared when the file output stream is created.

The file output stream may be created only if the current execution context is allowed, by the security manager and the underlying file system, to write to the specified file.

PARAMETERS

`append` If `true`, writes to the stream will append to the file; if `false`, the file is cleared first.

`fd` The non-`null` opened file descriptor of the file.

`file` The non-`null` `File` object of the file.

`filename` The non-`null` string name of the file.

EXCEPTIONS

`IOException`
If the file is not found or some other IO error occurred while attempting to open the file for writing.

`SecurityException`
The file cannot be opened for writing due to security reasons.

SEE ALSO `File`, `FileDescriptor`, `java.lang.SecurityManager.checkWrite()`.

EXAMPLE This example creates a file output stream for the file supplied to the command line. It appends "hello" to the file each time the program is run. See the class example also for usages of the other constructors.

```
import java.io.FileOutputStream;
import java.io.IOException;

class Main {
    public static void main (String[] args) {
        if (args.length != 1) {
            System.err.println("Usage: java Main <output_file>");
            System.exit(-1);
        }
        try {
            // create file in append mode
            FileOutputStream out = new FileOutputStream(args[0], true);
            byte[] buf = {'h', 'e', 'l', 'l', 'o', '\n'};
            out.write(buf);
            out.close();
        } catch (IOException e) {
            e.printStackTrace();
```

```
            }
        }
    }
```

finalize()

PURPOSE Called to close this file output stream when it is ready to be discarded.

SYNTAX `protected void finalize() throws IOException`

DESCRIPTION This method is called by the Java virtual machine when this stream is ready to be discarded. See `java.lang.Object.finalize()` for details.

OVERRIDES `java.lang.Object.finalize()`.

SEE ALSO `close()`, `System.gc()`, `System.runFinalization()`.

getFD()

PURPOSE Retrieves the file descriptor used by this file output stream.

SYNTAX `public final FileDescriptor getFD() throws IOException`

RETURNS The non-`null` file descriptor used by this file output stream.

EXCEPTIONS

`IOException`

If the file has already been closed and consequently no longer has a file descriptor.

SEE ALSO `FileDescriptor`.

EXAMPLE See `FileDescriptor.sync()`.

write()

PURPOSE Writes bytes to this file output stream.

SYNTAX

```
public void write(int oneByte) throws IOException
public void write(byte[] buffer) throws IOException
public void write(byte[] buffer, int offset, int count) throws
    IOException
```

DESCRIPTION The three forms of this method write bytes to this file output stream. The first writes a single byte (8 bits) to this file output stream. The low-order byte from `oneByte` is written to the stream. The second and third forms write bytes from the byte array buffer to this file output stream. If offset and count are specified, count number of bytes starting at index offset in buffer are written to this stream; otherwise, all of the bytes from buffer are written. All three forms of write() block until all of the bytes have been written to this stream.

PARAMETERS

buffer	The non-null byte array containing the bytes to be written.
count	The number of bytes to be written. 0 ≤ count ≤ buffer.length-offset.
offset	The index in buffer from which to start getting the bytes to be written. 0 ≤ offset < buffer.length.
oneByte	The byte to be written.

EXCEPTIONS

ArrayIndexOutOfBoundsException
If count or offset is outside of the specified bounds.

IOException
If an IO error occurred while attempting to write the bytes.

OVERRIDES OutputStream.write().

EXAMPLE See the class example.

FileReader

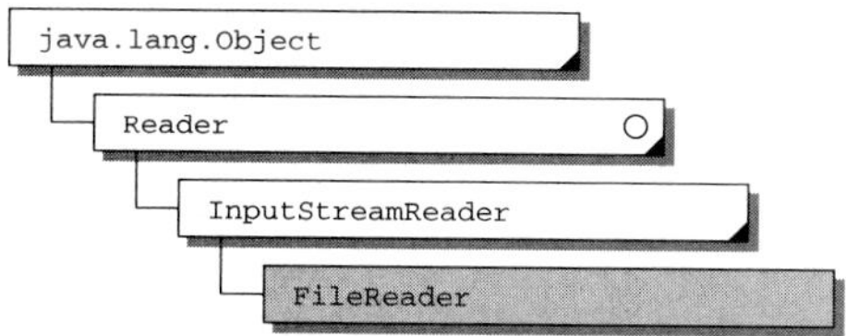

A B C D E F G H I J K L M N O P Q R S T U V W X Y Z

Syntax

```
public class FileReader extends InputStreamReader
```

Description

`FileReader` implements a character input stream, or *file reader*, for reading characters from a file (Figure 49).

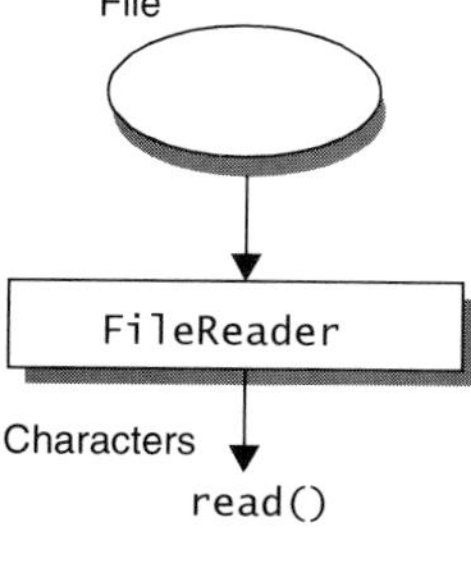

FIGURE 49: **`FileReader`.**

Usage

To read characters from a file, you create a `FileReader` using its filename, `File` object, or file descriptor; for example:

```
FileReader in = new FileReader("inputfile");
char[] buf = ...;
in.read(buf);
```

Default Byte Encoding

The file being read by this file reader is assumed to contain characters encoded using the platform-dependent default byte encoding. In the JDK 1.1, the default byte encoding is identified by the `file.encoding` system property. This property contains an *encoding identifier*; see `String.getBytes()` for a description of encoding identifers. If this system property is not defined, the default encoding identifier is "8859_1" (ISO-Latin-1). If the converter (class) for the default encoding identifier is not found, an ASCII encoding is used.

To read a file with a byte encoding other than the default, you should use `FileInputStream` with `InputStreamReader` and specify the encoding explicitly. For example, the following reader reads characters from a file encoded using the UTF-8 encoding:

```
InputStreamReader in = new InputStreamReader(
    new FileInputStream("inputfile"), "UTF8"));
```

FileInputStream versus FileReader

`FileInputStream` is meant for reading bytes (0–255) from a file. `FileReader` is a convenient class for reading characters from a file. If you are reading characters from a file with a particular encoding, you can use `FileInputStream` with `InputStreamReader` as shown previously.

MEMBER SUMMARY	
Constructor	
`FileReader()`	Constructs a `FileReader` instance.

See Also

`File`, `FileDescriptor`, `FileInputStream`, `FileWriter`, `java.lang.String.String()`.

Example

This example reads a file using a `FileReader` and echoes its contents to standard output.

```
import java.io.*;

class Main {
    public static void main(String[] args) {
        if (args.length != 1) {
            System.err.println("usage: java Main <inputfile>");
        }
        try {
            FileReader in = new FileReader(args[0]);
            Writer out = new PrintWriter(System.out);
            char[] buf = new char[512];
            int howmany;
            while ((howmany = in.read(buf)) >= 0) {
                out.write(buf, 0, howmany);
            }
            out.flush();
            out.close();
            in.close();
        } catch (FileNotFoundException e) {
            System.err.println(e);
        } catch (IOException e) {
            System.err.println(e);
        }
    }
}
```

FileReader()

PURPOSE Constructs a `FileReader` instance.

SYNTAX

```
public FileReader(String filename) throws FileNotFoundException
public FileReader(File file) throws FileNotFoundException
public FileReader(FileDescriptor fd)
```

DESCRIPTION There are three forms of the constructor for `FileReader`. The first form constructs a file reader for the file that has the name `filename`. `filename` is a platform-dependent name of the file. It can be an absolute or a relative pathname of the file. If absolute, it is resolved relative to the root of the file system. If relative, it is resolved relative to the current directory in which the Java program was started. See `File` for descriptions of absolute and relative filenames. The second form constructs a file reader for the file identified by the `File` object file. The third form constructs a file reader using the opened file descriptor `fd`.

The file reader may be constructed only if the current execution context is allowed, by the security manager and the underlying file system, to read the specified file.

PARAMETERS

`fd` The non-`null` opened file descriptor of the file.

`file` The non-`null` `File` object of the file.

`filename` The non-`null` string name of the file.

EXCEPTIONS

`FileNotFoundException`
If the file is not found.

`SecurityException`
If the file cannot be read due to security reasons.

SEE ALSO `File`, `FileInputStream`, `InputStreamReader`, `SecurityManager.checkRead()`.

EXAMPLE This example reads a specified number of lines from a file and echoes the lines to standard output.

```
import java.io.*;

class Main {
    public static void main(String[] args) {
        if (args.length != 2) {
            System.err.println("usage: java Main <inputfile> num");
        }
        int num = Integer.parseInt(args[1]);  // number of lines
        try {
            BufferedReader in =
                new BufferedReader(new FileReader(new File(args[0])));
            PrintWriter out = new PrintWriter(System.out);
            String str;
            while (num > 0 && (str = in.readLine()) != null) {
                out.println(str);
                --num;
            }
            out.flush();
            out.close();
            in.close();
        } catch (NumberFormatException e) {
            System.err.println(e);
        } catch (FileNotFoundException e) {
            System.err.println(e);
        } catch (IOException e) {
            System.err.println(e);
        }
    }
}
```

java.io

FileWriter

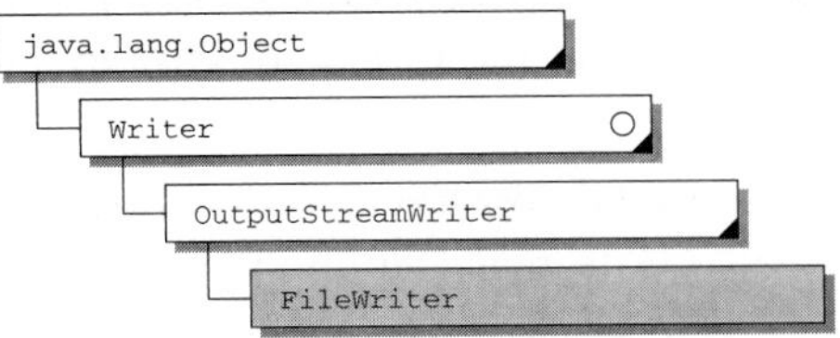

A B C D E F G H I J K L M N O P Q R S T U V W X Y Z

Syntax

```
public class FileWriter extends OutputStreamWriter
```

Description

`FileWriter` implements a character output stream, or *file writer*, for writing characters to a file. See Figure 50.

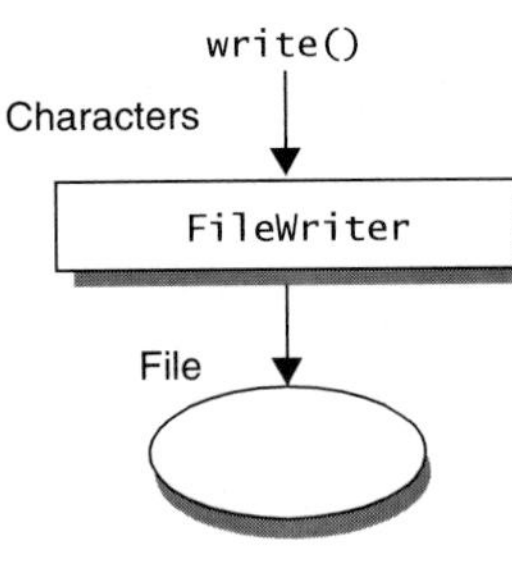

FIGURE 50: **`FileWriter`.**

Usage

To write characters to a file, you create a `FileWriter` using its filename, `File` object, or file descriptor; for example:

```
FileWriter out = new FileWriter("outputfile");
char[] buf = ...;
out.write(buf);
```

Default Byte Encoding

The characters written to the file writer are converted to their byte representations using the platform-dependent default byte encoding. In the JDK 1.1, the default byte encoding is identified by the `file.encoding` system property. This property contains an *encoding identifier*; see `String.getBytes()` for a description of encoding identifiers. If this system property is not defined, the default encoding identifier is "8859_1" (ISO-Latin-1). If the converter (class) for the default encoding identifier is not found, an ASCII encoding is used.

To use a byte encoding other than the default, you should use `FileOutputStream` with `OutputStreamWriter` and specify the encoding explicitly. For example, output written to the following `OutputStreamWriter` will result in those characters being converted to bytes using the UTF-8 encoding:

```
OutputStreamWriter out = new OutputStreamWriter(
    new FileOutputStream("outputfile"), "UTF8"));
```

FileOutputStream versus FileWriter

FileOutputStream is meant for writing bytes to a file. Its methods write bytes (0–255). FileWriter is for writing characters to a file. If you are writing characters to a file using a particular encoding, you can use FileOutputStream with OutputStreamWriter as shown previously.

MEMBER SUMMARY	
Constructor	
FileWriter()	Constructs a FileWriter instance.

See Also

File, FileDescriptor, FileOutputStream, FileReader, java.lang.String.getBytes().

Example

This example opens a file and writes a string to it. If the file already exists, the existing contents are removed first.

```
import java.io.*;

class Main {
    public static void main(String[] args) {
        if (args.length != 1) {
            System.err.println("usage: java Main <outputfile>");
            System.exit(-1);
        }

        try {
            FileWriter out = new FileWriter(args[0]);
            out.write("Java Class Libraries\n");
            out.flush();
            out.close();
        } catch (IOException e) {
            System.err.println(e);
        }
    }
}
```

FileWriter()

PURPOSE Constructs a `FileWriter` instance.

SYNTAX
```
public FileWriter(String fileName) throws IOException
public FileWriter(String fileName, boolean append) throws
   IOException
public FileWriter(File file) throws IOException
public FileWriter(FileDescriptor fd)
```

DESCRIPTION There are four forms of the constructor for `FileWriter`. The first two forms construct a file writer for the file that has the name `filename`. `filename` is a platform-dependent name of the file. It can be an absolute or a relative pathname of the file. If absolute, it is resolved relative to the root of the file system. If relative, it is resolved relative to the current directory in which the Java program was started. See `File` for descriptions of absolute and relative filenames.

The first form opens the file and erases any existing contents. The second form opens the file without erasing its contents; characters written to this writer are appended to the file. The third form constructs a file reader for the file identified by the `File` object file. The fourth form constructs a file reader using the opened file descriptor `fd`. These two forms open the file and erase any existing contents.

The file writer may be created only if the current execution context is allowed, by the security manager and the underlying file system, to create or append to the specified file.

PARAMETERS

`append` If `true`, opens the file for append; otherwise, existing contents of the file are erased.

`fd` The non-`null` opened file descriptor of the file.

`file` The non-`null` `File` object of the file.

`filename` The non-`null` string name of the file.

EXAMPLE

`IOException`
If the file is not found (i.e., intermediate directories are not found) or if some other IO error occurs.

`SecurityException`
If the file cannot be created or written to due to security reasons.

SEE ALSO `File`, `FileOutputStream`, `OutputStreamWriter`, `SecurityManager.checkWrite()`.

EXAMPLE This example appends a string to the specified file each time the program is run.

```
import java.io.*;

class Main {
    public static void main(String[] args) {
        if (args.length != 1) {
            System.err.println("usage: java Main <outputfile>");
            System.exit(-1);
        }

        try {
            FileWriter out = new FileWriter(args[0], true);
            out.write("Java Class Libraries\n");
            out.flush();
            out.close();
        } catch (IOException e) {
            System.err.println(e);
        }
    }
}
```

java.io

FilterInputStream

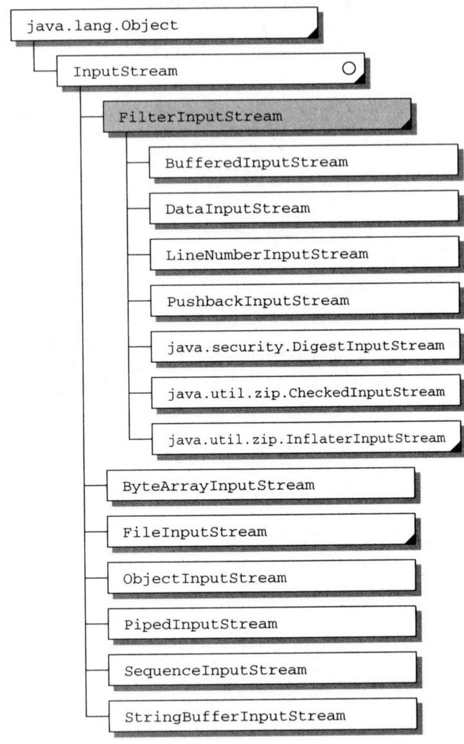

Syntax

```
public class FilterInputStream extends InputStream
```

Description

A *filter input stream* takes input from another stream and "filters" it so that when you read from this filter input stream, you get a filtered view of the input (see Figure 51). An example of a filter input stream is a stream that reads input and buffers it. Another example is a stream that reads from a stream and computes a checksum of the data read (`java.util.zip.CheckedInputStream`). In both cases, the filter input stream is adding functionality to the original stream. In the buffered stream case, the filter is providing buffering. In the checksum stream case, the filter is serving a computational function. Filter input streams can be composed with other filter input streams. For example, you can have a buffered stream that computes the checksum.

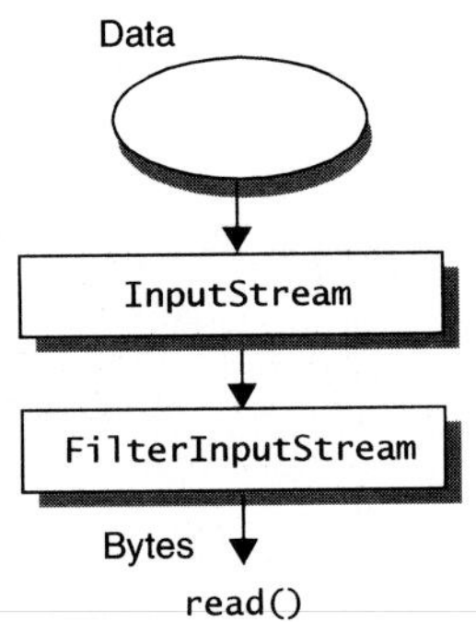

FIGURE 51: `FilterInputStream`.

Note the different stages at which filtering occurs for filter output streams and filter input streams. A filter output stream performs processing on the data *before* sending it to its eventual destination, while a filter input stream does processing *after* reading data from its original source.

The `FilterInputStream` class represents a filter input stream. A class extends `FilterInputStream` and overrides its input methods in order to add functionality to the stream that it is filtering.

FilterInputStream versus FilterReader

`FilterInputStream` is meant for byte streams. Its methods read bytes (0–255). `FilterReader` is for character input streams.

MEMBER SUMMARY	
Constructor	
`FilterInputStream()`	Constructs a `FilterInputStream` instance for an input stream.
Input Methods	
`read()`	Reads bytes from this filter input stream.
`skip()`	Skips bytes from this filter input stream.
Mark/Reset Methods	
`mark()`	Marks the current position in the filter input stream.
`markSupported()`	Determines whether this filter input stream supports mark/reset.
`reset()`	Resets the current read position to the last marked position.
Stream Methods	
`available()`	Determines the number of bytes that can be read without being blocked.
`close()`	Closes this filter input stream.
Protected Field	
`in`	The input stream that is being filtered.

See Also

`BufferedInputStream`, `DataInputStream`, `FilterOutputStream`, `FilterReader`, `FilterWriter`, `InputStream`, `LineNumberInputStream`, `PushbackInputStream`.

Example

This example defines a `ScrambleInputStream` class that XOR's its input using the hash code of a password string. Running the program on the output produced by the example in `Filter-OutputStream` produces the original data.

```
import java.io.*;

class ScrambleInputStream extends FilterInputStream {
    private byte[] p = new byte[4];
    int counter = 0;
    public ScrambleInputStream (String passwd, InputStream in) {
        super(in);
        // Compute hash code of password and store into 4 bytes.
        int pw = passwd.hashCode();
        p[0] = (byte) ((pw >>> 24) & 0xFF);
        p[1] = (byte) ((pw >>> 16) & 0xFF);
        p[2] = (byte) ((pw >>> 8) & 0xFF);
        p[3] = (byte) (pw & 0xFF);
    }

    public int read() throws IOException {
        int b = in.read();
        if (b < 0)
            return b;  // end-of-file

        b = ((byte)b ^ p[counter++]) &0xff;
        if (counter == 4)
            counter = 0;
        return b;
    }
}

class Main {
    public static void main(String[] args) {
        if (args.length != 3) {
            System.err.println("Usage: java Main <passwd> <input> <output>");
            System.exit(-1);
        }
        try {
            FileInputStream in = new FileInputStream(args[1]);
            FileOutputStream out = new FileOutputStream(args[2]);
            InputStream s1 = new ScrambleInputStream(args[0], in);
            for(int c = s1.read(); c > -1; c = s1.read()) {
                out.write(c);
            }
            s1.close();
            out.flush();
            out.close();
        } catch (IOException e) {
            System.out.println(e);
        }
    }
}
```

available()

PURPOSE Determines the number of bytes that can be read without being blocked.

SYNTAX `public int available() throws IOException`

DESCRIPTION This method returns the number of bytes that can be read from this filter input stream without being blocked. In the default implementation of `FilterInputStream`, this number is determined by the number of bytes available from the stream that is being filtered (`in`).

RETURNS The number of bytes that can be read without being blocked.

EXCEPTIONS

`IOException`

If an IO error occurred.

OVERRIDES `InputStream.available()`.

SEE ALSO `in`.

EXAMPLE See `InputStream.available()`.

close()

PURPOSE Closes this filter input stream.

SYNTAX `public void close() throws IOException`

DESCRIPTION This method closes this filter input stream. By default, it closes the stream that is being filtered (`in`). This, in turn, closes the next stream downstream, and so on. Hence, this method effectively closes this stream and all of the streams "downstream."

A subclass of `FilterInputStream` might need to release other resources related to the filter, depending on the nature of the filter.

EXCEPTIONS

`IOException`

If an IO error has occurred.

OVERRIDES `InputStream.close()`.

SEE ALSO `in`.

EXAMPLE See the class example.

FilterInputStream()

PURPOSE Constructs a `FilterInputStream` instance for an input stream.

SYNTAX `protected FilterInputStream(InputStream in)`

DESCRIPTION This method constructs a filter input stream for the input stream `in`. Data read from `in` is filtered by this new filter input stream before being returned by the `read()` method.

PARAMETERS

`in` The input stream to filter.

SEE ALSO `in`.

EXAMPLE See the class example.

in

PURPOSE The input stream that is being filtered.

SYNTAX `protected InputStream in`

DESCRIPTION This is the input stream with which this filter input stream has been created. It is the stream that this filter input stream reads from in order to satisfy the read/skip requests.

SEE ALSO `FilterInputStream()`.

EXAMPLE See the class example.

mark()

PURPOSE Marks the current position in the filter input stream.

SYNTAX `public synchronized void mark(int readlimit)`

DESCRIPTION This method marks the current position in the input stream so that a subsequent call to `reset()` will reposition the stream to this marked position. This allows subsequent `read()` calls to reread the same bytes that have already been read. `readlimit` is the number of bytes that can be read before the mark position becomes invalid. The default implementation uses the `mark()` method of the stream that is being filtered (`in`).

PARAMETERS

`readlimit` The number of bytes that can be read before the mark becomes invalid.

OVERRIDES `InputStream.mark()`.

SEE ALSO `in`, `markSupported()`, `reset()`.

EXAMPLE See `InputStream.mark()`.

markSupported()

PURPOSE Determines whether this filter input stream supports mark/reset.

SYNTAX
```
public boolean markSupported()
```

DESCRIPTION This method determines whether this filter input stream supports mark/reset. It returns `true` if mark/reset is supported and `false` otherwise. By default, whether mark/reset is supported is determined by the stream that is being filtered (`in`).

RETURNS `true` if mark/reset is supported; `false` otherwise.

OVERRIDES `InputStream.markSupported()`.

SEE ALSO `in`, `mark()`, `reset()`.

EXAMPLE See `InputStream.mark()`.

read()

PURPOSE Reads bytes from this filter input stream.

SYNTAX
```
public int read() throws IOException
public int read(byte[] buffer) throws IOException
public int read(byte[] buffer, int offset, int count) throws
    IOException
```

DESCRIPTION The three forms of this method read bytes from this filter input stream. They are usually overridden because a filter input stream typically performs some postprocessing after reading the bytes from the stream that it is filtering (`in`).

The first form reads a single byte (8 bits) from this filter input stream and returns it as a 32-bit `int`. The first 3 bytes of the `int` are set to `0`. `read()` blocks until a byte is available for reading from this input stream. If end-of-file is reached on this stream, `read()` returns `-1`.

The second and third forms read bytes from this filter input stream and store the bytes read into the `byte` array `buffer`. If `offset` and `count` are specified, `read()` reads at most `count` number of bytes from this stream and stores them in `buffer` starting at index `offset`. Otherwise, `read()` reads at most `buffer.length` number of bytes and stores them in `buffer` starting at index `0`.

read() returns the number of bytes actually read from this stream. If end-of-file is reached on this stream before any bytes are read, read() returns -1.

PARAMETERS

buffer The non-null byte array in which to store the bytes read.

count The number of bytes to read. 0 ≤ count ≤ buffer.length-offset.

offset The index in buffer at which to start storing the bytes read. 0 ≤ offset < buffer.length.

RETURNS The first form returns the byte read. The second and third forms return the actual number of bytes read. All forms return -1 if end-of-file is reached before any bytes are read.

EXCEPTIONS

ArrayIndexOutOfBoundsException

If count or offset is outside of the specified bounds.

IOException

If an IO error occurred while attempting to read.

OVERRIDES InputStream.read().

SEE ALSO in, skip().

EXAMPLE See the class example.

reset()

PURPOSE Resets the current read position to the last marked position.

SYNTAX `public synchronized void reset() throws IOException`

DESCRIPTION This method resets the current read position of this filter input stream to be the last marked position (the read position when mark() was last called). The default implementation invokes the reset() method of the stream that is being filtered (in).

EXCEPTIONS

IOException

If no mark has been set or if the mark is invalid.

OVERRIDES InputStream.reset().

SEE ALSO in, mark(), markSupported().

EXAMPLE See InputStream.mark().

skip()

PURPOSE Skips bytes from this filter input stream.

SYNTAX `public long skip(long count) throws IOException`

DESCRIPTION This method skips `count` number of bytes from this filter input stream. Bytes that are skipped will not be returned by subsequent `read()` calls (except if mark/reset is used). The default implementation skips `count` number of bytes from the stream being filtered (`in`). This method returns the number of bytes actually skipped.

PARAMETERS

`count` The number of bytes to skip.

RETURNS The actual number of bytes skipped.

EXCEPTIONS

`IOException`

If an IO error occurred.

OVERRIDES `InputStream.skip()`.

SEE ALSO `in`, `read()`.

EXAMPLE See `InputStream.skip()`.

java.io

FilterOutputStream

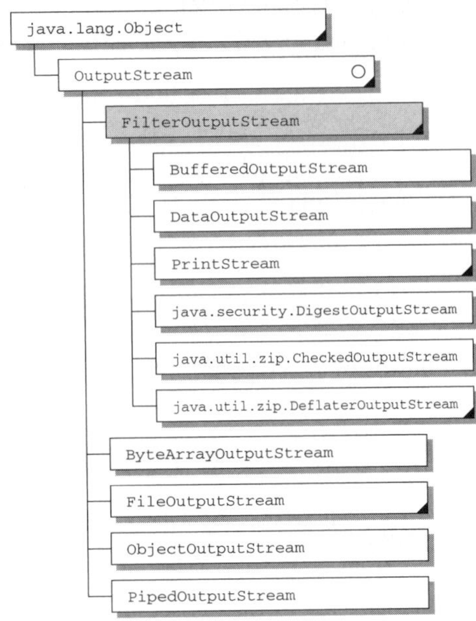

Syntax

```
public class FilterOutputStream extends OutputStream
```

Description

A *filter output stream* takes output to be written to a stream and "filters" it so that when you write to this filter output stream, the resulting output is "filtered" (see Figure 52). An example of a filter output stream is a stream that buffers output. Another example is a stream that computes the checksum of values based on bytes that flow through the stream (see `java.util.zip.CheckedOutputStream`). In each case, the filter output stream is adding functionality to the original stream. In the buffered stream case, the filter is providing buffering. In the checksum output stream case, the filter is serving a computational function.

write()
Bytes
FilterOutputStream
OutputStream
Storage

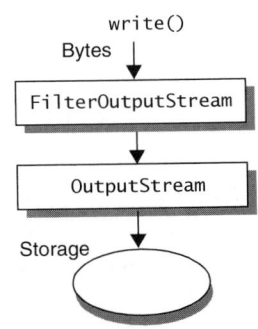

FIGURE 52: **`FilterOutputStream`.**

Filter output streams can be composed with other filter output streams. For example, you can compose a buffered stream with the checksum output stream to get a resulting stream that does buffering and computes the checksum.

Note the different stages at which filtering occurs for filter output streams and filter input streams. A filter output stream performs processing on the data *before* sending it out to its eventual destination, while a filter input stream does processing *after* reading data from its original source.

The `FilterOutputStream` class represents a filter output stream. A class extends `FilterOutputStream` and overrides its output methods in order to add functionality to the stream that it is filtering.

FilterOutputStream versus FilterWriter

`FilterOutputStream` is meant for byte streams. Its methods write bytes (0–255). `FilterWriter` is for character output streams.

MEMBER SUMMARY	
Constructor	
`FilterOutputStream()`	Constructs a `FilterOutputStream` instance for an output stream.
Output Methods	
`flush()`	Flushes this filter output stream.
`write()`	Writes bytes to this filter output stream.
Method for Closing Stream	
`close()`	Closes this filter output stream.
Protected Field	
`out`	The output stream that is being filtered.

See Also

`BufferedOutputStream`, `DataOutputStream`, `FilterInputStream`, `FilterWriter`, `OutputStream`, `PrintStream`.

Example

This example defines a `ScrambleOutputStream` class that XOR's its output using the hash code of a password string. Running the program on an input stream produces a scrambled version. Running the program again on the scrambled version produces the data contained in the original input stream. Alternatively, you can feed the scrambled version to the example in `FilterInputStream` to get back the original data.

```
import java.io.*;

class ScrambleOutputStream extends FilterOutputStream {
    private byte[] p = new byte[4];
    int counter = 0;
    public ScrambleOutputStream (String passwd, OutputStream out) {
```

```
            super(out);
            // Compute hash code of password and store into 4 bytes.
            int pw = passwd.hashCode();
            p[0] = (byte) ((pw >>> 24) & 0xFF);
            p[1] = (byte) ((pw >>> 16) & 0xFF);
            p[2] = (byte) ((pw >>> 8) & 0xFF);
            p[3] = (byte) (pw & 0xFF);
        }

        public void write(int b) throws IOException {
            out.write(((byte)b) ^ p[counter++]);
            if (counter == 4)
                counter = 0;
        }
    }

    class Main {
        public static void main(String[] args) {
            if (args.length != 3) {
                System.err.println("Usage: java Main <passwd> <input> <output>");
                System.exit(-1);
            }
            try {
                FileInputStream in = new FileInputStream(args[1]);
                FileOutputStream out = new FileOutputStream(args[2]);
                ScrambleOutputStream sout =
                    new ScrambleOutputStream(args[0], out);

                byte[] buf = new byte[512];
                int howmany;
                while ((howmany = in.read(buf)) > 0) {
                    sout.write(buf, 0, howmany);
                }
                in.close();
                sout.flush();
                sout.close();
            } catch (IOException e) {
                System.out.println(e);
            }
        }
    }
```

close()

PURPOSE Closes this filter output stream.

SYNTAX `public void close() throws IOException`

DESCRIPTION This method closes this filter output stream. By default, it closes the stream that is being filtered (out). This, in turn, closes the next stream downstream, and so on. Hence, this method effectively closes this stream and all of the streams "downstream."

A subclass of `FilterOutputStream` might need to release other resources related to the filter, depending on the nature of the filter.

EXCEPTIONS
`IOException`
If an IO error occurred.

OVERRIDES `OutputStream.close()`.

SEE ALSO `out`.

EXAMPLE See the class example.

FilterOutputStream()

PURPOSE Constructs a `FilterOutputStream` instance for an output stream.

SYNTAX `public FilterOutputStream(OutputStream out)`

DESCRIPTION This method constructs a filter output stream for the output stream `out`. Data written to this new stream is processed by this filter before being sent to `out`.

PARAMETERS
`out` The non-`null` output stream being filtered.

SEE ALSO `out`.

EXAMPLE See the class example.

flush()

PURPOSE Flushes this filter output stream.

SYNTAX `public void flush() throws IOException`

DESCRIPTION This method flushes any buffered bytes in this filter output stream. The default implementation simply flushes any bytes buffered by the stream being filtered (`out`). If this filter output stream does any buffering, `flush()` should be overridden to flush the buffered bytes as well.

EXCEPTIONS
`IOException`
If an IO error occurred.

OVERRIDES `OutputStream.flush()`.

SEE ALSO `BufferedOutputStream.flush()`, `out`.

EXAMPLE See the class example.

A B C D E F G H I J K L M N O P Q R S T U V W X Y Z

out

PURPOSE The output stream that is being filtered.

SYNTAX `protected OutputStream out`

DESCRIPTION This is the output stream with which this filter output stream was created. Data written to this filter output stream is processed by this filter output stream and then written to `out`.

SEE ALSO `FilterOutputStream()`.

EXAMPLE See the class example.

write()

PURPOSE Writes bytes to this filter output stream.

SYNTAX
```
public void write(int oneByte) throws IOException
public void write(byte[] buffer) throws IOException
public void write(byte[] buffer, int offset, int count) throws
    IOException
```

DESCRIPTION The three forms of this method write bytes to this filter output stream. They are usually overridden because a filter output stream typically performs some preprocessing before writing the bytes to the stream that it is filtering (`out`).

The first form of `write()` writes a single byte to this filter output stream. It writes the low-order byte from `oneByte`. The second form writes the bytes from the `byte` array `buffer` to this filter output stream. The third form writes `count` number of bytes starting at index `offset` from the `byte` array `buffer` to this filter output stream.

PARAMETERS

`buffer` The non-`null` `byte` array containing the bytes to be written.

`count` The number of bytes to write. `0` ≤ `count` ≤ `buffer.length-offset`.

`offset` The index in `buffer` from which to start getting the bytes to be written. `0` ≤ `offset` < `buffer.length`.

`oneByte` The byte to be written. The low-order byte of `oneByte` is written.

EXCEPTIONS

`ArrayIndexOutOfBoundsException`
If `count` or `offset` is outside of the specified bounds.

`IOException`
If an IO error occurred.

OVERRIDES `OutputStream.write()`.

EXAMPLE See the class example.

FilterReader

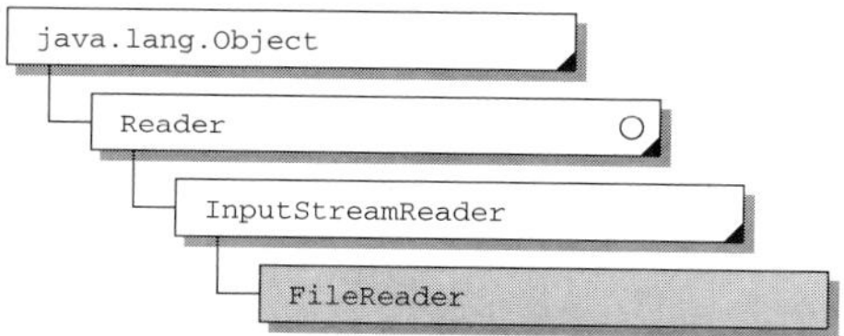

Syntax

```
public abstract class FilterReader extends Reader
```

Description

A *filter reader* is a character input stream that takes input from another character input stream and "filters" it so that when you read from this filter reader, you get a filtered view of the input (see Figure 53). A reader that reads input and buffers it is an example of a filter reader. Another example is a reader that reads Unicode characters from a character stream and turns them into localized characters. In both cases, the filter reader is adding functionality to the original reader. In the buffered reader case, the filter is providing buffering. In the localized reader case, the filter is serving a translation function. Filter readers can be composed with other filter readers. For example, you can have a buffered reader that translates Unicode characters into localized characters.

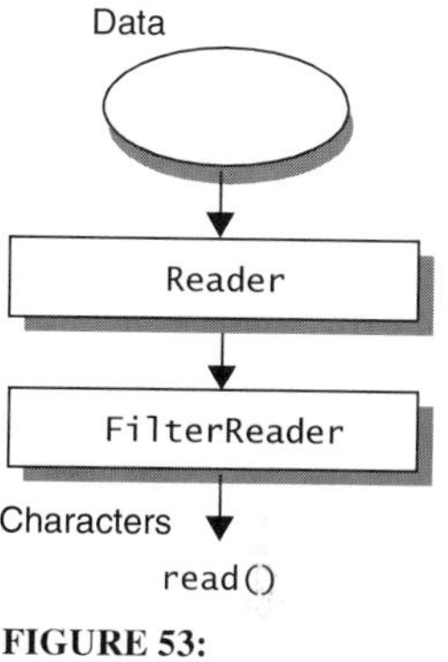

FIGURE 53: **`FilterReader`.**

Note the different stages at which filtering occurs for filter readers and filter writers. A filter writer performs processing on the stream *before* sending it to its eventual destination, while a filter reader does processing *after* reading characters from its original source.

Usage

The `FilterReader` class represents a filter reader. It is an abstract class that must be subclassed. A class extends `FilterReader` and overrides some or all of its methods in order to add functionality to the stream that it is filtering.

FilterInputStream versus FilterReader

`FilterInputStream` is meant for byte streams. Its methods read bytes (0–255). `FilterReader` is for character input streams.

See Also

`BufferedReader`, `FilterOutputStream`, `FilterWriter`, `InputStream`.

MEMBER SUMMARY	
Constructor	
`FilterReader()`	Constructs a filter reader for another reader.
Input Methods	
`read()`	Reads characters from this filter reader.
`skip()`	Skips characters from this filter reader.
Mark/Reset Methods	
`mark()`	Marks the current position in the filter reader
`markSupported()`	Determines whether this filter reader supports mark/reset.
`reset()`	Resets the current read position to the last marked position.
Stream Methods	
`close()`	Closes this filter reader.
`ready()`	Determines whether this filter reader is ready to be read.
Protected Field	
`in`	The reader that is being filtered.

Example

This example defines a `FilterReader` that skips every other character read from the reader.

```
import java.io.*;

// a filter reader that skips every other character in the stream

class SkipFilterReader extends FilterReader {
    public SkipFilterReader (Reader in) {
        super(in);
    }
    public int read() throws IOException {
        synchronized (lock) {
            int c = in.read();
            in.skip(1);
            return (c);
        }
    }
    public int read(char[] b, int off, int len)
        throws IOException {
            synchronized (lock) {
                char[] tmp = new char[len+len];

                int howmany = in.read(tmp);
                int real_count = off;
                for (int i = 0; i < howmany; i += 2) {
                    b[real_count++] = tmp[i];
                }
                return (real_count);
```

```
            }
        }

        public boolean markSupported() {
            return in.markSupported();
        }

        public void mark(int readlimit) throws IOException {
            in.mark(readlimit + readlimit);
        }
    }

    class Main {
        public static void main(String[] args) {
            if (args.length != 1) {
                System.err.println("Usage: java Main <input_file>");
                System.exit(-1);
            }
            try {
                FileReader f1 = new FileReader(args[0]);
                SkipFilterReader s1 = new SkipFilterReader(f1);

                for(int c = s1.read(); c > -1; c = s1.read()) {
                    System.out.print((char)c);
                }
                s1.close();
            } catch (IOException e) {
                System.out.println(e);
            }
        }
    }
```


close()

PURPOSE Closes this filter reader.

SYNTAX `public void close() throws IOException`

DESCRIPTION This method closes this filter reader. By default, it closes the reader that is being filtered (`in`), which in turn will close the next reader downstream, and so on. Consequently, this method effectively closes this reader and all of the readers "downstream."

A subclass of filter reader might need to release other resources related to the filter, depending on the nature of the filter.

EXCEPTIONS

`IOException`

If an IO error has occurred.

OVERRIDES `Reader.close()`.

SEE ALSO `in`.

EXAMPLE See the class example.

FilterReader()

PURPOSE Constructs a filter reader for another reader.

SYNTAX `protected FilterReader(Reader in)`

DESCRIPTION This method constructs a filter reader for the reader `in`. Characters read from `in` are filtered by this new filter reader before being returned by the `read()` method.

PARAMETERS
`in` The non-`null` reader to filter.

SEE ALSO `in`.

EXAMPLE See the class example.

in

PURPOSE The reader that is being filtered.

SYNTAX `protected Reader in`

DESCRIPTION This is the reader with which this filter reader has been created. It is the reader that this filter reader reads from in order to satisfy the read/skip requests.

SEE ALSO `FilterReader()`.

EXAMPLE See the class example.

mark()

PURPOSE Marks the current position in the filter reader.

SYNTAX `public synchronized void mark(int readlimit)`

DESCRIPTION This method marks the current position in the reader so that a subsequent call to `reset()` will reposition the reader to this marked position. This allows subsequent `read()` calls to reread the same characters that have already been read. `readlimit` is the number of characters that can be read before the mark position becomes invalid. The default implementation uses the `mark()` method of the reader that is being filtered (`in`).

PARAMETERS
`readlimit` The number of characters that can be read before the mark becomes invalid.

OVERRIDES `Reader.mark()`.

SEE ALSO `in`, `markSupported()`, `reset()`.

EXAMPLE This example uses `SkipFilterReader` from the class example. It marks the reader before starting and then, after reading the entire reader, resets it.

```
import java.io.*;

class Main {
    public static void main(String[] args) {
        if (args.length != 1) {
            System.err.println("Usage: java Main <input_file>");
            System.exit(-1);
        }
        try {
            char[] buf = {'h', 'h', 'e', 'e', 'l', 'l', 'l', 'l',
                          'o', 'o', '\n', '\n'};
            SkipFilterReader s1 =
                new SkipFilterReader(new CharArrayReader(buf));

            int howmany;
            if (s1.markSupported()) {
                System.out.println("marking");
                s1.mark(200);
            }
            int ch;
            while ((ch=s1.read()) >= 0) {
                System.out.print((char)ch);
            }
            if (s1.markSupported()) {
                System.out.println("resetting");
                s1.reset();
            }
            while ((ch=s1.read()) >= 0) {
                System.out.print((char)ch);
            }
            s1.close();
        } catch (IOException e) {
            System.out.println(e);
        }
    }
}
```

A B C D E F G H I J K L M N O P Q R S T U V W X Y Z

markSupported()

PURPOSE Determines whether this filter reader supports mark/reset.

SYNTAX `public boolean markSupported()`

DESCRIPTION This method determines whether this filter reader supports mark/reset. It returns `true` if mark/reset is supported and `false` otherwise. By default, whether mark/reset is supported is determined by the reader that is being filtered (`in`).

RETURNS `true` if mark/reset is supported; `false` otherwise.

OVERRIDES `Reader.markSupported()`.

SEE ALSO `in`, `mark()`, `reset()`.

EXAMPLE See `mark()`.

A B C D E F G H I J K L M N O P Q R S T U V W X Y Z

read()

PURPOSE Reads characters from this filter reader.

SYNTAX
```
public int read() throws IOException
public int read(char[] buffer, int offset, int count) throws
   IOException
```

DESCRIPTION The two forms of this method read characters from this filter reader. They are usually overridden because a filter reader typically performs some postprocessing after reading the characters from the reader that it is filtering (`in`).

The first form reads a single character from the reader `in`, filters it, and returns it as a 32-bit `int`. The high-order 2 bytes of the `int` are not used. `read()` blocks until a character is available for reading from `in`. If end-of-file is reached on this reader, `read()` returns -1.

The second form reads characters from this filter reader and stores the characters read into the `char` array `buffer`. `read()` reads at most `count` number of characters from this reader and stores them in `buffer` starting at index `offset`. `read()` returns the number of characters actually read from this reader. If end-of-file is reached on this reader before any characters are read, `read()` returns -1.

PARAMETERS

`buffer` The non-`null` `char` array in which to store the characters read.

`count` The number of characters to read. $0 \leq$ `count` $\leq$ `buffer.length-offset`.

`offset` The index in `buffer` at which to start storing the characters read. $0 \leq$ `offset` $<$ `buffer.length`.

RETURNS The first form returns the character read. The second form returns the actual number of characters read. Both forms return -1 if end-of-file is reached before any characters are read.

EXCEPTIONS

`ArrayIndexOutOfBoundsException`
If `count` or `offset` is outside of the specified bounds.

`IOException`
If an IO error occurred while attempting to read.

OVERRIDES `Reader.read()`.

SEE ALSO `in`, `skip()`.

EXAMPLE See the class example.

ready()

PURPOSE Determines whether this filter reader is ready to be read without being blocked.

SYNTAX `public boolean ready() throws IOException`

DESCRIPTION This method determines whether this reader is ready to be read. If `true`, the next `read()` will not block while waiting for input. If `false`, the next `read()` may or may not block. By default, this method returns `in.ready()`. A subclass of `FilterReader` should override this method to return `true` when this reader is ready to be read.

RETURNS `true` if this reader is ready to be read without being blocked; `false` if not ready or doesn't know.

EXCEPTIONS

`IOException`

If an IO occurred while attempting to make the determination (for example, if the reader has already been closed).

EXAMPLE See `Reader.ready()`.

reset()

PURPOSE Resets the current read position to the last marked position.

SYNTAX `public synchronized void reset() throws IOException`

DESCRIPTION This method resets the current read position of this filter reader to be the last marked position (the read position when `mark()` was last called). The default implementation invokes the `reset()` method of the reader being filtered (`in`).

EXCEPTIONS

`IOException`

If no mark has been set or if the mark is invalid.

OVERRIDES `Reader.reset()`.

SEE ALSO `in`, `mark()`, `markSupported()`.

EXAMPLE See `mark()`.

A B C D E F G H I J K L M N O P Q R S T U V W X Y Z

skip()

PURPOSE Skips characters from this filter reader.

SYNTAX `public long skip(long count) throws IOException`

DESCRIPTION This method skips `count` number of characters from this filter reader. Characters that are skipped will not be returned by subsequent `read()` calls (except if mark/reset is used). The default implementation skips `count` number of characters from the reader being filtered (`in`). This method returns the number of characters actually skipped.

PARAMETERS
`count` The number of characters to skip.

RETURNS The actual number of characters skipped.

EXCEPTIONS
`IOException`
If an IO error occurred.

OVERRIDES `Reader.skip()`.

SEE ALSO `in`, `read()`.

EXAMPLE See the class example.

FilterWriter

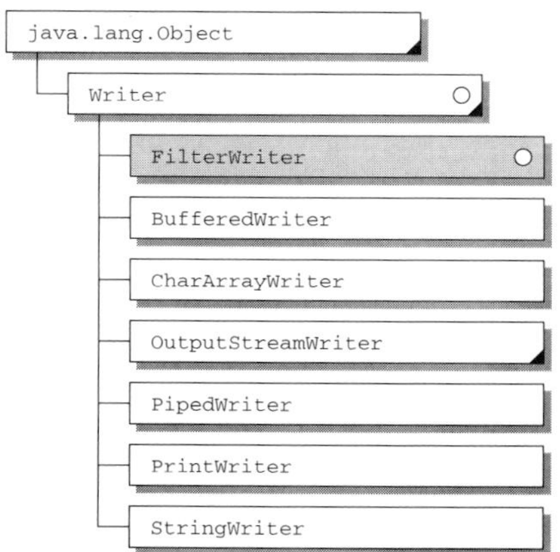

A B C D E F G H I J K L M N O P Q R S T U V W X Y Z

Syntax

```
public abstract class FilterWriter extends Writer
```

Description

A *filter writer* is a character output stream that "filters" output destined for another character output stream so that when you write to this filter writer, the resulting output is "filtered" (see Figure 54). An example of a filter writer is a writer that buffers its output. Another example is a writer that accepts Unicode characters written to it and translates them into localized characters. In each case, the filter writer is adding functionality to the original writer. In the buffered writer case, the filter writer is providing buffering. In the localized writer case, the filter writer is serving as a translator.

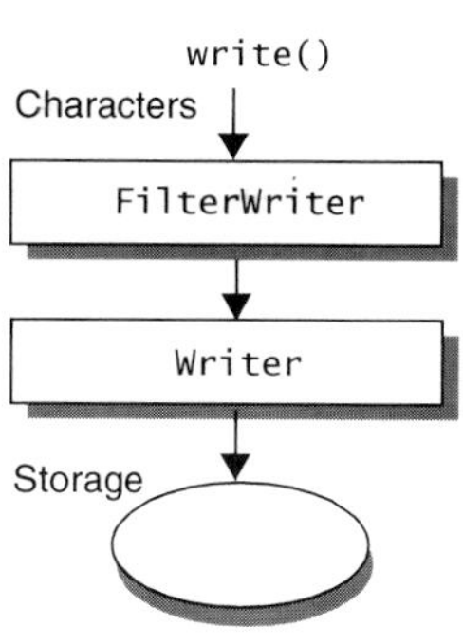

FIGURE 54: **`FilterWriter`.**

Filter writers can be composed with other filter writers; for example, a buffered writer that translates Unicode characters into localized characters.

Note the different stages at which filtering occurs for filter readers and filter writers. A filter writer performs processing on the stream *before* sending it out to its eventual destination. A filter reader does processing *after* reading characters from its original source.

The `FilterWriter` class represents a filter character output stream. A class extends `FilterWriter` and overrides its output methods in order to add functionality to the writer that it is filtering.

MEMBER SUMMARY	
Constructor	
`FilterWriter()`	Constructs a filter writer for another writer.
Output Methods	
`flush()`	Flushes this filter writer.
`write()`	Writes one or more characters to this filter writer.
Method for Closing the Stream	
`close()`	Closes this filter writer.
Protected Field	
`out`	The writer that is being filtered.

A B C D E F G H I J K L M N O P Q R S T U V W X Y Z

See Also

`BufferedWriter`, `FilterReader`, `OutputStream`, `Writer`.

Example

This example defines a `FilterWriter` for producing line-numbered output.

```
import java.io.*;

class LineNumberWriter extends FilterWriter {
    private int linenumber = 0;
    private boolean neednewline = true;
    public LineNumberWriter (Writer out) {
        super(out);
    }

    protected void newline() {
        synchronized (lock) {
            String prefix = ++linenumber + "\t";
            try {
                out.write(prefix);
            } catch (IOException e) {
                System.err.println(e);
            }
        }
    }

    public void write(int b) throws IOException {
        synchronized (lock) {
            if (neednewline) {
                newline();
                neednewline = false;
            }
            out.write(b);
            if (b == '\n') {
                neednewline = true;
```

```
            }
        }
    }
}

class Main {
    public static void main(String[] args) {
        if (args.length == 0) {
            System.err.println("java Main <input file>");
            System.exit(-1);
        }
        try {
            FileReader in = new FileReader(args[0]);
            LineNumberWriter out =
                new LineNumberWriter(new OutputStreamWriter(System.out));

            for (int c = in.read(); c > -1; c = in.read())
                out.write(c);
            out.flush();
            out.close();
        } catch (IOException e) {
            System.out.println(e);
        }
    }
}
```

close()

PURPOSE Closes this filter writer.

SYNTAX `public void close() throws IOException`

DESCRIPTION This method closes this filter writer. By default, it closes the writer that is being filtered (`out`), which in turn will close the next writer downstream, and so on. Hence, this method effectively closes this writer and all of the writers "downstream."

A subclass of filter writer might need to release other resources related to the filter, depending on the nature of the filter.

EXCEPTIONS

`IOException`

If an IO error occurred.

OVERRIDES `Writer.close()`.

SEE ALSO `out`.

EXAMPLE See the class example.

FilterWriter()

PURPOSE Constructs a filter writer for another writer.

SYNTAX `protected FilterWriter(Writer out)`

DESCRIPTION This method creates a filter writer for the writer `out`. Data written to this writer is processed by this filter before being sent to `out`.

PARAMETERS
`out` The non-`null` writer being filtered.

SEE ALSO `out`.

EXAMPLE See the class example.

flush()

PURPOSE Flushes this filter writer.

SYNTAX `public void flush() throws IOException`

DESCRIPTION This method flushes any buffered characters in this filter writer. The default implementation simply flushes any characters buffered by the writer being filtered (`out`). This, in turn, will flush the next writer downstream, and so on. Hence, this method effectively flushes this writer and all of the writers "downstream."

If this filter writer does any buffering, `flush()` should be overridden to flush the buffered characters as well.

EXCEPTIONS
`IOException`
If an IO error occurred.

OVERRIDES `Writer.flush()`.

SEE ALSO `BufferedWriter.flush()`, `out`.

EXAMPLE See the class example.

out

PURPOSE The writer that is being filtered.

SYNTAX `protected Writer out`

DESCRIPTION This is the writer with which this filter writer has been created. Characters written to this filter writer are processed by this filter writer and then written to `out`.

SEE ALSO `FilterWriter()`.

EXAMPLE See the class example.

write()

PURPOSE Writes one or more characters to this filter writer.

SYNTAX
```
public void write(int oneChar) throws IOException
public void write(char[] buffer, int offset, int count) throws
   IOException
public void write(String str, int offset, int count) throws
   IOException
```

DESCRIPTION The three forms of this method write characters to this filter writer. These methods are usually overridden because a filter writer typically performs some preprocessing before writing the characters to the writer that it is filtering (`out`).

The first form of `write()` writes a single character to this filter writer. It uses the low-order 2 bytes from `oneChar`. The second form writes `count` number of characters from the `char` array `buffer` starting at index `offset` to this filter writer. The third form writes `count` number of characters starting at index `offset` from the string `str` to this filter writer.

PARAMETERS

`buffer`	The non-`null` `char` array containing the characters to be written.
`count`	The number of characters to write. `0` ≤ `count` ≤ `buffer.length-offset` or `0` ≤ `count` ≤ `str.length()-offset`.
`offset`	The index in `buffer` from which to start getting the characters to be written. `0` ≤ `offset` < `buffer.length` or `0` ≤ `offset` < `str.length()`.
`oneChar`	The `char` to be written. The low-order 2 bytes from `oneChar` are used.

EXCEPTIONS

`ArrayIndexOutOfBoundsException`
If `count` or `offset` is outside of the specified bounds.

`IOException`
If an IO error occurred.

OVERRIDES `Writer.write()`.

EXAMPLE See the class example.

A B C D E F G H I J K L M N O P Q R S T U V W X Y Z

Float

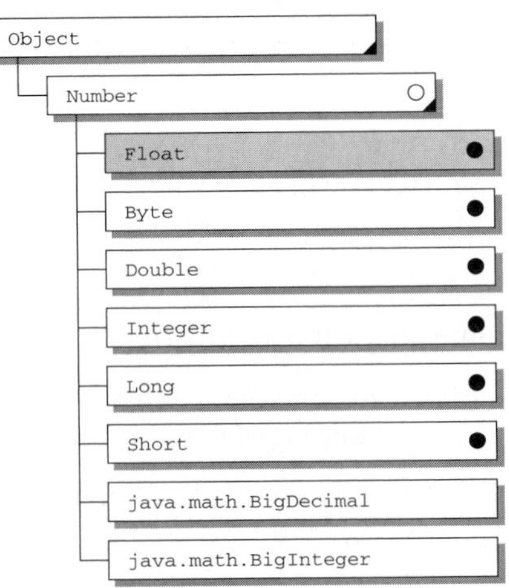

Syntax

```
public final class Float extends Number
```

Description

A `float` in Java is a 32-bit floating-point number. The `Float` class provides an object wrapper for the `float` data value. This wrapper allows floating-point numbers to be passed to methods in Java class libraries that accept Java objects as parameters. In addition, the `Float` class provides methods that convert values to and from `float`s. It also performs other operations on `float`s.

Usage

`Float` instances cannot be used in arithmetic expressions in place of `float`. For example, the following is not allowed:

```
Float f1 = new Float(243.34);
Float f2 = new Float(5);
Float f3 = f1 * f2;      // Illegal
```

To perform an arithmetic operation using a `Float` instance, you first must use access methods defined in the `Float` class to obtain its numeric value, as follows:

```
float f3 = f1.floatValue() * f2.floatValue();
double d1 = f1.floatValue() + f2.doubleValue();
```

MEMBER SUMMARY	
Constructor	
`Float()`	Constructs a `Float` instance using a number or a string.
Constant Fields	
`MAX_VALUE`	The maximum value a `float` can have.
`MIN_VALUE`	The smallest positive value a `float` can have.
`NaN`	The special Not-a-Number (`NaN`) value.
`NEGATIVE_INFINITY`	Negative infinity for a `float`.
`POSITIVE_INFINITY`	Positive infinity for a `float`.
`TYPE`	The `Class` object representing the primitive type `float`.
Number Methods	
`byteValue()`	Retrieves the value of this object as a `byte`.
`doubleValue()`	Retrieves the value of this object as a `double`.
`floatValue()`	Retrieves the value of this object as a `float`.
`intValue()`	Retrieves the value of this object as an `int`.
`longValue()`	Retrieves the value of this object as a `long`.
`shortValue()`	Retrieves the value of this object as a `short`.
Conversion Methods	
`floatToIntBits()`	Retrieves the bit representation of a `float`.
`intBitsToFloat()`	Retrieves the `float` corresponding to a given bit representation.
`toString()`	Generates the string representation of a `float` or a `Float` instance.
`valueOf()`	Creates a new `Float` instance using its string representation.
Comparison Methods	
`equals()`	Compares this object with another object for equality.
`isInfinite()`	Determines whether a `float` is infinitely large in magnitude.
`isNaN()`	Determines whether a `float` is the special Not-a-Number (`NaN`) value.
Hash Code Method	
`hashCode()`	Computes the hash code for this object.

See Also

`Byte`, `Double`, `Int`, `Number`, `Long`, `Short`.

byteValue()

PURPOSE Retrieves the value of this object as a `byte`.

SYNTAX `public byte byteValue()`

RETURNS This method retrieves the value of this object as a `byte` by casting its `float` value to a `byte`. If the `float` exceeds what a `byte` can accommodate, the sign of the `byte` might differ from that of the `float`. Their numeric values might be very different as a result of the cast.

SEE ALSO `doubleValue()`, `floatValue()`, `intValue()`, `longValue()`, `Number`, `shortValue()`.

EXAMPLE See `doubleValue()`.

A B C D E F G H I J K L M N O P Q R S T U V W X Y Z

doubleValue()

PURPOSE Retrieves the value of this object as a `double`.

SYNTAX `public double doubleValue()`

DESCRIPTION This method retrieves the value of this object by casting its `float` value to a `double` value.

RETURNS The value of this object as a `double`.

SEE ALSO `byteValue()`, `floatValue()`, `intValue()`, `longValue()`, `Number`, `shortValue()`.

EXAMPLE

```
Float fobj = new Float(0.47712f);

double dval = fobj.doubleValue(); // 0.4771200120449066
float fval = fobj.floatValue();   // 0.47712
int ival = fobj.intValue();       // round to 0
long lval = fobj.longValue();     // round to 0
byte bval = fobj.byteValue();     // round to 0
short sval = fobj.shortValue();   // round to 0
```

equals()

PURPOSE Compares this object with another object for equality.

SYNTAX `public boolean equals(Object obj)`

DESCRIPTION This method compares the `float` value of this object against that of the object `obj`. It returns `true` if the two values are equal. It returns `false` if the two values are not equal or if `obj` is `null` or not a `Float` object. This method considers two NaN float values to be equal in order for Float.equals() to be useful in hash tables. This is contrary to the IEEE specification.

PARAMETERS

obj — The possibly null object against which this object is compared.

RETURNS — true if obj has the same float value as this object; false otherwise.

OVERRIDES — Object.equals().

SEE ALSO — hashCode().

EXAMPLE

```
Float f1 = new Float(4.8123f);
Float f2 = new Float(4.8123f);

// Check whether the value of two Floats are equal
if (f1.equals(f2))
    System.out.println("equal");
```

Float()

PURPOSE — Constructs a Float object using a number or a string.

SYNTAX

```
public Float(float fval)
public Float(double dval)
public Float(String sval) throws NumberFormatException
```

DESCRIPTION — The three forms of this constructor construct instances of Float using either a floating-point number (fval or dval) or the string representation sval of a floating-point number. The format of str is described in valueOf().

PARAMETERS

dval — The double value used to construct this object.

fval — The float value used to construct this object.

sval — The non-null string representation of a float value.

EXCEPTIONS

NumberFormatException

If sval cannot be parsed into a float.

SEE ALSO — valueOf().

EXAMPLE

```
Float pi = new Float(3.14159f);        // using float
Float num = new Float(8.23e13);        // using double
if (num.equals(pi))
  ...
try {
    Float f = new Float("1.23");       // using string
        ...
} catch (NumberFormatException e) {
  ...
}
```

floatToIntBits()

PURPOSE Retrieves the bit representation of a `float` value.

SYNTAX `public static native int floatToIntBits(float value)`

DESCRIPTION A `float` is a 32-bit floating-point number. This method returns an `int` containing the bit representation of the `float` value `value`. The bit representation is the IEEE standard format for 32-bit floating-point numbers. This method is the inverse of `intBitsToFloat()`.

PARAMETERS

`value` The `float` value.

RETURNS An `int` containing the bit representation of `value`.

SEE ALSO `intBitsToFloat()`.

EXAMPLE

```
float fnum = 22.45915f;
int bitrepr = Float.floatToIntBits(fnum);      // get bit repr
float reconst = Float.intBitsToFloat(bitrepr); // reconstruct fnum

if (reconst == fnum) // should be true
    System.out.println("correct");
```

floatValue()

PURPOSE Retrieves the value of this object as a `float`.

SYNTAX `public float floatValue()`

RETURNS The value of this object as a `float`.

SEE ALSO `byteValue()`, `doubleValue()`, `intValue()`, `longValue()`, `Number`, `shortValue()`.

EXAMPLE See `doubleValue()`.

hashCode()

PURPOSE Computes the hash code for this object.

SYNTAX `public int hashCode()`

DESCRIPTION This method returns the hash code for this `Float` object. The code is calculated using the object's `float` value. Two `Float`s that have the same `float` value will have the same hash code. However, two `Float`s with the same hash code may not necessarily have the same `float` value.

RETURNS An `int` representing the hash code.

OVERRIDES `Object.hashCode()`.

SEE ALSO `equals()`, `java.util.Hashtable`.

EXAMPLE

```
Float fnum = new Float(1.61803f);
int hashval = fnum.hashCode();          // generate hash code
++hits[Math.abs(hashval%tabsize)];      // count hits
```

intBitsToFloat()

PURPOSE Retrieves the `float` corresponding to a given bit representation.

SYNTAX `public static native float intBitsToFloat(int bits)`

DESCRIPTION This method returns the `float` value corresponding to the bit representation `bits`. It is the inverse of the method `floatToIntBits()`.

PARAMETERS

`bits` The bits used to generate the `float` value.

RETURNS The `float` value represented by `bits`.

SEE ALSO `floatToIntBits()`.

EXAMPLE See `floatToIntBits()`.

intValue()

PURPOSE Retrieves the value of this object as an `int`.

SYNTAX `public int intValue()`

RETURNS This method retrieves the value of this object as an `int` by casting its `float` value to an `int`. If the `float` value exceeds what an `int` can accommodate, the sign of the `int` value might differ from that of the `float`. Their numeric values might be very different as a result of the cast.

DESCRIPTION The value of this object as an `int`.

SEE ALSO `byteValue()`, `doubleValue()`, `floatValue()`, `longValue()`, `Number`, `shortValue()`.

EXAMPLE See `doubleValue()`.

isInfinite()

PURPOSE Determines whether a `float` is infinitely large in magnitude.

SYNTAX
```
public boolean isInfinite()
public static boolean isInfinite(float value)
```

DESCRIPTION The first form of this method returns `true` if the `float` value of this `Float` object is infinitely large in magnitude. It returns `false` otherwise. The second form returns `true` if the `float` value `value` is infinitely large in magnitude. It returns `false` otherwise.

PARAMETERS

`value` The `float` to check for infinity.

RETURNS `true` if the `float` is infinitely large in magnitude; `false` otherwise.

SEE ALSO `NEGATIVE_INFINITY`, `POSITIVE_INFINITY`.

EXAMPLE
```
Float fnum = new Float(1.6878f);
...
if (fnum.isInfinite())          // method version
    throw new ArithmeticException();
if (Float.isInfinite(85.1f))    // class version
    break;
```

isNaN()

PURPOSE Determines whether a `float` is the special Not-a-Number (`NaN`) value.

SYNTAX
```
public boolean isNaN()
public static boolean isNan(float value)
```

DESCRIPTION The first form of this method returns `true` if the `float` value of this `Float` object is the special `NaN` value. It returns `false` otherwise. The second form returns `true` if the `float` value `value` is the `NaN`. It returns `false` otherwise.

PARAMETERS

`value` The `float` to check whether it is the `NaN`.

RETURNS `true` if the `float` is the `NaN`; `false` otherwise.

SEE ALSO `NaN`.

EXAMPLE
```
Float fnum = new Float(1.523E24f);
if (fnum.isNaN())                     // method version
    throw new ArithmeticException();
if (Float.isNaN(fnum.floatValue())) // class version
  ...
```

longValue()

PURPOSE Retrieves the value of this object as a `long`.

SYNTAX `public long longValue()`

DESCRIPTION This method retrieves the value of this object as a `long` by casting its `float` value to a `long` value.

RETURNS The value of this object as a `long`.

SEE ALSO `byteValue()`, `doubleValue()`, `floatValue()`, `intValue()`, `Number`, `shortValue()`.

EXAMPLE See `doubleValue()`.

A B C D E F G H I J K L M N O P Q R S T U V W X Y Z

MAX_VALUE

PURPOSE The maximum value a `float` can have.

SYNTAX `public static final float MAX_VALUE`

DESCRIPTION This constant represents the maximum value a `float` can have, which is `3.40282346638528860e+38`.

SEE ALSO `MIN_VALUE`.

EXAMPLE

```
// test if number is less than MAX_VALUE
float fnum = 3.1415927f;
if (fnum < Float.MAX_VALUE)
    fnum *= 100;
```

MIN_VALUE

PURPOSE The minimum value a `float` can have.

SYNTAX `public static final float MIN_VALUE`

DESCRIPTION This constant represents the smallest positive value a `float` can have, which is `1.40129846432481707e-45`.

SEE ALSO `MAX_VALUE`.

EXAMPLE

```
// test if number is greater than MIN_VALUE
float fnum = 2.71828f;
if (fnum > Float.MIN_VALUE)
    fnum = 1/fnum;
```

NaN

PURPOSE The special Not-a-Number (`NaN`) value.

SYNTAX `public static final float NaN`

DESCRIPTION This constant represents the special Not-a-Number (`NaN`). The value of `NaN` is not equal to anything, including `NaN` itself. However, for the value to be useful in hash tables, the `Float.equals()` method considers two `NaN`s equal, which is contrary to the IEEE specification. However, the equals operator (==) considers two `float` `NaN`s to be not equal. This is consistent with the IEEE specification.

SEE ALSO `isNaN()`.

EXAMPLE

```
float fnum = Float.NaN;
// test if number is Not-A-Number
if (Float.isNaN(fnum))                // succeeds
    System.out.println("correct");
if (Float.isNaN(Float.NaN))           // succeeds
    System.out.println("correct");

// A NaN is not equal to itself except when using equals()
if (fnum == Float.NaN)                // fails
    System.out.println("incorrect");
Float f1 = new Float(Float.NaN);
Float f2 = new Float(Float.NaN);
if (f1.equals(f2))                    // succeeds
    System.out.println("correct");
```

NEGATIVE_INFINITY

PURPOSE Negative infinity for a `float` value.

SYNTAX `public static final float NEGATIVE_INFINITY`

SEE ALSO `isInfinite()`, `POSITIVE_INFINITY`.

EXAMPLE

```
float fnum;
  ...
// reset to 0 if number reached neg infinity
if (fnum == Float.NEGATIVE_INFINITY)
    fnum = 0;
```

POSITIVE_INFINITY

PURPOSE Positive infinity for a `float` value.

SYNTAX `public static final float POSITIVE_INFINITY`

SEE ALSO `isInfinite()`, `NEGATIVE_INFINITY`.

EXAMPLE

```
float fnum;
  ...
// reset to 0 if number reached pos infinity
if (fnum == Float.POSITIVE_INFINITY)
    fnum = 0;
```

shortValue()

PURPOSE Retrieves the value of this object as a `short`.

SYNTAX `public short shortValue()`

RETURNS This method retrieves the value of this object as a `short` by casting its `float` value to a `short`. If the `float` value exceeds what a `short` can accommodate, the sign of the `short` value might differ from that of the `float`. Their numeric values might be very different as a result of the cast.

SEE ALSO `byteValue()`, `doubleValue()`, `floatValue()`, `intValue()`, `longValue()`, `Number`.

EXAMPLE See `doubleValue()`.

toString()

PURPOSE Generates the string representation for this object.

SYNTAX
```
public String toString()
public static String toString(float value)
```

DESCRIPTION The two forms of this method return the string representation of a `float` value. This first form returns the string representation of this `Float` object (basically the string form of its `float` value). The second form returns the string representation of the `float` value `value`.

The format of the string is a leading negative sign (if the number is negative) followed by a sequence of digits, a period character, more digits, and, optionally, an exponent. Special cases are made for `NaN`, `POSITIVE_INFINITY`, and

NEGATIVE_INFINITY. See *The Java Language Specification, First Edition*, Section 20.9.16, for a full description of the string representation.

PARAMETERS

value The float for which to generate the string representation.

RETURNS The string representation of value or the float value of this Float object.

OVERRIDES Object.toString().

SEE ALSO valueOf().

EXAMPLE

```
Float fnum = new Float(0.843f);
String str = fnum.toString();          // get string form of number
String str2 = Float.toString(1.523E24f);
String pstr = "The two floats are " + str + " and " + str2;
```


TYPE

PURPOSE The Class object representing the primitive type float.

SYNTAX public static final Class TYPE

DESCRIPTION This constant can be used where the Class object—float.class—of the primitive type float is required, such as for reflection. Although there are no restrictions on the use of Float.TYPE, the preferred syntax for naming the class is float.class.

SEE ALSO Class.

EXAMPLE

```
public static void main(String[] args) {
    Class c = Float.TYPE;
    System.out.println("TYPE: " + c);
    System.out.println("isPrimitive: " + c.isPrimitive());
    System.out.println("superclass: " + c.getSuperclass());
    try {
        Object obj = c.newInstance();  // ERROR
        System.out.println("float: " + obj);
    } catch (InstantiationException e) {
        e.printStackTrace();
    } catch (IllegalAccessException e) {
        e.printStackTrace();
    }
}
```

valueOf()

PURPOSE Creates a new `Float` object using its string representation.

SYNTAX `public static native Float valueOf(String str) throws NumberFormatException`

DESCRIPTION This method creates a new `Float` object by parsing the string `str` into a `float` value. The format of the string is

[*Sign*] *Digits* **.** [*Digits*] [*ExponentPart*]

[*Sign*] **.** *Digits* [*ExponentPart*]

where *Sign* is a negative sign, *Digits* is a sequence of digits from "0123456789," and *ExponentPart* is one of "e" or "E" followed by a signed integer. Details of this format are in *The Java Language Specification, First Edition*, Section 20.9.17. Leading and trailing whitespace characters in `str` are ignored.

PARAMETERS

`str` The string to be parsed.

RETURNS A new `Float` object with the `float` value of the number parsed from `str`.

SEE ALSO `toString()`.

EXCEPTIONS

`NumberFormatException`

If `str` cannot be parsed into a `float` value.

EXAMPLE

```
String str = "1.0871E3f";
try {
    Float r = Float.valueOf(str);
     ...
} catch (NumberFormatException e) {
    System.err.println("Could not convert string to number " + str);
}
```

Format

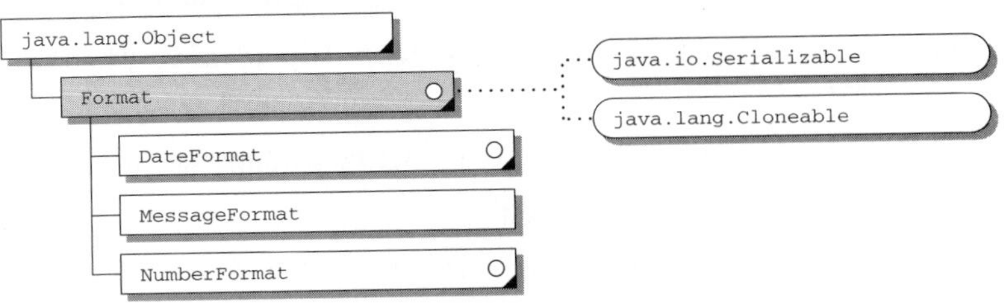

A B C D E F G H I J K L M N O P Q R S T U V W X Y Z

Syntax

```
public abstract class Format extends Object implements Serializable, Cloneable
```

Description

Dates and numbers are represented internally in a locale-independent way. For example, `Date` objects are kept as milliseconds since epoch (January 1, 1970 00:00:00 UTC). When these `Date` objects are printed or displayed, they must be converted to localized strings. The locale-specific parts of a date string, such as the time zone string, are separately imported from a locale-specific resource bundle.

The `format()` method converts the `Date` object from –604656780000 milliseconds to the form "Tuesday, November 3, 1997 9:47am CST" for the U. S. English locale. Figure 55 shows how the `format()` method of `Format` subclasses enables instances of `Number`, `Date`, `String`, and other objects to be formatted to locale-specific strings.

Conversely, the `parseObject()` method (and `parse()` method in subclasses) perform the reverse operation of parsing localized strings and converting them to `Number`, `Date`, and `String` objects. Figure 55 shows how the `parse()` method is complementary to `format()`. Any `String` formatted by `format()` is guaranteed to be parseable by `parseObject()`.

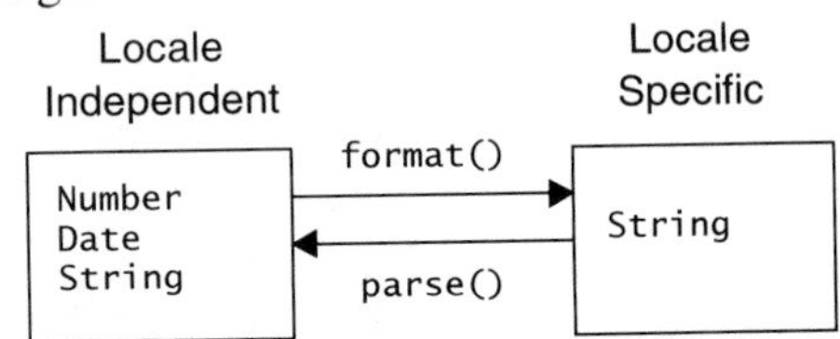

FIGURE 55: Formatting and parsing.

The `Format` class is the abstract superclass of the format family of classes. It defines the minimum operations that a format must implement. It provides the basic methods for formatting and parsing objects. Java provides three direct, concrete subclasses of `Format` for formatting dates, numbers, and messages, respectively: `DateFormat`, `NumberFormat`, and `MessageFormat`. Other subclasses specialize these.

The `MessageFormat` class allows the formatting of messages, which are strings visible to users. A message can mix strings generated with the `format()` method (such as `Date` and `Number` objects) with string literals (either hard-coded or imported from a resource bundle).

Usage: Subclassing

Concrete subclasses of `Format` *must* implement (or inherit implementations of) these two methods:

```
StringBuffer format(Object obj, StringBuffer appendBuf, FieldPosition pos)
Object parseObject(String sourceStr, ParsePosition pos)
```

Most immediate subclasses will also implement the following two methods:

- `getInstance()`, for getting a useful format object appropriate for the current locale
- `getInstance(Locale)`, for getting a useful format object appropriate for the specified locale

Some subclasses also may choose to implement other `getXxxInstance` methods for more specialized control. For example, the `NumberFormat` class provides `getPercentInstance()` and `getCurrencyInstance()` methods for getting specialized number formatters.

Subclasses of `Format` that allow programmers to create objects for locales (for example, using `getInstance(Locale)`) must also implement the following class method:

```
public static Locale[] getAvailableLocales()
```

And finally, subclasses may define a set of constants to identify the various fields in both the objects to be formatted and the resulting strings. Each constant is used to create a `FieldPosition` object that identifies the field and its position in the formatted result. Examples for dates are `YEAR_FIELD`, `MONTH_FIELD`, and `HOUR_FIELD`. Examples for numbers are `INTEGER_FIELD` and `FRACTION_FIELD`. These constants should be named *item*`_FIELD`, where *item* identifies the field.

Usage: Exceptions

During formatting, if the `format()` method is unsuccessful because it cannot format the type of object passed in, it throws an `IllegalArgumentException`. Otherwise, if there is something ill-formed about the object, `format()` returns the Unicode replacement character, `\uFFFD`.

During parsing, if there is no match, `parseObject(String)` throws a `ParseException`, while `parseObject(String, ParsePosition)` leaves the `ParsePosition index` member unchanged and returns `null`.

MEMBER SUMMARY	
Constructor	
`Format()`	Constructor called by subclasses.
Format and Parse Methods	
`format()`	Formats an object to produce a string.
`parseObject()`	Parses a string to produce an object.
Object Method	
`clone()`	Creates a copy of this format.

See Also

NumberFormat, DecimalFormat, ChoiceFormat, DateFormat, SimpleDateFormat, MessageFormat, ParsePosition, FieldPosition.

Example

This example creates a PhoneNumberFormat class that extends Format. It contains a format() method that formats a phone number string of the form "(123) 456-7890" to a Long, where "(123)" is the area code. The area code prefix and suffix are "(" and ")." The parse() method does the reverse by parsing a Long to such a string. This example is not internationalized; it works only for phone numbers in the U. S. format and is not customizable.

```
import java.text.*;

class PhoneNumberFormat extends Format implements Cloneable {
    // Constructor.
    public PhoneNumberFormat() {
    }

    // Prefix/Suffix setters and setters.
    public String getAreacodePrefix () {
        return areacodePrefix;
    }
    public void setAreacodePrefix (String newValue) {
        areacodePrefix = newValue;
    }
    public String getAreacodeSuffix () {
        return areacodeSuffix;
    }
    public void setAreacodeSuffix (String newValue) {
        areacodeSuffix = newValue;
    }

    // Signifies the position of the local part
    // of a formatted phone number should be returned.
    public static final int LOCALNUMBER_FIELD = 0;

    // Signifies that the position of the area
    // code part of a formatted phone number should be returned.
    public static final int AREACODE_FIELD = 1;

    // Implementation of the required format method.
    public final StringBuffer format(Object number,
                                     StringBuffer toAppendTo,
                                     FieldPosition pos) {
        if (number instanceof Long) {
            return format((Long)number);
        }
        else {
            throw new IllegalArgumentException("Cannot format " +
                                               " given Object as a Number");
        }
    }

    // Format the phone number.
    public final StringBuffer format(Long phonenumber) {
```

```
        StringBuffer pnString = new StringBuffer(phonenumber.toString());

        // Start from the right end inserting characters.

        // Insert hyphen into local phone number.
        pnString.insert(6, "-");

        // Insert space between area code and phone number.
        pnString.insert(3, " ");

        // Insert area code prefix/suffix.
        pnString.insert(3, getAreacodeSuffix());
        pnString.insert(0, getAreacodePrefix());

        return pnString;
    }

    // The required parseObject method.
    public final Object parseObject(String source,
                                    ParsePosition parsePosition) {
        return parse(source, parsePosition);
    }

    // Convenience parse method that returns a Long.
    public Long parse(String text) throws ParseException {
        ParsePosition parsePosition = new ParsePosition(0);
        Long phonenumber;

        phonenumber = (Long)parse(text, parsePosition);
        if (parsePosition.getIndex() == 0) {
            throw new ParseException("Unparseable number: \"" + text + "\"", 0);
        }
        return phonenumber;
    }

    // Convenience parse method that returns a Number.
    public Number parse(String text, ParsePosition status) {
        int start = status.getIndex();

        // Check for areacodePrefix in text.
        boolean gotAreacode = text.regionMatches(start, areacodePrefix, 0,
                                                 areacodePrefix.length());

        // Advance the start point past the prefix if it exists.
        if (gotAreacode) {
            start += areacodePrefix.length();
        }
        else return null;

        Long longResult = new Long(0);
        StringBuffer stringResult = new StringBuffer("");

        for (;start < text.length(); ++start) {

            // Get the first character.
            char ch = text.charAt(start);

            // Convert ch to a character object.
            Character chObj = new Character(ch);
```

```
                // If the character is a digit, add it to result.
                if (Character.isDigit(ch)) {
                    stringResult.append(ch);
                }
            }

            longResult = new Long(stringResult.toString());


            // Reset the index.
            if (gotAreacode) {
                status.setIndex(start + areacodeSuffix.length());
            }

            // Return final value.
            return (Number)longResult;
        }

        // Overrides hashCode
        public int hashCode() {
            return (((new Integer(areacodePrefix)).intValue() * 37
                   + (new Integer(areacodeSuffix)).intValue()));
        }

        // Overrides equals
        public boolean equals(Object obj) {
            if (this == obj) return true;
            if (getClass() != obj.getClass()) return false;
                    PhoneNumberFormat other = (PhoneNumberFormat) obj;
                    return (areacodePrefix == other.areacodePrefix
                    && areacodeSuffix == other.areacodeSuffix);
        }

        // Overrides Cloneable
        public Object clone() {
            PhoneNumberFormat other = (PhoneNumberFormat) super.clone();
            return other;
        }

        // Private constants used by equals() and hashcode()

        private String  areacodePrefix = "";
        private String  areacodeSuffix = "";
    }

    class Main {
        // Parse and print the phone number string.
        public static void printParse(PhoneNumberFormat pnf, String pnString) {
            System.out.println("Phone number to parse: " + pnString);

            // Parse inside a try block.
            try {
               System.out.println("Phone number as Long:  " + pnf.parse(pnString));
            } catch (ParseException pe) {
                System.out.println("Could not parse number " + pnString +
                          " with given area code prefix '" +
                          pnf.getAreacodePrefix() + "'");
            }
            // Print blank line.
            System.out.println("");
```

```
    }

    public static void main(String args[]) {
        // Create the phone number format and set its prefix/suffix.
        PhoneNumberFormat pnf = new PhoneNumberFormat();
        pnf.setAreacodePrefix("(");
        pnf.setAreacodeSuffix(")");

        // Parse two example strings to Longs.
        printParse(pnf, "(415) 856-3565");              // 4158563565
        printParse(pnf, "8563565");                     // Properly thows
                                                        // parse exception.

        // Format a Long to a string.
        Long pnLong = new Long(4158563565l);
        System.out.println("Number to format: " + pnLong);
        System.out.println("Formatted number: "
                          + pnf.format(pnLong));       // (415) 856-3565
    }
}
```

Output

```
Phone number to parse: (415) 856-3565
Phone number as Long:  4158563565

Phone number to parse: 8563565
Could not parse number 8563565 with given area code prefix '('

Number to format: 4158563565
Formatted number: (415) 856-3565
```

clone()

PURPOSE Creates a copy of this format.

SYNTAX `public Object clone()`

DESCRIPTION This method creates a copy of this format. Changing any value in the new format will not affect this instance.

RETURNS A non-`null` copy of this format.

OVERRIDES `java.lang.Object.clone()`.

EXAMPLE This example illustrates the use of `clone()` to copy a decimal format object. It then uses `equals()` to compare them and prints out `hashcode()`. Note that the copy has the same pattern as the original.

```
import java.text.NumberFormat;

class Main {

    public static void main(String args[]) {
```

```
            NumberFormat nf = NumberFormat.getInstance();

            // create string character iterator
            nf.setMinimumFractionDigits(5);
            System.out.println(nf.getMinimumFractionDigits());   // prints '5'

            // create a clone
            NumberFormat nfCopy = (NumberFormat)nf.clone();
            System.out.println(nfCopy.getMinimumFractionDigits());   // prints '5'

            if(nf.equals(nfCopy)) {
                System.out.println("Copy is equal to original");
            } else {
                System.out.println("Copy is not equal to original");
            }

            // compute hashcode
            int hc = nf.hashCode();
            System.out.println("Hash code is: " + hc);
        }
    }
```

Format()

PURPOSE Constructor called by subclasses.

SYNTAX `public Format()`

DESCRIPTION Do not call this constructor directly. Typically, the constructor of a subclass implicitly calls this constructor.

EXAMPLE See the class example.

format()

PURPOSE Formats an object to produce a string.

SYNTAX
```
public final String format(Object obj)
public abstract StringBuffer format(Object obj,
   StringBuffer appendBuf, FieldPosition pos)
```

DESCRIPTION This method formats the object `obj` to produce a string, which is appended to the buffer `appendBuf`. The `appendBuf` value is returned. Returning the full result allows chaining, as with `StringBuffer.append()`. If `appendBuf` is not specified, the produced string is simply returned.

The field position `pos` has absolutely no effect on the formatted result. Its purpose is to determine where in the string the range of characters are for a given field so that the strings can be aligned in a column on that particular field. If you don't care about column alignment, set `pos` to any valid field position. More on this later in this discussion.

Note that the three-parameter form of this method is an abstract method. Subclasses *must* implement this form (or inherit an implementation of it). Subclasses typically also implement variations of `format()` that take a particular object, such as a `Number` object:

```
StringBuffer format (Number obj, StringBuffer appendBuf)
```

Likewise, subclasses can implement a complementary `parse()` method that implements the reverse operation, such as parsing a string to a number:

```
Number parse (String str)
```

The field position works as follows. You create an instance of `FieldPosition` using the field constant for the field you want to align. For example, if you are formatting numbers and want to output them in a column and align the decimal separators, create the `FieldPosition` object with the field constant `NumberFormat.INTEGER_FIELD`. When you call `format()`, the begin and end index values of the field position `pos` are updated to the integer range in the resulting string. You next can use these values to get the length of the integer portion and then use that length to position the string horizontally. For an example of this, see the class example in the `FieldPosition` class.

PARAMETERS

`appendBuf` The string buffer in which the resulting string is to be appended.
`obj` The object to format.
`pos` A `FieldPosition` object whose field you want to eventually align in a column.

RETURNS The string passed in as `appendBuf` with the newly formatted string appended to it.

EXCEPTIONS

`IllegalArgumentException`
If the instance of `Format` cannot format the object passed in.

SEE ALSO `MessageFormat`, `FieldPosition`.

EXAMPLE See the class example.

parseObject()

PURPOSE Parses a string to an object.

SYNTAX
```
public Object parseObject(String sourceStr)
   throws ParseException
public abstract Object parseObject(String sourceStr,
   ParsePosition pos)
```

DESCRIPTION This method uses this `Format` object to parse the string `sourceStr`, starting at position `pos`, and converts that string to an object. Before calling this method, set the index of `pos` to where you want to start parsing the source string. If `pos` is not specified, the parsing begins at the start of the string.

This method has two syntax forms which have different exception handling. When faced with the same parse exception, the first form stops and throws a `ParseException`, while the second form continues parsing.

Parsing skips over whitespace and begins matching on the first non-whitespace character it finds. It compares that character with what the format expects to find. For example, a decimal format would expect a positive or negative prefix or, if none is defined, the start of a number. If this character matches, it updates the `ParsePosition` object with the new position and continues to the next character and so on until it has matched the expected format. If anywhere along the line the character does not match, the first syntax form throws a `ParseException`; the second form does not throw an exception.

Therefore, you can loop, continually using the current index of the updated `ParsePosition` object to iterate over potentially the entire string. Note that during parsing, leading whitespace is discarded (with a successful parse) and trailing whitespace is left as is.

Note that the `parseObject(String, ParsePosition)` form of this method is an abstract method. Subclasses *must* implement this form (or inherit an implementation of it).

This method is called `parseObject()` to denote that it can return any subclass of `Object`. A subclass of `Format` will typically implement a convenience method that returns a particular type of value. This avoids having to cast `Object` to that type. Since methods can't overload on return types, the convenience method cannot be called `parseObject()` and will instead typically be named `parse()`.

Any `parse()` method that does not take a field position should throw a `ParseException` when no text in the required format is at the start position.

Subclasses typically implement convenient variations of this method that return a particular object, such as parsing a string to a number:

```
Number parse (String str);
long parse (String str);
double parse (String str);
```

When implementing these methods, it's good to include the complementary convenience implementations as well:

```
String format (Number obj);
String format (long obj);
String format (double obj);
```

PARAMETERS

`pos` The parse position that determines where the parse begins.

`sourceStr` The string to be parsed.

RETURNS The possibly `null` object parsed from the string.

EXCEPTIONS

`ParseException`

If the specified string is invalid. Thrown only for the first form of `parseObject()`.

SEE ALSO `ParsePosition`.

EXAMPLE See the class example.

java.util

GregorianCalendar

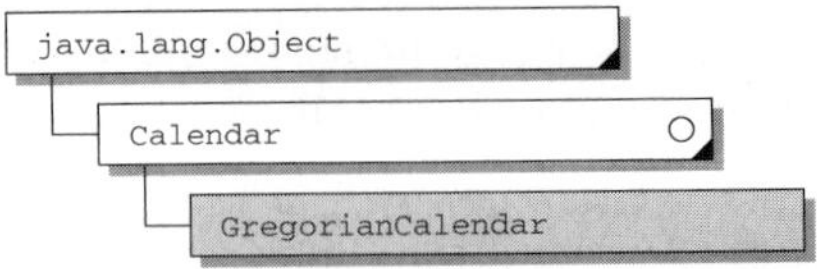

A B C D E F G H I J K L M N O P Q R S T U V W X Y Z

Syntax

```
public class GregorianCalendar extends Calendar
```

Description

The Gregorian calendar is the world's most widely used calendar system. The `GregorianCalendar` class is used to perform operations on dates under the Gregorian calendar system. A complete discussion of calendar classes in general is in the `Calendar` class. In fact, most of the documentation for this class is located in the `Calendar` class. Please refer to `Calendar` when using this class.

The implementation of this class is not historically accurate and should not be used to build historical calendars. However, it works fine for modern calendar calculations.

The current implementation handles dates from 4,716 B.C. up to 5,000,000 A.D. Dates outside of that range will throw an `IllegalArgumentException`.

The Change Date

The Gregorian calendar has two eras: B.C. and A.D. It also has a Gregorian change date (default: October 15, 1582 midnight), which represents the date on which the Gregorian calendar was instituted. This date can be modified for countries who instituted the date later. The calendar system in effect before this date was the Julian calendar system. The main effect of the change date is on how leap years are calculated. See `isLeapYear()` for details.

Usage

To use this class, you first construct a `GregorianCalendar` object. You can supply a locale and time zone if the default values (`Locale.getDefault()` and `TimeZone.getDefault()`) are not appropriate. The new `GregorianCalendar` object is initialized with the current date and time. You can set the object's current date and time either by calling the `set()` method or by calling `setTime()`.

After you've set the current date and time to the desired value, you then can query the values of the calendar fields (see `Calendar`). The following code creates a `GregorianCalendar` instance and gets a `Date` value from it.

```
Calendar xmas = new GregorianCalendar(1997, Calendar.DECEMBER, 25);
Date d = xmas.getTime();
```

MEMBER SUMMARY	
Constructor	
`GregorianCalendar()`	Constructs a `GregorianCalendar` instance.
Era Constants	
`AD`	Represents A.D. (Anno Domini).
`BC`	Represents B.C. (before Christ).
Date Modification Methods	
`add()`	Increments/decrements a calendar field.
`roll()`	Rolls a calendar field.
Comparison Methods	
`after()`	Determines if the time of this `GregorianCalendar` object is later than the time of another such object.
`before()`	Determines if the time of this `GregorianCalendar` object is before the time of another such object.
`isLeapYear()`	Determines if a year is a leap year.
Gregorian Change Methods	
`getGregorianChange()`	Retrieves the Gregorian calendar change date.
`setGregorianChange()`	Sets the Gregorian calendar change date.
Range Methods	
`getGreatestMinimum()`	Retrieves the greatest minimum value for a calendar field.
`getLeastMaximum()`	Retrieves the least maximum value for a calendar field.
`getMaximum()`	Retrieves the maximum value for a calendar field.
`getMinimum()`	Retrieves the minimum value for a calendar field.
Internal Calendar Computation Methods	
`computeFields()`	Computes the values for the calendar fields from this `GregorianCalendar` object's `Date` value.
`computeTime()`	Converts the calendar fields into a `Date` value.
Object Methods	
`equals()`	Determines if this Calendar object is equal to another object.
`hashCode()`	Computes the hash code for this object.

See Also

`Calendar`, `Date`, `java.text.DateFormat`, `java.text.SimpleDateFormat`, `TimeZone`.

Example

This example prints a textual mini-calendar to standard output when supplied with a month and year.

```
import java.text.*;
import java.util.*;

class Main {
    public static void main(String[] args) {
        if (args.length < 2) {
            System.out.println("Usage: java Main <1-based month> <year>");
            System.exit(1);
        }
        int month = Integer.parseInt(args[0])-1;
        int year = Integer.parseInt(args[1]);

        // Create a calendar object with the desired month and year.
        Calendar cal = new GregorianCalendar(year, month, 1);

        // Use SimpleDateFormat to get weekNames.
        cal.set(Calendar.DAY_OF_WEEK, cal.getFirstDayOfWeek());
        cal.set(Calendar.WEEK_OF_MONTH, 2);
        cal.clear(Calendar.DAY_OF_MONTH);
        do {
            SimpleDateFormat sdf = new SimpleDateFormat("E");
            String s = sdf.format(cal.getTime());

            // Only take the first two characters.
            if (s.length () > 2) {
                System.out.print(s.substring(0, 2) + " ");
            } else if (s.length () < 2) {
                System.out.print(s + "  ");
            } else {
                System.out.print(s + " ");
            }
            cal.roll(Calendar.DAY_OF_WEEK, true);
        } while (cal.get(Calendar.DAY_OF_WEEK) != cal.getFirstDayOfWeek());
        System.out.println();

        // Get the day of the week of the first day.
        cal.set(year, month, 1);
        int dayOfWeek = cal.get(Calendar.DAY_OF_WEEK);

        // Print blanks for the columns preceding the first day.
        for (int i=cal.getFirstDayOfWeek(); i<dayOfWeek; i++) {
            System.out.print("   ");
        }

        // Print the days.
        cal.set(Calendar.MONTH, month);
        for (int i=cal.getMinimum(Calendar.DAY_OF_MONTH);
                i<=cal.getMaximum(Calendar.DAY_OF_MONTH); i++) {
            cal.set(Calendar.DATE, i);

            // Make sure we haven't skipped to the next month.
            if (cal.get(Calendar.MONTH) != month) {
                break;
            }
```

```
                // If start of new week, print a newline.
                if (cal.get(Calendar.DAY_OF_WEEK) == cal.getFirstDayOfWeek()) {
                    System.out.println();
                }

                // Ensure that all number take up two character positions.
                if (i < 10) {
                    System.out.print(" ");
                }
                System.out.print(i + " ");
            }
            System.out.println();
        }
    }
```

Output

```
> java Main 3 2000

Su Mo Tu We Th Fr Sa
          1  2  3  4
 5  6  7  8  9 10 11
12 13 14 15 16 17 18
19 20 21 22 23 24 25
26 27 28 29 30 31
```


AD

PURPOSE Represents A.D. (Anno Domini).

SYNTAX `public static final int AD`

SEE ALSO `AD`, `Calendar.ERA`.

EXAMPLE See `Calendar.YEAR`.

add()

PURPOSE Increments/decrements a calendar field.

SYNTAX `public void add(int fld, int amount)`

DESCRIPTION This method increments the calendar field `fld` by `amount`. Modifying this field can also affect other calendar fields. For example, if the current date is January 31 and the `DATE` field is incremented by `1`, the month is changed to February.

The leniency of this `GregorianCalendar` object has no effect on this method. `fld` cannot be either `DST_OFFSET` or `ZONE_OFFSET`.

PARAMETERS

`amount`	The amount of date or time to be added to the field.
`fld`	One of the valid calendar field constants.

EXCEPTIONS

`IllegalArgumentException`
If `fld` is either `DST_OFFSET` or `ZONE_OFFSET`.

SEE ALSO `roll()`.

EXAMPLE `Calendar.add()`.

after()

PURPOSE Determines if the time of this `GregorianCalendar` object is later than the time of another such object.

SYNTAX `public boolean after(Object cal)`

DESCRIPTION This method returns `true` if `cal` is an instance of this `GregorianCalendar` object and `getTimeInMillis() > cal.getTimeInMillis()`. Note that the comparison is independent of the time zone.

As needed, this method recomputes the time fields of this `GregorianCalendar` object and `cal` using their calendar fields before doing the comparison.

PARAMETERS

`cal`	A possibly `null` object.

RETURNS `true` if this `GregorianCalendar` object's time is later than `cal`'s time.

EXCEPTIONS

`IllegalArgumentException`
If there is insufficient information to recompute the calendar fields of this `GregorianCalendar` object and `cal`.

SEE ALSO `before()`.

EXAMPLE See `Calendar.after()`.

BC

PURPOSE Represents B.C. (before Christ).

SYNTAX `public static final int BC`

SEE ALSO `AD, Calendar.ERA`.

EXAMPLE See `Calendar.YEAR`.

before()

PURPOSE Determines if the time of this `GregorianCalendar` object is before the time of another such object.

SYNTAX `public boolean before(Object cal)`

DESCRIPTION This method returns `true` if cal is an instance of this `GregorianCalendar` object and `getTimeInMillis() < cal.getTimeInMillis()`. Note that the comparison is independent of the time zone.

As needed, this method recomputes the time fields of this `GregorianCalendar` object and `cal` using their calendar fields before doing the comparison.

PARAMETERS

`cal` A possibly `null` object.

RETURNS `true` if this `GregorianCalendar` object's time is earlier than `cal`'s time.

EXCEPTIONS

`IllegalArgumentException`

If there is insufficient information to recompute the calendar fields of this `GregorianCalendar` object and `cal`.

SEE ALSO `after()`.

EXAMPLE See `Calendar.before()`.

computeFields()

PURPOSE Computes the values for the calendar fields from this `GregorianCalendar` object's `Date` value.

SYNTAX `protected void computeFields()`

DESCRIPTION This override implements an algorithm for converting the calendar fields into a single `Date` value. See `Calendar.computeFields()` for more details.

computeTime()

PURPOSE Converts the calendar fields into a `Date` value.

SYNTAX `protected void computeTime()`

DESCRIPTION This override implements an algorithm for converting the calendar fields into a single `Date` value. See `Calendar.computeTime()` for more details.

EXCEPTIONS

`IllegalArgumentException`
If insufficient calendar fields were set to determine a `Date` value or if the calendar is not lenient and a calendar field was out of bounds.

equals()

PURPOSE Determines if this `GregorianCalendar` object is equal to another object.

SYNTAX `public boolean equals(Object obj)`

DESCRIPTION This method returns `true` if `obj` is an instance of `GregorianCalendar` and its properties are identical to this instance. The properties that must be equal are the time and date, the lenient property, the first day-of-week, the minimal days-in-first-week, and the time zone.

PARAMETERS

`obj` A possibly `null` object.

RETURNS `true` if `obj` is equal to this object; `false` otherwise.

SEE ALSO `getFirstDayOfWeek()`, `getMinimalDaysInFirstWeek()`, `getTimeInMillis()`, `getTimeZone()`, `hashCode()`, `isLenient()`.

EXAMPLE

```
import java.util.*;

class Main {
    public static void main(String[] args) {
        GregorianCalendar cal1 = new GregorianCalendar();
        GregorianCalendar cal2 = (GregorianCalendar)cal1.clone();

        System.out.println(cal1.equals(null));                  // false
        System.out.println(cal1.equals(cal2));                  // true

        // Create one with a different time zone.
        cal2 = new GregorianCalendar(TimeZone.getTimeZone("GMT"));
        cal2.setTime(cal1.getTime());
        System.out.println(cal1.equals(cal2));                  // false
    }
}
```

getGreatestMinimum()

PURPOSE Retrieves the greatest minimum value for a calendar field.

SYNTAX `public int getGreatestMinimum(int calfield)`

DESCRIPTION This method retrieves the greatest minimum value for the calendar field `calfield`. For the Gregorian calendar, the results of this method are identical to `getMinimum()`.

PARAMETERS

`calfield` One of the valid calendar field constants.

RETURNS The greatest minimum value for the calendar field `calfield`.

SEE ALSO `getLeastMaximum()`, `getMaximum()`, `getMinimum()`.

EXAMPLE See `getMinimum()`.

getGregorianChange()

PURPOSE Retrieves the Gregorian calendar change date.

SYNTAX `public final Date getGregorianChange()`

DESCRIPTION This method retrieves the date on which the Julian calendar was replaced by the Gregorian calendar. The Gregorian change date affects how leap years are determined. See `setGregorianChange()` for `details()`.

The default change date is 00:00:00 local time, October 15, 1582.

RETURNS A non-`null` `Date` object containing the Gregorian change date.

SEE ALSO `setGregorianChange()`.

EXAMPLE See `isLeapYear()`.

getLeastMaximum()

PURPOSE Retrieves the least maximum value for a calendar field.

SYNTAX `public int getLeastMaximum(int calfield)`

DESCRIPTION This method retrieves the lowest maximum value for the calendar field `calfield`. For example, the lowest maximum value for the `DAY_OF_MONTH` field in a Gregorian calendar is `28`.

PARAMETERS

`calfield` One of the valid calendar field constants.

RETURNS The lowest maximum value for the calendar field `calfield`.

SEE ALSO `getGreatestMinimum()`, `getMaximum()`, `getMinimum()`.

EXAMPLE See `getMinimum()`.

getMaximum()

PURPOSE Retrieves the maximum value for a calendar field.

SYNTAX `public int getMaximum(int calfield)`

DESCRIPTION This method retrieves the maximum value for the calendar field `calfield`. For example, the maximum value for the `DAY_OF_MONTH` field is `31`.

PARAMETERS

`calfield` One of the valid calendar field constants.

RETURNS The maximum value for the calendar field `calfield`.

SEE ALSO `getGreatestMinimum()`, `getLeastMaximum()`, `getMinimum()`.

EXAMPLE See `getMinimum()`.

getMinimum()

PURPOSE Retrieves the minimum value for a calendar field.

SYNTAX `public int getMinimum(int calfield)`

DESCRIPTION This method retrieves the minimum value for the calendar field `calfield`. For example, the minimum value for the `DAY_OF_MONTH` field is `1`.

PARAMETERS

`calfield` One of the valid calendar field constants.

RETURNS The minimum value for the calendar field `calfield`.

SEE ALSO `getGreatestMinimum()`, `getLeastMaximum()`, `getMaximum()`.

EXAMPLE This example prints the minimum, greatest minimum, least maximum, and maximum values for all fields of the Gregorian calendar.

```
import java.util.*;

class Main {
    static int[] fieldValues = {
        Calendar.ERA, Calendar.YEAR, Calendar.MONTH, Calendar.DATE,
        Calendar.DAY_OF_MONTH, Calendar.DAY_OF_WEEK,
        Calendar.DAY_OF_WEEK_IN_MONTH, Calendar.DAY_OF_YEAR,
        Calendar.WEEK_OF_MONTH, Calendar.WEEK_OF_YEAR,
        Calendar.HOUR, Calendar.HOUR_OF_DAY, Calendar.AM_PM,
        Calendar.MILLISECOND, Calendar.MINUTE, Calendar.SECOND,
        Calendar.ZONE_OFFSET, Calendar.DST_OFFSET,};
    static String[] fieldNames = {
        "ERA", "YEAR", "MONTH", "DATE",
        "DAY_OF_MONTH", "DAY_OF_WEEK",
        "DAY_OF_WEEK_IN_MONTH", "DAY_OF_YEAR",
        "WEEK_OF_MONTH", "WEEK_OF_YEAR",
        "HOUR", "HOUR_OF_DAY", "AM_PM",
```

```
        "MILLISECOND", "MINUTE", "SECOND",
        "ZONE_OFFSET", "DST_OFFSET", };

    static void printField(String s) {
        System.out.print(" ");
        for (int i=0; i<12-s.length(); i++) {
            System.out.print(" ");
        }
        System.out.print(s);
    }

    public static void main(String[] args) {
        GregorianCalendar cal = new GregorianCalendar();

        System.out.println(
          "Field              minimum  greatestMin leastMaximum      maximum");
        for (int i=0; i<Calendar.FIELD_COUNT; i++) {
            printField(fieldNames[i]);
            printField(""+cal.getMinimum(fieldValues[i]));
            printField(""+cal.getGreatestMinimum(fieldValues[i]));
            printField(""+cal.getLeastMaximum(fieldValues[i]));
            printField(""+cal.getMaximum(fieldValues[i]));
            System.out.println();
        }
    }
}
```

Output

```
Field                minimum  greatestMin leastMaximum      maximum
         ERA               0            0            1            1
        YEAR               1            1      5000000      5000000
       MONTH               0            0           11           11
        DATE               1            1           28           31
DAY_OF_MONTH               1            1           28           31
 DAY_OF_WEEK               1            1            7            7
DAY_OF_WEEK_IN_MONTH      -1           -1            4            6
 DAY_OF_YEAR               1            1          365          366
WEEK_OF_MONTH              0            0            4            6
WEEK_OF_YEAR               0            0           53           54
        HOUR               0            0           11           12
 HOUR_OF_DAY               0            0           23           23
       AM_PM               0            0            1            1
 MILLISECOND               0            0          999          999
      MINUTE               0            0           59           59
      SECOND               0            0           59           59
 ZONE_OFFSET       -43200000    -43200000     43200000     43200000
```

GregorianCalendar()

PURPOSE Constructs a `GregorianCalendar` instance.

SYNTAX
```
public GregorianCalendar()
public GregorianCalendar(TimeZone zone)
public GregorianCalendar(Locale aLocale)
```

```
public GregorianCalendar(TimeZone zone, Locale aLocale)
public GregorianCalendar(int year, int month, int date)
public GregorianCalendar(int year, int month, int date, int hour,
   int minute)
public GregorianCalendar(int year, int month, int date, int hour,
   int minute, int second)
```

DESCRIPTION This constructor constructs a `Gregorian` instance. The new instance is not lenient.

If `zone` is not specified, it defaults to `TimeZone.getDefault()`. If `aLocale` is not specified, it defaults to `Locale.getDefault()`. If any of `year`, `month`, `date`, `hour`, `minute`, or `second` are not specified, they default to the value taken from the current time.

PARAMETERS

`aLocale`	A non-`null` `Locale` object.
`date`	The value used to set the `DATE` calendar field. `1` ≤ value ≤ `31`.
`hour`	The value used to set the `HOUR_OF_DAY` calendar field. `0` ≤ value ≤ `23`.
`minute`	The value used to set the `MINUTE` calendar field. `0` ≤ value ≤ `59`.
`month`	The value used to set the `MONTH` calendar field. Use the constants `Calendar.JANUARY`, `Calendar.FEBRUARY`, and so on, rather than directly using integers.
`second`	The value used to set the `SECOND` calendar field. `0` ≤ value ≤ `59`.
`year`	The value used to set the `YEAR` calendar field.
`zone`	A non-`null` `TimeZone` object.

EXAMPLE See the class example.

hashCode()

PURPOSE Computes the hash code for this object.

SYNTAX `public synchronized int hashCode()`

DESCRIPTION The `GregorianCalendar` object's hash code is an integer calculated using the `GregorianCalendar` object's first day-of-week and minimal days-in-first-week properties. Two equal `GregorianCalendar` objects will have the same hash code. However, unequal `GregorianCalendar` objects might also have the same hash code, although the hash code algorithm minimizes this possibility. The hash code is typically used as the key in a hash table.

RETURNS This object's hash code.

SEE ALSO `equals()`, `getFirstDayOfWeek()`, `getMinimalDaysInFirstWeek()`, `Hashtable`.

EXAMPLE See `Object.hashCode()`.

isLeapYear()

PURPOSE Determines if a year is a leap year.

SYNTAX `public boolean isLeapYear(int year)`

DESCRIPTION In the Gregorian calendar, a leap year is a year in which an extra day—February 29—is added to the year. Every year that is divisible by 4 is a leap. However, centennial years (years divisible by 100) are not leap years unless the year is also divisible by 400.

PARAMETERS

`year` A year.

RETURNS `true` if `year` is a leap year; `false` otherwise.

EXAMPLE This example prints some leap years before and after the Gregorian change date. In the Gregorian calendar, a centennial year is not a leap year unless it is divisible by 400. For example, the year 1400 and 1500 are leap years in the Julian calendar but not in the Gregorian calendar.

The example also uses `setGregorianChange()` to modify the Gregorian change date and demonstrate its effect on leap years. Notice how the set of leap years has changed.

```
import java.util.*;
import java.text.*;

class Main {
    public static void main(String[] args) {
        GregorianCalendar cal = new GregorianCalendar();
        int year = cal.get(Calendar.YEAR);

        // Julian Leap Years
        for (int i=1400; i<1582; i++) {
            if (cal.isLeapYear(i)) {
                System.out.print(i + " ");
            }
        }
        System.out.println();
// 1400 1404 1408 1412 1416 1420 1424 1428 1432 1436 1440 1444 1448 1452 1456
// 1460 1464 1468 1472 1476 1480 1484 1488 1492 1496 1500 1504 1508 1512 1516
// 1520 1524 1528 1532 1536 1540 1544 1548 1552 1556 1560 1564 1568 1572 1576
// 1580


        // Gregorian Leap Years
        for (int i=1582; i<1708; i++) {
            if (cal.isLeapYear(i)) {
                System.out.print(i + " ");
            }
        }
        System.out.println();
// 1584 1588 1592 1596 1600 1604 1608 1612 1616 1620 1624 1628 1632 1636 1640
// 1644 1648 1652 1656 1660 1664 1668 1672 1676 1680 1684 1688 1692 1696 1704
```

```
            // Modify the Gregorian cutover date to year 0.
            System.out.println(cal.getGregorianChange());
                                                // Thu Oct 04 17:00:00 PDT 1582
            cal.setGregorianChange(
                new GregorianCalendar(0, Calendar.JANUARY, 1).getTime());
            for (int i=1400; i<1582; i++) {
                if (cal.isLeapYear(i)) {
                    System.out.print(i + " ");
                }
            }
            System.out.println();
    // 1404 1408 1412 1416 1420 1424 1428 1432 1436 1440 1444 1448 1452 1456 1460
    // 1464 1468 1472 1476 1480 1484 1488 1492 1496 1504 1508 1512 1516 1520 1524
    // 1528 1532 1536 1540 1544 1548 1552 1556 1560 1564 1568 1572 1576 1580
        }
    }
```

roll()

PURPOSE Rolls a calendar field.

SYNTAX `public void roll(int fld, boolean up)`

DESCRIPTION This method increments or decrements the calendar field `fld` by `1`.

If `up` is `true` and `get(fld) == getMaximum(fld)`, the calendar field is set to `getMinimum(fld)`. If `up` is `false` and `get(fld) == getMinimum(fld)`, the calendar field is set to `getMaximum(fld)`. This process is called *rolling*.

Rolling this field can also affect other calendar fields. For example, if the current date is January 31 and the `WEEK_OF_MONTH` field is `5`, rolling up the `DATE` field causes the `WEEK_OF_MONTH` field to be `1`.

The leniency of this `Calendar` object has no effect on this method. `fld` cannot be either `DST_OFFSET` or `ZONE_OFFSET`.

PARAMETERS

`fld` One of the valid calendar field constants.

`up` If `true`, rolls the calendar field up; if `false`, rolls the calendar field down.

EXCEPTIONS

`IllegalArgumentException`
If `fld` is either `DST_OFFSET` or `ZONE_OFFSET`.

SEE ALSO `add()`.

EXAMPLE See `Calendar.roll()`.

setGregorianChange()

PURPOSE Sets the Gregorian calendar change date.

SYNTAX
```
public void setGregorianChange(Date date)
```

DESCRIPTION This method sets the date on which the Julian calendar was replaced by the Gregorian calendar. The Gregorian change date affects how leap years are determined. In particular, before the change date, all years divisible by 4 were considered leap years. After the change date, the same is `true`, except that centennial years (years divisible by 100) are not leap years unless the year is also divisible by 400.

The default change date is 00:00:00 local time, October 15, 1582.

PARAMETERS

`date` A non-`null` `Date` object.

SEE ALSO `getGregorianChange()`, `isLeapYear()`.

EXAMPLE See `isLeapYear()`.

java.util.zip
GZIPInputStream

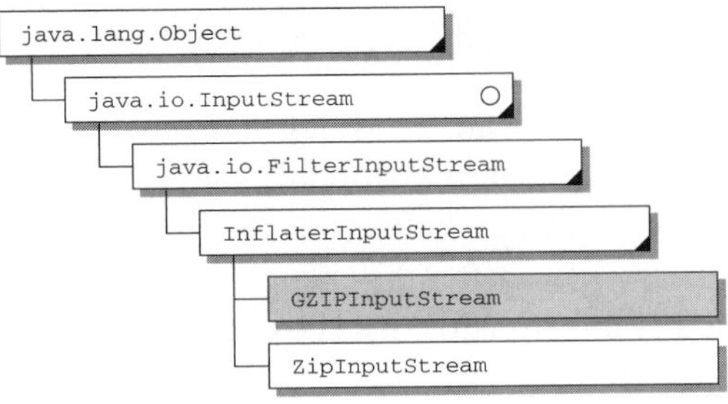

A B C D E F G H I J K L M N O P Q R S T U V W X Y Z

Syntax

```
public class GZIPInputStream extends InflaterInputStream
```

Description

The `GZIPInputStream` class implements an input stream filter for reading a GZIP compressed file and decompressing it. See `http://ds.internic.net/rfc/rfc1952.txt` for more information about the GZIP format.

This class uses the DEFLATE algorithm to decompress the compressed data. The `Deflater` and `Inflater` classes implement this algorithm. See these classes for more information.

A GZIP file uses the CRC-32 algorithm to compute a checksum of the uncompressed data. This algorithm is implemented by the `CRC32` class.

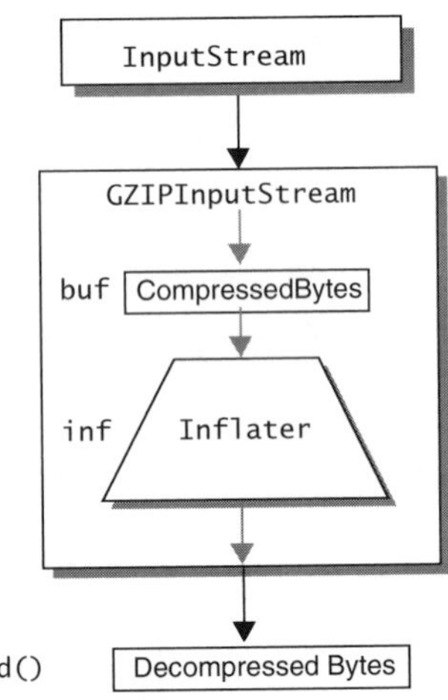

FIGURE 56: `GZIPInputStream`.

Usage

To use a GZIP input stream, you create a `GZIPInputStream` instance on an existing input stream that serves the compressed data. Then you call `read()` to retrieve the decompressed data. See Figure 56.

MEMBER SUMMARY	
Constructor	
`GZIPInputStream()`	Constructs a `GZIPInputStream` instance.
Stream Methods	
`close()`	Closes this GZIP input stream.
`read()`	Reads decompressed data from this GZIP input stream.

MEMBER SUMMARY	
Protected Fields	
crc	Holds the Checksum object used by this GZIP input stream.
eos	Indicates whether the end of this GZIP input stream has been reached.
Magic Constant	
GZIP_MAGIC	Identifies a GZIP file.

See Also

CRC32, java.io.FilterInputStream, GZIPOutputStream, Inflater.

Example

This example demonstrates how to use a GZIP input stream. It reads a GZIP file from its standard input, decompresses it, and writes it out to standard output.

```
import java.io.*;
import java.util.zip.*;

class Main {
    public static void main(String[] args) {
        try {
            GZIPInputStream is = new GZIPInputStream(System.in);
            byte[] buf = new byte[1024];
            int len;

            while ((len = is.read(buf)) > 0) {
                System.out.write(buf, 0, len);
            }
            is.close();
        } catch (Exception e) {
            e.printStackTrace();
        }
    }
}
```

close()

PURPOSE Closes this GZIP input stream.

SYNTAX `public void close() throws IOException`

DESCRIPTION This method closes this GZIP input stream. All input streams downstream are also closed. This GZIP input stream can no longer be used after this call.

EXCEPTIONS

`IOException`
If an IO error occurs while closing.

OVERRIDES `java.io.FilterInputStream.close()`.

SEE ALSO `java.io.InputStream.close()`.

EXAMPLE See the class example.

crc

PURPOSE Holds the `Checksum` object used by this GZIP input stream.

SYNTAX `protected CRC32 crc`

DESCRIPTION The GZIP input stream computes the checksum of the decompressed data in order to compare it with the checksum value embedded in the GZIP file. If the checksum values do not agree, an `IOException` is thrown by `read()`. The GZIP input stream uses a `CRC32` object to compute the CRC-32 checksum. The object is stored in this field.

SEE ALSO `Checksum`, `CRC32`.

EXAMPLE This example implements a subclass of `GZIPInputStream` in order to access the two protected fields, `crc` and `eos`. The program reads a GZIP compressed file from its standard input and writes the decompressed data to its standard output. The program then accesses the `Checksum` object used by the GZIP input stream to retrieve and print the checksum of the decompressed data.

```
import java.io.*;
import java.util.zip.*;

class Main {
    public static void main(String[] args) {
        try {
            MyGZIPInputStream is = new MyGZIPInputStream(System.in);
            byte[] buf = new byte[1024];
            int len;

            while (!is.getEos()) {
                len = is.read(buf);
                if (len > 0) {
                    System.out.write(buf, 0, len);
                }
            }
            is.close();
            System.err.println("\nThe checksum is: " +
                               is.getChecksum().getValue());
        } catch (Exception e) {
            e.printStackTrace();
        }
    }
```

```
}

class MyGZIPInputStream extends GZIPInputStream {
    MyGZIPInputStream(InputStream in) throws IOException {
        super(in);
    }
    boolean getEos() {
        return eos;
    }
    Checksum getChecksum() {
        return crc;
    }
}
```

A B C D E F G H I J K L M N O P Q R S T U V W X Y Z

eos

PURPOSE Indicates whether the end of this GZIP input stream has been reached.

SYNTAX `protected boolean eos`

DESCRIPTION This field is used internally by the GZIP input stream to implement its end-of-stream strategy. It is generally not useful to subclasses.

This field is set to `true` when the end-of-stream has been reached and a subsequent call to `read()` will return `-1`. However, if this field is `false`, a subsequent call to `read()` may still return `-1`. This means that the value of this field cannot replace the checking of the return value of `read()`.

SEE ALSO `read()`.

EXAMPLE See `crc`.

GZIP_MAGIC

PURPOSE Identifies a GZIP file.

SYNTAX `public final static int GZIP_MAGIC`

DESCRIPTION This constant must appear at the beginning of a GZIP file. It is used primarily as a quick check to determine if an arbitrary file is a GZIP file. Its value is `0x8b1f`.

EXAMPLE This example determines whether a file is a GZIP file by checking if its first 16 bits matches the GZIP magic number.

```
import java.io.*;
import java.util.zip.*;

class Main {
    public static void main(String[] args) {
```

```
            if (args.length != 1) {
                System.err.println("Usage: java Main <filename>");
            } else {
                try {
                    InputStream is = new FileInputStream(args[0]);

                    // Read the 16-bit value.
                    int magic = is.read() | (is.read() << 8);

                    if (magic == GZIPInputStream.GZIP_MAGIC) {
                        System.out.println("This is a GZIP file");
                    } else {
                        System.out.println("This is not a GZIP file.");
                        System.out.println("Its magic number is 0x" +
                            Integer.toHexString(magic) + " and not 0x" +
                            Integer.toHexString(GZIPInputStream.GZIP_MAGIC));
                    }
                    is.close();
                } catch (Exception e) {
                    e.printStackTrace();
                }
            }
        }
    }
```


GZIPInputStream()

PURPOSE
Constructs a `GZIPInputStream` instance.

SYNTAX
```
public GZIPInputStream(InputStream istream) throws IOException
public GZIPInputStream(InputStream in, int readsize) throws
    IOException
```

DESCRIPTION
This constructor creates a `GZIPInputStream` instance. It reads the header of the GZIP file. If the GZIP header is corrupted, an `IOException` is thrown.

An internal buffer (`InflaterInputStream.buf`) of size `readsize` is created to retrieve the compressed data read from `istream`. The new GZIP input stream's internal decompressor is applied over this buffer for decompression. See Figure 56. If `readsize` is not specified, it defaults to `512`.

This class internally uses an `Inflater` instance that does not use the ZLIB header. See `Inflater()` for more details.

PARAMETERS

`istream` A non-`null` input stream.

`readsize` The size of the buffer of compressed data to read from `istream`.

EXCEPTIONS

`IOException`
If an IO error occurs while reading the GZIP header.

SEE ALSO `java.io.IOException, java.io.InputStream.`

EXAMPLE See the class example.

read()

PURPOSE Reads decompressed data from this GZIP input stream.

SYNTAX `public int read(byte[] buf, int off, int len) throws IOException`

DESCRIPTION This method reads at most `len` decompressed bytes from this GZIP input stream and places them in `buf` starting at `buf[off]`. The blocking behavior of this method depends on the input streams from which it reads. In general, this method blocks until some bytes (possibly fewer than `len`) are read.

This method returns `-1` if the GZIP input stream has no more data to return.

PARAMETERS

`buf` The non-`null` buffer in which to store the data.

`len` The maximum number of bytes to read into `buf` starting at `buf[off]`. `0` ≤ `len` ≤ `buf.length-off`.

`off` The starting index in `buf` at which to store the data. `0` ≤ `off` < `buf.length`.

RETURNS The number of bytes read, or `-1` if the end-of-stream has been reached before any data is read.

EXCEPTIONS

`IOException`

If an IO error occurs while reading or if the GZIP file is corrupt.

OVERRIDES `InflaterInputStream.read().`

SEE ALSO `java.io.IOException.`

EXAMPLE See the class example.

GZIPOutputStream

```
java.lang.Object
  java.io.OutputStream
    java.io.FilterOutputStream
      DeflaterOutputStream
        GZIPOutputStream
        ZipOutputStream
```


Syntax

```
public class GZIPOutputStream extends DeflaterOutputStream
```

Description

The `GZIPOutputStream` class implements an output stream filter for creating a compressed file in GZIP format. For more information about the GZIP format, see `http://ds.internic.net/rfc/rfc1952.txt`.

This class uses the DEFLATE algorithm to compress the uncompressed data. The `Deflater` and `Inflater` classes implement this algorithm. See these classes for more information.

A GZIP file uses the CRC-32 algorithm to compute a checksum of the uncompressed data. This algorithm is implemented by the `CRC32` class.

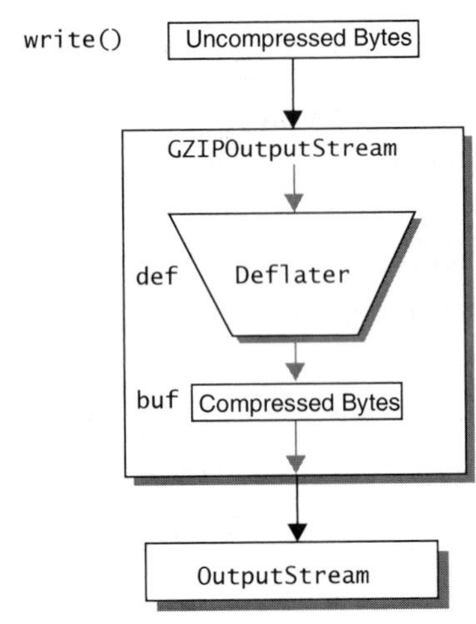

FIGURE 57: `GZIPOutputStream`.

Usage

To use a GZIP output stream, create a `GZIPOutputStream` instance on an existing output stream that will receive the compressed data. Then you write the uncompressed data to the GZIP output stream using `write()`. See Figure 57.

When all of the uncompressed data has been written into the GZIP output stream, it is necessary to call `close()` to force the GZIP trailing information to be written out. When another GZIP file is to be written to the same GZIP output stream, call `finish()` instead (see `finish()` for details).

See Also

`CRC32`, `Deflater`, `java.io.FilterOutputStream`, `GZIPInputStream`.

MEMBER SUMMARY	
Constructor	
`GZIPOutputStream()`	Creates a `GZIPOutputStream` instance.
Stream Methods	
`close()`	Writes the closing information of the GZIP file and closes this stream.
`finish()`	Writes the closing information of the GZIP file without closing this stream.
`write()`	Writes uncompressed data to this GZIP output stream.
CRC Field	
`crc`	Holds the `Checksum` object used by this GZIP output stream.

Example

This example is a variant of the `java.awt.Image` class example. It implements a thumbnail image viewer. You run this program by supplying it with the name of a graphics file or the name of a directory. If the former, the image in the graphics file is displayed. If the latter, all of the images (`.gif` and `.jpg` images) in the directory are displayed. See Figure 58.

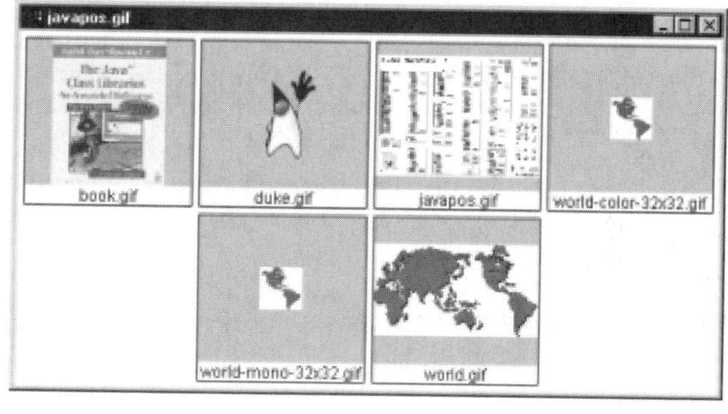

FIGURE 58: Thumbnail Image Viewer Using `GZIPOutputStream`.

To speed up the future display of the thumbnails, the program saves the thumbnails in a file in the same directory as the full images. The program uses the `PixelGrabber` class to retrieve the pixels of a thumbnail and then uses the `GZIPOutputStream` to compress the pixels. The compressed pixels are saved in a file that has the same name as the full image plus the extension `.imgz`.

When the program is started, it first locates all of the images in the directory. For each image, it checks whether an up-to-date thumbnail file exists for that image. It does this by appending the extension `.imgz` to the image filename and checking whether the file exists. If it does exist, the program uses a `GZIPInputStream` to first decompress the pixels and then use the `MemoryImageSource` class to recreate the thumbnail image from the decompressed pixels.

```
import java.awt.*;
import java.awt.event.*;
```

```
import java.awt.image.*;
import java.io.*;
import java.util.zip.*;

class Main extends Frame {
    int cellSize = 125;

    Main(File dir) {
        String[] filenames;

        if (dir.isDirectory()) {
            // If directory, get files.
            filenames = dir.list();
        } else {
            // Otherwise, only show one image.
            filenames = new String[1];
            filenames[0] = dir.getName();

            // Set dir to be the directory rather than the file.
            dir = new File(dir.getParent());
        }

        for (int i=0; i<filenames.length; i++) {
            if (filenames[i].toLowerCase().endsWith(".gif")
                || filenames[i].toLowerCase().endsWith(".jpg")) {

                // Create and add the thumbnail component.
                // File is relative to dir.
                Component c = new Thumbnail(new File(
                    dir.getAbsolutePath() + File.separator + filenames[i]));
                add(c);
                c.setSize(cellSize, cellSize);
            }
        }

        // Listen for events and layout.
        addWindowListener(new WindowEventHandler());
        setLayout(new FlowLayout());
        pack();
        show();
    }

    public Dimension getPreferredSize() {
        Insets insets = getInsets();
        int count = getComponentCount();
        int hgap = ((FlowLayout)getLayout()).getHgap();
        int vgap = ((FlowLayout)getLayout()).getVgap();

        // Maximum of 4 columns,
        int cols = Math.max(1, Math.min(count, 4));

        // The following code exactly determines the size
        // necessary to show all the thumbnails.
        Dimension d = new Dimension(
            cols*(cellSize+hgap) + hgap,
            ((count-1)/cols+1)*(cellSize+vgap) + vgap);

        // Don't forget the frame's insets.
        d.width += insets.left+insets.right;
        d.height += insets.top+insets.bottom;
```

```
        // Make sure it's not larger than the screen.
        Dimension screenDim = getToolkit().getScreenSize();
        d.width = Math.min(d.width, screenDim.width);
        d.height = Math.min(d.height, screenDim.height);
        return d;
    }

    class WindowEventHandler extends WindowAdapter {
        public void windowClosing(WindowEvent evt) {
            // Destroy the window.
            dispose();
        }
    }

    public static void main(String[] args) {
        File dir;

        if (args.length == 1) {
            dir = new File(args[0]);
        } else {
            dir = new File(".");
        }
        new Main(dir);
    }
}

class Thumbnail extends Canvas {
    File fullFile;
    Image fullImage;
    File thumbFile;
    Image thumbImage;
    String filename;
    boolean saveThumbnail;

    Thumbnail(File file) {
        fullFile = file;
        thumbFile = new File(file.getPath() + ".imgz");

        if (thumbFile.exists()
                && thumbFile.lastModified() > file.lastModified()) {
// -------------- Read compressed image ---------------
            System.out.print("Reading thumbnail " + thumbFile.getName() +
                             " ... ");
            try {
                ObjectInputStream is = new ObjectInputStream(
                    new GZIPInputStream(
                    new FileInputStream(thumbFile)));

                // Read the dimensions.
                Dimension dim = (Dimension)is.readObject();

                // Read the pixels into a pixel array.
                int[] pixels = (int[])is.readObject();

                // Convert the pixels into an image.
                thumbImage = getToolkit().createImage(
                    new MemoryImageSource(dim.width, dim.height, pixels,
                                          0, dim.width));
                System.out.println("done");
```

A B C D E F G H I J K L M N O P Q R S T U V W X Y Z

```
            } catch (Exception e) {
                System.out.println("failed");
            }
// ---------------------------------------------------------
        }
        if (thumbImage == null) {
            fullImage = getToolkit().getImage(file.getPath());
            saveThumbnail = true;
        }

        // Listen for mouse events.
        addMouseListener(new MouseEventHandler());
    }

    public void paint(Graphics g) {
        update(g);
    }
    public void update(Graphics g) {
        FontMetrics fm = g.getFontMetrics();
        int w = getSize().width;
        int h = getSize().height - fm.getHeight();
        int iw = 0;
        int ih = 0;

        // Create the thumbnail if it doesn't exist.
        if (thumbImage == null) {
            iw = fullImage.getWidth(this);
            ih = fullImage.getHeight(this);

            if (iw > 0 && ih > 0) {
                // Scale down if necessary.
                if (iw > h) {
                    ih = ih * w / iw;
                    iw = w;
                }
                if (ih > h && ih > 0) {
                    iw = iw * h / ih;
                    ih = h;
                }

                thumbImage = fullImage.getScaledInstance(iw, ih, 0);
            }
        } else {
            iw = thumbImage.getWidth(null);
            ih = thumbImage.getHeight(null);
        }
        if (iw > 0 && ih > 0) {
            // Clear background.
            g.setColor(Color.lightGray);
            g.fillRect(0, 0, w, h);

            // Center the image.
            boolean done =
                g.drawImage(thumbImage, (w-iw)/2, (h-ih)/2, iw, ih, this);
            if (done & saveThumbnail) {
// -------------- Write compressed image ---------------
                System.out.print("saving " + thumbFile.getName() + " ... ");
                try {
                    // Grab the pixels from the image.
                    ObjectOutputStream os = new ObjectOutputStream(
```

```
                        new GZIPOutputStream(
                        new FileOutputStream(thumbFile)));

                    // Write the dimensions of the image.
                    os.writeObject(new Dimension(iw, ih));

                    // Grab the image pixels and write them out.
                    int[] pixels = new int[iw * ih];
                    PixelGrabber pg =
                      new PixelGrabber(thumbImage, 0, 0, iw, ih, pixels, 0, iw);
                    pg.grabPixels();
                    os.writeObject(pixels);

                    os.close();
                    System.out.println("done");
                } catch (Exception e) {
                    System.out.println("failed");
                }
// ------------------------------------------------------
                saveThumbnail = false;
            }
        }
        // Draw the name.
        h = getSize().height;
        g.setColor(Color.black);
        g.clearRect(0, h, w, fm.getHeight());
        g.drawString(fullFile.getName(),
            (w-fm.stringWidth(fullFile.getName()))/2,
            h-fm.getHeight()+fm.getAscent());
        g.drawRect(0, 0, w-1, h-1);
    }

    class MouseEventHandler extends MouseAdapter {
        public void mousePressed(MouseEvent evt) {
            if (fullImage == null) {
                fullImage = getToolkit().getImage(fullFile.getPath());
            }
            new ImageViewer(fullImage, fullFile.getName());
        }
        public void mouseEntered(MouseEvent evt) {
            // Set the frame's title.
            findFrame().setTitle(filename);
        }
        public void mouseExited(MouseEvent evt) {
            // Clear the frame's title.
            findFrame().setTitle(null);
        }

        // Returns this component's frame.
        public Frame findFrame() {
            Component c = getParent();
            while (c != null && !(c instanceof Frame)) {
                c = c.getParent();
            }
            return (Frame)c;
        }
    }
}

class ImageViewer extends Frame {
```

```
        Image image;
        ImageViewer(Image image, String filename) {
            super(filename);
            this.image = image;

            try {
                MediaTracker tracker = new MediaTracker(this);
                tracker.addImage(image, 0);
                tracker.waitForAll(0);
            } catch (Exception e) {
                e.printStackTrace();
            }
            // Listen for events and show frame.
            addWindowListener(new WindowEventHandler());
            pack();
            show();
        }

        // Determine the size of the frame that will show the image.
        public Dimension getPreferredSize() {
            Insets insets = getInsets();

            return new Dimension(image.getWidth(null) + insets.left + insets.right,
                image.getHeight(null) + insets.top + insets.bottom);
        }

        public void paint(Graphics g) {
            g.drawImage(image, getInsets().left, getInsets().top, this);
        }

        class WindowEventHandler extends WindowAdapter {
            public void windowClosing(WindowEvent evt) {
                // Destroy the window.
                dispose();
            }
        }
    }
```


close()

PURPOSE Writes the closing information of the GZIP file and closes this stream.

SYNTAX `public void close() throws IOException`

DESCRIPTION This method calls `finish()` on this GZIP output stream and closes it. All output streams downstream are also closed. This GZIP output stream can no longer be used after this call.

EXCEPTIONS

`IOException`

If an IO error occurs while closing.

OVERRIDES `DeflaterOutputStream.close()`.

SEE ALSO `java.io.IOException`, `java.io.OutputStream.close()`, `finish()`.

EXAMPLE See the class example.

crc

PURPOSE Holds the Checksum object used by this GZIP output stream.

SYNTAX `protected CRC32 crc`

DESCRIPTION The GZIP output stream computes the checksum of the decompressed data and writes it out to the GZIP output stream when `finish()` is called on the GZIP output stream. The checksum is used when the GZIP file is read back using `GZIPInputStream`. If the checksum value of the stream does not agree with the checksum computed using contents of the GZIP file, an `IOException` is thrown by `GZIPInputStream.read()`. The GZIP output stream uses a `CRC32` object to compute the CRC-32 checksum. The object is stored in this field.

SEE ALSO `Checksum`, `CRC32`.

EXAMPLE This example implements a subclass of the `GZIPOutputStream` in order to access the `crc` protected field. The program reads uncompressed data from its standard input and writes the compressed data to its standard output. The program then accesses the `Checksum` object used by the GZIP output stream to retrieve and print out the checksum of the decompressed data.

```
import java.io.*;
import java.util.zip.*;

class Main {
    public static void main(String[] args) {
        try {
            MyGZIPOutputStream os = new MyGZIPOutputStream(System.out);
            byte[] buf = new byte[1024];
            int len;

            while ((len = System.in.read(buf)) > 0) {
                os.write(buf, 0, len);
            }
            os.close();
            System.err.println("\nThe checksum is: " +
                               os.getChecksum().getValue());
        } catch (Exception e) {
            e.printStackTrace();
        }
    }
}

class MyGZIPOutputStream extends GZIPOutputStream {
    MyGZIPOutputStream(OutputStream out) throws IOException {
        super(out);
    }
    Checksum getChecksum() {
        return crc;
    }
}
```

finish()

PURPOSE Writes the closing information of the GZIP file without closing this stream.

SYNTAX `public void finish() throws IOException`

DESCRIPTION This method must be called after all pieces of data have been written to this GZIP output stream. This method writes out necessary information that appears at the end of GZIP files.

This method should be used instead of `close()` if another GZIP file must be written to the same underlying output stream. In this case, a new GZIP output stream must be created on the underlying stream. An example of where this feature might be used is in a client/server application that delivers many GZIP files on the same connection.

EXCEPTIONS

`IOException`

If an IO error occurs while finishing the GZIP file.

OVERRIDES `DeflaterOutputStream.finish()`.

SEE ALSO `java.io.IOException`.

EXAMPLE This example demonstrates how to write more than one GZIP file on the same output stream. Each file specified on the command line is compressed in its own GZIP file. However, all of the GZIP files are concatenated into the same file.

```
import java.io.*;
import java.util.zip.*;

class Main {
    public static void main(String[] args) {
        if (args.length < 1) {
            System.err.println("Usage: java Main <filename>...");
            System.exit(1);
        }

        byte[] buf = new byte[1024];
        int len;
        try {
            GZIPOutputStream os = null;
            for (int i=0; i<args.length; i++) {
                // Open the input file.
                FileInputStream is = new FileInputStream(args[i]);

                // Create a new GZIP output stream on the same output stream.
                os = new GZIPOutputStream(System.out);

                // Transfer the data from the input file to the output file.
                while ((len = is.read(buf)) >= 0) {
                    os.write(buf, 0, len);
                }
```

```
                // Close the input file.
                is.close();

                // Write out GZIP trailer information.
                os.finish();
            }
            // Now it's safe to close.
            os.close();
        } catch (Exception e) {
            e.printStackTrace();
        }
    }
}
```


GZIPOutputStream()

PURPOSE Creates a `GZIPOutputStream` instance.

SYNTAX
```
public GZIPOutputStream(OutputStream out) throws IOException
public GZIPOutputStream(OutputStream out, int readsize) throws
   IOException
```

DESCRIPTION This constructor creates a `GZIPOutputStream` instance. It also writes the GZIP header to `out`.

An internal buffer (`DeflaterOutputStream.buf`) of size `readsize` is created to store the compressed data retrieved from the new GZIP output stream's internal deflater. The compressed data is then written to `out`. See Figure 57. If `readsize` is not specified, it defaults to `512`.

PARAMETERS

`out` A non-`null` output stream.

`readsize` The size of the buffer of compressed data to be retrieved from the deflater.

EXCEPTIONS

`IOException`

If an IO error has occurred.

SEE ALSO `java.io.IOException`, `java.io.OutputStream`.

EXAMPLE This is a simple example of how to use a GZIP output stream to compress a file. The program reads uncompressed data from its standard input and writes a GZIP compressed file to its standard output.

```
import java.util.zip.*;

class Main {
    public static void main(String[] args) {
        int len;
        byte[] buf = new byte[1024];
```

```
                try {
                    GZIPOutputStream os = new GZIPOutputStream(System.out);

                    while ((len = System.in.read(buf)) >= 0) {
                        os.write(buf, 0, len);
                    }
                    os.close();
                } catch (Exception e) {
                    e.printStackTrace();
                }
            }
        }
```


write()

PURPOSE Writes uncompressed data to this GZIP output stream.

SYNTAX
```
public synchronized void write(byte[] buf, int off, int len)
   throws IOException
```

DESCRIPTION This method write `len` bytes starting from `buf[off]` to this GZIP output stream. This method blocks until all of the bytes have been written to this output stream.

PARAMETERS

`buf` A non-`null` `byte` array containing the data to be written.

`len` The number of bytes to write starting from `buf[off]`. `0` ≤ `len` ≤ `buf.length-off`.

`off` The `0`-based index of the first byte in `buf` to write. `0` ≤ `off` < `buf.length`.

EXCEPTIONS

`IOException` If an IO error occurs while writing.

OVERRIDES `DeflaterOutputStream.write()`.

SEE ALSO `java.io.OutputStream.write()`.

EXAMPLE See the class example.

Hashtable

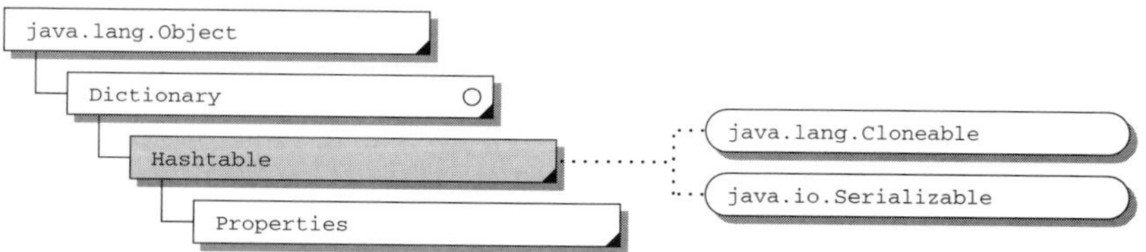

Syntax

```
public class Hashtable extends Dictionary implements Cloneable, Serializable
```

Description

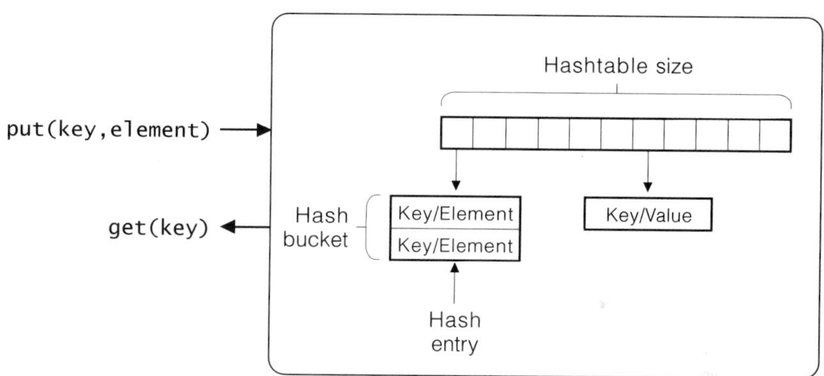

FIGURE 59: `Hashtable`.

The `Hashtable` class represents a *hash table*. A *hash table* consists of an array of *hash buckets*. Each hash bucket contains zero or more *hash table entries*. Each hash table entry consists of a *key/element* pair; neither the key nor the element can be `null`. When an entry is added to the hash table, its key is used to *hash* to one of the buckets in the hash table. The hash table entry is stored in the bucket. More than one key can hash to a single bucket, but a key always hashes to the same bucket (in a hash table of the same size). Keys that hash to the same bucket are said to *collide*. See Figure 59.

During the process of finding an entry in the hash table, the key is used to hash to the bucket in which its entry is located. If that bucket has more than one entry, the key is compared with the key of each entry (using `equals()`) to locate the right entry.

Hash Algorithm

The hash value of an object is obtained using its `hashCode()` method. The `Object` class defines a default implementation for `hashCode()` that uses the object's reference. Many classes override this default implementation to generate hash codes that are suited for themselves. For example, the `Number` subclasses (`Byte`, `Double`, `Long`, `Int`, `Float`, and `Short`) define `hashCode()` to be a function of the object's numeric value. The hash value of a key is used in combination with the hash table's size to determine in which bucket the entry is placed.

Using a prime number as the hash table's size helps distribute the entries among the different buckets (this is an artifact of the distribution algorithm used).

Hash Buckets

More than one key can hash to the same bucket. When that happens, the keys (and their elements) share the same bucket. When you search for a key, the hash algorithm is used to locate the bucket. Then a linear search is performed in the bucket to locate the entry that has the target key. (`equals()` is used when comparing keys for equality.) As the bucket grows larger, searching for a key in that bucket takes longer. A desirable characteristic of a hash table is that entries in it are distributed evenly among all of its buckets.

Extensibility and Load Factor

The hash table implementation is an *extensible hash table*. This means that as the hash table becomes full, it will grow automatically to accommodate all of the hash table entries. When a table grows to a larger size, all existing hash table entries must be rehashed using the new table size. Growing a table can be quite a costly operation, depending on the size of the table.

When you create a hash table, you can control when you want the table to grow by specifying a *load factor*. The load factor is the fraction of the number of entries in the hash table over the size of the hash table. When the hash table's load factor exceeds the load factor specified in its constructor, the table is grown. For example, a load factor of 0.5 means that when the table reaches half full (50%), it will be grown to its next size. A low load factor means the table will be grown when it is sparse, thereby leading to the probability of fewer collisions. A high load factor means the table will be grown when it is fairly full, thereby decreasing the number of times that the table is grown and saving the overhead of growing the table many times. However, a higher load factor means a higher probability of hash collisions. This leads to larger hash buckets.

A larger hash table size also means more memory is required. A small load factor means few of the buckets in the hash table are being used and, consequently, the hash table is not making efficient use of memory.

MEMBER SUMMARY	
Constructor	
`Hashtable()`	Constructs an empty `Hashtable` instance.
Dictionary Methods	
`elements()`	Retrieves a list of all elements in this hash table.
`isEmpty()`	Determines whether this hash table has any elements.
`get()`	Retrieves the element associated with a key from this hash table.
`keys()`	Retrieves a list of all keys in this hash table.
`put()`	Adds a key/element pair to this hash table.
`remove()`	Removes a key/element pair from this hash table.
`size()`	Retrieves the number of elements in this hash table.

MEMBER SUMMARY	
Hash Table Methods	
`clear()`	Removes all keys and elements from this hash table.
`contains()`	Determines whether an element is in this hash table.
`containsKey()`	Determines whether a key is in this hash table.
Object Override Methods	
`clone()`	Creates a clone of this hash table.
`toString()`	Generates the string representation of this hash table.
Protected Method	
`rehash()`	Rehashes the content of this hash table into a larger hash table.

See Also

`Dictionary`, `Enumeration`, `java.io.Serializable`, `java.lang.Object.equals()`, `java.lang.Object.hashCode()`.

Example

This example implements a juke box using `Hashtable`, with each element in `Hashtable` being a `Disc`. A disc consists of the title and singer of the song on the disc. The example creates the juke box, adds a few elements to it, displays its contents, searches it by name and content for a disc, and finally clears it. The `print()` method uses many of the `Dictionary` methods, including the enumeration ones, to print the contents of the juke box.

```
import java.util.Hashtable;
import java.util.Enumeration;

class Disc {
    public String title;
    public String singer;

    Disc(String t, String s) {
        title = t;
        singer = s;
    }
    public String toString() {
        return ("'" + title + "' by " + singer);
    }
}
class Main {
    // print the contents of the jukebox
    public static void print(String msg, Hashtable box, boolean all) {
        if (msg != null)
            System.out.print(msg + ": ");
        if (box.isEmpty())
            System.out.println("The juke box is empty");
        else {
```

```
                System.out.println("There are " + box.size()
                                   + " discs in the juke box:");
                for(Enumeration e = (all ? box.elements() : box.keys());
                    e.hasMoreElements();
                    System.out.println("\t" + e.nextElement()));
            }
        }
        public static void main (String[] args) {
            // create a jukebox with initial capacity of 13 and 0.5 load factor
            Hashtable jukebox = new Hashtable(13, 0.5f);
            Disc houndDog;

            jukebox.put("Hound Dog", houndDog = new Disc("Hound Dog", "Elvis"));
            jukebox.put("Yesterday", new Disc("Yesterday", "Beatles"));
            jukebox.put("On Top of the World",
                        new Disc("On Top of the World", "Carpenters"));
            jukebox.put("Only You", new Disc("Only You", "Platters"));

            print("jukebox after adding 4 titles", jukebox, true);

            // search by title
            System.out.println("Yesterday is " +
                (jukebox.containsKey("Yesterday") ? "" : "not ") +
                " in the jukebox");
            // search by content
            System.out.println(houndDog + " is " +
                (jukebox.contains(houndDog) ? "" : "not ") +
                " in the jukebox");

            // empty jukebox
            jukebox.clear();
            print("jukebox after clearing it", jukebox, true);
        }
    }
```

clear()

PURPOSE Removes all keys and elements from this hash table.

SYNTAX `public synchronized void clear()`

EXAMPLE See the class example.

clone()

PURPOSE Creates a clone of this hash table.

SYNTAX `public synchronized Object clone()`

DESCRIPTION This method creates a clone of this hash table by making a copy of the entire table and copies of all of the hash table entries. Each hash table entry contains references to the key and element of that entry; the key and element objects are *not* cloned. If you make changes to this hash table (e.g., add a new entry or delete an old one), such changes will not affect the new copy of the hash table. Conversely, if you make changes to the new copy of the hash table, such changes will not affect this original hash table. However, if you subsequently change the key or element object themselves, such changes are reflected in both the new and old hash tables (because the references will point to the modified objects).

RETURNS A copy of this hash table.

OVERRIDES `java.lang.Object.clone()`.

EXAMPLE See `get()`.

contains()

PURPOSE Determines whether an element is in this hash table.

SYNTAX `public synchronized boolean contains(Object obj)`

DESCRIPTION This method searches this hash table for an entry whose element is equal to `obj`. Equality is determined by using the `equals()` method. If such an entry is found, this method returns `true`; otherwise, it returns `false`. Searching for an element is an expensive operation. Its cost increases linearly with the number of entries in this hash table.

PARAMETERS
`obj` The non-`null` element for which to search.

RETURNS `true` if `obj` is an element in this hash table; `false` otherwise.

SEE ALSO `containsKey()`, `java.lang.Object.equals()`.

EXAMPLE See the class example.

containsKey()

PURPOSE Determines whether a key is in this hash table.

SYNTAX `public synchronized boolean containsKey(Object key)`

DESCRIPTION This method searches this hash table for an entry whose key is equal to `key`. Equality is determined using the `equals()` method. If such an entry is found, this method returns `true`; otherwise, it returns `false`.

PARAMETERS
`obj` The non-`null` key for which to search.

SEE ALSO `contains(), java.lang.Object.equals().`

EXAMPLE See the class example.

A B C D E F G H I J K L M N O P Q R S T U V W X Y Z

elements()

PURPOSE Retrieves a list of all elements in this hash table.

SYNTAX `public synchronized Enumeration elements()`

DESCRIPTION This method returns a list of all elements in this hash table in the form of an `Enumeration`. Methods in the `Enumeration` class can then be used to retrieve the elements from this list one at a time.

Whether modifications to this hash table during enumeration affect the results of the enumeration depends on where the modifications occur. For example, if a new key/element pair is added to the front of the hash table and the enumeration is nearing the end of the table, the newly added element will not be returned by this enumeration.

RETURNS A non-`null` enumeration of the elements in this table.

SEE ALSO `keys(), Enumeration.`

EXAMPLE See the class example.

get()

PURPOSE Retrieves the element associated with a key from this hash table.

SYNTAX `public synchronized Object get(Object key)`

DESCRIPTION This method retrieves the element associated with the key `key` in this hash table. If this hash table has no such key, `null` is returned.

PARAMETERS

`key` The non-`null` key for which to search.

RETURNS The element associated with `key`; `null` if `key` is not in this hash table.

SEE ALSO `put().`

EXAMPLE This example uses the `Disc` declaration in the class example. It creates a few entries in the juke box and then clones the box (`oldies`). After making changes to the original juke box, it checks that these changes have not affected the clone.

```
import java.util.Hashtable;
import java.util.Enumeration;
```

```
class Main {
    public static void main(String[] args) {
        Hashtable jukebox = new Hashtable(13, 0.5f);

        jukebox.put("Hound Dog", new Disc("Hound Dog", "Elvis"));
        jukebox.put("Yesterday", new Disc("Yesterday", "Beatles"));

        // Make a copy of it
        Hashtable oldies = (Hashtable)jukebox.clone();

        // find houndDog in jukebox
        System.out.println("looking for hounddog: " +
                           jukebox.get("Hound Dog"));
        System.out.println("removing it: " +
                           jukebox.remove("Hound Dog"));
        System.out.println("looking for it again: " +
                           jukebox.get("Hound Dog"));

        // find houndDog in oldies (should still be there)
        System.out.println("looking for hounddog in oldies: " +
                           oldies.get("Hound Dog"));
    }
}
```


Hashtable()

PURPOSE Constructs an empty `Hashtable` instance.

SYNTAX

```
public Hashtable()
public Hashtable(int initialSize)
public Hashtable(int initialSize, float loadFactor)
```

DESCRIPTION There are three forms of the constructor for `Hashtable`. The first creates a new hash table with the initial size of `101` buckets and a load factor of `0.75`. The second creates a new hash table with initial size `initialSize` and a load factor of `0.75`. The third form creates a new hash table with initial size `initialSize` and a load factor of `loadFactor`. When the hash table reaches the load specified by its load factor, it will automatically grow.

PARAMETERS

`initialCapacity`
The initial size of the hash table. It must be a positive value. The default capacity is `101`. It is a good idea to use a prime number as the size. This is because prime numbers help make the keys more evenly distributed in the hash table.

`loadFactor` A number in the range `0.0` (exclusive) and `1.0` (inclusive) stating how full the hash table should be before it is increased in size and rehashed. `1.0` means 100% full; `0.5` means 50% full. The smaller the load factor, the sooner the table will be increased. A small load factor also means that because the table is likely to be sparse, collisions (hashing a key to the same bucket) are less likely. Smaller buckets mean fewer comparisons are required before a key is found. Increasing the hash table size is a costly operation because it involves rehashing all existing entries in the hash table for the new table size. A larger load factor means the table should be fuller before it is increased and rehashed. `1.0` means that the table should be completely full before it is increased.

SEE ALSO `rehash()`.

EXAMPLE See the class example and `get()`.

isEmpty()

PURPOSE Determines whether this hash table has any elements.

SYNTAX `public boolean isEmpty()`

RETURNS `true` if this hash table has no elements; `false` otherwise.

EXAMPLE See the class example.

keys()

PURPOSE Retrieves a list of all keys from in hash table.

SYNTAX `public synchronized Enumeration keys()`

DESCRIPTION This method returns a list of all keys in this hash table in the form of an `Enumeration`. Methods in the `Enumeration` class can then be used to retrieve the keys from this list one at a time.

Whether modifications to this hash table during enumeration affect the results of the enumeration depends on where the modifications occur. For example, if a new key/element pair is added to the front of the hash table and the enumeration is nearing the end of the table, the newly added key will not be returned by this enumeration.

RETURNS A non-`null` enumeration of the keys in this hash table.

SEE ALSO `elements()`, `Enumeration`.

EXAMPLE See the class example.

put()

PURPOSE
Adds a key/element pair to this hash table.

SYNTAX
`public synchronized Object put(Object key, Object elem)`

DESCRIPTION
This method adds the entry consisting of the key `key` and element `elem` into this hash table. `key` is hashed to determine in which bucket of this hash table this entry will be placed. If `key` already is in this hash table, the old element associated with `key` is returned by this method. If `key` is not in this hash table, `null` is returned.

PARAMETERS

`elem`	The non-`null` element of the entry to add.
`key`	The non-`null` key of the entry to add.

RETURNS
The old element associated with `key`; `null` if `key` was not in this hash table.

SEE ALSO
`get()`.

EXAMPLE
See the class example and `get()`.

rehash()

PURPOSE
Rehashes the content of this hash table into a larger hash table.

SYNTAX
`protected void rehash()`

DESCRIPTION
When a new entry is added to the hash table (using `put()`), if the load factor (the number of entries in the table as a fraction of the total table size) exceeds that specified by the load factor argument in this hash table's constructor, the table is automatically increased in size by using `rehash()`. The new size is at least double the old size. After the table has been grown, all existing entries in the table are rehashed using this new table size and then placed into their new buckets.

A subclass of `Hashtable` can override this method if it does not want to use this rehash policy.

SEE ALSO
`Hashtable()`, `put()`.

remove()

PURPOSE Removes a key/element pair from this hash table.

SYNTAX `public synchronized Object remove(Object key)`

DESCRIPTION This method removes the key/element pair with key `key` from this hash table. It returns the element associated with `key`; if `key` is not present in this hash table, it returns `null`.

PARAMETERS

`key` The non-`null` key associated with the entry to remove.

RETURNS The element associated with `key`; `null` if `key` is not present.

SEE ALSO `put()`.

EXAMPLE See `put()`.

size()

PURPOSE Retrieves the number of elements in this hash table.

SYNTAX `public int size()`

RETURNS The number of elements in this hash table.

EXAMPLE See the class example.

toString()

PURPOSE Generates the string representation of this hash table.

SYNTAX `public synchronized String toString()`

DESCRIPTION The string representation of a hash table is a comma-separated list of all key/element pairs, with each key and element separated by an equals character (=).

RETURNS The non-`null` string representation of this hash table.

OVERRIDES `java.lang.Object.toString()`.

SEE ALSO `elements()`, `keys()`.

EXAMPLE

```
Hashtable tab = new Hashtable(13);

tab.put("Foo", new Integer(1245));
tab.put("Bar", new Float(5.4f));

System.out.println(tab.toString()); // "{Bar=5.4,Foo=1245}"
```

HttpURLConnection

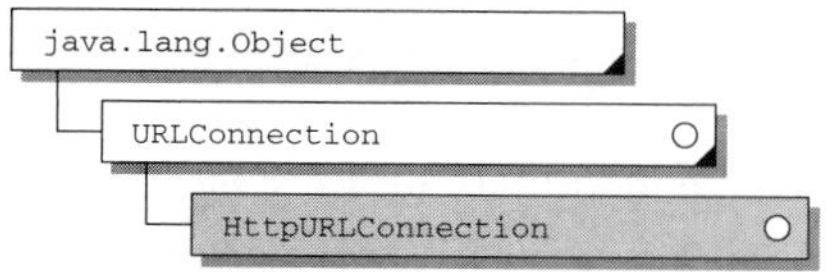

A B C D E F G H I J K L M N O P Q R S T U V W X Y Z

Syntax

```
abstract public class HttpURLConnection extends URLConnection
```

Description

HTTP is the Hypertext Transfer Protocol—a protocol for transmitting HTML documents and related resources. The `HttpURLConnection` class is an abstract subclass of `URLConnection` that contains methods and constants specific for the HTTP protocol. This protocol is described in detail in documents found at `http://www.w3.org/pub/WWW/Protocols/` and *RFC 2068*.

Usage

When the program calls `URL.getContent()` or `URL.openStream()`, these methods create a `URLConnection` for the URL and invoke methods on the `URLConnection`. The program can also call `URL.openConnection()`, which returns an instance of `URLConnection` for the URL. For all of these scenarios, the subclass of `URLConnection` returned is determined by the URL stream handler that corresponds to the protocol being requested in the URL. `HttpURLConnection` is a subclass of `URLConnection` and thus can be returned in places that return a `URLConnection`. See `URLStreamHandler` for a description of how URL stream handlers are selected.

When implementing a URL stream handler for the HTTP protocol, you can define `URLStreamHandler.openConnection()` to return a subclass of `HttpURLConnection`. To provide an implementation for `HttpURLConnection`, you must provide, at a minimum, implementations for the abstract methods—`connect()`, `disconnect()`, and `useProxy()`—and override the following methods in order to implement the HTTP protocol: `getInputStream()`, `getOutputStream()`, `getHeaderField()`, and `getHeaderFieldKey()`. See the class example.

Basic Elements of the Protocol

HTTP is a request/response protocol. A client sends a request to the server. The request contains a method token indicating the operation to be performed on the resource identified by the URL in the request. The method tokens are “OPTIONS”, “GET”, “HEAD”, “POST”, “PUT”, “DELETE”, and “TRACE”; note, these are case-sensitive. Brief descriptions of these tokens are found in Table 28. Detailed descriptions are found in the HTTP 1.1 document at the URL `http://www.w3.org/pub/WWW/Protocols/` and *RFC 2068*. The server processes the request and replies with a response.

The method token must be set before the connection is established (in other words, before invoking `connect()`). The default method token is "GET".

Token	Description
"DELETE"	Delete the resource identified in this request.
"GET"	Retrieve the resource identified in this request.
"HEAD"	Retrieve the header information associated with the resource identified in this request.
"OPTIONS"	Retrieve the options and/or requirements associated with the resource identified in this request.
"POST"	Send a request describing an action to be performed by the server.
"PUT"	Create or update the resource identified in this request using the information supplied in this request.
"TRACE"	Send the request to the server (through possible intermediaries) and then back to the sender.

TABLE 28: HTTP Request Method Tokens.

Proxies

The client and server may be communicating by way of intermediary agents called *proxies*. A proxy is a server that acts on behalf of the client to submit a request to the HTTP server. Proxies are used for many purposes; for example, for improving performance and for getting outside of the firewall of an internal network.

Redirects

The program uses `getResponseCode()` and `getResponseMessage()` to read the response from the server. One type of response that a server may send back is a *redirect*. Redirects have the response code `3xx`. This indicates to the client that the redirection information included in the response should be used to complete the request. The `HttpURLConnection` class contains methods to set and check whether redirects should be followed automatically by the HTTP connections. These are static methods to be applied to all HTTP connections, rather than just one instance of the connection.

Table 29 contains the constants defined in this class and used for HTTP response codes. They are described in detail in documents relating to HTTP 1.1 at the URL `http://www.w3.org/pub/WWW/Protocols/` and *RFC 2068*.

Constant	Value	Description
HTTP_ACCEPTED	202	The request has been accepted but not yet completed.
HTTP_BAD_GATEWAY	502	The server received an invalid response from another server when processing this request.
HTTP_BAD_METHOD	405	The method token specified in the request is invalid.
HTTP_BAD_REQUEST	400	The request was malformed.
HTTP_CLIENT_TIMEOUT	408	The server is not waiting for the client to complete the request.
HTTP_CONFLICT	409	The request could not be completed due to conflict with the current state of the resource.
HTTP_CREATED	201	A new resource has been created as requested (by a "POST" request).
HTTP_ENTITY_TOO_LARGE	413	The requested resource is too large to be processed by the server.
HTTP_FORBIDDEN	403	The server refuses to process the request.
HTTP_GATEWAY_TIMEOUT	504	The server timed-out while awaiting a response from another server when processing this request.
HTTP_GONE	410	The requested resource has been removed from the server with no forwarding information.
HTTP_INTERNAL_ERROR	501	The server does not support the requested operation.
HTTP_LENGTH_REQUIRED	411	The request must contain a content-length field in its header.
HTTP_MOVED_PERM	301	The requested resource has moved permanently to the location specified in the response.
HTTP_MOVED_TEMP	302	The requested resource has moved temporarily to the location specified in the response.
HTTP_MULT_CHOICE	300	The requested resource corresponds to multiple choices that can be gotten from the locations included in the response.
HTTP_NO_CONTENT	204	The request has been completed, but there is no new information to send back.
HTTP_NOT_ACCEPTABLE	406	The response to the request is not acceptable in terms of the request's "accept" headers.
HTTP_NOT_AUTHORITATIVE	203	The meta information in the header of the response may have come from a source other than the originating server.
HTTP_NOT_FOUND	404	The requested resource is not found.

Continued

TABLE 29: HTTP Response Codes.

Constant	Value	Description
HTTP_NOT_MODIFIED	304	The requested resource has not been changed since it was last requested by the client.
HTTP_OK	200	The operation succeeded. The information contained in the response depends on the request.
HTTP_PARTIAL	206	The server has completed the partial "GET" request for the resource requested.
HTTP_PAYMENT_REQUIRED	402	Reserved for future use.
HTTP_PRECON_FAILED	412	The request contained preconditions in its header that evaluated to `false` by the server.
HTTP_PROXY_AUTH	407	The request requires that user authentication be first supplied to the proxy.
HTTP_REQ_TOO_LONG	414	The URL of the request is too long to be processed by the server.
HTTP_RESET	205	The server has completed the request, and the client should reset the document viewer that caused the request to be sent in the first place.
HTTP_SEE_OTHER	303	The requested resource should be requested using the location specified in the response.
HTTP_SERVER_ERROR	500	The server encountered an internal server error.
HTTP_USE_PROXY	305	The requested resource should be requested using a proxy.
HTTP_UNAUTHORIZED	401	Either the request requires user authentication or authorization has been refused.
HTTP_UNSUPPORTED_TYPE	415	The request resource's format is not supported by the server.
HTTP_UNAVAILABLE	503	The server is currently unable to process the request.
HTTP_VERSION	505	The server does not support the version of the HTTP protocol specified in the request's header.

TABLE 29: HTTP Response Codes.

MEMBER SUMMARY	
Constructor	
`HttpURLConnection()`	Constructs an `HttpURLConnection` instance.
Request/Response-Related Methods	
`getRequestMethod()`	Retrieves the method token from the request.
`getResponseCode()`	Retrieves the response code from the response.
`getResponseMessage()`	Retrieves the response message from the HTTP response read from this connection.
`setRequestMethod()`	Sets the method token of the request.
Connection Methods	
`disconnect()`	Tears down the connection to the HTTP server.
`usingProxy()`	Determines whether this connection is going through a proxy.
Redirects (For All HTTP Connections)	
`getFollowRedirects()`	Determines whether HTTP connections automatically follow redirects.
`setFollowRedirects()`	Sets the connection to follow or not follow redirects automatically.
Protected Fields	
`method`	The method token of the request.
`responseCode`	The response code from the HTTP response.
`responseMessage`	The message associated with response code from the HTTP response.
HTTP Success Response Codes[a]	
`HTTP_OK`	(Value is `200`.) The operation succeeded.
`HTTP_CREATED`	(Value is `201`.) The resource created as requested (by a "POST" request).
`HTTP_ACCEPTED`	(Value is `202`.) The request was accepted but has not yet completed.
`HTTP_NOT_AUTHORITATIVE`	(Value is `203`.) The response header information came from a nonauthoritative source.
`HTTP_NO_CONTENT`	(Value is `204`.) The request completed successfully, but no new information is available.
`HTTP_RESET`	(Value is `205`.) The client should reset the document viewer that sent the request.
`HTTP_PARTIAL`	(Value is `206`.) The partial "GET" request completed.
HTTP Redirection Response Codes	
`HTTP_MULT_CHOICE`	(Value is `300`.) The requested resource can be gotten from multiple locations.

Continued

A B C D E F G H I J K L M N O P Q R S T U V W X Y Z

MEMBER SUMMARY

HTTP Redirection Response Codes *(Continued)*

HTTP_MOVED_PERM	(Value is 301.) The requested resource has moved permanently.
HTTP_MOVED_TEMP	(Value is 302.) The requested resource has moved temporarily.
HTTP_SEE_OTHER	(Value is 303.) Use another URL for locating resource.
HTTP_NOT_MODIFIED	(Value is 304.) The requested resource has not been changed since it was last requested.
HTTP_USE_PROXY	(Value is 305.) The requested resource should be requested using a proxy.

HTTP Client Error Response Codes

HTTP_BAD_REQUEST	(Value is 400.) A malformed request.
HTTP_UNAUTHORIZED	(Value is 401.) The request requires user authentication.
HTTP_PAYMENT_REQUIRED	(Value is 402.) Reserved for future use.
HTTP_FORBIDDEN	(Value is 403.) The server refused to process the request.
HTTP_NOT_FOUND	(Value is 404.) The requested resource was not found.
HTTP_BAD_METHOD	(Value is 405.) The method token specified in the request is invalid.
HTTP_NOT_ACCEPTABLE	(Value is 406.) The response cannot conform to "accept" headers in the request.
HTTP_PROXY_AUTH	(Value is 407.) User authentication to the proxy is required.
HTTP_CLIENT_TIMEOUT	(Value is 408.) The server timed-out while waiting for the client.
HTTP_CONFLICT	(Value is 409.) The request is in conflict with the state of the resource.
HTTP_GONE	(Value is 410.) The requested resource has been removed.
HTTP_LENGTH_REQUIRED	(Value is 411.) The request must specify a content-length field.
HTTP_PRECON_FAILED	(Value is 412.) The request contained preconditions that failed on the server.
HTTP_ENTITY_TOO_LARGE	(Value is 413.) The requested resource is too large.
HTTP_REQ_TOO_LONG	(Value is 414.) The URL of the request is too long.
HTTP_UNSUPPORTED_TYPE	(Value is 415.) The requested resource is in an unsupported format.

HTTP Server Error Response Codes

HTTP_SERVER_ERROR	(Value is 500.) Internal server error.
HTTP_INTERNAL_ERROR	(Value is 501.) The request is not supported.
HTTP_BAD_GATEWAY	(Value is 502.) Invalid response from the gateway.
HTTP_UNAVAILABLE	(Value is 503.) The server is currently unable to process the request.
HTTP_GATEWAY_TIMEOUT	(Value is 504.) The request to the gateway timed-out.
HTTP_VERSION	(Value is 505.) The protocol version is not supported.

a. To conserve space, these HTTP response code constants do not have member descriptions.

See Also

ContentHandler, URL, URLConnection, URLStreamHandler.

Example

This example defines a very simplistic HTTP client implemented using HttpURLConnection. It provides implementations for the abstract methods—connect(), disconnect(), and usingProxy()—and overrides some of the default methods in URLConnection (such as those providing for getting IO streams and reading headers) to implement the HTTP protocol.

```
import java.io.*;
import java.net.*;
import java.util.Hashtable;
import java.util.Vector;

public class HttpImpl extends HttpURLConnection {
    Socket sock = null;

    public HttpImpl(URL url) {
        super(url);
    }

    // Establishes connection to HTTP server and sends request
    // Implementation of abstract method defined in URLConnection
    public void connect() throws IOException {
        if (connected) {  // connected is defined in URLConnection
            return;
        }
        InetAddress dst = InetAddress.getByName(getURL().getHost());
        int port;
        if ((port = getURL().getPort()) == -1)
            port = 80;         // default port number for HTTP
        sock = new Socket(dst, port);
        OutputStream out = sock.getOutputStream();

        send(out, getRequestMethod() + " " + url.toString() +
            " HTTP/1.1\r\n");
        send(out, "\r\n");
        connected  = true;
    }

    // Disconnects from HTTP server.
    // Implementation of abstract method defined in HttpURLConnection
    public void disconnect() {
        if (sock != null) {
            try {
                sock.close();
            } catch (IOException e) {
            }
            sock = null;
        }
        connected = false;
    }

    // Implementation of abstract method defined in HttpURLConnection
    public boolean usingProxy() {
        return false; // this simple impl does not use proxy
```

```
    }

    // Override default provided in URLConnection
    public InputStream getInputStream() throws IOException {
        if (!connected) {
            connect();
        }
        return sock.getInputStream();
    }

    // Override default provided in URLConnection
    public OutputStream getOutputStream() throws IOException {
        if (!connected) {
            connect();
        }
        return sock.getOutputStream();
    }

    // Override default provided in URLConnection
    public String getHeaderField(int n) {
        getHeaders();
        if (n < headers.size()) {
            return getField((String)headers.elementAt(n));
        }
        return null;
    }

    // Override default provided in URLConnection
    public String getHeaderField(String key) {
        getHeaders();
        return (String)keys.get(key.toLowerCase());
    }

    // Override default provided in URLConnection
    public String getHeaderFieldKey(int n) {
        getHeaders();
        if (n < headers.size()) {
            return getKey((String)headers.elementAt(n));
        }
        return null;
    }

    // Helper routine to send a string to an output stream
    static void send(OutputStream out, String s) throws IOException {
        for (int i=0; i<s.length(); i++) {
            out.write((byte)s.charAt(i));
        }
        out.flush();
    }

    // Helper routine to read a newline-terminated string from input stream
    static String recv(InputStream in) throws IOException {
        String result = "";
        int c = in.read();

        while (c >= 0 && c != '\n') {
            if (c != '\r') {
                result += (char)c;
            }
            c = in.read();
```

```
        }
        return result;
    }

    // Helper routines for parsing header field
    private static final char keySeparator = ':';
    static String getKey(String str) {
        if (str == null)
            return null;
        int ind = str.indexOf(keySeparator);
        if (ind >= 0)
            return str.substring(0, ind).toLowerCase();
        return null;
    }

    static String getField(String str) {
        if (str == null)
            return null;
        int ind = str.indexOf(keySeparator);
        if (ind >= 0)
            return str.substring(ind+1).trim();
        else
            return str;
    }

    // Helper routine that reads header from HTTP connection
    Hashtable keys = new Hashtable();
    Vector headers = new Vector();
    boolean gotten = false;
    void getHeaders() {
        if (gotten)
            return;
        gotten = true;
        try {
            connect();
            InputStream in = sock.getInputStream();
            while (true) {
                String header = recv(in);
                if (header.length() == 0)
                    break;
                headers.addElement(header);
                String key = getKey(header);
                if (key != null) {
                    keys.put(key, getField(header));
                }
            }
        } catch (IOException e) {
            e.printStackTrace();
        }
    }
}
```

disconnect()

PURPOSE Tears down the connection to the HTTP server.

SYNTAX `public abstract void disconnect()`

DESCRIPTION This method needs to be implemented by subclasses of `HttpURLConnection`.

SEE ALSO `URLConnection.connect()`, `URLConnection.connected`.

EXAMPLE See the class example.

getFollowRedirects()

PURPOSE Determines whether HTTP connections automatically follow redirects.

SYNTAX `public static boolean getFollowRedirects()`

DESCRIPTION A redirect maps an existing URL to a new URL. When an HTTP request is sent to a server, the server can respond with a redirect (response code of `3xx`). HTTP connections should use this method to determine whether they should follow redirects. Whether redirects are automatically followed is controlled through the use of `setFollowRedirects()`. By default, the "follow redirects" setting is enabled.

RETURNS `true` if HTTP connections should automatically follow redirects; `false` otherwise.

SEE ALSO `setFollowRedirects()`.

EXAMPLE This code overrides the `URLConnection.getContent()` to deal with redirects. It examines the response code to check whether the response indicates a redirect. If so, the redirection is followed naively using `HttpImpl`.

```
public Object getContent() throws IOException {
        connect();  // make sure we're connected

        int code = getResponseCode(); // get response code
        if (getFollowRedirects() && (code/100) == 3) {
            String newLocation = getHeaderField("location");
            if (newLocation != null) {
                // Very simplistic assumption: use HTTP again
                HttpImpl n = new HttpImpl(new URL(newLocation));
                return n.getContent();
            }
        }
        // else just continue as before
        return super.getContent();
    }
```

getRequestMethod()

PURPOSE

Retrieves the request method of the request.

SYNTAX

```
public String getRequestMethod()
```

DESCRIPTION

This method retrieves the method token of the request that will be sent in this HTTP connection. The possible method tokens are described in Table 28. If no request method has been specified, the default is "GET".

RETURNS

The non-`null` method token of the request of this HTTP connection.

SEE ALSO

`method`, `setRequestMethod()`.

EXAMPLE

See the class example.

getResponseCode()

PURPOSE

Retrieves the response code from the HTTP response read from this connection.

SYNTAX

```
public int getResponseCode() throws IOException
```

DESCRIPTION

This method reads the response from this HTTP connection and extracts the response's response code as an integer. The response code is one of the constants listed in Table 29. For example, if the response is

```
HTTP/1.0 200 OK
```

the response code returned will be `200`.

Note that for this method to work, the methods `URLConnection.getHeaderField()` and `URLConnection.getHeaderFieldKey()` must be overridden to implement the HTTP protocol.

RETURNS

The response code read from this HTTP connection. `-1` if no valid response code could be read from the response. If valid, one of the response codes listed in Table 29.

EXCEPTIONS

`IOException`

If an error occurred while attempting to read the response from the HTTP connection.

SEE ALSO

`getResponseMessage()`.

EXAMPLE

See `getFollowRedirects()`.

getResponseMessage()

PURPOSE Retrieves the response message from the HTTP response read from this connection.

SYNTAX `public String getResponseMessage() throws IOException`

DESCRIPTION This method reads the response from this HTTP connection and extracts the message accompanying the response code. For example, if the response is

```
HTTP/1.0 200 OK
```

the response message would be "OK".

Note that for this method to work, the methods `URLConnection.getHeaderField()` and `URLConnection.getHeaderFieldKey()` must be overridden to implement the HTTP protocol.

RETURNS The non-`null` response message read from this HTTP connection; `null` if no valid response was read.

EXCEPTIONS
`IOException`
If an error occurred while attempting to read the response from the HTTP server.

SEE ALSO `getResponseCode()`, `java.io.IOException`.

HttpURLConnection()

PURPOSE Constructs an `HttpURLConnection` instance.

SYNTAX `protected HttpURLConnection (URL url)`

DESCRIPTION This constructor constructs an instance of `HttpURLConnection` for the URL `url`.

PARAMETERS
`url` The URL for which to open this HTTP connection.

SEE ALSO `URL`, `URLConnection()`.

EXAMPLE See the class example.

method

PURPOSE Method token of the request.

SYNTAX `protected String method`

DESCRIPTION This field contains the method token of the request to be sent for this HTTP connection. The method token should be accessed and changed using `getRequestMethod()` and `setRequestMethod()`. This field should not be manipulated directly. The default method token is "GET".

SEE ALSO `getRequestMethod()`, `setRequestMethod()`.

responseCode

PURPOSE Response code from the HTTP response.

SYNTAX `protected int responseCode`

DESCRIPTION This field contains the response code read from this HTTP connection as a result of invoking `getResponseCode()` or `getResponseMessage()`. Its value is initialized to `-1`. This field should not be manipulated directly.

SEE ALSO `getResponseCode()`, `responseMessage`.

responseMessage

PURPOSE Response message associated with the response code from the HTTP response.

SYNTAX `protected String responseMessage`

DESCRIPTION This field contains the message associated with the response code read from this HTTP connection as a result of invoking `getResponseCode()` or `getResponseMessage()`. This field should not be manipulated directly.

SEE ALSO `getResponseMessage()`, `responseCode`.

setFollowRedirects()

PURPOSE Sets the connection to follow or not follow redirects automatically.

SYNTAX `public static void setFollowRedirects(boolean auto)`

DESCRIPTION A redirect maps an existing URL to a new URL. When an HTTP request is sent to a server, the server can respond with a redirect (response code of `3xx`). HTTP connections should use this method to determine whether they should follow redirects. Whether redirects are automatically followed is controlled through the use of `setFollowRedirects()`. By default, the "follow redirects" setting is enabled.

This method can be executed only if allowed by the security manager. `SecurityManager.checkSetFactory()` is used for the check.

A
B
C
D
E
F
G
H
I
J
K
L
M
N
O
P
Q
R
S
T
U
V
W
X
Y
Z

PARAMETERS

`auto` `true` means to follow redirects automatically; `false` means not to follow redirects automatically.

EXCEPTIONS

`SecurityException`
If cannot change the "follow redirects" setting.

SEE ALSO `java.lang.SecurityManager.checkSetFactory()`.

EXAMPLE This example is to be used in conjunction with the modified `HttpImpl` class used in `getRequestMethod()`. If the `-l` flag is supplied to the program, redirects are followed; otherwise, they are not followed. See the `ContentHandlerFactory` class example for the definition of `SampleFactory` used in this example.

```
public class Main {
    public static void main(String[] args) {
        if (args.length == 0) {
            System.err.println("java Main [-l] <http url>");
            System.exit(-1);
        }

        String url = args[args.length-1];
        // -l means do follow redirects
        boolean redirect = (args.length == 2);
        HttpURLConnection.setFollowRedirects(redirect);

        // Configure system to use our own factory
        URLConnection.setContentHandlerFactory(new SampleFactory());

        try {
            // Directly use implementation to get
            HttpImpl conn = new HttpImpl(new URL(url));

            // Retrieve contents
            Object obj = conn.getContent();

            // Display what we've found
            System.out.println(obj);
        } catch (IOException e) {
            e.printStackTrace();
        }
    }
}
```

setRequestMethod()

PURPOSE Sets the method token of the request.

SYNTAX `public void setRequestMethod(String mtoken) throws ProtocolException`

DESCRIPTION The possible method tokens are described in Table 28. If `mtoken` is a string other than those presented in Table 28, an exception is thrown. If no request method has been specified, the default is "GET".

This method cannot be invoked if the connection has already been established.

PARAMETERS

`mtoken` The non-`null` string containing the method token to use for the request.

EXCEPTIONS

`ProtocolException`

If `mtoken` is not one of those listed in Table 29 or if the HTTP connection has already been established.

SEE ALSO `getRequestMethod()`, `method`.

EXAMPLE This example is to be used in conjunction with the `HttpImpl` class used in the class example. It sets the method token to be sent in the connection.

```
import java.net.*;
import java.io.*;

public class Main {
    public static void main(String[] args) {
        if (args.length != 2) {
            System.err.println("java Main <request> <http url>");
            System.exit(-1);
        }
        try {
            // Directly use implementation to get
            HttpImpl conn = new HttpImpl(new URL(args[1]));

            // Set method token
            conn.setRequestMethod(args[0]);

            // Retrieve contents
            Object obj = conn.getContent();

            // Print out header
            for (int i = 0; true; i++) {
                String h = conn.getHeaderField(i);
                String k = conn.getHeaderFieldKey(i);
                if (h == null) {
                    break;
                }
                if (k != null)
                    System.out.print(k + ": ");
                System.out.println(h);
            }
```

```
                // Display what we've found
                System.out.println(obj);
            } catch (IOException e) {
                e.printStackTrace();
            }
        }
    }
```


usingProxy()

PURPOSE Determines whether this connection is going through a proxy.

SYNTAX `public abstract boolean usingProxy()`

DESCRIPTION An implementation for this method must be provided by subclasses. For more information on the use of proxies, see the documents found at `http://www.w3.org/pub/WWW/Protocols/` and *RFC 2068*.

RETURNS `true` if the connection is going through a proxy; `false` otherwise.

EXAMPLE See the class example.

IllegalAccessError

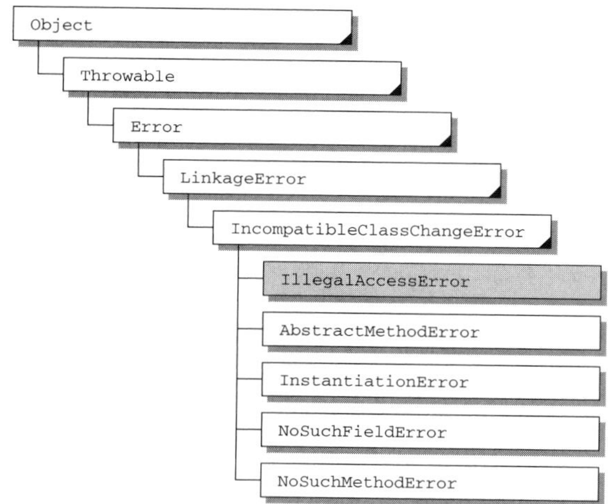

A B C D E F G H I J K L M N O P Q R S T U V W X Y Z

Syntax

```
public class IllegalAccessError extends IncompatibleClassChangeError
```

Description

`IllegalAccessError` is a runtime linkage error that is thrown when the program attempts to access a member of a class (field, member, or constructor) to which it does not have access. For example, this error will be thrown when the program tries to access a private or protected class or a private or protected method of a class. Normally, when you compile these classes, you get a compilation error pinpointing the problem so that a linkage error at runtime will not occur. However, the access problem could be introduced when classes of a program become inconsistent, for example if you were to make an incompatible change and then recompile only some of the program's classes.

`IllegalAccessError` and `IllegalAccessException` both report the same error; namely, the requested access cannot be made due to access restrictions declared by the class. `IllegalAccessError` is thrown by the Java virtual machine when it tries to perform the requested access. In contrast, `IllegalAccessException` is thrown when access is made explicitly via the program (for example, via the `Object.newInstance()` call).

`IllegalAccessError` should not be caught or declared in the `throws` clause of a method.

MEMBER SUMMARY	
Constructor	
`IllegalAccessError()`	Constructs an `IllegalAccessError` instance.

See Also

Error, IllegalAccessException, IncompatibleClassChangeError, LinkageError.

Example

In this example, an IllegalAccessError should be thrown when main() attempts to call A's constructor after A has been made private within pkg2. However, in Java 1.1.4 Main is able to access A even after the change, and thus the error is not thrown.

Main.java

```
import pkg2.A;

class Main {
    public static void main(String[] args) {
        System.out.println("IllegalAccessError example");
        A a = new A(10);
    System.out.println("a: " + a.add5());
    }
}
```

pkg2/A.java

```
package pkg2;

public class A {
    int a;
    public A(int i) {
        a = i;
        System.out.println("A created");
    }
    public int add5() {
        return a+=5;
    }
}
```

Modified pkg2/A.java

```
package pkg2;

class A {
    int a;
    A(int i) {
        a = i;
        System.out.println("A created");
    }
    int add5() {
        return a+=5;
    }
}
```

IllegalAccessError()

PURPOSE

Constructs an `IllegalAccessError` instance.

SYNTAX

```
public IllegalAccessError()
public IllegalAccessError(String msg)
```

DESCRIPTION

The two forms of this constructor construct an instance of `IllegalAccessError`. An optional string `msg` can be supplied that describes this particular instance of the error. If `msg` is not supplied, it defaults to `null`.

PARAMETERS

`msg` A possibly `null` string that gives details about this error.

SEE ALSO

`Throwable.getMessage()`.

java.lang
IllegalAccessException

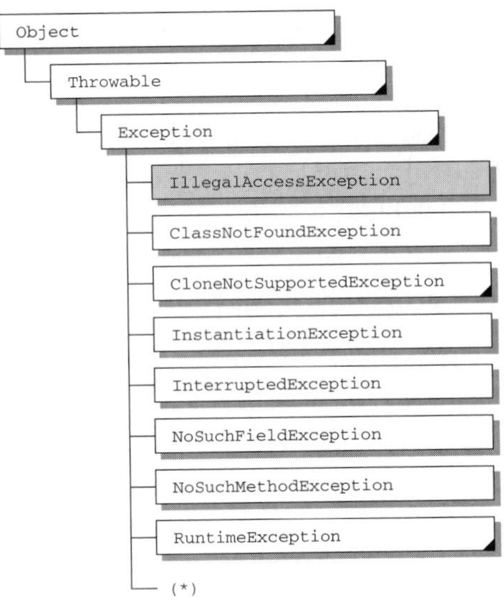

(*) 21 classes from other packages not shown.

A B C D E F G H I J K L M N O P Q R S T U V W X Y Z

Syntax

```
public class IllegalAccessException extends Exception
```

Description

`IllegalAccessException` is an exception that is thrown when the program attempts to access a member of a class (field, member, or constructor) to which it does not have access. For example, this exception will be thrown when the program tries to access a private or protected method of a class.

Normally, when you compile a program's classes, you get a compilation error pinpointing the problem. However, a program can use not only classes with which it has been compiled, but also other classes. It also can invoke methods on those classes through the use of class loaders and the methods in the `Class` and reflection classes. Classes and their methods accessed in this way are checked by the Java runtime just like other classes. Hence, an `IllegalAccessException` can arise if the caller does not have permission to access the fields, methods, or classes.

A method that throws `IllegalAccessException` must declare it or any of its superclasses in the method's `throws` clause.

MEMBER SUMMARY	
`IllegalAccessException()`	Constructs an `IllegalAccessException` instance.

See Also

`IllegalAccessError`, `Class.newInstance()`, `java.lang.reflect.Constructor.newInstance()`, `java.lang.reflect.Field.get()`, `java.lang.reflect.Field.getBoolean()`, `java.lang.reflect.Field.getByte()`, `java.lang.reflect.Field.getChar()`, `java.lang.reflect.Field.getDouble()`, `java.lang.reflect.Field.getFloat()`, `java.lang.reflect.Field.getInt()`, `java.lang.reflect.getLong()`, `java.lang.reflect.Field.getShort()`, `java.lang.reflect.Field.set()`, `java.lang.reflect.Field.setBoolean()`, `java.lang.reflect.Field.setByte()`, `java.lang.reflect.Field.setChar()`, `java.lang.reflect.Field.setDouble()`, `java.lang.reflect.Field.setFloat()`, `java.lang.reflect.Field.setInt()`, `java.lang.reflect.setLong()`, `java.lang.reflect.Field.setShort()`, `java.lang.reflect.Method.invoke()`.

Example

In this example, an `IllegalAccessException` is thrown when `main()` attempts to invoke `newInstance()` on class A because A's constructor is private.

Main.java

```
class Main {
    public static void main(String[] args) {
        System.out.println("IllegalAccessException example");
        try {
            Class c = Class.forName("A");
            Object a = c.newInstance();
        } catch (InstantiationException e) {
            e.printStackTrace();
        } catch (IllegalAccessException e) {
            e.printStackTrace();
        } catch (ClassNotFoundException e) {
            e.printStackTrace();
        }
    }
}
```

A.java

```
class A {
    private A() {
        System.out.println("A created");
    }
}
```

IllegalAccessException()

PURPOSE Constructs an `IllegalAccessException` instance.

SYNTAX

```
public IllegalAccessException()
public IllegalAccessException(String msg)
```

DESCRIPTION The two forms of this constructor construct an instance of `IllegalAccessException`. An optional string `msg` can be supplied that describes this particular instance of the exception. If `msg` is not supplied, it defaults to `null`.

PARAMETERS

`msg` A possibly `null` string that gives details about this exception.

SEE ALSO `Throwable.getMessage()`.

IllegalArgumentException

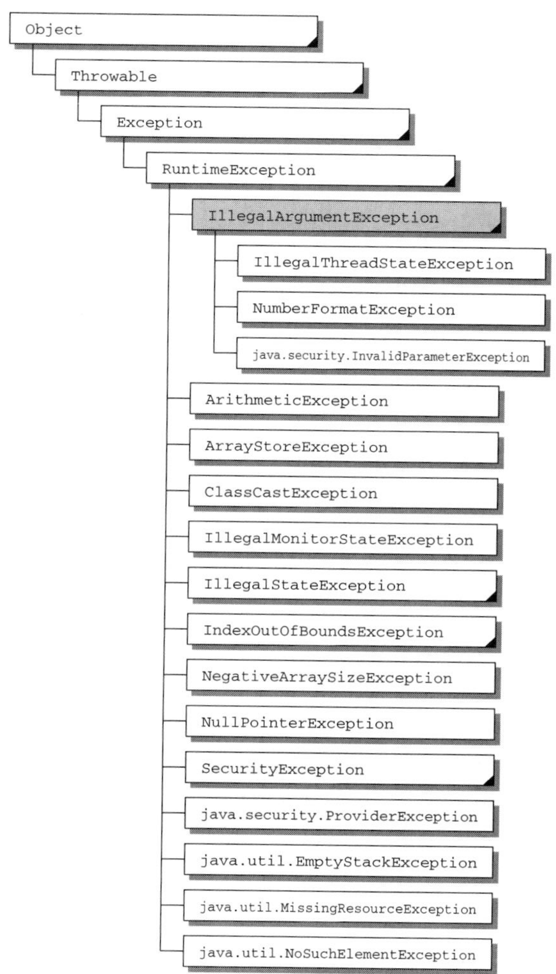

Syntax

```
public class IllegalArgumentException extends RuntimeException
```

Description

`IllegalArgumentException` is thrown by methods in the Java class libraries as well as by user-defined methods when they detect that any one of the arguments being supplied to the method is not valid. For example, a method that expects a positive number as an argument will throw an `IllegalArgumentException` if it receives a negative number.

`IllegalArgumentException` should not be caught or declared in the `throws` clause of a method.

MEMBER SUMMARY	
Constructor	
`IllegalArgumentException()`	Constructs an `IllegalArgumentException` instance.

See Also

`IllegalThreadStateException`, `NumberFormatException`, `RuntimeException`.

Example

This example defines a square root function that checks that its argument is nonnegative before taking its square root. It throws an `IllegalArgumentException` when `sqrt(-4)` is called.

```
class Main {
    static double sqrt(double i) throws IllegalArgumentException {
        if (i < 0)
            throw new IllegalArgumentException(
                "Cannot take square root of a negative number");

        return (Math.sqrt(i));
    }
    public static void main(String[] args) {
        System.out.println("IllegalArgumentException example");

        System.out.println(sqrt(-4));
    }
}
```

IllegalArgumentException()

PURPOSE — Constructs an `IllegalArgumentException` instance.

SYNTAX
```
public IllegalArgumentException()
public IllegalArgumentException(String msg)
```

DESCRIPTION — The two forms of this constructor construct an instance of `IllegalAccess-Exception`. An optional string `msg` can be supplied that describes this particular instance of the exception. If `msg` is not supplied, it defaults to `null`.

PARAMETERS
- `msg` — A possibly `null` string that gives details about this exception.

SEE ALSO — `Throwable.getMessage()`.

IllegalMonitorStateException

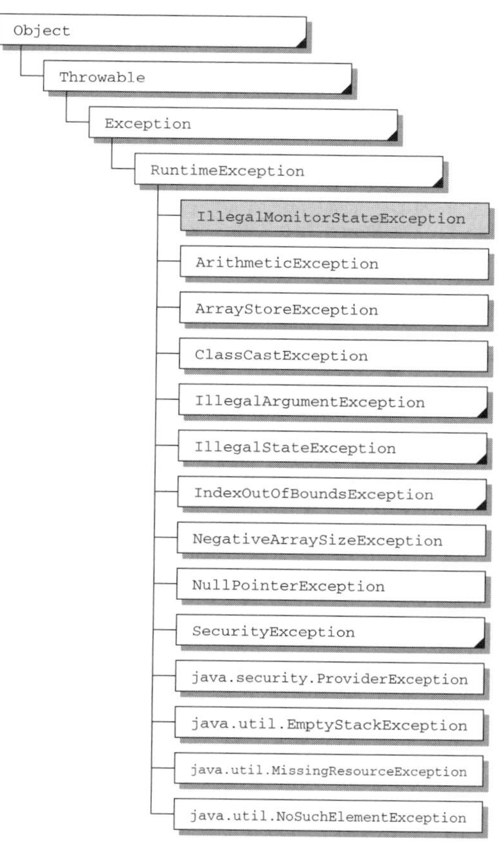

Syntax

```
class IllegalMonitorStateException extends RuntimeException
```

Description

`IllegalMonitorStateException` is thrown when the program attempts to use a synchronization method (`wait()` or `notify()`) on an object for which it does not have the monitor (lock).

`IllegalMonitorStateException` should not be caught or declared in the `throws` clause of a method.

MEMBER SUMMARY	
Constructor	
`IllegalMonitorStateException()`	Constructs an instance of `IllegalMonitorStateException`.

See Also

`Object.notify()`, `Object.notifyAll()`, `Object.wait()`, `RuntimeException`, `Thread`.

Example

The following code throws an `IllegalMonitorStateException` when it executes `a.wait()` because `wait()` is not being executed inside of a synchronized method or block.

```
class Main {
    public static void main(String[] args) {
        Integer a = new Integer(10);
        try {
            a.wait();
        } catch (InterruptedException e) {
            e.printStackTrace();
        }
    }
}
```

IllegalMonitorStateException()

PURPOSE
Constructs an `IllegalMonitorStateException` instance.

SYNTAX
```
public IllegalMonitorStateException()
public IllegalMonitorStateException(String msg)
```

DESCRIPTION
The two forms of this constructor construct an instance of `IllegalMonitorStateException`. An optional string `msg` can be supplied that describes this particular instance of the exception. If `msg` is not supplied, it defaults to `null`.

PARAMETERS
`msg` A possibly `null` string that gives details about this exception.

SEE ALSO
`Throwable.getMessage()`.

IllegalStateException

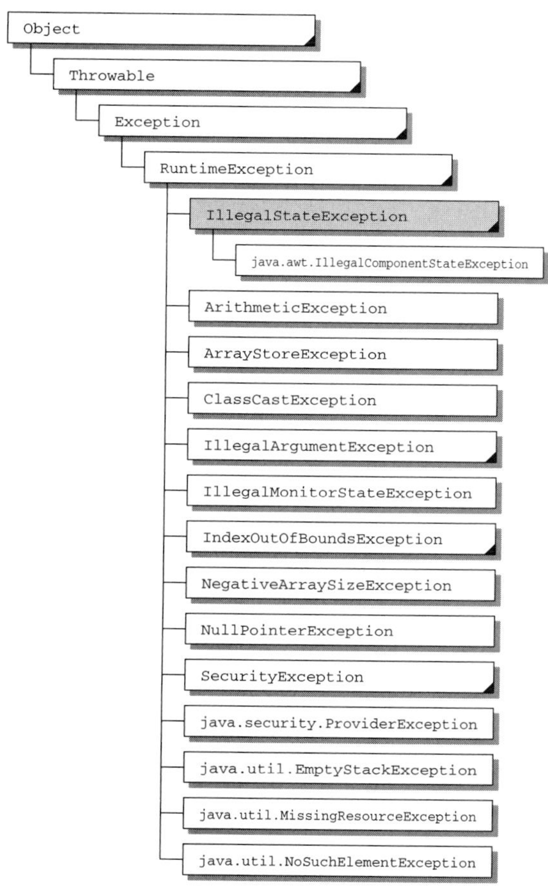

Syntax

```
public class IllegalStateException extends RuntimeException
```

Description

`IllegalStateException` is a runtime exception that is thrown when the program attempts to perform an operation on an object while the object is not in an appropriate state to perform the operation.

MEMBER SUMMARY	
Constructor	
`IllegalStateException()`	Constructs an `IllegalStateException` instance.

See Also

`java.awt.IllegalComponentStateException`.

Example

No classes in Java 1.1.4 throw `IllegalStateException` directly. Its subclass, `IllegalComponentStateException`, is thrown by methods in the AWT. See the class example of `java.awt.IllegalComponentStateException`.

IllegalStateException()

PURPOSE Constructs an `IllegalStateException` instance.

SYNTAX `public IllegalStateException()`

DESCRIPTION This constructor constructs an instance of `IllegalStateException`. An optional string `msg` can be supplied that describes this particular instance of the exception. If `msg` is not specified, it defaults to `null`.

PARAMETERS

`msg` The possibly `null` string that gives details about this exception.

SEE ALSO `Throwable.getMessage()`.

IllegalThreadStateException

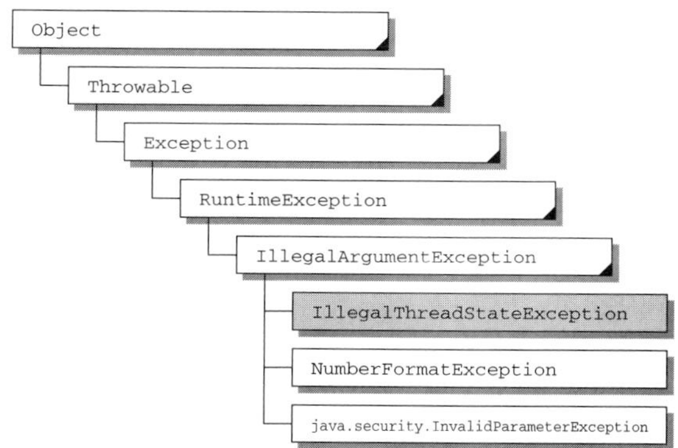

Syntax

```
public class IllegalThreadStateException extends IllegalArgumentException
```

Description

`IllegalThreadStateException` is an exception thrown by the runtime system when it detects that the program is attempting to perform an operation on a thread while the thread is in a state unsuitable for that operation. Table 30 lists the methods that can throw `IllegalThreadState-Exception` and the corresponding condition under which each throws the exception.

Method	Condition Under Which Exception Is Thrown
`Thread.countStackFrames()`	Thread is not suspended.
`Thread.setDaemon()`	Thread is already active.
`Thread.start()`	Thread has already started.
`ThreadGroup.destroy()`	Thread group is not empty or is already destroyed.
`ThreadGroup.ThreadGroup()`	Thread group has already been destroyed.

TABLE 30: Methods That Throw an `IllegalThreadStateException`.

`IllegalThreadStateException` should not be caught or declared in the `throws` clause of a method.

MEMBER SUMMARY	
Constructor	
`IllegalThreadStateException()`	Constructs an `IllegalThreadStateException` instance.

See Also

`IllegalArgumentException`, `RuntimeException`, `Thread.start()`, `Thread.countStackFrames()`, `Thread.setDaemon()`, `ThreadGroup.destroy()`, `ThreadGroup.ThreadGroup()`.

Example

This example throws `IllegalThreadStateException` when it attempts to call `start()` on the thread the second time:

```
import java.util.Date;

class T extends Thread {
    public void run() {
        System.out.println(new Date());
    }
}
class Main {
    public static void main(String[] args) {
        T th = new T();
        th.start();
        th.start(); // will raise IllegalThreadStateException
    }
}
```

IllegalThreadStateException()

PURPOSE: Constructs an `IllegalThreadStateException` instance.

SYNTAX:
```
public IllegalThreadStateException()
public IllegalThreadStateException(String msg)
```

DESCRIPTION: The two forms of this constructor construct an instance of `IllegalThreadStateException`. An optional string `msg` can be supplied that describes this particular instance of the exception. If `msg` is not specified, it defaults to `null`.

PARAMETERS

`msg`: A possibly `null` string that gives details about this exception.

SEE ALSO: `Throwable.getMessage()`.

IncompatibleClassChangeError

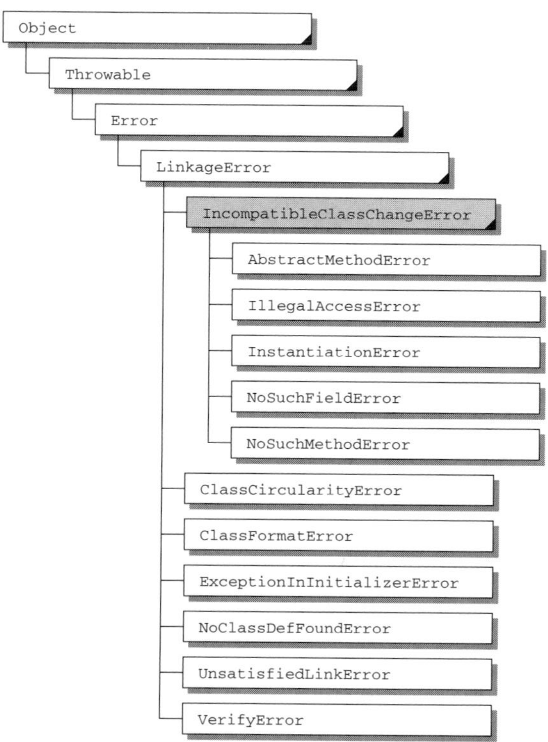

Syntax

```
public class IncompatibleClassChangeError extends LinkageError
```

Description

`IncompatibleClassChangeError` is the superclass of errors that occur when the Java virtual machine detects that the program is attempting to load or access a member of a class in a way that violates Java language rules.

Normally, such errors are caught by the compiler when the program is compiled. However, problems could be introduced when classes used by a program become inconsistent, for example if you were to make an incompatible change and then recompile only some of the classes.

`IncompatibleClassChangeError` should not be caught or declared in the `throws` clause of a method.

MEMBER SUMMARY	
Constructor	
`IncompatibleClassChangeError()`	Constructs an instance of `IncompatibleClassChangeError`.

A B C D E F G H I J K L M N O P Q R S T U V W X Y Z

See Also

`AbstractMethodError`, `Error`, `IllegalAccessError`, `InstantiationError`, `LinkageError`, `NoSuchFieldError`, `NoSuchMethodError`.

Example

See examples of subclasses.

IncompatibleClassChangeError()

PURPOSE Constructs an `IncompatibleClassChangeError` instance.

SYNTAX
```
public IncompatibleClassChangeError()
public IncompatibleClassChangeError(String msg)
```

DESCRIPTION The two forms of this constructor construct an instance of `IncompatibleClassChangeError`. An optional string `msg` can be supplied that describes this particular instance of the error. If `msg` is not supplied, it defaults to `null`.

PARAMETERS

`msg` A possibly `null` string that gives details about this error.

SEE ALSO `Throwable.getMessage()`.

IndexOutOfBoundsException

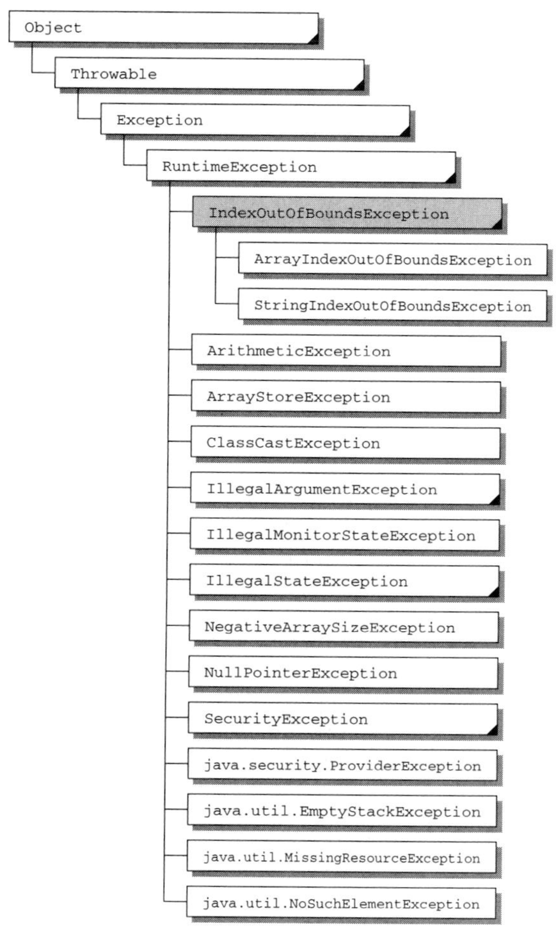

Syntax

```
public class IndexOutOfBoundsException extends RuntimeException
```

Description

`IndexOutOfBoundsException` is the superclass of exceptions thrown when the program attempts to use an index that is outside the bounds of the object that it is accessing. If the object is a `String`, a `StringIndexOutOfBoundsException` is thrown. If the object is an array, an `ArrayIndexOutOfBoundsException` is thrown.

`IndexOutOfBoundsException` should not be caught or declared in the `throws` clause of a method.

MEMBER SUMMARY	
Constructor	
`IndexOutOfBoundsException()`	Constructs an `IndexOutOfBoundsException` instance.

See Also

`ArrayIndexOutOfBoundsException`, `RuntimeException`, `StringIndexOutOfBoundsException`.

Example

See examples of subclasses.

IndexOutOfBoundsException()

PURPOSE Constructs an `IndexOutOfBoundsException` instance.

SYNTAX
```
public IndexOutOfBoundsException()
public IndexOutOfBoundsException(String msg)
```

DESCRIPTION The two forms of this constructor construct an instance of `IndexOutOfBoundsException`. An optional string `msg` can be supplied that describes this particular instance of the exception. If `msg` is not supplied, it defaults to `null`.

PARAMETERS

`msg` A possibly `null` string that gives details about this exception.

SEE ALSO `Throwable.getMessage()`.

InetAddress

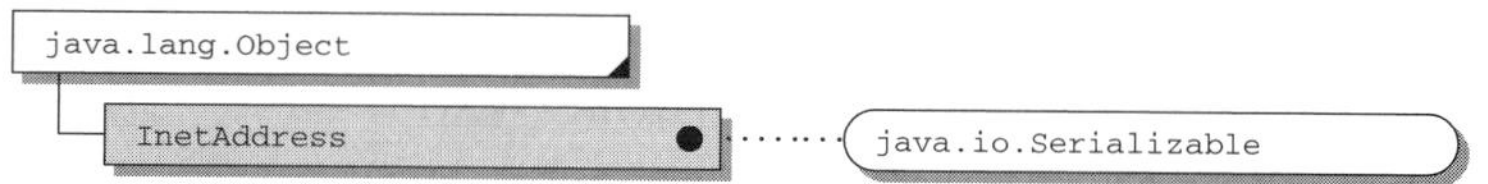

Syntax

```
public final class InetAddress implements Serializable
```

Description

The `InetAddress` class represents an *IP address*, a 32-bit unsigned number used by IP, the lower-level protocol on which protocols like UDP and TCP are built. An instance of an `InetAddress` consists of an IP address and its corresponding host name if the host name is determinable.

Dotted-String Notation

The 32-bit unsigned number of an IP address is actually four, 8-bit unsigned numbers. IP addresses are often written in a *dotted-string notation*, with each 8-bit number separated by a dot. An example of an IP address in dotted-string notation is `129.143.15.32`.

Host Name Resolution

Host name-to-Internet address *resolution* is accomplished through the use of a combination of local machine configuration information and network naming services such as the Internet Domain Name System (DNS) and Network Information Service (NIS). The particular naming service(s) being used is platform-dependent. For any host name, its corresponding IP address is returned.

Reverse host name resolution means that for any IP address, the host associated with the IP address is returned.

The `InetAddress` class provides methods to resolve host names to their Internet addresses and vice versa.

Multicast IP Address

Usually an IP address identifies a single host or network. This is called a *unicast* address. A *multicast* address identifies a *group* of hosts.

A special group of IP addresses is reserved for multicast addresses. Multicast addresses are in the range `224.0.0.1` to `239.255.255.255` (in other words, their first 4 bits are `1110`).

MEMBER SUMMARY	
Host Name Resolution Methods	
`getAllByName()`	Retrieves all of a host's IP addresses.
`getByName()`	Retrieves the IP address of a host.
`getLocalHost()`	Retrieves the IP address of the local host.
Field Access Methods	
`getAddress()`	Retrieves the IP address in network byte order from this IP address.
`getHostAddress()`	Retrieves the dotted-string form of the IP address.
`getHostName()`	Retrieves the host name associated with this IP address.
Multicast Method	
`isMulticastAddress()`	Determines whether this IP address is a multicast address.
Object Override Methods	
`equals()`	Compares this object with another object for equality.
`hashCode()`	Computes the hash code of this object.
`toString()`	Generates the string representation of this object.

A B C D E F G H I J K L M N O P Q R S T U V W X Y Z

See Also

`DatagramSocket`, `MulticastSocket`, `Socket`.

equals()

PURPOSE
Compares this object with another object for equality.

SYNTAX
`public boolean equals(Object obj)`

DESCRIPTION
This method compares this object with `obj` for equality. If `obj` is `null` or is not an object of class `InetAddress`, `equals()` returns `false`. If `obj` is of class `InetAddress` and has the same host name and IP address as this `InetAddress`, `equals()` returns `true`; otherwise, it returns `false`. If a machine has multiple names, instances of `InetAddress` for different names of that same machine are not equal. This is because they have different host names.

PARAMETERS
`obj` The object with which to compare. Can be `null`.

RETURNS
`true` if the objects are the same; `false` otherwise.

OVERRIDES
`java.lang.Object.equals()`.

SEE ALSO
`hashCode()`.

EXAMPLE This example defines a method `localHostP()` that returns `true` if the specified host name has the same `InetAddress` as the local host.

```
public static boolean localHostP(String hostname) {
    try {
        InetAddress target = InetAddress.getByName(hostname);
        return (target.equals(InetAddress.getLocalHost()));
    } catch (UnknownHostException e) {
        return (false);
    }
}
```


getAddress()

PURPOSE Retrieves the IP address in network byte order from this IP address.

SYNTAX `public byte[] getAddress()`

DESCRIPTION This method returns the IP address associated with this `InetAddress` object. The IP address is returned in a `byte` array in network byte order (i.e., highest-order IP number first, lowest-order IP number last). A 32-bit IP address has an array with 4 bytes. For example, the address `129.144.50.23` would be returned in a 4-element `byte` array with contents {`129`, `144`, `50`, `23`}.

RETURNS A non-`null` `byte` array with the IP address in network byte order.

EXAMPLE

```
try {
    byte [] addr = InetAddress.getLocalHost().getAddress();
    System.out.println("My address: " +
        (addr[0]&0xff) + "." + (addr[1]&0xff) + "." +
        (addr[2]&0xff) + "." + (addr[3]&0xff));
    System.out.println("Try again the easy way: " +
        InetAddress.getLocalHost().getHostAddress());
} catch (UnknownHostException e) {
    e.printStackTrace();
}
```

getAllByName()

PURPOSE Retrieves all of a host's IP addresses.

SYNTAX

```
public static InetAddress[] getAllByName(String host) throws
    UnknownHostException
```

DESCRIPTION This method retrieves all of the IP addresses for the machine with name `host`. (This process is called *host name resolution* and is described in the class description.) The ordering of the IP addresses in the array returned is not significant. A security exception is thrown if the calling thread is not allowed to resolve `host` to its IP address(es). Host names that have been looked up previously are cached and returned in subsequent calls.

If the first character of `host` is a digit, `host` is assumed to be the dotted-string representation of an IP address. An array is returned with one element containing the `InetAddress` instance that has `host` as its address. The host name of the `InetAddress` will be determined later on demand when `getHostName()` is called. No check is made regarding whether the calling thread is allowed to connect to the IP address.

A B C D E F G H I J K L M N O P Q R S T U V W X Y Z

PARAMETERS

`host` The host name to resolve or the IP address of the host. If `host` is `null` or an empty string, `UnknownHostException` is thrown.

RETURNS A non-`null` array of `InetAddress` objects.

EXCEPTIONS

`SecurityException`
If the resolution of `host` to its IP address(es) is not allowed due to security reasons.

`UnknownHostException`
If `host` is `null` or an empty string or it could not be resolved.

SEE ALSO `getByName()`, `getHostName()`, `Security.checkConnect()`.

EXAMPLE

```
String target = “java.sun.com”;
try {
    InetAddress[] alladdrs = InetAddress.getAllByName(target);
    for (int i = 0; i < alladdrs.length; i++)
        System.out.println(target + "[" + i + "] = " + alladdrs[i]);
} catch (UnknownHostException e) {
    System.err.println("Host not found: " + e);
}
```

getByName()

PURPOSE Retrieves the IP address of a host.

SYNTAX
```
public static InetAddress getByName(String host) throws
    UnknownHostException
```

DESCRIPTION This method retrieves the IP address of the machine with name `host`. (This process is called *host name resolution* and is described in the class description.) A security exception is thrown if the calling thread is not allowed to resolve `host` to an IP address. If `host` has multiple addresses, only one address is returned; which address is selected is platform-dependent. Host names that have been looked up previously are cached and returned in subsequent calls.

If `host` is `null`, the *loopback* address of this host is returned. The loopback address is an address that can be used to contact this machine (from within this machine) without going out to the network.

If the first character of `host` is a digit, `host` is assumed to be the dotted-string representation of an IP address. An `InetAddress` instance with `host` as its address is returned. The host name will be determined later on demand when `getHostName()` is invoked. No check is made regarding whether the calling thread is allowed to connect to the IP address.

PARAMETERS

`host` The host name to resolve or the IP address of the host. If `host` is `null`, this means the local machine.

EXCEPTIONS

`SecurityException`

If the resolution of `host` to an IP address is not allowed due to security reasons.

`UnknownHostException`

If `host` could not be resolved.

SEE ALSO `getAllByName()`, `getHostName()`, `Security.checkConnect()`.

EXAMPLE See `getHostName()`.

getHostAddress()

PURPOSE Retrieves the dotted-string form of the IP address.

SYNTAX `public String getHostAddress()`

RETURNS The IP address of this `InetAddress` object in dotted-string form (described in the class description).

SEE ALSO `getHostName()`.

EXAMPLE See `getAddress()`.

getHostName()

PURPOSE Retrieves the host name associated with this IP address.

SYNTAX `public String getHostName()`

DESCRIPTION If this `InetAddress` was created by passing the dotted-string representation of an IP address to `getByName()` or `getAllByName()`, the IP address is resolved to determine its host name. (This process is called *reverse host name resolution* and is described in the class description.) If this `InetAddress` was created by passing a host name parameter to `getByName()` or `getAllByName()`, that host name is returned.

The dotted-string form of the IP address is returned if the reverse host name resolution fails, or if the IP address does not have a corresponding host name, or if this thread is not allowed to perform the resolution due to security reasons.

RETURNS The host name associated with this IP address.

SEE ALSO `getByName()`, `getHostAddress()`, `SecurityManager.checkConnect()`.

EXAMPLE

```
try {
    InetAddress somehost = InetAddress.getByName(target);
    String somehostName = somehost.getHostName();
    if (target.equals(somehostName))
        System.out.println("same name");
    else
        System.out.println("target is different from host name");
} catch (UnknownHostException e) {
    System.err.println("Host not found: " + e);
}
```

getLocalHost()

PURPOSE Retrieves the IP address of the local host.

SYNTAX

```
public static InetAddress getLocalHost() throws
   UnknownHostException
```

DESCRIPTION If the security manager allows the current thread to create a socket connection to the local host using its host name, this method returns an `InetAddress` for the local host with that host name. If the security manager disallows this, an `InetAddress` for the *loopback* local host (i.e., with IP address `127.0.0.1`) is returned. The loopback address is an address that can be used to contact this machine (from within this machine) without going out to the network.

RETURNS The IP address of the local host.

EXCEPTIONS

`UnknownHostException`
If the host name of this machine cannot be resolved to an address.

SEE ALSO `getByName()`, `getAllByName()`, `SecurityManager.checkConnect()`.

EXAMPLE See `getAddress()`.

hashCode()

PURPOSE Computes the hash code of this object.

SYNTAX `public int hashCode()`

DESCRIPTION This method returns the hash code of this `InetAddress` object. The hash code of an `InetAddress` object is computed using its IP address.

RETURNS An `int` representing the hash code for this object.

OVERRIDES `java.lang.Object.hashCode()`.

SEE ALSO `equals()`, `java.util.Hashtable`.

EXAMPLE

```
int tabsize = 13;
int[] hits = new int[tabsize];
try {
    InetAddress addr = InetAddress.getByName(target);
    int hashval = addr.hashCode();          // generate hash code
    ++hits[Math.abs(hashval%tabsize)];  // count hits
} catch (UnknownHostException e) {
    System.err.println("Host not found: " + e);
}
```

isMulticastAddress()

PURPOSE Determines whether this IP address is a multicast address.

SYNTAX `public boolean isMulticastAddress()`

DESCRIPTION This method determines whether this `InetAddress` is an multicast address. See the class description for a description of multicast addresses.

RETURNS `true` if this is a multicast address; `false` otherwise.

SEE ALSO `MulticastSocket`.

toString()

PURPOSE Generates the string representation of this object.

SYNTAX `public String toString()`

DESCRIPTION The string representation of an `InetAddress` object consists of its host name and its IP address in dotted-string notation (e.g., `129.144.50.23`). The `toString()` method returns the string representation for this `InetAddress` object.

RETURNS The non-`null` string representation of this `InetAddress` object.

OVERRIDES `java.lang.Object.toString()`.

SEE ALSO `getHostAddress()`, `getHostName()`.

EXAMPLE

```
try {
    InetAddress myAddr = InetAddress.getLocalHost();
    System.out.println(myAddr.toString());        // hostname/a.b.c.d
} catch (UnknownHostException e) {
    System.err.println("Host not found: " + e);
}
```

Inflater

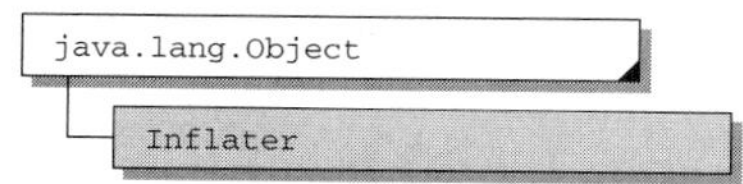

Syntax

```
public class Inflater
```

Description

The `Inflater` class is used to decompress a data stream that was compressed with the DEFLATE compression algorithm and data format. The `Deflater` class compresses data using the DEFLATE algorithm. The DEFLATE compression algorithm and data format are described in *RFC 1951*, which can be found at `http://ds.internic.net/rfc/rfc1951.txt`.

Usage

An inflater is typically used with the `InflaterOutputStream` class, which makes it convenient to decompress a stream of data.

To use an inflater to compress some data, you first need to create an `Inflater` instance. Then you supply some of the compressed data to the inflater by calling `setInput()`. After each call to `setInput()`, you must call `inflate()` to retrieve the decompressed data. You must continually call `inflate()` until `needsInput()` returns `true`.

After calling `inflate()`, you can check to see if you've reached the end of the stream by calling `finished()`.

MEMBER SUMMARY	
Constructor	
`Inflater()`	Constructs a `Inflater` instance.
Compression Method	
`inflate()`	Retrieves decompressed data from this inflater.
Stream Methods	
`end()`	Frees all internal resources used by this inflater.
`finalize()`	Called by Java virtual machine to clean up this inflater's state when it is ready to be discarded.
`finished()`	Determines if the end of the compressed data stream has been reached.
`needsInput()`	Determines if the input buffer is empty.
`reset()`	Resets this inflater so that it can be reused.
`setInput()`	Delivers compressed data to this inflater to decompress.

A B C D E F G H I J K L M N O P Q R S T U V W X Y Z

MEMBER SUMMARY

Get Property Methods	
`getAdler()`	Retrieves the current checksum value of the uncompressed data read so far.
`getRemaining()`	Determines the number of compressed bytes in the input buffer.
`getTotalIn()`	Retrieves the number of compressed bytes delivered to this inflater.
`getTotalOut()`	Retrieves the number of decompressed bytes read from this inflater.
Dictionary Methods	
`needsDictionary()`	Determines if a preset dictionary was used in the compressed data.
`setDictionary()`	Sets a prebuilt dictionary for decompression.

See Also

`Deflater`, `InflaterInputStream`.

Example

This example implements a simple client/server application. The client reads a string from standard input, compresses it, and delivers it to the server. The server decompresses the string and prints it.The client uses a prebuilt dictionary every other time it sends a message to the server.

Main.java

```
import java.io.*;
import java.net.*;
import java.util.zip.*;

class Main {
    static String dictionary =
        "byteshortintlongfloatdoubleclassinterfaceforifelse";

    public static void main(String[] args) {
        try {
            Socket socket = new Socket("localhost", 1200);
            BufferedReader in =
        new BufferedReader(new InputStreamReader(System.in));
            DataOutputStream os =
                new DataOutputStream(socket.getOutputStream());
            String line;
            int count = 0;

            while ((line = in.readLine()) != null) {
                Deflater def = new Deflater();
                DeflaterOutputStream dos = new DeflaterOutputStream(os, def);
```

```
                // Alternately set the dictionary to see its effects.
                if ((count++ % 2) == 0) {
                    def.setDictionary(dictionary.getBytes());
                    System.out.println("checksum of dictionary: " +
                                       def.getAdler());
                }

                // Write the length of the string.
                os.writeInt(line.length());

                // Write the string.
                dos.write(line.getBytes());

                // Finish it but don't close it.
                dos.finish();
            }
        } catch (Exception e) {
            e.printStackTrace();
        }
    }
}
```

Server.java

```
import java.io.*;
import java.net.*;
import java.util.zip.*;

public class Server extends Thread {
    static String dictionary =
        "byteshortintlongfloatdoubleclassinterfaceforifelse";

    public void run() {
        byte[] inbuf = new byte[128];
        Inflater inf = new Inflater();

        while (true) {
            try {
                Socket socket = serverSocket.accept();
                DataInputStream is =
                    new DataInputStream(socket.getInputStream());
                byte[] strbuf;

                while (true) {
                    int offset = 0;
                    long dictCRC = -1L;

                    try {
                        strbuf = new byte[is.readInt()];
                    } catch (EOFException e) {
                        // Connection is closed.
                        break;
                    }

                    // Continue until all of the string is decompressed.
                    while (!inf.finished()) {
                      // while(inf.getRemaining() == 0) {// could also be used.
                        if (inf.needsInput()) {
                            int len = is.read(inbuf);
                            inf.setInput(inbuf, 0, len);
```

```
                    }

                    // Check if the data was compressed with a
                    // pre-built dictionary.
                    if (inf.needsDictionary()) {
                        dictCRC = inf.getAdler();
                        inf.setDictionary(dictionary.getBytes());
                    }

                    // Retrieve the decompressed string.
                    offset +=
                        inf.inflate(strbuf, offset, strbuf.length-offset);
                }

                // Print details.
                System.out.println(new String(strbuf));
                System.out.print("  in: " + inf.getTotalIn());
                System.out.println("   " +
                    (dictCRC < 0 ? "" : "<"+dictCRC+">"));
                System.out.println("  out: " + inf.getTotalOut());
                System.out.println("  adler: 0x" +
                    Integer.toHexString(inf.getAdler()));
                System.out.println("----------------------------");
                inf.reset();
            }
        } catch (IOException e) {
            e.printStackTrace();
            inf.reset();
        } catch (Exception e) {
            e.printStackTrace();
            break;
        }
    }

    // Not necessary; shown here for demonstrative purposes.
    inf.end();
}

static ServerSocket serverSocket;

public static void main(String[] args) {
    try {
        // Create a server socket on port 1200 and start the server.
        serverSocket = new ServerSocket(1200);
        new Server().start();
    } catch (IOException e) {
        e.printStackTrace();
    }
}
}
```

Client Output

```
> java Main
interface
checksum of dictionary: 458036471
interface
```

Server Output

Notice that the entry that uses the dictionary (i.e., "in = 14") is slightly smaller.

```
> java Server
interface
  in: 14  <458036471>
  out: 9
  adler: 0x1
----------------------------
interface
  in: 17
  out: 9
  adler: 0x1
----------------------------
```

end()

PURPOSE Frees all internal resources used by this inflater.

SYNTAX `public synchronized native void end()`

DESCRIPTION This method discards any unprocessed input left in the inflater and frees all resources used by this inflater. After this method is called, this inflater can no longer be used.

This method is automatically called by `finalize()` when the garbage collector reclaims this `Inflater` instance.

SEE ALSO `finalize()`.

EXAMPLE See the class example.

finalize()

PURPOSE Called by Java virtual machine to clean up this deflater's state when it is ready to be discarded.

SYNTAX `protected void finalize()`

DESCRIPTION This method should not be called directly. It is automatically called by the Java virtual machine to finalize this `Inflater` instance before reclaiming its storage.

This method calls `end()` by default. If you override this method, you should call `end()` to ensure the internal resources are freed.

OVERRIDES `java.lang.Object.finalize()`.

SEE ALSO `end()`.

EXAMPLE See `Deflater.finalize()`.

finished()

PURPOSE Determines if the end of the compressed data stream has been reached.

SYNTAX `public synchronized boolean finished()`

DESCRIPTION If this method returns `true`, no more decompressed data is available. In particular, `setInput()` and `inflate()` should no longer be called. To reuse this inflater, call `reset()`.

RETURNS `true` if no more decompressed data is available; `false` otherwise.

SEE ALSO `inflate()`, `reset()`, `setInput()`.

getAdler()

PURPOSE Retrieves the current checksum value of the uncompressed data read so far.

SYNTAX `public synchronized native int getAdler()`

DESCRIPTION The algorithm used to compute the checksum value is ADLER-32. See `Adler32` for more details.

If this inflater needs a dictionary (i.e., `needsDictionary()` returns `true`), this method can be called to retrieve the checksum value of the dictionary. If the inflater and deflater use different dictionaries at different times, this checksum value can be used to determine which dictionary the deflater used.

The return value is invalid if this inflater was created with the `noHeader` option. See `Inflater()` for more details.

RETURNS The checksum value of the uncompressed data.

SEE ALSO `Adler32`.

EXAMPLE See the class example.

getRemaining()

PURPOSE Determines the number of compressed bytes in the input buffer.

SYNTAX `public synchronized int getRemaining()`

DESCRIPTION The `setInput()` method delivers to this inflater an input buffer filled with compressed data. This inflater reads bytes from this buffer every time `inflate()` is called. This method returns the number of bytes left in the input buffer that have not yet been decompressed.

`needsInput()` is equivalent to the expression `(getRemaining() == 0)`.

RETURNS The number of uncompressed bytes in the input buffer.

SEE ALSO `inflate()`, `needsInput()`, `setInput()`.

EXAMPLE See the class example.

getTotalIn()

PURPOSE Retrieves the number of compressed bytes delivered to this inflater.

SYNTAX

```
public synchronized native int getTotalIn()
```

DESCRIPTION This method returns the number of compressed bytes delivered to this inflater via the `setInput()` method call.

RETURNS The number of compressed bytes delivered to this inflater.

SEE ALSO `setInput()`.

EXAMPLE See the class example.

getTotalOut()

PURPOSE Retrieves the number of decompressed bytes read from this inflater.

SYNTAX

```
public synchronized native int getTotalOut()
```

DESCRIPTION This method returns the number of decompressed bytes read from this inflater via the `inflate()` method call.

RETURNS The number of decompressed bytes read from this inflater.

SEE ALSO `inflate()`.

EXAMPLE See the class example.

inflate()

PURPOSE Retrieves decompressed data from this inflater.

SYNTAX

```
public int inflate(byte[] buf) throws DataFormatException
public synchronized native int inflate(byte[] buf, int off, int
    len) throws DataFormatException
```

DESCRIPTION This method retrieves `len` decompressed bytes into `buf` starting at `buf[off]`. If `off` is not specified, it defaults to `0`. If `len` is not specified, it defaults to `buf.length`.

This method should be called after this inflater is given uncompressed data via `setInput()`. It should be called continually until `needsInput()` returns `true` and `finished()` returns `false`.

If the compressed data was compressed using a prebuilt dictionary (see `setDictionary()`), it is necessary to set the dictionary before calling this method.

PARAMETERS

`buf`	The non-`null` buffer into which the decompressed data is retrieved.
`len`	The maximum number of bytes to retrieve into `buf` starting at `buf[off]`. `0` ≤ `len` ≤ `buf.length-off`.
`off`	The `0`-based starting index of the data in `buf`. `0` ≤ `off` < `buf.length`.

RETURNS The number of decompressed bytes actually retrieved.

EXCEPTIONS

`DataFormatException`
If the compressed data is corrupted or invalid.

SEE ALSO `finished()`, `needsInput()`, `setInput()`.

EXAMPLE See the class example.

Inflater()

PURPOSE Constructs an `Inflater` instance.

SYNTAX

```
public Inflater()
public Inflater(boolean noHeader)
```

DESCRIPTION `noHeader` controls whether the inflater should expect a ZLIB header in the input stream (see the `Deflater` class description for more information about the ZLIB header). If `noHeader` is `true`, the inflater does not look for the ZLIB header.

The `Inflater` can read data compressed by the `Deflater`. However, the values of the `noHeader` parameters in both the deflater and inflater must match. That is, if the compressed data is written without a ZLIB header, the inflater must be created with `noHeader` as `true`.

If `noHeader` is not specified, it defaults to `false`.

PARAMETERS

`noHeader`	If `true`, the input stream does not contain the ZLIB header.

SEE ALSO `Deflater()`.

EXAMPLE See the class example.

needsDictionary()

PURPOSE Determines if a prebuilt dictionary was used in the compressed data.

SYNTAX `public synchronized boolean needsDictionary()`

DESCRIPTION This method should be called after the first call to `setInput()` and before the first call to `inflate()`. If this method returns `true`, a dictionary should be supplied to this inflater. See `setDictionary()` for details.

If this inflater was constructed with `noHeader` as `true` (see `Inflater()`), this method does not need to be called, since no dictionary will be included with the compressed data. (Unfortunately, if you do call it, it returns `true`.)

RETURNS `true` if the input data was compressed with a preset dictionary.

SEE ALSO `setDictionary()`.

EXAMPLE See the class example.

needsInput()

PURPOSE Determines if the input buffer is empty.

SYNTAX `public synchronized boolean needsInput()`

DESCRIPTION The input buffer is the `byte` array of compressed data supplied to `setInput()`. This method returns `false` as long as there are unread bytes in the input buffer.

Note that this method will return `true` if `finished()` returns `true`.

RETURNS `true` if the input buffer is empty; `false` otherwise.

SEE ALSO `setInput()`.

EXAMPLE See the class example.

reset()

PURPOSE Resets this inflater so that it can be reused.

SYNTAX `public synchronized native void reset()`

DESCRIPTION This method discards any data on which this inflater may be working. After this method is called, this inflater can be reused to inflate a new stream of data.

EXAMPLE See the class example.

setDictionary()

PURPOSE Sets a prebuilt dictionary for decompression.

SYNTAX
```
public synchronized native void setDictionary(byte[] buf)
public synchronized native void setDictionary(byte[] buf, int
   off, int len)
```

DESCRIPTION If the compressed input data was compressed using a prebuilt dictionary, it is necessary to give the same dictionary to this inflater. See `Deflater.setDictionary()` for more information about dictionaries.

This method must be called if `needsDictionary()` returns `true` and the compressed data has a ZLIB header (see `Inflater()` for more details).

This inflater copies `len` bytes in `buf`, starting from `buf[off]`, into its internal dictionary storage. Only the last 32K are used. If `off` is not specified, it defaults to `0`. If `len` is not specified, it defaults to `buf.length`.

If the compressor can use different prebuilt dictionaries to compress its data, it is possible to determine which one was used based on the checksum value of the dictionary. In particular, calling `getAdler()` returns the checksum value of the dictionary used by the compressor.

PARAMETERS

`buf`	A non-`null` `byte` array containing the prebuilt dictionary.
`len`	The number of bytes to use starting from `buf[off]`. `0` ≤ `len` ≤ `buf.length-off`. Only the last `0xFFFF` bytes are used.
`off`	The `0`-based index of the first byte in `buf` to use. `0` ≤ `off` < `buf.length`.

SEE ALSO `Deflater.setDictionary()`, `needsDictionary()`, `getAdler()`.

EXAMPLE See the class example.

setInput()

PURPOSE Delivers compressed data to this inflater to decompress.

SYNTAX
```
public synchronized void setInput(byte[] buf)
public synchronized void setInput(byte[] buf, int off, int len)
```

DESCRIPTION This method delivers `len` bytes starting from `buf[off]` to this inflater to decompress. If `off` is not specified, it defaults to `0`. If `len` is not specified, it defaults to `buf.length`.

All of the compressed data must be delivered to this inflater using this method call. After `setInput()` is called, `inflate()` must be called to retrieve the compressed data. In fact, `inflate()` must be called until `needsInput()` or `finished()` returns `true`.

This method should be called only if `needsInput()` returns `true` and `finished()` returns `false`.

PARAMETERS

`buf`	The non-`null` buffer containing the compressed data.
`len`	The number of bytes in buf starting at `buf[off]`. `0` ≤ `len` ≤ `buf.length-off`.
`off`	The `0`-based starting offset of the data in buf. `0` ≤ `off` < `buf.length`.

SEE ALSO `finished()`, `inflate()`, `needsInput()`.

EXAMPLE See the class example.

java.util.zip
InflaterInputStream

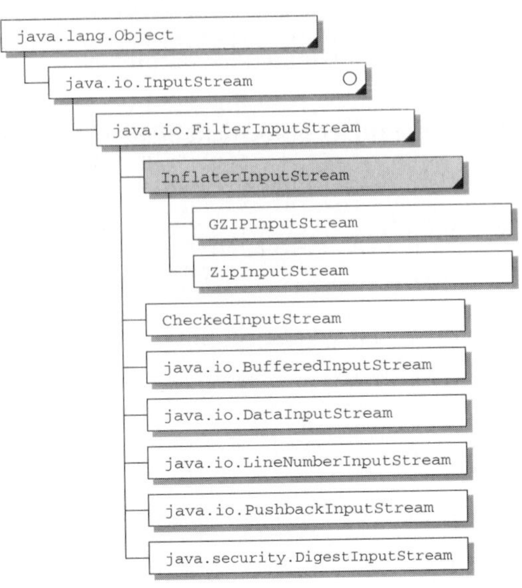

A B C D E F G H I J K L M N O P Q R S T U V W X Y Z

Syntax

```
public class InflaterInputStream extends FilterInputStream
```

Description

The `InflaterInputStream` class implements an input stream filter for decompressing data using the `Inflater` class. It makes it convenient to use an `Inflater` instance in a data streaming fashion. See the `Inflater` class for more information.

Usage

To use an inflater input stream, you create a new `InflaterInputStream` instance on an existing input stream that serves the compressed data. Then you call `read()` to retrieve the decompressed data. See Figure 60.

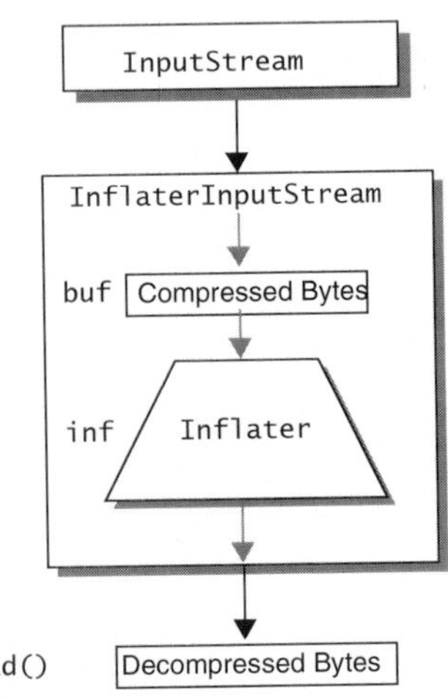

FIGURE 60: **`InflaterInputStream`.**

MEMBER SUMMARY	
Constructor	
`InflaterInputStream()`	Creates an `InflaterInputStream` instance.
Stream Methods	
`read()`	Reads decompressed data from this inflater input stream.
`skip()`	Discards decompressed data from this inflater input stream.
Protected Fields and Method	
`buf`	The buffer for delivering uncompressed data to the inflater.
`fill()`	Reads compressed data from the underlying input stream and decompresses it.
`inf`	The inflater used to decompress data.
`len`	The number of read bytes in `buf`.

A B C D E F G H I J K L M N O P Q R S T U V W X Y Z

See Also

`Inflater`, `java.io.FilterInputStream`

Example

This example uses the inflater input stream to decompress the pixels of an image as it is being deserialized.

See `DeflaterOuputStream` for an example that writes the serialized images read by this example.

Main.java

```
import java.awt.*;
import java.io.*;

class Main {
    public static void main(String[] args) {
        if (args.length < 1) {
            System.err.println("Usage: java Main <imagefile>...");
            System.exit(1);
        }

        for (int i=0; i<args.length; i++) {
            try {
                ObjectInputStream is = new ObjectInputStream(
                    new FileInputStream(args[i]));

                System.out.println("Reading " + args[i]);
                SerImage si = (SerImage)is.readObject();
                is.close();

                new ImageViewer(si.image);
            } catch (Exception e) {
                e.printStackTrace();
```

```
                }
            }
        }
    }

    class ImageViewer extends Frame {
        Image image;
        ImageViewer(Image image){
            this.image = image;
            pack();
            show();
        }

        // Determine the size of the frame that will show the image.
        public Dimension getPreferredSize() {
            Insets insets = getInsets();

            return new Dimension(image.getWidth(null) + insets.left + insets.right,
                image.getHeight(null) + insets.top + insets.bottom);
        }

        public void paint(Graphics g) {
            g.drawImage(image, getInsets().left, getInsets().top, this);
        }
    }
```

SerImage.java

```
import java.awt.*;
import java.awt.image.*;
import java.io.*;
import java.util.zip.*;

public class SerImage implements Serializable {
    transient Image image;

    public SerImage(String filename) {
        image = Toolkit.getDefaultToolkit().getImage(filename);

        // Create media tracker with dummy button
        MediaTracker tracker = new MediaTracker(new Button());
        try {
            tracker.addImage(image, 0);
            tracker.waitForAll(0);
        } catch (Exception e) {
            throw new IllegalArgumentException("Could not create image.");
        }
    }

    private void writeObject(ObjectOutputStream out) throws IOException {
        Dimension d = new Dimension(image.getWidth(null),
            image.getHeight(null));
        DeflaterOutputStream dos = new DeflaterOutputStream(out);
        ObjectOutputStream os = new ObjectOutputStream(dos);

        // Write the dimensions of the image.
        os.writeObject(d);

        // Grab the image pixels.
        int[] pixels = new int[d.width * d.height];
```

```
        PixelGrabber pg = new PixelGrabber(
            image, 0, 0, d.width, d.height, pixels, 0, d.width);
        try {
            pg.grabPixels();
        } catch (Exception e) {
            throw new IOException("Could not grab pixels.");
        }

        // Write the pixel data.
        os.writeObject(pixels);

        dos.finish();
    }

    private void readObject(ObjectInputStream in)
            throws IOException, ClassNotFoundException {
        ObjectInputStream is = new ObjectInputStream(
            new InflaterInputStream(in));

        // Read the Dimensions.
        Dimension d = (Dimension)is.readObject();

        // Read the pixels into a pixel array.
        int[] pixels = (int[])is.readObject();

        // Convert the pixels into an image.
        image = Toolkit.getDefaultToolkit().createImage(
            new MemoryImageSource(d.width, d.height, pixels, 0, d.width));
    }
}
```

buf

PURPOSE The buffer for delivering uncompressed data to the inflater.

SYNTAX `protected byte[] buf`

DESCRIPTION This buffer is used by this class to read compressed data from the underlying input stream and deliver it to the internal `Inflater` instance (see `inf`).

The size of this buffer is determined by a parameter to the constructor.

SEE ALSO `InflaterOutputStream()`, `fill()`.

fill()

PURPOSE Reads compressed data from the underlying input stream and decompresses it.

SYNTAX `protected void fill() throws IOException`

DESCRIPTION This method reads compressed data from the underlying input stream into `buf` (see `buf`) and gives it to the `Inflater` instance to decompress (see `inf`).

EXCEPTIONS

`IOException`
If an IO error occurs while reading from the underlying input stream.

SEE ALSO `buf`, `inf`.

inf

PURPOSE The inflater used to decompress data.

SYNTAX
```
protected Inflater inf
```

DESCRIPTION This field holds a reference to the `Inflater` instance that this inflater input stream uses to decompress the data read from this stream. This is the same `Inflater` instance that is supplied to the constructor.

SEE ALSO `Inflater`.

InflaterInputStream()

PURPOSE Creates an `InflaterInputStream` instance.

SYNTAX
```
public InflaterInputStream(InputStream in)
public InflaterInputStream(InputStream in, Inflater infl)
public InflaterInputStream(InputStream in, Inflater infl, int
    bufsize)
```

DESCRIPTION This constructor creates an inflater input stream around `in`. Reading data from this new inflater input stream will result in data's being read from `in` and decompressed by `infl`. `infl` is assigned to the protected field `inf` (see `inf`). If `infl` is not specified, `inf` is assigned a new instance of `Inflater`.

`bufsize` determines the size of the protected field `buf` (see `buf` for details). If `bufsize` is not specified, it defaults to `512`.

PARAMETERS

`bufsize` A nonnegative buffer size.
`in` A non-`null` input stream.
`infl` A non-`null` `Inflater` instance.

SEE ALSO `buf`, `inf`, `Inflater`.

EXAMPLE See the class example.

len

PURPOSE The number of read bytes in `buf`.

SYNTAX `protected int len`

DESCRIPTION This field holds the most recent number of bytes read by `fill()` from the underlying input stream.

SEE ALSO `fill()`.

read()

PURPOSE Reads decompressed data from this inflater input stream.

SYNTAX

```
public int read() throws IOException
public int read(byte[] buf, int off, int len) throws IOException
```

DESCRIPTION This method reads at most `len` decompressed bytes from this inflater input stream and places them in `buf` starting at `buf[off]`. The blocking behavior of this method depends on the input streams from which it reads. In general, this method blocks until some bytes (possibly fewer than `len`) are read.

This method returns `-1` if the inflater input stream has no more data to return or if the internal `Inflater` instance requires a dictionary (see `Inflater.needsDictionary()` for more details).

PARAMETERS

`buf` The non-`null` buffer in which to store the data.

`len` The maximum number of bytes to read into `buf` starting at `buf[off]`. `0` ≤ `len` ≤ `buf.length-off`.

`off` The `0`-based starting index of the data in `buf`. `0` ≤ `off` < `buf.length`.

RETURNS If `-1` is returned, the end of the stream is reached or a dictionary is needed. If no parameters are specified, the read byte is returned in the low-order byte of an `int`; otherwise, the number of read bytes is returned.

EXCEPTIONS

`IOException`
If an IO error occurs while reading.

`ZipException`
If a ZIP format error occurs while reading.

OVERRIDES `java.io.FilterInputStream.read()`.

SEE ALSO `java.io.IOException`.

EXAMPLE See the class example.

skip()

PURPOSE Discards decompressed data from this inflater input stream.

SYNTAX `public long skip(long n) throws IOException`

DESCRIPTION This method reads at most `n` decompressed bytes from this inflater input stream and discards them. `n` can be larger than the number of bytes in the stream; it simply returns the number of bytes skipped.

PARAMETERS

`n` The number of bytes to skip. If negative, `n` becomes `0`.

RETURNS The nonnegative number of bytes skipped.

EXCEPTIONS

`IOException`

If an IO error occurs while skipping bytes.

`ZipException`

If a ZIP file error occurs while skipping bytes.

OVERRIDES `java.io.FilterInputStream.skip()`.

SEE ALSO `java.io.IOException`.

EXAMPLE See `ZipInputStream.skip()`.

InputStream

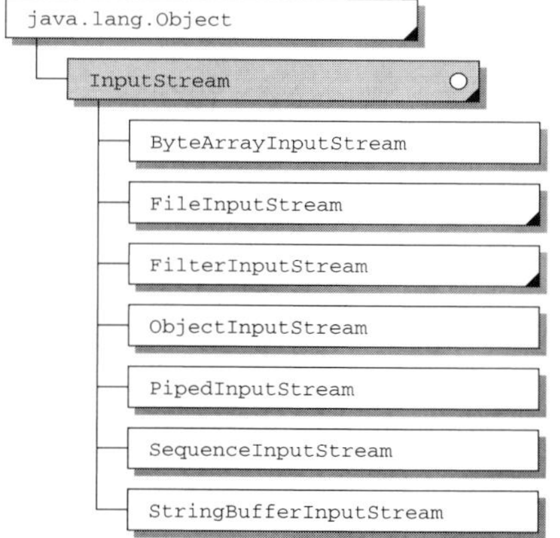

A B C D E F G H I J K L M N O P Q R S T U V W X Y Z

Syntax

```
public abstract class InputStream
```

Description

The `InputStream` class is the superclass of all byte input streams. It provides basic input methods for reading bytes from an input stream.

Usage

Subclasses of `InputStream` override some or all of these basic methods for implementing their particular type of input stream. Figure 61 shows that you can either read directly from a subclass of `InputStream` or read from an input stream through filters.

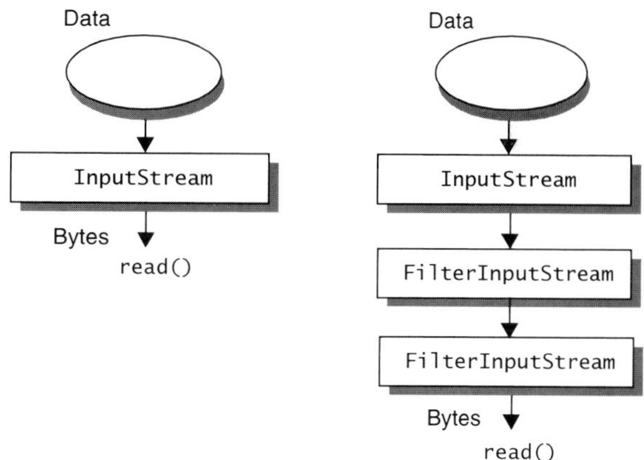

FIGURE 61: `InputStream`.

InputStream versus Reader

`InputStream` is meant for byte streams. Its `read()` method reads bytes (0–255). `Reader` is the superclass of all character-oriented input streams. You should use `Reader` and its subclass when the input is a stream of characters.

If you need to translate between byte streams and character streams, use `InputStream-Reader`. `InputStreamReader` translates bytes read from an input stream into characters using either a specified or default byte-to-character encoding.

Current Read Position and Mark/Reset

Each input stream has a current read position. As read operations occur, this current read position is incremented to reflect that the bytes have been read. In addition to conducting read operations, you also can skip bytes in the input stream. This is similar to reads, except that skipping a byte increments only the current read position; it does not return the byte skipped.

You can mark the current read position (using `mark()`) so that you can return to it (using `reset()`). This allows you to reread previously read bytes. Mark/reset is useful for implementing parsers. You can mark the current read position and then read ahead in the stream to determine what action to take next. After making that determination, you then can reset the read position to that mark and pass the stream onto the appropriate processor.

MEMBER SUMMARY	
Input Methods	
`read()`	Reads bytes from this input stream.
`skip()`	Skips bytes from this input stream.
Mark/Reset Methods	
`mark()`	Marks the current read position in the input stream.
`markSupported()`	Determines whether this input stream supports mark/reset.
`reset()`	Resets the current read position to be the last marked position.
Stream Methods	
`available()`	Determines the number of bytes that can be read without being blocked.
`close()`	Closes this input stream.

See Also

`InputStreamReader`, `IOException`, `OutputStream`, `Reader`.

Example

This example counts the number characters, words, and lines read from an input stream. Since it is dealing with characters, a better way to write this example is to use `Reader`.

```
import java.io.InputStream;
import java.io.IOException;
import java.io.FileInputStream;

class Main {
    public static void wordCount(InputStream in) {
        int bytecount = 0;
        int wordcount = 0;
        int linecount = 0;
```

```
        try {
            int c;
            boolean newspace = true;
            while ((c = in.read()) > -1) {
                ++bytecount;
                if (c == '\n' || c == '\r')
                    ++linecount;
                if (Character.isWhitespace((char)c)) {
                    if (newspace) {
                        ++wordcount;
                        newspace = false;
                    }
                } else {
                    newspace = true;
                }
            }
            in.close();
        } catch (IOException e) {
            e.printStackTrace();
        }
        System.out.println(linecount + " " + wordcount + " " + bytecount);
    }
    public static void main(String[] args) {
        if (args.length == 1) {
            try {
                wordCount(new FileInputStream(args[0]));
            } catch (IOException e) {
                e.printStackTrace();
            }
        } else {
            System.err.println("Usage: java Main <file>");
            System.exit(-1);
        }
    }
}
```

available()

PURPOSE Determines the number of bytes that can be read without being blocked.

SYNTAX `public int available() throws IOException`

DESCRIPTION This method returns the number of bytes that can be read without being blocked. The default implementation of this method simply returns `0`.

RETURNS The number bytes that can be read without being blocked.

EXCEPTIONS

`IOException`

If an IO error occurred.

EXAMPLE

```
Inputstream in = ...;
int howmany = in.available();
```

```
    if (howmany > 0) {
        byte[] buf = new byte[howmany];
        int count = in.read(buf);
        ...
    }
```

A B C D E F G H I J K L M N O P Q R S T U V W X Y Z

close()

PURPOSE Closes this input stream.

SYNTAX `public void close() throws IOException`

DESCRIPTION This method closes this input stream. The default implementation does not do anything. Subclasses of `InputStream` should override this method to release any resources (especially system resources) used by this input stream, such as file descriptors and sockets.

EXCEPTIONS

`IOException`

If an IO error occurred.

EXAMPLE See the class example.

mark()

PURPOSE Marks the current read position in the input stream.

SYNTAX `public synchronized void mark(int readlimit)`

DESCRIPTION This method marks the current position in the input stream so that a subsequent call to `reset()` will reposition the read position of the stream to this marked position. This marked position becomes invalid if you read more than `readlimit` number of bytes beyond it. The default implementation of `mark()` does nothing.

PARAMETERS

`readlimit` The number of bytes that can be read before this mark is invalidated.

SEE ALSO `markSupported()`, `reset()`.

EXAMPLE This is a slightly modified version of `URLConnection.guessContentTypeFromStream()`. It demonstrates the use of the `mark()/reset()` methods in probing the input stream to determine the content type and then resetting the stream so that the appropriate parser can complete the processing of the stream.

```
    static protected String guessContentType(InputStream is)
```

```
        throws IOException {
        if (is.markSupported()) {
            is.mark(6);
            int c1 = is.read();
            int c2 = is.read();
            int c3 = is.read();
            int c4 = is.read();
            int c5 = is.read();
            int c6 = is.read();
            is.reset();
            if (c1 == 'G' && c2 == 'I' && c3 == 'F' && c4 == '8')
                return "image/gif";
            if (c1 == '#' && c2 == 'd' && c3 == 'e' && c4 == 'f')
                return "image/x-bitmap";
            if (c1 == '!' && c2 == ' ' && c3 == 'X' &&
                c4 == 'P' && c5 == 'M' && c6 == '2')
                return "image/x-pixmap";
            if (c1 == '<')
                if (c2 == '!' || (c6 == '>'
                && (c2 == 'h' && (c3 == 't' && c4 == 'm' && c5 == 'l' ||
                                  c3 == 'e' && c4 == 'a' && c5 == 'd')
                    || c2 == 'b' && c3 == 'o' && c4 == 'd' && c5 == 'y')))
                return "text/html";
        }
        return null;
    }
```

markSupported()

PURPOSE Determines whether this input stream supports mark/reset.

SYNTAX `public boolean markSupported()`

DESCRIPTION This method returns `true` if this input stream supports mark/reset; it returns `false` otherwise. The default implementation returns `false` (i.e., mark/reset is not supported).

RETURNS `true` if this input stream supports mark/reset; `false` otherwise.

SEE ALSO `mark()`, `reset()`.

EXAMPLE See `mark()`.

read()

PURPOSE Reads bytes from this input stream.

SYNTAX
```
abstract public int read() throws IOException
public int read(byte[] buffer) throws IOException
public int read(byte[] buffer, int offset, int count) throws
    IOException
```

DESCRIPTION The three forms of this method read bytes from this input stream. The first form is an abstract method whose implementation is supplied by the subclasses of `InputStream`. The other two forms are implemented using this first form which reads a byte at a time. These two methods usually should be overridden to be more efficient than performing reads a byte at a time.

The second form reads `buffer.length` number of bytes from this input stream and stores those bytes into `buffer`. The third form reads `count` number of bytes from this input stream and stores those bytes into `buffer` starting at index `offset`.

PARAMETERS

`buffer` The non-`null` `byte` array in which the bytes read will be stored.

`count` The number of bytes to read. `0` ≤ `count` ≤ `buffer.length-offset`.

`offset` The index in `buffer` at which to start storing the bytes read. `0` ≤ `offset` < `buffer.length`.

RETURNS The first form returns the byte read. The second and third forms return the actual number of bytes read. All forms return `-1` if end-of-file is reached before any bytes are read.

EXCEPTIONS

`ArrayIndexOutOfBoundsException`
If `count` or `offset` is outside of the specified bounds.

`IOException`
If an IO error occurred.

SEE ALSO `mark()`, `reset()`, `skip()`.

EXAMPLE See the class example and `mark()`.

reset()

PURPOSE Resets the current read position to the last marked position.

SYNTAX `public synchronized void reset() throws IOException`

DESCRIPTION This method resets the current read position of this input stream to the last marked position. Subsequent invocations of `read()`/`skip()` will begin getting input from this marked position. The default implementation of `reset()` simply throws an `IOException`.

EXCEPTIONS

`IOException`
If the stream has not been marked or if the mark has been invalidated.

SEE ALSO `mark()`, `markSupported()`.

EXAMPLE See `mark()`.

skip()

PURPOSE Skips bytes from this input stream.

SYNTAX `public long skip(long count) throws IOException`

DESCRIPTION This method skips `count` number of bytes from this input stream. Skipped bytes will not be returned by subsequent `read()` calls (unless the read position has been changed using `reset()`).

The default implementation of `skip()` simply reads `count` number of bytes into a temporary buffer. This process is not efficient because a buffer must be allocated to store the bytes and the bytes need to be copied from this input stream to the buffer. Although `count` is a `long`, it is cast to an `int` when the temporary buffer is allocated. This method should be overridden by subclasses of `InputStream`.

PARAMETERS

`count` The number of bytes to skip.

RETURNS The actual number of bytes skipped.

EXCEPTIONS

`IOException`

If an IO error occurred.

EXAMPLE This example prints every other byte in the input stream.

```
static protected void skippy(InputStream in)
{
    try {
        int c;
        while ((c = in.read()) > -1) {
            System.out.print((char)c);
            if (in.skip(1) == 0)
                break;
        }
    } catch (IOException e) {
        e.printStackTrace();
    }
}
```

InputStreamReader

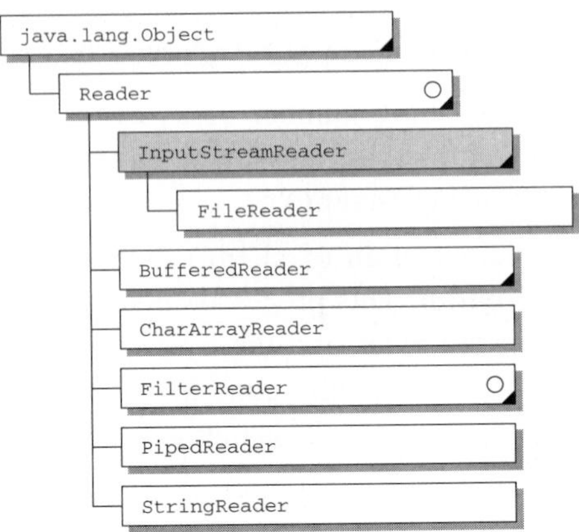

Syntax

```
public class InputStreamReader extends Reader
```

Description

The `InputStreamReader` class is used to convert a byte input stream into a character input stream.

Usage

You use an input stream reader by first creating an instance of it for a byte input stream. You then can read from the input stream reader using the `Reader` methods. See Figure 62.

The following example reads bytes from a file in UTF-8 format. The bytes are translated into Unicode characters using the converter corresponding to the "UTF8" encoding identifier.

```
InputStreamReader in = new InputStreamReader(
    new FileInputStream("inputfile", "UTF8"));
char[] buf = ...;
in.read(buf);
```

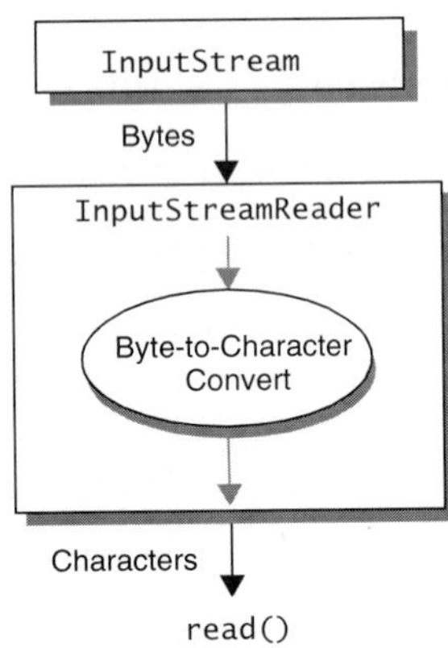

FIGURE 62: `InputStreamReader`.

Specifying the Byte Encoding to Use

The conversion of a sequence of bytes into Unicode characters is determined by the encoding specified implicitly or explicitly when the input stream reader is created. When you create the input stream reader, you specify the byte encoding using an *encoding identifier*. The encoding identifier is used to select the byte-to-character converter. See `String.String()` for a description of the encoding identifiers.

Instead of explicitly specifying an encoding, you also can omit the encoding identifier, in which case the input stream reader will use the platform-dependent default encoding. In the JDK 1.1, this default encoding is identified by the `file.encoding` system property. If this system property is not defined, the default encoding identifier is "8859_1" (ISO-Latin-1). If the converter (class) for the default encoding identifier is not found, an ASCII encoding is used.

Mechanics of the Character-to-Byte Conversion

The input stream reader reads bytes into a large internal buffer (8,192 bytes). As characters are requested from the reader (via the `read()` or `skip()` methods), the bytes are converted into Unicode characters. The encoding may consume 1 or more bytes to produce a single Unicode character.

Each time a character or a number of characters are read from the input stream reader, the conversion takes place. It is usually more efficient for a converter to convert a large sequence of bytes than a large number of small sequences. To avoid having the application worry about how many characters to read to an input stream reader in order to be more efficient, you can use a `BufferedReader` as a filter reader for `InputStreamReader`.

MEMBER SUMMARY

Constructor	
`InputStreamReader()`	Constructs an instance of `InputStreamReader`.
Input Method	
`read()`	Reads one or more characters from this reader.
Stream Methods	
`close()`	Closes this reader.
`ready()`	Determines whether this reader can be read without being blocked.
Character Encoding Method	
`getEncoding()`	Retrieves the string that identifies the encoding used for this reader.

See Also

`BufferedReader`, `InputStream`, `OutputStreamWriter`, `Reader`, `java.lang.String.String()`.

A B C D E F G H I J K L M N O P Q R S T U V W X Y Z

Example

This example reads a file with bytes encoded using UTF-8 and converts the bytes into a Unicode character string. The resulting string is displayed in a window. See Figure 63.

The input file was produced by the `Writer` class example. It contains the UTF-8 encoding for the two Unicode characters `\u597d` and `\u5929`.

FIGURE 63:
Reading UTF-8 from a File.

```
import java.io.*;
import java.awt.*;

class Main {
    public static void main(String[] args) {
        if (args.length != 1) {
            System.err.println(
                "Usage: java Main <input>");
            System.exit(-1);
        }
        try {
            Reader in = new BufferedReader(
                new InputStreamReader(new FileInputStream(args[0]), "UTF8"));

            StringBuffer buf = new StringBuffer();
            int ch;
            while ((ch = in.read()) > -1) {
                buf.append((char)ch);
            }
            in.close();
            new StringWin(buf.toString());
        } catch (IOException e) {
            e.printStackTrace();
        }
    }
}

class StringWin extends Frame {
    FontMetrics fontM;
    String str;

    StringWin(String str) {
        this.str = str;

        Font font = new Font("Monospaced", Font.BOLD, 72);
        fontM = getFontMetrics(font);
        setFont(font);

        // Calculate total width.
        int size = 0;
        for (int i = 0; i<str.length(); i++) {
            size += fontM.charWidth(str.charAt(i));
        }
        size += 2;

        // Set bounds and show.
        setSize(size, fontM.getHeight()+20);
        setLocation(getSize().width/2, getSize().height/2);
        show();
```

```
        }

        public void paint(Graphics g) {
            Insets insets = getInsets();
            int x = insets.left, y = insets.top;
            g.drawString(str, x, y+fontM.getAscent());
        }
    }
```


close()

PURPOSE Closes this reader.

SYNTAX `public void close() throws IOException`

DESCRIPTION This method closes this reader. It closes the input stream that it reads from and releases the resources—the converter and the buffer—used for byte-to-character conversions. Once this reader has been closed, you can no longer read from it or get its encoding.

This method is idempotent. That is, you can invoke it many times, but only the first invocation has any effect.

EXCEPTIONS

`IOException`

If an IO error occurs while closing this reader.

EXAMPLE See the class example.

getEncoding()

PURPOSE Retrieves the string that identifies the encoding used for this reader.

SYNTAX `public String getEncoding()`

DESCRIPTION When this reader was created, either it was created with an encoding identifier that specified the converter to use or the encoding was unspecified and the default was used (see the class description). The encoding identifier determines how bytes read from the underlying input stream are converted to characters that are returned by the `read()` method of this reader. See `String.String()` for details on this encoding identifier.

This method returns the string that identifies the encoding scheme being used for this reader.

RETURNS The possibly `null` string identifying the encoding being used by this reader. It is `null` if this reader has been closed.

SEE ALSO `java.lang.String.String()`.

EXAMPLE This example prints out the encoding for two input stream readers. One is created using an encoding identifier of "UTF8", and the other is created without an encoding identifier's being explicitly specified.

```
import java.io.*;

class Main {
    public static void main(String[] args) {
        if (args.length != 1) {
            System.err.println("Usage: java Main <input>");
            System.exit(-1);
        }
        try {
            InputStreamReader in1 =
                new InputStreamReader(new FileInputStream(args[0]), "UTF8");
            InputStreamReader in2 = new InputStreamReader(System.in);

            System.out.println("in1 encoding: " + in1.getEncoding()); // UTF8
            System.out.println("in2 encoding: " + in2.getEncoding()); // 8859_1
            in1.close();
            in2.close();
        } catch (IOException e) {
            e.printStackTrace();
        }
    }
}
```

InputStreamReader()

PURPOSE Constructs an instance of `InputStreamReader`.

SYNTAX
```
public InputStreamReader(InputStream in)
public InputStreamReader(InputStream in, String enc) throws
    UnsupportedEncodingException
```

DESCRIPTION There are two forms of the constructor for `InputStreamReader`. The first form constructs an instance of `InputStreamReader` that reads bytes from the input stream `in` and converts the bytes into characters using the default byte-to-character encoding (see the class description).

The second form uses the converter specified by `enc` to convert bytes read from `in` into characters. `enc` is a string that identifies the encoding scheme. See `String.String()` for more details on the acceptable values for this string.

PARAMETERS

`enc` The non-`null` string identifying the encoding to use when converting bytes read from `in` into characters.

`in` The non-`null` input stream from which to read.

EXCEPTIONS

`UnsupportedEncodingException`
If the encoding scheme specified by `enc` is not supported

SEE ALSO `java.lang.String.String()`.

EXAMPLE See the class example, `getEncoding()`.

A B C D E F G H I J K L M N O P Q R S T U V W X Y Z

read()

PURPOSE Reads one or more characters from this reader.

SYNTAX

```
public int read() throws IOException
public int read(char buf[], int offset, int count) throws
    IOException
```

DESCRIPTION This method reads characters from this reader. The first form reads one or more bytes from the underlying input stream and converts them into a Unicode character to be returned. Only the low-order 2 bytes of the `int` returned are used; the high-order 2 bytes are set to `0`. If end-of-stream is reached before any bytes are read, `-1` is returned.

The second form reads bytes from the input stream `in` and converts them into Unicode characters. It stores at most `count` number of such characters in the buffer `buf` starting at position `offset`. If end-of-stream is reached on the underlying byte input stream before any bytes are read, `-1` is returned.

The bytes read from the byte input stream are converted into characters using the encoding scheme specified (explicit or otherwise) in the constructor.

PARAMETERS

`buf` The non-`null` `char` array in which to store the characters read.
`count` The number of characters to read. `0` ≤ `count` ≤ `buf.length-offset`.
`offset` The index in `buf` at which to start storing the characters read. `0` ≤ `offset` < `buf.length`.

RETURNS The first form returns the character read. The second form returns the number of characters read. Both forms return `-1` if end-of-stream is reached before any characters are read.

EXCEPTIONS

`ArrayIndexOutOfBoundsException`
If `count` or `offset` is outside of the specified bounds.

`IOException`
If an IO error was encountered or the bytes read could not be converted into Unicode characters.

`InternalError`
If the byte-to-character converter malfunctions.

OVERRIDES `Reader.read()`.

EXAMPLE See the class example.

A B C D E F G H I J K L M N O P Q R S T U V W X Y Z

ready()

PURPOSE Determines whether this reader can be read without being blocked.

SYNTAX `public boolean ready() throws IOException`

DESCRIPTION This method returns `true` if there are bytes that this reader has read but not yet converted to characters. It also returns `true` is the input stream from which it is reading is ready to be read without being blocked.

Note: In Java 1.1.4, `ready()` returns `false` when end-of-stream is reached, even though the next `read()` will not block (it will return `-1`). This is a bug.

RETURNS `true` if this reader is ready to be read without being blocked.

EXCEPTIONS

`IOException`

If an IO error occurs while determining whether the stream that this read reads from is ready.

OVERRIDES `Reader.ready()`.

EXAMPLE See `Reader.ready()`.

InstantiationError

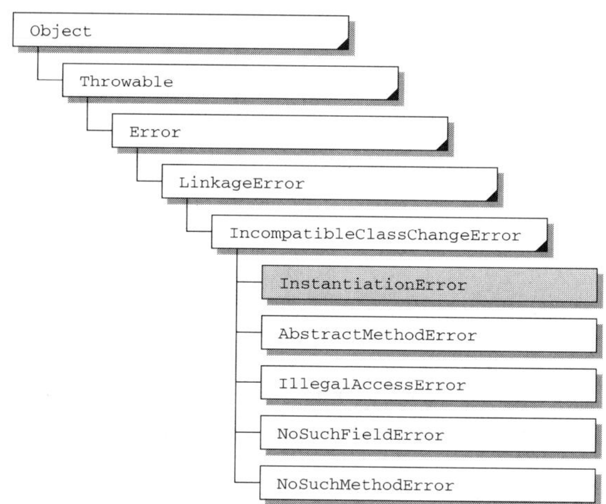

Syntax

`public class InstantiationError extends IncompatibleClassChangeError`

Description

`InstantiationError` is a runtime linkage error that is raised when the program attempts to instantiate an abstract class or an interface.

Normally, when you compile a program that attempts to invoke an abstract method, you get a compilation error pinpointing the problem so that a linkage error at runtime will not occur. However, the problem could be introduced when classes used by the program become inconsistent, for example if you were to make an incompatible change and then recompile only some of the classes.

`InstantiationError` and `InstantiationException` both report the same error; namely, that the class being instantiated is either an abstract class or an interface. They differ in that `InstantiationError` is thrown by the Java virtual machine when it detects this error when executing the program. In contrast, `InstantiationException` is thrown when the program explicitly attempts to instantiate an object and fails (e.g., via `Class.newInstance()`).

`InstantiationError` should not be caught or declared in the `throws` clause of a method.

MEMBER SUMMARY	
Constructor	
`InstantiationError()`	Constructs an `InstantiationError` instance.

See Also

`IncompatibleClassChangeError`, `InstantiationException`, `LinkageError`.

Example

In this example, class `A` and `A.method1()` used to have the following definition:

A.java

```
class A {
    public void method1(int i) {
        System.out.println(i);
    }
}
```

Main.java

```
class Main {
    public static void main(String[] args) {
        System.out.println("InstantiationError example");
        A a = new A();
        a.method1(0);
    }
}
```

Running `Main` after changing `A` as follows would throw `InstantiationError` because the Java runtime cannot instantiate an abstract method:

Modified A.java

```
abstract class A {
    abstract public void method1(int i);
}
```

InstantiationError()

PURPOSE	Constructs an `InstantiationError` instance.
SYNTAX	`public InstantiationError()` `public InstantiationError(String msg)`
DESCRIPTION	The two forms of this constructor construct an instance of `InstantiationError`. An optional string `msg` can be supplied that describes this particular instance of the error. If `msg` is not supplied, it defaults to `null`.
PARAMETERS	
`msg`	A possibly `null` string that gives details about this error.
SEE ALSO	`Throwable.getMessage()`.

InstantiationException

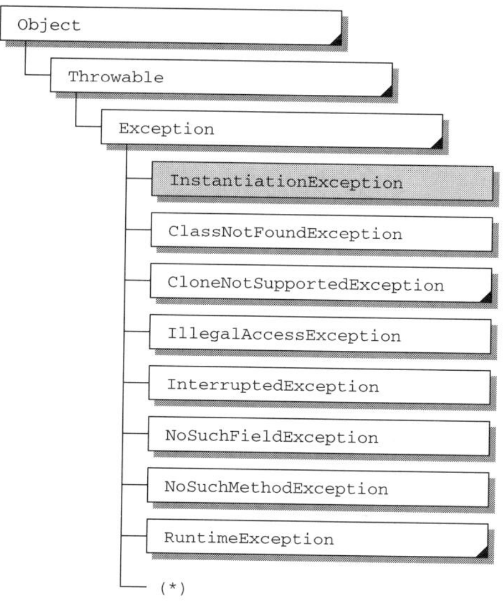

(*) 21 classes from other packages not shown.

Syntax

```
public class InstantiationException extends Exception
```

Description

`InstantiationException` is an exception that is thrown when the program attempts to instantiate an abstract class or an interface.

Normally, when you compile a program's classes, you get a compilation error pinpointing the problem. However, a program can use not only the classes with which it has been compiled, but also other classes. It also can invoke methods on them through the use of class loaders and the methods in the `Class` and reflection classes. Classes and their methods accessed in this way are checked by the Java runtime just like other classes. Hence, an `InstantiationException` can arise if one of these classes is an abstract class or an interface.

A method that throws `InstantiationException` must declare it or any of its superclasses in its `throws` clause.

MEMBER SUMMARY	
Constructor	
`InstantiationException()`	Constructs an `InstantiationException` instance.

See Also

`Class.newInstance()`, `InstantiationError`, `java.lang.reflect.Constructor.newInstance()`.

Example

In the following example, `InstantiationException` is thrown when `main()` attempts to invoke `newInstance()` on `A` because `A` is an interface:

Main.java

```
class Main {
    public static void main(String[] args) {
        System.out.println("InstantiationException example");
        try {
            Class c = Class.forName("A");
            Object a = c.newInstance();
        } catch (InstantiationException e) {
            e.printStackTrace();
        } catch (IllegalAccessException e) {
            e.printStackTrace();
        } catch (ClassNotFoundException e) {
            e.printStackTrace();
        }
    }
}
```

A.java

```
interface A {
    void methodX();
}
```

InstantiationException()

PURPOSE Constructs an `InstantiationException` instance.

SYNTAX
```
public InstantiationException()
public InstantiationException(String msg)
```

DESCRIPTION The two forms of this constructor construct an instance of `InstantiationException`. An optional string `msg` can be supplied that describes this particular instance of the exception. If `msg` is not supplied, it defaults to `null`.

PARAMETERS

`msg` A possibly `null` string that gives details about this exception.

SEE ALSO `Throwable.getMessage()`.

A B C D E F G H I J K L M N O P Q R S T U V W X Y Z

Integer

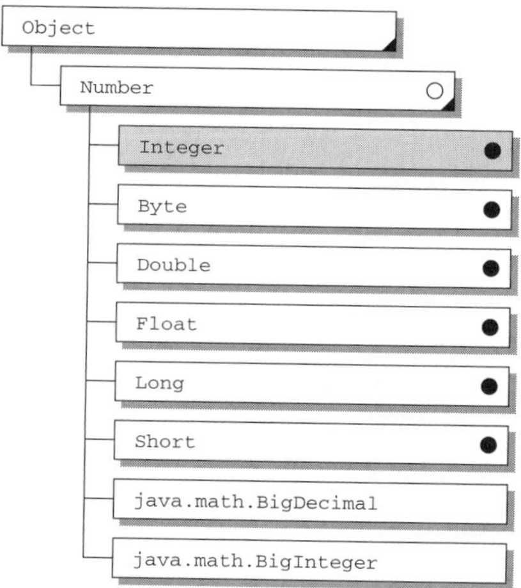

A B C D E F G H I J K L M N O P Q R S T U V W X Y Z

Syntax

```
public final class Integer extends Number
```

Description

An `int` in Java is a 32-bit signed integer. The `Integer` class provides an object wrapper for `int` data values. Doing this allows integers to be passed to methods in Java class libraries that accept Java objects as parameters. In addition, the `Integer` class provides methods that convert values to and from `int` values and perform other operations on `int` values.

Usage

`Integer` instances cannot be used in arithmetic expressions in place of `int`. For example, the following is not allowed:

```
Integer i1 = new Integer(50);
Integer i2 = new Integer(100);
Integer i3 = i1 * i2;       // Illegal
```

To perform arithmetic operations using an `Integer` instance, you first must use access methods defined in the `Integer` class to obtain its numeric value, as follows:

```
int i3 = i1.intValue() * i2.intValue();
long lnum = i1.longValue() + i2.intValue();
```

MEMBER SUMMARY	
Constructor	
`Integer()`	Constructs an `Integer` instance using an `int` value or a string.
Constant Fields	
`MAX_VALUE`	The maximum value an `int` can have.
`MIN_VALUE`	The minimum value an `int` can have.
`TYPE`	The `Class` object representing the primitive type `int`.
Number Methods	
`byteValue()`	Retrieves the value of this object as a `byte`.
`doubleValue()`	Retrieves the value of this object as a `double`.
`floatValue()`	Retrieves the value of this object as a `float`.
`intValue()`	Retrieves the value of this object as an `int`.
`longValue()`	Retrieves the value of this object as a `long`.
`shortValue()`	Retrieves the value of this object as a `short`.
Conversion Methods	
`decode()`	Parses the string representation of a 16-bit signed integer into an `Integer`.
`getInteger()`	Creates an `Integer` instance using the value of a system property.
`parseInt()`	Parses a string representation of an integer into an `int`.
`toBinaryString()`	Generates the string representation of an `int` as an unsigned binary number.
`toHexString()`	Generates the string representation of an `int` as an unsigned hexadecimal number.
`toOctalString()`	Generates the string representation of an `int` as an unsigned octal number.
`toString()`	Generates the string representation for an `int` or `Integer` instance.
`valueOf()`	Creates a new `Integer` instance using its string representation.
Object Methods	
`equals()`	Compares this object with another object for equality.
`hashCode()`	Computes the hash code for this object.

See Also

`Byte`, `Double`, `Float`, `Long`, `Number`, `Short`.

byteValue()

PURPOSE Retrieves the value of this object as a `byte`.

SYNTAX `public byte byteValue()`

DESCRIPTION This method retrieves the value of this object as a `byte` by casting its `int` value to a `byte` value.

RETURNS The value of this object as a `byte`.

SEE ALSO `doubleValue()`, `floatValue()`, `intValue()`, `longValue()`, `Number`, `shortValue()`.

EXAMPLE See `doubleValue()`.

decode()

PURPOSE Parses the string representation of a 32-bit signed integer into an `int`.

SYNTAX `public static Integer decode(String str) throws NumberFormatException`

DESCRIPTION The string may be in hexadecimal format (with a `0x` or `#` prefix), in octal format (with a zero character (`0`) prefix), or in decimal format (radix 10 digits preceded by an optional negative character (–)).

`decode()` is similar to `valueOf()`, except that `valueOf()` accepts a radix argument to determine the radix, while `decode()` examines the string's format in order to determine the radix. `decode()` also is similar to `parseInt()`, except that `parseInt()` returns an `int`, while `decode()` returns an `Integer` object and examines the string's format in order to determine the radix.

PARAMETERS

`str` The non-`null` string to parse.

EXCEPTIONS

`NumberFormatException`

If `str` cannot be parsed into a 32-bit signed integer of the specified radix.

SEE ALSO `Integer()`, `parseInt()`, `valueOf()`.

EXAMPLE This example uses `decode()` to convert some strings into `Integer` objects.

```
class Main {
    public static void main(String[] args) {
        try {
            Integer i_dec = Integer.decode("225");
            Integer i_oct = Integer.decode("065");      // octal
            Integer i_hex1 = Integer.decode("0x1f");    // hex
            Integer i_hex2 = Integer.decode("#1e");     // hex
```

```
            // Integer i_big = Integer.decode("1234123455555");// ERROR: too big

             System.out.println("parsed: " +
                 i_dec + "," + i_oct + "," + i_hex1 + ","  + i_hex2);
         } catch (NumberFormatException e) {
             e.printStackTrace();
         }
     }
 }
```


doubleValue()

PURPOSE Retrieves the value of this object as a `double`.

SYNTAX `public double doubleValue()`

DESCRIPTION This method retrieves the value of this object as a `double` by casting its `int` value to a `double` value.

RETURNS The value of this object as a `double`.

SEE ALSO `byteValue()`, `floatValue()`, `intValue()`, `longValue()`, `Number`, `shortValue()`.

EXAMPLE

```
Integer iobj = new Integer(855);

double dval = iobj.doubleValue(); // 855.0
float fval = iobj.floatValue();   // 855.0
int ival = iobj.intValue();       // 855
long lval = iobj.longValue();     // 855
byte bval = iobj.byteValue();     // 87
short sval = iobj.shortValue();   // 855
```

equals()

PURPOSE Compares this object with another object for equality.

SYNTAX `public boolean equals(Object obj)`

DESCRIPTION This method compares the `int` value of this object with that of `obj`. It returns `true` if the two values are equal; it returns `false` otherwise. It also returns `false` if `obj` is `null` or is not an `Integer` object.

PARAMETERS

`obj` The possibly `null` object against which this object will be compared.

RETURNS `true` if `obj` has the same `int` value as this object; `false` otherwise.

OVERRIDES `Object.equals()`.

SEE ALSO `hashCode()`.

EXAMPLE

```
Integer i1 = new Integer(192);
Integer i2 = new Integer(192);

// Check whether the value of two Integers are equal
if (i1.equals(i2))
    System.out.println("equal");
```

A B C D E F G H I J K L M N O P Q R S T U V W X Y Z

floatValue()

PURPOSE Retrieves the value of this object as a `float`.

SYNTAX `public float floatValue()`

DESCRIPTION This method returns the value of this object as a `float` by casting its `int` value to a `float` value.

RETURNS The value of this object as a `float`.

SEE ALSO `byteValue()`, `doubleValue()`, `intValue()`, `longValue()`, `Number`, `shortValue()`.

EXAMPLE See `doubleValue()`.

getInteger()

PURPOSE Creates an `Integer` object using the value of a system property.

SYNTAX

```
public static Integer getInteger(String prop)
public static Integer getInteger(String prop, int defval)
public static Integer getInteger(String prop, Integer defobj)
```

DESCRIPTION The three forms of this method find the system property identified by `prop` and return the property's value as an `Integer` object. The property's value must be an integer (in radix 10), a hexadecimal number, or an octal number. A hexadecimal number is prefixed with either `0x` or `#`. An octal number has a leading zero (`0`). If `prop` does not exist or if `prop`'s value is not a number in the format described here, the first form of this method returns `null`. In the same situation, the second form returns an `Integer` object constructed using `defval`, while the third form returns `defobj`.

PARAMETERS

`defobj` The possibly `null` default `Integer` object to return if `prop` does not exist.

`defval` The default `int` value to use for the resulting `Integer` object if `prop` does not exist.

`prop` The non-`null` string containing the name of the property.

RETURNS An `Integer` object containing the value of `prop` if it contains a valid integer. Otherwise, returns either `null` if the first form of the method is used or a default `Integer` object as determined by `defval` or `defobj`.

SEE ALSO `decode()`, `java.util.Properties`, `System.getProperty()`.

EXAMPLE

```
// set up properties
Properties props = System.getProperties();
props.put("os.maxusers", "250");     // radix 10 int property
props.put("os.maxfiles", "0xff");    // radix 16 int property
props.put("os.maxprinters", "#2a"); // radix 16 int property
props.put("os.maxfd", "065");        // radix 8 int property
props.put("os.version", "2.5.1");    // non-int property
System.setProperties(props);

// use the three forms of getInteger()
Integer maxusers = Integer.getInteger("os.maxusers");
Integer maxfiles = Integer.getInteger("os.maxfiles", 1024);
Integer maxprs = Integer.getInteger("os.maxprinters",
                                    new Integer(1));
Integer maxfd = Integer.getInteger("os.maxfd", 256);
Integer vers = Integer.getInteger("os.version", 1);
if (maxusers != null)
    System.out.println("max users: " + maxusers);
System.out.println("max files: " + maxfiles);
System.out.println("max printers: " + maxprs);
System.out.println("max fds: " + maxfd);
System.out.println("os version: " + vers);
```

hashCode()

PURPOSE Computes the hash code for this object.

SYNTAX `public int hashCode()`

DESCRIPTION This method returns the hash code for this `Integer` object. The code is calculated by using its `int` value. Two `Integers` with the same `int` value will have the same hash code and vice versa.

RETURNS An `int` representing the hash code.

OVERRIDES `Object.hashCode()`.

SEE ALSO `equals()`, `java.util.Hashtable`.

EXAMPLE

```
Integer inum = new Integer(3290);
int hashval = inum.hashCode();          // generate hash code
++hits[Math.abs(hashval%tabsize)];      // count hits
```

Integer()

PURPOSE — Constructs an `Integer` object using an `int` value or a string.

SYNTAX

```
public Integer(int value)
public Integer(String str) throws NumberFormatException
```

DESCRIPTION — The first form of this constructor constructs an `Integer` object using `value`. The second form parses `str`—the string representation of an integer in radix 10—and uses its numeric value to create the `Integer` object. The syntax of the string expected in `str` is the same as that used for `parseInt()`.

PARAMETERS

`str` — The non-`null` string representation of an integer in radix 10.

`value` — The numeric value to use as the object's value.

EXCEPTIONS

`NumberFormatException` — If `str` cannot be parsed into an `int`.

SEE ALSO — `decode()`, `parseInt()`, `valueOf()`.

EXAMPLE

```
Integer width = new Integer(240);         // using integer
try {
    Integer height = new Integer("360"); // using string
    int area = width.intValue() * height.intValue();
} catch (NumberFormatException e) {
  ...
}
```

intValue()

PURPOSE — Retrieves the value of this object as an `int`.

SYNTAX — `public int intValue()`

DESCRIPTION — This method retrieves the value of this object as an `int`.

RETURNS — The value of this object as an `int`.

SEE ALSO — `byteValue()`, `doubleValue()`, `floatValue()`, `longValue()`, `Number`, `shortValue()`.

EXAMPLE — See `doubleValue()`.

longValue()

PURPOSE Retrieves the value of this object as a `long`.

SYNTAX `public long longValue()`

DESCRIPTION This method returns the value of this object as a `long` value by casting its `int` value into a `long`.

RETURNS The value of this object as a `long`.

SEE ALSO `byteValue()`, `doubleValue()`, `floatValue()`, `intValue()`, `Number`, `shortValue()`.

EXAMPLE See `doubleValue()`.

MAX_VALUE

PURPOSE The maximum value an `int` can have.

SYNTAX `public static final int MAX_VALUE`

DESCRIPTION This constant represents the maximum value an `int` can have, which is `0x7fffffff`.

SEE ALSO `MIN_VALUE`.

EXAMPLE

```
// test if number is less than MAX_VALUE
int inum = 512;
if (inum < Integer.MAX_VALUE)
    inum += 16344;
```

MIN_VALUE

PURPOSE The minimum value an `int` can have.

SYNTAX `public static final int MIN_VALUE`

DESCRIPTION This constant represents the minimum value an `int` can have, which is `0x80000000`. This is a negative number.

SEE ALSO `MAX_VALUE`.

EXAMPLE

```
// test if number is greater than MIN_VALUE
int inum = -512;
if (inum > Integer.MIN_VALUE)
    inum *= 100;
```

parseInt()

PURPOSE
Parses the string representation of an integer into an `int`.

SYNTAX
```
public static int parseInt(String str) throws
    NumberFormatException
public static int parseInt(String str, int radix) throws
    NumberFormatException
```

DESCRIPTION
This method parses the string `str` into an integer and returns it as an `int`. If no radix is given, the radix used to parse `str` is 10. A negative integer has a leading negative (–) character; a positive integer consists only of digits in the specified radix.

`parseInt()` is similar to `valueOf()`, except that `parseInt()` returns an `int`, while `valueOf()` returns an `Integer` object. `parseInt()` also is similar to `decode()`, except that `decode()` returns an `Integer` object and examines the string's format in order to determine its radix. Note that strings with a `0x` or `#` prefix accepted by `decode()` are illegal in `parseInt()`, and the `0` prefix for denoting octal numbers is ignored by `parseInt()`. See the example.

PARAMETERS

`radix`
The radix to use when parsing `str`. `Character.MIN_RADIX` ≤ `radix` ≤ `Character.MAX_RADIX`.

`str`
The non-`null` string containing the integer.

RETURNS
An `int` containing the numeric value of the integer represented by `str`.

EXCEPTIONS

`NumberFormatException`
If `str` cannot be parsed into an integer of the specified radix.

SEE ALSO
`Character.MAX_RADIX`, `Character.MIN_RADIX`, `decode()`, `toString()`, `valueOf()`.

EXAMPLE
This example uses `parseInt()` to convert strings into `int`s. Note that octal strings acceptable to `decode()` are treated as decimal strings here and hexadecimal strings acceptable to `decode()` throw `NumberFormatException`.

```
class Main {
    public static void main(String[] args) {
        try {
            int i_dec = Integer.parseInt("25");           // decimal
            int i_oct = Integer.parseInt("65", 8);        // octal
            int i_hex1 = Integer.parseInt("1f", 16);      // hex
            int i_hex2 = Integer.parseInt("1e", 16);      // hex
            int i_oct2 = Integer.parseInt("033");         // leading 0 ignored
            // int i_hex3 = Integer.parseInt("0x1e");     // ERROR: format
            // int i_hex4 = Integer.parseInt("0x1e", 16);// ERROR: format

            System.out.println("parsed: " + i_dec + "," + i_oct + "," + i_hex1
                        + ","  + i_hex2 + "," + i_oct2);
```

```
            } catch (NumberFormatException e) {
                e.printStackTrace();
            }
        }
    }
```


shortValue()

PURPOSE Retrieves the value of this object as a `short`.

SYNTAX `public short shortValue()`

DESCRIPTION This method returns the value of this object as a `short` value by casting its `int` value into a `short`.

RETURNS The value of this object as a `short`.

SEE ALSO `byteValue()`, `doubleValue()`, `floatValue()`, `intValue()`, `Number`, `longValue()`.

EXAMPLE See `doubleValue()`.

toBinaryString()

PURPOSE Generates the string representation of an `int` as an unsigned binary number.

SYNTAX `public static String toBinaryString(int inum)`

DESCRIPTION This method returns the string representation of `inum` as an unsigned binary number (base 2). (Treating `inum` as an unsigned 32-bit number means that the highest-order bit is treated as `2^32` if `inum` is negative.) The string consists of digits from base 2 ("01") representing the numeric value of `inum`. If `inum` is `0`, "0" is the string representation; otherwise, leading zeros are not included in the string.

This method is equivalent to `toString(inum, 2)` only when `inum` is nonnegative. This is because `toString()` always treats `inum` as a signed number.

PARAMETERS

`inum` The `int` for which to generate the string representation.

RETURNS The non-`null` string representation of `inum` as an unsigned binary number.

SEE ALSO `parseInt()`, `toHexString()`, `toOctalString()`, `toString()`, `valueOf()`.

EXAMPLE This example shows the difference between using `toString()`, `toBinaryString()`, `toOctalString()`, and `toHexString()` on a negative number. The output of this program is shown after the code.

```
class Main {
    public static void main(String[] args) {
        int inum = -279436;
        System.out.println(Integer.toString(inum, 10));
        System.out.println(Integer.toString(inum, 2));
        System.out.println(Integer.toString(inum, 8));
        System.out.println(Integer.toString(inum, 16));

        System.out.println(Integer.toString(inum));
        System.out.println(Integer.toBinaryString(inum));
        System.out.println(Integer.toOctalString(inum));
        System.out.println(Integer.toHexString(inum));
    }
}
```

Output

```
-279436
-1000100001110001100
-1041614
-4438c
-279436
11111111111110111011110001110100
37776736164
fffbbc74
```


toHexString()

PURPOSE
: Generates the string representation of an `int` as an unsigned hexadecimal number.

SYNTAX
: `public static String toHexString(int inum)`

DESCRIPTION
: This method returns the string representation of `inum` as an unsigned hexadecimal number (radix 16). (Treating `inum` as an unsigned 32-bit number means that the highest-order bit is treated as `2^32` if `inum` is negative.) The string consists of digits from base 16 ("0123456789abcdef") representing the numeric value of `inum`. If `inum` is `0`, "0" is the string representation; otherwise, leading zeros are not included in the string.

This method is equivalent to `toString(inum, 16)` only when `lnum` is nonnegative. This is because `toString()` always treats `inum` as a signed number.

PARAMETERS

`inum`
: The `int` for which to generate the string representation.

RETURNS
: The non-`null` string representation of `inum` as an unsigned hexadecimal number.

SEE ALSO
: `parseInt()`, `toBinaryString()`, `toOctalString()`, `toString()`, `valueOf()`.

EXAMPLE
: See `toBinaryString()`.

toOctalString()

PURPOSE Generates the string representation of an `int` as an unsigned octal number.

SYNTAX `public static String toOctalString(int inum)`

DESCRIPTION This method returns the string representation of `inum` as an unsigned octal number (radix 8). (Treating `inum` as an unsigned 32-bit number means that the highest-order bit is treated as `2^32` if `inum` is negative.) The string consists of digits from base 8 ("01234567") representing the numeric value of `inum`. If `inum` is `0`, "0" is the string representation; otherwise, leading zeros are not included in the string.

This method is equivalent to `toString(inum, 8)` only when `inum` is nonnegative. This is because `toString()` always treats `inum` as a signed number.

PARAMETERS

`inum` The `int` for which to generate the string representation.

RETURNS The non-`null` string representation of `inum` as an unsigned octal number.

SEE ALSO `parseInt()`, `toBinaryString()`, `toHexString()`, `toString()`, `valueOf()`.

EXAMPLE See `toBinaryString()`.

toString()

PURPOSE Generates the string representation of an `int` or `Integer` object.

SYNTAX

```
public String toString()
public static String toString(int inum)
public static String toString(int inum, int radix)
```

DESCRIPTION The three forms of this method are used to generate a string representation of an `int`. The first form returns the string representation of the `int` value of this `Integer` object. The second form returns the string representation of `inum` in radix 10. The third form returns the string representation of `inum` in base `radix`.

The string consists of digits from the specified radix representing the numeric value of the number. If the number is negative, a leading negative sign (–) precedes the digits.

PARAMETERS

`inum` The `int` for which to generate the string representation.

`radix` The radix to use when generating the string representation. `Character.MIN_RADIX ≤ radix ≤ Character.MAX_RADIX`. If `radix` is outside this range, it defaults to 10.

RETURNS The non-`null` string representation of this `Integer` object, or `inum`.

OVERRIDES `Object.toString()`.

SEE ALSO `Character.MAX_RADIX`, `Character.MIN_RADIX`, `Integer.valueOf()`, `String.valueOf()`.

EXAMPLE See `toBinaryString()`.

TYPE

PURPOSE The `Class` object representing the primitive type `int`.

SYNTAX `public static final Class TYPE`

DESCRIPTION This constant can be used where the `Class` object—`int.class`—of the primitive type `int` is required, such as for reflection. Although there are no restrictions on the use of `Integer.TYPE`, the preferred syntax for naming the class is `int.class`.

SEE ALSO `Class`.

EXAMPLE

```
public static void main(String[] args) {
    Class c = Integer.TYPE;
    System.out.println("TYPE: " + c);
    System.out.println("isPrimitive: " + c.isPrimitive());
    System.out.println("superclass: " + c.getSuperclass());
    try {
        Object obj = c.newInstance();  // ERROR
        System.out.println("int: " + obj);
    } catch (InstantiationException e) {
        e.printStackTrace();
    } catch (IllegalAccessException e) {
        e.printStackTrace();
    }
}
```

valueOf()

PURPOSE Creates an `Integer` object using its string representation.

SYNTAX
```
public static Integer valueOf(String str) throws
    NumberFormatException
public static Integer valueOf(String str, int radix) throws
    NumberFormatException
```

DESCRIPTION This method parses the string `str` into an integer and return an `Integer` object constructed using the integer. If no radix is given, the radix used to parse `str` is

10. A negative integer has a leading negative (–) character; a positive integer consists only of digits in the specified radix.

`valueOf()` is similar to `parseInt()`, except that `parseInt()` returns an `int`, while `valueOf()` returns an `Integer` object. `valueOf` also is similar to `decode()`, except that `valueOf()` accepts a radix argument to determine the radix, while `decode()` examines the string's format in order to determine the radix. Note that strings with a `0x` or `#` prefix accepted by `decode()` are illegal in `valueOf()` and the `0` prefix for denoting octal numbers is ignored by `valueOf()`. See the example.

PARAMETERS

`radix` The radix to use when parsing `str`. `Character.MIN_RADIX` ≤ `radix` ≤ `Character.MAX_RADIX`.

`str` The non-`null` string containing the integer.

EXCEPTIONS

`NumberFormatException`
If `str` cannot be parsed into an integer of the specified radix.

SEE ALSO `Character.MAX_RADIX`, `Character.MIN_RADIX`, `decode()`, `parseInt()`, `toString()`.

EXAMPLE

```
class Main {
    public static void main(String[] args) {
        try {
            Integer i_dec = Integer.valueOf("25");           // decimal
            Integer i_oct = Integer.valueOf("65", 8);        // octal
            Integer i_hex1 = Integer.valueOf("1f", 16);      // hex
            Integer i_hex2 = Integer.valueOf("1e", 16);      // hex
           Integer i_oct2 = Integer.valueOf("033");         // leading 0 ignored
            // Integer i_hex3 = Integer.valueOf("0x1e");     // ERROR: format
            // Integer i_hex4 = Integer.valueOf("0x1e", 16);// ERROR: format

            System.out.println("parsed: " + i_dec + "," + i_oct + "," + i_hex1
                                   + ","  + i_hex2 + "," + i_oct2);
        } catch (NumberFormatException e) {
            e.printStackTrace();
        }
    }
}
```

InternalError

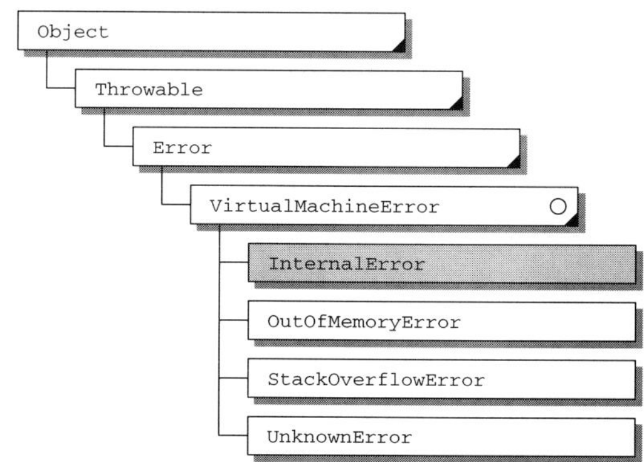

Syntax

`public class InternalError extends VirtualMachineError`

Description

`InternalError` is an error that is thrown when the Java virtual machine encounters an unrecoverable error that involves the virtual machine's internal logic (e.g., an unknown opcode).

`InternalError` should not be caught or declared in the `throws` clause of a method.

MEMBER SUMMARY	
Constructor	
`InternalError()`	Constructs an `InternalError` instance.

See Also

`Error`, `VirtualMachineError`.

InternalError()

PURPOSE Constructs an `InternalError` instance.

SYNTAX

```
public InternalError()
public InternalError(String msg)
```

DESCRIPTION This constructor constructs an instance of `InternalError`. An optional string `msg` can be supplied that describes this particular instance of the error. If `msg` is not supplied, it defaults to `null`.

PARAMETERS

`msg` A possibly `null` string that gives details about this error.

SEE ALSO `Throwable.getMessage()`.

InterruptedException

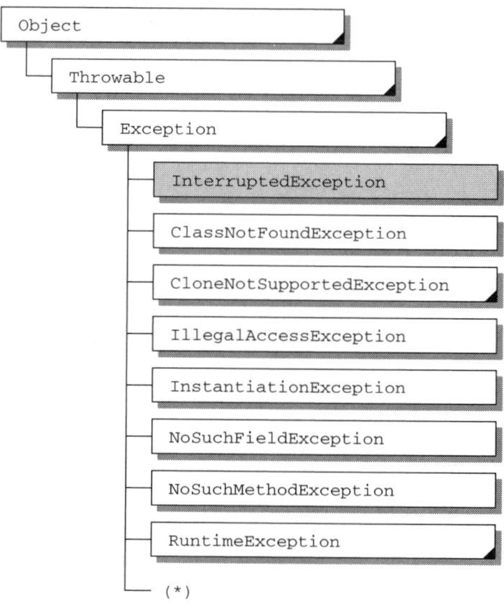

(*) 21 classes from other packages not shown.

Syntax

```
public class InterruptedException extends Exception
```

Description

`InterruptedException` is thrown when a thread interrupts another thread. Methods that cause a thread to block (such as `Object.wait()` and `Thread.sleep()`) require the thread to have a `try/catch` clause for the `InterruptedException` so that the thread can deal with its being interrupted.

A method that throws `InterruptedException` must declare it or any of its superclasses in its `throws` clause.

MEMBER SUMMARY	
Constructor	
`InterruptedException()`	Constructs an `InterruptedException` instance.

See Also

`Exception`, `Object.notify()`, `Object.notifyAll()`, `Object.wait()`, `Thread`.

Example

This example loops, printing out the message "This is a test" every 5 seconds. It must use a `try/catch` clause to catch the `InterruptedException` that might be thrown by `sleep()`.

```
class Main {
    public static void main(String[] args) {
        try {
            while (true) {
                System.out.println("This is a test");
                Thread.sleep(5000);
            }
        } catch (InterruptedException e) {
            System.out.println("Interrupted!");
        }
    }
}
```


InterruptedException()

PURPOSE Constructs an `InterruptedException` instance.

SYNTAX

```
public InterruptedException()
public InterruptedException(String msg)
```

DESCRIPTION This constructor constructs an instance of `InterruptedException`. An optional string `msg` can be supplied that describes this particular instance of the exception. If `msg` is not supplied, it defaults to `null`.

PARAMETERS

`msg` A possibly `null` string that gives details about this exception.

SEE ALSO `Throwable.getMessage()`.

java.io
InterruptedIOException

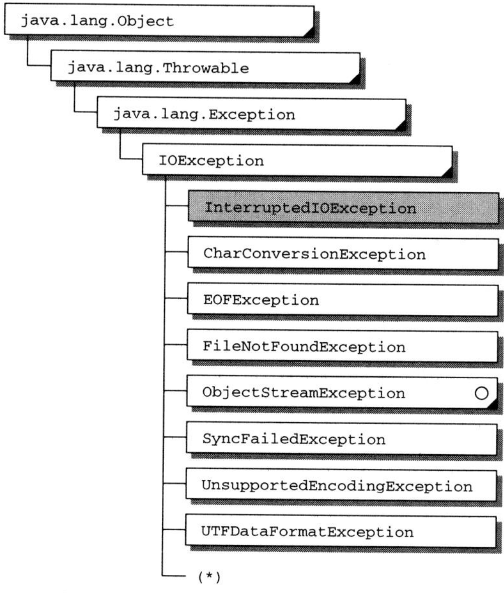

Syntax

`public class InterruptedIOException extends IOException`

Description

`InterruptedIOException` is an IO exception that is thrown when a program reading or writing to a stream receives an interrupt during its IO operation. This exception is also thrown when the socket time-out period on a datagram socket or socket expires before data is received from the socket.

A method that throws `InterruptedIOException` must declare it or any of its superclasses in the method's `throws` clause.

MEMBER SUMMARY	
Constructor	
`InterruptedIOException()`	Constructs an `InterruptedIOException` instance.
Field	
`bytesTransferred`	The number of bytes transferred before an interrupt.

See Also

`IOException`, `InterruptedException`, `java.net.DatagramSocket.receive()`, `java.net.DatagramSocketImpl.receive()`, `java.net.DatagramSocket.setSoTimeout()`, `java.net.Socket.setSoTimeout()`, `PipedInputStream`, `PrintStream`.

A B C D E F G H I J K L M N O P Q R S T U V W X Y Z

Example

This example creates a datagram socket with a time-out of 0.5 secs. It throws `InterruptedIOException` when 0.5 secs have elapsed without receiving any data from the datagram socket.

```
import java.io.*;
import java.net.*;

class Main {
    public static void main(String[] args) {
        try {
            DatagramSocket sock = new DatagramSocket(); // any port
            DatagramPacket dg = new DatagramPacket(new byte[128], 128);

            sock.setSoTimeout(500);
            sock.receive(dg);
        } catch (InterruptedIOException e) {
            System.out.println("interrupted IO: " + e);
        } catch (IOException e) {
            System.out.println(e);
        }
    }
}
```

bytesTransferred

PURPOSE The number of bytes transferred before an interrupt.

SYNTAX `public int bytesTransferred`

DESCRIPTION This field is typically set by the code that called the constructor. It is read by the code that catches `InterruptedIOException`. If not set, its default value is `0`.

InterruptedIOException()

PURPOSE Constructs an `InterruptedIOException` instance.

SYNTAX
```
public InterruptedIOException()
public InterruptedIOException(String msg)
```

DESCRIPTION The two forms of this constructor construct an instance of `InterruptedIOException`. An optional string `msg` can be supplied that describes this particular instance of the exception. If `msg` is not supplied, it defaults to `null`.

PARAMETERS

`msg` A possibly `null` string that gives details about this exception.

SEE ALSO `java.lang.Throwable.getMessage()`.

java.io
InvalidClassException

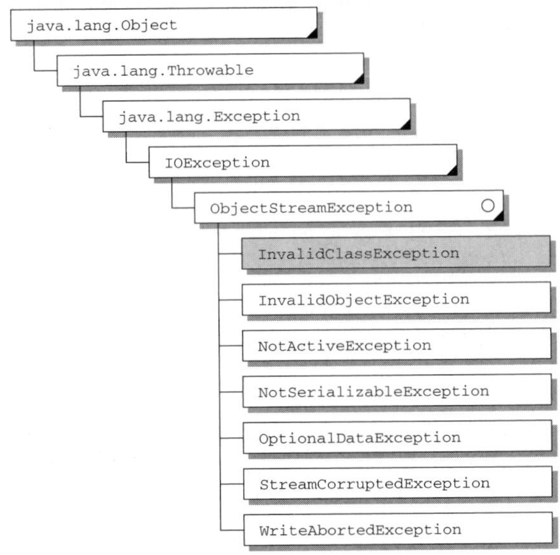

A B C D E F G H I J K L M N O P Q R S T U V W X Y Z

Syntax

```
public class InvalidClassException extends ObjectStreamException
```

Description

`InvalidClassException` is thrown when the program attempts to serialize or deserialize data from a stream and is unable to do so due to problems with the class of the object being serialized/deserialized. This exception can be thrown for one of the following reasons:

- The Stream Unique Identifier (SUID) of the class does not match that of the `Class` object loaded by the Java virtual machine.
- A serializable class's nonserializable superclass does not have an *accessible* constructor that takes no parameters or the nonserializable superclass cannot be instantiated using that constructor. The constructor is accessible if it is declared public, or protected, or has package scope and is in the same package as the subclass. See *The Java Language Specification, First Edition*, Section 6.6.1, for details on the definition of "accessible." [1]
- An externalizable class does not have a public constructor that takes no parameters or the class cannot be instantiated using that constructor.

1. In Java 1.1.4, this exception is thrown if the nonserializable superclass does not have a public constructor that takes no arguments. This is a bug.

- The program is attempting to serialize or deserialize an array of an unknown primitive type or a class with a field of an unknown primitive type.
- `ObjectInputStream.resolveClass()` was overridden such that it generated a class that does not have the same SUID and class name as that expected, or the class's implementation of the `Serializable` and `Externalizable` interfaces do not match, or the class has fields that are incompatible with those expected. In a future version of the JDK, the restriction on class name will be removed in order to support classes with different names (possibly in different packages) that are otherwise compatible..

MEMBER SUMMARY

Constructor	
`InvalidClassException()`	Constructs an instance of `InvalidClassException`.
Throwable Override Method	
`getMessage()`	Generates the detail message for this exception.

A B C D E F G H I J K L M N O P Q R S T U V W X Y Z

See Also

`ObjectInputStream.readObject()`, `ObjectOutputStream.writeObject()`.

Example

This example throws an `InvalidClassException` when `Class1` is being deserialized because `Class1`'s nonserializable superclass `Class2` does not have a constructor that takes no parameters.

```
import java.io.*;

class Main {
    public static void main(String[] args) {
        try {
            // Write object out
            FileOutputStream f = new FileOutputStream("Class1.ser");
            ObjectOutput out = new ObjectOutputStream(f);

            Class1 c1 = new Class1(10);
            out.writeObject(c1);
            out.flush();
            out.close();

            // Read it back
            FileInputStream f2 = new FileInputStream("Class1.ser");
            ObjectInputStream in = new ObjectInputStream(f2);
            Class1 cc1 = (Class1) in.readObject();
            in.close();

            System.out.println("c1.field1 " + cc1.field1);
```

```
            } catch (IOException e) {
                e.printStackTrace();
            } catch (ClassNotFoundException e) {
                e.printStackTrace();
            }
        }
    }

    class Class1 extends Class2 implements Serializable {
        int field1;
        transient int field2;

        public Class1(int ignore) {
            super(ignore);
            field1 = 10;
            field2 = -1;
        }
    }

    class Class2 {
        int field1;
        int field2;

        public Class2(int ignore) {}
    }
```

getMessage()

PURPOSE Generates the detail message for this exception.

SYNTAX `public String getMessage()`

DESCRIPTION The implementation of `Throwable.getMessage()` retrieves the detail message supplied with the constructor. This method overrides that implementation so that if a non-`null` class name was supplied with the constructor, the detail message is concatenated with the class name (separated by a semicolon character ;) and returned as the new detail message. If this exception was created with no class name or with a `null` class name, the detail message returned is the same as `Throwable.getMessage()`.

RETURNS The possibly `null` detail message of this exception. If `null`, a `null` class name and a `null` message was supplied in the exception's constructor.

OVERRIDES `java.lang.Throwable.getMessage()`.

InvalidClassException()

PURPOSE Constructs an instance of `InvalidClassException`.

SYNTAX

```
public InvalidClassException(String reason)
public InvalidClassException(String classname, String reason)
```

DESCRIPTION The two forms of this constructor construct an instance of `InvalidClassException`. The parameters of the constructor are used to create the detail message. If `classname` is not supplied, it defaults to `null`.

PARAMETERS

`classname` The string name of the class that had problems being serialized/deserialized.

`reason` A possibly `null` string describing why this exception is thrown.

SEE ALSO `getMessage()`.

java.io
InvalidObjectException

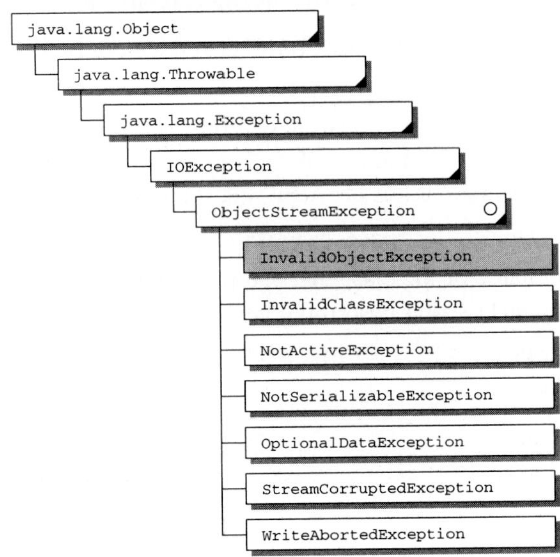

Syntax

```
public class InvalidObjectException extends ObjectStreamException
```

Description

An object's `readObject()` can call `ObjectInputStream.registerValidation()` to register a *validator* object to validate the object when it is deserialized. `readObject()` can register zero or more validators. The definition of whether an object is *valid* is determined by the validators. The `validateObject()` method of each validator is called in turn to validate the object. When a validator determines that the object is not valid, it throws an `InvalidObjectException`.

MEMBER SUMMARY<	
Constructor	
`InvalidObjectException()`	Constructs an instance of `InvalidObjectException`.

See Also

`ObjectInputStream.registerValidation()`, `ObjectInputValidation.validateObject()`.

Example

See `ObjectInputValidation`.

InvalidObjectException()

PURPOSE Constructs an instance of `InvalidObjectException`.

SYNTAX `public InvalidObjectException(String msg)`

DESCRIPTION This constructor constructs an instance of `InvalidObjectException` with an explanation `msg` of why the validation of the object failed.

PARAMETERS

`msg` A possibly `null` string describing why the validation failed.

SEE ALSO `java.lang.Throwable.getMessage()`.

java.lang.reflect
InvocationTargetException

A B C D E F G H I J K L M N O P Q R S T U V W X Y Z

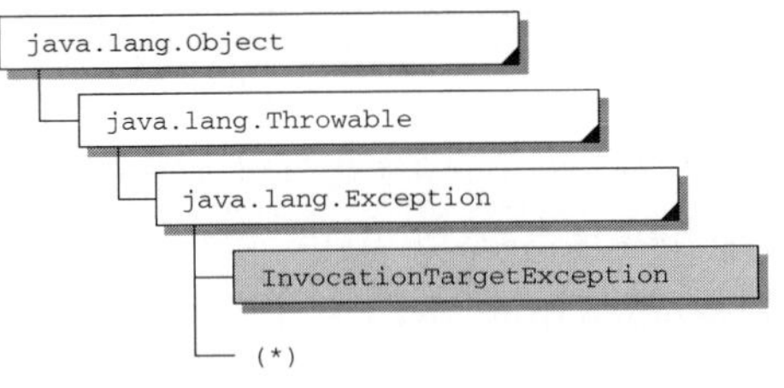

(*) 28 classes from other packages not shown.

Syntax

`public class InvocationTargetException extends Exception`

Description

`InvocationTargetException` is a wrapper for an exception which is produced by a *target* object in response to the invocation of a method or constructor. `InvocationTargetException` is thrown by `Method.invoke()` and `Constructor.newInstance()` when the invoked method or constructor throws an exception. This original exception can be retrieved from the `InvocationTargetException` by calling `getTargetException()`.

MEMBER SUMMARY	
Constructor	
`InvocationTargetException()`	Constructs an `InvocationTargetException` instance.
Wrapped Exception Method	
`getTargetException()`	Retrieves the exception wrapped by this `InvocationTargetException` instance.

See Also

`Method.invoke()`, `Constructor.newInstance()`.

Example

This example is a simple demonstration of how an `InvocationTargetException` can be thrown. Both the method and constructor throw an `IllegalArgumentException` when invoked. When the caller catches the `InvocationTargetException`, it can retrieve the original `IllegalArgumentException` by calling `getTargetException()`.

```
import java.lang.reflect.*;

class Main {
    Main() throws IllegalArgumentException {
        throw new IllegalArgumentException("not implemented yet");
    }
    static void m() throws IllegalArgumentException {
        throw new IllegalArgumentException("out to lunch");
    }

    public static void main(String[] args) {
        try {
            // Create the constructor object and create a new object.
            try {
                Constructor con =
                    Main.class.getDeclaredConstructor(new Class[] {});
                Object o = con.newInstance(new Object[] {});
            } catch (InstantiationException e) {
                e.printStackTrace();
            } catch (InvocationTargetException e) {
                e.getTargetException().printStackTrace();
            }

            // Create and invoke the method object.
            try {
                Method m = Main.class.getDeclaredMethod("m", new Class[] {});
                Object o = m.invoke(null, new Object[] {});
            } catch (InvocationTargetException e) {
                e.getTargetException().printStackTrace();
            }
        } catch (NoSuchMethodException e) {
            e.printStackTrace();
        } catch (IllegalAccessException e) {
            e.printStackTrace();
        }
    }
}
```

Output

```
> java Main
java.lang.IllegalArgumentException: not implemented yet
    at Main.<init>(Main.java:5)
    at Main.main(Main.java:19)
java.lang.IllegalArgumentException: out to lunch
    at Main.m(Main.java:8)
    at Main.main(Main.java:30)
```

getTargetException()

PURPOSE Retrieves the exception wrapped by this `InvocationTargetException` instance.

SYNTAX `public Throwable getTargetException()`

DESCRIPTION This method returns the exception that the invoked method or constructor threw.

It returns `null` if this exception object was created with a `null` exception (which is not typical).

RETURNS A possibly `null` exception object.

EXAMPLE See the class example.

InvocationTargetException()

PURPOSE Constructs an `InvocationTargetException` instance.

SYNTAX

```
protected InvocationTargetException()
public InvocationTargetException(Throwable exc)
public InvocationTargetException(Throwable exc, String msg)
```

DESCRIPTION This constructor is used by `Method.invoke()` and `Constructor.newInstance()` whenever the invoked method or constructor throws an exception. The exception is caught and supplied as the `exc` parameter to this constructor.

If `exc` is specified, `exc` should be the exception that the invoked method or constructor threw. If `exc` is not specified, it defaults to `null`.

If `msg` is specified, `msg` is a human-readable string that describes the reason for the exception. If `msg` is not specified, it defaults to `null`.

PARAMETERS

`exc` A possibly `null` exception object.

`msg` A possibly `null` message.

SEE ALSO `java.lang.Throwable.getMessage()`.

IOException

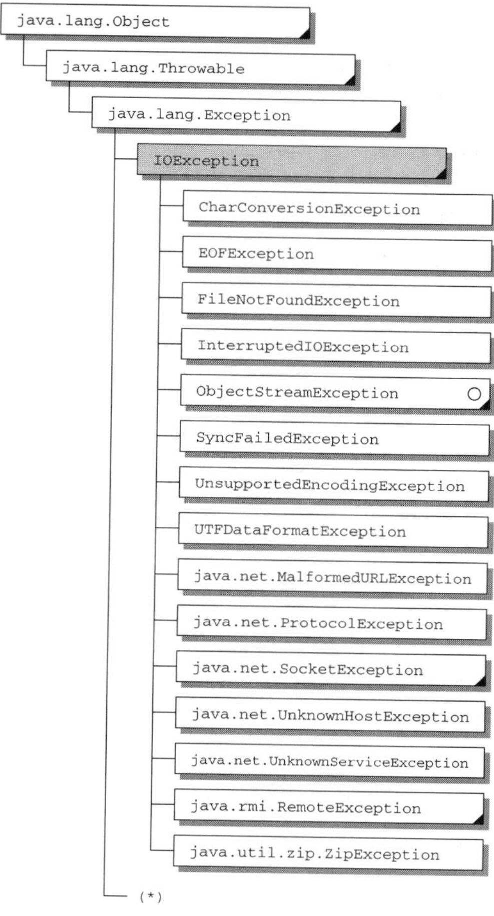

(*) 28 classes from other packages not shown.

Syntax

```
public class IOException extends Exception
```

Description

`IOException` and its subclasses are used to indicate that an exceptional condition has occurred with the input or output stream being operated on. A method that throws an `IOException` must declare it in its `throws` clause.

MEMBER SUMMARY	
Constructor	
`IOException()`	Constructs an `IOException` instance.

A B C D E F G H I J K L M N O P Q R S T U V W X Y Z

See Also

`EOFException`, `FileNotFoundException`, `InputStream`, `OutputStream`, `Reader`, `Writer`, `java.net.Socket`, `java.net.URLConnection`.

Example

See the use of `IOException` in the examples for `EOFException` and `FileNotFoundException`.

IOException()

PURPOSE Constructs an `IOException` instance.

SYNTAX

```
public IOException()
public IOException(String msg)
```

DESCRIPTION The two forms of this constructor construct an instance of `IOException`. An optional string `msg` can be supplied that describes this particular instance of the exception. If `msg` is not supplied, it defaults to `null`.

PARAMETERS

`msg` A possibly `null` string that gives details about this exception.

SEE ALSO `java.lang.Throwable.getMessage()`.

DEPRECATED LineNumberInputStream

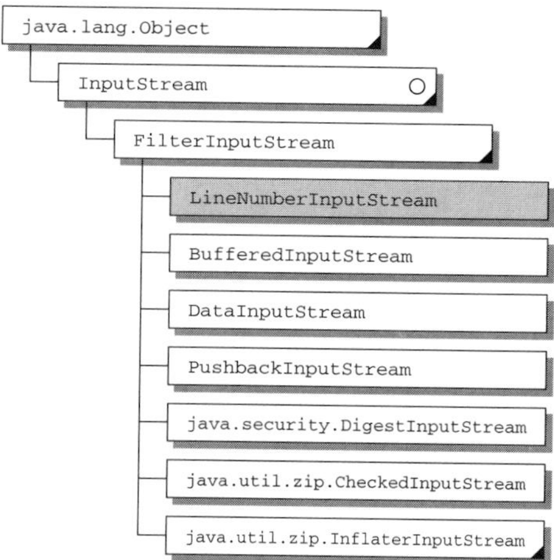

A B C D E F G H I J K L M N O P Q R S T U V W X Y Z

Note: Use of the LineNumberInputStream class is deprecated. Replace the usage of this class with LineNumberReader.

Syntax

```
public class LineNumberInputStream extends FilterInputStream
```

Description

A *line number input stream* is a filter input stream that counts the number of line terminators as data is read from the input stream that it is filtering. A line terminator is one of

- a newline character (`\n`),
- a carriage return character (`\r`), or
- a carriage return character followed by a newline character (`\r\n`).

The line number of the stream starts at 0 and is incremented as each line terminator is encountered.

Deprecation

The `LineNumberInputStream` class is used to represent a line number byte input stream. The usage of this class is deprecated because it assumes that a byte can be used to represent any character. This is not true in general for characters. `LineNumberReader` should be used instead. Replace the usage of `LineNumberInputStream`, as in

```
LineNumberInputStream in =
    new LineNumberInputStream(new FileInputStream("tmp"));
byte[] buf = ...;
while (in.read(buf) > 0) {
    ...
}
```

with

```
LineNumberReader in = new LineNumberReader(new FileReader("tmp"));
char[] buf = ...;
while (in.read(buf, 0, buf.length) > 0) {
    ...
}
```

A B C D E F G H I J K L M N O P Q R S T U V W X Y Z

MEMBER SUMMARY	
Deprecated Constructor	
`LineNumberInputStream()`	Replaced by `LineNumberReader.LineNumberReader()`.
Deprecated Input Methods	
`read()`	Replaced by `LineNumberReader.read()`.
`skip()`	Replaced by `LineNumberReader.skip()`.
Deprecated Mark/Reset Methods	
`mark()`	Replaced by `LineNumberReader.mark()`.
`reset()`	Replaced by `LineNumberReader.reset()`.
Deprecated Line Number Methods	
`getLineNumber()`	Replaced by `LineNumberReader.getLineNumber()`.
`setLineNumber()`	Replaced by `LineNumberReader.setLineNumber()`.
Deprecated Stream Method	
`available()`	Replaced by `BufferedReader.ready()`.

See Also

`FilterInputStream`, `InputStream`, `LineNumberReader`.

Example

This example echoes the input supplied to it and labels each line with its corresponding line number. The usage of `LineNumberInputStream` is deprecated. The second example that follows shows how to do the same thing using `LineNumberReader`.

Deprecated

```
import java.io.*;

class Old {
    // reads input from 'in' and writes the bytes out to 'out'
    // with line numbers on the left
    public static void echo(InputStream i, OutputStream o) {
        try {
            LineNumberInputStream in = new LineNumberInputStream(i);
```

```
            PrintStream out = new PrintStream(o);
            int c, oldLineNumber = 0, newLineNumber = 0;
            boolean writePrefix = true;

            while((c = in.read()) > -1) {
                if (writePrefix) {
                    out.print(newLineNumber+1);
                    out.write('\t');
                }
                out.write(c);
                if (writePrefix =
                    ((newLineNumber = in.getLineNumber()) != oldLineNumber))
                    oldLineNumber = newLineNumber;
            }
            in.close();                  // close streams
            out.close();
        } catch (IOException e) {
            e.printStackTrace();
        }
    }
    public static void main(String[] args) {
        try {
            InputStream in;
            if (args.length == 0)
                in = System.in;
            else
                in = new FileInputStream(args[0]);
            echo(in, System.out);
        } catch (IOException e) {
            e.printStackTrace();
        }
    }
}
```

Using LineNumberReader

```
import java.io.*;

class New {
    // reads input from 'in' and writes the characters out to 'out'
    // with line numbers on the left
    public static void echo(Reader i, Writer o) {
        try {
            LineNumberReader in = new LineNumberReader(i);
            PrintWriter out = new PrintWriter(o);
            int c, oldLineNumber = 0, newLineNumber = 0;
            boolean writePrefix = true;

            while((c = in.read()) > -1) {
                if (writePrefix) {
                    out.print(newLineNumber+1);
                    out.write('\t');
                }
                out.write(c);
                if (writePrefix =
                    ((newLineNumber = in.getLineNumber()) != oldLineNumber))
                    oldLineNumber = newLineNumber;
            }
            in.close();                  // close streams
            out.close();
```

```
            } catch (IOException e) {
                e.printStackTrace();
            }
        }
        public static void main(String[] args) {
            try {
                Reader in;
                if (args.length == 0)
                    in = new InputStreamReader(System.in);
                else
                    in = new FileReader(args[0]);
                echo(in, new OutputStreamWriter(System.out));
            } catch (IOException e) {
                e.printStackTrace();
            }
        }
    }
```

available() *DEPRECATED*

PURPOSE Replaced by `BufferedReader.ready()`.

SYNTAX `public int available() throws IOException`

RETURNS The number of bytes that can be read without being blocked.

EXCEPTIONS

`IOException`
If an IO error occurred.

OVERRIDES `FilterInputStream.available()`.

DEPRECATION This method returns the number of bytes that can be read without being blocked, which is determined by invoking `available()` on the underlying stream. The `LineNumberReader` class does not have a method that corresponds exactly to `available()`. Instead, the program should use `BufferedReader.ready()` (inherited by `LineNumberReader`) to determine whether the stream can be read without being blocked.

getLineNumber() *DEPRECATED*

PURPOSE Replaced by `LineNumberReader.getLineNumber()`.

SYNTAX `public int getLineNumber()`

RETURNS The current line number.

SEE ALSO `setLineNumber()`.

DEPRECATION See the class example for how to replace the usage of this method with `LineNumberReader.getLineNumber()`.

LineNumberInputStream() *DEPRECATED*

PURPOSE Replaced by `LineNumberRerader.LineNumberReader()`.

SYNTAX `public LineNumberInputStream(InputStream in)`

PARAMETERS

`in` The input stream for which to create the line number input stream.

SEE ALSO `FilterInputStream()`, `getLineNumber()`.

DESCRIPTION This constructor creates a new line number input stream for the input stream `in`. This line number input stream will count the line terminating characters (`\n`, `\r`, and `\n\r`) as input is read from `in`. Replace the usage of `LineNumberInputStream` with `LineNumberReader`. See the class description and the class example of how to do this replacement.

mark() *DEPRECATED*

PURPOSE Replaced by `LineNumberReader.mark()`.

SYNTAX `public void mark(int readlimit)`

PARAMETERS

`readlimit` The number of bytes that can be read before this mark becomes invalidated.

OVERRIDES `FilterInputStream.mark()`.

DEPRECATION This method marks the current read position and line number of this line number input stream so that a subsequent call to `reset()` will reset the read position to this marked position and line number.

Replace the usage of this deprecated method, as in

```
LineNumberInputStream in = ...;
in.mark(128);
...
in.reset();
```

with

```
LineNumberReader in = ...;
in.mark(128);
...
in.reset();
```

read() *DEPRECATED*

PURPOSE Replaced by `LineNumberReader.read()`.

SYNTAX

```
public int read() throws IOException
public int read(byte[] buffer, int offset, int count) throws
   IOException
```

A B C D E F G H I J K L M N O P Q R S T U V W X Y Z

PARAMETERS

buffer — The byte array in which to store the bytes read.

count — The number of bytes to read. 0 ≤ count ≤ buffer.length-offset.

offset — The index in buffer at which to start storing the bytes read. 0 ≤ offset < buffer.length.

RETURNS — The first form returns the byte (0–255) read; the second form returns the actual number of bytes read. All forms return -1 if end-of-file has been reached in the stream before any bytes have been read.

EXCEPTIONS

ArrayIndexOutOfBoundsException
If count or offset is outside of the specified bounds.

IOException
If an IO error occurred while attempting to read the bytes.

OVERRIDES — FilterInputStream.read().

DEPRECATION — This method reads bytes from the input stream, incrementing the line number if a line terminator is encountered. Replace the usage of this method using LineNumberReader.read(), as illustrated by the class example.

reset() *DEPRECATED*

PURPOSE — Replaced by LineNumberReader.reset().

SYNTAX — `public void reset() throws IOException`

EXCEPTIONS

IOException
If no mark has been previously set or if the mark has been invalidated.

OVERRIDES — FilterInputStream.reset().

DEPRECATION — This method resets the current read position to be the last marked position and resets the line number to be the line number of the last marked position. The usage of this method is deprecated. See mark() for an example of how to replace the usage of reset() with LineNumberReader.reset().

setLineNumber() *DEPRECATED*

PURPOSE — Replaced by LineNumberReader.setLineNumber().

SYNTAX — `public void setLineNumber(int lineNumber)`

PARAMETERS

lineNumber — The line number to which to set.

SEE ALSO getLineNumber().

DEPRECATION This method sets the current line number to be lineNumber. Replace then usage of this deprecated method, as in

```
LineNumberInputStream in = ...;
in.setLineNumber(20);
```

with

```
LineNumberReader in = ...;
in.setLineNumber(20);
```


skip()

DEPRECATED

PURPOSE Replaced by LineNumberReader.skip().

SYNTAX `public long skip(long count) throws IOException`

PARAMETERS

count The number of bytes to skip.

RETURNS The actual number of bytes skipped.

EXCEPTIONS

IOException

If an IO error occurred.

OVERRIDES FilterInputStream.skip().

DEPRECATION This method skips count number of bytes from this line number input stream and increments the line number as line terminators are encountered in the count number of bytes skipped. Replace the usage of this method, as in

```
LineNumberInputStream in = ...;
in.skip(10);
```

with

```
LineNumberReader in = ...;
in.skip(10);
```

java.io

LineNumberReader

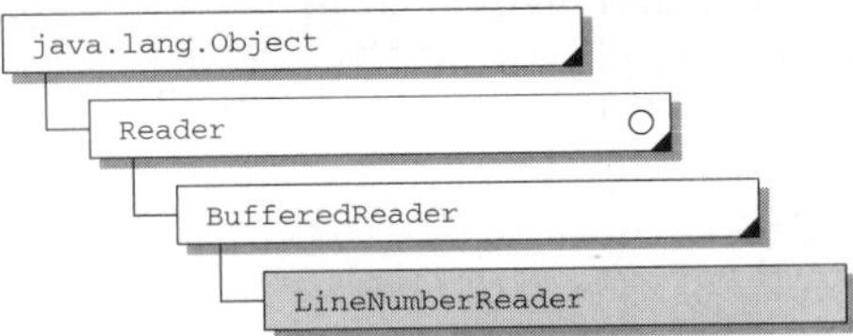

A B C D E F G H I J K L M N O P Q R S T U V W X Y Z

Syntax

```
public class LineNumberReader extends BufferedReader
```

Description

A *line number reader* is a filtered buffered reader that counts the number of line terminators as characters are read from the reader that it is filtering. See Figure 64. A line terminator is one of

- a newline character (`\n`),
- a carriage return character (`\r`), or
- a carriage return character followed by a newline character (`\r\n`).

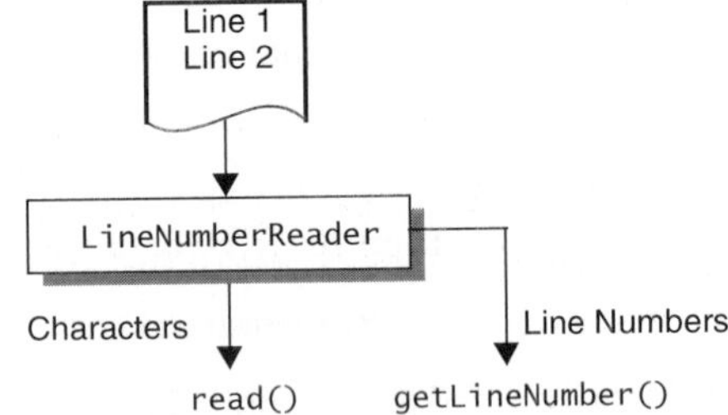

FIGURE 64: **`LineNumberReader`.**

The line number of the reader starts at 0 and is incremented as each line terminator is encountered through calls to `read()`, `readLine()`, or `skip()`.

The `LineNumberReader` class is used to represent a line number reader.

MEMBER SUMMARY	
Constructor	
`LineNumberReader()`	Constructs an instance of `LineNumberReader` for another reader.
Input Methods	
`read()`	Reads characters from this line number reader.
`readLine()`	Reads a line of characters from this line number reader.
`skip()`	Skips characters from this line number reader.
Mark/Reset Methods	
`mark()`	Marks the current read position in this line number reader.
`reset()`	Repositions the read position to the last marked position.

MEMBER SUMMARY	
Line Number Methods	
`getLineNumber()`	Retrieves the current line number.
`setLineNumber()`	Sets the current line number.

See Also

`FilterReader`.

Example

This example echoes the input supplied to it and labels each line with its corresponding line number.

```
import java.io.*;

class Main {
    // Reads input from 'in' and writes the characters out to 'out'
    // with line numbers on the left
    public static void echo(Reader i, Writer o) {
        try {
            LineNumberReader in = new LineNumberReader(i);
            PrintWriter out = new PrintWriter(o);
            String str;

        // Subtract one because readLine() already incremented line no.
            while((str = in.readLine()) != null) {
                out.println(in.getLineNumber()-1 + "\t" + str);
            }
            in.close();                  // close streams
            out.close();
        } catch (IOException e) {
            e.printStackTrace();
        }
    }
    public static void main(String[] args) {
        try {
            Reader in;
            if (args.length == 0)
                in = new InputStreamReader(System.in);
            else
                in = new FileReader(args[0]);
            echo(in, new OutputStreamWriter(System.out));
        } catch (IOException e) {
            e.printStackTrace();
        }
    }
}
```

getLineNumber()

PURPOSE Retrieves the current line number.

SYNTAX `public int getLineNumber()`

DESCRIPTION The line number is initially `0`. Characters on the first line (before any line terminator has been encountered) have a line number of 0. The line number is incremented after each line terminator is read or skipped. It can be changed using `setLineNumber()`.

RETURNS The current line number.

SEE ALSO `setLineNumber()`.

EXAMPLE This example reads characters and prints out the line number of each.

```
import java.io.*;

class Main {
    public static void echo(Reader i, Writer o) {
        try {
            LineNumberReader in = new LineNumberReader(i);
            PrintWriter out = new PrintWriter(o);
            int c;

            while((c = in.read()) > -1) {
                    out.print(in.getLineNumber());
                    out.write('\t');
                    out.write(c);
                    out.write('\n');
            }
            in.close();                    // close streams
            out.close();
        } catch (IOException e) {
            e.printStackTrace();
        }
    }
    public static void main(String[] args) {
        try {
            Reader in;
            if (args.length == 0)
                in = new InputStreamReader(System.in);
            else
                in = new FileReader(args[0]);
            echo(in, new OutputStreamWriter(System.out));
        } catch (IOException e) {
            e.printStackTrace();
        }
    }
}
```

LineNumberReader()

PURPOSE Constructs an instance of `LineNumberReader` for another reader.

SYNTAX
```
public LineNumberReader(Reader in)
public LineNumberReader(Reader in, int size)
```

DESCRIPTION The two forms of this constructor construct an instance of `LineNumberReader` for the reader `in`. The new line number reader will count the line terminating characters (`\n`, `\r`, and `\n\r`) as input is read from `in`.

The new line number reader is also a buffered reader. `size` specifies the size of the buffer to use. If unspecified, the default specified by `BufferedReader` (8192) is used.

PARAMETERS

`in` The non-`null` reader for which to create the line number reader.

`size` The nonnegative size of the buffer to use.

SEE ALSO `BufferedReader.BufferedReader()`, `getLineNumber()`.

EXAMPLE See the class example and `setLineNumber()`.

mark()

PURPOSE Marks the current read position in this line number reader.

SYNTAX
```
public void mark(int readlimit) throws IOException
```

DESCRIPTION This method marks the current read position and line number of this line number reader so that a subsequent call to `reset()` will reset the read position to this marked position and line number. `readlimit` number of characters can be read after this mark has been set. If you read more than `readlimit` number of characters, the mark becomes invalid.

`mark()` on this reader is always supported because it is a buffered reader.

PARAMETERS

`readlimit` The number of characters that can be read before this mark becomes invalidated.

EXCEPTIONS

`IOException`

If an IO error was encountered while marking `in`.

OVERRIDES `BufferedReader.mark()`.

SEE ALSO `Reader.markSupported()`, `reset()`.

EXAMPLE This example prints the number of lines and characters in a file and displays the first 100 characters of that file. It obtains the number of lines by skipping to the end of the file.

```
import java.io.*;

class Main {
    public static void main(String[] args) {
        if (args.length != 1) {
            System.err.println("Usage: java Main <inputfile>");
            System.exit(-1);
        }
        try {
            File f = new File(args[0]);
            LineNumberReader in = new LineNumberReader(new FileReader(f));

            int charcount = (int)f.length();
            in.mark(charcount); // mark at beginning of stream
            in.skip(charcount); // skip to end of buffer
            int linecount = in.getLineNumber();

            System.out.println("file:\t" + args[0] +
                               "\nlines:\t" + linecount +
                               "\nchars:\t" + charcount +
                               "\ncontent:");
            in.reset();
            char[] buf = new char[100];
            int howmany = in.read(buf);

            // Echo characaters
            for (int i = 0; i < howmany; i++)
                System.out.write(buf[i]);
            System.out.println();

            // Indicate whether there are more
            if (charcount >= 100)
                System.out.println("...");
            System.out.flush();        // flush output

            in.close();                // closes all "downstream" readers
        } catch (IOException e) {
            e.printStackTrace();
        }
    }
}
```

read()

PURPOSE Reads characters from this line number reader.

SYNTAX

```
public int read() throws IOException
public int read(char[] buffer, int offset, int count) throws
    IOException
```

DESCRIPTION The two forms of this method read characters from this line number reader. The first form reads and returns a single character from this line number reader, incrementing the line number if a line terminator has been encountered. The low-order 2 bytes of the `int` are used to represent the character; the high-order 2 bytes are not used. If a line terminator has been encountered, the character returned is the newline character (`\n`).

The second form reads `count` number of characters from this line number reader and stores them into the `char` array `buffer` starting at index `offset`. It returns the actual number of characters read. This second form also increments the line number as line terminators are encountered. It does this in the same way that the first form does. A multicharacter line terminator (`\r\n`) is treated as a single character (`\n`).

Characters are read starting from this reader's current read position, which is incremented after each character is read. The current read position can be changed using `mark()/reset()`.

PARAMETERS

`buffer` The non-`null` `char` array in which to store the characters read.
`count` The number of characters to read. `0` ≤ `count` ≤ `buffer.length-offset`.
`offset` The index in `buffer` at which to start storing the characters read. `0` ≤ `offset` < `buffer.length`.

RETURNS The first form returns the character read; the second form returns the actual number of characters read. Both forms return `-1` if end-of-stream has been reached before any characters have been read.

EXCEPTIONS

`ArrayIndexOutOfBoundsException`
If `count` or `offset` is outside of the specified bounds.

`IOException`
If an IO error occurred while attempting to read the characters from `in`.

OVERRIDES `BufferedReader.read()`.

SEE ALSO `getLineNumber()`, `mark()`, `reset()`, `skip()`.

EXAMPLE See the class example, `getLineNumber()`, `mark()`, `setLineNumber()`.

readLine()

PURPOSE Reads a line of characters from this line number reader.

SYNTAX `public String readLine() throws IOException`

DESCRIPTION This method reads a line of characters and returns it as a string. A line is defined as a sequence of characters terminated by a newline (`\n`), return (`\r`), newline-return (`\r\n`), or end-of-stream. The string does not include the line terminator character. This method blocks until a complete line has been read.

The read position and line number are updated accordingly.

RETURNS A `String` containing the contents of the line. `null` if no character is read before the end-of-stream is reached.

EXCEPTIONS

`IOException`

If an IO error occurs while attempting to read.

OVERRIDES `BufferedReader.readLine()`.

SEE ALSO `DataInputStream.readLine()`.

EXAMPLE See the class example.

reset()

PURPOSE Resets the read position to be the last marked position.

SYNTAX `public void reset() throws IOException`

DESCRIPTION This method resets the current read position to be the last marked position. It also resets the line number to be the line number of the last marked position. Subsequent invocations of the `read()`/`skip()` methods will begin getting input from this marked position. Subsequent invocations of `getLineNumber()` will return this reset line number.

`mark()`/`reset()` on this stream is always supported because it is a buffered reader.

EXCEPTIONS

`IOException`

If no mark has been previously set or if the mark has been invalidated.

OVERRIDES `BufferedReader.reset()`.

SEE ALSO `Reader.markSupported()`, `getLineNumber()`, `mark()`.

EXAMPLE See `mark()`.

setLineNumber()

PURPOSE Sets the current line number.

SYNTAX `public void setLineNumber(int lineNumber)`

DESCRIPTION This method sets the current line number to be `lineNumber`.

PARAMETERS

`lineNumber` The line number to which to set.

SEE ALSO `getLineNumber()`.

EXAMPLE This example is a variation of the class example. It prints the line number with each line but resets the line number for each new page.

```
import java.io.*;

class Main {
    public static void echo(Reader i, OutputStream o, int pagesize) {
        try {
            LineNumberReader in = new LineNumberReader(i);
            PrintWriter out = new PrintWriter(o);
            int lineno;

            String str;

            // Subtract one because readLine() already incremented line no.
            while((str = in.readLine()) != null) {
                lineno = in.getLineNumber();
                out.println(lineno-1 + "\t" + str);
                if (lineno >= pagesize) {
                    in.setLineNumber(0);
                }
            }
            in.close();                    // close streams
            out.close();
        } catch (IOException e) {
            e.printStackTrace();
        }
    }
    public static void main(String[] args) {
        try {
            Reader in;
            if (args.length == 0)
                in = new InputStreamReader(System.in);
            else
                in = new FileReader(args[0]);
            echo(in, System.out, 10);
        } catch (IOException e) {
            e.printStackTrace();
        }
    }
}
```

skip()

PURPOSE Skips characters from this line number reader.

SYNTAX `public long skip(long count) throws IOException`

DESCRIPTION This method skips `count` number of characters from this line number reader. The line number is incremented as line terminators are encountered in the `count` number of characters skipped. A multicharacter line terminator (`\r\n`) counts as a single character.

PARAMETERS

`count` The number of characters to skip.

RETURNS The actual number of characters skipped.

EXCEPTIONS

`IOException`

If an IO error occurred.

OVERRIDES `FilterInputStream.skip()`.

EXAMPLE See `mark()`.

LinkageError

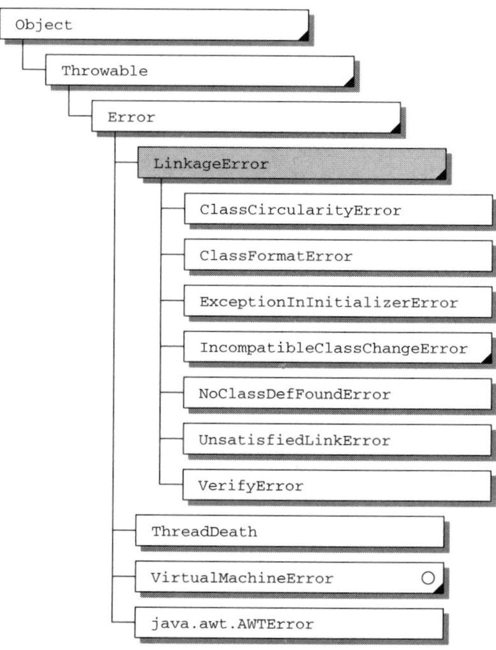

Syntax

```
public class LinkageError extends Error
```

Description

`LinkageError` and its subclasses of errors indicate that the classes that a class depends on have been changed in an incompatible way. This can happen if some of the classes were changed and compiled independently (not all of the classes were recompiled).

`LinkageError` and its subclasses should not be caught or declared in the `throws` clause of a method.

MEMBER SUMMARY	
Constructor	
`LinkageError()`	Constructs a `LinkageError` instance.

See Also

`ClassCircularityError`, `ClassFormatError`, `Error`, `IncompatibleClassChangeError`, `NoClassDefFoundError`, `UnsatisfiedLinkError`, `VerifyError`.

Example

See the examples of subclasses.

LinkageError()

PURPOSE
Constructs a `LinkageError` instance.

SYNTAX
```
public LinkageError()
public LinkageError(String msg)
```

DESCRIPTION
This constructor construct an instance of `LinkageError`. An optional string `msg` can be supplied that describes this particular instance of the error. If `msg` is not supplied, it defaults to `null`.

PARAMETERS
`msg` A possibly `null` string that gives details about this error.

SEE ALSO
`Throwable.getMessage()`.

ListResourceBundle

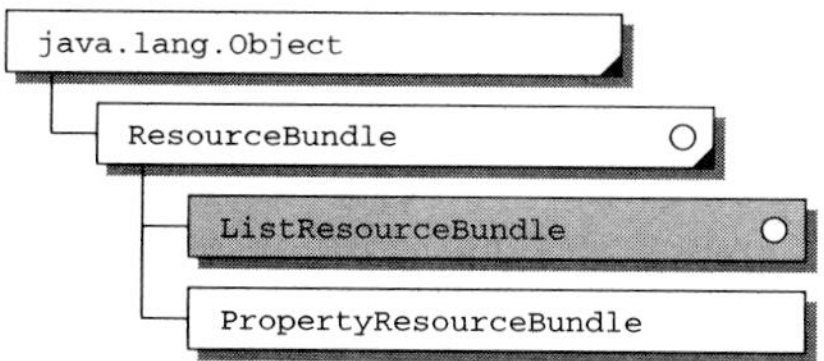

A B C D E F G H I J K L M N O P Q R S T U V W X Y Z

Syntax

`public abstract class ListResourceBundle extends ResourceBundle`

Description

A list resource bundle is a special type of resource bundle whose resource values are known at the time the resource bundle is instantiated. See the `ResourceBundle` class for complete information about resource bundles.

Usage

You do not typically retrieve resources directly with this class. Instead, resources are retrieved through the `ResourceBundle` class.

This class is meant for developers building resource bundles. To build a list resource bundle, you need to create a new class that extends `ListResourceBundle`. Then, you must override the `getContents()` method to return the entire contents of the resource bundle in a two-dimensional array.

MEMBER SUMMARY	
Resource Bundle Methods	
`getKeys()`	Creates an enumeration of the keys in this resource bundle.
`handleGetObject()`	Called to retrieve a resource from this resource bundle.
Protected Method	
`getContents()`	Called to retrieve the entire contents of this resource bundle.

See Also

`PropertyResourceBundle`, `ResourceBundle`.

Example

This example is a typical subclass of `ListResourceBundle`.

Main.java

```
import java.util.*;

class Main {
    public static void main(String[] args) {
        ResourceBundle bundle = ResourceBundle.getBundle("MyListResources");

        System.out.println(bundle.getString("key-1"));             // wombat
        System.out.println(bundle.getStringArray("key-2")[0]);     // apple
        System.out.println(bundle.getObject("key-3"));
                                                // java.awt.Point[x=1,y=2]
    }
}
```

MyListResources.java

```
import java.awt.*;
import java.util.*;

public class MyListResources extends ListResourceBundle {
    public Object[][] getContents() {
        return contents;
    }

    private Object[][] contents = {
        {"key-1", "wombat",},
        {"key-2", new String[]{"apple", "blueberry", "cantaloupe",}},
        {"key-3", new Point(1, 2),},
    };

/*
    // This is an alternate but equivalent way to create the content array.
    public Object[][] getContents() {
        Object[][] result = new Object[3][2];
        result[0][0] = "key-1";
        result[0][1] = "wombat";
        result[1][0] = "key-2";
        result[1][1] = new String[]{"apple", "blueberry", "cantaloupe",};
        result[2][0] = "key-3";
        result[2][1] = new Point(1, 2);
        return result;
    }
*/
}
```

getContents()

PURPOSE Called to retrieve the entire contents of this resource bundle.

SYNTAX `abstract protected Object[][] getContents()`

DESCRIPTION This method must be overridden by the subclass of this class. The result must be an array of two-element arrays. The first element of the array contains a key, and the second element contains the resource. The size of the first dimension is exactly the number of resources in this resource bundle.

The default implementation of this class calls this method once and loads the result into a hash table. This means that any changes to the values after this method call have no effect.

RETURNS A non-`null` array of two-element arrays containing the keys and resources of this resource bundle.

EXAMPLE See the class example.

getKeys()

PURPOSE Creates an enumeration of the keys in this resource bundle.

SYNTAX `public Enumeration getKeys()`

DESCRIPTION This method returns an enumeration containing the keys of all available resources in this resource bundle.

The default implementation of this method creates an enumeration on an internal hash table.

RETURNS A non-`null` enumeration of this resource bundle.

EXAMPLE See the `ResourceBundle` class example.

handleGetObject()

PURPOSE Called to retrieve a resource from this resource bundle.

SYNTAX `public final Object handleGetObject(String key)`

DESCRIPTION This method is called by the resource bundle framework (see `ResourceBundle`) to retrieve a resource from this resource bundle. This method is not meant to be called directly.

This method looks up `key` in an internal hash table that is initialized with the results from `getContents()`.

PARAMETERS

`key` A non-`null` case-sensitive string containing the name of the resource.

RETURNS The resource with the name key. `null` if not found.

SEE ALSO `ResourceBundle.getObject()`, `ResourceBundle.getString()`, `ResourceBundle.getStringArray()`, `ResourceBundle.parent`.

EXAMPLE See the `ResourceBundle` class example.

java.util
Locale

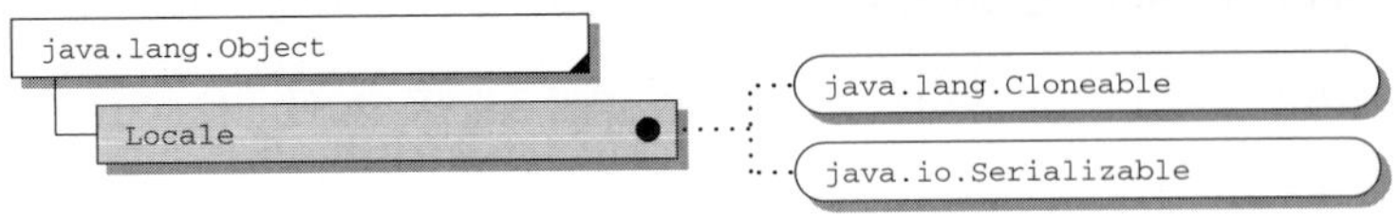

Syntax

```
public final class Locale implements Cloneable, Serializable
```

Description

A *locale* is Java's standard means of identifying a language for the purposes of internationalization and localization. All classes that support localization use the `Locale` class to determine in which language to display its information. For example, when the `DateFormat` class is asked to format a date, it will use the word "Monday" for an English locale and the word "Lundi" for a French locale.

There are often differences in conventions even within the same language. For example, currency in the French language is displayed differently in Canada and in France. To allow for this, a locale can also identify a particular country.

Finally, if there are further differences in conventions within a language used in one country, an application-specific *variant code* can be added to a locale to identify the difference. For example, if a country uses slightly different dialects in its northern and southern regions and your application needs to be localized to each dialect, you could define two variant codes such as `NORTH` and `SOUTH`. The variant code is arbitrary and completely application-specific.

A more typical use of the variant code is to identify differences due to the computing platform. For example, perhaps because of differences in fonts, a string may have to use different characters depending on whether the string is used on Windows or on Unix. Your application could then define two variant codes, `WIN` and `UNIX`.

In summary, a locale consists of three ordered pieces of information: a language code, a country code, and a variant code. See Figure 65. The language code is a two-letter lowercase ISO-639 code specifying a particular language. The country code is a two-letter uppercase ISO-3166 code specifying a particular country. The variant code is any application-specific string. A copy of ISO-639 is at `http://www.ics.uci.edu/pub/ietf/http/related/iso639.txt`. A copy of ISO-3166 is at `http://www.chemie.fu-berlin.de/diverse/doc/ISO_3166.html`.

Language	Country	Variant
en	US	UNIX

FIGURE 65: The Components of a Locale.

Usage: Creating Locales

If you are localizing your application for a locale that is not one of the predefined locales in the `Locale` class, you will have to create your own `Locale` object. New `Locale` objects are created using the `Locale` constructor. To use the constructor, you must specify at least a language code that identifies a particular language. The language code should be one of the two-letter lowercase ISO-639 language codes. If the locale is specific to a country, a two-letter uppercase ISO-3166 country code must be used. Finally, a variant code can be supplied to the constructor, if necessary.

A B C D E F G H I J K L M N O P Q R S T U V W X Y Z

Usage: Retrieving Locales

Classes that support internationalization typically have a method called `getAvailableLocales()` that returns all of the locales supported by that class. An example of such a class is `java.text.DateFormat`. You then can either check the list to see if your desired locale is supported or display the list to the user.

Locale Identifier

The *locale identifier* is a unique string representing a locale. It contains at least the language code (lowercase) of a locale. If the locale has a country code, the country code (uppercase) is appended to the locale identifier and separated from it by an underscore. Finally, if the locale also has a variant code, the variant code (uppercase) is appended to the locale identifier and separated from it by an underscore. An example of a locale identifier is `en_US_UNIX_SOLARIS`, where `en` is the language code, `US` is the country code, and `UNIX_SOLARIS` is the variant code.

The locale identifier is typically used to label localized resource bundles. In particular, the name of a resource bundle localized for a particular locale is the name of the resource bundle concatenated with the locale's locale identifier. An example of a resource bundle name is `ButtonLabelResources_en_US_UNIX_SOLARIS`, where `en_US_UNIX_SOLARIS` is the locale identifier.

The format of the locale identifier is important to how resource bundles are located. When a resource bundle is searched for, the full name of the resource bundle is used. If no resource bundles have that name, the rightmost underscore and subsequent characters are removed and the shortened name is used to locate a resource bundle. In the previous example, `_SOLARIS` is stripped off first, followed by`_UNIX`, then by `_US`, and finally by `_en`. The locale identifier is continually shortened until a resource bundle is found. See `ResourceBundle` for more information about this process.

Predefined Locales

Table 31 shows the details of all of the predefined locales in this class. The column headings are named after all of the getter methods available in this class. For example, "Display Name" is the information returned by the `getDisplayName()` method.

Constant	Display Name	Display Language	Language	ISO3 Language	Display Country	Country	ISO3 Country	Locale Identifier
CANADA	English (Canada)	English	en	eng	Canada	CA	CAN	en_CA
CANADA_FRENCH	French (Canada)	French	fr	fra	Canada	CA	CAN	fr_CA
CHINA	Chinese (China)	Chinese	zh	chs	China	CN	CHN	zh_CN
CHINESE	Chinese (China)	Chinese	zh	chs	China		CHN	zh
ENGLISH	English (United States)	English	en	eng	United States		USA	en
FRANCE	French (France)	French	fr	fra	France	FR	FRA	fr_FR
FRENCH	French (France)	French	fr	fra	France		FRA	fr
GERMAN	German (Germany)	German	de	deu	Germany		DEU	de
GERMANY	German (Germany)	German	de	deu	Germany	DE	DEU	de_DE
ITALIAN	Italian (Italy)	Italian	it	ita	Italy		ITA	it
ITALY	Italian (Italy)	Italian	it	ita	Italy	IT	ITA	it_IT
JAPAN	Japanese (Japan)	Japanese	ja	jpn	Japan	JP	JPN	ja_JP
JAPANESE	Japanese (Japan)	Japanese	ja	jpn	Japan		JPN	ja
KOREA	Korean (Korea)	Korean	ko	kor	Korea	KR	KOR	ko_KR
KOREAN	Korean (Korea)	Korean	ko	kor	Korea		KOR	ko
RPC	Chinese (China)	Chinese	zh	chs	China	CN	CHN	zh_CN
SIMPLIFIED_CHINESE	Chinese (China)	Chinese	zh	chs	China	CN	CHN	zh_CN
TAIWAN	Chinese (ROC)	Chinese	zh	cht	ROC	TW	TWN	zh_TW
TRADITIONAL_CHINESE	Chinese (ROC)	Chinese	zh	cht	ROC	TW	TWN	zh_TW
UK	English (United Kingdom)	English	en	eng	United Kingdom	GB	GBR	en_GB
US	English (United States)	English	en	eng	United States	US	USA	en_US

TABLE 31: Predefined Locales and Their Codes.

MEMBER SUMMARY	
Constructor	
`Locale()`	Constructs a `Locale` instance.
Getter Methods	
`getCountry()`	Retrieves this `Locale` object's two-letter country code.
`getDefault()`	Retrieves the default locale.
`getDisplayCountry()`	Retrieves a human-readable localized version of this `Locale` object's country code.
`getDisplayLanguage()`	Retrieves a human-readable localized version of this `Locale` object's language code.
`getDisplayName()`	Retrieves a human-readable localized version of this `Locale` object.
`getDisplayVariant()`	Retrieves a human-readable localized version of this `Locale` object's variant code.
`getISO3Country()`	Retrieves this `Locale` object's three-letter country code.
`getISO3Language()`	Retrieves this `Locale` object's three-letter ISO language code.
`getLanguage()`	Retrieves this `Locale` object's two-letter ISO language code.
`getVariant()`	Retrieves this `Locale` object's variant code.
Set Locale Method	
`setDefault()`	Sets the default locale.
Predefined Locales for Countries	
`CANADA`	Locale for Canada.
`CHINA`	Locale for China. Equivalent to `PRC`.
`FRANCE`	Locale for France.
`GERMANY`	Locale for Germany.
`ITALY`	Locale for Italy.
`JAPAN`	Locale for Japan.
`KOREA`	Locale for Korea.
`PRC`	Locale for People's Republic of China. Equivalent to `CHINA`.
`TAIWAN`	Locale for Taiwan.
`UK`	Locale for the United Kingdom.
`US`	Locale for the United States.
Predefined Locales for Languages	
`CANADA_FRENCH`	Locale for French-speaking Canada.
`CHINESE`	Locale for the Chinese language.
`ENGLISH`	Locale for the English language.
`FRENCH`	Locale for the French language.
`GERMAN`	Locale for the German language.
`ITALIAN`	Locale for the Italian language.
`JAPANESE`	Locale for the Japanese language.

Continued

MEMBER SUMMARY

Predefined Locales for Languages *(Continued)*

`KOREAN`	Locale for the Korean language.
`SIMPLIFIED_CHINESE`	Locale for Chinese in mainland China.
`TRADITIONAL_CHINESE`	Locale for Chinese in Taiwan.

Object Methods

`clone()`	Creates a clone of this `Locale` object.
`equals()`	Determines if this `Locale` object is equal to another object.
`hashCode()`	Computes the hash code for this `Locale` object.
`toString()`	Generates a string representing this `Locale` object.

See Also

`java.text.DateFormat`, `java.text.NumberFormat`, `ResourceBundle`.

Example

This example prints various details about each of the predefined locales. It also prints all of the locales supported by the `NumberFormat` class.

```
import java.util.*;
import java.text.*;

class Main {
    static void print(String name, Locale locale) {
        System.out.print(name);
        System.out.print(" " + locale.getDisplayName());

        System.out.print(" " + locale.getDisplayLanguage());
        System.out.print(" " + locale.getLanguage());
        System.out.print(" " + locale.getISO3Language());
        System.out.print(" " + locale.getDisplayCountry());
        System.out.print(" " + locale.getCountry());
        System.out.print(" " + locale.getISO3Country());
        System.out.print(" " + locale.getDisplayVariant());
        System.out.print(" " + locale.getVariant());

        System.out.println(" " + locale.toString());
    }

    public static void main(String[] args) {
        Locale locale = Locale.getDefault();
        //Locale.setDefault(Locale.ITALIAN);
        print("CANADA", Locale.CANADA);
        print("CANADA_FRENCH", Locale.CANADA_FRENCH);
        print("CHINA", Locale.CHINA);
        print("CHINESE", Locale.CHINESE);
        print("ENGLISH", Locale.ENGLISH);
        print("FRANCE", Locale.FRANCE);
```

```
        print("FRENCH", Locale.FRENCH);
        print("GERMAN", Locale.GERMAN);
        print("GERMANY", Locale.GERMANY);
        print("ITALIAN", Locale.ITALIAN);
        print("ITALY", Locale.ITALY);
        print("JAPAN", Locale.JAPAN);
        print("JAPANESE", Locale.JAPANESE);
        print("KOREA", Locale.KOREA);
        print("KOREAN", Locale.KOREAN);
        print("RPC", Locale.PRC);
        print("SIMPLIFIED_CHINESE", Locale.SIMPLIFIED_CHINESE);
        print("TAIWAN", Locale.TAIWAN);
        print("TRADITIONAL_CHINESE", Locale.TRADITIONAL_CHINESE);
        print("UK", Locale.UK);
        print("US", Locale.US);

        Locale[] locales = NumberFormat.getAvailableLocales();
        for (int i=0; i<locales.length; i++) {
            print("", locales[i]);
        }
    }
}
```

A B C D E F G H I J K L M N O P Q R S T U V W X Y Z

clone()

PURPOSE Creates a clone of this `Locale` object.

SYNTAX `public Object clone()`

DESCRIPTION This method creates a clone of this `Locale` object. The new object is identical to this one. Calling `equals()` on this object and the new object yields `true`.

RETURNS A non-`null` copy of this `Locale` object.

OVERRIDES `java.lang.Object.clone()`.

EXAMPLE This example clones the default locale and does a reference and `equals()` comparison.

```
import java.util.*;

class Main {
    public static void main(String[] args) {
        Locale defloc = Locale.getDefault();
        Locale loc = (Locale)defloc.clone();

        System.out.println((loc == defloc));              // false
        System.out.println((loc.equals(defloc)));         // true
    }
}
```

A B C D E F G H I J K L M N O P Q R S T U V W X Y Z

equals()

PURPOSE Determines if this `Locale` object is equal to another object.

SYNTAX `public boolean equals(Object obj)`

DESCRIPTION This method returns `true` only if `obj` is an instance of `Locale` and if the three components—language, country, and variant—are identical to those of this `Locale` object.

PARAMETERS

`obj` A possibly `null` object.

RETURNS `true` if `obj` is equal to this locale; `false` otherwise.

OVERRIDES `java.lang.Object.equals()`.

EXAMPLE See `java.lang.Object.equals()`.

getCountry()

PURPOSE Retrieves this `Locale` object's two-letter country code.

SYNTAX `public String getCountry()`

DESCRIPTION This method retrieves the two-letter uppercase country code used to construct this `Locale` object.

RETURNS A non-`null` string containing this `Locale` object's two-letter country code.

SEE ALSO `Locale()`.

EXAMPLE See the class example.

getDefault()

PURPOSE Retrieves the default locale.

SYNTAX `public static synchronized Locale getDefault()`

DESCRIPTION This method retrieves the most recent `Locale` object set by `setDefault()`. If `setDefault()` was never called, this method creates a `Locale` object and makes it the default. This method first determines the default language and country by calling `System.getProperty("user.language")` and `System.getProperty("user.region")`, respectively. If the `user.language` system property is not defined, "EN" is used. If `user.region` is not defined, "" is used.

Note: The returned `Locale` object should not be modified. The returned object is globally shared by all clients of the `Locale` class.

RETURNS A non-`null` `Locale` object containing the default locale.

SEE ALSO `java.lang.System.getProperty()`, `setDefault()`.

EXAMPLE See `setDefault()`.

getDisplayCountry()

PURPOSE Retrieves a human-readable localized version of this `Locale` object's country code.

SYNTAX
```
public final String getDisplayCountry()
public String getDisplayCountry(Locale inLocale)
```

DESCRIPTION This method retrieves a human-readable version of this `Locale` object's country code. The human-readable name is localized for the language specified in `inLocale`. If `inLocale` is not specified, the default locale is used.

If the country name cannot be translated into the language specified by `inLocale`, the country name is translated into the language specified in this `Locale` object.

PARAMETERS

`inLocale` A non-`null` `Locale` object.

RETURNS A non-`null` localized string of this locale's country code.

EXAMPLE This example prints the French translation for Germany. Since the Chinese translation for Germany is not available, Germany is printed in German.

```
import java.util.*;

class Main {
    public static void main(String[] args) {
        System.out.println(Locale.GERMAN.getDisplayCountry(Locale.FRENCH));
            // Allemagne

        System.out.println(Locale.GERMAN.getDisplayCountry(Locale.CHINA));
            // Deutschland
    }
}
```

getDisplayLanguage()

PURPOSE
Retrieves a human-readable localized version of this `Locale` object's language code.

SYNTAX
```
public final String getDisplayLanguage()
public String getDisplayLanguage(Locale inLocale)
```

DESCRIPTION
This method retrieves a human-readable version of this `Locale` object's language code. The human-readable name is localized for the language specified in `inLocale`. If `inLocale` is not specified, the default locale is used.

If the language name cannot be translated into the language specified by `inLocale`, the language name is translated into the language specified in this `Locale` object.

PARAMETERS

`inLocale` A non-`null` `Locale` object.

RETURNS
A non-`null` localized string of this locale's language code.

EXAMPLE
This example prints the French translation for German. Since the Chinese translation for German is not available, German is printed in German.

```
import java.util.*;

class Main {
    public static void main(String[] args) {
        System.out.println(Locale.GERMAN.getDisplayLanguage(Locale.FRENCH));
            // allemand

        System.out.println(Locale.GERMAN.getDisplayLanguage(Locale.CHINA));
            // Deutsch
    }
}
```

getDisplayName()

PURPOSE
Retrieves a human-readable localized version of this `Locale` object.

SYNTAX
```
public final String getDisplayName()
public String getDisplayName(Locale inLocale)
```

DESCRIPTION
This method retrieves a human-readable string of this `Locale` object. The string includes human-readable versions of this `Locale` object's language code, country code, and variant code. The human-readable string is localized for the language specified in `inLocale`. If `inLocale` is not specified, the default locale is used.

If the string cannot be translated into the language specified by `inLocale`, the string is translated into the language specified in this `Locale` object.

PARAMETERS

`inLocale` A non-`null` `Locale` object.

RETURNS A non-`null` localized string representation of this locale.

SEE ALSO `toString()`.

EXAMPLE This example prints the French translation for the `GERMAN` locale. Since the Chinese translation for the `GERMAN` locale is not available, it is instead printed in German.

```
import java.util.*;

class Main {
    public static void main(String[] args) {
        System.out.println(Locale.GERMAN.getDisplayName(Locale.FRENCH));
            // allemand (Allemagne)

        System.out.println(Locale.GERMAN.getDisplayName(Locale.CHINA));
            // Deutsch (Deutschland)
    }
}
```

getDisplayVariant()

PURPOSE Retrieves a human-readable localized version of this `Locale` object's variant code.

SYNTAX

```
public final String getDisplayVariant()
public String getDisplayVariant(Locale inLocale)
```

DESCRIPTION This method retrieves a human-readable version of this `Locale` object's variant code. The human-readable name is localized for the language specified in `inLocale`. If `inLocale` is not specified, the default locale is used.

If the variant name cannot be translated into the language specified by `inLocale`, the variant name is translated into the language specified in this `Locale` object.

Note: In Java 1.1.4, this method always returns the same variant code supplied to the constructor (after it has been converted to uppercase).

PARAMETERS

`inLocale` A non-`null` `Locale` object.

RETURNS A non-`null` localized string of this locale's variant code.

EXAMPLE

```
import java.util.*;

class Main {
    public static void main(String[] args) {
        Locale NORWAY = new Locale("no","NO");
        Locale NORWAY_NYNORSK = new Locale("no","NO","NY");

        System.out.println(NORWAY.getDisplayName());
            // Norwegian (Bokmal) (Norway)
        System.out.println(NORWAY.getDisplayVariant());
            //

        System.out.println(NORWAY_NYNORSK.getDisplayName());
            // Norwegian (Nynorsk) (Norway,NY)
        System.out.println(NORWAY_NYNORSK.getDisplayVariant());
            // NY
    }
}
```


getISO3Country()

PURPOSE Retrieves this `Locale` object's three-letter country code.

SYNTAX `public String getISO3Country() throws MissingResourceException`

DESCRIPTION This method retrieves this `Locale` object's three-letter country code. The complete list of valid three-letter ISO country codes is in ISO-3166. If this `Locale` object was not constructed with a valid or recognized language or country code, this method returns `getDefault().getISO3Country()`.

RETURNS A non-`null` string containing a three-letter country code.

EXCEPTIONS

`MissingResourceException`
If Java's resource bundle containing the ISO-3166 country codes cannot be found.

EXAMPLE See the class example.

getISO3Language()

PURPOSE Retrieves this `Locale` object's three-letter ISO language code.

SYNTAX `public String getISO3Language() throws MissingResourceException`

DESCRIPTION This method retrieves this `Locale` object's three-letter ISO language code. The complete list of valid three-letter ISO language codes is in ISO-3166. If this

Locale object was not constructed with a valid or recognized language or country code, this method returns `getDefault().getISO3Language()`.

RETURNS A non-null string containing a three-letter language code.

EXCEPTIONS

`MissingResourceException`

If Java's resource bundle containing the ISO-3166 language codes cannot be found.

EXAMPLE See the class example.

getLanguage()

PURPOSE Retrieves this Locale object's two-letter ISO language code.

SYNTAX `public String getLanguage()`

DESCRIPTION This method retrieves the two-letter lowercase language code used to construct this Locale object.

RETURNS A non-null string containing this Locale object's two-letter language code.

EXAMPLE See the class example.

getVariant()

PURPOSE Retrieves this Locale object's variant code.

SYNTAX `public String getVariant()`

DESCRIPTION This method retrieves this Locale object's variant code. The variant code is an application-specific code that typically is used to designate a platform. See the class description for more details. If this Locale object was constructed with a variant code, this method returns that code (after converting it to uppercase).

RETURNS A non-null (but possibly empty) string containing this Locale object's variant code.

EXAMPLE See the class example.

hashCode()

PURPOSE Computes the hash code for this Locale object.

SYNTAX `public synchronized int hashCode()`

DESCRIPTION This method computes the hash code for this `Locale` object.A locale's hash code is an integer that's calculated from the three locale components—language, country, and variant. Two locales whose components are equal will have the same hash code. However, unequal locales might also have the same hash code, although the hash code algorithm minimizes this possibility. The hash code is typically used as the key in a hash table.

For performance reasons, the hash code calculation is done only once and kept in a private field.

RETURNS An `int` representing this `Locale` object's hash code.

OVERRIDES `java.lang.Object.hashCode()`.

EXAMPLE See `java.lang.Object.hashCode()`.

Locale()

PURPOSE Construct a `Locale` instance.

SYNTAX

```
public Locale(String languageCode, String countryCode)
public Locale(String languageCode, String countryCode, String
    variantCode)
```

DESCRIPTION This constructor constructs a new `Locale` object that has the specified codes. `languageCode` should be one of the ISO-639 language codes; it is converted to lowercase. `countryCode` should be one of the two-letter ISO-3166 country codes; it is converted to uppercase. The `variantCode` can be any string and is converted to uppercase. This constructor simply stores the code strings; the strings are not checked to be valid codes.

If the locale is not country-specific, it must be "". If a `variantCode` is specified, `countryCode` must not be empty; otherwise the variant code is ignored.

PARAMETERS

`countryCode` A non-`null` possibly empty string containing a two-letter ISO-3166 country code.

`languageCode`
A non-`null` string containing a two-letter ISO-639 language code.

`variantCode` A non-`null` possibly empty string containing a variant code.

EXAMPLE This example demonstrates that the codes supplied to the constructor have their case adjusted.

```
import java.util.*;

class Main {
    public static void main(String[] args) {
        Locale l = new Locale("En", "Us", "Unix");
        System.out.println(l.getLanguage());    // en
        System.out.println(l.getCountry());     // US
        System.out.println(l.getVariant());     // UNIX
        System.out.println(l.toString());       // en_US_UNIX

        // Demonstrates a Java 1.1.4 bug where the variant is not displayed
        // if the country code is empty.
        l = new Locale("En", "", "Unix");
        System.out.println(l.getLanguage());    // en
        System.out.println(l.getCountry());     //
        System.out.println(l.getVariant());     // UNIX
        System.out.println(l.toString());       // en
    }
}
```

setDefault()

PURPOSE Sets the default locale.

SYNTAX `public static synchronized void setDefault(Locale newLocale)`

DESCRIPTION This method sets the default locale to be `newLocale`. `newLocale` can be retrieved later using `getDefault()`.

Changing the default locale is a global operation and affects all clients of the `Locale` class. All subsequent calls to `getDefault()` using this or any other `Locale` object results in `newLocale`.

PARAMETERS

`newLocale` A non-`null` `Locale` object.

SEE ALSO `getDefault()`, `java.lang.System.getProperty()`, `setTimeZone()`.

EXAMPLE This example demonstrates how to change the default locale. Changing the default locale is not a usual thing to do.

```
import java.util.*;

class Main {
    public static void main(String[] args) {
        // Get and print the real default.
        Locale locale = Locale.getDefault();
        System.out.println(locale.toString());              // en_US

        // Create a new locale.
        locale = new Locale("ab", "XY", "Solaris");
```

```
            // Make it the default.
            Locale.setDefault(locale);

            // Print the new default.
            System.out.println(locale.toString());          // ab_XY_Solaris
        }
    }
```

A B C D E F G H I J K L M N O P Q R S T U V W X Y Z

toString()

PURPOSE Generates a string representing this `Locale` object.

SYNTAX `public final String toString()`

DESCRIPTION This method concatenates this locale's two-letter language code and two-letter country code, separated by an underscore (_). The codes are the same values passed to the constructor (after their cases have been adjusted). For example, if this locale were created with language code "en" and country code "US", this method would return "en_US".

If this `Locale` object has a variant code, an underscore and the variant code is appended to the result. The variant code is the same value passed to the constructor (after it has been converted to uppercase). To continue the previous example, if the variant code was "UNIX", this method would return "en_US_UNIX".

The format returned by this method is used by classes such as `ResourceBundle` to search for localized resource bundles. See `ResourceBundle` for more information.

Note: Java 1.1.4 has a bug whereby if the country code is empty, the variant code will not appear in the returned string.

RETURNS A non-`null` string representing this Locale object.

OVERRIDES `java.lang.Object.toString()`.

EXAMPLE See the class example.

Long

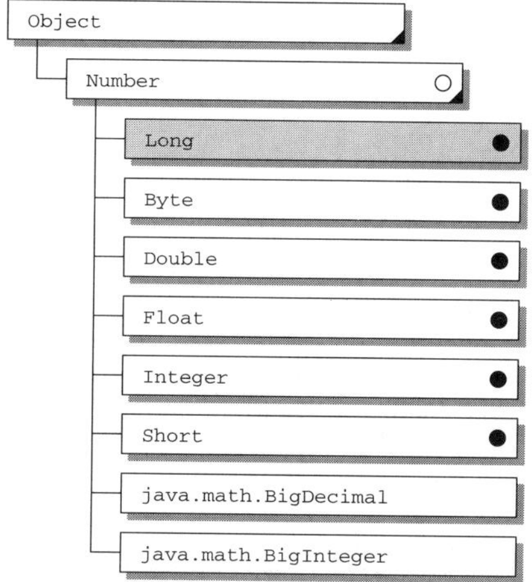

Syntax

```
public final class Long extends Number
```

Description

A `long` in Java is a 64-bit signed integer. The `Long` class provides an object wrapper for `long` data values. This allows `long` integers to be passed to methods in Java class libraries that accept Java objects as parameters. In addition, the `Long` class provides methods that convert values to and from `long`s and perform other operations on `long`s.

Usage

`Long` instances cannot be used in arithmetic expressions in place of `long`. For example, the following is not allowed:

```
Long l1 = new Long(193);
Long l2 = new Long(5);
Long l3 = l1 * l2;       // Illegal
```

To perform arithmetic operations using a `Long` instance, you first must use access methods defined in the `Long` class to obtain its numeric value, as follows:

```
long l3 = l1.longValue() * l2.longValue();
double d1 = l1.intValue() + l2.doubleValue();
```

MEMBER SUMMARY

Constructor	
`Long()`	Constructs a `Long` instance using a `long` or a string.
Constant Fields	
`MAX_VALUE`	The maximum value a `long` can have.
`MIN_VALUE`	The minimum value a `long` can have.
`TYPE`	The `Class` object representing the primitive type `long`.
Conversion Methods	
`getLong()`	Creates a `Long` object using the value of a system property.
`parseLong()`	Parses the string representation of an integer into a `long`.
`toBinaryString()`	Generates the string representation of a `long` as an unsigned binary number.
`toHexString()`	Generates the string representation of a `long` as an unsigned hexadecimal number.
`toOctalString()`	Generates the string representation of a `long` as an unsigned octal number.
`toString()`	Generates the string representation of a `long` or a `Long` object.
`valueOf()`	Creates a `Long` object using its string representation.
Number Methods	
`byteValue()`	Retrieves the value of this object as a `byte`.
`doubleValue()`	Retrieves the value of this object as a `double`.
`floatValue()`	Retrieves the value of this object as a `float`.
`intValue()`	Retrieves the value of this object as an `int`.
`longValue()`	Retrieves the value of this object as a `long`.
`shortValue()`	Retrieves the value of this object as a `short`.
Object Methods	
`equals()`	Compares this object with another object for equality.
`hashCode()`	Computes the hash code for this object.

See Also

`Byte`, `Double`, `Float`, `Integer`, `Number`, `Short`.

byteValue()

PURPOSE Retrieves the value of this object as a `byte`.

SYNTAX `public byte byteValue()`

DESCRIPTION This method returns the value of this object as a `byte` value by casting its `long` value to a `byte`.

RETURNS The value of this object as a `byte`.

SEE ALSO `doubleValue()`, `floatValue()`, `intValue()`, `longValue()`, `Number`, `shortValue()`.

EXAMPLE See `doubleValue()`.

doubleValue()

PURPOSE Retrieves the value of this object as a `double`.

SYNTAX `public double doubleValue()`

DESCRIPTION This method returns the value of this object as a `double` by casting its `long` value to a `double`.

RETURNS The value of this object as a `double`.

EXAMPLE

```
Long longobj = new Long(69121);

double dval = longobj.doubleValue(); // 69121.0
float fval = longobj.floatValue();   // 69121.0
int ival = longobj.intValue();       // 69121
long lval = longobj.longValue();     // 69121
byte bval = longobj.byteValue();     // 1
short sval = longobj.shortValue();   // 3685
```

equals()

PURPOSE Compares this object with another object for equality.

SYNTAX `public boolean equals(Object obj)`

DESCRIPTION This method compares the `long` value of this object with that of `obj`. It returns `true` if the two values are equal; it returns `false` otherwise. It also returns `false` if `obj` is `null` or is not a `Long` object.

PARAMETERS

`obj` The possibly `null` object against which this object is compared.

RETURNS `true` if the objects are the same; `false` otherwise.

OVERRIDES `Object.equals()`.

SEE ALSO `hashCode()`.

EXAMPLE

```
Long l1 = new Long(35661);
Long l2 = new Long(2341);

// Check whether the value of two Longs are equal
if (l1.equals(l2))
    System.out.println("equal");
```

A B C D E F G H I J K L M N O P Q R S T U V W X Y Z

floatValue()

PURPOSE Retrieves the value of this object as a `float`.

SYNTAX `public float floatValue()`

DESCRIPTION This method returns the value of this object as a `float` by casting its `long` value to a `float`.

RETURNS The value of this object as a `float`.

SEE ALSO `byteValue()`, `doubleValue()`, `intValue()`, `longValue()`, `Number`, `shortValue()`.

EXAMPLE See `doubleValue()`.

getLong()

PURPOSE Creates a `Long` object using the value of a system property.

SYNTAX

```
public static Long getLong(String prop)
public static Long getLong(String prop, long defval)
public static Long getLong(String prop, Long defobj)
```

DESCRIPTION The three forms of this method find the system property identified by `prop` and return the property's value as a `Long` object. The property's value must be an integer (in radix 10), a hexadecimal number, or an octal number. A hexadecimal number is prefixed by either `0x` or `#`. An octal number has a leading zero (`0`). If `prop` does not exist or if `prop`'s value is not a number in the format described here, the first form of this method returns `null`. In the same situation, the second form returns a `Long` object constructed using `defval`, while the third form returns `defobj`.

PARAMETERS

`defobj` The possibly `null` default `Long` object to return if `prop` does not exist.

`defval` The default `long` value to use for the resulting `Long` object if `prop` does not exist.

`prop` The name of the property.

RETURNS A `Long` object containing the value of `prop` if it contains a valid integer; otherwise, either `null` if the first form of the method is used or a default `Long` object as determined by `defval` or `defobj`.

SEE ALSO `java.util.Properties`, `System.getProperty()`.

EXAMPLE

```
// set up properties
Properties props = System.getProperties();
props.put("test.bignum", "1048576");        // radix 10 int property
props.put("test.bighex", "0xefffffffff"); // radix 16 int property
props.put("test.hex2", "#2");               // radix 16 int property
props.put("test.octal", "065");             // radix 8 int property
props.put("test.nonnum", "2.5.1");          // non-int property
System.setProperties(props);

// use the three forms of getInteger()
Long p1 = Long.getLong("test.bignum");
Long p2 = Long.getLong("test.bighex", 1024);
Long p3 = Long.getLong("test.hex2", new Long(0));
Long p4 = Long.getLong("test.octal", 256);
Long p5 = Long.getLong("test.nonnum", 1);

System.out.println("bignum: " + p1);
System.out.println("bighex: " + p2);
System.out.println("hex2: " + p3);
System.out.println("octal: " + p4);
System.out.println("nonnum: " + p5);
```

hashCode()

PURPOSE Computes the hash code for this object.

SYNTAX `public int hashCode()`

DESCRIPTION This method returns the hash code for this `Long` object. The code is calculated using its `long` value. Two `Long` objects with the same `long` value will have the same hash code, but two `Long` objects with the same hash code may not necessarily have the same `long` value.

RETURNS An `int` representing the object's hash code.

OVERRIDES `Object.hashCode()`.

SEE ALSO `equals()`, `java.util.Hashtable`.

EXAMPLE

```
Long lnum = new Long(3290);
int hashval = lnum.hashCode();      // generate hash code
++hits[Math.abs(hashval%tabsize)]; // count hits
```

intValue()

PURPOSE Retrieves the value of this object as an `int`.

SYNTAX `public int intValue()`

DESCRIPTION This method returns the value of this object as an `int` by casting its `long` value to an `int`.

RETURNS The value of this object as an `int`.

SEE ALSO `byteValue()`, `doubleValue()`, `floatValue()`, `longValue()`, `Number`, `shortValue()`.

EXAMPLE See `doubleValue()`.

Long()

PURPOSE Constructs a `Long` object using a `long` or a string.

SYNTAX
```
public Long(long value)
public Long(String str) throws NumberFormatException
```

DESCRIPTION The first form of this constructor constructs a `Long` object using `value`. The second form parses `str`—the string representation of a radix 10 integer—and uses its numeric value to create the `Long` object.

PARAMETERS

`str` The non-`null` string to be parsed into a `long`.

`value` The numeric value to use as the object's value.

EXCEPTIONS

`NumberFormatException`

If `str` cannot be parsed into an integer.

SEE ALSO `parseLong()`, `valueOf()`.

EXAMPLE
```
Long lobj = new Long(1024);           // using long
try {
    Long lobj2 = new Long("1048576"); // using string
    long div = lobj2.longValue() / lobj.longValue();
} catch (NumberFormatException e) {
  ...
}
```

A B C D E F G H I J K L M N O P Q R S T U V W X Y Z

longValue()

PURPOSE Retrieves the value of this object as a `long`.

SYNTAX `public long longValue()`

DESCRIPTION This method returns the value of this object as a `long` value.

RETURNS The value of this object as a `long`.

SEE ALSO `byteValue()`, `doubleValue()`, `floatValue()`, `intValue()`, `Number`, `shortValue()`.

EXAMPLE See `doubleValue()`.

MAX_VALUE

PURPOSE The maximum value a `long` can have.

SYNTAX `public static final long MAX_VALUE`

DESCRIPTION This constant represents the maximum value a `long` can have, which is `0x7fffffffffffffff`.

SEE ALSO `MIN_VALUE`.

EXAMPLE

```
// test if number is less than MAX_VALUE
long lnum = 512;
if (lnum < Long.MAX_VALUE)
    lnum *= 1000;
```

MIN_VALUE

PURPOSE The minimum value a `long` can have.

SYNTAX `public static final long MIN_VALUE`

DESCRIPTION This constant represents the minimum value a `long` can have, which is `0x8000000000000000`. This is a negative number.

SEE ALSO `MAX_VALUE`.

EXAMPLE

```
// test if number is greater than MIN_VALUE
long lnum = -512;
if (lnum > Long.MIN_VALUE)
    lnum -= 1000;
```

parseLong()

PURPOSE Parses the string representation of an integer into a `long`.

SYNTAX
```
public static long parseLong(String str) throws
    NumberFormatException
public static long parseLong(String str, int radix) throws
    NumberFormatException
```

DESCRIPTION The two forms of this method parse the string `str` into an integer and returns it as a `long`. If no radix is given, the radix used to parse `str` is 10. A negative integer has a leading negative (–) character. A positive integer consists only of the digits of the specified radix.

`parseLong()` is similar to `valueOf()`, except that `parseLong()` returns a `long`, while `valueOf()` returns a `Long` object.

PARAMETERS

`radix` The radix to use when parsing `str`. `Character.MIN_RADIX` ≤ `radix` ≤ `Character.MAX_RADIX`.

`str` The non-`null` string to be parsed.

RETURNS A `long` containing the numeric value of the integer represented by `str`.

EXCEPTIONS

`NumberFormatException`
If `str` cannot be parsed into an integer of the specified radix.

SEE ALSO `Character.MAX_RADIX`, `Character.MIN_RADIX`, `toString()`, `valueOf()`.

EXAMPLE
```
try {
    long lnum = Long.parseLong("8861212097");
    long hexnum = Long.parseLong("8a24fe3", 16);
} catch (NumberFormatException e) {
  ...
}
```

shortValue()

PURPOSE Retrieves the value of this object as a `short`.

SYNTAX
```
public short shortValue()
```

DESCRIPTION This method returns the value of this object as a `short` value by casting its `long` value to a `short`.

RETURNS The value of this object as a `short` by casting its `long` value to a `short`.

SEE ALSO `byteValue()`, `doubleValue()`, `floatValue()`, `intValue()`, `Number`, `longValue()`.

EXAMPLE See `doubleValue()`.

toBinaryString()

PURPOSE Generates the string representation of a `long` as an unsigned binary number.

SYNTAX `public static String toBinaryString(long lnum)`

DESCRIPTION This method returns the string representation of `lnum` as an unsigned binary number (base 2). (Treating `inum` as an unsigned 64-bit number means that the highest-order bit is treated as `2^64` if `inum` is negative.) The string consists of digits from base 2 ("01") representing the numeric value of `lnum`. If `inum` is `0`, "0" is the string representation; otherwise, leading zeros are not included in the string.

This method is equivalent to `toString(lnum, 2)` only when `lnum` is nonnegative. This is because `toString()` always treats `lnum` as a signed number.

PARAMETERS

`lnum` The `long` for which to generate the string representation.

RETURNS The non-`null` string representation of `lnum` as an unsigned binary number.

SEE ALSO `parseLong()`, `toHexString()`, `toOctalString()`, `toString()`, `valueOf()`.

EXAMPLE This example shows the difference between using `toString()`, `toBinaryString()`, `toOctalString()`, and `toHexString()` on a negative number. The output of this program is shown after the code.

```
class Main {
    public static void main(String[] args) {
        long lnum = -1234567890123l;
        System.out.println(Long.toString(lnum, 10));
        System.out.println(Long.toString(lnum, 2));
        System.out.println(Long.toString(lnum, 8));
        System.out.println(Long.toString(lnum, 16));

        System.out.println(Long.toString(lnum));
        System.out.println(Long.toBinaryString(lnum));
        System.out.println(Long.toOctalString(lnum));
        System.out.println(Long.toHexString(lnum));
    }
}
```

Output

```
-1234567890123
-10001111101110001111110110000010011001011
-21756176602313
```

```
-11f71fb04cb
-1234567890123
1111111111111111111111101110000010001110000001001111101100110101
1777777756021601175465
fffffee08e04fb35
```

A B C D E F G H I J K L M N O P Q R S T U V W X Y Z

toHexString()

PURPOSE Generates the string representation of a `long` as an unsigned hexadecimal number.

SYNTAX `public static String toHexString(long lnum)`

DESCRIPTION This method returns the string representation of `lnum` as an unsigned hexadecimal number (base 16). (Treating `inum` as an unsigned 64-bit number means that the highest-order bit is treated as `2^64` if `inum` is negative.) The string consists of digits from base 16 ("0123456789abcdef") representing the numeric value of `lnum`. If `inum` is `0`, "0" is the string representation; otherwise, leading zeros are not included in the string.

This method is equivalent to `toString(lnum, 16)` only when `lnum` is nonnegative. This is because `toString()` always treats `lnum` as a signed number.

PARAMETERS

`lnum` The `long` for which to generate the string representation.

RETURNS The non-`null` string representation of `lnum` as an unsigned hexadecimal number.

SEE ALSO `parseLong(), toBinaryString(), toOctalString(), toString(), valueOf().`

EXAMPLE See `toBinaryString()`.

toOctalString()

PURPOSE Generates the string representation of a `long` as an unsigned octal number.

SYNTAX `public static String toOctalString(long lnum)`

DESCRIPTION This method returns the string representation of `lnum` as an unsigned octal number (base 8). (Treating `inum` as an unsigned 64-bit number means that the highest-order bit is treated as `2^64` if `inum` is negative.) The string consists of digits from base 8 ("01234567") representing the numeric value of `lnum`. If `inum` is `0`, "0" is the string representation; otherwise, leading zeros are not included in the string.

This method is equivalent to toString(lnum, 8) only when lnum is nonnegative. This is because toString() always treats lnum as a signed number.

PARAMETERS

lnum — The long for which to generate the string representation.

RETURNS — The non-null string representation of lnum as an unsigned octal number.

SEE ALSO — parseLong(), toBinaryString(), toHexString(), toString(), valueOf().

EXAMPLE — See toBinaryString().

toString()

PURPOSE — Generates the string representation of a long or a Long object

SYNTAX

```
public String toString()
public static String toString(long lnum)
public static String toString(long lnum, int radix)
```

DESCRIPTION — The three forms of this method are used to generate the string representation of a long. The first form returns the string representation of the long value of this Long object. The second form returns the string representation of lnum in base 10. The third form returns the string representation of lnum in base radix.

The string consists of digits from the specified radix representing the numeric value of the number. If the number is negative, a leading negative sign (–) precedes the digits.

PARAMETERS

lnum — The number for which to generate the string representation.

radix — The radix to use when generating the string representation. Character.MIN_RADIX ≤ radix ≤ Character.MAX_RADIX. If radix is outside this range, it defaults to 10.

RETURNS — The non-null string representation of this Long object, or lnum.

OVERRIDES — Object.toString().

SEE ALSO — Character.MAX_RADIX, Character.MIN_RADIX, parseLong(), String.valueOf(), valueOf().

EXAMPLE

```
Long lnum = new Long(7981828);
String str = lnum.toString();                // get string form of Long obj
String str2 = Long.toString(312123412);      // string of number
String str3 = Long.toString(123318811, 16);  // string of hex
String pstr = "The three numbers are " + str + ", " + str2 + " ," + str3;
```

TYPE

PURPOSE The Class object representing the primitive type long.

SYNTAX `public static final Class TYPE`

DESCRIPTION This constant can be used where the Class object—long.class—of the primitive type long is required, such as for reflection. Although there are no restrictions on the use of Long.TYPE, the preferred syntax for naming the class is long.class.

SEE ALSO Class.

EXAMPLE

```
public static void main(String[] args) {
    Class c = Long.TYPE;
    System.out.println("TYPE: " + c);
    System.out.println("isPrimitive: " + c.isPrimitive());
    System.out.println("superclass: " + c.getSuperclass());
    try {
        Object obj = c.newInstance();  // ERROR
        System.out.println("short: " + obj);
    } catch (InstantiationException e) {
        e.printStackTrace();
    } catch (IllegalAccessException e) {
        e.printStackTrace();
    }
}
```

valueOf()

PURPOSE Creates a Long object using its string representation.

SYNTAX

```
public static Long valueOf(String str) throws
    NumberFormatException
public static Long valueOf(String str, int radix) throws
    NumberFormatException
```

DESCRIPTION These methods parse the string str into an integer and return a Long object constructed using the integer. If no radix is given, the radix used to parse str is 10. A negative integer has a leading negative (–) character. A positive integer consists only of digits in the specified radix.

valueOf() is similar to parseLong(), except that valueOf() returns a Long object, while parseLong() returns a long.

PARAMETERS

radix The radix to use when parsing str. Character.MIN_RADIX ≤ radix ≤ Character.MAX_RADIX.

str The string to be parsed.

EXCEPTIONS

`NumberFormatException`
If `str` cannot be parsed into an integer of the specified radix.

SEE ALSO `Character.MAX_RADIX`, `Character.MIN_RADIX`, `parseLong()`, `toString()`.

EXAMPLE

```
String str = "89618291243";
try {
    Long l1 = Long.valueOf(str);     // parse number in radix 10
    Long l2 = Long.valueOf(str, 16); // parse number in radix 16
     ...
} catch (NumberFormatException e) {
    System.err.println("Could not convert string to number " + str);
}
```

MalformedURLException

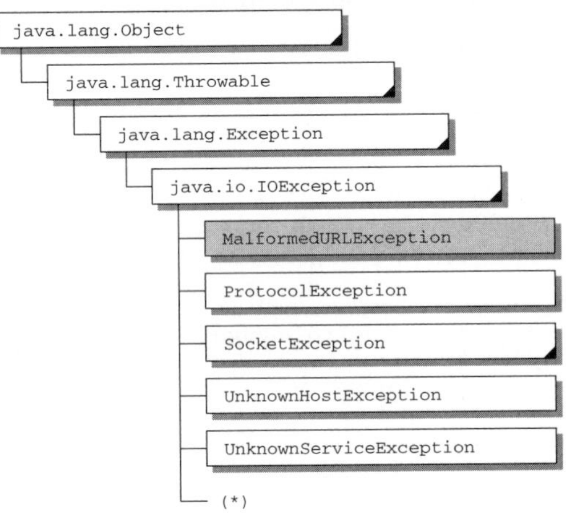

(*) 10 classes from other packages not shown.

A B C D E F G H I J K L M N O P Q R S T U V W X Y Z

Syntax

`public class MalformedURLException extends IOException`

Description

URL stands for *Uniform Resource Locator*. URLs are described in *RFC 1738*. A URL identifies the location of a resource on the World Wide Web. The `URL` class has constructors that allow you to create `URL` instances. If the arguments supplied to these constructors cannot be used to form a valid `URL`, a `MalformedURLException` is thrown.

A method that throws a `MalformedURLException` must declare it (or any of its superclasses) in the method's `throws` clause.

MEMBER SUMMARY	
Constructor	
`MalformedURLException()`	Constructs a `MalformedURLException` instance.

See Also

`java.io.IOException`, `URL`.

Example

This example throws a `MalformedURLException` when it attempts to create a `URL` with an unknown protocol `funnyProt`.

```
import java.net.URL;
import java.net.MalformedURLException;

class Main {
    public static void main(String[] args) {
        System.out.println("MalformedURLException example");
        try {
            URL url = new URL("funnyProt://www.test.com");
        } catch (MalformedURLException e) {
            e.printStackTrace();
        }
    }
}
```

MalformedURLException()

PURPOSE Constructs a `MalformedURLException` instance.

SYNTAX
```
public MalformedURLException()
public MalformedURLException(String msg)
```

DESCRIPTION The two forms of this constructor construct an instance of `MalformedURLException`. An optional string `msg` can be supplied that describes this particular instance of the exception. If `msg` is not supplied, it defaults to `null`.

PARAMETERS

`msg` A non-`null` string that gives details about this exception.

SEE ALSO `java.lang.Throwable.getMessage()`.

java.lang
Math

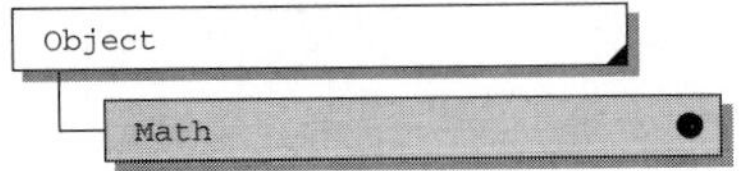

A B C D E F G H I J K L M N O P Q R S T U V W X Y Z

Syntax

```
public final class Math
```

Description

The `Math` class defines methods in the standard Math library. This library includes methods for calculating trigonometric functions, for rounding floating-point numbers into whole numbers, and for performing calculations using numbers. All methods and variables that this class defines are static.

This class cannot be subclassed or instantiated.

The ways by which these methods handle out-of-range or invalid results are platform-dependent.

See *The Java Language Specification, First Edition*, Section 20.11 for details of the semantics of the operations in this class.

MEMBER SUMMARY	
Constant Fields	
`E`	The value of *e*.
`PI`	The value of π.
Methods for Rounding	
`ceil()`	Rounds a number to the smallest whole number greater than or equal to it.
`floor()`	Rounds a number to the largest whole number less than or equal to it.
`rint()`	Rounds a floating-point number to its closest whole number.
`round()`	Rounds a floating-point number to a whole number and casts it to an `int` or `long`.
Methods for Trigonometry	
`acos()`	Calculates the arc cosine of a number.
`asin()`	Calculates the arc sine of a number.
`atan()`	Calculates the arc tangent of a number.
`atan2()`	Converts rectangular coordinates to polar coordinates.
`cos()`	Calculates the trigonometric cosine of an angle.
`sin()`	Calculates the trigonometric sine of an angle.
`tan()`	Calculates the trigonometric tangent of an angle.

MEMBER SUMMARY	
Other Methods	
`abs()`	Calculates the absolute value of a number.
`exp()`	Calculates the result of *e* raised to a specified power.
`IEEEremainder()`	Calculates the remainder of the division between two floating-point numbers.
`log()`	Calculates the natural logarithm of a number.
`max()`	Determines the greater of two numbers.
`min()`	Determines the smaller of two numbers.
`pow()`	Calculates the result of raising a number to a specified power.
`random()`	Generates a random number between 0.0 and 1.0.
`sqrt()`	Calculates the square root of a number.

abs()

PURPOSE
Calculates the absolute value of a number.

SYNTAX
```
public static int abs(int num)
public static long abs(long num)
public static float abs(float num)
public static double abs(double num)
```

DESCRIPTION
The forms of this method return the absolute value of `num` in the same data type as `num`. If `num` ≥ `0`, its absolute value is num. If `num` < `0`, then its absolute value is `-num`.

PARAMETERS

`num` The number of which to take the absolute value.

RETURNS
The absolute value of `num` in the same type as `num`.

EXAMPLE
```
int inum = 10;
long lnum = -2934;
float fnum = -0.1243f;
double dnum = 21341390.8;

// take the total of the absolute values
double sum = Math.abs(inum) + Math.abs(lnum) +
    Math.abs(fnum) + Math.abs(dnum);
```

acos()

PURPOSE Calculates the arc cosine of a number.

SYNTAX `public static native double acos(double x)`

DESCRIPTION This method returns the arc cosine of a number, `x`, where $-1 \le x \le 1$. The result is between $0 \le \operatorname{acos} x \le \pi$. If `x` is not in the range of `-1` to `1`, then the result is `NaN`.

PARAMETERS

`x` The cosine of an angle, where $-1 \le x \le 1$.

RETURNS The arc cosine of `x`, where $-1 \le x \le 1$; `Double.NaN` otherwise.

EXAMPLE

```
double x;
double alpha;
 ...
alpha = Math.acos(x);
```

asin()

PURPOSE Calculates the arc sine of a number.

SYNTAX `public static native double asin(double x)`

DESCRIPTION This method returns the arc sine of a number `x`, where $-1 \le x \le 1$. The result is between $-\pi/2 \le \operatorname{asin} x \le \pi/2$.

PARAMETERS

`x` The sine of an angle, where $-1 \le x \le 1$.

RETURNS The arc sine of `x`, where $-1 \le x \le 1$; `Double.NaN` otherwise.

EXAMPLE

```
double x;
double alpha;
 ...
alpha = Math.asin(x);
```

atan()

PURPOSE Calculates the arc tangent of a number.

SYNTAX `public static native double atan(double x)`

DESCRIPTION This method returns the arc tangent of a number `x`, where $-\infty < x < \infty$. The result is between $-\pi/2 < \operatorname{atan} x < \pi/2$.

A B C D E F G H I J K L M N O P Q R S T U V W X Y Z

PARAMETERS

`x` The tangent of an angle, where $-\infty < x < \infty$.

RETURNS The arc tangent of `x`.

EXAMPLE

```
double x;
double alpha; // place holder for atan(x)
  ...
if (x >= 0)
    alpha = (Math.PI / 2) - Math.atan(1 / x);
```

atan2()

PURPOSE Converts rectangular coordinates to polar coordinates.

SYNTAX `public static native double atan2(double y, double x)`

DESCRIPTION This method converts rectangular coordinates (x, y) to polar coordinates (r; θ). r is the radius vector, and θ is the vectorial angle. This method computes and returns the vectorial angle θ in the range –¼ to ¼. The radius vector can be computed using the formula $\sqrt{x^2 + y^2}$.

PARAMETERS

`x` The x part of the rectangular coordinates.

`y` The y part of the rectangular coordinates.

RETURNS The vectorial angle `0` in radians.

EXAMPLE

```
double x, y;
x = -2.33;
y = 0;
double alpha = Math.atan2(y, x); // == pi;
```

ceil()

PURPOSE Rounds a number to the smallest whole number greater than or equal to it.

SYNTAX `public static native double ceil(double x)`

DESCRIPTION This method returns the ceiling of `x`. This is the smallest whole number greater than or equal to `x`.

PARAMETERS

`x` The floating-point number being rounded.

RETURNS The ceiling of `x` as a `double`.

SEE ALSO `floor()`, `rint()`, `round()`.

EXAMPLE

```
double x = 879.327;
double ceilx = Math.ceil(x); // == 880
```

A B C D E F G H I J K L M N O P Q R S T U V W X Y Z

cos()

PURPOSE Calculates the trigonometric cosine of an angle.

SYNTAX `public static native double cos(double x)`

DESCRIPTION This method returns the cosine of the angle `x`.

PARAMETERS

`x` An angle measured in radians.

RETURNS The cosine of `x`.

EXAMPLE

```
// Calculate the cosine of a 60 degree angle
double angle = Math.PI / 3;
double cos = Math.cos(angle);
```

E

PURPOSE The value of *e*.

SYNTAX `public static final double E`

DESCRIPTION The floating-point representation (`double`) of the value of *e*, which is `2.7182818284590452354`.

EXAMPLE

```
// Calculate e**2
double e2 = Math.E * Math.E;
```

exp()

PURPOSE Calculates the result of *e* raised to a specified power.

SYNTAX `public static native double exp(double x)`

DESCRIPTION This method returns e^{x}.

PARAMETERS

`x` The power to which to raise *e*.

RETURNS e^{x}.

EXAMPLE

```
// Calculate e**pi
double ep = Math.exp(Math.PI);
```

floor()

PURPOSE Rounds a number to the largest whole number less than or equal to it.

SYNTAX `public static native double floor(double x)`

DESCRIPTION This method returns the floor of `x`. This is the largest whole number less than or equal to `x`.

PARAMETERS

`x` The floating-point number of which to take the floor.

RETURNS The floor of `x`.

SEE ALSO `ceil()`, `rint()`, `round()`.

EXAMPLE

```
double x = 879.327;
double floorx = Math.floor(x); // == 879
```

IEEEremainder()

PURPOSE Calculates the remainder of the division between two floating-point numbers.

SYNTAX `public static native double IEEEremainder(double f1, double f2)`

DESCRIPTION This method returns the remainder of dividing `f1` by `f2` as defined by IEEE754.

PARAMETERS

`f1` The dividend.

`f2` The divisor.

RETURNS The remainder.

EXAMPLE

```
double x = 8.892e20;
double y = 4.3109e3;
double rem = Math.IEEEremainder(x, y);
```

log()

PURPOSE Calculates the natural logarithm of a number.

SYNTAX `public static native double log(double x)`

DESCRIPTION This method returns $\log_e x$.

PARAMETERS

x The number of which to take the natural log. $x \geq 0$.

EXCEPTIONS

`ArithmeticException`
If $x < 0$.

EXAMPLE

```
double x = 1.383e2;
double natural_log = Math.log(x);
```

max()

PURPOSE Determines the greater of two numbers.

SYNTAX

```
public static int max(int x, int y)
public static long max(long x, long y)
public static float max(float x, float y)
public static double max(double x, double y)
```

DESCRIPTION The four forms of this method return the greater of the numbers x and y. There is a method for each of the numeric types `int`, `long`, `float`, and `double`.

PARAMETERS

x A number to be compared.

y A number to be compared.

RETURNS The greater of x and y.

SEE ALSO `min()`.

EXAMPLE

```
int i1 = 28, i2 = 3, imax, imin;
long l1 = 960876, l2 = 78768, lmax, lmin;
float f1 = 1.384f, f2 = -2.83e2f, fmax, fmin;
double d1 = -2.3498e18, d2 = 8.792e8, dmax, dmin;

imax = Math.max(i1, i2);
lmax = Math.max(l1, l2);
fmax = Math.max(f1, f2);
dmax = Math.max(d1, d2);

imin = Math.min(i1, i2);
lmin = Math.min(l1, l2);
```

```
fmin = Math.min(f1, f2);
dmin = Math.min(d1, d2);
```

min()

PURPOSE Determines the smaller of two numbers.

SYNTAX
```
public static int min(int x, int y)
public static long min(long x, long y)
public static float min(float x, float y)
public static double min(double x, double y)
```

DESCRIPTION The four forms of the method return the smaller of the numbers `x` and `y`. There is a method for each of the numeric types `int`, `long`, `float`, and `double`.

PARAMETERS

`x` A number to be compared.

`y` A number to be compared.

RETURNS The smaller of `x` and `y`.

SEE ALSO `max()`.

EXAMPLE See `max()`.

PI

PURPOSE The value of π.

SYNTAX
```
public static final double PI
```

DESCRIPTION The floating-point representation (`double`) of the value π, which is `3.14159265358979323846`.

EXAMPLE
```
public static double circleArea(double radius) {
    // area of a circle is pi*r**2
    return (Math.PI * Math.pow(radius, 2));
}
```

pow()

PURPOSE Calculates the result of raising a number to the specified power.

SYNTAX
```
public static native double pow(double x, double y)
```

DESCRIPTION This method returns x^y. If `x` is 0, then `y` must be greater than 0. If `x` is 0 or negative, then `y` must be a whole number.

PARAMETERS

x The number to raise.

y The power by which to raise x. Must be a whole number unless x is a nonzero, positive number.

RETURNS x^y.

EXCEPTIONS

`ArithmeticException`
If x = 0 and y ≤ 0.

`ArithmeticException`
If x ≤ 0 and y is not a whole number.

EXAMPLE

```
double pow1 = Math.pow(21.2, 2.5);
double pow2 = Math.pow(-12, 2); // == 144
double pow3 = Math.pow(2, -1);  // == 0.5
```

random()

PURPOSE Generates a random number between 0.0 and 1.0.

SYNTAX `public static synchronized double random()`

DESCRIPTION This method returns a random number between 0.0 and 1.0 using a *pseudorandom-number generator*. Random-number generators are often called pseudorandom-number generators because the numbers produced tend to repeat themselves after some number of calls.

RETURNS A pseudorandom number between 0.0 (inclusive) and 1.0 (exclusive).

SEE ALSO `Random`.

EXAMPLE

```
// Returns a number between 1 and 5 (inclusive)
public static short dice() {
    return (short)(Math.floor(Math.random() * 5) + 1);
}
```

rint()

PURPOSE Rounds a floating-point number to its closest whole number.

SYNTAX `public static native double rint(double x)`

DESCRIPTION This method rounds x to a whole number according to the IEEE754 rounding direction and returns it as a floating-point number (`double`). The rounding is to the closest whole number. If x is equally close to two whole numbers, the even whole number is returned. If x is already a whole number or if x is NaN or an infinity, x is returned.

PARAMETERS

x — The floating-point number to round.

RETURNS — The value of x rounded and returned as a double.

SEE ALSO — ceil(), floor(), round().

EXAMPLE

```
double round1 = Math.rint(21.345); // == 21
double round2 = Math.rint(21.534); // == 22
```

round()

PURPOSE — Rounds a floating-point number to its closest whole number and casts it to an int or long.

SYNTAX

```
public static int round(float x)
public static long round(double x)
```

DESCRIPTION — The two forms of this method round x to its closest whole number by first adding 0.5 to x, taking the floor of the result, and casting the result to an int or a long. A float is casted to an int; a double is casted to a long. When the resulting number does not fit into an int or a long, the result is that of Integer.MAX_VALUE or Integer.MIN_VALUE or of Long.MAX_VALUE or Long.MIN_VALUE, respectively.

PARAMETERS

x — The number to round.

RETURNS — The rounded-off whole number. If x is a float, the return type is an int. If x is a double, the return type is a long.

SEE ALSO — ceil(), floor(), round().

EXAMPLE

```
int round = Math.round(5.62e2f);      // == 562
long lround = Math.round(1243.45);    // == 1243
```

sin()

PURPOSE — Calculates the trigonometric sine of an angle.

SYNTAX

```
public static native double sin(double x)
```

DESCRIPTION — This method returns the trigonometric sine of the angle x.

PARAMETERS

x An angle measured in radians.

RETURNS The sine of x.

EXAMPLE

```
// Calculate the sine of a 30 degree angle
double angle = Math.PI / 6;
double sin = Math.sin(angle);
```

sqrt()

PURPOSE Calculates the square root of a number.

SYNTAX `public static native double sqrt(double x)`

DESCRIPTION This method returns the square root of the positive number x.

PARAMETERS

x The number of which to take the square root. x must be a positive number.

RETURNS The square root of x.

EXCEPTIONS

ArithmeticException
If x is negative.

EXAMPLE

```
double sqrt1 = Math.sqrt(2);
```

tan()

PURPOSE Calculates the trigonometric tangent of an angle.

SYNTAX `public static native double tan(double x)`

DESCRIPTION This method returns the trigonometric tangent of the angle x.

PARAMETERS

x An angle measured in radians.

RETURNS The tangent of x.

EXAMPLE

```
double angle = 3 * Math.PI / 4;
double tan = Math.tan(angle);
```

Member

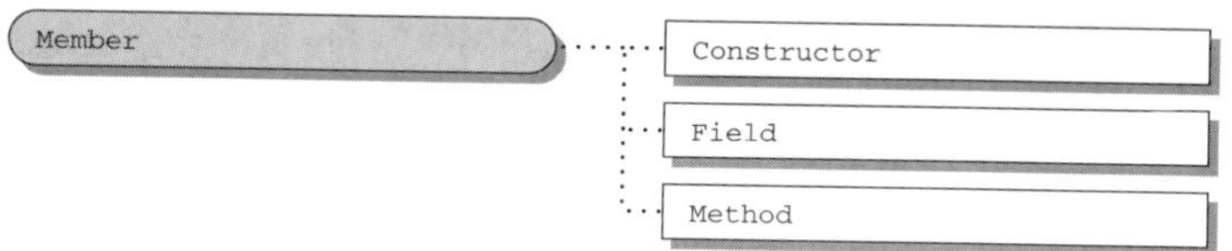

A B C D E F G H I J K L M N O P Q R S T U V W X Y Z

Syntax

```
public interface Member
```

Description

This interface is implemented by the classes `Field`, `Method`, and `Constructor`. This interface contains methods that are common to all three classes.

Note that in *The Java Language Specification*, the term *member* refers to fields and methods and not to constructors. However, a `Member` is an object which reflects a field, or a method, or a constructor. To avoid encouraging incorrect terminology, we use the official (*The Java Language Specification*) definition in our descriptions.

The Name

The name of a `Member` object is the string used to name the field, method, or constructor in the source code. All `Member` objects have a name.

The Modifiers

The modifiers of a `Member` object can be retrieved by using `getModifiers()` and methods in the `Modifier` class. Except for the access modifiers—`public`, `protected`, and `private`—the set of possible modifiers for a `Member` object depends on its actual type. Table 32 summarizes the modifier set for each `Member` object type.

`Member` Object Type	Valid Modifiers
`Field`	`public, protected, private, static, final, volatile, transient`
`Method`	`public, protected, private, abstract, static, final, synchronized, native`
`Constructor`	`public, protected, private`

TABLE 32: Valid Modifiers for `Member` Object Types.

The Declaring Class
The declaring class of a `Member` object is the class or interface that actually declares the field, method, or constructor. For example, if you create a method object on an inherited method, the declaring class of the new method object is set to the superclass that actually declares the method. See the class descriptions of `Field`, `Method`, and `Constructor` for more specific information on the declaring class.

MEMBER SUMMARY	
Member Constants	
`DECLARED`	The set of declared fields, methods, and constructors of a class or interface.
`PUBLIC`	The set of public inherited and declared fields, methods, and constructors of a class or interface.
Get Property Methods	
`getDeclaringClass()`	Retrieves this `Member` object's declaring class object.
`getModifiers()`	Retrieves the modifiers for this `Member`.
`getName()`	Retrieves this `Member` object's name.

See Also
`Constructor`, `Field`, `Method`, `Modifiers`.

Example
This example implements a program that prints out the names of all of the `public` and `protected` members of a class. The list includes members and constructors declared by the class and by all of its superclasses. The printed list represents all of the fields, methods, and constructors that a client or subclass of the class can override or use. It uses the `QuickSort` and `Comparator` classes from the `Array` class example.

```
import java.lang.reflect.*;
import java.util.*;

class Main {
    Main(Class c) {
        Member[] members;
        Vector v = new Vector();

        // Retrieve the members of class c and all its superclasses.
        while (c != null) {
            members = c.getDeclaredFields();
            for (int i=0; i<members.length; i++) {
                v.addElement(members[i]);
            }
```

```
            members = c.getDeclaredMethods();
            for (int i=0; i<members.length; i++) {
                v.addElement(members[i]);
            }

            members = c.getDeclaredConstructors();
            for (int i=0; i<members.length; i++) {
                v.addElement(members[i]);
            }
            c = c.getSuperclass();
        }

        // Keep only public and protected members and constructors.
        for (int i=v.size()-1; i>=0; i--) {
            int mods = ((Member)v.elementAt(i)).getModifiers();

            if (!Modifier.isPublic(mods) && !Modifier.isProtected(mods)) {
                v.removeElementAt(i);
            }
        }

        // Transfer the vector contents to an array.
        members = new Member[v.size()];
        for (int i=0; i<v.size(); i++) {
            members[i] = (Member)v.elementAt(i);
        }

        // Sort the array by member name.
        QuickSort.sort(members, new Compare());

        // Print the results.
        String lastEntry = null;
        for (int i=0; i<members.length; i++) {
            String name = members[i].getName();
            String newEntry = members[i].getDeclaringClass()+name;

            // Skip duplicate entries.
            if (newEntry.equals(lastEntry)) {
                continue;
            }
            lastEntry = newEntry;

            System.out.print(name);
            if (!(members[i] instanceof Field)) {
                System.out.print("()");
            } else {
                System.out.print("  ");
            }

            // Pad with spaces.
            for (int j=0; j<20-name.length(); j++) {
                System.out.print(" ");
            }

            // Print declaring class.
            System.out.println(" " + members[i].getDeclaringClass().getName());
        }
    }

    // Sort by member name.
```

```
    class Compare implements Comparator {
        public int compare(Object a, Object b) {
            String s1 = ((Member)a).getName();
            String s2 = ((Member)b).getName();
            return s1.compareTo(s2);
        }
    }

    public static void main(String[] args) {
        if (args.length != 1) {
            System.err.println("Usage: java Main <classname>");
        } else {
            try {
                new Main(Class.forName(args[0]));
            } catch (ClassNotFoundException e) {
                e.printStackTrace();
            }
        }
    }
}
```

Output

```
> java Main java.io.BufferedReader
clone()                 java.lang.Object
close()                 java.io.BufferedReader
close()                 java.io.Reader
equals()                java.lang.Object
finalize()              java.lang.Object
getClass()              java.lang.Object
hashCode()              java.lang.Object
java.io.BufferedReader() java.io.BufferedReader
java.io.Reader()        java.io.Reader
java.lang.Object()      java.lang.Object
lock                    java.io.Reader
mark()                  java.io.Reader
mark()                  java.io.BufferedReader
markSupported()         java.io.Reader
ready()                 java.io.Reader
markSupported()         java.io.BufferedReader
notify()                java.lang.Object
notifyAll()             java.lang.Object
read()                  java.io.Reader
read()                  java.io.BufferedReader
read()                  java.io.Reader
read()                  java.io.BufferedReader
ready()                 java.io.BufferedReader
reset()                 java.io.Reader
reset()                 java.io.BufferedReader
readLine()              java.io.BufferedReader
skip()                  java.io.BufferedReader
skip()                  java.io.Reader
toString()              java.lang.Object
wait()                  java.lang.Object
```

DECLARED

PURPOSE The set of declared fields, methods, and constructors of a class or interface.

SYNTAX `public static final int DECLARED`

DESCRIPTION This constant is used by only one method: `SecurityManager.checkMemberAccess()`. It is used internally by classes in the `java.lang.reflect` package. It is used to check if the client has permission to access the declared fields, methods, and constructors of a particular class.

SEE ALSO `PUBLIC, java.lang.SecurityManager.checkMemberAccess().`

EXAMPLE This example demonstrates how to check to see if you have access to a class's declared or public methods. The example also demonstrates how to override the security manager to deny all access.

```
import java.lang.reflect.*;

class Main {
    static void check(Class c) {
        SecurityManager sm = System.getSecurityManager();

        // Check public access.
        try {
            if (sm != null) {
                sm.checkMemberAccess(c, Member.PUBLIC);
            }
            System.out.print("You do ");
        } catch (SecurityException e) {
            System.out.print("You don't ");
        }
        System.out.println("have permission to access all public "
            + "inherited and declared fields, methods, and constructors "
            + "of " + c);

        // Check declared access.
        try {
            if (sm != null) {
                sm.checkMemberAccess(c, Member.DECLARED);
            }
            System.out.print("You do ");
        } catch (SecurityException e) {
            System.out.print("You don't ");
        }
        System.out.println("have permission to access all declared "
            + "fields, methods, and constructors "
            + "of " + c);

    }
    public static void main(String[] args) {
        // Access enabled.
        check(Main.class);

        System.setSecurityManager(new MySecurityManager());
        System.out.println();
```

```
            // Access disabled.
            check(Main.class);
        }
    }

    class MySecurityManager extends SecurityManager {
        public void checkMemberAccess(Class clazz, int which) {
            throw new SecurityException();
        }
    }
```


getDeclaringClass()

PURPOSE Retrieves this `Member` object's declaring class.

SYNTAX `public Class getDeclaringClass()`

DESCRIPTION The declaring class of a `Member` object is the class or interface that actually declares the field, method, or constructor.

RETURNS The non-`null` `Class` object of the declaring class of this `Member` object.

EXAMPLE See the class example.

getModifiers()

PURPOSE Retrieves the modifiers for this `Member` object.

SYNTAX `public int getModifiers()`

DESCRIPTION This method retrieves this `Member` object's set of modifiers, bit-encoded in an `int`. The possible list of method modifiers for a `Member` object depends on its type. To process the encoding, use the methods and constants in `Modifier`. See the class description for more details.

RETURNS An `int` representing the `Member` object's set of modifiers.

SEE ALSO `Modifier`.

EXAMPLE See the class example.

getName()

PURPOSE Retrieves this `Member` object's name.

SYNTAX `public String getName()`

DESCRIPTION The name of a `Member` object is the string used to name the field, method, or constructor in the source code.

RETURNS A non-`null` string containing this method object's name.

EXAMPLE See the class example.

PUBLIC

PURPOSE The set of public inherited and declared fields, methods, and constructors of a class or interface.

SYNTAX `public static final int PUBLIC`

DESCRIPTION This constant is used by only one method: `SecurityManager.checkMemberAccess()`. It is used internally by classes in the `java.lang.reflect` package. It is used to check if the client has permission to access the public inherited and declared fields, methods, and constructors of a particular class.

SEE ALSO `DECLARED`, `java.lang.SecurityManager.checkMemberAccess()`.

EXAMPLE See `DECLARED`.

java.text

MessageFormat

- java.lang.Object
  - Format
    - MessageFormat
    - DateFormat
    - NumberFormat

Syntax

```
public class MessageFormat extends Format
```

Description

The `MessageFormat` class provides a standard means of producing language-specific user messages that contain number, currency, percentages, date, time, and string variables. `MessageFormat` takes a set of objects, formats them to strings, and then inserts those strings into a pattern at the appropriate places to produce a string. This class uses the term "message" to mean text that is generally visible to an international set of users and hence is localized for each locale.

A user message can contain text interspersed with numbers, currency, percentages, dates, times, and string variables. An example of a text variable is in this statement: "She selected a <car>," where <car> can be replaced by "Ford" or "Chevrolet." In a specific locale, while the text and text variables typically require manual translation, the other parts (numbers, dates currency, percent) can be translated automatically by built-in locale-sensitive reformatting.

The `MessageFormat` class enables the separating out of the elements that need only be reformatted from the rest of the text. These elements can be variables so that messages can be constructed on the fly based on some current state, and word order can vary from one locale to another.

Usage

A message is based on a pattern made up of strings and variables. The variables are substituted into strings at format time. The variables can be

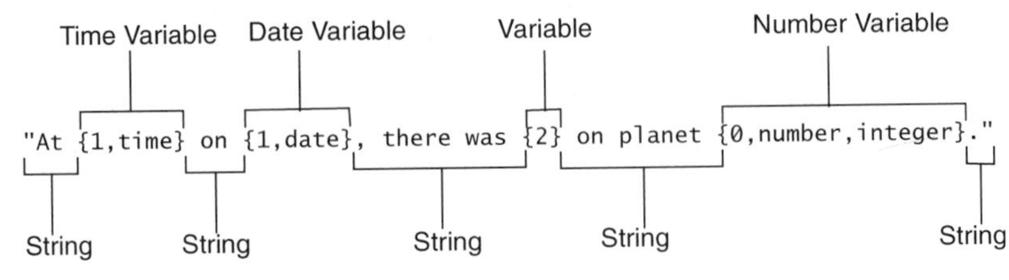

FIGURE 66: `MessageFormat`.

times, dates, numbers, or choices. The pattern itself is a string in which variables are denoted by braces, as shown in Figure 66.

The example in the figure formats to a message like the following (underlining is added to show where the variables are inserted):

```
At 12:30 PM on Jul 3, 2053, there was a disturbance in the Force on planet 7.
```

As shown in Figure 66, this pattern contains four variables. Each variable begins with an argument number (0–9) and can have an optional element format (`time`, `date`, `number`, or `choice`). The element format can itself contain a style, as in `{0,number,integer}`, where the style of `number` is `integer`. The element format indicates how the argument should be formatted.

Following are several ways to create a message format. In all cases, the arguments (if there are more than one) are set up in an array before calling `format()`.

1. Call the static method `MessageFormat.format(String pattern, Object arguments[])`, passing in a pattern and an array of arguments. This is quite straightforward and is the simplest approach, since it does not require explicitly creating an instance of `MessageFormat`. However, it does not give you access to the message format instance in case you want to apply a new pattern, locale, or set of formats. This is demonstrated later in alternative 1.
2. Create an instance of `MessageFormat`, passing in a pattern. Then call the nonstatic method `format(Object obj)`, which is inherited from `Format`, passing in the array of arguments. The pattern is formatted to a string, which is returned. This is equivalent to the next form—creating a new string buffer on the fly. This is demonstrated later in alternative 2.
3. Create an instance of `MessageFormat`, passing in a pattern. Then call the nonstatic method `format(Object arguments[], StringBuffer appendBuf, FieldPosition ignore)`. The pattern is formatted to a string, which is appended to `appendBuf`, and that result is returned.
4. If there is only one argument, a shortcut is to do the third approach but to call the method `format(Object singleArg, StringBuffer appendBuf, FieldPosition ignore)`.

The pattern can be either supplied when creating the `MessageFormat` instance or applied later by using the `applyPattern()` method. The arguments are always passed in with the `format()` method.

Each argument can have a format. You can supply the formats as an array, separate from the pattern, by using the `setFormats()` method.

Note: `MessageFormat` differs from most of the other `Format` classes in that you create a `MessageFormat` object with one of its constructors (not with a `getInstance`-style creation method).

Formatting: Alternative 1

This alternative first creates an array called `arguments` that holds objects to be formatted and output. The array includes an integer, a date, and a string. Then the static form of the `format()`

method is called, passing in a pattern and the argument array. The arguments from the array are called by the argument numbers 0, 1, and 2 in the pattern. The element formats time, date, and number determine how the arguments will be formatted. Typically, the pattern and any other locale-sensitive strings, such as the third argument, will come from resource bundles.

```
Object[] arguments = {
    new Integer(7),
    new Date(System.currentTimeMillis()),
    "disturbance was created"
};
// Call format() on a pattern.
String result = MessageFormat.format(
    "At {1,time} on {1,date}, a {2} on planet {0,number,integer}.",
    arguments);
```

Output

```
At 12:30 PM on Jul 3, 2053, a disturbance was created on planet 7.
```

Formatting: Alternative 2

This alternative first creates an array of size 2 to hold objects to be included in the formatted result. It then creates an instance of MessageFormat, passing in a pattern. Next, it uses the form of the format() method, inherited from the Format class, that takes an array of arguments.

```
Object[] arguments = {new Long(3), "MyDisk"};
MessageFormat form = new MessageFormat(
    "The disk {1} contains {0} file(s).");
System.out.println(form.format(arguments));
```

Output for various values in arguments

```
The disk MyDisk contains 0 file(s).
The disk MyDisk contains 1 file(s).
The disk MyDisk contains 1,273 file(s).
```

Message Pattern

The message pattern determines the type, style, and order of the variables in the message. The pattern can be passed in with the constructor or set with applyPattern(). The pattern is of this form:

```
messageFormatPattern := string ( "{" messageFormatElement "}" string )*
    messageFormatElement := argumentNumber { "," elementFormat }
        argumentNumber := "0".."9"
        elementFormat := "time" { "," datetimeStyle }
                       | "date" { "," datetimeStyle }
                       | "number" { "," numberStyle }
                       | "choice" { "," choiceStyle }
            datetimeStyle := "short"
                           | "medium"
                           | "long"
                           | "full"
                           | dateFormatPattern1
```

1. See “pattern” in SimpleDateFormat class.

```
numberStyle    := "currency"
                | "percent"
                | "integer"
                | numberFormatPattern¹
choiceStyle    := choiceFormatPattern²
```

A *variable* is a `messageFormatElement` enclosed within braces. Thus the `messageFormatElement` in the previous example of `1,time` corresponds to the variable `{1,time}`.

The argument number is an integer from 0 to 9, which corresponds to the arguments presented in an array to be formatted. This argument array is passed into the `format()` method.

If there is no `elementFormat`, then the argument must be a string type, which is substituted for at format time. If there is no `dateTimeStyle` or `numberStyle`, then the default format is used. (For example, `NumberFormat.getInstance` is used for numbers, `DateFormat.getTimeInstance` is used for time, and `DateFormat.getInstance` is used for date.)

In patterns, to include the brace as a literal character, use single quotation marks to quote the brace ({). A real single quotation mark is represented by two single marks (`''`). Inside a `messageFormatElement`, quoted elements are *not* removed. For example, `{1,number,'#',##}` will produce a number format with a literal pound-sign (#), thus formatting the number 12.34 to the string "#12,34".

If a pattern is used, then unquoted braces in the pattern, if any, must be balanced pairs. That is, "`ab {0} de`" and "`ab '}' de`" are okay, but "`ab {0'}' de`" and "`ab } de`" are not.

It is okay to have unused arguments in the array. With missing arguments, or arguments that are not of the right class for the specified format, a `ParseException` is thrown. First, `format()` checks to see if a `Format` object has been specified for the argument either in the pattern or with the `setFormats()` method. If so, then `format()` uses that `Format` object to format the argument. Otherwise, the argument is formatted based on the object's type. If the argument is a `Number` object, then `format` uses `NumberFormat.getInstance` to format the argument. If the argument is a `Date`, then `format()` uses `DateFormat.getDateTimeInstance` to format the argument. Otherwise, it uses the `toString()` method.

ChoiceFormat

For more sophisticated patterns, such as having the text be singular or plural to match its associated variable, you can use a `ChoiceFormat`:

```
import java.text.*;
import java.util.*;

class Main {
    static public void main(String[] args) {

        MessageFormat form = new MessageFormat("The disk {1} contains {0}.");
        double[] filelimits = {0,1,2};
        String[] filepart = {"no files","one file","{0,number} files"};
```

1. See "pattern" in `DecimalFormat` class.
2. See "pattern" in `ChoiceFormat` class.

```
            ChoiceFormat fileform = new ChoiceFormat(filelimits, filepart);
            form.setFormat(1,fileform);

            Object[] arguments = {null, null};

            arguments[1] = "MyDisk";

            arguments[0] = new Long(0);
            System.out.println(form.format(arguments));

            arguments[0] = new Long(1);
            System.out.println(form.format(arguments));

            arguments[0] = new Long(12373);
            System.out.println(form.format(arguments));
        }
    }
```

Output

```
> java Main
The disk MyDisk contains no files.
The disk MyDisk contains one file.
The disk MyDisk contains 12,373 files.
```

You can either generate the output programmatically, as in the above example, or by using a pattern (see `ChoiceFormat` for more information) as in this:

```
form.applyPattern(
"There {0,choice,0#are no files|1#is one file|1<are {0,number,integer} files}."
);
```

Note: The string produced by a `ChoiceFormat` in `MessageFormat` is treated specially. Occurrences of { are used to indicated subformats and cause recursion. If you create both a `MessageFormat` and `ChoiceFormat` programmatically (instead of using the string patterns), then be careful not to produce a format that recurses on itself, as doing this will cause an infinite loop.

Array of Formats

You can create an array of formats to use instead of supplying formats within the pattern. Each member of the array maps to a variable in the order in which it appears in the pattern. As with all arrays, the array keys are 0-based; these keys do *not* correspond to the argument numbering! It is necessary for the number of members in the format array to be equal to (or greater than) the number of variable items in the pattern; otherwise, an `ArrayIndexOutOfBoundsException` is thrown at runtime. In the future, `setLenient()` may added to allow fewer members in the format array.

Here is a sample format array for a locale `loc`:

```
Format[] formats = {
    DateFormat.getTimeInstance(DateFormat.DEFAULT, loc),
    DateFormat.getDateInstance(DateFormat.DEFAULT, loc),
    null,
    null,
    getIntegerFormat(loc)
};
```

When the `format()` method of `MessageFormat` is called, it calls the `format()` method of each member of the formats array, in turn, on the corresponding argument.

As an example of how the format array members map to the variables in a pattern, consider the pattern "`abc{2}def{3}ghi{0}`":

- `formats[0]` affects the *first* variable {2}.
- `formats[1]` affects the *second* variable {3}.
- `formats[2]` affects the *third* variable {0}.

Parsing

Parsing is the reverse operation of formatting—iterating over a string, recognizing formats, and converting those formats to an array of objects such as numbers, dates, and times. Parsing does not require that you start with an array of arguments. Instead, you start with an array of formats as defined by `setFormats()` and with a pattern. Then, calling `parse(String str, ParsePosition pos)` converts string `str` starting at position `pos` to the array of objects.

MEMBER SUMMARY

Constructor	
`MessageFormat()`	Constructs a `MessageFormat` instance with a string pattern.
Parse and Format Methods	
`format()`	Formats this message pattern to produce a string.
`getFormats()`	Gets the array of formats that are used on variables in a pattern.
`setFormat()`	Sets a format to be used on a variable in a pattern.
`setFormats()`	Sets an array of formats to be used on variables in a pattern.
`parse()`	Parses a string to an array of number, date, time, string, and other objects.
`parseObject()`	Parses a string to an object.
Pattern Methods	
`applyPattern()`	Applies a pattern to this message format.
`toPattern()`	Produces a string of the current pattern.
Locale Methods	
`getLocale()`	Retrieves the locale used by this message format.
`setLocale()`	Sets the locale for number and date formats in this message format.
Object Methods	
`clone()`	Creates a copy of this message format.
`equals()`	Compares this `MessageFormat` object with another object for equality.
`hashCode()`	Computes the hash code for this `MessageFormat` object.

See Also

java.util.Locale, Format, NumberFormat, DecimalFormat, ChoiceFormat.

Example

This example uses formatting alternative 2 discussed earlier in this class, except that it applies the pattern using applyPattern(). It contains a simple message in English and French. Each is stored in its own resource bundle. The word order is slightly different to show how the pattern can accept variables in different orders. The class MyResources is the resource bundle for the U. S. locale and is defined in the file MyResources.java. The class MyResources_fr is the resource bundle for the France locale and is in the file MyResources_fr.java. Notice that the date and time for the French printout is 9 hours later than the U. S. English printout; this reflects the time difference between California (where the virtual machine is running) and France.

Main.java

```
import java.text.MessageFormat;
import java.util.*;

class Main {
    static public void main(String[] args) {

        Locale[] locArray = {Locale.ENGLISH, Locale.FRENCH};

        for (int i = 0; i < locArray.length; ++i) {

            Locale loc = locArray[i];

            // Create a message format and set its locale.
            MessageFormat mf = new MessageFormat("");
            mf.setLocale(loc);

            // Diagnostics.
            System.out.println(mf.getLocale());

            // Create a resource bundle object and load the bundle.
            ResourceBundle myResources = null;
            myResources = ResourceBundle.getBundle("MyResources", loc);

            // Assign the first 4 objects from the bundle to an array.
            Object[] arguments = {
                new Integer(7),
                new Long(System.currentTimeMillis()),
                myResources.getString("color"),
                myResources.getString("animal"),
            };

            // Get the pattern from resource bundle and apply it to mf.
            mf.applyPattern(myResources.getString("pattern"));

            // Diagnostics.
            System.out.println(mf.toPattern());

            // Format the objects in the arguments array to a string.
            String result = mf.format(arguments);
```

```
            // Print the formatted string.
            System.out.println(result);
            System.out.println("");       // Blank line
        }
    }
}
```

MyResources.java

```
import java.util.ListResourceBundle;

public class MyResources extends ListResourceBundle {
    public Object[][] getContents() {
        return contents;
    }

    static final Object[][] contents = {
        // LOCALIZE THE FOLLOWING
        {"color", "blue"},
        {"animal", "dog"},
        {"pattern",
        "At {1,time} on {1,date}, a {2} {3} ate on Planet {0,number,integer}."}
        // END OF MATERIAL TO LOCALIZE
    };
}
```

MyResources_fr.java

```
import java.util.ListResourceBundle;

public class MyResources_fr extends ListResourceBundle {
    public Object[][] getContents() {
        return contents;
    }

    static final Object[][] contents = {
        // LOCALIZE THE FOLLOWING
        {"color", "bleu"},
        {"animal", "chien"},
        {"pattern",
         "A {1,time} le {1,date}, un {3} {2} a mangé sur la Planète {0,num-
ber,integer}."}
        // END OF MATERIAL TO LOCALIZE
    };
}
```

Output

```
> java Main
en
At {1,date,h:mm:ss a} on {1,date,dd-MMM-yy}, a {2} {3} ate on Planet {0,num-
ber,integer}.
At 11:34:49 AM on 15-Nov-97, a blue dog ate on Planet 7.

fr
A {1,date,HH:mm:ss} le {1,date,d MMM yy}, un {3} {2} a mangé sur la Planète
{0,number,integer}.
A 20:34:49 le 15 nov 97, un chien bleu a mangé sur la Planète 7.
```

applyPattern()

PURPOSE Applies a pattern to this message format.

SYNTAX `public void applyPattern(String newPattern)`

DESCRIPTION This method applies the string `pattern` to this message format. Typically, the pattern is localized. This pattern is used by the `format()` method to generate a string.

PARAMETERS

`newPattern` The string pattern to be applied.

EXAMPLE See the class example.

clone()

PURPOSE Creates a copy of this message format.

SYNTAX `public Object clone()`

DESCRIPTION This method makes a copy of this message format. The new message format has a complete copy of the pattern. Changing any value in the new message format will not affect the original instance.

RETURNS A non-`null` copy of this message format.

OVERRIDES `Format.clone()`.

EXAMPLE This example illustrates the use of `clone()` to copy a message format object. Note that the copy has the same pattern as the original.

```
import java.text.MessageFormat;

class Main {
    public static void main(String args[]) {

        // create message format
        MessageFormat df = new MessageFormat("The disk {1} contains {0}.");
        System.out.println("Original pattern: " + df.toPattern());

        // create a clone
        MessageFormat dfCopy = (MessageFormat)df.clone();
        System.out.println("Copy's pattern:   " + df.toPattern());

        // tests for equality
        if (df.equals(dfCopy)) {
            System.out.println("Clone is equal to original");
        }

        // compute hashcode
        int hc = df.hashCode();
        System.out.println("Hash code:        " + hc);
    }
}
```

Output

```
> java Main
Original pattern: The disk {1} contains {0}.
Copy's pattern:   The disk {1} contains {0}.
Clone is equal to original
Hash code:        -2068320632
```


equals()

PURPOSE Compares this `MessageFormat` object with another object for equality.

SYNTAX `public boolean equals(Object obj)`

DESCRIPTION This method compares this `MessageFormat` with `obj` for equality. If `obj` is a `MessageFormat` object and if it has the same pattern and locale values as this `MessageFormat`, the objects are equal and this method returns true. If the values are not equal or if `obj` is `null` or not a `MessageFormat` object, this method returns `false`.

PARAMETERS

`obj` A possibly `null` object.

RETURNS `true` if object `obj` is not `null` and is of type `MessageFormat` and is equal to this message format; `false` otherwise.

OVERRIDES `Object.equals()`.

SEE ALSO `hashCode()`.

EXAMPLE See `clone()`.

format()

PURPOSE Formats this message pattern to produce a string.

SYNTAX

```
public static String format(String pattern, Object arguments[])
public final StringBuffer format(Object arguments[],
   StringBuffer appendBuf, FieldPosition ignore)
public final StringBuffer format(Object singleArg,
   StringBuffer appendBuf, FieldPosition ignore)
```

DESCRIPTION The first form of this method is a convenience static method for the default locale that avoids explicit creation of an instance of `MessageFormat`. However, it doesn't allow further customization, such as setting the locale, changing the pattern, or setting formats. This method formats the variables (denoted by braces `{}`) with objects from the `arguments` array and inserts those formatted strings into the string `pattern`. Each variable begins with an argument number that corresponds to the index of the argument array. Therefore variable {1,time} formats argument[1] as a time object.

The second syntax form formats an array of objects according to the format's pattern and appends the resulting string to the string buffer appendBuf, which it also returns. The field position parameter is ignored. The pattern can be set before calling format(), either when calling the MessageFormat() constructor or with applyPattern().

The third syntax form is similar to the second, except that it formats a single object.

A fourth syntax form is inherited from the format class and allows the array of arguments to be passed in. It assumes the message format has already had the pattern applied to it. Its syntax is

```
public final String format(Object obj)
```

PARAMETERS

appendBuf	The string buffer in which the formatted text is appended.
arguments	The array of objects to be formatted and inserted into the pattern.
ignore	This field is ignored because messages do not have fields. Passes in null.
pattern	A localized string pattern.
singleArg	A single object to be formatted and inserted into the pattern.

OVERRIDES Format.format().

EXAMPLE This example demonstrates the second form of format() so that it can set the locale to French (this is not possible with the first form). It uses the same two resource files as the class example.

Main.java

```
import java.text.MessageFormat;
import java.util.*;

class Main {
    static public void main(String[] args) {

        Locale loc = Locale.FRENCH;

        // Create a message format and set its locale.
        MessageFormat mf = new MessageFormat("");
        mf.setLocale(loc);

        // Create a resource bundle object and load the bundle.
        ResourceBundle myResources = null;
        myResources = ResourceBundle.getBundle("MyResources", loc);

        // Assign the first 4 objects from the bundle to an array.
        Object[] arguments = {
            new Integer(7),
            new Long(System.currentTimeMillis()),
            myResources.getString("color"),
            myResources.getString("animal"),
```

```
        };

        // Create a string buffer for the format method result.
        StringBuffer strbuf = new StringBuffer("");

        // Get the pattern from resource bundle and apply it to mf.
        mf.applyPattern(myResources.getString("pattern"));

        // Format the objects in the arguments array to the string buffer.
        StringBuffer result = mf.format(arguments, strbuf, null);

        // Print the formatted string.
        System.out.println(result);
    }
}
```

Output

```
> java Main
A 22:30:20 le 15 nov 97, un chien bleu a mangé sur la Planète 7.
```


getFormats()

PURPOSE	Gets the array of formats that are used on variables in a pattern.
SYNTAX	`public Format[] getFormats()`
DESCRIPTION	This method returns the array of formats that are used on variables. See the class description for more about the array of formats.
RETURNS	The array of formats used on variables.
EXAMPLE	See `parse()`.

getLocale()

PURPOSE	Retrieves the locale used by this message format.
SYNTAX	`public Locale getLocale()`
DESCRIPTION	This method gets the locale of this message format. This locale is used for fetching localized formats for numbers, dates, times, currency, percentages, and integers that are part of an element format.
RETURNS	The locale used by this message format.
SEE ALSO	`setLocale()`.
EXAMPLE	See the class example.

hashCode()

PURPOSE Computes the hash code for this `MessageFormat` object.

SYNTAX `public int hashCode()`

DESCRIPTION This method computes the hash code for this `MessageFormat` object based on the pattern of this message format. Two `MessageFormat` objects with the same properties will have the same hash code. However, two `MessageFormat` objects that do not have the same properties might also have the same hash code, although the hash code algorithm minimizes this possibility. The hash code is typically used as the key in a hash table.

RETURNS The hash code of this `MessageFormat` object (an integer).

OVERRIDES `java.lang.Object.hashCode()`.

SEE ALSO `equals()`.

EXAMPLE See `clone()`.

MessageFormat()

PURPOSE Constructs a `MessageFormat` instance with a string pattern.

SYNTAX `public MessageFormat(String pattern)`

DESCRIPTION This constructor constructs an instance of `MessageFormat` with the `pattern` string for the default locale. The locale can be changed using `setLocale()`.

`MessageFormat` differs from most of the other `Format` classes in that you create a `MessageFormat` object with its constructor, rather than with a `getInstance` creation method. A creation method isn't necessary because `MessageFormat` doesn't require any complex setup for a given locale. In fact, the class `MessageFormat` doesn't implement any locale-specific behavior at all; it relies on the `NumberFormat` and `DateFormat` subclasses for that. Localized messages just need to be set up on a sentence-by-sentence basis.

PARAMETERS

`pattern` The string pattern to be formatted.

SEE ALSO `applyPattern()`.

EXAMPLE See the class example.

A B C D E F G H I J K L M N O P Q R S T U V W X Y Z

parse()

PURPOSE Parses a string to an array of number, date, time, string, and other objects.

SYNTAX
```
public Object[] parse(String sourceStr, ParsePosition pos)
public Object[] parse(String sourceStr) throws ParseException
```

DESCRIPTION This method parses the string.

Caveats: The parse may fail in a number of circumstances. For example:

- If one of the arguments does not occur in the pattern.
- If the format of an argument loses information, such as with a choice format, in which a large number formats to "many".
- It does not yet handle recursion (whereby the substituted strings contain `{n}` references).
- It will not always find a match (or the correct match) if some part of the parse is ambiguous. For example, if the pattern "`{1},{2}`" is used with the string arguments `{`"`a,b`", "`c`"`}`, it will format as "`a,b,c`". When the result is parsed, it will return `{`"`a`", "`b,c`"`}`.
- If a single argument is formatted twice in the string, then the later parse wins.

PARAMETERS

`pos` The parse position at which to begin parsing. After the parse is done, the index of this parse position is updated to the offset in the string at which the parse ended.

`sourceStr` The string to be parsed.

EXCEPTIONS

`ParseException`
If the string can't be parsed.

EXAMPLE This example parses the following French string into its component objects:

```
A 00:34:21 le 16 nov 97, un chief bleu a mangé sur la Planète 7.
```

using this pattern:

```
"A {1} le {1}, un {3} {2} a mangé sur la Planète {0}."
```

The example does this by creating an array of formats that correspond to the variables enclosed in braces. Then it uses `applyPattern()` to apply the pattern and `setFormats()` to apply the formats to the message format. Finally, it calls `parse()` to perform the conversion of the string to an array of objects. The array consists of the four arguments corresponding to `{0}`, `{1}`, `{2}`, and `{3}`. These arguments are an integer object (7), a date object (`00:34:21, 16 nov 97`), and two string objects ("`chien`", "`bleu`").

A B C D E F G H I J K L M N O P Q R S T U V W X Y Z

```
import java.text.*;
import java.util.*;
import java.io.*;

class Main {

    Main(String str) {

        System.out.println("input.txt:" + "\n" + str);

        Locale loc = Locale.FRENCH;

        // Create a message format and set its locale.
        MessageFormat mf = new MessageFormat("");
        mf.setLocale(loc);

        // Create a resource bundle object and load the bundle.
        ResourceBundle myResources = null;
        myResources = ResourceBundle.getBundle("MyResources", loc);

        // Get the pattern from resource bundle and apply it to mf.
        mf.applyPattern(myResources.getString("pattern"));

        // Create an array of formats corresponding to the
        // 5 variables in the pattern.
        Format[] formats = new Format[] {
            DateFormat.getTimeInstance(DateFormat.MEDIUM, loc),
            DateFormat.getDateInstance(DateFormat.MEDIUM, loc),
            null,
            null,
            getIntegerFormat(loc)
        };

        // Diagnostics.
        System.out.println("Pattern before applying formats: ");
        System.out.println(mf.toPattern() + "\n");

        // Set the formats for the pattern.
        mf.setFormats(formats);

        // Diagnostics.
        System.out.println("Pattern after applying formats: ");
        System.out.println(mf.toPattern() + "\n");

        // Parses the string to produced an array of objects.
        Object[] result = mf.parse(str, (new ParsePosition(0)));

        // Print the objects created from the parse.
        System.out.println("Objects resulting from parse: ");
        for (int i=0; (i<result.length) && (result[i] != null); i++) {
            printInColumn("result[" + i + "]: ", 12);
            printInColumn((result[i]).getClass(), 25);
            System.out.println(result[i]);
        }
    }

    static NumberFormat getIntegerFormat(Locale locale) {
        NumberFormat temp = NumberFormat.getInstance(locale);
        if (temp instanceof DecimalFormat) {
            DecimalFormat temp2 = (DecimalFormat) temp;
```

```
            temp2.setMaximumFractionDigits(0);
            temp2.setDecimalSeparatorAlwaysShown(false);
            temp2.setParseIntegerOnly(true);
        }
        return temp;
    }

    static void printInColumn(Object obj, int col) {
        System.out.print(obj);
        for (int p = obj.toString().length(); p < col; ++p) {
            System.out.print(" ");
        }
    }

    public static void main(String[] args) {
        // Accept a string as an argument
        if (args.length != 1) {
            System.err.println("This program parses a string");
            System.err.println("Usage: java Main input.txt");
            System.exit(1);
        }

        try {
            // Convert line endings to '\n' (not really necessary)
            // Read in the entire contents of the file.
            BufferedReader rd = new BufferedReader(new FileReader(args[0]));
            String line;
            StringBuffer sbuf = new StringBuffer();

            while ((line = rd.readLine()) != null) {
                sbuf.append(line);
                sbuf.append('\n');
            }
            rd.close();
            new Main(new String(sbuf));
        } catch (Exception e) {
            e.printStackTrace();
        }
    }
}
```

MyResources.java

```
import java.util.ListResourceBundle;

public class MyResources extends ListResourceBundle {
    public Object[][] getContents() {
        return contents;
    }

    static final Object[][] contents = {
        // LOCALIZE THE FOLLOWING
        {"pattern", "At {1} on {1}, a {2} {3} ate on Planet {0}."}
        // END OF MATERIAL TO LOCALIZE
    };
}
```

MyResources_fr.java

```
import java.util.ListResourceBundle;

public class MyResources_fr extends ListResourceBundle {
    public Object[][] getContents() {
        return contents;
    }

    static final Object[][] contents = {
        // LOCALIZE THE FOLLOWING
        {"pattern", "A {1} le {1}, un {3} {2} a mangé sur la Planète {0}."}
        // END OF MATERIAL TO LOCALIZE
    };
}
```

Output

```
> java Main input.txt
input.txt:
A 00:34:21 le 16 nov 97, un chien bleu a mangé sur la Planète 7.

Pattern before applying formats:
A {1} le {1}, un {3} {2} a mangé sur la Planète {0}.

Pattern after applying formats:
A {1,date,HH:mm:ss} le {1,date,d MMM yy}, un {3} {2} a mangé sur la Planète
{0,number,integer}.

Objects resulting from parse:
result[0]:  class java.lang.Long     7
result[1]:  class java.util.Date     Sat Nov 15 15:00:00 PST 1997
result[2]:  class java.lang.String   bleu
result[3]:  class java.lang.String   chien
```

parseObject()

PURPOSE Parses a string to an object.

SYNTAX `public Object parseObject(String sourceStr, ParsePosition pos)`

DESCRIPTION This method uses this format to parse the string `sourceStr`, starting at position `pos`, and converting that string to an object. Before calling this method, set the index of `pos` to where you want to start parsing the source string.

This method does not yet handle recursion (where the substituted strings contain `{n}` references).

PARAMETERS

`pos` The parse position that determines where the parse begins.

`sourceStr` The string to be parsed.

RETURNS The possibly `null` object parsed from the string.

OVERRIDES `Format.parseObject()`.

EXAMPLE See the class example in `Format` for an example of `parseObject()`.

setFormat()

PURPOSE
Sets a format to be used on a variable in a pattern.

SYNTAX
`public void setFormat(int variableNum, Format newFormat)`

DESCRIPTION
This method individually sets a format to use on a variable. This method must be applied *after* the pattern is applied. (Applying the pattern resets the formats to the default behavior.) However, if default formats will do, it is not necessary to call `setFormat()` at all, as the `format()` method will determine a format based on the type of the arguments.

PARAMETERS

`newFormat` The format to be applied to this variable.

`variableNum` The zero-based number of the variable in the pattern, counting in sequence from the beginning of the pattern. This number is independent of the argument number that appears as the first value in the message format element.

EXAMPLE
This example calls `setFormat()` to apply the formats to the message format `mf`.

```
import java.text.*;
import java.util.*;

class Main {
    static public void main(String[] args) {

        Locale loc = Locale.FRENCH;

        // Create a message format and set its locale.
        MessageFormat mf = new MessageFormat("");
        mf.setLocale(loc);

        // Create a resource bundle object and load the bundle.
        ResourceBundle myResources = null;
        myResources = ResourceBundle.getBundle("MyResources", loc);

        // Assign the first 4 objects from the bundle to an array.
        Object[] arguments = {
            new Integer(7),
            new Long(System.currentTimeMillis()),
            myResources.getString("color"),
            myResources.getString("animal"),
        };

        // Get the pattern from resource bundle and apply it to mf.
        mf.applyPattern(myResources.getString("pattern"));

        // Set the formats.
        mf.setFormat(0, DateFormat.getTimeInstance(DateFormat.SHORT, loc));
        mf.setFormat(1, DateFormat.getDateInstance(DateFormat.SHORT, loc));
        mf.setFormat(4, getIntegerFormat(loc));

        // Create a string buffer for the format method result.
        StringBuffer strbuf = new StringBuffer("");
```

```
            // Print the pattern.
            System.out.println("Pattern:");
            System.out.println(mf.toPattern() + "\n");

            // Format the objects in the arguments array to the string buffer.
            StringBuffer result = mf.format(arguments, strbuf, null);

            // Print the formatted string.
            System.out.println("Formatted result:");
            System.out.println(result);
        }

        static NumberFormat getIntegerFormat(Locale locale) {
            NumberFormat temp = NumberFormat.getInstance(locale);
            if (temp instanceof DecimalFormat) {
                DecimalFormat temp2 = (DecimalFormat) temp;
                temp2.setMaximumFractionDigits(0);
                temp2.setDecimalSeparatorAlwaysShown(false);
                temp2.setParseIntegerOnly(true);
            }
            return temp;
        }
    }
```

MyResources.java

```
    import java.util.ListResourceBundle;

    public class MyResources extends ListResourceBundle {
        public Object[][] getContents() {
            return contents;
        }

        static final Object[][] contents = {
            // LOCALIZE THE FOLLOWING
            {"color", "blue"},
            {"animal", "dog"},
            {"pattern", "At {1} on {1}, a {2} {3} ate on Planet {0}."}
            // END OF MATERIAL TO LOCALIZE
        };
    }
```

MyResources_fr.java

```
    import java.util.ListResourceBundle;

    public class MyResources_fr extends ListResourceBundle {
        public Object[][] getContents() {
            return contents;
        }

        static final Object[][] contents = {
            // LOCALIZE THE FOLLOWING
            {"color", "bleu"},
            {"animal", "chien"},
            {"pattern", "A {1} le {1}, un {3} {2} a mangé sur la Planète {0}."}
            // END OF MATERIAL TO LOCALIZE
        };
    }
```

Output

```
> java Main
Pattern:
A {1,date,HH:mm} le {1,date,dd/MM/yy}, un {3} {2} a mangé sur la Planète
{0,number,integer}.

Formatted result:
A 02:32 le 23/11/97, un chien bleu a mangé sur la Planète 7.
```


setFormats()

PURPOSE Sets an array of formats to be used on variables in a pattern.

SYNTAX `public void setFormats(Format[] newFormats)`

DESCRIPTION This method applies the array of format objects `newFormats` to this message format for use on variables in a pattern. The members of the array correspond to the variables in the pattern. The members apply to the variables in the order in which they appear in the pattern (rather than the argument number order). This method is used instead of supplying formats with a pattern. The `newFormats` array must have at least as many members as variables in the pattern. However, if default formats will do, it is not necessary to call `setFormats()` at all, as the `format()` method will determine a format based on the type of the arguments.

The `setFormats()` method must be applied *after* the pattern is applied. (Applying the pattern resets the formats to the default behavior.)

A pattern without formats contains variables that have only argument numbers, such as:

```
"A {1} le {1}, un {3} {2} a mangé sur la Planète {0}."
```

The format array for this pattern would have five members, one for each variable. To apply no format to a variable (such as a string), supply `null` for its format.

PARAMETERS

`newFormats` The array of format objects to be applied to the variables.

EXAMPLE See `parse()`.

setLocale()

PURPOSE Sets the locale for number and date formats in this message format.

SYNTAX `public void setLocale(Locale loc)`

DESCRIPTION This method sets the locale to `loc` for this message format. This locale is used for fetching formats for numbers, dates, times, currency, percentages, and integers that are part of an element format. An element format is part of a message pattern.

PARAMETERS

`loc` The locale for number formats that appear in element formats.

SEE ALSO `setPattern, getLocale().`

EXAMPLE See the class example.

toPattern()

PURPOSE Produces a string of the current pattern.

SYNTAX `public String toPattern()`

RETURNS The string pattern of this message format.

SEE ALSO `applyPattern().`

EXAMPLE See the class example.

Method

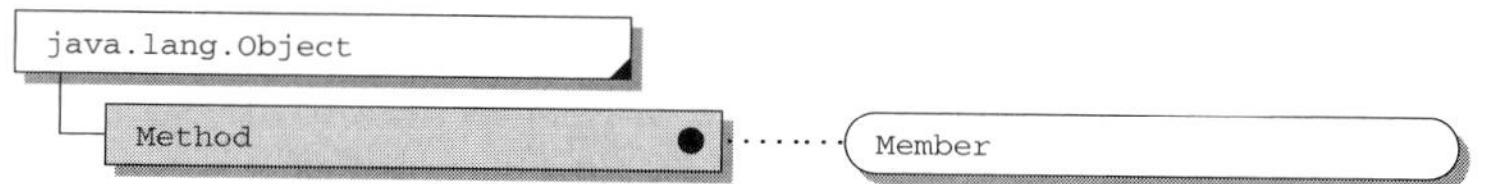

Syntax

```
public final class Method implements Member
```

Description

A `Method` object represents a method member of a class or interface. It can represent a static (class) or instance method. It further can be used to discover the method's list of attributes: its name, set of modifiers, return type, parameter types, and set of throwable exceptions. The `Method` object can also be used to invoke the method.

Usage

This class cannot be instantiated (since you can't create a method). Instead, you need first to obtain a `Class` object for the class that has the desired method. For example,

```
Class.forName("java.awt.Point")
```

or

```
java.awt.Point.class
```

With the class object, you call one of the methods in Table 33 to obtain a `Method` object for the desired method.

Method	Description
`Class.getMethod()`	Retrieves a `Method` object for a public inherited or declared method in a class.
`Class.getMethods()`	Retrieves `Method` objects for all public inherited or declared methods in a class.
`Class.getDeclaredMethod()`	Retrieves a `Method` object for a declared method in a class.
`Class.getDeclaredMethods()`	Retrieves `Method` objects for all declared methods in a class.

TABLE 33: Methods for Creating `Method` Objects.

A B C D E F G H I J K L M N O P Q R S T U V W X Y Z

The Name

The name of a `Method` object is the string used to name the method in the source code. For example, in the following method signature the name of the method is "random":

```
public double random()
```

All `Method` objects have a name.

The Modifiers

The modifiers of a method can be retrieved from a `Method` object by using `getModifiers()` and methods in the `Modifier` class. A method can have any of these five modifiers—`abstract`, `static`, `final`, `synchronized`, and `native`—and at most one access modifier: `public`, `protected`, or `private`. For example, in the following method signature the modifiers are `private`, `final`, and `synchronized`:

```
private final synchronized void append()
```

The Return Type

The return type of a `Method` object reflects the method's return type or lack of one and is represented by a `Class` object. If the method does not return a value, the reflected return type is `void.class`. For example, in the following method signature:

```
public static synchronized double random()
```

the return type is `double`, so the return type of the `Method` object is `double.class`.

The Parameter Types

The parameter types of a `Method` object are represented by an array of `Class` objects, one for each parameter. The first element of the array refers to the type of the first parameter, the second element refers to the type of the second parameter, and so on. For example, in the following method signature:

```
public boolean drawImage(Image img, int x, int y,
        ImageObserver obs);
```

an array with the following `Class` objects is produced:

```
java.awt.Image.class,
int.class,
int.class,
java.awt.ImageObserver.class
```

The Exception Types

The exception types of a `Method` object are represented by an array of `Class` objects, one for each declared exception. For example, in the following method signature:

```
public native Object invoke(Object obj, Object[] args)
    throws IllegalAccessException, IllegalArgumentException,
           InvocationTargetException
```

an array with the following `Class` objects is produced:

```
java.lang.IllegalAccessException.class,
java.lang.IllegalArgumentException.class,
java.lang.reflect.InvocationTargetException.class
```

The order of the elements in the array does not necessarily match the order in which the exceptions are declared.

The Declaring Class

The declaring class of a `Method` object is the class or interface that actually declares the method. For example, in the following code the declaring class of `D.m()` is `C`:

```
class C {
    int m() {};
}
class D extends C {
}
```

Because methods are inherited, they can appear in classes that do not explicitly declare them. In the previous example, a `Method` object reflecting `C.x` is equal to a `Method` object reflecting `D.x` because the two names refer to the same method. However, the two `Method` objects need not have identical references; you must use `equals()` to determine their equality.

When you retrieve a `Method` object for an inherited method in a class, the identity of that class is lost (i.e., it cannot be retrieved from the `Method` object); only the `Method` object's declaring class is available. However, if the class overrides the method, the returned `Method` object is associated with the most specific class that overrides the method.

MEMBER SUMMARY	
Invocation Method	
`invoke()`	Invokes the method represented by this `Method` object.
Attribute Methods	
`getDeclaringClass()`	Retrieves this `Method` object's declaring class object.
`getExceptionTypes()`	Retrieves this `Method` object's list of declared exceptions.
`getModifiers()`	Retrieves the method modifiers for this `Method` object.
`getName()`	Retrieves this `Method` object's name.
`getParameterTypes()`	Retrieves the types of each parameter in this `Method` object's parameter list.
`getReturnType()`	Retrieves this `Method` object's return type.
Object Methods	
`equals()`	Compares this `Method` object with another `Method` object.
`hashCode()`	Computes the hash code for this `Method` object.
Debugging Method	
`toString()`	Generates a string representing this `Method` object.

See Also

java.lang.Class, Modifiers.

Example

This example implements a program that prints all of the overridden methods of a class. That is, if the specified class has a method that overrides a method in one of its superclasses, the signature of that method is printed.

The heart of the example is the test for method signature equality (sameNameAndSignature()). Method.equals() cannot be used because it also checks that the declaring classes are identical.

This example uses getDeclaredMethods() to retrieves all public, protected, private and default (package) access methods of each class. getMethods() cannot be used in its place because getMethods() returns Method objects for every declared public and inherited public method, making it difficult to tell which methods are actually declared by the class. The use getDeclaredMethods() is subject to access checks by the security manager. Therefore an example such as this may not work in applets.

```
import java.lang.reflect.*;
import java.util.*;

class Main {
    Main(Class c) {
        Vector superMethods = new Vector();
        Method[] methods = c.getDeclaredMethods();

        // Retrieve the declared methods of c's superclasses.
        c = c.getSuperclass();
        while (c != null) {
            Method[] ms = c.getDeclaredMethods();
            for (int i=0; i<ms.length; i++) {
                superMethods.addElement(ms[i]);
            }
            c = c.getSuperclass();
        }

        // Compare each method in c with the methods in all of its superclasses.
        for (int i=0; i<methods.length; i++) {
            for (int j=0; j<superMethods.size(); j++) {
                Method m2 = (Method)superMethods.elementAt(j);

                if (sameNameAndSignature(methods[i], m2)) {
                    System.out.println(methods[i]);
                    System.out.println("   overrides "
                        + m2.getDeclaringClass().getName());
                    break;
                }
            }
        }
    }

    boolean sameNameAndSignature(Method m1, Method m2) {
        // Is either private?
```

```
        if (Modifier.isPrivate(m1.getModifiers())
            || Modifier.isPrivate(m2.getModifiers())) {
            return false;
        }

        // Are the names the same?
        if (!m1.getName().equals(m2.getName())) {
            return false;
        }

        // Get the parameter type lists.
        Class[] p1 = m1.getParameterTypes();
        Class[] p2 = m2.getParameterTypes();

        // Are the parameter list sizes the same?
        if (p1.length != p2.length) {
            return false;
        }

        // Are the types the same?
        for (int i=0; i<p1.length; i++) {
            if (p1[i] != p2[i]) {
                return false;
            }
        }
        return true;
    }

    public static void main(String[] args) {
        if (args.length != 1) {
            System.err.println("Usage: java Main <classname>");
        } else {
            try {
                new Main(Class.forName(args[0]));
            } catch (ClassNotFoundException e) {
                e.printStackTrace();
            }
        }
    }
}
```

Output

```
> java Main java.awt.Button
public void java.awt.Button.addNotify()
   overrides java.awt.Component
boolean java.awt.Button.eventEnabled(java.awt.AWTEvent)
   overrides java.awt.Component
protected void java.awt.Button.processEvent(java.awt.AWTEvent)
   overrides java.awt.Component
protected java.lang.String java.awt.Button.paramString()
   overrides java.awt.Component
```

equals()

PURPOSE Compares this `Method` object with another `Method` object.

SYNTAX `public boolean equals(Object obj)`

DESCRIPTION Two `Method` objects are equal only if both represent exactly the same method in the same class. Note that a `Method` object for an inherited method is indistinguishable from, and therefore equal to, one retrieved directly from its declaring class. However, if one method overrides another, they will not be equal. They will have the same name and signature but differing declaring classes.

PARAMETERS

`obj` A possibly `null` `Method` object.

OVERRIDES `java.lang.Object.equals()`.

SEE ALSO `hashCode()`.

EXAMPLE This example creates a number of `Method` objects and tests their equality. Notice that when a `Method` object is created on an inherited method, it is equal to the declared method (and in fact, the name of `dn` appears as `C.n`).

```
import java.lang.reflect.*;

class Main {
    public static void main(String[] args) {
        try {
            Method cm = C.class.getMethod("m", new Class[] {});
            Method cn = C.class.getMethod("n", new Class[] {});

            Method dm = D.class.getMethod("m", new Class[] {});
            Method dn = D.class.getMethod("n", new Class[] {});

            Method em = E.class.getMethod("m", new Class[] {});

            checkEquality(cm, dm);    // C.m != D.m
            checkEquality(cn, dn);    // C.n == C.n
            checkEquality(cm, em);    // C.m != E.m
        } catch (NoSuchMethodException ext) {
            ext.printStackTrace();
        }
    }

    public static void checkEquality(Method m1, Method m2) {
        System.out.print(m1.getDeclaringClass().getName()+"."+m1.getName());
        if (m1.equals(m2)) {
            System.out.print(" == ");
        } else {
            System.out.print(" != ");
        }
        System.out.println(m2.getDeclaringClass().getName()+"."+m2.getName());
    }
}
```

```
class C {
    public void m() {}
    public void n() {}
}
class D extends C {
    public void m() {}
}
class E {
    public void m() {};
}
```

getDeclaringClass()

PURPOSE Retrieves this `Method` object's declaring class.

SYNTAX `public Class getDeclaringClass()`

DESCRIPTION The declaring class of a `Method` object is the class or interface that actually declares the method. See the class description for more details.

RETURNS The non-`null` `Class` object of the declaring class of this `Method` object.

EXAMPLE See `equals()`.

getExceptionTypes()

PURPOSE Retrieves this `Method` object's list of declared exceptions.

SYNTAX `public Class[] getExceptionTypes()`

RETURNS A non-`null` array with a length equal to the number of declared exceptions in this method.

EXAMPLE This example implements a program that discovers and prints out methods that declare one or more specified exceptions. The program reads a text file of fully qualified class names and searches the methods in those classes.

```
import java.lang.reflect.*;
import java.io.*;
import java.util.*;

class Main {
    // Returns a non-null vector containing any methods that throw
    // at least one of the exceptions in excs.
    static Vector isThrows(Class c, Class[] excs) {
        Vector v = new Vector();
        Method[] methods = c.getDeclaredMethods();

        // Scan each method.
        for (int i=0; i<methods.length; i++) {
            Class[] es = methods[i].getExceptionTypes();
```

```
            // Scan each of the method's exceptions.
        search:
            for (int j=0; j<es.length; j++) {
              // Check against each of the user's specified list of exceptions.
                for (int k=0; k<excs.length; k++) {
                    if (es[j] == excs[k]) {
                        // Found a match.
                        v.addElement(methods[i]);
                        break search;
                    }
                }
            }
        }
        return v;
    }

    public static void main(String[] args) {
        if (args.length < 2) {
            System.err.println(
                "Usage: java Main <file of class names> <exception>...");
            System.exit(1);
        }

        try {
            Class[] exceptions = new Class[args.length-1];
            BufferedReader in = new BufferedReader(new FileReader(args[0]));

            // Create class objects for each of the specified exceptions.
            for (int i=1; i<args.length; i++) {
                exceptions[i-1] = Class.forName(args[i]);
            }

            // Read the input file and retrieve their Class objects.
            String classname = null;
            while ((classname = in.readLine()) != null) {
                Class c = Class.forName(classname);
                Vector v = isThrows(c, exceptions);

                for (int i=0; i<v.size(); i++) {
                    Method m = (Method)v.elementAt(i);
                    System.out.println(m.getDeclaringClass().getName()
                        + "." + m.getName() + "()");
                }
            }
        } catch (ClassNotFoundException e) {
            e.printStackTrace();
        } catch (IOException e) {
            e.printStackTrace();
        }
        System.exit(0);
    }
}
```

Output

```
> java Main input.txt java.lang.reflect.InvocationTargetException
java.lang.reflect.Method.invoke()
java.lang.reflect.Constructor.newInstance()
```

Input

```
java.lang.reflect.Method
java.lang.reflect.Array
java.lang.reflect.Member
java.lang.reflect.Constructor
```


getModifiers()

PURPOSE Retrieves the method modifiers for this `Method` object.

SYNTAX `public native int getModifiers()`

DESCRIPTION This method retrieves this `Method` object's set of method modifiers, bit-encoded in an `int`. The possible method modifiers are `public`, `protected`, `private`, `abstract`, `static`, `final`, `synchronized`, and `native`. To process the encoding, use the methods and constants in `Modifier`.

RETURNS An `int` representing the `Method` object's set of modifiers.

SEE ALSO `Modifier`.

EXAMPLE This example implements a program that prints all of the public methods (declared and inherited) of a class.

```
import java.lang.reflect.*;
import java.io.*;
import java.util.*;

class Main {
    Main(Class c) {
        Method methods[] = c.getMethods();

        for (int i=0; i<methods.length; i++) {
            int mods = methods[i].getModifiers() & ~Modifier.PUBLIC;
            if (mods != 0) {
                System.out.print(Modifier.toString(mods) + " ");
            }
            System.out.print(methods[i].getReturnType().getName());
            System.out.print(" ");
            System.out.println(methods[i].getName() + "()");
        }
    }

    public static void main(String[] args) {
        if (args.length != 1) {
            System.err.println("Usage: java Main <classname>");
        } else {
            try {
                new Main(Class.forName(args[0]));
            } catch (ClassNotFoundException e) {
                e.printStackTrace();
            }
        }
    }
}
```

Output

```
> java Main java.lang.reflect.Method
final native java.lang.Class getClass()
int hashCode()
boolean equals()
java.lang.String toString()
final native void notify()
final native void notifyAll()
final native void wait()
final void wait()
final void wait()
java.lang.Class getDeclaringClass()
java.lang.String getName()
native int getModifiers()
java.lang.Class getReturnType()
[Ljava.lang.Class; getParameterTypes()
[Ljava.lang.Class; getExceptionTypes()
native java.lang.Object invoke()
```


getName()

PURPOSE Retrieves this `Method` object's name.

SYNTAX `public String getName()`

DESCRIPTION The name of a `Method` object is the string used to name the method in the source code.

RETURNS A non-`null` string containing this `Method` object's name.

EXAMPLE See the class example.

getParameterTypes()

PURPOSE Retrieves the types of each parameter in this `Method` object's parameter list.

SYNTAX `public Class[] getParameterTypes()`

DESCRIPTION This method retrieves an array containing one class object for each of this method's parameters. The first element of the resulting array refers to the type of the first parameter, the second element refers to the type of the second parameter, and so on.

RETURNS A non-`null` array with a length equal to the number of parameters in this method.

EXAMPLE See the class example.

getReturnType()

PURPOSE Retrieves this `Method` object's return type.

SYNTAX `public Class getReturnType()`

DESCRIPTION This method retrieves the `Class` object representing this `Method` object's return type. If the method represented by this `Method` object does not return a value, then the return type is `void.class`.

RETURNS A non-`null` `Class` object representing this `Method` object's return type.

EXAMPLE This example prints out the class name of the return types for a few methods.

```
import java.lang.reflect.*;

class Main {
    Main() {
        Method[] methods = getClass().getDeclaredMethods();

        for (int i=0; i<methods.length; i++) {
            System.out.println(methods[i].getName() + ": "
                + methods[i].getReturnType().getName());
        }
    }

    void m1() {
    }
    int m2() {
        return 0;
    }
    Integer m3() {
        return new Integer(0);
    }
    String m4() {
        return "0";
    }

    public static void main(String[] args) {
        new Main();
    }
}
```

Output

```
m1: void
m2: int
m3: java.lang.Integer
m4: java.lang.String
main: void
```

hashCode()

PURPOSE Computes the hash code for this `Method` object.

SYNTAX `public int hashCode()`

DESCRIPTION The Method object's hash code is an integer that is calculated from the Method object's name and declaring class name. Two equal Method objects will have the same hash code. Note that unequal Method objects might also have the same hash code, although the hash code algorithm minimizes this possibility. The hash code is typically used as the key in a hash table.

RETURNS The Method object's hash code.

OVERRIDES `java.lang.Object.hashCode()`.

SEE ALSO `equals()`, `java.lang.Hashtable`.

EXAMPLE This example creates a Method object and inserts it into a hash table.

```
import java.awt.*;
import java.util.*;
import java.lang.reflect.*;

class Main {
    public static void main(String[] args) {
        Hashtable ht = new Hashtable();
        try {
            Method f = Method.class.getMethod("hashCode", new Class[] {});
            ht.put(f, f);
        } catch (NoSuchMethodException e) {
            e.printStackTrace();
        }
    }
}
```

invoke()

PURPOSE Invokes the method represented by this Method object.

SYNTAX
```
public native Object invoke(Object obj, Object[] args) throws
   IllegalAccessException, IllegalArgumentException,
   InvocationTargetException
```

DESCRIPTION `invoke()` is used to invoke the method represented by this Method object. If the method is nonstatic, then `obj` specifies the object whose method will be invoked; otherwise, `obj` is ignored.

`args` contains the values to be passed as parameters to the invoked method. `args.length` must be equal to the number of parameters accepted by the method. If a parameter type is primitive, the corresponding value in `args` must be wrapped in the appropriate object wrapper. For example, if the parameter type of the second parameter is `char`, then the second element of `args` must be a `Character` object.

args contains the values to be passed as arguments to the invoked method. args.length must be equal to the number of parameters accepted by the invoked method. If a parameter type is an object reference, the type of the corresponding value in args must be assignable to the parameter type. If a parameter type is primitive, the corresponding value in args must be an object wrapper of the appropriate type. When the value is unwrapped, it may be automatically widened. For example, if the type of the second parameter is int, args[1] must be an Integer, a Short, a Character, or a Byte. If args[1] is a Short, a Character, or a Byte, its unwrapped value is automatically widened to an int. More information about valid widening conversions are described in Table 27 in the Field class and *The Java Language Specification, First Edition*, Section 5.1.4. Automatic narrowing conversions are never done. If an attempt to widen a value to a parameter type fails, an IllegalArgumentException is thrown.

The return value of invoke() is the result returned by the invoked method. If the invoked method does not return a value (that is, its return type is void), invoke() returns null. Since null is also a valid return value by the invoked method, you cannot determine whether the invoked method returns a value based on invoke()'s return value. To determine if the invoked method is supposed to return a value, use getReturnType()

If the invoked method throws an exception, invoke() wraps the exception with InvocationTargetException and throws it. You can retrieve the exception that was thrown by the invoked method by calling InvocationTargetException.getTargetException().

The method that is actually invoked may not be the method declared in this Method object's declaring class. This can happen if the method has been overridden and obj's class is a subclass of this Method object's declaring class. In this case, the method declared in obj's class is invoked. For example, suppose class D extends class C and class D overrides a method m(). Calling invoke() on a Method object for C.m() when obj is an instance of D will invoke D.m(). The precise rules for determining which method to invoke are described in *The Java Language Specification, First Edition*, Section 15.11.4.4.

invoke() does not use the types of the arguments to select an overloading. It is always invoked on a specific overloading of the method, previously selected by a call to getMethod() or other means. The reflection package does not automatically choose between overloadings.

When invoke() is called, the Java virtual machine performs the access checks described in *The Java Language Specification, First Edition*, Section 6.6.1. These checks compare the identity of the caller of invoke() with the access permission and identity of the method being called. It is as if the caller of invoke() had a statically compiled call to the selected method. The access check takes into account both the accessibility of the method itself and the accessibility of its class.

It is a common error to attempt to invoke an overridden method by retrieving the overriding method from obj. This will not always work because the overriding method may be defined in a class inaccessible to the caller. See the second EXAMPLE section.

PARAMETERS

`args` The non-null array containing the argument values to be passed to the invoked method.

`obj` The possibly null object whose class inherits or declares this method.

EXCEPTIONS

`IllegalAccessException`
If the caller does not have permission to invoke this method; for example, if the method is private.

`IllegalArgumentException`
If the method being reflected is an instance method and obj's class does not inherit or declare the method, or if args is not compatible with the method's parameter type list (see the DESCRIPTION section), or if the caller does not have permission to access the class that overrides the method.

`InvocationTargetException`
If the invoked method throws an exception.

`NullPointerException`
If this method is an instance method and obj is null.

SEE ALSO getReturnType(), InvocationTargetException.getTargetException().

EXAMPLE This example demonstrates how to invoke methods. One method returns a value, while the other does not. This example also demonstrates that invoke() automatically wraps and unwraps primitive types in object wrappers.

Note that the call to "m2" on "new Integer(100)" does not invoke the overload form of m2 that accepts an int because the Method object was created for the form that accepts a double.

```
import java.lang.reflect.*;
import java.awt.*;

class Main {
    static void invoke(Object o, String name, Class[] params, Object[] args) {
        try {
            Method m = C.class.getDeclaredMethod(name, params);
            System.out.print(name + "() -> ");
            Object r = m.invoke(o, args);

            if (r != null) {
                System.out.println(r.getClass().getName()+": "+r);
```

```
            } else {
                System.out.println(m.getReturnType().getName()+": "+r);
            }
        } catch (NoSuchMethodException e) {
            e.printStackTrace();
        } catch (IllegalAccessException e) {
            e.printStackTrace();
        } catch (InvocationTargetException e) {
            e.getTargetException().printStackTrace();
        }
    }

    public static void main(String[] args) {
        C c = new C();

        // Demonstrate that if return type is primitive, it is wrapped
        // with an Object wrapper.
        invoke(c, "m1", new Class[] {}, new Object[] {});

        // Demonstrate that if parameter is primitive, must wrap with
        // Object wrapper.
        invoke(c, "m2", new Class[] {double.class},
                new Object[] {new Double(0)});

        // Demonstrate that an int value can be widened to a double.
        // Also demonstrate how to handle m2's exception.
        invoke(c, "m2", new Class[] {double.class},
                new Object[] {new Integer(100)});

        // Demonstrate that Button can be widened to Component.
        invoke(c, "m3", new Class[] {Component.class},
                new Object[] {new Button("OK")});

        // Demonstrate that even though the method object refers to C.m1(),
        // D.m1() will be called.
        D d = new D();
        invoke(d, "m1", new Class[] {}, new Object[] {});
    }
}

class C {
    double m1() {
        return 3.14;
    }
    void m2(double d) throws IllegalArgumentException {
        if (d > 50) {
            throw new IllegalArgumentException();
        }
    }
    void m2(int i) {
        System.out.println("*** NOT REACHED ***");
    }
    void m3(Component c) {
    }
}

class D extends C {
    double m1() {
        return 2*super.m1();
    }
}
```

Output

```
m1() -> java.lang.Double: 3.14
m2() -> void: null
m2() -> java.lang.IllegalArgumentException
        at C.m2(Main.java:56)
        at Main.invoke(Main.java:8)
        at Main.main(Main.java:38)
m3() -> void: null
m1() -> java.lang.Double: 6.28
```

EXAMPLE This example demonstrates how `invoke()` fails when it is invoked on a `Method` object reflecting a public method from a private class.

```
import java.lang.reflect.*;
import java.util.*;

class Main2 {
    public static void main(String[] args) throws Exception {
        Enumeration e = new Vector().elements();

        // RIGHT: m1 is a public method in a public interface.
        Class c1 = Enumeration.class;
        Method m1 = c1.getMethod("hasMoreElements", new Class[] {});
        System.out.println(m1.invoke(e, new Object[] {}));
                                                    // false

        // WRONG: m2 is a public method in a private class.
        Class c2 = e.getClass();
        Method m2 = c2.getMethod("hasMoreElements", new Class[] {});
        System.out.println(m2.invoke(e, new Object[] {}));
                                                    // IllegalAcessException
    }
}
```

toString()

PURPOSE Generates a string representing this `Method` object.

SYNTAX `public String toString()`

DESCRIPTION This method generates a string containing this `Method` object's name, return type, parameter types, set of modifiers, and set of declared exceptions, as well as the fully qualified name of the declaring class. The order of the modifiers matches the canonical order as defined in *The Java Language Specification*. The canonical ordering is `public`, `protected`, `private`, `abstract`, `static`, `final`, `synchronized`, and `native`.

OVERRIDES `java.lang.Object.toString()`.

EXAMPLE This example implements a program that takes a fully qualified class name, instantiates the corresponding class, and prints out all of the class's declared methods.

```
import java.lang.reflect.*;
import java.io.*;
import java.util.*;

class Main {
    Main(Class c) {
        Method methods[] = c.getDeclaredMethods();

        for (int i=0; i<methods.length; i++) {
            System.out.println(methods[i].toString());
        }
    }

    public static void main(String[] args) {
        if (args.length != 1) {
            System.err.println("Usage: java Main <classname>");
        } else {
            try {
                new Main(Class.forName(args[0]));
            } catch (ClassNotFoundException e) {
                e.printStackTrace();
            }
        }
    }
}
```

Output

```
> java Main java.lang.reflect.Method
public java.lang.Class java.lang.reflect.Method.getDeclaringClass()
public java.lang.String java.lang.reflect.Method.getName()
public native int java.lang.reflect.Method.getModifiers()
public java.lang.Class java.lang.reflect.Method.getReturnType()
public java.lang.Class[] java.lang.reflect.Method.getParameterTypes()
public java.lang.Class[] java.lang.reflect.Method.getExceptionTypes()
public boolean java.lang.reflect.Method.equals(java.lang.Object)
public int java.lang.reflect.Method.hashCode()
public java.lang.String java.lang.reflect.Method.toString()
public native java.lang.Object
java.lang.reflect.Method.invoke(java.lang.Object,java.lang.Object[])
throws  java.lang.IllegalAccessException,java.lang.IllegalArgumentException,
java.lang.reflect.InvocationTargetException
static java.lang.Class[] java.lang.reflect.Method.copy(java.lang.Class[])
```

java.util
MissingResourceException

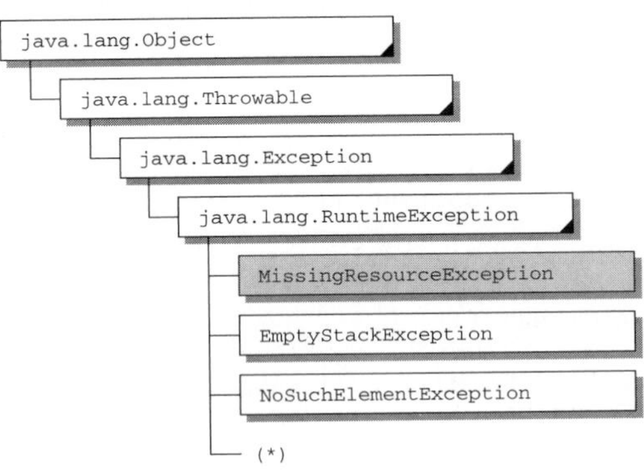

(*) 11 classes from other packages not shown.

A B C D E F G H I J K L M N O P Q R S T U V W X Y Z

Syntax

`public class MissingResourceException extends RuntimeException`

Description

This exception is thrown by the methods in `ResourceBundle` if either a resource bundle could not be found or a resource in a resource bundle could not be found.

MEMBER SUMMARY	
Constructor	
`MissingResourceException()`	Constructs a `MissingResourceException` instance.
Missing Resource Methods	
`getClassName()`	Retrieves the class name of a resource bundle.
`getKey()`	Retrieves the name of a resource.

See Also

`ResourceBundle`.

Example

This example demonstrates two situations that cause a `MissingResourceException` to be thrown. In the first situation, an attempt is made to load in a nonexistent resource bundle.

Notice that the key is empty. In the second situation, an attempt is made to retrieve a nonexistent resource.

Main.java

```
import java.util.*;

class Main {
    public static void main(String[] args) {
        // Non-existent bundle.
        try {
            ResourceBundle rb = ResourceBundle.getBundle("foo");
        } catch (MissingResourceException e) {
            System.out.println(e.getMessage());
                                    // can't find resource for foo_en_US
            System.out.println(e.getClassName());   // foo_en_US
            System.out.println("*"+e.getKey()+"*"); // **
        }

        // Non-existent resource.
        try {
            ResourceBundle rb = ResourceBundle.getBundle("data");
            rb.getString("foo");
        } catch (MissingResourceException e) {
            System.out.println(e.getMessage());     // Can't find resource
            System.out.println(e.getClassName());
                                    // java.util.PropertyResourceBundle
            System.out.println("*"+e.getKey()+"*"); // *foo*
        }
    }
}
```

data.properties

```
language=Java
```

getClassName()

PURPOSE Retrieves the class name of a resource bundle.

SYNTAX

```
Gets parameter passed by constructor.
public String getClassName()
```

DESCRIPTION This method returns the class name of the resource bundle that threw this exception. If the exception was thrown because a resource bundle could not be found, this method returns the name of the missing resource bundle.

RETURNS A non-`null` string containing the class name of a resource bundle.

SEE ALSO `ResourceBundle.getBundle()`, `ResourceBundle.getObject()`.

EXAMPLE See the class example.

getKey()

PURPOSE Retrieves the name of a resource.

SYNTAX `public String getKey()`

DESCRIPTION This method returns the name of the resource that could not be found. If the exception was thrown because a resource bundle could not be found, this method returns "".

RETURNS A non-`null` possibly empty string containing the name of a resource.

SEE ALSO `ResourceBundle.getObject()`.

EXAMPLE See the class example.

MissingResourceException()

PURPOSE Constructs a `MissingResourceException` instance.

SYNTAX
```
public MissingResourceException(String msg, String className,
   String key)
```

DESCRIPTION This constructor is used by the `ResourceBundle` class if either a resource bundle could not be found or a resource in a resource bundle could not be found. In the first case, `className` should be set to the name of the nonexistent resource bundle class and `key` should be set to "". In the second case, `className` should be set to the class name of the resource bundle and `key` should be set to the name of the nonexistent resource.

PARAMETERS

`className` A non-`null` string containing the class name of a resource bundle.
`key` A non-`null` possibly empty string containing the name of a resource.
`msg` A non-`null` string containing more details about the exception.

SEE ALSO `getClassName()`, `getKey()`, `java.lang.Throwable.getMessage()`.

Modifier

A B C D E F G H I J K L M N O P Q R S T U V W X Y Z

Syntax

```
public class Modifier
```

Description

The modifiers of a class, interface, field, method, or constructor (Java entities) are bit-encoded as an `int`. This class contains methods to process the encoding. Not all modifiers can appear on a Java entity. Table 34 summarizes the set of valid modifiers for the various Java entities.

Java Entity	Valid Modifiers	Modifier-Retrieval Method
Class	`public`[a], `abstract`, `final`	`Class.getModifiers()`
Constructor	`public`, `protected`, `private`	`Constructor.getModifiers()`
Field	`public`, `protected`, `private`, `static`, `final`, `volatile`, `transient`	`Field.getModifiers()`
Interface	`public`	`Class.getModifiers()`
Method	`public`, `protected`, `private`, `abstract`, `static`, `final`, `synchronized`, `native`	`Method.getModifiers()`

TABLE 34: Valid Modifiers for Java Entities.

a. In Java 1.1, a class can be private or protected, in addition to public. However, the reflection API does not present this view.

Note that although `interface` is treated like a modifier by this class, the term *modifier* in *The Java Language Specification* does not include it.

Usage

To use this class, you first need to retrieve the modifier set for a Java entity. Once you have the modifier set, you use the methods in this class to determine which modifiers are in the set. Table 34 shows the method to use to retrieve the modifiers for a particular Java entity.

A B C D E F G H I J K L M N O P Q R S T U V W X Y Z

MEMBER SUMMARY

Bit Mask Constants[a]	
`ABSTRACT`	Represents the `abstract` modifier (value `0x400`).
`FINAL`	Represents the `final` modifier (value `0x10`).
`INTERFACE`	Represents the `interface` modifier (value `0x200`).
`NATIVE`	Represents the `native` modifier (value `0x100`).
`PRIVATE`	Represents the `private` modifier (value `0x2`).
`PROTECTED`	Represents the `protected` modifier (value `0x4`).
`PUBLIC`	Represents the `public` modifier (value `0x1`).
`STATIC`	Represents the `static` modifier (value `0x8`).
`SYNCHRONIZED`	Represents the `synchronized` modifier (value `0x20`).
`TRANSIENT`	Represents the `transient` modifier (value `0x80`).
`VOLATILE`	Represents the `volatile` modifier (value `0x40`).
Query Methods	
`isAbstract()`	Determines if the modifier set includes the `abstract` modifier.
`isFinal()`	Determines if the modifier set includes the `final` modifier.
`isInterface()`	Determines if the modifier set includes the `interface` modifier.
`isNative()`	Determines if the modifier set includes the `native` modifier.
`isPrivate()`	Determines if the modifier set includes the `private` modifier.
`isProtected()`	Determines if the modifier set includes the `protected` modifier.
`isPublic()`	Determines if the modifier set includes the `public` modifier.
`isStatic()`	Determines if the modifier set includes the `static` modifier.
`isSynchronized()`	Determines if the modifier set includes the `synchronized` modifier.
`isTransient()`	Determines if the modifier set includes the `transient` modifier.
`isVolatile()`	Determines if the modifier set includes the `volatile` modifier.
Debugging Method	
`toString()`	Generates a string containing the printable representation of the modifier set.

a. To conserve space, these constants do not have a member description. See the corresponding query method for a description of the modifier.

See Also

`java.lang.Class`, `Constructor`, `Field`, `Member`, `Method`.

Example

This example implements a program that will go through all of the methods of some classes looking for a particular combination set of modifiers. The list of classes to try is supplied in a text file containing the fully qualified names of the classes.

The list of modifiers is specified on the command line. This set of modifiers is used to create a modifier mask, which in turn is applied to all of the method modifiers. If a match is found, the method signature is printed.

Note that the method `modifier2string()` produces the same output as `Modifier.toString()`. It is shown here only to demonstrate the use of the "is" methods.

```
import java.lang.reflect.*;
import java.io.*;
import java.util.*;

class Main {
    // Converts a modifier constant to its string representation.
    public static String modifier2string(int mod) {
        if (Modifier.isPublic(mod))          return "public";
        if (Modifier.isPrivate(mod))         return "private";
        if (Modifier.isProtected(mod))       return "protected";
        if (Modifier.isAbstract(mod))        return "abstract";
        if (Modifier.isStatic(mod))          return "static";
        if (Modifier.isFinal(mod))           return "final";
        if (Modifier.isTransient(mod))       return "transient";
        if (Modifier.isVolatile(mod))        return "volatile";
        if (Modifier.isNative(mod))          return "native";
        if (Modifier.isSynchronized(mod))    return "synchronized";
        if (Modifier.isInterface(mod))       return "interface";
        return "";
    }

    // Converts the string representation of a modifier to a modifier constant.
    public static int string2modifier(String s) {
        if (s.equals("public"))          return Modifier.PUBLIC;
        if (s.equals("private"))         return Modifier.PRIVATE;
        if (s.equals("protected"))       return Modifier.PROTECTED;
        if (s.equals("abstract"))        return Modifier.ABSTRACT;
        if (s.equals("static"))          return Modifier.STATIC;
        if (s.equals("final"))           return Modifier.FINAL;
        if (s.equals("transient"))       return Modifier.TRANSIENT;
        if (s.equals("volatile"))        return Modifier.VOLATILE;
        if (s.equals("native"))          return Modifier.NATIVE;
        if (s.equals("synchronized"))    return Modifier.SYNCHRONIZED;
        if (s.equals("interface"))       return Modifier.INTERFACE;
        return 0;
    }

    public static void main(String[] args) {
        if (args.length < 2) {
            System.err.println(
                "Usage: java Main <file of class names> <modifiers>...");
            System.exit(1);
        }

        // Get modifier set.
        int mod = 0;
```

```
            for (int i=1; i<args.length; i++) {
                int m = string2modifier(args[i]);
                mod |= m;
                // Could have simply used args[i];
                // this is done for demonstration purposes.
                System.out.println("   " + modifier2string(m));
            }
            System.out.println();

            try {
                // Create the input stream.
                BufferedReader is =
                    new BufferedReader(
                    new FileReader(args[0]));

                // Read the input file and retrieve their Class objects.
                String classname = null;
                while ((classname = is.readLine()) != null) {
                    // Get the class object and then all its methods.
                    Class c = Class.forName(classname);
                    Method[] methods = c.getDeclaredMethods();

                    // Scan each method looking for a modifier set match.
                    for (int i=0; i<methods.length; i++) {
                        Method m = (Method)methods[i];

                        if ((m.getModifiers() & mod) == mod) {
                            // Found a match so print the method signature.
                            System.out.println(m);
                        }
                    }
                }
            } catch (ClassNotFoundException e) {
                e.printStackTrace();
            } catch (IOException e) {
                e.printStackTrace();
            }
            System.exit(0);
        }
    }
```

Output

```
    > java Main input.txt private synchronized
        private
        synchronized
    private static synchronized int java.awt.EventQueue.nextThreadNum()
    private synchronized boolean java.awt.MediaTracker.checkAll(boolean,boolean)
    private synchronized int java.awt.MediaTracker.statusAll(boolean,boolean)
    private synchronized boolean java.awt.MediaTracker.checkID(int,boolean,
        boolean)
    private synchronized int java.awt.MediaTracker.statusID(int,boolean,boolean)
```

isAbstract()

PURPOSE Determines if the modifier set includes the `abstract` modifier.

SYNTAX `public static boolean isAbstract(int mod)`

DESCRIPTION An abstract method is a method without an implementation.

An abstract class cannot be instantiated; it must be subclassed in order to be used. Usually, a class is abstract because one or more of its methods is abstract.[1] However, an otherwise instantiable class can be made abstract in order to force the client to subclass the class (for example, `java.awt.event.WindowAdapter`). See *The Java Language Specification* for more details on the `abstract` modifier.

PARAMETERS

`mod` An `int` representing a set of modifiers.

RETURNS `true` if `mod` includes `ABSTRACT`.

EXAMPLE See the class example.

isFinal()

PURPOSE Determines if the modifier set includes the `final` modifier.

SYNTAX `public static boolean isFinal(int mod)`

DESCRIPTION A final field cannot be modified. A final method cannot be overridden. A final class cannot be subclassed. See *The Java Language Specification* for more details on the `final` modifier.

PARAMETERS

`mod` An `int` representing a set of modifiers.

RETURNS `true` if `mod` includes `FINAL`.

EXAMPLE See the class example.

isInterface()

PURPOSE Determines if the modifier set includes the `interface` modifier.

SYNTAX `public static boolean isInterface(int mod)`

1. A nonabstract class can contain an abstract member if that member is a class and not a method.

DESCRIPTION This method can be used on the modifiers retrieved from `Class.getModifiers()` to determine whether the `Class` object is associated with an interface. See *The Java Language Specification* for more details on interfaces.

PARAMETERS
`mod` An `int` representing a set of modifiers.

RETURNS `true` if `mod` includes `INTERFACE`.

EXAMPLE See the class example.

isNative()

PURPOSE Determines if the modifier set includes the `native` modifier.

SYNTAX `public static boolean isNative(int mod)`

DESCRIPTION A native method is a method that is implemented in platform-dependent code. See *The Java Language Specification* for more details on the `native` modifier.

PARAMETERS
`mod` An `int` representing a set of modifiers.

RETURNS `true` if `mod` includes `NATIVE`.

EXAMPLE See the class example.

isPrivate()

PURPOSE Determines if the modifier set includes the `private` modifier.

SYNTAX `public static boolean isPrivate(int mod)`

DESCRIPTION A private field, method, or constructor is accessible only to other methods and constructors inside the class. See *The Java Language Specification* for more details on the `private` modifier.

Although a Java class which is a member of another class can be private or protected, its reflected access permissions are adjusted to be default (instead of private) or public (instead of protected).

PARAMETERS
`mod` An `int` representing a set of modifiers.

RETURNS `true` if `mod` includes `PRIVATE`.

EXAMPLE See the class example.

isProtected()

PURPOSE Determines if the modifier set includes the `protected` modifier.

SYNTAX `public static boolean isProtected(int mod)`

DESCRIPTION A protected field, method, or constructor in a class is accessible only by the class itself, by classes in the same package as the class, and by subclasses of the class. See *The Java Language Specification* for more details on the `protected` modifier.

Although a Java class which is a member of another class can be private or protected, its reflected access permissions are adjusted to be default (instead of private) or public (instead of protected).

PARAMETERS

`mod` An `int` representing a set of modifiers.

RETURNS `true` if `mod` includes `PROTECTED`.

EXAMPLE See the class example.

isPublic()

PURPOSE Determines if the modifier set includes the `public` modifier.

SYNTAX `public static boolean isPublic(int mod)`

DESCRIPTION The `public` access specifier is the only modifier that can appear on all reflected Java entities. It specifies unrestricted access to the Java entity. See *The Java Language Specification* for more details on the `public` modifier.

Note that in Java source code, all entities, including classes, can also be marked private, protected, or static, but these attributes are removed at the time the class names are mangled for processing by the Java virtual machine and therefore are not reflected.

PARAMETERS

`mod` An `int` representing a set of modifiers.

RETURNS `true` if `mod` includes `PUBLIC`.

EXAMPLE See the class example.

isStatic()

PURPOSE Determines if the modifier set includes the `static` modifier.

SYNTAX `public static boolean isStatic(int mod)`

DESCRIPTION A static field is a field associated with a class and not an object; it is accessed using the notation *ClassName.fieldName* (for example, `java.lang.System.in`). A static method is a method that can be invoked without an instance of its declaring class; it is invoked using the notation *ClassName.methodName* (for example, `java.lang.System.getProperties()`). See *The Java Language Specification* for more details on the `static` modifier.

Although a Java class which is a member of another class can be marked static (turning it into a top-level class), its reflected access permissions are adjusted to be nonstatic.

PARAMETERS
`mod` An `int` representing a set of modifiers.

RETURNS `true` if `mod` includes `STATIC`.

EXAMPLE See the class example.

isSynchronized()

PURPOSE Determines if the modifier set includes the `synchronized` modifier.

SYNTAX `public static boolean isSynchronized(int mod)`

DESCRIPTION When a thread invokes a synchronized method, it first must acquire a lock. The lock is associated with the object. If that lock is not free, the thread must wait until it is free. Once the thread acquires the lock, no other thread can invoke the method until the first thread releases the lock (by returning from the method.) See *The Java Language Specification* for more details on the `synchronized` modifier.

PARAMETERS
`mod` An `int` representing a set of modifiers.

RETURNS `true` if `mod` includes `SYNCHRONIZED`.

EXAMPLE See the class example.

isTransient()

PURPOSE Determines if the modifier set includes the `transient` modifier.

SYNTAX `public static boolean isTransient(int mod)`

DESCRIPTION The values of transient fields in a class are not saved when the class is serialized. See *The Java Language Specification* for more details on the `transient` modifier.

PARAMETERS

`mod` An `int` representing a set of modifiers.

RETURNS `true` if `mod` includes `TRANSIENT`.

EXAMPLE See the class example.

isVolatile()

PURPOSE Determines if the modifier set includes the `volatile` modifier.

SYNTAX `public static boolean isVolatile(int mod)`

DESCRIPTION When two threads concurrently access a field, the language semantics allow each thread to maintain its own copy of the field. Only when a thread encounters a synchronized statement must it actually write its copy of the field into shared memory. Marking a field as volatile causes every modification to the field to be written into shared memory. See *The Java Language Specification* for more details on the `volatile` modifier.

PARAMETERS

`mod` An `int` representing a set of modifiers.

RETURNS `true` if `mod` includes `VOLATILE`.

EXAMPLE See the class example.

toString()

PURPOSE Generates a string containing the printable representation of the modifier set.

SYNTAX `public static String toString(int mod)`

DESCRIPTION This method generates a string containing the printable representation of the modifier set. It places the set of modifiers in `mod` in canonical order, which is `public`, `protected`, `private`, `abstract`, `static`, `final`, `transient`, `volatile`, `native`, and `synchronized`. `interface`, if it appears in `mod`, is placed last. The names of the modifiers are exactly those used in the Java language syntax. For example, if `isPublic(mod)` and `isAbstract(mod)` are both `true`, `toString()` will generate "public abstract".

PARAMETERS

`mod` An `int` representing a set of modifiers.

RETURNS A non-`null` string containing the printable representation of the modifiers in `mod`.

SEE ALSO `java.lang.Object.toString()`.

EXAMPLE See `Method.getModifiers()`.

MulticastSocket

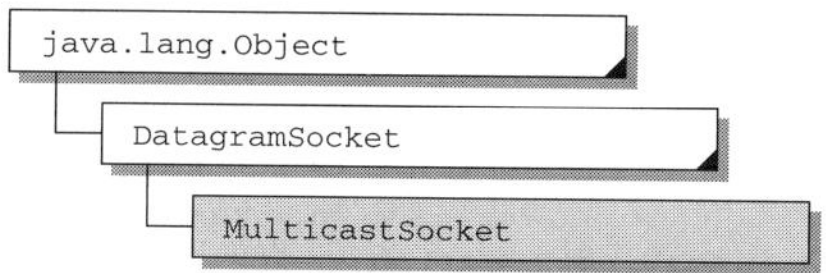

Syntax

```
public class MulticastSocket extends DatagramSocket
```

Description

A program can communicate with other programs on the network by sending a *single* datagram packet to a *multicast group* consisting of zero or more members. The group is identified by a *multicast address*—an IP address to which group members subscribe. A *multicast packet* is a datagram packet that contains a multicast address. The `MulticastSocket` class contains methods for sending and receiving multicast packets. You can also send multicast packets using the `DatagramSocket` class (see `DatagramSocket.send()`).

Multicast IP Addresses and Groups

A multicast group is identified by its multicast address. A special group of IP addresses is reserved for multicast addresses. Multicast addresses are in the range `224.0.0.1` to `239.255.255.255` (in other words, their first 4 bits are `1110`).

Multicast Packet Transmission and Time-to-Live

Whether a datagram packet is sent to a single-host address or a multicast group is determined by the address contained in the datagram packet. The socket from which the datagram packet is sent can be either a `DatagramSocket` or a `MulticastSocket` (see the class example). Using `MulticastSocket` allows you control over the socket settings (time-to-live and network interface usage).

A multicast packet has a *time-to-live*[1] value that specifies the transmission range of this multicast packet, as received by members of the multicast group in other networks. The higher the time-to-live value, the higher the potential coverage of the multicast packet. The time-to-live value can be set per multicast socket (via `setTTL()`) or be specified per packet using `MulticastSocket.send()`.

1. If the time-to-live value of a datagram packet is one, the datagram packet is transmitted using the local network multicast which reaches all immediately-neighboring members of the sender. If the datagram packet's time-to-live value is greater than one, the datagram packet is also forwarded by *multicast routers* to all other networks that have members of the multicast group. If the datagram packet's time-to-live value is greater than two, the datagram packet is again forwarded from those networks, and so on.

Receiving Multicast Packets

A multicast socket must first *join* a multicast group before it can receive multicast packets sent to the group. A multicast socket can join more than one group, but cannot join a group in which it is already a member. A multicast socket can *leave* a multicast group, after which it will no longer receive multicast packets sent to the multicast group. A multicast socket cannot leave a group in which it is not a member. See the `MListener` class in the class example.

Unlike with normal datagram sockets, the address (local port number and network interface) bound to the multicast socket can be reused by other threads of applications on the local machine. For example, you can have multiple applications create multicast sockets by using the same port number on the local machine. After joining the multicast group, they will all receive packets sent to the group.

Multicast Socket Implementation

The actual implementation of multicast sockets is supplied by a subclass of `DatagramSocketImpl` and is configurable by either the application or the user of the application. It is the same implementation used for `DatagramSocket`. See `DatagramSocket` for details.

MEMBER SUMMARY	
Constructor	
`MulticastSocket()`	Constructs a `MulticastSocket` instance for sending/receiving multicast packets.
Method for Communicating	
`send()`	Sends a datagram packet using this multicast socket.
Multicast Group Membership Methods	
`joinGroup()`	Adds this multicast socket to a multicast group.
`leaveGroup()`	Removes this multicast socket from a multicast group.
Methods That Affect Multicast Packet Transmission	
`getInterface()`	Retrieves the address of the network interface used for this multicast socket.
`getTTL()`	Retrieves the time-to-live for multicast packets sent from this multicast socket.
`setInterface()`	Sets the address of the network interface to be used for this multicast socket.
`setTTL()`	Sets the time-to-live for multicast packets sent from this multicast socket.

See Also

DatagramSocket, DatagramSocketImpl, InetAddress.

Example

This example contains two parts. One is a client program (Main.java) that sends multicast packets (constructed using text strings read from standard input) to a multicast address using DatagramSocket. The other is a server program (MListener.java) that receives multicast packets from the same multicast address and simply prints them to standard output.

You can start up one or more MListeners either on the same machine as Main or on different machines. MListener must be on a machine on the same subnet as Main because the default time-to-live (1) is used. See the modified version of Main in setTTL(), which allows you to set the time-to-live of the multicast packets sent from the socket. See also the modified version of Main in send(), which allows you to set the time-to-live on a per packet basis.

Main.java

```
import java.net.*;
import java.io.*;

class Main {
    public static void main(String[] args) {
        try {
            // Create a multicast address
            InetAddress group = InetAddress.getByName("228.1.2.3");
            int port = 1234;
            DatagramSocket socket = new DatagramSocket();

            // Read from standard input and send to group
            BufferedReader r =
                new BufferedReader(new InputStreamReader(System.in));
            String cmd;
            while ((cmd=r.readLine()) != null) {
                DatagramPacket packet =
                    new DatagramPacket(cmd.getBytes(), cmd.length(),
                                       group, port);
                socket.send(packet);
            }
            cmd = "BYE";
            DatagramPacket packet =
                new DatagramPacket(cmd.getBytes(), cmd.length(),
                                   group, port);
            socket.send(packet);
            socket.close();
        } catch (Exception e) {
            e.printStackTrace();
        }
    }
}
```

MListener.java

```
import java.net.*;
import java.io.*;
import java.util.Date;
```

```
public class MListener extends Thread {
    MulticastSocket msocket;
    InetAddress group;

    public MListener(String g, int port) {
        super();
        try {
            msocket = new MulticastSocket(port);
            group = InetAddress.getByName(g);
            msocket.joinGroup(group);
        } catch (IOException e) {
            e.printStackTrace();
            System.exit(-1);
        }
    }

    public void run() {
        while (true) {
            try {
                byte[] buf = new byte[1024];
                DatagramPacket packet = new DatagramPacket(buf, buf.length);
                msocket.receive(packet);

                String answer = new String(packet.getData(), 0,
                                           packet.getLength());
                System.out.println(new Date() + ":(" +
                                   answer.length() + ")" + answer);
                if (answer.equals("BYE")) {
                    msocket.leaveGroup(group); // Not necessary; for demo only
                    msocket.close();           // close() will also leave group
                    System.out.println("exiting...");
                    break;
                }
            } catch (IOException e) {
                e.printStackTrace();
            }
        }
    }

    public static void main(String[] args) {
        try {
            MListener m = new MListener("228.1.2.3", 1234);
            m.start();
        } catch (NumberFormatException e) {
            e.printStackTrace();
        }
    }
}
```

getInterface()

PURPOSE Retrieves the address of the network interface used for this multicast socket.

SYNTAX `public InetAddress getInterface() throws SocketException`

DESCRIPTION On a *multihomed* machine—a machine with multiple network interfaces, each having its own IP address—an application can choose the interface to use for sending multicast packets. This method retrieves the address of the network interface currently being used for this multicast socket. If `setInterface()` has not been called, the address defaults to the platform-dependent system default.

RETURNS The non-`null` network interface on the local machine being used for this multicast socket.

SEE ALSO `InetAddress`, `setInterface()`.

getTTL()

PURPOSE Retrieves the time-to-live for multicast packets sent from this multicast socket.

SYNTAX `public byte getTTL() throws IOException`

DESCRIPTION A multicast packet sent from this multicast socket has a *time-to-live* value that specifies the transmission range of the packet. See the class description for details. The default time-to-live value is determined by `setTTL()`. If `setTTL()` has never been invoked on this multicast socket, the default is obtained from this socket's `DatagramSocketImpl`. Most implementations use a default of one, which means to multicast on the local network.

`getTTL()` returns the default time-to-live value of packets sent from this multicast socket. You can override this default value on a per packet basis by using the form of `send()` that accepts a time-to-live value.

RETURNS The time-to-live for multicast packets sent from this multicast socket. `0` < time-to-live ≤ `0xFF`.

SEE ALSO `DatagramSocket.send()`, `DatagramSocketImpl.getTTL()`, `send()`, `setTTL()`.

EXAMPLE See `setTTL()`.

joinGroup()

PURPOSE Adds this multicast socket to a multicast group.

SYNTAX `public void joinGroup(InetAddress groupAddr) throws IOException`

DESCRIPTION A multicast group is identified by a multicast IP address in the range `224.0.0.1` to `239.255.255.255`. This method adds this multicast socket to the group identified by `groupAddr` so that packets sent to `groupAddr` can be received from this multicast socket.

A multicast socket can join more than one group, but cannot join a group in which it is already a member.

PARAMETERS

`groupAddr` The non-`null` multicast address of the multicast group to join.

EXCEPTIONS

`IOException`
If there is an error joining or if `groupAddr` is not a multicast address.

`SecurityException`
If the current execution context is not allowed to communicate with `groupAddr`.

SEE ALSO `DatagramSocketImpl.join()`, `InetAddress.isMulticastAddress()`, `java.io.IOException`, `java.lang.SecurityException`, `java.lang.SecurityManager.checkMulticast()`, `leaveGroup()`.

EXAMPLE See the class example.

leaveGroup()

PURPOSE Removes this multicast socket from a multicast group.

SYNTAX `public void leaveGroup(InetAddress groupAddr) throws IOException`

DESCRIPTION A multicast group is identified by a multicast IP address in the range `224.0.0.1` to `239.255.255.255`. This method removes this multicast socket from the group identified by `groupAddr` so that this multicast socket will not receive packets sent to `groupAddr`.

If this multicast socket is not a member of `groupAddr`, an exception is thrown.

PARAMETERS

`groupAddr` The non-`null` multicast address of the multicast group to leave.

EXCEPTIONS

`IOException`
If there is an error leaving or if `groupAddr` is not a multicast address.

SEE ALSO `DatagrmSocketImpl.leave()`, `java.io.IOException`, `java.lang.SecurityException`, `InetAddress.isMulticastAddress()`, `java.lang.SecurityManager.checkMulticast()`, `joinGroup()`.

EXAMPLE See the class example.

A B C D E F G H I J K L M N O P Q R S T U V W X Y Z

MulticastSocket()

PURPOSE Constructs a `MulticastSocket` instance for sending/receiving multicast packets.

SYNTAX
```
public MulticastSocket() throws IOException
public MulticastSocket(int port) throws IOException
```

DESCRIPTION This constructor creates a multicast socket and binds it to the local port `port`. If `port` is not supplied or if `port` is `0`, the new socket is bound to any locally available port. The use of certain ports is restricted, and the use of *any* port is permitted only if allowed by the security manager.

The multicast socket is bound to the address of any of the available network interface(s) on the local machine. Which network interface is selected is platform-dependent. The address can be changed subsequent to the creation of the socket using `setInterface()`.

Unlike normal datagram sockets, the local address (local port number and network interface) bound to the multicast socket can be reused by other threads of applications that are on the local machine. For example, you can have multiple applications create multicast sockets using the same port number on the local machine.

The default time-to-live for packets sent from this multicast socket is obtained from this socket's `DatagramSocketImpl`. Most implementations use a default of one, which means to multicast on the local network.. This default can be changed using `setTTL()` or be overridden on a per packet basis using `send()`.

PARAMETERS

`port` The local port to which to bind this multicast socket. `0` ≤ `port` ≤ `65535`. If `port` is `0` or unspecified, use any available port.

EXCEPTIONS

`IllegalArgumentException`
If `port` < `0` or `port` > `65535`.

`IOException`
If cannot create a multicast socket using `port`.

`SecurityException`
If cannot use `port` due to security reasons.

SEE ALSO `DatagramSocket()`, `java.lang.SecurityException`, `java.lang.SecurityManager.checkListen()`, `setInterface()`, `setTTL()`.

EXAMPLE See `send()`, `setTTL()`, and the class example.

A B C D E F G H I J K L M N O P Q R S T U V W X Y Z

send()

PURPOSE Sends a datagram packet using this multicast socket.

SYNTAX

```
public synchronized void send(DatagramPacket dgram, byte ttl)
   throws IOException
```

DESCRIPTION This method uses this multicast socket to send the datagram packet `dgram` to the destination address found inside `dgram`. If the destination is a multicast address, `ttl` overrides the default time-to-live for this socket and `dgram` is sent using a time-to-live value of `ttl` instead. (`DatagramSocket.send()` uses the default time-to-live value returned by `getTTL()`.) The default time-to-live value for this socket is otherwise unaffected by `ttl`. If the destination is not a multicast address, `ttl` is ignored.

This method can be executed only if the security manager permits communication with the destination specified in `dgram`.

PARAMETERS

`dgram` The non-`null` datagram packet to be sent.

`ttl` An unsigned 8-bit number specifying the time-to-live for `dgram`. `0` < `ttl` ≤ `0xFF`.

EXCEPTIONS

`IOException`

If an error occurred while setting the time-to-live or while sending the datagram packet.

`SecurityException`

If not allowed to communicate with the destination specified in `dgram` due to security reasons.

SEE ALSO `DatagramSocket.send()`, `DatagramSocket.receive()`, `java.io.IOException`, `java.lang.SecurityException`, `java.lang.SecurityManager.checkConnect()`, `java.lang.SecurityManager.checkMulticast()`.

EXAMPLE This is a modified version of the class example. Instead of using `DatagramSocket` to send multicast packets to a multicast address, this example uses `MulticastSocket`. If the line it reads from standard input is prefixed by an integer, the integer is used as the time-to-live value for the multicast packet constructed using that line.

To see this program in action, run `MListener` (from the class example) on various machines in networks of various distances from the machine running `Main`. Then, enter different time-to-live values and observe which `MListener` receives the multicast packets.

See `setTTL()` for another variation of this program.

```
import java.net.*;
import java.io.*;

class Main {
    public static void main(String[] args) {
        try {
            // Create a multicast address
            InetAddress group = InetAddress.getByName("228.1.2.3");
            int port = 1234;
            MulticastSocket socket = new MulticastSocket();

            // Read from standard input ttl and msg, then send to group
            BufferedReader r =
                new BufferedReader(new InputStreamReader(System.in));
            String cmd;
            byte ttl = 1; // default
            while ((cmd=r.readLine()) != null) {
                int where = cmd.indexOf(' ');
                if (Character.isDigit(cmd.charAt(0)) && where > 0) {
                    // Get TTL from input
                    ttl = Byte.parseByte(cmd.substring(0, where));
                    cmd = cmd.substring(where+1);
                }
                DatagramPacket packet =
                    new DatagramPacket(cmd.getBytes(), cmd.length(),
                                       group, port);
                socket.send(packet, ttl);
            }
            cmd = "BYE";
            DatagramPacket packet =
                new DatagramPacket(cmd.getBytes(), cmd.length(),
                                   group, port);
            socket.send(packet, ttl);
            socket.close();
        } catch (Exception e) {
            e.printStackTrace();
        }
    }
}
```

setInterface()

PURPOSE Sets the address of the network interface to be used for this multicast socket.

SYNTAX
```
public void setInterface(InetAddress addr) throws
   SocketException
```

DESCRIPTION On a multihomed machine—a machine with multiple network interfaces, each having its own IP address—an application can choose the interface to use for sending multicast packets. This method sets `addr` to be the network interface used by this multicast socket. If `setInterface()` has not been called, the address defaults to the platform-dependent system default.

PARAMETERS

`addr` The non-`null` address of the network interface to use.

EXAMPLE

`SocketException`
If a problem was encountered while attempting to set the address for this multicast socket.

SEE ALSO `getInterface()`.

setTTL()

PURPOSE Sets the time-to-live for multicast packets sent from this multicast socket.

SYNTAX
```
public void setTTL(byte ttl) throws IOException
```

DESCRIPTION A multicast packet sent from this multicast socket has a time-to-live value that specifies the transmission range of the packet. See the class description for deteails. The default time-to-live value is determined by this socket's `DatagramSocketImpl`. Most implementations use a default of one, which means to multicast on the local network.

This method sets to `ttl` the default time-to-live value of packets sent from this multicast socket. Subsequent calls to `getTTL()` will return this time-to-live value. Subsequent calls to `send()` will use this time-to-live value. You can override this default value on a per packet basis by using the form of `send()` that accepts a time-to-live value.

PARAMETERS

`ttl` An unsigned 8-bit number specifying the time-to-live for packets sent from this multicast socket. `0` < `ttl` ≤ `0xFF`.

EXCEPTIONS

`IOException`
If an IO error occurred while attempting to set the time-to-live of this multicast socket.

SEE ALSO `DatagramSocket.send()`, `DatagramSocketImpl.setTTL()`, `getTTL()`, `send()`.

EXAMPLE This is a modified version of the class example. Instead of using `DatagramSocket` to send multicast packets to a multicast address, this example uses `MulticastSocket`. It accepts a positive or negative number (`delta`) from the command line and uses that to augment the default time-to-live value. Note that the time-to-live value is an unsigned number and that certain values of `delta` will result in a `SocketException`.

To see this program in action, run `MListener` (from the class example) on various machines in networks of various distances from the machine running `Main`. Then, run `Main` using different values of delta and observe which `MListener` receives the multicast packets.

See `send()` for another variation of this program.

```
import java.net.*;
import java.io.*;

class Main {
    public static void main(String[] args) {
        if (args.length != 1) {
            System.err.println("java Main <ttl>");
            System.exit(-1);
        }
        byte delta = Byte.parseByte(args[0]);
        try {
            // Create a multicast address
            InetAddress group = InetAddress.getByName("228.1.2.3");
            int port = 1234;
            MulticastSocket socket = new MulticastSocket();
            socket.setTTL((byte)(socket.getTTL()+delta));

            // Read from standard input and send to group
            BufferedReader r =
                new BufferedReader(new InputStreamReader(System.in));
            String cmd;
            while ((cmd=r.readLine()) != null) {
                DatagramPacket packet =
                    new DatagramPacket(cmd.getBytes(), cmd.length(),
                                       group, port);
                socket.send(packet);
            }
            cmd = "BYE";
            DatagramPacket packet =
                new DatagramPacket(cmd.getBytes(), cmd.length(),
                                   group, port);
            socket.send(packet);
            socket.close();
        } catch (Exception e) {
            e.printStackTrace();
        }
    }
}
```

NegativeArraySizeException

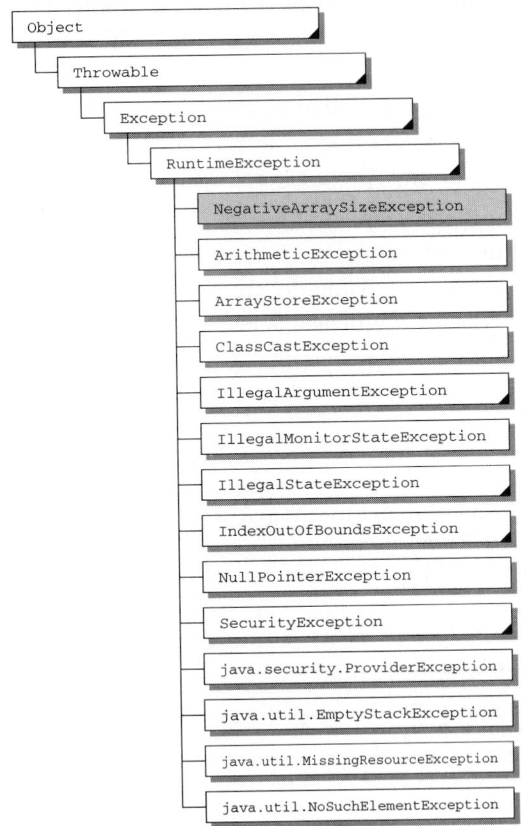

Syntax

```
public class NegativeArraySizeException extends RuntimeException
```

Description

`NegativeArraySizeException` is thrown when the program attempts to create an array with a negative size. It should not be caught or declared in the `throws` clause of a method.

MEMBER SUMMARY	
Constructor	
`NegativeArraySizeException()`	Constructs a `NegativeArraySizeException` instance.

See Also

RuntimeException.

Example

This example throws NegativeArraySizeException.

```
class Main {
    public static void main(String[] args) {
        System.out.println("NegativeArraySizeException example");
        int[] intArray = new int[-5];
        intArray[3] = 10;
    }
}
```

NegativeArraySizeException()

PURPOSE Constructs a NegativeArraySizeException instance.

SYNTAX

```
public NegativeArraySizeException()
public NegativeArraySizeException(String msg)
```

DESCRIPTION The two forms of this constructor construct an instance of NegativeArraySizeException. An optional string msg can be supplied that describes this particular instance of the exception. If msg is not supplied, it defaults to null.

PARAMETERS

msg A possibly null string that gives details about this exception.

SEE ALSO Throwable.getMessage().

NoClassDefFoundError

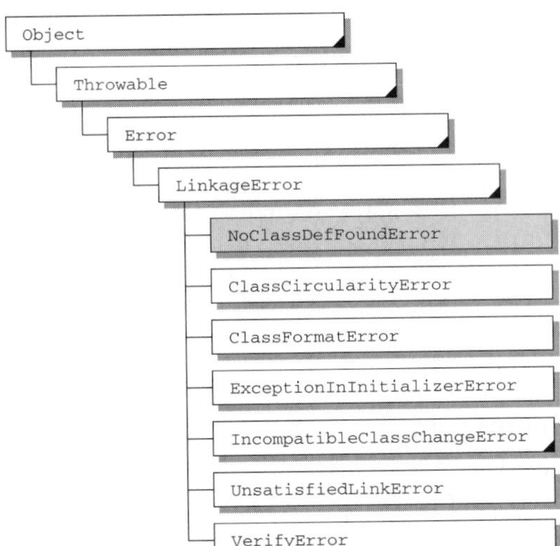

Syntax

```
public class NoClassDefFoundError extends LinkageError
```

Description

`NoClassDefFoundError` is a runtime linkage error that is thrown when the system's default class loader cannot find the class to load. Normally, when you compile a program's classes, you get a compilation error saying that the class is missing. However, if the class file was removed subsequent to compilation, then the runtime will not be able to find it, and so `NoClassDefFoundError` will be thrown.

`ClassNotFoundException` and `NoClassDefFoundError` both report the same error; namely, the requested class cannot be found. They differ in that `ClassNotFoundException` is an exception thrown by a program-defined class loader or the user's invocation of a method to find a class (such as the use of `Class.forName()` and `ClassLoader.findSystemClass()`). On the other hand, `NoClassDefFoundError` is a runtime linkage error thrown by the Java virtual machine when it is attempting to load and resolve class references.

`NoClassDefFoundError` should not be caught or declared in the `throws` clause of a method.

MEMBER SUMMARY	
Constructor	
`NoClassDefFoundError()`	Constructs a `NoClassDefFoundError` instance.

See Also

`ClassNotFoundException`, `ClassLoader.findSystemClass()`, `Error`, `LinkageError`.

Example

This example throws a `NoClassDefFoundError` if, after compilation of `Main.java`, the class file for `A` is deleted.

A.java

```
class A {
}
```

Main.java

```
class Main {
    public static void main(String[] args) {
        System.out.println("NoClassDefFoundError Example");
        A a = new A();
    }
}
```

NoClassDefFoundError()

PURPOSE: Constructs a `NoClassDefFoundError` instance.

SYNTAX:
```
public NoClassDefFoundError()
public NoClassDefFoundError(String msg)
```

DESCRIPTION: The two forms of this constructor construct an instance of `NoClassDefFoundError`. An optional string `msg` can be supplied that describes this particular instance of the error. If `msg` is not supplied, it defaults to `null`.

PARAMETERS

`msg` — A possibly `null` string that gives details about this error.

SEE ALSO: `Throwable.getMessage()`.

java.net

NoRouteToHostException

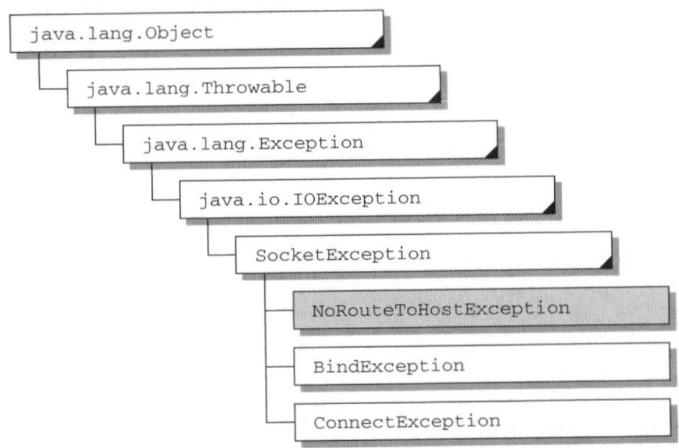

A B C D E F G H I J K L M N O P Q R S T U V W X Y Z

Syntax

```
public class NoRouteToHostException extends SocketException
```

Description

`NoRouteToHostException` is an exception that is thrown when the program attempts to connect a socket to a remote address and port. The failure may be a result of an intervening firewall or of an intermediate router being down.

This exception is different from `UnknownHostException`. With `UnknownHostException`, the host name could not be resolved to its address. With `NoRouteToHostException`, the host name can be resolved to its address, but no route can be found through the network to reach that address.

MEMBER SUMMARY	
Constructor	
`NoRouteToHostException()`	Constructs a `NoRouteToHostException` instance.

Example

This example opens a socket to the host specified in the command line. It will throw `NoRouteToHostException` if you specify an unreachable host (note that an unreachable host is different from a nonexistent host).

```
import java.net.Socket;
import java.io.IOException;
```

```
class Main {
  public static void main(String[] args) {
    if (args.length != 1) {
        System.out.println("usage: java Main <unreachable host or IPaddr>");
        System.exit(0);
     }
    try {
      Socket sock = new Socket(args[0], 25);
      System.out.println("socket created" + sock.toString());

      sock.close();
    } catch (IOException e) {
      e.printStackTrace();
    }
  }
}
```


NoRouteToHostException()

PURPOSE
Constructs a `NoRouteToHostException` instance.

SYNTAX
```
public NoRouteToHostException()
public NoRouteToHostException(String msg)
```

DESCRIPTION
This constructor constructs an instance of `NoRouteToHostException`. An optional string `msg` can be supplied that describes this particular instance of the exception. If no `msg` is supplied, it defaults to `null`.

PARAMETERS

`msg`
A possibly `null` string containing more details about the cause of this exception.

SEE ALSO
`java.lang.Throwable.getMessage()`.

NoSuchElementException

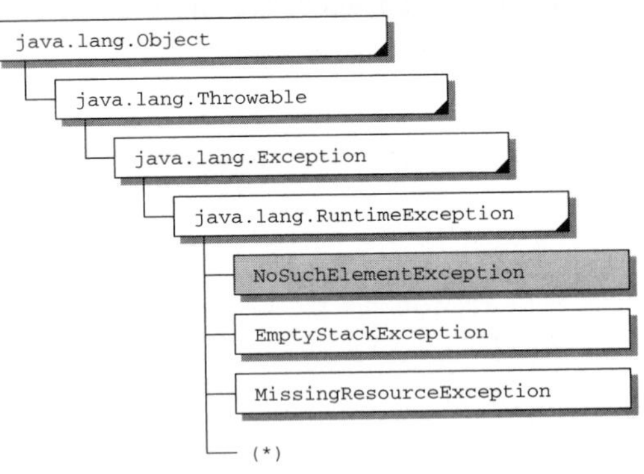

(*) 11 classes from other packages not shown.

A B C D E F G H I J K L M N O P Q R S T U V W X Y Z

Syntax

`public class NoSuchElementException extends RuntimeException`

Description

`NoSuchElementException` is a runtime exception that is thrown when the program attempts to access an element in an enumeration after the enumeration has finished.

`NoSuchElementException` should not be caught or declared in the `throws` clause of a method.

MEMBER SUMMARY	
Constructor	
`NoSuchElementException()`	Constructs a `NoSuchElementException` instance.

See Also

`Enumeration`, `java.lang.RuntimeException`.

Example

This example incorrectly avoids using `Enumeration.hasMoreElements()` and instead just loops, calling `Enumeration.nextElement()` until the enumeration has completed. After the enumeration has completed, a call to `Enumeration.nextElement()` throws a `NoSuchElementException`.

```
import java.util.Hashtable;
import java.util.Enumeration;

class Main {
    public static void main(String[] args) {
        Hashtable tab = new Hashtable(13);

        tab.put("Jones", "station wagon");
        tab.put("Smith", "race car");
        tab.put("Graham", "sedan");

        Enumeration e = tab.keys();
        Object elem;
        while ((elem = e.nextElement()) != null)
            System.out.println(elem);
    }
}
```

NoSuchElementException()

PURPOSE Constructs a `NoSuchElementException` instance.

SYNTAX

```
public NoSuchElementException()
public NoSuchElementException(String msg)
```

DESCRIPTION The two forms of this constructor construct an instance of `NoSuchElementException`. An optional string `msg` can be supplied that describes this particular instance of the exception. If `msg` is not supplied, it defaults to `null`.

PARAMETERS

`msg` A possibly `null` string that gives details about this exception.

SEE ALSO `java.lang.Throwable.getMessage()`.

java.lang
NoSuchFieldError

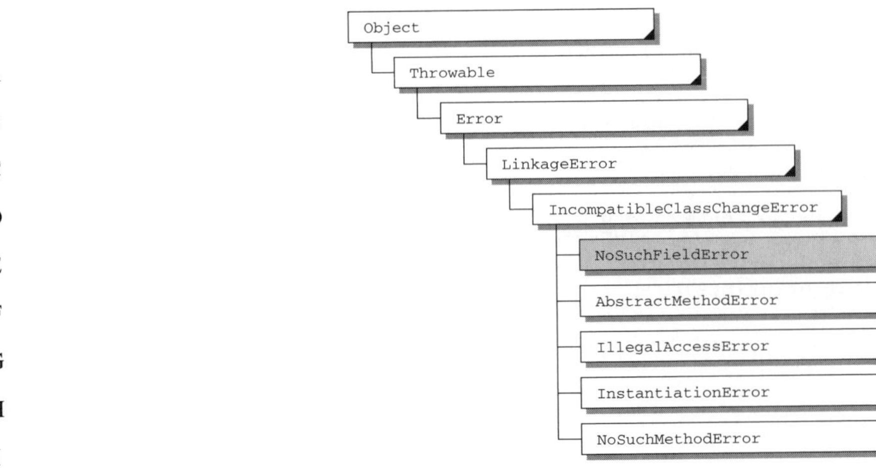

A B C D E F G H I J K L M N O P Q R S T U V W X Y Z

Syntax

```
public class NoSuchFieldError extends IncompatibleClassChangeError
```

Description

`NoSuchFieldError` is a runtime linkage error that is thrown when the program attempts to access a nonexistent field of a class. Normally, when you compile a program's classes, you get a compilation error pinpointing the problem so that a linkage error at runtime does not occur. However, this problem could be introduced when classes of a program become inconsistent, for example if you were to make an incompatible change and then recompile only some of the classes.

`NoSuchFieldError` and `NoSuchFieldException` both report the same error; namely, the requested field cannot be found. The difference is that `NoSuchFieldException` is an exception thrown by the user's invocation of reflection methods such as `Class.getField()` and `Class.getDeclaredField()`. On the other hand, `NoSuchFieldError` is a runtime linkage error thrown by the Java virtual machine when it is attempting to access a nonexistent field.

`NoSuchFieldError` should not be caught or declared in the `throws` clause of a method.

MEMBER SUMMARY	
Constructor	
`NoSuchFieldError()`	Constructs a `NoSuchFieldError` instance.

See Also

`IncompatibleClassChangeError`, `LinkageError`, `NoSuchMethodError`.

Example

In this example, when `fieldA` is deleted from class `A` and `A.java` is recompiled, the main program throws `NoSuchFieldError`.

Main.java

```
class Main {
    public static void main(String[] args) {
        System.out.println("NoSuchFieldError example");
        A a = new A();

        System.out.println(a.fieldA);
        System.out.println(a.fieldB);
    }
}
```

A.java

```
class A {
    public int fieldA = 100;
    public int fieldB = 200;
}
```

Modified A.java

```
class A {
//    public int fieldA = 100;
    public int fieldB = 200;
}
```

A B C D E F G H I J K L M N O P Q R S T U V W X Y Z

NoSuchFieldError()

PURPOSE: Constructs a `NoSuchFieldError` instance.

SYNTAX:
```
public NoSuchFieldError()
public NoSuchFieldError(String msg)
```

DESCRIPTION: The two forms of this constructor construct an instance of `NoSuchFieldError`. An optional string `msg` can be supplied that describes this particular instance of the error. If `msg` is not supplied, it defaults to `null`.

PARAMETERS

`msg` A non-`null` string that gives details about this error.

SEE ALSO: `Throwable.getMessage()`.

java.lang
NoSuchFieldException

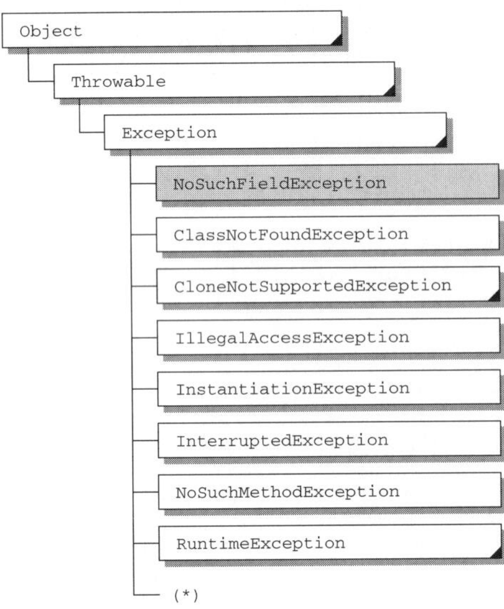

(*) 21 classes from other packages not shown.

A B C D E F G H I J K L M N O P Q R S T U V W X Y Z

Syntax

```
public class NoSuchFieldException extends Exception
```

Description

`NoSuchFieldException` is an exception that is thrown when the program attempts to access a nonexistent field of a class. Normally, when you compile a program's classes, you get a compilation error pinpointing the problem so that a linkage error at runtime does not occur. But in addition to linking to the classes with which the program is compiled, you also can dynamically link in classes and invoke methods on them through the use of class loaders and the reflection methods in the `Class` class. When the program attempts to access a nonexistent field in one of these classes, a `NoSuchFieldException` is thrown.

`NoSuchFieldError` and `NoSuchFieldException` both report the same error; namely, the requested field cannot be found. The difference is that `NoSuchFieldException` is an exception thrown by the user's invocation of reflection methods such as `Class.getField()` and `Class.getDeclaredField()`. On the other hand, `NoSuchFieldError` is a runtime linkage error thrown by the Java virtual machine when it is attempting to access a nonexistent field.

See Also

`Class.getField()`, `Class.getDeclaredField()`, `NoSuchFieldError`, `NoSuchMethodException`.

MEMBER SUMMARY	
Constructor	
`NoSuchFieldException()`	Constructs a `NoSuchFieldException` instance.

Example

In this example, `NoSuchFieldException` is thrown when the program attempts to access a nonexistent field `fieldA`.

```
class A {
//    public int fieldA = 100;
    public int fieldB = 200;
}

class Main {
    public static void main(String[] args) {
        System.out.println("NoSuchFieldException example");
        try {
            Class c = Class.forName("A");
            Object a = c.newInstance();
            System.out.println(c.getField("fieldA"));
        } catch (InstantiationException e) {
            e.printStackTrace();
        } catch (IllegalAccessException e) {
            e.printStackTrace();
        } catch (ClassNotFoundException e) {
            e.printStackTrace();
        } catch (NoSuchFieldException e) {
            e.printStackTrace();
        }
    }
}
```

NoSuchFieldException()

PURPOSE Constructs a `NoSuchFieldException` instance.

SYNTAX
```
public NoSuchFieldException()
public NoSuchFieldException(String msg)
```

DESCRIPTION The two forms of this constructor construct an instance of `NoSuchFieldException`. An optional string `msg` can be supplied that describes this particular instance of the error. If `msg` is not supplied, it defaults to `null`.

PARAMETERS

`msg` A possibly `null` string that gives details about this exception.

SEE ALSO `Throwable.getMessage()`.

NoSuchMethodError

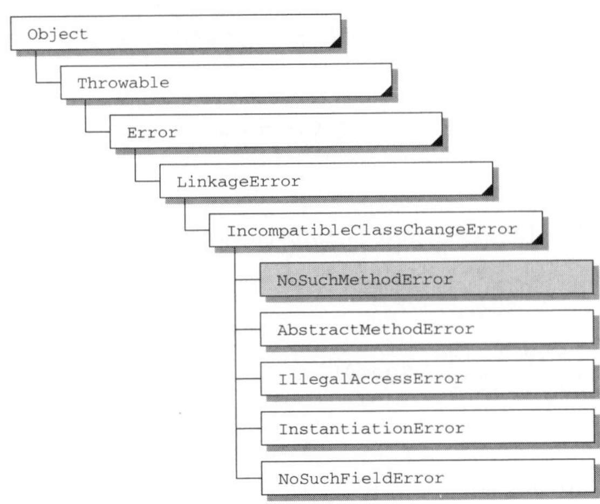

Syntax

```
public class NoSuchMethodError extends IncompatibleClassChangeError
```

Description

`NoSuchMethodError` is a runtime linkage error that is thrown when the program attempts to access a nonexistent method of a class. Normally, when you compile a program's classes, you get a compilation error pinpointing the problem so that a linkage error at runtime does not occur. However, this problem could be introduced when classes of a program become inconsistent, for example if you were to make an incompatible change and then recompile only some of the program's classes.

`NoSuchMethodError` and `NoSuchMethodException` both report the same error; namely, the requested method cannot be found. The difference is that `NoSuchMethodException` is an exception thrown by the user's invocation of reflection methods such as `Class.getConstructor()` or `Class.getMethod()`. On the other hand, `NoSuchMethodError` is a runtime linkage error thrown by the Java virtual machine when it is attempting to invoke a nonexistent method.

`NoSuchMethodError` should not be caught or declared in the `throws` clause of a method.

MEMBER SUMMARY	
Constructor	
`NoSuchMethodError()`	Constructs a `NoSuchMethodError` instance.

See Also

IncompatibleClassChangeError, LinkageError, NoSuchFieldError, NoSuchMethodException.

Example

In this example, when the methodA line is commented out in class A and A.java is recompiled, the main program raises a NoSuchMethodError.

Main.java

```
class Main {
    public static void main(String[] args) {
        System.out.println("NoSuchMethodError example");
        A a = new A();

        System.out.println(a.methodA());
        System.out.println(a.methodB());
    }
}
```

A.java

```
class A {
    public int methodA() { return 100; }
    public int methodB() { return 200; }
}
```

Modified A.java

```
class A {
//    public int methodA() { return 100; }
    public int methodB() { return 200; }
}
```

NoSuchMethodError()

PURPOSE Constructs a NoSuchMethodError instance.

SYNTAX

```
public NoSuchMethodError()
public NoSuchMethodError(String msg)
```

DESCRIPTION The two forms of this constructor construct an instance of NoSuchMethodError. An optional string msg can be supplied that describes this particular instance of the error. If msg is not supplied, it defaults to null.

PARAMETERS

msg A possibly null string that gives details about this error.

SEE ALSO Throwable.getMessage().

A B C D E F G H I J K L M N O P Q R S T U V W X Y Z

NoSuchMethodException

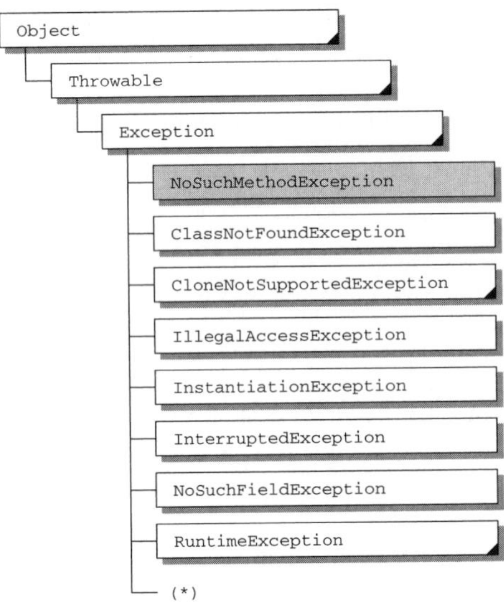

(*) 21 classes from other packages not shown.

A B C D E F G H I J K L M N O P Q R S T U V W X Y Z

Syntax

```
public class NoSuchMethodException extends Exception
```

Description

`NoSuchMethodException` is an exception that is thrown when the program attempts to access a nonexistent method of a class. Normally, when you compile a program's classes, you get a compilation error pinpointing the problem so that a linkage error at runtime does not occur. But in addition to linking the classes with which the program is compiled, you also can dynamically link in classes and invoke methods on them through the use of class loaders and the reflection methods in the `Class` class. When the program attempts to invoke a nonexistent method in one of these classes, a `NoSuchMethodException` is thrown.

`NoSuchMethodError` and `NoSuchMethodException` both report the same error; namely, the requested method cannot be found. The difference is that `NoSuchMethodException` is an exception thrown by the user's invocation of reflection methods such as `Class.getConstructor()` or `Class.getMethod()`. On the other hand, `NoSuchMethodError` is a runtime linkage error thrown by the Java virtual machine when it is attempting to invoke a nonexistent method.

MEMBER SUMMARY	
Constructor	
`NoSuchMethodException()`	Constructs a `NoSuchMethodException` instance.

See Also

`Class.getConstructor()`, `Class.getDeclaredConstructor()`, `Class.getDeclaredMethod()`, `Class.getMethod()`, `Class.newInstance()`, `NoSuchFieldException`, `NoSuchMethodError`.

Example

In this example, a `NoSuchMethodException` is thrown when `main()` attempts to invoke `newInstance()` on the class `A`. This happens because `A` does not have a constructor that accepts no arguments.

Main.java

```
class Main {
    public static void main(String[] args) {
        System.out.println("NoSuchMethodException example");
        try {
            Class c = Class.forName("A");
            Object a = c.newInstance();
        } catch (InstantiationException e) {
            e.printStackTrace();
        } catch (IllegalAccessException e) {
            e.printStackTrace();
        } catch (ClassNotFoundException e) {
            e.printStackTrace();
        }
    }
}
```

A.java

```
class A {
    public A(int i, int j) {
        System.out.println(i + j);
    }
}
```

NoSuchMethodException()

PURPOSE Constructs a `NoSuchMethodException` instance.

SYNTAX
```
public NoSuchMethodException()
public NoSuchMethodException(String msg)
```

DESCRIPTION The two forms of this constructor construct an instance of `NoSuchMethodException`. An optional string `msg` can be supplied that describes this particular instance of the exception. If `msg` is not supplied, it defaults to `null`.

PARAMETERS

`msg` A possibly `null` string that gives details about this exception.

SEE ALSO `Throwable.getMessage()`.

NotActiveException

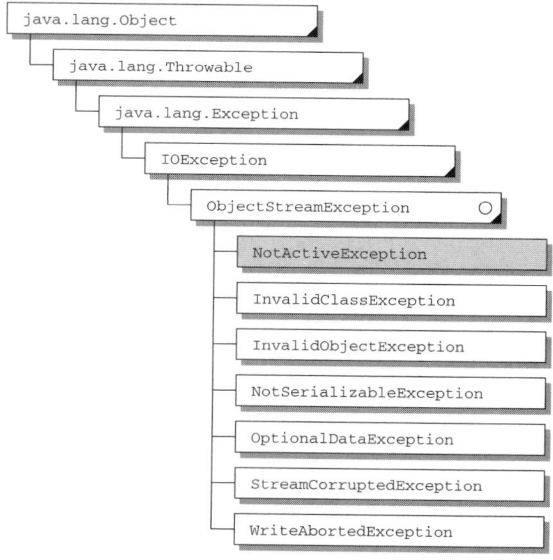

Syntax

`public class NotActiveException extends ObjectStreamException`

Description

A `NotActiveException` is thrown if the program tries to use one of the following methods when it is not trying to serializing or deserializing an object:

- `ObjectInputStream.defaultReadObject()`
- `ObjectInputStream.registerValidation()`
- `ObjectOutputStream.defaultWriteObject()`

The first two methods should be called only from within an object's `readObject()` method. `defaultWriteObject()` should be called only within an object's `writeObject()` method. If these methods are called from any other context, a `NotActiveException` is thrown.

MEMBER SUMMARY	
Constructor	
`NotActiveException()`	Constructs an instance of `NotActiveException`.

See Also

`ObjectInputStream.defaultReadObject()`, `ObjectInputStream.registerValidation()`, `ObjectOutputStream.defaultWriteObject()`.

A B C D E F G H I J K L M N O P Q R S T U V W X Y Z

Example

This example throws a `NotActiveException` when it attempts to use `ObjectOutput-Stream.defaultWriteObject()` from the main program.

```
import java.io.*;

class Main {
    public static void main(String[] args) {
        try {
            // Write object out
            FileOutputStream f = new FileOutputStream("Class1.ser");
            ObjectOutputStream out = new ObjectOutputStream(f);

            Class1 c1 = new Class1(10);
            out.defaultWriteObject();
            out.flush();
            out.close();
        } catch (IOException e) {
            e.printStackTrace();
        }
    }
}

class Class1 implements Serializable {
    int field1;
    transient int field2;

    public Class1(int ignore) {
        field1 = 10;
        field2 = -1;
    }
}
```

NotActiveException()

PURPOSE Constructs an instance of `NotActiveException`.

SYNTAX
```
public NotActiveException()
public NotActiveException(String msg)
```

DESCRIPTION The two forms of this constructor construct an instance of `NotActiveException`. An optional string `msg` can be supplied that describes this particular instance of the exception. If `msg` is not supplied, it defaults to `null`.

PARAMETERS

`msg` A possibly `null` string that gives details about this exception.

SEE ALSO `java.lang.Throwable.getMessage()`.

NotSerializableException

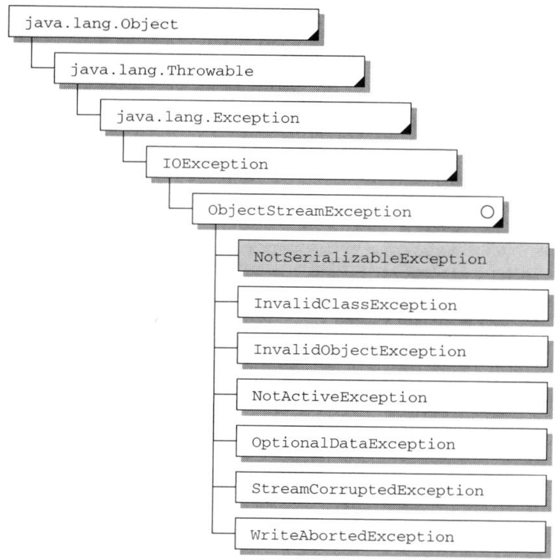

A B C D E F G H I J K L M N O P Q R S T U V W X Y Z

Syntax

```
public class NotSerializableException extends ObjectStreamException
```

Description

A `NotSerializableException` is thrown when `ObjectOutput.writeObject()` is given an object that implements neither `Serializable` nor `Externalizable`.

This exception can also be thrown intentionally by a class's `writeObject()` method to indicate that the class does not want to be serialized. Since the `Serializable` interface is inherited by all subclasses, this is the only way to selectively disable serialization.

MEMBER SUMMARY	
Constructor	
`NotSerializableException()`	Constructs an instance of `NotSerializableException`.

See Also

`ObjectOutput.writeObject()`, `ObjectOutputStream.writeObject()`.

A B C D E F G H I J K L M N O P Q R S T U V W X Y Z

Example

This example throws `NotSerializableException` when it attempts to serialize `Class1`, which does not implement the `Serializable` or `Externalizable` interfaces.

```
import java.io.*;

class Main {
    public static void main(String[] args) {
        try {
            FileOutputStream f = new FileOutputStream("Class1.ser");
            ObjectOutput out = new ObjectOutputStream(f);

            out.writeObject(new Class1(10, 20));
            out.flush();
            out.close();
        } catch (IOException e) {
            e.printStackTrace();
        }
    }
}

class Class1 {
    int field1;
    int field2;

    Class1(int one, int two) {
        field1 = one;
        field2 = two;
    }
}
```

NotSerializableException()

PURPOSE: Constructs an instance of `NotSerializableException`.

SYNTAX:

```
public NotSerializableException()
public NotSerializableException(String className)
```

DESCRIPTION: The two forms of this constructor construct an instance of `NotSerializableException`. If a non-`null` string `className` is supplied, it is used to construct the detail message of this exception (that returned by `Throwable.getMessage()`). If `className` is `null` or not supplied, the message is `null`.

PARAMETERS

`className` The possibly `null` name of the class that was being serialized.

SEE ALSO: `java.lang.Throwable.getMessage()`.

NullPointerException

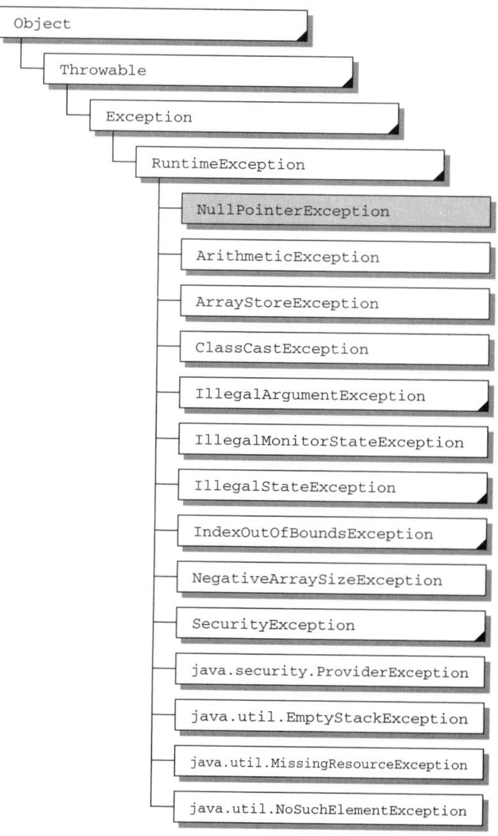

Syntax

```
public class NullPointerException extends RuntimeException
```

Description

`NullPointerException` is thrown when the program attempts to dereference a `null` object reference. A typical example of this is a method that expects an object reference as an argument but instead gets a `null`.

`NullPointerException` should not be caught or declared in the `throws` clause of a method.

MEMBER SUMMARY	
Constructor	
`NullPointerException()`	Constructs a `NullPointerException` instance.

A B C D E F G H I J K L M N O P Q R S T U V W X Y Z

See Also

`RuntimeException`.

Example

This example throws `NullPointerException` when `null` is passed to the `test()` method, which expects its argument to be non-`null`.

```
class Main {
    public static void test(Object obj) {
        System.out.println(obj.toString());
    }
    public static void main(String[] args) {
        System.out.println("NullPointerException example");
        test(null);
    }
}
```

NullPointerException()

PURPOSE Constructs a `NullPointerException` instance.

SYNTAX
```
public NullPointerException()
public NullPointerException(String msg)
```

DESCRIPTION The two forms of this constructor construct an instance of `NullPointerException`. An optional string `msg` can be supplied that describes this particular instance of the exception. If `msg` is not supplied, it defaults to `null`.

PARAMETERS

`msg` A possibly `null` string that gives details about this exception.

SEE ALSO `Throwable.getMessage()`.

Number

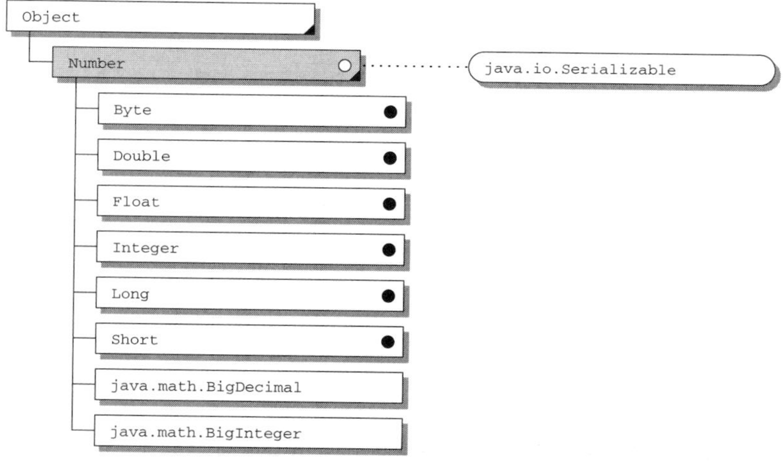

A B C D E F G H I J K L M N O P Q R S T U V W X Y Z

Syntax

```
public abstract class Number implements Serializable
```

Description

`Number` is an abstract superclass for numeric scalar types. `Byte`, `Integer`, `Short`, `Long`, `Float`, and `Double` are subclasses of `Number` that implement the abstract methods in the `Number` class for the basic numeric types—`byte`, `int`, `short`, `long`, `float`, and `double`, respectively—in Java.

The two classes in `java.math`—`BigDecimal` and `BigInteger`—also are subclasses of `Number`. This allows the numeric values to be retrieved from instances of these classes.

MEMBER SUMMARY	
Number Methods	
`byteValue()`	Retrieves the value of this object as a `byte`.
`doubleValue()`	Retrieves the value of this object as a `double`.
`floatValue()`	Retrieves the value of this object as a `float`.
`intValue()`	Retrieves the value of this object as an `int`.
`longValue()`	Retrieves the value of this object as a `long`.
`shortValue()`	Retrieves the value of this object as a `short`.

See Also

Byte, Double, Float, Integer, java.io.Serializable, java.math.BigDecimal, java.math.BigInteger, Long, Short.

Example

```
import java.util.Vector;
import java.util.Enumeration;

class Main {

 // Calculate the double sum of a vector of Number objects
    public static double doubleSum(Vector v) {
        double sum = 0;
        for (Enumeration e = v.elements();
             e.hasMoreElements();
             sum += ((Number)e.nextElement()).doubleValue());
        return (sum);
    }
    public static void main(String[] args) {
        Vector numvec = new Vector(6);

        // Prepare contents of vector
        numvec.addElement(new Integer(1995));
        numvec.addElement(new Double(6.4e3));
        numvec.addElement(new Integer(32));
        numvec.addElement(new Float(7.821e3f));
        numvec.addElement(new Double(22.32e2));
        numvec.addElement(new Byte((byte)12));
        numvec.addElement(new Short((short)1997));
        numvec.addElement(new Long(10424300));
        numvec.addElement(new java.math.BigDecimal("1923.19009"));
        numvec.addElement(new java.math.BigInteger("104243001231239879"));

        System.out.println("double total: " + doubleSum(numvec));
    }
}
```

byteValue()

PURPOSE Retrieves the value of this object as a byte.

SYNTAX `public abstract byte byteValue()`

DESCRIPTION This method returns the value of this object as a byte. If the value is not already a byte, this may involve casting.

RETURNS The value of this object as a byte.

EXAMPLE

```
// Calculate the byte sum of a vector of Number objects
public static int byteSum(Vector v) {
    byte sum = 0;
    for (Enumeration e = v.elements();
```

```
        e.hasMoreElements();
        sum += ((Number)e.nextElement()).byteValue())
        ;
    return (sum);
}
```

A B C D E F G H I J K L M N O P Q R S T U V W X Y Z

doubleValue()

PURPOSE Retrieves the value of this object as a `double`.

SYNTAX `public abstract double doubleValue()`

DESCRIPTION This method returns the value of this object as a `double`. If the value is not already a `double`, this may involve casting .

RETURNS The value of this object as a `double`.

EXAMPLE

```
// Calculate the double sum of a vector of Number objects
public static double doubleSum(Vector v) {
    double sum = 0;
    for (Enumeration e = v.elements();
         e.hasMoreElements();
         sum += ((Number)e.nextElement()).doubleValue())
        ;
    return (sum);
}
```

floatValue()

PURPOSE Retrieves the value of this object as a `float`.

SYNTAX `public abstract float floatValue()`

DESCRIPTION This method returns the value of this object as a `float`. If the value is not already a `float`, this may involve casting (and possibly a loss of precision).

RETURNS The value of this object as a `float`.

EXAMPLE

```
// Calculate the float sum of a vector of Number objects
public static float floatSum(Vector v) {
    float sum = 0;
    for (Enumeration e = v.elements();
         e.hasMoreElements();
         sum += ((Number)e.nextElement()).floatValue())
        ;
    return (sum);
}
```

intValue()

PURPOSE Retrieves the value of this object as an `int`.

SYNTAX `public abstract int intValue()`

DESCRIPTION This method returns the value of this object as an `int`. If the value is not already an `int`, this may involve casting and rounding (and possibly a loss of precision). Casting a number that does not fit into an `int` results in an `int` with the value of `-1`.

RETURNS The value of this object as an `int`.

EXAMPLE

```
// Calculate the int sum of a vector of Number objects
public static int intSum(Vector v) {
    int sum = 0;
    for (Enumeration e = v.elements();
         e.hasMoreElements();
         sum += ((Number)e.nextElement()).intValue())
        ;
    return (sum);
}
```

longValue()

PURPOSE Retrieves the value of this object as a `long`.

SYNTAX `public abstract long longValue()`

DESCRIPTION This method returns the value of this object as a `long`. If the value of this object is not already a whole number, this may involve rounding.

RETURNS The value of this object as a `long`.

EXAMPLE

```
// Calculate the long sum of a vector of Number objects
public static long longSum(Vector v) {
    long sum = 0;
    for (Enumeration e = v.elements();
         e.hasMoreElements();
         sum += ((Number)e.nextElement()).longValue())
        ;
    return (sum);
}
```

shortValue()

PURPOSE Retrieves the value of this object as a `short`.

SYNTAX `public abstract short shortValue()`

DESCRIPTION This method returns the value of this object as a `short`. If the value of this object is not already a whole number, this may involve rounding.

RETURNS The value of this object as a `short`.

EXAMPLE

```
// Calculate the short sum of a vector of Number objects
public static int shortSum(Vector v) {
    short sum = 0;
    for (Enumeration e = v.elements();
         e.hasMoreElements();
         sum += ((Number)e.nextElement()).shortValue())
        ;
    return (sum);
}
```

NumberFormat

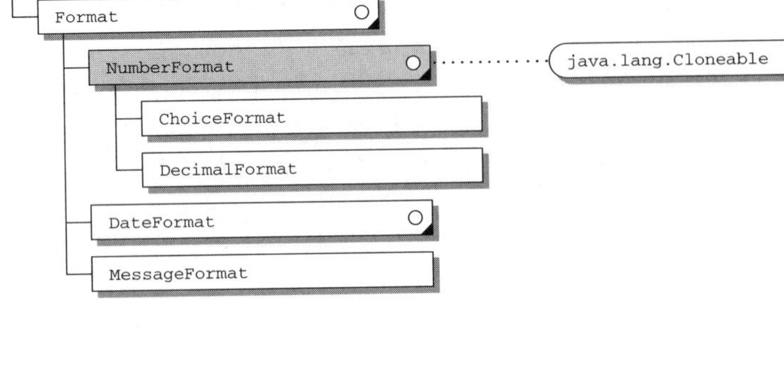

Syntax

```
public abstract class NumberFormat extends Format implements Cloneable
```

Description

`NumberFormat` is the abstract base class for all number formats. This class provides the interface for formatting and parsing numbers. `NumberFormat` also provides methods for determining which locales have number formats and what their names are.

`NumberFormat` helps you to format and parse numbers for any locale. Your code can be completely independent of the locale conventions for decimal points, thousands separators, even the particular decimal digits used, or whether the number format is even decimal. You can also display a number as a normal decimal number, as currency, or as a percentage:

```
1234.5        // Decimal number
$1,234.50     // U.S. currency
Fr1.234,50    // French currency
123450%       // Percent
```

Usage

To format a number for the current locale, use one of the creation class methods, such as:

```
myString = NumberFormat.getInstance().format(myNumber);
```

If you are formatting multiple numbers, it is more efficient to get the format once and use it multiple times so that the system doesn't have to fetch the information about the local language and country conventions multiple times:

```
NumberFormat nf = NumberFormat.getInstance();
for (int i = 0; i < a.length; ++i) {
    output.println(nf.format(myNumber[i]) + "; ");
}
```

To format a number for a different locale, specify it in the call to `getInstance`:

```
NumberFormat nf = NumberFormat.getInstance(Locale.FRENCH);
```

You can also use a NumberFormat to parse digits in a string and convert them into numbers:

```
myNumber = nf.parse(myString);
```

Use getInstance or getNumberInstance to get the normal number format. Use getCurrencyInstance to get the currency number format. And use getPercentInstance to get a format for displaying percentages. With this format, a fraction like 0.53 is displayed as 53%.

You can also control the display of numbers with such methods as setMinimumFractionDigits(). If you want even more control over the format or parsing, or you want to give your users more control, you can try casting the NumberFormat you get from the factory methods to a DecimalNumberFormat. This will work for the vast majority of locales. Just remember to test first using instanceof DecimalFormat in case you encounter an unusual number format. This is demonstrated in DecimalFormat.

The Minimum/Maximum Digits Properties

An easy way to limit the number of digits in a number is to set the *minimum* or *maximum* size of the integer or fraction part. This class provides four setters and four getters for setting these.

The Grouping Used Property

The *grouping used* property indicates whether a grouping separator is used during formatting and parsing:

```
1,234,567.89    Grouping separator used
1234567.89      Grouping separator not used
```

The ParsePosition Class

You can use forms of the parse methods with ParsePosition to allow you to progressively parse through pieces of a string After parseObject() or parseObject() is called, the index of the parse position is set to where in the string it stopped parsing. Therefore you can loop on parse, continually using the same parse position object, with its updated index, to iterate over potentially the entire string. If an error occurs, the index is left unchanged. Note that during parsing, leading whitespace is discarded (with a successful parse) and trailing whitespace is left as is.

The Parse Integer Only Property

When the *parse integer only* property is true, the parse() method will parse only the integer portion of numbers. That is, in the English locale, if parse() encounters "1234.56", it will return "1234", which is everything up to the decimal separator.

The FieldPosition Class

Variations of the format methods that contain FieldPosition allow you to align columns of numbers on the decimal separator or other characters. You can align numbers in two ways:

1. **Use monospaced font.** In this case, you use a monospaced font and pad with spaces for alignment. Given that you have a column of width C characters to hold the integer por-

tion, you first calculate the number of characters in the integer portion (I) and then insert the difference, C – I spaces, ahead of the integer. You do this by creating an instance of `FieldPosition` with the field set to `INTEGER_FIELD` and passing this into your `format()` call. After `format()` is called, the `FieldPosition` method `getEndIndex()` will be set to the index following the last character of the integer.

2. **Use proportional-spaced font.** To produce code that works with either monospaced or proportional-spaced fonts, you do not pad with spaces. Instead, you measure the width of the string in pixels from the start to `getEndIndex` (using `stringWidth()` from `FontMetrics`). Then you move the pen by `(desiredPixelWidth - widthToAlignmentPoint)` before drawing the text. This also works where there is no decimal separator, but there are possibly more characters at the end, such as with parentheses in negative numbers: "(12)" for –12.

MEMBER SUMMARY	
Constructor	
`NumberFormat()`	Constructor called by subclasses.
Creation Methods	
`getCurrencyInstance()`	Creates and returns a currency format for a locale.
`getInstance()`	Creates and returns the default number format for a locale.
`getNumberInstance()`	Creates and returns a general-purpose number format for a locale.
`getPercentInstance()`	Creates and returns a percentage format for a locale.
FieldPosition Constants	
`FRACTION_FIELD`	Signifies the fraction portion when creating a FieldPosition object.
`INTEGER_FIELD`	Signifies the integer portion when creating a FieldPosition object.
Format and Parse Methods	
`format()`	Formats a number to produce a string.
`parse()`	Parses a string to an instance of `Number`.
`parseObject()`	Parses a string to produce an object.
Parse Integer Methods	
`isParseIntegerOnly()`	Determines if this format parses only the integer portion of numbers.
`setParseIntegerOnly()`	Sets the property for parsing only integers.
Locale Method	
`getAvailableLocales()`	Get the set of `Locales` for which number formats are installed.

MEMBER SUMMARY	
Minimum/Maximum Digit Methods	
`getMaximumFractionDigits()`	Retrieves the maximum number of digits allowed in the fraction portion of a number.
`getMaximumIntegerDigits()`	Retrieves the maximum number of digits allowed in the integer portion of a number.
`getMinimumFractionDigits()`	Retrieves the minimum number of digits allowed in the fraction portion of a number.
`getMinimumIntegerDigits()`	Retrieves the minimum number of digits allowed in the integer portion of a number.
`setMaximumFractionDigits()`	Sets the maximum number of digits allowed in the fraction portion of a number.
`setMaximumIntegerDigits()`	Sets the maximum number of digits allowed in the integer portion of a number.
`setMinimumFractionDigits()`	Sets the minimum number of digits allowed in the fraction portion of a number.
`setMinimumIntegerDigits()`	Sets the minimum number of digits allowed in the integer portion of a number.
Grouping Methods	
`isGroupingUsed()`	Determines if the grouping separator is used with this format.
`setGroupingUsed()`	Sets the property for using group separators.
Object Methods	
`clone()`	Creates a copy of this number format.
`equals()`	Compares two `NumberFormat` objects for equality.
`hashCode()`	Computes the hash code for the number format.

See Also

`DecimalFormat`, `ChoiceFormat`.

Example

This example calls the four creation methods and then prints out their patterns and the results of formatting and parsing the number 1234.56.

```
import java.text.NumberFormat;
import java.text.DecimalFormat;
import java.util.Locale;
import java.text.ParseException;

class Main {
```

```
    public static void main(String[] args) {
        Locale loc = Locale.US;
        double myNumber = 1234.56;
        NumberFormat numform;
        DecimalFormat decform;
        int WIDTHCOL1 = 33;
        int WIDTHCOL2 = 29;
        int WIDTHCOL3 = 14;
        int WIDTHCOL0 = 10;

        printAlignColumn("COUNTRY:  ", 0);
        printAlignColumn(loc.getDisplayName(), 0);
        printAlignColumn("\n", 0);

        for (int j = 0; j < 4; ++j) {
            switch (j) {
            case 0:
                printAlignColumn("\n", 0);
                printAlignColumn("INSTANCE:", WIDTHCOL0);
                printAlignColumn("PATTERN", WIDTHCOL2);
                printAlignColumn("FORMATTED", WIDTHCOL3);
                printAlignColumn("PARSED\n", 0);
                break;
            case 1:
                printAlignColumn("\n", 0);
                printAlignColumn("NUMBER:", WIDTHCOL0);
                printAlignColumn("PATTERN", WIDTHCOL2);
                printAlignColumn("FORMATTED", WIDTHCOL3);
                printAlignColumn("PARSED\n", 0);
                break;
            case 2:
                printAlignColumn("\n", 0);
                printAlignColumn("PERCENT:", WIDTHCOL0);
                printAlignColumn("PATTERN", WIDTHCOL2);
                printAlignColumn("FORMATTED", WIDTHCOL3);
                printAlignColumn("PARSED\n", 0);
                break;
            default:
                printAlignColumn("\n", 0);
                printAlignColumn("CURRENCY:", WIDTHCOL0);
                printAlignColumn("PATTERN", WIDTHCOL2);
                printAlignColumn("FORMATTED", WIDTHCOL3);
                printAlignColumn("PARSED\n", 0);
                break;
            }

            printAlignColumn("", WIDTHCOL0);

            switch (j) {
            case 0:
              numform =
                 NumberFormat.getInstance(loc);          // 1,234.56
                break;
            case 1:
              numform =
                 NumberFormat.getNumberInstance(loc);    // 1,234.56
                break;
            case 2:
              numform =
                 NumberFormat.getPercentInstance(loc);   // 123,456%
```

```
                break;
            default:
              numform =
                 NumberFormat.getCurrencyInstance(loc); // $1,234.56
                break;
            }

                // Test before casting
            if (numform instanceof DecimalFormat) {

                // Cast to DecimalFormat
                decform = (DecimalFormat)numform;
                try {
                    // Print pattern.
                    printAlignColumn(decform.toPattern(), WIDTHCOL2);

                    // Print formatted number (a string).
                    printAlignColumn(decform.format(myNumber), WIDTHCOL3);

                } catch (IllegalArgumentException iae) { }

                try {

                    // Print parsed string (a number).
                  System.out.println(decform.parse(decform.format(myNumber)));

                } catch (ParseException pe) {
                  System.out.println("Parse exception");
                }
            }
        }
    }

    static void printAlignColumn(String str, int col) {
        System.out.print(str);
        for (int p = str.length(); p < col; ++p) {
            System.out.print(" ");
        }
    }
}
```

Output

```
> java Main
COUNTRY:  English (United States)

INSTANCE: PATTERN                      FORMATTED    PARSED
          #,##0.###                    1,234.56     1234.56

NUMBER:   PATTERN                      FORMATTED    PARSED
          #,##0.###                    1,234.56     1234.56

PERCENT:  PATTERN                      FORMATTED    PARSED
          #,##0%                       123,456%     1234.56

CURRENCY: PATTERN                      FORMATTED    PARSED
          $#,##0.00;($#,##0.00)        $1,234.56    1234.56
```

clone()

PURPOSE Creates a copy of this number format.

SYNTAX `public Object clone()`

DESCRIPTION This method makes a copy of this number format.

RETURNS A non-`null` copy of this number format.

OVERRIDES `Format.clone()`

EXAMPLE This example illustrates the use of `clone()` to copy a number format object. It then uses `equals()` to compare them and prints out `hashcode()`. Note that the copy is equal to the original.

```
import java.text.NumberFormat;

class Main {

    public static void main(String args[]) {

        // Create a number format.
        NumberFormat nf = NumberFormat.getInstance();

        // Set a property.
        nf.setMinimumFractionDigits(5);
        System.out.println(nf.getMinimumFractionDigits());   // prints '5'

        // Create a clone.
        NumberFormat nfCopy = (NumberFormat)nf.clone();
        System.out.println(nfCopy.getMinimumFractionDigits());   // prints '5'

        if(nf.equals(nfCopy)) {
            System.out.println("Copy is equal to original");
        } else {
            System.out.println("Copy is not equal to original");
        }

        // Compute hashcode.
        int hc = nf.hashCode();
        System.out.println("Hash code is: " + hc);
    }
}
```

equals()

PURPOSE Compares this `NumberFormat` object with another object for equality.

SYNTAX `public boolean equals(Object obj)`

DESCRIPTION This method compares this `NumberFormat` with the object `obj` for equality. If `obj` is a `NumberFormat` object and has the same properties as this `NumberFor-`

mat, the objects are equal and this method returns `true`. If the properties are not equal or if `obj` is `null` or not a `NumberFormat` object, this method returns `false`.

PARAMETERS

`obj`	A possibly `null` object.

RETURNS `true` if `obj` is equal to this object; `false` otherwise.

OVERRIDES `java.lang.Object.equals()`.

SEE ALSO `hashCode()`.

EXAMPLE See `clone()`.

format()

PURPOSE Formats a number to produce a string.

SYNTAX

```
public final String format(double number)
public final String format(long number)
public abstract StringBuffer format(double number,
   StringBuffer appendBuf, FieldPosition pos)
public abstract StringBuffer format(long number,
   StringBuffer appendBuf, FieldPosition pos)
public final StringBuffer format(Object number,
   StringBuffer appendBuf, FieldPosition pos)
```

DESCRIPTION This method formats the number `number` to produce a string, which is appended to the buffer `appendBuf`. The `appendBuf` value is returned. Returning the full result allows chaining, as with `StringBuffer.append()`. If `appendBuf` is not specified, the produced string is simply returned.

The field position `pos` has absolutely no effect on the formatted result. Its purpose is to determine where in the string the range of characters are for a given field so that the strings can be aligned in a column on that particular field. If you don't care about column alignment, set `pos` to any valid field position.

The field position works as follows. Create an instance of `FieldPosition` using the field constant for the field you want to align. For example, if you are formatting numbers and want to output them in a column and align the decimal separators, create the `FieldPosition` object with the field constant `NumberFormat.INTEGER_FIELD`. When you call `format()`, the begin and end indexes of the field position `pos` are updated to the integer range in the resulting string. You can use these values to get the length of the integer portion and then use that length to position the string horizontally. For an example of this, see the class example in the `FieldPosition` class.

PARAMETERS

`appendBuf`	The string buffer in which the resulting string is to be appended.
`number`	The number to format.
`pos`	A `FieldPosition` object whose field you want to eventually align in a column.

RETURNS The string passed in as `appendBuf` with the newly formatted string appended to it.

OVERRIDES `Format.format()`.

EXAMPLE See the class example.

FRACTION_FIELD

PURPOSE Signifies the fraction portion when creating a `FieldPosition` object.

SYNTAX `public static final int FRACTION_FIELD`

DESCRIPTION This constant is passed into the `FieldPosition` constructor to signify that the fraction part of this formatted number should be located. The `FieldPosition` object can then be passed into `format()`. The value of `FRACTION_FIELD` is `1`.

SEE ALSO `FieldPosition`.

EXAMPLE See the class example in `FieldPosition`.

getAvailableLocales()

PURPOSE Gets the set of `Locales` for which number formats are installed.

SYNTAX `public static Locale[] getAvailableLocales()`

DESCRIPTION This method gets the set of `Locale` instances for which `NumberFormat` instances are installed for this virtual machine.

RETURNS Array of available locale objects.

EXAMPLE See the class example for `DecimalFormat`.

getCurrencyInstance()

PURPOSE
Creates and returns a currency format for a locale.

SYNTAX
```
public static final NumberFormat getCurrencyInstance()
public static NumberFormat getCurrencyInstance(Locale loc)
```

RETURNS
A currency format for the locale `loc`. If `loc` is not specified, the format returned is for the current locale.

EXAMPLE
See the class example.

getInstance()

PURPOSE
Creates and returns a default number format for a locale.

SYNTAX
```
public static final NumberFormat getInstance()
public static NumberFormat getInstance(Locale loc)
```

DESCRIPTION
This method returns the default number format for the locale `loc`, which is one of the styles provided by the other creation methods: `getNumberInstance()`, `getCurrencyInstance()`, or `getPercentInstance()`. The actual format provided is locale-dependent.

When `loc` is omitted, this method returns the default number format for the default locale.

If this method returns a decimal format, the decimal format has the associated decimal format symbols for the same locale.

PARAMETERS

`loc`
The locale for the number format.

RETURNS
A number format for a locale.

EXAMPLE
See the class example.

getMaximumFractionDigits()

PURPOSE
Retrieves the maximum number of digits allowed in the fraction portion of a number.

SYNTAX
```
public int getMaximumFractionDigits()
```

RETURNS
The maximum number of digits allowed in the fraction portion of a number.

SEE ALSO
`setMaximumFractionDigits()`.

EXAMPLE
See `getMaximumIntegerDigits()`.

getMaximumIntegerDigits()

PURPOSE Retrieves the maximum number of digits allowed in the integer portion of a number.

SYNTAX `public int getMaximumIntegerDigits()`

RETURNS The maximum number of digits allowed in the integer portion of a number.

SEE ALSO `setMaximumIntegerDigits()`.

EXAMPLE This example creates a number format and sets the maximum and minimum number of digits for the integer and fraction portions. It then formats and parses two numbers: 123456.654321 and 123.321.

```
import java.text.NumberFormat;
import java.text.DecimalFormat;
import java.text.ParseException;
import java.util.Locale;

class Main {

    public static void main(String[] args) {
        Locale loc = Locale.US;
        double[] myNumber = {123456.654321, 123.321};
        NumberFormat numform;
        DecimalFormat decform;
        int WIDTHCOL1 = 35;
        int WIDTHCOL2 = 20;

        printAlignColumn("COUNTRY:  ", 0);
        printAlignColumn(loc.getDisplayName(), 0);
        printAlignColumn("\n", 0);

        numform =
            NumberFormat.getCurrencyInstance(loc);      // $1,234.56

        // Set the maximum number of integer digits
        numform.setMaximumIntegerDigits(5);
        println("getMaximumIntegerDigits:  "
                            + numform.getMaximumIntegerDigits());

        // Set the minimum number of integer digits
        numform.setMinimumIntegerDigits(4);
        println("getMinimumIntegerDigits:  "
                            + numform.getMinimumIntegerDigits());


        // Set the maximum number of fraction digits
        numform.setMaximumFractionDigits(5);
        println("getMaximumFractionDigits: "
                            + numform.getMaximumFractionDigits());

        // Set the minimum number of fraction digits
        numform.setMinimumFractionDigits(4);
        println("getMinimumFractionDigits: "
                            + numform.getMinimumFractionDigits());
```

```
        for(int i=0; i<2; ++i) {

            println("\nOriginal number: "
                                + Double.toString(myNumber[i]));

            // Print the headings
            printAlignColumn("\n", 0);
            println("CURRENCY");
            printAlignColumn("PATTERN", WIDTHCOL1);
            printAlignColumn("FORMATTED", WIDTHCOL2);
            printAlignColumn("PARSED\n", 0);

            // Test before casting
            if (numform instanceof DecimalFormat) {

                // Cast to DecimalFormat
                decform = (DecimalFormat)numform;
                try {
                    // Print pattern.
                    printAlignColumn(decform.toPattern(), WIDTHCOL1);

                    // Print formatted number (a string).
                    printAlignColumn(decform.format(myNumber[i]), WIDTHCOL2);

                } catch (IllegalArgumentException iae) { }

                try {

                    // Print parsed string (a number).
                    println(decform.parse(decform.format(myNumber[i])));

                } catch (ParseException pe) {
                    println("Parse exception");
                }
            }
        }
    }

    static void printAlignColumn(String str, int col) {
        System.out.print(str);
        for (int p = str.length(); p < col; ++p) {
            System.out.print(" ");
        }
    }

    static void println(Object obj) {
        System.out.println(obj);
    }
}
```

Output

```
COUNTRY:  English (United States)
getMaximumIntegerDigits:  5
getMinimumIntegerDigits:  4
getMaximumFractionDigits: 5
getMinimumFractionDigits: 4

Original number: 123456.654321
```

```
CURRENCY
PATTERN                          FORMATTED          PARSED
$#0,000.0000#;($#0,000.0000#)    $23,456.65432      23456.654319999998

Original number: 123.321

CURRENCY
PATTERN                          FORMATTED          PARSED
$#0,000.0000#;($#0,000.0000#)    $0,123.3210        123.32100000000001
```


getMinimumFractionDigits()

PURPOSE Retrieves the minimum number of digits allowed in the fraction portion of a number.

SYNTAX `public int getMinimumFractionDigits()`

RETURNS The minimum number of digits allowed in the fraction portion of a number.

SEE ALSO `setMinimumFractionDigits()`.

EXAMPLE See `getMaximumIntegerDigits()`.

getMinimumIntegerDigits()

PURPOSE Retrieves the minimum number of digits allowed in the integer portion of a number.

SYNTAX `public int getMinimumIntegerDigits()`

RETURNS The minimum number of digits allowed in the integer portion of a number.

SEE ALSO `setMinimumIntegerDigits()`.

EXAMPLE See `getMaximumIntegerDigits()`.

getNumberInstance()

PURPOSE Creates and returns a general-purpose number format for a locale.

SYNTAX
```
public static final NumberFormat getNumberInstance()
public static NumberFormat getNumberInstance(Locale loc)
```

DESCRIPTION Returns a general-purpose number format for a locale `loc`. If `loc` is omitted, the format returned is for the current locale.

PARAMETERS

`loc` The locale for the number format.

RETURNS A general-purpose number for a locale.

EXAMPLE See the class example.

getPercentInstance()

PURPOSE Creates and returns a percentage format for a locale.

SYNTAX
```
public static final NumberFormat getPercentInstance()
public static NumberFormat getPercentInstance(Locale loc)
```

DESCRIPTION Returns a percentage format for a locale `loc`. If `loc` is omitted, the format returned is for the current locale.

PARAMETERS

`loc` The locale for the number format.

EXAMPLE See the class example.

hashCode()

PURPOSE Computes the hash code for this `NumberFormat` object.

SYNTAX
```
public int hashCode()
```

DESCRIPTION This method computes the hash code for this `NumberFormat` object. Two `NumberFormat` objects with the same properties will have the same hash code. However, two `NumberFormat` objects that do not have the same properties might also have the same hash code, although the hash code algorithm minimizes this possibility. The hash code is typically used as the key in a hash table.

OVERRIDES `java.lang.Object.hashCode()`.

SEE ALSO `equals()`.

EXAMPLE See `clone()`.

INTEGER_FIELD

PURPOSE Signifies the integer portion when creating a `FieldPosition` object.

SYNTAX
```
public static final int INTEGER_FIELD
```

DESCRIPTION This constant is passed into the `FieldPosition` constructor to signify that the integer part of this formatted number should be located. The `FieldPosition` object can then be passed into `format()`. The value of `INTEGER_FIELD` is `0`.

SEE ALSO `FieldPosition`.

EXAMPLE See the class example in `FieldPosition`.

isGroupingUsed()

PURPOSE Determines if the grouping separator is used with this format.

SYNTAX `public boolean isGroupingUsed()`

RETURNS `true` if the grouping separator is used in this format; `false` otherwise.

SEE ALSO `setGroupingUsed()`.

EXAMPLE This example creates a number format and sets it to parse only integers and not use grouping separators.

```
import java.text.NumberFormat;
import java.text.DecimalFormat;
import java.text.ParseException;
import java.util.Locale;

class Main {

    public static void main(String[] args) {
        Locale loc = Locale.US;
        double myNumber = 1234.56;
        NumberFormat numform;
        DecimalFormat decform;
        int WIDTHCOL1 = 33;
        int WIDTHCOL2 = 29;
        int WIDTHCOL3 = 14;
        int WIDTHCOL0 = 10;

        printAlignColumn("COUNTRY:  ", 0);
        printAlignColumn(loc.getDisplayName(), 0);
        printAlignColumn("\n", 0);

        numform =
             NumberFormat.getCurrencyInstance(loc);      // $1,234.56

        // Set the format to parse only integers
        numform.setParseIntegerOnly(true);
        System.out.println("isParseIntegerOnly: "
                                          + numform.isParseIntegerOnly());

        // Set the format to not use grouping separator
        numform.setGroupingUsed(false);
        System.out.println("isGroupingUsed: "
                                          + numform.isGroupingUsed());
```

```
        // Print the headings
        printAlignColumn("\n", 0);
        printAlignColumn("CURRENCY:", WIDTHCOL0);
        printAlignColumn("PATTERN", WIDTHCOL2);
        printAlignColumn("FORMATTED", WIDTHCOL3);
        printAlignColumn("PARSED\n", 0);
        printAlignColumn("", WIDTHCOL0);

        // Test before casting
        if (numform instanceof DecimalFormat) {

            // Cast to DecimalFormat
            decform = (DecimalFormat)numform;
            try {
                // Print pattern.
                printAlignColumn(decform.toPattern(), WIDTHCOL2);

                // Print formatted number (a string).
                printAlignColumn(decform.format(myNumber), WIDTHCOL3);

            } catch (IllegalArgumentException iae) { }

            try {

                // Print parsed string (a number).
                System.out.println(decform.parse(decform.format(myNumber)));

            } catch (ParseException pe) {
                System.out.println("Parse exception");
            }
        }
    }

    static void printAlignColumn(String str, int col) {
        System.out.print(str);
        for (int p = str.length(); p < col; ++p) {
            System.out.print(" ");
        }
    }
}
```

isParseIntegerOnly()

PURPOSE Determines if this format parses only the integer portion of numbers.

SYNTAX `public boolean isParseIntegerOnly()`

RETURNS `true` if this format parses only the integer portion of numbers; `false` otherwise.

SEE ALSO `setParseIntegerOnly()`.

EXAMPLE See `isGroupingUsed()`.

NumberFormat()

PURPOSE Constructor called by subclasses.

SYNTAX `public NumberFormat()`

DESCRIPTION Do not call this constructor directly. This constructor constructs an instance of `NumberFormat`, and should only be called by subclasses. To create `NumberFormat` object, use the creation methods, such as `getInstance()`.

EXAMPLE No example for this constructor, since it is typically called implicitly from a subclass.

parse()

PURPOSE Parses a string to an instance of `Number`.

SYNTAX
```
public abstract Number parse(String sourceStr,
   ParsePosition pos)
public Number parse(String sourceStr) throws ParseException
```

DESCRIPTION Returns a `Long` if possible—that is, if the return value is within the range [`Long.MIN_VALUE`, `Long.MAX_VALUE`] and has no fraction part. Otherwise, this method returns a `Double`. If `IntegerOnly` is set, this method will stop at a decimal separator (or equivalent; for example, for rational numbers "`1 2/3`", it will stop after the `1`). This method does not throw an exception. If no object can be parsed, the index of `pos` is unchanged.

Omitting the parse position `pos` causes the parse to begin at the start of the `sourceStr`.

PARAMETERS
- `sourceStr` The string to be parsed.
- `pos` The parse position that determines where the parse begins.

RETURNS An instance of `Long` or `Double` with the parsed value. If the parse fails, the syntax form that takes `ParsePosition` returns `null`, while the form that takes only `String` throws a `ParseException`.

EXCEPTIONS
- `ParseException` If the specified string is invalid.

SEE ALSO `isParseIntegerOnly()`, `parseObject()`, `format()`.

EXAMPLE See the class example.

parseObject()

PURPOSE
Parses a string to produce an object.

SYNTAX
```
public final Object parseObject(String sourceStr, ParsePosition
   pos)
```

DESCRIPTION
This method uses this format to parse the string `sourceStr`, starting at position `pos`, and converts that string to an object. Before calling this method, set the index of `pos` to where you want to start parsing the source string. If `pos` is omitted, the parsing begins at the start of the string.

Parsing will skip over whitespace and begin matching on the first non-whitespace character found. It compares that character with what the format expects to find. For example, a decimal format would expect a positive or negative prefix or, if none is defined, the start of a number. If this character matches, it continues to the next character; otherwise, it throws a `ParseException`.

After `parseObject()` is called, the index of the parse position is set to where in the string it stopped parsing. Therefore you can loop on parse, continually using the same parse position to iterate over potentially the entire string. If an error occurs, the index is left unchanged. Note that during parsing, leading whitespace is discarded (with a successful parse) and trailing whitespace is left as is.

This method is called `parseObject()` to denote that it can return any subclass of `Object`. A subclass of `NumberFormat` will typically implement a convenience method that returns a particular type of value. This avoids having to cast `Object` to that type. Since methods can't overload on return types, the convenience method cannot be called `parseObject()` and will instead typically be named `parse()`.

Any `parse()` method that does not take a field position should throw a `ParseException` when no text in the required format is at the start position.

PARAMETERS

`pos` The parse position that determines where the parse begins.

`sourceStr` The string to be parsed.

RETURNS
The possibly `null` object parsed from the string.

OVERRIDES
`parseObject in class Format.`

EXAMPLE
See the class example in `Format` for an example of `parseObject()`.

A B C D E F G H I J K L M N O P Q R S T U V W X Y Z

setGroupingUsed()

PURPOSE Sets the property for using group separators.

SYNTAX `public void setGroupingUsed(boolean newValue)`

DESCRIPTION This method determines whether grouping will be used when formatting and parsing is performed. For example, in the English locale, with grouping on, the number 1234567 would typically be formatted as "`1,234,567`". The grouping separator as well as the size of each group is locale-dependent and is determined by `DecimalFormat` and `DecimalFormatSymbols` classes.

PARAMETERS

`newValue` If `true`, the format uses the grouping separator; if `false`, it does not.

SEE ALSO `isGroupingUsed()`.

EXAMPLE See `isGroupingUsed()`.

setMaximumFractionDigits()

PURPOSE Sets the maximum number of digits allowed in the fraction portion of a number.

SYNTAX `public void setMaximumFractionDigits(int maxFractionDigits)`

DESCRIPTION This method sets the maximum number of digits allowed in the fraction portion of a number for both formatting and parsing. If the number has more digits than `maxFractionDigits`, then the least-significant digits are truncated.

It must be `true` that `maxFractionDigits` ≥ `minFractionDigits`. If the new value for `maxFractionDigits` is less than the current value of `minFractionDigits`, then `minFractionDigits` will also be set to `maxFractionDigits`.

In the `DecimalFormat` class, this method is equivalent to calling `applyPattern()`, with `maxFractionDigits` number of digit characters (#) filling out the fraction field.

PARAMETERS

`maxFractionDigits`
The maximum number of digits in the fraction portion of a number.

SEE ALSO `getMaximumFractionDigits()`.

EXAMPLE See `getMaximumIntegerDigits()`.

setMaximumIntegerDigits()

PURPOSE Sets the maximum number of digits allowed in the integer portion of a number.

SYNTAX `public void setMaximumIntegerDigits(int maxIntegerDigits)`

DESCRIPTION This method sets the maximum number of digits allowed in the integer portion of a number for both formatting and parsing. If the number has more digits than `maxIntegerDigits`, then the *most*-significant digits are truncated!

It must be `true` that `maxIntegerDigits` ≥ `minIntegerDigits`. If the new value for `maxIntegerDigits` is less than the current value of `minIntegerDigits`, then `minIntegerDigits` will also be set to `maxIntegerDigits`.

Because this method truncates most-significant digits, it has no equivalent using `applyPattern()` in the `DecimalFormat` class.

PARAMETERS

`maxIntegerDigits`
The maximum number of digits in the integer portion of a number.

SEE ALSO `getMaximumIntegerDigits()`.

EXAMPLE See `getMaximumIntegerDigits()`.

setMinimumFractionDigits()

PURPOSE Sets the minimum number of digits allowed in the fraction portion of a number.

SYNTAX `public void setMinimumFractionDigits(int minFractionDigits)`

DESCRIPTION This method sets the minimum number of digits allowed in the fraction portion of a number for both formatting and parsing. If the number has fewer digits than `minFractionDigits`, then the remaining places are filled with zero digits (`0`) for that locale.

It must be `true` that `minFractionDigits` ≤ `maxFractionDigits`. If the new value for `minFractionDigits` exceeds the current value of `maxFractionDigits`, then `maxFractionDigits` will also be set to `minFractionDigits`.

In the `DecimalFormat` class, this method is equivalent to calling `applyPattern()` with `minFractionDigits` number of zero digit characters (`0`) filling out the fraction field.

PARAMETERS

`minFractionDigits`
The minimum number of digits in the fraction portion of a number.

SEE ALSO `getMinimumFractionDigits()`.

EXAMPLE See `getMaximumIntegerDigits()`.

setMinimumIntegerDigits()

PURPOSE Sets the minimum number of digits allowed in the integer portion of a number.

SYNTAX `public void setMinimumIntegerDigits(int minIntegerDigits)`

DESCRIPTION This method sets the minimum number of digits allowed in the integer portion of a number for both formatting and parsing. If the number has fewer digits than `minIntegerDigits`, then the remaining places are filled with zero digits (`0`) for that locale.

It must be `true` that `minIntegerDigits` ≤ `maxIntegerDigits`. If the new value for `minIntegerDigits` exceeds the current value of `maxIntegerDigits`, then `maxIntegerDigits` will also be set to `minIntegerDigits`.

In the `DecimalFormat` class, this method is equivalent to calling `applyPattern()` with `minIntegerDigits` number of zero digit characters (`0`) filling out the integer field.

PARAMETERS

`minIntegerDigits`
The minimum number of digits in the integer portion of a number.

SEE ALSO `getMinimumIntegerDigits()`.

EXAMPLE See `getMaximumIntegerDigits()`.

setParseIntegerOnly()

PURPOSE Sets the property for parsing only integers.

SYNTAX `public void setParseIntegerOnly(boolean value)`

DESCRIPTION This method sets whether numbers should be parsed as integers only. For example, in the English locale, with `value` set to `true`, the string "`1234.56`" is parsed as the integer value 1234, since parsing would stop at the decimal separator (.) character. The decimal separator character is locale-dependent and is determined in the `DecimalFormat` and `DecimalFormatSymbols` classes.

PARAMETERS

`value` If `true`, this format parses only integers; if `false`, it parses both the integer and fraction parts.

SEE ALSO `isParseIntegerOnly()`.

EXAMPLE See `isGroupingUsed()`.

NumberFormatException

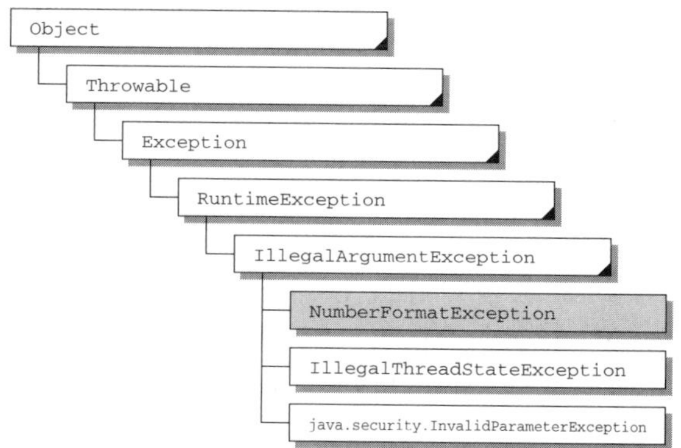

Syntax

```
public class NumberFormatException extends IllegalArgumentException
```

Description

`NumberFormatException` is an exception that is thrown when a method detects that the string representation of a number it is parsing is in an invalid format. The validity of the string's syntax is determined by each method. It could also be thrown by methods in user-supplied classes.

A method that throws `NumberFormatException` must declare it or any of its superclasses in the methods `throws` clause.

MEMBER SUMMARY	
Constructor	
`NumberFormatException()`	Constructs a `NumberFormatException` instance.

See Also

`Byte`, `Double`, `Float`, `IllegalArgumentException`, `Integer`, `java.awt.Color.decode()`, `java.math.BigDecimal`, `java.math.BigInteger`, `java.text.MessageFormat`, `Long`, `Short`.

Example

In this example, a `NumberFormatException` is thrown because the string representation of an integer cannot contain a dot character (.).

```
class Main {
    public static void main(String[] args) {
        System.out.println("NumberFormatException example");
        Integer inum = new Integer("36.5"); // format problem
    }
}
```


NumberFormatException()

PURPOSE Constructs a `NumberFormatException` instance.

SYNTAX
```
public NumberFormatException ()
public NumberFormatException (String msg)
```

DESCRIPTION The two forms of this constructor construct an instance of `NumberFormatException`. An optional string `msg` can be supplied that describes this particular instance of the exception. If `msg` is not specified, it defaults to `null`.

PARAMETERS

`msg` A possibly `null` string that gives details about this exception.

SEE ALSO `Throwable.getMessage()`.

Object

Syntax

```
public class Object
```

Description

The `Object` class is the ultimate superclass of all classes in Java; it is at the root of the Java class hierarchy. Every method defined in the `Object` class is available in all of its subclasses and hence in all objects in the system. Subclasses often override the implementation of some of these methods (such as `clone()`, `hashCode()`, and `equals()`).

Object Locking and Thread Synchronization

Each object has a *monitor* (or *lock*) associated with it. When a thread executes a synchronized method or a synchronized statement of that object, it grabs the monitor for that object. When the thread exits the method or statement, it releases the monitor. No two threads can grab an object's monitor at the same time. Hence, no two threads can enter a synchronized method or a statement for that object at the same time.

Multiple threads can synchronize access to an object with each other through the use of `wait()/notify()` calls. During execution, a thread may need to wait for a condition (related to the synchronized object that it is manipulating) to occur before continuing execution. As mentioned earlier, when a thread is executing a synchronized method or synchronized statement, it is holding the monitor for that object. The thread waits for the condition by calling `wait()` on the object, which has the effect of atomically releasing the monitor that it is holding. The waiting thread blocks until the condition that it is waiting for has been satisfied. Effectively, the waiting thread is waiting for the monitor of the object to be returned to it. When a thread determines that the condition on which the waiting thread is awaiting has been satisfied, it invokes `notify()` on the object. This unblocks the waiting thread and allows the unblocked thread to grab the object's monitor when it has a chance to run.

Monitors are reentrant. A thread that is holding the monitor of an object can grab the monitor again by calling another synchronized method or synchronized statement of that object. When the thread exits all of its synchronized methods and statements, the monitor is released. A `wait()` call will release the monitor completely, regardless of how many times the thread grabbed it.

MEMBER SUMMARY

Constructor

`Object()`	Constructs an instance of `Object`.

Synchronization Methods

`notify()`	Notifies a thread blocked on this object of a change in condition.
`notifyAll()`	Notifies all threads blocked on this object of a change in condition.
`wait()`	Causes a thread to wait until it is notified.

General Methods

`equals()`	Compares this object with another object for equality.
`getClass()`	Retrieves the `Class` object associated with this object.
`hashCode()`	Computes the hash code for this object.
`toString()`	Generates the string representation of this object.

Protected Methods

`clone()`	Creates a copy of this object.
`finalize()`	Called by Java virtual machine to clean up this object's state when it is ready to be discarded.

A B C D E F G H I J K L M N O P Q R S T U V W X Y Z

See Also

`Class`, `Cloneable`, `Hashtable`, `System.gc()`, `Thread`.

clone()

PURPOSE Creates a copy of this object.

SYNTAX

```
protected native Object clone() throws
   CloneNotSupportedException
```

DESCRIPTION `clone()` creates a copy of this object. The default implementation of `clone()` creates a new instance of this object's class, and the contents of this object are-*field-by-field-copied* into the new instance. For example, if you are cloning a tree object that has not overridden its `clone()` method, invoking `clone()` on the tree object will result simply in the root object of the tree being copied. The objects contained in the original tree will not be copied, but this newly cloned tree will point to those objects in the original tree. If any object in the original tree subsequently changes, those changes will be visible to the newly cloned tree.

A class whose `clone()` method should do more than just field-by-field-copy (for example, making clones of objects to which it refers) should override the clone() method to perform tasks specific to the cloning of that class. There is no requirement that the method use the default implementation of Object.clone().

It is common for cloneable classes to override clone() to make it public rather than protected. In this way, the clone() method can be accessed by other classes.

A class that is cloneable (regardless of whether it overrides clone()) should declare that it implements the Cloneable interface.

RETURNS A copy of this object.

EXCEPTIONS

CloneNotSupportedException

If this object uses the default implementation of Object.clone() to clone itself but does not support the Cloneable interface or if this object cannot be cloned.

OutOfMemoryError

If there is not enough memory to create the clone.

SEE ALSO Cloneable, CloneNotSupportedException.

EXAMPLE See the Cloneable class example.

equals()

PURPOSE Compares this object with another object for equality.

SYNTAX `public boolean equals(Object obj)`

DESCRIPTION This method compares this object with obj for equality. It returns true if the objects are equal; it returns false otherwise. The default implementation of equals() in the Object class defines equality between two objects as that of *object reference equivalence*. That is, two objects are equal if they refer to the same object (they have the same object reference). This is equivalent to the == Java operator.

Subclasses of Object often override equals() with their own definitions of equality. For example, the Number classes—Byte, Short, Integer, Long, Double, Float, BigDecimal, and BigInteger—define equality in terms of equality of the object's numeric value and its Class. If equals() is overridden, hashCode() should also be overridden so that two objects that are equal have the same hash code.

The runtime system uses equals() when storing an Object in a hash table.

PARAMETERS

obj The possibly null object against which to compare.

RETURNS true if this object is equal to obj; false otherwise.

SEE ALSO hashCode(), java.util.Hashtable.

EXAMPLE The Hashtable class uses hashCode() and equals() to locate an object in a hash table.

```
public class Hashtable extends Dictionary implements Cloneable {
    ...
    public synchronized Object get(Object key) {
        HashtableEntry tab[] = table;
        int hash = key.hashCode();
        int index = (hash & 0x7FFFFFFF) % tab.length;
        for (HashtableEntry e = tab[index] ; e != null ; e = e.next) {
            if ((e.hash == hash) && e.key.equals(key)) {
                return e.value;
            }
        }
        return null;
    }
}
```

finalize()

PURPOSE Called by Java virtual machine to clean up this object's state when it is ready to be discarded.

SYNTAX `protected void finalize() throws Throwable`

DESCRIPTION An object is ready to be discarded when the Java virtual machine determines that the object can no longer be accessed by any thread. Such an object is said to be ready for *finalization*. Finalization is the process of the virtual machine's invoking the object's finalize() method in order to "clean up" the object's state.

The virtual machine asynchronously and automatically runs the finalize() method of objects ready for finalization. Any uncaught exception thrown by this method during finalization is ignored, and the finalization terminates. You can use System.runFinalization() to explicitly ask the virtual machine to finalize methods ready to be discarded. It is important to note that there is no guarantee as to exactly when this method will be called; the virtual machine is not obligated to satisfy the request immediately. System.runFinalizersOnExit() is used to notify the virtual machine whether to run finalizers before the program exits. If a program is terminated abnormally (e.g., its process is killed), finalize() may not always be called by the virtual machine. See the example later in this discussion.

The finalize() method on an object will be called, at most, once by the virtual machine. If the program explicitly invokes finalize(), it has no effect on the automatic finalization—the virtual machine will still invoke finalize()

when the object is ready to be discarded. Once the virtual machine has finalized an object, the object is ready to be *garbage-collected* (i.e., its memory freed). If an object becomes "reincarnated" inside its own finalizer, the object's finalizer will not be called again.

By default, this method does nothing. Subclasses of `Object` should override this method if there are resources held by instances of the subclass that need to be freed. In such cases, the class should override this method to include code that releases the resources held by an instance. For example, each instance of the `Graphics` class is associated with a platform-dependent drawing context. Such classes should override `finalize()` to dispose of the native resource.

For more details on finalization, see *The Java Language Specification, First Edition*, Section 20.1.11, and *The Java Virtual Machine Specification*, Section 2.16.7.

SEE ALSO `System.gc()`, `System.runFinalization()`, `System.runFinalizersOnExit()`.

EXAMPLE This example shows a class `C` that overrides `finalize()` to print out a message. If you run the program with no arguments, `C`'s finalizer is not called by default when the program exits. If you run the program with one argument, `runFinalizersOnExit()` notifies the virtual machine and `C`'s finalizer is called before the program exits. If you run the program with two arguments and then type Ctrl-C to terminate the program abnormally, `C`'s finalizer is not called even though `runFinalizersOnExit()` was called with `true`.

```
class Main {
    public static void main(String[] args) {
        if (args.length > 0) {
            // Turn on finalizer.
            System.runFinalizersOnExit(true);
        }
        new C();

        // Keep busy until user hits Ctrl-C.
        if (args.length > 1) {
            long prod = 1;
            for (int i = 1; i < 1000000000; i++) {
                prod *= i;
            }
        }
    }

    static class C {
        C() {
            System.out.println("C created");
        }

        protected void finalize() {
            System.out.println("C finalized");
        }
    }
}
```

getClass()

PURPOSE Retrieves the `Class` object associated with this object.

SYNTAX `public final native Class getClass()`

DESCRIPTION Every object in Java is an instance of a class. For each class, Java maintains an immutable `Class` object containing information about the class. The `getClass()` method returns the `Class` object associated with this object.

RETURNS This object's non-`null` `Class` object.

SEE ALSO `Class`.

EXAMPLE

```
public static void printClassName(Object obj) {
    System.out.println("The class of " + obj + " is " +
                       obj.getClass().getName());
}
```

hashCode()

PURPOSE Computes the hash code for this object.

SYNTAX `public native int hashCode()`

DESCRIPTION Each `Object` in the Java system has a *hash code*, which is a *signed* number (`int`) that usually differs for different objects. The hash code of an object is used when storing the object in hash tables.

An object's hash code is computed by calling its `hashCode()` method. The algorithm used to compute a hash code can differ for different classes of objects; most algorithms are based on the values in the object. If `equals()` is `true` for two objects, both objects must have the same hash code. However, the converse is not always true; that is, two objects having the same hash code are not necessarily equal. Subclasses of `Object` override the default implementation of `hashCode()` if `hashCode()` wants to change the way hash codes are generated for its class of objects.

If `hashCode()` is overridden, `equals()` should also be overridden so that two objects that are equal have the same hash code.

RETURNS An `int` representing the hash code of the object.

SEE ALSO `equals()`, `java.util.Hashtable`.

EXAMPLE See `equals()`.

Object()

PURPOSE Constructs an instance of `Object`.

SYNTAX `public Object()`

EXAMPLE

```
Objects objs = new Object[3];
objs[0] = System.out;
objs[1] = "Java";
objs[2] = new Object();
```

notify()

PURPOSE Notifies a thread blocked on this object of a change in condition.

SYNTAX `public final native void notify()`

DESCRIPTION A thread notifies another thread of a change in condition related to this object by calling `notify()`. This method unblocks one of the waiting threads and allows the unblocked thread to grab the object's monitor when it has a chance to run. If there are multiple waiting threads, the choice of which thread is unblocked is implementation-dependent. Other threads waiting for the condition to change remain blocked until other `notify()` or `notifyAll()` calls are invoked or until their specified time-out periods (if any) expire. If no thread is waiting for that condition, `notify()` does nothing. No state is kept that a `notify()` was done on the object.

There is no guarantee that after a `notify()` call, a waiter is immediately awakened. In particular, control may be transferred to some other thread that may call `notify()` again.

The `notify()` method of an object can be called only by the thread holding the monitor for that object. In other words, a thread must hold this object's monitor before it can call its `notify()` method. Furthermore, the thread does not release the monitor until it exits the synchronized method/block from which `notify()` is called, and consequently, the waiting thread being notified cannot grab the monitor until that time. In other words, the location of `notify()` within the synchronized block is irrelevant.

EXCEPTIONS

`IllegalMonitorStateException`

If the thread invoking `notify()` is not holding the object's monitor.

SEE ALSO `wait()`, `notifyAll()`, `Thread`.

EXAMPLE This example illustrates the use of `wait()/notify()` in synchronizing access to a shared stack, defined by the class `Stack`. If the stack is full, `push()` waits until there is room in the stack before pushing another item onto the stack. If the stack is empty, `pop()` waits until there is an item on the stack to pop. If the stack was previously empty, push() notifies any thread that was waiting for an item to pop. If the stack was previously full, pop() notifies any thread that was waiting for space on the stack. The Retriever and Stacker classes are threads that, respectively, pop and push items onto the shared stack.

```
// A stack that has a 3 item limit
class Stack {
    static final int STACK_SIZE = 3;
    private int[] stack_store = new int[STACK_SIZE];
    private int stack_ptr = 0;

    // push item onto stack
    // If stack is full, wait until it has room
    synchronized public void push(int item) {
        while (stack_ptr >= STACK_SIZE) {
            try {
                wait();
            } catch (InterruptedException e) {
                // ignore
            }
        }
        if (stack_ptr == 0)
            notify();   // pop was awaiting stack to fill
        stack_store[stack_ptr++] = item;
    }

    // pop item off top of stack
    // If stack is empty, wait until it has item
    synchronized public int pop() {
        while (stack_ptr == 0) {
            try {
                wait();
            } catch (InterruptedException e) {
                // ignore
            }
        }
        if (stack_ptr >= STACK_SIZE)
            notify();  // push was awaiting stack to drain
        return(stack_store[--stack_ptr]);
    }
}

// Thread that loops, pushing items onto the stack, and then
// sleeping a random period of time
class Stacker extends Thread {
    Stack s;
    Stacker(Stack s) {
        super();
        this.s = s;
    }
    public void run() {
        while (true) {
            int rand = Math.round((float)((Math.random()* 6)));
            s.push(rand);
            System.out.println("push: " + rand);
            try {
                Thread.sleep(Math.round(Math.random()*100));
            } catch (InterruptedException e) {
```

```
            }
        }
    }
}

// Thread that loops, popping an item off the stack, and then
// sleeping a random period of time
class Retriever extends Thread {
    Stack s;
    Retriever(Stack s) {
        super();
        this.s = s;
    }
    public void run() {
        while (true) {
            int top = s.pop();
            System.out.println("pop: " + top);
            try {
                Thread.sleep(Math.round(Math.random()*100));
            } catch (InterruptedException e) {
            }
        }
    }
}

class Main {
    public static void main(String[] args) {
        Stack s = new Stack();  // create stack

        // create threads
        Thread rthread = new Retriever(s);
        Thread sthread = new Stacker(s);

        // start threads
        sthread.start();
        rthread.start();
    }
}
```


notifyAll()

PURPOSE Notifies all threads blocked on this object of a change in condition.

SYNTAX `public final native void notifyAll()`

DESCRIPTION `notifyAll()` notifies and unblocks all threads blocked on this object, waiting for a condition to change. If no thread is blocked on this object, `notifyAll()` does nothing. The calling thread must be holding the object's monitor.

EXCEPTIONS

`IllegalMonitorStateException`

If the thread invoking `notifyAll()` is not holding the object's monitor.

SEE ALSO `wait()`, `notify()`, `Thread`.

EXAMPLE

```
// wait until all workers are idle
while (workers_active > 0) {
    try {
        wait();
    } catch (InterruptedException e) {
        // ignore
    }
}
fillTaskList();
notifyAll();
```

A B C D E F G H I J K L M N O P Q R S T U V W X Y Z

toString()

PURPOSE Generates the string representation of this object.

SYNTAX `public String toString()`

DESCRIPTION This method returns the string representation of this object. By convention, all Java objects have a `toString()` method that returns the string representation of the object. This method is typically used for debugging purposes. Occasionally, this method is used to generate a string that is parsable by other methods and constructors (for example, the subclass of `Number`, including `BigInteger` and `BigDecimal`).

When an object appears in a string concentation operation (+), where a `String` is expected, the compiler automatically invokes the `toString()` method of that object to get its string representation.

All subclasses should override this method so that their string representations display information relevant for that class.

RETURNS The non-`null` string representation of this object.

EXAMPLE

```
class PhoneEntry {
    String name;
    String phoneNumber;
    ...
    public String toString() {
        return "name : " + name + " phone: " + phoneNumber;
    }
}
```

wait()

PURPOSE Causes a thread to wait until it is notified.

SYNTAX `public final void wait() throws InterruptedException`

```
public final void wait(long timeout) throws InterruptedException
public final void wait(long timeout, int nanos) throws
   InterruptedException
```

DESCRIPTION During the course of execution, a thread may need to wait for a condition related to this object to occur before continuing execution. It does this by calling `wait()`, which causes it to block until another thread invokes `notify()` on the object to indicate that the condition has been satisfied. The `wait()` method of an object can be called only by the thread holding the monitor for that object.

There are three forms of the `wait()` method. They vary in the time-out period to use for the wait. For all three forms, the wait can be interrupted by another thread (that invokes `interrupt()` on the thread). The first form of `wait()` blocks indefinitely until it has been notified. The second form blocks either until it has been notified or until `timeout` milliseconds has passed. A `timeout` of `0` means to wait indefinitely. The third form is like the second form, except that it allows more precision in the time-out period by allowing nanoseconds to be specified as part of the time-out period. A `timeout` and `nanos` of `0` mean to wait indefinitely.

`wait()` is usually called in a loop. This is because there is no guarantee that the reason the thread was unblocked was because of a change in the condition on which the thread has been waiting. The thread could have been unblocked due to an interrupt or an expired time-out period. `wait()` is typically used by including the `wait()` statement in the body of a `while` loop. The condition at the top of the `while` loop checks that the condition that the thread is waiting on has not changed. If the condition has changed, the `while` loop is exited. Otherwise, the thread continues with the `wait()` call inside the `while` loop. An example of this is shown in the `notify()` example.

PARAMETERS

`timeout` The maximum number of milliseconds to wait. `timeout` ≥ `0`.

`nanos` In addition to `timeout` milliseconds, wait `nanos` nanoseconds. `0` ≤ `nanos` ≤ `999999`. `nanos` is rounded to the nearest millisecond, unless `timeout` is `0`, in which case a nonzero `nanos` is treated as 1 millisecond.

EXCEPTIONS

`IllegalArgumentException`
If `timeout` < `0` or if `nanos` < `0` or `nanos` > `999999`.

`IllegalMonitorStateException`
If the thread invoking `wait()` is not the owner of the object's monitor.

`InterruptedException`
If another thread has interrupted this thread.

SEE ALSO `notify()`, `notifyAll()`, `Thread`.

EXAMPLE See `notify()`.

java.io
ObjectInput

Syntax

```
public interface ObjectInput extends DataInput
```

Description

`ObjectInput` is an interface that declares methods for reading in serialized objects and returning them as Java objects. It extends the `DataInput` interface, which contains declarations for methods that read in data values, and returns them as Java primitive data types.

MEMBER SUMMARY	
Input Methods	
`read()`	Reads one or more bytes from the `ObjectInput` object.
`readObject()`	Reads an object from the `ObjectInput` object.
`skip()`	Skips bytes from the `ObjectInput` object.
ObjectInput Methods	
`available()`	Determines the number of bytes that can be read for primitive data from the `ObjectInput` object.
`close()`	Closes the `ObjectInput` object.

See Also

`DataInput`, `ObjectInputStream`, `ObjectOutput`.

Example

See `ObjectInputStream`.

available()

PURPOSE Determines the number of bytes that can be read for primitive data from the `ObjectInput` object.

SYNTAX

```
public int available() throws IOException
```

RETURNS The number bytes that can be read for primitive data from this stream.

`IOException`

If an IO error is encountered while determining the number of available bytes.

EXAMPLE See `ObjectInputStream.skipBytes()`.

close()

PURPOSE Closes the `ObjectInput` object.

SYNTAX

```
public void close() throws IOException
```

DESCRIPTION This method releases any resources used by the `ObjectInput` object. After the object has been closed, invoking methods on it will throw an `IOException`.

EXCEPTIONS

`IOException`

If an IO error has occurred while closing the `ObjectInput` object.

EXAMPLE See the `InputStream` class example.

read()

PURPOSE Reads one or more bytes from the `ObjectInput` object.

SYNTAX

```
public int read() throws IOException
public int read(byte[] buf) throws IOException
public int read(byte[] buf, int off, int count) throws
   IOException
```

DESCRIPTION This method reads one or more bytes from the `ObjectInput` object. The first form reads a single byte and returns it as an `int`. The byte is in the low-order byte of the `int`; the high-order 3 bytes are set to `0`.

The second and third forms of this method reads `count` number of bytes from the `ObjectInput` object and stores the bytes read into the `byte` array `buf` starting at index `offset`. If `offset` and `count` are not specified, they default to `0` and `buf.length`, respectively.

If no byte is available to be read, this method blocks until a byte is available.

PARAMETERS

`buf`	The non-`null` `byte` array in which the bytes read will be stored.
`count`	The number of bytes to read. `0` ≤ `count` ≤ `buf.length-offset`.
`offset`	The index in `buf` at which to start storing the bytes read. `0` ≤ `offset` < `buf.length`.

RETURNS The first form returns the byte read; the second and third forms return the actual number of bytes read. All forms return `-1` if end-of-file is reached before any bytes are read.

EXCEPTIONS

`ArrayIndexOutOfBoundsException`
If `offset` or `count` is outside of the specified bounds.

`IOException`
If an IO error has occurred.

EXAMPLE See the `InputStream` class example.

readObject()

PURPOSE Reads an object from the `ObjectInput` object.

SYNTAX

```
public Object readObject() throws ClassNotFoundException,
    IOException
```

DESCRIPTION This method blocks until a complete object has been read from the `ObjectInput` object. The format of the data that constitutes the object read from the `ObjectInput` object is determined by the implementation of the `ObjectInput` object. For example, an `ObjectInputStream` object implements `readObject()` by using the serialized object's `readExternal()`, `readObject()`, or `defaultReadObject()` methods.

RETURNS The object read from the `ObjectInput` object. It is `null` if the next item in the stream is `null`.

EXCEPTIONS

`ClassNotFoundException`
If the class of the object being read cannot be found.

`EOFException`
If end-of-stream is reached on the `ObjectInput` object without reading an object.

`IOException`
If an IO error occurs while reading the object.

EXAMPLE See the `Serializable` class example.

skip()

PURPOSE
Skips bytes from the `ObjectInput` object.

SYNTAX
`public long skip(long count) throws IOException`

DESCRIPTION
This method skips `count` number of bytes from the `ObjectInput` object. Skipped bytes will not be returned or used by subsequent `read()` or `readObject()` calls. `ObjectInputStream.skipBytes()` uses `skip()` to skip primitive data in an object input stream. See `ObjectInputStream.skipBytes()` for details.

PARAMETERS

`count` The number of bytes to skip.

RETURNS
The actual number of bytes skipped.

EXCEPTIONS

`IOException`

If an IO error has occurred while attempting to skip `count` bytes.

SEE ALSO
`ObjectInputStream.skipBytes()`.

EXAMPLE
See `InputStream.skip()` and the usage of `skipBytes()` in `ObjectInputStream.skipBytes()`.

java.io

ObjectInputStream

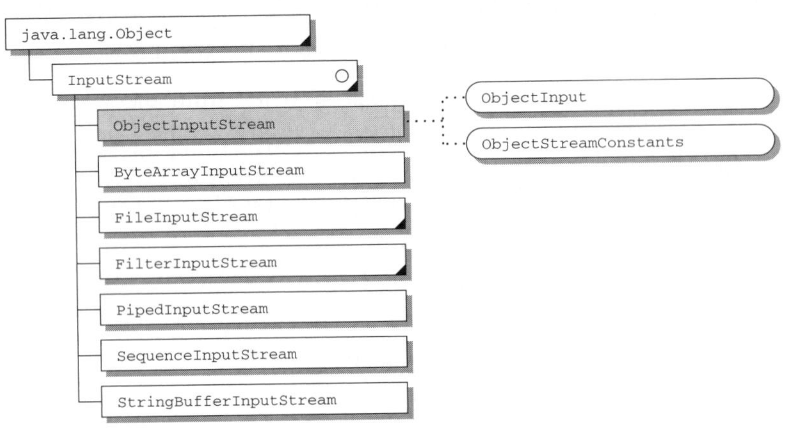

Syntax

```
public class ObjectInputStream extends InputStream implements ObjectInput,
    ObjectStreamConstants
```
[1]

Description

The `ObjectInputStream` class is used for deserializing primitive data and objects (including arrays and strings) read from an input stream. The data in the input stream was produced by using a corresponding `ObjectOutputStream`. See Figure 67.

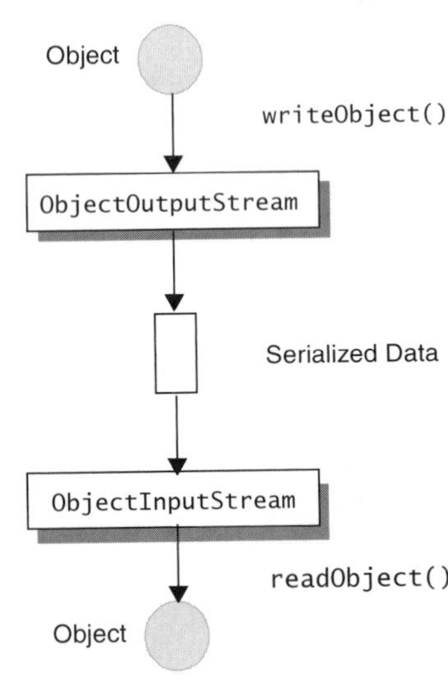

FIGURE 67: `ObjectInputStream` and `ObjectOutputStream`.

Usage

Classes that implement the `Serializable` or `Externalizable` interfaces can be serialized by using `ObjectOutputStream.writeObject()`, and deserialized by using `ObjectInputStream.readObject()`.

For example, suppose `ClassX` is serializable:

```
public class ClassX implements Serializable
{ ...
}
```

1. The `ObjectStreamConstants` interface is not accessible outside of the `java.io` package. The interface contains declarations for various constants used in object serialization.

You can serialize an instance of ClassX to an ObjectOutputStream and then read it back by using ObjectInputStream:

```
ObjectOutputStream out = ...;
out.writeObject(new ClassX());
ObjectInputStream in = ...
ClassX obj = (ClassX) in.readObject();
```

Deserialization

Data of primitive types is deserialized by using methods declared in the DataInput interface. Strings,[1] arrays, and objects are deserialized by using readObject(). The primitive data and objects must be deserialized in the same order in which they were written to the serialized stream. For example, if the serialized stream was produced by using the following sequence of writes:

```
out.writeInt(ival);
out.writeByte(bval);
out.writeChar(ch);
out.writeObject("Java");
out.writeObject(new Date());
```

then the corresponding read sequence to deserialize data from the serialized stream must be the following:

```
int ival = in.readInt();
byte bval = in.readByte();
char ch = in.readChar();
Object obj1 = in.readObject();
Object obj2 = in.readObject();
```

For serialized objects, you can use readObject() and then later determine its type by using the instanceof operator or the reflection APIs. For serialized primitive data, however, you must know the data type beforehand. DataInput read methods can be used only to read data written by using the corresponding DataOutput write method.

When an object is deserialized, the constructor that takes no parameters that is defined by the nonserializable superclass of the object is called to allocate an instance of the object. Then, starting with the highest ancestor serializable class (that closest to java.lang.Object) through each subclass to the most derived class, the corresponding readObject() method of each class, or ObjectInputStream.defaultRead-Object() if the class has not defined a readObject(), is invoked to restore the state of the object. See Serializable for more information about the serialization/deserialization process.

1. A string can be serialized either as an object by using writeObject() or as an UTF string by using writeUTF(). A string that was serialized as an object must be deserialized by using readObject(). A string that was serialized as an UTF string must be deserialized by using readUTF(). If a string is serialized as an UTF string multiple times to the same stream, it is written out to the stream multiple times. If a string is serialized as an object multiple times to the same stream, only one copy is serialized—the other copies are represented by a handle. Default serialization writes strings as objects, so the only way a string is written as a UTF string is if it is explicitly written into the stream by using writeUTF().

`ObjectInputStream.readObject()` may be invoked recursively when an object being deserialized references other objects that require deserialization.

See `http://java.sun.com/products/jdk/1.1/docs/guide/serialization/spec` for complete details on how objects are serialized and deserialized.

A B C D E F G H I J K L M N O P Q R S T U V W X Y Z

Multiple Occurrences of the Same Object

If an object occurs more than once in a serialized stream, its first occurrence is serialized. Subsequent occurrences use a *handle* to refer to the first occurrence. In this way, an object is serialized only once to the stream. When the stream is deserialized, the serialized form of the object is deserialized and recorded in an *object/handle cache*. Handles that refer to the serialized object are subsequently resolved to the previously deserialized object. As far as the caller invoking `readObject()` is concerned, there is no difference between the result returned for the first serialized form and those that were represented by using only a handle.

When a "reset" marker is encountered in the serialized stream (see `ObjectOutputStream`), the object/handle cache is cleared. As objects are later deserialized from the stream, they and their handles are added to the cache and multiple occurrences of the same object are processed as described previously. The reset marker also affects object and class substitution (`resolveObject()` and `resolveClass()`). To these methods, it is as if the deserialized stream was just opened.

ClassLoading

When data is deserialized into an object, the class for that object is loaded by using the class loader of the method invoking `readObject()`. You can use a different policy by overriding `resolveClass()`.

Other Customizations

An `ObjectInputStream` can be subclassed to perform special processing over the serialized data. Typically, the stream is produced by using a corresponding customized subclass of `ObjectOutputStream`. For example, you can add additional header information when producing the serialized stream (such as checksums) and process the special header when deserializing objects from the stream.

MEMBER SUMMARY

Constructor	
`ObjectInputStream()`	Constructs an instance of `ObjectInputStream`.
Methods Used by a Class's readObject()	
`defaultReadObject()`	Reads the serializable fields of the object being deserialized.
`registerValidation()`	Registers an object to be validated.

MEMBER SUMMARY	
Stream Customization Methods	
`enableResolveObject()`	Enables/disables this object input stream to replace objects read from this stream.
`readStreamHeader()`	Reads and verifies the stream header from the underlying input stream.
`resolveClass()`	Loads the local class represented by the class descriptor read from this object input stream.
`resolveObject()`	Replaces an object with another object during deserialization.
ObjectInput Methods	
`available()`	Determines the number of bytes that can be read for primitive data from this object input stream.
`close()`	Closes this object input stream.
`read()`	Reads one or more bytes from this object input stream.
`readObject()`	Reads an object from this object input stream.
DataInput Methods	
`readBoolean()`	Reads a `boolean` from this object input stream.
`readByte()`	Reads a `byte` from this object input stream.
`readChar()`	Reads a 16-bit Unicode `char` from this object input stream.
`readDouble()`	Reads a 64-bit `double` from this object input stream.
`readFloat()`	Reads a 32-bit `float` from this object input stream.
`readFully()`	Reads the requested number of bytes from this object input stream.
`readInt()`	Reads a 32-bit `int` from this object input stream.
`readLine()`	Reads in a sequence of bytes terminated by a line terminator.
`readLong()`	Reads a 64-bit `long` from this object input stream.
`readShort()`	Reads 16-bit `short` from this object input stream.
`readUnsignedByte()`	Reads an unsigned 8-bit `byte` from this object input stream.
`readUnsignedShort()`	Reads an unsigned 16-bit `short` from this object input stream.
`readUTF()`	Reads a Unicode string from this object input stream.
`skipBytes()`	Skips the requested number of bytes of primitive data from this object input stream.

See Also

`Externalizable`, `ObjectOutputStream`, `ObjectStreamClass`, `Serializable`.

Example

See the previous *Usage* example, `defaultReadObject()`, `readStreamHeader()`, `resolveObject()`, and `skipBytes()`.

available()

PURPOSE
Determines the number of bytes that can be read for primitive data from this object input stream.

SYNTAX
`public int available() throws IOException`

DESCRIPTION
This method returns the number of bytes available to be read for primitive data from this object input stream. If the next byte in this stream belongs to a serialized object, this method returns `0`. This method can be used by a program to find all of the objects in an object input stream. Such a program would use `available()` and `skipBytes()` to determine and skip segments of the stream that contain primitive data serialized directly to the stream.

RETURNS
The number of bytes that can be read for primitive data from this stream.

EXCEPTIONS
`IOException`
If an IO error occurs.

OVERRIDES
`InputStream.available()`.

SEE ALSO
`skipBytes()`.

EXAMPLE
See `skipBytes()`.

close()

PURPOSE
Closes this object input stream.

SYNTAX
`public void close() throws IOException`

DESCRIPTION
This method closes this object input stream by closing the underlying input stream.

EXCEPTIONS
`IOException`
If an IO error occurs.

OVERRIDES
`InputStream.close()`.

EXAMPLE
See `defaultReadObject()`.

defaultReadObject()

PURPOSE Reads the serializable fields of the object being deserialized.

SYNTAX

```
public final void defaultReadObject() throws IOException,
   ClassNotFoundException, NotActiveException
```

DESCRIPTION This method restores the serializable fields of the object being deserialized from this object input stream. In Java 1.1, the serializable fields of a class are all of its nontransient and nonstatic fields. This method is invoked automatically when deserializing an object whose class implements the `Serializable` interface but does not define a `readObject()` method. It can also be invoked explicitly from inside of an object's `readObject()` method, in which case, `defaultReadObject()` should be the first method in `readObject()` that reads from the stream. The order in which `readObject()` reads from the stream must match the writes of the corresponding `writeObject()`. If `defaultReadObject()` is invoked from outside of an object's `readObject()`, `NotActiveException` is thrown.

EXCEPTIONS

`ClassCastException`

If `resolveObject()` returns an object that is incompatible with the field being assigned by `defaultReadObject()`.

`ClassNotFoundException`

If the class of a field of the object being deserialized cannot be found. The class of the object being deserialized has already been found by the time `defaultReadObject()` is called.

`IOException`

If an IO error occurs while reading the object's fields from the underlying input stream.

`NotActiveException`

If this method is not invoked from within the object's `readObject()` method.

SEE ALSO `Serializable`.

EXAMPLE This example writes out an instance of `Class1` and reads it back. `Class1` is a serializable class that defines `readObject()` and `writeObject()` methods. `readObject()` calls `ObjectInputStream.defaultReadObject()` to restore its fields and then sets one field specially.

```
import java.io.*;
import java.util.Date;

class Main {
    public static void main(String[] args) {
        try {
            // Write class out
            FileOutputStream f = new FileOutputStream("Class1.ser");
```

```
                ObjectOutput out = new ObjectOutputStream(f);

                Class1 c1 = new Class1();
                c1.date = new Date();
                out.writeObject(c1);
                out.flush();
                out.close();

                // Read it back
                FileInputStream f2 = new FileInputStream("Class1.ser");
                ObjectInputStream in = new ObjectInputStream(f2);
                Class1 cc1 = (Class1) in.readObject();
                in.close();

                System.out.println("cc1.date " + cc1.date);
                System.out.println("cc1.restored " + cc1.restored);
            } catch (IOException e) {
                e.printStackTrace();
            } catch (ClassNotFoundException e) {
                e.printStackTrace();
            }
        }
    }

    class Class1 implements Serializable {
        transient boolean restored;
        public Date date;
        transient String str;

        private void readObject(ObjectInputStream in)
        throws IOException, ClassNotFoundException {
            in.defaultReadObject();
            restored = true;
        }

        // Does just default serialization
        private void writeObject(ObjectOutputStream out) throws IOException {
            out.defaultWriteObject();
        }
    }
```

enableResolveObject()

PURPOSE Enables/disables this object input stream to replace objects read from this stream.

SYNTAX

```
protected final boolean enableResolveObject(boolean enable)
    throws SecurityException
```

DESCRIPTION After an object has been read from this object input stream and before it is returned by `readObject()`, it can be replaced by another object by using `resolveObject()`. By default, `ObjectInputStream` does not allow this replacement. A subclass of `ObjectInputStream` must call `enableResolve-`

`Object()` with `true` in order to allow it. This method can be invoked only from an instance of an `ObjectInputStream` subclass that was loaded by a trusted class loader (for example, the default system class loader).

PARAMETERS

`enable` If `true`, allows objects read from this stream to be replaced. If `false`, objects read from this stream cannot be replaced.

RETURNS The previous setting before `enableResolveObject()` was invoked: `true` if replacement was previously enabled and `false` otherwise.

EXCEPTIONS

`SecurityException`

If `enable` is `true` and this stream was not loaded by using the default system class loader.

SEE ALSO `java.lang.ClassLoader`, `ObjectOutputStream.enableReplaceObject()`, `resolveObject()`.

EXAMPLE See `resolveObject()`.

ObjectInputStream()

PURPOSE Constructs an instance of `ObjectInputStream`.

SYNTAX
```
public ObjectInputStream(InputStream in) throws IOException,
   StreamCorruptedException
```

DESCRIPTION This method creates an instance of `ObjectInputStream` for the input stream `in`. The constructor must first read a *stream header* that verifies whether `in` contains serialized data written by an `ObjectOutputStream` and that this version of the `ObjectInputStream` implementation is compatible with the version of `ObjectOutputStream` used to write out the data. If this verification fails, a `StreamCorruptedException` is thrown. The constructor blocks until the header is completely read from `in`.

After the header has been verified, methods can be invoked on this newly created stream to read data from `in` and deserialized it into primitive data and objects expected by those methods.

PARAMETERS

`in` The non-`null` input stream from which to read the serialized data.

EXCEPTIONS

`IOException`

If an IO error occurs while reading from `in`.

`StreamCorruptedException`
If `in` does not contain a compatible version of serialized data format that can be read by this `ObjectInputStream` implementation.

SEE ALSO `DataInputStream.DataInputStream()`, `readStreamHeader()`.

EXAMPLE See `defaultReadObject()`.

A B C D E F G H I J K L M N O P Q R S T U V W X Y Z

read()

PURPOSE Reads one or more bytes from this object input stream.

SYNTAX

```
public int read() throws IOException
public int read(byte[] buffer, int offset, int count) throws
   IOException
```

DESCRIPTION This method reads one or more bytes from this object input stream. The first form reads a single byte and returns it in the low-order byte of an `int`. The second form reads `count` number of bytes and stores them into the `byte` array `buffer` starting at index `offset`. It returns the actual number of bytes read.

This method blocks if no bytes are available to be read. The requested number of bytes to be read (`count`) might not all be read if there are not that many bytes available. If you want to block waiting for all of the number of bytes requested, use `readFully()`.

This method can be used only to read bytes written by using one of the `DataOutput` write methods that write bytes. It is not valid to call this method if `available()` returns `0`.

PARAMETERS

- `buffer` The non-`null` `byte` array into which the data is stored.
- `count` The maximum number of bytes to read. `0` ≤ `count` ≤ `buffer.length-offset`.
- `offset` The index in `buffer` at which to start storing the bytes read. `0` ≤ `offset` < `buffer.length`.

RETURNS The first form returns the byte read in the low-order byte of the `int`. The second form returns the actual number of bytes read. `-1` is returned when no bytes are read because end-of-stream has been reached.

EXCEPTIONS

`ArrayIndexOutOfBoundsException`
If `count` or `offset` is outside the specified bounds.

`IndexOutOfBoundsException`
If `count` < `0`.

`IOException`
If an IO error occurs.

OVERRIDES `InputStream.read()`.

SEE ALSO `ObjectOutputStream.write()`, `ObjectOutputStream.writeByte()`, `readByte()`, `readLine()`, `readFully()`, `readUnsignedByte()`.

EXAMPLE See the `DataInputStream` class example.

A B C D E F G H I J K L M N O P Q R S T U V W X Y Z

readBoolean()

PURPOSE Reads a `boolean` from this object input stream.

SYNTAX `public boolean readBoolean() throws IOException`

DESCRIPTION This method reads a `boolean` value from this stream. A `boolean` is represented as a single byte. If the byte is nonzero, the `boolean` value is `true`. If the byte is `0`, the `boolean` value is `false`.

This method can be used only to read a `boolean` written by using `DataOutput.writeBoolean()`. It is not valid to call this method if `available()` returns `0`.

RETURNS The `boolean` value read (`true` or `false`).

EXCEPTIONS

`EOFException`

If end-of-file is reached while attempting to read from this stream.

`IOException`

If an IO error occurs while attempting to read from this stream.

SEE ALSO `DataInput.readBoolean()`, `ObjectOutputStream.writeBoolean()`.

EXAMPLE See the `DataInputStream` class example.

readByte()

PURPOSE Reads a `byte` from this object input stream.

SYNTAX `public byte readByte() throws IOException`

DESCRIPTION This method can be used only to read a byte written by using one of the `DataOutput` write methods that write bytes. It is not valid to call this method if `available()` returns `0`.

RETURNS The 8-bit `byte` read.

EXCEPTIONS

`EOFException`

If end-of-file is reached while attempting to read from this stream.

IOException
: If an IO error occurs while attempting to read from this stream.

SEE ALSO `DataInput.readByte()`, `ObjectOutputStream.writeByte()`, `ObjectOutputStream.writeBytes()`, `readUnsignedByte()`.

EXAMPLE See the `DataInputStream` class example.

readChar()

PURPOSE Reads a 16-bit Unicode `char` from this object input stream.

SYNTAX `public char readChar() throws IOException`

DESCRIPTION A Unicode `char` is represented by a 16-bit unsigned integer. This method reads a `char` by reading two consecutive bytes from this stream and interpreting those as a 16-bit unsigned integer (the first byte read is the high-order byte) to be used as the value of the `char`.

This method can be used only to read a `char` written by using `DataOutput.writeChar()` or `DataOutput.writeChars()`. It is not valid to call this method if `available()` returns `0`.

RETURNS The `char` read.

EXCEPTIONS

EOFException
: If end-of-file is reached while attempting to read from this stream.

IOException
: If an IO error occurs while attempting to read from this stream.

SEE ALSO `DataInput.readChar()`, `ObjectOutputStream.writeChar()`, `ObjectOutputStream.writeChars()`.

EXAMPLE See the `DataInputStream` class example.

readDouble()

PURPOSE Reads a 64-bit `double` from this object input stream.

SYNTAX `public double readDouble() throws IOException`

DESCRIPTION This method reads 8 bytes from this stream and returns the `double` value represented by the bits of those 8 bytes. The 8 bytes are in the format expected by `Double.longBitsToDouble()`.

This method can be used only to read a `double` written by using `DataOutput.writeDouble()`. It is not valid to call this method if `available()` returns `0`.

RETURNS The `double` value read.

EXCEPTIONS

`EOFException`

If end-of-file is reached while attempting to read from this stream.

`IOException`

If an IO error occurs while attempting to read from this stream.

SEE ALSO `DataInput.readDouble()`, `ObjectOutputStream.writeDouble()`, `java.lang.Double.longBitsToDouble()`.

EXAMPLE See the `DataInputStream` class example.

readFloat()

PURPOSE Reads a 32-bit `float` from this object input stream.

SYNTAX `public float readFloat() throws IOException`

DESCRIPTION This method reads 4 bytes from this stream and returns the `float` value represented by the bits of those 4 bytes. The 4 bytes are in the format expected by `Float.intBitsToFloat()`.

This method can be used only to read a `float` written by using `DataOutput.writeFloat()`. It is not valid to call this method if `available()` returns `0`.

RETURNS The `float` value read.

EXCEPTIONS

`EOFException`

If end-of-file is reached while attempting to read from this stream.

`IOException`

If an IO error occurs while attempting to read from this stream.

SEE ALSO `DataInput.readFloat()`, `ObjectOutputStream.writeFloat()`, `java.lang.Float.intBitsToFloat()`.

EXAMPLE See the class example.

readFully()

PURPOSE Reads the requested number of bytes from this object input stream.

SYNTAX
```
public void readFully(byte[] buffer) throws IOException
public void readFully(byte[] buffer, int offset, int count) throws
    IOException
```

DESCRIPTION This method reads bytes from this stream and copies them into the byte array buffer. If offset and count are specified, count bytes are read and placed into buffer starting at index offset. If they are not specified, buffer.length bytes are read and placed into buffer starting at index 0. This method will block waiting for all of the requested number of bytes to be read (either count or buffer.length).

This method can be used only to read bytes written by using one of the DataOutput write methods that write bytes. It is not valid to call this method if available() returns 0.

PARAMETERS

buffer The byte array into which the bytes are stored.

count The maximum number of bytes to read. 0 ≤ count ≤ buffer.length-offset.

offset The index in buffer at which to start storing the bytes read. 0 ≤ offset < buffer.length.

EXCEPTIONS

ArrayIndexOutOfBoundsException
If count or offset is outside of the specified bounds.

EOFException
If end-of-file is reached while attempting to read from this stream.

IOException
If an IO error occurs while attempting to read from this stream.

SEE ALSO DataInput.readFully(), read().

EXAMPLE See the DataInputStream class example.

readInt()

PURPOSE Reads a 32-bit int from this object input stream.

SYNTAX
```
public int readInt() throws IOException
```

DESCRIPTION This method reads 4 bytes from this stream and returns the int value represented by the bits of those 4 bytes. The higher-order bytes are read in order from this stream.

This method can be used only to read an `int` written by using `DataOutput.writeInt()`. It is not valid to call this method if `available()` returns `0`.

RETURNS The `int` value read.

EXCEPTIONS

`EOFException`

If end-of-file is reached while attempting to read from this stream.

`IOException`

If an IO error occurs while attempting to read from this stream.

SEE ALSO `DataInput.readInt()`, `ObjectOutputStream.writeInt()`.

EXAMPLE See the `DataInputStream` class example.

readLine()

PURPOSE Reads in a sequence of bytes terminated by a line terminator.

SYNTAX `String readLine() throws IOException`

DESCRIPTION A line is a sequence of bytes terminated by `\n`, `\r`, `\r\n`, or end-of-stream. Each byte read is converted to a character by filling the high-order byte of each character with `0`. This method blocks until a complete line has been read.

RETURNS A string containing the bytes of the line read (not including the line terminating character). `null` if no bytes are read before end-of-stream is reached.

Note: This method is deprecated in JDK 1.2.

EXCEPTIONS

`IOException`

If an IO error occurs.

SEE ALSO `DataInput.readLine()`, `readUTF()`.

readLong()

PURPOSE Reads a 64-bit `long` from this object input stream.

SYNTAX `public long readLong() throws IOException`

DESCRIPTION This method reads 8 bytes from this stream and returns the `long` value represented by the bits of those 8 bytes. The higher-order bytes are read in order from this stream.

This method can be used only to read a `long` written by using `DataOutput.writeLong()`. It is not valid to call this method if `available()` returns `0`.

RETURNS The `long` value read.

EXCEPTIONS

`EOFException`
If end-of-file is reached while attempting to read from this stream.

`IOException`
If an IO error occurs while attempting to read from this stream.

SEE ALSO `DataInput.readLong()`, `ObjectOutputStream.writeLong()`.

EXAMPLE See the `DataInputStream` class example.

A B C D E F G H I J K L M N O P Q R S T U V W X Y Z

readObject()

PURPOSE Reads an object from this object input stream.

SYNTAX
```
public final Object readObject() throws OptionalDataException,
    ClassNotFoundException, IOException
```

DESCRIPTION This method reads data from the underlying input stream, deserializes it into an object, and returns it to the caller. If the object's fields contain references to other objects, those objects and their references are also read and deserialized to form a complete graph of objects. Each object is deserialized by using one of the following methods of the class:

- `readExternal()` if the class implements `Externalizable`
- `defaultReadObject()` if the class implements `Serializable` but doesn't define a `readObject()` method
- `readObject()` if the class implements `Serializable` and defines a `readObject()` method

If this object input stream has enabled replacement of objects read from its stream, `resolveObject()` is invoked for each object as the object is deserialized. If this object input stream has any registered validation instances, those are invoked to validate the object(s) before this method returns. (See `registerValidation()`.)

If a class defines a `writeObject()` method that writes out its required data followed by its optional data, then the corresponding `readObject()` method must first invoke `defaultReadObject()` to deserialize the required data. Then it reads and deserializes any optional data. See `Serializable` for an explanation of required data and optional data.

If an exception is encountered during `readObject()`, the validity of the rest of the data in this object input stream is suspect and should not be used any further.

RETURNS The object read from this object input stream. `null` if the next object in this stream is `null`.

EXCEPTIONS

`ClassNotFoundException`

If the class of the object (or an object reachable from the object) being read and deserialized cannot be found. The exception's message will contain the name of the class that is not found.

`EOFException`

If end-of-stream is reached before an object can be read.

`InvalidClassException`

If the deserialized class cannot be restored—for example, if the constructor required is not accessible or nonexistent—or if the class cannot be instantiated.

`OptionalDataException`

If primitive data is found in the stream when an object was expected (i.e., if this method is invoked when a call to `available()` would return a nonzero value).

`StreamCorruptedException`

If the handle to a previously serialized object cannot be deserialized because the serialized object was not found in the stream, or if the class descriptor for the class is not in the stream, or if the stream's control data is otherwise inconsistent with its actual content.

`IOException`

If an IO error occurs while reading from the underlying input stream.

SEE ALSO `registerValidation()`, `resolveObject()`.

EXAMPLE See `defaultReadObject()` and `ObjectOutputStream.writeObject()`.

readShort()

PURPOSE Reads a 16-bit `short` from this stream.

SYNTAX `public short readShort() throws IOException`

DESCRIPTION This method reads 2 bytes from this stream and returns the `short` value represented by the bits of those 2 bytes. The higher-order byte is read first from this stream.

This method can be used only to read a `short` written by using `DataOutput.writeShort()`. It is not valid to call this method if `available()` returns `0`.

RETURNS The `short` value read.

EXCEPTIONS

`EOFException`

If end-of-file is reached while attempting to read from this stream.

`IOException`
If an IO error occurs while attempting to read from this stream.

SEE ALSO `DataInput.readShort()`, `ObjectOutputStream.writeShort()`, `readUnsignedShort()`.

EXAMPLE See the `DataInputStream` class example.

readStreamHeader()

PURPOSE Reads and verifies the stream header from the underlying input stream.

SYNTAX
```
protected void readStreamHeader() throws IOException,
   StreamCorruptedException
```

DESCRIPTION This method reads the *stream header* from the input stream passed to the `ObjectInputStream` constructor. The header consists of a *magic number*—a constant used to mark all serialized streams—and the version number of the serialization algorithm. Both of these numbers must match that supported by this `ObjectInputStream` instance. If they do not, a `StreamCorruptedException` is thrown.

A subclass can override this method to read and verify its own stream headers.

EXCEPTIONS

`IOException`
If an IO error occurs while reading from the underlying input stream.

`StreamCorruptedException`
If the stream does not contain a compatible version of serialized data format that can be read by this `ObjectInputStream` implementation.

SEE ALSO `ObjectOutputStream.writeStreamHeader()`.

EXAMPLE This example defines subclasses of `ObjectOutputStream` and `ObjectInputStream` that override `writeStreamHeader()` and `readStreamHeader()`, respectively, to add another verifier to check. In practice, a subclass might write some information in the header for verifying the integrity of the stream (such as a checksum) or passphrases/keys for decrypting the contents of the stream.

```
import java.io.*;
import java.util.Date;

class TestInputStream extends ObjectInputStream {
    TestInputStream(InputStream in)
        throws IOException, StreamCorruptedException {
        super(in);
    }

    protected void readStreamHeader()
```

```
        throws IOException, StreamCorruptedException {
        super.readStreamHeader();
        short my_magic = readShort();

        if (my_magic != TestOutputStream.TEST_MAGIC) {
            throw new StreamCorruptedException(
                "Stream not generated from TestOutputStream");
        }
    }
}

class TestOutputStream extends ObjectOutputStream {
    static final int TEST_MAGIC = 100;

    TestOutputStream(OutputStream out) throws IOException {
        super(out);
    }

    protected void writeStreamHeader() throws IOException {
        super.writeStreamHeader();
        writeShort(TEST_MAGIC);
    }
}

class Main {
    public static void main(String[] args) {
        try {
            // Write class out
            FileOutputStream f = new FileOutputStream("Date.ser");
            ObjectOutput out = new TestOutputStream(f);

            out.writeObject(new Date());
            out.flush();
            out.close();

            // Read it back
            FileInputStream f2 = new FileInputStream("Date.ser");

// Using a plain ObjectInputStream would throw StreamCorruptedException
//             ObjectInput in = new ObjectInputStream(f2);

            ObjectInput in = new TestInputStream(f2);
            Date d = (Date) in.readObject();
            in.close();

            System.out.println("answer: " + d);
        } catch (IOException e) {
            e.printStackTrace();
        } catch (ClassNotFoundException e) {
            e.printStackTrace();
        }
    }
}
```

readUnsignedByte()

PURPOSE Reads an unsigned 8-bit `byte` from this stream.

SYNTAX `public int readUnsignedByte() throws IOException`

DESCRIPTION This method reads a byte from this stream and returns it as the low-order byte in an `int`. The only difference between this method and `readByte()` is that this method returns the byte in an `int`, while `readByte()` returns the byte in a `byte`. Because `byte` is a signed type, the high-order bit will determine the sign of the value. When a byte is returned in an `int`, the high-order 3 bytes are unused (`0`). Consequently, the `int` value returned is always unsigned.

RETURNS An `int` containing the byte read.

EXCEPTIONS

`EOFException`
If end-of-file is reached while attempting to read from this stream.

`IOException`
If an IO error occurs while attempting to read from this stream.

SEE ALSO `DataInput.readUnsignedByte()`, `ObjectOutputStream.writeByte()`, `readByte()`.

EXAMPLE See the `DataInputStream` class example.

readUnsignedShort()

PURPOSE Reads an unsigned 16-bit `short` from this stream.

SYNTAX `public int readUnsignedShort() throws IOException`

DESCRIPTION This method reads 2 bytes from this stream and returns the unsigned integer value represented by the bits of those 2 bytes. The high-order byte is read first from this stream. The only difference between this method and `readShort()` is that this method returns the result as an `int`, while `readShort()` returns the result as a `short`.

Because `short` is a signed type, the high-order bit will determine the sign of the value. When a `short` is returned in an `int`, it occupies the low-order 2 bytes of the `int`; the high-order 2 bytes are unused (`0`). Consequently, the `int` value returned is always unsigned.

This method can be used only to read a `short` written by using `DataOutput.writeShort()`. It is not valid to call this method if `available()` returns `0`.

RETURNS An `int` containing the 16-bit `short` value read.

EXCEPTIONS

`EOFException`

If end-of-file is reached while attempting to read from this stream.

`IOException`

If an IO error occurs while attempting to read from this stream.

SEE ALSO `DataInput.readUnsignedShort()`, `ObjectOutputStream.writeShort()`, `readShort()`.

EXAMPLE See the `DataInputStream` class example.

readUTF()

PURPOSE Reads a Unicode string from this stream.

SYNTAX
```
public String readUTF() throws IOException
```

DESCRIPTION This method reads a Unicode string and returns it as a `String`.

UTF stands for Unicode Transfer Format. It is an encoding scheme for Unicode characters. The size of the string is specified in the encoded form. UTF strings are restricted to have an encoded length ≤ 65,535. See *The Java Language Specification, First Edition*, Section 22.1.15, for details about UTF.

RETURNS The Unicode string read as a `String`.

EXCEPTIONS

`EOFException`

If end-of-file is reached while attempting to read the string.

`IOException`

If an IO error occurs while attempting to read the string.

`UTFDataFormatException`

If the string being read is a malformed UTF string.

SEE ALSO `DataInput.readUTF()`, `ObjectOutputStream.writeUTF()`.

EXAMPLE See the `DataInputStream` class example.

registerValidation()

PURPOSE Registers an object to be validated.

SYNTAX
```
public synchronized void
    registerValidation(ObjectInputValidation obj, int prio)
    throws NotActiveException, InvalidObjectException
```

DESCRIPTION This method is called from within an object's `readObject()` method to register the object, `obj`, to call back in order to validate the object being read. The definition of whether an object is *valid* is determined by `obj`. Typically, `obj` needs access to the fields of the object in order to validate it. Hence, `obj` is usually either the object itself or an instance of an inner class that has access to the object's fields. However, this is not a requirement. A deserialized object can be validated by using any criteria, perhaps even in relation to other objects.

This stream maintains a prioritized queue of registered `ObjectInputValidation` objects. All objects being deserialized by this stream share the same prioritized queue. The `ObjectInputValidation` instance with the highest priority is invoked first.

A single invocation of `ObjectInputStream.readObject()` might cause a graph of objects to be deserialized. Validation is performed just before the top-level `ObjectInputStream.readObject()` invocation returns. Each object in the graph of objects with registered validators are validated at that point.

Note: In Java 1.1.4, once `obj` has been registered with this stream, it is never deregistered. In other words, it is never removed from the prioritized queue. Each top-level invocation of `readObject()` on this stream will invoke `obj.validateObject()`, even if the objects being read have nothing to do with the original class that defined the `readObject()` method from which `registerValidation()` was invoked.

PARAMETERS

`obj` The non-`null` object to receive the validation callback.

`prio` A number indicating the priority of this callback. The higher the value, the earlier it will be called amongst the registered callbacks. `0` is a good default.

EXCEPTIONS

`NotActiveException`
If this method is not called from within an object's `readObject()` method.

`InvalidObjectException`
If `obj` is `null`.

SEE ALSO `readObject()`.

EXAMPLE See the `ObjectInputValidation` class example.

resolveClass()

PURPOSE Loads the class represented by the class descriptor read from this object input stream.

SYNTAX

```
protected Class resolveClass(ObjectStreamClass desc) throws
   IOException, ClassNotFoundException
```

DESCRIPTION

When deserializing data into an object, `readObject()` requires the class of the corresponding object in order to do the deserialization. The identity of the class of the object is stored in the deserialized data in the form of a *class descriptor* (`ObjectStreamClass`). This descriptor is read by this stream and converted into an `ObjectStreamClass` instance.

`readObject()` calls `resolveClass()` in order to load the class of the object being deserialized.

`resolveClass()` loads the class identified by `desc`. By default, it loads the class with the class name `desc.getName()` by using the first non-`null` class loader up the execution stack from the method that called `readObject()`. If no non-`null` class loader is found, the default system class loader is used (see `ClassLoader`).

Each class used by deserialized objects in an `ObjectInputStream` is represented by a class descriptor in the stream. Each class descriptor is deserialized once, and the corresponding class is loaded only once. Later uses of the same class will use the class that has already been loaded. Hence, `resolveClass()` is invoked exactly once per class encountered in this object input stream. The exception to this rule is if a "reset" marker was encountered in the stream. In this case, the object/handle cache is cleared and thereafter `resolveClass()` will be invoked the first time each class descriptor is deserialized.

The returned `Class` instance must have the same class name and SUID as that of `desc`. Otherwise, `readObject()` throws an `InvalidClassException`. In a future version of the JDK, the restriction on class name will be removed in order to support classes that have different names (possibly in different packages) that are otherwise compatible.

A subclass of `ObjectInputStream` can override this method to use a different way of loading the class or to use a different class loader than the one selected by the default implementation. For example, when the object was serialized by using `ObjectOutputStream`, `annotateClass()` could have been called to add the byte codes of the class into the stream. Consequently, `resolveClass()` would read the byte codes from the object input stream in order to get an instance of the class instead of using a class loader identified from the execution stack.

PARAMETERS

`desc` The non-`null` class descriptor of the class to load.

RETURNS The non-`null` `Class` identified by `desc`.

EXCEPTIONS

`ClassNotFoundException`
If the class represented by `desc` cannot be found.

SEE ALSO `java.lang.ClassLoader`, `ObjectOutputStream.annotateClass()`, `ObjectStreamClass`.

EXAMPLE See `ObjectOutputStream.annotateClass()`.

resolveObject()

PURPOSE Replaces an object with another object during deserialization.

SYNTAX `protected Object resolveObject(Object obj) throws IOException`

DESCRIPTION When deserializing data into an object, `readObject()` allows a trusted subclass of `ObjectInputStream` to replace the object just deserialized with a compatible object. In Java 1.1, a trusted subclass is one that is loaded by using the default system class loader. For example, this mechanism could be used to replace an object with a newer implementation. `null` is an acceptable replacement. `readObject()` invokes `resolveObject()` in order to do the replacement.

`resolveObject()` method accepts the deserialized object `obj` and returns a replacement for it. If this object input stream has enabled the replacement of objects (see `enableResolveObject()`), `resolveObject()` is invoked after each object has been deserialized from this stream. The replacement replaces `obj` in the object/handle cache maintained by this stream.

A deserialized object appears in an object input stream only once; later occurrences of the object are represented by a *handle*. Hence, `resolveObject()` is invoked exactly once per deserialized object encountered in this stream. If a deserialized object has been replaced by another object, deserialization of the original object's handles also returns the replacement object (instead of the original deserialized object). Thus a deserialized object is replaced exactly once per stream, except when a "reset" marker is encountered in the stream. In this case, the object/handle cache is cleared and thereafter `resolveObject()` will be invoked the first time each object is deserialized.

The default implementation of `resolveObject()` returns `obj`. A subclass of `ObjectInputStream` can override this method to return another object. The overridden method, for example, might return a newer implementation or a subclass of `obj`. Since the replacement might be returned more than once by the `readObject()` method, the replacement must be compatible with all occurrences of `obj` in this object input stream. The replacement can be `null`, as long as that is compatible with all occurrences of `obj` (i.e., none of those occurrences required obj to be non-null). If the replacement is non-null, it must have all of the accessible fields and methods that obj had and be type-compatible with obj where it and its handles occur in the stream.

The subclass of ObjectInputStream that overrides resolveObject() controls which objects, if any, are replaced. If an object of an incompatible class is returned, a ClassCastException will be thrown from defaultReadObject() when the incompatible object is assigned to a field of a class.

PARAMETERS

obj The non-null object being replaced.

RETURNS The possibly null replacement object.

EXCEPTIONS

IOException

If an IO error is encountered while getting the replacement for obj.

SEE ALSO enableResolveObject().

EXAMPLE This example defines TestStream, a subclass of ObjectInputStream, which overrides resolveObject(), which, in turn, replaces instances of AncientClass with UpToDateClass.

```
import java.io.*;

class TestStream extends ObjectInputStream {
    TestStream(InputStream in) throws IOException, StreamCorruptedException {
        super(in);
        enableResolveObject(true);
    }

    protected Object resolveObject(Object obj) {
        if (obj instanceof AncientClass) {
            return new UpToDateClass(((AncientClass)obj).field1);
        }
        return obj; // otherwise just return original
    }
}

class AncientClass implements Serializable {
    int field1;

    AncientClass(int i) {
        field1 = i;
    }
    int doub() {
        System.out.println("Using addition");
        return (field1 += field1);
    }
}

class UpToDateClass extends AncientClass {
    UpToDateClass(int f) {
        super(f);
```

```
        }
        int doub() {
            System.out.println("Using shift");
            return (field1 <<= 1);
        }
    }

    class Main {
        public static void main(String[] args) {
            try {
                // Write class out
                FileOutputStream f = new FileOutputStream("Ancient.ser");
                ObjectOutput out = new ObjectOutputStream(f);

                AncientClass a = new AncientClass(10);
                System.out.println("first answer: " + a.doub());
                out.writeObject(a);
                out.flush();
                out.close();

                // Read it back
                FileInputStream f2 = new FileInputStream("Ancient.ser");
                TestStream in = new TestStream(f2);
                AncientClass aa = (AncientClass) in.readObject();
                in.close();

                System.out.println("after answer: " + aa.doub());
            } catch (IOException e) {
                e.printStackTrace();
            } catch (ClassNotFoundException e) {
                e.printStackTrace();
            }
        }
    }
```

skipBytes()

PURPOSE Skips the requested number of bytes of primitive data from this object input stream.

SYNTAX `public int skipBytes(int count) throws IOException`

DESCRIPTION This method skips `count` number of bytes from this object input stream. It blocks until all `count` number of bytes are skipped. It should be used only in conjunction with `OptionalDataException` or `available()` so as to skip primitive data. It should not be used to skip an arbitrary number of bytes from this stream.

PARAMETERS

`count` The number of bytes to be skipped.

RETURNS The actual number of bytes skipped.

EXCEPTIONS

`EOFException`

If end-of-file is reached while attempting to skip `count` number of bytes.

`IOException`

If an IO error occurs while attempting to skip `count` number of bytes.

SEE ALSO `available()`, `OptionalDataException`.

EXAMPLE This example finds all objects in a serialized stream by using `available()` and `skipBytes()`.

```
import java.io.*;
import java.util.*;

class Main {
    public static void main(String[] args) {

        try {
            // Produce serialization file
            FileOutputStream f = new FileOutputStream("test.ser");
            ObjectOutput out = new ObjectOutputStream(f);

            out.writeInt(100);
            out.writeByte(8);
            out.writeObject(new Date());
            out.writeDouble(10.3f);
            out.writeShort(99);
            out.writeObject("Java");
            out.writeObject(new Vector());
            out.close();

            // Read in serialization file
            FileInputStream f2 = new FileInputStream("test.ser");
            ObjectInputStream in = new ObjectInputStream(f2);

            while (true) {
                int primData = in.available();
                if (primData > 0) {
                    System.out.println("skipped " + in.skipBytes(primData));
                }
                System.out.println(in.readObject());
            }
        } catch (EOFException e) {
        } catch (IOException e) {
            e.printStackTrace();
        } catch (ClassNotFoundException e) {
            e.printStackTrace();
        }
    }
}
```

Output

```
> java Main
skipped: 5
Sat Dec 13 20:43:55 PST 1997
skipped: 10
Java
[]
```

ObjectInputValidation

ObjectInputValidation

A B C D E F G H I J K L M N O P Q R S T U V W X Y Z

Syntax

```
public interface ObjectInputValidation
```

Description

An object's `readObject()` method can invoke `ObjectInputStream.registerValidation()` in order to register *validator* objects to validate an object when it is deserialized. These validators are instances of `ObjectInputValidation`.

`ObjectInputStream` maintains a prioritized queue of registered validators. Validators for all objects being deserialized by an `ObjectOutputStream` instance share the same queue. The validator with the highest priority is invoked first.

Validation is performed by invoking the `validateObject()` method of a validator. The definition of whether an object is *valid* is determined by the validator. Typically, the validator needs access to the fields of the object in order to validate it. Consequently, the validator is usually either the object itself or an instance of an inner class that has access to the object's fields. However, this is not a requirement. A deserialized object can be validated using any criteria, perhaps even in relation to other objects.

A single invocation of `ObjectInputStream.readObject()` might cause a graph of objects to be deserialized. Validation is performed just before the top-level `ObjectInputStream.readObject()` invocation returns. Each object in the graph of objects with registered validators are validated.

Note: In Java 1.1.4, once a validator has been registered with an `ObjectInputStream` instance, it is never deregistered. Each invocation of `readObject()` on that stream will invoke the validator's `validateObject()` method.

MEMBER SUMMARY	
Validation Method	
`validateObject()`	Validates an object being deserialized.

See Also

`ObjectInputStream.registerValidation()`, `InvalidObjectException`.

Example

This example shows how `Class1.readObject()` calls `registerValidation()` to register the object itself in order to validate the deserialized object. The criteria used by this class is that both fields must be nonnegative.

```
import java.io.*;
import java.util.Date;

class Main {
    public static void main(String[] args) {
        try {
            // Write class out
            FileOutputStream f = new FileOutputStream("Class1.ser");
            ObjectOutput out = new ObjectOutputStream(f);

            Class1 c1 = new Class1(11, 22);
            out.writeObject(c1);
            out.writeObject(new Date());
            out.flush();
            out.close();

            // Read it back
            FileInputStream f2 = new FileInputStream("Class1.ser");
            ObjectInputStream in = new ObjectInputStream(f2);
            Class1 cc1 = (Class1) in.readObject();
            System.out.println("date: " + in.readObject());
            in.close();

            System.out.println(cc1.a + " " + cc1.b);
        } catch (IOException e) {
            e.printStackTrace();
        } catch (ClassNotFoundException e) {
            e.printStackTrace();
        }
    }
}

class Class1 implements Serializable, ObjectInputValidation {
    int a, b;

    public Class1(int aa, int bb) {
        a = aa;
        b = bb;
    }
    public void validateObject() throws InvalidObjectException {
        System.out.println("Validating object");
        if (a < 0 || b < 0) {
            throw new InvalidObjectException("Fields cannot be negative");
        }
    }
    private void readObject(ObjectInputStream in)
        throws IOException, ClassNotFoundException {
            in.registerValidation(this, 1);
            in.defaultReadObject();
    }
}
```

validateObject()

PURPOSE Validates an object being deserialized.

SYNTAX `public void validateObject() throws InvalidObjectException`

DESCRIPTION This method validates the object with which it has been registered. Different classes have different criteria for validation. Whether an object is valid is determined by the implementation of this method. If this method determines that the object is not valid, it throws an `InvalidObjectException`; otherwise, it just returns.

EXCEPTIONS

`InvalidObjectException`
If the validation of the object fails.

EXAMPLE See the class example.

ObjectOutput

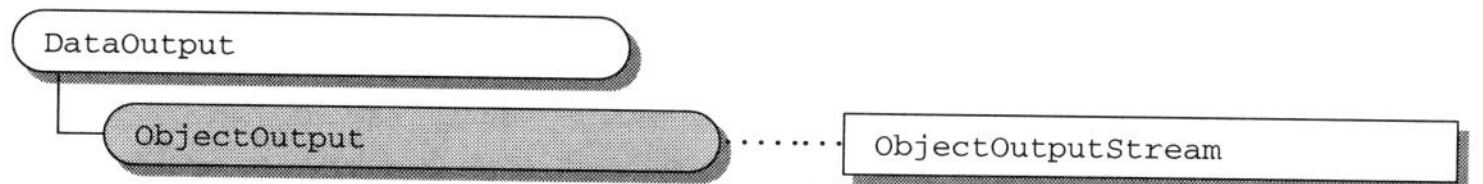

Syntax

```
public interface ObjectOutput extends DataOutput
```

Description

`ObjectOutput` is an interface that declares methods for writing serialized objects. `ObjectOutput` extends the `DataOutput` interface, which contains declarations for methods that write data of Java primitive types.

MEMBER SUMMARY

Output Methods	
`write()`	Writes one or more bytes to the `ObjectOutput` object.
`writeObject()`	Writes an object to the `ObjectOutput` object.
Object Methods	
`close()`	Closes the `ObjectOutput` object.
`flush()`	Flushes any buffered data the `ObjectOutput` object has.

See Also

`DataOutput`, `ObjectInput`, `ObjectOutputStream`.

Example

See `ObjectOutputStream`.

close()

PURPOSE Closes the `ObjectOutput` object.

SYNTAX `public void close() throws IOException`

DESCRIPTION This method releases any resources used by the `ObjectInput` instance. After the instance has been closed, invoking methods on it will throw a `IOException`.

EXCEPTIONS

`IOException`
If an IO error occurs while closing the `ObjectOutput` object.

EXAMPLE See `ObjectOutputStream.writeObject()`.

flush()

PURPOSE Flushes any buffered data the `ObjectOutput` object has.

SYNTAX `public void flush() throws IOException`

EXCEPTIONS

`IOException`
If an IO error occurs while flushing the `ObjectOutput` object.

EXAMPLE See `ObjectOutputStream.writeObject()`.

write()

PURPOSE Writes one or more bytes to the `ObjectOutput` object.

SYNTAX

```
public void write(int oneByte) throws IOException
public void write(byte buffer[]) throws IOException
public void write(byte buffer[], int offset, int count) throws
    IOException
```

DESCRIPTION The three forms of this method write bytes to the `ObjectOutput` object. The first form writes the low-order byte from `oneByte` to the object. The other two forms write `count` number of bytes from the `byte` array `buffer` starting at index `offset`. If `offset` and `count` are not specified, they default to `0` and `buffer.length` respectively.

PARAMETERS

`buffer` The non-`null` `byte` array containing data to be written.

A B C D E F G H I J K L M N O P Q R S T U V W X Y Z

count — The number of bytes from `buffer` to be written. 0 ≤ `count` ≤ `buffer.length-offset`.

offset — The index in `buffer` of the bytes to be written. 0 ≤ `offset` < `buffer.length`.

oneByte — The byte to be written. The low-order byte from `oneByte` is written.

EXCEPTIONS

`ArrayIndexOutOfBoundsException`
If `offset` or `count` is outside of the specified bounds.

`IOException`
If an IO error has occurred.

EXAMPLE — See the `OutputStream` class example.

writeObject()

PURPOSE — Writes an object to the `ObjectOutput` object.

SYNTAX

```
public void writeObject(Object obj) throws IOException
```

DESCRIPTION — This method blocks until `obj` has been written to the `ObjectOutput` object. The format and content of the data written to represent `obj` is determined by the implementation of the `ObjectOutput` object. For example, an `ObjectOutputStream` instance implements `writeObject()` by using the object's `writeExternal()`, `writeObject()`, or `defaultWriteObject()` method.

PARAMETERS

obj — The possibly `null` object to be written. If `null`, the representation for `null` is written to the `ObjectOutput` object.

EXCEPTIONS

`IOException`
If an IO error occurs while writing the object.

EXAMPLE — See the `Serializable` class example.

ObjectOutputStream

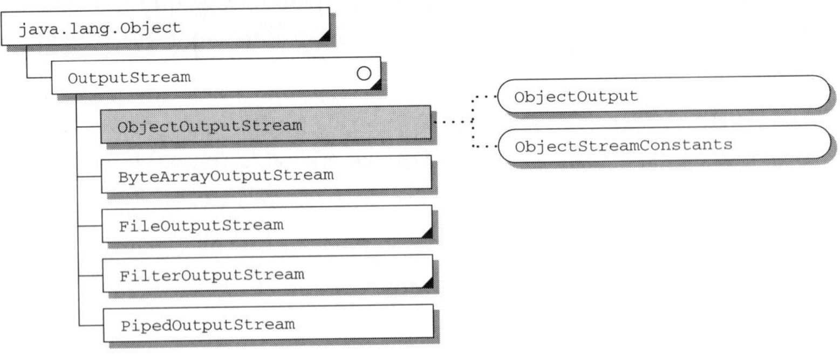

A B C D E F G H I J K L M N O P Q R S T U V W X Y Z

Syntax

```
public class ObjectOutputStream extends OutputStream implements ObjectOutput,
    ObjectStreamConstants
```
[1]

Description

The `ObjectOutputStream` class is used for serializing primitive data and objects (including arrays and strings) to an output stream. The serialized data can be read by a corresponding `ObjectInputStream`. See Figure 68.

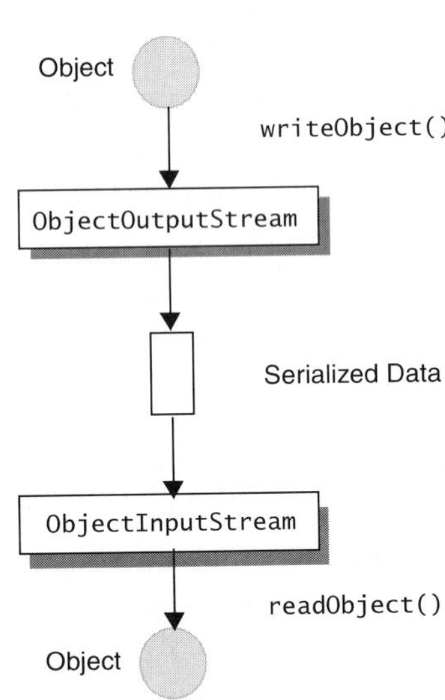

FIGURE 68: `ObjectInputStream` and `ObjectOutputStream`.

Usage

Classes that implement the `Serializable` or `Externalizable` interfaces can be serialized using `ObjectOutputStream.writeObject()` and deserialized using `ObjectInputStream.readObject()`.

For example, suppose `ClassX` is serializable:

```
public class ClassX implements Serializable
{
...
}
```

You can serialize an instance of `ClassX` to an `ObjectOutputStream` and then read it back using `ObjectInputStream`:

```
ObjectOutputStream out = ...;
out.writeObject(new ClassX());
```

1. The `ObjectStreamConstants` interface is not accessible outside of the `java.io` package. The interface contains declarations for various constants used in object serialization.

```
ObjectInputStream in = ...
ClassX obj = (ClassX) in.readObject();
```

Serialization

Primitive types are serialized using methods declared in the DataOutput interface. Strings,[1] arrays, and objects are serialized using writeObject(). If you serialize primitive data and objects to a stream, you must deserialize them in the same order in which they were written. For example, if the serialized stream was produced using the follow sequence of writes:

```
out.writeInt(ival);
out.writeByte(bval);
out.writeChar(ch);
out.writeObject("Java");
out.writeObject(new Date());
```

you must use the following read sequence to deserialize data from the serialized stream:

```
int ival = in.readInt();
byte bval = in.readByte();
char ch = in.readChar();
Object obj1 = in.readObject();
Object obj2 = in.readObject();
```

When an object is serialized, all of the objects that it references directly or indirectly are also serialized. If any object in that graph does not implement either the Serializable or Externalizable interfaces, a NotSerializableException is thrown. If an object's class has defined a writeObject() method, that method is used to serialize it. Otherwise, ObjectOutputStream.defaultWriteObject() is used. See Serializable for more information about the serialization and deserialization process.

If a class defines a writeObject() method, it is recommended that the method first write out the object's required data (using ObjectOutputStream.defaultWriteObject()). It should then write out any additional data—called *optional data*. Optional data may consists of primitive data and objects and is written out using methods in the ObjectOutputStream class.

ObjectOutputStream.writeObject() may be invoked recursively when an object being serialized references other objects that require serialization.

See http://java.sun.com/products/jdk/1.1/docs/guide/serialization/spec for complete details on how objects are serialized.

1. A string can be serialized either as an object by using writeObject() or as a UTF string by using writeUTF(). A string serialized as an object must be deserialized by using readObject(). A string serialized as an UTF string must be deserialized using readUTF(). A string serialized as an UTF string multiple times to the same stream is written out to the stream multiple times. In contrast, a string serialized as an object multiple times to the same stream has only one copy serialized; the other copies are represented via a handle. Default serialization writes strings as objects, so the only way a string is written as a UTF string is if it is explicitly written into the stream by using writeUTF().

A B C D E F G H I J K L M N O P Q R S T U V W X Y Z

Multiple Occurrences of the Same Object

The first time an object is serialized to an object output stream, its serialized data is written to the stream and a *handle* is generated for it. This object/handle pair is recorded in an *object/handle cache*. When the same object is serialized to the same stream, its handle is written to the stream. In this way, an object is serialized only once to the stream. There is no difference as far as the caller invoking `writeObject()` is concerned.

When an object output stream is *reset* (see the next section), the object/handle cache is cleared. As objects are later serialized to the stream, they and their handles are added to the cache and multiple occurrences of the same object are processed as described previously.

Resetting a Stream

You can *reset* an object output stream. This places a "reset" marker in the stream and clears the object/handle cache. When the reset marker is encountered in the serialized stream as it is being deserialized, the reader of the stream will clear its corresponding object/handle cache and start deserializing objects as if the stream was just opened.

Resetting a stream also affects object substitution (`replaceObject()`) and class annotation (`annotateClass()`) if these features have been enabled for this object output stream. These methods are invoked only once for the object or class being manipulated, except when the stream is reset. When the stream is reset, it is as if the stream was just opened. When the stream is deserialized, the reset marker also affects object and class substitution on the reader side (`ObjectInputStream.resolveObject()` and `ObjectInputStream.resolveClass()`).

The ability to reset an object output stream is important to an application that must maintain an open object output stream for a long period of time. An example of such an application is one that communicates with another application over the network using Remote Method Invocation (RMI). The reset allows serialized objects to be garbage-collected if they are no longer referred to by the application except via the reference in the object/handle cache. It also allows the application reading the serialized stream and reset marker to do the same. That is, it can clear its object/handle cache so that objects in it can be garbage-collected.

Customizations

An `ObjectOutputStream` can be subclassed to perform special processing. Such a customized stream must be read by a corresponding customized subclass of `ObjectInputStream`. For example, you can add additional header information when producing the serialized stream (such as checksums), process the special header when deserializing objects from the stream, and perform object substitution (i.e., replace an object being serialized with another object).

Class Information

When an object is serialized, the class for that object is recorded in the stream using a *class descriptor* (`ObjectStreamClass`). This class descriptor contains the class's fully qualified name and its Stream Unique Identifier (SUID). In addition, if the class implements `Serializable`, the class descriptor contains a list of the names and type names of the serializable fields of the class. In Java 1.1, the serializable fields of a class are all of its nontransient and nonstatic fields. If the class implements `Externalizable`, the class descriptor does not have this list. When that data is deserialized, the class descriptor must match that of the class loaded by the Java virtual machine that is performing the deserialization.

MEMBER SUMMARY

Constructor	
`ObjectOutputStream()`	Constructs an instance of `ObjectOutputStream`.
Method Used by a Class's writeObject()	
`defaultWriteObject()`	Writes the serializable fields of the class being serialized.
Stream Customization Methods	
`annotateClass()`	Writes information related to a class to this object output stream.
`enableReplaceObject()`	Enables/disables this object output stream to replace objects written to this stream.
`replaceObject()`	Replaces an object with another object during serialization.
`writeStreamHeader()`	Writes the stream header to the underlying output stream.
Stream Methods	
`close()`	Closes this object output stream.
`drain()`	Writes any buffered data to the underlying output stream.
`flush()`	Flushes this object output stream.
`reset()`	Resets the state of this object output stream.
ObjectOutput Methods	
`write()`	Writes one or more bytes to this object output stream.
`writeObject()`	Writes an object to this object output stream.
DataOutput Methods	
`writeBoolean()`	Writes a `boolean` to this object output stream.
`writeByte()`	Writes an 8-bit `byte` to this object output stream.
`writeBytes()`	Writes a string as a sequence of bytes to this object output stream.
`writeChar()`	Writes a 16-bit `char` to this object output stream.
`writeChars()`	Writes a string as a sequence of `char`s to this object output stream.
`writeDouble()`	Writes a 64-bit `double` to this object output stream.
`writeFloat()`	Writes a 32-bit `float` to this object output stream.
`writeInt()`	Writes a 32-bit `int` to this object output stream.
`writeLong()`	Writes a 64-bit `long` to this object output stream.
`writeShort()`	Writes a 16-bit `short` to this object output stream.
`writeUTF()`	Writes a string in UTF to this object output stream.

A B C D E F G H I J K L M N O P Q R S T U V W X Y Z

See Also

`Externalizable`, `ObjectInputStream`, `Serializable`.

Example

See `writeObject()`.

annotateClass()

PURPOSE Writes information related to a class to this object output stream.

SYNTAX

```
protected void annotateClass(Class cl) throws IOException
```

DESCRIPTION When `writeObject()` is serializing an object, it writes information related to the class of the object—its class descriptor (`ObjectStreamClass`)—into this object output stream. In addition, `writeObject()` calls `annotateClass()` to give its subclasses an opportunity to write other information related to the class.

For example, a subclass may override `annotateClass()` to write to this stream `cl`'s byte codes or a URL of the location of `cl`'s byte codes. If `annotateClass()` writes bytes to the stream, the `ObjectInputStream` class that deserializes the stream must override `resolveClass()` to read/consume the bytes written.

When an object is serialized to this object output stream, a class descriptor (`ObjectStreamClass`) corresponding to the object's class is also serialized to the stream. If there are multiple objects of the same class being serialized to this stream, the class descriptor is serialized only once. Subsequent occurrences of instances of the same class will use a handle to the serialized class descriptor. `annotateClass()` is invoked only when the class descriptor of a class is serialized. Hence, it is invoked only once for per class (i.e., it would not be invoked more than once for the same value of `cl`) until `reset()` is invoked on this stream. After this stream is reset, `annotateClass()` will be invoked again on `cl` if an instance of `cl` is again written to this stream.

`annotateClass()`, by default, does nothing.

PARAMETERS

`cl` The non-`null` class to annotate.

EXCEPTIONS

`IOException`
If an IO error occurs while writing class information for `cl`.

SEE ALSO `ObjectInputStream.resolveClass()`.

EXAMPLE This example shows the use of `ObjectInputStream.resolveClass()` and `annotateClass()`. `TestOutputStream` overrides `annotateClass()` and writes to the stream a file directory name of where class files are to be found. `TestInputStream` overrides `resolveClass()` to read the directory name from the stream and then uses `FileClassLoader` to load the class file. See the class example for `ClassLoader` for the source to `FileClassLoader`.

```
import java.io.*;
import java.util.Date;

class TestInputStream extends ObjectInputStream {
    TestInputStream(InputStream in)
        throws IOException, StreamCorruptedException {
        super(in);
    }

    protected Class resolveClass(ObjectStreamClass v)
        throws IOException, ClassNotFoundException {
            String classdir = readUTF();
            System.out.println("Loading class from directory " + classdir);
            ClassLoader cl = new FileClassLoader(classdir);
            return cl.loadClass(v.getName());
        }
}

class TestOutputStream extends ObjectOutputStream {
    String classdir;
    TestOutputStream(OutputStream out, String cd) throws IOException {
        super(out);
        classdir = cd;
    }

    protected void annotateClass(Class cl) throws IOException {
        System.out.println("Recording directory to load class " + classdir);
        writeUTF(classdir);
    }
}

class Main {
    public static void main(String[] args) {
        if (args.length != 1) {
            System.err.println("Usage: java Main <directory>");
            System.exit(-1);
        }
        try {
            // Write class out
            FileOutputStream f = new FileOutputStream("Class1.ser");
            ObjectOutput out = new TestOutputStream(f, args[0]);

            out.writeObject(new Class1());
            out.flush();
            out.close();

            // Read it back
            FileInputStream f2 = new FileInputStream("Class1.ser");

// Using a plain ObjectInputStream would throw StreamCorruptedException
```

```
//            ObjectInput in = new ObjectInputStream(f2);

            ObjectInput in = new TestInputStream(f2);
            Class1 c1 = (Class1) in.readObject();
            in.close();

            System.out.println("field1: " + c1.field1);
            System.out.println("field2: " + c1.field2);
            System.out.println("field3: " + c1.field3);
        } catch (IOException e) {
            e.printStackTrace();
        } catch (ClassNotFoundException e) {
            e.printStackTrace();
        }
    }
}

class Class1 implements Serializable {
    int field1;
    String field2;
    transient int field3;

    public Class1() {
        field1 = 10;
        field2 = "a string";
        field3 = -1;
    }
}
```

close()

PURPOSE Closes this object output stream.

SYNTAX `public void close() throws IOException`

DESCRIPTION This method writes any buffered output to the underlying output stream, flushes the stream, and then closes it.

EXCEPTIONS

`IOException`

If an I/O error occurs.

OVERRIDES `OutputStream.close()`.

SEE ALSO `drain()`, `flush()`.

EXAMPLE See `writeObject()`.

defaultWriteObject()

PURPOSE Writes the serializable fields of the class being serialized.

SYNTAX `public final void defaultWriteObject() throws IOException`

DESCRIPTION This method serializes and writes the serializable fields of the object being serialized to this object output stream. In Java 1.1, the serializable fields of a class are all of its nontransient and nonstatic fields. This method is invoked automatically when serializing an instance of a class that implements the `Serializable` interface, but it does not define a `writeObject()` method. It can also be invoked explicitly from inside an object's `writeObject()` method. In this case, `defaultWriteObject()` should be the first method that writes any data to this stream (see the *Serialization* section in the class description). If `defaultWriteObject()` is invoked from outside of `writeObject()`, a `NotActiveException` is thrown.

SEE ALSO `Serializable`.

EXAMPLE See `ObjectInputStream.defaultReadObject()`.

drain()

PURPOSE Writes any buffered data to the underlying output stream.

SYNTAX `protected void drain() throws IOException`

DESCRIPTION If there are any buffered data yet to be written to the underlying output stream, this method writes it out. Otherwise, this method does nothing.

EXCEPTIONS

`IOException`

If an IO error occurs while writing to the underlying output stream.

SEE ALSO `close()`, `flush()`.

enableReplaceObject()

PURPOSE Enables/disables this object output stream to replace objects written to this stream.

SYNTAX
```
protected final boolean enableReplaceObject(boolean enable)
   throws SecurityException
```

DESCRIPTION Before serializing an object to the underlying stream, `writeObject()` allows a subclass of `ObjectOutputStream` to replace the object with the value returned by `replaceObject()`. By default, `ObjectOutputStream` does not allow this replacement. A subclass of `ObjectOutputStream` must call `enableReplace-Object()` with `true` in order to allow this replacement. This method can be invoked only from an instance of a trusted `ObjectOutputStream` subclass. A trusted subclass is one that is loaded by using the default system class loader.

PARAMETERS

`enable` If `true`, allows objects written to this object output stream to be replaced. If `false`, objects written to this stream cannot be replaced.

RETURNS The previous setting before `enableReplaceObject()` was invoked. `true` if replacement was enabled; `false` otherwise.

EXCEPTIONS

`SecurityException`
If `enable` is `true` and this stream object was not loaded by using the default system class loader.

SEE ALSO `java.lang.ClassLoader`, `ObjectInputStream.enableResolveObject()`, `replaceObject()`.

EXAMPLE See `replaceObject()`.

flush()

PURPOSE Flushes this object output stream.

SYNTAX `public void flush() throws IOException`

DESCRIPTION This method calls `drain()` to write any buffered data to the underlying output stream and then flushes the stream.

EXCEPTIONS

`IOException`
If an IO error occurs while writing to or flushing the underlying output stream.

OVERRIDES `OutputStream.flush()`.

SEE ALSO `close()`, `drain()`.

EXAMPLE See `writeObject()`.

ObjectOutputStream()

PURPOSE Constructs an instance of `ObjectOutputStream`.

SYNTAX `public ObjectOutputStream(OutputStream out) throws IOException`

DESCRIPTION This constructor creates an instance of `ObjectOutputStream` that writes serialized data to the stream `out`. It writes the stream header (see `writeStreamHeader()`) to `out` and readies itself to accept objects and data to be serialized.

PARAMETERS

`out` The non-`null` output stream to which to write.

EXCEPTIONS

`IOException`

If an IO error occurs while writing to `out`.

SEE ALSO `ObjectInputStream.ObjectInputStream()`, `writeStreamHeader()`.

EXAMPLE See `writeObject()`.

replaceObject()

PURPOSE Replaces an object with another object during serialization.

SYNTAX `protected Object replaceObject(Object obj) throws IOException`

DESCRIPTION When serializing an object, `writeObject()` allows a trusted subclass of `ObjectOutputStream` to replace the object being serialized with another compatible object. A trusted subclass is one that is loaded by using the default system class loader. For example, this mechanism could be used to replace an object with a newer implementation. `writeObject()` invokes `replaceObject()` in order to do the replacement.

`replaceObject()` method accepts the object `obj` and returns a replacement for it. If this object output stream has enabled the replacement of objects (see `enableReplaceObject()`), `replaceObject()` is invoked before each object is to be serialized and written to the underlying output stream.

A serialized object appears in an object output stream only once; later occurrences of the object are represented by a *handle*. Hence, `replaceObject()` is invoke exactly once per serialized object written to this stream. If an object to be serialized has been replaced by another object, its handles in this stream will refer to the replacement. If `reset()` is invoked on the stream, `replaceObject()` will be invoked on `obj` again if `obj` is serialized after the reset.

The default implementation of `replaceObject()` returns `obj`. A subclass of `ObjectOutputStream` can override this method to return another object. The overridden method, for example, might return a newer implementation or a subclass of `obj`. If `obj` is written to the stream more than once, its replacement must be compatible with all occurrences of `obj`. The replacement can be `null`, as long as that is compatible with all occurrences of `obj` (i.e., none of those occurrences required `obj` to be non-`null`). If the replacement is non-`null`, it must have all of the accessible fields and methods that `obj` had and be type-compatible with `obj` where `obj` and its handles occur in the stream.

Note: In Java 1.1.4, returning `null` causes `ObjectOutputStream.writeObject()` to throw a `NullPointerException`.

The subclass of `ObjectOutputStream` controls which objects, if any, are replaced.

PARAMETERS

`obj` The non-`null` object to replace.

RETURNS The replacement object. Can be `null`.

EXCEPTIONS

`IOException`
If an IO error occurs.

SEE ALSO `enableReplaceObject()`, `ObjectInputStream.resolveObject()`.

EXAMPLE This example replaces instances of `TargetClass` with `NewClass`.

```
import java.io.*;

class TestStream extends ObjectOutputStream {
    TestStream(OutputStream out) throws IOException, StreamCorruptedException {
        super(out);
        enableReplaceObject(true);
    }

    protected Object replaceObject(Object obj) {
        if (obj instanceof TargetClass) {
            return new NewClass(((TargetClass)obj).field1);
        }
        return obj; // otherwise just return original
    }
}

class TargetClass implements Serializable {
    public int field1;

    TargetClass(int i) {
        field1 = i;
    }

    public String toString() {
        return (field1+"");
    }
}
```

```
class NewClass extends TargetClass {
    public int field2;
    NewClass(int i) {
        super(i);
        field2 = field1*2;
    }

    public String toString() {
        return ("field1: " + field1 + " field2: " + field2);
    }
}

class Main {
    public static void main(String[] args) {
        try {
            // Write class out
            FileOutputStream f = new FileOutputStream("Target.ser");
            ObjectOutputStream out = new TestStream(f);

            TargetClass a = new TargetClass(10);
            out.writeObject(a);
            out.flush();
            out.close();

            // Read it back
            FileInputStream f2 = new FileInputStream("Target.ser");
            ObjectInput in = new ObjectInputStream(f2);
            Object aa = in.readObject();
            in.close();

            System.out.println(aa);
        } catch (IOException e) {
            e.printStackTrace();
        } catch (ClassNotFoundException e) {
            e.printStackTrace();
        }
    }
}
```

reset()

PURPOSE Resets the state of this object output stream.

SYNTAX `public void reset() throws IOException`

DESCRIPTION As objects are written to this object output stream, this stream remembers the objects written and their classes so that multiple occurrences of an object or a class are serialized just once. Later occurrences use handles to refer to those objects already serialized.

`reset()` erases all state about previously serialized objects and classes. After a reset, writing an object that was serialized before the reset will cause the object to be serialized again. A "reset" marker is written to the underlying stream so that the corresponding `ObjectInputStream` will be reset at the same point. See the class description for more details.

EXCEPTIONS

`IOException`
If this stream is in the middle of serializing an object.

EXAMPLE This example serializes an instance of `Date` twice to one stream. It then serializes the same instance two times, separated by a reset. You can check the file sizes and contents to see that `Test2.ser` contains the serialized instance twice, whereas the `Test1.ser` contains the serialized instance only once.

```
import java.io.*;
import java.util.Date;

class Main {
    public static void main(String[] args) {
        try {
            // Write 2 instances of Date
            FileOutputStream f = new FileOutputStream("Test1.ser");
            ObjectOutputStream out = new ObjectOutputStream(f);

            Date d = new Date();
            out.writeObject(d);
            out.writeObject(d);
            out.flush();
            out.close();

            // Write 2 instances of Date, separated by reset()
            f = new FileOutputStream("Test2.ser");
            out = new ObjectOutputStream(f);

            out.writeObject(d);
            out.reset();
            out.writeObject(d);
            out.flush();
            out.close();
        } catch (IOException e) {
            e.printStackTrace();
        }
    }
}
```

write()

PURPOSE Writes one or more bytes to this object output stream.

SYNTAX
```
public void write(int oneByte) throws IOException
public void write(byte[] buffer) throws IOException
public void write(byte[] buffer, int offset, int count) throws
    IOException
```

DESCRIPTION The `write()` method writes the specified byte or bytes to this object output stream. The first form writes a single byte `oneByte` to this stream. Only the low-order byte of `oneByte` is used. The second and third forms write `count` bytes from the `byte` array `buffer` starting at index `offset` to this stream. If `offset` and `count` are not specified, they default to `0` and `buffer.length`, respectively.

PARAMETERS

`buffer` The non-`null` `byte` array containing data to be written.

`count` The number of bytes from `buffer` to be written. `0` ≤ `count` ≤ `buffer.length-offset`.

`offset` The index in `buffer` of the bytes to be written. `0` ≤ `offset` < `buffer.length`.

`oneByte` The byte to be written. The low-order byte from `oneByte` is written.

EXCEPTIONS

`ArrayIndexOutOfBoundsException`
If `count` or `offset` is outside of the specified bounds.

`IndexOutOfBoundsException`
If `count` < `0`.

`IOException`
If an IO error occurs while attempting to write to the stream.

OVERRIDES `OutputStream.write()`.

SEE ALSO `ObjectInputStream.readByte()`, `ObjectInputStream.readLine()`, `ObjectInputStream.readFully()`, `ObjectInputStream.readUnsignedByte()`, `writeByte()`, `writeBytes()`.

EXAMPLE See the `DataOutputStream` class example.

writeBoolean()

PURPOSE Writes a `boolean` to this object output stream.

SYNTAX `public void writeBoolean(boolean val) throws IOException`

DESCRIPTION This method writes the `boolean` value `val` to this object output stream. The output consists of a single byte whose value is `1` if `val` is `true` and `0` if `val` is `false`.

PARAMETERS

`val` The `boolean` value to be written.

EXCEPTIONS

`IOException`
If an IO error occurs while attempting to write to the stream.

SEE ALSO `DataOutput.writeBoolean()`, `ObjectInputStream.readBoolean()`.

EXAMPLE See the `DataOutputStream` class example.

A B C D E F G H I J K L M N O P Q R S T U V W X Y Z

writeByte()

PURPOSE Writes an 8-bit `byte` to this object output stream.

SYNTAX `public void writeByte(int val) throws IOException`

DESCRIPTION This method writes a `byte` to this object output stream. The output consists of a single byte whose value is the low-order byte of `val`.

PARAMETERS

`val` The `byte` value to be written.

EXCEPTIONS

`IOException`

If an IO error occurs while attempting to write to the stream.

SEE ALSO `DataOutput.writeByte()`, `ObjectInputStream.read()`, `ObjectInputStream.readByte()`, `ObjectInputStream.readFully()`, `ObjectInputStream.readLine()`, `ObjectInputStream.readUnsignedByte()`, `write()`.

EXAMPLE See the `DataOutputStream` class example.

writeBytes()

PURPOSE Writes a string as a sequence of bytes to this object output stream.

SYNTAX `public void writeBytes(String str) throws IOException`

DESCRIPTION This method writes the string `str` to this object output stream as a sequence of bytes (8 bits). Because a string consists of 16-bit Unicode `char` values, only the low-order 8 bits of each `char` are written; the high-order 8 bits are lost (and not written). Use `writeChar()` and `writeChars()` to write all 16 bits of a Unicode `char` or `char` string.

PARAMETERS

`str` The non-`null` string to be written.

EXCEPTIONS

`IOException`

If an IO error occurs while attempting to write to this stream.

SEE ALSO `DataOutput.writeBytes()`, `ObjectInputStream.read()`, `ObjectInputStream.readByte()`, `ObjectInputStream.readFully()`, `ObjectInputStream.readLine()`, `ObjectInputStream.readUnsignedByte()`, `write()`, `writeChar()`, `writeChars()`.

EXAMPLE See the `DataOutputStream` class example.

writeChar()

PURPOSE Writes a 16-bit `char` to this object output stream.

SYNTAX `public void writeChar(int val) throws IOException`

DESCRIPTION This method writes a 16-bit Unicode `char val` to this object output stream. Only the low-order 2 bytes of `val` are written; the high-order 2 bytes are ignored. The output consists of 2 bytes (high-order byte written first), which represent the Unicode value of `val`.

PARAMETERS

`val` The `char` value to be written.

EXCEPTIONS

`IOException`

If an IO error occurs while attempting to write to this stream.

SEE ALSO `BufferedWriter.write()`, `DataOutput.writeChar()`, `ObjectInputStream.readChar()`, `writeByte()`, `writeChars()`.

EXAMPLE See the `DataOutputStream` class example.

writeChars()

PURPOSE Writes a string as a sequence of `char`s to this object output stream.

SYNTAX `public void writeChars(String str) throws IOException`

DESCRIPTION This method writes the string `str` to this object output stream as a sequence of `chars` (16 bits). Each `char` written consists of 2 bytes (high-order byte written first), which represent its Unicode value.

PARAMETERS

`str` The non-`null` string to be written.

EXCEPTIONS

`IOException`

If an IO error occurs while attempting to write to this stream.

SEE ALSO `BufferedWriter.write()`, `DataOutput.writeChars()`, `ObjectInputStream.readChar()`, `writeChar()`, `writeBytes()`.

EXAMPLE See the `DataOutputStream` class example.

A B C D E F G H I J K L M N O P Q R S T U V W X Y Z

writeDouble()

PURPOSE Writes a 64-bit `double` to this object output stream.

SYNTAX `public void writeDouble(double val) throws IOException`

DESCRIPTION This method writes the `double` value `val` to this object output stream. The output generated consists of 8 bytes in the format produced by `Double.doubleToLongBits()`.

PARAMETERS
`val` The `double` value to be written.

EXCEPTIONS
`IOException`
If an IO error occurs while attempting to write to this stream.

SEE ALSO `DataOutput.writeDouble()`, `ObjectInputStream.readDouble()`, `java.lang.Double.doubleToLongBits()`.

EXAMPLE See the `DataOutputStream` class example.

writeFloat()

PURPOSE Writes a 32-bit `float` to this object output stream.

SYNTAX `public void writeFloat(float val) throws IOException`

DESCRIPTION This method writes the `float` value `val` to this object output stream. The output generated consists of 4 bytes in the format produced by `Float.floatToIntBits()`.

PARAMETERS
`val` The `float` value to be written.

EXCEPTIONS
`IOException`
If an IO error occurs while attempting to write.

SEE ALSO `DataOutput.writeFloat()`, `ObjectInputStream.readFloat()`, `java.lang.Float.floatToIntBits()`.

EXAMPLE See the `DataOutputStream` class example.

writeInt()

PURPOSE Writes a 32-bit `int` to this object output stream.

SYNTAX `public void writeInt(int val) throws IOException`

DESCRIPTION This method writes the `int` value `val` to this object output stream. The output generated consists of 4 bytes, highest-to-lowest byte order, that represent the value of `val`.

PARAMETERS

`val` The `int` value to be written.

EXCEPTIONS

`IOException`

If an IO error occurs while attempting to write to this stream.

SEE ALSO `DataOutput.writeInt()`, `ObjectInputStream.readInt()`.

EXAMPLE See the `DataOutputStream` class example.

writeLong()

PURPOSE Writes a 64-bit `long` to this object output stream.

SYNTAX `public void writeLong(long val) throws IOException`

DESCRIPTION This method writes the `int` value `val` to this object output stream. The output generated consists of 8 bytes, highest-to-lowest byte order, that represent the value of `val`.

PARAMETERS

`val` The `long` value to be written.

EXCEPTIONS

`IOException`

If an IO error occurs while attempting to write to this stream.

SEE ALSO `DataOutput.writeLong()`, `ObjectInputStream.readLong()`.

EXAMPLE See the `DataOutputStream` class example.

writeObject()

PURPOSE Writes an object to this object output stream.

SYNTAX `public final void writeObject(Object obj) throws IOException`

DESCRIPTION This method serializes `obj` and writes it to the underlying output stream. If `obj`'s fields contain references to other objects, those objects and their references are also serialized and written to the underlying output stream such that the entire graph of objects rooted at `obj` are serialized. The object is serialized using one of the following methods of the class:

- `writeExternal()` if the class implements `Externalizable`
- `defaultWriteObject()` if the class implements `Serializable` but doesn't define a `writeObject()` method
- `writeObject()` method if the class implements `Serializable` and does define a `writeObject()` method

If this object output stream has enabled the replacement of objects read from it, `replaceObject()` is invoked with `obj` before it is serialized.

If an exception is encountered during `writeObject()`, the validity of the entire object output stream is suspect and should not be used further.

A B C D E F G H I J K L M N O P Q R S T U V W X Y Z

PARAMETERS

`obj` The possibly `null` object to write. If `null`, `null` is written to the stream.

EXCEPTIONS

`InvalidClassException`
If the class of `obj` (or the class of one of the objects in the graph of objects rooted at `obj`) is an array of an unknown primitive type, or if the class's fields do not match those of the object being serialized.

`IOException`
If an IO error occurs while writing to the underlying output stream.

`NotSerializableException`
If `obj` or one of the objects that it references does not implement the `Serializable` (or `Externalizable`) interface.

EXAMPLE

This example writes out a `String`, a `Date` instance, `null`, and an `int` array using an `ObjectOutputStream`. It then reads these objects back using an `ObjectInputStream`.

```
import java.io.*;
import java.util.Date;

class Main {
    public static void main(String[] args) {
        try {
            // Write class out
            FileOutputStream f = new FileOutputStream("Test.ser");
            ObjectOutput out = new ObjectOutputStream(f);

            out.writeObject("Java Class Libraries");
            out.writeObject(new Date());
            out.writeObject(null);
            int[] ints = {1, 2, 3, 4, 5};
            out.writeObject(ints);
            out.flush();
            out.close();

            // Read it back
            FileInputStream f2 = new FileInputStream("Test.ser");
            ObjectInputStream in = new ObjectInputStream(f2);
            while (true) {
```

```
                try {
                    Object obj = in.readObject();
                    System.out.println(obj);
                } catch (EOFException e) {
                    System.out.println("done");
                    break;
                }
            }
            in.close();
        } catch (IOException e) {
            e.printStackTrace();
        } catch (ClassNotFoundException e) {
            e.printStackTrace();
        }
    }
}
```


writeShort()

PURPOSE
Writes a 16-bit `short` to this object output stream.

SYNTAX
`public void writeShort(int val) throws IOException`

DESCRIPTION
This method writes the `short` value `val` to this object output stream (the low-order 2 bytes of `val` are used). The output generated consists of 2 bytes, with the high-order byte written first.

PARAMETERS

`val`
The value to be written. The 2 low-order bytes of `val` are used as the value of the `short` to be written.

EXCEPTIONS

`IOException`
If an IO error occurs while attempting to write to this stream.

SEE ALSO
`DataOutput.writeShort()`, `ObjectInputStream.readShort()`, `ObjectInputStream.readUnsignedShort()`.

EXAMPLE
See the `DataOutputStream` class example.

writeStreamHeader()

PURPOSE
Writes the stream header to the underlying output stream.

SYNTAX
`protected void writeStreamHeader() throws IOException`

DESCRIPTION
The header consists of a *magic number*—a constant used to mark all serialized streams—and the version number of the serialization algorithm used. When the stream data is read by an `ObjectInputStream` instance, the header is

checked to ensure that the stream has not been corrupted and that both the input and output streams are using the same algorithm.

A subclass can override this method to write additional header information, such as checksums.

EXCEPTIONS

`IOException`
If an IO error occurs while writing to the underlying output stream.

SEE ALSO `ObjectInputStream.readStreamHeader()`.

EXAMPLE See `ObjectInputStream.readStreamHeader()`.

writeUTF()

PURPOSE Writes a string in UTF to this object output stream.

SYNTAX `public void writeUTF(String str) throws IOException`

DESCRIPTION This method writes a string `str` to this object output stream in UTF. UTF stands for Unicode Transfer Format, an encoding scheme for Unicode characters. UTF strings are restricted to have an encoded length ≤ 65535. See *The Java Language Specification, First Edition*, Section 22.2.14 for details on UTF.

PARAMETERS

`str` The non-`null` string to be written.

EXCEPTIONS

`IOException`
If an IO error occurs while attempting to write to this stream.

`UTFDataFormatException`
If the resulting UTF data size would exceed 65,535 bytes.

SEE ALSO `DataOutput.writeUTF()`, `ObjectInputStream.readUTF()`, `writeBytes()`, `writeChars()`.

EXAMPLE See the `ObjectOutputStream` class example.

ObjectStreamClass

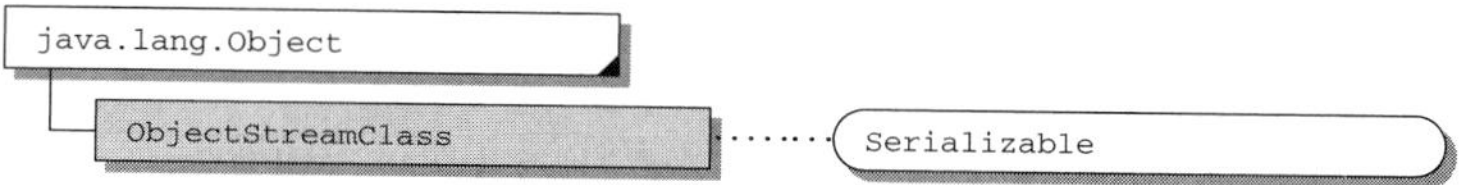

A B C D E F G H I J K L M N O P Q R S T U V W X Y Z

Syntax

```
public class ObjectStreamClass implements java.io.Serializable
```

Description

An `ObjectStreamClass` is a descriptor that describes a serializable class. It consists of the class's name and its Stream Unique Identifier (SUID). In addition, if the class implements `Serializable`, the class descriptor contains a list of the names and type names of the serializable fields of the class. In Java 1.1, the serializable fields of a class are all of its nontransient and nonstatic fields. If the class implements `Externalizable`, the class descriptor does not have this list. This descriptor is stored with a serialized object to identify the class of the serialized object.

`ObjectStreamClass` is itself serializable. If there is more than one object of the same class in a serialized stream, only one occurrence of the `ObjectStreamClass` for that class is serialized. Subsequent occurrences use a handle to the first occurrence, just as multiple occurrences of other serializable objects are handled. The exception is when the stream has been reset; see `ObjectOutputStream.reset()` for details.

Usage

`ObjectStreamClass` is used by the `ObjectInputStream` and `ObjectOutputStream` classes when they serialize and deserialize data.

Stream Unique Identifier

A class's SUID identifies the serialization format that instances of this class (and implementations that evolve from it) will have. You can explicitly declare a class's SUID by using the `serialver` command and use its output to declare a `serialVersionUID` field in the class. For example, the `Date` class has the following declaration:

```
private static final long serialVersionUID = 7523967970034938905L;
```

If a class has a `serialVersionUID` field, the class's corresponding `ObjectStreamClass` will have the value of this field. If a class does not have such a field, its SUID is generated by the Java virtual machine using the algorithm described in the Object Serialization specification at `http://java.sun.com/products/jdk/1.1/docs/guide/serialization/spec`.

See Also

`java.lang.Class`, `ObjectInputStream`, `ObjectOutputStream`.

MEMBER SUMMARY	
Lookup Method	
`lookup()`	Retrieves the descriptor for a class.
Get Methods	
`forClass()`	Retrieves the `Class` instance described by this descriptor.
`getName()`	Retrieves the name of the class described by this descriptor.
`getSerialVersionUID()`	Retrieves the SUID of the class described by this descriptor.
Object Method	
`toString()`	Generates the string representation of this descriptor.

Example

See method examples.

forClass()

PURPOSE Retrieves the `Class` instance described by this descriptor.

SYNTAX `public Class forClass()`

DESCRIPTION The class descriptor returned by `lookup()` always has an associated `Class` instance. So invoking `forClass()` on such an instance will always be non-`null`. The result of `forClass()` is usually `null` only when an object is in the midst of being deserialized from the stream and its `Class` has not been loaded yet.

RETURNS The `Class` instance that this descriptor represents. `null` if the class of this descriptor has not been set yet.

SEE ALSO `java.lang.Class`, `java.lang.Class.forName()`.

EXAMPLE

```
import java.io.ObjectStreamClass;
import java.io.Serializable;

class Main {
    public static void main(String[] args) {
        ObjectStreamClass desc1 = ObjectStreamClass.lookup(Class1.class);

        System.out.println(desc1.forClass());          // class Class1
        System.out.println(desc1.getName());           // Class1
        System.out.println(desc1.getSerialVersionUID());// -7143511112820278689
    }
}
```

getName()

PURPOSE Retrieves the name of the class described by this descriptor.

SYNTAX `public String getName()`

RETURNS The non-`null` fully qualified name of the class.

SEE ALSO `getSerialVersionUID()`, `ObjectInputStream.readObject()`, `ObjectInputStream.resolveClass()`.

EXAMPLE See `forClass()`.

getSerialVersionUID()

PURPOSE Retrieves the SUID of the class described by this descriptor.

SYNTAX `public long getSerialVersionUID()`

DESCRIPTION See the class description for more details on the SUID.

RETURNS The SUID of the class described by this descriptor.

SEE ALSO `getName()`.

EXAMPLE See `forClass()`.

lookup()

PURPOSE Retrieves the descriptor for a class.

SYNTAX `public static ObjectStreamClass lookup(Class cl)`

DESCRIPTION This method returns the descriptor for the class `cl` for a class loaded by the Java virtual machine. If `cl` does not implement `Serializable` or `Externalizable`, it returns `null`.

PARAMETERS

`cl` The non-`null` class for which to get the descriptor.

RETURNS The descriptor for `cl`; `null` if `cl` does not implement `Serializable` or `Externalizable`.

EXAMPLE

```
import java.io.ObjectStreamClass;
import java.io.Serializable;

class Main {
    public static void main(String[] args) {
        System.out.println(ObjectStreamClass.lookup(java.lang.String.class));
        System.out.println(ObjectStreamClass.lookup(Class1.class));
```

```
            System.out.println(ObjectStreamClass.lookup(Class2.class)); // null
        }
    }

    class Class1 implements Serializable {
        int field1;
        String field2;
        transient int field3;

        public Class1() {
            field1 = 10;
            field2 = "a string";
            field3 = -1;
        }
    }

    class Class2 {
        int fieldx;
    }
```

Output

```
> java Main
java.lang.String: static final long serialVersionUID = -6849794470754667710L;
Class1: static final long serialVersionUID = -7143511112820278689L;
null
```

toString()

PURPOSE Generates the string representation of this descriptor.

SYNTAX `public String toString()`

DESCRIPTION The string representation consists of the class's name and its SUID in the form that can be used within a Java program. This string is the same output produced by the `serialver` command.

RETURNS A non-`null` string describing this `ObjectStreamClass`.

OVERRIDES `java.lang.Object.toString()`.

EXAMPLE

```
import java.io.ObjectStreamClass;
import java.io.Serializable;

class Main {
    public static void main(String[] args) {
        System.out.println(ObjectStreamClass.lookup(java.util.Date.class));
        System.out.println(ObjectStreamClass.lookup(Class1.class));
    }
}

class Class1 implements Serializable {
    int field1;
    String field2;
```

```
    transient int field3;

    public Class1() {
        field1 = 10;
        field2 = "a string";
        field3 = -1;
    }
}
```

Output

```
> java Main
java.util.Date: static final long serialVersionUID = 7523967970034938905L;
Class1: static final long serialVersionUID = -7143511112820278689L;
```

java.io

ObjectStreamException

A B C D E F G H I J K L M N O P Q R S T U V W X Y Z

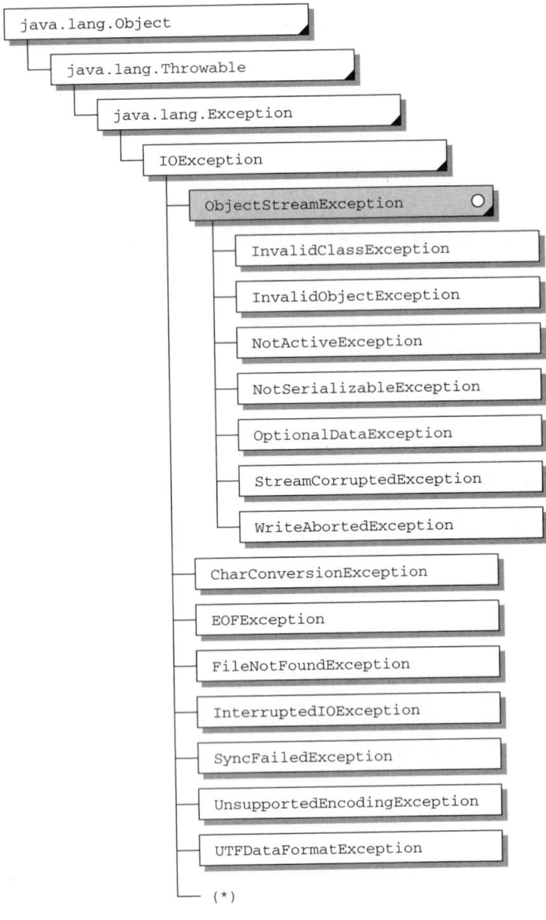

(*) 7 classes from other packages not shown.

Syntax

```
public abstract class ObjectStreamException extends IOException
```

Description

`ObjectStreamException` is the superclass of all serialization-related exceptions. Typically, when any of the `ObjectStreamException` subclasses is thrown, the state of the object input or output stream is such that it probably cannot be used further.

MEMBER SUMMARY	
Constructor	
`ObjectStreamException()`	Constructs an instance of `ObjectStreamException`.

See Also

`InvalidObjectException`, `NotActiveException`, `NotSerializableException`, `OptionalDataException`, `StreamCorruptedException`, `WriteAbortedException`.

Example

See the subclasses for examples.

ObjectStreamException()

PURPOSE Constructs an instance of `ObjectStreamException`.

SYNTAX

```
protected ObjectStreamException()
protected ObjectStreamException(String msg)
```

DESCRIPTION The two forms of this constructor construct an instance of `ObjectStream-Exception`. An optional string `msg` can be supplied to give further details about the exception. For example `msg` may be a class name that indicates the class of the object that had problems being serialized/deserialized. If `msg` is not supplied, it defaults to `null`.

PARAMETERS

`msg` A possibly `null` string containing a detail message.

SEE ALSO `java.lang.Throwable.getMessage()`.

Observable

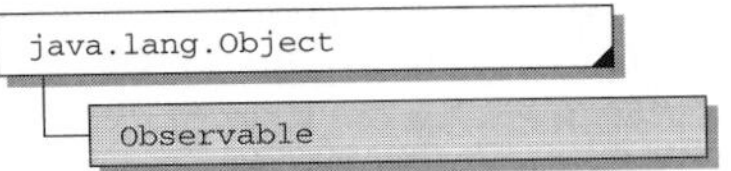

Syntax

```
public class Observable
```

Description

An *observable* is an object that holds some data. An *observer* is an object that monitors changes to the data in an observable object. You can associate a set of observers with an observable object (see Figure 69(a)). When a change is made to this observable object (see Figure 69(b)), the set of observers are notified of the change (see Figure 69(c)). Typically, a change in this observable object results in some state changes in, or action by, the observers. Each observer must implement the `Observer` interface, but it otherwise is unrestricted as to its implementation. You can have observers of different subclasses observing the same observable object.

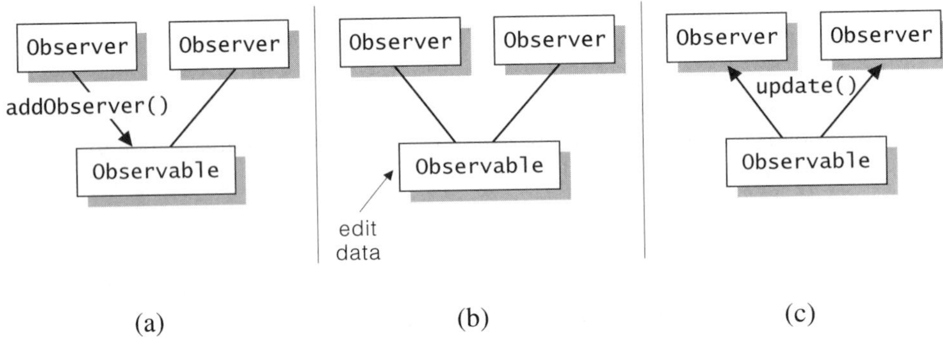

FIGURE 69: Observable and Observer Objects.

The observable object must be a subclass of the `Observable` class. An example of an observable object is the balance of a bank account. Observers of that observable could be an overdraft monitor, a financial advising tool, and the account owner's beeper. Whenever the balance is updated, you notify these three objects of the change (perhaps including the account's delta as part of the arguments passed to notify these observers).

An Observable's Changed State

Each observable object has a state that records whether this object has changed. This state is either "changed" or "unchanged" and is set using `setChanged()` or `clearChanged()`, respectively. The typical sequence of steps are as follows:

1. Make changes to the data of an observable object.
2. Call `setChanged()` on the object to indicate that it has changed.
3. Notify observers of the change (using `notifyObservers()`), thereby automatically calling `clearChanged()`.

MEMBER SUMMARY	
Constructor	
`Observer()`	Creates a `Observable` instance.
Observer Management Methods	
`addObserver()`	Adds an observer for this observable.
`countObservers()`	Determines the number of observers observing this observable.
`deleteObserver()`	Deletes an observer for this observable.
`deleteObservers()`	Deletes all observers for this observable.
Observable Status Change Methods	
`clearChanged()`	Records that this observable has not changed.
`hasChanged()`	Determines whether this observable has changed.
`notifyObservers()`	Notifies observers that this observable has changed.
`setChanged()`	Records that this observable has changed.

A B C D E F G H I J K L M N O P Q R S T U V W X Y Z

See Also

`Observer`.

Example

This example contains one observable—(`ColorObservable`)—and two observers, `Statistician` and `Echoer`, that track objects as their colors change. `Statistician` maintains an array that counts the number of times an object has been accessed. `Echoer` prints out information about the change that has been made. The example in `addObserver()` shows how these observers are added and used.

```
import java.util.Observer;
import java.util.Observable;

// Observer that counts number of times the Integer 'arg' has been accessed
class Statistician implements Observer {
    private int[] counts;
    Statistician(int array_size) {
        counts = new int[array_size];
    }
    public void update(Observable o, Object arg) {
        Integer int_obj = (Integer)arg;
        if (int_obj.intValue() < counts.length)
            ++counts[int_obj.intValue()];
```

```
        }
        public void report() {
            System.out.println("Record of changes: ");
            for (int i = 0; i < counts.length; i++)
                System.out.println(ColorObservable.colorName(i) + ": " + counts[i]);
        }
    }

    // Observer that prints out arg each time that it is accessed
    class Echoer implements Observer {
        int current_color;
        public void update(Observable o, Object arg) {
            int new_color = ((Integer)arg).intValue();
            System.out.println("Changing from " +
                                   ColorObservable.colorName(current_color) +
                                   " to " +
                                   ColorObservable.colorName(new_color));
            current_color = new_color;
        }
    }

    class ColorObservable extends Observable {
        public static String colorName(int i) {
            switch (i) {
            case 1: return ("Red");
            case 0: return ("White");
            case 2: return ("Blue");
            default: return (null);
                }
        }
        public void changeColor(int i) {
            setChanged();
            notifyObservers(new Integer(i));
            clearChanged(); // not necessary; notifyObservers() already clears it
        }
    }
```

addObserver()

PURPOSE Adds an observer for this observable.

SYNTAX `public synchronized void addObserver(Observer obs)`

DESCRIPTION This method adds the observer `obs` as an observer for this observable. If there are already observers for this observable, `obs` is added to the list of observers. `obs` is notified of changes in this observable.

PARAMETERS

`obs` The non-`null` observer to add.

SEE ALSO `deleteObserver()`, `notifyObservers()`.

EXAMPLE This example uses the classes in the `Observable` and `Observer` classes examples. It first creates the observable (`colors`) and then creates and adds the observers (`Statistician` and `Echoer`) for it. After performing some changes to the observable item, it prints a summary and then removes first one, and then all, of the observers.

```
import java.util.Observable;
import java.util.Observer;

class Main {
    final static int white = 0;
    final static int red = 1;
    final static int blue = 2;

    public static void main(String[] args) {
        ColorObservable colors = new ColorObservable();
        Statistician counter = new Statistician(3);

        // Assign Observers
        colors.addObserver(counter);
        colors.addObserver(new Echoer());
        System.out.println("Number of observers: " + colors.countObservers());

        // Make changes to Observable
        colors.changeColor(blue);
        colors.changeColor(white);
        colors.changeColor(red);
        colors.changeColor(blue);

        counter.report();

        // Remove one Observer
        colors.deleteObserver(counter);
        System.out.println("Number of observers: " + colors.countObservers());
        // Remove all Observers
        colors.deleteObservers();
        System.out.println("Number of observers: " + colors.countObservers());
    }
}
```

A B C D E F G H I J K L M N O P Q R S T U V W X Y Z

clearChanged()

PURPOSE Records that this observable has not changed.

SYNTAX `protected synchronized void clearChanged()`

DESCRIPTION This method clears the changed state recorded for this observable. If this observable was recorded earlier as having been changed, this method resets that state to "unchanged."

This method is the inverse of `setChanged()`.

SEE ALSO `hasChanged()`, `setChanged()`.

EXAMPLE See the class example.

A B C D E F G H I J K L M N **O** P Q R S T U V W X Y Z

countObservers()

PURPOSE Determines the number of observers for this observable.

SYNTAX `public synchronized int countObservers()`

RETURNS The number of observers observing this observable.

SEE ALSO `addObserver()`, `deleteObserver()`.

EXAMPLE See `addObserver()`.

deleteObserver()

PURPOSE Deletes an observer for this observable.

SYNTAX `public synchronized void deleteObserver(Observer obs)`

DESCRIPTION This method deletes the observer `obs` from the observers observing this observable. This method does nothing if `obs` is not one of the observers for this observable.

This method is the inverse of `addObserver()`.

PARAMETERS

`obs` The non-`null` observer to delete.

SEE ALSO `addObserver()`, `deleteObservers()`.

EXAMPLE See `addObserver()`.

deleteObservers()

PURPOSE Deletes all observers for this observable.

SYNTAX `public synchronized void deleteObservers()`

SEE ALSO `deleteObserver()`.

EXAMPLE See `addObserver()`.

hasChanged()

PURPOSE Determines whether this observable has changed.

SYNTAX `public synchronized boolean hasChanged()`

DESCRIPTION An observable's changed state is set and cleared using `setChanged()` and `clearChanged()`, respectively. `hasChanged()` returns this observable's change state. It returns `true` if the observable has changed and `false` if the observable has not changed.

RETURNS `true` if this observable has changed; `false` if it has not changed.

SEE ALSO `clearChanged()`, `setChanged()`.

EXAMPLE See the class example.

A B C D E F G H I J K L M N O P Q R S T U V W X Y Z

notifyObservers()

PURPOSE Notifies observers that this observable has changed.

SYNTAX
```
public void notifyObservers()
public void notifyObservers(Object arg)
```

DESCRIPTION If this observable has changed, this method notifies its observers of the change and the changed state of this observable is cleared. The object `arg` is passed to each observer as part of the notification process. If `arg` is not specified, it defaults to `null`.

If this observable has not changed, this method does nothing.

PARAMETERS

`arg` The possibly `null` argument to be passed to the observers when notifying them.

SEE ALSO `clearChanged()`, `hasChanged()`, `Observer.update()`, `setChanged()`.

EXAMPLE See the class example.

setChanged()

PURPOSE Records that this observable has changed.

SYNTAX
```
protected synchronized void setChanged()
```

DESCRIPTION This method is the inverse of `clearChanged()`.

SEE ALSO `clearChanged()`, `hasChanged()`, `notifyObservers()`.

EXAMPLE See the class example.

Observer

Observer

A B C D E F G H I J K L M N O P Q R S T U V W X Y Z

Syntax

```
public interface Observer
```

Description

An *observable* is an object that holds some data. An *observer* is an object that monitors changes to the data in an observable object. You can associate a set of observers with an observable object (see Figure 70(a)). When a change is made to this observable object (see Figure 70(b)), the set of observers are notified of the change (see Figure 70(c)). Typically, a change in this observable object results in some state changes in, or action by, the observers. Each observer must implement the `Observer` interface, but it otherwise is unrestricted as to its implementation. You can have observers of different subclasses observing the same observable object.

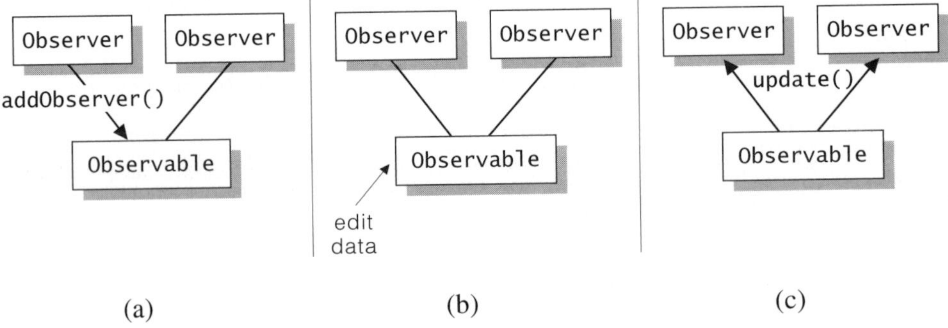

FIGURE 70: Observable and Observer Objects.

An example of an observable object is the balance of a bank account. Observers of that observable could be an overdraft monitor, a financial advising tool, and the account owner's beeper. Whenever the balance is updated, you notify these three objects of the change (perhaps including the account's delta as part of the arguments passed to notify these observers). Doing this will cause the `update()` method of each observer to be invoked to react to the change. The overdraft monitor object (which is an observer) will check whether the change in the account caused the new balance to fall below zero, and if so, it will take action to automatically transfer funds to cover the overdraft.

MEMBER SUMMARY	
Observer Method	
`update()`	Updates this observer using the supplied information.

A B C D E F G H I J K L M N O P Q R S T U V W X Y Z

See Also

`Observable`.

Example

This example implements a class for walking a directory of files. The `FileWalker` class uses the `Observer` interface and the `Observable` class to notify observers each time it encounters a file. To use the `FileWalker` class, you must implement the `Observer` interface and implement the `update()` method.

The main program walks the directory specified on the command line and prints all of the files in that directory tree. If the `-d` option is supplied, the names of directories are also printed.

```
import java.io.*;
import java.util.*;
import java.util.zip.*;

class Main implements Observer {
    Main(File dir, boolean includeDirectories) {
        FileWalker fw = new FileWalker();

        fw.addObserver(this);
        fw.walk(dir, includeDirectories);
    }

    // Simply print out the name of the file.
    public void update(Observable o, Object arg) {
        File f = (File)arg;
        try {
            System.out.println(f.getCanonicalPath());
        } catch (IOException e) {
            e.printStackTrace();
        }
    }

    public static void main(String[] args) {
        if (args.length < 1 || args.length > 2) {
            System.err.println("Usage: java Main <directory> [-d]");
            System.exit(1);
        }
        boolean includeDirectories = args.length == 2 && args[1].equals("-d");
        new Main(new File(args[0]), includeDirectories);
    }
}

class FileWalker extends Observable {
    // If includeDirectories is false, the walker does not notify the observers
```

```
    // when it encounters a directory. Encountered files are always reported.
    void walk(File dir, boolean includeDirectories) {
        if (dir.isDirectory()) {
            if (includeDirectories) {
                setChanged();
                notifyObservers(dir);
            }
            String[] filenames = dir.list();

            // Recursively walk all subdirectories.
            if (filenames != null) {
                for (int i=0; i<filenames.length; i++) {
                    walk(new File(dir, filenames[i]), includeDirectories);
                }
            }
        } else {
            setChanged();
            notifyObservers(dir);
        }
    }
}
```

update()

PURPOSE Updates this observer using the supplied information.

SYNTAX `void update(Observable observed, Object arg)`

DESCRIPTION This method updates this observer, which is observing the object `observed`. This observer is notified that `observed` has changed and that `arg` is the argument that accompanies this notification. Each class that implements the `Observer` interface must supply an implementation for this method.

PARAMETERS

`arg` The possibly `null` argument to supply to this observer when updating it.

`observed` The non-`null` observed object that has changed.

SEE ALSO `Observable.notifyObservers()`, `Observable.setChanged()`.

EXAMPLE See the class example.

OptionalDataException

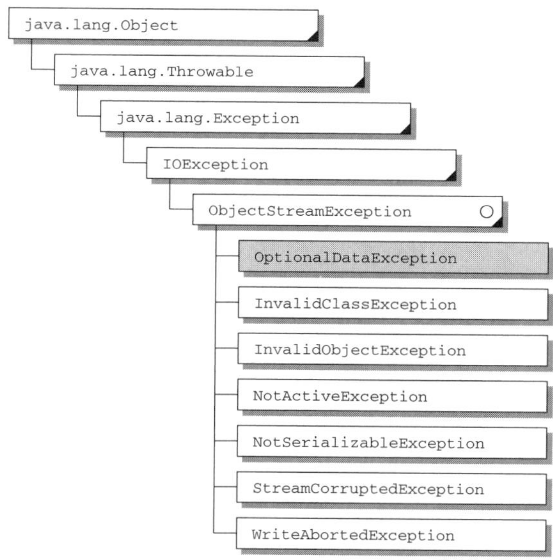

Syntax

```
public class OptionalDataException extends ObjectStreamException
```

Description

A `OptionalDataException` is thrown by `readObject()` when it encounters serialized primitive data instead of a serialized object.

Object serialization uses this exception to skip data written by an evolved version of `writeObject()` that an older version of `readObject()` does not know exists. A program can use this exception to find all of the objects in an object input stream (see the example).

Note that the `OptionalDataException` class has only constructors that are accessible within the `java.io` package. It does not have a constructor that a class outside of that package can use.

MEMBER SUMMARY	
Fields	
`eof`	Indicates whether there is more primitive data available.
`length`	Holds the number of bytes of primitive data.

See Also

`ObjectInputStream.available()`, `ObjectInputStream.readObject()`, `ObjectInputStream.skipBytes()`.

Example

This example uses `OptionalDataException` to read all of the serialized objects from an object input stream.

```
import java.io.*;
import java.util.*;

class Main {
    public static void main(String[] args) {

        try {
            // Produce serialization file
            FileOutputStream f = new FileOutputStream("test.ser");
            ObjectOutput out = new ObjectOutputStream(f);

            out.writeInt(100);
            out.writeByte(8);
            out.writeObject(new Date());
            out.writeDouble(10.3f);
            out.writeShort(99);
            out.writeObject("Java");
            out.writeObject(new Vector());
            out.close();

            // Read in serialization file
            FileInputStream f2 = new FileInputStream("test.ser");
            ObjectInputStream in = new ObjectInputStream(f2);

            while (true) {
                try {
                    System.out.println(in.readObject());
                                // 1st time: Sat Dec 13 20:43:55 PST 1997
                                // 2nd time: Java
                                // 3rd time: []
                } catch (OptionalDataException ode) {
                    if (ode.eof) {
                        in.close();
                        break;
                    }
                    // Skip primitive data
                    in.skipBytes(ode.length);
                } catch (EOFException e) {
                    in.close();
                    break;
                }
            }
        } catch (IOException e) {
            e.printStackTrace();
        } catch (ClassNotFoundException e) {
            e.printStackTrace();
        }
    }
}
```

eof

PURPOSE Indicates whether there is more primitive data available.

SYNTAX `public boolean eof`

DESCRIPTION If `eof` is `true`, it means that there is no more data in the buffered part of the object input stream.

EXAMPLE See the class example.

length

PURPOSE Holds the number of bytes of primitive data.

SYNTAX `public int length`

DESCRIPTION This field is set to the number of bytes of primitive data that are found in the object input stream at the point at which bytes for a serialized object are expected. This value can be passed to `ObjectInputString.skipBytes()` to skip this block of primitive data to find the next object in the stream.

EXAMPLE See the class example.

java.lang
OutOfMemoryError

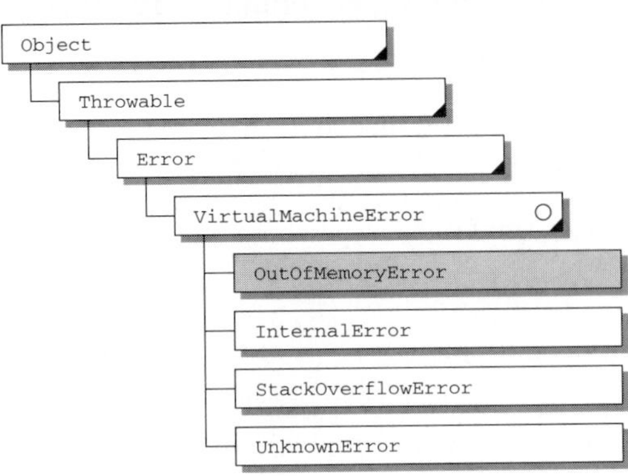

A B C D E F G H I J K L M N **O** P Q R S T U V W X Y Z

Syntax

```
public class OutOfMemoryError extends VirtualMachineError
```

Description

`OutOfMemoryError` is an unrecoverable error raised by the Java virtual machine when no more memory is available for continuing the execution of the program. It should not be caught or declared in the `throws` clause of a method.

MEMBER SUMMARY	
Constructor	
`OutOfMemoryError()`	Constructs an `OutOfMemoryError` instance.

See Also

`Error`, `VirtualMachineError`.

OutOfMemoryError()

PURPOSE
Constructs an `OutOfMemoryError` instance.

SYNTAX
```
public OutOfMemoryError()
public OutOfMemoryError(String msg)
```

DESCRIPTION
The two forms of this constructor constructs an instance of `OutOfMemoryError`. An optional string `msg` can be supplied that describes this particular instance of the error. If `msg` is not supplied, it defaults to `null`.

PARAMETERS

`msg` A possibly `null` string that gives details about this error.

SEE ALSO
`Throwable.getMessage()`.

OutputStream

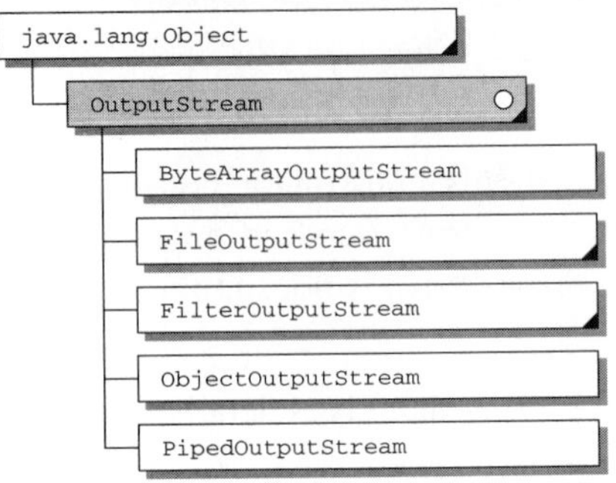

A B C D E F G H I J K L M N O P Q R S T U V W X Y Z

Syntax

```
public abstract class OutputStream
```

Description

The `OutputStream` class is the superclass of all byte output streams. It provides basic output methods for writing bytes to an output stream.

Usage

Subclasses of `OutputStream` override some or all of these basic methods for implementing their particular type of output stream. Figure 71 shows that you can either write directly to a subclass of `OutputStream` or write to an output stream through filters.

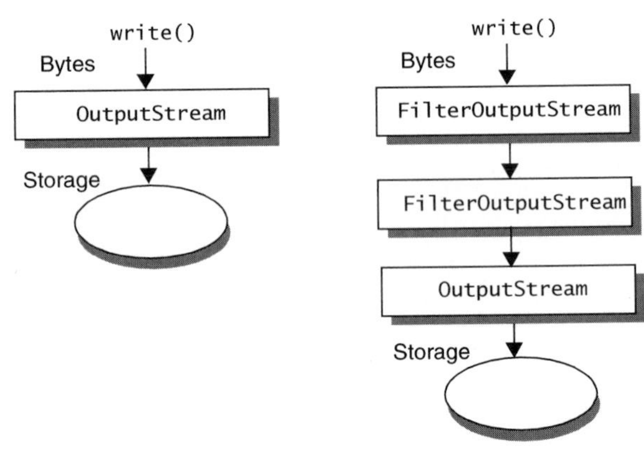

FIGURE 71: `OutputStream` and `FilterOutputStream`.

OutputStream versus Writer

`OutputStream` is meant for byte streams. Its `write()` methods writes bytes (0–255). `Writer` is the superclass of all character-oriented output streams. You should use `Writer` and its subclass when creating character streams.

If you need to translate between character streams and byte streams, use `OutputStreamWriter`. `OutputStreamWriter` translates characters into their byte encodings using either a specified or default character-to-byte encoding.

MEMBER SUMMARY

Output Method

`write()`	Writes bytes to this output stream.

Stream Methods

`close()`	Closes this output stream.
`flush()`	Flushes any buffered bytes from this output stream.

See Also

`InputStream`, `IOException`, `OutputStreamWriter`, `Writer`.

Example

This example shows an `echo()` method that takes input from an input stream and writes the bytes read directly to an output stream.

```
import java.io.*;

class Main {
    // reads input from 'in' and writes the bytes out to 'out'
    public static void echo(InputStream in, OutputStream out) {
        try {
            int c;
            while((c = in.read()) > -1)
                out.write(c);
            out.flush();                    // flush output

            in.close();                     // close streams
            out.close();
        } catch (IOException e) {
            e.printStackTrace();
        }
    }
    public static void main(String[] args) {
        try {
            InputStream in;
            if (args.length == 0)
                in = System.in;
            else
                in = new FileInputStream(args[0]);
            echo(in, System.out);
        } catch (IOException e) {
            e.printStackTrace();
        }
    }
}
```

A B C D E F G H I J K L M N O P Q R S T U V W X Y Z

close()

PURPOSE Closes this output stream.

SYNTAX `public void close() throws IOException`

DESCRIPTION This method closes this output stream. The default implementation does nothing.

Subclasses of `OutputStream` should override this method to first flush the stream and then release any resources (especially system resources) used by this output stream, such as file descriptors and network connections. Once the stream has been closed, invoking methods on it should throw an `IOException`.

EXCEPTIONS

`IOException`

If an IO error occurred.

EXAMPLE See the class example.

flush()

PURPOSE Flushes any buffered bytes from this output stream.

SYNTAX `public void flush() throws IOException`

DESCRIPTION Some output streams buffer the bytes written to them. `flush()` writes out any buffered bytes. The default implementation of `flush()` does nothing.

EXCEPTIONS

`IOException`

If an IO error occurred.

EXAMPLE See the class example.

write()

PURPOSE Writes bytes to this output stream.

SYNTAX

```
public void write(int oneByte) throws IOException
public void write(byte[] buffer) throws IOException
public void write(byte[] buffer, int offset, int count) throws
   IOException
```

DESCRIPTION The three forms of this method write bytes to this output stream. The first form is an abstract method whose implementation is supplied by the subclasses of `OutputStream`. It writes the lowest-order byte from `oneByte` to this output stream. The other two forms are implemented using this first form and consequently should usually be overridden to be more efficient than performing writes a byte at a time. The second form writes `buffer.length` number of bytes from the `byte` array `buffer` to this output stream. The third form writes `count` number of bytes from the `byte` array `buffer`, starting at index `offset`, to this output stream.

A B C D E F G H I J K L M N O P Q R S T U V W X Y Z

PARAMETERS

`buffer`	The non-`null` `byte` array containing the bytes to be written.
`count`	The number of bytes to write. `0` ≤ `count` ≤ `buffer.length-offset`.
`offset`	The index in `buffer` at which to start getting bytes to be written. `0` ≤ `offset` < `buffer.length`.
`oneByte`	The byte to be written.

EXCEPTIONS

`ArrayIndexOutOfBoundsException`

If `count` or `offset` is outside of the specified bounds.

`IOException`

If an IO error occurred while attempting to write.

EXAMPLE

This example reimplements the `echo()` method in the class example. It writes the bytes into a buffer and then, when the buffer becomes full, writes the buffer to the output stream.

```
public static void echo(InputStream in, OutputStream out) {
    try {
        int c, i = 0;
        byte[] buffer = new byte[1024]; // buffer for bytes
        while((c = in.read()) > -1) {
            if (i < buffer.length)
                buffer[i++] = (byte)c;  // get lowest order byte
            else {
                out.write(buffer);
                out.flush();            // flush output
                i = 0;                  // reset
            }
        }
        // write remaining bytes
        if (i > 0) {
            out.write(buffer, 0, i);
        }
        in.close();                     // close streams
        out.close();
    } catch (IOException e) {
        e.printStackTrace();
    }
}
```

java.io

OutputStreamWriter

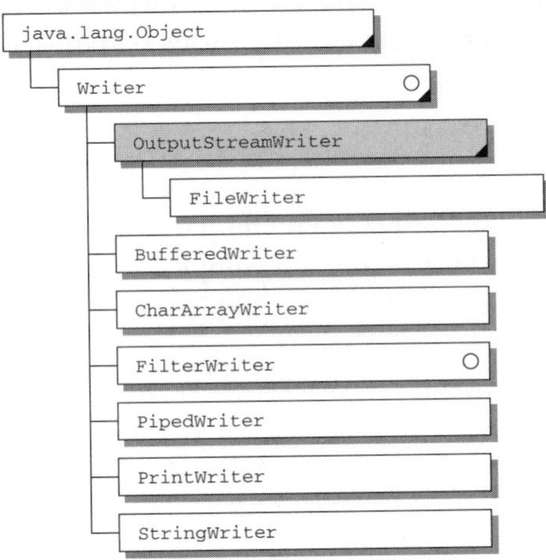

A B C D E F G H I J K L M N O P Q R S T U V W X Y Z

Syntax

```
public class OutputStreamWriter extends Writer
```

Description

The `OutputStreamWriter` class is used to convert a character output stream into a byte output stream.

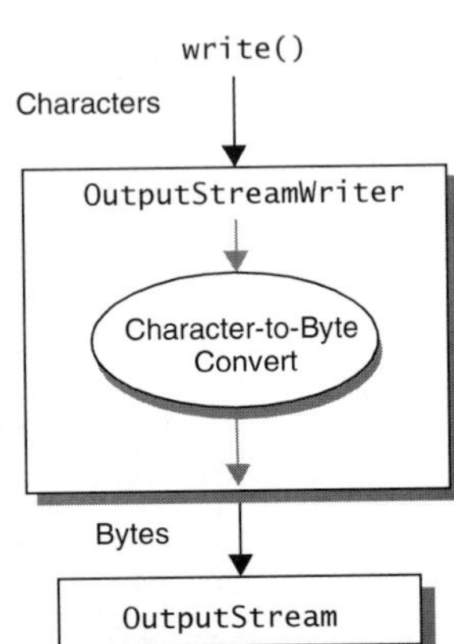

FIGURE 72: **`OutputStreamWriter.`**

Usage

You use an output stream writer by first creating an instance of it for a byte output stream. You can then write to the writer using the `Writer` methods. See Figure 72.

The following example writes characters to a file using UTF-8 encoding. The characters are translated into bytes using the converter corresponding to the "UTF8" encoding identifier.

```
OutputStreamWriter out = new OutputStreamWriter(
    new FileOutputStream("outputfile", "UTF8"));
out.write("This is a test");
```

Specifying the Byte Encoding to Use

The conversion of Unicode characters to its byte encoding is determined by the encoding specified implicitly or explicitly when the output stream writer is created. When you create the output stream writer, you specify the byte encoding using an *encoding identifier.* The encoding identifier is used to select the character-to-byte converter. See `String.getBytes()` for a description of the encoding identifiers.

Instead of explicitly specifying an encoding, you can create an output stream writer that uses the platform-dependent default encoding by using `OutputStreamWriter's` public constructor that takes no parameters. In the JDK 1.1, this default encoding is identified by the `file.encoding` system property. If this system property is not defined, the default encoding identifier is "8859_1" (ISO-Latin-1). If the converter (class) for the default encoding identifier is not found, an ASCII encoding is used.

Mechanics of the Character-to-Byte Conversion

When characters are written to an output stream writer, they are converted into their corresponding byte encoding and stored in a large internal buffer (8192 bytes). The encoding may represent a single character as one or more bytes. When the internal buffer becomes full or when `flush()` is invoked on this writer, the contents of the buffer are written to the underlying byte output stream.

Each time characters are written to the output stream writer, the conversion takes place. It is usually more efficient for a converter to convert a large sequence of characters than a large number of small sequences. To avoid having the application worry about how many characters to write to an output stream writer in order to be more efficient, you can use a `BufferedWriter` as a filter writer for `OutputStreamWriter`.

MEMBER SUMMARY

Constructor	
`OutputStreamWriter()`	Constructs an `OutputStreamWriter` instance.
Output Method	
`write()`	Writes one or more characters to this writer.
Stream Methods	
`close()`	Closes this writer.
`flush()`	Flushes this writer.
Character Encoding Method	
`getEncoding()`	Retrieves the string identifying the encoding used for this writer.

See Also

`BufferedWriter`, `InputStreamReader`, `OutputStream`, `String.getBytes()`, `Writer`.

Example

This program accepts from the command line an encoding identifier and a output filename. It creates an `OutputStreamWriter` using the encoding identifier for the output file and writes a message to it. If no converter is found for the encoding identifier, it throws `UnsupportedEncodingException`. For a list of encoding identifiers to try, see `String.getBytes()`.

A B C D E F G H I J K L M N O P Q R S T U V W X Y Z

```
import java.io.*;

class Main {
    public static void main(String[] args) {
        if(args.length != 2) {
            System.err.println("Usage: java Main <enc> <outputfile>");
        }
        try {
            BufferedWriter out = new BufferedWriter(new OutputStreamWriter(
                new FileOutputStream(args[1]), args[0]));

            out.write("This is a test");
            out.newLine();
            out.write('H');
            char[] buf = {'e', 'l', 'l', 'o'};
            out.write(buf);
            out.newLine();

            out.flush(); // for illustration only; close() will flush
            out.close();
        } catch (UnsupportedEncodingException e) {
            e.printStackTrace();
        } catch (IOException e) {
            e.printStackTrace();
        }
    }
}
```

close()

PURPOSE Closes this writer.

SYNTAX `public void close() throws IOException`

DESCRIPTION This method closes this writer. It first flushes its internal buffer and the underlying byte output stream. It then closes the byte output stream and releases resources—the converter and the buffer—used for the character-to-byte conversions.

Once this writer has been closed, you can no longer write to it or get its encoding. This method is idempotent; that is, you can invoke it many times but only the first invocation has any effect.

EXCEPTIONS

`IOException`

If an IO error occurs while closing this writer.

OVERRIDES `Writer.close()`.

SEE ALSO `flush()`.

EXAMPLE See the class example.

flush()

PURPOSE Flushes this writer.

SYNTAX `public void flush() throws IOException`

DESCRIPTION This writer maintains an internal buffer in which it stores bytes that have been converted from characters but not yet written to the underlying byte output stream. This internal buffer's contents are written out when the buffer gets full or when `flush()` is invoked on this writer.

This method flushes this writer by flushing its internal buffer and then flushing the underlying byte output stream.

EXCEPTIONS

`IOException`

If an IO error occurs.

OVERRIDES `Writer.flush()`.

EXAMPLE See the class example.

getEncoding()

PURPOSE Retrieves the string identifying the encoding used for this writer.

SYNTAX `public String getEncoding()`

DESCRIPTION When this writer was created, either it was created with an encoding identifier specifying the converter to use or the encoding was unspecified and a default was chosen (see the class description). The encoding identifier determines how characters written to this writer are converted into bytes to be written to the underlying byte output stream. See `String.getBytes()` for details on this encoding identifier.

This method returns the string that identifies the encoding scheme being used for this writer.

RETURNS A string identifying the encoding scheme used by this writer. It is `null` if this writer has been closed.

SEE ALSO `java.lang.String.getBytes()`.

EXAMPLE

```
import java.io.*;

class Main {
    public static void main(String[] args) {
        if (args.length != 1) {
            System.err.println("Usage: java Main <outputfile>");
            System.exit(-1);
        }
        try {
            OutputStreamWriter o1 =
                new OutputStreamWriter(new FileOutputStream(args[0]), "UTF8");
            OutputStreamWriter o2 = new OutputStreamWriter(System.out);

            System.out.println("o1 encoding: " + o1.getEncoding()); // UTF8
            System.out.println("o2 encoding: " + o2.getEncoding()); // 8859_1
            o1.close();
            o2.close();
        } catch (IOException e) {
            e.printStackTrace();
        }
    }
}
```

OutputStreamWriter()

PURPOSE Constructs an `OutputStreamWriter` instance.

SYNTAX

```
public OutputStreamWriter(OutputStream out)
public OutputStreamWriter(OutputStream out, String enc) throws
   UnsupportedEncodingException
```

DESCRIPTION There are two forms of the constructor for `OutputStreamWriter`. The first form creates an instance of `OutputStreamWriter` that converts characters written to it into their byte encoding using the default character-to-byte converter (see the class description).

The second form uses the converter specified by `enc` to convert characters written to the newly created writer into their byte encodings. See `String.getBytes()` for details on `enc`.

The converted bytes are written to the byte output stream `out`.

PARAMETERS

`enc` The non-`null` string identifying the encoding to use when converting characters into bytes.

`out` The non-`null` output stream to write the bytes.

EXCEPTIONS

`UnsupportedEncodingException`
If the encoding specified by `enc` is not supported

SEE ALSO `java.lang.String.getBytes()`.

EXAMPLE See the class example.

write()

A B C D E F G H I J K L M N O P Q R S T U V W X Y Z

PURPOSE Writes one or more characters to this writer.

SYNTAX

```
public void write(int oneChar) throws IOException
public void write(char[] buf, int offset, int count) throws
   IOException
public void write(String str, int offset, int count) throws
   IOException
```

DESCRIPTION This method writes characters to this writer. The first form writes a single character—the low-order 2 bytes of `oneChar`—to this writer. The second form writes `count` number of characters from the `char` buffer `buf` starting at index `offset` to this writer. The third form writes `count` number of characters from the string `str` starting at index `offset` to this writer.

When these characters are written to this writer, they are converted into their corresponding byte encoding (as specified in the constructor) and stored in an internal buffer. When the buffer becomes full or when `flush()` is invoked on this writer, the contents of the buffer are written to the underlying byte output stream.

PARAMETERS

`buf` The non-`null` `char` array containing the characters to be written.

`count` The number of characters to write. `0` ≤ `count` ≤ `buf.length-offset` (or `0` ≤ `count` ≤ `str.length()-offset`).

`offset` The index in `buf` or `str` at which to start fetching the characters to be written. `0` ≤ `offset` < `buf.length` or `0` ≤ `offset` < `str.length()`.

`oneChar` The low-order 2 bytes of `oneChar` are written to this writer.

`str` The non-`null` string containing the characters to be written.

EXCEPTIONS

`ArrayIndexOutOfBoundsException`
If `count` or `offset` is outside of the specified bounds.

`CharConversionException`
If the internal buffer being used for the conversion is too small and consequently, the characters cannot be converted properly.

`IOException`
If an IO error occurs

EXAMPLE See the class example.

ParseException

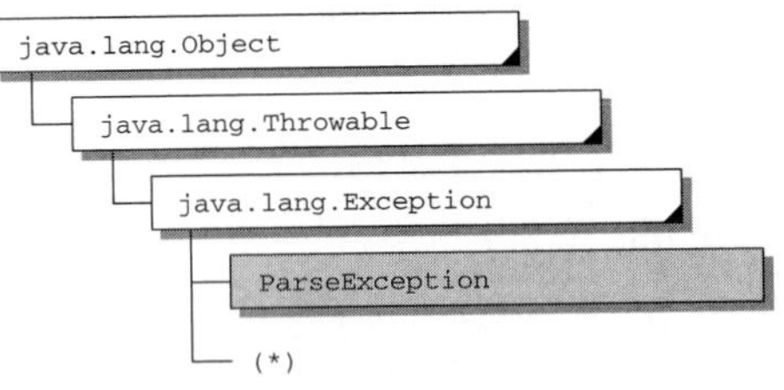

(*) 28 classes from other packages not shown.

Syntax

```
public class ParseException extends Exception
```

Description

`ParseException` is an exception that is thrown when an unexpected error has been encountered while parsing a string.

MEMBER SUMMARY	
Constructor	
`ParseException()`	Constructs a `ParseException` instance with the specified detail message and offset.
Getter Method	
`getErrorOffset()`	Retrieves the position in the string where the error occurred.

See Also

`Exception`, `Format`, `FieldPosition`.

Example

This example parses a short date passed in on the command line. To execute this example, pass in a short date string on the command line, such as `java Main 1/1/98`. In this example, `1/1/98` is a properly formed short date that is parsed to a `Date` object. A `ParseException` is thrown if the string to be parsed is of the wrong form. For example, `Jan-1-98` throws a parse exception because the short date requires the month to be an integer and forward slashes (/) to be the separators.

```
import java.text.*;
import java.io.*;
import java.util.*;

class Main {

    // Create a date format.
    static DateFormat dateForm = DateFormat.getDateInstance(DateFormat.SHORT);

    Main (String str) {
        // Print out original text passed in.
    System.out.println("String: " + str);

        // Parse the text for a short date.
        parseDate(str);
    }

    static void parseDate(String str) {
        int beginParseIndex;
        int endParseIndex;
        Date d = null;

        // Parse the string for a date.
        try {
            d = dateForm.parse(str);
        } catch (ParseException pe) {
           System.out.println("Parse error at offset: " + pe.getErrorOffset());
        }

        // Format the date to a string for printout.
        if (d != null) {
            System.out.println("\nParsed the string for the short date:");
            System.out.print("Date:   ");
            System.out.println(dateForm.format(d));
        }
    }

    public static void main(String[] args) {

        // Accept a date string as an argument
        if (args.length != 1) {
            System.err.println("This program parses text for dates");
            System.err.println("Usage: java Main <shortdate>");
            System.exit(1);
        }

        new Main(new String(args[0]));
    }
}
```

Output

```
> java Main Jan-1-98
String: Jan-1-98
Parse error at offset: 0
```

ParseException()

PURPOSE Constructs a `ParseException` instance with the specified detail message and offset.

SYNTAX `public ParseException(String msg, int errorOffset)`

DESCRIPTION This constructor constructs a `ParseException` with the detail message `msg` and integer `errorOffset`. The detail message is a string that describes this particular exception. The `errorOffset` is the position in the string where the parsing error occurred.

PARAMETERS

`errorOffset` The position in the string where the parsing error occurred.

`msg` The possibly null detail message.

SEE ALSO `java.lang.Throwable.getMessage()`.

getErrorOffset()

PURPOSE Retrieves the position in the string where the parse error occurred.

SYNTAX `public int getErrorOffset()`

RETURNS The position in the string where the parse error occurred.

EXAMPLE See the class example.

java.text
ParsePosition

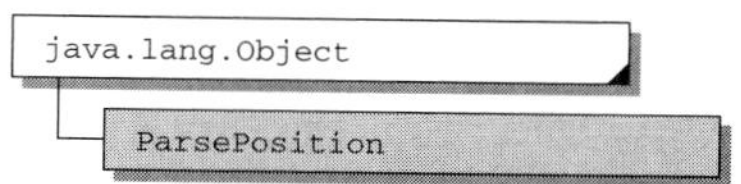

Syntax

```
public class ParsePosition extends Object
```

Description

Parsing is the operation of recognizing a pattern of digits in a string and returning it as a number object.

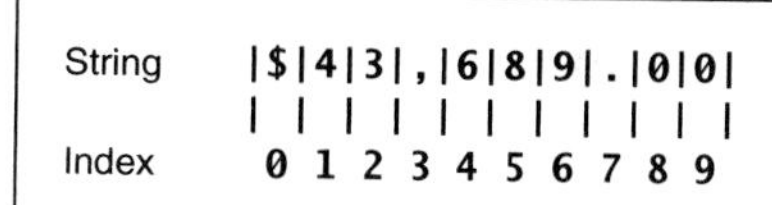

FIGURE 73: `ParsePosition`.

`ParsePosition` is a simple class used by `Format` and its subclasses to keep track of the current position in a string during parsing. The index property records the current position. See Figure 73. By design, as you parse through a string with different `Format` objects, all `Format` objects can use the same `ParsePosition`.

A `ParsePosition` object is not locale-sensitive, since it tracks Unicode characters.

The classes that use a `ParsePosition` object include `Format` and its subclasses. For example, the `parseObject()` method takes a `ParsePosition` object, as does the `parse()` method in `NumberFormat` and all of its subclasses `DecimalFormat`, `DateFormat`, `SimpleDateFormat`, and `MessageFormat`.

Usage

You use the constructor `ParsePosition()` to create a `ParsePosition` object, supplying the position at which you want to begin parsing. Use `0` to parse from the start of the string. Then pass this object in to the `parse()` or `parseObject()` method. A `ParsePosition` object is used both for input and output. That is, parsing of a string begins at the index of the `ParsePosition` object and ends by updating that index to the offset in the string at which the parse ended.

Index

The *index* is the offset in the string at which the parse is currently located. This position can indicate not only where the last parse ended but also where the next parse will begin.

MEMBER SUMMARY	
Constructor	
`ParsePosition()`	Constructs a `ParsePosition` instance that has an initial index.
Parse Methods	
`getIndex()`	Retrieves the current parse position.
`setIndex()`	Sets the current parse position.

A B C D E F G H I J K L M N O P Q R S T U V W X Y Z

See Also

`Format.`

Example

This example takes any text file as its input and then finds and prints out all decimal numbers, currency numbers, and percentages in the text. It first creates three different number formats (`decimalForm`, `currencyForm`, and `percentForm`) and then reads in the text file. Next, it uses the `parse()` method to scan through the file three times, each time looking for and printing out a different form of the number: decimal number, currency, and percentage.

```
import java.text.*;
import java.io.*;
import java.util.*;

class Main {

    // Create a parse position object for tracking the parse.
    static ParsePosition parsePos = new ParsePosition(0);

    // Create three number formats.
    static NumberFormat decimalForm  = NumberFormat.getInstance();
    static NumberFormat currencyForm = NumberFormat.getCurrencyInstance();
    static NumberFormat percentForm  = NumberFormat.getPercentInstance();

    // Createfour date formats.
    static DateFormat shortDateForm  =
          DateFormat.getDateInstance(DateFormat.SHORT, Locale.US);
    static DateFormat medDateForm =
          DateFormat.getDateInstance(DateFormat.MEDIUM, Locale.US);
    static DateFormat longDateForm =
          DateFormat.getDateInstance(DateFormat.LONG, Locale.US);
    static DateFormat fullDateForm =
          DateFormat.getDateInstance(DateFormat.FULL, Locale.US);

   Main (String str) {
       // Print out original text.
       System.out.println(str):

       // Parse through text for numbers.
       System.out.println("All Decimals Numbers ");
```

```
        parseNum(str, ".");
        System.out.println("\nCurrency ");
        parseNum(str, "$");
        System.out.println("\nPercent ");
        parseNum(str, "%");

        // Parse through text for dates.
        System.out.println("\nShort Date");
        parseNum(str, "short");
        System.out.println("\nMedium Date");
        parseNum(str, "med");
        System.out.println("\nLong Date");
        parseNum(str, "long");
        System.out.println("\nFull Date");
        parseNum(str, "full");
    }

    static void parseNum(String str, String t) {
        int beginParseIndex;
        int endParseIndex;
        Number num = null;
        Date date = null;

        while (parsePos.getIndex() < str.length()) {

            beginParseIndex = parsePos.getIndex();

            // Parse the string starting at parsePos.
            if (t.equals(".")) {
                // Find decimal number beginning at parsePos.
                num = decimalForm.parse(str, parsePos);
            } else if (t.equals("$")) {
                // Find currency beginning at parsePos.
                num = currencyForm.parse(str, parsePos);
            } else if (t.equals("%")) {
                // Find percentage beginning at parsePos.
                num = percentForm.parse(str, parsePos);
            } else if (t.equals("short")) {
                // Find short-style date beginning at parsePos.
                date = shortDateForm.parse(str, parsePos);
            } else if (t.equals("med")) {
                // Find medium-style date beginning at parsePos.
                date = medDateForm.parse(str, parsePos);
            } else if (t.equals("long")) {
                // Find long-style date beginning at parsePos.
                date = longDateForm.parse(str, parsePos);
            } else if (t.equals("full")) {
                // Find full-style date beginning at parsePos.
                date = fullDateForm.parse(str, parsePos);
            } else {
                System.err.println("Error: Bad character.");
                System.exit(1);
            }
            endParseIndex = parsePos.getIndex();

            if (num != null) {
                System.out.print("Index: " + beginParseIndex + "  ");
                System.out.println("Number: " + num);
            }
```

```
                if (date != null) {
                    System.out.print("Index: " + beginParseIndex + "  ");
                    System.out.println("Date:   " + date);
                }
                parsePos.setIndex(endParseIndex + 1);
            }
            // Reset parse position to 0 for next loop.
            parsePos.setIndex(0);
        }

        public static void main(String[] args) {

            // Accept an input text file
            if (args.length != 1) {
                System.err.println("This program parses thru text for numbers");
                System.err.println("Usage: java Main <filename>");
                System.exit(1);
            }
            try {
                // Read the text into a buffered reader
                // with '\n' for newlines
                BufferedReader rd = new BufferedReader(new FileReader(args[0]));
                String line;
                StringBuffer sbuf = new StringBuffer();

                while ((line = rd.readLine()) != null) {
                    sbuf.append(line);
                    sbuf.append('\n');
                }
                rd.close();

                // Call the constructor Main with the input string
                new Main(new String(sbuf));

            } catch (Exception e) {
                e.printStackTrace();
            }
        }
    }
```

Output

```
Jan 1, 1998.  It's hard to find a system under $1200 that is 100%-reliable.
The current price of $1,100.00 does not include 3 required $50 add-ons.
The price is going up 10 - 15% on November 3, 1998 at 5:25pm.  Wait for 12/31/
98.

All Decimals Numbers
Index: 4  Number: 1
Index: 7  Number: 1998
Index: 48  Number: 1200
Index: 61  Number: 100
Index: 98  Number: 1100.0
Index: 124  Number: 3
Index: 136  Number: 50
Index: 170  Number: 10
Index: 175  Number: 15
Index: 191  Number: 3
Index: 194  Number: 1998
Index: 202  Number: 5
```

```
Index: 204  Number: 25
Index: 220  Number: 12
Index: 223  Number: 31
Index: 226  Number: 98

Currency
Index: 47  Number: 1200
Index: 97  Number: 1100.0
Index: 135  Number: 50

Percent
Index: 61  Number: 1.0
Index: 175  Number: 0.15

Short Date
Index: 220  Date:   Thu Dec 31 00:00:00 PST 1998

Medium Date

Long Date
Index: 0  Date:   Thu Jan 01 00:00:00 PST 1998
Index: 182  Date:   Tue Nov 03 00:00:00 PST 1998

Full Date
```

getIndex()

PURPOSE Retrieves the current parse position.

SYNTAX `public int getIndex()`

DESCRIPTION This method retrieves the current parse position. When passed into a parse method, this position is the index of the character at which parsing will begin. On output, it is the index of the character that follows the last character parsed.

RETURNS The current parse position as a character index.

SEE ALSO `setIndex()`.

EXAMPLE See the class example.

ParsePosition()

PURPOSE Constructs a ParsePosition instance that has an initial index.

SYNTAX `public ParsePosition(int index)`

DESCRIPTION This method creates an instance of `ParsePosition` with its initial character index set to `index`. Parsing will begin at this character index.

PARAMETERS

`index` The character index at which to begin parsing.

EXAMPLE See the class example.

setIndex()

PURPOSE Sets the current parse position.

SYNTAX `public void setIndex(int index)`

DESCRIPTION This method sets the current parse position to the character index given by `index`.

PARAMETERS

`index` The character index at which to begin parsing.

SEE ALSO `getIndex()`.

EXAMPLE See the class example.

PipedInputStream

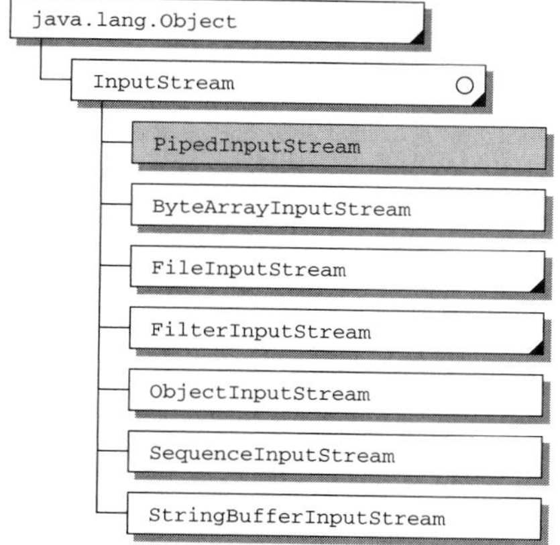

A B C D E F G H I J K L M N O P Q R S T U V W X Y Z

Syntax

```
public class PipedInputStream extends InputStream
```

Description

When writing a program, you may sometimes find it useful to be able to use a *pipe* as a communications stream between two threads. One thread communicates with another thread by sending output to the pipe. The other thread receives data from its counterpart by reading data from the pipe. Such a paradigm is useful when the threads have a producer/consumer relationship and the best way to transfer data between the two threads is via a pipe. For example, in a process-monitoring program, one thread could be collecting raw data from various monitoring devices and sending the data through a pipe to another thread. The other thread would then read data from the pipe and process the raw data in order to update status indicators.

Usage

The `PipedInputStream` class is used to provide a byte input stream to a pipe. A `PipedInputStream` is connected with a `PipedOutputStream` to create a pipe, whereby one thread can send data to the pipe while another thread reads the data from the pipe (see Figure 74).

Bytes are read in the order in which they were written. The pipe buffers any unread bytes. When the pipe becomes full, the writing thread blocks until there is

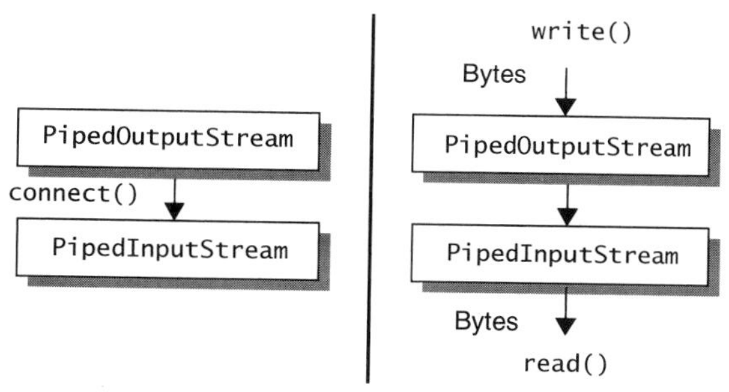

FIGURE 74: `PipedInputStream` and `PipedOutputStream`.

room in the pipe to write more bytes. If the pipe is empty, the reading thread blocks until there are bytes in the pipe to be read.

PipedInputStream versus PipedReader

`PipedInputStream` and `PipedOutputStream` are designed for a pipe of bytes. Use `Piped-Reader` and `PipedWriter` when a piped character stream is required.

MEMBER SUMMARY	
Constructor	
`PipedInputStream()`	Constructs a `PipedInputStream` instance.
Input Method	
`read()`	Reads bytes from this piped input stream.
Pipe Methods	
`available()`	Determines the number of bytes that can be read from the pipe without being blocked.
`close()`	Closes this piped input stream.
`connect()`	Connects this piped input stream to a piped output stream.
Protected Constants, Fields, and Method	
`buffer`	Buffer used to hold data in a pipe.
`in`	Index of where the next byte written to this pipe will be stored.
`out`	Index of where the next byte read from this pipe will be retrieved.
`PIPE_SIZE`	Default pipe size in bytes.
`receive()`	Stores a byte into the pipe.

See Also

`InputStream`, `PipedOutputStream`, `PipedReader`, `PipedWriter`.

Example

This example illustrates the use of piped input and output streams for two threads to communicate with each other. The `RunningAverage` thread is a thread that reads from the input stream a sequence of numbers and computes its running average. The `NumberGenerator` is a thread that generates a sequence of numbers and writes it to an output stream. This particular implementation uses `Random()` to generate the numbers, but one could imagine other data generators, such as speedometers and temperature sensors.

```
import java.io.*;
import java.util.Random;
```

```
// reads numbers from input stream and compute running average
class RunningAverage extends Thread {
    private DataInputStream in;
    double total = 0;
    long count = 0;

    public RunningAverage(InputStream i) {
        in = new DataInputStream(i);
    }
    public void run() {
        while (true) {
            try {
                double num = in.readDouble();
                total += num;
                count++;
                System.out.println(count + ": " + num + " avg = "
                                   + total/count);
            } catch (IOException e) {
                e.printStackTrace();
            }
        }
    }
}
class NumberGenerator extends Thread {
    private DataOutputStream out;
    private Random gen = new Random();
    private final long RANGE = 10000;

    public NumberGenerator(OutputStream o) {
        out = new DataOutputStream(o);
    }
    public void run() {
        while (true) {
            try {
                double num = gen.nextFloat() * RANGE;
                out.writeDouble(num);
                out.flush();
                sleep(500);  // sleep for 500 milliseconds
            } catch (IOException e) {
                e.printStackTrace();
            } catch (InterruptedException e) {
                e.printStackTrace();
            }
        }
    }
}
class Main {
    public static void main(String[] args) {
        try {
            PipedOutputStream producer = new PipedOutputStream();
            PipedInputStream consumer = new PipedInputStream(producer);

            RunningAverage avg = new RunningAverage(consumer);
            NumberGenerator gen = new NumberGenerator(producer);

            gen.start();
            avg.start();
        } catch (IOException e) {
            e.printStackTrace();
        }
    }
}
```

available()

PURPOSE
: Determines the number of bytes that can be read from this pipe without being blocked.

SYNTAX
: `public synchronized int available() throws IOException`

DESCRIPTION
: This method determines the number of bytes that have been written to the pipe but not yet read. It is the size of the pipe (1024 bytes) if the pipe is full.

RETURNS
: The number of bytes that can be read from this pipe without being blocked. `0` if this pipe has not been connected yet.

EXCEPTIONS

`IOException`
: If an IO error occurred.

OVERRIDES
: `InputStream.available()`.

EXAMPLE
: See `InputStream.available()`.

buffer

PURPOSE
: Buffer used to hold data in a pipe.

SYNTAX
: `protected byte[] buffer`

DESCRIPTION
: This is a `byte` array of 1024 bytes used for holding data written to the pipe. The indices `in` and `out` are used to track the location in the buffer of where to store and read the next byte, respectively. Bytes are read in the order in which they were written.

SEE ALSO
: `in`, `out`, `receive()`, `read()`.

close()

PURPOSE
: Closes this piped input stream.

SYNTAX
: `public void close() throws IOException`

DESCRIPTION
: This method closes this piped input stream. Once the stream has been closed, you can no longer read from it. If you subsequently attempt to write to the piped output stream to which this piped input stream is connected, an `IOException` is thrown.

EXCEPTIONS

`IOException`

If an IO error occurred.

OVERRIDES `InputStream.close()`.

SEE ALSO `read()`.

EXAMPLE See `connect()`.

connect()

PURPOSE Connects this piped input stream to a piped output stream.

SYNTAX `public void connect(PipedOutputStream src) throws IOException`

DESCRIPTION This method connects this piped input stream to the piped output stream `src`. Once the two streams are connected, output written to `src` can be read from this piped input stream by using `read()`. If this piped input stream has already been connected, an `IOException` is thrown.

PARAMETERS

`src` The non-`null` output stream to which to connect.

EXCEPTIONS

`IOException`

If this piped input stream was previously connected or if an IO error occurred while attempting to connect this stream to `src`.

SEE ALSO `PipedInputStream()`, `PipedOutputStream.connect()`.

EXAMPLE This example is a modification of the class example. It connects the pipe explicitly using `connect()` and runs for only 5 seconds before terminating the threads and closing the streams.

```
import java.io.*;

class Main {
    public static void main(String[] args) {
        try {
            PipedOutputStream producer = new PipedOutputStream();
            PipedInputStream consumer = new PipedInputStream();

            consumer.connect(producer);        // connect pipes

            RunningAverage avg = new RunningAverage(consumer);
            NumberGenerator gen = new NumberGenerator(producer);

            gen.start();                // start threads
            avg.start();

            try {
```

```
            Thread.sleep(5000);  // sleep for 5 seconds
        } catch (InterruptedException e) {
        }

        gen.stop();               // stop threads
        avg.stop();

        producer.close();         // close streams
        consumer.close();
    } catch (IOException e) {
        e.printStackTrace();
    }
  }
}
```

A B C D E F G H I J K L M N O P Q R S T U V W X Y Z

in

PURPOSE Index of where the next byte written to this pipe will be stored.

SYNTAX `protected int in`

DESCRIPTION This field is an index into `buffer` indicating where the next byte that is written to this pipe will be stored. If `in` is -1, the pipe is empty and the next byte will be stored at index `0`. Otherwise, the next byte is stored at index `in`. After a byte is stored, `in` is incremented. When `in` reaches the end of `buffer` (`buffer.length`), it loops around to `0`. If `buffer` is full (`in == out`), the byte is not stored until one is read from the pipe.

SEE ALSO `buffer`, `out`, `receive()`.

out

PURPOSE Index of where the next byte read from this pipe will be retrieved.

SYNTAX `protected int out`

DESCRIPTION This field is an index into `buffer` indicating where the next byte that is read from this pipe will be retrieved. `out` starts at `0` and is incremented each time after a byte is read. When `out` reaches the end of `buffer` (`buffer.length`), it loops to `0`. If `buffer` is empty (`in == -1`), the read blocks until a byte is written to the pipe.

SEE ALSO `buffer`, `in`, `receive()`.

PIPE_SIZE

PURPOSE Default pipe size in bytes.

SYNTAX `protected static final int PIPE_SIZE`

DESCRIPTION The default pipe size is 1024. This is the size with which `buffer` is created.

SEE ALSO `buffer`, `in`, `out`.

PipedInputStream()

PURPOSE Constructs a `PipedInputStream` instance.

SYNTAX

```
public PipedInputStream ()
public PipedInputStream (PipedOutputStream src) throws IOException
```

DESCRIPTION There are two forms of this constructor for `PipedInputStream`. The first form constructs a piped input stream that is not connected to any piped output stream. Before this piped input stream can be used, it must be connected to a piped output stream using `connect()`. The second form constructs a piped input stream that is connected to the piped output stream `src`. Output from `src` can be read from this newly created piped input stream.

PARAMETERS

`src` The non-`null` output stream to which to connect.

EXCEPTIONS

`IOException`

If `src` is already connected or an IO error occurred while attempting to connect this new stream to `src`.

SEE ALSO `connect()`, `PipedOutputStream`.

EXAMPLE See the class example and `connect()`.

read()

PURPOSE Reads bytes from this piped input stream.

SYNTAX

```
public synchronized int read() throws IOException
public synchronized int read(byte[] buffer, int offset, int count)
   throws IOException
```

DESCRIPTION The two forms of this method read bytes from this piped input stream. The first form reads a single byte from this piped input stream and returns it as an `int` (the lowest-order byte of the `int`). The second form reads `count` number of bytes from this piped input stream and stores it into the `byte` array `buffer` starting at index `offset`.

The bytes read are obtained from the piped output stream to which this piped input stream is connected. If no input is available yet, `read()` waits until some input is available.

If the corresponding piped output stream is closed before any bytes are read, `-1` is returned for both forms of this method.

PARAMETERS

`buffer` The non-`null` `byte` array in which to store the bytes read.

`count` The number of bytes to read. `0` ≤ `count` ≤ `buffer.length-offset`.

`offset` The index in `buffer` at which to start storing the bytes read. `0` ≤ `offset` < `buffer.length`.

RETURNS The first form returns the byte read; the second form returns the actual number of bytes read. Both forms return `-1` when end-of-stream is reached before any bytes are read.

EXCEPTIONS

`ArrayOutOfBoundsException`
If `count` or `offset` is outside of the specified ranges.

`IOException`
If this piped input stream has already been closed or if the thread that is writing to the connecting piped output stream is no longer alive (it died without closing the output stream).

OVERRIDES `InputStream.read()`.

SEE ALSO `PipedOutputStream.write()`.

EXAMPLE See the class example.

receive()

PURPOSE Stores a byte into the pipe.

SYNTAX
```
protected synchronized void receive(int oneByte) throws
    IOException
```

DESCRIPTION This method is called by `PipedOutputStream.write()` when it writes bytes to the pipe. It stores a single byte—the lowest-order byte of `oneByte`—into `buffer` at the index pointed to by the index `in`. Bytes are read in the order in which they are written into `buffer`.

PARAMETERS

`oneByte` The lowest-order byte of `oneByte` is stored into the pipe.

EXCEPTIONS

`InterruptedIOException`

If the pipe is full and the current thread is interrupted while waiting for space to free up in the pipe.

`IOException`

If the thread that was reading from this pipe is no longer alive (it died without closing the piped input stream).

SEE ALSO `buffer`, `in`, `out`, `PIPE_SIZE`, `PipedOutputStream.write()`.

PipedOutputStream

```
java.lang.Object
└ OutputStream
  ├ PipedOutputStream
  ├ ByteArrayOutputStream
  ├ FileOutputStream
  ├ FilterOutputStream
  └ ObjectOutputStream
```

A B C D E F G H I J K L M N O P Q R S T U V W X Y Z

Syntax

`public class PipedOutputStream extends OutputStream`

Description

When writing a program, you may sometimes find it useful to be able to use a *pipe* as a communications stream between two threads. One thread communicates with another thread by sending output to the pipe. The other thread receives data from its counterpart by reading data from the pipe. Such a paradigm is useful when the threads have a producer/consumer relationship and the best way to transfer data between the two threads is via a pipe. For example, in a process-monitoring program, one thread could be collecting raw data from various monitoring devices and sending the data through a pipe to another thread. The other thread would then read data from the pipe and process the raw data in order to update status indicators.

Usage

The `PipedOutputStream` class is used to provide a byte output stream to a pipe. A `PipedInputStream` is connected with a `PipedOutputStream` to create a pipe, whereby one thread can send data to the pipe while another thread reads the data from the pipe. (See Figure 75.)

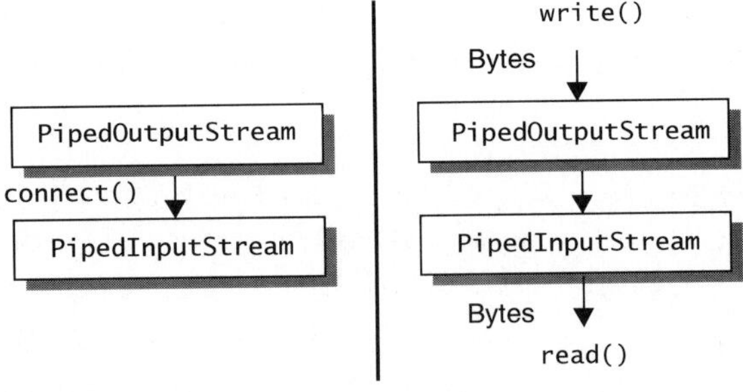

FIGURE 75: **`PipedInputStream` and `PipedOutputStream`.**

Bytes are read in the order in which they were written. The pipe buffers any unread bytes. When the pipe becomes full, the writing thread blocks until there is room in the pipe to write more bytes. If the pipe is empty, the reading thread blocks until there are bytes in the pipe to be read.

PipedOutputStream versus PipedWriter

`PipedInputStream` and `PipedOutputStream` are designed for a pipe of bytes. Use `Piped-Reader` and `PipedWriter` when a piped character stream is required.

MEMBER SUMMARY

Constructor

`PipedOutputStream()`	Constructs a `PipedOutputStream` instance.

Output Method

`write()`	Writes bytes to this piped output stream.

Pipe Methods

`close()`	Closes this piped output stream.
`connect()`	Connects this piped output stream to a piped input stream.
`flush()`	Notifies the piped input stream readers that bytes can be read from this pipe.

See Also

`OutputStream`, `PipedInputStream`, `PipedReader`, `PipedWriter`.

Example

See the class example of `PipedInputStream`.

close()

PURPOSE Closes this piped output stream.

SYNTAX `public void close() throws IOException`

DESCRIPTION This method closes this piped output stream. Once the stream has been closed, you can no longer send data to it. After the rest of the data that's in the pipe has been read, the thread reading from the corresponding piped input stream will receive a `-1` return code, indicating that the piped has been closed.

This method does nothing if the pipe has not been connected.

EXCEPTIONS

`IOException`

If an IO error occurred while closing the stream.

OVERRIDES `OutputStream.close()`.

SEE ALSO `PipedInpuStream.read()`, `write()`.

EXAMPLE See `PipedInputStream.connect()`.

A B C D E F G H I J K L M N O P Q R S T U V W X Y Z

connect()

PURPOSE Connects this piped output stream to a piped input stream.

SYNTAX `public void connect(PipedInputStream dest) throws IOException`

DESCRIPTION This method connects this piped output stream to the piped input stream `dest`. Data written to this piped output stream can be read from `dest`.

PARAMETERS

`dest` The piped input stream to which to connect.

EXCEPTIONS

`IOException`

If either this piped output stream or `dest` is already connected.

SEE ALSO `PipedInputStream.connect()`, `PipedOutputStream`.

EXAMPLE This example is a modification of the one in `PipedInputStream.connect()`. Instead of invoking `connect()` on the `PipedInputStream`, call `connect()` on the `PipedOutputStream`. Both ways produce the same effect.

```
import java.io.*;
class Main {
    public static void main(String[] args) {
        try {
            PipedOutputStream producer = new PipedOutputStream();
            PipedInputStream consumer = new PipedInputStream();

            producer.connect(consumer);        // connect pipe
              ...
```

flush()

PURPOSE Notifies the piped input stream readers that bytes can be read from this pipe.

SYNTAX `public synchronized void flush() throws IOException`

DESCRIPTION This method does nothing if the pipe has not been connected.

EXCEPTIONS

`IOException`

If an IO error occurred while notifying the readers.

OVERRIDES `OutputStream.flush()`.

EXAMPLE See the `PipedInputStream` class example.

PipedOutputStream()

PURPOSE Constructs a `PipedOutputStream` instance.

SYNTAX
```
public PipedOutputStream()
public PipedOutputStream(PipedInputStream dest) throws
   IOException
```

DESCRIPTION There are two forms of the constructor for `PipedOutputStream`. The first form constructs a piped output stream that is not connected to any piped input stream. Before this piped output stream can be used, it must be connected to a piped input stream using `connect()`. The second form constructs a piped output stream that is connected to the piped input stream `dest`. Output from this newly created piped output stream can be read from `dest`.

PARAMETERS

`dest` The input stream to which to connect.

EXCEPTIONS

`IOException`

If `dest` is already connected to another piped output stream.

SEE ALSO `connect()`, `PipedInputStream`.

EXAMPLE See the class examples of `PipedInputStream` and `PipedInputStream.connect()`.

write()

PURPOSE Writes bytes to this piped output stream.

SYNTAX
```
public void write(int oneByte) throws IOException
public void write(byte[] buffer, int offset, int count) throws
   IOException
```

DESCRIPTION The two forms of this method write bytes to this piped output stream. The first form writes a single byte to this stream. The byte written is the lowest-order byte of `oneByte`. The second form writes `count` number of bytes from the `byte` array `buffer`, starting at index `count`.

The bytes written to this piped output stream can be read by the piped input stream to which this output stream is connected. Bytes that are not yet read are buffered by the pipe. If the pipe becomes full, `write()` blocks until there is room in the pipe to write more bytes.

PARAMETERS

`buffer` The non-`null` `byte` array containing the bytes to be written.

`count` The number of bytes to write. `0` ≤ `count` ≤ `buffer.length-offset`.

`offset`	The index in `buffer` at which to start getting the bytes for writing. `0` ≤ `offset` < `buffer.length`.
`oneByte`	The lowest-order byte in `oneByte` is written.

EXCEPTIONS

`ArrayIndexOutOfBoundsException`
If `count` or `offset` is outside of the specified bounds.

`InterruptedIOException`
If the pipe is full and the current thread is interrupted while waiting for space to free up in the pipe.

`IOException`
If the thread that was reading from the pipe is no longer alive (it died without closing the piped input stream).

`NullPointerException`
If you try to write to this stream before it has been connected.

OVERRIDES `connect()`, `PipedOutputStream()`, `OutputStream.write()`.

SEE ALSO `PipedInputStream.read()`, `PipedInputStream.receive()`.

EXAMPLE See the class example of `PipedInputStream`.

PipedReader

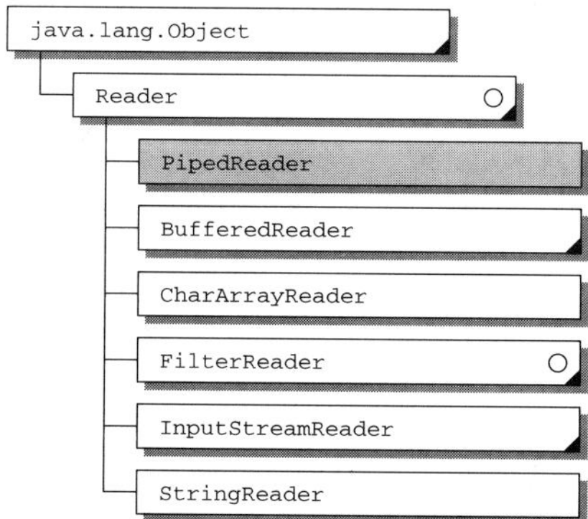

Syntax

```
public class PipedReader extends Reader
```

Description

A *pipe* is a useful programming paradigm for communication between two threads. See `PipedInputStream` for more on the use of pipes. The `PipedReader` class is used to provide a character input stream to a pipe. It is paired with `PipedWriter`, which writes characters to the pipe.

Usage

A piped reader is connected to a piped writer to create a pipe. One thread writes characters to the pipe while the other thread reads the characters from the pipe. See Figure 76. Characters are read in the order in which they were written. The pipe buffers any unread characters. When the pipe becomes full, the writing thread blocks until there is room in the pipe to write more characters. If the pipe is empty, the reading thread blocks until there are characters in the pipe to be read.

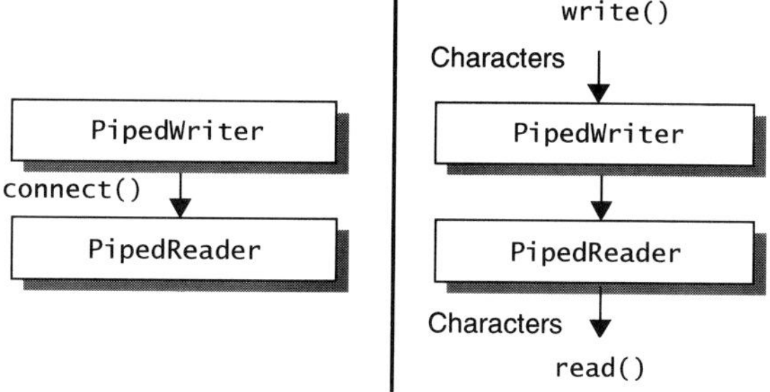

FIGURE 76: `PipedReader` and `PipedWriter`.

PipedReader versus PipedInputStream

A piped reader is like a piped input stream, except that a reader reads characters, while an input stream reads bytes. In Java 1.1.4, `PipedReader` is implemented using a `PipedInput-Stream`, using 2 bytes to encode each character.

MEMBER SUMMARY	
Constructor	
`PipedReader()`	Constructs a `PipedReader` instance.
Input Method	
`read()`	Reads characters from this piped reader.
Pipe Methods	
`close()`	Closes this piped reader.
`connect()`	Connects this piped reader to a piped writer.

See Also

`PipedInputStream`, `PipedOutputStream`, `PipedWriter`.

Example

This example illustrates the use of a piped reader and a piped writer. The `CharGenerator` generates characters between "a" and "z" and writes each to the pipe. The `VowelCounter` thread reads characters from the pipe and counts the number of vowels encountered.

```
import java.io.*;
import java.util.Random;

// reads characters from pipe and counts vowels
class VowelCounter extends Thread {
    private Reader in;
    int vowels = 0;

    public VowelCounter(Reader in) {
        this.in = in;
    }
    static boolean isVowel(char c) {
        switch (c) {
        case 'a':
        case 'e':
        case 'i':
        case 'o':
        case 'u':
            return true;
        }
        return false;
    }
    public void run() {
        int ch;
        try {
            while ((ch = in.read()) >= 0) {
                if (isVowel((char)ch)) {
                    vowels++;
                }
                // Prints letter and how many vowels counted so far
```

```
                System.out.print((char)ch + " " + vowels + " ");
            }
            in.close();
        } catch (IOException e) {
            e.printStackTrace();
        }
    }
}
class CharGenerator extends Thread {
    private Writer out;
    private Random gen = new Random();

    public CharGenerator(Writer out) {
        this.out = out;
    }
    public void run() {
        while (true) {
            try {
                // generate a character between 'a' and 'z'
                char ch = (char)('a' + Math.abs(gen.nextInt())%26);
                out.write(ch);
                out.flush();
                sleep(1000);  // sleep for 1 sec
            } catch (IOException e) {
                e.printStackTrace();
            } catch (InterruptedException e) {
                e.printStackTrace();
            }
        }
    }
}
class Main {
    public static void main(String[] args) {
        try {
            PipedWriter producer = new PipedWriter();
            PipedReader consumer = new PipedReader(producer);

            VowelCounter v = new VowelCounter(consumer);
            CharGenerator g = new CharGenerator(producer);

            v.start();
            g.start();
        } catch (IOException e) {
            e.printStackTrace();
        }
    }
}
```

close()

PURPOSE Closes this piped reader.

SYNTAX `public void close() throws IOException`

DESCRIPTION This method closes this piped reader. Once this reader has been closed, you can no longer read from it. This method is idempotent. That is, you can invoke it many times, but only the first invocation has any effect.

EXCEPTIONS

`IOException`
If an IO error occurs while closing this piped reader.

SEE ALSO `read()`.

EXAMPLE See the class example.

connect()

PURPOSE Connects this piped reader to a piped writer.

SYNTAX

```
public void connect(PipedWriter src) throws IOException
```

DESCRIPTION This method connects this piped reader to the piped writer `src`. Once these are connected, output written to `src` can be read from this piped reader by using `read()`.

PARAMETERS

`src` The non-`null` piped writer to which to connect.

EXCEPTIONS

`IOException`
If this reader has been closed, or if `src` has been closed, or if this reader is already connected.

EXAMPLE See the similar usage of `PipedInputStream.connect()`.

PipedReader()

PURPOSE Constructs a `PipedReader` instance.

SYNTAX

```
public PipedReader()
public PipedReader(PipedWriter src) throws IOException
```

DESCRIPTION There are two forms of this constructor. The first form constructs a piped reader that is not connected to any piped writer. Before this piped reader can be used, it must be connected to a piped writer using `connect()`.

The second form constructs a piped reader that is connected to the piped writer `src`. Output written to src can be read from this piped reader.

PARAMETERS

`src` The non-`null` piped writer to which to connect.

EXCEPTIONS

`IOException`

If `src` has been closed or if `src` has already been connected.

EXAMPLE See the class example.

read()

PURPOSE Reads characters from this piped reader.

SYNTAX
```
public int read(char buf[], int offset, int count) throws
   IOException
```

DESCRIPTION This method reads `count` number of characters from this piped reader and stores them into the `char` array `buf` starting at index `offset`. The characters read are obtained from the piped writer to which this piped reader is connected. If no input is available, `read()` waits until some is.

If the corresponding piped writer has been closed before any characters have been read, `-1` is returned.

The other `read()` methods in `Reader` are implemented using this method. For example, invoking `read()` with no parameters returns a single character from the pipe (as shown in the class example).

PARAMETERS

`buf` The non-`null` `char` array in which to store the characters read.

`count` The number of characters to read. `0` ≤ `count` ≤ `buf.length-offset`.

`offset` The index in `buf` at which to start storing characters. `0` ≤ `offset` < `buf.length`.

RETURNS The number of characters read, or –1 if the end of the corresponding piped writer has been closed.

EXCEPTIONS

`ArrayIndexOutOfBoundsException`

If `count` or `offset` is outside of the specified bounds.

`IOException`

If this piped reader has been closed or if the thread that is writing to the connecting piped writer is no longer alive (it died without closing).

EXAMPLE See the class example.

java.io

PipedWriter

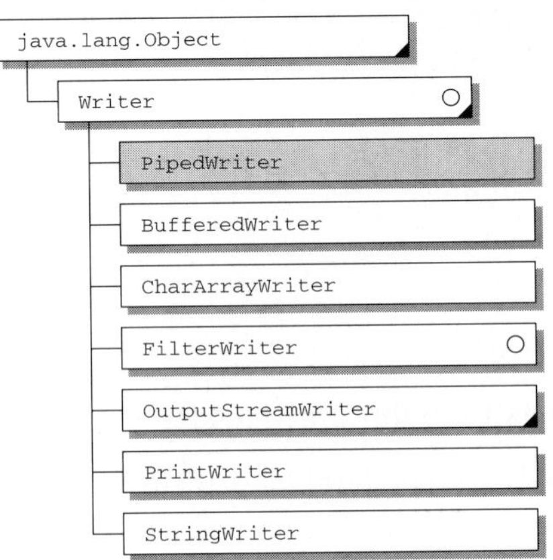

Syntax

`public class PipedWriter extends Writer`

Description

A *pipe* is a useful programming paradigm for communication between two threads. See `PipedInputStream` for more on the use of pipes. The `PipedWriter` class is used to provide a character output stream for a pipe. It is paired with `PipedReader`, which reads characters from the pipe.

Usage

A piped writer is connected to a piped reader to create a pipe. One thread writes characters to the pipe while the other thread reads the characters from the pipe. See Figure 77. Characters are read in the order in which they were written. The pipe buffers any unread characters. When the pipe becomes full, the writing thread blocks until there is room in the pipe to write more characters. If the pipe is empty, the reading thread blocks until there are characters in the pipe to be read.

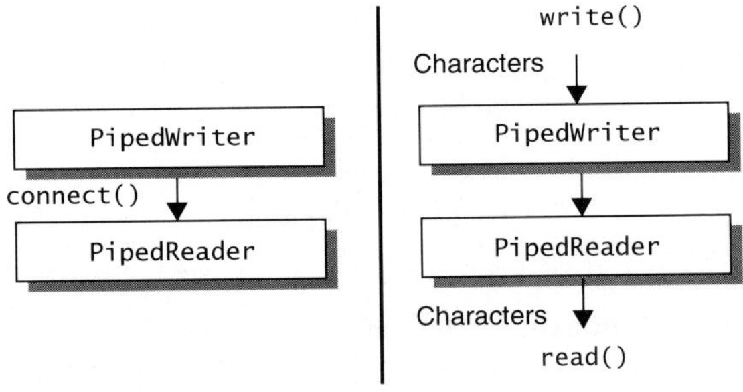

FIGURE 77: **`PipedReader` and `PipedWriter`.**

PipedWriter versus PipedOutputStream

A piped writer is like a piped output stream, except that a writer writes characters, while an output stream writes bytes. In Java 1.1.4, `PipedWriter` is implemented using a `PipedOutputStream`, using 2 bytes to encode each character.

MEMBER SUMMARY	
Constructor	
`PipedWriter()`	Constructs a `PipedWriter` instance.
Output Methods	
`write()`	Writes characters to this piped writer.
Pipe Methods	
`close()`	Closes this piped writer.
`connect()`	Connects this piped writer to a piped reader.
`flush()`	Flushes this piped writer.

See Also

`PipedInputStream`, `PipedOutputStream`, `PipedWriter`.

Example

See `PipedReader`.

close()

PURPOSE
Closes this piped writer.

SYNTAX
`public void close() throws IOException`

DESCRIPTION
This method closes this piped writer. Once this writer has been closed, you can no longer write to it. This method is idempotent. That is, you can invoke it many times, but only the first invocation has any effect.

EXCEPTIONS

`IOException`

If an IO error occurs while closing this piped writer.

EXAMPLE
See `Reader.close()`.

A B C D E F G H I J K L M N O P Q R S T U V W X Y Z

connect()

PURPOSE Connects this piped writer to a piped reader.

SYNTAX `public void connect(PipedReader sink) throws IOException`

DESCRIPTION This method connects this piped writer to the piped reader `sink`. Characters written to this writer can be read from `sink`.

PARAMETERS

`sink` The non-`null` piped reader to which to connect.

EXCEPTIONS

`IOException`

If this writer has been closed, or if `sink` has been closed, or if `sink` has already been connected.

EXAMPLE See the similar usage of `PipedOutputStream.connect()`.

flush()

PURPOSE Flushes this piped writer.

SYNTAX `public void flush() throws IOException`

DESCRIPTION This method flushes this writer by notifying threads that are reading from the corresponding piped reader that characters in the pipe are waiting to be read.

EXCEPTIONS

`IOException`

If this piped writer has been closed.

EXAMPLE See the `PipedReader` class example.

PipedWriter()

PURPOSE Constructs a `PipedWriter` instance.

SYNTAX
```
public PipedWriter()
public PipedWriter(PipedReader sink) throws IOException
```

DESCRIPTION There are two forms of this constructor. The first form constructs a piped writer that is not connected to any piped reader. Before this piped writer can be used, it must be connected to a piped reader using `connect()`.

The second form constructs a piped writer that is connected to the piped reader `sink`. Characters written to this newly created piped writer can be read from `sink`.

PARAMETERS

`sink` The non-`null` piped reader to connect.

EXCEPTIONS

`IOException`

If `sink` has been closed or if `sink` has already been connected.

EXAMPLE See the `PipedReader` class example.

write()

PURPOSE Writes characters to this piped writer.

SYNTAX
```
public void write(char buffer[], int offset, int count) throws
    IOException
```

DESCRIPTION This method writes to this piped writer `count` number of characters from the `char` array `buffer` starting at index `offset`.

The characters written to this piped writer can be read from the piped reader connected to this writer. Characters not yet read from the piped reader are buffered in the pipe. If the pipe becomes full, `write()` blocks until there is room in the pipe to write more characters.

The other `write()` methods in `Writer` are implemented using this method. For example, invoking `write()` with a single character (`int`) writes a single character to the pipe (as shown in the `PipedReader` class example).

PARAMETERS

`buffer` The non-`null` `char` array containing the characters to be written.

`count` The number of characters to write. `0` ≤ `count` ≤ `buffer.length-offset`.

`offset` The index in `buffer` at which to start getting the characters for writing. `0` ≤ `offset` < `buffer.length`.

EXCEPTIONS

`ArrayIndexOutOfBoundsException`

If `count` or `offset` is outside of the specified bounds.

`InterruptedIOException`

If the pipe is full and the current thread is interrupted while waiting for space to free up in the pipe.

`IOException`

If this piped writer has already been closed or if the thread that was reading from the pipe is no longer alive (it died without closing the piped input stream).

`NullPointerException`

If you try to write to this writer before it has been connected.

EXAMPLE See the `PipedReader` class example.

PrintStream

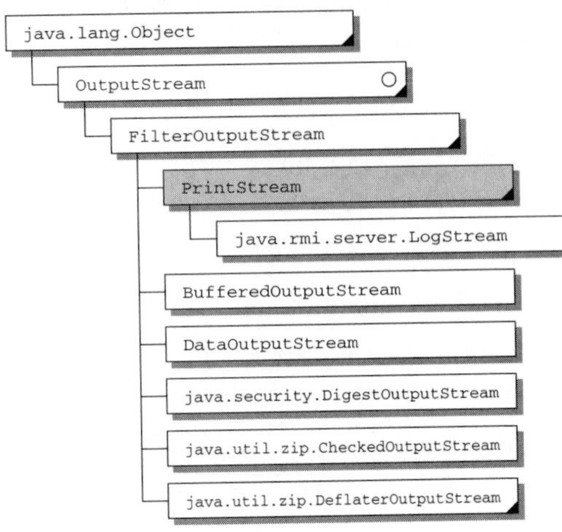

A B C D E F G H I J K L M N O P Q R S T U V W X Y Z

Syntax

```
public class PrintStream extends FilterOutputStream
```

Description

A *print stream* is a filter stream that accepts Java data values and writes out their string representations as a byte stream. The characters in the string representation are converted into bytes using a platform-dependent default byte encoding. Figure 78 shows a print stream accepting an `int`, a `char`, and a string.

FIGURE 78: **`PrintStream`.**

Usage

`PrintStream` has a set of `print()` and `println()` methods that accept Java objects and Java primitive types and prints their string representations. Typically, you use a print stream to generate output to be displayed to users. `System.out` and `System.err` are examples of print streams commonly used in programs:

```
System.out.print("Hello There!");
System.err.println(new Date());
```

Default Byte Encoding

The byte encoding to use when converting characters to bytes is platform-dependent. In the JDK 1.1, the default byte encoding is identified by the `file.encoding` system property. This property contains an *encoding identifier*; see `String.getBytes()` for a description of encoding identifiers. If this system property is not defined, the default encoding identifier is

"8859_1" (ISO-Latin-1). If the converter (class) for the default encoding identifier is not found, an ASCII encoding is used.

To use a byte encoding other than the default, you should use `PrintWriter` with `OutputStreamWriter` and specify the encoding explicitly. For example, output written to the following `PrintWriter` will result in those characters being converted to bytes by using the Big5 encoding:

```
PrintWriter out = new PrintWriter(
    new OutputStreamWriter(byteStream, "Big5"));
```

PrintStream versus PrintWriter

`PrintStream` is meant for byte-oriented output—the stream that it is filtering is a byte output stream. `System.out` and `System.err` are examples of print streams that are commonly used, but they are intended only for debugging and backward compatibility.

When you need to create an output stream for printing, you should use the `PrintWriter` class so that printing can proceed without the output's first being converted to a byte encoding.

Automatic Flushing

When creating a print stream, you can specify whether you want the stream to be flushed each time a line of output is terminated (via the `println()` methods) and when a line terminator is encountered in the stream. Such streams have the advantage that output written to them need not be explicitly flushed. Their disadvantage is that the operations on the stream take longer due to the flushing.

Both `System.out` and `System.err` are, by default, autoflush streams.

Exceptions

IO operations can throw IO exceptions. For ease-of-use and convenience, the methods in the `PrintStream` class do not throw IO exceptions. Instead, the stream maintains a flag to indicate whether an IO exception has been encountered. The application can check this flag (using `checkError()`) if it needs to find out whether an IO operation on the print stream has thrown an exception.

MEMBER SUMMARY

Output Methods

`print()`	Prints a data value to this print stream.
`println()`	Prints a data value followed by a line separator to this print stream.
`write()`	Writes bytes to this print stream.

Error-Checking Methods

`checkError()`	Determines whether this stream has had any exceptions.
`setError()`	Records that this stream has encountered an IO exception.

Continued

MEMBER SUMMARY	
Stream Methods	
close()	Closes this print stream.
flush()	Flushes any buffered output from this print stream.
Deprecated Constructor	
PrintStream()	Replaced by PrintWriter().

A B C D E F G H I J K L M N O P Q R S T U V W X Y Z

See Also

BufferedWriter.newLine(), PrintWriter, OutputStream, String.getBytes(), String.valueOf(), System.err, System.out.

Example

This example shows how different data types can be passed as arguments to print() and println().

```
import java.io.PrintStream;
import java.util.Date;

class Main {
    public static void main(String[] args) {
        String str = "abc";
        char[] chs = new char[str.length()];
        str.getChars(0, str.length(), chs, 0);

        System.out.print(new Date());          // Printing objects
        System.out.println(new Date());        // date

        System.out.print(str);                 // String
        System.out.println(str);
        System.out.print(chs);                 // char[]
        System.out.println(chs);
        System.out.print(' ');                 // char
        System.out.println(' ');
        System.out.print(5);                   // int
        System.out.println(5);
        System.out.print(5L);                  // long
        System.out.println(5L);
        System.out.print(1.23f);               // float
        System.out.println(1.23f);
        System.out.print(1.23);                // double
        System.out.println(1.23);
        System.out.print(true);                // boolean
        System.out.println(true);

        // flush stream and check if we got any errors from those
        // print() and println() calls
        if (System.out.checkError()) {
            System.err.println("Got errors printing");
            System.exit(-1);
```

```
        }

        // can also 'write' to a print stream
        System.out.write('A');
        byte[] b = str.getBytes();
        System.out.write(b, 0, b.length);
        System.out.flush();// not needed; close() will flush
        System.out.close();
    }
}
```

A B C D E F G H I J K L M N O P Q R S T U V W X Y Z

checkError()

PURPOSE Determines whether this stream has had any exceptions.

SYNTAX `public boolean checkError()`

DESCRIPTION This method flushes any buffered output from this print stream. It then returns a `boolean` value indicating whether an exception occurred earlier on this print stream. None of the output methods throw exceptions. When these output methods encounter an `IOException`, they record that the exception has occurred, but they do not throw it to the caller. The caller can check whether the output method succeeded by invoking `checkError()`. Once an exception has occurred, any subsequent call to `checkError()` on this print stream will always return `true`, regardless of which output method recorded the exception.

RETURNS `true` if this print stream encountered an exception; `false` otherwise.

SEE ALSO `close()`, `flush()`, `setError()`, `write()`.

EXAMPLE See the class example.

close()

PURPOSE Closes this print stream.

SYNTAX `public void close()`

DESCRIPTION This method closes this print stream by closing the underlying output stream. This, in turn, will close the next stream downstream, and so on. Hence, this method effectively closes this stream and all of the streams "downstream."

If an `IOException` is thrown while the stream is being closed, this fact is recorded and can be checked later using `checkError()`.

OVERRIDES `FilterOutputStream.close()`.

SEE ALSO `checkError()`, `FilterOutputStream`, `PrintStream()`.

EXAMPLE See the class example.

A B C D E F G H I J K L M N O P Q R S T U V W X Y Z

flush()

PURPOSE Flushes any buffered output from this print stream.

SYNTAX `public void flush()`

DESCRIPTION This method flushes any buffered output from this print stream by flushing the underlying output stream. This, in turn, will flush the next stream downstream, and so on. Hence, this method effectively flushes this stream and all of the streams "downstream."

If an `IOException` is thrown while the stream is being flushed, this fact is recorded and can be checked later using `checkError()`.

OVERRIDES `FilterOutputStream.flush()`.

SEE ALSO `checkError()`, `PrintStream()`.

EXAMPLE See the class example.

print()

PURPOSE Prints a data value to this print stream.

SYNTAX

```
public void print(boolean bool)
public void print(int inum)
public void print(long lnum)
public void print(float fnum)
public void print(double dnum)
public void print(Object obj)
public void print(String str)
public void print(char ch)
public void print(char[] charArray)
```

DESCRIPTION The nine forms of this method print a data value to this print stream. `String.valueOf()` is used on the data value to obtain its string representation. The output is generated by converting this string representation to its byte representation using the platform's default byte encoding. See the class description and `String.getBytes()` for details.

The data is written to the underlying output stream using `write()`. If this print stream is an autoflush stream and the string representation of the data value being written contains a line separator, the stream is automatically flushed.

PARAMETERS

`bool` The `boolean` value (`true` or `false`) to print.

`ch` The `char` value to print.

`charArray` The non-`null` `char` array to print.

`dnum`	The `double` value to print.
`fnum`	The `float` value to print.
`inum`	The `int` value to print.
`lnum`	The `long` value to print.
`obj`	The object to print (`null` is accepted).
`str`	The string to print (`null` is accepted).

SEE ALSO `flush()`, `java.lang.String.getBytes()`, `java.lang.String.valueOf()`, `write()`.

EXAMPLE See the class example.

println()

PURPOSE Prints a data value followed by a line separator to this print stream.

SYNTAX

```
public void println()
public void println(boolean bool)
public void println(int inum)
public void println(long lnum)
public void println(float fnum)
public void println(double dnum)
public void println(Object obj)
public void println(String str)
public void println(char ch)
public void println(char[] charArray)
```

DESCRIPTION The first form of this method prints a line separator. The other nine forms print to this print stream a data value followed by a line separator. `String.valueOf()` is used on the data value to obtain its string representation. The output is generated by converting this string representation to its byte representation using the platform's default character-to-byte encoding. See the class description and `String.getBytes()` for details.

The line separator printed is defined by the system property `line.separator`. On Solaris, it is `\n`; on Windows NT, it is `\r\n`.

The data is written to the underlying output stream using `write()`. If this print stream is an autoflush stream, the output is flushed automatically after it has been written.

PARAMETERS

`bool`	The `boolean` value (`true` or `false`) to print.
`ch`	The `char` value to print.
`charArray`	The non-`null` `char` array to print.
`dnum`	The `double` value to print.

`fnum`	The `float` value to print.
`inum`	The `int` value to print.
`lnum`	The `long` value to print.
`obj`	The object to print (`null` is accepted).
`str`	The string to print (`null` is accepted).

SEE ALSO `flush()`, `print()`, `java.lang.String.getBytes()`, `java.lang.String.valueOf()`, `write()`.

EXAMPLE See the class example and `PrintStream()`.

PrintStream() *DEPRECATED*

PURPOSE Replaced by `PrintWriter()`.

SYNTAX
```
public PrintStream(OutputStream out)
public PrintStream(OutputStream out, boolean autoflush)
```

PARAMETERS

`autoflush` `true` means this print stream will automatically flush output after each line separator is written. `false` means no automatic flushing will be performed.

`out` The non-`null` output stream for which to create the print stream filter.

DEPRECATION Character output should be displayed using `PrintWriter`. Replace the usage of these deprecated constructors, as in

```
OutputStream out = ...;
PrintStream p1 = new PrintStream(out);
PrintStream p2 = new PrintStream(out, true);
p2.println("Hello");
```

with the usage of `PrintWriter`, as in

```
PrintWriter p1 = new PrintWriter(out);
PrintWriter p2 = new PrintWriter(out, true);
p2.println("Hello");
```

setError()

PURPOSE Records that this stream has encountered an IO exception.

SYNTAX `protected setError()`

DESCRIPTION This method is used by subclasses to indicate that an `IOException` was thrown while writing to the underlying output stream was occurring. The application can check whether an exception occurred by using `checkError()`. There is no method to clear the error. Once an exception has occurred, any subsequent call to `checkError()` on this print stream will always return `true`, regardless of which output method recorded the exception.

SEE ALSO `checkError()`.

write()

PURPOSE

Writes bytes to this print stream.

SYNTAX

```
public void write(int oneByte)
public void write(byte[] buffer, int offset, int count)
```

DESCRIPTION

The two forms of this method write bytes to this print stream. The first form writes a single byte (the low-order byte in `oneByte`). If this print stream is an autoflush stream and `oneByte` is the line separator character (`\n`), the stream is flushed.

The second form writes to this print stream `count` number of bytes from the `byte` array `buffer`, starting at index `offset`. If this print stream is an autoflush stream, it flushes the stream. The bytes are written to the underlying output stream. If an `IOException` is thrown during the write, this fact is recorded and can be checked by using `checkError()`.

PARAMETERS

`buffer` The non-`null` `byte` array containing the bytes to write.

`count` The number of bytes to write. `0` ≤ `count` ≤ `buffer.length-offset`.

`offset` The index in `buffer` at which to start getting the bytes to write. `0` ≤ `offset` < `buffer.length`.

`oneByte` The low-order byte of `oneByte` is written.

EXCEPTIONS

`ArrayIndexOutOfBoundsException`

If `count` or `offset` is outside of the specified bounds.

OVERRIDES

`FilterOutputStream.write()`.

SEE ALSO

`checkError()`, `print()`, `println()`.

EXAMPLE

See the class example.

PrintWriter

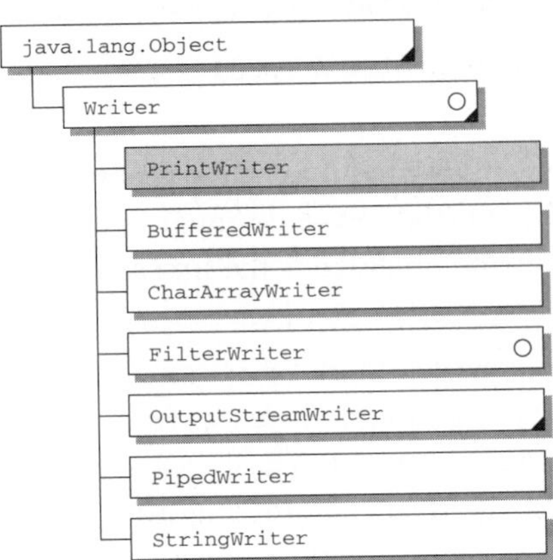

Syntax

```
public class PrintWriter extends Writer
```

Description

A *print writer* is a character output stream, or *writer*, that accepts Java data values and writes out their string representations as characters. Figure 79 shows a print writer accepting an `int`, a `char`, and a string. It also shows that the output can be written to either a byte output stream or to another writer.

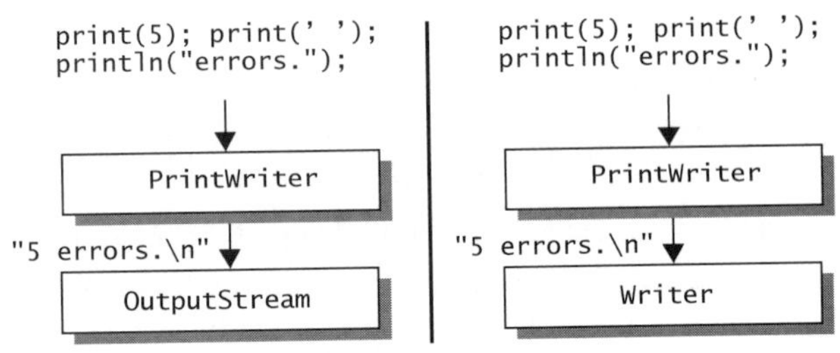

FIGURE 79: `PrintWriter`.

Usage

`PrintWriter` has a set of `print()` and `println()` methods that accept Java objects and Java primitive types and prints their string representations. Typically, you use a print writer to generate output to be displayed to users.

```
Writer wr = ...;
PrintWriter out = new PrintWriter(wr);
out.print("Hello There!");
```

Using PrintWriter for Byte Output

A `PrintWriter` can also be created for a byte output stream (`OutputStream`). In that case, the characters are converted into bytes using a platform-dependent default byte encoding. In the JDK 1.1, the default byte encoding is identified by the `file.encoding` system property. This property contains an *encoding identifier*; see `String.getBytes()` for a description of encoding identifiers. If this system property is not defined, the default encoding identifier is "8859_1" (ISO-Latin-1). If the converter (class) for the default encoding identifier is not found, an ASCII encoding is used.

To use a byte encoding other than the default, you should use `OutputStreamWriter` and specify the encoding explicitly. For example, output written to the following `PrintWriter` will result in those characters being converted to bytes by using the Big5 encoding:

```
PrintWriter out = new PrintWriter(
    new OutputStreamWriter(byteStream, "Big5"));
```

PrintStream versus PrintWriter

`PrintStream` is meant for byte-oriented output—the stream that it is filtering is a byte output stream. `System.out` and `System.err` are examples of print streams that are commonly used, but they are intended only for debugging and backward compatibility.

When you need to create an output stream for printing, you should use the `PrintWriter` class so that printing can proceed without the output's first being converted to a byte encoding. Even if you need to write characters to a byte stream, you should use the `PrintWriter` constructor that accepts an output stream. (The usage of the `PrintStream` constructors is deprecated.)

Automatic Flushing

When creating a print writer, you can specify whether you want the writer to be flushed each time a line of output is terminated via the `println()` methods. Such writers have the advantage that output written to them need not be explicitly flushed. Their disadvantage is that the operations on the writer take longer due to the flushing. Note that the writer is *not* flushed when a line terminator is encountered in the data; it is flushed only when `println()` is used. This differs from `PrintStream`, which flushes the stream also when a line terminator is encountered.

Exceptions

IO operations can throw `IOExceptions`. For ease-of-use and convenience, the methods in the `PrintWriter` class do not throw any IO exceptions. Instead, the writer maintains a flag to indicate whether any IO exceptions have been encountered. The application can check this flag (using `checkError()`) if it needs to find out whether an IO operation on the print writer has thrown an exception.

MEMBER SUMMARY

Constructor

`PrintWriter()`	Constructs a `PrintWriter` instance.

Output Methods

`print()`	Prints a data value to this print writer.
`println()`	Prints a data value followed by a newline to this print writer.
`write()`	Writes characters to this print writer.

Error-Checking Methods

`checkError()`	Determines whether this writer has had any exceptions.
`setError()`	Records that this writer has encountered an IO exception.

Close Methods

`close()`	Closes this print writer.
`flush()`	Flushes any buffered output from this print writer.

A B C D E F G H I J K L M N O P Q R S T U V W X Y Z

See Also

`BufferedWriter.newLine()`, `PrintStream`.

Example

This example shows how different data types can be passed as an argument to `print()` and `println()`.

```
import java.io.PrintWriter;
import java.io.FileWriter;
import java.io.IOException;
import java.util.Date;

class Main {
    public static void main(String[] args) {
        String str = "abc";
        char[] chs = new char[str.length()];
        str.getChars(0, str.length(), chs, 0);

        PrintWriter out;
        try {
            out = new PrintWriter(new FileWriter(args[0]));
        } catch (IOException e) {
            System.err.println(e);
            return;
        }

        out.print(new Date());          // Printing objects
        out.println(new Date());        // date

        out.print(str);                 // String
```

```
            out.println(str);
            out.print(chs);                 // char[]
            out.println(chs);
            out.print(' ');                 // char
            out.println(' ');
            out.print(5);                   // int
            out.println(5);
            out.print(5L);                  // long
            out.println(5L);
            out.print(1.23f);               // float
            out.println(1.23f);
            out.print(1.23);                // double
            out.println(1.23);
            out.print(true);                // boolean
            out.println(true);

            // flush and check if we got any errors from those
            // print() and println() calls
            if (out.checkError()) {
                System.err.println("Got errors printing");
                System.exit(-1);
            }

            // can also 'write' to a print writer
            out.write('A');
            out.write(str);
            char[] buf = str.toCharArray();
            out.write(buf, 0, buf.length);
            out.flush();    // not needed; close() will flush
            out.close();
        }
    }
```

checkError()

PURPOSE Determines whether this writer has had any exceptions.

SYNTAX `public boolean checkError()`

DESCRIPTION This method flushes any buffered output from this print writer. It then returns a `boolean` value indicating whether an exception occurred earlier on this print writer. None of the output methods throw exceptions. When these output methods encounter an `IOException`, they record that the exception occurred, but they do not throw it to the caller. The caller can check whether the output method succeeded by invoking `checkError()`. Once an exception has occurred, any subsequent call to `checkError()` on this print writer will always return `true`, regardless of which output method recorded the exception.

RETURNS `true` if this print writer encountered an exception; `false` otherwise.

SEE ALSO `close()`, `flush()`, `write()`.

EXAMPLE See the class example.

close()

PURPOSE Closes this print writer.

SYNTAX `public void close()`

DESCRIPTION This method closes this print writer by closing the underlying output stream or writer. If an `IOException` is thrown while the underlying stream or writer is being closed, this fact is recorded and can be checked later by using `checkError()`. If this writer has already been closed, this method does nothing.

SEE ALSO `checkError()`.

EXAMPLE See the class example.

flush()

PURPOSE Flushes any buffered output from this print writer.

SYNTAX `public void flush()`

DESCRIPTION This method flushes any buffered output from this print writer. If an `IOException` is thrown while this writer is being flushed, this fact is recorded and can be checked later by using `checkError()`.

SEE ALSO `checkError()`.

EXAMPLE See the class example.

print()

PURPOSE Prints a data value to this print writer.

SYNTAX

```
public void print(boolean bool)
public void print(int inum)
public void print(long lnum)
public void print(float fnum)
public void print(double dnum)
public void print(Object obj)
public void print(String str)
public void print(char ch)
public void print(char[] charArray)
```

DESCRIPTION The nine forms of this method print a data value to this print writer. The output generated is the string representation of the data value to be printed. `String.valueOf()` is used on the data value to obtain its string representation. The data is written to the underlying writer by using `write()`.

PARAMETERS

`bool`	The `boolean` value (`true` or `false`) to print.
`ch`	The `char` value to print.
`charArray`	The non-`null` `char` array to print.
`dnum`	The `double` value to print.
`fnum`	The `float` value to print.
`inum`	The `int` value to print.
`lnum`	The `long` value to print.
`obj`	The object to print (`null` is accepted).
`str`	The string to print (`null` is accepted).

SEE ALSO `flush()`, `java.lang.String.valueOf()`, `write()`.

EXAMPLE See the class example.

println()

PURPOSE Prints a data value followed by a newline to this print writer.

SYNTAX

```
synchronized public void println(boolean bool)
synchronized public void println(int inum)
synchronized public void println(long lnum)
synchronized public void println(float fnum)
synchronized public void println(double dnum)
synchronized public void println(Object obj)
synchronized public void println(String str)
synchronized public void println(char ch)
synchronized public void println(char[] charArray)
```

DESCRIPTION The nine forms of this method print a data value followed by a newline to this print writer. The output generated is the string representation of the data value to be printed. `String.valueOf()` is used on the data value to obtain its string representation.

The data is written to the underlying writer by using `write()`. If this print writer is an autoflush writer, the output is automatically flushed after it has been written.

PARAMETERS

`bool`	The `boolean` value (`true` or `false`) to print.
`ch`	The `char` value to print.
`charArray`	The non-`null` `char` array to print.
`dnum`	The `double` value to print.
`fnum`	The `float` value to print.
`inum`	The `int` value to print.

`lnum`	The `long` value to print.
`obj`	The object to print (`null` is accepted).
`str`	The string to print (`null` is accepted).

SEE ALSO `flush(), java.lang.String.valueOf(), write().`

EXAMPLE See the class example.

PrintWriter()

PURPOSE Constructs a `PrintWriter` instance.

SYNTAX
```
public PrintWriter(Writer wr)
public PrintWriter(Writer wr, boolean autoflush)
public PrintWriter(OutputStream out)
public PrintWriter(OutputStream out, boolean autoflush)
```

DESCRIPTION There are four forms of this constructor for `PrintWriter`.

The first two forms construct a print writer for the writer `wr`. If `autoflush` is `true`, output sent to this print writer is automatically flushed when `println()` is used. If `autoflush` is `false` or unspecified, no automatic flushing is done.

The last two forms construct a print writer for the output stream `out`. The constructor uses `OutputStreamWriter` to create a writer for `out` that uses the default byte encoding (see `OutputStreamWriter` for details). Characters written to this newly created writer will be converted by using this byte encoding and then written to `out`. If `autoflush` is `true`, output sent to this print writer is automatically flushed when `println()` is used. If `autoflush` is `false` or unspecified, no automatic flushing is done.

PARAMETERS

`autoflush`	`true` means this print writer will automatically flush output when `println()` is used. `false` means no automatic flushing will be performed.
`out`	The byte output stream for which to create the print writer.
`wr`	The writer for which to create the print writer.

SEE ALSO `flush(), OutputStream.`

EXAMPLE This example creates a print writer using `System.out`, a byte output stream.

```
import java.io.PrintWriter;

class Main {
    public static void main(String[] args) {
        // Create a writer for a byte output stream
        PrintWriter out = new PrintWriter(System.out);
        out.println("Hello There!");
        out.close();
    }
}
```

setError()

PURPOSE Records that this writer has encountered an IO exception.

SYNTAX

```
protected setError()
```

DESCRIPTION This method is used by subclasses to indicate that an `IOException` was thrown while writing to the underlying writer was occurring. The application can check whether an exception occurred by using `checkError()`. There is no method to clear the error. Once an exception has occurred, any subsequent call to `checkError()` on this print stream will always return `true`, regardless of which output method recorded the exception.

SEE ALSO `checkError()`.

write()

PURPOSE Writes characters to this print writer.

SYNTAX

```
public void write(int oneChar)
public void write(char[]buf)
public void write(char[]buf, int offset, int count)
public void write(String str)
public void write(String str, int offset, int count)
```

DESCRIPTION The five forms of this method write characters to this print writer. The first form of the method writes a single character to this writer. The low-order 2 bytes of `oneChar` are written.

The second and third forms write characters to this writer from the array `buf` as specified by `offset` and `count`. If `offset` and `count` are not specified, the entire buffer is written.

The last two forms write the characters from a string to this writer. If `offset` and `count` are specified, the range of characters in `str` specified by `offset` and `count` are written. Otherwise, the entire string `str` is written.

The characters are written to this writer's underlying byte output stream or writer. If the destination is a byte output stream, the characters are first converted to their byte encodings (see `PrintWriter()`). If an `IOException` is thrown during the write, this fact is recorded and can be checked by using `checkError()`.

PARAMETERS

`buf` The non-`null` `char` array containing the characters to be written.

`count` The number of characters to write. `0` ≤ `count` ≤ `buf.length-offset` (or `0` ≤ `count` ≤ `str.length()-offset`).

`offset`	The index in `buf` or `str` at which to start fetching the characters to be written. $0 \le$ `offset` $<$ `buf.length` or $0 \le$ `offset` $<$ `str.length()`.
`oneChar`	The low-order 2 bytes of `oneChar` are written to the writer.
`str`	The non-`null` string containing the characters to be written.

EXCEPTIONS

`ArrayIndexOutOfBoundsException`
If `count` or `offset` is outside of the specified bounds.

OVERRIDES `Writer.write()`.

SEE ALSO `checkError()`.

EXAMPLE See the class example.

Process

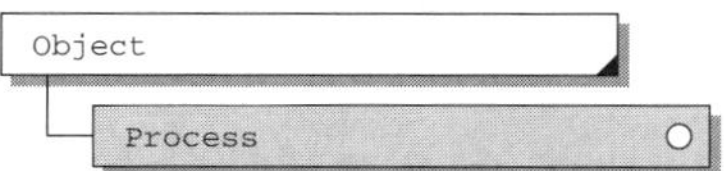

Syntax

```
public abstract class Process
```

Description

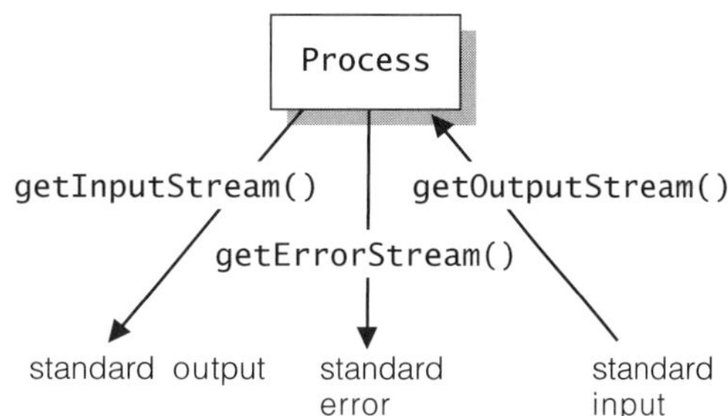

FIGURE 80: Communicating with a `Process` through Standard IO.

Java allows a program to spawn processes to execute *system programs* (*commands*). System programs are programs found in the native operating system on which Java is running. The `Runtime` class contains various `exec()` methods for executing system programs. An `exec()` method spawns a process to execute the specified program and returns to the caller a `Process` object that contains information about the process just created. This information includes how to communicate with the process through its standard IO streams (see Figure 80), stop the process, and retrieve the exit status of the process.

The `Process` class is an abstract class that defines methods that all subclasses of `Process` must support. Subclasses of `Process` (such as implementations for Windows or UNIX) define specific implementations for these methods.

A process is destroyed when all references to its associated `Process` object have been dropped. There is no requirement that the process execute asynchronously with the existing Java process.

MEMBER SUMMARY	
Methods for Communicating with the Process	
`getErrorStream()`	Retrieves an input stream for reading error output from the process.
`getInputStream()`	Retrieves an input stream for reading output from the process.
`getOutputStream()`	Retrieves an output stream for sending data to the process.
Process Management Methods	
`destroy()`	Destroys the process.
`exitValue()`	Retrieves the exit value of the process.
`waitFor()`	Waits for the process to terminate.

See Also

`InputStream, OutputStream, Runtime.exec(), System.`

Example

This example lists the output of the UNIX command `ls`.

```
import java.io.*;

class Main {
    public static void main(String[] args) {
        // some code that captures output from 'ls'
        try {
            String cmd = "ls";
            Process child = Runtime.getRuntime().exec(cmd);
            InputStream in = child.getInputStream();
            int c;
            // echo output of 'ls'
            while ((c = in.read()) != -1) {
                System.out.print((char)c);
            }
            in.close();
            // Wait for subprocess to exit
            try {
                child.waitFor();
            } catch (InterruptedException e) {
                e.printStackTrace();
            }
            // Display exit status of subprocess
            System.out.println("child exited with " + child.exitValue());
        } catch (IOException e) {
            System.err.println(e);
        }
    }
}
```

destroy()

PURPOSE Destroys the process.

SYNTAX `abstract public void destroy()`

DESCRIPTION A process can be destroyed at any time before it is completed. This is done by invoking a `destroy()` method on the `Process` object associated with the process. Any streams obtained from the process are invalidated when the process is destroyed.

EXAMPLE This example executes the `ls` program, reads five lines from its output, and then destroys the process.

```
import java.io.*;
```

```
class Main {
    public static void main(String[] args) {
        try {
            String cmd = "ls";
            // read first 5 lines from 'ls' and then destroy process
            Process child = Runtime.getRuntime().exec(cmd);
            InputStream in = child.getInputStream();
            int c, newline = 0;
            // read first 5 lines and then stop
            while ((c = in.read()) != -1 && newline < 5) {
                char ch = (char)c;
                System.out.print(ch);
                if (ch == '\n')
                    ++newline;
            }
            in.close();
            child.destroy(); // destroy process
        } catch (IOException e) {
            System.err.println(e);
        }
    }
}
```


exitValue()

PURPOSE Retrieves the exit value of the process.

SYNTAX `abstract public int exitValue()`

DESCRIPTION When a process terminates, it records the status of the system program just completed. This status is referred to as the *exit value* of the process. An exit status of `0` indicates success; all other exit values indicate failure. The meaning of nonzero exit values is program- and platform-dependent. This method returns the exit value of a process. If `exitvalue()` is called before the process has terminated, an `IllegalThreadStateException` is thrown.

RETURNS The exit value of the process. `0` means the program executed successfully; otherwise, the program failed.

EXCEPTIONS

`IllegalThreadStateException`

If the process has not yet terminated.

SEE ALSO `System.exit()`.

EXAMPLE This example executes the `ls` command, waits for the command to terminate, and reports the execution status of the command by examining the command's exit value.

```
import java.io.*;

class Main {
    public static void main(String[] args) {
        // some code that captures output from 'ls'
        try {
            String cmd = "ls";
            Process child = Runtime.getRuntime().exec(cmd);

            // Wait for child to finish
            try {
                child.waitFor();
            } catch (InterruptedException e) {
            }
            // Display exit status of subprocess
            int status = child.exitValue();
            if (status == 0)
                System.out.println("process successfully completed.");
            else
                System.out.println("process exited with " + status);
        } catch (IOException e) {
            System.err.println(e);
        }
    }
}
```

getErrorStream()

PURPOSE Retrieves an input stream for reading error output from the process.

SYNTAX `abstract public InputStream getErrorStream()`

DESCRIPTION The standard IO of a process consists of an input stream, an output stream, and an error stream. The error stream is an output stream generated by the process to display information about erroneous conditions. `getErrorStream()` allows the caller to obtain an input stream connected to this error stream. This allows the caller to then use methods like `InputStream.read()` to obtain the output sent by the process to the error steam.

There is only one error stream per process. Hence, multiple calls to `getErrorStream()` return the same `InputStream` object.

This stream is typically unbuffered.

RETURNS An input stream for reading error output from the process.

EXAMPLE This example executes the `ls` command on a nonexistent directory and hence forces a failure. It reads, from the error output stream of the command, the error reported by the command.

```
import java.io.*;
```

```
class Main {
    public static void main(String[] args) {
        try {
            String cmd = "ls";
            Process child = Runtime.getRuntime().exec(cmd + " /notthere");
            // get error output from child process
            InputStream child_err = child.getErrorStream();
            int c;
            while ((c = child_err.read()) != -1) {
                System.out.print((char)c);
            }
            child_err.close();
        } catch (IOException e) {
            System.err.println(e);
        }
    }
}
```


getInputStream()

PURPOSE Retrieves an input stream for reading output from the process.

SYNTAX `abstract public InputStream getInputStream()`

DESCRIPTION The standard IO of a process consists of an input stream, an output stream, and an error stream. The output stream is where the process sends output intended for display to the user. `getInputStream()` allows the caller to obtain an input stream that is connected to this output stream. This allows the caller to then use methods like `InputStream.read()` on the input stream to obtain the output of the process.

There is only one standard output stream per process. Hence, multiple calls to `getInputStream()` return the same `InputStream` object.

This stream is typically *buffered*, which means output generated by the process is stored until it is read (from this stream).

RETURNS An input stream for reading output from the process.

EXAMPLE This example executes the `ls` command and echoes the command's output.

```
import java.io.*;

class Main {
    public static void main(String[] args) {
        try {
            String cmd = "ls";
            Process child = Runtime.getRuntime().exec(cmd);
            // get output from child process
            InputStream child_in = child.getInputStream();
            int c;
            while ((c = child_in.read()) != -1) {
                System.out.print((char)c);
            }
```

```
            child_in.close();
        } catch (IOException e) {
            System.err.println(e);
        }
    }
}
```


getOutputStream()

PURPOSE Retrieves an output stream for sending data to the process.

SYNTAX `abstract public OutputStream getOutputStream()`

DESCRIPTION The standard IO of a process consists of an input stream, an output stream, and an error stream. The input stream is where the process reads its input from the user. `getOutputStream()` allows the caller to obtain an output stream that is connected to this input stream. This allows the caller to then use methods like `OutputStream.write()` to send data to the process.

There is only one standard input stream per process. Hence, multiple calls to `getOutputStream()` return the same `OutputStream` object.

This stream is typically *buffered*, which means data sent to this stream is stored until the process reads it.

RETURNS An output stream for feeding input to the process.

EXAMPLE This example executes the `cat` command and sends "hello world!" to `cat` by opening an output stream to it.

```
import java.io.*;

class Main {
    public static void main(String[] args) {
        try {
            String cmd = "cat";
            Process child = Runtime.getRuntime().exec(cmd);
            // stream for feeding input to child process
            PrintWriter out = new PrintWriter(child.getOutputStream());
            out.println("hello world!");
            out.close();
        } catch (IOException e) {
            System.err.println(e);
        }
    }
}
```

waitFor()

PURPOSE Waits for the process to terminate.

SYNTAX `abstract public int waitFor() throws InterruptedException`

DESCRIPTION A program can wait for its process to terminate using `waitFor()`. If the process has already terminated, the exit value of the process is returned. If the process has not terminated, this call blocks until the process terminates and returns the process's exit value.

RETURNS The exit value of the process. An exit value of `0` indicates the process executed successfully; all other values indicate failure.

EXCEPTIONS

`InterruptedException`

If another thread has interrupted this thread while it is waiting.

SEE ALSO `exitValue()`.

EXAMPLE This example executes the `ls` command, waits for the command to terminate, and reports the execution status of the command by examining the command's exit value returned by `waitFor()`.

```
import java.io.*;

class Main {
    public static void main(String[] args) {
        try {
            String cmd = "ls";
            Process child = Runtime.getRuntime().exec(cmd);
            // Wait for child to finish
            int status;
            try {
                status = child.waitFor();
            } catch (InterruptedException e) {
                status = -1;
            }
            // Display exit status of subprocess
            if (status == 0)
                System.out.println("process successfully completed.");
            else
                System.out.println("process exited with " + status);
        } catch (IOException e) {
            System.err.println(e);
        }
    }
}
```

java.util
Properties

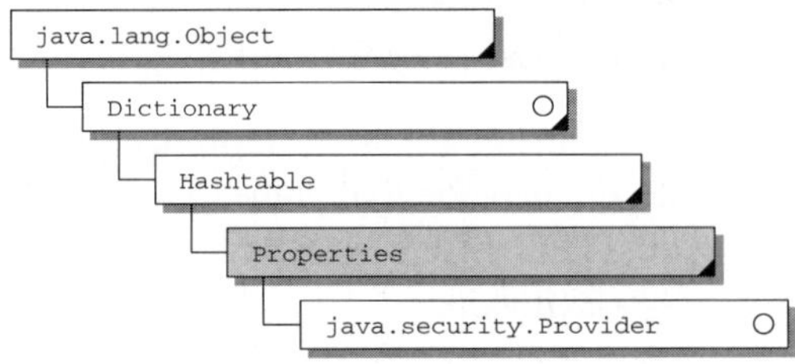

A B C D E F G H I J K L M N O P Q R S T U V W X Y Z

Syntax

```
public class Properties extends Hashtable
```

Description

The `Properties` class is used to represent a *properties list*. Each item on the list is called a *property* and consists of a *property name* and a *property value*. Each property name and property value is a Unicode string. If the properties list is to be used only internally within the Java program, there are no restrictions on the format of these strings. If the properties list is to be loaded or stored from IO streams, then syntactic rules apply that the property names and values must follow. These rules are described in the following section, "Formats of Properties." Also, some programs may have conventions for naming properties and their values.

Defaults

Each instance of the `Properties` class actually contains two properties lists: a *main* properties list and a *default* properties list. When you create a new `Properties` instance, you can supply a default properties list. This list is consulted when a requested property is not found in the main properties list. It also is a `Properties` instance, so it therefore can contain its own list of defaults. You can use this support of default properties lists to chain together properties lists.

Properties can be loaded from and saved into IO streams. Properties loaded from a stream are added to the main properties list. Since `Properties` is a subclass of `Hashtable`, you can also use methods from the `Hashtable` class to add and remove items from a `Properties` instance. Such changes affect the main properties list, not the default properties list. To make changes to the default properties list, perform the `Properties` methods directly on the reference of the default properties list.

System Properties

The `System` class uses `Properties` to represent *system properties*, which are information about the system and environment in which the Java program is running. Examples of system properties are the name of the user running the Java program, the version of the Java interpreter being used, and the name of the operating system on which the Java program is running. A complete list of the system properties is given in Table 35.

Property Name	Description
`java.version`	Java version number.
`java.vendor`	Java vendor-specific information.
`java.vendor.url`	Java vendor URL.
`java.home`	Directory name of where Java software has been installed.
`java.class.version`	Java class version number.
`java.class.path`	The setting of `CLASSPATH`.
`os.name`	Name of the operating system.
`os.arch`	Machine architecture.
`os.version`	Release version of the operating system.
`file.separator`	String used in file pathnames to separate directories.
`path.separator`	String used to separate components in a path variable.
`line.separator`	String used to separate lines.
`user.name`	User's account name.
`user.home`	Pathname of user's home directory.
`user.dir`	Pathname of user's current working directory.

TABLE 35: Java System Properties.

The Java system properties have a hierarchical naming convention for its property names; for example, "`user.name`", "`user.home`", and "`java.vendor`".

The class libraries contain methods that will parse the strings of system property values into Java data types (`Boolean.getBoolean()`, `Integer.getInteger()`, `Long.getLong()`, `Color.getColor()`, and `Font.getFont()`).

Formats of Properties

A property consists of a property name and a property value. A property name can contain any Unicode character except for the following:

equals (`=`)
colon (`:`)
space
newline (`\n`)
tab (`\t`)
return (`\r`)

The property value is a Unicode string. A backslash, newline, return, or tab that appears in the string is encoded by writing the character as *two* characters. For example, a newline (`\n`) is represented by two characters: a backslash (`\`) followed by the letter `n`. A property value cannot be `null`. If a property name does not have a corresponding value, the result is as if the property does not exist.

A properties list can be read from an input stream. The input stream can use localized character sets, but when they are read in, they are translated into Unicode. Conversely, a properties list can be written out to an output stream. The Java runtime will attempt to write out the list using the localized character set, if it is appropriate. If the properties are not being written out to a localized stream, a character that is not in the printable range is encoded using its Unicode value. Such a value has the format "`\u`*dddd*", where *d* is a hexadecimal character (one of `0–9`, `a–e`, `A–E`) (see `Character`). If the properties are written out to a localized stream, the Unicode characters will be translated to their localized representation by the localized stream.

When a properties list is written out, the property name is separated by an equals character (=). Each property name /property value pair is written on a single line and terminated by a newline character.

When a properties list is read in, lines beginning with the hash character (#) or the exclamation character (!) are treated as comment lines and are ignored (no property name/value are derived from them). Empty lines (those containing only whitespace characters, newlines, or returns) are also ignored. If a property name appears on a line with no property value, the property value is `null`.

Following is an example of an output file containing a properties list. It was generated using `Properties.save()` (see the example in `load()`).

```
#/* testing */
#Fri Oct 17 00:29:31 CDT 1997
user.language=en
java.home=q:\\jdk1.1.4\\bin\\..
java.vendor.url.bug=http://java.sun.com/cgi-bin/bugreport.cgi
awt.toolkit=sun.awt.windows.WToolkit
file.encoding.pkg=sun.io
java.version=1.1.4
file.separator=\\
line.separator=\r\n
user.region=US
file.encoding=8859_1
java.vendor=Sun Microsystems Inc.
user.timezone=CST
user.name=jcl
os.arch=x86
os.name=Windows NT
java.vendor.url=http://www.sun.com/
user.dir=q:\\users\\jcl\\book\\util\\properties
java.class.path=.;q:\\jdk1.1.4\\bin\\..\\classes;q:\\jdk1.1.4\\bin\\..\\lib\\c
lasses.zip;q:\\jdk1.1.4\\bin\\..\\lib\\classes.jar;q:\\jdk1.1.4\\bin\\..\\lib\
\rt.jar;q:\\jdk1.1.4\\bin\\..\\lib\\i18n.jar
java.class.version=45.3
os.version=4.0
path.separator=;
user.home=q:\\users\\jcl
```

MEMBER SUMMARY	
Constructor	
`Properties()`	Constructs a new properties list.
Property Methods	
`getProperty()`	Retrieves the value of a property in this properties list.
`list()`	Writes this properties list to a print output stream or writer.
`load()`	Reads properties from an input stream and adds them to this properties list.
`propertyNames()`	Retrieves the list of property names from this properties list.
`save()`	Writes this properties list to an output stream.
Protected Field	
`defaults`	The default properties.

See Also

`Hashtable`, `java.lang.System.getProperties()`.

defaults

PURPOSE The default properties.

SYNTAX `protected Properties defaults`

DESCRIPTION This field contains the default properties for this properties list. It is an optional argument supplied to the `Properties()` constructor. If the constructor was called with no defaults, `defaults` is `null`.

`getProperty()` will search `defaults` when the requested property is not found in the main properties list.

SEE ALSO `getProperty()`, `Properties()`.

EXAMPLE This example shows the use of `defaults` in the implementation of `getProperty()`.

```
public String getProperty(String key) {
    String val = (String)super.get(key);
        return ((val == null) && (defaults != null)) ?
                defaults.getProperty(key) : val;
    }
```

getProperty()

PURPOSE Retrieves the value of a property in this properties list.

SYNTAX
```
public String getProperty(String propName)
public String getProperty(String propName, String defVal)
```

DESCRIPTION The two forms of this method find the property with the name `propName` from this properties list and return the property's value as a string. If `propName` is not in the main properties list, the default properties list, if any, associated with this properties list is searched. If `propName` is still not found and no `defVal` is specified, `null` is returned. If `propName` is not found and `defVal` is specified, `defVal` is returned.

PARAMETERS

`defVal` A possibly `null` string containing the default value to return if `propName` is not found.

`propName` The non-`null` name of the property to retrieve.

RETURNS The value associated with `propName` if `propName` is found; otherwise, `defVal`. If `defVal` is not specified, `null`.

SEE ALSO `Boolean.getBoolean()`, `Color.getColor()`, `defaults`, `Font.getFont()`, `Integer.getInteger()`, `Long.getLong()`, `System.getProperty()`.

EXAMPLE
```
// Look for property
System.out.println("java.version: " +
                   props.getProperty("java.version"));

// Look for property with default
System.out.println("notthere: " +
                   props.getProperty("notthere", "default"));
```

list()

PURPOSE Writes this list of properties to a print output stream or writer.

SYNTAX
```
public void list(PrintStream out)
public void list(PrintWriter writer)
```

DESCRIPTION This method writes this list of properties to the print output stream `out` or to the printer writer `wr`. Unlike `save()`, *both* the default properties list and the main properties list are printed. If a property appears in both lists, only the one in the main list is printed.

A B C D E F G H I J K L M N O P Q R S T U V W X Y Z

Each property is printed, one per line, in the format

```
propertyName=propertyValue
```

If the property value is too long (over 40 characters), only a prefix of it is printed. No special provisions are made for special characters (like newlines and returns). The format of the output generated by this method is not the same as that generated by `save()` and cannot be read in using `load()`.

PARAMETERS

`out` The non-`null` print output stream to print the properties.

`wr` The non-`null` print writer to use for printing the properties.

SEE ALSO `PrintStream`, `save()`.

EXAMPLE See the `load()` example also.

```
Properties props_copy = new Properties(props); // Make copy
props.list(System.out);                        // print out
```

load()

PURPOSE Reads properties from an input stream and adds them to this properties list.

SYNTAX `public synchronized void load(InputStream in) throws IOException`

DESCRIPTION This method reads properties from the input stream `in` and adds them to this properties list's main properties list (i.e., not to the default list). If a property being added already exists in the main properties list, the newly added property's value overrides the existing value. These properties override any corresponding properties in the default properties list (but do not change the properties in the default properties list). The format of the data in the input stream is expected to be in the format described in the `Properties` class description. If the data contains two properties with the same name, the last one to be loaded overrides the previously loaded one.

Because `Properties` is a subclass of `Hashtable`, `Hashtable.put()` can also be used to add to the properties list.

PARAMETERS

`in` The non-`null` input stream from which to read.

EXCEPTIONS

`IOException`

If an IO error occurred when reading from `in`.

SEE ALSO `Hashtable.put()`, `save()`.

EXAMPLE

```
Properties props = new Properties();  // empty list

Properties sysprops = System.getProperties();

try {
    FileOutputStream out = new FileOutputStream("/tmp/props");
    sysprops.save(out, "/* testing */");
    FileInputStream in = new FileInputStream("/tmp/props");

    props.load(in);

    System.out.println("Got properties from /tmp/props");
    props.list(System.out);
} catch (IOException e) {
    System.out.println(e);
}
```

Properties()

PURPOSE
Constructs a new properties list.

SYNTAX
```
public Properties()
public Properties(Properties defs)
```

DESCRIPTION
There are two forms of the constructor for the `Properties` class. The first form creates an empty properties list with no default properties list. The second form creates an empty main properties list with default `defs`. If a requested property is not found in the main properties list, the properties list in `defs` is searched. Modifications to the contents of `defs` subsequent to calling this constructor will be visible to this `Properties` instance.

PARAMETERS
`defs` The possibly `null` default properties list.

SEE ALSO
`defaults`, `getProperty()`, `load()`.

EXAMPLE
See `list()` and `load()`.

propertyNames()

PURPOSE
Retrieves the list of property names from this properties list.

SYNTAX
```
public Enumeration propertyNames()
```

DESCRIPTION
This method returns the property names of all properties in the main properties list and default properties list in this properties list. If there are duplicates in the main and default lists, the properties in the default list are overridden.

Modifications made to either list during enumeration do not affect the enumeration.

If you are interested only in the properties in the main properties list, you can use `Hashtable.keys()` to get the property names of all properties in the main properties list.

RETURNS An enumeration of all property names in this properties list.

SEE ALSO `Hashtable.keys()`.

EXAMPLE

```
// Enumeration properties
for (Enumeration e = props.propertyNames();
     e.hasMoreElements();
     System.out.println("\t" + (String)e.nextElement()));
```

save()

PURPOSE Writes this properties list to an output stream.

SYNTAX `public synchronized void save(OutputStream out, String comment)`

DESCRIPTION This method writes this properties list to the output stream `out`. Only the main properties list is written. If the string `comment` is not `null`, it is written out as the first line in the stream as a comment preceded by a hash character (#). Before the properties are written, a comment with the current time of day is written out to the stream. The properties are then written out in the format described in the `Properties` class description.

PARAMETERS

`comment` The possibly `null` comment to write to the stream.

`out` The non-`null` output stream to which to write.

SEE ALSO `list()`, `load()`.

EXAMPLE See `load()`.

java.util
PropertyResourceBundle

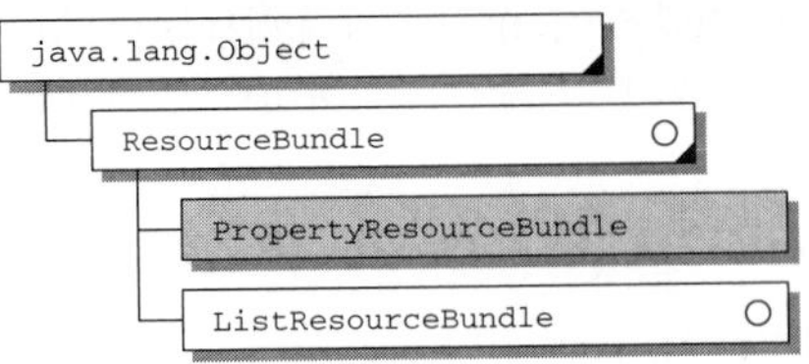

A B C D E F G H I J K L M N O P Q R S T U V W X Y Z

Syntax
`public class PropertyResourceBundle extends ResourceBundle`

Description
A property resource bundle is a special type of resource bundle whose values are stored in a properties file (see `Properties`). See the `ResourceBundle` class for complete information on resource bundles.

Usage
This class is not typically used directly by the programmer. This class is used by the `ResourceBundle.getBundle()` method when it encounters a properties file. See the `ResourceBundle` class description for more details.

MEMBER SUMMARY	
Constructor	
`PropertyResourceBundle()`	Constructs a `PropertyResourceBundle` instance.
Resource Bundle Methods	
`getKeys()`	Creates an enumeration of the keys in this resource bundle.
`handleGetObject()`	Called to retrieve a resource from this resource bundle.

See Also
`ListResourceBundle`, `ResourceBundle`.

Example
For a typical example of how this class is used by `ResourceBundle.getBundle()`, see the `ResourceBundle` class example. The example here demonstrates how to directly create a property resource bundle when needed.

```
import java.util.*;
import java.io.*;

class Main {
    public static void main(String[] args) {
        try {
            FileInputStream is = new FileInputStream("data.properties");

            PropertyResourceBundle bundle = new PropertyResourceBundle(is);
            is.close();

            System.out.println(bundle.getString("key-1"));
            System.out.println(bundle.getString("key-2"));
        } catch (Exception e) {
            System.out.println(e);
        }
    }
}
```

getKeys()

PURPOSE Creates an enumeration of the keys in this resource bundle.

SYNTAX `public Enumeration getKeys()`

DESCRIPTION This method returns an enumeration containing the keys of all available resources in this resource bundle.

The default implementation of this method creates an enumeration on an internal hash table.

RETURNS A non-`null` enumeration of this resource bundle.

EXAMPLE See the `ResourceBundle` class example.

handleGetObject()

PURPOSE Called to retrieve a resource from this resource bundle.

SYNTAX `public final Object handleGetObject(String key)`

DESCRIPTION This method is called by the resource bundle framework (see `ResourceBundle`) to retrieve a resource from this resource bundle. This method is not meant to be called directly.

This method looks up `key` in an internal hash table initialized by the `PropertyResourceBundle` constructor.

PARAMETERS

`key` A non-`null` case-sensitive string containing the name of the resource.

RETURNS The resource with the name `key`. `null` if not found.

SEE ALSO `ResourceBundle.getObject()`, `ResourceBundle.getString()`, `ResourceBundle.getStringArray()`, `ResourceBundle.parent`.

EXAMPLE See the `ResourceBundle` class example.

A B C D E F G H I J K L M N O P Q R S T U V W X Y Z

PropertyResourceBundle()

PURPOSE Constructs a `PropertyResourceBundle` instance.

SYNTAX
```
public PropertyResourceBundle (InputStream stream) throws
    IOException
```

DESCRIPTION This constructor constructs a property resource bundle and initializes it with the information from `stream`. It initializes an internal hash table containing all of the resources contained by processing `stream`. The format of stream is detailed in the `Properties` class description.

PARAMETERS

`stream` A non-`null` input stream.

EXCEPTIONS

`IOException`

If an IO error occurred while reading the properties from `stream`.

SEE ALSO `java.io.IOException`, `Properties`.

EXAMPLE See the class example.

ProtocolException

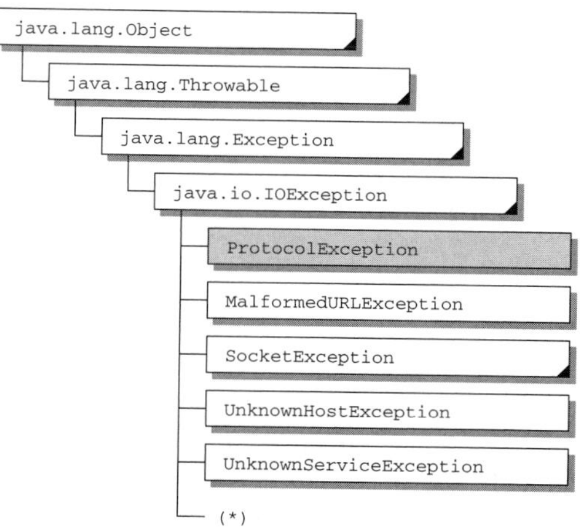

A B C D E F G H I J K L M N O P Q R S T U V W X Y Z

Syntax

```
public class ProtocolException extends IOException
```

Description

`ProtocolException` is an IO exception that is thrown when an attempt is made to connect a socket of the wrong type (stream versus nonstream) or to indicate an unexpected data exchange that violates the protocol in question. For example, an attempt to connect a datagram socket to a protocol that accepts only streams would result in a `ProtocolException` being thrown. Sending data or controls not expected by a particular protocol would result in a `ProtocolException` being thrown.

A method that throws a `ProtocolException` must declare it or any of its superclasses in the method's `throws` clause.

MEMBER SUMMARY	
Constructor	
`ProtocolException()`	Constructs a `ProtocolException` instance.

See Also

`java.io.IOException`, `SocketImpl.connect()`, `SocketException`.

Example

See the use of `ProtocolException` in the `URLConnection` class example.

ProtocolException()

PURPOSE — Constructs a `ProtocolException` instance.

SYNTAX

```
public ProtocolException()
public ProtocolException(String host)
```

DESCRIPTION — The two forms of this constructor construct an instance of `ProtocolException`. An optional string `host` can be supplied. Typically, `host` is the name of the remote machine to which the socket is attempting to connect, but it can be any arbitrary message. `host` is used to construct the message returned by `Throwable.getMessage()`. If `host` is not supplied, it defaults to `null`.

PARAMETERS

`host` — The possibly `null` machine name for which this exception was thrown.

SEE ALSO — `java.lang.Throwable.getMessage()`.

PushbackInputStream

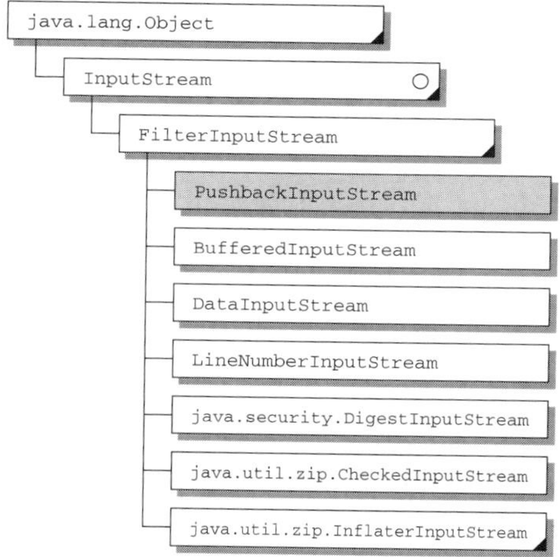

Syntax

```
public class PushbackInputStream extends FilterInputStream
```

Description

A *pushback input stream* is a filter stream that allows bytes to be "pushed back" to (or unread from) the stream. For example, you can read some bytes and then push them back onto the stream so that the next read operation will retrieve the bytes that were pushed back. In Figure 81, the character "a" is read once, then pushed back, and then read again. This capability is useful when building parsers that need to read ahead in the stream in order to decide how to process the stream.

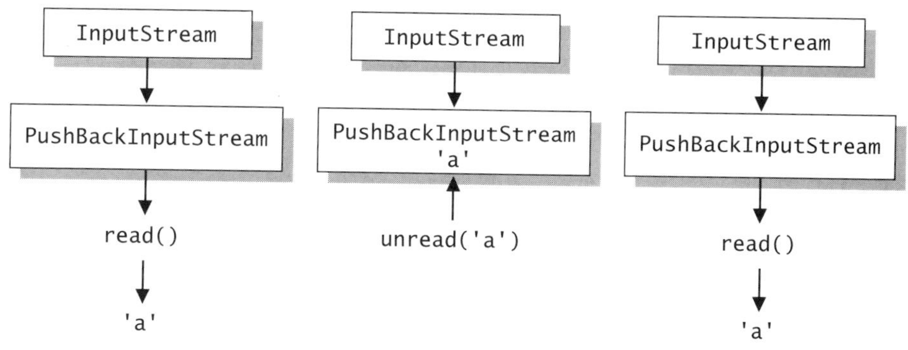

FIGURE 81: **`PushbackInputStream`.**

Pushing Back Bytes

`PushbackInputStream` implements a pushback input stream that has a buffer (`buf`) of a program-specified size. The buffer's size determines the maximum number of pushed-back bytes in its stream. The buffer is used as a stack—bytes that are most recently pushed back are read first. See Figure 82.

When the buffer becomes full, no more bytes can be pushed back until one or more of the pushed back bytes have been read.

When the buffer is empty, bytes are read from the stream that this pushback input stream filters.

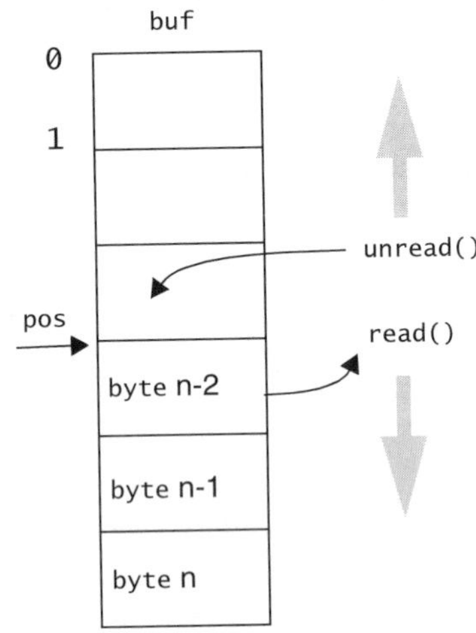

FIGURE 82: How Bytes Are Pushed Back.

PushbackInputStream versus PushbackReader

`PushbackInputStream` is meant for byte streams. Its read/unread methods deal with bytes (0–255). `PushbackReader` is meant for character-oriented input streams. Its read/unread methods deal with `char` values. You should use `PushbackReader` when the input is a character stream (for example, when writing a parser).

MEMBER SUMMARY	
Constructor	
`PushbackInputStream()`	Constructs a `PushbackInputStream` instance for an input stream.
Input Methods	
`read()`	Reads bytes from this pushback input stream.
`unread()`	Pushes back one or more bytes.
Stream Methods	
`available()`	Determines the number of bytes that can be read without blocking.
`markSupported()`	Determines whether this pushback input stream supports mark/reset.
Protected Fields	
`buf`	The buffer containing the unread bytes.
`pos`	The position in `buf` from which to read the next pushed-back byte.

See Also

BufferedInputStream, FilterInputStream, InputStream, PushbackReader.

Example

This example shows how a pushback input stream is used to categorize the bytes read from a stream: those with values less than 128 and the rest. There are two read methods: readGroupOne() and readGroupTwo(). Each of these keeps reading from the input stream until it encounters a byte that does not belong to its group. At this point, it will push back the byte onto the stream for the other read method to process.

```
import java.io.*;
import java.util.Vector;

class Main {
    static int countOne = 0;
    static int countTwo = 0;

    public static void main(String[] args) {
        if (args.length != 1) {
            System.err.println("usage: java Main <input>");
            System.exit(-1);
        }
        try {
            PushbackInputStream pushin = new PushbackInputStream(
                new FileInputStream(args[0]));
            boolean eof;
            while (true) {
                if (eof = readGroupOne(pushin))
                    break;
                if (eof = readGroupTwo(pushin))
                    break;
            }
            System.out.println("ones: " + countOne + " twos: " + countTwo);
        } catch (IOException e) {
            e.printStackTrace();
        }
    }
    private static boolean readGroupOne(PushbackInputStream in) {
        int c = -1;
        int i = 0;
        try {
            c = in.read();
            for (i = 0; c >= 0; i++) {
                if (c < 128) {
                    in.unread(c);
                    break;
                }
                c = in.read();
            }
        } catch (IOException e) {
        }
        countOne += i;
        return (c == -1);
    }
    private static boolean readGroupTwo(PushbackInputStream in) {
```

```
            int c = -1;
            int i = 0;
            try {
                c = in.read();
                for (i = 0; c >= 0; i++) {
                    if (c >= 128) {
                        in.unread(c);
                        break;
                    }
                    c = in.read();
                }
            } catch (IOException e) {
            }
            countTwo += i;
            return (c == -1);
        }
    }
```


available()

PURPOSE Determines the number of bytes that can be read without being blocked.

SYNTAX `public int available() throws IOException`

DESCRIPTION This method returns the number of bytes that can be read without being blocked. This number includes the number of bytes that have been pushed back (if any), plus the number of bytes available from the stream that this pushback input stream is filtering.

RETURNS The number of bytes that can be read without being blocked.

EXCEPTIONS

`IOException`

If an IO error occurred while attempting to determine the number of bytes available from the stream being filtered.

OVERRIDES `FilterInputStream.available()`.

EXAMPLE This example uses a pushback input stream to examine the header of a file. It uses the length of the file and this header information to determine which parser to use.

```
try {
    PushbackInputStream pushin =
        new PushbackInputStream(new FileInputStream(args[0]));
    if (pushin.available() > CLASSC_LIMIT) {
        // read header (first byte) to find out format
        int c = pushin.read();
        if (c >= 0)
            pushin.unread(c);  // let parsers deal with it
        switch (c) {
        case CLASSA:
```

```
            classAParser(pushin);
            break;
        case CLASSB:
            classBParser(pushin);
        }
    } else {
        classCParser(pushin);
    }
    pushin.close();
} catch (IOException e) {
    e.printStackTrace();
}
```


buf

PURPOSE The buffer containing the unread bytes.

SYNTAX `protected byte[] buf`

DESCRIPTION This `byte` array contains the bytes that have been pushed back. It is created by the `PushbackInputStream` constructors. See the class description for information about how it is used.

This field is not used directly by the application. The application uses `read()` and `unread()` to remove/add bytes from/to this `byte` array.

SEE ALSO `pos`, `read()`, `unread()`.

markSupported()

PURPOSE Determines whether this pushback input stream supports mark/reset.

SYNTAX `public boolean markSupported()`

DESCRIPTION Pushback input streams do not support mark/reset. This method always returns `false` for pushback input streams.

RETURNS `false`.

OVERRIDES `FilterInputStream.markSupported()`.

SEE ALSO `InputStream.mark()`, `InputStream.markSupported()`, `InputStream.reset()`.

EXAMPLE

```
PushbackInputStream pushin = new PushbackInputStream(System.in);
if (pushin.markSupported())
    System.out.println("Mark for pushback is supported");
else
    System.out.println("Mark for pushback is not supported");
```

A B C D E F G H I J K L M N O P Q R S T U V W X Y Z

pos

PURPOSE The position in buf from which to read the next pushed back byte.

SYNTAX `protected int pos`

DESCRIPTION This field contains the index in `buf` of the next pushed-back byte to read. If `buf` contains no pushed-back bytes, `pos` is `buf.length`. If `buf` is full with pushed-back bytes, `pos` is `0`. See the class description for more about how `pos` is used to make `buf` behave like a stack.

This field is not used directly by the application. The application uses `read()` and `unread()` to remove/add bytes from/to `buf` and, as a side effect, updates `pos`.

SEE ALSO `buf, unread(), read().`

PushbackInputStream()

PURPOSE Constructs a `PushbackInputStream` instance for an input stream.

SYNTAX
```
public PushbackInputStream(InputStream in)
public PushbackInputStream(InputStream in, int size)
```

DESCRIPTION This constructor creates a new pushback input stream for the input stream `in`. `size` specifies the size of the buffer to create to hold the pushed-back bytes. If `size` is not specified, it defaults to `1`.

When you read from this new pushback input stream, it reads from `in`, except when you have previously "pushed back" bytes to this pushback stream using `unread()`. In that case, the pushed-back bytes are returned before new bytes are read from `in`.

PARAMETERS
- `in` The non-`null` input stream for which this pushback input stream is created.
- `size` The size of the buffer to create for holding the pushed-back bytes. `size` ≥ `0`.

SEE ALSO `FilterInputStream, read(), unread().`

EXAMPLE See the class example, `available()`, and `markSupported()`.

read()

PURPOSE Reads bytes from this pushback input stream.

SYNTAX
```
public int read() throws IOException
public int read(byte[] buffer, int offset, int count) throws
    IOException
```

DESCRIPTION This method reads bytes from this pushback input stream. If there are bytes that have been previously pushed back (`unread()`), these are "read" first before other bytes are read from the stream being filtered. See the class description for details.

The first form of this method reads the next byte from this pushback input stream and returns it as an `int`. The high-order 3 bytes of the `int` are set to `0`. The second form of this method reads `count` number of bytes from this pushback input stream and stores the bytes in the `byte` array `buffer` starting at index `offset`. Depending on how many bytes were requested and how many pushed-back bytes there are, the bytes that are stored into `buffer` may be a mix of pushed-back bytes and bytes read from the stream being filtered. This method returns the total number of bytes read.

PARAMETERS

`buffer` The non-`null` `byte` array in which to store the bytes read.

`count` The number of bytes to read. `0` ≤ `count` ≤ `buffer.length-offset`.

`offset` The index in `buffer` at which to start storing the bytes read. `0` ≤ `offset` < `buffer.length`.

RETURNS The first form returns the byte read; the second form returns the number of bytes read. Both forms return `-1` if end-of-stream has been reached before any bytes have been read.

EXCEPTIONS

`ArrayIndexOutOfBoundsException`
If `count` or `offset` is outside of the specified bounds.

`IOException`
If an IO error occurred.

OVERRIDES `FilterInputStream.read()`.

SEE ALSO `unread()`.

EXAMPLE See the class example.

unread()

PURPOSE Pushes back one or more bytes.

SYNTAX

```
public void unread(int oneByte) throws IOException
public void unread(byte[] buffer) throws IOException
public void unread(byte[] buffer, int offset, int count) throws
    IOException
```

DESCRIPTION This method pushes back one or more bytes to this pushback input stream by storing them into the field `buf`. See the class description for details.

The first form of this method pushes back the low-order byte of oneByte to this pushback input stream. The immediate next read() call on this pushback input stream will return oneByte first before returning other pushed-back bytes or bytes read from the stream being filtered.

The second and third forms of this method push back count number of bytes from buffer starting at index offset. If count and offset are not specified, they default to buffer.length and 0, respectively. The bytes from buffer are pushed back such that the bytes are subsequently read back in the following order:

```
buffer[offset], buffer[offset+1], ...
```

Note that this is the exact opposite order as that achieved by pushing them a byte at a time, as follows:

```
for (int i = 0; i < buffer.length; i++) {
    in.unread(buffer[i]);
}
```

PARAMETERS

buffer	The non-null byte array containing bytes to be pushed back.
count	The number of bytes to push back. 0 ≤ count ≤ buffer.length-offset.
offset	The index in buffer at which to get the bytes to be pushed back. 0 ≤ offset < buffer.length.
oneByte	The byte to push back.

EXCEPTIONS

ArrayIndexOutOfBoundsException
: If count or offset is outside of the specified bounds.

IOException
: If an attempt is made to push back bytes when the buffer holding the pushed-back bytes (buf) is already full.

SEE ALSO buf, pos, read().

EXAMPLE This is a silly program that pushes "hello" to the head of the stream to demonstrate pushing back an array of bytes using unread(). See the class example for the use of unread() on a single byte.

```
import java.io.*;

class Main {
    public static void main(String[] args) {
        // Create a pb input stream with buf size of 10
        PushbackInputStream in = new PushbackInputStream(System.in, 10);

        byte[] buf = {'h', 'e', 'l', 'l', 'o', '\n'};
        try {
            in.unread(buf);
            int c;
```

```
            // Echo contents of pb stream to standard out.
            while ((c=in.read()) >= 0) {
                System.out.print((char)c);// hello ...
            }
            System.out.println();
        } catch (IOException e) {}
    }
}
```

java.io

PushbackReader

```
java.lang.Object
  └ Reader
      └ FilterReader
          └ PushbackReader
```


Syntax

```
public class PushbackReader extends FilterReader
```

Description

A *pushback reader* is a filter reader (filter character stream) that allows characters to be "pushed back" (or unread) from the stream. For example, you can read some characters and subsequently push them back onto the stream so that the next read operation will retrieve the characters that were pushed back. This capability is useful when building parsers that need to read ahead in order to decide how to process the input.

Pushing Back Characters

`PushbackReader` implements a pushback reader that has a buffer of a program-specified size. The buffer's size determines the maximum number of pushed-back characters the reader will allow. The buffer is used as a stack—characters that are most recently pushed back are read first. See Figure 83.

When the buffer becomes full, no more characters can be pushed back until one or more of the pushed-back characters have been read.

When the buffer is empty, characters are read from the reader that this pushback reader filters.

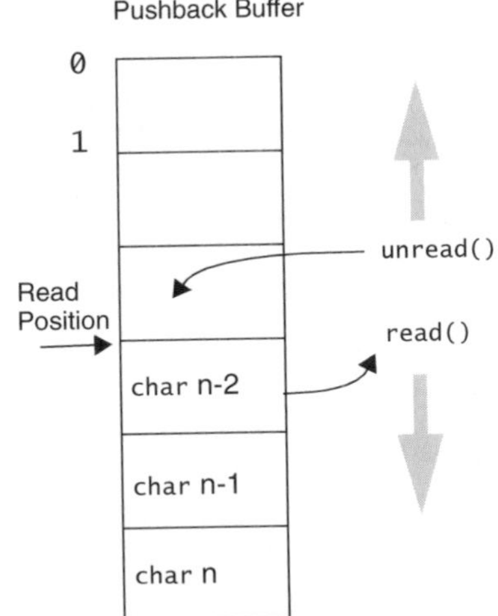

FIGURE 83: How Characters Are Pushed Back.

PushbackInputStream versus PushbackReader

`PushbackInputStream` is meant for byte streams. Its read/unread methods deal with bytes (0–255). `PushbackReader` is meant for character-oriented input streams. Its read/unread methods deal with `char` values. You should use `PushbackReader` when the input is a character stream (for example, when writing a parser).

MEMBER SUMMARY	
Constructor	
`PushbackReader()`	Creates a `PushbackReader` instance.
Input Methods	
`read()`	Reads one or more characters from this pushback reader.
`unread()`	Pushes back one or more characters.
Stream Methods	
`ready()`	Determines whether this pushback reader is ready to be read without being blocked.
`close()`	Closes this pushback reader.
Mark/Reset Method	
`markSupported()`	Determines whether this pushback reader supports mark/reset.

See Also

`BufferedReader`, `PushbackInputStream`.

Example

This example shows how a pushback reader is used to parse a sequence of numeric or string tokens. There are two parsing methods: `readNumber()` and `readString()`. Each of these keeps reading until it encounters a character that does not belong to its token. At this point, it will push back the character for the other parser to read.

```
import java.io.*;
import java.util.Vector;

class Main {
    public static void main(String[] args) {
        if (args.length != 1) {
            System.err.println("Usage: java Main <input>");
            System.exit(-1);
        }
        Vector vec = new Vector();
        try {
            PushbackReader in = new PushbackReader(new FileReader(args[0]));
            boolean eof;
            while (true) {
                if (eof = readNumber(in, vec))
                    break;
                if (eof = readString(in, vec))
                    break;
            }
            in.close();
        } catch (IOException e) {
            System.err.println(e);
```

```
        }
        System.out.println(vec);
    }
    private static boolean readNumber(PushbackReader in, Vector vec) {
        StringBuffer sb = new StringBuffer();
        int c = -1;
        // read number
        try {
            for (c = in.read(); c >= 0; c = in.read()) {
                if (Character.isDigit((char)c)) {
                    sb.append((char)c);
                } else if (Character.isWhitespace((char )c)) {
                    break;
                } else {
                    in.unread(c);
                    break;
                }
            }
        } catch (IOException e) {
        }
        if (sb.length() > 0)
            vec.addElement(Integer.valueOf(sb.toString()));
        return (c == -1);
    }
    private static boolean readString(PushbackReader in, Vector vec) {
        StringBuffer sb = new StringBuffer();
        int c = -1;
        try {
            for (c = in.read(); c >= 0; c = in.read()) {
                if (Character.isDigit((char)c)) {
                    in.unread(c);
                    break;
                } else if (Character.isWhitespace((char )c))
                    break;
                else
                    sb.append((char)c);
            }
        } catch (IOException e) {
        }
        vec.addElement(sb.toString());
        return (c == -1);
    }
}
```

close()

PURPOSE Closes this pushback reader.

SYNTAX `public void close() throws IOException`

DESCRIPTION This method closes this pushback reader. It releases the pushback buffer that it was using and closes the underlying reader. This, in turn, will close the next reader downstream, and so on. Hence, this method effectively closes this reader and all of the readers "downstream."

EXCEPTIONS

`IOException`

If an IO error occurs while attempting to close the underlying reader.

OVERRIDES `FilterReader.close()`.

EXAMPLE See the class example.

markSupported()

PURPOSE Determines whether this pushback reader supports mark/reset.

SYNTAX `public boolean markSupported()`

DESCRIPTION Pushback readers do not support mark/reset. This method always returns `false` for pushback readers.

RETURNS `false`.

OVERRIDES `FilterReader.markSupported()`.

SEE ALSO `Reader.mark()`, `Reader.markSupported()`, `Reader.reset()`.

EXAMPLE See `FilterReader.mark()`.

PushbackReader()

PURPOSE Creates a `PushbackReader` instance.

SYNTAX

```
public PushbackReader(Reader in)
public PushbackReader(Reader in, int size)
```

DESCRIPTION This constructor creates a new pushback reader for the reader `in`. `size` specifies the size of the buffer to create to hold the pushed back characters. If `size` is not specified, it defaults to `1`.

When you read from this new pushback reader, it reads from `in`, except when you have previously "pushed back" characters to this pushback reader by using `unread()`. In that case, the pushed-back characters are returned before new characters are read from `in`.

PARAMETERS

`in` The non-`null` reader from which characters will be read.

`size` The size of the pushback buffer. `size` ≥ `0`.

SEE ALSO `read()`, `unread()`.

EXAMPLE See the class example.

read()

PURPOSE Reads one or more characters from this pushback reader.

SYNTAX
```
public int read() throws IOException
public int read(char buffer[], int offset, int count) throws
   IOException
```

DESCRIPTION This method reads characters from this pushback reader. If there are characters that have been previously pushed back (`unread()`), these are "read" first before other characters are read from the underlying reader. See the class description for details.

The first form of this method reads the next character from this pushback reader and returns it as an `int`. The high-order 2 bytes of the `int` are set to `0`. The second form of this method reads `count` number of characters from this pushback reader and stores the characters into the `char` array `buffer` starting at index `offset`. Depending on how many characters were requested and how many pushed-back characters there are, the characters that are stored into `buffer` may be a mix of pushed-back characters and characters read from the underlying reader. This method returns the total number of characters read.

PARAMETERS

`buffer` The non-`null` `char` array containing characters to be pushed back.

`count` The number of characters to push back. `0` ≤ `count` ≤ `buffer.length-offset`.

`offset` The index in `buffer` at which to get the characters to be pushed back. `0` ≤ `offset` < `buffer.length`.

`oneChar` The character to push back.

RETURNS The first form returns the character read; the second form returns the number of characters read. Both forms return `-1` if end-of-stream has been reached before any characters have been read.

EXCEPTIONS

`ArrayIndexOutOfBoundsException`
If `count` or `offset` is outside of the specified bounds.

`IOException`
If reader has already been closed or if an error was encountered while attempting to read from the underlying reader.

OVERRIDES `FilterReader.read()`.

SEE ALSO `unread()`.

EXAMPLE See the class example.

ready()

PURPOSE Determines whether this pushback reader is ready to be read without being blocked.

SYNTAX
```
public boolean ready() throws IOException
```

RETURNS `true` if there are unread characters in the pushback buffer or if the underlying reader is ready to be read without being blocked; `false` otherwise.

EXCEPTIONS

`IOException`

If this reader has already been closed.

OVERRIDES `FilterReader.ready()`.

SEE ALSO `Reader.ready()`.

EXAMPLE See `Reader.ready()`.

unread()

PURPOSE Pushes back one or more characters.

SYNTAX
```
public void unread(int oneChar) throws IOException
public void unread(char buffer[]) throws IOException
public void unread(char buffer[], int offset, int count) throws
    IOException
```

DESCRIPTION This method pushes back one or more characters to this pushback reader and stores them into the pushback buffer to be returned in subsequent calls to `read()`.

The first form of this method pushes back the low-order 2 bytes of `oneChar` to this pushback reader. The immediate next `read()` call on this pushback reader will return `oneChar` first before returning other pushed-back characters or characters read from the underlying reader.

The second and third forms of this method push back `count` number of characters from `buffer` starting at index `offset`. If `count` and `offset` are not specified, they default to `buffer.length` and `0`, respectively. The characters from `buffer` are pushed back such that the characters are subsequently read back in the following order:

```
buffer[offset], buffer[offset+1], ...
```

Note that this is the exact opposite order as that achieved by pushing them one character at a time, as follows:

```
for (int i = 0; i < buffer.length; i++) {
    in.unread(buffer[i]);
}
```

PARAMETERS

`buffer`	The non-`null` `char` array containing characters to be pushed back.
`count`	The number of characters to push back. $0 \le$ `count` $\le$ `buffer.length-offset`.
`offset`	The index in `buffer` at which to get the characters to be pushed back. $0 \le$ `offset` $<$ `buffer.length`.
`oneChar`	The character to push back.

EXCEPTIONS

`ArrayIndexOutOfBoundsException`
If `count` or `offset` is outside of the specified bounds.

`IOException`
If the pushback buffer is full, or if this reader has already been closed, or if some other I/O error occurs

SEE ALSO `read()`.

EXAMPLE This is a silly program that pushes "numéro" to the head of the reader to demonstrate pushing back an array of `char` using `unread()`. See the class example for the use of `unread()` on a single `char`.

```
import java.io.*;

class Main {
    public static void main(String[] args) {
        // Create a pushback reader with buf size of 10
        PushbackReader in = new PushbackReader(
            new InputStreamReader(System.in), 10);

        char[] buf = {'n', 'u', 'm', '\u00e9', 'r', 'o'};

        try {
            in.unread(buf);     // next chars read are buf[0], buf[1]
            int c;
            // Echo contents of reader to standard out.
            while ((c=in.read()) >= 0) {
                System.out.print((char)c);      // numero ...
            }
            System.out.println();
        } catch (IOException e) {}
    }
}
```

Random

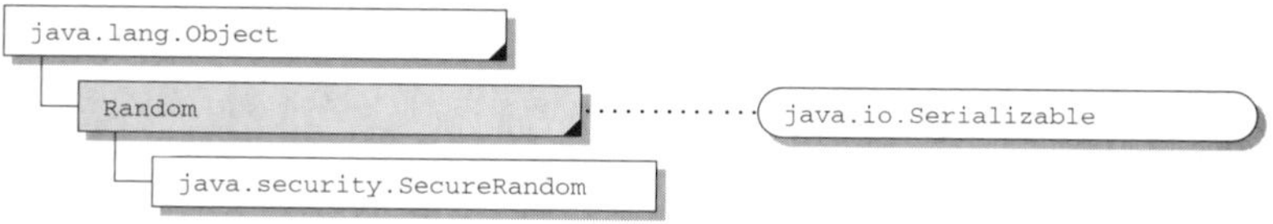

Syntax

```
public class Random implements Serializable
```

Description

A *random-number generator* produces a sequence of numbers that are picked randomly from among a set or range of numbers. The appearance of a number at a particular position in this sequence is purely random. A *pseudorandom-number generator* produces a sequence of *pseudorandom numbers*. A pseudorandom-number generator is created with a *seed*. Two pseudorandom-number generators that have been created with the same seed value will produce two identical sequences of pseudorandom numbers. Consequently, pseudorandom numbers are not really random numbers in the true sense. Rather, they exhibit randomness within any *single* sequence of pseudorandom numbers of a given seed.

The `Random` class is used to represent a pseudorandom-number generator for generating a sequence of pseudorandom numbers. You create a pseudorandom-number generator by giving it a seed. The generator uses the seed in the algorithm for generating the pseudorandom numbers.

Distribution of Pseudorandom Numbers

The numbers returned by the pseudorandom-number generator are of two distributions. One is *uniform distribution*. This means the numbers are uniformly distributed between the target range of numbers. For example, if the range is between 0.0 (inclusive) and 1.0 (exclusive), the numbers returned will be uniformly distributed between 0.0 and 1.0. The probability of returning any number in this range is equal. This is the distribution used for `nextDouble()`, `nextFloat()`, `nextInt()`, and `nextLong()`.

The second distribution is the *Gaussian distribution*. This is a bell-curved distribution with a mean of 0.0 and a standard deviation of 1.0.

MEMBER SUMMARY	
Constructor	
`Random()`	Constructs a pseudorandom-number generator.
Seed Method	
`setSeed()`	Sets the seed of this pseudorandom-number generator.
Generation Methods	
`nextBytes()`	Generates the next pseudorandom, uniformly distributed sequence of bytes.
`nextDouble()`	Generates the next pseudorandom, uniformly distributed `double` value.
`nextFloat()`	Generates the next pseudorandom, uniformly distributed `float` value.
`nextGaussian()`	Generates the next pseudorandom, Gaussian-distributed `double` value.
`nextInt()`	Generates the next pseudorandom, uniformly distributed `int` value.
`nextLong()`	Generates the next pseudorandom, uniformly distributed `long` value.
Protected Method	
`next()`	Generates the next pseudorandom number in the sequence.

See Also

`java.io.Serializable`, `java.lang.Math.random()`.

Example

This example uses the pseudorandom-number generator to simulate a sequence of roulette spins. The pseudorandom-number generator is first created with the current time of day. When the dealer is changed, the generator is given a new seed (based on the new current time of day). The test program makes 20 spins and then changes the dealer and does 20 more spins.

```
import java.util.Random;
class Roulette {
    Random generator = new Random();
    // Spin the wheel and return a string (00, 0, 1-36)
    String spin() {
        int rand = generator.nextInt();
        int num = Math.abs(rand % 38);

        switch (num) {
        case 37: return ("00");
        case 36: return ("0");
        default: return (Integer.toString(num + 1)); // 1- 36 inclusive
        }
    }
    // Use a new seed when we change dealer
    void changeDealer() {
        generator.setSeed(System.currentTimeMillis());
```

```
        }
    }
    class Main {
        public static void main(String[] args) {
            Roulette r = new Roulette();

            // Spin 20 times
            for (int i = 0; i < 20; i++)
                System.out.println(i + ": " + r.spin());

            // change dealer
            r.changeDealer();

                // Spin 20 times again
            for (int i = 0; i < 20; i++)
                System.out.println(i + ": " + r.spin());
        }
    }
```

A B C D E F G H I J K L M N O P Q R S T U V W X Y Z

next()

PURPOSE Generates the next pseudorandom number in the sequence.

SYNTAX `protected synchronized int next(int bits)`

DESCRIPTION This method is used by all the "next" methods as the basis for generating the next pseudorandom number in the sequence. It calculates the next "seed" value of this sequence using the current "seed" value. It then returns a result calculated using the new seed and `bits`.

A subclass of `Random` can override this method to control the algorithm used for the pseudorandom-number generator used by all of the "next" methods.

PARAMETERS

`bits` The number of low-order bits in the result that will be random.

RETURNS The next pseudorandom number in the sequence.

SEE ALSO `nextBytes()`, `nextDouble()`, `nextFloat()`, `nextInt()`, `nextDouble()`, `nextGaussian()`.

EXAMPLE This example defines a subclass of `Random` that provides additional methods.

```
import java.util.Random;

// Subclass that also has sequence generators for byte and short.
class NRandom extends Random {
    NRandom() {
    }

    NRandom(long seed) {
        super(seed);
    }
```

```
        public byte nextByte() {
            return (byte)next(8);    // Random low-order 8 bits
        }

        public short nextShort() {  // Random low-order 16 bits
            return (short)next(16);
        }
    }

    class Main {
        public static void main(String[] args) {
            NRandom rand = new NRandom(1997);

            // Let's see what the byte sequence looks like.
            for (int i = 0; i < 20; i++) {
                System.out.print(rand.nextByte() + " ");
            }
            System.out.println("\n");

            // Reset seed and try the short sequence.
            rand.setSeed(1997);
            for (int i = 0; i < 20; i++) {
                System.out.print(rand.nextShort() + " ");
            }
            System.out.println("\n");
        }
    }
```

nextBytes()

PURPOSE Generates the next pseudorandom, uniformly distributed sequence of bytes.

SYNTAX `public void nextBytes(byte[] buf)`

DESCRIPTION This method generates a random sequence of bytes and updates `buf` with them.

PARAMETERS

`buf` The non-`null` byte array in which to put the pseudorandom bytes.

SEE ALSO `next()`.

EXAMPLE

```
import java.util.Random;

class Main {
    public static void main(String args[]) {
        Random rand = new Random();

        byte[] b1 = new byte[1];
        rand.nextBytes(b1);
        System.out.println(b1[0]);

        byte[] b2 = new byte[2];
        rand.nextBytes(b2);
        System.out.println(b2[0] + " " + b2[1]);
```

```
        byte[] b3 = new byte[3];
        rand.nextBytes(b3);
        System.out.println(b3[0] + " " + b3[1] + " " + b3[2]);

        byte[] b10 = new byte[10];
        rand.nextBytes(b10);
        for (int i = 0; i < b10.length; i++) {
            System.out.print(b10[i] + " ");
        }
        System.out.println("\n");

        byte[] b50 = new byte[50];
        rand.nextBytes(b50);
        for (int i = 0; i < b50.length; i++) {
            System.out.print(b50[i] + " ");
        }
    }
}
```


nextDouble()

PURPOSE Generates the next pseudorandom, uniformly distributed `double` value.

SYNTAX `public double nextDouble()`

RETURNS A `double` x, where `0.0` $\leq x <$ `1.0`.

SEE ALSO `nextFloat()`.

EXAMPLE This example generates a sequence of random `double` values.

```
for(int i = 0; i < n; i++)
    System.out.println(rand.nextDouble());
```

nextFloat()

PURPOSE Generates the next pseudorandom, uniformly distributed `float` value.

SYNTAX `public float nextFloat()`

DESCRIPTION Generates a pseudorandom, uniformly distributed `float` value between 0.0 and 1.0.

RETURNS A `float` x, where `0.0` $\leq x <$ `1.0`.

SEE ALSO `nextDouble()`.

EXAMPLE

```
if (rand.nextFloat() < 0.5)
        System.out.print("heads");
else
        System.out.print("tails");
```

nextGaussian()

PURPOSE Generates the next pseudorandom, Gaussian-distributed `double` value.

SYNTAX `synchronized public double nextGaussian()`

DESCRIPTION This method generates a pseudorandom, Gaussian-distributed `double` value with mean 0.0 and standard deviation 1.0.

RETURNS A pseudorandom, Gaussian-distributed `double` value x, where `0.0` $\leq x <$ `1.0`.

SEE ALSO `nextDouble()`.

EXAMPLE This example prints out a sequence of `n` pseudorandom Gaussian values.

```
for(int i = 0; i < n; i++)
    System.out.println(rand.nextGaussian());
```

nextInt()

PURPOSE Generates the next pseudorandom, uniformly distributed `int` value.

SYNTAX `public int nextInt()`

RETURNS An `int` value that ranges over all possible `int` values (positive and negative).

SEE ALSO `java.lang.Integer.MAX_VALUE`, `java.lang.Integer.MIN_VALUE`, `next()`, `nextLong()`.

EXAMPLE See the class example.

nextLong()

PURPOSE Generates the next pseudorandom ,uniformly distributed `long` value.

SYNTAX `public long nextLong()`

RETURNS A `long` in the range of all positive and negative `long` values.

SEE ALSO `java.lang.Long.MAX_VALUE`, `java.lang.Long.MIN_VALUE`, `next()`, `nextInt()`.

EXAMPLE This example prints out a sequence of `n` pseudorandom `long` values.

```
for(int i = 0; i < n; i++)
    System.out.println(rand.nextLong());
```

Random()

PURPOSE Creates a pseudorandom-number generator.

SYNTAX

```
public Random()
public Random(long seed)
```

DESCRIPTION There are two forms of the constructor for `Random()`. The first constructs a pseudorandom-number generator using the current time of day as the seed. The second constructs a pseudorandom-number generator using the number `seed`. In both cases, the seed can be replaced later by using `setSeed()` to reset the generator and to start a new sequence using the new seed.

PARAMETERS

`seed` The seed to use for generating a sequence of pseudorandom numbers.

SEE ALSO `setSeed()`.

EXAMPLE See the class example.

```
Random time_based = new Random();
Random seed_based = new Random(41991);
```

setSeed()

PURPOSE Sets the seed of this pseudorandom-number generator.

SYNTAX

```
synchronized public void setSeed(long seed)
```

DESCRIPTION This method resets this pseudorandom-number generator and sets its seed to be `seed`. This seed is used to generate a new sequence of pseudorandom numbers for satisfying subsequent "next" calls. Doing this is effectively the same as creating a pseudorandom-number generator.

PARAMETERS

`seed` The seed to use for generating a sequence of pseudorandom numbers.

SEE ALSO `next()`, `Random()`.

EXAMPLE See the class example.

java.io

RandomAccessFile

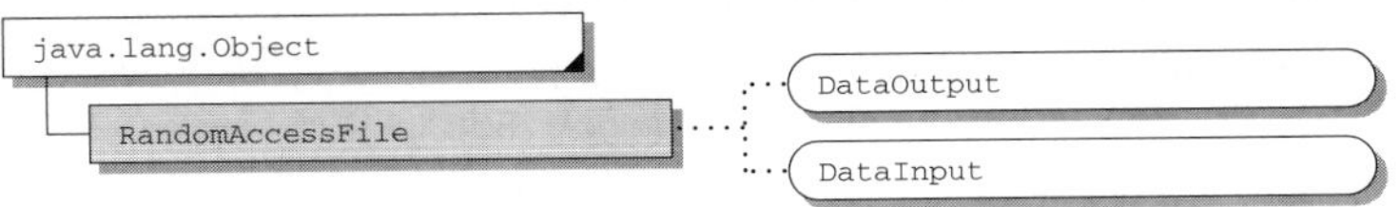

A
B
C
D
E
F
G
H
I
J
K
L
M
N
O
P
Q
R
S
T
U
V
W
X
Y
Z

Syntax

```
public class RandomAccessFile implements DataOutput, DataInput
```

Description

A random-access file is a file in which you can point anywhere in the file and perform IO operations on the file at that point. The `RandomAccessFile` class represents a random-access file. It provides methods for setting the *current file pointer* (the position in the file where the IO will be effected). It also provides methods defined in the `DataInput` and `DataOutput` interfaces to allow primitive data values to be read from and written to the file.

MEMBER SUMMARY	
Constructor	
`RandomAccessFile()`	Constructs a `RandomAccessFile` instance.
Random Access Methods	
`getFilePointer()`	Retrieves the current file pointer of this file.
`seek()`	Sets the file pointer of this file.
Input Methods	
`read()`	Reads bytes from this file.
`readBoolean()`	Reads a `boolean` from this file.
`readByte()`	Reads an 8-bit `byte` from this file.
`readChar`	Reads a 16-bit `char` from this file.
`readDouble()`	Reads a 64-bit `double` from this file.
`readFloat()`	Reads a 32-bit `float` from this file.
`readFully()`	Reads the requested number of bytes from this file, blocking until all bytes are read.
`readInt()`	Reads a 32-bit `int` from this file.
`readLine()`	Reads a line from this file.
`readLong()`	Reads a 64-bit `long` from this file.
`readShort()`	Reads a 16-bit `short` from this file.
`readUnsignedByte()`	Reads an unsigned 8-bit `byte` from this file.
`readUnsignedShort()`	Reads an unsigned 16-bit `short` from this file.
`readUTF()`	Reads a Unicode string in UTF from this file.
`skipBytes()`	Skips bytes from this file.

MEMBER SUMMARY

Output Methods	
`write()`	Writes bytes to this file.
`writeBoolean()`	Writes a `boolean` to this file.
`writeByte()`	Writes an 8-bit `byte` to this file.
`writeBytes()`	Writes a string to this file as a sequence of `bytes`.
`writeChar()`	Writes a 16-bit `char` to this file.
`writeChars()`	Writes a string to this file as a sequence of 16-bit `chars`.
`writeDouble()`	Writes a 64-bit `double` to this file.
`writeFloat()`	Writes a 32-bit `float` to this file.
`writeInt()`	Writes a 32-bit `int` to this file.
`writeLong()`	Writes a 64-bit `long` to this file.
`writeShort()`	Writes a 16-bit `short` to this file.
`writeUTF()`	Writes a string in UTF to this file.
Information Methods	
`length()`	Determines the number of bytes in this file.
`getFD()`	Retrieves the file descriptor of this file.
Close Method	
`close()`	Closes this file.

A B C D E F G H I J K L M N O P Q R S T U V W X Y Z

See Also

`DataInput`, `DataInputStream`, `DataOutput`, `DataOutputStream`, `File`, `FileDescriptor`.

Example

This example opens a random-access file for writing, writes using the different write methods, and then reads the data back using the read methods.

```
import java.io.*;

class Main {
    public static void main(String[] args) {
        if (args.length != 1) {
            System.err.println(
                "Usage: java Main <output file>");
            System.exit(-1);
        }
        try {
            RandomAccessFile raf = new RandomAccessFile(args[0], "rw");

            char a = 'a';
            byte b = 2;
            String c = "abc";
```

```
                short d = 4;
                byte[] b2 = {'a', 'b', 'c'};

                // write some stuff out
                long file_start = raf.getFilePointer();
                raf.write(b);
                raf.write(b2, 0, b2.length);
                raf.writeBoolean(true);
                raf.writeChar(a);
                raf.writeBytes(c);
                raf.writeChars(c);
                raf.writeDouble(123.456);
                raf.writeFloat(123.456f);
                raf.writeInt(678);
                raf.writeLong(678l);
                raf.writeShort(d);
                raf.writeUTF(c);
                raf.writeUTF("abc\n");
                raf.write(b);
                raf.writeShort(d);

                System.out.println("Length of file: " + raf.length());

                // read the stuff back
                raf.seek(file_start);

                b2 = new byte[1];
                b = raf.readByte();
                System.out.println("Byte: " + b);
                raf.read(b2);
                System.out.println("Byte[0]: " + (char)b2[0]);
                raf.read(b2, 0, b2.length);
                System.out.println("Byte[0]: " + (char)b2[0]);
                int ub = raf.readUnsignedByte();
                System.out.println("Unsigned Byte: " + b);
                System.out.println("Boolean: " + raf.readBoolean());
                a = raf.readChar();
                System.out.println("Char: " + a);

                byte[] b3 = new byte[3];
                raf.readFully(b3);
                System.out.println("readFully: " + (char)b3[0] + (char)b3[1] +
                                   (char)b3[2]);
                raf.skipBytes(6); // skip string 'abc'
                double d1 = raf.readDouble();
                float f1 = raf.readFloat();
                int i = raf.readInt();
                long l = raf.readLong();
                short s = raf.readShort();
                String str = raf.readUTF();
                ub = raf.readUnsignedByte();
                int us = raf.readUnsignedShort();
                System.out.println("UTF String" + str);

                raf.close();
            } catch (IOException e) {
                System.err.println(e);
            }
        }
    }
```

close()

PURPOSE Closes this file.

SYNTAX `public native void close() throws IOException`

DESCRIPTION This method closes this random-access file. It releases any resources, such as file descriptors, used by this file.

EXCEPTIONS

`IOException`

If an IO error occurred while attempting to close this file.

EXAMPLE See the class example.

getFD()

PURPOSE Retrieves the file descriptor used by this file.

SYNTAX `public final FileDescriptor getFD() throws IOException`

DESCRIPTION When this `RandomAccessFile` is constructed, it is opened and assigned a file descriptor to use for accessing the file (from the underlying file system). This method returns this file descriptor.

RETURNS The non-`null` file descriptor used by this file.

EXCEPTIONS

`IOException`

If this file has already been closed.

SEE ALSO `FileDescriptor`.

getFilePointer()

PURPOSE Retrieves the current file pointer of this file.

SYNTAX `public native long getFilePointer() throws IOException`

DESCRIPTION The current file pointer is the position in the file at which the next read/write method will operate. For example, if the file is opened for read, the current file pointer is the position at which the next byte from the file will be read. If the file is opened for writing, the current file pointer is the position at which the bytes will be written. The current file pointer is incremented after each read/write/skip and is set using `seek()`.

RETURNS The current file pointer of this file.

EXCEPTIONS

`IOException`
If an IO error occurred while retrieving the current file pointer.

SEE ALSO `seek(), skipBytes(), read*(), write*().`

EXAMPLE See the class example.

length()

PURPOSE Determines the number of bytes in this file.

SYNTAX
```
public native long length() throws IOException
```

DESCRIPTION This method returns the number of bytes between the beginning of the file and the end of the file.

RETURNS The number of bytes in this file.

EXCEPTIONS

`IOException`
If an IO error occurred.

EXAMPLE See the class example.

RandomAccessFile()

PURPOSE Constructs a `RandomAccessFile` instance.

SYNTAX
```
public RandomAccessFile(String fileName, String mode) throws
    IOException
public RandomAccessFile(File file, String mode) throws IOException
```

DESCRIPTION There are two forms of the constructor for `RandomAccessFile`. The first form constructs an instance of `RandomAccessFile` for the file with the file pathname `fileName`. The second form constructs an instance of `RandomAccessFile` for the file as described by the `File` instance `file`. When the `RandomAccessFile` instance is created, it opens the file specified in the mode as specified by the string `mode`. `mode` can be "r," which means to open the file in read-only mode, or "rw," which means to open the file in read-write mode. Any other values of `mode` will raise an `IllegalArgumentException`.

The file can be opened only if allowed by the security manager.

PARAMETERS

`file` The non-`null` `File` of the file to open.
`fileName` The non-`null` string name of the file to open.
`mode` The non-`null` access mode ("r" or "rw").

EXCEPTIONS

`IOException`
If an IO error occurred while attempting to open the specified file.

`IllegalArgumentException`
If `mode` is neither "r" nor "rw".

`SecurityException`
If the file could not be opened in the mode specified due to security reasons.

SEE ALSO `FileDescriptor`, `SecurityManager.checkRead()`, `SecurityManager.checkWrite()`.

EXAMPLE See the class example.

read()

PURPOSE Reads bytes from this file.

SYNTAX

```
public int read() throws IOException
public int read(byte[] buffer) throws IOException
public int read(byte[] buffer, int offset, int count) throws
   IOException
```

DESCRIPTION The three forms of this method read bytes from this file. The first form reads a single byte and returns it in the lowest-order byte of an `int`. The other two forms read bytes and store them in `buffer`. If `offset` and `count` are specified, `count` bytes are read and placed into `buffer` starting at index `offset`. If these are not specified, `buffer.length` bytes are read and placed into `buffer` starting at index `0`. These methods might block if no bytes are available to be read. The requested number of bytes to be read (either `count` or `buffer.length`) might not all be read if there are not that many bytes available. If you want to block waiting for all of the number of bytes requested, use `readFully()`.

PARAMETERS

`buffer` The non-`null` `byte` array to store the bytes read.

`count` The number of bytes to read. `0` ≤ `count` ≤ `buffer.length-offset`.

`offset` The index in `buffer` at which to start storing the bytes read. `0` ≤ `offset` ≤ `buffer.length`.

RETURNS The first form of `read()` returns the byte read; the other two forms return the actual number of bytes read. All forms return `-1` when end-of-file has been reached before any bytes have been read.

EXCEPTIONS

`IOException`
If an IO error has occurred.

SEE ALSO `DataInput.read()`, `readByte()`, `readBytes()`, `readFully()`, `readLine()`, `readUnsignedByte()`.

EXAMPLE See the class example.

readBoolean()

PURPOSE Reads a `boolean` from this file.

SYNTAX `public final boolean readBoolean() throws IOException`

DESCRIPTION This method reads a `boolean` value from this random-access file. A `boolean` is represented as a single byte. If the byte is nonzero, the `boolean` value is `true`. If the byte is zero, the `boolean` value is `false`.

RETURNS The `boolean` value read (`true` or `false`).

EXCEPTIONS

`EOFException`
If end-of-file was reached while attempting to read from this file.

`IOException`
If an IO error occurred while attempting to read from this file.

SEE ALSO `DataInput.readBoolean()`, `writeBoolean()`.

EXAMPLE See the class example.

readByte()

PURPOSE Reads an 8-bit `byte` from this file.

SYNTAX `public final byte readByte() throws IOException`

RETURNS The 8-bit `byte` read.

EXCEPTIONS

`EOFException`
If end-of-file was reached while attempting to read from this file.

`IOException`
If an IO error occurred while attempting to read from this file.

SEE ALSO `DataInput.readByte()`, `writeByte()`, `writeBytes()`, `readUnsignedByte()`.

EXAMPLE See the class example.

readChar()

PURPOSE Reads a 16-bit `char` from this file.

SYNTAX `public final char readChar() throws IOException`

DESCRIPTION A Unicode `char` is represented by a 16-bit unsigned integer. This method reads a `char` by reading two consecutive bytes from this random-access file and interpreting them as a 16-bit unsigned integer (the first byte read is the high-order byte) to be used as the value of the `char`.

RETURNS The `char` read.

EXCEPTIONS

`EOFException`

If end-of-file was reached while attempting to read from this file.

`IOException`

If an IO error occurred while attempting to read from this file.

SEE ALSO `DataInput.readChar()`, `writeChar()`, `writeChars()`.

EXAMPLE See the class example.

readDouble()

PURPOSE Reads a 64-bit `double` from this file.

SYNTAX `public final double readDouble() throws IOException`

DESCRIPTION This method reads 8 bytes from this random-access file and returns the `double` value represented by the bits of those 8 bytes.

RETURNS The `double` value read.

EXCEPTIONS

`EOFException`

If end-of-file was reached while attempting to read from this file.

`IOException`

If an IO error occurred while attempting to read from this file.

SEE ALSO `DataInput.readDouble()`, `java.lang.Double.longBitsToDouble()`, `writeDouble()`.

EXAMPLE See the class example.

readFloat()

PURPOSE Reads a 32-bit `float` from this file.

SYNTAX `public final float readFloat() throws IOException`

DESCRIPTION This method reads 4 bytes from the random-access file and returns the `float` value represented by the bits of those 4 bytes.

RETURNS The `float` value read.

EXCEPTIONS

`EOFException`
If end-of-file was reached while attempting to read from this file.

`IOException`
If an IO error occurred while attempting to read from this file.

SEE ALSO `DataInput.readFloat()`, `java.lang.Float.intBitsToFloat()`, `writeFloat()`.

EXAMPLE See the class example.

readFully()

PURPOSE Reads the requested number of bytes from this file, blocking until all bytes are read.

SYNTAX

```
public final void readFully(byte[] buffer) throws IOException
public final void readFully(byte[] buffer, int offset, int count)
   throws IOException
```

DESCRIPTION The two forms of this method read bytes from this random-access file and copy them into the `byte` array `buffer`. If `offset` and `count` are specified, `count` bytes are read and placed into `buffer` starting at index `offset`. If these are not specified, `buffer.length` bytes are read and placed into `buffer` starting at index `0`. These methods will block waiting for all of the requested number of bytes to be read (either `count` or `buffer.length`).

PARAMETERS

`buffer` The non-`null` `byte` array into which the data is read.
`count` The maximum number of bytes to read. `0` ≤ `count` ≤ `buffer.length-offset`.
`offset` The index in `buffer` at which to start putting the bytes read. `0` ≤ `offset` < `buffer.length`.

EXCEPTIONS

`EOFException`
If end-of-file was reached while attempting to read from this file.

`IOException`

If an IO error occurred while attempting to read from this file.

SEE ALSO `DataInput.readFully()`.

EXAMPLE See the class example.

readInt()

PURPOSE Reads a 32-bit `int` from this file.

SYNTAX `public final int readInt() throws IOException`

DESCRIPTION This method reads 4 bytes from this random-access file and returns the `int` value represented by the bits of those 4 bytes. The higher-order bytes are read in order from the file.

RETURNS The `int` value read.

EXCEPTIONS

`EOFException`

If end-of-file was reached while attempting to read from this file.

`IOException`

If an IO error occurred while attempting to read from this file.

SEE ALSO `DataInput.readInt()`, `writeInt()`.

EXAMPLE See the class example.

readLine()

PURPOSE Reads a line from this file.

SYNTAX `public final String readLine() throws IOException`

DESCRIPTION This method reads a line from this random-access file and returns it as a string. A line is defined as a sequence of bytes terminated by an `\n` or end-of-file. The string does not include the line terminator character.

RETURNS A string copy of a line read from this file; `null` if no character is read before end-of-file is reached.

EXCEPTIONS

`IOException`

If an IO error occurred while attempting to read from this stream.

SEE ALSO `DataInput.readLine()`, `writeBytes()`.

EXAMPLE See the class example.

readLong()

PURPOSE Reads a 64-bit `long` from this file.

SYNTAX `public final long readLong() throws IOException`

DESCRIPTION This method reads 8 bytes from this random-access file and returns the `long` value represented by the bits of those 8 bytes. The higher-order bytes are read in order from the file.

RETURNS The `long` value read.

EXCEPTIONS

`EOFException`
If end-of-file was reached while attempting to read from this file.

`IOException`
If an IO error occurred while attempting to read from this file.

SEE ALSO `DataInput.readLong()`, `writeLong()`.

EXAMPLE See the class example.

readShort()

PURPOSE Reads a 16-bit `short` from this file.

SYNTAX `public final short readShort() throws IOException`

DESCRIPTION This method reads 2 bytes from this random-access file and returns the `short` value represented by the bits of those 2 bytes. The higher-order byte is read first from the file.

RETURNS The `short` value read.

EXCEPTIONS

`EOFException`
If end-of-file was reached while attempting to read from this stream.

`IOException`
If an IO error occurred while attempting to read from this stream.

SEE ALSO `DataInput.readShort()`, `readUnsignedShort()`, `writeShort()`.

EXAMPLE See the class example.

readUnsignedByte()

PURPOSE Reads an unsigned 8-bit `byte` from this file.

SYNTAX `public final int readUnsignedByte() throws IOException`

DESCRIPTION This method reads a byte from this random-access file and returns it as the lowest byte in an `int`. The only difference between this method and `readByte()` is that this method returns the byte in an `int`, while `readByte()` returns the byte in a `byte`. Because `byte` is a signed type, the highest-order bit determines the sign of the value. When a byte is returned in an `int`, the higher-order 3 bytes are unused (`0`). Hence, the `int` value returned is always unsigned.

RETURNS An `int` containing the byte read.

EXCEPTIONS

`EOFException`

If end-of-file was reached while attempting to read from this stream.

`IOException`

If an IO error occurred while attempting to read from this stream.

SEE ALSO `DataInput.readUnsignedByte()`, `readByte()`, `writeByte()`.

EXAMPLE See the class example.

readUnsignedShort()

PURPOSE Reads an unsigned 16-bit `short` from this file.

SYNTAX `public final int readUnsignedShort() throws IOException`

DESCRIPTION This method reads 2 bytes from this random-access file and returns the unsigned integer value represented by the bits of those 2 bytes. The higher-order byte is read first from the input stream. The only difference between this method and `readShort()` is that this method returns the result as an `int`, while `readShort()` returns the result as a `short`. Because `short` is a signed type, the highest-order bit will determine the sign of the value. When a `short` is returned in an `int`, it occupies the lower-order 2 bytes of the `int`; the higher-order 2 bytes are unused (`0`). Hence, the `int` value returned is always unsigned.

RETURNS An `int` containing the 16-bit `short` value read.

EXCEPTIONS

`EOFException`

If end-of-file was reached while attempting to read from this stream.

`IOException`

If an IO error occurred while attempting to read from this stream.

SEE ALSO `DataInput.readUnsignedShort()`, `readShort()`, `writeShort()`.

EXAMPLE See the class example.

readUTF()

PURPOSE Reads a Unicode string in UTF from this file.

SYNTAX `public final String readUTF() throws IOException`

DESCRIPTION This method reads a Unicode string and returns it as a `String`. UTF stands for *Unicode Transfer Format*, an encoding scheme for Unicode characters. You write a string to a file using `writeUTF()` and read it back using `readUTF()`. UTF strings are restricted to have an encoded length ≤ 65535.

See *The Java Language Specification, First Edition*, Section 22.1.15, for details of UTF.

RETURNS The non-`null` Unicode string read as a `String`.

EXCEPTIONS

`EOFException`
If end-of-file was reached while attempting to read the string.

`IOException`
If an IO error occurred while attempting to read the string.

`UTFDataFormatException`
If the string being read is not in UTF.

SEE ALSO `DataInput.readUTF()`, `writeUTF()`.

EXAMPLE See the class example.

seek()

PURPOSE Sets the file pointer of this file.

SYNTAX `public native void seek(long pos) throws IOException`

DESCRIPTION This method sets the current file pointer of this random-access file to be `pos`. Subsequent read/write/skip operations will operate on the file starting at this new file pointer.

PARAMETERS

`pos` The absolute position to which to set the file pointer.

EXCEPTIONS

`EOFException`
If `pos` is beyond the end of the file.

IOException

If an IO error occurred.

SEE ALSO `getFilePointer()`.

EXAMPLE See the class example.

skipBytes()

PURPOSE Skips bytes from this file.

SYNTAX
```
public int skipBytes(int count) throws IOException
```

DESCRIPTION This method skips `count` number of bytes from this random-access file. It updates the current file pointer to reflect the number of bytes skipped. This method returns the actual number of bytes skipped.

PARAMETERS

`count` The number of bytes to skip.

RETURNS The actual number of bytes skipped.

EXCEPTIONS

EOFException

If end-of-file is reached before `count` bytes have been skipped.

IOException

If an IO error occurred.

SEE ALSO `seek()`.

EXAMPLE See the class example.

write()

PURPOSE Writes bytes to this file.

SYNTAX
```
public void write(int oneByte) throws IOException
public void write(byte[] buffer) throws IOException
public void write(byte[] buffer, int offset, int count) throws
    IOException
```

DESCRIPTION The three forms of the `write()` method write the specified byte or bytes to this file. The first form writes a single byte `oneByte` to this file. The second form writes all of the bytes from `buffer` to this file. The third form writes `count` bytes from the `byte` array `buffer` starting at index `offset` to this stream.

PARAMETERS

`buffer`	The non-`null` `byte` array containing bytes to be written.
`count`	The number of bytes from `buffer` to write. `0` ≤ `count` ≤ `buffer.length-offset`.
`offset`	The index in `buffer` of the bytes to be written. `0` ≤ `offset` < `buffer.length`.
`oneByte`	The byte to be written.

EXCEPTIONS

`IOException`
If an IO error occurred while attempting to write.

SEE ALSO `DataOutput.write()`, `readByte()`, `readLine()`, `readFully()`, `readUnsignedByte()`, `writeByte()`, `writeBytes()`.

EXAMPLE See the class example.

writeBoolean()

PURPOSE Writes a `boolean` to this file.

SYNTAX `public final void writeBoolean(boolean val) throws IOException`

DESCRIPTION This method writes the `boolean` value `val` to this file. The output consists of a single byte whose value is `1` if `val` is `true` and `0` if `val` is `false`.

PARAMETERS

`val`	The `boolean` to be written.

EXCEPTIONS

`IOException`
If an IO error occurred while attempting to write.

SEE ALSO `DataOutput.writeBoolean()`, `readBoolean()`.

EXAMPLE See the class example.

writeByte()

PURPOSE Writes an 8-bit `byte` to this file.

SYNTAX `public final void writeByte(int val) throws IOException`

DESCRIPTION This method writes the 8-bit byte (in the lowest-order byte of `val`) to this file. The output consists of a single byte whose value is the lowest-order byte of `val`.

PARAMETERS

`val` The byte value to be written.

EXCEPTIONS

`IOException`

If an IO error occurred while attempting to write.

SEE ALSO `DataOutput.writeByte(), read(), readByte(), readFully(), readLine(), readUnsignedByte(), write().`

EXAMPLE See the class example.

writeBytes()

PURPOSE Writes a string to this file as a sequence of bytes.

SYNTAX `public final void writeBytes(String str) throws IOException`

DESCRIPTION This method writes the string `str` to this file as a sequence of bytes (8 bits). Because a string consists of 16-bit Unicode `char` values and the output is only 8-bit bytes, the high-order bytes of the `char` values are lost (and not written). Use `writeChar()` and `writeChars()` to write all 16 bits of a Unicode `char` or `char` string.

PARAMETERS

`str` The non-`null` string to be written.

EXCEPTIONS

`IOException`

If an IO error occurred while attempting to write.

SEE ALSO `DataOutput.writeBytes(), read(), readByte(), readFully(), readLine(), readUnsignedByte(), writeChar(), writeChars().`

EXAMPLE See the class example.

writeChar()

PURPOSE Writes a 16-bit `char` to this file.

SYNTAX `public final void writeChar(int val) throws IOException`

DESCRIPTION This method writes a 16-bit Unicode `char val` to this file. Only the lower-order 2 bytes of `val` are written. The output consists of two bytes (higher-order written first), which represent the Unicode value of `val`.

PARAMETERS

`val` The `char` value to be written.

EXCEPTIONS

`IOException`

If an IO error occurred while attempting to write.

SEE ALSO `DataOutput.writeChar(), readChar(), writeByte(), writeChars().`

EXAMPLE See the class example.

A B C D E F G H I J K L M N O P Q R S T U V W X Y Z

writeChars()

PURPOSE Writes a string to this file as a sequence of 16-bit `chars`.

SYNTAX `public final void writeChars(String str) throws IOException`

DESCRIPTION This method writes the string `str` to the output stream as a sequence of `chars` (16 bits). Each `char` written consists of 2 bytes (higher-order written first), which represent its Unicode value.

PARAMETERS

`str` The non-`null` string to be written.

EXCEPTIONS

`IOException`

If an IO error occurred while attempting to write.

SEE ALSO `DataOutput.writeChars(), readChar(), writeBytes(), writeChar(), writeUTF().`

EXAMPLE See the class example.

writeDouble()

PURPOSE Writes a 16-bit `double` to this file.

SYNTAX `public final void writeDouble(double val) throws IOException`

DESCRIPTION This method writes the `double` value `val` to this file. The output generated consists of 8 bytes, which make up the bit representation of `val`.

PARAMETERS

`val` The `double` value to be written.

EXCEPTIONS

`IOException`

If an IO error occurred while attempting to write.

SEE ALSO `DataOutput.writeDouble()`, `readDouble()`, `Double.doubleToLongBits()`.

EXAMPLE See the class example.

writeFloat()

PURPOSE Writes a 32-bit `float` to this file.

SYNTAX `public final void writeFloat(float val) throws IOException`

DESCRIPTION This method writes the `float` value `val` to this file. The output generated consists of 4 bytes, which make up the bit representation of `val`.

PARAMETERS

`val` The `float` value to be written.

EXCEPTIONS

`IOException`

If an IO error occurred while attempting to write.

SEE ALSO `DataOutput.writeFloat()`, `readFloat()`, `Float.floatToIntBits()`.

EXAMPLE See the class example.

writeInt()

PURPOSE Writes a 32-bit `int` to this file.

SYNTAX `public final void writeInt(int val) throws IOException`

DESCRIPTION This method writes the `int` value `val` to this file. The output generated consists of 4 bytes, in highest-to-lowest byte order, which represent the value of `val`.

PARAMETERS

`val` The `int` value to be written.

EXCEPTIONS

`IOException`

If an IO error occurred while attempting to write.

SEE ALSO `DataOutput.writeInt()`, `readInt()`.

EXAMPLE See the class example.

writeLong()

PURPOSE Writes a 64-bit `long` to this file.

SYNTAX `public final void writeLong(long val) throws IOException`

DESCRIPTION This method writes the `long` value `val` to this file. The output generated consists of 8 bytes, in highest-to-lowest byte order, which represent the value of `val`.

PARAMETERS

`val` The `long` value to be written.

EXCEPTIONS

`IOException`

If an IO error occurred while attempting to write.

SEE ALSO `DataOutput.writeLong()`, `readLong()`.

EXAMPLE See the class example.

writeShort()

PURPOSE Writes a 16-bit `short` to this file.

SYNTAX `public final void writeShort(int val) throws IOException`

DESCRIPTION This method writes the `short` value `val` to this file (the lower-order 2 bytes of `val` are used). The output generates 2 bytes, with the higher-order byte written first.

PARAMETERS

`val` The value to be written. The two lower-order bytes of `val` are used as the value of the `short` to be written.

EXCEPTIONS

`IOException`

If an IO error occurred while attempting to write.

SEE ALSO `DataOutput.writeShort()`, `readShort()`, `readUnsignedShort()`.

EXAMPLE See the class example.

writeUTF()

PURPOSE Writes a string in UTF to this file.

SYNTAX `public final void writeUTF(String str) throws IOException`

DESCRIPTION This method writes a string `str` to this file in UTF. UTF stands for *Unicode Transfer Format*, an encoding scheme for Unicode characters. You write a string to a file using the `writeUTF()` method and read it back using `readUTF()`. UTF strings are restricted to have an encoded length ≤ 65535. See *The Java Language Specification, First Edition*, Section 22.2.14, for details on UTF.

PARAMETERS

`str` The non-`null` string to be written.

EXCEPTIONS

`IOException`

If an IO error occurred while attempting to write.

`UTFDataFormatException`

If the resulting UTF data size would exceed 65,535 bytes.

SEE ALSO `DataOutput.writeUTF()`, `readUTF()`, `writeBytes()`, `writeChars()`.

EXAMPLE See the class example.

java.io

Reader

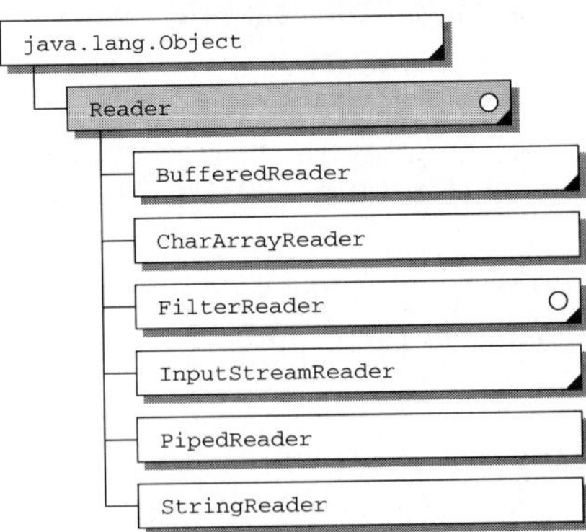

A B C D E F G H I J K L M N O P Q R S T U V W X Y Z

Syntax

```
public abstract class Reader
```

Description

The `Reader` class is the superclass of all character input streams, or *readers*. It provides basic input methods for reading characters from an input stream.

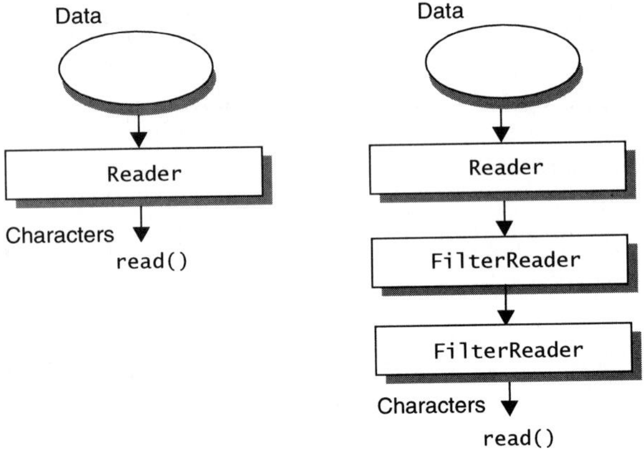

FIGURE 84: `Reader`.

Usage

Subclasses of `Reader` override some or all of these basic methods for implementing their particular type of reader. Concrete subclasses must provide implementations for the methods `read(char[], int, int)` and `close()`. Figure 84 shows that you can either read directly from a subclass of `Reader` or read from a reader through filters.

Current Read Position and Mark/Reset

Each reader has a current read position. As read operations occur, this current read position is incremented to reflect that the characters have been read. In addition to conducting read operations, you can also skip characters in the reader. This is similar to reads, except that skipping a character increments only the current read position; it does not return the character read.

You can mark the current read position (using `mark()`) so that you can return to it (using `reset()`). This allows you to reread previously read characters. Mark/reset is useful for implementing parsers. You can mark the current read position and then read ahead in the writer to determine what action to take next. After making that determination, you then can reset the read position to that marker and pass the reader onto the appropriate processor.

Reader versus InputStream
`Reader` is for processing character input streams. `InputStream` is intended for processing byte input streams. `InputStream`'s `read()` methods read bytes (0–255).

If you need to translate between byte streams and character streams, use `InputStreamReader`. `InputStreamReader` translates bytes read from an input stream into characters using either a specified or default byte-to-character encoding.

MEMBER SUMMARY	
Constructor	
`Reader()`	Constructs a `Reader` instance.
Input Methods	
`read()`	Reads one or more characters from this reader.
`skip()`	Skip characters from this reader.
Mark/Reset Methods	
`mark()`	Marks the current read position in this reader.
`markSupported()`	Determines whether this reader supports mark/reset.
`reset()`	Resets the current read position to be the last marked position.
Stream Methods	
`close()`	Closes this reader.
`ready()`	Determines whether this reader is ready to be read without being blocked.
Synchronization Field	
`lock`	Holds the object used to synchronize operations on this reader.

See Also

`BufferedReader`, `CharArrayReader`, `FileReader`, `FilterReader`, `InputStream`, `InputStreamReader`, `LineNumberReader`, `PipedReader`, `PushbackReader`, `StringReader`, `Writer`.

Example

This example counts the number characters, words, and lines read using a reader.

```
import java.io.*;

class Main {
    public static void wordCount(Reader in) {
        int charcount = 0;
        int wordcount = 0;
        int linecount = 0;
        try {
            int c;
            boolean newspace = true;
            while ((c = in.read()) > -1) {
                ++charcount;
                if (c == '\n' || c == '\r')
                    ++linecount;
                if (Character.isWhitespace((char)c)) {
                    if (newspace) {
                        ++wordcount;
                        newspace = false;
                    }
                } else {
                    newspace = true;
                }
            }
            in.close();
        } catch (IOException e) {
            e.printStackTrace();
        }
        System.out.println(linecount + " " + wordcount + " " + charcount);
    }
    public static void main(String[] args) {
        if (args.length == 1) {
            try {
                wordCount(new FileReader(args[0]));
            } catch (IOException e) {
                e.printStackTrace();
            }
        } else {
            System.err.println("Usage: java Main <file>");
            System.exit(-1);
        }
    }
}
```

close()

PURPOSE
: Closes this reader.

SYNTAX
: `abstract public void close() throws IOException`

DESCRIPTION
: This method must be implemented by any concrete subclass of `Reader`. The implementation should release any resources (especially system resources) used by this reader, such as file descriptors.

`close()` is idempotent. That is, you can invoke it many times, but only the first invocation has any effect. Once a reader has been closed, except for the `close()` method, attempts to invoke other methods on the reader will throw an `IOException`.

EXCEPTIONS

`IOException`
: If an IO error occurs while attempting to close this reader.

EXAMPLE
: See the class example.

lock

PURPOSE
: Holds the object used to synchronize operations on this reader.

SYNTAX
: `protected Object lock`

DESCRIPTION
: This field is used whenever an operation on this reader needs to be synchronized against access by multiple threads. Instead of defining the method to be synchronized, or using `this` as the lock, the method should use

```
synchronized (lock) {
    ...
}
```

The `Reader` constructor that accepts no arguments assigns `lock` to this instance of `Reader`. The other `Reader` constructor accepts an object, which is then assigned to this field to serve as the lock for operations on this `Reader`.

SEE ALSO
: `Reader()`.

EXAMPLE
: See the class example.

mark()

PURPOSE Marks the current read position in this reader.

SYNTAX `public void mark(int readLimit) throws IOException`

DESCRIPTION This method marks the current position in this reader so that a subsequent call to `reset()` will reposition the read position of the reader to this marked position. This marked position becomes invalid (i.e. `reset()` may not work) if you read more than `readlimit` number of characters beyond this marked position.

The default implementation of this method throws an `IOException`. A subclass of `Reader` that supports mark/reset must override this method.

PARAMETERS

`readLimit` The number of characters that can be read before this mark is invalidated.

SEE ALSO `markSupported()`, `reset()`.

EXCEPTIONS

`IOException`

If this reader does not support `mark()`, or if this reader has already been closed, or if some other IO error occurs.

EXAMPLE See `FilterReader.mark()`.

markSupported()

PURPOSE Determines whether this reader supports mark/reset.

SYNTAX `public boolean markSupported()`

DESCRIPTION This method returns `true` if this reader supports mark/reset; `false` otherwise. See the class description for an explanation of mark/reset. The default implementation returns `false` (i.e., mark/reset is not supported).

RETURNS `true` if this reader supports mark/reset; `false` otherwise.

SEE ALSO `mark()`, `reset()`.

EXAMPLE See `FilterReader.mark()`.

read()

PURPOSE
Reads one or more characters from this reader.

SYNTAX
```
abstract public int read(char buf[], int offset, int count)
   throws IOException
public int read() throws IOException
public int read(char buf[]) throws IOException
```

DESCRIPTION
The three forms of this method read characters from this reader. The first form reads some characters from this reader and stores them into the region in `buf` specified by `offset` and `count`. It returns the number of characters read, or `-1` if the end of the reader was encountered before any characters were read. This is an abstract method whose implementation must be provided by `Reader`'s concrete subclasses.

The default implementations of the second and third forms of this method are implemented using this first form.

The second form reads a single character from this reader and returns it as an `int` (the high-order 2 bytes are `0`). It is implemented using the first form by allocating a one-character array and using that to read the single character. If the end of the reader is reached before a character can be read, `-1` is returned.

The third form reads characters into `buf` and stores them starting at index `0`.

PARAMETERS

`buf` The non-`null` `char` array in which characters read are stored.

`count` The maximum number of characters to read. `0` ≤ `count` ≤ `buf.length`.

`offset` The index in `buf` at which to start storing the characters read. `0` ≤ `offset` < `buf.length`.

RETURNS
The first form returns the character read; the second and third forms return the actual number of characters read. All forms return `-1` if end-of-file is reached before any characters are read.

EXCEPTIONS

`ArrayIndexOutOfBoundsException`
If `count` or `offset` is outside of the specified bounds.

`IOException`
If this reader has been closed or if an IO error was encountered while attempting to read characters from this reader.

EXAMPLE
See the class example.

Reader()

PURPOSE Constructs a `Reader` instance.

SYNTAX
```
protected Reader()
protected Reader(Object lock)
```

DESCRIPTION The two forms of the constructor creates an instance of `Reader`. The difference between the two is the object used for synchronizing subsequent method invocations on the `Reader` instance. The first form uses the `Reader` instance itself as the synchronizing object. The second form uses `lock` as the lock as the synchronizing object.

PARAMETERS

`lock` The non-`null` object to used for synchronized blocks.

SEE ALSO `lock`.

A B C D E F G H I J K L M N O P Q R S T U V W X Y Z

ready()

PURPOSE Determines whether this reader is ready to be read without being blocked.

SYNTAX
```
public boolean ready() throws IOException
```

DESCRIPTION This method determines whether this reader is ready to be read. If `true`, the next `read()` will not block waiting for input. If `false`, the next `read()` may or may not block. By default, this method returns `false`. A subclass of `Reader` should override this method to return `true` when this reader is ready to be read.

This method is useful to applications that do not want to block waiting for input. Input streams and readers that wait on external devices like files cannot be interrupted while inside `read()` (they do not respond to `Thread.interrupt()`). To make such threads interruptible, you can use `ready()` before doing `read()`. See the example.

RETURNS `true` if this reader is ready to be read without being blocked; `false` if not ready or don't know.

EXCEPTIONS

`IOException`

If an IO error occurred while attempting to make the determination (for example, if the reader has already been closed).

EXAMPLE This example reads only from a reader when it will not block.

Note: In Java 1.1.4, `FileReader` does not implement `ready()` correctly when end-of-file is encountered, so this example does not work with files.

```
import java.io.*;

class Main {
    public static void main(String[] args) {
        if (args.length != 1) {
            System.err.println("Usage: java Main <file>");
            System.exit(-1);
        }
        try {
//          BufferedReader in = new BufferedReader(new FileReader(args[0]));
//          Reader in = new FileReader(args[0]);
            Reader in = new BufferedReader(new StringReader("This is a test"));
            char[] buf = new char[512];
            int howmany;
            while (true) {
                if (in.ready()) {
                    howmany = in.read(buf);
                    if (howmany <= 0) {
                        break;
                    } else {
                        System.out.println(new String(buf, 0, howmany));
                    }
                } else {
                    try {
                        Thread.sleep(1000);
                    } catch (InterruptedException e) {
                        // Thread.currentThread().interrupt();
                        System.err.println(e);
                        break;
                    }
                }
            }
            in.close();
        } catch (IOException e) {
            e.printStackTrace();
        }
    }
}
```


reset()

PURPOSE Resets the current read position to be the last marked position.

SYNTAX `public void reset() throws IOException`

DESCRIPTION This method resets the current read position of this reader to the last marked position. Subsequent invocations of `read()/skip()` will begin getting input from this marked position. If this reader has not been marked, `reset()`'s behavior is implementation-dependent. For example, `StringReader` will reset the reader to the start of the string if `mark()` has not been called. A subclass of `Reader` that supports mark/reset must override this method.

The default implementation of this method throws an `IOException`.

EXCEPTIONS

`IOException`
If this reader has not been marked and the mark is required, or if the mark has been invalidated, or if this reader does not support `reset()`, or if this reader has already been closed, or if some other IO error occurs

EXAMPLE See `FilterReader.mark()`.

A B C D E F G H I J K L M N O P Q R S T U V W X Y Z

skip()

PURPOSE Skips characters from this reader.

SYNTAX `public long skip(long count) throws IOException`

DESCRIPTION This method skips `count` number of characters from this reader. Skipped characters will not be returned by subsequent `read()` calls (unless the read position is changed using `reset()`).

The default implementation of `skip()` allocates a buffer that may be reused for skipping characters and then reads the characters into the buffer without returning them. Multiple reads may be necessary to skip all `count` characters. If no character is available to be read yet, `skip()` will wait until one or more characters become available. A subclass may override `skip()` if it has other ways of skipping characters.

PARAMETERS

`count` The number of characters to skip.

RETURNS The nonnegative number of characters actually skipped.

EXCEPTIONS

`IOException`
If an IO error occurs.

EXAMPLE See the `FilterReader` class example.

ResourceBundle

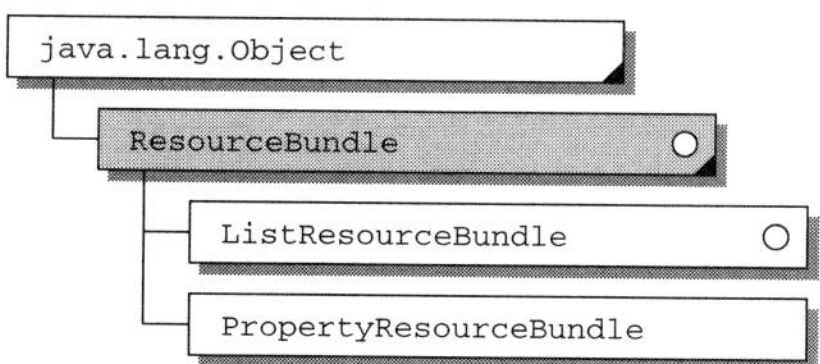

Syntax

```
abstract public class ResourceBundle
```

Description

A *resource bundle* is a set of resources such as strings, numbers, audio clips, and images. A resource can be any subclass of `Object` (hence, the primitive types cannot be resources). Every resource in a resource bundle has a unique case-sensitive name (a string), called the *key*, which is used to retrieve the resource from the resource bundle.

A resource bundle is a live Java object that holds the resources. Retrieving a resource involves calling a method provided by the resource bundle. Moreover, each resource bundle is typically implemented by a different class. For example, you could bundle all audio clips in the resource bundle represented by a class called `AudioResourceBundle` and all images by one called `ImageResourceBundle`. However, there is a special case in which there is no need to declare a new Java class to handle resources that are stored in a properties file (see `Properties`); see `getBundle()` for details.

This design may seem to be tedious and heavyweight, but it does allow for a lot of flexibility in where and how the resources are actually stored. For example, you could define a resource bundle that fetches the resources from a server on the Internet.

Resource Bundles for Localization

The resource bundle is Java's primary mechanism for localizing applications. In particular, an application should store all of its localizable resources in resource bundles. This makes it possible to create a version of the application for a particular locale by duplicating the set of resource bundles (with slightly different names) and then replacing the resources with localized versions. There is a set of rules for naming the localized resource bundles that make it possible to avoid modifying the application at all. These rules are explained shortly. A compiler, for example, should store all of its error messages in a resource bundle. To build a version of the compiler for another locale, all one needs to do is copy the resource bundle and translate all the error messages. There is no need to modify the compiler.

Resource bundles not only support the localization of an application but also allow an application to support multiple locales simultaneously if desired. In other words, an application is not "locked" into a particular locale at start-up. Instead, it is free to use the resource bundles of one or more supported locales at any time and dynamically switch between locales if desired.

Resource Bundle Names

The name of a resource bundle class has two parts—the *base name* and the *locale identifier.* The base name is any valid Java class name, for example, `ErrorResources`. The locale identifier consists of three parts—the language code, the country code, and a variant code—each separated by an underscore character. An example of a locale identifier is `en_US_MAC`, where `en` is the language code, `US` is the country code, and `MAC` is the variant code. The complete resource bundle class name would then be `ErrorResources_en_US_MAC`. For more information about these codes, see `Locale`.

When an application is being built, the localized resources are placed in resource bundles whose names do not include a locale identifier. For example, a compiler's error messages might be placed in `ErrorResources` and the names for its compilation options placed in `OptionResources`. These resource bundles are called the *default resource bundles.* The language used in the default resource bundles can be anything you choose. However, when an application is started in a locale for which you have not built a localized version, the resources in the default resource bundles are used.

To build a localization for a particular language, append the two-character language code (see `Locale`) onto the resource bundle's base name, separated by an underscore character. For example, to build a German version of our example, you would create two new resource bundles called `ErrorResources_de` and `OptionResource_de`. Typically, all of the resources contained in the default resource bundles would be copied and translated in these German resource bundles. For example, a resource called `OK_LABEL` might be "Ok" in the default resource and "Gut" in the German resource bundle.

It is actually not necessary to copy all of the resources from the default resource bundle into the localized bundle. It is necessary only to copy the ones whose translations are different. For example, a resource for a version number would be the same for all locales.

Note: It is important that the keys for the localized resources be identical to the ones used in the default resource bundles (that is, the keys must not be localized).

If necessary, the resource bundle could be further localized for a particular country. In this case, the name of the language-localized resource bundle is appended with the two-character country code (see `Locale`) separated by an underscore character. For example, to provide a localization for Swiss German, the resource bundle name would be `ErrorResources_de_CH` and `OptionResource_de_CH`, where `CH` is the country code for Switzerland.

Finally, if the resources in a resource bundle have to be different for different dialects or platforms, the resource bundle can be further localized to a dialect/platform. For example, a resource may have special character codes depending on whether the resource bundle was used on Windows or on Unix. These platform-dependent localizations are called *variants* (see `Locale` for more details). The variant name is an arbitrary string that is decided by the application. However, when used, it is appended onto the resource bundle class name after the two-character country code and separated by an underscore character. An example of a resource bundle class name with a variant is `ErrorResources_de_CH_WIN`. A variant can also have a hierarchy, with each component in the hierarchy separated by an underscore character. For example, `ErrorResources_de_CH_WIN` might have two child variants:

- `ErrorResources_de_CH_WIN_95`
- `ErrorResources_de_CH_WIN_311`

Note: It is not valid to omit a language code if a country code is used. It also is not valid to leave out either the language code or country code if a variant is used.

Locating a Resource Bundle

To retrieve a bundle, two pieces of information are required: the fully qualified base name of the resource bundle and a locale identifier. These two strings are concatenated together, separated by an underscore character, to form a class name. An attempt is then made to load a class with that class name (using the default system class loader). An example of such a class name is `pkg.MyResources_ja_JP`, where `pkg.MyResources` is the fully qualified base name and `ja_JP` is the locale identifier.

If a class with the class name cannot be loaded or instantiated, the class name then is successively shortened until a resource bundle class is successfully loaded and instantiated. The shortening process goes like this. First, the complete class name—base name plus the desired locale identifier—is used. If this fails, the locale identifier is continually shortened by removing the rightmost underscore and subsequent characters until a resource bundle class is successfully loaded and instantiated. If this fails, the process starts again using the locale identifier of the default locale (see `Locale.getDefault()`).

To demonstrate the sequence of class names attempted, here's an example using a base name of `pkg.MyResources` and a desired locale of `Locale.JAPAN` with a `WIN_95` variant. The default locale is `Local.ENGLISH`.

1. `pkg.MyResources_jp_JA_WIN_95`
2. `pkg.MyResources_jp_JA_WIN`
3. `pkg.MyResources_jp_JA`
4. `pkg.MyResources_jp`
5. `pkg.MyResources`
6. `pkg.MyResources_en_US`
7. `pkg.MyResources_en`

Note: If a class name names a class file but the class file cannot be loaded or instantiated for any reason, the class name is skipped and the next class name is tried.

Properties Files

Whenever a class name fails to produce a resource bundle object, a check is made to see if a properties file (see `Properties`) with the same name exists. In particular, the class name is appended with the string ".properties". If such a file exists, a `PropertyResourceBundle` object is created for that properties file (see `PropertyResourceBundle` for more details.)

A B C D E F G H I J K L M N O P Q R S T U V W X Y Z

To demonstrate more concretely the sequence of files attempted, here's an example using a base name of `pkg.MyResources` and a desired locale of `Locale.JAPAN` with a `WIN_95` variant. The default locale is `Locale.ENGLISH`.

1. class `pkg.MyResources_jp_JA_WIN_95`
2. file `pkg.MyResources_jp_JA_WIN_95.properties`
3. class `pkg.MyResources_jp_JA_WIN`
4. file `pkg.MyResources_jp_JA_WIN.properties`
5. class `pkg.MyResources_jp_JA`
6. file `pkg.MyResources_jp_JA.properties`
7. class `pkg.MyResources_jp`
8. file `pkg.MyResources_jp.properties`
9. class `pkg.MyResources`
10. file `pkg.MyResources.properties`
11. class `pkg.MyResources_en_US`
12. file `pkg.MyResources_en_US.properties`
13. class `pkg.MyResources_en`
14. file `pkg.MyResources_en.properties`

A B C D E F G H I J K L M N O P Q R S T U V W X Y Z

Resource Bundle Parent Relationship

Whenever a resource bundle object is successfully loaded and instantiated, a search is made to see if the bundle has a *parent*. If the parent exists, it is also loaded and instantiated. The result is a chain of resource bundles.

In the search for a parent, the locale identifier is successively shortened and if a resource bundle class is successfully loaded and instantiated, that class becomes the parent. For example, the parent of a resource bundle called `MyResources_jp_JA` is `MyResources_jp` and the parent of `MyResources_jp` is `MyResources`.

Note: If shortening the desired locale identifier fails to yield a parent for a resource bundle, the search for a parent using the default locale identifier is halted.

The parent chain of resource bundles is used when retrieving a resource. In particular, if a resource bundle does not have a resource, the parent chain is automatically climbed, with each resource bundle checked along the way for the desired resource. If one is found, it is immediately returned.

Usage: Using a Resource Bundle

To obtain a resource bundle for the default locale or for a particular locale, use `getBundle()`. With the returned resource bundle, you can retrieve a resource by calling one of the three resource retrieval methods: `getObject()`, `getString()`, or `getStringArray()`.

Usage: Making a Resource Bundle

There are several ways to make a resource bundle. First, if the resources for a resource bundle are all strings, the resources can be placed in a properties file, thus the need to write a new resource bundle class is avoided.

Second, if the resources are all objects that can be initialized when the resource bundle is instantiated, you can subclass the `ListResourceBundle` class and provide an implementation for the abstract method `getContents()` to return the entire set of resources as an array. See `ListResourceBundle` for more details.

If the resources are not known at the time of resource bundle instantiation, a new resource bundle must be declared. A declared resource bundle class must be a subclass of `ResourceBundle` and implement two abstract methods: `getKeys()` and `handleGetObject()`. The class itself must be public and have a public constructor with no parameters.

MEMBER SUMMARY	
Resource Bundle Search and Creation Method	
`getBundle()`	Loads and instantiates a resource bundle.
Resource Retrieval Methods	
`getKeys()`	Retrieves an enumeration of the keys in this resource bundle.
`getObject()`	Retrieves a resource from this resource bundle or a parent resource bundle.
`getString()`	Retrieves a string resource from this resource bundle or a parent resource bundle.
`getStringArray()`	Retrieves a string array resource from this resource bundle or a parent resource bundle.
`handleGetObject()`	Called to retrieve a resource from this resource bundle.
Parent Field and Method	
`parent`	Holds the parent of this resource bundle.
`setParent()`	Called to set the parent for this bundle.

See Also

`ListResourceBundle`, `Properties`, `PropertyResourceBundle`.

Example

This example demonstrates several important characteristics of resource bundles. First, the resource bundles are declared in a package called `pkg`. Note that the class name supplied to `getBundle()` includes the package name.

Second, three resource bundles are declared and exist in a parent chain. Note that whenever a resource is retrieved, the search begins at the end of the chain (`MyResourceBundle_ja_JP`) and continues up the parent chain until a resource is found.

Third, note that the implementation of the `getKeys()` method in all but the default resource bundle calls and returns the `getKeys()` method of its parent.

Finally, the example loads two properties file, also in a parent chain. Note that the base name used in the call to `getBundle()` includes the package name but not the ".properties" suffix.

pkg/Main.java

```
package pkg;

import java.util.*;

class Main {
    public static void main(String[] args) {
        ResourceBundle rb = ResourceBundle.getBundle(
            "pkg.MyResourceBundle", Locale.FRENCH);

        // The French locale is not available so the default result
        // bundle is used.
        // Print it to prove it.
        System.out.println(rb.getClass());           // MyResourceBundle

        rb = ResourceBundle.getBundle("pkg.MyResourceBundle", Locale.JAPAN);

        // The Japan locale is available so it is used.
        System.out.println(rb.getClass());           // MyResourceBundle_ja_JP

        // Print the available keys.
        for (Enumeration e=rb.getKeys(); e.hasMoreElements(); ) {
            System.out.println(e.nextElement());     // animal food version
        }

        System.out.println(rb.getStringArray("food")[0]);      // sushi
        System.out.println(rb.getString("animal"));            // bird
        System.out.println(rb.getObject("version"));           // 42

        // The following automatically creates a ResourceBundle object for a
        // properties file.  The name of the properties file is data.properties.
        rb = ResourceBundle.getBundle("pkg.data", Locale.JAPAN);
        System.out.println(rb.getObject("p1"));                // data_ja
    }
}
```

pkg/MyResourceBundle.java

```
package pkg;

import java.util.*;

public class MyResourceBundle extends ResourceBundle {

    public Object handleGetObject(String key) {
        if (key.equals("animal")) {
            return "bear";
        } else if (key.equals("food")) {
            return new String[]{"hamburger", "pizza", "apple pie"};
        } else if (key.equals("version")) {
            return new Integer(42);
        }
        return null;
    }
```

```
        String[] keys = {"animal", "food", "version"};
        public Enumeration getKeys() {
            return new Enumeration() {
                int count;

                public boolean hasMoreElements() {
                    return count < keys.length;
                }

                public Object nextElement() {
                    if (count < keys.length) {
                        return keys[count++];
                    }
                    throw new NoSuchElementException("Enumeration");
                }
            };
        }
    }
```

pkg/MyResourceBundle_ja.java

```
    package pkg;

    import java.util.*;

    public class MyResourceBundle_ja extends ResourceBundle {
        public Object handleGetObject(String key) {
            if (key.equals("animal")) {
                return "bird";
            } else if (key.equals("food")) {
                return new String[]{"rice"};
            }
            return null;
        }

        public Enumeration getKeys() {
            if (parent != null) {
                return parent.getKeys();
            }
            return null;
        }
    }
```

pkg/MyResourceBundle_ja_JP.java

```
    package pkg;

    import java.util.*;

    public class MyResourceBundle_ja_JP extends ResourceBundle {
        public Object handleGetObject(String key) {
            if (key.equals("food")) {
                return new String[]{"sushi", "udon", "tempura"};
            }
            return null;
        }

        public Enumeration getKeys() {
            if (parent != null) {
                return parent.getKeys();
```

```
            }
            return null;
        }
    }
```

pkg/data.properties

```
p1 = data.properties
```

pkg/data_ja.properties

```
p1 = data_ja.properties
```


getBundle()

PURPOSE
Loads and instantiates a resource bundle.

SYNTAX

```
public static final ResourceBundle getBundle(String baseName)
   throws MissingResourceException
public static final ResourceBundle getBundle(String baseName,
   Locale locale)
```

DESCRIPTION
This method is used to find, load, and instantiate a resource bundle class. It is also used to load properties files (see `Properties`). See the class description for complete details on how this method locates resource bundles.

If `locale` is not specified, it defaults to `Locale.getDefault()`.

The returned resource bundles are cached by this class. This means that a resource bundle that has already been loaded will not be loaded again.

PARAMETERS

`baseName` The non-`null` fully qualified base name of the resource bundle.

`locale` A non-`null` `Locale` object.

RETURNS
A non-`null` `ResourceBundle` object.

EXCEPTIONS

`MissingResourceException`
If a resource bundle cannot be found, loaded, or instantiated.

SEE ALSO
`Locale`.

EXAMPLE
See the class example.

getKeys()

PURPOSE
Retrieves an enumeration of the keys in this resource bundle.

SYNTAX
`public abstract Enumeration getKeys()`

DESCRIPTION
This method returns an enumeration containing the keys of all available resources in this resource bundle.

In general, only the topmost parent of a chain of the resource bundles needs to create the `Enumeration` object. All other resource bundles should simply call and return the `getKeys()` method of its parent. The following is a typical implementation of a non-topmost parent resource bundle.

```
public Enumeration getKeys() {
    if (parent != null) {
        return parent.getKeys();
    }
    return null;
}
```

RETURNS
A non-`null` enumeration of this resource bundle.

EXAMPLE
See the class example.

getObject()

PURPOSE
Retrieves a resource from this resource bundle or a parent resource bundle.

SYNTAX
```
public final Object getObject(String key) throws
    MissingResourceException
```

DESCRIPTION
This method is used to retrieve the resource with the name `key` from this resource bundle. If this resource bundle does not have a resource with the name `key`, each parent of this resource bundle, starting with the closest parent, is searched until one is found or there are no more parents.

This method is not typically overridden by a resource bundle to return a resource. Rather, the method called `handleGetObject()` is the method that should be overridden to return the resource.

PARAMETERS
`key`
A non-`null` case-sensitive string containing the name of the resource.

RETURNS
A non-`null` object.

EXCEPTIONS
`MissingResourceException`
If a resource with the name `key` cannot be found.

SEE ALSO
`getString()`, `getStringArray()`, `handleGetObject()`, `parent`.

EXAMPLE
See the class description.

getString()

PURPOSE Retrieves a string resource from this resource bundle or a parent resource bundle.

SYNTAX
```
public final String getString(String key) throws
    MissingResourceException
```

DESCRIPTION This method is used to retrieve the string resource with the name `key` from this resource bundle. If this resource bundle does not have a resource with the name `key`, each parent of this resource bundle, starting with the closest parent, is searched until one is found or there are no more parents.

This method is not typically overridden by a resource bundle to return a resource. Rather, the method called `handleGetObject()` is the method that should be overridden to return the resource.

The implementation of this method calls `getObject()` and casts the result to a `String`.

PARAMETERS

`key` A non-`null` case-sensitive string containing the name of the resource.

RETURNS A non-`null` string.

EXCEPTIONS

`MissingResourceException`
If a resource with the name `key` cannot be found.

SEE ALSO `getObject()`, `getStringArray()`, `handleGetObject()`, `parent`.

EXAMPLE See the class description.

getStringArray()

PURPOSE Retrieves a string array resource from this resource bundle or a parent resource bundle.

SYNTAX
```
public final String[] getStringArray(String key) throws
    MissingResourceException
```

DESCRIPTION This method is used to retrieve the string array resource with the name key from this resource bundle. If this resource bundle does not have a resource with the name key, each parent of this resource bundle, starting with the closest parent, is searched until one is found or there are no more parents.

This method is not typically overridden by a resource bundle to return a resource. Rather, the method called `handleGetObject()` is the method that should be overridden to return the resource.

The implementation of this method calls `getObject()` and casts the result to a string array.

PARAMETERS

`key` A non-`null` case-sensitive string containing the name of the resource.

RETURNS A non-`null` string array.

EXCEPTIONS

`MissingResourceException`

If a resource with the name `key` cannot be found.

SEE ALSO `getObject()`, `getString()`, `handleGetObject()`, `parent`.

EXAMPLE See the class description.

handleGetObject()

PURPOSE Called to retrieve a resource from this resource bundle.

SYNTAX

```
protected abstract Object handleGetObject(String key) throws
    MissingResourceException
```

DESCRIPTION This method must be overridden by the subclass to return the resource with the name `key`. If there is no resource with that name, this method must return `null`.

If this resource bundle does not contain the resource named `key`, there is no need for this method to search its list of parents. It is the responsibility of this method's caller, `getObject()`, to search the list of parents.

PARAMETERS

`key` A non-`null` case-sensitive string containing the name of the resource.

RETURNS The resource with the name `key`; `null` if not found.

SEE ALSO `getObject()`, `getString()`, `getStringArray()`, `parent`.

EXAMPLE See the class example.

parent

PURPOSE Holds the parent of this resource bundle.

SYNTAX

```
protected ResourceBundle parent
```

DESCRIPTION This field, if not `null`, refers to the parent of this resource bundle. See the class description for more information about parents. This field is used by `getObject()` as it searches the parent list of resource bundles for resources. If `null`, this resource bundle does not have a parent.

SEE ALSO `getObject()`.

EXAMPLE See the class example.

setParent()

PURPOSE Called to set the parent for this bundle.

SYNTAX `protected void setParent(ResourceBundle p)`

DESCRIPTION This method sets the parent of this resource bundle to `p`. If a call to `getObject()` is made on this resource bundle and this resource bundle does not have the desired resource, the search continues to the resource bundle `p`. See the class description for more information about parents.

This method is called by `getBundle()` as it builds its parent list of resource bundles. The default implementation of this method simply sets the parent field to `p`. In general, there is no need to override this method.

PARAMETERS

`p` The non-`null` parent of this resource bundle.

SEE ALSO `getObject()`.

EXAMPLE See the class description.

RuleBasedCollator

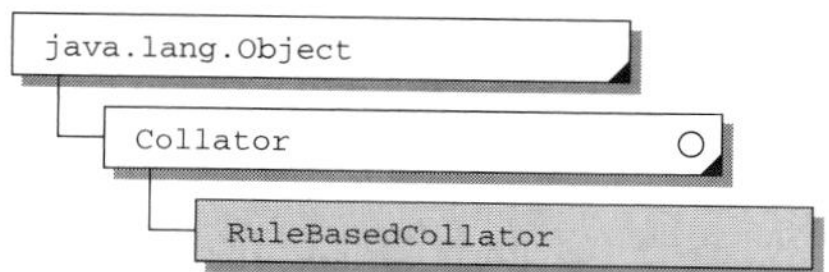

Syntax

```
public class RuleBasedCollator extends Collator
```

Description

The `RuleBasedCollator` class is a concrete subclass of `Collator` that performs locale-sensitive string comparison. You use this class to build searching and alphabetical sorting routines for natural language text. The term *collate* means to determine the proper sort sequence for two or more strings.

The comparison is determined by a rules table for each locale. Java comes with rules tables for many locales. You can customize any of these rules tables as you desire.

Usage: Predefined Rules

Normally, to create a `RuleBasedCollator` object, you use the `Collator` creation method `getInstance()`. The following code creates a `RuleBasedCollator` object that has predefined collation rules for the chosen locale:

```
Collator myCollator = Collator.getInstance(Locale.FRENCH);
System.out.println(myCollator.getClass());       // RuleBasedCollator
if ( myCollator.compare("abc", "ABC") < 0 ) {
    System.out.println("abc is less than ABC");
} else {
    System.out.println("abc is greater than ABC");
}
```

See the `Collator` class for more information about sorting and searching.

Usage: Custom Rules

To create a `RuleBasedCollator` object with specialized collation rules tailored to your needs, you construct the `RuleBasedCollator` directly, passing in the rules as a `String` object. For example:

```
String simpleRules = "< a < b < c < d";
RuleBasedCollator mySimple = new RuleBasedCollator(simpleRules);
```

You can modify an existing set of rules by using `getRules()` to get the rules from a `RuleBasedCollator` object of a particular locale:

```
// Get en_US Collator rules
RuleBasedCollator en_USCollator =
    (RuleBasedCollator)Collator.getInstance(Locale.US);
// Add a characters to sort before English characters
// Suppose the last character before the first base letter 'a' in
// the English collation rule is \u2212
String addedRules = "& \u2212 < \u3041, \u3042 < \u3043, \u3044";
RuleBasedCollator myNewCollator =
    new RuleBasedCollator(en_USCollator.getRules() + addedRules);
```

The collation rules are converted to an internal rules table used by the `compare()` method when comparing two strings. The following sections describe how to write and customize collation rules.

Collation Rules

The collation rules use the following grammar:

```
collationRules := rule *
rule := modifier
      | relation text-argument
      | reset text-argument
```

As indicated, the `collationRules` are composed of any number of `rule` elements. Each `rule` can take any of three forms: a `modifier`, a `relation`, or a `reset`, where the latter two each has a `text-argument`. Notice that a rule cannot begin with a `text-argument`. Ignorable characters are described later rather than included in this grammar.

The following are the elements of the rules:

- **Text-Argument:** A *text-argument* is any sequence of characters not separated by whitespace, excluding the special characters used in a modifier, relation, and reset form (that is, excluding `@ < ; ,` and `=`). To use a special character in its original or usual meanings, put it within single quotation marks (such as `'&'` for ampersand). Here is the entire range of special characters:

```
\u0009 - \u000d
\u0020 - \u002f
\u003a - \u0040
\u005b - \u0060
\u007b - \u007e
```

- **Modifier:** Only one modifier character currently exists:
  '`@`', which indicates that accents are sorted backwards, as in French.
- **Relation:** The relations are the following characters, each followed by a text argument:
  '<': Text argument is greater as a letter difference (primary strength).
  ';': Text argument is greater as an accent difference (secondary strength).
  ',': Text argument is greater as a case difference (tertiary strength).
  '=': Text argument is equal.
- **Reset**: There is a single reset character, which is followed by a text-argument:
  '&': This character indicates that the next rule follows the position where reset's text-argument appears earlier in the rules. The reset character is used primarily for contractions and expansions anywhere in the collation rules. However, it can also be used to add a modifi-

A B C D E F G H I J K L M N O P Q R S T U V W X Y Z

cation at the end of a set of rules that affects characters that appear previously in the rules. This is described next in “Customizing the Rules.” See Figure 85.

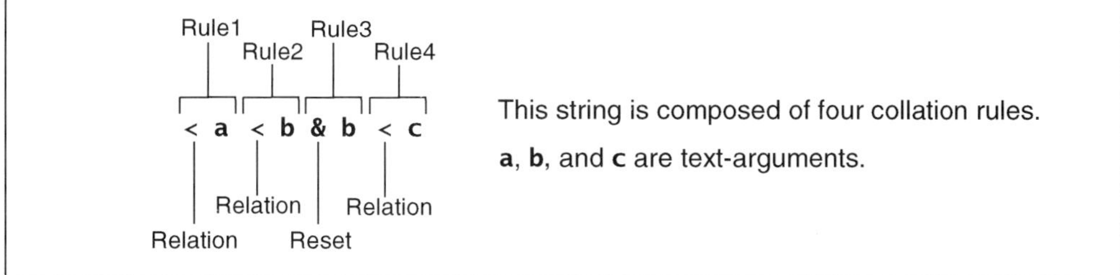

FIGURE 85: Rules Containing a Reset Character.

Customizing the Rules

You can concatenate rule strings together to customize them. When appending rules of the form “`< arg`”, this simply means the text argument `arg` is sorted after all of the other characters. Using the reset character, you can also add rules at the end that override earlier rules, rather than simply add characters to the end of the sorting.

For example, in traditional Spanish, the “ch” combination should sort between the characters “c” and “d”. (The default Spanish locale does not use this rule as of JDK 1.1.6.) To add this rule to the English sorting rules, do this:

```
< a < b < c < d < e < f & c < ch
```

According to these rules, “a” sorts first, then “b”, then “c”, and so on, until the reset character ‘&’ indicates that the next rule (`< ch`) immediately follows reset’s text-argument (`c`) position. This is equivalent to the following:

```
< a < b < c < ch < d < e < f
```

The “Rule Modification Example” later gives another example.

Equivalency

The following are equivalent ways of expressing the same thing. Notice they all begin with a relation character.

```
< a < b < c
< a < b & b < c
< a < c & a < b
```

The order is important, as the subsequent item goes immediately after the text-argument. These examples can be expressed in words, as follows:

- `< a < b < c`
  “a” comes first, then “b,” and then “c.”

- `< a < b & b < c`
  "a" comes first, then "b," and then the reset character '&' indicates that the next rule (`< c`) immediately follows the position to where reset's text-argument (`b`) would be sorted. Hence, this is equivalent to the first rule.
- `< a < c & a < b`
  "a" comes first, "c" is next, and the reset character '&' indicates that the next rule (`< b`) immediately follows the position at which the reset text-argument (`a`) would be sorted. So this, too, is the equivalent to the first rule.

The following are not equivalent to each other:

```
< a < b & a < c
< a < c & a < b
```

Reset Character

When including the reset character, either its text-argument must be present earlier in the sequence or some initial substring of the text-argument must be present earlier in the sequence. So the following is invalid because the reset argument `z` does not also appear to the left of the reset character ('&'):

```
< a < b & z < c
```

The following is valid, since the initial character `a` in the reset argument `ae` *does* appear to the left of the reset character ('&'):

```
< a < b & ae < e
```

Expansion

Expansion is the process of sorting a character as if it were expanded to two characters. In the previous example, "e" is sorted as if it were expanded to two characters: "a" followed by an "e."

In traditional German "ä" (a-umlaut) is sorted as though it expands to two characters. This is expressed as these rules:

```
< a & ae ; ä < b
```

Expressed in words, this can be described as: "a" sorts first, then "ä" sorts as an accent difference from "ae," and then "b" sorts last.

Contraction

In traditional Spanish "ch" is treated as though it contracts to a single character. This is expressed as these rules:

```
< c < ch < d
```

which would cause these words to sort as follows:

```
car cyanide churo day
```

Ignorable Characters

An *ignorable character* is a character that is removed from consideration for sorting at the `PRIMARY` level but is considered significant at the `SECONDARY` or `TERTIARY` level, depending on whether ";" or "," was used in the rules. You can think of an ignorable character as being removed from the word when a comparison is performed. A character is made ignorable by placing it ahead of the first < relation character (separated by other relation characters). In other words, if the first relation is not <, then all of the text-arguments up to the first < are ignorable. For example:

```
, - < a < b
```

The comma "," is the first relation character, and it has "-" as its text-argument. This rule makes "-" an ignorable character, as in the word "black-birds." In many languages, most accents are ignorable.

Normalization and Accents

A `Collator` object automatically normalizes text internally to separate accents from base characters where possible. This is done both when processing the rules and when comparing two strings. `Collator` also uses the Unicode canonical mapping to ensure that combining sequences are sorted properly. (For more information, see the print version of *The Unicode Standard, Version 2.0,* at `http://www.awl.com/cseng/titles/0-201-48345-9/`.)

Most languages that use accents sort them in a consistent fashion immediately after the unmodified base character. This can be achieved by making the accents ignorable and putting them in the right order at the beginning of the collation rules. When this is done, only special cases like the traditional German "ä" need to be handled by explicit rules.

Errors

The following are errors:

- A relation or reset character not followed by a text-argument (for example, the character "<" in "`a < , b`").
- A reset character whose text-argument (or an initial substring of its text-argument) is not already in the sequence (for example, the character "e" in "`a < b & e < f`").
- A text-argument not preceded by either a reset or relation character (for example, the character "c" in "`a < b c < d`"). *Note:* This is currently not an error in JDK 1.1.6 and earlier. The rule "`a < b c < d`" is currently treated as "`a < bc < d`".

These errors cause `RuleBasedCollator` to throw a `ParseException`.

Example: Simple Rules

Here is an example with unrealistically simple rules:

```
< a < b < c < d
```

Usually, to create a `RuleBasedCollator` object, you use the `Collator` creation method `getInstance()`. However, to create a `RuleBasedCollator` object with specialized rules tailored to

A B C D E F G H I J K L M N O P Q R S T U V W X Y Z

your needs, you instead construct a RuleBasedCollator instance with the rules contained in a String object. For example:

```
String simpleRules = "< a < b < c < d";
RuleBasedCollator mySimple = new RuleBasedCollator(simpleRules);
```

Example: Norwegian Rules

To give a richer example of the complete rules for a locale, here are the Norwegian rules:

```
String norwegianRules = "< a,A < b,B < c,C < d,D < e,E < f,F < g,G < h,H" +
"< i,I < j,J < k,K < l,L < m,M < n,N < o,O < p,P < q,Q < r,R < s,S < t,T" +
"< u,U < v,V < w,W < x,X < y,Y < z,Z" +
    "< \u00E5=a\u030A,\u00C5=A\u030A" +
    ";aa,AA < \u00E6,\u00C6 < \u00F8,\u00D8";

RuleBasedCollator myNorwegian = new RuleBasedCollator(norwegianRules);
```

Combining Collators

Combining Collator objects is as simple as concatenating strings. A rule located later in a string overrides an earlier rule. Here's an example that combines two Collator objects from two different locales:

```
// Create an en_US Collator object
RuleBasedCollator en_USCollator =
    (RuleBasedCollator) Collator.getInstance(new Locale("en", "US", ""));
// Create a da_DK Collator object
RuleBasedCollator da_DKCollator =
    (RuleBasedCollator) Collator.getInstance(new Locale("da", "DK", ""));

// Combine the two rules.
// First, get the collation rules from en_USCollator
String en_USRules = en_USCollator.getRules();
// Second, get the collation rules from da_DKCollator
String da_DKRules = da_DKCollator.getRules();
RuleBasedCollator newCollator =
    new RuleBasedCollator(en_USRules + da_DKRules);
// newCollator has the combined rules
```

Example: Rule Modification

In another interesting example, create a new RuleBasedCollator object that makes changes to an existing table. You do this by concatenating the added rules to the end of the existing rules and passing that into the constructor. The added rules will take precedence, because they are added to the end of the string. For example, add "& C < ch, cH, Ch, CH" to the en_USRules (from the previous example) to create new rules:

```
// Create a new Collator object with additional rules
String addedRules = "& C < ch, cH, Ch, CH";
RuleBasedCollator myCollator =
    new RuleBasedCollator(en_USRules + addedRules);
// myCollator contains the new rules
```

Example: Accent Reordering

The following example demonstrates how to change the order of nonspacing accents. The `oldRules` sets up accents in a particular order. The `addOn` string changes the order of the circumflex (`\u0302`) and umlaut (`\u0308`) accents:

```
// old rule
String oldRules = "=\u0301;\u0300;\u0302;\u0308"    // main accents
                + "< a , A ; ae, AE ; \u00e6 , \u00c6"
                + "< b , B < c, C < e, E & C < d, D";
// change the order of accent characters
String addOn = "& \u0300 ; \u0308 ; \u0302";
RuleBasedCollator myCollator = new RuleBasedCollator(oldRules + addOn);
```

Example: Primary Ordering

This example shows how to put new primary ordering in before the default setting. For example, in Japanese `Collator`, you can sort English characters either before or after Japanese characters:

```
// get en_US Collator rules
RuleBasedCollator en_USCollator =
    (RuleBasedCollator)Collator.getInstance(Locale.US);
// add a few Japanese character to sort before English characters
// suppose the last character before the first base letter 'a' in
// the English collation rule is \u2212
String jaString = "& \u2212 < \u3041, \u3042 < \u3043, \u3044";
RuleBasedCollator myJapaneseCollator = new
RuleBasedCollator(en_USCollator.getRules() + jaString);
```

Restrictions

For efficiency, `RuleBasedCollator` has the following restrictions (other subclasses may be used for more complex languages):

- If French secondary ordering is specified, it is applied to all rules in a `RuleBasedCollator` object; it cannot be specified only for certain characters.
- All non-mentioned Unicode characters are at the end of the collation order.

A B C D E F G H I J K L M N O P Q R S T U V W X Y Z

MEMBER SUMMARY	
Constructor	
`RuleBasedCollator()`	Constructs a `RuleBasedCollator` instance.
Comparison Method	
`compare()`	Compares two strings according to this `RuleBasedCollator` object's rules and returns an integer indicating which should be sorted first.

Continued

MEMBER SUMMARY	
Iterator Method	
`getCollationElementIterator()`	Retrieves the `CollationElementIterator` object for a string.
Collation Method	
`getCollationKey()`	Transforms a string into a `CollationKey` object for bitwise comparison with other `CollationKey` objects.
Rule Method	
`getRules()`	Retrieves the rules string for this `RuleBasedCollator` object.
Object Methods	
`clone()`	Standard override; no change in semantics.
`equals()`	Compares this `RuleBasedCollator` object with another object for equality.
`hashCode()`	Computes the hash code for this `RuleBasedCollator`.

See Also

`Collator`, `CollationElementIterator`.

Example

This example compares and sorts the lines read in from a file.

```
import java.text.Collator;
import java.util.Locale;
import java.io.*;

class Main {

    Main (String[] array) {
        Locale loc = Locale.FRENCH;
        String tmp;

        // Create an instance of a subclass of collator.
        Collator collator = Collator.getInstance(loc);

        // Find out what kind of subclass it is.
        System.out.println(collator.getClass() + "\n");
                                    // java.text.RuleBasedcollator
        // Sort and print the array.
        sortArray(collator, array);
        printArray(array);
    }
```

```
// Sort strings.
public static void sortArray(Collator collator, String[] strArray) {
    String tmp;
    // Sort the string array.
    for (int i = 0; i < strArray.length; i++) {
        for (int j = i + 1; j < strArray.length; j++) {
            // Compare members of the array two at a time.
            if( collator.compare(strArray[i], strArray[j] ) > 0 ) {
                //swap strArray[i] and strArray[j]
                tmp = strArray[i];
                strArray[i] = strArray[j];
                strArray[j] = tmp;
            }
        }
    }
}

// Print the contents of an array
static void printArray(String[] a) {
    for (int i = 0; i < a.length; i++) {
        if (a[i].length() == 0) {
            System.out.println("(empty)" + "  ");
        } else {
            if (a[i] == null) {
                System.out.println("(null)" + "  ");
            } else {
                System.out.println(a[i] + "  ");
            }
        }
    }
}

public static void main(String[] args) {
    // Accept a string as an argument
    if (args.length != 1) {
        System.err.println("This program sorts lines in a file");
        System.err.println("Usage: java Main input.txt");
        System.exit(1);
    }

    try {
        // Read in the entire contents of the file.
        BufferedReader rd = new BufferedReader(new FileReader(args[0]));
        String line;

        // Create a temporary array of a big size.
        String[] tmpArray = new String[100];

        int i = 0;
        while ((line = rd.readLine()) != null) {
            tmpArray[i] = line;
            ++i;
        }
        rd.close();

        // Create a new array of the right size.
        String[] newArray = new String[i];
        System.arraycopy(tmpArray, 0, newArray, 0, i);
```

```
                // Call the constructor passing in the array.
                new Main(newArray);

            } catch (Exception e) {
                e.printStackTrace();
            }
        }
    }
```

Output

```
> java Main input.txt
class java.text.RuleBasedCollator

Cinnamon
dogs
Doug
friends
Lady
Linda
pêche
péché
pécher
pêcher
toad
toed
tofu
töne
tots
```

clone()

PURPOSE Creates a copy of this `RuleBasedCollator` object.

SYNTAX `public Object clone()`

DESCRIPTION This method makes a copy of this `RuleBasedCollator` object. The new `RuleBasedCollator` object is a complete copy of the original, including its properties. Changing any value in the new `RuleBasedCollator` object will not affect the original instance.

RETURNS A copy of this `RuleBasedCollator` object.

OVERRIDES `Collator.clone()`.

EXAMPLE This example illustrates the use of `clone()` to copy a `RuleBasedCollator` object. Note that the copy has the same rules as the original.

```
import java.text.RuleBasedCollator;
import java.text.ParseException;

class Main {
    public static void main(String args[]) {
```

```
        // Create a simple collator rule.
        String rules = "< a < b < c < d";

        // Create a rule-based collator.
        try {
            RuleBasedCollator rbc = new RuleBasedCollator(rules);

            // Create a clone and print its rule string.
            RuleBasedCollator rbcCopy = (RuleBasedCollator)rbc.clone();
            System.out.println("Copy's rules:" + "\n" + rbc.getRules());

            // Tests for equality.
            if (rbc.equals(rbcCopy)) {
                System.out.println("Clone is equal to original");
            }

            // Compute hashcode.
            int hc = rbc.hashCode();
            System.out.println("Hash code:        " + hc);

        } catch (ParseException pe) {
            System.out.println("Parse exception for rules");
        }
    }
}
```

compare()

PURPOSE — Compares two strings according to this `RuleBasedCollator` object's rules and returns an integer indicating which should be sorted first.

SYNTAX — `public int compare(String source, String target)`

DESCRIPTION — This method compares the `source` string to the `target` string character-by-character according to the collation rules for this `RuleBasedCollator` object. It returns an integer that is less than, equal to, or greater than `0`, depending on whether `source` is less than, equal to, or greater than the `target` string.

For a one-time comparison, this method has the best performance. If a given string will be involved in multiple comparisons, `CollationKey.compareTo()` has the best performance. See the `CollationKey` class description for an example using `CollationKey`.

PARAMETERS

`source` — A string to compare.

`target` — A string to compare.

RETURNS — An `int` whose value is less than `0` if `source` is less than `target`, `0` if `source` and `target` are equal, and greater than `0` if `source` is greater than `target`.

OVERRIDES — `Collator.compare()`.

EXAMPLE — See the class example.

equals()

PURPOSE Compares this `RuleBasedCollator` object with another object for equality.

SYNTAX `public boolean equals(Object obj)`

DESCRIPTION This method compares this `RuleBasedCollator` object with the object `obj` for equality. If `obj` is a `RuleBasedCollator` object and if it has the same strength, decomposition mode, and rule strings as this `RuleBasedCollator` object, the objects are equal and this method returns `true`. If those values are not equal or if `obj` is `null` or not a `RuleBasedCollator` object, this method returns `false`.

PARAMETERS

`obj` A possibly `null` object with which to compare.

RETURNS `true` if this `RuleBasedCollator` object is equal to `obj`; `false` otherwise.

OVERRIDES `Collator.equals()`.

SEE ALSO `hashCode()`.

EXAMPLE See `clone()`.

getCollationElementIterator()

PURPOSE Retrieves the `CollationElementIterator` object for a string.

SYNTAX

```
public CollationElementIterator
   getCollationElementIterator(String source)
```

DESCRIPTION You call this method explicitly only when you want to create your own collation rules that need access to the particular values of the primary, secondary, and tertiary orders (as described in `CollationElementIterator`). When you call `compare()` on a built-in `Collator` object, such as `RuleBasedCollator`, `CollationElementIterator` objects are created automatically for you for each string to be compared.

This method creates and returns an instance of `CollationElementIterator` for the locale-specific `source` string. This iterator is used to walk through each character of the string according to the rules of this `RuleBasedCollator` object. Use the iterator to return the sort-order properties of the positioned character. The order properties of a character define how a character is collated by the given `Collation` object.

PARAMETERS

`source` The string to be compared.

RETURNS The instance of `CollationElementIterator` for the `source` string.

SEE ALSO CollationElementIterator.

EXAMPLE See the class example in the CollationElementIterator class.

getCollationKey()

PURPOSE Transforms a string into a CollationKey object for bitwise comparison with other CollationKey objects.

SYNTAX `public CollationKey getCollationKey(String source)`

DESCRIPTION This method transforms the source string into a series of bits (in an instance of CollationKey) that can be compared bitwise, using compareTo(), with other CollationKey instances. The rules for this conversion are based on this Collator object's collation rules. When multiple comparisons are involved, a CollationKey instance with compareTo() provides better performance than compare() when strings are involved in multiple comparisons. Two strings to be compared with compareTo() must be generated from the same RuleBasedCollator object. This method can be overridden in a subclass.

PARAMETERS

source The string to be transformed into a CollationKey object and compared.

OVERRIDES Collator.getCollationKey().

RETURNS The instance of CollationKey for the source string. If the source string is null, a null CollationKey object is returned.

EXAMPLE This example uses getCollationKey() to convert strings into CollationKey objects and then calls compareTo() from CollationKey to compare them.

```
import java.text.Collator;
import java.text.CollationKey;
import java.util.Locale;

class Main {
    public static void main(String args[]) {
        Locale loc = Locale.FRENCH;

        // Create an instance of a subclass of collator.
        Collator collator = Collator.getInstance(loc);

        // Find out what kind of subclass it is.
        System.out.println(collator.getClass());
                                    // java.text.RuleBasedcollator

        // Set up strings to sort.
        String s1 = "ABC";
        String s2 = "abc";
        String tmp;
        String[] array = new String[] { s1, s2 };
```

```
            // Create collation keys from the two strings.
            CollationKey ck1 = collator.getCollationKey(s1);
            CollationKey ck2 = collator.getCollationKey(s2);

            // Compare two strings in the array and sort them.
            if( ck1.compareTo(ck2) > 0 ) {
                tmp = array[0];
                array[0] = array[1];
                array[1] = tmp;
            }
            printArray(array);
        }

        // Print the contents of a 1-dimensional array
        static void printArray(Object[] a) {
            for (int i=0; i<a.length; i++) {
                if (a[i].toString().length() == 0) {
                    System.out.print("(empty)" + "  ");
                } else {
                    System.out.println(a[i] + "  ");
                }
            }
        }
    }
```

getRules()

PURPOSE Retrieves the rules string for this `RuleBasedCollator` object.

SYNTAX `public String getRules()`

RETURNS The collation rules from which this `RuleBasedCollator` object was created.

EXAMPLE See the constructor `RuleBasedCollator()`.

hashCode()

PURPOSE Computes the hash code for this `RuleBasedCollator` object.

SYNTAX `public int hashCode()`

DESCRIPTION This method computes the hash code for this `RuleBasedCollator` object based on the rules of this `RuleBasedCollator` object. Two `RuleBasedCollator` objects with the same rules will have the same hash code. However, two `RuleBasedCollator` objects that do not have the same rules might also have the same hash code, although the hash code algorithm minimizes this possibility. The hash code is typically used as the key in a hash table.

RETURNS The `RuleBasedCollator` object's hash code, an integer.

OVERRIDES `Collator.hashCode()`.

SEE ALSO `equals()`.

EXAMPLE See `clone()`.

RuleBasedCollator()

PURPOSE Constructs a `RuleBasedCollator` instance.

SYNTAX `public RuleBasedCollator(String rules) throws ParseException`

DESCRIPTION This constructor constructs an instance of `RuleBasedCollator`, building a collation table from the `rules` passed in. This instance can then be used to compare strings. For a localized instance of `RuleBasedCollator`, call `Collator.getInstance()` instead, which can accept a locale as a parameter.

PARAMETERS

`rules` A string that defines the collation rules for this `RuleBasedCollator` object.

EXCEPTIONS

`ParseException`

A format exception is thrown if the build process of the rules fails. For example, the rule "a < b c < d" will throw this exception.

SEE ALSO `java.util.Locale`.

EXAMPLE This example first creates simple rules and then creates an instance of `RuleBasedCollator`, passing in those rules. It then sorts an array of strings using `compare()`.

```
import java.text.RuleBasedCollator;
import java.text.ParseException;

class Main {
    public static void main(String args[]) {

        // Create a simple collator rule.
        String rules = ("< a,A < b,B < c,C < d,D < e,E < f,F " +
                        "< g,G < h,H < i,I < j,J < k,K < l,L " +
                        "< m,M < n,N < o,O < p,P < q,Q < r,R " +
                        "< s,S < t,T < u,U < v,V < w,W < x,X " +
                        "< y,Y < z,Z");

        // Set up strings to sort.
        String s0 = "Linda";
        String s1 = "Doug";
        String s2 = "Cinnamon";
        String s3 = "Lady";
        String tmp;
        String[] array = new String[] { s0, s1, s2, s3 };

        // Create a rule-based collator.
        try {
            RuleBasedCollator rbc = new RuleBasedCollator(rules);
```

```
            // Print the rule string.
            System.out.println("Rules:" + "\n" + rbc.getRules());

            // Sort and print the array.
            sortArray(rbc, array);
            printArray(array);

        } catch (ParseException pe) {
            System.out.println("Parse exception for rules");
        }
    }

    // Sort strings.
    public static void sortArray(RuleBasedCollator collator,
                                          String[] strArray) {
        String tmp;
        // Sort the string array.
        for (int i = 0; i < strArray.length; i++) {
            for (int j = i + 1; j < strArray.length; j++) {
                // Compare members of the array two at a time.
                if( collator.compare(strArray[i], strArray[j] ) > 0 ) {
                    //swap strArray[i] and strArray[j]
                    tmp = strArray[i];
                    strArray[i] = strArray[j];
                    strArray[j] = tmp;
                }
            }
        }
    }

    // Print the contents of an array
    static void printArray(Object[] a) {
        System.out.println("\n" + "Sorted array:");
        for (int i = 0; i < a.length; i++) {
            if (a[i].toString().length() == 0) {
                System.out.print("(empty)" + "  ");
            } else {
                System.out.println(a[i] + "  ");
            }
        }
    }
}
```

Output

```
> java Main
Rules:
< a , A
< b , B
< c , C
< d , D
< e , E
< f , F
< g , G
< h , H
< i , I
< j , J
< k , K
< l , L
```

```
< m , M
< n , N
< o , O
< p , P
< q , Q
< r , R
< s , S
< t , T
< u , U
< v , V
< w , W
< x , X
< y , Y
< z , Z

Sorted array:
Cinnamon
Doug
Lady
Linda
```

Runnable

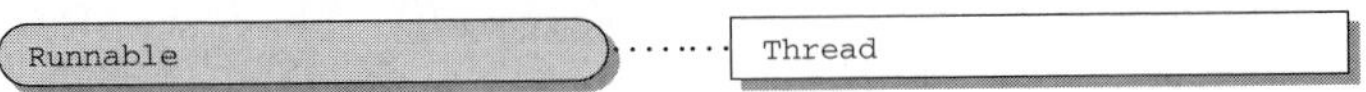

A B C D E F G H I J K L M N O P Q R S T U V W X Y Z

Syntax

```
public interface Runnable
```

Description

When defining a new thread, you typically define a class that subclasses `Thread`. When you create an instance of that class, a new thread is created. When you start that thread, it runs the code in the class's `run()` method. For example, the following code defines a class that prints a message every second:

```
// class that prints out "Lights On!" every second
class ThreadTest extends Thread {
    public void run() {
        while (true) {
            System.out.println("Lights On!");
            try {
                sleep(1000);
            } catch (InterruptedException e) {
                // ignore
            }
        }
    }
}
  ...
// create ThreadTest thread
ThreadTest tt = new ThreadTest();
tt.start();          // start thread
```

However, in some cases, you cannot or do not want a class to subclass `Thread`. Java is a language that supports single inheritance. Perhaps you want a class to inherit from something that is functionally similar to the class that you are defining. In that case, you declare the class to implement the `Runnable` interface and provide an implementation for the single `run()` method of the `Runnable` interface.

Usage

A class that implements `Runnable` provides a definition for `run()`, which contains the code that a thread will execute. To have a thread execute this code, you first create an instance of that class. Then you pass this instance as an argument to one of the `Thread` constructors. The `run()` method defined by this class will then be executed when the thread starts running. The following code is functionally equivalent to the previous `ThreadTest` example, except that it is implemented by declaring a class that is *not* a subclass of `Thread`. Instead, it implements the `Runnable` interface directly.

```
// class that prints out "Lights On!" every second
class RunTest implements Runnable {
    public void run() {
        while (true) {
            System.out.println("Lights On!");
            try {
                Thread.sleep(1000);
            } catch (InterruptedException e) {
                // ignore
            }
        }
    }
}
  ...
// create thread with 'RunTest' object
Thread tr = new Thread(new RunTest(), "runtest");
tr.start();          // start thread
```

MEMBER SUMMARY	
Abstract Method	
`run()`	Defines the code to be run.

See Also

`Thread`.

run()

PURPOSE Defines the code to be run.

SYNTAX `public abstract void run()`

DESCRIPTION This method is executed when a `Runnable` object is executed by a thread. A class that implements `Runnable` or a class that is a subclass of `Thread` must provide an implementation for `run()`.

SEE ALSO `Thread`, `Thread.run()`.

EXAMPLE See the class example.

Runtime

Syntax

```
public class Runtime
```

Description

This class defines methods in the Runtime library. It contains methods that perform environment- and system-related functions, such as those for loading libraries, executing system programs, turning on tracing, and performing garbage-collection.

This class cannot be instantiated.

Usage

You get a reference to an instance of Runtime by calling getRuntime(), as follows:

```
Runtime rt = Runtime.getRuntime();
```

You can then invoke methods on this Runtime object, as follows:

```
// display amount of free and total memory
System.out.println("free " + rt.freeMemory() +
                   " total " + rt.totalMemory());
```

The System class provides shortcuts to many of the methods in this class. For example the following two lines are equivalent.

```
Runtime.getRuntime().runFinalization();
System.runFinalization();
```

MEMBER SUMMARY	
Getting the Runtime Instance	
getRuntime()	Retrieves the reference to the Runtime object.
Memory Management Methods	
freeMemory()	Retrieves an approximation of the number of free bytes in the Java system memory.
gc()	Runs the garbage collector.
runFinalization()	Runs the finalize() method of objects that are pending finalization.
runFinalizersOnExit()	Enables/disables finalization when the program exits.
totalMemory()	Retrieves the total number of bytes in the Java system memory.

MEMBER SUMMARY	
Debugging Methods	
`traceInstructions()`	Enables/disables the tracing of instructions.
`traceMethodCalls()`	Enables/disables the tracing of method calls.
General Methods	
`exec()`	Executes a platform-dependent program.
`exit()`	Causes the virtual machine to exit.
`load()`	Loads a dynamic library when given its full pathname.
`loadLibrary()`	Loads a dynamic library when given its library name.
Deprecated Methods	
`getLocalizedInputStream()`	Replaced by `InputStreamReader` and `BufferedReader`.
`getLocalizedOutputStream()`	Replaced by `OutputStreamWriter` and `BufferedWriter`.

See Also

`System`.

exec()

PURPOSE Executes a platform-dependent program.

SYNTAX

```
public Process exec(String prog) throws IOException
public Process exec(String prog, String[] envp) throws IOException
public Process exec(String[] progarray) throws IOException
public Process exec(String[] progarray, String[] envp) throws
    IOException
```

DESCRIPTION This method executes the platform-dependent program specified by `prog` or `progarray[0]`. The program may be specified using a platform-dependent absolute pathname or as a platform-dependent command name found using the platform-dependent search path. On Windows for example, a command can be specified without its filename extension (e.g., `.exe`).

`exec()` returns a `Process` object, which has methods for obtaining the standard input, standard output, and standard error of the newly created process.

This method can be executed only if permitted by the security manager.

PARAMETERS

`envp`	A possibly `null` array containing environment variable settings to use when executing the system program. Each string in this array has the format *variable_name=value*. The syntaxes of the variable names and values are platform-dependent.
`prog`	The non-`null` pathname of the program to execute.
`progarray`	`progarray[0]` contains the pathname of the program to be executed; arguments to the program are supplied in the rest of `progarray`. `progarray` cannot be `null`.

RETURNS A (non-`null`) `Process` object representing the process created for the execution of the platform-dependent program.

EXCEPTIONS

`IOException`
: `program` or `progarray[0]` does not name a valid program.

`SecurityException`
: If the currently executing thread is not allowed to execute the specified program.

SEE ALSO `Process`, `SecurityManager.checkExec()`.

EXAMPLE

```
try {
    // set up command, arguments, and environment variables
    String[] progarray = new String[2];
    String[] envp = new String[1];
    String prog = "/bin/ls";
    progarray[0] = prog;
    progarray[1] = "/";
    envp[0] = "TERM=vt100";

    Process p1 = rt.exec(prog);                 // '/bin/ls'
    Process p2 = rt.exec(prog, envp);           // '(TERM=vt100; ls)'
    Process p3 = rt.exec(progarray);            // '/bin/ls /'
    Process p4 = rt.exec(progarray, envp);      // '(TERM=vt100; ls /)'
  ...
} catch (IOException e) {
    System.err.println("exec error:" + e);
}
```

exit()

PURPOSE Cause the virtual machine to exit.

SYNTAX `public void exit(int status)`

DESCRIPTION This method causes the virtual machine to terminate with the exit code `status`. All running threads are terminated. All resources associated with the process, such as threads and file descriptors, are released. This method does not return.

This method can be executed only if permitted by the security manager.

Note: This method should be used with caution because it terminates the virtual machine. Consider using `return` or `throw` to recover from an error. Use `exit()` only when you really mean for the virtual machine to exit.

PARAMETERS

`status` The exit status. A value of `0` indicates success; all other values indicate failure.

EXCEPTIONS

`SecurityException`
If the currently executing thread is not allowed to terminate the program for security reasons.

SEE ALSO `SecurityManager.checkExit()`.

EXAMPLE This example checks that an argument is passed to the program. If no argument is passed, the program exits with a status code of `-1`.

```
class Main {
    public static void main(String[] args) {
        if (args.length != 1) {
            System.err.println("usage: java Main <arg>");
            Runtime.getRuntime().exit(-1);
        }
        System.out.println(args[0]);
    }
}
```

freeMemory()

PURPOSE Retrieves an approximation of the number of free bytes in the Java system memory.

SYNTAX `public native long freeMemory()`

DESCRIPTION This method returns an approximation of the number of free bytes available in the Java runtime system. Additional free memory might be obtained by calling `runFinalization()` or `gc()`, depending on whether there are any objects that need to be finalized or garbage-collected.

RETURNS An approximation of the number of free bytes in system memory.

SEE ALSO `gc()`, `Object.finalize()`, `runFinalization()`, `totalMemory()`.

EXAMPLE

```
// display amount of free and total memory
System.out.println("free " + rt.freeMemory() +
                   " total " + rt.totalMemory());
```


gc()

PURPOSE Runs the garbage collector.

SYNTAX `public native void gc()`

DESCRIPTION An object is ready to be discarded when the Java virtual machine determines that the object can no longer be accessed by any thread. Such an object is said to be ready for *finalization*. Finalization is the process of the virtual machine's invoking the object's `finalize()` method in order to "clean up" the object's state. Once an object has been finalized, it is ready to be *garbage-collected*.

The system's garbage collector is run asynchronously and automatically by the Java virtual machine to free memory tied up in objects that have been finalized. The particular algorithm used for garbage-collection is implementation-dependent. You can give an indication to the system that you want the garbage collector to run by invoking the `gc()` method. Doing this, however, does not guarantee that the garbage collector will run immediately; a call to `gc()` acts only as a hint to the system.

SEE ALSO `Object.finalize()`, `runFinalization()`.

EXAMPLE

```
Runtime rt = Runtime.getRuntime();
 ...
rt.gc();        // indicate that Garbage Collector should run
```

getLocalizedInputStream() *DEPRECATED*

PURPOSE Replaced by `InputStreamReader` and `BufferedReader`.

SYNTAX `public InputStream getLocalizedInputStream(InputStream in)`

PARAMETERS

`in` The input stream for which to create the localized stream.

RETURNS `in`

DEPRECATION This method does not do any localization; it just returns `in`. To obtain a stream that turns localized characters read from `in` into Unicode characters, use `InputStreamReader` and `BufferedReader`, as follows:

```
BufferedReader u = new
BufferedReader(new InputStreamReader(in));
```

This code creates a reader that reads bytes (encoded using the platform's default encoding) from the stream `in` and translates those bytes into Unicode characters.

SEE ALSO `java.io.BufferedReader`, `java.io.InputStreamReader`.

getLocalizedOutputStream() *DEPRECATED*

PURPOSE Replaced by `OutputStreamWriter` and `BufferedWriter`.

SYNTAX `public OutputStream getLocalizedOutputStream(OutputStream out)`

PARAMETERS

`out` The output stream for which to create the localized stream.

RETURNS `out`

DEPRECATION This method does not do any localization; it just returns `out`. To obtain a stream that takes Unicode characters and writes them to `out` as localized characters, use `OutputStreamWriter` and `BufferedWriter`, as follows:

```
BufferedWriter u = new
    BufferedWriter(new OutputStreamWriter(out));
```

This code creates a writer that translates the Unicode characters written to it into localized characters using the platform's default (localized) encoding and then writes the encoded data to `out`.

SEE ALSO `java.io.BufferedWriter`, `java.io.InputStreamWriter`.

getRuntime()

PURPOSE Retrieves the reference to the `Runtime` object.

SYNTAX `public static Runtime getRuntime()`

DESCRIPTION A reference to the `Runtime` object is required to invoke the runtime library methods. This method returns the reference to `Runtime` object. There is only one instance of the `Runtime` object per program.

RETURNS A non-`null` reference to the `Runtime` object.

SEE ALSO `System.getRuntime()`.

EXAMPLE

```
Runtime rt = Runtime.getRuntime();
```

load()

PURPOSE Loads a dynamic library when given its full pathname.

SYNTAX `public synchronized void load(String pathname)`

DESCRIPTION This method loads the dynamic library named by the absolute filename `pathname`. The syntax of `pathname` is platform-dependent. Loading a library makes the symbols and functions exported by that library available to the program. This can be used to support native methods. See *The Java Tutorial, First Edition*, Lessons 26 and 27, for details on native methods.

`load()` is idempotent. That is, once a library has been loaded, calling `load()` or `loadLibrary()` on it again results in no action.

If you use `load()` from `java_g`, it will automatically insert `_g` before the `.so`. For example, if `pathname` is `/usr/lib/libabc.so`, `java_g` will look for `/usr/lib/libabc_g.so`; `/usr/lib/libabc.so` will not be consulted.

A library can be loaded only if permitted by the security manager.

PARAMETERS

`pathname` The non-`null` absolute pathname of the library.

EXCEPTIONS

`OutOfMemoryError`
If the library could not be loaded due to insufficient memory in the system.

`SecurityException`
If the currently executing thread is not permitted to load `pathname`.

`UnsatisfiedLinkError`
If `pathname` does not name a library or the library could not be linked successfully (for example, because of unresolved references).

SEE ALSO `loadLibrary()`, `SecurityManager.checkLink()`.

EXAMPLE This example shows the usage of `load()` in a static initializer for providing the implementation of the native method `abcMethod()`.

```
class Abc {
    public native Object abcMethod(Object args);

    static {
        Runtime.getRuntime().load("/export/lib/libabc.so");
    }
}
```

loadLibrary()

PURPOSE Loads a dynamic library when given its library name.

SYNTAX `public synchronized void loadLibrary(String libname)`

DESCRIPTION

This method loads in the dynamic library, `libname`, that it finds in the directory or directories specified by the platform-dependent library search path. On Solaris and Windows, the library search path is specified by the environment variable `LD_LIBRARY_PATH`.

Loading a library makes the symbols and functions exported by that library available to the program. This can be used to support native methods. See *The Java Tutorial, First Edition*, Lessons 26 and 27, for details on native methods.

`loadLibrary()` is idempotent. That is, once a library has been loaded, calling `loadLibrary()` or `load()` on it again results in no action.

If you use `loadLibrary()` from `java_g`, it will automatically add "`_g`" to the library name. In other words, "`_g`" is inserted before the "`.so`" or "`.dll`." For example, if `libname` is `libabc.so`, `java_g` will look for `libabc_g.so`; `libabc.so` will not be consulted.

A library can be loaded only if permitted by the security manager.

PARAMETERS

`libname` The non-`null` name of the library.

EXCEPTIONS

`OutOfMemoryError`

If the library could not be loaded due to insufficient memory in the system.

`SecurityException`

If the currently executing thread is not permitted to load `libname`.

`UnsatisfiedLinkError`

If the library does not exist or the library could not be linked successfully (for example, as a result of unresolved references).

SEE ALSO `load()`, `SecurityManager.checkLink()`.

EXAMPLE

This example shows the usage of `loadLibrary()` in a static initializer for providing the implementation of the native method `abcMethod()`.

```
class Abc {
    public native Object abcMethod(Object args);

    static {
        Runtime.getRuntime().loadLibrary("abc");
    }
}
```

runFinalization()

PURPOSE Runs the `finalize()` method of any objects that are pending finalization.

SYNTAX `public native void runFinalization()`

DESCRIPTION An object is ready to be discarded when the Java virtual machine determines that the object can no longer be accessed by any thread. Such an object is said to be ready for *finalization*. Finalization is the process of the virtual machine's invoking the object's `finalize()` method in order to "clean up" the object's state.

The virtual machine asynchronously and automatically runs the `finalize()` method of objects ready for finalization. Any uncaught exception thrown by this method during finalization is ignored and the finalization terminates. You can use `System.runFinalization()` to explicitly ask the virtual machine to finalize methods that are ready to be discarded. However, this is only a request and the virtual machine is not obligated to satisfy the request immediately.

The `finalize()` method on an object will be called only once by the virtual machine. If the program explicitly invokes `finalize()`, this has no effect on the automatic finalization—the virtual machine will still invoke `finalize()` when the object is ready to be discarded. Once the virtual machine has finalized an object, the object is ready to be *garbage-collected* (i.e., its memory is freed).

See *The Java Language Specification, First Edition*, Section 20.1.11, and *The Java Virtual Machine Specification*, Section 2.16.7, for more details on finalization.

SEE ALSO `gc()`, `Object.finalize()`, `runFinalizersOnExit()`.

EXAMPLE

```
rt.runFinalization();        // run finalize() methods
```

runFinalizersOnExit()

PURPOSE Enables/disables finalization when the program exits.

SYNTAX `public native void runFinalizersOnExit(boolean run)`

DESCRIPTION An object is ready to be discarded when the Java virtual machine determines that the object can no longer be accessed by any thread. Such an object is said to be ready for *finalization*. Finalization is the process of the virtual machine's invoking the object's `finalize()` method in order to "clean up" the object's state.

The virtual machine asynchronously and automatically runs the `finalize()` method of objects ready for finalization. Any uncaught exception thrown by this method during finalization is ignored, and the finalization terminates. You can use `System.runFinalization()` to explicitly ask the virtual machine to finalize methods ready to be discarded. The `finalize()` method on an object will be called only once by the virtual machine. If the program explicitly invokes `finalize()`, this has no effect on the automatic finalization—the virtual machine will still invoke `finalize()` when the object is ready to be discarded.

By default, when a program exits, objects ready for finalization are not finalized; the program simply exits. You can ask the system to finalize objects that are ready to be finalized before the program exits by calling `runFinalizersOnExit()` with an argument of `true`. This method can be run only if the currently executing thread is allowed by the security manager to call `exit()`.

If a program is terminated abnormally (e.g., its process is killed), finalization may not always occur, regardless of whether `runFinalizersOnExit()` was called. See the `Object.finalize()` example.

See *The Java Language Specification, First Edition*, Section 20.1.11, and *The Java Virtual Machine Specification*, Section 2.16.7, for more details on finalization.

PARAMETERS

`run` — `true` means finalize objects pending finalization before exiting; `false` means finalization need not be run upon exit.

EXCEPTIONS

`SecurityException`
If the currently executing thread cannot call `exit()`.

SEE ALSO `gc()`, `Object.finalize()`, `runFinalization()`, `SecurityManager.checkExit()`.

EXAMPLE This example asks that finalization be done before the program exits, and then exits the program. See `Object.finalize()` for another example of using `runFinalizersOnExit()`.

```
Runtime rt = Runtime.getRuntime();
rt.runFinalizersOnExit(true);
rt.exit(0);
```

totalMemory()

PURPOSE Retrieves the total number of bytes in the Java system memory.

SYNTAX `public native long totalMemory()`

RETURNS The number of bytes of total memory available in the Java system.

SEE ALSO `freeMemory()`.

EXAMPLE See `freeMemory()`.

traceInstructions()

PURPOSE Enables/disables the tracing of instructions.

SYNTAX `public native void traceInstructions(boolean on)`

DESCRIPTION This method turns the tracing of byte code instructions on and off. When tracing is set to *on*, each byte code instruction that is executed, as well as all entries and exits from method calls, are displayed to standard error output. A voluminous amount of output is generated when tracing is set to *on*. For a less-detailed trace of your program, use `traceMethodCalls()`.

`traceInstructions()` can be used for debugging your Java program when using `java_g`; it does nothing when the normal `java` interpreter is used.

PARAMETERS

`on` If `true`, turns tracing on; otherwise, turns tracing off.

SEE ALSO `traceMethodCalls()`.

EXAMPLE

```
// trace all instructions executed for creating Date instance
rt.traceInstructions(true);         // trace on
Date d = new Date();
rt.traceInstructions(false);        // trace off
```

traceMethodCalls()

PURPOSE Enables/disables the tracing of method calls.

SYNTAX `public native void traceMethodCalls(boolean on)`

DESCRIPTION This method turns the tracing of method calls on and off. When tracing is set to *on*, output is displayed to standard error output each time a method is entered or exited, showing the name of the method involved. For more-detailed information about the execution of your program, use `traceInstructions()`.

`traceMethodCalls()` can be used for debugging your Java program when using `java_g`; it does nothing when the normal `java` interpreter is used.

PARAMETERS

`on` If `true`, turns tracing on; otherwise, turns tracing off.

SEE ALSO `traceInstructions()`.

EXAMPLE

```
// trace all methods executed for creating Date instance
rt.traceMethodCalls(true);         // trace on
Date d = new Date();
rt.traceMethodCalls(false);        // trace off
```

RuntimeException

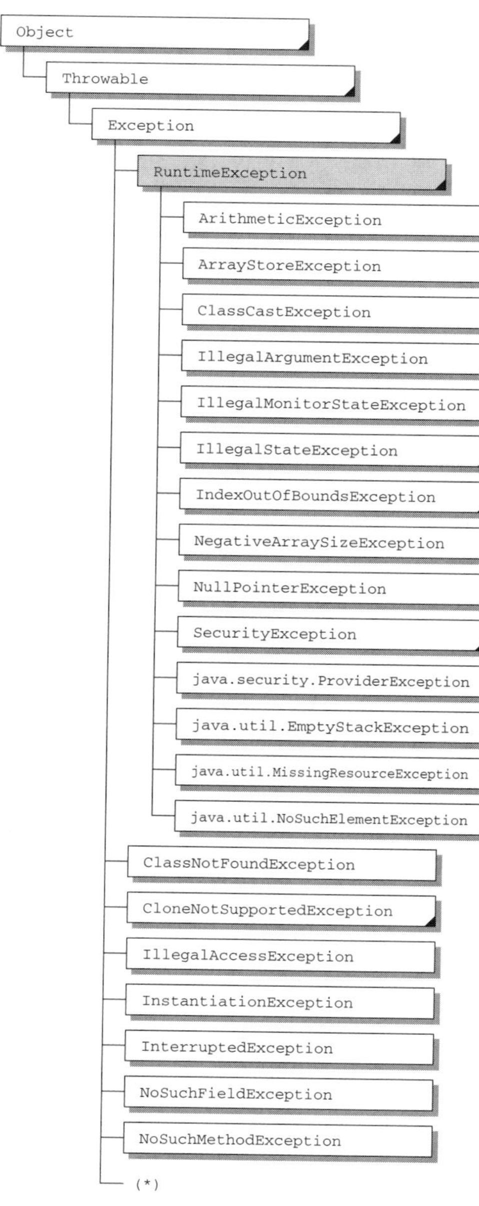
Object
Throwable
Exception
RuntimeException
ArithmeticException
ArrayStoreException
ClassCastException
IllegalArgumentException
IllegalMonitorStateException
IllegalStateException
IndexOutOfBoundsException
NegativeArraySizeException
NullPointerException
SecurityException
java.security.ProviderException
java.util.EmptyStackException
java.util.MissingResourceException
java.util.NoSuchElementException
ClassNotFoundException
CloneNotSupportedException
IllegalAccessException
InstantiationException
InterruptedException
NoSuchFieldException
NoSuchMethodException
(*)

(*) 21 classes from other packages not shown.

Syntax

```
public class RuntimeException extends Exception
```

Description

`RuntimeException` and its subclasses are exceptions thrown by the Java runtime. They indicate unrecoverable conditions indicative of programming errors. Consequently, they should not be declared in the `throws` clause of a method. Nor should they be caught using `try/catch` statements. These exceptions should be allowed to percolate to the top level of the user's program, where they will be dealt with by the Java runtime system. The Java runtime system displays to the user executing the faulty program a stack trace of where the `RuntimeException` occurred. User programs should not subclass `RuntimeException` or its subclasses; these are reserved for the Java runtime system.

A B C D E F G H I J K L M N O P Q R S T U V W X Y Z

MEMBER SUMMARY	
Constructor	
`RuntimeException()`	Constructs a `RuntimeException` instance.

See Also

`ArithmeticException`, `ArrayStoreException`, `ClassCastException`, `Exception`, `IllegalArgumentException`, `IllegalStateException`, `IndexOutOfBoundsException`, `NegativeArraySizeException`, `NullPointerException`, `SecurityException`.

Example

See examples of subclasses of `RuntimeException`.

RuntimeException()

PURPOSE
Constructs a `RuntimeException` instance.

SYNTAX
```
public RuntimeException()
public RuntimeException(String msg)
```

DESCRIPTION
The two forms of this constructor construct an instance of `RuntimeException`. An optional string `msg` can be supplied that describes this particular instance of the exception. If `msg` is not supplied, it defaults to `null`.

PARAMETERS
`msg` A possibly `null` string that gives details about this exception.

SEE ALSO
`Throwable.getMessage()`.

SecurityException

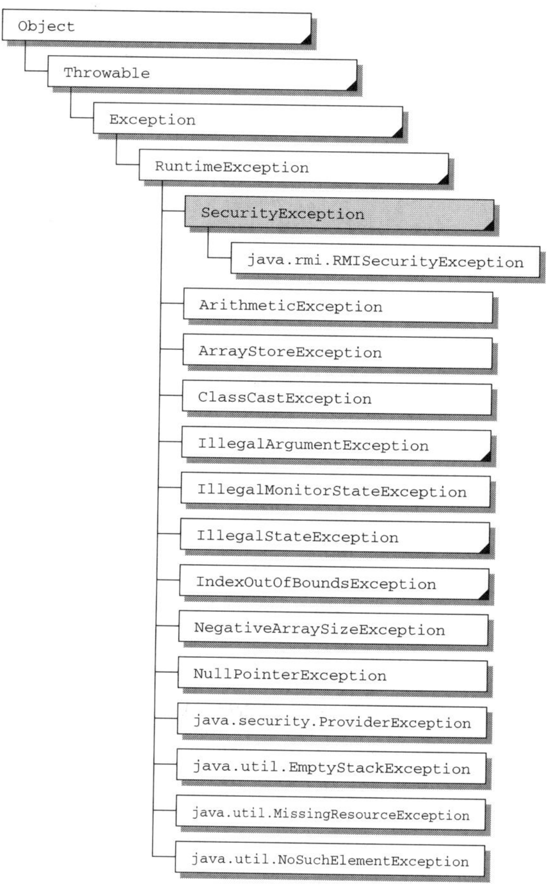

Syntax

```
public class SecurityException extends RuntimeException
```

Description

`SecurityException` is a runtime exception that is thrown by the Java runtime library when a method cannot be executed for security reasons. Throwing of a `SecurityException` indicates that the program has violated security constraints on the system.

`SecurityException` is a runtime exception and should not be caught or declared in the `throws` clause of a method.

MEMBER SUMMARY	
Constructor	
`SecurityException()`	Constructs a `SecurityException` instance.

A B C D E F G H I J K L M N O P Q R S T U V W X Y Z

See Also

`SecurityManager`.

Example

Here are some examples of methods that throw `SecurityException`:

```
protected SecurityManager() {
    if (System.getSecurityManager() != null) {
        throw new SecurityException("can't create SecurityManager");
    }
}
public void checkConnect(String host, int port) {
    if (port > 1024)
        throw new SecurityException();
}
```

SecurityException()

PURPOSE Constructs a `SecurityException` instance.

SYNTAX

```
public SecurityException()
public SecurityException(String msg)
```

DESCRIPTION The two forms of this constructor construct an instance of `SecurityException`. An optional string `msg` can be supplied that describes this particular instance of the exception. If `msg` is not supplied, it defaults to `null`.

PARAMETERS

`msg` A possibly `null` string that gives details about this exception.

SEE ALSO `Throwable.getMessage()`.

SecurityManager

A B C D E F G H I J K L M N O P Q R S T U V W X Y Z

Syntax

```
public abstract class SecurityManager
```

Description

A security manager enforces security policies related to what a program is allowed to do. Some of these policies concern inspection of the execution stack, access to local files, access to system properties, and permission to execute system commands.

The Java runtime system, by default, does not use a security manager. This means there are no security checks on any operation and all operations are allowed. However, applications like Web browsers typically define a security manager and use `System.setSecurityManager()` to install it. Only one security manager can be installed. Once installed, it cannot be replaced.

Permission Checking

When you define a security manager, you must override some or all of the permission checking methods, depending on the policies the security manager enforces. With the exception of `checkTopLevelWindow()`, all of these methods, by default, simply throw `SecurityException`, meaning the operation is not allowed for security reasons. For example, if your security manager wants to allow the program to be able to read any file (that is, any allowed by the underlying operating system), then it must supply its own implementation for `checkRead()`, as follows:

```
public void checkRead(String filename) {
}
public void checkRead(FileDescriptor fd) {
}
```

These two methods override the existing implementations of `checkRead()` and permit any file to be read. If all other policies are to remain unchanged, then these are the only method definitions your security manager must supply.

When you override a check method, that method should set the protected variable `inCheck` to `true` to indicate that a check is in progress and set it to `false` before exiting the check method. A check method may make calls to code outside the security manager. It may be necessary for the outside code to take special action depending on whether it is performing a security check. Such code can use `getInCheck()` to determine whether it is being called from a check method in the security manager. Note that code that sets `inCheck` and then calls methods that depend on the behavior of `getInCheck()` should be synchronized so that the same code cannot be executed concurrently by two threads. This is necessary to prevent one thread from setting `inCheck` and unintentionally allowing another thread to take advantage of the fact that `getInCheck()` is `true` in order to bypass other necessary security checks.

Current Execution Context

When permission checks are made, they are always done with respect to the *current execution context*, sometimes called the current *security context*. The current execution context is a platform-dependent collection of information that the system has about the currently executing thread (including the thread group to which it belongs, the identity of the user executing the Java program, and the machine on which the Java program is executing). The information in the current execution context can be used by the security manager to do permission checks.

Execution Stack Information

The *execution stack* is a record of the method calls that were made from the main program to the current method. It indicates all of the methods that are in progress and pending termination of the current method call. For example, if `main()` calls `foo()`, which in turn calls `bar()`, the execution stack, when executing inside `bar()`, would be `bar() -> foo() -> main()`. For some methods to perform some of the permission checking, they may need to inspect the execution stack to find out information about the current execution context. The `SecurityManager` class provides protected methods that can be used by subclasses of `SecurityManager` for this purpose.

MEMBER SUMMARY

Constructor	
`SecurityManager()`	Constructs a `SecurityManager` instance.
Permission Checking Methods	
`checkAccept()`	Determines if allowed to accept a socket connection.
`checkAccess()`	Determines if allowed to modify a thread or thread group.
`checkAwtEventQueueAccess()`	Determines if allowed to access the AWT system event queue.
`checkConnect()`	Determines if allowed to establish a socket connection.
`checkCreateClassLoader()`	Determines if allowed to create a class loader.
`checkDelete()`	Determines if allowed to delete a file.
`checkExec()`	Determines if allowed to execute a platform-dependent program.
`checkExit()`	Determines if allowed to exit the virtual machine.
`checkLink()`	Determines if allowed to load and link in a library.
`checkListen()`	Determines if allowed to bind to a local port.

MEMBER SUMMARY

`checkMemberAccess()`	Determines if allowed to access reflection objects of members of a class.
`checkMulticast()`	Determines if allowed to join, leave, or send data to a multicast address.
`checkPackageAccess()`	Determines if allowed to access a package.
`checkPackageDefinition()`	Determines if allowed to add class definitions to a package.
`checkPrintJobAccess()`	Determines if allowed to submit a print job.
`checkPropertiesAccess()`	Determines if allowed to read and update the system properties.
`checkPropertyAccess()`	Determines if allowed to access a system property.
`checkRead()`	Determines if allowed to read a file.
`checkSecurityAccess()`	Determines if allowed to perform a specified security-related action.
`checkSetFactory()`	Determines if allowed to set the networking-related object factories.
`checkSystemClipboardAccess()`	Determines if allowed to read or write to the system clipboard.
`checkTopLevelWindow()`	Determines if allowed to create a top-level window.
`checkWrite()`	Determines if allowed to write to a file.
Methods for Checking Security Manager's State	
`getInCheck()`	Determines whether there is a security check in progress.
`getSecurityContext()`	Retrieves a security context for performing security checks.
`getThreadGroup()`	Retrieves the default thread group to use when creating threads.
Methods and Field for Examining the Execution Stack	
`classDepth()`	Finds the first occurrence of a class on the execution stack.
`classLoaderDepth()`	Finds the first occurrence of a class created by a class loader on the execution stack.
`currentClassLoader()`	Finds the topmost class loader on the execution stack.
`currentLoadedClass()`	Finds the topmost class with a class loader on the execution stack.
`getClassContext()`	Retrieves the context of the execution stack.
`inCheck`	Records whether there is a security check in progress.
`inClass()`	Determines whether a class is on the execution stack.
`inClassLoader()`	Determines whether a class loader is on the execution stack.

See Also

java.rmi.RMISecurityManager, System.getSecurityManager(), System.setSecurityManager().

checkAccept()

PURPOSE Determines if allowed to accept a socket connection.

SYNTAX

```
public void checkAccept(String host, int port)
```

DESCRIPTION This method determines whether the current execution context is allowed to accept a socket connection from the machine `host` on the remote port `port`.

PARAMETERS

`host` The non-`null` machine name to check. The syntax of the name is platform-dependent. For example, if the machine has an Internet host name, `host` could be a domain-qualified name like `foobar.widget.com` or a nonqualified name like `foobar`.

`port` The remote port number to check.

EXCEPTIONS

`SecurityException`
If the connection cannot be accepted due to security reasons.

SEE ALSO `checkListen()`, `checkRead()`, `checkWrite()`, `java.net.ServerSocket.accept()`.

checkAccess()

PURPOSE Determines if allowed to modify a thread or thread group.

SYNTAX

```
public void checkAccess(Thread thrd)
public void checkAccess(ThreadGroup thrdGroup)
```

DESCRIPTION The first form of this method determines whether the current execution context is allowed to modify the thread `thrd`. Modifications include stopping, suspending, and resuming the thread and changing its priority, name, and daemon status.

The second form of this method determines whether the current thread is allowed to modify the thread group `thrdGroup`. Modifications include stopping, suspending, resuming, and destroying threads in the thread group, joining the thread group, and changing the thread group's daemon status and maximum priority.

PARAMETERS

`thrd` The non-`null` thread to be checked.

`thrdGroup` The non-`null` thread group to be checked.

EXCEPTIONS

`SecurityException`

If the current thread is not allowed to modify `thrd` or `thrdGroup` for security reasons.

SEE ALSO `Thread.checkAccess()`, `Thread.resume()`, `Thread.setDaemon()`, `Thread.setName()`, `Thread.setPriority()`, `Thread.stop()`, `Thread.suspend()`, `Thread.Thread()`, `ThreadGroup.checkAccess()`, `ThreadGroup.destroy()`, `ThreadGroup.setDaemon()`, `ThreadGroup.setMaxPriority()`, `ThreadGroup.setPriority()`, `ThreadGroup.resume()`, `ThreadGroup.stop()`, `ThreadGroup.suspend()`, `ThreadGroup.ThreadGroup()`.

checkAwtEventQueueAccess()

PURPOSE Determines if allowed to access the AWT system event queue.

SYNTAX `public void checkAwtEventQueueAccess()`

DESCRIPTION This method determines whether the current execution context is allowed to accept a socket connection from the machine `host` on the remote port `port`.

The AWT system uses a single *system event queue* for posting events (see `java.awt.Toolkit.getSystemEventQueue()`). The system event queue can include not only events generated by the AWT, but also system events that are added programmatically.

Depending on the AWT toolkit implementation, applets running on the same virtual machine may not necessarily share the same system event queue.

This method checks whether the currently executing context can get a reference to the system event queue. Gaining a reference to the system event queue has security implications. This is because with the reference, you can read the queue's contents or post events to it.

EXCEPTIONS

`SecurityException`

If the system event queue cannot be accessed due to security reasons.

SEE ALSO `java.awt.EventQueue`, `java.awt.Toolkit.getSystemEventQueue()`.

checkConnect()

PURPOSE Determines if allowed to establish a socket connection.

SYNTAX
```
public void checkConnect(String host, int prt)
public void checkConnect(String host, int prt, Object ctx)
```

DESCRIPTION The two forms of this method check whether the current execution context is allowed to establish a connection to the port `prt` on the machine `host`. If `prt` is -1, this method checks whether the resolution of `host` to an IP address is allowed. If a context `ctx` is specified, the security manager determines whether *both* the current execution context and `ctx` are allowed to establish the connection.

PARAMETERS

`ctx` The non-`null` additional context to check.
`host` The non-`null` machine name to check.
`prt` The port to check. If `prt` is -1, checks whether the resolution of `host` to an IP address is allowed.

EXCEPTIONS

`SecurityException`
If the connection cannot be established for security reasons.

SEE ALSO `java.net.DatagramSocket.getLocalAddress()`, `java.net.DatagramSocket.send()`, `java.net.DatagramSocket.receive()`, `getSecurityContext()`, `java.net.InetAddress.getByName()`, `java.net.InetAddress.getHostName()`, `java.net.InetAddress.getAllByName()`, `java.net.MulticastSocket.send()`, `java.net.Socket.Socket()`.

checkCreateClassLoader()

PURPOSE Determines if allowed to create a class loader.

SYNTAX
```
public void checkCreateClassLoader()
```

DESCRIPTION This method determines whether the current execution context is allowed to create a class loader.

EXCEPTIONS

`SecurityException`
If a class loader cannot be created due to security reasons.

SEE ALSO `ClassLoader.ClassLoader()`.

checkDelete()

PURPOSE Determines if allowed to delete a file.

SYNTAX `public void checkDelete(String fileName)`

DESCRIPTION This method determines whether the current execution context is allowed to delete the file `fileName`. Implementers should use the canonical form of `fileName` in order to unambiguously identify the file being checked.

PARAMETERS

`fileName` The non-`null` system-dependent filename to check.

EXCEPTIONS

`SecurityException`

If `fileName` cannot be deleted for security reasons.

SEE ALSO `java.io.File.delete()`, `java.io.File.getCanonicalPath()`.

checkExec()

PURPOSE Determines if allowed to execute a platform-dependent program.

SYNTAX `public void checkExec(String prog)`

DESCRIPTION This method determines whether the current execution context is allowed to execute the platform-dependent program `prog`. Executing platform-dependent programs has security implications because certain programs can make unexpected and sometimes undesirable updates to the system environment.

PARAMETERS

`prog` The non-`null` platform-dependent name of the program to check. `prog` may be an absolute filename naming the program or a program name to be searched in the invoker's program execution path.

EXCEPTIONS

`SecurityException`

If `prog` cannot be executed for security reasons.

SEE ALSO `Process`, `Runtime.exec()`.

checkExit()

PURPOSE Determines if allowed to exit the virtual machine.

SYNTAX `public void checkExit(int stat)`

DESCRIPTION This method determines whether the current execution context is allowed to exit the virtual machine with status `stat`. Exiting the virtual machine has security implications because it effectively stops the entire Java program. The exit status is significant because it is sometimes used by other programs to check whether a program executed correctly.

PARAMETERS

`stat` The exit status to check.

EXCEPTIONS

`SecurityException`
If the virtual machine cannot be exited with `stat` for security reasons.

SEE ALSO `Runtime.exit()`.

checkLink()

PURPOSE Determines if allowed to load and link a library.

SYNTAX `public void checkLink(String lib)`

DESCRIPTION This method determines whether the current execution context is allowed to load and link the library `lib` into the system. Loading libraries has security implications because it makes the symbols being exported by the libraries visible to the program. This could possibly result in the overriding of the definition of symbols (to be loaded in the future) of functions that have security importance, such as functions for getting passwords, resolving host names, and getting machine licenses.

PARAMETERS

`lib` A non-`null` string containing either the filename or library name of the library to load.

EXCEPTIONS

`SecurityException`
If `lib` cannot be loaded for security reasons.

SEE ALSO `Runtime.load()`, `Runtime.loadLibrary()`.

checkListen()

PURPOSE Determines if allowed to bind to a local port.

SYNTAX `public void checkListen(int lport)`

DESCRIPTION This method determines whether the current execution context is allowed to bind to the local port `lport`.

PARAMETERS

`lport` The local port to check.

EXCEPTIONS

`SecurityException`

If `lport` cannot be bound due to security reasons.

SEE ALSO `java.net.DatagramSocket.DatagramSocket()`, `java.net.MulticastSocket.MulticastSocket()`, `java.net.ServerSocket.ServerSocket()`.

checkMemberAccess()

PURPOSE Determines if allowed to access the reflection objects of members of a class.

SYNTAX `public void checkMemberAccess(Class cl, int mtype)`

DESCRIPTION This method determines whether the current execution context is allowed to access the reflection objects of members of type `mtype` from the class or interface `cl`. Note that "access" is orthogonal to the access control specified in the program using the `public`, `protected`, and `private` modifiers. `checkMemberAccess()` is used by the security manager to check whether the currently executing context should be allowed to obtain the reflection objects of the constructors, methods, and fields of `cl`.

`mtype` specifies the type of members to check. `mtype` that is `Member.DECLARED` means check whether access to reflection objects of members declared in `cl` is allowed. `mtype` that is `Member.PUBLIC` means check whether access to reflection objects of public (inherited and declared) members of `cl` is allowed.

PARAMETERS

`cl` The non-`null` class or interface being checked.

`mtype` The type of members being checked. It is one of `Member.DECLARED` or `Member.PUBLIC`.

EXCEPTIONS

`SecurityException`

If reflection objects of members of type `mtype` from class or interface `cl` cannot be accessed due to security reasons.

SEE ALSO `Class.getConstructor()`, `Class.getConstructors()`, `Class.getDeclaredClasses()`, `Class.getDeclaredConstructors()`, `Class.getDeclaredConstructor()`, `Class.getDeclaredField()`, `Class.getDeclaredFields()`, `Class.getDeclaredMethod()`, `Class.getDeclaredMethods()`, `Class.getField()`, `Class.getFields()`, `Class.getMethod()`, `Class.getMethods()`, `java.lang.reflect.Member.DECLARED`, `java.lang.reflect.Member.PUBLIC`.

checkMulticast()

PURPOSE Determines if allowed to use join, leave, or send to a multicast address.

SYNTAX

```
public void checkMulticast(InetAddress maddr)
public void checkMulticast(InetAddress maddr, byte ttl)
```

DESCRIPTION A program can communicate with other programs on the network by sending a *single* datagram packet to a *multicast group* comprising zero or more members. The group is identified by a *multicast address*—an IP address to which group members subscribe. The `MulticastSocket` class contains methods for sending and receiving IP multicast packets.

This method determines whether the current execution context is allowed to join, leave, or send data to the IP multicast address `maddr`.

If `ttl` is specified, it means to check whether the current execution context is allowed to send datagram packets to members of the group `maddr` using a time-to-live value of `ttl`.[1] A higher value of `ttl` means more network resources will be used. If `ttl` is not specified, it is the default time-to-live value of datagram packets sent from the socket. If the program has not changed the default, most socket implementations use a default of one, which means to multicast on the local network.

PARAMETERS

`maddr` The non-`null` multicast group address to check.

`ttl` The transmission range of datagram packets that will be used.

EXCEPTIONS

`SecurityException`
If a multicast address for `maddr` (and `ttl`) cannot be used due to security reasons.

1. If the time-to-live value of a datagram packet is one, the datagram packet is transmitted using the local network multicast which reaches all immediately-neighboring members of the sender. If the datagram packet's time-to-live value is greater than one, the datagram packet is also forwarded by *multicast routers* to all other networks that have members of the multicast group. If the datagram packet's time-to-live value is greater than two, the datagram packet is again forwarded from those networks, and so on.

SEE ALSO `java.net.DatagramSocket.send()`, `java.net.DatagramSocketImpl`, `java.net.MulticastSocket.getTTL()`, `java.net.MulticastSocket.joinGroup()`, `java.net.MulticastSocket.leaveGroup()`, `java.net.MulticastSocket.send()`, `java.net.MulticastSocket.setTTL()`.

A B C D E F G H I J K L M N O P Q R S T U V W X Y Z

checkPackageAccess()

PURPOSE Determines if allowed to access a package.

SYNTAX `public void checkPackageAccess(String pkg)`

DESCRIPTION This method determines whether the current execution context is allowed to access the package `pkg`. Note that "access" is orthogonal to the access control specified in the program using the `public`, `protected`, and `private` modifiers.

This method is not used internally by the JDK. It is intended to be used by Web browsers to control which packages applets can access.

PARAMETERS

`pkg` The non-`null` name of the package to check (e.g., "java.io").

EXCEPTIONS

`SecurityException`

If `pkg` cannot be accessed due to security reasons.

checkPackageDefinition()

PURPOSE Determines if allowed to add class definitions to a package.

SYNTAX `public void checkPackageDefinition(String pkg)`

DESCRIPTION This method determines whether the current execution context is allowed to add class or interface definitions to the package `pkg`. Class definitions in the same package can access package-private classes, interfaces, and members. Applications might want to restrict such access for security reasons.

This method is not used internally by the JDK. It is intended to be used by Web browsers to control whether an applet is allowed to add definitions to classes or interfaces to existing packages. For example, a browser might not allow applets to have classes in the "java.lang" and "sun.net" packages.

PARAMETERS

`pkg` The non-`null` name of the package to check (e.g., "java.io").

EXCEPTIONS

`SecurityException`
If class definitions cannot be added to `pkg` due to security reasons.

A B C D E F G H I J K L M N O P Q R S T U V W X Y Z

checkPrintJobAccess()

PURPOSE Determines if allowed to submit a print job.

SYNTAX

```
public void checkPrintJobAccess()
```

DESCRIPTION This method determines whether the current execution context is allowed to submit a print job.

This method is not used internally by the JDK. It is intended to be used by applications such as Web browsers to control whether an applet is allowed to use printer resources in the application's environment.

EXCEPTIONS

`SecurityException`
If not allowed to submit a print job.

checkPropertiesAccess()

PURPOSE Determines if allowed to read and update the system properties.

SYNTAX

```
public void checkPropertiesAccess()
```

DESCRIPTION This method determines whether the current execution context is allowed to access the system properties. This method controls both the reading and updating of system properties.

EXCEPTIONS

`SecurityException`
If the system properties cannot be accessed due to security reasons.

SEE ALSO `checkPropertyAccess()`, `java.util.Properties`, `System.getProperties()`, `System.setProperties()`.

checkPropertyAccess()

PURPOSE Determines if allowed to access a system property .

SYNTAX

```
public void checkPropertyAccess(String prop)
public void checkPropertyAccess(String prop, String defval)
```

DESCRIPTION The two forms of this method determine whether the current execution context is allowed to access the system property `prop`. If `defval` is supplied, a check is made to see whether `defval` is allowed to be returned as the default value for `prop` if `prop` does not exist.

Note: The form of this method that accepts `defval` as an argument does not exist in Java 1.1.

PARAMETERS

`defval` The possibly `null` default value for `prop` to check.

`prop` The non-`null` system property to check.

EXCEPTIONS

`SecurityException`

If `prop` cannot be accessed due to security reasons.

SEE ALSO `checkPropertiesAccess()`, `java.util.Properties`, `System.getProperty()`.

checkRead()

PURPOSE Determines if allowed to read a file.

SYNTAX

```
public void checkRead(FileDescriptor fd)
public void checkRead(String fileName)
public void checkRead(String fileName, Object ctx)
```

DESCRIPTION The three forms of this method check whether the current execution context is allowed to read the specified file. The first form determines whether the security manager allows reading from the open file descriptor, `fd`. This is useful for checking objects such as sockets that more commonly have file descriptors rather than filenames.

The other two forms check whether the current execution context is allowed to read the file named `fileName`. If `ctx` is supplied, both the current execution context and `ctx` must be allowed to read `fileName`.

Implementers should use the canonical form of `fileName` in order to unambiguously identify the file being checked (for example by using `File.getCanonicalPath()`).

PARAMETERS

`ctx` The non-`null` additional execution context to be checked.

`fd` The non-`null` file descriptor of the file to check.

`fileName` The non-`null` system-dependent filename to check.

EXCEPTIONS

`SecurityException`

If `fileName` or `fd` cannot be read due to security reasons.

SEE ALSO java.io.File.canRead(), java.io.File.exists(), java.io.File.getCanonicalPath(), java.io.File.isDirectory(), java.io.File.isFile(), java.io.File.lastModified(), java.io.File.length(), java.io.File.list(), java.io.FileInputStream.FileInputStream(), java.io.RandomAccessFile.RandomAccessFile().

checkSecurityAccess()

PURPOSE Determines if allowed to perform a specified security-related action.

SYNTAX `public void checkSecurityAccess(String action)`

DESCRIPTION The `Identity` and `Security` classes use this method to check whether the caller is allowed to invoke the methods defined in their classes. This method is intended only for use within the JDK.

PARAMETERS

`action` A non-`null` string specifying the security-related action to check. The format of the string is unspecified and meant for internal use only.

EXCEPTIONS

`SecurityException`
If not allowed to perform the security-related action `action`.

SEE ALSO java.security.Identity.setPublicKey(), java.security.Identity.setInfo(), java.security.Identity.addCertificate(), java.security.Identity.removeCertificate(), java.security.Identity.toString(), java.security.Security.insertProviderAt(), java.security.Security.removeProvider(), java.security.Security.getProviders(), java.security.Security.getProvider(), java.security.Security.getProperty(), java.security.Security.setProperty().

checkSetFactory()

PURPOSE Determines if allowed to set the networking-related object factories.

SYNTAX `public void checkSetFactory()`

DESCRIPTION The networking classes use the concept of a *factory* to allow different underlying implementations to be used at the discretion of the Java program. A `Foo` factory is an object that generates instances of class `Foo`. There are factories for sockets, URL protocol handlers, and URL content handlers. The program can set a particular factory *once* during the life of the program. This factory defines the implementation for that class for the rest of the program.

`checkSetFactory()` determines whether the current execution context is allowed to set networking-related object factories.

EXCEPTIONS

`SecurityException`

If not allowed to set any networking-related object factory due to security reasons.

SEE ALSO `java.net.HttpURLConnection.setFollowRedirects()`, `java.net.ServerSocket.setSocketFactory()`, `java.net.Socket.setSocketImplFactory()`, `java.net.URL.setURLStreamHandlerFactory()`, `java.net.URLConnection.setContentHandlerFactory()`, `java.rmi.server.RMISocketFactory.setSocketFactory()`.

checkSystemClipboardAccess()

PURPOSE Determines if allowed to read or write to the system clipboard.

SYNTAX `public void checkSystemClipboardAccess()`

DESCRIPTION The system clipboard allows data to be transferred between Java programs and native programs. `Toolkit.getSystemClipboard()` is an abstract method that retrieves the system clipboard. Its implementation should call `checkSystemClipboardAccess()` to determine whether the caller can access the system clipboard.

EXCEPTIONS

`SecurityException`

If not allowed to access the system clipboard.

SEE ALSO `java.awt.datatransfer.Clipboard`, `java.awt.Toolkit.getSystemClipboard()`.

checkTopLevelWindow()

PURPOSE Determines if allowed to create a top-level window.

SYNTAX `public boolean checkTopLevelWindow(Object window)`

DESCRIPTION This method determines whether the current execution context is allowed to create the top-level window `window`. Creating top-level windows has security implications because a program may impersonate security-related applications (e.g., login windows) and mislead the user to supply security-sensitive information (e.g., passwords).

`checkTopLevelWindow()` returns `false` if the window creation is allowed, but the window must have visual warnings that it is a window generated by the Java program. The method returns `true` if creation is allowed without restrictions. To disallow the creation entirely, `checkTopLevelWindow()` should throw a `SecurityException`. The default implementation of this method simply returns `false`.

PARAMETERS

`window` The non-`null` new window being created.

RETURNS `true` if top-level windows can be created without restrictions; `false` if top-level windows should be created with an accompanying visual warning.

EXCEPTIONS

`SecurityException`
If `window` cannot be created due to security reasons.

SEE ALSO `java.awt.Window.Window()`.

checkWrite()

PURPOSE Determines if allowed to write to a file.

SYNTAX

```
public void checkWrite(FileDescriptor fd)
public void checkWrite(String fileName)
```

DESCRIPTION The two forms of this method determine whether the current execution context is allowed to write to the file named `fileName` or to the open file descriptor `fd`. `fd` is useful for checking objects such as sockets that more commonly have file descriptors rather than filenames. Implementers should use the canonical form of `fileName` in order to unambiguously identify the file being checked.

PARAMETERS

`fd` The non-`null` file descriptor to check.
`fileName` The non-`null` system-dependent filename to check.

EXCEPTIONS

`SecurityException`
If `fd` or `fileName` cannot be written to for security reasons.

SEE ALSO `java.io.File.canWrite()`, `java.io.File.getCanonicalPath()`, `java.io.File.mkdir()`, `java.io.File.mkdirs()`, `java.io.File.renameTo()`, `java.io.FileOutputStream.FileOutputStream()`, `java.io.RandomAccessFile.RandomAccessFile()`.

classDepth()

PURPOSE

Finds the first occurrence of a class on the execution stack.

SYNTAX

`protected native int classDepth(String className)`

DESCRIPTION

By convention, the current stack frame is on "top" of the execution stack; it has position `0`. The oldest stack frame is on the "bottom" of the execution stack. This is a utility method for security managers. It searches the current execution stack starting from the top, looking for a stack frame that is executing a method of the class `className`. If such a stack frame is found, its position is returned; otherwise, `-1` is returned.

Note: This method is deprecated in JDK1.2.

PARAMETERS

`className` The non-`null` fully qualified name of the class for which to look.

RETURNS

The position of the stack frame found; `-1` if not found.

EXAMPLE

This example creates two different execution stacks and shows the class depth values of classes on those stacks. Since the `classDepth()` method is protected, it cannot be called directly. Hence, this example creates a subclass of `SecurityManager` with a public method that provides access to the `classDepth()` method.

```
public class Main {
    public static void main(String[] args) {
        MySecurityManager sm = new MySecurityManager();

        System.setSecurityManager(sm);
        sm.printClassDepth("C");                         // -1
        sm.printClassDepth("MySecurityManager");         // 0
        sm.printClassDepth("Main");                      // 1

        C.printClassDepth("C");                          // 1
        C.printClassDepth("MySecurityManager");          // 0
        C.printClassDepth("Main");                       // 2
    }
}

class MySecurityManager extends SecurityManager {
    public void printClassDepth(String name) {
        System.out.println(classDepth(name));
    }
}

class C {
    static void printClassDepth(String name) {
        ((MySecurityManager)
         System.getSecurityManager()).printClassDepth(name);
    }
}
```

classLoaderDepth()

PURPOSE Finds the first occurrence of a class created by a class loader on the execution stack.

SYNTAX `protected native int classLoaderDepth()`

DESCRIPTION By convention, the current stack frame is on "top" of the execution stack; it has position `0`. The oldest stack frame is on the "bottom" of the execution stack. This is a utility method for security managers. It searches the current execution stack starting from the top, looking for a stack frame that is executing a method of a class that was created with a class loader other than the default system class loader. If such a stack frame is found, its position is returned; otherwise, `-1` is returned.

Note: This method is deprecated in JDK1.2.

RETURNS The topmost stack frame that is executing a method whose class was created with a class loader.

SEE ALSO `ClassLoader`, `currentClassLoader()`, `inClassLoader()`.

currentClassLoader()

PURPOSE Finds the topmost class loader on the execution stack.

SYNTAX `protected native ClassLoader currentClassLoader()`

DESCRIPTION This method searches the current execution stack of the current thread for a stack frame that is executing a method of a class created by a class loader other than the default system class loader. If such a stack frame is found, the class loader for the class is returned.

RETURNS The class loader for the most recent stack frame that is executing a method of a class created by a class loader. `null` is returned if such a stack frame does not exist.

SEE ALSO `ClassLoader`, `classLoaderDepth()`, `inClassLoader()`.

currentLoadedClass()

PURPOSE Finds the topmost class with a class loader on the execution stack.

SYNTAX `protected native Class currentLoadedClass()`

DESCRIPTION This method searches the current execution stack of the current thread for a stack frame that is executing a method of a class created by a class loader other than the default system class loader. If such a stack frame is found, the class is returned.

RETURNS The class of the most recent stack frame that is executing a method of a class created by a class loader. `null` is returned if such a stack frame does not exist.

SEE ALSO `ClassLoader`, `classLoaderDepth()`, `currentClassLoader()`, `inClassLoader()`.

getClassContext()

PURPOSE Retrieves the context of the execution stack.

SYNTAX `protected native Class[] getClassContext()`

DESCRIPTION This is a utility method for security managers. It scans the current execution stack and determines the class of the method being invoked in each stack frame. For each class, its `Class` object is returned.

RETURNS A non-`null` array containing the `Class` objects of the methods on the execution stack. Index `0` holds the `Class` object of the method in the most recent stack frame.

EXAMPLE This example prints out the context for an execution stack. Since the `getClassContext()` method is protected, it cannot be called directly. Hence, this example creates a subclass of `SecurityManager` that has a public method that provides access to the `getClassContext()` method.

```
public class Main {
    public static void main (String[] args) {
        System.setSecurityManager(new MySecurityManager());

        C.printContext();
    }
}

class MySecurityManager extends SecurityManager {
    public void printContext() {
        Class[] c = getClassContext();

        for (int i=0; i<c.length; i++) {
            System.out.println(c[i]);
        }
    }
}

class C {
    static void printContext() {
        ((MySecurityManager)
            System.getSecurityManager()).printContext();
    }
}
```

Output

```
class MySecurityManager
class C
class Main
```


getInCheck()

PURPOSE Determines whether there is a security check in progress.

SYNTAX `public boolean getInCheck()`

DESCRIPTION If a check method in the security manager needs to call code outside of the security manager, the outside code may need to know whether it is being executed inside a check in order to take special action. The outside code can call this method in order to make that determination.

Note: Code that sets `inCheck` and then calls methods that depend on the behavior of `getInCheck()` should be synchronized so that the same code cannot be executed concurrently by two threads. This is necessary to prevent one thread from setting `inCheck` and unintentionally allowing another thread to take advantage of the fact that `getInCheck()` is `true` in order to bypass other necessary security checks.

Note: This method is deprecated in JDK1.2.

RETURNS `true` if a security check is in progress; `false` otherwise.

SEE ALSO `inCheck`.

getSecurityContext()

PURPOSE Retrieves a security context for performing security checks.

SYNTAX `public Object getSecurityContext()`

DESCRIPTION This method returns the current execution context. This is an implementation-dependent `Object` that encapsulates enough information about the current execution environment to perform subsequent security checks.

RETURNS The current execution context.

getThreadGroup()

PURPOSE Retrieves the default thread group to use when creating threads.

SYNTAX `public ThreadGroup getThreadGroup()`

DESCRIPTION This method is used when creating a new thread without specifying a thread group. The default implementation of this method is

```
Thread.currentThread().getThreadGroup();
```

It can be overridden by the security manager to return a different default.

RETURNS The thread group to use when creating threads without specifying a thread group.

SEE ALSO `ThreadGroup`.

inCheck

PURPOSE Records whether there is a security check in progress.

SYNTAX `protected boolean inCheck`

DESCRIPTION If a subclass of security manager overrides one of the check methods, the overridden check method should set `inCheck` to `true` to indicate that a security check is in progress. Also, it should set `inCheck` to `false` before exiting the method to indicate that it is no longer doing a security check.

Note: Code that sets `inCheck` and then calls methods that depend on the behavior of `getInCheck()` should be synchronized so that the same code cannot be executed concurrently by two threads. This is necessary to prevent one thread from setting `inCheck` and unintentionally allowing another thread to take advantage of the fact that `getInCheck()` is `true` in order to bypass other necessary security checks.

Note: This field is deprecated in JDK1.2.

SEE ALSO `getInCheck()`.

inClass()

PURPOSE Determines whether a class is on the execution stack.

SYNTAX `protected boolean inClass(String className)`

DESCRIPTION This method determines whether the class `className` is on the current execution stack.

Note: This method is deprecated in JDK1.2.

PARAMETERS

`className` The non-`null` name of the class for which to look.

RETURNS `true` if `className` is on the execution stack; `false` otherwise.

SEE ALSO `classDepth()`.

inClassLoader()

PURPOSE Determines whether a class loader is on the execution stack.

SYNTAX `protected boolean inClassLoader()`

DESCRIPTION This method searches the current execution stack of the current thread for a stack frame that is executing a method of a class created by a class loader other than the default system class loader.

Note: This method is deprecated in JDK1.2.

RETURNS `true` if some class on the execution stack has been created by a class loader; `false` otherwise.

SEE ALSO `ClassLoader`, `currentClassLoader()`.

A B C D E F G H I J K L M N O P Q R S T U V W X Y Z

SecurityManager()

PURPOSE Constructs a `SecurityManager` object.

SYNTAX `protected SecurityManager()`

DESCRIPTION This method constructs a `SecurityManager` object. If no security manager has been previously set, this newly created object can be installed as the security manager by calling `System.setSecurityManager()`. If a security manager has already been set, a `SecurityException` is thrown, since a new security manager cannot be created if a security manager is already installed.

EXCEPTIONS

`SecurityException`
If a security manager has already been set or if a security manager cannot be created.

SEE ALSO `System.getSecurityManager()`, `System.setSecurityManager()`.

SequenceInputStream

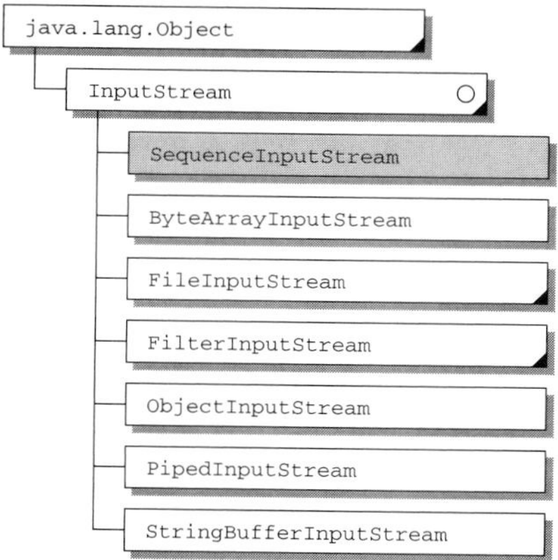

A
B
C
D
E
F
G
H
I
J
K
L
M
N
O
P
Q
R
S
T
U
V
W
X
Y
Z

Syntax

```
public class SequenceInputStream extends InputStream
```

Description

The `SequenceInputStream` class is used to represent a *sequence input stream*. A sequence input stream is a stream in which the contents of the input stream is composed of the contents of an ordered list of input streams. You create a sequence input stream by giving it a list of input streams, as show in Figure 86.

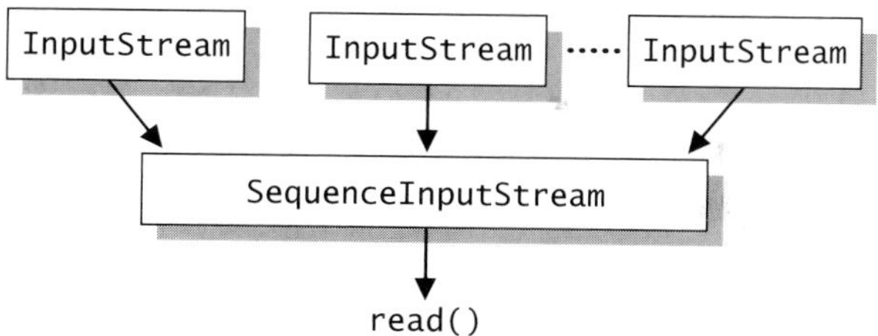

FIGURE 86: `SequenceInputStream`.

When reading from the sequence input stream, you start reading from the first input stream. Then, when data is exhausted from that stream, you go on to the next input stream in the sequence, and so on, until the entire list of input streams has been exhausted. To the reader reading from the sequence input stream, there is no visible boundary as the sequence input stream moves from one input stream to the next. It is as if the sequence input stream is one whole stream.

For example, you can use a sequence input stream to process data spread over multiple files by creating a sequence input stream that consists of `FileInputStreams` for those files (see the class example).

MEMBER SUMMARY	
Constructor	
`SequenceInputStream()`	Constructs an instance of `SequenceInputStream` using multiple streams.
Input Method	
`read()`	Reads bytes from this sequence input stream.
Stream Methods	
`available()`	Determines the number of bytes that can be read from the currently active stream without being blocked.
`close()`	Closes this sequence input stream.

A B C D E F G H I J K L M N O P Q R S T U V W X Y Z

See Also

`InputStream`.

Example

This example shows how `SequenceInputStream` can be used to implement a program that takes a list of filenames and prints their contents to standard output (this works similarly to the Unix `cat` command).

```
import java.io.SequenceInputStream;
import java.io.FileInputStream;
import java.io.IOException;
import java.util.Vector;

class Main {
    // This implements a form of 'cat' that echoes all files named
    // on command line to standard output
    public static void main(String[] args) {
        try {
            Vector streams = new Vector(args.length);
            for (int i = 0; i < args.length; i++)
                streams.addElement(new FileInputStream(args[i]));

            SequenceInputStream in =
                new SequenceInputStream(streams.elements());

            byte[] b = new byte[256];
            int howmany;
            while ((howmany = in.read(b)) > 0)
                for(int i = 0; i < howmany; i++)
                    System.out.print((char)b[i]);
            System.out.flush();
            in.close();
        } catch (IOException e) {
            e.printStackTrace();
        }
    }
}
```

available()

PURPOSE
Determines the number of bytes that can be read from the currently active stream without being blocked.

SYNTAX
`public int available() throws IOException`

DESCRIPTION
The currently active stream of this sequence input stream is the stream from which bytes are currently being read. This method returns the result of invoking `available()` on that currently active stream. If there is no currently active stream (i.e., all streams have been exhausted), this method returns `0`.

RETURNS
The number of bytes available from the currently active stream.

EXCEPTIONS
`IOException`
If an IO error occurred while invoking `available()` on the currently active stream.

SEE ALSO
`InputStream.available()`.

EXAMPLE
See `InputStream.available()`.

close()

PURPOSE
Closes this sequence input stream.

SYNTAX
`public void close() throws IOException`

DESCRIPTION
This method closes this sequence input stream by closing all input streams in its sequence that have not yet been closed.

EXCEPTIONS
`IOException`
If an IO error occurred while attempting to close the input streams in its sequence.

OVERRIDES
`InputStream.close()`.

EXAMPLE
See the class example.

read()

PURPOSE Reads bytes from this sequence input stream.

SYNTAX
```
public int read() throws IOException
public int read(byte[] buffer, int offset, int count) throws
    IOException
```

DESCRIPTION The two forms of this method read bytes from this sequence input stream. The first form reads a single byte (0–255) from this sequence input stream and returns it. The second form reads `count` number of bytes from this sequence input stream and stores the bytes read into the `byte` array `buffer`, starting at index `offset`. It returns the number of bytes actually read.

Bytes read from this sequence input stream are read from the current input stream of this sequence. When end-of-file is reached on the current input stream, the stream is closed. The next stream in the sequence becomes current, and bytes are then read from it. When end-of-file has been reached on all input streams of this sequence input stream, both forms of `read()` return -1.

PARAMETERS

`buffer` The non-`null` `byte` array in which to store the bytes read.

`count` The number of bytes to read. `0` ≤ `count` ≤ `buffer.length-offset`.

`offset` The index in `buffer` at which to start storing the bytes read. `0` ≤ `offset` < `buffer.length`.

RETURNS The first form of `read()` returns the byte read. The second form returns the number of bytes read. Both forms return -1 if end-of-stream has been reached on all input streams.

EXCEPTIONS

`ArrayIndexOutOfBoundsException`
If `count` or `offset` is outside of the specified bounds.

`IOException`
If an IO error occurred.

OVERRIDES `InputStream.read()`.

EXAMPLE See the class example.

SequenceInputStream()

PURPOSE Constructs an instance of `SequenceInputStream` using multiple streams.

SYNTAX

```
public SequenceInputStream(InputStream s1, InputStream s2)
public SequenceInputStream(Enumeration streams)
```

DESCRIPTION The first form of this constructor constructs a sequence using the input streams `s1` and `s2`. Bytes read from this new sequence input stream are first read from `s1` until end-of-file is reached on the stream. Then bytes are read from `s2`. The second form constructs a sequence using the list of input streams in the enumeration `streams`. When bytes are read from this new sequence input stream, the streams are read in the same order in which they appear in the enumeration.

PARAMETERS

`s1` The non-`null` first input stream to use for this sequence input stream.
`s2` The non-`null` second input stream to use for this sequence input stream.
`streams` The non-`null` list of streams to use for this sequence input stream.

SEE ALSO `java.util.Enumeration`, `InputStream`.

EXAMPLE See the class example.

Serializable

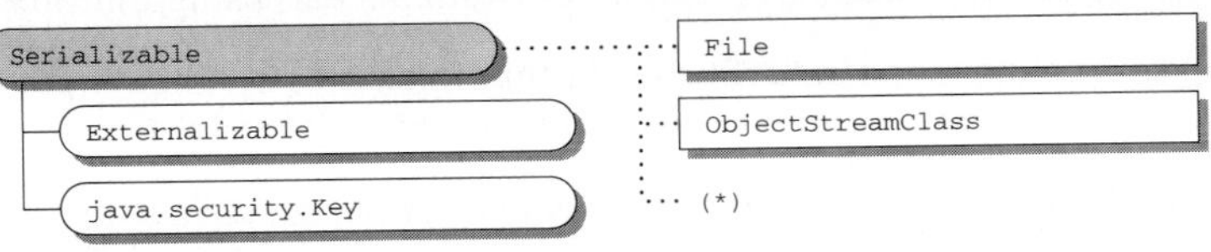

A B C D E F G H I J K L M N O P Q R S T U V W X Y Z

Syntax

```
public interface Serializable
```

Description

To *serialize* an object means to convert its state into a byte stream in such a way that the byte stream can be reconverted back into a copy of the object. See Figure 87. Not all objects can be serialized. An object that can be serialized is *serializable*. A Java object is serializable if its class or any of its superclasses implement the `Serializable` interface or its subinterface `Externalizable`.

Deserialization is the process of converting the serialized form of an object back into a copy of the object.

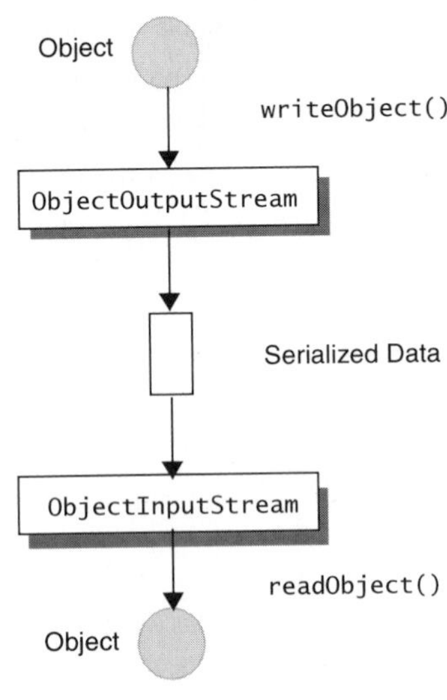

FIGURE 87: Object Serialization and Deserialization.

Usage

To make objects of a class serializable, you declare the class to implement the `Serializable` interface.

```
public class ClassX implements Serializable
{
...
}
```

This will make `ClassX` serializable. You can serialize an instance of `ClassX` to an `ObjectOutputStream` and then read it back by using `ObjectInputStream`.

```
ObjectOutputStream out = ...;
out.writeObject(new ClassX());
ObjectInputStream in = ...
ClassX obj = (ClassX) in.readObject();
```

Default Serialization

By default, a class (or any of its superclasses) that is declared to implement the `Serializable` interface is serialized by writing out its *serializable fields*. In Java 1.1, the serializable fields of a class are all of its nontransient and nonstatic fields. This applies to all public, protected, package, and private fields. The serializable fields are written out automatically by using `ObjectOutputStream.defaultWriteObject()` when the object is serialized and read in by using `ObjectInputStream.defaultReadObject()` when the object is deserialized. The data written out using `ObjectOutputStream.defaultWriteObject()` is called *required data.* A class can declare customized serialization methods instead of, or in addition to, these defaults. This is discussed in the next section.

A serialized field that is of a primitive type is serialized using the corresponding method in `DataOutputStream`. A field that contains a `String` instance is serialized just like any other object (using `defaultWriteObject()`). A field that is not one of the primitive types must contain an object that is serializable. If the field is `null`, its class need not be serializable. If the field contains an object that is not serializable, `NotSerializableException` is thrown. When the field's object is serialized, that object's fields are in turn serialized. Thus the entire graph of objects referred to directly or indirectly by the original object being serialized are serialized as well. If an object is referred to more than once in this graph, only the first occurrence is serialized; subsequent occurrences use a *handle* to refer to the first serialized form. A field that is an array is serialized by serializing its size and each element of the array in a manner identical to that described for individual fields.

Complete details on the serialization/deserialization algorithm is described in the document `http://java.sun.com/products/jdk/1.1/docs/guide/serialization/spec`.

Customized Serialization

A class can override the default serialization/deserialization by defining the following two methods:

```
private void writeObject(ObjectOutputStream out) throws IOException;
private void readObject(ObjectInputStream in) throws IOException,
    ClassNotFoundException;
```

If defined by a class, `writeObject()` is automatically invoked when instances of that class are serialized. `writeObject()` serializes the state of an object by invoking write operations on the stream `out` (see `ObjectOutputStream` for details). The implementation can choose the fields and any additional state it writes to `out`. It is recommended that `writeObject()` first write out the object's required data (by using `ObjectOutputStream.defaultWriteObject()`), although this is not a requirement. Any data written out by `writeObject()` in addition to the required data is called *optional data.* Optional data may consist of primitive data and objects and is written out by using methods in the `ObjectOutputStream` class. See Figure 88.

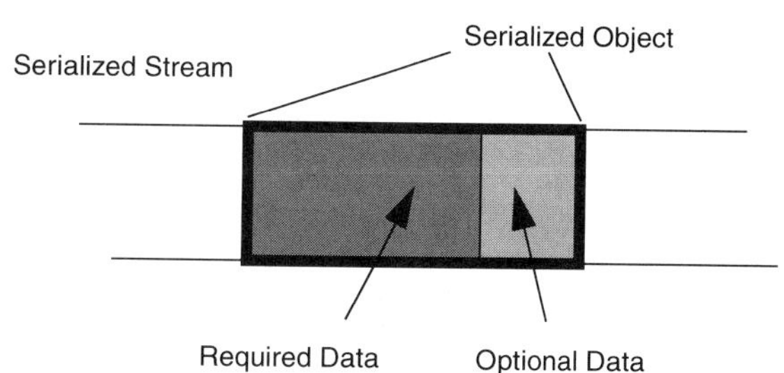

FIGURE 88: Required Data and Optional Data.

If defined by a class, `readObject()` is automatically invoked when instances of that class are deserialized. `readObject()` deserializes an object by reading from the stream `in` (see `ObjectInputStream` for details). `readObject()` must be able to restore the object written by `writeObject()` and therefore the implementations of both must be coordinated and compatible with each other. If `writeObject()` wrote out required data followed by optional data, then `readObject()` must first invoke `ObjectInputStream.defaultReadObject()` to read in the required data and then invoke methods in the `ObjectInputStream` class to read in the optional data.

An object that overrides `writeObject()` also typically overrides `readObject()` and vice versa. However, this is not strictly required. The only requirement is that serialization and deserialization of the object are reversible. For example, an object might override only `readObject()` because it wants to add validation tests (see `ObjectInputValidation`); there is no need to override `writeObject()` because the format of the serialize form has not been altered.

Nonserializable Superclasses

`Object` is the superclass of all classes. Instances of `Object` are not serializable. This means that there must be a class that is not serializable at some point in the class hierarchy of any serializable class.

A serializable class that extends a nonserializable superclass can be deserialized only if the superclass has an *accessible* constructor that accepts no parameters. The constructor is accessible from its subclass if it is declared public, protected, or has package scope when the superclass occurs in the same package as the subclass. For more details on accessibility, see *The Java Language Specification, First Edition*, Section 6.6.1. If the nonserializable superclass does not have an accessible constructor that takes no parameters, an `InvalidClassException` is thrown when the serialized state of such object is deserialized.[1]

The serializable class is serialized by using its corresponding `writeObject()` method, if it has one, or by using `ObjectInputStream.defaultWriteObject()`. The latter does not serialize the state of the nonserializable superclass. `writeObject()` may serialize the state (fields) of its superclass, but it is not required to do so. `writeObject()` does not have special privileges as far as the Java language is concerned and therefore can serialize only accessible fields of its superclass.

When the serialized state of such an object is deserialized, first, the nonserializable superclass's constructor that takes no parameters is called. This constructor must be accessible; otherwise, `InvalidClassException` is thrown. Next, the serializable class's fields are restored by calling the serializable subclass's `readObject()`, if it has defined one, or by calling `ObjectInputStream.defaultReadObject()`.

1. In Java 1.1.4, the nonserializable superclass's constructor that accepts no parameters must be public in order for the deserialization to work.

Effect of Subclassing

All subclasses of a serializable class are also serializable. Each class need concern itself only with its own state, not with that of its superclasses or subclasses. Serialization and deserialization of the state associated with an object's superclasses and subclasses are done automatically by `ObjectOutputStream.writeObject()` and `ObjectInputStream.readObject()`.

When an object is serialized, the highest ancestor superclass that is serializable is identified. Starting with this superclass, the corresponding `writeObject()` method of the superclass or `ObjectOutputStream.defaultWriteObject()` is used to serialize its state. Then, for each derived class of that superclass through to the class of the object being serialized, each class's corresponding `writeObject()` or `ObjectOutputStream.defaultWriteObject()` is invoked.

When an object is deserialized, a similar, reverse, process occurs. The constructor that takes no parameters of the nonserializable superclass of the object is called to allocate an instance of the object. Then, starting with the highest ancestor serializable class (that closest to `java.lang.Object`) through all the derived classes to the class of the object, the corresponding `readObject()` method of each class, or `ObjectInputStream.defaultReadObject()` if the class has not declared a `readObject()`, is invoked to restore the state of the derived class.

A Serialized Object's Class

When an object is serialized, in addition to the data that is serialized (by using either `writeObject()` or `ObjectOutputStream.defaultWriteObject()`) pertaining to the object's state, a *class descriptor* (`ObjectStreamClass`) is also recorded to identify the class of the object. This class descriptor consists of the class's fully qualified name and its *Stream Unique Identifier*, or SUID (discussed in the next section). In addition, if the class implements `Serializable`, the class descriptor contains a list of the names and type names of the class's serializable fields.[1]

Notice that although the class descriptor uniquely identifies a class, it does not contain information about where or how to load class files containing the byte codes of the class and its superclasses. When the serialized state of an object is deserialized, the Java virtual machine performing the deserialization must be able to obtain and load the class files of the corresponding class (and superclasses). If it cannot locate or load the class files, `defaultReadObject()` and `readObject()` will throw a `ClassNotFoundException`.

The system/subsystem that is using serialization/deserialization determines the mechanism to use for locating and loading the associated class files. For example, Remote Method Invocation (RMI) is a system that enables a Java program running on one Java virtual machine to invoke methods on Java objects located on another Java virtual machine. It uses serialization/deserialization to transmit objects between Java virtual machines. It defines its own mechanism for specifying where to locate and load class files required for deserializing objects. In another example, a persistent object store might use a different mechanism for class loading when it is deserializing objects from the store.

1. If the class implements `Externalizable`, the class descriptor does not have this list.

Evolution of Classes and Versioning

When you serialize an object, you are basically recording its state in a form that can be retrieved outside of the environment in which it was originally created. When the state is eventually deserialized, its new environment might be very different than the original in terms of the version of the Java virtual machine and the class libraries and class files available.

The serialized state contains a SUID that uniquely identifies the serialization version of the class. The SUID is a 64-bit number generated by applying the Secure Hash Algorithm (SHA-1) to a stream consisting of the class's name, its modifiers, its interfaces, its field names, and its method name and signatures. The exact algorithm is described in the `http://java.sun.com/products/jdk/1.1/docs/guide/serialization/spec`. That document also describes in detail the changes that can be made to a class so that its serialized form remains compatible.

A serializable class need not explicitly declare its SUID. If it does not declare one, the Java virtual machine will generate one for it automatically by using the algorithm described previously. However, if the class is subsequently changed, you must declare a SUID for it in order to maintain serialization compatibility. To maintain compatibility with the version prior to the change, you should generate a SUID using the class for which you want to maintain compatibility. To do this, use the `serialver` command with one or more class name. You need to set the class path appropriately in order for `serialver` to find the class. This produces a 64-bit number that you then use to add a static `serialVersionUID` field to the class. If the class already declares a `serialVersionUID` field, this value is displayed instead of a new one's being generated.

Here are some results of running `serialver` on a class that already has a `serialVersionUID` field and on one that does not.

```
> serialver java.util.Date
java.util.Date: static final long serialVersionUID = 7523967970034938905L;
> set CLASSPATH=.
> serialver Class1
Class1:    static final long serialVersionUID = 3118887714304291189L;
```

You can then use this result and add it to your class as follows. In the `Class1.java` file, you would add the line:

```
private static final long serialVersionUID = 3118887714304291189L;
```

Default serialization automatically takes care of class evolution. For example, if you add additional serializable fields to an evolved serializable class, default serialization will skip data written by an evolved version of `writeObject()` that an older version of `readObject()` does not know exists. With *customized* serialization, the serializable class must take care of maintaining compatibility of changes to the optional data portion of its serialized form.

For additional information on class evolution and versioning see `http://java.sun.com/products/jdk/1.1/docs/guide/serialization/spec`.

Security Considerations

Declaring a class to be serializable enables code that has a reference to an object of that class to be serialized into a form that could be examined and used outside of the environment in which it was originally created. If a class contains sensitive information, the class can prevent such information from being serialized by declaring such fields transient. If a class is such that it could be misused outside of the context in which it was created, the class should not be declared serializable. For more details on security-related issues relating to serializable objects, see `http://java/sun.com/products/jdk/1.1/docs/guide/serialization/spec`.

See Also

`Externalizable`, `ObjectInputStream`, `ObjectOutputStream`.

Example

This example declares two serializable classes: `Class1` and `Class2`. `Class1` uses the default serialization methods, while `Class2` defines its own `writeObject()` and `readObject()` methods.

The main program serializes an instance of each of these and writes them out to separate files. It then recreates the objects by reading their serialized forms back in.

```
import java.io.*;

class Main {
    public static void main(String[] args) {
        try {
            // Write them out
            FileOutputStream f = new FileOutputStream("Class1.ser");
            ObjectOutput out = new ObjectOutputStream(f);

            out.writeObject(new Class1());
            out.flush();
            out.close();

            f = new FileOutputStream("Class2.ser");
            out = new ObjectOutputStream(f);
            out.writeObject(new Class2());
            out.flush();
            out.close();

            // Read them back
            FileInputStream f2 = new FileInputStream("Class1.ser");
            ObjectInputStream in = new ObjectInputStream(f2);
            Class1 cc1 = (Class1) in.readObject();
            in.close();

            f2 = new FileInputStream("Class2.ser");
            in = new ObjectInputStream(f2);
            Class2 cc2 = (Class2) in.readObject();
            in.close();
            System.out.println("c2.field1 " + cc2.field1);
```

```
            } catch (IOException e) {
                e.printStackTrace();
            } catch (ClassNotFoundException e) {
                e.printStackTrace();
            }
        }
    }
```

ServerSocket

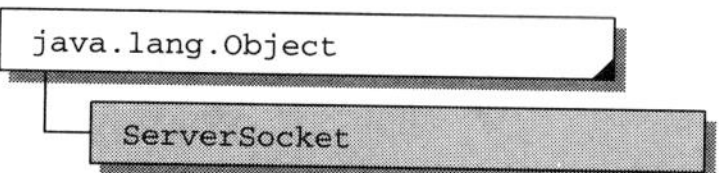

Syntax

```
public class ServerSocket
```

Description

A *socket* is a communications endpoint. A *server socket* is an endpoint (used by the server) in a connection-oriented protocol. The server uses a server socket to listen for connection requests from clients.[1] When the server socket receives a connection request, the server socket creates a new socket for communicating with the client. The server socket itself is not involved further in communicating with the client.

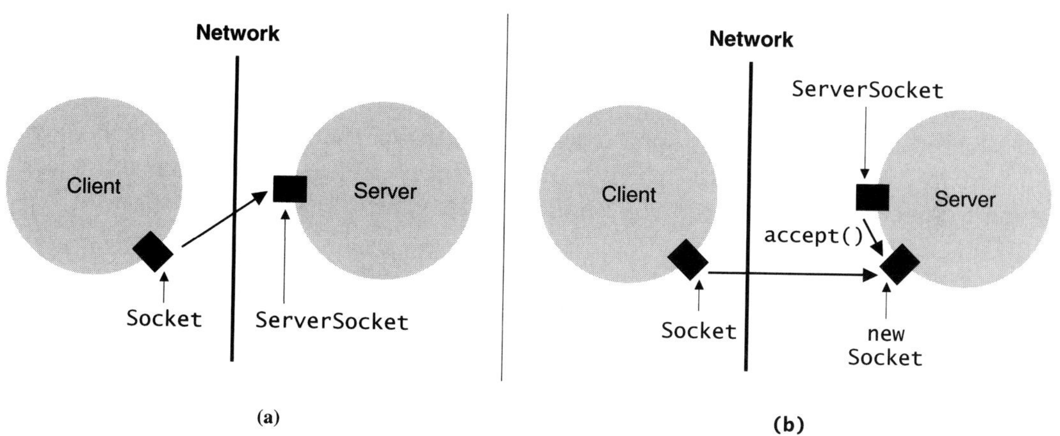

FIGURE 89: **Socket (a) and ServerSocket (b).**

Usage

In a client/server application, the server typically creates a server socket and binds it to a well-known port. Clients learn of this well-known port either by convention or through a naming service that maps service names to port numbers. This server then listens on this well-known port for connection requests. Any connection requests made to this server are then queued.

1. While the server is listening for a connection, the thread that's running the server is blocked until a connection request arrives.

The client sends a connection request to the server (see Figure 89a). The server accepts the request by creating a new socket. This establishes a connection between the client's socket and this new socket through which the client and server can communicate with each other (see Figure 89b). The original well-known port is still open for accepting new connections. New connection requests that arrive while the server is interacting with clients are queued until the server is ready to accept them. The class example illustrates the use of these methods.

A B C D E F G H I J K L M N O P Q R S T U V W X Y Z

Server Socket Implementation Factory

The actual implementation of server sockets is supplied by a subclass of `SocketImpl`. When the application creates an instance of `ServerSocket`, a corresponding instance of `SocketImpl` is created. The particular subclass of `SocketImpl` to use is determined by the *server socket implementation factory* installed by the application that is using `setSocketFactory()`. The factory is responsible for creating instances of `SocketImpl` to be used by server sockets. There can be only one server socket implementation factory installed in a program at any one time. Once installed, the factory cannot be replaced. If no factory is installed, the `PlainSocketImpl` class[1] is used.

Use of server socket implementation factories allows the application to choose its socket implementation depending on the security properties of the network, such as its firewall implementation.

Socket Time-Out Period

By default, when the server waits for a connection, the server waits indefinitely until a connection arrives. The application can specify a time-out period for the server socket such that the server will block only until either a connection arrives or the time-out period expires.

MEMBER SUMMARY	
Constructor	
`ServerSocket()`	Constructs a server socket and binds it to the specified local port.
Communications Methods	
`accept()`	Accepts a connection request on this server socket.
`close()`	Closes this server socket.
Socket Information Methods	
`getInetAddress()`	Retrieves the local IP address used by this server socket.
`getLocalPort()`	Retrieves this server socket's local port.
`toString()`	Generates the string representation of this object.

1. `PlainSocketImpl` is a `java.net` package-private implementation of sockets with no security checks. It does implement SOCKS Version 4.

MEMBER SUMMARY	
Socket Time-Out Methods	
`getSoTimeout()`	Retrieves the time-out period of this server socket.
`setSoTimeout()`	Sets the time-out period of this server socket.
Socket Implementation Methods	
`implAccept()`	Accepts a connection on this server socket using a new socket.
`setSocketFactory()`	Sets the system's server socket implementation factory.

See Also

`DatagramPacket`, `DatagramSocket`, `Socket`, `SocketImpl`, `SocketImplFactory`.

Example

This example implements a "talk" program. It demonstrates how to set up a two-way communication link between two Java programs. See Figure 90.

When the program is invoked with one parameter, the program behaves as the server. The parameter is the port number to which the server will bind. The server creates a server socket and waits for a connection. The server also prints out the port number to which it is bound. This is useful when the specified port number is `0` (which means bind to any locally available port number).

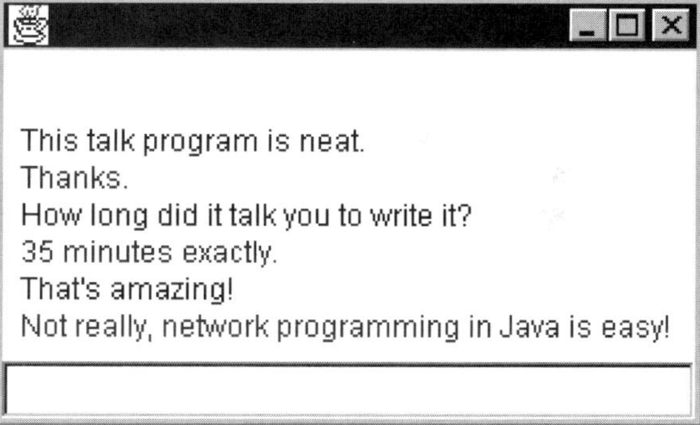

FIGURE 90: "Talk" Program.

When the program is invoked with two parameters, the program behaves as the client. The client creates a socket to connect the given host name and port number.

For example, to start the server, you could type

```
> java Main 0
port: 2818
```

To start the client, type

```
> java Main localhost 2818
```

The reason for the new lines array in the `append()` method is to avoid a race condition that can arise if a new line is added while the lines are being painted. The strategy to avoid the race condition is to add to the `newLines` vector and have the painter thread copy `newLine` to lines. In this way, only one method (the `paint()` method) ever modifies lines.

```
import java.awt.*;
import java.awt.event.*;
import java.io.*;
import java.net.*;
import java.util.*;

class Main extends Frame implements ActionListener, Runnable {
    TtyCanvas tty = new TtyCanvas();
    TextField input = new TextField();
    DataInputStream in;
    DataOutputStream out;

    Main(InputStream in, OutputStream out) {
        this.in = new DataInputStream(in);
        this.out = new DataOutputStream(out);

        // Add components.
        add(tty, BorderLayout.CENTER);
        add(input, BorderLayout.SOUTH);
        input.addActionListener(this);

        // Display frame.
        setSize(400, 300);
        show();

        // Start the network reading thread.
        new Thread(this).start();
    }

    public void actionPerformed(ActionEvent evt) {
        if (evt.getSource() == input) {
            try {
                // Send the line to the other program and then display it.
                out.writeUTF(input.getText());
                tty.append(input.getText(), Color.blue);
            } catch (Exception e) {
                tty.append("Connection broken", Color.red);
            }
            input.setText(null);
        }
    }

    public void run() {
        try {
            while (true) {
                // Wait for a line from the other program.
                String line = in.readUTF();
                tty.append(line, Color.black);
            }
        } catch (Exception e) {
            tty.append("Connection broken", Color.red);
        }
    }

    public static void main(String[] args) {
        Socket socket = null;

        try {
            if (args.length == 1) {
                // Server
```

```
            ServerSocket ssocket = new ServerSocket(
                Integer.parseInt(args[0]));
            System.out.println("port: " + ssocket.getLocalPort());
            socket = ssocket.accept();
        } else if (args.length == 2) {
            // Client
            socket = new Socket(args[0], Integer.parseInt(args[1]));
        } else {
            System.err.println("server: java Main <port>");
            System.err.println("client: java Main <hostname> <port>");
            System.exit(1);
        }

        new Main(socket.getInputStream(), socket.getOutputStream());
    } catch (Exception e) {
        e.printStackTrace();
    }

  }
}

// This class implements a simple text display that can
// display lines with different colors.
class TtyCanvas extends Component {
    // Vector of current lines.
    Vector lines = new Vector();

    // Vector of new lines.
    Vector newLines = new Vector();

    synchronized void append(String s, Color c) {
        newLines.addElement(new TtyLine(s, c));
        repaint();
    }

    public void paint(Graphics g) {
        synchronized (this) {
            // Transfer new lines into lines.
            while (newLines.size() > 0) {
                lines.addElement(newLines.elementAt(0));
                newLines.removeElementAt(0);
            }

            // Keep at most the last 50 lines.
            while (lines.size() > 50) {
                lines.removeElementAt(0);
            }
        }

        FontMetrics fm = g.getFontMetrics();
        int margin = fm.getHeight()/2;
        int w = getSize().width;
        int y = getSize().height-fm.getHeight()-margin;

        // Paint all the lines bottom up.
        for (int i=lines.size()-1; i>=0; i--) {
            TtyLine tl = (TtyLine)lines.elementAt(i);
            g.setColor(tl.c);
            g.drawString(tl.s, margin, y+fm.getAscent());
            y -= fm.getHeight();
```

```
            }
        }
    }

    // Convenient class to hold a string and its color.
    class TtyLine {
        String s;
        Color c;
        TtyLine(String s, Color c) {
            this.s = s;
            this.c = c;
        }
    }
```

A B C D E F G H I J K L M N O P Q R S T U V W X Y Z

accept()

PURPOSE Accepts a connection request on this server socket.

SYNTAX `public Socket accept() throws IOException`

DESCRIPTION `accept()` retrieves the first connection request from the queue of pending requests and creates a new socket to handle that connection. The new socket is used to read and write data to and from the socket at the other end of the connection. The new socket is closed when the connection is terminated. This server socket remains open for accepting further connection requests and queues them for future processing.

If there are no pending connection requests, `accept()` blocks until a request arrives or until the time-out period of this server socket has expired.

`accept()` creates an instance of `Socket` and invokes `implAccept()` with it. To use a subclass of `Socket` (such as an SSL socket) for accepting connections, you should override `accept()` so that it invokes `implAccept()` using an instance of the `Socket` subclass.

RETURNS A new non-`null` socket for communicating with the socket at the other end of the connection.

EXCEPTIONS

`InterruptedIOException`
If the time-out period for this server socket has expired before a connection arrives. This server socket is still usable for accepting future connections.

`IOException`
If an IO error occurs while waiting for the connection.

`SecurityException`
If it cannot accept a connection from the sending socket due to security reasons.

SEE ALSO getSoTimeout(), implAccept(), java.io.InterruptedIOException, java.io.IOException, java.lang.SecurityManager.checkAccept(), setSoTimeout(), SocketImpl.accept().

EXAMPLE This example illustrates a server that uses multiple threads to accept connections, thereby allowing concurrent handling of requests. It consists of two classes: the main server ClockServer and ClockWorker. A request to the server returns the worker id (its thread name) followed by the current time of day.

```
import java.net.*;
import java.io.*;
import java.util.Date;

class Main {
    static final int date_port = 1258;  // pick a port that server can use

    public static void getDate(InetAddress dst, int port) {
        try {
            Socket client = new Socket(dst, port);
            BufferedReader in = new BufferedReader(
                new InputStreamReader(client.getInputStream()));
            System.out.println(in.readLine());
            client.close();
        } catch (IOException e) {
            e.printStackTrace();
        }
    }

    public static void main(String[] args) {
        // start server
        ClockServer srv = new ClockServer(date_port);

        try {
            InetAddress dst = InetAddress.getLocalHost();

            for (int i = 0; i < 10; i++)
                getDate(dst, date_port);
        } catch (UnknownHostException e) {
                System.err.println("Host not found: " + e);
        }
    }
}

// Server spawns worker thread to handle each connection
class ClockServer extends Thread {
    private ServerSocket srvSock = null;
    public ClockServer(int port) {
        try {
            srvSock = new ServerSocket(port, 5); // backlog of 5
            System.err.println("Server Socket: " + srvSock.toString());
            System.err.println("Socket is connected to: " +
                                srvSock.getInetAddress());
            System.err.println("Local port: " + srvSock.getLocalPort());
            // Set thread to be "daemon" so that the program can exit
            // without having to kill the thread.
            setDaemon(true);
            start();
```

```
            } catch (IOException e) {
                e.printStackTrace();
            }
        }
        public void run() {
            Socket sock;
            while (true) {
                try {
                    sock = srvSock.accept();
                    (new ClockWorker(sock)).start();
                } catch (IOException e) {
                    e.printStackTrace();
                }
            }
        }

        // Override finalize() to close server socket
        protected void finalize() {
            if (srvSock != null) {
                try {
                    srvSock.close();
                } catch (IOException e) {
                    e.printStackTrace();
                }
                srvSock = null;
            }
        }
    }

    // Worker that determines date and sends back to server
    class ClockWorker extends Thread {
        private Socket sock;
        public ClockWorker(Socket ss) {
            super();
            sock = ss;
        }
        public void run() {
            try {
                BufferedWriter out = new BufferedWriter(
                    new OutputStreamWriter(sock.getOutputStream()));
                String answer = Thread.currentThread().getName() + ": " +
                    (new Date()).toString() + "\n";
                out.write(answer, 0, answer.length());
                out.flush();
                sock.close();
            } catch (IOException e) {
                e.printStackTrace();
            }
        }
    }
```

close()

PURPOSE Closes this server socket.

SYNTAX `public void close() throws IOException`

DESCRIPTION A server socket should be closed when it is no longer needed. Closing the server socket frees up resources associated with the socket (e.g., file descriptors and socket descriptors) and allows the port that was bound to the socket to be reused. After a server socket has been closed, the server cannot accept connections from it. Any attempts by a client to connect to it will fail.

EXCEPTIONS

`IOException`

If an IO error occurred when closing the socket.

SEE ALSO `java.io.IOException`, `SocketImpl.close()`.

EXAMPLE See `accept()`.

getInetAddress()

PURPOSE Retrieves the local IP address used by this server socket.

SYNTAX `public InetAddress getInetAddress()`

DESCRIPTION When you create a server socket, you can specify the local IP address to use. This is useful for a multihomed host—a machine with more than one network interface, each having its own IP address. If you do not specify the local address to use, it defaults to the platform-dependent system default.

`getInetAddress()` returns the local address being used for this server socket.

RETURNS The local address used by this server socket.

SEE ALSO `InetAddress`, `ServerSocket()`, `SocketImpl.getInetAddress()`.

EXAMPLE See `accept()`.

getLocalPort()

PURPOSE Retrieves this server socket's local port.

SYNTAX `public int getLocalPort()`

DESCRIPTION When a server socket is created, you can specify the local port to use or leave it to the system to select any available ports. `getLocalPort()` returns this port number (whether specified by you or selected by the system).

RETURNS This server socket's port number.

SEE ALSO `ServerSocket()`, `SocketImpl.getLocalPort()`.

EXAMPLE See the class example.

getSoTimeout()

PURPOSE Retrieves the time-out period of this server socket.

SYNTAX `public synchronized int getSoTimeout() throws SocketException`

DESCRIPTION A server socket's time-out period specifies the maximum number of milliseconds that `accept()` will block when waiting for a connection. If the time-out period is `0`, `accept()` will block indefinitely for a connection. If the time-out period is greater than `0`, subsequent invocations of `accept()` will unblock either when a connection arrives within the time-out period or when `InterruptedIOException` is thrown when the time-out period expires.

`getSoTimeout()` retrieves the time-out period of this datagram socket.

RETURNS A nonnegative number specifying the maximum number of milliseconds that `accept()` will block. If `0`, `accept()` will block indefinitely while waiting for a connection.

EXCEPTIONS

`SocketException`
If an error occurs while attempting to get the socket's time-out period.

SEE ALSO `accept()`, `setSoTimeout()`, `SocketImpl.getOption()`, `SocketException`.

EXAMPLE See `setSoTimeout()`.

implAccept()

PURPOSE Accepts a connection on this server socket using a new socket.

SYNTAX `protected final void implAccept(Socket s) throws IOException`

DESCRIPTION `accept()` creates an instance of `Socket` and invokes `implAccept()` with it. To use a subclass of `Socket` (such as an SSL socket) for accepting connections, you should override `accept()` and invoke `implAccept()` using an instance of the subclass.

PARAMETERS

`s` A new non-`null` socket. When `implAccept()` returns, `s` will be connected for communicating with the socket at the other end of the connection

EXCEPTIONS

`InterruptedIOException`
If the time-out period for this server socket has expired before a connection is made. This server socket is still usable for accepting future connections.

`IOException`
If an IO error occurs while waiting for the connection.

`SecurityException`

If it cannot accept a connection from the client due to security reasons.

SEE ALSO `accept()`, `getSoTimeout()`, `java.io.InterruptedIOException`, `java.io.IOException`, `java.lang.SecurityManager.checkAccept()`, `setSoTimeout()`, `SocketImpl.accept()`.

EXAMPLE This implementation shows the use of `implAccept()` in implementing a subclass of `Socket`.

```
import java.net.ServerSocket;
import java.net.Socket;
import java.io.IOException;

class FooSocket extends Socket {
    FooSocket() {
        // Do some FooSocket-specific things.
    }
}
class FooServerSocket extends ServerSocket {
    public FooServerSocket(int port) throws IOException {
        super(port);
    }

  public Socket accept() throws IOException {
      // Create a new FooSocket for each accept.
      FooSocket s = new FooSocket();

      // Pass newly created socket to use for accepting connection.
      implAccept(s);

      // Return connected socket.
      return s;
    }
}
```

ServerSocket()

PURPOSE Constructs a server socket and binds it to the specified local port.

SYNTAX

```
public ServerSocket(int port) throws IOException
public ServerSocket(int port, int backlog) throws IOException
public ServerSocket(int port, int backlog, InetAddress localAddr)
   throws IOException
```

DESCRIPTION The three forms of this constructor construct a server socket. The socket is bound to the local port `port` and local address `localAddr`. Once a server socket has been created, you can accept connections to it by using `accept()`.

If `port` is `0`, the server socket is bound to any locally available port. The use of certain ports is restricted (e.g., those well-known ports for Internet protocols such as FTP, Telnet, and SMTP), and use of *any* port is permitted only if allowed by the security manager. To determine which port is being used for this server socket, use `getLocalPort()`.

`localAddr` is useful when creating a server socket on a multihomed host—a machine with more than one network interface, each having its own IP address. `localAddr` specifies which one of the multiple addresses of the local machine to use. If `localAddr` is not specified, it defaults to the platform-dependent system default. To determine which local address is being used for this server socket, use `getInetAddress()`.

`backlog` specifies the maximum number of pending connections that this server socket can have. If `backlog` is not specified, it defaults to `50`. When `backlog` number of connections are pending, clients making further requests for connections will fail with `IOException`.

PARAMETERS

`backlog` The maximum number of pending connections this server socket can have.
`localAddr` The possibly `null` local address to use for this server socket.
`port` The local port to which to bind this server socket. `0` ≤ `port` ≤ `65535`. If `port` is `0`, use any available port.

EXCEPTIONS

`IllegalArgumentException`
If `port` < `0` or `port` > `65535`.

`IOException`
If an IO error occurred while creating the socket.

`SecurityException`
If `port` cannot be used due to security reasons.

SEE ALSO `accept()`, `java.lang.SecurityManager.checkListen()`, `java.lang.IllegalArgumentException`, `java.io.IOException`, `setSocketFactory()`, `SocketImpl.create()`, `SocketImpl.bind()`, `SocketImpl.listen()`.

EXAMPLE See `accept()` and the class example.

setSocketFactory()

PURPOSE Sets the system's server socket implementation factory.

SYNTAX

```
public static synchronized void
    setSocketFactory(SocketImplFactory factory) throws
    IOException
```

DESCRIPTION The actual implementation of server sockets is supplied by a subclass of `SocketImpl` created using the *server socket implementation factory.* This method sets `factory` to be the server socket implementation factory. `factory` is responsible for creating an instance of (subclass of) `SocketImpl` whenever a new server socket is created.

`setSocketFactory()` can be executed only if permitted to do so by the security manager. If permitted, it can be executed only once during the lifetime of the application.

Note that this is the factory for *server* sockets. The factory for creating sockets for use by `accept()` is controlled using `Socket.setSocketImplFactory()`.

PARAMETERS

`factory` The non-`null` server socket implementation factory to use.

EXCEPTIONS

`IOException`
If an IO error occurred while setting the factory.

`SecurityException`
If not allowed to set the socket implementation factory due to security reasons.

`SocketException`
If a socket implementation factory has already been set.

SEE ALSO `java.lang.SecurityManager.checkSetFactory()`, `java.io.IOException`, `Socket.setSocketImplFactory()`, `SocketImpl`, `SocketImplFactory`.

EXAMPLE This example sets the server socket implementation factory for server sockets to be `DebugSocketImplFactory` (see the class example of `SocketImplFactory` for the definition of `DebugSocketImplFactory`).

```
try {
    ServerSocket.setSocketFactory(new DebugSocketImplFactory());
} catch (IOException e) {
    e.printStackTrace();
}
```

setSoTimeout()

PURPOSE Sets the time-out period of this server socket.

SYNTAX
```
public synchronized void setSoTimeout(int timeout) throws
    SocketException
```

DESCRIPTION A server socket's time-out period specifies the maximum number of milliseconds that `accept()` will block when waiting for a connection to arrive. If the time-out period is `0`, `accept()` will block indefinitely for a connection. If the time-out period is greater than `0`, subsequent invocations of `accept()` will unblock either when a connection arrives within the time-out period or when `InterruptedIOException` is thrown when the time-out period expires.

`setSoTimeout()` sets the time-out period of this server socket and affects only subsequent `accept()` calls.

PARAMETERS

`timeout` A nonnegative number specifying the maximum number of milliseconds that `accept()` will block. If `0`, `accept()` will block indefinitely when waiting for a connection.

EXCEPTIONS

`SocketException`
If an error occurred while attempting to set the socket's time-out period.

SEE ALSO `getSoTimeout()`, `SocketException`, `SocketImpl.setOption()`.

EXAMPLE This is a modified version of the `ClockServer` class in the `accept()` example. This `ClockServer` is single-threaded and displays a message whenever no connection is received within a specified time-out period. It demonstrates the usage of the `setSoTimeout()` and `getSoTimeout()` methods.

```
class ClockServer extends Thread {
    private ServerSocket srvSock = null;
    public ClockServer(int port, int timeout) {
        super();
        try {
            srvSock = new ServerSocket(port, 5); // backlog = 5
            // set timeout for future accept() calls;
            srvSock.setSoTimeout(timeout);
            setDaemon(true);
            start();
        } catch (IOException e) {
            e.printStackTrace();
        }
    }
    public void run() {
        while (true) {
            try {
                Socket sock = srvSock.accept();
                BufferedWriter out = new BufferedWriter(
                    new OutputStreamWriter(sock.getOutputStream()));
                String answer = Thread.currentThread().getName() + ": " +
                    (new Date()).toString() + "\n";
                out.write(answer, 0, answer.length());
                out.flush();
                sock.close();
            } catch (InterruptedIOException e) {
                try {
                    System.err.println("No requests for: " +
                                       srvSock.getSoTimeout() + "ms.");
                } catch (IOException et) {
                  // exception from getSoTimeOut()
                    et.printStackTrace();
                }
            } catch (IOException e) {
                e.printStackTrace();
            }
        }
```

```
        }
        // Close socket when done
        protected void finalize() {
            if (srvSock != null) {
                try {
                    srvSock.close();
                } catch (IOException e) {
                    e.printStackTrace();
                }
                srvSock = null;
            }
        }
    }
```

A B C D E F G H I J K L M N O P Q R S T U V W X Y Z

toString()

PURPOSE Generates the string representation of this object.

SYNTAX `public String toString()`

DESCRIPTION The string representation of a server socket consists of its local address and local port number. `toString()` returns the string representation for this server socket.

RETURNS The string representation of this server socket.

OVERRIDES `java.lang.Object.toString()`.

SEE ALSO `getInetAddress()`, `getLocalPort()`.

EXAMPLE See `accept()`.

java.lang

Short

- Object
  - Number
    - Short
    - Byte
    - Double
    - Float
    - Integer
    - Long
    - java.math.BigDecimal
    - java.math.BigInteger

Syntax

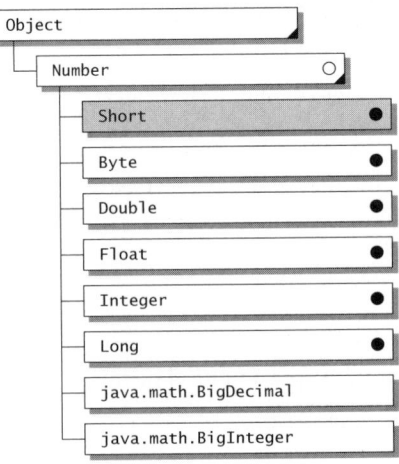

```
public final class Short extends Number
```

Description

A `short` in Java is a 16-bit signed integer. The `Short` class provides an object wrapper for `short` data values. This allows `short`s to be passed to methods in Java class libraries that accept Java objects as parameters. In addition, the `Short` class provides methods that convert values to and from `short` values.

Usage

`Short` instances are used to pass `short` values to methods that accept Java objects as parameters. They cannot be used in arithmetic expressions in place of `short`. For example, the following is not allowed:

```
Short s1 = new Short((short)10);
Short s2 = new Short((short)-2);
Short s3 = s1 + s2; // Illegal
```

To perform arithmetic operations using a `Short` instance, you first must use access methods defined in the `Short` class to obtain its numeric value, as follows:

```
short s3 = s1.shortValue() * s2.shortValue();
double d1 = s1.doubleValue() + s2.shortValue();
```

MEMBER SUMMARY

Constructor	
`Short()`	Constructs a `Short` instance using a `short` value or a string.
Number Methods	
`byteValue()`	Retrieves the value of this object as a `byte`.
`doubleValue()`	Retrieves the value of this object as a `double`.
`floatValue()`	Retrieves the value of this object as a `float`.
`intValue()`	Retrieves the value of this object as an `int`.
`longValue()`	Retrieves the value of this object as a `long`.
`shortValue()`	Retrieves the value of this object as a `short`.
`short`-Related Constants	
`MAX_VALUE`	The maximum value a `short` can have.
`MIN_VALUE`	The minimum value a `short` can have.
`TYPE`	The `Class` object representing the primitive type `short`.
String Conversion Constants	
`decode()`	Parses the string representation of a 16-bit signed integer into a `Short`.
`parseShort()`	Parses the string representation of an integer into a `short`.
`toString()`	Generates the string representation of a `short` or `Short` object.
`valueOf()`	Creates a `Short` object using its string representation.
Object Methods	
`equals()`	Compares this object with another object for equality.
`hashCode()`	Computes the hash code for this object.

See Also

`Byte`, `Double`, `Float`, `Long`, `Integer`, `Number`.

byteValue()

PURPOSE Retrieves the value of this object as a `byte`.

SYNTAX `public byte byteValue()`

DESCRIPTION This method returns the value of this object as a `byte` by casting its value to a `byte`.

RETURNS The value of this object as a `byte`.

SEE ALSO `doubleValue(), floatValue(), intValue(), longValue(), shortValue().`

EXAMPLE See `doubleValue()`.

A B C D E F G H I J K L M N O P Q R S T U V W X Y Z

decode()

PURPOSE Parses the string representation of a 16-bit signed integer into a `Short`.

SYNTAX `public static Short decode(String str) throws NumberFormatException`

DESCRIPTION The string may be in hexadecimal format (with a `0x` or `#` prefix), in octal format (with a zero character (`0`) prefix), or in decimal format (radix 10 digits preceded by an optional negative sign (-)).

`decode()` is similar to `valueOf()`, except that `valueOf()` accepts a radix argument to determine the radix, while `decode()` examines the string's format so as to determine the radix. `decode()` also is similar to `parseShort()`, except that `parseShort()` returns a short, while `decode()` returns a `Short` object and `decode()` examines the string's format so as to determine the radix.

PARAMETERS

`str` The non-`null` string to parse.

EXCEPTIONS

`NumberFormatException`
If `str` cannot be parsed into a 16-bit signed integer of the specified radix.

SEE ALSO `Short(), parseShort(), valueOf().`

EXAMPLE This example uses `decode()` to convert some strings into `Short` objects.

```
class Main {
    public static void main(String[] args) {
        try {
            Short s_dec = Short.decode("225");
            Short s_oct = Short.decode("065");       // octal
            Short s_hex1 = Short.decode("0x1f");     // hex
            Short s_hex2 = Short.decode("#1e");      // hex
            // Short s_big = Short.decode("55555");  // ERROR: too big

            System.out.println("parsed: " +
                s_dec + "," + s_oct + "," + s_hex1 + ","  + s_hex2);
        } catch (NumberFormatException e) {
            e.printStackTrace();
        }
    }
}
```

doubleValue()

PURPOSE Retrieves the value of this object as a `double`.

SYNTAX `public double doubleValue()`

DESCRIPTION This method returns the value of this object as a `double` by casting its value to a `double`.

RETURNS The value of this object as a `double`.

SEE ALSO `byteValue()`, `floatValue()`, `intValue()`, `longValue()`, `shortValue()`.

EXAMPLE

```
Short sobj = new Short((short)118);

byte bval = sobj.byteValue();     // 118.0
double dval = sobj.doubleValue(); // 118.0
float fval = sobj.floatValue();   // 118
int ival = sobj.intValue();       // 118
long lval = sobj.longValue();     // 118
short sval = sobj.shortValue();   // 118
```

equals()

PURPOSE Compares this object with another object for equality.

SYNTAX `public boolean equals(Object obj)`

DESCRIPTION This method compares the `short` value of this object with that of `obj`. It returns `true` if the two values are equal; it returns `false` otherwise. It also returns `false` if `obj` is `null` or is not a `Short` object.

PARAMETERS

`obj` The possibly `null` object against which this object is compared.

RETURNS `true` if `obj` has the same short value as this object; `false` otherwise.

OVERRIDES `Object.equals()`.

SEE ALSO `hashCode()`.

EXAMPLE

```
Short s1 = new Short((short)92);
Short s2 = new Short((short)92);

// Check whether the value of two Shorts are equal
if (s1.equals(s2))
    System.out.println("equal");
```

floatValue()

PURPOSE Retrieves the value of this object as a `float`.

SYNTAX `public float floatValue()`

DESCRIPTION This method returns the value of this object as a `float` by casting its value to a `float`.

RETURNS The value of this object as a `float`.

SEE ALSO `byteValue()`, `doubleValue()`, `intValue()`, `longValue()`, `shortValue()`.

EXAMPLE See `doubleValue()`.

hashCode()

PURPOSE Computes the hash code for this object.

SYNTAX `public int hashCode()`

DESCRIPTION The hash code for this object is calculated using its `short` value. Two `Short` objects with the same `short` value will have the same hash code.

RETURNS An `int` representing the hash code.

OVERRIDES `Object.hashCode()`.

SEE ALSO `equals()`, `java.util.Hashtable`.

EXAMPLE

```
Short s0 = new Short((short)39);
int hashval = s0.hashCode();          // generate hash code
++hits[Math.abs(hashval%tabsize)];    // count hits
```

intValue()

PURPOSE Retrieves the value of this object as an `int`.

SYNTAX `public int intValue()`

DESCRIPTION This method returns the value of this object as an `int` by casting its value to an `int`.

RETURNS The value of this object as an `int`.

SEE ALSO `byteValue()`, `doubleValue()`, `floatValue()`, `longValue()`, `shortValue()`.

EXAMPLE See `doubleValue()`.

longValue()

PURPOSE Retrieves the value of this object as a `long`.

SYNTAX `public long longValue()`

DESCRIPTION This method returns the value of this object as a `long` by casting its value to a `long`.

RETURNS The value of this object as a long.

SEE ALSO `byteValue()`, `doubleValue()`, `floatValue()`, `intValue()`, `shortValue()`.

EXAMPLE See `double()`.

MAX_VALUE

PURPOSE The maximum value a `short` can have.

SYNTAX `public static final short MAX_VALUE`

DESCRIPTION This constant represents the maximum value a `short` can have, which is `32767`.

SEE ALSO `MIN_VALUE`.

EXAMPLE

```
// test if number is less than MAX_VALUE
short s0 = 32;
if (s0 < Short.MAX_VALUE)
    s0 += 500;
```

MIN_VALUE

PURPOSE The minimum value a `short` can have.

SYNTAX `public static final short MIN_VALUE`

DESCRIPTION This constant represents the minimum value a `short` can have, which is `-32768`.

SEE ALSO `MAX_VALUE`.

EXAMPLE

```
// test if number is greater than MIN_VALUE
short s0 = -12;
if (s0 > Short.MIN_VALUE)
    s0 -= 5;
```

parseShort()

PURPOSE
Parses the string representation of an integer into a short.

SYNTAX
```
public static short parseShort(String str) throws
    NumberFormatException
public static short parseShort(String str, int radix) throws
    NumberFormatException
```

DESCRIPTION
This method parses the string str into an integer and returns it as a short. If no radix is given, the radix used to parse str is 10. A positive integer consists of digits in the specified radix; a negative integer has a leading negative sign (-) in addition to digits in the specified radix.

parseShort() is similar to valueOf(), except that parseShort() returns a short, while valueOf() returns a Short object. parseShort() also is similar to decode(), except that decode() returns a Short object and examines the string's format so as to determine its radix. Note that strings with a 0x or # prefix accepted by decode() are illegal in parseShort(), and the 0 prefix for denoting octal numbers is ignored by parseShort(). See the example.

PARAMETERS

radix
The radix to use when parsing str. Character.MIN_RADIX ≤ radix ≤ Character.MAX_RADIX.

str
The non-null string containing the integer.

RETURNS
A short containing the numeric value of the integer represented by str.

EXCEPTIONS

NumberFormatException
If str cannot be parsed into a 16-bit signed integer of the specified radix.

SEE ALSO
Character.MAX_RADIX, Character.MIN_RADIX, decode(), toString(), valueOf().

EXAMPLE
This example uses parseShort() to convert strings into short values. Note that octal strings acceptable to decode() are treated as decimal strings here, and hexadecimal strings acceptable to decode() throw NumberFormatException.

```
class Main {
    public static void main(String[] args) {
        try {
            short s_dec = Short.parseShort("25");           // decimal
            short s_oct = Short.parseShort("65", 8);        // octal
            short s_hex1 = Short.parseShort("1f", 16);      // hex
            short s_hex2 = Short.parseShort("1e", 16);      // hex
            short s_oct2 = Short.parseShort("033");         // leading 0 ignored
            // short s_hex3 = Short.parseShort("0x1e");     // ERROR: format
            // short s_hex4 = Short.parseShort("0x1e", 16);// ERROR: format
            // short s_big = Short.parseShort("55555");     // ERROR: too big
```

```
            System.out.println("parsed: " + s_dec + "," + s_oct + "," + s_hex1
                               + ","  + s_hex2 + "," + s_oct2);
        } catch (NumberFormatException e) {
            e.printStackTrace();
        }
    }
}
```

A B C D E F G H I J K L M N O P Q R S T U V W X Y Z

Short()

PURPOSE
Constructs a Short object using a short value or a string.

SYNTAX
```
public Short(short value)
public Short(String str) throws NumberFormatException
```

DESCRIPTION
This first form of this constructor constructs a Short object using value. The second form parses str—the string representation of an integer—and uses its numeric value to create the Short object. The string consists of a sequence of digits in radix 10 and an optional negative sign (-) as a prefix to indicate a negative number.

PARAMETERS

str
The non-null string representation of an integer in radix 10.

value
The numeric value to use as the object's value.

EXCEPTIONS

NumberFormatException
If str cannot be parsed into an 16-bit signed integer.

SEE ALSO
decode(), parseShort(), valueOf().

EXAMPLE
```
Short width = new Short((short)12); // using integer
try {
    Short height = new Short("22"); // using string
    int area = width.intValue() * height.shortValue();
} catch (NumberFormatException e) {
    ...
}
```

shortValue()

PURPOSE
Retrieves the value of this object as a short.

SYNTAX
```
public short shortValue()
```

DESCRIPTION
This method returns the value of this object as a short.

RETURNS The value of this object as a `short`.

SEE ALSO `byteValue()`, `doubleValue()`, `floatValue()`, `intValue()`, `Number`, `longValue()`.

EXAMPLE See `doubleValue()`.

toString()

PURPOSE Generates the string representation of a `short` or `Short` object.

SYNTAX
```
public String toString()
public static String toString(short sval)
```

DESCRIPTION The first form of this method returns the string representation of the `short` value of this `Short` object. The second form returns the string representation of the value `sval`. For both forms, the radix 10 is used.

The string consists of digits from the specified radix representing the numeric value of the number. If the number is negative, a leading negative sign (–) precedes the digits.

PARAMETERS
`sval` The `short` value for which to generate the string representation.

RETURNS The non-`null` string representation of this `Short` object, or `sval`.

OVERRIDES `Object.toString()`.

SEE ALSO `decode()`, `parseShort()`, `String.valueOf()`, `valueOf()`.

EXAMPLE
```
class Main {
    public static void main(String[] args) {
        short sval = 12;
        Short sobj = new Short((short)34); // cast to short needed

        System.out.println(Short.toString(sval));
        System.out.println(sobj.toString());
    }
}
```

TYPE

PURPOSE The `Class` object representing the primitive type `short`.

SYNTAX `public static final Class TYPE`

DESCRIPTION This constant can be used where the `Class` object—`short.class`—of the primitive type `short` is required, such as for reflection. Although there are no restrictions on the use of `Short.TYPE`, the preferred syntax for naming the class is `short.class`.

SEE ALSO `Class`.

EXAMPLE

```
public static void main(String[] args) {
    Class c = Short.TYPE;
    System.out.println("TYPE: " + c);
    System.out.println("isPrimitive: " + c.isPrimitive());
    System.out.println("superclass: " + c.getSuperclass());
    try {
        Object obj = c.newInstance();  // ERROR
        System.out.println("short: " + obj);
    } catch (InstantiationException e) {
        e.printStackTrace();
    } catch (IllegalAccessException e) {
        e.printStackTrace();
    }
}
```


valueOf()

PURPOSE Creates a `Short` object using its string representation.

SYNTAX

```
public static Short valueOf(String str) throws
    NumberFormatException
public static Short valueOf(String str, int radix) throws
    NumberFormatException
```

DESCRIPTION This method parses the string `str` into an integer and returns a `Short` object constructed using the integer. If no radix is given, the radix 10 is used. A positive integer consists of digits in the specified radix. A negative integer has a leading negative sign (–) followed by digits in the specified radix.

`valueOf` is similar to `parseShort()`, except that `parseShort()` returns a `short`, while `valueOf()` returns a `Short` object. `valueOf` also is similar to `decode()`, except that `valueOf()` accepts a radix argument to determine the radix, while `decode()` examines the string's format so as to determine the radix. Note that strings with a `0x` or `#` prefix accepted by `decode()` are illegal in `valueOf()`, and the `0` prefix for denoting octal numbers is ignored by `valueOf()`. See the example.

PARAMETERS

`radix` The radix to use when parsing `str`. `Character.MIN_RADIX` ≤ `radix` ≤ `Character.MAX_RADIX`.

`str` The non-`null` string containing the integer.

EXCEPTIONS

NumberFormatException
If str cannot be parsed into a 16-bit signed integer of the specified radix.

SEE ALSO Character.MAX_RADIX, Character.MIN_RADIX, decode(), parseShort(), String.valueOf(), toString().

EXAMPLE This example uses valueOf() to convert strings into Short objects. Note that octal strings acceptable to decode() are treated as decimal strings here and hexadecimal strings acceptable to decode() throw NumberFormatException.

```
class Main {
    public static void main(String[] args) {
        try {
            Short s_dec = Short.valueOf("25");          // decimal
            Short s_oct = Short.valueOf("65", 8);       // octal
            Short s_hex1 = Short.valueOf("1f", 16);     // hex
            Short s_hex2 = Short.valueOf("1e", 16);     // hex
            Short s_oct2 = Short.valueOf("033");        // leading 0 ignored
            // Short s_hex3 = Short.valueOf("0x1e");    // ERROR: format
            // Short s_hex4 = Short.valueOf("0x1e", 16);// ERROR: format
            // Short s_big = Short.valueOf("55555");// ERROR: too big

            System.out.println("parsed: " + s_dec + "," + s_oct + "," + s_hex1
                             + ","  + s_hex2 + "," + s_oct2);
        } catch (NumberFormatException e) {
            e.printStackTrace();
        }
    }
}
```

SimpleDateFormat

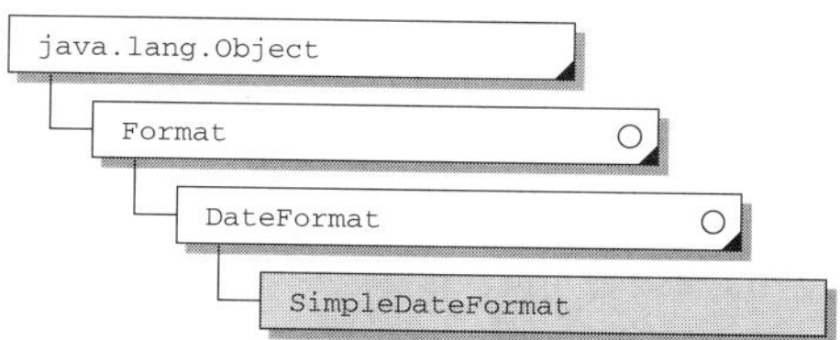

Syntax

```
public class SimpleDateFormat extends DateFormat
```

Description

`SimpleDateFormat` is a concrete class for formatting and parsing dates in a locale-sensitive manner. It allows for formatting (milliseconds to text), parsing (text to milliseconds), and normalization (described in the `DateFormat` class).

Usage

`SimpleDateFormat` allows you to choose any user-defined pattern for date-time formatting. However, you are encouraged to create a date-time formatter with either `getInstance()`, `getTimeInstance()`, `getDateInstance()`, or `getDateTimeInstance()` in `DateFormat`. Each of these class methods can return a date-time formatter initialized with a default format pattern. You can modify the format pattern using the desired `applyPattern` methods. For more information on using these methods, see `DateFormat`.

For time zones that have no names, this class use the string "GMT+*hours:minutes*" (where the + sign indicates time zones ahead of and to the east of Greenwich, England) or the string "GMT–*hours:minutes*" (where the minus sign indicates time zones behind and to the west of Greenwich).

The calendar defines the first day of the week, the first week of the year, whether hours are zero based or not (0 versus 12 or 24), and the time zone. There is one common decimal format to handle all of the numbers; the digit count is handled programmatically according to the pattern.

Not all locales support `SimpleDateFormat`. For full generality, use the creation methods in the `DateFormat` class.

Pattern

To specify the date or time format, use a pattern string. A *pattern* is a shorthand specification made up of pattern letters for formatting properties of a date and is represented as a string. The *pattern letters* are shown in Table 36. The pattern is similar to that used in spreadsheet applications for formatting dates. Here's a simple pattern for a time and date, along with the formatted result:

```
Pattern:   "h:mm a MMM d, yyyy"
Result:    4:08 PM Feb 10, 1962
```

The number of pattern letters used in sequence determines the format—in general, the more letters, the longer the resulting string. Fewer letters generally produces an abbreviation. For example, a month can be specified as a number with `M` or `MM` but as a string with `MMM` or `MMMM`.

	Pattern Letter	Meaning	Presentation	Example	
				Pattern	Result
Date	`d`	Day in month	Number only	`d` `dd`	`5` `05`
	`D`	Day in year	Number only	`D`	`89`
	`F`	Day of week in month	Number only	`F`	`2` (2nd Wed in July)

	`E`	Day in week	Text only	`E`
				`EEE`
				`EEEE`
					`Tues`
					`Tues`
					`Tuesday`

	`w`	Week in year	Number only	`w`	`27`
	`W`	Week in month	Number only	`W`	`2`

	`M`	Month in year	Text or Number	`MM`
				`MMM`
				`MMMM`
					`07` (7th month)
					`Jul`
					`July`

	`y`	Year	Number only	`yy` `yyyy`	`97` `1997`
	`G`	Era designator	Text only	`G`	`AD`
Time	`K`	Hour in A.M./P.M. (0–11)	Number only	`K`	`0`
	`h`	Hour in A.M./P.M. (1–12)	Number only	`hh`	`12`
	`k`	Hour in day (1–24)	Number only	`k`	`24`
	`H`	Hour in day (0–23)	Number only	`H`	`0`
	`m`	Minute in hour	Number only	`m`	`30`
	`s`	Second in minute	Number only	`s`	`55`
	`S`	Millisecond	Number only	`S`	`978`
	`a`	A.M./P.M. marker	Text only	`a`	`PM`
	`z`	Time zone	Text only	`z` `zzzz`	`PST` `Pacific Standard Time`
Text	`'...'`	Quoted text			
	`''`	Single quote char '			

TABLE 36: Pattern Letters for the `SimpleDateFormat` Class.

A B C D E F G H I J K L M N O P Q R S T U V W X Y Z

A pattern can be localized or not. A localized pattern in French uses "j" (for "jour") to represent the day of the month, while English uses "d."

The pattern is used both for formatting and parsing. During formatting, it determines what the resulting string will look like. During parsing, it determines what pattern of digits and other characters in a string will be recognized and converted to a `Date` object.

Table 36 indicates whether the result is text only, number only, or either text or number, as follows:

- **Text Only.** If a text-only pattern letter is repeated one, two, or three times, use an abbreviated form. If the pattern letter is repeated four or more times, use the full form.
- **Number Only.** If a pattern letter is presented only as a number, the number of pattern letters determines the minimum number of digits. If the number is shorter than the pattern, leading zeros are added to this number of digits. The year is handled specially; that is, 'yy' means the year will be truncated to two digits.
- **Text or Number.** If a pattern letter can be presented as text or a number, a one- or two-letter pattern produces a number; three or more letters produce text.

Any characters in the pattern that are not in the ranges of [`'a'..'z'`] and [`'A'..'Z'`] are treated as quoted text. For instance, characters like the colon (`:`), period (`.`), space, hash sign (`#`), and at-sign (`@`) will appear in the resulting date-time text even when they are not embraced within single quotes.

A pattern containing any invalid pattern letter will result in a thrown exception during formatting or parsing.

Table 37 shows some example patterns and typical resulting strings.

Format Pattern	U.S. Locale Result
`"yyyy.MM.dd G 'at' hh:mm:ss z"`	`1996.07.10 AD at 15:08:56 PDT`
`"EEE, MMM d, ''yy"`	`Wed, July 10, '96`
`"h:mm a"`	`4:08 PM`
`"H:mm"`	`16:08`
`"hh 'o''clock' a, zzzz"`	`12 o'clock PM, Pacific Daylight Time`
`"K:mm a, z"`	`0:00 PM, PST`
`"yyyyy.MMMMM.dd GGG hh:mm aaa"`	`1996.July.10 AD 12:08 PM`

TABLE 37: Pattern Examples Using the U.S. Locale.

A.M./P.M. Time

When using the "`hour in am/pm`" pattern letter "`h`", you should use the A.M./P.M. marker "`a`", as follows:

```
h:mm a
2:30 PM
```

Note that for this format `h:mm a`, when parsing text for a P.M. time, such as `2:30PM`, if the A.M./P.M. marker is missing, the number will parse as an A.M. time, as you might expect.

Dates and Times

To create a date or time, use either the `Date` or `GregorianCalendar` classes. Also see the `Calendar` class for related information.

MEMBER SUMMARY

Constructors	
`SimpleDateFormat()`	Constructs a `SimpleDateFormat` instance with a pattern for a locale.
Pattern Methods	
`applyLocalizedPattern()`	Assigns a localized pattern to this `SimpleDateFormat` object.
`applyPattern()`	Assigns a nonlocalized pattern to this `SimpleDateFormat` object.
`toLocalizedPattern()`	Produces a string of the current localized pattern.
`toPattern()`	Produces a string of the current nonlocalized pattern.
Format and Parse Methods	
`format()`	Formats a `Date` object to produce a string.
`parse()`	Parses a date-time string to produce a `Date` object.
DateFormatSymbols Methods	
`getDateFormatSymbols()`	Retrieves the instance of `DateFormatSymbols` for this `SimpleDateFormat` object.
`setDateFormatSymbols()`	Sets an instance of `DateFormatSymbols` to this `SimpleDateFormat` object.
Object Methods	
`clone()`	Creates a copy of this `SimpleDateFormat` object.
`equals()`	Compares this `SimpleDateFormat` object with another object for equality.
`hashCode()`	Computes the hash code of this `SimpleDateFormat` object.

See Also

Calendar, GregorianCalendar, TimeZone, DateFormat, DateFormatSymbols, DecimalFormat.

Example 1

This example uses the SimpleDateFormat() constructor to create a date.

```
import java.text.SimpleDateFormat;
import java.util.*;

class Main1 {
    // Set column widths.
    static int NARROW = 12;
    static int WIDE = 42;

    // Create the date January 3, 1956
    static Date date =
        (new GregorianCalendar(1956, Calendar.JANUARY, 3, 2, 5)).getTime();

    // Create a date format.
    static SimpleDateFormat[] sdf = new SimpleDateFormat[] {
                            new SimpleDateFormat ("", Locale.US),
                            new SimpleDateFormat ("", Locale.FRENCH),
                            new SimpleDateFormat ("", Locale.GERMAN),
                           new SimpleDateFormat ("", new Locale("cs", "CZ")),
                            new SimpleDateFormat ("", Locale.ITALY)
                        };

    public static void main(String[] args) {

        System.out.println("Date:    " + date + "\n");

        System.out.println("PATTERN     US                          " +
                          "FRENCH     GERMAN       CZECH        ITALIAN");

        System.out.println("LETTER      EXAMPLE                     " +
                          "EXAMPLE    EXAMPLE      EXAMPLE      EXAMPLE");

                                        // US          FRENCH
                                        // EXAMPLE     EXAMPLE
        formatPatternLetters("d");        // 3           3
        formatPatternLetters("dd");       // 03          03
        formatPatternLetters("D");        // 3           3
        formatPatternLetters("DD");       // 03          03
        formatPatternLetters("F");        // 1           1
        formatPatternLetters("FF");       // 01          01
        formatPatternLetters("E");        // Tue         mar
        formatPatternLetters("EE");       // Tue         mar
        formatPatternLetters("EEE");      // Tue         mar
        formatPatternLetters("EEEE");     // Tuesday     mardi
        formatPatternLetters("w");        // 1           2
        formatPatternLetters("ww");       // 01          02
        formatPatternLetters("W");        // 1           2
        formatPatternLetters("WW");       // 01          02
        formatPatternLetters("M");        // 1           1
        formatPatternLetters("MM");       // 01          01
        formatPatternLetters("MMM");      // Jan         jan
```

```
formatPatternLetters("MMMM");   // January   janvier
formatPatternLetters("y");      // 56        56
formatPatternLetters("yy");     // 56        56
formatPatternLetters("yyy");    // 56        56
formatPatternLetters("yyyy");   // 1956      1956
formatPatternLetters("yyyyy");  // 01956     1956
formatPatternLetters("G");      // AD        ap. J.-C.
formatPatternLetters("GG");     // AD        ap. J.-C.
formatPatternLetters("GGG");    // AD        ap. J.-C.
formatPatternLetters("K");      // 2         11
formatPatternLetters("KK");     // 02        11
formatPatternLetters("h");      // 2         11
formatPatternLetters("hh");     // 02        11
formatPatternLetters("H");      // 2         11
formatPatternLetters("HH");     // 02        11
formatPatternLetters("m");      // 5         5
formatPatternLetters("mm");     // 05        05
formatPatternLetters("s");      // 0         0
formatPatternLetters("ss");     // 00        00
formatPatternLetters("S");      // 0         0
formatPatternLetters("SS");     // 00        00
formatPatternLetters("a");      // AM        AM
formatPatternLetters("aa");     // AM        AM
formatPatternLetters("aaa");    // AM        AM
formatPatternLetters("z");      // PST       GMT+01:00
formatPatternLetters("zz");     // PST       GMT+01:00
formatPatternLetters("zzz");    // PST       GMT+01:00
formatPatternLetters("zzzz");   // Pacific Standard Time  GMT+01:00

System.out.println();

System.out.print("PATTERNS");
System.out.print(" ------------------------------------------ ");
System.out.println("LOCALE  " + "\n");

formatPattern("EEEE, MMMM d, yyyy", 0);            // US
            // Tuesday, January 3, 1956

formatPattern("EEEE d MMMM yyyy", 1);              // FRENCH
            // mardi 3 janvier 1956

formatPattern("EEE, MMM d, ''yy", 0);              // US
            // Tue, Jan 3, '56

formatPattern("EEE d MMM yy", 1);                  // FRENCH
            // mar 3 jan 56

formatPattern("h:mm a z", 0);                      // US
            // 2:05 AM PST

formatPattern("k'H'mm z", 1);                      // FRENCH
            // 11H05 GMT+01:00

formatPattern("h 'o''clock' a, zzzz", 0);          // US
            // 2 o'clock AM, Pacific Standard Time

formatPattern("h 'heures' zzzz", 1);               // FRENCH
            // 11 heures GMT+01:00

formatPattern("yyyy.MM.dd G 'at' hh:mm:ss z" , 0);  // US
```

```
                // 1956.02.03 AD at 02:05:00 PST

        formatPattern("yyyy.MM.dd G 'à' kk:mm:ss z" , 1);   // FRENCH
                // 1956.02.03 AD à  02:05:00 GMT+01:00
    }

    public static void formatPatternLetters(String pattern) {
        sdf[0].applyPattern(pattern);
        System.out.print(pattern);
        int currentColumnTextWidth = pattern.length();
        String example;
        int narrowTmp;

        // Apply the pattern.
        for (int loc = 0; loc < sdf.length; loc++) {
            sdf[loc].applyPattern(pattern);

            // Add more space for "Pacific Standard Time"
            if (loc == 1) {
                narrowTmp = NARROW + 11;
            } else {
                narrowTmp = NARROW;
            }
            // Print spaces for the example date.
            printSpaces(narrowTmp - currentColumnTextWidth);

            // Format and print the example date.
            example = sdf[loc].format(date);
            System.out.print(example);

            currentColumnTextWidth = example.length();
        }
        System.out.println();
    }

    public static void formatPattern(String pattern, int localeIndex) {
        sdf[0].applyPattern(pattern);
        System.out.print("Pattern:  " + pattern);
        int currentColumnTextWidth = pattern.length();
        String example;
        String localeString = "";

        // Apply the pattern.
        sdf[localeIndex].applyPattern(pattern);

        // Space over for the example date.
        printSpaces(WIDE - currentColumnTextWidth);

        switch (localeIndex) {
            case 0:  localeString = "US      "; break;
            case 1:  localeString = "FRENCH  "; break;
            case 2:  localeString = "GERMAN  "; break;
            case 3:  localeString = "CZECH   "; break;
            case 4:  localeString = "ITALIAN "; break;
        }
        System.out.println(localeString);

        // Format and print the example date.
        example = sdf[localeIndex].format(date);
        System.out.println("Example:  " + example);
```

```
            System.out.println();
        }

        public static void printSpaces(int count) {
            for (int i = 0; i < count; i++) {
                System.out.print(" ");
            }
        }
    }
```


Output

```
Date:    Tue Jan 03 02:05:00 PST 1956

PATTERN    US             FRENCH        GERMAN        CZECH         ITALIAN
LETTER     EXAMPLE        EXAMPLE       EXAMPLE       EXAMPLE       EXAMPLE
d          3              3             3             3             3
dd         03             03            03            03            03
D          3              3             3             3             3
DD         03             03            03            03            03
F          1              1             1             1             1
FF         01             01            01            01            01
E          Tue            mar           Di            Út            mar
EE         Tue            mar           Di            Út            mar
EEE        Tue            mar           Di            Út            mar
EEEE       Tuesday        mardi         Dienstag      Útery         martedì
w          1              2             1             1             1
ww         01             02            01            01            01
W          1              2             1             1             1
WW         01             02            01            01            01
M          1              1             1             1             1
MM         01             01            01            01            01
MMM        Jan            jan           Jan           I             gen
MMMM       January        janvier       Januar        Leden         gennaio
y          56             56            56            56            56
yy         56             56            56            56            56
yyy        56             56            56            56            56
yyyy       1956           1956          1956          1956          1956
yyyyy      1956           1956          1956          1956          1956
G          AD             ap. J.-C.     n. Chr.       po Kr.        dopo Cristo
GG         AD             ap. J.-C.     n. Chr.       po Kr.        dopo Cristo
GGG        AD             ap. J.-C.     n. Chr.       po Kr.        dopo Cristo
K          2              11            11            11            11
KK         02             11            11            11            11
h          2              11            11            11            11
hh         02             11            11            11            11
H          2              11            11            11            11
HH         02             11            11            11            11
m          5              5             5             5             5
mm         05             05            05            05            05
s          0              0             0             0             0
ss         00             00            00            00            00
S          0              0             0             0             0
SS         00             00            00            00            00
a          AM             AM            AM            AM            AM
aa         AM             AM            AM            AM            AM
aaa        AM             AM            AM            AM            AM
z          PST            GMT+01:00     GMT+01:00     GMT+01:00     GMT+01:00
zz         PST            GMT+01:00     GMT+01:00     GMT+01:00     GMT+01:00
```

```
zzz          PST                        GMT+01:00   GMT+01:00   GMT+01:00   GMT+01:00
zzzz         Pacific Standard Time      GMT+01:00   GMT+01:00   GMT+01:00   GMT+01:00

PATTERNS ------------------------------------------ LOCALE

Pattern:  EEEE, MMMM d, yyyy                           US
Example:  Tuesday, January 3, 1956

Pattern:  EEEE d MMMM yyyy                             FRENCH
Example:  mardi 3 janvier 1956

Pattern:  EEE, MMM d, ''yy                             US
Example:  Tue, Jan 3, '56

Pattern:  EEE d MMM yy                                 FRENCH
Example:  mar 3 jan 56

Pattern:  h:mm a z                                     US
Example:  2:05 AM PST

Pattern:  k'H'mm z                                     FRENCH
Example:  11H05 GMT+01:00

Pattern:  h 'o''clock' a, zzzz                         US
Example:  2 o'clock AM, Pacific Standard Time

Pattern:  h 'heures' zzzz                              FRENCH
Example:  11 heures GMT+01:00

Pattern:  yyyy.MM.dd G 'at' hh:mm:ss z                 US
Example:  1956.01.03 AD at 02:05:00 PST

Pattern:  yyyy.MM.dd G 'à' kk:mm:ss z                  FRENCH
Example:  1956.01.03 ap. J.-C. à 11:05:00 GMT+01:00
```

Example 2

This example uses the `SimpleDateFormat()` constructor to create a date.

```
import java.text.SimpleDateFormat;
import java.util.*;

class Main2 {
    public static void main(String[] args) {

        Locale locale = Locale.FRENCH;

        // Create a date formatter.
        SimpleDateFormat formatter =
            new SimpleDateFormat ("dd.MM.yyyy 'à' H:mm:ss zzzz", locale);

        // Format the current time.
        String dateString = formatter.format(new Date());
        System.out.println(dateString + "\n");
                                   // 27.11.1997 à 5:44:10 GMT+01:00
    }
}
```

Example 3

This example uses a method from DateFormat, the getDateTimeInstance() method, to create the date. This is a more general solution because not all locales support SimpleDateFormat. This method creates an instance of SimpleDateFormat for many Western languages. However, for locales for which no subclass of DateFormat is defined, it does nothing.

```
import java.text.SimpleDateFormat;
import java.text.DateFormat;
import java.util.*;

class Main3 {
    public static void main(String[] args) {

        Locale locale = Locale.FRENCH;

        // Create an instance of DateFormat.
        DateFormat df = DateFormat.getDateTimeInstance(DateFormat.SHORT,
                                              DateFormat.SHORT, locale);

        if (df instanceof SimpleDateFormat) {
            SimpleDateFormat formatter = (SimpleDateFormat)df;

            // Apply a pattern.
            formatter.applyPattern("yyyy.MM.dd 'at' hh:mm:ss a zzz");

            // Format the current time.
            String dateString = formatter.format(new Date());
            System.out.println(dateString + "\n");
                                      // 1997.11.27 at 05:44:10 AM GMT+01:00
        }
    }
}
```

applyLocalizedPattern()

PURPOSE Assigns a localized pattern to this SimpleDateFormat object.

SYNTAX `public void applyLocalizedPattern(String pattern)`

DESCRIPTION This method applies the pattern string to this SimpleDateFormat object. The pattern is assumed to be in a notation localized to this SimpleDateFormat object (typically specified in the constructor).

PARAMETERS

pattern A localized pattern string.

EXAMPLE This example assigns both the nonlocalized and localized versions of the same pattern to show that their effects are identical for the same SimpleDateFormat object. In this case, the locale is France.

```
import java.text.SimpleDateFormat;
import java.text.ParseException;
import java.util.*;

class Main {

    public static void main(String[] args) {

//      String dateString = "dd.MM.yyyy 'à' H:mm:ss zzzz"

        Locale loc = Locale.FRENCH;

        System.out.println("Locale:                    " + loc.getDisplayName());

        Date date = new Date();

        // Create a date formatter.
        SimpleDateFormat dateformat =
            new SimpleDateFormat ("", loc);

        System.out.println("\napplyPattern ---------------------------");

        dateformat.applyPattern("dd.MMM.yyyy - H:mm:ss zzz");

        System.out.println("toLocalizedPattern:  "
            + dateformat.toLocalizedPattern());

        System.out.println("toPattern:           "
            + dateformat.toPattern());

        System.out.println("format:              "
            + dateformat.format(date));

        System.out.println("\napplyLocalizedPattern ------------------");

        dateformat.applyLocalizedPattern("jj.nnn.aaaa - H:mm:ss zzz");

        System.out.println("toLocalizedPattern:  "
            + dateformat.toLocalizedPattern());

        System.out.println("toPattern:           "
            + dateformat.toPattern());

        System.out.println("format:              "
            + dateformat.format(date));
    }
}
```

Output

```
Locale:                French (France)

applyPattern ---------------------------
toLocalizedPattern:    jj.nnn.aaaa - H:mm:ss zzz
toPattern:             dd.MMM.yyyy - H:mm:ss zzz
format:                27.nov.1997 - 5:15:29 GMT+01:00

applyLocalizedPattern ------------------
toLocalizedPattern:    jj.nnn.aaaa - H:mm:ss zzz
toPattern:             dd.MMM.yyyy - H:mm:ss zzz
format:                27.nov.1997 - 5:15:29 GMT+01:00
```

applyPattern()

PURPOSE Assigns a nonlocalized pattern to this `SimpleDateFormat` object.

SYNTAX `public void applyPattern(String pattern)`

DESCRIPTION This method applies the string `pattern` to this decimal format. The pattern is assumed to be in a nonlocalized notation. The properties of this pattern can also be changed individually through the various setter methods.

PARAMETERS

`pattern` A localized pattern string.

EXAMPLE See `applyLocalizedPattern()`.

clone()

PURPOSE Creates a copy of this `SimpleDateFormat` object.

SYNTAX `public Object clone()`

DESCRIPTION This method makes a copy of this `SimpleDateFormat` object. The new `SimpleDateFormat` object has a copy of the original pattern. Changing any value in the new `SimpleDateFormat` object will not affect the original instance.

RETURNS A copy of this `SimpleDateFormat` object.

OVERRIDES `clone() in class DateFormat.`

EXAMPLE This example illustrates the use of `clone()` to copy a `SimpleDateFormat` object. Note that the copy has the same pattern as the original.

```
import java.text.SimpleDateFormat;

class Main {
    public static void main(String args[]) {

        // Create decimal format.
        SimpleDateFormat sdf = new SimpleDateFormat("MMM dd, yyyy");
        System.out.println("Original pattern: " + sdf.toPattern());

        // Create a clone.
        SimpleDateFormat sdfCopy = (SimpleDateFormat)sdf.clone();
        System.out.println("Copy's pattern:   " + sdf.toPattern());

        // Tests for equality.
        if (sdf.equals(sdfCopy)) {
            System.out.println("Clone is equal to original");
        }
```

```
        // Compute hashcode.
        int hc = sdf.hashCode();
        System.out.println("Hash code:        " + hc);
    }
}
```

Output

```
Original pattern: MMM dd, yyyy
Copy's pattern:   MMM dd, yyyy
Clone is equal to original
Hash code:        1224263791
```

A B C D E F G H I J K L M N O P Q R S T U V W X Y Z

equals()

PURPOSE Compares this `SimpleDateFormat` object with another object for equality.

SYNTAX `public boolean equals(Object obj)`

DESCRIPTION This method compares this `SimpleDateFormat` object with another object for equality. If `obj` is a `SimpleDateFormat` object and if it has the pattern as this `SimpleDateFormat` object, the objects are equal and this method returns `true`. If the patterns are not equal or if `obj` is `null` or is not a `SimpleDateFormat` object, the method returns `false`.

PARAMETERS

`obj` A possibly `null` object with which to compare.

RETURNS `true` if the objects are equal; `false` otherwise.

OVERRIDES `DateFormat.equals()`.

SEE ALSO `hashCode()`.

EXAMPLE See `clone()`.

format()

PURPOSE Formats a `Date` object to produce a string.

SYNTAX `public StringBuffer format(Date date, StringBuffer appendBuf, FieldPosition pos)`

DESCRIPTION This method formats a `Date` object to produce a string, which is appended to the buffer `appendbuf`. The `appendBuf` value is returned. Returning the full result allows chaining. If `appendBuf` is omitted, the produced string is simply returned.

The field position pos has absolutely no effect on the formatted result. Its purpose is to determine where in the string the range of characters are for a given field so that the strings can be aligned in a column on that particular field. If you don't care about column alignment, set pos to any valid field position.

The field position works as follows. You create an instance of `FieldPosition` using the field constant for the field you want to align. For example, if you are formatting dates and want to output them in a column and align the months, create the `FieldPosition` object with the constant `DateFormat.MONTH_FIELD`. When you call `format()`, the begin and end index values of the field position `pos` are updated to the month range in the resulting string. You can then use these values to get the length of the month portion and then use that length to position the string horizontally. For an example of this, see the class example in the `FieldPosition` class.

PARAMETERS

`appendBuf`	The string buffer to which the resulting string is to be appended.
`date`	A `Date` object to be converted to a string.
`pos`	A `FieldPosition` object whose field you want to eventually align in a column.

RETURNS The formatted date-time string.

OVERRIDES `DateFormat.format()`.

SEE ALSO `DateFormat`.

EXAMPLE See the class examples.

getDateFormatSymbols()

PURPOSE Retrieves the instance of `DateFormatSymbols` for this `SimpleDateFormat` object.

SYNTAX `public DateFormatSymbols getDateFormatSymbols()`

DESCRIPTION This method gets the `DateFormatSymbols` object, which allows access to all of the user strings that make up dates and times, plus the symbols for the date-time pattern.

RETURNS A copy of the `DateFormatSymbols` object associated with this `SimpleDateFormat` object.

EXAMPLE See `setDateFormatSymbols()`.

hashCode()

PURPOSE
Computes the hash code of this `SimpleDateFormat` object.

SYNTAX
`public int hashCode()`

DESCRIPTION
This method computes the hash code for this `SimpleDateFormat` based on the pattern of this `SimpleDateFormat` object. Two `SimpleDateFormat` objects with the same properties will have the same hash code. However, two `SimpleDateformat` objects that do not have the same properties might also have the same hash code, although the hash code algorithm minimizes this possibility. The hash code is typically used as the key in a hash table.

RETURNS
The `SimpleDateFormat` object's hash code, an integer.

OVERRIDES
`DateFormat.hashCode()`.

SEE ALSO
`equals()`.

EXAMPLE
See `clone()`.

parse()

PURPOSE
Parses a date-time string to produce a `Date` object.

SYNTAX
`public Date parse(String sourceStr, ParsePosition pos)`

DESCRIPTION
This method parses a string starting at the parse position `pos` looking for the pattern of this date format. If this pattern is found at that position, an instance of `Date` is produced and the begin index of the parse position is updated to this position. If this pattern is not found, it returns `null` and the parse position does not advance.

For example, the string "07/10/96 4:50 PM, PDT" will be parsed into an instance of `Date` that is equivalent to `new Date(837039928046)`.

By default, parsing is lenient. That is, if, for example, the input is January 32, the parse will still succeed, treating the date as February 1. Clients may insist on strict adherence to the format by calling `setLenient(false)`.

Omitting the parse position `pos` causes the parse to begin at the start of `sourceStr`.

PARAMETERS

`pos`
The parse position that determines where the parse begins. If `parse()` succeeds, the begin index is updated to the position at which parsing terminated.

`sourceStr`
The string to be parsed.

RETURNS An instance of `Date`, or `null` if the input could not be parsed.

OVERRIDES `DateFormat.parse()`.

SEE ALSO `DateFormat`.

EXAMPLE This example parses a string to produce a `Date` object. Also see `parse()` in the `DateFormat` class for an example using `DateFormat`.

```
import java.text.SimpleDateFormat;
import java.text.ParsePosition;
import java.util.*;

class Main {
    public static void main(String[] args) {
        Locale locale = Locale.FRENCH;

        // Create a date formatter.
        SimpleDateFormat formatter =
            new SimpleDateFormat ("dd.MM.yyyy 'à' H:mm:ss zzzz", locale);

        // Specify a date string.
        String dateString = "27.11.1997 à 16:30:00 GMT+01:00";

        // Parse a string into a Date.
        ParsePosition pos = new ParsePosition(0);
        Date currentTime = formatter.parse(dateString, pos);

        // Format the date to a string and print it out.
        System.out.println(formatter.format(currentTime) + "\n");
                                        // 27.11.1997 à 16:30:00 GMT+01:00
    }
}
```

setDateFormatSymbols()

PURPOSE Sets an instance of `DateFormatSymbols` to this `SimpleDateFormat` object.

SYNTAX `public void setDateFormatSymbols(DateFormatSymbols symbols)`

DESCRIPTION This method sets the `DateFormatSymbols` object associated with this `SimpleDateFormat` object. This allows modifying the user strings that make up dates and times, plus the symbols for the date-time pattern.

PARAMETERS

`symbols` An instance of `DateFormatSymbols` for this `SimpleDateFormat` object.

EXAMPLE This example modifies the `DateFormatSymbols` object by setting the short month strings to be all uppercase.

```
import java.text.DateFormatSymbols;
import java.text.SimpleDateFormat;
import java.util.*;

class Main {
    public static void main(String[] args) {

        // Create a date formatter.
        SimpleDateFormat dateformat =
            new SimpleDateFormat ();

        // Create an instance of DateFormatSymbols.
        DateFormatSymbols dfs = new DateFormatSymbols();

        // Modify the short month string to be all uppercase.
        dfs.setShortMonths(new String[]
                    {"JAN", "FEB", "MAR", "APR", "MAY", "JUN",
                     "JUL", "AUG", "SEP", "OCT", "NOV", "DEC"});

        // Apply pattern.
        dateformat.applyPattern("dd-MMM-yyyy - H:mm:ss zzzz");

        // Apply the symbols to this date format.
        dateformat.setDateFormatSymbols(dfs);

        // Format the current time.
        String dateString = dateformat.format(new Date());
        System.out.println(dateString + "\n");
                                 // "27-NOV-1997 - 5:44:47 GMT+01:00"

        // Get and print out the first short month string.
        String month = dateformat.getDateFormatSymbols().getShortMonths()[0];
        System.out.println(month);       // "JAN"
    }
}
```

SimpleDateFormat()

PURPOSE Constructs a `SimpleDateFormat` instance with a pattern for a locale.

SYNTAX

```
public SimpleDateFormat()
public SimpleDateFormat(String pattern)
public SimpleDateFormat(String pattern, Locale loc)
public SimpleDateFormat(String pattern,
   DateFormatSymbols symbols)
```

DESCRIPTION These constructors create a `SimpleDateFormat` using a nonlocalized string `pattern` in the locale `loc`, with a locale-specific `DateFormatSymbols` object `symbols`. Omitting the locale `loc` uses the default locale; omitting the pattern uses the default pattern, omitting the `symbols` uses the default `DateFormatSymbols` object for the locale.

Note: Not all locales support `SimpleDateFormat`. For full generality, use the creation methods in the `DateFormat` class. This is illustrated in class example 2.

PARAMETERS

`loc`	The locale for this `SimpleDateFormat` object.
`pattern`	The pattern string to be applied to the new `SimpleDateFormat` object.
`symbols`	The locale-specific symbols to be used by this `SimpleDateFormat` object.

SEE ALSO `DateFormat`.

EXAMPLE See the class examples.

toLocalizedPattern()

PURPOSE Produces a string of the current localized pattern.

SYNTAX `public String toLocalizedPattern()`

DESCRIPTION This method synthesizes a localized pattern string that represents the current pattern of this `SimpleDateFormat` object. It uses the locale of the `SimpleDateFormat` instance. This string should be used when displaying the pattern to a native user so that familiar symbols will be displayed.

RETURNS The localized string pattern for this decimal format.

EXAMPLE See `applyLocalizedPattern()`.

toPattern()

PURPOSE Produces a string of the current nonlocalized pattern.

SYNTAX `public String toPattern()`

DESCRIPTION This method synthesizes a nonlocalized pattern string that represents the current state of this `SimpleDateFormat` object. This pattern is independent of locales, so it can be applied to a `SimpleDateFormat` object in any locale by using `applyPattern()`.

This pattern happens to coincide with the pattern of the U.S. locale.

RETURNS The nonlocalized string pattern for this decimal format.

EXAMPLE See `applyLocalizedPattern()`.

SimpleTimeZone

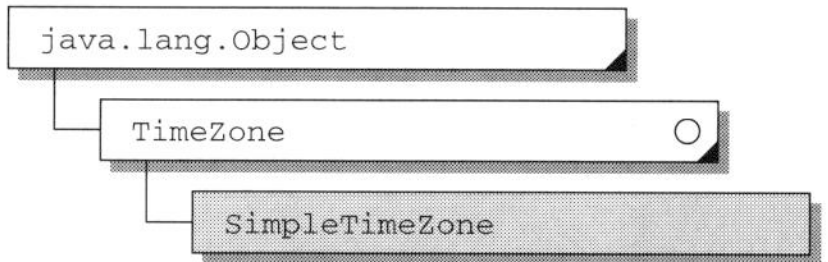

Syntax

```
public class SimpleTimeZone extends TimeZone
```

Description1559

`SimpleTimeZone` is a concrete subclass of `TimeZone` and represents a time zone for use with a Gregorian calendar. `SimpleTimeZone` implements daylight savings time rules of the form "start on the 1st Sunday in April." `SimpleTimeZone` cannot handle other rules such as ones of the form "start on March 4th"; a different `TimeZone` subclass is needed for this.

Usage

This class is useful only if you are creating new time zones—not a typical thing to do. This class is used primarily by the `TimeZone` class, which creates and manages a `SimpleTimeZone` object for each time zone.

To create a `SimpleTimeZone` object, you have to supply an ID (a three-character label for the time zone) and a raw offset (the number of milliseconds by which this time zone differs from Greenwich Mean Time, GMT). You can then specify a starting and ending date for daylight savings time.

Daylight Savings Time

Daylight savings time was introduced during World War I in order to conserve fuel for production of electricity for lighting. Under this system, the time is advanced one hour sometime in the spring. In the United States, daylight savings time begins on the first Sunday in April and ends on the last Sunday in October.

Standard time refers to the time when daylight savings time is not in effect. For example, noon on July 4 in PST (Pacific Standard Time) is 11 A.M. in standard time. This is because July 4 in PST is within the daylight savings time period.

When the start time of daylight savings time is being specified, it is important to note that the time is specified in standard time rather than daylight savings time. For example, suppose daylight savings time is to start at 2 A.M. standard time. This means that when the clock is at 1:59:59 A.M. and advances by a second, the time immediately becomes 3 A.M.

The end time of daylight savings time is also specified in standard time. For example, suppose daylight savings time is to end at 2 A.M. standard time. This means that when the clock is at 2:59:59 A.M. and advances by a second, the time immediately becomes 2 A.M.

Daylight Savings Time Start Year

By default, the daylight savings time rules are assumed to apply in all years. However, if necessary, it possible to set the actual year in which daylight savings time takes effect by calling `setStartYear()`. This means dates before the daylight savings time start year are never within a daylight savings time period.

A B C D E F G H I J K L M N O P Q R S T U V W X Y Z

MEMBER SUMMARY	
Constructor	
`SimpleTimeZone()`	Constructs a `SimpleTimeZone` instance.
Daylight Savings Time Methods	
`inDaylightTime()`	Determines if a particular date falls in this time zone's daylight savings time period.
`setEndRule()`	Sets the daylight savings time ending rule.
`setStartRule()`	Sets the daylight savings time starting rule.
`setStartYear()`	Sets the year in which daylight savings time takes effect.
`useDaylightTime()`	Determines if this `SimpleTimeZone` object has a daylight savings time period.
Time Offset Methods	
`getOffset()`	Retrieves the time difference (in daylight savings time) of this time zone from GMT.
`getRawOffset()`	Retrieves the time difference (in standard time) of this time zone from GMT.
`setRawOffset()`	Sets the time difference from GMT.
Object Methods	
`clone()`	Creates a clone of this `SimpleTimeZone` object.
`equals()`	Determines if this `SimpleTimeZone` object is equal to another object.
`hashCode()`	Computes the hash code for this `SimpleTimeZone` object.

See Also

`Calendar`, `TimeZone`.

Example

This example demonstrates the creation of a new time zone complete with its own daylight savings time period. The created time zone uses the raw offset of the default time zone. The daylight savings time period of the new time zone is calculated to be exactly 10 seconds in the future and ends 20 seconds in the future.

In calculating the start of daylight saving time, an hour must be subtracted from the start time. This is because the start time must be specified relative to daylight savings time rather than to standard time.

A thread is created to monitor the time as it enters and leaves daylight savings time.

```
import java.util.*;
import java.text.*;

class Main extends Thread {
    static SimpleTimeZone tz;

    public static void main(String[] args) {
        // See example description.
        int BUG_WORKAROUND = 60*60*1000;

        // Create a new SimpleTimeZone object with the name JAV.
        // Use the local raw offset.
        tz = new SimpleTimeZone(TimeZone.getDefault().getRawOffset(), "JAV");

        Calendar calendar = Calendar.getInstance();

        // Determine the number of milliseconds so far today.
        int todayMillis = calendar.get(Calendar.HOUR)*60*60*1000
            + calendar.get(Calendar.MINUTE)*60*1000
            + calendar.get(Calendar.SECOND)*1000;

        // If PM, add another 12 hours.
        if (calendar.get(Calendar.AM_PM) == Calendar.PM) {
            todayMillis += 12*60*60*1000;
        }

        // Set the start of daylight savings time 10 seconds from now.
        tz.setStartRule(
            calendar.get(Calendar.MONTH),
            calendar.get(Calendar.DAY_OF_WEEK_IN_MONTH),
            calendar.get(Calendar.DAY_OF_WEEK),
            todayMillis + 10000);

        // Set the end of daylight savings time 20 seconds from now.
        tz.setEndRule(
            calendar.get(Calendar.MONTH),
            calendar.get(Calendar.DAY_OF_WEEK_IN_MONTH),
            calendar.get(Calendar.DAY_OF_WEEK),
            todayMillis + 20000 + BUG_WORKAROUND);

        // Start a thread to monitor the time.
        new Main().start();
    }

    public void run() {
        DateFormat formatter =
            new SimpleDateFormat("MMM dd HH:mm:ss zzz", Locale.US);
        formatter.setTimeZone(tz);

        while (true) {
            try {
                // Get the current time and date.
                Date date = new Date();
```

```
                    // Print current time.
                    System.out.print( (tz.inDaylightTime(date) ?
                        "Daylight Savings Time - " : "Standard Time         - "));
                    System.out.println(formatter.format(date));

                    // Sleep for 3 seconds.
                    Thread.sleep(3000);
                } catch (Exception e) {
                    e.printStackTrace();
                }
            }
        }
    }
```

Output

```
Standard Time         - Oct 06 16:42:04 GMT-08:00
Standard Time         - Oct 06 16:42:07 GMT-08:00
Standard Time         - Oct 06 16:42:10 GMT-08:00
Daylight Savings Time - Oct 06 17:42:13 GMT-07:00
Daylight Savings Time - Oct 06 17:42:16 GMT-07:00
Daylight Savings Time - Oct 06 17:42:19 GMT-07:00
Daylight Savings Time - Oct 06 17:42:22 GMT-07:00
Standard Time         - Oct 06 16:42:25 GMT-08:00
Standard Time         - Oct 06 16:42:28 GMT-08:00
```

clone()

PURPOSE Creates a clone of this `SimpleTimeZone` object.

SYNTAX `public Object clone()`

DESCRIPTION The new object is identical to this one. In particular, calling `equals()` on this object and the new object yields `true`.

RETURNS A non-`null` copy of this `SimpleTimeZone` object.

OVERRIDES `TimeZone.clone()`.

EXAMPLE See `TimeZone.clone()`.

equals()

PURPOSE Determines if this `SimpleTimeZone` object is equal to another object.

SYNTAX `public boolean equals(Object obj)`

DESCRIPTION This method returns if `obj` is a `SimpleTimeZone` object and its values are identical to this one. Two `SimpleTimeZone` objects are equal if the ID and daylight savings time rules are identical. See `setStartRule()` and `setEndRule()` for details about the values involved in the daylight savings time rules.

PARAMETERS

`obj`	The possibly `null` `SimpleTimeZone` object to compare.

RETURNS `true` if `obj` has identical values to this object; `false` otherwise.

OVERRIDES `java.lang.Object.equals()`.

SEE ALSO `endStartRule()`, `hashCode()`, `setStartRule()`.

EXAMPLE See `java.lang.Object.equals()`.

getOffset()

PURPOSE Retrieves the time difference (in daylight savings time) of this time zone from GMT.

SYNTAX

```
public int getOffset(int era, int year, int month, int day, int
   dayOfWeek, int millis)
```

DESCRIPTION The offset is the number of milliseconds by which the time zone differs from GMT for a particular point in time as specified by the six parameters. It takes into account daylight savings time. For example, in January, the offset for PST is –8 hours. In May, the offset for PST is -7 hours.

This method returns the raw offset (see `getRawOffset()`) if `year` is less than the daylight savings time start year (see `setStartYear()`) or if `era` is `GregorianCalendar.BC`.

PARAMETERS

`era`	A Gregorian calendar era, which can be either `GregorianCalendar.BC` or `GregorianCalendar.AD`.
`year`	A year.
`month`	`Calendar.JANUARY` ≤ `month` ≤ `Calendar.DECEMBER`.
`day`	The day in the month. `1` ≤ `day` ≤ `31`.
`dayOfWeek`	The day of the week. `Calendar.SUNDAY` ≤ `dayOfWeek` ≤ `Calendar.SATURDAY`.
`milliseconds`	The number of milliseconds from midnight in standard time.

RETURNS The number of milliseconds by which this time zone differs from GMT taking into account daylight savings time.

OVERRIDES `TimeZone.getOffset()`.

SEE ALSO `getRawOffset()`, `GregorianCalendar`.

A B C D E F G H I J K L M N O P Q R S T U V W X Y Z

getRawOffset()

PURPOSE Retrieves the time difference (in standard time) of this time zone from GMT.

SYNTAX `public int getRawOffset()`

DESCRIPTION The raw offset is the number of milliseconds by which this time zone differs from GMT. For example, PST differs by -8*1000*60*60 milliseconds from GMT. The raw offset is based on standard time—the effects of daylight savings time are ignored.

The raw offset can be added to the time at GMT to obtain the local time. For an offset that takes into account daylight savings time, see `getOffset()`.

RETURNS The number of milliseconds by which this time zone differs from GMT in standard time.

OVERRIDES `TimeZone.getRawOffset()`.

EXAMPLE See `TimeZone.getAvailableIDs()`.

hashCode()

PURPOSE Computes the hash code for this `SimpleTimeZone` object.

SYNTAX `public synchronized int hashCode()`

DESCRIPTION The simple hash code is an integer that's calculated using the start and end month, start and end day, start and end day-of-week, start and end time, and raw offset. Two `SimpleTimeZone` objects that are equal have the same hash code. However, unequal `SimpleTimeZone` objects might also have the same hash code, although the hash code algorithm minimizes this possibility. The hash code is typically used as the key in a hash table.

RETURNS The `SimpleTimeZone` object's hash code.

OVERRIDES `java.lang.Object.hashCode()`.

SEE ALSO `equals()`.

EXAMPLE See `java.lang.Object.hashCode()`.

inDaylightTime()

PURPOSE Determines if a particular date falls in this time zone's daylight savings time period.

SYNTAX `public boolean inDaylightTime(Date date)`

DESCRIPTION

This method determines if `date` falls within the daylight savings time period for this time zone.

Note: There are some issues to keep in mind regarding a date that coincides exactly with the start and end of daylight savings time. See the class description for details.

PARAMETERS

`date` A non-`null` date representing a point in time.

RETURNS `true` if `date` falls within this time zone's daylight savings period; `false` otherwise.

OVERRIDES `TimeZone.inDaylightTime()`.

EXAMPLE See the class example.

setEndRule()

PURPOSE Sets the daylight savings time ending rule.

SYNTAX

```
public void setEndRule(int month, int dayOfWeekInMonth, int
    dayOfWeek, int time)
```

DESCRIPTION

This method sets the end of daylight savings time for this `TimeZone` object. The four parameters together specify the time (in standard time) on which daylight savings time ends.

The type of starting rule that this class can handle must have the form like this: "last Sunday in October at 2 A.M. in standard time." This class cannot handle other types of starting rules, such as "September 4th."

`month` specifies the starting month; for example, `Calendar.APRIL`. `dayOfWeek` specifies one of the 7 days of the week; for example. `Calendar.SUNDAY`. `dayOfWeekInMonth` specifies the *n*th week in the month; for example, `1` means the first week of the month. `dayOfWeekInMonth` can also be negative; for example `-1` means the last week of the month. `dayOfWeekInMonth` cannot be `0`.

`time` is the number of milliseconds after midnight. It is important to note that the time is specified in daylight savings time rather than standard time. For example, suppose `time` was 2 A.M. (2*60*60*1000). Then when the clock is at 2:59:59 A.M.and advances by a second, the time immediately becomes 2 A.M.

When a daylight savings time period is being set, both this method and `setStartRule()` must be used. Otherwise, the effects are undefined. After this method is called, `useDaylightTime()` returns `true`.

Note: In Java 1.1.4, this method has a off-by-one-hour bug. To work around this bug, add 1 hour (that is, 60*60*1000 milliseconds) to the time.

PARAMETERS

`month` The daylight savings time starting month. `Calendar.JANUARY` ≤ `month` ≤ `Calendar.DECEMBER`.

`dayOfWeekInMonth`
The *n*th week of the month.
`dayOfWeekInMonth` ≥ 1 or `dayOfWeekInMonth` ≤ -1.

`dayOfWeek` The daylight savings time starting day-of-week. `Calendar.SUNDAY` ≤ `dayOfWeek` ≤ `Calendar.SATURDAY`.

`time` The daylight savings time starting time. `0` ≤ `time` ≤ `24*60*60*1000`.

SEE ALSO `setStartRule()`.

EXAMPLE See the class example.

setRawOffset()

PURPOSE Sets the time difference from GMT.

SYNTAX `public void setRawOffset(int offsetMillis)`

DESCRIPTION This method sets the raw offset of this `SimpleTimeZone` object to `offsetMillis`. The raw offset is an integer that specifies the number of milliseconds by which a time zone differs from GMT. For example, PST differs by -8*1000*60*60 milliseconds from GMT. The raw offset is based on standard time—the effects of daylight savings time are ignored.

PARAMETERS

`offsetMillis` The number of milliseconds by which this time zone differs from GMT. May be negative.

SEE ALSO `getOffset()`, `getRawOffset()`.

EXAMPLE See `TimeZone.clone()`.

setStartRule()

PURPOSE
Sets the daylight savings time starting rule.

SYNTAX
```
public void setStartRule(int month, int dayOfWeekInMonth, int
   dayOfWeek, int time)
```

DESCRIPTION
This method sets the start of daylight savings time for this `SimpleTimeZone` object. The four parameters together specify a particular day and time (in standard time) on which daylight savings time should start.

The type of starting rule that this class can handle must have the form like this: "1st Sunday in April at 2 A.M. in standard time." This class cannot handle other types of starting rules, such as "March 4th."

`month` specifies the starting month; for example, `Calendar.APRIL`. `dayOfWeek` specifies one of the 7 days of the week; for example. `Calendar.SUNDAY`. `dayOfWeekInMonth` specifies the *n*th week in the month; for example, `1` means the first week of the month. `dayOfWeekInMonth` can also be negative; for example `-1` means the last week of the month. `dayOfWeekInMonth` cannot be `0`.

`time` is the number of milliseconds after midnight. It is important to note that the time is specified in daylight savings time rather than standard time. For example, suppose `time` was 2 A.M. (2*60*60*1000). When the clock is at 1:59:59 A.M. and advances by a second, the time immediately becomes 3 A.M.

When a daylight savings time period is being set, both this method and `setEndRule()` must be used. Otherwise, the effects are undefined. After this method is called, `useDaylightTime()` returns `true`.

PARAMETERS

`month`
The daylight savings starting month. `Calendar.JANUARY` ≤ `month` ≤ `Calendar.DECEMBER`.

`dayOfWeekInMonth`
The *n*th week of the month.
`dayOfWeekInMonth` ≥ `1` or `dayOfWeekInMonth` ≤ `-1`.

`dayOfWeek`
The daylight savings time starting day-of-week.
`Calendar.SUNDAY` ≤ `dayOfWeek` ≤ `Calendar.SATURDAY`.

`time`
The daylight savings time starting time after midnight.
`0` ≤ `time` ≤ `24*60*60*1000`.

SEE ALSO
`setEndRule()`.

EXAMPLE
See the class example.

setStartYear()

PURPOSE Sets the year in which daylight savings time takes effect.

SYNTAX `public void setStartYear(int startYear)`

DESCRIPTION Sets the year in which daylight savings time takes effect to `startYear`. Any time before `startYear` will never be in daylight savings time.

By default, the daylight savings time start year is `0`. After this method is called, `useDaylightTime()` returns `true`.

PARAMETERS

`startYear` The year in which daylight savings time takes effect.

EXAMPLE This example tests whether July 4, 1000 PST is in the daylight savings time period. It is. The PST time zone is then modified so that the starting year for daylight savings time is 1500. After this call, July 4, 1000 PST is no longer in the daylight savings time period.

```
import java.util.*;

class Main {
    public static void main(String[] args) {
        // Daylight savings for PST is between April and October.
        SimpleTimeZone tz = (SimpleTimeZone)TimeZone.getTimeZone("PST");

        // Create an arbitrary point in time.
        Calendar cal = new GregorianCalendar(1000, Calendar.JULY, 4);

        // In daylight savings.
        System.out.println(tz.inDaylightTime(cal.getTime()));    // true

        // Set an abitrary year in which daylight saving time takes effect.
        tz.setStartYear(1500);

        // Not in daylight savings.
        System.out.println(tz.inDaylightTime(cal.getTime()));    // false
    }
}
```

SimpleTimeZone()

PURPOSE Constructs a `SimpleTimeZone` instance.

SYNTAX

```
public SimpleTimeZone(int rawOffset, String ID)
public SimpleTimeZone(int rawOffset, String ID, int startMonth,
   int startDayOfWeekInMonth, int startDayOfWeek, int startTime,
   int endMonth, int endDayOfWeekInMonth, int endDayOfWeek, int
   endTime)
```

DESCRIPTION The two forms of this constructor construct a new instance of `SimpleTimeZone`. `rawOffset` is the number of milliseconds this time zone differs from GMT. For example, PST differs by -8*1000*60*60 milliseconds from GMT. The raw offset is based on standard time (that is, the effects of daylight savings time is ignored.)

`ID` is the time-zone ID for this new time zone. The ID is three characters long. For example, the ID of the Pacific Standard Time time zone is "PST."

`startMonth`, `startDayOfWeekInMonth`, `startDayOfWeek`, and `startTime` together specify the start of daylight savings time. See `setStartRule()` for details on what these parameters mean.

`endMonth`, `endDayOfWeekInMonth`, `endDayOfWeek`, and `endTime` together specify the end of daylight savings time. See `setEndRule()` for details on what these parameters mean.

When the first form of the constructor is used, the new time zone is assumed not to have a daylight savings time; `useDaylightTime()` returns `false`. When the second form of the constructor is used, `useDaylightTime()` returns `true`.

By default, the daylight savings time start year is `0`.

PARAMETERS

`endMonth` The daylight savings time starting month. `Calendar.JANUARY` ≤ `month` ≤ `Calendar.DECEMBER`.

`endDayOfWeekInMonth`
The *n*th week of the month. `endDayOfWeekInMonth` ≥ 1 or `endDayOfWeekInMonth` ≤ -1.

`endDayOfWeek`
The daylight savings time starting day-of-week. `Calendar.SUNDAY` ≤ `endDayOfWeek` ≤ `Calendar.SATURDAY`.

`endTime` The daylight savings time starting time. 0 ≤ `endTime` ≤ `24*60*60*1000`.

`ID` A non-`null` three-character string containing the ID of the time zone.

`rawOffset` The number of milliseconds by which this time zone differs from GMT. May be negative.

`startMonth` The daylight savings time starting month. `Calendar.JANUARY` ≤ `startMonth` ≤ `Calendar.DECEMBER`.

startDayOfWeekInMonth
: The *n*th week of the month. `dayOfWeekInMonth` ≥ 1 or `startDayOfWeekInMonth` ≤ -1.

startDayOfWeek
: The daylight savings time starting day-of-week. `Calendar.SUNDAY` ≤ `startDayOfWeek` ≤ `Calendar.SATURDAY`.

startTime
: The daylight savings time starting time. `0` ≤ `startTime` ≤ `24*60*60*1000`.

EXAMPLE See the class example.

useDaylightTime()

PURPOSE Determines if this `SimpleTimeZone` object has a daylight savings time period.

SYNTAX `public boolean useDaylightTime()`

DESCRIPTION In general, this method returns `true` if this `SimpleTimeZone` object has a daylight savings time period. More precisely, this method returns `true` if one of the following occurs:

- This object was created by the constructor with the daylight savings time parameters.
- `setStartRule()` was called.
- `setEndRule()` was called.
- `setYear()` was called.

RETURNS `true` if this `SimpleTimeZone` object has a daylight savings time period; `false` otherwise.

OVERRIDES `TimeZone.useDaylightTime()`.

EXAMPLE See `TimeZone.getAvailableIDs()`.

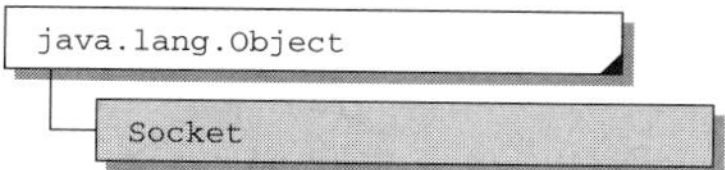

Syntax

```
public class Socket
```

Description

A *socket* is a communications endpoint. The Socket class is used to represent a socket to be used for connection-oriented (streaming) protocols. The DatagramSocket class is used for connection-less protocols.

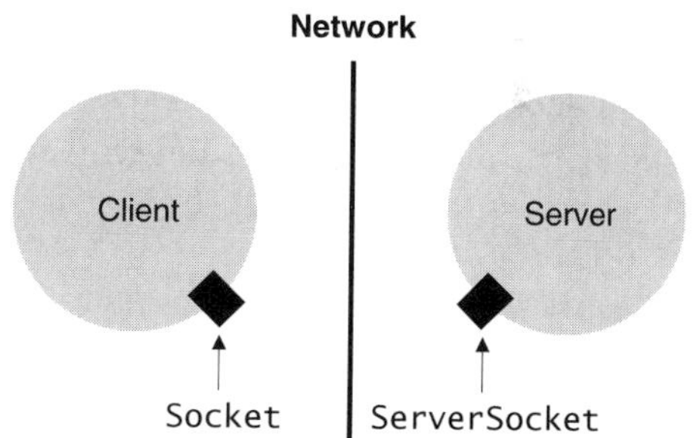

FIGURE 91: **Socket and ServerSocket.**

Usage

In a client/server application, the server creates a server socket and uses it to accept connection requests. See Figure 91. When a request arrives, the server socket creates a new socket in order to communicate with the client. The client communicates with the server by creating a socket with the server's address and port number. The client can then create IO streams with the socket in order to receive from and/or send data to the server.

Socket Implementation Factory

The actual implementation of sockets is supplied by a subclass of `SocketImpl`. When the application creates an instance of `Socket`, a corresponding instance of `SocketImpl` is created. The particular subclass of `SocketImpl` to use is determined by the *socket implementation factory* installed by the application by calling `setSocketImplFactory()`. The factory is responsible for creating instances of `SocketImpl` to be used by sockets. There can be only one socket implementation factory installed in a program at any one time. Once installed, the factory cannot be replaced. If no factory is installed, the `PlainSocketImpl` class[1] is used.

The use of socket implementation factories allows the application to choose its socket implementation depending on the security properties of the network, such as its firewall implementation.

1. `PlainSocketImpl` is a `java.net` package-private implementation of sockets with no security checks. It does implement SOCKS Version 4.

Socket Options

Once a socket has been created, you can set various options on the socket. These options include its socket time-out period, its linger-on-close time-out period, and whether to use Nagle's algorithm for TCP data coalescing. The `Socket` class has methods for getting and setting these socket options.

Socket Time-Out Period

Reading data from a socket sometimes requires waiting, if the socket's peer has not yet sent the data. A socket's time-out period specifies the maximum number of milliseconds that a read operation will block when waiting for data. If the time-out period is `0`, a read operation will block indefinitely until the requested data arrives. If the time-out period is greater than `0`, a read operation will unblock either when the requested data arrives within the time-out period or when `InterruptedIOException` is thrown when the time-out period expires.

A socket's time-out period is set using `setSoTimeout()` and retrieved using `getSoTimeout()`. The default setting is determined by the socket implementation being used.

TCP Data Coalescing

To avoid the overhead and possible congestion of sending many small packets, many TCP implementations use Nagle's algorithm to delay sending a new packet until the receiver acknowledges its receipt of the previously sent packet. During the wait for this acknowledgment, data submitted for the next transmission is coalesced into a single packet. Nagle's algorithm is effective for lowering the number of small packets sent when the total transmission and acknowledgment time of the packet is high (such as with wide-area networks). Some applications, however, require that the small chunks of data that they send be sent as quickly as possible; they cannot afford the delay imposed by Nagle's algorithm. An example is an interactive client/server application in which the user enters small bits of data at a time (such as mouse actions) and expects visual feedback (generated by the server in response to the user's data) as quickly as possible.

Nagle's algorithm is enabled and disabled by using `setTcpNoDelay()`; its setting is retrieved by using `getTcpNoDelay()`. The default setting is determined by the socket implementation being used.

Linger-on-Close

The *linger-on-close* option affects how a socket behaves when it closes. If the linger-on-close option has been disabled, `close()` returns immediately and an attempt is made to deliver any data that has been queued but not yet sent to the socket's peer. If the linger-on-close option has been enabled on a socket, `close()` blocks until any data that has been queued for transmission has been sent to the socket's peer or until the linger time-out period has expired. If the linger time-out period expires before all data is sent, the socket will be closed forcibly and any data not yet sent will be discarded. If linger-on-close has been enabled with a zero linger time-out period, `close()` returns immediately and discards any queued data.

A socket's linger-on-close option is controlled using `setSoLinger()` and retrieved using `getSoLinger()`. The default setting is determined by the socket implementation being used.

MEMBER SUMMARY	
Constructor	
`Socket()`	Constructs a stream socket to the specified destination.
Communications Methods	
`close()`	Closes the socket.
`getInputStream()`	Creates an input stream for this socket.
`getOutputStream()`	Creates an output stream to this socket.
Socket Information Methods	
`getInetAddress()`	Retrieves the remote IP address to which this socket is connected.
`getLocalAddress()`	Retrieves the local IP address used by this socket.
`getLocalPort()`	Retrieves this socket's local port.
`getPort()`	Retrieves this socket's remote port.
`toString()`	Generates the string representation of this object.
Socket Option Methods	
`getSoLinger()`	Retrieves the linger-on-close time-out period of this socket.
`getSoTimeout()`	Retrieves the time-out period of this socket.
`getTcpNoDelay()`	Determines whether this socket is using Nagle's algorithm.
`setSoLinger()`	Sets the linger-on-close time-out period of this socket.
`setSoTimeout()`	Sets the time-out period of this socket.
`setTcpNoDelay()`	Enables or disables Nagle's algorithm on this socket.
Socket Implementation Method	
`setSocketImplFactory()`	Sets the system's client socket implementation factory.

See Also

`DatagramSocket`, `ServerSocket`, `SocketImpl`, `SocketImplFactory`.

Example

This example implements a new-mail checker. It implements just enough of the POP3 protocol (see *RFC 1225* at `http://ds.internic.net/rfc/rfc1225.txt`) to determine if there are any unread messages in a POP3 server. If new unread messages are detected (or if a protocol error occurs), a window is displayed containing a message. See Figure 92.

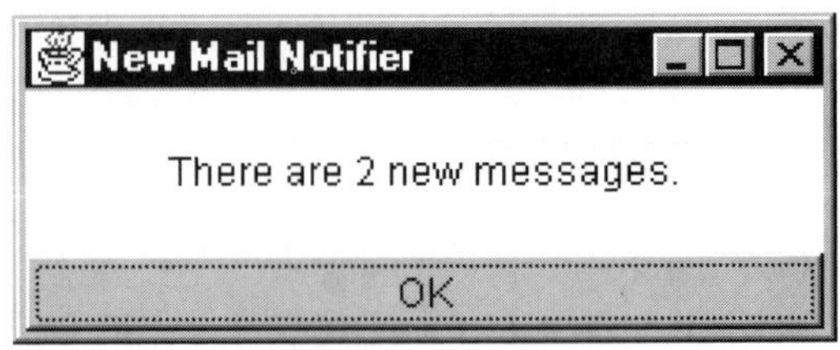

FIGURE 92: Mail Notifier.

A thread is created that checks the server every 10 minutes. Each time the thread checks, it creates a socket to the server and then sends out four commands: USER, PASS, STAT, and QUIT. The server's reply to the STAT command contains the number of unread messages.

One useful enhancement to this program is to play a sound file instead of displaying a message when new unread messages are detected.

For a simpler example of using sockets, see `getInputStream()`.

```
import java.awt.*;
import java.awt.event.*;
import java.net.*;
import java.io.*;
import java.util.*;

class Main extends Frame implements ActionListener, Runnable {
    static final int DELAY_MS = 10 * 60 * 1000;    // 10 minutes.

    // The number of new messages in the POP3 server.
    int numMessages;

    // Socket parameters.
    String hostname;
    String user;
    String password;
    int port;

    // Components.
    Label message = new Label("", Label.CENTER);
    Button okBtn = new Button("OK");

    Main(String user, String hostname, String password, int port) {
        super("New Mail Notifier");
        this.user = user;
        this.hostname = hostname;
        this.password = password;
        this.port = port;

        // Create user interface.
        add(message, BorderLayout.CENTER);
        add(okBtn, BorderLayout.SOUTH);
        okBtn.addActionListener(this);
        setSize(250, 100);

        (new Thread(this)).start();
```

```
    }

    public void actionPerformed(ActionEvent evt) {
        setVisible(false);
    }

    public void run() {
        while (true) {
            Socket socket = null;

            try {
                socket = new Socket(hostname, port);
                BufferedInputStream is = new BufferedInputStream(
                    socket.getInputStream());
                BufferedOutputStream os = new BufferedOutputStream(
                    socket.getOutputStream());
                String line;

                // Skip welcome message.
                recv(is);

                send(os, "USER " + user + "\r\n");
                if (error(line = recv(is))) {
                    continue;
                }

                send(os, "PASS " + password + "\r\n");
                if (error(line = recv(is))) {
                    continue;
                }

                send(os, "STAT\r\n");
                if (error(line = recv(is))) {
                    continue;
                }

                // Retrieve number of messages from STAT command.
                StringTokenizer st = new StringTokenizer(line);
                st.nextToken();    // skip +OK
                int m = Integer.parseInt(st.nextToken());
                if (m != numMessages) {
                    if (m > numMessages) {
                        message.setText("There are "+m+" new messages.");
                        show();
                        toFront();
                    }
                    numMessages = m;
                }

                send(os, "QUIT");
            } catch (Exception e) {
                e.printStackTrace();
            } finally {
                if (socket != null) {
                    try {
                        socket.close();
                    } catch (IOException e) {
                        e.printStackTrace();
                    }
                }
```

```
            }

            // Sleep
            try {
                Thread.sleep(DELAY_MS);
            } catch (Exception e) {
                e.printStackTrace();
            }
        }
    }

    // Display an error message if the reply does not start with a '+'.
    boolean error(String msg) {
        if (msg.charAt(0) != '+') {
            message.setText("ERROR: "+msg);
            show();
            return true;
        }
        return false;
    }

    // Sends a string to the POP3 server.
    void send(OutputStream os, String s) throws IOException {
        for (int i=0; i<s.length(); i++) {
            os.write((byte)s.charAt(i));
        }
        os.flush();
    }

    // Receives a reply from the POP3 server.
    String recv(InputStream is) throws IOException {
        String result = "";
        int c = is.read();

        while (c >= 0 && c != '\n') {
            if (c != '\r') {
                result += (char)c;
            }
            c = is.read();
        }
        return result;
    }

    public static void main(String[] args) {
        if (args.length < 3) {
            System.err.println("Usage: java Main <user> <host> "
                + "<password> [port]");
            return;
        }

        if (args.length > 3) {
            new Main(args[0], args[1], args[2], Integer.parseInt(args[3]));
        } else {
            new Main(args[0], args[1], args[2], 110);
        }
    }
}
```

close()

PURPOSE Closes this socket.

SYNTAX `public synchronized void close() throws IOException`

DESCRIPTION Because sockets are a limited system resource, a socket should be closed when it is no longer needed. Closing a socket frees up resources associated with the socket (e.g., streams, file descriptors, and socket descriptors) and allows the ports that were bound to the socket to be reused. You cannot send or receive data from a socket once it has been closed.

The behavior of `close()` is affected by the *linger-on-close* option, described in the class description.

EXCEPTIONS

`IOException`

If an IO error occurred when closing the socket.

SEE ALSO `getSoLinger()`, `setSoLinger()`, `java.io.IOException`, `SocketImpl.close()`.

EXAMPLE See `getInputStream()`.

getInetAddress()

PURPOSE Retrieves the remote IP address to which this socket is connected.

SYNTAX `public InetAddress getInetAddress()`

RETURNS The non-`null` address of this socket's remote host.

SEE ALSO `getPort()`, `SocketImpl.getInetAddress()`.

EXAMPLE

```
public static void socketDetails(Socket s) {
    System.out.println("Socket description " + s.toString());
    System.out.println("Destination: " + s.getInetAddress() + "/" +
                        s.getPort());
    System.out.println("Source: " + s.getLocalAddress() + "/" +
                        s.getLocalPort());
}
```

getInputStream()

PURPOSE Creates an input stream for this socket.

SYNTAX `public InputStream getInputStream() throws IOException`

DESCRIPTION This method creates an input stream for this socket so that you can read data from this socket. By using filter streams, you can compose this stream with input streams that have other properties. For example, filtering could be used to obtain the data in the expected format or to improve the performance of the stream by buffering so that not all reads require direct interaction with the socket. Data sent by the remote host to this socket can be read from this input stream. Input streams and output streams can coexist on a socket.

Once a socket has been closed, any input streams created from it are also closed. Attempting to read from an input stream of a closed socket raises an IO exception.

The behavior of read operations on an input stream associated with a socket is affected by the socket's time-out period, which is described in more detail in the class description.

RETURNS A non-`null` input stream that allows reading data from the socket.

SEE ALSO `getOutputStream()`, `getSoTimeout()`, `java.io.BufferedInputStream`, `java.io.FilterInputStream`, `java.io.InputStream`, `setSoTimeout()`, `SocketImpl.getInputStream()`.

EXAMPLE This example is a client-side routine that creates a connection to a destination and reads and echoes the data from the input stream.

```
public static void echoer(InetAddress dst, int port) {
    try {
        Socket client = new Socket(dst, port);
        InputStream in = client.getInputStream();

        for (int ch = in.read(); ch > 0; ch = in.read()) {
            System.out.print((char)ch);
        }
        client.close();
    } catch (IOException e) {
        e.printStackTrace();
    }
}
```

getLocalAddress()

PURPOSE Retrieves the local IP address used by this socket.

SYNTAX `public InetAddress getInetAddress()`

DESCRIPTION When you create a socket, you can specify the local IP address to use. This is useful for a multihomed host—a machine with more than one network interface, each having its own IP address. If you do not specify the local address to use, it defaults to the platform-dependent system default.

`getLocalAddress()` returns the local address being used for this socket.

RETURNS The non-`null` local IP address used by this socket.

SEE ALSO `InetAddress`, `getLocalPort()`, `ServerSocket()`, `SocketImpl.getInetAddress()`.

EXAMPLE See `getInetAddress()`.

getLocalPort()

PURPOSE Retrieves this socket's local port.

SYNTAX `public int getLocalPort()`

DESCRIPTION When a socket is created, you can specify the local port to use or leave it to the system to select any available port. `getLocalPort()` returns this port number (whether specified by you or selected by the system).

RETURNS The port being used for this socket on the local machine.

SEE ALSO `DatagramPacket.getPort()`, `getInetAddress()`, `getLocalAddress()`, `getPort()`, `SocketImpl.getLocalPort()`.

EXAMPLE See `getInetAddress()`.

getOutputStream()

PURPOSE Creates an output stream to this socket.

SYNTAX `public OutputStream getOutputStream() throws IOException`

DESCRIPTION This method creates an output stream to this socket so that you can send data to the remote host connected to this socket. By using filter streams, you can compose this stream with output streams that have other properties. For example, filtering could be used to send the data in the desired format or to improve the performance of the stream by buffering the data so that not all output operations interact directly with the socket. Data sent to this stream can be read from the other endpoint of the socket (by using `getInputStream()`). Input streams and output streams can coexist on a socket.

Once a socket has been closed, any output streams created from it are also closed. Attempting to send data to an output stream of a closed socket throws an `IOException`.

RETURNS An output stream for sending data to the remote host.

SEE ALSO `getInputStream()`, `java.io.BufferedOutputStream`, `java.io.FilterOutputStream`, `java.io.OutputStream`, `SocketImpl.getOutputStream()`.

EXAMPLE

```
// write string to socket
public static void writeToSocket(Socket s, String msg) {
    try {
        OutputStream out = s.getOutputStream();
        if (out != null) {
            byte[] ob = msg.getBytes();
            out.write(ob);
            out.flush();
            // close() will happen when socket gets closed
        }
    } catch (IOException e) {
        System.err.println("Had problems with writing to socket: " + e);
    }
}
```

getPort()

PURPOSE Retrieves this socket's remote port.

SYNTAX `public int getPort()`

DESCRIPTION A socket has two endpoints. Each endpoint is identified by the IP address of the machine to which it is connected and the port on the machine being used. This method returns the port that is being used by this socket on the remote machine to send and receive data.

RETURNS The port being used for the socket on the remote machine.

SEE ALSO `getInetAddress()`, `getLocalPort()`, `SocketImpl.getPort()`.

EXAMPLE See `getInetAddress()`.

A B C D E F G H I J K L M N O P Q R S T U V W X Y Z

getSoLinger()

PURPOSE Retrieves the linger-on-close time-out period of this socket.

SYNTAX `public int getSoLinger() throws SocketException`

DESCRIPTION This method retrieves the *linger-on-close* time-out period of this socket. The linger-on-close option is described in the class description.

RETURNS The maximum number of milliseconds that `close()` will block; `-1` if linger-on-close has been disabled for this socket.

EXCEPTIONS

`SocketException`

If an error occurred while attempting to get the socket's linger-on-close time-out period.

SEE ALSO `setSoLinger()`, `SocketImpl.getOption()`, `SocketException`.

EXAMPLE See `setSoLinger()`.

getSoTimeout()

PURPOSE Retrieves the time-out period of this socket.

SYNTAX `public synchronized int getSoTimeout() throws SocketException`

DESCRIPTION This method retrieves the *time-out* period of this socket. A socket's time-out period specifies the maximum number of milliseconds that a read operation on the socket will block while waiting for data. It is described in more detail in the class description.

RETURNS A nonnegative number specifying the maximum number of milliseconds that a read operation will block. If `0`, a read operation will block indefinitely until the requested data arrives.

EXCEPTIONS

`SocketException`

If an error occurs while attempting to get the socket's time-out period.

SEE ALSO `setSoTimeout()`, `SocketImpl.getOption()`, `SocketException`.

EXAMPLE See `setSoTimeout()`.

getTcpNoDelay()

PURPOSE Determines whether this socket is using Nagle's algorithm.

SYNTAX `public boolean getTcpNoDelay() throws SocketException`

DESCRIPTION This method determines whether Nagel's algorithm is being used for this socket. Nagle's algorithm for TCP data coalescing is described in the class description.

RETURNS `true` if Nagle's algorithm has been disabled; `false` otherwise.

EXCEPTIONS

`SocketException`
If an error occurred while attempting to get the Nagle's algorithm option of the socket.

SEE ALSO `setTcpNoDelay()`, `SocketImpl.getOption()`, `SocketException`.

EXAMPLE See `setTcpNoDelay()`.

setSocketImplFactory()

PURPOSE Sets the system's client socket implementation factory.

SYNTAX
```
public static synchronized void
    setSocketImplFactory(SocketImplFactory factory) throws
    IOException
```

DESCRIPTION The actual implementation of sockets is supplied by a subclass of `SocketImpl` that is created by the socket implementation factory installed by the application. This method sets `factory` to be the socket implementation factory. `factory` is responsible for creating an instance of (subclasses of) `SocketImpl` whenever a new socket is created.

`setSocketImplFactory()` can be executed only if permitted to do so by the security manager. If it is permitted, it can be executed only once during the application's lifetime.

PARAMETERS

`factory` The non-`null` socket implementation factory to use.

EXCEPTIONS

`IOException`
If an IO error occurred while setting the socket implementation factory.

`SecurityException`
If not allowed to set the socket implementation factory due to security reasons.

`SocketException`
If a socket implementation factory has already been defined.

SEE ALSO `java.io.IOException`, `java.lang.SecurityManager.checkSetFactory()`, `Socket()`, `SocketImpl`, `SocketImplFactory`.

EXAMPLE See the `SocketImplFactory` class example for a definition of `DebugSocketImplFactory`.

```
try {
    Socket.setSocketImplFactory(new DebugSocketImplFactory());
} catch (IOException e) {
    System.out.println("Cannot set Socket factory: " + e);
}
```


setSoLinger()

PURPOSE Sets the linger-on-close time-out period of this socket.

SYNTAX
```
public void setSoLinger(boolean on, int timeout) throws
   SocketException
```

DESCRIPTION The linger-on-close option is described in the class description. If `on` is `true`, this socket's linger-on-close option is enabled and its linger-on-close time-out period is set to `timeout` milliseconds. If `on` is `false`, this socket's linger-on-close option is disabled and `timeout` is ignored.

PARAMETERS

`on` If `true`, enable the linger-on-close option; if `false`, disable the linger-on-close option.

`timeout` A nonnegative number specifying the maximum number of milliseconds that `close()` will block until the socket is forcibly closed. If `0`, `close()` will return immediately. `timeout` is ignored if `on` is `false`.

EXCEPTIONS

`SocketException`

If an error occurred while attempting to set the socket's linger-on-close time-out period.

SEE ALSO `close()`, `getSoLinger()`, `SocketException`, `SocketImpl.setOption()`.

EXAMPLE This is a modified version of the `getInputStream()` example that demonstrates the use of `setSoLinger()` and `getSoLinger()`.

```
public static void lingerEchoer(InetAddress dst, int port, int lingerTimeout)
{
    try {
      Socket client = new Socket(dst, port);

      System.out.println("Original linger option: " +
                         client.getSoLinger() + "ms");
```

```
        // enable linger-on-close option and set linger timeout period
        client.setSoLinger(true, lingerTimeout);

        System.out.println("Updated linger option: " +
                           client.getSoLinger() + "ms");

        InputStream in = client.getInputStream();

        for (int ch = in.read(); ch > 0; ch = in.read()) {
          System.out.print((char)ch);
        }

        // close is affected by setting of linger-on-close above
        client.close();
      } catch (IOException e) {
        e.printStackTrace();
      }
    }
```


setSoTimeout()

PURPOSE Sets the time-out period of this socket.

SYNTAX `public synchronized void setSoTimeout(int timeout) throws SocketException`

DESCRIPTION A socket's time-out period specifies the maximum number of milliseconds that a read operation on the socket will block when waiting for data. It is described in more detail in the class description.

PARAMETERS

`timeout` A nonnegative number specifying the maximum number of milliseconds that a read operation will block. If `0`, a read operation will block indefinitely until the requested data arrives.

EXCEPTIONS

`SocketException`
If an error occurred while attempting to set the socket's time-out period.

SEE ALSO `getSoTimeout()`, `SocketException`, `SocketImpl.setOption()`.

EXAMPLE This is a modified version of the `getInputStream()` example. Instead of just creating a socket and echoing the data received, this example sets a time-out period on the socket and keeps track of how many attempts have timed-out. Note that even though the socket times-out, it is still usable for subsequent read operations.

```
    public static void impatientEchoer(InetAddress dst, int port,
                                       int timeout, int retries) {
      try {
        Socket client = new Socket(dst, port);
```

```
        client.setSoTimeout(timeout); // set socket timeout period
        System.out.println("Setting maximum waiting period to " +
                           client.getSoTimeout() + "ms");
        InputStream in = client.getInputStream();

        for (int i=0; i <retries; i++) {
          try {
            for (int ch = in.read(); ch > 0; ch = in.read()) {
              System.out.print((char)ch);
            }
            break;
          } catch (InterruptedIOException timedout) {
            System.err.println("Timedout on try " + i);
            // try again, socket and stream are still valid
          }
        }
        client.close();
      } catch (IOException e) {
        e.printStackTrace();
      }
    }
```

setTcpNoDelay()

PURPOSE Enables or disables Nagle's algorithm on this socket.

SYNTAX `public void setTcpNoDelay(boolean on) throws SocketException`

DESCRIPTION The socket option for Nagle's algorithm for TCP data coalescing is described in the class description. `setTcpNoDelay()` disables the use of Nagle's algorithm if `on` is `true` and enables its use if `on` is `false`.

PARAMETERS

`on` If `true`, disables Nagle's algorithm; if `false`, enables Nagle's algorithm.

EXCEPTIONS

`SocketException`

If an error occurred while attempting to set the Nagle's algorithm option of the socket.

SEE ALSO `getTcpNoDelay()`, `SocketException`, `SocketImpl.setOption()`.

EXAMPLE In this example, before data is written to the output stream of the socket, `setTcpNoDelay()` is invoked on the socket to disable Nagle's algorithm.

```
Socket sock = srvSock.accept();

System.out.println("Socket's original nodelay setting:" +
                   (sock.getTcpNoDelay() ? "on" : "off"));

// enable Tcp no-delay (disable Nagle's algorithm)
sock.setTcpNoDelay(true);
```

```
System.out.println("Socket's updated nodelay setting:" +
                   (sock.getTcpNoDelay() ? "on" : "off"));

OutputStream out = sock.getOutputStream();
String answer = (new Date()).toString();
byte[] b = answer.getBytes();
out.write(b, 0, b.length);
out.write('\n');
out.flush();
sock.close();
```


Socket()

PURPOSE Constructs a stream socket to the specified destination.

SYNTAX

```
public Socket(String hostName, int dstPort) throws
   UnknownHostException, IOException
public Socket(InetAddress dstAddr, int dstPort) throws IOException
public Socket(String hostName, int dstPort, InetAddress localAddr,
   int localPort) throws UnknownHostException, IOException
public Socket(InetAddress dstAddr, int dstPort, InetAddress
   localAddr, int localPort) throws IOException
protected Socket()
protected Socket(SocketImpl impl) throws SocketException
```

DEPRECATED
```
public Socket(String hostName, int port, boolean stream) throws
   UnknownHostException, IOException
```

DEPRECATED
```
public Socket(InetAddress dst, int port, boolean stream) throws
   IOException
```

The four public forms of this constructor construct a stream socket for communicating with the specified destination. The destination can be specified using either the host name `hostName` of the remote machine or the IP address `dstAddr` of the remote machine. In either case, you must specify the port `dstPort` to use on the remote machine. After creating a socket, you can set options on the socket and create IO streams for it so that you can communicate with the destination. When you no longer need the socket, be sure to close it to free up resources associated with it. You can create a socket to the destination specified (the target machine's IP address and port number) only if allowed to do so by the security manager.

If `localPort` is `0` or unspecified, the socket is bound to any locally available port. The use of certain ports is restricted (for example, those well-known ports for Internet protocols such as FTP, Telnet, and SMTP) and the use of *any* port is permitted only if allowed by the security manager.

`localAddr` is useful when creating a socket on a multihomed host—a machine with more than one network interface, each having its own IP address. `local-`

Addr specifies which one of the multiple addresses of the local machine to use. If localAddr is not specified, it defaults to the platform-dependent system default. To determine which local address is being used for this socket, use getLocalAddress().

The two protected forms of this constructor are called by subclasses of Socket to create an unconnected socket using a socket implementation. If impl is specified, it is used for the socket's implementation. If impl is not specified, a new socket implementation is created using the socket implementation factory installed. If no factory has been installed, a new instance of PlainSocketImpl[1] is used.

A B C D E F G H I J K L M N O P Q R S T U V W X Y Z

PARAMETERS

dstAddr	The destination's IP address.
dstPort	The destination's port number. 0 ≤ dstPort ≤ 65535.
hostName	The non-null destination's host name.
impl	The non-null socket implementation to use for this socket.
localAddr	The possibly null local IP address to which to bind the socket. If localAddr is not specified, use any local address.
localPort	The local port number to which to bind the socket. 0 ≤ localPort ≤ 65535. If localPort is 0 or not specified, use any available port
stream	true means create a stream socket; false means create a datagram socket.

RETURNS A new socket for communicating with the remote host.

EXCEPTIONS

IOException
If an IO error occurred while creating the socket.

SecurityException
If the connection to the destination cannot be made due to security reasons.

UnknownHostException
If hostName cannot be resolved (that is, its IP address cannot be found).

DEPRECATION In Java 1.0, the Socket class supports both datagram sockets or stream (connection-oriented) sockets. Two forms of its constructor allowed a stream argument to be supplied. If stream is true, a stream socket is created; otherwise, a datagram socket is created. These the two forms of the constructor are deprecated. To create stream sockets, use the corresponding forms without the stream argument:

```
Socket s = new Socket(host, dstPort);
Socket s2 = new Socket(dstAddr, dstPort);
```

1. PlainSocketImpl is a java.net package-private implementation of sockets with no security checks. It does implement SOCKS Version 4.

For datagram sockets, use the DatagramSocket class to create the socket and then specify the address of the destination in the datagram packet:

```
DatagramSocket s = new DatagramSocket();
DatagramPacket packet = new DatagramPacket(buf, count, dstAddr,
    dstPort);
s.send(packet);    // send packet to (dstAddr, dstPort)
s.receive(packet); // receive packet from (dstAddr, dstPort)
```

SEE ALSO BindException, ConnectException, DatagramSocket, java.io.IOException, java.lang.SecurityManager.checkConnect(), NoRouteToHostException, setSoLinger(), setSoTimeout(), setTcpNoDelay(), setSocketImpl.create(), SocketImpl.connect().

EXAMPLE This example illustrates various ways of creating a socket. socketDetails() is defined in the toString() example.

```
try {
    // Connect to hostname, port = 9 ('discard' port)
    Socket sock = new Socket(target, 9);
    socketDetails(sock);
    writeToSocket(sock, "this is a test");
    sock.close();

    // This time use InetAddr
    InetAddress dstAddr = InetAddress.getByName(target);
    Socket sock2 = new Socket(dstAddr, 9);
    socketDetails(sock2);
    writeToSocket(sock2, "this is a test");
    sock2.close();

    // This time specify local address and local port to use
    InetAddress localAddr = InetAddress.getLocalHost();  // pick any
    int localPort = 1500;
    Socket sock3 = new Socket(dstAddr, 9, localAddr, localPort);
    socketDetails(sock3);
    writeToSocket(sock3, "this is a test");
    sock3.close();

    // Do the same thing using a host name instead of InetAddr
    Socket sock4 = new Socket(target, 9, localAddr, 2001);
    socketDetails(sock4);
    writeToSocket(sock4, "this is a test");
    sock4.close();
} catch (IOException e) {
    e.printStackTrace();
}
```

toString()

PURPOSE Generates the string representation of this object.

SYNTAX `public String toString()`

DESCRIPTION The string representation of a socket consists of its remote IP address and port and its local port. `toString()` returns the representation of this socket.

RETURNS The non-`null` string representation of this socket.

OVERRIDES `java.lang.Object.toString()`.

SEE ALSO `getInetAddress()`, `getLocalPort()`, `getPort()`.

EXAMPLE

```
public static void socketDetails(Socket s) {
    System.out.println("Socket description " + s.toString());
    System.out.println("Destination: " + s.getInetAddress() + "/" +
        s.getPort());
    System.out.println("Source: " + s.getLocalAddress() + "/" +
        s.getLocalPort());
}
```

java.net
SocketException

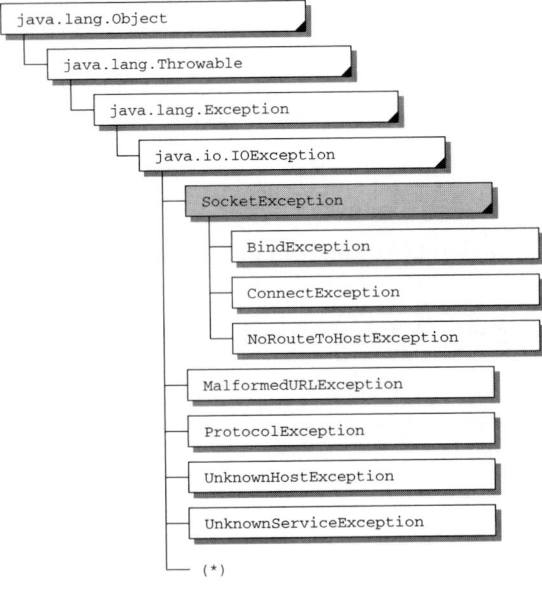

(*) 10 classes from other packages not shown.

A B C D E F G H I J K L M N O P Q R S T U V W X Y Z

Syntax

```
public class SocketException extends IOException
```

Description

`SocketException` is an exception that is thrown when the program attempts to create a socket, to manipulate a socket's options, or to set a program's socket factory when one has already been set.

A method that throws `SocketException` must declare it or any of its superclasses in the method's `throws` clause.

MEMBER SUMMARY	
Constructor	
`SocketException()`	Constructs a `SocketException` instance.

See Also

DatagramSocket, java.io.IOException, ProtocolException, ServerSocket, Socket, SocketImpl.

Example

This example throws a SocketException when it attempts set the time-to-live value of a multicast socket to an unacceptable value.

```
import java.net.MulticastSocket;
import java.io.IOException;

class Main {
    public static void main(String[] args) {
        try {
            // Set the time-to-live to something outrageous.
            MulticastSocket sock = new MulticastSocket();
            sock.setTTL((byte)127); // OK
            sock.setTTL((byte)128); // Not OK (arg is treated as unsigned)
            sock.close();
        } catch (IOException e) {
            e.printStackTrace();
        }
    }
}
```

SocketException()

PURPOSE Constructs a SocketException instance.

SYNTAX

```
public SocketException()
public SocketException(String msg)
```

DESCRIPTION The two forms of this constructor construct an instance of SocketException. An optional string msg can be supplied that describes this particular instance of the exception. If msg is not specified, it defaults to null.

PARAMETERS

msg A possibly null string that gives details about this exception.

SEE ALSO java.lang.Throwable.getMessage().

SocketImpl

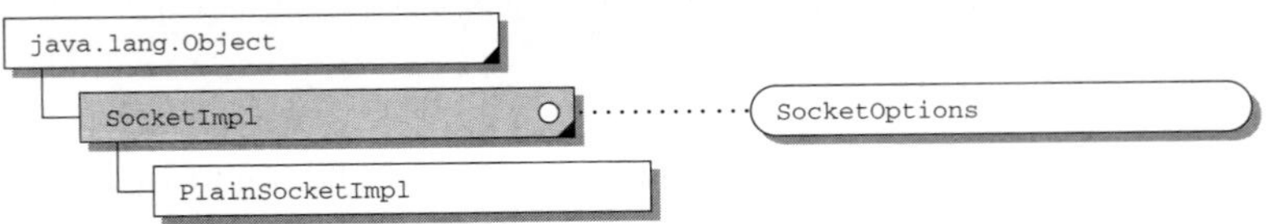

Syntax

```
public abstract class SocketImpl implements SocketOptions
```

Description

The Java programmer uses the methods in the `Socket` and `ServerSocket` classes to write applications that communicate with each other using stream sockets. Java allows a program (such as a Web browser) to choose its socket implementation depending on the security properties of the network, such as its firewall implementation. It does this by defining a socket implementation class, `SocketImpl`, which is used by the `Socket` and `ServerSocket` classes. It is a subclass (provided by the program) of `SocketImpl` that provides the actual implementation for sockets.

`SocketImpl` is designed for implementing stream sockets. For datagram sockets, use `DatagramSocketImpl`.

Usage

The methods in `SocketImpl` are invoked from `Socket` and `ServerSocket` and are not invoked directly by the program.

To provide a socket implementation, you provide a subclass of `SocketImpl` that contains implementations for the abstract methods declared in `SocketImpl`. (See the class example.)

Socket and Server Socket Implementation Factories

The particular subclass of `SocketImpl` to use is determined by *socket implementation factories* installed by the application. The program uses `Socket.setSocketImplFactory()` to install the factory for `Socket` and uses `ServerSocket.setSocketFactory()` to set the factory for `ServerSocket`. A program can have different factories for `Socket` and `ServerSocket`. However, there can be only one socket implementation factory and one server socket implementation factory installed in a program at any one time. Once installed, the factories cannot be replaced. If no factory is installed, the `PlainSocketImpl` class[1] is used.

1. `PlainSocketImpl` is a `java.net` package-private implementation of sockets with no security checks. It does implement SOCKS Version 4.

Changing Socket State

The first step for a client that is using a socket is to create an unconnected socket. A socket must be connected before it is used. Once it is connected, you can get IO streams on it in order to send and/or receive data. When you no longer need the socket, you must close it in order to free this limited resource.

A server must first create an unconnected server socket and bind its own address to it. It then listens on the socket for connection requests and queues them as they arrive. It accepts a connection request by creating a new socket to communicate with the client, while keeping the original server socket open for listening for and queueing more connection requests. The server must close each new socket created for accepting a connection.

MEMBER SUMMARY	
Methods for Changing Socket State (Abstract)	
`accept()`	Accepts a connection request for this socket.
`bind()`	Binds this socket to the local port.
`close()`	Closes this socket.
`connect()`	Connects this socket to a destination.
`create()`	Creates a new unconnected socket.
`listen()`	Listens for connection requests on this stream socket.
Methods for Communicating via Sockets (Abstract)	
`available()`	Determines the number of bytes that can be read from this socket without blocking.
`getInputStream()`	Creates an input stream for this socket.
`getOutputStream()`	Creates an output stream for this socket.
Socket Information Fields	
`address`	The IP address to which this socket is connected.
`fd`	This socket's file descriptor.
`localport`	This socket's local port number.
`port`	This socket's remote port number.
Socket Information Methods	
`getFileDescriptor()`	Retrieves the file descriptor used by this socket.
`getInetAddress()`	Retrieves the IP address to which this socket is connected.
`getLocalPort()`	Retrieves this socket's local port number.
`getPort()`	Retrieves this socket's remote port number.
`toString()`	Generates the string representation of this object.

See Also

`DatagramSocket`, `DatagramSocketImpl`, `ServerSocket`, `Socket`, `SocketImplFactory`.

Example

The JDK contains a package-private class `PlainSocketImpl` that implements sockets by using native methods that have no security checks. This is the implementation that is used when no socket implementation factory has been set. Typically, the application (e.g., a Web browser) installs its own socket implementation factory for security reasons, so this default implementation is not used. `PlainSocketImpl` gives you a good idea of how to build socket implementations. The following example extends `PlainSocketImpl` to give some debugging output. Because this new class is being added to the `java.net` package, the class file for the following must be installed in `$JAVA_HOME/classes/java/net`:

```
package java.net;

import java.io.*;
import java.net.PlainSocketImpl;

/**
 * Wrapper around default socket implementation that
 * provides debugging information.
 */

public class DebugSocketImpl extends PlainSocketImpl
{
    protected synchronized void create(boolean stream) throws IOException {
        System.err.println("Creating " +
                           (stream ? "virtual circuit" : "datagram") +
                           " socket.");
        super.create(stream);
    }

    protected void connect(String host, int port)
        throws UnknownHostException, IOException
    {
        System.err.println("Connecting to " + host + " at port " + port);
        super.connect(host, port);
    }

    protected void connect(InetAddress address, int port) throws IOException {
        System.err.println("Connect to " + address + " at port " + port);
        super.connect(address, port);
    }

    protected synchronized void bind(InetAddress address, int lport)
        throws IOException
    {
        System.err.println("Binding " + address + " at local port " + lport);
        super.bind(address, lport);
    }

    protected synchronized void listen(int count) throws IOException {
        System.err.println("Listening for " + count + " msec");
        super.listen(count);
    }

    protected synchronized void accept(SocketImpl s) throws IOException {
        System.err.println("Accepting connection for " + s.toString());
        super.accept(s);
```

```
    }

    protected synchronized InputStream getInputStream() throws IOException {
        System.err.println("Returning input stream for this socket");
        return super.getInputStream();
    }

    protected synchronized OutputStream getOutputStream() throws IOException {
        System.err.println("Returning output stream for this socket");
        return super.getOutputStream();
    }

    protected synchronized void close() throws IOException {
        System.err.println("Closing socket");
        super.close();
    }

    protected synchronized void finalize() throws IOException {
        System.err.println("Finalizing socket");
        super.finalize();
    }
}
```


accept()

PURPOSE Accepts a connection request for this socket.

SYNTAX `protected abstract void accept(SocketImpl newSocket) throws IOException`

DESCRIPTION This method accepts the next pending connection request on this socket using `newSocket`. If there are no pending connection requests, `accept()` blocks until one arrives.

You must create `newSocket` (typically using the server socket implementation factory) before invoking `accept()`. `accept()` should invoke `newSocket.create()` and fill in the IP address, port numbers, and file descriptor fields of `newSocket` when the connection is made. After `accept()` returns, `newSocket` can be used to send and receive data to and from the remote host of the accepted connection request. When the connection is terminated, `newSocket` must be closed. This socket remains available for listening and queueing pending connection requests.

PARAMETERS

`newSocket` The new socket created for establishing the accepted connection request.

EXCEPTIONS

`IOException`

If an IO error occurred while accepting the next connection request.

SEE ALSO `java.io.IOException`.

EXAMPLE This example shows how an existing socket implementation creates a socket implementation for accepting a new connection request.

```
SocketImpl impl = factory.createSocketImpl();
impl.create(true);                    // create stream socket
impl.address = new InetAddress();     // use package private constructor
impl.fd = new FileDescriptor();
this.accept(impl);    // accept connection req and fill in address, ports, fd
```

address

PURPOSE The IP address to which this socket is connected.

SYNTAX `protected InetAddress address`

DESCRIPTION For a client stream socket, `address` is the IP address of this socket's remote host. For a server stream socket (the one on which the server is listening), `address` is the local machine's IP address to which the socket is bound.

SEE ALSO `getAddress()`.

EXAMPLE See `accept()`.

available()

PURPOSE Determines the number of bytes that can be read from this socket without blocking.

SYNTAX `protected abstract int available() throws IOException`

RETURNS The number of bytes that can be read without blocking.

EXCEPTIONS

`IOException`
If an error occurred while determining the number of bytes.

SEE ALSO `getInputStream()`.

EXAMPLE

```
SocketImpl impl = factory.createSocketImpl();
    ...
System.out.println("Bytes available from socket: " +
    impl.available());
```

bind()

PURPOSE Binds this socket to the local port.

SYNTAX
```
protected abstract void bind(InetAddress localAddr, int
    localPort) throws IOException
```

DESCRIPTION After a stream socket has been created, it must be bound to a local address and port before it can listen for connections. This method binds this socket to the port `localPort` on the local machine and the local address `localAddr`. Use of certain ports is restricted (e.g., those well-known ports for Internet protocols such as FTP, Telnet, and SMTP).

PARAMETERS

`localPort` The local port number to use for this socket. `0` ≤ `localPort` ≤ `65535`. If `lport` is `0`, any available port is used.

`localAddr` The non-`null` IP address of this machine to use.

EXCEPTIONS

`IOException`

If an IO error occurred while attempting to bind this socket to `localAddr` and `localPort`.

SEE ALSO `java.io.IOException, listen(), ServerSocket.ServerSocket()`.

EXAMPLE The following code fragment shows the typical steps involved in setting up a server socket:

```
SocketImpl impl = factory.createSocketImpl();
impl.create(true);
impl.bind(InetAddress.getLocalHost(), port);
impl.listen(queueSize);
```

close()

PURPOSE Closes this socket.

SYNTAX
```
protected abstract void close() throws IOException
```

DESCRIPTION This method closes this socket. A `close()` method typically frees up the resources used for this socket, such as its file descriptor, streams, and port numbers.

EXCEPTIONS

`IOException`

If an IO error occurred when closing the socket.

SEE ALSO `ServerSocket.close(), Socket.close()`.

EXAMPLE See `connect()`.

connect()

PURPOSE Connects this socket to a destination.

SYNTAX
```
protected abstract void connect(String hostName, int port) throws
   IOException
protected abstract void connect(InetAddress dst, int port) throws
   IOException
```

DESCRIPTION After a socket has been created, it must be connected to a destination before it can be used. `connect()` connects this socket to the port `port` on the machine named by `hostName` or on the machine with IP address `dst`. After a socket has been connected, the socket can then send and receive data.

For a stream socket, `connect()` typically attempts to contact the destination as part of the operation.

PARAMETERS

`dst` The IP address of the remote host.

`hostName` The name of the remote host.

`port` The port on the remote host. $0 \le$ `port` ≤ 65535.

EXCEPTIONS

`IOException`
If an IO error occurred while attempting to connect to the destination.

SEE ALSO `create()`, `getInputStream()`, `getOutputStream()`, `Socket.Socket()`.

EXAMPLE This code fragment shows how a client creates a socket to a destination (`destHost`, `destPort`).

```
SocketImpl impl = factory.createSocketImpl();
impl.create(true); // create in "stream" mode
impl.connect(destHost, destPort);
...                  // use the socket
impl.close();
```

create()

PURPOSE Creates a new unconnected socket.

SYNTAX
```
protected abstract void create(boolean stream) throws IOException
```

DESCRIPTION This method creates a stream socket if `stream` is `true`; otherwise, it creates a datagram socket. Creation of a socket typically involves allocating a file descriptor to be used for the socket.

A socket must be connected before any data may be sent or received on it.

DEPRECATION Use of `Socket` for datagram sockets is deprecated. `SocketImpl` can provide support for datagram sockets, but the recommended approach is to use `DatagramSocket` and `DatagramSocketImpl`.

PARAMETERS

`stream` `true` means create a stream socket; `false` means create a datagram socket.

EXCEPTIONS

`IOException`

If an IO error occurred during the creation of the stream.

SEE ALSO `bind()`, `connect()`, `DatagramSocket.DatagramSocket()`, `ServerSocket.ServerSocket()`, `Socket.Socket()`.

EXAMPLE See `accept()`.

fd

PURPOSE This socket's file descriptor.

SYNTAX `protected FileDescriptor fd`

SEE ALSO `getFileDescriptor()`.

EXAMPLE See `accept()`.

getFileDescriptor()

PURPOSE Retrieves the file descriptor used by this socket.

SYNTAX `protected FileDescriptor getFileDescriptor()`

DESCRIPTION A socket typically has a file descriptor that is used for doing IO. This method returns the file descriptor associated with this socket.

RETURNS This socket's file descriptor.

SEE ALSO `fd`, `getInputStream()`, `getOutputStream()`, `java.io.FileDescriptor`.

EXAMPLE This code fragment prints information about a socket.

```
System.out.println("fd: " + impl.getFileDescriptor());
System.out.println("inetAddr: " + impl.getInetAddress());
System.out.println("port: " + impl.getPort());
System.out.println("local port: " + impl.getLocalPort());
```

A B C D E F G H I J K L M N O P Q R S T U V W X Y Z

getInetAddress()

PURPOSE Retrieves the IP address to which this socket is connected.

SYNTAX `protected InetAddress getInetAddress()`

DESCRIPTION For a client stream socket, `getInetAddress()` returns the IP address of this socket's remote host. For a server stream socket (the one on which the server is listening), `getInetAddress()` returns the local machine's IP address used for binding this socket.

RETURNS The IP address to which this socket is connected.

SEE ALSO `address`, `InetAddress`, `Socket.getInetAddress()`, `ServerSocket.getInetAddress()`.

EXAMPLE See `getFileDescriptor()`.

getInputStream()

PURPOSE Creates an input stream for this socket.

SYNTAX
```
protected abstract InputStream getInputStream() throws
   IOException
```

DESCRIPTION After a socket has been connected, you can receive data from it by first creating an input stream for it and then reading data from this input stream. A typical implementation would use the file descriptor of this socket for creating its input stream.

RETURNS An input stream for receiving data from this socket.

EXCEPTIONS

`IOException`
If an IO error occurred while creating the input stream.

SEE ALSO `getOutputStream()`, `java.io.InputStream`, `java.io.IOException`, `Socket.getInputStream()`.

EXAMPLE See the class example.

getLocalPort()

PURPOSE Retrieves this socket's local port number.

SYNTAX `protected int getLocalPort()`

RETURNS This socket's local port number.

SEE ALSO `localport`, `ServerSocket.getLocalPort()`.

EXAMPLE See `getFileDescriptor()`.

getOutputStream()

PURPOSE Creates an output stream for this socket.

SYNTAX
```
protected abstract OutputStream getOutputStream() throws
   IOException
```

DESCRIPTION After a socket has been connected, you can send data to the socket by first creating an output stream to it and then sending data to this output stream. `getOutputStream()` creates an output stream for this socket. A typical implementation would use the file descriptor of this socket for creating its output stream.

RETURNS An output stream for sending data to the remote host.

EXCEPTIONS

`IOException`

If an IO error occurred while creating the output stream.

SEE ALSO `getInputStream()`, `java.io.IOException`, `java.io.OutputStream`, `Socket.getOutputStream()`.

EXAMPLE See the class example.

getPort()

PURPOSE Retrieves this socket's remote port number.

SYNTAX
```
protected int getPort()
```

RETURNS This socket's remote port number.

SEE ALSO `port`, `Socket.getPort()`.

EXAMPLE See `getFileDescriptor()`.

listen()

PURPOSE Listens for connection requests on this stream socket.

SYNTAX `protected abstract void listen(int backlog) throws IOException`

DESCRIPTION After a stream socket has been created and bound, the `listen()` call is used to set the socket into "listening" mode. In this mode, connection set-up requests sent to this socket are queued until the server is ready to accept them. `backlog` specifies the maximum number of pending connections this socket can have. When this socket has `backlog` number of pending connection requests, clients attempting to make further connections to this socket will fail with an `IOException`.

`listen()` can be invoked only on stream sockets; it does not apply to datagram sockets. Typically, `listen()` is invoked, then `accept()` is called in a loop to accept process connections as they arrive.

PARAMETERS

`backlog` The maximum number of pending connection requests this socket can have.

EXCEPTIONS

`IOException`

If an IO error occurred while listening for connections.

SEE ALSO `accept()`, `java.io.IOException`, `ServerSocket.ServerSocket()`.

EXAMPLE See `bind()`.

localport

PURPOSE This socket's local port number.

SYNTAX `protected int localport`

SEE ALSO `getLocalPort()`.

EXAMPLE

```
SocketImpl impl = factory.createSocketImpl();
    ...
System.out.println("Local port:" + impl.localport);
System.out.println("Remote port: " + impl.port);
```

port

PURPOSE This socket's remote port number.

SYNTAX `protected int port`

SEE ALSO `getPort()`.

EXAMPLE See `localport`.

toString()

PURPOSE Generates the string representation of this object.

SYNTAX `public String toString()`

DESCRIPTION The string representation of a socket consists of its destination address (IP address plus remote port number) and the local port number being used for the socket. `toString()` returns the string representation of this socket.

RETURNS The non-`null` string representation of this socket.

OVERRIDES `java.lang.Object.toString()`.

SEE ALSO `getInetAddress()`, `getLocalPort()`, `getPort()`.

EXAMPLE

```
SocketImpl impl = factory.createSocketImpl();
System.out.println("This is what a newly created SocketImpl looks like: "
    + impl.toString());
```

java.net
SocketImplFactory

SocketImplFactory

A B C D E F G H I J K L M N O P Q R S T U V W X Y Z

Syntax

```
public interface SocketImplFactory
```

Description

The `SocketImplFactory` interface defines a factory for `SocketImpl` instances. It is used by the socket classes to create socket implementations that implement various policies.

Socket Implementations

In socket programming, Java programs use the methods in the `Socket` and `ServerSocket` classes. Java allows a program (such as a Web browser) to choose its socket implementation depending on the security properties of the network, such as its firewall implementation. To do this, it defines a socket implementation class, `SocketImpl`, which is used by the `Socket` and `ServerSocket` classes. It is a subclass (provided by the program) of `SocketImpl` that provides the actual implementation for sockets.

Socket Implementation Factories

The particular subclass of `SocketImpl` to use is determined by *socket implementation factories* installed by the application. The program uses `Socket.setSocketImplFactory()` to install the factory for `Socket` and uses `ServerSocket.setSocketFactory()` to set the factory for `ServerSocket`. A program can have different factories for `Socket` and `ServerSocket`. However, there can be only one socket implementation factory and one server socket implementation factory installed in a program at any one time. Once installed, the factories cannot be replaced. If no factory is installed, the `PlainSocketImpl` class (a `java.net` package-private socket implementation) is used.

MEMBER SUMMARY	
Implementation Creation Method	
`createSocketImpl()`	Creates a socket implementation.

See Also

`ServerSocket.setSocketFactory()`, `Socket.setSocketImplFactory()`, `SocketImpl`.

Example

This example defines a socket implementation factory `DebugSocketImplFactory` that creates and returns a new instance of `DebugSocketImpl` for each request to create a new socket implementation. See the class example of `SocketImpl` for the definition of `DebugSocketImpl`, and see `ServerSocket.setSocketFactory()` for how to set the socket factory to be `DebugSocketImplFactory`.

```
import java.net.SocketImplFactory;
import java.net.SocketImpl;

public class
DebugSocketImplFactory implements SocketImplFactory {
    public SocketImpl createSocketImpl() {
        return new DebugSocketImpl();
    }
}
```

createSocketImpl()

PURPOSE	Creates a socket implementation.
SYNTAX	`SocketImpl createSocketImpl()`
DESCRIPTION	This method creates an instance of `SocketImpl`. It is used by the constructors in `ServerSocket` and `Socket` when instances of `ServerSocket` and `Socket` classes, respectively, are created.
SEE ALSO	`ServerSocket.ServerSocket()`, `Socket.Socket()`.
EXAMPLE	See the class example.

java.util
Stack

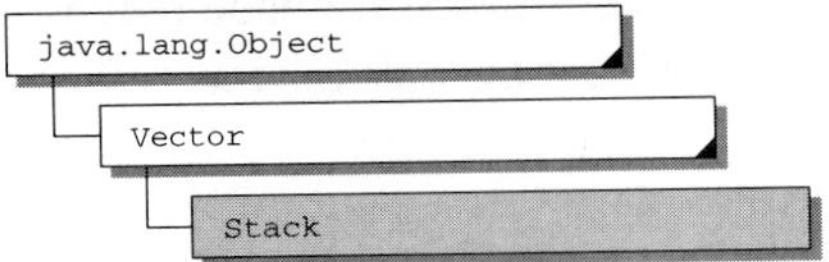

Syntax

```
public class Stack extends Vector
```

Description

The `Stack` class represents a last-in/first-out (LIFO) stack of objects. It provides methods for popping and pushing possibly `null` objects onto the stack. There is no limit to the size of the stack. If you try to pop objects from an empty stack, an `EmptyStackException` will be raised. See Figure 93.

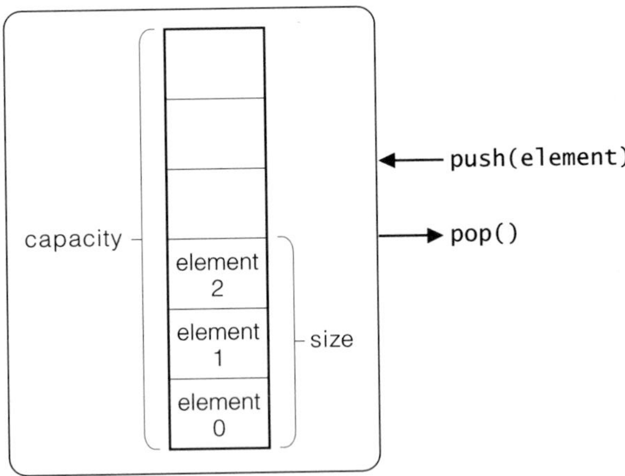

FIGURE 93: `Stack`.

MEMBER SUMMARY	
Stack Methods	
`empty()`	Determines whether this stack is empty.
`peek()`	Retrieves the top object of this stack without removing it.
`pop()`	Removes the top object from this stack.
`push()`	Pushes an object onto the top of this stack.
`search()`	Searches for an object on this stack.

See Also

`EmptyStackException`, `Vector`.

Example

This example uses a stack to maintain a stack of newspapers. A newspaper that is pushed on top of another newspaper must first be removed (popped) before the newspaper beneath it can be removed. This example shows the use of the various methods in the `Stack` class.

```
import java.util.Stack;
import java.util.Date;
import java.util.EmptyStackException;

class Newspaper {
    Date date;
    String publisher;
    Newspaper(String pub, Date d) {
        date = d;
        publisher = pub;
    }
    Newspaper(String pub) {
        this(pub, new Date()); // use today's date
    }
    public String toString() {
        return (publisher + " " + date);
    }
}
class Main {
    public static void main(String[] args) {
        Stack newspapers = new Stack();

        Newspaper NYT = new Newspaper("New York Times");
        Newspaper SJM = new Newspaper("San Jose Mercury News");
        Newspaper SFC = new Newspaper("San Francisco Chronicle");
        Newspaper WSJ = new Newspaper("Wall Street Journal");

        // push onto stack
        newspapers.push(NYT);
        newspapers.push(SJM);
        newspapers.push(SFC);

        int where = newspapers.search(SJM);
        System.out.println(SJM + " is at the " + where + " position");

        where = newspapers.search(WSJ);
        if (where > 0)
            System.out.println(WSJ + " is at the " + where + " position");
        else
            System.out.println(WSJ + " is not on the stack");

        try {
            Newspaper top = (Newspaper) newspapers.peek();
            System.out.println("Top contains " + top);

            do {
                top = (Newspaper) newspapers.pop();
                System.out.println("Popped off " + top);
            } while (!newspapers.empty());

        } catch (EmptyStackException e) {
            System.out.println("Trying to go beyond bottom of stack");
        }
    }
}
```

empty()

PURPOSE Determines whether this stack is empty.

SYNTAX `public boolean empty()`

RETURNS `true` if this stack is empty; `false` otherwise.

EXAMPLE See the class example.

peek()

PURPOSE Retrieves the top object from this stack without removing it.

SYNTAX `public synchronized Object peek()`

RETURNS The top object from this stack; `null` if the top object is `null`.

EXCEPTIONS

`EmptyStackException`
If this stack is empty.

SEE ALSO `pop()`.

EXAMPLE See the class example.

pop()

PURPOSE Removes the top object of this stack.

SYNTAX `public synchronized Object pop()`

DESCRIPTION This method removes the top object from this stack and returns it.

RETURNS The top object from this stack; `null` if the top object is `null`.

EXCEPTIONS

`EmptyStackException`
If this stack is empty.

SEE ALSO `peek()`, `push()`.

EXAMPLE See the class example.

push()

PURPOSE Pushes an object onto the top of this stack.

SYNTAX `public Object push(Object obj)`

DESCRIPTION This method pushes the object `obj` onto the top of this stack and returns `obj`.

PARAMETERS

`obj` The possibly `null` object to push.

RETURNS `obj`.

SEE ALSO `peek()`, `pop()`.

EXAMPLE See the class example.

search()

PURPOSE Searches for an object on this stack.

SYNTAX `public synchronized int search(Object obj)`

DESCRIPTION This method searches for the object `obj` on this stack. If `obj` is on this stack, this method returns its position on the stack as measured from the top of the stack. For example, if `obj` is at the top of the stack, its position is 1; if `obj` is next to the top on the stack, its position is 2, and so on. If `obj` is not on this stack, `-1` is returned. If more than one instance of `obj` is on the stack, the position of the one closest to the top of the stack is returned.

PARAMETERS

`obj` The object for which to search. `obj` cannot be `null`.

RETURNS The position of `obj` on the stack (1 is top of stack); `-1` if `obj` is not found.

EXAMPLE See the class example.

java.lang
StackOverflowError

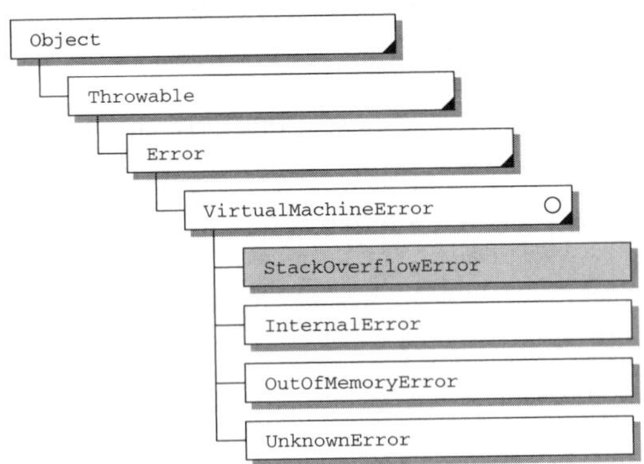

A B C D E F G H I J K L M N O P Q R S T U V W X Y Z

Syntax

```
public class StackOverflowError extends VirtualMachineError
```

Description

When the Java virtual machine executes a program, the execution environment (e.g., parameters and variables) of each method that it calls is placed on an execution stack. For example, if method `A` was to call method `B`, which in turn would call method `C`, the execution stack would contain {`C, B, A`}. `StackOverflowError` is an unrecoverable error raised by the Java virtual machine when the execution stack overflows as it is attempting to execute a method. Usually, this indicates a problem with the calling sequence of methods, rather than a problem with the limit of the execution stack. For example, a nonterminating, tail-recursive program would overflow the stack because the execution stack cannot be infinitely large.

`StackOverflowError` should not be caught or declared in the `throws` clause of a method.

MEMBER SUMMARY	
Constructor	
`StackOverflowError()`	Constructs a `StackOverflowError` instance.

See Also

`Error`, `VirtualMachineError`.

Example

This example throws a `StackOverflowError` because the calling sequence never terminates.

```
class Main {
    public static void method1() {
        method2();
    }
    public static void method2() {
        method1();
    }
    public static void main(String[] args) {
        System.out.println("StackOverflowError example");
        method1();
    }
}
```


StackOverflowError()

PURPOSE Constructs a `StackOverflowError` instance.

SYNTAX
```
public StackOverflowError()
public StackOverflowError(String msg)
```

DESCRIPTION The two forms of this constructor construct an instance of `StackOverflowError`. An optional string `msg` can be supplied that describes this particular instance of the error. If `msg` is not supplied, it defaults to `null`.

PARAMETERS

`msg` A possibly `null` string that gives details about this error.

SEE ALSO `Throwable.getMessage()`.

java.io

StreamCorruptedException

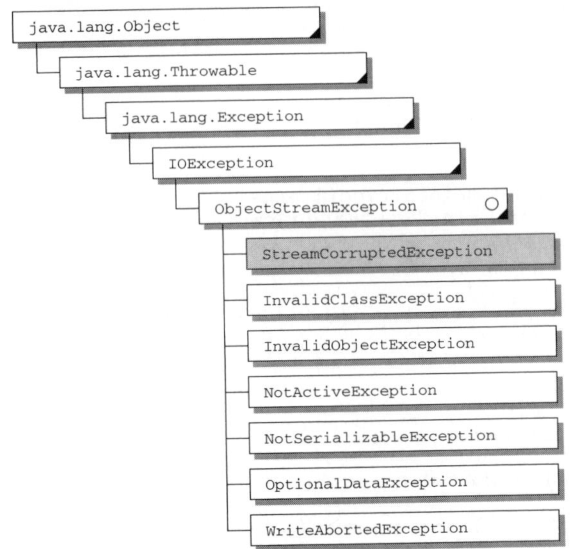

A B C D E F G H I J K L M N O P Q R S T U V W X Y Z

Syntax

```
public class StreamCorruptedException extends ObjectStreamException
```

Description

A `StreamCorruptedException` is thrown when it cannot read an object from the object input stream because control information in the stream does not match the data in the stream. It is thrown by `ObjectInputStream.readObject()` and the `ObjectInputStream` constructor.

This exception is thrown when one of the following occurs.

- The stream contains a handle to a serialized object that is not found in the stream
- The serialized object is that of a class whose serialized class descriptor is not found in the stream, the serialized data for an object ends abruptly before the entire object is deserialized, or end-of-stream is encountered before the entire object is deserialized

MEMBER SUMMARY	
Constructor	
`StreamCorruptedException()`	Constructs an instance of `StreamCorruptedException`.

See Also

ObjectInputStream.

Example

This example throws StreamCorruptedException when it creates an ObjectInputStream for a file that does not contain serialized data.

```
import java.io.*;

class Main {
    public static void main(String[] args) {
        try {
            // Try to create an ObjectInputStream for
            // a non-object stream.
            FileInputStream f2 = new FileInputStream("Main.class");
            ObjectInputStream in = new ObjectInputStream(f2);
            System.out.println(in.readObject());
            in.close();
        } catch (IOException e) {
            e.printStackTrace();
        } catch (ClassNotFoundException e) {
            e.printStackTrace();
        }
    }
}
```

A B C D E F G H I J K L M N O P Q R S T U V W X Y Z

StreamCorruptedException()

PURPOSE: Constructs an instance of StreamCorruptedException.

SYNTAX:
```
public StreamCorruptedException()
public StreamCorruptedException(String msg)
```

DESCRIPTION: The two forms of this constructor construct an instance of StreamCorruptedException. An optional string msg can be supplied that describes this particular instance of the exception. If msg is not specified, it defaults to null.

PARAMETERS

msg: A possibly null string containing the detail message.

SEE ALSO: java.lang.Throwable.getMessage().

StreamTokenizer

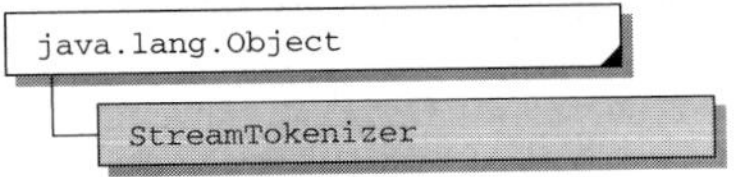

A B C D E F G H I J K L M N O P Q R S T U V W X Y Z

Syntax

```
public class StreamTokenizer
```

Description

The `StreamTokenizer` class reads from an input stream to produce a stream of tokens (see Figure 94). The input stream is parsed according to the syntax defined by the stream tokenizer. The stream tokenizer is defined using the syntactic elements defined in Table 38.

By default, the stream tokenizer defines various settings for characters that are word characters, characters that are whitespace characters, and so on. You can customize your stream tokenizer by changing these settings using the methods provided by the `StreamTokenizer` class.

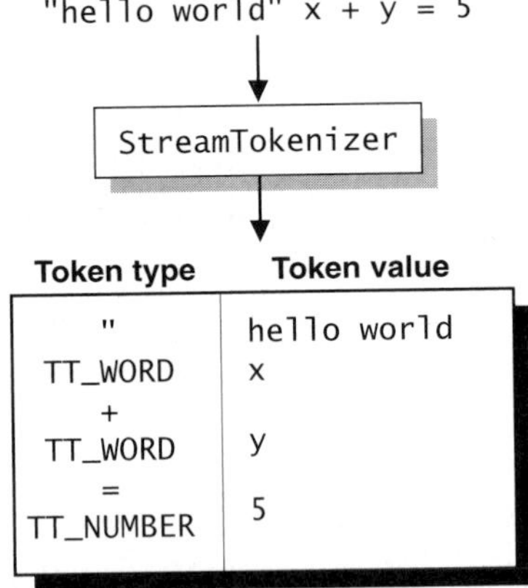

FIGURE 94: **`StreamTokenizer`.**

Syntactic Element	Description
Number	A sequence of digits characters of a double-precision floating-point number.
Word	A sequence of consecutive word characters delimited by whitespace characters.
String	A sequence of characters delimited by matching quote characters.
Comment	Characters that are for comments only and not parsed as tokens.
EOF	Indicates that an end-of-file has been reached on the stream.
EOL	Indicates that an end-of-line has been encountered in the stream.
Whitespace	Whitespace characters are used to separate word tokens from word tokens and number tokens from number tokens.

TABLE 38: **Syntactic Elements of a Stream Tokenizer.**

Usage

You use the stream tokenizer first by calling its constructor to create it. Then you call various syntax-specifying methods to customize it. Finally, you call `nextToken()` in a loop to parse the stream into tokens.

Byte Streams versus Character Streams

The stream tokenizer can be constructed using either an `InputStream` or a `Reader`. The `InputStream` form is deprecated because it does not, in general, convert bytes to characters properly. Each byte read from the input stream is treated as a character in the range 0–255. Characters read from the reader can span the range of valid Unicode characters. Characters with a `char` value greater than 255 are always treated as "word" characters only. You cannot specify that such characters be treated as numbers, ordinary characters, comments, or quotes.

MEMBER SUMMARY	
Constructor	
`StreamTokenizer()`	Constructs a `StreamTokenizer` instance for an input stream.
Syntax-Specifying Methods	
`commentChar()`	Specifies a character as the start of a single-line comment.
`eolIsSignificant()`	Specifies whether an end-of-line is recognized as a token.
`lowerCaseMode()`	Specifies whether word tokens are automatically made lowercase.
`ordinaryChar()`	Specifies a character as being ordinary.
`ordinaryChars()`	Specifies characters in a range as being ordinary.
`parseNumbers()`	Specifies that digit characters are used for number tokens.
`quoteChar()`	Specifies a character as a quote character.
`resetSyntax()`	Resets the syntax table so that all characters are ordinary.
`slashSlashComments()`	Specifies whether to recognize C++-style comments.
`slashStarComments()`	Specifies whether to recognize C-style comments.
`whitespaceChars()`	Specifies that characters in this range are whitespace characters.
`wordChars()`	Specifies that characters in this range are word characters.
Parsing Methods	
`lineno()`	Retrieves the current input line number.
`pushBack()`	Pushes back a token onto the input stream.
`nextToken()`	Parses a token from the input stream.
Token Fields	
`nval`	The numeric value of the number token.
`sval`	The string value of the word or string token.
`ttype`	The type of the token returned.

Continued

MEMBER SUMMARY	
Token Type Constants	
`TT_EOF`	The end-of-file token type.
`TT_EOL`	The end-of-line token type.
`TT_NUMBER`	The number token type.
`TT_WORD`	The word token type.
Description Method	
`toString()`	Generates the string representation of the token.

See Also

`StringTokenizer`.

Example

This example uses the stream tokenizer to parse a list of key/value pairs and places those pairs into a hash table. The key is separated from the value using either whitespace characters or an equals character (=).

```
import java.util.Hashtable;
import java.io.*;

class KeyValue {
    public static void parser(Reader in, Hashtable h) {
        StreamTokenizer p = new StreamTokenizer(in);

        // key values are separated by white spaces or '='
        p.whitespaceChars('=', '=');
        int c;
        String key = null;
        boolean errFlag = false;
        boolean expecting_value = false;
        try {
        out:
            while (true) {
                c = p.nextToken();
                switch (c) {
                case StreamTokenizer.TT_EOF:
                    break out;
                case StreamTokenizer.TT_EOL:
                    // should not see this because we didn't make
                    // EOL significant
                    System.err.println("warning: unexpected EOL token");
                    break;
                case StreamTokenizer.TT_NUMBER:
                    if (expecting_value) {
                        h.put(key, new Double(p.nval));
                        expecting_value = false;
                    } else {
                        // cannot have numeric keys
```

```
                    errFlag = true;
                    break out;
                }
                break;
            case StreamTokenizer.TT_WORD:
                if (expecting_value) {
                    h.put(key, p.sval);
                    expecting_value = false;
                } else {
                    expecting_value = true;
                    key = p.sval;
                }
                break;
            default:
                errFlag = true;
                break out;
            }
        }
        if (errFlag)
            System.err.println("Error encountered around '" + key +"'");
    } catch (IOException e) {
        e.printStackTrace();
    }
}
public static void main(String[] args) {
    Hashtable h = new Hashtable();
    parser(new InputStreamReader(System.in), h);
    System.out.println(h.toString());
}
}
```


commentChar()

PURPOSE
Specifies a character as the start of a single-line comment.

SYNTAX
`public void commentChar(int ch)`

DESCRIPTION
This method specifies that the character `ch` is used to denote the start of a single-line comment. When `ch` is encountered in the input stream, all characters between `ch` and the end of the line are treated as a single-line comment. Comments are not returned by the parser (`nextToken()`).

There can be many such comment characters. By default, the forward slash character (/) is a comment character.

PARAMETERS

`ch`
The character to be used as the start of a single-line comment. If `ch` < `0` or `ch` > `255`, this method does nothing.

SEE ALSO
`nextToken()`, `slashSlashComments()`, `slashStarComments()`.

EXAMPLE
This example shows the different ways that comments can be specified to the stream tokenizer. This example turns on both // and /* comments. It also uses

to begin single-line comments. The default / comment character must be turned off in order for /* comments to be recognized.

```
import java.io.*;

class Main {
    public static void main(String[] args) {
        try {
            StreamTokenizer tokens = new StreamTokenizer(
                new InputStreamReader(System.in));
            // turn off single slash as comment char, this is required
            // for slashStar comments to work properly
            tokens.ordinaryChar('/');
            tokens.slashStarComments(true);
            tokens.slashSlashComments(true);

            tokens.commentChar('#');
            int c;
        out:
            while (true) {
                switch (c=tokens.nextToken()) {
                case StreamTokenizer.TT_EOF:
                    break out;
                case StreamTokenizer.TT_EOL:
                    System.out.print("\n" + tokens.lineno() + "\t");
                    break;
                case StreamTokenizer.TT_NUMBER:
                    System.out.println("Number: " + tokens.nval);
                    break;
                case StreamTokenizer.TT_WORD:
                    System.out.println("Identifier: " + tokens.sval);
                    break;
                }
            }
        } catch (IOException e) {
            e.printStackTrace();
        }
    }
}
```

eolIsSignificant()

PURPOSE Specifies whether an end-of-line is recognized as a token.

SYNTAX `public void eolIsSignificant(boolean eolSign)`

DESCRIPTION This method specifies whether end-of-line characters are significant. If they are, then when an end-of-line (one of \n, \r, or \r\n) is encountered, the token type TT_EOL is returned in ttype. If they are not significant, end-of-line characters are treated as whitespace characters. If eolSign is true, end-of-line characters are significant; if eolSign is false, end-of-line characters are not significant. By default, they are not significant.

PARAMETERS

`eolSign` — `true` means end-of-lines are significant; `false` means end-of-lines are treated as whitespaces.

SEE ALSO `nextToken()`, `TT_EOL`, `ttype`.

EXAMPLE See `nextToken()`.

lineno()

PURPOSE Retrieves the current input line number.

SYNTAX `public int lineno()`

RETURNS The current input line number.

EXAMPLE See `nextToken()`.

lowerCaseMode()

PURPOSE Specifies whether word tokens are automatically made lowercase.

SYNTAX `public void lowerCaseMode(boolean lower)`

DESCRIPTION This method specifies whether word tokens parsed from this stream will automatically be made lowercase before being returned. If `lower` is `true`, word tokens (`sval`) are made lowercase before being returned in `sval`. If `lower` is `false`, the case of characters in word tokens is left unchanged. By default, the case is left unchanged.

PARAMETERS

`lower` — `true` means automatically make word tokens lowercase; `false` means leave word tokens as is.

SEE ALSO `java.lang.String.toLowerCase()`, `sval`, `TT_WORD`.

EXAMPLE See `nextToken()`.

nextToken()

PURPOSE Parses a token from the input stream.

SYNTAX `public int nextToken() throws IOException`

DESCRIPTION This method parses the next token in the input stream. It uses the syntax as specified by the program to determine what defines a token. `nextToken()`

returns the token type of the token or the character read from the stream (this is the same as the value of `ttype`). If the token type is `TT_NUMBER`, the value of the token is returned in `nval`. If the token type is `TT_WORD` or one of the quote characters, the value of the token is returned in `sval`. `TT_EOL` indicates an end-of-line has been encountered; `TT_EOF` indicates an end-of-file has been encountered in the stream. If the return value is none of `TT_NUMBER`, `TT_WORD`, `TT_EOL`, or `TT_EOF`, it is the character read from the input stream.

RETURNS The token type of the next token (one of `TT_NUMBER`, `TT_WORD`, `TT_EOL`, or `TT_EOF`) or the next character in the input stream.

EXCEPTIONS

`IOException`
If an IO error occurred while attempting to read the next token.

SEE ALSO `nval`, `sval`, `TT_EOF`, `TT_EOL`, `TT_NUMBER`, `TT_WORD`, `ttype`.

EXAMPLE See also the class example, `commentChar()`, and `parseNumbers()`. This example demonstrates the use of `nextToken()` and various syntax specifiers. To have digit characters be treated as word characters, you first must reset the syntax and then add back the word characters and whitespace characters.

```
import java.io.*;

class Main {
    public static void main(String[] args) {
        try {
            StreamTokenizer tokens = new StreamTokenizer(
                new InputStreamReader(System.in));

            tokens.resetSyntax();
            tokens.wordChars('0', '9');        // make digit chars word chars
            tokens.wordChars('a', 'z');
            tokens.wordChars('A', 'Z');
            tokens.eolIsSignificant(true);
            tokens.quoteChar('"');             // " is quoted string delimiter
            tokens.whitespaceChars(0, ' ');
            tokens.whitespaceChars('$', '$');  // treat $ as white space
            tokens.lowerCaseMode(true);        // turn tokens to lowercase
            int c;
        out:
            while (true) {
                switch (c=tokens.nextToken()) {
                case StreamTokenizer.TT_EOF:
                    break out;
                case StreamTokenizer.TT_EOL:
                    System.out.print("\n" + tokens.lineno() + "\t");
                    break;
                case StreamTokenizer.TT_NUMBER:
                    // unexpected because we made digit chars words
                    System.err.println(
                        "warning: unexpected number: " + tokens.nval);
                    break;
                case StreamTokenizer.TT_WORD:
```

```
                    System.out.println("Identifier: " + tokens.sval);
                    break;
                case '"':
                    System.out.println("Quoted String: " + tokens.sval);
                    break;
                default:
                    System.out.println("Default: " + (char)c);
                }
            }
        } catch (IOException e) {
            e.printStackTrace();
        }
    }
}
```


nval

PURPOSE The numeric value of the number token.

SYNTAX `public double nval`

DESCRIPTION This field stores the numeric value of the token being returned by `nextToken()`. Numeric tokens are returned only if the syntax specifies that digit characters should be treated as numbers. Otherwise, digit characters are treated as ordinary characters.

SEE ALSO `nextToken()`, `parseNumbers()`, `TT_NUMBER`.

EXAMPLE See the class example, `commentChar()`, and `nextToken()`.

ordinaryChar()

PURPOSE Specifies a character as being ordinary.

SYNTAX `public void ordinaryChar(int ch)`

DESCRIPTION This method specifies that the character `ch` is ordinary. When `ch` is encountered in the input stream, it is not treated as a word character, comment, string, whitespace character, or number character. It is simply returned as is by `nextToken()`.

All other characters not set by the `StreamTokenizer` constructor are, by default, ordinary characters. You can call `ordinaryChar()` or `ordinaryChars()` several times to set different ranges of characters to be ordinary characters. You can set a character that is an ordinary character to be some other type of character by calling `wordChars()` or other syntax-specifying methods.

PARAMETERS

ch — The character to be classified as ordinary. If `ch` < `0` or `ch` > `255`, this method does nothing.

SEE ALSO — `ordinaryChars()`, `StreamTokenizer()`.

EXAMPLE — See `commentChar()`.

A B C D E F G H I J K L M N O P Q R S T U V W X Y Z

ordinaryChars()

PURPOSE — Specifies characters in a range as being ordinary.

SYNTAX — `public void ordinaryChars(int low, int hi)`

DESCRIPTION — This method specifies that the characters in the range of Unicode characters `low` to `hi`, inclusive, are ordinary. Any of these characters encountered in the input stream will not be treated as a word character, comment, string, whitespace character, or number character. They are simply returned as is by `nextToken()`.

All other characters with `char` values in the range 0–255, inclusive, that have not been set by the `StreamTokenizer` constructor are, by default, ordinary characters. Characters with `char` values outside of this range are word characters and cannot be set to ordinary characters.

You can call `ordinaryChar()` or `ordinaryChars()` several times to set different ranges of characters to be ordinary characters. You can set a character that is an ordinary character to be some other type of character by calling `wordChars()` or other syntax-specifying methods.

PARAMETERS

hi — The last Unicode character in the range of ordinary characters. Inclusive. If `hi` > `255`, 255 is used as the upper limit in the range.

low — The first Unicode character in the range of ordinary characters. Inclusive. If `low` < `0`, 0 is used as the lower limit in the range.

SEE ALSO — `ordinaryChar()`, `StreamTokenizer()`.

EXAMPLE — See the use of `ordinaryChar()` in the `commentChar()` example for an example of a similar usage.

parseNumbers()

PURPOSE — Specifies that digit characters are used for number tokens.

SYNTAX — `public void parseNumbers()`

DESCRIPTION

This method specifies that the digit characters (0–9, period (.), and minus (–)) are to be used in constructing number tokens. Digit characters also can appear as part of a word if they occur in the second or higher position of the word. When a number token (any double-precision floating-point number) is encountered in the input stream, `nextToken()` returns `tt_number` and sets the field `nval` to be the numeric value of the token. Once `parseNumbers()` has been invoked, the only way to undo its effects (i.e., specify that digit characters are not to be used for number tokens) is to call `ordinaryChar()` or `wordChars()` explicitly on those characters.

The default `StreamTokenizer` constructor calls `parseNumbers()`.

SEE ALSO

`nextToken()`, `nval`, `tt_number`.

EXAMPLE

This example recognizes only numbers as tokens. All other nonwhitespace characters are not returned as tokens but are treated as individual characters.

```
import java.io.*;

class Main {
    public static void main(String[] args) {
        try {
            StreamTokenizer tokens = new StreamTokenizer(
                new InputStreamReader(System.in));

            tokens.resetSyntax();               // turn off everything else
            tokens.parseNumbers();
            tokens.whitespaceChars(0, ' ');     // must put spaces back

            int c;
        out:
            while (true) {
                c = tokens.nextToken();
                switch (tokens.ttype) {         // same as value of 'c'
                case StreamTokenizer.TT_EOF:
                    break out;
                case StreamTokenizer.TT_NUMBER:
                    System.out.println(tokens.toString());
                    break;
                case StreamTokenizer.TT_WORD:
                    System.err.println(
                        "warning: unexpected identifier: " + tokens.sval);
                    break;
                default:
                    System.out.println("Default: " + (char)c);
                }
            }
        } catch (IOException e) {
            e.printStackTrace();
        }
    }
}
```

pushBack()

PURPOSE Pushes back a token onto the input stream.

SYNTAX `public void pushBack()`

DESCRIPTION This method pushes back the last token obtained via `nextToken()` onto the input stream. The next call to `nextToken()` will return this same token. Calling `pushBack()` consecutive times has the same effect as calling it once.

SEE ALSO `nextToken()`.

EXAMPLE This example shows part of an expression parser that uses `pushBack()`.

```
public static Node parseExpr(StreamTokenizer tokens) throws IOException {
        Node left, op, right;
        int c = tokens.nextToken();
        switch (c) {
        case '(':
                left = parseToken(tokens);
                op = parseToken(tokens);
                right = parseToken(tokens);
                if (tokens.nextToken() != (int)')')  {
                    System.err.print("Unbalanced parenthesis");
                    return (null);
                }
                return new Node(op, left, right);
        default:
                tokens.pushBack();
                return (parseToken(tokens));
        }
    }
    public static Node parseToken(StreamTokenizer tokens)
        throws IOException {
            switch (tokens.nextToken()) {
            case StreamTokenizer.TT_EOF:
                return (null);
            case StreamTokenizer.TT_NUMBER:
                return (new Node(tokens.ttype, tokens.nval));
            case StreamTokenizer.TT_WORD:
                return (new Node(tokens.ttype, tokens.sval));
            case '+':
            case '-':
            case '*':
            case '/':
                return (new Node(Node.TT_OPERATOR, (char)tokens.ttype));
            case '(':
                tokens.pushBack();
                return (parseExpr(tokens));
            }
            return (null);
    }
```

quoteChar()

PURPOSE
Specifies a character as a quote character.

SYNTAX
`public void quoteChar(int ch)`

DESCRIPTION
This method specifies that the character `ch` is a quote character. `ch` will delimit the start and end of a string token. When `nextToken()` encounters `ch`, all characters appearing between the starting and ending `ch`, exclusive, are returned as a string token in `sval`. The quoted string can also be terminated by a line or file terminator.

`nextToken()` itself returns `ch` (`ttype` is also set to `ch`). There can be multiple quote characters in the syntax, but the same character must be used to delimit a single string token. Other such characters that appear within a string token are not treated as quote characters for that string token.

If the backslash character (\) is encountered after the starting quote character `ch`, it is treated as the escape character for the sequence of characters to follow. The escape sequence is mapped to its corresponding `char` value according to Table 39.

Character Sequence	char Value
`\000-\377`	Octal number (e.g., `\377` is `0xff`)
`\a`	`0x7`
`\b`	`\b` (backspace)
`\f`	`0xC`
`\n`	`\n` (newline)
`\r`	`\r` (return)
`\t`	`\t` (tab)
`\v`	`0xB`

TABLE 39: Mapping of Escaped Character Sequences to a `char` Value.

PARAMETERS

`ch`
The character to be used as a quote character. If `ch` < `0` or `ch` > `255`, this method does nothing.

SEE ALSO
`nextToken(), sval.`

EXAMPLE
See `nextToken()`.

A B C D E F G H I J K L M N O P Q R S T U V W X Y Z

resetSyntax()

PURPOSE Resets the syntax table so that all characters are ordinary.

SYNTAX `public void resetSyntax()`

SEE ALSO `ordinaryChar()`, `ordinaryChars()`.

EXAMPLE See `nextToken()`, `parseNumbers()`.

A B C D E F G H I J K L M N O P Q R S T U V W X Y Z

slashSlashComments()

PURPOSE Specifies whether to recognize C++-style comments.

SYNTAX `public void slashSlashComments(boolean cpp)`

DESCRIPTION A C++-style comment is delimited by two consecutive forward slash characters (/) and the end of the line. `slashSlashComments()` is used to specify whether the parser should recognize C++-style comments. If `cpp` is `true`, double slashes are recognized as the start of comments; otherwise, they are not treated as the start of comments.

Note that, by default, the single forward slash (/) is a comment character. This means that turning on C++-style comments does nothing because the first slash is recognized as a comment character and the rest of the line is treated as a comment. `slashSlashComments()` is useful only if the slash character has been explicitly turned into a word character or an ordinary character.

PARAMETERS

`cpp` `true` means recognize C++-style comments; `false` means do not recognize C++-style comments.

SEE ALSO `commentChar()`, `nextToken()`, `slashStarComments()`.

EXAMPLE See `commentChar()`.

slashStarComments()

PURPOSE Specifies whether to recognize C-style comments.

SYNTAX `public void slashStarComments(boolean cp)`

DESCRIPTION A C-style comment is delimited by the string "`/*`" and the string ("`*/`"). Any characters that occur between "`/*`" and "`*/`" are treated as comments. `slashStarComments()` is used to specify whether the parser should recognize C-style comments. If `cp` is `true`, C-style comments are recognized; otherwise, "`/*`" strings are not treated specially.

Note that, by default, the single forward slash (/) is a comment character. This means that turning on C-style comments does not work by default because the first slash is recognized as a comment character and the rest of the line is treated as a comment. `slashStarComments()` works only if the slash character has been explicitly turned into a word character or an ordinary character.

PARAMETERS

`cp` — `true` means recognize C-style comments; `false` means do not recognize C-style comments.

SEE ALSO — `commentChar()`, `nextToken()`, `slashStarComments()`.

EXAMPLE — See `commentChar()`.

StreamTokenizer()

PURPOSE — Constructs a `StreamTokenizer` instance for an input stream.

SYNTAX

```
public StreamTokenizer(Reader reader)
```

DEPRECATED

```
public StreamTokenizer (InputStream in)
```

DESCRIPTION — The constructor for `StreamTokenizer` constructs a stream tokenizer for the input stream `in`. The default settings are as follows:

- a–z, A–Z, and characters with Unicode values 160–255 are word characters.
- Forward slash (/) is a comment character.
- Characters with Unicode values 0–32 are whitespace characters (this includes, among others, the space, escape, newline (\n), carriage return (\r), backspace, and delete).
- Single quote (') and double quote (") are quote characters.
- 0–9, period (.), and minus (-) are digit characters.

To override these defaults, call the appropriate syntax specifier methods after the stream tokenizer has been created.

PARAMETERS

`in` — The non-`null` input stream for which to create the stream tokenizer.

`reader` — The non-`null` character input stream for which to create the stream tokenizer.

SEE ALSO — `commentChar()`, `eolIsSignificant()`, `parseNumbers()`, `ordinaryChar()`, `quoteChar()`, `resetSyntax()`, `slashSlashComments()`, `slashStarComments()`, `whiteSpaceChars()`, `wordChars()`.

EXAMPLE — See the class example, `commentChar()`, `nextToken()`, and `parseNumbers()`.

sval

PURPOSE The string value of the word or string token.

SYNTAX `public String sval`

DESCRIPTION When `nextToken()` encounters a word token or a quoted string, it sets `sval` to be the word token or quoted string. For the quoted string, the beginning and ending quote characters are not included in `sval`.

The contents of this field are unspecified unless `nextToken()` indicates that it has encountered a word token or a quoted string. When that happens, `sval` contains a non-`null` string.

SEE ALSO `nextToken()`, `quoteChar()`, `TT_WORD`, `wordChars()`.

EXAMPLE See the class example, `commentChar()`, and `nextToken()`.

toString()

PURPOSE Generates the string representation of the token.

SYNTAX `public String toString()`

DESCRIPTION This method returns the string representation of the token that `nextToken()` just returned (i.e., the token most recently parsed). It consists of a string description of the token and the line number at which the token occurred in the input stream.

RETURNS The non-`null` string representation of the token.

OVERRIDES `java.lang.Object.toString()`.

EXAMPLE See `parseNumbers()`.

TT_EOF

PURPOSE The end-of-file token.

SYNTAX `public static final int TT_EOF`

DESCRIPTION This constant field represents the end-of-file token. It is returned by `nextToken()` when the end-of-file has been reached on the input stream.

SEE ALSO `nextToken()`, `ttype`.

EXAMPLE See the class example, `commentChar()`, `nextToken()`, and `parseNumbers()`.

TT_EOL

PURPOSE The end-of-line token.

SYNTAX `public static final int TT_EOL`

DESCRIPTION This constant field represents the end-of-line token. It is returned by `nextToken()` when an end-of-line has been encountered in the input stream *and* if end-of-line has been made significant via `eolIsSignificant()`.

SEE ALSO `eolIsSignificant()`, `nextToken()`, `ttype`.

EXAMPLE See the class example, `commentChar()`, and `nextToken()`.

TT_NUMBER

PURPOSE The number token type.

SYNTAX `public static final int TT_NUMBER`

DESCRIPTION This constant field represents the number token type. It is returned by `nextToken()` when a number token has been encountered in the input stream. When `nextToken()` returns `TT_NUMBER`, it sets `nval` to be the numeric value of the token. `nextToken()` recognizes number tokens only if `parseNumbers()` has been called (it is called by default in the `StreamTokenizer` constructor).

SEE ALSO `nextToken()`, `nval`, `parseNumbers()`, `StreamTokenizer()`, `ttype`.

EXAMPLE See the class example, `commentChar()`, `nextToken()`, and `parseNumbers()`.

TT_WORD

PURPOSE The word token type.

SYNTAX `public static final int TT_WORD`

DESCRIPTION This constant field represents the word token type. It is returned by `nextToken()` when a word token has been encountered in the input stream. When `nextToken()` returns `TT_WORD`, it sets `sval` to be the value of the word token. `nextToken()` recognizes word tokens by setting word characters via calls to `wordChars()`. Some default word characters are set, by default, in the `StreamTokenizer` constructor.

SEE ALSO `nextToken()`, `sval`, `StreamTokenizer()`, `wordChars()`, `ttype`.

EXAMPLE See the class example, `commentChar()`, `nextToken()`, and `parseNumbers()`.

ttype

PURPOSE The type of the token returned.

SYNTAX `public int ttype`

DESCRIPTION This field holds the type of the token parsed by `nextToken()`. It is identical to the value returned by `nextToken()`. Its value is one of `TT_EOF`, `TT_EOL`, `TT_NUMBER`, or `TT_WORD`, or the character just read from the input stream token if it is none of the special characters recognized by the tokenizer.

SEE ALSO `nextToken()`, `quoteChar()`, `TT_EOF`, `TT_EOL`, `TT_NUMBER`, `TT_WORD`.

EXAMPLE See `parseNumbers()`.

whitespaceChars()

PURPOSE Specifies characters in this range are whitespace characters.

SYNTAX `public void whitespaceChars(int low, int hi)`

DESCRIPTION This method specifies that the characters with Unicode value `low` to Unicode value `hi` are to be treated as whitespace characters. Whitespace characters are used to separate word tokens and number tokens.

By default, the `StreamTokenizer` constructor sets the characters with Unicode values 0–32 to be whitespace characters (this includes, among other characters, the space, escape, newline (\n), carriage return (\r), backspace, and delete). You can call `whitespaceChars()` several times to set different ranges of characters to be whitespace characters. You can reset a character that is a whitespace character to be some other type of character by calling `ordinaryChar()` or other syntax-specifying methods.

PARAMETERS

`hi` The last Unicode character in the range of whitespace characters. Inclusive. If `hi` > `255`, 255 is used as the upper limit in the range.

`low` The first Unicode character in the range of whitespace characters. Inclusive. If `low` < `0`, 0 is used as the lower limit in the range.

SEE ALSO `eolIsSignificant()`, `nextToken()`, `StreamTokenizer()`.

EXAMPLE See the class example, `nextToken()`, and `parseNumbers()`.

wordChars()

PURPOSE Specifies that characters in this range are word characters.

SYNTAX `public void wordChars(int low, int hi)`

DESCRIPTION This method specifies that the characters with Unicode value `low` to Unicode value `hi` should be treated as word characters. A word consists of a word character, followed by consecutive word or digit characters. Words are separated by whitespaces, end-of-lines, or an end-of-file. When `nextToken()` encounters a word, it returns `TT_WORD` and sets `sval` to be the word just parsed.

By default, the `StreamTokenizer` constructor sets the characters a–z, A–Z, and characters with Unicode values 160–255 to be word characters. Also, all characters with Unicode value `>255` are word characters. Calls to `wordChars()` are cumulative. You can call `wordChars()` several times to set different ranges of characters to be word characters. You can reset a character that is a word character to be some other type of character by calling `ordinaryChar()` or other syntax-specifying methods.

PARAMETERS

`hi` The last Unicode character in the range of word characters. Inclusive. If `hi` > `255`, `255` is used as the upper limit in the range.

`low` The first Unicode character in the range of word characters. Inclusive. If `low` < `0`, 0 is used as the lower limit in the range.

SEE ALSO `nextToken()`, `sval`, `TT_WORD`, `whitespaceChars()`.

EXAMPLE See `nextToken()`.

java.lang
String

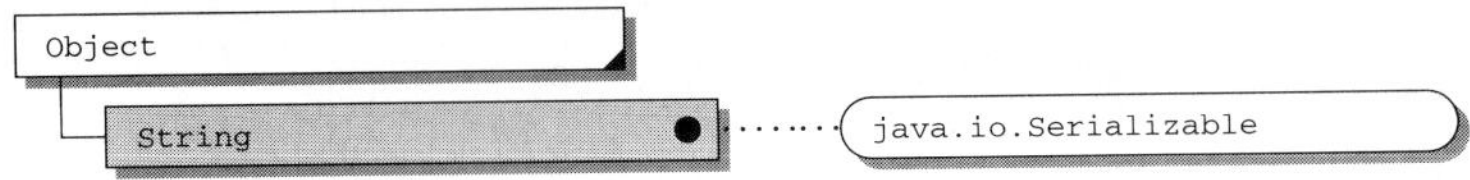

A
B
C
D
E
F
G
H
I
J
K
L
M
N
O
P
Q
R
S
T
U
V
W
X
Y
Z

Syntax

```
public final class String implements Serializable
```

Description

The `String` class is used to represent a sequence of characters. Once the class is created, its contents cannot be modified. The `String` class contains methods for examining and searching the contents of a `String` and methods for creating new `Strings` using existing `String` objects and other data types.

Creating New Strings

The `String` class provides methods for creating new `String` objects by using other `String` objects or other data types. There are also methods that take an existing `String` and create a variation of that `String`. For example, the `toLowerCase()` method takes an existing `String` and creates a new version of it in which all of the characters are converted to lowercase.

The Java language supports not only these methods but also the creation of `String` objects using `String` constants and the concatenation operator (+). For example, in the following, `str1` and `str2` are equivalent and `str3` and `str4` are equivalent:

```
String str1 = "abc";
char data[] = {'a', 'b', 'c'};
String str2 = new String(data);

String str3 = str1.concat(str2);
String str4 = str1 + str2;
```

Note that these methods all create a *new, immutable* `String` object.

Character and Substring Searches

The `String` class provides methods that do character and substring searches. Character positions (or *indices*) within a `String` range from 0 to $n - 1$, where n is the number of characters in the string. An index of `0` is the position of the first character; an index of $n - 1$ is the position of the last character in the `String`.

Strings to Other Representations

The `String` class provides methods for converting strings to and from other representations. You can pass a `byte` array containing bytes representing characters in a non-Unicode encoding to the `String` constructor and have those bytes be converted into a Unicode string. You can also get from a `String` a `byte` array containing bytes in a specified encoding (see `getBytes()`).

MEMBER SUMMARY

Constructor	
`String()`	Constructs a new `String` object using characters from a character array, `byte` array, or `String`.
Methods for Creating New Strings	
`concat()`	Creates a string that is the concatenation of two strings.
`copyValueOf()`	Creates a string using characters from a character array.
`replace()`	Creates a string by replacing all occurrences of a character with another character.
`substring()`	Creates a string that is a substring of this string.
`toLowerCase()`	Creates a string by turning all characters of this string into lowercase.
`toUpperCase()`	Creates a string by turning all characters of this string into uppercase.
`trim()`	Creates a string by trimming leading and trailing whitespace characters from this string.
`valueOf()`	Creates the string representation of a data value.
Comparison Methods	
`compareTo()`	Compares this string to another string for equality and Unicode ordering.
`equals()`	Compares this string with another object for equality.
`equalsIgnoreCase()`	Performs a case-insensitive comparison of this string with another string.
Search Methods	
`endsWith()`	Determines whether this string ends with a specified suffix.
`indexOf()`	Finds the first occurrence of a character or substring within this string.
`lastIndexOf()`	Finds the last occurrence of a character or substring within this string.
`regionMatches()`	Determines whether a region of this string matches a region of another string.
`startsWith()`	Determines whether this string starts with a specified prefix.
Conversion Methods	
`charAt()`	Retrieves the character at an index.
`getBytes()`	Retrieves the byte encoding of the characters in this string.

Continued

MEMBER SUMMARY

Conversion Methods	
`getChars()`	Copies characters from this string into the specified character array.
`toCharArray()`	Creates a character array containing the characters from this string.
`toString()`	Generates the string representation of this object.
Object Methods	
`hashCode()`	Computes the hash code for this object.
`intern()`	Retrieves this string from the "string pool."
`length()`	Retrieves the number of characters in this string.

A B C D E F G H I J K L M N O P Q R S T U V W X Y Z

See Also

`java.io.UnsupportedEncodingException`, `java.io.Serializable`, `StringBuffer`.

charAt()

PURPOSE Retrieves the character at an index.

SYNTAX `public char charAt(int index)`

DESCRIPTION This method returns the character at the position, `index`, of this `String` object.

PARAMETERS

`index` The character position. `0` ≤ `index` < `length()`.

RETURNS The character at position `index`.

EXCEPTIONS

`StringIndexOutOfBoundsException`

If `index` < `0` or `index` ≥ `length()`.

EXAMPLE

```
// method that returns true if 'str' contains a white
// space character
public static boolean hasWhiteSpace(String str) {
    for (int i = 0; i < str.length(); i++) {
        if (Character.isWhitespace(str.charAt(i)))
            return (true);
    }
    return (false);
}
```

compareTo()

PURPOSE Compares this string to another string for equality and Unicode ordering.

SYNTAX `public int compareTo(String str)`

DESCRIPTION This method compares this string with the string `str`, character-by-character, according to Unicode ordering. It returns an integer indicating whether the two strings are equal and, if they are not, the ordering of the two strings. If the two strings are identical (they have the same length and the same characters in the same order), this method returns `0`. Otherwise, it returns a negative value if the difference—i.e., the first different character—of this string precedes that of `str` in the Unicode code set. A negative value is also returned if this string is a prefix of `str`. `compareTo()` returns a positive value if the difference of `str` precedes that of this string in the Unicode code set. A positive value is also returned if `str` is a prefix of this string. For roman character sets, the positive and negative return values could be used to order strings alphabetically.

PARAMETERS

`str` The non-`null` string to be compared.

RETURNS `0` if the strings are identical. A negative value if the difference of this string is lower in the Unicode code set than that of `str`. A positive value if the difference of this string is higher in the Unicode code set.

SEE ALSO `equals()`, `equalsIgnoreCase()`.

EXAMPLE

```
String str = "this is a test";

int r1 = str.compareTo("this is a test and more"); // negative (str shorter)
int r2 = str.compareTo("this is not a test");      // negative ('a' < 'n')
int r3 = str.compareTo("this is a test");          // 0
int r4 = str.compareTo("no, this is not a test");  // positive ('t' > 'n')
int r5 = str.compareTo("this");                    // positive (str longer)
```

concat()

PURPOSE Creates a string that is the concatenation of two strings.

SYNTAX `public String concat(String str)`

DESCRIPTION This method creates a new `String` object whose content is the string concatenation of this string and `str`. If `str` is an empty string (has a length of 0), this `String` object is simply returned. A new `String` object is not created because no concatenation is required.

PARAMETERS

`str` The non-`null` string to be concatenated to the end of this string to make a new string.

RETURNS A new `String` object that is the concatenation of this string and `str`.

EXAMPLE

```
String str1 = "abc";

String str2 = str1.concat("cde"); // "abccde"
String str3 = str1 + "cde";       // "abccde"
```

copyValueOf()

PURPOSE Creates a `String` using characters from a character array.

SYNTAX

```
public static String copyValueOf(char[] data)
public static String copyValueOf(char[] data, int offset, int
   count)
```

DESCRIPTION The two forms of this method create a new `String` object using characters from the character array `data`. The first form copies the characters from the entire array `data` for creating the new string. The second form copies `count` characters starting at position `offset` within `data`. Changes to `data` after the creation of the string do not affect the contents of the new string.

`copyValueOf()` is equivalent to the `String()` constructor and `valueOf()` (the forms that take a `char` array as an argument).

PARAMETERS

`count` The number of characters from `data` to copy. `count` ≥ `0`.

`data` The non-`null` character array from which to copy the characters.

`offset` The position of the first character in `data` to copy. `0` ≤ `offset` < `length()`.

RETURNS A new non-`null` `String` object whose content is a copy of the characters from `data` (or a subset of it as specified by `offset` and `count`).

EXCEPTIONS

`ArrayIndexOutOfBoundsException`
If `offset` or `count` are outside the bounds of `data`.

SEE ALSO `getBytes()`, `String()`, `valueOf()`.

EXAMPLE

```
char data[] = {'a', 'b', 'c'};
String abc = String.copyValueOf(data);
String bc = String.copyValueOf(data, 1, 2);
System.out.println("copy " + abc + " " + bc);
data[2] = 'e';  // updating 'data' doesn't affect abc or bc
System.out.println("copy after " + abc + " " + bc);
```

endsWith()

PURPOSE Determines whether this string ends with a specified suffix.

SYNTAX `public boolean endsWith(String suffix)`

DESCRIPTION This method determines whether this string ends with the string `suffix`. It returns `true` if this string ends with `suffix`; it returns `false` otherwise.

PARAMETERS

`suffix` The non-`null` suffix to be compared.

RETURNS `true` if this string ends with `suffix`; `false` otherwise.

SEE ALSO `startsWith()`.

EXAMPLE

```
// method that checks whether 'file' has correct suffix
// to be Java source file
public static boolean validSrcFilename(String file) {
    return (file.endsWith(".java"));
}
```

equals()

PURPOSE Compares this string with another object for equality.

SYNTAX `public boolean equals(Object obj)`

DESCRIPTION This method compares this `String` object with `obj`. It returns `true` if `obj` is another `String` containing a string of the same length and with the same sequence of characters as this string; it returns `false` otherwise. It also returns `false` if `obj` is `null` or if `obj` is not a `String` object.

PARAMETERS

`obj` The possibly `null` object to be compared.

RETURNS `true` if `obj` is equal to this `String` object; `false` otherwise.

OVERRIDES `Object.equals()`.

SEE ALSO `compareTo()`, `equalsIgnoreCase()`, `hashCode()`, `regionMatches()`.

EXAMPLE

```
String abc = "abc";
String str = new String(abc);
if (str.equals(abc))
    System.out.println("correct");
```

equalsIgnoreCase()

PURPOSE Performs a case-insensitive comparison of this string with another string.

SYNTAX `public boolean equalsIgnoreCase(String str)`

DESCRIPTION This method performs a case-insensitive comparison of this string with another string `str`. It returns `true` if the two strings are equal when case is ignored; it returns `false` otherwise (including if `str` is `null`). The strings are considered equal if they have the same length, contain the same sequence of characters, and differ only in the case of the characters.

PARAMETERS

`str` The possibly `null` string to be compared.

RETURNS `true` if the strings are equal when case is ignored; `false` otherwise.

SEE ALSO `compareTo()`, `equals()`, `regionMatches()`.

EXAMPLE

```
String abc = "abc";
String str = new String("ABC");
if (str.equalsIgnoreCase(abc))
    System.out.println("correct");
```

getBytes()

PURPOSE Retrieves the byte encoding of the characters in this string.

SYNTAX

```
public byte[] getBytes() throws UnsupportedEncodingException
public byte[] getBytes(String enc) throws
    UnsupportedEncodingException
```

DEPRECATED

```
public void getBytes(int srcOffset, int srcEnd, byte[] dst, int
    dstOffset)
```

DESCRIPTION This method retrieves the byte encoding of the characters of this string, from index `srcOffset` (inclusive) to index `srcEnd` (exclusive). The encoding scheme used is specified using the encoding identifier `enc`. If `enc` is not specified, a platform-dependent default encoding is used.[1] The size of the resulting `byte` array depends on the encoding used.

`enc` is a string that identifies the encoding scheme. Table 40 lists the encoding identifiers that comes with JavaSoft's standalone JDK1.1. The exact list

1. In the JDK1.1, this default encoding is identified by the `file.encoding` system property. If this system property is not defined, the default encoding identifier is "8859_1" (ISO-Latin-1). If the class for the converter cannot be loaded, an ASCII encoding is used.

of encoding identifiers available is platform-dependent. You also can name some of these encodings using their IANA standard names. For example, you can use "ISO-Latin-1" or "ISO-8859-1" to mean the ISO Latin 1 character encoding instead of using "8859_1".

8859_1	8859_2	8859_3	8859_4
8859_5	8859_6	8859_7	8859_8
8859_9	Big5	CNS11643	Cp037
Cp1006	Cp1025	Cp1026	Cp1046
Cp1097	Cp1098	Cp1112	Cp1122
Cp1123	Cp1124	Cp1250	Cp1251
Cp1252	Cp1253	Cp1254	Cp1255
Cp1256	Cp1257	Cp1258	Cp1381
Cp1383	Cp273	Cp277	Cp278
Cp280	Cp284	Cp285	Cp297
Cp33722	Cp420	Cp424	Cp437
Cp500	Cp737	Cp775	Cp838
Cp850	Cp852	Cp855	Cp856
Cp857	Cp860	Cp861	Cp862
Cp863	Cp864	Cp865	Cp866
Cp868	Cp869	Cp870	Cp871
Cp874	Cp875	Cp918	Cp921
Cp922	Cp930	Cp933	Cp935
Cp937	Cp939	Cp942	Cp948
Cp949	Cp950	Cp964	Cp970
EUCJIS	GB2312	GBK	ISO2022CN_CNS
ISO2022CN_GB	ISO2022KR	JIS	KOI8_R
KSC5601	MS874	MacArabic	MacCentralEurope
MacCroatian	MacCyrillic	MacDingbat	MacGreek
MacHebrew	MacIceland	MacRoman	MacRomania
MacSymbol	MacThai	MacTurkish	MacUkraine
SJIS	UTF8	Unicode	UnicodeBig
UnicodeBigUnmarked		UnicodeLittle	
UnicodeLittleUnmarked			

TABLE 40: Character to Byte Encoding Identifiers.

A B C D E F G H I J K L M N O P Q R S T U V W X Y Z

PARAMETERS

`dst`	The non-`null` destination array.
`dstOffset`	The inclusive start offset in `dst` into which to copy characters. `0` ≤ `dstOffset` < `dst.length`.
`enc`	The non-`null` string identifying the encoding to use when converting the characters from this string into bytes.
`srcEnd`	The exclusive index of the character in this string at which to stop copying. 0 ≤ `srcEnd` ≤ `length()`. `srcOffset` ≤ `srcEnd`.
`srcOffset`	The inclusive index of the character in this string at which to start copying. 0 ≤ `srcOffset` < `length()`. `srcOffset` ≤ `srcEnd`.

EXCEPTIONS

`ArrayIndexOutOfBoundsException`
If `srcOffset` or `srcEnd` or `dstOffset` is outside the bounds specified.

`UnsupportedEncodingException`
If no byte-to-character converted for `enc` can be found.

DEPRECATION The third form of this method translates the characters of this string, from index `srcOffset` (inclusive) to index `srcEnd` (exclusive), to the byte array `dst` starting at `dstOffset` in `dst`. Since `dst` is a `byte` array, the 16-bit Unicode characters of this string are cast into 8-bit bytes when copied into `dst`. The top 8 bits of the Unicode character are ignored; the lower 8 bits are used for the byte. This translation technique is not generally correct and usage of this form of the method is deprecated. Replace such usage, as in

```
String str = ...;
byte[] b = new byte[str.length()];
str.getBytes(0, str.length(), b, 0);
```

with

```
String str = ...;
try {
    byte[] b = str.getBytes();
} catch (UnsupportedEncodingException e) {
    e.printStackTrace();
}
```

SEE ALSO `getChars()`, `java.io.UnsupportedEncodingException`, `String()`.

EXAMPLE

```
class Main {
    public static void main(String[] args) {
        String str = new String("num\u00e9ro");

        try {
            byte[] def = str.getBytes();
            byte[] utf = str.getBytes("UTF8");

            // print out contents of byte arrays
            for (int i = 0; i < def.length; i++) {
                System.out.println("[" + i + "]:" + def[i]);
            }
```

```
            System.out.println("-----");
            for (int i = 0; i < utf.length; i++) {
                System.out.println("[" + i + "]:" + utf[i]);
            }
            System.out.println("-----");

            // Reconstruct strings using byte arrays
            String defstr = new String(def);
            String utfstr = new String(utf, "UTF8");

            System.out.println("default: " + defstr);
            System.out.println("utf8: " + utfstr);

        } catch (java.io.UnsupportedEncodingException e) {
            e.printStackTrace();
        }
    }
}
```

getChars()

PURPOSE Copies characters from this string into the specified character array.

SYNTAX `public void getChars(int srcOffset, int srcEnd, char[] dst, int dstOffset)`

DESCRIPTION This method copies the characters of this string, from index `srcOffset` (inclusive) to index `srcEnd` (exclusive), to the character array `dst`, starting at `dstOffset` in `dst`. The character at `srcOffset` is copied, but the character at `srcEnd` is not.

PARAMETERS

`dst` The (non-`null`) destination array.

`dstOffset` The inclusive start offset in `dst` at which to copy characters. `0` ≤ `dstOffset` < `dst.length`.

`srcEnd` The exclusive index of the character in this string at which to stop copying. `0` ≤ `srcEnd` ≤ `length()` and `srcOffset` ≤ `srcEnd`.

`srcOffset` The index of the character in this string at which to start copying. 0 ≤ `srcOffset` < `length()` and `srcOffset` ≤ `srcEnd`.

EXCEPTIONS

`ArrayIndexOutOfBoundsException`

If `srcOffset` or `srcEnd` or `dstOffset` are outside the specified bounds.

SEE ALSO `getBytes()`, `toCharArray()`.

EXAMPLE

```
// method that splits a string into two and returns the head
public static String firstHalf(String str) {
    int half = str.length() / 2;
    char[] buf = new char[half];
    str.getChars(0, half, buf, 0);
    return (new String(buf));
}
```

hashCode()

PURPOSE Computes the hash code for this object.

SYNTAX `public int hashCode()`

DESCRIPTION This method generates the hash code for this `String` object. This hash code is calculated using the object's character values. Two strings with the same string value (characters) have the same hash code. However, two strings with the same hash code may not necessarily have the same string values.

RETURNS An `int` representing the hash code of this object.

OVERRIDES `Object.hashCode()`.

SEE ALSO `equals()`, `java.util.Hashtable`.

EXAMPLE

```
// Keep track of hits on hash code
String str = "this is a test";
int hashval = str.hashCode();         // get hash code for str
++hits[Math.abs(hashval%tabsize)];   // count hits
```

indexOf()

PURPOSE Finds the first occurrence of a character or substring within this string.

SYNTAX

```
public int indexOf(int ch)
public int indexOf(int ch, int offset)
public int indexOf(String str)
public int indexOf(String str, int offset)
```

DESCRIPTION The four forms of this method return the index within this string of the first occurrence of the given character `ch` or substring `str`. If `offset` is specified, the characters within this string that are considered during the search are those between `offset` and the end of this string (`length()-1`). If `offset` is not specified, this string is searched in its entirety. If `ch` or `str` does not occur in the specified portion of this string, this method returns `-1`.

If `str` is the empty string, `0` is returned. For example, `"abc".indexOf("")` returns `0`.

PARAMETERS

`ch`	The character for which to search.
`offset`	The index in this string from which to start the search. The search is performed in the region between `offset` (inclusive) and the end of the string. If `offset` < `0`, an `offset` of `0` is used. If `offset` ≥ `length()`, `-1` is returned.
`str`	The substring for which to search. `str` must not be `null`.

RETURNS The index of the first occurrence of `ch` or `str`; `-1` if not found. Note that this number is relative to the start of this string.

SEE ALSO `lastIndexOf()`.

EXAMPLE

```
class Main {
    public static void main(String[] args) {
        String s = "Madam, I'm Adam";

        System.out.println(s.indexOf('\''));          // 8
        System.out.println(s.indexOf('\'', 8));       // 8
        System.out.println(s.indexOf('\'', 9));       // -1
        System.out.println(s.indexOf('a', 100));      // -1
        System.out.println(s.indexOf('X'));           // -1

        // Retrieve the first word.
        System.out.println(
            s.substring(0, s.indexOf(' ')));          // Madam,
    }
}
```

intern()

PURPOSE Retrieves this string from the "string pool."

SYNTAX `public native String intern()`

DESCRIPTION A "string pool" is maintained by the system. `intern()` returns this string from the string pool if it is already in the string pool. Otherwise, it adds it to the string pool first and then returns the string.

Two `String` objects with the same `intern()` result are guaranteed to be equal. Two `String` objects that are equal have the same `intern()` result. Consequently, you can use `intern()` to test for equality, instead of using the more expensive `equals()`.

RETURNS The non-`null` string representation from the string pool.

EXAMPLE

```
String s1 = new String("def");
String s2 = new String("abc");
...
if (s1.intern() == s2.intern()) ...
```

lastIndexOf()

PURPOSE
Finds the last occurrence of a character or substring within this string.

SYNTAX
```
public int lastIndexOf(char ch)
public int lastIndexOf(char ch, int offset)
public int lastIndexOf(String str)
public int lastIndexOf(String str, int offset)
```

DESCRIPTION
The four forms of this method return the index within this string of the last occurrence of the given character `ch` or substring `str`. If `offset` is specified, the characters within this string that are considered during the search are those between the start of the string and the index `offset`. If `offset` is not specified, this string is searched in its entirety. The search is performed backwards starting at `offset` (if specified) or the end of the string towards the front of the string. If the `ch` or `str` does not occur in the specified portion of this string, this method returns `-1`.

If `str` is the empty string, `this.length()` is returned. For example, `"abc".lastIndexOf("")` returns 3.

PARAMETERS

`ch` The character for which to search.

`offset` The index at which to start the reverse search. The search is performed in the region between `0` and `offset` (inclusive) of this string. `0` ≤ `offset` < `length()`; if `offset` is not in this range, `-1` is returned.

`str` The non-`null` substring for which to search.

RETURNS
The index of the last occurrence of `ch` or `str`; `-1` if not found. Note that this number is relative to the start of this string.

SEE ALSO
`indexOf()`.

EXAMPLE
```
class Main {
    public static void main(String[] args) {
        String s = "Madam, I'm Adam";

        System.out.println(s.lastIndexOf('\''));        // 8
        System.out.println(s.lastIndexOf('\'', 8));     // 8
        System.out.println(s.lastIndexOf('\'', 7));     // -1
        System.out.println(s.lastIndexOf('a', -1));     // -1
        System.out.println(s.lastIndexOf('X'));         // -1

        // Retrieve the last word.
        System.out.println(
            s.substring(s.lastIndexOf(' ')+1));         // Adam
    }
}
```

length()

PURPOSE Retrieves the number of characters in the string.

SYNTAX `public int length()`

RETURNS The number of characters in this string.

EXAMPLE See `charAt()`.

regionMatches()

PURPOSE Determines whether a region of this string matches a region of another string.

SYNTAX
```
public boolean regionMatches(int offset1, String str2, int
   offset2, int count)
public boolean regionMatches(boolean ignoreCase, int offset1,
   String str2, offset2, int count)
```

DESCRIPTION The two forms of this method determine whether a region of this string as specified by `offset1` and `count` matches the region of another string, `str2`, as specified by `offset2` and `count`. If `ignoreCase` is specified and is set to `true`, uppercase characters are considered equivalent to their corresponding lowercase characters. Otherwise, the match is based on a character-by-character comparison.

PARAMETERS

`count`	The number of characters in the region to match. `count` ≥ `0`.
`ignoreCase`	If `true`, case is ignored; otherwise, case is considered.
`offset1`	The start of the region in this string. `0` ≤ `offset1` < `length()`.
`offset2`	The start of the region in `str2`. `0` ≤ `offset2` < `str2.length()`.
`str2`	The non-`null` string to be compared.

RETURNS `true` if the regions match; `false` otherwise. `false` is also returned if the regions as specified by `offset1` and `count` or `offset2` and `count` are outside the bounds of their respective string object.

SEE ALSO `compareTo()`, `equals()`, `equalsIgnoreCase()`.

EXAMPLE
```
String s1 = "this is a test";
String s2 = "testing";
String s3 = "Testing";
int testLoc = s1.indexOf("test", 0);
if (testLoc >= 0) {
    if (s1.regionMatches(testLoc, s2, 0, 4))
        System.out.println("regions match");
    // try again using case-insensitive match
    if (s1.regionMatches(true, testLoc, s3, 0, 4))
        System.out.println("regions match when case ignored");
}
```

replace()

PURPOSE Creates a string by replacing all occurrences of a character with another character.

SYNTAX `public String replace(char oldChar, char newChar)`

DESCRIPTION This method creates a new `String` object that is a copy of this string, except that all occurrences of `oldChar` are replaced with `newChar`.

PARAMETERS

`newChar` The character that replaces the old character.

`oldChar` The character to be replaced.

RETURNS A new `String` object with `oldChar` replaced with `newChar`.

EXAMPLE

```
// method that replaces blanks with '#'
public static String blanksWithHash(String str) {
    return (str.replace(' ', '#'));
}
```

startsWith()

PURPOSE Determines whether this string starts with a specified prefix.

SYNTAX `public boolean startsWith(String prefix)`
`public boolean startsWith(String prefix, int offset)`

DESCRIPTION The two forms of this method determine whether this string starts with the given string `prefix`. It returns `true` if this string starts with `prefix`; it returns `false` otherwise. If `offset` is specified, `prefix` is compared against this string starting at index `offset`. If `offset` is not specified, the comparison is done starting at index `0`.

PARAMETERS

`offset` The index of this string at which to start the comparison. `0` ≤ `offset` < `length()`.

`prefix` The non-`null` prefix substring for which to search.

RETURNS `true` if this string starts with `prefix`; `false` otherwise. `false` is also returned if `offset` is outside the bounds of this string.

SEE ALSO `endsWith()`.

EXAMPLE This example is a method that parses a string of octal, hexadecimal, or decimal numbers. Any string that starts with "`0x`" or "`#`" denotes a hexadecimal string, while any string that starts with "`0`" denotes an octal string. All other strings are considered to denote decimal numbers.

```
// Method that parses string of octal, hex, or decimal number
public static int parseNumber(String str) throws NumberFormatException {
    if (str.startsWith("0x")) {
        return Integer.parseInt(str.substring(2), 16);
    }
    if (str.startsWith("#")) {
        return Integer.parseInt(str.substring(1), 16);
        }
    if (str.startsWith("0")) {
        return Integer.parseInt(str.substring(1), 8);
        }
    return Integer.parseInt(str, 10);
}
```

String()

PURPOSE Constructs a new `String` object using characters from a character array, `byte` array, or `String`.

SYNTAX

```
public String()
public String(String src)
public String(StringBuffer buffer)
public String(char[] charArray)
public String(char[] charArray, int offset, int count)
public String(byte[] byteArray)
public String(byte[] byteArray, int offset, int count)
public String(byte[] byteArray, String enc) throws
    UnsupportedEncodingException
public String(byte[] byteArray, int offset, int count, String enc)
    throws UnsupportedEncodingException
```

DEPRECATED `public String(byte[] asciiArray, int hibyte)`

DEPRECATED `public String(byte[] asciiArray, int hibyte, int offset, int count)`

DESCRIPTION The `String` class has nine constructors (and two deprecated ones). Each creates an immutable `String` object by using characters from the arguments supplied. Any modifications to the arguments after the `String` object has been constructed do not affect the `String` object.

You can create an empty string using the first form of the constructor. It takes no arguments.

You also can create a new string from an existing string, `src`, using the second form. The result is a new `String` object that is a copy of `src`.

You can create a new string by supplying the constructor with a `StringBuffer`, `buffer`. The result is a new `String` object whose value is that of `buffer`. If `buffer` is subsequently modified, a new copy of `buffer` is created for the updates so that the modifications do not affect the string already created.

The fourth and fifth forms of the constructor allow you to create a string using characters from a character array, `charArray`. You can specify a region of `charArray` to copy characters from by using `offset` and `count`. Otherwise, characters from the entire `charArray` are copied.

You also can create a string using bytes from a `byte` array, `byteArray` (forms six to nine of the method). The bytes in `byteArray` are converted to Unicode characters using the byte-to-character converter for the encoding scheme specified by `enc`. If `enc` is not specified, the platform-dependent default encoding is used.[1] `offset` and `count` are used to specify that `count` number of bytes starting at index `offset` in the byte array `byteArray` are to be used for creating the string. Note that the number of characters in the resulting `String` may not be `count` because the number depends on the encoding, which may translate several bytes into a single character.

`enc` is a string that identifies the encoding scheme. Table 41 lists the encoding identifiers that come with JavaSoft's standalone JDK1.1. The exact list of encoding identifiers available is platform-dependent. You can also name some of these encodings using their IANA standard names. For example, you can use "ISO-Latin-1" or "ISO-8859-1" to mean the ISO Latin 1 character encoding instead of using "8859_1".

8859_1	8859_2	8859_3	8859_4
8859_5	8859_6	8859_7	8859_8
8859_9	Big5	CNS11643	Cp037
Cp1006	Cp1025	Cp1026	Cp1046
Cp1097	Cp1098	Cp1112	Cp1122
Cp1123	Cp1124	Cp1250	Cp1251
Cp1252	Cp1253	Cp1254	Cp1255
Cp1256	Cp1257	Cp1258	Cp1381
Cp1383	Cp273	Cp277	Cp278
Cp280	Cp284	Cp285	Cp297
Cp33722	Cp420	Cp424	Cp437
Cp500	Cp737	Cp775	Cp838
Cp850	Cp852	Cp855	Cp856
Cp857	Cp860	Cp861	Cp862

TABLE 41: Byte to Character Encoding Identifiers.

1. In the JDK1.1, this default encoding is identified by the `file.encoding` system property. If this system property is not defined, the default encoding identifier is "8859_1" (ISO-Latin-1). If the class for the converter cannot be loaded, an ASCII encoding is used.

Cp863	Cp864	Cp865	Cp866
Cp868	Cp869	Cp870	Cp871
Cp874	Cp875	Cp918	Cp921
Cp922	Cp930	Cp933	Cp935
Cp937	Cp939	Cp942	Cp948
Cp949	Cp950	Cp964	Cp970
EUCJIS	GB2312	GBK	ISO2022CN
ISO2022KR	JIS	JISAutoDetect	KOI8_R
KSC5601	MS874	MacArabic	MacCentralEurope
MacCroatian	MacCyrillic	MacDingbat	MacGreek
MacHebrew	MacIceland	MacRoman	MacRomania
MacSymbol	MacThai	MacTurkish	MacUkraine
SJIS	UTF8	Unicode	UnicodeBig
UnicodeLittle			

TABLE 41: Byte to Character Encoding Identifiers.

PARAMETERS

`asciiArray` The non-`null` `byte` array from which to copy the lower 8-bit bytes.

`buffer` The non-`null` `StringBuffer` from which to get characters. `buffer` must not be `null`.

`byteArray` The non-`null` `byte` array containing the bytes to be converted into characters.

`charArray` The non-`null` character array from which to copy characters.

`count` The number of elements from the array to use. `count` ≥ `0`.

`enc` The non-`null` string identifying the encoding to use when converting the bytes to Unicode.

`hibyte` The top 8 bits to pad each byte with when making a 16-bit Unicode `char` value.

`offset` The offset into `charArray` or `byteArray` to start copying.
`0` ≤ `offset` ≤ (`charArray.length - count`), or
`0` ≤ `offset` ≤ (`byteArray.length - count`), or
`0` ≤ `offset` ≤ (`asciiArray.length - count`).

`src` The non-`null` `String` object from which to copy.

EXCEPTIONS

`UnsupportedEncodingException`
If no byte-to-character converter is found for the encoding identified by `enc`.

`StringIndexOutOfBoundsException`
If `count` < `0`, or if `offset` < 0, or if `offset` > (`charArray.length - count`), or
if `offset` > (`byteArray.length - count`), or
if `offset` > (`asciiArray.length - count`).

DEPRECATION Usage of the forms of this method that accepts `asciiArray` is deprecated. These forms do not properly convert bytes into characters in general. Replace the usage of these forms of the constructor, as in

```
byte[] b = ...;
String s1 = new String(b, 0); // use 0 for padding upper byte
String s2 = new String(b, 0, 3, 6);
```

with

```
byte[] b = ...;
String s1 = new String(b); // use default byte-to-char converter
String s2 = new String(b, 3, 6);
```

SEE ALSO `copyValueOf()`, `getBytes()`, `java.io.UnsupportedEncodingException`, `valueOf()`.

EXAMPLE

```
String s1 = new String();                // empty string
String s2 = "abc";                       // use constant
String s3 = new String(s2);              // copy from String

s2 = "def";                              // won't affect s3


char[] charArray = {'a', 'b', 'c'};      // copy from char array
String s4 = new String(charArray);       // "abc"

charArray[1] = 'B';                      // won't affect s4
String s5 = new String(charArray, 1, 1);// "B"

// translate from byte array, using default encoding
byte[] byteArray = {'a', 'b', 'c'};
String s6 = new String(byteArray);       // "abc"

byteArray[1] = 'x';                      // won't affect s6
String s7 = new String(byteArray, 1, 1);// "x"

String s8 = null;
try {
    // translate from byte array, using  utf-8 encoding
    byte[] utfbuf = {(byte)110, (byte)117, (byte)109,
                          (byte)-61, (byte)-87, (byte)114, (byte)111};
    s8 = new String(utfbuf, "UTF8");
} catch (UnsupportedEncodingException e) {
    e.printStackTrace();
}

// copy from StringBuffer
StringBuffer buf = new StringBuffer("xyz");
String s9 = new String(buf);

buf.setLength(1); // update to buf won't affect s8
```

substring()

PURPOSE Creates a string that is a substring of this string.

SYNTAX
```
public String substring(int offset)
public String substring(int offset, int endIndex)
```

DESCRIPTION The two forms of this method create a new string that is a substring of this string. The substring starts at the index `offset` and ends at the index `endIndex`. The character at `offset` is included in the substring, but the character at `endIndex` is not. The characters copied are those between `offset` and `endIndex-1` inclusive.

PARAMETERS

`endIndex` The ending index, exclusive. `0` ≤ `endindex` ≤ `length()` and `offset` ≤ `endIndex`.

`offset` The beginning index, inclusive. `0` ≤ `offset` < `length()`. and `offset` ≤ `endIndex`.

RETURNS A new non-`null` string that is a substring of this string in the range (`offset`, `endIndex-1`) inclusive.

EXCEPTIONS

`StringIndexOutOfBoundsException`
If `offset` or `endIndex` is outside the bounds specified.

EXAMPLE See `indexOf()`, `startsWith()`.

toCharArray()

PURPOSE Creates a character array using characters from this string.

SYNTAX
```
public char[] toCharArray()
```

DESCRIPTION This method creates a new `char` array using the sequence of characters from this string.

RETURNS A non-`null` `char` array containing the characters of this string.

SEE ALSO `getChars()`.

EXAMPLE

```
// return an upper case version of a string
public static String turnUpper(String str) {
    char[] contents = str.toCharArray();
    for(int i = 0; i < contents.length; i++) {
        contents[i] = Character.toUpperCase(contents[i]);
    }
    return (new String(contents));
}
```

A B C D E F G H I J K L M N O P Q R S T U V W X Y Z

toLowerCase()

PURPOSE Creates a string by turning all characters in this string into lowercase.

SYNTAX
```
public String toLowerCase()
public String toLowerCase(Locale loc)
```

DESCRIPTION This method creates a new string that has the same sequence of characters as this string, except that all of the characters are in their lowercase forms as determined by the specified locale `loc`. If `loc` is not specified, the platform-dependent default locale is used.

PARAMETERS

`loc` The non-`null` locale to use when doing the conversion to lowercase.

RETURNS A new non-`null` string with all characters in lowercase.

SEE ALSO `Character.toLowerCase()`, `toUpperCase()`.

EXAMPLE
```
// creates new string with all lower case
System.out.println("This is a test".toLowerCase()); // "this is a test"
```

toString()

PURPOSE Generates the string representation of this object.

SYNTAX
```
public String toString()
```

RETURNS This string.

OVERRIDES `Object.toString()`.

EXAMPLE
```
String s1 = "abc";
String s2 = s1.toString();
// s2 is just reference of s1
if (s1 == s2)
    System.out.println("same thing");
```

toUpperCase()

PURPOSE Creates a string by turning all characters in this string into uppercase.

SYNTAX
```
public String toUpperCase()
public String toUpperCase(Locale loc)
```

DESCRIPTION This method creates a string that has the same sequence of characters as this string, except that all of the characters are in their uppercase forms as determined by the specified locale `loc`. If `loc` is not specified, the platform-dependent default locale is used.

PARAMETERS

`loc` The non-`null` locale to use when doing the conversion to uppercase.

RETURNS A new non-`null` string with all characters in uppercase.

SEE ALSO `Character.toUpperCase()`, `toLowerCase()`.

EXAMPLE

```
// creates new string with all upper case
System.out.println("This is a test".toUpperCase()); // "THIS IS A TEST"
```

trim()

PURPOSE Creates a new string by trimming any leading and trailing whitespace characters from this string.

SYNTAX `public String trim()`

DESCRIPTION This method creates a new string that has the same sequence of characters as this string, except that any leading and trailing whitespace characters have been removed. The definition of whitespace character is any Unicode character less than or equal to `\u0020`.

RETURNS A new non-`null` string with any leading and trailing whitespaces removed.

SEE ALSO `Character.isWhitespace()`.

EXAMPLE

```
String s1 = "  Start and end.  ";
String s2 = s1.trim(); // "Start and end."
```

valueOf()

PURPOSE Creates the string representation of a data value.

SYNTAX

```
public static String valueOf(boolean bool)
public static String valueOf(char ch)
public static String valueOf(int inum)
public static String valueOf(long lnum)
public static String valueOf(float fnum)
public static String valueOf(double dnum)
```

```
public static String valueOf(Object obj)
public static String valueOf(char[] data)
public static String valueOf(char[] data, int offset, count)
```

DESCRIPTION The nine forms of this method create the string representation of an object or a data value. After the string has been created, any modifications to the arguments do not affect the string already created.

PARAMETERS

`bool`	The `boolean` value (`true` or `false`) for which to create the string.
`ch`	The `char` value for which to create the string.
`count`	The number of characters to copy from `data`.
`data`	The non-`null` `char` array for which to create the string.
`dnum`	The `double` value for which to create the string.
`fnum`	The `float` value for which to create the string.
`inum`	The `int` value for which to create the string.
`lnum`	The `long` value for which to create the string.
`obj`	The possibly `null` object for which to create the string. If `null`, the result is "null."
`offset`	The index in `data` from which to start copying. `offset` must be in the range from `0` to `data.length-1` (inclusive).

RETURNS A new non-`null` `String` object that represents the data value.

SEE ALSO `copyValueOf()`, `Boolean.toString()`, `Byte.toString()`, `Character.toString()`, `Double.toString()`, `Float.toString()`, `Integer.toString()`, `Long.toString()`, `Short.toString()`, `Object.toString()`.

EXAMPLE

```
int inum = 512;
long lnum = Long.MAX_VALUE;
double dnum = 123.123e54;
float fnum = 3.1243f;
Object obj1 = null;
Object obj2 = new Vector();

String s1 = String.valueOf(true); // "true"
String s2 = String.valueOf('A');  // "A"
String s3 = String.valueOf(inum); // "512"
String s4 = String.valueOf(lnum); // "9223372036854775807"
String s5 = String.valueOf(dnum); // "1.23123e+56"
String s6 = String.valueOf(fnum); // "3.1243"
String s7 = String.valueOf(obj1); // "null"
String s8 = String.valueOf(obj2); // "[]"

char[] charArray = {'a', 'b', 'c'};
String s9 = String.valueOf(charArray);  // "abc"
charArray[1] = 'B'; // won't affect s9
```

StringBuffer

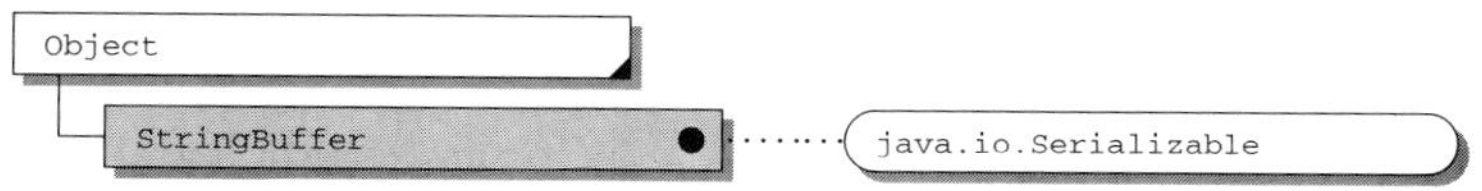

A B C D E F G H I J K L M N O P Q R S T U V W X Y Z

Syntax

```
public final class StringBuffer implements Serializable
```

Description

The `String` class is used to create immutable `String` objects. Each time you update a string, a new `String` object is created. A more efficient way to deal with these updates is to store a string in a `StringBuffer`, make updates to it until a `String` form is needed, and then use the `StringBuffer` to create a `String` object.

The `StringBuffer` class implements a buffer for characters that allows updates and allows the buffer to grow and shrink as needed to accommodate the updates. The Java compiler uses `StringBuffer` to implement the + operator. For example,

```
"a" + 4 + "c"
```

is compiled to

```
new StringBuffer().append("a").append(4).append("c").toString()
```

Capacity

When you create a `StringBuffer`, you can create it with a *capacity*. A capacity is the amount of storage that has been allocated for the string buffer (see Figure 95). If you know approximately how big your string is going to be, you can supply that number as the capacity so that the string buffer does not have to expand each time more characters are added to it. After a `StringBuffer` has been created, you can set its capacity at any time by calling `ensureCapacity()`.

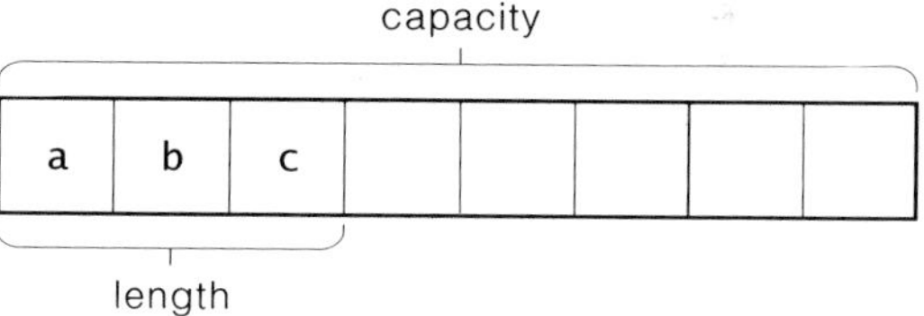

FIGURE 95: `StringBuffer`.

MEMBER SUMMARY	
Constructor	
`StringBuffer()`	Constructs a `StringBuffer` instance.
Update Methods	
`append()`	Appends the string representation of an object or data value to this string buffer.
`insert()`	Inserts the string representation of an object or data value into this string buffer.
`reverse()`	Reverses the order of characters in this string buffer.
`setCharAt()`	Replaces a character in this string buffer.
`setLength()`	Truncates or expands this string buffer.
Access Methods	
`charAt()`	Retrieves a character from this string buffer.
`getChars()`	Copies a region of this string buffer to a character array.
Capacity and Length Methods	
`capacity()`	Retrieves the current capacity of this string buffer.
`ensureCapacity()`	Ensures that the capacity of this string buffer is at least a specified amount.
`length()`	Retrieves the number of characters in this string buffer.
String Method	
`toString()`	Generates the string representation of this object.

See Also

`ByteArrayOutputStream`, `CharArrayReader`, `CharArrayWriter`, `String`.

append()

PURPOSE Appends the string representation of an object or data value to this string buffer.

SYNTAX

```
public StringBuffer append(boolean bool)
public synchronized StringBuffer append(char ch)
public StringBuffer append(int inum)
public StringBuffer append(long lnum)
public StringBuffer append(float fnum)
public StringBuffer append(double dnum)
public synchronized StringBuffer append(Object obj)
public synchronized StringBuffer append(String str)
```

```
public synchronized StringBuffer append(char[] data)
public synchronized StringBUffer append(char[] data, int offset,
   int count)
```

DESCRIPTION

Each of the ten forms of this method appends the string representation of its argument to this string buffer and returns the reference to the (updated) string buffer. The string buffer is automatically expanded as needed to accommodate additional characters. The data is copied into the string buffer, so any subsequent modifications to the arguments do not affect the string buffer. For example, subsequent changes to `data` will not affect the string buffer.

Although some forms of the method do not have the `synchronized` modifier, they eventually call a version of `append()` that does have the `synchronized` modifier, thus ensuring that all updates to the string buffer are done one at a time.

PARAMETERS

`bool`	The `boolean` whose string representation to append.
`ch`	The character to append.
`count`	The number of characters from `data` to use.
`data`	The non-`null char` array for getting characters to append.
`dnum`	The `double` whose string representation to append.
`fnum`	The `float` whose string representation to append.
`inum`	The `int` whose string representation to append.
`lnum`	The `long` whose string representation to append.
`obj`	The possibly `null` object whose string representation to append. If `null`, the string “null” is appended.
`offset`	The index (inclusive) in `data` from which to start getting characters. `0` ≤ `offset` < `data.length`.
`str`	The possibly `null` string to append. If `null`, append the string “null”.

RETURNS

The non-`null` updated `StringBuffer`, *not* a new one.

SEE ALSO

`insert()`, `ensureCapacity()String.valueOf()`.

EXAMPLE

```
int inum = 512;
long lnum = Long.MAX_VALUE;
double dnum = 123.123e54;
float fnum = 3.1243f;
char sep = ' ';
Object obj1 = null;
Object obj2 = new Vector();
char[] charArray = {'a', 'b', 'c'};
StringBuffer buf = new StringBuffer(100);

// Keep appending all the data types above to buf
buf.append(inum).append(sep).append(lnum).append(sep);
buf.append(dnum).append(sep).append(dnum).append(sep);
buf.append(obj1).append(sep).append(obj2);
```

```
buf.append(sep).append(charArray);
buf.append(sep).append(charArray, 1, 2);
```


capacity()

PURPOSE Retrieves the current capacity of this string buffer.

SYNTAX `public int capacity()`

DESCRIPTION A *capacity* is the amount of storage that has been allocated for the string buffer. It differs from the *length* of the string buffer, which is the actual number of characters in the string buffer. If the number of characters to be added to the string buffer during an update exceeds the string buffer's capacity, the string buffer's capacity is increased to accommodate the additional characters. You can set the capacity either when creating the string buffer or at any time after creation by calling `ensureCapacity()`. `capacity()` returns the current capacity of this string buffer.

RETURNS The current capacity of this string buffer.

SEE ALSO `ensureCapacity()`, `length()`, `StringBuffer()`.

EXAMPLE

```
StringBuffer s0 = new StringBuffer();
StringBuffer s1 = new StringBuffer(20);
StringBuffer s2 = new StringBuffer("this is a test");

// capacity is different from length
// for s0 (cap 16, len 0)
// for s1 (cap 20, len 0),
// for s2 (cap 16+14, len 14)
System.out.println("s0: capacity " + s0.capacity() + " length " + s0.length());
System.out.println("s1: capacity " + s1.capacity() + " length " + s1.length());
System.out.println("s2: capacity " + s2.capacity() + " length " + s2.length());
```

charAt()

PURPOSE Retrieves a character from this string buffer.

SYNTAX `public synchronized char charAt(int index)`

DESCRIPTION This method returns the character at the index `index` of this string buffer.

PARAMETERS

`index` The index of the character to retrieve. `0` ≤ `index` < `length()`.

RETURNS The character at `index`.

EXCEPTIONS

`StringIndexOutOfBoundsException`

If `index` is outside the range specified.

SEE ALSO `getChars()`, `setCharAt()`.

EXAMPLE

```
// Count null characters in buffer
public static int countNullChars(StringBuffer buf)
{
    int count = 0;
    for (int i = 0; i < buf.length(); i++) {
        if (buf.charAt(i) == '\0')
            ++count;
    }
    return (count);
}
```

A B C D E F G H I J K L M N O P Q R S T U V W X Y Z

ensureCapacity()

PURPOSE Ensures that the capacity of the string buffer is at least a specified amount.

SYNTAX `public synchronized void ensureCapacity(int minimumCapacity)`

DESCRIPTION A *capacity* is the amount of storage that has been allocated for the string buffer. It differs from the *length* of the string buffer, which is the actual number of characters in the string buffer. If the number of characters to be added to the string buffer during an update exceeds the string buffer's capacity, the string buffer's capacity is increased to accommodate the additional characters. If you know the approximate expected size of the final string, you should set the capacity of the string buffer to that number to decrease the number of times the capacity must be increased. You can set the capacity either when creating the string buffer or at any time after creation by calling `ensureCapacity()`. `ensureCapacity()` ensures that the capacity of the string buffer is at least `minimumCapacity`. If the capacity is less than `minimumCapacity`, it is increased to `minimumCapacity`. If the capacity is already at or greater than `minimumCapacity`, the capacity is left unchanged.

PARAMETERS

`minimumCapacity`

The minimum desired capacity.

SEE ALSO `capacity()`.

EXAMPLE

```
StringBuffer s1 = new StringBuffer("this is a test");
String filler = new String("simple yet powerful");

s1.ensureCapacity(10); // no op, already cap > 10
```

```
s1.ensureCapacity(100);

// buffer need not be expanded for following operations
s1.append(filler).append(filler).append(filler);
```


getChars()

PURPOSE Copies a region of the string buffer to a character array.

SYNTAX
```
public synchronized void getChars(int srcOffset, int srcEnd,
   char[] dst, int dstOffset)
```

DESCRIPTION This method copies the characters in the region specified by the starting index `srcOffset` (inclusive) and the ending index `srcEnd` (exclusive) of this string buffer into the character array `dst`, starting at the array's `dstBegin` index. If `srcOffset` ≥ `srcEnd`, no characters are copied.

PARAMETERS

`dst` The non-`null` `char` array into which to copy the characters.

`dstOffset` The index in `dst` to which to start copying. `0` ≤ `dstOffset` < `dst.length`.

`srcEnd` The index in this string buffer at which to stop copying (exclusive). `0` ≤ `srcEnd` ≤ `length()`.

`srcOffset` The index in this string buffer to start copying (inclusive). `0` ≤ `srcOffset` < `length()`.

EXCEPTIONS

`StringIndexOutOfBoundsException`
If `srcOffset` or `srcEnd` is outside the bounds of this string buffer.

`ArrayIndexOutOfBoundsException`
If `dstOffset` is outside the bounds of `dst`.

SEE ALSO `charAt()`.

EXAMPLE

```
// Make a copy of StringBuffer
public static StringBuffer copyStringBuffer(StringBuffer buf) {
    char[] data = new char[buf.length()];
    buf.getChars(0, buf.length(), data, 0);
    StringBuffer answer = new StringBuffer(buf.length());
    answer.append(data);
    return (answer);
}
```

insert()

PURPOSE

Inserts the string representation of an object or data value into this string buffer.

SYNTAX

```
public StringBuffer insert(int offset, boolean bool)
public synchronized StringBuffer insert(int offset, char ch)
public StringBuffer insert(int offset, int inum)
public StringBuffer insert(int offset, long lnum)
public StringBuffer insert(int offset, float fnum)
public StringBuffer insert(int offset, double dnum)
public synchronized StringBuffer insert(int offset, Object obj)
public synchronized StringBuffer insert(int offset, String str)
public synchronized StringBuffer insert(int offset, char[] data)
```

DESCRIPTION

Each of the nine forms of this method inserts the string representation of its argument into this string buffer starting at index `offset`. Any characters occurring at or greater than `offset` are placed after the newly added characters. A call to `insert()` with an `offset` of `length()` is equivalent to a call to `append()`. This method returns the reference to the (updated) string buffer. The string buffer is automatically expanded as needed to accommodate additional characters. The data is copied into the string buffer, so any subsequent modifications to the arguments do not affect the string buffer. For example, subsequent changes to `data` will not affect the string buffer.

Although some forms of the method do not have the `synchronized` modifier, they eventually call a version of `insert()` that does have the `synchronized` modifier, thus ensuring that all updates to the string buffer are done one at a time.

PARAMETERS

`bool` The `boolean` whose string representation to insert.

`ch` The character to insert.

`data` The non-`null` `char` array for getting characters to insert.

`dnum` The `double` whose string representation to insert.

`fnum` The `float` whose string representation to insert.

`inum` The `int` whose string representation to insert.

`lnum` The `long` whose string representation to insert.

`obj` The possibly `null` object whose string representation to insert. If `null`, the string "null" is inserted.

`offset` The index in this string buffer at which to start the insertion. `0` ≤ `offset` ≤ `length()`.

`str` The non-`null` string to insert.

RETURNS

The updated `StringBuffer`, *not* a new one.

EXCEPTIONS

`StringIndexOutOfBoundsException`
If `offset` is not in the range of `0` to `length()`.

SEE ALSO `append()`, `ensureCapacity()String.valueOf()`.

A B C D E F G H I J K L M N O P Q R S T U V W X Y Z

EXAMPLE

```
int inum = 512;
long lnum = Long.MAX_VALUE;
double dnum = 123.123e54;
float fnum = 3.1243f;
char sep = ' ';
Object obj1 = null;
Object obj2 = new Vector();
char[] charArray = {'a', 'b', 'c'};
StringBuffer buf = new StringBuffer(100);

// Keep inserting at head of buffer all the data types above
buf.insert(0, inum).insert(0, sep).insert(0, lnum).insert(0, sep);
buf.insert(0, dnum).insert(0, sep).insert(0, dnum).insert(0, sep);
buf.insert(0, obj1).insert(0, sep).insert(0, obj2);
buf.insert(0, sep).insert(0, charArray);
```

length()

PURPOSE Retrieves the number of characters in this string buffer.

SYNTAX `public int length()`

RETURNS The number of characters in this string buffer.

SEE ALSO `capacity()`, `setLength()`.

EXAMPLE See `capacity()`.

reverse()

PURPOSE Reverses the order of characters in this string buffer.

SYNTAX `public synchronized StringBuffer reverse()`

RETURNS The non-`null` updated `StringBuffer`, *not* a new one.

EXAMPLE

```
class Main {
    public static void main(String[] args) {
        StringBuffer sb = new StringBuffer("abcde");

        sb.reverse();
        System.out.println(sb);   // "edcba"
    }
}
```

setCharAt()

PURPOSE Replaces a character in this string buffer.

SYNTAX `public synchronized void setCharAt(int index, char ch)`

DESCRIPTION This method replaces the character at the index `index` of this string buffer with the character `ch`.

PARAMETERS

`index` The index of the character to update. `0` ≤ `index` < `length()`.

`ch` The character to use.

EXCEPTIONS

`StringIndexOutOfBoundsException`

If `index` is not in the range specified.

SEE ALSO `charAt()`.

EXAMPLE

```
// Set null characters in buffer to '#'
public static void markNullChars(StringBuffer buf)
{
    for (int i = 0; i < buf.length(); i++) {
        if (buf.charAt(i) == '\0')
            buf.setCharAt(i, '#');
    }
}
```

setLength()

PURPOSE Truncates or expands this string buffer.

SYNTAX `public synchronized void setLength(int newLength)`

DESCRIPTION This method sets the length of this string buffer to `newLength`. If `newLength` is less than the current length of the string buffer, the string buffer is truncated. Characters located at an index at or greater than `newLength` are lost. If `newLength` is greater than the current length of the string buffer, the newly added region is filled with null characters (`\0`).

PARAMETERS

`newLength` The new length of the string buffer. `newLength` ≥ `0`.

EXCEPTIONS

`StringIndexOutOfBoundsException`

If `newLength` is negative.

EXAMPLE

```
StringBuffer s1 = new StringBuffer("this is a test");
```

```
// expand buffer
s1.setLength(20);
System.out.println(s1 + "(" + s1.length() + ")"); // added null chars

// truncate buffer
s1.setLength(4);
System.out.println(s1 + "(" + s1.length() + ")"); // "this"
```

A B C D E F G H I J K L M N O P Q R S T U V W X Y Z

StringBuffer()

PURPOSE Constructs a new `StringBuffer` instance.

SYNTAX
```
public StringBuffer()
public StringBuffer(int capacity)
public StringBuffer(String str)
```

DESCRIPTION The `StringBuffer` class has three constructors. The first takes no arguments; it creates an empty `StringBuffer` with a default capacity of 16. The second creates an empty `StringBuffer` that has the initial capacity of `capacity`. The third takes a string, `str`, as the argument and creates a new `StringBuffer` by copying the characters from `str` into the new string buffer.

PARAMETERS

`capacity` The initial capacity of this string buffer.

`str` The non-`null` initial value of the string buffer.

SEE ALSO `capacity()`, `ensureCapacity()`.

EXAMPLE See `capacity()`.

toString()

PURPOSE Generates the string representation of this object.

SYNTAX
```
public String toString()
```

DESCRIPTION This method returns a new `String` object that shares the internal string buffer of this `StringBuffer` object. The `StringBuffer` class enforces a copy-on-write policy on this shared buffer so that when this string buffer is updated in the future, a copy will be made to accommodate the new updates without affecting the `String` already returned.

RETURNS A new non-`null` `String` object that shares the internal string buffer of this `StringBuffer` object.

OVERRIDES `Object.toString()`.

EXAMPLE See `append()`.

DEPRECATED StringBufferInputStream

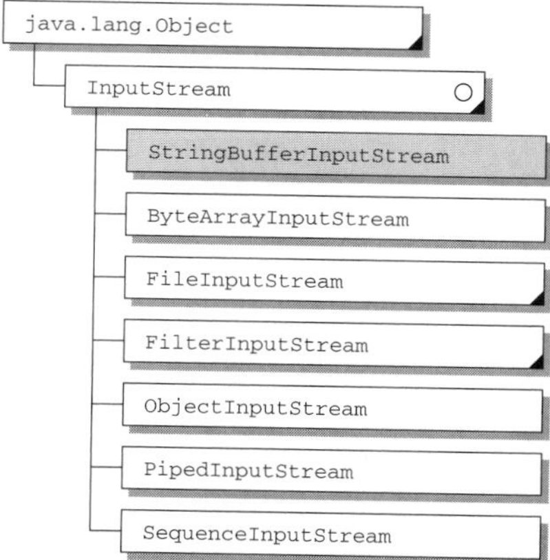

Note: The use of the StringBufferInputStream class is deprecated. Replace the usage of this class with StringReader.

Syntax

```
public class StringBufferInputStream extends InputStream
```

Description

The `StringBufferInputStream` class allows a string to be used as an input stream.

Deprecation

`StringBufferInputStream` removes the high-order byte of a character when "reading" a character from the string. This generally does not properly convert a character into its byte representation.

Replace the usage of `StringBufferInputStream`, as in:

```
StringBufferInputStream in =
    new StringBufferInputStream("this is a string");
byte[] buf = ...;
while (in.read(buf) > 0) {
    ...
}
```

with `StringReader`, as in:

```
StringReader in = new StringReader("this is a string");
char[] buf = ...;
while (in.read(buf, 0, buf.length) > 0) {
    ...
}
```

MEMBER SUMMARY	
Deprecated Constructor	
`StringBufferInputStream()`	Replaced by `StringReader.StringReader()`.
Deprecated Input Methods	
`read()`	Replaced by `StringReader.read()`.
`skip()`	Replaced by `StringReader.skip()`.
Deprecated Stream Methods	
`available()`	Replaced by `StringReader.ready()`.
`reset()`	Replaced by `StringReader.reset()`.
Deprecated Protected Fields	
`buffer`	The string in which data for this stream is stored.
`count`	The total number of characters in this string.
`pos`	The current read position of this stream.

See Also

`ByteArrayInputStream`, `InputStream`, `StringBuffer`, `StringReader`.

Example

The following code uses a string buffer input stream to read its input from either the command line or standard input. The usage of string buffer input stream is deprecated. The second example that follows shows doing the same thing using `StringReader`.

Deprecated

```
import java.io.StringBufferInputStream;
import java.io.InputStream;
import java.io.IOException;

class Old {
    private static long rand(InputStream in) {
        long sum = 0;
        try {
            int c;
            while ((c = in.read()) >= 0)
                sum += c;
        } catch (IOException e) {
        }
        return sum;
    }
    public static void main(String[] args) {
        InputStream in;
        // if no string specified in command line, read from standard in
        if (args.length != 1) {
            in = System.in;
        } else {
```

```
            in = new StringBufferInputStream(args[0]);
        }

        System.out.println(rand(in));
    }
}
```

Using StringReader

```
import java.io.*;

class New {
    private static long rand(Reader in) {
        long sum = 0;
        try {
            int c;
            while ((c = in.read()) >= 0)
                sum += c;
        } catch (IOException e) {
        }
        return sum;
    }
    public static void main(String[] args) {
        Reader in;
        // if no string specified in command line, read from standard in
        if (args.length != 1) {
            in = new InputStreamReader(System.in);
        } else {
            in = new StringReader(args[0]);
        }

        System.out.println(rand(in));
    }
}
```


available() *DEPRECATED*

PURPOSE Replaced by `StringReader.ready()`.

SYNTAX `public synchronized int available()`

RETURNS The number of bytes available in this stream.

OVERRIDES `InputStream.available()`.

DEPRECATION This method returns the number of bytes available in this string buffer input stream, which is the number of characters yet to be read from this stream. Replace the usage of the `StringBufferInputStream` class with `StringReader`. The `StringReader` class does not have a method corresponding directly to `available()`. Because of a bug in the JDK, `StringReader.ready()` always returns true and therefore cannot be used as a replacement for `StringBufferInputStream.available()`.

A B C D E F G H I J K L M N O P Q R S T U V W X Y Z

buffer

DEPRECATED

PURPOSE The string in which data for this stream is stored.

SYNTAX `protected String buffer`

DEPRECATION Replace the usage of the `StringBufferInputStream` class with `StringReader`. The `StringReader` class does not allow subclasses to manipulate its internal state by changing fields.

SEE ALSO `count`, `pos`.

count

DEPRECATED

PURPOSE The total number of characters in this string.

SYNTAX `protected int count`

DEPRECATION Replace the usage of the `StringBufferInputStream` class with `StringReader`. The `StringReader` class does not allow subclasses to manipulate its internal state by changing fields.

SEE ALSO `buffer, pos`.

pos

DEPRECATED

PURPOSE The current read position of this stream.

SYNTAX `protected int pos`

DEPRECATION Replace the usage of the `StringBufferInputStream` class with `StringReader`. The `StringReader` class does not allow subclasses to manipulate its internal state by changing fields.

SEE ALSO `buffer, count, read(), reset(), skip()`.

read()

DEPRECATED

PURPOSE Replaced by `StringReader.read()`.

SYNTAX
```
public synchronized int read()
public synchronized int read(byte[] buffer, int offset, int count)
```

PARAMETERS

- `buffer` The non-`null` `byte` array in which to store the bytes read.
- `count` The number of bytes to read. $0 \leq$ `count` $\leq$ `buffer.length-offset`.
- `offset` The index in `buffer` at which to start storing the bytes read. $0 \leq$ `offset` $<$ `buffer.length`.

RETURNS The first form returns the byte read (0–255); the second form returns the actual number of bytes read. Both forms return `-1` when end-of-string has been reached.

EXCEPTIONS

`ArrayIndexOutOfBoundsException`

If `count` or `offset` is outside of the specified bounds.

OVERRIDES `InputStream.read()`.

DEPRECATION The two forms of this method read bytes from this string buffer input stream. The first form reads the next character from this string buffer input stream and returns it as an `int` after removing the character's high-order byte. The higher-order 3 bytes of the `int` are 0 and are unused. The second form reads the next `count` number of characters from this string buffer input stream and stores the bytes in the `byte` array `buffer` starting at index `offset`. Only the lower-order byte of each character is stored in `buffer`; the higher-order byte is ignored. This method does not in general properly convert a character to its byte representation. See the class description and class example for how to replace the usage of this method with `StringReader.read()`.

reset()

DEPRECATED

PURPOSE Replaced by `StringReader.reset()`.

SYNTAX `public synchronized void reset()`

OVERRIDES `InputStream.reset()`.

DEPRECATION This method resets the current read position to `0` so that subsequent `read()` and `skip()` calls will get characters from the beginning of the string. Replace the usage of `StringBufferInputStream` with `StringReader` and the usage of `reset()` with `StringReader.reset()`.

skip()

DEPRECATED

PURPOSE Replaced by `StringReader.skip()`.

SYNTAX `public synchronized long skip(long count)`

PARAMETERS

`count` The number of characters to skip. If `n` < `0`, `0` is returned.

RETURNS The actual number of characters skipped.

OVERRIDES `InputStream.skip()`.

DEPRECATION This method skips `count` number of characters from this string buffer input stream. It increments the current read position by `count` so that subsequent `read()/skip()` calls will not read those characters just skipped. Replace the usage of `StringBufferInputStream` with `StringReader` and the usage of `skip()` with `StringReader.skip()`.

StringBufferInputStream() *DEPRECATED*

PURPOSE Replaced by `StringReader.StringReader()`.

SYNTAX `public StringBufferInputStream(String str)`

PARAMETERS

`str` The non-`null` string to use for the new input stream. It is not copied.

DESCRIPTION This constructor creates a new string buffer input stream using the string `str` as data for the stream. The initial current read position (`pos`) of the stream is `0` (the beginning of `str`), and there are `str.length` (`count`) number of characters in this stream. Replace the usage of `StringBufferInputStream` with `StringReader`. See the class description and the class example for how to do this replacement.

java.text

StringCharacterIterator

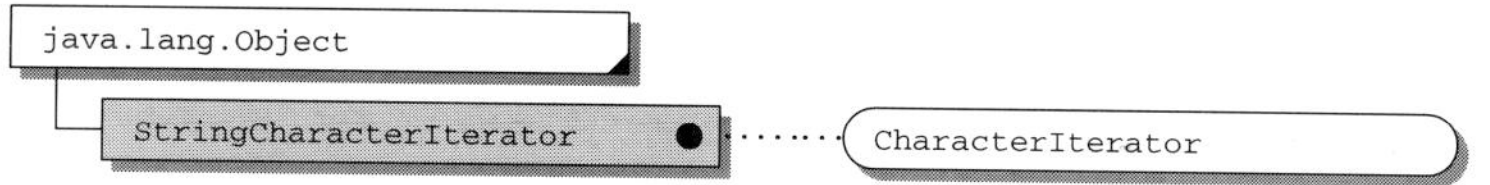

Syntax

```
public final class StringCharacterIterator extends Object implements
    CharacterIterator
```

Description

`StringCharacterIterator` is a class for iterating forward and backward over a string of Unicode characters. This class enables moving about within a range of text and returning individual characters or their index values. See Figure 96.

```
|N|o|w| |i|s| |t|h|e| |t|i|m|e|
  0 1 2 3 4 5 6 7 8 9 10
  |          |          |
first()   current()   last()
```

FIGURE 96: `StringCharacterIterator`.

You use `StringCharacterIterator` for iterator operations on `String` where you want the additional benefit of having those same operations also work on text held in classes other than `String`. For example, the `BreakIterator` class can perform boundary analysis not only on text that is stored in a `String` object, but also on text that is in a fictitious `DatabaseText` class stored on a remote database. This is possible because `StringCharacterIterator` implements `CharacterIterator` for accessing the characters in a `String` object. See `CharacterIterator` for more details.

The `StringCharacterIterator` class defines a cursor and the ability to limit its motion to a subrange of the string. The cursor tracks the current position in the text. The iterator's movement methods can control the position of the cursor, jumping either to an absolute position or relative to the current position. These methods can return the character or its index at the new position. Iteration can be restricted to a contiguous subrange of characters.

Usage

When you create a string character iterator, you call a constructor and specify the string that it iterates over and the initial cursor position. You also specify the subrange, if desired. This subrange includes characters that have index values from `getBeginIndex()` through `getEndIndex() - 1`. The index of the current character can be retrieved by calling `getIndex()`.

Calling a movement method on the iterator causes its cursor to move to the specified position in that subrange. The methods `next()` and `previous()` move relative to the current position. If either method would move the cursor beyond either end of the subrange, the method instead returns `StringCharacterIterator.DONE` (documented in `CharacterIterator`), thereby signaling that the iterator has reached the end of the subrange. The methods `first()`, last(), and setIndex(int) move to absolute positions that are independent of the current position. All five movement methods return the character at the new position. The getter methods with names containing "index" return index values: getBeginIndex(), getEndIndex(), and getIndex().

Note: A known bug in JDK 1.1.5 and earlier versions is that the method next() has a peculiar behavior. That is, after it reaches the end of the subrange and returns DONE, continuing to call it causes it to mistakenly continue incrementing the current position well beyond the index of the last character. In contrast, the method previous() stops at the start of the range. This has been fixed in JDK 1.1.6.

Index

The position of each character is identified by its *index*, which is 0-based, starting with the very first character in the string, independent of any subrange. Thus a given character has a fixed index regardless of the begin and end index values of the subrange.

Subrange

An iterator can be created to iterate either over the entire string or over a restricted *subrange*. The constructor StringCharacterIterator(String text, int begin, int end, int pos) creates a StringCharacterIterator object that iterates across the subrange begin to end, instead of the entire string.

When an iterator has a restricted range, it cannot move the current index outside that subrange of text. To be precise, the iterator allows the current index to travel over the range from getBeginIndex() to getEndIndex() – 1.

The end of the subrange is an interesting case in that the integer returned by getEndIndex() is the index of the first character *following* the end of the iterable subrange. Another way of looking at this is that the subrange includes the first character getBeginIndex() and excludes the last character getEndIndex(). Thus, if the text subrange can iterate over character index 5 to 10 inclusive, getEndIndex() returns 11. This means that if you want to iterate to the end of the string, you use the string's length for the ending index.

StringCharacterIterator has no methods for setting a subrange. The range can be set only once—when the iterator is created.

Cursor and Current Index

The *current index* is the index at which the iterator is currently positioned in the string. This position is marked by an imaginary *cursor*, just ahead of the character at the current index and positioned between characters. Calling the movement methods moves the cursor and current index from one position to another, in either direction. This cursor is conceptually the same as the caret described in TextComponent, except it is not visible.

MEMBER SUMMARY	
Constructor	
`StringCharacterIterator()`	Constructs a `StringCharacterIterator` instance.
Movement Methods	
`first()`	Moves the index to the beginning of the text subrange and retrieves the character at that position.
`last()`	Moves the index to the end of the text subrange and retrieves the character at that position.
`next()`	Increments the index by 1 and retrieves the character at the new index.
`previous()`	Decrements the index by 1 and retrieves the character at the new index.
`setIndex(int)`	Moves the index to a position and retrieves the character at the new index.
Character and Index Getter Methods	
`current()`	Retrieves the character at the current index.
`getIndex()`	Retrieves the current index.
`getBeginIndex()`	Retrieves the index at the beginning of the text subrange.
`getEndIndex()`	Retrieves the index at the end of the text subrange.
Comparison Method	
`equals()`	Compares this `StringCharacterIterator` object with another object for equality.
Object Methods	
`clone()`	Creates a copy of this string character iterator.
`hashCode()`	Computes the hash code for this `StringCharacterIterator` object.

See Also

`CharacterIterator`.

Example

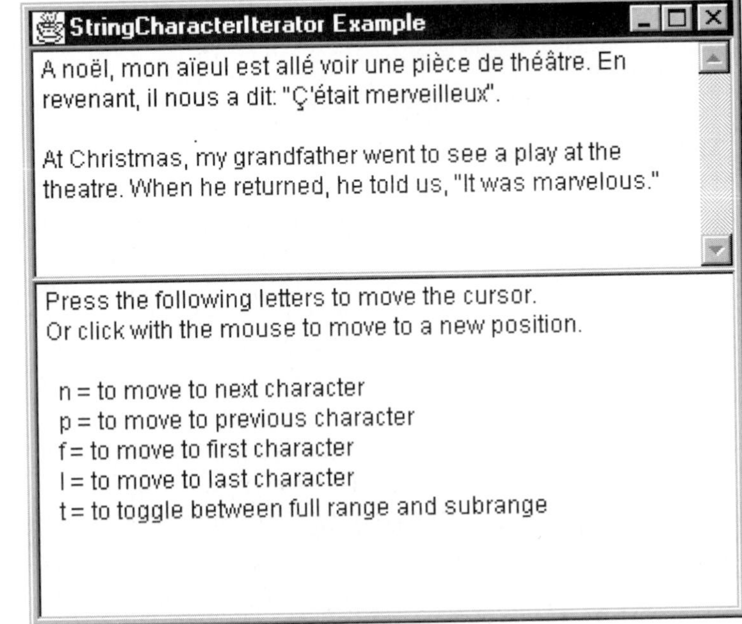

FIGURE 97: Using `StringCharacterIterator`.

This example demonstrates the different ways a string character iterator can move through text. When you run this program, supply a filename of a text file you want to display and iterate over, such as `input.txt`. The full text is initially highlighted, with the cursor at position 0. Press the letters n (next), p (previous), f (first) and l (last) to move the cursor. See Figure 97.

To toggle between iterating over the full range and subrange, press "t." (The subrange is highlighted in Solaris but not in Windows.) Notice that if you click in the text but *outside* of the subrange, then pressing a movement key properly causes an `IllegalArgumentException`. This is because the iterator is trying to set the current index to a value outside of its subrange. Click inside of the subrange for a valid value. Values are printed in the console window. This example enables you to go one character past the end of the subrange or range so that you can see the diagnostic "DONE" appear.

```
import java.awt.*;
import java.awt.event.*;
import java.io.*;
import java.util.*;
import java.text.StringCharacterIterator;

class Main extends Frame {
    TextArea textArea =
        new TextArea("", 20, 50, TextArea.SCROLLBARS_VERTICAL_ONLY);
    TextArea message =
        new TextArea("", 10, 50, TextArea.SCROLLBARS_NONE);

    StringCharacterIterator sci = null;
    StringCharacterIterator sci1 = null;
    StringCharacterIterator sci2 = null;
    boolean subrangeflag = false;

    Main(String s, String sNative) {
        super("StringCharacterIterator Example");
```

```
    // Set the text and create the iterator.
    textArea.setText(s);
    sci1 = new StringCharacterIterator(sNative);

    // Create the subrange iterator.
    int end = (int)Math.round (0.7 * sNative.length());
    int begin  = (int)Math.round (0.3 * sNative.length());

    // Diagnostics:
    System.out.println("start of subrange: " + begin);
    System.out.println("end of subrange:   " + end);

    sci2 = new StringCharacterIterator(sNative, begin, end, begin);

    // Set the initial iterator.
    sci = sci1;

    // Display the instructions
    message.setText(
      "Press the following letters to move the cursor.\n" +
      "Or click with the mouse to move to a new position.\n" +
      "\n" +
      "  n = to move to next character\n" +
      "  p = to move to previous character\n" +
      "  f = to move to first character\n" +
      "  l = to move to last character\n" +
      "  t = to toggle between full range and subrange\n"
    );

    message.setEditable(false);

    // Create text area and listen for key events.
    add(textArea, BorderLayout.CENTER);
    add(message, BorderLayout.SOUTH);
    textArea.addKeyListener(new KeyEventHandler());

    setSize(400, 400);
    show();
    textArea.select(sci.getBeginIndex(), sci.getEndIndex() - 1);
    textArea.setCaretPosition(sci.getIndex());
}

class KeyEventHandler extends KeyAdapter {
    public void keyPressed(KeyEvent evt) {

        // In case the user clicks, get the caret position.
        int caret = textArea.getCaretPosition();

        // Set the iterator to match the caret.
        if (subrangeflag) {
            if (caret < (sci.getEndIndex() - 1)) {
                sci.setIndex(caret);
            }
        } else {
            if (caret < textArea.getText().length()) {
                sci.setIndex(caret);
            }
        }
        char rtn = '_';
```

```
            // Branch according to key pressed.
            switch (Character.toLowerCase(evt.getKeyChar())) {
              case 'n':
                  //  Workaround for bug in next().
                  if (sci.getIndex() < sci.getEndIndex()) {
                      rtn = sci.next();
                  }
                  break;
              case 'p':
                  rtn = sci.previous();
                  break;
              case 'f':
                  rtn = sci.first();
                  break;
              case 'l':
                  rtn = sci.last();
                  break;
              case 't':
                  // Toggle between range and subrange.

                  if (subrangeflag) {
                      sci = sci1;
                      subrangeflag = false;
                  } else {
                      sci = sci2;
                      subrangeflag = true;
                  }

                  // Diagnostics:
                  System.out.println("");
                  System.out.println("getBeginIndex:   " + sci.getBeginIndex());
                  System.out.println("getEndIndex:     " + sci.getEndIndex());

                  // Highlight the range.
                  textArea.select(sci.getBeginIndex(), sci.getEndIndex() - 1);
                  break;
            }

            // Set the caret position.
            textArea.setCaretPosition(sci.getIndex());

            // Diagnostics:
            System.out.println("");
            System.out.println("current:      " + sci.current());
            System.out.println("getIndex:     " + sci.getIndex());
            if (rtn == StringCharacterIterator.DONE) {
                System.out.println("character:    " + "DONE");
            } else {
                System.out.println("character:    " + rtn);
            }

            evt.consume();
        }
    }

    public static void main(String[] args) {
        if (args.length != 1) {
            System.err.println("Usage: java Main <filename>");
            System.exit(1);
        }
```

```
        try {
            // To workaround a TextArea bug, create two versions
            // of the text:
            // - one with '\n' for newlines (to display in text area)
            // - the other with native newlines (to iterate over)
            // Read in the entire contents of the file.
            BufferedReader rd = new BufferedReader(new FileReader(args[0]));
            String sep = System.getProperty("line.separator");
            String line;
            StringBuffer sbuf = new StringBuffer();
            StringBuffer sbufNative = new StringBuffer();

            while ((line = rd.readLine()) != null) {
                sbuf.append(line);
                sbuf.append('\n');
                sbufNative.append(line);
                sbufNative.append(sep);
            }
            rd.close();
            new Main(new String(sbuf), new String(sbufNative));
        } catch (Exception e) {
            e.printStackTrace();
        }
    }
}
```

clone()

PURPOSE Creates a copy of this string character iterator.

SYNTAX `public Object clone()`

DESCRIPTION This method makes a copy of this string character iterator. The copy points to the same text and has the same current index as the original.

OVERRIDES `java.lang.Object.clone()`.

RETURNS A copy of this string character iterator.

EXAMPLE This example demonstrates the use of `clone()` to copy a string character iterator. Note that the copy has the same `getIndex()` value (6) and current character (“w”) as the original.

```
import java.text.StringCharacterIterator;

class Main {

    public static void main(String args[]) {

        String str = "Hello world";

        // create string character iterator
        StringCharacterIterator iter = new StringCharacterIterator(str, 6);
        printValues(iter);          // prints '6' and 'w'
```

```
            // create a clone
            StringCharacterIterator iterCopy =
                (StringCharacterIterator)iter.clone();
            printValues(iterCopy);      // prints '6' and 'w'

            if(iter.equals(iterCopy)) {
                System.out.println("Copy is equal to original");
            } else {
                System.out.println("Copy is not equal to original");
            }

            // compute hashcode
            int hc = iter.hashCode();
            System.out.println("Hash code is: " + hc);
        }

        public static void printValues(StringCharacterIterator it) {
            System.out.println(it.getIndex());
            System.out.println(it.current());
        }
    }
```

Output

```
> java Main
6
w
6
w
Copy is equal to original
Hash code is: -1596494559
```

current()

PURPOSE Retrieves the character at the current index.

SYNTAX `public char current()`

DESCRIPTION This method gets the character at the current index. This is the same index returned by `getIndex()`. This method does not move the current index.

Note: In JDK 1.1.x, this method throws `StringIndexOutOfBoundsException` if the text subrange you're trying to iterate over is empty (that is, if `getBeginIndex()` and `getEndIndex()` return the same value). This is considered a bug. Starting with JDK 1.2, `it` will return `DONE`, rather than throw an error. Because it is a change in semantics, it will not be fixed in the JDK 1.1.x series.

RETURNS The character at the current index.

EXAMPLE See `next()`.

equals()

PURPOSE Compares this `StringCharacterIterator` object with another object for equality.

SYNTAX `public boolean equals(Object obj)`

DESCRIPTION This method compares this `StringCharacterIterator` object with the object `obj` for equality. If `obj` is a `StringCharacterIterator` object and if it has the same text, current index, and range as this `StringCharacterIterator` object, the objects are equal and this method returns `true`. If those values are not equal or if `obj` is `null` or not a `StringCharacterIterator` object, this method returns `false`.

PARAMETERS

`obj` The string character iterator with which to be compared.

RETURNS `true` if the given `obj` is equal to this `StringCharacterIterator` instance; `false` otherwise.

OVERRIDES `java.lang.Object.equals()`.

SEE ALSO `hashCode()`.

EXAMPLE See `clone()`.

first()

PURPOSE Moves the index to the beginning of the text subrange and retrieves the character at that position.

SYNTAX `public char first()`

DESCRIPTION This method moves the current index to the beginning of the text subrange and returns the character at that position. This new index is the same as that returned by `getBeginIndex()`.

Note: In JDK 1.1.x, this method throws `StringIndexOutOfBoundsException` if the text subrange you're trying to iterate over is empty (that is, if `getBeginIndex()` and `getEndIndex()` return the same value). This is considered a bug. Starting with JDK 1.2, `it` will return `DONE`, rather than throw an error. Because it is a change in semantics, it will not be fixed in the JDK 1.1.x series.

RETURNS The first character in the text subrange.

SEE ALSO `getBeginIndex()`.

EXAMPLE See `next()`.

getBeginIndex()

PURPOSE Retrieves the index at the beginning of the text subrange.

SYNTAX `public int getBeginIndex()`

DESCRIPTION This method returns the index at the beginning of the iterable text subrange. It does not move the current index.

RETURNS The index at which the text subrange begins.

SEE ALSO `first()`.

EXAMPLE See `next()`.

getEndIndex()

PURPOSE Retrieves the index at the end of the text subrange.

SYNTAX `public int getEndIndex()`

DESCRIPTION This method retrieves the index of the first character following the end of the text subrange. Thus, if the text subrange includes characters with index `5` to `10`, this method returns `11`. This method does not move the current index.

Note: A known bug in JDK 1.1.5 and earlier versions is that the method `next()` has a peculiar behavior. That is, after it reaches the end of the subrange and returns `DONE`, continuing to call it causes it to mistakenly continue incrementing the current position well beyond the index of the last character. Therefore, `getEndIndex()` has no upper limit. This is fixed in JDK 1.1.6.

RETURNS The index at which the text subrange ends.

EXAMPLE See `next()`.

getIndex()

PURPOSE Retrieves the current index.

SYNTAX `public int getIndex()`

DESCRIPTION This method gets the current index without moving it.

RETURNS The current index.

EXAMPLE See `next()`.

hashCode()

PURPOSE
Computes the hash code for this `StringCharacterIterator` object.

SYNTAX
```
public int hashCode()
```

DESCRIPTION
This method computes the hash code of this `StringCharacterIterator` object based on the string, current index value, begin range value, and end range value. Two `StringCharacterIterator` objects with the same properties will have the same hash code. However, two `StringCharacterIterator` objects that do not have the same properties might also have the same hash code, although the hash code algorithm minimizes this possibility. The hash code is typically used as the key in a hash table.

RETURNS
The string character iterator's hash code, an integer.

OVERRIDES
`java.lang.Object.hashCode()`.

SEE ALSO
`equals()`.

EXAMPLE
See `clone()`.

last()

PURPOSE
Moves the index to the end of the text subrange and retrieves the character at that position.

SYNTAX
```
public char last()
```

DESCRIPTION
This method moves the current index to the end of the text subrange and returns the character at that position. This new index is the same as that returned by `getEndIndex() - 1`.

Note: In JDK 1.1.x, this method throws `StringIndexOutOfBoundsException` if the text subrange you're trying to iterate over is empty (that is, if `getBegin-Index()` and `getEndIndex()` return the same value). This is considered a bug. Starting with JDK 1.2, `it` will return `DONE`, rather than throw an error. Because it is a change in semantics, it will not be fixed in the JDK 1.1.x series.

RETURNS
The last character in the text subrange.

EXAMPLE
See `next()`.

next()

PURPOSE Increments the index by 1 and retrieves the character at the new index.

SYNTAX `public char next()`

DESCRIPTION This method increments the current index by 1 and returns the character at the new index. If the iterator attempts to increment past the end of the text subrange, the current index remains at that position and a value of `StringCharacterIterator.DONE` is returned (documented in `CharacterIterator`).

Note: A known bug in JDK 1.1.5 and earlier versions is that the method `next()` has a peculiar behavior. That is, after it reaches the end of the subrange and returns `DONE`, continuing to call it causes it to mistakenly continue incrementing the current position well beyond the index of the last character. In contrast, the method `previous()` stops at the start of the range. This is fixed in JDK 1.1.6.

Note: In JDK 1.1.x, this method throws `StringIndexOutOfBoundsException` if the text subrange you're trying to iterate over is empty (that is, if `getBeginIndex()` and `getEndIndex()` return the same value). This is considered a bug. Starting with JDK 1.2, `it` will return `DONE`, rather than throw an error. Because it is a change in semantics, it will not be fixed in the JDK 1.1.x series.

RETURNS The character at the new index, or `StringCharacterIterator.DONE`.

SEE ALSO `CharacterIterator.DONE`.

EXAMPLE This example demonstrates all of the movement methods. It also shows the value of the index at the last character (20) and the end of the range (21) and tests for the value `DONE`.

```
import java.text.StringCharacterIterator;

class Main {
    public static void main(String args[]) {

        String str =  "We want to thank you.";
        String str2 = "   |<-SUBRANGE-->|   ";

        // create string character iterator
        StringCharacterIterator sci =
                           new StringCharacterIterator(str, 3, 17, 11);

        System.out.println("'sci' is the string character iterator ");
        System.out.println("'|' is positioned ahead of the current index");
        System.out.println("                              " + str2);

        char rtn = sci.current();
        System.out.print("sci.current():        ");
        printOutChar(sci, str, rtn);

        rtn = sci.next();
```

```
        System.out.print("sci.next():          ");
        printOutChar(sci, str, rtn);

        rtn = sci.previous();
        System.out.print("sci.previous():      ");
        printOutChar(sci, str, rtn);

        rtn = sci.setIndex(sci.getEndIndex() - 2);
        System.out.print("sci.setIndex(" + (sci.getEndIndex() - 2) + "):    ");
        printOutChar(sci, str, rtn);

        rtn = sci.next();
        System.out.print("sci.next():          ");
        printOutChar(sci, str, rtn);

        rtn = sci.next();
        System.out.print("sci.next():          ");
        printOutChar(sci, str, rtn);

        rtn = sci.first();
        System.out.print("sci.first():         ");
        printOutChar(sci, str, rtn);

        rtn = sci.last();
        System.out.print("sci.last():          ");
        printOutChar(sci, str, rtn);

        int i = sci.getIndex();
        System.out.print("sci.getIndex():      ");
        printOutInt(sci, str, i);

        i = sci.getBeginIndex();
        System.out.print("sci.getBeginIndex(): ");
        printOutInt(sci, str, i);

        i = sci.getEndIndex();
        System.out.print("sci.getEndIndex():   ");
        printOutInt(sci, str, i);
    }

    // Print the text with a separator '|' at the current position
    public static void printOutChar(StringCharacterIterator iter,
                                    String str, char rtn) {
        printFirstPart(iter, str);
        if (rtn == StringCharacterIterator.DONE)
            System.out.println("   returns " + "DONE");
        else
            System.out.println("   returns \"" + rtn + "\"");
    }

    // Print the text with a separator '|' at the current position
    public static void printOutInt(StringCharacterIterator iter,
        String str, int rtn) {
        printFirstPart(iter, str);
        if (rtn == StringCharacterIterator.DONE)
            System.out.println("   returns " + "DONE");
        else
            System.out.println("   returns \"" + rtn + "\"");
    }
```

```
    public static void printFirstPart(StringCharacterIterator iter, String str) {
        int pos = iter.getIndex();
        System.out.print("\"" + str.substring(0,pos));
        System.out.print("|");
        System.out.print(str.substring(pos,str.length()) + "\"");
    }
}
```

Output

```
> java Main
'sci' is the string character iterator
'|' is positioned ahead of the current index
                          |<-SUBRANGE-->|
sci.current():       "We want to |thank you."   returns "t"
sci.next():          "We want to t|hank you."   returns "h"
sci.previous():      "We want to |thank you."   returns "t"
sci.setIndex(15):    "We want to than|k you."   returns "k"
sci.next():          "We want to thank| you."   returns " "
sci.next():          "We want to thank |you."   returns DONE
sci.first():         "We |want to thank you."   returns "w"
sci.last():          "We want to thank| you."   returns " "
sci.getIndex():      "We want to thank| you."   returns "16"
sci.getBeginIndex(): "We want to thank| you."   returns "3"
sci.getEndIndex():   "We want to thank| you."   returns "17"
```

previous()

PURPOSE Decrements the index by 1 and retrieves that character at the new index.

SYNTAX `public char previous()`

DESCRIPTION This method decrements the current index by 1 and returns the character at the new index. If the iterator attempts to decrement past the beginning of its range, `getBeginIndex()`, the current index remains at that position and a value of `StringCharacterIterator.DONE` is returned (documented in `CharacterIterator`).

Note: In JDK 1.1.x, this method throws `StringIndexOutOfBoundsException` if the text subrange you're trying to iterate over is empty (that is, if `getBeginIndex()` and `getEndIndex()` return the same value). This is considered a bug. Starting with JDK 1.2, `it` will return `DONE`, rather than throw an error. Because it is a change in semantics, it will not be fixed in the JDK 1.1.x series.

RETURNS The character at the new index, or `StringCharacterIterator.DONE`.

SEE ALSO `CharacterIterator.DONE`.

EXAMPLE See `next()`.

setIndex()

PURPOSE Moves the index to a position and retrieves that character at that new index.

SYNTAX `public char setIndex(int idx)`

DESCRIPTION This method sets the current index to `idx` and returns the character at that new index. If a value outside of the subrange is passed in, it throws an error. (It does not return `CharacterIterator.DONE`.)

Note: In JDK 1.1.x, the call `iterator.setIndex(iterator.getEndIndex())` throws an exception. This is considered a bug. Starting with JDK 1.2, this will be a valid call. Because it is a change in semantics, it will not be fixed in the JDK 1.1.x series.

PARAMETERS

`idx` Index to which to move the current index. It is necessary that `begin <= idx < end` or an `IllegalArgumentException` is thrown. The values `begin` and `end` are arguments passed into the constructor `StringCharacterIterator()`. *Note*: In JDK 1.1.x, a value of `idx` equal to `end` is invalid. This is considered a bug. Starting in JDK 1.2 it will be valid.

RETURNS The character at the new index, or `StringCharacterIterator.DONE`.

EXCEPTIONS

`IllegalArgumentException`
If `idx` is outside of its valid range.

EXAMPLE See `next()`.

StringCharacterIterator()

PURPOSE Constructs a `StringCharacterIterator` instance.

SYNTAX
```
public StringCharacterIterator(String text)
public StringCharacterIterator(String text, int pos)
public StringCharacterIterator(String text, int begin, int end,
   int pos)
```

DESCRIPTION This constructor constructs a string character iterator to iterate over the string `text`, sets the current index to the value `pos`, and restricts the iterator to the range from `begin` to `end`. If `pos` is not specified, it defaults to `0`. If `begin` and `end` are not specified, they default to `0` and `text.length()`, thereby enabling iteration over the full string.

Note: Contrary to convention, the second parameter in the second and third syntax forms of this method are not the same. The pos parameter is unexpectedly in the last position in the third form, rather than the second position.

PARAMETERS

`begin` Index of the character in the string where the iterator begins. It is necessary that `begin` ≥ `0` or an `IllegalArgumentException` is thrown. Throwing an exception may change in future versions.

`end` Index of the character in the string following the last character where the iterator ends. It is necessary that `begin` ≤`end` ≤ `text.length()` or an `IllegalArgumentException` is thrown.

`pos` Initial value of the current index. It is necessary that `begin` ≤ `pos` ≤ `end` or an `IllegalArgumentException` is thrown.

`text` The non-`null` string to be iterated over.

EXCEPTIONS

`IllegalArgumentException`
If `begin`, `pos`, or `end` is outside of its valid range. Throwing an exception for this condition may change in a future version.

EXAMPLE This example demonstrates all three constructors. For each constructor, it prints out the text over the entire range of its iterator, inserting a vertical bar "|" character to the left of the character where the current index is located.

The first two lines of output show the entire text, with different current index values. The third line of output shows the text subrange from positions 6 to 9.

```
import java.text.StringCharacterIterator;

class Main {
    public static void main(String args[]) {

        String str = "Hello big world";

        // Use one-argument constructor
        StringCharacterIterator iter1 =
            new StringCharacterIterator(str);
        printRange(iter1, str);

        // Use two-argument constructor
        StringCharacterIterator iter2 =
            new StringCharacterIterator(str, 6);
        printRange(iter2, str);

        // Use three-argument constructor
        StringCharacterIterator iter3 =
            new StringCharacterIterator(str, 6, 9, 6);
        printRange(iter3, str);
    }

    // Print the full range of the iterator
    // with a separator '|' at the current index
```

```
    public static void printRange(StringCharacterIterator iter, String src) {
        int pos = iter.getIndex();
        System.out.print(src.substring(iter.getBeginIndex(),pos));
        System.out.print("|");
        System.out.println(src.substring(pos,iter.getEndIndex()));
    }
}
```

Output

```
> java Main
|Hello big world
Hello |big world
|big
```

java.lang
StringIndexOutOfBoundsException

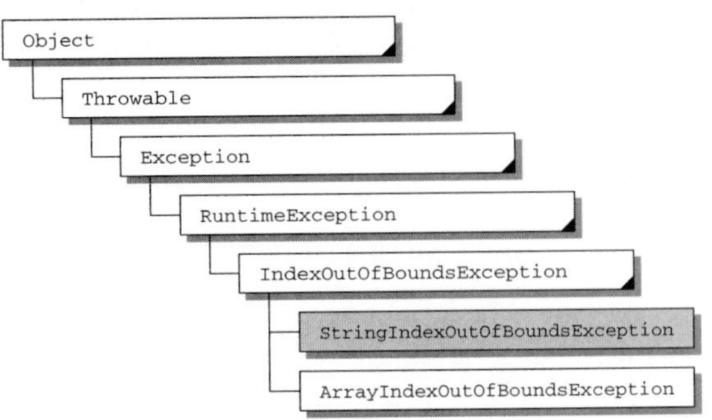

A B C D E F G H I J K L M N O P Q R **S** T U V W X Y Z

Syntax

`public class StringIndexOutOfBoundsException extends IndexOutOfBoundsException`

Description

`StringIndexOutOfBoundsException` is a runtime exception that is thrown when the program attempts to access a character within a `String` using an index that is not within the bounds of the `String`. Because `String` indices use a zero-based numbering scheme, the index is either negative or a number greater than or equal to the string's length.

`StringIndexOutOfBoundsException` is a runtime exception that should not be caught or declared in the `throws` clause of a method.

MEMBER SUMMARY	
Constructor	
`StringIndexOutOfBoundsException()`	Constructs an instance of `StringIndexOutOfBoundsException`.

See Also

`IndexOutOfBoundsException`, `RuntimeException`.

Example

This example generates a `StringIndexOutOfBoundsException`.

```
class Main {
    public static void main(String[] args) {
        System.out.println("StringIndexOutOfBoundsException example");
```

```
        String str = "abc";
        System.out.println(str.charAt(3));
    }
}
```


StringIndexOutOfBoundsException()

PURPOSE Constructs a `StringIndexOutOfBoundsException` instance.

SYNTAX
```
public StringIndexOutOfBoundsException()
public StringIndexOutOfBoundsException(int idx)
public StringIndexOutOfBoundsException(String msg)
```

DESCRIPTION The three forms of this constructor construct an instance of `StringIndexOutOfBoundsException`. An optional string `msg` can be supplied that describes this particular instance of the exception. Alternatively, the index `idx` that caused the exception can be supplied to the constructor, which will use `idx` to construct a message for describing this exception. If neither `idx` nor `msg` is supplied, the message defaults to `null`.

PARAMETERS

`idx` The index that caused the exception.

`msg` A possibly `null` string that gives details about this exception.

SEE ALSO `Throwable.getMessage()`.

java.io

StringReader

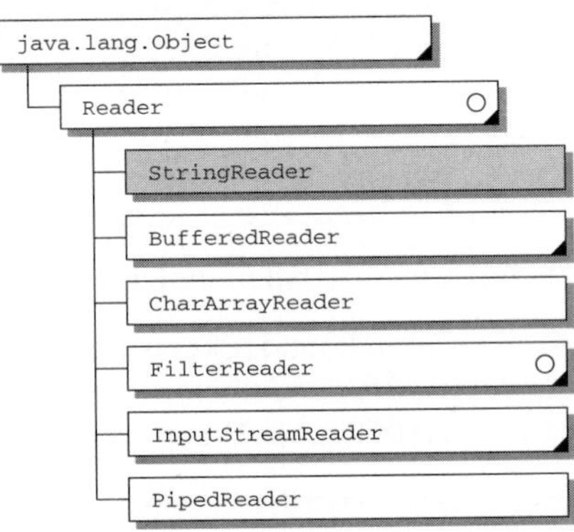

Syntax

```
public class StringReader extends Reader
```

Description

The `StringReader` class allows a string to be used as an character input stream. For example, you can turn a string into an character input stream (reader) so that you can read characters from that reader. Figure 98 shows an example of this. The string "This is a string" is turned into a `StringReader`. A `read()` of the first four characters from this reader produces the string "This".

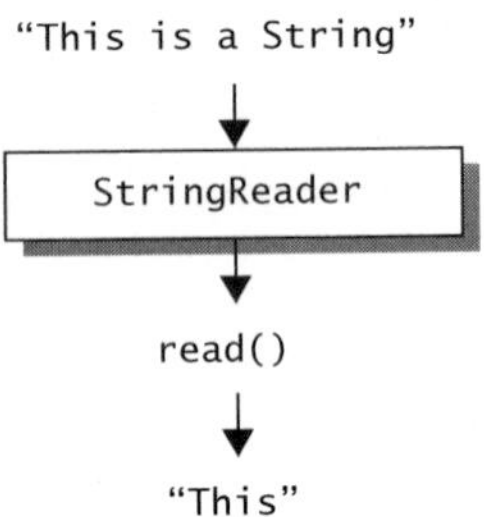

FIGURE 98: `StringReader.`

MEMBER SUMMARY	
Constructor	
`StringReader()`	Constructs a `StringReader` instance using a string.
Input Methods	
`read()`	Reads characters from this reader.
`skip()`	Skips characters from this reader.
Mark/Reset Methods	
`mark()`	Marks the current read position in the reader.
`markSupported()`	Determines whether this reader supports mark/reset.
`reset()`	Resets the read position to the previously marked position.

MEMBER SUMMARY	
Stream Methods	
`close()`	Closes this reader.
`ready()`	Determines whether this reader is ready to be read.

See Also

`ByteArrayInputStream`, `CharArrayReader`, `Reader`, `StringBuffer`, `StringWriter`.

Example

The following code reads its input from either the command line (using a string reader) or standard input.

```
import java.io.*;

class Main {
    private static long rand(Reader in) {
        long sum = 0;
        try {
            int c;
            while ((c = in.read()) >= 0)
                sum += c;
        } catch (IOException e) {
        }
        return sum;
    }
    public static void main(String[] args) {
        Reader in;
        // if no string specified in command line, read from standard in
        if (args.length != 1) {
            in = new InputStreamReader(System.in);
        } else {
            in = new StringReader(args[0]);
        }

        System.out.println(rand(in));
        try {
            in.close();
        } catch (IOException e) {}
    }
}
```

A B C D E F G H I J K L M N O P Q R S T U V W X Y Z

close()

PURPOSE Closes this reader.

SYNTAX `public void close()`

DESCRIPTION After this reader has been closed, you can no longer read from it. This method is idempotent. That is, you can invoke it many times, but only the first invocation has any effect.

OVERRIDES `Reader.close()`

EXAMPLE See the class example.

mark()

PURPOSE Marks the current read position in this reader.

SYNTAX `public void mark(int readlimit) throws IOException`

DESCRIPTION This method marks the current position in this reader so that a subsequent call to `reset()` will reposition the read position of the reader to this marked position.

PARAMETERS

`readlimit` This parameter is ignored.

EXCEPTIONS

`IOException`

If this reader has already been closed.

OVERRIDES `Reader.mark()`.

SEE ALSO `markSupported()`, `reset()`.

EXAMPLE The following code reads its input from either the command line (using a string reader) or standard input. If the reader supports mark/reset, a preview of the reader is displayed before the complete contents of the reader. The preview is available if the input is supplied from the command line, but it is not available from standard input because standard input does not support mark/reset.

```
import java.io.*;

class Main {
    private static void preview(Reader in) {
        try {
            if (in.markSupported()) {
                in.mark(0);                        // readlimit ignored
                char[] buf = new char[5];
                in.read(buf);                      // read characters
                in.reset();                        // reset to beginnning
```

```
                System.out.println("preview: " + new String(buf));
            }
        } catch (IOException e) {
        }
    }
    private static void showAll(Reader in) {
        try {
            char[] buf = new char[512];
            int howmany;
            while ((howmany=in.read(buf)) > 0) {
                System.out.print(new String(buf, 0, howmany));
            }
        } catch (IOException e) {
        }
    }
    public static void main(String[] args) {
        Reader in;
        // if no string specified in command line, read from standard in
        if (args.length != 1) {
            in = new InputStreamReader(System.in);
        } else {
            in = new StringReader(args[0]);
        }
        preview(in);
        showAll(in);
        try {
            in.close();
        } catch (IOException e) {}
    }
}
```

markSupported()

PURPOSE Determines whether this reader supports mark/reset.

SYNTAX `public boolean markSupported()`

DESCRIPTION A string reader supports mark/reset. This method always returns `true`.

RETURNS `true`.

OVERRIDES `Reader.markSupported()`.

SEE ALSO `mark()`, `reset()`.

EXAMPLE See `mark()`.

read()

PURPOSE Reads characters from this reader.

SYNTAX
```
public int read() throws IOException
public int read(char[] buffer, int offset, int count) throws
    IOException
```

DESCRIPTION The two forms of this method read characters from this string reader. The first form reads the next character from this reader and returns it as an `int` (the higher-order 2 bytes are 0 and unused). The second form reads the next `count` number of characters from this reader and stores the characters in the `char` array `buffer` starting at index `offset`.

The next character read is determined by the current read position, which is incremented as characters are read from the reader. It can be changed using `mark()/reset()`.

PARAMETERS

`buffer` The non-`null` `char` array in which to store the characters read.

`count` The number of characters to read. `0` ≤ `count` ≤ `buffer.length-offset`.

`offset` The index in `buffer` at which to start storing the characters read. `0` ≤ `offset` < `buffer.length`.

RETURNS The first form returns the character read; the second form returns the actual number of characters read. Both forms return `-1` when end-of-string has been reached.

EXCEPTIONS

`ArrayIndexOutOfBoundsException`
If `count` or `offset` is outside of the specified bounds.

`IOException`
If this reader has already been closed.

OVERRIDES `Reader.read()`.

SEE ALSO `mark()`, `reset()`, `skip()`.

EXAMPLE See `mark()`.

ready()

PURPOSE Determines whether this reader is ready to be read.

SYNTAX `public boolean ready()`

DESCRIPTION This method always returns `true`, even when the reader has been closed.

RETURNS `true`.

OVERRIDES `Reader.ready()`.

SEE ALSO `close()`.

EXAMPLE

```
StringReader in = new StringReader("Java Class Libraries");
System.out.println(in.ready()); // true
```


reset()

PURPOSE Resets the read position to the previously marked position.

SYNTAX `public void reset() throws IOException`

DESCRIPTION This method resets the current read position to the previously marked position so that subsequent `read()` and `skip()` calls will get characters from that position. If `mark()` has not been called, the reader is reset to the beginning of the string.

EXCEPTIONS

`IOException`

If this reader has already been closed.

OVERRIDES `Reader.reset()`.

SEE ALSO `mark()`, `markSupported()`.

EXAMPLE See `mark()`.

skip()

PURPOSE Skips characters from this reader.

SYNTAX `public long skip(long count) throws IOException`

DESCRIPTION This method skips `count` number of characters from this reader. It increments the current read position by `count` so that subsequent `read()/skip()` calls will not read those characters just skipped.

PARAMETERS

`count` The number of characters to skip. If `count` < `0`, no characters are skipped.

RETURNS The actual number of characters skipped.

EXCEPTIONS

`IOException`

If this reader has already been closed.

OVERRIDES `Reader.skip()`.

SEE ALSO `read()`.

StringReader()

PURPOSE Constructs a `StringReader` instance using a string.

SYNTAX `public StringReader(String str)`

DESCRIPTION This constructor constructs a new string reader using the string `str` as data for the reader. The initial current read position of the reader is `0` (the beginning of `str`), and there are `str.length` number of characters in this reader.

PARAMETERS

`str` The non-`null` string to use for the new reader. It is not copied.

EXAMPLE See the class example.

StringTokenizer

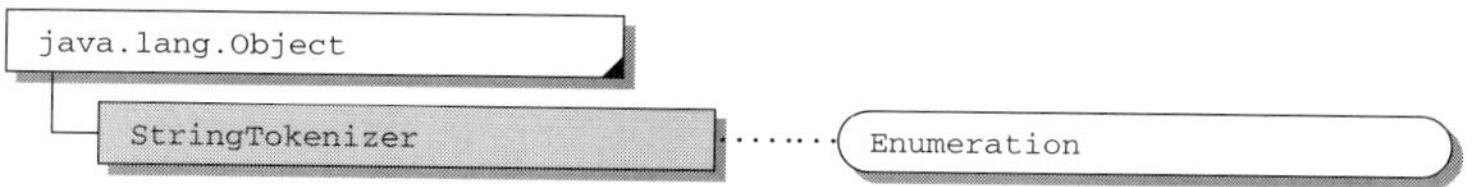

Syntax

```
public class StringTokenizer implements Enumeration
```

Description

The `StringTokenizer` class is for parsing a string into a sequence of *tokens*. A token is a string of characters separated by *delimiter characters* (or simply *delimiters*). An instance of a `StringTokenizer` is created with a string, a set of delimiters, and a flag indicating whether delimiters are to be returned as tokens. The delimiters can be replaced any time after the `StringTokenizer` has been created. The default delimiters are the whitespace characters (space, tab, newline, and return).

Usage

The following example shows a tokenizer that parses a string using the default delimiters (Figure 99):

```
String s = "99 cups of Java";
StringTokenizer parser =
    new StringTokenizer(s);
try {
    while(parser.hasMoreTokens()) {
         System.out.println(
            parser.nextToken());
    }
} catch (NoSuchElementException e) {
    System.out.println(e);
}
```

This example produces the following output:

```
99
cups
of
Java
```

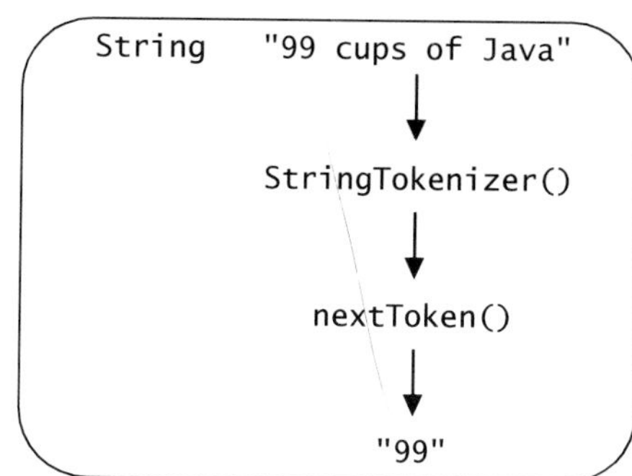

FIGURE 99: `StringTokenizer`.

`StringTokenizer` implements the `Enumeration` interface. This means you can pass an instance of `StringTokenizer` to methods that accept enumerations. You can use the enumeration methods to enumerate the tokens in a `StringTokenizer`.

The following example shows a tokenizer that parses a string using the semicolon character (;) as the delimiter:

```
String s = "c:\\windows\\command;c:\\dos;c:\\bin;c:\\util";
StringTokenizer parser = new StringTokenizer(s, ";");
```

```
try {
    while(parser.hasMoreTokens()) {
        System.out.println(parser.nextToken());
    }
} catch (NoSuchElementException e) {
    System.out.println(e);
}
```

It produces the following output:

```
c:\windows\command
c:\dos
c:\bin
c:\util
```

MEMBER SUMMARY	
Constructor	
`StringTokenizer()`	Constructs a `StringTokenizer` instance.
Parsing Methods	
`countTokens()`	Determines the number of tokens remaining in this string tokenizer.
`hasMoreTokens()`	Determines whether this string tokenizer has any more tokens.
`nextToken()`	Retrieves the next token in this string tokenizer.
Enumeration Methods	
`hasMoreElements()`	Determines whether this string tokenizer has any more tokens.
`nextElement()`	Retrieves the next token in this string tokenizer.

See Also

`Enumeration`, `StreamTokenizer`.

countTokens()

PURPOSE Determines the number of tokens remaining in this string tokenizer.

SYNTAX `public int countTokens()`

DESCRIPTION This method returns the number of tokens remaining in this string tokenizer. This is the number of times `nextToken()` can be called before it raises a `NoSuchElementException`. `countTokens()` does not affect the current position of the string tokenizer or the value returned by subsequent calls to `nextToken()`.

RETURNS The number of tokens remaining.

SEE ALSO `hasMoreTokens()`, `nextToken()`.

EXAMPLE This example shows a tokenizer that treats the delimiters as tokens. The output of this example follows its code.

```
String s = "a = b + c, d = e.";
StringTokenizer parser = new StringTokenizer(s, ",.", true);
System.out.println("There are " + parser.countTokens() + " tokens");
try {
    while (parser.hasMoreTokens()) {
        System.out.println(parser.nextToken());
    }
} catch (NoSuchElementException e) {
    e.printStackTrace();
}
```

Output

```
There are 4 tokens
a = b + c
,
 d = e
.
```

hasMoreElements()

PURPOSE Determines whether this string tokenizer has any more tokens.

SYNTAX `public boolean hasMoreElements()`

DESCRIPTION This method determines whether this string tokenizer has any more tokens. It is the same as `hasMoreTokens()`. It is provided for the `Enumeration` interface implemented by `StringTokenizer`.

RETURNS `true` if there are more tokens; `false` otherwise.

SEE ALSO `Enumeration.hasMoreElements()`, `hasMoreTokens()`.

EXAMPLE See the class example.

hasMoreTokens()

PURPOSE Determines whether this string tokenizer has any more tokens.

SYNTAX `public boolean hasMoreTokens()`

DESCRIPTION This method checks this string tokenizer to see if it has any more unparsed tokens. It updates the current position of the string tokenizer to be at the starting position of the next token. If it is already at the start of the next token, the current position is not changed.

RETURNS `true` if there are more tokens; `false` otherwise.

SEE ALSO `countTokens()`, `hasMoreElements()`.

EXAMPLE See the class example.

nextElement()

PURPOSE Retrieves the next token in this string tokenizer.

SYNTAX
```
public Object nextElement()
```

DESCRIPTION This method retrieves the next token in this string tokenizer. It is the same as `nextToken()`. It is provided for the `Enumeration` interface implemented by `StringTokenizer`.

RETURNS A non-`null` string containing the next token in this string tokenizer.

EXCEPTIONS

`NoSuchElementException`
If there are no more tokens in this string tokenizer.

SEE ALSO `Enumeration.nextElement()`, `nextToken()`.

EXAMPLE See the class example.

nextToken()

PURPOSE Retrieves the next token in this string tokenizer.

SYNTAX
```
public String nextToken()
public String nextToken(String delims)
```

DESCRIPTION The two forms of the method return the next token in this string tokenizer, delimited by any of the delimiters associated with this string tokenizer. If `delims` is specified, `nextToken()` first sets the delimiters of this string tokenizer to be `delims` and then returns the next token in its string delimited by any character in `delims`. `delims` will be used for subsequent `nextToken()` calls until it is replaced by another set of delimiters.

If this string tokenizer was created with `retDelim` set to `true`, any delimiter that is encountered in its string is also returned as a token, one character at a time. If it was created with `retDelim` set to `false`, delimiters are not returned as tokens.

PARAMETERS

`delims` A non-`null` string containing the delimiters to use for this string tokenizer.

RETURNS A non-null string containing the next token in this string tokenizer.

EXCEPTIONS

`NoSuchElementException`

If there are no more tokens in this string tokenizer.

SEE ALSO `nextElement()`, `StringTokenizer()`.

EXAMPLE This example shows the use of `nextElement()` to parse a quoted string. Initially, the tokenizer uses blanks and the single quotation mark character as delimiters. When it encounters the single quotation mark character, it uses only that character as the delimiter. In this way, you can have embedded blanks within the quoted string. Once the quoted string has been parsed, the tokenizer switches back to accepting both blanks and single quotation mark characters as delimiters. The output of this example follows its code.

```
String s = "frontstuff 'Welcome to our Home' endstuff";
StringTokenizer parser = new StringTokenizer(s, " '", true);
String token, new_delimiter = null;
boolean look_for_matching_quote = false;
try {
    while (parser.hasMoreTokens()) {
        if (new_delimiter != null) {
            token = parser.nextToken(new_delimiter);
            new_delimiter = null;
        } else {
            token = parser.nextToken();
        }
        if (token.equals(" "))
            continue;
        if (token.equals("'")) {
            if (look_for_matching_quote) {
                new_delimiter = " '";
                look_for_matching_quote = false;
            } else {
                new_delimiter = "'";  // can have embedded blanks
                look_for_matching_quote = true;
            }
        } else {
            System.out.println(token);
        }
    }
} catch (NoSuchElementException e) {
    e.printStackTrace();
}
```

Output

```
frontstuff
Welcome to our Home
endstuff
```

StringTokenizer()

PURPOSE
Constructs a `StringTokenizer` instance.

SYNTAX

```
public StringTokenizer(String str)
public StringTokenizer(String str, String delims)
public StringTokenizer(String str, String delims, boolean
   retDelim)
```

DESCRIPTION
There are three forms of the constructor for `StringTokenizer`. The first form creates a string tokenizer for the string `str` with delimiters " `\t\n\r`" (blank, tab, newline, and return). Delimiters that occur in `str` are not returned as tokens.

The second form creates a string tokenizer for the string `str` with delimiters in the string `delims`. Delimiters that occur in `str` are not returned as tokens.

The third form creates a string tokenizer for the string `str` with delimiters in the string `delims`. If `retDelim` is `true`, delimiters that occur in `str` are returned as tokens; if `retDelim` is `false`, delimiters are not returned.

PARAMETERS

`delims` A non-`null` string containing the delimiters for this tokenizer. Each character in `delims` is used to delimit tokens that occur in `str`.

`retDelim` If `true`, the delimiters will be returned as a token a character at a time as they are encountered; if `false`, the delimiters will not be returned as tokens.

`str` The non-`null` string to parse for this string tokenizer.

SEE ALSO
`nextToken()`.

EXAMPLE
See the class examples and `count()`, `nextToken()` for examples.

StringWriter

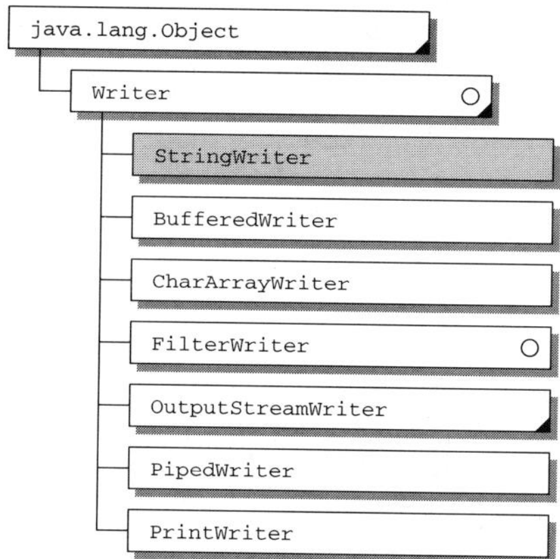

Syntax

```
public class StringWriter extends Writer
```

Description

`StringWriter` implements a character output stream that uses a `StringBuffer` to store the characters written to it. You can subsequently request that the characters written to it be returned as a string. This is helpful when you want to capture output from methods that operate on writers in the form of a string. See Figure 100.

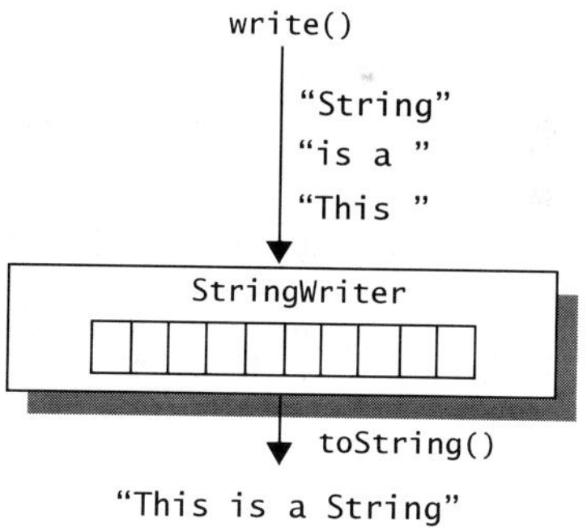

FIGURE 100: `StringWriter`.

CharArrayWriter and ByteArrayOutputStream

Classes that perform similar functions are `CharArrayWriter` and `ByteArrayOutputStream`. Instead of writing to a `StringBuffer`, `CharArrayWriter` writes to a `char` array. `ByteArrayOutputStream` provides similar functionality for `byte` arrays.

MEMBER SUMMARY	
Constructor	
`StringWriter()`	Constructs a `StringWriter` instance.
Output Method	
`write()`	Writes one or more characters to this string writer.
Externalizing Methods	
`getBuffer()`	Retrieves the contents of this writer as a `StringBuffer`.
`toString()`	Retrieves the contents of this writer as a `String`.
Stream Methods	
`close()`	This method does nothing.
`flush()`	This method does nothing.

A B C D E F G H I J K L M N O P Q R S T U V W X Y Z

See Also

`ByteArrayOutputStream`, `CharArrayWriter`, `java.lang.String`, `java.lang.StringBuffer`, `StringReader`.

Example

This example creates a `StringWriter` and then writes a string and some characters to it. It then retrieves the contents of the writer.

```
import java.io.*;

class Main {
    public static void main(String[] args) {
        StringWriter out = new StringWriter();

        out.write("Java Class Libraries");
        for (char ch = 'a'; ch < 'z'; ch++ ) {
            out.write(ch);
            out.write(' ');
        }
        System.out.println(out.toString());
// Java Class Librariesa b c d e f g h i j k l m n o p q r s t u v w x y z
    }
}
```

close()

PURPOSE This method does nothing.

SYNTAX `public void close()`

DESCRIPTION This method implements the abstract method declared in `Writer`.

SEE ALSO `Writer.close()`.

flush()

PURPOSE This method does nothing.

SYNTAX `public void flush()`

DESCRIPTION This method implements the abstract method declared in `Writer`.

SEE ALSO `Writer.flush()`.

getBuffer()

PURPOSE Retrieves the contents of this writer as a `StringBuffer`.

SYNTAX `public StringBuffer getBuffer()`

DESCRIPTION This writer's internal `StringBuffer` is returned. Any characters subsequently written to this writer are reflected in the returned buffer, and any changes made to the buffer by the caller are reflected in this writer.

RETURNS The `StringBuffer` used by this string writer.

SEE ALSO `toString()`.

EXAMPLE This example retrieves the contents of a string writer as a `StringBuffer` and then makes changes to the `StringBuffer`. Note that this has a direct impact on the string writer.

```
import java.io.*;

class Main {
    public static void main(String[] args) {
        StringWriter out = new StringWriter();

        out.write("Java Class Libraries");
        for (char ch = 'a'; ch < 'z'; ch++ ) {
            out.write(ch);
            out.write(' ');
        }
        StringBuffer buf = out.getBuffer();
        buf.reverse();  // Make a change to the StringBuffer

        System.out.println(out.toString()); // writer is affected
// y x w v u t s r q p o n m l k j i h g f e d c b aseirarbiL ssalC avaJ

    }
}
```

StringWriter()

PURPOSE Constructs a `StringWriter` instance.

SYNTAX
```
public StringWriter()
protected StringWriter(int initialSize)
```

DESCRIPTION The public constructor constructs an instance of `StringWriter`. It creates a `StringBuffer` with a default size of 16 to hold characters written to this writer. The protected constructor constructs an instance of `StringWriter` that has a string buffer size of `initialSize`. The `StringBuffer` of the newly created writer will grow automatically as the number of characters written to it exceeds the initial buffer size.

The lock of this reader is assigned to the `StringBuffer` being used for this writer. (See `Writer.lock`.)

PARAMETERS

`initialSize` The initial size to use when creating the internal `StringBuffer`.

SEE ALSO `Writer.lock`, `Writer.Writer()`.

EXAMPLE See the class example.

toString()

PURPOSE Retrieves the contents of this string writer as a string.

SYNTAX `public String toString()`

DESCRIPTION This method creates a string using the contents of this string writer. The string that is returned is a snapshot of the current contents of this writer. It is not affected by any subsequent changes to this writer.

RETURNS The non-`null` string representing the contents of this writer.

OVERRIDES `java.lang.Object.toString()`.

SEE ALSO `java.lang.String.String()`, `getBuffer()`.

EXAMPLE See the class example.

write()

PURPOSE

Writes one or more characters to this string writer.

SYNTAX

```
public void write(int oneChar)
public void write(char[] buffer, int offset, int count)
public void write(String str)
public void write(String str, int offset, int count)
```

DESCRIPTION

The `write()` method writes one or more characters to this string writer. The first form of `write()` writes a single character `oneChar` to this writer. The other forms write `count` characters from the `char` array `buffer` or string `str` starting at index `offset` to this writer. If `offset` and `count` are not specified, they default to `0` and `str.length()`, respectively.

The characters are written to the writer starting at the current write position. The current write position is incremented to reflect the new characters written. The internal `StringBuffer` used to hold the contents of the writer expands dynamically as required to hold all of the new data.

PARAMETERS

`buffer` The non-`null` `char` array containing the characters to be written.

`count` The number of characters from `buffer` or `str` to be written.
`0` ≤ `count` ≤ `buffer.length-offset` or `0` ≤ `count` ≤ `str.length()-offset`.

`offset` The index in `buffer` or `str` of the first character to be written.
`0` ≤ `offset` < `buffer.length` or 0 ≤ `offset` < `str.length()`.

`oneChar` The character to be written. The low-order 2 bytes of `oneChar` are used.

`str` The non-`null` string containing the characters to be written.

EXCEPTIONS

`ArrayIndexOutOfBoundsException`
If `count` or `offset` is outside of the specified bounds.

OVERRIDES

`Writer.write()`.

EXAMPLE

See the class example.

java.io
SyncFailedException

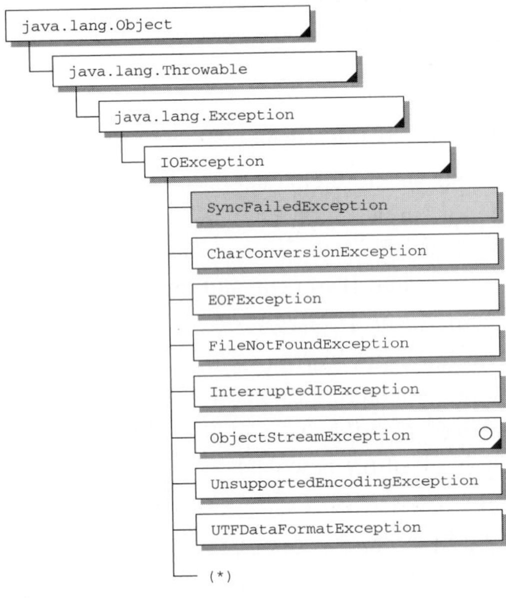

Syntax

`public class SyncFailedException extends IOException`

Description

`SyncFailedException` is thrown when the `FileDescriptor.sync()` method cannot be completed successfully. See `FileDescriptor.sync()` for details.

MEMBER SUMMARY	
Constructor	
`SyncFailedException()`	Constructs a `SyncFailedException` instance.

See Also

`FileDescriptor.sync()`.

Example

This is a code fragment showing `SyncFailedException` being caught in a call to `FileDescriptor.sync()`.

```
FileOutputStream out = ...;
try {
    out.getFD().sync();    // Commit changes to disk
} catch (SyncFailedException se) {
    System.err.println("sync failed: " + se);
}
```

SyncFailedException()

PURPOSE Constructs an `SyncFailedException` instance.

SYNTAX `public SyncFailedException(String msg)`

DESCRIPTION This constructor constructs an instance of `SyncFailedException`. `msg` gives more details about this particular instance of this exception. If `msg` is not supplied, it defaults to `null`.

PARAMETERS

`msg` A possibly `null` string that gives details about this exception.

SEE ALSO `java.lang.Throwable.getMessage()`.

java.lang
System

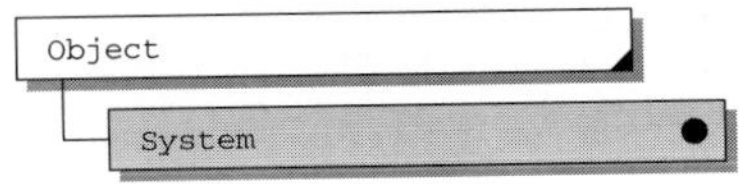

A B C D E F G H I J K L M N O P Q R S T U V W X Y Z

Syntax

```
public final class System
```

Description

The `System` class provides a collection of methods for examining and manipulating system-related information in a platform-independent manner. These methods include support for standard IO, memory management, and system properties.

This class cannot be instantiated or subclassed.

Standard IO

The `System` class provides support for user-level IO. Three open streams are associated with the three standard open files: input, output, and error output. The standard input stream is used by the program to read character data from the user who is running the program. The standard output stream is used by the program to print text output for display to the user; for example:

```
System.out.println("Hello World!");
```

The standard error output stream is used by the program to print error messages to the user.

The `System` class provides methods to change these standard IO streams.

Security

A security manager enforces security policies related to what a program is allowed to do. Some of these policies concern which class loaders to use, inspection of the execution stack, access to local files, access to system properties, and permission to execute system programs. The `System` class allows the program to set these policies by defining which security manager to use.

The Java runtime system, by default, does not use a security manager. However, applications such as Web browsers typically define a security manager and use `System.setSecurityManager()` to install it. Only one security manager can be installed. Once installed, it cannot be replaced.

Runtime

The `System` class provides methods for performing runtime-related functions, such as loading libraries and memory management. These methods are also available directly from the `Runtime` class; the `System` class methods are just short forms of the same methods.

For example, calling

```
System.gc();
```

is equivalent to calling

```
Runtime.getRuntime().gc();
```

A B C D E F G H I J K L M N O P Q R S T U V W X Y Z

System Properties

A *system property* is a key-value pair that the Java runtime defines to describe the user, system environment, and Java system. Table 42 lists the default system properties. Other properties also can be made available to a Java program via the -D option to the Java interpreter. For example, running the interpreter as follows:

```
java -Dmyenviron=abc Main
```

adds the property myenviron with value abc to the list of properties visible to the program Main.

The System class provides methods that allow you to get all or selected properties, as well as a method to update the list of properties. The ability to read or update any system property is controlled by the security manager.

Property Name	Description
java.version	Java version number.
java.vendor	Java vendor-specific information.
java.vendor.url	Java vendor URL.
java.home	Name of the directory in which the Java software has been installed.
java.class.version	Java class version number.
java.class.path	Setting of CLASSPATH plus default path (see ClassLoader).
os.name	Name of the operating system.
os.arch	Machine architecture.
os.version	Release version of the operating system.
file.separator	String used in file pathnames to separate directories.
path.separator	String used to separate components in a path variable.
line.separator	String used to separate lines.
user.name	User's account name.
user.home	Pathname of user's home directory.
user.dir	Pathname of user's current working directory.

TABLE 42: Java System Properties.

MEMBER SUMMARY

Standard IO	
`err`	Standard error output stream.
`in`	Standard input stream.
`out`	Standard output stream.
`setErr()`	Sets the standard error output stream.
`setIn()`	Sets the standard input stream.
`setOut()`	Sets the standard output stream.
Security Methods	
`getSecurityManager()`	Retrieves the reference to the security manager.
`setSecurityManager()`	Sets the system's security manager.
Runtime Methods	
`exit()`	Exits the virtual machine.
`gc()`	Runs the garbage collector.
`load()`	Loads a dynamic library when given its full pathname.
`loadLibrary()`	Loads a dynamic library when given its library name.
`runFinalization()`	Runs the finalization method of objects that are pending finalization.
`runFinalizersOnExit()`	Enables/disables finalization when the program exits.
System Properties	
`getProperties()`	Retrieves the list of system properties.
`getProperty()`	Retrieves the named system property.
`setProperties()`	Updates the list of system properties.
Array Method	
`arraycopy()`	Copies a region of one array to another.
Time Method	
`currentTimeMillis()`	Retrieves the current time in milliseconds.
Object Method	
`identityHashCode()`	Returns `Object.hashCode()` for an object.
Deprecated Method	
`getenv()`	Replaced by `getProperty()`.

See Also

`java.io.InputStream`, `java.io.OutputStream`, `java.io.PrintStream`, `java.util.Date`, `java.util.Properties`, `Runtime`, `SecurityManager`.

arraycopy()

PURPOSE Copies a region of one array to another.

SYNTAX
```
public static native void arraycopy(Object src, int srcOffset,
    Object dst, int dstOffset, int count)
```

DESCRIPTION This method copies a region of one array, `src`, beginning at the array cell at `srcOffset`, to another array, `dst`, beginning at the array cell at `dstOffset`. `count` cells are copied. This method does not allocate memory for the destination array `dst`. The memory must already be allocated.

PARAMETERS

`count`	The number of cells to copy.
`dst`	The non-`null` array into which to copy.
`dstOffset`	The first cell in `dst` into which to copy.
`src`	The non-`null` array from which to copy.
`srcOffset`	The first cell in `src` from which to copy.

EXCEPTIONS

`ArrayIndexOutOfBoundsException`
: `count`, `dstOffset`, or `srcOffset` are specified in such a way that the copy would cause access of data outside array bounds.

`ArrayStoreException`
: If an element in the `src` array could not be stored into the destination array due to a type mismatch.

EXAMPLE
```
// Implementation of String.getChars().
public void getChars(int srcBegin, int srcEnd, char dst[], int dstBegin) {
    System.arraycopy(value, offset + srcBegin, dst, dstBegin,
        srcEnd - srcBegin);
}
```

A B C D E F G H I J K L M N O P Q R S T U V W X Y Z

currentTimeMillis()

PURPOSE Retrieves the current time in milliseconds.

SYNTAX
```
public static native long currentTimeMillis()
```

DESCRIPTION This method returns the current time in milliseconds GMT since *epoch* (00:00:00 UTC, January 1, 1970). It is a signed 64-bit integer, so it will not overflow until the year 292,280,995.

RETURNS The current time in milliseconds.

SEE ALSO `java.util.Date`.

EXAMPLE

```
// Create a Date object using today's date
Date today = new Date(System.currentTimeMillis());
System.out.println("Today: " + today.toString());
```

A B C D E F G H I J K L M N O P Q R S T U V W X Y Z

err

PURPOSE Standard error output stream.

SYNTAX `public final static PrintStream err`

DESCRIPTION The standard error output stream is used by the program to print messages to the user concerning errors about program execution. This is separate from the standard output stream, which is intended for normal, expected output to the user of the program.

`err` is a *print stream*. This means you can send data values like integers to it and those data values will be automatically converted into strings for printing. The strings are then converted automatically to their byte representations using the platform's default character-to-byte encoding (see `String.getBytes()`).

By default, `err` is also an *auto-flush, buffered* stream. This means output sent to it is stored and written out only when the buffer is full, or when the buffer is explicitly flushed, or when a line separator is written.

You can change the default error stream using `setErr()`.

SEE ALSO `java.io.BufferedOutputStream`, `java.io.PrintStream`, `out`, `setErr()`.

EXAMPLE

```
public static void usage() {
    System.err.println("Usage: testprog <username> <age>");
    System.exit(-1);
}
```

exit()

PURPOSE Exits the virtual machine.

SYNTAX `public void exit(int status)`

DESCRIPTION This method is equivalent to `Runtime.getRuntime().exit()`. All threads are terminated, and the executing program is halted.

Note: This method should be used with caution because it terminates the virtual machine. Consider using `return` or `throw` to recover from an error. Use `exit()` only when you really mean for the virtual machine to exit.

PARAMETERS

`status` The exit status. A value of `0` indicates success; all other values indicate failure.

SEE ALSO `runFinalizersOnExit()`, `Runtime.exit()`, `SecurityManager.checkExit()`.

EXAMPLE See `err`.

gc()

PURPOSE Runs the garbage collector.

SYNTAX `public static void gc()`

DESCRIPTION This method is equivalent to `Runtime.getRuntime().gc()`.

SEE ALSO `Runtime.gc()`.

EXAMPLE

```
System.gc(); // indicate that garbage collector should run
```

getEnv() *DEPRECATED*

PURPOSE Replaced by `getProperty()`.

SYNTAX `public static String getenv(String name)`

DEPRECATION To get information about the environment, use `getProperty()`. In addition to adding standard system properties, you can add properties that are visible to the program via the `-D` option to the `java` command. See the class description for details.

This method simply throws an `Error` when you try to use it.

getProperties()

PURPOSE Retrieves the list of system properties.

SYNTAX `public static Properties getProperties()`

DESCRIPTION This method returns the list of system properties currently defined. These include the standard system properties listed in Table 42, as well as any environment variables set via the `-D` option to the `java` command (see the example given in the class description). Any changes, additions, or removals are made to the system properties via the `setProperties()` method will also be reflected in the list of properties returned.

The system properties can be accessed only if permitted by the security manager.

RETURNS The non-`null` list of system properties currently defined.

SEE ALSO `getProperty()`, `java.util.Properties`, `SecurityManager.checkPropertiesAccess()`, `setProperties()`.

EXAMPLE

```
Properties props = System.getProperties(); // get list of properties
// Print properties using Enumeration
for (Enumeration enum = props.propertyNames(); enum.hasMoreElements();) {
    String key = (String)enum.nextElement();
    System.out.println(key + " = " + (String)(props.get(key)));
}
```

getProperty()

PURPOSE Retrieves the named system property.

SYNTAX

```
public static String getProperty(String property)
public static String getProperty(String property, String defval)
```

DESCRIPTION The two forms of this method retrieve the system property identified by `property` and return the property's value as a string. If the property does not exist, the first form of this method returns `null`. The second form returns `defval` in the same situation.

The system property can be accessed only if permitted by the security manager.

PARAMETERS

`defval` The possibly `null` default value to return if `property` does not exist.

`property` The non-`null` name of the property.

RETURNS The string value of `property` if `property` names a system property; otherwise, `defval`, or `null` if `defval` is not supplied.

SEE ALSO `Boolean.getBoolean()`, `Integer.getInteger()`, `getProperties()`, `java.awt.Color.getColor()`, `java.awt.Font.getFont()`, `java.util.Properties`, `Long.getLong()`, `SecurityManager.checkPropertyAccess()`, `setProperties()`.

EXAMPLE

```
// get user's home directory
String homeDir = System.getProperty("user.home");
// If 'outDir' not found, use 'homeDir' as default
String outDir = System.getProperty("testdir", homeDir);
```

getSecurityManager()

PURPOSE Retrieves the reference to the security manager.

SYNTAX `public static SecurityManager getSecurityManager()`

DESCRIPTION This method allows you to get a reference to the current security manager. If no security manager has been set, this method returns `null`. Otherwise, you can use the returned reference to perform various security-related checks (e.g., permission to do IO to files and permission to launch system programs).

RETURNS The reference to the security manager if it has been set; `null` otherwise.

SEE ALSO `SecurityManager`, `setSecurityManager()`.

EXAMPLE

```
// Implementation of Thread.checkAccess()
public final void checkAccess() {
    SecurityManager security = System.getSecurityManager();
    if (security != null) {
        security.checkAccess(this);
    }
}
```

identityHashCode()

PURPOSE Returns `Object.hashCode()` for an object.

SYNTAX `public static native int identityHashCode(Object obj);`

DESCRIPTION This method returns the nonoverridden `Object.hashCode()` for object `obj`. Even if `obj` has overridden `hashCode()`, the `hashCode()` from the base class `Object` is used. If `obj` is `null`, `0` is returned.

PARAMETERS

`obj` The possibly `null` object for which to return the hash code.

RETURNS `Object.hashCode()` for `obj`; `0` if `obj` is `null`.

SEE ALSO `Object.hashCode()`.

in

PURPOSE Standard input stream.

SYNTAX `public final static InputStream in`

DESCRIPTION The standard input stream is used by the program to read character data from the user. By default, `in` is a *buffered* input stream, meaning input from the user is kept in a buffer until it is read by the program. You can change the standard input stream by using `setIn()`.

SEE ALSO `err, java.io.BufferedInputStream, java.io.InputStream, out, setIn()`.

EXAMPLE

```
// reads a line from standard input
public static String getLine() {
    StringBuffer buf = new StringBuffer(80);
    int c;
    try {
        while ((c = System.in.read()) != -1) {
            char ch = (char) c;
            if (ch == '\n')
                break;
            buf.append(ch);
        }
    } catch (IOException e) {
        System.err.println(e);
    }
    return (buf.toString());
}
```

load()

PURPOSE Loads a dynamic library when given its full pathname.

SYNTAX `public static void load(String pathname)`

DESCRIPTION This method is equivalent to `Runtime.getRuntime().load()`.

PARAMETERS

`pathname` The non-`null` absolute pathname of the library to load.

EXCEPTIONS

`OutOfMemoryError`
If the library could not be loaded due to insufficient memory in the system.

`SecurityException`
If the currently executing thread is not permitted to load `pathname`.

`UnsatisfiedLinkError`
If `pathname` does not name a library or the library could not be linked successfully (for example, because of unresolved references).

SEE ALSO `loadLibrary(), Runtime.load()`.

EXAMPLE See a similar usage at `Runtime.load()`.

loadLibrary()

PURPOSE Loads a dynamic library when given its library name.

SYNTAX `public static void loadLibrary(String libname)`

DESCRIPTION This method is equivalent to `Runtime.getRuntime().loadLibrary()`.

PARAMETERS

`libname` The non-`null` name of the library.

EXCEPTIONS

`OutOfMemoryError`
If the library could not be loaded due to insufficient memory in the system.

`SecurityException`
If the currently executing thread is not permitted to load `libname`.

`UnsatisfiedLinkError`
If the library does not exist or the library could not be linked successfully (for example, as a result of unresolved references).

SEE ALSO `load()`, `Runtime.loadLibrary()`.

EXAMPLE See a similar usage at `Runtime.loadLibrary()`.

out

PURPOSE Standard output stream.

SYNTAX `public static PrintStream out`

DESCRIPTION The standard output stream is used by the program to print text output for display to the user.

`out` is a *print stream*. This means you can send data values like integers to it and those data values will be automatically converted into strings for printing. The strings are then converted automatically to their byte representation using the platform's default character-to-byte encoding (see `String.getBytes()`).

By default, `out` is also an *auto-flush, buffered* stream. This means output sent to it is stored and written out only when the buffer is full, or when the buffer is explicitly flushed, or when a line separator is written.

To change the standard output, use `setOut()`.

SEE ALSO `err`, `in`, `java.io.BufferedOutputStream`, `java.io.PrintStream`.

EXAMPLE See `getProperties()`.

runFinalization()

PURPOSE Runs the finalization method of objects that are pending finalization.

SYNTAX `public static void runFinalization()`

DESCRIPTION This method is equivalent to `Runtime.getRuntime().runFinalization()`.

SEE ALSO `gc()`, `runFinalizersOnExit()`, `Runtime.runFinalization()`.

EXAMPLE

```
System.runFinalization();
```

runFinalizersOnExit()

PURPOSE Enables/disables finalization when the program exits.

SYNTAX `public native void runFinalizersOnExit(boolean run)`

DESCRIPTION This method is equivalent to `Runtime.getRuntime().runFinalizersOnExit()`.

SEE ALSO `gc()`, `runFinalization()`, `Runtime.runFinalizersOnExit()`.

EXAMPLE

```
System.runFinalizersOnExit(true);
```

setErr()

PURPOSE Sets the standard error output stream.

SYNTAX `public final static void setErr(PrintStream newErr)`

DESCRIPTION The standard error output stream is used by the program to print messages to the user concerning errors about program execution. This method sets the standard error stream to be `newErr`. After this method has been executed, the value of `err` is `newErr`.

This method can be executed only if permitted by the security manager.

PARAMETERS

`newErr` The non-`null` new standard error output stream.

SEE ALSO `err`, `SecurityManager.checkExec()`.

EXAMPLE

```
System.setIn(new java.io.FileInputStream("myinputfile"));
System.setOut(new PrintStream(new java.io.FileOutputStream("myoutputfile")));
System.setErr(new PrintStream(
    new java.io.FileOutputStream("myerrinputfile")));
```

```
System.out.println("Hello there file");      // using new out
System.err.println("Hello there err file");  // using new err
```

setIn()

PURPOSE
: Sets the standard input stream.

SYNTAX
: `public final static void setIn(InputStream newIn)`

DESCRIPTION
: The standard input stream is used by the program to accept input from the user. This method sets the standard input stream to be `newIn`. After this method has been executed, the value of `in` is `newIn`.

  This method can be executed only if permitted by the security manager.

PARAMETERS

`newIn`
: The non-`null` new standard input stream.

SEE ALSO
: `newIn, SecurityManager.checkExec().`

setOut()

PURPOSE
: Sets the standard output stream.

SYNTAX
: `public final static void setOut(OutputStream newOut)`

DESCRIPTION
: The standard output stream is used by the program to print output for display to the user. This method sets the standard output stream to be `newOut`. After this method has been executed, the value of `out` is `newOut.`

  This method can be executed only if permitted by the security manager.

PARAMETERS

`newOut`
: The non-`null` new standard output stream.

SEE ALSO
: `out, SecurityManager.checkExec().`

setProperties()

PURPOSE
: Updates the list of system properties.

SYNTAX
: `public static void setProperties(Properties props)`

DESCRIPTION
: This method replaces the existing list of system properties with the new list, `props`. The list may contain deletions from and modifications and additions to the current list.

The system properties can be changed only if permitted by the security manager.

PARAMETERS

`props` The non-`null` new list of system properties. If `null`, subsequent `getProperty()` and related methods throw `NullPointerException`.

SEE ALSO `getProperties()`, `getProperty()`, `java.util.Properties`, `SecurityManager.checkPropertiesAccess()`.

EXAMPLE

```
Properties props = System.getProperties();
// Add 'outDir' property
props.put("outDir", "/tmp");
// overwrites System properties with new properties
System.setProperties(props);
```

setSecurityManager()

PURPOSE Sets the system's security manager.

SYNTAX `public static void setSecurityManager(SecurityManager s)`

DESCRIPTION This method sets the security manager of the current program to `s`. Once set to a non-`null` value, the security manager cannot be replaced. `s` set to `null` means that no security manager is being installed.

PARAMETERS

`s` The possibly `null` security manager.

EXCEPTIONS

`SecurityException`
If the security manager has already been set to a non-`null` value.

SEE ALSO `getSecurityManager()`, `SecurityManager`.

EXAMPLE See `SecurityManager.classDepth()`.

Thread

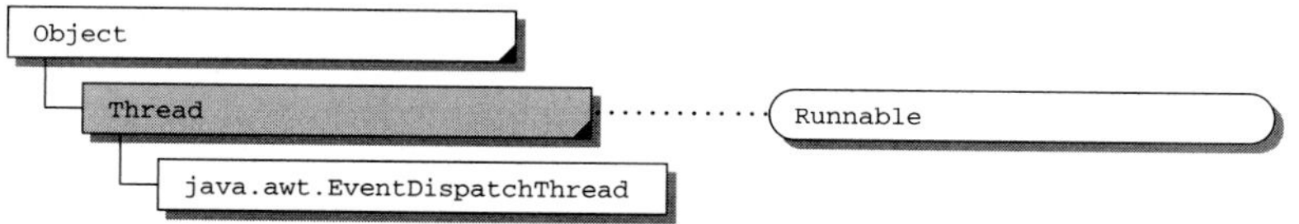

A B C D E F G H I J K L M N O P Q R S T U V W X Y Z

Syntax

```
public class Thread implements Runnable
```

Description

A *thread* is a single sequential flow of control within a process. A single process can have multiple concurrently executing threads. For example, a process may have a thread reading input from the user, while at the same time another thread is updating a database containing the user's account balance, while at the same time a third thread is updating the display with the latest stock quotes. Such a process is called a *multithreaded process*; the program from which this process executes is called a *multithreaded program.*

The `Thread` class is used to represent a thread and includes methods to control the execution state of a thread.

Usage

To create a new thread of execution, you first declare a new class that is a subclass of `Thread` and override the `run()` method with code that you want executed in this thread:

```
class PrimeThread extends Thread {
  public void run() {
       // compute primes...
  }
}
```

You then create an instance of this subclass, followed by a call to the `start()` method. That method will execute the `run()` method defined by this subclass:

```
PrimeThread pThread = new PrimeThread();
pThread.start();
...
```

You can achieve this same effect by having the class directly implement the `Runnable` interface:

```
class Primes implements Runnable {
  public void run() {
       // compute primes...
  }
}
```

To create a thread to execute this `run()` method, do the following:

```
Primes p = new Primes();
Thread pThread = new Thread(p);
pThread.start();
...
```


Thread Priorities

Each thread has a priority that is used by the Java runtime in scheduling threads for execution. A thread that has a higher priority than another thread is typically scheduled ahead of the other thread. However, the way thread priorities precisely affect scheduling is platform-dependent. In some systems, priority-based scheduling is guaranteed, while in others, priorities act only as hints to the scheduler. Therefore you should not depend on priorities in designing your program.

A thread inherits its priority from the thread that created it. A thread's priority can be changed subsequent to the thread's creation at any time using the `setPriority()` method in the `Thread` class, if allowed by the security manager.

User Threads and Daemon Threads

Each thread has a *daemon* status that indicates whether the thread is a *user* thread or a *daemon* thread. User and daemon threads are the same in all but one respect. That is, a Java program will terminate only when all user threads have stopped running. In contrast, the program will stop regardless of how many daemon threads are still running. Examples of daemon threads are the garbage-collector thread and the finalization thread. An example of a user thread is the one that executes `main()` in a Java program.

A thread inherits its daemon status from the thread that created it. This status can be changed after creation but before the thread has started. After a thread has been started, its daemon status cannot be changed.

Thread Groups

A *thread group* contains a set of threads and thread groups. It is the means by which you can organize threads into logical units for security and organizational reasons. When a thread is created, it is added to a thread group. The thread group either is specified as an argument to the thread's constructor or is, by default, the thread group specified by the security manager. (See `Thread()` for details.)

Thread State and Synchronization between Threads

When a thread is started, its state is *active*. Its state remains active until it has terminated execution or is stopped. An active thread can be executing or suspended. When a thread is first started, it starts executing its `run()` method. The `Thread` class provides methods for you to suspend an executing thread, to resume execution of a suspended thread, and to stop a thread completely (it can no longer run unless it is restarted at the beginning of its `run()` method). These methods can be invoked only if allowed by the security manager.

In addition to these methods in the `Thread` class, you also can control the execution of a thread by using synchronization methods available in the `Object` class (`wait()`/`notify()`).

Interrupts

A thread can send an *interrupt* to another thread. This sets the interrupted flag in the target thread to indicate that it has been interrupted. The target thread can then check for this flag at its discretion and react appropriately.

Interrupting a thread that is blocked while calling a method that is declared to throw `InterruptedException` will cause the thread to throw `InterruptedException`. When `InterruptedException` is thrown, the thread's interrupted flag is cleared.

MEMBER SUMMARY

Constructor	
`Thread()`	Constructs a `Thread` instance.
Thread Property Fields and Method	
`getName()`	Retrieves this thread's name.
`getPriority()`	Retrieves this thread's priority.
`getThreadGroup()`	Retrieves this thread's thread group.
`isDaemon()`	Determines if this thread is a daemon thread.
`MAX_PRIORITY`	The maximum priority that a thread can have.
`MIN_PRIORITY`	The minimum priority that a thread can have.
`NORM_PRIORITY`	The default priority that is assigned to the first user thread.
`setDaemon()`	Changes this thread's daemon status.
`setName()`	Changes this thread's name.
`setPriority()`	Changes this thread's priority.
Thread State Methods	
`destroy()`	Destroys this thread without any cleanup.
`isAlive()`	Determines if this thread is active.
`join()`	Waits for this thread to terminate.
`resume()`	Resumes the execution of this thread.
`run()`	The actual body of this thread.
`sleep()`	Causes the currently executing thread to sleep for a period of time.
`start()`	Starts the execution of this thread.
`stop()`	Stops the execution of this thread.
`suspend()`	Suspends the execution of this thread.
`yield()`	Causes the currently executing thread object to yield to other threads.
Interrupt Methods	
`interrupt()`	Sends an interrupt to this thread.
`interrupted()`	Determines if the currently executing thread has been interrupted.
`isInterrupted()`	Determines if this thread has been interrupted.

Continued

MEMBER SUMMARY	
Stack Frame Methods	
`countStackFrames()`	Counts the number of stack frames in this thread.
`dumpStack()`	Prints a snapshot of the current execution stack trace.
Security Method	
`checkAccess()`	Checks whether the currently executing thread is allowed to modify this thread.
Current Thread Methods	
`activeCount()`	Estimates the number of active threads in the current thread's threadgroup and its subgroup.
`currentThread()`	Retrieves the currently executing thread.
`enumerate()`	Enumerates the active threads in the currently executing thread's thread group.
Description Method	
`toString()`	Generates a string representation of the thread.

A B C D E F G H I J K L M N O P Q R S T U V W X Y Z

See Also

`Object`, `Runnable`, `ThreadGroup`, `SecurityManager`.

Example

This example implements a thread viewer that shows all of the threads in the system at a certain point in time. See Figure 101. The thread viewer updates the list of threads every 5 seconds. The thread viewer can be paused and resumed by clicking the Pause button at the top of the frame.

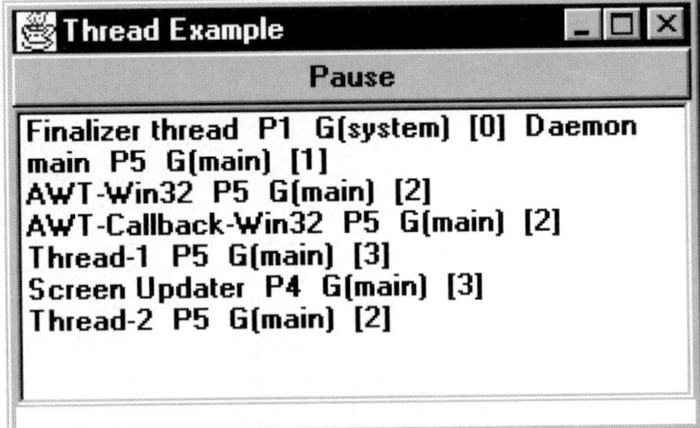

FIGURE 101: Thread Viewer.

A thread can be stopped (via the `stop()` method) by clicking the thread name in the list. If the thread that is stopped is one of the `Main` class's thread, a message is printed on `System.out`.

In the `ThreadViewer` class, the `actionPerformed()` and `updateList()` methods are synchronized because they share several fields. This prevents the two methods from seeing inconsistent values in the shared fields.

```
import java.awt.*;
import java.awt.event.*;

class Main implements Runnable {
    public static void main(String args[] ) {
        try {
            new ThreadViewer();

            // periodically create a thread just to keep things interesting
            while (true) {
                Thread.sleep((int)Math.floor(Math.random()*5000));
                (new Thread(new Main())).start();
            }
        } catch (Exception e) {
            e.printStackTrace();
        }
    }
    public void run() {
        try {
            Thread.sleep(5000);
        } catch (Exception e) {
            e.printStackTrace();
        } catch (ThreadDeath e) {
            System.out.println(Thread.currentThread().getName() +
                " has been stopped!");
        }
    }
}

class ThreadViewer extends Frame implements Runnable, ActionListener {
    Thread timerThread;

    // List of all threads in the system.
    Thread[] threads;

    // List component containing all the threads in the system.
    List threadList = new List();

    ThreadViewer() {
        super("Thread Example");
        add(threadList, BorderLayout.CENTER);
        Button b;
        add(b = new Button("Pause"), BorderLayout.NORTH);
        b.addActionListener(this);
        threadList.addActionListener(this);

        setSize(300, 300);
        show();
        timerThread = new Thread(this);
        timerThread.start();
    }

    public synchronized void actionPerformed(ActionEvent evt) {
        String cmd = evt.getActionCommand();
        if (evt.getSource() == threadList) {
            Thread t = threads[threadList.getSelectedIndex()];
            try {
                t.checkAccess();
                t.stop();
            } catch (SecurityException e) {
```

```
                System.out.println("No permission to stop thread " +
                    t.getName());
            }
        } else if ("Pause".equals(cmd)) {
            timerThread.suspend();
            ((Button)evt.getSource()).setLabel("Resume");
        } else if ("Resume".equals(cmd)) {
            timerThread.resume();
            ((Button)evt.getSource()).setLabel("Pause");
        }
    }

    public void run() {
        try {
            while (timerThread == Thread.currentThread()) {
                updateList();
                Thread.sleep(5000);
            }
        } catch (Exception e) {
            e.printStackTrace();
        }
    }

    synchronized void updateList() {
        // Find the root thread group
        ThreadGroup rootGrp = Thread.currentThread().getThreadGroup();

        while (rootGrp.getParent() != null) {
            rootGrp = rootGrp.getParent();
        }

        threads = new Thread[rootGrp.activeCount()];
        int count = rootGrp.enumerate(threads, true);

        threadList.removeAll();
        for (int i=0; i<count; i++) {
            Thread t = threads[i];

            threadList.addItem(t.getName()
                + "  P" + t.getPriority()
                + "  G(" + t.getThreadGroup().getName() + ")"
                + "  [" + t.countStackFrames() + "]"
                + "  " + (t.isDaemon() ? "Daemon" : "")
                + "  " + (t.isInterrupted() ? "" : "Interrupted")
                + "  " + (t.isAlive() ? "" : "NotAlive"));
        }
    }
}
```

activeCount()

PURPOSE Estimates the number of active threads in the current thread's thread group and its subgroups.

SYNTAX `public static int activeCount()`

DESCRIPTION This method estimates the number of active threads in the currently executing thread's thread group and its subgroups. This is only an estimate because during this call, threads might be added to or removed from the thread group or its subgroups.

SEE ALSO `currentThread()`, `getThreadGroup()`, `isAlive()`, `ThreadGroup`.

EXAMPLE See the class example.

checkAccess()

PURPOSE Checks whether the currently executing thread is allowed to modify this thread.

SYNTAX `public void checkAccess()`

DESCRIPTION This method checks whether the security manager allows the currently executing thread to modify this thread. Modifications that require access checking include changing the state of the thread (e.g., suspend/resume) and changing the properties associated with a thread (its daemon status and priority).

EXCEPTIONS

`SecurityException`

If the currently executing thread is not allowed to modify this thread due to security reasons.

SEE ALSO `currentThread()`, `resume()`, `SecurityManager.checkAccess()`, `setDaemon()`, `setName()`, `setPriority()`, `stop()`, `suspend()`, `Thread()`,`ThreadGroup.checkAccess()`.

EXAMPLE See the class example.

countStackFrames()

PURPOSE Counts the number of stack frames in this thread.

SYNTAX `public native int countStackFrames()`

DESCRIPTION This method returns the number of stack frames in this thread. The thread must be suspended when this method is called.

RETURNS The number of stack frames in this thread.

EXCEPTIONS

`IllegalThreadStateException`

If this thread is not suspended.

SEE ALSO `suspend()`.

EXAMPLE See the class example.

currentThread()

PURPOSE Retrieves the currently executing thread.

SYNTAX `public static native Thread currentThread()`

RETURNS The reference to the currently executing thread.

EXAMPLE See the class example.

destroy()

PURPOSE Destroys this thread without any cleanup.

SYNTAX `public void destroy()`

DESCRIPTION This method destroys this thread without any cleanup. It removes the thread from its thread group. Any monitors the thread has locked remain locked.

Note: In Java 1.1.4, `destroy()` has not been implemented. Invoking `destroy()` on a thread does nothing.

SEE ALSO `isActive()`, `stop()`.

dumpStack()

PURPOSE Prints a snapshot of the current execution stack trace.

SYNTAX `public static void dumpStack()`

DESCRIPTION A debugging procedure to print a stack trace for the current `Thread` to `System.err`.

SEE ALSO `currentThread()`, `System.err`, `Throwable.printStackTrace()`.

EXAMPLE This example simply calls a method recursively. On the tenth recursion, `dumpStack()` is called to print a stack trace. The output of this program is shown following the code.

```
class Main {
    static void method(int i) {
        if (i == 10) {
            Thread.currentThread().dumpStack();
        } else {
            method(++i);
        }
    }

    public static void main(String args[]) {
        method(0);
    }
}
```

Output

```
java.lang.Exception: Stack trace
        at java.lang.Thread.dumpStack(Thread.java:884)
        at Main.method(Main.java:4)
        at Main.method(Main.java:6)
        at Main.method(Main.java:6)
        at Main.method(Main.java:6)
        at Main.method(Main.java:6)
        at Main.method(Main.java:6)
        at Main.method(Main.java:6)
        at Main.method(Main.java:6)
        at Main.method(Main.java:6)
        at Main.method(Main.java:6)
        at Main.method(Main.java:6)
        at Main.main(Main.java:11)
```

enumerate()

PURPOSE Enumerates the active threads in the currently executing thread's thread group.

SYNTAX `public static int enumerate(Thread[] threads)`

DESCRIPTION This method recursively enumerates the active threads in the currently executing thread's thread group and its subgroups. It copies into the array `threads` the references to these active threads. You can use `activeCount()` to estimate the size of the array `threads` to allocate before calling `enumerate()`.

PARAMETERS

`threads` An existing array into which to copy the references.

RETURNS The number of active threads in the current thread's thread group and its subgroups.

SEE ALSO `activeCount()`, `currentThread()`, `getThreadGroup()`, `isAlive()`, `ThreadGroup`.

EXAMPLE See the class example.

getName()

PURPOSE Retrieves this thread's name.

SYNTAX `public final String getName()`

DESCRIPTION Each thread is given a name when it is created. A thread's name can be changed subsequent to the thread's creation at any time by using `setName()`. `getName()` returns the name of this thread.

RETURNS This thread's name.

SEE ALSO	`Thread(), setName().`
EXAMPLE	See the class example.

getPriority()

PURPOSE Retrieves the thread's priority.

SYNTAX `public final int getPriority()`

DESCRIPTION Each thread has a priority that is used by the Java runtime in scheduling threads for execution. A thread that has a higher priority than another thread is typically scheduled ahead of the other thread. However, the way thread priorities precisely affect scheduling is platform-dependent. In some systems, priority-based scheduling is guaranteed, while in others, priorities act only as hints to the scheduler.

A thread inherits its priority from the thread that created it. A thread's priority can be changed subsequent to the thread's creation at any time by using `setPriority()`. `getPriority()` returns this thread's priority.

RETURNS This thread's priority.

SEE ALSO `MAX_PRIORITY, MIN_PRIORITY, NORM_PRIORITY, setPriority().`

EXAMPLE See the class example.

getThreadGroup()

PURPOSE Retrieves this thread's thread group.

SYNTAX `public final ThreadGroup getThreadGroup()`

DESCRIPTION A *thread group* contains a set of threads and thread groups. It is the means by which you can organize threads into logical units for security and organizational reasons. When a thread is created, it is added to a thread group. The thread group either is specified as an argument to the thread's constructor or is the thread group specified by the security manager. If no security manager is installed, the thread group is, by default, the same thread group as that of the creating thread.

`getThreadGroup()` returns this thread's thread group.

RETURNS This thread's thread group.

SEE ALSO `SecurityManager.getThreadGroup(), Thread(), ThreadGroup.`

EXAMPLE See the class example.

interrupt()

PURPOSE Sends an interrupt to this thread.

SYNTAX `public void interrupt()`

DESCRIPTION A thread can send an *interrupt* to another thread by calling `interrupt()` on it. This sets the interrupted flag in the target thread to indicate that it has been interrupted. The target thread can then check for this flag at its discretion using `interrupted()` or `isInterrupted()`.

If a thread is calling a method that is declared to throw `InterruptedException` (such as `sleep()`), calling `interrupt()` on it will cause it to throw `InterruptedException`, which will wake up the thread and clear its interrupted flag.

SEE ALSO `interrupted()`, `isInterrupted()`, `InterruptedException`.

EXAMPLE This example tests the use of the `interrupt()` method. The main thread sleeps a random number of milliseconds and then interrupts a worker thread. The worker thread is either `Sleeper` (if the program is run with no argument) or `Counter` (if the program is run with an argument). The `Sleeper` thread is a thread that loops, sleeping for 2-second intervals. The `Counter` thread loops, generating a sum until either the computation is complete or it has been interrupted.

When the `Sleeper` thread uses `isInterrupted()` to check whether it has been interrupted, the answer is always `false`. This is because the `Sleeper`'s `sleep()` method is interrupted by the fact that `InterruptedException` is thrown; this clears its interrupted flag.

The `Counter` thread's calls to `isInterrupted()` will depend on the state of its interrupted flag. The `Counter` thread uses `interrupted()` to clear the interrupted flag before the next iteration.

```
import java.util.Random;

class Main {
    public static void main(String[] args) {
        Thread t;

        if (args.length > 0) {
            t = new Counter();
        } else {
            t = new Sleeper();
        }

        t.start();

        Random rand = new Random();
        while (true) {
            int p = Math.abs(rand.nextInt()%5000);
```

```
                System.out.println("wake up worker in " + p + "ms");
                try {
                    Thread.sleep(p);
                } catch (InterruptedException e) {
                    System.out.println("main interrupted");
                }
                t.interrupt();
            }
        }
    }

    class Sleeper extends Thread {
        public void run() {
            while (true) {
                try {
                    Thread.sleep(2000);
                    System.out.println("sleeper woke up");
                } catch (InterruptedException e) {
                    System.out.println("sleeper interrupted (1): "
                        + isInterrupted());
                    System.out.println("sleeper interrupted");
                }
                System.out.println("sleeper interrupted (2): " + isInterrupted());
            }
        }
    }

    class Counter extends Thread {
        public void run() {
            while (true) {

                long sum = 0;
                for (int i = 0; i< 1000000 && !isInterrupted(); i++) {
                    sum += i;
                }
                System.out.println("Sum: " + sum);

                System.out.println("isInterrupted (0): " + isInterrupted());
                System.out.println("isInterrupted (1): " + isInterrupted());

                System.out.println("interrupted(0): " + interrupted());
                // First call should have cleared it.
                System.out.println("interrupted (1): " + interrupted());

            }
        }
    }
```

interrupted()

PURPOSE Determines if the currently executing thread has been interrupted.

SYNTAX `public static boolean interrupted()`

DESCRIPTION A thread can send an *interrupt* to another thread by calling `interrupt()` on it. This sets the interrupted flag in the target thread to indicate that it has been interrupted. The target thread can then check for this flag at its discretion and react appropriately.

You can check whether the currently executing thread has been interrupted by using `interrupted()`. Doing this has the side effect of clearing the interrupted flag; hence, this is *not* equivalent to `currentThread().isInterrupted()`. This method returns `true` if the currently executing thread has been interrupted; it returns `false` otherwise.

If a thread is calling a method that is declared to throw `InterruptedException` (such as `sleep()`), calling `interrupt()` on it will cause it to throw `InterruptedException`. Doing this will wake the thread up and clear its interrupted flag. Calling `interrupted()` after `InterruptedException` is thrown will return `false`, since the interrupted flag has already been cleared.

RETURNS `true` if the currently executing thread has been interrupted; `false` otherwise.

SEE ALSO `currentThread()`, `interrupt()`, `InterruptedException`, `isInterrupted()`.

EXAMPLE See `interrupt()`.

isAlive()

PURPOSE Determines if this thread is active.

SYNTAX `public final native boolean isAlive()`

DESCRIPTION A thread that has been started is *active*. It remains active until it has been stopped or destroyed. This method returns `true` if this thread is active.

RETURNS `true` if this thread is active; `false` otherwise.

SEE ALSO `activeCount()`, `destroy()`, `start()`, `stop()`.

EXAMPLE See the class example.

isDaemon()

PURPOSE Determines if this thread is a daemon thread.

SYNTAX `public final boolean isDaemon()`

DESCRIPTION Each thread has a *daemon* status that indicates whether the thread is a *user* thread or a *daemon* thread. User and daemon threads are the same in all but one respect. That is, a Java program will terminate only when all user threads have stopped running. The program will stop regardless of how many daemon threads are still running. Examples of daemon threads are the garbage-collector thread and the finalization thread. An example of a user thread is the one that executes `main()` in a Java program.

A thread inherits its daemon status from the thread that created it. This status can be changed after creation—but before the thread has started—by using `setDaemon()`. You can determine the daemon status of a thread by calling `isDaemon()`. This method returns `true` if this thread is a daemon thread.

RETURNS `true` if this thread is a daemon thread; `false` if this thread is a user thread.

SEE ALSO `setDaemon()`, `Thread()`.

EXAMPLE See the class example.

isInterrupted()

PURPOSE Determines if this thread has been interrupted.

SYNTAX `public boolean isInterrupted()`

DESCRIPTION A thread can send an *interrupt* to another thread by calling `interrupt()` on it. This sets the interrupted flag in the target thread to indicate that it has been interrupted. The target thread can then check for this flag at its discretion and react appropriately.

You can check whether this thread has been interrupted by using `isInterrupted()`. This does not clear the thread's interrupted flag.

This method returns `true` if this thread has been interrupted; it returns `false` otherwise.

If a thread is calling a method that is declared to throw `InterruptedException` (such as `sleep()`), calling `interrupt()` on it will cause it to throw `InterruptedException`. Doing this will wake up the thread and clear its interrupted flag. Calling `isInterrupted()` after the `InterruptedException` is thrown will return `false`, since the interrupted flag has already been cleared.

RETURNS `true` if this thread has been interrupted; `false` otherwise.

SEE ALSO `interrupt()`, `interrupted()`, `InterruptedException`.

EXAMPLE See `interrupt()`.

join()

PURPOSE

Waits for this thread to terminate.

SYNTAX

```
public final void join() throws InterruptedException
public final synchronized void join(long timeout) throws
   InterruptedException
public final synchronized void join(long timeout, int nanos)
   throws InterruptedException
```

DESCRIPTION

The three forms of this method cause the currently executing thread to wait until this thread has terminated (stopped). The currently executing thread blocks until any one of the following events occurs:

- The currently executing thread has been interrupted.
- This thread has terminated.
- The time-out specified has expired.

The time-out period to wait is specified in milliseconds. If finer granularity is desired, you can supply a nanosecond count `nanos`. If no time-out period has been specified or if the time-out period is `0`, the currently executing thread waits indefinitely for the other two events to occur.

PARAMETERS

`timeout` The time to wait in milliseconds.

`nanos` Additional nanoseconds to wait. `0` ≤ `nanos` ≤ `999999`. `nanos` is rounded to the nearest millisecond, unless `millis` is `0`, in which case a nonzero `nanos` is treated as 1 millisecond.

EXCEPTIONS

`IllegalArgumentException`

If `timeout` < `0`, or `nanos` < `0`, or `nanos` > `999999`.

`InterruptedException`

If the currently executing thread has been interrupted.

SEE ALSO

`destroy()`, `Object.wait()`, `sleep()`, `stop()`.

EXAMPLE

This example illustrates the use of worker threads and priorities. In this example, one worker is created for every priority level. Each worker does exactly the same amount of work; the only difference is their priority levels. The output of this program (shown following the code) shows that higher-priority threads (priority 9) are much more productive that lower-priority threads (priority 1).

```
class Main {
    public static void main(String args[] ) {
        // Create a slot for each priority level.
        Worker[] workers =
            new Worker[Thread.MAX_PRIORITY-Thread.MIN_PRIORITY];
```

```
            // Create the workers.
            for (int i=0; i<workers.length; i++) {
                workers[i] = new Worker(Thread.MIN_PRIORITY+i);
                workers[i].start();
            }

            // Now wait for them to terminate.
            for (int i=workers.length-1; i >= 0; i--) {
                try {
                    workers[i].join();
                } catch (Exception e) {
                    e.printStackTrace();
                }
                System.out.println(workers[i].getName() + ": " +
                    workers[i].time + " ms");
            }
        }
    }

    class Worker extends Thread {
        // Record current time.
        long time = System.currentTimeMillis();

        Worker(int priority) {
            setPriority(priority);
            setName("Worker-"+priority);
        }

        public void run() {
            // Here is where the work gets done.
            String s = "";
            for (int i=0; i<1024; i++) {
                s += i;
            }

            // Record time.
            time = System.currentTimeMillis() - time;
        }
    }
```

Output

```
Worker-9: 491 ms
Worker-8: 481 ms
Worker-7: 811 ms
Worker-6: 791 ms
Worker-5: 1122 ms
Worker-4: 1432 ms
Worker-3: 1392 ms
Worker-2: 1833 ms
Worker-1: 1642 ms
```

MAX_PRIORITY

PURPOSE The maximum priority a thread can have.

SYNTAX `public final static int MAX_PRIORITY`

DESCRIPTION The maximum priority a thread can have is `10`.

SEE ALSO `getPriority()`, `MIN_PRIORITY`, `NORM_PRIORITY`, `setPriority()`.

EXAMPLE See `join()`.

MIN_PRIORITY

PURPOSE The minimum priority that a thread can have.

SYNTAX `public final static int MIN_PRIORITY`

DESCRIPTION The minimum priority that a thread can have is `1`.

SEE ALSO `getPriority()`, `MAX_PRIORITY`, `NORM_PRIORITY`, `setPriority()`.

EXAMPLE See `join()`.

NORM_PRIORITY

PURPOSE The default priority that is assigned to the first user thread.

SYNTAX `public final static int NORM_PRIORITY`

DESCRIPTION `NORM_PRIORITY` is the priority assigned to the first user thread created by the system. The value of `NORM_PRIORITY` is `5`.

SEE ALSO `getPriority()`, `MAX_PRIORITY`, `MIN_PRIORITY`, `setPriority()`.

resume()

PURPOSE Resumes execution of this thread.

SYNTAX `public final void resume()`

DESCRIPTION This method causes this suspended thread to resume execution. It can be executed only if permitted by the security manager. If you resume a thread that has not been suspended, no action is taken.

Note: This method is deprecated in JDK1.2.

EXCEPTIONS

`SecurityException`

If the currently executing thread is not allowed to modify this thread due to security reasons.

SEE ALSO `checkAccess()`, `suspend()`, `stop()`, `ThreadGroup.resume()`.

EXAMPLE See the class example.

run()

PURPOSE The actual body of this thread.

SYNTAX `public void run()`

DESCRIPTION This method defines the actual body of this thread. This is what the thread executes when it is started. You must either override this method by subclassing class `Thread` or create the thread with a `Runnable` target, which defines the `run()` method to execute.

SEE ALSO `Runnable, start(), stop().`

EXAMPLE See the class example.

A B C D E F G H I J K L M N O P Q R S T U V W X Y Z

setDaemon()

PURPOSE Changes the daemon status of this thread.

SYNTAX `public final void setDaemon(boolean status)`

DESCRIPTION Each thread has a *daemon* status that indicates whether the thread is a *user* thread or a *daemon* thread. User and daemon threads are the same in all but one respect. That is, a Java program terminates only when all user threads have stopped running. The program will stop regardless of how many daemon threads are still running. Examples of daemon threads are the garbage-collector thread and the finalization thread. An example of a user thread is the one that executes `main()` in a Java program.

A thread inherits its daemon status from the thread that created it. This status can be changed after creation—but before the thread has started—by using `setDaemon()`. Once the thread has been started, you cannot change its daemon status. If `status` is `true`, the thread becomes a daemon thread. If `status` is `false`, the thread becomes a user thread.

`setDaemon()` can be executed only if permitted by the security manager.

PARAMETERS

`status` `true` means this thread becomes a daemon thread; `false` means this thread becomes a user thread.

EXCEPTIONS

`IllegalThreadStateException`
If this thread is active (i.e., it has been started).

`SecurityException`
If the currently executing thread is not allowed to modify this thread due to security reasons.

SEE ALSO `checkAccess(), isDaemon(), start(), Thread().`

EXAMPLE This example creates a server thread (which does not do anything particularly useful) that continually waits for a socket connection. However, the server thread is made a daemon thread so that when the main program terminates, the server thread does not prevent the program from terminating.

```
import java.net.*;
class Main {
    public static void main(String[] args ) {
        (new Waiter()).start();

        try {
            Thread.sleep(5000);    // Wait 5 seconds.
        } catch (InterruptedException e) {
            e.printStackTrace();
        }
    }
}

class Waiter extends Thread {
    Waiter() {
        setDaemon(true);
    }

    public void run() {
        try {
            ServerSocket socket = new ServerSocket(2000);
            while (true) {
                Socket s = socket.accept();
                System.out.println("got a connection");
            }
        } catch (Exception e) {
            e.printStackTrace();
        }
    }
}
```

setName()

PURPOSE Changes this thread's name.

SYNTAX `public final void setName(String name)`

DESCRIPTION Each thread is given a name when it is created. A thread's name can be changed after the thread's creation at any time by using `setName()`. This method changes the name of this thread to `name`. It can be executed only if permitted by the security manager.

PARAMETERS

`name` The new name of this thread. `name` cannot be `null`.

EXCEPTIONS

`SecurityException`
If the currently executing thread is not allowed to modify this thread due to security reasons.

SEE ALSO `checkAccess()`, `getName()`, `Thread()`, `toString()`.

EXAMPLE See `join()`.

A B C D E F G H I J K L M N O P Q R S T U V W X Y Z

setPriority()

PURPOSE Changes this thread's priority.

SYNTAX
```
public final void setPriority(int newPriority)
```

DESCRIPTION Each thread has a priority that is used by the Java runtime in scheduling threads for execution. A thread that has a higher priority than another thread is typically scheduled ahead of the other thread. However, the way thread priorities precisely affect scheduling is platform-dependent. In some systems, priority-based scheduling is guaranteed, while in others, priorities act only as hints to the scheduler.

A thread inherits its priority from the thread that created it. A thread's priority can be changed subsequent to the thread's creation at any time by using `setPriority()`. `setPriority()` sets this thread's priority to `newPriority`. If `newPriority` is greater than the thread group's maximum priority, the thread group's maximum is used as the new priority.

This method can be executed only if permitted by the security manager.

PARAMETERS

`newPriority` The new priority the thread is to have. `MIN_PRIORITY` ≤ `newPriority` ≤ `MAX_PRIORITY`.

EXCEPTIONS

`IllegalArgumentException`
If `newPriority` is not within the range of `MIN_PRIORITY` to `MAX_PRIORITY`.

`SecurityException`
If the currently executing thread is not allowed to modify this thread due to security reasons.

SEE ALSO `checkAccess()`, `getPriority()`, `MAX_PRIORITY`, `MIN_PRIORITY`, `NORM_PRIORITY`, `ThreadGroup.getMaxPriority()`, `ThreadGroup.setMaxPriority()`.

EXAMPLE See `join()`.

sleep()

PURPOSE
Causes the currently executing thread to sleep for a period of time.

SYNTAX
```
public static native void sleep(long timeout) throws
   InterruptedException
public static void sleep(long timeout, int nanos) throws
   InterruptedException
```

DESCRIPTION
This method causes the currently executing thread to sleep for `timeout` milliseconds. For finer granularity of the time-out period, you can supply a nanosecond count `nanos`.

The thread that is put to sleep remains in active state, but it is not scheduled to run until the time-out period has expired. It can be interrupted from its sleep by another thread.

PARAMETERS

`timeout` The length of time to sleep, in milliseconds. `timeout` ≥ `0`.

`nanos` Additional nanoseconds to sleep. `0` ≤ `nanos` ≤ `999999`. `nanos` is rounded to the nearest millisecond, unless `timeout` is `0`, in which case a nonzero `nanos` is treated as 1 millisecond.

EXCEPTIONS

`IllegalArgumentException`
If `timeout` < `0`, or `nanos` < `0`, or `nanos` > `999999`.

`InterruptedException`
If another thread has interrupted the currently executing thread while the latter was sleeping.

SEE ALSO
`currentThread()`, `interrupt()`, `suspend()`.

EXAMPLE
See the class example, `setDaemon()`, and `stop()`.

start()

PURPOSE
Starts execution of this thread.

SYNTAX
```
public synchronized native void start()
```

DESCRIPTION
This method starts execution of this thread by calling the `run()` method associated with this thread. The state of this thread is set to *active*.

`start()` returns immediately.

EXCEPTIONS

`IllegalThreadStateException`
The thread was already started.

SEE ALSO `activeCount()`, `isActive()`, `run()`, `stop()`.

EXAMPLE See the class example.

stop()

PURPOSE Stops the execution of this thread.

SYNTAX

```
public final void stop()
public final synchronized void stop(Throwable e)
```

DESCRIPTION The two forms of this method stop the execution of this thread. A thread that has been stopped is no longer active and is removed from its thread group.

Normally, to stop a thread you call `stop()` with no arguments. Doing this causes the error `ThreadDeath` to be thrown. The Java runtime then catches this error and completes the termination. You can also call `stop()` with a `Throwable` object `e`, but this is rarely done unless you want to terminate the thread abnormally. If `e` is not an instance of `ThreadDeath` or its subclasses, it is not caught by the Java runtime. The uncaught exception is thrown to the top-level error handler, which prints out a stack trace of `e`.

When a thread is stopped, it terminates immediately and any locks it is holding are released. Releasing locks in such an abnormal manner typically leads to unintended program behavior. The `stop()` method should be used only with great caution.

This method can be executed only if permitted by the security manager.

Note: This method is deprecated in JDK1.2.

PARAMETERS

`e` The object to be thrown when stopping this thread.

EXCEPTIONS

`SecurityException`
If the currently executing thread is not allowed to stop this thread due to security reasons.

SEE ALSO `checkAccess()`, `activeCount()`, `isActive()`, `start()`, `ThreadDeath`, `ThreadGroup.stop()`, `ThreadGroup.uncaughtException()`, `Throwable`.

EXAMPLE This example implements a framework for measuring the performance of Java operations. A thread, called the *timer*, is created to perform a certain test. The timer thread executes the test by running an operation in a very tight loop. The timer thread doesn't check whether it should be terminated. Instead, the creator of the timer thread calls `stop()` on the timer thread to terminate it. The text following the code shows the output of the example when run on a 200MHz Pentium running Windows NT.

```
class Main {
    public static void main(String args[]) {
        for (int i=0; i<Timer.NUM_TESTS; i++) {
            Timer timer = new Timer(i);
            long time = System.currentTimeMillis();
            double usPerOp;

            try {
                timer.start();
                Thread.sleep(5000);     // Wait 5 seconds.

                time = System.currentTimeMillis() - time;
                usPerOp = time * 1000.0 / timer.count;
                System.out.println(timer.label + ": " + usPerOp + " us/op");

                timer.stop();           // Stop the thread.

                Thread.sleep(1000);     // Wait a second for it to terminate.
            } catch (InterruptedException e) {
                e.printStackTrace();
            }
        }
    }
}

class Timer extends Thread {
    static int NUM_TESTS = 6;
    int count;
    int testType;
    String label;

    Timer(int testType) {
        this.testType = testType;
    }

    public void run() {
        switch (testType) {
          case 0:
            label = "i++";
            while (true) {
                count++;
            }
          case 1:
            label = "Non-synchronized method call";
            while (true) {
                nonSynchronizedMethod();
                count++;
            }
          case 2:
            label = "Synchronized method call";
            while (true) {
                synchronizedMethod();
                count++;
            }
          case 3:
            label = "Math.random()";
            while (true) {
                Math.random();
                count++;
            }
```

```
                case 4:
                  label = "Thread.interrupted";
                  while (true) {
                       interrupted();
                       count++;
                  }
                case 5:
                  label = "Thread.sleep(60)";
                  while (true) {
                       try {
                           Thread.sleep(60);
                       } catch (InterruptedException e) {
                           e.printStackTrace();
                       }
                       count++;
                  }
            }
        }

        synchronized void synchronizedMethod() {
        }

        void nonSynchronizedMethod() {
        }
    }
```

Output

```
i++: 2.22373 us/op
Non-synchronized method call: 4.39275 us/op
Synchronized method call: 22.3401 us/op
Math.random(): 101.539 us/op
Thread.interrupted: 6.31886 us/op
Thread.sleep(60): 68493.2 us/op
```

suspend()

PURPOSE Suspends the execution of this thread.

SYNTAX `public final void suspend()`

DESCRIPTION This method suspends the execution of this thread. When a thread has been suspended, it cannot run until it is resumed via a call to `resume()`. A thread that is suspended is still marked *active*. If you suspend a thread that has already been suspended, no action is taken.

Note that a suspended thread still holds all of the locks it acquired. Hence, thread suspension can be a source of deadlocks in multithreaded programs and should be used only with great caution.

This method can be executed only if permitted by the security manager.

Note: This method is deprecated in JDK1.2.

EXCEPTIONS

`SecurityException`

If the currently executing thread is not allowed to suspend this thread due to security reasons.

SEE ALSO `checkAccess()`, `countStackFrames()`, `resume()`, `stop()`,`ThreadGroup.suspend()`.

EXAMPLE See the class example.

A B C D E F G H I J K L M N O P Q R S T U V W X Y Z

Thread()

PURPOSE Constructs a `Thread` instance.

SYNTAX

```
public Thread()
public Thread(Runnable target)
public Thread(String threadName)
public Thread(ThreadGroup group, Runnable target)
public Thread(ThreadGroup group, String threadName)
public Thread(Runnable target, String threadName)
public Thread(ThreadGroup group, Runnable target, String
   threadName)
```

DESCRIPTION A `Thread` instance is created with three, optional arguments: its name, a `Runnable` object whose `run()` method will be the core of this thread, and the thread group `group` to which the new thread is to be added. The thread is created with the name `threadName`. If you do not supply a name for the thread, the thread will be created with an automatically generated name. If you supply `target`, the thread will run the `run()` method defined by `target` when it starts. If you do not supply a `Runnable` object, the `run()` method that will be used is that defined by the new thread itself. If you do not supply a thread group, the new thread will be added to the same thread group as the currently executing thread if no security manager has been installed or if the security manager's `getThreadGroup()` method returns `null`. If the security manager's `getThreadGroup()` returns a non-`null` thread group, the new thread is added to that group. If you supply a thread group `group` in which to add the new thread, the currently executing thread must be permitted by the security manager to access and update `group`.

When a thread is created, its status is *inactive*. It remains that way until a `start()` method has been invoked on it. At that time, its state is changed to *active* and the thread starts running. When a thread is created, its daemon status and priority are the same as those of the currently executing thread. These can be changed using `setDaemon()` and `setPriority()`, respectively, before the thread has been started.

PARAMETERS

`group`	The thread group to which the new thread will be added. If `null`, the new thread is added to the same thread group as the currently executing thread.
`target`	The object whose `run()` method will be called.
`threadName`	The name of the new thread. `threadName` cannot be `null`.

EXCEPTIONS

`SecurityException`
If the currently executing thread is not allowed to create a new thread and place it in the specified group due to security reasons.

SEE ALSO `checkAccess()`, `currentThread()`, `run()`, `Runnable`, `SecurityManager.getThreadGroup()`, `setDaemon()`, `setPriority()`, `start()`, `ThreadGroup`.

EXAMPLE See the class example.

toString()

PURPOSE Generates the string representation of this thread.

SYNTAX `public String toString()`

DESCRIPTION The string representation of a thread includes the thread's name, priority, and thread group. `toString()` returns this string representation.

RETURNS The string representation of a thread.

OVERRIDES `Object.toString()`.

EXAMPLE See `Object.toString()`.

yield()

PURPOSE Causes the currently executing thread to yield to other threads.

SYNTAX `public static native void yield()`

DESCRIPTION This method causes the currently executing thread to yield to other runnable threads for execution. This causes another runnable thread to execute. If no other runnable thread is found, the currently executing thread continues to execute.

On some platforms, a thread that goes into a continuous loop takes control of the processor, thus starving other threads. So that this does not happen, such threads should call the `yield()` method to relinquish the processor to some other thread.

SEE ALSO `currentThread()`, `resume()`, `stop()`, `suspend()`.

EXAMPLE This example demonstrates the effect of the `yield()` method by creating several worker threads that perform intensive computation work. To show that a worker has just started running, the worker constantly checks a static field to see if it was the last running thread. If it wasn't, it prints its identification number to indicate that it is now running. Every worker thread does some amount of work and then prints an asterisk just before calling `yield()`.

The output of this program is shown below the code. Notice that just after an asterisk, a new thread starts to run. Also, notice that once in a while a thread can be preempted even without a call to `yield()`.

```
class Main {
    public static void main(String args[] ) {
        for (int i=0; i<10; i++) {
            (new Worker(i)).start();
        }
    }
}

class Worker extends Thread {
    int id;
    static int lastRunningWorker;

    Worker(int id) {
        this.id =  id;
    }

    public void run() {
        int i = 0;

        // Here is where the work gets done.
        while (true) {
            synchronized (this) {
                if (id != lastRunningWorker) {
                    System.out.print(id);
                    lastRunningWorker = id;
                }
            }
            if (i++ % 100 == 0) {
                System.out.print("*");
                Thread.yield();
            }
        }
    }
}
```

Output

```
*1*0*2*1*0*3*2*0*4*3*2*1*0*5*4*3*2*1*0*6*5
*4*3*2*1*0*7*6*5*4*3*2*1*08*7*6*5*4*3*2*1*0
*9*8*7*6*4*3*2*1*0*9*8*7*6*5*4*3*2*1*0*9*8
*7*6*5*4*
```

java.lang
ThreadDeath

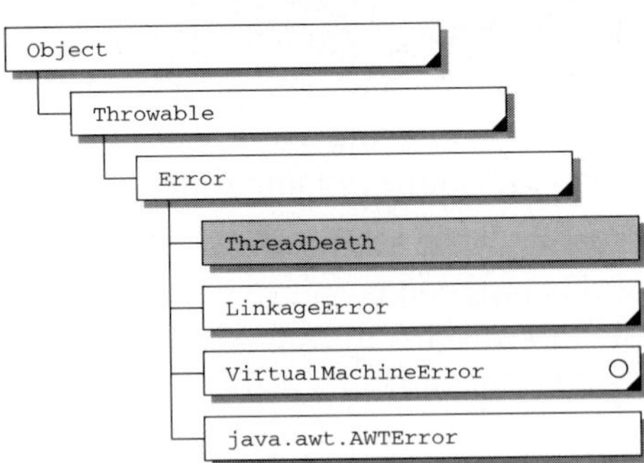

A B C D E F G H I J K L M N O P Q R S T U V W X Y Z

Syntax

`public class ThreadDeath extends Error`

Description

When a program invokes `Thread.stop()` with no argument, the thread's execution is stopped and a `ThreadDeath` error is thrown. The Java virtual machine catches this error and completes the termination (e.g., it frees system resources such as monitors used by the thread). `ThreadDeath` is explicitly caught by the program only if the program needs to do some special clean-up for the thread. After `ThreadDeath` has been caught, it must be rethrown so that it will be caught by the Java virtual machine to complete the thread termination.

You can declare subclasses of `ThreadDeath` for `Thread.stop()` to throw so as to indicate any special processing required for cleaning up a thread. Any error or exception thrown by `Thread.stop()` must be a subclass of `ThreadDeath`.

`ThreadDeath` is a special subclass of `Error`. Other subclasses of `Error` generated by the Java virtual machine indicate unrecoverable errors that cause the program to terminate. `ThreadDeath`, on the other hand, indicates only that a thread has been destroyed; the program continues to run with other existing threads.

See Also

`Error`, `Thread.stop()`, `ThreadGroup.uncaughtException()`.

Example

See `ThreadGroup.uncaughtException()`.

ThreadGroup

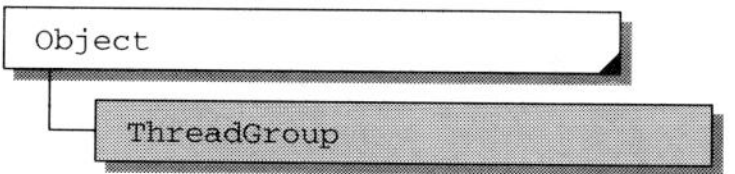

Syntax

```
public class ThreadGroup
```

Description

The `ThreadGroup` class represents a group of threads. A thread group can contain a set of threads and other thread groups (see Figure 102). A thread or thread group can be in at most one thread group. Thread groups allow you to organize groups so that you can manipulate the group of threads as a whole. For example, you can set the maximum priority of a thread group and suspend and resume all threads in a group.

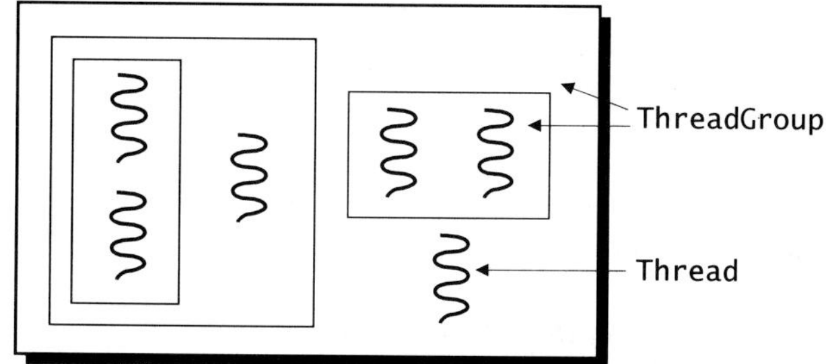

FIGURE 102: `ThreadGroup`.

Security

You also can use thread groups to control manipulation of thread state between groups, provided this is a policy enforced by the security manager. For example, the security manager's policy may allow a thread to access threads in its own thread group but not in its parent's. The policies and restrictions regarding which thread group can manipulate which other thread group depend on the security manager in place.

Maximum Priority

A thread group's *maximum priority* places an upper bound on the priority to which threads and thread groups in this thread group can be set. When a thread group is created, its maximum priority is that of its parent thread group. This maximum can subsequently be lowered if permitted by the security manager.

Daemon Thread Groups

A *daemon* thread group is automatically destroyed when it becomes empty (contains no more threads or thread groups). A thread group that is not a daemon thread group must be destroyed explicitly. When a thread group is created, it inherits the daemon status of its parent thread group. You can change a thread group's daemon status subsequent to creation by using `setDaemon()`.

There is no relationship between daemon thread groups and daemon threads.

MEMBER SUMMARY

Constructor	
`ThreadGroup()`	Constructs a `ThreadGroup` instance.
ThreadGroup Property Methods	
`getMaxPriority()`	Retrieves the maximum priority of this thread group.
`getName()`	Retrieves the name of this thread group.
`getParent()`	Retrieves the parent thread group of this thread group.
`isDaemon()`	Determines if this thread group is a daemon thread group.
`parentOf()`	Determines if this thread group is an ancestor of another group.
`setDaemon()`	Changes the daemon status of this thread group.
`setMaxPriority()`	Sets the maximum priority of this thread group and its subgroup.
ThreadGroup State Methods	
`activeCount()`	Estimates the number of active threads in this thread group.
`activeGroupCount()`	Estimates the number of active thread groups in this thread group.
`enumerate()`	Enumerates the threads or thread groups in this thread group.
`isDestroyed()`	Determines whether this thread group has been destroyed.
`list()`	Prints the threads and thread groups in this thread group.
Thread State Methods	
`allowThreadSuspension()`	Enables/disables whether this thread group's threads can be suspended due to low memory in the virtual machine.
`destroy()`	Destroys this thread group and its subgroups.
`resume()`	Resumes all of the threads in this thread group and its subgroups.
`stop()`	Stops all of the threads in this thread group and its subgroups.
`suspend()`	Suspends all of the threads in this thread group and its subgroups.
Security Method	
`checkAccess()`	Determines if allowed to modify this thread group.
Thread Exit Handling Method	
`uncaughtException()`	Handles a thread exit from this thread group due to an uncaught exception.
Description Method	
`toString()`	Generates the string representation of this thread group.

See Also

`Thread`, `SecurityManager`.

Example

This example implements a thread group viewer that shows all thread groups in the system at a certain point in time. The thread viewer updates the list of thread groups every 5 seconds. The thread group viewer can be paused and resumed by clicking the Pause button at the top of the frame. See Figure 103.

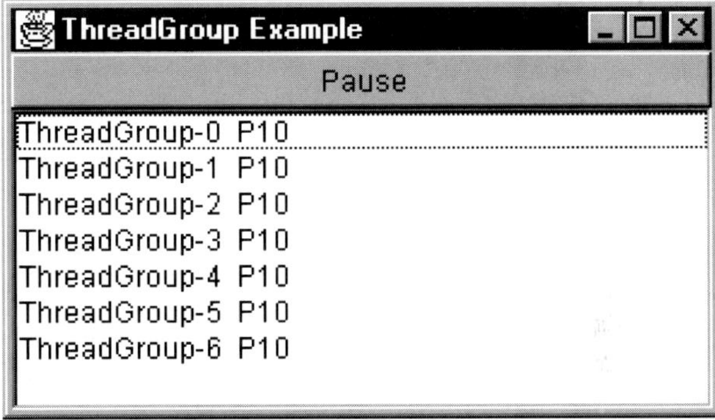

FIGURE 103: Thread Group Viewer.

A thread group can be destroyed by clicking the thread group name in the list. In this example, the `handleEvent()` method first interrupts all of the threads in the thread group and then waits for them to be stopped.

In the `ThreadViewer` class, the `actionPerformed()` and `updateList()` methods are synchronized because they share a number of fields. Doing this prevents the two methods from seeing inconsistent values in the shared fields.

```
import java.awt.*;
import java.awt.event.*;

class Main implements Runnable {
    public static void main(String args[] ) {
        try {
            new ThreadGViewer();          // Create the thread viewer

            // periodically create a thread group just to
            // keep things interesting
            for (int i=0; ; i++) {
                // Create a new thread group.
                ThreadGroup grp = new ThreadGroup("ThreadGroup-"+i);

                // And create a new thread in the thread group.
                (new Thread(grp, new Main())).start();

                Thread.sleep((int)Math.floor(Math.random()*5000));
            }
        } catch (Exception e) {
            e.printStackTrace();
        }
    }

    public void run() {
        try {
            while (true) {
```

```
                    // Check if this thread has been interrupted.
                    if (Thread.currentThread().isInterrupted()) {
                        break;
                    }
                    Thread.sleep(500);
                }
            } catch (Exception e) {
                e.printStackTrace();
            }
        }
    }

class ThreadGViewer extends Frame implements Runnable, ActionListener {
    Thread timerThread;

    // List of all thread groups in the system.
    ThreadGroup[] groups;

    // List component containing all the thread groups in the system.
    List threadList = new List();

    ThreadGViewer() {
        super("ThreadGroup Example");
        add(threadList, BorderLayout.CENTER);
        Button b;
        add(b = new Button("Pause"), BorderLayout.NORTH);
        b.addActionListener(this);
        threadList.addActionListener(this);

        setSize(300, 300);
        show();
        timerThread = new Thread(this);
        timerThread.start();
    }

    public void actionPerformed(ActionEvent evt) {
        String cmd = evt.getActionCommand();
        if ("Pause".equals(cmd)) {
            timerThread.suspend();
            ((Button)evt.getSource()).setLabel("Resume");
        } else if ("Resume".equals(cmd)) {
            timerThread.resume();
            ((Button)evt.getSource()).setLabel("Pause");
        } else if (evt.getSource() == threadList) {
            ThreadGroup grp = groups[threadList.getSelectedIndex()];
            try {
                grp.checkAccess();

                if (grp.isDestroyed()) {
                    System.out.println(grp + " already destroyed");
                    return;
                }

                // Interrupt & then wait until all threads have stopped.
                Thread[] threads = new Thread[grp.activeCount()];
                int count = grp.enumerate(threads, false);
                for (int i=0; i<count; i++) {
                    threads[i].interrupt();
                    threads[i].join();
                }
```

```
                // Now destroy the group.
                grp.destroy();
            } catch (InterruptedException e) {
                e.printStackTrace();
            } catch (SecurityException e) {
                System.out.println("No permission to stop thread " +
                    grp.getName());
            }
        }
    }

    public void run() {
        try {
            while (timerThread == Thread.currentThread()) {
                updateList();
                Thread.sleep(5000);
            }
        } catch (Exception e) {
            e.printStackTrace();
        }
    }

    synchronized void updateList() {
        ThreadGroup curGrp = Thread.currentThread().getThreadGroup();
        ThreadGroup[] grps = new ThreadGroup[curGrp.activeGroupCount()];
        int count = curGrp.enumerate(grps, true);

        groups = new ThreadGroup[count];
        threadList.removeAll();
        int j = 0;
        for (int i=0; i<count; i++) {
            if (Thread.currentThread().getThreadGroup().parentOf(grps[i])) {
                ThreadGroup grp = grps[i];

                threadList.addItem(grp.getName()
                    + "  P" + grp.getMaxPriority()
                    + "  " + (grp.isDaemon() ? "Daemon" : ""));
                groups[j++] = grp;
            }
        }
    }
}
```

activeCount()

PURPOSE Estimates the number of active threads in this thread group.

SYNTAX `public int activeCount()`

DESCRIPTION This method returns an estimate of the number of active threads in this thread group and its subgroups. This includes (recursively) all descendents of this thread group. It is only an estimate because during this call, threads might have been added to or removed from this thread group or its subgroups.

RETURNS An estimate of the total number of active threads in this thread group and its subgroups.

SEE ALSO `activeGroupCount()`, `enumerate()`, `list()`.

EXAMPLE See the class example.

activeGroupCount()

PURPOSE Estimates the number of thread groups in this thread group.

SYNTAX `public int activeGroupCount()`

DESCRIPTION This method returns an estimate of the number of thread groups in this thread group and its subgroups. It is only an estimate because during this call, thread groups might have been added to or removed from this thread group or its subgroups.

RETURNS An estimate of the total number of thread groups in this thread group and its subgroups.

SEE ALSO `activeCount()`, `enumerate()`, `list()`.

EXAMPLE See the class example.

allowThreadSuspension()

PURPOSE Enables/disables whether this thread group's threads can be suspended due to low memory in the virtual machine.

SYNTAX `public boolean allowThreadSuspension(boolean allow)`

DESCRIPTION This method enables or disables the ability of the virtual machine to suspend this thread group's threads when the virtual machine is low on memory. If `allow` is `true`, this thread group's threads can be suspended. If `allow` is `false`, this thread group's threads cannot be suspended and any threads that are currently suspended due to low memory are unsuspended.

A thread group inherits this property (whether the virtual machine can suspend its threads if the virtual machine is low on memory) from its parent at the time the thread group is created. This property has no effect on the suspension of this thread group's threads via the `suspend()` call.

PARAMETERS
`allow` `true` means suspension can occur; `false` means suspension cannot occur.

RETURNS `true`.

checkAccess()

PURPOSE Determines if allowed to modify this thread group.

SYNTAX `public final void checkAccess()`

DESCRIPTION This method checks if the currently executing thread is allowed to modify this thread group. Modifications that require access checking include changing the state of the threads within the group (e.g., suspend/resume) and changing the properties of the thread group (its daemon status and maximum priority).

EXCEPTIONS

`SecurityException`

If the currently executing thread is not allowed to modify this thread group due to security reasons.

SEE ALSO `destroy()`, `resume()`, `SecurityManager.checkAccess()`, `setDaemon()`, `setMaxPriority()`, `stop()`, `suspend()`, `ThreadGroup()`.

EXAMPLE See the class example.

destroy()

PURPOSE Destroys this thread group and its subgroups.

SYNTAX `public final void destroy()`

DESCRIPTION This method destroys this thread group and its subgroups and removes this thread group from its parent's thread group. A thread group can be destroyed only if it and all of its subgroups contain no more threads.

EXCEPTIONS

`IllegalThreadStateException`

If this thread group is not empty or if it has already been destroyed.

`SecurityException`

If the currently executing thread is not allowed to destroy this thread group due to security reasons.

SEE ALSO `isDaemon()`, `setDaemon()`.

EXAMPLE See the class example.

enumerate()

PURPOSE Enumerates the threads or thread groups in this thread group.

SYNTAX
```
public int enumerate(Thread[] threads)
public int enumerate(Thread[] threads, boolean recurse)
public int enumerate(ThreadGroup[] groups)
public int enumerate(ThreadGroup[] groups, boolean recurse)
```

DESCRIPTION The four forms of this method enumerate the threads or thread groups in this thread group.

The first two forms enumerate the threads in this group. `enumerate()` copies to the array `threads` the references of the `Thread` objects in this group. `recurse` specifies whether to recursively enumerate the threads in the subgroups of this thread group. If `recurse` is `true`, the subgroups are enumerated. If `recurse` is `false`, only this thread group is enumerated. If `recurse` is not specified, subgroups are enumerated. `threads` must have been allocated before `enumerate()` is called. If `threads` is too small to hold all of the references, then when it becomes full, the enumeration terminates. You can use `activeCount()` to estimate the size of `threads`.

The last two forms enumerate the thread groups in this group. `enumerate()` copies to the array `groups` the references of the `ThreadGroup` objects in this group. `recurse` specifies whether to recursively enumerate the thread groups in the subgroups of this thread group. If `recurse` is `true`, the subgroups are enumerated. If `recurse` is `false`, only this thread group is enumerated. If `recurse` is not specified, subgroups are enumerated. `groups` must have been allocated before calling `enumerate()`. If `groups` is too small to hold all of the references, then when it becomes full, the enumeration terminates. You can use `activeGroupCount()` to estimate the size of `groups`.

PARAMETERS

`groups` An existing array to hold the references to `ThreadGroup` objects.

`recurse` Whether to enumerate recursively the subgroups of this thread group. `true` means to recursively enumerate subgroups; `false` means enumerate on this thread group, not on its subgroups.

`threads` An existing array to hold the references to `Thread` objects.

RETURNS The number of references filled in `groups` or `threads`.

SEE ALSO `activeCount()`, `activeGroupCount()`, `list()`.

EXAMPLE See the class example.

getMaxPriority()

PURPOSE Retrieves the maximum priority of this thread group.

SYNTAX `public final int getMaxPriority()`

DESCRIPTION A thread group's maximum priority places an upper bound on the priority to which threads and thread groups in this thread group can be set. When a thread is created, its priority is set to that of the thread that created it and is not limited by the thread group's maximum priority. The thread group's maximum priority is checked only when the thread's priority is set by using `Thread.setPriority()`.

When a thread group is created, its maximum priority is that of its parent thread group. This maximum can later be lowered by using `setMaxPriority()` if permitted by the security manager.

`getMaxPriority()` returns the maximum priority of this thread group.

RETURNS The maximum priority of this thread group.

SEE ALSO `setMaxPriority()`, `Thread.setPriority()`, `ThreadGroup()`.

EXAMPLE See the class example.

getName()

PURPOSE Retrieves the name of this thread group.

SYNTAX `public final String getName()`

RETURNS The name of this thread group.

SEE ALSO `ThreadGroup()`.

EXAMPLE See the class example.

getParent()

PURPOSE Retrieves the parent thread group of this thread group.

SYNTAX `public final ThreadGroup getParent()`

RETURNS The parent of this thread group. `null` if this thread group is the first thread group created in the system.

SEE ALSO `parentOf()`, `ThreadGroup()`.

EXAMPLE See the `Thread` class example.

isDaemon()

PURPOSE Determines if this thread group is a daemon thread group.

SYNTAX `public final boolean isDaemon()`

DESCRIPTION A *daemon* thread group is automatically destroyed when it becomes empty (contains no more threads or thread groups). A thread group that is not a daemon thread group must be destroyed explicitly using `destroy()`. When a thread group is created, it inherits the daemon status of its parent thread group. You can change a thread group's daemon status using `setDaemon()`.

`isDaemon()` returns `true` if this thread group is a daemon thread group. It returns `false` if this thread group is not a daemon thread group.

There is no relationship between daemon thread groups and daemon threads.

RETURNS `true` if this thread group is daemon; `false` otherwise.

SEE ALSO `destroy()`, `setDaemon()`, `ThreadGroup()`.

EXAMPLE See the class example.

isDestroyed()

PURPOSE Determines whether this thread group has been destroyed.

SYNTAX `public synchronized boolean isDestroyed()`

RETURNS `true` if this thread group has been destroyed; `false` otherwise.

SEE ALSO `destroy()`.

EXAMPLE See the class example.

list()

PURPOSE Prints the threads and thread groups in this thread group.

SYNTAX `public void list()`

DESCRIPTION This method prints all of the threads and thread groups in this thread group to `System.out`. This includes (recursively) all descendents of this thread group. This method is useful for debugging.

SEE ALSO `enumerate()`, `System.out`.

EXAMPLE This example simply creates a set of nested thread groups and then calls `list()`. The output of this program follows the following code.

```
import java.awt.*;
class Main {
    public static void main(String args[] ) {
        ThreadGroup grp = Thread.currentThread().getThreadGroup();

        for (int i=0; i<5; i++) {
            // Create a new thread group.
            ThreadGroup g = new ThreadGroup(grp, "group-"+i);

            grp = g;
        }
        Thread.currentThread().getThreadGroup().list();
    }
}
```

Output

```
java.lang.ThreadGroup[name=main,maxpri=10]
    Thread[main,5,main]
    java.lang.ThreadGroup[name=group-0,maxpri=10]
        java.lang.ThreadGroup[name=group-1,maxpri=10]
            java.lang.ThreadGroup[name=group-2,maxpri=10]
                java.lang.ThreadGroup[name=group-3,maxpri=10]
                    java.lang.ThreadGroup[name=group-4,maxpri=10]
```

parentOf()

PURPOSE Determines if this thread group is an ancestor of another group.

SYNTAX `public final boolean parentOf(ThreadGroup group)`

DESCRIPTION This method determines whether this thread group is equal to `group` or is an *ancestor* of `group`. This thread group is an ancestor of `group` if this thread group is `group`'s parent, or `group`'s parent's parent, and so on.

PARAMETERS

`group` The thread group to check.

RETURNS `true` if this thread group is equal to or is an ancestor of `group`; `false` otherwise.

SEE ALSO `getParent()`, `ThreadGroup()`.

EXAMPLE See the class example.

resume()

PURPOSE Resumes all of the threads in this thread group and its subgroups.

SYNTAX `public final void resume()`

DESCRIPTION This method can be executed only if permitted by the security manager.

Note: This method is deprecated in JDK1.2.

EXCEPTIONS

SecurityException
If the currently executing thread is not allowed to modify this thread group due to security reasons.

SEE ALSO `checkAccess()`, `stop()`, `suspend()`, `Thread.resume()`, `Thread.stop()`, `Thread.suspend()`.

EXAMPLE See the class example.

setDaemon()

PURPOSE Changes the daemon status of this thread group.

SYNTAX `public final void setDaemon(boolean daemon)`

DESCRIPTION A *daemon* thread group is automatically destroyed when it becomes empty (contains no more threads or thread groups). A thread group that is not a daemon thread group must be destroyed explicitly using `destroy()`. When a thread group is created, it inherits the daemon status of its parent thread group. You can change a thread group's daemon status using `setDaemon()`. If `daemon` is `true`, the thread group becomes a daemon thread group. If `daemon` is `false`, the thread group becomes a non-daemon thread group.

There is no relationship between daemon thread groups and daemon threads.

PARAMETERS

`daemon` `true` changes the thread group to a daemon thread group; `false` changes the thread group to a non-daemon thread group.

EXCEPTIONS

SecurityException
If the currently executing thread is not allowed to modify this thread group due to security reasons.

SEE ALSO `destroy()`, `isDaemon()`.

EXAMPLE This example creates a daemon thread group that contains a number of threads. When the threads in the thread group terminate, so does the thread group.

```
class Main {
    public static void main(String args[] ) {
        ThreadGroup grp = new ThreadGroup("Group");

        grp.setDaemon(true);
        // Create a few workers
        for (int i=0; i<5; i++) {
            (new Worker(grp)).start();
        }
    }
}
```

```
class Worker extends Thread {
    Worker(ThreadGroup grp) {
        super(grp, "Worker");
    }

    public void run() {
        try {
            Thread.sleep((int)Math.floor(Math.random()*5000));
            System.out.println("done");
        } catch (Exception e) {
            e.printStackTrace();
        }
    }
}
```

setMaxPriority()

PURPOSE Sets the maximum priority of this thread group and its subgroups.

SYNTAX `public final void setMaxPriority(int pri)`

DESCRIPTION A thread group's maximum priority places an upper bound on the priority to which threads and thread groups in this thread group can be set. When a thread is created, its priority is set to that of the thread that created it and is not limited by the thread group's maximum priority. The thread group's maximum priority is checked only when the thread's priority is set by using `Thread.setPriority()`. When a thread group is created, its maximum priority is that of its parent thread group.

`setMaxPriority()` lowers the maximum priority of this thread group and its subgroups to `pri`. `pri` is limited to the inclusive range `Thread.MIN_PRIORITY` and the current maximum. If `pri` is greater than the current maximum, the maximum remains unchanged.

`setMaxPriority()` does not change the priorities of threads that are already in this thread group and its subgroups, even if those priorities are higher than `pri`. However, if the priorities of these threads are subsequently changed (by using `Thread.setPriority()`), the new thread group maximum priority will apply.

This method can be executed only if permitted by the security manager.

PARAMETERS

`pri` The maximum priority of this group.

EXCEPTIONS

`SecurityException`

If the currently executing thread is not allowed to modify this thread group due to security reasons.

SEE ALSO `checkAccess()`, `getMaxPriority()`, `Thread.MAX_PRIORITY`, `Thread.MIN_PRIORITY`, `Thread.setPriority()`, `ThreadGroup()`.

EXAMPLE See `suspend()`.

stop()

PURPOSE Stops all of the threads in this thread group and its subgroups.

SYNTAX `public final void stop()`

DESCRIPTION When a thread is stopped, it terminates immediately and any locks it is holding are released. Releasing locks in such an abnormal manner typically leads to unintended program behavior. The `stop()` method should be used only with great caution.

This method can be executed only if permitted by the security manager.

Note: This method is deprecated in JDK1.2.

EXCEPTIONS

`SecurityException`
If the currently executing thread is not allowed to stop this thread group due to security reasons.

SEE ALSO `checkAccess()`, `resume()`, `suspend()`, `Thread.resume()`, `Thread.stop()`, `Thread.suspend()`.

EXAMPLE See `uncaughtException()`.

suspend()

PURPOSE Suspends all of the threads in this thread group and its subgroups.

SYNTAX `public final void suspend()`

DESCRIPTION Note that a suspended thread still holds all of the locks it acquired. Hence, thread suspension can be a source of deadlocks in multithreaded programs and so should be used only with great caution.

This method can be executed only if permitted by the security manager.

Note: This method is deprecated in JDK1.2.

EXCEPTIONS

`SecurityException`
If the currently executing thread is not allowed to suspend this thread group due to security reasons.

SEE ALSO `checkAccess()`, `resume()`, `stop()`, `Thread.resume()`, `Thread.stop()`, `Thread.suspend()`.

EXAMPLE This example creates two thread groups: one whose maximum priority is normal (`hiGroup`) and one whose maximum priority is minimum (`loGroup`). See Figure 104. Two threads are created in each group. The example also creates a frame with two labels, one for each group. The labels are used to show the progress of the threads.

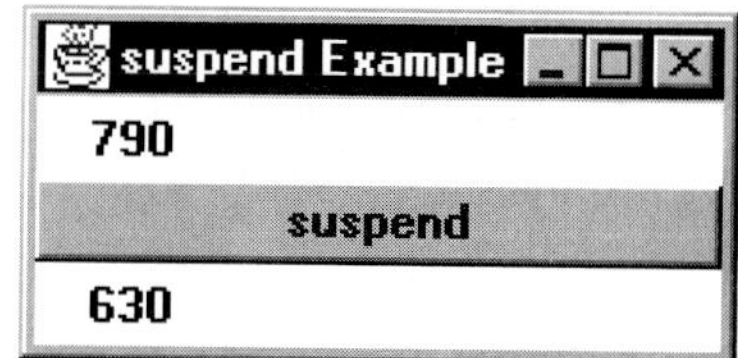

FIGURE 104: `Threadgroup.suspend()`.

The threads in the `hiGroup` will get more work done than will the threads in the `loGroup`. Clicking the suspend button in the frame will suspend the `hiGroup`, thus resulting in all of the processor cycles being given to the threads in the `loGroup`.

```
import java.awt.*;
import java.awt.event.*;

class Main extends Frame implements ActionListener {
    Label loLabel = new Label();
    Label hiLabel = new Label();
    ThreadGroup hiGroup = new ThreadGroup("High");
    ThreadGroup loGroup = new ThreadGroup("Low");

    Main() {
        super("suspend Example");

        // Limit the priority in the lo priority thread group.
        loGroup.setMaxPriority(Thread.MIN_PRIORITY);

        // Add a few threads.
        (new Worker(hiGroup, hiLabel)).start();
        (new Worker(hiGroup, hiLabel)).start();
        (new Worker(loGroup, loLabel)).start();
        (new Worker(loGroup, loLabel)).start();

        add(hiLabel, BorderLayout.NORTH);
        add(loLabel, BorderLayout.SOUTH);
        Button b;
        add(b = new Button("suspend"), BorderLayout.CENTER);
        b.addActionListener(this);

        pack();
        show();
    }

    public synchronized void actionPerformed(ActionEvent evt) {
        String cmd = evt.getActionCommand();
        if ("suspend".equals(cmd)) {
            hiGroup.suspend();
            ((Button)evt.getSource()).setLabel("resume");
        } else if ("resume".equals(cmd)) {
```

```
                hiGroup.resume();
                ((Button)evt.getSource()).setLabel("suspend");
            }
        }

        static public void main(String[] args) {
            new Main();
        }
    }

    class Worker extends Thread {
        Label label;

        Worker(ThreadGroup group, Label label) {
            super(group, "Worker");
            this.label = label;
        }

        public void run() {
            try {
                for (int i=0; ; i++) {
                    if (i % 10 == 0) {
                        label.setText(""+i);
                    }
                    Thread.sleep(16);
                }
            } catch (Exception e) {
                e.printStackTrace();
            }
        }
    }
```

ThreadGroup()

PURPOSE Constructs a ThreadGroup instance.

SYNTAX

```
public ThreadGroup()
public ThreadGroup(String name)
public ThreadGroup(ThreadGroup parent, String name)
```

DESCRIPTION ThreadGroup has three constructors. By default, the new thread group is created in the same thread group as the currently executing thread. You can specify that it be created in a different thread group by supplying a thread group parent. A thread group can be added to another thread group only if permitted by the security manager.

PARAMETERS

name The name of the new thread group being created. name can be null.

parent The thread group in which to create this new thread group. parent must not be null.

EXCEPTIONS

`IllegalArgumentException`
If the parent thread group has already been destroyed.

`SecurityException`
If the currently executing thread is not allowed to create this thread group in the parent due to security reasons.

SEE ALSO `checkAccess()`, `Thread.currentThread()`, `Thread.getThreadGroup()`.

EXAMPLE See the class example.

toString()

PURPOSE Generates the string representation of this thread group.

SYNTAX `public String toString()`

DESCRIPTION The string representation of a thread group consists of the `ThreadGroup` class name, the thread group's name, and its maximum priority. `toString()` returns this string representation.

RETURNS The string representation of this thread group.

OVERRIDES `Object.toString()`.

SEE ALSO `getMaxPriority()`, `getName()`.

EXAMPLE See `Object.toString()`.

uncaughtException()

PURPOSE Handles a thread exit from this thread group due to an uncaught exception.

SYNTAX `public void uncaughtException(Thread thrd, Throwable e)`

DESCRIPTION When the thread `thrd` from this thread group throws an exception or error that has not been caught, `uncaughtException()` is called by the Java runtime to handle it. Normally, when a thread is destroyed, a `ThreadDeath` error is thrown. `uncaughtException()` checks to determine whether `e` is a subclass of `ThreadDeath`. If it is not, `uncaughtException()` prints a stack trace of `e`.

PARAMETERS

`e` The uncaught exception.

`thrd` The thread that threw `e`.

SEE ALSO `stop()`, `Thread.stop()`, `ThreadDeath`, `Throwable.printStackTrace()`.

EXAMPLE This example defines a thread group that overrides the `uncaughtException()` method. A thread is created in this group and then later stopped (via the `stop()` method). Since the thread does not catch `ThreadDeath` (which is thrown because of the `stop()`), the `uncaughtException()` method is invoked. The output generated by this program is after the following code:

```
class Main implements Runnable {
    public static void main(String args[]) {
        MainThreadGroup mtg = new MainThreadGroup("MainThreadGroup");
        Thread thread = new Thread(mtg, new Main());

        thread.start();

        // Wait 1 second ...
        try {
            Thread.sleep(1000);

            // And then stop the thread.
            thread.stop();
        } catch (InterruptedException e) {
            e.printStackTrace();
        }
    }

    public void run() {
        try {
            Thread.sleep(2000);
        } catch (Exception e) {
            e.printStackTrace();
        }
    }
}

class MainThreadGroup extends ThreadGroup {
    MainThreadGroup(String name) {
        super(name);
    }

    public void uncaughtException(Thread t, Throwable e) {
        System.out.println("UNCAUGHT EXCEPTION by " + t.getName());
        e.printStackTrace();
    }
}
```

Output

```
UNCAUGHT EXCEPTION by Thread-1
java.lang.ThreadDeath
    at Main.run(Main.java:21)
    at java.lang.Thread.run(Thread.java:294)
```

java.lang
Throwable

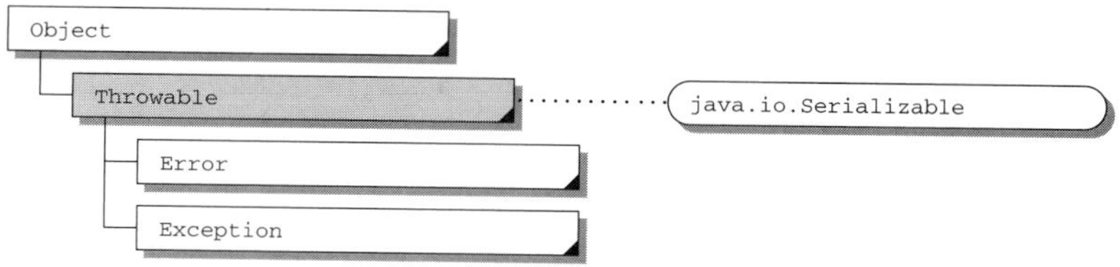

A B C D E F G H I J K L M N O P Q R S T U V W X Y Z

Syntax

```
public class Throwable implements Serializable
```

Description

The `Throwable` class is the superclass for `Error` and `Exception`, which in turn are the superclasses for all other system- and user-defined exceptions. Exception for specially system-defined errors and runtime exceptions, the Java language requires any method that throws an instance of `Throwable` or its subclasses to declare the throwable in its `throws` clause as part of the method's declaration. Any method that calls such a method must either catch the throwable using `try/catch` statements or declare it in its own `throws` clause. The Java compiler will generate a compilation error for any code that does not follow these rules.

Usage

The following is an example of how to catch a throwable. In your programs, however, instead of using `Throwable` directly you should use the `Exception` class hierarchy when defining, throwing, or catching exceptions.

```
try {
    int a[] = new int[2];
    a[4]= 3;
} catch (Throwable e) {
    System.err.println("exception msg: " + e.getMessage());
    System.err.println("exception string: " + e.toString());
    e.printStackTrace();
}
```

Information in a Throwable

When you create a throwable, it contain three pieces of information:

1. The class name of the throwable
2. A snapshot of the current execution stack
3. An optional string describing the details of this particular throwable

The class name indicates the type of the throwable. The stack trace is useful for pinpointing where the throwable was thrown. The optional string can be used to provide additional details about the throwable. For example, if the throwable is associated with a file, the filename could be supplied as this string.

MEMBER SUMMARY	
Constructor	
`Throwable()`	Constructs an instance of `Throwable`.
Stack Trace Methods	
`fillInStackTrace()`	Fills in the execution stack trace of this throwable.
`printStackTrace()`	Prints this throwable and its stack trace.
Message Methods	
`getLocalizedMessage()`	Retrieves the localized message associated with this throwable.
`getMessage()`	Retrieves the string with which this throwable was created.
Description Method	
`toString()`	Generates the string representation of this throwable.

A B C D E F G H I J K L M N O P Q R S T U V W X Y Z

See Also

`Error`, `Exception`.

fillInStackTrace()

PURPOSE Fills in the execution stack trace of this throwable.

SYNTAX `public native Throwable fillInStackTrace()`

DESCRIPTION An instance of `Throwable` is created with a snapshot of the current stack trace. If the throwable is not thrown at the same point at which it was created or if the throwable is to be rethrown, `fillInStackTrace()` can be called to update this snapshot to the current stack trace so that it reflects exactly where the throwable was thrown.

RETURNS The `Throwable` itself.

SEE ALSO `Throwable.printStackTrace()`.

EXAMPLE

```
Exception e = ...;
int a, b, c;
... // do some computation using a, b, and c

// Fill in stack trace to indicate that e is being thrown at this point.
throw e.fillInStackTrace();
```

getLocalizedMessage()

PURPOSE Retrieves the localized message associated with this throwable.

SYNTAX `public String getMessage()`

DESCRIPTION When you create an instance of `Throwable`, you can associate with it a string that describes details of the throwable. `getMessage()` returns this string. `getLocalizedMessage()`, by default, returns the result of `getMessage()`. It can be overriden to return the localized version of the message.

RETURNS The localized version of the string that this throwable was created with; `null` if this throwable was not created with a string.

SEE ALSO `Throwable()`, `getMessage()`, `toString()`.

getMessage()

PURPOSE Retrieves the string with which this throwable was created.

SYNTAX `public String getMessage()`

DESCRIPTION When you create an instance of `Throwable`, you can associate with it a string describing details of the throwable. This could be, for example, a filename or the string representation of a number. `getMessage()` returns this string. This string also is included in the throwable's string representation generated by `toString()`.

RETURNS The string that this throwable was created with; `null` if this throwable was not created with a string.

SEE ALSO `getLocalizedMessage()`, `Throwable()`, `toString()`.

EXAMPLE

```
try {
    FileInputStream out = new FileInputStream(args[0]);
...
} catch (IOException e) {
    System.err.println("cannot create stream: " + e.getMessage());
}
```

printStackTrace()

PURPOSE Prints this throwable and its stack trace.

SYNTAX

```
public void printStackTrace()
public void printStackTrace(PrintStream s)
public void printStackTrace(PrintWriter wr)
```

DESCRIPTION A throwable has associated with it a stack trace. You can display this stack track using `printStackTrace()`. By default, the output is sent to `System.err`. If you supply a `PrintStream` argument `s`, the output will go to `s`. If you supply a `PrintWriter` argument `wr`, the output will go to `wr`.

PARAMETERS

`s` The print stream to which to send the output.

`wr` The printer writer to which to send the output.

SEE ALSO `fillInStackTrace()`, `java.io.PrintStream`, `java.io.PrintWriter`, `System.err`, `Throwable()`.

EXAMPLE

```
try {
    Long lobj2 = new Long("1048L576"); // using string
} catch (NumberFormatException e) {
    e.printStackTrace();              // output goes to System.err
    e.printStackTrace(System.out);    // send trace to stdout too
}
```

Throwable()

PURPOSE Constructs an instance of `Throwable`.

SYNTAX

```
public Throwable()
public Throwable(String message)
```

DESCRIPTION The two forms of this constructor construct a `Throwable` instance and records in it the current stack trace. If the string `message` is supplied to the constructor, it is recorded with the throwable. `message` is then included with the string representation of the throwable (the one generated by `toString()`). `message` can be retrieved from the throwable using `getMessage()`. If `message` is not supplied, it defaults to `null`.

The snapshot of the stack trace recorded in the throwable can be displayed using `printStackTrace()`. The stack trace can be updated at any time using `fillInStackTrace()`.

PARAMETERS

`message` The possibly `null` string to associate with the throwable.

SEE ALSO `fillInStackTrace()`, `getMessage()`, `printStackTrace()`, `toString()`.

EXAMPLE

```
// Implementation of FileInputStream.getFD()
public final FileDescriptor getFD() throws IOException {
    if (fd != null) return fd;
    throw new IOException();
}
// Implementation of FileInputStream constructor
```

```
public FileInputStream(String name) throws FileNotFoundException {
    SecurityManager security = System.getSecurityManager();
    if (security != null) {
        security.checkRead(name);
    }
    try {
        fd = new FileDescriptor();
        open(name);
    } catch (IOException e) {
        throw new FileNotFoundException(name);
    }
}
```


toString()

PURPOSE Generates the string representation of this throwable.

SYNTAX `public String toString()`

DESCRIPTION The string representation of a throwable includes its class name and the string with which the throwable was created (if any). `toString()` returns this string representation.

RETURNS The string representation of this object.

OVERRIDES `Object.toString()`.

SEE ALSO `getMessage()`, `printStackTrace()`.

EXAMPLE

```
try {
    FileInputStream out = new FileInputStream(args[0]);
...
} catch (IOException e) {
    System.err.println(e.toString());
}
```

java.util
TimeZone

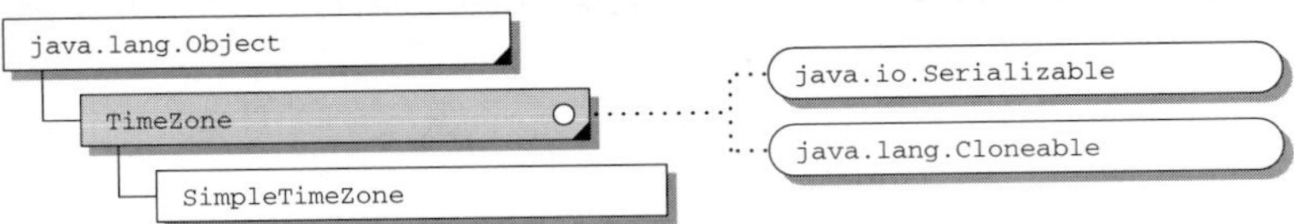

A
B
C
D
E
F
G
H
I
J
K
L
M
N
O
P
Q
R
S
T
U
V
W
X
Y
Z

Syntax

```
abstract public class TimeZone implements Serializable, Cloneable
```

Description

A `TimeZone` object represents a time zone. It is used to compute the local time based on a time relative to Greenwich Mean Time (GMT). A `TimeZone` object also contains daylight savings time information.

The `TimeZone` class is an abstract class designed to be the superclass of different kinds of `TimeZone` objects. `TimeZone` objects can differ in the type of calendar used to interpret dates and in the rules that determine the daylight savings time period. For example, Java 1.1 provides one `TimeZone` subclass called `SimpleTimeZone`. `SimpleTimeZone` uses a Gregorian calendar (see `GregorianCalendar`) and its daylight savings time rules can only be of the form "start on the 1st Sunday in April." `SimpleTimeZone` cannot handle rules of the form "start on March 4th"; a different `TimeZone` subclass is needed for this.

Usage

This class is used primarily to retrieve `TimeZone` objects for a time zone. For example, to get the `TimeZone` object for the local time zone, call `getDefault()`. To get the `TimeZone` object for GMT, call `getTimeZone("GMT")`. You can then query the returned `TimeZone` object for information about the time zone, or you can use the object in other classes such as `Calendar`.

It is not usual to create your own `TimeZone` objects. This class has a predefined set of `TimeZone` objects and does not provide a means to register new `TimeZone` objects. You can retrieve the available `TimeZone` objects by calling `getAvailableIDs()`.

Time Zones and The Raw Offset

Earth is divided into 24 standard time zones, one time zone per 15° of longitude. The time is advanced by one hour for each time zone east of Greenwich, England, and delayed by one hour for each time zone west of Greenwich. The time zone that contains Greenwich is called Greenwich Mean Time (GMT).

The time difference of a time zone as compared to GMT is called the *raw offset*. More precisely, the raw offset refers to the number of milliseconds by which a time zone differs from GMT. For example, PST (Pacific Standard Time) differs by -8 hours (or -8*1000*60*60 milliseconds) from GMT. The raw offset is based on standard time (that is, the effects of daylight savings time are ignored.)

There are actually more than 24 time zones. Some time zones have a raw offset that is not a multiple of an hour. For example, the raw offset of MET (Middle East Time) is 3.5 hours. Also, a time zone may have the same raw offset but different daylight savings time periods. Table 43 lists all of the time zones available in this class. The raw offsets are also shown. Each time zone has an uppercase three-character ID (an acronym for the time zone's name).

ID	Raw Offset	Name
MIT	−11	Midway Islands Time
HST	−10	Hawaii Standard Time
AST	−9	Alaska Standard Time
PST	−8	Pacific Standard Time
PNT	−7	Phoenix Standard Time
MST	−7	Mountain Standard Time
CST	−6	Central Standard Time
EST	−5	Eastern Standard Time
IET	−5	Indiana Eastern Standard Time
PRT	−4	Puerto Rico and US Virgin Islands Time
CNT	−3.5	Canada Newfoundland Time
AGT	−3	Argentina Standard Time
BET	−3	Brazil Eastern Time
CAT	−1	Central African Time
GMT	0	Greenwich Mean Time
ECT	1	European Central Time
EET	1	Eastern European Time
ART	2	(Arabic) Egypt Standard Time
EAT	3	Eastern African Time
MET	3.5	Middle East Time
NET	4	Near East Time
PLT	5	Pakistan Lahore Time
IST	5.5	India Standard Time
BST	6	Bangladesh Standard Time
VST	7	Vietnam Standard Time
CTT	8	China Taiwan Time
JST	9	Japan Standard Time

Continued

TABLE 43: Time Zone IDs and their Raw Offsets from GMT.

ID	Raw Offset	Name
ACT	9.5	Australia Central Time
AET	10	Australia Eastern Time
SST	11	Solomon Standard Time
NST	12	New Zealand Standard Time

TABLE 43: Time Zone IDs and their Raw Offsets from GMT.

The Default Time Zone

The default (or local) time zone is the time zone in which the Java virtual machine is running. It is based on the value of the `user.timezone` system property. The default time zone can be retrieved by calling `getDefault()`.

Standard and Daylight Savings Times

Although there are methods that support daylight savings time, the actual rules are implemented by subclasses. The methods in this class allow you to determine if the time zone has a daylight savings time period and whether a particular date falls within that period.

Java 1.1 provides one subclass of this class called `SimpleTimeZone`. See `SimpleTimeZone` for an implementation of a particular type of daylight savings time rule.

MEMBER SUMMARY	
ID Methods	
`getAvailableIDs()`	Retrieves all available time zone IDs.
`getID()`	Retrieves this `TimeZone` object's ID.
`setID()`	Sets the ID for this `TimeZone` object.
`getDefault()`	Retrieves the default `TimeZone` object.
`getTimeZone()`	Retrieves the `TimeZone` object for a time zone.
`inDaylightTime()`	Determines if a particular date falls in this time zone's daylight savings time period.
`setDefault()`	Sets the default time zone.
`useDaylightTime()`	Determines if this `TimeZone` object has a daylight savings time period.
Offset Methods	
`getOffset()`	Retrieves the time difference (observing daylight savings time) of this time zone from GMT.
`getRawOffset()`	Retrieves the time difference (in standard time) of this time zone from GMT.
`setRawOffset()`	Sets the time difference from GMT.
Object Method	
`clone()`	Creates a clone of this `TimeZone` object.

See Also

GregorianCalendar, SimpleTimeZone.

Example

This example is a travel clock that shows the time in two different time zones. The choice component at the bottom of the display is used to select the "AWAY" time zone. See Figure 105.

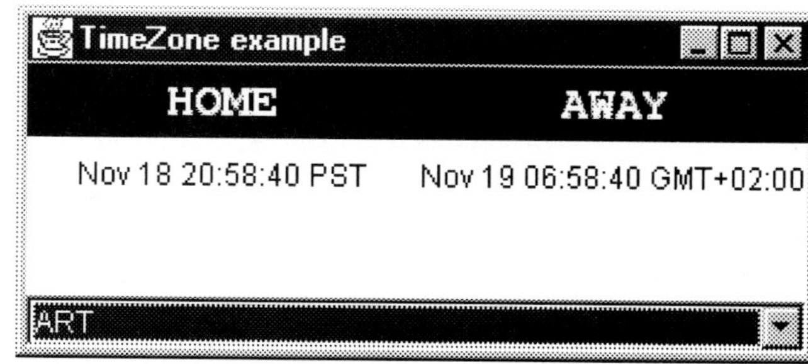

FIGURE 105: Travel Clock.

```
import java.awt.*;
import java.awt.event.*;
import java.util.*;
import java.text.*;

class Main extends Frame implements Runnable, ItemListener {
    Label home = new Label("", Label.CENTER);
    Label away = new Label("", Label.CENTER);
    Choice tzCh = new Choice();

    Main() {
        super("TimeZone example");

        Panel p = new Panel(new GridLayout(0, 2));
        p.add(createHeader("  HOME  "));
        p.add(createHeader("  AWAY  "));
        p.add(home);
        p.add(away);
        add(p, BorderLayout.NORTH);

        String[] ids = TimeZone.getAvailableIDs();
        for (int i=0; i<ids.length; i++) {
            tzCh.add(ids[i]);
        }

        add(tzCh, BorderLayout.SOUTH);
        tzCh.addItemListener(this);

        new Thread(this).start();
        setSize(300, 200);
        show();
    }

    String getDate(Date date, TimeZone tz) {
        DateFormat formatter
            = new SimpleDateFormat("MMM dd HH:mm:ss zzz", Locale.US);
        formatter.setTimeZone(tz);
        return formatter.format(date);
    }
```

```
        Label createHeader(String s) {
            Label l = new Label(s, Label.CENTER);
            l.setFont(new Font("Monospaced", Font.BOLD, 18));
            l.setBackground(Color.black);
            l.setForeground(Color.white);
            return l;
        }

        TimeZone curTz = TimeZone.getDefault();


        public void itemStateChanged(ItemEvent evt) {
            curTz = TimeZone.getTimeZone((String)evt.getItem());
        }

        public void run() {
            try {
                Date date = new Date();
                TimeZone homeTz = TimeZone.getDefault();

                while (true) {
                    date.setTime(System.currentTimeMillis());
                    home.setText(getDate(date, homeTz));
                    away.setText(getDate(date, curTz));
                    Thread.sleep(5000);
                }
            } catch (Exception e) {
                e.printStackTrace();
            }
        }

        public static void main(String[] args) {
            new Main();
        }
    }
```

clone()

PURPOSE Creates a clone of this `TimeZone` object.

SYNTAX `public Object clone()`

DESCRIPTION This method creates a clone of this `TimeZone` object. The new object is identical to this one. In particular, calling `equals()` on this object and the new object yields `true`.

RETURNS A non-`null` copy of this `TimeZone` object.

OVERRIDES `java.lang.Object.clone()`.

EXAMPLE This example creates a time zone based on the local time zone. The name is changed to “JAV” and the raw offset is advanced by 30 minutes.

```
import java.util.*;
import java.text.*;

class Main {
    static String getDate(Date date, TimeZone tz) {
        DateFormat formatter
            = new SimpleDateFormat("MMM dd HH:mm:ss zzz", Locale.US);
        formatter.setTimeZone(tz);
        return formatter.format(date);
    }

    public static void main(String[] args) {
        TimeZone tz = (TimeZone)TimeZone.getDefault().clone();

        System.out.println(getDate(new Date(), tz));

        // Change the time zone ID.
        tz.setID("JAV");

        // Advance the offset by 30 minutes.
        tz.setRawOffset(tz.getRawOffset() + 1000*60*60/2);

        System.out.println(getDate(new Date(), tz));
    }
}
```

Output

```
> java Main
Sep 27 08:39:18 PDT
Sep 27 09:09:19 GMT-06:30
```

getAvailableIDs()

PURPOSE Retrieves all available time zone IDs.

SYNTAX

```
public static synchronized String[] getAvailableIDs()
public static synchronized String[] getAvailableIDs(int
   rawOffset)
```

DESCRIPTION This method retrieves all available time zone IDs. If `rawOffset` is specified, this method returns all time zone IDs whose raw offsets match `rawOffset`. If `rawOffset` is not specified, this method returns all available time zone IDs.

Use `getTimeZone()` to retrieve a `TimeZone` object for a particular time zone ID.

RETURNS A non-`null` array of strings, each containing a time zone ID.

EXAMPLE This example prints all available time zone IDs. For each time, it also prints its raw offset, the GMT offset relative to the current time, and whether the current time is in daylight savings time. The daylight savings time information is printed only if the time zone has a daylight savings time period.

A `BigDecimal` object is used to convert the millisecond time offsets to hours. This is done to gain full control over how the value appears (`double` values have trailing zeroes and exponents.)

```
import java.util.*;
import java.math.*;

class Main {
    // Converts a time offset (in milliseconds) to hours.
    static String convertToHours(int time) {
        BigDecimal n = BigDecimal.valueOf(time);
        n = n.setScale(10);
        n = n.divide(BigDecimal.valueOf(60*60*1000), BigDecimal.ROUND_DOWN);

        // Get rid of trailing zeroes.
        int scale = n.scale();
        while (scale >= 0) {
            try {
                n = n.setScale(--scale, BigDecimal.ROUND_UNNECESSARY);
            } catch (ArithmeticException e) {
                break;
            }
        }

        // Pad the result out to 7 spaces.
        //String result = n.toString();
        String result = "" + n;
        int len = 7-result.length();
        for (int i=0; i<len; i++) {
            result += " ";
        }
        return result;
    }

    public static void main(String[] args) {
        String[] ids = TimeZone.getAvailableIDs();

        // Print header.
        System.out.println("ID  Raw Offset    Offset   Daylight Savings");

        // Print info.
        for (int i=0; i<ids.length; i++) {
            Calendar cal = Calendar.getInstance();
            SimpleTimeZone tz = (SimpleTimeZone)TimeZone.getTimeZone(ids[i]);

            System.out.print(ids[i] + "      "
                + convertToHours(tz.getRawOffset()) + "      "
                + convertToHours(tz.getOffset(
                    cal.get(Calendar.ERA),
                    cal.get(Calendar.YEAR),
                    cal.get(Calendar.MONTH),
                    cal.get(Calendar.DAY_OF_MONTH),
                    cal.get(Calendar.DAY_OF_WEEK),
                    cal.get(Calendar.MILLISECOND))) + "      ");

            if (tz.useDaylightTime()) {
                System.out.print(tz.inDaylightTime(cal.getTime()));
            }
```

```
            System.out.println();
        }
    }
}
```

Output

```
ID  Raw Offset    Offset   Daylight Savings
GMT    0           0
ECT    1           2          true
EET    2           3          true
ART    2           2          false
EAT    3           3
MET    3.5         3.5
NET    4           4
PLT    5           5
IST    5.5         5.5
BST    6           6
VST    7           7
CTT    8           8
JST    9           9
ACT    9.5         9.5        false
AET    10          10         false
SST    11          11
NST    12          13         true
MIT    -11         -11
HST    -10         -10
AST    -9          -8         true
PST    -8          -7         true
PNT    -7          -7
MST    -7          -6         true
CST    -6          -5         true
EST    -5          -4         true
IET    -5          -5
PRT    -4          -4
CNT    -3.5        -2.5       true
AGT    -3          -3
BET    -3          -2         true
CAT    -1          -1
```

getDefault()

PURPOSE Retrieves the default `TimeZone` object.

SYNTAX `public static synchronized TimeZone getDefault()`

DESCRIPTION This method returns the most recent `TimeZone` object set by `setDefault()`. If `setDefault()` was never called, this method creates a `TimeZone` object and makes it the default. This method first determines the default time zone ID by calling `System.getProperty("user.timezone")`. If the `user.timezone` system property is not defined, the time zone ID "GMT" is used. It then calls `getTimeZone()` using the time zone ID and makes the resulting `TimeZone` object the default time zone.

Note: The returned `TimeZone` object should not be modified. The returned object is globally shared by all clients of the `TimeZone` class.

RETURNS A non-null TimeZone object containing the default time zone.

SEE ALSO java.lang.System.getProperty(), setDefault, setTimeZone().

EXAMPLE See setDefault().

getID()

PURPOSE Retrieves this TimeZone object's ID.

SYNTAX `public String getID()`

RETURNS The non-null three-character string containing the ID of this TimeZone object. See Table 43.

EXAMPLE See setDefault().

getOffset()

PURPOSE Retrieves the time difference (observing daylight savings time) of this time zone from GMT.

SYNTAX
```
abstract public int getOffset(int era, int year, int month, int
    day, int dayOfWeek, int milliseconds)
```

DESCRIPTION The offset is the number of milliseconds by which the time zone differs from GMT for a particular point in time as specified by the six parameters. The offset takes into account daylight savings time. For example, in January, the offset for PST is –8 hours. In May, the offset for PST is –7 hours.

PARAMETERS

day	The day in the month. 1 ≤ day ≤ 31.
dayOfWeek	The day of the week. Calendar.SUNDAY ≤ dayOfWeek ≤ Calendar.SATURDAY.
era	A Gregorian calendar era, which can be either GregorianCalendar.BC or GregorianCalendar.AD.
milliseconds	The number of milliseconds from midnight in standard time.
month	Calendar.JANUARY ≤ month ≤ Calendar.DECEMBER.
year	The year.

RETURNS The number of milliseconds by which this time zone differs from GMT, taking into account daylight savings time.

SEE ALSO getRawOffset(), GregorianCalendar.

EXAMPLE See getAvailableIDs().

getRawOffset()

PURPOSE Retrieves the time difference (in standard time) of this time zone from GMT.

SYNTAX `abstract public int getRawOffset()`

DESCRIPTION The raw offset is the number of milliseconds by which this time zone differs from GMT. For example, PST differs by -8*1000*60*60 milliseconds from GMT. The raw offset is based on standard time—the effects of daylight savings time are ignored.

The raw offset can be added to the time at GMT to obtain the local time. For an offset that takes into account daylight savings time, see `getOffset()`.

RETURNS The number of milliseconds by which this time zone differs from GMT in standard time.

SEE ALSO `getOffset()`.

EXAMPLE See `getAvailableIDs()`.

getTimeZone()

PURPOSE Retrieves the `TimeZone` object for a time zone.

SYNTAX `public static synchronized TimeZone getTimeZone(String ID)`

DESCRIPTION This method retrieves the `TimeZone` object for a time zone. `ID` should be one of the ID's returned by `getAvailableIDs()`. If not, `null` is returned.

By default, the daylight savings time rules are assumed to apply in all years. However, if necessary, it possible to set the actual year in which daylight savings time took effect by calling `setStartYear()`.

Note: The returned `TimeZone` object should not be modified. The returned object is globally shared by all clients of the `TimeZone` class.

Note: In Java 1.1.4, this method returns only `SimpleTimeZone` objects.

PARAMETERS

`ID` A possibly `null` three-character string containing a time zone ID.

RETURNS A non-`null` `TimeZone` object.

SEE ALSO `getAvailableIDs()`.

EXAMPLE See the class example.

inDaylightTime()

PURPOSE Determines if a particular date falls in this time zone's daylight savings time period.

SYNTAX `abstract public boolean inDaylightTime(Date date)`

DESCRIPTION This method determines if `date` falls within the daylight savings time period for this time zone.

Note: There are some issues to keep in mind regarding a date that coincides exactly with the start and end of daylight savings time. See the `SimpleTimeZone` class description for details.

PARAMETERS

`date` A non-`null` date representing a point in time.

RETURNS `true` if `date` falls within this time zone's daylight savings time period; `false` otherwise.

EXAMPLE See the `SimpleTimeZone` class example.

setDefault()

PURPOSE Sets the default time zone.

SYNTAX `public static synchronized void setDefault(TimeZone tz)`

DESCRIPTION This method sets the default time zone to be `tz`. `tz` can be retrieved later using `getDefault()`.

Changing the default time zone is a global operation and affects all clients of the `TimeZone` class. All subsequent calls to `getDefault()` using this or any other `TimeZone` object result in `tz`.

PARAMETERS

`tz` A non-`null` `TimeZone` object.

SEE ALSO `getDefault()`, `java.lang.System.getProperty()`, `setTimeZone()`.

EXAMPLE This example demonstrates how to change the default time zone. Changing the default time zone is not a usual thing to do.

```
import java.util.*;

class Main {
    static void printDefaultTimeZone() {
        TimeZone tz = TimeZone.getDefault();

        System.out.println(tz.getID() + " " + tz.getRawOffset());
    }
```

```
    public static void main(String[] args) {
        // Print real default.
        printDefaultTimeZone();

        // Replace the default time zone (not a typical thing to do.)
        TimeZone tz = new SimpleTimeZone(1234567, "FOO");
        TimeZone.setDefault(tz);

        // Print new default.
        printDefaultTimeZone();
    }
}
```

setID()

PURPOSE Sets the ID for this `TimeZone` object.

SYNTAX `public void setID(String ID)`

DESCRIPTION This method sets the ID for this `TimeZone` object. `ID` is the time zone ID for this new time zone. The ID is three characters long. For example, the ID of the Pacific Standard Time time zone is "PST".

Note: This method should not be called on `TimeZone` objects obtained by the `getTimeZone()` or `getDefault()` methods. These methods return objects that are globally shared by all clients of the `TimeZone` class.

PARAMETERS

`ID` A non-`null` three-character string containing the ID of the time zone.

EXAMPLE See `clone()`.

setRawOffset()

PURPOSE Sets the time difference from GMT.

SYNTAX `abstract public void setRawOffset(int offsetMillis)`

DESCRIPTION This method sets the raw offset of this `TimeZone` object to `offsetMillis`. The raw offset is an integer that specifies the number of milliseconds by which a time zone differs from GMT. For example, PST differs by -8*1000*60*60 milliseconds from GMT. The raw offset is based on standard time—the effects of daylight savings time are ignored.

PARAMETERS

`offsetMillis`
The number of milliseconds by which this time zone differs from GMT. May be negative.

SEE ALSO `getOffset()`, `getRawOffset()`.

EXAMPLE See `clone()`.

useDaylightTime()

PURPOSE Determines if this `TimeZone` object has a daylight savings time period.

SYNTAX `abstract public boolean useDaylightTime()`

RETURNS `true` if this `TimeZone` object has a daylight savings time period; `false` otherwise.

EXAMPLE See `getAvailableIDs()`.

TooManyListenersException

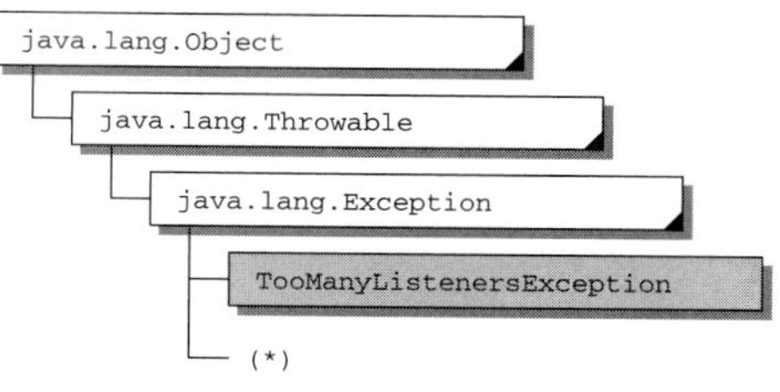

Syntax

`public class TooManyListenersException extends Exception`

Description

When an *event source* does not support multiple listeners, its add listener registration method must declare a `TooManyListenersException` in its `throws` clause. This exception should be thrown if the program attempts to register a listener with an event source, but a listener is already registered.

See `EventObject` for more details on event sources, event objects, and event listeners.

MEMBER SUMMARY	
Constructor	
`TooManyListenersException()`	Constructs a `TooManyListenersException` instance.

See Also

`EventListener`, `EventObject`.

Example

This example is adapted from the `EventObject` class example. It is modified so that any single listener can be registered for tick events from a `Timer` object. (This isn't a particularly useful thing to do and is done here only for demonstrative purposes.)

```
import java.util.*;

class Main implements TickListener {
    Main() {
        Timer timer = new Timer(3000);
```

```
        try {
            timer.addTickListener(this);
        } catch (TooManyListenersException e) {
            e.printStackTrace();
        }
    }

    // Called whenever timer ticks.
    public void ticked(TickEvent evt) {
        System.out.println(evt.getTime());
    }

    public static void main(String[] args) {
        new Main();
    }
}

class Timer extends Thread {
    int period;
    TickListener listener;

    Timer(int periodMillis) {
        period = periodMillis;
        start();
    }

    // Listener registration methods.
    void addTickListener(TickListener listener)
        throws TooManyListenersException {
        if (listener != null) {
            throw new TooManyListenersException();
        }
    }
    void removeTickListener(TickListener listener) {
        listener = null;
    }

    public void run() {
        while (true) {
            try {
                // This avoids a race condition
                TickListener l = listener;

                // Deliver a TickEvent to the listeners.
                if (l != null) {
                    l.ticked(new TickEvent(this));
                }

                Thread.sleep(period);
            } catch (Exception e) {
                e.printStackTrace();
            }
        }
    }
}

class TickEvent extends EventObject {
    long time;
```

```
    TickEvent(Object source) {
        super(source);
        time = System.currentTimeMillis();
    }

    long getTime() {
        return time;
    }
}

interface TickListener {
    void ticked(TickEvent evt);
}
```

TooManyListenersException()

PURPOSE Constructs a `TooManyListenersException` instance.

SYNTAX

```
public TooManyListenersException()
public TooManyListenersException(String msg)
```

DESCRIPTION The two forms of this constructor construct an instance of `TooManyListeners-Exception`. An optional string `msg` can be supplied that describes this particular instance of the exception. If `msg` is not supplied, it defaults to `null`.

PARAMETERS

`msg` A possibly-`null` string describing the reason for the exception.

SEE ALSO `java.lang.Throwable.getMessage()`.

EXAMPLE See the class example.

java.lang
UnknownError

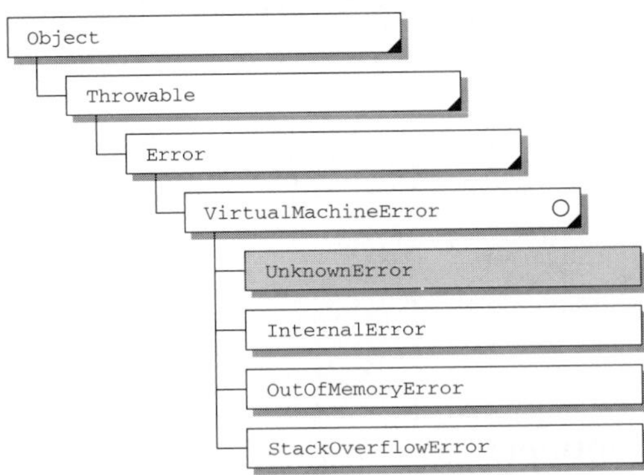

A B C D E F G H I J K L M N O P Q R S T U V W X Y Z

Syntax

```
public class UnknownError extends VirtualMachineError
```

Description

`UnknownError` is an error that is thrown when the Java virtual machine encounters an unrecoverable error that does not fit into any of the other error subclasses. It should not be caught or declared in the `throws` clause of a method.

MEMBER SUMMARY	
Constructor	
`UnknownError()`	Constructs an `UnknownError` instance.

See Also

`Error`, `VirtualMachineError`.

UnknownError()

PURPOSE Constructs an `UnknownError` instance.

SYNTAX
```
public UnknownError()
public UnknownError(String msg)
```

DESCRIPTION

This constructor constructs an instance of `UnknownError`. An optional string `msg` can be supplied that describes this particular instance of the error. If `msg` is not supplied, it defaults to `null`.

PARAMETERS

`msg` A possibly `null` string that gives details about this error.

SEE ALSO

`Throwable.getMessage()`.

java.net
UnknownHostException

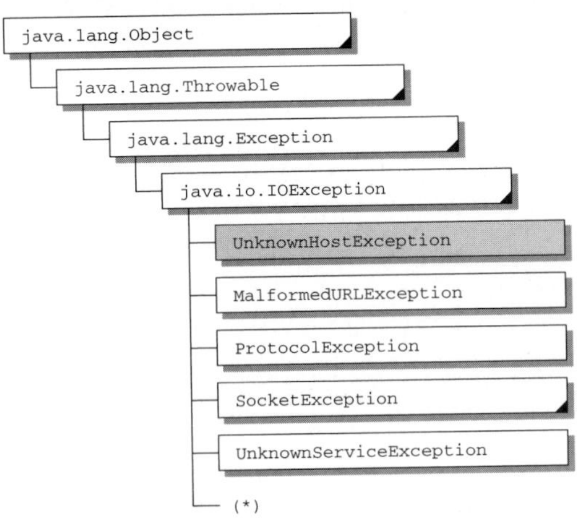

(*) 10 classes from other packages not shown.

A B C D E F G H I J K L M N O P Q R S T **U** V W X Y Z

Syntax

```
public class UnknownHostException extends IOException
```

Description

`UnknownHostException` is an IO exception that is thrown when the name of a machine (host) cannot be resolved to an address. Such name resolution capability is required by the `InetAddress` and `URL` classes.

A method that throws `UnknownHostException` must declare it or any of its superclasses in the method's `throws` clause.

MEMBER SUMMARY	
Constructor	
`UnknownHostException()`	Constructs an `UnknownHostException` instance.

See Also

`IOException`, `InetAddress`, `URL`.

Example

This example generates an `UnknownHostException` when trying to resolve the host name `NeverFindThis`.

```
import java.net.InetAddress;
import java.net.UnknownHostException;

class Main {
    public static void main(String[] args) {
        System.out.println("UnknownHostException example");
        try {
            InetAddress someAddr = InetAddress.getByName("NeverFindThis");
        } catch (UnknownHostException e) {
            System.err.println("Cannot resolve: " + e);
        }
    }
}
```

UnknownHostException()

PURPOSE Constructs an `UnknownHostException` instance.

SYNTAX

```
public UnknownHostException()
public UnknownHostException(String host)
```

DESCRIPTION The two forms of this constructor construct an instance of `UnknownHostException`. An optional string `host` containing the name of the machine can be supplied. If `host` is not supplied, it defaults to `null`.

PARAMETERS

`host` The possibly `null` string containing the name of machine for which this exception was thrown. This is used as the message for the exception (returned by `getMessage()`).

SEE ALSO `java.lang.Throwable.getMessage()`.

java.net

UnknownServiceException

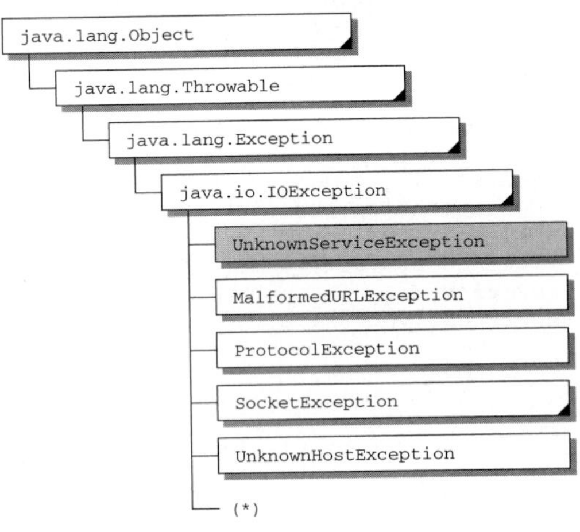

A B C D E F G H I J K L M N O P Q R S T U V W X Y Z

Syntax

```
public class UnknownServiceException extends IOException
```

Description

`UnknownServiceException` is an IO exception that is thrown when a URL connection does not support a particular service. Examples of services that a URL connection may support are reading from the connection as an input stream, writing to the connection as an output stream, and getting MIME-typed content from the connection.

A method that throws `UnknownServiceException` must declare it or any of its superclasses in the method's `throws` clause.

MEMBER SUMMARY	
Constructor	
`UnknownServiceException()`	Constructs an `UnknownServiceException` instance.

See Also

`java.io.IOException`, `URLConnection`.

Example

This example throws an `UnknownServiceException` when it attempts to get an output stream for a `file` URL.

```
import java.net.*;
import java.io.IOException;
import java.io.OutputStream;

class Main {
    public static void main(String[] args) {
        try {
            URL u = new URL(
                "file://localhost/export/home/java/api/packages.html");
            URLConnection conn = u.openConnection();

            OutputStream out = conn.getOutputStream();
        } catch (UnknownServiceException e) {
            System.err.println("Cannot get output stream: "+ e);
        } catch (IOException e) {
            e.printStackTrace();
        }
    }
}
```

UnknownServiceException()

PURPOSE Constructs an `UnknownServiceException` instance.

SYNTAX
```
public UnknownServiceException()
public UnknownServiceException(String msg)
```

DESCRIPTION This constructor constructs an instance of `UnknownServiceException`. An optional string `msg` can be supplied that describes this particular instance of the exception. If `msg` is not supplied, it defaults to `null`.

PARAMETERS

`msg` A possibly `null` string that gives details about this exception. This is used as the message for the exception (returned by `getMessage()`).

SEE ALSO `java.lang.Throwable.getMessage()`.

UnsatisfiedLinkError

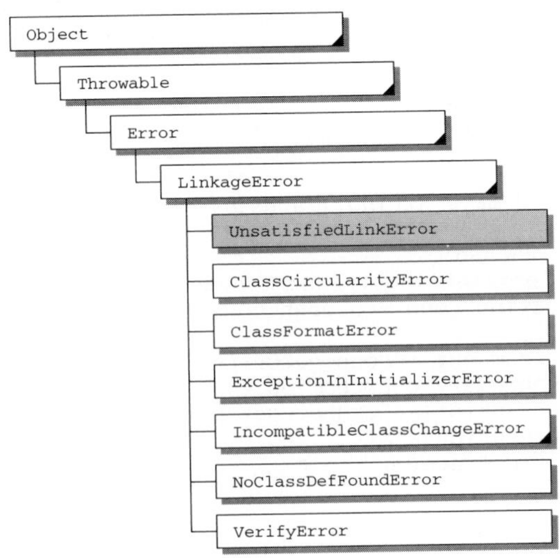

Syntax

```
public class UnsatisfiedLinkError extends LinkageError
```

Description

`UnsatisfiedLinkError` is a runtime linkage error that is thrown when a library cannot be loaded and linked successfully. This can occur, for example, if the requested library does not exist, or, if it does exist, it contains unresolved references that prevent it from being successfully loaded.

`UnsatisfiedLinkError` is an unrecoverable error that should not be caught or declared in the `throws` clause of a method.

MEMBER SUMMARY	
Constructor	
`UnsatisfiedLinkError()`	Constructs an `UnsatisfiedLinkError` instance.

See Also

`LinkageError`, `Runtime.load()`, `Runtime.loadLibrary()`, `System.load()`, `System.loadLibrary()`.

Example

This example throws an UnsatisfiedLinkError.

```
class Main {
    public static void main(String[] args) {
        System.out.println("UnsatisfiedLinkError example");

        System.load("NeverFindThisOne"); // link error
    }
}
```


UnsatisfiedLinkError()

PURPOSE
Constructs an UnsatisfiedLinkError instance.

SYNTAX
```
public UnsatisfiedLinkError()
public UnsatisfiedLinkError(String msg)
```

DESCRIPTION
The two forms of this constructor construct an instance of UnsatisfiedLinkError. An optional string msg can be supplied that describes this particular instance of the error. If msg is not supplied, it defaults to null.

PARAMETERS

msg
A possibly null string that gives details about this error.

SEE ALSO
Throwable.getMessage().

UnsupportedEncodingException

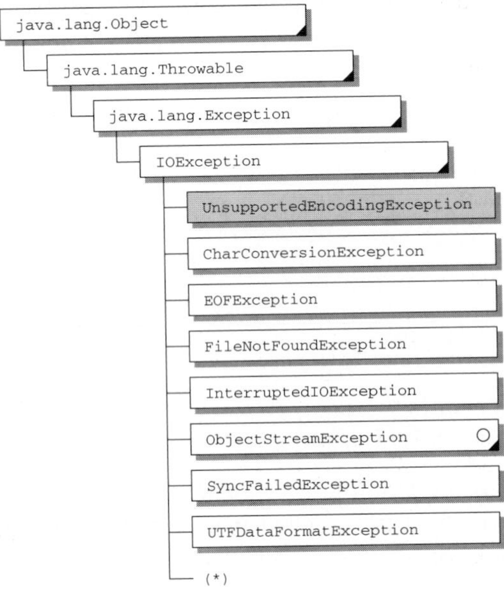

(*) 7 classes from other packages not shown.

Syntax

```
public class UnsupportedEncodingException extends IOException
```

Description

Some methods allow bytes to be converted into Unicode characters and vice versa. Using an *encoding identifier*, they specify the encoding to use for the conversion. See `String.String()` for a description of encoding identifiers. When the encoding identifier supplied to these methods does not name a valid encoding (i.e., the classes needed for the conversion are not found), `UnsupportedEncodingException` is thrown.

MEMBER SUMMARY	
Constructor	
`UnsupportedEncodingException()`	Constructs an `UnsupportedEncodingException` instance.

See Also

`ByteArrayOutputStream.toString()`, `InputStreamReader.InputStreamReader()`, `OutputStreamWriter.OutputStreamWriter()`, `String.getBytes()`, `String.String()`.

Example

This example throws an `UnsupportedEncodingException` when `String.getBytes()` is given a bogus encoding identifier.

```
import java.io.*;

class Main {
    public static void main(String[] args) {
        try {
            String str = "This is a test";
            byte[] buf = str.getBytes("NonExistentEnc");
        } catch (UnsupportedEncodingException e) {
            e.printStackTrace();
        }
    }
}
```

UnsupportedEncodingException()

PURPOSE Constructs a `UnsupportedEncodingException` instance.

SYNTAX
```
public UnsupportedEncodingException()
public UnsupportedEncodingException(String msg)
```

DESCRIPTION The two forms of this constructor construct an instance of `UnsupportedEncodingException`. An optional string `msg` can be supplied that describes this particular instance of the exception. If `msg` is not supplied, it defaults to `null`.

PARAMETERS

`msg` A possibly `null` string that gives details about this exception.

SEE ALSO `java.lang.Throwable.getMessage()`.

java.net
URL

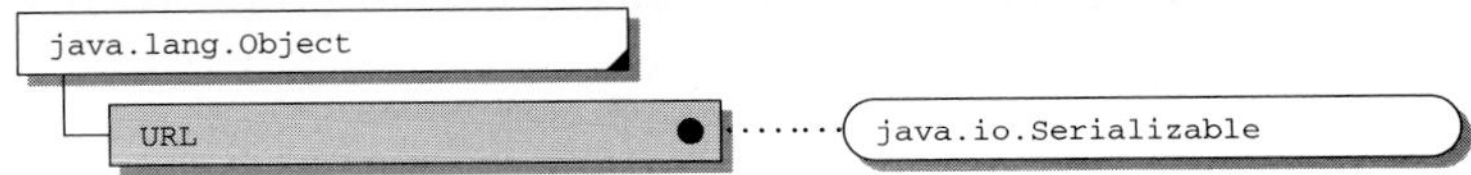

A B C D E F G H I J K L M N O P Q R S T U V W X Y Z

Syntax

```
public final class URL implements Serializable
```

Description

A *Uniform Resource Locator* (*URL*) is a string that specifies the location of a resource on the World Wide Web. The specification of a URL's syntax and semantics are described in *RFC 1738*.

In general, a URL consists of the following components (in order of their appearance in the URL):

protocol — An identifier that specifies which Internet protocol to use to access the resource. Examples of such protocol identifiers are `http`, `ftp`, `gopher`, `news`, `telnet`, and `mailto`.

host name — The name of a host or domain to contact to access the resource. Examples of these are `ds.internic.net`, `localhost`, and `jupiter`.

port number — The port number on the host to which to connect. It usually is optional. Most protocols have a default port number. For example, the default port number for HTTP is `80`; the default port number for Telnet is `23`.

filename — Identifies the file or directory on the file system exported by the host that contains the resource. Examples of filenames are `pub/beta/product.zip` and `apidocs/`. A trailing slash in the name indicates a directory.

reference — HTTP URLs may contain fragment identifiers—also called *anchors*—that name fragments of the document named by the filename of the URL. For example, suppose the document `notice.html` contains

```
<A name=READMEFIRST>
```

In the URL `http://jupiter/notice.html#READMEFIRST`, the reference (anchor) is `READMEFIRST`. The URL would access the fragment of `notice.html` starting at the anchor marked with the label.

Here is an example of a complete URL:

```
http://ds.internic.net:80/rfc/rfc1738.txt
```

This URL uses the HTTP protocol and will contact the host `ds.internic.net` using port `80` to access the file `rfc/rfc1738.txt`. For more information on URLs, read the document named by this URL.

Usage

The `URL` class represents a URL and provides methods to construct and obtain components of the URL (its protocol identifier, host name, port number, and so on). In addition, it provides methods that, after a URL has been created, can be used to retrieve the resource identified by the URL. It also supports lower-level methods such as opening a connection or IO streams to the server that is managing the resource identified by the URL. Figure 106 shows the use of the `URL` and `URLConnection` classes for accessing Web services.

The following code shows how a URL is typically used:

```
URL u =
    new URL("http://java.sun.com/");
Object obj = u.getContent();
```

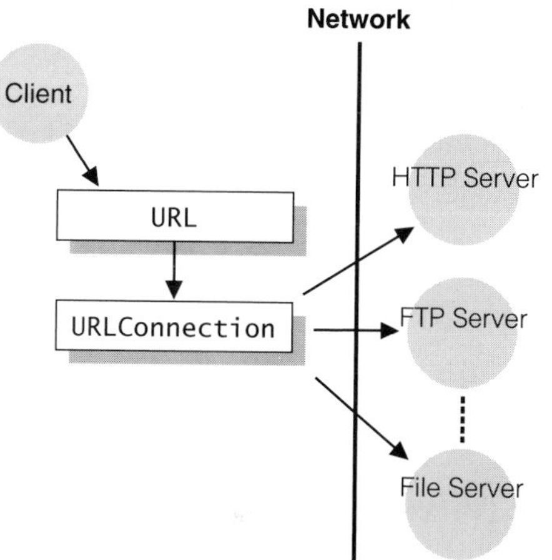

FIGURE 106: Use of `URL` and `URLConnection` to Access Web Services.

First, a `URL` instance is created for the resource. Second, the resource is retrieved using the `getContent()` method.

URL Stream (Protocol) Handlers

Associated with each URL is a *URL stream* (or *protocol*) *handler*. A URL stream handler is responsible for implementing the protocol associated with the URL. For example, there is a HTTP stream handler for URLs with the `http` protocol identifier.

The Java runtime itself provides a handful of stream handlers (e.g., HTTP and FTP) and allows new stream handlers to be added dynamically.

URL Stream Handler Factory

A *URL stream handler factory* is responsible for creating an instance of `URLStreamHandler` when it is supplied with a protocol identifier. The factory controls which implementations are selected for the protocol identifiers, as well as which protocols are supported.

The program uses `setURLStreamHandlerFactory()` to select the stream handler factory to use (if permitted to do so by the security manager). This method sets the stream handler factory for the program. Once set, the factory cannot be replaced.

Default Policy for Creating Stream Handlers

If no stream handler factory has been installed, the system searches for a class that has the class name

packagePrefix "." *protocol* "." Handler

packagePrefix is obtained from the system property `java.protocol.handler.pkgs`, which is a |-separated list of package prefixes. *protocol* is the protocol identifier (e.g., `http` or `ftp`). If the class is not found using these package prefixes, the package prefix `sun.net.www.protocol` is tried. For example, if the `java.protocol.handler.pkgs` system property contains "com.widget|com.wiz" and the protocol identifier is `http`, the system will attempt to load each of the following classes in turn until one is successfully instantiated:

```
com.widget.http.Handler
com.wiz.http.Handler
sun.net.www.protocol.http.Handler
```

If no class can be instantiated in this way, `MalformedURLException` is thrown.

MEMBER SUMMARY	
Constructor	
`URL()`	Constructs a `URL` instance.
Field Access Methods	
`getFile()`	Retrieves this URL's filename.
`getHost()`	Retrieves this URL's host name.
`getPort()`	Retrieves this URL's port number.
`getProtocol()`	Retrieves this URL's protocol identifier.
`getRef()`	Retrieves this URL's reference.
`set()`	Sets the fields of this URL.
Communications Methods	
`getContent()`	Retrieves the content pointed to by this URL.
`openConnection()`	Opens this URL's connection.
`openStream()`	Opens an input stream to this URL's connection.
Comparison Methods	
`equals()`	Compares two URLs for equality.
`sameFile()`	Determines whether two URLs point to the same file.
Hash Code Method	
`hashCode()`	Computes the hash code for this URL object.
Description Methods	
`toExternalForm()`	Generates the string representation of this URL.
`toString()`	Generates the string representation of this URL.
Factory Method	
`setURLStreamHandlerFactory()`	Sets the URL stream handler factory for this application.

See Also

ContentHandler, ContentHandlerFactory, java.io.InputStream, URLConnection, URLStreamHandler, URLStreamHandlerFactory.

Example

This example implements a "spider" program that returns all URLs reachable from a given URL (root URL) at a given depth. The program reads the HTML file at a URL and recursively finds all links from that HTML file.

The Spider class uses the Observer and Observable classes to report every new URL that it discovers. It uses a thread to traverse the URL tree so that calling the walk() method does not block the caller. A depth of 0 shows only those links in the root URL.

```
import java.net.*;
import java.io.*;
import java.util.*;

class Main implements Observer {
    Main(String u, int depth) {
        try {
            URL url = new URL(Spider.adjustIfDir(u));
            Spider spider = new Spider(url, depth);

            spider.addObserver(this);
            spider.thread.join(); // Wait for spider to finish.
        } catch (MalformedURLException e) {
        } catch (InterruptedException e) {
        }
    }

    // This method is called immediately whenever the spider
    // discovers a new URL.  It should return as quickly as
    // possible since it is holding up the spider.
    public void update(Observable o, Object arg) {
        SpiderArgs warg = (SpiderArgs)arg;
        for (int i=0; i<warg.depth; i++) {
            System.out.print("    ");
        }
        System.out.println(warg.dst);
    }

    public static void main(String[] args) {
        if (args.length != 2) {
            System.err.println("Usage: java Main <url> <depth>");
        } else {
            new Main(args[0], Integer.parseInt(args[1]));
        }
    }
}

class Spider extends Observable implements Runnable {
    Hashtable walked = new Hashtable();
    int maxDepth;
    URL homeURL;
    String host;
    int port;
```

```
Thread thread;

Spider(URL url, int depth) {
    homeURL = url;
    maxDepth = depth;
    host = url.getHost();
    port = getPort(url);

    // Start spider thread.
    thread = new Thread(this);
    thread.start();
}

void walk(URL url, int curDepth) throws IOException {
    Vector v = findLinks(url);

    // Remove duplicates
    for (int i=v.size()-1; i>=0; i--) {
        try {
            URL ur = new URL(url, (String)v.elementAt(i));
            if (walked.get(ur) != null
                    || !ur.getProtocol().equals("http")
                    || !(getPort(ur) == port)
                    || !ur.getHost().equals(host)) {
                v.removeElementAt(i);
            } else {
                walked.put(ur, ur);
                setChanged();
                notifyObservers(new SpiderArgs(url, ur, curDepth));
            }
        } catch (MalformedURLException e) {
        }
    }

    // Now walk each of the links in url.
    if (curDepth < maxDepth) {
        for (int i=0; i<v.size(); i++) {
            URL ur = null;
            try {
                ur = new URL(url, (String)v.elementAt(i));
                walk(ur, curDepth + 1);
            } catch (MalformedURLException e) {
            } catch (IOException e) {
                System.out.println("*** " + url + " -> " + ur);
            }
        }
    }
}

// Finds all the links in 'url' and returns them in a vector.
Vector findLinks(URL url) throws IOException {
    Vector v = new Vector();
    BufferedReader in = new BufferedReader(
        new InputStreamReader(url.openStream()));
    String line;
    String lineLC;

    while ((line = in.readLine()) != null) {
        while (line != null) {
            int p = line.indexOf("<a ");
```

```
                if (p < 0) {
                    p = line.indexOf("<A ");
                    if (p < 0) {
                        break;
                    }
                }

                // Make sure the > is on the same line.
                int q = 0;
                while ((q=line.indexOf(">", p)) < 0) {
                    String l = in.readLine();
                    if (l == null) { // EOF reached.
                        return v;
                    }
                    line += l;
                }
                String u = getLink(in, line, p);

                if (u != null && u.length() > 0) {
                    v.addElement(adjustIfDir(u));
                }
                // Continue looking for links on the line.
                line = line.substring(q+1);
            }
        }
        in.close();
        return v;
    }

    // Returns the port number of 'url'.  If the port number is
    // not defined, returns the default HTTP port number.
    int getPort(URL url) {
        int p = url.getPort();
        if (p == -1) {
            p = 80;
        }
        return p;
    }

    // This method implements a heuristic for URLs that are probably
    // directories.  If the last component of the URL does not contain
    // a dot and does not end with a "/", then it is explicitly
    // converted to a directory by appending a "/".
    static String adjustIfDir(String s) {
        int p = s.lastIndexOf("/") + 1;

        if (!s.endsWith("/") && s.indexOf(".", p) < 0) {
            s += "/";
        }
        return s;
    }

    // Extracts the <a> tag from s and then returns the remainder of
    // the line.
    String getLink(BufferedReader in, String s, int p)
            throws IOException {
        int e;

        // Find the href attribute.
        p = s.indexOf("href=");
```

```
            if (p < 0) {
                p = s.indexOf("HREF=");
                if (p < 0) {
                    // No href so skip the tag.
                    return null;
                }
            }

            // Skip the "href="
            p += 5;
            int q = -1;
            if (s.charAt(p) == '"') {
                p++;
                q = s.indexOf('"', p);
            } else {
                q = s.indexOf(' ', p);
                int q2 = s.indexOf('>', p);
                if (Math.min(q, q2) < 0 && Math.max(q, q2) >= 0) {
                    // If one is > 0 and the other < 0, use the > 0 one.
                    q = Math.max(q, q2);
                }

                // Use the smaller of the two.
                q = Math.min(q, q2);
            }

            // Could not complete the href tag for some reason
            // so skip the tag.
            if (q < 0) {
                return null;
            }
            s = s.substring(p, q);

            // Remove the reference, if any.
            p = s.indexOf('#');
            if (p == 0) {
                return null;
            } else if (p > 0) {
                s = s.substring(0, p);
            }
            return s;
        }

        public void run() {
            try {
                walk(homeURL, 0);
            } catch (IOException e) {
                System.out.println("*** " + homeURL);
            }
        }
    }

    class SpiderArgs {
        SpiderArgs(URL src, URL dst, int depth) {
            this.src = src;
            this.dst = dst;
            this.depth = depth;
        }
```

```
        URL src;
        URL dst;
        int depth;
    }
```

equals()

PURPOSE Compares two URLs for equality.

SYNTAX `public boolean equals(Object obj)`

DESCRIPTION Two URLs are considered equal if they are both of class `URL` and they both have the same protocol identifier, host name, port number, filename, and reference. `equals()` returns `true` if `obj` is equal to this URL; it returns `false` otherwise.

This method is different from `sameFile()` in that `sameFile()` accepts only an instance of `URL` as an argument and `sameFile()` does not check the references of the URLs.

PARAMETERS

`obj` The object against which to compare.

RETURNS `true` if `obj` is the same URL as this URL; `false` otherwise.

OVERRIDES `java.lang.Object.equals()`.

SEE ALSO `hashCode()`, `sameFile()`.

EXAMPLE

```
try {
    URL u1 = new URL("http://java.sun.com:80/new.html");
    URL u2 = new URL("http://java.sun.com/new.html");
    URL u3 = new URL("http://java.sun.com/new.html#_top_");
    // u1 and u2 are not the same because of 'port'
    System.out.println(u1 + (u1.equals(u2)? " is " : " is not ") +
                       "the same as " + u2);
    // u2 and u3 are not the same because fragments are different
    System.out.println(u3 + (u3.equals(u2)? " is " : " is not ") +
                       "the same as " + u2);
} catch (MalformedURLException e) {
    e.printStackTrace();
}
```

getContent()

PURPOSE Retrieves the content pointed to by this URL.

SYNTAX `public final Object getContent() throws IOException`

DESCRIPTION This method retrieves the content identified by this URL by first opening a connection to the destination named by the URL (if it has not been opened already) and then getting its content. The mechanisms used for getting the content are particular to the protocol and the content handler for that protocol. The use of various content handlers is configurable by the application through the use of the ContentHandlerFactory. Figure 107 shows the use of getContent() on an HTTP URL to retrieve a GIF image.

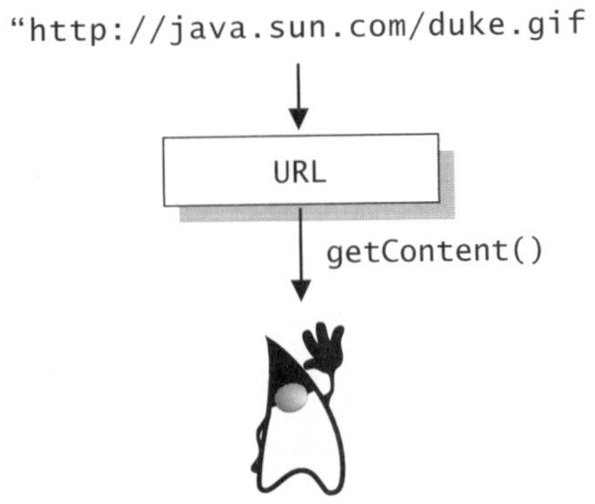

FIGURE 107: `URL.getContent()`.

RETURNS The non-null object representing the content identified by this URL.

EXCEPTIONS

IOException

If an IO error has occurred while attempting to get the content identified by this URL.

SEE ALSO `ContentHandler`, `ContentHandlerFactory`, `URLConnection.getContent()`.

EXAMPLE See `URL()`, `URLStreamHandler`.

getFile()

PURPOSE Retrieves this URL's filename.

SYNTAX `public String getFile()`

DESCRIPTION The URLs for many protocols, such as FTP and HTTP, contain a file component that names a file or directory within the file system exported by the host of the URL. getFile() returns the file component of this URL.

RETURNS A non-null string containing this URL's filename/directory name.

SEE ALSO `URL()`.

EXAMPLE

```
import java.net.*;
import java.io.*;
```

```
class Main {
    public static void main(String[] args) {
        try {
            URL u = new URL("http://java.sun.com/new.html#_top_");
            String protocol = u.getProtocol(); // "http"
            String host = u.getHost();  // "java.sun.com"
            int port = u.getPort();     // -1 (unspecified)
            String file = u.getFile();  // new.html
            String frag = u.getRef();   // _top_

            System.out.println(protocol + "|" + host + "|" + port + "|"
                + file + "|" + frag);
        } catch (MalformedURLException e) {
            e.printStackTrace();
        }
    }
}
```

getHost()

PURPOSE Retrieves this URL's host name.

SYNTAX `public String getHost()`

DESCRIPTION A URL contains the name of a host to contact to access the resource. This method returns the name of this host.

RETURNS A non-`null` string containing this URL's host name.

SEE ALSO `URL()`.

EXAMPLE See `getFile()`.

getPort()

PURPOSE Retrieves this URL's port number.

SYNTAX `public int getPort()`

DESCRIPTION A connection to the host of this URL is made to a particular port number. This method returns the port number that this URL's connection uses. `-1` means the default port number for this URL's protocol will be used.

RETURNS This URL's port number. If `-1`, uses the default port number for this protocol.

SEE ALSO `URL()`.

EXAMPLE This example demonstrates that if the port is not specified in the URL, `getPort()` returns `-1`. Otherwise, it returns the specified port number.

```
import java.net.*;

class Main {
    public static void main(String[] args) {
        try {
            URL url = new URL("http://java.sun.com");
            System.out.println(url.getPort());    // -1

            url = new URL("http://java.sun.com:123");
            System.out.println(url.getPort());    // 123

            url = new URL("ftp://java.sun.com:456");
            System.out.println(url.getPort());    // 456
        } catch (MalformedURLException e) {
            e.printStackTrace();
        }
    }
}
```

getProtocol()

PURPOSE Retrieves this URL's protocol identifier.

SYNTAX `public String getProtocol()`

DESCRIPTION The first component of a URL is its protocol identifier. It is the first identifier in the URL string that precedes a colon character (:). The protocol identifier is a string that names the Internet protocol to use to access the resource. Examples of identifiers of common protocols found in URLs are `http`, `gopher`, `ftp`, `news`, `telnet`, and `mailto`. `getProtocol()` returns this protocol identifier.

RETURNS The non-`null` string containing this URL's protocol identifier.

SEE ALSO `URL()`.

EXAMPLE This example demonstrates the use of `getProtocol()`. It also shows that the URL constructor throws an exception if it does not have a handler for the specified protocol identifier.

```
import java.net.*;

class Main {
    public static void main(String[] args) {
        try {
            URL url = new URL("http://java.sun.com");
            System.out.println(url.getProtocol());    // http

            url = new URL("ftp://java.sun.com");
            System.out.println(url.getProtocol());    // ftp

            // The following causes a MalformedURLException
            // since there is no protocol handler for foobar.
            url = new URL("foobar://java.sun.com");
```

```
        } catch (MalformedURLException e) {
          e.printStackTrace();
        }
    }
}
```


getRef()

PURPOSE Retrieves this URL's reference.

SYNTAX `public String getRef()`

DESCRIPTION The reference field of a URL is the substring that appears after the # character. This character may not necessarily be used in all protocols. For HTTP URLs, it is called a *fragment identifier* or *anchor*. It refers to a named location within the document named by the filename component of the URL. `getRef()` returns this fragment identifier.

The reference field can be specified only when the URL constructor that takes a URL string (`spec`) is used. If the URL is constructed by passing the protocol identifier, host name, and filename (and optionally the port number) as separate arguments, the reference is not parsed from the file component.

RETURNS This URL's reference; `null` if this URL does not have a reference.

SEE ALSO `URL()`.

EXAMPLE See `getFile()`.

hashCode()

PURPOSE Computes the hash code for this URL object.

SYNTAX `public int hashCode()`

DESCRIPTION This method returns the hash code for this URL object. The code is computed using the hash code of its protocol identifier, the hash code of its hostname, and the hash code of its file. This means that two URLs with the same protocol identifier, hostname, and file fields, but with different port or reference fields, will have the same hash code.

RETURNS An `int` that represents the hash code of this URL object.

OVERRIDES `java.lang.Object.hashCode()`.

SEE ALSO `equals()`, `java.util.Hashtable`, `sameFile()`.

EXAMPLE

```
try {
    int[] hits = new int[1023];
    URL u = new URL("http://java.sun.com/");
    int hashval = u.hashCode();
    ++hits[Math.abs(hashval%hits.length)];  // count hits
} catch (MalformedURLException e) {
    e.printStackTrace();
}
```

A B C D E F G H I J K L M N O P Q R S T U V W X Y Z

openConnection()

PURPOSE Opens a connection to the location identified by this URL.

SYNTAX `public URLConnection openConnection() throws IOException`

DESCRIPTION This method opens a connection to the location identified by this URL. First, the stream handler for this URL's protocol is created and then `openConnection()` is invoked on the handler to establish the connection.

The methods `getContent()` and `openStream()` invoke `openConnection()` in order to establish a connection to the URL.

RETURNS A non-`null` connection to the location identified by this URL.

EXCEPTIONS

`IOException`

If an IO exception occurred while attempting to open a connection to this URL.

SEE ALSO `getContent()`, `java.io.IOException`, `openStream()`, `URLConnection`, `URLStreamHandler`.

EXAMPLE

```
try {
    URL u = new URL("file://localhost/app/java1.1/index.html");
    System.out.println("host of URL is " + u.getHost());
    URLConnection uconn = u.openConnection();
    Object content = uconn.getContent();
    if (content != null) {
        System.out.println("class: " + content.getClass());
        System.out.println("obj: " + content);
    }
} catch (MalformedURLException e) {
    e.printStackTrace();
} catch (IOException e) {
    e.printStackTrace();
}
```

openStream()

PURPOSE Opens an input stream to this URL's connection.

SYNTAX `public final InputStream openStream() throws IOException`

DESCRIPTION This method returns an input stream for reading from the connection of this URL. If this URL's connection is not open, `openStream()` will open it before attempting to retrieve the stream. Closing this URL's connection also closes this input stream.

RETURNS The non-`null` input stream of this URL's connection.

EXCEPTIONS

`IOException`

If an IO exception occurred while attempting to open the input stream.

SEE ALSO `java.io.InputStream`, `java.io.IOException`, `openConnection()`.

EXAMPLE See `URL()`.

sameFile()

PURPOSE Determines whether two URLs point to the same file.

SYNTAX `public boolean sameFile(URL other)`

DESCRIPTION This method determines whether two URLs point to the same file. All components of the URL (protocol identifier, host name, port number, and filename) must be equal. The reference component of the URL (i.e., the one following the # character) is excluded from the comparison.

PARAMETERS

`other` The URL against which to compare. `other` cannot be `null`.

RETURNS `true` if `other` and this URL both point to the same file; `false` otherwise.

SEE ALSO `equals()`, `URL()`.

EXAMPLE

```
try {
    URL u1 = new URL("http://java.sun.com:80/new.html");
    URL u2 = new URL("http://java.sun.com/new.html");
    URL u3 = new URL("http://java.sun.com/new.html#_top_");
    // u1 and u2 are not the same because of 'port'
    System.out.println(u1 + (u1.sameFile(u2)? " is " : " is not ") +
                       "the same as " + u2);
    // u2 and u3 are the same because fragment is ignored
    System.out.println(u2 + (u2.sameFile(u3)? " is " : " is not ") +
                       "the same as " + u3);

} catch (MalformedURLException e) {
    e.printStackTrace();
}
```

set()

PURPOSE Sets the fields of this URL.

SYNTAX
```
protected void set(String protocol, String host, int port, String
    file, String ref)
```

DESCRIPTION Subclasses of `URLStreamHandler` use this method to set the various fields of a URL. URL fields are otherwise constant after creation.

PARAMETERS

- `file` The non-`null` filename on `host`.
- `host` The non-`null` string containing the name of the host to which to connect.
- `port` The port number to which to connect.
- `protocol` The non-`null` string containing the protocol identifier.
- `ref` Additional arguments for operating on `file`.

SEE ALSO `URL()`, `URLStreamHandler`.

setURLStreamHandlerFactory()

PURPOSE Sets the URL stream handler factory for this application.

SYNTAX
```
public static synchronized void
    setURLStreamHandlerFactory(URLStreamHandlerFactory factory)
```

DESCRIPTION A *URL stream handler* is responsible for implementing the protocol of this URL. A *URL stream handler factory* is responsible for creating instances of URL stream handlers. This method sets `factory` to be the stream handler factory for this application. It can be executed only if permitted by the security manager. If permitted, it can be executed only once during the lifetime of the application.

PARAMETERS

- `factory` The non-`null` URL stream handler factory to use.

EXCEPTIONS

- `Error` If the URL stream handler factory has already been defined.
- `SecurityException`
  If not allowed to set the factory due to security reasons.

SEE ALSO `java.lang.Error`, `java.lang.SecurityException`, `java.lang.SecurityManager.checkSetFactory()`, `URLStreamHandler`, `URLStreamHandlerFactory`.

EXAMPLE See `URLConnection`, `URLStreamHandler`, and `URLStreamHandlerFactory` for related examples.

```
import java.io.IOException;
import java.net.*;

class Main {
    public static void main(String[] args) {
        URL.setURLStreamHandlerFactory(new TestFactory());
        String host = "localhost";
        if (args.length > 0)
            host = args[0];
        try {
            URL u = new URL("date://" + host);
            Object content = u.getContent();

            if (content != null) {
                System.out.println("class: " + content.getClass());
                System.out.println("obj: " + content);
            }
        } catch (MalformedURLException e) {
            e.printStackTrace();
        } catch (IOException e) {
            e.printStackTrace();
        }
    }
}
```

toExternalForm()

PURPOSE Generates the string representation of this `URL`.

SYNTAX `public String toExternalForm()`

DESCRIPTION This method returns the string representation of this URL. Typically, this consists of the protocol identifier, host name, port numbers, and filename fields of the URL. All fields except the protocol identifier may be displayed in a protocol-dependent format. This method is identical to `toString()`. The result of this method can be used to construct an instance of `URL` equal to this `URL` instance. See the `toString()` example.

RETURNS The non-`null` string representation of this URL.

SEE ALSO `toString()`, `URL()`, `URLStreamHandler.toExternalForm()`.

EXAMPLE

```
try {
    URL u = new URL("http", "java.sun.com", 80, "new.html");
    if (u.toString().equals(u.toExternalForm()))
        System.out.println("external form is same as string form");
    else
        System.out.println("external form is different");
} catch (MalformedURLException e) {
    e.printStackTrace();
}
```

toString()

PURPOSE Generates the string representation of this URL.

SYNTAX `public String toString()`

DESCRIPTION The string representation of a URL consists of its protocol identifier and a protocol-dependent string representation of the rest of the URL. `toString()` returns this string representation. It is identical to `toExternalForm()`. The result of this method can be used to construct an instance of `URL` equal to this `URL` instance. See example.

RETURNS The non-`null` string representation of this URL.

OVERRIDES `java.lang.Object.toString()`.

SEE ALSO `toExternalForm()`, `URL()`.

EXAMPLE

```
import java.net.*;

class Main {
    public static void main(String[] args) {
        try {
            URL u = new URL("http://java.sun.com/new.html#_top_");
            System.out.println(u.equals(new URL(u.toString()))); // true
        } catch (MalformedURLException e) {
            e.printStackTrace();
        }
    }
}
```

URL()

PURPOSE Constructs a `URL` instance.

SYNTAX

```
public URL(String protocol, String host, int port, String file)
    throws MalformedURLException
public URL(String protocol, String host, String file) throws
    MalformedURLException
public URL(String spec) throws MalformedURLException
public URL(URL context, String spec) throws MalformedURLException
```

DESCRIPTION The four forms of the constructor of the `URL` class construct a `URL` instance from the information supplied. The first two forms create a URL for the protocol with identifier `protocol` to host `host` at the port number `port`. If `port` is not supplied or if it is `-1`, the default port number for `protocol` is used. For example, for the HTTP protocol, the default port is `80`. `file` specifies the pathname and any arguments to use after reaching the host. `file` is parsed into a file pathname and arguments (if any) that occur after the hash character (#) (these are recorded as the *reference* of the URL).

The last two forms construct a URL by parsing the URL string `spec`. An example of `spec` is `http://www.widget.com/cgi-bin/123.cgi#urllist`. This string gets parsed into a URL with host `www.widget.com`, default port `-1`, file `cgi-bin/123.cgi`, and reference `urllist`.

If `spec` is a relative URL and if `context` is specified and non-`null`, `context` identifies the context in which to parse `spec` and construct the new URL. If `spec` is an absolute URL (as in the previous example), `context` is ignored. If `context` is not specified or is `null`, `spec` must be an absolute URL. For example, if `context` is the URL `http://www.widget.com/cgi-bin/` and `spec` is `formX`, the new URL will be `http://www.widget.com/cgi-bin/formX`.

Once a URL has been constructed, you can then open a connection to the location pointed to by the URL and read the data from that location.

Each URL instance has associated with it a URL stream handler. If a stream handler cannot be created for the protocol identified by the URL, a `MalformedURLException` is thrown.

PARAMETERS

`context`	The possibly `null` context in which to interpret `spec` if `spec` is a relative URL. If `null`, `spec` must be an absolute URL.
`file`	The non-`null` file pathname (and any arguments) to use after reaching the host.
`host`	The non-`null` string containing the name of the host to which to connect.
`port`	The port number to use.
`protocol`	The non-`null` string containing the protocol identifier.
`spec`	The non-`null` URL string to parse.

EXCEPTIONS

`MalformedURLException`
If the protocol identifier (either `protocol` or that identifier determined from `spec`) is unspecified (`null`) or a stream handler could not be found for it.

SEE ALSO `openConnection()`, `getContent()`, `URLStreamHandler.parseURL()`.

EXAMPLE

```
try {
    String protocol = "file";
    String host = "localhost";
    int port = 0;
    String file = "/app/java1.1/index.html";
    URL u1 = new URL(protocol, host, port, file);
    URL u2 = new URL(protocol, host, file);
    URL u3 = new URL(protocol + "://" + host + "/");
    URL u4 = new URL(u3, file + "#_top_");
```

```
            Object content = u4.getContent();
            if (content != null) {
                System.out.println("class: " + content.getClass());
                System.out.println("obj: " + content);
            }

            InputStream in = u4.openStream();
            if (in != null) {
                for(int c = in.read(); c > 0; c = in.read()) {
                    System.out.print((char)c);
                }
            }
        } catch (MalformedURLException e) {
            e.printStackTrace();
        } catch (IOException e) {
            e.printStackTrace();
        }
```

URLConnection

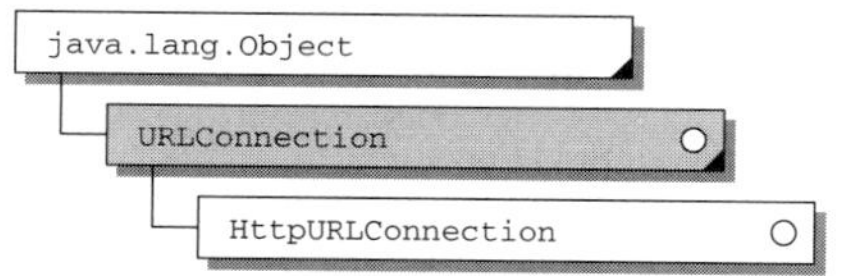

Syntax

```
abstract public class URLConnection
```

Description

The `URLConnection` class represents an active connection to the resource identified by a URL. It is an abstract class that must be subclassed to provide an implementation of `connect()`.

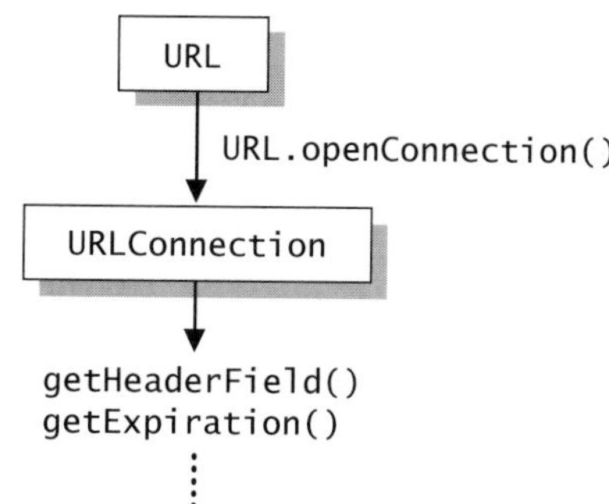

FIGURE 108: **`URLConnection`.**

Usage

`URLConnection` can be used directly or indirectly by a program. When the program calls `URL.getContent()` or `URL.openStream()`, these methods create a `URLConnection` for the URL and invoke methods on the `URLConnection`.

The program can also call `URL.openConnection()`, which returns an instance of `URLConnection` for the URL. It then can invoke methods directly on the `URLConnection` instance.

For both of these scenarios, the subclass of `URLConnection` returned is determined by the URL stream handler that corresponds to the protocol being requested in the URL. See `URLStreamHandler` for a description of how URL stream handlers are selected.

When implementing the URL stream handler for a particular protocol, you define `URLStreamHandler.openConnection()` to return a subclass of `URLConnection` specific for that protocol. To provide an implementation for `URLConnection`, you must, at a minimum, provide an implementation for the `connect()` abstract method. Most likely, you will also need to override the following methods in order to implement the protocol: `getInputStream()`, `getOutputStream()`, `getHeaderField()`, and `getHeaderFieldKey()`.

Life Cycle of a URLConnection

A `URLConnection` object goes through the following steps in its lifetime:

1. The `URLConnection` object is created for a particular URL.
2. (*optional*) Various options or characteristics about the URL connection are set.
3. A connection is established to the host destination named by the URL that is using the specified protocol.

4. A request is constructed using the information in the URL, the properties and characteristics of the connection, and information about the user and the client environment that are making the request. The request is sent through the connection to the destination.
5. A response is received from the connection. Headers describing the response and its content are decoded and returned to the caller.
6. The connection is closed.

Step 2 is accomplished through the use of the many get and set methods provided by the `URLConnection` class. These settings can be changed only prior to the establishment of the connection. The implementation of `connect()` has responsibility for Steps 3–4. Step 5 is performed by the various methods for getting header fields and `getContent()`, whose particular implementation is determined by the type of content to be obtained.

Although this class could be used for other protocols, as is evident by the methods supported by `URLConnection`, it is designed to support HTTP in particular.

URL Stream (Protocol) Handlers

`URLConnection` is an abstract class, so what provides the actual implementations for `URLConnection`? The answer is URL stream (or protocol) handlers. Different protocols, by definition, specify different ways in which the client and server of a connection interact. Consequently, individual URL stream handlers (instances of `URLStreamHandler`) define their own subclass of `URLConnection`. They also create their own instances of a `URLConnection` in response to a request to open a connection to the resource specified by a given URL.

The selection of the particular implementation of URL stream handlers used by a program is configurable by the program. See the `URLStreamHandler` class description for details.

useCaches

Some protocols support caching of documents. Occasionally, it is necessary to bypass the cache; for example, when reloading the document upon explicit directions from the user (e.g., support for the Reload button in a Web browser). When the `useCaches` flag is set on a connection, caches can be used by the stream handler; otherwise, caches are bypassed. An enabled `useCaches` does not mean the stream handler *will* use caches. Some stream handlers do not use them at all. This flag indicates only that *if* the stream handler does support caching, then it is allowed to use caches. This flag does not affect stream handlers that have no caching support.

The `URLConnection` class provides methods for setting and getting the default value of this flag that all new URL connections will have. It also provides methods for getting and setting this flag for individual connections. Note that this flag can be set only before the connection has been established. Once the connection has been established, attempting to change the `useCaches` flag results in an error.

The `useCaches` setting is consulted when the stream handler is constructing the request header (if caching is relevant for that protocol).

If-Modified-Since

For efficiency, some protocols allow reuse of documents even if the uncached copy (on the server) has been modified. This reuse is allowed within some specified grace period. The time when the document must be refetched is called the *If-Modified-Since* time. Documents that have been modified before this time are not refetched. Documents that have been modified after this time must be refetched.

The `URLConnection` class provides methods for setting this modification time limit for a connection.

The If-Modified-Since setting is consulted when the stream handler is constructing the request header (if the If-Modified-Since time is relevant for that protocol).

allowUserInteraction

Some connections require interaction with the user. For example, the user might need to fill in fields in a form or enter a password for a particular connection. The `URLConnection` class provides an `allowUserInteraction` `boolean` field and set/get methods for determining whether such interaction is allowed. This setting is consulted when the response is being processed.

HTTP Request Headers

The HTTP protocol is described in detail in documents found at `http://www.w3.org/pub/WWW/Protocols/` and *RFC 2068*. An HTTP request consists of the *method* to apply to the object named by a URL, a *header*, and *content*. The header contains *request header fields* that indicate to the server certain information about the client making the request, as well as information about the request itself. These fields are encoded in *RFC 822* header style. A summary of the request header fields is given in Table 44.

`Accept:` *`type/subtype`*	List of MIME content types acceptable to the client.
`Accept-Encoding:` *`type`*	List of data encoding types acceptable to the client.
`Accept-Language:` *`lang`*	List of languages preferred by the client.
`Authorization:` *`authinf`*	User authentication information and encryption scheme.
`Charge-To:` *`accountInf`*	Account information (format TBD).
`Content-Length:` *`length`*	Length of the content, in bytes.
`Content-Type:` *`type/subtype`*	MIME content type of this message.
`From:` *`email_address`*	E-mail address of the user making the request.
`If-Modified-Since:` *`date`*	Directs that if the document requested hasn't changed since `date`, don't send it.
`Pragma:` *`server_directive`*	Special instructions to the server (e.g., `no-cache`).
`Referer:` *`URL`*	URL of the document from which this request originated.
`User-Agent:` *`product/vers`*	Product name and version number of the client software.

TABLE 44: HTTP Request Header Fields.

The `Accept`, `Accept-Encoding`, and `Accept-Language` fields are semicolon-separated lists and may appear more than once in the header. If the `Accept` field is absent, the client is assumed to be able to accept `text/plain` and `text/html`. All of these fields are optional.

The `useCaches` flag of the `URLConnection` class can be used to construct the no-cache `Pragma` field. The connection's If-Modified-Since time is used to construct the `If-Modified-Since` header field. Other header fields can be constructed using the get/set request property methods.

HTTP Response Header

Once an HTTP request has been sent through the URL connection, the server at the other end of the connection sends back an HTTP response. This response consists of the HTTP version number and a status code for the request. This is followed by (applicable) response header fields, which are given in Table 45,[1] and then by the response data.

`Allowed:` *`method method ...`*	List of request methods the user is allowed to issue for this URL.
`Content-Encoding:` *`type`*	Encoding of this response message (e.g., `x-compress or x-gzip`).
`Content-Language:` *`lang`*	Language in which this response message is written.
`Content-Length:` *`length`*	Length of this response message in bytes.
`Content-Transfer-Encoding:` *`type`*	Encoding used for the MIME messages (the default is 8-bit character encoding).
`Content-Type:` *`type/subtype`*	MIME content type of this document.
`Cost: TBS`	Cost of retrieving this document.
`Date:` *`date`*	Creation time (in GMT) of this document.
`Derived-From:` *`verid`*	Version of the document from which this document is derived.
`Expires:` *`date`*	Time (in GMT) at which this document expires and should be refetched.
`Last-Modified:` *`date`*	Last modified time (in GMT) of this document.
`Message-ID:` *`URI`*	Unique identifier for this message.
`Public:` *`method*`*	List of request methods anyone is allowed to issue for this URL.
`Title:` *`string`*	Title of this document.
`URI:` *`url`*	URI or URL of this document.
`Version:` *`verid`*	String identifying the version of this document.

TABLE 45: HTTP Response Header Fields.

1. This list is obtained from the HTTP/1.1 draft. There may be differences between this list and that of HTTP/1.0.

`WWW-Authenticate: auth`	Encryption and authorization schemes the server wants to use.
`WWW-Link: href`	HTML link reference of this document.

TABLE 45: HTTP Response Header Fields.

The `URLConnection` class provides methods that retrieve the common header fields (such as content types, length, and date) and generic methods for retrieving arbitrary header fields.

For a full discussion of the HTTP protocol, see *RFC 2068* and documents at

`http://www.w3.org/hypertext/WWW/Protocols/`

Content Handlers

Once a response header has been retrieved from a URL connection, its content must be processed. The header information (more specifically, `Content-Type`) is used to determine which content handler to invoke to process the content. If the `Content-Type` header field is missing from the response or if the field contains the wrong type, some heuristics are applied to "guess" the type of the response.

The `getContent()` method, whose implementation is provided by individual content handlers, processes the response data and generates an object of the appropriate type. For example, response data that is an image gets turned into an object of class `Image`. Typically, the program invokes `URL.getContent()`, which opens the URL connection and invokes `URLConnection.getContent()`.

The selection of the particular implementation of content handlers used by a program is configurable by the program. See the class description of `ContentHandler` for a description of how content handlers are selected.

MEMBER SUMMARY

Constructor	
`URLConnection()`	Constructs a URL connection.
Connection Establishment Field and Method	
`connect()`	Establishes this URL connection.
`connected`	Indicates whether a connection has been established to this URL.
Content Processing Field and Methods	
`fileNameMap`	Map for translating filenames to content types.
`getContent()`	Retrieves the content of this URL as an object.
`getInputStream()`	Creates an input stream for reading from this URL connection.

Continued

MEMBER SUMMARY

Content Processing Field and Methods *(Continued)*	
`getOutputStream()`	Creates an output stream for writing to this URL connection.
`setContentHandlerFactory()`	Sets the content handler factory for this application.
`guessContentTypeFromName()`	Guesses the content type by looking at the filename extension.
`guessContentTypeFromStream()`	Guesses the content type by inspecting the content of the document.
Response Header Methods	
`getContentEncoding()`	Retrieves the content encoding type of the response data.
`getContentLength()`	Retrieves the content length of the response data.
`getContentType()`	Retrieves the content type of the response data.
`getDate()`	Retrieves the creation date of the response data.
`getExpiration()`	Retrieves the expiration date of the response data.
`getHeaderField()`	Retrieves a header field from the response.
`getHeaderFieldDate()`	Retrieves a response header field and parses its value as a GMT date.
`getHeaderFieldInt()`	Retrieves a response header field and parses its value as an integer.
`getHeaderFieldKey()`	Retrieves the *n*th header field name at the specified position in the response header.
`getLastModified()`	Retrieves the last modification date of the response data.
Request Header Methods	
`getDefaultRequestProperty()`	Retrieves the default value of a request header field for future connections.
`getRequestProperty()`	Retrieves the value of a request header field for this URL connection.
`setDefaultRequestProperty()`	Sets the default value of a request header field for new connections.
`setRequestProperty()`	Sets the value of a request header field for this URL connection.
Cache Field and Methods	
`getDefaultUseCaches()`	Determines whether new URL connections, by default, may use caches.
`getUseCaches()`	Determines whether this URL connection allows caches to be used.
`setDefaultUseCaches()`	Sets the default cache usage flag for new connections.

MEMBER SUMMARY

`setUseCaches()`	Sets the cache usage flag of this URL connection.
`useCaches`	Indicates whether this URL connection allows the use of caches.
If-Modified-Since Field and Methods	
`getIfModifiedSince()`	Retrieves the modification time that forces refetching of the document.
`ifModifiedSince`	Indicates that documents modified after this time must be refetched.
`setIfModifiedSince()`	Sets the modification time that forces refetching of the document.
User Interaction Field and Methods	
`allowUserInteraction`	Indicates whether user interaction is allowed for this URL connection.
`getAllowUserInteraction()`	Determines whether this URL connection allows user interaction.
`getDefaultAllowUserInteraction()`	Determines whether new URL connections, by default, allow user interaction.
`setAllowUserInteraction()`	Sets the user interaction flag for this URL connection.
`setDefaultAllowUserInteraction()`	Sets the default user interaction flag for new connections.
User IO Fields and Methods	
`doInput`	Indicates whether this URL connection will be used for input.
`doOutput`	Indicates whether this URL connection will be used for output.
`getDoInput()`	Determines whether this URL connection intends to do any input.
`getDoOutput()`	Determines whether output is planned to this URL connection.
`setDoInput()`	Sets the indication of whether input from this URL connection is planned.
`setDoOutput()`	Sets the indication of whether output to this URL connection is planned.
URL Field and Method	
`url`	The URL of this URL connection.
`getURL()`	Retrieves the URL of this URL connection.
Description Method	
`toString()`	Generates the string representation of this object.

See Also

ContentHandler, ContentHandlerFactory, URL, URL.getContent(), URL.setURLStreamHandlerFactory, URLStreamHandler, URLStreamHandlerFactory.

Example

This example shows an implementation of a URLConnection for the Internet daytime protocol (port 13), which uses UDP to return the time of day in a string in GMT format.

DateURLConnection defines two methods: connect() and getContent(). connect() makes a connection to the host named in the URL, while getContent() reads the current date from the host and returns the answer in the form of a Date object. getContent() overrides the URLConnection.getContent() because it does not handle the content in the same style as HTTP does. Most methods in URLConnection, such as those related to content headers and IO streams, are not relevant for this simple protocol.

See related examples in URLStreamHandler, URLStreamHandlerFactory, and URL.setURLStreamHandlerFactory() for how a program makes use of DateURLConnection.

```
import java.net.*;
import java.io.*;
import java.util.Date;
import java.text.DateFormat;
import java.text.ParseException;

public class DateURLConnection extends URLConnection {
    DatagramSocket sock = null;
    public DateURLConnection(URL u) {
        super(u);
    }
    public void connect() throws IOException {
        if (connected) {
            return;
        }
        InetAddress dst = InetAddress.getByName(getURL().getHost());
        byte[] outbuf = new byte[1];
        outbuf[0] = '\n';
        int port;
        if ((port = getURL().getPort()) == -1)
            port = 13;         // daytime

        DatagramPacket request =
            new DatagramPacket(outbuf, outbuf.length, dst, port);
        try {
            sock = new DatagramSocket();
            sock.send(request);
            connected = true;
        } catch (SocketException e) {
            sock = null;
            throw e;
        }
    }
    // Override instead letting content handler be selected
    // based on content-type
    public Object getContent() throws IOException {
        if (!connected)
```

```
            connect();

        byte[] inbuf = new byte[256];  // default size
        DatagramPacket reply = new DatagramPacket(inbuf, inbuf.length);
        sock.receive(reply);
        sock.close();
        sock = null;
        connected = false;
        String dateStr = new String(reply.getData());
        if (dateStr != null) {
            try {
                DateFormat df = DateFormat.getDateInstance(DateFormat.FULL);
                return (df.parse(dateStr));
            } catch (ParseException e) {
                System.err.println("Date string: " + dateStr);
                e.printStackTrace();
            }
        }
        throw new ProtocolException("Not conforming to date protocol");
    }
}
```

allowUserInteraction

PURPOSE Indicates whether user interaction is allowed for this URL connection.

SYNTAX `protected boolean allowUserInteraction`

DESCRIPTION This field records whether this URL connection allows interaction with the user. See the class description for details. If `allowUserInteraction` is `true`, interaction is allowed; if `false`, interaction is not allowed. The default value for `allowUserInteraction` is `false` unless the default has been modified earlier in the program via `setDefaultAllowUserInteraction()`. `getDefaultAllowUserInteraction()` can be used to examine the default setting of `allowUserInteraction`.

This field should be accessed and manipulated through the `getAllowUserInteraction()` and `setAllowUserInteraction()` methods, respectively.

SEE ALSO `getDefaultAllowUserInteraction()`, `getAllowUserInteraction()`, `setDefaultAllowUserInteraction()`, `setAllowUserInteraction()`.

RETURNS `true` if this URL connection allows user interaction; `false` otherwise.

connect()

PURPOSE Establishes this URL connection.

SYNTAX `abstract public void connect() throws IOException`

DESCRIPTION After a `URLConnection` object has been created and (optionally) after various options (such as `useCaches` and `allowUserInteraction`) have been set, the connection can be established via a call to `connect()`. The implementation of this abstract method is provided by the subclass of `URLConnection`, which in turn is provided by the `URLStreamHandler` for the protocol identified in the URL of this connection.

The connection is established to the host and port number identified in the URL. A request is then sent to the connection. The request consists of information derived from the rest of the URL, option settings on this connection, and user and client information. The particulars of the request depend on the protocol. A response is then returned from the connection. `connect()` is responsible for getting the connection to a state in which a subsequent call to `getContent()` will retrieve the content of the response as an object. The steps required to achieve this are protocol-dependent.

Certain methods will call `connect()` automatically if their semantics are such that they make sense only after `connect()` has been called (e.g., `getContent()`, `getContentLength()`, and `getInputStream()`).

The implementation of `connect()` should be idempotent; that is, if a connection has already been established, `connect()` does nothing. After a connection has been successfully established, `connect()` should set the field `connected` to `true`.

EXCEPTIONS

`IOException`

If an IO error occurred while attempting to establish the connection.

SEE ALSO `connected`, `java.io.IOException`, `URLStreamHandler`.

EXAMPLE See the class example.

connected

PURPOSE Indicates whether a connection has been established to this URL.

SYNTAX `protected boolean connected`

A B C D E F G H I J K L M N O P Q R S T U V W X Y Z

DESCRIPTION A URL connection is first created and then connected. This field records whether this URL connection has been connected. If it has been, `connected` is `true`; otherwise, it is `false`.

SEE ALSO `connect()`.

EXAMPLE See the class example.

doInput

PURPOSE Indicates whether this URL connection will be used for input.

SYNTAX `protected boolean doInput`

DESCRIPTION A URL connection can be used for input, output, or both. This field records whether this URL connection will be used for input. By default, it is `true`.

This field should be examined and manipulated through the use of the methods `getDoInput()` and `setDoInput()`, respectively.

SEE ALSO `getDoInput()`, `setDoInput()`.

doOutput

PURPOSE Indicates whether this URL connection will be used for output.

SYNTAX `protected boolean doOutput`

DESCRIPTION A URL connection can be used for input, output, or both. This field records whether this URL connection will be used for output. By default, it is `false`.

This field should be examined and manipulated through the use of the methods `getDoOutput()` and `setDoOutput()`, respectively.

SEE ALSO `getDoOutput()`, `setDoOutput()`.

fileNameMap

PURPOSE Map for translating filenames to content types.

SYNTAX `public static FileNameMap fileNameMap`

DESCRIPTION This map is used by `guessContentTypeFromName()` to determine the MIME content type of an object from its filename extension. Its value is set by the subclass of `URLConnection`.

SEE ALSO `FileNameMap`, `guessContentTypeFromName()`.

getAllowUserInteraction()

PURPOSE
Determines whether this URL connection allows user interaction.

SYNTAX
`public boolean getAllowUserInteraction()`

DESCRIPTION
This method returns a `boolean` flag indicating whether this URL connection allows user interaction. This flag can be changed prior to the connection's being established (before `connect()` is called) by using `setAllowUserInteraction()`. See the class description for more details on this flag.

RETURNS
`true` if this URL connection allows user interaction; `false` otherwise.

SEE ALSO
`getDefaultAllowUserInteraction()`, `setDefaultAllowUserInteraction()`, `setDefaultAllowUserInteraction()`, `allowUserInteraction`.

getContent()

PURPOSE
Retrieves the content of this URL as an object.

SYNTAX
`public Object getContent() throws IOException`

DESCRIPTION
The implementation of this method is determined by the content handler selected for the content type of the response (obtained from the response header). The implementation is determined dynamically using system configuration. See the `ContentHhandler` class for a description of how the content handler implementation is selected.

`getContent()` returns an object whose class is determined by its content type. For example, a content with type "image/gif" might generate an object of subclass of `java.awt.Image`; a content with type "text/plain" might generate an object of class `String`. The `instanceof` operator should be used to determine the class of the object.

RETURNS
The non-`null` object representing the content of this URL connection.

EXCEPTIONS
`IOException`
If an IO error occurred while retrieving the content.

SEE ALSO
`ContentHandler`, `ContentHandlerFactory`, `java.io.IOException`, `setContentHandlerFactory()`.

EXAMPLE
See the class example. Instead of using explicit content handlers, this example overrides `getContent()` to produce a result (a `Date` object) directly.

getContentEncoding()

PURPOSE Retrieves the content encoding type of the response data.

SYNTAX `public String getContentEncoding()`

DESCRIPTION This method returns the content encoding type of the response data. The encoding type is obtained by examining the `Content-Encoding` header field in the response header. Currently, only two encodings are used in HTTP: `x-compress` and `x-gzip`. This method returns `null` if the `Content-Encoding` header field is not in the response.

This method requires an appropriate implementation of `getHeaderField()` to process the header fields.

RETURNS An identifier specifying how the response data is encoded; `null` if this was not specified in the response.

SEE ALSO `getContentType()`.

getContentLength()

PURPOSE Retrieves the content length of the response data.

SYNTAX `public int getContentLength()`

DESCRIPTION This method returns the content length of the response data, in bytes. The length is obtained by examining the `Content-Length` header field in the response header. If the header does not contain a `Content-Length` header field, this method returns `-1`.

This method requires an appropriate implementation of `getHeaderField()` to process the header fields.

RETURNS The length of the response data, in bytes; `-1` if unknown.

SEE ALSO `getContentType()`.

getContentType()

PURPOSE Retrieves the content type of the response data.

SYNTAX `public String getContentType()`

DESCRIPTION This method returns the MIME type of the response data. The MIME type is specified in the `Content-Type` header field and has the form *type/subtype*. For example, "text/html" has type "text" and subtype "html". If no `Content-Type` header field is found, this method returns `null`.

This method requires an appropriate implementation of `getHeaderField()` to process the header fields.

RETURNS The MIME content type of the response data; `null` if unknown.

SEE ALSO `guessContentTypeFromName()`, `guessContentTypeFromStream()`.

getDate()

PURPOSE Retrieves the creation date of the response data.

SYNTAX `public long getDate()`

DESCRIPTION This method returns the creation date of the response data by examining the `Date` header field in the response. If no `Date` header field is found, it returns `0`.

This method requires an appropriate implementation of `getHeaderField()` in order to process the header fields.

RETURNS The creation date in number of milliseconds since epoch; `0` if unknown.

SEE ALSO `getExpiration()`, `getLastModified()`, `java.util.Date`.

getDefaultAllowUserInteraction()

PURPOSE Determines whether new URL connections, by default, allow user interaction.

SYNTAX `public static boolean getDefaultAllowUserInteraction()`

DESCRIPTION This method returns a `boolean` flag indicating whether new URL connections may, by default, allow user interaction. This may not necessarily be the same as what this URL connection allows. `getAllowUserInteraction()` can be used to find out whether this URL connection allows user interaction. See the class description for more details on this flag.

RETURNS `true` if new connections allow user interaction by default; `false` if new connections do not allow user interaction by default.

SEE ALSO `getAllowUserInteraction()`, `setDefaultAllowUserInteraction()`, `setAllowUserInteraction()`, `allowUserInteraction`.

getDefaultRequestProperty()

PURPOSE Retrieves the default value of a request header field for future connections.

SYNTAX `public static String getDefaultRequestProperty(String field)`

DESCRIPTION — This method returns the default value of the request header field `field` that will be used for future URL connections. When a new URL connection is created, it gets initialized with these default request header fields. Table 44 contains examples of request header fields. This method returns `null` if `field` does not have a default value.

The default implementation of this method returns `null`. It must be overridden by protocol implementations that support default request properties.

PARAMETERS

`field` — The name of the request header field.

RETURNS — The default value of `field`; `null` if it does not have a default value.

SEE ALSO — `setDefaultRequestProperty()`.

getDefaultUseCaches()

PURPOSE — Determines whether new URL connections may, by default, use caches.

SYNTAX

```
public boolean getDefaultUseCaches()
```

DESCRIPTION — This method returns a `boolean` flag indicating whether new URL connections may, by default, use caches. This may not necessarily be the same as what this URL connection allows. `getUseCaches()` can be used to find out whether this URL connection may use caches.

RETURNS — `true` if new connections may use caches by default; `false` otherwise.

SEE ALSO — `getUseCaches()`, `setDefaultUseCaches()`, `setUseCaches()`, `useCaches`.

getDoInput()

PURPOSE — Determines whether this URL connection intends to do any input.

SYNTAX

```
public boolean getDoInput()
```

DESCRIPTION — This method returns a `boolean` flag indicating whether this URL connection intends to do any input. This flag can be changed only prior to the connection's being established (before `connect()` is called) by using `setDoInput()`.

RETURNS — `true` if this URL connection intends to do input; `false` otherwise.

SEE ALSO — `setDoInput()`, `doInput`.

getDoOutput()

PURPOSE Determines whether this URL connection intends to do any output.

SYNTAX `public boolean getDoOutput()`

DESCRIPTION This method returns a `boolean` flag indicating whether this URL connection intends to do any output. This flag can be changed only prior to the connection's being established (before `connect()` is called) by using `setDoOutput()`.

RETURNS `true` if this URL connection intends to do output; `false` otherwise.

SEE ALSO `setDoOutput()`, `doOutput`.

getExpiration()

PURPOSE Retrieves the expiration date of the response data.

SYNTAX `public long getExpiration()`

DESCRIPTION This method returns the expiration date of the response data by examining the `Expires` header field in the response. If no such field is found, it returns `0`. This date can be used by systems that implement caching to know when the data needs to be flushed from the cache.

This method requires an appropriate implementation of `getHeaderField()` to process the header fields.

RETURNS The expiration date in number of milliseconds since epoch; `0` if unknown.

SEE ALSO `Date`. `getDate()`, `getLastModified()`.

getHeaderField()

PURPOSE Retrieves a header field from the response header.

SYNTAX

```
public String getHeaderField(int posn)
public String getHeaderField(String key)
```

DESCRIPTION This method retrieves a header field from the response header.

The first form returns the value of the header field at position `posn`. If there are fewer than `posn` fields, this method returns `null`. This method can be used in conjunction with `getHeaderFieldKey()` to iterate through all of the response header fields in the message.

The second form returns the value of the header field identified by `key`. If no such field exists, it returns `null`. Whether the character case of `key` is case-sensitive or case-insensitive depends on the `URLConnection` implementation.

The default implementation of this method returns `null`. It must be overridden by protocol implementations that support reading header fields from the connection.

PARAMETERS

`key` The identifier of the header field to fetch.

`posn` The position of the header field value to fetch; the first field has position 0.

RETURNS The value of the header field specified; `null` if no such header field exists.

SEE ALSO `getHeaderFieldDate()`, `getHeaderFieldInt()`, `getHeaderFieldKey()`.

EXAMPLE Suppose the header contains the following fields and the subclass of `URLConnection` overrode `getHeaderField()` with an appropriate implementation:

```
HTTP/1.0 200 OK
Content-type: text/html
Content-length: 1224
```

Then the following would occur:

`getHeaderField(0)` would return "HTTP/1.0 200 OK".

`getHeaderField(1)` would return "text/html".

`getHeaderField(2)` would return "1223".

`getHeaderField("Content-type")` would return "text/html".

getHeaderFieldDate()

PURPOSE Retrieves a response header field and parses its value as a GMT date.

SYNTAX `public long getHeaderFieldDate(String field, long default)`

DESCRIPTION This method retrieves the response header field from the response with name `field` and parses its value as a GMT date. It then returns this date value as the number of milliseconds since epoch. If `field` is not found, `default` is returned.

This method requires an appropriate implementation of `getHeaderField()` to process the header fields.

This method can be overridden by implementations that support preparsed headers and hence bypass the parsing altogether.

PARAMETERS

`default` The value to return if `field` is not in the response header.

`field` The name of the header field.

RETURNS The date value (in number of milliseconds since epoch) of the header field `field`; `default` if `field` is not found in the response header or if the value of `field` cannot be parsed into a date.

SEE ALSO `Date, getHeaderField(), getHeaderFieldInt().`

getHeaderFieldInt()

PURPOSE Retrieves a response header field and parses its value as an integer.

SYNTAX `public int getHeaderFieldInt(String field, int default)`

DESCRIPTION This method retrieves the response header field with name `field`, parses its value as an integer, and returns that value as an `int`. If `field` is not found, `default` is returned.

This method requires an appropriate implementation of `getHeaderField()` to process the header fields.

This method can be overridden by implementations that support preparsed headers and hence bypass the parsing altogether.

PARAMETERS

`default` The value to return if `field` is not in the response header.

`field` The name of the header field.

RETURNS The value of the header field `field` as an `int`; `default` if `field` is not found in the response header or if the value of `field` cannot be parsed into an `int`.

SEE ALSO `getHeaderField(), getHeaderFieldDate().`

getHeaderFieldKey()

PURPOSE Retrieves the *n*th header field name at the specified position in the response header.

SYNTAX `public String getHeaderFieldKey(int posn)`

DESCRIPTION This method returns the name of the header field at position `posn` from the response header (e.g., "content-type"). If there are fewer than `posn` fields, this method returns `null`. Note that some fields have no key, in which case an empty string is returned (see example). This method can be used in conjunction with `getHeaderField()` to iterate through all of the response header fields in the message.

The default implementation of this method returns `null`. It must be overridden by protocol implementations that support reading header fields from the connection.

PARAMETERS

`posn` The position of the header field to fetch; the first field has position `0`.

RETURNS The name of the header field at position `posn`; `null` if there are fewer than `posn` fields.

SEE ALSO `getHeaderFieldDate()`, `getHeaderFieldInt()`, `getHeaderField()`.

EXAMPLE Suppose the header contains the following fields and the subclass of `URLConnection` overrode `getHeaderField()` with an appropriate implementation, as follows:

```
HTTP/1.0 200 OK
Content-type: text/html
Content-length: 1224
```

Then the following would occur:

`getHeaderFieldKey(0)` would return "".

`getHeaderFieldKey(1)` would return "Content-type".

`getHeaderFieldKey(2)` would return "Content-length".

getIfModifiedSince()

PURPOSE Retrieves the modification time that forces refetching of the document.

SYNTAX `public long getIfModifiedSince()`

DESCRIPTION This method returns the If-Modified-Since time of this URL connection (if the protocol associated with this URL connection makes use of If-Modified-Since times). This time is placed in the request header to indicate to the server that it should skip returning the document if the document has not been modified since the If-Modified-Since time. This value can be set and modified prior to the connection's being established (before `connect()` is called) by using `setIfModifiedSince()`.

This method requires an appropriate implementation of `getHeaderField()` in order to process the header fields.

RETURNS The If-Modified-Since time of this URL connection in milliseconds since epoch.

SEE ALSO `ifModifiedSince`, `java.util.Date`, `setIfModifiedSince()`.

getInputStream()

PURPOSE Creates an input stream for reading from this URL connection.

SYNTAX `public InputStream getInputStream() throws IOException`

DESCRIPTION This method creates an input stream from this URL connection. By default, it throws `UnknownServiceException`. It must be overridden by protocol implementations that support reading input from the connection. This method should establish a connection with the server of the URL, if one has not been established yet.

RETURNS A non-`null` input stream for reading from the connection.

EXCEPTIONS

`UnknownServiceException`
This protocol does not support input.

SEE ALSO `getContent()`, `getOutputStream()`, `java.io.InputStream`, `java.io.IOException`.

getLastModified()

PURPOSE Retrieves the last modification date of the response data.

SYNTAX `public long getLastModified()`

DESCRIPTION This method returns the last modification date of the response data by examining the `Last-Modified` header field in the response. If no `Last-Modified` header field is found, it returns `0`.

This method requires an appropriate implementation of `getHeaderField()` to process the header fields.

RETURNS The last modified date in number of milliseconds since epoch; `0` if unknown.

SEE ALSO `java.util.Date`, `getDate()`, `getExpiration()`.

getOutputStream()

PURPOSE Creates an output stream for writing to this URL connection.

SYNTAX `public OutputStream getOutputStream() throws IOException`

DESCRIPTION This method creates an output stream for writing to this URL connection. By default, it throws `UnknownServiceException`. It must be overridden by protocol implementations that support writing to the connection. This method should establish a connection to the server of the URL, if one has not been established yet.

RETURNS A non-`null` output stream for writing to this URL connection.

EXCEPTIONS

`UnknownServiceException`
This protocol does not support output.

SEE ALSO `getContent()`, `getInputStream()`, `java.io.IOException`.

getRequestProperty()

PURPOSE Retrieves the value of a request header field for this URL connection.

SYNTAX
```
public String getRequestProperty(String field)
```

DESCRIPTION This method returns the value of the request header field `field`. If there is no value for `field`, this method returns `null`. Table 44 contains examples of request header fields. The value of `field` can be changed prior to the connection's being established (before `connect()` is called) by using `setRequestProperty()`. This method cannot be called after the connection has already been established.

The default implementation of this method returns `null`. It must be overridden by protocol implementations that support reading header fields from the request.

RETURNS The value of `field`; `null` if not found.

EXCEPTIONS

`IllegalAccessError`
If the connection has already been established.

SEE ALSO `getDefaultRequestProperty()`, `setDefaultRequestProperty()`, `setRequestProperty()`.

getURL()

PURPOSE Retrieves the URL of this URL connection.

SYNTAX
```
public URL getURL()
```

DESCRIPTION This method returns the URL of this URL connection. It is set initially by the `URLConnection` constructor and typically remains unchanged for the duration of the connection.

RETURNS The non-`null` URL for this URL connection.

SEE ALSO `url`, `URLConnection()`.

getUseCaches()

PURPOSE Determines whether this URL connection allows caches to be used.

SYNTAX `public boolean getUseCaches()`

DESCRIPTION This method returns a `boolean` flag indicating whether this URL connection allows caches to be used. This flag can be changed prior to the connection's being established (before `connect()` is called) by using `setUseCaches()`.

RETURNS `true` if this URL connection can use caches; `false` otherwise.

SEE ALSO `getDefaultUseCaches()`, `setDefaultUseCaches()`, `setUseCaches()`, `useCaches`.

guessContentTypeFromName()

PURPOSE Guesses the content type by looking at the filename extension.

SYNTAX `protected static String guessContentTypeFromName(String url)`

DESCRIPTION This method extracts the file pathname component of the URL string `url` and examines the filename extension of that pathname to determine the content type of the document named by that URL. Any fragment identifier (the identifier follows the #) is removed from the URL in order to find the filename extension. For example, a filename extension of `.html` or `.htm` results in the content-type of "text/html"; a filename extension of `.jpeg` or `.jpg` results in the content type of "image/jpeg".

`getContentType()` should be used to determine the content type of the response. However, sometimes the `Content-Type` header field is not present. Hence, this heuristic must be used to guess its type.

PARAMETERS

`url` The non-`null` URL string to use for guessing.

RETURNS The MIME type deduced from the filename extension; `null` if the method cannot guess.

SEE ALSO `fileNameMap`, `FileNameMap.getContentTypeFor()`, `getContentType()`, `guessContentTypeFromStream()`.

guessContentTypeFromStream()

PURPOSE Guesses the content type by inspecting the content of the document.

SYNTAX
```
public static String
   guessContentTypeFromStream(InputStream stream)
   throws IOException
```

DESCRIPTION This method is used to guess the content type of a document by inspecting its content. The bytes at the beginning of the document are examined loosely. The document is accessed via the input stream `stream`. `stream` must support `mark()` and `reset()` in order for this method to work. You can use `BufferedInputStream` as one of the filters to `stream` in order to enable `mark()/reset()` support.

This method is used in two cases. In the first, the document is lacking a `Content-Type` header field. In the second, the document contains an incorrect header field and `guessContentTypeFromName()` is not sufficient because of the use of nonstandard filename extensions. Use of this method allows the system to be able to recover from these problems.

PARAMETERS

`stream` The non-`null` stream to read to inspect the content. The stream must support `mark()/reset()`.

RETURNS The MIME type deduced from the content of the stream; `null` if the method cannot guess.

EXCEPTIONS

`IOException`

If an IO error occurred while reading from `stream`.

SEE ALSO `getContentType()`, `guessContentTypeFromName()`, `java.io.BufferedInputStream`, `java.io.InputStream`, `java.io.IOException`.

ifModifiedSince

PURPOSE Indicates that documents modified after this time must be refetched.

SYNTAX `protected long ifModifiedSince`

DESCRIPTION This field records the time after which a document requested must be refetched for this URL connection. Its value is the number of milliseconds since epoch.

This field should be accessed and updated through the use of `getIfModifiedSince()` and `setIfModifiedSince()`, respectively.

SEE ALSO `Date`, `getIfModifiedSince()`, `setIfModifiedSince()`.

setAllowUserInteraction()

PURPOSE Sets the user interaction flag for this URL connection.

SYNTAX `public void setAllowUserInteraction(boolean allows)`

DESCRIPTION This method is used to indicate whether this URL connection allows user interaction. It can be invoked after the URL connection has been created but before the connection has been established (i.e., before `connect()` has been invoked on it). See the class description for more details on this flag.

PARAMETERS

`allows` A `boolean` flag indicating whether to allow user interaction. `true` means allow user interaction; `false` means do not allow user interaction.

EXCEPTIONS

`IllegalAccessError`
If this method is called after the connection has already been established.

SEE ALSO `allowUserInteraction`, `getDefaultAllowUserInteraction()`, `getAllowUserInteraction()`, `java.lang.IllegalAccessError`, `setDefaultAllowUserInteraction()`.

setContentHandlerFactory()

PURPOSE Sets the content handler factory for this application.

SYNTAX

```
public static synchronized void
   setContentHandlerFactory(ContentHandlerFactory factory)
```

DESCRIPTION A *content handler* processes the content in the response data of a URL connection and generates an object representing that data. The actual implementation of content handlers is supplied by a subclass of `ContentHandler` and is configurable by the application. See the `ContentHandler` class for details.

A *content handler factory* is responsible for creating an instance of (subclasses of) `ContentHandler`. This method sets `factory` to be the content handler factory. It can be executed only if permitted by the security manager. If permitted, it can be executed only once during the lifetime of the application.

PARAMETERS

`factory` The content handler factory to use.

EXCEPTIONS

`Error` If the content handler factory has already been defined.

`SecurityException`
If not allowed to set the factory due to security reasons.

SEE ALSO `ContentHandler`, `ContentHandlerFactory`, `java.lang.SecurityException`, `java.lang.SecurityManager.checkSetFactory()`.

EXAMPLE This example sets the content handler factory to be `SampleFactory`. (See related examples at `ContentHandler` and `ContentHandlerFactory`.)

```
class Main {
    public static void main(String[] args) {

        if (args.length != 1) {
            System.err.println("Usage: java Main <URL>");
            System.exit(1);
        }

        // Configure system to use our own factory
        URLConnection.setContentHandlerFactory(new SampleFactory());
        try {
            URL url = new URL(args[0]);

            Object obj = url.getContent();
            if (obj != null) {
                 System.out.println("class: " + obj.getClass());
                 System.out.println("obj: " + obj);
            }
        } catch (MalformedURLException e) {
            e.printStackTrace();
        } catch (IOException e) {
            e.printStackTrace();
        }
    };
}
```

setDefaultAllowUserInteraction()

PURPOSE Sets the default user interaction flag for new connections.

SYNTAX `public static void setDefaultAllowUserInteraction(boolean allows)`

DESCRIPTION This method sets the default flag for whether new URL connections allow user interaction. It applies to all new URL connections; it does not apply to this URL connection, since this URL connection has already been created. The allow user interaction status of this URL connection can be modified only via `setAllowUserInteraction()`. See the class description for more details on this flag.

PARAMETERS

`allows` A `boolean` flag indicating whether to allow user interaction by default for all new URL connections. `true` means allow user interaction; `false` means do not allow user interaction.

SEE ALSO `allowUserInteraction`, `getDefaultAllowUserInteraction()`, `getAllowUserInteraction()`, `setAllowUserInteraction()`.

setDefaultRequestProperty()

PURPOSE Sets the default value of a request header field for new connections.

SYNTAX
```
public static void setDefaultRequestProperty(String field,
   String value)
```

DESCRIPTION This method sets the default value of the request header field `field` to be `value`. When a URL connection is created, it gets initialized with these request header fields. This call does not affect request header field settings already in place for the current URL connection. Table 44 contains examples of request header fields.

The default implementation of this method does nothing. It must be overridden by protocol implementations that support the setting of default request properties.

PARAMETERS

`field` The non-`null` name of the request header field.
`value` The non-`null` value of the request header field.

SEE ALSO `getDefaultRequestProperty()`, `getRequestProperty()`, `setRequestProperty()`.

setDefaultUseCaches()

PURPOSE Sets the default cache usage flag for new connections.

SYNTAX
```
public void setDefaultUseCaches(boolean useCaches)
```

DESCRIPTION This method sets the default flag for whether new URL connections may use caches. It applies to all new URL connections; it does not apply to the current URL connection, since this URL connection has already been created. This URL connection's cache usage can be modified only via `setUseCaches()`.

PARAMETERS

`useCaches` A `boolean` flag indicating whether to use caches by default for all new URL connections. `true` means use caches; `false` means do not use caches.

SEE ALSO `getDefaultUseCaches()`, `getUseCaches()`, `setUseCaches()`, `useCaches`.

A B C D E F G H I J K L M N O P Q R S T U V W X Y Z

setDoInput()

PURPOSE Sets the indication of whether input from this URL connection is planned.

SYNTAX `public void setDoInput(boolean enable)`

DESCRIPTION This method sets an indication of whether input from this URL connection is planned. It updates the field `doInput` with the value of the argument `enable`. If `enable` is `true`, input is expected; if `enable` is `false`, input is not expected.

PARAMETERS

`enable` Whether input from this URL connection is planned.

EXCEPTIONS

`IllegalAccessError`

If this URL connection has already been connected.

SEE ALSO `doInput`, `getDoInput()`, `java.lang.IllegalAccessError`, `setDoOutput()`.

setDoOutput()

PURPOSE Sets the indication of whether output to this URL connection is planned.

SYNTAX `public void setDoOutput(boolean enable)`

DESCRIPTION This method sets an indication of whether output to this URL connection is planned. It updates the field `doOutput` with the value of the argument `enable`. If `enable` is `true`, output is expected; if `enable` is `false`, output is not expected.

PARAMETERS

`enable` Whether output to this URL connection is planned.

EXCEPTIONS

`IllegalAccessError`

If this URL connection has already been established.

SEE ALSO `doOutput`, `getDoOutput()`, `java.lang.IllegalAccessError`, `setDoInput()`.

setIfModifiedSince()

PURPOSE Sets the modification time that forces refetching of the document.

SYNTAX `public void setIfModifiedSince(long time)`

DESCRIPTION This method is used to set the If-Modified-Since time of this URL connection to `time`. This time is used to set the `If-Modified-Since` request header field to indicate to the server to not send the document unless it has been modified since `time`. It can be invoked after the URL connection has been created but before the connection has been established (i.e., before `connect()` has been invoked on it).

PARAMETERS

`time` The If-Modified-Since time for this URL connection in the number of milliseconds since epoch.

EXCEPTIONS

`IllegalAccessError`

If this method is called after the connection has already been established.

SEE ALSO `getIfModifiedSince()`, `ifModifiedSince`, `java.lang.IllegalAccessError`.

setRequestProperty()

PURPOSE Sets the value of a request header field for this URL connection.

SYNTAX `public void setRequestProperty(String field, String value)`

DESCRIPTION This method sets the value of the request header field `field` to `value`. Table 44 contains examples of request header fields. The value of `field` can be changed prior to the connection's being established (before `connect()` is called). This method affects only the current URL connection; it cannot be called after the connection has already been established.

The default implementation of this method does nothing. It must be overridden by protocol implementations that support the setting of header fields in the request.

PARAMETERS

`field` The non-`null` name of the request header field.

`value` The non-`null` value of the request header field.

EXCEPTIONS

`IllegalAccessError`

If this method is called after the connection has already been established.

SEE ALSO `getDefaultRequestProperty()`, `setDefaultRequestProperty()`, `getRequestProperty()`.

setUseCaches()

PURPOSE Sets the cache usage flag of this URL connection.

SYNTAX `public void setUseCaches(boolean useCaches)`

DESCRIPTION This method is used to indicate whether this URL connection may use caches. It can be invoked after the URL connection has been created but before the connection has been established (i.e., before `connect()` has been invoked on it).

PARAMETERS

`useCaches` A `boolean` flag indicating whether to use caches. `true` means use caches; `false` means do not use caches.

EXCEPTIONS

`IllegalAccessError`

If this method is called after the connection has already been established.

SEE ALSO `getDefaultUseCaches()`, `getUseCaches()`, `java.lang.IllegalAccessError`, `setDefaultUseCaches()`, `useCaches`.

toString()

PURPOSE Generates the string representation of this object.

SYNTAX `public String toString()`

DESCRIPTION This method returns the string representation of this URL connection. The string representation of a URL connection consists of the name of the `URLConnection` class (usually a subclass specific for a particular protocol) and the URL of the connection.

RETURNS The non-`null` string representation of this URL connection.

OVERRIDES `java.lang.Object.toString()`.

url

PURPOSE The URL of this URL connection.

SYNTAX `protected URL url`

DESCRIPTION This field is used to hold the URL of this URL connection. It is set initially by the `URLConnection` constructor and typically remains unchanged for the duration of the connection.

SEE ALSO `getURL()`, `URLConnection()`.

URLConnection()

PURPOSE Constructs a URL connection.

SYNTAX `protected URLConnection (URL url)`

DESCRIPTION This constructor creates a `URLConnection` object for the URL `url`. The constructor is protected and is typically called by the URL stream handler for a particular protocol (from its `openConnection()` method). After a `URLConnection` has been created, a connection can be made to the destination of `url` by invoking `connect()`.

PARAMETERS

`url` The URL for which to create the connection.

SEE ALSO `connect()`, `URLStreamHandler.openConnection()`.

EXAMPLE See the class examples for `HttpURLConnection` and `URLStreamHandler`.

useCaches

PURPOSE Indicates whether this URL connection allows the use of caches.

SYNTAX `protected boolean useCaches`

DESCRIPTION This field records whether this URL connection allows the use of caches. If `useCaches` is `true`, caching is allowed; if `false`, caches are bypassed. The default value for `useCaches` is `true` unless the default has been modified earlier in the program via `setDefaultUseCaches()`. `getDefaultUseCaches()` can be used to examine the default setting of `useCaches`.

This field should be accessed and manipulated through the `getUseCaches()` and `setUseCaches()` methods, respectively.

SEE ALSO `getDefaultUseCaches()`, `getUseCaches()`, `setDefaultUseCaches()`, `setUseCaches()`.

URLEncoder

java.lang.Object
 └ URLEncoder

Syntax

`public class URLEncoder`

Description

The `URLEncoder` class provides a method for encoding a string in the format required by the `application/x-www-form-urlencoded` MIME content type.

URL Character Encoding

A URL consists of a sequence of (8-bit) characters that must meet certain requirements in terms of their "displayability" in different media (newspaper, electronic protocols, and so on). There is an encoding scheme defined for URLs to meet these requirements. Basically, all characters in a URL are drawn from a restricted subset of the printable U. S.-ASCII character set. Nonprintable characters, plus those that are printable but considered unsafe or reserved, must be encoded by a triplet consisting of a percent character (%) followed by two hexadecimal digit characters representing the hexadecimal ISO-Latin-1 code of the character.

For example, the hash character (#) is an unsafe character. Instead of the # character appearing as is in a URL, it must be encoded as the triplet `%23` (23 is the character code for #).

Here are the characters that may appear unencoded in a URL:

alphanumeric characters and `$ - _ . + ! , * ()` '

These characters also can be encoded, in which case, they have the same meaning as when unencoded. For example, `B` and `%42` both mean `B`.

Following are the unsafe characters:

`{ } | \ ^ ~ [ ]` ' space `< >` " `# %`

These must be encoded when they appear in a URL.

A reserved character that appears unencoded in a URL has the special meaning for which it was reserved. When encoded, that character is "escaped" and does not hold the special meaning. Following are the reserved characters:

`; / ? : @ = &`

The nonprintable characters have the character codes `80-ff`, `00-1f`, and `7f`. These must be encoded when they appear in a URL. For example, a string

```
c=us/o=widget/ou=engineering
```

will appear encoded in a URL as

```
c%3dus%2fo%3dwidget%2fou%3dengineering
```

The application/x-www-form-urlencoded MIME Content Type

When the content type of a message is `application/x-www-form-urlencoded`, the content is a string of URL-encoded `FORM` name/value arguments used in the HTTP protocol. In this encoding, name/value pairs are listed in the string, with each pair separated by an ampersand (&) character. Each name/value pair has the format *name=value*. Names and values must follow the URL character encoding scheme described earlier in this section, except that blank characters are replaced by the plus (+) character.

The following is an example of a string in `x-www-form-urlencoded` format:

```
country=Canada&province=Manitoba
```

This string consists of two name/value pairs: `country=Canada` and `province=Manitoba`.

The following is another example of a string in this format:

```
country=United+States&state=Ohio
```

This string consists of two name/value pairs: `country=United States` and `state=Ohio`. The blank character in "`United States`" has been replaced with a +.

Usage

The `URLEncoder` class provides a method that encodes a string in `x-www-form-urlencoded` format. The string is expected to be the name or value in the name/value of a `FORM` argument. For example, `United States` gets encoded as `United+States`, but `a=b` gets encoded as `a%3db`. Each name and each value should be encoded separately. See Figure 109.

The implementation of this method is conservative in that even some allowable characters are encoded with the % triplet.

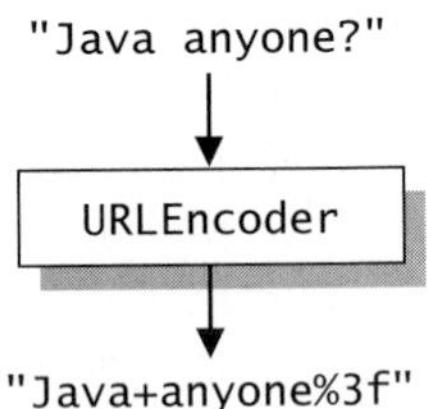

FIGURE 109: `URLEncoder`.

MEMBER SUMMARY	
Encode Method	
`encode()`	Encodes a string in `x-www-form-urlencoded` format.

See Also

`URL`, `URLConnection`.

encode()

PURPOSE Encodes a string in `x-www-form-urlencoded` format.

SYNTAX `public static String encode(String str)`

DESCRIPTION This method encodes the string `str` as if it were a name or value expected by the `x-www-form-urlencoded` format. Alphanumeric characters and any of the characters `-` `_` `.` and `*` appear as is, but all other characters are encoded using the % hexadecimal code triplet.

PARAMETERS

`str` The non-`null` string to be encoded.

RETURNS The non-`null` string encoded in `x-www-form-urlencoded` format.

EXAMPLE

```
import java.net.URLEncoder;

class Main {
    public static void main(String[] args) {
        String x500name = new String("c=us/o=sun/ou=eng");

        String u1 = URLEncoder.encode(x500name);
        System.out.println(u1);        // "c%3dus%2fo%3dsun%2fou%3deng"

        String u2 = URLEncoder.encode("Open Sesame");
        System.out.println(u2);        // "Open+Sesame"

    }
}
```

java.net
URLStreamHandler

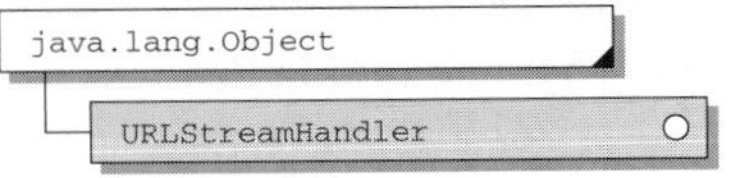

A B C D E F G H I J K L M N O P Q R S T U V W X Y Z

Syntax

```
public abstract class URLStreamHandler
```

Description

Associated with each URL is a *URL stream* (or *protocol*) *handler*. A URL stream handler is responsible for implementing the protocol associated with the URL. For example, there is a HTTP stream handler for URLs with the `http` protocol identifier.

The Java runtime itself provides a handful of stream handlers (e.g., HTTP and FTP) and allows new stream handlers to be added dynamically.

Usage

A URL stream handler is created indirectly each time the program creates an instance of the `URL` class. Only the `URL` class implementation invokes methods on the `URLStreamHandler` class; these methods are not invoked directly by the program.

A URL stream handler implements a particular protocol and provides methods to open a connection to the service identified in the URL using that protocol. All subclasses of `URLStreamHandler` must provide an implementation for `openConnection()`, which returns a protocol-specific `URLConnection` object for communicating with the service identified in the URL.

URL Stream Handler Factory

A *URL stream handler factory* is responsible for creating an instance of `URLStreamHandler` when it is supplied with a protocol identifier. The factory controls which implementations are selected for the protocol identifiers, as well as which protocols are supported.

The program uses `URL.setURLStreamHandlerFactory()` to select the stream handler factory to use (if permitted to do so by the security manager). This method sets the stream handler factory for the program. Once set, the factory cannot be replaced.

Default Policy for Creating Stream Handlers

If no stream handler factory has been installed, the system searches for a class that has the class name

packagePrefix "." *protocol* "." Handler

packagePrefix is obtained from the system property `java.protocol.handler.pkgs`, which is a `|`-separated list of package prefixes. *protocol* is the protocol identifier (e.g., `http` or `ftp`). If the class is not found using these package prefixes, the package prefix `sun.net.www.protocol` is tried. For example, if the `java.protocol.handler.pkgs` system property contains "com.widget|com.wiz" and the protocol identifier is `http`, the system will attempt to load each of the following classes in turn until one is successfully instantiated:

```
com.widget.http.Handler
com.wiz.http.Handler
sun.net.www.protocol.http.Handler
```

If no class can be instantiated in this way, `MalformedURLException` is thrown.

MEMBER SUMMARY	
Communications Method (Abstract)	
`openConnection()`	Creates a connection to the service identified in a URL.
URL Methods	
`parseURL()`	Parses a string URL into a URL object using the syntax of this protocol.
`setURL()`	Sets the components of a URL using the given arguments.
`toExternalForm()`	Generates the string representation of a URL using the syntax of this protocol.

See Also

`URL`, `URLConnection`, `URLStreamHandlerFactory`.

Example

This example shows an implementation of a `URLStreamHandler` that supports URL connections that use `dateURLConnection`. See related examples at `URL.setURLStreamHandlerFactory()`, `URLConnection`, and `URLStreamHandlerFactory`.

```
import java.net.*;
import java.io.IOException;

// given host name, communicates with host via the daytime port

public class TestdateHandler extends URLStreamHandler {
    protected URLConnection openConnection(URL u) throws IOException {
        return new DateURLConnection(u);
    }
}
```

openConnection()

PURPOSE Creates a connection to the service identified in a URL.

SYNTAX
```
abstract protected URLConnection openConnection(URL url) throws
    IOException
```

DESCRIPTION This method creates a connection to the service identified in the URL `url`. The service is typically identified by the host name and port number specified in the URL. The implementation of this method is protocol-specific and must be provided by a subclass of `URLStreamHandler`. The connection created also is protocol-specific. Subsequent communication over this connection is achieved using the methods defined in the abstract class `URLConnection`.

This method is invoked by `URL.openConnection()`. When providing an implementation for this method, you should declare the method `public` so that it can be accessed by the `URL` class.

PARAMETERS
`url` The non-`null` URL for which to create a connection.

RETURNS A non-`null` protocol-specific connection to the service identified by the URL.

EXCEPTIONS
`IOException`
If an IO error occurred while attempting to create the connection.

SEE ALSO `URL`, `URLConnection`.

EXAMPLE See the class example.

parseURL()

PURPOSE Parses a URL string into a `URL` object using the syntax of this protocol.

SYNTAX
```
protected void parseURL(URL url, String spec, int startIndex, int
    endIndex)
```

DESCRIPTION This method parses the URL string `spec` into a `URL` object `url` using the syntax of this protocol. Any existing components in `url` not overridden by new components in `spec` remain unchanged. This allows a context to be specified in `url` prior to the calling of `parseURL()`. `startIndex` and `endIndex` specify the range of characters in `spec` that should be parsed. This substring should not include the protocol. For example, an acceptable string would be "//java.sun.com/products/jndi/".

This method's default implementation uses the URL syntax for HTTP URLs. Most other URL protocol families also follow this syntax. If this protocol has a different syntax, then its protocol handler must override this method. This method is called by the `URL` constructor.

PARAMETERS

`endIndex`	The ending index of `spec` at which to stop parsing, exclusive. `0` ≤ `endIndex` ≤ `spec.length()`.
`startIndex`	The beginning index of `spec` at which to start parsing, inclusive. `0` ≤ `startIndex` < `spec.length()`.
`spec`	The non-`null` URL string to parse.
`url`	The non-`null` `URL` object to update.

SEE ALSO `toExternalForm()`, `URL()`.

setURL()

PURPOSE Sets the components of a URL using the given arguments.

SYNTAX
```
protected void setURL(URL url, String protocol, String host, int
   port, String file, String ref)
```

DESCRIPTION This method sets the components of the URL `url` using the given arguments `protocol`, `host`, `port`, `file`, and `ref`.

PARAMETERS

`file`	The non-`null` file pathname of the URL.
`host`	The non-`null` host name of the URL.
`port`	The port of the URL. `-1` means to use the protocol's default port.
`protocol`	The non-`null` string containing the protocol identifier.
`ref`	The possibly `null` reference (fragment identifier) of the URL.
`url`	The non-`null` URL to update.

SEE ALSO `URL()`, `URL.set()`.

toExternalForm()

PURPOSE Generates the string representation of a URL using the syntax of this protocol.

SYNTAX
```
protected String toExternalForm(URL url)
```

DESCRIPTION This method generates the string representation of a URL using the syntax of this protocol. By default, the syntax used is that of HTTP URLs. This consists of the protocol name, host name, port number (if explicitly specified; used instead of the protocol's default port number), the file pathname, and, if present, the fragment identifier (reference). Appropriate separators (//, #, and so on) are used to separate these components according to the HTTP syntax.

If this protocol's syntax differs from the HTTP URL syntax, then the protocol handler should override this method. This method is called by `URL.toExternalForm()` (and consequently `URL.toString()`). The result of this method should be such that it can be used to construct an instance of `URL` that is equal to `url`, that it can be parsed using `parseURL()`, and whose URL stream handler is `this`.

PARAMETERS

`url` The non-`null` URL for which to generate the string representation.

RETURNS The non-`null` string representation of the (fully qualified) URL `url`.

SEE ALSO `parseURL()`, `URL.toExternalForm()`.

URLStreamHandlerFactory

URLStreamHandlerFactory

Syntax

```
public interface URLStreamHandlerFactory
```

Description

A *URL stream handler factory* is responsible for creating *URL stream handlers*, which are objects that implement protocols associated with URLs. Each time an instance of `URL` is created, a URL stream handler is created for it. For example, when you create a `URL` instance for the URL string `http://java.sun.com`, a URL stream handler for the protocol with identifier "http" is created.

Usage

An application such as a Web browser installs a URL stream handler factory in order to control the types of URLs and protocols supported, as well as to control the implementations of the protocols. It does this by creating an object that implements the `URLStreamHandlerFactory` interface and installing it, as follows:

```
URLStreamHandlerFactory factory = new SampleFactory();
URL.setURLStreamHandlerFactory(factory);
```

Subsequent invocations of the `URL` constructor will automatically create URL stream handlers using this factory.

URL Stream (Protocol) Handlers

Associated with each URL is a *URL stream* (or *protocol*) *handler*. A URL stream handler is responsible for implementing the protocol associated with the URL. For example, there is a HTTP stream handler for URLs with the `http` protocol identifier.

The Java runtime itself provides a handful of stream handlers (e.g., HTTP and FTP) and allows new stream handlers to be added dynamically.

URL Stream Handler Factory

A *URL stream handler factory* is responsible for creating an instance of `URLStreamHandler` when supplied with a protocol identifier. The factory controls which implementations are selected for the protocol identifiers, as well as which protocols are supported.

The program uses `URL.setURLStreamHandlerFactory()` to select the stream handler factory that is to be used (if permitted to do so by the security manager). This method sets the stream handler factory for the program. Once set, the factory cannot be replaced.

If no URL stream handler factory has been installed, the program uses the default policy for locating URL stream handlers described in the `URL` class description.

MEMBER SUMMARY	
Handler Creation Method	
`createURLStreamHandler()`	Creates a URL stream handler for a protocol.

Example

This example shows a `URLStreamHandlerFactory` that uses its own algorithm for constructing the class name of the handler requested. Handlers that have been previously located are cached in a hash table.

See related examples at `URL.setURLStreamHandlerFactory()`, `URLConnection`, and `URLStreamHandler`.

```
import java.net.*;
import java.util.Hashtable;

public class TestFactory implements URLStreamHandlerFactory {
    static Hashtable handlers = new Hashtable();

    public URLStreamHandler createURLStreamHandler(String protocol) {
        // try cached handlers first
        URLStreamHandler handler = (URLStreamHandler)handlers.get(protocol);
        if (handler == null) {
            String className = "Test" + protocol + "Handler";
            try {
                handler = (URLStreamHandler)Class.
                    forName(className).newInstance();
            } catch (ClassNotFoundException e) {
                handler = null;                  // not found
            } catch (Exception e) {
                // all other exceptions, print out problem
                e.printStackTrace();
                handler = null;
            }

            if (handler != null)
                handlers.put(protocol, handler); // put into cache
        }
        return (handler);
    }
}
```

createURLStreamHandler()

PURPOSE Creates a URL stream handler for a protocol.

SYNTAX `URLStreamHandler createURLStreamHandler(String protocol)`

DESCRIPTION This method creates a `URLStreamHandler` instance for the protocol identifier `protocol`. If a URL stream handler cannot be created, returns `null`.

PARAMETERS

`protocol` The non-`null` string containing the protocol identifier (e.g., "http", "telnet", or "ftp"). The identifier is usually lowercase.

RETURNS A possibly `null` stream handler for `protocol`.

SEE ALSO `URL`, `URLStreamHandler`.

EXAMPLE See the class example.

UTFDataFormatException

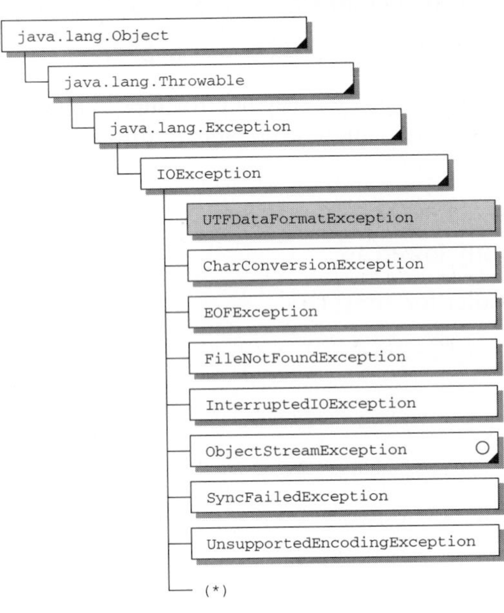

(*) 7 classes from other packages not shown.

A B C D E F G H I J K L M N O P Q R S T U V W X Y Z

Syntax

```
public class UTFDataFormatException extends IOException
```

Description

UTF stands for *Unicode Transfer Format*. It is an encoding scheme for Unicode characters. When writing a string to a data stream, a program uses `DataOutputStream.writeUTF()`. It reads it back using `DataInputStream.readUTF()`. If `DataInputStream.readUTF()` encounters a malformed UTF string, it throws a `UTFDataFormatException`.

See *The Java Language Specification, First Edition*, Sections 22.1.15 and 22.2.14, for more details on UTF.

A method that throws `UTFDataFormatException` must declare it or any of its superclasses in the method's `throws` clause.

MEMBER SUMMARY	
Constructor	
`UTFDataFormatException()`	Constructs a `UTFDataFormatException` instance.

See Also

DataInputStream.readUTF(), DataOutputStream.writeUTF(), IOException, RandomAccessFile.readUTF(), RandomAccessFile.writeUTF().

Example

This example throws a UTFDataFormatException when it attempts to read a UTF string (that has been purposely mangled).

```
import java.io.*;

class Main {
    public static void main(String[] args) {
        if (args.length != 1) {
            System.err.println(
                "Usage: java Main <temp output file>");
            System.exit(-1);
        }
        try {
            // write it out
            FileOutputStream fout = new FileOutputStream(args[0]);
            DataOutputStream out = new DataOutputStream(fout);
            String str = "This is a test\n";
            out.writeDouble(10.02); // introduce bogus value
            out.writeUTF(str);
            out.close();

            // read it back
            FileInputStream fin = new FileInputStream(args[0]);
            DataInputStream in = new DataInputStream(fin);

            System.out.println(in.readUTF());
        } catch (UTFDataFormatException e) {
            System.err.println("UTF error");
            e.printStackTrace();
        } catch (IOException e) {
            e.printStackTrace();
        }
    }
}
```


UTFDataFormatException()

PURPOSE — Constructs a UTFDataFormatException instance.

SYNTAX
```
public UTFDataFormatException()
public UTFDataFormatException(String msg)
```

DESCRIPTION — The two forms of this constructor construct an instance of UTFDataFormatException. An optional string msg can be supplied that describes this particular instance of the exception. If msg is not supplied, it defaults to null.

PARAMETERS

msg — A possibly null string that gives details about this exception.

SEE ALSO — java.lang.Throwable.getMessage().

java.util
Vector

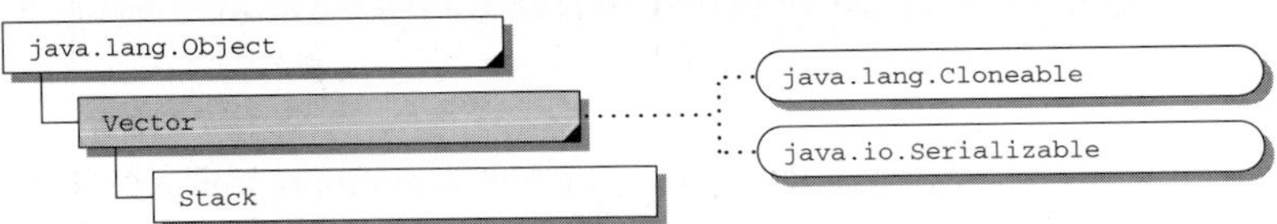

A
B
C
D
E
F
G
H
I
J
K
L
M
N
O
P
Q
R
S
T
U
V
W
X
Y
Z

Syntax

```
public class Vector implements Cloneable, Serializable
```

Description

The `Vector` class represents an expansible array consisting of an array of objects called *elements*. You manipulate a vector much like an array. They differ only in that you can add objects to a vector and the vector will grow automatically to accommodate the new objects. You can also shrink a vector, whereas you cannot shrink an array. Elements can be `null`, but the search methods in `Vector` class do not accept `null` as an argument.[1]

Vector Capacity

A *capacity* is the amount of storage that has been allocated for a vector. It differs from the *size* of a vector, which is the actual number of elements in the vector. If the number of elements added to a vector exceeds the vector's capacity, its capacity will be automatically increased to accommodate the additional elements. By default, the capacity is doubled when it needs to be increased. When you create the vector, you can set the initial capacity as well as the amount by which the capacity increases. The capacity can be changed any time after creation by calling `ensureCapacity()`.

MEMBER SUMMARY	
Constructor	
`Vector()`	Constructs an empty `Vector` instance.
Access Methods	
`contains()`	Determines whether an object is in this vector.
`copyInto()`	Copies the references of the elements of this vector into an array.
`elementAt()`	Retrieves the element at the specified index in this vector.
`elements()`	Generates a list of the elements in this vector.
`firstElement()`	Retrieves the first element in this vector.
`indexOf()`	Searches for an object in this vector.

1. JDK 1.2's `Vector` allows searching for `null` elements.

MEMBER SUMMARY	
`isEmpty()`	Determines whether this vector is empty.
`lastElement()`	Retrieves the last element in this vector.
`lastIndexOf()`	Searches for an object starting from the end of this vector.
`size()`	Determines the number of elements in this vector.
Update Methods	
`addElement()`	Adds an element to the end of this vector.
`insertElementAt()`	Inserts an element in this vector.
`removeAllElements()`	Removes all elements from this vector.
`removeElement()`	Removes an element from this vector.
`removeElementAt()`	Removes the element at the specified index from this vector.
`setElementAt()`	Replaces the element at the specified index in this vector.
`setSize()`	Truncates or expands this vector.
Vector Capacity Methods	
`capacity()`	Determines the current capacity of this vector.
`ensureCapacity()`	Ensures that this vector has at least the specified capacity.
`trimToSize()`	Trims this vector's capacity to be the same as the vector's size.
Object Methods	
`clone()`	Creates a clone of this vector.
`toString()`	Generates the string representation for this vector.
Protected Fields	
`capacityIncrement`	The size of the increment to use when growing the capacity of this vector.
`elementCount`	The number of elements in `elementData`.
`elementData`	The buffer in which elements of this vector are stored.

See Also

`java.io.Serializable`, `StringBuffer`.

Example

`Vector` is useful when you do not know ahead of time the number of elements in an object. This example shows how `Vector` can be used to read in a file of lines and write out the lines in reverse order.

```
import java.util.Vector;
import java.util.Enumeration;
import java.io.*;

class Main {
```

```
    // reads in a file of lines and writes the lines out in reverse order
    public static void main (String[] args) {
        if (args.length != 2) {
            System.err.println("Usage: Main inputfile outputfile");
            System.exit(1);
        }
        try {
            BufferedReader in = new BufferedReader(new FileReader(args[0]));
            Vector buf = new Vector(100);
            String str;
            while ((str = in.readLine()) != null)
                buf.addElement(str);
            in.close();

            BufferedWriter out = new BufferedWriter(new FileWriter(args[1]));
            for (int i = buf.size()-1; i >=0; i--) {
                str = (String)buf.elementAt(i);
                out.write(str, 0, str.length());
                out.write('\n');
            }
            out.close();
        } catch (IOException e) {
            e.printStackTrace();
        }
    }
    }
```

addElement()

PURPOSE Adds an element to the end of this vector.

SYNTAX `public final synchronized void addElement(Object obj)`

DESCRIPTION This method adds the element `obj` to the end of this vector. The capacity of this vector is automatically increased if necessary to accommodate the new element. If `obj` is `null`, it cannot later be searched by using `contains()`, `indexOf()`, or `lastIndexOf()` and it cannot be removed by using `removeElement()`

PARAMETERS
`obj` The possibly `null` element to add.

SEE ALSO `ensureCapacity()`.

EXAMPLE See the class example, `copy()`, and `toString()`.

capacity()

PURPOSE Determines the current capacity of this vector.

SYNTAX `public final int capacity()`

DESCRIPTION The capacity of a vector indicates how much space has been allocated for it. See the class description for details.

RETURNS The current capacity of this vector.

SEE ALSO `ensureCapacity()`, `size()`, `Vector()`.

EXAMPLE This example ensures that `capacity()` can hold `len` elements before they are added.

```
if (v.capacity() - v.size() < len )
    v.ensureCapacity(len+v.size());
for (int i = 0; i < len; i++)
    v.addElement(obj[i]);
```

capacityIncrement

PURPOSE The size of the increment to use when growing the capacity of this vector.

SYNTAX `protected int capacityIncrement`

DESCRIPTION This field is set when this vector is first created. Its default value is `0`, which means to double the capacity each time this vector is grown. It is an argument to its constructor.

SEE ALSO `capacity()`, `ensureCapacity()`, `Vector()`.

EXAMPLE The following is an excerpt from the JDK. It illustrates the use of the protected variables `capacityIncrement`, `elementCount`, and `elementData`.

```
public final synchronized void ensureCapacity(int minCapacity) {
    int oldCapacity = elementData.length;
    if (minCapacity > oldCapacity) {
        Object oldData[] = elementData;
        int newCapacity = (capacityIncrement > 0) ?
            (oldCapacity + capacityIncrement) : (oldCapacity * 2);
        if (newCapacity < minCapacity) {
            newCapacity = minCapacity;
        }
        elementData = new Object[newCapacity];
        System.arraycopy(oldData, 0, elementData, 0, elementCount);
    }
}
```

clone()

PURPOSE Creates a clone of this vector.

SYNTAX `public synchronized Object clone()`

DESCRIPTION This method creates a clone of this vector. The size, capacity, and capacity increment of the new vector are the same as those of the original. The references to the objects in this vector are copied to the new vector, but the objects themselves are not cloned. Adding and deleting elements from this vector does not affect the new vector, and vice versa.

RETURNS A new non-`null` copy of this vector.

OVERRIDES `java.lang.Object.clone()`.

SEE ALSO `java.lang.Cloneable`.

EXAMPLE See `setSize()`.

contains()

PURPOSE Determines whether an object is in this vector.

SYNTAX `public final boolean contains(Object obj)`

DESCRIPTION This method searches this vector for the object `obj`. It returns `true` if `obj` is an element in this vector; it returns `false` otherwise. `obj.equals()` is used when comparing `obj` with the elements for equality.

PARAMETERS
`obj` The non-`null` object for which to search.

RETURNS `true` if `obj` is in this vector; `false` otherwise.

SEE ALSO `indexOf()`, `lastIndexOf()`, `java.lang.Object.equals()`.

EXAMPLE See `copyInto()`.

copyInto()

PURPOSE Copies the reference of the elements of this vector into an array.

SYNTAX `public final synchronized void copyInto(Object[] objArray)`

DESCRIPTION This method copies the reference of the elements of this vector into the array `objArray`. The elements themselves are not copied.

PARAMETERS

objArray — The non-null array into which to copy.

SEE ALSO — clone().

EXAMPLE — This example takes an array of strings, adds and removes strings as requested, and returns an updated string array. It first creates a Vector of the original strings and then uses the Vector operations to add and remove items. After the modifications have been made, it uses copyInto() to get the data back into an array of string form.

```
public static String[] filter(String[] master,
                              String[] additions,
                              String[] deletions) {
    // make rough estimate of size needed
    Vector vec =
        new Vector(master.length+additions.length-deletions.length);
    for (int i = 0; i < master.length; i++)
        vec.addElement(master[i]);

    for (int i = 0; i < deletions.length; i ++)
        vec.removeElement(deletions[i]);

    for (int i = 0; i < additions.length; i++)
        if (!vec.contains(additions[i]))
            vec.addElement(additions[i]);

    String[] newmaster = new String[vec.size()];
    vec.copyInto((Object[])newmaster);
    return (newmaster);
}
```

elementAt()

PURPOSE — Retrieves the element at the specified index in this vector.

SYNTAX — `public final synchronized Object elementAt(int idx)`

PARAMETERS

idx — The 0-based index of the element to retrieve. 0 ≤ idx < size().

RETURNS — The element at the index idx from this vector. null if the element happens to be null.

EXCEPTIONS

ArrayIndexOutOfBoundsException
If idx < 0 or idx ≥ size().

SEE ALSO — element(), size().

EXAMPLE This example uses `elementAt()` to enumerate the objects in a vector for printing. Also see the class example and `insertElementAt()`.

```
public static void printVec(String msg, Vector vec) {
    if (msg != null)
        System.out.println(msg);
    if (vec.isEmpty())
        System.out.println("Empty vector");
    else
        for (int i=0; i < vec.size(); i++)
            System.out.println(vec.elementAt(i));
}
```

elementCount

PURPOSE The number of elements in `elementData`.

SYNTAX `protected int elementCount`

DESCRIPTION This field keeps track of the number of elements in `elementData`. It is decremented when an element is removed and incremented when an element is added. This is the value returned by `size()`.

SEE ALSO `addElement()`, `elementData`, `insertElementAt()`, `removeElement()`, `removeAllElements()`, `size()`.

EXAMPLE See `capacityIncrement`.

elementData

PURPOSE The buffer in which elements of this vector are stored.

SYNTAX `protected Object[] elementData`

DESCRIPTION This field is the array that contains the elements of this vector. It is grown automatically when it becomes full or can be grown manually by using `ensureCapacity()`.

SEE ALSO `capacity()`, `capacityIncrement`, `ensureCapacity()`.

EXAMPLE See `capacityIncrement`.

elements()

PURPOSE Generates a list of the elements in this vector.

SYNTAX `public final synchronized Enumeration elements()`

DESCRIPTION This method generates a list of all elements in this vector and returns the list as an `Enumeration`. The methods in the `Enumeration` class can subsequently be used to retrieve objects from this list one at a time. Any changes to this vector may be visible in this enumeration, depending on where the changes were made and how far the enumeration has proceeded.

This is one way of enumerating the elements in a vector. The other way is to use `elementAt()` in a `for` loop.

RETURNS A non-`null` enumeration of the elements in this vector.

SEE ALSO `elementAt()`, `Enumeration`.

EXAMPLE This example shows how to use `Enumeration` to print the elements of a vector. See the example for `elementAt()` for another way of doing the same thing.

```
public static void printVec2(String msg, Vector vec) {
    if (msg != null)
        System.out.println(msg);
    if (vec.isEmpty())
        System.out.println("Empty vector");
    else {
        Enumeration e = vec.elements();
        while (e.hasMoreElements())
             System.out.println("\t" + e.nextElement());
    }
}
```

ensureCapacity()

PURPOSE Ensures that this vector has at least the specified capacity.

SYNTAX `public final synchronized void ensureCapacity(int minCap)`

DESCRIPTION If you know approximately the expected size of the final vector, you should set the capacity of this vector to the expected size to minimize the number of times that the capacity must be increased. You can set the capacity either at the time this vector is created or at any time after creation by calling `ensureCapacity()`. `ensureCapacity()` ensures that the capacity of this vector is at least `minCap`. If the current capacity is less than `minCap`, it is increased to `minCap`. If the current capacity is already at or greater than `minCap`, the capacity is left unchanged.

PARAMETERS

`minCap` The minimum capacity this vector should have.

SEE ALSO `capacity()`.

EXAMPLE See `capacity()`.

firstElement()

PURPOSE Retrieves the first element of this vector.

SYNTAX `public final synchronized Object firstElement()`

RETURNS The first element in this vector; `null` if the first element happens to be `null`.

EXCEPTIONS

`NoSuchElementException`
If this vector is empty.

SEE ALSO `elementAt()`, `isEmpty()`, `lastElement()`.

EXAMPLE This example swaps the first element of a vector with its last element.

```
public static void swapFirstLast(Vector vec) {
    try {
        Object fst = vec.firstElement();
        Object lst = vec.lastElement();
        vec.setElementAt(lst, 0);
        vec.setElementAt(fst, vec.size()-1);
    } catch (NoSuchElementException e) {
        System.out.println(e);
    }
}
```

indexOf()

PURPOSE Searches for an object in this vector.

SYNTAX `public final int indexOf(Object obj)`
`public final synchronized int indexOf(Object obj, int idx)`

DESCRIPTION This method searches for the object `obj` in this vector. If `idx` is specified, the search begins at the index `idx` toward the end of this vector. If `idx` is not specified, the search begins at index `0`. A comparison of `obj` with the elements in this vector uses `Object.equals()` to test for equality.

PARAMETERS

`idx` The index in this vector at which to start the search. `idx` ≥ `0`.

`obj` The non-`null` object for which to search.

RETURNS The index of `obj` in this vector; `-1` if `obj` is not in this vector in the range specified.

SEE ALSO `contains()`, `lastIndexOf()`, `java.lang.Object.equals()`.

EXAMPLE This example replaces the first occurrence of an object `target` in a vector `vec` with another object `sub`.

```
public static boolean replaceFirst(Vector vec, Object target, Object sub) {
    int loc = vec.indexOf(target);
    if (loc >= 0) {
        vec.setElementAt(sub, loc);
        return (true);
    }
    return (false);
}
```

A B C D E F G H I J K L M N O P Q R S T U V W X Y Z

insertElementAt()

PURPOSE Inserts an element in this vector.

SYNTAX `public final synchronized void insertElementAt(Object obj, int idx)`

DESCRIPTION This method inserts object `obj` at index `idx` in this vector. The element that used to be at `idx` and all elements with an index greater than `idx` are shifted up by one index position (toward the end of this vector). The size of this vector is increased by 1. When `idx` is equal to `size()`, this method is the same as `addElement()`. If `obj` is `null`, it cannot later be searched by using `contains()`, `indexOf()`, or `lastIndexOf()` and it cannot be removed by using `removeElement()`.

PARAMETERS

`idx` The `0`-based index in this vector at which to insert `obj`. 0 ≤ `idx` ≤ `size()`.

`obj` The possibly `null` object to insert.

EXCEPTIONS

`ArrayIndexOutOfBoundsException`

If `idx` < `0` or `idx` > `size()`.

SEE ALSO `addElement()`, `size()`.

EXAMPLE This example replaces the first occurrence of the object `obj` in the vector `vec` with all of the elements from the vector `replacement`.

```
public static boolean replaceElementWithVec(Vector vec, Object obj,
                                            Vector replacement)
{
    int ind = vec.indexOf(obj);
    if (ind < 0)
        return (false);

    // Remove existing element and insert vector
    vec.removeElementAt(ind);
    for(int i = 0; i < replacement.size(); i++)
        vec.insertElementAt(replacement.elementAt(i), ind++);
    return (true);
}
```

isEmpty()

PURPOSE Determines whether this vector is empty.

SYNTAX `public final boolean isEmpty()`

RETURNS `true` if this vector is empty; `false` otherwise.

SEE ALSO `size()`.

EXAMPLE See `elementAt()` and `elements()`.

lastElement()

PURPOSE Retrieves the last element in this vector.

SYNTAX `public final synchronized Object lastElement()`

RETURNS The last element in this vector; `null` if the last element happens to be `null`.

EXCEPTIONS

`NoSuchElementException`
If this vector is empty.

SEE ALSO `elementAt()`, `firstElement()`, `size()`.

EXAMPLE See `firstElement()`.

lastIndexOf()

PURPOSE Searches for an object starting from the end of this vector.

SYNTAX

```
public final int lastIndexOf(Object obj)
public final synchronized int lastIndexOf(Object obj, int idx)
```

DESCRIPTION This method searches for the object `obj` in this vector. If `idx` is specified, the search begins at the index `idx` toward the start of this vector. If `idx` is not specified, the search begins at index `size()-1`. A comparison of `obj` with the elements in this vector uses `Object.equals()` to test for equality.

PARAMETERS

`idx` The `0`-based index in this vector at which to start the backward search. `idx` < `size()`.

`obj` The non-`null` object for which to search.

RETURNS The index of `obj` in this vector; `-1` if `obj` is not in this vector in the search range specified.

SEE ALSO `contains()`, `indexOf()`, `java.lang.Object.equals()`.

EXAMPLE This method replaces the last occurrence of the object `target` in the vector `vec` with another object `sub`.

```
public static boolean replaceLast(Vector vec, Object target, Object sub) {
    int loc = vec.lastIndexOf(target);
    if (loc >= 0) {
        vec.setElementAt(sub, loc);
        return (true);
    }
    return (false);
}
```

removeAllElements()

PURPOSE Removes all elements from this vector.

SYNTAX `public final synchronized void removeAllElements()`

DESCRIPTION This method removes all elements from this vector and leaves the vector empty. The size of the vector becomes `0`, but the capacity of this vector remains unchanged.

SEE ALSO `capacity()`, `isEmpty()`, `size()`.

EXAMPLE

```
public static void clearVec(Vector vec) {
    vec.removeAllElements();        // remove all elements
    vec.trimToSize();               // reclaim space
}
```

removeElement()

PURPOSE Removes an element from this vector.

SYNTAX `public final synchronized boolean removeElement(Object obj)`

DESCRIPTION This method removes the element `obj` from this vector. If `obj` is not found in this vector, this method returns `false`; otherwise, it returns `true`. A comparison of `obj` with the elements in this vector uses `Object.equals()` to test for equality. If `obj` occurs more than once, only the first occurrence (from the beginning of the vector) is removed.

When `obj` is removed, all elements located at an index greater than where `obj` was are shifted down (toward the head of this vector). The size of this vector is decremented by 1.

PARAMETERS

`obj` The non-`null` object to remove.

RETURNS `true` if `obj` is removed; `false` if `obj` is not in this vector.

SEE ALSO `java.lang.Object.equals()`, `removeAllElements()`, `removeElementAt()`, `size()`.

EXAMPLE See `copyInto()`.

removeElementAt()

PURPOSE Removes the element at the specified index from this vector.

SYNTAX `public final synchronized void removeElementAt(int idx)`

DESCRIPTION This method removes the element at index `idx` from this vector. Elements at an index greater than `idx` are shifted down (toward the head of this vector). The size of this vector is decremented by 1.

PARAMETERS

`idx` The `0`-based index of the element to remove. `0` ≤ `idx` < `size()`.

EXCEPTIONS

`ArrayIndexOutOfBoundsException`
If `idx` < `0` or `idx` ≥ `size()`.

SEE ALSO `removeElement()`, `removeAllElements()`, `size()`.

EXAMPLE See `insertElementAt()`.

setElementAt()

PURPOSE Replaces the element at the specified index in this vector.

SYNTAX `public final synchronized void setElementAt(Object obj, int idx)`

DESCRIPTION This method replaces the element at index `idx` of this vector with the object `obj`. If `obj` is `null`, it cannot later be searched by using `contains()`, `indexOf()`, or `lastIndexOf()` and it cannot be removed by using `removeElement()`.

PARAMETERS

`idx` The `0`-based index of the element to replace. `0` ≤ `idx` < `size()`.

`obj` The possibly `null` object with which to replace the element.

EXCEPTIONS

`ArrayIndexOutOfBoundsException`

If `idx` < `0` or `idx` ≥ `size()`.

SEE ALSO `size()`.

EXAMPLE See `firstElement()`, `indexOf()`, `lastIndexOf()`.

setSize()

PURPOSE Truncates or expands this vector.

SYNTAX `public final synchronized void setSize(int newSize)`

DESCRIPTION This method sets the size of this vector to `newSize`. If `newSize` is less than the current size of this vector, the vector is truncated. Elements located at an index at or greater than `newSize` are lost. If `newSize` is greater than the current length of this vector, the newly added region is filled with `null`. `size()` becomes `newSize`.

PARAMETERS

`newSize` The new size of this vector. `newSize` ≥ `0`.

EXCEPTIONS

`ArrayIndexOutOfBoundsException`

If `newSize` < `0`.

SEE ALSO `size()`.

EXAMPLE This method creates a vector that has the first `n` elements of a vector `orig`.

```
public static Vector vecNCopy(Vector orig, int n) {
    Vector vec = (Vector)orig.clone();
    vec.setSize(n);
    return (vec);
}
```

size()

PURPOSE Determines the number of elements in this vector.

SYNTAX `public final int size()`

DESCRIPTION This method determines the number of elements in this vector. Each time an element is added or removed, this number changes correspondingly.

RETURNS The number of elements in this vector.

SEE ALSO `capacity()`, `elementCount`, `lastElement()`, `setSize()`.

EXAMPLE This example creates an array from a Vector.

```
static Object toArray(Vector v, Class c) {
    Object result = Array.newInstance(c, v.size());
    for (int i=0; i<v.size(); i++) {
        Array.set(result, i, v.elementAt(i));
    }
    return result;
}
```


toString()

PURPOSE Generates the string representation for this vector.

SYNTAX `public final synchronized String toString()`

DESCRIPTION The string representation of a vector is a comma-separated list of all of the elements in the vector. The elements are listed from index `0` to index `size()-1`. `toString()` returns this string representation.

RETURNS The non-`null` string representation of this vector.

OVERRIDES `java.lang.Object.toString()`.

SEE ALSO `elements()`.

EXAMPLE

```
Vector v = new Vector(10);
v.addElement("a");
v.addElement("b");
v.addElement("c");
v.addElement("d");
v.addElement("e");
v.addElement("f");
System.out.println(v.toString());  // [a, b, c, d, e, f]
```

trimToSize()

PURPOSE Trims this vector's capacity to be the same as the vector's size.

SYNTAX `public final synchronized void trimToSize()`

DESCRIPTION This method trims the capacity of this vector to its size. It removes the currently unused storage from this vector. If an object is subsequently added, the capacity will be increased.

SEE ALSO `capacity()`, `ensureCapacity()`, `size()`.

EXAMPLE See `removeAllElements()`.

Vector()

PURPOSE Constructs an empty vector.

SYNTAX

```
public Vector()
public Vector(int initCap)
public Vector(int initCap, int capIncrement)
```

DESCRIPTION The `Vector` class has three forms of the constructor. The first form takes no arguments. It constructs an empty vector with a default capacity of 10. The second form constructs an empty vector with the initial capacity of `initCap`. Vectors created using these two forms increase their capacity as needed by doubling their existing capacity. The third form constructs an empty vector with the initial capacity of `initCap` and capacity increment of `capIncrement`. When additional capacity is needed, the existing capacity is increased by `capIncrement`.

PARAMETERS

`capIncrement`
The amount by which to grow when additional capacity is needed.

`initCap` The initial capacity of this vector. `initCap` ≥ `0`.

SEE ALSO `capacity()`, `capacityIncrement`, `ensureCapacity()`.

EXAMPLE See the class example, `copyInto()`, and `toString()`.

VerifyError

Syntax

```
public class VerifyError extends LinkageError
```

Description

When a class is to be loaded (by using either the system's default class loader or a user-defined class loader), its class definition must be verified before it is installed. This verification involves ensuring that all method names and signatures are valid, all field names and signatures are valid, and no final methods or classes are being overridden. If any of these verifications fail, the Java virtual machine throws a `VerifyError`.

`VerifyError` should not be caught or declared in the `throws` clause of a method.

MEMBER SUMMARY	
Constructor	
`VerifyError()`	Constructs a `VerifyError` instance.

See Also

`LinkageError`.

VerifyError()

PURPOSE
Constructs a `VerifyError` instance.

SYNTAX
```
public VerifyError()
public VerifyError(String msg)
```

DESCRIPTION
The two forms of this constructor construct an instance of `VerifyError`. An optional string `msg` can be supplied that describes this particular instance of the exception. If `msg` is not supplied, it defaults to `null`.

PARAMETERS

`msg` A possibly `null` string that gives details about this error.

SEE ALSO
`Throwable.getMessage()`.

java.lang
VirtualMachineError

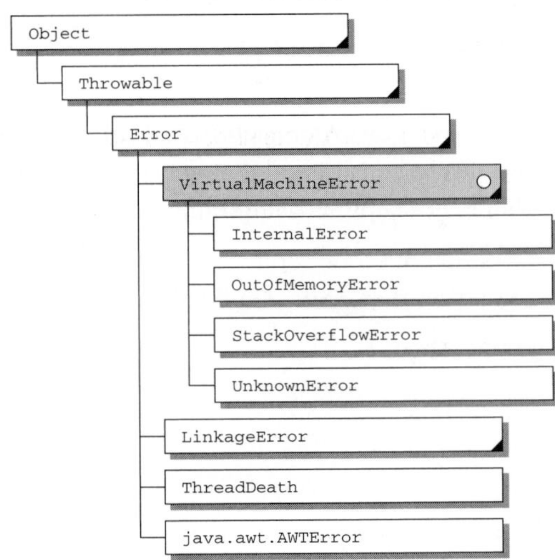

A B C D E F G H I J K L M N O P Q R S T U V W X Y Z

Syntax

```
abstract public class VirtualMachineError extends Error
```

Description

`VirtualMachineError` and its subclasses of errors indicate that the Java virtual machine has encountered an unrecoverable error or has ran out of system resources required to continue execution.

`VirtualMachineError` and its subclasses should not be caught or declared in the `throws` clause of a method.

MEMBER SUMMARY	
Constructor	
`VirtualMachineError()`	Constructs a `VirtualMachineError` instance.

See Also

`Error`, `InternalError`, `OutOfMemoryError`, `StackOverflowError`, `UnknownError`.

VirtualMachineError()

PURPOSE Constructs a `VirtualMachineError` instance.

SYNTAX
```
public VirtualMachineError()
public VirtualMachineError(String msg)
```

DESCRIPTION The two forms of this constructor construct an instance of `VirtualMachineError`. An optional string `msg` can be supplied that describes this particular instance of the error. If msg is not supplied, it defaults to `null`.

PARAMETERS

`msg` A possibly `null` string that gives details about this error.

SEE ALSO `Throwable.getMessage()`.

java.lang
Void

A B C D E F G H I J K L M N O P Q R S T U V W X Y Z

Syntax

```
public final class Void
```

Description

void is used in the Java language to denote that a method has no return value. The Void class contains a single constant—TYPE—used to represent the Class object for void. This constant is equivalent to void.class and is returned by the method Method.getReturnType() to indicate that the method being reflected does not have of a return value.

The Void class cannot be subclassed or instantiated.

MEMBER SUMMARY	
Constant	
TYPE	The Class object representing void.

See Also

Class, java.lang.reflect.Method.getReturnType().

TYPE

PURPOSE The Class object representing void.

SYNTAX `public static final Class TYPE`

DESCRIPTION This constant is the Class object—void.class—which represents void. Although there are no restrictions on the use of Void.TYPE, the preferred syntax for naming the class is void.class.

SEE ALSO Class.

EXAMPLE

```
public static void main(String[] args) {
    Class c = Void.TYPE;
    System.out.println("TYPE: " + c);
```

```
    System.out.println("isPrimitive: " + c.isPrimitive());
    System.out.println("superclass: " + c.getSuperclass());
    try {
        Object obj = c.newInstance();  // ERROR
        System.out.println("obj: " + obj);
    } catch (InstantiationException e) {
        e.printStackTrace();
    } catch (IllegalAccessException e) {
        e.printStackTrace();
    }
}
```

java.io
WriteAbortedException

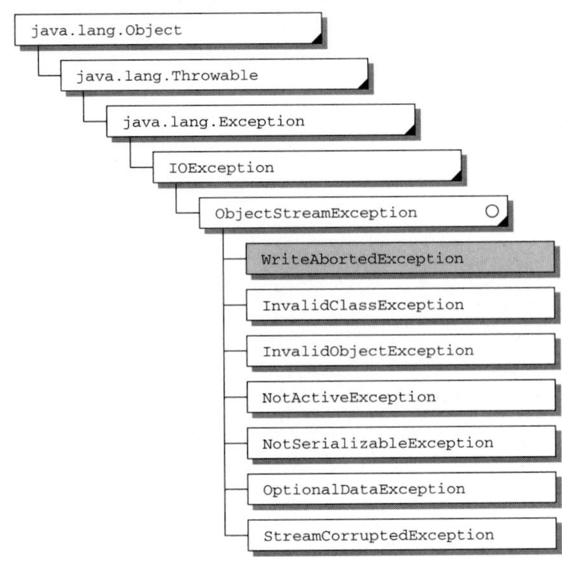

A B C D E F G H I J K L M N O P Q R S T U V W X Y Z

Syntax

```
public class WriteAbortedException extends ObjectStreamException
```

Description

`WriteAbortedException` is thrown by `ObjectInputStream.readObject()` when the stream from which it is reading indicates that serialization has been aborted because the writer encountered an exception while serializing.

MEMBER SUMMARY	
Constructor	
`WriteAbortedException()`	Constructs an instance of `WriteAbortedException`.
Field	
`detail`	Holds the exception that caused the serialization to be aborted.
Override Throwable Method	
`getMessage()`	Generates the detail message describing this exception.

See Also

ObjectInputStream.readObject().

Example

This example throws WriteAbortedException when reading from a serialization stream that was aborted due to a NotSerializableException.

```
import java.io.*;
import java.util.Date;

class Main {
    public static void main(String[] args) {
        try {
            // Write class out
            FileOutputStream f = new FileOutputStream("Test.ser");
            ObjectOutputStream out = new ObjectOutputStream(f);
            out.writeObject("Java Class Libraries");
            out.writeObject(new Date());
            out.flush();
            out.writeObject(new ClassX()); // not serializable
            out.close();
        } catch (IOException e) {
            System.err.println(e);
        }

        try {
            // Read it back
            FileInputStream f2 = new FileInputStream("Test.ser");
            ObjectInputStream in = new ObjectInputStream(f2);
            while (true) {
                try {
                    Object obj = in.readObject();
                    System.out.println(obj);
                } catch (EOFException e) {
                    System.out.println("done");
                    break;
                }
            }
            in.close();
        } catch (IOException e) {
            e.printStackTrace();
        } catch (ClassNotFoundException e) {
            e.printStackTrace();
        }
    }
}

class ClassX {
    int fieldx;
}
```

detail

PURPOSE Holds the exception that caused the serialization to be aborted.

SYNTAX `public Exception detail`

DESCRIPTION This field is set by the constructor.

getMessage()

PURPOSE Generates the detail message describing this exception.

SYNTAX `public String getMessage()`

DESCRIPTION If this exception was created with a non-`null` cause exception, that exception's string representation is included in the detail message. Otherwise, the detail message is the `msg` parameter to the constructor.

RETURNS The possibly `null` string describing this exception.

OVERRIDES `java.lang.Throwable.getMessage()`.

WriteAbortedException()

PURPOSE Constructs an instance of `WriteAbortedException`.

SYNTAX `public WriteAbortedException(String msg, Exception rootCause)`

DESCRIPTION This constructor constructs an instance of `WriteAbortedException` with the detail message `msg` and the exception `rootCause`.

PARAMETERS

`msg` The possibly `null` string containing details about this exception.

`rootCause` The exception that caused the serialization to be aborted.

SEE ALSO `java.lang.Throwable.getMessage()`.

Writer

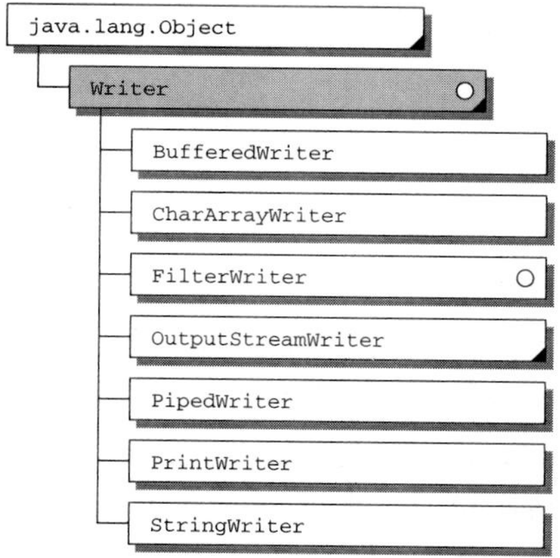

Syntax

```
public abstract class Writer
```

Description

The `Writer` class is the superclass of all character output streams. It provides basic output methods for writing characters to an output stream.

Usage

Subclasses of `Writer` override some or all of these basic methods for implementing their particular type of writer. Concrete subclasses must provide implementations for the abstract methods `write(char[], int, int)`, `close()`, and `flush()`. Figure 110 shows that you can either write directly to a subclass of `Writer` or write to a writer through filters.

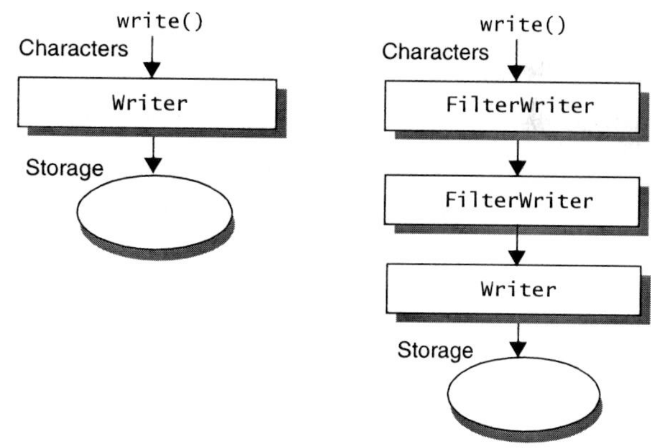

FIGURE 110: `Writer` and `FilterWriter`.

Writer versus OutputStream

`Writer` is for writing to character output streams. `OutputStream` is intended for processing byte output streams. `OutputStream`'s `write()` methods write bytes (0–255).

If you need to translate between character streams and byte streams, use OutputStreamWriter. OutputStreamWriter can be used to translate characters into their byte representations using either a specified or default character-to-byte encoding.

MEMBER SUMMARY	
Constructor	
Writer()	Constructs a Writer instance.
Output Method	
write()	Writes one or more characters to this writer.
Character Stream Methods	
close()	Closes this writer.
flush()	Flushes any buffered characters from this writer.
Synchronization Field	
lock	Holds the object used to synchronize operations on this writer.

See Also

IOException, OutputStream, OutputStreamWriter, Reader.

Example

This example writes a string of Unicode characters to a file using UTF-8 encoding. You can use the InputStreamReader class example to display the Unicode string stored in this file.

```
import java.io.*;

class Main {
    public static void main(String[] args) {
        if (args.length != 1) {
            System.out.println("Usage: java Main <output>");
            System.exit(-1);
        }
        String str = "\u597d\u5929";  // beautiful day

        try {
            Writer out =
                new OutputStreamWriter(new FileOutputStream(args[0]), "UTF8");

            out.write(str);
            out.flush();  // not necessary because close() already does it
            out.close();
        } catch (IOException e) {
            e.printStackTrace();
        }
    }
}
```

close()

PURPOSE Closes this writer.

SYNTAX `abstract public void close() throws IOException`

DESCRIPTION This method must be implemented by any concrete subclass of `Writer`. The implementation should first flush the writer and then release any resources (such as file descriptors and especially system resources) used by this writer.

`close()` is idempotent. That is, you can invoke it many times, but only the first invocation has any effect. Once a writer has been closed, attempts to invoke other methods, except for the `close()` method, on the writer will throw an `IOException`.

EXCEPTIONS

`IOException`

If an IO error occurs while closing the writer.

EXAMPLE See the class example.

flush()

PURPOSE Flushes any buffered characters from this writer.

SYNTAX `abstract public void flush() throws IOException`

DESCRIPTION This method must be implemented by concrete subclasses of `Writer`. Some writers buffer the characters written to them. `flush()` writes out any buffered characters.

EXCEPTIONS

`IOException`

If this writer has already been closed or if some other IO error occurs.

EXAMPLE See the class example.

lock

PURPOSE Holds the object used to synchronize operations on this writer.

SYNTAX `protected Object lock`

DESCRIPTION This field is used whenever an operation on this writer needs to be synchronized against access by multiple threads. Instead of the method to be synchronized being defined or `this` being used as the lock, the method should use

```
synchronized (lock) {
    ...
}
```

The `Writer` constructor that accepts no arguments assigns `lock` to this instance of `Writer`. The other `Writer` constructor accepts an object that is then assigned to this field to serve as the lock for operations on this `Writer`.

SEE ALSO `Writer()`.

EXAMPLE See the `FilterWriter` class example.

write()

PURPOSE Writes one or more characters to this writer.

SYNTAX

```
abstract public void write(char[] buf, int offset, int count)
    throws IOException
public void write(int oneChar) throws IOException
public void write(char buf) throws IOException
public void write(String str) throws IOException
public void write(String str, int offset, int count) throws
    IOException
```

DESCRIPTION This method writes one or more characters to this writer.

The first form writes to this writer the range of characters from the array `buf` as specified by `offset` and `count`. This is an abstract method whose implementation must be provided by concrete `Writer` subclasses. The other forms of this method are implemented using this first form.

The second form writes a single character to this writer. The low-order 2 bytes of `oneChar` are written. The third form is the same as the first form, with `offset` set to `0` and `count` set to `buf.length`.

The last two forms write the characters from a string to this writer. If `offset` and `count` are specified, the range of characters in `str` specified by `offset` and `count` are written. Otherwise, the entire string `str` is written.

PARAMETERS

- `buf` The non-`null` `char` array containing the characters to be written.
- `count` The number of characters to write. `0` ≤ `count` ≤ `buf.length-offset` (or `0` ≤ `count` ≤ `str.length()-offset`).
- `offset` The index in `buf` or `str` at which to start fetching the characters to be written. `0` ≤ `offset` < `buf.length` or `0` ≤ `offset` < `str.length()`.
- `oneChar` The low-order 2 bytes of `oneChar` are written to the writer.
- `str` The non-`null` string containing the characters to be written.

EXCEPTIONS

`ArrayIndexOutOfBoundsException`
: If `count` or `offset` is outside of the specified bounds.

`IOException`
: If this writer has been closed or if some other IO error occurs.

EXAMPLE See the class example.

A B C D E F G H I J K L M N O P Q R S T U V W X Y Z

Writer()

PURPOSE Constructs a `Writer` instance.

SYNTAX

```
protected Writer()
protected Writer(Object lock)
```

DESCRIPTION The two forms of the constructor construct an instance of `Writer`. The difference between the two is the object used for synchronizing subsequent method invocations on the `Writer` instance. The first form uses the `Writer` instance itself as the synchronizing object. The second form uses `lock` as the lock as the synchronizing object.

PARAMETERS

`lock` The non-`null` object to use for synchronized blocks.

SEE ALSO `lock`.

EXAMPLE See the `FilterWriter` class example.

ZipEntry

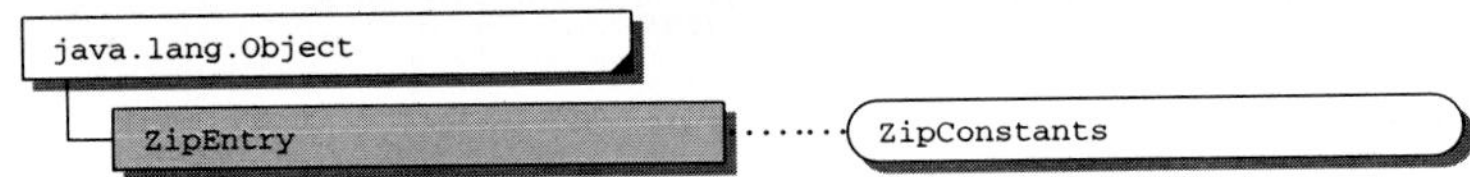

A B C D E F G H I J K L M N O P Q R S T U V W X Y Z

Syntax

```
public class ZipEntry implements ZipConstants
```
[1]

Description

The `ZipEntry` class is used to represent a ZIP entry in a ZIP file. A ZIP entry is used to described a piece of compressed (or uncompressed) data stored in the ZIP file. There is one ZIP entry for every independent piece of data in the ZIP file. A ZIP entry contains such information as the time the data was last modified and the data's compressed and uncompressed sizes. Table 46 summarizes the ZIP entry's properties.

The format of a ZIP file is described in detail in the document at `ftp://ftp.uu.net/pub/archiving/zip/doc/appnote-970531-pk.zip`.

Property	Description
Name	The name of the ZIP entry can be any arbitrary string, but it should be unique with respect to all of the other ZIP entries in the ZIP file. However, the name is typically the relative pathname of a file. The specification of these relative pathnames is described in the document at `ftp://ftp.uu.net/pub/archiving/zip/doc/appnote-970531-pk.zip`.
Data	The ZIP entry data is the actual data to be stored in the ZIP file. This data may or may not be compressed. The purpose of the ZIP entry is to hold information about this data, such as its size and last modification time.
Comment	The comment is an arbitrary string containing a description of the data. It is optional.
Compressed Size	If the data is compressed, this property contains the compressed size of the ZIP entry data. If the data is not compressed, this property contains the uncompressed size of the data.

TABLE 46: `ZipEntry` Properties.

1. The `ZipConstants` interface is not accessible outside of the `java.util.zip` package. The interface contains declarations for various constants used in the ZIP-related classes.

Property	Description
Compression Method	In the case of reading from a ZIP file, the compression method indicates whether the ZIP entry data is compressed. In the case of writing to a ZIP file, the compression method specifies whether the ZIP entry data should be compressed.
CRC	The CRC holds the checksum value of the uncompressed ZIP entry data. It is computed using the CRC-32 algorithm. See `CRC32` for more details.
Extra	This is a `byte` array containing extra information about the ZIP entry data. This property allows the ZIP format to be extended in the future and still be compatible with older ZIP files.
Size	This is the size of the uncompressed data.
Time	This is the last modification time of the data. Typically, the data is retrieved from a file and this property is set to the last modification time of the file.

TABLE 46: `ZipEntry` Properties.

Usage

When a ZIP file is read, the `ZipEntry` class is used in conjunction with either `ZipInputStream` or `ZipFile`. When writing a ZIP file, this class is used in conjunction with `ZipOutputStream`. See these classes for more details.

Directory ZIPEntries

A ZIP entry whose name ends with the forward slash (/) is considered to be a directory ZIP entry. The interpretation of a directory ZIP entry is application-specific. For example, a directory unzipping program would create a file directory for each directory ZIP entry.

MEMBER SUMMARY

Constructor	
`ZipEntry()`	Constructs a `ZipEntry` instance.
Get Property Methods	
`getComment()`	Retrieves the comment string for this entry.
`getCompressedSize()`	Retrieves the compressed size of this ZIP entry's data.
`getCrc()`	Retrieves the checksum value for the uncompressed form of this ZIP entry's data.
`getExtra()`	Retrieves any extra information associated with this ZIP entry.
`getMethod()`	Retrieves the compression method of this ZIP entry.
`getName()`	Retrieves this ZIP entry's name.
`getSize()`	Retrieves the uncompressed size of this ZIP entry's data.
`getTime()`	Retrieves the last modification time of this ZIP entry.
`isDirectory()`	Determines if this ZIP entry is a directory.

Continued

MEMBER SUMMARY	
Set Property Methods	
`setComment()`	Sets the optional comment string for this ZIP entry.
`setCrc()`	Sets the checksum value for this ZIP entry.
`setExtra()`	Sets optional extra information for this ZIP entry.
`setMethod()`	Sets the compression method for this ZIP entry.
`setSize()`	Sets the uncompressed size of this ZIP entry data.
`setTime()`	Sets the last modification time of this ZIP entry.
Compression Method Constants	
`DEFLATED`	Compression-method constant for compressed entries.
`STORED`	Compression-method constant for uncompressed entries.
Debugging Method	
`toString()`	Generates a string representation of this ZIP entry object.

A B C D E F G H I J K L M N O P Q R S T U V W X Y Z

See Also

`ZipFile`, `ZipInputStream`, `ZipOutputStream`.

Example

This example implements a program that prints information about every ZIP entry in a ZIP file. You can control which of the ZIP entry properties to print by specifying one or more single character switches on the command line.

The program uses the `ZipFile` class to retrieve the ZIP entries in a ZIP file. This ensures that all of the ZIP entry information will be available. If a `ZipInputStream` was used, the ZIP entry data would have to be read (or skipped) before all of the ZIP entry data was available.

```
import java.io.*;
import java.text.*;
import java.util.*;
import java.util.zip.*;

class Main {
    public static void main(String[] args) {
        if (args.length != 2) {
            System.err.println("Usage: java Main <ntsScCed> <zip filename>");
            System.err.println("    n - name");
            System.err.println("    t - modified time");
            System.err.println("    c - comment");
            System.err.println("    C - CRC");
            System.err.println("    s - compressed size");
            System.err.println("    S - size");
            System.err.println("    e - extra");
            System.err.println("    d - is directory");
            System.exit(1);
        }
```

```
        try {
            ZipFile zipfile = new ZipFile(args[1]);

            for (Enumeration e=zipfile.entries(); e.hasMoreElements() ;) {
                printEntry((ZipEntry)e.nextElement(), args[0]);
            }
        } catch (IOException e) {
            e.printStackTrace();
        }
    }

    static void printEntry(ZipEntry ze, String options) {
        for (int i=0; i<options.length(); i++) {
            switch (options.charAt(i)) {
              case 'n':
                System.out.print(ze.getName());
                break;
              case 't':
                System.out.print(DateFormat.getDateTimeInstance(
                    DateFormat.SHORT,
                    DateFormat.SHORT).format(new Date(ze.getTime())));
                break;
              case 'c':
                System.out.print(ze.getComment());
                break;
              case 'C':
                System.out.print(ze.getCrc());
                break;
              case 's':
                System.out.print(ze.getCompressedSize());
                break;
              case 'S':
                System.out.print(ze.getSize());
                break;
              case 'e':
                byte[] extra = ze.getExtra();
                for (int j=0; j<extra.length; j++) {
                    System.out.println(Integer.toHexString(extra[j]));
                }
                break;
              case 'd':
                System.out.print(ze.isDirectory());
                break;
            }
            if (i < options.length() - 1) {
                System.out.print('\t');
            }
        }
        System.out.println();
    }
}
```

DEFLATED

PURPOSE Compression-method constant for compressed entries.

SYNTAX `public static final int DEFLATED`

DESCRIPTION If this ZIP entry is used to write out data, this constant (value `8`) specifies that the ZIP entry data should be compressed. If this ZIP entry is created while a ZIP file is being read, this constant specifies that the ZIP entry data is compressed.

SEE ALSO `STORED`, `ZipOutputStream.setMethod()`.

EXAMPLE See `ZipOutputStream.finish()`.

getComment()

PURPOSE Retrieves the comment string for this entry.

SYNTAX `public String getComment()`

DESCRIPTION If there is no comment string for this entry, `null` is returned.

RETURNS A possibly `null` string containing a comment for this ZIP entry.

SEE ALSO `setComment()`.

EXAMPLE See the class example.

getCompressedSize()

PURPOSE Retrieves the compressed size of this ZIP entry's data.

SYNTAX `public long getCompressedSize()`

DESCRIPTION After a ZIP entry object is obtained from either a `ZipFile` or `ZipInputStream` object, this method can be used to retrieve the compressed size of the ZIP entry data.

The compressed size for a new ZIP entry object is `-1`.

RETURNS The compressed size of this ZIP entry's data, or `-1` if not known.

EXAMPLE See the class example.

getCrc()

PURPOSE Retrieves the checksum value for the uncompressed form of this ZIP entry's data.

SYNTAX `public long getCrc()`

DESCRIPTION After a ZIP entry object is obtained from either a `ZipFile` or `ZipInputStream` object, this method can be used to retrieve the checksum value of the uncompressed form of the ZIP entry's data.

The algorithm used to compute the checksum value is CRC-32. See `CRC32` for more information.

The checksum value for a new ZIP entry object is `-1`.

RETURNS The checksum value size of this ZIP entry's uncompressed data, or `-1` if not known.

EXAMPLE See the class example.

getExtra()

PURPOSE Retrieves any extra information associated with this ZIP entry.

SYNTAX `public byte[] getExtra()`

DESCRIPTION After a ZIP entry object is obtained from either a `ZipFile` or `ZipInputStream` object, this method can be used to retrieve any extra information associated with the ZIP entry. The main purpose of the extra information is to allow for future extensions and still be compatible with older ZIP files.

If no extra information is available, `null` is returned.

RETURNS A possibly `null` array of bytes.

EXAMPLE See the class example.

getMethod()

PURPOSE Retrieves the compression method of this ZIP entry.

SYNTAX `public int getMethod()`

DESCRIPTION The compression method specifies whether the ZIP entry data is compressed. A return value of `STORED` indicates that the ZIP entry data is not compressed. A return value of `DEFLATED` indicates that the ZIP entry data is compressed.

The compression method for a new ZIP entry object is `-1`.

RETURNS One of `STORED`, `DEFLATED`, or `-1`.

EXAMPLE See the class example.

getName()

PURPOSE Retrieves this ZIP entry's name.

SYNTAX `public String getName()`

DESCRIPTION The name of the ZIP entry can be any arbitrary string, but it is usually the relative pathname of a file. The name of a ZIP entry must be unique with respect to all other ZIP entries in a ZIP file. A ZIP entry whose name ends with the forward slash (/) is considered to be a directory ZIP entry. See the class description for details.

RETURNS A non-`null` string contain this ZIP entry's name.

EXAMPLE See the class example.

getSize()

PURPOSE Retrieves the uncompressed size of this ZIP entry's data.

SYNTAX `public long getSize()`

DESCRIPTION After a ZIP entry object is obtained from either a `ZipFile` or `ZipInputStream` object, this method can be used to retrieve the uncompressed size of the ZIP entry's data.

The size value for a new ZIP entry object is `-1`.

RETURNS The uncompressed size of this ZIP entry's data, or `-1` if not known.

EXAMPLE See the class example.

getTime()

PURPOSE Retrieves the last modification time of this ZIP entry.

SYNTAX `public long getTime()`

DESCRIPTION This method returns the last modification time of the ZIP entry data. If the data was retrieved from a file, the returned time is typically the last modification time of the file. The resulting time value is in Universal Time format. See the `Date` class for more information on this format.

If the property was never set, `-1` is returned.

RETURNS A time value in Universal Time format, or `-1` if not initialized.

SEE ALSO `java.util.Date`.

EXAMPLE See the class example.

isDirectory()

PURPOSE Determines if this ZIP entry is a directory.

SYNTAX `public boolean isDirectory()`

DESCRIPTION A ZIP entry whose name ends with a forward slash (/) is considered a directory ZIP entry. The interpretation of a directory ZIP entry is application-specific. For example, a directory unzipping program would create a file directory for each directory ZIP entry.

RETURNS `true` if this ZIP entry's name indicates that this entry is a directory ZIP entry; `false` otherwise.

EXAMPLE See the class example.

setComment()

PURPOSE Sets the optional comment string for this ZIP entry.

SYNTAX `public void setComment(String comment)`

DESCRIPTION This method sets a comment string for this ZIP entry. The comment string is included with the ZIP entry in a ZIP file when `ZipOutputStream.putNextEntry()` is called.

Only the lower byte of each character in the comment is stored.

The comment string for a new ZIP entry object is `null`.

PARAMETERS

`comment` A possibly `null` string. If `comment` is non-`null`, `comment.length()` ≤ `65535` (`0xFFFF`).

EXCEPTIONS

`IllegalArgumentException`

If `comment.length()` > 65535 (`0xFFFF`).

EXAMPLE See the `ZipOutputStream` class example.

setCrc()

PURPOSE Sets the checksum value for this ZIP entry.

SYNTAX `public void setCrc(long crc)`

DESCRIPTION The checksum value of this ZIP entry's uncompressed data must be computed using the CRC-32 algorithm (see CRC32).

The checksum value does not need to be set if the ZIP entry data is to be compressed; the ZIP output stream will automatically compute this information. However, supplying this information before the ZIP entry data is written out makes this information available when the ZIP file is read sequentially. See `ZipOutputStream.putNextEntry()` for more details.

The checksum value must be set if ZIP entry data is to be uncompressed. See `STORED` for more details.

PARAMETERS

`crc` The checksum value of the uncompressed ZIP entry data.

EXCEPTIONS

`IllegalArgumentException`
If `crc` < `0` or `crc` > `0xFFFFFFFF`.

EXAMPLE See `ZipOutputStream.finish()`.

setExtra()

PURPOSE Sets optional extra information for this ZIP entry.

SYNTAX `public void setExtra(byte[] extra)`

DESCRIPTION The extra information for a ZIP entry is used to allow the ZIP format to be extended in the future and still be compatible with older ZIP files.

PARAMETERS

`extra` A possibly `null` byte array. If `extra` is non-`null`, `extra.length` ≤ `65535 (0xFFFF)`.

EXCEPTIONS

`IllegalArgumentException`
If `extra.length > 65535 (0xFFFF)`.

EXAMPLE See the `ZipOutputStream` class example.

setMethod()

PURPOSE Sets the compression method for this ZIP entry.

SYNTAX `public void setMethod(int m)`

DESCRIPTION The compression method specifies whether the ZIP entry data should be compressed. If `m` is `STORED`, the ZIP entry data will not be compressed. If `m` is `DEFLATED`, the ZIP entry data will be compressed.

PARAMETERS

`m` Must be either the `DEFLATED` or `STORED` compression method constant.

EXCEPTIONS

`IllegalArgumentException`
If `m` is neither `STORED` nor `DEFLATED`.

EXAMPLE See the `ZipOutputStream` class example.

setSize()

PURPOSE Sets the uncompressed size of this ZIP entry data.

SYNTAX `public void setSize(long sz)`

DESCRIPTION The size does not need to be set if the ZIP entry data is to be compressed; the ZIP output stream will automatically compute this information. However, supplying this information before the ZIP entry data is written out makes this information available when the ZIP file is read sequentially. See `ZipOutputStream.putNextEntry()` for more details.

The size must be set if ZIP entry data is to be uncompressed. See `STORED` for more details.

PARAMETERS

`sz` The uncompressed size of the ZIP entry data. $0 \le sz \le$ `0xFFFFFFFF`.

EXCEPTIONS

`IllegalArgumentException`
If $sz < 0$ or $sz >$ `0xFFFFFFFF`.

EXAMPLE See `ZipOutputStream.finish()`.

setTime()

PURPOSE Sets the last modification time of this ZIP entry.

SYNTAX `public void setTime(long t)`

DESCRIPTION This method sets the last modification time of the ZIP entry. If the data is retrieved from a file, this property is typically set to the last modification time of the file.

The format of `t` is Universal Time, which is described in the `Date` class.

PARAMETERS

`t` A time value in Universal Time format.

SEE ALSO java.util.Date.

EXAMPLE See the `ZipOutputStream` class example.

STORED

PURPOSE Cmpression-method constant for uncompressed entries.

SYNTAX `public static final int STORED`

DESCRIPTION If this ZIP entry is used to write out data, this constant (value `0`) specifies that the ZIP entry data should not be compressed. If this ZIP entry is created while a ZIP file is being read, this constant specifies that the ZIP entry data is not compressed.

When this compression method is used, the size and checksum values for this ZIP entry must be set before it can be used to write a ZIP entry. See `ZipOutputStream.putNextEntry()` for more details.

SEE ALSO `DEFLATED`, `ZipOutputStream.setMethod()`.

EXAMPLE See `ZipOutputStream.finish()`.

toString()

PURPOSE Generates a string representation of this ZIP entry object.

SYNTAX `public String toString()`

DESCRIPTION This method returns the name of this ZIP entry object.

RETURNS A non-`null` string containing the ZIP entry's name.

OVERRIDES `java.lang.Object.toString()`.

SEE ALSO `getName()`.

EXAMPLE See `java.lang.Object.toString()`.

ZipEntry()

PURPOSE Constructs a `ZipEntry` instance.

SYNTAX `public ZipEntry(String zname)`

DESCRIPTION This constructor creates a ZIP entry with the name `zname`. Only the lower byte of each character in `zname` is used in the name.

The comment string and extra data properties are set to `null`. All other properties have the value `-1`.

PARAMETERS

`zname` A non-`null` string containing the ZIP entry name. Only the lower byte of each character is used. `zname.length()` ≤ `65535 (0xFFFF)`.

EXCEPTIONS

`NullPointerException`
If `zname` is `null`.

`IllegalArgumentException`
If `zname.length` > `65535` (`0xFFFF`) characters.

EXAMPLE See the class example.

ZipException

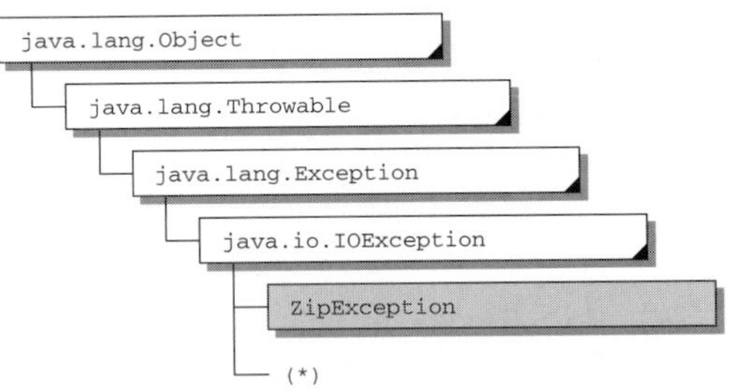

(*) 14 classes from other packages not shown.

A B C D E F G H I J K L M N O P Q R S T U V W X Y Z

Syntax

```
public class ZipException extends IOException
```

Description

The `ZipException` exception is thrown by various classes that read and write files in the ZIP format. These classes include `ZipFile`, `ZipInputStream`, and `ZipOutputStream`. `ZipException` is thrown if the read data is not in the ZIP format or if an error occurs while creating a ZIP file.

MEMBER SUMMARY	
Constructor	
`ZipException()`	Constructs a `ZipException` instance.

See Also

`ZipFile`, `ZipInputStream`, `ZipOutputStream`.

Example

This example is a simple demonstration of how a `ZipException` can be thrown. In the first case, `ZipFile` is used to open a file that is not in the ZIP format. In the second case, an improperly initialized ZIP entry is written to a ZIP output stream. When data is written uncompressed (`STORED`), the size and checksum value of the ZIP entry must be initialized.

```
import java.io.*;
import java.util.zip.*;
```

```
class Main {
    //
    public static void main(String[] args) {
        try {
            ZipFile zis = new ZipFile(args[0]);
        } catch (ZipException e) {
            System.err.println("Not a ZIP file.");
        } catch (Exception e) {
            e.printStackTrace();
        }

        try {
            ZipOutputStream zos = new ZipOutputStream(
                new FileOutputStream("test"));
            ZipEntry ze = new ZipEntry("test");
            ze.setMethod(ZipEntry.STORED);

            zos.putNextEntry(ze);
        } catch (ZipException e) {
            System.err.println("Failed to write the zip file.");
        } catch (Exception e) {
            e.printStackTrace();
        }


    }
}
```

ZipException()

PURPOSE — Constructs a `ZipException` instance.

SYNTAX

```
public ZipException()
public ZipException(String msg)
```

DESCRIPTION — The two forms of this constructor construct an instance of `ZipException`. An optional string `msg` can be supplied that describes this particular instance of the exception. If `msg` is not supplied, it defaults to `null`.

PARAMETERS

`msg` — A possibly `null` message containing details that caused the exception.

SEE ALSO — `java.lang.Throwable.getMessage()`.

java.util.zip
ZipFile

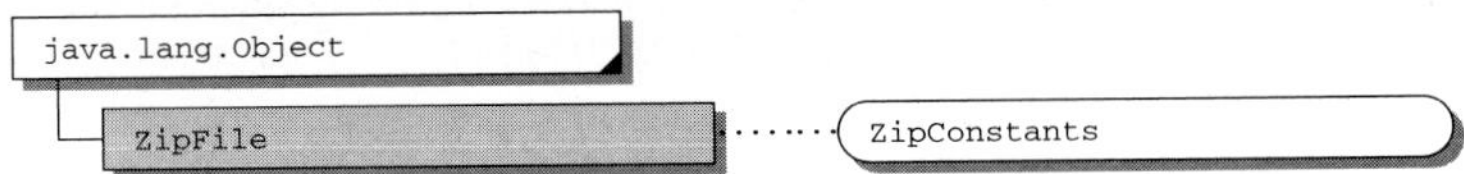

A
B
C
D
E
F
G
H
I
J
K
L
M
N
O
P
Q
R
S
T
U
V
W
X
Y
Z

Syntax

```
public class ZipFile implements ZipConstants
```
[1]

Description

The `ZipFile` class is used to read the contents of a ZIP file. It does not support the ability to create a new ZIP file. Instead, use `ZipOutputStream` to create a new ZIP file. The `ZipOutputStream` class example shows how this is done.

The format of a ZIP file is described in detail in the documents at `ftp://ftp.uu.net/pub/archiving/zip/doc/`. `ZipFile` uses the DEFLATE compression algorithm described in *RFC 1951* at `http://ds.internic.net/rfc/rfc1951.txt`.

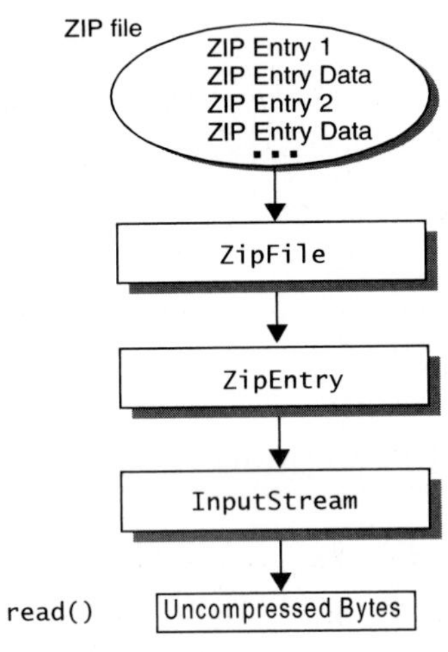

FIGURE 111: `ZipFile` and `ZipEntry`.

Usage

To use this class, you supply a `File` object or the filename of the ZIP file to the `ZipFile()` constructor. If the constructor succeeds, you can then visit all of the ZIP entries by calling `entries()`. To read the ZIP entry data, call `getInputStream()` to obtain an input stream that will deliver the uncompressed data. See Figure 111.

ZIP Entries

A ZIP file consists of one or more compressed (or uncompressed) pieces of data. Each piece of data is represented by a *ZIP entry*. The ZIP entry contains information about the data, such as its uncompressed size, its checksum value, and its location in the ZIP file.

This class opens up the ZIP file and reads all of its ZIP entries into memory. Only the value in the ZIP entry is read into memory, not the data that it describes. One `ZipEntry` object is created for each ZIP entry. If more than one ZIP entry has the same name, only one of the ZIP entries is retained. See `ZipEntry` for more details on the contents of a ZIP entry object.

1. The `ZipConstants` interface is not accessible outside of the `java.util.zip` package. This interface contains declarations for various constants used in the ZIP-related classes.

This class does not support any operations that change the set of ZIP entry objects in a ZIP file. That is, ZIP entry objects are never created or destroyed. The methods `entries()` and `getEntry()` return the actual objects maintained by a ZIP file object, so they should not be modified.

MEMBER SUMMARY	
Constructor	
`ZipFile()`	Opens a ZIP file.
ZIP File Methods	
`close()`	Closes this ZIP file object.
`getName()`	Retrieves the ZIP file's name.
ZIP Entry Methods	
`entries()`	Creates an enumeration of all of the ZIP entries.
`getEntry()`	Retrieves a ZIP entry.
`getInputStream()`	Creates an input stream on the contents represented by a ZIP entry.

See Also

`ZipEntry`, `ZipInputStream`, `ZipOutputStream`.

Example

This example demonstrates both how to open and read the contents of a ZIP file and how to create a new one. It implements a program that allows you to delete ZIP entries from a ZIP file.

After opening the ZIP file, this program displays all of the ZIP entry names in a list component. You then use the list component to select and delete entries from the list. To rewrite the ZIP file without the deleted ZIP entries, press the Save and Exit button. See Figure 112.

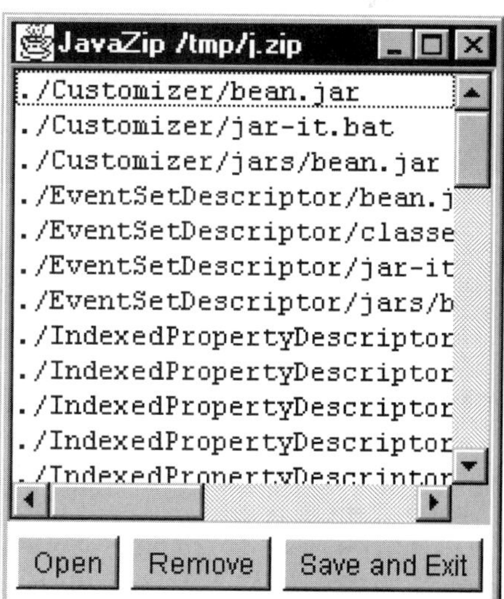

FIGURE 112: ZIP File Viewer.

The program also allows you to view the decompressed data associated with a ZIP entry. To do this, select the ZIP entry in the list component and press the Open button. This program uses a variation of the `QuickSort` class from the `java.lang.reflect.Array` class example to sort the ZIP entries by name. This variation uses a `Vector` instead of an array.

```
import java.awt.*;
import java.awt.event.*;
import java.io.*;
import java.util.*;
import java.util.zip.*;

class Main extends Frame implements ActionListener {
    String zipFilename;
    ZipFile zipfile;

    // Vector of zip entries.
    Vector entries = new Vector();

    // Components.
    List entryList = new List();
    Button removeBtn = new Button("Remove");
    Button saveBtn = new Button("Save and Exit");
    Button openBtn = new Button("Open");

    Main(String zipFilename) throws IOException {
        this.zipFilename = zipFilename;
        zipfile = new ZipFile(zipFilename);
        setTitle("JavaZip " + zipfile.getName());

        // Get the entries into a vector.
        for (Enumeration e=zipfile.entries(); e.hasMoreElements();) {
            entries.addElement((ZipEntry)e.nextElement());
        }

        // Sort the vector.
        QuickSort.sort(entries, new QuickSortCompare());

        // Add sorted entries to list component.
        for (int i=0; i<entries.size(); i++) {
            ZipEntry ze = (ZipEntry)entries.elementAt(i);
            entryList.add(ze.getName());
        }

        // Layout components.
        entryList.setFont(new Font("Monospaced", Font.PLAIN, 12));
        add(entryList, BorderLayout.CENTER);

        // Set up the buttons along the bottom.
        Panel p = new Panel(new FlowLayout());
        p.add(openBtn);
        p.add(removeBtn);
        p.add(saveBtn);
        add(p, BorderLayout.SOUTH);

        // Listen for events.
        openBtn.addActionListener(this);
        removeBtn.addActionListener(this);
        saveBtn.addActionListener(this);
        addWindowListener(new WindowEventHandler());

        setSize(300, 400);
        show();
    }

    class QuickSortCompare implements Comparator {
```

```
    public int compare(Object o1, Object o2) {
        return ((ZipEntry)o1).getName().
                  compareTo(((ZipEntry)o2).getName());
    }
}

class WindowEventHandler extends WindowAdapter {
    public void windowClosing(WindowEvent e) {
        dispose();
        System.exit(1);
    }
}

public void actionPerformed(ActionEvent evt) {
    if (evt.getSource() == removeBtn) {
        int sel = entryList.getSelectedIndex();
        if (sel >= 0) {
            entryList.delItem(sel);
            entries.removeElementAt(sel);
        }
    } else if (evt.getSource() == saveBtn) {
        try {
            // First save the new zip file in a file called "temp".
            File outfile = new File("temp");
            ZipOutputStream os =
                new ZipOutputStream(new FileOutputStream(outfile));

            // Write all remaining entries to the new zip file.
            for (int i=0; i<entries.size(); i++) {
                ZipEntry ze = (ZipEntry)entries.elementAt(i);
                InputStream is = zipfile.getInputStream(ze);

                // Status information.
                System.out.println(ze.getName());

                // Copy data from input stream to output stream.
                os.putNextEntry(new ZipEntry(ze.getName()));
                os.putNextEntry(ze);
                copy(is, os);
                is.close();
            }

            os.close();
            zipfile.close();

            // Now rename the temp file to the original file.
            outfile.renameTo(new File(zipFilename));
            System.exit(0);
        } catch (IOException e) {
            e.printStackTrace();
        }
    } else if (evt.getSource() == openBtn) {
        int sel = entryList.getSelectedIndex();
        if (sel >= 0) {
            try {
                ZipEntry ze = (ZipEntry)entries.elementAt(sel);
                byte[] buf = new byte[(int)ze.getSize()];
                InputStream is = zipfile.getInputStream(ze);
                int len = 0, off = 0;
```

```
                    // Read the entire contents.
                    while (off < buf.length
                          && (len = is.read(buf, off, buf.length-off)) >= 0) {
                        off += len;
                    }
                    is.close();
                    new TextViewer(new String(buf), ze.getName());
                } catch (Exception e) {
                    e.printStackTrace();
                }
            }
        }
    }

    // Copy data from is to os.
    void copy(InputStream is, OutputStream os) throws IOException {
        byte[] buf = new byte[1024];
        int len;

        while ((len = is.read(buf)) >= 0) {
            os.write(buf, 0, len);
        }
    }

    public static void main(String[] args) {
        if (args.length != 1) {
            System.err.println("Usage: java Main <zip filename>");
        } else {
            try {
                new Main(args[0]);
            } catch (IOException e) {
                e.printStackTrace();
            }
        }
    }
}

// This frame is used to view the decompressed data of a zip entry.
class TextViewer extends Frame {
    TextViewer(String text, String name) {
        super(name);

        // Create and add the text area.
        TextArea ta = new TextArea(text);
        add(ta, BorderLayout.CENTER);

        // Listen for events and show frame.
        addWindowListener(new WindowEventHandler());
        setSize(300, 300);
        show();
    }

    class WindowEventHandler extends WindowAdapter {
        public void windowClosing(WindowEvent evt) {
            // Destroy the window.
            dispose();
        }
    }
}
```

close()

PURPOSE Closes this ZIP file object.

SYNTAX `public void close() throws IOException`

DESCRIPTION This method closes the ZIP file object. The ZIP file object cannot be reopened; instead, you need to create a new `ZipFile` instance. After this call, no other `ZipFile` operations can be made on this ZIP file object.

EXCEPTIONS

`IOException`

If an IO error occurs while closing the ZIP file object.

SEE ALSO `java.io.IOException.`

EXAMPLE See the class example.

entries()

PURPOSE Creates an enumeration of all of the ZIP entries.

SYNTAX `public Enumeration entries()`

DESCRIPTION The returned enumeration is used to access all of the ZIP entries in a ZIP file. Unlike with ZIP entry objects returned by the `ZipInputStream` class, the size, compressed size, and checksum value of these ZIP entry objects are initialized with the correct values.

The ZIP entry objects returned by the enumeration are the actual ZIP entry objects maintain by this ZIP file and should not be modified.

RETURNS A non-`null` enumeration object.

SEE ALSO `java.util.Enumeration.`

EXAMPLE See the class example.

getEntry()

PURPOSE Retrieves a ZIP entry.

SYNTAX `public ZipEntry getEntry(String zname)`

DESCRIPTION This method returns the ZIP entry with the name `zname`. If none is found, `null` is returned.

Unlike with ZIP entry objects returned by the `ZipInputStream` class, the size, compressed size, and checksum value of these ZIP entry objects are initialized with the correct values.

The returned ZIP entry object is the actual ZIP entry object maintain by this ZIP file and should not be modified.

PARAMETERS

`zname` The non-`null` name of the ZIP entry.

RETURNS A possibly `null` ZIP entry with the name `zname`.

getInputStream()

PURPOSE Creates an input stream on the contents represented by a ZIP entry.

SYNTAX
```
public InputStream getInputStream(ZipEntry ze) throws
    IOException
```

DESCRIPTION Every ZIP entry represents a sequence of compressed or uncompressed data. This method creates an input stream that will deliver that data. The bytes flowing from the input stream are uncompressed.

RETURNS A non-`null` input stream that will deliver `ze`'s data.

PARAMETERS

`ze` The non-`null` ZIP entry.

EXCEPTIONS

`ZipException`
If a ZIP format error occurs while creating the input stream.

`IOException`
If an IO error occurs while creating the input stream.

SEE ALSO `java.io.IOException`, `java.io.InputStream`.

EXAMPLE See the class example.

getName()

PURPOSE Retrieves the ZIP file's name.

SYNTAX `public String getName()`

DESCRIPTION The name is the ZIP file's filename. If a filename was specified in the constructor, that filename is returned. Otherwise, a `File` object was specified in the constructor and the returned name is the result of calling `getPath()` on that `File` object. Note that this is the name of the ZIP file object, not a ZIP entry filename.

RETURNS A non-`null` string containing the filename of the ZIP file.

SEE ALSO `java.io.File.getPath()`.

EXAMPLE See the class example.

ZipFile()

PURPOSE Opens a ZIP file.

SYNTAX

```
public ZipFile(String fname) throws IOException
public ZipFile(File f) throws ZipException, IOException
```

DESCRIPTION This method opens a ZIP file and reads in all of its ZIP entries. See the class description for more details on reading ZIP entries. If `fname` is specified, it is the ZIP file's filename. If `f` is specified, it is a file object on the ZIP file.

If `fname` is specified, `fname` becomes the ZIP file's name; otherwise, `f.getPath()` becomes the ZIP file's name. Use `getName()` to retrieve the ZIP file's name.

PARAMETERS

`f` The non-`null` file object to be opened for reading.

`fname` A non-`null` string containing the filename of the ZIP file.

EXCEPTIONS

`ZipException`

If a ZIP format error occurs while reading the ZIP entries.

`IOException`

If an IO error occurs while opening the ZIP file.

SEE ALSO `close()`, `getName()`, `java.io.IOException`.

EXAMPLE See the class example.

ZipInputStream

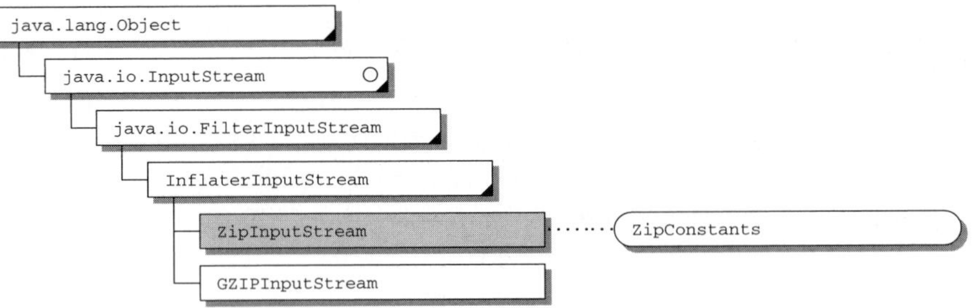

Syntax

`public class ZipInputStream extends InflaterInputStream implements ZipConstants`[1]

Description

The `ZipInputStream` class implements an input stream filter for reading a ZIP file. See `ZipFile` for more information on the format of a ZIP file.

A ZIP file differs from a GZIP file (see `GZIPInputStream`) in that a GZIP file contains only one piece of data, while a ZIP file can contain multiple pieces of data. Each piece is called a *ZIP entry data*. Each ZIP entry data can be either compressed or uncompressed and is preceded by a *ZIP entry*, which is a description of the ZIP entry data.

The ZIP input stream uses the DEFLATE compression algorithm to decompress data. This algorithm is implemented by the `Inflater` class. See `Inflater` for more information.

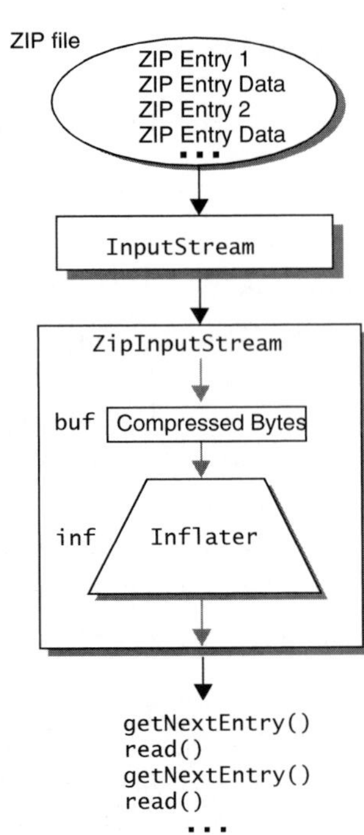

FIGURE 113: `ZipInputStream`.

Usage

A new ZIP input stream must first be created on an existing input stream. Before reading a ZIP entry data from the stream, you first must call `getNextEntry()` to obtain a new `ZipEntry` object, which contains information about the ZIP entry data that follows. You then read the actual data from the stream by calling `read()`. To read another

1. The `ZipConstants` interface is not accessible outside of the `java.util.zip` package. This interface contains declarations for various constants used in the ZIP-related classes.

piece of data from the ZIP input stream, you must restart the process by calling `getNextEntry()`. See Figure 113.

MEMBER SUMMARY	
Constructor	
`ZipInputStream()`	Constructs a `ZipInputStream` instance.
Entry Methods	
`closeEntry()`	Closes the current ZIP entry.
`getNextEntry()`	Reads the next ZIP entry from this ZIP input stream.
Stream Methods	
`close()`	Closes this ZIP input stream.
`read()`	Reads decompressed data from this ZIP input stream.
`skip()`	Discards decompressed data from this ZIP input stream.

A B C D E F G H I J K L M N O P Q R S T U V W X Y Z

See Also

`Inflater`, `java.io.InputStream`, `ZipOutputStream`.

Example

This example reads a ZIP file from standard input and prints the last 128 bytes of the printable file. If the file is not printable, the string "UNPRINTABLE" is printed instead.

For each ZIP entry, the program determines the uncompressed size of the input and skips all but the last `128` bytes. It then prints the remaining 128 bytes.

Note that this program requires that the size, compressed size, and checksum values appear in front of the ZIP entry data, which may not always be the case. In some cases, this information won't be available until the ZIP entry data has been read. See `ZipOutputStream.putNextEntry()` for more details.

```
import java.io.*;
import java.util.zip.*;

class Main {
    public static void main(String[] args) {
        try {
            ZipInputStream is = new ZipInputStream(System.in);
            ZipEntry ze;
            byte[] buf = new byte[128];
            int len;

            while ((ze = is.getNextEntry()) != null) {
                System.out.println("---------- " + ze);

                // Determine the number of bytes to skip and skip them.
```

```
                    int skip = (int)ze.getSize() - 128;
                    while (skip > 0) {
                        skip -= is.skip(Math.min(skip, 512));
                    }

                    // Read the remaining bytes and if it's printable, print them.
                    out: while ((len = is.read(buf)) >= 0) {
                        for (int i=0; i<len; i++) {
                            if ((buf[i]&0xFF) >= 0x80) {
                                System.out.println("**** UNPRINTABLE ****");

                                // This isn't really necessary since getNextEntry()
                                // automatically calls it.
                                is.closeEntry();

                                // Get the next zip entry.
                                break out;
                            }
                        }
                        System.out.write(buf, 0, len);
                    }
                }
                is.close();
            } catch (Exception e) {
                e.printStackTrace();
            }
        }
    }
```

close()

PURPOSE Closes this ZIP input stream.

SYNTAX `public void close() throws IOException`

DESCRIPTION This method closes this ZIP input stream. All input streams downstream are also closed. This ZIP input stream can no longer be used after this call.

EXCEPTIONS

`IOException`

If an IO error occurs while closing.

SEE ALSO `java.io.InputStream.close()`.

EXAMPLE See the class example.

closeEntry()

PURPOSE Closes the current ZIP entry.

SYNTAX `public void closeEntry() throws IOException`

DESCRIPTION This method closes the current ZIP entry and discards any unread data associated with the current ZIP entry.

It is usually unnecessary to call this method directly, since two other methods—`getNextEntry()` and `close()`—call this method automatically.

EXCEPTIONS

`IOException`

If an IO error occurs while closing the entry.

`ZipException`

If a ZIP file error occurs while closing the entry.

EXAMPLE See the class example.

getNextEntry()

PURPOSE Reads the next ZIP entry from this ZIP input stream.

SYNTAX `public ZipEntry getNextEntry() throws IOException`

DESCRIPTION This method creates a new `ZipEntry` object, initializes it with the ZIP entry information read from this ZIP input stream, and returns the `ZipEntry` object. When no more ZIP entries are available, `null` is returned. However, if this ZIP input stream contains another ZIP file, calling this method again will retrieve the first ZIP entry in the new ZIP file.

The size, compressed size, and checksum value of this ZIP entry object may or may not be initialized. Whether they are depends on if this information was made available in front of the ZIP entry data in the ZIP file (see `ZipOutputStream.putNextEntry()` for more details). If this information is not available, it will be made available only after all of the ZIP entry data is read. If this information is needed before the ZIP entry data is read, use the `ZipFile` class.

RETURNS A ZIP entry. If `null`, there are no more ZIP entries in the ZIP input stream.

EXCEPTIONS

`IOException`

If an IO error occurs while retrieving the next ZIP entry.

`ZipException`

If a ZIP file error occurs while retrieving the next ZIP entry.

EXAMPLE See the class example.

read()

PURPOSE Reads decompressed data from this ZIP input stream.

SYNTAX `public int read(byte[] buf, int off, int len) throws IOException`

DESCRIPTION This method reads at most `len` bytes from this ZIP input stream and places them in `buf` starting at `buf[off]`. The bytes are uncompressed.

The blocking behavior of this method depends on the input streams from which it reads. In general, this method blocks until some bytes (possibly fewer than `len`) are read.

This method returns `-1` if the ZIP input stream has no more data to return.

PARAMETERS

`buf` The non-`null` buffer in which to store the data.

`len` The maximum number of bytes to read into `buf` starting at `buf[off]`. `0` ≤ `len` ≤ `buf.length-off`.

`off` The `0`-based starting offset of the data in `buf`. `0` ≤ `off` < `buf.length`.

RETURNS The number of bytes read, or `-1` if the end-of-stream has been reached.

EXCEPTIONS

`IOException`
If an IO error occurs while reading or if the ZIP file is corrupt.

`ZipException`
If a ZIP file error occurs while reading.

OVERRIDES `InflaterInputStream.read()`.

EXAMPLE See the class example.

skip()

PURPOSE Discards decompressed data from this ZIP input stream.

SYNTAX `public long skip(long n) throws IOException`

DESCRIPTION This method reads at most `n` decompressed bytes from this ZIP input stream and discards them. `n` can be larger than the number of bytes in the stream; it simply returns the number of bytes skipped.

PARAMETERS

`n` The number of bytes to skip. If negative, `n` becomes `0`.

RETURNS The nonnegative number of bytes skipped.

EXCEPTIONS

`IOException`
: If an IO error occurs while opening the ZIP file.

`ZipException`
: If a ZIP file error occurs while reading the ZIP header.

OVERRIDES `InflaterInputStream.skip()`.

EXAMPLE See the class example.

A B C D E F G H I J K L M N O P Q R S T U V W X Y Z

ZipInputStream()

PURPOSE Constructs a `ZipInputStream` instance.

SYNTAX `public ZipInputStream(InputStream in)`

DESCRIPTION This constructor creates a `ZipInputStream` instance. It reads the header of the ZIP file. If the ZIP header is corrupted, an `IOException` is thrown.

This class internally uses an `Inflater` instance that does not use the ZLIB header. See `Inflater()` for more details.

PARAMETERS

`in` A non-`null` input stream.

EXCEPTIONS

`IOException`
: If an IO error occurs while opening the ZIP file.

`ZipException`
: If a ZIP file error occurs while reading the ZIP header.

SEE ALSO `java.io.InputStream`.

EXAMPLE See the class example.

java.util.zip
ZipOutputStream

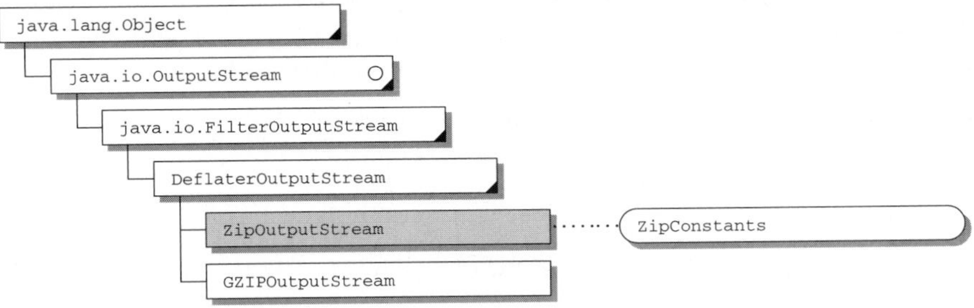

Syntax

```
public class ZipOutputStream extends DeflaterOutputStream implements
    ZipConstants1
```

Description

The `ZipOutputStream` class implements an output stream filter for creating a ZIP file. See `ZipFile` for more information on the format of a ZIP file.

A ZIP file differs from a GZIP file (see `GZIPOutputStream`) in that a GZIP file contains only one piece of data, while a ZIP file can contain multiple pieces of data. Each piece of data in a ZIP file can be either compressed or uncompressed.

The ZIP output stream uses the DEFLATE compression algorithm to compress data. This algorithm is implemented by the `Deflater` class. See `Deflater` for more information.

Usage

A new ZIP output stream first must be created on an existing output stream. Before writing a piece of data to the stream, you first must create a `ZipEntry` object, fill it with details about the data, and then write it into the ZIP output stream using `putNextEntry()`. How to initialize a ZIP entry is described in `putNextEntry()`.

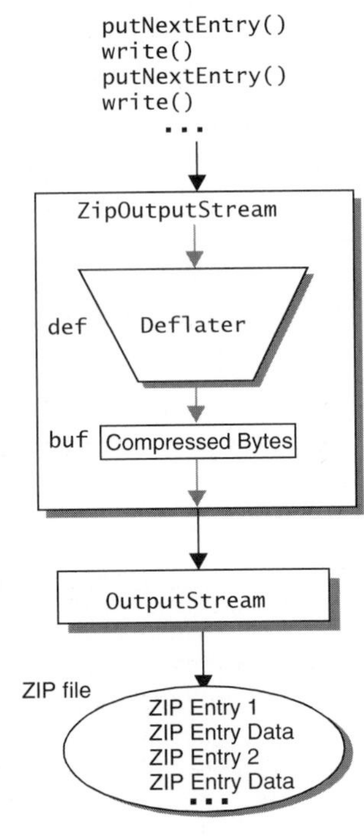

FIGURE 114: `ZipOutputStream`.

1. The `ZipConstants` interface is not accessible outside of the `java.util.zip` package. This interface contains declarations for various constants used in the ZIP-related classes.

After writing the ZIP entry, you write the actual data to the stream by calling `write()`. To write another piece of data to the stream, you must restart the process by creating a new `ZipEntry` object, one that has a different name.

When all of the uncompressed data has been written to the ZIP output stream, `close()` must be called to force the ZIP trailing information to be written out. See Figure 114. When another ZIP file is to be written to the same ZIP output stream, `finish()` is called instead (see `finish()` for details).

The Comment String

You can associate a comment string with a ZIP file. The comment string is typically a short description of the ZIP file contents. At the moment, there is no way to retrieve the comment string. Appropriate methods in `ZipFile` and `ZipInputStream` will be added in the next release of Java.

Note that this comment string differs from ZIP entry comments.

Default Compression Method

The ZIP output stream maintains a default compression method value that controls whether data flowing through the stream will be compressed and which algorithm to use to compress the data. At the moment, only the DEFLATE compression algorithm is supported.

The default compression method value is used only if the compression method for ZIP entry has not been set; the compression method specified in a ZIP entry always takes precedence. The default compression method can be changed at any time.

Compression Level

The ZIP output stream can compress data at ten different levels. The compression level allows you to trade time for a smaller compressed file. In other words, at the lowest level (level `0`), the compression algorithm runs the fastest but results in the worst compression ratio. At the highest level (level `9`), the compression algorithm runs the slowest, thereby providing the best compression ratio.

MEMBER SUMMARY

Constructor	
`ZipOutputStream()`	Constructs a `ZipOutputStream` instance.
Compression Method Constants	
`DEFLATED`	Specifies that entries are to be compressed.
`STORED`	Specifies that entries are to be uncompressed.
Entry Methods	
`closeEntry()`	Closes the current ZIP entry.
`putNextEntry()`	Writes a ZIP entry into this ZIP output stream.

Continued

MEMBER SUMMARY	
Property Methods	
`setComment()`	Sets a comment for the ZIP file.
`setLevel()`	Sets the compression level for this ZIP output stream.
`setMethod()`	Sets the default compression method.
Stream Methods	
`close()`	Writes the closing information of the ZIP file and closes this stream.
`finish()`	Writes the closing information of the ZIP file without closing this stream.
`write()`	Writes data to this ZIP output stream to be compressed.

See Also

`java.io.OutputStream`, `ZipFile`, `ZipInputStream`.

Example

This example implements a program that compresses a directory into a single ZIP file. The program allows you to specify one or more patterns that determine which files are saved. If patterns are specified, the filename must end with one of the specified patterns in order for it to be saved.

The `FileWalker` class is used to walk a directory tree. It uses the `Observer/Observable` classes to notify the example program of all files it discovers.

Main.java

```
import java.io.*;
import java.util.*;
import java.util.zip.*;

class Main implements Observer {
    ZipOutputStream zos;
    String[] patterns;
    File dir;

    Main(String dirname, String outFilename, String[] patterns) {
        dir = new File(dirname);
        this.patterns = patterns;

        try {
            // Create zip output stream.
            zos = new ZipOutputStream(new FileOutputStream(outFilename));

            // Start walking the file system.
            FileWalker fw = new FileWalker();
            fw.addObserver(this);
            fw.walk(new File(dirname), false);
```

```
            zos.close();
        } catch (IOException e) {
            e.printStackTrace();
        }
    }

    // This method is called for each file that the file walker discovers.
    public void update(Observable o, Object arg) {
        File f = (File)arg;
        byte[] buf = new byte[1024];
        int len;

        try {
            if (match(f.getName(), patterns)) {
                ZipEntry ze = new ZipEntry(convertToZIPName(f));
                FileInputStream is = new FileInputStream(f);

                // Initialize entry with the file's last modified time.
                ze.setTime(f.lastModified());

                // These statements are for demonstrative purposes
                // and not necessary.
                ze.setMethod(ZipEntry.DEFLATED);
                ze.setComment(f.getCanonicalPath());
                ze.setExtra(new byte[]{(byte)'X'});

                // Add the zip entry.
                zos.putNextEntry(ze);

                // Now read and write the zip entry data.
                while ((len = is.read(buf)) >= 0) {
                    zos.write(buf, 0, len);
                }

                // This isn't necessary since the next call to putNextEntry()
                // will close the zip entry.
                zos.closeEntry();

                System.out.println(ze.getName() + " ("
                    + ze.getCompressedSize()*100/ze.getSize() + "%)");

                is.close();
            }
        } catch (IOException e) {
            e.printStackTrace();
        }
    }

    // Returns true if s matches one of the patterns.
    boolean match(String s, String[] patterns) {
        if (patterns.length == 0) {
            return true;
        } else {
            for (int i=0; i<patterns.length; i++) {
                if (s.endsWith(patterns[i])) {
                    return true;
                }
            }
        }
```

```
            return false;
        }

        // Converts f's pathname to a form acceptable to ZIP files.
        String convertToZIPName(File f) throws IOException {
            String root = dir.getCanonicalPath();
            String pname = f.getCanonicalPath();
            String rootname =
                root.substring(root.lastIndexOf(File.separatorChar) + 1);

            pname = pname.substring(root.length() + 1);
            pname = pname.replace(File.separatorChar, '/');
            return rootname + "/" + pname;
        }

        public static void main(String[] args) {
            if (args.length < 2) {
                System.err.println(
                    "Usage: java Main <directory> <output file> [<pattern1>...]");
            } else {
                // Retrieve patterns, if any.
                String[] patterns = new String[args.length-2];
                for (int i=2; i<args.length; i++) {
                    patterns[i-2] = args[i];
                }
                new Main(args[0], args[1], patterns);
            }
        }
    }
```

FileWalker.java

```
import java.io.*;
import java.util.*;
import java.util.zip.*;

class FileWalker extends Observable {
    void walk(File dir, boolean includeDirectories) {
        if (dir.isDirectory()) {
            if (includeDirectories) {
                setChanged();
                notifyObservers(dir);
            }
            String[] filenames = dir.list();

            if (filenames != null) {
                for (int i=0; i<filenames.length; i++) {
                    walk(new File(dir, filenames[i]), includeDirectories);
                }
            }
        } else {
            setChanged();
            notifyObservers(dir);
        }
    }
}
```

close()

PURPOSE Writes the closing information of the ZIP file and closes this stream.

SYNTAX `public void close() throws IOException`

DESCRIPTION This method calls `finish()` on this ZIP output stream and closes it. All output streams downstream are also closed. This ZIP output stream can no longer be used after this call.

EXCEPTIONS

`ZipException`
If a ZIP file error occurs while closing.

`IOException`
If an IO error occurs while closing.

OVERRIDES `DeflaterOutputStream.close()`.

SEE ALSO `java.io.IOException`, `java.io.OutputStream.close()`, `finish()`.

EXAMPLE See the class example.

closeEntry()

PURPOSE Closes the current ZIP entry.

SYNTAX `public void closeEntry() throws IOException`

DESCRIPTION This method must be used immediately after all of the data for a ZIP entry has been written. It writes out in a ZIP file necessary information that appears at the end of each ZIP entry.

If the current ZIP entry's three properties—size, compressed size, and checksum value—were initialized when the entry was entered into the ZIP output stream via `putNextEntry()`, this method checks to see if those values are accurate. If they are incorrect, this method throws a `ZipException`.

If the current ZIP entry's three properties were not initialized, this method sets them. For example, after this method call, you can determine the compressed size of the data by calling `ZipEntry.getCompressedSize()`.

It is usually unnecessary to call this method directly, since other methods—`putNextEntry()`, `finish()`, and `close()`—automatically call this method.

EXCEPTIONS

`ZipException`
If a ZIP file error occurs while closing the entry.

`IOException`
If an IO error occurs while closing the entry.

SEE ALSO `close()`, `finish()`, `java.io.IOException`, `putNextEntry()`.

EXAMPLE See the class example.

DEFLATED

PURPOSE Specifies that entries are to be compressed.

SYNTAX `public static final int DEFLATED`

DESCRIPTION This constant (value 8) is used in conjunction with `setMethod()` to set the default compression method. `DEFLATED` specifies that subsequent ZIP entries should be compressed. See `setMethod()` for more details.

SEE ALSO `setMethod()`, `STORED`.

EXAMPLE See `finish()`.

finish()

PURPOSE Writes the closing information of the ZIP file without closing this stream.

SYNTAX `public void finish() throws IOException`

DESCRIPTION This method must be called after all pieces of data have been written to this ZIP output stream. It writes out necessary information that appears at the end of ZIP files. This ZIP output stream can no longer be used after this call.

This method should be used instead of `close()` if it is necessary to write another ZIP file to the same underlying output stream. In this case, a new ZIP output stream must be created on the underlying stream. An example of where this feature might be used is in a client/server application that delivers many ZIP files on the same connection.

This method will call `closeEntry()` if the previous ZIP entry was not already closed.

EXCEPTIONS

`ZipException`
If a ZIP file error occurs while finishing the ZIP file.

`IOException`
If an IO error occurs while finishing the ZIP file.

OVERRIDES `DeflaterOutputStream.finish()`.

SEE ALSO `java.io.IOException`.

EXAMPLE This example demonstrates how to write two ZIP files on the same output stream. After all of the data of the first ZIP file (which only has one entry) has been written, `finish()` is called to write out the closing information of the first ZIP file. For the second ZIP file to be written, the first ZIP output stream is discarded and a new ZIP output stream is created. After all of the data for the second ZIP file is written, `close()` is called to complete the ZIP file and close all of the output streams.

The example also demonstrates how to set the default compression methods. Notice that when the `STORED` compression method is used, it is necessary to initialize the ZIP entry with size and checksum values.

```
import java.util.zip.*;

class Main {
    public static void main(String[] args) {
        if (args.length != 1) {
            System.err.println("Usage: java Main <string>");
        } else {
            try {
                String str = args[0];
            // Write uncompressed zip file.
                ZipOutputStream os = new ZipOutputStream(System.out);
                os.setMethod(ZipOutputStream.STORED);
                os.setComment("uncompressed");

                // Create entry.
                ZipEntry ze = new ZipEntry(str);
                ze.setSize(str.length());

                // Determine the checksum of the string.
                CRC32 crc = new CRC32();
                crc.update(str.getBytes(), 0, str.length());
                ze.setCrc(crc.getValue());

                // Write entry and data.
                os.putNextEntry(ze);
                os.write(str.getBytes(), 0, str.length());

                // Finish the zip output stream without closing it
                // so we can write a new zip file.
                os.finish();

            // Write compressed zip file.
                // Create a new zip output stream on the same output stream.
                os = new ZipOutputStream(System.out);
                os.setMethod(ZipOutputStream.DEFLATED);
                os.setComment("compressed");

                // Write entry and data.
                os.putNextEntry(new ZipEntry(str));
                os.write(str.getBytes(), 0, str.length());

                // Now it's safe to close.
                os.close();
            } catch (Exception e) {
                e.printStackTrace();
            }
        }
    }
}
```

putNextEntry()

PURPOSE Writes a ZIP entry into this ZIP output stream.

SYNTAX `public void putNextEntry(ZipEntry ze) throws IOException`

DESCRIPTION A ZIP file consists of one or more pieces of data. Each piece of data in the ZIP file is described by a ZIP entry, which must accompany the data. In particular, a ZIP entry must precede the data that it describes. This method writes the ZIP entry `ze` into the ZIP output stream, thereby preparing the stream for the data that will follow. See `ZipEntry` for more information about ZIP entries.

The name of `ze` must be different from all ZIP entries previous written to this output stream.

If the modification time of `ze` is not set, the current time is used.

If the compression method of `ze` is not set, the actual compression method used to write the ZIP data is the default compression method of this ZIP output stream.

If the compression method is `STORED`, the size and checksum of `ze` must be set. The ZIP output stream tracks both the size and checksum of the data as it is being written to the stream. If these values do not match the ones in `ze`, a `ZipException` is thrown.

If the compression method is `DEFLATED`, the size, compressed size, and checksum values of `ze` may or may not be set. If not set, the ZIP output stream automatically determines them. If set, the ZIP output stream verifies the values when `ze` is closed. If any one of these three fields is not set, all three are considered to be not set.

The ZIP format allows the size, compressed size, and checksum information to appear before or after the actual data. If this information has been set in `ze`, the information will appear before the actual data; otherwise, the information appears after the actual data. In the later case, if a `ZipInputStream` is used to read the ZIP file, this information won't be available in the ZIP entry returned by `ZipInputStream.getNextEntry()`. Only after the ZIP entry data has been read will the information be available in the ZIP entry.

PARAMETERS

`ze` A non-`null` ZIP entry.

EXCEPTIONS

`IOException`
If an IO error occurs while writing the ZIP entry.

`ZipException`
If `ze` is not properly initialized.

EXAMPLE See the class example.

setComment()

PURPOSE Sets a comment for the ZIP file.

SYNTAX `public void setComment(String comment)`

DESCRIPTION There is currently no method for getting the comment back from the ZIP file. Note that this comment string differs from ZIP entry comments.

PARAMETERS

`comment` A non-`null` string containing a comment. `comment.length()` ≤ 65535 (`0xFFFF`).

EXCEPTIONS

`IllegalArgumentException`

If `comment.length()` > 65535 (`0xFFFF`).

EXAMPLE See `finish()`.

setLevel()

PURPOSE Sets the compression level for this ZIP output stream.

SYNTAX `public void setLevel(int lvl)`

DESCRIPTION This method sets the compression level for subsequent ZIP entries whose compression method is `DEFLATED`; the compression level is ignored if the ZIP entry's compression method is `STORED`.

The ZIP output stream can compress data at ten different levels. Generally, compression runs the fastest at the lowest level (level `0`), but this yields the worst compression ratio. On the other hand, compression runs the slowest at the highest level (level `9`), thereby yielding the best compression ratio.

Note: this method does not work in Java 1.1.4. In particular, this method does not change the compression level from `Deflater.DEFAULT_COMPRESSION`.

PARAMETERS

`lvl` The compression level that must be in the range `Deflater.NO_COMPRESSION` (value `0`) and `Deflater.BEST_COMPRESSION` (value `9`) or `Deflater.DEFAULT_COMPRESSION` (value `-1`).

EXCEPTIONS

`IllegalArgumentException`

If the compression level is invalid.

EXAMPLE This example is a simple demonstration of the use of `setLevel()`. It implements a program that compresses a file at all available compression levels. For each compression level, it prints the compressed size and the time it took to compress the file.

```
import java.io.*;
import java.util.zip.*;

class Main {
    // Compresses the input stream to the output stream.
    static void zipit(InputStream is, OutputStream out, int level)
                        throws ZipException, IOException {
        // Create the entry and output streams.
        ZipOutputStream os = new ZipOutputStream(out);
        ZipEntry ze = new ZipEntry("test");

        int len = 0;
        int readCount = 0;
        byte[] buf = new byte[1024];
        long time = System.currentTimeMillis();

        // Set compression level and write entry.
        os.setLevel(level);
        os.putNextEntry(ze);

        // Write data.
        while ((len = is.read(buf)) >= 0) {
            os.write(buf, 0, len);
            readCount += len;
        }
        os.close();

        System.out.println("    time: " +
            (System.currentTimeMillis()-time) + "ms");
        System.out.println("input size: " + readCount +
            "    level: " + level);
        System.out.println("    compressed size: " + ze.getCompressedSize());
    }

    public static void main(String[] args) {
        if (args.length != 1) {
            System.err.println("Usage: java Main <filename>");
        } else {
            try {
                OutputStream os = new NullOutputStream();

                zipit(new FileInputStream(args[0]), os,
                    Deflater.DEFAULT_COMPRESSION);
                zipit(new FileInputStream(args[0]), os,
                    Deflater.NO_COMPRESSION);
                for (int i=Deflater.BEST_SPEED;
                    i<=Deflater.BEST_COMPRESSION; i++) {
                    zipit(new FileInputStream(args[0]), os, i);
                }
            } catch (Exception e) {
                e.printStackTrace();
            }
        }
    }
}
```

```
class NullOutputStream extends OutputStream {
    public void write(int b) {
    }
    public void write(byte[] buf, int off, int len) {
    }
}
```


setMethod()

PURPOSE Sets the default compression method.

SYNTAX `public void setMethod(int m)`

DESCRIPTION This method sets the default compression method for this ZIP output stream. The default compression method is used by subsequent ZIP entries whose compression method property has not been set. This method should be called just before a ZIP entry is written into this ZIP output stream.

PARAMETERS

`m` Must be either the `DEFLATED` or `STORED` compression method constants.

EXCEPTIONS

`IllegalArgumentException`

If `m` is neither `DEFLATED` nor `STORED`.

SEE ALSO See `DEFLATED`, `finish()`, `STORED`.

EXAMPLE See `finish()`.

STORED

PURPOSE Specifies that entries are to be uncompressed.

SYNTAX `public static final int STORED`

DESCRIPTION This constant (value `0`) is used in conjunction with `setMethod()` to set the default compression method. `STORED` specifies that subsequent ZIP entries should be uncompressed. See `setMethod()` for more details.

SEE ALSO `DEFLATED`, `setMethod()`.

EXAMPLE See `finish()`.

write()

PURPOSE
Writes data to this ZIP output stream to be compressed.

SYNTAX
```
public synchronized void write(byte[] buf, int off, int len)
   throws IOException
```

DESCRIPTION
This method writes `len` bytes, starting from `buf[off]`, to this ZIP output stream. This method blocks until all of the bytes have been written to this output stream.

PARAMETERS

`buf` A non-`null` `byte` array containing the data to be written.

`len` The number of bytes to write starting from `buf[off]`. `0` ≤ `len` ≤ `buf.length-off`.

`off` The `0`-based index of the first byte in `buf` to write. `0` ≤ `off` < `buf.length`.

EXCEPTIONS

`ZipException`
If a ZIP file error occurs while writing.

`IOException`
If an IO error occurs while writing.

OVERRIDES
`DeflaterOutputStream.write()`.

SEE ALSO
`java.io.IOException`, `java.io.OutputStream.write()`.

EXAMPLE
See the class example.

ZipOutputStream()

PURPOSE
Constructs a `ZipOutputStream` instance.

SYNTAX
```
public ZipOutputStream(OutputStream out)
```

DESCRIPTION
This constructor creates a new ZIP output stream on `out`. When all data has been written to the ZIP output stream, it is necessary to call either `finish()` to complete the ZIP file or `close()` to complete the ZIP file and close `out`. See the class description for more information on how to use a ZIP output stream.

The default compression method is `DEFLATED`. The default compression level is `Deflater.DEFAULT_COMPRESSION`.

PARAMETERS

`out` A non-`null` output stream.

SEE ALSO
`close()`, `DEFLATED`, `finish()`, `setMethod()`, `STORED`.

EXAMPLE
See the class example.

Index

12-hour clock
- Calendar.AM; 243
- Calendar.AM_PM; 244
- Calendar.HOUR; 262
- Calendar.HOUR_OF_DAY; 263
- Calendar.PM; 267
- DateFormat.AM_PM_FIELD; 588

A

absolute
- abs()
  - BigDecimal; 79
  - BigInteger; 103
  - Math; 1085
- pathname
  - File.getAbsolutePath(); 790
  - File.getCanonicalPath(); 791
  - testing, File.isAbsolute(); 794
- value
  - BigDecimal.abs(); 79
  - BigInteger.abs(); 103
  - Math.abs(); 1085

abstract
- ABSTRACT, Modifier; 1144
- AbstractMethodError; 39
  - package, java.lang; 39
- methods, AbstractMethodError; 39
- modifier, testing for
  - Modifier.isAbstract(); 1147

accents
- term description, RuleBasedCollator; 1451

accept()
- FilenameFilter; 815
- ServerSocket; 1520
- SocketImpl; 1595

access control
- errors, IllegalAccessError; 939
- exceptions, IllegalAccessException; 942
- threads, permission check
  - Thread.checkAccess(); 1729

accessibility
- bibliographic reference
  - InvalidClassException; 1022
  - Serializable; 1510
- field
  - bibliographic references, Field; 752
  - Field; 752
- term description, InvalidClassException; 1022

acos()
- *See Also* trigonometric functions
- Math; 1086

activexxx methods
- activeCount()
  - Thread; 1728
  - ThreadGroup; 1755
- activeGroupCount(), ThreadGroup; 1756

AD
- GregorianCalendar; 885

adding
- add()
  - BigDecimal; 80
  - BigInteger; 104
  - Calendar; 242
  - GregorianCalendar; 885
- addElement(), Vector; 1864
- addObserver(), Observable; 1292

address(es)
- address, SocketImpl; 1596
- datagram, retrieving
  - DatagramSocketImpl.peek(); 523
- datagram packet, setting
  - DatagramPacket.setAddress(); 504
- datagram packets, source
  - DatagramPacket.getAddress(); 502
- datagram socket, retrieving
  - DatagramSocket.getLocalAddress(); 510
- datagram socket, binding
  - DatagramSocketImpl.bind(); 519

address(es) *(continued)*
IP
representation of, InetAddress; 957
retrieving for a local host
InetAddress.getLocalHost(); 962
retrieving host name for
InetAddress.getHostName(); 961
retrieving
InetAddress.getAddress(); 959
InetAddress.getAllByName(); 959
InetAddress.getByName(); 960
InetAddress.getHostAddress(); 961
ServerSocket.getInetAddress(); 1523
Socket.getInetAddress(); 1577
Socket.getLocalAddress(); 1579
socket, retrieving
SocketImpl.getInetAddress(); 1600
socket, SocketImpl.address; 1596
string representation
InetAddress.toString(); 963
multicast
DatagramSocket; 506
IP addresses reserved for, InetAddress; 957
socket, retrieving
MulticastSocket.getInterface(); 1157
testing for
InetAddress.isMulticastAddress(); 963
ADLER-32 algorithm
See Also algorithms
Adler32; 41
getValue(); 43
package, java.util.zip; 41
reset(); 43
update(); 44
checksum value, retrieving
Deflater.getAdler(); 688
Inflater.getAdler(); 970
after()
Calendar; 242
Date; 565
GregorianCalendar; 886
algorithms
ADLER-32
Adler32; 41
retrieving checksum value
Deflater.getAdler(); 688
Inflater.getAdler(); 970
checksum
Adler32; 41
CRC32; 493
compression, DEFLATE; 679
CRC-32
CRC32; 493
setting checksum value
ZipEntry.setCrc(); 1899
retrieving checksum value
ZipEntry.getCrc(); 1896
DEFLATE
GZIPInputStream; 896
URL, ZipFile; 1906
ZipEntry.DEFLATED; 1895
ZipFile; 1906
ZipOutputStream; 1920
hash, Hashtable; 913
MD5, ClassLoader; 414
message digest, ClassLoader; 414
Nagle's
determining if used
Socket.getTcpNoDelay(); 1582
enabling/disabling
Socket.setTcpNoDelay(); 1585
Socket; 1572
serialization/deserialization, Serializable; 1509
SHA, ClassLoader; 414
SHA-1, SUID relationship to, Serializable; 1512
aligning
dates, *Table*, DateFormat; 582
numbers, NumberFormat; 1193
allowxxx methods
allowThreadSuspension()
ThreadGroup; 1756
allowUserInteraction, URLConnection; 1827
AM/PM
AM, Calendar; 243
AM_PM, Calendar; 244
AM_PM_FIELD, DateFormat; 588
property
DateFormatSymbols; 611
setting, DateFormatSymbols.setAmPmStrings(); 621
retrieving, DateFormatSymbols.getAmPmStrings(); 618
term description, SimpleDateFormat; 1544
analysis
boundary, BreakIterator; 154

AND logical operation
See Also logical operations
and()
BigInteger; 104
BitSet; 138
andNot(), BigInteger; 105
annotation
annotateClass(), ObjectOutputStream; 1266
append()
StringBuffer; 1656
applying
applyLocalizedPattern()
DecimalFormat; 638
SimpleDateFormat; 1550
applyPattern()
ChoiceFormat; 356
DecimalFormat; 640
MessageFormat; 1110
SimpleDateFormat; 1552
APRIL
Calendar, *Table*; 233
arc
See Also trigonometric functions
cosine, Math.acos(); 1086
sine, Math.asin(); 1086
tangent, Math.atan(); 1086
archives
signed, ClassLoader; 414
term description, ClassLoader; 414
areFieldsSet
Calendar; 244
arguments
exceptions, IllegalArgumentException; 945
arithmetic
See Also mathematics; numbers; trigonometric functions
ArithmeticException; 45
package, java.lang; 45
array(s)
See Also data structures; vectors
Array; 47
get(); 51
getBoolean(); 53
getByte(); 54
getChar(); 55
getDouble(); 56
getFloat(); 57
getInt(); 58
getLength(); 59
getLong(); 60
getShort(); 61
newInstance(); 62
package, java.lang.reflect; 47
set(); 63
setBoolean(); 63
setByte(); 65
setChar(); 66
setDouble(); 66
setFloat(); 67
setInt(); 67
setLong(); 68
setShort(); 69
arraycopy(), System; 1713
ArrayIndexOutOfBoundsException; 70
package, java.lang; 70
ArrayStoreException; 72
package, java.lang; 72
boolean
modifying, Array.setBoolean(); 65
retrieving elements from
Array.getBoolean(); 53
byte
converting collation key to
CollationKey.toByteArray(); 445
modifying, Array.setByte(); 65
reading into, DataInputStream.read(); 537
retrieving elements from, Array.getByte(); 54
byte streams
ByteArrayInputStream; 216
ByteArrayOutputStream; 224
calendar field set state, Calendar.isSet; 264
character, retrieving elements from
Array.getChar(); 55
character streams
CharArrayReader; 315
CharArrayWriter; 323
component type, retrieving
Class.getComponentType(); 372
component types
Array; 47
for Get and Set methods, *Tables*, Array; 48
copying, System.arraycopy(); 1713
copying vector references into
Vector.copyInto(); 1866
creating, Array.newInstance(); 62
days property, DateFormatSymbols; 612
elements, retrieving, Array.get(); 51
eras property, DateFormatSymbols; 612

array(s) *(continued)*
exceptions
ArrayIndexOutOfBoundsException; 70
ArrayStoreException; 72
IndexOutOfBoundsException; 955
NegativeArraySizeException; 1164
floating point
Array.getFloat(); 57
modifying
Array.setDouble(); 66
Array.setFloat(); 67
retrieving elements from
Array.getDouble(); 56
of formats, in message patterns
MessageFormat; 1106
integer
modifying
Array.setInt(); 67
Array.setLong(); 68
Array.setShort(); 69
retrieving elements from
Array.getInt(); 58
Array.getLong(); 60
Array.getShort(); 61
length, retrieving, Array.getLength(); 59
limits, ChoiceFormat; 346
retrieving, ChoiceFormat.getLimits(); 360
modifying, Array.set(); 63
months property, DateFormatSymbols; 612
numerical, setting element to character value
Array.setChar(); 66
as objects, Array; 47
string, resource, retrieving
ResourceBundle.getStringArray(); 1444
strings, ChoiceFormat; 346
retrieving, ChoiceFormat.getFormats(); 360
testing for, Class.isArray(); 399
time zone property, DateFormatSymbols; 612
type descriptors for
Class; 366
Table, Class; 367
vector relationship to, Vector; 1862
asin()
See Also trigonometric functions
Math; 1086
atan()
See Also trigonometric functions
Math; 1086
atan2()
See Also trigonometric functions
Math; 1087
AUGUST
Calendar, *Table*; 233
available()
BufferedInputStream; 178
ByteArrayInputStream; 218
FileInputStream; 809
FilterInputStream; 837
InputStream; 985
LineNumberInputStream; 1036
ObjectInput; 1227
ObjectInputStream; 1234
PipedInputStream; 1326
PushbackInputStream; 1386
SequenceInputStream; 1505
SocketImpl; 1596
StringBufferInputStream; 1667
AWT (Abstract Window Toolkit)
See Also "The Java Class Libraries, Second Edition, Volume 2"
event queue access, permission determination
SecurityManager.checkAwtEventQueue-Access(); 1485

B

base
See Also radix
digit characters, Character; 282
BC
GregorianCalendar; 886
beans
See Also "The Java Class Libraries, Second Edition, Volume 2"
Java, signature conventions used by
EventObject; 732
before()
Calendar; 245
Date; 565
GregorianCalendar; 887
best
BEST_COMPRESSION, Deflater; 683
BEST_SPEED, Deflater; 684
big decimal values
See Also numbers
BigDecimal; 74
abs(); 79
add(); 80

compareTo(); 82
divide(); 83
doubleValue(); 84
equals(); 84
floatValue(); 85
hashCode(); 85
intvalue(); 86
longValue(); 86
max(); 87
min(); 87
movePointLeft(); 88
movePointRight(); 88
multiply(); 89
negate(); 90
package, java.math; 74
ROUND_CEILING; 90
ROUND_DOWN; 90
ROUND_FLOOR; 91
ROUND_HALF_DOWN; 91
ROUND_HALF_EVEN; 92
ROUND_HALF_UP; 92
ROUND_UNNECESSARY; 93
ROUND_UP; 92
scale(); 93
setScale(); 94
signum(); 95
subtract(); 96
toBigInteger(); 96
toString(); 96
valueOf(); 97
string representation, generating
BigDecimal.toString(); 96

big integer values
See Also numbers
big decimal value conversion to
BigDecimal.toBigInteger(); 96
BigInteger; 99
abs(); 103
add(); 104
and(); 104
andNot(); 105
bitCount(); 108
bitLength(); 108
clearBit(); 109
compareTo(); 110
divide(); 111
divideAndRemainder(); 112
doubleValue(); 113
equals(); 113
flipBit(); 114
floatValue(); 114
gcd(); 115
getLowestSetBit(); 116
hashCode(); 116
intValue(); 117
isProbablePrime(); 117
longValue(); 118
max(); 118
min(); 119
mod(); 119
modInverse(); 120
modPow(); 121
multiply(); 122
negate(); 123
not(); 123
or(); 124
package, java.math; 99
pow(); 124
remainder(); 125
setBit(); 126
shiftLeft(); 127
shiftRight(); 127
signum(); 128
subtract(); 128
testBit(); 129
toByteArray(); 130
toString(); 131
valueOf(); 132
xor(); 132
bit representation, BigInteger; 100
string representation, generating
BigInteger.toString(); 131

binary number
string representation, generating
Integer.toBinaryString(); 1010
Long.toBinaryString(); 1077

binding
bind()
DatagramSocketImpl; 519
SocketImpl; 1597
BindException; 134
package, java.net; 134
datagram socket
DatagramSocketImpl.bind(); 519

bit representation
big integers, BigInteger; 100
clearing a bit, BigInteger.clearBit(); 109

bit representation *(continued)*
counting zeroes or ones
BigInteger.bitCount(); 108
creating a byte array from
BigInteger.toByteArray(); 130
finding the rightmost
BigInteger.getLowestSetBit(); 116
flipping a bit in, BigInteger.flipBit(); 114
generating, Double.doubleToLongBits(); 712
generating double from
Double.longBitsToDouble(); 716
generating float from
Float.intBitsToFloat(); 865
length, determining
BigInteger.bitLength(); 108
retrieving, Float.floatToIntBits(); 864
setting a bit, BigInteger.setBit(); 126
shifting
left, BigInteger.shiftLeft(); 127
right, BigInteger.shiftRight(); 127
testing for bits set, BigInteger.testBit(); 129
bit sets
big integer use as, BigInteger; 100
BitSet; 136
and(); 138
clear(); 139
clone(); 139
equals(); 140
get(); 140
hashCode(); 141
package, java.util; 136
set(); 141
size(); 142
toString(); 143
xor(); 143
BitSet, or(); 141
clearing a bit in, BitSet.clear(); 139
cloning, BitSet.clone(); 139
retrieving a bit from, BitSet.get(); 140
setting a bit in, BitSet.set(); 141
size, BitSet.size(); 142
string representation, generating
BitSet.toString(); 143
bit vector
See bit sets
bitxxx methods
bitCount(), BigInteger; 108
bitLength(), BigInteger; 108
boolean
arrays
modifying, Array.setBoolean(); 65
retrieving elements from
Array.getBoolean(); 53
Boolean; 144
booleanValue(); 146
FALSE; 147
package, java.lang; 144
TRUE; 148
Class object that represents primitive type
Boolean.TYPE; 149
equality, testing for, Boolean.equals(); 146
fields
modifying, Field.setBoolean(); 766
retrieving values of, Field.getBoolean(); 757
object wrappers, Boolean; 144
reading
DataInput.readBoolean(); 527
DataInputStream.readBoolean(); 538
ObjectInputStream.readBoolean(); 1239
RandomAccessFile.readBoolean(); 1412
string representation, generating
Boolean.toString(); 148
writing
DataOutput.writeBoolean(); 547
DataOutputStream.writeBoolean(); 556
ObjectOutputStream.writeBoolean();
1275
RandomAccessFile.writeBoolean(); 1420
boundary
analysis, BreakIterator; 154
character, break iterator, retrieving
BreakIterator.getCharacterInstance();
165
first, retrieving position
BreakIterator.first(); 163
following, retrieving position
BreakIterator.following(); 163
last, retrieving position
BreakIterator.last(); 171
line-break, boundary, break iterator, retrieving
BreakIterator.getLineInstance(); 165
next, retrieving position
BreakIterator.next(); 172
position, BreakIterator; 153
previous, retrieving position
BreakIterator.previous(); 174
rules, BreakIterator; 153

term description
BreakIterator; 153
BreakIterator.previous(); 174
text, setting a new string to be scanned
BreakIterator.setText(); 175
user character, determining
CollationElementIterator; 436
word-break, creating break iterator for
BreakIterator.getWordInstance(); 171
breaks
BreakIterator; 150
clone(); 161
current(); 162
first(); 163
following(); 163
getAvailableLocales(); 164
getCharacterInstance(); 165
getLineInstance(); 165
getSentenceInstance(); 169
getText(); 169
getWordInstance(); 171
last(); 171
next(); 172
package, java.text; 150
previous(); 174
setText(); 175
term description, BreakIterator; 150
buffers
buf
BufferedInputStream; 179
BufferedOutputStream; 187
ByteArrayInputStream; 218
ByteArrayOutputStream; 226
CharArrayReader; 317
CharArrayWriter; 325
DeflaterOutputStream; 698
InflaterInputStream; 979
PushbackInputStream; 1387
buffer
PipedInputStream; 1326
StringBufferInputStream; 1668
BufferedInputStream; 176
available(); 178
buf; 179
count; 180
mark(); 180
marklimit; 181
markpos; 181
markSupported(); 181
package, java.io; 176
pos; 182
read(); 182
reset(); 183
skip(); 183
BufferedOutputStream; 185
buf; 187
count; 188
flush(); 188
package, java.io; 185
write(); 189
BufferedReader; 190
close(); 193
mark(); 194
markSupported(); 194
package, java.io; 190
read(); 195
readLine(); 196
ready(); 196
reset(); 197
skip(); 197
BufferedWriter; 199
close(); 202
flush(); 202
newLine(); 203
package, java.io; 199
write(); 203
byte array
ByteArrayInputStream.buf; 218
ByteArrayOutputStream.buf; 226
bytes stored in, number of
BufferedOutputStream.count; 188
character, CharArrayReader.buf; 317
compressed data
DeflaterOutputStream.buf; 698
InflaterInputStream.buf; 979
flushing
DataOutputStream.flush(); 555
ObjectOutput.flush(); 1260
input, determining if empty
Deflater.needsInput(); 689
Inflater.needsInput(); 973
input stream
BufferedInputStream.buf; 179
CharArrayWriter.buf; 325
PipedInputStream.buffer; 1326
PushbackInputStream.buf; 1387
number of bytes in
InflaterInputStream.len; 981

buffers *(continued)*
output stream, BufferedOutputStream.buf; 187
read position, BufferedInputStream.pos; 182
retrieving, StringWriter.getBuffer(); 1705
streams
BufferedOutputStream; 185
concept description; 6
input, BufferedInputStream; 176
string
capacity retrieval
StringBuffer.capacity(); 1658
retrieving characters from
StringBuffer.charAt(); 1658
StringBuffer; 1655
vector element, Vector.elementData; 1868
writing, ObjectOutputStream.drain(); 1269
bytes
arrays
converting collation key to
CollationKey.toByteArray(); 445
creating from the big integer bits
BigInteger.toByteArray(); 130
modifying, Array.setByte(); 65
retrieving elements from, Array.getByte(); 54
Byte; 205
byteValue(); 207
decode(); 207
doubleValue(); 208
equals(); 209
floatValue(); 209
hashCode(); 209
intValue(); 210
longValue(); 210
MAX_VALUE; 210
MIN_VALUE; 211
package, java.lang; 205
parseByte(); 211
shortValue(); 212
toString(); 213
TYPE(); 213
valueOf(); 214
ByteArrayInputStream; 216
available(); 218
buf; 218
count; 219
mark; 219
mark(); 220
markSupported(); 221
package, java.io; 216
pos; 221
read(); 221
reset(); 222
skip(); 223
ByteArrayOutputStream; 224
buf; 226
count; 227
package, java.io; 224
reset(); 227
size(); 228
toByteArray(); 228
toString(); 229
write(); 229, 230
writeTo(); 231
bytesTransferred
InterruptedIOException; 1020
byteValue()
Byte; 207
Double; 711
Float; 862
Integer; 1003
Long; 1070
Number; 1188
Short; 1531
character conversion to
InputStreamReader; 991
OutputStreamWriter; 1309
to character encoding identifiers, *Table*
String.startsWith(); 1648
character to byte encoding identifiers, *Table*
String; 1639
codes
ClassLoader; 418
compiler control, Compiler; 470
creating class objects from
ClassLoader.defineClass(); 418
default encoding, FileReader; 827
fields
modifying, Field.setByte(); 767
retrieving values of, Field.getByte(); 758
flushing
BufferedOutputStream.flush(); 188
OutputStream.flush(); 1306
OutputStreamWriter.flush(); 1311
PipedOutputStream.flush(); 1334
PipedWriter.flush(); 1344
PrintStream.flush(); 1350
PrintWriter.flush(); 1358
Writer.flush(); 1889

input buffer, number of
  BufferedInputStream.count; 180
  ByteArrayInputStream.count; 219
input stream
  reading, CheckedInputStream.read(); 337
  skipping, CheckedInputStream.skip(); 338
number written
  DataOutputStream.written; 561
output buffer, number of
  ByteArrayOutputStream.count; 227
output stream, writing
  CheckedOutputStream.write(); 341
pseudorandom-numbers, generating
  Random.nextBytes(); 1402
pushing back
  PushbackInputStream.unread(); 1389
read position, ByteArrayInputStream.pos; 221
reading
  ByteArrayInputStream.read(); 221
  DataInput.readByte(); 527
  DataInput.readUnsignedByte(); 531
  DataInputStream.read(); 537
  DataInputStream.readByte(); 538
  DataInputStream.readUnsignedByte(); 543
  FileInputStream.read(); 811
  FilterInputStream.read(); 839
  number available for
    BufferedInputStream.available(); 178
    ByteArrayInputStream.available(); 218
    FileInputStream.available(); 809
  ObjectInputStream.readByte(); 1239
  PushbackInputStream.read(); 1388
  RandomAccessFile.read(); 1411
  RandomAccessFile.readByte(); 1412
  RandomAccessFile.readUnsignedByte(); 1417
  SequenceInputStream.read(); 1505
  total number requested
    DataInput.readFully(); 529
    DataInputStream.readFully(); 540
    RandomAccessFile.readFully(); 1414
retrieving
  as byte array, ByteArrayOutputStream.toByte-Array(); 228
  number of
    ByteArrayOutputStream.size(); 228
    DataOutputStream.size(); 555
retrieving object value as
  Double.byteValue(); 711
  Float.byteValue(); 862
  Integer.byteValue(); 1003
  Long.byteValue(); 1070
  Number.byteValue(); 1188
  Short.byteValue(); 1531
skipping
  BufferedInputStream.skip(); 183
  ByteArrayInputStream.skip(); 223
  DataInput.skipBytes(); 533
  DataInputStream.skipBytes(); 545
  FileInputStream.skip(); 812
  FilterInputStream.skip(); 841
  InputStream.skip(); 989
  ObjectInputStream.skipBytes(); 1254
socket, determining number available
  SocketImpl.available(); 1596
streams
  BufferedInputStream; 176
  ByteArrayInputStream; 216
  ByteArrayOutputStream; 224
  InputStream; 983
  OutputStream; 1304
  PipedInputStream; 1323
  PipedOutputStream; 1332
  PrintStream; 1346
  PushbackInputStream; 1383
  SequenceInputStream; 1503
string representation, generating
  Byte.toString(); 213
term description, Byte; 205
transferred before an interrupt
  InterruptedIOException.bytesTransferred; 1020
unsigned, reading
  ObjectInputStream.readUnsignedByte(); 1248
writing
  BufferedOutputStream.write(); 189
  DataOutput.write(); 547
  DataOutput.writeByte(); 548
  DataOutput.writeBytes(); 548
  DataOutputStream.write(); 555
  DataOutputStream.writeByte(); 557
  DataOutputStream.writeBytes(); 557
  FileOutputStream.write(); 825
  FilterOutputStream.write(); 846
  ObjectOutputStream.write(); 1274

bytes *(continued)*
- writing
  - ObjectOutputStream.writeByte(); 1276
  - OutputStream.write(); 1306
  - PipedOutputStream.write(); 1335
  - PrintStream.write(); 1353
  - PrintWriter stream use for; 1354
  - RandomAccessFile.write(); 1419
  - RandomAccessFile.writeByte(); 1420
  - RandomAccessFile.writeBytes(); 1421
  - to another stream
    - ByteArrayOutputStream.writeTo; 231
  - to byte array
    - ByteArrayOutputStream.write(); 230

C

C++ language
- comments, specifying
  - StreamTokenizer.slashSlashComments(); 1626

C language
- comments, specifying
  - StreamTokenizer.slashStarComments(); 1626

caching
- determining whether connection permits
  - URLConnection.getUseCaches(); 1840
- document, protocol support, URLConnection; 1820
- URL connection
  - flag, setting
    - URLConnection.setDefaultUseCaches(); 1844
    - URLConnection.setUseCaches(); 1846
  - testing for permitted use
    - URLConnection.useCaches; 1848
    - URLConnection.getUseCaches(); 1840
    - URLConnection.getDefaultUseCaches(); 1833

calendar(s)
- *See Also* date(s)
- Calendar; 232
  - add(); 242
  - after(); 242
  - AM; 243
  - AM_PM; 244
  - areFieldsSet; 244
  - before(); 245
  - clear(); 246
  - clone(); 247
  - complete(); 247
  - computeFields(); 248
  - computeTime(); 248
  - DATE; 249
  - Date relationship to; 232
  - DAY_OF_MONTH; 249
  - DAY_OF_WEEK; 250
  - DAY_OF_WEEK_IN_MONTH; 250
  - DAY_OF_YEAR; 251
  - DST_OFFSET; 251
  - equals(); 252
  - ERA; 252
  - FIELD_COUNT; 253
  - fields; 253
  - get(); 254
  - getAvailableLocales(); 254
  - getFirstDayOfWeek(); 258
  - getGreatestMinimum(); 258
  - getInstance(); 258
  - getLeastMaximum(); 258
  - getMaximum(); 259
  - getMinimalDaysInFirstWeek(); 260
  - getMinimum(); 260
  - getTime(); 260
  - getTimeInMillis(); 261
  - getTimeZone(); 261
  - HOUR; 262
  - HOUR_OF_DAY; 263
  - instantiating, Calendar.getInstance(); 258
  - internalGet(); 263
  - isSet(); 264
  - isSet; 264
  - isTimeSet; 264
  - MILLISECOND; 265
  - MINUTE; 265
  - MONTH; 266
  - package, java.util; 232
  - PM; 267
  - roll(); 267
  - SECOND; 268
  - set(); 269
  - setFirstDayOfWeek(); 272
  - setLenient(); 273
  - setMinimalDaysInFirstWeek(); 274
  - setTime(); 274
  - setTimeInMillis(); 275
  - setTimeZone(); 275
  - time; 275
  - WEEK_OF_MONTH; 275

WEEK_OF_YEAR; 279
YEAR; 280
ZONE_OFFSET; 281
calendar, DateFormat; 588
fields
Calendar; 233
Calendar.AM; 243
Calendar.AM_PM; 244
Calendar.getMinimum(); 260
Calendar.WEEK_OF_MONTH; 275
Calendar.WEEK_OF_YEAR; 279
Calendar.YEAR; 280
Calendar.ZONE_OFFSET; 281
clearing, Calendar.clear(); 246
computing
Calendar.complete(); 247
Calendar.computeFields(); 248
GregorianCalendar.computeFields(); 887
constant
Calendar.DATE; 249
Calendar.DAY_OF_MONTH; 249
Calendar.DAY_OF_WEEK; 250
Calendar.DAY_OF_WEEK_IN_MONTH; 250
Calendar.DAY_OF_YEAR; 251
Calendar.DST_OFFSET; 251
Calendar.ERA; 252
Calendar.HOUR; 262
Calendar.HOUR_OF_DAY; 263
Calendar.MILLISECOND; 265
Calendar.MINUTE; 265
Calendar.MONTH; 266
Calendar.SECOND; 268
converting to Date value
GregorianCalendar.computeTime(); 887
incrementing/decrementing
Calendar.add(); 242
Calendar.roll(); 267
GregorianCalendar.add(); 885
GregorianCalendar.roll(); 894
number of, Calendar.FIELD_COUNT; 253
retrieving, Calendar.get(); 254
retrieving current value
Calendar.internalGet(); 263
retrieving greatest minimum value
Calendar.getGreatestMinimum(); 258
GregorianCalendar.getGreatest-Minimum(); 888
retrieving least maximum value
Calendar.getLeastMaximum(); 259
GregorianCalendar.getLeast-Maximum(); 889
retrieving maximum value
Calendar.getMaximum(); 259
GregorianCalendar.getMaximum(); 890
retrieving minimum value
Calendar.getMinimum(); 260
GregorianCalendar.getMinimum(); 890
setting,
Calendar.set(); 269
Calendar.setFirstDayOfWeek(); 272
Calendar.setLenient(); 273
Calendar.setMinimalDaysInFirst-Week(); 274
Calendar.setTime(); 274
Calendar.setTimeInMillis(); 275
Calendar.setTimeZone(); 275
state array, Calendar.isSet; 264
testing if set, Calendar.isSet(); 264
updating steps, *Table*, Calendar.set(); 270
value array, Calendar.fields; 253
GregorianCalendar; 882
AD; 885
add(); 885
after(); 886
BC; 886
before(); 887
computeFields(); 887
computeTime(); 887
equals(); 888
getGreatestMinimum(); 888
getGregorianChange(); 889
getLeastMaximum(); 889
getMaximum(); 890
getMinimum(); 890
hashCode(); 892
isLeapYear(); 893
package, java.util; 882
roll(); 894
setGregorianChange(); 895
Julian
retrieving date replaced by Gregorian
GregorianCalendar.getGregorian-Change(); 889
setting date replaced by Gregorian
GregorianCalendar.setGregorian-Change(); 895

calendar(s) *(continued)*
leniency, Calendar; 233
retrieving, DateFormat.getCalendar(); 595
setting, DateFormat.setCalendar(); 604
systems, Calendar; 232
canxxx methods
canRead(), File; 786
canWrite(), File; 786
Canada
CANADA, Locale; 1056
CANADA_FRENCH, Locale; 1056
predefined locale codes, *Table*, Locale; 1056
canonical
CANONICAL_DECOMPOSITION, Collator; 453
decomposition
collation order, Collator; 450
Collator.CANONICAL_DECOMPOSITION; 453
pathname, File.getCanonicalPath(); 791
capacity
capacity()
StringBuffer; 1658
Vector; 1865
capacityIncrement, Vector; 1865
retrieving for a string buffer
StringBuffer.capacity(); 1658
string buffer, setting
StringBuffer.ensureCapacity(); 1659
term description, StringBuffer; 1655
vector
determining, Vector.capacity(); 1865
minimum, specifying
Vector.ensureCapacity(); 1869
setting increment size
Vector.capacityIncrement(); 1865
Vector; 1862
vectors, trimming to size
Vector.trimToSize(); 1876
case
character, Character; 283
insensitive comparison
String.equalsIgnoreCase(); 1638
lowercase, specifying
StreamTokenizer.lowerCaseMode(); 1619
lowercase conversion
String.toLowerCase(); 1652
uppercase conversion
String.toUpperCase(); 1652
casting
exceptions, ClassCastException; 407
to SimpleDateFormat, DateFormat; 581
ceiling
See Also mathematics
ceil(), Math; 1087
Math.ceil(); 1087
character(s)
array, closing, CharArrayReader.close(); 318
array, creating from a string
String.toCharArray(); 1651
arrays, retrieving elements from
Array.getChar(); 55
availability testing
CharArrayReader.ready(); 321
base, BreakIterator; 151
boundary
analysis, BreakIterator; 154
break iterator, retrieving
BreakIterator.getCharacter-
Instance(); 165
BreakIterator; 150
to byte conversion
InputStreamReader; 991
OutputStreamWriter; 1309
byte to character encoding identifiers, *Table*
String.startsWith(); 1648
Character; 282
charValue(); 286
digit(); 286
equals(); 287
forDigit(); 287
getNumericValue(); 288
getType(); 288
hashCode(); 290
isDefined(); 290
isDigit(); 290
isIdentifierIgnorable(); 291
isISOControl(); 292
isJavaIdentifierPart(); 292
isJavaIdentifierStart(); 293
isJavaLetter(); 294
isJavaLetterOrDigit(); 294
isLetter(); 295
isLetterOrDigit(); 296
isLowerCase(); 296
isSpace(); 297
isSpaceChar(); 297
isTitleCase(); 297
isUnicodeIdentifierPart(); 298
isUnicodeIdentifierStart(); 299

isUpperCase(); 299
isWhitespace(); 300
MAX_RADIX; 300
MAX_VALUE; 301
MIN_RADIX; 301
MIN_VALUE; 301
package, java.lang; 282
toLowerCase(); 302
toTitleCase(); 302
toUpperCase(); 302
TYPE; 304
CharacterIterator; 305
clone(); 310
current(); 310
DONE; 311
first(); 311
getBeginIndex(); 311
getEndIndex(); 312
getIndex(); 312
last(); 312
next(); 312
package, java.text; 305
previous(); 313
setIndex(); 313
CharArrayReader; 315
buf; 317
close(); 318
count; 318
mark(); 318
markPos; 319
markSupported(); 320
package, java.io; 315
pos; 320
read(); 320
ready(); 321
reset(); 322
skip(); 322
CharArrayWriter; 323
buf; 325
close(); 326
count; 326
flush(); 326
package, java.io; 323
reset(); 326
size(); 327
toCharArray(); 328
toString(); 329
write(); 329
writeTo(); 330
charAt()
String; 1634
StringBuffer; 1658
CharConversionException; 331
package, java.io; 331
charValue(), Character; 286
combining
BreakIterator; 151
sequence, BreakIterator; 151
comment, specifying
StreamTokenizer.commentChar(); 1617
conversion, exception
CharConversionException; 331
copying from a string buffer
StringBuffer.getChars(); 1660
copying from string into character array
String.getChars(); 1641
creating strings from
String.copyValueOf(); 1636
current, retrieving
StringCharacterIterator.current(); 1678
digit
retrieving
DecimalFormatSymbols.getDigit(); 670
setting
DecimalFormatSymbols.setDigit(); 674
Unicode, *Table*, Character; 291
digit representation by
Character.forDigit(); 287
encoding
URLEncoder; 1849
URLEncoder.encode(); 1851
fields
modifying, Field.setChar(); 769
retrieving values of, Field.getChar(); 758
finding first occurrence in a string
String.indexOf(); 1642
finding last occurrence in a string
String.lastIndexOf(); 1643
first
retrieving
CharacterIterator.first(); 311
StringCharacterIterator.first(); 1679
retrieving index of
FieldPosition.getBeginIndex(); 778
flushing
BufferedWriter.flush(); 202
CharArrayWriter.flush(); 326

character(s) *(continued)*
ignorable, RuleBasedCollator; 1451
input, number of, CharArrayReader.count; 318
ISO-LATIN1
Character.isLetter(); 295
Character.isLetterOrDigit(); 296
iteration over, CollationElementIterator; 435
iterator, retrieving
BreakIterator.getText(); 169
last
retrieving
CharacterIterator.last(); 312
StringCharacterIterator.last(); 1681
retrieving index of
FieldPosition.getEndIndex(); 781
lowercase
Character.isLowerCase(); 296
Character.toLowerCase(); 302
next, retrieving
CharacterIterator.next(); 312
StringCharacterIterator.next(); 1682
ordinary
resetting syntax for
StreamTokenizer.resetSyntax(); 1626
specifying
StreamTokenizer.ordinaryChar(); 1621
StreamTokenizer.ordinaryChars(); 1622
StreamTokenizer.ordinaryChar(); 1621
output, number of, CharArrayWriter.count; 326
position in a field, FieldPosition; 775
previous, retrieving
CharacterIterator.previous(); 313
StringCharacterIterator.previous(); 1684
pushing back, PushbackReader.unread(); 1397
quote, specifying
StreamTokenizer.quoteChar(); 1625
read position, CharArrayReader.pos; 320
reading
BufferedReader.read(); 195
CharArrayReader.read(); 320
DataInput.readChar(); 528
DataInputStream.readChar(); 538
FileReader; 827
ObjectInputStream.readChar(); 1240
PushbackReader.read(); 1396
RandomAccessFile.readChar(); 1413
Reader.read(); 1431
StringReader.read(); 1693
replacing, StringBuffer.setCharAt(); 1663
reset, RuleBasedCollator; 1450
retrieving
as char array
CharArrayWriter.toCharArray(); 328
CharacterIterator.setIndex(); 313
CollationElementIterator.next(); 438
number of, CharArrayWriter.size(); 327
StringCharacterIterator.setIndex(); 1685
retrieving from a string, String.charAt(); 1634
retrieving from a string buffer
StringBuffer.charAt(); 1658
reversing order of
StringBuffer.reverse(); 1662
skipping
BufferedReader.skip(); 197
FilterReader.skip(); 854
LineNumberReader.skip(); 1048
Reader.skip(); 1434
StringReader.skip(); 1695
space, Character.isSpaceChar(); 297
streams
BufferedReader; 190
BufferedWriter; 199
FileReader; 827
FilterReader; 847
FilterWriter; 855
input, CharArrayReader; 315
InputStreamReader; 990
LineNumberReader; 1040
output, CharArrayWriter; 323
OutputStreamWriter; 1308
PipedReader; 1337
PipedWriter; 1342
PrintWriter; 1354
PushbackReader; 1392
Reader; 1426
StringReader; 1690
StringWriter; 1703
Writer; 1887
string representation, generating
Character.toString(); 302
StringCharacterIterator; 1671
substring searches with, String; 1632
titlecase
Character.isTitleCase(); 297
Character.toTitleCase(); 302
to byte encoding identifiers, *Table*, String; 1639
Unicode, BreakIterator; 151

uppercase
Character.isUpperCase(); 299
Character.toUpperCase(); 303
user, Unicode characters compared with
BreakIterator; 152
values, setting numerical array element to,
Array.setChar(); 66
whitespace, Character.isWhitespace(); 300
as whitespace
StreamTokenizer.whitespaceChars; 1630
as words, StreamTokenizer.wordChars; 1631
writing
BufferedWriter.write(); 203
CharArrayWriter.write(); 329
DataOutput.writeChar(); 548
DataOutput.writeChars(); 549
DataOutputStream.writeChar(); 558
DataOutputStream.writeChars(); 558
FileWriter; 830
FilterWriter.write(); 859
ObjectOutputStream.writeChar(); 1277
OutputStreamWriter.write(); 1313
PipedWriter.write(); 1345
PrintWriter.write(); 1361
RandomAccessFile.writeChar(); 1421
RandomAccessFile.writeChars(); 1422
StringWriter.write(); 1707
to another writer
CharArrayWriter.writeTo; 330
Writer.write(); 1890

checking
checkAccept(), SecurityManager; 1484
checkAccess()
SecurityManager; 1484
Thread; 1729
ThreadGroup; 1757
checkAwtEventQueueAccess()
SecurityManager; 1485
checkConnect(), SecurityManager; 1486
checkCreateClassLoader()
SecurityManager; 1486
checkDelete(), SecurityManager; 1487
checkError()
PrintStream; 1349
PrintWriter; 1357
checkExec(), SecurityManager; 1487
checkExit(), SecurityManager; 1488
checkLink(), SecurityManager; 1488
checkListen(), SecurityManager; 1489
checkMemberAccess()
SecurityManager; 1489
checkMulticast(), SecurityManager; 1490
checkPackageAccess()
SecurityManager; 1491
checkPackageDefinition()
SecurityManager; 1491
checkPrintJobAccess()
SecurityManager; 1492
checkPropertiesAccess()
SecurityManager; 1492
checkPropertyAccess()
SecurityManager; 1492
checkRead(), SecurityManager; 1493
checkSecurityAccess()
SecurityManager; 1494
checkSetFactory(), SecurityManager; 1494
checkSystemClipboardAccess()
SecurityManager; 1495
checkTopLevelWindow()
SecurityManager; 1495
checkWrite(), SecurityManager; 1496

checksum
algorithms
Adler32; 41
CRC32; 493
CheckedInputStream; 333
getChecksum(); 337
package, java.util.zip; 333
read(); 337
skip(); 338
CheckedOutputStream; 339
getChecksum(); 341
package, java.util.zip; 339
write(); 341
Checksum; 343
getValue(); 345
package, java.util.zip; 343
reset(); 345
update(); 345
concept description; 37
CRC-32, ZipEntry.getCrc(); 1896
resetting
Checksum.reset(); 345
CRC32.reset(); 495
retrieving
CheckedInputStream.getChecksum(); 337
CheckedOutputStream.getChecksum(); 341
Checksum.getValue(); 345
CRC32.getValue(); 495

checksum *(continued)*
term description, Checksum; 343
updating
Adler32.update(); 44
Checksum.update(); 345
CRC32.update(); 495
value, retrieving
Adler32.getValue(); 43
Deflater.getAdler(); 688
Inflater.getAdler(); 970
China
CHINA, Locale; 1056
CHINESE, Locale; 1056
Chinese, predefined locale codes, *Table* Locale; 1056
predefined locale codes, *Table*, Locale; 1056
choice
ChoiceFormat
applyPattern(); 356
clone(); 358
equals(); 359
format(); 360
getFormats(); 360
getLimits(); 360
hashCode(); 361
nextDouble(); 361
package, java.text; 346
parse(); 362
previousDouble(); 363
setChoices(); 363
toPattern(); 364
ChoiceFormat, message pattern use MessageFormat; 1105
class(es)
BigDecimal, java.math package; 74
BigInteger, java.math package; 99
Class; 365
forName(); 370
getClasses(); 371
getClassLoader(); 372
getComponentType(); 372
getConstructor(); 373
getConstructors(); 375
getDeclaredClasses(); 375
getDeclaredConstructor(); 376
getDeclaredConstructors(); 377
getDeclaredField(); 379
getDeclaredFields(); 380
getDeclaredMethod(); 381
getDeclaredMethods(); 383
getDeclaringClass(); 384
getField(); 385
getFields(); 386
getInterfaces(); 388
getMethod(); 389
getMethods(); 390
getModifiers(); 392
getName(); 393
getResource(); 393
getResourceAsStream(); 396
getSigners(); 398
getSuperclass(); 399
isArray(); 399
isAssignableFrom(); 400
isInstance(); 401
isInterface(); 402
isPrimitive(); 403
newInstance(); 404
object, primitive type wrappers, *Table*; 368
object that represents boolean primitive type Boolean.TYPE; 149
object that represents byte primitive type Byte.TYPE; 213
object that represents char primitive type Character.TYPE; 304
object that represents double primitive type Double.TYPE; 719
object that represents float primitive type Float.TYPE; 870
object that represents int primitive type Integer.TYPE; 1013
object that represents long primitive type Long.TYPE; 1080
object that represents short primitive type Short.TYPE; 1538
object that represents void, Void.TYPE; 1882
package, java.lang; 365
toString(); 405
Class.getDeclaringClass(); 384
Class objects, retrieving Class.getClasses(); 371
ClassCastException; 407
package, java.lang; 407
ClassCircularityError; 409
package, java.lang; 409
classDepth(), SecurityManager; 1496
ClassFormatError; 411
package, java.lang; 411

ClassLoader; 413
defineClass(); 418
findLoadedClass(); 419
findSystemClass(); 420
getResource(); 421
getResourceAsStream(); 421
getSystemResource(); 422
getSystemResourceAsStream(); 422
loadClass(); 423
package, java.lang; 413
resolveClass(); 425
setSigners(); 425
classLoaderDepth(), SecurityManager; 1498
ClassNotFoundException; 426
package, java.lang; 426
compiling
Compiler.compileClass(); 471
Compiler.compileClasses(); 471
descriptor
ObjectInputStream.resolveClass(); 1251
ObjectOutputStream; 1264
errors, NoClassDefFoundError; 1166
exceptions, ClassNotFoundException; 426
files
bibliographic reference, ClassLoader; 413
ClassLoader; 413
linking, ClassLoader.resolveClass(); 425
loaders
concepts and overview, ClassLoader; 413
creating, permission determination
SecurityManager.checkCreateClass-Loader(); 1486
default system, ClassLoader; 413
on stack, testing for
SecurityManager.inClassLoader(); 1502
retrieving, Class.getClassLoader(); 372
loading
ClassLoader; 413
ClassLoader.findSystemClass(); 420
ClassLoader.loadClass(); 423
objects
characteristics and overview, Class; 365
creating, ClassLoader.defineClass(); 418
Boolean.TYPE; 149
Byte.TYPE; 213
Character.TYPE; 304
Double.TYPE; 719
Float.TYPE; 870
Integer.TYPE; 1013
Long.TYPE; 1080
retrieving; 367
Object.getClass(); 1220
Short.TYPE; 1538
Void.TYPE; 1882
retrieving
Class objects
Class.getDeclaredClasses(); 375
Class objects for, Class.getClasses(); 371
ClassLoader.findLoadedClass(); 419
root; 13
on stack, testing for
SecurityManager.inClass(); 1501
valid modifiers for, *Table*, Modifier; 1143
clearing
clear()
BitSet; 139
Calendar; 246
Hashtable; 916
clearBit(), BigInteger; 109
clearChanged(), Observable; 1293
clipboard
accessing, permission determination, Security-Manager.checkSystemClipboardAccess(); 1495
cloning
bit sets, BitSet.clone(); 139
calendars, Calendar.clone(); 247
clone()
BitSet; 139
BreakIterator; 161
Calendar; 247
CharacterIterator; 310
ChoiceFormat; 358
Collator; 454
DateFormat; 589
DateFormatSymbols; 616
DecimalFormat; 642
DecimalFormatSymbols; 668
Format; 877
Hashtable; 916
Locale; 1059
MessageFormat; 1110
NumberFormat; 1198
Object; 1216
RuleBasedCollator; 1456
SimpleDateFormat; 1552
SimpleTimeZone; 1562

cloning *(continued)*
clone()
StringCharacterIterator; 1677
TimeZone; 1778
Vector; 1866
Cloneable; 428
package, java.lang; 428
CloneNotSupportedException; 431
package, java.lang; 431
concepts and overview, Cloneable; 428
exceptions, CloneNotSupportedException; 431
hash tables, Hashtable.clone(); 916
locales, Locale.clone(); 1059
objects, Object.clone(); 1216
SimpleTimeZone.clone(); 1562
time zones
SimpleTimeZone.clone(); 1562
TimeZone.clone(); 1778
vectors, Vector.clone(); 1866
closing
close()
BufferedReader; 193
BufferedWriter; 202
CharArrayReader; 318
CharArrayWriter; 326
DatagramSocket; 509
DatagramSocketImpl; 519
DeflaterOutputStream; 698
FileInputStream; 809
FileOutputStream; 823
FilterInputStream; 837
FilterOutputStream; 844
FilterReader; 849
FilterWriter; 857
GZIPInputStream; 897
GZIPOutputStream; 908
InputStream; 986
InputStreamReader; 993
ObjectInput; 1227
ObjectInputStream; 1234
ObjectOutput; 1260
ObjectOutputStream; 1268
OutputStream; 1306
OutputStreamWriter; 1310
PipedInputStream; 1326
PipedOutputStream; 1333
PipedReader; 1339
PipedWriter; 1343
PrintStream; 1349
PrintWriter; 1358
PushbackReader; 1394
RandomAccessFile; 1409
Reader; 1429
SequenceInputStream; 1505
ServerSocket; 1522
Socket; 1577
SocketImpl; 1597
StringReader; 1692
StringWriter; 1704
Writer; 1889
ZipFile; 1911
ZipInputStream; 1916
ZipOutputStream; 1925
closeEntry()
ZipInputStream; 1917
ZipOutputStream; 1925
FileInputStream, finalize(); 810
FileOutputStream, finalize(); 825
code
response
HttpURLConnection.responseCode; 935
retrieving
HttpURLConnection.getResponse-Code(); 933
collation
classes that implement; 31
CollationElementIterator; 434
next(); 438
NULLORDER; 439
package, java.text; 434
primaryOrder(); 439
reset(); 439
secondaryOrder(); 440
tertiaryOrder(); 440
CollationKey; 441
compareTo(); 444
equals(); 444
getSourceString(); 445
hashCode(); 445
package, java.text; 441
toByteArray(); 445
Collator; 447
CANONICAL_DECOMPOSITION; 453
clone(); 454
compare(); 455
equals(); 456
FULL_DECOMPOSITION; 456
getAvailableLocales(); 457

getCollationKey(); 458
getDecomposition(); 459
getInstance(); 460
getStrength(); 460
hashCode(); 460
IDENTICAL; 461
NO_DECOMPOSITION; 461
package, java.text; 447
PRIMARY; 462
SECONDARY; 462
setDecomposition; 463
setStrength; 467
TERTIARY; 469
concept description; 27
element, CollationElementIterator; 434
errors, RuleBasedCollator; 1451
keys
CollationKey; 441
transforming a string into
RuleBasedCollator.getCollationKey(); 1459
order, CollationElementIterator; 434
RuleBasedCollator; 1447
term description
Collator; 447
RuleBasedCollator; 1447

collision
hash table, Hashtable; 913

combining
Collator objects, RuleBasedCollator; 1452
COMBINING_SPACING_MARK, Character, *Table*; 289

commands
command(), Compiler; 470
spawning processes to run, Process; 1363

comments
C++ language, specifying, StreamTokenizer.slashSlashComments(); 1626
C language, specifying, StreamTokenizer.slashStarComments(); 1626
commentChar(), StreamTokenizer; 1617
ObjectOutputStream.annotateClass(); 1266
retrieving, ZipEntry.getComment(); 1896
setting
ZipEntry.setComment(); 1899
ZipOutputStream.setComment(); 1929
specifying character that starts
StreamTokenizer.commentChar(); 1617
as token element, *Table*, StreamTokenizer; 1614
ZipOutputStream; 1920

comparing
BigDecimal.compareTo(); 82
BigInteger.compareTo(); 110
compare()
Collator; 455
RuleBasedCollator; 1457
compareTo()
BigDecimal; 82
BigInteger; 110
CollationKey; 444
String; 1635
with consideration for all differences
Collator.IDENTICAL; 461
with consideration for primary differences
Collator.PRIMARY; 462
with consideration for secondary and greater differences, Collator.SECONDARY; 462
strings, locale-sensitive, Collator; 447

compiler
commands, sending, Compiler.command(); 470
compileClass(), Compiler; 471
compileClasses(), Compiler; 471
Compiler; 470
command(); 470
compileClass(); 471
compileClasses(); 471
enable(); 472
package, java.lang; 470
concept description; 16
disabling, Compiler.disable(); 472
enabling, Compiler.enable(); 472

complete()
Calendar; 247

component types
array
Array; 47
retrieving, Class.getComponentType(); 372

compression
algorithms, Deflater; 679
compressed bytes, retrieving number of
Inflater.getTotalIn(); 971
compressed data
delivering, Inflater.setInput(); 974
determining availability
Deflater.finished(); 688
Inflater.finished(); 970
retrieving number of bytes
Deflater.getTotalOut(); 689

compression *(continued)*
compressed data
writing to output stream
DeflaterOutputStream.write(); 700
compressed entries, ZipEntry.DEFLATED; 1895
concept description; 37
data
Deflater; 679
writing to output stream
DeflaterOutputStream.deflate(); 699
decompressed data
discarding
InflaterInputStream.skip(); 982
discarding, ZipInputStream.skip(); 1918
reading, InflaterInputStream.read(); 981
reading, ZipInputStream.read(); 1918
retrieving number of bytes
Inflater.getTotalOut(); 971
decompressing data
InflaterInputStream.fill(); 979
DEFLATE algorithm use, ZipOutputStream; 1920
deflater used for
DeflaterOutputStream.def; 698
DeflaterOutputStream; 695
determining number of compressed bytes remaining
Inflater.getRemaining(); 970
dictionary, setting
Deflater.setDictionary(); 690
Inflater.setDictionary(); 974
finishing
Deflater.finish(); 687
DeflaterOutputStream.finish(); 700
GZIP format
GZIPInputStream; 896
GZIPOutputStream; 902
Inflater; 965
InflaterInputStream; 976
level
default, Deflater.DEFAULT_COMPRESSION; 684
fastest, Deflater.BEST_SPEED; 684
setting, Deflater.setLevel(); 692
smallest, Deflater.BEST_COMPRESSION; 683
levels
Deflater; 679
ZipOutputStream; 1920
method
retrieving, ZipEntry.getMethod(); 1897
setting
ZipEntry.setMethod(); 1901
ZipOutputStream.setMethod(); 1931
retrieving compressed data
Deflater.deflate(); 685
retrieving decompressed data
Inflater.inflate(); 971
specifying, ZipOutputStream.DEFLATED; 1926
specifying none, Deflater.NO_COMPRESSION; 690
strategy
default, Deflater.DEFAULT_STRATEGY; 684
Deflater; 680
Deflater.FILTERED; 687
Huffman encoding specification
Deflater.HUFFMAN_ONLY; 689
setting, Deflater.setStrategy(); 693
uncompressed bytes, retrieving number of
Deflater.getTotalIn(); 688
uncompressed data
retrieving, Deflater.setInput(); 691
specifying, ZipOutputStream.STORED; 1931
uncompressed entries, ZipEntry.STORED; 1902
uncompressed size
retrieving, ZipEntry.getSize(); 1898
setting, ZipEntry.setSize(); 1901
zip entry specification, Deflater.DEFLATED; 685
ZipEntry; 1892
ZLIB library, URL, Deflater; 679
computexxx methods
computeFields()
Calendar; 248
GregorianCalendar; 887
computeTime()
Calendar; 248
GregorianCalendar; 887
concatenation
concat(), String; 1635
strings, String.concat(); 1635
connection
connect()
PipedInputStream; 1327
PipedOutputStream; 1334
PipedReader; 1340
PipedWriter; 1344
SocketImpl; 1598
URLConnection; 1828
connected, URLConnection; 1828

ConnectException; 473
  package, java.net; 473
CONNECTOR_PUNCTUATION, Character, *Table*; 289
protocols
  connection-oriented, DatagramPacket; 499
  connectionless, DatagramPacket; 499
request
  server socket, acceptance
    ServerSocket.accept(); 1520
    ServerSocket.implAccept(); 1524
  socket, acceptance
    SocketImpl.accept(); 1595
  stream socket, listening for
    SocketImpl.listen(); 1602
URL
  cache flag, setting
    URLConnection.setDefaultUseCaches(); 1844
    URLConnection.setUseCaches(); 1846
  content, retrieving
    URLConnection.getContent(); 1830
  creating input stream for
    URLConnection.getInputStream(); 1838
  determining if caching permitted
    URLConnection.getUseCaches(); 1840
  establishing
    URLConnection.connect(); 1828
  input, setting
    URLConnection.setDoInput(); 1844
  input, testing for
    URLConnection.getDoInput(); 1833
  opening
    URL.openConnection(); 1812
    URLStreamHandler.openConnection(); 1854
  output, setting
    URLConnection.setDoOutput(); 1845
  output, testing for
    URLConnection.getDoOutput(); 1834
  request header field, retrieving value of
    URLConnection.getRequestProperty(); 1839
  request header field, setting default value
    URLConnection.setDefaultRequestProperty(); 1844
  request header field, setting
    URLConnection.setRequestProperty(); 1846
  retrieving, URLConnection.getURL(); 1839
  status, URLConnection.connected; 1828
  string representation
    URLConnection.toString(); 1847
  testing for cache use
    URLConnection.getDefaultUseCaches(); 1833
  URL for, URLConnection.url; 1847
  URLConnection; 1819
  URLConnection.allowUserInteraction; 1827
  user interaction flag, setting
    URLConnection.setDefaultAllowUserInteraction(); 1843
  user interaction, testing for
    URLConnection.getDefaultAllowUserInteraction(); 1832
    URLConnection.getAllowUserInteraction(); 1830
constants
  calendar, *Table*, Calendar; 234
constructor(s)
  Constructor; 475
    creating an instance of
      Constructor.newInstance(); 483
    equals(); 479
    getDeclaringClass(); 480
    getExceptionTypes(); 480
    getModifiers(); 481
    getName(); 481
    getParameterTypes(); 481
    hashCode(); 482
    newInstance(); 483
    package, java.lang.reflect; 475
    toString(); 485
  declaring class, Member; 1096
  representation of, Constructor; 475
  retrieving
    Class.getConstructor(); 373
    Class.getConstructors(); 375
    Class.getDeclaredConstructor(); 376
    Class.getDeclaredConstructors(); 377
  valid modifiers for, *Table*, Modifier; 1143
containsxxx methods
  contains()
    Hashtable; 917
    Vector; 1866
  containsKey(), Hashtable; 917

content
ContentHandler; 487
getContent(); 489
package, java.net; 487
ContentHandlerFactory; 490
createContentHandler(); 492
package, java.net; 490
handler
ContentHandler; 487
ContentHandlerFactory; 490
ContentHandlerFactory.createContentHandler(); 492
handler factory
ContentHandler; 487
ContentHandlerFactory; 490
handlers, URLConnection; 1823
retrieving, ContentHandler.getContent(); 489
type
ContentHandler; 487
ContentHandlerFactory; 490
mapping filenames into, FileNameMap; 816
URL connection, retrieving
URLConnection.getContent(); 1830
URL encoding type
retrieving
URLConnection.getContentEncoding(); 1831
URLConnection.getContentType(); 1831
URL length, retrieving
URLConnection.getContentLength(); 1831
context
current execution, SecurityManager; 1482
contraction
term description, RuleBasedCollator; 1450
control
characters (ISO), testing for
Character.isISOControl(); 292
CONTROL, Character, *Table*; 289
loop, Enumeration; 723
conventions
signature, EventObject; 732
conversion
array, Array; 47
big decimal values to big integers
BigDecimal.toBigInteger(); 96
of big decimal values to floating point
BigDecimal.doubleValue(); 84
BigDecimal.floatValue(); 85
of big decimal values to integers
BigDecimal.intvalue(); 86
BigDecimal.longValue(); 86
of big integers to floating point
BigInteger.doubleValue(); 113
BigInteger.floatValue(); 114
of calendar fields into date value
Calendar.computeTime(); 248
character-to-byte
InputStreamReader; 991
OutputStreamWriter; 1309
characters, exception
CharConversionException; 331
of date value into calendar fields
Calendar.computeFields(); 248
field, Field; 750
coordinates
converting rectangular to polar
Math.atan2(); 1087
copying
bit sets, BitSet.clone(); 139
bypassing
BufferedReader; 191
writing, BufferedWriter; 200
copyInto(), Vector; 1866
copyValueOf(), String; 1636
objects, Object.clone(); 1216
cosine
See Also trigonometric functions
Math.cos(); 1088
counting
count
BufferedInputStream; 180
BufferedOutputStream; 188
ByteArrayInputStream; 219
ByteArrayOutputStream; 227
CharArrayReader; 318
CharArrayWriter; 326
StringBufferInputStream; 1668
countObservers(), Observable; 1294
countStackFrames(), Thread; 1729
countTokens(), StringTokenizer; 1698
country(s)
decimal formatting examples
DecimalFormat; 636
ISO code, retrieving
Locale.getISO3Country(); 1064
locale code, retrieving
Locale.getCountry(); 1060
Locale.getDisplayCountry(); 1061

CRC-32 algorithm
See Also algorithms
checksum
calculation in, GZIPInputStream; 896
object, GZIPInputStream.crc; 898
object, GZIPOutputStream.crc; 909
retrieving, ZipEntry.getCrc(); 1896
checksum value, setting
ZipEntry.setCrc(); 1899
crc
GZIPInputStream; 898
GZIPOutputStream; 909
CRC32; 493
getValue(); 495
package, java.util.zip; 493
reset(); 495
update(); 495
creating, locale(s), Locale; 1054
create()
DatagramSocketImpl; 519
SocketImpl; 1598
createContentHandler()
ContentHandlerFactory; 492
createSocketImpl()
SocketImplFactory; 1605
createURLStreamHandler()
URLStreamHandlerFactory; 1859
currency
CURRENCY_SYMBOL, Character, *Table*; 289
format, creating for a locale
NumberFormat.getCurrencyInstance(); 1201
current
current()
BreakIterator; 162
CharacterIterator; 310
StringCharacterIterator; 1678
currentClassLoader()
SecurityManager; 1498
currentLoadedClass()
SecurityManager; 1498
currentThread(), Thread; 1730
currentTimeMillis(), System; 1713
index, CharacterIterator; 306
position
BreakIterator; 155
BreakIterator.current(); 162
cursor
imaginary
CharacterIterator; 306
StringCharacterIterator; 1672
term description, BreakIterator; 155
cycles
class inheritance, ClassCircularityError; 409

D

daemon
thread, setting, Thread.setDaemon(); 1740
thread group
setting, ThreadGroup.setDaemon(); 1762
ThreadGroup; 1751
threads
testing for, Thread.isDaemon(); 1735
Thread; 1724
DASH_PUNCTUATION
Character, *Table*; 289
data
boolean, Boolean; 144
compression
Deflater; 679
DeflaterOutputStream; 695
writing to output stream
DeflaterOutputStream.deflate(); 699
DataFormatException; 497
package, java.util.zip; 497
DataInput; 526
package, java.io; 526
readBoolean(); 527
readByte(); 527
readChar(); 528
readDouble(); 528
readFloat(); 528
readFully(); 529
readInt(); 529
readLine(); 530
readLong(); 530
readShort(); 531
readUnsignedByte(); 531
readUnsignedShort(); 521
readUTF(); 532
skipBytes(); 533
DataInputStream; 534
package, java.io; 534
read(); 537
readBoolean(); 538
readByte(); 538

data *(continued)*
DataInputStream
readChar(); 538
readDouble(); 539
readFloat(); 539
readFully(); 540
readInt(); 541
readLine(); 541
readLong(); 542
readShort(); 543
readUnsignedByte(); 543
readUnsignedShort(); 544
readUTF(); 544
skipBytes(); 545
DataOutput; 546
package, java.io; 546
write(); 547
writeBoolean(); 547
writeByte(); 548
writeBytes(); 548
writeChar(); 548
writeChars(); 549
writeDouble(); 549
writeFloat(); 550
writeInt(); 550
writeLong(); 550
writeShort(); 551
writeUTF(); 551
DataOutputStream; 552
flush(); 555
package, java.io; 552
size(); 555
write(); 555
writeBoolean(); 556
writeByte(); 557
writeBytes(); 557
writeChar(); 558
writeChars(); 558
writeDouble(); 558
writeFloat(); 559
writeInt(); 559
writeLong(); 560
writeShort(); 560
writeUTF(); 561
written; 561
determining number of bytes available
ObjectInput.available(); 1227
ObjectInputStream.available(); 1234
exceptions, DataFormatException; 497
printing
PrintStream.print(); 1350
PrintWriter.print(); 1358
streams, concept description; 3
datagram(s)
address, retrieving
DatagramSocketImpl.peek(); 523;
multicast
time-to-live, retrieving
MulticastSocket.getTTL(); 1157
time-to-live, setting
MulticastSocket.setTTL(); 1162
packets
address, setting
DatagramPacket.setAddress(); 504
data, DatagramPacket.getData(); 502
DatagramPacket; 499
DatagramPacket.getAddress(); 502
DatagramPacket.getData(); 502
DatagramPacket.getLength(); 503
DatagramPacket.getPort(); 503
DatagramPacket, package, java.net; 499
DatagramPacket.setAddress(); 504
DatagramPacket.setLength(); 504
DatagramPacket.setPort(); 505
length, retrieving
DatagramPacket.getLength(); 503
length, setting
DatagramPacket.setLength(); 504
port, retrieving
DatagramPacket.getPort(); 503
port, setting
DatagramPacket.setPort(); 505
setting data, DatagramPacket.setData(); 504
source address
DatagramPacket.getAddress(); 502
receiving
DatagramSocket.receive(); 512
DatagramSocketImpl.receive(); 524
sending
DatagramSocket.send(); 512
DatagramSocketImpl.send(); 524
sockets
address, retrieving
DatagramSocket.getLocalAddress(); 510
closing
DatagramSocket.close(); 509
DatagramSocketImpl.close(); 519

creating
DatagramSocketImpl.create(); 519
DatagramSocket; 506
DatagramSocket.close(); 509
DatagramSocket.getLocalAddress(); 510
DatagramSocket.getLocalPort(); 510
DatagramSocket.getSoTimeout(); 511
DatagramSocket, package, java.net; 506
DatagramSocket.receive(); 512
DatagramSocket.send(); 512
DatagramSocket.setSoTimeout(); 514
DatagramSocketImpl; 516
DatagramSocketImpl.bind(); 519
DatagramSocketImpl.close(); 519
DatagramSocketImpl.create(); 519
DatagramSocketImpl.fd; 520
DatagramSocketImpl.getFileDescriptor(); 520
DatagramSocketImpl.getLocalPort(); 521
DatagramSocketImpl.getTTL(); 521
DatagramSocketImpl.join(); 522
DatagramSocketImpl.leave(); 522
DatagramSocketImpl.localPort; 523
DatagramSocketImpl
package, java.net; 516
DatagramSocketImpl.peek(); 523
DatagramSocketImpl.receive(); 524
DatagramSocketImpl.send(); 524
DatagramSocketImpl.setTTL(); 525
file descriptor, DatagramSocketImpl.fd; 520
file descriptor, retrieving
DatagramSocketImpl.getFileDescriptor(); 520
joining a multicast group
DatagramSocketImpl.join(); 522
leaving a multicast group
DatagramSocketImpl.leave(); 522
multicast packets, setting
DatagramSocketImpl.setTTL(); 525
port, DatagramSocketImpl.localPort; 523
port, retrieving
DatagramSocket.getLocalPort(); 510
DatagramSocketImpl.getLocalPort(); 521
time-out period, retrieving
DatagramSocket.getSoTimeout(); 511
term description, DatagramPacket; 499

date(s)
See Also calendar(s)
aligning, *Table*, DateFormat; 582
calendar used by, DateFormat.calendar; 588
change
retrieving, GregorianCalendar.getGregorianChange(); 889
setting, GregorianCalendar.setGregorianChange(); 895
checking against DST time period
SimpleTimeZone.inDaylightTime(); 1564
creating
DateFormat.getDateInstance(); 595
DateFormat.getDateTimeInstance(); 596
DateFormat.getInstance(); 596
creation, retrieving
URLConnection.getDate(); 1832
Date; 562
after(); 565
before(); 565
converting calendar fields to
GregorianCalendar.computeTime(); 887
equals(); 567
getDate(); 568
getDay(); 570
getHours(); 570
getMinutes(); 570
getMonth(); 570
getSeconds(); 570
getTime(); 571
getTimezoneOffset(); 571
getYear(); 572
hashCode(); 572
package, java.util; 562
parse(); 572
setDate(); 574
setHours(); 575
setMinutes(); 575
setMonth(); 576
setSeconds(); 576
setTime(); 577
setYear(); 577
toGMTString(); 578
toLocaleString(); 578
toString(); 578
UTC(); 579
DATE, Calendar; 249
DATE_FIELD, DateFormat; 590
Date relationship to Calendar; 232

date(s) *(continued)*
DateFormat; 580
AM_PM_FIELD; 588
calendar; 588
clone(); 589
DATE_FIELD; 590
DAY_OF_WEEK_FIELD; 591
DAY_OF_WEEK_IN_MONTH_FIELD; 591
DAY_OF_YEAR_FIELD; 591
DEFAULT; 591
equals(); 592
ERA_FIELD; 592
format(); 592
FULL; 594
getAvailableLocales(); 595
getCalendar(); 595
getDateInstance(); 595
getDateTimeInstance(); 596
getInstance(); 596
getNumberFormat(); 596
getTimeInstance(); 597
getTimeZone(); 597
hashCode(); 597
HOUR_OF_DAY0_FIELD; 598
HOUR_OF_DAY1_FIELD; 598
HOUR0_FIELD; 598
HOUR1_FIELD; 599
isLenient(); 599
LONG; 599
MEDIUM; 600
MILLISECOND_FIELD; 600
MINUTE_FIELD; 600
MONTH_FIELD; 600
numberFormat; 601
package, FRACTION_FIELD; 580
parse(); 601
parseObject(); 604
SECOND_FIELD; 604
setCalendar(); 604
setLenient(); 605
setNumberFormat(); 606
setTimeZone(); 607
SHORT; 608
TIMEZONE_FIELD; 608
WEEK_OF_MONTH_FIELD; 609
WEEK_OF_YEAR_FIELD; 608
YEAR_FIELD; 609
DateFormatSymbols; 610
clone(); 616
equals(); 618
getAmPmStrings(); 618
getEras(); 618
getLocalPatternChars(); 618
getMonths(); 619
getShortMonths(); 619
getShortWeekdays(); 619
getWeekdays(); 620
getZoneStrings(); 620
hashCode(); 620
package, FRACTION_FIELD; 610
setAmPmStrings(); 621
setEras(); 623
setLocalPatternChars(); 623
setMonths(); 623
setShortMonths(); 624
setShortWeekdays(); 624
setWeekdays(); 624
setZoneStrings(); 624
default, DateFormat.DEFAULT; 591
determining
Date.after(); 565
Date.before(); 565
displaying, Date; 563
expiration, URLConnection.getExpiration(); 1834
fields, FieldPosition; 774
format
retrieving, SimpleDateFormat.getDateFormatSymbols(); 1554
setting, SimpleDateFormat.setDateFormatSymbols(); 1556
formatting
Calendar; 233
pattern, SimpleDateFormat; 1541
styles, *Table*, DateFormat; 582
GMT, parsing response header field as
URLConnection.getHeaderFieldDate(); 1835
locale-sensitive formatting, Format; 872
long style, DateFormat.LONG; 599
medium-length style, DateFormat.MEDIUM; 600
modification, retrieving
URLConnection.getLastModified(); 1838
modifying, Date; 563
normalizing, DateFormat; 583

parsing
DateFormat.parse(); 601
DateFormat.parseObject(); 604
short style, DateFormat.SHORT; 608
SimpleDateFormat; 1541
applyLocalizedPattern(); 1550
applyPattern(); 1552
casting DateFormat to; 581
clone(); 1552
equals(); 1553
format(); 1553
getDateFormatSymbols(); 1554
hashCode(); 1555
parse(); 1555
setDateFormatSymbols(); 1556
toPattern(); 1558
specifying, Date; 563
string, parsing, SimpleDateFormat.parse(); 1555
string representation, generating,
SimpleDateFormat.toLocalized-Pattern(); 1558
Date.toString(); 578
testing for DST
TimeZone.inDaylightTime(); 1784
unabbreviated pattern, DateFormat.FULL; 594
value
computing,
Calendar.getTime(); 260
Calendar.getTimeInMillis(); 261
ContentHandlerFactory; 492
converting calendar fields into
Calendar.computeTime(); 248
recomputing, Calendar.complete(); 247

day(s)
DAY_OF_MONTH, Calendar; 249
DAY_OF_WEEK, Calendar; 250
DAY_OF_WEEK_FIELD, DateFormat; 591
DAY_OF_WEEK_IN_MONTH, Calendar; 250
DAY_OF_WEEK_IN_MONTH_FIELD
DateFormat; 591
DAY_OF_YEAR, Calendar; 251
DAY_OF_YEAR_FIELD, DateFormat; 591
day-of-week
calendar constants, *Table*, Calendar; 234
first, retrieving
Calendar.getFirstDayOfWeek(); 258
HOUR_OF_DAY0_FIELD, DateFormat; 598
HOUR_OF_DAY1_FIELD, DateFormat; 598
names of, accessing, DateFormatSymbols; 610
property, DateFormatSymbols; 612

daylight savings time
See DST (daylight savings time)

debugging
tracing
instructions
Runtime.traceInstructions(); 1476
method calls
Runtime.traceMethodCalls(); 1476

DECEMBER
Calendar, *Table*; 233

decimal
DECIMAL_DIGIT_NUMBER, Character, *Table*; 289
DecimalFormat; 626
applyLocalizedPattern(); 638
applyPattern(); 640
clone(); 642
equals(); 645
format(); 645
getDecimalFormatSymbols(); 647
getGroupingSize(); 650
getMultiplier(); 651
getNegativePrefix(); 651
getNegativeSuffix(); 651
getPositivePrefix(); 651
getPositiveSuffix(); 652
hashCode(); 652
isDecimalSeparatorAlwaysShown(); 652
package, java.text; 626
parse(); 653
setDecimalFormatSymbols(); 655
setDecimalSeparatorAlwaysShown(); 657
setGroupingSize(); 658
setMultiplier(); 659
setNegativePrefix(); 661
setNegativeSuffix(); 661
setPositivePrefix(); 661
setPositiveSuffix(); 662
toLocalizedPattern(); 662
toPattern(); 662
DecimalFormatSymbols; 665
clone(); 668
equals(); 670
getDecimalSeparator(); 670
getDigit(); 670
getGroupingSeparator(); 671
getInfinity(); 671
getMinusSign(); 671
getNan(); 671
getPatternSeparator(); 672

decimal *(continued)*
DecimalFormatSymbols
getPercent(); 672
getPerMill(); 672
getZeroDigit(); 673
hashCode(); 673
package, java.text; 665
setDecimalSeparator(); 673
setDigit(); 674
setGroupingSeparator(); 676
setInfinity(); 676
setMinusSign(); 677
setNaN(); 677
setPatternSeparator(); 677
setPercent(); 678
setPerMill(); 678
setZeroDigit(); 678
multiplier
DecimalFormat; 632
retrieving
DecimalFormat.getMultiplier(); 651
setting
DecimalFormat.setMultiplier(); 659
point
moving to the left
BigDecimal.movePointLeft(); 88
moving to the right
BigDecimal.movePointRight(); 88
separator
DecimalFormat; 632
determining, DecimalFormat.isDecimal-SeparatorAlwaysShown(); 652
retrieving, DecimalFormatSymbols.get-DecimalSeparator(); 670
setting
DecimalFormat.setDecimalSeparator-AlwaysShown(); 657
DecimalFormatSymbols.setDecimal-Separator(); 673
DECLARED
Member; 1099
declaring class
constructor
Constructor; 476
Member; 1096
creating an instance of
Constructor.newInstance(); 483
fields
Field; 750
retrieving, Field.getDeclaringClass(); 759
member, retrieving
Member.getDeclaringClass(); 1100
methods
Method; 1125
retrieving
Method.getDeclaringClass(); 1129
retrieving
Constructor.getDeclaringClass(); 480
decode()
Byte; 207
Integer; 1003
Short; 1532
decomposition
canonical
collation order, Collator; 450
Collator.CANONICAL_DECOMPOSITION; 453
full, collation order, Collator; 450
FULL_DECOMPOSITION, Collator; 456
mode
collation order, Collator; 450
retrieving
Collator.getDecomposition(); 459
setting, Collator.setDecomposition; 463
NO_DECOMPOSITION, Collator; 461
preventing, Collator.NO_DECOMPOSITION; 461
decompression
concept description; 38
default(s)
DEFAULT, DateFormat; 591
DEFAULT_COMPRESSION, Deflater; 684
DEFAULT_STRATEGY, Deflater; 684
defaultReadObject()
ObjectInputStream; 1235
defaults, Properties; 1373
defaultWriteObject()
ObjectOutputStream; 1269
properties
Properties; 1370
Properties.defaults; 1373
time zone
retrieving, TimeZone.getDefault(); 1781
setting, TimeZone.setDefault(); 1784
time zones, TimeZone; 1776
defineClass()
ClassLoader; 418
DEFLATE algorithm
See Also algorithms
as compression algorithm used by
GZIPInputStream; 896
GZIPOutputStream; 902

def, DeflaterOutputStream; 698
deflate(), DeflaterOutputStream; 699
DEFLATED
ZipEntry; 1895
ZipOutputStream; 1926
Deflater; 679
BEST_COMPRESSION; 683
BEST_SPEED; 684
DEFAULT_COMPRESSION; 684
DEFAULT_STRATEGY; 684
deflate(); 685
DEFLATED; 685
end(); 686
FILTERED; 687
finalize(); 687
finish(); 687
finished(); 688
getAdler(); 688
getTotalIn(); 688
getTotalOut(); 689
HUFFMAN_ONLY; 689
needsInput(); 689
NO_COMPRESSION; 690
package, java.util.zip; 679
reset(); 690
setDictionary(); 690
setInput(); 691
setLevel(); 692
setStrategy(); 693
DeflaterOutputStream; 695
buf; 698
close(); 698
def; 698
deflate(); 699
finish(); 700
package, java.util.zip; 695
write(); 700
URL, ZipFile; 1906
ZIP output stream use, ZipOutputStream; 1920

deleting
delete(), File; 787
deleteObserver(), Observable; 1294
deleteObservers(), Observable; 1294

delimiters
term description, StringTokenizer; 1697

descriptors
Class instance, retrieving
ObjectStreamClass.forClass(); 1284
file
socket, retrieving
SocketImpl.getFileDescriptor(); 1599
socket, SocketImpl.fd; 1599
retrieving, ObjectStreamClass.lookup(); 1285
serializable class, term description
ObjectStreamClass; 1283
string representation, generating
ObjectStreamClass.toString(); 1286
type, Class; 366

deserialization
See serialization

destroy()
Process; 1364
Thread; 1730
ThreadGroup; 1757

detail
WriteAbortedException; 1886

dictionary(s)
compression
setting, Deflater.setDictionary(); 690
setting, Inflater.setDictionary(); 974
compression algorithm use, Deflater; 679
determining if used
Inflater.needsDictionary(); 973
Dictionary; 702
elements(); 705
get(); 706
isEmpty(); 706
keys(); 706
package, java.util; 702
put(); 707
remove(); 707
size(); 708
term description, Dictionary; 702

digests
term description, ClassLoader; 414

digits
character for a pattern
retrieving
DecimalFormatSymbols.getDigit(); 670
setting
DecimalFormatSymbols.setDigit(); 674
character representation
Character.forDigit(); 287
characters
Character; 282
Unicode, *Table*, Character; 291
conversion radix

digits *(continued)*
conversion radix
Character.MAX_RADIX; 300
Character.MIN_RADIX; 301
digit(), Character; 286
maximum
in a fraction, setting, NumberFormat.set-MaximumFractionDigits(); 1210
integer, setting, NumberFormat.setMaximum-IntegerDigits(); 1211
retrieving
NumberFormat.getMaximumInteger-Digits(); 1202
minimum
fraction, setting, NumberFormat.setMinimum-FractionDigits(); 1211
integer, setting, NumberFormat.set-MinimumIntegerDigits(); 1212
retrieving
NumberFormat.getMinimumFraction-Digits(); 1204
NumberFormat.getMinimumInteger-Digits(); 1204
new tail, BigDecimal; 75
NumberFormat, maximum; 1193
properties, minimum, NumberFormat; 1193
testing for
Character.isDigit(); 290
Character.isLetterOrDigit(); 296
zero
retrieving, DecimalFormatSymbols.getZero-Digit(); 673
setting, DecimalFormatSymbols.setZero-Digit(); 678
directories
creating
File.mkdir(); 797
File.mkdirs(); 798
listing files in, File.list(); 796
parent, retrieving pathname, File.getParent(); 792
separator character
File.separator; 800
File.separatorChar; 801
testing for, File.isDirectory(); 794
ZIP entry, determining
ZipEntry.isDirectory(); 1899
ZIP files, format, ZipEntry; 1893
disabling
disable(), Compiler; 472
enableReplaceObject()
ObjectOutputStream; 1269
enableResolveObject()
ObjectInputStream; 1236
disconnect()
HttpURLConnection; 932
distribution
pseudorandom-number, Random; 1399
division
divide()
BigDecimal; 83
BigInteger; 111
divideAndRemainder(), BigInteger; 112
remainder from, BigInteger.remainder(); 125
DNS (Internet Domain Name System)
term description, InetAddress; 957
doxxx methods
doInput, URLConnection; 1829
doOutput, URLConnection; 1829
document
headers
ContentHandler; 487
ContentHandlerFactory; 490
DONE
BreakIterator; 162
CharacterIterator; 311
dotted-string notation
term description, InetAddress; 957
double floating-point numbers
arrays
modifying, Array.setDouble(); 66
retrieving elements from
Array.getDouble(); 56
converting big
decimal values to
BigDecimal.doubleValue(); 84
integers to, BigInteger.doubleValue(); 113
Double; 709
byteValue(); 711
doubleToLongBits(); 712
doubleValue(); 712
equals(); 713
floatValue(); 713
hashCode(); 714
intValue(); 714
isInfinite(); 714
isNaN(); 715
longBitsToDouble(); 716

longValue(); 716
MAX_VALUE; 716
MIN_VALUE; 717
NaN; 717
NEGATIVE_INFINITY; 718
package, java.lang; 709
POSITIVE_INFINITY; 718
shortValue(); 718
toString(); 719
TYPE; 719
valueOf(); 720
doubleToLongBits(), Double; 712
doubleValue()
BigDecimal; 84
BigInteger; 113
Byte; 208
Double; 712
Float; 862
Integer; 1004
Long; 1071
Number; 1189
Short; 1533
fields
modifying, Field.setDouble(); 769
retrieving values of, Field.getDouble(); 759
next, retrieving, ChoiceFormat.nextDouble(); 361
nextDouble(), ChoiceFormat; 361
previous, retrieving
ChoiceFormat.previousDouble(); 363
pseudorandom-number, generating
Random.nextDouble(); 1403
reading
DataInput.readDouble(); 528
DataInputStream.readDouble(); 539
ObjectInputStream.readDouble(); 1240
RandomAccessFile.readDouble(); 1413
writing
DataOutput.writeDouble(); 549
DataOutputStream.writeDouble(); 558
ObjectOutputStream.writeDouble(); 1278
RandomAccessFile.writeDouble(); 1422

drain()
ObjectOutputStream; 1269

DSA
ClassLoader support; 414

DST (daylight savings time)
See Also time
calendar field constant
Calendar.DST_OFFSET; 251
checking date against DST time period
SimpleTimeZone.inDaylightTime(); 1564
checking for
SimpleTimeZone.useDaylightTime(); 1570
DST_OFFSET, Calendar; 251
setting
end rule
SimpleTimeZone.setEndRule(); 1565
start rule
SimpleTimeZone.setStartRule(); 1567
starting year
SimpleTimeZone.setStartYear(); 1568
term description, SimpleTimeZone; 1559
testing for
TimeZone.inDaylightTime(); 1784
TimeZone.useDaylightTime(); 1786
time difference
retrieving, TimeZone.getOffset(); 1782
setting, TimeZone.useDaylightTime(); 1785
time zones, TimeZone; 1776

dumpStack()
Thread; 1730

E

***e* constant**
E, Math; 1088
Math.E; 1088
raising to a power, Math.exp(); 1088

elements
array, setting, Array.set(); 63
dictionary
adding, Dictionary.put(); 707
associated with a key, retrieving
Dictionary.get(); 706
determining how many
Dictionary.size(); 708
Dictionary; 702
removing, Dictionary.remove(); 707
retrieving, Dictionary.elements(); 705
testing for, Dictionary.isEmpty(); 706
elementAt(), Vector; 1867
elementCount, Vector; 1868
elementData, Vector; 1868

elements *(continued)*
elements()
Dictionary; 705
Hashtable; 918
Vector; 1868
enumeration
loop control with, Enumeration; 723
retrieving, Enumeration.nextElement(); 724
testing for
Enumeration.hasMoreElements(); 724
exceptions, NoSuchElementException; 1170
hash table
adding, Hashtable.put(); 921
associated with a key, retrieving
Hashtable.get(); 918
Hashtable; 913
removing
Hashtable.clear(); 916
Hashtable.remove(); 922
retrieving list of, Hashtable.elements(); 918
retrieving number of, Hashtable.size(); 922
testing for
Hashtable.contains(); 917
Hashtable.isEmpty(); 920
vector
adding, Vector.addElement(); 1864
determining number of
Vector.elementCount; 1868
inserting, Vector.insertElementAt(); 1871
listing, Vector.elements(); 1868
removing
Vector.removeAllElements(); 1873
Vector.removeElement(); 1873
Vector.removeElementAt(); 1874
replacing, Vector.setElementAt(); 1874
retrieving
Vector.elementAt(); 1867
Vector.firstElement(); 1870
Vector.lastElement(); 1872
testing for
Vector.contains(); 1866
Vector.isEmpty(); 1872
Vector; 1862
empty
empty(), Stack; 1608
EmptyStackException; 721
package, java.util; 721
enabling
enable(), Compiler; 472
enableResolveObject()
ObjectInputStream; 1236
enableReplaceObject()
ObjectOutputStream; 1269
ENCLOSING_MARK
Character, *Table*; 289
encoding
encode(), URLEncoder; 1851
identifier
retrieving
InputStreamReader.getEncoding(); 993
OutputStreamWriter.getEncoding(); 1311
UnsupportedEncodingException; 1798
end
end()
Deflater; 686
Inflater; 969
END_PUNCTUATION, Character, *Table*; 289
endsWith(), String; 1637
end-of-file (EOF)
token, StreamTokenizer.TT_EOF; 1628
as token element, *Table*, StreamTokenizer; 1614
end-of-line (EOL)
as token, specifying
StreamTokenizer.eolIsSignificant(); 1618
token, StreamTokenizer.TT_EOL; 1629
as token element, *Table*, StreamTokenizer; 1614
English
ENGLISH, Locale; 1056
predefined locale codes, *Table*, Locale; 1056
ensureCapacity()
StringBuffer; 1659
Vector; 1869
entries()
ZipFile; 1911
enumeration
enumerate()
Thread; 1731
ThreadGroup; 1758
Enumeration; 723
hasMoreElements(); 724
nextElement(); 724
package, java.util; 723
environment management
Runtime; 1466

eof
OptionalDataException; 1301
EOFException; 725
package, java.io; 725
eolIsSignificant()
StreamTokenizer; 1618
eos
GZIPInputStream; 899
epoch
term description, Date; 562
equality
BigDecimal.equals(); 84
BigInteger.equals(); 113
BitSet.equals(); 140
boolean values, testing for
Boolean.equals(); 146
Byte.equals(); 209
Calendar.equals(); 252
Character.equals(); 287
Constructor.equals(); 479
Date.equals(); 567
Double.equals(); 713
equals()
BigDecimal; 84
BigInteger; 113
BitSet; 140
Boolean; 146
Byte; 209
Calendar; 252
Character; 287
ChoiceFormat; 359
CollationKey; 444
Collator; 456
Constructor; 479
Date; 567
DateFormat; 592
DateFormatSymbols; 618
DecimalFormat; 645
DecimalFormatSymbols; 670
Double; 713
Field; 754
File; 788
Float; 862
GregorianCalendar; 888
Integer; 1004
Locale; 1060
Long; 1071
MessageFormat; 1111
Method; 1128
NumberFormat; 1198
Object; 1217
RuleBasedCollator; 1458
Short; 1533
SimpleDateFormat; 1553
SimpleTimeZone; 1562
String; 1637
StringCharacterIterator; 1679
URL; 1807
equalsIgnoreCase(), String; 1638
equivalent expressions, in
RuleBasedCollator; 1449
Field.equals(); 754
file, File.equals(); 788
Float.equals(); 862
GregorianCalendar.equals(); 888
InetAddress.equals(); 958
Integer.equals(); 1004
Locale.equals(); 1060
Method.equals(); 1128
Object.equals(); 1217
SimpleTimeZone.equals(); 1562
String.compareTo(); 1635
String.equals(); 1637
String.equalsIgnoreCase(); 1638
String.intern(); 1643
string regions, String.regionMatches(); 1645
URL, testing, URL.sameFile(); 1813
URL.equals(); 1807
eras
ERA, Calendar; 252
ERA_FIELD, DateFormat; 592
GregorianCalendar.AD; 885
GregorianCalendar.BC; 886
property
DateFormatSymbols; 612
setting, DateFormatSymbols.setEras(); 623
retrieving
DateFormatSymbols.getEras(); 618
errors
AbstractMethodError; 39
ClassCircularityError; 409
ClassFormatError; 411
collation, RuleBasedCollator; 1451
concept description; 16
err
FileDescriptor; 804
System; 1714

errors *(continued)*
Error; 727
package, java.lang; 727
error stream, System.err; 1714
IllegalAccessError; 939
IncompatibleClassChangeError; 953
InstantiationError; 997
InternalError; 1015
LinkageError; 1049
NoClassDefFoundError; 1166
NoSuchFieldError; 1172
NoSuchMethodError; 1176
OutOfMemoryError; 1302
parsing, retrieving location of
ParseException.getErrorOffset(); 1316
StackOverflowError; 1610
standard
FileDescriptor; 802
FileDescriptor.err; 804
streams, Process.getErrorStream(); 1366
ThreadDeath; 1750
Throwable; 1769
UnknownError; 1790
UnsatisfiedLinkError; 1796
VerifyError; 1878
VirtualMachineError; 1880

event(s)
AWT event queue access, permission determination
SecurityManager.checkAwtEventQueue-Access(); 1485
EventListener; 729
package, java.util; 729
EventObject; 731
getSource(); 735
package, java.util; 731
source; 735
toString(); 735
listener
EventListener; 729
EventObject; 731
object
EventObject; 731
string representation, generating
EventObject.toString(); 735
source
EventListener; 729
EventObject; 731
EventObject.source; 735
registering, EventObject; 732
retrieving, EventObject.getSource(); 735

exceptions
ArithmeticException; 45
ArrayIndexOutOfBoundsException; 70
ArrayStoreException; 72
BindException; 134
CharConversionException; 331
checking for, PrintWriter.checkError(); 1357
ClassCastException; 407
ClassNotFoundException; 426
CloneNotSupportedException; 431
ConnectException; 473
DataFormatException; 497
directly inherited from Exception
concept discussion; 18
EmptyStackException; 721
EOFException; 725
Exception; 737
package, java.lang; 737
ExceptionInInitializerError; 741
getException(); 742
package, java.lang; 741
FileNotFoundException; 819
formatting
IllegalArgumentException, Format; 873
IllegalAccessException; 942
IllegalArgumentException; 945
IllegalMonitorStateException; 947
IllegalStateException; 949
IllegalThreadStateException; 951
IndexOutOfBoundsException; 955
initialization
ExceptionInInitializerError; 741
retrieving, ExceptionInInitializer-Error.getException(); 742
InstantiationException; 999
InterruptedException; 1017
InterruptedIOException; 1019
InvalidClassException; 1022
InvalidObjectException; 1026
InvocationTargetException; 1028
IOException; 1031
java.net; 25
MalformedURLException; 1082
MissingResourceException; 1140
NegativeArraySizeException; 1164
NoRouteToHostException; 1168
NoSuchElementException; 1170
NoSuchFieldException; 1174
NoSuchMethodException; 1178
NotActiveException; 1181

NotSerializableException; 1183
NullPointerException; 1185
NumberFormatException; 1213
ObjectStreamException; 1288
OptionalDataException; 1299
ParseException; 1314
ProtocolException; 1381
recording
PrintStream.setError(); 1352
PrintWriter.setError(); 1361
retrieving, InvocationTargetException.getTargetException(); 1030
RuntimeException; 1477
SecurityException; 1479
SocketException; 1590
StreamCorruptedException; 1612
StringIndexOutOfBoundsException; 1688
SyncFailedException; 1708
testing for, PrintStream.checkError(); 1349
Throwable; 1769
TooManyListenersException; 1787
types
constructor, Constructor; 476
methods, Method; 1124
methods, retrieving
Method.getExceptionTypes(); 1129
retrieving
Constructor.getExceptionTypes(); 480
UnknownHostException; 1792
UnknownServiceException; 1794
UnsupportedEncodingException; 1798
UTFDataFormatException; 1860
WriteAbortedException; 1884

execution
alternatives to subclassing
Thread, Runnable; 1464
current context, SecurityManager; 1482
exec(), Runtime; 1467
platform-dependent, Runtime.exec(); 1467
platform-dependent programs
permission determination
SecurityManager.checkExec(); 1487
Runnable; 1464
Runnable.run(); 1464
stack
finding first occurrence of a class
SecurityManager.checkDepth(); 1497
SecurityManager; 1482
thread
starting, Thread.start(); 1743
stopping, Thread.stop(); 1744
suspending, Thread.suspend(); 1745
yielding, Thread.yield(); 1748
Thread.run(); 1740

exists()
File; 788

exit
exit()
Runtime; 1468
System; 1714
exitValue(), Process; 1365
finalization running
Runtime.runFinalizersOnExit(); 1474
System.runFinalizersOnExit(); 1720
thread, handling
ThreadGroup.uncaughtException(); 1767
value, Process.exitValue(); 1365
virtual machine
permission determination
SecurityManager.checkExit(); 1488
Runtime.exit(); 1468

expansion
term description, RuleBasedCollator; 1450

exponent
e constant, Math.exp(); 1088
exp(), Math; 1088

extensibility
hash table, Hashtable; 914
vectors as extensible arrays, Vector; 1862

externalization
Externalizable; 743
package, java.io; 743
readExternal(); 747
writeExternal(); 747
security considerations
Externalizable; 745
URL, Externalizable; 745
term description, Externalizable; 743, 744

F

factory
content handler
ContentHandler; 487
ContentHandlerFactory; 490
setting, URLConnection.setContentHandlerFactory(); 1842

factory *(continued)*
server socket implementation
ServerSocket; 1516
setting
ServerSocket.setSocketFactory(); 1526
setting, permission determination
SecurityManager.checkSetFactory(); 1494
socket implementation
creating, SocketImplFactory.createSocketImpl(); 1605
setting
Socket.setSocketImplFactory(); 1582
Socket; 1571
SocketImpl; 1592
SocketImplFactory; 1604
term description
SecurityManager.checkSetFactory(); 1494
URL stream handler
creating
URLStreamHandlerFactory.createURLStreamHandler(); 1859
setting, URL.setURLStreamHandlerFactory(); 1814
URL; 1801
URLStreamHandler; 1852
URLStreamHandlerFactory; 1857

false
Boolean.FALSE; 147
FALSE, Boolean; 147

fd
DatagramSocketImpl; 520
SocketImpl; 1599

FEBRUARY
Calendar, *Table*; 233

field(s)
AM_PM_FIELD, DateFormat; 588
boolean
modifying, Field.setBoolean(); 766
retrieving values of, Field.getBoolean(); 757
byte
modifying, Field.setByte(); 767
retrieving values of, Field.getByte(); 758
Calendar; 233
calendar
AM value, Calendar.AM; 243
Calendar.AM_PM; 244
Calendar.getMinimum(); 260
Calendar.WEEK_OF_MONTH; 275
Calendar.WEEK_OF_YEAR; 279
Calendar.YEAR; 280
Calendar.ZONE_OFFSET; 281
clearing, Calendar.clear(); 246
computing
Calendar.complete(); 247
Calendar.computeFields(); 248
GregorianCalendar.computeFields(); 887
constant
Calendar.DATE; 249
Calendar.DAY_OF_MONTH; 249
Calendar.DAY_OF_WEEK; 250
Calendar.DAY_OF_WEEK_IN_MONTH; 250
Calendar.DAY_OF_YEAR; 251
Calendar.DST_OFFSET; 251
Calendar.ERA; 252
Calendar.HOUR_OF_DAY; 263
Calendar.MILLISECOND; 265
Calendar.MINUTE; 265
Calendar.MONTH; 266
Calendar.SECOND; 268
converting to Date value
GregorianCalendar.computeTime(); 887
DatagramPacket; 499
incrementing/decrementing
Calendar.add(); 242
Calendar.roll(); 267
GregorianCalendar.add(); 885
GregorianCalendar.roll(); 894
number of, Calendar.FIELD_COUNT; 253
retrieving, Calendar.get(); 254
retrieving current value
Calendar.internalGet(); 263
retrieving greatest minimum value
Calendar.getGreatestMinimum(); 258
GregorianCalendar.getGreatestMinimum(); 888
retrieving least maximum value
Calendar.getLeastMaximum(); 259
GregorianCalendar.getLeastMaximum(); 889

retrieving maximum value
Calendar.getMaximum(); 259
GregorianCalendar.getMaximum(); 890
retrieving minimum value
Calendar.getMinimum(); 260
GregorianCalendar.getMinimum(); 890
setting
Calendar.set(); 268
Calendar.setFirstDayOfWeek(); 272
Calendar.setLenient(); 273
Calendar.setMinimalDaysInFirst-Week(); 274
Calendar.setTime(); 274
Calendar.setTimeInMillis(); 275
Calendar.setTimeZone(); 275
state array, Calendar.isSet; 264
testing if set, Calendar.isSet(); 264
value array, Calendar.fields; 253
character
modifying, Field.setChar(); 769
retrieving values of, Field.getChar(); 758
clear flag, Calendar.areFieldsSet; 244
DATE_FIELD, DateFormat; 590
DAY_OF_WEEK_FIELD, DateFormat; 591
DAY_OF_WEEK_IN_MONTH_FIELD
DateFormat; 591
DAY_OF_YEAR_FIELD, DateFormat; 591
declaring class, retrieving
Field.getDeclaringClass(); 759
ERA_FIELD, DateFormat; 592
errors, NoSuchFieldError; 1172
exceptions, NoSuchFieldException; 1174
Field; 749
equals(); 754
get(); 756
getBoolean(); 757
getByte(); 758
getChar(); 758
getDeclaringClass(); 759
getDouble(); 759
getFloat(); 760
getInt(); 761
getLong(); 761
getModifiers(); 762
getName(); 763
getShort(); 763
getType(); 764
hashCode(); 764
package, java.lang.reflect; 749
set(); 765
setBoolean(); 766
setByte(); 767
setChar(); 769
setDouble(); 769
setFloat(); 770
setInt(); 771
setLong(); 771
setShort(); 772
toString(); 773
FIELD_COUNT, Calendar; 253
FieldPosition; 774
getBeginIndex(); 778
getEndIndex(); 781
getField(); 781
NumberFormat use; 1193
package, java.text; 774
fields, Calendar; 253
floating point
modifying
Field.setDouble(); 769
Field.setFloat(); 770
retrieving values of
Field.getDouble(); 759
Field.getFloat(); 760
FRACTION_FIELD, NumberFormat; 1200
HOUR_OF_DAY0_FIELD, DateFormat; 598
HOUR_OF_DAY1_FIELD, DateFormat; 598
HOUR0_FIELD, DateFormat; 598
HOUR1_FIELD, DateFormat; 599
HTTP request header, *Table*
URLConnection; 1821
HTTP response header, *Table*
URLConnection; 1822
identifier
FieldPosition.getField(); 781
retrieving, FieldPosition.getField(); 781
integer
modifying
Field.setInt(); 771
Field.setLong(); 771
Field.setShort(); 772
retrieving values of
Field.getInt(); 761
Field.getLong(); 761
Field.getShort(); 763
INTEGER_FIELD, NumberFormat; 1205
MILLISECOND_FIELD, DateFormat; 600
MINUTE_FIELD, DateFormat; 600

field(s) *(continued)*
modifier, retrieving, Field.getModifiers(); 762
MONTH_FIELD, DateFormat; 600
name, retrieving values of, Field.getName(); 763
representation of, Field; 749
request header
retrieving value of, URLConnection.getRequestProperty(); 1839
setting default value, URLConnection.setDefaultRequestProperty(); 1844
setting, URLConnection.setRequestProperty(); 1846
response header
parsing as GMT date, URLConnection.getHeaderFieldDate(); 1835
parsing as integer, URLConnection.getHeaderFieldInt(); 1836
retrieving as key, URLConnection.getHeaderFieldKey(); 1836
retrieving
Class.getDeclaredField(); 379
Class.getDeclaredFields(); 380
Class.getField(); 385
Class.getFields(); 386
SECOND_FIELD, DateFormat; 604
serializable
reading, ObjectInputStream.defaultReadObject(); 1235
term description, Serializable; 1508
writing, ObjectOutputStream.defaultWriteObject(); 1269
string representation, generating, Field.toString(); 773
TIMEZONE_FIELD, DateFormat; 608
type, retrieving, Field.getType(); 764
types, for Get and Set methods, *Tables* Calendar; 259
URL, setting, URL.set(); 1814
URL request header, retrieving value, URLConnection.getDefaultRequestProperty(); 1832
valid modifiers for, *Table*, Modifier; 1143
value, modifying, Field.set(); 765
value, retrieving, Field.get(); 756
WEEK_OF_MONTH_FIELD, DateFormat; 609
WEEK_OF_YEAR_FIELD, DateFormat; 608
YEAR_FIELD, DateFormat; 609

file(s)
absolute pathname
File.getAbsolutePath(); 790
class
bibliographic reference, ClassLoader; 413
ClassLoader; 413
closing
FileInputStream.close(); 809
FileInputStream.finalize(); 810
FileOutputStream.close(); 823
FileOutputStream.finalize(); 825
RandomAccessFile.close(); 1409
concept description; 4
current file pointer
RandomAccessFile; 1406
retrieving
RandomAccessFile.getFilePointer(); 1409
setting, RandomAccessFile.seek(); 1418
deleting
File.delete(); 787
permission determination
SecurityManager.checkDelete(); 1487
descriptors
datagram socket
DatagramSocketImpl.fd; 520
datagram socket, retrieving
DatagramSocketImpl.getFileDescriptor(); 520
FileDescriptor; 802
retrieving
RandomAccessFile.getFD(); 1409
FileInputStream.getFD(); 811
FileOutputStream.getFD(); 825
socket, SocketImpl.fd; 1599
socket, retrieving
SocketImpl.getFileDescriptor(); 1599
directories
creating,
File.mkdir(); 797
File.mkdirs(); 798
listing files in, File.list(); 796
retrieving pathname of parent
File.getParent(); 792
separator character
File.separator; 800
File.separatorChar; 801
testing for, File.isDirectory(); 794

equality testing, File.equals(); 788
exceptions
  EOFException; 725
  FileNotFoundException; 819
existence status, File.exists(); 788
File; 782
  canRead(); 786
  canWrite(); 786
  delete(); 787
  equals(); 788
  exists(); 788
  getAbsolutePath(); 790
  getCanonicalPath(); 791
  getName(); 792
  getParent(); 792
  getPath(); 793
  hashCode(); 793
  isAbsolute(); 794
  isDirectory(); 794
  isFile(); 795
  lastModified(); 796
  length(); 796
  list(); 796
  mkdir(); 797
  mkdirs(); 798
  package, java.io; 782
  pathSeparator; 798
  pathSeparatorChar; 799
  renameTo(); 799
  separator; 800
  separatorChar; 801
  toString(); 801
FileDescriptor; 802
  err; 804
  in; 804
  out; 804
  package, java.io; 802
  sync(); 804
  valid(); 805
FileInputStream; 807
  available(); 809
  close(); 809
  finalize(); 810
  getFD(); 811
  package, java.io; 807
  read(); 811
  skip(); 812
FileNotFoundException; 819
  package, java.io; 819
FileOutputStream; 821
  close(); 823
  finalize(); 825
  getFD(); 825
  package, java.io; 821
  write(); 825
FileReader; 827
  package, java.io; 827
FileWriter; 830
  package, java.io; 830
flushing, FileDescriptor.sync(); 804
hashcode, File.hashCode(); 793
modification time, retrieving
    File.lastModified(); 796
pathname, retrieving, File.getPath(); 793
RandomAccessFile; 1406
read status, File.canRead(); 786
reading
  FileReader; 827
  permission determination
    SecurityManager.checkRead(); 1493
  RandomAccessFile.read(); 1411
renaming, File.renameTo(); 799
resource bundle properties
  ResourceBundle; 1437
size
  RandomAccessFile.length(); 1410
  retrieving, File.length(); 796
streams, FileOutputStream; 821
testing for, File.isFile(); 795
write status, File.canWrite(); 786
writing
  FileWriter; 830
  permission determination
    SecurityManager.checkWrite(); 1496

filenames
  extension, determining content type from
    URLConnection.guessContentTypeFrom-Stream(); 1841
  File; 782
  FilenameFilter; 814
    accept(); 815
    package, java.io; 814
  FileNameMap; 816
    getContentTypeFor(); 817
    package, java.net; 816
  fileNameMap, URLConnection; 1829
  mapping to content types
    FileNameMap; 816
    URLConnection.fileNameMap; 1829

filenames *(continued)*
MIME type, determining
FileNameMap.getContentTypeFor(); 817
retrieving, File.getName(); 792
testing for filter acceptance
FilenameFilter.accept(); 815
URL, retrieving, URL.getFile(); 1808
as URL component, URL; 1800
fill
fill(), InflaterInputStream; 979
fillInStackTrace(), Throwable; 1770
filters
filename, FilenameFilter; 814
FILTERED, Deflater; 687
FilterInputStream; 834
available(); 837
close(); 837
in; 838
mark(); 838
markSupported(); 839
package, java.io; 834
read(); 839
reset(); 840
skip(); 841
FilterOutputStream; 842
close(); 844
flush(); 845
out; 846
package, java.io; 842
write(); 846
FilterReader; 847
close(); 849
in; 850
mark(); 850
markSupported(); 851
package, java.io; 847
read(); 852
ready(); 853
reset(); 853
skip(); 854
FilterWriter; 855
close(); 857
flush(); 858
out; 858
package, java.io; 855
write(); 859
input stream, creating
ZipFile.getInputStream(); 1912
streams
CheckedOutputStream; 339
checksum, CheckedInputStream; 333
concept description; 5
DataInputStream; 534
DataOutputStream; 552
DeflaterOutputStream; 695
FilterInputStream; 834
FilterOutputStream; 842
FilterWriter; 855
InflaterInputStream; 979
PrintStream; 1346
final modifier
FINAL, Modifier; 1144
testing for, Modifier.isFinal(); 1147
finalization
finalize()
Deflater; 687
FileInputStream; 810
FileOutputStream; 825
Inflater; 969
Object; 1218
Inflater.finalize(); 969
Object.finalize(); 1218
Runtime.runFinalization(); 1473
Runtime.runFinalizersOnExit(); 1474
System.runFinalization(); 1720
System.runFinalizersOnExit(); 1720
virtual machine, Deflater.finalize(); 687
findxxx methods
findLoadedClass(), ClassLoader; 419
findSystemClass(), ClassLoader; 420
finishing
compression
DeflaterOutputStream.finish(); 700
finish()
Deflater; 687
DeflaterOutputStream; 699
GZIPOutputStream; 910
ZipOutputStream; 1926
finished()
Deflater; 688
Inflater; 970
first
first()
BreakIterator; 163
CharacterIterator; 311
StringCharacterIterator; 1679
firstElement(), Vector; 1870

flipping bits
BigInteger.flipBit(); 114
flipBit(), BigInteger; 114
floating-point numbers
arrays
Array.setFloat(); 67
modifying, Array.setDouble(); 66
retrieving elements from
Array.getDouble(); 56
Array.getFloat(); 57
converting big
decimal values to
BigDecimal.doubleValue(); 84
BigDecimal.floatValue(); 85
integers to
BigInteger.doubleValue(); 113
BigInteger.floatValue(); 114
double, Byte.doubleValue(); 208
fields
modifying
Field.setDouble(); 769
Field.setFloat(); 770
retrieving values of
Field.getDouble(); 759
Field.getFloat(); 760
Float; 860
byteValue(); 862
doubleValue(); 862
equals(); 862
floatToIntBits(); 864
floatValue(); 864
hashCode(); 864
intBitsToFloat(); 865
intValue(); 865
isInfinite(); 866
isNaN(); 866
longValue(); 867
MAX_VALUE; 867
MIN_VALUE; 867
NaN; 868
NEGATIVE_INFINITY; 868
package, java.lang; 860
POSITIVE_INFINITY; 869
shortValue(); 869
toString(); 869
TYPE; 870
valueOf(); 871
floatToIntBits(), Float; 864
floatValue()
BigDecimal; 85
BigInteger; 114
Byte; 209
Double; 713
Float; 864
Integer; 1005
Long; 1072
Number; 1189
Short; 1534
pseudorandom-number, generating
Random.nextDouble(); 1403
Random.nextFloat(); 1403
reading
DataInput.readDouble(); 528
DataInput.readFloat(); 528
DataInputStream.readDouble(); 539
DataInputStream.readFloat(); 539
ObjectInputStream.readFloat(); 1241
RandomAccessFile.readDouble(); 1413
RandomAccessFile.readFloat(); 1414
retrieving object value as
Double.doubleValue(); 712
Double.floatValue(); 713
Float.doubleValue(); 862
Float.floatValue(); 864
Integer.doubleValue(); 1004
Integer.floatValue(); 1005
Long.doubleValue(); 1071
Long.floatValue(); 1072
Number.doubleValue(); 1189
Number.floatValue(); 1189
Short.doubleValue(); 1533
Short.floatValue(); 1534
rounding
Math; 1084
to nearest whole number
Math.rint(); 1092
Math.round(); 1093
string representation, generating
Double.toString(); 719
Float.toString(); 869
wrappers
Double; 709
Float; 860
writing
DataOutput.writeDouble(); 549
DataOutput.writeFloat(); 550
DataOutputStream.writeDouble(); 558
DataOutputStream.writeFloat(); 559
ObjectOutputStream.writeFloat(); 1278
RandomAccessFile.writeDouble(); 1422
RandomAccessFile.writeFloat(); 1423

floor()
Math; 1089
flush()
BufferedOutputStream; 188
BufferedWriter; 202
CharArrayWriter; 326
DataOutputStream; 555
FilterOutputStream; 845
FilterWriter; 858
ObjectOutput; 1260
ObjectOutputStream; 1270
OutputStream; 1306
OutputStreamWriter; 1311
PipedOutputStream; 1334
PipedWriter; 1344
PrintStream; 1350
PrintWriter; 1358
StringWriter; 1705
Writer; 1889
following()
BreakIterator; 163
fonts
character display importance
DecimalFormatSymbols; 667
number alignment issues, NumberFormat; 1193
forxxx methods
forClass(), ObjectStreamClass; 1284
forDigit(), Character; 287
forName(), Class; 370
format(ting)
array of, retrieving
MessageFormat.getFormats(); 1113
ChoiceFormat; 346
class
class loader definition, ClassLoader; 413
ClassFormatError; 411
classes that implement; 29
concept description; 27
DateFormat; 580
DateFormatSymbols; 610
dates, DateFormat.format(); 592
DecimalFormat; 626
exceptions
DataFormatException; 497
IllegalArgumentException, Format; 873
ZipException; 1904
Format; 872
FORMAT, Character, *Table*; 289
format()
ChoiceFormat; 360
DateFormat; 592
DecimalFormat; 645
Format; 878
MessageFormat; 1111
NumberFormat; 1199
SimpleDateFormat; 1553
MessageFormat; 1102
number, NumberFormatException; 1213
NumberFormat; 1192
numbers, NumberFormat.format(); 1199
properties, Properties; 1371
SimpleDateFormat; 1541
strings, ChoiceFormat; 346
styles, *Table*, DateFormat; 582
time, DateFormat.format(); 592
fractions
FRACTION_FIELD, NumberFormat; 1200
lost, BigDecimal; 75
maximum digits
retrieving, NumberFormat.getMaximum-FractionDigits(); 1201
setting, NumberFormat.setMaximum-FractionDigits(); 1210
minimum digits
retrieving, NumberFormat.getMinimum-IntegerDigits(); 1204
setting, NumberFormat.setMinimum-FractionDigits(); 1211
France
FRANCE, Locale; 1056
predefined locale codes, *Table*, Locale; 1056
freeing
freeMemory(), Runtime; 1469
resources
Deflater.end(); 686
Inflater.end(); 969
French
FRENCH, Locale; 1056
predefined locale codes, *Table*, Locale; 1056
FRIDAY
Calendar, *Table*; 233
full
FULL, DateFormat; 594
FULL_DECOMPOSITION, Collator; 456

G

garbage collector
  Runtime.gc(); 1470
  System.gc(); 1715
Gaussian
  distribution
    pseudorandom-number generation
      Random.nextGaussian(); 1404
    pseudorandom-number, Random; 1399
gc()
  Runtime; 1470
  System; 1715
gcd (greatest common denominator)
  computing for big integers
    BigInteger.gcd(); 115
  gcd(), BigInteger; 115
German
  GERMAN, Locale; 1056
  predefined locale codes, *Table*, Locale; 1056
Germany
  GERMANY, Locale; 1056
  predefined locale codes, *Table*, Locale; 1056
getxxx methods
  get()
    Array; 51
    BitSet; 140
    Calendar; 254
    Dictionary; 706
    Field; 756
    Hashtable; 918
  get methods
    valid array types, *Table*, Array; 48
    valid field types, *Table*, Field; 751
  getAbsolutePath(), File; 790
  getAddress()
    DatagramPacket; 502
    InetAddress; 959
  getAdler()
    Deflater; 688
    Inflater; 970
  getAllByName(), InetAddress; 959
  getAllowUserInteraction()
    URLConnection; 1830
  getAmPmStrings(), DateFormatSymbols; 618
  getAvailableIDs(), TimeZone; 1779
  getAvailableLocales()
    BreakIterator; 164
    Calendar; 254
    Collator; 457
    DateFormat; 595
    NumberFormat; 1200
  getBeginIndex()
    CharacterIterator; 311
    FieldPosition; 778
    StringCharacterIterator; 1680
  getBoolean()
    Array; 53
    Boolean; 147
    Field; 757
  getBuffer(), StringWriter; 1705
  getBundle(), ResourceBundle; 1442
  getByName(), InetAddress; 960
  getByte()
    Array; 54
    Field; 758
  getBytes(), String; 1638
  getCalendar(), DateFormat; 595
  getCanonicalPath(), File; 791
  getChar()
    Array; 55
    Field; 758
  getCharacterInstance()
    BreakIterator; 165
  getChars()
    String; 1641
    StringBuffer; 1660
  getChecksum()
    CheckedInputStream; 337
    CheckedOutputStream; 341
  getClass(), Object; 1220
  getClassContext(), SecurityManager; 1499
  getClasses(), Class; 371
  getClassLoader(), Class; 372
  getClassName()
    MissingResourceException; 1141
  getCollationElementIterator()
    RuleBasedCollator; 1458
  getCollationKey()
    Collator; 458
    RuleBasedCollator; 1459
  getComment(), ZipEntry; 1896
  getComponentType(), Class; 372
  getCompressedSize(), ZipEntry; 1896
  getConstructor(), Class; 373
  getConstructors(), Class; 375
  getContent()
    ContentHandler; 489
    URL; 1807
    URLConnection; 1830

getxxx methods *(continued)*
getContentEncoding(), URLConnection; 1831
getContentLength(), URLConnection; 1831
getContents(), ListResourceBundle; 1052
getContentType(), URLConnection; 1831
getContentTypeFor(), FileNameMap; 817
getCountry(), Locale; 1060
getCrc(), ZipEntry; 1896
getCurrencyInstance(), NumberFormat; 1201
getData(), DatagramPacket; 502
getDate()
Date; 568
URLConnection; 1832
getDateFormatSymbols()
SimpleDateFormat; 1554
getDateInstance(), DateFormat; 595
getDateTimeInstance(), DateFormat; 596
getDay(), Date; 570
getDecimalFormatSymbols()
DecimalFormat; 647
getDecimalSeparator()
DecimalFormatSymbols; 670
getDeclaredClasses(), Class; 375
getDeclaredConstructor(), Class; 376
getDeclaredConstructors(), Class; 377
getDeclaredField(), Class; 379
getDeclaredFields(), Class; 380
getDeclaredMethod(), Class; 381
getDeclaredMethods(), Class; 383
getDeclaringClass()
Class; 384
Constructor; 480
Field; 759
Member; 1100
Method; 1129
getDecomposition(), Collator; 459
getDefault()
Locale; 1060
TimeZone; 1781
getDefaultAllowUserInteraction()
URLConnection; 1832
getDefaultRequestProperty()
URLConnection; 1832
getDefaultUseCaches()
URLConnection; 1833
getDigit(), DecimalFormatSymbols; 670
getDisplayCountry(), Locale; 1061
getDisplayLanguage(), Locale; 1062
getDisplayName(), Locale; 1062
getDisplayVariant(), Locale; 1063
getDoInput(), URLConnection; 1833
getDoOutput(), URLConnection; 1834
getDouble()
Array; 56
Field; 759
getEncoding()
InputStreamReader; 993
OutputStreamWriter; 1311
getEndIndex()
CharacterIterator; 312
FieldPosition; 781
StringCharacterIterator; 1680
getEntry(), ZipFile; 1912
getenv(), System; 1715
getEras(), DateFormatSymbols; 618
getErrorOffset(), ParseException; 1316
getErrorStream(), Process; 1366
getException()
ExceptionInInitializerError; 742
getExceptionTypes()
Constructor; 480
Method; 1129
getExpiration(), URLConnection; 1834
getExtra(), ZipEntry; 1897
getFD()
FileInputStream; 811
FileOutputStream; 825
RandomAccessFile; 1409
getField()
Class; 385
FieldPosition; 781
getFields(), Class; 386
getFile(), URL; 1808
getFileDescriptor()
DatagramSocketImpl; 520
SocketImpl; 1599
getFilePointer(), RandomAccessFile; 1409
getFirstDayOfWeek(), Calendar; 258
getFloat()
Array; 57
Field; 760
getFollowRedirects()
HttpURLConnection; 932
getFormats()
ChoiceFormat; 360
MessageFormat; 1113
getGreatestMinimum()
Calendar; 258
GregorianCalendar; 888
getGregorianChange()
GregorianCalendar; 889

getGroupingSeparator()
DecimalFormatSymbols; 671
getGroupingSize(), DecimalFormat; 650
getHeaderField(), URLConnection; 1834
getHeaderFieldDate(), URLConnection; 1835
getHeaderFieldInt(), URLConnection; 1836
getHeaderFieldKey(), URLConnection; 1836
getHost(), URL; 1809
getHostAddress(), InetAddress; 961
getHostName(), InetAddress; 961
getHours(), Date; 570
getID(), TimeZone; 1782
getIfModifiedSince(), URLConnection; 1837
getInCheck(), SecurityManager; 1500
getIndex()
CharacterIterator; 312
ParsePosition; 1321
StringCharacterIterator; 1680
getInetAddress()
ServerSocket; 1523
Socket; 1577
SocketImpl; 1600
getInfinity(), DecimalFormatSymbols; 671
getInputStream()
Process; 1367
Socket; 1578
SocketImpl; 1600
URLConnection; 1838
ZipFile; 1912
getInstance()
Calendar; 258
Collator; 460
DateFormat; 596
NumberFormat; 1201
getInt()
Array; 58
Field; 761
getInteger(), Integer; 1005
getInterface(), MulticastSocket; 1157
getInterfaces(), Class; 388
getISO3Country(), Locale; 1064
getISO3Language(), Locale; 1064
getKey(), MissingResourceException; 1142
getKeys()
ListResourceBundle; 1053
PropertyResourceBundle; 1379
ResourceBundle; 1443
getLanguage(), Locale; 1065
getLastModified(), URLConnection; 1838
getLeastMaximum()
Calendar; 259
GregorianCalendar; 889
getLength()
Array; 59
DatagramPacket; 503
getLimits(), ChoiceFormat; 360
getLineInstance(), BreakIterator; 165
getLineNumber()
LineNumberInputStream; 1036
LineNumberReader; 1042
getLocalAddress()
DatagramSocket; 510
Socket; 1579
getLocale(), MessageFormat; 1113
getLocalHost(), InetAddress; 962
getLocalizedInputStream(), Runtime; 1470
getLocalizedMessage(), Throwable; 1771
getLocalizedOutputStream(), Runtime; 1471
getLocalPatternChars()
DateFormatSymbols; 618
getLocalPort()
DatagramSocket; 510
DatagramSocketImpl; 521
ServerSocket; 1523
Socket; 1579
SocketImpl; 1600
getLong()
Array; 60
Field; 761
Long; 1072
getLowestSetBit(), BigInteger; 116
getMaximum()
Calendar; 259
GregorianCalendar; 890
getMaximumFractionDigits()
NumberFormat; 1201
getMaximumIntegerDigits()
NumberFormat; 1202
getMaxPriority(), ThreadGroup; 1759
getMessage()
InvalidClassException; 1024
Throwable; 1771
WriteAbortedException; 1886
getMethod()
Class; 389
ZipEntry; 1897
getMethods(), Class; 390
getMinimalDaysInFirstWeek()
Calendar; 260

getxxx methods *(continued)*
getMinimum()
Calendar; 260
GregorianCalendar; 890
getMinimumFractionDigits()
NumberFormat; 1204
getMinimumIntegerDigits()
NumberFormat; 1204
getMinusSign(), DecimalFormatSymbols; 671
getMinutes(), Date; 570
getModifiers()
Class; 392
Constructor; 481
Field; 762
Member; 1100
Method; 1131
getMonth(), Date; 570
getMonths(), DateFormatSymbols; 619
getMultiplier(), DecimalFormat; 651
getName()
Class; 393
Constructor; 481
Field; 763
File; 792
Member; 1101
Method; 1132
ObjectStreamClass; 1285
Thread; 1731
ThreadGroup; 1759
ZipEntry; 1898
ZipFile; 1913
getNaN(), DecimalFormatSymbols; 671
getNegativePrefix(), DecimalFormat; 651
getNegativeSuffix(), DecimalFormat; 651
getNextEntry(), ZipInputStream; 1917
getNumberFormat(), DateFormat; 596
getNumberInstance(), NumberFormat; 1204
getNumericValue(), Character; 288
getObject(), ResourceBundle; 1443
getOffset()
SimpleTimeZone; 1563
TimeZone; 1782
getOutputStream()
Process; 1368
Socket; 1579
SocketImpl; 1601
URLConnection; 1838
getParameterTypes()
Constructor; 481
Method; 1132
getParent()
File; 792
ThreadGroup; 1759
getPath(), File; 793
getPatternSeparator()
DecimalFormatSymbols; 672
getPercent(), DecimalFormatSymbols; 672
getPercentInstance(), NumberFormat; 1205
getPerMill(), DecimalFormatSymbols; 672
getPort()
DatagramPacket; 503
Socket; 1580
SocketImpl; 1601
URL; 1809
getPositivePrefix(), DecimalFormat; 651
getPositiveSuffix(), DecimalFormat; 652
getPriority(), Thread; 1732
getProperties(), System; 1715
getProperty()
Properties; 1374
System; 1716
getProtocol(), URL; 1810
getRawOffset()
SimpleTimeZone; 1564
TimeZone; 1783
getRef(), URL; 1811
getRemaining(), Inflater; 970
getRequestMethod(), HttpURLConnection; 933
getRequestProperty(), URLConnection; 1839
getResource()
Class; 393
ClassLoader; 421
getResourceAsStream()
Class; 396
ClassLoader; 421
getResponseCode(), HttpURLConnection; 933
getResponseMessage()
HttpURLConnection; 933
getReturnType(), Method; 1133
getRules(), RuleBasedCollator; 1460
getRuntime(), Runtime; 1471
getSeconds(), Date; 570
getSecurityContext()
SecurityManager; 1500
getSecurityManager(), System; 1717
getSentenceInstance(), BreakIterator; 169
getSerialVersionUID()
ObjectStreamClass; 1285

getShort()
  Array; 61
  Field; 763
getShortMonths(), DateFormatSymbols; 619
getShortWeekdays()
  DateFormatSymbols; 619
getSigners(), Class; 398
getSize(), ZipEntry; 1898
getSoLinger(), Socket; 1581
getSoTimeout()
  DatagramSocket; 511
  ServerSocket; 1524
  Socket; 1581
getSource(), EventObject; 735
getSourceString(), CollationKey; 445
getStrength(), Collator; 460
getString(), ResourceBundle; 1444
getStringArray(), ResourceBundle; 1444
getSuperclass(), Class; 399
getSystemResource(), ClassLoader; 422
getSystemResourceAsStream()
  ClassLoader; 422
getTargetException()
  InvocationTargetException; 1030
getTcpNoDelay(), Socket; 1582
getText(), BreakIterator; 169
getThreadGroup()
  SecurityManager; 1500
  Thread; 1732
getTime()
  Calendar; 260
  Date; 571
  ZipEntry; 1898
getTimeInMillis(), Calendar; 261
getTimeInstance(), DateFormat; 597
getTimeZone()
  Calendar; 261
  DateFormat; 597
  TimeZone; 1783
getTimezoneOffset(), Date; 571
getTotalIn()
  Deflater; 688
  Inflater; 971
getTotalOut()
  Deflater; 689
  Inflater; 971
getTTL()
  DatagramSocketImpl; 521
  MulticastSocket; 1157
getType()
  Character; 288
  Field; 764
getURL(), URLConnection; 1839
getUseCaches(), URLConnection; 1840
getValue()
  Adler32; 43
  Checksum; 345
  CRC32; 495
getVariant(), Locale; 1065
getWeekdays(), DateFormatSymbols; 620
getWordInstance(), BreakIterator; 171
getYear(), Date; 572
getZeroDigit(), DecimalFormatSymbols; 673
getZoneStrings(), DateFormatSymbols; 620
GMT (Greenwich Mean Time)
  See Also time
  date, parsing response header field as
    URLConnection.getHeaderFieldDate(); 1835
  term description, TimeZone; 1774
  time difference
    retrieving
      SimpleTimeZone.getOffset(); 1563
      SimpleTimeZone.getRawOffset(); 1564
      TimeZone.getOffset(); 1782
      TimeZone.getRawOffset(); 1783
    setting
      SimpleTimeZone.setRawOffset(); 1566
      TimeZone.setRawOffset(); 1785
Greenwich Mean Time
  See GMT (Greenwich Mean Time)
GregorianCalendar; 882
  See Also calendar(s); date(s)
  AD; 885
  add(); 885
  after(); 886
  BC; 886
  before(); 887
  computeFields(); 887
  computeTime(); 887
  equals(); 888
  getGreatestMinimum(); 888
  getGregorianChange(); 889
  getLeastMaximum(); 889
  getMaximum(); 890
  getMinimum(); 890
  hashCode(); 892
  isLeapYear(); 893
  roll(); 894
  setGregorianChange(); 895

grouping
separator
determining if used
NumberFormat.isGroupingUsed(); 1206
property, NumberFormat; 1193
retrieving, DecimalFormatSymbols.get-GroupingSeparator(); 671
setting
DecimalFormatSymbols.setGrouping-Separator(); 676
NumberFormat.setGroupingUsed(); 1210
size
DecimalFormat; 632
retrieving, DecimalFormat.getGrouping-Size(); 650
setting, DecimalFormat.setGrouping-Size(); 658
used property, NumberFormat; 1193
groups-thread
enumerating active threads in
Thread.enumerate(); 1731
retrieving, Thread.getThreadGroup(); 1732
Thread; 1724
guessxxx methods
guessContentTypeFromStream()
URLConnection; 1841
guessContentTypeFromName()
URLConnection; 1840
GZIP format
file identifier
GZIPInputStream.GZIP_MAGIC; 899
GZIP_MAGIC, GZIPInputStream; 899
GZIPInputStream; 896
close(); 897
crc; 898
eos; 899
GZIP_MAGIC; 899
package, java.util.zip; 896
read(); 901
GZIPOutputStream; 902
close(); 908
crc; 909
finish(); 910
package, java.util.zip; 902
write(); 912
URL
GZIPInputStream; 896
GZIPOutputStream; 902
ZIP file differences
ZipInputStream; 1914
ZipOutputStream; 1920

H

handlers
content
ContentHandler; 487
ContentHandlerFactory.create-ContentHandler(); 492
factory, setting, URLConnection.set-ContentHandlerFactory(); 1842
URLConnection; 1823
handleGetObject()
ListResourceBundle; 1053
PropertyResourceBundle; 1379
ResourceBundle; 1445
serialization, ObjectInputStream; 1232
stream
FileNameMap; 816
URL, HttpURLConnection use; 923
URL, URLStreamHandler; 1852
URL
protocol, URLConnection; 1820
stream, URLConnection; 1820
URL stream, factory
URL; 1801
URLStreamHandlerFactory; 1857
creating, URLStreamHandlerFactory.cre-ateURLStreamHandler(); 1859
setting, URL.setURLStreamHandler-Factory(); 1814
hasxxx methods
hasChanged(), Observable; 1294
hasMoreElements()
Enumeration; 724
StringTokenizer; 1699
hasMoreTokens(), StringTokenizer; 1699
hashing
algorithm, Hashtable; 913
buckets, Hashtable; 913, 914
hashCode()
BigDecimal; 85
BigInteger; 116
BitSet; 141
Boolean; 147
Byte; 209
Character; 290
ChoiceFormat; 361

CollationKey; 445
Collator; 460
Constructor; 482
Date; 572
DateFormat; 597
DateFormatSymbols; 620
DecimalFormat; 652
DecimalFormatSymbols; 673
Double; 714
Field; 764
File; 793
Float; 864
GregorianCalendar; 892
InetAddress; 963
Integer; 1006
Locale; 1066
Long; 1073
MessageFormat; 1114
Method; 1133
NumberFormat; 1205
Object; 1220
RuleBasedCollator; 1460
Short; 1534
SimpleDateFormat; 1555
SimpleTimeZone; 1564
String; 1642
StringCharacterIterator; 1681
URL; 1811

hashCode, System.identityHashCode(); 1717

Hashtable; 913
clear(); 916
clone(); 916
contains(); 917
containsKey(); 917
elements(); 918
extensibility; 914
get(); 918
isEmpty(); 920
keys(); 920
load factor; 914
package, java.util; 913
put(); 921
rehash(); 921
remove(); 922
size(); 922
string representation, generating; 922
toString(); 922

rehashing, Hashtable.rehash(); 921

header
document
ContentHandler; 487
ContentHandlerFactory; 490

hexadecimal number
string representation, generating
Integer.toHexString(); 1011
Long.toHexString(); 1078

host
exceptions, UnknownHostException; 1792
IP address, retrieving
InetAddress.getLocalHost(); 962
name
as URL component, URL; 1800
retrieving for an IP address
InetAddress.getHostName(); 961
retrieving, URL.getHost(); 1809
name resolution, InetAddress; 957

hour(s)
HOUR, Calendar; 262
HOUR_OF_DAY, Calendar; 263
HOUR_OF_DAY0_FIELD, DateFormat; 598
HOUR_OF_DAY1_FIELD, DateFormat; 598
HOUR0_FIELD.DateFormat; 598
HOUR1_FIELD.DateFormat; 599

HTTP (Hypertext Transfer Protocol)
connection, constructing, HttpURL-Connection.httpURLConnection(); 934
documentation for, (URL)
HttpURLConnection; 923
HTTP_ACCEPTED
HttpURLConnection, *Table*; 925
HTTP_BAD_GATEWAY
HttpURLConnection, *Table*; 925
HTTP_BAD_METHOD
HttpURLConnection, *Table*; 924
HTTP_BAD_REQUEST
HttpURLConnection, *Table*; 925
HTTP_CLIENT_TIMEOUT
HttpURLConnection, *Table*; 925
HTTP_CONFLICT
HttpURLConnection, *Table*; 925
HTTP_CREATED
HttpURLConnection, *Table*; 925
HTTP_ENTITY_TOO_LARGE
HttpURLConnection, *Table*; 925
HTTP_FORBIDDEN
HttpURLConnection, *Table*; 925
HTTP_GATEWAY_TIMEOUT
HttpURLConnection, *Table*; 925

HTTP (Hypertext Transfer Protocol) *(continued)*
HTTP_GONE, HttpURLConnection, *Table*; 925
HTTP_INTERNAL_ERROR
HttpURLConnection, *Table*; 925
HTTP_LENGTH_REQUIRED
HttpURLConnection, *Table*; 925
HTTP_MOVED_PERM
HttpURLConnection, *Table*; 925
HTTP_MOVED_TEMP
HttpURLConnection, *Table*; 925
HTTP_MULT_CHOICE
HttpURLConnection, *Table*; 925
HTTP_NO_CONTENT
HttpURLConnection, *Table*; 925
HTTP_NOT_ACCEPTABLE
HttpURLConnection, *Table*; 925
HTTP_NOT_AUTHORITATIVE
HttpURLConnection, *Table*; 925
HTTP_NOT_FOUND
HttpURLConnection, *Table*; 925
HTTP_NOT_MODIFIED
HttpURLConnection, *Table*; 926
HTTP_OK, HttpURLConnection, *Table*; 926
HTTP_PARTIAL, HttpURLConnection, *Table*; 926
HTTP_PAYMENT_REQUIRED
HttpURLConnection, *Table*; 926
HTTP_PRECON_FAILED
HttpURLConnection, *Table*; 926
HTTP_PROXY_AUTH
HttpURLConnection, *Table*; 926
HTTP_RESET, HttpURLConnection, *Table*; 926
HTTP_SEE_OTHER
HttpURLConnection, *Table*; 926
HTTP_SERVER_ERROR
HttpURLConnection, *Table*; 926
HTTP_UNAUTHORIZED
HttpURLConnection, *Table*; 926
HTTP_UNAVAILABLE
HttpURLConnection, *Table*; 926
HTTP_UNSUPPORTED_TYPE
HttpURLConnection, *Table*; 926
HTTP_USE_PROXY
HttpURLConnection, *Table*; 926
HTTP_VERSION, HttpURLConnection, *Table*; 926
HttpURLConnection; 923
disconnect(); 932
getFollowRedirects(); 932
getRequestMethod(); 933
getResponseCode(); 933
getResponseMessage(); 934
HTTP_ACCEPTED, *Table*; 926
HTTP response codes, *Table*; 926
httpURLConnection(); 934
method; 935
package, java.net; 923
responseCode; 935
responseMessage; 935
setFollowRedirects(); 935
setRequestMethod(); 937
usingProxy(); 938
method token, HttpURLConnection.method; 935
request header
fields, *Table*, URLConnection; 1821
URLConnection; 1821
request method tokens
HttpURLConnection, *Table*; 924
response codes, HttpURLConnection, *Table*; 924
response header
fields, *Table*, URLConnection; 1822
URLConnection; 1822
response message, retrieving
HttpURLConnection.getResponse-Message(); 934
server, disconnecting
HttpURLConnection.disconnect(); 932
term definition and description
HttpURLConnection; 923

Huffman coding
compression strategy, specification,
Deflater.HUFFMAN_ONLY; 689
HUFFMAN_ONLY, Deflater; 689

I

IO
See Also file(s); input; output; stream(s)
error stream, Process.getErrorStream(); 1366
exceptions
CharConversionException; 331
EOFException; 725
FileNotFoundException; 819
InterruptedIOException; 1019
IOException; 1031
ProtocolException; 1381
SyncFailedException; 1708
UnknownHostException; 1792
UnknownServiceException; 1794
UnsupportedEncodingException; 1798
UTFDataFormatException; 1860
input stream, Process.getOutputStream(); 1368
IOException; 1031
package, java.io; 1031
output stream, Process.getInputStream(); 1367

standard
error stream
Process.getErrorStream(); 1366
System.err; 1714
System.setErr(); 1720
input stream
Process.getOutputStream(); 1368
System.in; 1717
System.setIn(); 1721
output stream
Process.getInputStream(); 1367
System.out; 1719
System.setOut(); 1721
System; 1710

IDENTICAL
Collator; 461

identifiers
byte to character encoding, *Table*, String.startsWith(); 1648
character to byte encoding, *Table*, String; 1639
encoding
retrieving,
InputStreamReader.getEncoding(); 993
OutputStreamWriter.getEncoding(); 1311
UnsupportedEncodingException; 1798
GZIP file, GZIPInputStream.GZIP_MAGIC; 899
ignorable characters
Table, Character; 291
testing for
Character.isIdentifierIgnorable(); 291
Java
Character; 283
Character.isJavaIdentifierPart(); 292
Character.isJavaIdentifierStart(); 293
locale
Locale; 1055
resource bundles, ResourceBundle; 1436
ResourceBundle, locale(s); 1436
SUID (Stream Unique Identifier), term description
Externalizable; 743
ObjectOutputStream; 1264
ObjectStreamClass; 1283
Serializable; 1511
time zone
retrieving
TimeZone.getAvailableIDs(); 1779
TimeZone.getID(); 1782
setting, TimeZone.setID(); 1785
time zones, *Table*, TimeZone; 1775
Unicode
Character; 283
Character.isUnicodeIdentifierPart(); 298
Character.isUnicodeIdentifierStart(); 299

identityHashCode()
System; 1717

IEEE
754 standard
Math.IEEEremainder(); 1089
rounding, Math.rint(); 1092
IEEEremainder(), Math; 1089

ifModifiedSince
URLConnection; 1841

ignorable characters
for Java and Unicode identifiers
Table, Character; 291
testing for
Character.isIdentifierIgnorable(); 291
term description, RuleBasedCollator; 1451

illegalxxx errors and exceptions
IllegalAccessError; 939
package, java.lang; 939
IllegalAccessException; 942
package, java.lang; 942
IllegalArgumentException; 945
package, java.lang; 945
IllegalMonitorStateException; 947
package, java.lang; 947
IllegalStateException; 949
package, java.lang; 949
IllegalThreadStateException; 951
package, java.lang; 951

implAccept()
ServerSocket; 1524

inxxx fields
in
FileDescriptor; 804
FilterInputStream; 838
FilterReader; 850
PipedInputStream; 1328
System; 1717
inCheck, SecurityManager; 1501

inxxx methods
inClass(), SecurityManager; 1501
inClassLoader(), SecurityManager; 1502
inDaylightTime()
SimpleTimeZone; 1564
TimeZone; 1784
IncompatibleClassChangeError; 953
package, java.lang; 953
index
character position, FieldPosition; 775
current
CharacterIterator; 306
StringCharacterIterator; 1672
indexOf()
String; 1642
Vector; 1870
IndexOutOfBoundsException; 955
package, java.lang; 955
parsing
ParsePosition; 1317
retrieving, ParsePosition.getIndex(); 1321
setting, ParsePosition.setIndex(); 1322
term description
CharacterIterator; 306
StringCharacterIterator; 1672
text subrange
beginning, retrieving, StringCharacter-Iterator.getBeginIndex(); 1680
current, retrieving, StringCharacter-Iterator.getIndex(); 1680
end, retrieving, StringCharacter-Iterator.getEndIndex(); 1680
InetAddress; 957
equals(); 958
getAddress(); 959
getAllByName(); 959
getByName(); 960
getHostAddress(); 961
getHostName(); 961
getLocalHost(); 962
hashCode(); 963
isMulticastAddress(); 963
package, java.net; 957
toString(); 963
infinity
formatting, DecimalFormat; 633
negative
Double.NEGATIVE_INFINITY; 718, 868
rounding towards
BigDecimal.ROUND_FLOOR; 91
positive
Double.POSITIVE_INFINITY; 718
Float.POSITIVE_INFINITY; 869
rounding towards
BigDecimal.ROUND_CEILING; 90
string representation
retrieving, DecimalFormatSymbols.get-Infinity(); 671
setting, DecimalFormatSymbols.set-Infinity(); 676
testing for
Double.isInfinite(); 714
Float.isInfinite(); 866
value, not possible with BigDecimal; 75
inflater
inf, InflaterInputStream; 980
inflate(), Inflater; 971
Inflater; 965
end(); 969
finalize(); 969
finished(); 970
getAdler(); 970
getRemaining(); 970
getTotalIn(); 971
getTotalOut(); 971
inflate(); 971
needsDictionary(); 973
needsInput(); 973
package, java.util.zip; 965
reset(); 973
setDictionary(); 974
setInput(); 974
InflaterInputStream; 979
buf; 979
fill(); 980
inf; 980
len; 981
package, java.util.zip; 976
read(); 981
skip(); 982
InflaterInputStream.inf; 980
resetting, Inflater.reset(); 973
inheritance
cycles, ClassCircularityError; 409
initialization
exceptions
ExceptionInInitializerError; 741

input
buffer
determining if empty
Deflater.needsInput(); 689
Inflater.needsInput(); 973
bytes, number available for reading
BufferedInputStream.available(); 178
data, DataInput; 526
InputStream; 983
available(); 985
close(); 986
mark(); 986
markSupported(); 987
package, java.io; 983
read(); 987
reset(); 988
skip(); 989
InputStreamReader; 990
close(); 993
getEncoding(); 993
package, java.io; 990
read(); 995
ready(); 996
standard
FileDescriptor; 802
FileDescriptor.in; 804
streams
buffered, BufferedInputStream; 176
BufferedReader; 190
ByteArrayInputStream; 216
CharArrayReader; 315
checksum, CheckedInputStream; 333
creating for URL connection
URLConnection.getInputStream(); 1838
creating
Socket.getInputStream(); 1578
ZipFile.getInputStream(); 1912
DataInputStream; 534
FileInputStream; 807
FilterInputStream; 834
FilterReader; 847
for reading error output
Process.getErrorStream(); 1366
for reading output
Process.getInputStream(); 1367
GZIPInputStream; 896
InflaterInputStream; 976
InputStream; 983
InputStreamReader; 990
LineNumberReader; 1040
ObjectInputStream; 1230
PipedInputStream; 1323
PipedReader; 1337
Process.getOutputStream(); 1368
PushbackInputStream; 1383
PushbackReader; 1392
Reader; 1426
reading, CheckedInputStream.read(); 337
retrieving resources as
Class.getResourceAsStream(); 396
SequenceInputStream; 1503
skipping bytes
BufferedInputStream.skip(); 183
CheckedInputStream.skip(); 338
socket, creating
SocketImpl.getInputStream(); 1600
StringReader; 1690
URL connection, opening
URL.openStream(); 1813
ZipInputStream; 1914
URL, URLConnection.doInput; 1829
URL connection
setting, URLConnection.setDoInput(); 1844
testing for
URLConnection.getDoInput(); 1833
insertxxx methods
insert(), StringBuffer; 1661
insertElementAt(), Vector; 1871
instantiation
Constructor declaring class
Constructor.newInstance(); 483
creating instances, Constructor; 475
errors, InstantiationError; 997
exceptions, InstantiationException; 999
instances
creating, Class.newInstance(); 404
testing for, Class.isInstance(); 401
InstantiationError; 997
package, java.lang; 997
InstantiationException; 999
package, java.lang; 999

integer(s)
See Also big decimal values; big integer values
arrays
modifying
Array.setInt(); 67
Array.setLong(); 68
Array.setShort(); 69
retrieving elements from
Array.getInt(); 58
Array.getLong(); 60
Array.getShort(); 61
converting big decimal values into
BigDecimal.intvalue(); 86
BigDecimal.longValue(); 86
converting big integer values into
BigInteger.intValue(); 117
BigInteger.longValue(); 118
creating big integer from
BigInteger.valueOf(); 132
fields
modifying
Field.setInt(); 771
Field.setLong(); 771
Field.setShort(); 772
retrieving values of
Field.getInt(); 761
Field.getLong(); 761
Field.getShort(); 763
intBitsToFloat(), Float; 865
Integer; 1001
byteValue(); 1003
decode(); 1003
doubleValue(); 1004
equals(); 1004
floatValue(); 1005
getInteger(); 1005
hashCode(); 1006
intValue(); 1007
longValue(); 1008
MAX_VALUE; 1008
MIN_VALUE; 1008
package, java.lang; 1001
parseInt(); 1009
shortValue(); 1010
toBinaryString(); 1010
toHexString(); 1011
toOctalString(); 1012
toString(); 1012
TYPE; 1013
valueOf(); 1013
INTEGER_FIELD, NumberFormat; 1205
Integer object creation using system properties
Integer.getInteger(); 1005
intValue()
BigDecimal; 86
BigInteger; 117
Byte; 210
Double; 714
Float; 865
Integer; 1007
Long; 1074
Number; 1189
Short; 1534
Long object creation using system properties,
Long.getLong(); 1072
maximum digits
retrieving, NumberFormat.getMaximum-FractionDigits(); 1202
setting, NumberFormat.setMaximumInteger-Digits(); 1211
minimum digits
retrieving, NumberFormat.getMinimum-IntegerDigits(); 1204
setting, NumberFormat.setMinimumInteger-Digits(); 1212
parsing response header field as
URLConnection.getHeaderFieldInt(); 1836
parsing string representation into a short
Short.decode(); 1532
portion of FieldPosition object
NumberFormat.INTEGER_FIELD; 1205
pseudorandom-number, generating
Random.nextInt(); 1404
Random.nextLong(); 1404
reading
DataInput.readInt(); 529
DataInput.readLong(); 530
DataInput.readShort(); 531
DataInput.readUnsignedShort(); 532
DataInputStream.readInt(); 541
DataInputStream.readLong(); 542
DataInputStream.readShort(); 543
DataInputStream.readUnsignedShort(); 544
ObjectInputStream.readInt(); 1242
ObjectInputStream.readLong(); 1243

ObjectInputStream.readUnsigned-
Short(); 1248
RandomAccessFile.readInt(); 1415
RandomAccessFile.readLong(); 1416
RandomAccessFile.readShort(); 1416
RandomAccessFile.readUnsignedShort(); 1417

retrieving object value as an int
BigDecimal.intvalue(); 86
BigInteger.intValue(); 117
Double.intValue(); 714
Float.intValue(); 865
Integer.intValue(); 1007
Long.intValue(); 1074
Number.intValue(); 1189
Short.intValue(); 1534

retrieving object value as a long
BigDecimal.longValue(); 86
BigInteger.longValue(); 118
Byte.longValue(); 210
Double.longValue(); 716
Float.longValue(); 867
Integer.longValue(); 1008
Long.longValue(); 1075
Number.longValue(); 1190
Short.longValue(); 1535

retrieving object value as a short
Byte.shortValue(); 212
Double.shortValue(); 718
Integer.shortValue(); 1010
Number.shortValue(); 1190
Long.shortValue(); 1076

string representation, generating
Byte.toString(); 213
Integer.toString(); 1012
Long.toString(); 1079
Short.toString(); 1538

wrappers
Byte; 205
Integer; 1001
Long; 1069
Short; 1530

writing
DataOutput.writeInt(); 550
DataOutput.writeLong(); 550
DataOutput.writeShort(); 551
DataOutputStream.writeInt(); 559
DataOutputStream.writeLong(); 560
DataOutputStream.writeShort(); 560
ObjectOutputStream.writeInt(); 1278
ObjectOutputStream.writeLong(); 1279
ObjectOutputStream.writeShort(); 1281
RandomAccessFile.writeInt(); 1423
RandomAccessFile.writeLong(); 1424
RandomAccessFile.writeShort(); 1424

interaction
user, flag for determining if URL connection permits
URLConnection.allowUserInteraction; 1827
setting, URLConnection.setAllowUser-
Interaction(); 1842
testing for
URLConnection.getAllowUser-
Interaction(); 1830
URLConnection.getDefaultAllowUser-
Interaction(); 1832

interface(s)
INTERFACE, Modifier; 1144
modifier, testing for
Modifier.isInterface(); 1147
network, setting address of,
MulticastSocket.setInterface(); 1162
retrieving, Class.getInterfaces(); 388
testing for, Class.isInterface(); 402
valid modifiers for, *Table*, Modifier; 1143

intern()
String; 1643

InternalError; 1015
package, java.lang; 1015

internalGet()
Calendar; 263

internationalization
See Also locale(s)
classes that implement; 34

Internet
RFC 1738, URLs described in
MalformedURLException; 1082

interrupts
See Also errors; events; exceptions
interrupt(), Thread; 1733
interrupted(), Thread; 1734
InterruptedException; 1017
package, java.lang; 1017
InterruptedIOException; 1019
bytesTransferred; 1020
package, java.io; 1019
isInterrupted(), Thread; 1734
term description, Thread; 1725

interrupts *(continued)*
thread
sending, Thread.interrupt(); 1733
testing for
Thread.interrupted(); 1734
Thread.isInteruppted(); 1736
invalid
InvalidClassException; 1022
package, java.io; 1022
InvalidObjectException; 1026
package, java.io; 1026
inversion
BigInteger.not(); 123
invoking methods
InvocationTargetException; 1028
getTargetException(); 1030
package, java.lang.reflect; 1028
invoke(), Method; 1134
Method.invoke(); 1134
IP (Internet Protocol) address
representation of, InetAddress; 957
retrieving
for a local host
InetAddress.getLocalHost(); 962
host name for
InetAddress.getHostName(); 961
InetAddress.getAddress(); 959
InetAddress.getAllByName(); 959
InetAddress.getByName(); 960
InetAddress.getHostAddress(); 961
ServerSocket.getInetAddress(); 1523
Socket.getInetAddress(); 1577
Socket.getLocalAddress(); 1579
socket
retrieving
SocketImpl.getInetAddress(); 1600
SocketImpl.address; 1596
string representation
InetAddress.toString(); 963
isxxx methods
isAbsolute(), File; 794
isAbstract(), Modifier; 1147
isAlive(), Thread; 1735
isArray(), Class; 399
isAssignableFrom(), Class; 400
isDaemon()
Thread; 1735
ThreadGroup; 1760
isDecimalSeparatorAlwaysShown()
DecimalFormat; 652
isDefined(), Character; 290
isDestroyed(), ThreadGroup; 1760
isDigit(), Character; 290
isDirectory()
File; 794
ZipEntry; 1899
isEmpty()
Dictionary; 706
Hashtable; 920
Vector; 1872
isFile(), File; 795
isFinal(), Modifier; 1147
isGroupingUsed(), NumberFormat; 1206
isIdentifierIgnorable(), Character; 291
isInfinite()
Double; 714
Float; 866
isInstance(), Class; 401
isInterface()
Class; 402
Modifier; 1147
isInterrupted(), Thread; 1736
isISOControl(), Character; 292
isJavaIdentifierPart(), Character; 292
isJavaIdentifierStart(), Character; 293
isJavaLetter(), Character; 294
isJavaLetterOrDigit(), Character; 294
isLeapYear(), GregorianCalendar; 893
isLenient()
Calendar; 264
DateFormat; 599
isLetter(), Character; 295
isLetterOrDigit(), Character; 296
isLowerCase(), Character; 296
isMulticastAddress(), InetAddress; 963
isNaN()
Double; 715
Float; 866
isNative(), Modifier; 1148
isParseIntegerOnly(), NumberFormat; 1207
isPrimitive(), Class; 403
isPrivate(), Modifier; 1148
isProbablePrime(), BigInteger; 117
isProtected(), Modifier; 1149
isPublic(), Modifier; 1149
isSet(), Calendar; 264
isSet, Calendar; 264
isSpace(), Character; 297
isSpaceChar(), Character; 297
isStatic(), Modifier; 1150

isSynchronized(), Modifier; 1150
isTimeSet, Calendar; 264
isTitleCase(), Character; 297
isTransient(), Modifier; 1151
isUnicodeIdentifierPart(), Character; 298
isUnicodeIdentifierStart()
Character; 299
isUpperCase(), Character; 299
isVolatile(), Modifier; 1151
isWhitespace(), Character; 300
ISO (International Standards Organization)
control characters
Character.isISOControl(); 292
country code, retrieving
Locale.getISO3Country(); 1064
language code
Locale.getISO3Language(); 1064
retrieving, Locale.getLanguage(); 1065
LATIN1 characters
testing for
Character.isLetter(); 295
Character.isLetterOrDigit(); 296
Italian
ITALIAN, Locale; 1056
predefined locale codes, *Table*, Locale; 1056
Italy
ITALY, Locale; 1056
predefined locale codes, *Table*, Locale; 1056
iteration
break, BreakIterator; 150
BreakIterator; 150
character, retrieving
BreakIterator.getText(); 169
CharacterIterator; 305
classes that implement; 31
CollationElementIterator; 434
concept description; 28
resetting iterators
CollationElementIterator.reset(); 439
retrieving CollationElementIterator
RuleBasedCollator.getCollation-ElementIterator(); 1458
StringCharacterIterator; 1671

J

JANUARY
Calendar, *Table*; 233
Japan
JAPAN, Locale; 1056
predefined locale codes, *Table*, Locale; 1056
Japanese
JAPANESE, Locale; 1056
predefined locale codes, *Table*, Locale; 1056
JAR (Java Archive)
term description, ClassLoader; 414
Java
class hierarchy, Object class as root of; 1215
identifiers
Character; 283
Character.isIdentifierIgnorable(); 291
Character.isJavaIdentifierPart(); 292
Character.isJavaIdentifierStart(); 293
modifiers, retrieving
Class.getModifiers(); 392
system properties, *Table*, System; 1711
java.io package; 1
BufferedInputStream; 176
BufferedOutputStream; 185
BufferedReader; 190
BufferedWriter; 199
ByteArrayInputStream; 216
ByteArrayOutputStream; 224
CharArrayReader; 315
CharArrayWriter; 323
CharConversionException; 331
data streams, concept description; 3
DataInput; 526
DataInputStream; 534
DataOutput; 546
DataOutputStream; 552
EOFException; 725
Externalizable; 743
File; 782
FileDescriptor; 802
FileInputStream; 807
FilenameFilter; 814
FileNotFoundException; 819
FileOutputStream; 821
FileReader; 827
files, concept description; 3
FileWriter; 830
FilterInputStream; 834
FilterOutputStream; 842

java.io package *(continued)*
FilterReader; 847
FilterWriter; 855
InputStream; 983
InputStreamReader; 990
InterruptedIOException; 1019
InvalidClassException; 1022
InvalidObjectException; 1026
IOException; 1031
LineNumberInputStream; 1033
LineNumberReader; 1040
NotActiveException; 1181
NotSerializableException; 1183
ObjectInput; 1226
ObjectInputStream; 1230
ObjectInputValidation; 1256
ObjectOutput; 1259
ObjectOutputStream; 1262
ObjectStreamClass; 1283
ObjectStreamException; 1288
OptionalDataException; 1299
OutputStream; 1304
OutputStreamWriter; 1308
PipedInputStream; 1323
PipedOutputStream; 1332
PipedReader; 1337
PipedWriter; 1342
PrintStream; 1346
PrintWriter; 1354
PushbackInputStream; 1383
PushbackReader; 1392
RandomAccessFile; 1406
Reader; 1426
SequenceInputStream; 1503
Serializable; 1508
serialization, concept description; 3
StreamCorruptedException; 1612
StreamTokenizer; 1614
StringBufferInputStream; 1665
StringReader; 1690
StringWriter; 1703
SyncFailedException; 1708
UnsupportedEncodingException; 1798
WriteAbortedException; 1884
Writer; 1887
java.lang package; 10
AbstractMethodError; 39
ArithmeticException; 45
ArrayIndexOutOfBoundsException; 70
ArrayStoreException; 72
Boolean; 144
Byte; 205
Character; 282
Class; 365
ClassCastException; 407
ClassCircularityError; 409
ClassFormatError; 411
ClassLoader; 413
ClassNotFoundException; 426
Cloneable; 428
CloneNotSupportedException; 431
Compiler; 470
Double; 709
Exception; 737
ExceptionInInitializerError; 741
Float; 860
IllegalAccessError; 939
IllegalAccessException; 942
IllegalArgumentException; 945
IllegalMonitorStateException; 947
IllegalStateException; 949
IllegalThreadStateException; 951
IncompatibleClassChangeError; 953
IndexOutOfBoundsException; 955
InstantiationError; 997
InstantiationException; 999
Integer; 1001
InternalError; 1015
InterruptedException; 1017
LinkageError; 1049
Long; 1069
Math; 1084
NegativeArraySizeException; 1164
NoClassDefFoundError; 1166
NoSuchFieldError; 1172
NoSuchFieldException; 1174
NoSuchMethodError; 1176
NoSuchMethodException; 1178
NullPointerException; 1185
Number; 1187
Object; 1215
OutOfMemoryError; 1302
overview; 12
Process; 1363
Runnable; 1464
Runtime; 1466
RuntimeException; 1477
SecurityException; 1479

SecurityManager; 1481
Short; 1530
StackOverflowError; 1610
String; 1632
StringBuffer; 1655
StringIndexOutOfBoundsException; 1688
System; 1710
Thread; 1723
ThreadDeath; 1750
ThreadGroup; 1751
Throwable; 1769
UnknownError; 1790
UnsatisfiedLinkError; 1796
VerifyError; 1878
VirtualMachineError; 1880
Void; 1882

java.lang.reflect package; 19
Array; 47
Constructor; 475
Field; 749
InvocationTargetException; 1028
Member; 1095
Method; 1123
Modifier; 1143

java.math package; 21
BigDecimal; 74
BigInteger; 99

java.net package; 22
BindException; 134
ConnectException; 473
ContentHandler; 487
ContentHandlerFactory; 490
DatagramPacket; 499
DatagramSocket; 506
DatagramSocketImpl; 516
FileNameMap; 816
HttpURLConnection; 923
InetAddress; 957
MalformedURLException; 1082
MulticastSocket; 1153
NoRouteToHostException; 1168
ProtocolException; 1381
ServerSocket; 1515
Socket; 1571
SocketException; 1590
SocketImpl; 1592
SocketImplFactory; 1604
UnknownHostException; 1792
UnknownServiceException; 1794
URL; 1800
URLConnection; 1819
URLEncoder; 1849
URLStreamHandler; 1852
URLStreamHandlerFactory; 1857

java.text package; 26
BreakIterator; 150
CharacterIterator; 305
ChoiceFormat; 346
CollationElementIterator; 434
CollationKey; 441
Collator; 447
DateFormat; 580
DateFormatSymbols; 610
DecimalFormat; 626
DecimalFormatSymbols; 665
FieldPosition; 774
Format; 872
MessageFormat; 1102
NumberFormat; 1192
ParseException; 1314
ParsePosition; 1317
RuleBasedCollator; 1447
SimpleDateFormat; 1541
StringCharacterIterator; 1671

java.util package; 32
BitSet; 136
Calendar; 232
data structures; 33
Date; 562
Dictionary; 702
EmptyStackException; 721
Enumeration; 723
EventListener; 729
EventObject; 731
GregorianCalendar; 882
Hashtable; 913
ListResourceBundle; 1051
Locale; 1054
MissingResourceException; 1140
NoSuchElementException; 1170
Observable; 1290
Observer; 1296
Properties; 1370
PropertyResourceBundle; 1378
Random; 1399
ResourceBundle; 1435
SimpleTimeZone; 1559
Stack; 1606

java.util package *(continued)*
StringTokenizer; 1697
TimeZone; 1774
TooManyListenersException; 1787
Vector; 1862
java.util.zip package; 36
Adler32; 41
CheckedInputStream; 333
CheckedOutputStream; 339
Checksum; 343
CRC32; 493
DataFormatException; 497
Deflater; 679
DeflaterOutputStream; 695
GZIPInputStream; 896
GZIPOutputStream; 902
Inflater; 965
InflaterInputStream; 976
ZipEntry; 1892
ZipFile; 1906
ZipInputStream; 1914
ZipOutputStream; 1920
joinxxx methods
join()
DatagramSocketImpl; 522
Thread; 1737
joinGroup(), MulticastSocket; 1158
JRE (Java Runtime Environment)
term description, ClassLoader; 415
Julian calendar
date replaced by Gregorian
retrieving, GregorianCalendar.get-GregorianChange(); 889
setting, GregorianCalendar.setGregorian-Change(); 895
JULY
Calendar, *Table*; 233
JUNE
Calendar, *Table*; 233

K

keys
collation
CollationKey; 441
comparing, CollationKey.compareTo(); 444
retrieving source string
CollationKey.getSourceString(); 445
transforming a string into
Collator.getCollationKey(); 458
RuleBasedCollator.getCollation-Key(); 1459
dictionary
adding, Dictionary.put(); 707
Dictionary; 702
dictionary element associated with, retrieving
Dictionary.get(); 706
list of, retrieving, Dictionary.keys(); 706
removing, Dictionary.remove(); 707
hash table
adding, Hashtable.put(); 921
Hashtable; 913
removing, Hashtable.clear(); 916
removing, Hashtable.remove(); 922
retrieving list of, Hashtable.keys(); 920
testing for, Hashtable.containsKey(); 917
keys()
Dictionary; 706
Hashtable; 920
resource bundle
enumerating
ListResourceBundle.getKeys(); 1053
PropertyResourceBundle.getKeys(); 1379
keys, enumerating
ResourceBundle.getKeys(); 1443
retrieving response header as
URLConnection.getHeaderFieldKey(); 1836
Korea
KOREA, Locale; 1056
predefined locale codes, *Table*, Locale; 1056
Korean
KOREAN, Locale; 1056
predefined locale codes, *Table*, Locale; 1056

L

language(s)
C++, specifying comment token
StreamTokenizer.slashSlashComments(); 1626
C, specifying comment token
StreamTokenizer.slashSlashComments(); 1626
ISO code
Locale.getISO3Language(); 1064
retrieving, Locale.getLanguage(); 1065

Latin-based, ordering strength, *Table*
Collator; 448
locale code, retrieving
Locale.getDisplayLanguage(); 1062
lastxxx methods
last()
BreakIterator; 171
CharacterIterator; 312
StringCharacterIterator; 1681
lastElement(), Vector; 1872
lastIndexOf()
String; 1644
Vector; 1872
lastModified(), File; 796
Latin-based languages
ordering strength, *Table*, Collator; 448
leap year
testing for
GregorianCalendar.isLeapYear(); 893
leavexxx methods
leave(), DatagramSocketImpl; 522
leaveGroup(), MulticastSocket; 1158
length
bit representation, determining
BigInteger.bitLength(); 108
datagram packet
retrieving
DatagramPacket.getLength(); 503
setting, DatagramPacket.setLength(); 504
len, InflaterInputStream; 981
length()
File; 796
RandomAccessFile; 1410
String; 1645
StringBuffer; 1662
length, OptionalDataException; 1301
leniency
Calendar; 233
calendar, setting, Calendar.setLenient(); 273
date normalization controlled by, DateFormat; 583
determining if set, DateFormat.isLenient(); 599
setting, DateFormat.setLenient(); 605
term description, DatagramPacket; 499
testing for, Calendar.isLenient(); 264
letters
LETTER_NUMBER, Character, *Table*; 289
testing for
Character.isLetter(); 295
Character.isLetterOrDigit(); 296
libraries
linking, permission determination
SecurityManager.checkLink(); 1488
loading
permission determination
SecurityManager.checkLink(); 1488
Runtime.load(); 1471
Runtime.loadLibrary(); 1472
System.load(); 1718
System.loadLibrary(); 1719
Math; 1084
Runtime; 1466
life cycle
URL, URLConnection; 1819
limits
array of, retrieving
ChoiceFormat.getLimits(); 360
limits array, ChoiceFormat; 346
lines
-breaks
boundary analysis, BreakIterator; 155
boundary, break iterator, retrieving
BreakIterator.getLineInstance(); 165
input line number, retrieving
LineNumberReader.getLineNumber(); 1042
StreamTokenizer.lineno(); 1619
LINE_SEPARATOR, Character, *Table*; 289
lineno(), StreamTokenizer; 1619
LineNumberInputStream; 1033
available(); 1036
getLineNumber(); 1036
mark(); 1037
package, java.io; 1033
read(); 1037
reset(); 1038
setLineNumber(); 1038
skip(); 1039
LineNumberReader; 1040
mark(); 1043
package, java.io; 1040
read(); 1045
readLine(); 1046
reset(); 1046
setLineNumber(); 1047
skip(); 1048
printing
PrintStream.println(); 1351
PrintWriter.println(); 1359

lines *(continued)*
reading
DataInput.readLine(); 530
DataInputStream.readLine(); 541
ObjectInputStream.readLine(); 1243
RandomAccessFile.readLine(); 1415
separator, writing
BufferedWriter; 200
BufferedWriter.newLine(); 203
linger-on-close
term description, Socket; 1572
time-out period
retrieving, Socket.getSoLinger(); 1581
setting, Socket.setSoLinger(); 1583
linking
classes
bibliographic reference, Class-Loader.resolveClass(); 425
ClassLoader.resolveClass(); 425
errors, AbstractMethodError; 39
libraries, permission determination
SecurityManager.checkLink(); 1488
LinkageError; 1049
package, java.lang; 1049
list(s)
list()
File; 796
Properties; 1374
ThreadGroup; 1760
ListResourceBundle; 1051
getContents(); 1052
getKeys(); 1053
handleGetObject(); 1053
package, java.util; 1051
properties
Properties; 1370
writing, Properties.list(); 1374
resource bundles, ListResourceBundle; 1051
vector elements, generating
Vector.elements(); 1868
listener(s)
event
EventListener; 729
EventObject; 731
exceptions, TooManyListenersException; 1787
listen(), SocketImpl; 1602
loading
classes
ClassLoader; 413
ClassLoader.findSystemClass(); 420
ClassLoader.loadClass(); 423
concepts and overview, ClassLoader; 413
ObjectInputStream.resolveClass(); 1250
deserialized objects, term description
ObjectInputStream; 1232
hash table load factor, Hashtable; 914
libraries
permission determination
SecurityManager.checkLink(); 1488
Runtime.load(); 1471
Runtime.loadLibrary(); 1472
System.load(); 1718
System.loadLibrary(); 1719
load()
Properties; 1375
Runtime; 1471
System; 1718
loadClass(), ClassLoader; 423
loadLibrary()
Runtime; 1472
System; 1719
properties, Properties.load(); 1375
locale(s)
accessing date-time formatting strings
DateFormatSymbols; 610
break iterators and, BreakIterator; 153
classes that are sensitive to; 28
classes that implement; 34
creating, a Collator for
Collator.getInstance(); 460
currency format, creating
NumberFormat.getInstance(); 1201
date format, SimpleDateFormat; 1541
date-time pattern characters, retrieving
DateFormatSymbols.getLocalPattern-Chars(); 618
decimal format
examples, DecimalFormat; 636
symbols, *Table*, DecimalFormatSymbols; 665
default
retrieving, Locale.getDefault(); 1060
setting, Locale.setDefault(); 1067
-dependent properties, Calendar; 234
identifier, resource bundles
ResourceBundle; 1436

Locale; 1054
clone(); 1059
equals(); 1060
getCountry(); 1060
getDefault(); 1060
getDisplayCountry(); 1061
getDisplayLanguage(); 1062
getDisplayName(); 1062
getDisplayVariant(); 1063
getISO3Country(); 1064
getISO3Language(); 1064
getLanguage(); 1065
getVariant(); 1065
hashCode(); 1066
package, java.util; 1054
setDefault(); 1067
toString(); 1068
localized
messages, retrieving
Throwable.getLocalizedMessage(); 1771
vs. nonlocalized patterns, DecimalFormat; 631
number format
creating
NumberFormat.getInstance(); 1201
NumberFormat.getNumberInstance(); 1204
retrieving
NumberFormat.getAvailableLocales(); 1200
pattern
generating string representation
SimpleDateFormat.toLocalizedPattern(); 1558
localized, applying
DecimalFormat.applyLocalizedPattern(); 639
SimpleDateFormat.applyLocalizedPattern(); 1550
predefined, codes, *Table*, Locale; 1056
resource bundles for, ResourceBundle; 1435
retrieving
BreakIterator.getAvailableLocales(); 164
Calendar.getAvailableLocales(); 254
Collator.getAvailableLocales(); 457
DateFormat.getAvailableLocales(); 595
MessageFormat.getLocale(); 1113
setting, MessageFormat.setLocale(); 1122
-specific
formatting data in, Format; 872
messages, formatting, MessageFormat; 1102
number representation, DecimalFormat; 626
numbers, formatting, NumberFormat; 1192
parsing and formatting, dates and time
DateFormat; 580
string comparison, Collator; 447
strings, searching through
CollationElementIterator; 434
string representation, generating,
Locale.toString(); 1068
term description, Locale; 1054
localization
See locale(s)
localPort
DatagramSocketImpl; 523
localport
SocketImpl; 1602
locks
See Also synchronization
exceptions
IllegalMonitorStateException; 947
lock
Reader; 1429
Writer; 1890
term description, Object; 1215
thread synchronization with, Object; 1215
logarithm
log(), Math; 1090
natural, Math.log(); 1090
logical operations
AND
BigInteger.and(); 104
BitSet.and(); 138
with inverse, BigInteger.andNot(); 105
inversion, BigInteger.not(); 123
OR
BigInteger.or(); 124
BitSet.or(); 141
XOR
BigInteger.xor(); 132
BitSet.xor(); 143
long integer(s)
See Also integer(s)
arrays
modifying, Array.setLong(); 68
retrieving elements from, Array.getLong(); 60

long integer(s) *(continued)*
converting big
decimal values to
BigDecimal.longValue(); 86
integers into, BigInteger.longValue(); 118
creating big integer from
BigInteger.valueOf(); 132
fields
modifying, Field.setLong(); 771
retrieving values of, Field.getLong(); 761
Long; 1069
byteValue(); 1070
doubleValue(); 1071
equals(); 1071
floatValue(); 1072
getLong(); 1072
hashCode(); 1073
intValue(); 1074
longValue(); 1075
MAX_VALUE; 1075
MIN_VALUE; 1075
package, java.lang; 1069
parseLong(); 1076
shortValue(); 1076
toBinaryString(); 1077
toHexString(); 1078
toOctalString(); 1078
toString(); 1079
TYPE; 1080
valueOf(); 1080
LONG, DateFormat; 599
longBitsToDouble(), Double; 716
longValue()
BigDecimal; 86
BigInteger; 118
Byte; 210
Double; 716
Float; 867
Integer; 1008
Long; 1075
Number; 1190
Short; 1535
pseudorandom-number, generating
Random.nextLong(); 1404
reading
DataInput.readLong(); 530
DataInputStream.readLong(); 542
ObjectInputStream.readLong(); 1243
RandomAccessFile.readLong(); 1416
retrieving object as a long
Byte.longValue(); 210
wrappers, Long; 1069
writing
DataOutput.writeLong(); 550
DataOutputStream.writeLong(); 560
ObjectOutputStream.writeLong(); 1279
RandomAccessFile.writeLong(); 1424
lookup()
ObjectStreamClass; 1285
loops
control, Enumeration; 723
lost fraction
term description, BigDecimal; 75
lowercase
converting to, Character.toLowerCase(); 302
LOWERCASE_LETTER, Character, *Table*; 289
lowerCaseMode(), StreamTokenizer; 1619
specifying
StreamTokenizer.lowerCaseMode(); 1619
testing for, Character.isLowerCase(); 296

M

magic number
GZIP, GZIPInputStream.GZIP_MAGIC; 899
serialization, term description
ObjectInputStream.readStream-
Header(); 1246
ObjectOutputStream.writeStream-
Header(); 1281
MalformedURLException; 1082
package, java.net; 1082
mapping
filenames into content type, FileNameMap; 816
MARCH
Calendar, *Table*; 233
mark(ing)
current position
BufferedReader.mark(); 194
ByteArrayInputStream.mark(); 220
CharArrayReader.mark(); 318
FilterInputStream.mark(); 838
FilterReader.mark(); 850
InputStream.mark(); 986
LineNumberReader.mark(); 1043
Reader.mark(); 1430
StringReader.mark(); 1692
ENCLOSING_MARK, Character, *Table*; 289

input stream
maximum read-ahead allowed
BufferedInputStream.marklimit; 181
position
BufferedInputStream.mark(); 180
BufferedInputStream.markpos; 181
CharArrayReader.markPos; 319
testing for, BufferedInputStream.markSupported(); 181
mark()
BufferedInputStream; 180
BufferedReader; 194
ByteArrayInputStream; 220
CharArrayReader; 318
FilterInputStream; 838
FilterReader; 850
InputStream; 986
LineNumberInputStream; 1037
LineNumberReader; 1043
Reader; 1430
StringReader; 1692
mark, ByteArrayInputStream; 219
markedPos, CharArrayReader; 319
marklimit, BufferedInputStream; 181
markpos, BufferedInputStream; 181
markSupported()
BufferedInputStream; 181
BufferedReader; 194
ByteArrayInputStream; 221
CharArrayReader; 320
FilterInputStream; 839
FilterReader; 851
InputStream; 987
PushbackInputStream; 1387
PushbackReader; 1395
Reader; 1430
StringReader; 1693
NON_SPACING_MARK, Character, *Table*; 289
position of, ByteArrayInputStream.mark; 219
stream
BufferedInputStream; 177
BufferedReader; 191
testing for support of
BufferedReader.markSupported(); 194
ByteArrayInputStream.markSupported(); 221
CharArrayReader.markSupported(); 320
FilterInputStream.markSupported(); 839
FilterReader.markSupported(); 851
InputStream.markSupported(); 987
PushbackInputStream.markSupported(); 1387
PushbackReader.markSupported(); 1395
Reader.markSupported(); 1430
StringReader.markSupported(); 1693

mathematics
See Also trigonometric functions
java.math package
BigDecimal; 74
BigInteger; 99
Math; 1084
abs(); 1085
acos(); 1086
asin(); 1086
atan(); 1086
atan2(); 1087
ceil(); 1087
cos(); 1088
E; 1088
exp(); 1088
floor(); 1089
IEEEremainder(); 1089
log(); 1090
max(); 1090
min(); 1091
package, java.lang; 1084
PI; 1091
pow(); 1091
random(); 1092
rint(); 1092
round(); 1093
sin(); 1093
sqrt(); 1094
tan(); 1094
Math library, Math; 1084
MATH_SYMBOL, Character, *Table*; 289

maximum
digits
in a fraction, setting, NumberFormat.setMaximumFractionDigits(); 1210
integer, setting, NumberFormat.setMaximumIntegerDigits(); 1211
property, NumberFormat; 1193
retrieving,
NumberFormat.getMaximumFractionDigits(); 1201
NumberFormat.getMaximumIntegerDigits(); 1202

maximum *(continued)*
max()
BigDecimal; 87
BigInteger; 118
Math; 1090
MAX_PRIORITY, Thread; 1738
MAX_RADIX
Character; 300
Character, *Table*; 289
MAX_VALUE
Byte; 210
Character; 301
Character, *Table*; 289
Double; 716
Float; 867
Integer; 1008
Long; 1075
Short; 1535
of two
big decimal values, BigDecimal.max(); 87
big integer values, BigInteger.max(); 118
numbers, Math.max(); 1090
MAY
Calendar, *Table*; 233
MD5 algorithm
term description, ClassLoader; 414
MEDIUM
DateFormat; 600
member(s)
declared, constant, Member.DECLARED; 1099
declaring class, retrieving
Member.getDeclaringClass(); 1100
Member; 1095
DECLARED; 1099
getDeclaringClass(); 1100
getModifiers(); 1100
getName(); 1101
package, java.lang.reflect; 1095
PUBLIC; 1101
modifier, retrieving
Member.getModifiers(); 1100
modifiers
Member; 1095
Table, Member; 1095
name, retrieving, Member.getName(); 1101
names, Member; 1095
public, constant referring to, Member.PUBLIC; 1101
reflection objects, access permission determination
SecurityManager.checkMemberAccess(); 1489
representation of, Member; 1095
memory
errors, OutOfMemoryError; 1302
free, determining how much
Runtime.freeMemory(); 1469
garbage collector
Runtime.gc(); 1470
System.gc(); 1715
in-memory streams; 7
classes, *See* ByteArrayInputStream; ByteArrayOutputStream; CharArrayReader; CharArrayWriter; StringReader; StringWriter
total, determining how much
Runtime.totalMemory(); 1475
message(s)
digest algorithm, ClassLoader; 414
format, creating, MessageFormat; 1103
formatting strings for, ChoiceFormat; 346
locale-sensitive formatting, Format; 872
localized, retrieving
Throwable.getLocalizedMessage(); 1771
MessageFormat; 1102
clone(); 1110
equals(); 1110
format(); 1111
getFormats(); 1111
getLocale(); 1113
hashCode(); 1114
package, java.text; 1102
parse(); 1115
parseObject(); 1118
setFormat(); 1119
setFormats(); 1121
setLocale(); 1122
toPattern(); 1122
parsing, MessageFormat; 1115
pattern, MessageFormat; 1104
patterns, formatting
MessageFormat.format(); 1111
retrieving, Throwable.getMessage(); 1771
term description, MessageFormat; 1102
method(s)
abstract, AbstractMethodError; 39
declaring class
Method; 1125
retrieving
Method.getDeclaringClass(); 1129
errors, NoSuchMethodError; 1176

exception types
Method; 1124
retrieving
Method.getExceptionTypes(); 1129
exceptions, NoSuchMethodException; 1178
invoking, Method.invoke(); 1134
Method; 1123
equals(); 1128
getDeclaringClass(); 1129
getExceptionTypes(); 1129
getModifiers(); 1131
getParameterTypes(); 1132
getReturnType(); 1133
hashCode(); 1133
invoke(); 1134
package, java.lang.reflect; 1123
toString(); 1138
method, HttpURLConnection; 935
modifier, Method; 1124
modifiers, retrieving
Method.getModifiers(); 1131
name
Method; 1123
retrieving, Method.getName(); 1132
parameter types
Method; 1124
retrieving
Method.getParameterTypes(); 1132
representation of, Method; 1123
retrieving
Class.getDeclaredMethod(); 381
Class.getDeclaredMethods(); 383
Class.getMethod(); 389
Class.getMethods(); 390
return type
Method; 1124
retrieving, Method.getReturnType(); 1133
string representation, Method.toString(); 1138
tracing calls
Runtime.traceMethodCalls(); 1476
valid modifiers for, *Table*, Modifier; 1143

milliseconds
MILLISECOND, Calendar; 265
MILLISECOND_FIELD, DateFormat; 600

MIME type
See Also content, type
ContentHandler; 487
ContentHandlerFactory; 490
of a filename, determining
FileNameMap.getContentTypeFor(); 817
mapping filenames into, FileNameMap; 816
URL, URLEncoder; 1849

minimum
digits
fraction, setting, NumberFormat.setMinimum-FractionDigits(); 1211
integer, setting, NumberFormat.setMinimum-IntegerDigits(); 1212
property, NumberFormat; 1193
retrieving, NumberFormat.getMinimumFrac-tionDigits(); 1204
retrieving, NumberFormat.getMinimum-IntegerDigits(); 1204
min()
BigDecimal; 87
BigInteger; 119
Math; 1091
MIN_PRIORITY, Thread; 1739
MIN_RADIX
Character; 301
Character, *Table*; 289
MIN_VALUE
Byte; 211
Character; 289, 301
Double, *Table*; 717
Float; 867
Integer; 1008
Long; 1075
Short; 1535
of two
big decimal values, BigDecimal.min(); 87
big integer values, BigInteger.min(); 119
numbers, Math.min(); 1091

minus sign
retrieving, DecimalFormatSymbols.getMinus-Sign(); 671
setting character for, DecimalFormat-Symbols.setMinusSign(); 677

minutes
MINUTE, Calendar; 265
MINUTE_FIELD, DateFormat; 600

MissingResourceException; 1140
getClassName(); 1141
getKey(); 1142
package, java.util; 1140

mkdirxxx methods
mkdir(), File; 797
mkdirs(), File; 798
modxxx methods
mod(), BigInteger; 119
modInverse(), BigInteger; 120
modPow(), BigInteger; 121
modifier(s)
abstract, testing for
Modifier.isAbstract(); 1147
bit mask constants
Modifier.ABSTRACT; 1144
Modifier.FINAL; 1144
Modifier.INTERFACE; 1144
Modifier.NATIVE; 1144
Modifier.PRIVATE; 1144
Modifier.PROTECTED; 1144
Modifier.PUBLIC; 1144
Modifier.STATIC; 1144
Modifier.SYNCHRONIZED; 1144
Modifier.TRANSIENT; 1144
Modifier.VOLATILE; 1144
for classes, *Table*, Modifier; 1143
constructor, Constructor; 475, 476
for constructors, *Table*, Modifier; 1143
field
Field; 750
retrieving, Field.getModifiers(); 762
for fields, *Table*, Modifier; 1143
final, testing for, Modifier.isFinal(); 1147
interface, testing for
Modifier.isInterface(); 1147
for interfaces, *Table*, Modifier; 1143
member
Member; 1095
retrieving, Member.getModifiers(); 1100
Table, Member; 1095
method, retrieving
Method.getModifiers(); 1131
methods, Method; 1124
for methods, *Table*, Modifier; 1143
Modifier; 1143
ABSTRACT; 1144
FINAL; 1144
INTERFACE; 1144
isAbstract(); 1147
isFinal(); 1147
isInterface(); 1147
isNative(); 1148
isPrivate(); 1148
isProtected(); 1149
isStatic(); 1150
isSynchronized(); 1150
isTransient(); 1151
isVolatile(); 1151
NATIVE; 1144
package, java.lang.reflect; 1143
PRIVATE; 1144
PROTECTED; 1144
PUBLIC; 1144
STATIC; 1144
SYNCHRONIZED; 1144
toString(); 1151
TRANSIENT; 1144
VOLATILE; 1144
MODIFIER_LETTER, Character, *Table*; 289
MODIFIER_SYMBOL, Character, *Table*; 289
native, testing for, Modifier.isNative(); 1148
private, testing for, Modifier.isPrivate(); 1148
protected, testing for
Modifier.isProtected(); 1149
public, testing for, Modifier.isPublic(); 1149
representation of, Modifier; 1143
retrieving
Class.getModifiers(); 392
Constructor.getModifiers(); 481
static, testing for, Modifier.isStatic(); 1150
string representation
BigInteger, Modifier.toString(); 1151
synchronized, testing for
Modifier.isSynchronized(); 1150
transient, testing for
Modifier.isTransient(); 1151
valid, *Table*, Modifier; 1143
volatile, testing for
Modifier.isVolatile(); 1151
modulus
calculating, BigInteger.mod(); 119
multiplicative inverse, calculating
BigInteger.modInverse(); 120
power, calculating, BigInteger.modPow(); 121
MONDAY
Calendar, *Table*; 233
monitors
exceptions
IllegalMonitorStateException; 947
thread synchronization with, Object; 1215

months
calendar constants, *Table*, Calendar; 234
DAY_OF_WEEK_IN_MONTH_FIELD, DateFormat; 591
MONTH, Calendar; 266
MONTH_FIELD, DateFormat; 600
names of, accessing, DateFormatSymbols; 610
property
DateFormatSymbols; 612
retrieving
DateFormatSymbols.getMonths(); 619
DateFormatSymbols.getShortMonths(); 619
setting
DateFormatSymbols.setMonths(); 623
DateFormatSymbols.setShortMonths(); 624
WEEK_OF_MONTH_FIELD, DateFormat; 609
movexxx methods
movePointLeft(), BigDecimal; 88
movePointRight(), BigDecimal; 88
multicast
access and use, permission determination
SecurityManager.checkMulticast(); 1490
address, testing for
InetAddress.isMulticastAddress(); 963
addresses, IP addresses reserved for
InetAddress; 957
concept description, DatagramSocket; 506
datagrams
DatagramPacket; 499
MulticastSocket; 1153;
time-to-live, retrieving
MulticastSocket.getTTL(); 1157
time-to-live, setting
MulticastSocket.setTTL(); 1162
group
adding multicast socket to
MulticastSocket.joinGroup(); 1158
joining, DatagramSocketImpl.join(); 522
leaving, DatagramSocketImpl.leave(); 522
removing multicast socket from
MulticastSocket.leaveGroup(); 1158
IP addresses and groups, MulticastSocket; 1153
MulticastSocket; 1153
getInterface(); 1157
getTTL(); 1157
joinGroup(); 1158
leaveGroup(); 1158
package, java.net; 1153
send(); 1160
setInterface(); 1162
setTTL(); 1162
packets
time-to-live, retrieving
DatagramSocketImpl.getTTL(); 521
time-to-live, setting
DatagramSocketImpl.setTTL(); 525
sending, MulticastSocket.send(); 1160
socket
adding to multicast group
MulticastSocket.joinGroup(); 1158
removing from multicast group
MulticastSocket.leaveGroup(); 1158
sending datagram
MulticastSocket.send(); 1160
sockets
address, retrieving
MulticastSocket.getInterface(); 1157
implementation, MulticastSocket; 1154
term description
and discussion; 506
DatagramPacket; 499
time-to-live, MulticastSocket; 1153
multiplication
of big decimal values
BigDecimal.multiply(); 89
of big integers, BigInteger.multiply(); 122
decimal, DecimalFormat; 632
decimal multiplier
retrieving
DecimalFormat.getMultiplier(); 651
setting
DecimalFormat.setMultiplier(); 659
modular multiplicative inverse, calculating
BigInteger.modInverse(); 120
multiply()
BigDecimal; 89
BigInteger; 122
multithreading
term description, Thread; 1723

N

Nagle's algorithm
- *See Also* algorithms
- determining if used
  - Socket.getTcpNoDelay(); 1582
- enabling/disabling
  - Socket.setTcpNoDelay(); 1585
- term description, Socket; 1572

name(s)
- base, resource bundles, ResourceBundle; 1436
- class objects, retrieving, Class.getName(); 393
- constructor, Constructor; 476
- field, Field; 750
- fields, retrieving values of, Field.getName(); 763
- fully qualified, retrieving
  - Constructor.getName(); 481
- host
  - resolution, InetAddress; 957
  - retrieving for an IP address
    - InetAddress.getHostName(); 961
- locale, retrieving
  - Locale.getDisplayName(); 1062
- member
  - Member; 1095
  - retrieving, Member.getName(); 1101
- methods
  - Method; 1123
  - retrieving, Method.getName(); 1132
- properties
  - Properties; 1370
  - retrieving
    - Properties.propertyNames(); 1376
- resource, retrieving
  - MissingResourceException.getKey(); 1142
- resource bundle, retrieving
  - MissingResourceException.getClassName(); 1141
- resource bundles, ResourceBundle; 1436
- retrieving
  - ObjectStreamClass.getName(); 1285
- thread, setting, Thread.setName(); 1741
- thread group, retrieving
  - ThreadGroup.getName(); 1759
- threads, retrieving, Thread.getName(); 1731
- ZIP entry, retrieving, ZipEntry.getName(); 1898
- ZIP file, retrieving, ZipFile.getName(); 1913

NaN (Not-a-Number)
- Double.NaN; 717
  - Float; 868
- formatting, DecimalFormat; 633
- NaN
  - Double; 717
  - Float; 868
- string representation
  - retrieving
    - DecimalFormatSymbols.getNaN(); 671
  - setting
    - DecimalFormatSymbols.setNaN(); 677
- testing for
  - Double.isNaN(); 715
  - Float.isNaN(); 866
- value, not possible with BigDecimal; 75

native modifier
- NATIVE, Modifier; 1144
- testing for, Modifier.isNative(); 1148

natural logarithm
- Math.log(); 1090

needs
- needsDictionary(), Inflater; 973
- needsInput()
  - Deflater; 689
  - Inflater; 973

negation
- big decimal values, BigDecimal.negate(); 90
- big integer values, BigInteger.negate(); 123
- negate()
  - BigDecimal; 90
  - BigInteger; 123
- NEGATIVE_INFINITY
  - Double; 718
  - Float; 868
- NegativeArraySizeException; 1164
  - package, java.lang; 1164
- numbers
  - DecimalFormat; 632
  - retrieving for, DecimalFormat.getNegativePrefix(); 651
  - retrieving suffix for, DecimalFormat.getNegativeSuffix(); 651
  - setting negative prefix, DecimalFormat.setNegativePrefix(); 661
  - setting negative suffix, DecimalFormat.setNegativeSuffix(); 661
- patterns, DecimalFormat; 629

networks
content handler, factory
ContentHandlerFactory; 490
content handlers, ContentHandler; 487
exceptions
BindException; 134
ConnectException; 473
MalformedURLException; 1082
NoRouteToHostException; 1168
ProtocolException; 1381
SocketException; 1590
UnknownHostException; 1792
UnknownServiceException; 1794
factory setting, permission determination
SecurityManager.checkSetFactory(); 1494
interface, setting address of
MulticastSocket.setInterface(); 1162
new tail digit
term description, BigDecimal; 75
newxxx methods
newInstance()
Array; 62
Class; 404
Constructor; 483
newLine(), BufferedWriter; 203
newline
writing, BufferedWriter.newLine(); 203
nextxxx methods
next()
BreakIterator; 172
CharacterIterator; 312
CollationElementIterator; 438
Random; 1401
StringCharacterIterator; 1682
nextBytes(), Random; 1402
nextDouble()
ChoiceFormat; 361
Random; 1403
nextElement()
Enumeration; 724
StringTokenizer; 1700
nextFloat(), Random; 1403
nextGaussian(), Random; 1404
nextInt(), Random; 1404
nextLong(), Random; 1404
nextToken()
StreamTokenizer; 1619
StringTokenizer; 1700
NIS (Network Information Service)
term description, InetAddress; 957
noxxx fields
NO_COMPRESSION, Deflater; 690
NO_DECOMPOSITION, Collator; 461
Noxxx errors and exceptions
NoClassDefFoundError; 1166
package, java.lang; 1166
NoRouteToHostException; 1168
package, java.net; 1168
NoSuchElementException; 1170
package, java.util; 1170
NoSuchFieldError; 1172
package, java.lang; 1172
NoSuchFieldException; 1174
package, java.lang; 1174
NoSuchMethodError; 1176
package, java.lang; 1176
NoSuchMethodException; 1178
package, java.lang; 1178
NON_SPACING_MARK
Character, *Table*; 289
NORM_PRIORITY
Thread; 1739
normalization
term description, DateFormat; 583
text, RuleBasedCollator; 1451
not()
BigInteger; 123
not
NotActiveException; 1181
package, java.io; 1181
NotSerializableException; 1183
package, java.io; 1183
notation
dotted-string, InetAddress; 957
notification
notify(), Object; 1221
notifyAll(), Object; 1223
notifyObservers(), Observable; 1295
Object.notify(); 1221
Object.notifyAll(); 1221
NOVEMBER
Calendar, *Table*; 233
null
NULLORDER, CollationElementIterator; 439
NullPointerException; 1185
package, java.lang; 1185

number(s)
- *See Also* mathematics
- absolute value, Math.abs(); 1085
- binary
  - Integer.toBinaryString(); 1010
  - Long.toBinaryString(); 1077
- decimal, formatting
  - DecimalFormat.format(); 645
- fields, FieldPosition; 774
- format
  - DateFormat.numberFormat; 601
  - NumberFormatException; 1213
  - retrieving
    - DateFormat.getNumberFormat(); 596
  - setting
    - DateFormat.setNumberFormat(); 606
- formatting
  - NumberFormat; 1192
  - NumberFormat.format(); 1199
- greater of two, Math.max(); 1090
- grouping size
  - DecimalFormat; 632
  - retrieving
    - DecimalFormat.getGroupingSize(); 650
  - setting
    - DecimalFormat.setGroupingSize(); 658
- hexadecimal
  - Integer.toHexString(); 1011
  - Long.toHexString(); 1078
- integer, BigInteger representation of; 99
- lesser of two, Math.min(); 1091
- locale-sensitive formatting, Format; 872
- negative
  - DecimalFormat; 632
  - retrieving prefix for, DecimalFormat.getNegativePrefix(); 651
  - retrieving suffix for, DecimalFormat.getNegativeSuffix(); 651
  - setting negative prefix, DecimalFormat.setNegativePrefix(); 661
  - setting negative suffix, DecimalFormat.setNegativeSuffix(); 661
- Number; 1187
  - byteValue(); 1188
  - doubleValue(); 1189
  - floatValue(); 1189
  - intValue(); 1190
  - longValue(); 1190
  - package, java.lang; 1187
  - shortValue(); 1190
- number format locales, retrieving
  - NumberFormat.getAvailableLocales(); 1200
- NumberFormat; 1192
  - clone(); 1198
  - equals(); 1198
  - format(); 1199
  - FRACTION_FIELD; 1200
  - getAvailableLocales(); 1200
  - getCurrencyInstance(); 1201
  - getInstance(); 1201
  - getMaximumFractionDigits(); 1201
  - getMaximumIntegerDigits(); 1202
  - getMinimumFractionDigits(); 1204
  - getMinimumIntegerDigits(); 1204
  - getNumberInstance(); 1204
  - getPercentInstance(); 1205
  - hashCode(); 1205
  - INTEGER_FIELD; 1205
  - isGroupingUsed(); 1206
  - isParseIntegerOnly(); 1207
  - package, java.text; 1192
  - parse(); 1208
  - parseObject(); 1209
  - setGroupingUsed(); 1210
  - setMaximumFractionDigits(); 1210
  - setMaximumIntegerDigits(); 1211
  - setMinimumFractionDigits(); 1211
  - setMinimumIntegerDigits(); 1212
  - setParseIntegerOnly(); 1212
- numberFormat, DateFormat; 601
- NumberFormatException; 1213
  - package, java.lang; 1213
- octal
  - Integer.toOctalString(); 1012
  - Long.toOctalString(); 1078
- parsing
  - NumberFormat.parse(); 1208
  - ParsePosition; 1317
- parsing a string to, ChoiceFormat.parse(); 362
- positive
  - DecimalFormat; 632
  - retrieving prefix for, DecimalFormat.getPositivePrefix(); 651
  - retrieving suffix for, DecimalFormat.getPositiveSuffix(); 652
  - setting positive prefix, DecimalFormat.setPositivePrefix(); 661
  - setting positive suffix, DecimalFormat.setPositiveSuffix(); 661

power, Math.pow(); 1091
radix, Character.MIN_RADIX; 301
raising to a power, Math.pow(); 1091
random, Math.random(); 1092
rational, BigDecimal representation of; 74
scalar types, Number; 1187
square root, Math.sqrt(); 1094
string representation, locale-sensitive
DecimalFormat; 626
token, StreamTokenizer.TT_NUMBER; 1629
as token element, *Table*, StreamTokenizer; 1614
tokens, specifying digits as
StreamTokenizer.parseNumbers(); 1622
nval
StreamTokenizer; 1621

O

objects(s)
Class, Object.getClass(); 1220
cloning, Object.clone(); 1216
event
EventObject; 731
string representation, generating
EventObject.toString(); 735
formatting as strings, Format.format(); 878
generating, from URL
ContentHandler.getContent(); 489
locking and thread synchronization, Object; 1215
making cloneable, Cloneable; 428
member types, modifiers for, *Table*, Member; 1095
Object
clone(); 1216
equals(); 1217
finalize(); 1218
getClass(); 1220
hashCode(); 1220
notify(); 1221
notifyAll(); 1223
package, java.lang; 1215
toString(); 1224
wait(); 1224
object/handle cache, term description
ObjectInputStream; 1232
ObjectInput; 1226
available(); 1227
close(); 1227
package, java.io; 1226
read(); 1227
readObject(); 1228
skip(); 1229
ObjectInputStream; 1230
available(); 1234
close(); 1234
defaultReadObject(); 1235
enableResolveObject(); 1236
package, java.io; 1230
read(); 1238
readBoolean(); 1239
readByte(); 1239
readChar(); 1240
readDouble(); 1240
readFloat(); 1241
readFully(); 1242
readInt(); 1242
readLine(); 1243
readLong(); 1243
readObject(); 1244
readShort(); 1245
readStreamHeader(); 1246
readUnsignedByte(); 1248
readUnsignedShort(); 1248
readUTF(); 1249
registerValidation(); 1249
resolveClass(); 1250
resolveObject(); 1252
skipBytes(); 1254
ObjectInputValidation; 1256
package, java.io; 1256
validateObject(); 1258
ObjectOutput; 1259
close(); 1260
flush(); 1260
package, java.io; 1259
write(); 1260
writeObject(); 1261
ObjectOutputStream; 1262
annotateClass(); 1266
close(); 1268
defaultWriteObject(); 1269
drain(); 1269
enableReplaceObject(); 1269
flush(); 1270
package, java.io; 1262
replaceObject(); 1271
reset(); 1273
write(); 1274
writeBoolean(); 1275
writeByte(); 1276

objects(s) *(continued)*
ObjectOutputStream
writeBytes(); 1276
writeChar(); 1277
writeChars(); 1277
writeDouble(); 1278
writeFloat(); 1278
writeInt(); 1278
writeLong(); 1279
writeObject(); 1279
writeShort(); 1281
writeStreamHeader(); 1281
writeUTF(); 1282
ObjectStreamClass; 1283
forClass(); 1284
getName(); 1285
getSerialVersionUID(); 1285
lookup(); 1285
package, java.io; 1283
toString(); 1285
ObjectStreamException; 1288
package, java.io; 1288
parsing strings to
Format.parseObject(); 880
MessageFormat.parseObject(); 1118
wrappers, Boolean; 144
observable
adding observer
Observable.addObserver(); 1292
changed state
determining
Observable.hasChanged(); 1294
notifying observers
Observable.notifyObservers(); 1295
recording, Observable.setChanged(); 1295
clearing changed state
Observable.clearChanged(); 1293
Observable; 1290
addObserver(); 1292
clearChanged(); 1293
countObservers(); 1294
deleteObserver(); 1294
deleteObservers(); 1294
hasChanged(); 1294
notifyObservers(); 1295
package, java.util; 1290
setChanged(); 1295
term description
Observable; 1290
Observer; 1296
observers
adding, Observable.addObserver(); 1292
deleting
Observable.deleteObserver(); 1294
Observable.deleteObservers(); 1294
determining number of
Observable.countObservers(); 1294
notifying
Observable.notifyObservers(); 1295
Observer; 1296
package, java.util; 1296
update(); 1298
term description
Observable; 1290
Observer; 1296
updating, Observer.update(); 1298
octal number
string representation, generating
Integer.toOctalString(); 1012
Long.toOctalString(); 1078
OCTOBER
Calendar, *Table*; 233
offset
time zone, TimeZone; 1774
opening
openConnection()
URL; 1812
URLStreamHandler; 1854
openStream(), URL; 1813
OptionalDataException; 1299
eof; 1301
length; 1301
package, java.io; 1299
OR logical operation
See Also logical operations
or()
BigInteger; 124
BitSet; 141
ordering
collation, CollationElementIterator; 434
determining
Calendar.after(); 242
Calendar.before(); 245
GregorianCalendar.after(); 886
GregorianCalendar.before(); 887
reversing, StringBuffer.reverse(); 1662
strength, Collator; 448
Unicode, String.compareTo(); 1635

ordinaryxxx methods
ordinaryChar(), StreamTokenizer; 1621
ordinaryChars(), StreamTokenizer; 1622
OTHERxxx fields
OTHER_LETTER, Character, *Table*; 289
OTHER_NUMBER, Character, *Table*; 289
OTHER_PUNCTUATION, Character, *Table*; 289
OTHER_SYMBOL, Character, *Table*; 289
out
FileDescriptor; 804
FilterOutputStream; 846
FilterWriter; 858
PipedInputStream; 1328
System; 1719
OutOfMemoryError; 1302
package, java.lang; 1302
output
data, DataOutput; 546
OutputStream; 1304
close(); 1306
flush(); 1306
package; 1304
write(); 1306
OutputStreamWriter; 1308
close(); 1310
flush(); 1311
getEncoding(); 1311
package; 1308
write(); 1313
standard
FileDescriptor; 802
FileDescriptor.out; 804
stream
CheckedOutputStream; 339
creating for URL connection
URLConnection.getOutputStream(); 1838
GZIPOutputStream; 902
writing, CheckedOutputStream.write(); 341
streams
BufferedOutputStream; 185
BufferedWriter; 199
ByteArrayOutputStream; 224
CharArrayWriter; 323
creating, Socket.getOutputStream(); 1579
DataOutputStream; 552
DeflaterOutputStream; 695
FileOutputStream; 821
FilterOutputStream; 842
FilterWriter; 855
for writing input
Process.getOutputStream(); 1368
ObjectOutputStream; 1262
OutputStream; 1304
OutputStreamWriter; 1308
PipedOutputStream; 1332
PrintStream; 1346
PrintWriter; 1354
Process.getInputStream(); 1367
retrieving
SocketImpl.getOutputStream(); 1601
StringWriter; 1703
Writer; 1887
URL, URLConnection.doOutput; 1829
URL connection
setting
URLConnection.setDoOutput(); 1845
testing for
URLConnection.getDoOutput(); 1834

P

packages
See Also java.io; java.lang; java.lang.reflect; java.math; java.net; java.text; java.util; java.util.zip
accessing, permission determination, SecurityManager.checkPackageAccess(); 1491
modifying, permission determination, SecurityManager.checkPackageDefinition(); 1491
packets
datagram
address, setting
DatagramPacket.setAddress(); 504
data, DatagramPacket.getData(); 502
DatagramPacket; 499
length, retrieving
DatagramPacket.getLength(); 503
length, setting
DatagramPacket.setLength(); 504
port, retrieving
DatagramPacket.getPort(); 503
port, setting
DatagramPacket.setPort(); 505
setting data, DatagramPacket.setData(); 504
source address
DatagramPacket.getAddress(); 502

packets *(continued)*
multicast
time-to-live, retrieving
DatagramSocketImpl.getTTL(); 521
time-to-live, setting
DatagramSocketImpl.setTTL(); 525
term description, DatagramPacket; 499
PARAGRAPH_SEPARATOR
Character, *Table*; 289
parameter types
constructor, Constructor; 476
method, retrieving
Method.getParameterTypes(); 1132
methods, term definition, Method; 1124
retrieving
Constructor.getParameterTypes(); 481
parent
parent, ResourceBundle; 1445
parentOf(), ThreadGroup; 1761
resource bundle
ResourceBundle.parent; 1445
retrieving
ResourceBundle.setParent(); 1446
resource bundle relationship
ResourceBundle; 1438
thread group
determining, ThreadGroup.parentOf(); 1761
retrieving, ThreadGroup.getParent(); 1759
parsing
concept description; 27
dates, DateFormat; 580
error, retrieving location of
ParseException.getErrorOffset(); 1316
exception, ParseException; 1314
index
retrieving, ParsePosition.getIndex(); 1321
setting, ParsePosition.setIndex(); 1322
integers
determining, NumberFormat.isParse-IntegerOnly(); 1207
setting, NumberFormat.setParse-IntegerOnly(); 1212
message formats, MessageFormat; 1107
numbers
NumberFormat.parse(); 1208
ParsePosition; 1317
parse()
ChoiceFormat; 362
Date; 572
DateFormat; 601
DecimalFormat; 653
MessageFormat; 1115
NumberFormat; 1208
SimpleDateFormat; 1555
parseByte(), Byte; 211
ParseException; 1314
package, java.text; 1314
parseInt(), Integer; 1009
parseLong(), Long; 1076
parseNumbers(), StreamTokenizer; 1622
parseObject()
DateFormat; 604
Format; 880
MessageFormat; 1118
NumberFormat; 1209
ParsePosition; 1317
getIndex(); 1321
NumberFormat use; 1193
package, java.text; 1317
setIndex(); 1322
parseShort(), Short; 1536
parseURL(), URLStreamHandler; 1854
setting leniency, DateFormat.setLenient(); 605
streams for building parsers; 8
classes, *See* PushbackInputStream; PushbackReader; StreamTokenizer
strings
ChoiceFormat; 348
into tokens, StringTokenizer; 1697
NumberFormat.parseObject(); 1209
term description, DateFormat; 581
time, DateFormat; 580
tokens
StreamTokenizer; 1614
StreamTokenizer.nextToken(); 1619
path variables
separator character
File.pathSeparatorChar; 799
separator string, File.pathSeparator; 798
term description, File.pathSeparator; 798
pathname
absolute
File.getAbsolutePath(); 790
File.getCanonicalPath(); 791
testing, File.isAbsolute(); 794
canonical, File.getCanonicalPath(); 791
retrieving, File.getPath(); 793

pathSeparatorxxx fields
pathSeparator, File; 798
pathSeparatorChar, File; 799
patterns
applying
ChoiceFormat.applyPattern(); 356
DecimalFormat.applyLocalized-Pattern(); 638
DecimalFormat.applyPattern(); 640
MessageFormat.applyPattern(); 1110
SimpleDateFormat.applyLocalized-Pattern(); 1550
SimpleDateFormat.applyPattern(); 1552
constructing, ChoiceFormat; 348
date-time formatting, SimpleDateFormat; 1541
decimal format
DecimalFormat; 627
symbols used with, *Table* DecimalFormat; 630
decimal format symbols, *Table* DecimalFormatSymbols; 665
digit character
retrieving
DecimalFormatSymbols.getDigit(); 670
setting
DecimalFormatSymbols.setDigit(); 674
letters, *Table*, SimpleDateFormat; 1542
local pattern character property
DateFormatSymbols; 610
retrieving, DateFormatSymbols.get-LocalPatternChars(); 618
setting, DateFormatSymbols.setLocal-PatternChars(); 623
Table, DateFormatSymbols; 611
localized
applying, SimpleDateFormat.apply-LocalizedPattern(); 1550
generating string representation, SimpleDate-Format.toLocalizedPattern(); 1558
vs. nonlocalized, DecimalFormat; 631
message
formatting, MessageFormat.format(); 1111
MessageFormat; 1104
nonlocalized
applying, SimpleDateFormat.apply-Pattern(); 1552
generating string representation for, Decimal-Format.toLocalizedPattern(); 662
generating string representation, SimpleDate-Format.toPattern(); 1558
separator
retrieving, DecimalFormatSymbols.get-PatternSeparator(); 672
setting, DecimalFormatSymbols.set-PatternSeparator(); 677
string formatting, ChoiceFormat; 347
string representation, generating
ChoiceFormat.toPattern(); 364
DecimalFormat.toPattern(); 662
MessageFormat.toPattern(); 1122
term description, DecimalFormat; 628
unabbreviated style, for date or time
DateFormat.FULL; 594
variables
retrieving formats
MessageFormat.getFormats(); 1113
setting format for
MessageFormat.setFormat(); 1119
setting format for
MessageFormat.setFormats(); 1121
peek()
DatagramSocketImpl; 523
Stack; 1608
percent
character
retrieving, DecimalFormatSymbols.get-Percent(); 672
setting DecimalFormatSymbols.set-Percent(); 678
decimal multiplier
DecimalFormat; 632
retrieving
DecimalFormat.getMultiplier(); 651
setting
DecimalFormat.setMultiplier(); 659
locale format, creating
NumberFormat.getPercentInstance(); 1205
permill
character
retrieving, DecimalFormatSymbols.get-PerMill(); 672
setting, DecimalFormatSymbols.set-PerMill(); 678
decimal multiplier
DecimalFormat; 632
retrieving
DecimalFormat.getMultiplier(); 651
setting
DecimalFormat.setMultiplier(); 659

permission control
thread group suspension
ThreadGroup.allowThreadSuspension(); 1756
PGP
ClassLoader support; 414
PI constant
Math.PI; 1091
PI, Math; 1091
pipes
closing
PipedOutputStream.close(); 1333
PipedReader.close(); 1339
PipedWriter.close(); 1343
connecting
PipedInputStream.connect(); 1327
PipedOutputStream.connect(); 1334
PipedReader.connect(); 1340
PipedWriter.connect(); 1344
default size
PipedInputStream.PIPE_SIZE; 1329
flushing
PipedOutputStream.flush(); 1334
PipedWriter.flush(); 1344
location of next byte
to be retrieved, PipedInputStream.out; 1328
to be stored, PipedInputStream.in; 1328
PIPE_SIZE, PipedInputStream; 1329
PipedInputStream; 1323
available(); 1326
buffer; 1326
close(); 1326
connect(); 1327
in; 1328
out; 1328
package, java.io; 1323
PIPE_SIZE; 1329
read(); 1329
receive(); 1330
PipedOutputStream; 1332
close(); 1333
connect(); 1334
flush(); 1334
package, java.io; 1332
write(); 1335
PipedReader; 1337
close(); 1339
connect(); 1340
package, java.io; 1337
read(); 1341
PipedWriter; 1342
close(); 1343
connect(); 1344
flush(); 1344
package, java.io; 1342
write(); 1345
reading
PipedInputStream.read(); 1329
PipedReader.read(); 1341
streams; 7
PipedInputStream; 1323
PipedOutputStream; 1332
PipedReader; 1337
PipedWriter; 1342
term description, PipedInputStream; 1323
writing
PipedInputStream.receive(); 1330
PipedOutputStream.write(); 1335
PipedWriter.write(); 1345
platform-dependent
execution, Runtime.exec(); 1467
PM
Calendar; 267
pointers
null, NullPointerException; 1185
polar coordinates
converting rectangular to, Math.atan2(); 1087
pop()
Stack; 1608
ports
binding socket to, SocketImpl.bind(); 1597
binding to a local port, permission determination, SecurityManager.checkListen(); 1489
datagram packet
retrieving, DatagramPacket.getPort(); 503
setting, DatagramPacket.setPort(); 505
datagram socket
DatagramSocketImpl.localPort; 523
binding, DatagramSocketImpl.bind(); 519
retrieving
DatagramSocket.getLocalPort(); 510
DatagramSocketImpl.getLocalPort(); 521
number
as URL component, URL; 1800
retrieving, URL.getPort(); 1809
port, SocketImpl; 1603
retrieving
ServerSocket.getLocalPort(); 1523

socket
retrieving
Socket.getLocalPort(); 1579
Socket.getPort(); 1580
SocketImpl.getLocalPort(); 1600
SocketImpl.getPort(); 1601
SocketImpl.localport; 1602
SocketImpl.port; 1603
position
current, BreakIterator; 155
current read
BufferedInputStream.mark(); 180
BufferedInputStream.markpos; 181
BufferedInputStream.pos; 182
BufferedReader.mark(); 194
ByteArrayInputStream.mark(); 220
ByteArrayInputStream.mark; 219
ByteArrayInputStream.pos; 221
CharArrayReader.mark(); 318
CharArrayReader.markPos; 319
CharArrayReader.pos; 320
FilterInputStream.mark(); 838
FilterInputStream.reset(); 840
FilterReader.mark(); 850
InputStream; 985
InputStream.mark(); 986
LineNumberReader.mark(); 1043
marking
BufferedInputStream.mark(); 180
BufferedReader.mark(); 194
ByteArrayInputStream.mark(); 220
CharArrayReader.mark(); 318
CharArrayReader.markPos; 319
FilterInputStream.mark(); 838
FilterReader.mark(); 850
InputStream.mark(); 986
LineNumberReader.mark(); 1043
Reader.mark(); 1430
StringReader.mark(); 1692
PushbackInputStream.pos; 1388
Reader; 1426
resetting
BufferedInputStream.reset(); 183
BufferedReader.reset(); 197
ByteArrayInputStream.reset(); 222
ByteArrayOutputStream.reset(); 227
CharArrayReader.reset(); 322
CharArrayWriter.reset(); 326
FilterInputStream.reset(); 840
FilterReader.reset(); 853
InputStream.reset(); 988
LineNumberReader.setLineNumber(); 1047
Reader.reset(); 1433
StringReader.reset(); 1695
StringReader.mark(); 1692
pos
BufferedInputStream; 182
ByteArrayInputStream; 221
CharArrayReader; 320
PushbackInputStream; 1388
StringBufferInputStream; 1668
text boundary
first, retrieving, BreakIterator.first(); 163
following, retrieving
BreakIterator.following(); 163
positive
numbers
DecimalFormat; 632
retrieving prefix for, DecimalFormat.getPositivePrefix(); 651
retrieving suffix for, DecimalFormat.getPositiveSuffix(); 652
setting positive prefix, DecimalFormat.setPositivePrefix(); 661
setting positive suffix, DecimalFormat.setPositiveSuffix(); 662
patterns, DecimalFormat; 629
POSITIVE_INFINITY
Double; 718
Float; 869
power
pow()
BigInteger; 124
Math; 1091
raising a big integer to, BigInteger.pow(); 124
raising a number to, Math.pow(); 1091
PRC
Locale; 1056
precision
BigDecimal; 74
BigInteger; 99
predefined
Locale, locale(s); 1055
previous
previous()
BreakIterator; 174
CharacterIterator; 313
StringCharacterIterator; 1684
previousDouble(), ChoiceFormat; 363

primary
collation order
CollationElementIterator; 435
Latin-based languages, *Table*, Collator; 448
retrieving, CollationElement-Iterator.primaryOrder(); 439
PRIMARY, Collator; 462
primaryOrder()
CollationElementIterator; 439
primes
testing for
BigInteger.isProbablePrime(); 117
primitive types
Class objects for, *Table*
Class.isPrimitive(); 403
data input as, DataInput; 526
data output as, DataOutput; 546
string representation, *Table*, Class; 366
testing for, Class.isPrimitive(); 403
type descriptors for, *Table*, Class; 366
wrappers
Boolean; 149
Character; 282
Double; 709
Float; 860
Integer; 1001
Long; 1069
Short; 1530
Table, Class; 368
printing
permission determination, Security-Manager.checkPrintJobAccess(); 1492
print()
PrintStream; 1350
PrintWriter; 1358
println()
PrintStream; 1351
PrintWriter; 1359
printStackTrace(), Throwable; 1771
PrintStream; 1346
checkError(); 1349
close(); 1349
flush(); 1350
package, java.io; 1346
print(); 1350
println(); 1351
setError(); 1352
write(); 1353
PrintWriter; 1354
checkError(); 1357
close(); 1358
flush(); 1358
package, java.io; 1354
print(); 1358
println(); 1359
setError(); 1361
write(); 1361
priorities
maximum, ThreadGroup; 1751
thread
default, Thread.NORM_PRIORITY; 1739
maximum, Thread.MAX_PRIORITY; 1738
minimum, Thread.MIN_PRIORITY; 1739
retrieving, Thread.getPriority(); 1732
setting, Thread.setPriority(); 1742
Thread; 1724
thread group
maximum
ThreadGroup.getMaxPriority(); 1759
setting
ThreadGroup.setMaxPriority(); 1763
private modifier
PRIVATE, Modifier; 1144
testing for, Modifier.isPrivate(); 1148
PRIVATE_USE
Character, *Table*; 289
processes
concepts and overview, Process; 1363
destroying, Process.destroy(); 1364
error output stream handling
Process.getErrorStream(); 1366
exit value retrieval, Process.exitValue(); 1365
input stream handling
Process.getOutputStream(); 1368
multithreaded, Thread; 1723
output stream handling
Process.getInputStream(); 1367
Process
getErrorStream(); 1366
getInputStream(); 1367
getOutputStream(); 1368
package, java.lang; 1363
waitFor(); 1369
waiting for termination, Process.waitFor(); 1369
programs
multithreaded, Thread; 1723
system, spawning processes to run, Process; 1363

properties
AM/PM strings, DateFormatSymbols; 611
collation order strengths
CollationElementIterator; 435
Collator; 448
days, DateFormatSymbols; 612
defaults, Properties; 1370
digit, minimum, NumberFormat; 1193
eras, DateFormatSymbols; 612
formats, Properties; 1371
grouping separator used, NumberFormat; 1193
list
Properties; 1370
saving, Properties.save(); 1377
writing
Properties.list(); 1374
Properties.save(); 1377
loading, Properties.load(); 1375
local pattern character
DateFormatSymbols; 610
Table, DateFormatSymbols; 611
months, DateFormatSymbols; 612
name
Properties; 1370
retrieving
Properties.propertyNames(); 1376
NumberFormat, maximum; 1193
Properties; 1370
defaults; 1374
getProperty(); 1374
list(); 1374
load(); 1375
package, java.util; 1370
propertyNames(); 1376
save(); 1377
propertyNames(), Properties; 1376
PropertyResourceBundle; 1378
getKeys(); 1379
handleGetObject(); 1379
package, java.util; 1378
resource bundle
PropertyResourceBundle; 1378
ResourceBundle; 1437
retrieving, Properties.getProperty(); 1373
system
access permission determination, Security-Manager.checkPropertiesAccess(); 1492
access permission determination, Security-Manager.checkPropertyAccess(); 1492
creating Integer object using Integer.getInteger(); 1005
creating Long object using Integer.getInteger(); 1008
Properties; 1370
retrieving boolean value Boolean.getBoolean(); 147
retrieving named System.getProperty(); 1716
retrieving, System.getProperties(); 1715
setting, System.setProperties(); 1721
System; 1711
Table, Properties; 1371
Table, System; 1711
time zone, DateFormatSymbols; 612
value, Properties; 1370
ZIP files, *Table*, ZipEntry; 1892
protected modifier
PROTECTED, Modifier; 1144
testing for, Modifier.isProtected(); 1149
protocols
See Also HTTP (Hypertext Transfer Protocol); IP (Internet Protocol) address; TCP (Transmission Control Protocol)
connection-oriented, DatagramPacket; 499
connectionless, DatagramPacket; 499
identifier, retrieving, URL.getProtocol(); 1810
ProtocolException; 1381
package, java.net; 1381
URL, handlers, URLConnection; 1820
as URL component, URL; 1800
proxies
determining if used
HttpURLConnection.usingProxy(); 938
term description, HttpURLConnection; 924
pseudorandom-number
generating
bytes, Random.nextBytes(); 1402
floating point
Random.nextDouble(); 1403
Random.nextFloat(); 1403
Gaussian, Random.nextGaussian(); 1404
integer
Random.nextInt(); 1404
Random.nextLong(); 1404
Random.next(); 1401
generator, Random; 1399
setting the seed, Random.setSeed(); 1405

public
members, constant referring to
Member.PUBLIC; 1101
PUBLIC
Member; 1101
Modifier; 1144
testing for, Modifier.isPublic(); 1149
push()
Stack; 1609
pushback
pushBack(), StreamTokenizer; 1624
PushbackInputStream; 1383
available(); 1386
buf; 1387
markSupported; 1387
package, java.io; 1383
pos; 1388
read(); 1388
unread(); 1389
PushbackReader; 1392
close(); 1394
markSupported(); 1395
package, java.io; 1392
read(); 1396
ready(); 1397
unread(); 1397
streams, PushbackReader; 1392
term description, PushbackInputStream; 1383
putxxx methods
put()
Dictionary; 707
Hashtable; 921
putNextEntry(), ZipOutputStream; 1928

Q

quote
character, specifying
StreamTokenizer.quoteChar(); 1625
quoteChar(), StreamTokenizer; 1625
quotient
BigInteger.divideAndRemainder(); 112

R

radius vector
Math.atan2(); 1087
radix
digit characters, Character; 282
digit to/from number conversion
Character.MAX_RADIX; 300
Character.MIN_RADIX; 301
random
number generator
Math.random(); 1092
Random; 1399
pseudorandom-number generator, Random; 1399
Random; 1399
next(); 1401
nextBytes(); 1402
nextDouble(); 1403
nextFloat(); 1403
nextGaussian(); 1404
nextInt(); 1404
nextLong(); 1404
package, java.util; 1399
setSeed(); 1405
random(), Math; 1092
RandomAccessFile; 1406
close(); 1409
getFD(); 1409
getFilePointer(); 1409
length(); 1410
package, java.io; 1406
read(); 1411
readBoolean(); 1412
readByte(); 1412
readChar(); 1413
readDouble(); 1413
readFloat(); 1414
readFully(); 1414
readInt(); 1415
readLine(); 1415
readLong(); 1416
readShort(); 1416
readUnsignedByte(); 1417
readUnsignedShort(); 1417
readUTF(); 1418
seek(); 1418
skipBytes(); 1419
write(); 1419
writeBoolean(); 1420
writeByte(); 1420
writeBytes(); 1421
writeChar(); 1421
writeChars(); 1422
writeDouble(); 1422
writeFloat(); 1423
writeInt(); 1423
writeLong(); 1424
writeShort(); 1424
writeUTF(); 1425

ranges
pattern, ChoiceFormat; 348
rational numbers
BigDecimal representation of; 74
readers
BufferedReader; 190
CharArrayReader; 315
FilterReader; 847
InputStreamReader; 990
LineNumberReader; 1040
PipedReader; 1337
PushbackReader; 1392
Reader; 1426
close(); 1429
lock; 1429
mark(); 1430
markSupported(); 1430
package, java.io; 1426
read(); 1431
reset(); 1433
skip(); 1434
StringReader; 1690
reading
availability testing
BufferedReader.ready(); 196
CharArrayReader.ready(); 321
FileInputStream.available(); 809
FilterInputStream.available(); 837
FilterReader.ready(); 853
InputStream.available(); 985
InputStreamReader.ready(); 996
PipedInputStream.available(); 1326
PushbackInputStream.available(); 1386
PushbackReader.ready(); 1397
Reader.ready(); 1432
SequenceInputStream.available(); 1505
StringReader.ready(); 1694
FileReader; 827
FilterReader; 847
read()
BufferedInputStream; 182
BufferedReader; 195
ByteArrayInputStream; 221
CharArrayReader; 320
CheckedInputStream; 337
DataInputStream; 537
FileInputStream; 811
FilterInputStream; 839
FilterReader; 852
GZIPInputStream; 901
InflaterInputStream; 981
InputStream; 987
InputStreamReader; 995
LineNumberInputStream; 1037
LineNumberReader; 1045
ObjectInput; 1227
ObjectInputStream; 1238
PipedInputStream; 1329
PipedReader; 1341
PushbackInputStream; 1388
PushbackReader; 1396
RandomAccessFile; 1411
Reader; 1431
SequenceInputStream; 1505
StringBufferInputStream; 1668
StringReader; 1694
ZipInputStream; 1918
read limit
BufferedInputStream; 177
BufferedReader; 191
readBoolean()
DataInput; 527
DataInputStream; 538
ObjectInputStream; 1239
RandomAccessFile; 1412
readByte()
DataInput; 527
DataInputStream; 538
ObjectInputStream; 1239
RandomAccessFile; 1412
readChar()
DataInput; 528
DataInputStream; 538
ObjectInputStream; 1240
RandomAccessFile; 1413
readDouble()
DataInput; 528
DataInputStream; 539
ObjectInputStream; 1240
RandomAccessFile; 1413
Reader; 1426
close(); 1429
lock; 1429
mark(); 1430
markSupported(); 1430
read(); 1431
ready(); 1432
reset(); 1433
skip(); 1434

reading *(continued)*
- readExternal(), Externalizable; 747
- readFloat()
  - DataInput; 528
  - DataInputStream; 539
  - ObjectInputStream; 1241
  - RandomAccessFile; 1414
- readFully()
  - DataInput; 529
  - DataInputStream; 540
  - ObjectInputStream; 1242
  - RandomAccessFile; 1414
- readInt()
  - DataInput; 529
  - DataInputStream; 541
  - ObjectInputStream; 1242
  - RandomAccessFile; 1415
- readLine()
  - BufferedReader; 196
  - DataInput; 530
  - DataInputStream; 541
  - LineNumberReader; 1046
  - ObjectInputStream; 1243
  - RandomAccessFile; 1415
- readLong()
  - DataInput; 530
  - DataInputStream; 542
  - ObjectInputStream; 1243
  - RandomAccessFile; 1416
- readObject()
  - ObjectInput; 1228
  - ObjectInputStream; 1244
- readShort()
  - DataInput; 531
  - DataInputStream; 543
  - ObjectInputStream; 1245
  - RandomAccessFile; 1416
- readStreamHeader()
  - ObjectInputStream; 1246
- readUnsignedByte()
  - DataInput; 531
  - DataInputStream; 543
  - ObjectInputStream; 1248
  - RandomAccessFile; 1417
- readUnsignedShort()
  - DataInput; 532
  - DataInputStream; 544
  - ObjectInputStream; 1248
  - RandomAccessFile; 1417
- readUTF()
  - DataInput; 532
  - DataInputStream; 544
  - ObjectInputStream; 1249
  - RandomAccessFile; 1418
- ready(), Reader; 1432
- stream, input, CheckedInputStream.read(); 337

receive()
- DatagramSocket; 512
- DatagramSocketImpl; 524
- PipedInputStream; 1330

rectangular coordinates
- converting to polar, Math.atan2(); 1087

redirects
- automatically following
  - determining, HttpURLConnection.getFollowRedirects(); 932
  - setting, HttpURLConnection.setFollowRedirects(); 935
- term description, HttpURLConnection; 924

reference
- URL, retrieving, URL.getRef(); 1811
- as URL component, URL; 1800

references
- Runtime object, accessing
  - Runtime.getRuntime(); 1471

reflection
- *See* java.lang.reflect package

regionMatches()
- String; 1645

registering
- registerValidation()
  - ObjectInputStream; 1249

rehash()
- Hashtable; 921

release
- resources, Deflater.end(); 686

remainder
- BigInteger.divideAndRemainder(); 112
- floating-point division
  - Math.IEEEremainder(); 1089
- from big integer division
  - BigInteger.remainder(); 125
- remainder(), BigInteger; 125

removexxx methods
- remove()
  - Dictionary; 707
  - Hashtable; 922
- removeAllElements(), Vector; 1873
- removeElement(), Vector; 1873
- removeElementAt(), Vector; 1874

renameTo()
File; 799
replacing
replace(), String; 1646
replaceObject(), ObjectOutputStream; 1271
representation
converting strings to and from, String; 1632
request
method
retrieving, HttpURLConnection.getRequest-Method(); 933
setting method token, HttpURLConnection.setRequestMethod(); 937
resetting
character, RuleBasedCollator; 1450
checksum
Checksum.reset(); 345
CRC32.reset(); 495
reset()
Adler32; 43
BufferedInputStream; 183
BufferedReader; 197
ByteArrayInputStream; 222
ByteArrayOutputStream; 227
CharArrayReader; 322
CharArrayWriter; 326
Checksum; 345
CollationElementIterator; 439
CRC32; 495
Deflater; 690
FilterInputStream; 840
FilterReader; 853
Inflater; 973
InputStream; 988
LineNumberInputStream; 1038
LineNumberReader; 1046
ObjectOutputStream; 1273
Reader; 1433
StringBufferInputStream; 1669
StringReader; 1695
resetSyntax(), StreamTokenizer; 1626
streams, term description
ObjectOutputStream; 1264
resolution
host name, InetAddress; 957
resolveClass()
ClassLoader; 425
ObjectInputStream; 1250
resolveObject(), ObjectInputStream; 1252
resource(s)
bundles
base name, ResourceBundle; 1436
creating, ResourceBundle; 1438
enumerating keys
ListResourceBundle.getKeys(); 1053
PropertyResourceBundle.getKeys(); 1379
enumerating
ResourceBundle.getKeys(); 1443
instantiating
ResourceBundle.getBundle(); 1442
list, ListResourceBundle; 1051
loading, ResourceBundle.getBundle(); 1442
locating, ResourceBundle; 1437
name, retrieving, MissingResourceException.getClassName(); 1141
names, ResourceBundle; 1436
parent relationship, ResourceBundle; 1438
parent, ResourceBundle.parent; 1445
parent, retrieving
ResourceBundle.setParent(); 1446
properties files, ResourceBundle; 1437
PropertyResourceBundle; 1378
ResourceBundle; 1435
retrieving contents
ListResourceBundle.getContents(); 1052
retrieving resource from
ListResourceBundle.handleGetObject(); 1053
ResourceBundle.getObject(); 1443
PropertyResourceBundle.handleGetObject(); 1379
retrieving, ResourceBundle; 1437
using, ResourceBundle; 1438
variants, ResourceBundle; 1436
exceptions, MissingResourceException; 1140
freeing
Deflater.end(); 686
Inflater.end(); 969
name, retrieving
MissingResourceException.getKey(); 1142
ResourceBundle; 1435
getBundle(); 1442
getKeys(); 1443
getObject(); 1443
getString(); 1444

resource(s) *(continued)*
ResourceBundle
getStringArray(); 1444
handleGetObject(); 1445
locale(s); 1435
package, java.util; 1435
parent; 1445
setParent(); 1446
retrieving
as input stream
Class.getResourceAsStream(); 396
Class.getResource(); 393
ClassLoader.getResource(); 421
ClassLoader.getResourceAsStream(); 421
ClassLoader.getSystemResource(); 422
ClassLoader.getSystemResourceAs-Stream(); 422
from resource bundle, ListResource-Bundle.handleGetObject(); 1053
PropertyResourceBundle.handleGet-Object(); 1379
ResourceBundle.getObject(); 1443
ResourceBundle.handleGetObject(); 1445
string
array, retrieving, ResourceBundle.get-StringArray(); 1444
retrieving
ResourceBundle.getString(); 1444
system, ClassLoader; 415
term description, ClassLoader; 415
response
code
HTTP protocol, *Table*; 924
HttpURLConnection.responseCode; 935
retrieving, HttpURLConnection.get-ResponseCode(); 933
message
HttpURLConnection.responseMessage; 935
retrieving, HttpURLConnection.get-ResponseMessage(); 934
responseCode, HttpURLConnection; 935
responseMessage, HttpURLConnection; 935
resume()
Thread; 1739
ThreadGroup; 1761
retrieving
Locale, locale(s); 1055
return type
method, retrieving, Method.getReturnType(); 1133
methods, Method; 1124
reverse()
StringBuffer; 1662
reversed host name resolution
term description, InetAddress; 957
RFC 1950
ZLIB header, URL, Deflater; 680
RFC 1951
URL
Deflater; 679
ZipFile; 1906
RFC 2045
specifying document header with
ContentHandler; 487
ContentHandlerFactory; 490
RFC 2046
specifying content type with
ContentHandler; 487
ContentHandlerFactory; 490
rint()
Math; 1092
RMI (Remote Method Invocation)
as application requiring object output stream resetting
ObjectOutputStream; 1264
Serializable; 1511
roll()
Calendar; 267
GregorianCalendar; 894
root classes; 13
rounding
away from zero, BigDecimal.ROUND_UP; 93
floating-point numbers, Math; 1084
Math.ceil(); 1087
Math.floor(); 1089
Math.rint(); 1092
Math.round(); 1093
modes, *Table*, BigDecimal; 75
with no loss of precision
BigDecimal.ROUND_UNNECESSARY; 93
round(), Math; 1093
ROUND_CEILING, BigDecimal; 90
ROUND_DOWN, BigDecimal; 90
ROUND_FLOOR, BigDecimal; 91
ROUND_HALF_DOWN, BigDecimal; 91
ROUND_HALF_EVEN, BigDecimal; 92

ROUND_HALF_UP, BigDecimal; 92
ROUND_UNNECESSARY, BigDecimal; 93
ROUND_UP, BigDecimal; 93
term description, BigDecimal; 75
towards
nearest neighbor
BigDecimal.ROUND_HALF_DOWN; 91
BigDecimal.ROUND_HALF_EVEN; 92
BigDecimal.ROUND_HALF_UP; 92
negative Infinity
BigDecimal.ROUND_FLOOR; 91
positive Infinity
BigDecimal.ROUND_CEILING; 90
zero, BigDecimal.ROUND_DOWN; 90
RSA
ClassLoader support; 414
rules
boundary, BreakIterator; 153
examples of, RuleBasedCollator; 1451
modifying, RuleBasedCollator; 1452
restrictions, RuleBasedCollator; 1453
retrieving
RuleBasedCollator.getRules(); 1460
RuleBasedCollator; 1447
clone(); 1456
compare(); 1457
equals(); 1458
getCollationElementIterator(); 1458
getCollationKey(); 1459
getRules(); 1460
hashCode(); 1460
package, java.text; 1447
runtime
class loaders, ClassLoader; 413
errors, AbstractMethodError; 39
exceptions; 17
ArithmeticException; 45
ArrayIndexOutOfBoundsException; 70
ArrayStoreException; 72
ClassCastException; 407
IllegalArgumentException; 945
IllegalMonitorStateException; 947
IllegalStateException; 949
IllegalThreadStateException; 951
IndexOutOfBoundsException; 955
NegativeArraySizeException; 1164
NullPointerException; 1185
NumberFormatException; 1213
RuntimeException; 1477
StringIndexOutOfBoundsException; 1688
functions related to, System; 1710
JRE (Java Runtime Environment)
ClassLoader; 415
run()
Runnable; 1465
Thread; 1740
runFinalization()
Runtime; 1473
System; 1720
runFinalizersOnExit()
Runtime; 1474
System; 1720
Runnable; 1464
package, java.lang; 1464
Runtime; 1466
exec(); 1467
exit(); 1468
freeMemory(); 1469
gc(); 1470
getLocalizedInputStream(); 1470
getLocalizedOutputStream(); 1471
getRuntime(); 1471
load(); 1471
loadLibrary(); 1472
package, java.lang; 1466
runFinalization(); 1473
runFinalizersOnExit(); 1474
totalMemory(); 1475
traceInstructions(); 1476
traceMethodCalls(); 1476
RuntimeException; 1477
package, java.lang; 1477

S

sameFile()
URL; 1813
SATURDAY
Calendar, *Table*; 233
save()
Properties; 1377
scalar numeric types
Number; 1187
scale
big decimal values, modifying
BigDecimal.setScale(); 94
retrieving, BigDecimal.scale(); 93
term description, BigDecimal; 74

searching
language-sensitive
CollationElementIterator; 436
locale-sensitive, Collator; 448
search(), Stack; 1609
String; 1632
secondary
collation order
CollationElementIterator; 435
CollationElementIterator.secondary-Order(); 440
Latin-based languages, *Table*, Collator; 448
SECONDARY, Collator; 462
secondaryOrder()
CollationElementIterator; 440
seconds
SECOND, Calendar; 268
SECOND_FIELD.DateFormat; 604
Secure Hash Algorithm (SHA-1)
SUID relationship to, Serializable; 1512
security
actions, permission determination, Security-Manager.checkSecurityAccess(); 1493
check
SecurityManager.inCheck(); 1501
testing for
SecurityManager.getInCheck(); 1500
class loader enforcement, ClassLoader; 413
concept description; 15
context, SecurityManager.getSecurity-Context(); 1500
exceptions, SecurityException; 1479
externalization considerations
Externalizable; 745
URL, Externalizable; 745
manager
concepts and overview
SecurityManager; 1481
retrieving
System.getSecurityManager(); 1717
SecurityManager; 1481
System.setSecurityManager(); 1722
policies, System; 1710
reflection issues; 19
SecurityException; 1479
package, java.lang; 1479
SecurityManager; 1481
checkAccept(); 1484
checkAccess(); 1484
checkAwtEventQueueAccess(); 1485
checkConnect(); 1486
checkCreateClassLoader(); 1486
checkDelete(); 1487
checkExec(); 1487
checkExit(); 1488
checkLink(); 1488
checkListen(); 1489
checkMemberAccess(); 1489
checkMulticast(); 1490
checkPackageAccess(); 1491
checkPackageDefinition(); 1491
checkPrintJobAccess(); 1492
checkPropertiesAccess(); 1492
checkPropertyAccess(); 1492
checkRead(); 1493
checkSecurityAccess(); 1494
checkSetFactory(); 1494
checkSystemClipboardAccess(); 1495
checkTopLevelWindow(); 1495
checkWrite(); 1496
classDepth(); 1497
classLoaderDepth(); 1498
currentClassLoader(); 1498
currentLoadedClass(); 1498
getClassContext(); 1499
getInCheck(); 1500
getSecurityContext(); 1500
getThreadGroup(); 1500
inCheck(); 1501
inClass(); 1501
inClassLoader(); 1502
package, java.lang; 1481
serialization considerations
Serializable; 1513
URL, Serializable; 1513
signature specifications, ClassLoader support; 414
thread group, ThreadGroup; 1751
seed
generator, Random; 1399
setting, Random.setSeed(); 1405
seek()
RandomAccessFile; 1418
send()
DatagramSocket; 512
DatagramSocketImpl; 524
MulticastSocket; 1160

sentence(s)
boundary
analysis, BreakIterator; 154
BreakIterator.getSentenceInstance(); 169
separators
decimal
DecimalFormat; 632
determining, DecimalFormat.isDecimalSeparatorAlwaysShown(); 652
retrieving, DecimalFormatSymbols.getDecimalSeparator(); 670
setting, DecimalFormat.setDecimalSeparatorAlwaysShown(); 657
setting, DecimalFormatSymbols.setDecimalSeparator(); 673
grouping
property, NumberFormat; 1193
retrieving, DecimalFormatSymbols.getGroupingSeparator(); 671
setting, DecimalFormatSymbols.setGroupingSeparator(); 676
setting, NumberFormat.setGroupingUsed(); 1210
line
writing
BufferedWriter; 200
BufferedWriter.newLine(); 203
pattern
retrieving, DecimalFormatSymbols.getPatternSeparator(); 672
setting, DecimalFormatSymbols.setPatternSeparator(); 677
separator, File; 800
separatorChar, File; 801
SEPTEMBER
Calendar, *Table*; 233
sequence(s)
SequenceInputStream; 1503
available(); 1505
close(); 1505
package, java.io; 1503
read(); 1505
UTF-encoded
reading
DataInput.readUTF(); 532
DataInputStream.readUTF(); 544
RandomAccessFile.readUTF(); 1418
writing
DataOutput.writeUTF(); 551
DataOutputStream.writeUTF(); 561
RandomAccessFile.writeUTF(); 1425
serialization
classes, *See* DataInput; DataInputStream; DataOutput; DataOutputStream; Externalizable; ObjectInput; ObjectInputStream; ObjectInputValidation; ObjectOutput; ObjectOutputStream; ObjectStreamClass; Serializable
concept description; 4
deserialization
ObjectInputStream; 1230
replacing objects during, ObjectInputStream.resolveObject(); 1252
term description
ObjectInputStream; 1231
Serializable; 1508
URL, Serializable; 1509
validation of an object during, ObjectInputValidation.validateObject(); 1258
exceptions
InvalidClassException; 1022
InvalidObjectException; 1026
NotActiveException; 1181
NotSerializableException; 1183
ObjectStreamException; 1288
OptionalDataException; 1299
StreamCorruptedException; 1612
WriteAbortedException; 1884
object state
Externalizable.writeExternal(); 747
replacing objects during, ObjectOutputStream.replaceObject(); 1271
security considerations, Serializable; 1513
Serializable, package, java.io; 1508
SUID (Stream Unique Identifier), term description
Externalizable; 743
ObjectOutputStream; 1264
ObjectStreamClass; 1283
Serializable; 1511
term description
Externalizable; 743
ObjectOutputStream; 1263
Serializable; 1508
WriteAbortedException; 1884

server(s)
ServerSocket; 1515
accept(); 1520
close(); 1522
getInetAddress(); 1523
getLocalPort(); 1523
getSoTimeout(); 1524
implAccept(); 1524
package, java.net; 1515
setSocketFactory(); 1526
setSoTimeout(); 1527
toString(); 1529
socket, string representation
ServerSocket.toString(); 1529
sockets
connection request acceptance
ServerSocket.accept(); 1520
ServerSocket.implAccept(); 1524
ServerSocket; 1515
setxxx methods
set()
Array; 63
BitSet; 141
Calendar; 269
Field; 765
URL; 1814
setAddress(), DatagramPacket; 504
setAllowUserInteraction()
URLConnection; 1842
setAmPmStrings(), DateFormatSymbols; 621
setBit(), BigInteger; 126
setBoolean()
Array; 65
Field; 766
setByte()
Array; 65
Field; 767
setCalendar(), DateFormat; 604
setChanged(), Observable; 1295
setChar()
Array; 66
Field; 769
setCharAt(), StringBuffer; 1663
setChoices(), ChoiceFormat; 363
setComment()
ZipEntry; 1899
ZipOutputStream; 1929
setContentHandlerFactory()
URLConnection; 1842
setCrc(), ZipEntry; 1899
setDaemon()
Thread; 1740
ThreadGroup; 1762
setData(), DatagramPacket; 504
setDate(), Date; 574
setDateFormatSymbols()
SimpleDateFormat; 1556
setDecimalFormatSymbols()
DecimalFormat; 655
setDecimalSeparator()
DecimalFormatSymbols; 673
setDecimalSeparatorAlwaysShown()
DecimalFormat; 657
setDecomposition(), Collator; 463
setDefault()
Locale; 1067
TimeZone; 1784
setDefaultAllowUserInteraction()
URLConnection; 1843
setDefaultRequestProperty()
URLConnection; 1844
setDefaultUseCaches()
URLConnection; 1844
setDictionary()
Deflater; 690
Inflater; 974
setDigit(), DecimalFormatSymbols; 674
setDoInput(), URLConnection; 1844
setDoOutput(), URLConnection; 1845
setDouble()
Array; 66
Field; 769
setElementAt(), Vector; 1874
setEndRule(), SimpleTimeZone; 1565
setEras(), DateFormatSymbols; 623
setErr(), System; 1720
setError()
PrintStream; 1352
PrintWriter; 1361
setExtra(), ZipEntry; 1900
setFirstDayOfWeek(), Calendar; 272
setFloat()
Array; 67
Field; 770
setFollowRedirects()
HttpURLConnection; 935
setFormat(), MessageFormat; 1119
setFormats(), MessageFormat; 1121
setGregorianChange()
GregorianCalendar; 895

setGroupingSeparator()
DecimalFormatSymbols; 676
setGroupingSize(), DecimalFormat; 658
setGroupingUsed(), NumberFormat; 1210
setHours(), Date; 575
setID(), TimeZone; 1785
setIfModifiedSince(), URLConnection; 1845
setIn(), System; 1721
setIndex()
CharacterIterator; 313
ParsePosition; 1322
StringCharacterIterator; 1685
setInfinity(), DecimalFormatSymbols; 676
setInput()
Deflater; 691
Inflater; 974
setInt()
Array; 67
Field; 771
setInterface(), MulticastSocket; 1162
setLength()
DatagramPacket; 504
StringBuffer; 1663
setLenient()
Calendar; 273
DateFormat; 605
setLevel()
Deflater; 692
ZipOutputStream; 1929
setLineNumber()
LineNumberInputStream; 1038
LineNumberReader; 1047
setLocale(), MessageFormat; 1122
setLocalPatternChars()
DateFormatSymbols; 623
setLong()
Array; 68
Field; 771
setMaximumFractionDigits()
NumberFormat; 1210
setMaximumIntegerDigits()
NumberFormat; 1211
setMaxPriority(), ThreadGroup; 1763
setMethod()
ZipEntry; 1901
ZipOutputStream; 1931
setMinimalDaysInFirstWeek()
Calendar; 274
setMinimumFractionDigits()
NumberFormat; 1211
setMinimumIntegerDigits()
NumberFormat; 1212
setMinusSign(), DecimalFormatSymbols; 677
setMinutes(), Date; 575
setMonth(), Date; 576
setMonths(), DateFormatSymbols; 623
setMultiplier(), DecimalFormat; 659
setName(), Thread; 1741
setNaN(), DecimalFormatSymbols; 677
setNegativePrefix(), DecimalFormat; 661
setNegativeSuffix(), DecimalFormat; 661
setNumberFormat(), DateFormat; 606
setOut(), System; 1721
setParent(), ResourceBundle; 1446
setParseIntegerOnly(), NumberFormat; 1212
setPatternSeparator()
DecimalFormatSymbols; 677
setPercent(), DecimalFormatSymbols; 678
setPerMill(), DecimalFormatSymbols; 678
setPort(), DatagramPacket; 505
setPositivePrefix(), DecimalFormat; 661
setPositiveSuffix(), DecimalFormat; 662
setPriority(), Thread; 1742
setProperties(), System; 1721
setRawOffset()
SimpleTimeZone; 1566
TimeZone; 1785
setRequestMethod()
HttpURLConnection; 937
setRequestProperty(), URLConnection; 1846
setScale(), BigDecimal; 94
setSeconds(), Date; 576
setSecurityManager(), System; 1722
setSeed(), Random; 1405
setShort()
Array; 69
Field; 772
setShortMonths(), DateFormatSymbols; 624
setShortWeekdays()
DateFormatSymbols; 624
setSigners(), ClassLoader; 425
setSize()
Vector; 1875
ZipEntry; 1901
setSocketFactory(), ServerSocket; 1526
setSocketImplFactory(), Socket; 1582
setSoLinger(), Socket; 1583
setSoTimeout()
DatagramSocket; 514
ServerSocket; 1527
Socket; 1584

setxxx methods *(continued)*
setStartRule(), SimpleTimeZone; 1567
setStartYear(), SimpleTimeZone; 1568
setStrategy(), Deflater; 693
setStrength(), Collator; 467
setTcpNoDelay(), Socket; 1585
setText(), BreakIterator; 175
setTime()
Calendar; 274
Date; 577
ZipEntry; 1901
setTimeInMillis(), Calendar; 275
setTimeZone()
Calendar; 275
DateFormat; 607
setTTL()
DatagramSocketImpl; 525
MulticastSocket; 1162
setURL(), URLStreamHandler; 1855
setURLStreamHandlerFactory(), URL; 1814
setUseCaches(), URLConnection; 1846
setWeekdays(), DateFormatSymbols; 624
setYear(), Date; 577
setZeroDigit(), DecimalFormatSymbols; 678
setZoneStrings(), DateFormatSymbols; 624
valid array types, *Table*, Array; 48
valid field types, *Table*, Field; 751
SHA-1 (Secure Hash Algorithm)
SUID relationship to, Serializable; 1512
term description, ClassLoader; 414
shiftxxx methods
shiftLeft(), BigInteger; 127
shiftRight(), BigInteger; 127
short integer(s)
See Also integer(s)
arrays
modifying, Array.setShort(); 69
retrieving elements from
Array.getShort(); 61
fields
modifying, Field.setShort(); 772
retrieving values of, Field.getShort(); 763
reading
DataInput.readShort(); 531
DataInput.readUnsignedShort(); 532
DataInputStream.readShort(); 543
DataInputStream.readUnsignedShort(); 544
ObjectInputStream.readShort(); 1245
ObjectInputStream.readUnsignedShort(); 1248
RandomAccessFile.readShort(); 1416
RandomAccessFile.readUnsignedShort(); 1417
retrieving object value as
Double.shortValue(); 718
Short; 1530
byteValue(); 1531
decode(); 1532
doubleValue(); 1533
equals(); 1533
floatValue(); 1534
hashCode(); 1534
intValue(); 1534
longValue(); 1535
MAX_VALUE; 1535
MIN_VALUE; 1535
package, java.lang; 1530
parseShort(); 1536
shortValue(); 1537
toString(); 1538
TYPE; 1538
valueOf(); 1539
SHORT, DateFormat; 608
short, retrieving object value as
Float.shortValue(); 869
Integer.shortValue(); 1010
Long.shortValue(); 1076
Number.shortValue(); 1190
shortValue()
Byte; 212
Double; 718
Float; 869
Integer; 1010
Long; 1076
Number; 1190
Short; 1537
writing
DataOutput.writeShort(); 551
DataOutputStream.writeShort(); 560
ObjectOutputStream.writeShort(); 1281
RandomAccessFile.writeShort(); 1424
sign
big decimal value, determining
BigDecimal.signum(); 95
bits, bit representation, BigInteger; 100
determining, BigInteger.signum(); 128

minus
retrieving, DecimalFormatSymbols.getMinusSign(); 671
setting character for, DecimalFormatSymbols.setMinusSign(); 677

signature
conventions, EventObject; 732
specifications, ClassLoader support; 414

signers
recording, ClassLoader.setSigners(); 425
retrieving, Class.getSigners(); 398

signum()
BigDecimal; 95
BigInteger; 128

simple
SimpleDateFormat; 1541
applyLocalizedPattern(); 1550
applyPattern(); 1552
casting to DateFormat; 581
clone(); 1552
equals(); 1553
format(); 1553
getDateFormatSymbols(); 1554
hashCode(); 1555
package, java.text; 1541
parse(); 1555
setDateFormatSymbols(); 1556
toPattern(); 1558
SimpleTimeZone; 1559
clone(); 1562
equals(); 1562
getOffset(); 1563
getRawOffset(); 1564
hashCode(); 1564
inDaylightTime(); 1564
package, java.util; 1559
setEndRule(); 1565
setRawOffset(); 1566
setStartRule(); 1567
setStartYear(); 1568
SIMPLIFIED_CHINESE, Locale; 1056

sine
See Also trigonometric functions
Math.sin(); 1093

size()
BitSet; 142
ByteArrayOutputStream; 228
CharArrayWriter; 327
DataOutputStream; 555
Dictionary; 708
Hashtable; 922
Vector; 1875

skipping
skip()
BufferedInputStream; 183
BufferedReader; 197
ByteArrayInputStream; 223
CharArrayReader; 322
CheckedInputStream; 338
FileInputStream; 812
FilterInputStream; 841
FilterReader; 854
InflaterInputStream; 982
InputStream; 989
LineNumberInputStream; 1039
LineNumberReader; 1048
ObjectInput; 1229
Reader; 1434
StringBufferInputStream; 1669
StringReader; 1695
ZipInputStream; 1918
skipBytes()
DataInput; 533
DataInputStream; 545
ObjectInputStream; 1254
RandomAccessFile; 1419

slashSlashComments()
StreamTokenizer; 1626

slashStarComments()
StreamTokenizer; 1626

sleep
sleep(), Thread; 1743
threads, Thread.sleep(); 1743

sockets
binding to port, SocketImpl.bind(); 1597
bytes, determining number available
SocketImpl.available(); 1596
classes that implement; 23
closing
Socket.close(); 1577
SocketImpl.close(); 1597
connection
permission determination
SecurityManager.checkAccept(); 1484
SecurityManager.checkConnect(); 1486
request acceptance, SocketImpl.accept(); 1595
to a destination, SocketImpl.connect(); 1598
creating, SocketImpl.create(); 1598

sockets *(continued)*
- datagram
  - address, retrieving
    - DatagramSocket.getLocalAddress(); 510
  - binding, DatagramSocketImpl.bind(); 519
  - closing
    - DatagramSocket.close(); 509
    - DatagramSocketImpl.close(); 519
  - creating
    - DatagramSocketImpl.create(); 519
  - DatagramSocket; 506
  - file descriptor, retrieving, DatagramSocketImpl.getFileDescriptor(); 520
  - joining a multicast group
    - DatagramSocketImpl.join(); 522
  - leaving a multicast group
    - DatagramSocketImpl.leave(); 522
  - port, DatagramSocketImpl.localPort; 523
  - port, retrieving
    - DatagramSocket.getLocalPort(); 510
    - DatagramSocketImpl.getLocalPort(); 521
  - time-out period
    - DatagramSocket; 507
    - retrieving, DatagramSocket.getSoTimeout(); 511
    - setting, DatagramSocket.setSoTimeout(); 514
- file descriptors
  - retrieving
    - SocketImpl.getFileDescriptor(); 1599
  - SocketImpl.fd; 1599
- input stream, creating
  - Socket.getInputStream(); 1578
  - SocketImpl.getInputStream(); 1600
- IP address
  - retrieving
    - Socket.getInetAddress(); 1577
    - Socket.getLocalAddress(); 1579
    - SocketImpl.getInetAddress(); 1600
  - SocketImpl.address; 1596
- linger-on-close, Socket; 1572
- multicast
  - adding to multicast group
    - MulticastSocket.joinGroup(); 1158
  - address, retrieving, MulticastSocket.getInterface(); 1157
  - removing from multicast group
    - MulticastSocket.leaveGroup(); 1158
  - sending datagram
    - MulticastSocket.send(); 1160
- options, Socket; 1572
- output stream, creating
  - Socket.getOutputStream(); 1579
  - SocketImpl.getOutputStream(); 1601
- port
  - retrieving
    - Socket.getLocalPort(); 1579
    - Socket.getPort(); 1580
    - SocketImpl.getLocalPort(); 1600
    - SocketImpl.getPort(); 1601
  - SocketImpl.localport; 1602
  - SocketImpl.port; 1603
- server
  - closing, ServerSocket.close(); 1522
  - connection request acceptance
    - ServerSocket.accept(); 1520
  - IP address, retrieving
    - ServerSocket.getInetAddress(); 1523
  - port, retrieving
    - ServerSocket.getLocalPort(); 1523
  - ServerSocket; 1515
  - string representation
    - ServerSocket.toString(); 1529
  - time-out period, retrieving
    - ServerSocket.getSoTimeout(); 1524
  - time-out periods, setting
    - ServerSocket.setSoTimeout(); 1527
- Socket; 1571
  - close(); 1577
  - getInetAddress(); 1577
  - getInputStream(); 1578
  - getLocalAddress(); 1579
  - getLocalPort(); 1579
  - getOutputStream(); 1579
  - getPort(); 1580
  - getSoLinger(); 1581
  - getSoTimeout(); 1581
  - getTcpNoDelay(); 1582
  - package, java.net; 1571
  - setSocketImplFactory(); 1582
  - setSoLinger(); 1583
  - setSoTimeout(); 1584
  - setTcpNoDelay(); 1585
  - toString(); 1589

SocketException; 1590
package, java.net; 1590
SocketImpl; 1592
accept(); 1595
address(); 1596
available(); 1596
bind(); 1597
close(); 1597
connect(); 1598
create(); 1598
fd; 1599
getFileDescriptor(); 1599
getInetAddress(); 1600
getInputStream(); 1600
getOutputStream(); 1601
getPort(); 1601
listen(); 1602
localport; 1602
package, java.net; 1592
port; 1603
toString(); 1603
SocketImplFactory; 1604
createSocketImpl(); 1605
package, java.net; 1604
state, modifying, SocketImpl; 1593
stream, connection request, listening for
SocketImpl.listen(); 1602
string representation, generating
Socket.toString(); 1589
SocketImpl.toString(); 1603
term description
ServerSocket; 1515
Socket; 1571
time-out period
linger-on-close
retrieving, Socket.getSoLinger(); 1581
setting, Socket.setSoLinger(); 1583
setting, Socket.setSoTimeout(); 1584
Socket; 1572
Socket.getSoTimeout(); 1581

sorting
collation order
CollationElementIterator; 435
Collator; 448
keys, CollationKey; 441
locale-sensitive, Collator; 447

source
event
EventListener; 729
EventObject; 731
EventObject.source; 735
registering, EventObject; 732
retrieving, EventObject.getSource(); 735
source, EventObject; 735

space
character, Character; 283
SPACE_SEPARATOR, Character, *Table*; 289
testing for, Character.isSpaceChar(); 297

specifications
signature, ClassLoader support; 414

square root
Math.sqrt(); 1094
sqrt(), Math; 1094

stacks
class loader on, testing for
SecurityManager.inClassLoader(); 1502
class on, testing for
SecurityManager.inClass(); 1502
context
SecurityManager.getClassContext(); 1499
empty, testing for, Stack.empty(); 1608
errors, StackOverflowError; 1610
exceptions, EmptyStackException; 721
execution
finding first occurrence of a class
SecurityManager.checkDepth(); 1497
SecurityManager; 1482
finding first occurrence of a class, created by class loader
SecurityManager.classLoaderDepth(); 1498
finding topmost class loader
SecurityManager.currentClassLoader(); 1498
finding topmost class with a class loader
SecurityManager.currentLoadedClass(); 1498
peeking, Stack.peek(); 1608
popping, Stack.pop(); 1608
printing
Thread.dumpStack(); 1730
Throwable.printStackTrace(); 1771
pushing, Stack.push(); 1609
searching, Stack.search(); 1609

stacks *(continued)*
Stack; 1606
empty(); 1608
package, java.util; 1606
peek(); 1608
pop(); 1608
push(); 1609
search(); 1609
StackOverflowError; 1610
package, java.lang; 1610
term description, Stack; 1606
thread, Thread.countStackFrames(); 1729
trace, filling in
Throwable.fillInStackTrace(); 1770
standard IO
error
FileDescriptor; 802
FileDescriptor.err; 804
error stream
Process.getErrorStream(); 1366
setting, System.setErr(); 1720
System.err; 1714
input
FileDescriptor; 802
FileDescriptor.in; 804
input stream
Process.getOutputStream(); 1368
System.in; 1717
System.setIn(); 1721
output
FileDescriptor; 802
FileDescriptor.out; 804
output stream
Process.getInputStream(); 1367
System.out; 1719
System.setOut(); 1721
term description, System; 1710
standard time
term description, SimpleTimeZone; 1559
time difference, retrieving
TimeZone.getRawOffset(); 1783
time zones, TimeZone; 1776
start
start(), Thread; 1743
START_PUNCTUATION, Character, *Table*; 289
startsWith(), String; 1646
state
active, Thread; 1724
calendar fields, Calendar.isSet; 264
exceptions
IllegalStateException; 949
IllegalThreadStateException; 951
finalization
Object.finalize(); 1218
Runtime.runFinalization(); 1473
System.runFinalization(); 1720
System.runFinalizersOnExit(); 1720
object
reading
Externalizable.readExternal(); 747
serializing
Externalizable.writeExternal(); 747
observable
clearing, Observable.clearChanged(); 1293
notifying observers
Observable.notifyObservers(); 1295
Observable; 1290
recording, Observable.setChanged(); 1295
resetting, ObjectOutputStream.reset(); 1273
socket, modifying, SocketImpl; 1593
threads, Thread; 1724
static modifier
STATIC, Modifier; 1144
testing for, Modifier.isStatic(); 1150
status
file descriptor, validity testing
FileDescriptor.valid(); 805
files
existence, File.exists(); 788
read permission, File.canRead(); 786
write permission, File.canWrite(); 786
process exit value, Process.exitValue(); 1365
stopping
stop()
Thread; 1744
ThreadGroup; 1764
thread groups, ThreadGroup.stop(); 1764
STORED
ZipEntry; 1902
ZipOutputStream; 1931
strategy
compression
Deflater.FILTERED; 687
Huffman encoding specification,
Deflater.HUFFMAN_ONLY; 689

streams
buffered, concept description; 6
byte
BufferedInputStream; 176
BufferedOutputStream; 185
ByteArrayInputStream; 216
ByteArrayOutputStream; 224
InputStream; 983
OutputStream; 1304
PipedInputStream; 1323
PipedOutputStream; 1332
PrintStream; 1346
PushbackInputStream; 1383
SequenceInputStream; 1503
to character stream converters; 5
character
BufferedReader; 190
BufferedWriter; 199
byte stream to character stream converters; 5
CharArrayReader; 315
CharArrayWriter; 323
FileReader; 827
FileWriter; 830
FilterReader; 847
FilterWriter; 855
InputStreamReader; 990
LineNumberReader; 1040
OutputStreamWriter; 1308
PipedReader; 1337
PipedWriter; 1342
PrintWriter; 1354
PushbackReader; 1392
Reader; 1426
StringReader; 1690
StringWriter; 1703
Writer; 1887
data, concept description; 3
error, Process.getErrorStream(); 1366
exception
EOFException; 725
StreamCorruptedException; 1612
filter
CheckedOutputStream; 339
checksum, CheckedInputStream; 333
concept description; 5
FilterInputStream; 834
FilterOutputStream; 842
FilterReader; 847
FilterWriter; 855
PrintStream; 1346
handler
URL, HttpURLConnection use; 923
URL, URLStreamHandler; 1852
handlers, FileNameMap; 816
header
reading, ObjectInputStream.readStreamHeader(); 1246
term description, ObjectInputStream.readStreamHeader(); 1246
writing, ObjectOutputStream.writeStreamHeader(); 1281
in-memory; 7
classes, *See* ByteArrayInputStream; ByteArrayOutputStream; CharArrayReader; CharArrayWriter; StringReader; StringWriter
input
buffered, BufferedInputStream; 176
BufferedReader; 190
ByteArrayInputStream; 216
CharArrayReader; 315
checksum, CheckedInputStream; 333
creating for URL connection URLConnection.getInputStream(); 1838
creating, Socket.getInputStream(); 1578
creating, ZipFile.getInputStream(); 1912
DataInputStream; 534
FileInputStream; 807
FilterInputStream; 834
FilterReader; 847
for reading error output Process.getErrorStream(); 1366
for reading output Process.getInputStream(); 1367
GZIPInputStream; 896
InflaterInputStream; 976
InputStream; 983
InputStreamReader; 990
LineNumberReader; 1040
ObjectInputStream; 1230
PipedInputStream; 1323
PipedReader; 1337
Process.getOutputStream(); 1368
PushbackInputStream; 1383
PushbackReader; 1392
Reader; 1426
reading, CheckedInputStream.read(); 337
retrieving resources as Class.getResourceAsStream(); 396
SequenceInputStream; 1503

streams *(continued)*
input
skipping bytes
CheckedInputStream.skip(); 338
socket, creating
SocketImpl.getInputStream(); 1600
StringReader; 1690
URL connection, opening
URL.openStream(); 1813
ZipInputStream; 1914
mark, BufferedInputStream; 177
output
buffered, BufferedOutputStream; 185
BufferedWriter; 199
ByteArrayOutputStream; 224
CharArrayWriter; 323
CheckedOutputStream; 339
closingDeflaterOutputStream.close(); 698
creating for URL connection
URLConnection.getOutputStream(); 1838
creating, Socket.getOutputStream(); 1579
DataOutputStream; 552
DeflaterOutputStream; 695
FilterOutputStream; 842
FilterWriter; 855
for writing input
Process.getOutputStream(); 1368
GZIPOutputStream; 902
ObjectOutputStream; 1262
OutputStream; 1304
OutputStreamWriter; 1308
PipedOutputStream; 1332
PipedWriter; 1342
PrintStream; 1346
PrintWriter; 1354
Process.getInputStream(); 1367
socket, creating
SocketImpl.getOutputStream(); 1601
StringWriter; 1703
Writer; 1887
writing, CheckedOutputStream.write(); 341
pipes; 7
PipedInputStream; 1323
PipedOutputStream; 1332
PipedReader; 1337
PipedWriter; 1342
pushback
PushbackInputStream; 1383
PushbackReader; 1392
resetting, term description
ObjectOutputStream; 1264
retrieving resources as
ClassLoader.getResourceAsStream(); 421
ClassLoader.getSystemResourceAsStream(); 422
sockets, connection request, listening for
SocketImpl.listen(); 1602
StreamCorruptedException; 1612
package, java.io; 1612
StreamTokenizer; 1614
commentChar(); 1617
eolIsSignificant(); 1618
lineno(); 1619
lowerCaseMode(); 1619
nextToken(); 1619
nval; 1621
ordinaryChar(); 1621
ordinaryChars(); 1622
package, java.io; 1614
parseNumbers(); 1622
pushBack(); 1624
quoteChar(); 1625
resetSyntax(); 1626
slashSlashComments(); 1626
slashStarComments(); 1626
sval; 1628
toString(); 1628
TT_EOF; 1628
TT_EOL; 1629
TT_NUMBER; 1629
TT_WORD; 1629
ttype; 1630
whitespaceChars; 1630
wordChars; 1631
string
StringReader; 1690
StringWriter; 1703
SUID (Stream Unique Identifier), term description
Externalizable; 743
ObjectOutputStream; 1264
ObjectStreamClass; 1283
Serializable; 1511
superclasses, concept description; 5

URL handler
URL; 1801
URLConnection; 1820
factory, URLStreamHandlerFactory; 1857
creating
URLStreamHandlerFactory.create-URLStreamHandler(); 1859
setting
URL.setURLStreamHandlerFactory(); 1814

strength
collation order
CollationElementIterator; 435
Collator; 448
setting, Collator.setStrength; 467
minimum level, retrieving
Collator.getStrength(); 460

string(s)
appending to, StringBuffer.append(); 1656
array
resource, retrieving, ResourceBundle.get-StringArray(); 1444
retrieving, ChoiceFormat.getFormats(); 360
buffer
capacity retrieval, StringBuffer.capacity(); 1658
capacity setting, StringBuffer.ensure-Capacity(); 1659
retrieving characters from
StringBuffer.charAt(); 1658
StringBuffer; 1655
byte encoding, String.getBytes(); 1638
class objects
representation, Class; 365
retrieving, Class.getName(); 393
collation
classes that implement; 31
concept description; 27
collation key source, retrieving
CollationKey.getSourceString(); 445
comparing
collation key use, CollationKey; 441
Collator.compare(); 455
RuleBasedCollator.compare(); 1457
concatenating, String.concat(); 1635
concepts and overview, String; 1632
copying characters from
a string buffer
StringBuffer.getChars(); 1660
String.getChars(); 1641
creating
from a data value, String.valueOf(); 1653
objects from
BigDecimal.valueOf(); 97
Boolean.valueOf(); 149
Byte.valueOf(); 214
Double.valueOf(); 720
Float.valueOf(); 871
Integer.valueOf(); 1013
Long.valueOf(); 1080
String.valueOf(); 1653
Short.valueOf(); 1539
String.copyValueOf(); 1636
date-time, parsing, DateFormat.parseObject(); 604
encoding, URLEncoder.encode(); 1851
end-of-string indicator
CollationElementIterator.NULLORDER; 439
equality testing, String.intern(); 1643
exceptions
IndexOutOfBoundsException; 955
StringIndexOutOfBoundsException; 1688
finding first occurrence, String.indexOf(); 1642
formatting, ChoiceFormat; 346
formatting date or time
DateFormat.format(); 592
formatting objects as, Format.format(); 878
generating
BigDecimal.toString(); 96
BigInteger.toString(); 131
BitSet.toString(); 143
Boolean.toString(); 148
Byte.toString(); 213
ByteArrayOutputStream.toString(); 229
Character.toString(); 302
CharArrayWriter.toString(); 329
Class.toString(); 405
Constructor.toString(); 485
Date.toString(); 578
Double.toString(); 719
EventObject.toString(); 735
Field.toString(); 773
File.toString(); 801
Float.toString(); 869

string(s) *(continued)*
generating
for a pattern
ChoiceFormat.toPattern(); 364
MessageFormat.toPattern(); 1122
Hashtable.toString(); 922
InetAddress.toString(); 963
Integer.toBinaryString(); 1010
Integer.toString(); 1012
Locale.toString(); 1068
Long.toBinaryString(); 1077
Long.toString(); 1079
Method.toString(); 1138
Modifier.toString(); 1151
nonlocalized pattern, DecimalFormat.toLocalizedPattern(); 662
Object.toString(); 1224
ObjectStreamClass.toString(); 1286
pattern, DecimalFormat.toPattern(); 662
representation from an object, String.toString(); 1652
ServerSocket.toString(); 1529
Short.toString(); 1538
SimpleDateFormat.toLocalizedPattern(); 1558
SimpleDateFormat.toPattern(); 1558
Socket.toString(); 1589
SocketImpl.toString(); 1603
StreamTokenizer.toString(); 1628
String.toString(); 1652
StringBuffer.toString(); 1664
StringWriter.toString(); 1706
Thread.toString(); 1748
ThreadGroup.toString(); 1767
Throwable.toString(); 1773
URL.toExternalForm(); 1815
URL.toString(); 1816
URLConnection.toString(); 1847
URLStreamHandler.toExternalForm(); 1855
Vector.toString(); 1876
ZipEntry.toString(); 1902
infinity
retrieving, DecimalFormatSymbols.getInfinity(); 671
setting, DecimalFormatSymbols.setInfinity(); 676
inserting into, StringBuffer.insert(); 1661
iteration
classes that implement; 31
concept description; 28
length
accessing, String.length(); 1645
accessing, StringBuffer.length(); 1662
setting, StringBuffer.setLength(); 1663
locale-sensitive comparison, Collator; 447
NaN
retrieving
DecimalFormatSymbols.getNaN(); 671
setting
DecimalFormatSymbols.setNaN(); 677
number, local-sensitive, DecimalFormat; 626
parsing
Byte.decode(); 207
Byte.parseByte(); 211
ChoiceFormat.parse(); 362
Format.parseObject(); 880
Integer.decode(); 1003
Integer.parseInt(); 1009
into numbers, ParsePosition; 1317
Long.parseLong(); 1076
MessageFormat.parseObject(); 1118
NumberFormat.parseObject(); 1209
ParseException; 1314
Short.decode(); 1532
Short.parseShort(); 1536
StringTokenizer; 1697
prefix, String.startsWith(); 1646
primitive type representation, *Table*, Class; 366
reading, DataInputStream.readUTF(); 544
replacing characters in, String.replace(); 1646
resource, retrieving
ResourceBundle.getString(); 1444
retrieving
characters from
CollationElementIterator.next(); 438
String.charAt(); 1634
Class objects, Class.forName(); 370
from the string pool, String.intern(); 1643
ResourceBundle.getString(); 1444
reversing character order
StringBuffer.reverse(); 1662
serialization, term description
ObjectInputStream; 1231
serialization of, ObjectOutputStream; 1263
streams
StringReader; 1690
StringWriter; 1703

String; 1632
- charAt(); 1634
- compareTo(); 1635
- concat(); 1635
- copyValueOf(); 1636
- endsWith(); 1637
- equals(); 1637
- equalsIgnoreCase(); 1638
- getBytes(); 1638
- getChars(); 1641
- hashCode(); 1642
- indexOf(); 1642
- intern(); 1643
- lastIndexOf(); 1644
- length(); 1645
- package, java.lang; 1632
- regionMatches(); 1645
- replace(); 1646
- startsWith(); 1646
- substring(); 1651
- toCharArray(); 1651
- toLowerCase(); 1652
- toString(); 1652
- toUpperCase(); 1652
- trim(); 1653
- valueOf(); 1653

StringBuffer; 1655
- append(); 1656
- capacity(); 1658
- charAt(); 1658
- ensureCapacity(); 1659
- getChars(); 1660
- insert(); 1661
- length(); 1662
- package, java.lang; 1655
- reverse(); 1662
- setCharAt(); 1663
- setLength(); 1663
- toString(); 1664

StringBufferInputStream; 1665
- available(); 1667
- buffer; 1668
- count; 1668
- package, java.io; 1665
- pos; 1668
- read(); 1668
- reset(); 1669
- skip(); 1669

StringCharacterIterator; 1671
- clone(); 1677
- current(); 1678
- equals(); 1679
- first(); 1679
- getBeginIndex(); 1680
- getEndIndex(); 1680
- getIndex(); 1680
- hashCode(); 1681
- last(); 1681
- next(); 1682
- package, java.text; 1671
- previous(); 1684
- setIndex(); 1685

StringIndexOutOfBoundsException; 1688
- package, java.lang; 1688

StringReader; 1690
- close(); 1692
- mark(); 1692
- markSupported(); 1693
- package, java.io; 1690
- read(); 1694
- ready(); 1694
- reset(); 1695
- skip(); 1695

strings array, ChoiceFormat; 346

StringTokenizer; 1697
- countTokens(); 1698
- hasMoreElements(); 1699
- hasMoreTokens(); 1699
- nextElement(); 1700
- nextToken(); 1700
- package, java.util; 1697

StringWriter; 1703
- getBuffer(); 1705
- package, java.io; 1703
- write(); 1707

substring creation, String.substring(); 1651

suffix determination, String.endsWith(); 1637

text, setting, BreakIterator.setText(); 175

as token element, *Table*, StreamTokenizer; 1614

token value, StreamTokenizer.sval; 1628

transforming into collation key
- Collator.getCollationKey(); 458
- RuleBasedCollator.getCollationKey(); 1459

trimming whitespace, String.trim(); 1653

string(s) *(continued)*
Unicode
reading
DataInput.readUTF(); 532
DataInputStream.readUTF(); 544
ObjectInputStream.readUTF(); 1249
RandomAccessFile.readUTF(); 1418
writing
DataOutput.writeUTF(); 551
DataOutputStream.writeUTF(); 561
ObjectOutputStream.writeUTF(); 1282
RandomAccessFile.writeUTF(); 1425
updating in place, StringBuffer; 1655
URL, parsing into an object
URLStreamHandler.parseURL(); 1854
writing
DataOutput.writeUTF(); 551
DataOutputStream.writeUTF(); 561
ObjectOutputStream.writeBytes(); 1276
ObjectOutputStream.writeChars(); 1277
RandomAccessFile.writeBytes(); 1421
RandomAccessFile.writeChars(); 1422
subrange
term description
CharacterIterator; 306
StringCharacterIterator; 1672
substring()
String; 1651
subtraction
big decimal values, BigDecimal.subtract(); 96
big integer values, BigInteger.subtract(); 128
SUID (Stream Unique Identifier)
retrieving, ObjectStreamClass.getSerialVersionUID(); 1285
term description
Externalizable; 743
ObjectOutputStream; 1264
ObjectStreamClass; 1283
Serializable; 1511
SUNDAY
Calendar, *Table*; 233
superclass(es)
retrieving, Class.getSuperclass(); 399
testing for, Class.isAssignableFrom(); 400
SURROGATE
Character, *Table*; 289
suspension
suspend()
Thread; 1745
ThreadGroup; 1764
thread group
permission control, ThreadGroup.allowThreadSuspension(); 1756
ThreadGroup.suspend(); 1764
sval
StreamTokenizer; 1628
symbols
date format, DateFormatSymbols; 610
decimal format
DecimalFormat; 631
retrieving, DecimalFormat.getDecimalFormatSymbols(); 647
setting, DecimalFormat.setDecimalSeparatorAlwaysShown(); 655
Table, DecimalFormat; 630
Table, DecimalFormatSymbols; 665
synchronization
locks
Reader.lock; 1429
Writer.lock; 1890
sync(), FileDescriptor; 804
SyncFailedException; 1708
package, java.io; 1708
SYNCHRONIZED, Modifier; 1144
testing for, Modifier.isSynchronized(); 1150
thread
Object; 1215
Thread; 1724
syntax
resetting, StreamTokenizer.resetSyntax(); 1626
system
See Also ClassLoader; Process; Runtime
clipboard, access permission determination
SecurityManager.checkSystemClipboardAccess(); 1495
concepts and overview, System; 1710
event queue access, permission determination
SecurityManager.checkAwtEventQueueAccess(); 1485
management, Runtime; 1466
programs, spawning processes to run
Process; 1363

properties
access permission determination
SecurityManager.checkProperties-Access(); 1492
SecurityManager.checkProperty-Access(); 1492
creating Integer object using
Integer.getInteger(); 1005
creating Long object using
Long.getInteger(); 1072
Properties; 1370
retrieving boolean value
Boolean.getBoolean(); 147
retrieving named
System.getProperty(); 1716
retrieving, System.getProperties(); 1715
setting, System.setProperties(); 1721
System; 1711
Table, Properties; 1371
Table, System; 1711
resources, ClassLoader; 415
System; 1710
arraycopy(); 1713
currentTimeMillis(); 1713
err(); 1714
exit(); 1714
gc(); 1715
getEnv(); 1715
getProperties(); 1715
getProperty(); 1716
getSecurityManager(); 1717
identityHashCode(); 1717
in(); 1717
load(); 1718
loadLibrary(); 1719
out(); 1719
package, java.lang; 1710
runFinalization(); 1720
runFinalizersOnExit(); 1720
setErr(); 1720
setIn(); 1721
setOut(); 1721
setProperties(); 1721
setSecurityManager(); 1722

T

tail digit
new, BigDecimal; 75
Taiwan
predefined locale codes, *Table*, Locale; 1056
TAIWAN, Locale; 1056
tangent
See Also trigonometric functions
Math.tan(); 1094
target
exceptions
InvocationTargetException; 1028
retrieving, InvocationTarget-Exception.getTargetException(); 1030
TCP (Transmission Control Protocol)
Nagle's algorithm use, Socket; 1572
termination
process, waiting for, Process.waitFor(); 1368
tertiary
collation order
CollationElementIterator; 435
CollationElementIterator.tertiary-Order(); 440
Collator.TERTIARY; 469
Latin-based languages, *Table*, Collator; 448
TERTIARY, Collator; 469
tertiaryOrder()
CollationElementIterator; 440
testBit()
BigInteger; 129
text
See Also character(s); java.text package; string(s)
boundary, BreakIterator.previous(); 174
character iterator, retrieving
BreakIterator.getText(); 169
end of, BreakIterator.DONE; 162
end of text indicator, CharacterIterator.DONE; 311
index
CharacterIterator; 306
retrieving
CharacterIterator.getIndex; 312
setting
CharacterIterator.setIndex(); 313
StringCharacterIterator.setIndex(); 1685

text *(continued)*
- subrange
  - retrieving index at beginning of
    - CharacterIterator.getBeginIndex; 311
  - retrieving index at end of
    - CharacterIterator.getEndIndex; 312

thread groups
- access control, monitoring
  - ThreadGroup.checkAccess(); 1757
- active
  - estimating
    - ThreadGroup.activeGroupCount(); 1756
  - threads, estimating
    - ThreadGroup.activeCount(); 1755
- concepts and overview, ThreadGroup; 1751
- daemon
  - term description, ThreadGroup; 1751
  - testing for, ThreadGroup.isDaemon(); 1760
- destroyed, testing for
  - ThreadGroup.isDestroyed(); 1760
- destroying, ThreadGroup.destroy(); 1757
- enumerating
  - active threads in, Thread.enumerate(); 1731
  - ThreadGroup.enumerate(); 1758
- listing, ThreadGroup.list(); 1760
- name, retrieving, ThreadGroup.getName(); 1759
- parent, retrieving
  - ThreadGroup.getParent(); 1759
- priorities, maximum
  - ThreadGroup.getMaxPriority(); 1759
- retrieving
  - SecurityManager.getThreadGroup(); 1500
  - Thread.getThreadGroup(); 1732
- suspension, permission control
  - ThreadGroup.allowThreadSuspension(); 1756
- term description, Thread; 1724
- ThreadGroup; 1751
  - activeCount(); 1755
  - activeGroupCount(); 1756
  - allowThreadSuspension(); 1756
  - checkAccess(); 1757
  - destroy(); 1757
  - enumerate(); 1758
  - getMaxPriority(); 1759
  - getName(); 1759
  - getParent(); 1759
  - isDaemon(); 1760
  - isDestroyed(); 1760
  - list(); 1760
  - package, java.lang; 1751
  - parentOf(); 1761
  - resume(); 1761
  - setDaemon(); 1762
  - setMaxPriority(); 1763
  - stop(); 1764
  - suspend(); 1764
  - toString(); 1767
  - uncaughtException(); 1767

threads
- *See Also* Runnable
- access, permission check
  - Thread.checkAccess(); 1729
- active
  - enumerating, Thread.enumerate(); 1731
  - estimating for a thread group
    - ThreadGroup.activeCount(); 1755
  - testing for, Thread.isAlive(); 1735
  - Thread; 1724
  - Thread.activeCount(); 1728
- body of, Thread.run(); 1740
- concepts and overview, Thread; 1723
- current, retrieving
  - Thread.currentThread(); 1730
- daemon
  - setting, Thread.setDaemon(); 1740
  - testing for, Thread.isDaemon(); 1735
  - Thread; 1724
- destroying, without cleanup
  - Thread.destroy(); 1730
- errors, ThreadDeath; 1750
- exceptions
  - IllegalThreadStateException; 951
  - InterruptedException; 1017
- execution
  - resuming, Thread.resume(); 1739
  - starting, Thread.start(); 1743
  - stopping, Thread.stop(); 1744
  - suspending, Thread.suspend(); 1745
  - yielding, Thread.yield(); 1748
- interrupt
  - sending, Thread.interrupt(); 1733
  - testing for, Thread.interrupted(); 1734
  - testing for, Thread.isInterrupted(); 1736
  - Thread; 1725
- modification of, permission determination
  - SecurityManager.checkAccess(); 1484

name
  retrieving, Thread.getName(); 1731
  setting, Thread.setName(); 1741
notification
  Object.notify(); 1221
  Object.notifyAll(); 1223
pipe streams, *See* pipes
priority
  default, Thread.NORM_PRIORITY; 1739
  maximum, Thread.MAX_PRIORITY; 1738
  minimum, Thread.MIN_PRIORITY; 1739
  retrieving, Thread.getPriority(); 1732
  setting, Thread.setPriority(); 1742
  Thread; 1724
sleep, Thread.sleep(); 1743
stack frames
  Thread.countStackFrames(); 1729
string representation, generating
  ThreadGroup.toString(); 1767
synchronization of, Object; 1215
term description, Thread; 1723
Thread; 1723
  activeCount(); 1728
  checkAccess(); 1729
  countStackFrames(); 1729
  currentThread(); 1730
  destroy(); 1730
  dumpStack(); 1730
  enumerate(); 1731
  getName(); 1731
  getPriority(); 1732
  getThreadGroup(); 1732
  interrupt(); 1733
  interrupted(); 1734
  isAlive(); 1735
  isDaemon(); 1735
  isInterrupted(); 1736
  join(); 1737
  MAX_PRIORITY; 1738
  MIN_PRIORITY; 1739
  NORM_PRIORITY; 1739
  package, java.lang; 1723
  resume(); 1739
  run(); 1740
  setDaemon(); 1740
  setName(); 1741
  setPriority(); 1742
  sleep(); 1743
  start(); 1743
  stop(); 1744
  suspend(); 1745
  toString(); 1748
  yield(); 1748
thread group
  determining, ThreadGroup.parentOf(); 1761
  resuming, ThreadGroup.resume(); 1761
  setting daemon status
    ThreadGroup.setDaemon(); 1762
in a thread group
  enumerating
    ThreadGroup.enumerate(); 1758
  listing, ThreadGroup.list(); 1760
ThreadDeath; 1750
  package, java.lang; 1750
user, Thread; 1724
waiting
  suspension, Object.wait(); 1224
  termination, Thread.join(); 1737

Throwable; 1769
  fillInStackTrace(); 1770
  getLocalizedMessage(); 1771
  getMessage(); 1771
  package, java.lang; 1769
  printStackTrace(); 1771
  string representation, generating
    Throwable.toString(); 1773
  toString(); 1773

THURSDAY
  Calendar, *Table*; 233

time
  See Also DST (Daylight Savings Time); GMT (Greenwich Mean Time)
  12-hour clock, DateFormat.AM_PM_FIELD; 588
  AM/PM strings, DateFormatSymbols; 611
  calendar field, setting, Calendar.setTime(); 274
  Calendar.HOUR; 262
  Calendar.HOUR_OF_DAY; 263
  Calendar.MILLISECOND; 265
  Calendar.MINUTE; 265
  Calendar.SECOND; 268
  Calendar.time; 275
  creating
    DateFormat.getDateTimeInstance(); 596
    DateFormat.getTimeInstance(); 597
  date value, computing
    Calendar.getTime(); 260
    Calendar.getTimeInMillis(); 261

time *(continued)*
daylight savings, calendar field constant
Calendar.DST_OFFSET; 251
default, DateFormat.DEFAULT; 591
difference
retrieving
SimpleTimeZone.getOffset(); 1563
SimpleTimeZone.getRawOffset(); 1564
TimeZone.getOffset(); 1782
TimeZone.getRawOffset(); 1783
setting
SimpleTimeZone.setRawOffset(); 1566
TimeZone.setRawOffset(); 1785
TimeZone.useDaylightTime(); 1785
displaying, Date; 563
format
retrieving, SimpleDateFormat.getDate-FormatSymbols(); 1554
setting, SimpleDateFormat.setDate-FormatSymbols(); 1556
formatting
DateFormat; 580
styles, *Table*, DateFormat; 582
formatting pattern, SimpleDateFormat; 1541
long style, DateFormat.LONG; 599
medium-length style, DateFormat.MEDIUM; 600
modification
retrieving
URLConnection.getIfModifiedSince(); 1837
ZipEntry.getTime(); 1898
setting
URLConnection.setIfModifiedSince(); 1845
ZipEntry.setTime(); 1901
modifying, Date; 563
ordering
Calendar.after(); 242
Calendar.before(); 245
GregorianCalendar.after(); 886
GregorianCalendar.before(); 887
parsing
DateFormat.parse(); 601
DateFormat.parseObject(); 604
retrieving
Date.getTime(); 571
System.currentTimeMillis(); 1713
setting, Date.setTime(); 577
short style, DateFormat.SHORT; 608
SimpleDateFormat; 1541
specifying, Date; 563
standard time, SimpleTimeZone; 1559
string, parsing, SimpleDateFormat.parse(); 1555
testing if set, Calendar.isTimeSet; 264
time, Calendar; 275
time-out period
DatagramSocket; 507
linger-on-close, retrieving
Socket.getSoLinger(); 1581
retrieving
DatagramSocket.getSoTimeout(); 511
ServerSocket.getSoTimeout(); 1524
ServerSocket; 1516
setting
DatagramSocket.setSoTimeout(); 514
ServerSocket.setSoTimeout(); 1527
Socket.setSoLinger(); 1583
Socket.setSoTimeout(); 1584
Socket.getSoTimeout(); 1581
sockets, Socket; 1572
time-to-live
multicast datagrams, setting
MulticastSocket.setTTL(); 1162
multicast packets, retrieving
DatagramSocketImpl.getTTL(); 521
multicast packets, setting
DatagramSocketImpl.setTTL(); 525
MulticastSocket; 1153;
retrieving, MulticastSocket.getTTL(); 1157
TimeZone; 1774
clone(); 1778
getAvailableIDs(); 1779
getDefault(); 1781
getID(); 1782
getOffset(); 1782
getRawOffset(); 1783
getTimeZone(); 1783
inDaylightTime(); 1784
package, java.util; 1774
setDefault(); 1784
setID(); 1785
setRawOffset(); 1786
useDaylightTime(); 1786
TIMEZONE_FIELD.DateFormat; 608
unabbreviated pattern, DateFormat.FULL; 594

zone
Calendar; 233, 234
Calendar.ZONE_OFFSET; 281
DateFormat.TIMEZONE_FIELD; 608
default, retrieving
TimeZone.getDefault(); 1781
identifiers, retrieving
TimeZone.getAvailableIDs(); 1779
TimeZone.getID(); 1782
identifiers, *Table*, TimeZone; 1775
offset, TimeZone; 1774
property, DateFormatSymbols; 612
property, setting
DateFormatSymbols.setZoneStrings(); 624
retrieving
Calendar.getTimeZone(); 261
DateFormat.getTimeZone(); 597
TimeZone.getTimeZone(); 1783
setting
Calendar.setTimeZone(); 275
DateFormat.setTimeZone(); 607
SimpleTimeZone; 1559
strings, accessing, DateFormatSymbols; 610
TimeZone; 1774

titlecase
converting to, Character.toTitleCase(); 302
testing for, Character.isTitleCase(); 297
TITLECASE_LETTER, Character, *Table*; 289

toxxx methods
toBigInteger(), BigDecimal; 96
toBinaryString()
Integer; 1010
Long; 1077
toByteArray()
BigInteger; 130
ByteArrayOutputStream; 228
CollationKey; 445
toCharArray()
CharArrayWriter; 328
String; 1651
toExternalForm()
URL; 1815
URLStreamHandler; 1855
toGMTString(), Date; 578
toHexString()
Integer; 1011
Long; 1078
toLocaleString(), Date; 578
toLocalizedPattern()
DecimalFormat; 662
SimpleDateFormat; 1558
toLowerCase()
Character; 302
String; 1652
toOctalString()
Integer; 1012
Long; 1078
toPattern()
ChoiceFormat; 364
DecimalFormat; 662
MessageFormat; 1122
SimpleDateFormat; 1558
toString()
BigDecimal; 96
BigInteger; 131
BitSet; 143
Boolean; 148
Byte; 213
ByteArrayOutputStream; 229
Character; 302
CharArrayWriter; 329
Class; 405
Constructor; 485
Date; 578
Double; 719
EventObject; 735
Field; 773
File; 801
Float; 869
Hashtable; 922
InetAddress; 963
Integer; 1012
Locale; 1068
Long; 1079
Method; 1138
Modifier; 1151
Object; 1224
ObjectStreamClass; 1286
ServerSocket; 1529
Short; 1538
Socket; 1589
SocketImpl; 1603
StreamTokenizer; 1628
String; 1652
StringBuffer; 1664
StringWriter; 1706
Thread; 1748
ThreadGroup; 1767

toxxx methods *(continued)*
toString()
Throwable; 1773
URL; 1816
URLConnection; 1847
Vector; 1876
ZipEntry; 1902
toTitleCase(), Character; 302
toUpperCase()
Character; 303
String; 1652
tokens
counting, StringTokenizer.countTokens(); 1698
creating, StreamTokenizer; 1614
elements that are, *Table*, StreamTokenizer; 1614
end-of-file, StreamTokenizer.TT_EOF; 1628
end-of-line, StreamTokenizer.TT_EOL; 1629
number, StreamTokenizer.TT_NUMBER; 1629
numbers, specifying digits as
StreamTokenizer.parseNumbers(); 1622
numeric value, StreamTokenizer.nval; 1621
parsing
StreamTokenizer; 1614
StreamTokenizer.nextToken(); 1619
strings into, StringTokenizer; 1697
pushing back, StreamTokenizer.pushBack(); 1624
retrieving
StringTokenizer.nextElement(); 1700
StringTokenizer.nextToken(); 1700
string representation, generating
StreamTokenizer.toString(); 1628
string value, StreamTokenizer.sval; 1628
syntactic elements, *Table*
StreamTokenizer; 1614
term description, StringTokenizer; 1697
testing for
StringTokenizer.hasMoreElements(); 1699
StringTokenizer.hasMoreTokens(); 1699
type of, StreamTokenizer.ttype; 1630
word, StreamTokenizer.TT_WORD; 1629
TooManyListenersException; 1787
package, java.util; 1787
totalMemory()
Runtime; 1475
tracing
instructions
Runtime.traceInstructions(); 1476
method calls
Runtime.traceMethodCalls(); 1476
stack, filling in
Throwable.fillInStackTrace(); 1770
traceInstructions(), Runtime; 1476
traceMethodCalls(), Runtime; 1476
TRADITIONAL_CHINESE
Locale; 1056
transient modifier
testing for, Modifier.isTransient(); 1151
TRANSIENT, Modifier; 1144
trigonometric functions
See Also mathematics
arc cosine, Math.acos(); 1086
arc sine, Math.asin(); 1086
arc tangent, Math.atan(); 1086
cosine, Math.cos(); 1088
Math; 1084
sine, Math.sin(); 1093
tangent, Math.tan(); 1094
trimxxx methods
trim(), String; 1653
trimToSize(), Vector; 1876
true
Boolean.TRUE; 148
TRUE, Boolean; 148
TTxxx fields
TT_EOF, StreamTokenizer; 1628
TT_EOL, StreamTokenizer; 1629
TT_NUMBER, StreamTokenizer; 1629
TT_WORD, StreamTokenizer; 1629
ttype
StreamTokenizer; 1630
TUESDAY
Calendar, *Table*; 233
types
array, for Get and Set methods, *Tables*, Array; 48
component, of arrays, Array; 47
content
determining from document contents
URLConnection.guessContentTypeFromStream(); 1841
determining from filename extension
URLConnection.guessContentTypeFromName(); 1840
mapping filenames into, FileNameMap; 816

descriptors, Class; 366
exception
  methods, retrieving
    Method.getExceptionTypes(); 1129
  retrieving
    Constructor.getExceptionTypes(); 480
field
  Field; 750
  for Get and Set methods, *Tables*
    Calendar; 259
fields, retrieving, Field.getType(); 764
MIME, of a filename, determining
  FileNameMap.getContentTypeFor(); 817
object, member, modifiers for, *Table*
  Member; 1095
parameter
  constructor, Constructor; 476
  method, retrieving
    Method.getParameterTypes(); 1132
  methods, Method; 1124
primitive
  Class; 366
  reading data as, DataInput; 526
  string representation, *Table*, Class; 366
  testing for, Class.isPrimitive(); 403
  type descriptors for, *Table*, Class; 366
  wrappers, Double; 709
  wrappers, Float; 860
  wrappers for, *Table*, Class; 368
  wrappers, Integer; 1001
  wrappers, Long; 1069
  wrappers, Short; 1530
  writing data as, DataOutput; 546
return
  method, retrieving
    Method.getReturnType(); 1133
  methods, Method; 1124
scalar numeric, Number; 1187
TYPE
  Boolean; 149
  Byte; 213
  Character; 304
  Double; 719
  Float; 870
  Integer; 1013
  Long; 1080
  Short; 1538
  Void; 1882
URL content encoding, retrieving
  URLConnection.getContentEncoding(); 1831

U

U.S. English
  decimal format symbols, *Table*
    DecimalFormatSymbols; 665
UK
  predefined locale codes, *Table*, Locale; 1056
  UK, Locale; 1056
UNASSIGNED
  Character, *Table*; 289
uncaughtException()
  ThreadGroup; 1767
UNDECIMBER
  Calendar, *Table*; 233
unicast
  concept description, DatagramSocket; 506
  DatagramPacket, DatagramPacket; 499
  term description, DatagramPacket; 499
Unicode
  byte conversion to
    InputStreamReader; 991
    OutputStreamWriter; 1309
  canonical mapping, RuleBasedCollator; 1451
  category
    determining, Character.getType(); 288
    types, *Table*; 289
  characters
    attributes, URL, Character; 282
    bibliographic reference, Character; 282
    BreakIterator; 151
    decomposing
      Collator.FULL_DECOMPOSITION; 456
    iterating over
      StringCharacterIterator; 1671
    user characters compared with
      BreakIterator; 152
  decimal format symbols, *Table*
    DecimalFormatSymbols; 665
  definition, testing for
    Character.isDefined(); 290
  digit characters, *Table*, Character; 291
  identifiers
    Character; 283
    Character.isIdentifierIgnorable(); 291
    Character.isUnicodeIdentifierPart(); 298
    Character.isUnicodeIdentifierStart(); 299

Unicode *(continued)*
numeric values, retrieving
Character.getNumericValue(); 288
ordering, String.compareTo(); 1635
reading
DataInput.readUTF(); 532
DataInputStream.readUTF(); 544
RandomAccessFile.readUTF(); 1418
space, Character.isSpaceChar(); 297
standard
decomposition, Collator; 450
string comparison, CollationKey; 441
Standard, URL, RuleBasedCollator; 1451
string, reading
ObjectInputStream.readUTF(); 1249
text, including in format strings
ChoiceFormat; 347
UTF, writing
ObjectOutputStream.writeUTF(); 1282
writing
DataOutput.writeUTF(); 551
DataOutputStream.writeUTF(); 561
RandomAccessFile.writeUTF(); 1425
uniform
distribution, pseudorandom-number, Random; 1399
Unknownxxx errors and exceptions
UnknownError; 1790
package, java.lang; 1790
UnknownHostException; 1792
package, java.net; 1792
UnknownServiceException; 1794
package, java.net; 1794
unread()
PushbackInputStream; 1389
PushbackReader; 1397
UnsatisfiedLinkError; 1796
package, java.lang; 1796
UnsupportedEncodingException; 1798
package, java.io; 1798
updating
checksum
Checksum.update(); 345
CRC32.update(); 495
update()
Adler32; 44
Checksum; 345
CRC32; 495
Observer; 1298
uppercase
converting to, Character.toUpperCase(); 303
testing for, Character.isUpperCase(); 299
UPPERCASE_LETTER, Character, *Table*; 289
URL (Uniform Resource Locator)
character encoding, URLEncoder; 1849
classes that implement; 24
connection
cache flag, setting
URLConnection.setDefaultUse-Caches(); 1844
URLConnection.setUseCaches(); 1846
caching, testing for permitted use
URLConnection.useCaches; 1848
content, retrieving
URLConnection.getContent(); 1830
creating input stream for
URLConnection.getInputStream(); 1838
creating output stream for
URLConnection.getOutputStream(); 1838
establishing
URLConnection.connect(); 1828
expiration date
URLConnection.getExpiration(); 1834
input, setting
URLConnection.setDoInput(); 1844
input, testing for
URLConnection.getDoInput(); 1833
opening
URL.openConnection(); 1812
URLStreamHandler.openConnection(); 1854
output, setting
URLConnection.setDoOutput(); 1845
output, testing for
URLConnection.getDoOutput(); 1834
request header field, setting default value
URLConnection.setDefaultRequest-Property(); 1844
URLConnection.setRequestProperty(); 1846
retrieving, URLConnection.getURL(); 1839
status, URLConnection.connected; 1828
string representation
URLConnection.toString(); 1847
testing for cache use
URLConnection.getDefaultUse-Caches(); 1833

URL for, URLConnection.url; 1847
URLConnection; 1819
URLConnection.allowUserInteraction; 1827
user interaction, testing for
URLConnection.getAllowUser-Interaction(); 1830
content
encoding type, retrieving
URLConnection.getContentEncoding(); 1831
URLConnection.getContentType(); 1831
length, retrieving
URLConnection.getContentLength(); 1831
contents, retrieving, URL.getContent(); 1807
equality, testing, URL.sameFile(); 1813
exceptions, UnknownServiceException; 1794
externalization security considerations
Externalizable; 745
fields, setting, URL.set(); 1814
filename, retrieving, URL.getFile(); 1808
generating objects from
ContentHandler.getContent(); 489
GZIP format
GZIPInputStream; 896
GZIPOutputStream; 902
host name, retrievingURL.getHost(); 1809
input, URLConnection.doInput; 1829
input stream, URL connection, opening, URL.open-Stream(); 1813
life cycle, URLConnection; 1819
output, URLConnection.doOutput; 1829
port number, retrieving, URL.getPort(); 1809
protocol handlers, URLConnection; 1820
protocol identifier, retrieving
URL.getProtocol(); 1810
reference, retrieving, URL.getRef(); 1811
request header, field, retrieving value
URLConnection.getDefaultRequest-Property(); 1832
response header, field, retrieving
URLConnection.getHeaderField(); 1834
RFC 1950, Deflater; 680
RFC 1951
Deflater; 679
ZipFile; 1906
serialization security considerations
Serializable; 1513
serialization/deserialization, Serializable; 1509
setting, URLStreamHandler.setURL(); 1855
stream handler
factory, URL; 1801
HttpURLConnection use; 923
URL; 1801
stream handler factory
creating, URLStreamHandlerFac-tory.createURLStreamHandler(); 1859
URLStreamHandlerFactory; 1857
stream handlers
FileNameMap use; 816
URLConnection; 1820
string, parsing into an object
URLStreamHandler.parseURL(); 1854
string representation, generating
URL.toExternalForm(); 1815
URL.toString(); 1816
URLStreamHandler.toExternalForm(); 1855
term description
MalformedURLException; 1082
URL; 1800
Unicode characters attributes, Character; 282
Unicode Standard, RuleBasedCollator; 1451
URL; 1800
equals(); 1807
getContent(); 1807
getFile(); 1808
getHost(); 1809
getPort(); 1809
getProtocol(); 1810
getRef(); 1811
hashCode(); 1811
openConnection(); 1812
openStream(); 1813
package, java.net; 1800
sameFile(); 1813
set(); 1814
setURLStreamHandlerFactory(); 1814
toExternalForm(); 1815
toString(); 1816
url, URLConnection; 1847
URLConnection; 1819
allowUserInteraction; 1827
connect(); 1828
connected; 1828
doInput; 1829
doOutput; 1829

URL (Uniform Resource Locator) *(continued)*
URLConnection
fileNameMap; 1829
getAllowUserInteraction(); 1830
getContent(); 1830
getContentEncoding(); 1831
getContentLength(); 1831
getContentType(); 1831
getDate(); 1832
getDefaultAllowUserInteraction(); 1832
getDefaultRequestProperty(); 1832
getDefaultUseCaches(); 1833
getDoInput(); 1833
getDoOutput(); 1834
getExpiration(); 1834
getHeaderField(); 1834
getHeaderFieldDate(); 1835
getHeaderFieldInt(); 1836
getHeaderFieldKey(); 1836
getIfModifiedSince(); 1837
getInputStream(); 1838
getLastModified(); 1838
getOutputStream(); 1838
getRequestProperty(); 1839
getURL(); 1839
getUseCaches(); 1840
guessContentTypeFromStream(); 1841
ifModifiedSince(); 1841
package, java.net; 1819
setAllowUserInteraction(); 1842
setContentHandlerFactory(); 1842
setDefaultAllowUserInteraction(); 1843
setDefaultRequestProperty(); 1844
setDefaultUseCaches(); 1844
setDoInput(); 1844
setDoOutput(); 1845
setIfModifiedSince(); 1845
setRequestProperty(); 1846
setUseCaches(); 1846
toString(); 1847
url; 1847
useCaches; 1848
URLEncoder; 1849
encode(); 1851
package, java.net; 1849
URLStreamHandler
openConnection(); 1854
package, java.net; 1852
parseURL(); 1854
setURL(); 1855
toExternalForm(); 1855
URLStreamHandlerFactory; 1857
createURLStreamHandler(); 1859
package, java.net; 1857
versioning, Serializable; 1512
ZIP file format
ZipEntry; 1892
ZipFile; 1906
ZLIB library, Deflater; 679
US (United States)
predefined locale codes, *Table*, Locale; 1056
US, Locale; 1056
useCaches flag
term description, URLConnection; 1820
URL connection use, testing for, URLConnection.getDefaultUseCaches(); 1833
URLConnection; 1848
useDaylightTime()
SimpleTimeZone; 1570
TimeZone; 1786
user
characters, Unicode characters compared with, BreakIterator; 152
interaction
determining if URL connection permits
URLConnection.allowUserInteraction(); 1827
flag, setting
URLConnection.setDefaultAllowUserInteraction(); 1843
URLConnection.setAllowUserInteraction(); 1842
URL connection, testing for
URLConnection.getAllowUserInteraction(); 1830
URLConnection.getDefaultAllowUserInteraction(); 1832
threads, Thread; 1724
usingProxy()
HttpURLConnection; 938
UTC (Coordinated Universal Time)
term description, Date; 562
UTC(), Date; 579
UTF (Unicode Transfer Format)
reading
DataInput.readUTF(); 532
DataInputStream.readUTF(); 544
ObjectInputStream.readUTF(); 1249
RandomAccessFile.readUTF(); 1418

writing
DataOutput.writeUTF(); 551
DataOutputStream.writeUTF(); 561
ObjectOutputStream.writeUTF(); 1282
RandomAccessFile.writeUTF(); 1425
UTFDataFormatException; 1860
package, java.io; 1860

V

validation
registering objects for
ObjectInputStream.registerValidation(); 1249
term description, ObjectInputValidation; 1256
valid(), FileDescriptor; 805
validateObject(), ObjectInputValidation; 1258
validator
term description, InvalidObjectException; 1026
values
See Also big decimal values; big integer values; floating-point values; numbers; primitive types; types
absolute, computing, BigInteger.abs(); 103
big integer, BigInteger.valueOf(); 132
data
reading as primitive types, DataInput; 526
writing as primitive types, DataOutput; 546
exit, Process.exitValue(); 1365
field
Field; 750
retrieving, Field.get(); 756
maximum
Byte.MAX_VALUE; 210
Character.MAX_VALUE(); 301
Double.MAX_VALUE; 716
Float.MAX_VALUE; 867
Integer.MAX_VALUE; 1008
Long.MAX_VALUE; 1075
Short.MAX_VALUE; 1535
minimum
Byte.MIN_VALUE; 211
Character.MIN_VALUE; 301
Double.MIN_VALUE; 717
Float.MIN_VALUE; 867
Integer.MIN_VALUE; 1008
Long.MIN_VALUE; 1075
Short.MIN_VALUE; 1535
NaN
Double.NaN; 717
Float.NaN; 868
numeric, Character.digit(); 286
properties, Properties; 1370
retrieving object as a double
Double.doubleValue(); 712
Float.doubleValue(); 862
Integer.doubleValue(); 1004
Long.doubleValue(); 1071
Number.doubleValue(); 1189
Short.doubleValue(); 1533
retrieving object as a float
Long.floatValue(); 1072
Number.floatValue(); 1189
Short.floatValue(); 1534
retrieving object as a long
Byte.longValue(); 210
Double.longValue(); 716
Float.longValue(); 867
Integer.longValue(); 1008
Long.longValue(); 1075
Number.longValue(); 1190
Short.longValue(); 1535
retrieving object as a short
Double.shortValue(); 718
Float.shortValue(); 869
Integer.shortValue(); 1010
Number.shortValue(); 1190
Short.shortValue(); 1537
retrieving object as an int
Byte.intValue(); 210
Integer.intValue(); 1007
Long.intValue(); 1074
Number.intValue(); 1189
Short.intValue(); 1534
valueOf()
BigDecimal; 97
BigInteger; 132
Boolean; 149
Byte; 214
Double; 720
Float; 871
Integer; 1013
Long; 1080
Short; 1539
String; 1653

values *(continued)*
wrappers for primitive types
Byte; 205
Character; 282
Double; 709
Float; 860
Integer; 1001
Long; 1069
Short; 1530
variable(s)
message pattern, MessageFormat; 1105
pattern
retrieving formats
MessageFormat.getFormats(); 1113
setting format for
MessageFormat.setFormat(); 1119
MessageFormat.setFormats(); 1121
variant code
Locale, locale(s); 1054
locale
retrieving
Locale.getDisplayVariant(); 1063
Locale.getVariant(); 1065
variants
resource bundles, ResourceBundle; 1436
vector(s)
angle, Math.atan2(); 1087
bit, *See* BitSet
capacity
determining, Vector.capacity(); 1865
minimum, specifying
Vector.ensureCapacity(); 1869
setting increment size
Vector.capacityIncrement(); 1865
trimming to size, Vector.trimToSize(); 1876
Vector; 1862
elements
determining number of
Vector.elementCount; 1868
inserting, Vector.insertElementAt(); 1871
listing, Vector.elements(); 1868
removing
Vector.removeAllElements(); 1873
Vector.removeElement(); 1873
Vector.removeElementAt(); 1874
replacing, Vector.setElementAt(); 1874
retrieving
Vector.elementAt(); 1867
Vector.firstElement(); 1870
Vector.lastElement(); 1872
testing for
Vector.contains(); 1866
Vector.isEmpty(); 1872
Vector; 1862
searching
Vector.indexOf(); 1870
Vector.lastIndexOf(); 1872
size
changing, Vector.setSize(); 1875
determining, Vector.size(); 1875
string representation, generating
Vector.toString(); 1876
term description, Vector; 1862
Vector; 1862
addElement(); 1864
capacity(); 1865
capacityIncrement(); 1865
clone(); 1866
contains(); 1866
copyInto(); 1866
elementAt(); 1867
elementCount; 1868
elementData; 1868
elements(); 1868
firstElement(); 1870
indexOf(); 1870
insertElementAt(); 1871
isEmpty(); 1872
lastElement(); 1872
lastIndexOf(); 1872
package, java.util; 1862
removeAllElements(); 1873
removeElement(); 1873
removeElementAt(); 1874
setElementAt(); 1874
setSize(); 1875
size(); 1875
toString(); 1876
trimToSize(); 1876
VerifyError; 1878
package, java.lang; 1878
versioning
serialization issues
Externalizable; 743
Serializable; 1512
URL, Serializable; 1512

virtual machine
errors
InternalError; 1015
OutOfMemoryError; 1302
VirtualMachineError; 1880
exit, permission determination
SecurityManager.checkExit(); 1488
exiting
Runtime.exit(); 1468
System.exit(); 1714
finalization, Deflater.finalize(); 687
VirtualMachineError; 1880
package, java.lang; 1880
Void; 1882
package, java.lang; 1882
TYPE; 1882
volatile modifier
testing for, Modifier.isVolatile(); 1151
VOLATILE, Modifier; 1144

W

waiting
for process termination, Process.waitFor(); 1368
thread
suspension, Object.wait(); 1224
termination, Thread.join(); 1737
wait(), Object; 1224
waitFor(), Process; 1368
WEDNESDAY
Calendar, *Table*; 233
week(s)
calendar constants, *Table*, Calendar; 234
DAY_OF_WEEK_FIELD, DateFormat; 591
DAY_OF_WEEK_IN_MONTH_FIELD, DateFormat; 591
first day-of-week, retrieving
Calendar.getFirstDayOfWeek(); 258
first week in the year, retrieving minimal number of days
Calendar.getMinimalDaysInFirstWeek(); 260
names of days, accessing
DateFormatSymbols; 610
WEEK_OF_MONTH, Calendar; 275
WEEK_OF_MONTH_FIELD.DateFormat; 609
WEEK_OF_YEAR, Calendar; 279
WEEK_OF_YEAR_FIELD, DateFormat; 608
weekdays
property
retrieving
DateFormatSymbols.getShortWeekdays(); 619
DateFormatSymbols.getWeekdays(); 620
setting
DateFormatSymbols.setShortWeekdays(); 624
DateFormatSymbols.setWeekdays(); 624
whitespace
characters as
StreamTokenizer.whitespaceChars; 1630
testing for, Character.isWhitespace(); 300
as token element, *Table*, StreamTokenizer; 1614
whitespaceChars(), StreamTokenizer; 1630
windows
creating, permission determination
SecurityManager.checkTopLevelWindow(); 1495
words
boundary, analysis, BreakIterator; 154
-break boundary, creating break iterator for
BreakIterator.getWordInstance(); 171
characters as, StreamTokenizer.wordChars; 1631
token, StreamTokenizer.TT_WORD; 1629
as token element, *Table*, StreamTokenizer; 1614
wordChars(), StreamTokenizer; 1631
wrappers
Boolean; 144
Byte; 205
Character; 282
concept description; 15
Double; 709
Float; 860
Integer; 1001
Long; 1069
Number; 1187
primitive types, *Table*, Class; 368
Short; 1530
Void; 1882
writers
buffered, BufferedWriter; 199
BufferedWriter; 199
CharArrayWriter; 323
FileWriter; 830
FilterWriter; 855
OutputStreamWriter; 1308

writers *(continued)*
PipedWriter; 1342
PrintWriter; 1354
StringWriter; 1703
Writer; 1887
close(); 1889
flush(); 1889
lock; 1890
package, java.io; 1887
write(); 1890
writing
buffers, ObjectOutputStream.drain(); 1269
compressed data, to output stream
DeflaterOutputStream.write(); 700
compressed data writing to output stream
DeflaterOutputStream.deflate(); 699
files
FileWriter; 830
permission determination
SecurityManager.checkWrite(); 1496
object information
ObjectOutputStream.annotateClass(); 1266
output stream, CheckedOutputStream.write(); 341
property list
Properties.list(); 1374
Properties.save(); 1377
serializable fields, ObjectOutputStream.defaultWriteObject(); 1269
serialized objects, ObjectOutput; 1259
write()
BufferedOutputStream; 189
BufferedWriter; 203
ByteArrayOutputStream; 230
CharArrayWriter; 329
CheckedOutputStream; 341
DataOutput; 547
DataOutputStream; 555
DeflaterOutputStream; 699
FileOutputStream; 825
FilterOutputStream; 846
FilterWriter; 859
GZIPOutputStream; 912
ObjectOutput; 1260
ObjectOutputStream; 1274
OutputStream; 1306
OutputStreamWriter; 1313
PipedOutputStream; 1335
PipedWriter; 1345
PrintStream; 1353
PrintWriter; 1361
RandomAccessFile; 1419
StringWriter; 1707
Writer; 1890
ZipOutputStream; 1932
WriteAbortedException; 1884
package, java.io; 1884
writeBoolean()
DataOutput; 547
DataOutputStream; 556
ObjectOutputStream; 1275
RandomAccessFile; 1420
writeByte()
DataOutput; 548
DataOutputStream; 557
ObjectOutputStream; 1276
RandomAccessFile; 1420
writeBytes()
DataOutput; 548
DataOutputStream; 557
ObjectOutputStream; 1276
RandomAccessFile; 1421
writeChar()
DataOutput; 548
DataOutputStream; 558
ObjectOutputStream; 1277
RandomAccessFile; 1421
writeChars()
DataOutput; 549
DataOutputStream; 558
ObjectOutputStream; 1277
RandomAccessFile; 1422
writeDouble()
DataOutput; 549
DataOutputStream; 558
ObjectOutputStream; 1278
RandomAccessFile; 1422
writeExternal(), Externalizable; 747
writeFloat()
DataOutput; 550
DataOutputStream; 559
ObjectOutputStream; 1278
RandomAccessFile; 1423
writeInt()
DataOutput; 550
DataOutputStream; 559
ObjectOutputStream; 1278
RandomAccessFile; 1423

writeLong()
DataOutput; 550
DataOutputStream; 560
ObjectOutputStream; 1279
RandomAccessFile; 1424
writeObject()
ObjectOutput; 1261
ObjectOutputStream; 1279
writeShort()
DataOutput; 551
DataOutputStream; 560
ObjectOutputStream; 1281
RandomAccessFile; 1425
writeStreamHeader(), ObjectOutputStream; 1281
writeTo()
ByteArrayOutputStream; 231
CharArrayWriter; 330
writeUTF()
DataOutput; 551
DataOutputStream; 561
ObjectOutputStream; 1282
RandomAccessFile; 1425
written, DataOutputStream; 561

X

XOR logical operation
See Also logical operations
xor()
BigInteger; 132
BitSet; 143

Y

years
DAY_OF_YEAR_FIELD, DateFormat; 591
first week in the year, retrieving minimal number of days, Calendar.getMinimalDaysIn-FirstWeek(); 260
leap, testing for
GregorianCalendar.isLeapYear(); 893
WEEK_OF_YEAR_FIELD.DateFormat; 608
YEAR, Calendar; 280
YEAR_FIELD.DateFormat; 609
yield()
Thread; 1748

Z

zero
digit
retrieving, DecimalFormatSymbols.get-ZeroDigit(); 673
setting, DecimalFormatSymbols.set-ZeroDigit(); 678
rounding towards, BigDecimal.ROUND_DOWN; 90
ZIP files
bibliographic reference, ClassLoader; 414
compressed size
ZipEntry.getCompressedSize(); 1896
compression specification
Deflater.DEFLATED; 685
concept description; 37
decompressed data
discarding, ZipInputStream.skip(); 1918
reading, ZipInputStream.read(); 1918
exceptions, ZipException; 1904
format
directory, ZipEntry; 1892
URL, ZipEntry; 1892
URL, ZipFile; 1906
GZIP file differences
ZipInputStream; 1914
ZipOutputStream; 1920
information
closing
ZipOutputStream.close(); 1925
ZipOutputStream.finish(); 1926
retrieving, ZipEntry.getExtra(); 1897
setting, ZipEntry.setExtra(); 1900
input stream, closing
ZipInputStream.close(); 1916
levels, setting
ZipOutputStream.setLevel(); 1929
opening, ZipFile.ZipFile(); 1913
properties, *Table*, ZipEntry; 1892
term description, ClassLoader; 414
writing, ZipOutputStream.write(); 1932
ZIP entry
closing
ZipInputStream.closeEntry(); 1917
ZipOutputStream.closeEntry(); 1925
enumeration, ZipFile.entries(); 1912
format URL, ZipFile; 1906
retrieving
ZipFile.getEntry(); 1912
ZipInputStream.getNextEntry(); 1917

ZIP files *(continued)*
ZIP entry
writing
ZipOutputStream.putNextEntry(); 1928
ZipEntry; 1892
DEFLATED; 1895
getComment(); 1896
getCompressedSize(); 1896
getCrc(); 1896
getExtra(); 1897
getMethod(); 1897
getName(); 1898
getSize(); 1898
getTime(); 1898
isDirectory(); 1899
package, java.util.zip; 1892
setComment(); 1899
setCrc(); 1899
setExtra(); 1900
setMethod(); 1901
setSize(); 1901
setTime(); 1901
STORED; 1902
toString(); 1902
ZipException; 1904
package, java.util.zip; 1904
ZipException; 1904
ZipFile; 1906
close(); 1911
entries(); 1911
getEntry(); 1912
getInputStream(); 1912
getName(); 1913
package, java.util.zip; 1906
ZipInputStream; 1914
close(); 1916
closeEntry(); 1917
getNextEntry(); 1917
package, java.util.zip; 1914
read(); 1918
skip(); 1918
ZipOutputStream; 1920
close(); 1925
closeEntry(); 1925
DEFLATED; 1926
finish(); 1926
package, java.util.zip; 1920
putNextEntry(); 1928
setComment(); 1929
setLevel(); 1929
setMethod(); 1931
STORED; 1931
write(); 1932
ZLIB
compression library, URL, Deflater; 679
header, Deflater; 680
zone
time
Calendar; 234
Calendar.ZONE_OFFSET; 281
retrieving, Calendar.getTimeZone(); 261
setting, Calendar.setTimeZone(); 275
ZONE_OFFSET, Calendar; 281

The Addison-Wesley Java™ Series

ISBN 0-201-31006-6

ISBN 0-201-31007-4

ISBN 0-201-63458-9

ISBN 0-201-31003-1

ISBN 0-201-31002-3

ISBN 0-201-63451-1

ISBN 0-201-63453-8

ISBN 0-201-63459-7

ISBN 0-201-30995-5

ISBN 0-201-63456-2

ISBN 0-201-69581-2

ISBN 0-201-63452-X

ISBN 0-201-32576-4

Please see our web site (http://www.awl.com/cseng/javaseries) for more information on these titles.